official guides to quality

self-catering
holiday homes
2005

visit **Britain**
publishing

Contents

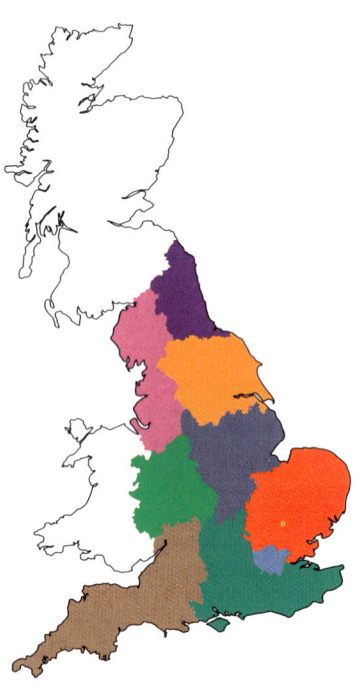

The guide that gives you more	5
A great choice of quality-rated accommodation	6
Ratings and awards	8
National Accessible Scheme	10
How do we arrive at a star rating?	12
Accommodation entries explained	13
Inspiring ideas for a short break	14
Enjoy England Excellence Awards	19
Accommodation maps	22

The guide is divided into **10 sections** (see opposite)

Self-catering agencies	393
Complete listing of all VisitBritain assessed self-catering properties	399
Complete listing of all VisitBritain assessed boat accommodation	725
The National Quality Assurance Standard	730
General advice and information	731
About the guide entries	734
Travel information by car and by train	736
A selection of events for 2005	738
In which region is the county I wish to visit?	744
National Accessible Scheme index	746
Town index	751

VisitBritain

VisitBritain is the organisation created to market Britain to the rest of the world, and England to the British. Formed by the merger of the British Tourist Authority and the English Tourism Council, its mission is to build the value of tourism by creating world-class destination brands and marketing campaigns.

It will also build partnerships with – and provide insights to – other organisations which have a stake in British and English tourism.

Above Brunt Knott Farm Holiday Cottages, Staveley **Right, from top** take a city break in Nottingham; Old Brantrake, Eskdale

Accommodation, places to visit and information

London	36
England's Northwest	46
Cumbria – The Lake District	58
Northumbria	96
Yorkshire	120
Heart of England	160
East Midlands	186
East of England	214
South East England	252
South West England	292

Enjoy England official guides to **quality**

welcome
to the new and fully updated edition of the **Enjoy England** guide to self-catering accommodation

The guide that gives you more
This Enjoy England guide is packed with information from where to stay, to how to get there and what to do. In fact, everything you need to know to Enjoy England.

Quality accommodation
Choose from a wide choice of quality-assured accommodation to suit all budgets and tastes. This guide contains an exclusive listing of all self-catering and boat accommodation participating in VisitBritain's National Quality Assurance Standard.

Visitor attractions
Ideas for places to visit, highlighting those receiving our quality assurance marque, are detailed in each regional section.

Tourist Information Centres
For local information call a Tourist Information Centre. Telephone numbers are shown in the blue bands next to the place names in accommodation entries.

Guides and maps
We list free and saleable tourism publications available from regional tourism organisations.

Finding accommodation is easy
Regional listings
The guide is divided into 10 regional areas, and accommodation is listed alphabetically by place name within each region. Additionally ALL VisitBritain assessed self-catering and boat accommodation is listed in the back of the guide.

Colour maps
Use the colour maps, starting on page 22, to find the location of all accommodation featured in the regional sections. Then refer to the town index at the back of the guide to find the page number. The index also includes tourism areas such as the New Forest or the Cotswolds.

The official guide to quality self-catering accommodation in **England**.

Left The Olde Rectory, Whitbourne **Right, from top** Snape Maltings, Snape; take a stroll by the river in Ross-on-Wye

Enjoy England official guides to quality

A great choice of quality-rated accommodation

In this new, fully updated Enjoy England guide, you'll find details of every accommodation establishment in England that has been quality assessed by VisitBritain's own assessors under the National Quality Assurance Standard.

This scheme covers nearly every type of accommodation and on these pages we give you a taste of the quality and variety to be found in this guide.

Our professional assessors visit each establishment unannounced and on at least an annual basis. Wherever appropriate to the accommodation type they stay overnight and thoroughly test the food and hospitality.

In the regional sections you'll find either standard or enhanced accommodation entries (see page 734) for which properties have paid and have supplied details such as descriptions and prices.

You'll also find lots of ideas for short breaks and longer stays whatever your tastes, interests and budget – and you can book in confidence knowing that your accommodation has been thoroughly checked and rated for quality before you make your booking.

Left Clippesby Hall, Clippesby **Right, from top** Brunt Knott Farm Holiday Cottages, Staveley; Old Brantrake, Eskdale; Bosinver Farm Cottages, St Austell

You'll find over **10,000** places to stay, all quality assessed.

Enjoy England official guides to quality

Ratings and awards – your reliable guide to quality

Reliable, rigorous, easy to use – VisitBritain's ratings and awards system will help you choose with confidence. All the accommodation in this guide has been assessed and awarded a rating for quality by VisitBritain, so you can be sure that the accommodation you choose will meet your expectations. Visitor attractions can also receive a special quality marque.

These are the ratings and awards to look for:

Star ratings
Establishments are awarded a rating of one to five stars based on a combination of quality of facilities and services provided. VisitBritain has over 50 trained assessors who visit properties every year, generally on a day visit arranged in advance with the owner.

They award ratings based on the overall level of quality and ensure that all requirements are met. There are strict guidelines to ensure every property is assessed to the same criteria. High standards of cleanliness are a major requirement; heating, lighting, comfort and convenience are also part of the assessment.

National Accessible Scheme
Establishments with a National Accessible rating provide access and facilities for guests with visual, hearing and mobility impairment (see page 10).

Enjoy England Excellence Awards
The Oscars of the English tourism industry, these awards are run by VisitBritain in association with England's regional tourism organisations. There are 10 categories including Self-Catering Holiday of the Year (see page 19).

Visitor Attraction Quality Assurance
To receive this award, attractions must achieve high standards in all aspects of the visitor experience, from initial telephone enquiries to departure, customer services to catering, as well as all facilities and activities. All participating attractions are visited every year by trained assessors.

Above Blaize Cottages, Lavenham **Right** The Olde Rectory, Whitbourne

One to five stars

The star ratings reflect the quality that you're looking for when booking accommodation. All properties have to meet an extensive list of minimum requirements to take part in the scheme. From there, increased levels of quality apply.

The more stars, the higher the overall level of quality you can expect. Establishments at higher rating levels also have to meet additional requirements for facilities.

The brief explanation of the star ratings for self-catering accommodation outlined below shows what is included at each rating level (note that each rating also includes what is provided at a lower star rating).

★ An acceptable overall level of quality with adequate furniture, furnishings and fittings.

★★ A good overall level of quality. All units are self-contained.

★★★ A good to very good overall level of quality with good standards of maintenance and decoration. Ample space and good-quality furniture. All double beds have access from both sides. Microwave.

★★★★ An excellent overall level of quality with very good care and attention to detail throughout. Access to a washing machine and drier if it is not provided in the unit, or a 24-hour laundry service.

★★★★★ An exceptional overall level of quality with high levels of décor, fixtures and fittings, with personal touches. Excellent standards of management efficiency and guest services.

Many self-catering establishments have a range of accommodation units in the building or on the site, and in some cases the individual units may have different star ratings. In such cases, the entry shows the range available.

Further information about the standard, as well as details of the rating standard for boat accommodation, can be found at the back of this guide.

When you're looking for a place to stay, you need a rating system you can trust.

VisitBritain's ratings give a clear guide to what to expect, in an easy-to-understand form. Properties are visited annually by trained, impartial assessors, so you can be confident that your accommodation has been thoroughly checked and rated for quality before you make your booking.

Enjoy England official guides to **quality**

VisitBritain's National Accessible Scheme

VisitBritain's National Accessible Scheme for accommodation includes standards for hearing and visually impaired guests in addition to standards for guests with mobility impairment.

Accommodation taking part in the National Accessible Scheme include appropriate symbols (as shown opposite) in their guide entry. See the index at the back of the guide for a full list of self-catering accommodation which has received the National Accessible rating.

VisitBritain has a variety of accessible accommodation in its scheme, and the different accessible ratings will help you choose the one that best suits your needs.

When you see one of the symbols, you can be sure that the accommodation has been thoroughly assessed against demanding criteria. If you have additional needs or special requirements we strongly recommend that you make sure these can be met by your chosen establishment before you confirm your booking.

The criteria VisitBritain and national and regional tourism organisations have adopted do not necessarily conform to British Standards or to Building Regulations. They reflect what the organisations understand to be acceptable to meet the practical needs of guests with mobility or sensory impairments.

National Accessible Scheme ratings are also shown on the full list of establishments at the back of this guide.

All accommodation is **assessed** against demanding criteria.

Left Stonecroft and Swallows Nest, Cockfield **Right, from top** Forge Mill Farm Cottages, Middlewich; Cliff Farm Cottage, Lincoln

Access symbols

Mobility
LEVEL 1 – Typically suitable for a person with sufficient mobility to climb a flight of steps but who would benefit from fixtures and fittings to aid balance.

LEVEL 2 – Typically suitable for a person with restricted walking ability and for those who may need to use a wheelchair some of the time.

LEVEL 3 – Typically suitable for a person who depends on the use of a wheelchair and transfers unaided to and from the wheelchair in a seated position.

LEVEL 4 – Typically suitable for a person who depends on the use of a wheelchair in a seated position. They can require personal/mechanical assistance to aid transfer (eg carer, hoist).

Hearing Impairment
LEVEL 1 – Minimum entry requirements to meet the National Accessible Standards for guests with hearing impairment, from mild hearing loss to profoundly deaf.

LEVEL 2 – Recommended (Best Practice) additional requirements to meet the National Accessible Standards for guests with hearing impairment, from mild hearing loss to profoundly deaf.

Visual Impairment

LEVEL 1 – Minimum entry requirements to meet the National Accessible Standards for visually impaired guests.

LEVEL 2 – Recommended (Best Practice) additional requirements to meet the National Accessible Standards for visually impaired guests.

The National Accessible Scheme forms part of the Tourism for All Campaign that is being promoted by VisitBritain and national and regional tourism organisations. Additional help and guidance on finding suitable holiday accommodation for those with special needs can be obtained from:

**Tourism for All UK
(formerly Holiday Care Service)
Hawkins Suite, Enham Place,
Enham Alamein, Andover,
Hampshire SP11 6JS**

Admin/consultancy: 0845 124 9974
Information helpline: 0845 124 9971
(9-5 Mon, Tue and 9-1 Wed-Fri)
Reservation/Friends: 0845 124 9973
Fax: 0845 124 9972
Minicom: 0845 124 9976
Email: info@holidaycare.org
Web: www.tourismforall.info

How do we arrive at a star rating?

VisitBritain has more than 50 trained assessors throughout England who visit properties annually, generally on a day visit arranged in advance with the owner.

They award ratings based on the overall level of quality and ensure that all requirements are met. There are strict guidelines to ensure every property is assessed to the same criteria. High standards of cleanliness are a major requirement; heating, lighting, comfort and convenience are also part of the assessment.

The assessor's role

An assessor takes into account everything a guest will experience. This includes:

- how the initial enquiry is dealt with
- the brochure or information supplied
- the arrival procedure
- help and contact for guests during their stay
- the quality of the accommodation and facilities.

In fact all aspects which contribute to the overall comfort and convenience for guests who may hire the property for a holiday or short break. During their visit assessors will take into consideration the quality and condition of all the fixtures and fittings. Most importantly excellent standards of cleanliness are noted.

Personal touches which give a homely and welcoming feeling are encouraged. Spaciousness and convenience of use is also part of the assessment, related to the number of people who can be accommodated. The quality of information provided about places to visit, where to eat and how to operate equipment is all taken into account. To attract the highest star rating everything must be of an exceptional standard, both inside and outside the property.

At the end of the visit the assessor will advise the owner of the star rating they have awarded, discussing the reasons why, as well as suggesting areas for improvement. So you can see it's a very thorough process to ensure that when you book accommodation with a particular star rating you can be confident it will meet your expectations. After all, meeting customer expectations is what makes happy guests.

Above, from left Middletown Farm Cottages, Upleadon; Old Brantrake, Eskdale Right Clippesby Hall, Clippesby

Accommodation entries explained

Each accommodation entry contains detailed information to help you decide if it is right for you. This information has been provided by the proprietors themselves, and our aim has been to ensure that it is as objective and factual as possible. To the left of the establishment name you will find the star rating.

At-a-glance symbols at the end of each entry give you additional information on services and facilities – a key can be found on the back cover flap. Keep this open to refer to as you read.

Trained VisitBritain **assessors** visit properties annually.

Sample enhanced entry

1. Listing under town or village with map reference
2. VisitBritain star rating
3. Number of units and how many they sleep
4. Accessible rating where applicable
5. Colour picture for enhanced entries
6. Description
7. At-a-glance facility symbols
8. Establishment name, postal town and booking details
9. Prices per unit per week for low and high season
10. Indicates when the establishment is open and payment accepted
11. Special promotions (enhanced entries only)

Enjoy England official guides to **quality**

13

Inspiring ideas for a short break

Relax and unwind. Go on! You owe it to **yourself**.

Give the humdrum the heave-ho with a break in one of these distinctive holiday homes. From love nests for two to country manors for 25, you'll find plenty of ideas for a break with a difference. Many places have special short-stay promotions and weekend deals too, perfect for last-minute escapes – look out for more offers, highlighted in red in the guide.

Be a sport

Sporty types will love an active break. Practise your swing on a golf break at **Rogue's and Rascal's Barn,** Sheringham, playing at the nearby Sheringham and Royal Cromer courses. **Romsey Oak Cottages,** Wingfield, offers special deals for tennis breaks with professional coaching. Try coarse fishing on the private lake at the **Cyder House and Cheese House,** Lacock, or fly-fishing on the river Dove in the Peak District National Park at **Dove Cottage,** Alstonefield.

Art for art's sake

Have a go at photography, watercolours, mosaics, cartooning and lots more in Devon – **Lower Campscott Farm,** Lee, and **Widmouth Farm,** Ilfracombe, have joined forces to provide a wide range of creative courses with expert tuition. At **Shatton Hall Farm,** Bamford in the Peak District, courses include Art in Nature, working in and out of the studio with two local artists. At **Brentwood Farm Cottages,** Burton-in-Lansdale, the traditional skills of hedge laying and walling are surprisingly relaxing.

Romantic retreats

Re-kindle the old spark on a break somewhere really special. **The Grove,** Lavenham, is an oasis of calm with eight cottages furnished in a bohemian style with antiques, original art and contemporary touches. In idyllic Exmoor National Park, **Royal Castle Lodge,** Lynton, a picturesque thatched Swiss chalet style cottage, is the perfect hideaway for two. Romance and small children don't usually mix, but the **Garden Flat, Ramsey House,** Salisbury, has the solution. The owner of this glamorous haven of stylish vintage furniture, chandeliers and Venetian mirrors offers a baby-sitting service too. Breaks at elegant Georgian townhouse **19a Lindum Hill,** Lincoln, include a welcome hamper with champagne and chocolates. Get away from it all at peaceful **Blaize Cottages,** Lavenham, equipped with a welcoming fire and romantic CDs and DVDs.

Great getaways

You don't always have to stay a whole week – bargain short breaks are often available, especially at the last minute and in the autumn and winter. For reduced-rate, short-stay breaks and stand-by weekend deals, try **Apartment 5,** Burgh Island Causeway, Bigbury-on-Sea, right on the beach, or the typical Cornish stone and slate cottages at **The Laurels Holiday Park** in Padstow and **The Schoolhouse,** Cambridge, a charming early Victorian villa just three miles from the city centre. Short breaks at **Cruck and Wolfscote Cottages,** Hartington, include a farm and nature trail through unspoilt Peak District landscapes.

Big is beautiful

Looking for somewhere big enough for a family celebration or an old friends' reunion? **The Manor House,** St Issey, sleeps up to 25 people and offers a great choice of activities, from surf dude weekends to canoeing, cycling and rock climbing, all with highly qualified, licensed instructors. The five cottages at **Mayrose Farm,** Helstone, also sleep 25 and you'll have exclusive use of the outdoor heated swimming pool too.

Left, from top Blaize Cottages, Lavenham; Mayrose Farm, Helstone; Rogue's and Rascal's Barn, Sheringham; Shatton Hall Farm, Bamford

Enjoy England official guides to quality

Lakelovers

For the ultimate in Lakeland holidays, Lakelovers have it all, from traditional farmhouses sleeping up to 14 steeped in character, to luxury modern apartments sleeping 2, complete with private tennis facilities. Over 200 retreats to choose from. We pride ourselves on hand picking individual properties equipped to the highest standard to suit every taste and pocket. We include FREE leisure club membership with every holiday. Short breaks also available.

Belmont House, Lake Road, Bowness-on-Windermere, Cumbria LA23 3BJ
t: 015394 88855   f: 015394 88857   e: bookings@lakelovers.co.uk   www.lakelovers.co.uk

---

TAKE A
cottage
WITH
BEAMS
IN A
village
NEAR THE
SEA

DISCOVER the hidden beauty of England, Wales and Scotland from the comfort and charm of a Hoseasons Country Cottage.

Some have beams and thatch, others indoor pools and games rooms and every one is a well equipped home from home. Choose from a fisherman's cottage by the sea to a converted farmhouse in the heart of the countryside. Our colour brochure offers over 1600 delightful cottages, many of which welcome pets.

Send for your free copy.

CALL 0870 902 3112
Quote: C0017 or book online at
www.hoseasons.co.uk

Hoseasons
Country Cottages

Best of both worlds –
South Coast and New Forest

Both of our self-catering holiday parks are set in peaceful, unspoilt parkland in the beautiful South Coast area.

There are comprehensive leisure facilities available and great entertainment for the whole family.

Pamper yourself in our new 'Reflections' Day Spa at Shorefield Country Park or explore Britain's latest National Park - the New Forest.

For a really memorable family holiday

For full details, ask for our brochure or browse on-line.

01590 648331
e-mail: holidays@shorefield.co.uk

Shorefield Country Park
Shorefield Road, Milford on Sea, Hampshire SO41 0LH

Oakdene Forest Park
St. Leonards, Ringwood, Hampshire BH24 2RZ

Ref. WTS

www.shorefield.co.uk

Follow the **stars** for the assurance of a rating system you know you can trust

During 2003/4 VisitBritain introduced new Quality Assurance Standards for water-based accommodation. These standards, covering Cruisers, Narrow Boats and Hotel Boats, have been developed to give customers the re-assurance that real efforts have been made to set, maintain and improve standards in boat accommodation, not only in terms of fixtures and fittings but also in areas such as cleanliness, comfort, hospitality, efficiency and service provided.

Craft are assessed annually by trained, impartial assessors, so you can be confident that your accommodation has been thoroughly checked and rated before you make a booking.

Look out for the star ratings

VisitBritain star ratings will give you a clear and trustworthy guide as to what you can expect. Five grades of award reflect the range of quality standards and facilities provided by a craft and they are indicated by a simple one to five stars system. The final rating is awarded after assessing a combination of facilities and the overall quality of the accommodation – so the more stars, the higher the overall level of quality and comfort you can expect.

For more information and to find out which operators have attained a quality rating, look on:
www.waterwayholidaysuk.com

enjoyEngland™
Excellence Awards

Enjoy England Excellence Awards are all about blowing English tourism's trumpet and telling the world what a fantastic place England is to visit, whether it's for a day trip, a weekend break or a fortnight's holiday.

The Awards, now in their 6th year, are run by Enjoy England in association with England's regional tourism organisations. This year there are 10 categories including Self-Catering Holiday of the Year, Visitor Attraction of the Year, and an award for the best tourism website.

The winners of the 2004 Self-Catering Holiday of the Year Award are:

- **Gold winner:**
  The Thatched Cottage Company,
  Otterton, Devon
- **Silver winners:**
  Wolfen Mill Country Retreats, Lancashire
  Shoreline Cottages, Leeds

Winners of the 2005 awards will receive their trophies at a ceremony on 19 April 2005. The day will celebrate excellence in tourism in England.

For more information about the Enjoy England Excellence Awards visit www.visitengland.com

Right, from top The Thatched Cottage Company receiving their award from HRH The Duke of Kent; Shoreline Cottages, Leeds

Follow the stars...

and wake up with a different view each morning!

Hire a country cottage that moves.

Self drive hire boats from the quality operators listed in this guide are all tourist board assessed just like cottages, so you can be sure of quality accommodation and service. Modern boats have all the facilities of a cottage – comfortable beds, cookers, fridges, tv's, central heating and often more.

Why not try self catering with a difference – hire a boat on Britain's unique, restful and attractive waterways. It really is the fastest way of slowing down and getting away from the roads and motorways. Get close to nature. See the wildlife at first hand. Enjoy the heritage, the scenery, the country villages and pubs! Work the locks, travel the tunnels and aqueducts, and enjoy the most peaceful holiday you have ever had!

★★★★ CRUISER

★★★★ NARROW BOAT

Freedom Holiday Homes

Self-catering accommodation throughout Kent & East Sussex

Enjoy the freedom of choice with our superb range of quality self-catering holiday accommodation in cottages, barn conversions, granaries, Oast Houses and apartments throughout the beautiful counties of Kent and East Sussex.

Our friendly, professional staff who have extensive local knowledge can offer something for everyone: – hidden attractions, rich heritage, National Trust properties, castles and beautiful gardens. Rural or coastal locations.

Some pet-friendly properties. All are VisitBritain graded. Mini-breaks as well as longer stays available out of season – subject to availability. Rentals from £140pw - £1200pw.

**15 High Street, Cranbrook, Kent, TN17 3EB   Tel: 01580 720770   Fax: 01580 720771
Email: mail@freedomholidayhomes.co.uk   www.freedomholidayhomes.co.uk**

WE OFFER THE *widest choice* OF HOLIDAY COTTAGES, INCLUDING THE *ideal one* FOR YOU

There's nothing quite like a cottage holiday in Britain, and there's no better way to enjoy one than with Country Holidays.

With over 4,000 VisitBritain graded cottages throughout the UK, you're sure to find the ideal one for you. And as many of our properties also accept pets none of your family need miss out. For only £20 per pet per week or short break you can save yourself the hassle and expense of boarding fees too.

With many properties also available for 2, 3 or 4 night short breaks, Country Holidays offers the perfect way to escape at any time of year.

So whether you want to stay in a fisherman's cottage by the sea, or a converted barn in the heart of the countryside, Country Holidays offers all the choice you need.

Look & book:
www.country-holidays.co.uk

For your free copy of our 2005 brochure call:
0870 336 7226

Country Holidays
BRITAIN'S FAVOURITE COTTAGE HOLIDAYS

MAP 1

Location Maps

Every place name featured in the regional accommodation sections of this Enjoy England guide has a map reference to help you locate it on the maps which follow. For example, to find Colchester, Essex, which has 'Map ref 3B2', turn to Map 3 and refer to grid square B2.

All place names appearing in the regional sections are shown in black type on the maps. This enables you to find other places in your chosen area which may have suitable accommodation – the town index (at the back of this guide) gives page numbers.

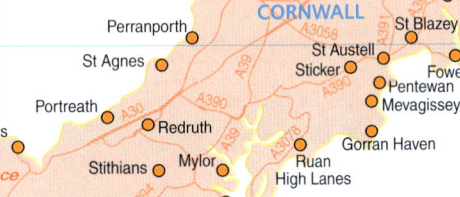

Key to regions: South West England

MAP 1

All place names in black offer accommodation in this guide.

MAP 2

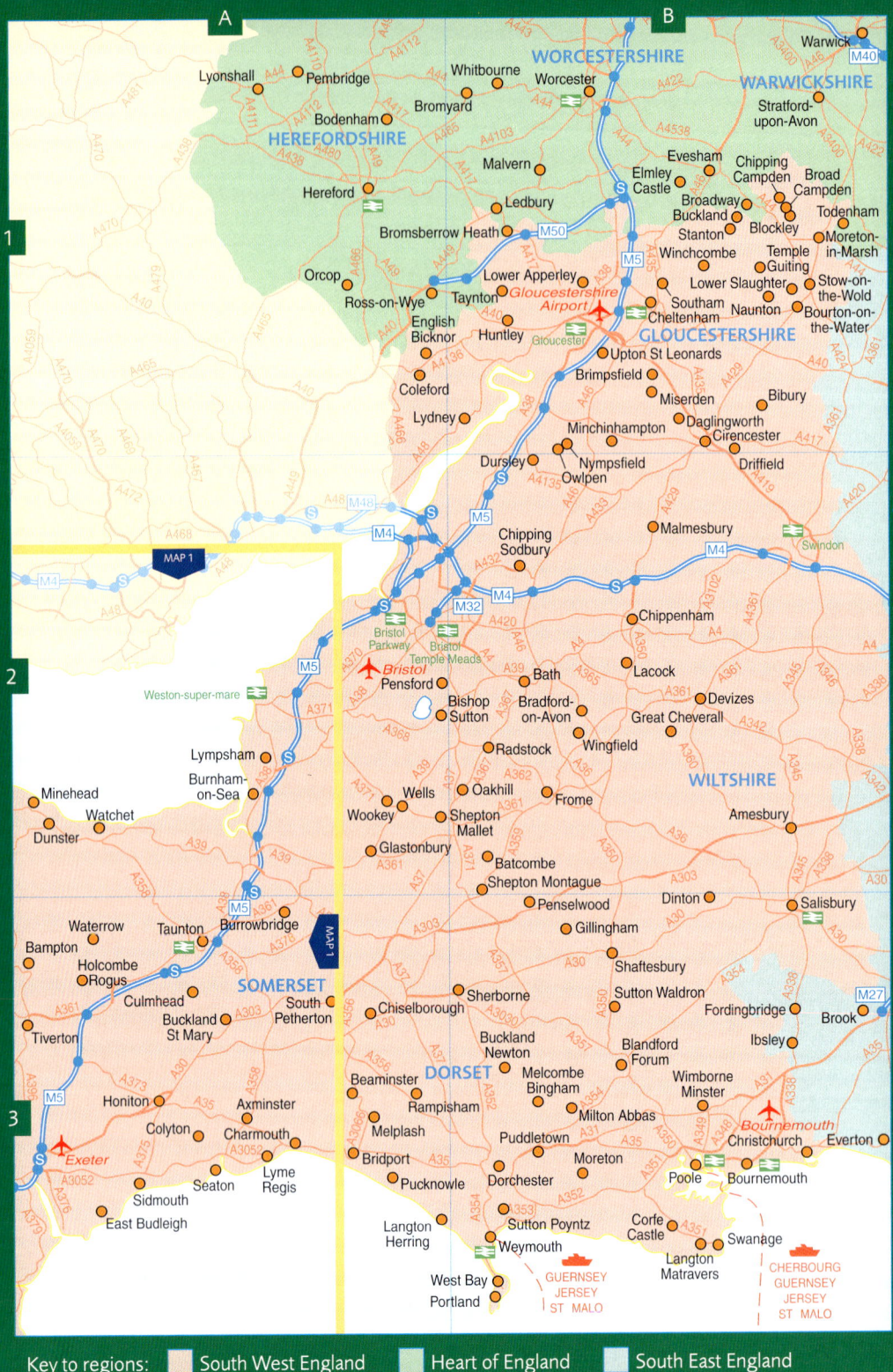

Key to regions: South West England | Heart of England | South East England

MAP 2

MAP 3

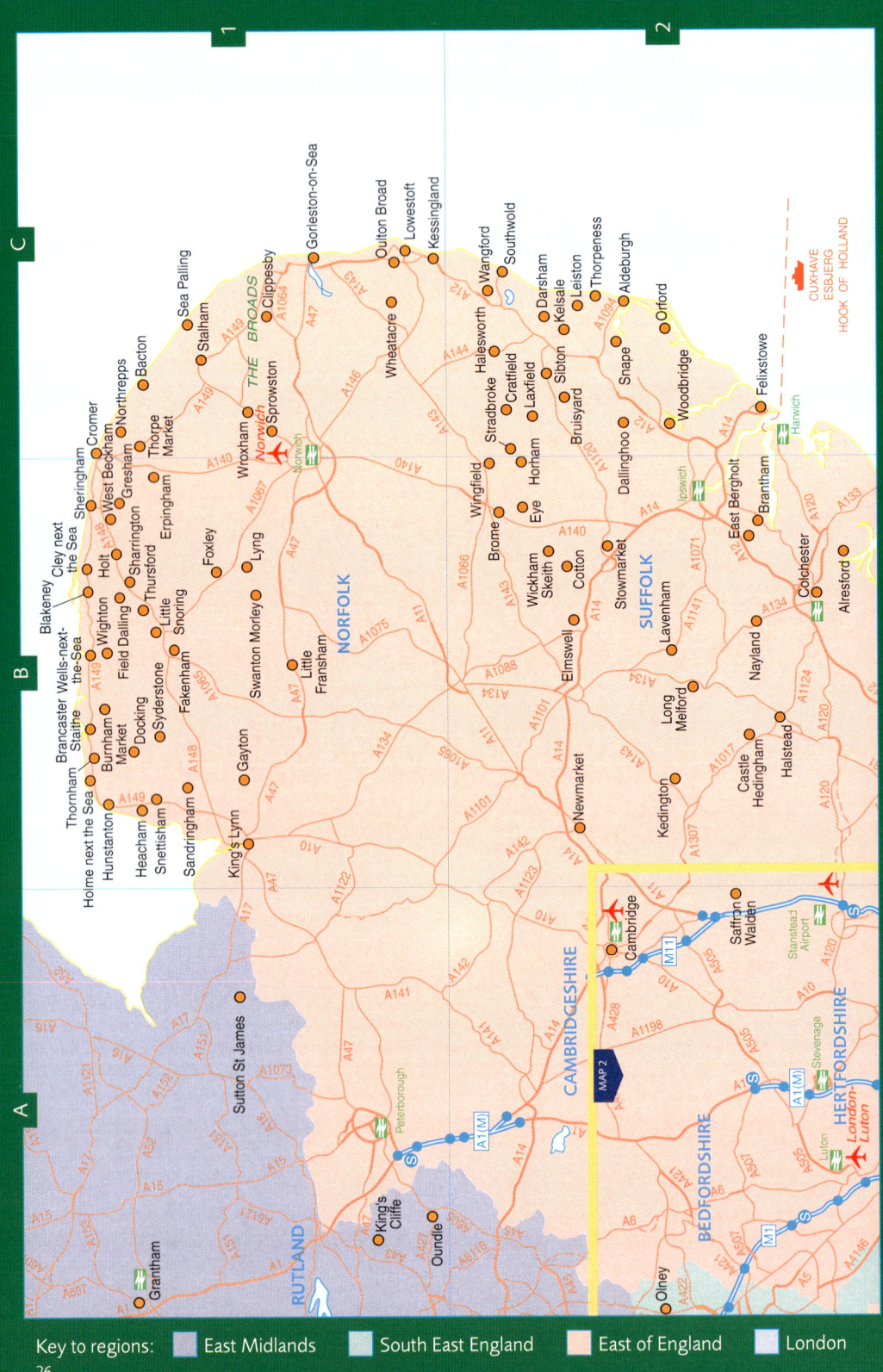

Key to regions: East Midlands | South East England | East of England | London

26

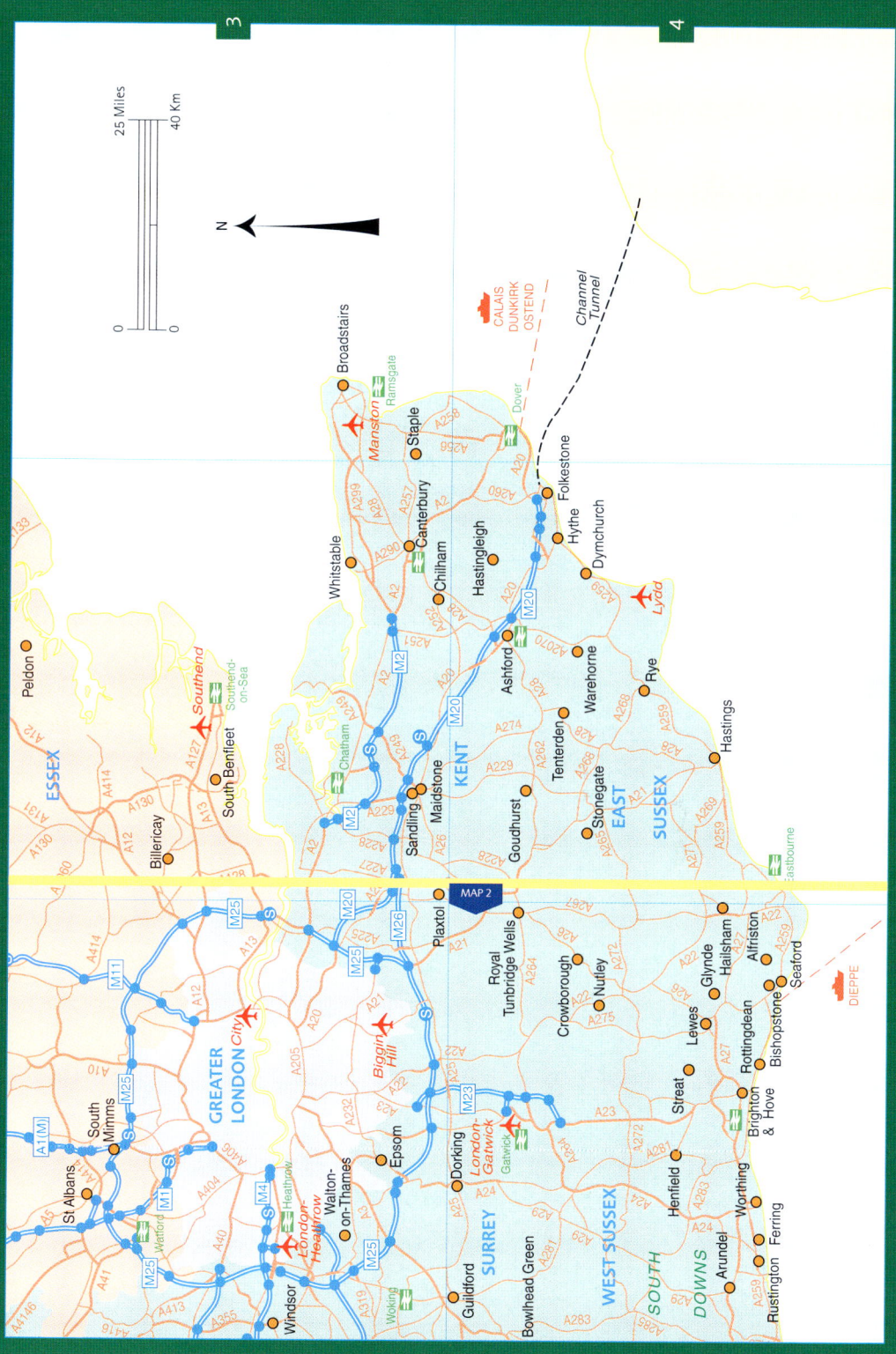

MAP 3

All place names in black offer accommodation in this guide.

MAP 4

Key to regions: Heart of England | England's Northwest including Cumbria | Yorkshire | East Midlands

MAP 4

East of England
All place names in black offer accommodation in this guide.

MAP 5

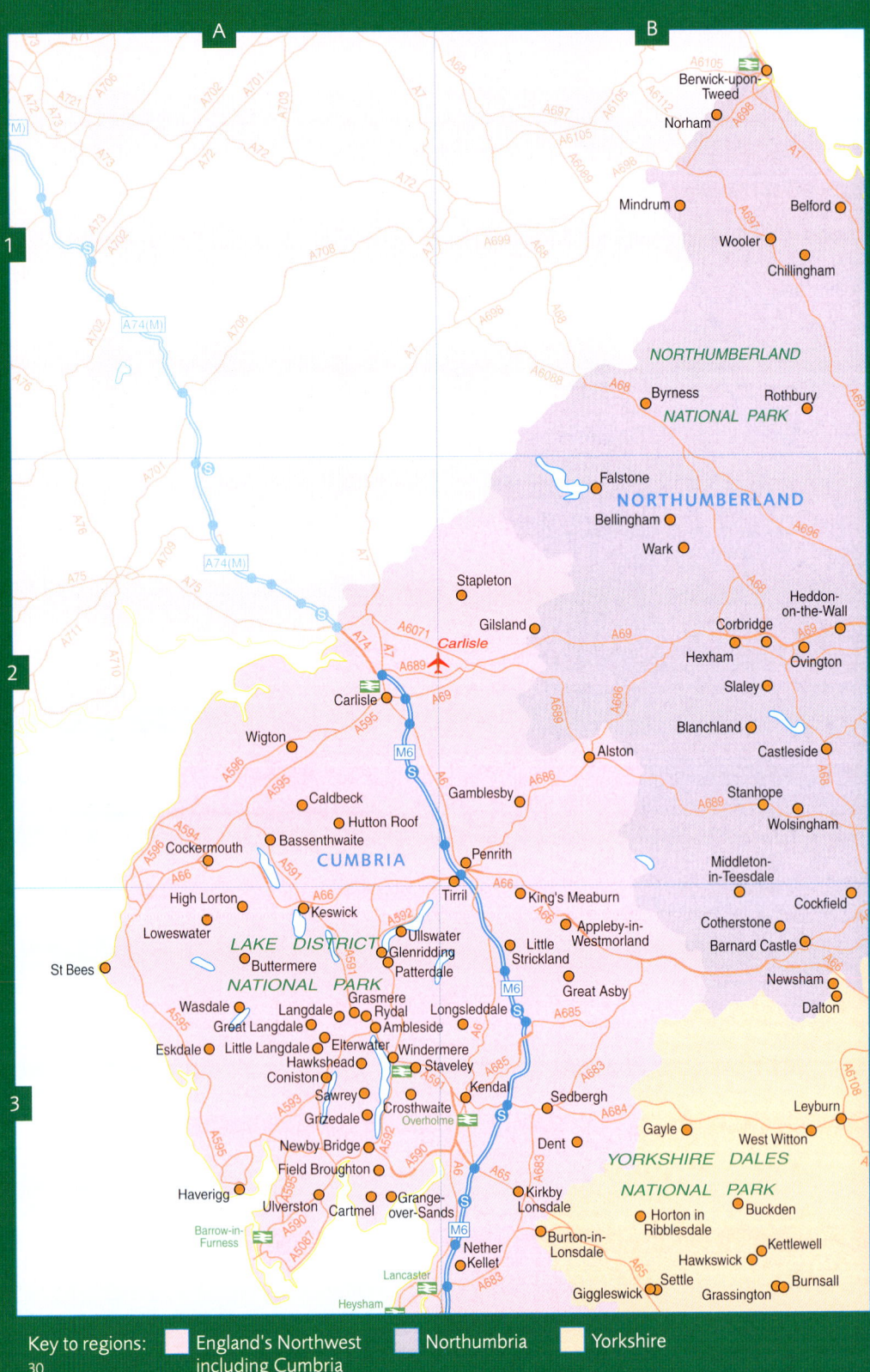

Key to regions: England's Northwest including Cumbria | Northumbria | Yorkshire

30

MAP 6

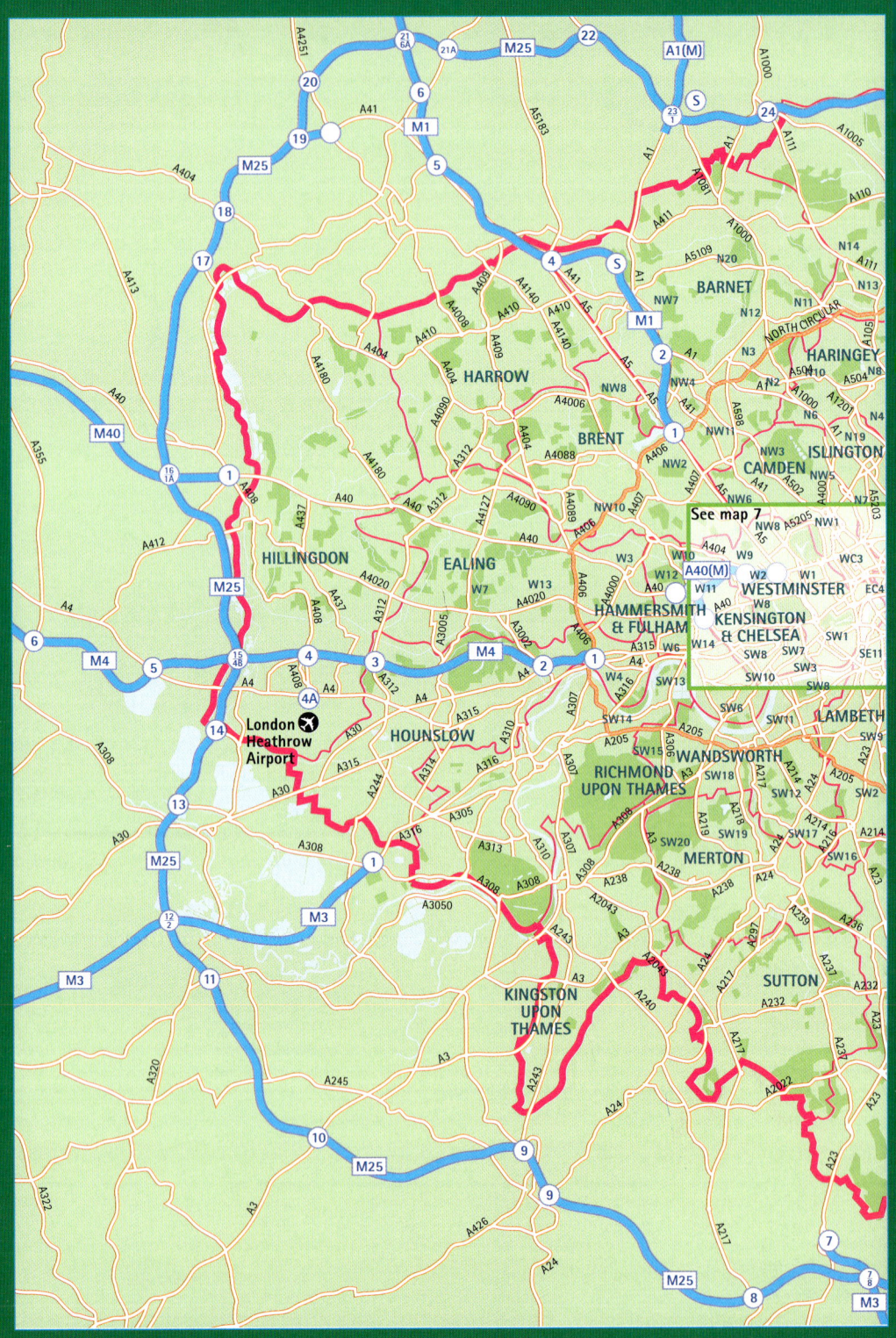

MAP 6

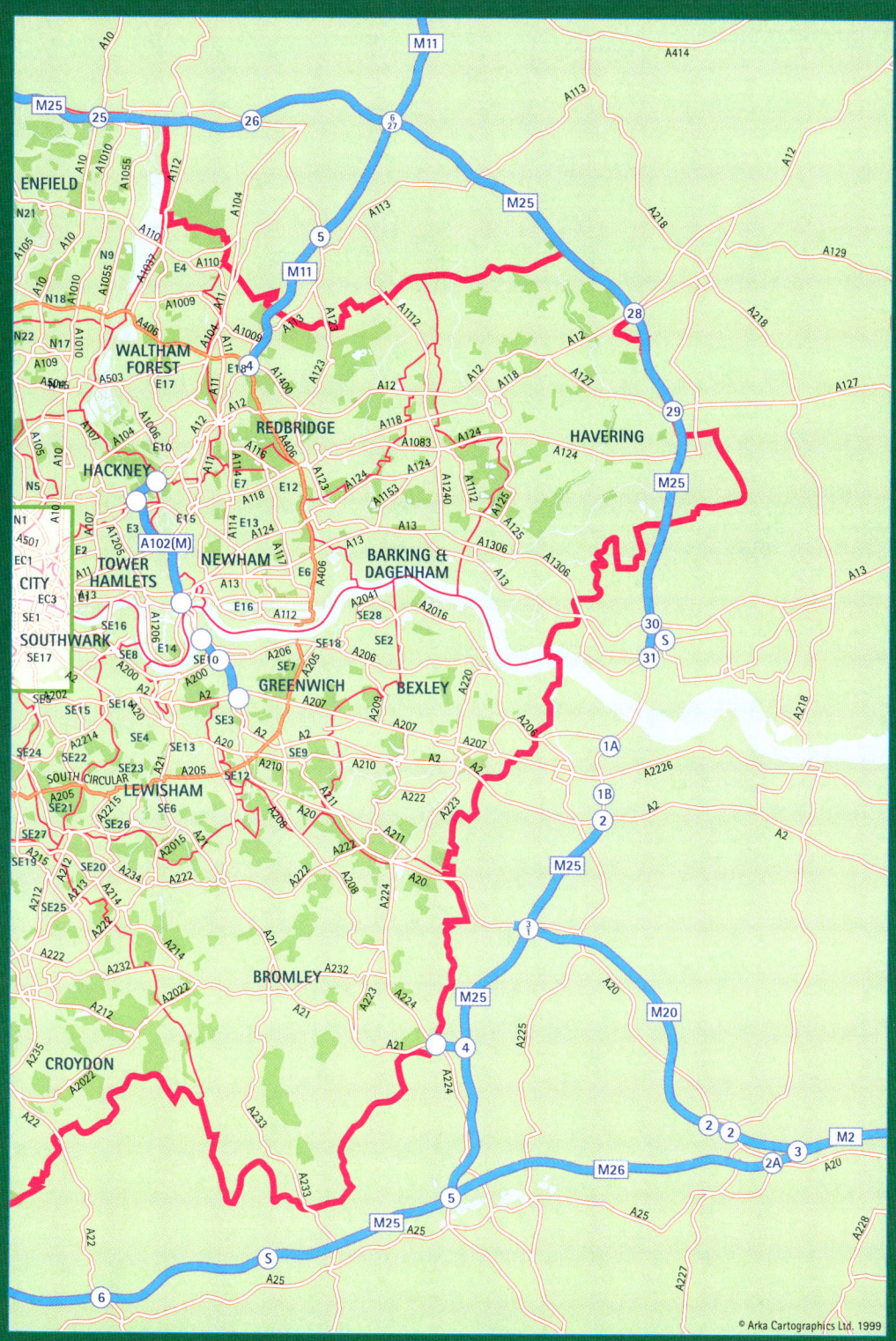

33

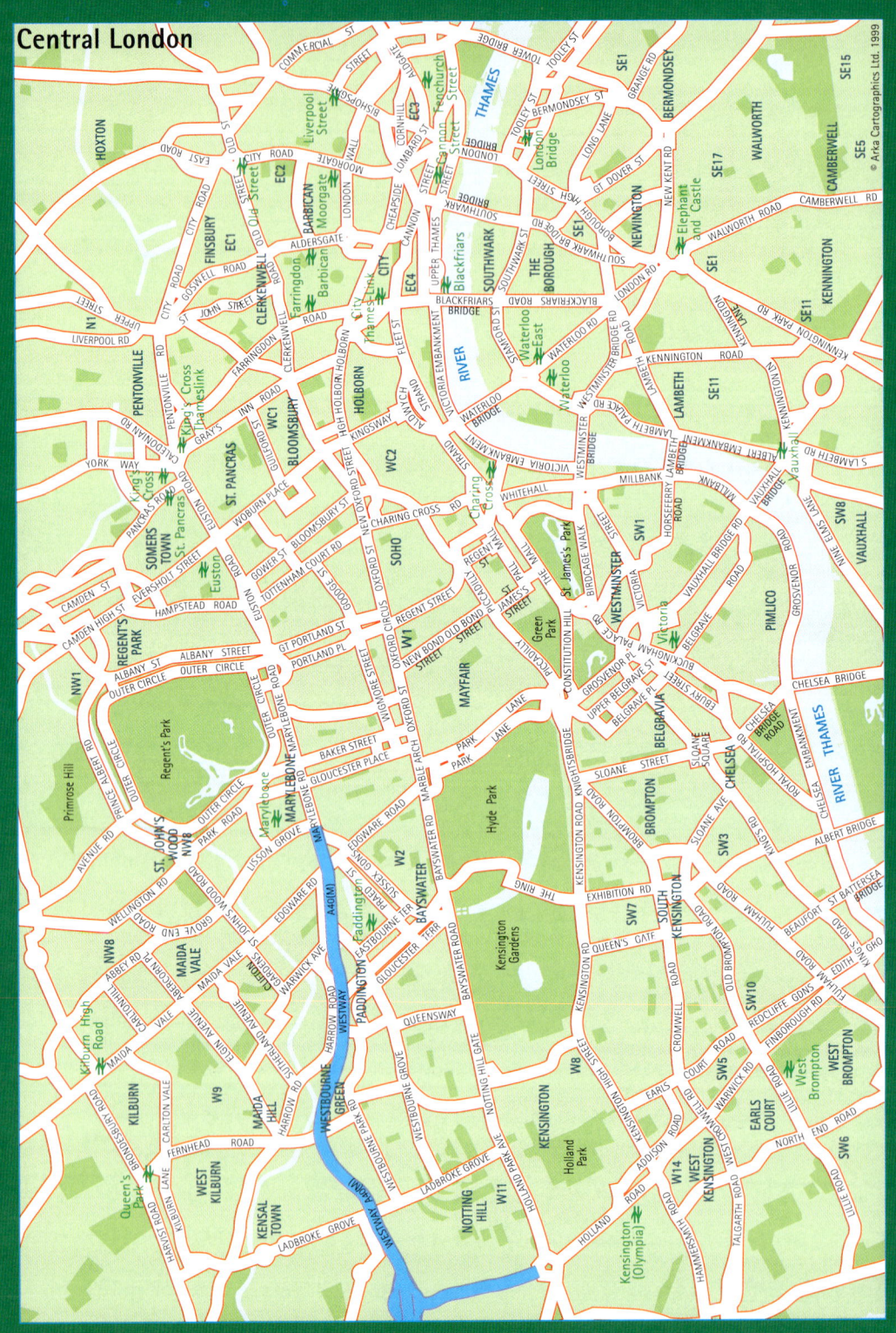

Finding **accommodation**
is as easy as **1 2 3**

Enjoy England official guides to quality accommodation make it quick and easy to find a place to stay. There are several ways to use this guide.

1 TOWN INDEX
The town index at the back lists all the places with accommodation featured in the regional sections. The index gives a page number where you can find full accommodation and contact details.

2 COLOUR MAPS
All the place names in black on the colour maps at the front have an entry in the regional sections. Refer to the town index for the page number where you will find one or more establishments offering accommodation in your chosen town or village.

3 ACCOMMODATION LISTING
Contact details for all VisitBritain assessed accommodation throughout England, together with their national star rating are given in the listing section of this guide. Establishments with a full entry in the regional sections are shown in blue. Look in the town index for the page number on which their full entry appears.

London is a **unique mix** of historical and contemporary. There's always something new and **exciting** to experience.

London

Looking for some inspiration? Here are a few ideas to get you started in London. **experience** Dragon Boat racing – 20 people, a 40-foot-long boat and a drummer. **discover** your artistic side in five new suites at the Victoria & Albert Museum. **explore** the Thames by bike, on foot or on a barge. **relax** on a 40-minute trip around Kew Gardens on the Kew Explorer.

THE REGION
Greater London, comprising the 32 London Boroughs

CONTACT
▶ VISIT LONDON
6th Floor, 2 More London Riverside,
London SE1 2RR
T: (020) 7234 5800
F: (020) 7378 6525
www.visitlondon.com

LONDON

One of the most dynamic and cosmopolitan cities in the world, London is a unique mix of the historical and the contemporary. Enjoy the peace of the many parks, or soak up the buzz and bustle of the busy West End. There's always something new and exciting to experience.

Park life

London's parks and gardens are an oasis of pleasure. Delight in regal Regent's Park and watch a play in the open-air theatre; go swimming on tranquil Hampstead Heath; or play a round of golf in rolling Richmond Park.

For more outdoor entertainment get tickets for Shakespeare's Globe near Southwark Bridge. Audiences at this theatre sit in a gallery or stand in the yard, just as they did 400 years ago. Royal connections are everywhere and Clarence House – the London residence of the Prince of Wales – recently opened to the public for the first time.

Culture capital

Get a flavour of London's opulence in the private rooms of Burlington House. Restored to their original 18th-century glory, they house some of the Royal Academy's finest works. More paintings and art can be viewed at the Hayward Gallery and Barbican, and at the Saatchi Gallery on the South Bank. The Thames is inextricably linked with London's fortunes and you can discover its dramatic 2000-year history at the newly opened Museum in Docklands. Also new is the UK's first Fashion and Textile Museum, dedicated to contemporary works.

Follow the thread, and take in the Vivienne Westwood exhibition at the V&A. If you enjoy classical music, the Handel House Museum celebrates Handel's life and works in his finely restored house at 25 Brook Street.

Lucky dip

For two weeks every summer tennis fever takes hold as Wimbledon hosts the world's most famous tournament. When the covers go back on, you can still enjoy a taste of the action at the Wimbledon Lawn Tennis Museum. Turn your attention to shopping, and you'll find London hits the mark – from Harrods, with its famous food hall, to major new developments at Kingly Court and Duke of York Square. And if you enjoy fine dining with plenty of variety, there really is no better place. Every taste is catered for: from Japanese to Russian, and from restaurants run for the stars – like the fashionable Ivy – to those run by the stars, like Jamie Oliver's Fifteen.

Getting around

Travel in London is easy as the city has a massive transport network: Underground trains, buses, taxis, riverboats and trams, as well as connections to national rail services. Whether touring the sights in the centre of town or exploring areas at the edge of the city, you'll find yourself within easy distance of transport links.

Left, from top set your watch by Big Ben; journey towards Buckingham Palace; share in the excitement of the capital at Trafalgar Square **Right** Yeoman Warder stands guard

Enjoy England official guides to quality

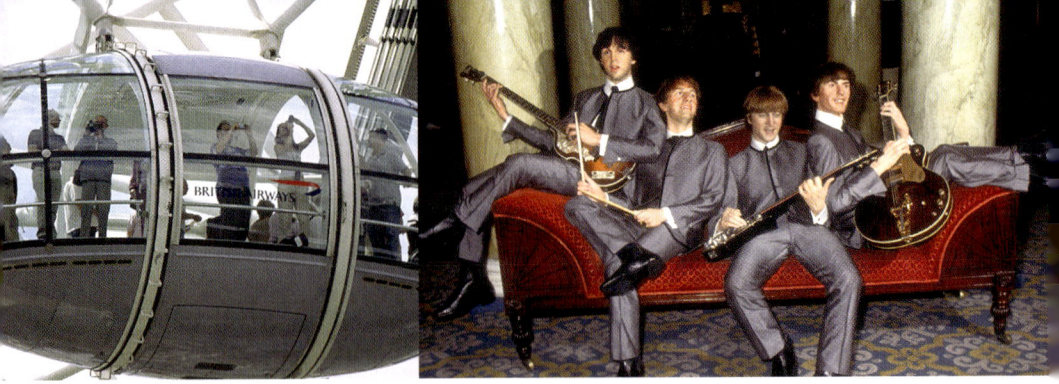

Places to visit

 Awarded VisitBritain's Quality Assured Visitor Attraction marque.

Bank of England Museum
Threadneedle Street, EC2R 8AH
Tel: (020) 7601 5491
www.bankofengland.co.uk/museum
Marvel at ancient gold bars, historic bank notes and documents belonging to famous, past customers like Horatio Nelson and George Washington – just a few of the exhibits in the nation's central bank.

BBC Television Centre Tours
BBC Television Centre, Wood Lane, W12 7RJ
Tel: 0870 603 0304
www.bbc.co.uk/tours
Go behind the scenes at the BBC. Your tour will be planned around what is happening on the day, and may include the News Centre, dressing rooms and studios.

British Airways London Eye
Jubilee Gardens, South Bank, SE1 7PB
Tel: 0870 500 0600
www.ba-londoneye.com
From your glass pod on the world's largest observation wheel you'll enjoy the most spectacular views of London – see over 55 famous landmarks in just 30 minutes.

British Library
Euston Road, NW1 2OB
Tel: (020) 7412 7332
www.bl.uk
Visit the UK's national library and browse galleries displaying famous written and printed works, including the Magna Carta, Shakespeare's first folio and a da Vinci notebook.

The British Museum
Great Russell Street, WC1B 3DG
Tel: (020) 7323 8299
www.thebritishmuseum.ac.uk
One of the great museums of the world, showing the works of man from prehistoric to modern times with collections drawn from all over the globe.

Cabinet War Rooms
Clive Steps, King Charles Street, SW1A 2AQ
Tel: (020) 7930 6961
www.iwm.org.uk
Experience the atmosphere in the underground headquarters used by Winston Churchill and the British Government during World War II. Includes Cabinet Room, Transatlantic Telephone Room and Map Room.

Hampton Court Palace
Hampton Court, East Molesey
Tel: 0870 752 7777
www.hrp.org.uk
Step back into history at the oldest Tudor palace in England. The many attractions include the State Apartments and King's Apartments, Tudor kitchens, tennis courts and maze.

Handel House Museum
Brook Street, W1K 4HB
Tel: (020) 7495 1685
www.handelhouse.org
Home to composer George Frideric Handel from 1723 until his death in 1759, the Museum celebrates his life with live music and special exhibitions in an evocative 18th century setting.

Imperial War Museum
Lambeth Road, SE1 6HZ
Tel: (020) 7416 5000
www.iwm.org.uk
This national museum is dedicated to the history of 20thC warfare, with exhibits ranging from tanks and aircraft to personal letters, plus films and sound recordings.

Kensington Palace State Apartments
Kensington Gardens, W8 4PX
Tel: 0870 751 5170
www.hrp.org.uk
Tread where royalty have passed and view the King's Apartment, magnificent Old Master paintings and the Royal Ceremonial Dress Collection, with dresses worn by the Queen and Princess Diana.

This is just a selection of attractions available. Contact any Tourist Information Centre in London for more ideas.

LONDON

Kew Gardens (Royal Botanic Gardens)
Kew, Richmond
Tel: (020) 8332 5655
www.kew.org
121-ha (300-acre) garden in a beautiful setting by the River Thames with stunning vistas, six magnificent glasshouses and over 30,000 plants from all over the world.

The London Dungeon
Tooley Street, SE1 2SZ
Tel: (020) 7403 7221
www.thedungeons.com
This historic horror experience is dead good fun! Descend into the dark Dungeon, relive the Great Fire of London, unmask Jack the Ripper and take the Boat ride to Hell.

London Wetland Centre
Queen Elizabeth's Walk, Barnes, SW13 9WT
Tel: (020) 8409 4400
www.wwt.org.uk
Spot hundreds of birds and other wildlife in this newly created nature reserve of over 40 ha (105 acres) of wetland habitats, developed on the site of disused Victorian reservoirs.

London Zoo
Regent's Park, NW1 4RY
Tel: (020) 7722 3333
www.londonzoo.co.uk
For an action-packed day out, why not escape the stress of city life and visit the amazing animals at the world-famous London Zoo.

London's Transport Museum
Covent Garden Piazza, WC2E 7BB
Tel: (020) 7379 6344
www.ltmuseum.co.uk
The history of transport for everyone, from spectacular vehicles, special exhibitions, actors and guided tours to film shows, gallery talks and children's craft workshops.

Madame Tussauds and the London Planetarium
Marylebone Road, NW1 5LR
Tel: 0870 400 3000
www.madame-tussauds.com
Come face-to-face with your heros in this world-famous collection of wax figures. Themed settings include The Garden Party, Superstars, The Grand Hall, The Chamber of Horrors and The Spirit of London.

Museum of London
London Wall, EC2Y 5HN
Tel: 0870 444 3851
www.museumoflondon.org.uk
Over 2000 years of London's history come alive here, with highlights including the Roman Gallery, Victorian shops, the Great Fire Experience and Elizabethan jewellery.

National Army Museum
Royal Hospital Road, Chelsea, SW3 4HT
Tel: (020) 7730 0717
www.national-army-museum.ac.uk
Learn the story of the British soldier in peace and war, through five centuries. Exhibits range from paintings to uniforms and from the English Civil War to Kosovo.

National Gallery
Trafalgar Square, WC2N 5DN
Tel: (020) 7747 2885
www.nationalgallery.org.uk
Observe stunning works by Botticelli, Leonardo da Vinci, Rembrandt, Gainsborough, Turner, Renoir, Cezanne and Van Gogh in this absorbing gallery, displaying Western European painting from about 1250 to 1900.

National Maritime Museum
Greenwich, SE10 9NF
Tel: (020) 8312 6565
www.nmm.ac.uk
Understand an island's seafaring heritage – Britain's world-wide influence explained through its explorers, traders, migrants and naval power. Features on ship models, costume, and ecology of the sea.

Natural History Museum
Cromwell Road, SW7 5BD
Tel: (020) 7942 5000
www.nhm.ac.uk
Discover the wonders of the natural world from 'Creepy-Crawlies' to dinosaurs, earthquakes to ecology, through hundreds of interactive exhibits.

Royal Air Force Museum Hendon
Grahame Park Way, Hendon, NW9 5LL
Tel: (020) 8205 2266
www.rafmuseum.org
Fly with the best on the Simulator ride! While waiting to take off, take in an amazing display; aircraft, film shows, interactives and more.

Royal Observatory Greenwich
Greenwich, SE10 9NF
Tel: (020) 8858 4422
www.nmm.ac.uk
Museum of time and space and site of the Greenwich Meridian. Working telescopes and planetarium, timeball, Wren's Octagon Room and intricate clocks and computer simulations.

The Saatchi Gallery
County Hall, South Bank, SE1 2SZ
Tel: (020) 7823 2363
www.saatchi-gallery.co.uk
Contemplate contemporary art from the famous Saatchi collection, with shows by the Chapman brothers, Tracey Emin, Damien Hirst and Sarah Lucas.

Left take a flight on the London Eye; face-to-face with The Beatles at Madame Tussauds

Places to visit

 Awarded VisitBritain's Quality Assured Visitor Attraction marque.

St Paul's Cathedral
St Paul's Churchyard, EC4M 8AD
Tel: (020) 7246 8348
www.stpauls.co.uk
Experience the splendour of Wren's famous cathedral church of the diocese of London, incorporating the Crypt, Ambulatory and Whispering Gallery.

Science Museum
Exhibition Road, SW7 2DD
Tel: 0870 870 4868
www.sciencemuseum.org.uk
See, touch and experience the major scientific advances of the last 300 years at the largest museum of its kind in the world.

Shakespeare's Globe Exhibition and Tour
New Globe Walk, Bankside, SE1 9DT
Tel: (020) 7902 1500
www.shakespeares-globe.org
A fascinating introduction to the world-famous Globe Theatre and daily existence in Shakespeare's London, brought vividly to life by a story-teller guide.

Somerset House
Strand, WC2R 1LA
Tel: (020) 7845 4600
www.somerset-house.org.uk
Home to the Courtauld Institute's collection of world-famous paintings, the Gilbert Collection of decorative art and the Hermitage Rooms, containing treasures from Russia's Hermitage Museum.

Tate Britain
Millbank, SW1P 4RG
Tel: (020) 7887 8008
www.tate.org.uk
The national gallery of British art from the Tudors to the Turner Prize, including works by Constable, Gainsborough and Turner, through to Hodgkin, Moore and Hockney.

Tate Modern
Bankside, SE1 9TG
Tel: (020) 7887 8008
www.tate.org.uk
For aspiring connoisseurs of modern art, Britain's national museum houses major works by Matisse, Picasso and Rothko as well as contemporary works by Richard Deacon, Mariko Mori and Gerhard Richter.

Theatre Museum
Russell Street, WC2E 7PA
Tel: (020) 7943 4700
www.theatremuseum.org
The museum's galleries explore British theatre and performers from Shakespeare's time, brought to life with imaginative exhibitions and events.

Tower of London
Tower Hill, EC3N 4AB
Tel: 0870 756 6060
www.hrp.org.uk
Chat with a Beefeater and see the legendary ravens. The Tower of London spans 900 years of British history and displays the nation's Crown Jewels, regalia and armoury robes.

Victoria and Albert Museum
Cromwell Road, SW7 2RL
Tel: (020) 7942 2000
www.vam.ac.uk
The V&A holds one of the world's largest and most diverse collections of the decorative arts, dating from 3000BC to the present day.

Vinopolis – London's Wine Tasting Visitor Attraction
Bank End, SE1 9BU
Tel: 0870 241 4040
www.vinopolis.co.uk
One of the few attractions where guests grow merrier as they walk through! Discover wine cultures from around the world and the origins of the art of winemaking.

Above hi-tech discovery at the Science Museum; take time out at the Tate Modern

This is just a selection of attractions available. Contact any Tourist Information Centre in London for more ideas.

LONDON

Visit London

6th Floor, 2 More London Riverside,
London SE1 2RR
T: (020) 7234 5800 F: (020) 7378 6525
www.visitlondon.com

Need more information?

Call '0870 1 LONDON' **for the following:**

A London tourist information pack

Tourist information on London – speak to
an expert for information and advice on museums, galleries, attractions, riverboat trips, sightseeing tours, theatre, shopping, eating out and much more!

Accommodation reservations

Or visit one of London's Tourist Information Centres listed overleaf.

Which part of London?
The majority of tourist accommodation is situated in the central parts of London and is therefore very convenient for most of the city's attractions and nightlife.

However, there are many establishments in outer London which provide other advantages, such as easier parking. In the accommodation pages which follow, you will find establishments listed under INNER LONDON (covering the E1 to W14 London Postal Area) and OUTER LONDON (covering the remainder of Greater London). Colour maps 6 and 7 at the front of the guide show place names and London Postal Area codes and will help you to locate accommodation in your chosen area of London.

Travel information

By road:
Major trunk roads into London include: A1, M1, A5, A10, A11, M11, A13, A2, M2, A23, A3, M3, A4, M4, A40, M40, A41, M25 (London orbital). London Transport is responsible for running London's bus services and the underground rail network. (020) 7222 1234 (24-hour telephone service; calls answered in rotation).

By rail:
Main rail termini: Victoria/Waterloo/Charing Cross – serving the South/South East; King's Cross – serving the North East; Euston – serving the North West/Midlands; Liverpool Street – serving the East; Paddington – serving the Thames Valley/West.

Enjoy England official guides to quality

Tourist Information Centres

Inner London

Britain and London Visitor Centre
1 Regent Street, Piccadilly Circus, SW1Y 4XT
Open: Mon 0930-1830, Tue-Fri 0900-1830, Sat & Sun 1000-1600; Jun-Oct, Sat 0900-1700.

Greenwich TIC
Pepys House, 2 Cutty Sark Gardens,
Greenwich, SE10 9LW
Tel: 0870 608 2000 Fax: (020) 8853 4607
Open: Daily 1000-1700.

Lewisham TIC
Lewisham Library, 199-201 Lewisham High Street, SE13 6LG
Tel: (020) 8297 8317 Fax: (020) 8297 9241
Open: Mon 1000-1700, Tue-Fri 0900-1700,
Sat 1000-1600.

London Visitors Centre
Arrivals Hall, Waterloo International Terminal, SE1 7LT
Open: Daily 0830-2230.

Southwark TIC
Vinoplois, 1 Bank End, SE1 9BU
Tel: (020) 7357 9168
Open: Tues-Sun 1000-1800.

Outer London

Bexley Hall Place TIC
Bourne Road, Bexley, Kent, DA5 1PQ
Tel: (01322) 558676 Fax (01322) 522921
Open: Mon-Sat 1000-1630, Sun 1400-1730.

Croydon TIC
Katharine Street, Croydon, CR9 1ET
Tel: (020) 8253 1009 Fax: (020) 8253 1008
Open: Mon-Wed & Fri 0900-1800, Thu 0930-1800,
Sat 0900-1700, Sun 1400-1700.

Harrow TIC
Civic Centre, Station Road,
Harrow, HA1 2XF
Tel: (020) 8424 1103 Fax: (020) 8424 1134
Open: Mon-Fri 0900-1700.

Hillingdon TIC
Central Library, 14-15 High Street, Uxbridge, UB8 1HD
Tel: (01895) 250706 Fax: (01895) 239794
Open: Mon, Tue & Thu 0930-2000, Wed 0930-1730,
Fri 1000-1730, Sat 0930-1600.

Hounslow TIC
The Treaty Centre, High Street, Hounslow, TW3 1ES
Tel: 0845 456 2929 Fax: 0845 456 2904
Open: Mon, Tues & Thurs 0930-2000,
Wed, Fri & Sat 0930-1730, Sun 1130-1600.

Kingston TIC
Market House, Market Place,
Kingston upon Thames, KT1 1JS
Tel: (020) 8547 5592 Fax: (020) 8547 5594
Open: Mon-Sat 1000-1700.

Richmond TIC
Old Town Hall, Whittaker Avenue,
Richmond, TW9 1TP
Tel: (020) 8940 6899 Fax: (020) 8940 6899
Open: Mon-Sat 1000-1700;
May-Sep, Sun 1030-1330.

Swanley TIC
London Road, Swanley, BR8 7AE
Tel: (01322) 614660 Fax: (01322) 666154
Open: Mon-Thu 0930-1730, Fri 0930-1800,
Sat 0900-1600.

Twickenham TIC
The Atrium, Civic Centre, York Street, Twickenham,
Middlesex, TW1 3BZ
Tel: (020) 8891 7272; Fax: (020) 8891 7738
Open: Mon-Thu 0900-1715, Fri 0900-1700.

Above experience the splendour of St Paul's Cathedral; explore the underwater world at the London Aquarium

LONDON

Where to stay in
London

Entries in this region are listed under Inner London (postcode areas E1 to W14) and Outer London (the remainder of Greater London).

Please refer to the colour location maps 6 and 7 at the front of this guide.

Accommodation symbols
Symbols give useful information about services and facilities. Inside the back cover flap you can find a key to these symbols. Keep it open for easy reference.

INNER LONDON
LONDON N7

★★★
2 Units
Sleeping 1–5

CARENA HOLIDAY ACCOMMODATION
London N7
Contact: Mr M Chouthi, 98 St George's Avenue, London N7 0AH
T: (020) 7607 7453
F: (020) 7607 7453
E: deo.chouthi@btopenworld.com

OPEN All Year

Low season per wk
£300.00–£500.00
High season per wk
£350.00–£550.00

In quiet road with free street parking. Comfortable apartments with a range of quality facilities and services. Perfectly positioned for easy access to London.

LONDON SE10

★★★★
1 Unit
Sleeping 1–4

HARBOUR MASTER'S HOUSE
London SE10
Contact: Mr Chris French
T: (020) 8293 9597
E: harbourmaster@lineone.net
I: website.lineone.net/~harbourmaster

OPEN All Year

Low season per wk
£525.00–£595.00
High season per wk
£525.00–£595.00

Superb self-contained flat, part of the historic Harbour Master's house (Grade II Listed). Situated on attractive riverside enclave on the Thames in maritime Greenwich.

LONDON SW18

★★★★
2 Units
Sleeping 1–8

BEAUMONT APARTMENTS
London SW18
Contact: Mr Alan Afriat, 24 Combemartin Road, London SW18 5PR
T: (020) 8789 2663
F: (020) 8265 5499
E: alan@beaumont-london-apartments.co.uk
I: www.beaumont-london-apartments.co.uk

OPEN All Year

Payment accepted: Amex, Delta, Mastercard, Switch, Visa, Euros

Low season per wk
£470.00–£650.00
High season per wk
£510.00–£780.00

Well-appointed flats in leafiest suburb within 25 minutes of West End. Close to zone 3 underground, Wimbledon tennis and convenient for A3, M4, M41, M25, Heathrow, Gatwick.

 Ratings All accommodation in this guide has been rated, or is awaiting a rating, by a trained VisitBritain assessor.

LONDON

LONDON SW20

★★★-★★★★★
2 Units
Sleeping 6

THALIA & HEBE HOLIDAY HOMES
London SW20
Contact: Peter and Ann Briscoe-Smith, Thalia and Hebe Holiday Homes, 150 Westway, London SW20 9LS
T: (020) 8542 0505
E: peter@briscoe-smith.org.uk
I: www.briscoe-smith.org.uk/thalia

OPEN All Year

Low season per wk
£550.00–£650.00
High season per wk
£550.00–£650.00

Thalia and Hebe are both three-bedroomed houses in the residential suburban area of West Wimbledon. Home from home, with easy access to central London.

LONDON W1

★★-★★★★
10 Units
Sleeping 2–6

TUSTIN HOLIDAY FLATS
London W1
Contact: Mr Bruce Tunstin, P C Tustin and Co Limited, 94 York Street, London W1H 1QX
T: (020) 7723 9611
F: (020) 7724 0224
E: pctustinuk@btconnect.com
I: www.pctustin.com

OPEN All Year except Christmas and New Year
Payment accepted: Mastercard, Visa

Low season per wk
£360.00–£670.00
High season per wk
£370.00–£680.00

Fully furnished self-contained flats in central London, offering easy access to Oxford Street, places of interest and public transport.

LONDON W5

★★★★
3 Units
Sleeping 2–6

CLARENDON HOUSE APARTMENTS
London W5
Contact: Mrs A Pedley, 48 Ranelagh Road, Ealing, London W5 5RJ
T: (020) 856 70314
F: (020) 856 63241
E: clarendon.house@lineone.net
I: www.clarendonhouseapartments.co.uk

OPEN All Year
Payment accepted: Delta, Mastercard, Switch, Visa

Low season per wk
£425.00–£775.00
High season per wk
£425.00–£775.00

Ealing is a vibrant suburb with great shops, restaurants and cafes. Apartments in good locations with free parking. Great transport links, convenient for Heathrow.

LONDON W13

★★★
4 Units
Sleeping 1–4

APARTMENTS WEST LONDON

London W13
Contact: Mr W G Smith, Apartments West London, 94 Gordon Road, Ealing, London W13 8PT
T: (020) 8566 8187
F: (020) 8566 7670
E: info@apartmentswestlondon.com
I: www.apartmentswestlondon.com

Attractive, fully equipped apartments for holiday and business travellers. Located in tree-lined residential street. Ealing Broadway underground station, lively bars, restaurants, shopping malls and supermarkets within walking distance. Unrestricted parking. Fast tube connection to all London's tourist attractions and Heathrow Airport. Easy access to M40/M4 motorways.

OPEN All Year
Payment accepted: Delta, Mastercard, Switch, Visa

Low season per wk
£336.00–£528.00
High season per wk
£353.00–£528.00

Quality Assurance Standard

Star ratings and awards were correct at time of going to press but are subject to change. Please check at the time of booking.

LONDON

OUTER LONDON
BECKENHAM

★★-★★★
8 Units
Sleeping 2–6

OAKFIELD APARTMENTS
Beckenham
Contact: Mr Deane, Oakfield Apartments, Flat 1,
107 South Eden Park Road, Beckenham BR3 3AX
T: (020) 8658 4441 & 8658 9198
E: john@oakfield.co.uk
I: www.oakfield.co.uk

Victorian mansion with a large garden in a semi-rural setting, three minutes' walk to Eden Park rail station, 25 minutes by rail or 14km by road to central London. Mr and Mrs Deane live on the premises and welcome children but not pets.

OPEN All Year
Payment accepted:
Mastercard, Switch, Visa

Low season per wk
£250.00–£625.00
High season per wk
£250.00–£625.00

PINNER

★★★★
1 Unit
Sleeping 4–5

MOSS COTTAGE
Pinner
T: (020) 8868 5507
F: (020) 8868 5507
E: info@moss-lane-cottages.com
I: www.moss-lane-cottages.com

This self-contained wing of a 17thC building has been renovated to provide quality accommodation in a traditional setting just 12 miles from central London. Conveniently located for shops, restaurants, underground, rail and bus services, Heathrow airport and M25. Spacious bedrooms, bathroom with shower, kitchen with laundry facilities, central heating, private patio.

OPEN All Year
Payment accepted:
Mastercard, Visa

Short breaks available during low season.

Low season per wk
£650.00–£700.00
High season per wk
£700.00–£800.00

Quality Assurance Standard
For an explanation of the quality and facilities represented by the stars please refer to the front of this guide. A more detailed explanation can be found in the information pages at the back.

Explore **fashionable** Manchester, **nautical** Liverpool and **bustling** Blackpool.

England's Northwest

Looking for some inspiration? Here are a few ideas to get you started in England's Northwest. **experience** the atmosphere of anticipation at the Grand National. **discover** the most exciting modern art gallery outside London at Tate Liverpool. **explore** the varied coastline with its unspoilt estuaries and seaside entertainment. **relax** and watch the world go by on a canal-boat holiday through the beautiful Cheshire countryside.

THE REGION
Cheshire, Greater Manchester, Lancashire, Merseyside and Cumbria – The Lake District (see page 58)

CONTACT
▸ **ENGLAND'S NORTHWEST**
www.visitenglandsnorthwest.com
Cheshire and Warrington Tourism Board
T: (01244) 346543 www.visit-cheshire.com
The Lancashire & Blackpool Tourist Board
T: (01257) 226600 www.lancashiretourism.com
or www.visitblackpool.com
Marketing Manchester – The Tourist Board for Greater Manchester
T: (0161) 237 1010
www.destinationmanchester.com
The Mersey Partnership – The Tourist Board for Merseyside
T: (0151) 227 2727 www.visitliverpool.com

ENGLAND'S NORTHWEST

Explore Cumbria's soaring peaks, with their mirror-perfect reflections in the waters of the lakes (see page 58), or discover the rounded hills and plains of Cheshire. Relax on inland waterways or on Lancashire's sandy beaches. Experience the buzz and excitement of Manchester and Liverpool or the thrill of a rollercoaster ride in Blackpool – it's all possible in England's Northwest.

A black-and-white picture

Tour through the Cheshire countryside and you'll come across pretty black-and-white timbered buildings like 15th-century Little Moreton Hall. At Lyme Park you might get a sense of déjà vu – it was the setting for BBC's Pride and Prejudice. Relax on Cheshire's waterways and experience the thrill as you rise up on the giant Anderton Boat Lift or let a Roman centurion guide you around the walled city of Chester, with its two-tier shops known as The Rows, and the Dewa Roman Experience.

A city reborn

Take in Manchester's amazing vistas from the top of the all-glass Urbis before visiting the museum below. This is just one of 50 fascinating free museums and stunning art galleries in the Greater Manchester area. Head for the Quays and the paintings of LS Lowry or the stunning Imperial War Museum North. Indulge yourself in the city's many restaurants, cafés and bars, in particular the Curry Mile. Or there's music and theatre, festivals and carnivals, superb shopping and, of course, football!

Capital of Culture

More choices to make when you visit Liverpool, named European Capital of Culture 2008. And you can see why. You've hit the jackpot with the largest collection of national museums and galleries outside London. Dine and dance, listen to music, shop 'til you drop, enjoy the theatre and, of course, search out the Beatles' haunts. For a sporting experience, walk through the tunnel to the sound of the crowd at Anfield or test your riding skills on the Grand National simulator at Aintree.

Fairways and candy floss

Like to be active? England's Golf Coast stretches for miles from the Wirral to Cumbria and boasts over 40 links courses to test all handicaps, but for non-golfers there's wonderful walks along stunning beaches or inland on the footpaths of the Forest of Bowland. You'll enjoy historic Lancaster and Preston's National Football Museum, but if it's thrills you want, Blackpool's the place. Take in the spectacular views from the Tower, scream with excitement on the white-knuckle rides of the Pleasure Beach, build sandcastles on the beach or ride a tram along the seafront.

Left, from top feel the thunder of hooves at the Grand National, Aintree; reflections of Liverpool; wander around the gardens at Arley Hall, Northwich **Right** watch the sun go down over Morecambe Bay

Enjoy England official guides to quality

47

Places to visit

Awarded VisitBritain's Quality Assured Visitor Attraction marque.

Albert Dock
Liverpool, Merseyside
Tel: (0151) 708 7334
www.albertdock.com
Something for everyone at Britain's largest Grade I Listed historic building. Restored four-sided dock including shops, bars, restaurants, entertainment, Maritime Museum, Tate Gallery and marina.

Arley Hall and Gardens
Northwich, Cheshire
Tel: (01565) 777353
www.arleyhallandgardens.com
Early Victorian country house set in 5ha (12 acres) of magnificent gardens, with a 15thC Grade I tithe barn. Plant nursery, gift shop and restaurant. A plantsman's paradise!

The Beatles Story Ltd
Albert Dock, Liverpool, Merseyside
Tel: (0151) 709 1963
www.beatlesstory.com
Award-winning visitor attraction revealing the many chapters of The Beatles story. Relive the group's early days in Hamburg, and the heady days of the Cavern Club.

Beeston Castle (English Heritage)
Chapel Lane, Beeston, Cheshire
Tel: (01829) 260464
www.english-heritage.org.uk
Soak up the history at this ruined 13thC castle set on top of the Peckforton Hills, with dramatic views of the surrounding countryside. Exhibitions are also held telling of the castle's past.

Blackpool Pleasure Beach
Ocean Boulevard, Blackpool, Lancashire
Tel: 0870 444 5566
www.blackpoolpleasurebeach.com
Endless fun for all! Blackpool Pleasure Beach offers over 145 rides and attractions, plus spectacular shows.

Blackpool Tower and Circus
The Promenade, Blackpool, Lancashire
Tel: (01253) 622242
www.blackpooltower.co.uk
A world of entertainment – inside Blackpool Tower you'll find the UK's best circus, the famous Tower Ballroom, Jungle Jim's Playground, Tower Top Ride and Undersea World.

Boat Museum
South Pier Road, Ellesmere Port, Cheshire
Tel: (0151) 355 5017
www.boatmuseum.org.uk
Brush up on the history of the canals at this historic dock complex on the Shropshire Union Canal. Home to the UK's largest collection of inland waterway craft, Power Hall, Pump House and seven exhibitions of industrial heritage.

Botany Bay Villages and Puddletown Pirates
Canal Mill, Chorley, Lancashire
Tel: (01257) 261220
www.botanybay.co.uk
A shopping, leisure and heritage experience including Puddletown Pirates, the largest indoor adventure play centre in the Northwest.

Bridgemere Garden World
Bridgemere, Cheshire
Tel: (01270) 521100
www.bridgemere.co.uk
Inspiration for greenfingers – 10 fascinating hectares (25 acres) of plants, gardens, greenhouses and a shop. Over 20 different display gardens, incorporating many Chelsea Flower Show Gold Medal winners.

Camelot Theme Park
Park Hall Road, Charnock Richard, Lancashire
Tel: (01257) 453044
www.camelotthemepark.co.uk
The Magical Kingdom of Camelot, voted Lancashire's Family Attraction of the Year 2002, is a world of thrilling rides, fantastic entertainment and family fun.

This is just a selection of attractions available. Contact any Tourist Information Centre in the region for more ideas.

ENGLAND'S NORTHWEST

Chester Zoo
Chester, Cheshire
Tel: (01244) 380280
www.chesterzoo.org.uk
Observe over 7000 animals in spacious and natural enclosures at one of Europe's leading conservation zoos. Now featuring the 'Tsavo' African Black Rhino Experience.

Croxteth Hall and Country Park
Croxteth Hall Lane, Liverpool, Merseyside
Tel: (0151) 228 5311
www.croxteth.co.uk
An Edwardian stately home set in 200ha (500 acres) of countryside, featuring a Victorian walled garden and large collection of rare, farm animal breeds.

Dunham Massey Hall Park and Garden (National Trust)
Altrincham, Cheshire
Tel: (0161) 941 1025
www.nationaltrust.org.uk
Spend the day at this 18thC mansion, with furniture, paintings and silver, set in a wooded deer park with a 10-ha (25-acre) informal garden.

East Lancashire Railway
Bolton Street Station, Bury, Lancashire
Tel: (0161) 764 7790
www.east-lancs-rly.co.uk
Journey back in time on this steam-hauled railway running along the Irwell Valley, north from Bury to Ramsbottom and Rawtenstall. Spectacular views of the West Pennine Moor.

Gawsworth Hall
Gawsworth, Cheshire
Tel: (01260) 223456
www.gawsworthhall.com
Beautiful, Tudor, half-timbered manor house with tilting ground. Inside are pictures, sculpture and furniture. Book your seat at one of the summer plays performed in the open-air theatre.

Gulliver's World Family Theme Park
Off Shackleton Close, Warrington, Cheshire
Tel: (01925) 444888
www.gulliversfun.co.uk
A theme park for the whole family, offering over 50 rides and attractions from log flumes to roller-coasters and dinosaurs. Suitable for children aged two and over.

Jodrell Bank Visitor Centre
Lower Withington, Macclesfield, Cheshire
Tel: (01477) 571339
www.jb.man.ac.uk/scicen
Home of the Lovell radio telescope, plus 3D theatre, small exhibition, observational pathway and 14-ha (35-acre) arboretum. Shop and space café.

Knowsley Safari Park
Prescot, Merseyside
Tel: (0151) 430 9009
www.knowsley.com
Enjoy, if you dare, a five-mile safari through 200ha (500 acres) of rolling countryside and see the world's wildest animals roaming free.

Lady Lever Art Gallery
Port Sunlight Village, Higher Bebington, Cheshire
Tel: (0151) 478 4136
www.ladyleverartgallery.org.uk
A chance to admire the 1st Lord Leverhulme's magnificent collection of British paintings dating from 1750-1900, British furniture, Wedgwood pottery and oriental porcelain.

Lyme Park (National Trust)
Disley, Stockport
Tel: (01663) 762023
www.nationaltrust.org.uk
Set in a country estate of over 550ha (1377 acres) of moorland, woodland and park, this magnificent house will appeal to those who appreciate Elizabethan, Georgian and Regency architecture.

Macclesfield Silk Museum
The Heritage Centre, Macclesfield, Cheshire
Tel: (01625) 613210
www.silk-macclesfield.org
Set in the former Sunday School built for child workers in the silk industry, the museum tells the story of silk in Macclesfield through an award-winning audio-visual programme.

Merseyside Maritime Museum
Albert Dock, Liverpool, Merseyside
Tel: (0151) 478 4499
www.merseysidemaritimemuseum.org.uk
The museum tells the story of one of the world's greatest ports and the people who used it, reflecting the international importance of Liverpool as a gateway to the world.

The Museum of Science & Industry in Manchester
Liverpool Road, Manchester
Tel: (0161) 832 2244
www.msim.org.uk
Get interactive in the brand new Xperiment gallery, see the wheels of industry turning in the Power Hall and marvel at the planes that made history in the Air and Space Hall.

The National Football Museum
Deepdale Stadium, Preston, Lancashire
Tel: (01772) 908442
www.nationalfootballmuseum.com
The history of football at your fingertips with hands-on exhibits and the magnificent FIFA collection, the finest collection of historic football memorabilia in the world.

Left take a ride to the top of Blackpool Tower; admire the collection at Lady Lever Art Gallery, Port Sunlight

Enjoy England official guides to quality

Places to visit

Awarded VisitBritain's Quality Assured Visitor Attraction marque.

Norton Priory Museum and Gardens
Tudor Road, Runcorn, Cheshire
Tel: (01928) 569895
www.nortonpriory.org
Medieval priory remains with a purpose-built museum, St Christopher's statue, sculpture trail and award-winning walled garden, all set in 15ha (38 acres) of beautiful gardens.

Pleasureland Theme Park
Marine Drive, Southport, Merseyside
Tel: 0870 220 0204
www.pleasureland.uk.com
Over 100 rides and attractions, including the classic Cyclone coaster, TRAUMAtizer and the Lucozade Space Shot. Not for the fainthearted!

Quarry Bank Mill (National Trust)
Styal, Cheshire
Tel: (01625) 527468
www.quarrybankmill.org.uk
A Georgian water-powered cotton spinning mill with five floors of award-winning displays and demonstrations and 120ha (300 acres) of parkland surroundings.

Sandcastle Tropical Waterworld
South Promenade, Blackpool, Lancashire
Tel: (01253) 343602
www.sandcastle-waterworld.co.uk
Prepare to get wet ... complete with wave pool, fun pools, giant water flumes, sauna, white-knuckle water slides, children's safe harbour, play area, catering, bar shops and amusements.

Sea Life Blackpool
The Promenade, Blackpool, Lancashire
Tel: (01253) 621258
www.sealifeeurope.com
Experience the enchanting world of the Amazon, one of the world's greatest rainforests, featuring electric eels and piranhas, and discover the lost city of Atlantis.

Smithills Hall
Smithills Dean Road, Bolton, Lancashire
Tel: (01204) 332377
www.smithills.org
Budding historians will appreciate one of the oldest manor houses in Lancashire. Smithills Hall has a great hall dating back to the 14thC, plus 16thC and Victorian additions.

Tate Liverpool
Albert Dock, Liverpool, Merseyside
Tel: (0151) 702 7400
www.tate.org.uk/liverpool/
Exhibiting the National Collection of Modern Art, Tate Liverpool is well worth a visit.

Tatton Park (National Trust)
Knutsford, Cheshire
Tel: (01625) 534400
www.tattonpark.org.uk
Fine Georgian mansion full of art treasures and furniture with a garden, traditional working farm and Tudor manor house, all set in a 400-ha (1000-acre) deer park.

Wigan Pier
Trencherfield Mill, Wigan
Tel: (01942) 323666
www.wiganmbc.gov.uk
With old favourites 'The Way We Were' and 'Victorian Schoolroom', plus the new attraction 'The Museum of Memories', our social history is explored in Wigan Pier's unique style.

Wildfowl and Wetland Trust Martin Mere
Burscough, Lancashire
Tel: (01704) 895181
www.wwt.org.uk
Twenty-hectare (50-acre) landscaped Waterfowl Gardens, home to over 1600 ducks, geese and swans, including some of the world's rarest and most endangered species.

Above the inspired Trois Danseusses by Pablo Picasso, Tate Liverpool; enjoy the high life on Blackpool's Central Pier
Right marvel at The Lowry arts centre, The Quays, Salford

50   This is just a selection of attractions available. Contact any Tourist Information Centre in the region for more ideas.

England's Northwest
www.visitenglandsnorthwest.com

There are various publications and guides about England's Northwest available from the following Tourist Boards:

Cheshire and Warrington Tourism Board
Grosvenor Park Lodge, Grosvenor Park Road
Chester CH1 1QQ
T: (01244) 346543
E: info@cwtb.co.uk
www.visit-cheshire.com

The Lancashire & Blackpool Tourist Board
St Georges House, St Georges Street
Chorley PR7 2AA
T: (01257) 226600
Brochure request: (01772) 533369
E: info@lancashiretourism.com
www.lancashiretourism.com or www.visitblackpool.com

Marketing Manchester – The Tourist Board for Greater Manchester
Churchgate House, 56 Oxford Street
Manchester M1 6EU
T: (0161) 237 1010
Brochure request: 0870 609 3013
F: (0161) 228 2960
E: Manchester_visitor_centre@notes.manchester.gov.uk
www.destinationmanchester.com

The Mersey Partnership – The Tourist Board for Merseyside
12 Princes Parade, Liverpool L3 1BG
T: (0151) 227 2727
F: (0151) 227 2325
Overseas: 00 44 151 709 8111
Tourist Information Centre: (0151) 709 3285
Accommodation booking service: 0845 601 1125
E: info@visitliverpool.com
www.visitliverpool.com

Travel information

By road:
Motorways intersect within the region which has the best road network in the country. Travelling north or south use the M6, and east or west the M62.

By rail:
Most Northwest coastal resorts are connected to InterCity routes with trains from many parts of the country, and there are through trains to major cities and towns.

ENGLAND'S NORTHWEST

Where to stay in
England's Northwest

All place names in the blue bands, under which accommodation is listed, are shown on the maps at the front of this guide.

A complete listing of all VisitBritain assessed accommodation covered by this guide appears at the back.

Accommodation symbols
Symbols give useful information about services and facilities. Inside the back cover flap you can find a key to these symbols. Keep it open for easy reference.

BLACKPOOL, Blackpool Map ref 4A1 *Tourist Information Centre Tel: (01253) 478222*

★★-★★★
4 Units
Sleeping 1–4

DONANGE
Blackpool
Contact: Mrs Myra Hasson, Donange,
29 Holmfield Road, Blackpool FY2 9TB
T: (01253) 355051
E: don-ange@bushinternet.com
I: www.donange.cjb.net

OPEN All Year

Low season per wk
£80.00–£150.00
High season per wk
£140.00–£195.00

Select holiday apartments 150 yards Queens Promenade. High standard of cleanliness assured. Tea/sugar/towels provided. Standard beds. A friendly welcome awaits. Families, couples, Senior Citizens.

★★-★★★
51 Units
Sleeping 2–8

GRAND HOTEL HOLIDAY FLATS
Blackpool
Contact: Mr Smith, Station Road, Blackpool FY4 1EU
T: (01253) 343741
F: (01253) 408228
I: www.grandholidayflats.co.uk

OPEN All Year except Christmas and New Year
Payment accepted: Mastercard, Switch, Visa

Low season per wk
£123.00–£458.00
High season per wk
£194.00–£540.00

A large complex of self-contained holiday flats and en suite hotel rooms with heated indoor pool and licensed bar lounge.

BRINSCALL, Lancashire Map ref 4A1

★★★
1 Unit
Sleeping 5–8

MOORS VIEW COTTAGE
Chorley
Contact: Mrs Sheila Smith, Four Seasons Guest House,
9 Cambridge Road, Thornton, Cleveleys FY5 1EP
T: (01253) 853537 & 07747 808406
F: (01624) 662190

OPEN All Year
Payment accepted: Euros

Low season per wk
Min £300.00
High season per wk
£335.00–£395.00

Situated amid lovely countryside adjacent to canal, motorways, market towns and coast, this fully equipped cottage comprises two bedrooms and excellent bedsettee, luxury bathroom, separate shower and toilet, large through lounge and dining area, oak kitchen, off-road parking, large rear garden and sun room. Fuel, power and linen included.

ENGLAND'S NORTHWEST

CHESTER, Cheshire Map ref 4A2 *Tourist Information Centre Tel: (01244) 402111*

★★★
2 Units
Sleeping 2-6

CITY WALLS APARTMENTS
Chester
Contact: Mr Rod Cox, 1 City Walls, Rufus Court, Chester CH1 2JG
T: (01244) 313400
F: (01244) 400414

Modern, second floor apartments, both with courtyard and garden views, parking, near everything. Large studio (one double bed) and two-bedroom (two doubles) in award-winning courtyard, half built 1990, half 1750, nestling on the city walls, housing craft shops, book shops, restaurants and Alexander's Jazz Bar. Everything included.

OPEN All Year

Payment accepted: Mastercard, Switch, Visa, Euros

Short breaks if late availability (3 weeks ahead) only. Ring for prices.

Studio: £250.00 all year except Christmas and New Year
2 bed: £350.00 all year except Christmas and New Year

★★★
1 Unit
Sleeping 1-4

KINGSWOOD COACH HOUSE
Chester
Contact: Mrs C Perry, Kingswood Coach House, Parkgate Road, Kingswood, Chester CH1 6JS
T: (01244) 851204
F: (01244) 851244
E: caroline.m.perry@btopenworld.com

OPEN All Year

Low season per wk
£170.00-£190.00
High season per wk
£200.00-£220.00

Ideal for couples. Large bedroom, fitted kitchen, living room, toilet and shower. Garden and patio, off-road parking. Close to bus route. Near Wales and Wirral.

★★
1 Unit
Sleeping 1-6

LITTLE MAYFIELD
Hoole Village
Contact: Mr Michael John Cullen, Mayfield House, Warrington Road, Hoole Village CH2 4EX
T: (01244) 300231
F: (01244) 300231

Low season per wk
£190.00-£260.00
High season per wk
£190.00-£260.00

Self-contained wing of William IV house set in three acres of garden with hard tennis court. Spacious rooms. Seven minutes from Chester city centre.

CHIPPING, Lancashire Map ref 4A1

★★★-★★★★★
4 Units
Sleeping 2-8

RAKEFOOT BARN
Nr Clitheroe
Contact: Mrs Gifford, Rakefoot Farm, Thornley Road, Nr Clitheroe BB7 3LY
T: (01995) 61332
F: (01995) 61296
E: info@rakefootfarm.co.uk
I: www.rakefootfarm.co.uk

OPEN All Year

Low season per wk
Min £100.00
High season per wk
Max £575.00

Converted barn, original features, woodburners, en suites. Family farm. Forest of Bowland, Chipping/Clitheroe. Past winner NWTB Silver Award. Properties interlinked when required. Also B&B.

CONGLETON, Cheshire Map ref 4B2 *Tourist Information Centre Tel: (01260) 271095*

★★★★
1 Unit
Sleeping 1-4

YEW TREE FARM COTTAGE
Congleton
Contact: Ann Syson, Yew Tree Farm Cottage, North Rode, Congleton CW12 2PF
T: (01260) 223547
E: syson@ukonline.co.uk

OPEN All Year

Low season per wk
£210.00-£225.00
High season per wk
£245.00-£295.00

The farm cottage adjoins the 300-year-old farmhouse. Spacious lounge/dining room, double bedroom, twin bedroom, modern bathroom, fitted kitchen. Views to Peak District.

53

ENGLAND'S NORTHWEST

HIGH LANE, Greater Manchester Map ref 4B2

★★★
1 Unit
Sleeping 1–6

TY COCH
Stockport
Contact: Jane Beard, 1 Huron Crescent, Lakeside, Cardiff CF23 6DT
T: (02920) 761888
E: townsendsom@hotmail.com

OPEN All Year

Low season per wk
Min £226.00
High season per wk
Min £389.00

Two bedroomed bungalow. The kitchen has all facilities with televisions in the lounge and bedrooms.

KNUTSFORD, Cheshire Map ref 4A2 Tourist Information Centre Tel: (01565) 632611

★★★★
5 Units
Sleeping 1–6

DANEBURY SERVICED APARTMENTS
Knutsford
Contact: Mr Stephen & Mrs Pauline West, Danebury Apartments, 8 Tabley Road, Knutsford WA16 0NB
T: (01565) 755219
E: info@daneburyapartments.co.uk
I: www.daneburyapartments.co.uk

OPEN All Year
Payment accepted: Mastercard, Visa

Low season per wk
£365.00–£575.00
High season per wk
£365.00–£575.00

Set in the town's conservation area, these self-contained apartments have been thoughtfully created from an Edwardian property of character. Choice of one, two or three bedrooms with fully equipped kitchens, bathrooms, lounge/dining areas and parking spaces. Only a stroll from the pretty town of Knutsford's restaurants, bars and boutiques.

LIVERPOOL, Merseyside Map ref 4A2 Tourist Information Centre Tel: 0906 680 6886 (25p per min)

★★★★
2 Units
Sleeping 1–8

TRAFALGAR WAREHOUSE APARTMENTS
Liverpool
Contact: Mr Ray Gibson, 25 Rosedale Road, Liverpool L18 5JD
T: (0151) 7344924 & 07715 118419
F: (0151) 7344924

OPEN All Year
Payment accepted: Mastercard, Switch, Visa, Euros

Low season per wk
£400.00–£600.00
High season per wk
£500.00–£700.00

Two fully-furnished apartments, character features, open plan contemporary fittings. Two double bedrooms, one of which is on the mezzanine floor. Luxurious bathroom with jacuzzi.

LYTHAM ST ANNES, Lancashire Map ref 4A1 Tourist Information Centre Tel: (01253) 725610

★★★
4 Units
Sleeping 1–5

MERLEWOOD HOLIDAY APARTMENTS
Lytham St Annes
Contact: Sharon, Merlewood Holiday Apartments, 383 Clifton Drive North, Lytham St Annes FY8 2PA
T: (01253) 726082

OPEN All Year

Low season per wk
£175.00–£250.00
High season per wk
£200.00–£275.00

Self-contained apartments for couples/families. Separate kitchens and bedrooms, sea views, 50yds from promenade and town centre. Private parking.

MACCLESFIELD, Cheshire Map ref 4B2 Tourist Information Centre Tel: (01625) 504114

★★★
1 Unit
Sleeping 6

MILL HOUSE FARM COTTAGE
Macclesfield
Contact: Mrs Lynne Whittaker, Mill House Farm, Bosley, Macclesfield SK11 0NZ
T: (01260) 226265
I: http://www.geocities.com/farm_cottage

OPEN All Year except Christmas and New Year

Low season per wk
£165.00–£185.00
High season per wk
£185.00–£275.00

Comfortable, spacious cottage on 130-acre dairy farm bordering the Peak District. Beautiful surrounding countryside and convenient for Alton Towers, Potteries, Chester, Manchester Airport.

ENGLAND'S NORTHWEST

MANCHESTER, Greater Manchester Map ref 4B1 *Tourist Information Centre Tel: (0161) 234 3157*

★★★★
108 Units
Sleeping 1–4

THE PLACE APARTMENT HOTEL
Piccadilly, Manchester
Contact: Ms Clare Johnson, The Place Apartment Hotel,
Ducie Street, Piccadilly M1 2TP
T: (0161) 778 7500
F: (0161) 778 7507
E: reservations@theplaceforliving.com
I: www.theplacehotel.com

OPEN All Year

Payment accepted: Amex,
Delta, Diners, Mastercard,
Switch, Visa

Low season per wk
£560.00–£2,000.00
High season per wk
£700.00–£2,300.00

Luxury Grade II Listed building with contemporary loft-style apartments. One-and two-bedroom apartments available. Modern and stylish. Right in Manchester city centre.

MANCHESTER AIRPORT

See under Knutsford, Manchester, Stockport

MIDDLEWICH, Cheshire Map ref 4A2

★★★–★★★★★
2 Units
Sleeping 4–5

Barn, newly converted to a high standard to create beautiful cottages. Located in a peaceful situation, ideal for a long-weekend break, peaceful holiday or business trip. Forge Masters is the larger cottage and is suitable for the partially disabled. Millers is smaller but has its own special charm. Equipped with all modern conveniences.

FORGE MILL FARM COTTAGES
Warmingham
Contact: Mrs Susan Moss, Forge Mill Farm Cottages,
Forge Mill Farm, Forge Mill Lane, Warmingham,
Middlewich CW10 0HQ
T: (01270) 526204
F: (01270) 526204
E: forgemill2@msn.com

OPEN All Year

3-night stays available all year.

Low season per wk
£200.00–£420.00

NANTWICH, Cheshire Map ref 4A2 *Tourist Information Centre Tel: (01270) 610983*

★★★
2 Units
Sleeping 2–6

BANK FARM COTTAGES
Hough
Contact: Margaret Vaughan, Bank Farm Cottages,
Newcastle Road, Hough, Nr Crewe CW2 5JG
T: (01270) 841809
F: (01270) 841809

OPEN All Year

Payment accepted: Euros

Low season per wk
£250.00–£300.00
High season per wk
£300.00–£350.00

Charming holiday cottages created from Victorian farm buildings, furnished to a high standard. Full gas central heating, washing machines, microwaves. Ample parking. Excellent base for North Wales potteries.

NETHER KELLET, Lancashire Map ref 5B3

★★★
1 Unit
Sleeping 4

THE APARTMENT
Nether Kellet
Contact: Mr Richardson, 10 Meadowcroft,
Nether Kellet, Carnforth LA6 1HN
T: (01524) 734969 & 736331

OPEN All Year

Low season per wk
Min £155.00
High season per wk
Min £235.00

One-bedroomed, self-contained flat with extensive, private gardens in peaceful, rural village. Secluded cul-de-sac location.

 **Accessibility** Look for the symbols which indicate National Accessible Scheme standards for hearing and visually impaired guests in addition to standards for guests with mobility impairment. You can find an index of all scheme participants at the back of this guide.

ENGLAND'S NORTHWEST

OLDHAM, Greater Manchester Map ref 4B1 *Tourist Information Centre Tel: (0161) 627 1024*

★★★
1 Unit
Sleeping 1–5

CLIFTON COTTAGE
Greenfield
Contact: Mrs Wood, 113 Chew Valley Road, Greenfield,
Saddleworth, Oldham OL3 7JJ
T: (01457) 872098
F: (01457) 870760
E: ced117@aol.com

OPEN All Year

Low season per wk
Min £250.00
High season per wk
Min £250.00

Fully modernised country terraced cottage. One double and one single bedroom plus double bed settee in lounge. Heating, electricity and linen included.

RIBBLE VALLEY

See under Chipping

SOUTHPORT, Merseyside Map ref 4A1 *Tourist Information Centre Tel: (01704) 533333*

★★★★
2 Units
Sleeping 1–6

MARTIN LANE FARMHOUSE HOLIDAY COTTAGES
Burscough
Contact: Mrs Stubbs, Martin Lane Farmhouse,
Martin Lane, Burscough L40 8JH
T: (01704) 893527
F: (01704) 893527
E: mlfhc@btinternet.com
I: www.martinlanefarmhouse.btinternet.co.uk

OPEN All Year
Payment accepted: Euros

10% discount on 2-week bookings.

Low season per wk
£150.00–£325.00
High season per wk
£225.00–£395.00

Beautiful, award-winning country cottages, nestling in the rich arable farmland of West Lancashire and just four miles from Southport and the seaside. Our cottages have a friendly, relaxed, family atmosphere. The ideal base for visiting all the North West's major attractions.

★★★
5 Units
Sleeping 2–6

SANDY BROOK FARM
Southport
Contact: Mr Core, Sandy Brook Farm,
52 Wyke Cop Road, Scarisbrick, Southport PR8 5LR
T: (01704) 880337
F: (01704) 880337
E: sandybrookfarm@lycos.co.uk

OPEN All Year

Low season per wk
£120.00–£150.00
High season per wk
£230.00–£300.00

Converted barn offering self-catering apartments furnished in traditional style with all modern amenities. Three-and-a-half miles from Southport in rural area of Scarisbrick. Adapted apartment for disabled guests.

STOCKPORT, Greater Manchester Map ref 4B2 *Tourist Information Centre Tel: (0161) 474 4444*

★★★
1 Unit
Sleeping 1–6

LAKE VIEW
Marple Bridge
Contact: Mrs M Sidebottom, Shire Cottage, Benches Lane,
Marple Bridge, Stockport SK6 5RY
T: (01457) 866536
F: (01457) 866536
E: monica@lakeviewscstockport6.fsbusiness.co.uk

OPEN All Year

Low season per wk
£250.00–£300.00
High season per wk
£350.00–£450.00

Peaceful well-equipped bungalow with magnificent views overlooking Etherow Country Park near Peak District. All rooms on ground floor. Open fire in lounge. Central heating throughout. Electricity on 50p meter, first £6.00 free. Small garden. Parking available. Easy access to Peak District, Manchester and country houses. Restaurant and pub food five minutes away.

56

ENGLAND'S NORTHWEST

TOSSIDE, Lancashire Map ref 4A1

★★★★

5 Units
Sleeping 4–12

PRIMROSE COTTAGE, JENNY WREN, WAGTAIL, SWALLOWS, LOWER GILL FARM HOUSE
Skipton
Contact: Mr Roger Wales, Holiday Cottages (Yorkshire), Water Street, Skipton BD23 1PB
T: (01756) 700510
E: brochure@holidaycotts.co.uk
I: www.holidaycotts.co.uk

OPEN All Year
Payment accepted: Mastercard, Switch, Visa

Low season per wk
£258.00–£443.00
High season per wk
£450.00–£910.00

Superb cottages with heated indoor pool, games room, tennis court and play area. Surrounded by open countryside.

Use your *i*s

There are more than 550 Tourist Information Centres throughout England offering friendly help with accommodation and holiday ideas as well as suggestions of places to visit and things to do. You'll find addresses in the local phone book.

Awesome views and calm lakes; the **great outdoors** doesn't get much **grander** than in Cumbria.

Cumbria – The Lake District

Looking for some inspiration? Here are a few ideas to get you started in Cumbria – The Lake District. **experience** Roman history along Hadrian's Wall. **discover** the narrow gauge steam railway running through the Eskdale Valley. **explore** England's highest mountain and deepest lake – Scafell Pike and Wastwater. **relax** on a romantic break in a lakeside hotel.

CONTACT
▸ **CUMBRIA TOURIST BOARD**
Ashleigh, Holly Road,
Windermere, Cumbria LA23 2AQ
T: (015394) 44444
F: (015394) 44041
E: info@golakes.co.uk
www.golakes.co.uk
www.lakedistrictoutdoors.co.uk

CUMBRIA – THE LAKE DISTRICT

Rewarding walks, energetic climbs, awesome views and calm lakes: Cumbria offers a spectacular variety of pursuits and a refreshing quality of life. Roman remains, outdoor adventure, colourful gardens and good food and drink will ensure you're fully satisfied with your stay.

Floral inspiration

Visit in springtime to see the hosts of golden daffodils that inspired Wordsworth to write his famous poem 200 years ago. In Cockermouth you can visit his birthplace and see the garden he loved so much. A new centre near Grasmere houses Wordsworth's books, manuscripts, paintings and drawings, and includes a space for poetry reading. Explore the magnificent grounds surrounding 800-year-old Muncaster Castle, wander through the national award-winning gardens at Holker Hall or let the children run free in the lakeside parkland of Fell Foot Country Park.

High excitement

The great outdoors doesn't get much grander than the Lake District where you can experience some of the best walking and outdoor activities in England. Go Ape! on a forest adventure course, go sailing, rock climbing or paragliding. Walk alongside Hadrian's Wall – you'll find spectacular views and a visitor centre explaining its 1800 year history at Birdoswald Roman Fort, set high on a spur overlooking the river Irthing.

Then discover the diverse wildlife, scenic qualities and world-class geological heritage which has earned the North Pennines its status as the first European Geopark in Britain. For something more leisurely take a cruise across one of the many lakes. Lake Windermere is the most popular, with a 10-mile boat trip in wonderful scenery.

Festivals and food

Cumbria is awash with festivals and events, including the Barrow Festival of the Sea, the Whitehaven Maritime Festival, Words by the Water, the Lake District Summer Music Festival and a variety of country shows. If you're a connoisseur of local produce, don't miss The Cumbria and Lake District Food and Drink Festival including a series of events at award-winning Rheged – The Village in the Hill – where you can sample the excellent and diverse range of food from across the county.

Left, from top top take a scenic drive along a Cumbrian country lane, Haweswater Beck; deserted coastline, St Bees; discover the world of Wordsworth at Dove Cottage, Grasmere
Right a gentle stroll, Ashness Bridge

Enjoy England official guides to quality

Places to visit

Awarded VisitBritain's Quality Assured Visitor Attraction marque.

Aquarium of the Lakes
Lakeside, Newby Bridge, Cumbria
Tel: (01539) 530153
www.aquariumofthelakes.co.uk
Set on the southern shores of Lake Windermere, this fascinating aquarium is the UK's largest collection of freshwater fish, with over 30 naturally themed displays.

The Beacon
West Strand, Whitehaven, Cumbria
Tel: (01946) 592302
www.thebeacon-whitehaven.co.uk
Award-winning attraction and museum telling the story of historic Whitehaven, superbly situated overlooking the Georgian harbour.

Birdoswald Roman Fort
Gilsland, Cumbria
Tel: (01697) 747602
www.birdoswaldromanfort.org
Remains of a Roman fort on one of the best parts of Hadrian's Wall with excellent views of the Irthing Gorge. Exhibition, shop, tearoom and excavations.

Brantwood, Home of John Ruskin
Coniston, Cumbria
Tel: (015394) 41396
www.brantwood.org.uk
Discover a wealth of things to do at Brantwood, the most beautifully situated house in the Lake District, and home of John Ruskin from 1872 until 1900.

Cars of the Stars Motor Museum
Standish Street, Keswick, Cumbria
Tel: (017687) 73757
www.carsofthestars.com
See many famous TV and film vehicles including the Batmobile, Chitty Chitty Bang Bang, the James Bond Aston Martin, Herbie and Thunderbird's FAB 1.

The Dock Museum
North Road, Barrow-in-Furness, Cumbria
Tel: (01229) 894444
www.dockmuseum.org.uk
A spectacular modern museum built over an original Victorian dry dock. Galleries include multi-media interactive exhibits and impressive ship models.

Dove Cottage and Wordsworth Museum
Town End, Grasmere, Cumbria
Tel: (015394) 35544
www.wordsworth.org.uk
Wordsworth's home during his most creative period. Cottage guided tours, original manuscripts in the museum and contemporary art in the 3ºW art gallery.

Eden Ostrich World
Langwathby, Cumbria
Tel: (01768) 881771
www.ostrich-world.com
Meet ostriches and many other animals. Also enjoy the tearoom, hayloft galleries, play areas, including soft play mania, riverside walk, Zebroid foal and a sheep milking parlour.

Gleaston Water Mill
Gleaston, Ulverston, Cumbria
Tel: (01229) 869244
www.watermill.co.uk
A truly rural experience – a water cornmill, artefacts, traditions, folklore, great home-cooked food, and of course, the acclaimed Pig's Whisper country store.

Heron Glass
Ulverston, Cumbria
Tel: (01229) 581121
www.herongiftware.com
Displays of making hand-blown glass giftware and lead crystal, plus the Gateway to Furness Exhibition, which provides a fascinating snapshot of the history of the Furness Peninsula. Lighthouse café and restaurant.

This is just a selection of attractions available. Contact any Tourist Information Centre in the region for more ideas.

CUMBRIA – THE LAKE DISTRICT

Hill Top (National Trust)
Near Sawrey, Ambleside, Cumbria
Tel: (015394) 36269
www.nationaltrust.org.uk
Beatrix Potter wrote many of her popular Peter Rabbit stories and other books in this charming little house which still contains her own china and furniture.

Holker Hall and Gardens
Cark in Cartmel, Cumbria
Tel: (015395) 58328
www.holker-hall.co.uk
An impressive historic house with new Victorian wing, award-winning formal and woodland gardens, deer park, motor museum, adventure playground, café and gift shop.

Jennings Brothers plc
The Castle Brewery, Cockermouth, Cumbria
Tel: 0845 129 7185
www.jenningsbrewery.co.uk
Take a guided tour of this traditional brewery and sample the ales in the Old Cooperage Bar.

The Lake District Coast Aquarium Maryport
South Quay, Maryport, Cumbria
Tel: (01900) 817760
www.lakedistrict-coastaquarium.co.uk
Independent aquarium with over 35 displays, including walk-over ray pool and hands-in rock pool. Largest collection of native marine species in Cumbria.

The Lake District Visitor Centre
Brockhole, Windermere, Cumbria
Tel: (015394) 46601
www.lake-district.gov.uk
An Edwardian house on the shores of Windermere with extensive landscaped gardens and stunning views. Lake cruises, adventure playground, walks, events and activities.

Lakeland Motor Museum
Holker Hall and Gardens, Cark in Cartmel, Cumbria
Tel: (015395) 58509
www.lakelandmotormuseum.co.uk
Over 25,000 exhibits including rare motoring automobilia, a 1930s garage re-creation and the Campbell Legend Bluebird Exhibition.

Lakeland Sheep and Wool Centre
Egremont Road, Cockermouth, Cumbria
Tel: (01900) 822673
www.sheep-woolcentre.co.uk
Live farm show including cows, sheep, dogs and geese, all displaying their working qualities. Large gift shop and licensed café/restaurant. All weather attraction.

Lakeland Wildlife Oasis
Hale, Cumbria
Tel: (015395) 63027
www.wildlifeoasis.co.uk
A wildlife exhibition where both living animals and hands-on displays are used to illustrate evolution in the animal kingdom. Includes gift shop and café.

Lakeside and Haverthwaite Railway
Haverthwaite Station, Ulverston, Cumbria
Tel: (015395) 31594
Standard-gauge steam railway operating a daily seasonal service through the beautiful Leven Valley. Steam and diesel locomotives on display.

Levens Hall
Levens, Cumbria
Tel: (015395) 60321
www.levenshall.co.uk
Elizabethan home of the Bagot family with 13thC pele tower, world-famous topiary gardens, Bellingham Buttery, Potting Shed gift shop, plant centre and play area.

Muncaster Castle, Gardens, Owl Centre and Meadow Vole Maze
Ravenglass, Cumbria
Tel: (01229) 717614
www.muncaster.co.uk
Historic haunted castle with the most beautifully situated Owl Centre in the world. See the birds fly, picnic in the gardens, visit the Pennington family home.

Rheged – The Village in the Hill
Redhills, Penrith, Cumbria
Tel: (01768) 868000
www.rheged.com
Award-winning Rheged is home to a giant cinema screen showing four movies daily, the only international Everest Exhibition, speciality shops, indoor play area and café.

The Rum Story
Lowther Street, Whitehaven, Cumbria
Tel: (01946) 592933
www.rumstory.co.uk
The world's first exhibition depicting the unique and dramatic story of the UK rum trade, set in the original Jefferson's wine merchant premises.

Rydal Mount and Gardens
Rydal, Cumbria
Tel: (015394) 33002
www.rydalmount.co.uk
Nestling between the majestic fells, Lake Windermere and Rydal Water lies the most beloved home of William Wordsworth from 1813-1850.

Left still waters, Ambleside; spellbinding views at Borrowdale

Enjoy England official guides to quality

Places to visit

Awarded VisitBritain's Quality Assured Visitor Attraction marque.

Sellafield Visitors Centre
Sellafield, Cumbria
Tel: (01946) 727027
www.sparkingreaction.info
Sellafield's new exhibition, produced and written by the Science Museum in London, explores the complex issues around nuclear power.

Sizergh Castle and Garden (National Trust)
Sizergh, Kendal, Cumbria
Tel: (015395) 60070
www.nationaltrust.org.uk
The Strickland family home for 750 years with 14thC pele tower, 15thC great hall, 16thC wings and Stuart connections. Rock garden, rose garden, daffodils.

South Tynedale Railway
Railway Station, Alston, Cumbria
Tel: (01434) 381696
www.strps.org.uk
Narrow-gauge steam and diesel railway along part of the route of the former Alston to Haltwhistle branch line, through the beautiful scenery of the South Tynedale valley.

Steam Yacht Gondola (National Trust)
Pier Cottage, Coniston, Cumbria
Tel: (015394) 41288
www.nationaltrust.org.uk/gondola
View Coniston Water from the elegant, Victorian steam-powered yacht Gondola, now completely renovated with an opulently-upholstered saloon.

Theatre by the Lake
Lakeside, Keswick, Cumbria
Tel: (017687) 74411
www.theatrebythelake.com
Year-round programme of drama, music, dance and comedy, with a summer season of plays, Christmas and Easter shows and festivals of film, literature and jazz.

Tullie House Museum and Art Gallery
Castle Street, Carlisle, Cumbria
Tel: (01228) 534781
www.tulliehouse.co.uk
Georgian mansion housing a magnificent pre-Raphaelite collection, Victorian childhood gallery, 1689 fireplace and Jacobean oak staircase.

Ullswater 'Steamers'
Penrith, Cumbria
Tel: (017684) 82229
www.ullswater-steamers.co.uk
Relax and enjoy a beautiful Ullswater cruise with walks and picnic areas. Boat services operating all year round.

Windermere Lake Cruises
Lakeside, Newby Bridge, Cumbria
Tel: (015395) 31188
www.windermere-lakecruises.co.uk
Steamers and launches sail daily throughout the year between Ambleside, Lakeside and Bowness. Seasonal sailings to Brockhole, Lakeside and Haverthwaite Steam Railway and Aquarium of the Lakes.

Windermere Steamboats & Museum
Rayrigg Road, Bowness-on-Windermere, Cumbria
Tel: (015394) 45565
www.steamboat.co.uk
A wealth of interest and information about life on bygone Windermere. Regular steam launch trips, vintage vessels and classic motorboats. Model boat pond, lakeside picnic area.

The World of Beatrix Potter Attraction
The Old Laundry, Bowness-on-Windermere, Cumbria
Tel: (015394) 88444
www.hop-skip-jump.com
The life and works of Beatrix Potter brought to life, with three dimensional scenes from the delightful children's stories.

Above great views from the Settle to Carlisle Railway, Dent; the centre of town, Keswick. **Right** stunning scenery at Ullswater

This is just a selection of attractions available. Contact any Tourist Information Centre in the region for more ideas.

CUMBRIA – THE LAKE DISTRICT

Cumbria Tourist Board

Ashleigh, Holly Road, Windermere, Cumbria LA23 2AQ
T: (015394) 44444 F: (015394) 44041
E: info@golakes.co.uk
www.golakes.co.uk   www.lakedistrictoutdoors.co.uk

The following publications are available from Cumbria Tourist Board:

Cumbria – The Lake District Holidays & Breaks Guide (free) T: 0870 513 3059

The Hidden Treasures of Cumbria Guide (free) T: 0870 070 2199

The Gardens, Parks and Wildlife of Cumbria – The Lake District (free) T: (015394) 44444

The Caravan and Camping Guide of Cumbria – the Lake District (free) T: (015394) 44444

The Taste District Food & drink guide (free) T: (015394) 44444

Events Listing (free) T: (015394) 44444

Travel information

By road:
The M1/M6/M25/M40 provide a link with London and the South East and the M5/M6 provide access from the South West. The M6 links the Midlands and North West and the M62/M6 links the East of England and Yorkshire. Approximate journey time from London is five hours, from Manchester one hour 30 minutes.

By rail:
From London (Euston) to Oxenholme (Kendal) takes approximately three hours 30 minutes. From Oxenholme (connecting station for all main line trains) to Windermere takes approximately 20 minutes. From Carlisle to Barrow-in-Furness via the coastal route, with stops at many of the towns in between, takes approximately two hours. Trains from Edinburgh to Carlisle take approximately two hours 15 minutes. The historic Settle-Carlisle line also runs through the county bringing passengers from Yorkshire via the Eden Valley.

www.golakes.co.uk/transport.html

Enjoy England official guides to quality

CUMBRIA – THE LAKE DISTRICT

Cumbrian Cottages

2 Lonsdale Street
Carlisle
CA1 1DB

Choose from the largest and best choice of over 500 graded, quality cottages in the Lake District and Cumbria. Our experienced and friendly staff will be delighted to help you find your perfect holiday retreat.

Visit our website for more information or contact us for a free colour brochure.

Telephone: 01228 599950
e-mail: enquiries@cumbrian-cottages.co.uk
www.cumbrian-cottages.co.uk

Opening Hours 9am–9pm Sunday to Friday 9am–5.30pm Saturday

Heart of the Lakes & Cottage Life

Fisherbeck Mill, Old Lake Road, Ambleside, LA22 0DH

330 properties sleeping 2 - 12
Weekly Prices range from £200 - £2000

★★ - ★★★★★

Lakeland's Premier Holiday Letting Agency

For the best selection of self-catering homes in the very heart of England's beautiful Lake District.

Prime locations include Ambleside, Grasmere, Langdale, Keswick, Ullswater etc.

All properties include free leisure club membership. Call us now or visit our informative website.

Tel: 015394 32321 or Fax: 015394 33251
www.heartofthelakes.co.uk
e-mail: info@heartofthelakes.co.uk

Open all year round
Credit Cards: Visa, Access, Switch, Delta

INVESTOR IN PEOPLE

CUMBRIA – THE LAKE DISTRICT

Where to stay in Cumbria – The Lake District

All place names in the blue bands, under which accommodation is listed, are shown on the maps at the front of this guide.

A complete listing of all VisitBritain assessed accommodation covered by this guide appears at the back.

Accommodation symbols
Symbols give useful information about services and facilities. Inside the back cover flap you can find a key to these symbols. Keep it open for easy reference.

ALSTON, Cumbria Map ref 5B2

 ★★★★
4 Units
Sleeping 2–14

ROCK HOUSE ESTATE
Alston
Contact: Mr Paul & Mrs Carol Huish, Valley View,
Rock House Estate, Nenthead, Alston CA9 3NA
T: (01434) 382684
F: (01434) 382685
E: Paul@RockHouseEstate.co.uk
I: www.RockHouseEstate.co.uk

OPEN All Year

Low season per wk
£250.00–£700.00
High season per wk
£350.00–£1,200.00

Luxurious cottages, from a cosy cottage for two up to a farmhouse for 14, all set in 100-acre estate in the beautiful, unspoilt North Pennines.

AMBLESIDE, Cumbria Map ref 5A3 *Tourist Information Centre Tel: (015394) 32582*

 ★★★
1 Unit
Sleeping 4

BIRCH COTTAGE
Ambleside
Contact: Dr Nash, 47 Goring Road, Bounds Green,
London N11 2BT
T: (020) 8888 1252 & (0115) 969 2190
E: birch@vithani.freeserve.co.uk

OPEN All Year

Low season per wk
Min £200.00
High season per wk
Max £400.00

Delightful 200-year-old traditional stone cottage in a quiet hamlet with mountain views. Five minutes' walk to village centre. Comfortably furnished, well equipped. No smokers.

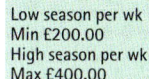

At-a-glance symbols

Symbols at the end of each entry give useful information about services and facilities. A key to symbols can be found inside the back cover flap. Keep this open for easy reference.

CUMBRIA – THE LAKE DISTRICT

AMBLESIDE continued

CHESTNUTS, BEECHES AND THE GRANARY
Ambleside
Contact: Mr Benson, High Sett, Sun Hill Lane, Windermere LA23 1HJ
T: (015394) 42731
F: (015394) 42731
E: sbenson@talk21.com
I: www.accommodationlakedistrict.com

★★★★
3 Units
Sleeping 4–6

Charming cottages and a bungalow converted from a former coach house and tack room, furnished to a high standard. Set in idyllic surroundings overlooking Lake Windermere with panoramic views of the Lakeland mountains. High Wray is a quiet hamlet between Ambleside and Hawkshead, an ideal base for walking/touring.

OPEN All Year

3-night stays available low season.

Low season per wk
£250.00–£550.00
High season per wk
£250.00–£550.00

DOWER HOUSE COTTAGE
Ambleside
Contact: Mrs Margaret Rigg, Dower House Cottage, Dower House, Wray Castle, Ambleside LA22 0JA
T: (015394) 33211
F: (015394) 33211

★★★
1 Unit
Sleeping 5

Self-catering cottage with two bedrooms, large kitchen, dining room, large sitting room, bathroom. French windows opening onto terrace and gardens.

Low season per wk
£268.00–£355.00
High season per wk
£406.00–£516.00

Confirm your booking You are advised to confirm your booking in writing.

THE LAKELAND COTTAGE COMPANY

• • • **Choose** from our portfolio of over 70 characterful VisitBritain inspected cottages

• • • **Plan** what to do and where to go with our Lakeland Life Guide

• • • **Explore** lakes walks and cottages with our wonderful virtual tours

• • • **Call** us for friendly advice in choosing your ideal holiday home

See it all and more on our award winning website
or call for our full colour brochure

www.lakelandcottagecompany.com
Telephone 0870 442 5826   e-mail john@lakelandcottageco.com

WOODSIDE   CHARNEY ROAD   CUMBRIA   THE LAKE DISTRICT   LA11 6BP

CUMBRIA – THE LAKE DISTRICT

AMBLESIDE continued

★★★★
12 Units
Sleeping 2–8

THE LAKELANDS
Ambleside
Contact: Jackie Kingdom, The Lakelands, Lower Gale, Ambleside LA22 0BD
T: (015394) 33777
F: (015394) 31301
E: lakeland@globalnet.co.uk
I: www.the-lakelands.com

OPEN All Year
Payment accepted: Delta, Mastercard, Switch, Visa

Low season per wk
£255.00–£575.00
High season per wk
£425.00–£835.00

Self-catering apartments at The Lakelands, set in a unique position overlooking Ambleside with unspoilt views of the surrounding fells. Furnished with quality in mind. Private leisure centre available for use of guests.

★★★★
1 Unit
Sleeping 1–4

THE ROCK SHOP FLAT
Ambleside
Contact: Ms Louise Burhouse, Burhouse Ltd, Quarmby Mills, Tanyard Road, Oakes, Huddersfield HD3 4YD
T: (01484) 485104
F: (01484) 460036
E: flat@rock-shop.co.uk
I: www.rock-shop.co.uk/flat

OPEN All Year
Payment accepted: Mastercard, Switch, Visa

Low season per wk
£198.00–£490.00
High season per wk
£208.00–£640.00

Beautiful flat, recently refurbished to very high standard, double and twin, dvd, cd, barbeque area. Central Ambleside, close to shops, restaurants, pubs and cinema.

★★★
1 Unit

SCANDALE BRIDGE COTTAGE
Ambleside
Contact: Mr Derek Sweeney, Kings Head Hotel, Thirlspot, Keswick CA12 4TN
T: (017687) 72393
F: (017687) 72309
E: stay@lakedistrictinns.co.uk
I: www.lakedistrictinns.co.uk

A beautifully furnished, period Lakeland-stone house on the edge of Ambleside, fully equipped to be your country home from home in the Lake District. Mature, private gardens with river frontage, ample parking. This is a wonderful base for touring the Lake District.

Low season per wk
£250.00–£500.00
High season per wk
£500.00–£800.00

★★-★★★★★
67 Units
Sleeping 2–14

See Ad p84

WHEELWRIGHTS HOLIDAY COTTAGES
Ambleside
Contact: Mr Bass, Wheelwrights, Elterwater, Ambleside LA22 9HS
T: (015394) 37635
F: (015394) 37618
E: enquiries@wheelwrights.com
I: www.wheelwrights.com

For nearly 30 years Wheelwrights has been letting some of the very best cottages set in the most beautiful scenery in central Lakes. For more information please visit our website or telephone. 'Escape to the beauty of the Lakes'.

OPEN All Year
Payment accepted: Delta, Mastercard, Switch, Visa

Low season per wk
£150.00–£1,500.00
High season per wk
£350.00–£2,300.00

Short breaks available autumn, winter and early spring. See website for details.

67

CUMBRIA – THE LAKE DISTRICT

APPLEBY-IN-WESTMORLAND, Cumbria Map ref 5B3 Tourist Information Centre Tel: (017683) 51177

★★★★
2 Units
Sleeping 2–6

GLEBE HAYLOFT AND GLEBE STABLE
Appleby-in-Westmorland
Contact: Mr Martin Wardle, Goosemire Cottages,
Bateman Fold Barn, Crook, Nr Kendal LA8 8LN
T: (015395) 68102
F: (015395) 68104
E: goosemirecottage@aol.com
I: www.glebeholidays.co.uk

OPEN All Year

Low season per wk
£200.00–£255.00
High season per wk
£320.00–£405.00

Spacious, high-quality barn conversion in peaceful, attractive village. Stables suitable for disabled. Pets welcome. Short breaks.

★★★
1 Unit
Sleeping 4–5

LONG MARTON STATION
Appleby-in-Westmorland
Contact: David and Madeleine Adams, The Station,
Milburn Road, Long Marton, Appleby-in-Westmorland
CA16 6BU
T: (0161) 775 5669
E: info@LongMartonStation.fsnet.co.uk
I: www.LongMartonStation.co.uk

OPEN All Year
Payment accepted: Euros

Low season per wk
£200.00–£280.00
High season per wk
£280.00–£360.00

Long Marton Station, on the spectacular Settle-Carlisle Railway in the unspoilt Eden Valley between the Lakes and the Pennines, occupies a commanding position just outside the village. Lounge (original marble fireplace), dining room, kitchen, bathroom (plus shower), double bedroom with cot, twin bedroom. All inclusive (even firewood!), welcome pack on arrival. Pets by arrangement.

BASSENTHWAITE, Cumbria Map ref 5A2

★★★
1 Unit
Sleeping 5

THE GRANARY
Wigton
Contact: Margaret Crooks, Road Farm, Ruthwaite,
Ireby, Wigton CA7 1HG
T: (016973) 71524
E: mcrooks.roadfarm@btopenworld.com

OPEN All Year

Low season per wk
£260.00–£320.00
High season per wk
£320.00–£430.00

Barn conversion in a quiet hamlet. Open views of Skiddaw and Calbeck Fells and only three miles from Bassenthwaite Lake. Central for lakes, coast, Scottish Borders and Hadrian's Wall.

★★★★
5 Units
Sleeping 2–6

IRTON HOUSE FARM
Cockermouth
Contact: Mr & Mrs Almond, Isel, Cockermouth
CA13 9ST
T: (017687) 76380
E: almond@farmersweekly.net
I: www.irtonhousefarm.com

OPEN All Year
Payment accepted:
Mastercard, Switch, Visa,
Euros

Low season per wk
Min £295.00
High season per wk
Max £385.00

Immaculate, spacious properties, all furnished to a high specification. Shopping at Keswick and Cockermouth. Superb views, walks and places of interest. Prices are for two people.

Credit card bookings

If you book by telephone and are asked for your credit card number it is advisable to check the proprietor's policy should you cancel your reservation.

CUMBRIA – THE LAKE DISTRICT

BUTTERMERE, Cumbria Map ref 5A3

★★★★
6 Units
Sleeping 2–6

Superbly situated, surrounded by fells in Area of Outstanding Natural Beauty. Each apartment is furnished to a high standard. All modern facilities. Dogs welcome.

BRIDGE HOTEL SELF CATERING APARTMENTS
Cockermouth
Contact: Mr John McGuire, Bridge Hotel, Buttermere, Cockermouth CA13 9UZ
T: (017687) 70252
F: (017687) 70215
I: www.bridge-hotel.com

OPEN All Year
Payment accepted: Mastercard, Switch, Visa

Low season per wk
Min £210.00
High season per wk
Max £650.00

★★★★
1 Unit
Sleeping 2–4

Situated at the foot of Melbreak on a working farm. Looking towards Crummock Water, luxury, cosy 16thC cottage. Boasts all modern facilities.

LANTHWAITE GREEN FARM COTTAGE
Cockermouth
Contact: Mr John McGuire, Bridge Hotel, Buttermere, Cockermouth CA13 9UZ
T: (017687) 70252
F: (017687) 70215
E: enquiries@bridge-hotel.com
I: www.bridge-hotel.com

OPEN All Year
Payment accepted: Mastercard, Switch, Visa

Low season per wk
Min £210.00
High season per wk
Max £650.00

CALDBECK, Cumbria Map ref 5A2

★★★★
1 Unit
Sleeping 1–3

THE BARN, MANOR COTTAGE
Wigton
Contact: Mrs Ann Wade, The Barn, Manor Cottage, Fellside, Caldbeck, Wigton CA7 8HA
T: (016974) 78214
E: walterwade@tiscali.co.uk

Converted barn with pine beams, nestling in the Caldbeck Fells in unspoilt Northern Lakeland. Comfortable, well equipped. Panoramic views with garden and patio opening onto fells.

Low season per wk
£160.00–£220.00
High season per wk
£220.00–£300.00

CARLISLE, Cumbria Map ref 5A2 *Tourist Information Centre Tel: (01228) 625600*

★★★★
1 Unit
Sleeping 1–4

A spacious, tastefully furnished and well-equipped cottage adjoining a Georgian Listed house in a village location three miles from historic Carlisle city. Village amenities include a shop, post office and pub serving good food. Relax on the patio or visit the beautiful Lake District, Hadrian's Wall and the Scottish Borders.

WEST COTTAGE
Carlisle
Contact: Mrs Allison Stamper, Cringles, Cumwhinton, Carlisle CA4 8DL
T: (01228) 561600

OPEN All Year

Open all year. Short breaks available.

Low season per wk
£210.00–£250.00
High season per wk
£300.00–£395.00

CUMBRIA – THE LAKE DISTRICT

CARTMEL, Cumbria Map ref 5A3

★★★★
1 Unit
Sleeping 2–8

GRANGE END COTTAGES
Grange-over-Sands
Contact: Mr Simon Cleasby, 45 The Row, Silverdale, Lancashire LA5 0UG
T: (01524) 702955 & 07770 301709
E: simoncleasby@aol.com
I: www.holidaycottagescumbria.com

A charming and luxurious 18thC Georgian cottage. Oak beams and inglenook fireplace, thick stone walls, and lavishly furnished with antiques, four-poster bed. One mile from historic Cartmel village with 12thC priory, cobbled streets and four great pubs. Lake Windermere is only a 10-minute drive. Plenty of walks right from the doorstep of the cottage.

OPEN All Year

Payment accepted: Delta, Mastercard, Switch, Visa, Euros

Low season per wk
£280.00–£380.00
High season per wk
£480.00–£680.00

Short breaks available, except during school holidays.

COCKERMOUTH, Cumbria Map ref 5A2 *Tourist Information Centre Tel: (01900) 822634*

★★★
1 Unit
Sleeping 1–6

37 KIRKGATE
Cockermouth
Contact: Mr Nelson & Mrs Valerie Chicken, 39 Kirkgate, Cockermouth CA13 9PJ
T: (01900) 823236
F: (01900) 825983
E: valandnelson@btopenworld.com
I: www.37kirkgate.com

Low season per wk
Min £200.00
High season per wk
Max £300.00

An ideal base for touring Cumbria, this spacious and comfortable three-bedroomed Georgian house overlooks tree-lined, cobbled area of Kirkgate.

CONISTON, Cumbria Map ref 5A3

★★★★
2 Units
Sleeping 6

1 AND 2 ASH GILL COTTAGES
Torver, Coniston
Contact: Mrs Dorothy Cowburn, Lyndene, Pope Lane, Whitestake, Preston PR4 4JR
T: (01772) 612832

Set amidst the rolling hills surrounding Coniston Water, the houses are equipped to the highest standard. Ample parking, gardens and patios. Central heating throughout for the cooler months. Excellent base for walking, touring, watersports and pony trekking.

OPEN All Year

Low season per wk
Max £310.00
High season per wk
Max £460.00

★★★★
7 Units
Sleeping 2–16

BANK GROUND FARM COTTAGES
Coniston
Contact: Mrs Lucy Batty, Bank Ground Farm Cottages, Bank Ground, Coniston LA21 8AA
T: (015394) 41264
F: (015394) 41900
I: www.bankground.com

'Storybook' cottages, with Arthur Ransome's Swallows and Amazons being both written and filmed here. A mere 150yds from the properties' own 0.5-mile stretch of Coniston shoreline, they command uninterrupted views over the lake to Coniston village and its magnificent backdrop of Lakeland fells. Ideal for all outdoor activities.

OPEN All Year

Payment accepted: Delta, Mastercard, Switch, Visa

Low season per wk
Min £245.00
High season per wk
Max £3,250.00

Mini-breaks available late Oct-mid Feb (excl Christmas and New Year).

CUMBRIA – THE LAKE DISTRICT

CONISTON continued

★★★
1 Unit
Sleeping 5

1 FAR END COTTAGES
Coniston
Contact: Mrs Andrea Batho, High Hollin Bank, Coniston LA21 8AG
T: (015394) 41680
E: a.batho@virgin.net
I: www.cottagescumbria.com

This charming, Grade II Listed cottage is in a lovely, peaceful location at the foot of the fell, close to the village and the lake. It is furnished and equipped to a high standard. There is an open fire in the cosy sitting room and delightful views from the front rooms.

OPEN All Year

Low season per wk
£198.00–£297.00
High season per wk
£324.00–£423.00

★★★
1 Unit
Sleeping 8

5 HOLME GROUND COTTAGES
Coniston
Contact: Mrs Kate Bradshaw, The Rookery, Oaklands, Riding Mill NE44 6AR
T: (01434) 682526
E: rookery1@tiscali.co.uk

Tranquilly located, traditionally built (1860s), former quarryman's cottage in (rarely fully occupied) terrace of eight. Cosy and comfortable with double-glazing and open fire. Rates include coal and electricity throughout the year. Well-equipped home from home surrounded by woodland and fell with attractive views. Enjoy great family fun and walking straight from the doorstep.

OPEN All Year

Free linen supplied (up to 4 people) for certain weeks low season.

Low season per wk
£225.00–£290.00
High season per wk
£350.00–£455.00

★★★
1 Unit

SHELT GILL
Coniston
Contact: Mrs Rosalind Dean, 9 The Fairway, Sheffield S10 4LX
T: (0114) 230 8077
F: (0114) 230 8077
E: holiday@sheltgill.co.uk
I: www.sheltgill.co.uk

Medieval cottage with a view of Lake Coniston from the timbered living room, a stream in the garden and easy access to hill walks.

OPEN All Year

Payment accepted: Euros

Low season per wk
Min £190.00
High season per wk
Max £400.00

★★–★★★★★
8 Units
Sleeping 2–6

THURSTON HOUSE & THURSTON VIEW
Coniston
Contact: Mr & Mrs Jefferson, 21 Chale Green, Harwood, Bolton BL2 3NJ
T: (01204) 419261
E: alan@jefferson99.freeserve.co.uk
I: www.jefferson99.freeserve.co.uk

Thurston View: lovely stone cottage with superb views. Sorry, no pets/smoking in cottage. Short walk to village centre. Parking for one car. Thurston House: large Victorian house converted into individual apartments. Quiet location close to village centre. Private parking at rear of property.

OPEN All Year

Short breaks may be available – please phone for details.

Low season per wk
£90.00–£245.00
High season per wk
£150.00–£380.00

CUMBRIA – THE LAKE DISTRICT

CROSTHWAITE, Cumbria Map ref 5A3

★★★★
3 Units
Sleeping 1–7

GREENBANK
Kendal
Contact: Jackie Gaskell, Crosthwaite, Kendal LA8 8JD
T: (015395) 68598
E: greenbank@nascr.net
I: www.greenbank-cumbria.co.uk

OPEN All Year

Low season per wk
£150.00–£615.00

Delightfully appointed holiday homes, extremely welcoming to canine companions. Access to wonderful, quiet walks from your doorstep. Perfect peace.

DENT, Cumbria Map ref 5B3

★★★
2 Units
Sleeping 4

MIDDLETON'S COTTAGE AND FOUNTAIN COTTAGE
Sedbergh
Contact: Mr & Mrs Ayers, The Old Rectory, Litlington, Polegate BN26 5RB
T: (01323) 870032
F: (01323) 870032
E: candpayers@mistral.co.uk
I: www.dentcottages.co.uk

Modernised mid-17thC cottages in centre of small, quaint village, comfortably furnished and decorated to high standards. Quiet, unspoilt Dentdale offers a good base for walking, touring and exploring the Yorkshire Dales or the Lake District, with Kendal and Hawes nearby. Brochure available. Open all year.

OPEN All Year

Short breaks from Oct-Mar, weekend or mid-week. Any combination, subject to availability.

Low season per wk
£185.00–£235.00
High season per wk
£245.00–£290.00

ELTERWATER, Cumbria Map ref 5A3

★★★
2 Units
Sleeping 1–4

LANE ENDS COTTAGES
Ambleside
Contact: Mrs Rice, Fellside, 3 & 4 Lane Ends, Elterwater, Ambleside LA22 9HN
T: (015394) 37678

OPEN All Year

Low season per wk
Min £200.00
High season per wk
Max £380.00

Family-run stone-built cottages with open fireplaces. In a peaceful setting in Great Langdale on the edge of the common, with views of the surrounding fells.

★★★
2 Units
Sleeping 3–4

WISTARIA COTTAGE AND 3 MAIN STREET
Ambleside
Contact: Mr Geoffrey & Mrs Doreen Beardmore, 2 Beech Drive, Kidsgrove, Stoke-on-Trent ST7 1BA
T: (01782) 783170
F: (01782) 783170
E: geoff.doreen.beardmore@ntlword.com

OPEN All Year

Low season per wk
£308.00–£331.00
High season per wk
£358.00–£411.00

Traditional 18thC cottages near village centre. Tastefully renovated, well equipped. Serviced and maintained by owners. Warm and comfortable, off-peak heating, open fires. Fell and valley walking.

Use your *i*s

There are more than 550 Tourist Information Centres throughout England offering friendly help with accommodation and holiday ideas as well as suggestions of places to visit and things to do. You'll find addresses in the local phone book.

CUMBRIA – THE LAKE DISTRICT

ESKDALE, Cumbria Map ref 5A3

★★★★
2 Units
Sleeping 1–6

THE CHALETS
Boot, Eskdale
Contact: Philip Hayden & Lisa Borrowdale, The Chalets, Boot, Eskdale CA19 1TF
T: (019467) 23128
E: info@thechalets.co.uk
I: www.thechalets.co.uk

Recently renovated to a high standard, The Chalets offer spacious, homely accommodation. Leading from the living room is a south-facing deck with views over the mature riverside gardens. Perfect for the lakes. Climb a different mountain every day or relax surrounded by stunning scenery.

OPEN All Year

Flexible short breaks available Nov-Feb. Any combination of days to suit your plans.

Low season per wk
£220.00–£320.00
High season per wk
£320.00–£450.00

★★★
4 Units
Sleeping 2–6

FISHERGROUND FARM HOLIDAYS
Holmrook
Contact: Mrs Hall, Fisherground Farm Holidays, Fisherground Farm, Eskdale, Holmrook CA19 1TF
T: (01946) 723319
E: holidays@fisherground.co.uk
I: www.fisherground.co.uk

Fisherground is a lovely traditional hill farm, offering accommodation in cottages and pine lodges. Ideal for walkers, nature lovers, dogs and children. We have a games room, an adventure playground, raft ponds and even our own station on the miniature Ravenglass and Eskdale Railway!

OPEN All Year

Short breaks available Nov-Mar.

Low season per wk
£225.00–£330.00
High season per wk
£350.00–£540.00

★★★★★
1 Unit
Sleeping 8

LONGRIGG GREEN
Holmrook
Contact: Mrs Christine Carter, Forest How, Eskdale, Holmrook CA19 1TR
T: (019467) 23201
F: (019467) 23190
E: fcarter@easynet.co.uk
I: www.longrigg.green.btinternet.co.uk

OPEN All Year

Low season per wk
£320.00–£505.00
High season per wk
£505.00–£725.00

Spacious, detached house with garden and stream. Four bedrooms, jacuzzi whirlpool bath, conservatory, log fire, drying room. Steam railway, pub and shop nearby. Brochure available.

★★★★
1 Unit
Sleeping 2–6

OLD BRANTRAKE
Eskdale
Contact: Mr Tyson, Old Brantrake, Brant Rake, Eskdale, Holmrook CA19 1TT
T: (019467) 23340
F: (019467) 23340
E: tyson@eskdale1.demon.co.uk

17thC Listed farmhouse in a quiet rural setting; ideal for walking, exploring the central fells or touring. Restored to high standard, three bedrooms, sleeping up to six, with two WCs, bath and shower, modern kitchen and woodfire. In winter short lets (minimum three nights) are also available. Brochure.

OPEN All Year

Low season per wk
£250.00–£350.00
High season per wk
£365.00–£475.00

CUMBRIA – THE LAKE DISTRICT

FIELD BROUGHTON, Cumbria Map ref 5A3

★★★★
1 Unit
Sleeping 1–4

THE BYRE
Grange-over-Sands
Contact: Mrs Penny Crowe, The Byre,
Broughton House Farm, Grange-over-Sands LA11 6HN
T: (015395) 36577
E: p_crowe@talk21.com
I: http://lakedistrictcottage.mysite.freeserve.com

OPEN All Year

Low season per wk
Min £250.00
High season per wk
Max £400.00

A two-bedroom newly converted cottage, open plan on split levels, lounge, dining room/kitchen with doors to private patio.

GAMBLESBY, Cumbria Map ref 5B2

★★★–★★★★★
4 Units
Sleeping 2–6

CHURCH COURT COTTAGES
Penrith
Contact: Mark Cowell, Church Villa, Gamblesby,
Penrith CA10 1HR
T: (01768) 881682
F: (01768) 889055
E: markcowell@tiscali.co.uk
I: www.gogamblesby.co.uk

OPEN All Year
Payment accepted: Euros

Low season per wk
£165.00–£299.00
High season per wk
£249.00–£595.00

Well-equipped sandstone cottages set round a beautiful courtyard and garden in tranquil, picturesque Gamblesby in the unspoilt North Pennines. Fifteen minutes from Penrith and the M6.

GILSLAND, Cumbria Map ref 5B2

★★★
1 Unit
Sleeping 4

WORKING DALES PONY CENTRE
Brampton
Contact: Mr & Mrs Parker, Working Dales Pony Centre,
Clarks Hill Farm, Gilsland, Brampton CA8 7DF
T: (016977) 47208
E: Dales_Logger@clarkshill.fsnet.co.uk
I: www.daleslogger.com

OPEN All Year

Low season per wk
Min £350.00
High season per wk
£350.00–£400.00

Barn converted to a high standard situated on a traditional Cumberland farm close to Hadrian's Wall. Spectacular scenery. Rare breeds of animals kept.

GLENRIDDING, Cumbria Map ref 5A3

★★★★
4 Units
Sleeping 2–6

FELL VIEW HOLIDAYS
Penrith
Contact: Mr & Mrs Burnett, Fell View Holidays, Fell View,
Grisedale Bridge, Penrith CA11 0PJ
T: (017684) 82342 & (017688) 67420
F: (017688) 67420
E: enquiries@fellviewholidays.com
I: www.fellviewholidays.com

Situated at the south end of Lake Ullswater with wonderful views of the mountains and lake, our well-appointed cottages and apartments are in our own gardens and grounds where there is an abundance of wildlife and places to sit and relax. You can also walk through our wildflower meadows to the river.

OPEN All Year

Low season per wk
£212.00–£275.00
High season per wk
£293.00–£440.00

GRANGE-OVER-SANDS, Cumbria Map ref 5A3 *Tourist Information Centre Tel: (015395) 34026*

★★★
1 Unit
Sleeping 2–4

CORNERWAYS BUNGALOW
Grange-over-Sands
Contact: Mrs Eunice Rigg, Prospect House,
Barber Green, Grange-over-Sands LA11 6HU
T: (015395) 36329

Low season per wk
£250.00–£325.00
High season per wk
£325.00–£375.00

Pleasant bungalow in quiet situation, with double and twin bedroom. All-round views, private garden with parking. Ideal base for touring Lake District. Personal supervision. Open March to November.

CUMBRIA – THE LAKE DISTRICT

GRANGE-OVER-SANDS continued

★★★
1 Unit
Sleeping 1–6

DYER DENE
Grange-over-Sands
Contact: Mrs Andrews, 121 Dorchester Road, Garstang, Preston PR3 1FE
T: (01995) 602769
E: dyerdene@fish.co.uk
I: www.dyerdene.com

Comfortable cottage in tranquil valley. Beautiful views and excellent local walking. Garage-cum-games room and garden. Ideal for children. Radiators in all bedrooms. On arrival, the peace is immediate. Unload, put the kettle on and relax with a log fire in winter or in the secluded garden in summer.

OPEN All Year

Open all year round. 3-night stays (minimum) available Nov-mid-Mar also 7 days over New Year.

Low season per wk
Min £200.00
High season per wk
Max £390.00

GRASMERE, Cumbria Map ref 5A3

★★★★
1 Unit
Sleeping 2–12

BRAMRIGG HOUSE
Grasmere
Contact: Mr Derek Sweeney, Lakeland Inns & Cottages, Kings Head Hotel, Thirlspot, Keswick CA12 4TN
T: (017687) 72393
F: (017687) 72309
I: www.lakedistrictinns.co.uk

Spacious, detached house with sweeping views from its elevated position over the Vale of Grasmere. Beautifully furnished with ample parking and mature gardens. A true country home in the Lake District.

OPEN All Year

Low season per wk
£500.00–£800.00
High season per wk
£1,000.00–£2,200.00

★★★★
3 Units
Sleeping 2–5

BROADRAYNE FARM COTTAGES
Grasmere
Contact: Mrs Jo Dennison Drake, Broadrayne Farm Cottages, Broadrayne Farm, Grasmere, Ambleside LA22 9RU
T: (015394) 35055
F: (015394) 35733
E: jo@grasmere-accommodation.co.uk
I: www.grasmere-accommodation.co.uk

With dramatic mountains, gentle rolling fells, glorious lakes and peaceful valleys, Broadrayne Farm is at the very heart of the Lake District, superbly located for wonderful views. The atmospheric traditional farm properties have been lovingly renovated with today's creature comforts, including open coal fires, central heating and off-street parking. Pets welcome by arrangement.

OPEN All Year
Payment accepted: Mastercard, Switch, Visa

A week booked in the year allows 10% off a second week booked in March (excl Easter holidays).

Low season per wk
£245.00–£275.00
High season per wk
£408.00–£565.00

★★★
3 Units
Sleeping 2–5

LAKE VIEW HOLIDAY APARTMENTS
Ambleside
Contact: Mr Stephen & Mrs Michelle King, Lake View Holiday Apartments, Lake View Drive, Grasmere, Ambleside LA22 9TD
T: (015394) 35167
I: www.lakeview-grasmere.com

Tranquil setting close to village centre. Lakeshore access. Well equipped including TV/VCR/CD. Some recently refurbished, all with baths and showers. Many varied walks from the door.

OPEN All Year
Payment accepted: Delta, Mastercard, Switch, Visa

Low season per wk
Min £99.00
High season per wk
Max £391.00

75

CUMBRIA – THE LAKE DISTRICT

GRASMERE continued

1 Unit
Sleeping 2–4

In a peaceful riverside location, a short, level stroll to village shops, pubs and restaurants, our spacious ground floor garden apartment has two double en suite bedrooms, lounge with access to garden patio, large fully equipped kitchen/dining room. All services and linen included. Sorry, no pets, non-smoking.

ROTHAY LODGE GARDEN APARTMENT
Grasmere
Contact: Mrs Lindsay Rogers, 54A Trevor Road, West Bridgford, Nottingham NG2 6FT
T: (0115) 923 2618
F: (0115) 923 3984
I: www.rothay-lodge.co.uk

OPEN All Year

Low season per wk
£300.00–£380.00
High season per wk
£380.00–£575.00

---

1 Unit
Sleeping 2–5

A personal welcome awaits you at this attractive Lakeland house furnished to a high standard. Ideal situation on village outskirts, within minutes of local amenities. Three bedrooms, large, modern kitchen, dining room, comfortable lounge with magnificent views of fells. Spacious, yet cosy and warm in winter (coal fire optional). Attractive garden.

SILVERGARTH
Grasmere
Contact: Mrs Susan Coward, Silvergarth, 1 Low Riddings, Grasmere, Ambleside LA22 9QY
T: (015394) 35828
F: (015394) 35828
E: cowards.silvergarth@btinternet.com
I: www.cowards.silvergarth.btinternet.co.uk

OPEN All Year

Low season per wk
£165.00–£290.00
High season per wk
£345.00–£420.00

GREAT ASBY, Cumbria Map ref 5B3

3 Units
Sleeping 2–5

SCALEBECK HOLIDAY COTTAGES
Appleby-in-Westmorland
Contact: Keith & Diane, Scalebeck, Great Asby, Appleby-in-Westmorland CA16 6TH
T: (01768) 351006
F: (01768) 353532
E: mail@scalebeckholidaycottages.com
I: www.scalebeckholidaycottages.com

Self-catering cottages in barn conversion. Secluded valley, abundant wildlife. Non-smokers, pets welcome, games room, open all year.

OPEN All Year

Low season per wk
£220.00–£290.00
High season per wk
£290.00–£440.00

GREAT LANGDALE, Cumbria Map ref 5A3

6 Units
Sleeping 4–6

ELTERWATER HALL
Ambleside
Contact: Mrs Kath Morton, The Langdale Estate, Great Langdale, Ambleside LA22 9JD
T: (015394) 38012
F: (015394) 37394
E: sales@langdale.co.uk
I: www.langdale.co.uk

Elterwater Hall is situated in its own grounds and forms part of the award-winning Langdale Estate, with its hotel and country club a short walk away.

OPEN All Year
Payment accepted: Amex, Delta, Mastercard, Switch, Visa, Euros

Low season per wk
£585.00–£790.00
High season per wk
£995.00–£1,435.00

CUMBRIA – THE LAKE DISTRICT

GREAT LANGDALE continued

★★★★
10 Units
Sleeping 4–8

LANGDALE ESTATE CHAPEL STILE APARTMENTS
Ambleside
Contact: Mrs Kath Morton, Langdale Estate Chapel Stile Apartments, The Langdale Estate, Great Langdale, Ambleside LA22 9JD
T: (015394) 38012
F: (015394) 37394
E: sales@langdale.co.uk
I: www.langdale.co.uk

OPEN All Year

Payment accepted: Amex, Delta, Mastercard, Switch, Visa, Euros

Low season per wk
£465.00–£665.00
High season per wk
£790.00–£1,020.00

Chapel Stile is situated next to Wainwrights Inn and forms part of the award-winning Langdale Estate, with its hotel and country club a short walk away.

★★★★★
81 Units
Sleeping 4–8

LANGDALE ESTATE LODGES
Ambleside
Contact: Mrs Kath Morton, Langdale Estate Lodges, Great Langdale, Ambleside LA22 9JD
T: (015394) 38012
F: (015394) 37394
E: sales@langdale.co.uk
I: www.langdale.co.uk

OPEN All Year

Payment accepted: Amex, Delta, Mastercard, Switch, Visa, Euros

Low season per wk
£530.00–£825.00
High season per wk
£865.00–£1,585.00

Formerly an old gunpowder mill for the Elterwater Gunpowder Company and now a hotel and lodge complex, with a leisure centre and all facilities attached.

GRIZEDALE, Cumbria Map ref 5A3

★★★
2 Units
Sleeping 2–6

HIGH DALE PARK BARN
Ulverston
Contact: Mr Peter Brown, High Dale Park Farm, High Dale, Ulverston LA12 8LJ
T: (01229) 860226
I: www.lakesweddingmusic.com

Delightfully situated, south-facing, 17thC converted barn attached to owner's farmhouse. Wonderful views down quiet, secluded valley, surrounded by beautiful, broadleaf woodland, rich in wildlife. Oak beams, log fire, central heating, patio. Hawkshead and Beatrix Potter's house three miles.

OPEN All Year

Short breaks available minimum 2 nights.

Low season per wk
Min £195.00
High season per wk
Max £670.00

HAVERIGG, Cumbria Map ref 5A3

★★★★★
1 Unit
Sleeping 1–4

LAZEY COTTAGE
Millom
Contact: Mrs Gloria Parsons and Mrs P Jenkinson, Orchard House, The Hill, Millom LA18 5HE
T: (01229) 772515 & 773291

OPEN All Year

Low season per wk
£225.00–£270.00
High season per wk
£295.00–£450.00

Lovely well-equipped seaside cottage overlooking Haverigg's harbour and beaches. Water-skiing, fishing, golf, walking, shops and pubs nearby. Excellent touring base for the Lake District.

HAWKSHEAD, Cumbria Map ref 5A3

★★★★
1 Unit
Sleeping 1–6

BEN FOLD
Ambleside
Contact: Mrs Anne Gallagher, Hideaways, The Minstrels Gallery, The Square Hawkshead, Ambleside LA22 0NZ
T: (015394) 42435
F: (015394) 36178
E: bookings@lakelandhideaways.co.uk
I: www.lakeland-hideaways.co.uk

OPEN All Year

Low season per wk
£250.00–£375.00
High season per wk
£375.00–£465.00

Detached character cottage in a quiet rural location with open fires. Private parking and garden.

CUMBRIA – THE LAKE DISTRICT

HAWKSHEAD continued

★★★–★★★★★
8 Units
Sleeping 2–6

BROOMRIGGS
Ambleside
Contact: Mrs Wilson, Nr Sawrey, Hawkshead, Ambleside LA22 0JX
T: (015394) 36280
E: broomriggs@zoom.co.uk
I: www.broomriggs.co.uk

OPEN All Year

3-night stays available.

Low season per wk
£150.00–£250.00
High season per wk
£200.00–£480.00

Large country house converted into comfortable apartments, set in 100 acres of gardens, woodlands and lake frontage with rowing boats. All apartments have views of Esthwaite Water and surrounding fells. Located one mile from Hawkshead on the B5286 to Windermere ferry. Within easy access of all areas of the Lake District.

★★★
9 Units
Sleeping 2–6

THE CROFT HOLIDAY FLATS
Ambleside
Contact: Mrs Barr, The Croft Holiday Flats, North Lonsdale Road, Hawkshead, Ambleside LA22 0NX
T: (015394) 36374
F: (015394) 36544
E: enquiries@hawkshead-croft.com
I: www.hawkshead-croft.com

OPEN All Year

Payment accepted: Delta, Mastercard, Switch, Visa

Low season per wk
£190.00–£300.00
High season per wk
£315.00–£435.00

Large house, with garden and private parking, converted into holiday flats. In village of Hawkshead on B5286 from Ambleside.

★★★★
1 Unit
Sleeping 1–8

HIGH ORCHARD
Ambleside
Contact: Mrs Anne Gallagher, Hideaways, The Minstrels Gallery, The Square, Hawkshead, Ambleside LA22 0NZ
T: (015394) 42435
F: (015394) 36178
E: bookings@lakeland-hideaways.co.uk
I: www.lakeland-hideaways.co.uk

OPEN All Year

Low season per wk
£495.00–£625.00
High season per wk
£710.00–£920.00

A spacious detached Victorian house in an elevated position. With lake views and a short walk from Hawkshead.

★★★
1 Unit

MEADOW VIEW
Ambleside
Contact: Blakes Country Cottages, Spring Mill, Earby BB94 0AA
T: 08700 708090
F: 08705 851150
I: www.blakes-cottages.co.uk

OPEN All Year

Payment accepted: Amex, Delta, Mastercard, Switch, Visa

Low season per wk
£205.00–£251.00
High season per wk
£305.00–£434.00

Three hundred-year-old cottage in the centre of Hawkshead. Entrance hall, bathroom, twin bedroom, double bedroom with wash basin and separate wc, kitchen and living accommodation. Central heating.

Important note Information on accommodation listed in this guide has been supplied by the proprietors. As changes may occur you are advised to check details at the time of booking.

CUMBRIA – THE LAKE DISTRICT

HAWKSHEAD continued

★★★★
2 Units
Sleeping 2–5

A superb barn conversion set amid stunning countryside. A quiet location within easy reach of Hawkshead village. Cosy, comfortable interior, furnished to a very high standard – all home comforts. Log fires. An excellent base for walking, cycling and sightseeing. Delightful private garden. Off-road parking. Lovely views.

THE OLD BARN & BARN END COTTAGE
Ambleside
Contact: Mrs Anne Gallagher, Hideaways,
The Minstrels Gallery, The Square, Hawkshead, Ambleside
LA22 0NZ
T: (015394) 42435
F: (015394) 36178
E: bookings@lakeland-hideaways.co.uk
I: www.lakeland-hideaways.co.uk

OPEN All Year

Short breaks available autumn, winter and early spring.

Low season per wk
£220.00–£375.00
High season per wk
£340.00–£445.00

★★–★★★★★
67 Units
Sleeping 2–14

See Ad p84

For nearly 30 years Wheelwrights has been letting some of the very best cottages set in the most beautiful scenery in central Lakes. For more information please visit our website or telephone. 'Escape to the beauty of the Lakes'.

WHEELWRIGHTS HOLIDAY COTTAGES
Ambleside
Contact: Mr Bass, Wheelwrights, Elterwater, Ambleside
LA22 9HS
T: (015394) 37635
F: (015394) 37618
E: enquiries@wheelwrights.com
I: www.wheelwrights.com

OPEN All Year
Payment accepted: Delta, Mastercard, Switch, Visa

Short breaks available autumn, winter and early spring. See website for details.

Low season per wk
£150.00–£1,500.00
High season per wk
£350.00–£2,300.00

HIGH LORTON, Cumbria Map ref 5A3

★★★★
1 Unit
Sleeping 2

Traditional Lakeland barn with exposed beams, converted to quality accommodation. In beautiful Lorton Vale, overlooking local fells. Close to Keswick and northern Lakes. Warm in winter, light and sunny in summer. Situated in the midst of superb walking country. All prices include electricity, central heating and linen. Tennis courts nearby.

HOLEMIRE HOUSE BARN
Cockermouth
Contact: Mrs Angela Fearfield, Holemire House Barn,
Holemire House, High Lorton, Cockermouth CA13 9TX
T: (01900) 85225
E: enquiries@lakelandbarn.co.uk
I: www.lakelandbarn.co.uk

OPEN All Year

Low season per wk
£225.00–£245.00
High season per wk
£260.00–£375.00

 Enjoy England official guides to quality
Please mention this guide when making your booking.

CUMBRIA – THE LAKE DISTRICT

HUTTON ROOF, Cumbria Map ref 5A2

★★★★★
4 Units
Sleeping 2–20

CARROCK COTTAGES
Penrith
Contact: Mr Malcolm & Mrs Gillian Iredale, Carrock House, Howhill, Penrith CA11 0XY
T: (01768) 484111
F: (01768) 488850
E: info@carrockcottages.co.uk
I: www.carrockcottages.co.uk

Luxury in a quiet rural location near the lovely villages of Hesket Newmarket, Caldbeck and Greystoke. Explore the northern Lake District or head north to historic Carlisle and on to Hadrian's Wall. Restaurants, fell walking and other activities. A warm welcome guaranteed.

OPEN All Year

Payment accepted: Amex, Delta, Mastercard, Switch, Visa

Low season per wk £325.00–£1,295.00
High season per wk £355.00–£1,895.00

15% discount on second week of stay.

KENDAL, Cumbria Map ref 5B3 Tourist Information Centre Tel: (01539) 725758

★★★
1 Unit
Sleeping 2–4

BARKINBECK COTTAGE
Kendal
Contact: Mrs A Hamilton, Barkin House, Gatebeck, Kendal LA8 0HX
T: (015395) 67122
E: ann@barkin.fsnet.co.uk
I: www.barkinbeck.co.uk

Converted barn in beautiful, peaceful countryside between Lakes and Dales, an ideal base for touring and walking. Log fire, owner maintained. Adapted for disabled.

OPEN All Year

Low season per wk £220.00–£275.00
High season per wk £275.00–£320.00

★★★-★★★★★
9 Units
Sleeping 2–9

FIELD END BARNS & SHAW END MANSION
Kendal
Contact: Mr & Mrs Robinson, Field End Barns & Shaw End Mansion, Patton, Kendal LA8 9DU
T: (01539) 824220
F: (01539) 824464
E: robinson@fieldendholidays.co.uk
I: www.fieldendholidays.co.uk

Field End Barns and Shaw End Mansion are set on a 200-acre estate in a beautiful location. The Barns provide award-winning cottages of character with own private gardens, exposed oak beams and open fireplaces. Shaw End Mansion contains four spacious and elegant apartments in a restored Georgian mansion.

OPEN All Year

Payment accepted: Amex, Mastercard, Switch, Visa

Low season per wk £195.00–£230.00
High season per wk £240.00–£470.00

Short breaks from 2 nights available most of the year, prices from £95.

KESWICK, Cumbria Map ref 5A3 Tourist Information Centre Tel: (017687) 72645

★★★★
1 Unit
Sleeping 1–6

BANNERDALE
Keswick
Contact: Ms Hazel Hutton, Springs Farm, Keswick CA12 4AN
T: 07816 824253
F: (017687) 72546
E: info@bannerdale.co.uk
I: www.bannerdale.co.uk

OPEN All Year

Low season per wk £340.00–£420.00
High season per wk £420.00–£810.00

Situated at the foot of Walla Crag in the heart of the Lake District, this luxurious accommodation boasts magnificent uninterrupted views of the surrounding meadows and mountains.

CUMBRIA – THE LAKE DISTRICT

KESWICK continued

★★★–★★★★★
3 Units
Sleeping 1–4

BELLE VUE
Keswick
Contact: Mrs Lexie Ryder, Hillside, Portinscale, Keswick CA12 5RS
T: (017687) 71065
E: lexieryder@hotmail.com

Close to the heart of Keswick, this lovely Lakeland-stone residence has been superbly converted, providing very spacious, comfortable, well-appointed suites. Fell-top views from lounges of Catbells and Newlands Valley. Carefully owner maintained. Ideally located with Derwentwater and the famous Theatre by the Lake a short walk away.

OPEN All Year

Short breaks available Nov–Mar, minimum 3 nights. Reductions given for 2 people.

Low season per wk
£100.00–£200.00
High season per wk
£220.00–£350.00

★★★
1 Unit
Sleeping 2–5

3 CATHERINE COTTAGES
Keswick
Contact: Mr Peter & Mrs Margaret Hewitson, 17 Cedar Lane, Cockermouth CA13 9HN
T: (01900) 828039
E: peter.hewitson1@btinternet.com

Cottage in a quiet area near Fitz Park, five minutes' walk from the shops. Owner maintained. Car park. Phone or email for brochure.

OPEN All Year

Low season per wk
£180.00–£225.00
High season per wk
£225.00–£300.00

★★★
1 Unit
Sleeping 1–4

THE COTTAGE
Newlands Valley, Keswick
Contact: Mrs Margaret Beaty, The Cottage, Birkrigg, Newlands Valley, Keswick CA12 5TS
T: (017687) 78278

Comfortable oak-beamed cottage, adjoining farmhouse. Very pleasantly situated with excellent view. Five miles from Keswick between Braithwaite and Buttermere, in the peaceful Newlands Valley.

OPEN All Year

Low season per wk
Min £180.00
High season per wk
Max £320.00

★★★★
4 Units
Sleeping 2–8

CROFT HOUSE HOLIDAYS
Keswick
Contact: Mrs Jan Boniface, Croft House Holidays, Croft House, Applethwaite, Keswick CA12 4PN
T: (017687) 73693
E: holidays@crofthouselakes.co.uk
I: www.crofthouselakes.co.uk

Escape to stunning, panoramic views of Derwentwater and Borrowdale. Peaceful, rural locations in Applethwaite village, nestling at the foot of Skiddaw, just over one mile from Keswick – but a world away. Cottage and ground floor apartment in a Victorian country house. Two further cottages. Fell walks from the door.

OPEN All Year

Short breaks (minimum 2 nights) Nov–Mar (excl Christmas and New Year). Special 2-person rates.

Low season per wk
£220.00–£405.00
High season per wk
£390.00–£700.00

★★★★★
2 Units
Sleeping 1–4

CROFTLANDS COTTAGES
Keswick
Contact: Mrs Susan McGarvie, Croftlands Cottages, Croftlands, Thornthwaite, Keswick CA12 5SA
T: (017687) 78300
F: (017687) 78300
E: robmcgarvie@lineone.net
I: www.croftlands-cottages.co.uk

Outstanding, luxuriously appointed cottages with magnificent fell views, logburning stoves, old beams and antiques. All bedrooms en suite. Walks from the doorstep. Keswick five minutes' drive away.

OPEN All Year

Low season per wk
£235.00–£285.00
High season per wk
£435.00–£485.00

CUMBRIA – THE LAKE DISTRICT

KESWICK continued

★★★★★
1 Unit
Sleeping 2

DERWENT COTTAGE MEWS
Keswick
Contact: Mrs Susan Newman, Derwent Cottage Mews, Portinscale, Keswick CA12 5RF
T: (017687) 74838
E: enquiries@dercott.demon.co.uk
I: www.dercott.demon.co.uk

Derwent Cottage Mews is a spacious first floor, one-bedroomed apartment in the former stable block adjoining Derwent Cottage. This secluded house is set in landscaped gardens in the quiet village of Portinscale, one mile from Keswick. It is tastefully and comfortably furnished to a high standard and fully equipped.

OPEN All Year

Payment accepted: Delta, Mastercard, Switch, Visa, Euros

Any 3 consecutive days at a cost of £75pn reducing to £50pn during winter months, subject to availability.

Low season per wk
£320.00–£380.00
High season per wk
£430.00–£460.00

★★★
4 Units
Sleeping 1–6

DERWENT HOUSE AND BRANDELHOWE
Keswick
Contact: Mr & Mrs Oliver Bull, Derwent House Holidays, Stone Heath, Hilderstone ST15 8SH
T: (01889) 505678
F: (01889) 505679
I: www.dhholidays-lakes.com

Traditional stone and slate Lakeland building of character in village on north shore of Derwentwater one mile from Keswick. Comfortable, well-equipped holiday suites, one retaining old cottage grate and range and another open beams. Various views over lake and to Skiddaw. Ideal centre for walking and resting.

OPEN All Year

Short breaks available Nov-Mar. Minimum 2 nights.

Low season per wk
£110.00–£205.00
High season per wk
£230.00–£340.00

★★★★
19 Units
Sleeping 2–6

DERWENT MANOR
Keswick
Contact: Mrs C Denwood, Derwent Manor, Portinscale, Keswick CA12 5RE
T: (017687) 72538
F: (017687) 71002
E: info@derwentwater-hotel.co.uk
I: www.derwent-manor.co.uk

Enjoy village life at this former gentleman's residence. Refurbished to provide some of the most comfortable and well-equipped apartments available, or one-bedroomed cottage within grounds. Many extras including Sunday lunch, entry to local leisure club. Pets welcome. Lake on your doorstep, with 16 acres of conservation grounds.

OPEN All Year

Payment accepted: Amex, Delta, Mastercard, Switch, Visa

Short breaks subject to availability.

Low season per wk
£225.00–£450.00
High season per wk
£390.00–£630.00

Location Complete addresses for properties are not given and the town(s) listed may be a distance from the actual establishment. Please check the precise location at the time of booking.

82

CUMBRIA – THE LAKE DISTRICT

KESWICK continued

★★★★
5 Units
Sleeping 1–4

LOW BRIERY HOLIDAY VILLAGE
Keswick
Contact: Mr Michael Atkinson, Low Briery Holiday Village, Penrith Road, Keswick CA12 4RN
T: (017687) 72044
F: (017687) 72044
I: www.keswick.uk.com

OPEN All Year
Payment accepted: Delta, Mastercard, Switch, Visa

Low season per wk
£340.00–£395.00
High season per wk
£525.00–£595.00

Chalets beside the river Greta with magnificent views. Well-equipped properties offering comfortable accommodation in a choice setting.

★★★
2 Units
Sleeping 4–12

ORCHARD BARN
Keswick
Contact: Mr & Mrs Hall, Fisherground Farm, Eskdale CA19 1TF
T: (01946) 723319
E: holidays@fisherground.co.uk
I: www.orchardhouseholidays.co.uk

Superb family house with fabulous views. Aga, central heating, laundry, freezer, video etc. Huge lounge, fully-equipped kitchen, two bathrooms. Large garden. Pets welcome. Ideal for family or walking groups. Brochure on request, or see our website.

OPEN All Year

Short breaks available Oct–May, minimum 3 nights.

Low season per wk
£450.00–£650.00
High season per wk
£790.00–£1,090.00

KING'S MEABURN, Cumbria Map ref 5B3

★★★–★★★★★
4 Units
Sleeping 3–6

LYVENNET COTTAGES
Penrith
Contact: Mrs Margaret & Wendy & Janet Addison, Lyvennet Cottages, Keld, King's Meaburn, Penrith CA10 3BS
T: (01931) 714226
F: (01931) 714598
E: info@lyvennetcottages.co.uk
I: www.lyvennetcottages.co.uk

Attractive, well-furnished cottages in quiet village, overlooking the beautiful Lyvennet Valley and Lakeland hills. Some log fires in winter. Fishing, fuel and linen inclusive. Children and pets welcome. Good pub. Own woodland walks and bird-watching. Bring your own horse – excellent livery or grass. Ideal centre for Lakes, Dales, Hadrian's Wall and Scottish Borders.

OPEN All Year

Short breaks available Oct–Mar (excl Christmas and New Year). Minimum 3 nights.

Low season per wk
£185.00–£275.00
High season per wk
£285.00–£460.00

KIRKBY LONSDALE, Cumbria Map ref 5B3 Tourist Information Centre Tel: (015242) 71437

★★★★
3 Units

SELLET HALL COTTAGES
Carnforth
Contact: Mrs Hall, Sellet Hall Cottages, Sellet Hall, Hosticle Lane, Carnforth LA6 2QF
T: (01524) 271865
E: sellethall@hotmail.com
I: www.sellethall.com

Unique cottages converted from 17thC barn set in the grounds of Sellet Hall, surrounded by open countryside and complemented by far-distance views over the Lune Valley, Trough of Bowland and Yorkshire Dales. All have log fires, fitted kitchens, dishwasher, microwave etc. Own gardens, patio and parking.

OPEN All Year

Short breaks, subject to availability, (excl Christmas and New Year). Pets welcome.

Low season per wk
£275.00–£350.00
High season per wk
£350.00–£500.00

83

CUMBRIA – THE LAKE DISTRICT

LANGDALE, Cumbria Map ref 5A3

★★★

2 Units
Sleeping 2–5

2 & 7 LINGMOOR VIEW

Langdale, Ambleside
Contact: Mr Batho, High Hollin Bank, Coniston LA21 8AG
T: (015394) 41680
E: a.batho@virgin.net
I: www.cottagescumbria.com

Traditional, stone-built, Lakeland cottages situated in peaceful, unspoilt valley. Ideal position for fell and valley walking, 0.5 miles from village shop and pub. Cosy country interior with open fire and original features. Modern fitted kitchen, sitting room, bathroom and two bedrooms. Sunny aspect with magnificent views across hills.

OPEN All Year

Special long-weekend-break prices available during low season.

Low season per wk
£198.00–£282.00
High season per wk
£303.00–£387.00

WEB

www.visitengland.com

Log on for information and inspiration. The latest information on places to visit, events and quality assessed accommodation.

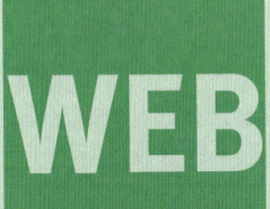

Wheelwrights
Lake District Holiday Cottages

For over a quarter of a century, we have been letting some of the best cottages in the Lake District, all of which are set in stunning scenery. Based in Elterwater, in the heart of magnificent Great Langdale, we are surrounded by the beauty of the mountains and the lakes and would like to share it with you! Whether you are just wanting a romantic short break for two or a really good family holiday, do give us a call to discuss your options. As a small company, we pride ourselves on our personal service and ability to find the right cottage for all occasions.

For detailed descriptions of all our properties go to:
www.wheelwrights.com
e-mail: enquiries@wheelwrights.com
Or telephone our office and talk to one of our friendly staff on:
Tel: 015394 37635
Fax: 015394 37618

Escape to the beauty of the lakes

CUMBRIA – THE LAKE DISTRICT

LANGDALE continued

★★★–★★★★★★
2 Units
Sleeping 2–10

MEADOW BANK
Elterwater
Contact: Pat & Robert Locke, Elterwater Investments Ltd,
17 Shay Lane, Hale Barns, Altrincham WA15 8NZ
T: (0161) 904 9445
F: (0161) 904 9877
E: lockemeadow@aol.com
I: www.langdalecottages.co.uk

OPEN All Year

4-night winter mid-week breaks for the price of 2 (Chalet £100, House £250-300).

Low season per wk
£220.00–£650.00
High season per wk
£320.00–£1,500.00

In the centre of the unspoilt village of Elterwater, Meadow Bank has fine views towards the beck and fells. It is an exceptional property, completely renovated and beautifully furnished throughout. The house has four bedrooms and three bathrooms. There is also the Garden Chalet. Leisure Club facilities are included.

LITTLE LANGDALE, Cumbria Map ref 5A3

★★★
1 Unit
Sleeping 2–5

HIGHFOLD COTTAGE
Ambleside
Contact: Mrs Blair, 8 The Glebe, Chapel Stile, Ambleside LA22 9JT
T: (015394) 37686
I: www.highfoldcottage.co.uk

OPEN All Year

Low season per wk
£220.00–£280.00
High season per wk
£280.00–£375.00

Comfortable, well-equipped cottage, set in magnificent scenery. Ideally situated for walking and touring. Open fires, central heating. Pets and children welcome. Personally maintained.

LITTLE STRICKLAND, Cumbria Map ref 5B3

★★★★
1 Unit
Sleeping 2–3

SPRING BANK
Penrith
Contact: Mrs Joan Ostle, Meadowfield, Little Strickland, Penrith CA10 3EG
T: (01931) 716346
E: springbank17@hotmail.com
I: www.holidaycumbria.co.uk

OPEN All Year

Low season per wk
Max £200.00
High season per wk
Max £300.00

Modern, king/twin-bedded bungalow in quiet location. Easy access to Lakes, Dales and Eden Valley. Satisfied clients reflect quality accommodation/location. Brochure available.

LONGSLEDDALE, Cumbria Map ref 5B3

★★★
1 Unit
Sleeping 2–4

THE COACH HOUSE
Kendal
Contact: Mrs Farmer, The Coach House, Capplebarrow House, Longsleddale, Kendal LA8 9BB
T: (01539) 823686
E: jenyfarmer@aol.com
I: www.capplebarrowcoachhouse.co.uk

OPEN All Year

Low season per wk
£150.00–£170.00
High season per wk
£170.00–£225.00

Stone-built, converted coach house with ground floor shower room and bedroom and open staircase to first floor kitchen and lounge. Excellent views.

Map references The map references refer to the colour maps at the front of this guide. The first figure is the map number; the letter and figure which follow indicate the grid reference on the map.

CUMBRIA – THE LAKE DISTRICT

LOWESWATER, Cumbria Map ref 5A3

1 Unit
Sleeping 8

THE COACH HOUSE
Loweswater
Contact: Mrs Naomi Kerr, Looking Stead, Cockermouth CA13 0RS
T: (01900) 85660
E: lookingstead@aol.com
I: www.cottageguide.co.uk/loweswater/index.html

This four-bedroomed converted coach house has views of Crummock Water and the surrounding fells, and is situated in a lovely unexploited valley. The house is close to other buildings, and has a spacious garden. Three bathrooms, a laundry area and a drying cabinet make it ideal for relaxed holidays.

OPEN All Year

Low season per wk
£340.00–£450.00
High season per wk
£500.00–£1,000.00

NEWBY BRIDGE, Cumbria Map ref 5A3

1 Unit
Sleeping 2–4

WOODLAND COTTAGE
Newby Bridge
Contact: Mr Peter Newton, Fellside Lodge, Newby Bridge Caravan Park, Canny Hill, Newby Bridge LA12 8NF
T: (015395) 31030
F: (015395) 30105
E: info@cumbriancaravans.co.uk
I: www.cumbriancaravans.co.uk

OPEN All Year except Christmas and New Year

Payment accepted: Delta, Mastercard, Switch, Visa, Euros

Low season per wk
£230.00–£375.00
High season per wk
£375.00–£520.00

Detached cottage with two en suite bedrooms, in own private gardens within the award-winning Newby Bridge Caravan Park. All on one level.

PATTERDALE, Cumbria Map ref 5A3

1 Unit
Sleeping 15

BROAD HOW
Patterdale
Contact: Country Holidays
T: 0870 197 0600
I: www.country-holidays.co.uk

Beautiful, large, 1850s' family house, sensitively and comfortably modernised. Log fire, piano, pool table, books and games. In stunning Lakeland scenery, one mile from Ullswater with its steamer service (April to October), sailing, swimming etc. Marvellous fell walking, and within easy reach of small towns for non-walkers. Property number 8478.

OPEN All Year

Low season per wk
£1,049.00–£1,304.00
High season per wk
£1,586.00–£2,004.00

Special breaks

Many establishments offer special promotions and themed breaks. These are highlighted in red. (All such offers are subject to availability.)

CUMBRIA – THE LAKE DISTRICT

PENRITH, Cumbria Map ref 5B2 *Tourist Information Centre Tel: (01768) 867466*

★★★★
2 Units
Sleeping 6–26

BRACKEN BANK LODGE & BRACKEN BANK COTTAGE
Penrith
Contact: Mrs Hilary Burton, Bracken Bank Lodge & Bracken Bank Cottage, Lazonby, Penrith CA10 1AX
T: (01768) 898241
F: (01768) 898221
E: info@brackenbank.co.uk
I: www.brackenbank.co.uk

This famous shooting lodge, dating from the 17thC, is traditionally furnished with four-poster beds, log fires, antiques and oil paintings. The lodge's facilities include a snooker room and traditional English bar. The 700-acre private estate boasts deer, red squirrel, lakes and a wealth of sporting facilities. Catering can be provided by arrangement.

OPEN All Year

Lodge: 3 nights £3400, sleeping up to 26 people.

Cottage:
Low season per wk
£296.00–£350.00
High season per wk
£350.00–£480.00

★★★★
5 Units
Sleeping 3–8

WETHERAL COTTAGES
Penrith
Contact: Mr John Lowrey, Great Salkeld, Penrith CA11 9NA
T: (01768) 898779
E: wetheralcottages@btopenworld.com
I: www.wetheralcottages.co.uk

Charming, well-equipped sandstone cottages clustered amongst attractive gardens with large grassed area. Situated in Eden Valley on the edge of a quiet country village with pub. Easy access to the amenities of the Lake District, northern England and southern Scotland. Walking, cycling, golf, swimming and fishing nearby. Prices fully inclusive.

OPEN All Year

Payment accepted: Mastercard, Switch, Visa, Euros

Short breaks available Nov 04-Easter 05. 3-night weekend breaks or 4-night mid-week breaks.

Low season per wk
£200.00–£400.00
High season per wk
£400.00–£700.00

RYDAL, Cumbria Map ref 5A3

★★★
1 Unit
Sleeping 2–6

HALL BANK COTTAGE
Rydal, Ambleside
Contact: Mrs Janet Horne, Rydal Estate, Carter Jonas, 52 Kirkland, Kendal LA9 5AP
T: (01539) 814902
F: (01539) 729587
E: janet.horne@carterjonas.co.uk

Delightful, 17thC detached cottage set centrally within a large rural estate, held by one family since 1480. Spacious, yet cosy with log fire. Large private garden and ample off-road parking. Superb location at foot of Nab Scar. Historic Rydal Mount, Rydal Hall and gardens immediately adjacent.

OPEN All Year

Short breaks available.

Low season per wk
£250.00–£475.00
High season per wk
£550.00–£575.00

Quality Assurance Standard
Star ratings and awards were correct at time of going to press but are subject to change. Please check at the time of booking.

87

CUMBRIA – THE LAKE DISTRICT

ST BEES, Cumbria Map ref 5A3

★★★
1 Unit
Sleeping 6

TARN FLATT COTTAGE
Sandwith, Whitehaven
Contact: Mrs Janice Telfer, Tarn Flatt Cottage,
Sandwith, Whitehaven CA28 9UX
T: (01946) 692162
E: stay@tarnflattfarm.co.uk
I: www.tarnflattfarm.co.uk

OPEN All Year

Low season per wk
Min £295.00
High season per wk
Min £395.00

Charming three-bedroomed cottage with panoramic sea views. Quiet location.

SAWREY, Cumbria Map ref 5A3

★★★
1 Unit
Sleeping 1–4

DERWENTWATER COTTAGE
Ambleside
Contact: Mrs Anne Gallagher, The Minstrels Gallery,
The Square, Hawkshead, Ambleside LA22 0NZ
T: (015394) 42435
F: (015394) 36178
E: bookings@lakeland-hideaways.co.uk
I: www.lakeland-hideaways.co.uk

OPEN All Year

Short breaks available autumn, winter and early spring.

Low season per wk
£230.00–£340.00
High season per wk
£380.00–£430.00

Family-run self-catering accommodation consisting of traditional farm buildings converted into attractive apartments and cottages in beautiful rural setting. Sunny terraces overlooking private paddock. Access to private lakeshore. Free coarse and trout fishing. Log fires, cosy and comfortable, excellent base for walking, cycling and sightseeing.

★★★★★
1 Unit
Sleeping 1–7

SAWREY STABLES
Ambleside
Contact: Mrs Anne Gallagher, Hideaways,
The Minstrels Gallery, The Square, Hawkshead,
Ambleside LA22 0NZ
T: (015394) 42435
F: (015394) 36178
E: bookings@lakeland-hideaways.co.uk
I: www.lakeland-hideaways.co.uk

OPEN All Year

Low season per wk
£495.00–£625.00
High season per wk
£710.00–£920.00

Superb, luxury, five-star cottage above Lake Windermere. Complete with Aga, jacuzzi bath, open fire. Peaceful, yet with excellent local amenities.

SEDBERGH, Cumbria Map ref 5B3

★★★★
2 Units
Sleeping 2–14

FELL HOUSE
Sedbergh
Contact: Mr Stephen Wickham, 14 Home Meadows,
Billericay CM12 9HQ
T: (01277) 652746 & 07974 028901
E: steve@higround.co.uk
I: www.higround.co.uk

OPEN All Year

Low season per wk
£150.00–£850.00
High season per wk
£230.00–£1,110.00

Luxurious character warehouse conversion with linked, self-contained flat. Spacious living areas, tastefully furnished. Quiet, but very close to pubs, shops, restaurant. Weekend bookings taken.

Accessibility Look for the symbols which indicate National Accessible Scheme standards for hearing and visually impaired guests in addition to standards for guests with mobility impairment. You can find an index of all scheme participants at the back of this guide.

CUMBRIA – THE LAKE DISTRICT

SEDBERGH continued

★★★★
1 Unit
Sleeping 2–8

THE MOUNT
Sedbergh
Contact: Mrs Suzan Sedgwick, Howgill Lane, Sedbergh LA10 5HE
T: (015396) 20252
E: lockbank@uk4free.net
I: www.holidaysedbergh.co.uk

Spacious well-equipped centrally heated farmhouse, can accommodate two families or four couples in four bedrooms comfortably. Ideal for exploring Lake District and Yorkshire Dales. Open fires, private gardens and ample parking. Linen, towels, gas, electric are included as are the cot and highchair. Local amenities 0.5 miles.

OPEN All Year

Short breaks and discounts available. Phone or see our website for details.

Low season per wk
£280.00–£530.00
High season per wk
£530.00–£1,000.00

STAPLETON, Cumbria Map ref 5B2

★★★
1 Unit
Sleeping 8–10

DROVE COTTAGE
Carlisle
Contact: Mr Kenneth & Mrs Anne Hope, Drove Inn Public House, Roweltown, Stapleton CA6 6LB
T: (01697) 748202
F: (01697) 748054
E: droveinn@hotmail.com

Our first floor cottage adjoins our busy 'Country Inn' which is family run with an excellent reputation for food – established 29 years! The cottage has a lounge/fitted kitchen, three twin rooms – one with extra futon – and one double room. Bathroom, shower room and one en suite room. Beautiful countryside location.

OPEN All Year
Payment accepted: Delta, Mastercard, Switch, Visa

Low season per wk
£150.00–£200.00
High season per wk
£200.00–£250.00

STAVELEY, Cumbria Map ref 5A3

★★★
4 Units
Sleeping 2–5

BRUNT KNOTT FARM HOLIDAY COTTAGES
Kendal
Contact: Mr William & Mrs Margaret Beck, Brunt Knott Farm, Staveley, Kendal LA8 9QX
T: (01539) 821030
F: (01539) 821221
E: margaret@bruntknott.demon.co.uk
I: www.bruntknott.demon.co.uk

Cosy cottages on small, secluded 17thC hill farm. Peaceful, elevated fellside location with superb panoramic views over Lakeland fells. Five miles from Windermere/Kendal. Cycling/lovely walks from your doorstep. Central heating. Three cottages with woodburner/open fire. Parking. Laundry facilities. Winter short breaks available. Brochure available.

OPEN All Year

Low season per wk
£200.00–£230.00
High season per wk
£305.00–£430.00

Credit card bookings
If you book by telephone and are asked for your credit card number it is advisable to check the proprietor's policy should you cancel your reservation.

CUMBRIA – THE LAKE DISTRICT

TIRRIL, Cumbria Map ref 5B2

★★★★
5 Units
Sleeping 1–9

TIRRIL FARM COTTAGES
Penrith
Contact: Mr David Owens, Tirril Farm Cottages, Tirril View, Penrith CA10 2JE
T: (01768) 864767
F: (01768) 864767
E: enquiries@tirrilfarmcottages.co.uk
I: www.tirrilfarmcottages.co.uk

Easily accessible two miles from Ullswater, these tasteful barn conversions enjoy a quiet courtyard setting with outstanding views over the fells. Tirril is an attractive village with prize winning pub/restaurant. Ideal for visiting the lakes and Eden Valley. Short breaks welcome.

OPEN All Year
Payment accepted: Euros

Low season per wk
£120.00–£450.00
High season per wk
£190.00–£890.00

ULLSWATER, Cumbria Map ref 5A3

★★★
4 Units
Sleeping 1–5

LAND ENDS
Penrith
Contact: Ms Barbara Holmes, Land Ends, Watermillock, Nr Ullswater, Penrith CA11 0NB
T: (017684) 86438
F: (017684) 86959
E: infolandends@btinternet.com
I: www.landends.co.uk

For those seeking total relaxation, Land Ends is ideal. Only one mile from Ullswater, our detached log cabins have a peaceful, fellside location in 25-acre grounds with two pretty lakes, red squirrels, ducks and wonderful birdlife. Inside, exposed logs and comfortable furnishings give a cosy, rustic appeal. Dogs welcome.

OPEN All Year

Short breaks available Oct–Mar.

Low season per wk
£235.00–£325.00
High season per wk
£290.00–£510.00

★★-★★★
17 Units
Sleeping 2–6

PATTERDALE HALL ESTATE
Penrith
Contact: Ms Sue Kay, Patterdale Hall Estate, Estate Office, Glenridding, Penrith CA11 0PJ
T: (017684) 82308
F: (017684) 82867
E: mail@patterdalehallestate.com
I: www.patterdalehallestate.com

Between Helvellyn and Ullswater, the private 300-acre estate with private foreshore, woodland and gardens offers a range of comfortable, centrally heated, self-catering properties all in an idyllic and relaxing setting. Perfect for leisurely holidays, ideally situated for outdoor activities, an excellent base from which to explore the Lake District.

OPEN All Year
Payment accepted: Delta, Mastercard, Switch, Visa

Short breaks available Nov–mid-Mar or any time if booked within a fortnight of arrival date (subject to availability).

Low season per wk
£149.00–£247.00
High season per wk
£287.00–£475.00

Important note Information on accommodation listed in this guide has been supplied by the proprietors. As changes may occur you are advised to check details at the time of booking.

CUMBRIA – THE LAKE DISTRICT

ULLSWATER continued

5 Units
Sleeping 6–14

160-acre hill livestock farm. Properties overlook Ullswater and have colour TV, freezer, central heating, dishwasher and clothes washing and drying facilities. Private access to lake, visitors may bring own boats and horses (motor boats, sailing dinghies, canoes, mountain bikes for hire). Horses available for riding.

SWARTHBECK FARM HOLIDAY COTTAGES
Penrith
Contact: Mr & Mrs Parkin, Swarthbeck Farm Holiday Cottages, Swarthbeck Farm, Howtown, Penrith CA10 2ND
T: (017684) 86432
E: whparkin@ukonline.co.uk
I: www.horseholidaysincumbria.co.uk

OPEN All Year
Payment accepted: Euros

Low season per wk
£200.00–£500.00
High season per wk
£250.00–£1,200.00

ULVERSTON, Cumbria Map ref 5A3 Tourist Information Centre Tel: (01229) 587120

★★-★★★★
3 Units
Sleeping 2–6

THE FALLS
Ulverston
Contact: Mrs Cheetham and Mrs Unger, Mansriggs, Ulverston LA12 7PX
T: (01229) 583781
I: www.thefalls.co.uk

OPEN All Year

Low season per wk
£200.00–£350.00
High season per wk
£260.00–£490.00

17thC farmstead in beautiful surroundings, converted into holiday homes in traditional Lakeland style. Resident proprietors. Children and dogs welcome.

WASDALE, Cumbria Map ref 5A3

★★★
1 Unit
Sleeping 2–6

SUNDIAL COTTAGE
Wasdale
Contact: Mr Michael & Mrs Christine McKinley, Sundial Cottage, Galesyke, Wasdale CA20 1ET
T: (01946) 726267

OPEN All Year

Low season per wk
£200.00–£350.00
High season per wk
£300.00–£495.00

Unique, well-equipped, self-contained cottage in large riverside grounds. Situated in the middle of Wasdale.

★★★
3 Units
Sleeping 1–20

WOODHOW FARM COTTAGES
Seascale
Contact: Dr Kaminski, The Squirrels, 55 Broadway, Cheadle SK8 1LB
T: (0161) 428 9116
E: woodhow_farm@kaminsk.fsnet.co.uk
I: www.kaminski.fsnet.co.uk

OPEN All Year

Low season per wk
£300.00–£380.00
High season per wk
£470.00–£600.00

Grade II Listed, centrally heated, four-bedroom, beamed farmhouse and converted byres in 210 acres of beautiful countryside including tarn. Lovely setting. Woodburning stoves.

Town index

This can be found at the back of the guide. If you know where you want to stay the index will give you the page number listing accommodation in your chosen town, city or village.

CUMBRIA – THE LAKE DISTRICT

WIGTON, Cumbria Map ref 5A2

1 Unit
Sleeping 1–8

FOXGLOVES
Westward
Contact: Mr & Mrs Kerr, Foxgloves, Greenrigg Farm, Westward, Wigton CA7 8AH
T: (016973) 42676
F: (016973) 42676
E: kerr_greenrigg@hotmail.com

OPEN All Year

Short breaks and mid-week breaks.

Low season per wk
£200.00–£252.00
High season per wk
£398.00–£425.00

Spacious, well-equipped, comfortable cottage on a working farm. Superlative setting and views, large kitchen/dining room, Aga, lounge, open fire, storage heaters, TV/video, dishwasher, three bedrooms, bathroom, shower room. Linen, towels, electricity, logs and coal inclusive. Children and pets very welcome. Extensive garden. Horse grazing and stabling available.

WINDERMERE, Cumbria Map ref 5A3 Tourist Information Centre Tel: (015394) 46499

2 Units
Sleeping 2–6

THE ABBEY COACH HOUSE
Windermere
Contact: Mrs Pamela Bell, The Abbey Coach House, St Mary's Park, Windermere LA23 1AZ
T: (015394) 44027
F: (015394) 44027
E: abbeycoach@aol.com
I: www.oas.co.uk/ukcottages

OPEN All Year

3-night breaks available Nov-Mar (excl Christmas and New Year).

Low season per wk
£130.00–£295.00
High season per wk
£250.00–£445.00

This former Victorian coach house offers an excellent location of a ground floor apartment and bungalow in quiet, private grounds. Only a short walk to the lake and Windermere town. Extensive gardens with ample parking. Within easy reach of all amenities. Ideal for families or retired.

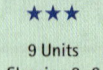
9 Units
Sleeping 2–6

BIRTHWAITE EDGE
Windermere
Contact: Mr Bruce Dodsworth, Birthwaite Road, Windermere LA23 1BS
T: (015394) 42861
I: www.lakedge.com

OPEN All Year except Christmas

Payment accepted: Mastercard, Switch, Visa, Euros

Low season per wk
£180.00–£260.00
High season per wk
£300.00–£530.00

Birthwaite Edge is the perfect holiday base from which to explore the north of England. Public transport and bus tours nearby. Set in an exclusive area 10 minutes' stroll from Windermere village and lake. Central for restaurants, cafes and inns. Resident proprietors guarantee comfortable, clean apartments. No smoking or pets.

1 Unit
Sleeping 6–7

CANONS CRAIG
Windermere
Contact: Mr A or Mrs L Salter, 52 Bromleigh Drive, Stoke, Coventry CV2 5LX
T: (024) 7645 7141
E: dougie@freeneasy.net
I: web.ukonline.co.uk/dougiedoo/Index.htm

OPEN All Year

Low season per wk
£280.00–£375.00
High season per wk
£375.00–£520.00

Traditional Lakeland-stone-built accommodation within easy walking distance of Lake Windermere and amenities. Membership of Parklands Leisure Club included. Ideal base for a relaxing holiday.

CUMBRIA – THE LAKE DISTRICT

WINDERMERE continued

★★★
6 Units
Sleeping 2–8

CANTERBURY FLATS
Windermere
Contact: Mr & Mrs Zuniga, Bowness Holidays,
131 Radcliffe New Road, Manchester M45 7RP
T: (0161) 796 3896
F: (0161) 272 1841
E: info@bownesslakelandholidays.co.uk
I: www.bownesslakelandholidays.co.uk

OPEN All Year

Low season per wk
£170.00–£340.00
High season per wk
£285.00–£520.00

Wonderful location. Apartments in the centre of the village, close to all amenities. Full membership of private leisure club, indoor swimming complex. Short breaks available.

★★★★
1 Unit
Sleeping 1–4

GAVEL COTTAGE
Windermere
Contact: Screetons, 25 Bridgegate, Howden, Goole
DN14 7AA
T: (01430) 431201
F: (01430) 432114
E: howden@screetons.co.uk
I: screetons.co.uk

Secluded period cottage situated in an elevated position close to the marina. Tastefully furnished, Gavel Cottage offers a quiet, comfortable holiday retreat. Fully-equipped accommodation comprising entrance hall, open-plan area including lounge with open fire, dining area and kitchen, two bedrooms, bathroom, large garden and summer house. Member Burnside Leisure Centre.

OPEN All Year

Low season per wk
£235.00–£395.00
High season per wk
£395.00–£475.00

Check the maps
The colour maps at the front of this guide show all the cities, towns and villages for which you will find accommodation entries. Refer to the town index to find the page on which they are listed.

3,4 & 7 night breaks with FREE use of our own private leisure club. Bistro & Bar. Holiday & annual moorings.

WINDERMERE MARINA VILLAGE
info@wmv.co.uk
www.wmv.co.uk
Call FREE
0800 262902

Luxury Cottages in the heart of the LAKE DISTRICT

93

CUMBRIA – THE LAKE DISTRICT

WINDERMERE continued

★★★
4 Units
Sleeping 2–5

HELM FARM
Windermere
Contact: Mrs J Marsden, Matson Ground Estate Co Ltd, Estate Office, Matson Ground, Windermere LA23 2NH
T: (015394) 45756
F: (015394) 47892
E: info@matsonground.co.uk
I: www.matsonground.co.uk

Helm Farm is very quiet whilst being only a few minutes from Windermere and Bowness. Footpaths lead from the door across wooded farmland. Three of the four units have wood fires. Helm Lune, the largest, sleeps five. Helm Mint, the smallest, is a compact, studio-style apartment for two.

OPEN All Year

Payment accepted: Delta, Mastercard, Switch, Visa, Euros

Low season per wk
£125.00–£375.00
High season per wk
£180.00–£550.00

★★★
4 Units
Sleeping 2–6

LANGDALE VIEW HOLIDAY APARTMENTS
Windermere
Contact: Mrs Julie Marsh, 112 Craig Walk, Bowness-on-Windermere, Windermere LA23 3AX
T: (015394) 46655
E: enquiries@langdale-view.co.uk
I: www.langdale-view.co.uk

Attractive, comfortable holiday apartments with car parking. Quiet, elevated position very close to village centre, lake, steamers, shops and restaurants.

OPEN All Year

Payment accepted: Delta, Mastercard, Switch, Visa

Low season per wk
£175.00–£230.00
High season per wk
£275.00–£430.00

★★★
3 Units
Sleeping 1–2

WINSTER HOUSE
Windermere
Contact: Mrs Shirley Jump, Winster House, Sunny Bank Road, Windermere LA23 2EN
T: (015394) 44723
E: enquiries@winsterhouse.co.uk
I: www.winsterhouse.co.uk

Private parking and use of secluded garden. Five minutes' walk to shops and restaurants, 10 minutes' walk to Lake Windermere. Brochure available.

OPEN All Year

Low season per wk
£185.00–£210.00
High season per wk
£225.00–£250.00

Country Code Always follow the Country Code

- Enjoy the countryside and respect its life and work
- Guard against all risk of fire • Fasten all gates • Keep your dogs under close control • Keep to public paths across farmland • Use gates and stiles to cross fences, hedges and walls • Leave livestock, crops and machinery alone • Take your litter home • Help to keep all water clean • Protect wildlife, plants and trees • Take special care on country roads • Make no unnecessary noise.

enjoyEngland™
official guides to quality

Hotels, Townhouses, Travel Accommodation and Restaurants with Rooms in England 2005
£10.99

Bed & Breakfasts, Guesthouses, Small Hotels, Farmhouses, Inns, Campus Accommodation and Hostels in England 2005
£11.99

Self-Catering Holiday Homes and Boat Accommodation in England 2005
£11.99

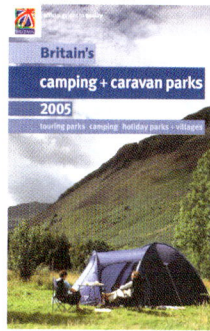

Touring Parks, Camping, Holiday Parks and Villages in Britain 2005
£8.99

Somewhere Special in England 2005
£8.99

Families and Pets Welcome in England 2005
£11.99

INFORMATIVE • EASY TO USE • GREAT VALUE FOR MONEY

The guides include:
- **Accommodation entries packed with information**
- **Full colour maps**
- **Places to visit**
- **Tourist Information Centres**

From all good bookshops or by mail order from:

**VisitBritain Fulfilment Centre,
c/o Westex Ltd, 7 St Andrews Way,
Devons Road, Bromley-by-Bow, London E3 3PA
Tel: 0870 606 7204
Fax: (020) 7987 6505
Email: fulfilment@visitbritain.org**

Invigorate your senses and free your mind. There's so much **diversity** in this corner of England you'll want to come back for **more**.

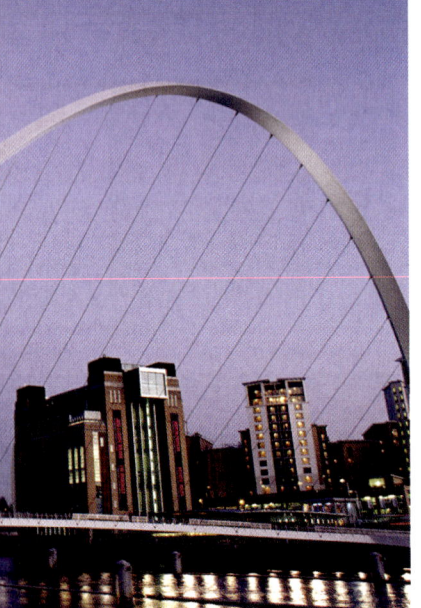

Northumbria

Looking for some inspiration? Here are a few ideas to get you started in Northumbria. **experience** the splendour of Alnwick Castle and Garden or Sunderland Museum & Winter Gardens, one of the finest new hothouses in the country. **discover** Hartlepool Historic Quay, a museum dedicated to seafaring experiences at the time of Nelson and Trafalgar. **explore** Roman remains along the Hadrian's Wall Path National Trail. **relax** and unwind in the sanctuary of senses at Seaham Hall, Excellence in England 2004 Small Hotel of the Year, Silver Winner.

THE REGION
County Durham, Tees Valley, Tyne and Wear (including NewcastleGateshead), Northumberland (including Hadrian's Wall Country)

CONTACT
▸ One NORTHEAST TOURISM TEAM
Aykley Heads,
Durham DH1 5UX
T: (0191) 375 3050
F: (0191) 386 0899
www.visitnorthumbria.com

NORTHUMBRIA

Northumbria will stir your soul and relax your mind. Enjoy lively cities with fantastic nightlife, discover the sheer beauty of empty beaches and breathtaking countryside and get the taste for Craster kippers. There's so much diversity in this corner of England you'll want to come back for more.

Feel the city vibe

Shop in designer outlets or splash out in one of Europe's biggest indoor shopping complexes, the MetroCentre. Head for Eldon Square or Northumberland Street in Newcastle for all the major high street names. At weekends, the clubs, pubs and restaurants are buzzing and eating out is a favourite pastime for city visitors, with a host of international flavours on offer. Enjoy your choice of cuisine from tapas to teriyaki before stepping out to sample world-class entertainment. Take in a show from the Royal Shakespeare Company, a smash-hit West End musical or one of the latest films. Check out the magnificent Angel of the North, the inspiring BALTIC Centre for Contemporary Art, the Biscuit Factory and the amazing Gateshead Millennium Bridge to return home culturally hip.

Relax and indulge

The north-east air will invigorate your senses and free your mind as you walk through picture-postcard vistas. Miles and miles of empty sandy beaches are overlooked by stunning castles, and picturesque villages are dotted along the unspoilt coastline. Reflect and reminisce on your favourite moments in quaint pubs. Absorb the region's distinctiveness from bespoke handmade jewellery to medieval fairs and music festivals.

Stroll around Durham City with its amazing castle and cathedral or visit Beamish, The North of England Open Air Museum, which re-creates the years of 1825 and 1913. Then join in the exciting hustle and bustle of the farmers' markets where you can indulge in local specialities like Northumberland hill lamb, cheese and a wide range of exotic jams and jellies.

Activity Utopia

Outdoor life is a big part of Northumbria. With two National Parks, two Areas of Outstanding Natural Beauty, acres of forests and Europe's biggest man-made lake at Kielder, it's the perfect place to enjoy your favourite activities, from walking to horse-riding. And remember to keep your eyes peeled for abundant wildlife – from otters to puffins. Championship-standard golf courses will challenge your game and the C2C cycle route will test your determination. There are plenty of relaxing cycle routes too, suitable for families or those wanting a bit of gentle exercise, with a rewarding pub meal to round off your adventure.

Left, from top unwind at Seaham Hall and Serenity Spa, Seaham; imposing Alnwick Castle; NewcastleGateshead Quaysides **Right** shoreside at Saltburn

Enjoy England official guides to quality

Places to visit

Awarded VisitBritain's Quality Assured Visitor Attraction marque.

Alnwick Castle
Alnwick, Northumberland
Tel: (01665) 510777
www.alnwickcastle.com
Imposing Alnwick Castle is the largest inhabited castle in England after Windsor Castle. It has been home of the Percys, Dukes of Northumberland, since 1309 and a film location for the Harry Potter movies.

Alnwick Garden
Alnwick, Northumberland
Tel: (01665) 511350
www.alnwickgarden.com
Take pleasure in this beautiful 5-ha (12-acre) garden with dramatic grand cascade, rose garden, ornamental garden with over 15,000 plants, water features and woodland walk.

BALTIC Centre for Contemporary Art
South Shore Road, Gateshead, Tyne and Wear
Tel: (0191) 478 1810
www.balticmill.com
Don't miss this major international centre for contemporary art with an ever changing programme of exhibitions in five galleries plus artists' studios, cinema and Rooftop Restaurant with stunning views.

Bamburgh Castle
Bamburgh, Northumberland
Tel: (01668) 214515
www.bamburghcastle.com
Stand in awe at this magnificent coastal castle, completely restored in 1900. Collections of china, porcelain, furniture, paintings, arms and armour.

Beamish The North of England Open Air Museum
Beamish, County Durham
Tel: (0191) 370 4000
www.beamish.org.uk
Plenty to see and do here – wander around the town, colliery village, working farm, Pockerley Manor and 1825 railway, recreating life in the North East in the early 1800s and 1900s.

Bede's World
Jarrow, Tyne and Wear
Tel: (0191) 489 2106
www.bedesworld.co.uk
Discover the exciting world of the Venerable Bede, early-medieval Europe's greatest scholar. Church, monastic site, museum with exhibitions and recreated Anglo-Saxon farm.

Blue Reef Aquarium
Grand Parade, Tynemouth, Tyne and Wear
Tel: (0191) 258 1031
www.bluereefaquarium.co.uk
Marvel at more than 30 living displays exploring the drama of the North Sea and the dazzling beauty of a spectacular coral reef with its own underwater tunnel.

Bowes Museum
Barnard Castle, County Durham
Tel: (01833) 690606
www.bowesmuseum.org.uk
Outstanding collections of art, ceramics and textiles – take the time to call into this world-class visitor attraction and centre for major exhibitions.

Captain Cook Birthplace Museum
Stewart Park, Marton, Middlesbrough, Cleveland
Tel: (01642) 311211
www.captaincook-ne.co.uk
Discover why Captain Cook is the world's most famous navigator and explorer, and shudder at the hardships of life below decks in the 18thC.

Cherryburn: Thomas Bewick Birthplace Museum
Cherryburn, Station Bank, Stocksfield, Northumberland
Tel: (01661) 843276
Birthplace cottage of artist Thomas Bewick (1700) and farmyard, with a printing house using original printing blocks. Introductory exhibition of his life, work and countryside.

98 This is just a selection of attractions available. Contact any Tourist Information Centre in the region for more ideas.

NORTHUMBRIA

Chesters Roman Fort (Cilurnum) Hadrian's Wall
Chollerford, Humshaugh, Northumberland
Tel: (01434) 681379
www.english-heritage.org.uk
Hear the rumble of distant hooves in the remains of this fort built for 500 cavalrymen. Five gateways, barrack blocks, commandant's house and headquarters, and the finest military bath house in Britain to explore.

Chillingham Castle
Chillingham, Northumberland
Tel: (01668) 215359
www.chillingham-castle.com
Be sure to avoid the torture chamber in this medieval fortress with Tudor additions, shop, dungeon, tearoom, woodland walks, furnished rooms and topiary garden.

Cragside House, Gardens and Estate (National Trust)
Cragside, Rothbury, Northumberland
Tel: (01669) 620333
www.nationaltrust.org.uk
Revolutionary home of Lord Armstrong, Victorian inventor and landscape genius – as amazing today as it was then. House, gardens, red squirrels, woodland and lakeside walks.

Discovery Museum
Blandford House, Newcastle upon Tyne, Tyne and Wear
Tel: (0191) 232 6789
www.twmuseums.org.uk
A wide variety of experiences for all the family to enjoy. Check out the Newcastle Story, Live Wires, Science Maze and Fashion Works.

Dunstanburgh Castle (English Heritage)
Craster, Alnwick, Northumberland
Tel: (01665) 576231
www.english-heritage.org.uk
Feel the drama in the romantic ruins of this extensive 14thC castle built by Thomas, Earl of Lancaster. In a stunning coastal setting on 30.5m (100ft) cliffs.

Durham Castle
Durham, County Durham
Tel: (0191) 334 4106
www.durhamcastle.com
This fine example of a motte-and-bailey castle, founded in 1072, evokes a real sense of history. The Norman chapel dates from 1080 and the kitchens and great hall from 1499 and 1284 respectively.

Durham Cathedral
Durham, County Durham
Tel: (0191) 386 4266
www.durhamcathedral.co.uk
Thought by many to be the finest example of Norman church architecture in England. Contains the tombs of St Cuthbert and The Venerable Bede.

Guisborough Priory
Church Street, Guisborough, Cleveland
Tel: (01287) 633801
Remains of a priory for Augustinian canons founded by Robert de Brus in AD1119, in the grounds of Guisborough Hall. A sanctuary from busy market day shopping.

Hall Hill Farm
Lanchester, County Durham
Tel: (01388) 731333
www.hallhillfarm.co.uk
Family fun set in attractive countryside with an opportunity to see and touch the animals at close quarters. Farm trailer ride, gift shop, tearoom, picnic and play area.

Hartlepool Historic Quay
Maritime Avenue, Hartlepool, Cleveland
Tel: (01429) 860006
www.destinationhartlepool.com
Hartlepool Historic Quay is an exciting reconstruction of a seaport of the 1800s with buildings and lively quayside, authentically reconstructed.

Housesteads Roman Fort, Hadrian's Wall (English Heritage)
Haydon Bridge, Northumberland
Tel: (01434) 344363
www.english-heritage.org.uk
Best preserved and most impressive of the Roman forts. Vercovicium was a five-acre fort for an extensive 800 civil settlement. See the only example of a Roman hospital.

Killhope, The North of England Lead Mining Museum
Cowshill, County Durham
Tel: (01388) 537505
www.durham.gov.uk/killhope
Don a hard hat and go underground at Britain's most complete lead mining site. Mine tours available, 34ft diameter waterwheel, reconstruction of Victorian machinery, miner's lodging and woodland walks.

Life Science Centre
Centre for Life, Newcastle upon Tyne, Tyne and Wear
Tel: (0191) 243 8223
www.lifesciencecentre.org.uk
Meet your four billion-year-old family, explore what makes us all different, test your brain power and enjoy the thrill of the crazy motion ride.

Lindisfarne Castle (National Trust)
Holy Island, Northumberland
Tel: (01289) 389244
www.nationaltrust.org.uk
Built in 1550 and perched atop a rocky crag, this miniature castle was converted into a private home for Edward Hudson by the architect Sir Edwin Lutyens in 1903.

Left majestic Bamburgh Castle; picturesque Kielder

Places to visit

Awarded VisitBritain's Quality Assured Visitor Attraction marque.

Locomotion The National Railway Museum at Shildon
Soho Cottages, Shildon, County Durham
Tel: (01388) 777999
www.locomotion.uk.com
Get on the right track at Shildon Railway Village. Free admission to visitors who will be able to view 60 vehicles, a workshop and education centre. Shop and refreshments.

National Glass Centre
Liberty Way, Sunderland, Tyne and Wear
Tel: (0191) 515 5555
www.nationalglasscentre.com
A unique attraction presenting the best in contemporary glass. Watch live glass-making demostrations by master craftspeople or attend classes and workshops.

Nature's World at the Botanic Centre
Ladgate Lane, Acklam, Middlesbrough, Cleveland
Tel: (01642) 594895
www.naturesworld.org.uk
Pioneering eco-experience, with new futuristic Hydroponicum and Eco centre, plus demonstration gardens, wildlife pond, white garden, environmental exhibition hall, shop and tearoom.

Otter Trust's North Pennines Reserve
Vale House Farm, Bowes, County Durham
Tel: (01833) 628339
www.ottertrust.org.uk/pennine.htm
Animal lovers will delight in this branch of the famous Otter Trust. Spot Asian and British otters, red and fallow deer and rare breeds of farm animals in this 93-ha (230-acre) wildlife reserve.

Raby Castle
Staindrop, County Durham
Tel: (01833) 660202
www.rabycastle.com

Dramatic medieval castle, home of Lord Barnard's family since 1626, with deer park, walled gardens, carriage collection, adventure playground, shop and tearoom.

South Shields Museum and Art Gallery
Ocean Road, South Shields, Tyne and Wear
Tel: (0191) 456 8740
www.twmuseums.org.uk
Discover how the area's development has been influenced by its natural and industrial past through lively displays in this recently refurbished museum.

Wallington House, Walled Garden and Grounds (National Trust)
Wallington, Morpeth, Northumberland
Tel: (01670) 773600
www.nationaltrust.org.uk
17thC country house set in 40ha (100 acres) of lawns, lakes and woodlands, with beautiful walled garden and conservatory.

Washington Old Hall
The Avenue, Washington, Tyne and Wear
Tel: (0191) 416 6879
Home to George Washington's ancestors from 1183 to 1399, the manor remained in the family until 1613 and was saved in 1936.

Wet 'N Wild
Rotary Way, North Shields, Tyne and Wear
Tel: (0191) 296 1333
www.wetnwild.co.uk
Tropical indoor water park, a fun water playground providing the wildest and wettest indoor rapids experience. Whirlpools, slides and meandering lazy river. Don't forget your towel!

Wildfowl and Wetlands Trust
Washington Pattinson, Washington, Tyne and Wear
Tel: (0191) 416 5454
www.wwt.org.uk
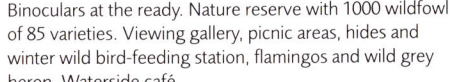
Binoculars at the ready. Nature reserve with 1000 wildfowl of 85 varieties. Viewing gallery, picnic areas, hides and winter wild bird-feeding station, flamingos and wild grey heron. Waterside café.

Above contemporary day out at BALTIC Centre for Contemporary Art, Gateshead; inviting countryside near Ireshopeburn
Right shopping spree in the MetroCentre, Newcastle upon Tyne

This is just a selection of attractions available. Contact any Tourist Information Centre in the region for more ideas.

NORTHUMBRIA

One NorthEast Tourism Team
Aykley Heads, Durham DH1 5UX
T: (0191) 375 3050 F: (0191) 386 0899
www.visitnorthumbria.com

The following publications are available from One NorthEast Tourism Team unless otherwise stated:

Northumbria 2005 – information on the region, including hotels, bed and breakfast and self-catering accommodation, caravan and camping parks, attractions, shopping, eating and drinking.

Group Travel Guide – packed with everything tour planners need to know when planning a group visit – group hotels, attractions, destinations, itinerary suggestions, Blue Badge Guides, coach parking locations and events.

Educational Visits Guide – information for teachers planning school visits including attractions with links to National Curriculum subjects, suitable accommodation, itinerary suggestions and events.

Northumbria's Top Tours – a selection of themed itineraries offering suggestions for day tours, short breaks and long stay holidays which can be tailored to suit the needs of the group.

Cycle Northumbria – for information on day rides, traffic free trails and challenging routes call (0191) 375 3044 for your free cycling guide.

Travel information

By road:
The north/south routes on the A1 and A19 thread the region as does the A68. East/west routes like the A66 and A69 easily link with the western side of the country. Within Northumbria you will find fast, modern interconnecting roads between all the main centres, a vast network of scenic, traffic-free country roads to make motoring a pleasure and frequent local bus services operating to all towns and villages.

By rail:
London to Edinburgh InterCity service stops at Darlington, Durham, Newcastle and Berwick upon Tweed. Trains make the journey between London and Newcastle in around three hours. The London to Middlesbrough journey (changing at Darlington) takes three hours. Birmingham to Darlington just under three hours. Bristol to Durham five hours and Sheffield to Newcastle just over two hours. Direct services operate to Newcastle from Liverpool, Manchester, Glasgow and Carlisle. Regional services to areas of scenic beauty operate frequently, allowing the traveller easy access. The Tyne & Wear Metro makes it possible to travel to many destinations within the Tyneside area, such as Gateshead, South Shields, Whitley Bay, Sunderland, Newcastle City Centre and Newcastle International Airport, in minutes.

Enjoy England official guides to quality

NORTHUMBRIA

Where to stay in
Northumbria

All place names in the blue bands, under which accommodation is listed, are shown on the maps at the front of this guide.

A complete listing of all VisitBritain assessed accommodation covered by this guide appears at the back.

Accommodation symbols
Symbols give useful information about services and facilities. Inside the back cover flap you can find a key to these symbols. Keep it open for easy reference.

ALNMOUTH, Northumberland Map ref 5C1

1 Unit
Sleeping 1–6

CURLEW'S CALLING
Alnmouth
Contact: Alan and Sheila Worsley, Curlew's Calling,
Rear of 10 Riverside Road, Alnmouth, Alnwick
NE66 2SD
T: (01665) 830888
F: (01665) 830888

OPEN All Year

Low season per wk
£280.00–£360.00
High season per wk
£460.00–£560.00

Fully furnished, centrally heated, three-bedroom flat 50yds from beach. Area of Outstanding Natural Beauty, walking, bird-watching, golf. Phone or write for brochure.

★★–★★★
3 Units
Sleeping 5

WOODEN FARM HOLIDAY COTTAGES
Alnmouth
Contact: Mr Farr, Wooden Farm Holiday Cottages,
Lesbury, Alnmouth, Alnwick NE66 2TW
T: (01665) 830342

OPEN All Year

Low season per wk
Max £190.00
High season per wk
Max £250.00

Stone-built cottages in a quiet farm setting, overlooking the coast and the picturesque village of Alnmouth. Only four miles from Alnwick Castle/Garden.

ALNWICK, Northumberland Map ref 5C1 *Tourist Information Centre Tel: (01665) 510665*

1 Unit
Sleeping 1–2

GREEN BATT STUDIO
Alnwick
Contact: Mrs Clare Mills, 1 Percy Street, Alnwick
NE66 1AE
T: (01665) 602742
E: paul@mills84.freeserve.co.uk

OPEN All Year

Low season per wk
£180.00–£200.00
High season per wk
£200.00–£250.00

Second floor studio apartment in a quiet conservation area, yet only 100m from town centre. Friendly hosts live on ground floor. Well-equipped accommodation, welcome pack provided.

Location Complete addresses for properties are not given and the town(s) listed may be a distance from the actual establishment. Please check the precise location at the time of booking.

NORTHUMBRIA

ALNWICK continued

★★★
1 Unit
Sleeping 1–5

THE PEBBLE
Alnwick
Contact: Clare Laughton, Okelands, Pickhurst Road, Chiddingfold GU8 4TS
T: (01428) 683941
F: (01428) 683967
E: anthony.laughton@soc.soton.ac.uk

OPEN All Year

Low season per wk
£230.00–£250.00
High season per wk
£450.00–£500.00

Spacious, comfortable, semi-detached cottage. Parking and lockable garage. Ideal base for exploring beautiful coast, castles and moors. Nearby farm shop.

★★★–★★★★★
13 Units
Sleeping 1–12

17thC farmhouse, cottages and beautifully appointed chalets complemented by excellent facilities – indoor heated swimming pool, health club, steam room, sauna, sunshower, beauty therapist, games room, tennis, riding, fishing and adventure playground. Situated between Alnwick and Heritage Coast. A warm, personal welcome.

VILLAGE FARM
Alnwick
Contact: Mrs Crissy Stoker, Town Foot Farm, Shilbottle, Alnwick NE66 2HG
T: (01665) 575591
F: (01665) 575591
E: crissy@villagefarmcottages.co.uk
I: www.villagefarmcottages.co.uk

OPEN All Year
Payment accepted: Visa

2/3-night stays available Nov-Easter (excl Christmas, New Year and half-terms).

Low season per wk
£140.00–£395.00
High season per wk
£250.00–£980.00

BAMBURGH, Northumberland Map ref 5C1

★★★–★★★★★
16 Units
Sleeping 3–12

ADDERSTONE HALL COUNTRY COTTAGES
Bamburgh
Contact: Dr David Ratliff, Country Cottages, Adderstone Hall, Market Place, Belford NE70 7NE
T: (01668) 213543
F: (01668) 213787
E: davidratliff1@hotmail.com
I: www.adderstonehall.co.uk

OPEN All Year

Low season per wk
£120.00–£450.00
High season per wk
£250.00–£1,200.00

Adderstone Hall Estate, a country retreat near Bamburgh and Belford, offers good self-catering period cottages, facilities for one to six double bedrooms.

★★★–★★★★★
4 Units
Sleeping 2–6

BRADFORD COUNTRY COTTAGES
Belford
Contact: Mr L W Robson, Bradford Country Cottages, Bradford House, Bamburgh, Belford NE70 7JT
T: (01668) 213432
F: (01668) 213891
E: lwrob@tiscali.co.uk
I: www.bradford-leisure.co.uk

OPEN All Year
Payment accepted: Delta, Mastercard, Switch, Visa

Low season per wk
£200.00–£400.00
High season per wk
£400.00–£600.00

Four stone built cottages in a rural setting, two miles from Bamburgh village, full central heating and facilities, access to swimming pool included in tariff.

Map references The map references refer to the colour maps at the front of this guide. The first figure is the map number; the letter and figure which follow indicate the grid reference on the map.

103

NORTHUMBRIA

BAMBURGH continued

★★★★
5 Units
Sleeping 2–8

DUKESFIELD FARM HOLIDAY COTTAGES
Bamburgh
Contact: Mrs Maria Eliana Robinson, The Glebe, Radcliffe Road, Bamburgh NE69 7AE
T: (01668) 214456
F: (01668) 214354
E: eric_j_robinson@compuserve.com
I: www.secretkingdom.com/dukes/field.htm

Situated just outside Bamburgh village, this attractive farmsteading offers easy access to coast, castle, beach and golf course. Spacious yet cosy cottages with first-class kitchens and bathrooms. Own paddocks. Children and pets welcome. Ample parking. An ideal base for walking and exploring Northumberland's Heritage Coast.

OPEN All Year
Payment accepted: Euros

Low season per wk
£295.00–£495.00
High season per wk
£495.00–£925.00

Special 2-person weekly prices and short breaks available.

★★★★★
2 Units
Sleeping 2–8

GLEBE HOUSE AND GLEBE COTTAGE
Bamburgh
Contact: Mrs Maria Eliana Robinson, The Glebe, Radcliffe Road, Bamburgh NE69 7AE
T: (01668) 214456
F: (01668) 214354
E: eric_j_robinson@compuserve.com
I: www.secretkingdom.com/glebe/house.htm

In Bamburgh village, this lovely 18thC vicarage has stunning views of church, castle and sea. Glebe House is spacious and well furnished with full central heating included. First-class kitchen. Children welcome. Large, peaceful, private gardens. Separate cottage also available with ground floor bedrooms and private patio.

OPEN All Year
Payment accepted: Euros

Low season per wk
£325.00–£675.00
High season per wk
£595.00–£1,100.00

Special 2-person prices and short breaks available.

★★★★
1 Unit
Sleeping 4

HARELAW HOUSE
Bamburgh
Contact: Mr Robert Turnbull, Church House, New Road, Chatton NE66 5PU
T: (01668) 215494
F: (01668) 215494
E: harelaw@fsmail.net
I: www.harelawhouse.ntb.org.uk

Spacious, fully equipped house in historic Bamburgh, five minutes from castle, village green, wide sandy beaches, restaurants, pubs, teashops. Open-plan dining room/kitchen, woodburning stove. South facing conservatory, landscaped garden. Double and twin bedrooms, cosy living room, colour TV, video. Shower room, loos upstairs and downstairs. Electricity, linen included in price.

OPEN All Year

Low season per wk
Min £300.00
High season per wk
Max £500.00

Quality Assurance Standard
Star ratings and awards are explained at the back of this guide.

NORTHUMBRIA

BAMBURGH continued

★★★★
1 Unit
Sleeping 12

THE OLD COACH HOUSE
Bamburgh
Contact: Carolynn & David Croisdale-Appleby,
Abbotsholme, Hervines Road, Amersham HP6 5HS
T: (01494) 725194
F: (01494) 725474
E: croisdaleappleby@aol.com
I: www.selfcateringluxury.co.uk

Nestling in the centre of beautiful Bamburgh village, this 200-year-old stone cottage, Bamburgh's prettiest, is beautifully furnished and equipped. Close to fabulous beach. Views of the dramatic castle. Two beamed reception rooms, dining room, conservatory, farmhouse kitchen, five bedrooms, two bathrooms, patio, private garden, parking.

OPEN All Year

Short breaks available Nov-Mar. Weekend breaks, 3 nights, Fri-Mon; mid-week breaks, 4 nights, Mon-Fri.

Low season per wk
£547.00–£865.00
High season per wk
£865.00–£1,336.00

★★★★
16 Units
Sleeping 2–6

OUTCHESTER & ROSS FARM COTTAGES
Belford
Contact: Mrs Shirley McKie, 1 Cragview Road, Belford NE70 7NT
T: (01668) 213336
F: (01668) 219385
E: enquiry@rosscottages.co.uk
I: www.rosscottages.co.uk

Ross is in a superb location near the sea between Bamburgh and Holy Island – really 'away from it all'. Outchester Manor Cottages won the Northumbria Tourist Board 'Pride of Northumbria Award' for self-catering cottages in 2001. Please phone/fax for our colour brochure, or visit our website.

OPEN All Year

Low season per wk
£220.00–£395.00
High season per wk
£309.00–£659.00

★★★★★
3 Units
Sleeping 2–28

WAREN LEA HALL
Bamburgh
Contact: Carolynn & David Croisdale-Appleby,
Abbotsholme, Hervines Road, Amersham HP6 5HS
T: (01494) 725194
F: (01494) 725474
E: croisdaleappleby@aol.com
I: www.selfcateringluxury.co.uk

Imposing, spacious country house on shore of Budle Bay at Waren Mill near Bamburgh in two acres of waters-edge parkland. Breathtaking, panoramic views of Lindisfarne and the Cheviots. The holiday homes can be booked individually or together. Waren Lea Hall enjoys an unrivalled location with easy access for walking, golf, fishing etc.

OPEN All Year

Short breaks available from Nov-Mar. Weekend breaks, 3 nights, Fri-Mon. Mid-week breaks, 4 nights, Mon-Fri.

Low season per wk
£208.00–£1,646.00
High season per wk
£353.00–£2,044.00

Quality Assurance Standard
Star ratings and awards were correct at time of going to press but are subject to change. Please check at the time of booking.

NORTHUMBRIA

BARNARD CASTLE, County Durham Map ref 5B3 *Tourist Information Centre Tel: (01833) 690909*

★★★★
2 Units
Sleeping 2–5

STAINDROP HOUSE MEWS & THE ARCHES
Staindrop, Darlington
Contact: Mrs Dorothy Walton, Staindrop House,
14 Front Street, Darlington DL2 3NH
T: (01833) 660951
E: shmholidays@hotmail.com

Converted stable units comprising one/two reception rooms, bathroom, shower room, fitted kitchen and small balcony. The unit with two reception rooms also has a beamed ceiling. Pretty countryside village. Use of large, landscaped garden with children's play area. All linen provided. Sorry, no smoking or pets in Arches unit.

OPEN All Year

Coal fire (first bucket of coal free). Bottle of wine in fridge.

Low season per wk
£180.00–£220.00
High season per wk
£270.00–£415.00

★★★
1 Unit

WACKFORD SQUEERS COTTAGE
Barnard Castle
Contact: Mr John Braithwaite, Wackford Squeers Cottage, Wodencroft, Cotherstone, Barnard Castle DL12 9UQ
T: (01833) 650032
F: (01833) 650909

OPEN All Year

Low season per wk
£150.00–£220.00
High season per wk
£250.00–£270.00

Open-beamed cottage on quiet Teesdale farm in unspoilt countryside. Easy access long-distance paths. Easy drive to Lakes and Yorkshire Dales.

BEADNELL, Northumberland Map ref 5C1

★★★
1 Unit
Sleeping 8

BEECHLEY
Chathill
Contact: Mrs Deborah Baker, 22 Upper Green Way, Tingley, Wakefield WF3 1TA
T: (0113) 218 9176
F: (0113) 218 9176
E: deb_n_ade@hotmail.com

OPEN All Year except Christmas and New Year

Low season per wk
£350.00–£400.00
High season per wk
£450.00–£550.00

A four-bedroomed, centrally heated house on the seafront. Modern fitted kitchen, enclosed rear garden, sea view from all bedrooms. Fuel and linen included.

★★★-★★★★★
7 Units
Sleeping 2–5

TOWN FARM COTTAGES
Seahouses
Contact: Mr & Mrs Thompson, South Lodge, Morpeth NE65 9JA
T: (01665) 604110
F: (01670) 786188
E: paul.thompson@marishalthompson.co.uk
I: www.northumberland-holidays.com

17thC stable block converted to cottages and apartments. Close to the sea and beaches, ideal for exploring lovely Northumbria. Easy walk to beach. Short distance to beautiful Bamburgh Castle and Holy Isle. Seahouses and Farne Isle three miles. Alnwick Gardens and Castle easily accessible, plus Heritage Coast and National Park.

OPEN All Year

Short breaks available in low season.

Low season per wk
£120.00–£220.00
High season per wk
£220.00–£435.00

Visitor attractions For ideas on places to visit refer to the introduction at the beginning of this section. Look out for the VisitBritain Quality Assured Visitor Attraction signs.

NORTHUMBRIA

BEAMISH, County Durham Map ref 5C2

★★★
4 Units
Sleeping 2

CHAPEL HOUSE STUDIO APARTMENTS
Newcastle upon Tyne
Contact: Mr MacLennan, Chapel House, Causey Row,
Marley Hill, Newcastle upon Tyne NE16 5EJ
T: (01207) 290992

OPEN All Year

Low season per wk
Min £160.00
High season per wk
Min £175.00

Studio apartments located on a quiet country lane overlooking farmland. Beamish Museum and Tanfield Railway are a short drive away and the MetroCentre can be reached in 20 minutes.

BELFORD, Northumberland Map ref 5B1

★★★
3 Units
Sleeping 2-6

3, 4 AND 5 SWINHOE COTTAGES
Belford
Contact: Mrs Valerie Nixon, Swinhoe Farm House,
Belford NE70 7LJ
T: (01668) 213370
I: www.swinhoecottages.co.uk

OPEN All Year

Low season per wk
£145.00-£300.00
High season per wk
£355.00-£395.00

Well-equipped cottages on working farm. Many walks including St Cuthbert's Cave. Approximately 10 minutes' drive from Bamburgh, with its sandy beaches, and Holy Island.

BELLINGHAM, Northumberland Map ref 5B2 Tourist Information Centre Tel: (01434) 220616

★★★★
2 Units
Sleeping 2-4

BOAT FARM COTTAGES
Hexham
Contact: Mrs Young, Boat Farm, Bellingham, Hexham
NE48 2AR
T: (01434) 220989
E: barbaraattheboat@hotmail.com
I: www.boatfarm.co.uk

OPEN All Year

Low season per wk
Min £175.00
High season per wk
Max £350.00

Quiet, peaceful location one mile from Bellingham village on banks of North Tyne. Excellent location for exploring Kielder, Hadrian's Wall, Northumberland National Park.

★★★★
1 Unit
Sleeping 2-5

CONHEATH COTTAGE
Hexham
Contact: Mrs Zaina Riddle, Blakelaw Farm, Bellingham,
Hexham NE48 2EF
T: (01434) 220250
F: (01434) 220250
E: stay@conheath.co.uk
I: www.conheath.co.uk

OPEN All Year

Low season per wk
Min £200.00
High season per wk
Max £375.00

Quiet, semi-detached cottage. Stunning views. Very well equipped and comfortable. Centrally heated with open fire. Garden with accessories. Beautiful indoor heated swimming pool. Ideal location.

★★★★
4 Units
Sleeping 2-8

RIVERDALE COURT
Hexham
Contact: John and Iben Cocker, Riverdale Court,
Bellingham, Hexham NE48 2JT
T: (01434) 220254
F: (01434) 220457
I: www.riverdalehall.demon.co.uk

Nestling alongside Riverdale Hall Hotel with splendid views over the North Tyne river and Dunterley Fells (Pennine Way). Guests have free use of hotel pool, sauna and cricket field. There is a charge for salmon fishing. All apartments have either a balcony or patio area.

OPEN All Year

Payment accepted: Amex, Delta, Diners, Mastercard, Switch, Visa, Euros

3-and 4-day bookings accepted – from £120.

Low season per wk
£230.00-£290.00
High season per wk
£380.00-£460.00

107

NORTHUMBRIA

BERWICK-UPON-TWEED, Northumberland Map ref 5B1 *Tourist Information Centre Tel: (01289) 330733*

★★★
1 Unit
Sleeping 1–5

BROADSTONE COTTAGE
Berwick-upon-Tweed
Contact: Mr Edward Chantler, Broadstone Farm,
Grafty Green, Maidstone ME17 2AT
T: (01622) 850207
F: (01622) 851750

OPEN All Year

Low season per wk
£130.00–£180.00
High season per wk
£190.00–£350.00

Village cottage. Ideal centre for touring, walking, fishing holidays. Twenty minutes beach. Shops, pubs nearby. Full central heating. Bathroom with shower.

BISHOP MIDDLEHAM, County Durham Map ref 5C2

★★★
1 Unit
Sleeping 1–8

BEE EATER COTTAGE
Bishop Middleham
Contact: Mrs Daphne Anderson, Farnless Farm Cottage,
Bishop Middleham DL17 9EB
T: (0191) 377 1428
I: www.bee-eater-cottage.co.uk

OPEN All Year

Low season per wk
Min £280.00
High season per wk
Max £550.00

Ornithologists' paradise! Working farm with lake and spectacular views. Neighbouring nature reserve (Site of Special Scientific Interest) and golf course. Well situated for Northumbria/Yorkshire.

BLANCHLAND, Northumberland Map ref 5B2

★★
2 Units
Sleeping 4

BOLTSBURN HOLIDAY COTTAGES
Consett
Contact: Mr Cecil Ernest Davison, Bolts Brae,
10 Watergate Road, Consett DH8 9QS
T: (01207) 583076

Low season per wk
Min £170.00
High season per wk
Min £170.00

Self-contained cottages in picturesque countryside, two miles Blanchland, 10 miles Hexham. Hadrian's Wall, Beamish Museum, Durham Cathedral all within driving distance. Open May to September.

BOULMER, Northumberland Map ref 5C1

★★★★
1 Unit
Sleeping 2–4

NORTH COTTAGE
Alnwick
Contact: Mrs Madeleine Frater, North Cottage,
Boulmer, Alnwick NE66 3BX
T: (01665) 577308
E: madeleine_frater@hotmail.com
I: www.northcottage.boulmer.co.uk

OPEN All Year
Payment accepted: Euros

Low season per wk
£280.00–£365.00
High season per wk
£395.00–£525.00

Charming, detached, stone cottage in unspoilt fishing village. Stunning views of the sea with beach at garden wall. Private garden, parking and secure storage shed.

BYRNESS, Northumberland Map ref 5B1

★★★★
1 Unit
Sleeping 4

THE OLD SCHOOL HOUSE
Newcastle upon Tyne
Contact: Dales Holiday Cottages, Carleton Business Park,
Sandylands Business Centre, Carleton New Road, Skipton
BD23 2DG
T: (01756) 799821
F: (01756) 797012

OPEN All Year

Low season per wk
Min £214.00
High season per wk
Min £367.00

On Pennine Way with views over Kielder Forest Park. Northumbrian single-storey, stone cottage under slate. Exterior restored in vernacular style. Interior remodelled in pine with attic bedrooms and modern facilities. Spacious and cosy with oil-fired Rayburn for central heating and cooking. Excellent for touring Borders and Cheviot Hills.

 Prices Please check prices and other details at the time of booking.

NORTHUMBRIA

CASTLESIDE, County Durham Map ref 5B2

★★–★★★★
3 Units
Sleeping 1–5

THE COTTAGE, THE DAIRY & THE FORGE
Consett
Contact: Mr & Mrs Elliot, Derwent Grange Farm,
Consett DH8 9BN
T: (01207) 508358
E: ekelliot@aol.com

OPEN All Year

Low season per wk
£200.00–£225.00
High season per wk
£225.00–£250.00

Charming cottages converted from farm buildings, set on a working sheep farm, provide a serene, relaxing holiday. Access to wonderful countryside and tourist attractions. Friendly hosts.

CHATHILL, Northumberland Map ref 5C1

★★
1 Unit
Sleeping 1–5

NEWSTEAD COTTAGE
Chathill
Contact: Mrs Riddell, Newstead Cottage,
Newstead Farm, Chathill NE67 5LH
T: (01665) 589263

Low season per wk
Min £200.00
High season per wk
£300.00–£350.00

A mixed farm, four miles from unspoilt beaches. Ideal for touring. Castles, golf courses and the famous Alnwick Gardens within a 10-mile radius. Open March-November.

CHILLINGHAM, Northumberland Map ref 5B1

★★★
8 Units
Sleeping 2–7

CHILLINGHAM CASTLE
Alnwick
Contact: Chillingham Castle, Chillingham, Alnwick
NE66 5NJ
T: (01668) 215359
F: (01668) 215463
E: enquiries@chillingham-castle.com
I: www.chillingham-castle.com

OPEN All Year
Payment accepted:
Mastercard, Switch, Visa

Low season per wk
£271.00–£543.00
High season per wk
£542.00–£1,053.00

In the heart of a medieval castle with stunning views of formal gardens and Cheviot Hills or in the romantic wing overlooking the valley and stream.

COCKFIELD, County Durham Map ref 5B3

★★★★
2 Units
Sleeping 4–5

Award-winning cottages on a working livestock farm. Both cottages beautifully renovated and decorated to an exceptionally high standard. Beams, log fires, gas barbecue, own gardens and parking. Close to Durham City, Northumberland, Lakes, Hadrian's Wall. Pets and children most welcome, childminding available. Children's equipment, fuels, electric, linens and towels all included.

STONECROFT AND SWALLOWS NEST

Bishop Auckland
Contact: Mrs Alison Tallentire, Low Lands Farm, Cockfield,
Bishop Auckland DL13 5AW
T: (01388) 718251
F: (01388) 718251
E: info@farmholidaysuk.com
I: www.farmholidaysuk.com

OPEN All Year

Mid-week and weekend breaks available out of season. Open Christmas and New Year.

Low season per wk
£150.00–£200.00
High season per wk
£225.00–£340.00

Accessibility Look for the symbols which indicate National Accessible Scheme standards for hearing and visually impaired guests in addition to standards for guests with mobility impairment. You can find an index of all scheme participants at the back of this guide.

NORTHUMBRIA

CORBRIDGE, Northumberland Map ref 5B2

★★★★
1 Unit
Sleeping 6

OSWALD COTTAGE
Corbridge
Contact: Mrs Harriman, Swarden House,
Kyloe House Farm, Newcastle upon Tyne NE18 0BB
T: (01661) 852909
F: (01661) 854106
E: paul.harriman@littonproperties.co.uk

Exceptional 18thC double-fronted large stone cottage. Carved external Latin inscription 'To the good all things are good' reflects interior ambience, beams and open fire. In heart of historic village but quiet. Stone's throw from river and superb local shops. Lovely patio garden. Perfect, winter or summer.

OPEN All Year

Weekends available.

Low season per wk
£250.00–£350.00
High season per wk
£350.00–£500.00

★★★
1 Unit
Sleeping 4

WEST FELL COTTAGE
Corbridge
Contact: Mrs Smith, West Fell House, Corbridge
NE45 5RZ
T: (01434) 632044

Two-bedroomed farm cottage near Dilston Castle and convenient for Corbridge and the Roman Wall.

OPEN All Year

Low season per wk
£100.00–£150.00
High season per wk
£200.00–£245.00

COTHERSTONE, County Durham Map ref 5B3

★★★
1 Unit
Sleeping 4–6

FARTHINGS
Barnard Castle
Contact: Mr Christopher John Bainbridge, Glen Leigh,
Cotherstone, Barnard Castle DL12 9QW
T: (01833) 650331

Comfortable stone-built bungalow overlooking village green. Two bedrooms (double and twin), gas central heating, living room fire. Well equipped and decorated.

OPEN All Year

Low season per wk
Min £100.00
High season per wk
Max £280.00

CRAMLINGTON, Northumberland Map ref 5C2

★★★★
3 Units
Sleeping 2–4

BURRADON FARM COTTAGES
Cramlington
Contact: Mrs Judith Younger, Burradon Farm Cottages,
Burradon Farm, Cramlington NE23 7ND
T: (0191) 268 3203
E: judy_younger@burradonfarm.freeserve.co.uk
I: www.burradonfarm.freeserve.co.uk

Burradon Farm is located only a few miles from the spectacular Northumbrian coastline and within easy reach of the cultural heritage and dynamic centre which is Newcastle-upon-Tyne. The new barn conversions have become characterful, high-quality cottages boasting every amenity and facility to ensure an enjoyable visit.

OPEN All Year

Payment accepted: Amex, Delta, Mastercard, Switch, Visa

3/4-night stays welcomed, all year round.

Low season per wk
£225.00–£270.00
High season per wk
£285.00–£420.00

110

NORTHUMBRIA

DARLINGTON, Darlington Map ref 5C3 *Tourist Information Centre Tel: (01325) 388666*

★★★–★★★★★
3 Units
Sleeping 2–10

HIGH HOUSE FARM COTTAGES
Darlington
Contact: Mr Harry & Mrs Peggy Wood,
High House Farm, Houghton-le-Side, Darlington
DL2 2UU
T: (01388) 834879
F: (01388) 834879
E: wood@houghtonleside.fsnet.co.uk
I: www.farmstaynorth.co.uk / www.highhousefarm.com

OPEN All Year
Payment accepted: Euros

Low season per wk
£150.00–£250.00
High season per wk
£240.00–£340.00

Panoramic views across Teesdale. Home of Fairisle Shetland sheep and Aymara alpacas. Smithy, Granary and Coach House conversions, with original features plus all mod cons.

★★★
1 Unit
Sleeping 4–6

PEGASUS COTTAGE
Darlington
Contact: Mr Stuart & Mrs Denise Chapman, Pegasus Cottage, 4 Tees View, Hurworth Place, Darlington
DL2 2DH
T: (01325) 722542
F: (01325) 722542
E: stuart1948@msn.com
I: www.pegasuscottage.co.uk

OPEN All Year
Payment accepted: Delta, Mastercard, Switch, Visa

Low season per wk
£230.00–£280.00
High season per wk
£280.00–£330.00

Converted stable block of a Grade II Listed building, c1850. Local mayor's Design Award winner 1995. Set in small village three miles from Darlington.

DURHAM, County Durham Map ref 5C2 *Tourist Information Centre Tel: (0191) 384 3720*

★★★★
1 Unit
Sleeping 1–5

BOURNE COTTAGE
Durham
Contact: Mrs Judith Heron, Bourne House Farm,
Church Villas, Shadforth, Durham DH6 1LQ
T: (0191) 372 0730
F: (0191) 372 0730
E: judithheron@aol.com
I: www.bournecottagedurham.com

OPEN All Year

Low season per wk
Min £250.00
High season per wk
Min £350.00

Beautiful, detached, stone-built cottage situated in idyllic, rural location approximately five miles east of Durham City. Durham coast, Yorkshire and Northumberland within easy reach.

★★
2 Units
Sleeping 2–3

26A AND 26B HALLGARTH STREET
Durham
Contact: Ms Sue Pitts, 27 Hallgarth Street, Durham
DH1 3AT
T: (0191) 384 1611

Low season per wk
Min £285.00
High season per wk
Max £285.00

Situated in a late-Georgian terrace, Grade II Listed. Half a mile from the market-place, five minutes from Durham Cathedral. Well equipped and comfortable. Open July to October.

★★★★
1 Unit
Sleeping 2–4

THE OLD POWER HOUSE
Chester-le-Street
Contact: Mrs Anne Hall, The Old Power House,
Garden Cottage, Southill Hall, Chester-le-Street DH3 4EQ
T: (0191) 387 3001
F: (0191) 389 3569
E: g.s.hall@talk21.com

OPEN All Year

Low season per wk
£200.00–£250.00
High season per wk
£250.00–£340.00

Recently redeveloped former power house set in walled garden of old hall, providing compact two-bedroomed country cottage set in three acres of landscaped gardens. Idyllic location midway between Durham City (three miles) and Chester-le-Street (three miles). Newcastle, Sunderland and MetroCentre (Gateshead) within 25 minutes' drive.

111

NORTHUMBRIA

DURHAM continued

★★★
4 Units
Sleeping 3-6

STOWHOUSE FARM COTTAGES
Durham
Contact: Mr Peter Swinburne, Stowhouse Farm Cottages, Stowhouse Farm, Old Cornsay, Durham DH7 9EN
T: (0191) 373 9990

Cosy stone cottages set on a peaceful, isolated, working hill farm with beautiful views over valley, wood and fell. Set well off any road yet easily accessible to historic Durham City, the Roman Wall, Teesdale, Weardale and the coast of Northumberland. Quiet village with friendly pub and restaurant 0.5 miles away.

OPEN All Year

Payment accepted: Mastercard, Visa

Low season per wk £170.00–£260.00
High season per wk £290.00–£450.00

EDLINGHAM, Northumberland Map ref 5C1

★★★★
1 Unit
Sleeping 5

HAZELNUTHOUSE
Edlingham
Contact: Ms Hazel Bennett, 61 Portsmouth Road, Guildford GU2 4BS
T: (01483) 569346
F: (01483) 569346
E: hazelnuthouse@dial.pipex.com
I: www.bigfoot.com/~hazelnuthouse

Traditional Northumbrian stone-built cottage. Panoramic views of moorland valley. Three bedrooms, lounge, kitchen/diner, luxury bathroom, log stove, double glazing and central heating. Open April to October.

Low season per wk £300.00–£350.00
High season per wk £425.00–£450.00

EMBLETON, Northumberland Map ref 5C1

★★-★★★★★
8 Units
Sleeping 2-7

DOXFORD FARM COTTAGES
Chathill
Contact: Mrs Sarah Shell, Doxford Farm Cottages, Doxford Farm, Doxford, Chathill NE67 5DY
T: (01665) 579348 & 579477
F: (01665) 579331
E: doxfordfarm@hotmail.com
I: www.doxfordfarmcottages.com

Set in wooded countryside four miles from sea, on a working mixed farm. Well equipped and furnished cottages with central heating and open fires. Wildlife trail, woodland walks. Doxford Country Store is nearby, with coffee shop, gift shop, country clothing and art gallery. Ideal base for Northumberland's castles and coastline and Alnwick Gardens.

OPEN All Year

Payment accepted: Amex, Mastercard, Switch, Visa

Low season per wk £175.00–£350.00
High season per wk £325.00–£525.00

3-night stays available Oct-Mar (excl Christmas and New Year).

Check the maps

The colour maps at the front of this guide show all the cities, towns and villages for which you will find accommodation entries. Refer to the town index to find the page on which they are listed.

NORTHUMBRIA

EMBLETON continued

★★★
4 Units
Sleeping 2–4

17thC coach house converted to cottages in the quiet village of Embleton. An easy walk to the superb Embleton Beach and Dunstanburgh Castle. Ideal for exploring lovely Northumbria, the Heritage Coastline, Holy Island, Alnwick Castle and gardens and the National Park.

DUNSTANBURGH CASTLE COURTYARD COTTAGES
Alnwick
Contact: Mrs Allison Licence, 6A Greensfield Court, Alnwick NE66 2DE
T: (01665) 604110
F: (08702) 414339
E: paul.thompson@marishalthompson.co.uk
I: www.northumberland-holidays.co.uk

OPEN All Year

Short breaks available in low season.

Low season per wk £120.00–£220.00
High season per wk £220.00–£435.00

FALSTONE, Northumberland Map ref 5B2

★★★★
1 Unit

Station Cottage has recently been converted from the old station waiting room into a small, cosy, very comfortable, one-double-bedroomed cottage. Located on the old disused Border Counties railway line, near the centre of the village, it offers beautiful views across the valley. Close to Kielder Water and Forest.

STATION COTTAGE
Falstone
Contact: Mrs June Banks, Station House, Falstone, Hexham NE48 1AB
T: (01434) 240311

OPEN All Year

Short breaks available.

Low season per wk Min £175.00
High season per wk Max £300.00

HAMSTERLEY FOREST

See under Barnard Castle, Stanhope, Wolsingham

HEDDON-ON-THE-WALL, Northumberland Map ref 5B2

★★★
1 Unit
Sleeping 2–7

2 EAST TOWN HOUSE
Newcastle upon Tyne
Contact: Mr Ridley & Mrs Beryl Amos,
1 East Town House, Heddon-on-the-Wall,
Newcastle upon Tyne NE15 0DR
T: (01661) 852277
F: (01661) 853063

OPEN All Year

Low season per wk £240.00–£260.00
High season per wk £330.00–£380.00

Stone-built, well-equipped house furnished to a high standard, in historic village on Hadrian's Wall. Only six miles to Newcastle, 20 minutes from Hexham.

Quality Assurance Standard

For an explanation of the quality and facilities represented by the stars please refer to the front of this guide. A more detailed explanation can be found in the information pages at the back.

NORTHUMBRIA

HEXHAM, Northumberland Map ref 5B2 *Tourist Information Centre Tel: (01434) 652220*

★★★★★
1 Unit
Sleeping 2–4

SAMMY'S PLACE
Hexham
Contact: Mr T A Sisterson, High Mead, Leazes Lane,
Hexham NE46 3AE
T: (01434) 604656
F: (01434) 604656
E: relax@sammyshideaway.com
I: www.sammyshideaway.com

OPEN All Year

Low season per wk
Min £235.00
High season per wk
£350.00–£450.00

Beautifully appointed two-bedroomed apartment, with both rooms being en suite. The property is situated in the heart of historic Hexham in Hadrian's Wall country.

See display advertisement below

HOLY ISLAND, Northumberland Map ref 5C1

★★★
2 Units
Sleeping 4

FARNE COURT COTTAGES, FARNE VIEW COTTAGE
Holy Island
Contact: Mrs Batty, Waterside House,
Dalton by Lockerbie DG11 1AT
T: (01387) 840122
E: angelabatty@ukonline.co.uk

OPEN All Year

Low season per wk
£210.00–£325.00
High season per wk
£325.00–£500.00

18thC cottages in private courtyard setting. Stone built, one with private garden. Very well equipped and furnished, cosy in winter.

KIELDER FOREST

See under Bellingham, Falstone, Wark

MIDDLETON-IN-TEESDALE, County Durham Map ref 5B3 *Tourist Information Centre Tel: (01833) 641001*

★★★
1 Unit
Sleeping 2–6

COUNTRY COTTAGE
Middleton-in-Teesdale
Contact: Mr Burman, 1 Thorn Road, Bramhall,
Stockport SK7 1HG
T: (0161) 860 7123
E: enquiries@robinburman.com

OPEN All Year

Low season per wk
Min £150.00
High season per wk
Max £350.00

200-year-old cottage in quiet, peaceful location with superb views, surrounded by farmland. Excellent walking countryside.

★★★
1 Unit
Sleeping 2

FIRETHORN COTTAGE
Middleton-in-Teesdale, Barnard Castle
Contact: Mrs June Thompson, Cutbush Farmhouse,
Hardingham Road, Norwich NR9 4LY
T: (01953) 850364

OPEN All Year

Low season per wk
£110.00–£130.00
High season per wk
£140.00–£180.00

Stone-built lead miner's cottage, one up/one down, flagstone floors, traditional rag rugs, beamed ceilings. Superb walking, fishing, pubs and restaurants.

 Symbols The symbols in each entry give information about services and facilities. A key to these symbols appears at the back of this guide.

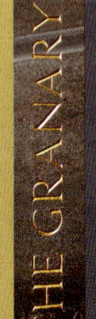

Grade II Listed building formerly the granary for a local farm. Completely refurbished in 2003. Facilities include 2 TVs one of which is widescreen, Freeview, DVD/video and hi-fi. Living, dining, sunroom, 3 beds, 2 baths, kitchen with dishwasher/dryer. Secluded/private drive with ample parking. Delightful gardens with lovely views.

For bookings please contact:
E: eileenwilley@lineone.net
T: 01434 607314 F: 01434 607864

NORTHUMBRIA

MIDDLETON-IN-TEESDALE continued

★★★
1 Unit
Sleeping 1–7

NORTH WYTHES HILL
Middleton-in-Teesdale, Barnard Castle
Contact: Mrs Eileen Dent, Wythes Hill, Middleton-in-Teesdale, Barnard Castle DL12 0NX
T: (01833) 640349
E: eileendent@teesdaleonline.co.uk

OPEN All Year

Low season per wk
£175.00–£225.00
High season per wk
£300.00–£400.00

Recently renovated farmhouse on Pennine Way. Very comfortable. Peace and quiet guaranteed. Lovely walking area. Plenty of wildlife and flowers.

MINDRUM, Northumberland Map ref 5B1

★★★
1 Unit
Sleeping 2–8

THE LONGKNOWE
Mindrum
Contact: Jo Andrews, 10 Yerbury Road, London N19 4RL
T: (020) 7281 9679
E: longknowe@hotmail.com
I: www.cottageguide.co.uk/longknowe

An old hunting kennels in the heart of the Cheviots. It has been completely renovated by its present owners. Aga, open fires, great views, wonderful stars, walking from doorstep. Four bedrooms. Ideal for children and families. Can be let at substantial discount to couples and smaller families (two bedrooms).

OPEN All Year

Weekend and mid-week breaks available all year except late Jun to early Sep, Christmas and New Year.

Low season per wk
£225.00–£300.00
High season per wk
£375.00–£550.00

MORPETH, Northumberland Map ref 5C2 Tourist Information Centre Tel: (01670) 500700

★★★★
1 Unit
Sleeping 6–12

BARNACRE
Morpeth
Contact: Mrs Linda Rudd, Warren Cottage, Longhirst Village, Morpeth NE61 3LX
T: (01670) 790116
E: linda@mrudd.fslife.co.uk

OPEN All Year

Low season per wk
£450.00–£650.00
High season per wk
£700.00–£1,100.00

Barn conversion, spacious accommodation, village location. Five bedrooms, three bathrooms, two lounges, dining room, conservatory, games room, large garden. Ideal for family gatherings.

NEWCASTLE UPON TYNE, Tyne and Wear Map ref 5C2 Tourist Information Centre Tel: (0191) 277 8000

★★★
1 Unit
Sleeping 1–6

135 AUDLEY ROAD
Newcastle upon Tyne
Contact: Miss Linda Wright, 137 Audley Road, South Gosforth, Newcastle upon Tyne NE3 1QH
T: (0191) 285 6374
E: lkw@audleyender.fsnet.co.uk
I: www.audleyender.fsnet.co.uk

OPEN All Year

Low season per wk
£200.00–£300.00
High season per wk
£200.00–£300.00

Self-contained flat, close to shops and Metro and with easy access to city centre. All amenities.

NEWTON-BY-THE-SEA, Northumberland Map ref 5C1

★★★★
5 Units
Sleeping 2–8

LINK HOUSE FARM
Alnwick
Contact: Mrs Jayne Hellmann, The Granary, Link House Farm, Alnwick NE66 3DF
T: (01665) 576820
F: (01665) 576821
E: jayne.hellman@virgin.net

Converted stone-built cottages/houses on working farm. About one-minute walk from picturesque, clean, sandy beach. Peacocks and aviaries. No pets please.

OPEN All Year except Christmas and New Year

Low season per wk
£220.00–£365.00
High season per wk
£500.00–£890.00

NORTHUMBRIA

NEWTON-BY-THE-SEA continued

★★★★
1 Unit
Sleeping 2–6

SEAWINDS
Alnwick
Contact: Miss Jo Park, Low Buston Hall, Warkworth,
Morpeth NE65 0XY
T: (01665) 714805
F: (01665) 711345
E: jopark@farming.co.uk
I: www.buston.co.uk/seawinds.htm

OPEN All Year

Low season per wk
£275.00–£450.00
High season per wk
£450.00–£650.00

Former fisherman's cottage, 200 yards from sandy beach. Home-from-home with two ground floor bedrooms and bathroom. Excellent opportunity for families, bird-watchers, walkers and golfers.

NORHAM, Northumberland Map ref 5B1

★★★
1 Unit
Sleeping 2–10

THE BOATHOUSE
Norham
Contact: Mrs Mair Chantler, Great Humphries Farm,
Grafty Green, Maidstone ME17 2AX
T: (01622) 859672
F: (01622) 859672
E: chantler@humphreys46.fsnet.co.uk
I: www.recommended-cottages.co.uk

OPEN All Year

Low season per wk
Min £400.00
High season per wk
Min £800.00

Period 18thC cottage with frontage to river Tweed. Spacious and well-equipped with spectacular views over surrounding countryside. Fishing can be arranged, subject to availability. Well-fitted kitchen.

OVINGTON, Northumberland Map ref 5B2

★★★★
1 Unit
Sleeping 2–4

WESTGARTH COTTAGE
Prudhoe
Contact: Mrs Claire Graham, Stonecroft, Ovington
NE42 6EB
T: (01661) 832202

OPEN All Year

Low season per wk
£260.00–£300.00
High season per wk
£300.00–£400.00

Attractive stone-built cottage in a small, peaceful village surrounded by beautiful countryside, near the historic towns of Hexham and Corbridge.

ROTHBURY, Northumberland Map ref 5B1

★★★★
1 Unit
Sleeping 1–4

THE OLD TELEPHONE EXCHANGE
Rothbury
Contact: Mrs K Scott-Foreman, Sunnyville Cottage,
Backcrofts, Rothbury, Morpeth NE65 7XY
T: (01669) 621858
E: info@theoldtelephoneexchange.com
I: www.theoldtelephoneexchange.com

OPEN All Year

Low season per wk
£184.00–£210.00
High season per wk
£255.00–£300.00

A cleverly converted cottage in the village centre, yet quietly tucked away. Close to the hills, and the coast is only a 20-mile drive away.

★★★★★
1 Unit
Sleeping 2–4

THE PELE TOWER
Morpeth
Contact: Mr David Malia, Whitton, Rothbury, Morpeth
NE65 7RL
T: (01669) 620410
F: (01669) 621006
E: davidmalia@aol.com
I: www.thepeletower.com

OPEN All Year
Payment accepted:
Mastercard, Visa

Low season per wk
Min £250.00
High season per wk
Max £630.00

19thC wing of Northumbrian pele tower, origins 1380. Includes whirlpool bath, dishwasher, satellite TV and video. Mountain bikes. Sorry, no smoking and no pets.

Credit card bookings

If you book by telephone and are asked for your credit card number it is advisable to check the proprietor's policy should you cancel your reservation.

NORTHUMBRIA

ROTHBURY continued

★★★★
5 Units

RIVERSIDE LODGE
Morpeth
Contact: Mr Eric Jensen, Edgecombe, Hillside Road, Morpeth NE65 7PT
T: (01669) 620464
F: (01669) 621031
E: eric.jensen@virgin.net
I: www.theriversidelodge.com

Tastefully converted, stone-built schoolhouse overlooking the River Coquet. Fully equipped one- or two-bedroomed units. Coal fires, on-site parking, perfect centre for Northumberland National Park, walking, riding, fishing. Coast and beaches within easy reach. Situated in the beautiful town of Rothbury which provides ample shopping and eating facilities.

OPEN All Year
Payment accepted: Euros

Low season per wk £180.00–£280.00
High season per wk £250.00–£450.00

SEAHOUSES, Northumberland Map ref 5C1 Tourist Information Centre Tel: (01665) 720884

★★★
4 Units
Sleeping 1–3

CLIFF HOUSE COTTAGES
Seahouses
Contact: Mrs Jackie Forsyth, c/o Beadnell House, Beadnell NE67 5AT
T: (01665) 720161
E: wts.info@cliffhousecottages.co.uk
I: www.cliffhousecottages.co.uk

Cottages in their own courtyard, close to the harbour. Within yards of the village and the county's most beautiful beaches and castles. An ideal base for walking, cycling, golfing etc. All cottages: one bedroom, lounge/kitchen/diner, shower room. Communal laundry room. Private parking. Linen and electricity included.

OPEN All Year
Payment accepted: Amex, Delta, Mastercard, Switch, Visa

Low season per wk £192.00–£300.00
High season per wk £250.00–£375.00

★★★★
1 Unit
Sleeping 1–6

THE LOBSTER POTS
Seahouses
Contact: Julia Steel
T: (0113) 239 1130
E: julia@thelobsterpots.co.uk
I: www.thelobsterpots.co.uk

OPEN All Year

Low season per wk £225.00–£300.00
High season per wk £325.00–£450.00

Beautifully furnished holiday home with sea views. Situated only five minutes' walk from breathtaking coastline. Ideal for children with enclosed garden and toys. Dogs welcome.

★★★
1 Unit
Sleeping 1–8

LYNBANK
Seahouses
Contact: Mrs Louise Donaldson, 4 Broad Road, Seahouses NE68 7UP
T: (01665) 721066
F: (01665) 721066
E: islandproperties@uk6.net
I: www.dalfaber-lynbank.ntb.org.uk

OPEN All Year

Low season per wk £250.00–£350.00
High season per wk £360.00–£400.00

Clean, comfortable house, central location. Off-road parking, secure gardens with patio. Pets allowed, children welcome.

 Colour maps Colour maps at the front of this guide pinpoint all places under which you will find accommodation listed.

NORTHUMBRIA

SLALEY, Northumberland Map ref 5B2

★★★
1 Unit
Sleeping 1–5

COMBHILLS FARM
Hexham
Contact: Mrs Ogle, Slaley, Hexham NE47 0AQ
T: (01434) 673475
F: (01434) 673778
E: m.ogle@lineone.net

OPEN All Year

Low season per wk
£180.00–£200.00
High season per wk
£200.00–£280.00

Comfortable, well-equipped, centrally heated cottage on working family farm. Centrally located for Newcastle, Durham, MetroCentre and Hadrian's Wall. Beautiful countryside for walking. Ample parking.

STANHOPE, County Durham Map ref 5B2 Tourist Information Centre Tel: (01388) 527650

★★
1 Unit
Sleeping 8

PRIMROSE COTTAGE
Bishop Auckland
Contact: Mrs Dickson, Northumbria Byways, Unit 2, Brampton Business Centre, The Irthing Centre, Union Lane, Brampton CA8 1BX
T: (016977) 41600
F: (016977) 41800

Large, stone-built, three-bedroomed cottage in England's last great wilderness, yet with all modern conveniences and within walking distance of shops, tourist information centre, banks etc. The cottage is in a high position with superb views of Weardale. Two separate central heating systems and double glazing throughout ensure comfort.

OPEN All Year

Payment accepted: Delta, Mastercard, Switch, Visa

Short breaks available (special conditions apply).

Low season per wk
£225.00–£260.00
High season per wk
£280.00–£370.00

WARK, Northumberland Map ref 5B2

★★★★
1 Unit
Sleeping 2–6

THE HEMMEL
Hexham
Contact: Mrs Nichol, The Hemmel, Hetherington, Wark, Hexham NE48 3DR
T: (01434) 230260
F: (01434) 230260
E: alan_nichol@hotmail.com
I: www.hetheringtonfarm.co.uk

OPEN All Year

Low season per wk
£260.00–£300.00
High season per wk
£350.00–£460.00

Excellent converted farm building, all mod cons. Lovely rural setting close to Hadrian's Wall. Ideal walking, touring or relaxing holiday. Well recommended.

WARKWORTH, Northumberland Map ref 5C1

★★★★
3 Units
Sleeping 2–5

BUSTON FARM HOLIDAY COTTAGES
Warkworth
Contact: Miss Jo Park, Low Buston Hall, Warkworth, Morpeth NE65 0XY
T: (01665) 714805
F: (01665) 711345
E: stay@buston.co.uk
I: www.buston.co.uk

OPEN All Year

Low season per wk
£210.00–£285.00
High season per wk
Min £435.00

Stone farm cottages, all with original character. Newly refurbished, home from home, excellent opportunity for families, bird-watchers, walkers and golfers.

NB **Important note** Information on accommodation listed in this guide has been supplied by the proprietors. As changes may occur you are advised to check details at the time of booking.

NORTHUMBRIA

WHITLEY BAY, Tyne and Wear Map ref 5C2 Tourist Information Centre Tel: (0191) 200 8535

★★★
6 Units
Sleeping 2–6

SEAFRONT APARTMENTS
Cullercoats
Contact: Mrs Rosemary Webb, Seafront Apartments,
46 Beverley Terrace, Cullercoats, North Shields NE30 4NU
T: 07977 203379
E: stay@seafront.info
I: www.seafront.info

OPEN All Year

Low season per wk
£170.00–£310.00
High season per wk
£210.00–£390.00

Smart, warm apartments, superb coastal location, some with unrivalled views over picturesque Cullercoats Bay. Whitley Bay, Cullercoats and Tynemouth's magnificent beaches have cleanliness awards. Doorstep buses. Newcastle Metro, food shops, varied restaurants within three minutes' walk. Ideal base for business/leisure, Hadrian's Wall, Durham, Alnwick, Beamish, Northumbria's castles, MetroCentre.

WOLSINGHAM, County Durham Map ref 5B2

★★★
2 Units
Sleeping 4

ARDINE AND ELVET COTTAGES
Bishop Auckland
Contact: Mrs Gardiner, 3 Melbourne Place,
Wolsingham, Bishop Auckland DL13 3EQ
T: (01388) 527538

OPEN All Year

Low season per wk
Min £145.00
High season per wk
Max £223.00

Cosy, two-bedroomed terraced cottages overlooking small village green in old part of Wolsingham. Excellent walking and touring centre.

★★★
1 Unit
Sleeping 7

WHITFIELD HOUSE COTTAGE
Bishop Auckland
Contact: Mrs Margaret Shepheard, 25 Front Street,
Wolsingham, Bishop Auckland DL13 3DF
T: (01388) 527466
E: enquiries@whitfieldhouse.clara.net
I: www.whitfieldhouse.clara.net

OPEN All Year

Low season per wk
£200.00–£250.00
High season per wk
£250.00–£410.00

Spacious accommodation in part of an attractive Queen Anne house. Near the centre of this small town, in a designated Area of Outstanding Natural Beauty.

WOOLER, Northumberland Map ref 5B1

★★★
1 Unit
Sleeping 6

ROSE COTTAGE
Wooler
Contact: Mrs Christine Andrews, 1 Littleworth Lane,
Esher KT10 9PF
T: (01372) 464284
F: (01372) 467715
E: andrews@playfactors.demon.co.uk

Low season per wk
£220.00–£280.00
High season per wk
£300.00–£350.00

Two-bedroomed old stone cottage on edge of National Park. An open fire makes it ideal for autumn and summer breaks. Sun room, sitting room, modern kitchen, garden.

At-a-glance symbols

Symbols at the end of each entry give useful information about services and facilities. A key to symbols can be found inside the back cover flap. Keep this open for easy reference.

119

This **proud** corner of England boasts **heritage**, **hills** and **lively cities** with a **cutting-edge** arts scene.

Yorkshire

Looking for some inspiration? Here are a few ideas to get you started in Yorkshire. **experience** life as a Viking at JORVIK – The Viking City. **discover** the story of the world's oceans on a dramatic underwater journey at The Deep in Kingston upon Hull. **explore** the most beautiful corners of The Yorkshire Dales National Park via 26 pubs on The Inn Way. **relax** at the Turkish Baths & Health Spa in Harrogate for that elusive feeling of total wellbeing.

THE REGION
Yorkshire and North & North East Lincolnshire

CONTACT
▸ **YORKSHIRE TOURIST BOARD**
312 Tadcaster Road,
York YO24 1GS
T: (01904) 707070
(24-hour brochure line)
F: (01904) 701414
E: info@ytb.org.uk
www.yorkshirevisitor.com

YORKSHIRE

England's biggest county boasts heritage, hills and historical grandeur. Dramatic abbeys, picturesque villages, modern art, local and international cuisine: you'll find them all in this proud corner of England.

Green and pleasant land

For diverse landscape and inspiring scenery, Yorkshire really takes the biscuit. Relax in over 1000 square miles of National Parks (The Yorkshire Dales, the North York Moors and the Peak District) as well as the Pennines and a stretch of Heritage Coast, or cycle the Trans Pennine Trail to enjoy spectacular views.

At Xscape in Castleford you can put your climbing, skiing and skating skills to the test. Sheffield Winter Garden is an impressive cathedral of plants, creating a temperate green world in the city centre.

Huge heritage

Yorkshire's rich cultural and industrial heritage has given rise to an incredible number of historic houses, castles, abbeys and gardens. Fountains Abbey & Studley Royal Water Garden is rightly a World Heritage Site, and Harewood House and Whitby Abbey offer more treasures to discover. For atmosphere alone, impressive Rievaulx Abbey and Castle Howard are well worth a visit and give a glimpse of what life was like in days gone by. Stunning stained glass and 1000 years of history may entice you to York Minster, the largest medieval Gothic cathedral in northern Europe. And for free family entertainment, visit the National Railway Museum which tells the story of the train. Peep inside royal carriages with sumptuous bedrooms and dining rooms. Or plan an experimental day out at Magna – the UK's first science adventure centre.

For a more spiritual experience take a tour of Epworth Old Rectory, the house where John Wesley, founder of the Methodist Church, grew up.

Cultural landscape

Yorkshire boasts lively cities with a cutting-edge arts scene. If you're an opera buff, Leeds is home to Opera North. You'll also find top-class entertainment at the two theatres of the West Yorkshire Playhouse. In Bradford, the National Museum of Photography, Film & Television is the most visited museum outside London – which should come as no surprise since Yorkshire has been the inspiration for some of England's greatest films, books and TV series. Visit the locations for yourself as you explore the living sets of Emmerdale, The Full Monty, Wuthering Heights, Jane Eyre and, most recently, Calendar Girls. For modern culture, Bradford, Sheffield and Leeds are shopping heaven.

Left, from top ornate architecture at Castle Howard, York; the enchanting Yorkshire Dales; shopping in the Corn Exchange, Leeds **Right** the past comes to life at JORVIK Viking Festival, York

Enjoy England official guides to quality

Places to visit

Awarded VisitBritain's Quality Assured Visitor Attraction marque.

Beningbrough Hall & Gardens (National Trust)
Beningbrough, York
Tel: (01904) 470666
www.nationaltrust.org.uk
Contemplate 100 pictures from the National Portrait Gallery hung in this final example of a Baroque house, built in 1716. Victorian laundry, potting shed and restored walled garden.

Bolton Abbey Estate
Bolton Abbey, Skipton, North Yorkshire
Tel: (01756) 718009
www.boltonabbey.com
Ruins of 12thC priory in a park setting by the river Wharfe. Feeling energetic? Walk some of the 80 miles of footpaths through spectacular scenery. Tearooms, nature trails, fishing.

Colour Museum
Perkin House, Bradford, West Yorkshire
Tel: (01274) 390955
www.sdc.org.uk
Ever wondered how colours came about? The only museum of its kind in Europe, dedicated to the history, development and technology of colour.

Cusworth Hall Museum of South Yorkshire Life
Cusworth Hall, Doncaster, South Yorkshire
Tel: (01302) 782342
Georgian mansion in landscaped park containing displays illustrating everyday life in South Yorkshire over the last 200 years, from childhood to costumes and transport.

The Deep
Hull
Tel: (01482) 381000
www.thedeep.co.uk
Glimpse the world's oceans from the beginning of time and into the future using interactives and live aquaria exhibits, including the world's deepest underwater tunnel. Spellbinding.

Eureka! The Museum for Children
Discovery Road, Halifax, West Yorkshire
Tel: (01422) 330069
www.eureka.org.uk
The first museum of its kind designed especially for children up to the age of 12 – stimulate all the senses as you touch, listen, feel, and smell as well as look.

Flamingo Land Theme Park, Zoo and Holiday Village
Kirby Misperton, North Yorkshire
Tel: (01653) 668287
www.flamingoland.co.uk
One-price family fun park with over 100 attractions and six shows. Europe's largest privately owned zoo and only triple looping coaster, Magnum Force. Feel your heart race!

Fountains Abbey and Studley Royal Water Garden (National Trust)
Ripon, North Yorkshire
Tel: (01765) 608888
www.fountainsabbey.org.uk
Stunning, World Heritage Site including the largest monastic ruin in Britain, founded by Cistercian monks in 1132. Landscaped garden laid between 1720-40 with lake, water garden, temples and deer park.

Freeport Hornsea Outlet Village
Rolston Road, Hornsea, East Riding of Yorkshire
Tel: (01964) 534211
www.freeporthornsea.com
Set in landscaped gardens with over 40 quality high-street names all selling stock with discounts of up to 50%, plus licensed restaurant and leisure attractions. Shop until you drop!

Helmsley Castle (English Heritage)
Helmsley, York
Tel: (01439) 770442
www.english-heritage.org.uk/yorkshire
Explore the changing military defences of this castle with its 12thC keep, Tudor mansion and spectacular earthworks cut from solid rock. Exhibitions and excavated artefacts.

This is just a selection of attractions available. Contact any Tourist Information Centre in the region for more ideas.

YORKSHIRE

Last of the Summer Wine Exhibition
Huddersfield Road, Holmfirth, Huddersfield
Tel: (01484) 681408
www.summerwineexhibition.com
Check out the collection of photographs and memorabilia commemorating the world's longest running television comedy series, Last of the Summer Wine.

Leeds City Art Gallery
The Headrow, Leeds
Tel: (0113) 247 8248
www.leeds.gov.uk/artgallery
Art gallery containing British paintings, sculptures, prints and drawings of the 19th/20thC. Henry Moore gallery with permanent collection of 20thC sculpture.

Lightwater Valley
North Stainley, North Yorkshire
Tel: 0870 458 0040
www.lightwatervalley.net
Hang onto your hat! Set in 70ha (175 acres) of parkland, Lightwater Valley features white-knuckle rides and attractions for all the family, shopping, a restaurant and picnic areas.

Magna
Sheffield Road, Rotherham, South Yorkshire
Tel: (01709) 720002
www.magnatrust.org.uk
The UK's first Science Adventure Centre set in the vast Templeborough steelworks in Rotherham. Amusement guaranteed with giant interactives.

Mother Shipton's Cave & the Petrifying Well
Prophecy Lodge, Knaresborough, North Yorkshire
Tel: (01423) 864600
www.mothershipton.co.uk
Beware the prophecies of Mother Shipton! Her birthplace cave and the Petrifying Well are the oldest tourist attractions in Britain, opened in 1630. Well, museum, playground and 12 acres of riverside grounds.

National Fishing Heritage Centre
Alexandra Dock, Grimsby, North East Lincolnshire
Tel: (01472) 323345
www.nelincs.gov.uk/Tourism/Attractions
Sign on as a crew member and experience the reality of life on a deep-sea trawler. Interactive games and displays.

National Museum of Photography, Film & Television
Bradford, West Yorkshire
Tel: 0870 701 0200
www.nmpft.org.uk
Ten, free, interactive galleries will take you on a tour of the past, present and future of photography, film and television. Catch a screening at the spectacular 3D IMAX cinema.

National Railway Museum
Leeman Road, York
Tel: (01904) 621261
www.nrm.org.uk
The story of the train is brought to life in a great day out for all the family. Three enormous galleries to explore with interactive exhibits and working engines.

Newby Hall & Gardens
Ripon, North Yorkshire
Tel: (01423) 322583
www.newbyhall.com
Late 17thC house with additions, interior by Robert Adam, classical sculpture, Gobelins tapestries, 10ha (25 acres) of gardens, miniature railway, children's adventure garden.

North Yorkshire Moors Railway
Pickering, North Yorkshire
Tel: (01751) 472508
www.northyorkshiremoorsrailway.com
Jump aboard Britain's most popular heritage railway travelling through the beautiful North York Moors National Park.

Nunnington Hall (National Trust)
Nunnington, York
Tel: (01439) 748283
www.nationaltrust.org.uk
Large 17thC manor house situated on banks of river Rye. With hall, bedrooms, nursery and Carlisle collection of miniature rooms. Watch out for the haunted maid's room.

Piece Hall
Halifax, West Yorkshire
Tel: (01422) 358087
www.calderdale.gov.uk
Built in 1779 and restored in 1976, this Grade I Listed building forms a unique and striking monument to the wealth and importance of the wool trade.

Ripley Castle
Ripley, North Yorkshire
Tel: (01423) 770152
www.ripleycastle.co.uk
An adventure through English history, Ripley Castle, home to the Ingilby family since 1308, is set in the heart of a delightful estate with Victorian walled gardens, deer park and pleasure grounds.

Royal Armouries Museum
Armouries Drive, Leeds
Tel: (0113) 220 1916
www.armouries.org.uk
Traverse more than 3000 years of history covered by over 8000 spectacular items of arms and armour, jousting displays and falconry, all in stunning surroundings.

Left dramatic ruins of Fountains Abbey, Ripon; awe-inspiring Hardraw Force, Wensleydale

Enjoy England official guides to quality

Places to visit

Awarded VisitBritain's Quality Assured Visitor Attraction marque.

Sea Life and Marine Sanctuary
Scalby Mills, Scarborough, North Yorkshire
Tel: (01723) 373414
www.sealifeeurope.com
Meet creatures that live in and around the oceans of the British Isles, ranging from starfish to sharks. The comic inhabitants of the penguin sanctuary will no doubt keep you amused.

Sheffield Botanical Gardens
Clarkehouse Road, Sheffield
Tel: (0114) 267 6196
www.sbg.org.uk
Extensive gardens with over 5500 species of plants and Grade II Listed garden pavilion. Fully restored and containing a temperate plant collection.

Skipton Castle
Skipton, South Yorkshire
Tel: (01756) 792442
www.skiptoncastle.co.uk
Skipton was the last Royalist stronghold in the North during the Civil War and is one of the best preserved, complete medieval castles in England. A formidable fortification!

Thackray Museum
Beckett Street, Leeds
Tel: (0113) 244 4343
www.thackraymuseum.org
Award-winning collections and interactive displays bring to life the history of medicine from a Victorian operating theatre to the wonders of modern surgery. Not for the squeamish.

Thirsk Museum
Kirkgate, Thirsk, North Yorkshire
Tel: (01845) 527707
www.thirskmuseum.org
Exhibits of local life, industry and cricket memorabilia. The building was the home of Thomas Lord, founder of Lords cricket ground in London.

Thrybergh Country Park
Doncaster Road, Thrybergh, South Yorkshire
Tel: (01709) 850353
Twenty-eight hectare (70-acre) country park with a vast lake and bird reserve. Fly-fishing. Caravan and camping site. Take a picnic and contemplate the scenery.

The World of James Herriot
Kirkgate, Thirsk, North Yorkshire
Tel: (01845) 524234
www.worldofjamesherriot.org
Visit the original home and surgery of vet and author James Herriot, with 1950s themed rooms and the Austin Seven car used in the TV series.

Wensleydale Cheese Visitor Centre
Wensleydale Creamery, Hawes, North Yorkshire
Tel: (01969) 667664
www.wensleydale.co.uk
Observe Wensleydale cheese being made by hand and sample a range of cheeses too. Museum, shop and café.

York Minster
Deangate, York
Tel: (01904) 557200
www.yorkminster.org
Simply awe-inspiring, York Minster is the largest medieval gothic cathedral in northern Europe, and a treasure house of 800 years of stained glass. Take the audio tour to discover 2000 years of history.

Yorkshire Lavender
Terrington, York
Tel: (01653) 648430
www.lavenderland.co.uk
Probably Europe's most northerly lavender farm. Discover the many varieties of lavender and be amazed at their versatile uses.

Above spoilt for choice in York; journey through English history at Ripley Castle **Right** experience the age of steam on board the North York Moors Railway

This is just a selection of attractions available. Contact any Tourist Information Centre in the region for more ideas.

YORKSHIRE

Yorkshire Tourist Board
312 Tadcaster Road, York YO24 1GS
T: (01904) 707070 (24-hour brochure line) F: (01904) 701414
E: info@ytb.org.uk
www.yorkshirevisitor.com

The following publications are available from Yorkshire Tourist Board:

Yorkshire Visitor Guide – information on Yorkshire and Northern Lincolnshire, including hotels, self-catering, camping and caravan parks. Also attractions, shops, restaurants and major events

For information about Yorkshire outdoors, heritage breaks and seasonal breaks in Yorkshire, please visit www.yorkshirevisitor.com

Travel information

By road:
Motorways: M1, M62, M606, M621, M18, M180, M181, A1(M). Trunk roads: A1, A19, A57, A58, A59, A61, A62, A63, A64, A65, A66.

By rail:
InterCity services to Bradford, Doncaster, Harrogate, Kingston upon Hull, Leeds, Sheffield, Wakefield and York. Frequent regional railway services city centre to city centre including Manchester Airport service to Scarborough, York and Leeds.

Enjoy England official guides to quality

YORKSHIRE

Where to stay in
Yorkshire

All place names in the blue bands, under which accommodation is listed, are shown on the maps at the front of this guide.

A complete listing of all VisitBritain assessed accommodation covered by this guide appears at the back.

Accommodation symbols
Symbols give useful information about services and facilities. Inside the back cover flap you can find a key to these symbols. Keep it open for easy reference.

AMPLEFORTH, North Yorkshire Map ref 5C3

★★★★
1 Unit
Sleeping 1–4

Attractive stone cottage on the edge of National Park, enjoying splendid views. Immaculate decorative order throughout. Price fully inclusive. Close to village amenities. Superb eating hostelries locally. Ideally situated for walking, moors, coast. Twenty miles York, 10 miles Castle Howard. Non-smoking establishment. Personal attention by resident owners.

HILLSIDE COTTAGE
York
Contact: Mrs Pam Noble, Hillside, West End, Ampleforth, York YO62 4DY
T: (01439) 788303
F: (01439) 788303
E: hillsidecottage@westend-ampleforth.co.uk
I: www.cottageguide.co.uk/hillsidecottage

OPEN All Year

Low season per wk
£190.00–£230.00
High season per wk
£250.00–£310.00

BARMBY MOOR, East Riding of Yorkshire Map ref 4C1

★★★★
1 Unit
Sleeping 1–6

This pretty, three-bedroomed, converted Victorian coach house overlooks open countryside. Warm and cosy in winter, it is ideally situated in a picturesque village on the edge of the Wolds, only 12 miles from York and convenient for the coast and moors. Pubs, shops and restaurants nearby.

NORTHWOOD HOUSE
York
Contact: Mrs Gregory, Northwood House, St Helens Square, Barmby Moor, York YO42 4HF
T: (01759) 302305
E: annjgregory@hotmail.com
I: www.northwoodcoachhouse.co.uk

OPEN All Year
Payment accepted: Euros

Short breaks (3 days), bookable 28 days in advance, 60% normal weekly rate.

Low season per wk
£360.00–£400.00
High season per wk
£400.00–£600.00

YORKSHIRE

BARNOLDBY-LE-BECK, North East Lincolnshire Map ref 4D1

★★★★
3 Units
Sleeping 2–6

GRANGE FARM COTTAGES & RIDING SCHOOL
Grimsby
Contact: Ms Jo & Sue Jenkins, Grange Farm Cottages & Riding School, Waltham Road, Barnoldby-le-Beck, Grimsby DN37 0AR
T: (01472) 822216
F: (01472) 233550
E: sueuk4000@netscape.net
I: www.grangefarmcottages.com

OPEN All Year

Low season per wk
£175.00–£250.00
High season per wk
£275.00–£325.00

The holiday cottages are equipped with one double and one twin room. Take advantage of our all-weather-surface riding school, with fully qualified instructors.

BARTON-UPON-HUMBER, North Lincolnshire Map ref 4C1

★★★
3 Units
Sleeping 4

PASTURE HOUSE FISHERIES
Barton-upon-Humber
Contact: Mrs Martine Smith, Pasture House Fisheries Ltd, Pasture Road North, Barton-upon-Humber DN18 5RB
T: (01652) 636369
F: (01652) 636369
E: pasturehousefish@aol.com
I: www.pasturehouse.co.uk

OPEN All Year

Low season per wk
£195.00–£280.00
High season per wk
£350.00

Authentic timber cabins built and furbished to a very high specification. Overlooking well-stocked fishing lakes and idyllic rural settings.

BRIDLINGTON, East Riding of Yorkshire Map ref 5D3 Tourist Information Centre Tel: (01262) 673474

★★★★
3 Units
Sleeping 2–8

BAY SIDE HOLIDAYS
Bridlington
Contact: Mr Barry & Mrs Anne Hatfield,
c/o 25 Victoria Road, Bridlington YO15 2AT
T: (01262) 609431
F: (01262) 609431
E: bayside.bridlington@virgin.net
I: www.baysideholidays.co.uk

OPEN All Year
Payment accepted: Delta, Mastercard, Switch, Visa

Low season per wk
£275.00–£550.00
High season per wk
£395.00–£750.00

Superb for family holidays, off-season breaks! Individual houses in select locations, close to beach/town centre. Also luxury bungalow, just yards from sea, in beautiful Sewerby Village.

★-★★★
4 Units
Sleeping 1–5

HIGHCLIFFE HOLIDAY APARTMENTS
Bridlington
Contact: Mrs Pat Willcocks, Highcliffe Holiday Apartments, 19 Albion Terrace, Bridlington YO15 2PJ
T: (01262) 674127

On the seafront, south facing, only 50 metres from sandy beach and promenade. All apartments have uninterrupted views along the beach to the harbour. Ideal position for main shopping centre, restaurants and Leisure World complex. Fully equipped, with high standard of furnishing, each with own private bathroom facilities.

OPEN All Year

Low season per wk
£100.00–£220.00
High season per wk
£230.00–£350.00

Location Complete addresses for properties are not given and the town(s) listed may be a distance from the actual establishment. Please check the precise location at the time of booking.

YORKSHIRE

BUCKDEN, North Yorkshire Map ref 5B3

12 Units
Sleeping 1–6

DALEGARTH AND THE GHYLL COTTAGES
Buckden
Contact: Mr David & Mrs Susan Lusted, 9 Dalegarth, Buckden, Skipton BD23 5JU
T: (01756) 760877
F: (01756) 760877
E: info@dalegarth.co.uk
I: www.dalegarth.co.uk

Ramblers, amblers and tourers alike will appreciate Dalegarth and The Ghyll cottages, Buckden, acclaimed for quality, comfort and location, being sited on the Dales Way in the idyllic surroundings of Upper Wharfedale's unspoilt countryside. Additionally, private sauna, spa baths, mini-gym and indoor heated swimming pool help promote relaxation and enjoyment.

OPEN All Year

Payment accepted: Delta, Mastercard, Switch, Visa

Weekend/mid-week mini-breaks available, Nov-pre-Easter (excl Christmas and New Year).

Low season per wk
£345.00–£378.00
High season per wk
£595.00–£655.00

BURNSALL, North Yorkshire Map ref 5B3

1 Unit

THE SYCAMORES
Skipton
Contact: Mrs Sheila Carr, Moor Green Farm, Threshfield, Skipton BD23 5NR
T: (01756) 752435
F: (01756) 752435
E: carr@totalise.co.uk

A large, family cottage overlooking the village green and river. Well equipped, open fire in lounge. Patio with furniture and barbecue. Ideal for any time of year. Excellently situated for walking/touring the Dales.

OPEN All Year

Weekends and short breaks available Oct-Mar.

Low season per wk
£185.00–£225.00
High season per wk
£260.00–£450.00

BURTON-IN-LONSDALE, North Yorkshire Map ref 5B3

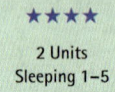
2 Units
Sleeping 1–5

BRENTWOOD FARM COTTAGES
Burton-in-Lonsdale
Contact: Mrs Anita Taylor, Barnoldswick Lane, Burton-in-Lonsdale LA6 3LZ
T: (015242) 62155
F: (015242) 62155
E: info@brentwoodfarmcottages.co.uk
I: www.brentwoodfarmcottages.co.uk

Relax in a spacious, yet cosy, new barn conversion located in a tranquil setting on a working dairy farm. Centrally situated for the Lake District, Yorkshire Dales, Lune Valley and Forest of Bowland. Ingleton waterfalls walk, three peaks and show caves nearby. Private walking and fishing on site. Brochure available.

OPEN All Year

Payment accepted: Delta, Mastercard, Switch, Visa

Winter short breaks available. Seasonal hedge laying and walling and computer tuition available on request.

Low season per wk
Min £225.00
High season per wk
Max £470.00

Map references
Map references apply to the colour maps at the front of this guide.

YORKSHIRE

BURTON LEONARD, North Yorkshire Map ref 5C3

★★★★
5 Units
Sleeping 1–6

PARK HOUSE HOLIDAY COTTAGES
Harrogate
Contact: Mr Russell Hammond, Park House,
Station Lane, Burton Leonard, Harrogate HG3 3RX
T: (01765) 677387
I: www.parkhouseholidays.com

OPEN All Year

Payment accepted:
Mastercard, Visa

Low season per wk
£185.00–£245.00
High season per wk
£355.00–£425.00

Spacious, comfortable and well-presented cottages converted from farm building. Large garden and playing field. Ideal base for exploring Yorkshire Dales and Moors. Near Harrogate.

COMMONDALE, North Yorkshire Map ref 5C3

★★★
3 Units
Sleeping 2–6

FOWL GREEN FARM
Whitby
Contact: Mrs Susan Muir, Fowl Green Farm, Commondale,
Whitby YO21 2HN
T: (01287) 660742
E: info@fowlgreenfarm.com
I: www.fowlgreenfarm.com

Three 18thC rough-stone pigsties and barn, converted to combine original features with 21stC comfort, set on a traditional hill sheep farm with footpaths and picnic sites across the farmland. The cottages are accesible to all, having ground floor bedroom, adapted bath/shower facilities and outside patio, barbecues and garden areas.

OPEN All Year

Short breaks available – minimum 2 nights.

Low season per wk
£140.00–£350.00
High season per wk
£180.00–£540.00

CROPTON, North Yorkshire Map ref 5C3

★★★★
7 Units
Sleeping 2–12

BECKHOUSE COTTAGES
Pickering
Contact: Mrs Smith, Beckhouse Farm, Cropton,
Pickering YO18 8ER
T: (01751) 417235
F: (01751) 417218
E: beckhousecottages@hotmail.com
I: www.beckhousecottages.co.uk

OPEN All Year

Low season per wk
£170.00–£400.00
High season per wk
£270.00–£950.00

Working farm, keeping mostly horses for carriage driving and breeding. Private gardens. Beautiful walking countryside. Handy for forest, moors and sea. Winter breaks available.

DALTON, North Yorkshire Map ref 5B3

★★★
1 Unit
Sleeping 4

KEEPERS COTTAGE
Dalton
Contact: Dorothy Lewis, Keepers Cottage, Dalton Hall,
Dalton, Richmond DL11 7GU
T: (01833) 621446
E: yaz66@dial.pipex.com

OPEN All Year except Christmas

Payment accepted: Euros

Low season per wk
£220.00–£290.00
High season per wk
£300.00–£370.00

Lovingly restored Georgian gamekeeper's cottage. Lounge, eat-in kitchen, two bedrooms. Beautiful views across open countryside.

DANBY, North Yorkshire Map ref 5C3

★★★
1 Unit
Sleeping 6

BLACKMIRES FARM
Whitby
Contact: Mrs Gillian Rhys, Blackmires Farm,
Danby Head, Danby, Whitby YO21 2NN
T: (01287) 660352
E: gl.rhys@freenet.co.uk

OPEN All Year except Christmas

Low season per wk
£275.00–£350.00
High season per wk
£350.00–£400.00

Stone cottage adjoining farmhouse. Two bedrooms and bathroom on ground floor, twin bedroom upstairs. Three miles from Danby village in North Yorkshire National Park.

YORKSHIRE

DRIFFIELD, East Riding of Yorkshire Map ref 4C1

★★★
2 Units

MANOR FARM COTTAGES
Driffield
Contact: Mr & Mrs Byass, Manor Farm Cottages,
North Dalton Manor, North Dalton, Driffield YO25 9UX
T: (01377) 217324
F: (01377) 217840
E: lanpulses@aol.com

OPEN All Year

Low season per wk
£175.00–£250.00
High season per wk
£250.00–£375.00

Fully modernised Georgian cottages in pretty village. Ideal for exploring York, Beverley and east coast. Moors and many stately homes within easy driving distance.

FILEY, North Yorkshire Map ref 5D3

★★–★★★★
10 Units
Sleeping 2–7

BEACH HOLIDAY FLATS
Filey
Contact: Mr David Tindall, 9-10 The Beach, Filey YO14 9LA
T: (01723) 513178
E: anntindall@aol.com
I: www.thebeach-holidayflats.co.uk

Probably the best position on the east coast, 25yds from the seafront, fabulous views over Filey Brigg, Bempton Rocks and Flamborough Head. We pride ourselves on the quality of our decor, fixtures and fittings, cleanliness and hospitality. The perfect location for your east coast holiday. Filey – gem of the Yorkshire coast.

OPEN All Year

Low season per wk
£135.00–£205.00
High season per wk
£215.00–£535.00

★★★
5 Units
Sleeping 1–5

THE COTTAGES
Filey
Contact: Mr & Mrs David Teet, The Cottages,
Muston Grange, Muston Road, Filey YO14 0HU
T: (01723) 516620
F: (01723) 516620
I: www.mustongrangefiley.co.uk

OPEN All Year
Payment accepted: Delta, Mastercard, Switch, Visa, Euros

Low season per wk
£265.00–£325.00
High season per wk
£400.00–£495.00

Situated between Muston and Filey, the cottages are a range of converted traditional ex-farm buildings providing quality accommodation in a private courtyard setting.

GARTON-ON-THE-WOLDS, East Riding of Yorkshire Map ref 4C1

★★★
1 Unit
Sleeping 1–4

ROLELLA
Driffield
Contact: Mr Garvey, 10 Main Street, Garton-on-the-Wolds, Driffield YO25 3ET
T: (01377) 253656 & 257570
F: (01377) 241408
E: stella@sssiteservices.co.uk

OPEN All Year

Low season per wk
Min £150.00
High season per wk
Min £200.00

Delightful, cosy barn conversion in village location on the Wolds. Ideal base to explore East and North Yorkshire. Cities, beaches, museums and moorlands are all close by.

GAYLE, North Yorkshire Map ref 5B3

★★
1 Unit
Sleeping 4–6

GAYLE FARMHOUSE
Hawes
Contact: Ms H Cook, Dales Holiday Cottages, Ref 636,
Carleton Business Park, Carleton New Road, Skipton
BD23 2AA
T: (01756) 799821
F: (01756) 797012
I: www.dalesholcot.com

OPEN All Year except Christmas and New Year
Payment accepted: Delta, Mastercard, Switch, Visa

Low season per wk
Min £280.00
High season per wk
£371.00–£450.00

Comfortable stone-built holiday cottage in the heart of Wensleydale close to the Pennine Way. Ideal for families. Well-behaved pets welcome.

 Ratings All accommodation in this guide has been rated, or is awaiting a rating, by a trained VisitBritain assessor.

YORKSHIRE

GIGGLESWICK, North Yorkshire Map ref 5B3

★★★★
1 Unit
Sleeping 6

IVY COTTAGE
Giggleswick
Contact: Fiona Moody, Dales Holiday Cottages, Ref 629, Carleton Business Park, Carleton New Road, Skipton BD23 2AA
T: (01756) 799821
F: (01756) 797012
I: www.dalesholcot.com

OPEN All Year

Low season per wk
£270.00–£380.00
High season per wk
£380.00–£460.00

Immaculate and well-appointed stone cottage at heart of lively Dales village, minutes from supermarket and rail station. Church, two inns and local transport close by.

GILLING WEST, North Yorkshire Map ref 5C3

★★★★
5 Units
Sleeping 2–10

Magnificent properties converted from traditional stone barns situated in idyllic courtyard setting, overlooking delightful open countryside. An ideal base from which to explore Swaledale and surrounding area.

GILLING OLD MILL COTTAGES
Richmond
Contact: Mr Hugh & Mrs Joyce Bird, Gilling Old Mill Cottages, Waters Lane, Gilling West, Richmond DL10 5JD
T: (01748) 822771
F: (01748) 821734
E: admin@yorkshiredales-cottages.com
I: www.yorkshiredales-cottages.com

OPEN All Year
Payment accepted: Euros

Low season per wk
£167.00–£460.00
High season per wk
£220.00–£700.00

GRASSINGTON, North Yorkshire Map ref 5B3 Tourist Information Centre Tel: (01756) 752774

★★★
1 Unit
Sleeping 4

GARRS HOUSE APARTMENT
Skipton
Contact: Mr Malcolm & Mrs Ann Wadsworth, 25 Watson Road, Blackpool FY4 1EG
T: (01253) 404726
E: mw001F3365@blueyonder.co.uk

OPEN All Year

Low season per wk
£125.00–£160.00
High season per wk
£210.00–£260.00

Large first floor apartment in the centre of the village overlooking the square. Lounge/diner, kitchen and two en suite bedrooms. Fully equipped.

★★★
1 Unit
Sleeping 1–4

Our warm and comfortable first-floor apartment is just 50m from the cobbled village square. It has original oak beams and living flame gas fire in the spacious lounge. Two large bedrooms, one double and one twin, bed linen provided. Large, full kitchen. Bathroom has bath and separate shower. Brochure available.

6A GARRS LANE
Skipton
Contact: Mr Borrill, The Fish Shop, Garrs Lane, Grassington, Skipton BD23 5AT
T: 07709 313716
E: paborrill@supanet.com
I: www.grassingtonapartment.co.uk

2/3-night stays available, Oct-Feb (excl Christmas and New Year).

Low season per wk
£225.00–£250.00
High season per wk
Max £250.00

Map references The map references refer to the colour maps at the front of this guide. The first figure is the map number; the letter and figure which follow indicate the grid reference on the map.

131

YORKSHIRE

GRASSINGTON continued

★★★★
1 Unit

MANNA COTTAGE
Skipton
Contact: Mrs Sheila Carr, Moor Green Farm, Tarns Lane,
Threshfield, Skipton BD23 5NR
T: (01756) 752435
F: (01756) 752435
E: carr@totalise.co.uk
I: www.yorkshirenet.co.uk/stayat/mannacottage

Low season per wk
£170.00–£200.00
High season per wk
£270.00–£370.00

An 18thC former lead miner's cottage which has been renovated to show many original features. Cosy and comfortable. Parking. Excellent facilities.

★★★★
1 Unit
Sleeping 2–6

SUNNYSIDE COTTAGE
Grassington
Contact: Mrs Carolyn Butt, Garris Lodge, Rylstone,
Skipton BD23 6LJ
T: (01756) 730391 & 07720 294391
E: info@cosycottages.com
I: www.cosycottages.com

OPEN All Year

Low season per wk
£250.00–£300.00
High season per wk
£400.00–£570.00

Beautiful 300-year-old barn conversion. Ideally situated overlooking open fields, yet only 150m from the quaint old cobbled village square.

GREAT AYTON, North Yorkshire Map ref 5C3

★★★★
2 Units
Sleeping 4–6

THE OLD STABLES
Great Ayton
Contact: Mrs Catherine Hawman, Park House,
Easby Hall, Easby, Great Ayton TS9 6JQ
T: (01642) 722560
E: theoldstables@btopenworld.com

OPEN All Year

Low season per wk
£290.00–£400.00
High season per wk
£400.00–£550.00

Victorian former coach house situated on a private country estate. Spacious, well-equipped cottages with antique furnishings. Comfortable base for exploring North York Moors and coast.

GREAT LANGTON, North Yorkshire Map ref 5C3

★★★★
1 Unit
Sleeping 2–6

STANHOW BUNGALOW
Northallerton
Contact: Mary Furness, Stanhow Farm, Great Langton,
Northallerton DL7 0TJ
T: (01609) 748614
F: (01609) 748614
E: mary.stanhow@freenet.co.uk

OPEN All Year

Low season per wk
£225.00–£450.00
High season per wk
£450.00–£520.00

Peaceful, relaxing, in interesting countryside, lovely views. Detached, three bedrooms. Central for Dales, Moors, 'Herriot' Country, close to villages, market towns, historic cities. Personally supervised. Brochure available.

GROSMONT, North Yorkshire Map ref 5D3

★★★★
1 Unit
Sleeping 2–5

VALLEY VIEW COTTAGE
Grosmont, Whitby
Contact: Mrs Maggie Andrews, 5 New Houses, Eskdaleside,
Whitby YO22 5PP
T: (01582) 462257
E: magsandrews@hotmail.com
I: www.valleyviewcottage.co.uk

OPEN All Year

Low season per wk
£300.00–£480.00
High season per wk
£480.00–£600.00

Beautifully restored cottage, idyllically situated in spectacular countryside overlooking the Esk valley. Three bedrooms (two double, one en suite; one single), main bathroom, sitting room (woodburning stove), fully equipped kitchen (dishwasher, washing machine, tumble-drier). Large double-aspect dining area, TV/DVD/video. Private gardens, patio, dining area, parking.

132

YORKSHIRE

HALIFAX, West Yorkshire Map ref 4B1 *Tourist Information Centre Tel: (01422) 368725*

★★★★
2 Units
Sleeping 2–4

CHERRY TREE COTTAGES
Halifax
Contact: Stan & Elaine Shaw, Cherry Tree Cottages, Wall Nook, Barkisland, Halifax HX4 0BL
T: (01422) 372662
F: (01422) 372662
E: cherrytree@yorkshire-cottages.co.uk
I: www.yorkshire-cottages.co.uk

Warm, comfortable, stone-built cottages set in two acres of natural woodland/heather garden with superb Pennine views and direct access to open countryside and footpaths. Close to a quiet Calderdale village with good pubs and restaurants nearby. Ideal location for exploring Bronte country and Pennine Yorkshire. Pets and children welcome.

OPEN All Year
Payment accepted: Delta, Mastercard, Visa

Short breaks available, minimum 3 nights. Check our website for late availability.

Low season per wk
£280.00–£285.00
High season per wk
£385.00–£415.00

HARROGATE, North Yorkshire Map ref 4B1 *Tourist Information Centre Tel: (01423) 537300*

★★★★
5 Units
Sleeping 2–6

APARTMENTS OF DISTINCTION
Harrogate
Contact: Graham and Amanda Lloyd, Muncaster House, 18 Swan Road, Harrogate HG1 2SA
T: (01423) 538742
F: (01423) 538765
E: info@harrogateholidayapartments.co.uk
I: www.harrogateholidayapartments.co.uk

OPEN All Year
Payment accepted: Amex, Delta, Diners, Mastercard, Switch, Visa

Low season per wk
£210.00–£310.00
High season per wk
£320.00–£470.00

Luxurious apartments in Harrogate, offering excellent facilities and a high degree of comfort. Good parking and accessibility to town centre and Yorkshire's many attractions.

★★★★
23 Units
Sleeping 2–4

ASHNESS APARTMENTS
Harrogate
Contact: Mr Spinlove & Miss H Spinlove, Ashness Apartments, 15 St Marys Avenue, Harrogate HG2 0LP
T: (01423) 526894
F: (01423) 700038
E: office@ashness.com
I: www.ashness.com

High-quality apartments, superbly situated in a nice, quiet road of fine Victorian townhouses very near the town centre of Harrogate. Excellent shops, restaurants and cafes are a short walk away through Montpellier Gardens with the Stray and Valley Gardens just around the corner.

OPEN All Year
Payment accepted: Amex, Delta, Mastercard, Switch, Visa

Short breaks available from £60pn, minimum 2 nights.

Low season per wk
£280.00–£370.00
High season per wk
£340.00–£480.00

Use your *i*

There are more than 550 Tourist Information Centres throughout England offering friendly help with accommodation and holiday ideas as well as suggestions of places to visit and things to do. You'll find addresses in the local phone book.

133

YORKSHIRE

HARROGATE continued

★★★★
10 Units
Sleeping 2–8

BRIMHAM ROCKS COTTAGES
Harrogate
Contact: Mrs Martin, Brimham Rocks Cottages,
High North Farm, Fellbeck, Harrogate HG3 5EY
T: (01765) 620284
F: (01765) 620477
E: brimham@nascr.net
I: www.brimham.co.uk

OPEN All Year

Short breaks at 66% of weekly rate.

Low season per wk
£300.00–£450.00
High season per wk
£500.00–£700.00

Overlooking Brimham Rocks and with views of up to 60 miles, these individual cottages are ideally situated to explore both Dales and Moors, York, Ripon, Harrogate, Leeds and the east coast. Converted from old farm buildings, the cottages are warm, cosy, comfortable and decorated with flair and imagination. A warm welcome guaranteed.

★★★★
2 Units
Sleeping 2–10

DAYS2GO.COM
Harrogate
Contact: Mrs Kish, days2go.com, Harrogate
T: (01423) 780661
F: (01423) 780661
E: info@days2go.com
I: www.days2go.com

OPEN All Year
Payment accepted: Euros

Low season per wk
£185.00–£259.00
High season per wk
£330.00–£850.00

Cosy Dales cottages with multi-fuel stoves and newly fitted kitchens. Also elegantly refurbished Victorian property sleeping eight to 10. Walking distance to Harrogate.

★★★★
3 Units
Sleeping 5

DINMORE COTTAGES
Harrogate
Contact: Mrs Susan Chapman, Dovecote Cottage,
Dinmore House, Pateley Bridge Road, Burnt Yates,
Harrogate HG3 3ET
T: (01423) 770860
F: (01423) 770860
E: aib@dinmore-cottages.freeserve.co.uk
I: www.dinmore-cottages.co.uk

OPEN All Year
Payment accepted: Euros

Low season per wk
£240.00–£325.00
High season per wk
£395.00–£580.00

Award-winning Dales cottages converted from 17thC farmstead. Peaceful situation, breathtaking views over Nidderdale, a protected Area of Outstanding Natural Beauty. Only seven miles to spa town of Harrogate, close to York and Herriot country. Ideal for walkers and bird-watchers and for touring and sightseeing in the Yorkshire Dales.

WEB

www.visitengland.com
Log on for information and inspiration. The latest information on places to visit, events and quality assessed accommodation.

YORKSHIRE

HARROGATE continued

★★★
60 Units
Sleeping 2–10

From luxury apartments in Harrogate centre to cosy cottages in the heart of the Yorkshire Dales, Harrogate Holiday Cottages will find you the perfect home from home. Ideal for a holiday or business trip or for visiting friends. Pets welcome (additional charge). Ideal for families.

HARROGATE HOLIDAY COTTAGES

Harrogate
Contact: Mrs Alison Hartwell, Harrogate Holiday Cottages, Crimple Head House, Beckwithshaw, Harrogate HG3 1QU
T: (01423) 523333
F: (01423) 526683
E: info@harrogateholidays.co.uk
I: www.harrogateholidays.co.uk

OPEN All Year

Short breaks.

Low season per wk
£190.00–£400.00
High season per wk
£250.00–£780.00

★★★
1 Unit
Sleeping 1–3

MOOR VIEW COTTAGE
Harrogate
Contact: Mrs Sweeting, 45 Kingsley Drive, Harrogate HG1 4TH
T: (01423) 885498
I: www.mvcottage.netfirms.com

Moor View Cottage is a delightful, fully furnished, two-bedroomed cottage, 10 minutes' walk from Harrogate Conference Centre and town shops. Shorter stays available.

OPEN All Year

Low season per wk
£175.00–£210.00
High season per wk
£210.00–£245.00

★★★
4 Units
Sleeping 2–10

Three miles from central Harrogate and one mile from Follifoot, these traditional country estate properties share a tranquil, sheltered position surrounded by fields and woodland. Approached by a private estate road, each well-equipped and comfortable cottage has countryside views, garden and car parking. Ground floor accommodation is available. Open March to October.

RUDDING ESTATE COTTAGES

Harrogate
Contact: Rudding Estate Cottages, Haggs Farm, Haggs Road, Follifoot, Harrogate HG3 1EQ
T: (01423) 844844
F: (01423) 844803
E: info@rudding.com
I: www.rudding.com

Payment accepted: Delta, Mastercard, Switch, Visa, Euros

Low season per wk
£255.00–£520.00
High season per wk
£380.00–£900.00

Special breaks

Many establishments offer special promotions and themed breaks. These are highlighted in red. (All such offers are subject to availability.)

135

YORKSHIRE

HARROGATE continued

★★★
14 Units
Sleeping 2–7

RUDDING HOLIDAY PARK
Harrogate
Contact: Mr Martin Hutchinson, Rudding Park, Harrogate HG3 1JH
T: (01423) 870439
F: (01423) 870859
E: holiday-park@ruddingpark.com
I: www.ruddingpark.com

OPEN All Year

Payment accepted: Delta, Mastercard, Switch, Visa, Euros

Receive £20 off your booking if you mention this advert when making your reservation.

Low season per wk
Min £260.00
High season per wk
Max £810.00

Choose from our traditional stone-built houses in the beautiful grounds of Rudding Park or our timber lodges set in delightful woodland clearings with many overlooking a small lake. Three miles south of Harrogate, Deer House family pub, shop, swimming pool, children's playground, games room, 18-hole golf course and driving range.

HAWKSWICK, North Yorkshire Map ref 5B3

★★★★★
1 Unit
Sleeping 9

REDMIRE FARM
Skipton
Contact: Mr Neil Tomlinson, Shaw Farm, Shaw Lane, Oxenhope BD22 9QL
T: (01535) 648791
F: (01535) 643671
E: neil@mckeighley.co.uk
I: www.redmire-farm.com

OPEN All Year

Low season per wk
£500.00–£700.00
High season per wk
£700.00–£1,600.00

Recently renovated, detached, Grade II Listed farmhouse dating from 1711. Idyllically situated in the heart of the Dales National Park.

HAWORTH, West Yorkshire Map ref 4B1 Tourist Information Centre Tel: (01535) 642329

★★★★
1 Unit
Sleeping 1–4

HERON COTTAGE
Keighley
Contact: Mr Richard & Mrs Jan Walker, Heron Cottage, Vale Barn, Mytholmes Lane, Haworth, Keighley BD22 0EE
T: (01535) 648537
E: jan_w@tinyworld.co.uk

OPEN All Year

Payment accepted: Euros

Low season per wk
Min £235.00
High season per wk
Min £375.00

Comfortable cottage in peaceful location beside River Worth. Set in paddocks and woodland with abundant walks. Haworth village and steam trains nearby. Also Yorkshire Dales.

★★★★
3 Units
Sleeping 1–6

HEWENDEN MILL COTTAGES
Cullingworth
Contact: Mrs Janet Emanuel, W Lancaster & Co Ltd, Hewenden Mill, Cullingworth, Bradford BD13 5BP
T: (01535) 274259
F: (01535) 273943
E: info@hewendenmillcottages.co.uk
I: www.hewendenmillcottages.co.uk

OPEN All Year

Payment accepted: Mastercard, Switch, Visa

Short breaks our speciality: 3-night weekend and 4-night mid-week (excl Bank Holidays).

Low season per wk
£200.00–£250.00
High season per wk
£240.00–£450.00

Ideally located in idyllic Bronte country, our cottages provide a perfect base for exploring northern England. Set in 10 acres of ancient woodland, they form part of an old water-mill complex and have been recently renovated to provide luxury, self-catering accommodation. Ideal for lovers of walking, wildlife and Wuthering Heights!

YORKSHIRE

HEBDEN BRIDGE, West Yorkshire Map ref 4B1 *Tourist Information Centre Tel: (01422) 843831*

★★★
1 Unit
Sleeping 3-4

3 BIRKS HALL COTTAGE
Hebden Bridge
Contact: Mrs Wilkinson, 1 Birks Hall Cottage,
Upper Birks, Cragg Vale, Hebden Bridge HX7 5SB
T: (01422) 882064

OPEN All Year

Low season per wk
£110.00-£140.00
High season per wk
£140.00-£190.00

Country cottage with two bedrooms, bathroom, kitchen and lounge with Georgian windows. In a small, picturesque village near the Pennine centre of Hebden Bridge.

HELMSLEY, North Yorkshire Map ref 5C3

★★★★
1 Unit
Sleeping 1-4

TOWNEND COTTAGE
Beadlam
Contact: Mrs Margaret Begg, Townend Farmhouse,
High Lane, Beadlam, Nawton, York YO62 7SY
T: (01439) 770103
E: margaret.begg@ukgateway.net
I: www.visityorkshire.com

Originally part of an 18thC farmhouse, this is a very warm, comfortable, two-bedroomed stone cottage with oak beams. Situated off the main road in village three miles from charming market town of Helmsley. Ideal for walking or touring moors, coast and York. Central heating and log fire included in price.

OPEN All Year

Low season per wk
Min £190.00
High season per wk
£285.00-£350.00

HEPTONSTALL, West Yorkshire Map ref 4B1

★★
3 Units
Sleeping 1-6

5 DRAPER CORNER
Slack Bottom
Contact: Mrs Taylor, 4 Northfield Terrace,
Hebden Bridge HX7 7NG
T: (01422) 844323

OPEN All Year

Low season per wk
£190.00-£240.00
High season per wk
£240.00-£340.00

Delightful 18thC cottage overlooking spectacular moorland/National Park views. Easy access to cities and Dales. Author's home when in England, furnished with personal antiques, books, pictures.

HOLMFIRTH, West Yorkshire Map ref 4B1 *Tourist Information Centre Tel: (01484) 222444*

★★★★
1 Unit
Sleeping 1-4

CUISH COTTAGES
Holmfirth
Contact: Mrs Mairi Binns, 5 Cliff Hill Court, Holmfirth
HD9 1JF
T: (01484) 682722
E: martin@crepes.freeserve.co.uk

OPEN All Year

Low season per wk
£250.00-£350.00
High season per wk
£350.00-£550.00

Grade II Listed cottage with light and spacious two-bedroomed accommodation featuring king-size beds and stone-mullioned windows. Exposed beams, gardens and waterfall. Parking, pets.

HORTON-IN-RIBBLESDALE, North Yorkshire Map ref 5B3 *Tourist Information Centre Tel: (01729) 860333*

★★★
1 Unit
Sleeping 1-5

BLIND BECK HOLIDAY COTTAGE
Settle
Contact: Mrs Huddleston, Blind Beck Holiday Cottage,
Horton-in-Ribblesdale, Settle BD24 0HT
T: (01729) 860396
E: h.huddleston@daelnet.co.uk
I: www.blindbeck.co.uk

OPEN All Year

Low season per wk
£200.00-£250.00
High season per wk
£250.00-£320.00

This 17thC cottage is full of character, in the centre of the Three Peaks area and near the Settle-Carlisle railway.

Confirm your booking You are advised to confirm your booking in writing.

YORKSHIRE

HUNMANBY, North Yorkshire Map ref 5D3

★★★
7 Units
Sleeping 2–7

ORCHARD FARM HOLIDAY VILLAGE
Filey
Contact: Mrs Sharon Dugdale, Orchard Farm Holiday Village, Stonegate, Hunmanby, Filey YO14 0PU
T: (01723) 891582
F: (01723) 891582
E: s.dugdale@virgin.net

OPEN All Year except Christmas and New Year

Low season per wk £180.00–£280.00
High season per wk £490.00–£620.00

Self-contained cottages forming part of Orchard Farm Holiday Village with facilities including indoor heated pool, fishing lake and shop.

HUTTON-LE-HOLE, North Yorkshire Map ref 5C3

★★★
2 Units
Sleeping 2–4

WATERSWALLOW COTTAGE & SWALLOW BARN
York
Contact: Mrs Barbara Grabowski, Halfway House, Hutton-le-Hole, York YO62 6UQ
T: (01751) 431596
F: (01751) 431596
E: waterswallow.cottage@virgin.net

OPEN All Year

Low season per wk £250.00–£300.00
High season per wk £300.00–£390.00

Both cottages are full of charm and character with spectacular views over the adjacent valley situated in the National Park.

KETTLEWELL, North Yorkshire Map ref 5B3

★★★★
4 Units
Sleeping 1–4

FOLD FARM COTTAGES
Skipton
Contact: Mrs Barbara Lambert, Fold Farm, Kettlewell, Skipton BD23 5RH
T: (01756) 760886
F: (01756) 760464
E: info@foldfarm.co.uk
I: www.foldfarm.co.uk

OPEN All Year

Low season per wk £200.00–£300.00
High season per wk £290.00–£440.00

Stone-built cottages beside village stream, close to farmhouse. Beamed ceilings, open coal fires, fully-fitted kitchens. Private off-road parking. Easy walk to pubs, shops and church.

KIRKBYMOORSIDE, North Yorkshire Map ref 5C3

★★★★
1 Unit
Sleeping 6

CHERRY VIEW COTTAGE
York
Contact: Mrs Drinkel, Starfitts Lane, Kirkbymoorside, York YO62 7JF
T: (01751) 431714

Cottage set at edge of farm, breathtaking views across Vale of Pickering. Spacious and self-contained, three-bedroomed accommodation, furnished to a high standard. Lawned garden, ample parking. Pets welcome by prior arrangement.

OPEN All Year

Low season per wk £280.00–£290.00
High season per wk £350.00–£425.00

Town index

This can be found at the back of the guide. If you know where you want to stay the index will give you the page number listing accommodation in your chosen town, city or village.

YORKSHIRE

KIRKBYMOORSIDE continued

★★★★
2 Units
Sleeping 2-4

Sympathetically restored stable mews cottages in 18thC watermill complex on the river Dove. Well-appointed accommodation with linen and towels, TV, video, mini hi-fi and central heating included. Bed and bath downstairs, living room upstairs. Garden and barbecue. Meals in the millhouse by arrangement.

THE CORNMILL
Kirkbymoorside
Contact: Mr Chris & Mrs Karen Tinkler, The Cornmill, Kirby Mills, Kirkbymoorside, York YO62 6NP
T: (01751) 432000
F: (01751) 432300
E: cornmill@kirbymills.demon.co.uk
I: www.kirbymills.demon.co.uk

OPEN All Year
Payment accepted: Mastercard, Switch, Visa

Low season per wk
£250.00-£325.00
High season per wk
Max £325.00

★★★★
1 Unit
Sleeping 1-5

Situated in a quiet location, The Retreat nestles in the heart of the cobbled Ryedale market town of Kirkbymoorside, gateway to the North York Moors. This well-appointed luxury apartment, with its charming beamed ceilings, is fully equipped providing quality contents and tasteful furnishings suiting the more discerning visitor.

THE RETREAT APARTMENT
Kirkbymoorside
Contact: Mrs A J Schulze, Mill Cottage, The Grange, Sinnington, York YO62 6RB
T: (01751) 430806
F: (01751) 430369
E: kingfisher.mill@virgin.net
I: www.the-retreat-yorkshire.co.uk

OPEN All Year

Low season per wk
£210.00-£250.00
High season per wk
£250.00-£390.00

★★★★
2 Units
Sleeping 4

Historic barn conversions on farmstead (originally an old mill and tannery) giving panoramic views over moorland edge, and immediate access to field and woodland walks. Warm, roomy accommodation with excellent-quality furnishings and fittings. A wealth of beams and original stone and brick features. 'Comfort' is the key word.

SURPRISE VIEW COTTAGE & FIELD BARN COTTAGE
Kirkbymoorside
Contact: Mrs Ruth Wass, Sinnington Lodge, Sinnington, York YO62 6RB
T: (01751) 431345
F: (01751) 433418
E: info@surpriseviewcottages.co.uk
I: www.surpriseviewcottages.co.uk

OPEN All Year

Short breaks available Nov-Mar – 3-night stay (excluding Christmas and half-terms).

Low season per wk
£200.00-£280.00
High season per wk
£300.00-£380.00

Quality Assurance Standard
Star ratings and awards were correct at time of going to press but are subject to change. Please check at the time of booking.

YORKSHIRE

KNARESBOROUGH, North Yorkshire Map ref 4B1

★★★★
1 Unit
Sleeping 1–2

THE GRANARY
Knaresborough
Contact: Mrs Rachel Thornton, Gibbet House Farm, Farnham Lane, Farnham, Knaresborough HG5 9JP
T: (01423) 862325 & 07970 000068
F: (01423) 862271

Traditional, converted granary adjacent to farmhouse. Situated in 30 acres of parkland with stunning views of the Nidderdale Valley. Furnished to a high standard. Five miles Harrogate, two miles Knaresborough. Central for Dales, Yorkshire Coast, 'Herriot' and 'Heartbeat' country. The perfect setting for a peaceful and comfortable holiday.

OPEN All Year

Payment accepted: Euros

Short breaks available. 3-night stays Oct–Mar.

Low season per wk
£210.00–£230.00
High season per wk
£235.00–£260.00

LEALHOLM, North Yorkshire Map ref 5C3

★★★
3 Units
Sleeping 3–6

GREENHOUSES FARM COTTAGES
Whitby
Contact: Mr & Mrs Nick Eddleston, Greenhouses Farm, Greenhouses, Lealholm, Whitby YO21 2AD
T: (01947) 897486
F: (01947) 897486
E: n_eddleston@yahoo.com
I: www.greenhouses-farm-cottages.co.uk

Stone and pantile cottages converted from traditional farm buildings, providing well-equipped, comfortable, centrally heated accommodation. The lounges have solid fuel stoves and colour TVs. The kitchens are all equipped with electric cooker, microwave, washing machine and pleasant dining area. In beautiful moorland hamlet within North York Moors National Park, nine miles Whitby.

OPEN All Year

Low season per wk
£203.00–£250.00
High season per wk
£352.00–£536.00

LEVEN, East Riding of Yorkshire Map ref 4C1

★★★★
2 Units
Sleeping 1–4

LEVEN PARK LAKE
Beverley
Contact: Mr Graham & Mrs Lisa Skinner, Leven Park Lake, South Street, Leven, Beverley HU17 5NY
T: (01964) 544510
I: www.levenparklake.co.uk

Idyllic lakeside setting, two-bedroomed log cabins with private parking on a 3.5-acre lake in eight acres of landscaped gardens and woodland. Each cabin is set on the lakeside with its own private fishing. An ideal base for bird-watching, visiting Beverley, The Deep in Hull and east coast.

OPEN All Year

Short breaks available for a relaxing, long weekend or mid-week break.

Low season per wk
£240.00–£300.00
High season per wk
£350.00–£450.00

Accessibility Look for the symbols which indicate National Accessible Scheme standards for hearing and visually impaired guests in addition to standards for guests with mobility impairment. You can find an index of all scheme participants at the back of this guide.

YORKSHIRE

LEYBURN, North Yorkshire Map ref 5B3 *Tourist Information Centre Tel: (01969) 623069*

★★★–★★★★★
6 Units
Sleeping 2–6

Stone-built period cottages and self-contained apartments form a secluded courtyard only 80m from Leyburn market place. Ample private parking, ideal touring and walking centre.

DALES VIEW HOLIDAY HOMES
Leyburn
Contact: Messrs Chilton, Dales View Holiday Homes, Jenkins Garth, Leyburn DL8 5SP
T: (01969) 623707
F: (01969) 623707
E: daleshols@aol.com
I: www.daleshols.co.uk

OPEN All Year

Short breaks available Oct–Apr.

Low season per wk
£140.00–£250.00
High season per wk
£250.00–£350.00

LITTLE THIRKLEBY, North Yorkshire Map ref 5C3

★★★★
6 Units
Sleeping 2–6

Luxury beamed cottages surrounding pretty landscaped courtyard. Exclusive use of new indoor swimming pool, spa bath and sauna. Wonderful location overlooking the White Horse of Kilburn. Ideally situated for visiting Yorkshire's coast, Dales, North York Moors and City of York. Many local attractions including James Herriot Museum, Thirsk.

OLD OAK COTTAGES
Thirsk
Contact: Mrs Tattersall, Old Oak Cottages, High House Farm, Little Thirkleby, Thirsk YO7 2BB
T: (01845) 501258
F: (01845) 501258
E: amanda@oldoakcottages.com
I: www.oldoakcottages.com

OPEN All Year

Mid-week and weekend breaks available Oct-Mar (excl Christmas, New Year and half-term).

Low season per wk
Min £250.00
High season per wk
Max £850.00

MALTON, North Yorkshire Map ref 5D3 *Tourist Information Centre Tel: (01653) 600048*

★★★★
1 Unit
Sleeping 2–3

A cosy, two-bedroomed, fully-equipped old farm cottage, caringly modernised to a very high standard, situated in the heart of rural Ryedale. Ideally located, being central to the North York Moors, Yorkshire Wolds, east coast seaside and the old City of York. Price includes logs and coal for multi-fuel stove.

SWANS NEST COTTAGE
Malton
Contact: Mrs Yvonne Dickinson, Abbotts Farm House, Ryton, Malton YO17 6SA
T: (01653) 694970
E: swansnestcottage@hotmail.com
I: www.uk-holiday-cottages.co.uk/swans-nest

OPEN All Year

Payment accepted: Delta, Mastercard, Switch, Visa, Euros

Mid-week and weekend breaks generally available.

Low season per wk
£205.00–£275.00
High season per wk
£305.00–£355.00

Credit card bookings
If you book by telephone and are asked for your credit card number it is advisable to check the proprietor's policy should you cancel your reservation.

141

YORKSHIRE

MASHAM, North Yorkshire Map ref 5C3

★★★★
2 Units
Sleeping 2–4

DALES VIEW COTTAGES
Ripon
Contact: Mr H Moyes, Dales View Cottages, Fearby, Masham, Ripon HG4 4NF
T: (01765) 688820
E: hrmoyes@aol.com

Two recently renovated Grade II Listed barn conversions. Set around the picturesque village green of Fearby. With splendid retained features like exposed beams, hand-made limestone fireplaces and luxury fitted bathrooms. With power showers, gold fittings and quality traditional kitchens, they make a splendid and relaxing place to stay.

OPEN All Year

Short breaks of 3 days available Oct-Mar or at short notice, subject to availability.

Low season per wk
£250.00–£300.00
High season per wk
£350.00–£425.00

MIDDLEHAM, North Yorkshire Map ref 5C3

★★★
1 Unit
Sleeping 1–6

THE COTTAGE
Middleham
Contact: Mr P Ralph, 1 New Hall Road, Chesterfield S40 1HE
T: (01246) 224260

Spacious cottage with three bedrooms (one double, one twin and one single plus large sofa bed). Separate dining room and kitchen, fully-appointed bathroom plus wc.

OPEN All Year

Low season per wk
£250.00–£300.00
High season per wk
£300.00–£350.00

NEWSHAM, North Yorkshire Map ref 5B3

★★★★
1 Unit
Sleeping 2–6

DYSON HOUSE BARN
Richmond
Contact: Mr & Mrs Clarkson, Dyson House, Newsham, Richmond DL11 7QP
T: (01833) 627365
E: dysonbarn@tinyworld.co.uk
I: www.cottageguide.co.uk/dysonhousebarn

Between Richmond and Barnard Castle this spacious, well-equipped, converted farm barn makes an ideal base for touring Teesdale, Swaledale, North Yorkshire, Durham and Cumbria. Retaining many original features there are three large bedrooms, one ground floor with shower room. Patio with barbecue. Two public house/restaurants, 10 minutes' walk. Brochure available.

OPEN All Year

Short stays available 6 Nov-31 Mar (excl school holidays), minimum 2 nights.

Low season per wk
£210.00–£440.00
High season per wk
£360.00–£440.00

NORTH DALTON, East Riding of Yorkshire Map ref 4C1

★★★
1 Unit
Sleeping 3–4

OLD COBBLERS COTTAGE
Driffield
Contact: Miss Chris Wade, 2 Star Row, North Dalton, Driffield YO25 9UR
T: (01377) 217523 & 217662
F: (01377) 217754
E: chris@adastey.demon.co.uk

19thC, mid-terraced, oak-beamed cottage overlooking picturesque pond in a peaceful and friendly farming village, between York and Yorkshire's Heritage Coast. Ideally located for walking, visiting the coast, historic houses, races at York and Beverley or just relaxing. Excellent inn/restaurant adjacent, shops 1.5 miles. Pets welcome.

OPEN All Year
Payment accepted: Mastercard, Switch, Visa

Short breaks available, 3 nights (excl Christmas, New Year, Easter and Bank Holidays).

Low season per wk
£140.00–£200.00
High season per wk
£225.00–£310.00

YORKSHIRE

NORTHALLERTON, North Yorkshire Map ref 5C3 *Tourist Information Centre Tel: (01609) 776864*

★★★
1 Unit
Sleeping 1–5

2 SUMMERFIELD COTTAGE
Northallerton
Contact: Mrs Sally Holmes, Summerfield House Farm,
Welbury, Northallerton DL6 2SL
T: (01609) 882393
F: (01609) 882393
E: sallyhholmes@aol.com

OPEN All Year

Low season per wk
£120.00–£170.00
High season per wk
£170.00–£250.00

Enjoy the peaceful surroundings of this well-appointed, three-bedroomed farm cottage. Superb views over open countryside. Central for Yorkshire Dales, Moors, 'Herriot' country and York.

NORTON, North Yorkshire Map ref 5D3

★★★★
1 Unit

ANSON HOUSE
Malton
Contact: Mrs Susan Camacho, Star Cottage,
Welham Road, Norton, Malton YO17 9DU
T: (01653) 694916
F: (01653) 694901
I: www.ansonhouseholidays.co.uk

OPEN All Year

Payment accepted: Euros

Low season per wk
£250.00–£350.00
High season per wk
£400.00–£495.00

New, luxury two-bedroomed en suite cottage on horse racing/stud complex next to 27-hole golf course. One mile town centre, bus/train stations, shops, pubs. Gallops visits.

OXENHOPE, West Yorkshire Map ref 4B1

★★★
1 Unit
Sleeping 2–3

YATE COTTAGE
Keighley
Contact: Mrs Jean M M Dunn, Yate House, Yate Lane,
Oxenhope, Keighley BD22 9HL
T: (01535) 643638
I: www.uk-holiday-cottages.co.uk/yatecottage

OPEN All Year except
Christmas and New Year

Low season per wk
£100.00–£120.00
High season per wk
£160.00–£200.00

18thC cottage adjoining Yate House, a 'yeoman' house of striking architectural appearance. South-facing view over beautiful garden to hills. No short breaks.

PICKERING, North Yorkshire Map ref 5D3 *Tourist Information Centre Tel: (01751) 473791*

Rating
Applied For

1 Unit

AMELIA COTTAGE
Pickering
Contact: Mr Paul Hickabottom, 16 The Parade,
Pearson Park, Hull HU5 2UH
T: (01482) 441175
F: (01482) 441175
E: hotham@hothamshipping.co.uk

OPEN All Year

Payment accepted: Euros

Low season per wk
Min £200.00
High season per wk
Max £350.00

Traditional cottage, exposed beams, open fire, full central heating, fitted kitchen, bathroom/shower. Enclosed garden, quiet yet close to centre.

★★★★-★★★★★★
8 Units
Sleeping 2–4

Award-winning stone cottages with heated indoor pool, sauna, children's play area, gardens and paddock. Delightful location in quiet village on edge of Moors National Park. Also convenient for coast and York. The cottages are in a courtyard setting backing onto fields. Brochure available.

BEECH FARM COTTAGES

Pickering
Contact: Mrs Pat Massara, Beech Farm Cottages, Wrelton,
Pickering YO18 8PG
T: (01751) 476612
F: (01751) 475032
E: holiday@beechfarm.com
I: www.beechfarm.com

OPEN All Year

Payment accepted: Amex,
Delta, Mastercard, Switch,
Visa, Euros

Low season per wk
£255.00–£720.00
High season per wk
£530.00–£1,735.00

4-times winner of Yorkshire
Tourist Board's 'Self-Catering
Holiday of the Year' award.
Short-listed for 2004 award.

143

YORKSHIRE

PICKERING continued

★★★★
8 Units
Sleeping 1–11

EASTHILL FARM HOUSE AND GARDENS
Pickering
Contact: Mrs Diane Stenton, Easthill Farm House, Wilton Road, Thornton Dale, Pickering YO18 7QP
T: (01751) 474561
E: info@easthill-farm-holidays.co.uk
I: www.easthill-farm-holidays.co.uk

Beautifully equipped/furnished farmhouse divided into apartments (separate entrances) with adjoining cottage. Also four pine lodges (one fully wheelchair accessible) nestled in woodland bordering landscaped gardens. Enjoy all-weather tennis, jacuzzi, putting, barbecue, play areas, games room and some farm animals. Friendly, personal supervision throughout. Central for North York Moors, forestry, coast and York.

OPEN All Year

Payment accepted: Delta, Mastercard, Switch, Visa, Euros

Low season per wk
£180.00–£335.00
High season per wk
£370.00–£920.00

Short breaks available. Finalist in White Rose 'Self-Catering Holiday of the Year' award.

★★★★
3 Units
Sleeping 4–6

LET'S HOLIDAY
Pickering
Contact: Mr John Wicks, Let's Holiday, Mel House, Newton-on-Rawcliffe, Pickering YO18 8QA
T: (01751) 475396
F: (01751) 475396
E: holiday@letsholiday.com
I: www.letsholiday.com

Comfortable and fully equipped offering indoor pool, spa and sauna, and set in extensive level grounds at the heart of our National Park village. Paddocks and stabling for DIY livery. Village pub, play area and duck pond nearby. Perfect for exploring North York Moors, the coast and City of York.

OPEN All Year

Payment accepted: Delta, Mastercard, Switch, Visa

Low season per wk
£255.00–£315.00
High season per wk
£555.00–£720.00

Low season short breaks: 2 or 3 nights over the weekend and 4 nights for the price of 3 mid-week.

★★★
1 Unit
Sleeping 5

11 POTTER HILL
Pickering
Contact: Mr Michael Jones, Cheeseboard, 26 Royal Hill, London SE10 8RT
T: (020) 8305 0401
F: (020) 8305 0401
E: michael@cheese-board.co.uk

OPEN All Year

Payment accepted: Amex, Mastercard, Switch, Visa

Low season per wk
Min £245.00
High season per wk
Min £435.00

This newly renovated family home is perfectly located in the pretty market town of Pickering. It has two double and one single bedroom. Pets welcome.

Country Code Always follow the Country Code

• Enjoy the countryside and respect its life and work • Guard against all risk of fire • Fasten all gates • Keep your dogs under close control • Keep to public paths across farmland • Use gates and stiles to cross fences, hedges and walls • Leave livestock, crops and machinery alone • Take your litter home • Help to keep all water clean • Protect wildlife, plants and trees • Take special care on country roads • Make no unnecessary noise.

YORKSHIRE

PICKERING continued

★★★★
6 Units
Sleeping 2–8

SANDS FARM COTTAGES
Pickering
Contact: Mr Michael & Mrs Susan Parkin & Mrs Price, Sands Farm Cottages, Wilton, Pickering YO18 7JY
T: (01751) 474405
E: info@sandsfarmcottages.co.uk
I: www.sandsfarmcottages.co.uk

Converted chapel and farm buildings set in 17 acres of farmland. Romantic honeymoon cottage for two people. Chapel has four en suite bedrooms. Additional cottages sleep four or six. Only four miles from Pickering town centre. Close to Dalby Forest and North Yorkshire Moors. Hot tubs in some units.

OPEN All Year

Payment accepted: Delta, Mastercard, Switch, Visa

Open all year including Christmas and New Year. Short breaks available winter months.

Low season per wk
£240.00–£550.00
High season per wk
£320.00–£1,000.00

★★★
1 Unit
Sleeping 4

UPPER CARR CHALET AND TOURING PARK
Pickering
Contact: Mr Martin Harker, Upper Carr Chalet and Touring Park, Upper Carr Lane, Malton Road, Pickering YO18 7JP
T: (01751) 473115
F: (01751) 473115
E: harker@uppercarr.demon.co.uk
I: www.uppercarr.demon.co.uk

Payment accepted: Delta, Mastercard, Switch, Visa

Low season per wk
£190.00–£210.00
High season per wk
£220.00–£400.00

Quiet family park near the North York Moors National Park, forest and coast. Country pub serving meals, and golf course opposite. Pets' corner.

RAVENSCAR, North Yorkshire Map ref 5D3

★★★–★★★★★
3 Units
Sleeping 2–4

SMUGGLERS ROCK COUNTRY HOUSE
Scarborough
Contact: Mrs Sharon Gregson, Smugglers Rock Country House, Staintondale Road, Ravenscar, Scarborough YO13 0ER
T: (01723) 870044
E: info@smugglersrock.co.uk
I: www.smugglersrock.co.uk

Beautiful cottages furnished to a very high standard and fully equipped for maximum comfort and relaxation. Situated in the North York Moors National Park with wonderful views, the cottages are an ideal base for country and coastal holidays. B&B also available.

OPEN All Year

3 night breaks available Oct–Mar.

Low season per wk
£204.00–£259.00
High season per wk
£416.00–£524.00

Check the maps

The colour maps at the front of this guide show all the cities, towns and villages for which you will find accommodation entries. Refer to the town index to find the page on which they are listed.

YORKSHIRE

ROBIN HOOD'S BAY, North Yorkshire Map ref 5D3

★★★-★★★★★
5 Units
Sleeping 3–5

FARSYDE FARM COTTAGES
Whitby
Contact: Mrs Angela Green, Farsyde Farm Cottages, Robin Hood's Bay, Whitby YO22 4UG
T: (01947) 880249
F: (01947) 880877
E: farsydestud@talk21.com
I: www.farsydefarmcottages.co.uk

Adjacent to Robin Hood's Bay village, beach and Boggle Hole via field/woodland paths, the stone and pantile cottages, permanently heated in cooler months, have attractive gardens. Magnificent panoramic views. Mistal Cottage guests enjoy private swimming (chalet pool). Horses/mountain bikes. Farm animals. Parking. Whitby six miles. Scarborough 16 miles. York 50 miles.

OPEN All Year

Short breaks in autumn, winter and spring. Minimum 2 nights. Special offers for bookings of 2 weeks or longer.

Low season per wk
£160.00–£350.00
High season per wk
£325.00–£600.00

★★★
1 Unit
Sleeping 2–4

LINGERS HILL
Whitby
Contact: Mrs Frances Harland, Lingers Hill Farm, Thorpe Lane, Robin Hood's Bay, Whitby YO22 4TQ
T: (01947) 880608

Cosy character cottage situated on the edge of the village at Robin Hood's Bay. Close to amenities, ideal walking and cycling area. Lovely views.

OPEN All Year

Low season per wk
£180.00–£230.00
High season per wk
£250.00–£325.00

★★★-★★★★★
5 Units
Sleeping 2–10

SOUTH HOUSE FARMHOUSE & COTTAGES
Whitby
Contact: Mrs Nealia Pattinson, South House Farmhouse & Cottages, Mill Beck, Fylingthorpe, Whitby YO22 4UQ
T: (01947) 880243
F: (01947) 880243
E: kmp@bogglehole.fsnet.co.uk
I: www.southhousefarm.co.uk

Situated in 180 acres of farmland near Robin Hood's Bay. Wonderful walks in National Park. Beach 0.5 miles. Super refurbished farmhouse, and luxury cottages. Large garden. Parking.

OPEN All Year

Low season per wk
£180.00–£800.00
High season per wk
£225.00–£1,000.00

SCARBOROUGH, North Yorkshire Map ref 5D3 Tourist Information Centre Tel: (01723) 373333

★
1 Unit
Sleeping 2–8

HYDEAWAY HAVEN
Scarborough
Contact: Mr & Mrs John Hyde, 18 Roslyn Close, Broxbourne EN10 7DA
T: (01992) 465509
F: (020) 8270 6451
E: hydehaven@ntlworld.com

Terraced house, centrally situated for both bays and all amenities. Sleeps eight plus cot. All linen provided.

OPEN All Year

Low season per wk
£180.00–£350.00
High season per wk
£300.00–£420.00

★★★★
7 Units
Sleeping 2–12

KILLERBY OLD HALL
Scarborough
Contact: Mrs Margery Middleton, Killerby Old Hall, Killerby, Cayton, Scarborough YO11 3TW
T: (01723) 583799
F: (01723) 583799
I: www.killerby.com

Holiday in Killerby Old Hall (ancient manor-house) or one of six cottages in a courtyard setting amid four acres of grounds. Convenient for country or coast.

OPEN All Year

Payment accepted: Delta, Mastercard, Switch, Visa

Low season per wk
£290.00–£900.00
High season per wk
£500.00–£2,100.00

YORKSHIRE

SCARBOROUGH continued

★★★★
1 Unit
Sleeping 1–4

LENDAL HOUSE
Scarborough
Contact: Mrs Petra Scott, Lendal House,
34 Trafalgar Square, Scarborough YO12 7PY
T: (01723) 372178
E: info@lendalhouse.co.uk
I: www.lendalhouse.co.uk

OPEN All Year

Low season per wk
£250.00–£300.00
High season per wk
£350.00–£400.00

Luxury, self-contained ground floor flat with four-poster bed. Near cricket ground, five minutes' walk to North Bay Beach, town centre, also great for walks on North Yorkshire moors.

★★★
2 Units
Sleeping 2–6

SPIKERS HILL COUNTRY COTTAGES
Scarborough
Contact: Mrs Janet Hutchinson, Spikers Hill Country Cottages, Spikers Hill Farm, Cockrah Road, West Ayton, Scarborough YO13 9LB
T: (01723) 862537
F: (01723) 865511
E: janet@spikershill.ndo.co.uk
I: www.spikershill.ndo.co.uk

OPEN All Year except Christmas and New Year

Low season per wk
£170.00–£320.00
High season per wk
£370.00–£500.00

Delightful cottages with beautiful view on a private 600-acre farm in North York Moors National Park. Ideal for countryside and coast (Scarborough five miles).

★★★★
9 Units
Sleeping 1–9

National winners of VisitBritain 'England for Excellence' award for Best Self-Catering Holiday of the Year. Superb indoor heated swimming pool, jacuzzi and sauna. Stunning panoramic sea views and beautiful countryside on edge of National Park. Lovely, award-winning gardens. Parking. Furnished Teddy Bear's cottage and picnic park. York one hour, Whitby 30 minutes.

WREA HEAD COUNTRY COTTAGES

Scarborough
Contact: Mr Steve Marshall, Wrea Head Country Cottages, Barmoor Lane, Scalby, Scarborough YO13 0PG
T: (01723) 375844
F: (01723) 375911
E: ytb@wreahead.co.uk
I: www.wreahead.co.uk

OPEN All Year
Payment accepted:
Mastercard, Switch, Visa

Excellent-value short breaks available from 30 Oct 2004 to 19 Mar 2005, including 4 nights for the price of 3.

Low season per wk
£255.00–£550.00
High season per wk
£325.00–£1,375.00

SETTLE, North Yorkshire Map ref 5B3 *Tourist Information Centre Tel: (01729) 825192*

★★★
1 Unit
Sleeping 4

HAZEL COTTAGE
Settle
Contact: Mrs Jennie Crawford
T: (01274) 832368
E: rogercrawford@greenclough.freeserve.co.uk
I: www.geocities.com/moorsideuk/

High season per wk
£210.00–£350.00

Pleasant garden cottage, close to The Green, in a picturesque village in the Yorkshire Dales. Parking is by The Green. Open week before Easter-end of Oct. Small charge for towels.

Important note Information on accommodation listed in this guide has been supplied by the proprietors. As changes may occur you are advised to check details at the time of booking.

147

YORKSHIRE

SHEFFIELD, South Yorkshire Map ref 4B2 *Tourist Information Centre Tel: (0114) 221 1900*

★★★
1 Unit
Sleeping 1–5

FOXHOLES FARM
Sheffield
Contact: Rachel Hague, Parkside adjacent to Prospect Farm, Bradfield, Sheffield S6 6LJ
T: (0114) 285 1551
F: (0114) 285 1559
E: hagueplant@farmersweekly.net

OPEN All Year
Payment accepted: Euros

Low season per wk
Max £350.00
High season per wk
Max £350.00

This Grade II Listed building lies in a rural and particularly tranquil area overlooking the historical and picturesque villages of High and Low Bradfield.

★★★★
1 Unit
Sleeping 1–6

HANGRAM LANE FARMHOUSE
Sheffield
Contact: Mrs Clark, Hangram Lane Farmhouse, Hangram Lane Grange, Hangram Lane, Sheffield S11 7TQ
T: (0114) 230 3570
F: (0114) 230 6573

OPEN All Year

Low season per wk
£282.00–£293.75
High season per wk
£340.75–£352.50

Comfortable, modernised farmhouse comprising large kitchen, dining room, lounge, one double bedroom, two twin-bedded rooms, bathroom and toilet. Two minutes' drive from the Peak District, shops and eating places.

SIGGLESTHORNE, East Riding of Yorkshire Map ref 4D1

★★★★
1 Unit
Sleeping 1–4

PEGGY'S COTTAGE
Nr Hornsea
Contact: Jude Collingwood, Peggy's Cottage, Nr Hornsea HU11 5QH
T: (01964) 535395
E: p.collingwood@btinternet.com

OPEN All Year
Payment accepted: Euros

Low season per wk
£150.00–£200.00
High season per wk
£200.00–£300.00

Once a stable, now a comfortable and pretty cottage enjoying a peaceful, rural setting four miles from the sea and Hornsea Mere.

SKIPTON, North Yorkshire Map ref 4B1 *Tourist Information Centre Tel: (01756) 792809*

★★★-★★★★★
7 Units
Sleeping 1–4

Peaceful, tastefully converted farm cottages in open countryside, one mile from castle and historic market town of Skipton. Suitable for disabled.

CAWDER HALL COTTAGES
Skipton
Contact: Mr Graham Pearson, Cawder Hall Cottages, Cawder Lane, Skipton BD23 2TD
T: (01756) 791579
F: (01756) 797036
E: info@cawderhallcottages.co.uk
I: www.cawderhallcottages.co.uk

OPEN All Year
Payment accepted: Amex, Delta, Mastercard, Switch, Visa

Low season per wk
£140.00–£250.00
High season per wk
£220.00–£380.00

★★★
1 Unit
Sleeping 2–5

DALESTONE
Skipton
Contact: Mr Malcolm & Mrs Ann Wadsworth, 25 Watson Road, Blackpool FY4 1EG
T: (01253) 404726
E: mw001f3365@blueyonder.co.uk

OPEN All Year

Low season per wk
£145.00–£180.00
High season per wk
£245.00–£295.00

A three-bedroomed house with separate lounge and dining room, private, mature gardens and garage. Quiet area close to the town centre.

 Enjoy England official guides to quality
Please mention this guide when making your booking.

148

YORKSHIRE

SKIPTON continued

★★★
1 Unit
Sleeping 6

7 PASTURE ROAD
Skipton
Contact: Mr J S & Mrs C Lunnon, 17 Cherry Tree Way, Rossendale BB4 4JZ
T: (01706) 230653
E: chris.lunnon@barlo.co.uk
I: www.cjlunnon.co.uk

OPEN All Year

Low season per wk
£190.00–£245.00
High season per wk
£295.00–£415.00

Detached, Victorian, stone-built house in quiet location on edge of Yorkshire Dales National Park. Three bedrooms, separate dining room. Spacious and comfortably furnished. Rent includes heating, linen and electricity. Village amenities include shop, post office, playground, two pubs. Ideal base for walking or touring. Pets and families welcome.

STAINTONDALE, North Yorkshire Map ref 5D3

★★★
4 Units
Sleeping 1–6

WHITE HALL FARM HOLIDAY COTTAGES
Scarborough
Contact: Mr James & Mrs Celia White, White Hall Farm Holiday Cottages, White Hall Farm, Staintondale, Scarborough YO13 0EY
T: (01723) 870234
E: celia@white66.fsbusiness.co.uk
I: www.whitehallcottages.co.uk

OPEN All Year

Low season per wk
£165.00–£240.00
High season per wk
£280.00–£450.00

Peace and tranquillity found on 170-acre sheep farm with stunning coastal and rural views. Ten minutes' walk from the Cleveland Way. Plenty of walks from the door amid cliffs, woodland and streams. 'Home from home', highly equipped, welcoming cottages. Ample parking. Pets made welcome.

STAITHES, North Yorkshire Map ref 5C3

★★
1 Unit
Sleeping 4

GLENCOE
Staithes
Contact: Mr David Purdy, Church Street, Kirkbymoorside, York YO62 6AZ
T: (01751) 431452

OPEN All Year

Low season per wk
£200.00–£240.00
High season per wk
£240.00–£300.00

Cosy, harbourside, mid-terrace former fisherman's cottage in a picturesque fishing village steeped in history. Open fire. Two bedrooms. Close beach, shops, pubs, restaurants.

THIRSK, North Yorkshire Map ref 5C3 Tourist Information Centre Tel: (01845) 522755

★★★
2 Units

BRIAR COTTAGE & BRAMBLE COTTAGE
Thirsk
Contact: Audrey Saye, Thirsk YO7 2QA
T: (01845) 597309
E: jim.dickinson@btinternet.com

OPEN All Year

Low season per wk
Min £250.00
High season per wk
Max £350.00

Two unique one-bedroomed cottages situated at the base of Sutton Bank in the heart of Herriot Country. Natural water supply.

★★★
1 Unit

THE OLD SCHOOL HOUSE
Thirsk
Contact: Mrs Gabrielle Readman, Catton, Thirsk YO7 4SG
T: (01845) 567308

OPEN All Year

Low season per wk
£130.00–£160.00
High season per wk
£160.00–£210.00

Formerly the village school. Two bedrooms, one double with a single bed and one twin-bedded, all ground floor. Pets welcome by prior arrangement only.

149

YORKSHIRE

TICKTON, East Riding of Yorkshire Map ref 4C1

★★★
1 Unit
Sleeping 1–7

BRIDGE HOUSE COTTAGE
Beverley
Contact: Mr Peter White & Ms Adele Wilkinson, Bridge House Cottage, Hull Bridge House, Weel Road, Tickton, Beverley HU17 9RY
T: (01964) 542355
E: alw@amj.co.uk

OPEN All Year

Low season per wk
£250.00–£300.00
High season per wk
£300.00–£350.00

Riverside cottage with excellent facilities. Three bedrooms, gas central heating, all linen included, private riverbank and garden. A warm welcome is assured.

TODMORDEN, West Yorkshire Map ref 4B1 Tourist Information Centre Tel: (01706) 818181

★★★
1 Unit
Sleeping 4

THE COTTAGE
Todmorden
Contact: Mr & Mrs Bentham, The Cottage, Causeway East Farmhouse, Lee Bottom Road, Todmorden OL14 6HH
T: (01706) 815265
E: andrew@bentham5.freeserve.co.uk

OPEN All Year

Low season per wk
£140.00–£170.00
High season per wk
£170.00–£200.00

Part of a 17thC farmhouse beneath the Pennine Way. Ideal for walking and touring.

TOTLEY RISE, South Yorkshire Map ref 4B2

★★★★
1 Unit
Sleeping 1–4

SWALLOW COTTAGE
Sheffield
Contact: Mrs D Hill-Pickford, Swallow Cottage, Bents Farm, Penny Lane, Totley Rise, Sheffield S17 3AZ
T: (0114) 236 7806
I: www.swallowcottage.com

OPEN All Year

Low season per wk
£250.00–£363.00
High season per wk
£364.00–£439.00

Beautiful character converted stone barn. Well equipped, spacious yet cosy with logburning stove. Surrounded by countryside. Bordering Derbyshire and yet close to the city.

WEST WITTON, North Yorkshire Map ref 5B3

★★★
1 Unit
Sleeping 2–4

Swallows Rest nestles at the foot of Pen Hill and is a newly converted hay barn. Many of the original features have been retained. The detached one-bedroom cottage provides a high quality of accommodation. This is the ideal location for a romantic break, walking or touring the dales.

ARNOLDS HOLIDAY COTTAGES
Leyburn
Contact: Mr and Mrs Arnold, Chantry Farmhouse, Main Street, West Witton, Leyburn DL8 4LU
T: (01969) 624303
F: (01969) 624303
E: holidaycottage2004@yahoo.com
I: www.arnoldsholidaycottages.com

OPEN All Year

Weekend and mid-week breaks may be available.

Low season per wk
£215.00–£310.00
High season per wk
£260.00–£410.00

Quality Assurance Standard

For an explanation of the quality and facilities represented by the stars please refer to the front of this guide. A more detailed explanation can be found in the information pages at the back.

YORKSHIRE

WHASHTON, North Yorkshire Map ref 5C3

★★★-★★★★★

3 Units
Sleeping 4-6

Enjoy a break in one of our beautifully converted, cosy cottages with wonderful views over open countryside. Peaceful, rural location with easy access to Richmond and Dales. The Dairy and Parlour have a double and twin, and High Barn has one double en suite and two twin bedrooms. All have comfy lounges, fully-equipped kitchen, dining area, patios and car parking.

MOUNT PLEASANT FARM
Richmond
Contact: Mrs Pittaway, Mount Pleasant Farm, Whashton, Richmond DL11 7JP
T: (01748) 822784
F: (01748) 822784
E: info@mountpleasantfarmhouse.co.uk
I: www.mountpleasantfarmhouse.co.uk

OPEN All Year

Low season per wk
£210.00-£600.00
High season per wk
£600.00-£700.00

WHITBY, North Yorkshire Map ref 5D3 Tourist Information Centre Tel: (01947) 602674

★★★★

12 Units
Sleeping 2-6

Bright, spacious, contemporary apartments set in a beautifully restored 18thC building. Situated around a peaceful, award-winning courtyard. Convenient for harbour, beach and all local amenities. Private, off-street parking. Our commitment is to provide superior-quality accommodation for your holiday.

DISCOVERY ACCOMMODATION
Whitby
Contact: Mrs Pam Gilmore, Discovery Accommodation, 11 Silver Street, Whitby YO21 3BX
T: (01947) 821598
F: (01947) 600406
E: info@discoveryaccommodation.com
I: www.discoveryaccommodation.com

OPEN All Year

Payment accepted: Delta, Mastercard, Switch, Visa, Euros

10% discount for guests re-booking.

Low season per wk
£300.00-£450.00
High season per wk
£350.00-£550.00

Location Complete addresses for properties are not given and the town(s) listed may be a distance from the actual establishment. Please check the precise location at the time of booking.

Shoreline Cottages

Shoreline Cottages won a Silver Award in the 'Self-Catering Holiday of the Year' category of the National Excellence in England Tourism Awards 2004 for its eighteen quality character cottages in and around Whitby. They all have four or five star ratings and have been beautifully furnished and styled throughout by an interior designer. You can choose from a variety of cottages of various sizes and locations. While some are cosy and compact, reflecting their origins as fishermen's cottages, others are more spacious and literally next door to each other.

Contact: Sue Brooks, PO Box 135, LEEDS, LS14 3XJ
Telephone: 0113 244 8410 Facsimile: 0113 244 9826

18 Units sleeping 2-8, OPEN All year round
2005 GUIDE PRICES
Low Season per week: £400 - £800;
High Season per week: £550 - £1260

Email: reservations@shoreline-cottages.com Web: www.shoreline-cottages.com

YORKSHIRE

WHITBY continued

EAST CLIFF COTTAGES, HARDWICK COTTAGE

★★★
1 Unit
Sleeping 6

A charming Grade II Listed fisherman's cottage at the foot of the famous 199 steps, right in the heart of old Whitby. The cottage has lots of character and great views of Whitby from all windows. Private, sunny yard. Parking available.

Whitby
Contact: Dr Thornton, Brookhouse, Dam Lane, Leavening, Malton YO17 9SF
T: (01653) 658249
E: enquiries@seasideholiday.co.uk
I: www.seasideholiday.co.uk

OPEN All Year

Weekends and part weeks are available Sep-Mar.

Low season per wk
£190.00–£455.00
High season per wk
£250.00–£490.00

At-a-glance symbols

Symbols at the end of each entry give useful information about services and facilities. A key to symbols can be found inside the back cover flap. Keep this open for easy reference.

RIVER ESK APARTMENTS

Brand new 2004, luxury riverside apartments (one ground floor – ideal for disabled access). Superbly located in a prime position, in the heart of Whitby. Boasting magnificent aspect overlooking the upper harbour and abbey. Personal parking, riverside walkways, intercom access and lift. Apartments are sited alongside the harbour to the right of the vista view.

Mrs Pauline Foran
River Esk Apartments Spital Bridge, Whitehall Landing Whitby YO22 4AE
T: (01947) 811264
E: foran9827@freeserve.co.uk

www.river-esk-apartments.co.uk

YORKSHIRE

WHITBY continued

★★-★★★★★
8 Units
Sleeping 2-7

SWALLOW HOLIDAY COTTAGES
Whitby
Contact: Mr & Mrs McNeil, Long Lease Farm, Hawsker, Whitby YO22 4LA
T: (01947) 603790
I: www.swallowcottages.co.uk

Swallow Cottages, regarded by many as the premier rural cottages in the area, converted Listed buildings and others in two groups. Ample parking. Some wheelchair-friendly. Situated in North Yorkshire Moors National Park. All have stunning views. Two miles to Whitby centre. Short breaks available in winter.

OPEN All Year

Payment accepted: Delta, Mastercard, Switch, Visa

Low season per wk £125.00–£395.00
High season per wk £215.00–£515.00

★★★
1 Unit
Sleeping 1-6

WHITE HORSE COTTAGE
Whitby
Contact: Mr George & Mr Steven Walker, The Shakespeare Inn, 120 Eldon Road, Rotherham S65 1RD
T: (01709) 367031

Grade II Listed building with period features situated at the rear of the Old White Horse and Griffin pub. New pine beds. Gas fired central heating.

OPEN All Year

Low season per wk £150.00–£230.00
High season per wk £230.00–£310.00

★★★-★★★★★
12 Units
Sleeping 1-8

WHITE ROSE HOLIDAY COTTAGES
Whitby
Contact: Mrs June Roberts, Greenacres, Brook Park, Briggswath, Whitby YO21 1RT
T: (01947) 810763
F: (01947) 811739
I: www.whiterosecottages.co.uk

New habourside apartments in Whitby and village properties in Sleights. Tastefully decorated and furnished for your pleasure and comfort. Centrally heated. Available all year. Ideal for coast/country. We aim to please with our quality accommodation and friendly customer service.

OPEN All Year

Reduced rates for autumn/winter breaks. Cosy, festively decorated properties for Christmas/New Year.

Low season per wk £180.00–£395.00
High season per wk £200.00–£700.00

WILSILL, North Yorkshire Map ref 5C3

★★★★
1 Unit
Sleeping 1-4

MANOR FARM BARN
Harrogate
Contact: Mr William & Mrs Kellie LaBonte, Wilsill, Harrogate HG3 5EB
T: (01423) 711386
F: (01423) 711069
E: b.labonte@btopenworld.com

Quiet, detached newly-converted barn by river Nidd and Nidderdale Way. Fantastic countryside views set in farmland. Children's play area.

OPEN All Year

Low season per wk £250.00–£300.00
High season per wk £300.00–£350.00

Map references
The map references refer to the colour maps at the front of this guide. The first figure is the map number; the letter and figure which follow indicate the grid reference on the map.

153

YORKSHIRE

YORK, York Map ref 4C1 *Tourist Information Centre Tel: (01904) 621756*

★★★★★
1 Unit
Sleeping 2-8

ABBEYGATE HOUSE
York
Contact: Mr & Mrs Halliday, 1 Grange Drive, Horsforth, Leeds LS18 5EQ
T: (0113) 258 9833

Superior new Georgian-style townhouse situated on the prestigious Bishops Wharf riverside development overlooking the medieval City walls and only a few minutes' walk from the city centre. Stunning new fully equipped shaker-style dining kitchen. Spacious lounge with four luxurious leather sofas and south-facing balcony. Jacuzzi bath. Private parking.

OPEN All Year
Payment accepted: Mastercard, Visa

Short breaks available. Discounts for smaller groups.

Low season per wk
Min £295.00

★★★
1 Unit
Sleeping 1-6

ACER BUNGALOW
York
Contact: Mrs Sandra Wreglesworth, The Acer Hotel, 52 Scarcroft Hill, York YO24 1DE
T: (01904) 653839
F: (01904) 677017
E: info@acerhotel.co.uk
I: www.acerbungalow.co.uk

High-quality accommodation – delightful bungalow situated in quiet area one mile from city centre and attractions. Comfort and good housekeeping are guaranteed. Power, heating, bed linen and towels are provided free. The bungalow is furnished to a high standard and is well equipped. Lovely gardens, and patio with seating and lighting.

OPEN All Year
Payment accepted: Euros

Short breaks available low season. Special discounts during less-busy periods. Please telephone (01904) 653839 for details of our special offers.

Low season per wk
£250.00-£350.00
High season per wk
£400.00-£485.00

★★★
1 Unit
Sleeping 1-4

BARBICAN MEWS
York
Contact: Mrs Helen Jones, Homefinders Holidays, 11 Walmgate, York YO1 9TX
T: (01904) 632660
F: (01904) 615388
E: agents@homefindersholidays.co.uk
I: www.homefindersholidays.co.uk

Barbican Mews is situated in the centre of York overlooking the walls. It has one double bedroom and one with bunk beds. There is also a very comfortable lounge with dining table and chairs. Outside it has a private paved patio with table etc, and there is also private parking.

OPEN All Year
Payment accepted: Amex, Mastercard, Switch, Visa, Euros

Low season per wk
£240.00-£330.00
High season per wk
£350.00-£400.00

Quality Assurance Standard
Star ratings and awards were correct at time of going to press but are subject to change. Please check at the time of booking.

YORKSHIRE

YORK continued

★★★★★
2 Units
Sleeping 1–2

THE BLUE ROOMS
York
Contact: Ms Lorraine Woodmansey, 4 Franklins Yard, Fossgate, York YO1 9TN
T: (01904) 673990
F: (01904) 658147
E: blue-rooms@blue-bicycle.co.uk
I: www.thebluebicycle.com

Overlooking the river Foss, The Blue Rooms occupy a secluded mews position and are equipped to the very highest standards. They offer luxury, convenience, privacy and comfort for that short romantic break or business trip. You will be welcomed on arrival with a bottle of champagne and fresh fruit basket with our compliments.

OPEN All Year
Payment accepted: Delta, Mastercard, Switch, Visa

Low season per wk
£500.00–£1,050.00
High season per wk
£500.00–£1,050.00

★★★
1 Unit
Sleeping 1–6

1 CLOISTERS WALK
York
Contact: Mrs Helen Jones, 11 Walmgate, York YO1 9TX
T: (01904) 632660
F: (01904) 651388
E: agents@homefindersholidays.co.uk
I: www.homefindersholidays.co.uk

Cloisters Walk is very central for shopping and sightseeing. The garden is beautiful and very private. Suitable for a couple or family.

OPEN All Year
Payment accepted: Amex, Mastercard, Switch, Visa, Euros

Low season per wk
£245.00–£335.00
High season per wk
£355.00–£395.00

★★★★
1 Unit
Sleeping 1–4

CRAMBECK COURT
York
Contact: Mrs Helen Jones, Homefinders Holidays, 11 Walmgate, York YO1 9TX
T: (01904) 632660
F: (01904) 651388
E: agents@homefindersholidays.co.uk
I: www.homefindersholidays.co.uk

Crambeck Court is a very attractive, first-floor flat in the centre of York. It has an en suite shower room and a main bathroom in the hall. The lounge has DVD, TV, CD player and video.

OPEN All Year
Payment accepted: Amex, Mastercard, Switch, Visa, Euros

Low season per wk
£365.00–£465.00
High season per wk
£485.00–£505.00

Rating Applied For
1 Unit
Sleeping 1–2

21 EMPERORS WHARF
Skeldergate
Contact: Mrs Helen Jones, 11 Walmgate, York YO1 9TX
T: (01904) 632660
F: (01904) 651388
E: agents@homefindersholidays.co.uk
I: www.homesfindersholidays.co.uk

Emperors Wharf is a modern flat at the river Ouse and has a balcony overlooking a pleasant garden. The fixtures and fittings are of a very high standard and it is near all the attractions in York – no need to use your car. Parking is enclosed in basement.

OPEN All Year
Payment accepted: Amex, Mastercard, Switch, Visa, Euros

Low season per wk
£240.00–£330.00
High season per wk
£350.00–£390.00

YORKSHIRE

YORK continued

★★★

1 Unit
Sleeping 1–4

17 ESCRICK STREET
York
Contact: Mrs Helen Jones, Homefinders Holidays,
11 Walmgate, York YO1 9TX
T: (01904) 632660
F: (01904) 651388
E: agents@homefindersholidays.co.uk
I: www.homefindersholidays.co.uk

Escrick Street is a very nice townhouse with one double and one twin bedroom. It is fully equipped and very close to the centre and shops. It has private parking.

OPEN All Year

Payment accepted: Amex, Mastercard, Switch, Visa, Euros

Low season per wk
£245.00–£335.00
High season per wk
£355.00–£395.00

Rating Applied For

1 Unit
Sleeping 1–5

THE JUNIPER
York
Contact: Mrs Helen Jones, 11 Walmgate, York YO1 9TX
T: (01904) 632660
F: (01904) 651388
E: agents@homefindersholidays.co.uk
I: www.homefindersholidays.co.uk

The Juniper is a most unusual modern garden flat in a renovated period townhouse. It has been very tastefully decorated with high-quality furnishings and is convenient for all tourist attractions and station. There is on-street parking.

OPEN All Year

Payment accepted: Amex, Mastercard, Switch, Visa, Euros

Low season per wk
£370.00–£470.00
High season per wk
£510.00–£610.00

★★★

8 Units
Sleeping 2–8

MERRICOTE COTTAGES
York
Contact: Mr Andrew Williamson, Merricote Cottages,
Malton Road, York YO32 9TL
T: (01904) 400256
F: (01904) 400846
E: merricote@hotmail.com
I: www.merricote-holiday-cottages.co.uk

Beautiful spot from which to explore the historic city of York (three miles), moors and coast. The cottages and bungalows are well appointed. Many amenities nearby.

OPEN All Year

Low season per wk
£200.00–£300.00
High season per wk
£360.00–£610.00

Rating Applied For

1 Unit
Sleeping 1–4

MINSTER VIEW
York
Contact: Mrs Helen Jones, 11 Walmgate, York YO1 9TX
T: (01904) 632660
F: (01904) 651388
E: agents@homefindersholidays.co.uk
I: www.homefindersholidays.co.uk

Minster View is a luxuriously appointed, two-bedroom apartment in the prestigious Stonegate Court development in the shadow of the Minster. No expense has been spared to create a magnificent, relaxing, contemporary environment. Secure, private terraces encourage outdoor living, and safe parking is near.

OPEN All Year

Payment accepted: Amex, Mastercard, Switch, Visa, Euros

Low season per wk
£370.00–£470.00
High season per wk
£510.00–£610.00

Quality Assurance Standard
Star ratings and awards are explained at the back of this guide.

YORKSHIRE

YORK continued

★★★★
1 Unit
Sleeping 1–4

145 MOUNT VALE
York
Contact: Mrs Helen Jones, Homefinders Holidays, 11 Walmgate, York YO1 9TX
T: (01904) 632660
F: (01904) 651388
E: agents@homefindersholidays.co.uk
I: www.homefindersholidays.co.uk

OPEN All Year

Payment accepted: Amex, Mastercard, Switch, Visa, Euros

Low season per wk
£245.00–£335.00
High season per wk
£355.00–£395.00

Mount Vale is a beautiful cottage with patio and garden where you have the best of both worlds as it is only 15 minutes' walk to the centre and Minster etc. It has one double and one twin bedroom and has a super atmosphere.

★★★★★
1 Unit
Sleeping 1–4

NUMBER 22 BOOTHAM TERRACE
York
Contact: Mrs Helen Jones, Homefinders Holidays, 11 Walmgate, York YO1 9TJ
T: (01904) 632660
F: (01904) 651388
E: agents@homefindersholidays.co.uk
I: www.homefindersholidays.co.uk

OPEN All Year

Payment accepted: Amex, Mastercard, Switch, Visa, Euros

Low season per wk
£365.00–£465.00
High season per wk
£485.00–£600.00

Bootham Terrace is a superb house; it has lots of room and is beautifully furnished and decorated. There is a large lounge and separate dining room. It has a very nice garden to sit in and is very central.

★★★★★
1 Unit
Sleeping 1–2

43 POSTERN CLOSE
York
Contact: Mr Gordon & Mrs Hilary Jones, 2 Chalfonts, York YO24 1EX
T: (01904) 702043
F: (01904) 702043
E: hilary@yorkcloisters.com
I: www.yorkcloisters.com

OPEN All Year

Payment accepted: Delta, Mastercard, Switch, Visa

Low season per wk
£310.00–£380.00
High season per wk
£440.00–£500.00

Stylish first floor apartment with lift, near to the city centre. The sitting room and balcony overlook the river Ouse. The corner site creates larger accommodation than many properties in the development, having a beautifully equipped separate dining kitchen with river views and a spacious bedroom with dressing area.

★★★★
1 Unit
Sleeping 1–2

44 POSTERN CLOSE
York
Contact: Mrs Christine Turner, Meadowcroft, Millfield, Willingham, Cambridge CB4 5HD
T: (01954) 201218
E: c.turner@gurdon.cam.ac.uk
I: www.yorkholidayflat.co.uk

OPEN All Year

Low season per wk
Min £290.00
High season per wk
Min £325.00

Double-bedroomed, self-contained riverside apartment within prestigious Bishops Wharf development. Five minutes walking distance from city centre. Sitting/dining room, small balcony, new kitchen, bathroom, parking space.

YORKSHIRE

YORK continued

★★★
1 Unit
Sleeping 1–5

29 RICHARDSON STREET
York
Contact: Mrs Helen Jones, Homefinders Holidays, 11 Walmgate, York YO1 9TX
T: (01904) 632660
F: (01904) 651388
E: agents@homefindersholidays.co.uk
I: www.homefindersholidays.co.uk

This is a very comfortable family house, a short walk from town and close to Rowntrees Park and shops. It has one double, one twin and one single room and there is also a futon if necessary.

OPEN All Year
Payment accepted: Amex, Mastercard, Switch, Visa, Euros

Low season per wk
£245.00–£335.00
High season per wk
£355.00–£395.00

★★★★
3 Units
Sleeping 1–2

SHAMBLES HOLIDAY APARTMENTS
York
Contact: Mr & Mrs Fletcher, Shambles Holiday Apartments, The Art Shop, 27-27A Shambles, York YO1 7LX
T: (01904) 623898
F: (01904) 671283
E: shamblesholiday-york@tinyworld.co.uk

Grade II Listed Georgian building in York's most famous medieval street, The Shambles. Adjacent open-air market and all city-centre facilities. No car parking.

OPEN All Year
Payment accepted: Delta, Mastercard, Switch, Visa

Low season per wk
Min £195.00
High season per wk
Max £395.00

★★★
5 Units
Sleeping 1–6

SPARROW HALL COTTAGES
Scrayingham
Contact: Mr Nick & Mrs Pam Gaunt, Sparrow Hall Cottages, Sparrow Hall, Scrayingham, York YO41 1JE
T: (01759) 372917
E: holidays@yorkcott-pool.freeuk.com
I: www.yorkcott-pool.freeuk.com

Central location in North Yorkshire. Within easy reach of historic York (11 miles to centre), North York Moors, coast and Dales. Well-equipped character cottages with log fires and private gardens. Indoor heated swimming pool open all year round. Ideal for couples and families. Peaceful rural location. Riding one mile.

OPEN All Year
Payment accepted: Delta, Mastercard, Switch, Visa, Euros

Low season per wk
£250.00–£300.00
High season per wk
£500.00–£640.00

Short breaks available Nov-mid-Mar. 3-night stay £187–£242. Christmas and New Year weeks £485–£599 per week.

★★★★
1 Unit
Sleeping 1–4

414 WESTGATE
York
Contact: Mrs Helen Jones, Homefinders Holidays, 11 Walmgate, York YO1 9TX
T: (01904) 632660
F: (01904) 651388
E: agents@homefindersholidays.co.uk
I: www.homefindersholidays.co.uk

Westgate is a stunning, fourth-floor apartment in a six-storey block situated near the station and town. Lift, concierge on site, main bedroom with en suite, family bathroom, fully fitted kitchen.

OPEN All Year
Payment accepted: Amex, Mastercard, Switch, Visa, Euros

Low season per wk
£365.00–£465.00
High season per wk
£485.00–£605.00

YORKSHIRE

YORK continued

★★★★
1 Unit
Sleeping 1–2

Woodsmill Quay is on the riverside and is a beautiful flat with one bedroom, which overlooks the Ouse. There is private parking and it is in the centre of York.

24 WOODSMILL QUAY
York
Contact: Mrs Helen Jones, Homefinders Holidays, 11 Walmgate, York YO1 9TX
T: (01904) 632660
F: (01904) 651388
E: agents@homefindersholidays.co.uk
I: www.homefindersholidays.co.uk

OPEN All Year

Payment accepted: Amex, Mastercard, Switch, Visa, Euros

Low season per wk
£245.00–£335.00
High season per wk
£355.00–£385.00

★★★★-★★★★★★
16 Units
Sleeping 2–7

YORK LAKESIDE LODGES
York
Contact: Mr Manasir, York Lakeside Lodges Ltd, Moor Lane, York YO24 2QU
T: (01904) 702346
F: (01904) 701631
E: neil@yorklakesidelodges.co.uk
I: www.yorklakesidelodges.co.uk

OPEN All Year

Low season per wk
£220.00–£355.00
High season per wk
£470.00–£705.00

Self-catering lodges and cottages in mature parkland around large fishing lake. Superstore across the road, coach to York centre every 10 minutes.

Use your *i*s

There are more than 550 Tourist Information Centres throughout England offering friendly help with accommodation and holiday ideas as well as suggestions of places to visit and things to do. You'll find addresses in the local phone book.

159

Explore at your leisure the **extensive canal** and river networks that are a legacy of the region's **industrial heritage**.

Heart of England

Looking for some inspiration? Here are a few ideas to get you started in the Heart of England. **experience** a Shakespeare play, performed in the great bard's birthplace. **discover** medieval history inside the ramparts of Warwick Castle. **explore** black-and-white villages in Shropshire and Herefordshire. **relax** with a drink at a canalside café in Birmingham's Brindleyplace.

THE REGION
Black Country, Herefordshire, Shropshire, Staffordshire, Warwickshire, Birmingham, Worcestershire

CONTACT
▸ **HEART OF ENGLAND TOURISM**
Larkhill Road, Worcester WR5 2EZ
T: (01905) 761100
F: (01905) 763450
www.visitheartofengland.com

HEART OF ENGLAND

The Heart of England is full of contrasts – you'll find England's second-largest city, historic towns, cathedrals, mighty battlements and ruined castles. Search out the region's industrial past or thrill to the excitement of a white-knuckle ride.

Big city buzz

Hit the pavements of Birmingham and you feel it instantly. The buzz of a great city. Start in the Bullring, the city's newly created retail experience the size of 26 football pitches in the centre of town! A stimulating glass-covered environment where you can shop, eat or just be. At one end is the bizarre, shimmering Selfridges building covered in over 15,000 aluminium-spun disks. Then head for the canalside bars and restaurants of Brindleyplace or the historic Jewellery Quarter.

Or opt for Coventry instead. A thousand years of history have left their imprint on the city, from the superb 14th-century guildhall to streets of timber-framed buildings and soaring church spires. But it's never been a city content to just look backwards. It boasts architect Sir Basil Spence's extraordinary modern cathedral and, like Birmingham, it is renewing and re-fashioning its city centre. With two world-renowned motor museums and the majestic ruins of medieval Kenilworth Castle in the surrounding area, you're guaranteed a great city break.

On the trail

By contrast, your jeans and trainers can feel rather out of place against the higgledy-piggledy backdrop of Tudor half-timbered buildings in the historic towns of Shrewsbury and Worcester. For more beautiful buildings, follow a trail of black-and-white villages in Shropshire and Herefordshire – they make wonderful photographs!

Or in spring, signposts will guide you through the stunning pink-and-white froth of the Blossom Trail, threading its way through the thousands of orchards in the Vale of Evesham.

In search of history

Head for Stratford-upon-Avon, Shakespeare's birthplace. With five houses associated with the bard, there is almost too much to see. Browse the antique shops before thrilling to a production performed by the Royal Shakespeare Company, the greatest exponent of his works. Then make your way to Warwick. Massive, brooding, battle-scarred. The temperature seems to drop and the hairs on the back of your neck rise as you enter England's bloody past inside the impenetrable ramparts of Warwick Castle.

Spend a day at Ironbridge Gorge, wandering among its many fascinating museums or at the Black Country Museum where electric tramcars and trolleybuses transport you back in time to the canalside village to watch costumed craftsmen bring the buildings to life with their local knowledge, practical skills and unique Black Country humour.

If it's historic houses and gardens that interest you, you're spoilt for choice in the Heart of England. Visit the great mansion at Shugborough, begun in 1693, or stroll through the parkland and woodlands of Trentham Gardens, both in Staffordshire.

Food for thought

Feeling hungry? Then you should visit the pretty market town of Ludlow on the Welsh borders. Here in the shadow of Ludlow Castle, are some of the best restaurants in the UK, and specialist food shops bursting with luscious British produce such as Evesham Asparagus.

Left, from top pedal your way around the region; peaceful countryside, Shropshire; reflecting on history, Ironbridge

Places to visit

Awarded VisitBritain's Quality Assured Visitor Attraction marque.

Acton Scott Historic Working Farm
Wenlock Lodge, Acton Scott, Shropshire
Tel: (01694) 781306
www.actonscottmuseum.co.uk
Living history in the Shropshire Hills. This working farm demonstrates farming and rural life in south Shropshire at the close of the 19thC.

Alton Towers
Alton, Staffordshire
Tel: 0870 520 4060
www.altontowers.com
Experience the thrills and excitement of Britain's No 1 theme park with rides and attractions such as Air, Oblivion, Nemesis, Congo River Rapids, Log Flume and the Tweenies live show.

Amazing Hedge Puzzle
The Jubilee Park, Symonds Yat, Herefordshire
Tel: (01600) 890360
Loose yourself in this traditional hedge maze, created to celebrate the Queen Elizabeth Jubilee in 1977. Visit the world's only hands-on interactive Museum of Mazes.

AZTEC Watersports
The Spring Holiday Park, Lower Moor, Worcestershire
Tel: (01386) 860013
An ideal learning environment with safe, shallow, clean, spring water and professional instructors for windsurfing, sailing, canoeing and lots more.

Birmingham Botanical Gardens and Glasshouses
Westbourne Road, Edgbaston, West Midlands
Tel: (0121) 454 1860
www.birminghambotanicalgardens.org.uk
Six hectares (15 acres) of ornamental gardens and glasshouses featuring the widest range of plants in the Midlands from tropical rainforest to arid desert. Aviaries with exotic birds, and a children's play area.

Black Country Living Museum
Tipton Road, Dudley, West Midlands
Tel: (0121) 557 9643
www.bclm.co.uk
Wander around original shops and houses, ride on a tramcar or fairground swingboat, chat by the coal-fired kitchen ranges, go down the mine or just soak up the atmosphere.

Cadbury World
Linden Road, Bournville, West Midlands
Tel: (0121) 451 4180
www.cadburyworld.co.uk
Indulge in the story of Cadbury's chocolate which includes a chocolate-making demonstration. Enjoy attractions for all ages, with free samples, free parking, shop and restaurant.

Coventry Cathedral
Priory Street, Coventry, West Midlands
Tel: (024) 7652 1200
www.coventrycathedral.org
This glorious 20thC cathedral rises above the stark ruins of the medieval cathedral which was destroyed in 1940. The visitor centre includes audio-visual shows.

Coventry Transport Museum
Hales Street, Coventry, West Midlands
Tel: (024) 7683 2425
www.mbrt.co.uk
A fascinating collection of cars and commercial vehicles from 1896, cycles from 1818, motorcycles from 1920 and Thrust 2 and Thrust SSC land speed record cars.

The Crystal Glass Centre
Churton House, Audnam, West Midlands
Tel: (01384) 354400
See the best of British and European crystal on show. The exhibition reveals the history of glass from its earliest days to the present.

---

162   This is just a selection of attractions available. Contact any Tourist Information Centre in the region for more ideas.

HEART OF ENGLAND

Drayton Manor Family Theme Park
Tamworth, Staffordshire
Tel: 0870 872 5252
www.draytonmanor.co.uk
Over 100 rides and attractions featuring some of the biggest, wettest and scariest rides around, including Apocalypse, the world's first stand up tower drop.

Droitwich Spa Brine Baths Complex
St Andrews Road, Droitwich, Worcestershire
Tel: (01905) 794894
www.brinebath.co.uk
Try a unique experience – floating weightless in natural Droitwich brine. Spa treatments plus fitness and health facilities such as physiotherapy, hydrotherapy and sports injury.

The Elgar Birthplace Museum
Crown East Lane, Lower Broadheath, Worcestershire
Tel: (01905) 333224
www.elgarfoundation.org
Country cottage birthplace of Sir Edward Elgar and the new Elgar Centre, giving a fascinating insight into his life, music, family, friends, musical development and inspirations.

Farncombe Estate Centre
Broadway, Worcestershire
Tel: 0845 230 8590
www.farncombeestate.co.uk
Music, writing, art, singing, meditation and yoga are just a selection of courses available for all throughout the year on this 120-ha (300-acre) private estate in the beautiful Cotswolds.

Hoar Park Craft Village and Antiques Centre
Hoar Park Farm, Nuneaton, Warwickshire
Tel: (024) 7639 4433
Craft and Antiques Centre, Garden Centre, Children's Farm, licensed restaurant, country walks, fishing pools and children's play area will keep you entertained. Regular craft and antique fairs are also held.

Ikon Gallery
Oozells Square, Brindleyplace, Birmingham
Tel: (0121) 248 0708
www.ikon-gallery.co.uk
One of Europe's foremost contemporary art galleries, presenting the work of national and international artists within an innovative educational framework.

Ironbridge Gorge Museums
Coalbrookdale, Telford, Shropshire
Tel: (01952) 435900
www.ironbridge.org.uk
See the world's first cast-iron bridge and visit the Museum of the Gorge, Tar Tunnel, Jackfield Tile Museum, Coalport China Museum, Rosehill House, Blists Hill Victorian Town and Iron and Enginuity Museum.

Ludlow Castle (ruin)
Castle Square, Ludlow, Shropshire
Tel: (01584) 873355
www.ludlowcastle.com
A former royal castle, these impressive ruins date from the 11th to the 16thC. It includes towers, a great hall and chambers as well as a shop and gallery.

Mamble Craft Centre Limited
Hall Farm, Mamble, Worcestershire
Tel: (01299) 832834
www.mamblecraftcentre.co.uk
Craft centre consisting of four workshops, gallery, tearoom, gift shop and courses room, housed in 17thC barns on an ancient medieval site with stunning views of Clee Hills.

Manor Farm Animal Centre and Donkey Sanctuary
Manor Farm, East Leake, Leicestershire
Tel: (01509) 852525
www.manorfarmanimalcentre.co.uk
A wide variety of animals and birds, small donkey sanctuary, nature trail, willow dens, adventure playgrounds, art and activity centre and straw maze will keep the family entertained.

National Sea Life Centre
The Water's Edge, Birmingham
Tel: (0121) 643 6777
www.sealifeeurope.com
Come face-to-face with hundreds of fascinating sea creatures from sharks to shrimps. Discover the pioneering seahorse breeding programme, and watch otters in their enclosure.

Newnham Paddox Gardens and Art Park
Newnham Paddox House, Monks Kirby, Warwickshire
Tel: (01788) 833513
www.newnhampaddox.com
12-ha (30-acre) open-air sculpture gallery set in idyllic 18thC landscaped park created by Capability Brown with woods, rare trees and lakes. Sculpture to view or buy.

Royal Brierley Crystal Experience
Tipton Road, Dudley, West Midlands
Tel: (0121) 530 5600
www.royalbrierley.com
Factory tours to see crystal being hand-made. Museum, factory shopping and attractive coffee shop open all year.

Secret Hills – The Shropshire Hill Discovery Centre
School Road, Craven Arms, Shropshire
Tel: (01588) 676000
www.shropshireonline.gov.uk/discover.nsf
All-weather, all-year-round family fun day out. Enjoy a simulated balloon ride over the Shropshire Hills and see the famous Shropshire mammoth. Café and shop.

Left tickle your taste buds at Cadbury World, Bournville; make a splash at Drayton Manor, Tamworth

Places to visit

Awarded VisitBritain's Quality Assured Visitor Attraction marque.

Severn Valley Railway
The Railway Station, Bewdley, Worcestershire
Tel: (01299) 403816
www.svr.co.uk
Take a ride on the standard-gauge steam railway running 16 miles between Kidderminster, Bewdley and Bridgnorth. Also see the collection of locomotives and passenger coaches.

Shakespeare's Birthplace
Henley Street, Stratford-upon-Avon, Warwickshire
Tel: (01789) 2040161
www.shakespeare.org.uk
Visit the world-famous house where William Shakespeare was born in 1564 and where he grew up. See the highly acclaimed Shakespeare Exhibition.

Shugborough Estate (National Trust)
Shugborough, Milford, Staffordshire
Tel: (01889) 881388
www.staffordshire.gov.uk/shugborough
18thC mansion with fine collections of furniture, paintings, silver and ceramics. Gardens and park with neo-classical monuments plus a Georgian farmstead and servants' quarters.

The Snowdome Leisure Island
River Drive, Tamworth, Staffordshire
Tel: 0870 500 0011
www.snowdome.co.uk
Real snow centre where you can ski, snowboard and toboggan indoors. Tuition and equipment provided. Bars, restaurants and other leisure activities available.

Walsall Arboretum
Lichfield Street, Walsall, West Midlands
Tel: (01922) 653148
www.walsallarboretum.co.uk
Picturesque Victorian park with over 70ha (170 acres) of gardens, lakes and parkland. Home to the famous Walsall Illuminations lights and laser show each autumn.

Walsall Leather Museum
Littleton Street West, Walsall, West Midlands
Tel: (01922) 721153
www.walsall.gov.uk/leathermuseum
Award-winning working museum in the saddlery and leathergoods 'capital' of Britain. Watch skilled craftsmen and women at work in this restored Victorian leather factory.

Warwick Castle
Warwick, Warwickshire
Tel: 0870 442 2000
www.warwick-castle.co.uk
Meet Warwick the Kingmaker in this mighty medieval castle with state rooms, armoury, dungeon, torture chamber and the Mill and Engine House attraction.

The Wedgwood Visitor Centre
Barlaston, Stoke-on-Trent, Staffordshire
Tel: (01782) 204218
www.thewedgwoodvisitorcentre.com
New £4.5 million visitor centre showing centuries of craftmanship on a plate. Audio-guided tour includes exhibition and demonstration areas. Shop and restaurants.

West Midland Safari and Leisure Park
Spring Grove, Bewdley, Worcestershire
Tel: (01299) 402114
www.wmsp.co.uk
See Britain's only pride of rare white lions. There's something for everyone: drive-through safari, pets corner, reptile house, sea lion theatre, hippo lakes, and family amusement rides.

Worcester Cathedral
College Green, Worcester, Worcestershire
Tel: (01905) 611002
www.cofe-worcester.org.uk
England's loveliest cathedral, with royal tombs, Medieval cloisters, an ancient crypt and magnificent Victorian stained glass. Refreshments and gift shop. Disabled access.

Above imposing Worcester Cathedral; state dining at Warwick Castle **Right** view a glass figure of Shakespeare in Stratford-upon-Avon

164   This is just a selection of attractions available. Contact any Tourist Information Centre in the region for more ideas.

HEART OF ENGLAND

Heart of England Tourism
Larkhill Road, Worcester WR5 2EZ
T: (01905) 761100 F: (01905) 763450
www.visitheartofengland.com

The following publications are available from Heart of England Tourism

Bed & Breakfast Touring Map including Camping and Caravan Parks 2005

Escape 2005/6 (Accommodation in the Heart of England)

Visit the Heart of England 2005 (Attractions in the Heart of England)

Travel information

By road:
Britain's main motorways (M1/M6/M5) meet in the Heart of England; the M40 links with the M42 south of Birmingham while the M4 provides fast access from London to the south of the region. These road links ensure that the Heart of England is more accessible by road than any other region in the UK.

By rail:
The Heart of England is served by an excellent rail network. InterCity rail services are fast and frequent from London and other major cities into the region. Trains run from Euston to Birmingham, Coventry, Rugby; from Paddington to the Cotswolds, Stratford-upon-Avon and Worcester; and from Marylebone to Birmingham and Stourbridge. From the main stations a network of regional routes takes you around the Heart of England.

Enjoy England official guides to quality

HEART OF ENGLAND

Where to stay in Heart of England

All place names in the blue bands, under which accommodation is listed, are shown on the maps at the front of this guide.

A complete listing of all VisitBritain assessed accommodation covered by this guide appears at the back.

Accommodation symbols

Symbols give useful information about services and facilities. Inside the back cover flap you can find a key to these symbols. Keep it open for easy reference.

ADMASTON, Staffordshire Map ref 4B3

★★★★
6 Units
Sleeping 2–10

Beautiful new barn conversions in quiet location overlooking Blithfield Reservoir. Close to Alton Towers and Peak District. Fishing, walking, birdwatching. Excellent pubs within two miles.

BLITHFIELD LAKESIDE BARNS
Rugeley
Contact: Mr Richard Brown, St Stephens Hill Farm, Steenwood Lane, Admaston, Rugeley WS15 3NQ
T: (01889) 500458
F: (01889) 500288
E: reser2000@aol.com
I: www.blithfieldlakesidebarns.co.uk

OPEN All Year

Low season per wk
£200.00–£500.00
High season per wk
£400.00–£900.00

ALL STRETTON, Shropshire Map ref 4A3

★★★
1 Unit
Sleeping 1–4

An environmentally friendly converted pottery in Area of Outstanding Natural Beauty. Ideal for walking or sightseeing. En suite shower room and lavatory, separate lavatory for guests using sofa bed. Woodburning stove, central heating, utility room, solar water heating, combo TV/DVD, treehouse and swing. Welcome wine and grocery pack.

THE POTTERY
All Stretton
Contact: Mr Chris Cotter, Overbatch House, Castle Hill, All Stretton SY6 6JX
T: (01694) 723511
F: (01694) 722397
E: chrisjcotter@yahoo.co.uk
I: www.churchstretton.co.uk/acpottery.htm

OPEN All Year

Short stays available (minimum 2 nights). Reduced rates for midweek breaks.

Low season per wk
£225.00–£250.00
High season per wk
Max £300.00

HEART OF ENGLAND

ALSTONEFIELD, Staffordshire Map ref 4B2

★★★★-★★★★★
2 Units

ANCESTRAL BARN & CHURCH FARM COTTAGE
Ashbourne
Contact: Mrs Sue Fowler, Ancestral Barn & Church Farm Cottage, Church Farm, Ashbourne DE6 2AD
T: (01335) 310243
F: (01335) 310243
E: sue@dovedalecottages.fsnet.co.uk
I: www.dovedalecottages.co.uk

OPEN All Year

Low season per wk
£320.00–£440.00
High season per wk
£550.00–£750.00

Idyllic country cottage, cosy and warm, nestling in a truly peaceful setting. Also our Ancestral Barn with luxurious canopy beds (two king-size), all en suite bathrooms, full of old world charm, character and medieval ambience, with polished floors, rich colours and antiques. Rambles from door to Dales. Organic farm near Dovedale.

★★★★★
1 Unit
Sleeping 5–6

DOVE COTTAGE FISHING LODGE
Ashbourne
Contact: Mrs M Hignett, Foxleaze Court, Preston, Cirencester GL7 5PS
T: (01285) 655875
F: (01285) 655885
E: info@dovecottages.co.uk
I: www.dovecottages.co.uk

OPEN All Year

2-rods fishing on River Dove (Apr-Oct). Short breaks available Oct-Apr (excl Christmas and New Year).

Low season per wk
£300.00–£580.00
High season per wk
£870.00–£1,130.00

Situated in a beautiful and idyllic part of Wolfscote Dale, enjoying stunning views along the River Dove. Relax in a comfortable and highly maintained family home. Let us spoil you with fires laid daily, welcome grocery basket, fresh bread, electric blankets and hand cream. Large gardens, toys, videos and ride-ons.

ALTON, Staffordshire Map ref 4B2

★★-★★★
6 Units
Sleeping 2–8

THE RADDLE INN
Stoke-on-Trent
Contact: Mr Wilkinson, The Raddle Inn, Quarry Bank, Stoke-on-Trent ST10 4HQ
T: (01889) 507278
F: (01889) 507520
I: www.logcabin.co.uk

OPEN All Year

Payment accepted: Amex, Delta, Mastercard, Switch, Visa, Euros

Low season per wk
£200.00–£350.00
High season per wk
£250.00–£450.00

A public house/restaurant, set in the countryside, with a log cabin overlooking Croxden Abbey.

Use your *i*s

There are more than 550 Tourist Information Centres throughout England offering friendly help with accommodation and holiday ideas as well as suggestions of places to visit and things to do. You'll find addresses in the local phone book.

167

HEART OF ENGLAND

ATHERSTONE, Warwickshire Map ref 4B3

★★★★
6 Units
Sleeping 1–7

HIPSLEY FARM COTTAGES
Atherstone
Contact: Mrs Ann Prosser, Waste Farm, Hurley, Atherstone
CV9 2LR
T: (01827) 872437
F: (01827) 875433
E: ann@hipsley.co.uk
I: www.hipsley.co.uk

OPEN All Year

Payment accepted: Delta, Mastercard, Switch, Visa, Euros

Low season per wk
£260.00–£450.00
High season per wk
£295.00–£575.00

Superb cottages carefully converted from old farm barns, each individually furnished to highest standards. Full central heating and all linen and towels included, fully equipped laundry. Enjoy the putting green, barbecue, lovely farm walks. Within easy reach of theatres, castles, cathedrals and museums of Stratford, Warwick, Lichfield and Birmingham.

BEWDLEY, Worcestershire Map ref 4A3 Tourist Information Centre Tel: (01299) 404740

★★★★
1 Unit
Sleeping 1–5

PEACOCK COACH HOUSE
Bewdley
Contact: Mrs Prisca Hall, Peacock House, Lower Park, Bewdley DY12 2DP
T: (01299) 400149
E: priscahall@hotmail.com

OPEN All Year

Low season per wk
£285.00–£345.00
High season per wk
£385.00–£450.00

Restored 17thC oak-beamed coach house, five minutes from Bewdley town centre and River Severn. Private walled garden with patio and barbecue.

★★★
1 Unit
Sleeping 1–8

RIVERVIEW COTTAGE
Bewdley
Contact: Mr & Mrs Giles, The Lodge, Station Road, Bewdley DY12 1BT
T: (01299) 403481
E: jgilesm81@aol.com
I: www.riverview-bdy.co.uk

OPEN All Year

Low season per wk
£220.00–£270.00
High season per wk
£250.00–£400.00

A 14thC, Grade II Listed cottage on the riverside. Three bedrooms, fully equipped and comfortably furnished. Five minutes' walk from the town centre.

BISHOP'S CASTLE, Shropshire Map ref 4A3

★★★★
1 Unit
Sleeping 4

MOUNT COTTAGE
Bishop's Castle
Contact: Mrs Heather Willis, Bull Lane, Bishop's Castle SY9 5DA
T: (01588) 638288
F: (01588) 638288
E: adamheather@btopenworld.com
I: www.mountcottage.co.uk

OPEN All Year

Low season per wk
Max £195.00
High season per wk
£250.00–£320.00

Converted 17thC barn. Very short walk to town. Well-equipped, modern fitted kitchen. Bathroom/wc with over-bath shower and second wc. Beams throughout.

Accessibility Look for the symbols which indicate National Accessible Scheme standards for hearing and visually impaired guests in addition to standards for guests with mobility impairment. You can find an index of all scheme participants at the back of this guide.

HEART OF ENGLAND

BODENHAM, Herefordshire Map ref 2A1

3 Units
Sleeping 1–5

BODENHAM FORGE
Bodenham, Hereford
Contact: Mrs Mary Nickols, Bodenham Forge, The Forge, Bodenham, Hereford HR1 3JZ
T: (01568) 797144
E: sgnickols@yahoo.co.uk
I: www.bodenhamforge.co.uk

Outstanding accommodation, ten minutes' walk from super pub food. Picturesque, orchard setting, next to river, on edge of a conservation village with country walks. Hampton Court gardens, Black and White village trail, city of Hereford all within easy reach. Ludlow, Hay-on-Wye a little further. A lovely place to stay.

OPEN All Year

Two night stays often available.

Low season per wk
£175.00–£295.00
High season per wk
£300.00–£395.00

BORESFORD, Herefordshire Map ref 4A3

1 Unit
Sleeping 1–7

HICKS FARM HOLIDAYS-ROSE COTTAGE
Boresford
Contact: Mrs Susan Bywater, Hicks Farm, Boresford, Presteigne LD8 2NB
T: (01544) 260237
E: holidays@hicksfarm.fsbusiness.co.uk
I: www.stmem.com/rosecottage

OPEN All Year

Low season per wk
£475.00–£515.00
High season per wk
£600.00–£695.00

Hideaway on our quiet farm set amidst breathtaking, unspoilt countryside. Our 18thC detached cottage is homely and superbly equipped, perfect for a truly relaxing holiday.

BRIDGNORTH, Shropshire Map ref 4A3   *Tourist Information Centre Tel: (01746) 763257*

5 Units
Sleeping 2–9

BULLS HEAD COTTAGES
Bridgnorth
Contact: Mr David Baxter, The Bulls Head, Chelmarsh, Bridgnorth WV16 6BA
T: (01746) 861469
F: (01746) 862646
E: dave@bullshead.fsnet.co.uk
I: www.virtual-shropshire.co.uk/bulls-head-inn

Superbly furnished cottage with stone feature walls. Fully equipped, centrally heated. Quiet location near owner's 17thC inn. Ideally situated for visiting the many places of interest nearby. Choice of other cottages/apartments (three on ground floor). Short breaks available.

OPEN All Year

Payment accepted:
Mastercard, Switch, Visa

Low season per wk
£185.00–£270.00
High season per wk
£210.00–£465.00

---

1 Unit
Sleeping 1–2

THE GRANARY
Bridgnorth
Contact: Mrs Sarah Allen, The Granary, The Old Vicarage, Ditton Priors, Bridgnorth WV16 6SQ
T: (01746) 712272
F: (01746) 712288
E: allens@oldvicditton.freeserve.co.uk

OPEN All Year

Low season per wk
Min £130.00
High season per wk
Min £180.00

Farm granary in unspoilt South Shropshire countryside. Bridgnorth within easy reach, Ludlow 16 miles. Studio sitting room, bedroom, kitchen, bathroom. Excellent walking.

Credit card bookings
If you book by telephone and are asked for your credit card number it is advisable to check the proprietor's policy should you cancel your reservation.

169

HEART OF ENGLAND

BRIDGNORTH continued

★★★★
1 Unit
Sleeping 4

JACOB'S COTTAGE
Bridgnorth
Contact: Mrs Gilly Wooldridge, 2 Allscott, Nr Worfield, Bridgnorth WV15 5JX
T: (01746) 716687
F: (01746) 716687
I: www.virtual-shropshire.co.uk/jacob

Delightful Georgian cottage in conservation area. A unique and individual town hideaway, tastefully renovated, decorated and furnished, Five minutes' stroll to Severn Valley Stream Railway, river, shops and pubs. All linen, towels and every other necessity provided. Warm, cosy and beautifully equipped. Children and pets welcome. Parking permit supplied.

OPEN All Year
Payment accepted: Euros

Low season per wk
£200.00–£225.00
High season per wk
£275.00–£375.00

BROADWAY, Worcestershire Map ref 2B1

★★★
1 Unit
Sleeping 1–2

HESTERS HOUSE
Broadway
Contact: Mrs Liz Dungate, Inglenook, Brokengate Lane, Denham, Uxbridge UB9 4LA
T: (01895) 834357
F: (01895) 832904
E: pdungate@aol.com

Charming, oak-beamed, end of terrace cottage with small courtyard, fronting Broadway High Street. A delightful, cosy home from which to tour Cotswolds. Prices include gas and electricity.

OPEN All Year except Christmas and New Year

Low season per wk
Min £195.00
High season per wk
£225.00–£250.00

BROMSGROVE, Worcestershire Map ref 4B3 Tourist Information Centre Tel: (01527) 831809

★★★
1 Unit
Sleeping 1–4

EAST VIEW APARTMENT
Bromsgrove
Contact: Mrs Alma Westwood, East View Apartment, Little Shortwood, Brockhill Lane, Tardebigge, Bromsgrove B60 1LU
T: (01527) 63180
F: (01527) 63180
E: westwoodja@hotmail.com

Comfortable apartment in 17thC cottage in beautiful countryside. 10 minutes M5/M42. Convenient for many local places of interest. Birmingham 30 minutes. Ideal for holidays/business.

OPEN All Year except Christmas
Payment accepted: Euros

Low season per wk
Min £145.00
High season per wk
Max £200.00

BROMYARD, Herefordshire Map ref 2B1 Tourist Information Centre Tel: (01432) 260280

★★★★
3 Units
Sleeping 2–6

BOYCE HOLIDAY COTTAGES
Bromyard
Contact: Alison Richards, Boyce Holiday Cottages, Boyce Farm, Stanford Bishop, Worcester WR6 5UB
T: (01886) 884248
F: (01886) 884187
E: ah.richards@btopenworld.com

Beautifully converted former stone farm buildings, with vaulted ceilings and original oak beams. Colour brochure available. Coarse fishing available on premises.

OPEN All Year

Low season per wk
£188.00–£291.00
High season per wk
£288.00–£471.00

CHURCH STRETTON, Shropshire Map ref 4A3

★★
1 Unit
Sleeping 4

BROOK HOUSE COTTAGE
Church Stretton
Contact: Mr & Mrs J Worley, Rosehill, Chestnut Walk, Felcourt, East Grinstead RH19 2LB
T: (01342) 870444

Located below Wenlock Edge, five miles west of Much Wenlock. Adjoins farmhouse, having its own entrance, parking and large garden. Open May to October.

Payment accepted: Euros

Low season per wk
Min £125.00
High season per wk
Min £225.00

HEART OF ENGLAND

CHURCH STRETTON continued

★★★★
2 Units
Sleeping 4-5

Part of an 18thC farm courtyard, sited next to an oak-framed threshing barn. The cottages are tastefully furnished, retaining many original beams and features, and with magnificent views of Wenlock Edge. Ideally suited to those seeking the real 'heart of the country'. Sorry, no smoking or pets.

GRANARY COTTAGE AND THE LONG BARN
Church Stretton
Contact: Mr & Mrs Kirkwood, Granary Cottage and The Long Barn, Lower Day House, Church Preen, Church Stretton SY6 7LH
T: (01694) 771521
E: bookings@lowerdayhouse.com
I: www.lowerdayhouse.com

OPEN All Year

Short breaks available from end Oct-Easter.

Low season per wk
£200.00–£240.00
High season per wk
£240.00–£375.00

★★★★
1 Unit
Sleeping 1-3

A pretty barn conversion in beautiful, quiet countryside. Views to the nearby Stretton Hills offering excellent walking and touring opportunities. Large, comfortable furnished living room and well-equipped kitchen. Exposed beams in the spacious, galleried, double bedroom. Easy access to Ludlow, Shrewsbury and Church Stretton, with good local restaurants.

LEASOWES COTTAGE
Shrewsbury
Contact: Mrs Margaret Harris, Leasowes, Watling Street, Longnor, Shrewsbury SY5 7QG
T: (01694) 751351
E: paul-harris@c-stretton.fsnet.co.uk
I: www.virtual-shropshire.co.uk/leasowes

Payment accepted: Euros

3-night stays available Apr-Sep.

Low season per wk
£185.00–£235.00
High season per wk
£240.00–£280.00

★★★
7 Units
Sleeping 1-4

LONGMYND HOTEL
Church Stretton
Contact: Mr Chapman, Longmynd Hotel, Cunnery Road, Church Stretton SY6 6AG
T: (01694) 722244
F: (01694) 722718
E: reservations@longmynd.co.uk
I: www.longmynd.co.uk

OPEN All Year

Payment accepted: Amex, Delta, Diners, Mastercard, Switch, Visa

Low season per wk
£175.00–£270.00
High season per wk
£245.00–£415.00

The hotel offers restaurant meals, afternoon tea, bar snacks and use of swimming pool, sauna, pitch 'n' putt and croquet lawn.

★★★
1 Unit
Sleeping 1-4

THE SAPLING AT OAKWOOD COTTAGE
Church Stretton
Contact: Mrs Jan Oram, Oakwood Cottage, Marshbrook, Church Stretton SY6 6RG
T: (01694) 781347
E: oakwoodcottage01@aol.com

OPEN All Year

Low season per wk
Min £150.00
High season per wk
Min £250.00

A beautifully decorated and furnished self-contained annex for up to four adults. Ground floor bedrooms, views from lounge, large garden. Fully equipped kitchen.

Important note Information on accommodation listed in this guide has been supplied by the proprietors. As changes may occur you are advised to check details at the time of booking.

HEART OF ENGLAND

CHURCH STRETTON continued

1 Unit
Sleeping 1–2

THE STABLES
Church Stretton
Contact: Mrs Maureen Burd, Station House,
Church Stretton SY6 6AX
T: (01694) 722057
I: www.chruchstretton.co.uk/acburd.htm

The Stables is a cosy, carefully furnished, beamed cottage, designed for one couple. Close to all amenities in an Area of Outstanding Natural Beauty. Situated in a quiet cul-de-sac with accessible and unrestricted walks over open hills and National Trust land from the doorstep. This is the best of both worlds!

OPEN All Year

Low season per wk
Min £250.00
High season per wk
Min £315.00

COTSWOLDS

See under Broadway

See also Cotswolds in the South East England and South West England sections

CRAVEN ARMS, Shropshire Map ref 4A3

2 Units
Sleeping 2–4

SWALLOWS NEST AND ROBIN'S NEST
Craven Arms
Contact: Mrs Caroline Morgan, Strefford Hall,
Craven Arms SY7 8DE
T: (01588) 672383
E: strefford@btconnect.com
I: www.streffordhall.co.uk

Set in the lovely South Shropshire countryside, surrounded by fields and close to Wenlock Edge, this stable conversion consists of Swallow's Nest, which is on the ground floor and is suitable for less mobile visitors, and Robin's Nest, which is on the first floor. Each offers one double en suite, fitted kitchen and large sitting/dining room.

OPEN All Year
Payment accepted: Euros

Low season per wk
Min £180.00
High season per wk
Max £260.00

ELMLEY CASTLE, Worcestershire Map ref 2B1

1 Unit
Sleeping 1–2

THE COTTAGE MANOR FARM HOUSE
Pershore
Contact: Mr & Mrs Brian and Pat Lovett, The Cottage Manor Farm House, Main Street, Elmley Castle, Pershore WR10 3HS
T: (01386) 710286
F: (01386) 710112

OPEN All Year

Low season per wk
£130.00–£160.00
High season per wk
£170.00–£190.00

Small cottage attached to original village farmhouse and beautiful garden, at the foot of Bredon Hill. Excellent for trekking and touring the Cotswolds and Malverns.

WEB

www.visitengland.com
Log on for information and inspiration. The latest information on places to visit, events and quality assessed accommodation.

HEART OF ENGLAND

EVESHAM, Worcestershire Map ref 2B1 Tourist Information Centre Tel: (01386) 446944

★★★★
1 Unit
Sleeping 2–6

Delightful Grade II Listed thatched black and white cottage with many traditional and original period features. Spacious, tastefully furnished, all modern facilities. Large enclosed garden, patio area, garden furniture. Private and peacefully situated. Ample parking. Ideal touring base. Family supervised. No pets. Brochures available.

THATCHERS END
Evesham
Contact: Mr & Mrs Wilson, 60 Pershore Road, Evesham WR11 2PQ
T: (01386) 446269
F: (01386) 446269
E: trad.accom@virgin.net
I: http://freespace.virgin.net/trad.accom

OPEN All Year
Payment accepted: Amex, Delta, Diners, Mastercard, Switch, Visa, Euros

Low season per wk
£340.00–£450.00
High season per wk
£450.00–£550.00

FOREST OF DEAN
See South West England section

HEREFORD, Herefordshire Map ref 2A1 Tourist Information Centre Tel: (01432) 268430

★★★★
1 Unit
Sleeping 6

Formerly the medieval watergate of Hereford Castle, Castle Cliffe provides luxury riverside accommodation. Period furnishings throughout, open fires and private, south-facing garden with beautiful views. Recently fitted kitchen and wonderful atmospheric bathroom. Set in historic parkland with town centre, cathedral and local amenities four minutes' walk.

CASTLE CLIFFE EAST
Hereford
Contact: Mr Mark Hubbard and Mr P Wilson, Castle Cliffe West, 14 Quay Street, Hereford HR1 2NH
T: (01432) 272096
E: mail@castlecliffe.net
I: www.castlecliffe.net

OPEN All Year

Short breaks available all year. Claim a 10% discount by mentioning 'Where to Stay' or VisitBritain.

Low season per wk
£350.00–£550.00
High season per wk
£600.00–£850.00

★★★★
1 Unit
Sleeping 1–3

Much-praised wing of owners' detached house in pleasant surroundings and pretty garden with ancient cider mill. Situated on city fringe with rural views, close to church, pub, shop and bus service, it is 30 minutes' walk into the city centre. Comfortable and peaceful, for non-smokers only.

RUSHFORD
Hereford
Contact: Mrs Roberts, Rushford, 7 Belle Bank Avenue, Hereford HR4 9RL
T: (01432) 273380
F: (01432) 273380

OPEN All Year except Christmas and New Year

Low season per wk
£120.00–£150.00
High season per wk
£180.00–£200.00

Location Complete addresses for properties are not given and the town(s) listed may be a distance from the actual establishment. Please check the precise location at the time of booking.

173

HEART OF ENGLAND

IRONBRIDGE, Shropshire Map ref 4A3 Tourist Information Centre Tel: (01952) 884391

★★★
1 Unit
Sleeping 4

LANGDALE COTTAGE
Ironbridge
Contact: Mr Keith Blight, 30 Kingswood Place, Boundary Walk, Knowle, Fareham PO17 5FQ
T: (01329) 830171

This comfortable, two-bedroomed restored 19thC cottage is situated in the beautiful Ironbridge Gorge just 0.5 miles from the famous Iron Bridge. It is an ideal base for exploring the town and the World Heritage museum sites as well as the ancient towns and hills of surrounding Shropshire.

OPEN All Year

Low season per wk
£150.00–£210.00
High season per wk
£265.00–£325.00

KENILWORTH, Warwickshire Map ref 4B3 Tourist Information Centre Tel: (01926) 748900

★★★★
2 Units
Sleeping 1–4

JACKDAW COTTAGE AND WREN'S NEST
Kenilworth
Contact: Mrs Lynn Grierson, The White Bungalow, 6 Canterbury Close, Kenilworth CV8 2PU
T: (01926) 855616
F: (01926) 513189
E: kgrierson@ukonline.co.uk

Cosy, well-furnished old world cottages in conservation area, on edge of historic town. Picturesque setting near castle. Convenient for Stratford, Warwick, Cotswolds, NEC and NAC.

OPEN All Year

Low season per wk
£250.00–£310.00
High season per wk
£340.00–£380.00

★★★
1 Unit
Sleeping 6

THE LITTLE BARN
Kenilworth
Contact: Mrs Oliver, Crewe Farm Barns, Crewe Lane, Kenilworth CV8 2LA
T: (01926) 850692

Tastefully converted barn in a secluded yard.

High season per wk
Max £300.00

KENLEY, Shropshire Map ref 4A3

★★★★
2 Units
Sleeping 2–4

NO 1 & 2 COURTYARD COTTAGES
Shrewsbury
Contact: Mrs Annabel Gill, Lower Springs Farm, Courtyard Cottages, Shrewsbury SY5 6PA
T: (01952) 510841
F: (01952) 510841
E: a-gill@lineone.net
I: www.courtyardcottages.com

Immaculate, recently converted cottages with exposed oak beams. Large garden and stocked trout pools in lovely, peaceful valley with panoramic views of Wenlock Edge.

OPEN All Year

Low season per wk
£200.00–£375.00
High season per wk
£225.00–£400.00

Special breaks

Many establishments offer special promotions and themed breaks. These are highlighted in red. (All such offers are subject to availability.)

HEART OF ENGLAND

LEAMINGTON SPA, Warwickshire Map ref 4B3 *Tourist Information Centre Tel: (01926) 742762*

★★★★
1 Unit
Sleeping 1–2

BARN OWL COTTAGE
Leamington Spa
Contact: Mrs Beatrice Norman, Fosseway Barns, Fosse Way, Offchurch, Leamington Spa CV33 9BQ
T: (01926) 614647
F: (01926) 614647
E: bnorman@fossebarn.prestel.co.uk
I: barnowlcottage.co.uk

Superbly appointed luxury cottage in delightful rural setting close to Warwick, Stratford and the Cotswolds. Tastefully decorated living/dining room, modern, well-equipped fitted kitchen and attractive twin-bedded room. Delightful, landscaped cottage garden with patio. Open views and nearby public right of way.

OPEN All Year
Payment accepted: Euros

Short breaks available. 10% discount if booking 2 weeks.

Low season per wk
£225.00–£270.00
High season per wk
£270.00–£335.00

★
2 Units
Sleeping 3–5

BLACKDOWN FARM COTTAGES
Leamington Spa
Contact: Mr & Mrs R Solt, Blackdown Farm, Sandy Lane, Leamington Spa CV32 6QS
T: (01926) 422522
F: (01926) 450996
E: bobby@solt.demon.co.uk

OPEN All Year

Low season per wk
£150.00–£250.00
High season per wk
£200.00–£350.00

Cottages converted from farm buildings, in the countryside between Leamington Spa and Kenilworth. Convenient for Shakespeare country, Warwick, Coventry and the Cotswolds.

★★★★
4 Units
Sleeping 2–7

FURZEN HILL FARM
Leamington Spa
Contact: Mrs Christine Whitfield, Furzen Hill Farm, Cubbington Heath, Leamington Spa CV32 7UJ
T: (01926) 424791
F: (01926) 424791

OPEN All Year

Low season per wk
Min £190.00
High season per wk
Max £375.00

Cottages at Cubbington, ideally situated for Warwick, Stratford-upon-Avon and NEC. Large garden. Use of hard tennis court.

LEDBURY, Herefordshire Map ref 2B1 *Tourist Information Centre Tel: (01531) 636147*

★★★
1 Unit
Sleeping 2–5

COACH HOUSE APARTMENT
Ledbury
Contact: Mr & Mrs Williams, Ross Road, Ledbury HR8 2LP
T: (01531) 631199
F: (01531) 631476
E: leadon.house@amserve.net
I: www.leadonhouse.net

OPEN All Year
Payment accepted: Amex, Mastercard, Switch, Visa, Euros

Low season per wk
£175.00–£225.00
High season per wk
£245.00–£325.00

Former coach house in the attractive themed grounds of Leadon House Hotel. High-quality 2001 conversion provides comfortable and spacious ground floor accommodation.

Map references The map references refer to the colour maps at the front of this guide. The first figure is the map number; the letter and figure which follow indicate the grid reference on the map.

HEART OF ENGLAND

LEDBURY continued

★★★–★★★★★
5 Units
Sleeping 2–5

WHITE HOUSE COTTAGES
Ledbury
Contact: Mrs Marianne Hills, White House Cottages, The White House, Aylton, Ledbury HR8 2RQ
T: (01531) 670349
F: (01531) 670057
E: hills1477@aol.com
I: www.whitehousecottages.co.uk

Aylton, a conservation area, is four miles from Ledbury. The cottages, former farm buildings, are set within the mature grounds of owner's 17thC property. An excellent centre for exploring the Wye Valley, the Malverns, Forest of Dean, the Welsh Borders and the cathedral cities of Hereford, Gloucester and Worcester.

OPEN All Year

3-night short breaks available all year, subject to certain booking restrictions. Please ring for details.

Low season per wk
£159.00–£232.00
High season per wk
£309.00–£452.00

LEEK, Staffordshire Map ref 4B2 Tourist Information Centre Tel: (01538) 483741

★★★★
1 Unit
Sleeping 4

WREN COTTAGE
Leek
Contact: Mr Robert & Mrs Elizabeth Lowe, Rudyard, Leek ST13 8PR
T: (01260) 226341
F: (01260) 226341
E: fairboroughs@talk21.co.uk
I: www.fairboroughs.co.uk

Converted 16thC barn on working beef/sheep farm. High specification. Historic features. Panoramic views. Fully heated. Convenient for Peak District, Potteries, Alton Towers. Manchester Airport 45 minutes.

OPEN All Year

Low season per wk
Min £150.00
High season per wk
Max £375.00

LEINTWARDINE, Herefordshire Map ref 4A3

★★★
1 Unit
Sleeping 2–4

OAK COTTAGE
Craven Arms
Contact: Mrs Vivienne Faulkner, 24 Watling Street, Craven Arms SY7 0LW
T: (01547) 540629
F: (01547) 540181
E: fmjones@skg.co.uk

16thC, Grade II Listed, timber-framed cottage, carefully restored and equipped, in borderland village on River Teme. Glorious walking, fishing, good food. You can even coracle.

OPEN All Year

Low season per wk
£200.00–£210.00
High season per wk
£220.00–£300.00

★★–★★★★
2 Units
Sleeping 2–11

OAKLANDS FARM
Craven Arms
Contact: Mrs Sally Ann Swift, Kinton, Leintwardine, Craven Arms SY7 0LT
T: (01547) 540635
E: mrpaswift@aol.co.uk

Lovely conversion of a traditional barn offering excellent cottages in a perfect walking location. Views over the River Teme. Ideal for a peaceful escape. Short breaks available.

OPEN All Year

Low season per wk
£210.00–£300.00
High season per wk
£280.00–£430.00

LUDLOW, Shropshire Map ref 4A3 Tourist Information Centre Tel: (01584) 875053

★★★★
1 Unit
Sleeping 6

THE AVENUE FLAT
Ludlow
Contact: Mr Meredith, The Avenue Flat, The Avenue, Ashford Carbonell, Ludlow SY8 4DA
T: (01584) 831616
E: ronmeredithavenue@talk21.com

Second floor of large, attractive, peaceful country residence set in six acres. Completely independent access with fine views and very comfortable, well-equipped accommodation.

OPEN All Year

Low season per wk
£130.00–£200.00
High season per wk
£200.00–£320.00

HEART OF ENGLAND

LUDLOW continued

BRIBERY COTTAGE
★★★
1 Unit

Ludlow
Contact: Mr Richard & Mrs Juliet Caithness, 2 Dinham, Ludlow SY8 1EJ
T: (01584) 872828
F: (01584) 872828
E: richard.caithness@virgin.net
I: www.virtual-shropshire.co.uk/bribery-cottage

OPEN All Year

Low season per wk
Min £145.00
High season per wk
Min £260.00

Three-storey terraced house, c1830 and a Grade II Listed building, set in historic surroundings near market square and castle. Rear conservatory leads into attractive walled garden.

CHURCH BANK
★★
1 Unit
Sleeping 5

Ludlow
Contact: Mrs Rosemary Laurie, Church Bank, Burrington, Ludlow SY8 2HT
T: (01568) 770426
E: laurie2502@lineone.net

Low season per wk
£170.00–£190.00
High season per wk
£200.00–£220.00

This stone cottage lies in a beautiful, peaceful valley near River Teme. There are excellent walks on the hills and forest trails. Wildlife abounds. Historic Ludlow is five winding miles away. Large, comfortable sitting room with woodburner and many books. Dinner can be provided by arrangement. Available March to October.

GOOSEFOOT BARN COTTAGES
★★★★
3 Units
Sleeping 4–6

Craven Arms
Contact: Mrs Sally Loft, Goosefoot Barn Cottages, Pinstones, Diddlebury, Craven Arms SY7 9LB
T: (01584) 861326
E: sally@goosefoot.freeserve.co.uk
I: www.goosefootbarn.co.uk

OPEN All Year

Short breaks available, minimum 2 nights. Winter special offers.

Low season per wk
£190.00–£260.00
High season per wk
£320.00–£440.00

Converted in 2000 from stone and timbered barns, the cottages are individually decorated and equipped to the highest standards. Each cottage has en suite facilities and private garden or seating area. Situated in a secluded valley with walks from the doorstep through beautiful Corvedale. Ideally located for exploring South Shropshire.

THE GRANARY
★★★
1 Unit
Sleeping 1–3

Craven Arms
Contact: Mr & Mrs Mercer, The Granary, Tana Leas Farm, Craven Arms SY7 9DZ
T: (01584) 823272
F: (01584) 823272
E: r.mercer@tinyworld.co.uk
I: www.southshropshire.org.uk/granary

Low season per wk
£195.00–£210.00
High season per wk
£210.00–£235.00

Recently refurbished converted granary in Area of Outstanding Natural Beauty. Ideal for quiet holiday. Ludlow six miles. Second property in Ludlow's historic Broad Street. Open all year.

 Visitor attractions For ideas on places to visit refer to the introduction at the beginning of this section. Look out for the VisitBritain Quality Assured Visitor Attraction signs.

HEART OF ENGLAND

LUDLOW continued

★★★★
1 Unit
Sleeping 1–4

HAZEL COTTAGE
Craven Arms
Contact: Mrs Rachel Sanders, Duxmoor Farm,
Craven Arms SY7 9BQ
T: (01584) 856342
F: (01584) 856696
E: RachelSanders@mac.com
I: www.stmem.com/hazelcottage

OPEN All Year

Short breaks available.

Low season per wk
Min £195.00
High season per wk
Max £410.00

Unspoilt period cottage, retaining its original features, with antiques. It comprises a living room with Victorian range (working perfectly), dining room, kitchen, hall, Victorian bathroom, two bedrooms with washbasins. Set in its own peaceful and private cottage garden with beautiful, panoramic views of the surrounding countryside. Five miles north of historic Ludlow.

★★★★
1 Unit
Sleeping 6

MARYVALE LODGE
Ludlow
Contact: Mrs Alison Cundall, Palmers House,
7 Corue Street, Ludlow SY8 1DB
T: (01584) 878353
F: (01584) 873010
E: mail@maryvalecottages.co.uk
I: www.maryvalecottages.co.uk

OPEN All Year

Payment accepted: Euros

Low season per wk
Max £400.00
High season per wk
Max £600.00

Detached, well-appointed house situated in scenic and peaceful location right in the heart of Ludlow. Features stunning woodland views.

★★
1 Unit
Sleeping 1–4

POST HORN COTTAGE
Ludlow
Contact: Ms Helen Davis, 32 Leamington Drive,
Chilwell, Nottingham NG9 5LJ
T: (0115) 922 2383

OPEN All Year

Low season per wk
£160.00–£210.00
High season per wk
£210.00–£250.00

Charming two-storey cottage in historic town-centre building with exposed beams and small, private patio. In quiet courtyard off Broad Street.

LYONSHALL, Herefordshire Map ref 2A1

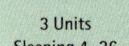

★★★★–★★★★★★
3 Units
Sleeping 4–26

FIELD COTTAGE, THE SHERRIFFS & GARDENERS COTTAGE
Kington
Contact: Mrs Joanna Hilditch, Whittern Farms Ltd,
Lyonshall, Kington HR5 3JA
T: (01544) 340241
F: (01544) 340253
E: info@whiteheronproperties.com
I: www.whiteheronproperties.com

OPEN All Year

Payment accepted:
Mastercard, Switch, Visa

Low season per wk
Min £350.00
High season per wk
Max £2,700.00

Charming properties set in remote Herefordshire countryside, all recently refurbished in opulent style with open fires or logburners. Field Cottage is in a panoramic orchard setting. Gardeners Cottage is in the old estate walled garden. The Sherriffs, a Listed Queen Anne house, is spacious and comfortable with large, mature gardens.

 Prices Please check prices and other details at the time of booking.

HEART OF ENGLAND

MALVERN, Worcestershire Map ref 2B1 *Tourist Information Centre Tel: (01684) 892289*

★★★
1 Unit
Sleeping 1–4

THE COACH HOUSE
Great Malvern
Contact: Mrs Jill Jones, 58 North Malvern Road,
Malvern WR14 4LX
T: (01684) 569562
E: jjmalvern@onetel.com

OPEN All Year

Low season per wk
£215.00–£295.00
High season per wk
£330.00–£365.00

Detached, turn-of-the-century coach house conversion in the heart of Great Malvern. Set in a secluded garden.

★★★
3 Units
Sleeping 2–6

THE DELL HOUSE
Malvern
Contact: Mr Ian Burrage, The Dell House, Green Lane,
Malvern Wells, Malvern WR14 4HU
T: (01684) 564448
F: (01684) 893974
E: burrage@dellhouse.co.uk
I: www.dellhouse.co.uk

OPEN All Year

Low season per wk
£175.00–£250.00
High season per wk
£295.00–£450.00

The apartments form the wing of the Regency main house, with the Coach House across its cobbled courtyard, all set in two acres of mature grounds.

MILWICH, Staffordshire Map ref 4B2

★★★★
2 Units
Sleeping 4–6

SUMMERHILL FARM
Stafford
Contact: Mrs Patricia Milward, Summerhill Farm,
Summer Hill, Milwich, Stafford ST18 0EL
T: (01889) 505546
F: (01889) 505692
E: p.milward@btinternet.com
I: www.summerhillfarmapartment.co.uk

OPEN All Year

Low season per wk
£126.00–£141.00
High season per wk
£141.00–£294.00

Fully-equipped apartments, close to Alton Towers, Peak District, Shugborough Hall and Wedgwood. Indoor heated swimming pool at owner's discretion.

MINSTERLEY, Shropshire Map ref 4A3

★★★
1 Unit
Sleeping 3

OVENPIPE COTTAGE
Shrewsbury
Contact: Mr & Mrs A Thornton, Tankerville Lodge,
Stiperstones, Shrewsbury SY5 0NB
T: (01743) 791401
F: (01743) 792305
E: tankervillelodge@supanet.com

OPEN All Year
Payment accepted: Euros

Low season per wk
£100.00–£160.00
High season per wk
£160.00–£190.00

Attractively restored barn in peaceful countryside setting close to Stiperstones nature reserve and Long Mynd in dramatic Shropshire hills. Superb walking, touring. Shop, inn nearby.

MUCH WENLOCK, Shropshire Map ref 4A3

★★★
1 Unit
Sleeping 1–4

QUEEN STREET
Much Wenlock
Contact: Mrs Elizabeth Ann Williams, 68 Church Hill,
Penn, Wolverhampton WV4 5JD
T: (01902) 341399
E: williams_letting@hotmail.com

OPEN All Year except Christmas

Low season per wk
£170.00–£210.00
High season per wk
£250.00–£280.00

Secluded detached cottage in heart of small medieval market town. Spacious comfortable rooms; sunny walled garden. Short walk to Priory, museum, Tourist Information Centre, shops and pubs.

Quality Assurance Standard

Star ratings and awards were correct at time of going to press but are subject to change. Please check at the time of booking.

HEART OF ENGLAND

OAKAMOOR, Staffordshire Map ref 4B2

★★★
1 Unit
Sleeping 1–3

THE ANNEXE AT THE OLD FURNACE
Oakamoor
Contact: Annette and John Higgins, The Annexe at The Old Furnace, Greendale, Oakamoor ST10 3AP
T: (01538) 703331
I: www.oldfurnace.co.uk

OPEN All Year

Low season per night
Min £30.00
High season per night
£30.00–£50.00

Set in magnificent countryside by a stream in Dimmingsdale; ideal for walking, cycling, bird-watching etc. Three single beds. Short breaks all year. High standard.

ORCOP, Herefordshire Map ref 2A1

★★★★
3 Units
Sleeping 2–5

THE BURNETT FARMHOUSE
Hereford
Contact: Mr & Mrs Gooch, The Burnett Farmhouse, Hereford HR2 8SF
T: (01981) 540999
F: (01981) 540999
E: burnett.farmhouse@talk21.com
I: www.burnettfarmhouse.co.uk

OPEN All Year

Payment accepted: Amex, Delta, Diners, Mastercard, Switch, Visa

Short breaks available all year round.

Low season per wk
£215.00–£270.00
High season per wk
£325.00–£425.00

Set in magnificent rolling countryside, these beautifully renovated farm buildings, with oak beams and old world charm, adjoin The Burnett Farmhouse. Far-reaching views across Orcop Valley to Garway Hill. Excellent base to discover the Wye Valley, Forest of Dean, Brecon Beacons, Malvern Hills, Welsh borders. Ideal walking/painting/wildlife. Payment by credit card welcomed.

PEAK DISTRICT

See under Alstonefield

See also Peak District in the East Midlands section

PEMBRIDGE, Herefordshire Map ref 2A1

★★★
2 Units
Sleeping 1–4

THE GRANARY AND THE DAIRY
Leominster
Contact: Mrs Owens, The Grove, Leominster HR6 9HP
T: (01544) 388268
F: (01544) 388154

OPEN All Year

Low season per wk
£170.00–£270.00
High season per wk
£270.00–£320.00

Attractive barn conversions in 200-acre farm in secluded valley near black and white villages, Offa's Dyke and Mortimer Trail. Friendly farm atmosphere. Children and pets welcome.

★★
1 Unit
Sleeping 5

ROWENA COTTAGE
Leominster
Contact: Mrs Diana Malone, The Cottage, Holme, Newark NG23 7RZ
T: (01636) 672914
E: dianamalone56@hotmail.com

OPEN All Year

Short breaks available out of school holidays. Minimum of 2 nights for £90.

Low season per wk
Min £200.00
High season per wk
Max £360.00

Charming black and white 16thC cottage with open fire and storage heaters in the picturesque village of Pembridge on the River Arrow. An ideal centre for the countless attractions of the Border country, Welsh Marches, Herefordshire, Shropshire and Offa's Dyke. Local shops and pubs. Fishing, riding, cycling and gliding nearby.

 Enjoy England official guides to quality
Please mention this guide when making your booking.

HEART OF ENGLAND

PRIORS HARDWICK, Warwickshire Map ref 2C1

Rating Applied For

1 Unit
Sleeping 1–2

PEPPERPOT LODGE
Contact: Mrs Prophet, School Cottage, London End, Southam CV47 7SL
T: (01327) 262015
F: (01327) 264663

OPEN All Year

Low season per wk
£130.00–£150.00
High season per wk
£150.00–£180.00

Tastefully appointed self-catering flat for two people. Annexe to 'chocolate box' thatched cottage, surrounded by wonderful countryside. Children up to 10 years.

ROSS-ON-WYE, Herefordshire Map ref 2A1 *Tourist Information Centre Tel: (01989) 562768*

★★★

2 Units
Sleeping 2–4

THE GAME LARDERS AND THE OLD BAKEHOUSE
Ross-on-Wye
Contact: Miss Anthea McIntyre, Wythall Estate, Ross-on-Wye HR9 5SD
T: (01989) 562688
F: (01989) 763225
E: wythall@globalnet.co.uk
I: www.wythallestate.co.uk

Self-contained cottages in the wing of a 16thC manor-house in a secluded setting with garden, duck pond and wooded grounds. You will enjoy peace and quiet here and see an abundance of wildlife. Well equipped and furnished in period style, the cottages are warm and comfortable.

OPEN All Year

Short breaks available Oct–Mar. 3-night stay.

Low season per wk
£210.00–£290.00
High season per wk
£250.00–£400.00

★★★★

1 Unit
Sleeping 1–2

OLD CIDER HOUSE
Ross-on-Wye
Contact: Mrs Heather Jackson, Lowcop, Glewstone, Ross-on-Wye HR9 6AN
T: (01989) 562827
F: (01989) 563877
E: man.of.ross.ltd@farming.co.uk

OPEN All Year

Low season per wk
£190.00–£220.00
High season per wk
£220.00–£260.00

Old cider house on fruit farm in Wye Valley, converted to character cottage with beams and antique furniture. Overlooking apple orchards. Warm in winter.

RUGBY, Warwickshire Map ref 4C3 *Tourist Information Centre Tel: (01788) 534970*

★★★★★

1 Unit
Sleeping 4–6

THE SADDLERY
Rugby
Contact: Mrs Heckford, Manor Farm, Brooks Close, Willoughby, Rugby CV23 8BY
T: (01788) 890256
E: office@thesaddlery.org.uk
I: thesaddlery.org.uk

A converted saddlery of the highest standard with luxurious accommodation. Tastefully furnished and centrally heated throughout. Situated in a quiet village on working farm in courtyard. Private parking and patio. Ideal location on Warwicks/Northants border. Close to Warwick, Stratford-upon-Avon, Leamington Spa, Silverstone and Althorpe.

OPEN All Year

Low season per wk
£350.00–£380.00
High season per wk
£380.00–£520.00

Credit card bookings
If you book by telephone and are asked for your credit card number it is advisable to check the proprietor's policy should you cancel your reservation.

HEART OF ENGLAND

SHREWSBURY, Shropshire Map ref 4A3 *Tourist Information Centre Tel: (01743) 281200*

★★
1 Unit
Sleeping 1–4

INGLENOOK
Shrewsbury
Contact: Mrs J.M Mullineux, Fach-Hir, Brooks,
Welshpool SY21 8QP
T: (01686) 650361

OPEN All Year

Low season per wk
£80.00–£100.00
High season per wk
£200.00–£250.00

Bungalow in peaceful surroundings, three miles from the centre of historic Shrewsbury town. Ample parking alongside. Gardens and lawn.

★★★★
1 Unit
Sleeping 1–4

YEWS BARN
Shrewsbury
Contact: Ms Hiorns, 5 Humbers Way, Telford TF2 8LH
T: (01952) 605915
E: gpassant@aol.com
I: www.yewsbarn.co.uk

OPEN All Year

Low season per wk
£155.00–£245.00
High season per wk
£205.00–£295.00

Romantic getaway. You'll experience an overwhelming sense of peace in Shropshire's beautiful countryside. Luxury abode with spa bath and four-poster bed – the ultimate treat.

STOKE-ON-TRENT, Stoke-on-Trent Map ref 4B2 *Tourist Information Centre Tel: (01782) 236000*

★★★★
1 Unit
Sleeping 11–14

FIELD HEAD FARM HOUSE HOLIDAYS
Stoke-on-Trent
Contact: Ms Janet Hudson, Stoney Rock Farm, Waterhouses, Stoke-on-Trent ST10 3LH
T: (01538) 308352
F: (01538) 308352
E: janet@field-head.co.uk
I: www.field-head.co.uk

OPEN All Year

Bargain mid-week breaks, short breaks, late-booking discount.

Low season per wk
£560.00–£1,190.00
High season per wk
£560.00–£1,190.00

Grade II Listed farmhouse situated within the southern Peak District and the Staffordshire moorlands. Set in beautiful, secluded surroundings close to Dovedale and the Manifold Valley. Ideal country for the walker, horse-rider or cyclist. Well equipped, Sky TV, spa, bath, pets' corner. Alton Towers 15-minute drive. All pets and horses welcome.

STRATFORD-UPON-AVON, Warwickshire Map ref 2B1 *Tourist Information Centre Tel: 0870 160 7930*

★★★★
1 Unit
Sleeping 1–4

55 BULL STREET
Stratford-upon-Avon
Contact: Mr John Barlow, JSB Consulting Ltd,
2 Old Town, Statford-upon-Avon CV37 6BG
T: (01789) 268378
F: (01789) 268715
E: info@55bullstreet.com
I: www.55bullstreet.com

OPEN All Year

Low season per wk
£250.00–£350.00
High season per wk
£400.00–£500.00

Victorian townhouse, furnished to high standards throughout. Two bedrooms, separate bathroom, ground floor utility/shower room. Mature enclosed rear garden.

Important note Information on accommodation listed in this guide has been supplied by the proprietors. As changes may occur you are advised to check details at the time of booking.

182

HEART OF ENGLAND

STRATFORD-UPON-AVON continued

★★★
1 Unit
Sleeping 1-3

CHESTNUT COTTAGE
Stratford-upon-Avon
Contact: Mrs Joyce Rush, Gospel Oak House,
Gospel Oak Lane, Pathlow, Stratford-upon-Avon
CV37 0JA
T: (01789) 292764

OPEN All Year except
Christmas and New Year

Low season per wk
Min £190.00
High season per wk
£220.00–£250.00

Set in splendid, secluded grounds by woodland, with far-reaching views. Well appointed, attractively furnished, ample parking. Two and a half miles from Stratford-upon-Avon.

★★★
1 Unit
Sleeping 1-5

FOSBROKE COTTAGE
Bidford-on-Avon
Contact: Mrs Susan Swift, 4 High Street, Bidford-on-Avon, Alcester B50 4BU
T: (01789) 772327
E: mark@swiftvilla.fsnet.co.uk
I: www.smoothhound.co.uk/hotels/fosbroke.html

OPEN All Year

Low season per wk
£230.00–£320.00
High season per wk
£395.00–£450.00

Attractive Grade II Listed cottage in riverside village. Modern comforts and facilities combined with original period features. Ten minutes from Stratford.

UPPER HULME, Staffordshire Map ref 4B2

★★★
1 Unit
Sleeping 2-4

FIELD HOUSE COTTAGE
Leek
Contact: Mr David Roberts, Field House Cottage, Upper Hulme, Leek ST13 8TZ
T: (01538) 300023
F: (01538) 300023
E: lesleyroberts@field-house.fsnet.co.uk

OPEN All Year

Low season per wk
Min £200.00
High season per wk
Min £300.00

A two-bedroom stone cottage in secluded location near Hencloud and The Roaches. Ideal for walkers and climbers.

WARWICK, Warwickshire Map ref 2B1 Tourist Information Centre Tel: (01926) 492212

★★★
1 Unit
Sleeping 1-4

COPES FLAT
Warwick
Contact: Mrs Draisey, Forth House, 44 High Street, Warwick CV34 4AX
T: (01926) 401512
F: (01926) 490809
E: info@forthhouseuk.co.uk
I: www.forthhouseuk.co.uk

OPEN All Year
Payment accepted: Delta, Mastercard, Switch, Visa, Euros

Low season per wk
£220.00–£250.00
High season per wk
£250.00–£320.00

Secluded, town centre, self-contained coach house flat. Sitting room/dining room, bedroom, bathroom, kitchen, telephone. Adjacent to castle, close to restaurants. Large roof garden. Non-smokers only, please.

WELLINGTON, Telford and Wrekin Map ref 4A3

★★★★
1 Unit
Sleeping 4

THE COACH HOUSE
Wrockwardine
Contact: Mrs Fellows, Old Vicarage, Wrockwardine, Telford TF6 5DG
T: (01952) 244859
F: (01952) 255066
E: mue@mfellows0.freeserve.co.uk
I: www.the-coach-house-wrockwardine.co.uk

OPEN All Year

Low season per wk
£240.00–£350.00
High season per wk
£350.00–£400.00

Detached private house providing centrally heated, two-bedroomed accommodation. Pleasant location, surrounded by farms yet close to Ironbridge, Shrewsbury and the Welsh Marches.

Location Complete addresses for properties are not given and the town(s) listed may be a distance from the actual establishment. Please check the precise location at the time of booking.

HEART OF ENGLAND

WETTON, Staffordshire Map ref 4B2

★★★★-★★★★★

6 Units
Sleeping 4–8

WETTON BARNS HOLIDAY COTTAGES
Wetton
Contact: Mrs T Reason, Chatsworth Estate Office, Bakewell DE45 1PJ
T: (01246) 565379
F: (01246) 583464
E: wettonbarns@chatsworth.org
I: www.chatsworth.org

OPEN All Year

Low season per wk
£300.00–£500.00
High season per wk
£480.00–£810.00

Three traditional barns on the Chatsworth Estate at Wetton have been converted and furnished under the supervision of the Dowager Duchess of Devonshire into six attractive and well-equipped cottages. Wonderful walks in the Manifold and Dove valleys. Free entry to Chatsworth House and Gardens (for weekly bookings) when open.

WHITBOURNE, Herefordshire Map ref 2B1

★★★

1 Unit
Sleeping 2–11

CRUMPLEBURY FARMHOUSE
Worcester
Contact: Mrs Anne Evans, Crumplebury Farmhouse, Worcester WR6 5SG
T: (01886) 821534
F: (01886) 821534
E: a.evans@candaevans.fsnet.co.uk
I: www.whitbourne-estate.co.uk

OPEN All Year

Low season per wk
£330.00–£850.00
High season per wk
£330.00–£595.00

Owner-maintained, comfortable and cosy five-bedroomed farmhouse on family farm. Ideal reunions, family gatherings, walking. Enclosed garden. Quiet. Wheelchair access. Coarse fishing available.

WORCESTER, Worcestershire Map ref 2B1 Tourist Information Centre Tel: (01905) 726311

★★★

1 Unit
Sleeping 2–6

LITTLE LIGHTWOOD FARM
Worcester
Contact: Mrs Rogers, Hazeldene, Little Lightwood Farm, Lightwood Lane, Cotheridge, Worcester WR6 5LT
T: (01905) 333236
F: (01905) 333236
E: lightwood.holidays@virgin.net
I: www.lightwoodfarm.co.uk

OPEN All Year

Low season per wk
£175.00–£275.00
High season per wk
£275.00–£400.00

Working farm with delightful views of Malvern Hills. Just off the A44 Worcester to Leominster road, 3.5 miles from Worcester.

WYE VALLEY

See under Hereford, Ross-on-Wye

WYTHALL, Worcestershire Map ref 4B3

★★★-★★★★★

7 Units
Sleeping 4–6

INKFORD COURT COTTAGES
Whythall
Contact: Mr Bedford, Inkford Court Cottages, Alcester Road, Whythall B47 6DL
T: (01564) 822304
F: (01564) 829618

OPEN All Year

Low season per wk
£195.00–£325.00
High season per wk
£200.00–£365.00

Cottages, part of a restoration and conversion of 18thC period farm buildings, set in 6.5 acres. Ideally located for Heart of England.

Map references The map references refer to the colour maps at the front of this guide. The first figure is the map number; the letter and figure which follow indicate the grid reference on the map.

What makes the **perfect break?**

Big city buzz or peaceful country panoramas? Take a fresh look at England and you may be surprised that everything is here on your very own doorstep. Where will you go? Make up your own mind and enjoy England in all its diversity.

experience... remember paddling on sandy beaches, playing Poohsticks in the forest, picnics at open-air concerts, tearooms offering home-made cakes... **discover...** make your own journey of discovery through England's cultural delights: surprising contrasts between old and new, traditional and trend-setting, time-honoured and contemporary...
explore... while you're reading this someone is drinking in lungfuls of fresh air on a hillside with heart-stopping views or wandering through the maze that can be in the garden of a stately home or tugging on the sails of a boat skimming across a lake... **relax...** no rush to do anything or be anywhere, time to immerse yourself in your favourite book by a roaring log fire or glide from a soothing massage to a refreshing facial, ease away the tension...

to enjoy England...

visit**england**.com™

With over **2,000** years of heritage, a **lively art** and events programme and a **thriving** pub culture.

East Midlands

Looking for some inspiration? Here are a few ideas to get you started in the East Midlands. **experience** food from around the world in Nottingham. **discover** the hidden gardens at Belvoir Castle. **explore** the limestone caves of the Peak District. **relax** on a boat on the Grand Union Canal.

THE REGION
Leicestershire and Rutland, Lincolnshire, Northamptonshire, Nottinghamshire, Peak District and Derbyshire

CONTACT
▸ **EAST MIDLANDS TOURISM**
www.enjoyeastmidlands.com
Leicestershire and Rutland
www.goleicestershire.com
Lincolnshire
www.visitlincolnshire.com
Northamptonshire
www.enjoynorthamptonshire.com
Nottinghamshire
www.experiencenottinghamshire.com
Peak District and Derbyshire
www.derbyshirethepeakdistrict.com
www.visitpeakdistrict.com

EAST MIDLANDS

Do you love that adrenalin rush or are you more into a laid back holiday? Whether your idea of perfect happiness is cave diving or watching the world go by very slowly from a canal-boat, you will find it in the East Midlands.

Break out in the city

East Midlands' cities make perfect short breaks. Visit Lincoln's cathedral and castle and then absorb the vibrant atmosphere along Brayford waterfront as the city comes to life. With a lively art and events programme, you can indulge in all your favourite pleasures. While here sample some Lincolnshire plumbread and Lincolnshire Poacher cheeses.

Or go in search of Robin Hood, and the story of lace-making in Nottingham. A medieval city with a thoroughly modern heart, Nottingham is one of the clubbing capitals of the Midlands and has more bars, restaurants and clubs than you've had hot cappuccinos.

In Leicester, get a flavour of the city in Belgrave Road, a street saturated in colourful silks, saris and spices and enjoy the buzz of the lively, covered market – just the place to sample a tasty Melton Mowbray pork pie, or Stilton and Red Leicester cheeses.

You are guaranteed a warm welcome in the great multicultural city of Derby, bursting with entertainment venues, museums, parks and shops. Fans of real ale should come in July for the annual CAMRA festival.

Wealth and power

Wealth and power simply ooze from the very foundations of great houses like Elizabethan Hardwick Hall and Chatsworth House, the Palace of the Peaks, where the gardens are as magnificent as the house. Nearby, taste some delicious Bakewell pudding in the village where it originated. Other fantastic gardens from all periods include Althorp (the final resting place of Princess Diana) and Belvoir Castle where you'll find the hidden Spring Gardens.

On the waterfront

Get the wind in every kind of sail along the Lincolnshire coast; water-ski or row at the National Watersports Centre at Holme Pierrepont in Nottinghamshire or try white-water rafting at Nene Whitewater Centre. Something less energetic? Stroll around the shore and watch the activity at Rutland Water, one of the largest man-made lakes in Western Europe, or take a gentle cruise on the Grand Union Canal, the river Nene or Soar. Discover special wildlife habitats throughout the intricate waterways of the Lincolnshire Fens. The Fens Discovery Centre at Spalding explains how man overcame nature and tamed the inhospitable marshland.

Plenty of activity

Walking, cycling, climbing, potholing. Enjoy them all in the East Midlands. Completing even a small section of the Pennine Way Long Distance Footpath will lift your spirits and make you crave for more and what could be more appropriate than to bowl through the picturesque Derwent Valley, a World Heritage Site, on a bike, one of its most important inventions.

Left, from top Robin Hood statue, Nottingham; drifting along the Grand Union Canal, Stoke Bruerne; be amazed at Chatsworth House in the Peak District

Enjoy England official guides to quality

Places to visit

 Awarded VisitBritain's Quality Assured Visitor Attraction marque.

78 Derngate
Northampton
Tel: (01604) 603407
www.78derngate.org.uk
Discover the Charles Ronnie Mackintosh designed interior and supporting exhibition, including life and work of patron WJ Bassett-Lowke, maker of engineering models. Strictly by pre-booked timed entry only.

American Adventure
Ilkeston, Derbyshire
Tel: 0845 330 2929
www.americanadventure.co.uk
Action and entertainment for all ages, including The Missile white-knuckle rollercoaster, Europe's tallest skycoaster and the world's wettest log flume.

Belton House, Park and Gardens (National Trust)
Belton, Lincolnshire
Tel: (01476) 566116
www.nationaltrust.org.uk
Magnificent restoration country house, with fine plasterwork ceilings and woodcarvings, portraits and oriental porcelain. Formal gardens, orangery and landscaped park.

Belvoir Castle
Belvoir, Leicestershire
Tel: (01476) 871002
www.belvoircastle.com
Enjoy magnificent views of the Vale of Belvoir. Art treasures include works by Poussin, Rubens, Holbein and Reynolds. See also the Queen's Royal Lancers display.

Berzerk Leisure
Moulton Park, Northamptonshire
Tel: (01604) 647213
Large indoor activity centre featuring inflatables, ballpons and slides, where children aged 12 months to 10 years will enjoy letting off steam. Restaurant and ample free parking.

Bosworth Battlefield Visitor Centre and Country Park
Sutton Cheney, Leicestershire
Tel: (01455) 290429
www.leics.gov.uk
Site of the Battle of Bosworth Field between Richard II and Henry VII in 1485. Explore the visitor centre with models, exhibitions, flags, armour, a film theatre and illustrated battle trails.

Brocks Hill Environment Centre and Country Park
Oadby, Leicester
Tel (0116) 271 4514
www.brockshill.co.uk
Be amazed at this environmentally friendly building promoting energy efficiency and sustainability set in 67 acres of country park. Play area, café and human sundial.

Butlins
Skegness, Lincolnshire
Tel: (01754) 762311
www.butlinsonline.co.uk
A feast of fun, magic and laughter with the Redcoats, Skyline Pavilion, Toyland, Sub Tropical Waterworld, tenpin bowling and entertainment centre with live shows.

Chatsworth House, Garden, Farmyard & Adventure Playground
Chatsworth, Derbyshire
Tel: (01246) 582204
www.chatsworth.org
One of the great Treasure Houses of England. More than 30 richly decorated rooms, garden with fountains, a cascade and maze. Farmyard and Adventure Playground.

Conkers: at the Heart of the National Forest
Near Ashby, Leicestershire
Tel: (01283) 216633
www.visitconkers.com
Innovative indoor exhibitions, including the Tree Top Adventure Walk, are complemented by 120-acres of trails, sculpture and habitats. Restaurants, shops and crafts, plus fantastic playpark and a train. Year-round activities.

EAST MIDLANDS

Crich Tramway Village
Crich, Derbyshire
Tel: (01773) 854321
www.tramway.co.uk
A collection of over 70 trams from Britain and overseas from 1873-1969 with tram rides, a period street scene, depots, a power station, workshops and exhibitions.

Denby Pottery Visitor Centre
Denby, Derbyshire
Tel: (01773) 740799
www.denbypottery.co.uk
See how pottery is made on one of the daily factory tours. Museum, Denby and Dartington Crystal factory shops, garden centre, gift shop, Cookery Emporium and Courtyard Restaurant.

The Galleries of Justice
Shire Hall, Nottingham
Tel: (0115) 952 0555
www.galleriesofjustice.org.uk
An atmospheric experience of justice over the ages located in and around an original 19thC courthouse and county gaol, brought to life by live actors.

Great Central Railway
Great Central Station, Loughborough
Tel: (01509) 230726
www.greatcentralrailway.com
Britain's only double track, mainline heritage railway running through eight miles of scenic Leicestershire countryside.

Grimsthorpe Castle, Park and Gardens
Bourne, Lincolnshire
Tel: (01778) 591205
www.grimsthorpe.co.uk
Visit the castle which features four periods of architecture and a collection of 18thC portraits and furniture. Young children will enjoy the adventure playground and can help feed the reed deer.

Gulliver's Kingdom
Matlock Bath, Derbyshire
Tel: (01629) 580540
www.gulliversfun.co.uk
Enjoy a great family day out at this theme park with rides and attractions including Little Switzerland, Fantasy Terrace, Royal Cave, chair lift and a cycle monorail.

Hartsholme Country Park
Skellingthorpe Road, Lincoln
Tel: (01522) 873577
Woodland, lakes and open grassland with a visitor centre and ranger service. Nearby is a local nature reserve, Swanholme Park.

The Heights of Abraham Cable Cars, Caverns and Hilltop Park
Matlock Bath, Derbyshire
Tel: (01629) 582365
www.heights-of-abraham.co.uk
A spectacular cable car ride takes you to the summit where, within the grounds, there are a wide variety of attractions for young and old alike. Gift shop and coffee shop.

Horse World
Market Rasen, Lincolnshire
Tel: (01673) 849967
See horses at work, rest and play with forest walks, a conservation area, educational visits, riding and hacking.

Indian Chief Cruises
The Boat Inn, Stoke Bruerne, Northamptonshire
Tel: (01604) 862428
www.boatinn.co.uk
Cruises on the Grand Union canal for up to 40 passengers, sailing through Northamptonshire countryside, through the famous Blisworth tunnel or up a flight of seven locks.

Lincoln Castle
Castle Hill, Lincoln
Tel: (01522) 511068
www.lincolnshire.gov.uk/lincolncastle
Walk the walls of this medieval castle, view the Magna Carta exhibition and reconstructed Westgate, experience a prison chapel, and enjoy popular events throughout the summer.

Lincoln Cathedral
Minster Yard, Lincoln
Tel: (01522) 544544
www.lincolncathedral.com
A medieval Gothic cathedral of outstanding historical and architectural merit. Must-sees include Katherine Swynford's tomb, St Hugh's Shrine and the Lincoln Imp.

Making It! Discovery Centre
Mansfield, Nottinghamshire
Tel: (01623) 473297
www.makingit.org.uk
Interactive galleries describing the process of making things. You can design and make a model to take away.

Midland Railway-Butterley
Butterley Station, Butterley, Derbyshire
Tel: (01773) 747674
Over 50 steam and diesel locomotives and over 100 items of historic Midland and LMS rolling stock with a steam-hauled passenger service, museum site, country and farm park.

Above left step back in time at Bosworth Battlefield, Sutton Cheney; drop in at Rockingham Castle

Enjoy England official guides to **quality**

Places to visit

 Awarded VisitBritain's Quality Assured Visitor Attraction marque.

Peak District Mining Museum
Matlock Bath, Derbyshire
Tel: (01629) 583834
www.peakmines.co.uk
A large exhibition illustrating 3500 years of lead mining with displays on geology, mines and miners, tools and engines. Go underground and pan for gold and other minerals.

Rockingham Castle
Rockingham, Northamptonshire
Tel: (01536) 770240
www.rockinghamcastle.com
An Elizabethan house within the walls of a Norman castle with fine pictures and china, extensive views and gardens with roses, a tilting lawn and an ancient yew hedge.

Royal Crown Derby Visitor Centre
Osmaston Road, Derby
Tel: (01332) 712800
www.royal-crown-derby.co.uk
A museum of Derby and Royal Crown Derby china dating from 1750. Take a guided tour of the working factory and see demonstrations of key skills. Museum, demonstrations and factory shop open daily.

Safari Parties at Grange Wood Zoo
Grangewood, Netherseal, Derbyshire
Tel: (01283) 760541
www.safari-parties.co.uk
Small rainforest zoo situated at Netherseal in Derbyshire, with a collection of small exotic rainforest animals, birds, reptiles and insects birds, mammals, reptiles and insects. Parties, open days and events.

The Seal Sanctuary
Mablethorpe, Lincolnshire
Tel: (01507) 473146
A wildlife sanctuary in gardens and natural dunes with the emphasis on Lincolnshire wildlife, past and present, and the Seal Trust Wildlife Hospital.

Skegness Natureland Seal Sanctuary
Skegness, Lincolnshire
Tel: (01754) 764345
www.skegnessnatureland.co.uk
Sanctuary for seals and baby seals, many rescued from beaches around the Wash, plus penguins, aquarium, crocodiles, snakes, terrapins, scorpions, tropical birds, butterflies and pets.

Snibston Discovery Park
Coalville, Leicestershire
Tel: (01530) 278444
www.leics.gov.uk/museums
An all-weather and award-winning science and technology heritage museum exploring Leicestershire's industrial past, where visitors can get 'hands-on'.

Twycross Zoo
Twycross, Leceistershire
Tel: (01827) 880250
www.twycrosszoo.com
A zoo with gorillas, orang-utans, chimpanzees, a modern gibbon complex, elephants, lions, giraffes, a reptile house, pets' corner and rides.

The Workhouse
Southwell, Nottinghamshire
Tel: (01636) 817250
www.nationaltrust.org.uk/workhouse
Explore the segregated rooms, stairways and the master's quarters of the best surviving workhouse in England. Built in 1824, it was a prototype for similar 'welfare' institutions throughout the country.

The Yard Gallery
Wollaton Hall, Nottingham
Tel: (0115) 915 3920
www.nottinghamcity.gov.uk
A vibrant art gallery housed in an old stableblock, hosting an exciting programme of contemporary art exhibitions exploring themes of natural history and science.

Above admire the views at Rushup Edge, the Peak District; admire Belvoir Castle, Leicestershire

This is just a selection of attractions available. Contact any Tourist Information Centre in the region for more ideas.

EAST MIDLANDS

East Midlands Tourism
Apex Court, City Link,
Nottingham NG2 4LA
www.enjoyeastmidlands.com

Further publications are available from the following organisations:

Experience Nottinghamshire
www.experiencenottinghamshire.com
Nottingham and Nottinghamshire Short Break and Visitor Guide
Nottingham and Nottinghamshire Places to visit

Peak District and Derbyshire
www.derbyshirethepeakdistrict.com or
www.visitpeakdistrict.com
Peak District Walking Guide
Peak District Visitor Guide
Savour the Flavour of the Peak District
Derbyshire – the Peak District Visitor Guide
Derbyshire – the Peak District Attractions Guide

Lincolnshire
www.visitlincolnshire.com
Visit Lincolnshire - Places to stay
Tastes of Lincolnshire
Visit Lincolnshire – Things to do
Visit Lincolnshire – Great days out
Visit Lincolnshire – Gardens and Nurseries

Northamptonshire Tourism
www.enjoynorthamptonshire.com
Enjoy Northamptonshire Visitor Guide

Leicestershire and Rutland
www.goleicestershire.com
Leicestershire 05
Cream of Leicestershire and Rutland
Rutland Guide

Travel information

The central location of the East Midlands makes it easily accessible from all parts of the UK.

By road:
From the North and South, the M1 bisects the East Midlands with access to the region from junctions 14 through to 31. The A1 offers better access to the eastern part of the region, particularly Lincolnshire and Rutland. From the west the M69, M/A42 and A50 provide easy access.

By rail:
The region is well served by three main line operators – GNER, Midland Mainline and Virgin, each offering direct services from London and the north of England and Scotland to the East Midlands' major cities and towns. East/west links are provided by Central Trains, offering not only access to the region but also travel within it.

By air:
Nottingham East Midlands airport is located centrally in the region, with scheduled domestic flights from Aberdeen, Belfast, Edinburgh, Glasgow, Isle of Man and the Channel Islands. Manchester, Birmingham, Luton, Stansted and Humberside airports also offer domestic scheduled routes with easy access to the region by road and rail.

Enjoy England official guides to quality

EAST MIDLANDS

Where to stay in
East Midlands

All place names in the blue bands, under which accommodation is listed, are shown on the maps at the front of this guide.

A complete listing of all VisitBritain assessed accommodation covered by this guide appears at the back.

Accommodation symbols
Symbols give useful information about services and facilities. Inside the back cover flap you can find a key to these symbols. Keep it open for easy reference.

ASHBOURNE, Derbyshire Map ref 4B2 *Tourist Information Centre Tel: (01335) 343666*

32 Units
Sleeping 2–8

Set in the former grounds of Sandybrook Hall, an elegant 19thC manor-house with woodland walks and wonderful views. Luxurious, fully equipped pine lodges furnished to the highest standards. Heated indoor swimming pool, indoor and outdoor play areas, restaurant and bar.

SANDYBROOK COUNTRY PARK
Ashbourne
Contact: Reception, Sandybrook Country Park, Buxton Road, Ashbourne DE6 2AQ
T: (01335) 300000
F: (01335) 342679
E: enquiries@pinelodgeholidays.co.uk
I: www.pinelodgeholidays.co.uk/sandybrook.ihtml

OPEN All Year

Payment accepted: Delta, Mastercard, Switch, Visa

Low season per wk
£250.00–£560.00
High season per wk
£390.00–£950.00

Mid-week and weekend breaks available all year round (excl Christmas and New Year). More offers upon application.

Town index
This can be found at the back of the guide. If you know where you want to stay the index will give you the page number listing accommodation in your chosen town, city or village.

EAST MIDLANDS

ASHBOURNE continued

★★★★★
1 Unit
Sleeping 2-4

You are invited to a luxury 18thC detached stone barn conversion on a beautiful four-acre estate. Enjoy exclusive use of the opulent indoor swimming pool and jacuzzi. Breathtaking views of the mountains at Dovedale. Ideally located for walking, cycling, watersports, Alton Towers and many historic houses.

THORPE CLOUD VIEW COTTAGE
Ashbourne
Contact: Mr Ray Neilson, Thorpe Cloud View Cottage, Thorpe House, Thorpe, Ashbourne DE6 2AW
T: (01335) 350215
E: rayneilson@aol.com
I: www.thorpecloudview.com

OPEN All Year

Low season per wk
£190.00–£225.00
High season per wk
£275.00–£390.00

ASHBY-DE-LA-ZOUCH, Leicestershire Map ref 4B3 Tourist Information Centre Tel: (01530) 411767

★★★
1 Unit
Sleeping 6

BADGER'S SETT
Ashby-de-la-Zouch
Contact: Aileen Wood, 16 Sandpiper Close, South Beach, Blyth NE24 3QN
T: (01670) 367723 & 07718 905251
E: graham-aileen@16sandpiper.freeserve.co.uk
I: www.badgers-sett.com

OPEN All Year

Low season per wk
£180.00–£190.00
High season per wk
£220.00–£285.00

Comfortable, modern, three-bedroom semi-detached house with small enclosed garden. All mod-cons. On outskirts of Ashby-de-la-Zouch.

★★★★
1 Unit
Sleeping 2-4

Luxuriously appointed barn conversion incorporating minstrels' gallery. Both double bedrooms en suite. On working farm including 130 acres of woodland walks. Easy access to M42, NEC, Calke Abbey and Castle Donington Park/Airport.

NORMAN'S BARN
Ashby-de-la-Zouch
Contact: Mrs Isabel Stanley, Ingles Hill Farm, Burton Road, Ashby-de-la-Zouch LE65 2TE
T: (01530) 412224
E: isabel_stanley@hotmail.com
I: www.normansbarn.co.uk

OPEN All Year

Low season per wk
£255.00–£395.00
High season per wk
£295.00–£450.00

BAKEWELL, Derbyshire Map ref 4B2 Tourist Information Centre Tel: (01629) 813227

★★★★
1 Unit
Sleeping 6

EDGE VIEW
Bakewell
Contact: Mrs Gillian Rogers, Penylan, Monyash Road, Bakewell DE45 1FG
T: (01629) 813336
F: (01629) 813336

OPEN All Year

Low season per wk
£270.00–£300.00
High season per wk
£300.00–£395.00

Three-bedroomed bungalow, with two bedrooms and bathroom/toilet on ground floor. Extensive views. Lawn, garden, ample off-road parking. Lock-up garage. Owner maintained.

Quality Assurance Standard
Star ratings and awards were correct at time of going to press but are subject to change. Please check at the time of booking.

EAST MIDLANDS

BAKEWELL continued

★★★
2 Units
Sleeping 6

SPOUT FARM
Bakewell
Contact: Mrs Ena Patterson, The Bungalow, Elton, Matlock DE4 2BY
T: (01629) 650358

Barn conversion with original stonework, beams and logburning stove, standing in spacious grounds with ponds, pool and abundant wildlife. Magnificent views over unspoilt scenery. Convenient for many attractions including Haddon and Chatsworth. Surrounded by pretty villages and superb walking country. Total peace and seclusion.

OPEN All Year
Payment accepted: Euros

Short breaks available Oct-Mar, 3 nights minimum (excl Christmas and New Year).

Low season per wk £200.00–£235.00
High season per wk £285.00–£360.00

BAMFORD, Derbyshire Map ref 4B2

★★★★
3 Units
Sleeping 1–6

SHATTON HALL FARM
Hope Valley
Contact: Mrs Angela Kellie, Shatton Hall Farm, Bamford, Hope Valley S33 0BG
T: (01433) 620635
F: (01433) 620689
E: ahk@peakfarmholidays.co.uk
I: www.peakfarmholidays.co.uk

Comfortable barn-converted cottages, each with own garden or terrace, on this 'out of the way', beautifully situated farmstead, with good access. Waymarked woodland walks, trout lake, tennis court and gardens of interest, open National Garden Scheme. Each cottage has double and twin-bedded rooms and good size living areas with open fires.

OPEN All Year
Payment accepted: Amex, Mastercard, Switch, Visa, Euros

Recently converted barn suitable for art, craft and special-interest groups.

Low season per wk £250.00–£275.00
High season per wk £300.00–£425.00

BASLOW, Derbyshire Map ref 4B2

★★★★★
1 Unit
Sleeping 2–4

GOOSE GREEN COTTAGE
Bakewell
Contact: Mr & Mrs Levick, 19 Peascliffe Drive, Grantham NG31 8EN
T: (01476) 571025 & 07979 004979
E: levick2@btopenworld.com
I: www.peakdistrict-nationalpark.com

Charming cottage in a delightful setting only 20yds from a medieval packhorse bridge. The footpath gives direct access to Chatsworth Park. Cosy, comfortable accommodation comprising: one double bedroom with en suite toilet and hand basin, sitting room with sofa bed, bathroom, dining room and fully equipped kitchen.

OPEN All Year

Short breaks available 3/4-night stay.

Low season per wk Min £225.00
High season per wk Max £370.00

Accessibility Look for the symbols which indicate National Accessible Scheme standards for hearing and visually impaired guests in addition to standards for guests with mobility impairment. You can find an index of all scheme participants at the back of this guide.

194

EAST MIDLANDS

BASLOW continued

★★★★
1 Unit
Sleeping 1–4

HALL COTTAGE
Bakewell
Contact: Mr & Mrs Griffiths, Beechcroft, School Lane, Bakewell DE45 1RZ
T: (01246) 582900
F: (01246) 583675
E: hallcottage@btinternet.com

OPEN All Year

Low season per wk
£270.00–£290.00
High season per wk
£300.00–£360.00

Small stone barn, tastefully restored. Beamed ceilings, fireplace. Quiet location in oldest part of village. Walking distance to shops, pubs, restaurants, Chatsworth and open countryside.

BEESBY, Lincolnshire Map ref 4D2

★★★
1 Unit
Sleeping 6

WALK VILLA
Alford
Contact: Sue & Joanne, Manor Farm, Beesby, Alford LN13 0JG
T: (01507) 450323 & 450392
E: j0anne66@yahoo.com

Countryside house with full central heating and open fire. Views over arable fields and green pasture. Rural village setting, parking for three cars. Feature half-tester bed complete with drapes. Beautifully equipped kitchen. Close to market town of Alford and four miles from the beach.

OPEN All Year

Short breaks available.

Low season per wk
£220.00–£330.00
High season per wk
£330.00–£425.00

BELCHFORD, Lincolnshire Map ref 4D2

★★★★
6 Units
Sleeping 2–26

POACHERS HIDEAWAY
Horncastle
Contact: Mr Andrew Tuxworth, Poachers Hideaway, Flintwood Farm, Belchford, Horncastle LN9 6QN
T: (01507) 533555
F: (01507) 534264
E: andrewtuxworth@poachershideaway.com
I: poachershideaway.com

In an isolated valley with outstanding views, cottages converted from traditional Lincolnshire barns. Equipped to a very high standard, each cottage has its own individual look. Direct access to public footpaths and bridleway, sauna, jacuzzi, 150 acres to roam. A hidden treasure waiting to be discovered.

OPEN All Year

Payment accepted: Mastercard, Switch, Visa

Short breaks and seasonal offers available. Contact Sally for discounted, last-minute bookings - 07774 890677.

Low season per wk
£150.00–£350.00
High season per wk
£290.00–£623.00

Country Code Always follow the Country Code
• Enjoy the countryside and respect its life and work • Guard against all risk of fire • Fasten all gates • Keep your dogs under close control • Keep to public paths across farmland • Use gates and stiles to cross fences, hedges and walls • Leave livestock, crops and machinery alone • Take your litter home • Help to keep all water clean • Protect wildlife, plants and trees • Take special care on country roads • Make no unnecessary noise.

195

EAST MIDLANDS

CALDECOTT, Rutland Map ref 4C3

★★★
1 Unit
Sleeping 1–5

MAGNOLIA COTTAGE
Caldecott
Contact: Mel Hudson, 22 Main Street, Caldecott, Market Harborough LE16 8RS
T: (01536) 771357
E: enquiries@rutland-cottages.co.uk
I: www.rutland-cottages.co.uk

OPEN All Year

Open Christmas and New Year. 2/3-night weekend breaks. Special rates for long-term stays.

Low season per wk
£185.00–£225.00
High season per wk
£225.00–£285.00

A traditional stone-built forester's cottage in Rutland, overlooking the hilltop Castle of Rockingham. The cottage offers a high standard of accommodation, off-street private parking and attractive gardens bordering the surrounding unspoilt countryside. An ideal location for walking, cycling, fishing, bird watching or just relaxing in this 'Secret England'.

★★★
1 Unit
Sleeping 1–8

WISTERIA COTTAGE
Caldecott
Contact: Mel Hudson, 22 Main Street, Caldecott, Market Harborough LE16 8RS
T: (01536) 771357
E: wisteria@rutland-cottages.co.uk
I: www.rutland-cottages.co.uk

OPEN All Year

Open Christmas and New Year. 2/3-night weekend breaks. Special rates for long-term stays.

Low season per wk
£150.00–£350.00
High season per wk
£185.00–£450.00

A charming stone-built cottage in historic Rutland, overlooking the rolling hills of the Welland valley. The cottage can be used as one or two dwellings, offering high-quality accommodation, a secluded garden and secure parking – an ideal location for water-sports, walking, cycling, fishing and bird-watching.

CARSINGTON, Derbyshire Map ref 4B2

★★★–★★★★★
17 Units
Sleeping 2–10

KNOCKERDOWN HOLIDAY COTTAGES
Ashbourne
Contact: Ms Cathy Lambert, Knockerdown, Ashbourne DE6 1NQ
T: (01629) 540525
F: (01629) 540525
E: cathy@knockerdown-cottages.co.uk
I: www.derbyshireholidaycottages.co.uk

OPEN All Year

Payment accepted: Delta, Diners, Mastercard, Switch, Visa

Low season per wk
£290.00–£759.00
High season per wk
£330.00–£2,000.00

Adjacent to village inn. Indoor pool, sauna, gym, outdoor play area. Central for both Derbyshire and Staffordshire's many attractions. Five minutes to beautiful Carsington Reservoir.

CHESTERFIELD, Derbyshire Map ref 4B2 Tourist Information Centre Tel: (01246) 345777

★★★★
1 Unit
Sleeping 1–5

PLOUGHMANS COTTAGE
Chesterfield
Contact: Mr & Mrs Fry, Ploughmans Cottage, Low Farm, Main Road, Marsh Lane, Chesterfield S21 5RH
T: (01246) 435328
E: ploughmans.cottage@virgin.net

OPEN All Year

Payment accepted: Euros

Short breaks available Oct-Mar (excl Christmas).

Low season per wk
£200.00–£240.00
High season per wk
Min £250.00

Fresh eggs from our hens, kisses from our llamas, skylarks and woodland walks. This delightful cottage is carefully and attractively maintained. It has a fenced garden with orchard, lawns, flower beds, patio and sandpit. Lovely open views and many places of interest within easy reach.

196

EAST MIDLANDS

COMBS, Derbyshire Map ref 4B2

★★★★★
1 Unit
Sleeping 1-2

Situated within the Peak District National Park and enjoying spectacular views, this cottage is finished and furnished to a very high standard whilst retaining original oak beams and many other interesting features. Ideal location for walking, golfing, the theatre (Buxton) or simply as an idyllic hideaway.

PYEGREAVE COTTAGE
High Peak
Contact: Mr Noel & Mrs Rita Pollard, Pyegreave Cottage, Combs, High Peak SK23 9UX
T: (01298) 813444
F: (01298) 815381
E: n.pollard@allenpollard.co.uk
I: www.holidayapartments.org

OPEN All Year

Payment accepted: Amex, Diners, Mastercard, Switch, Visa, Euros

Low season per wk
£260.00-£310.00
High season per wk
£330.00-£395.00

CURBAR, Derbyshire Map ref 4B2

★★★★
1 Unit
Sleeping 4

Romantic, luxury, detached stone cottage. Beautifully furnished. Range cooking. Real fire. Delightful private garden with sun terrace and barbecue. Peaceful village location with good local pubs. Ideal for walkers, explorers of Peak District delights.

JACK'S COTTAGE
Hope Valley
Contact: Mrs North, Green Farm, Hope Valley S32 3YH
T: (01433) 630120
F: (01433) 631829
E: enquiries@peakdistrictholiday.co.uk
I: www.peakdistrictholiday.co.uk

OPEN All Year

Short breaks available throughout the year, minimum 2 nights.

Low season per wk
£340.00-£430.00
High season per wk
£490.00-£550.00

★★★★★
1 Unit
Sleeping 2-6

Historic, detached character home amidst quiet Peak District village. Tastefully furnished and spacious. Two bathrooms, luxury kitchen, range cooker, real log fire, superb private garden. Excellent location for walking, climbing, fishing, exploring and dining out.

THE MULLIONS
Hope Valley
Contact: Mrs North, Green Farm, Hope Valley S32 3YH
T: (01433) 630120
F: (01433) 631829
E: enquiries@peakdistrictholiday.co.uk
I: www.peakdistrictholidays.co.uk

OPEN All Year

Short breaks available throughout the year, minimum 2 nights.

Low season per wk
£480.00-£860.00
High season per wk
£600.00-£750.00

★★★
2 Units
Sleeping 2-6

UPPER BARN AND LOWER BARN
Hope Valley
Contact: Mr & Mrs Pierce, Upper Barn and Lower Barn, Orchard House, Curbar, Hope Valley S32 3YJ
T: (01283) 631885
F: (0114) 290 3309
E: info@curbarcottages.com
I: www.curbarcottages.com

OPEN All Year
Payment accepted: Euros

Low season per wk
£165.00-£190.00
High season per wk
£220.00-£275.00

A recent conversion of 200-year-old barn into two cottages. Linked to let as one if required.

EAST MIDLANDS

EDALE, Derbyshire Map ref 4B2

★★★★
3 Units
Sleeping 2–5

OLLERBROOK COTTAGES
Edale, Hope Valley
Contact: Mrs Paula Greenlees, Ollerbrook Cottages, Middle Ollerbrook House, Ollerbrook, Hope Valley S33 7LG
T: (01433) 670083
I: www.ollerbrook-cottages.co.uk

OPEN All Year

Low season per wk £250.00–£330.00
High season per wk £445.00–£610.00

Luxury, 17thC gritstone cottages set in the heart of the Edale Valley. Original features including log fires. Walks from the door. Stunning, panoramic views.

ELKINGTON, Northamptonshire Map ref 4C3

★★★★
2 Units
Sleeping 1–4

MANOR FARM
Elkington
Contact: Elkington Farm Partnership, Manor Farm, Northampton NN6 6NH
T: (01858) 575245
F: (01858) 575213

OPEN All Year

Low season per wk £350.00–£450.00
High season per wk £350.00–£450.00

A Listed barn conversion in a historic hamlet. Easy access to the M1, M6, A14 and places of importance in the Midlands.

ELTON, Derbyshire Map ref 4B2

★★★★
1 Unit
Sleeping 3

SWALLOW COTTAGE
Elton
Contact: Mrs Lois Clark, 51 Telegraph Street, Cottenham, Cambridge CB4 8QU
T: (01954) 251004 & 07932 644287
E: lois@swallow-cottage.co.uk
I: www.swallow-cottage.co.uk

Charming character cottage in small village within the Peak District National Park about five miles south west of Bakewell. Accommodates three in a double and single bedroom. Gas central heating and gas stove in the lounge. Well equipped throughout. Ideal centre for all activities and attractions. Fabulous views. Highly recommended by all our guests.

OPEN All Year

Short breaks available Oct–Mar (excl Christmas and New Year) and at short notice. Minimum three nights.

Low season per wk £190.00–£260.00
High season per wk £260.00–£330.00

FROGGATT, Derbyshire Map ref 4B2

★★★★★
1 Unit
Sleeping 4

BRIDGEFOOT COTTAGE
Hope Valley
Contact: Mrs Marsha North, Green Farm, Curbar, Hope Valley S32 3YH
T: (01433) 630120
E: enquiries@peakdistrictholiday.co.uk
I: www.peakdistrictholiday.co.uk

Historic detached stone cottage on the banks of the river Derwent. Central village location. Good walking and good local pubs. Beautifully furnished. Oak beams, antiques, four-poster bed, Aga, real log fires. Romantic luxury. Ideal for fishermen, bird-watchers and those in search of perfect peace.

OPEN All Year

Low season per wk £430.00–£510.00
High season per wk £550.00–£680.00

Credit card bookings

If you book by telephone and are asked for your credit card number it is advisable to check the proprietor's policy should you cancel your reservation.

EAST MIDLANDS

GONALSTON, Nottinghamshire Map ref 4C2

1 Unit
Sleeping 1–2

THE STUDIO COTTAGE
Nottingham
Contact: Mike and Ann Carradice, The Studio Cottage, Hill House, Gonalston, Nottingham NG14 7JA
T: (0115) 966 4551
E: carradice@btinternet.com
I: www.carradice.btinternet.co.uk

A charming, beautifully appointed, centrally heated cottage, facing the croquet lawn of a country house, which overlooks the Trent and Dover Beck valleys. Ideal for exploring Robin Hood country, the Dukeries, the Vale of Belvoir and Nottingham, Lincoln, Newark and the nearby minster town of Southwell.

OPEN All Year
Payment accepted: Euros

3/4-night stays available throughout the year: £100-£190 depending on dates.

Low season per wk
£160.00–£190.00
High season per wk
Min £240.00

GRANTHAM, Lincolnshire Map ref 3A1 *Tourist Information Centre Tel: (01476) 406166*

1 Unit
Sleeping 4

BELVOIR COTTAGE
Grantham
Contact: Mrs Ursula Soar, Old Millhouse, Branston Road, Eaton, Grantham NG32 1SF
T: (01476) 870797

OPEN All Year
Payment accepted: Switch

Low season per wk
£195.00–£295.00
High season per wk
£350.00–£550.00

Listed stable conversion with winding stream in beautiful valley. Abundant wildlife, kingfishers, barn owls, badgers. Ideal for walking, cycling, private fishing nearby. Local country pubs serving meals.

GREAT CARLTON, Lincolnshire Map ref 4D2

★★★
1 Unit
Sleeping 5

WILLOW FARM
Louth
Contact: Mr James Clark, Willow Farm, Great Carlton, Louth LN11 8JT
T: (01507) 338540

OPEN All Year

Low season per wk
£140.00–£180.00
High season per wk
£200.00–£250.00

Comprising two double and one single bedrooms. Fly and coarse fishing available on site. Touring caravans welcome by arrangement.

GREAT HUCKLOW, Derbyshire Map ref 4B2

★★★★
1 Unit
Sleeping 2–4

SOUTH VIEW COTTAGE
Great Hucklow
Contact: Mrs Waterhouse, Holme Cottage, Windmill, Great Hucklow, Buxton SK17 8RE
T: (01298) 871440
E: mo@mmwaterhouse.demon.co.uk
I: www.cottageguide.co.uk/southviewcottage

OPEN All Year except Christmas and New Year

Low season per wk
£250.00–£280.00
High season per wk
£280.00–£320.00

Modernised country cottage in the hamlet of Windmill in the middle of the Peak District. Owner maintained. Furnished and decorated to a high standard. No smoking. Lock-up garage.

Check the maps

The colour maps at the front of this guide show all the cities, towns and villages for which you will find accommodation entries. Refer to the town index to find the page on which they are listed.

EAST MIDLANDS

HAGWORTHINGHAM, Lincolnshire Map ref 4D2

★★★★
1 Unit
Sleeping 2-4

KINGFISHER LODGE
Spilsby
Contact: Mr Nick Bowser, E W Bowser & Son Ltd,
The Estate Office, Boston PE22 0AA
T: (01205) 870210 & 07970 128531
F: (01205) 870602
E: office@ewbowser.com

A private wildlife haven in Tennyson country, this new and beautifully designed lakeside lodge has spectacular views over the Wolds and Alder Valley Lake. Enjoy the fishing, the unusual flora and fauna, go walking/cycling/riding or simply unwind and enjoy the beautiful tranquil setting. Good shops, restaurants and local attractions nearby.

OPEN All Year

Short breaks from £295.

Low season per wk
£540.00-£625.00
High season per wk
£715.00-£735.00

HARTINGTON, Derbyshire Map ref 4B2

1 Unit
Sleeping 5

CHURCH VIEW
Buxton
Contact: Miss Bassett, Digmer, Hartington, Buxton
SK17 0AQ
T: (01298) 84660

Stone-built cottage with lawns to the front and side. Storage heaters. Spacious, comfortable interior. Lounge, dining room, utility room, recently fitted kitchen. Three bedrooms, upstairs bathroom consisting of bath, toilet, wash basin and new walk-in shower. Open fire optional. Close to amenities. Owner maintained. Established 21 years.

Low season per wk
£170.00-£195.00
High season per wk
£195.00-£250.00

4 Units
Sleeping 2-7

CRUCK & WOLFSCOTE COTTAGES
Buxton
Contact: Mrs Jane Gibbs, Cruck & Wolfscote Cottages,
Wolfscote Grange Farm, Hartington, Buxton SK17 0AX
T: (01298) 84342
E: wolfscote@btinternet.com
I: www.wolfscotegrangecottages.co.uk

The unique setting overlooking Dove Valley/Dale with miles of rolling countryside and picture views sells Wolfcote cottages as the perfect place to stay. Cruck Cottage – an oak-beamed hideaway. 'No neighbours, only sheep'. Swallows Cottage – en suites, spa bathroom. Both offer comfort and character. Farm trail with freedom to roam. Central to Peak District.

OPEN All Year

Private farm trail weekend and short breaks available (especially Oct-Easter).

Low season per wk
£180.00-£200.00
High season per wk
£480.00-£560.00

Important note Information on accommodation listed in this guide has been supplied by the proprietors. As changes may occur you are advised to check details at the time of booking.

200

EAST MIDLANDS

HARTINGTON continued

★★★★–★★★★★
2 Units
Sleeping 2–12

Recently renovated, this tastefully furnished four-bedroom, typical Derbyshire-stone cottage, with adjacent two-bedroom luxury apartment, is situated in the heart of the picturesque Peak District village of Hartington. Both are spacious, yet cosy. Ideal for touring, walking, cycling and visiting stately homes. Alton Towers within easy reach.

DALESCROFT COTTAGE AND APARTMENT
Hartington
Contact: Mr Brian Leese, Bishops Grange, Bishops Lane, Buxton SK17 6UP
T: (01298) 24263
E: mail@dalescroft.co.uk
I: www.dalescroft.co.uk

OPEN All Year

Low season per wk
£265.00–£395.00
High season per wk
£425.00–£695.00

★★★★
2 Units
Sleeping 6

Spacious cottage with three bedrooms, dining room, lounge, ground floor bathroom, upstairs shower room/WC and garden. In a pretty village near amenities, shops and restaurants. Also second property. Owner maintained, established 20 years.

1 STALEY COTTAGE AND VICTORIA HOUSE
Buxton
Contact: Mr & Mrs Oliver, Carr Head Farm, Penistone, Sheffield S36 7GA
T: (01226) 762387

OPEN All Year

Low season per wk
£300.00–£350.00
High season per wk
£350.00–£500.00

HATHERSAGE, Derbyshire Map ref 4B2

★★★★
1 Unit
Sleeping 2–6

Luxury converted 16thC barn. Three bedrooms, all en suite, large comfortable lounge, fully-equipped kitchen, magnificent views, patio and garden.

THE OLD BARN
Hope Valley
Contact: Kathleen Stewart, Booths Farm, Sheffield Road, Hope Valley S32 1DA
T: (01433) 650667
F: (01433) 650667
I: www.theoldbarn.co.uk

OPEN All Year

Short breaks: £80pn Oct-Apr (excl Christmas and New Year); £100pn Apr-Oct. All minimum 3 nights.

Low season per wk
£450.00–£500.00
High season per wk
£550.00–£700.00

★★★
1 Unit
Sleeping 4–6

PAT'S COTTAGE
Sheffield
Contact: Mr John Drakeford, 110 Townhead Road, Sheffield S17 3GB
T: (0114) 236 6014 & 07850 200711
F: (0114) 236 6014
E: johnmdrakeford@hotmail.com
I: www.patscottage.co.uk

OPEN All Year

Low season per wk
£235.00–£325.00
High season per wk
£240.00–£340.00

An attractive 18thC stone cottage, sympathetically refurbished, retaining original features including black beams. On the edge of the Peak District, close to Hathersage and the city of Sheffield.

EAST MIDLANDS

HATHERSAGE continued

★★★
1 Unit
Sleeping 4

ST MICHAEL'S COTTAGE
Hope Valley
Contact: Miss Turton, Saint Michael's Environmental Education Centre, Main Road, Hope Valley S32 1BB
T: (01433) 650309
F: (01433) 650089
E: stmichaels@education.nottscc.gov.uk
I: www.eess.org.uk

OPEN All Year

Low season per wk
£180.00–£210.00
High season per wk
£250.00–£330.00

Cosy character cottage with one double and one twin bedroom. Dramatic scenery, walks from the door, close to all amenities.

HORSINGTON, Lincolnshire Map ref 4D2

★★★
1 Unit
Sleeping 4

WAYSIDE COTTAGE
Horsington, Woodhall Spa
Contact: Mr Ian & Mrs Jane Williamson, 72 Mill Lane, Horsington, Woodhall Spa LN10 6QZ
T: (01526) 353101
E: janewill89@hotmail.com
I: www.cottagesdirect.com

OPEN All Year
Payment accepted: Euros

Low season per wk
£170.00–£200.00
High season per wk
£175.00–£210.00

Cottage bungalow in rural setting in sleepy Horsington, central to the county for exploring. Many walks.

KING'S CLIFFE, Northamptonshire Map ref 3A1

★★★
1 Unit
Sleeping 1–2

MALTINGS COTTAGE
Peterborough
Contact: Mrs Jenny Dixon, 19 West Street, King's Cliffe, Peterborough PE8 6XA
T: (01780) 470365
F: (01780) 470623

Cosy stone cottage situated in centre of beautiful historic village with shops, pub and post office. Attractively furnished and well equipped. Central heating. Surrounded by stately homes, all within 45 minutes' drive. Wonderful rolling countryside for walking. Near Rutland Water for sailing and bird-watching. Rockingham Motor Speedway six miles.

OPEN All Year

Low season per wk
Min £130.00
High season per wk
£200.00–£250.00

KNIVETON, Derbyshire Map ref 4B2

★★★★
1 Unit
Sleeping 2–4

WILLOW BANK
Ashbourne
Contact: Mrs Vaughan, Willow Bank, Kniveton, Ashbourne DE6 1JJ
T: (01335) 343308
F: (01335) 347859
E: willowbank@kniveton.net
I: www.kniveton.net

OPEN All Year

Low season per wk
£275.00–£300.00
High season per wk
£350.00–£400.00

Luxurious, recently fitted ground floor accommodation, one double bedroom, one twin. An acre of garden, summerhouse, stream, barbecue, lovely views. Pretty Peak District village, Ashbourne 15 minutes.

Location Complete addresses for properties are not given and the town(s) listed may be a distance from the actual establishment. Please check the precise location at the time of booking.

EAST MIDLANDS

LAMBLEY, Nottinghamshire Map ref 4C2

1 Unit
Sleeping 4

Five miles north-east of Nottingham. Beamed cottage with garden. Two bedrooms – one double/one twin. TV/video, dishwasher, washer/dryer. Private parking.

DICKMAN'S COTTAGE
Nottingham
Contact: Mr William Marshall Smith, Springsyde, Birdcage Walk, Otley LS21 3HB
T: (01943) 462719
F: (01943) 850925
E: marshallsmithuk@hotmail.com
I: http://mywebpage.netscape.com/wmarshallsmith/default.html

OPEN All Year
Payment accepted: Euros

Low season per wk
Min £170.00
High season per wk
Min £250.00

LEICESTER, Leicestershire

See display advertisement below

LINCOLN, Lincolnshire Map ref 4C2 Tourist Information Centre Tel: (01522) 873213

1 Unit
Sleeping 1–3

BURTON MEWS
Lincoln
Contact: Mrs Karen Rastall, 30 Burton Road, Lincoln LN1 3LB
T: (01522) 524990
F: (01522) 560845
E: karen@rastallandco.com

OPEN All Year
Payment accepted: Euros

High season per wk
Min £420.00

Comfortable, well-equipped townhouse with enclosed garden. Minutes from historic area of Lincoln and close to shops, restaurants and bars. Single nights and weekends available.

Quality Assurance Standard

For an explanation of the quality and facilities represented by the stars please refer to the front of this guide. A more detailed explanation can be found in the information pages at the back.

CROSSWAYS COUNTRY HOLIDAYS

The Heart of the Shires is steeped in history and boasts much of England's most beautiful countryside, architecture and fabulous tourist attractions. The peaceful atmosphere at Crossways Cottage means you get quality time to prepare your holiday day by day without the stress and hassle of coach tours.

For details of availabilty, accommodation and rates, please contact Carol Mac directly on T: 01455 239261 or 07946 421123 (mobile)
Lutterworth Road, Burbage, Leicestershire, LE10 3AH
E: user@burbage60.fsnet.co.uk or www.crossways-holidays.com

203

EAST MIDLANDS

LINCOLN continued

★★★★
1 Unit
Sleeping 4

CLIFF FARM COTTAGE

North Carlton
Contact: Mrs Rae Marris, Cliff Farm, North Carlton, Lincoln
LN1 2RP
T: (01522) 730475
E: rae.marris@farming.co.uk
I: www.cliff-farm-cottage.co.uk

Combine the historic cathedral city of Lincoln with the tranquility of the countryside. Charming cottage coverted from traditional 19thC farm buildings. Situated three miles north of city on a working arable farm with panoramic views over the Trent Valley. Spacious, well-appointed accommodation. Relax in secluded garden. Wheelchair friendly. Warm welcome assured.

OPEN All Year

Short breaks available – minimum stay 3 nights.

Low season per wk
Min £270.00
High season per wk
Max £340.00

★★★★
1 Unit
Sleeping 4–6

D'ISNEY PLACE COTTAGE

Lincoln
Contact: Judy or Sarah, D'isney Place Cottage, Lincoln
LN2 4AA
T: (01522) 542411
F: (01522) 511321
E: info@disneyplacehotel.co.uk

The accommodation comprises a double, en suite room and a twin-bedded room with shower en suite, dining/kitchen, large sitting room with double doors leading to conservatory and garden.

OPEN All Year

Low season per wk
Min £350.00
High season per wk
Min £350.00

★★★★
1 Unit
Sleeping 1–5

19A LINDUM HILL

Lincoln
Contact: Mr Stuart Richardson, Elder House, The Green, Welbourn, Lincoln LN5 0NJ
T: (01400) 272793 & 07957 622583
E: therichardsons@lindumhill.fsnet.co.uk
I: www.lindum-hill.co.uk

Sympathetically and tastefully restored, graceful, Georgian residence retaining many period features with well-proportioned, comprehensively equipped kitchen/dining room and a cosy and relaxing living room. Overlooked by the cathedral and castle and the cultural quarter known as the Bailgate, home to the city's premier pubs and restaurants.

OPEN All Year

Payment accepted: Euros

Welcome hamper that includes tea, coffee, sugar, milk, champagne and chocolates.

Low season per wk
£200.00–£300.00
High season per wk
£300.00–£400.00

At-a-glance symbols

Symbols at the end of each entry give useful information about services and facilities. A key to symbols can be found inside the back cover flap. Keep this open for easy reference.

EAST MIDLANDS

LINCOLN continued

★★★
1 Unit
Sleeping 2

MARTINGALE COTTAGE
Lincoln
Contact: Mrs Patsy Pate, 19 East Street, Nettleham,
Lincoln LN2 2SL
T: (01522) 751795
E: patsy.pate@ntlworld.com

An 18thC stone cottage near the centre of the attractive village of Nettleham, 2.5 miles from Lincoln. Very comfortable, well-equipped accommodation with private parking. Use of owner's spacious, secluded garden. Good local shops and pubs, post office and library. Picturesque beckside and bus service to Lincoln. A warm welcome awaits.

OPEN All Year

Low season per wk
Min £130.00
High season per wk
Max £190.00

★★★★
2 Units
Sleeping 2–4

OLD VICARAGE COTTAGES
Nettleham
Contact: Mrs Susan Downs, The Old Vicarage, East Street,
Lincoln LN2 2SL
T: (01522) 750819
F: (01522) 750819
E: susan@oldvic.net

Delightful old stone cottages offering spacious accommodation, equipped with everything you need – including a whirlpool bath – private gardens and off-road parking/garage. Close to the centre of this award-winning village with shops, pubs, green and picturesque beckside. Good bus service. Four miles from Lincoln – the perfect holiday location.

OPEN All Year

Low season per wk
Max £145.00
High season per wk
Max £295.00

★★★
1 Unit
Sleeping 4

PINGLES COTTAGE
Lincoln
Contact: Mrs Sutcliffe, Pingles Cottage, Grange Farm,
Broxholme, Lincoln LN1 2NG
T: (01522) 702441

Well-equipped, secluded, cosy cottage with private garden and ample parking, only six miles from historic Lincoln and within easy reach of trunk roads (A57, A1500). Free-range hens' eggs and lamb are produced on the 100-acre organic farm. A good variety of wildlife regularly visits the garden.

OPEN All Year

Winter breaks; Nov-Easter, 3 nights £165.

Low season per wk
Min £275.00
High season per wk
Max £320.00

Use your *i*s

There are more than 550 Tourist Information Centres throughout England offering friendly help with accommodation and holiday ideas as well as suggestions of places to visit and things to do. You'll find addresses in the local phone book.

EAST MIDLANDS

LINCOLN continued

★★★
3 Units
Sleeping 1–2

SAINT CLEMENTS
Lincoln
Contact: Mrs Gill Marshall, Saint Clements, Langworthgate, Lincoln LN2 4AD
T: (01522) 538087
F: (01522) 560642
E: jroywood@aol.com
I: www.stayatstclements.co.uk

OPEN All Year

Low season per wk
Min £140.00
High season per wk
Min £200.00

Well-equipped, centrally heated apartments in comfortable Victorian rectory: one is twin-bedded, two are doubles. Situated down quiet drive lined with mature trees. Cathedral views and only five minutes' walk from historic up-hill area. Plenty of car parking. A peaceful retreat in the heart of the city. Short breaks when available.

★★★★
1 Unit
Sleeping 2–4

THE STABLE
Lincoln
Contact: Mr Jerry & Chris Scott, Sunnyside, Lincoln Road, Brattleby, Lincoln LN1 2SQ
T: (01522) 730561
E: jmsco@lineone.net
I: www.lincolncottages.co.uk

OPEN All Year

4 nights for the price of 3 in low season.

Low season per wk
£185.00–£240.00
High season per wk
£265.00–£350.00

300-year-old cottage of character converted from a former stone and pantile stable. Peace and tranquillity in a conservation village yet only six miles from the historic cathedral city of Lincoln. Tastefully furnished and decorated. Own enclosed cottage garden and views over open fields.

LITTON, Derbyshire Map ref 4B2

★★★
1 Unit
Sleeping 1–6

CROSS VIEW
Litton
Contact: Mrs Rowan-Olive, 44 Burnham Road, St Albans AL1 4QW
T: (01727) 844169
E: enquiries@cross-view.co.uk
I: www.cross-view.co.uk

OPEN All Year except Christmas and New Year

Short breaks available Oct–May (excl school half-terms, school holidays and Bank Holiday weekends).

Low season per wk
£210.00–£240.00
High season per wk
£270.00–£295.00

18thC stone cottage with traditional coal fire and modern comforts, including dishwasher and freezer. It faces the green in Litton, a small, peaceful village with excellent pub and community shop. Fine views and beautiful walking country. Accessible for Tideswell, Chatsworth, Haddon Hall, Bakewell and Buxton.

LOUTH, Lincolnshire Map ref 4D2 *Tourist Information Centre Tel: (01507) 609289*

★★★–★★★★★
5 Units
Sleeping 2–6

ASHWATER HOUSE
Louth
Contact: Mrs Holly Mapletoft, Ashpot Cottage, Willow Drive, Louth LN11 0AH
T: 0845 126 0322
E: enquiries@ashwaterhouse.co.uk
I: www.ashwaterhouse.co.uk

OPEN All Year

Low season per wk
£175.00–£205.00
High season per wk
£370.00–£440.00

Cottages and log cabins, each with a view of fishing lake and woodland, surrounded by open countryside, on the edge of Louth. Coarse fishing and an exclusive health and leisure club are complimentary.

EAST MIDLANDS

LOUTH continued

★★★★
3 Units
Sleeping 1–5

CANAL FARM COTTAGES
Louth
Contact: Mr & Mrs Richard Drinkel, Canal Farm, Austen Fen, Grainthorpe, Louth LN11 0NX
T: (01472) 388825
F: (01472) 388825
E: canalfarm@ukhome.net
I: www.canalfarmcottages.co.uk

Comfortable well-equipped canalside converted barns in a peaceful location. Lovely views. Near north Lincolnshire coast and Wolds. Ideal for walkers, cyclists and nature lovers, coastal nature reserves nearby. Many visitor attractions for families and the Georgian market town of Louth close by. Children and pets welcome.

OPEN All Year
Payment accepted: Delta, Mastercard, Switch, Visa

Short breaks available Oct–Apr, minimum 2 night stay – competitive rates.

Low season per wk
£210.00–£250.00
High season per wk
£315.00–£350.00

Rating Applied For

18 Units
Sleeping 1–6

KENWICK WOODS
Louth
Contact: Kenwick Woods, Kenwick Estate, Louth LN11 8NR
T: (01507) 608806 & 353003
F: (01507) 608027
E: enquiries@kenwick-park.co.uk
I: www.kenwickwoods.com

Luxurious Scandinavian lodges. Set in mature woodland on the select and exclusive Kenwick Park Estate in the Lincolnshire wolds Area of Outstanding Natural Beauty with superb leisure, golf, hotel and dining facilities to enjoy.

Payment accepted: Amex, Delta, Mastercard, Switch, Visa, Euros

34% off the weekly price for 3 nights Fri-Mon. 25% off the weekly price for 4 nights Mon-Fri (excl 22 Dec 2005 Jan 2006).

Low season per wk
£325.00–£550.00
High season per wk
£490.00–£795.00

MATLOCK, Derbyshire Map ref 4B2 Tourist Information Centre Tel: (01629) 583388

★★★★
1 Unit
Sleeping 2–4

CLEMATIS COTTAGE
Matlock
Contact: Mr J Lomas, Middle Hills Farm, Grange Mill, Matlock DE4 4HY
T: (01629) 650368
F: (01629) 650368
E: l.lomas@btinternet.com
I: www.peakdistrictfarmhols.co.uk

Comfortable cottage with magnificent views, patio, parquet floors, beams, rose arches. The cottage is designed for wheelchair users and the less able.

OPEN All Year

Low season per wk
Max £300.00
High season per wk
Max £400.00

www.visitengland.com

Log on for information and inspiration. The latest information on places to visit, events and quality assessed accommodation.

EAST MIDLANDS

MATLOCK continued

★★★-★★★★★
87 Units
Sleeping 2–8

DARWIN FOREST COUNTRY PARK
Matlock
Contact: Reception, Darwin Forest Country Park, Darley Moor, Two Dales, Matlock DE4 5LN
T: (01629) 732428
F: (01629) 735015
E: enquiries@pinelodgeholidays.co.uk
I: www.pinelodgeholidays.co.uk/darwin_forest.ihtml

Set in stunning woodland in the beautiful Derbyshire countryside, the perfect base from which to explore the Peak District. Luxurious, fully-equipped Pinelodges furnished to the highest standards. Indoor swimming pool, mini-golf and tennis, indoor and outdoor play areas, pub and restaurant with takeaway. Convenient shop, wine store and launderette.

OPEN All Year

Payment accepted: Delta, Mastercard, Switch, Visa

Mid-week and weekend breaks available all year round (excl Christmas and New Year). More offers upon application.

Low season per wk
£250.00–£560.00
High season per wk
£390.00–£950.00

★★★★
10 Units
Sleeping 4–7

DARWIN LAKE
Darley Moor, Matlock
Contact: Miss Nikki Manning, Peak Village Ltd, Darwin Lake, Jaggers Lane, Darley Moor, Matlock DE4 5LH
T: (01629) 735859
F: (01629) 735859
E: enquiries@darwinlake.co.uk
I: www.darwinlake.co.uk

Set in 10 acres of private, wooded grounds surrounding Darwin Lake, these superb, luxury, stone-built cottages provide a perfect setting for a tranquil, relaxing holiday, or for exploring the Peaks and Dales. Bustling market towns, stately homes, quaint villages and many family attractions. Village shops and pub two miles. Pets welcome in selected cottages.

OPEN All Year

Payment accepted: Mastercard, Switch, Visa

Larger detached cottages also available. Short breaks of 3 and 4 nights available (excl peak times). Late booking discount.

Low season per wk
£270.00–£480.00
High season per wk
£600.00–£1,076.00

★★★★
1 Unit
Sleeping 1–5

EAGLE COTTAGE
Matlock
Contact: Mrs Mary Prince, Haresfield House, Keeling Lane, Birchover, Matlock DE4 2BL
T: (01629) 650634
E: maryprince@msn.com
I: www.cressbrook.co.uk/youlgve/eagle/

A quiet end cottage in the centre of a small Peak District village having two pubs and a shop. The village is surrounded by a network of public footpaths and stunning scenery in an Area of Outstanding Natural Beauty. Many attractions, including stately Chatsworth House and Haddon Hall, are nearby.

OPEN All Year

Low season per wk
£190.00–£220.00
High season per wk
£250.00–£260.00

Symbols The symbols in each entry give information about services and facilities. A key to these symbols appears at the back of this guide.

EAST MIDLANDS

MIDDLETON-BY-YOULGREAVE, Derbyshire Map ref 4B2

★★★★
1 Unit
Sleeping 6

HOLLY HOMESTEAD COTTAGE
Bakewell
Contact: Mr David & Mrs Valerie Edge, Ridgeway House, Hillcliff Lane, Turnditch, Belper DE56 2EA
T: (01773) 550754
E: daveedge@turnditch82.freeserve.co.uk
I: www.holly-homestead.co.uk

Character cosy Grade II Listed cottage, 250 years old, provides comfortable accommodation in a beautiful and peaceful village. Excellent central base for exploring, walking and cycling the Peak Park, particularly Bradford Dale, Limestone Way, High Peak Trail. Chatsworth and Haddon Hall are close by. Cycle storage. Pets welcome.

OPEN All Year

Low season per wk
£250.00–£300.00
High season per wk
£380.00–£500.00

MONYASH, Derbyshire Map ref 4B2

★★★★
2 Units
Sleeping 2–5

SHELDON COTTAGES
Bakewell
Contact: Mrs Louise Fanshawe, Sheldon House, Chapel Street, Monyash, Bakewell DE45 1JJ
T: (01629) 813067
F: (01629) 815768
E: steveandlou.fanshawe@virgin.net
I: www.sheldoncottages.co.uk

Detached, self-catering cottage and flat in the heart of the Peak District; ideal for touring and walking. Dogs welcome in cottage by arrangement.

OPEN All Year

Low season per wk
£255.00–£261.00
High season per wk
£439.00–£450.00

NETTLEHAM, Lincolnshire Map ref 4C2

★★★★
1 Unit
Sleeping 2–4

THE STABLES
Lincoln
Contact: Mrs Annette Dickens, Northfield Farm, Scothern Road, Nettleham, Lincoln LN2 2TX
T: (01673) 861866
F: (01673) 862629
E: info@sunwish.com
I: www.sunwish.com

Cosy farm cottage located beside a private pond in the grounds of our home. Very well equipped. Village shops and pubs nearby.

OPEN All Year

Low season per wk
Min £250.00
High season per wk
Min £350.00

NORTHAMPTON, Northamptonshire Map ref 2C1 Tourist Information Centre Tel: (01604) 838800

★★★
1 Unit
Sleeping 1–9

MILL BARN COTTAGE
Northampton
Contact: Mr Roger Wolens, Mill Barn Cottage, The Mill House, Mill Lane, Northampton NN6 0NR
T: (01604) 810507
F: (01604) 810507
I: www.themillbarn.free-online.co.uk

A centuries-old riverside barn converted into a fully-equipped cottage, retaining all the original stone and oak-beam features. Unlimited access to gardens, river, barbecue etc. Private and secluded but offering easy access to major tourist attractions. Well equipped including microwave, dishwasher, washer/dryer, TV, video. Babysitting available. Six miles Northampton.

OPEN All Year

Special short-break and weekend rates from £50pn.

Low season per wk
Min £150.00
High season per wk
Max £450.00

 Colour maps Colour maps at the front of this guide pinpoint all places under which you will find accommodation listed.

EAST MIDLANDS

NOTTINGHAM, Nottingham Map ref 4C2 *Tourist Information Centre Tel: (0115) 915 5330*

★★★★
2 Units
Sleeping 1–4

WOODVIEW COTTAGES
Owthorpe
Contact: Mrs Judith Morley, Newfields Farm, Owthorpe, Nottingham NG12 3GF
T: (01949) 81279
F: (01949) 81279
E: enquiries@woodviewcottages.co.uk
I: www.woodviewcottages.co.uk

Idyllic cottages set in picturesque gardens with wood view surrounded by open countryside. Recently converted and tastefully furnished to complement the exposed beams/stonework. Well-equipped kitchen/comfortable living area/two bedrooms/bath/shower. Ideal touring/walking base. Located 20 minutes from Nottingham (eight miles)/Leicester on the edge of the Vale of Belvoir.

OPEN All Year

Short breaks available, minimum 3 nights.

Low season per wk
£350.00–£400.00
High season per wk
£400.00–£550.00

OLD BOLINGBROKE, Lincolnshire Map ref 4D2

★★★★
1 Unit
Sleeping 3

1 HOPE COTTAGE
Old Bolingbroke
Contact: Mr & Mrs Taylor, Clowery Cottage, Craypool Lane, Scothern, Lincoln LN2 2UU
T: (01673) 861412
F: (01673) 863336
E: no1hopecottage@aol.com
I: www.no1hopecottage.co.uk

Enjoy visiting this well-appointed country cottage, located in a quiet, royal village complete with castle ruins. Explore rolling Lincolnshire Wolds, nearby seaside or historic Lincoln and a host of market towns. Walking, cycling, fishing, nature reserves nearby – or just enjoy the peace and quiet!

OPEN All Year

Short breaks available. Contact us for late availability discounts.

Low season per wk
£185.00–£215.00
High season per wk
£245.00–£310.00

OUNDLE, Northamptonshire Map ref 3A1 *Tourist Information Centre Tel: (01832) 274333*

★★★★
1 Unit
Sleeping 1–4

THE BOLT HOLE
Oundle
Contact: Mrs Anita Spurrell, Rose Cottage, 70 Glapthorne Road, Oundle, Peterborough PE8 4PT
T: (01832) 272298 & 07850 388109
E: nanda@spurrell.ocs-uk.com

Well-appointed bungalow in quiet cul-de-sac, near town centre and countryside. Lounge/diner, fitted kitchen. Garden room/second bedroom. Double bedroom with large en suite shower. Separate cloaks/utility room. Basic stores/fresh breakfast ingredients supplied. Fenced rear garden with patio, lawn, vegetables and herbs. Parking on private drive outside front door.

OPEN All Year

Low season per wk
Min £280.00
High season per wk
Min £280.00

Map references The map references refer to the colour maps at the front of this guide. The first figure is the map number; the letter and figure which follow indicate the grid reference on the map.

210

EAST MIDLANDS

PARWICH, Derbyshire Map ref 4B2

★★★★★
1 Unit
Sleeping 1–2

TOM'S BARN
Ashbourne
Contact: Mr & Mrs J Fuller-Sessions, Tom's Barn, Orchard Farm, Parwich, Ashbourne DE6 1QB
T: (01335) 390519
E: tom@orchardfarm.demon.co.uk
I: www.tomsbarn.co.uk

A warm, welcoming, imaginatively restored and beautifully equipped 18thC limestone barn attached to the owners' home in the Peak Park village of Parwich. Tom's Barn is ideally situated for walking, watersports, antique shopping, good pubs and food, sightseeing or simply unwinding in peace.

OPEN All Year

Low season per wk
£250.00–£400.00
High season per wk
£300.00–£450.00

PEAK DISTRICT

See under Ashbourne, Bakewell, Bamford, Baslow, Edale, Froggatt, Great Hucklow, Hartington, Hathersage, Litton, Middleton-by-Youlgreave, Monyash, Parwich

See also Peak District in Heart of England section

SHERWOOD FOREST

See under Gonalston, Southwell

SOUTH COCKERINGTON, Lincolnshire Map ref 4D2

★★★
3 Units
Sleeping 2–4

WEST VIEW COTTAGES
Louth
Contact: Mr Richard Nicholson and Mrs Judith Hand, West View, South View Lane, Louth LN11 7ED
T: (01507) 327209
E: richard@nicholson55.freeserve.co.uk

Beautifully converted, single-storey farm buildings tastefully decorated to a high standard. Ideally located in a quiet village with the market town of Louth four miles away. There are numerous quiet beaches along the coast (six miles). Suitable walking and cycling routes are close by. Come and relax in pleasant surroundings.

OPEN All Year

Low season per wk
£200.00–£250.00
High season per wk
£250.00–£300.00

SOUTHWELL, Nottinghamshire Map ref 4C2

★★★
2 Units
Sleeping 2–6

THE HAYLOFT AND LITTLE TITHE
Southwell
Contact: Mrs Wilson, Lodge Farm, Morton, Southwell NG25 0XH
T: (01636) 830497
I: www.lodgebarns.co.uk

Situated on working farm in country village of Morton, these 18thC barn conversions offer you a high standard of self-contained facilities. Twin-bedded rooms, each with shower room, fully fitted kitchen, lounge. Set in an orchard courtyard and farmland. Within walking distance of village shop, local pubs and River Trent.

OPEN All Year

Low season per wk
£175.00–£300.00
High season per wk
£175.00–£300.00

211

EAST MIDLANDS

STANTON-ON-THE-WOLDS, Nottinghamshire Map ref 4C2

★★★★
1 Unit
Sleeping 6

FOXCOTE COTTAGE
Stanton-on-the-Wolds, Keyworth
Contact: Mrs Joan Hinchley, Hill Farm (Foxcote),
Melton Road, Stanton-on-the-Wolds, Keyworth
NG12 5PJ
T: (0115) 937 4337
F: (0115) 937 4337

OPEN All Year

Low season per wk
Min £450.00
High season per wk
Min £450.00

Situated on the edge of the Vale of Belvoir, the cottage overlooks open countryside, with views of a lake, and is set in a private, well-maintained garden.

SUTTON ST JAMES, Lincolnshire Map ref 3A1

★★★★
2 Units
Sleeping 4

FOREMANS BRIDGE CARAVAN PARK
Spalding
Contact: Mrs Ann Negus, Foreman's Bridge Caravan
Park, Sutton Road, Spalding PE12 0HU
T: (01945) 440346
F: (01945) 440346
I: www.foremans.bridge.co.uk

OPEN All Year

Low season per wk
£175.00–£240.00
High season per wk
£199.00–£289.00

Two holiday cottages, one suitable for the disabled, and seven luxury static caravans set in rural location adjacent to tranquil fen waterway. Ideal for fishing.

SWADLINCOTE, Derbyshire Map ref 4B3

★★★
1 Unit
Sleeping 1–5

BARNE COTTAGE
Swadlincote
Contact: Mrs M Fallon, Ivy Cottage, 96 Woodville Road,
Hartshorne, Swadlincote DE11 7EX
T: (01283) 221511
F: 0845 458 9632
E: mim@mims-holidaylets.co.uk
I: www.mims-holidaylets.co.uk

OPEN All Year

Low season per wk
£170.00–£195.00
High season per wk
£195.00–£275.00

Comfortable, homely and spacious cottage. Small village location. Beautiful countryside and many tourist attractions nearby. Excellent touring centre, convenient for motorways and Midlands airports.

TOWCESTER, Northamptonshire Map ref 2C1

★★★★
1 Unit
Sleeping 5

LODGE COTTAGE
Slapton, Nr Towcester
Contact: Mrs June Webster, Slapton Lodge, Slapton,
Towcester NN12 8PE
T: (01327) 860221
E: cjpht@aol.com

Cosy, three-bedroomed detached cottage with own garden, formerly the gatehouse to the owners' 17thC country house, set in 20 acres of parkland in which guests are welcome to wander. Use of tennis court and swimming pool by arrangement. Many attractions within easy drive – sightseeing or shopping!

OPEN All Year

Ring for late-availability
2/3-night breaks.

Low season per wk
Max £350.00
High season per wk
Max £595.00

WHALEY BRIDGE, Derbyshire Map ref 4B2

★★★★
2 Units
Sleeping 2–6

COTE BANK COTTAGES
High Peak
Contact: Mrs Pamela Broadhurst, Cote Bank Cottages,
Buxworth, Whaley Bridge, High Peak SK23 7NP
T: (01663) 750566
F: (01663) 750566
E: cotebank@btinternet.com
I: www.cotebank.co.uk

OPEN All Year

Payment accepted: Delta,
Mastercard, Switch, Visa

Low season per wk
£230.00–£300.00
High season per wk
£390.00–£600.00

Warm and welcoming cottages on a traditional hill farm, with marvellous views and log fires. Close to village amenities and wonderful walks from the door.

EAST MIDLANDS

WHALEY BRIDGE continued

★★★★★
2 Units
Sleeping 6–8

HORWICH BARNS
High Peak
Contact: Mr Colin MacQueen, Peak Cottages,
Strawberry Lee Lane, Totley Bents, Sheffield S17 3BA
T: (0114) 262 0777
F: (0114) 262 0666
I: www.peakcottages.com

OPEN All Year

Payment accepted: Amex, Delta, Diners, Mastercard, Switch, Visa, Euros

Low season per wk
£341.00–£418.00
High season per wk
£597.00–£720.00

Located on the edge of the High Peak, Horwich Barns (including Our Spring Cottage and Felton Brook Cottage) have recently been renovated to provide very high-quality accommodation.

WITHERN, Lincolnshire Map ref 4D2

★★★
6 Units
Sleeping 2–6

PARK FARM HOLIDAYS
Alford
Contact: Mrs E H Burkitt, Park Farm Holidays, Aby Road, Withern, Alford LN13 0DF
T: (01507) 450331
F: (01507) 450331
E: alan@park-farm25.fsnet.co.uk

OPEN All Year

Low season per wk
£150.00–£265.00
High season per wk
£220.00–£330.00

Situated just off the Wolds, seven miles from the sea. Two cottages on private road, four log cabins in woodland nearby. One mile from the village. Very peaceful. Good walking and cycling country. All are fully equipped and centrally heated. Birds and wildlife are all around.

WOODHALL SPA, Lincolnshire Map ref 4D2

★★
1 Unit
Sleeping 4

MILL LANE COTTAGE
Woodhall Spa
Contact: Mr Ian & Mrs Jane Williamson, 72 Mill Lane, Horsington, Woodhall Spa LN10 6QZ
T: (01526) 353101
E: janewill89@hotmail.com
I: www.skegness.net/woodhallspa.htm

OPEN All Year
Payment accepted: Euros

Low season per wk
£170.00–£190.00
High season per wk
£175.00–£200.00

Renovated cottage down quiet residential lane. Walks to river and pub. Cottage has all amenities, sports can be catered for.

★★★★
1 Unit
Sleeping 2–6

OLD FORGE COTTAGE
Woodhall Spa
Contact: Mr David Mawer, 47 Witham Road, Woodhall Spa LN10 6RG
T: (01526) 353813
F: (01526) 353996
E: tanyamawer@hotmail.com
I: www.oldforgecottage.co.uk

OPEN All Year

Low season per wk
Min £220.00
High season per wk
Min £300.00

Beautifully converted blacksmith's forge, with original beams and high ceilings. Cosy and comfortable surroundings with private decking area in garden. Central village location.

YARDLEY GOBION, Northamptonshire Map ref 2C1

★★
1 Unit
Sleeping 4

THE STABLE
Towcester
Contact: Mr Alan Paine, Old Wharf Farm, The Wharf, Towcester NN12 7UE
T: (01908) 542293
F: (01908) 542293

OPEN All Year

Low season per wk
Min £250.00
High season per wk
Min £300.00

Self-contained stable cottage in rural, canal-side location, built about 1850 by former French prisoners of war. Accommodation on ground and first floors.

(8)

Map references
Map references apply to the colour maps at the front of this guide.

A **quarter** of England's market towns are crammed into this **fertile corner** of the country.

East of England

Looking for some inspiration? Here are a few ideas to get you started in the East of England. **experience** classic flying legends at the Imperial War Museum Duxford. **discover** how Nelson came to be England's greatest naval hero at the Nelson Museum. **explore** the countryside that inspired Constable on the 81-mile Essex Way. **relax** while the children build sandcastles on the beach.

THE REGION
Bedfordshire, Cambridgeshire, Essex, Hertfordshire, Norfolk, Suffolk

CONTACT
▸ **EAST OF ENGLAND TOURIST BOARD**
Toppesfield Hall, Hadleigh,
Suffolk IP7 5DN
T: 0870 225 4800
F: 0870 225 4890
E: information@eetb.org.uk
www.visiteastofengland.com

EAST OF ENGLAND

The gently rolling countryside, historic market towns, traditional seaside resorts and unspoilt coastline of the East of England make it quintessentially English. Sailors, cyclists, hikers and bird-watchers will find it a natural haven.

Spinning wheels

With cycle tracks running along former railway lines, around reservoirs and through forests, this is the place to be on two wheels. Hire a bike and go where the mood takes you: follow specially-tailored cycle tours down quiet country lanes, or along one of the many cycle routes such as the Fens Cycle Way, the Suffolk Coastal Cycle Route or the Norfolk Coast Cycleway. Special maps are also available to guide you round a choice of Discovery Routes. The level terrain in the East of England means the views – and not the hills! – will take your breath away, making it perfect for cyclists of all ages.

Traditional England

A quarter of England's market towns are crammed into this fertile corner of the country that has somehow resisted the relentless march of time. Wander around colourful market stalls and take your pick of the local produce, experience the timeless atmosphere of the ancient market town of Woburn, visit Cromwell's birthplace at Huntingdon or make a bid at an antiques auction in Coggeshall. Many traditional crafts, such as glassblowing, can still be seen at Barleylands Craft Village in Billericay.

For aviation history visit the Imperial War Museum at Duxford, home to a fascinating display of historic aircraft including Spitfires and Gulf War jets – some of which still fly – as well as tanks and guns. For true wartime spirit, get along to one of the nostalgic events at Twinwood Airfield in 2005.

Left, from top take-off at the Shuttleworth Collection, Biggleswade; family fun in Southwold; admire Norwich Cathedral **Right** traditional entertainment in Great Yarmouth

Sail away

Over 250 miles of coastline and more than 50 rivers make this the ideal place for boating, sailing and fishing. Experience the calm of the reed-fringed waterways in the Norfolk Broads and enjoy the unique panorama of rivers and dykes in the Fens. The area is renowned for bird-watching, with plenty of wildlife to observe all year round at Minsmere, Titchwell, Berney Marshes and the Ouse Washes. The journey continues where rivers meet the sea. At the Norfolk Nelson Museum in Great Yarmouth the new interactive below-decks experience shows you how seamen lived in the 1800s. All along the coast there are many more places to stay and discover. From intimate fishing villages to the bustling seaside resorts of Felixstowe, Southend-on-Sea and Great Yarmouth, you're sure to find your ideal holiday destination.

Enjoy England official guides to quality   215

Places to visit

 Awarded VisitBritain's Quality Assured Visitor Attraction marque.

Audley End House and Park (English Heritage)
Audley End, Saffron Walden, Essex
Tel: (01799) 522399
www.english-heritage.org.uk
Palatial Jacobean house remodelled in the 18th-19thC with a magnificent great hall featuring 17thC plaster ceilings. Rooms and furniture by Robert Adam and park by Capability Brown.

Banham Zoo
The Grove, Banham, Norfolk
Tel: (01953) 887771
www.banhamzoo.co.uk
A wildlife spectacular which will take you on a journey to experience tigers, leopards and zebra plus some of the world's most exotic, rare and endangered animals.

Barleylands Craft Village and Farm Centre
Barleylands Road, Billericay, Essex
Tel: (01268) 290219
www.barleylands.co.uk
Stroll around over 20 impressive individual specialist workshops, including blacksmiths and glassblowing. Cuddle a rabbit and feed the animals.

Blickling Hall (National Trust)
Blickling, Norfolk
Tel: (01263) 738030
www.nationaltrust.org.uk
Jacobean redbrick mansion with garden, orangery, parkland and lake. Spectacular long gallery and interesting collections of furniture, pictures and books.

Bure Valley Railway: Aylsham Station
Norwich Road, Aylsham, Norfolk
Tel: (01263) 733858
www.bvrw.co.uk
A 15-inch narrow-gauge steam railway covering nine miles of track from Wroxham in the heart of the Norfolk Broads to the bustling market town of Aylsham.

Colchester Castle
Colchester, Essex
Tel: (01206) 282939
www.colchestermuseums.org.uk
A Norman keep on the foundations of a Roman temple. The archaeological material includes much on Roman Colchester (Camulodunum). Exciting hands-on displays.

Colchester Zoo
Maldon Road, Stanway, Colchester, Essex
Tel: (01206) 331292
www.colchester-zoo.co.uk
Zoo with 200 species and some of the best cat and primate collections in the UK, 24ha (60 acres) of gardens and lakes, award-winning animal enclosures and picnic areas.

Ely Cathedral
Chapter House, Ely, Cambridgeshire
Tel: (01353) 667735
www.cathedral.ely.anglican.org
One of England's finest cathedrals with guided tours and tours of the Octagon and West Tower. Monastic precincts, brass rubbing centre and The Stained Glass Museum.

Fritton Lake Country World
Church Lane, Fritton, Norfolk
Tel: (01493) 488208
www.frittonlake.co.uk
A 100-ha (250-acre) centre with a children's assault course, adventure playground, golf, fishing, boating, wildfowl, heavy horses, cart rides, falconry and flying displays.

Hatfield House, Park and Gardens
Hatfield, Hertfordshire
Tel: (01707) 287010
www.hatfield-house.co.uk
A magnificent Jacobean house, childhood home of Queen Elizabeth I and now home of the Marquess of Salisbury. Exquisite formal gardens, model soldiers and park trails.

216 This is just a selection of attractions available. Contact any Tourist Information Centre in the region for more ideas.

EAST OF ENGLAND

Hedingham Castle
Castle Hedingham, Essex
Tel: (01787) 460261
www.hedinghamcastle.co.uk
The finest Norman keep in England, built in 1140 by the de Veres, Earls of Oxford. Visited by Kings Henry VII and VIII and Queen Elizabeth I and besieged by King John.

Holkham Hall
Wells-next-the-Sea, Norfolk
Tel: (01328) 710227
www.holkham.co.uk
A classic 18thC Palladian-style mansion. Part of a great agricultural estate and a living treasure house of artistic and architectural history along with a bygones collection.

Ickworth House, Park and Gardens (National Trust)
The Rotunda, Horringer, Suffolk
Tel: (01284) 735270
www.nationaltrust.org.uk
An extraordinary oval house begun in 1795. View fine paintings, a beautiful collection of Georgian silver, an Italian garden and stunning parkland.

Imperial War Museum Duxford
Duxford, Cambridgeshire
Tel: (01223) 835000
www.iwm.org.uk
With its airshows, unique history and atmosphere, Duxford combines the sights, sounds and power of aircraft.

Knebworth House, Gardens and Park
Knebworth, Hertfordshire
Tel: (01438) 812661
www.knebworthhouse.com
15thC manor house, altered in the 19thC, with a Jacobean banquet hall and collections of manuscripts and portraits. Formal gardens, parkland and adventure playground.

Marsh Farm Country Park
Marsh Farm Road, South Woodham Ferrers, Essex
Tel: (01245) 321552
www.marshfarmcountrypark.co.uk
Working farm with sheep, a pig unit, free-range chickens, milking demonstrations, indoor and outdoor adventure play areas, nature reserve, walks, picnic area and pets' corner.

National Horseracing Museum and Tours
High Street, Newmarket, Suffolk
Tel: (01638) 667333
www.nhrm.co.uk
Award-winning display of the people and horses involved in racing's amazing history. Minibus tours of the gallops, stables and equine pool. Test your skills on the horse simulator in the hands-on gallery.

National Stud
Newmarket, Suffolk
Tel: (01638) 663464
www.nationalstud.co.uk
A conducted tour which includes top thoroughbred stallions, mares and foals, and gives an insight into the day-to-day running of a modern stud farm.

Norfolk Lavender Limited
Caley Mill, Heacham, Norfolk
Tel: (01485) 570384
www.norfolk-lavender.co.uk
Lavender is distilled from the flowers grown here and the oil is made into a wide range of gifts. There is a slide show when the distillery is not in action.

Norwich Cathedral
The Close, Norwich, Norfolk
Tel: (01603) 218321
www.cathedral.org.uk
A Norman cathedral dating from 1096 with 14thC roof bosses depicting bible scenes from Adam and Eve to the Day of Judgement. Shop and restaurant.

Oliver Cromwell's House
St Marys Street, Ely, Cambridgeshire
Tel: (01353) 662062
www.eastcambs.gov.uk
Explore the family home of Oliver Cromwell with its 17thC kitchen, parlour, Cromwell's study and a haunted bedroom. Tourist Information Centre, souvenirs and gift shop.

Peter Beales Roses
London Road, Attleborough, Norfolk
Tel: (01953) 454707
www.classicroses.co.uk
Large, world-famous collection of roses featuring over 1100 rare, unusual and beautiful varieties of which more than 250 are unique.

Pleasure Beach
South Beach Parade, Great Yarmouth, Norfolk
Tel: (01493) 844585
www.pleasure-beach.co.uk
Seafront leisure park with over 70 rides including Rollercoaster, Terminator, log flume, Twister, monorail, galloping horses, caterpillar, ghost train and fun house.

The Royal Air Force Air Defence Radar Museum
RAF Neatishead, Norwich, Norfolk
Tel: (01692) 633309
www.radarmuseum.co.uk
Discover the history of the development and use of radar in the UK and overseas from 1935 to date. Winner of the Regional Visitor Attraction (under 100,000 visitors), National Silver Award.

Left re-enactment of the past at Hedingham Castle; enjoy a visit to Holkham Hall, Wells-next-the-Sea

Enjoy England official guides to **quality**

Places to visit

Awarded VisitBritain's Quality Assured Visitor Attraction marque.

RSPB Minsmere Nature Reserve
Westleton, Suffolk
Tel: (01728) 648281
www.rspb.org.uk/reserves/minsmere
This RSPB reserve is located on the Suffolk coast with bird-watching hides and trails, year-round events and guided walks. Visitor centre with a large shop and welcoming tearoom.

Sainsbury Centre for Visual Arts
University of East Anglia, Norwich, Norfolk
Tel: (01603) 593199
www.uea.ac.uk/scva
Housed in a breathtaking Norman Foster building, the Sainsbury Collection includes works by artists such as Picasso, Bacon and Henry Moore, alongside art from across cultures and time.

Sandringham
Sandringham, Norfolk
Tel: (01553) 612908
www.sandringhamestate.co.uk
The country retreat of HM The Queen. A delightful house set in 24ha (60 acres) of grounds and lakes, with a museum of royal vehicles and memorabilia.

Shuttleworth Collection
Old Warden Aerodrome, Biggleswade, Bedfordshire
Tel: (01767) 627288
www.shuttleworth.org
A unique historical collection of aircraft – from a 1909 Bleriot to a 1942 Spitfire in flying condition – plus cars in running order dating from an 1898 Panhard.

Somerleyton Hall and Gardens
Somerleyton, Suffolk
Tel: (01502) 730224
www.somerleyton.co.uk
Early Victorian stately mansion in Anglo-Italian style, with lavish features and fine state rooms. Beautiful 5-ha (12-acre) gardens, with historic yew hedge maze. Gift shop.

Stondon Museum
Station Road, Henlow Camp, Bedfordshire
Tel: (01462) 850339
www.transportmuseum.co.uk
A museum with transport exhibits from the early 1900s to the 1980s. The largest private collection in England of bygone vehicles from the beginning of the century.

Thursford Collection
Thursford Green, Thursford, Norfolk
Tel: (01328) 878477
A live musical show with nine mechanical organs and a Wurlitzer show starring Robert Wolfe, plus fairground rides and traction engines.

Wimpole Hall and Home Farm (National Trust)
Arrington, Hertfordshire
Tel: (01223) 206000
www.wimpole.org
A 18thC house with a yellow drawing room by Sir John Soane, set in a landscaped park with a folly and Chinese bridge. Home Farm has a rare breeds centre.

Woburn Abbey
Woburn, Bedforshire
Tel: (01525) 290666
www.woburnabbey.co.uk
18thC Palladian mansion, altered by Henry Holland, the Prince Regent's architect, containing collections of English silver, French and English furniture and Old Master paintings.

Woburn Safari Park
Woburn Park, Woburn, Bedfordshire
Tel: (01525) 290407
www.woburnsafari.co.uk
Drive through the safari park with 30 species of animals in natural groups just a windscreen's width away, then venture into the action-packed Wild World Leisure Area.

Above bright lights in Great Yarmouth; come face-to face with a tiger at Woburn Safari Park **Right** Sandringham, HM The Queen's country retreat

218 This is just a selection of attractions available. Contact any Tourist Information Centre in the region for more ideas.

EAST OF ENGLAND

East of England Tourist Board
Toppesfield Hall, Hadleigh, Suffolk IP7 5DN
T: 0870 225 4800 F: 0870 225 4890
E: information@eetb.org.uk
www.visiteastofengland.com

The following publications are available from the East of England Tourist Board:

Great days out in the East of England 2005 – an information-packed A5 guide featuring all you need to know about places to visit and things to see and do in the East of England. From historic houses to garden centres, from animal collections to craft centres – this guide has it all, including film and TV locations, city, town and village information, events, shopping, car tours plus lots more! (£4.50 excl p&p).

England's Cycling Country – the East of England offers perfect cycling country – from quiet country lanes to ancient trackways. This free publication promotes the many Cycling Discovery Maps that are available to buy (£1.50 excl p&p), as well as providing useful information for anyone planning a cycling tour of the region.

Travel information

By road:
The region is easily accessible. From London and the south via the A1(M), M11, M25, A10, M1, A46 and A12. From the north via the A1(M), A15, A5, M1 and A6. From the west via the A14, A47, A421, A428, A418, A41, A422, A17 and A427.

By rail:
Regular fast trains run to all major cities and towns in the region. London stations which serve the region are Liverpool Street, Kings Cross, Fenchurch Street, St Pancras, London Marylebone and London Euston. Bedford, Luton and St Albans are on the Thameslink line which runs to Kings Cross and on to London Gatwick Airport. There is also a direct link between London Stansted Airport and Liverpool Street. Through the Channel Tunnel, there are trains direct from Paris and Brussels to Waterloo Station, London. A short journey on the Underground will bring passengers to those stations operating services into the East of England. Further information on rail journeys in the East of England can be obtained on 0845 748 4950.

Enjoy England official guides to quality

EAST OF ENGLAND

Where to stay in East of England

All place names in the blue bands, under which accommodation is listed, are shown on the maps at the front of this guide.

A complete listing of all VisitBritain assessed accommodation covered by this guide appears at the back.

Accommodation symbols
Symbols give useful information about services and facilities. Inside the back cover flap you can find a key to these symbols. Keep it open for easy reference.

ALDEBURGH, Suffolk Map ref 3C2 *Tourist Information Centre Tel: (01728) 453637*

★★★★
1 Unit
Sleeping 3

CRAGSIDE
Aldeburgh
Contact: Mrs Lesley Valentine, Rookery Farm, Cratfield, Halesworth IP19 0QE
T: (01986) 798609
F: (01986) 798609
E: j.r.valentine@btinternet.com

OPEN All Year

Short breaks available Oct-Mar. Minimum 3-night stay.

Low season per wk
£210.00–£270.00
High season per wk
£270.00–£385.00

Deceptively spacious accommodation in large house on Crag Path, recently completely refurbished. Twenty yards sea. Well equipped for a really comfortable holiday with two TVs, microwave, dishwasher, washer/dryer, telephone/answerphone, inglenook fireplaces. Cosy for winter with central heating, down duvets, electric blankets. No pets and no children, please.

 Ratings All accommodation in this guide has been rated, or is awaiting a rating, by a trained VisitBritain assessor.

DAY LAUNCHES & CRUISERS

Barnes Brinkcraft
For all-year-round broads holidays
- Boats available for 2-10 persons • Easy to board
- Hourly, Daily, Weekly • Heated all-weather day launches
- Riverside Lodges available all-year-round for up to 16 people

Telephone: 01603 782625

Riverside Road, Wroxham, Norfolk NR12 8UD
email: bookings@barnesbrinkcraft.co.uk www.barnesbrinkcraft.co.uk

EAST OF ENGLAND

ALDEBURGH continued

★★★
1 Unit
Sleeping 12–15

ORLANDO
Aldeburgh
Contact: Mr Peter Hatcher, Martlesham Hall, Church Lane, Woodbridge IP12 4PQ
T: (01394) 382126
F: (01394) 278600
E: orlando@hatcher.co.uk
I: www.hatcher.co.uk/orlando

OPEN All Year

Low season per wk
£800.00–£1,000.00
High season per wk
£1,300.00–£1,600.00

Orlando is a spacious, six-bedroom house adjacent to the beach with magnificent, panoramic views of the sea. The house is well equipped with all modern facilities. Open-plan kitchen with Aga and dining area. Two living rooms on two floors, four bathrooms. Ideal for three families.

★★★★
1 Unit
Sleeping 1–4

RIVER COTTAGE
Iken Cliff
Contact: Kate Kilburn, River Cottage, Iken Cliff, Woodbridge IP12 2EN
T: (01728) 688267
F: (01728) 688267
E: dkilburn@cmpinformation.com

OPEN All Year

Low season per wk
£250.00–£300.00
High season per wk
£350.00–£400.00

A semi-detached cottage on the banks of the Alde estuary, between Snape Maltings and Aldeburgh – one of the most spectacular views in East Anglia.

ALRESFORD, Essex Map ref 3B2

★★★
1 Unit
Sleeping 1–2

CREEK LODGE
Colchester
Contact: Mrs Patricia Mountney, Ford Lane, Colchester
CO7 8BE
T: (01206) 825411

Low season per wk
Min £150.00
High season per wk
Min £230.00

Tranquil riverside cottage set in extensive landscaped gardens, perfectly situated for sailing, walking and bird-watching. Only five miles from historic Colchester.

BACTON, Norfolk Map ref 3C1

★★★★
1 Unit
Sleeping 6

SWISS COTTAGE
Bacton
Contact: Mrs Linda Weinberg, Buehl Str 6, 8113 Boppelsen, Switzerland
T: 00 41 1844 2222
F: 00 41 1840 0222
E: info@swissonthebeach.com
I: www.swissonthebeach.com

OPEN All Year

Short breaks available on request.

Low season per wk
£340.00–£450.00
High season per wk
£550.00–£720.00

Few properties enjoy sea and sand views at such close proximity. With just a few steps to a quiet sandy beach, this recently built brick and flint cottage is within easy reach of the Norfolk Broads. The spacious conservatory and open-plan continental-style living accommodation enhance this idyllic location.

Quality Assurance Standard
Star ratings and awards were correct at time of going to press but are subject to change. Please check at the time of booking.

EAST OF ENGLAND

★★★★★
1 Unit
Sleeping 2–6

THE PUMP HOUSE APARTMENT
Billericay
Contact: Mr John Bayliss, Pump House, Church Street, Great Burstead, Billericay CM11 2TR
T: (01277) 656579
F: (01277) 631160
E: johnwbayliss@btinternet.com
I: www.thepumphouseapartment.co.uk

The apartment is on two floors and luxuriously furnished, with air conditioning. The accommodation comprises two living rooms, fully-fitted kitchen/diner and the option of one, two or three bedrooms with one, two or three bath/shower rooms. Guests have use of heated outdoor pool (May to September), hot tub, gazebo and gardens. Personal supervision.

OPEN All Year

Payment accepted: Amex, Mastercard, Switch, Visa, Euros

Low season per wk
£425.00–£890.00
High season per wk
£550.00–£990.00

5% discount for stays of 4 weeks/10% discount for stays of 8 weeks against 2/3-bedroom options.

Norfolk Cottage Holidays.com

Selection of self catering, owner managed holiday cottages, tucked away in Norfolk villages. Perfect for the Broads, Coast, Norwich and Great Yarmouth.

Visit our Web Site for full details
www.NorfolkCottageHolidays.com

Book Early
08456 444018
calls charged at local rate

Open All Year 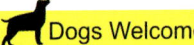 Dogs Welcome 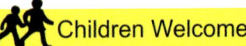 Children Welcome 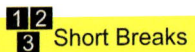 Short Breaks

EAST OF ENGLAND

BLAKENEY, Norfolk Map ref 3B1

★★★
1 Unit
Sleeping 3-8

THE TANNING HOUSE
Blakeney
Contact: Mrs Brigid Pope, The Lodge, Back Lane,
Blakeney, Holt NR25 7NR
T: (01263) 740477
F: (01263) 741356
E: enquiries@marinershillcottages.com
I: www.marinershillcottages.com

OPEN All Year

Low season per wk
£165.00–£475.00
High season per wk
£565.00–£765.00

Barn conversion in quiet cul-de-sac facing the harbour. Open log fires, ample parking. Local amenities. Ideal for golf, bird-watching, sailing, riding, walking.

BRANCASTER STAITHE, Norfolk Map ref 3B1

★★★
2 Units
Sleeping 2-6

VISTA & CARPENTERS COTTAGES
Brancaster Staithe
Contact: Mrs Gloria Smith, Dale View, Main Road,
Brancaster Staithe, King's Lynn PE31 8BY
T: (01485) 210497
F: (01485) 210497

OPEN All Year

Short breaks (weekend and mid-week) available during low season or at short notice; minimum 3 nights.

Low season per wk
£210.00–£300.00
High season per wk
£300.00–£750.00

These lovely cottages enjoy one of the best views along the Norfolk coast (see picture). Walking down the cottage gardens you meet the saltmarsh and the Norfolk coastal path. The cottages have exposed beams and open fires as well as central heating throughout. Close to amenities. Pets welcome.

BRANTHAM, Suffolk Map ref 3B2

★★★★
1 Unit
Sleeping 6

BRANTHAM HALL
Manningtree
Contact: Ms Caroline Williams, Brantham Lodge,
Brantham, Manningtree CO11 1PT
T: (01473) 327090
F: (01473) 327090
E: hwilliams@branmann.freeserve.co.uk

OPEN All Year

Short breaks available except Jul and Aug.

Low season per wk
Max £300.00
High season per wk
£400.00–£600.00

18thC cottage on South Suffolk farm overlooking Stour estuary (bird-watching). Full of character, two narrow staircases, four walk-through bedrooms. Enclosed garden, paved terrace. Footpaths to Flatford, Dedham and Shotley Peninsula. Peaceful spot, but pubs, shops and Alton Water nearby. Easy access to Ipswich, Colchester and Suffolk coast.

Special breaks

Many establishments offer special promotions and themed breaks. These are highlighted in red. (All such offers are subject to availability.)

EAST OF ENGLAND

BROME, Suffolk Map ref 3B2

★★★★
1 Unit
Sleeping 1–4

THE HOMESTEAD BARN
Eye
Contact: Mr David & Mrs Diana Downes, The Homestead Barn, The Homestead, Brome, Eye IP23 8AE
T: (01379) 870489
E: www.dianadownes@hotmail.com

Delightful Grade II Listed converted barn with exposed beams. Situated on smallholding, in small village within easy reach of coast. Central to Norwich, Bury St Edmunds, Ipswich. Large fenced garden/patio. Secure parking. Two bedrooms. Fully equipped kitchen. Comfortable sitting room. Available all year round.

OPEN All Year

Short breaks available Oct–Mar. Minimum 3 nights. £100.

Low season per wk £200.00–£250.00
High season per wk £250.00–£350.00

BRUISYARD, Suffolk Map ref 3C2

★★★★
1 Unit
Sleeping 20

BRUISYARD HALL
Saxmundham
Contact: Mr Robert Rous, The Country House, Dennington, Woodbridge IP13 8AU
T: (01728) 638712
F: (01728) 638712
E: dennington@farmline.com
I: www.bruisyardhall.co.uk

Once a priory of the Poor Clares, this beautiful Grade II Listed house now provides all the comforts for a family holiday in secluded countryside with meadows to the front and moat and fish behind. Some en suite rooms. Ideal for weekend house parties. Also available for mid-week breaks.

OPEN All Year

Weekend house parties – all months except Aug.

Low season per wk Min £2,400.00
High season per wk Max £5,000.00

BURNHAM MARKET, Norfolk Map ref 3B1

★★★
1 Unit
Sleeping 6

BARLEY COTTAGE
Burnham Market
Contact: Mr Andrew & Mrs Susan Watley, 26 Mount Crescent, Brentwood CM14 5DB
T: (01277) 218116
E: a.s.watley@btinternet.com

Beamed flint Maltings cottage. Peaceful location but just one minute from village green, restaurants and specialist shops. Close to beautiful Norfolk Heritage Coast.

OPEN All Year

Low season per wk £240.00–£380.00
High season per wk £325.00–£525.00

★★★
1 Unit
Sleeping 4

FUCHSIA COTTAGE
King's Lynn
Contact: Mr Tinsley, 6 The Green, Stanhoe, King's Lynn PE31 8QE
T: (01485) 518896
E: tinsley.co@virgin.net

A terraced Victorian cottage in rural surroundings in Stanhoe near picturesque Burnham Market. Ideally located for visiting nature reserves, beaches and other places of interest.

OPEN All Year

Low season per wk £175.00–£255.00
High season per wk £255.00–£380.00

Credit card bookings
If you book by telephone and are asked for your credit card number it is advisable to check the proprietor's policy should you cancel your reservation.

EAST OF ENGLAND

CAMBRIDGE, Cambridgeshire Map ref 2D1 *Tourist Information Centre Tel: (01223) 322640*

★★★★
3 Units
Sleeping 2-5

HOME FROM HOME APARTMENTS
Cambridge
Contact: Mrs Fasano, Home From Home Apartments,
78 Milton Road, Cambridge CB4 1LA
T: (01223) 323555
F: (01223) 277612
E: homefromhome@tesco.net
I: www.homefromhomecambridge.co.uk

Low season per wk
£350.00–£490.00
High season per wk
£420.00–£560.00

Victorian house centrally located to river and colleges. Apartments are fully equipped and furnished to a high standard, with home from home hospitality.

★★★★
1 Unit
Sleeping 1-8

A wonderful Victorian headmaster's house situated in an unspoilt village four miles from Cambridge city centre. Three/four bedrooms, two bathrooms, garden room, patio garden. Beautiful interior, very well equipped. Local riverside walks and traditional pubs. A full brochure on request.

THE SCHOOL HOUSE
Cambridge
Contact: Mr Terry & Mrs Nicola Mann, The School House,
High Street, Horningsea, Cambridge CB5 9JG
T: (01223) 440077
F: (01223) 441414
E: schoolhse1@aol.com
I: schoolhouse-uk.com

OPEN All Year except
Christmas and New Year

Payment accepted: Delta, Mastercard, Switch, Visa, Euros

Low season per wk
£300.00–£600.00
High season per wk
£400.00–£650.00

Weekend breaks can be offered.

CASTLE HEDINGHAM, Essex Map ref 3B2

★★★★
2 Units

Rosemary Farm is situated in a quiet country lane within view of Hedingham Castle, former home of the De Veres, Earls of Oxford, and is a convenient base for visiting the many nearby attractions. Cottages in barn conversion offering lounge, kitchen, one and two bedrooms, shower/toilet, tiled flooring throughout, patio area, parking.

ROSEMARY FARM
Halstead
Contact: Mr Garry Ian Henderson, Rosemary Lane,
Castle Hedingham, Nr Halstead CO9 3AJ
T: (01787) 461653

OPEN All Year

Low season per wk
Min £200.00
High season per wk
Max £327.00

Town index

This can be found at the back of the guide. If you know where you want to stay the index will give you the page number listing accommodation in your chosen town, city or village.

225

EAST OF ENGLAND

CLEY NEXT THE SEA, Norfolk Map ref 3B1

★★★
1 Unit
Sleeping 1–7

ARCHWAY COTTAGE
Holt
Contact: Mrs Vickey Jackson, 3A Brickendon Lane, Hertford SG13 8NU
T: (01992) 511303 & 503196
F: (01992) 511303

Pretty 18thC flint cottage, well furnished and comfortable, with four bedrooms, two bathrooms and garage. Near village centre, bird sanctuaries and the sea. Also Chantry, another similar cottage in Wells-next-the-Sea. Illustrated brochures available for both cottages.

OPEN All Year

Low season per wk
£200.00–£300.00
High season per wk
£350.00–£500.00

CLIPPESBY, Norfolk Map ref 3C1

★★★
3 Units
Sleeping 2–6

CLIPPESBY HALL
Clippesby
Contact: Mrs Jean Lindsay, Clippesby Hall, Hall Road, Clippesby, Great Yarmouth NR29 3BL
T: (01493) 367800
F: (01493) 367809
E: holidays@clippesby.com
I: www.clippesby.com

Discover Clippesby Hall's pine lodges and park. Set in the heart of the Norfolk Broads National Park, it's a great holiday area. Great for cycling, bird-watching and boating. Great rivers, beaches and broads, plus numerous tourist attractions. Clippesby Hall's park holds a Bellamy Gold Award for conservation. Ask for colour brochure.

OPEN All Year

Payment accepted: Amex, Delta, Mastercard, Switch, Visa

Short breaks available Sep-beginning of Jul.

Low season per wk
£399.00–£499.00
High season per wk
£679.00–£799.00

COLCHESTER, Essex Map ref 3B2 Tourist Information Centre Tel: (01206) 282920

★★★
1 Unit
Sleeping 5

50 ROSEBERY AVENUE
Colchester
Contact: Mrs Webb, 51 Rosebery Avenue, Colchester CO1 2UP
T: (01206) 866888
E: rosebery.avenue@ntlworld.com

Modernised house in quiet town-centre location. Castle, park, shops, museums and sports centre within walking distance. Ideal for east coast. Bus/trains close by.

OPEN All Year

Low season per wk
£200.00–£220.00
High season per wk
£240.00–£270.00

COTTON, Suffolk Map ref 3B2

★★★★
3 Units
Sleeping 1–3

CODA COTTAGES
Stowmarket
Contact: Mrs Kate Sida-Nicholls, Poplar Farm, Dandy Corner, Cotton, Stowmarket IP14 4QX
T: (01449) 780076
F: (01449) 780280
I: www.codacottages.co.uk

A 17thC barn with original features has been converted into cottages set around a shared courtyard surrounded by the owner's farmland in mid-Suffolk. Each cottage has exposed beams, wooden floors and open brickwork as well as all the modern accessories needed for a very comfortable stay.

OPEN All Year

Short breaks available all year.

Low season per wk
£155.00–£225.00
High season per wk
£235.00–£350.00

EAST OF ENGLAND

CRATFIELD, Suffolk Map ref 3C2

★★★★
1 Unit
Sleeping 2–6

CHERRY TREES
Halesworth
Contact: Mrs Chris Knox, Cratfield Hall, Halesworth
IP19 0DR
T: (01379) 586709
F: (01379) 588033
E: J.L.Knox@farming.co.uk
I: www.cratfield-hall.co.uk

OPEN All Year

Short breaks available (excl summer holidays).

Low season per wk
£190.00–£350.00
High season per wk
£200.00–£420.00

A chalet/bungalow situated in Suffolk with an enclosed garden set well back from the road and in the grounds of a working farm. Facilities for children. Pets welcome.

CROMER, Norfolk Map ref 3C1 Tourist Information Centre Tel: (01263) 512497

★★
1 Unit

CLIFF HOLLOW
Cromer
Contact: Miss L Willins, Cliff Hollow,
35 Overstrand Road, Cromer NR27 0AL
T: (01263) 512447
F: (01263) 512447

Low season per wk
Min £200.00
High season per wk
Min £250.00

Family home, secluded area, own garden, four bedrooms, combined bathroom/wc, lounge, dining room and kitchen. Cot and highchair.

DALLINGHOO, Suffolk Map ref 3C2

★★★★
2 Units
Sleeping 5

THE CARPENTER'S SHOP AT ROBINS NEST
Woodbridge
Contact: Mr Robert Blake, 1A Moorfield Road,
Woodbridge IP12 4JN
T: (01394) 382565 & 07907 773545
F: (01394) 389370
E: robert@blake4110.fsbusiness.co.uk

OPEN All Year

Low season per wk
£248.00–£306.00
High season per wk
£306.00–£650.00

16thC cottage and separate converted carpenter's shop, in quiet rural position overlooking countryside. Restored to a high standard. Ideal base for many local tourist attractions.

DARSHAM, Suffolk Map ref 3C2

★★★
2 Units
Sleeping 2–4

THE GRANARY & THE MALLARDS
Saxmundham
Contact: Mrs S Bloomfield, The Granary & The Mallards,
Priory Farm, Darsham, Saxmundham IP17 3QD
T: (01728) 668459

OPEN All Year

Low season per wk
£150.00–£275.00
High season per wk
£275.00–£425.00

Traditional 18thC Granary, carefully restored to retain its unusual, oak-beamed design and providing comfortable, well-equipped accommodation. Newly converted cart lodge and stables adjoining The Granary, providing ground floor accommodation with easy access (rating to be confirmed). Situated in picturesque Suffolk countryside within easy reach of the coast and heathlands.

Important note Information on accommodation listed in this guide has been supplied by the proprietors. As changes may occur you are advised to check details at the time of booking.

EAST OF ENGLAND

DOCKING, Norfolk Map ref 3B1

★★★★★
2 Units
Sleeping 4–7

NORFOLK HOUSE & COURTYARD COTTAGE
Docking
Contact: Mr Tim & Mrs Liz Witley, 17 Peddars Way South, Ringstead PE36 5LF
T: (01485) 525341
F: (01485) 532715
E: info@escapetonorfolk.com

Victorian townhouse and character cottage. Luxurious accommodation fully equipped with every comfort. Individually and tastefully designed rooms in period or traditional Norfolk style with numerous curios, artworks and homely touches. Bedrooms en suite or with hand basins. A warm welcome, log fires, fresh flowers, music room with keyboard. Quality assurance.

OPEN All Year
Payment accepted: Euros

Last-minute holidays at reduced rate. Winter breaks Nov-Mar from £175. Phone for tariff.

Low season per wk
Min £280.00
High season per wk
Min £395.00

EAST BERGHOLT, Suffolk Map ref 3B2

★★★
1 Unit
Sleeping 4

WOODSTOCK WING WOODSTOCK
Colchester
Contact: Mr Keith & Mrs Janet Alcoe, Woodstock Wing Woodstock, Gaston Street, East Bergholt, Colchester CO7 6SD
T: (01206) 298724
E: janetandkeith@familyalcoe.fsnet.co.uk

OPEN All Year

Low season per wk
Min £250.00
High season per wk
£250.00–£260.00

Close to centre of picturesque village, John Constable's birthplace. Ideal location to explore Suffolk and beyond. Comfortably furnished, all facilities, parking. Brochure available on request.

ELMSWELL, Suffolk Map ref 3B2

★★★★★
1 Unit
Sleeping 8

OAK FARM
Bury St Edmunds
Contact: Mr & Mrs Dyball, Willow Farm, Ashfield Road, Elmswell, Bury St Edmunds IP30 9HG
T: (01359) 240263
F: (01359) 240263

Oak Farm is a spacious beamed farmhouse, superbly renovated, extended and equipped, in rural surroundings. It is one mile from A14 dual carriageway and makes an excellent centre for exploring East Anglia or relaxing in a comfortable, peaceful environment with all the family.

OPEN All Year

Low season per wk
£480.00–£500.00
High season per wk
£500.00–£725.00

ERPINGHAM, Norfolk Map ref 3B1

★★★
5 Units
Sleeping 2–7

GRANGE FARM
Norwich
Contact: Mrs Jane Bell, Scarrow Beck Farm, Erpingham, Norwich NR11 7QU
T: (01263) 761241
F: (01263) 761241
E: jez.bell@btinternet.com
www.grangefarmholidays.co.uk

A 17thC farmhouse and converted period buildings around a courtyard, all in large garden in the middle of an 80-acre farm beside a river. Heated indoor swimming pool. Open Christmas and New Year.

OPEN All Year

Weekends (up to 4 nights) from £136 in low season.

Low season per wk
£200.00–£376.00
High season per wk
£328.00–£576.00

228

EAST OF ENGLAND

EYE, Suffolk Map ref 3B2

★★★★
4 Units
Sleeping 2–6

ATHELINGTON HALL
Eye
Contact: Mr Peter Havers, Athelington Hall, Horham, Eye IP21 5EJ
T: (01728) 628233
F: (01379) 384491
E: peter@logcabinholidays.co.uk
I: www.logcabinholidays.co.uk

OPEN All Year
Payment accepted: Amex, Delta, Diners, Mastercard, Switch, Visa, Euros

Low season per wk
£175.00–£199.00
High season per wk
£475.00–£500.00

Situated in an idyllic location, surrounding area is a haven for wildlife and birds with many unspoilt areas to explore. Breathtaking Suffolk Heritage Coast, only 25 minutes away.

FAKENHAM, Norfolk Map ref 3B1

★★★–★★★★★
14 Units
Sleeping 2–7

Superbly equipped cottages in eight acres of secluded grounds. Leisure centre with heated indoor pool, sauna, solarium and games room. Animal farm, children's play area, tennis court and enchanted wood. Plenty to do for adults and children with Norfolk's wonderful beaches a short drive away. Pets welcome.

IDYLLIC COTTAGES AT VERE LODGE
Fakenham
Contact: Jackie Nelson, Idyllic Cottages at Vere Lodge, South Raynham, Fakenham NR21 7HE
T: (01328) 838261
F: (01328) 838300
E: major@verelodge.co.uk
I: www.idylliccottages.co.uk

OPEN All Year
Payment accepted: Delta, Mastercard, Switch, Visa

Short breaks available.

Low season per wk
£320.00–£616.00
High season per wk
£659.00–£1,491.00

★★★★
1 Unit
Sleeping 1–8

Brimming with character, this pretty, well-equipped home wraps you in its cosy, comfortable interior. Nestled in a secluded, rambling flower garden, Pollywiggle Cottage lies on the fringe of a tranquil village 15 miles from long, sandy beaches. A wealth of attractions and amenities are within an easy drive.

POLLYWIGGLE COTTAGE
Nr Fakenham
Contact: Mrs Marilyn Farnham-Smith, 79 Earlham Road, Norwich NR2 3RE
T: (01603) 471990
F: (01603) 612221
E: marilyn@pollywigglecottage.co.uk
I: www.pollywigglecottage.co.uk

OPEN All Year

Small-party reductions and short breaks available – minimum 3 nights, during non-peak times.

Low season per wk
£360.00–£550.00
High season per wk
£480.00–£800.00

FELIXSTOWE, Suffolk Map ref 3C2 Tourist Information Centre Tel: (01394) 276770

★★★
1 Unit
Sleeping 1–4

FLAT 2
Felixstowe
Contact: Mrs Gwen Lynch, Cedar House, 20 The Close, Tattingstone, Ipswich IP9 2PD
T: (01473) 328729

OPEN All Year

Low season per wk
£140.00–£170.00
High season per wk
£170.00–£210.00

Two-bedroomed, first floor flat with balcony overlooking the sea. In quiet area and within walking distance of the town centre, with own parking space.

 Confirm your booking You are advised to confirm your booking in writing.

EAST OF ENGLAND

FELIXSTOWE continued

★★★
1 Unit
Sleeping 1–4

HONEYPOT COTTAGE
Ipswich
Contact: Mrs Theresa Adams, Deben Lodge, Falkenham,
Ipswich IP10 0RA
T: (01394) 448564
E: adams99@btinternet.com

OPEN All Year

Low season per wk
£165.00–£195.00
High season per wk
£230.00–£275.00

Comfortable, well-equipped cottage in delightful, peaceful, rural location near River Deben, five miles from Felixstowe. Ideal walking, cycling and bird-watching area. Short breaks available.

FIELD DALLING, Norfolk Map ref 3B1

★★★★
1 Unit
Sleeping 1–5

EASTCOTE COTTAGE
Field Dalling
Contact: Mrs Sally Grove, Eastcote Cottage, Holt Road,
Field Dalling, Holt NR25 7LE
T: (01328) 830359
E: sally@eastcotecottage.co.uk
I: www.eastcotecottage.co.uk

OPEN All Year

3-night stays available
Oct-Jan (excl Christmas and
New Year).

Low season per wk
£300.00–£400.00
High season per wk
£400.00–£500.00

An excellent renovation offering rural charm in relaxing and snug surroundings. Tastefully decorated and furnished. Fully equipped with all mod cons. Underfloor heating throughout plus woodburner. Secure private garden with patio, garden furniture and barbecue. Two bathrooms, pets considered. Tennis court available. Ample off-road parking.

FOXLEY, Norfolk Map ref 3B1

★★-★★★★
12 Units
Sleeping 3–7

MOOR FARM STABLE COTTAGES
Dereham
Contact: Mr Paul Davis, Moor Farm, Foxley, Dereham
NR20 4QN
T: (01362) 688523
F: (01362) 688523
E: moorfarm@aol.com
I: www.moorfarmstablecottages.co.uk

OPEN All Year

2/3-night breaks available
(mid-week or weekend)
Sep-May. 5 nights
Christmas/New Year.

Low season per wk
£190.00–£400.00
High season per wk
£280.00–£575.00

Located on working farm, a courtyard of two- and three-bedroomed self-catering chalets, all fully equipped and centrally heated, two specially adapted for disabled. Ideally situated for coast, Broads, Norwich, Sandringham. 365 acres of mature woodland adjoining owners' farm to walk. Fishing available close by. Pets welcome.

Country Code Always follow the Country Code
• Enjoy the countryside and respect its life and work • Guard against all risk of fire • Fasten all gates • Keep your dogs under close control • Keep to public paths across farmland • Use gates and stiles to cross fences, hedges and walls • Leave livestock, crops and machinery alone • Take your litter home • Help to keep all water clean • Protect wildlife, plants and trees • Take special care on country roads • Make no unnecessary noise.

EAST OF ENGLAND

GAYTON, Norfolk Map ref 3B1

★★★
1 Unit
Sleeping 1–4

FIELD VIEW
King's Lynn
Contact: Mr & Mrs Steel, Aramir, Lynn Road, Gayton, King's Lynn PE32 1QJ
T: (01553) 636813

Set in the very popular rural village of Gayton, this well-presented, semi-detached, two-bedroomed cottage is an ideal base for exploring all Norfolk has to offer. Ample off-road parking and unspoilt views over open countryside. The village boasts many amenities, including two highly recommended public houses.

OPEN All Year

Low season per wk
£150.00–£195.00
High season per wk
£195.00–£275.00

GORLESTON-ON-SEA, Norfolk Map ref 3C1

★★★
1 Unit
Sleeping 4

MANOR COTTAGE
Gorleston, Great Yarmouth
Contact: Mrs Margaret Ward, North Manor House, 12 Pier Plain, Gorleston, Great Yarmouth NR31 6PE
T: (01493) 669845
F: (01493) 669845
E: manorcottage@wardm4.fsnet.co.uk
I: www.wardm4.fsnet.co.uk

OPEN All Year except Christmas and New Year

Low season per wk
£150.00–£220.00
High season per wk
£220.00–£280.00

Edwardian two-bedroomed cottage attached to manor-house. Quiet location between high street, beach and harbour. Parking. Near Yarmouth, Lowestoft, Broads and nature reserves.

GRESHAM, Norfolk Map ref 3B1

★★
2 Units
Sleeping 3–4

ASTALOT AND AVALON COTTAGES
Lower Gresham
Contact: Mrs Jennifer Murray, Mariners Hard, High Street, Cley, Holt NR25 7RX
T: (01263) 740404
F: (01263) 740404

OPEN All Year

Low season per wk
£150.00–£230.00
High season per wk
£240.00–£320.00

Attractive, adjoining flint/brick cottages over 160 years old. Completely renovated. Warm and very comfortable with small, enclosed gardens. Dogs welcome. Sea two miles. Electricity included.

HALESWORTH, Suffolk Map ref 3C2

★★★★
4 Units
Sleeping 2–6

BUCKS FARM
Halesworth
Contact: Mrs Bradshaw, Bucks Farm, Halesworth IP19 0LX
T: (01986) 784216
F: (01986) 784216
E: jo@bucksfarm.freeuk.com
I: www.bucksfarm-holidays.co.uk

Attractive barn conversions around a sunny, south-facing courtyard. Situated in a pleasant rural location on a farm with chickens, ducks, goats and donkeys. Dishwashers provided. Indoor heated swimming pool open all year. Children's play area and games room. Southwold and the coast 10 miles, Halesworth, 1.5 miles. Babysitting offered. Pets accepted.

OPEN All Year

Short breaks: end Oct-end Mar, minimum 3 nights. Open Christmas and New Year.

Low season per wk
Min £290.00
High season per wk
Max £795.00

 Enjoy England official guides to quality
Please mention this guide when making your booking.

231

EAST OF ENGLAND

HALSTEAD, Essex Map ref 3B2

★★★★
1 Unit
Sleeping 2–9

FROYZ HALL BARN
Halstead
Contact: Mrs Judi Butler, Froyz Hall Farm, Halstead
CO9 1RS
T: (01787) 476684
F: (01787) 474647
E: judibutler@dsl.pipex.com
I: www.froyzhallbarn.co.uk

OPEN All Year

Low season per wk
£450.00–£550.00
High season per wk
£700.00–£850.00

Beautifully converted granary barn (2500 sq ft) set on country estate two miles from Halstead, where you can enjoy swimming (summer), tennis, woodland walks and fishing. This peaceful location is on the doorstep of Constable Country, and within easy reach of Cambridge and Colchester.

HEACHAM, Norfolk Map ref 3B1

★★
5 Units
Sleeping 4

CEDAR SPRINGS CHALETS
Heacham
Contact: Mr Michael & Mrs Ann Chestney,
35 The Street, West Raynham, Fakenham NR21 7EY
T: (01328) 838341
F: (01328) 838341

Low season per wk
£85.00–£115.00
High season per wk
£125.00–£180.00

2-bedroomed chalets on quiet garden site 300 yards from beach. No dogs, please. Conservation Area of Outstanding Natural Beauty. Sandringham within 6 miles. Open 1 April to 30 September.

HOLME NEXT THE SEA, Norfolk Map ref 3B1

★★★★
1 Unit
Sleeping 8

BROOK BUNGALOW
Hunstanton
Contact: Mrs Whitsed, 8 Holme Close, Ailsworth,
Peterborough PE5 7AQ
T: (01733) 380028
F: (01733) 380028
E: john@jwhitsed.freeserve.co.uk
I: www.cottageguide.co.uk

Low season per wk
£395.00–£595.00
High season per wk
£595.00–£795.00

Spacious, well-appointed three-bedroomed modern bungalow, standing in own secluded gardens. En suite facilities, off-road parking, village location, five minutes to sand and sea.

HOLT, Norfolk Map ref 3B1

★★★
1 Unit
Sleeping 4

5 CARPENTERS COTTAGES
Holt
Contact: Mr Christopher Knights,
The Hollies Farmhouse, Rushmere, Lowestoft NR33 8EP
T: (01502) 742022 & (01493) 842289
F: (01502) 742022

Low season per wk
£200.00–£250.00
High season per wk
£300.00–£375.00

Attractive 18thC flint and pantile cottage with gravelled garden area, on the edge of a pleasant market town four miles from the coast.

HORHAM, Suffolk Map ref 3B2

★★★
2 Units
Sleeping 2–5

ALPHA COTTAGES
Eye
Contact: Mr & Mrs Brian Cooper, The Street, Horham,
Eye IP21 5DX
T: (01379) 384424
F: (01379) 384424

OPEN All Year

Low season per wk
£211.00–£260.00
High season per wk
£464.00–£508.00

Beautifully converted, well-equipped cottages in the heart of rural East Anglia. Fenced garden, patio with meadow and play equipment. Leisure facilities and good inns two miles.

EAST OF ENGLAND

HUNSTANTON, Norfolk Map ref 3B1 *Tourist Information Centre Tel: (01485) 532610*

★★★
1 Unit
Sleeping 5

MINNA COTTAGE
Hunstanton
Contact: Mr Tony Cassie, 21 The Green, Hunstanton
PE36 5AH
T: (01485) 532448
E: tonycassie@btconnect.com
I: www.minnacottage.com

OPEN All Year

Low season per wk
Min £315.00
High season per wk
Max £445.00

This fully modernised coachman's cottage provides comfortable, private accommodation for five adults and one baby. Views of the 'Wash'. Convenient for shops, 200yds to beach.

KEDINGTON, Suffolk Map ref 3B2

★★★★
1 Unit
Sleeping 2–4

THE COTTAGE AT ROWANS
Haverhill
Contact: Mrs Cheryl Owen, Rowans House,
Calford Green, Kedington, Haverhill CB9 7UN
T: (01440) 702408
F: (01440) 702408
E: cheryl@owen41.supanet.com
I: www.where2stay-uk/html/thecottageatrowans.html

OPEN All Year

Payment accepted: Euros

Low season per wk
£175.00–£250.00
High season per wk
£280.00–£350.00

Spacious, bright, well-appointed, one-bedroomed cottage and double-sprung sofa bed. Cosy in winter. Stour Valley walks, golf and antique hunting nearby. Garden and patio.

KELSALE, Suffolk Map ref 3C2

★★★★
4 Units

EAST GREEN FARM COTTAGES
Saxmundham
Contact: Mr Robbie & Mrs Claire Gawthrop, East Green,
Kelsale, Saxmundham IP17 2PH
T: (01728) 602316
F: (01728) 604408
E: claire@eastgreenproperty.co.uk
I: www.eastgreencottages.co.uk

Between Southwold and Aldeburgh and only two miles from the beautiful Heritage Coast. The Granary, The Old Stables, The Hayloft and The Dairy are charming, spacious, fully equipped, converted barns set in the grounds of a 500-year-old farmhouse. Thirteen acres of paddocks, horses, tennis court and outdoor swimming pool. Tennis coaching available.

OPEN All Year

Short breaks and weekends available from £145.

Low season per wk
Min £245.00
High season per wk
Min £599.00

Norfolk Holiday Homes

Visit this lovely area in one of our self-catering coastal or country holiday homes. Over 50 to choose from and all VisitBritain graded.

Pets, Children, Disabled, all welcome.

62 Westgate, Hunstanton, PE36 5EL
T: 01485 534267 24 Hours F: 01485 535230
E: shohol@birdsnorfolkholidayhomes.co.uk
FREE BROCHURE
www.norfolkholidayhomes-birds.co.uk

233

EAST OF ENGLAND

KESSINGLAND, Suffolk Map ref 3C1

★★★
1 Unit
Sleeping 4

CHURCH ROAD
Lowestoft
Contact: Mr James Rayment, 28 Woollards Lane, Great Shelford, Cambridge CB2 5LZ
T: (01223) 843048

OPEN All Year except Christmas and New Year

Low season per wk
£155.00–£200.00
High season per wk
£200.00–£260.00

Traditional, terraced, modernised cottage. Fully fitted kitchen including microwave oven, large lounge/diner with colour TV, and porch. One double and one twin room, bathroom/toilet.

★★★
1 Unit
Sleeping 4–5

KEW COTTAGE
Lowestoft
Contact: Mrs Joan Gill, 46 St Georges Avenue, Northampton NN2 6JA
T: (01604) 717301
F: (01604) 791424
E: b.s.g@btopenworld.com

Modernised, two-bedroomed semi-detached cottage in the middle of village, 10 minutes' walk from the sea. Large back garden with patio area. Norfolk Broads three miles, Lowestoft three miles, Southwold five miles.

Low season per wk
£180.00–£190.00
High season per wk
£190.00–£260.00

KING'S LYNN, Norfolk Map ref 3B1 Tourist Information Centre Tel: (01553) 763044

★★★
1 Unit
Sleeping 1–4

THE STABLES TOO
King's Lynn
Contact: Ms Sue O'Brien, The Stables Too, 35A Goodwins Road, King's Lynn PE30 5QX
T: (01553) 774638
E: mikeandsueobrien@hotmail.com
I: www.cottageguide.co.uk/thestablestoo

Attractive converted Victorian stable with courtyard sitting area. Surprisingly secluded position, yet only a short walk into town. Convenient for Sandringham, coast, Broads, Cambridge and Norwich.

OPEN All Year

Low season per wk
£175.00–£220.00
High season per wk
£220.00–£285.00

LAVENHAM, Suffolk Map ref 3B2

★★★★★
2 Units
Sleeping 2–4

BLAIZE COTTAGES
Lavenham
Contact: Carol & Jim Keohane, Blaize House, Church Street, Lavenham, Sudbury CO10 9QT
T: (01787) 247402
F: (01787) 247402
E: info@blaizecottages.com
I: www.blaizecottages.com

Blaize Barn and Lady Cottage are luxury cottages in the heart of Lavenham, England's finest medieval village. Both cottages are within 200m of excellent pubs, restaurants and village shops.

OPEN All Year

Payment accepted: Delta, Mastercard, Switch, Visa, Euros

3-day weekend breaks or 4-day mid-week breaks throughout the year. Romantic breaks and gift vouchers available.

Low season per wk
£300.00–£400.00
High season per wk
£450.00–£640.00

234

EAST OF ENGLAND

LAVENHAM continued

★★★★
6 Units
Sleeping 2–6

THE GROVE
Lavenham
Contact: Mr Mark Scott, The Grove, Edwardstone, Lavenham CO10 5PP
T: (01787) 211115
E: mark@grove-cottages.co.uk
I: www.grove-cottages.co.uk

Enjoy the romance of your own 300-year-old farm cottage – oak beams, open log fires, period furniture, ducks, roses and a touch of luxury. Our cottages are close to the lovely medieval Suffolk village of Lavenham – just two hours from London. Bikes free and canoes available.

OPEN All Year

Payment accepted: Delta, Diners, Mastercard, Switch, Visa

Our cosy cottages make up The Grove Farm, bookable for 2-15 guests, from 2-night short breaks upwards. Pets welcome.

Low season per wk
£259.00–£447.00
High season per wk
£385.00–£776.00

★★★
1 Unit
Sleeping 2–6

OLD WETHERDEN HALL
Ipswich
Contact: Mrs Julie Elsden, Old Wetherden Hall, Hitcham, Ipswich IP7 7PZ
T: (01449) 740574
F: (01449) 740574
E: farm@wetherdenhall.force9.co.uk
I: www.oldwetherdenhall.co.uk

15thC oak-beamed house, enclosed moated site on arable farm. Beautiful secluded setting, large garden, abundance of wildlife. Inglenook fireplace.

Low season per wk
Min £200.00
High season per wk
Max £400.00

LAXFIELD, Suffolk Map ref 3C2

★★★
2 Units
Sleeping 6

THE LOOSE BOX & THE OLD STABLES
Laxfield
Contact: Mr John & Mrs Jane Reeve, Laxfield Leisure Ltd, High Street, Laxfield IP13 8DU
T: (01986) 798019
F: (01986) 798155
E: laxfieldleisure@talk21.com
I: www.villastables.co.uk

OPEN All Year

Low season per wk
£185.00–£325.00
High season per wk
£285.00–£435.00

The Loose Box and Old Stables are Listed properties in the village centre. Superb modern conversions retaining all their character.

★★★★
1 Unit
Sleeping 1–5

MEADOW COTTAGE
Woodbridge
Contact: Mr William Ayers, Quinton House, Gorhams Mill Lane, Laxfield, Woodbridge IP13 8DN
T: (01986) 798345
F: (01986) 798345
E: will.ayers@btinternet.com

Pretty Victorian cottage offering spacious accommodation in the centre of Laxfield. Ideal base for exploring Suffolk's Heritage Coast or the heart of Suffolk. Extremely well appointed, the cottage is cosy and comfortable all year round and overlooks peaceful meadowland. Two pubs/restaurants within 100yds.

OPEN All Year

Free first basket of logs for woodburner from 1/10/04 to 1/4/05; further logs available from owner.

Low season per wk
£220.00–£420.00
High season per wk
£280.00–£480.00

235

EAST OF ENGLAND

LEISTON, Suffolk Map ref 3C2

1 Unit
Sleeping 2–3

THE STUDIO COTTAGE
Leiston
Contact: Mrs Janet Lister, Ivy Cottage, Eastbridge, Leiston IP16 4SG
T: (01728) 833034
F: (01728) 833034

Peaceful, detached studio cottage. Luxury furnished and equipped. Perfect for bird-watching and walking, own parking area off the lane. Stunning interior with pine beams, woodburning stove and logs supplied. Terracotta tiled floor with rugs. South-facing veranda with table and chairs, overlooking fields.

OPEN All Year

Low season per wk
£210.00–£225.00
High season per wk
£225.00–£275.00

LITTLE FRANSHAM, Norfolk Map ref 3B1

★★★★-★★★★★★
2 Units
Sleeping 4–7

LYONS GREEN & LITTLE FLINT
East Dereham
Contact: Mrs Jenny Mallon, Fransham Farm Co Ltd, The Old Hall, Little Fransham, East Dereham NR19 2AD
T: (01362) 687649
F: (01362) 687419
E: office@franshamfarm.co.uk
I: www.franshamfarm.co.uk

OPEN All Year

Low season per wk
£230.00–£420.00
High season per wk
£420.00–£820.00

Superior holiday cottages, unique setting overlooking own gardens and lakes. Beautifully furnished, open fires. Ideally situated mid-Norfolk, easy access North Norfolk coast and Broads. Short breaks November to March.

LITTLE SNORING, Norfolk Map ref 3B1

★★★★
1 Unit
Sleeping 5

JEX FARM BARN
Fakenham
Contact: Mr Stephen Harvey, Jex Farm, Fakenham NR21 0JJ
T: (01328) 878257
F: (01328) 878257
E: stephenharvey@supanet.com
I: www.broadland.com/jexfarmbarn.html

OPEN All Year

Low season per wk
£220.00–£270.00
High season per wk
£285.00–£540.00

Spacious detached barn conversion overlooking meadows. Exposed beams and wooden floors with woodburner and patio in private garden.

LONG MELFORD, Suffolk Map ref 3B2

1 Unit
Sleeping 4

HOPE COTTAGE
Sudbury
Contact: Ms S Jamil, Hill Farm Cottage, Duffs Hill, Glemsford, Sudbury CO10 7PP
T: (01787) 282338 & 07970 808701
F: (01787) 282338
E: sns.jam@tesco.net
I: www.hope-cottage-suffolk.co.uk

Delightful Grade II Listed flint cottage in the heart of this historic and picturesque village. Recently renovated, retaining many traditional features. Attractively furnished to high levels of comfort. Secluded garden backing onto meadowlands. All amenities in the village are close by, including restaurants and shops.

OPEN All Year

Short breaks available all year (subject to availability in high season).

Low season per wk
Min £230.00
High season per wk
Max £370.00

Quality Assurance Standard
Star ratings and awards are explained at the back of this guide.

EAST OF ENGLAND

LOWESTOFT, Suffolk Map ref 3C1

★★
1 Unit
Sleeping 5–6

LOWESTOFT HOLIDAY FLAT
Lowestoft
Contact: Mrs Courtauld, Pyes Hall, London Road,
Wrentham, Beccles NR34 7HL
T: (01502) 675209
E: mcourtauld@onetel.net.uk

OPEN All Year

Low season per wk
£140.00–£250.00
High season per wk
£250.00–£350.00

Spacious flat, ideal for families and large groups. Three bedrooms, two bathrooms, kitchen, utility room, large, sunny front room. Close to pier, beaches and shops.

★★★
1 Unit
Sleeping 5

SUFFOLK SEASIDE & BROADLANDS
Lowestoft
Contact: Mrs Collecott, 282 Gorleston Road, Oulton,
Lowestoft NR32 3AJ
T: (01502) 564396

OPEN All Year

Low season per wk
£180.00–£375.00

Beautifully furnished, well-equipped bungalow with conservatory, garden and garage. Two bedrooms, two bathrooms, sitting room, dining room and large, fully-fitted kitchen.

LYNG, Norfolk Map ref 3B1

★★★
1 Unit
Sleeping 5

UTOPIA PARADISE
Norwich
Contact: Mrs Suzan Jarvis, The Mallards, Farman Close,
Lyng, Norwich NR9 5RD
T: (01603) 870812
E: holidays@utopia-paradise.co.uk

OPEN All Year
Payment accepted: Euros

Low season per wk
Min £250.00
High season per wk
Max £365.00

A traditional cottage situated besides a mixed coarse fishing lake in a picturesque village. Shop and pub within 5-minutes' walk. Norwich 13 miles.

NAYLAND, Suffolk Map ref 3B2

★★★★–★★★★★★
9 Units
Sleeping 2–8

Extensive wooded grounds in Suffolk's rolling Constable country with marvellous views make ours a wonderful location. Charming villages and gardens to explore – not far from the sea. Heated indoor pool, sauna, tennis, fishing, animals and playground. Pets welcome. East of England Self-Catering Holiday of the Year 2003.

GLADWINS FARM
Colchester
Contact: Mrs Pauline Dossor, Gladwins Farm, Harpers Hill,
Nayland, Colchester CO6 4NU
T: (01206) 262261
F: (01206) 263001
E: gladwinsfarm@aol.com
I: www.gladwinsfarm.co.uk

OPEN All Year
Payment accepted: Delta,
Mastercard, Switch, Visa

Low season per wk
£245.00–£715.00
High season per wk
£490.00–£1,590.00

Short breaks Oct-Easter.
3-night weekends or 4-night
mid-week breaks at 70%
full-week rate.

NEWMARKET, Suffolk Map ref 3B2 *Tourist Information Centre Tel: (01638) 667200*

★★★★
1 Unit
Sleeping 2

SWALLOWS REST
Newmarket
Contact: Mrs Gill Woodward, Swallows Rest,
6 Ditton Green, Woodditton, Newmarket CB8 9SQ
T: (01638) 730823
E: gillian@swallowsrest.f9.co.uk

OPEN All Year except
Christmas and New Year

Low season per wk
£170.00–£200.00
High season per wk
£200.00–£240.00

Comfortable annexe off owners' secluded property in quiet, rural village three miles from Newmarket. Own entrance and garden. Pub with food 400yds. Country walks. Cambridge 20 minutes.

NORFOLK BROADS

See under Clippesby, Gorleston-on-Sea, Lowestoft, Oulton Broad, Sprowston, Stalham, Wroxham

237

EAST OF ENGLAND

NORTHREPPS, Norfolk Map ref 3C1

★★★★
2 Units
Sleeping 4–6

TORRIDON & YEOMANS COTTAGE
Cromer
Contact: Mrs Youngman, Shrublands Farm, Northrepps, Cromer NR27 0AA
T: (01263) 579297
F: (01263) 579297
E: youngman@farming.co.uk
I: www.broadland.com/torridon

The property was built in 1963 for the present owner. It is spacious and very well equipped. Sleeps six plus one cot. Prices all inclusive. We are 1.5 miles from the coast and only 30 minutes from Norwich. Ideal for a family holiday.

OPEN All Year
Payment accepted: Delta, Mastercard, Switch, Visa

Low season per wk
£200.00–£250.00
High season per wk
£450.00–£510.00

Short breaks available, min 3 nights, Nov-Mar.

ORFORD, Suffolk Map ref 3C2

★★★
1 Unit
Sleeping 2

THE CART LODGE STUDIO APARTMENT
Woodbridge
Contact: Mrs Susan Crane, The White House, Ferry Road, Sudbourne, Woodbridge IP12 2BQ
T: (01394) 450033
F: (01394) 450033
E: jasmcrane@aol.com

High season per wk
Max £350.00

A recently built, self-contained studio apartment of a very high standard offering split-level/open-plan accommodation complete with all modern facilities. Located in the quiet countryside.

★★★
1 Unit
Sleeping 5

47 DAPHNE ROAD
Orford
Contact: Mrs Sheila Hitchcock, Church Farm Cottage, Ferry Road, Sudbourne, Woodbridge IP12 2BP
T: (01394) 450714
F: (01394) 450714
E: barryhitchcock@tesco.com

OPEN All Year

Low season per wk
£185.00–£275.00
High season per wk
£300.00–£385.00

Delightful three-bedroomed Edwardian cottage in centre of village. Quiet road with unrestricted parking. Electric heating and open fire. Near Woodbridge, Aldeburgh and Minsmere. Cots and highchairs by arrangement.

★★★
1 Unit
Sleeping 2–4

VESTA COTTAGE
Orford
Contact: Mrs Penny Kay, Orford, Woodbridge IP12 2NQ
T: (01394) 450652
F: (01394) 450097
E: kaycottages@pobox.com
I: www.vestacottage.co.uk

OPEN All Year

Low season per wk
£290.00–£325.00
High season per wk
£380.00–£410.00

Attractive two-bedroom (double and double-bunk) cottage with garden. Next to medieval friary, near Orford Castle and Quay. Suit sailors, bird-watchers, walkers, etc.

Location Complete addresses for properties are not given and the town(s) listed may be a distance from the actual establishment. Please check the precise location at the time of booking.

EAST OF ENGLAND

OULTON BROAD, Suffolk Map ref 3C1

2 Units
Sleeping 1–6

A spacious, yet cosy, one-bedroom, second floor apartment in converted Maltings. Also a well-appointed mews house with south-facing patio garden overlooking Oulton Broad. Quiet location and private parking. Enjoy 10% discount at the Crooked Barn, a 2-Rosette restaurant, when staying in either property.

MALTINGS HOLIDAY ACCOMMODATION
Lowestoft
Contact: Miss Caroline Sterry, c/o Ivy House Country Hotel, Ivy Lane, Oulton Broad, Lowestoft NR33 8HY
T: (01502) 501353
F: (01502) 501539
E: etc@ivyhousefarm.co.uk
I: www.ivyhousefarm.co.uk

OPEN All Year

Payment accepted: Amex, Delta, Diners, Mastercard, Switch, Visa, Euros

Short breaks available throughout the year.

Low season per wk
£160.00–£335.00
High season per wk
£225.00–£525.00

PELDON, Essex Map ref 3B3

1 Unit

Self-catering annexe to a converted barn-type property, in four acres. Five Lakes Country Club golf 10 minutes, Colchester 10 minutes, beach five minutes. Brochure available. Rose Barn Cottage is 50yds from the famous Peldon Rose Inn, a 600-year-old inn with a renowned kitchen.

ROSE BARN COTTAGE
Colchester
Contact: Mrs Ariette Everett, Mersea Road/Colchester Road, Peldon, Colchester CO5 7QJ
T: (01206) 735317
F: (01206) 735311
E: everettaj@aol.com

OPEN All Year except Christmas and New Year

Winter long-term £225 per week.

Low season per wk
£250.00–£300.00
High season per wk
£320.00–£425.00

SAFFRON WALDEN, Essex Map ref 2D1 Tourist Information Centre Tel: (01799) 510444

1 Unit
Sleeping 6

NEWHOUSE FARM
Saffron Walden
Contact: Mrs E Redcliffe, Newhouse Farm, Walden Road, Radwinter, Saffron Walden CB10 2SP
T: (01799) 599211
F: (01799) 599037
E: emmaredcliffe@hotmail.com

OPEN All Year

Low season per wk
£300.00–£350.00
High season per wk
£350.00–£400.00

Elizabethan/Georgian farmhouse surrounded by 60 acres of meadows. The traditional yard is where two brick buildings have been converted to provide attractive and cosy accommodation.

Check the maps

The colour maps at the front of this guide show all the cities, towns and villages for which you will find accommodation entries. Refer to the town index to find the page on which they are listed.

EAST OF ENGLAND

ST ALBANS, Hertfordshire Map ref 2D1 *Tourist Information Centre Tel: (01727) 864511*

★★★★
1 Unit
Sleeping 2

THE HOLLIES
St Albans
Contact: Mrs Anne Newbury, 11 Spencer Place, Sandridge, St Albans AL4 9DW
T: (01727) 859845
E: martin.newbury@ntlworld.co.uk

Delightful, self-contained, ground floor annexe attached to owner's home. Pretty double bedroom, shower room/wc and sunny kitchen/ diner. The lounge has French doors onto patio leading to large, peaceful garden which guests are welcome to enjoy. Close to countryside yet only 2.5 miles from historic St Albans.

OPEN All Year

Low season per wk
Max £300.00
High season per wk
Max £300.00

SANDRINGHAM, Norfolk Map ref 3B1

★★★★
1 Unit
Sleeping 7

FOLK ON THE HILL
Dersingham
Contact: Mrs L Skerritt, Mill Cottage, Mill Road, Dersingham, King's Lynn PE31 6HY
T: (01485) 544411
E: lili@skerritt-euwe.freeserve.co.uk

Delightfully converted 18thC coach house, set in large gardens, close to the North Norfolk coast with local facilities only 0.5 miles. A luxurious holiday barn for all seasons with four bedrooms, three bathrooms, games room, woodburner, barbecue. Ideal for children, and pets welcome. Popular beach hut at Old Hunstanton.

OPEN All Year

Short breaks available.

Low season per wk
£440.00–£485.00
High season per wk
£555.00–£815.00

SEA PALLING, Norfolk Map ref 3C1

★★★
1 Unit
Sleeping 1–4

SPRING COTTAGE
Norwich
Contact: Mrs Jane Davidson, Priory Barn,
Sea Palling Road, Ingham, Norwich NR12 0TW
T: (01692) 582346

OPEN All Year

Low season per wk
£225.00–£295.00
High season per wk
£375.00–£450.00

Charming cosy cottage, minutes from Blue Flag beaches. Ideal for the Broads. Four poster, wood burner, dogs welcome.

SHARRINGTON, Norfolk Map ref 3B1

★★★★
1 Unit
Sleeping 2–4

GARDEN COTTAGE
Sharrington
Contact: Mrs R M Kimmins, Chequers, Bale Road,
Sharrington, Melton Constable NR24 2PG
T: (01263) 860308
E: rkimmins@netcomuk.co.uk

OPEN All Year except Christmas and New Year

Low season per wk
£180.00–£220.00
High season per wk
£300.00–£360.00

New, super-comfortable conversion of 18thC building overlooking large, quiet garden of period private house. Sleeps two to four in double and twin rooms.

Map references The map references refer to the colour maps at the front of this guide. The first figure is the map number; the letter and figure which follow indicate the grid reference on the map.

EAST OF ENGLAND

SHERINGHAM, Norfolk Map ref 3B1

★★★★
2 Units
Sleeping 4–5

ROGUE'S AND RASCAL'S BARNS
Norwich
Contact: Mrs Clare Wilson, Grove Farm, Back Lane, Roughton, Norwich NR11 8QR
T: (01263) 761594
F: (01263) 761605
E: enquiries@grove-farm.com
I: www.grovefarm.com

Between the Norfolk Broads and the coast at Cromer, Grove Farm is an ideal hideaway to discover North Norfolk. Close to Holt, with its antique shops, clothes boutiques and deli's, Blickling and Felbrigg Halls. Golf, riding, sailing, tennis, cycling, walks all available locally. Bed and breakfast accommodation in main farmhouse.

OPEN All Year

Payment accepted: Delta, Mastercard, Switch, Visa, Euros

Low season per wk £480.00–£500.00
High season per wk £520.00–£560.00

3-night breaks with golf at Sheringham and Royal Cromer.

★★★★
2 Units
Sleeping 4

VICTORIA COURT
Sheringham
Contact: Mr Graham Simmons, Camberley, 62 Cliff Road, Sheringham NR26 8BJ
T: (01263) 823101
F: (01263) 821433
E: graham@camberleyguesthouse.co.uk
I: www.camberleyguesthouse.co.uk

Immaculate, fully equipped apartments enjoying excellent coastal and sea views. Direct access to beach. Safe parking in own grounds.

OPEN All Year

Low season per wk £205.00–£380.00
High season per wk £395.00–£470.00

SIBTON, Suffolk Map ref 3C2

★★★★
1 Unit
Sleeping 1–5

CARDINAL COTTAGE
Saxmundham
Contact: Mr & Mrs Eric Belton, Cardinal Cottage, Pouy Street, Sibton, Saxmundham IP17 2JH
T: (01728) 660111
E: jan.belton@btopenworld.com
I: www.cardinalcottageholidays.co.uk

Delightfully cosy, period timber-framed cottage with spectacular beams. Three bedrooms, sitting room, dining room, kitchen and bathroom, all fully equipped to high standard. Enclosed private garden, with car park. Close Heritage Coast, Minsmere, Aldeburgh and Southwold. Ideal base for walkers and bird-watchers, or those after a quiet country retreat.

OPEN All Year

Payment accepted: Delta, Mastercard, Switch, Visa

Low season per wk £200.00–£330.00
High season per wk £340.00–£520.00

Quality Assurance Standard

For an explanation of the quality and facilities represented by the stars please refer to the front of this guide. A more detailed explanation can be found in the information pages at the back.

EAST OF ENGLAND

SNAPE, Suffolk Map ref 3C2

★★★-★★★★★
4 Units
Sleeping 2-6

SNAPE MALTINGS
Snape
Contact: Mrs Melaine Thurston, Snape Maltings, Snape Bridge, Snape, Saxmundham IP17 1SR
T: (01708) 688303
F: (01708) 688930
E: accom@snapemaltings.co.uk
I: www.snapemaltings.co.uk

Snape Maltings is a unique collection of Victorian granaries and malthouses set on the River Alde – now housing a variety of shops, galleries and restaurants, and famous as home to the Aldeburgh Festival. The cottages and flat have been tastefully converted to make an ideal base for touring the Suffolk coast.

OPEN All Year

Payment accepted: Amex, Delta, Mastercard, Switch, Visa

Low season per wk
£275.00-£465.00
High season per wk
£385.00-£650.00

SNETTISHAM, Norfolk Map ref 3B1

★★★★
1 Unit
Sleeping 1-4

CURSONS COTTAGE
King's Lynn
Contact: Mrs Averil Campbell, Craven House, Lynn Road, Snettisham, King's Lynn PE31 7LW
T: (01485) 541179
F: (01485) 543259
E: ian.averilcampbell@btinternet.com
I: www.cottageguide.co.uk/cursonscottage

Attractive and comfortable stone cottage in centre of by-passed village. Near Sandringham and north-west Norfolk Heritage Coastline. Sensitively modernised to retain character.

OPEN All Year
Payment accepted: Euros

Low season per wk
£200.00-£275.00
High season per wk
£300.00-£395.00

SOUTH BENFLEET, Essex Map ref 3B3

★★★
1 Unit
Sleeping 1-4

ALICE'S PLACE
Benfleet
Contact: Mr & Mrs Millward, 43 Danesfield, South Benfleet SS7 5EE
T: (01268) 756283
F: (01268) 756283
E: info@alices-place.co.uk
I: www.alices-place.co.uk

Spacious two-bedroom bungalow with family-size hot tub. Walking distance of shops, railway station and country park. Easy access to seafront, London and all attractions.

OPEN All Year

Low season per wk
£400.00-£450.00
High season per wk
£450.00-£500.00

SOUTH MIMMS, Hertfordshire Map ref 2D1

★★-★★★
2 Units
Sleeping 2-6

THE BLACK SWAN
Potters Bar
Contact: Mr Marsterson, 62-64 Blanche Lane, Potters Bar EN6 3PD
T: (01707) 644180
F: (01707) 642344

Cottage and self-contained flats, 16thC Listed building. Rail connections at Potters Bar and London Underground at Barnet allow travel to London within 45 minutes.

OPEN All Year

Low season per wk
£185.00-£220.00
High season per wk
£250.00-£300.00

SOUTHWOLD, Suffolk Map ref 3C2

★★★★
1 Unit
Sleeping 1-3

THE COTTAGE
Southwold
Contact: Mr Thomas, 2 Pier Court, Pier Avenue, Southwold IP18 6BL
T: (01502) 723561

Lounge/diner, one twin and one single bedroom, bathroom, cloakroom, radio and TV/video. Fully fitted kitchen with washer/drier, fridge, freezer and microwave.

OPEN All Year

Low season per wk
£190.00-£230.00
High season per wk
£280.00-£300.00

EAST OF ENGLAND

SOUTHWOLD continued

★★★
1 Unit
Sleeping 1–4

GARDEN COTTAGE
Southwold
Contact: Mr & Mrs Wigg, 162 Hall Road, Oulton Broad, Lowestoft NR32 3NR
T: (01502) 568580
F: (01502) 568580

OPEN All Year

Low season per wk
£315.00–£395.00
High season per wk
£400.00–£510.00

A very appealing, tastefully furnished, two-bedroomed, ground-floor cottage, set in pretty herb and rose patio garden. One double- and one twin-bedded room offering comfortable accommodation. Garden Cottage is 50yds from the seafront, and Southwold's pier, shops and amenities are within easy walking distance.

★★★
1 Unit
Sleeping 2–6

HORSESHOE COTTAGE
Southwold
Contact: Ms Claire Guppy & Mrs J Tallon,
9 Trinity Street, Southwold IP18 6JH
T: (01502) 724033
F: (01502) 725168
E: sales@southwold-holidays.co.uk
I: www.southwold-holidays.co.uk

OPEN All Year
Payment accepted:
Mastercard, Visa

Low season per wk
£295.00–£365.00
High season per wk
£360.00–£600.00

A comfortable family house with views over South Green. Near to sea, shops and common. Small rear yard. Open fire. New kitchen/bathroom. Weekend breaks available.

★★
1 Unit
Sleeping 1–4

THE LITTLE BLUE HOUSE
Southwold
Contact: Mrs Diana Wright, The Kiln, The Folley,
Colchester CO2 0HZ
T: (01206) 738003

OPEN All Year

Low season per wk
£265.00–£300.00
High season per wk
£300.00–£430.00

Small, cosy cottage close to shops and seafront with an attractive enclosed paved garden at the rear. Sleeps two adults and two children.

★★★
1 Unit
Sleeping 2

THE NEST
Southwold
Contact: Mrs Daphne Hall, 98 High Street, Southwold
IP18 6DP
T: (01502) 723292
F: (01502) 724794
E: haadnams_lets@ic24.net
I: www.thenest-southwold.info

OPEN All Year

Low season per wk
£230.00–£260.00
High season per wk
£330.00–£430.00

Centrally located on one of Southwold's prettiest greens, near the lighthouse and beach, a peaceful, cosy hideaway with sea views. Well equipped and double-glazed throughout.

★★★★
2 Units
Sleeping 1–6

POPLAR HALL
Southwold
Contact: Mrs Anna Garwood, Poplar Hall,
Frostenden Corner, Frostenden, Nr Southwold
NR34 7JA
T: (01502) 578549
I: www.southwold.ws/poplar-hall

OPEN All Year

Low season per wk
£180.00–£350.00
High season per wk
£300.00–£420.00

Poplar Hall Cottage and Lofthouse are well-equipped and beautifully appointed and have their own gardens and patios, private parking and cycle store. Situated 3.5 miles from Southwold.

 Visitor attractions For ideas on places to visit refer to the introduction at the beginning of this section. Look out for the VisitBritain Quality Assured Visitor Attraction signs.

243

EAST OF ENGLAND

SOUTHWOLD continued

2 Units
Sleeping 5–9

WHITEHOUSE BARNS
Nr Southwold
Contact: Mrs Penelope Roskell-Griffiths,
66 Queen Elizabeth's Walk, London N16 5UQ
T: (020) 8802 6258
E: peneloperoskell@yahoo.co.uk
I: www.whitehousebarns.co.uk

Beautiful architect-converted barns in very peaceful location with spectacular views over Blyth estuary. Set in two acres of land, in an Area of Outstanding Natural Beauty, they are ideal for families, walkers and bird-watchers. Southwold and Walberswick sandy beaches four miles. Woodburning stoves, underfloor heating. Spacious play-barn, baby-sitting service.

OPEN All Year

Short breaks available. Reductions for couples mid-week, registered disabled and late bookings.

Low season per wk
£285.00–£460.00
High season per wk
£480.00–£725.00

SPROWSTON, Norfolk Map ref 3C1

★★
1 Unit
Sleeping 1–4

HOLME
Sprowston
Contact: Mrs P Guyton, 2 Recreation Ground Road, Sprowston, Norwich NR7 8EN
T: (01603) 465703

OPEN All Year

Low season per wk
£145.00–£170.00
High season per wk
£180.00–£230.00

Traditional, detached bungalow two miles north of Norwich. Non-smoking accommodation consists of two twin bedrooms, lounge, kitchen/diner, bathroom. Enclosed garden with patio furniture.

STALHAM, Norfolk Map ref 3C1

★★
1 Unit
Sleeping 2–4

144 BROADSIDE CHALET PARK
Norwich
Contact: Mr Crawford, 5 Collingwood Avenue, Surbiton KT5 9PT
T: (020) 8337 4487
F: (020) 8337 4487
E: crawfcall@aol.com
I: www.norfolkholiday.co.uk

OPEN All Year

Payment accepted: Euros

Low season per wk
£80.00–£140.00
High season per wk
£170.00–£265.00

South-facing, detached chalet in landscaped park, with pleasant lawns for quiet relaxation or where children may play safely. Swimming pool, licensed club, shop. Four miles to Blue Flag beach.

★★★
1 Unit
Sleeping 2–4

CHAPELFIELD COTTAGE FLAT
Norwich
Contact: Mr Gary Holmes, Chapelfield Cottage Flat, Chapel Field, Stalham, Norwich NR12 9EN
T: (01692) 582173
F: (01692) 583009
E: gary@cinqueportsmarine.freeserve.co.uk
I: www.norfolkbroads.com/chapelfield

OPEN All Year except Christmas

Low season per wk
£200.00–£250.00
High season per wk
£250.00–£300.00

Holiday apartment, part of Norfolk cottage, ideal for couples or small family. Tranquil location close to river, only 10 minutes' from Stalham. Lounge, kitchen, bathroom, bedroom.

Quality Assurance Standard
Star ratings and awards were correct at time of going to press but are subject to change. Please check at the time of booking.

EAST OF ENGLAND

STOWMARKET, Suffolk Map ref 3B2 *Tourist Information Centre Tel: (01449) 676800*

★★★★
5 Units
Sleeping 2

BARN COTTAGES
Stowmarket
Contact: Mrs Tydeman, Goldings, East End Lane, Stonham Aspal, Stowmarket IP14 6AS
T: (01449) 711229
E: maria@barncottages.co.uk
I: www.barncottages.co.uk

Immaculate, spacious cottages for two people amidst four acres of peaceful and tranquil surroundings in the heart of the Suffolk countryside. Cottages fully equipped and owner maintained. Ideally situated for exploring Constable country, Lavenham, Southwold and the Heritage Coast.

OPEN All Year

Low season per wk
£165.00–£265.00
High season per wk
£265.00–£315.00

STRADBROKE, Suffolk Map ref 3C2

★★★★
1 Unit
Sleeping 2–7

CORNHOUSE COTTAGE
Eye
Contact: Mrs Charmaine Cooper, Cornhouse Cottage, Hepwood Lodge, Wilby Road, Stradbroke, Eye IP21 5JN
T: (01379) 384256
F: (01379) 384256
E: cornhouse@hepwoodcottages.co.uk
I: www.hepwoodcottages.co.uk

OPEN All Year

Low season per wk
£250.00–£300.00
High season per wk
£350.00–£450.00

Enjoy peace, quiet and comfort. Fully equipped kitchen/diner, lounge (with sofa bed) and bathroom downstairs. Two en suite bathrooms and shower room via spiral staircase. Garden.

SWANTON MORLEY, Norfolk Map ref 3B1

★★★
3 Units
Sleeping 4–5

TEAL, HERON & GREBE COTTAGE
Dereham
Contact: Mrs Sally Marsham, Waterfall Farm, Worthing Road, Swanton Morley, East Dereham NR20 4QD
T: (01362) 637300
F: (01362) 637300
E: waterfallfarm@tesco.net

Situated in a peaceful area of mid-Norfolk, the cottages have been converted from old farm buildings into beautiful holiday homes and are an ideal base for exploring Norfolk. Spacious, well-equipped accommodation with underfloor central heating. With a play area and small animals to see, it is ideal for children.

OPEN All Year

New for 2005 – heated indoor swimming pool – open all year. Nightly stays available. Fishing locally – permits provided.

Low season per wk
Min £185.00
High season per wk
Max £315.00

SYDERSTONE, Norfolk Map ref 3B1

★★★★
1 Unit
Sleeping 2

HARROW BARN
Syderstone
Contact: Miss Catherine Ringer, Buildings Farm, Creake Road, Syderstone, King's Lynn PE31 8SH
T: (01485) 578287
F: (01485) 576030
E: chringeris@hotmail.com
I: www.norfolk-holiday-cottages.co.uk/cottage/harrowbarn.html

OPEN All Year

Low season per wk
£295.00–£325.00
High season per wk
£335.00–£375.00

Rural retreat on arable farm. Single-storey barn, carefully converted giving character full consideration. Vaulted ceilings, exposed beams, woodburner, level access. Stunning countryside views. Green lane walks.

245

EAST OF ENGLAND

THORNHAM, Norfolk Map ref 3B1

1 Unit
Sleeping 5

1 MALTHOUSE COTTAGES
Hunstanton
Contact: Mrs Rigby, 6 Church Hill, Castor,
Peterborough PE5 7AU
T: (01733) 380399
F: (01733) 380399
E: leslierigby@castor.freeserve.co.uk

OPEN All Year

Low season per wk
£195.00–£231.00
High season per wk
£250.00–£450.00

Charming, traditional Norfolk cottage with open fire in lovely coastal village with three pubs and beautiful beach. Area renowned for sailing, walking, birdwatching and golfing.

THORPE MARKET, Norfolk Map ref 3C1

★★★★

2 Units
Sleeping 2–4

Poppylands and Puddleduck cottages are one- and two-bedroom cottages set in their own gardens. Fully equipped with colour TV, microwave. Situated four miles from the fishing village of Cromer with its Blue Ribbon beach and only 16 miles from the historical city of Norwich.

POPPYLANDS & PUDDLEDUCK

Norwich
Contact: Jena Castleton, Poppy Cottage, Thorpe Market, Norwich NR11 8AJ
T: (01263) 833219
E: poppylandholiday@aol.com
I: www.bravura.com

OPEN All Year

Christmas bookings available.

Low season per wk
£250.00–£275.00
High season per wk
£375.00–£450.00

THORPENESS, Suffolk Map ref 3C2

★★★★

11 Units
Sleeping 2–10

THE COUNTRY CLUB APARTMENTS
Leiston
Contact: Reception, Thorpeness Hotel & Golf Club,
Lakeside Avenue, Leiston IP16 4NH
T: (01728) 452176
F: (01728) 453868
E: info@thorpeness.co.uk
I: www.thorpeness.co.uk

OPEN All Year
Payment accepted: Delta, Mastercard, Switch, Visa

Low season per wk
£242.00–£550.00
High season per wk
£462.00–£856.00

Family apartments and houses, some with sea views. Beach, cycling and wonderful walks make up this perfect holiday. Discounted golf, discounted tennis excluding July and August.

★★★

1 Unit
Sleeping 12

A true family holiday in this wonderfully eccentric 'fantasy unmatched in England'. The House in the Clouds has five bedrooms, three bathrooms and unrivalled views from the 'Room at the Top'. Play billiards, snooker, table tennis, tennis and boules. Overlooking sea, golf course and Meare. Bird-watching on RSPB reserves.

THE HOUSE IN THE CLOUDS

Leiston
Contact: Mrs Le Comber, 4 Hinde House, 14 Hinde Street,
London W1U 3BG
T: (020) 7224 3615
F: (020) 7224 3615
E: houseintheclouds@btopenworld.com
I: www.houseintheclouds.co.uk

OPEN All Year

Low season per wk
£1,650.00–£1,920.00
High season per wk
£2,000.00–£2,450.00

 Prices Please check prices and other details at the time of booking.

EAST OF ENGLAND

THURSFORD, Norfolk Map ref 3B1

★★★
1 Unit
Sleeping 5

HAYLOFT
Fakenham
Contact: Mrs Ann Green, Old Coach House, Fakenham NR21 0BD
T: (01328) 878273

On a small, 64-acre working farm, 10 miles from the unspoilt North Norfolk coast. Overlooking rolling grazing land, this unique 16thC hayloft conversion offers warmth and comfort in peaceful surroundings with owner's home across the courtyard.

OPEN All Year
Payment accepted: Euros

Low season per wk
£295.00–£300.00
High season per wk
£300.00–£420.00

WANGFORD, Suffolk Map ref 3C2

★★★
1 Unit
Sleeping 1–4

CORNER COTTAGE
Wangford
Contact: Mrs Paula Mather, Harrogate
T: (01423) 525305

OPEN All Year

Low season per wk
£200.00–£250.00
High season per wk
£250.00–£300.00

Delightful modernised cottage offering four sleeping with off-street parking, situated in sleepy village of Wangford, 4 miles from Southwold. Leaflet available, tel (01423) 525305.

WELLS-NEXT-THE-SEA, Norfolk Map ref 3B1

★★★
1 Unit
Sleeping 4

HONEYPOT COTTAGE
Wells-next-the-Sea
Contact: Mrs Joan Price, Shingles, Southgate Close, Wells-next-the-Sea NR23 1HG
T: (01328) 711982
F: (01328) 711982
E: walker.al@talk21.com
I: www.wells-honeypot.co.uk

OPEN All Year

Low season per wk
£220.00–£350.00
High season per wk
£350.00–£440.00

Offering comfortable accommodation on the picturesque North Norfolk coast with quaint shopping streets and harbour within easy walking distance. Ideally situated for bird-watching, walking, sightseeing etc.

★★★
1 Unit
Sleeping 2–4

13 TUNNS YARD
Wells-next-the-Sea
Contact: Ms Jean Clitheroe, 14 Shop Lane, Wells-next-the-Sea NR23
T: (01328) 711362 & 07880 871733
E: jean@theoldexchange.fsnet.co.uk
I: www.the1950shop.com/accommodation.htm

This modern self-contained apartment is situated in a quiet mews just off the historic quay and close to the centre. You will find the apartment very clean and comfortable with everything you need for an enjoyable holiday. A perfect base for bird-watching, coastal path walking, exploring, or simply relaxing.

OPEN All Year
Payment accepted: Euros

Low season per wk
£200.00–£300.00
High season per wk
£325.00–£400.00

Accessibility Look for the symbols which indicate National Accessible Scheme standards for hearing and visually impaired guests in addition to standards for guests with mobility impairment. You can find an index of all scheme participants at the back of this guide.

247

EAST OF ENGLAND

WEST BECKHAM, Norfolk Map ref 3B1

★★★
1 Unit
Sleeping 4

MERRY COTTAGE
Sheringham
Contact: Mrs Mo Teeuw, 20 High Street, Spalding
PE12 6QB
T: (01406) 370012
E: mo@moteeuw.co.uk
I: www.moteeuw.co.uk

OPEN All Year

Low season per wk
Min £195.00
High season per wk
Max £395.00

Cosy flint cottage in a peaceful rural setting. Furnished to a high standard. This lovely cottage has several period features including beams and inglenook fireplace with woodburning stove. The large, secluded garden offers peace and privacy. Five minutes' walk from Sheringham Park. Ample off-road parking.

WHEATACRE, Norfolk Map ref 3C1

★★★
1 Unit
Sleeping 4–11

BLUEBELL COTTAGE
Beccles
Contact: Mrs Vera Thirtle, Playters Old Farm, Church Road, Ellough, Beccles NR34 7TN
T: (01502) 712325
F: (01502) 712325
E: thirtle.playters@virgin.net
I: www.bluebellcottages.com

OPEN All Year

Low season per wk
£350.00–£400.00
High season per wk
£400.00–£500.00

Ideal situation for enjoying all Norfolk and Suffolk can offer. Beaches, countryside, historical towns, cities and more. Quiet location within easy reach of lively Great Yarmouth and Lowestoft.

WICKHAM SKEITH, Suffolk Map ref 3B2

★★★
1 Unit
Sleeping 1–4

THE NETUS BARN
Eye
Contact: Mrs Joy Homan, Street Farm, Wickham Skeith, Eye IP23 8LP
T: (01449) 766275
E: joygeoff@homansf.freeserve.co.uk

OPEN All Year

Low season per wk
£185.00–£225.00
High season per wk
£250.00–£265.00

Single-storey period barn, well-equipped kitchen-cum-living room, bathroom (shower), two twin bedrooms, disabled friendly, parking, patio garden. Rural views. Dogs welcome.

WIGHTON, Norfolk Map ref 3B1

★★★
1 Unit
Sleeping 1–5

MALTHOUSE
Wighton
Contact: Mrs Linden Green, Copys Green, Wells-next-the-Sea NR23 1NY
T: (01328) 820204
F: (01328) 820175
E: t.b.green@lineone.net

OPEN All Year

Low season per wk
£225.00–£250.00
High season per wk
£300.00–£400.00

Three-bedroomed flint cottage. Quiet location, three miles from sea. Open log fire plus central heating. Garden, parking, free fuel, electricity and linen.

At-a-glance symbols

Symbols at the end of each entry give useful information about services and facilities. A key to symbols can be found inside the back cover flap. Keep this open for easy reference.

EAST OF ENGLAND

WINGFIELD, Suffolk Map ref 3B2

★★★★
1 Unit
Sleeping 2–4

BEECH FARM MALTINGS
Diss
Contact: Mrs Rosemary Gosling, Beech Farm, Eye
IP21 5RG
T: (01379) 586630
F: (01379) 586630
E: maltings.beechfarm@virgin.net
I: www.beech-farm-maltings.co.uk

OPEN All Year

Low season per wk
£233.00–£291.00
High season per wk
£269.00–£375.00

Discover East Anglia from this secluded, spacious, converted Maltings which offers versatile, warehouse-style, first-floor accommodation. Fully equipped. Oil-fired central heating. Peaceful, rural, garden, parking. Walking, cycling, golf, fishing or just relaxing. Perfect base for exploring Heritage Coast (Aldeburgh, Southwold, Orford, Sutton Hoo), North Norfolk Coast/Broads. Something for everyone.

WOODBRIDGE, Suffolk Map ref 3C2 *Tourist Information Centre Tel: (01394) 382240*

★★★
1 Unit
Sleeping 4

THE COACH HOUSE
Framsden
Contact: Ms Nicola Deller, Hill House, Mill Hill, Framsden, Stowmarket IP14 6HB
T: (01473) 890891
E: nicoladeller@yahoo.com
I: www.accommodationsuffolk.co.uk

OPEN All Year

Low season per wk
£220.00–£250.00
High season per wk
£250.00–£325.00

In glorious Suffolk countryside, close to many walks and attractions. Exceptionally spacious and well-equipped. Lovely views. Shared garden. Modern kitchen. Walk to village pub.

★★★★
4 Units
Sleeping 2–8

WINDMILL LODGES
Woodbridge
Contact: Mrs Katie Coe, Windmill Lodges, Red House Farm, Saxtead, Woodbridge IP13 9RD
T: (01728) 685338
F: (01728) 684850
E: holidays@windmilllodges.co.uk
I: www.windmilllodges.co.uk

OPEN All Year

Payment accepted: Amex, Delta, Mastercard, Switch, Visa

Low season per wk
£184.00–£300.00
High season per wk
£403.00–£750.00

Authentic log cabins set around a small, private fishing lake in the heart of the beautiful Suffolk countryside. Each lodge features a private, outdoor hot tub. Guests have use of covered, heating swimming pool. A village location, within easy reach of local attractions and coast.

Off-peak short breaks available (weekend – 3 nights, or mid-week – 4 nights).

WROXHAM, Norfolk Map ref 3C1

★★★★
9 Units
Sleeping 4–9
See also ad p220

DAISY BROAD LODGES
Wroxham
Contact: Mr Daniel Thwaites, Riverside Road, Wroxham, Norwich NR12 8UD
T: (01603) 782625
F: (01603) 784072
E: daniel@barnesbrinkcraft.co.uk
I: www.barnesbrinkcraft.co.uk

OPEN All Year

Payment accepted: Delta, Mastercard, Switch, Visa

Low season per wk
£243.00–£511.00
High season per wk
£660.00–£1,193.00

Latest units new for 2003, river frontage. First floor living area and balcony allows for superb views. Two minutes' walk from Wroxham village. Daylaunch FOC (not July/August).

EAST OF ENGLAND

WROXHAM continued

★★★★
2 Units
Sleeping 2–6

Delightful, popular cottages in stunning, peaceful surroundings. Beautifully furnished to a high standard with all the facilities you need. Log fires and four-poster bed. Enjoy walks, relax, feed the fish, watch the sunsets.

NUTMEG & PLUM TREE COTTAGES
Norwich
Contact: Mrs Jane Pond, East View Farm, Stone Lane, Ashmanhaugh, Norwich NR12 8YW
T: (01603) 782225 & 07831 258258
F: (01603) 782225
E: john.pond@tinyworld.co.uk
I: www.eastviewfarm.co.uk

OPEN All Year

3-night stays available Oct-Apr (excl Christmas and New Year).

Low season per wk
£180.00–£422.00
High season per wk
£242.00–£642.00

★★★★
6 Units
Sleeping 2–6

Exclusive cottage conversions, beautifully furnished, providing outstandingly comfortable and well-appointed accommodation. Indoor swimming pool, spa, solarium, play area and games room. Perfectly situated for coast, countryside, local pubs by the river in Cotishall, stately homes and the lovely city of Norwich, a short drive away. We have it all!

OLD FARM COTTAGES
Norwich
Contact: Mrs Kay Paterson, Old Farm Cottages, Tunstead, Norwich NR12 8HS
T: (01692) 536612
F: (01692) 536612
E: mail@oldfarmcottages.fsnet.co.uk
I: www.oldfarmcottages.com

Low season per wk
Max £465.00
High season per wk
£465.00–£800.00

Country Code Always follow the Country Code

• Enjoy the countryside and respect its life and work • Guard against all risk of fire • Fasten all gates • Keep your dogs under close control • Keep to public paths across farmland • Use gates and stiles to cross fences, hedges and walls • Leave livestock, crops and machinery alone • Take your litter home • Help to keep all water clean • Protect wildlife, plants and trees • Take special care on country roads • Make no unnecessary noise.

Finding **accommodation** is as easy as **1 2 3**

Enjoy England official guides to quality accommodation make it quick and easy to find a place to stay. There are several ways to use this guide.

1

TOWN INDEX
The town index at the back lists all the places with accommodation featured in the regional sections. The index gives a page number where you can find full accommodation and contact details.

2

COLOUR MAPS
All the place names in black on the colour maps at the front have an entry in the regional sections. Refer to the town index for the page number where you will find one or more establishments offering accommodation in your chosen town or village.

3

ACCOMMODATION LISTING
Contact details for all VisitBritain assessed accommodation throughout England, together with their national star rating are given in the listing section of this guide. Establishments with a full entry in the regional sections are shown in blue. Look in the town index for the page number on which their full entry appears.

Flamboyant towns and cities blend **retail therapy** with **history** and **culture**.

South East England

Looking for some inspiration? Here are a few ideas to get you started in South East England. **experience** the world-famous Henley Royal Regatta. **discover** the nation's naval heritage at Historic Dockyards in Chatham or Portsmouth. **explore** the beautiful South Downs Way between Eastbourne and Winchester. **relax** with a glass of English wine at Tenterden Vineyard.

THE REGION
Berkshire, Buckinghamshire, East Sussex, Hampshire, Isle of Wight, Kent, Oxfordshire, Surrey, West Sussex

CONTACT
▸ TOURISM SOUTH EAST
40 Chamberlayne Road,
Eastleigh, Hampshire SO50 5JH
T: (023) 8062 5505
F: (023) 8062 0010
E: enquiries@tourismse.com
www.visitsoutheastengland.com

SOUTH EAST ENGLAND

Set sail beside chalk-white cliffs or drift inland through historic towns and cities such as Oxford and Canterbury. Walk the rolling downlands, then stretch out and soak up the sun on golden sands and shingle bays. Wild ponies tug at the grass on village greens in the tranquil New Forest.

Café culture

Step out in any of the major towns or cities of the South East to experience the history that has made each one unique. Enjoy the arts that have enriched it, the culture that has shaped it, the food and drink that keeps us all so nicely nourished! And of course there is the shopping, hard to match elsewhere.

You'll find a tempting choice of excellent cafés and restaurants in the South East. In many of the historic cities and towns, such as Windsor, Oxford and Canterbury, some of the age-old buildings have been given a new lease of life. Now they are cool cafés, restaurants and bars, all stripped floors and neat furnishings and it's great that they can continue to be an everyday part of our lives.

Green fingers

Blessed with a rich soil and a favourable climate, the South East has been home to many of Britain's top gardens for centuries. Explore the region's parklands and enjoy classic designs by famous landscapers – then marvel at the contemporary gardens laid out by modern masters. Be inspired by the variety and the rich tapestry of colours that change with the seasons.

You're spoilt for choice if you enjoy visiting stately homes and castles, set in magnificent surroundings. They are in abundance. Blenheim Palace, Churchill's birthplace in Oxfordshire, for example, has over 2000 acres of landscaped parkland while Hever Castle in Kent, childhood home of Anne Boleyn, boasts Tudor Gardens with a yew-hedge maze.

Go with the flow!

The South East is packed to the gunnels with maritime heritage and plays host to many flagship SeaBritain events. Soak up the fascinating history of seafaring in Portsmouth or Chatham, and watch great sporting events like the Henley Royal Regatta and Cowes Week. Brighton's seawater was once medically prescribed – offering so much fun in the sun, perhaps it still should be!

Stride out along the Thames Path National Trail through rural Oxfordshire to Henley, sit on the banks of the Thames, and enjoy a spot of fishing. Try your hand at rowing, punting or canoeing or take to the water yourself and enjoy a boat ride from Windsor, Wallingford or Oxford to see a different perspective of the towns and cities along the Thames.

Left, from top a gentle day on the river, Oxfordshire; be entertained on Brighton beach; admire the State Rooms at Blenheim Palace, Woodstock **Right** picturesque gardens of Scotney Castle, Lamberhurst

Places to visit

Awarded VisitBritain's Quality Assured Visitor Attraction marque.

Alfriston Clergy House (National Trust)
The Tye, Alfriston, East Sussex
Tel: (01323) 870001
www.nationaltrust.org.uk
A beautiful thatched medieval hall house, the first building to be acquired by the National Trust in 1896. Idyllic riverside setting, pretty cottage garden and charming gift shop.

Amberley Working Museum
Houghton Bridge, Amberley, West Sussex
Tel: (01798) 831370
www.amberleymuseum.co.uk
Touch the past at this open-air industrial history centre in a chalk quarry. Working craftsmen, narrow-gauge railway, early buses, working machines and other exhibits. Nature trail/visitor centre.

Arundel Wildfowl and Wetlands Centre
Mill Road, Arundel, West Sussex
Tel: (01903) 883355
www.wwt.org.uk
Get nose to beak with nature! Over 24ha (60 acres) of ponds, lakes and reedbeds, home to hundreds of wetland birds and wildlife. Restaurant, gift shop, wildlife art gallery.

Basingstoke Canal Visitor Centre
Mytchett Place Road, Mytchett, Surrey
Tel: (01252) 370073
www.basingstoke-canal.org.uk
Soak up the peace and tranquillity on one of the most beautiful waterways in the country. Canal visitor centre offers information, boat trips, narrowboat hire, floating art gallery and tearoom.

Battle Abbey and Battlefield (English Heritage)
High Street, Battle, East Sussex
Tel: (01424) 773792
www.english-heritage.org.uk
Atmospheric ruins of the abbey founded by William the Conqueror on the site of the 1066 Battle of Hastings. Look out over the battlefields and imagine the scene.

Bentley Wildfowl and Motor Museum
Bentley, Halland, East Sussex
Tel: (01825) 840573
www.bentley.org.uk
Something for everyone – over 1000 wildfowl in parkland with lakes, a motor museum with vintage cars, house with antique furniture and collection of wildlife paintings, children's play facilities and woodland walk.

Birdworld
Holt Pound, Farnham, Surrey
Tel: (01420) 22140
www.birdworld.co.uk
Ten and a half hectares (26 acres) of gardens and parkland with an impressive collection of birds. Seashore walk, penguin island, aquarium, children's farm and tropical walk. Heron theatre with regular shows.

Blenheim Palace
Woodstock, Oxfordshire
Tel: 0870 060 2080
www.blenheimpalace.com
Home of the Duke of Marlborough and birthplace of Sir Winston Churchill. Designed by Vanbrugh in the English baroque style with magnificent state rooms. Stunning parkland by Capability Brown.

Bletchley Park
The Mansion, Milton Keynes, Buckinghamshire
Tel: (01908) 640404
www.bletchleypark.org.uk
Learn about the secret history of Bletchley Park and its pioneering WWII codebreakers Alan Turing and Dilly Knox, as shown in the major film Enigma.

Borde Hill Garden
Balcombe Road, Haywards Heath, West Sussex
Tel: (01444) 450326
www.bordehill.co.uk
A plantsman's paradise with rare trees and shrubs amassed by the great plant collectors from all corners of the world. Formal and informal garden rooms. Woodland and parkland walks.

SOUTH EAST ENGLAND

Broadlands
Romsey, Hampshire
Tel: (01794) 505010
www.broadlands.net
Experience part of English history in this magnificent 18thC house, home of the late Lord Mountbatten. Superb views across river Test, Mountbatten exhibition and audiovisual presentation.

Brooklands Museum
Brooklands Road, Weybridge, Surrey
Tel: (01932) 857381
www.brooklandsmuseum.com
Evoking thrills on land or in the air, this original 1907 motor racing circuit was the birthplace of British motorsport and aviation. Collection of historic racing and sports cars, and aircraft. Motoring village and Grand Prix exhibition.

Charleston
Firle, East Sussex
Tel: (01323) 811265
www.charleston.org.uk
Charming farmhouse home of Vanessa Bell and Duncan Grant of the Bloomsbury Set, with interiors and furniture decorated by the artists. Traditional walled garden.

Chartwell (National Trust)
Mapleton Road, Westerham, Kent
Tel: (01732) 866368
www.nationaltrust.org.uk
Delightful home of Sir Winston Churchill, still much as he left it. Enter his study and studio, and visit the museum rooms with gifts, uniforms and photos. Garden, Golden Rose Walk, lakes and exhibition.

Dover Castle and Secret Wartime Tunnels (English Heritage)
Dover, Kent
Tel: (01304) 211067
www.english-heritage.org.uk
Secret tunnels bring wartime activities vividly to life at one of the most powerful medieval fortresses in Western Europe. St Mary-in-Castro Saxon church, Roman lighthouse and Henry II Great Keep.

Drusillas Park
Alfriston, East Sussex
Tel: (01323) 874100
www.drusillas.co.uk
All whole day's entertainment awaits at Drusillas. Known as the best small zoo in England with animals in natural habitats. Playland is masses of fun for children from three to 12 – they'll insist you return!

English Wine Centre
Alfriston, East Sussex
Tel: (01323) 870164
www.weddingwine.co.uk
Connoisseurs or not, the English Wine Centre will appeal to lovers of wine. It stocks a large selection of wines (English and world) plus beers and ciders. Tours and tastings available.

Explosion! Museum of Naval Firepower
Priddy's Hard, Gosport, Hampshire
Tel: (023) 9250 5600
www.explosion.org.uk
The amazing story of naval firepower, from gunpowder to the Exocet, in an exciting new visitor experience for all the family, on the shores of Portsmouth Harbour.

Goodwood House
Goodwood, West Sussex
Tel: (01243) 755040
www.goodwood.co.uk
Magnificent Regency house, home of the Dukes of Richmond, set on one of the world's finest sporting estates. Major collection of paintings, fine furnishings, tapestries and porcelain.

Hastings Castle and 1066 Story
West Hill, Hastings, East Sussex
Tel: (01424) 781112
www.discoverhastings.co.uk
Enter the dungeons carved out of rock and tread the fragmentary remains of this Norman castle set high on West Hill. 1066 Story audiovisual interpretation centre in siege tent.

Hatchlands Park (National Trust)
East Clandon, Surrey
Tel: (01483) 222482
www.nationaltrust.org.uk
Built in 1758 and set in a Repton park, Hatchlands has splendid interiors by Robert Adam and houses the Cobbe collection of keyboard musical instruments. Gertrude Jekyll garden.

High Beeches Woodland & Water Gardens
Handcross, West Sussex
Tel: (01444) 400589
www.highbeeches.com
Unearth the pleasures of the peaceful, landscaped woodland and water gardens with many rare plants, tree trail, wildflower meadow, spring bulbs and glorious autumn colour.

Left experience English history at Broadlands, Romsey; be inspired by Duncan Grant's fireplace at Charleston, Firle

Places to visit

Awarded VisitBritain's Quality Assured Visitor Attraction marque.

Isle of Wight Zoo, Home of the Tiger Sanctuary and Lemurland
Sandown, Isle of Wight
Tel: (01983) 403883
www.isleofwightzoo.com
This seafront zoo specialises in breeding and caring for some of the planet's most severely threatened creatures. Admire some of the most beautiful and dangerous tigers, big cats and primates.

Kent & East Sussex Railway
Tenterden Town Station, Tenterden, Kent
Tel: (01580) 765155
www.kesr.org.uk
Designed with the enthusiast in mind, a full-size heritage railway. Restored Edwardian stations, 14 steam engines, Victorian coaches and Pullman carriages. Museum. Children's play area.

National Motor Museum
John Montagu Building, Beaulieu, Hampshire
Tel: (01590) 612345
www.beaulieu.co.uk
Motoring memories abound in this museum with over 250 exhibits dating from 1896. Also Palace House, Wheels Experience, Beaulieu Abbey ruins and a display of monastic life.

Painshill Park
Portsmouth Road, Cobham, Surrey
Tel: (01932) 868113
www.painshill.co.uk
Unique, award-winning restoration of England's Georgian heritage. Discover true peace and inspiration in this 65-ha (160-acre) landscaped park created by Charles Hamilton.

Port Lympne Wild Animal Park, Mansion and Gardens
Aldington Road, Lympne, Kent
Tel: (01303) 264647
www.howletts.net
Take a trip on the safari trailer and see many rare and endangered species, including the largest herd of captive-bred black rhino in the world outside Africa.

Portsmouth Historic Dockyard
Porter's Lodge, Portsmouth,
Tel: (023) 9286 1533
www.historicdockyard.co.uk
Too much on offer for just one day out – Action Stations, Mary Rose, HMS Victory, HMS Warrior 1860, Royal Naval Museum, Warships by water harbour tours, Dockyard Apprentice exhibition.

Royal Marines Museum
Southsea, Hampshire
Tel: (023) 9281 9385
www.royalmarinesmuseum.co.uk
The history of the intrepid Royal Marines, 1664 to present day, set in what was one of the most stately Officers' Messes in England. Jungle and trench warfare sight and sound exhibitions among others.

Royal Navy Submarine Museum
Haslar Jetty Road, Gosport, Hampshire
Tel: (023) 9252 9217
www.rnsubmus.co.uk
Learn all there is to know about the Royal Navy Submarine Service, with models of submarines from earliest days to present nuclear age, including HM Submarine No 1 and midget submarines.

Above keeping guard at Windsor Castle; relax on the Basingstoke Canal **Right** a fun-filled visit to Portsmouth Historic Dockyard

256   This is just a selection of attractions available. Contact any Tourist Information Centre in the region for more ideas.

SOUTH EAST ENGLAND

St Mary's House and Gardens
Bramber, West Sussex
Tel: (01903) 816205
www.stmarysbramber.co.uk
A medieval timber-framed Grade I house with rare 16thC wall-leather, fine panelled rooms and a unique painted room. Enchanting topiary gardens and Victorian Secret Gardens.

Scotney Castle Garden and Estate (National Trust)
Lamberhurst, Kent
Tel: (01892) 891081
www.nationaltrust.org.uk
Romantic gardens created around the ruins of a 14thC moated castle containing exhibitions. Gardens created by the Hussey family with shrubs, winding paths and superb views.

South of England Rare Breeds Centre
Highlands Farm, Woodchurch, Kent
Tel: (01233) 861493
www.rarebreeds.org.uk
Visit this working farm and see the large collection of rare and traditional farm breeds. Home to the Tamworth Two. Woodland walks and children's play activities.

The Savill Garden, Windsor Great Park
Wick Lane, Windsor, Berkshire
Tel: (01753) 847518
www.savillgarden.co.uk
Woodland garden with formal rose gardens and herbaceous borders. Something of interest and beauty to behold in all seasons. Plant centre, gift shop, restaurant.

Ventnor Botanic Garden and Visitor Centre
The Undercliff Drive, Ventnor, Isle of Wight
Tel: (01983) 855397
www.botanic.co.uk
Escape overseas in nine hectares (22 acres) of world-themed gardens including Mediterranean, The Americas and New Zealand. Visitor centre, gift shop, café, two semi-permanent exhibitions and plant sales.

Weald and Downland Open Air Museum
Singleton, West Sussex
Tel: (01243) 811348
www.wealddown.co.uk
Rescued and rebuilt, a fascinating insight into dwellings from the past with over 45 historic buildings spanning more than 500 years, including a medieval farmstead, 17thC watermill and Tudor kitchen.

West Dean Gardens
West Dean, West Sussex
Tel: (01243) 818210
www.westdean.org.uk
Historic garden with specimen trees, 300ft pergola, rustic summerhouses and restored walled kitchen garden with splendid Victorian glasshouses. Parkland and arboretum walks.

Winchester Cathedral
The Close, Winchester, Hampshire
Tel: (01962) 857225
www.winchester-cathedral.org.uk
Magnificent medieval cathedral with a soaring Gothic nave. Inside are ancient and modern art treasures, 12thC illuminated Winchester Bible, Jane Austen's tomb, crypt and chapels.

Windsor Castle
Windsor, Berkshire
Tel: (020) 7766 7304
www.royal.gov.uk
Fit for a queen! Official residence of HM The Queen and royal residence for nine centuries. State apartments contain treasures from the Royal Collection as well as Queen Mary's Doll's House.

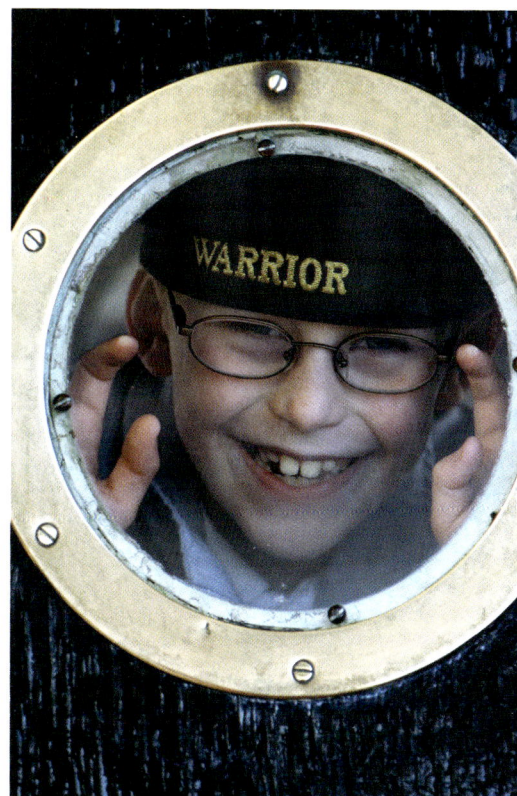

Enjoy England official guides to quality

Tourism South East

40 Chamberlayne Road, Eastleigh, Hampshire SO50 5JH
T: (023) 8062 5505 F: (023) 8062 0010
E: enquiries@tourismse.com
www.visitsoutheastengland.com

Travel information

By road:
From the north east – M1 & M25; the north west – M6, M40 & M25; the west and Wales – M4 & M25; the east – M25; the south west – M5, M4 & M25; London – M25, M2, M20, M23, M3, M4 or M40.

By rail:
Regular services from London's Charing Cross, Victoria, Waterloo and Waterloo East stations to all parts of the South East. Further information on rail journeys in the South East can be obtained on 0845 748 4950.

The following publications are available from Tourism South East:

Escape into the Countryside
Waterside
Cities
Horse Racing
Gardens
Great Value Touring Guide
Great Days Out
Regional Visitor Guide

Right wander around Nymans Gardens, Handcross

SOUTH EAST ENGLAND

Where to stay in
South East England

All place names in the blue bands, under which accommodation is listed, are shown on the maps at the front of this guide.

A complete listing of all VisitBritain assessed accommodation covered by this guide appears at the back.

Accommodation symbols
Symbols give useful information about services and facilities. Inside the back cover flap you can find a key to these symbols. Keep it open for easy reference.

ABINGDON, Oxfordshire Map ref 2C1 *Tourist Information Centre Tel: (01235) 522711*

★★★★
3 Units
Sleeping 2–5

BROOK FARM
Drayton, Abingdon
Contact: Mrs Pam Humphrey, Brook Farm, Abingdon
OX14 4EZ
T: (01235) 820717
F: (01235) 820262
E: info@brookfarmcottages.com
I: www.brookfarmcottages.co.uk

OPEN All Year

Low season per wk
£275.00–£300.00
High season per wk
£370.00–£390.00

Two-bedroom cottages, tastefully furnished, with own courtyard gardens. Centrally positioned for Stratford. Easy access to London, the Cotswolds and Oxford.

Quality Assurance Standard

For an explanation of the quality and facilities represented by the stars please refer to the front of this guide. A more detailed explanation can be found in the information pages at the back.

Completely private, spacious, self contained, professionally designed contemporary luxury apartment, annexed to a large country house. Set in an Area of Outstanding Natural Beauty in the heart of the Chilterns. Wonderful views and walks. Within easy reach of Speen, Amersham, Marlow and Henley. The apartment consists of a double en suite bedroom, hall, sitting room and kitchen.

HIGH GABLES Naphill, High Wycombe, Buckinghamshire
T: 01494 562 591 F: 01494 562 592 E: zacharydesign@btconnect.com

SOUTH EAST ENGLAND

ABINGDON continued

★★★–★★★★★
6 Units
Sleeping 2–10

KINGFISHER BARN HOLIDAY COTTAGES
Culham, Abingdon
Contact: Sarah, Culham, Abingdon OX14 3NN
T: (01235) 537538
F: (01235) 537538
E: info@kingfisherbarn.com
I: www.kingfisherbarn.com

Nestling in the Oxfordshire countryside, we offer impressive cottages and lodges with original stonework and exposed beams. Beautifully furnished and fully equipped with own garden area. Ideal for everybody to enjoy. The town centre and River Thames are a short walk away.

OPEN All Year
Payment accepted: Amex, Mastercard, Switch, Visa

Wedding package available. Ideal for family reunions and group bookings.

Low season per wk
£310.00–£985.00
High season per wk
£403.00–£1,804.00

ADDERBURY, Oxfordshire Map ref 2C1 *Tourist Information Centre Tel: (01295) 259855*

★★★★
1 Unit
Sleeping 2

HANNAH'S COTTAGE AT FLETCHER'S
Banbury
Contact: Mrs Charlotte Holmes, Fletchers, High Street, Adderbury, Banbury OX17 3LS
T: (01295) 810308
E: charlotteaholmes@hotmail.com
I: www.holiday-rentals.com

OPEN All Year except Christmas and New Year
Payment accepted: Euros

Low season per wk
£240.00–£270.00
High season per wk
£270.00–£300.00

Hannah's, a recently restored Victorian garden cottage which incorporates a former hayloft as first floor lounge, is cosy and quiet although in the centre of this lovely village.

Best of Brighton & Sussex Cottages
Fully furnished flats, houses, cottages and apartments throughout the City of Brighton & Hove and in East and West Sussex from Eastbourne to Chichester. Lettings available for periods of three days to three months.
T: 01273 308779 F: 01273 390211
E: enquiries@bestofbrighton.co.uk
www.bestofbrighton.co.uk www.eastbourneapartments.com

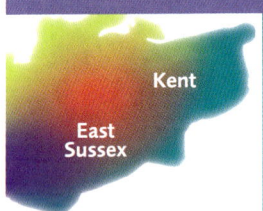

Fairhaven Holiday Homes
Friendly, knowledgeable people to help you to choose your holiday home from our wide range of high quality properties of all types in the countryside and on the coasts of Kent and Sussex.
T: 08452 304334 F: 01634 570157
E: enquiries@fairhaven-holidays.co.uk
www.fairhaven-holidays.co.uk

Garden of England Cottages
Small family agency offering high quality holiday homes in Kent and East Sussex. Short breaks to long lets with fully inclusive prices – no hidden extras. On-line booking and availability.
T: 01732 369168 Fax: 01732 358817
E: holidays@gardenofenglandcottages.co.uk
www.gardenofenglandcottages.co.uk

These independent agencies co-operate as The Southeast Association of Self Catering Agencies to offer visitors a wide choice of holiday properties in the South East of England and all participate in the VisitBritain 'Star' grading scheme.

SOUTH EAST ENGLAND

ALFRISTON, East Sussex Map ref 2D3

★★★
1 Unit
Sleeping 2–3

WINTON BARN
Alfriston
Contact: Mrs Fay Smith, Winton Barn, Winton Street, Alfriston, Polegate BN26 5UJ
T: (01323) 870407
F: (01323) 870407

OPEN All Year except Christmas and New Year

Low season per wk
£195.00–£210.00
High season per wk
£210.00–£250.00

A Listed building converted from a Sussex barn 50 years ago. Lovely views. Ideal for walking. Within easy reach of Eastbourne, Brighton, Lewes and Glyndebourne.

(15)

ALVERSTOKE, Hampshire Map ref 2C3

★★
1 Unit
Sleeping 6

28 THE AVENUE
Alverstoke
Contact: Mr Martin Lawson, 18 Upper Paddock Road, Watford WD19 4DZ
T: (01923) 244042
F: (01923) 244042
E: martinlawson8400@aol.com

Low season per wk
£325.00–£370.00
High season per wk
£370.00–£400.00

Three-bedroomed house with pleasant garden, 10 minutes from Stokes Bay. Opportunities for fishing, sailing and windsurfing. Close to Portsmouth, Southampton and New Forest.

AMERSHAM, Buckinghamshire Map ref 2D1

★★★★
1 Unit
Sleeping 8

This fine 15thC residence, in the heart of Amersham old town, boasts a large dining room with 16thC wall paintings, a fully equipped kitchen, comfortable, high-quality living room and a four-poster bed in the master bedroom. Free car parking. Approximately one mile from London Underground station.

CHILTERN COTTAGES

Amersham
Contact: Mr Stephen Hinds, Hill Farm Lane, Chalfont St. Giles HP8 4NT
T: (07973) 737107
F: (01494) 872421
E: bookings@chilterncottages.org.uk
I: www.chilterncottages.org.uk

OPEN All Year

Payment accepted: Delta, Mastercard, Switch, Visa, Euros

Low season per wk
Min £800.00
High season per wk
£1,000.00–£1,200.00

Short breaks bookings permitted 2 months before start date. Price: weekly rate less 10% per day not used.

ARUNDEL, West Sussex Map ref 2D3 *Tourist Information Centre Tel: (01903) 882268*

★★★
2 Units
Sleeping 4

THE COACHMAN'S FLAT AND THE COTTAGE
Slindon, Arundel
Contact: Mrs Jan Fuente, The Coachman's Flat and The Cottage, Mill Lane House, Arundel BN18 0RP
T: (01243) 814440
F: (01243) 814436
E: jan.fuente@btopenworld.com
I: www.mill-lane-house.co.uk

OPEN All Year

Low season per wk
£260.00–£350.00
High season per wk
£340.00–£420.00

Flat and cottage in 17thC property. Views to coast. In National Trust village on South Downs. Use of large gardens. Animals by arrangement. Children welcome.

ASHDOWN FOREST

See under Nutley

Important note Information on accommodation listed in this guide has been supplied by the proprietors. As changes may occur you are advised to check details at the time of booking.

SOUTH EAST ENGLAND

ASHFORD, Kent Map ref 3B4 *Tourist Information Centre Tel: (01233) 629165*

★★★
6 Units
Sleeping 1–4

EVERSLEIGH WOODLAND LODGES
Ashford
Contact: Mrs Drury, Eversleigh House, Hornash Lane,
Ashford TN26 1HX
T: (01233) 733248
F: (01233) 733248
E: cjdrury@freeuk.com
I: www.eversleighlodges.co.uk

OPEN All Year
Payment accepted:
Mastercard, Visa

Low season per wk
£245.00–£385.00
High season per wk
£400.00–£585.00

Spacious, detached lodges in woodland setting. Heated indoor swimming pool, games room, gymnasium, solarium, gardens. Easy access south coast, London, Canterbury, Channel ports and tunnel.

BARNHAM, West Sussex Map ref 2C3

★★★
2 Units
Sleeping 1–10

WEST COTTAGE & PADDOCK BARN
Barnham
Contact: Mrs Karen Blackman, Barnham Court Farm,
Barnham PO22 0BP
T: (01243) 553223
F: (01243) 553223

OPEN All Year

Low season per wk
£370.00–£878.00
High season per wk
£505.00–£1,595.00

This renovated 19thC cottage stands in a secluded garden in the peaceful countryside just four miles from a sandy beach. Arundel and Chichester nearby.

BEAULIEU, Hampshire Map ref 2C3

★★★
1 Unit
Sleeping 2–7

IVY COTTAGE
Brockenhurst
Contact: Mr & Mrs Gibb, 28 Church Street,
Littlehampton BN17 5PX
T: (01903) 715595
F: (01903) 719176
E: gibb28@breathemail.net

Low season per wk
Min £400.00
High season per wk
Max £595.00

Comfortable, well-equipped, four-bedroomed holiday cottage between Beaulieu and Lymington, with direct access to open forest. Village shop and pub nearby. Open March-October.

BEMBRIDGE, Isle of Wight Map ref 2C3

★★★
1 Unit
Sleeping 10

NINE
Bembridge
Contact: Mrs Betty Cripps, High Point, Brook Green,
Cuckfield RH17 5JJ
T: (01444) 454474

OPEN All Year

Low season per wk
£210.00–£340.00
High season per wk
£350.00–£800.00

Ideal holiday home 400yds from sea. Five double bedrooms, sun parlour, good garden. TV, video, washing machine/drier, dishwasher, fridge/freezer. Parking. Dogs welcome.

★★★
2 Units
Sleeping 4–6

PRINCESSA COTTAGE & COASTWATCH COTTAGE
Bembridge
Contact: Mrs Hargreaves, 1 Norcott Drive, Bembridge
PO35 5TX
T: (01983) 874403
F: (01983) 874403
E: ssnharg@aol.com
I: www.islandbreaks.co.uk

OPEN All Year

Low season per wk
£325.00–£500.00
High season per wk
£460.00–£645.00

Former coastguard cottages near sandy beach, rock pools at low tide. Well furnished, equipped to high standard. Private parking and gardens. Linen provided.

★★
1 Unit
Sleeping 4

WILL-O-COTT
Bembridge
Contact: Mrs Betty Cripps, High Point, Brook Green,
Cuckfield RH17 5JJ
T: (01444) 454474

OPEN All Year

Low season per wk
£130.00–£180.00
High season per wk
£210.00–£250.00

Chalet-type bungalow, with pleasant garden, three minutes from sea.

SOUTH EAST ENGLAND

BISHOPSTONE, East Sussex Map ref 2D3 *Tourist Information Centre Tel: (01323) 897426*

★★★
1 Unit
Sleeping 1–5

144 NORTON COTTAGE
Seaford
Contact: Mrs Carol Collinson, Norton Farm,
Bishopstone, Seaford BN25 2UW
T: (01323) 897544
F: (01323) 897544
E: norton.farm@farmline.com
I: members.farmline.com/collinson

OPEN All Year

Low season per wk
£130.00–£150.00
High season per wk
£150.00–£300.00

Comfortably furnished, semi-detached cottage situated on a working farm in a peaceful, rural location on the South Downs. Ideal for touring South East.

BOWLHEAD GREEN, Surrey Map ref 2C2

★★
1 Unit
Sleeping 1–2

THE BARN FLAT
Godalming
Contact: Mrs Grace Ranson, Bowlhead Green Farm,
Bowlhead Green, Godalming GU8 6NW
T: (01428) 682687
E: Ranson@Bowlhead.fsnet.co.uk

OPEN All Year

Low season per wk
Min £120.00
High season per wk
Max £140.00

In delightful hamlet, 16thC barn conversion with exposed oak beams. Attractive, small, self-contained flat overlooking farmhouse garden. Double sofa bed, kitchenette, shower and wc. No pets.

BRIGHSTONE, Isle of Wight Map ref 2C3

★★★
10 Units
Sleeping 2–8

CHILTON FARM COTTAGES
Newport
Contact: Mrs Susan Fisk, Chilton Farm, Chilton Lane,
Newport PO30 4DS
T: (01983) 740338
F: (01983) 741370
E: info@chiltonfarm.co.uk
I: www.chiltonfarm.co.uk

OPEN All Year

Payment accepted: Euros

Low season per wk
£156.00–£400.00
High season per wk
£400.00–£750.00

Attractive stone cottages on our 800-acre dairy farm. Set in beautiful countryside close to the sea. Two tennis courts, barbecue. A warm welcome assured.

★★★★
1 Unit
Sleeping 4

2 THE GRANARY
Brighstone
Contact: Teresa Herd, 22 Westrope Way, Bedford
MK41 7YU
T: (01234) 328664 & 07795 078049
E: info@2thegranary.co.uk
I: http://2thegranary.co.uk

Charming Grade II Listed granary beside quiet lane on edge of pretty village, Brighstone, 0.5 miles from sea. Converted in 1990, furnished to high standard with views of countryside from first-floor living area. Beautiful enclosed garden complete with patio and furniture. Short distance to village pubs and shops.

OPEN All Year

Prices/availability of short breaks upon request.

Low season per wk
£250.00–£400.00
High season per wk
£420.00–£690.00

Use your *i*s

There are more than 550 Tourist Information Centres throughout England offering friendly help with accommodation and holiday ideas as well as suggestions of places to visit and things to do. You'll find addresses in the local phone book.

SOUTH EAST ENGLAND

BRIGHTON & HOVE, Brighton & Hove Map ref 2D3 *Tourist Information Centre Tel: 0906 711 2255*

★★★
23 Units
Sleeping 1–6

BRIGHTON HOLIDAY FLATS
Brighton
Contact: Veronica Cronin, English Language & Holiday Bureau, 327 Portland Road, Hove BN3 5SE
T: (01273) 410595 & 410944
F: (01273) 412662
E: office@cronin-accommodation.co.uk
I: www.cronin-accommodation.co.uk

Self-catering apartments in a prime seafront location in the heart of Brighton. Near The Lanes, numerous restaurants, shops and entertainment. New (within the same complex) for 2005: a luxury three-bedroomed apartment with full-panorama sea views.

OPEN All Year

Payment accepted: Delta, Mastercard, Switch, Visa, Euros

Low season per wk
£240.00–£700.00
High season per wk
£315.00–£1,300.00

★★★★★
1 Unit
Sleeping 2–6

KILCOLGAN PREMIER BUNGALOW
Rottingdean
Contact: Mr J C St George, 22 Baches Street, London N1 6DL
T: (020) 7250 3678
F: (020) 7250 1955
E: jc.stgeorge@virgin.net

Welcome to excellence in self-catering accommodation. Exceptional, detached, three-bedroomed bungalow comprehensively equipped, with emphasis on comfort. Secluded, landscaped garden overlooking farmland. Garage parking for two vehicles. Accessible to the disabled. Rottingdean is a delightful seaside village with seafront and promenade, four miles from Brighton. Ideal, quiet retreat. Pets by arrangement (small charge).

OPEN All Year

Payment accepted: Euros

Short breaks, minimum 3-night stay, possible during low season, terms on request. Excludes Christmas and New Year.

Low season per wk
£550.00–£650.00
High season per wk
£650.00–£800.00

★★
1 Unit
Sleeping 4

UPPER MARKET STREET
Brighton
Contact: Ms Marcia Stanton, 4 King Charles Road, Surbiton KT5 8PY
T: (020) 8979 1792
F: (020) 8399 6639

Lovely, fully equipped studio apartment with entrance patio. Central location, close to seafront, shopping, entertainment and public transport facilities.

Low season per wk
£225.00–£250.00

www.visitengland.com
Log on for information and inspiration. The latest information on places to visit, events and quality assessed accommodation.

264

SOUTH EAST ENGLAND

BROADSTAIRS, Kent Map ref 3C3 *Tourist Information Centre Tel: (01843) 865650*

★★★★
1 Unit
Sleeping 2–6

FISHERMAN'S COTTAGE
Broadstairs
Contact: Ms Linda Spillane, 5 Union Square, Broadstairs CT10 1EX
T: (020) 8672 4150
E: linda.spillane@virgin.net
I: www.fishermanscottagebroadstairs.co.uk

Delightfully converted, four-storey, Grade II Listed, flint cottage in Broadstairs conservation area. One minute to harbour and beach. The cottage has three bedrooms, a well-equipped kitchen and spacious living areas. The floors are linked by a wooden spiral staircase – see virtual tour on our website.

OPEN All Year

Low season per wk
£305.00–£430.00
High season per wk
£470.00–£625.00

BROCKENHURST, Hampshire Map ref 2C3

★★★
1 Unit
Sleeping 1–5

BROOKLEY DAIRY
Brockenhurst
Contact: Mrs Tracey Boulton, Mayfield, 77 Burley Road, Bockhampton, Christchurch BH23 7AJ
T: (01425) 672013
F: (01425) 672013
E: tracey.boulton@btopenworld.com

Brookley Dairy is a delightful, two-bedroomed apartment situated in the centre of Brockenhurst. Ideal accommodation for touring the New Forest.

OPEN All Year

Low season per wk
Min £295.00
High season per wk
Max £350.00

BROOK, Hampshire Map ref 2B3 *Tourist Information Centre Tel: (023) 8028 2269*

★★★
1 Unit
Sleeping 6–8

WITTENSFORD LODGE
Lyndhurst
Contact: Ms Carol Smith, 14 Hunts Mead, Billericay CM12 9JA
T: (01277) 623997
F: (01277) 634976
E: mbmcarol@dircon.co.uk
I: www.wittensfordlodge.freeservers.com

Detached cottage set in woodland with 0.33-acre garden. Superb base for touring this lovely area.

OPEN All Year

Low season per wk
Min £300.00
High season per wk
Min £500.00

CANTERBURY, Kent Map ref 3B3 *Tourist Information Centre Tel: (01227) 378100*

★★★★
1 Unit
Sleeping 8

CANTERBURY HOLIDAY LETS
Canterbury
Contact: Mrs Kathryn Nevell, 4 Harbledown Park, Harbledown, Canterbury CT2 8NR
T: (01227) 763308
F: (01227) 763308
E: rnevell@aol.com

Five-bedroomed, detached, well-equipped accomodation. Sports facilities and woodland walks. Half a mile to nature reserve, 1.5 miles from city centre. Open July and August.

High season per wk
£400.00–£500.00

★★★-★★★★★
7 Units
Sleeping 2–19

KNOWLTON COURT
Canterbury
Contact: Miss Amy Froggatt, The Estate Office, Knowlton Court, Canterbury CT3 1PT
T: (01304) 842402
F: (01304) 842403
E: knowlton.cottages@farmline.com
I: www.knowltoncourt.co.uk

Elizabethan house and former farm cottages. Golf courses at Sandwich, Channel Tunnel at Folkestone, port of Dover and cathedral city of Canterbury all easily accessible.

OPEN All Year
Payment accepted: Delta, Mastercard, Switch, Visa

Low season per wk
£200.00–£1,200.00
High season per wk
£340.00–£2,000.00

265

SOUTH EAST ENGLAND

CANTERBURY continued

★★★★
3 Units
Sleeping 1-3

ORIEL LODGE
Canterbury
Contact: Mr Keith Rishworth, Oriel Lodge,
3 Queens Avenue, Canterbury CT2 8AY
T: (01227) 462845
F: (01227) 462845
E: info@oriel-lodge.co.uk
I: www.oriel-lodge.co.uk

OPEN All Year
Payment accepted: Delta, Mastercard, Switch, Visa

Low season per wk
£220.00-£280.00
High season per wk
£280.00-£390.00

High-grade apartments in a lovely Edwardian house, set in a tree-lined residential area with private parking, five minutes' walk from the city centre.

★★★★
1 Unit
Sleeping 1-4

ST MARY'S COTTAGE
Canterbury
Contact: Mr R Allcorn, Abberley House,
115 Whitstable Road, Canterbury CT2 8EF
T: (01227) 450265
F: (01227) 478626
E: r.allcorn@discovercanterbury.com

OPEN All Year

Low season per wk
£250.00-£360.00
High season per wk
£360.00-£465.00

St Mary's Cottage is spacious, well decorated, and provides all your needs for your holidays. Situated in a quiet road within the city walls, with a reserved parking space. Close to bus and rail stations. A real 'home from home'. Ask for a leaflet.

CAVERSFIELD, Oxfordshire Map ref 2C1

★★★
1 Unit
Sleeping 1-6

GROOMS COTTAGE
Caversfield
Contact: Mr Albert Phipps, Banbury Road, Caversfield,
Bicester OX27 8TG
T: (01869) 249307
F: (01869) 249307
E: odette@phippscottage.co.uk
I: www.phippscottage.co.uk

OPEN All Year

Low season per wk
Min £325.00
High season per wk
Max £400.00

Detached two-bedroomed cottage with pretty secluded garden. Luxury furnishings, exposed beams, original bread oven. Bathroom with shower.

CHICHESTER, West Sussex Map ref 2C3 Tourist Information Centre Tel: (01243) 775888

★★★★
1 Unit
Sleeping 1-6

5 CALEDONIAN ROAD
Chichester
Contact: Miss Victoria Chubb, 33 Hillier Road, London
SW11 6AX
T: (020) 7924 5446 & 07786 674195
E: victoriachubb@hotmail.com
I: www.visitsussex.org/caledonianroad

OPEN All Year

Low season per wk
£275.00-£350.00
High season per wk
£300.00-£425.00

Recently-restored old townhouse with high-quality, contemporary interior in quiet road. Modern kitchen, real fire, books and games. Patio garden. City centre three minutes' walk. Ideal for beach or exploring the South Downs, Goodwood and evenings at theatre, cinema, restaurants. Wonderful location, summer or winter.

Location Complete addresses for properties are not given and the town(s) listed may be a distance from the actual establishment. Please check the precise location at the time of booking.

266

SOUTH EAST ENGLAND

CHICHESTER continued

★★★★
1 Unit
Sleeping 1–6

CORNERSTONES
Chichester
Contact: Mrs Higgins, Greenacre, Goodwood Gardens, Chichester PO20 1SP
T: (01243) 839096
E: vjrmhiggins@hotmail.com
I: www.visitsussex.org/cornerstones

Built in local style. Two bedrooms upstairs, one downstairs. Bathroom and separate shower room. Village south of Chichester. Easy walking distance to pub/restaurant, church and post office/shop. Central heating. Equipped/furnished to a high standard. Garaging for two cars. Enclosed gardens with patio, tables and chairs. No smoking. Brochure available.

OPEN All Year
Payment accepted: Euros

Low season per wk
£385.00–£555.00
High season per wk
£555.00–£645.00

★★★★
1 Unit
Sleeping 1–2

CYGNET COTTAGE
Chichester
Contact: Mrs Higgins, Greenacre, Goodwood Gardens, Chichester PO20 1SP
T: (01243) 839096
E: vjrmhiggins@hotmail.com
I: www.visitsussex.org/cygnetcottage

Distinctive, detached, modernised one-bedroomed cottage. Village south of Chichester. Within easy walking distance of pub/restaurant, church, village post office/shop. Equipped and furnished to a high standard. Gas central heating. Off-road parking. Sun-trap patio with table and chairs. No smoking. Brochure available.

Payment accepted: Euros

Short breaks available Oct-Apr. Minimum 3 nights.

Low season per wk
£215.00–£285.00
High season per wk
£285.00–£330.00

★★★
5 Units
Sleeping 2–5

HUNSTON MILL
Chichester
Contact: Mr & Mrs Potter, Selsey Road, Chichester PO20 1AU
T: (01243) 783375
F: (01243) 785179
E: hunstonmillcottages@bushinternet.com
I: www.hunstonmill.co.uk

18thC windmill and adjoining buildings converted into comfortable holiday homes, set in nearly an acre of attractive gardens with putting and barbecue. Situated in the country between the historic city of Chichester and the sea, with views over farmland, golf course and to the Downs.

OPEN All Year

Low season per wk
£220.00–£348.00
High season per wk
£291.00–£499.00

Map references The map references refer to the colour maps at the front of this guide. The first figure is the map number; the letter and figure which follow indicate the grid reference on the map.

267

SOUTH EAST ENGLAND

CHICHESTER continued

★★★★
2 Units
Sleeping 14

POPLARS FARM HOUSE
Chichester
Contact: Mr & Mrs T Kinross, Batchmere Road, Almodington, Chichester PO20 7LD
T: (01243) 514969
F: (01243) 512081
E: poplarsfarmhouse@tiscali.co.uk
I: www.poplarsfarmhouse.co.uk

Set in 2.5 acres, well back from the road, a 17thC farmhouse and dairy cottage conversion. The farmhouse sleeps eight in four bedrooms, the dairy cottage sleeps six in three bedrooms. Each unit has two bathrooms. The farmhouse has an Aga kitchen and a dining room to seat 14.

OPEN All Year
Payment accepted: Amex, Delta, Mastercard, Switch, Visa

Low season per wk
£500.00–£700.00
High season per wk
£900.00–£1,250.00

CHILHAM, Kent Map ref 3B3 Tourist Information Centre Tel: (01227) 378100

★★★★
2 Units
Sleeping 2

MONCKTON COTTAGES
Canterbury
Contact: Mrs Helen Kirwan, Monckton Cottages, Mountain Street, Chilham, Canterbury CT4 8DG
T: (01227) 730256
F: (01227) 732423
E: monckton@rw-kirwan.demon.co.uk

Charming, peaceful cottages in 15thC manor set in three acres. Picturesque setting on North Downs Way alongside Chilham Castle's parkland. Perfect for walking, exploring ancient woodland, chalk downs, Tudor village, castles. Canterbury six miles. Own large gardens, oak beams, inglenook fire/woodburning stove. Immaculate, well equipped. New bathrooms/kitchen installed 2002. Detailed brochure.

OPEN All Year

Low season per wk
£160.00–£240.00
High season per wk
£240.00–£290.00

COTSWOLDS

See under Finstock

See also Cotswolds in Heart of England and South West England sections

CROWBOROUGH, East Sussex Map ref 2D2

★★★★
2 Units
Sleeping 2–4

CLEEVE LODGE
Crowborough
Contact: Mr Edward & Mrs Nina Sibley, The Old House, Harlequin Lane, Crowborough TN6 1HS
T: (01892) 654331
E: nina@the-old-house.co.uk
I: www.the-old-house.co.uk

Delightful Victorian self-catering lodge in East Sussex. Separate end of period property dating back to 1700s. Fully equipped with lovely views.

OPEN All Year

Low season per wk
£205.00–£265.00
High season per wk
£265.00–£340.00

DORKING, Surrey Map ref 2D2

★★★
2 Units
Sleeping 2–4

BULMER FARM
Dorking
Contact: Mrs Gill Hill, Bulmer Farm, Holmbury St Mary, Dorking RH5 6LG
T: (01306) 730210

30-acre beef farm. Single-storey units converted from 17thC farm building. Two-person unit, suitable for disabled, and four-person unit together form a courtyard to the farmhouse.

OPEN All Year

Low season per wk
£240.00–£320.00
High season per wk
£290.00–£380.00

SOUTH EAST ENGLAND

DORKING continued

★★★
1 Unit
Sleeping 1–2

MILTON BROOK COTTAGE
Dorking
Contact: Mrs Susan Scarrott, Milton Brook Cottage, Westcott Road, Dorking RH4 3PU
T: (01306) 877256
E: abacusue@aol.com

OPEN All Year
Payment accepted: Euros

High season per wk
Max £275.00

Studio accommodation in a detached annexe to an 18thC cottage with its back gate leading into a bluebell wood. Easy walk to town.

DYMCHURCH, Kent Map ref 3B4

★★★★★
1 Unit
Sleeping 2–8

DYMCHURCH HOUSE
Dymchurch
Contact: Mrs J Uden, 53 Crescent Road, Sidcup DA15 7HW
T: (020) 8300 2100
E: dymchurchhouse@btopenworld.com

OPEN All Year

Low season per wk
£350.00–£500.00
High season per wk
£650.00–£800.00

Luxury, spacious detached property in a prime position. Equipped to a very high standard. Ideal for its superb sandy beach accessed directly via footpath. Indoor swimming pool, the famous miniature railway and village with its children's amusement park are all within easy walking distance. Excellent location for visiting tourist attractions.

EMSWORTH, Hampshire Map ref 2C3

★★★★
1 Unit
Sleeping 2–6

DELTA HOUSE
Emsworth
Contact: Mr Ben Francis, Flat 1, 38 Mayfield Road, London N8 9LP
T: (020) 8340 8074
E: www.deltahouse-emsworth.co.uk
I: www.deltahouse-emsworth.co.uk

OPEN All Year

Low season per wk
£275.00–£350.00
High season per wk
£360.00–£500.00

Delta House is a spacious three-bedroom townhouse located in the centre of the beautiful fishing village of Emsworth. Located 100 metres from the harbour.

EPSOM, Surrey Map ref 2D2

★★★
1 Unit
Sleeping 1–5

7 GREAT TATTENHAMS
Epsom
Contact: Mrs Mary Willis, 7 Great Tattenhams, Epsom KT18 5RF
T: (01737) 354112

OPEN All Year

Low season per wk
£170.00–£195.00
High season per wk
£220.00–£245.00

Modern, spacious, comfortably furnished first floor flat. A good touring centre for London and the South East. Superstore nearby.

Special breaks

Many establishments offer special promotions and themed breaks. These are highlighted in red. (All such offers are subject to availability.)

269

SOUTH EAST ENGLAND

EVERTON, Hampshire Map ref 2B3

1 Unit
Sleeping 1–8

2 UPLAY COTTAGES
Lymington
Contact: Ms Jacquie Taylor, Centre Lane, Everton, Lymington SO41 0JP
T: (01590) 641810
F: (01590) 671325
E: booking@halcyonholidays.com
I: www.halcyonholidays.com

A beautifully refurbished, comfortable Edwardian cottage set in the heart of the village with shops, pub, coast and forest nearby. Larger cottages/two-person studio in Lymington and Brockenhurst with direct forest access, large gardens, open fires, antique furniture. Detailed information and pictures on website.

OPEN All Year

Payment accepted: Amex, Delta, Mastercard, Switch, Visa

Low season per wk
£294.00–£420.00
High season per wk
£332.00–£695.00

Mid-week/weekend bookings. 70% off-peak discount for 1-2 persons. Available all year round.

EXTON, Hampshire Map ref 2C3 Tourist Information Centre Tel: (023) 8083 3333

5 Units
Sleeping 1–5

BEACON HILL FARM COTTAGES
Southampton
Contact: Mrs C Dunford, The Farm Office, Manor Farm, Beacon Hill Lane, Warnford Road, Southampton SO32 3NW
T: (01730) 829724
F: (01730) 829833
E: chris@martin4031.freeserve.co.uk
I: www.beaconhillcottages.co.uk

Cottages in a converted barn, formerly part of a working farm. Idyllic setting, stunning views of Meon Valley farmland.

OPEN All Year

Low season per wk
£250.00–£350.00
High season per wk
£250.00–£470.00

FAREHAM, Hampshire Map ref 2C3 Tourist Information Centre Tel: (01329) 221342

1 Unit
Sleeping 4

MANOR CROFT
Fareham
Contact: Mr Thomson, Manor Croft, Church Path, Fareham PO16 7DT
T: (01329) 280750
F: (01329) 280750
E: mcc-feedback@btconnect.com
I: www.manor-croft-health.co.uk/visitor_accom_1.htm

Delightful English Heritage Grade II Listed building. Spacious apartment which combines original Victorian character features with modern comforts. Town centre location. Excellent local facilities including shopping centre, restaurants, pubs, leisure facilities etc. Ideal for south coast holiday base or business visitors. Short or long stays welcome.

OPEN All Year

Payment accepted: Delta, Mastercard, Switch, Visa, Euros

£60.00 per night – min 3 night stay

Short breaks available – minimum 3 nights – any start date.

Quality Assurance Standard
Star ratings and awards were correct at time of going to press but are subject to change. Please check at the time of booking.

SOUTH EAST ENGLAND

FARNHAM, Surrey Map ref 2C2 *Tourist Information Centre Tel: (01252) 715109*

3 Units
Sleeping 2–5

HIGH WRAY
Farnham
Contact: Mrs Alexine G N Crawford, High Wray,
73 Lodge Hill Road, Farnham GU10 3RB
T: (01252) 715589
F: (01252) 715746
E: crawford@highwray73.co.uk

Two ground-floor flats ideal for wheelchair users. Dorcy has double and triple bedrooms, kitchen/dining room and wheel-in shower. Rose has similar facilities with twin bed/sitting room. Open plan studio with barn roof in corner of large garden sleeps two in gallery plus double sofa bed in living area.

OPEN All Year

Low season per wk
£175.00–£350.00
High season per wk
£200.00–£450.00

---

33 Units
Sleeping 2–6

TILFORD WOODS
Farnham
Contact: Mr Ede, Tilford Woods, Tilford Road, Tilford, Farnham GU10 2DD
T: (01252) 792199
F: (01252) 797040
I: www.tilfordwoods.co.uk

Tilford Woods comprises one- to three-bedroom, fully fitted and equipped, luxury timber lodges. The one-bedroom 'Cobbett' lodges have a four-poster bed, en suite bathroom with sauna, spa and outside hot tub. Tilford Woods is the ideal base for exploring the wonderful surrounding countryside and the many local attractions.

OPEN All Year
Payment accepted: Delta, Mastercard, Switch, Visa

Short breaks available.

Low season per wk
£380.00–£440.00
High season per wk
£620.00–£750.00

FERRING, West Sussex Map ref 2D3

1 Unit
Sleeping 2–4

LAMORNA GARDENS
Ferring
Contact: Mrs Elsden & Mary Fitzgerald, Ferring-by-Sea, Worthing BN12 5QD
T: (01903) 238582 & 07860 699268
F: (01903) 230266

Spacious, detached bungalow situated on the seafront, just three miles from Worthing. Supermarket and tearooms six minutes' walk. Non-smokers only.

OPEN All Year
Payment accepted: Euros

Low season per wk
£350.00
High season per wk
£400.00–£500.00

FINSTOCK, Oxfordshire Map ref 2C1

1 Unit
Sleeping 4–5

WYCHWOOD
Chipping Norton
Contact: Mrs Bodil Grain, 40 School Road, Oxford OX7 3DJ
T: (01993) 868249
E: bgrain@wychwoodcottage.co.uk
I: www.wychwoodcottage.co.uk

A 17thC cottage, set in quiet village on edge of Cotswolds. Sleeps four plus cot.

OPEN All Year

Low season per wk
£200.00–£250.00
High season per wk
£250.00–£350.00

Accessibility Look for the symbols which indicate National Accessible Scheme standards for hearing and visually impaired guests in addition to standards for guests with mobility impairment. You can find an index of all scheme participants at the back of this guide.

SOUTH EAST ENGLAND

FOLKESTONE, Kent Map ref 3B4 Tourist Information Centre Tel: (01303) 258594

★★–★★★★★
14 Units
Sleeping 2–10

THE GRAND
Folkestone
Contact: Mr Michael Stainer, The Grand, The Leas, Folkestone CT20 2XL
T: (01303) 222222
F: (01303) 220220
E: info@grand.uk.com
I: www.grand.uk.com

The Grand is a fine Listed building situated on The Leas, the world-famous grassy cliff-top promenade running from the town centre along the southern side of the spacious and gracious west end of Folkestone. It enjoys uninterrupted views across the ever-changing seascape to France.

OPEN All Year

Payment accepted: Delta, Mastercard, Switch, Visa, Euros

Short breaks, Mon-Fri or Fri-Mon: low season – min £60, max £140; high season – min £125, max £255.

Low season per wk
£90.00–£295.00
High season per wk
£190.00–£460.00

FORDINGBRIDGE, Hampshire Map ref 2B3

★★★★–★★★★★★★
8 Units
Sleeping 2–18

BURGATE MANOR FARM HOLIDAYS
Fordingbridge
Contact: Mrs Bridget Stallard, Burgate Manor Farm Holidays, Burgate Manor Farm, Fordingbridge SP6 1LX
T: (01425) 653908
F: (01425) 653908
E: info@newforestcottages.com
I: www.newforestcottages.com

New Forest/Avon Valley. Small-and medium-sized farm cottages and large, newly-converted, galleried, beamed barn. Short walk pub/restaurant. Games barn. Fishing. Grazing. Beach 15 miles.

OPEN All Year

Low season per wk
£256.00–£1,134.00
High season per wk
£342.00–£2,839.00

★★★
1 Unit
Sleeping 4

GLENCAIRN
Damerham, Fordingbridge
Contact: Mrs Tiller, 2 Fernlea, Fordingbridge SP6 1PN
T: (01425) 652506

Detached cottage in pleasant, friendly village close to New Forest. Comfortably furnished and well maintained. Three bedrooms, well-equipped kitchen, large, quiet garden. Brochure available. Open March to October and Christmas.

Low season per wk
£210.00–£320.00
High season per wk
£320.00–£430.00

FRESHWATER, Isle of Wight Map ref 2C3

★★★
29 Units
Sleeping 2–7

FARRINGFORD HOTEL
Freshwater
Contact: Miss Hollyhead, Farringford Hotel, Bedbury Lane, Freshwater PO40 9PE
T: (01983) 752500
F: (01983) 756515
E: enquiries@farringford.co.uk
I: www.farringford.co.uk

Once the home of Alfred Lord Tennyson, now a country-style house with self-catering units of three different styles to suit individual needs. Set within 35 acres of mature pastureland incorporating a 9-hole par 3 golf course, tennis, outdoor heated pool, Bistro Bar and bowls.

OPEN All Year

Payment accepted: Amex, Delta, Mastercard, Switch, Visa, Euros

Fully inclusive Christmas packages available. Ferry-inclusive deals available. Subsidised child and pet rates available.

Low season per wk
£259.00–£480.00
High season per wk
£637.00–£786.00

SOUTH EAST ENGLAND

FRESHWATER continued

★★★
1 Unit
Sleeping 4

LITTLE RABBITS
Freshwater
Contact: Mrs Helen Long, Windrush, Yarmouth
PO41 0TA
T: (01983) 761506
E: hugh7@bushinternet.com

Low season per wk
Min £170.00
High season per wk
Max £310.00

Delightful bungalow in an exclusive development overlooking open landscape with The Needles and Solent to side and rear. Ideal base to explore this lovely island. Open March to October.

GLYNDE, East Sussex Map ref 2D3 *Tourist Information Centre Tel: (01273) 483448*

★★★★
8 Units
Sleeping 2–32

CABURN COTTAGES
Lewes
Contact: Mr & Mrs Philip Norris, Caburn Cottages,
Ranscombe Farm, Lewes BN8 6AA
T: (01273) 858062
I: www.caburncottages.co.uk

OPEN All Year

Low season per wk
£180.00–£600.00
High season per wk
£180.00–£650.00

Eight flint and brick cottages on working farm. Very comfortable. Non-smoking. Downland walks. Close to Glyndebourne, Lewes and Brighton. Friendly welcome.

GODSHILL, Isle of Wight Map ref 2C3

★★★
1 Unit
Sleeping 1–2

MILK PAN FARM
Ventnor
Contact: Mr Tony & Mrs Leila Morrish, Milk Pan Farm,
Bagwick Lane, Godshill, Ventnor PO38 3JY
T: (01983) 840570
E: tony@milkpanfarm.co.uk
I: www.milkpanfarm.co.uk

OPEN All Year

Low season per wk
£100.00–£200.00
High season per wk
£220.00–£310.00

Small, family-run farm, set in country lane, offering self-catering accommodation for a couple in a newly constructed part of the main farm bungalow.

GOUDHURST, Kent Map ref 3B4

★★★★
5 Units
Sleeping 2–7

THREE CHIMNEYS FARM
Cranbrook
Contact: Mrs Marion Fuller, Three Chimneys Farm,
Bedgebury Road, Goudhurst, Cranbrook TN17 2RA
T: (01580) 212175
F: (01580) 212175
E: marionfuller@threechimneysfarm.co.uk
I: www.threechimneysfarm.co.uk

OPEN All Year

Payment accepted: Amex,
Delta, Mastercard, Switch,
Visa

Low season per wk
£250.00–£450.00
High season per wk
£310.00–£675.00

80-acre mixed farm. Spacious cottages in a beautiful location, very quiet but not isolated.

GREAT MILTON, Oxfordshire Map ref 2C1 *Tourist Information Centre Tel: (01865) 726871*

★★★★
6 Units
Sleeping 2–5

VIEWS FARM BARNS
Oxford
Contact: Mr & Mrs Peers, Views Farm Barns,
Views Farm, Great Milton, Oxford OX44 7NW
T: (01844) 279352
F: (01844) 279362
E: info@viewsfarmbarns.co.uk
I: www.viewsfarmbarns.co.uk

OPEN All Year

Payment accepted:
Mastercard, Switch, Visa,
Euros

Low season per wk
£240.00–£290.00
High season per wk
£370.00–£435.00

400-acre arable and mixed farm. Converted stable block forming well-appointed holiday flats. Close to Oxford and the M40. Superb views of Thame Valley.

Credit card bookings

If you book by telephone and are asked for your credit card number it is advisable to check the proprietor's policy should you cancel your reservation.

SOUTH EAST ENGLAND

GUILDFORD, Surrey Map ref 2D2 Tourist Information Centre Tel: (01483) 444333

★★★
1 Unit
Sleeping 2–6

LAVENDER
Guildford
Contact: Mr & Mrs Liew, Mandarin, Pewley Point,
Pewley Hill, Guildford GU1 3SP
T: (01483) 506819
F: (01483) 506819
E: shirleyliew9@hotmail.com

OPEN All Year

Low season per wk
£430.00–£470.00
High season per wk
£430.00–£470.00

Well-presented, fully furnished, comfortable house, conveniently situated in town centre, close to high street shops, river, theatre, leisure facilities and railway station. Airports 40 minutes.

★★
20 Units
Sleeping 4–5

UNIVERSITY OF SURREY
Guildford
Contact: University of Surrey, Guildford GU2 7XH
T: (01483) 689157
F: (01483) 579266
E: conferences@surrey.ac.uk
I: www.surrey.ac.uk/conferences

Payment accepted: Delta, Mastercard, Switch, Visa

Low season per wk
£350.00–£410.00
High season per wk
£350.00–£410.00

Modern, self-contained accommodation for self-catering holidays on attractive campus. One mile from Guildford centre. Ideal base to enjoy London and South East England. Open June, July and August.

HAILSHAM, East Sussex Map ref 2D3

★★★–★★★★★
5 Units
Sleeping 4–11

Spacious oast house, cottages and wing of Tudor manor in extensive grounds. Hard tennis court, indoor heated pool, sauna, jacuzzi, badminton. Children and pets welcome. Prices shown are for the cottages. Oast house is £1200-£1525.

PEKES
Chiddingly
Contact: Ms Eva Morris, 124 Elm Park Mansions,
Park Walk, London SW10 0AR
T: (020) 7352 8088
F: (020) 7352 8125
E: pekes.afa@virgin.net
I: www.pekesmanor.com

OPEN All Year
Payment accepted: Switch

Off peak and short breaks available (excl school holidays). Cottages £230-£605, oast house £775-£900.

Low season per wk
Min £325.00
High season per wk
Max £1,020.00

HASTINGLEIGH, Kent Map ref 3B4 Tourist Information Centre Tel: (01233) 629165

★★★★
1 Unit
Sleeping 1–2

Stable conversion displaying beams and original features, yet offering all modern amenities. Situated in Area of Outstanding Natural Beauty with excellent walks from front door, including the North Downs Way. Within easy reach of Canterbury, Eurostar terminals, Channel ports of Dover and Folkestone, plus many places of historic interest.

STAPLE FARM
Ashford
Contact: Mr & Mrs Martindale, Staple Farm, Hastingleigh,
Ashford TN25 5HF
T: (01233) 750248
F: (01233) 750249

Low season per wk
Min £250.00
High season per wk
Min £350.00

Symbols The symbols in each entry give information about services and facilities. A key to these symbols appears at the back of this guide.

274

SOUTH EAST ENGLAND

HASTINGS, East Sussex Map ref 3B4 *Tourist Information Centre Tel: (01424) 781111*

★★★
1 Unit
Sleeping 4

ROSE HOUSE
Hastings
Contact: Mrs Susan Hill, 1 Beauport Gardens,
St Leonards-on-Sea, Hastings TN37 7PQ
T: (01424) 754812
F: (01424) 754812
E: hillbusybee@aol.com

OPEN All Year
Payment accepted:
Mastercard, Switch, Visa

Low season per wk
Min £195.00
High season per wk
Max £295.00

Home from home, fully furnished flat, short walking distance to all attractions. One bedroom, en suite shower, on-road parking.

HAYLING ISLAND, Hampshire Map ref 2C3

★★★
1 Unit
Sleeping 1–6

7 FAIRLIGHT CHALETS
Hayling Island
Contact: Mrs Janet Bulmer, 9 Whitethorn Road,
Hayling Island PO11 9LS
T: (023) 9246 0309

OPEN All Year

Low season per wk
£180.00–£220.00
High season per wk
Min £380.00

The chalet sleeps four to six. It has two toilets, bath, separate shower, washing machine, tumble drier, TV/video. Parking for four vehicles. Very quiet location. 10 minutes' walk to beach and shops. Pets welcome.

HENFIELD, West Sussex Map ref 2D3

★★★
2 Units
Sleeping 3–5

NEW HALL COTTAGE & NEW HALL HOLIDAY FLAT
Henfield
Contact: Mrs Marjorie Carreck, New Hall Cottage & New Hall Holiday Flat, New Hall, New Hall Lane, Henfield BN5 9YJ
T: (01273) 492546

OPEN All Year

Short breaks available. Nov-Mar: £110 for 2 nights, each extra night £30. Apr-Oct: £130 for 2 nights, each extra night £40.

Low season per wk
£180.00–£280.00
High season per wk
£300.00–£340.00

Self-contained flat and 17thC cottage attached to manor-house. Set in 3.5 acres of mature gardens and surrounded by farmland. Within easy reach of famous Sussex gardens, Nymans, High Beeches, Wakehurst Place, Leonardslee, and less than an hour from Wisley. Or visit the towns of Brighton, Arundel, Lewes and Chichester, the South Downs and the coast.

Millers
SELF-CATERING HOLIDAY ACCOMMODATION
HAYLING ISLAND, HAMPSHIRE

Self-Catering houses, bungalow's and flats near the seafront. Free colour brochure.

19 Mengham Road, Hayling Island, Hampshire PO11 9BG
T: 023 9246 5951
E: rentals@haylingproperty.co.uk   W: www.haylingproperty.co.uk

275

SOUTH EAST ENGLAND

HOVE
See under Brighton & Hove

HYTHE, Kent Map ref 3B4

★★★
1 Unit
Sleeping 4

HYTHE PERIOD COTTAGE
Hythe
Contact: Mrs Sophie James, 73 Donald Street, Roath,
Cardiff CF24 4TL
T: (029) 2048 0667
E: sophie-james123@hotmail.com

Low season per wk
Min £250.00
High season per wk
Max £360.00

Lovely 18thC family cottage with character. Near sea, indoor swimming pool and shops. Large secluded garden, open fire, own garage. Well-behaved pets welcome.

IBSLEY, Hampshire Map ref 2B3

★★★★★
1 Unit
Sleeping 6

CHOCOLATE BOX COTTAGE
Ringwood
Contact: Mrs Higham
T: 07768 075761
I: www.chocolateboxcottage.co.uk

OPEN All Year

Low season per wk
£500.00–£625.00
High season per wk
£625.00–£750.00

Beautiful 'chocolate box' cottage set in 0.5-acre grounds, on the edge of the New Forest. High-standard accommodation. Pets welcome. Smoking permitted.

ISLE OF WIGHT
See under Bembridge, Brighstone, Brook, Freshwater, Godshill, Porchfield, Ryde, Sandown, Seaview, Totland Bay, Wroxall

See display advertisement below

LEE ON THE SOLENT, Hampshire Map ref 2C3

★★★
1 Unit
Sleeping 5–6

THE CHART HOUSE
Lee on the Solent
Contact: Mr Brook White, 6 Cambridge Road,
Lee on the Solent PO13 9DH
T: (023) 9255 4145
F: (023) 9255 3847
E: marion_kinnear-white@talk21.com
I: www.brook.white1.btinternet.co.uk

OPEN All Year

Low season per wk
£265.00–£340.00
High season per wk
£380.00–£420.00

Comfortable, detached, three-bedroomed family home, close to seafront. Enclosed patio/garden. Off-road parking. Private indoor heated pool available by arrangement.

LEWES, East Sussex Map ref 2D3 Tourist Information Centre Tel: (01273) 483448

★★★
1 Unit
Sleeping 1–4

5 BUCKHURST CLOSE
Lewes
Contact: Mrs S Foulds, 66 Houndean Rise, Lewes
BN7 1EJ
T: (01273) 474755
F: (01273) 474755

OPEN All Year

Low season per wk
£200.00–£220.00
High season per wk
£220.00–£250.00

Modern terraced house, fully equipped. Small garden, parking space. Easy walking distance to town. Five minutes' drive to station or Glyndebourne.

Island Cottage Holidays
ISLE OF WIGHT

VisitBritain ★★★ – ★★★★

Low season (October-May)
£135-£595

High season (June-September)
£198-£1,225

T:(01929) 480080
F:(01929) 481070
E:enq@islandcottageholidays.com
I:www.islandcottageholidays.com

Short breaks also available.

Charming cottages in delightful rural surroundings and close to the sea. Beautiful views - attractive gardens - some with swimming pools. Situated throughout the Isle of Wight. Properties sleeping 1-12.

SOUTH EAST ENGLAND

LOCKS HEATH, Hampshire Map ref 2C3 *Tourist Information Centre Tel: (023) 8083 3333*

★★★★
1 Unit
Sleeping 2

STEPPING STONES
Southampton
Contact: Mrs Barbara Habens, Stepping Stones,
126 Locks Heath Park Road, Locks Heath, Southampton
SO31 6LZ
T: (01489) 572604
E: jimhabens@aol.com
I: http://members.lycos.co.uk/selfcateringannexe/

OPEN All Year

Low season per wk
Min £250.00
High season per wk
Min £250.00

One-bedroom annexe adjoining owners' bungalow. Very high-standard accommodation in a delightful, secluded garden. Easy reach of historic Portsmouth and Winchester, New Forest, Bournemouth etc.

LYMINGTON, Hampshire Map ref 2C3

★★★
1 Unit
Sleeping 2–5

FIR TREE COTTAGE
Lymington
Contact: Mrs Saword, 1 Merlewood Court,
Lyon Avenue, New Milton BH25 6AP
T: (01425) 617219

OPEN All Year

Low season per wk
£200.00–£260.00
High season per wk
£265.00–£430.00

Period cottage 1.5 miles from open forest. Enclosed garden, good for pets and children. Traditional furnishings, books, fitted carpets, double glazing, toys.

★★★★
1 Unit
Sleeping 1–4

NO.17 SOUTHAMPTON ROAD
Lymington
Contact: Miss Julie Stevens & Andrew Baxendine,
Elm Cottage, Pilley Bailey, Lymington SO41 5QT
T: (01590) 676445
E: juleestevens@aol.com
I: www.17southamptonroad.co.uk

OPEN All Year

Low season per wk
£300.00–£400.00
High season per wk
£400.00–£600.00

Beautifully presented three-bedroom Georgian townhouse. Close proximity to shops, restaurants and pretty town quay. Secluded patio garden. Isle of Wight ferry nearby. Welcome pack.

★★★★
1 Unit
Sleeping 4

SILK COTTAGE
Lymington
Contact: Mrs Anne Paterson, Silkhouse,
77 Lower Buckland Road, Lymington SO41 9DR
T: (01590) 688797
F: (01590) 688797
E: anne@silkcottage.com
I: www.silkcottage.com

Low season per wk
£400.00–£500.00
High season per wk
£500.00–£650.00

Pretty, brand-new cottage close to New Forest. Double upstairs, twin downstairs, both with en suite bathroom/shower room. Quiet, comfortable and well equipped. Ideal holiday/work base.

★★★★
4 Units
Sleeping 6–8

SOLENT REACH MEWS
Lymington
Contact: Ms Denise Farmer, Solent Reach Mews,
Lower Pennington Lane, Lymington SO41 8AN
T: (01590) 671648
F: (01590) 689244
E: enquiries@hurstviewleisure.co.uk
I: www.solentreachmews.co.uk

OPEN All Year
Payment accepted: Visa

Low season per wk
£500.00–£700.00
High season per wk
£600.00–£900.00

Modern cottage complex of high quality set in farmland near the Solent and Lymington. Excellent stress-free property.

Important note Information on accommodation listed in this guide has been supplied by the proprietors. As changes may occur you are advised to check details at the time of booking.

277

SOUTH EAST ENGLAND

LYMINGTON continued

★★★★
1 Unit
Sleeping 4

WATERFORD COTTAGE
Lymington
Contact: Mrs Sally Sargeaunt, 33 Barton Court Avenue,
Barton On Sea, New Milton BH25 7EP
T: (01425) 628970
F: (01425) 620399

OPEN All Year

Low season per wk
£290.00–£310.00
High season per wk
£350.00–£480.00

Attractive modernised cottage in quiet location between town/marina. Courtyard garden and off-road parking. Short walk to shops, restaurants, pubs. Double bedroom en suite and twin bedroom.

LYNDHURST, Hampshire Map ref 2C3 *Tourist Information Centre Tel: (023) 8028 2269*

★★★★
1 Unit
Sleeping 4

HOLLY COTTAGE
Lyndhurst
Contact: Mr & Mrs F S Turner, Greensward,
The Crescent, Ashurst, Southampton SO40 7AQ
T: (023) 8029 2374
F: (023) 8029 2374
E: sam@turner402.fsnet.co.uk
I: http://mysite.wanadoo-members.co.uk/hollycottnewforest

OPEN All Year except
Christmas and New Year

Low season per wk
£295.00–£390.00
High season per wk
£390.00–£499.00

Cosy, comfortably furnished 19thC cottage 50 yards from forest. Personally renovated and maintained by local owner. Children welcome. No short breaks.

★★★★
5 Units
Sleeping 2–7

PENNY FARTHING HOTEL & COTTAGES
Lyndhurst
Contact: Mike/Linda/Sue, Penny Farthing Hotel & Cottages, Romsey Road, Lyndhurst SO43 7AA
T: (023) 8028 4422
F: (023) 8028 4488
I: www.pennyfarthinghotel.co.uk

OPEN All Year

Payment accepted: Amex,
Delta, Diners, Mastercard,
Switch, Visa, Euros

Low season per wk
£650.00–£850.00
High season per wk
£725.00–£1,250.00

Our contemporary, modern interiors give guests the benefit of comfortable living areas within the heart of the New Forest. All properties are completely refurbished. Linen provided, washing machines, TVs, stereo/CD players and parking. Ideally situated in Lyndhurst village (Southampton nine miles/18 minutes, Bournemouth 25 miles/35 minutes). See website for all properties.

MAIDENHEAD, Windsor and Maidenhead Map ref 2C2 *Tourist Information Centre Tel: (01628) 796502*

★★★★
4 Units
Sleeping 2–4

COURTYARD COTTAGES
Maidenhead
Contact: Mrs Carol Bardo, Moor Farm, Ascot Road,
Maidenhead SL6 2HY
T: (01628) 633761
F: (01628) 636167
E: moorfm@aol.com
I: www.moorfarm.com

OPEN All Year

Payment accepted: Euros

Low season per wk
£360.00–£420.00
High season per wk
£360.00–£480.00

A 35-acre farm with easy access to London, Windsor and Ascot. Cottages converted from traditional farm buildings and furnished with antique pine. Bed and breakfast also available.

MAIDSTONE, Kent Map ref 3B3 *Tourist Information Centre Tel: (01622) 602169*

★★
1 Unit
Sleeping 1–3

LAVENDER COTTAGE
Maidstone
T: (01622) 850287
E: lavender@nascr.net
I: www.oas.co.uk/ukcottages/lavender

Low season per wk
Min £180.00
High season per wk
£225.00–£265.00

17thC, oak-beamed, two-bedroomed cottage. Log fire, fully equipped. In pretty village, close to Leeds Castle with easy access to M20, Channel Tunnel and ports and London.

278

SOUTH EAST ENGLAND

MILFORD ON SEA, Hampshire Map ref 2C3

★★★
1 Unit

WINDMILL COTTAGE
Lymington
Contact: Mrs Perham, Danescourt, 14 Kivernell Road, Milford on Sea, Lymington SO41 0PQ
T: (01590) 643516
F: (01590) 641255

Three-bedroomed, Georgian-style house in select residential area close to village, sea and the New Forest.

OPEN All Year

Low season per wk
£215.00–£255.00
High season per wk
£265.00–£530.00

MOLLINGTON, Oxfordshire Map ref 2C1 *Tourist Information Centre Tel: (01295) 259855*

★★★–★★★★★
3 Units
Sleeping 2–8

THE STABLES, THE SHIPPON, THE BYRE-ANITA'S HOLIDAY COTTAGES
Banbury
Contact: Mr Darrel & Mrs Anita Gail Jeffries, Anita's Holiday Cottages, The Yews, Church Farm, Banbury OX17 1AZ
T: (01295) 750731
F: (01295) 750731

Converted from an old cow byre, these cottages are superbly finished to a high standard. Situated in the lovely village of Mollington, within walking distance of the pub. Central to Oxford, Stratford-on-Avon, Blenheim, Warwick and Cotswolds. Lovely walks and cycling, even fishing close by.

OPEN All Year

Short breaks available on request.

Low season per wk
£140.00–£395.00
High season per wk
£240.00–£695.00

MORETON, Oxfordshire Map ref 2C1 *Tourist Information Centre Tel: (01844) 212834*

★★★★
4 Units
Sleeping 2–7

MEADOWBROOK FARM HOLIDAY COTTAGES
Thame
Contact: Mrs Diana Wynn, Meadowbrook Farm Holiday Cottages, Moreton, Thame OX9 2HY
T: (01844) 212116
F: (01844) 217503
E: rdwynn@ukonline.co.uk

Characterful, spacious and luxury cottages. Comfortable furnishings, exposed beams and features. Private gardens, ample parking. Peaceful retreat in Area of Outstanding Natural Beauty. Situated in pretty hamlet without passing traffic. Walking to Thame (15 minutes) and walks on farm to ponds with ducks, Koi fish and plenty of wildlife.

OPEN All Year

Low season per wk
£200.00–£365.00
High season per wk
£350.00–£450.00

NAPHILL, Buckinghamshire

See display advertisement on page 259

NEW FOREST

See under Beaulieu, Brockenhurst, Brook, Fordingbridge, Godshill, Hythe, Lymington, Lyndhurst, Milford on Sea, Sway

SOUTH EAST ENGLAND

NEWBURY, West Berkshire Map ref 2C2 *Tourist Information Centre Tel: (01635) 30267*

★★★-★★★★★
2 Units
Sleeping 2–6

YAFFLES
Newbury
Contact: Mr Tony & Mrs Jean Bradford, Yaffles,
Red Shute Hill, Thatcham RG18 9QH
T: (01635) 201100
F: (01635) 201100
E: yaffles@ukonline.co.uk
I: www.cottagesdirect.com/yaffles & www.ukonline.co.uk/yaffles

OPEN All Year

Low season per wk
£250.00–£360.00
High season per wk
£250.00–£360.00

Comfortable, secluded, self-contained garden flat and studio set in spacious, peaceful grounds just north of Newbury yet near junction 13 of M4. Prices are for two people.

NORTH NEWINGTON, Oxfordshire Map ref 2C1 *Tourist Information Centre Tel: (01295) 259855*

★★★★
1 Unit
Sleeping 2–4

HERRIEFF'S COTTAGE
Banbury
Contact: Mrs Mary T Bentley, Herrieff's Farmhouse,
The Green, North Newington, Banbury OX15 6AF
T: (01295) 738835
F: (01295) 738835
E: mary@herrieffsfarm.freeserve.co.uk
I: www.herrieffsfarm.freeserve.co.uk

OPEN All Year
Payment accepted: Euros

Low season per wk
£180.00–£200.00
High season per wk
£300.00–£330.00

Grade II Listed, converted cow shed located on the Oxfordshire cycleway in a quiet, unspoilt village, offering a very high standard of comfort.

NUTLEY, East Sussex Map ref 2D3

★★-★★★★
10 Units
Sleeping 1–5

Former smallholding overlooking open countryside and Ashdown Forest. Shower room, kitchen/diner/lounge. Fully equipped. Wheelchair, pet and smoker-friendly cottages available. Spare campbeds. Ideally situated for London, castles, gardens and coast. Both Friday and Saturday turn around.

WHITEHOUSE FARM HOLIDAY COTTAGES
Nutley
Contact: Mr K Wilson, Whitehouse Farm,
Horney Common, Nutley, Uckfield TN22 3EE
T: (01825) 712377
F: (01825) 712377
E: keith.g.r.wilson@btinternet.com
I: www.streets-ahead.com/whitehousefarm

OPEN All Year
Payment accepted:
Mastercard, Visa

Low season per wk
£249.00–£449.00
High season per wk
£336.00–£449.00

OLNEY, Milton Keynes Map ref 2C1

★★★★
2 Units
Sleeping 4

Beautifully situated at the end of a long drive with lovely views over open farmland, these cottages are comfortable and homely with their own garden, patio and parking. Ideal central location for many tourist attractions, with easy access to Milton Keynes, Northampton and Bedford. Olney market town just 1.5 miles.

HYDE FARM COTTAGES
Olney
Contact: Mrs Penny Reynolds, Hyde Farm Cottages,
Warrington Road, Olney MK46 4DU
T: (01234) 711223
F: (01234) 714305
E: accomm@thehyde.fsbusiness.co.uk

OPEN All Year

Low season per wk
Min £300.00
High season per wk
Min £400.00

 Colour maps Colour maps at the front of this guide pinpoint all places under which you will find accommodation listed.

SOUTH EAST ENGLAND

OWSLEBURY, Hampshire Map ref 2C3 *Tourist Information Centre Tel: (01962) 840500*

★★★
1 Unit

THE FO'C'SLE
Winchester
Contact: Mrs Barbara Crabbe, Little Lodge, Hensting Lane, Owslebury, Winchester SO21 1LE
T: (01962) 777887
F: (01962) 777781

OPEN All Year
Payment accepted: Euros

Low season per wk
Min £200.00
High season per wk
Min £200.00

Large open plan apartment, separate shower and toilet. Down quiet country lane one hour from London. Simply but comfortably furnished. Ideal for weekend break.

OXFORD, Oxfordshire Map ref 2C1 *Tourist Information Centre Tel: (01865) 726871*

★★★
1 Unit
Sleeping 2–4

Comfortable self-catering accommodation in a stylish and modern apartment within 2km of the city centre. Fully furnished and decorated to a high standard, situated in a quiet location close to Oxford colleges and parks.

WEEKLY HOME
Oxford
Contact: Mr Kelvin Fowler, Weekly Home, Gordon House, 276 Banbury Road, Oxford OX2 7ED
T: (01865) 557555 & 07870 234725
F: (01865) 557545
E: info@weeklyhome.com
I: www.weeklyhome.com

OPEN All Year
Payment accepted: Delta, Mastercard, Switch, Visa

Low season per wk
Min £350.00
High season per wk
Min £460.00

PANGBOURNE, West Berkshire Map ref 2C2 *Tourist Information Centre Tel: (0118) 956 6226*

★★★
1 Unit
Sleeping 5

Picturebook brick and flint thatched cottage on 300-acre beef and arable farm. Ideal base for visiting London, Oxford, Stonehenge and Stratford, and for sightseeing in the Thames Valley, Chilterns, Cotswolds and beyond. A warm and friendly home from home for a holiday to remember. Please telephone for quickest response.

BRAMBLY THATCH
Reading
Contact: Mr & Mrs Hatt, Merricroft Farming, Ref Brambly Thatch, Goring Heath, Reading RG8 7TA
T: (0118) 984 3121
F: (0118) 984 4662
E: hatts@merricroft.demon.co.uk

OPEN All Year
Payment accepted: Mastercard, Switch, Visa

Pay by credit card free of charge if you mention this advert. Also special monthly rates in winter.

Low season per wk
Max £395.00
High season per wk
Max £425.00

PLAXTOL, Kent Map ref 2D2 *Tourist Information Centre Tel: (01732) 450305*

★★★
1 Unit
Sleeping 1–6

GOLDING HOP FARM COTTAGE
Sevenoaks
Contact: Mrs Jacqueline Vincent, Bewley Lane, Plaxtol, Sevenoaks TN15 0PS
T: (01732) 885432
F: (01732) 885432
E: info@goldinghopfarm.com
I: www.goldinghopfarm.com

OPEN All Year

Low season per wk
£220.00–£270.00
High season per wk
£270.00–£420.00

12-acre cobnut farm. South-facing cottage with garden and all modern conveniences. Quiet position but not isolated.

Map references The map references refer to the colour maps at the front of this guide. The first figure is the map number; the letter and figure which follow indicate the grid reference on the map.

281

SOUTH EAST ENGLAND

PORCHFIELD, Isle of Wight Map ref 2C3

★★★★
1 Unit
Sleeping 6

SQUIRRELS
Newport
Contact: Mrs Bridget Lewis, Channers Ltd,
Blackbridge Brook House, Main Road, Ryde PO33 4DR
T: (01983) 884742
E: bridget.lewis@btinternet.com

An individually designed house full of character. Attractively and comfortably equipped for up to six. It has three bedrooms, one en suite. Beautifully appointed, well-equipped kitchen. Open fire with logs. Enclosed garden with decking, barbecue and seating. Set in well-positioned, quiet village with local pub close by.

OPEN All Year

Reduction for low occupancy and short breaks during low season.

Low season per wk
Min £300.00
High season per wk
Max £775.00

PORTSMOUTH & SOUTHSEA, Portsmouth Map ref 2C3 *Tourist Information Centre Tel: (023) 9282 6722*

★★★
6 Units

ATLANTIC APARTMENTS
Southsea
Contact: Mrs Dawn Sait, Atlantic Apartments,
61A Festing Road, Southsea PO4 0NQ
T: (023) 9282 3606
F: (023) 9229 7046
I: www.portsmouth-apartments.co.uk/atlantic.htm

OPEN All Year

Low season per wk
£150.00–£300.00
High season per wk
£200.00–£320.00

Situated in one of the most attractive areas of Southsea, only a few yards from the canoe lake and seafront. All apartments are fully self-contained. Large car park.

★★★★
1 Unit
Sleeping 1–4

GREENHAYS BUSINESS/HOLIDAY ACCOMMODATION
Portsmouth
Contact: Mrs Christine Martin, Greenhays Business/
Holiday Accommodation, 10 Helena Road, Portsmouth
PO4 9RH
T: (023) 9273 7590
F: (023) 9273 7590

OPEN All Year except
Christmas and New Year

Low season per wk
Min £250.00
High season per wk
£320.00–£395.00

Luxury and modern two-bedroomed apartment. 150m from the sea, shops and nightlife. Quiet residential road. Two miles from Gun Wharf.

★★★
10 Units
Sleeping 1–3

LAKESIDE HOLIDAY & BUSINESS APARTMENTS
Southsea
Contact: Mrs Hamza, 5 Helena Road, Southsea
PO4 9RH
T: 07810 436981
I: www.lakesidesouthsea.com

OPEN All Year

Payment accepted: Amex,
Mastercard, Switch, Visa,
Euros

Low season per wk
£180.00–£200.00
High season per wk
£200.00–£260.00

Self-catering apartments in lovely detached house, two minutes' walk to sea, rose gardens, bowling greens and lake. Open all year, parking available, rear garden.

★★★
6 Units
Sleeping 1–7

OCEAN APARTMENTS
Southsea
Contact: Mrs Dawn Sait, 8-10 St Helens Parade,
Southsea PO4 0RW
T: (023) 9273 4233
F: (023) 9229 7046
I: www.portsmouth-apartments.co.uk

OPEN All Year

Payment accepted:
Mastercard, Visa, Euros

Low season per wk
£140.00–£400.00
High season per wk
£250.00–£600.00

Imposing seafront building with magnificent views. Recently refurbished. Very spacious one-to four-bedroomed self-contained apartments, lift, private car parking. Executive suites available.

Quality Assurance Standard
Star ratings and awards were correct at time of going to press but are subject to change. Please check at the time of booking.

SOUTH EAST ENGLAND

ROTTINGDEAN, Brighton & Hove Map ref 2D3 *Tourist Information Centre Tel: 0906 711 2255*

★★★★★
1 Unit
Sleeping 2–6

KILCOLGAN PREMIER BUNGALOW
Rottingdean, Brighton
Contact: Mr J C St George, 22 Baches Street, London N1 6DL
T: (020) 7250 3678
F: (020) 7250 1955
E: jc.stgeorge@virgin.net

OPEN All Year
Payment accepted: Euros

Low season per wk
£550.00–£650.00
High season per wk
£650.00–£800.00

Well appointed, detached, three-bedroom quality bungalow. Spacious, comfortable accommodation, comprehensively equipped. Peaceful location. Picturesque coastal village. Accessible to disabled. An ideal seaside retreat. Brighton four miles.

ROYAL TUNBRIDGE WELLS, Kent Map ref 2D2 *Tourist Information Centre Tel: (01892) 515675*

★★★
2 Units
Sleeping 2–4

FORD COTTAGE
Royal Tunbridge Wells
Contact: Mrs Wendy Cusdin, Ford Cottage, Linden Park Road, Royal Tunbridge Wells TN2 5QL
T: (01892) 531419
E: FordCottage@tinyworld.co.uk
I: www.fordcottage.co.uk

Ford Cottage is a picturesque Victorian cottage three minutes' walk from the Pantiles. Self-contained studio flats with own front doors, fully fitted kitchens, en suites and showers. Off-street parking. Ideal for visiting many local gardens, castles and historic houses.

OPEN All Year except Christmas and New Year
Payment accepted: Euros

Short breaks available – terms on request.

Low season per wk
£220.00–£290.00
High season per wk
£275.00–£325.00

(1)

★★★
1 Unit
Sleeping 4

22 HAWKENBURY MEAD
Royal Tunbridge Wells
Contact: Mr R H Wright
T: (01892) 536977
F: (01892) 536200
E: rhwright1@aol.com

OPEN All Year
Payment accepted: Mastercard, Switch, Visa, Euros

Low season per wk
£180.00–£190.00
High season per wk
Min £240.00

A charming furnished cottage that can accommodate up to three or four people, set on the outskirts of the historic spa town of Royal Tunbridge Wells.

★★★★
6 Units
Sleeping 2–4

ITARIS PROPERTIES LIMITED
Royal Tunbridge Wells
Contact: Mrs Angela May, Itaris Properties Limited, 12 Mount Ephraim, Royal Tunbridge Wells TN4 8AS
T: (01892) 511065
F: (01892) 540171
E: enquiries@itaris.co.uk
I: www.itaris.co.uk

OPEN All Year

Low season per wk
£245.00–£280.00
High season per wk
£364.00–£390.00

Royal Tunbridge Wells is surrounded by beautiful and unspoilt countryside and is the ideal location for a short break or relaxing holiday. Our self-contained and fully equipped holiday apartments are situated in the very heart of Tunbridge Wells within walking distance of its many amenities.

Accessibility
Look for the symbols which indicate National Accessible Scheme standards for hearing and visually impaired guests in addition to standards for guests with mobility impairment. You can find an index of all scheme participants at the back of this guide.

SOUTH EAST ENGLAND

RUSTINGTON, West Sussex Map ref 2D3

★★★
1 Unit
Sleeping 2–4

SEAWAY
Rustington
Contact: Mrs Millidge, 25 Evelyn Avenue, Rustington
BN16 2EJ
T: (01903) 772548

OPEN All Year

Low season per wk
£230.00–£260.00
High season per wk
£320.00–£360.00

Detached two-bedroomed bungalow with beamed ceilings, comfortably furnished lounge, kitchen/diner, utility room and large garden. Near village shops and 10 minutes from sea.

RYDE, Isle of Wight Map ref 2C3 Tourist Information Centre Tel: (01983) 813818

★★★–★★★★★
2 Units
Sleeping 2–3

CLAVERTON HOUSE
Ryde
Contact: Dr Hartwig Metz, Claverton House,
12 The Strand, Ryde PO33 1JE
T: (01983) 613015
F: (01983) 613015
E: clavertonhouse@aol.com

OPEN All Year

Payment accepted: Euros

Low season per wk
£150.00–£200.00
High season per wk
£250.00–£300.00

Beautiful holiday residence at Ryde's seafront, overlooking the Solent. Ten minutes' walk to town centre, bus station and passenger ferries.

RYE, East Sussex Map ref 3B4 Tourist Information Centre Tel: (01797) 226696

★★★
3 Units
Sleeping 2

BOAT HOUSE
Rye
Contact: Mr Melville-Brown, 107 Crescent Drive South, Woodingdean, Brighton BN2 6SB
T: 07803 189031
E: chris@ryeholidays.co.uk
I: www.ryeholidays.co.uk

Quality riverside apartments on private quayside. These superb, split-level apartments with mahogany-decked balconies provide delightful views of passing yachts and Romney Marsh beyond. Within five minutes' walk of medieval Rye. Our website offers many pictures.

OPEN All Year

Short breaks available Nov-Easter.

Low season per wk
£195.00–£280.00
High season per wk
£280.00–£370.00

★★★★
1 Unit
Sleeping 2–6

FROGLETS COTTAGE
Rye
Contact: Mrs Brenda Haines, Little Frogs, Rye Road, Newenden, Cranbrook TN18 5PL
T: (01797) 252011
E: brenda@curtishaines.co.uk
I: www.froglets.uk.com

OPEN All Year

Payment accepted: Delta, Mastercard, Switch, Visa

Low season per wk
£225.00–£295.00
High season per wk
£395.00–£525.00

A characterful Grade II Listed cottage, comfortably sleeping six, in the heart of the conservation area and attracting many return visitors.

Town index

This can be found at the back of the guide. If you know where you want to stay the index will give you the page number listing accommodation in your chosen town, city or village.

SOUTH EAST ENGLAND

SANDLING, Kent Map ref 3B3 Tourist Information Centre Tel: (01622) 602169

★★★★
2 Units
Sleeping 6–8

Tastefully fully furnished and equipped cottages converted from former stables and coach house located next to an historical country manor-house made famous in Charles Dickens' 'The Pickwick Papers'. Conveniently located in Kent, only 50 minutes by rail/car to London, and in a beautiful country setting.

DINGLEY COTTAGE & DELL COTTAGE
Maidstone
Contact: Mr Robert Lawty, Cobtree Manor House, Forstal Road, Maidstone ME14 3AX
T: (01622) 671160
F: (01622) 750378
E: Enquiries@cobtreemanor.co.uk
I: www.cobtreemanor.co.uk

OPEN All Year

Payment accepted: Mastercard, Switch, Visa

Low season per wk £380.00–£450.00
High season per wk £495.00–£700.00

SANDOWN, Isle of Wight Map ref 2C3 Tourist Information Centre Tel: (01983) 813818

★★★★
3 Units
Sleeping 2–6

BRACKLA APARTMENTS
Sandown
Contact: Mrs Lindsay Heinrich, Brackla Apartments, 7 Leed Street, Sandown PO36 9DA
T: (01983) 403648
E: enquire@brackla-apartments.co.uk
I: www.brackla-apartments.co.uk

OPEN All Year

Low season per wk £260.00–£295.00
High season per wk £650.00–£690.00

Victorian property, tastefully converted, with all modern conveniences. Situated in a quiet area close to beach, shops, restaurants and station. Totally non-smoking.

★★★★
1 Unit
Sleeping 6

Apartment 2 Ocean View is a self-contained lower half of a former Victorian guesthouse with a large, private sun terrace and access directly onto Sandown beach, three double bedrooms, two with en suite, and a family bathroom with spa bath. Large lounge, kitchen/diner and separate utility room.

OCEAN VIEW APARTMENT 2
Sandown
Contact: Mr Clive Pettit, 125 High Street, Canvey Island SS8 7RF
T: (01268) 691444
F: (01268) 691444
E: oceanview@onthebeachiow.freeserve.co.uk
I: www.onthebeachiow.co.uk

OPEN All Year

Payment accepted: Mastercard, Switch, Visa

Low season per wk £235.00–£275.00
High season per wk £450.00–£700.00

SEAFORD, East Sussex Map ref 2D3 Tourist Information Centre Tel: (01323) 897426

★★★★
1 Unit
Sleeping 1–5

2 KINGSWAY COURT
Seaford
Contact: Mrs Pauline Gower, 6 Sunningdale Close, Southdown Road, Seaford BN25 4PF
T: (01323) 895233
E: sific@bgower.f9.co.uk

OPEN All Year

Payment accepted: Euros

Low season per wk £250.00–£350.00
High season per wk £350.00–£400.00

Fully equipped, spacious, semi-detached house. Gardens, balcony, parking. Five minutes from sea, open country, station and town centre. One single and two double bedrooms.

Credit card bookings
If you book by telephone and are asked for your credit card number it is advisable to check the proprietor's policy should you cancel your reservation.

285

SOUTH EAST ENGLAND

SEAVIEW, Isle of Wight Map ref 2C3

★★★
1 Unit
Sleeping 1–6

1 POND LANE
Seaview
Contact: Mrs Sara Capon, 11 Circular Road, Elmfield, Ryde
PO33 1AL
T: (01983) 564267
F: (01983) 564267
E: smcapon@aol.com

OPEN All Year

Low season per wk
Min £186.00
High season per wk
Max £546.00

Detached property set in a large garden with off-road parking. Situated on the outskirts of the tranquil village of Seaview, the beach is only a two-minute stroll with local shops, boutiques and restaurants within easy walking distance. A well-equipped cottage, open all year round, offering comfortable, homely accommodation.

SOUTHSEA
See under Portsmouth & Southsea

STAPLE, Kent Map ref 3C3 Tourist Information Centre Tel: (01227) 378100

★★★★
1 Unit
Sleeping 1–4

PIGLET PLACE
Canterbury
Contact: Mr Richard & Mrs Bronwen Barber,
Greengage Cottage, Lower Road, Barnsole, Canterbury
CT3 1LG
T: (01304) 813321
F: (01304) 812312
E: richbarber@lineone.net
I: www.pigletplace.co.uk

OPEN All Year

Low season per wk
£250.00–£350.00
High season per wk
£350.00–£500.00

Piglet Place is a converted barn. Two bedrooms, one en suite, one bathroom, lounge and kitchen/diner. Private woodland, secure parking, outdoor solar-heated swimming pool.

(7)

STONEGATE, East Sussex Map ref 3B4

★★★★★
1 Unit
Sleeping 4

COOPERS FARM COTTAGE
Stonegate
Contact: Ms Jane Howard, Coopers Farm Cottage,
Coopers Farm, Stonegate TN5 7EH
T: (01580) 200386
E: jane@coopersfarmstonegate.co.uk
I: www.coopersfarmstonegate.co.uk

OPEN All Year except Christmas

From Nov-Mar: £200 for the weekend or a 4-night, mid-week break.

Low season per wk
£350.00–£450.00
High season per wk
£450.00–£650.00

Coopers Cottage combines the charm of an ancient building – huge inglenook fireplace and a wealth of beams – with the comforts of 21st-century living. Enjoy the peace and seclusion of this traditional working farm situated in the High Weald Area of Outstanding Natural Beauty. Horses welcome.

Country Code Always follow the Country Code
• Enjoy the countryside and respect its life and work • Guard against all risk of fire • Fasten all gates • Keep your dogs under close control • Keep to public paths across farmland • Use gates and stiles to cross fences, hedges and walls • Leave livestock, crops and machinery alone • Take your litter home • Help to keep all water clean • Protect wildlife, plants and trees • Take special care on country roads • Make no unnecessary noise.

SOUTH EAST ENGLAND

STREAT, West Sussex Map ref 2D3

★★★
1 Unit
Sleeping 4

THE GOTE LODGE
Streat
Contact: Mrs Caroline Tower, The Gote Lodge, Streat, Hassocks BN6 8RN
T: (01273) 890976
F: (01273) 891656
E: tower@gote.freeserve.co.uk

OPEN All Year

Low season per wk
£325.00–£375.00
High season per wk
£350.00–£400.00

Lovely flint cottage in walled garden below the South Downs Way. Log fire, central heating, games room, children welcome. Ten minutes from historic town of Lewes.

SWAY, Hampshire Map ref 2C3

★★★
1 Unit
Sleeping 6

HACKNEY PARK
Lymington
Contact: Mrs Helen Beale, Hackney Park, Mount Pleasant Lane, Lymington SO41 8LS
T: (01590) 682049

OPEN All Year

Low season per wk
Min £190.00
High season per wk
Max £380.00

Modern, spacious and comfortable, self-contained apartment (more bedrooms available if required) in tranquil setting with delightful forest views. Excellent touring, walking and horse-riding area.

TENTERDEN, Kent Map ref 3B4

★★★★
2 Units
Sleeping 4–5

MEADOW COTTAGE & TAMWORTH COTTAGE
Tenterden
Contact: Mrs Cooke, Great Prawls Farm, Stone In Oxney, Tenterden TN30 7HB
T: (01797) 270539
E: info@prawls.co.uk
I: www.prawls.co.uk

OPEN All Year

Low season per wk
Min £200.00
High season per wk
Max £450.00

Lovely, detached, single-storey cottages on peaceful grass farm with views in Area of Outstanding Natural Beauty. Sandy beaches, medieval Rye and Tenterden 15 minutes. Castles, National Trust properties, bird reserves and steam trains nearby – France for a day trip! Personally supervised. Central heating. Short breaks. Brochure. See website for photos/prices/booking form.

★★★★
1 Unit
Sleeping 5

QUINCE COTTAGE
Tenterden
Contact: Mrs Heather E S Crease, Laurelhurst, 38 Ashford Road, Tenterden TN30 6LL
T: (01580) 765636
E: quincott@zetnet.co.uk
I: www.quincecottage.co.uk

OPEN All Year
Payment accepted: Euros

5% discount on bookings for 2 or more consecutive weeks. Short breaks (minimum 3 nights) possible Oct-Mar.

Low season per wk
£250.00–£365.00
High season per wk
£410.00–£460.00

Listed, beamed cottage on residential side of tree-lined high street. Comfortable home from home. One single, two double bedrooms, cot available. Rear secluded courtyard. Close to all amenities, including steam railway and leisure centre. Children welcome. Sorry no pets, no smoking. Good centre for exploring Kent and East Sussex. Brochure available.

SOUTH EAST ENGLAND

THAME, Oxfordshire Map ref 2C1 *Tourist Information Centre Tel: (01844) 212834*

★★★★
1 Unit
Sleeping 6

THE HOLLIES
Thame
Contact: Ms Julia Tanner, Little Acre, 4 High Street,
Thame OX9 7AT
T: (01844) 281423
E: info@theholliesthame.co.uk
I: www.theholliesthame.co.uk

OPEN All Year

Low season per wk
£350.00–£450.00

Beautifully appointed, luxury cottage-style bungalow with peaceful gardens, situated in a secluded backwater near the oldest part of Thame, five minutes' walk from the centre of our historic market town.

TOTLAND BAY, Isle of Wight Map ref 2C3

★★★
1 Unit
Sleeping 6

STONEWIND FARM
Totland Bay
Contact: Mrs Pat Hayles, Barn Cottage, Middleton,
Freshwater PO40 9RW
T: (01983) 752912
F: (01983) 752912

OPEN All Year

Low season per wk
Min £225.00
High season per wk
Max £500.00

Charming two-bedroomed farmhouse, in peaceful area with fine views. Central heating, fully equipped kitchen. Electricity, linen, towels provided. Secluded gardens with barbecue.

TUNBRIDGE WELLS

See under Royal Tunbridge Wells

WALTON-ON-THAMES, Surrey Map ref 2D2

★★★★
1 Unit
Sleeping 1–3

GUEST WING
Walton-on-Thames
Contact: Mr Richard Dominy, Guest Wing,
30 Mayfield Gardens, Walton-on-Thames KT12 5PP
T: (01932) 241223

OPEN All Year

Low season per wk
£245.00–£300.00
High season per wk
£300.00–£330.00

Attractive, two-bedroomed, self-contained wing of neo-Georgian house in residential cul-de-sac, adjacent to Walton station. Ideal for London, Hampton Court, Windsor and motorway network.

WAREHORNE, Kent Map ref 3B4

★★★★
1 Unit
Sleeping 1–2

TUCKERS FARM
Warehorne
Contact: Mrs Bernadette Restorick, Tuckers Farm,
Warehorne, Ashford TN26 2ER
T: (01233) 733433 & 07796 878733
F: (01233) 733700
E: prestorick@aol.com

OPEN All Year
Payment accepted: Euros
Short breaks: Mar-Oct by arrangement. 3 or 4 nights.

Low season per wk
£160.00–£180.00
High season per wk
£260.00–£280.00

In a stunningly beautiful location near Tenterden, this tastefully refurbished luxury studio offers country lovers a tranquil haven. Cool in summer or snug in winter with woodburner, cooks' kitchen or seasonal specialities prepared by the owners. Local fine dining, birds, wild flowers and country walks complete this rural gem.

Important note Information on accommodation listed in this guide has been supplied by the proprietors. As changes may occur you are advised to check details at the time of booking.

SOUTH EAST ENGLAND

WEST MARDEN, West Sussex Map ref 2C3 Tourist Information Centre Tel: (01243) 775888

★★★★
1 Unit
Sleeping 2–5

CABRAGH COTTAGE
Chichester
Contact: Mrs Lesley Segrave, Cabragh House, West Marden, Chichester PO18 9EJ
T: (023) 9263 1267
E: lsegrave@tinyworld.co.uk

This attractive former coach house offers excellent self-catering accommodation in a lovely woodland setting of 65 acres where peacocks freely roam. There are many public footpaths in the vicinity and four delightful country pubs ten minutes away. There are also many places of interest nearby.

OPEN All Year

Low season per wk
£380.00–£495.00
High season per wk
£535.00–£640.00

WHITSTABLE, Kent Map ref 3B3 Tourist Information Centre Tel: (01227) 275482

★★★
1 Unit
Sleeping 1–6

HARBOUR REST
Whitstable
Contact: Mr & Mrs Avery-Smith, 21 Argyle Road, Whitstable CT5 1JS
T: (01227) 261449 & 07932 410343

A spacious three-bed flat (one en suite) with garden five minutes from harbour, beach, town centre. Off-street parking. Market day Thursdays. Senior citizens 10% discount.

OPEN All Year
Payment accepted: Euros

Low season per wk
£250.00–£350.00
High season per wk
£400.00–£600.00

WINCHESTER, Hampshire Map ref 2C3 Tourist Information Centre Tel: (01962) 840500

★★★★★
1 Unit
Sleeping 4

GYLEEN
Winchester
Contact: Mr Paul & Mrs Elizabeth Tipple, 9 Mount View Road, Oliver's Battery, Winchester SO22 4JJ
T: (01962) 861918
F: 08700 542801
E: pauliz@tipple.demon.co.uk
I: www.cottageguide.co.uk/gyleen

Detached, secluded, well-equipped, two-bedroom bungalow set in large, peaceful, mature garden overlooking golf course. Two miles west of Winchester on a bus route. Ample parking in drive.

OPEN All Year

Low season per wk
£288.00–£382.00
High season per wk
£393.00–£423.00

★★★
1 Unit
Sleeping 2–4

MALLARD COTTAGE
Winchester
Contact: Mrs Tricia Simpkin, Mallard Cottage, 64 Chesil Street, Winchester SO23 0HX
T: (01962) 853002
F: (01962) 853002
E: mallardsimpkin@aol.com
I: www.mallardcottage.co.uk

Self-contained annexe to Georgian cottage. Two bedrooms, two shower rooms, sitting/dining room. Fully fitted kitchen. Utility room. Welcome hamper. On-site parking. Delightfully peaceful riverside garden. Historic heart of city five minutes' walk. Heated summer-house. Perfect touring base. Portsmouth nearby. Central London 59 minutes by train.

OPEN All Year
Payment accepted: Mastercard, Switch, Visa

Low season per wk
Min £385.00
High season per wk
Min £485.00

 Map references
Map references apply to the colour maps at the front of this guide.

289

SOUTH EAST ENGLAND

WINDSOR, Windsor and Maidenhead Map ref 2D2 *Tourist Information Centre Tel: (01753) 743900*

★★
3 Units
Sleeping 1–18

DORNEY HOLIDAY APARTMENTS
Windsor
Contact: Sarah Everitt, Dorney Holiday Apartments,
Nr Windsor SL4 6QQ
T: (01753) 827037
F: (01753) 855022
E: enquiries@troppo.uk.com
I: www.troppo.uk.com

OPEN All Year
Payment accepted: Delta, Mastercard, Switch, Visa, Euros

Low season per wk
£350.00–£665.00
High season per wk
£350.00–£665.00

Three apartments set in rural location. Close to Windsor Legoland, Dorney Lake, trains to London. Rowers welcome. Book by the night £50–£95.

★★★
1 Unit
Sleeping 1–4

FLAT 6 THE COURTYARD
Windsor
Contact: Mr Gavin Gordon, 5 Temple Mill Island, Marlow SL7 1SG
T: (01628) 824267
F: (01628) 828949
E: gavingordon@totalise.co.uk
I: www.windsor-selfcatering.co.uk

OPEN All Year

Low season per wk
Min £475.00
High season per wk
Min £525.00

An elegant, well-equipped, first floor (lift) apartment centrally situated in a quiet courtyard almost opposite Windsor Castle. One double and one twin bedroom. With direct access to Windsor High Street, the many restaurants, excellent shops, Theatre Royal and castle are only minutes away. London approximately 30 minutes. Exclusive parking.

 Ratings All accommodation in this guide has been rated, or is awaiting a rating, by a trained VisitBritain assessor.

The Castle Mews Apartment
Church Street, Windsor

Situated in the charming cobbled back streets by Windsor Castle, this delightful apartment is well presented throughout. A wonderful, central place to stay with great restaurants and pubs nearby, it has one double bedroom and a double sofa bed in the living room, a galley style kitchen and a good sized bathroom. Prices from £425 to £525 per week.

- Private car parking space
- TV / DVD + movies / Radio/CD player
- Microwave and washing machine
- Hairdryer + Ironing facilities
- Bath / electric shower
- All linen and bath towels supplied

 **royalwindsorlets.com**

01628 632092 | 01344 887613 | bookings@royalwindsorlets.com

SOUTH EAST ENGLAND

WORTHING, West Sussex Map ref 2D3 *Tourist Information Centre Tel: (01903) 221307*

★★
10 Units
Sleeping 2–8

8 MARINERS WALK
Rustington
Contact: Mrs A Wright, Promenade Holiday Homes,
44 Nepcote Lane, Findon BN14 0SL
T: (01903) 877047
F: (01903) 877047
I: www.promenadeholidayhomes.co.uk

OPEN All Year
Payment accepted:
Mastercard, Switch, Visa

Low season per wk
£190.00–£360.00
High season per wk
£295.00–£605.00

Houses, bungalows and flats available, some with direct sea views from an historic Georgian terrace. Rustington and Worthing areas.

★★
4 Units
Sleeping 2–4

TORRINGTON HOLIDAY FLATS
Worthing
Contact: Mrs Elsden & Mary Fitzgerald, Torrington
Holiday Flats, 60 Manor Road, Worthing BN11 4SL
T: (01903) 238582 & 07860 699268
F: (01903) 230266
I: www.visitsussex.org/torrington

OPEN All Year
Payment accepted: Euros

Low season per wk
£180.00–£200.00
High season per wk
£250.00–£280.00

Handsome Edwardian house in quiet conservation area, close to sea and shops. Spacious, well-furnished flats in excellent condition.

WROXALL, Isle of Wight Map ref 2C3

★★★–★★★★★
7 Units
Sleeping 2–9

APPULDURCOMBE HOLIDAY COTTAGES
Ventnor
Contact: Mrs Jane Owen, Appuldurcombe Farm,
Appuldurcombe Road, Wroxall, Ventnor PO38 3EW
T: (01983) 840188
F: (01983) 840188
I: www.appuldurcombe.co.uk

OPEN All Year
Payment accepted: Amex,
Mastercard, Switch, Visa

Low season per wk
£250.00–£300.00
High season per wk
£300.00–£1,100.00

Individual stone cottages around 300-acre historic estate with superb views, good walking and cycling. Free entry Appuldurcombe House and Falconry Centre. See each cottage's availability on website.

Country Code Always follow the Country Code

• Enjoy the countryside and respect its life and work

• Guard against all risk of fire • Fasten all gates • Keep your dogs under close control • Keep to public paths across farmland • Use gates and stiles to cross fences, hedges and walls • Leave livestock, crops and machinery alone • Take your litter home • Help to keep all water clean • Protect wildlife, plants and trees • Take special care on country roads • Make no unnecessary noise.

A mix of **sandy** beaches and **sheltered** bays, **wild moors,** buzzing nightlife and **relaxing** resorts.

South West England

Looking for some inspiration? Here are a few ideas to get you started in South West England. **experience** the amazing surfing championships at Newquay. **discover** The Lost Gardens of Heligan, 80 acres of the largest garden restoration project in Europe. **explore** the origins of life to the ends of the earth at Wildwalk, one of At-Bristol's three magical attractions **relax** in a honey-coloured Cotswolds village.

THE REGION
Bristol & Bath, Cornwall & the Isles of Scilly, Devon, Dorset, Gloucestershire & the Cotswolds, Somerset, Wiltshire

CONTACT
▸ SOUTH WEST TOURISM
Woodwater Park,
Exeter EX2 5WT
T: 0870 442 0880
www.visitsouthwest.co.uk

SOUTH WEST ENGLAND

Awe-inspiring cliffs, warm sandy beaches, rolling farmland and wild moors, buzzing nightlife and relaxing resorts: the many faces of the South West ensure every visitor is enthralled, and every visit is as different as you want it be.

Sand, surf and seals

The South West coast is always a popular holiday choice with its mix of safe, sandy beaches, sheltered bays and wilder stretches that are perfect for watersports. If you're a novice there are plenty of places to learn – try Bude, Croyde or Woolacombe for surfing or Poole for windsurfing and sailing. Check out the progress of Torquay's waterfront which is currently undergoing a £21 million facelift. Or watch penguins, seals and puffins in the re-created environment at Living Coasts. Divers can even explore an artificial reef which has been created off the coast in Whitsand Bay, Cornwall.

Dramatic coasts and moors

Enjoy breathtaking views along the South West Coast Path, a 630-mile continuous coastal trail. For the less adventurous there are plenty of shorter strolls in the National Parks of Exmoor and Dartmoor. Or if you don't feel like getting out of the car at all, the Royal Forest route is a 20-mile car trail designed to take visitors around the prettiest parts of the Forest of Dean.

In Dorset and East Devon, the Jurassic Coast Natural World Heritage Site offers a unique voyage back in time through 185 million years of the earth's history. Exposed rocks along 95 miles of beautiful coastline reveal the secrets of the past.

Good at any time

The sub-tropical climate of the South West ensures an early spring each year. Be among the first to catch a glimpse of the colourful buds as they burst into flower at Tresco Abbey Gardens on the Isles of Scilly, or at Westonbirt Arboretum with its acres of bluebells, giant rhododendrons and azaleas. All year round a visit to the Eden Project promises colour and fragrance, including a tropical rainforest. In Falmouth, be sure to visit the National Maritime Museum Cornwall. Interactive displays, small boats and windows looking under the ocean will bring out the sea salt in your blood! After a day's exploring, enjoy a meal of fresh, local ingredients home-cooked in a local pub. Or try an exciting new restaurant, such as Damien Hirst's at 11 The Quay, Ilfracombe. For a souvenir of your stay, visit Bristol Blue Glass where you can see glass pieces being blown in the traditional way.

Left, from top explore and discover At-Bristol; admire the great and ancient circle of Stonehenge; tranquil surroundings at the Roman Baths in Bath **Right** life's a beach in Newquay

Enjoy England official guides to quality

Places to visit

Awarded VisitBritain's Quality Assured Visitor Attraction marque.

At-Bristol
Anchor Road, Bristol
Tel: 0845 345 1235
www.at-bristol.org.uk
For the interactive adventure of a lifetime, visit At-Bristol's three award-winning attractions – Explore, Wildwalk and the IMAX Theatre. Amazing experiences every day.

Atwell-Wilson Motor Museum Trust
Calne, Wiltshire
Tel: (01249) 813119
www.atwell-wilson.org
Impressive motor museum with vintage, post-vintage and classic cars, including American models. Classic motorbikes. A 17thC water meadow walk. Play area.

Babbacombe Model Village
Hampton Avenue, Babbacombe, Devon
Tel: (01803) 315315
www.babbacombemodelvillage.co.uk
Over 400 models, many with sound and animation, set in award-winning gardens. See modern towns, villages and rural areas, and Aquaviva, a light, laser, sound and water show. An enchanting experience.

Bristol City Museum & Art Gallery
Queen's Road, Bristol
Tel: (0117) 922 3571
www.bristol-city.gov.uk/museums
An outstanding museum housing a diverse range of objects from sea dinosaurs to magnificent art. Dynamic temporary exhibitions complement the museum's vast permanent collections. Guaranteed to inspire.

Bristol Zoo Gardens
Clifton, Bristol
Tel: (0117) 974 7300
www.bristolzoo.org.uk
See over 300 species of wildlife from the smallest, rarest tortoise to the largest ape, in beautiful gardens. Voted Zoo of the Year by the Good Britain Guide 2004.

Buckland Abbey
Yelverton, Devon
Tel: (01822) 853607
www.nationaltrust.org.uk
Originally a Cistercian monastery, then home of Sir Francis Drake. Ancient buildings, exhibitions, herb garden, Elizabethan garden, craft workshops and estate walks.

Cheddar Caves and Gorge
Cheddar, Somerset
Tel: (01934) 742343
www.cheddarcaves.co.uk
Beautiful caves located in Cheddar Gorge. Stand in awe at Gough's Cave with its cathedral-like caverns and Cox's Cave with stalagmites and stalactites. Also The Crystal Quest fantasy adventure.

Children's Farm and Smugglers Barn
New Barn Road, Abbotsbury, Dorset
Tel: (01305) 871130
www.abbotsbury-tourism.co.uk
For those wet days, a soft play, undercover adventure with a smuggling theme for children under 11 years. Other activities include rabbit and guinea pig cuddling. Pony rides (extra charge).

Combe Martin Wildlife and Dinosaur Park
Combe Martin, Devon
Tel: (01271) 882486
www.dinosaur-park.com
The land that time forgot. A subtropical paradise with hundreds of birds and animals, and animatronics dinosaurs, so real they're alive!

Compton Acres
Canford Cliffs Road, Poole, Dorset
Tel: (01202) 700778
www.comptonacres.co.uk
Surprise, drama, romance and delight at every turn. Ten distinctive gardens of the world – themes include Italian, Japanese and Roman. Restaurants, craft centre and extensive retail development.

This is just a selection of attractions available. Contact any Tourist Information Centre in the region for more ideas.

SOUTH WEST ENGLAND

Cotswold Farm Park
Guiting Power, Gloucestershire
Tel: (01451) 850307
www.cotswoldfarmpark.co.uk
Fun on the farm! Observe 50 flocks and herds of British rare breeds of farm animals and watch seasonal farming demonstrations. Children's activities, café and gift shop.

Crealy Adventure Park
Sidmouth Road, Clyst St Mary, Devon
Tel: (01395) 233200
www.crealy.co.uk
Crealy offers an unforgettable day packed with magic, fun and adventure for all the family, with exciting rides, all-weather attractions and the friendliest animals.

Dairyland Farm World
Tresillian Barton, Summercourt, Cornwall
Tel: (01872) 510146
www.dairylandfarmworld.com
Meet lots of beautiful animals, including lambs, rabbits, donkeys and llamas, and have a go milking Clarabelle the Cybercow. Adventure playground, country life museum, nature trail.

Eden Project
Bodelva, St Austell, Cornwall
Tel: (01726) 811911
www.edenproject.com
An unforgettable experience in a breathtaking, epic location. Eden is a gateway into the fascinating world of plants and people.

Exmoor Falconry & Animal Farm
West Lynch Farm, Allerford, Somerset
Tel: (01643) 862816
www.exmoorfalconry.co.uk
Creatures galore – farm animals, rare breeds, pets corner, birds of prey and owls. Fabulous flying displays daily. Historic farm buildings. Short activity breaks.

Flambards Village
Culdrose Manor, Helston, Cornwall
Tel: (01326) 573404
www.flambards.co.uk
Let your imagination lead you through the lamp-lit streets of a full-size reconstuction of a Victorian village with 50 fully stocked shops, homes, carriages and fashions. Also Britain in the Blitz wartime street, historic aircraft, science centre and rides.

Heale Garden & Plant Centre
Middle Woodford, Wiltshire
Tel: (01722) 782504
Mature traditional garden with shrubs, musk and other roses, and kitchen garden. Authentic Japanese teahouse in water garden with magnolias and acers. Snowdrops and aconites in winter. Heavenly.

Jamaica Inn & Daphne du Maurier Smuggling Museum
Jamaica Inn Courtyard, Bolventor, Cornwall
Tel: (01566) 86250
www.jamaicainn.co.uk
High on wild and beautiful Bodmin Moor, visit the famous Jamaica Inn featuring the Daphne du Maurier smuggling museum.

Kingston Lacy (National Trust)
Wimborne Minster, Dorset
Tel: (01202) 883402
www.nationaltrust.org.uk
17thC house designed for Sir Ralph Bankes by Sir Roger Pratt, altered in 19thC. Outstanding collection of paintings, 100-ha (250-acre) wooded park, herd of Devon cattle.

Longleat
Warminster, Wiltshire
Tel: (01985) 844400
www.longleat.co.uk
One not to miss – Elizabethan stately home and safari park plus a wonderland of 10 family attractions. World's Longest Hedge Maze, Safari Boats, Pets Corner, Longleat railway and Adventure Castle.

The Lost Gardens of Heligan
Heligan, Pentewan, Cornwall
Tel: (01726) 845100
www.heligan.com
Justifiably nominated the Nation's Favourite Garden by viewers of BBC Gardener's World. This world-famous restoration now extends to over 80ha (200 acres) of superb working Victorian gardens.

Lyme Regis Philpot Museum
Bridge Street, Lyme Regis, Dorset
Tel: (01297) 443370
www.lymeregismuseum.co.uk
Lots of good tales to tell from fossils to geology, local history and literary connections – the story of Lyme in its landscape.

Left visit Buckland Abbey in Yelverton, the home of Sir Francis Drake; journey through gardens of the world at Compton Acres, Poole

Enjoy England official guides to quality

Places to visit

Awarded VisitBritain's Quality Assured Visitor Attraction marque.

National Marine Aquarium
Rope Walk, Plymouth
Tel: (01752) 600301
www.national-aquarium.co.uk
A fascinating journey through an amazing underwater world in Britain's biggest aquarium. Discover a mountain stream, wave tank and Caribbean reef complete with sharks.

Newquay Zoo
Trenance Park, Newquay, Cornwall
Tel: (01637) 873342
www.newquayzoo.co.uk
A modern award-winning zoo, where you can have fun and learn at the same time. Hundreds of animals in sub-tropical lakeside gardens.

Oceanarium
Pier Approach, Bournemouth
Tel: (01202) 311993
www.oceanarium.co.uk
Take a thrilling voyage across the oceans of the world to discover a dazzling array of underwater life from elegant seahorses to sinister sharks.

Paignton Zoo Environmental Park
Totnes Road, Paignton, Devon
Tel: (01803) 697500
www.paigntonzoo.org.uk
One of England's largest zoos with over 1200 animals in the beautiful setting of 30ha (75 acres) of botanical gardens. An educational experience for all the family.

Plant World
St Marychurch Road, Newton Abbot, Devon
Tel: (01803) 872939
www.plantworld-devon.co.uk
One and a half hectares (4 acres) of gardens including the unique map of the world gardens and cottage garden. Panoramic views. Comprehensive nursery of rare and more unusual plants.

Powderham Castle
Kenton, Devon
Tel: (01626) 890243
www.powderham.co.uk
Built c1390, restored in 18thC, with Georgian interiors, china, furnishings and paintings. Home of the Courtenays for over 600 years. Take time to enjoy the fine views across the deer park and river Exe.

Roman Baths
Pump Room, Bath
Tel: (01225) 477785
www.romanbaths.co.uk
The birthplace of Bath, one of the country's finest ancient monuments. Wonder at the great Roman temple and bathing complex built around natural hot springs almost 2000 years ago.

St Michael's Mount
Marazion, Cornwall
Tel: (01736) 710507
www.stmichaelsmount.co.uk
A must for every visitor to the area, this atmospheric island with 14thC castle, was originally the site of a Benedictine chapel. Reached by foot, or ferry at high tide in summer.

Steam – Museum of the Great Western Railway
Kemble Drive, Swindon, Wiltshire
Tel: (01793) 466646
www.steam-museum.org.uk
Displays celebrating the Great Western Railway include footplate access on locomotives, detailed reconstructions of life on the railways, people's stories, film and interactive displays.

Above be spooked by the Witch of Wookey at Wookey Hole Caves and Papermill at Wookey Hole; celebrate the Great Western Railway at Steam – Museum of the Great Western Railway **Right** be inspired at the Tate St Ives

This is just a selection of attractions available. Contact any Tourist Information Centre in the region for more ideas.

SOUTH WEST ENGLAND

Stonehenge
Amesbury, Wiltshire
Tel: (01980) 624715
www.english-heritage.org.uk
A real sense of mysticism at this dramatic prehistoric monument, built as a ceremonial centre 5000 years ago. It was remodelled several times in the next 1500 years.

Stourhead House and Garden (National Trust)
Stourton, Wiltshire
Tel: (01747) 841152
www.nationaltrust.org.uk
World-famous landscaped garden laid out c1741-80, with lakes, temples, rare trees and plants. Palladian mansion with magnificent interiors, fine paintings and Chippendale furniture.

The Tank Museum
Bovington, Dorset
Tel: (01929) 405096
www.tankmuseum.co.uk
You can't fail to be impressed by the world's finest display of armoured fighting vehicles from World War I tanks to Challenger, the latest main battle tank of the British Army.

Tate St Ives
Porthmeor Beach, St Ives, Cornwall
Tel: (01736) 796226
www.tate.org.uk
Opened in 1993, the gallery offers a unique introduction to modern art. Changing displays focus on St Ives' renowned modern movement. Major contemporary exhibitions.

Teignmouth Museum
French Street, Teignmouth, Devon
Tel: (01626) 777041
www.lineone.net/~teignmuseum/
A truly local museum whose exhibits include a 16thC cannon and artefacts from Armada wreck, c1920s pier machines and c1877 cannon.

Tintagel Castle (English Heritage)
Tintagel, Cornwall
Tel: (01840) 770328
www.english-heritage.org.uk/tintagel
Awe-inspiring, romantic and a place of Arthurian legend. A medieval ruined castle on wild, wind-swept coast, built largely in 13thC by Richard, Earl of Cornwall.

Totnes Costume Museum – Devonshire Collection of Period Costume
Bogan House, Totnes, Devon
Tel: (01803) 863821
This museum in Bogan House, an historic merchant's house, shows a new exhibition of costumes and accessories each season.

Woodlands Leisure Park
Blackawton, Devon
Tel: (01803) 712598
www.woodlandspark.com
All-weather fun guaranteed with this unique combination of indoor and outdoor attractions – three water coasters, toboggan run, indoor venture centre with rides. Falconry and animals.

Wookey Hole Caves and Papermill
Wookey Hole, Somerset
Tel: (01749) 672243
www.wookey.co.uk
Spectacular caves, the legendary home of the Witch of Wookey. Spooky! Working Victorian paper mill including Old Penny Arcade, Magical Mirror Maze and Cave Diving Museum.

WWT Slimbridge Wetlands Centre
Slimbridge, Gloucestershire
Tel: (01453) 891900
www.wwt.org.uk
Founded by Sir Peter Scott, the centre is home to over 2300 waterbirds of 180 different species. £6.2 million visitor centre, 17m (55ft) observation tower, hides and heated observatory.

South West Tourism

Woodwater Park, Exeter EX2 5WT
T: 0870 442 0880
www.visitsouthwest.co.uk

Travel information

By road:
The region is easily accessible from London, the South East, the North and Midlands by the M6/M5 which extends just beyond Exeter, where it links in with the dual carriageways of the A38 to Plymouth, A380 to Torbay and the A30 into Cornwall. The North Devon Link Road A361 joins junction 37 with the coast of North Devon and the A39, which then becomes the Atlantic Highway into Cornwall.

By rail:
The main towns in the South West are served throughout the year by fast, direct and frequent rail services from all over the country. Trains operate from London (Paddington) to Chippenham, Swindon, Bath, Bristol, Weston-super-Mare, Taunton, Exeter, Plymouth and Penzance, and also from Scotland, the North East and the Midlands to the South West.

A service runs from London (Waterloo) to Exeter, via Salisbury, Yeovil and Crewkerne. Sleeper services operate between Devon and Cornwall and London as well as between Bristol and Glasgow and Edinburgh. Motorail services operate from strategic points to key South West locations.

Visit the following websites for further information on South West England:

www.visitsouthwest.co.uk

www.sw-watersports.com

www.accessiblesouthwest.co.uk

www.swcp.org.uk

Also available from South West Tourism:

Trencherman's Restaurant Guide

Right majestic views across Dartmoor

SOUTH WEST ENGLAND

Where to stay in
South West England

All place names in the blue bands, under which accommodation is listed, are shown on the maps at the front of this guide.

A complete listing of all VisitBritain assessed accommodation covered by this guide appears at the back.

Accommodation symbols
Symbols give useful information about services and facilities. Inside the back cover flap you can find a key to these symbols. Keep it open for easy reference.

ABBOTSHAM, Devon Map ref 1C1

3 Units
Sleeping 5–14

Barn conversions and 17thC cottage with fitted carpets throughout. Horseshoe Barn sleeps eight plus two cots. Ground floor bedroom with adjacent shower/basin/wc. Corn House sleeps five to six plus cot. (Security doors between cottages to sleep 14 adults and three infants). Bowood Cottage sleeps six plus cot. Ample parking space.

BOWOOD FARM COTTAGES
Bideford
Contact: Toad Hall Cottages, Elliot House, Church Street, Kingsbridge TQ7 1BY
T: (01548) 853089
F: (01548) 853086
E: thc@toadhallcottages.com
I: www.toadhallcottages.com

OPEN All Year

Payment accepted: Delta, Mastercard, Switch, Visa, Euros

Low season per wk
£201.00–£288.00
High season per wk
£565.00–£747.00

ALLERFORD, Somerset Map ref 1D1

1 Unit
Sleeping 2–6

Delightful character National Trust cottage on a traditional working farm, surrounded by beautiful scenery. Old beams, log fire, cosy, clean and comfortable. Situated near Allerford, Minehead, and central for exploring the Exmoor coast and countryside. Many attractions nearby. Village shops, pubs and restaurants five minutes' drive away. Colour brochure available.

ORCHARD COTTAGE
Allerford
Contact: Mrs Diana Williams, Orchard Cottage, Brandish Street Farm, Allerford, Minehead TA24 8HR
T: (01643) 862383

OPEN All Year

Low season per wk
£260.00–£300.00
High season per wk
£320.00–£350.00

299

SOUTH WEST ENGLAND

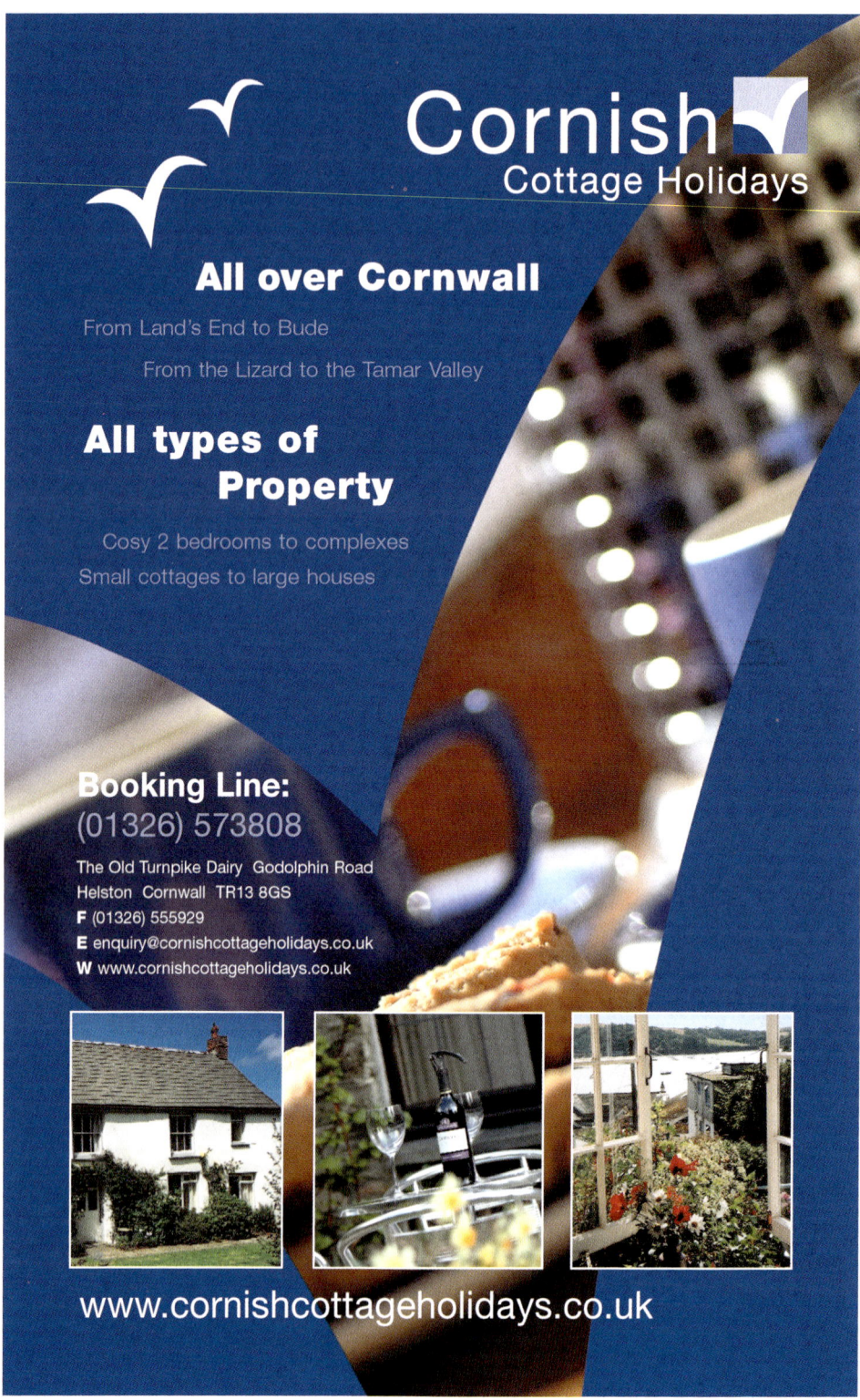

SOUTH WEST ENGLAND

ALLERFORD continued

★★★
5 Units
Sleeping 2–6

THE PACK HORSE
Minehead
Contact: Mr Brian & Mrs Linda Garner, The Pack Horse, Allerford, Minehead TA24 8HW
T: (01643) 862475
F: (01643) 862475
I: www.thepackhorse.net

Idyllic location in picturesque National Trust village, alongside shallow river Aller, overlooking an ancient packhorse bridge. Our comfortable apartments, sleeping two to three persons, suite and cottage, sleeping up to six persons, are perfectly situated to explore Exmoor, the coast and countryside. Local shop, private parking, pubs and restaurants within a mile.

OPEN All Year

2-and 3-night breaks available Oct-Jun from £105.

Low season per wk
£210.00–£295.00
High season per wk
£320.00–£465.00

Check the maps
The colour maps at the front of this guide show all the cities, towns and villages for which you will find accommodation entries. Refer to the town index to find the page on which they are listed.

500 superb cottages
The finest selection of cottages throughout Devon, Cornwall, Somerset & Dorset Choose from both rural and coastal locations, many also providing excellent facilities.

Telephone for FREE colour brochure

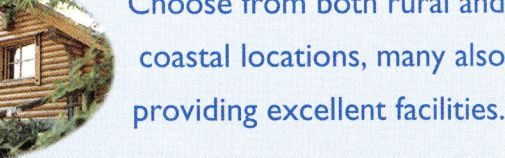

www.farmcott.co.uk

SOUTH WEST ENGLAND

AMESBURY, Wiltshire Map ref 2B2 *Tourist Information Centre Tel: (01980) 622833*

★★★★
1 Unit
Sleeping 2–4

THE COTTAGE
Salisbury
Contact: Mrs Joan Robathan, The Cottage, Maddington House, Maddington Street, Shrewton, Salisbury SP3 4JD
T: (01980) 620406
E: rsrobathan@freenet.co.uk
I: www.maddingtonhouse.co.uk

Pretty village with three pubs, shop, post office, doctors' surgeries, garage (newspapers) is within walking distance. Nearest train station Salisbury – 10 miles. Bus stop 100m. Local attractions include Stonehenge 2.5 miles, Wilton, Longleat, Broadlands, Winchester, Devizes, Avebury and New Forest etc. Bath, Oxford, Portsmouth and Windsor are all within one hour's drive.

OPEN All Year

2/3 night stays available Oct-May (excl Christmas and New Year).

Low season per wk
£230.00–£270.00
High season per wk
£370.00–£400.00

ASHBURTON, Devon Map ref 1C2

★★★–★★★★★
7 Units
Sleeping 2–12

WOODER MANOR HOLIDAY HOMES
Widecombe-in-the-Moor
Contact: Mrs Angela Bell, Wooder Manor Holiday Homes, Widecombe-in-the-Moor, Dartmoor, Newton Abbot TQ13 7TR
T: (01364) 621391
F: (01364) 621391
E: angela@woodermanor.com
I: www.woodermanor.com

Cottages nestled in picturesque valley in Dartmoor National Park. Peaceful location, beautiful views of woodland, moors and granite tors. Explore Devon, Dartmoor, the coast, National Trust properties and attractions. Clean and very well-equipped. Gardens. Off-road parking. Good food at two local inns 0.5 and 0.75 miles. Colour brochure.

OPEN All Year

Payment accepted: Delta, Mastercard, Switch, Visa

Short breaks available.

Low season per wk
Min £160.00
High season per wk
Max £1,000.00

★★★★
2 Units
Sleeping 2–6

WREN & ROBIN COTTAGES
Newton Abbot
Contact: Mrs Margaret Phipps, New Cott Farm, Poundsgate, Newton Abbot TQ13 7PD
T: (01364) 631421
F: (01364) 631421
E: enquiries@newcott-farm.co.uk
I: www.newcott-farm.co.uk

Enjoy Dartmoor National Park with tors, moors, tiny villages. Stress free, plenty of fresh air. Wren/Robin Cottages are peacefully situated and beautifully furnished. Prices all inclusive.

OPEN All Year

Payment accepted: Delta, Mastercard, Switch, Visa

Low season per wk
Min £220.00
High season per wk
Max £450.00

ASHWATER, Devon Map ref 1C2

★★★
6 Units
Sleeping 2–16

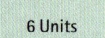

BRADDON COTTAGES AND FOREST
Ashwater
Contact: Mr George & Mrs Anne Ridge, Ashwater, Beaworthy EX21 5EP
T: (01409) 211350
E: holidays@braddoncottages.co.uk
I: www.braddoncottages.co.uk

For country lovers, cottages in secluded location. Games field, adults' snooker and children's games rooms. Wood fires, licensed shop. Colour brochure, extensive website.

OPEN All Year

Payment accepted: Delta, Mastercard, Switch, Visa, Euros

Low season per wk
£65.00–£195.00
High season per wk
£225.00–£1,100.00

SOUTH WEST ENGLAND

AXMINSTER, Devon Map ref 1D2

★★★★
1 Unit
Sleeping 1–4

BECKFORD COTTAGE
Axminster
Contact: Mrs Jill Bellamy, Dalwood, Axminster EX13 7HQ
T: (01404) 881641
F: (01404) 881108
I: www.beckford-cottage.co.uk

Very comfortable lodge set in nine-acre secluded gardens and grounds bordered by River Yarty. Bathroom with power shower. Central heating. Axminster 10 minutes. Lovely drives to nearby Dorset Heritage and South Devon Coast. Perfect setting for a really peaceful break. Own patio with barbecue and garden table. Much bird-life.

OPEN All Year except Christmas

Low season per wk
£275.00–£375.00
High season per wk
£380.00–£550.00

BAMPTON, Devon Map ref 1D1

★★★★
5 Units
Sleeping 2–6

THREE GATES FARM
Tiverton
Contact: Mrs Alison Spencer, Three Gates Farm, Huntsham, Tiverton EX16 7QH
T: (01398) 331280
F: (01398) 332476
E: threegatesfarm@hotmail.com
I: www.threegatesfarm.co.uk

Relax in one of our excellent converted barns, in the beautiful Devonshire countryside. Spend hours in our superb indoor heated pool, sauna or fitness room. Play in the grounds, with play tower and games rooms. The perfect place to unwind and explore the beaches, river valleys and attractions of Devon.

OPEN All Year

Short breaks available Oct–May (except school holidays).

Low season per wk
£140.00–£295.00
High season per wk
£315.00–£870.00

★★★
1 Unit

WONHAM BARTON
Tiverton
Contact: Clifford Williams & Anne McLean Williams, Wonham Barton, Bampton, Tiverton EX16 9JZ
T: (01398) 331312
F: (01398) 331312
I: www.wonham-country-holidays.co.uk

From friendly accommodation overlooking Exe Valley, conveniently explore secretive, historic Devon, rolling moorlands and dramatic coastlines; enjoy country pursuits and leisurely cream teas. Savour 300 tranquil acres, glimpsing Exmoor red deer, soaring buzzards and traditional shepherding; share romantic scenes from TV drama and 'Landgirls' filmed here. Tell us when you're coming!

OPEN All Year
Payment accepted: Mastercard, Visa

Short breaks available Oct–Mar. Min 2 nights. Prices on request. Dogs accepted by arrangement.

Low season per wk
£185.00–£335.00
High season per wk
£335.00–£390.00

Location Complete addresses for properties are not given and the town(s) listed may be a distance from the actual establishment. Please check the precise location at the time of booking.

SOUTH WEST ENGLAND

BARNSTAPLE, Devon Map ref 1C1 *Tourist Information Centre Tel:* **(01271) 375000**

★★★★
2 Units
Sleeping 2–10

HARTPIECE FARM
Barnstaple
Contact: Mr Chris Baker, c/o JFA Ltd, Riverside, Mill Lane, Taplow, Maidenhead SL6 0AA
T: (01628) 637111
F: (01628) 773030
E: chris@hartpiece.co.uk
I: www.hartpiece.co.uk

Ancient Devon longhouse in 90 acres of hedgerow with period features and picturesque views. Elegant, cosy accommodation with real fires and hot tub. Unspoilt Exmoor and North Devon offer year-round walking, gardens, bird-watching, golfing, fishing, surfing. Two miles from Barnstaple for all amenities, theatre and famous Pannier Market for traditional foodstuffs.

OPEN All Year

Payment accepted: Mastercard, Switch, Visa, Euros

Weekend breaks and non-standard weeks accepted.

Low season per wk
£275.00–£785.00
High season per wk
£375.00–£1,175.00

★★★
1 Unit
Sleeping 1–6

LOWER YELLAND FARM
Barnstaple
Contact: Mr Peter Day, Lower Yelland Farm, Yelland, Barnstaple EX31 3EN
T: (01271) 860101
E: pday@loweryellandfarm.co.uk
I: www.loweryellandfarm.co.uk

Built in 1658, modernised in 1990. Adjacent to RSPB Bird Sanctuary and Tarka Trail (footpath and cycle path). Borders River Taw. Ideal centre for touring North Devon. Good access to motorway. Sandy beach at Instow one mile. Winner of Golden Achievement Award of Excellence for Devon Retreat of the Year.

OPEN All Year

Low season per wk
Max £215.00
High season per wk
Max £650.00

BATCOMBE, Somerset Map ref 2B2

★★★★
1 Unit
Sleeping 1–5

THE COACH HOUSE AT BOORDS FARM
Shepton Mallet
Contact: Mr Michael & Mrs Anne Page, Batcombe, Shepton Mallet BA4 6HD
T: (01749) 850372
F: (01749) 850372
E: boordsfarm@michaelp.demon.co.uk
I: www.boordsfarm.co.uk

Recently converted coach house in grounds of 16thC thatched farmhouse equipped to high standard for comfort. Rural setting on edge of beautiful village. Twin and double bedrooms, each with own bathroom. Woodburning stove, central heating. Local walks, good touring location for Stourhead, Longleat, Bath, Wells. Short walk to excellent pub.

OPEN All Year

Short breaks available. Flexible changeover days on all lengths of bookings.

Low season per wk
£350.00–£375.00
High season per wk
£410.00–£420.00

Map references The map references refer to the colour maps at the front of this guide. The first figure is the map number; the letter and figure which follow indicate the grid reference on the map.

SOUTH WEST ENGLAND

BATH, Bath and North East Somerset Map ref 2B2 *Tourist Information Centre Tel: 0906 711 2000 (50p per minute)*

★★★★★
5 Units
Sleeping 2–4

GREYFIELD FARM COTTAGES
Bristol
Contact: Mrs June Merry, Greyfield Farm Cottages, Greyfield Road, High Littleton, Bristol BS39 6YQ
T: (01761) 471132
F: (01761) 471132
E: june@greyfieldfarm.com
I: www.greyfieldfarm.com

OPEN All Year

Payment accepted: Euros

Low season per wk
£195.00–£280.00
High season per wk
£310.00–£420.00

Quality cottages set in peaceful, private location with panoramic views of Mendips. Use of sauna, hot tub, fitness centre, gingerbread house and video library included. Brochure available.

★★★★★
2 Units
Sleeping 2–8

SHEYLORS FARM
Corsham
Contact: Mrs S Sanders, Sheylors Farm, Sheylors Barn, Ashley, Box, Corsham SN13 8AN
T: (01225) 743922
F: (01225) 743998
E: sam@sheylorsfarm.co.uk
I: www.sheylorsfarm.co.uk

Three miles from Bath. Two listed stables converted to a very high standard within a historic farm site. Set in 12-acres of protected pastures in the heart of the Wiltshire countryside. Access to Castle Combe, Lacock, Stonehenge, Bradford-on-Avon, many NT properties, golf, walks, village pub.

OPEN All Year

Short breaks available. Please telephone or email for details.

Low season per wk
£257.00–£422.00
High season per wk
£405.00–£741.00

★★★–★★★★★
2 Units
Sleeping 1–4

SPRING FARM HOLIDAY COTTAGES
Bath
Contact: Mrs Sue Brown, Spring Farm Holiday Cottages, Carlingcott, Peasedown St John, Bath BA2 8AP
T: (01761) 435524
F: (01761) 439461
I: www.springfarmcottages.co.uk

The main farmhouse (owner's residence) is a Grade II Listed 17thC farmhouse. The holiday cottages are converted from a Victorian dairy and 17thC milking parlour.

OPEN All Year

Payment accepted: Euros

Low season per wk
£235.00–£350.00
High season per wk
£350.00–£425.00

BEAMINSTER, Dorset Map ref 2A3

★★★
3 Units
Sleeping 4

GREENS CROSS FARM
Beaminster
Contact: Mr David & Mrs Lora Baker, Greens Cross Farm, Stoke Road, Beaminster DT8 3JL
T: (01308) 862661
E: greenscross@btopenworld.com

OPEN All Year

Low season per wk
£100.00–£250.00
High season per wk
£220.00–£310.00

Well-equipped holiday units within walking distance of Beaminster in heart of Dorset and close to coast. Short winter breaks. Field for horse.

Quality Assurance Standard
Star ratings and awards were correct at time of going to press but are subject to change. Please check at the time of booking.

SOUTH WEST ENGLAND

BEAMINSTER continued

★★★★
1 Unit
Sleeping 6

ORCHARD END
Beaminster
Contact: Mrs Wallbridge, Watermeadow House, Bridge Farm, Beaminster DT8 3PD
T: (01308) 862619
F: (01308) 862619
E: enquiries@watermeadowhouse.co.uk
I: www.watermeadowhouse.co.uk

OPEN All Year
Payment accepted: Mastercard, Switch, Visa, Euros

Low season per wk
£210.00–£320.00
High season per wk
£400.00–£500.00

280-acre dairy and livestock farm. Working dairy farm in a quiet village nine miles from the coast. Good walking country and near the Kingcombe Centre and Dorset Trust land.

★★★★
1 Unit
Sleeping 2–3

STABLE COTTAGE
Beaminster
Contact: Mrs Diana Clarke, Meerhay Manor, Beaminster DT8 3SB
T: (01308) 862305
F: (01308) 863972
E: meerhay@aol.com
I: www.meerhay.co.uk

OPEN All Year

Low season per wk
Min £150.00
High season per wk
Min £375.00

New ground floor conversion of old barn in grounds of old manor. Wheelchair accessible. 40 acres farmland, plantsman's garden, tennis court, stabling. Seven miles coast, idyllic setting.

BERRYNARBOR, Devon Map ref 1C1

★★★–★★★★★
4 Units
Sleeping 2–8

Near golden sands with sea and coastal views. Heated, covered swimming pool in a suntrap enclosure, gardens and games room with pool table, table tennis, football machine. Tree-house on two levels. Free pony rides, ball pond and bouncy castle, 14-acre recreation field and dog walk. For colour brochure phone Jayne.

SMYTHEN FARM COASTAL HOLIDAY COTTAGES
Ilfracombe
Contact: Mr & Ms Thompson & Elstone, Symthen, Sterridge Valley, Berrynarbor, Ilfracombe EX34 9TB
T: (01271) 882875
F: (01271) 882875
E: jayne@smythenfarmholidaycottages.co.uk
I: www.smythenfarmholidaycottages.co.uk

OPEN All Year

Low season per wk
£95.00–£267.00
High season per wk
£267.00–£848.00

BIBURY, Gloucestershire Map ref 2B1

★★★–★★★★★
4 Units
Sleeping 1–4

Set within secluded courtyard and gardens adjacent to the owners' home. A two-minute walk to pubs, shops and two stunning riverside hotels/restaurants in the centre of the village. Secure off-road parking.

BIBURY HOLIDAY COTTAGES
Cirencester
Contact: Mrs J Hedgeland, Bibury Holiday Cottages, Coln Court, Arlington, Cirencester GL7 5NL
T: (01285) 740314
F: (01285) 740314
E: info@biburyholidaycottages.com
I: www.biburyholidaycottages.com

OPEN All Year
Payment accepted: Delta, Mastercard, Switch, Visa

Low season per wk
£220.00–£250.00
High season per wk
£320.00–£380.00

3-and 4-night short breaks available all year round.

SOUTH WEST ENGLAND

 BIBURY continued

★★★★
2 Units
Sleeping 4

Situated in this picturesque village, these delightful cottages offer tastefully furnished, spacious accommodation. Equipped to a high standard to include all the comforts of home. Heating, linen and electricity included. Private parking. No smoking/pets. An ideal centre for touring Cotswolds and surrounding areas.

COTTESWOLD HOUSE COTTAGES

Bibury
Contact: Mrs Judith Underwood, Cotteswold House, Bibury, Cirencester GL7 5ND
T: (01285) 740609
F: (01285) 740609
E: cotteswold.house@btconnect.com
I: http://home.btconnect.com/cotteswold.house

OPEN All Year

Payment accepted: Mastercard, Visa

Low season per wk
Min £240.00
High season per wk
Max £375.00

 BIDEFORD, Devon Map ref 1C1 *Tourist Information Centre Tel: (01237) 477676*

★★★
1 Unit
Sleeping 2

COACHMANS COTTAGE
Bideford
Contact: Mr Tom & Mrs Sue Downie, Coachmans Cottage, Monkleigh, Bideford EX39 5JR
T: (01805) 623670
E: tom.downie@ukonline.co.uk
I: www.creamteacottages.co.uk

OPEN All Year

Payment accepted: Delta, Mastercard, Switch, Visa

Low season per wk
£130.00–£160.00
High season per wk
£160.00–£240.00

Charming character cottage in courtyard setting, within easy reach of national parks and beaches. Price includes cream tea on arrival, linen and fuel for woodburner.

 BIGBURY-ON-SEA, Devon Map ref 1C3

★★★★★
1 Unit
Sleeping 1–6

Luxury modern ground floor apartment set into cliff with panoramic southerly views from large patio. Facilities include pool, gym, sauna, cafe/bar, grassy cliff-top grounds and direct access to beautiful large sandy beach and coastal path. Popular for surfing and near golf course and village shop/post office.

APARTMENT 5, BURGH ISLAND CAUSEWAY

Kingsbridge
Contact: Helpful Holidays, Mill Street, Chagford, Devon TQ13 8AW
T: (01647) 433593
F: (01647) 433694
E: help@helpfulholidays.com
I: www.helpfulholidays.com

OPEN All Year

Payment accepted: Delta, Mastercard, Switch, Visa

Low season per wk
£392.00–£863.00
High season per wk
£931.00–£1,302.00

Bargain weekend and short-stay breaks available in autumn and winter months.

★★★★
1 Unit
Sleeping 1–6

FERRYCOMBE
Bigbury-on-Sea
Contact: Mrs Juliet Fooks, 15 Mouchotte Close, Biggin Hill, Westerham TN16 3ES
T: 07050 030231

OPEN All Year

Low season per wk
£200.00–£400.00
High season per wk
£300.00–£800.00

Unique, old Devon-stone barn in small courtyard with private gardens. Spectacular sea views of Bigbury Bay with its sandy beaches. Ideal for the family with children.

 Confirm your booking You are advised to confirm your booking in writing.

SOUTH WEST ENGLAND

BISHOP SUTTON, Bath and North East Somerset Map ref 2A2

★★★★
1 Unit
Sleeping 4–6

THE TREBARTHA
Bristol
Contact: Edward & Sally Catchpole, The Trebartha, The Street, Bishop Sutton, Bristol BS39 5UU
T: (01275) 333845
E: sally@thetrebartha.co.uk
I: www.thetrebartha.co.uk

OPEN All Year
Payment accepted: Euros

Low season per wk
Min £300.00
High season per wk
Min £400.00

Well-equipped, self-contained annexe in peaceful countryside; wonderful views; ideal base walking, cycling, fishing and touring; 30 minutes from Bath, Bristol and Wells.

BLANDFORD FORUM, Dorset Map ref 2B3 Tourist Information Centre Tel: (01258) 454770

★★★
4 Units
Sleeping 1–6

THE LODGE, THE STABLE, PLUMTREE COTTAGE AND JASMINE COTTAGE
Blandford Forum
Contact: Mrs Penny Cooper, Dairy House Farm, Woolland, Blandford Forum DT11 0EY
T: (01258) 817501
F: (01258) 818060
E: penny.cooper@farming.co.uk
I: www.self-cateringholidays4u.co.uk

OPEN All Year
Payment accepted: Mastercard, Switch, Visa

Low season per wk
£150.00–£200.00
High season per wk
£300.00–£650.00

Wonderful base from which to explore Dorset's superb scenery. Seventeen acres of woodland. Coarse fishing. A haven for children. Pets welcome.

BLOCKLEY, Gloucestershire Map ref 2B1

★★★★
9 Units
Sleeping 2–6

LOWER FARM COTTAGES
Moreton-in-Marsh
Contact: Mrs Katie Batchelor, Lower Farm Cottages, Lower Farmhouse, Moreton-in-Marsh GL56 9DP
T: (01386) 700237
F: (01386) 700237
E: lowerfarm@hotmail.com
I: www.lower-farm.co.uk

OPEN All Year

Winter breaks. Short breaks in season at short notice, subject to availability.

Low season per wk
£256.00–£393.00
High season per wk
£369.00–£660.00

Converted barns and typical Cotswold cottages in an idyllic setting on the edge of this pretty village, ideally situated to explore the numerous attractions of the Cotswolds, including Stratford, castles, gardens and wildlife parks. Cottages tastefully furnished with a blend of antique and new furnishings, together with modern facilities.

BOSCASTLE, Cornwall Map ref 1B2

★★★★
5 Units
Sleeping 4–6

CARGURRA FARM
Boscastle
Contact: Mrs Gillian Elson, Cargurra Farm, Hennett, St Juliot, Boscastle PL35 0BT
T: (01840) 261206
F: (01840) 261206
E: gillian@cargurra.co.uk
I: www.cargurra.co.uk

OPEN All Year
Payment accepted: Delta, Mastercard, Switch, Visa

Low season per wk
£140.00–£295.00
High season per wk
£300.00–£540.00

Secluded farm setting within the beautiful Valency Valley where Thomas Hardy met his love. A well-appointed, traditional cottage with log fire and central heating. Spacious gardens with barbecue, games room with pool and table tennis. Private road, ample parking. Country and coastal walks. Also, cottages converted from Victorian barn.

SOUTH WEST ENGLAND

BOSCASTLE continued

★★★★
2 Units
Sleeping 2–4

Luxurious apartments, adjacent to 18thC farmhouse, standing in 12-acre grounds, finished to a high standard. Tranquil location with distant sea views, near to Boscastle Harbour, Tintagel, Trebarwith, Strand, Polzeath, Port Isaac. Stunning coastal walks, beautiful sandy beaches, Cornish villages, galleries, craft shops, restaurants, pubs, pottery and museums.

VENN DOWN FARMHOUSE APARTMENTS
Boscastle
Contact: Mrs Diane Bentall, Venn Down Farmhouse, Minster, Boscastle PL35 0EG
T: (01840) 250599
F: (01840) 250599
E: venndownfarmhouse@uk2.net
I: www.venndownfarmhouse.co.uk

OPEN All Year

Payment accepted: Amex, Delta, Mastercard, Switch, Visa, Euros

Please call (01840) 250599 for special promotions or send an email for further details.

Low season per wk
£200.00–£395.00
High season per wk
£430.00–£525.00

BOURNEMOUTH, Bournemouth Map ref 2B3 *Tourist Information Centre Tel: (01202) 451700*

★★★
4 Units
Sleeping 2–6

THE BLACK HOUSE
Bournemouth
Contact: The Black House, 51 Carbery Avenue, Bournemouth BH6 3LN
T: 07855 280191
F: (01202) 483555
E: theblackhouse@hotmail.com
I: www.theblackhouse.co.uk

OPEN All Year

Low season per wk
£295.00–£495.00
High season per wk
£655.00–£895.00

Self-contained apartments in former boat-builder's house dating back two centuries. Stunning location on the sandspit at Mudeford/Christchurch. Breathtaking views.

BOURTON-ON-THE-WATER, Gloucestershire Map ref 2B1 *Tourist Information Centre Tel: (01451) 820211*

★★★★
2 Units
Sleeping 6

OXLEIGH COTTAGES
Cheltenham
Contact: Mrs Barbara Smith, 12 Moore Road, Bourton on-the-Water, Cheltenham GL54 2AZ
T: 07773 474108
E: cdsmith.annexe@fsmail.net

OPEN All Year

Low season per wk
£320.00–£405.00
High season per wk
£435.00–£800.00

Spacious 3-bedroomed cottages fully-equipped, four-poster beds. Private patios, lawned rear gardens. Situated on quiet road within walking distance of shops and restaurants.

BOVEY TRACEY, Devon Map ref 1D2

★★★★
1 Unit
Sleeping 1–12

WARMHILL FARM
Newton Abbot
Contact: W B Marnham, Hennock, Bovey Tracey, Newton Abbot TQ13 9QH
T: (01626) 833229
E: marnham@agriplus.net

OPEN All Year

Low season per wk
£380.00–£680.00
High season per wk
£950.00–£1,200.00

100-acre working farm. Superb thatched farmhouse in Dartmoor National Park. Ideal for moor and sea. Spacious and comfortable, with many old features preserved.

Accessibility Look for the symbols which indicate National Accessible Scheme standards for hearing and visually impaired guests in addition to standards for guests with mobility impairment. You can find an index of all scheme participants at the back of this guide.

SOUTH WEST ENGLAND

BRADFORD-ON-AVON, Wiltshire Map ref 2B2 *Tourist Information Centre Tel: (01225) 865797*

★★★★★
2 Units
Sleeping 11

FAIRFIELD BARNS
Atworth
Contact: Mr Taff & Mrs Gilly Thomas, Fairfield Barns, Bradford Road, Atworth SN12 8HZ
T: (01225) 703585 & 07768 625868
F: 0870 051490
E: gilly@fairfieldbarns.com
I: www.fairfieldbarns.com

In a quiet village close to Bath, two luxurious barn conversions, enjoying panoramic rural views of the Wiltshire countryside. Superbly equipped, woodburning stoves, beamed throughout, en suite bedrooms have exotic foreign theme. Indoor swimming pool, gym, tennis court, sauna and children's adventure playground. Children especially welcome. Perfect touring, sightseeing location.

OPEN All Year
Payment accepted: Mastercard, Switch, Visa

Short breaks available Oct-Mar. 3-night weekend stays or 4 nights mid-week.

Low season per wk
£465.00–£610.00
High season per wk
£680.00–£1,100.00

BRATTON, Somerset Map ref 1D1

8 Units
Sleeping 2–11

WOODCOMBE LODGES
Minehead
Contact: Mrs Hanson, Woodcombe Lodges, Bratton Lane, Minehead TA24 8SQ
T: (01643) 702789 & 07860 667325
F: (01643) 702789
E: nicola@woodcombelodge.co.uk
I: www.woodcombelodge.co.uk

Timber lodges and stone cottages in a tranquil, rural setting on the edge of Exmoor National Park. Standing in a beautiful, 2.5-acre garden with wonderful views towards the wooded slopes of Exmoor. Minehead's seafront, harbour, shops etc 1.5 miles. Close to Dunster, Selworthy, Porlock and many local beauty spots.

OPEN All Year
Payment accepted: Mastercard, Switch, Visa

Short breaks available Nov-Easter, minimum 3 nights.

Low season per wk
£160.00–£550.00
High season per wk
£250.00–£1,100.00

BRAYFORD, Devon Map ref 1C1

★★
1 Unit
Sleeping 6

MUXWORTHY COTTAGE
Barnstaple
Contact: Mrs G M Bament, Muxworthy Farm, Brayford, Barnstaple EX32 7QP
T: (01598) 710342

Secluded old world cottage in idyllic rural location, fully equipped. Warm and cosy in winter with woodburning stove. Unspoilt countryside, ideal for a peaceful and relaxing holiday in the heart of Exmoor. Weekends and short breaks available.

OPEN All Year

Low season per wk
Min £150.00
High season per wk
Max £300.00

Credit card bookings
If you book by telephone and are asked for your credit card number it is advisable to check the proprietor's policy should you cancel your reservation.

SOUTH WEST ENGLAND

BRIDPORT, Dorset Map ref 2A3 Tourist Information Centre Tel: (01308) 424901

★★★
5 Units
Sleeping 2–6

CONISTON HOLIDAY APARTMENTS
Bridport
Contact: Mrs Jackie Murphy, Coniston Holiday Apartments, Coniston House, Victoria Grove, Bridport DT6 3AE
T: (01308) 424049
F: (01308) 424049

OPEN All Year

Low season per wk
Min £100.00
High season per wk
Max £475.00

Spacious, self-contained, fully equipped apartments with summer swimming pool. Play area, gardens and garage parking. Overlooking Dorset hills, only two minutes' walk to market town, one mile to sea.

★★★
23 Units
Sleeping 1–6

HIGHLANDS END HOLIDAY PARK
Bridport
Contact: Mr Martin Cox, Highlands End Holiday Park, Eype, Bridport DT6 6AR
T: (01308) 422139
F: (01308) 425672
E: holidays@wdlh.co.uk
I: www.wdlh.co.uk

Payment accepted: Delta, Mastercard, Switch, Visa

Low season per wk
£175.00–£300.00
High season per wk
£440.00–£540.00

Flats in secluded grounds, 150m from entrance to select holiday park on West Dorset Heritage coastline. Indoor swimming pool. Pitch and putt.

BRIMPSFIELD, Gloucestershire Map ref 2B1

★★★
1 Unit
Sleeping 4

BRIMPSFIELD FARMHOUSE (WEST WING)
Gloucester
Contact: Mrs Valerie Partridge, Brimpsfield Farmhouse (West Wing), Brimpsfield Farm, Brimpsfield, Gloucester GL4 8LD
T: (01452) 863568

OPEN All Year except Christmas

Low season per wk
£180.00–£200.00
High season per wk
Min £300.00

Self-contained modern annexe adjoining farmhouse comfortably furnished and well equipped, village location, central Cotswolds, well placed for touring and walking.

BRIXHAM, Torbay Map ref 1D2 Tourist Information Centre Tel: 0906 680 1268 (Premium rate number)

★★★★★
10 Units

Luxury waterfront apartments with panoramic sea views and private balcony. Own parking. Close to beach and town.

BLUE CHIP VACATIONS – MOORINGS REACH
Brixham
Contact: Blue Chip Vacations, 3 Marina Walk, Berry Head Road, Brixham TQ5 9AF
T: (01803) 855282
F: (01803) 881029
E: info@bluechipdevelopments.com
I: www.bluechipvacations.com

OPEN All Year
Payment accepted: Amex, Delta, Mastercard, Switch, Visa

Low season per wk
£295.00–£400.00
High season per wk
£520.00–£795.00

Quality Assurance Standard

For an explanation of the quality and facilities represented by the stars please refer to the front of this guide. A more detailed explanation can be found in the information pages at the back.

SOUTH WEST ENGLAND

BRIXHAM continued

★★★★★
1 Unit
Sleeping 4

CAPTAIN'S QUARTERS
Brixham
Contact: Mrs Gretchen Tricker, The Hill House, 23 St Peter's Hill, Brixham TQ5 9TE
T: (01803) 857937
E: gtricker@aol.com
I: www.brixhamhistorichouses.co.uk

Grade II Listed, 19thC sea captain's house and walled garden with panoramic view of town and bay. Antiques and oriental carpets provide luxury accommodation for four adults. Two bedrooms, two baths, utility room, living room, dining room and gourmet kitchen. Large library, jacuzzi, colour TVs and satellite.

OPEN All Year

Payment accepted: Mastercard, Switch, Visa

Short breaks available Oct–Apr – 3-night minimum. Last-minute booking.

Low season per wk
Max £390.00
High season per wk
Max £720.00

★★
6 Units
Sleeping 1–5

DEVONCOURT HOLIDAY FLATS
Brixham
Contact: Mr Robin Hooker, Devoncourt Holiday Flats, Berry Head Road, Brixham TQ5 9AB
T: (01803) 853748
F: (01803) 855775
E: robinhooker@devoncoast.com
I: www.devoncourt.net

Panoramic sea views from your balcony and lounge over Torbay, Brixham harbour and marina. The beach is opposite, only 50m. Each flat is fully self-contained, with colour TV, full cooker, fully carpeted. Private gardens. Car park. Children, pets and credit cards welcome. For colour brochure telephone (01803) 853748 or 07050 853748.

OPEN All Year

Payment accepted: Delta, Mastercard, Switch, Visa, Euros

10% discount for Senior Citizens.

Low season per wk
£150.00–£220.00
High season per wk
£300.00–£560.00

★★★★★
1 Unit
Sleeping 5

GULLS' NEST
Brixham
Contact: Mrs Gretchen Tricker, The Hill House, 23 St Peter's Hill, Brixham TQ5 9TE
T: (01803) 857937
F: (01803) 857937
E: gtricker@aol.com
I: www.brixhamhistorichouses.co.uk

18thC fisherman's cottage. Renovated in 2003, this airy, minimalist interior in a palate of grey, white and black takes its inspiration from the light and graceful gulls. Three bedrooms, two bathrooms, living room, dining room and shaker-style kitchen. Aerial-like views of the bay and gateway to 'The Best of the West'.

OPEN All Year

Payment accepted: Mastercard, Switch, Visa

Short breaks available Oct–Apr – 3-night minimum. Last-minute booking.

Low season per wk
Max £390.00
High season per wk
Max £720.00

Important note Information on accommodation listed in this guide has been supplied by the proprietors. As changes may occur you are advised to check details at the time of booking.

312

SOUTH WEST ENGLAND

BROAD CAMPDEN, Gloucestershire Map ref 2B1

★★★
1 Unit
Sleeping 1–6

LION COTTAGE
Chipping Campden
Contact: Mrs Barbara Rawcliffe, Lion Cottage,
Broad Campden, Chipping Campden GL55 6UR
T: (01386) 840077

OPEN All Year

Low season per wk
£235.00–£270.00
High season per wk
£290.00–£360.00

Cotswold-stone cottage, beamed ceilings, open fireplace, open plan sitting, dining, kitchen areas, one twin, one double, one single bedroom. Bathroom, shower room. Lock-up garage.

BROMSBERROW HEATH, Gloucestershire Map ref 2B1

★★★★
1 Unit
Sleeping 6

HONEYSUCKLE COTTAGE
Ledbury
Contact: Wendy Hooper, Greenlands, Bromsberrow Heath, Ledbury HR8 1PG
T: (01531) 650360
E: ws.hooper@btopenworld.com

Three-bedroomed detached cottage in own private gardens. Beautifully furnished and well-equipped accommodation. Village location in delightful Herefordshire countryside providing easy access to Malvern Hills, Forest of Dean, Gloucester, Hereford and Worcester. Ideal touring base or just relax in comfort.

OPEN All Year

Low season per wk
£310.00–£460.00
High season per wk
£590.00–£680.00

BUCKLAND, Gloucestershire Map ref 2B1

★★★★
2 Units
Sleeping 2–10

HILLSIDE COTTAGE AND THE BOTHY
Buckland
Contact: Mr Edmondson, Burhill, Buckland, Broadway WR12 7LY
T: (01386) 853426
F: (01386) 833211
E: bob.e@tesco.net
I: www.burhill.co.uk

OPEN All Year
Payment accepted: Delta, Mastercard, Switch, Visa

Low season per wk
£310.00–£554.00
High season per wk
£324.00–£618.00

Delightful restored stone cottages in quiet Cotswold village. Both cottages have central heating, use of gardens and use of indoor heated pool.

BUCKLAND NEWTON, Dorset Map ref 2B3

★★★★
3 Units
Sleeping 4

DOMINEYS COTTAGES
Dorchester
Contact: Mrs Jeanette Gueterbock, Domineys Cottages, Domineys Yard, Buckland Newton, Dorchester DT2 7BS
T: (01300) 345295
F: (01300) 345596
E: cottages@domineys.com
I: www.domineys.com

Delightful, Victorian, two-bedroomed cottages, comfortably furnished and equipped and maintained to highest standards. Surrounded by beautiful gardens with patios. Heated summer swimming pool. Peaceful location on village edge in heart of Hardy's Dorset. Well situated for touring Wessex, walking and country pursuits. Regret no pets. Children 5+ and babies welcome.

OPEN All Year

Low season per wk
£200.00–£350.00
High season per wk
£350.00–£480.00

Enjoy England official guides to quality
Please mention this guide when making your booking.

313

SOUTH WEST ENGLAND

BUCKLAND ST MARY, Somerset Map ref 1D2

★★★★
1 Unit
Sleeping 2-4

THE APARTMENT
Chard
Contact: Mr Roy Harkness, Hillside Guest
Accommodation, Buckland St Mary, Chard TA20 3TQ
T: (01460) 234599
F: (01460) 234599
E: royandmarge@hillsidebsm.freeserve.co.uk
I: www.theaa.com/hotels/103591.html

OPEN All Year

Low season per wk
£135.00-£155.00
High season per wk
£180.00-£235.00

Tastefully extended Victorian cottage on the edge of Blackdown Hills (off A303), bordering South Somerset and North Devon. Comfortable and quiet. Ideal for Lyme, Exmoor, Dartmoor, Quantocks.

BUDE, Cornwall Map ref 1C2 Tourist Information Centre Tel: (01288) 354240

★★★★
1 Unit
Sleeping 6

BITHECUTT COTTAGE
Bude
Contact: Christine, Bude EX23 8EN
T: (01288) 352199
E: mikejur@aol.com

OPEN All Year

Low season per wk
Min £285.00
High season per wk
Max £750.00

Delightful three-bedroom, two-bathroom terraced cottage. Refurbished and equipped to very high standard. Easy walking distance of beaches, town, coastal path, canal and amenities.

★★★★
7 Units
Sleeping 2-6

GLEBE HOUSE COTTAGES
Holsworthy
Contact: Mr & Mrs Varley, Glebe House Cottages Limited, Bridgerule, Holsworthy EX22 7EW
T: (01288) 381272
E: etc@glebehousecottages.co.uk
I: www.glebehousecottages.co.uk

OPEN All Year
Payment accepted: Delta, Mastercard, Switch, Visa

Short breaks available most of the year (excl school summer holidays).

Low season per wk
£250.00-£550.00
High season per wk
£415.00-£865.00

Beautiful period cottages with exposed beams, some four-poster beds, en suite facilities and double spa baths. Set in five acres of tranquil countryside on Grade II Listed Georgian estate but only 10 minutes' drive to Bude and sandy beaches. Cellar bar and restaurant serving superb, home-cooked food. Baby-listening monitors.

★★-★★★★★
8 Units
Sleeping 2-8

IVYLEAF BARTON COTTAGES
Bude
Contact: Mr Robert Barrett, Ivyleaf Barton Cottages, Ivyleaf Hill, Bude EX23 9LD
T: (01288) 321237
F: (01288) 321937
E: info@ivyleafbarton.co.uk
I: www.ivyleafbarton.co.uk

OPEN All Year
Payment accepted: Delta, Mastercard, Switch, Visa

Special offers for Nov-Mar.

Low season per wk
£200.00-£750.00
High season per wk
£300.00-£1,350.00

Cottages converted from stone barns, well equipped and cosy in winter with focal point fires. Two sleeping two people, one sleeping three, two sleeping four, two sleeping seven and one sleeping eight. Own tennis court and adjacent golf course. Three miles to Bude. Short breaks welcome.

 Quality Assurance Standard
Star ratings and awards are explained at the back of this guide.

SOUTH WEST ENGLAND

BUDE continued

★★★
7 Units
Sleeping 2–6

LANGFIELD MANOR
Bude
Contact: Mr Keith Freestone, Langfield Manor, Broadclose, Bude EX23 8DP
T: (01288) 352415
E: info@langfieldmanor.co.uk
I: www.langfieldmanor.co.uk

Quality apartments within fine Edwardian house. Games room with full-sized snooker table, pool and table-tennis tables. Three minutes' walk to the shops and 10 to beautiful sandy beaches, yet peacefully situated in delightful, sheltered, south-facing gardens with heated outdoor swimming pool. Golf course adjacent.

OPEN All Year
Payment accepted: Mastercard, Switch, Visa

Low season per wk
£175.00–£330.00
High season per wk
£300.00–£750.00

★★★
1 Unit
Sleeping 2–9

PENHALT FARM
Bude
Contact: Mr Den & Mrs Jennie Marks, Widemouth Bay, Poundstock, Bude EX23 0DG
T: (01288) 361210
F: (01288) 361210
I: www.holidaybank.co.uk/penhaltfarm

Spectacular sea and country views. The farmhouse has comfortable accommodation with enclosed garden. Ample parking. Close to coastal footpath. Ideal for walking, surfing and touring the North Cornwall coast and countryside. Outside children's play area.

OPEN All Year except Christmas

Reduced rates for smaller parties Sep-Easter.

Low season per wk
Min £150.00
High season per wk
Max £675.00

Escape...
to 6 traditional Cornish stone cottages set in 33 wild & beautiful acres!

Trelay Farm Cottages
SELF-CATERING
St Gennys, Bude, Cornwall

Tel: 01840 230378
www.trelayfarm.co.uk

Everything you'd expect - plus lots more - relaxed quality, rich carved wood, special treasures, friendly animals & secret places - Perfect at any time of year

SOUTH WEST ENGLAND

BUDE continued

★★★★
3 Units
Sleeping 2–10

WOODLANDS FARM
Bude
Contact: Mrs S M Webb, Woodlands Farm, Woodford, Bude EX23 9HU
T: (01288) 331689
F: (01288) 331689
E: woodlandsholiday@aol.com
I: www.woodlandsfarmholidays.co.uk

Special cottages sleeping two, seven and 10 set in peaceful and tranquil 100-acre estate. Spectacular views over open countryside yet only 10 minutes' drive to stunning sandy beaches of north Cornish coastline. Indoor heated pool and games room.

OPEN All Year

Short breaks available early and late season.

Low season per wk
£250.00–£750.00
High season per wk
£480.00–£1,700.00

BURNHAM-ON-SEA, Somerset Map ref 1D1 *Tourist Information Centre Tel: (01278) 787852*

★★★
1 Unit
Sleeping 1–2

KINGSWAY
Burnham-on-Sea
Contact: Land & Law, PO Box 24930, London SE23 2YD
T: (020) 8699 1000
F: (020) 8699 1022

OPEN All Year

Low season per wk
£140.00–£180.00
High season per wk
Min £210.00

Ideally located, beautiful, contemporary and comfortable one-bedroom apartment – large bedroom – coolest whites – wood floors – Italian bathroom suite/thermostatic shower. Ten minutes to shops/beach.

★★★-★★★★★
4 Units
Sleeping 2–9

PROSPECT FARM
Highbridge
Contact: Mrs Gillian Wall, Strowlands, East Brent, Highbridge TA9 4JH
T: (01278) 760507

17thC tastefully restored country cottages set amidst flower gardens and surrounded by the natural West Country beauty of the Somerset Levels, near the legendary Brent Knoll, with remains of Iron Age and Roman settlements. Two miles junction 22 M5, three miles Burnham-on-Sea. Variety of small farm animals and pets. Children welcome.

OPEN All Year

Special tariffs quoted for mid-week and weekend breaks in low season.

Low season per wk
£80.00–£125.00
High season per wk
£255.00–£485.00

BURROWBRIDGE, Somerset Map ref 1D1

★★★
1 Unit
Sleeping 2

HILLVIEW
Bridgwater
Contact: Mrs Rosalind Griffiths, Hillview, Stanmoor Road, Burrowbridge, Bridgwater TA7 0RX
T: (01823) 698308
F: (01823) 698308

OPEN All Year

Low season per wk
Min £140.00
High season per wk
Min £175.00

Compact bungalow, fully equipped and centrally heated, in its own grounds. Conservatory. Short breaks available in low season.

Location Complete addresses for properties are not given and the town(s) listed may be a distance from the actual establishment. Please check the precise location at the time of booking.

SOUTH WEST ENGLAND

CAMELFORD, Cornwall Map ref 1B2

★★★★
5 Units
Sleeping 1–6

Two-bedroom, stone-built cottages sleeping four adults and two children, with a very high specification throughout, situated within this quiet holiday park with 31 acres of beautiful woodland and meadows. Facilities include an outdoor heated pool, bar, restaurant and more! Close to the coast/beach and to Bodmin Moor.

JULIOT'S WELL HOLIDAY PARK
Camelford
Contact: Mrs Kim Boundy, Juliot's Well Holiday Park, Camelford PL32 9RF
T: (01840) 213302
F: (01840) 212700
E: juliotswell@holidaysincornwall.net
I: www.holidaysincornwall.net

OPEN All Year

Payment accepted: Delta, Mastercard, Switch, Visa

Low season per wk
£199.00–£399.00
High season per wk
£469.00–£699.00

CHAPEL AMBLE, Cornwall Map ref 1B2

★★★★
3 Units
Sleeping 2–7

HOMELEIGH FARM
Wadebridge
Contact: Mrs Ann Rees, Homeleigh Farm, Chapel Amble, Wadebridge PL27 6EU
T: (01208) 812411
F: (01208) 815045
I: www.eclipse.co.uk/homeleigh

OPEN All Year

Low season per wk
£200.00–£400.00
High season per wk
£250.00–£850.00

Two-and three-bedroomed converted farm cottages in traditional Cornish stone, on edge of village, 1.5 miles off A39.

CHARMOUTH, Dorset Map ref 1D2

★★★
2 Units
Sleeping 2–4

LITTLE CATHERSTON FARM
Charmouth
Contact: Mrs R J White, Little Catherston Farm, Charmouth, Bridport DT6 6LZ
T: (01297) 560550
I: www.catherstonfarm-bungalows.co.uk

OPEN All Year

Low season per wk
£120.00–£195.00
High season per wk
£200.00–£230.00

Our holiday bungalows are self-contained and comfortably furnished. There are beautiful views of Charmouth and the sea.

★★★
1 Unit
Sleeping 4

THE POPLARS
Charmouth
Contact: Mrs Jane Pointing, The Poplars, Wood Farm Caravan Park, Axminster Road, Bridport DT6 6BT
T: (01297) 560697
F: (01297) 561243
E: holiday@woodfarm.co.uk
I: www.woodfarm.co.uk

Low season per wk
£220.00–£300.00
High season per wk
£300.00–£480.00

With breathtaking views and superb facilities, The Poplars offers spacious, comfortable accommodation specifically designed for disabled guests. See our Heritage Coast and spectacular rural scenery.

Map references The map references refer to the colour maps at the front of this guide. The first figure is the map number; the letter and figure which follow indicate the grid reference on the map.

SOUTH WEST ENGLAND

CHARMOUTH continued

1 Unit
Sleeping 7

SHADOWS
Bridport
Contact: I Ward, Shadows, Lower Sea Lane, Charmouth, Bridport DT6 6LW
T: (01297) 489609
F: (01297) 489609

Charming bungalow, minutes' level walk to sea and village. Spacious, secluded garden. Sunroom. Parking for two cars.

OPEN All Year

Low season per wk
£200.00–£250.00
High season per wk
£450.00–£600.00

CHEDDAR, Somerset Map ref 1D1

5 Units
Sleeping 2–5

HOME FARM COTTAGES
Winscombe
Contact: Mr Chris Sanders, Home Farm Cottages, Barton, Winscombe BS25 1DX
T: (01934) 842078
F: (01934) 842500
E: enquiries@homefarmcottages.com
I: www.homefarmcottages.com

Characterful, beamed, converted farm buildings, providing an ideal place to relax and an excellent base for Cheddar, Bath, Wells, Bristol and Weston-super-Mare. Many lovely walks in the area and comfortable, well-equipped cottages to return to. Set in two acres adjacent to farmhouse.

OPEN All Year
Payment accepted: Delta, Mastercard, Switch, Visa

Short breaks available.

Low season per wk
£220.00–£270.00
High season per wk
£350.00–£540.00

3 Units
Sleeping 2–3

SPRING COTTAGES
Cheddar
Contact: Mrs Jennifer Buckland, Spring Cottages, Spring Cottage, Venns Gate, Cheddar BS27 3LW
T: (01934) 742493
F: (01934) 742493
E: buckland@springcottages.co.uk
I: www.springcottages.co.uk

Charming one-bedroomed cottages in converted barn in two acres of gardens/grounds between the Mendip Hills and Somerset Levels. The famous Cheddar Gorge and caves are within walking distance. Ideally situated for touring the West Country. Nearby opportunities for most sports/interests. No smoking. Ample off-road parking. Dogs by arrangement.

OPEN All Year
Payment accepted: Mastercard, Switch, Visa

See our website for special offers.

Low season per wk
£210.00–£265.00
High season per wk
£265.00–£305.00

4 Units
Sleeping 1–4

SUNGATE HOLIDAY APARTMENTS
Cheddar
Contact: Mrs M M Fieldhouse, Pyrenmount, Parsons Way, Winscombe BS25 1BU
T: (01934) 842273
F: (01934) 844994
E: sunholapart@aol.com

OPEN All Year

Low season per wk
£112.00–£140.00
High season per wk
Max £168.00

Delightful apartments in beautiful Listed Georgian house. Well furnished and equipped. In the centre of Cheddar village. Well-behaved children and pets welcome.

SOUTH WEST ENGLAND

CHELTENHAM, Gloucestershire Map ref 2B1 *Tourist Information Centre Tel: (01242) 522878*

★★★
1 Unit
Sleeping 4

BAKERY COTTAGE
Gotherington
Contact: Mrs Weller, Wortheal House, Southam Lane,
Cheltenham GL52 3NY
T: (01242) 236765

OPEN All Year

High season per wk
£200.00–£350.00

Cotswold-stone cottage, gas central heating, lounge, kitchen/diner, shower and bath. Two twin bedrooms and patio.

★★★★
3 Units
Sleeping 8–10

HOLMER COTTAGES
Cheltenham
Contact: Mrs Jill Collins, Holmer Cottages,
Haines Orchard, Woolstone, Cheltenham GL52 9RG
T: (01242) 672848
F: (01242) 672848
E: holmercottages@talk21.com
I: www.cottageguide.co.uk/holmercottages

OPEN All Year
Payment accepted: Euros

Low season per wk
£190.00–£260.00
High season per wk
£290.00–£370.00

Numbers 1 and 2 are Edwardian cottages each with its own garden. Number 3 is an independent wing of the owner's house, suitable for disabled.

★★★
2 Units
Sleeping 2–4

SPRING HILL STABLE COTTAGES
Cheltenham
Contact: Mrs Smail, Spring Hill, Cheltenham GL54 4DU
T: (01242) 890263
F: (01242) 890266

Charming, fully-equipped cottages sleeping two to four. Situated in open countryside, close to the Cotswold village of Compton Abdale.

OPEN All Year

Low season per wk
£190.00–£335.00
High season per wk
£245.00–£355.00

CHIPPENHAM, Wiltshire Map ref 2B2 *Tourist Information Centre Tel: (01249) 706333*

★★★★
2 Units
Sleeping 4–6

OLIVEMEAD FARM HOLIDAYS
Chippenham
Contact: Mrs Suzanne Candy, Olivemead Farm,
Olivemead Lane, Chippenham SN15 4JQ
T: (01666) 510205
F: (01666) 510864
E: olivemeadfarmholidays@tesco.net
I: www.olivemeadfarmholidays.com

Imagine two delightful, comfortable, well-equipped cottages on a working farm, converted to offer the luxuries of modern living but retaining traditional features. Bed settees available for extra guests. Perfectly positioned for days out in Wiltshire, Bath and the Cotswolds. Convenient M4. Brochure available.

OPEN All Year
Payment accepted: Amex, Delta, Diners, Mastercard, Switch, Visa

Low season per wk
£200.00–£300.00
High season per wk
£350.00–£450.00

Quality Assurance Standard
Star ratings and awards were correct at time of going to press but are subject to change. Please check at the time of booking.

319

SOUTH WEST ENGLAND

CHIPPING CAMPDEN, Gloucestershire Map ref 2B1

★★★★
1 Unit
Sleeping 1–3

HONEYSUCKLE COTTAGE
Blockley
Contact: Mrs Kate Daly, 13 Serpentine Road, Harborne, Birmingham B17 9RD
T: (0121) 426 6310 & 07905 497211
F: (0121) 426 6310
E: stjohn.daly@virgin.net
I: www.thecountrycottage.co.uk

Delightful stone cottage, situated in Blockley, a very pretty, unspoilt village between Chipping Campden and Stow-on-the-Wold. The stone-walled lounge has exposed beams and a woodburning stove. It is furnished to an exceptionally high standard, which includes a new custom-built kitchen. There are magnificent country walks on doorstep.

OPEN All Year

Short breaks available on request.

Low season per wk
£230.00–£350.00
High season per wk
£350.00–£450.00

★★★★
1 Unit
Sleeping 6

ORCHARD COTTAGE
Saintbury
Contact: Ms Sheila Rolland, Campden Cottages, Folly Cottage, Paxford, Chipping Campden GL55 6XG
T: (01386) 593315
F: (01386) 593057
E: info@campdencottages.co.uk
I: www.campdencottages.co.uk

A 16thC Cotswold-stone cottage overlooking beautiful, peaceful countryside. Chipping Campden or Broadway three miles. Many original features including exposed beams, flagstone floor downstairs, wood floors upstairs, inglenook fireplace in sitting room (with logs supplied), separate dining room, three bedrooms, two bathrooms. Garden, barbecue, parking. We regret no dogs.

OPEN All Year
Payment accepted: Mastercard, Switch, Visa

Short breaks out of season/close to date – minimum 3 nights. Other cottages available Chipping Campden/Broadway area – sleeping 2-7.

Low season per wk
Min £450.00
High season per wk
Max £725.00

CHIPPING SODBURY, South Gloucestershire Map ref 2B2

★★★
1 Unit
Sleeping 8

TAN HOUSE FARM COTTAGE
Bristol
Contact: Mrs James, Tan House Farm, Tanhouse Lane, Yate, Bristol BS37 7QL
T: (01454) 228280
F: (01454) 228777

OPEN All Year

Low season per wk
Min £250.00
High season per wk
Max £270.00

Cottage situated on the edge of the Cotswolds. Full oil-fired central heating with open fireplace if required. Parking. Rear view overlooks own fishing lake. Children and dogs welcome.

Accessibility Look for the symbols which indicate National Accessible Scheme standards for hearing and visually impaired guests in addition to standards for guests with mobility impairment. You can find an index of all scheme participants at the back of this guide.

SOUTH WEST ENGLAND

CHISELBOROUGH, Somerset Map ref 2A3

★★★★
1 Unit
Sleeping 4

Golden hamstone cottage in quiet, picturesque village. Lovely countryside with wonderful walks. Many NT properties and gardens nearby. Ideal touring area. Two bedrooms and bathroom with shower, well-equipped kitchen overlooking pretty cottage garden, comfortable sitting room with logburning stove, colour TV and video. Linen provided. Brochure available.

ONE FAIR PLACE
Chiselborough
Contact: Mrs Adrienne Wright, 39 The Avenue, Crowthorne RG45 6PB
T: (01344) 772461
F: (01344) 778389
E: info@somersetcottageholidays.co.uk
I: www.somersetcottageholidays.co.uk

OPEN All Year

Short breaks available Oct–Mar, minimum 2 nights.

Low season per wk
£190.00–£230.00
High season per wk
£260.00–£350.00

CHRISTCHURCH, Dorset Map ref 2B3 Tourist Information Centre Tel: (01202) 471780

★★★★
1 Unit
Sleeping 10

RIVERBANK HOUSE
Christchurch
Contact: Mr Terry Hayden, Riverbank House,
5 Swan Green, Willow Way, Christchurch BH23 1JJ
T: (01202) 828487
F: (01202) 828487
E: handbleisure@amserve.net
I: riverbankholidays.co.uk

OPEN All Year

Low season per wk
£580.00–£790.00
High season per wk
£790.00–£1,300.00

Three-storey, south-facing property fronting River Stour. Magnificent views. Available mooring. Family accommodation for up to 10. Outdoor hot spa overlooking the river.

★★★
8 Units
Sleeping 1–6

Select individual holiday houses on the river Stour sleeping up to six people, each with a balcony and patio overlooking private gardens and river. Ample car parking, riverside picnic and BBQ area. Ideally situated for riverside walks, Priory Church, Quay, shops, safe sandy beaches, the New Forest, golfing and horse riding.

RIVERSIDE PARK
Christchurch
Contact: Mrs Lisa Booth, Riverside Park,
Paddlegrade Limited, 28 Willow Way, Christchurch BH23 1JJ
T: (01202) 471090
E: holidays@riversidepark.biz
I: www.riversidepark.biz

OPEN All Year

Short breaks available Oct–mid-Mar (excl Christmas and New Year). Minimum stay 3 nights.

Low season per wk
£229.00–£470.00
High season per wk
£247.00–£723.00

At-a-glance symbols

Symbols at the end of each entry give useful information about services and facilities. A key to symbols can be found inside the back cover flap. Keep this open for easy reference.

SOUTH WEST ENGLAND

CHUDLEIGH, Devon Map ref 1D2

★★★
3 Units
Sleeping 2-6

COOMBESHEAD FARM
Newton Abbot
Contact: Mr Robert & Mrs Anne Smith, Coombeshead Farm, Combeshead Cross, Chudleigh, Newton Abbot TQ13 0NQ
T: (01626) 853334
E: anne-coombeshead@supanet.com

Low season per wk
£180.00–£300.00
High season per wk
£320.00–£400.00

Comfortable cottages converted from stone barns. On non-working farm. Quiet but not isolated. Between Dartmoor and sea. Market town Newton Abbot six miles. Torquay and Paignton 12 miles. Teignmouth and Dawlish eight miles, Exeter 10 miles. Local shops, takeaways and pubs one mile. Owners in residence. Open March to January.

★★★
1 Unit
Sleeping 1-4

SILVER COTTAGE
Newton Abbot
Contact: Mr Eric Gardner, 75 Old Exeter Street, Chudleigh, Newton Abbot TQ13 0JX
T: (01626) 854571
F: (01626) 854571
E: ejgardner@care4free.net

OPEN All Year

Low season short breaks from £78. Discounts for Senior Citizens. Brochure and details upon request. Book early for Silver Cottage.

Low season per wk
£130.00–£235.00
High season per wk
£265.00–£295.00

Delightful character cottage ideally situated for shops, country walks and surrounding attractions of Dartmoor, Teignmouth, Torbay, Plymouth (Maritime Museum), Paignton (Zoo) and the seaside towns of Dawlish and Torquay, and of special interest The Eden Project with restaurants, cafes and picnic areas – whatever the weather – within easy distance via A38.

CHULMLEIGH, Devon Map ref 1C2

★★★★
1 Unit
Sleeping 2

DEER COTT
Chulmleigh
Contact: Mr & Mrs George Simpson, Deer Cott, Middle Garland, Chulmleigh EX18 7DU
T: (01769) 580461
F: (01769) 580461
E: enquiries@deercott.co.uk
I: www.deercott.co.uk

OPEN All Year

Low season per wk
Min £217.00
High season per wk
£231.00–£378.00

Discover the peace and beauty of the Devonshire countryside and relax in comfortable accommodation offering every convenience for two at any time of the year. In a park-like setting of 20 acres within the Devon heartland, handy for the moors and shores. Amenities at South Molton/Barnstaple a short drive away.

CIRENCESTER, Gloucestershire Map ref 2B1 Tourist Information Centre Tel: (01285) 654180

★★★
1 Unit
Sleeping 2

THE TALLET
Cirencester
Contact: Mrs Susan Spivey, Cirencester GL7 5PR
T: (01285) 653405
F: (01285) 651152
E: howard@theoldfarmhouse.fsbusiness.co.uk

Payment accepted: Euros

Low season per wk
Min £170.00
High season per wk
Max £240.00

An attractive Cotswold barn conversion approached by outside stone steps. Beams in all rooms overlooking farmland with a small number of livestock. Perfect for touring.

322

SOUTH WEST ENGLAND

CIRENCESTER continued

★★★★★
1 Unit
Sleeping 10–12

THE TALLET COTTAGE
Cirencester
Contact: Mrs Arbuthnott, The Tallet, Calmsden, Cirencester GL7 5ET
T: (01285) 831437
F: (01285) 831437
E: vanessa@thetallet.demon.co.uk
I: www.thetallet.co.uk

Large part of a lovingly restored country house, beautifully sited in the midst of sweeping, secluded countryside. Each room is beautifully decorated and is complete with en suite bathroom.

OPEN All Year
Payment accepted: Visa

Low season per wk
£790.00–£850.00
High season per wk
£860.00–£990.00

COLEFORD, Gloucestershire Map ref 2A1 Tourist Information Centre Tel: (01594) 812388

★★★
1 Unit
Sleeping 6

32 TUDOR WALK
Coleford
Contact: Mr Beale, 82 Park Road, Christchurch, Coleford GL16 7AZ
T: (01594) 832061

Set 100yds from the Forest of Dean in its own garden, on a flat site with off-road parking. Ideal for relaxing, walking and cycling in the forest. Three-bedroomed bungalow sleeps six people. All services provided. Golf courses and leisure facilities nearby. Well-behaved dogs welcome.

OPEN All Year

Low season per wk
£180.00–£200.00
High season per wk
£220.00–£300.00

COLYTON, Devon Map ref 1D2

★★★★
5 Units
Sleeping 2–8

SMALLICOMBE FARM
Colyton
Contact: Mrs Todd, Smallicombe Farm, Colyton EX24 6BU
T: (01404) 831310
F: (01404) 831431
E: maggie_todd@yahoo.com
I: www.smallicombe.com

Relax in award-winning converted barns, with superb rural views yet close to the World Heritage coastline. Roam over 70 acres of pasture and ancient woodland abounding with wildlife and enjoy the sights and sounds of the countryside. Visit our Ruby Devon cattle, Dorset Down sheep or prize-winning, rare-breed pigs.

OPEN All Year
Payment accepted: Visa

Short breaks: Nov-Mar from £99 per couple. Special monthly rates Nov-Mar. Winter breaks for groups up to 20.

Low season per wk
£165.00–£295.00
High season per wk
£325.00–£725.00

COMBE MARTIN, Devon Map ref 1C1

★★★★
6 Units
Sleeping 1–6

YETLAND FARM COTTAGES
Ilfracombe
Contact: Alan & Alison Balcombe, Yetland Farm Holiday Cottages, Berry Down, Combe Martin, Ilfracombe EX34 0NT
T: (01271) 883655
F: (01271) 883655
E: enquiries@yetlandcottages.co.uk
I: www.yetlandcottages.co.uk

Luxury, well-equipped barn conversions set around a courtyard on the edge of Exmoor in a quiet, rural location. Dogs welcome. All linen provided.

OPEN All Year
Payment accepted: Delta, Mastercard, Switch, Visa

Low season per wk
£197.00–£515.00
High season per wk
£369.00–£692.00

323

SOUTH WEST ENGLAND

CONSTANTINE BAY, Cornwall Map ref 1B2

★★–★★★★★
31 Units
Sleeping 2–6

TREVOSE GOLF & COUNTRY CLUB
Padstow
Contact: Miss Angela Wise, Trevose Golf & Country Club, Constantine Bay, Padstow PL28 8JB
T: (01841) 520208
F: (01841) 521057
E: info@trevose-gc.co.uk
I: www.trevose-gc.co.uk

OPEN All Year
Payment accepted: Mastercard, Switch, Visa, Euros

Low season per wk £390.00–£690.00
High season per wk £770.00–£1,290.00

One of England's most beautiful golf resorts with lovely views and 27 holes of superb golf (plus a short course).

CORFE CASTLE, Dorset Map ref 2B3

★★★★
3 Units

SCOLES MANOR
Wareham
Contact: Mr & Mrs Peter Bell, Scoles Manor, Kingston, Corfe Castle, Wareham BH20 5LG
T: (01929) 480312
F: (01929) 481237
E: peter@scoles.co.uk
I: www.scoles.co.uk

OPEN All Year

Low season per wk £225.00–£375.00
High season per wk £580.00–£1,050.00

Scoles Manor Barns are next to historic Scoles Manor (Listed Grade II) and have been converted into beautifully appointed units. They are in a superb rural setting with 30 acres of meadows and woodlands and spectacular views over Corfe Castle and the Purbeck countryside.

COTSWOLDS

See under Bibury, Blockley, Bourton-on-the-Water, Broad Campden, Cheltenham, Chipping Campden, Cirencester, Daglingworth, Dursley, Lower Slaughter, Minchinhampton, Miserden, Moreton-in-Marsh, Naunton, Nympsfield, Owlpen, Stanton, Stow-on-the-Wold, Temple Guiting, Upton St Leonards, Winchcombe

See also Cotswolds in Heart of England and South East England sections

COVERACK, Cornwall Map ref 1B3

★★★
1 Unit
Sleeping 1–2

14 COVERACK HEADLAND
Helston
Contact: Mrs Anne Bradley-Smith, Dorland Cottage, The Mint, Church Lane, Bletchingley, Redhill RH1 4LP
T: (01883) 743442
F: (01883) 743442

OPEN All Year

Low season per wk £160.00–£290.00
High season per wk £300.00–£360.00

Beautiful two-person apartment. Panoramic sea views. Linen supplied, TV, VCR and tennis court.

CRACKINGTON HAVEN, Cornwall Map ref 1C2

★★★★
6 Units
Sleeping 4–8
See Ad p315

TRELAY FARM HOLIDAY COTTAGES
Bude
Contact: Mr Robert Watson, Trelay Farm Holiday Cottages, St Gennys, Bude EX23 0NJ
T: (01840) 230378
F: (01840) 230423
E: info@trelayfarm.co.uk
I: www.trelayfarm.co.uk

OPEN All Year

We can cater for wedding parties.

Low season per wk £245.00–£555.00
High season per wk £555.00–£1,150.00

Escape deep into the Cornish countryside. Trelay farm has traditional Cornish-stone cottages, set in 33 wild and beautiful acres. Everything you'd expect plus lots more to discover – rich carved wood, special treasures, friendly animals and secret places. Enjoy our health spa. Perfect at any time of year.

324

SOUTH WEST ENGLAND

CRACKINGTON HAVEN continued

★★★
5 Units
Sleeping 2–6

Delightful cottages standing in three acres of lawn and woodland at the end of a private, tree-lined drive in peaceful, rural setting. Five miles from beach at Crackington Haven. Excellent touring base for North Cornish coast. Pets welcome. Open all year, with log fires for those colder evenings.

TRENANNICK COTTAGES
Launceston
Contact: Ms Lorraine Harrison, Trenannick Farm House, Warbstow, Launceston PL15 8RP
T: (01566) 781443
F: (01566) 781443
E: lorraine.trenannick@i12.com
I: www.trenannickcottages.co.uk

OPEN All Year

Short breaks and special reduced rates for small parties available Oct–Mar (excl school holidays).

Low season per wk
£130.00–£200.00
High season per wk
£200.00–£525.00

CROYDE, Devon

See display advertisement below

Credit card bookings
If you book by telephone and are asked for your credit card number it is advisable to check the proprietor's policy should you cancel your reservation.

Your first visit won't be your last adventure.

The largest selection of Visit Britain Inspected holiday cottages in North Devon.

Choose from over 250 cottages, sleeping from 1 to 12, some with swimming pools.

www.marsdens.co.uk
for information and 24 hour on line booking

For a free brochure, contact holidays@marsdens.co.uk, phone 01271 813777 or write 2 The Square, Braunton, Devon EX33 2JB

325

SOUTH WEST ENGLAND

CULMHEAD, Somerset Map ref 1D2

★★★
3 Units
Sleeping 2–6

CULMHEAD HOUSE
Culmhead, Taunton
Contact: Mr Timothy & Mrs Susan Rodgers, Culmhead House, Culmhead, Taunton TA3 7DU
T: (01823) 421073
I: www.culmheadhouse.com

This beautiful Victorian manor-house is set amidst 10 acres of glorious parkland. The suites are well equipped and guests are free to wander/explore the grounds with wooded areas and sleepy corners. Croquet, badminton and a trampoline are available or simply relax, unwind and enjoy this unique atmosphere. Pets welcome by arrangement.

OPEN All Year

Weekend and short breaks available in Maple, Beech and Mimosa.

Low season per wk
£180.00–£400.00
High season per wk
£280.00–£650.00

DAGLINGWORTH, Gloucestershire Map ref 2B1

★★★★
1 Unit
Sleeping 2

CORNER COTTAGE
Cirencester
Contact: Mrs Mary Bartlett, 23 Farm Court, Daglingworth, Cirencester GL7 7AF
T: (01285) 653478
F: (01285) 653478

Well-equipped, cosy cottage in small village. All inclusive tariff. No hidden extras. All you need to provide is yourselves, your food, clothes and transport.

OPEN All Year

Low season per wk
Min £215.00
High season per wk
Min £215.00

DARTMEET, Devon Map ref 1C2

★★★★
1 Unit
Sleeping 2–4

COACHMAN'S COTTAGE
Dartmeet
Contact: Mr John Evans, Coachman's Cottage, Hunters Lodge, Dartmeet, Princetown PL20 6SG
T: (01364) 631173
E: mail@dartmeet.com
I: www.dartmeet.com

In the heart of Dartmoor National Park, this granite cottage, recently converted from an old coach house, enjoys a breathtaking view of the Dart Valley and surrounding tors. Fully equipped kitchen/dining room. Spacious bedrooms can be arranged as double or twin. Immediate access to riverbank, woodland and open moorland.

OPEN All Year

Payment accepted: Amex, Delta, Mastercard, Switch, Visa, Euros

Short breaks available (excl school holidays).

Low season per wk
£210.00–£255.00
High season per wk
£320.00–£370.00

DARTMOOR

See under Ashburton, Bovey Tracey, Dartmeet, Moretonhampstead, Okehampton, Tavistock

DARTMOUTH, Devon Map ref 1D3 Tourist Information Centre Tel: (01803) 834224

★★★–★★★★★
5 Units
Sleeping 2–6

THE OLD BAKEHOUSE
Dartmouth
Contact: Mrs Sylvia Ridalls, The Old Bakehouse, 7 Broadstone, Dartmouth TQ6 9NR
T: (01803) 834585
F: (01803) 834585
E: gparker@pioneer.ps.co.uk
I: www.oldbakehousedartmouth.co.uk

Character cottages, some with beams and old stone fireplaces. In a conservation area, two minutes from historic town centre and river. Free parking. Beach 15 minutes' drive.

OPEN All Year

Low season per wk
£245.00–£400.00
High season per wk
£350.00–£695.00

SOUTH WEST ENGLAND

DELABOLE, Cornwall Map ref 1B2

★★★★
1 Unit
Sleeping 2-6

THE MILL HOUSE
Delabole
Contact: Richard & Rebecca Daglish, The Mill House,
Helland Barton, Delabole PL33 9ED
T: (01840) 212526
F: (01840) 212526
E: richard@daglish8141.freeserve.co.uk
I: www.themill-house.co.uk

OPEN All Year

Low season per wk
£375.00-£450.00
High season per wk
£450.00-£725.00

Converted mill house, large sitting room on first floor with stunning views. Beautiful coastal/inland walks. Situated on working farm at end of private road.

DEVIZES, Wiltshire Map ref 2B2 Tourist Information Centre Tel: (01380) 729408

★★★★
3 Units
Sleeping 2-4

THE OLD STABLES
Devizes
Contact: Mr Jon & Mrs Judy Nash, The Old Stables,
Tichborne's Farm, Etchilhampton, Devizes SN10 3JL
T: (01380) 862971
F: (01380) 862971
E: info@tichbornes.co.uk
I: www.tichbornes.co.uk

OPEN All Year

Payment accepted: Amex, Delta, Mastercard, Switch, Visa

Low season per wk
Max £224.00
High season per wk
Max £448.00

Single-storey cottages, converted from former stables, within a courtyard setting in an Area of Outstanding Natural Beauty on the edge of Pewsey Vale.

★★★★
1 Unit
Sleeping 1-5

OWLS COTTAGE
Devizes
Contact: Mrs Gill Whittome, Owls Cottage,
48 White Street, Easterton, Devizes SN10 4PA
T: (01380) 818804
F: (01380) 818804
E: gill_whittome@yahoo.co.uk
I: www.owlscottage.homestead.com

OPEN All Year

Payment accepted: Euros

Low season per wk
£220.00-£295.00
High season per wk
Max £440.00

Superior quality cottage in peaceful, rural location, outstanding downland views. Excellent walking, White Horse way, Wiltshire cycle way, bird-watching. Ideal for Stonehenge and Bath. Brochure.

DINTON, Wiltshire Map ref 2B3

★★★★
1 Unit
Sleeping 1-5

THE COTTAGE, MARSHWOOD FARM
Salisbury
Contact: Mrs Fiona Lockyer, Marshwood Farm, Dinton,
Salisbury SP3 5EI
T: (01722) 716334
F: (01722) 716334

OPEN All Year

Low season per wk
£300.00-£400.00
High season per wk
£350.00-£400.00

Comfortable cottage attached to 17thC farmhouse overlooking fields and woodland. Ideal for touring and exploring Wiltshire towns, countryside and places of interest.

DORCHESTER, Dorset Map ref 2B3 Tourist Information Centre Tel: (01305) 267992

★★★★-★★★★★★
20 Units
Sleeping 2-10

Converted brick and stone barns, tastefully furnished in cottage style and fully heated. Also beautifully appointed houses with dishwasher, washing machine/dryer, en suite facilities. Some cottages for couples, others sleeping up to ten. Superb indoor heated pool, games and fitness facilities, two 'en tout cas' (all-weather) hard tennis courts.

GREENWOOD GRANGE FARM COTTAGES
Dorchester
Contact: Mr R P O'Brien, Greenwood Grange,
Higher Bockhampton, Dorchester DT2 8QH
T: (01305) 268874
E: enquiries@greenwoodgrange.co.uk
I: www.greenwoodgrange.co.uk

OPEN All Year

Payment accepted: Delta, Mastercard, Switch, Visa

Low season per wk
£320.00-£1,054.00
High season per wk
£713.00-£2,445.00

SOUTH WEST ENGLAND

DRIFFIELD, Gloucestershire Map ref 2B1

★★★★
1 Unit
Sleeping 1–4

THE STABLES
Cirencester
Contact: Margaret Smith, The Grange, Driffield, Cirencester GL7 5PY
T: (01285) 850641
E: simonsmith@thegrangedriffield.freeserve.co.uk

This spacious stable conversion is situated in a quiet rural village yet only five miles from Cirencester and two miles from Cotswold Water Parks. Furnished to a high standard and immaculately maintained with sofa bed in lounge. Owners live opposite property. No pets.

OPEN All Year except Christmas and New Year

Low season per wk
£195.00–£215.00
High season per wk
£295.00–£315.00

DUNSTER, Somerset Map ref 1D1

★★★–★★★★★
2 Units
Sleeping 2–4

CEDAR HOUSE COTTAGES
Minehead
Contact: Mr David & Mrs Christine Holmes, Cedar House Cottages, Cedar House, Old Cleeve, Minehead TA24 6HH
T: (01984) 640437
F: (01984) 640437
E: enquiries@cedarhousesomerset.co.uk
I: www.cedarhousesomerset.co.uk

Peacefully located in 1.5-acre garden of Edwardian country house, a spacious, one-bedroomed bungalow and two-bedroomed, self-contained bungalow annexe overlooking apple orchards and magnificent countryside. Both cosy properties are fully central heated and double-glazed. Ideal base for walkers, West Somerset Railway and coastline. Owners resident on site.

OPEN All Year

Payment accepted: Amex, Mastercard, Switch, Visa

Low season per wk
£185.00–£275.00
High season per wk
£290.00–£350.00

★★★
1 Unit
Sleeping 1–4

POUND
Minehead
Contact: Mrs Sherrin, The Bungalow, Orchard Road, Minehead TA24 6NW
T: (01643) 821366
F: (01643) 821366

16thC thatched cottage with own private garden. Centrally heated, linen and electricity included. Cot and high chair available. Pets welcome.

OPEN All Year

Low season per wk
Min £175.00
High season per wk
Min £320.00

DURSLEY, Gloucestershire Map ref 2B2

★★★
1 Unit
Sleeping 1–4

BADGERS MEAD DOWNHOUSE FARM
Dursley
Contact: Mrs Maureen Marsh, Badgers Mead Downhouse Farm, Springhill, Upper Cam, Dursley GL11 5HQ
T: (01453) 546001
E: marsh52@clara.co.uk

Spacious self-contained wing of a Listed 18thC Cotswold farmhouse, situated in quiet rural location overlooking own lawn with ample parking. Convenient for Slimbridge and Westonbirt.

OPEN All Year

Low season per wk
£147.00–£181.00
High season per wk
£202.00–£303.00

Important note Information on accommodation listed in this guide has been supplied by the proprietors. As changes may occur you are advised to check details at the time of booking.

328

SOUTH WEST ENGLAND

DURSLEY continued

★★★
1 Unit
Sleeping 1–4

TWO SPRINGBANK
Dursley
Contact: Mrs Jones, 32 Everlands, Cam, Dursley
GL11 5NL
T: (01453) 543047
E: lhandfaj32lg@surefish.co.uk

OPEN All Year

Low season per wk
£141.00–£180.00
High season per wk
£186.00–£225.00

Victorian mid-terraced cottage, in a pleasant rural location near to a 14thC village church with open fields to rear and within easy reach of Cotswold Way.

EAST ALLINGTON, Devon Map ref 1C3

★★★★
7 Units
Sleeping 2–12

PITT FARM
Totnes
Contact: Mr Christopher & Mrs Denise Bates, Pitt Farm, Green Lane, East Allington, Totnes TQ9 7QD
T: (01548) 521234
F: (01548) 521518
E: info@pitt-farm.co.uk
I: www.pitt-farm.co.uk

Beautifully converted traditional farm buildings set in 10 acres of peaceful countryside, providing well-equipped, spacious and private cottages. Ideally located for exploring South Devon's coast, countryside, moors and towns. Facilities include indoor pool, sauna, tennis court, games room and children's play area.

OPEN All Year
Payment accepted: Mastercard, Switch, Visa

Low season per wk
£244.00–£900.00
High season per wk
£464.00–£1,920.00

Short breaks available (excl school holidays).

EAST BUDLEIGH, Devon Map ref 1D2

★★★★
1 Unit
Sleeping 6–8

BROOK COTTAGE
Budleigh Salterton
Contact: Mrs Jo Simons, Foxcote, Noverton Lane, Prestbury, Cheltenham GL52 5BB
T: (01242) 574031
E: josimons@tesco.net
I: www.BrookCottageBudleigh.co.uk

Spacious thatched cottage. Two showers and bathroom. Beaches, walking, golf, karting, bird-watching, riding nearby – but the cottage is so comfortable it's a pleasure to be indoors. Two living rooms with TVs, one for the adults, and a snug, with sofa bed, for the children! Visit our website for more photos.

OPEN All Year
Payment accepted: Euros

Low season per wk
£245.00–£335.00
High season per wk
£520.00–£675.00

Reduced-rate winter breaks for 3-night stays with or without linen (excl Christmas and New Year).

ENGLISH BICKNOR, Gloucestershire Map ref 2A1

★★★
2 Units
Sleeping 2–6

UPPER TUMP FARM
Eastbach
Contact: Mrs Merrett, Upper Tump Farm, Tump Lane, Eastbach, Coleford GL16 7EU
T: (01594) 860072

Converted barn and granary. Close to Symonds Yat and river Wye. Quiet location with lovely views. Ideal for walkers with ramblers' footpath on-site. Croquet lawn. Woodburning stove in barn. Microwave, plus conventional ovens. Barbecue available. On-site parking. Electricity for heating and lighting included. Pets welcome.

OPEN All Year

Low season per wk
£145.00–£180.00
High season per wk
£170.00–£280.00

SOUTH WEST ENGLAND

EXETER, Devon Map ref 1D2 *Tourist Information Centre Tel: (01392) 265700*

★★★★
7 Units

BUSSELLS FARM COTTAGES
Exeter
Contact: Lucy and Andy Hines, Bussells Farm Cottages, Bussells Farm, Huxham, Exeter EX5 4EN
T: (01392) 841238
F: (01392) 841345
E: bussellsfarm@aol.com
I: www.bussellsfarm.co.uk

High-quality barn-conversion cottages, heated outdoor swimming pool, adventure playground, well-equipped games room and excellent coarse fishing in the private lakes. We offer a wonderful base from which to explore the beautiful Exe Valley, Dartmoor, the South Devon beaches and the ancient city of Exeter.

OPEN All Year
Payment accepted: Delta, Mastercard, Switch, Visa

3-night stays available. Low season discounts for 1 or 2 people. Pets welcome.

Low season per wk
£330.00–£500.00
High season per wk
£560.00–£795.00

★★★★★
1 Unit
Sleeping 4

COACH HOUSE FARM
Exeter
Contact: Mr John & Miss Polly Bale, Coach House Farm, Moor Lane, Broadclyst, Exeter EX5 3JH
T: (01392) 461254
F: (01392) 460931
E: selfcatering@mpprops.co.uk

Surrounded by the National Trust Killerton estate, the converted stables of our Victorian coach house provide comfortable ground floor accommodation (no steps) with private entrance and garden overlooking sheep meadows. Working arable and sheep farm. Spectacular East Devon coastline, Exmoor, Dartmoor and Exeter are easily reached. Good access from M5/A30.

OPEN All Year
Payment accepted: Delta, Mastercard, Switch, Visa, Euros

Low season per wk
£185.00–£350.00
High season per wk
£410.00–£520.00

★★★★
1 Unit
Sleeping 1–4

THE GARDEN HOUSE
Exeter
Contact: Mr Hugh & Mrs Anna Evans, The Garden House, Anne's Park, Cowley, Exeter EX5 5EN
T: (01392) 211286
E: anna@realcakes.co.uk
I: www.exeterholidayhouse.co.uk

This is a charming, rural hideaway set in a spectacular plantsman's garden within easy reach of Exeter. A prime location for exploring the South West.

OPEN All Year except Christmas and New Year

Low season per wk
£250.00–£340.00
High season per wk
£310.00–£540.00

★★★★
2 Units
Sleeping 2–6

REGENT HOUSE
Nr Exeter
Contact: Mrs Jewel Goss, Regent House, The Strand, Starcross, Exeter EX6 8PA
T: (01626) 891947
F: (01626) 899126
E: regenthouse@eclipse.co.uk
I: www.selfcateringflats.co.uk

Luxury self-catering holiday flats. Boating, walking, wildlife. Linen, towels, TV and parking all inclusive. Sea views. Look at our website. Long and short lets.

OPEN All Year
Payment accepted: Amex, Delta, Diners, Mastercard, Switch, Visa, Euros

Low season per wk
£190.00–£210.00
High season per wk
£195.00–£580.00

Visitor attractions For ideas on places to visit refer to the introduction at the beginning of this section. Look out for the VisitBritain Quality Assured Visitor Attraction signs.

SOUTH WEST ENGLAND

EXFORD, Somerset Map ref 1D1

★★★
1 Unit
Sleeping 6

2 AUCTION FIELD COTTAGES
Minehead
Contact: Mr & Mrs Batchelor, Bulbarrow Farm,
Bulbarrow, Blandford Forum DT11 0HQ
T: (01258) 817801
F: (01258) 817004

OPEN All Year

Low season per wk
£210.00–£260.00
High season per wk
£260.00–£360.00

Available all year. Short walk from village. Superb woodland and moorland walking. Very well equipped, comfortable and relaxing. An ideal base for exploring Exmoor.

EXMOOR

See under Allerford, Bratton, Brayford, Combe Martin, Dunster, Exford, Lynton, Minehead, North Molton, Parracombe, Porlock, Simonsbath, West Anstey

FALMOUTH, Cornwall Map ref 1B3 Tourist Information Centre Tel: (01326) 312700

★★★
6 Units
Sleeping 2–5

GOOD-WINDS APARTMENTS
Falmouth
Contact: Mrs Jean Goodwin, Good-Winds Apartments,
13 Stratton Terrace, Falmouth TR11 2SY
T: (01326) 313200
F: (01326) 313200
E: goodwinds13@aol.com

OPEN All Year
Payment accepted: Euros

Low season per wk
£185.00–£355.00
High season per wk
£365.00–£445.00

Modern two-bedroomed apartments. All have balconies with marvellous views over the harbour, river Pen and the quaint fishing village of Flushing. Town walking distance.

FOREST OF DEAN

See under Coleford, English Bicknor, Lydney

 Prices Please check prices and other details at the time of booking.

Local colour
Lots of character
and lots to see and do

Superb 2 & 3 bedroom cottages set in a beautiful wooded valley in an area of outstanding natural beauty. Close to the historic maritime town of Falmouth.

Within walking distance of safe, sandy beaches. A short car journey to the Eden Project and Cornwall's fabulous Gardens.

Open all year.

Early and late short breaks available.

Maen Valley, Falmouth, TR11 5BJ
Tel : 01326 312190
Fax : 01326 211120

PENDRA LOWETH
VILLAGE of GARDENS

www.pendraloweth.co.uk

New Bar & Leisure Centre open now!

331

SOUTH WEST ENGLAND

FOWEY, Cornwall Map ref 1B3 Tourist Information Centre Tel: (01726) 833616

★★★★
4 Units
Sleeping 4–7

THE SQUARE RIG
Fowey
Contact: Mrs Stuart, Ladybird House, 26 The Avenue,
Birmingham B45 9AL
T: (0121) 457 6664
F: (0121) 457 6685
E: info@sqrighol.co.uk
I: www.sqrighol.co.uk

Low season per wk
£274.00–£388.00
High season per wk
£666.00–£981.00

Waterside flats on the beautiful Fowey estuary. All flats have balconies with river views. We offer boating facilities, games room and in-house launderette.

FROME, Somerset Map ref 2B2 Tourist Information Centre Tel: (01373) 467271

★★★★–★★★★★★
10 Units
Sleeping 2–22

EXECUTIVE HOLIDAYS
Frome
Contact: Mr R A Gregory, Executive Holidays,
Whitemill Farm, Iron Mills Lane, Frome BA11 2NR
T: (01373) 452907 & 07860 147525
F: (01373) 453253
E: info@executiveholidays.co.uk
I: www.executiveholidays.co.uk

OPEN All Year
Payment accepted:
Mastercard, Visa

Low season per wk
£180.00–£1,540.00
High season per wk
£370.00–£3,200.00

16thC mill and cottage, courtyard cottages and 16thC farmhouse. Country setting in own grounds with private trout stream. Twelve miles from Bath. Free brochure on request.

GILLINGHAM, Dorset Map ref 2B3

★★★★
1 Unit
Sleeping 6

MEADS FARM
Gillingham
Contact: June Wallis, Meads Farm, Stour Provost,
Gillingham SP8 5RX
T: (01747) 838265
F: (01258) 821123

OPEN All Year

Low season per wk
£235.00–£350.00
High season per wk
£385.00–£440.00

Meads Bungalow is a spacious, very well-equipped accommodation enjoying outstanding views over the Blackmore Vale. Situated one mile A30 in lovely village. Shaftesbury with its famous Gold Hill is nearby and within easy reach are Bournemouth, Weymouth and Bath. Over one mile of coarse fishing, quarter acre of lawns.

★★★★
1 Unit
Sleeping 2

WOOLFIELDS BARN
Gillingham
Contact: Mr & Mrs Thomas, Woolfields Barn,
Woolfields Farm, Milton on Stour, Gillingham SP8 5PX
T: (01747) 824729
F: (01747) 824986
E: OThomas453@aol.com
I: www.woolfieldsbarn.co.uk

OPEN All Year

Low season per wk
Min £180.00
High season per wk
Max £270.00

Fully-equipped barn conversion. Extremely comfortable and peaceful. Centrally heated. Linen provided.

Location Complete addresses for properties are not given and the town(s) listed may be a distance from the actual establishment. Please check the precise location at the time of booking.

332

SOUTH WEST ENGLAND

GLASTONBURY, Somerset Map ref 2A2 Tourist Information Centre Tel: (01458) 832954

★★★★
8 Units
Sleeping 2–6

Delightful cottages converted from a Listed farmhouse and barns. Set in eight acres of garden, apple orchards and meadows. The cottages have old world charm and country-style decor. There is also an indoor heated swimming pool. Beautiful views of the Somerset Levels and Mendip hills. Central for many places of interest.

MIDDLEWICK HOLIDAY COTTAGES
Glastonbury
Contact: Mr Martin & Mrs Shirley Kavanagh, Middlewick Holiday Cottages, Wick Lane, Middlewick, Glastonbury BA6 8JW
T: (01458) 832351
F: (01458) 832351
E: info@middlewickholidaycottages.co.uk
I: www.middlewickholidaycottages.co.uk

OPEN All Year

Payment accepted: Mastercard, Switch, Visa

Short breaks Oct–Mar.

Low season per wk
£175.00–£340.00
High season per wk
£235.00–£721.00

GORRAN HAVEN, Cornwall Map ref 1B3

★★★★
1 Unit
Sleeping 2–8

Four-bedroom, split level, detached bungalow sleeping up to eight. Any combination of bedrooms can be booked. Spacious lounge with open fireplace, video and satellite TV. Well-equipped kitchen with electric cooker, dishwasher, fridge/freezer, microwave etc. Separate dining room. Sea views with enclosed garden, 500m from beach harbour/shops.

MORWENNA HOUSE
St Austell
Contact: Mrs Pamela Kendall, 39 Perhaver Park, Gorran Haven, St Austell PL26 6NZ
T: (01726) 843015
I: morwennaholidays.co.uk

OPEN All Year

Payment accepted: Delta, Mastercard, Switch, Visa

Short breaks available Nov–Mar.

Low season per wk
£290.00–£450.00
High season per wk
£470.00–£900.00

GREAT CHEVERELL, Wiltshire Map ref 2B2

★
1 Unit
Sleeping 1–4

DOWNSWOOD
Devizes
Contact: Mrs Ros Shepherd, Downswood, Devizes SN10 5TW
T: (01380) 813304

Seven-acre stud farm. Annexe to small country house. Gardens, lovely surroundings. Adjacent to Salisbury Plain and ideal for touring, walking or riding (horses welcome).

OPEN All Year

Low season per wk
Max £200.00
High season per wk
Max £250.00

HELSTON, Cornwall Map ref 1B3 Tourist Information Centre Tel: (01326) 565431

★★★
5 Units
Sleeping 2–4

TRELAWNEY HOUSE SELF CATERING HOLIDAYS
Helston
Contact: Mr E J Cardnell, Gunwalloe, Helston TR12 7QB
T: (01326) 240260
F: (01326) 240260
E: ejcardnell@aol.com

Payment accepted: Euros

Beautiful, quiet location with spectacular sea/rural views. Close to beaches, coastal walks and golf. Ideally situated for exploring the secrets of the Lizard Peninsula. Open Easter to October.

Low season per wk
£170.00–£190.00
High season per wk
£340.00–£360.00

Symbols The symbols in each entry give information about services and facilities. A key to these symbols appears at the back of this guide.

SOUTH WEST ENGLAND

HELSTONE, Cornwall Map ref 1B2

★★★–★★★★★
5 Units

MAYROSE FARM
Camelford
Contact: Mrs Jane Maunder, Helstone, Camelford
PL32 9RN
T: (01840) 213509
F: (01840) 213509
E: info@mayrosefarmcottages.co.uk
I: www.mayrosefarmcottages.co.uk

Off quiet country lane, Cornish-stone farm cottages overlooking 18 acres of fields with views down picturesque Allen Valley. Cosy whitewashed interiors, some logburners. Linen and towels provided. Heated outdoor pool, friendly farm animals for the children. Close to coast and moor.

OPEN All Year

Payment accepted: Mastercard, Visa, Euros

Ideal for family reunions, group holidays etc. Catering help available. Short breaks available Oct-Mar.

Low season per wk
£270.00–£550.00
High season per wk
£600.00–£800.00

HIGHAMPTON, Devon Map ref 1C2

★★★★
1 Unit
Sleeping 2–3

NO 10 LAKEVIEW RISE
Beaworthy
Contact: Mr Peter & Mrs Margery Mathews, Kimberley, Bridge Street, Great Kimble, Aylesbury HP17 9TN
T: (01844) 347204
E: margejulepete@aol.com
I: www.lakeviewrise.com

One-bedroom bungalow, one of 14 properties set in 3.5 acres of terraced gardens. Beautiful countryside views overlooking Dartmoor. Indoor swimming pool and sauna. Fishing lake. Children's play area. Complete refurbishment. Thirty minutes from Bude and Dartmoor. Leaflet on request.

OPEN All Year

Payment accepted: Amex, Delta, Mastercard, Switch, Visa

Low season per wk
£190.00–£355.00
High season per wk
£320.00–£417.00

HOLCOMBE ROGUS, Devon Map ref 1D2

★★★★
1 Unit
Sleeping 1–2

WHIPCOTT HEIGHTS
Wellington
Contact: Mrs Gallagher, Whipcott Heights, Wellington
TA21 0NA
T: (01823) 672339
F: (01823) 672339
E: bookings@oldlimekiln.freeserve.co.uk

OPEN All Year

Low season per wk
Max £195.00
High season per wk
Max £365.00

A well-appointed one-bedroomed accommodation set on a hill overlooking thousands of acres of countryside and the Grand Western Canal. Five minutes junction 26/27 of the M5.

Use your *i*s

There are more than 550 Tourist Information Centres throughout England offering friendly help with accommodation and holiday ideas as well as suggestions of places to visit and things to do. You'll find addresses in the local phone book.

SOUTH WEST ENGLAND

HOLSWORTHY, Devon Map ref 1C2

★★★-★★★★★

10 Units
Sleeping 4–6

Tastefully converted self-catering cottages. Peaceful, quiet surroundings in central location. Games room with pool table, table tennis, outdoor adventure play area and vast area of grassland. Seated patio area with barbecue. Squash on site. Nine miles to sandy beach. Golf, fishing, horseriding, cycling and walking all nearby.

THORNE MANOR HOLIDAY COTTAGES
Holsworthy
Contact: Mr Julian & Mrs Angela Plank, Thorne Manor, Holsworthy EX22 7JD
T: (01409) 253342
E: thornemanor@ex227jd.freeserve.co.uk
I: thornemanor.co.uk

OPEN All Year

Short breaks available Oct-Mar. Minimum 2-night stay.

Low season per wk
£200.00–£280.00
High season per wk
£380.00–£600.00

HONITON, Devon Map ref 1D2 Tourist Information Centre Tel: (01404) 43716

★★★★★

1 Unit
Sleeping 6

Nestling in beautiful Blackdown Hills, this award-winning cottage offers three large en suite bedrooms, a fantastic farmhouse kitchen opening on to picnic/barbecue/play area with unbeatable views. Large, comfortable sitting room with log fire/Sky programmes. Explore Blackdown Hills, Dartmoor, Exmoor, Jurassic coastline. Fish free in our off-stream trout pond.

THE HAYBARTON
Honiton
Contact: Mrs Wells, Bidwell Farm, Honiton EX14 9PP
T: (01404) 861122
F: 0870 055496
E: pat@bidwellfarm.co.uk
I: www.bidwellfarm.co.uk

OPEN All Year

Payment accepted: Euros

On-stream pond – free trout fishing. B&B available – see website.

Low season per wk
£245.00–£450.00
High season per wk
£450.00–£680.00

★★★★★

7 Units
Sleeping 2–8

Grade II Listed Red Doors Farm forms an enchanting, private hamlet nestling in the Blackdown Hills, an Area of Outstanding Natural Beauty. The cottages are perfect for both family holidays and couples looking for a relaxing break. Luxury indoor pool, games room and children's play area.

RED DOORS FARM
Honiton
Contact: Mr Chris Shrubb, Red Doors Farm, Beacon, Honiton EX14 4TX
T: (01404) 890067
F: (01404) 890067
E: info@reddoors.co.uk
I: www.reddoors.co.uk

OPEN All Year

3-or 4-night breaks available Oct-Mar.

Low season per wk
£395.00–£750.00
High season per wk
£695.00–£1,500.00

Map references The map references refer to the colour maps at the front of this guide. The first figure is the map number; the letter and figure which follow indicate the grid reference on the map.

SOUTH WEST ENGLAND

HOPE COVE, Devon Map ref 1C3

★★★★★
3 Units
Sleeping 4–6

BOLBERRY FARM COTTAGES
Bolberry, Salcombe
Contact: Mrs Hazel Hassall, Bolberry Farm Cottages, Bolberry, Malborough, Kingsbridge TQ7 3DY
T: (01548) 561384
E: info@bolberryfarmcottages.co.uk
I: www.bolberryfarmcottages.co.uk

Luxury two- and three-bedroom, tasteful barn conversion cottages. Each individually designed, retaining true character whilst creating modern, high-quality living accommodation. Hand-crafted furniture, TV, video, washer/dryer, dishwasher. Full central heating and coal-effect gas open fire. Enclosed garden, car park and pet/boot wash area.

OPEN All Year
Payment accepted: Delta, Mastercard, Switch, Visa

Short breaks 'out of season'; discount off evening meals taken at our nearby Port Light hotel.

Low season per wk
£330.00–£425.00
High season per wk
£540.00–£725.00

★★★
1 Unit
Sleeping 1–6

SANDERLINGS
Kingsbridge
Contact: Mrs Diana Middleton, Reading Road, Woodley, Reading RG5 3DB
T: (0118) 969 0958
E: diana_middleton@yahoo.com

OPEN All Year

Low season per wk
£190.00–£330.00
High season per wk
£375.00–£600.00

This detached holiday bungalow is situated on the outskirts of the seaside village of Hope Cove. It is approximately six miles from Kingsbridge and Salcombe; particularly suitable for families and those who enjoy the outdoors.

★★★
1 Unit
Sleeping 6

SEASCAPE
Hope Cove
Contact: Mrs Hazel Kolb, 57 The Whiteway, Cirencester GL7 2HQ
T: (01285) 654781
F: (01285) 654781
E: kolb@btinternet.com
I: www.englishholidayhouses.co.uk

OPEN All Year

Low season per wk
£149.00–£279.00
High season per wk
£369.00–£625.00

Luxury bungalow. Spacious lounge, dining room/conservatory. Sea views and views of National Trust Bolt Tail from lounge and sun terrace. Fully-equipped kitchen. Private garden. Garden furniture. Three bedrooms – one king-size double, two twins. Few minutes' walk to village centre, shop, beaches, harbour, coastal path. Beautiful area, walks. Brochure.

WEB

www.visitengland.com

Log on for information and inspiration. The latest information on places to visit, events and quality assessed accommodation.

SOUTH WEST ENGLAND

HOPE COVE continued

★★★
7 Units
Sleeping 2–7

THORNLEA MEWS HOLIDAY COTTAGES
Salcombe
Contact: Mr John & Mrs Ann Wilton, Thornlea Mews Holiday Cottages, Hope Cove, Salcombe TQ7 3HB
T: (01548) 561319
F: (01548) 561319
E: thornleamews@ukonline.co.uk
I: www.thornleamews-holidaycottages.co.uk

Large flat, mews cottages and split-level bungalows in pretty, south-facing garden, 400 yards from the beach. Superb cliff walks, swimming and sailing. Kingsbridge and Salcombe 10 minutes' drive. Windsurfing and riding nearby. Wide range of good restaurants and pubs in the locality

Short breaks available in the low season.

Low season per wk
£105.00–£485.00
High season per wk
£158.00–£610.00

HUNTLEY, Gloucestershire Map ref 2B1

★★★
1 Unit
Sleeping 6

THE VINEARY
Gloucester
Contact: Mrs Ann Snow, The Vineary, Vinetree Cottage, Solomons Tump, Gloucester GL19 3EB
T: (01452) 830006

OPEN All Year

Low season per wk
£160.00–£200.00
High season per wk
£200.00–£260.00

The Vineary is a self-catering annexe to Vinetree Cottage in a quiet country lane with open views. Easy access to shop, post office and country inns.

ILFRACOMBE, Devon Map ref 1C1 Tourist Information Centre Tel: (01271) 863001

★★★
10 Units
Sleeping 2–6

WIDMOUTH FARM COTTAGES
Ilfracombe
Contact: Mrs Elizabeth Sansom, Widmouth Farm Cottages, Watermouth, Ilfracombe EX34 9RX
T: (01271) 863743
F: (01271) 866479
E: holidays@widmouthfarmcottages.co.uk
I: www.widmouthfarmcottages.co.uk

Delightful cottages, some early 1800s (including a unique round barn conversion), set in 35 acres of National Heritage coastland with private beach. The coastal footpath borders our land and the views are stunning. Easily accessible. Activities for all ages. Grocery and meal-delivery services. Pets welcome.

OPEN All Year
Payment accepted: Delta, Mastercard, Switch, Visa

Residential craft and hobby courses Oct–May (brochure available). Open and decorated for Christmas and New Year.

Low season per wk
£195.00–£340.00
High season per wk
£370.00–£750.00

Special breaks

Many establishments offer special promotions and themed breaks. These are highlighted in red. (All such offers are subject to availability.)

SOUTH WEST ENGLAND

KINGSBRIDGE, Devon Map ref 1C3 Tourist Information Centre Tel: (01548) 853195

★★★
2 Units
Sleeping 4–5

DAIRYMANS CORNER AND SHEPHERDS REST
Kingsbridge
Contact: Mrs Anne Rossiter, Burton Farmhouse & Garden Room Restaurant, Galmpton, Kingsbridge TQ7 3EY
T: (01548) 561210
F: (01548) 562257
I: www.burtonfarm.co.uk

Situated in a pretty hamlet, adjoining farmland, these cob and slate cottages are five miles from Kingsbridge, three miles from the sailing haunt of Salcombe and one mile from Hope Cove/Thurleston. Recently refurbished, retaining many original features. Guests welcome to enjoy farm activities (five minutes' walk). Meals available.

OPEN All Year
Payment accepted: Amex, Delta, Diners, Mastercard, Switch, Visa

Low season per wk
£120.00–£350.00
High season per wk
£495.00–£625.00

★★★
2 Units
Sleeping 2–4

READS FARM
Kingsbridge
Contact: Mrs Pethybridge, Reads Farm, Loddiswell, Kingsbridge TQ7 4RT
T: (01548) 550317
F: (01548) 550317

Flats are part of farmhouse in an Area of Outstanding Natural Beauty. Farmland adjoins River Avon. Fishing. Heated swimming pool. No through traffic. Open April to September.

Low season per wk
£150.00–£250.00
High season per wk
£300.00–£390.00

LACOCK, Wiltshire Map ref 2B2

★★★★
2 Units
Sleeping 2–5

CYDER HOUSE AND CHEESE HOUSE
Lacock
Contact: Mr Philip & Mrs Susan King, Cyder House and Cheese House, Wick Farm, Wick Lane, Lacock, Chippenham SN15 2LU
T: (01249) 730244
F: (01249) 730072
E: kingsilverlands2@btinternet.com
I: www.cheeseandcyderhouses.co.uk

Tastefully converted, beamed farm building with many original features, 1.5 miles from National Trust village. Each house has three bedrooms. Cyder has woodburning stove. Private garden with furniture and barbecue. Good location for Bath (12 miles), Stonehenge, Stourhead, Longleat and Wiltshire Chalk Horses.

OPEN All Year
Payment accepted: Visa

Anglers welcome at our coarse-fishing lake. Short breaks low season.

Low season per wk
£220.00–£360.00
High season per wk
£360.00–£615.00

LANGPORT, Somerset Map ref 1D1

★★★★
1 Unit
Sleeping 1–4

LAUREL WHARF
Langport
Contact: Mr John Neale, Laurel Wharf, C/o Laurel Cottage, Westport, Langport TA10 0BN
T: (01460) 281713
E: laurelwharf@hotmail.com
I: www.laurelwharf.co.uk

Exceptional Regency, Listed Wharf building in idyllic rural location offering spacious, well-equipped accommodation with stone walls, open beams and panoramic views. Balcony overlooking canal.

OPEN All Year
Payment accepted: Amex, Delta, Mastercard, Switch, Visa, Euros

Low season per wk
£180.00–£265.00
High season per wk
£275.00–£400.00

SOUTH WEST ENGLAND

LANGTON HERRING, Dorset Map ref 2A3

★★★★★
1 Unit
Sleeping 8

This 17thC cottage on Dorset's Jurassic coast has been tastefully modernised, providing three double and two single bedrooms. The sitting room has an inglenook with woodburning stove, and the fully fitted kitchen is complete with Aga. The gardens include a secure walled area with patio and barbecue facilities.

HIGHER FARM COTTAGE
Weymouth
Contact: Mr Peter Cropper, Zephen Properties Limited, Somerton Randle Farm, Somerton TA11 7HW
T: (01458) 274767
F: (01458) 274901
E: peter@zephen.com
I: www.zephen.com

OPEN All Year

Low season per wk
£500.00–£850.00
High season per wk
£850.00–£1,000.00

★★★★★
1 Unit
Sleeping 6

This period cottage has been fully modernised whilst retaining its original features. The accommodation provides three double bedrooms, sitting room with inglenook and woodburner, fully fitted dining, kitchen and utility room. There is a garden with patio and barbecue. This beautiful area offers great beaches and miles of walking.

SAINT ANTHONY'S COTTAGE
Weymouth
Contact: Mr Peter Cropper, Zephen Properties Limited, Somerton Randle Farm, Somerton TA11 7HW
T: (01458) 274767
F: (01458) 274901
E: peter@zephen.com
I: www.zephen.com

OPEN All Year

Low season per wk
£375.00–£640.00
High season per wk
£640.00–£750.00

LANGTON MATRAVERS, Dorset Map ref 2B3

★★★
1 Unit
Sleeping 4–5

The village of Langton Matravers is built almost entirely of the local Purbeck stone. The flat in Garfield House is spacious, traditionally furnished and homely. It has spectacular views to the Purbeck Hills, over the sea to the Isle of Wight, and is a 10-minute-walk to the Jurassic coastline.

FLAT 5 GARFIELD HOUSE
Nr Swanage
Contact: Susan Inge, Flat A, 147 Holland Road, London W14 8AS
T: (020) 7602 4945
E: sueinge@hotmail.com
I: www.langton-matravers.co.uk

OPEN All Year

Low season per wk
£210.00–£280.00
High season per wk
£280.00–£350.00

Quality Assurance Standard
Star ratings and awards were correct at time of going to press but are subject to change. Please check at the time of booking.

SOUTH WEST ENGLAND

LANGTON MATRAVERS continued

★★★
1 Unit
Sleeping 2–6

5 NORTH STREET
Swanage
Contact: Mrs Ann Garratt, High Street, Brasted, Westerham TN16 1JE
T: (01959) 565145

OPEN All Year

Low season per wk
£220.00–£330.00
High season per wk
£415.00–£550.00

A charming, attractively furnished mid-19thC Purbeck stone cottage in a quiet lane with private parking. Views of the Purbeck Hills. Langton Matravers is within walking distance of Dancing Ledge, a feature of the Dorset and east Devon coast, which has been awarded World Heritage status.

★★★★
1 Unit
Sleeping 1–6

WESTVIEW HOUSE
Swanage
Contact: Lodge Farm
T: (01788) 560193
F: (01788) 550603
E: alec@lodgefarm.com
I: www.westview.co.uk

OPEN All Year
Payment accepted: Amex, Delta, Mastercard, Switch, Visa, Euros

Low season per wk
£320.00–£450.00
High season per wk
£450.00–£700.00

Carefully converted stonemason's cottage in the heart of the Jurassic Coast. Fabulous for family, walking or cycling holidays or just to escape!

LANREATH-BY-LOOE, Cornwall Map ref 1C2

6 Units
Sleeping 3–7

THE OLD RECTORY
Looe
Contact: Mr & Mrs Duncan, The Old Rectory, Looe PL13 2NU
T: (01503) 220247
F: (01503) 220108
E: info@oldrectory-lanreath.co.uk
I: www.oldrectory-lanreath.co.uk

OPEN All Year
Payment accepted: Delta, Mastercard, Switch, Visa, Euros

Low season per wk
£150.00–£235.00
High season per wk
£340.00–£550.00

Gracious Georgian mansion with spacious, fully-equipped apartments. Enjoy large, beautiful, secluded gardens with heated swimming pool. Edge of picturesque, tranquil village offering all amenities – set in breathtaking countryside only minutes from pretty fishing villages and beaches. Many superb stately homes and beautiful gardens to visit. Parking for eight cars.

Town index
This can be found at the back of the guide. If you know where you want to stay the index will give you the page number listing accommodation in your chosen town, city or village.

340

SOUTH WEST ENGLAND

LAUNCESTON, Cornwall Map ref 1C2 *Tourist Information Centre Tel: (01566) 772321*

★★★★
8 Units
Sleeping 2–8

BAMHAM FARM COTTAGES
Launceston
Contact: Mrs Jackie Chapman, Bamham Farm Cottages, Higher Bamham Farm, Launceston PL15 9LD
T: (01566) 772141
F: (01566) 775266
E: jackie@bamhamfarm.co.uk
I: www.bamhamfarm.co.uk

Individually-designed cottages, ideally situated in beautiful countryside one mile from Launceston, the ancient capital of Cornwall, dominated by its Norman castle. The north and south coasts are easily accessible as are both Dartmoor and Bodmin Moor. Facilities include a heated indoor swimming pool, sauna, solarium, video recorders and trout fishing.

OPEN All Year

Payment accepted: Delta, Mastercard, Switch, Visa

For special offers see our website.

Low season per wk
£220.00–£320.00
High season per wk
£415.00–£1,135.00

★★★–★★★★★
4 Units
Sleeping 2–4

LANGDON FARM HOLIDAY COTTAGES
Launceston
Contact: Mrs Rawlinson, Langdon Farm Holiday Cottages, Langdon Farm, Boyton, Launceston PL15 8NW
T: (01566) 785389
E: g.f.rawlinson@btinternet.com
I: www.langdonholidays.com

OPEN All Year
Payment accepted: Euros

Low season per wk
£120.00–£260.00
High season per wk
£230.00–£350.00

One- and two-bedroom, well-equipped cottages, four-poster beds, countryside setting, near pub, 10 miles from sea. Easy drive to Eden Project. Short breaks available.

★★★
1 Unit
Sleeping 2–6

SWALLOWS
Launceston
Contact: Mrs Kathryn Broad, Swallows, Lower Dutson Farm, Dutson, Launceston PL15 9SP
T: (01566) 776456
F: (01566) 776456
E: francis.broad@farm-cottage.co.uk
I: www.farm-cottage.co.uk

OPEN All Year

Low season per wk
£185.00–£255.00
High season per wk
£275.00–£575.00

Well-equipped cottage with two bathrooms, walks, fishing on traditional Cornish farm. Central for coasts and beaches, Moors and National Trust properties. Lovely garden centre 400m.

LEE, Devon Map ref 1C1

★★★–★★★★★
8 Units
Sleeping 2–8

LOWER CAMPSCOTT FARM
Ilfracombe
Contact: Mrs Margaret Cowell, Lower Campscott Farm, Lee, Ilfracombe EX34 8LS
T: (01271) 863479
F: (01271) 867639
E: holidays@lowercampscott.co.uk
I: www.lowercampscott.co.uk

Charming, tastefully furnished character cottages converted from our farm buildings. Everything supplied to make your stay special. Also holiday homes and lodge. Peaceful farm setting with views across the Bristol Channel. Lee and Woolacombe beaches are easily accessible.

OPEN All Year

Payment accepted: Delta, Switch, Visa

Short breaks available out of school holidays. Residential craft and hobby courses Oct 04–May 05.

Low season per wk
£160.00–£320.00
High season per wk
£370.00–£970.00

341

SOUTH WEST ENGLAND

LISKEARD, Cornwall Map ref 1C2

★★★
2 Units
Sleeping 2–5

LODGE BARTON
Liskeard
Contact: Mrs Hodin, Lodge Barton, Lamellion, Liskeard
PL14 4JX
T: (01579) 344432
F: (01579) 344432
E: lodgebart@aol.com
I: www.selectideas.co.uk/lodgebarton

OPEN All Year

Low season per wk
£150.00–£160.00
High season per wk
£200.00–£510.00

Idyllic farm setting with river valley and woods. Sunny character cottages, well equipped and within easy reach of beaches and moors.

★★★★
3 Units
Sleeping 2–6

LOWER TRENGALE FARM
Liskeard
Contact: Mr Brian & Mrs Terri Shears, Lower Trengale Farm, Trengale, Liskeard PL14 6HF
T: (01579) 321019
F: (01579) 321432
E: enquiries@trengale.co.uk
I: www.trengale.co.uk

Set in six acres of rolling countryside our cottages are fully equipped, ensuring your stay will be relaxed and enjoyable. If it's hot, you can cook on your own gas barbecue, if not, curl up in front of the woodburner or play table tennis or pool in the games room.

OPEN All Year
Payment accepted: Delta, Mastercard, Switch, Visa

Low season per wk
£210.00–£260.00
High season per wk
£540.00–£650.00

Short breaks available off-peak. Couples-only discount. Christmas and New Year specials, art courses run in studio.

LITTLE TORRINGTON, Devon Map ref 1C2

★★★★
3 Units
Sleeping 4–14

CREAM TEA COTTAGES
Torrington
Contact: Mr Tom & Mrs Sue Downie, Staddon House, Monkleigh, Bideford EX39 5JR
T: (01805) 623670
E: tom.downie@ukonline.co.uk
I: www.creamteacottages.co.uk

Set in a lovely location, these cottages are converted barns dating back to the 1700s. They retain many original features but are renovated to modern standards. The properties all have French windows opening onto their own patios. There is also a play and picnic area for children.

OPEN All Year
Payment accepted: Delta, Mastercard, Switch, Visa

Low season per wk
£135.00–£330.00
High season per wk
£330.00–£550.00

Special prices for out of season 3-night or weekend breaks. Please ring for details.

LIVERTON, Devon Map ref 1D2

★★★
2 Units
Sleeping 5

LOOKWEEP FARM COTTAGES
Newton Abbot
Contact: Mr John & Mrs Helen Griffiths, Lookweep Farm Cottages, Liverton, Newton Abbot TQ12 6HT
T: (01626) 833277
F: (01626) 834312
E: holidays@lookweep.co.uk
I: www.lookweep.co.uk

OPEN All Year
Payment accepted: Amex, Delta, Mastercard, Switch, Visa

Low season per wk
£265.00–£365.00
High season per wk
£420.00–£550.00

Attractive, well-equipped stone cottages with swimming pool in tranquil Dartmoor setting surrounded by open farmland and woods. Two miles from Bovey Tracey and Haytor.

SOUTH WEST ENGLAND

LOOE, Cornwall Map ref 1C3

★★★★★

8 Units
Sleeping 2–6

BARCLAY HOUSE COTTAGES
Looe
Contact: Mr Barclay, Barclay House Cottages,
St Martins Road, Looe PL13 1LP
T: (01503) 262929
F: (01503) 262632
E: info@barclayhouse.co.uk
I: www.barclayhouse.co.uk

OPEN All Year
Payment accepted: Amex, Mastercard, Switch, Visa

Low season per wk
£250.00–£500.00
High season per wk
£500.00–£1,400.00

Luxury, award-winning holiday cottages. Breathtaking views over the Looe River valley. Five minutes' walk to harbour, town and beaches. Superb award-winning restaurant and bar/lounge on site.

★★★★

3 Units
Sleeping 4–5

Warm, welcoming and peaceful, these tastefully converted barns on a working farm nestle deep in beautiful Cornish countryside, yet are near the famous beaches and fishing harbours of Looe, Polperro and Fowey. Walking, fishing, wonderful houses and gardens are easily available, or just relax in comfort. Very wheelchair friendly.

BOCADDON HOLIDAY COTTAGES
Looe
Contact: Mrs Alison Maiklem, Bocaddon Holiday Cottages, Lanreath, Looe PL13 2PG
T: (01503) 220192
F: (01503) 220192
E: bocaddon@aol.com
I: www.bocaddon.com

OPEN All Year

Short breaks available Oct–Mar.

Low season per wk
£160.00–£270.00
High season per wk
£280.00–£500.00

★★★★–★★★★★

5 Units
Sleeping 2–8

Set deep in unspoilt countryside, with a large garden and exceptional sea views, these delightful stone cottages on an award-winning farm are just one mile from the beach and three miles from the fishing port of Looe. The Granary Restaurant is on site.

BUCKLAWREN FARM
Looe
Contact: Mrs Henly, Bucklawren Farm, St Martins, Looe PL13 1NZ
T: (01503) 240738
F: (01503) 240481
E: bucklawren@btopenworld.com
I: www.bucklawren.com

OPEN All Year
Payment accepted: Delta, Mastercard, Switch, Visa

Short breaks from Nov-Apr (excl Christmas and New Year).

Low season per wk
£150.00–£250.00
High season per wk
£250.00–£900.00

Country Code Always follow the Country Code

• Enjoy the countryside and respect its life and work • Guard against all risk of fire • Fasten all gates • Keep your dogs under close control • Keep to public paths across farmland • Use gates and stiles to cross fences, hedges and walls • Leave livestock, crops and machinery alone • Take your litter home • Help to keep all water clean • Protect wildlife, plants and trees • Take special care on country roads • Make no unnecessary noise.

SOUTH WEST ENGLAND

LOOE continued

★★★★
35 Units
Sleeping 1–8

See Ad below

CRYLLA VALLEY COTTAGES
Saltash
Contact: Mr M Walsh, Crylla Valley Cottages,
Notter Bridge, Saltash PL12 4RN
T: (01752) 851133
F: (01752) 851666
E: sales@cryllacottages.co.uk
I: www.cryllacottages.co.uk

Award-winning cottages and bungalows in beautiful riverside setting between Looe and Plymouth. Eighteen acres of grounds and attractive flower gardens. Play area. Ideal for fishing, golf, walking, riding, sailing, town and coast, visiting historic houses and gardens, and touring Cornwall and Devon. Country inn close by for good food.

OPEN All Year
Payment accepted: Delta, Mastercard, Switch, Visa

Free leisure membership to nearby Golf and Country Club: 3 pools, gym, sauna, jacuzzi, racquets and reduced golf rates.

Low season per wk
£160.00–£277.00
High season per wk
£267.00–£738.00

Accessibility Look for the symbols which indicate National Accessible Scheme standards for hearing and visually impaired guests in addition to standards for guests with mobility impairment. You can find an index of all scheme participants at the back of this guide.

Our award winning cottages & bungalows are nestled in 18 acres of flower gardens, lawns and handsome woodlands, alongside the River Lyhner. It's a truly beautiful spot, yet so convenient for town & coast, and exploring Devon & Cornwall. You can be assured of a warm welcome.

Our visitors enjoy FREE LEISURE MEMBERSHIP to nearby St Mellion International Golf & Country Club. This gives FREE use of: 3 swimming pools, gym, jacuzzi, steam room, squash, tennis & badminton facilities.

● Choice of 1,2 and 3 bedroom accommodation ● Reduced golf rates
Quality children's play area ● Country Inn nearby serving good food ● Free salmon and trout fishing ● Fifteen minutes from choice of sandy beaches
● Supermarket shopping and town of Saltash are within easy reach
● Short breaks available ● Open all year

AWARD WINNERS

FREE membership to nearby St Mellion International - swimming pool.

For your colour brochure and tariff please contact:
Crylla Valley Cottages, Notter Bridge, Nr. Saltash, Cornwall PL12 4RN
Telephone: (01752) 851133   Fax: (01752) 851666
Website: www.cryllacottages.co.uk
E-mail: sales@cryllacottages.co.uk

344

SOUTH WEST ENGLAND

LOOE continued

★★★★
2 Units
Sleeping 4

PENVITH COTTAGES
Looe

Contact: Mrs Beatrix Windle, 118 Horsham Road, Cranleigh GU6 8DY
T: (01483) 277894
E: beatrix@talk21.com
I: www.penvithcottages.co.uk

Penvith Cottages are situated in a lovely rural setting, with patio and paddock looking out across open countryside. The cottages are only a three mile drive from the fishing port of Looe, with its sandy beach and traditional inns and restaurants. The Eden Project is only 40 minutes away.

OPEN All Year

Low season per wk
£170.00–£280.00
High season per wk
£330.00–£490.00

★★★★
10 Units
Sleeping 4–8

ROCK TOWERS APARTMENTS
Looe

Contact: Mr Clive Dixon, Cornish Collection Ltd, 73 Bodrigan Road, Barbican, Looe PL13 1EH
T: (01503) 262736
F: (01503) 262736
E: cornishcol@aol.com
I: www.cornishcollection.co.uk

Situated in a commanding position right on the seafront in Looe, these apartments provide high-quality accommodation with a very high level of facilities. The views from each apartment are stunning, and the location is an ideal base for exploring the rest of Cornwall and South Devon.

OPEN All Year

Payment accepted: Delta, Mastercard, Switch, Visa, Euros

Low season per wk
£195.00–£495.00
High season per wk
£305.00–£855.00

5% discount Nov-Mar (excl Christmas and New Year) if you quote this advertisement.

★★★★
6 Units
Sleeping 2–6

TALEHAY
Looe

Contact: Mr Paul Brumpton, Talehay, Tremaine, Pelynt, Looe PL13 2LT
T: (01503) 220252
F: (01503) 220252
E: paul@talehay.co.uk
I: www.talehay.co.uk

Tastefully converted and very comfortable stone holiday cottages set around 17thC non-working farmstead. Set in unspoilt, peaceful countryside with breathtaking coastal walks/beaches nearby. Close to Eden Project, Lost Gardens of Heligan and many National Trust properties. An ideal base for exploring the many varied delights of Cornwall.

OPEN All Year

Payment accepted: Amex, Delta, Diners, Mastercard, Switch, Visa

Low season per wk
£150.00–£400.00
High season per wk
£280.00–£700.00

Short breaks available Oct-Mar (excl Christmas and New Year), minimum 2 nights.

Credit card bookings

If you book by telephone and are asked for your credit card number it is advisable to check the proprietor's policy should you cancel your reservation.

SOUTH WEST ENGLAND

LOOE continued

★★★★★
12 Units
Sleeping 2–8

Enchanting 18thC cottages for romantics near the sea in beautiful Looe river valley. Your own delightful private English cottage garden with breathtaking views to the river. Exclusively furnished, antiques, crackling fires, candlelit meals, dishwashers, four-poster beds and crisp white linen. Horse riding, tennis and beautiful heated swimming pool.

TREWORGEY COTTAGES
Looe
Contact: Mr Bevis & Mrs Linda Wright, Treworgey Cottages, Duloe, Liskeard PL14 4PP
T: (01503) 262730
F: (01503) 263757
E: treworgey@enterprise.net
I: www.cornishdreamcottages.co.uk

OPEN All Year
Payment accepted: Delta, Mastercard, Switch, Visa

Short breaks available Nov-Easter (excl Christmas and New Year).

Low season per wk
£256.00–£395.00
High season per wk
£750.00–£1,845.00

LOSTWITHIEL, Cornwall Map ref 1B2

★★★–★★★★★
8 Units
Sleeping 1–6

Charming selection of Georgian estate cottages nestling in the Fowey Valley with two delightful waterside properties. Cottages with leaded-light windows, crackling log fires, four-poster bed and glass-topped well. Parkland, river frontage and boat. Woodland and riverside walks from your cottage door. So much more than just a cottage!

LANWITHAN MANOR, FARM & WATERSIDE COTTAGES
Lostwithiel
Contact: Mr Edward-Collins, Lanwithan Cottages, Lanwithan Road, Lostwithiel PL22 0LA
T: (01208) 872444
F: (01208) 872444
I: www.lanwithancottages.co.uk

OPEN All Year

Short breaks out of season. Reduced green fees. Pets accepted in some cottages.

Low season per wk
Min £190.00
High season per wk
Max £790.00

LOWER APPERLEY, Gloucestershire Map ref 2B1

★★★★★
1 Unit
Sleeping 1–8

Recently converted from a 300-year-old barn, this outstanding property has four double bedrooms, is attractively furnished throughout and offers every amenity in a spacious, light and airy environment. Private, secure garden with outstanding views to the Cotswold Hills. Well placed for exploring both the Cotswolds and Wye Valley.

ROFIELD BARN
Nr Tewkesbury
Contact: Mrs Hazel Lewis, Rofield Barn, Lower Apperley, Gloucester GL19 4DR
T: (01452) 780323
F: (01452) 780777
E: jeremy@tewkbury.freeserve.co.uk
I: www.rofieldbarn.com

OPEN All Year
Payment accepted: Euros

3-night stays available Oct-Mar (excl Christmas and New Year).

Low season per wk
£675.00–£750.00
High season per wk
£750.00–£995.00

Colour maps Colour maps at the front of this guide pinpoint all places under which you will find accommodation listed.

SOUTH WEST ENGLAND

LOWER SLAUGHTER, Gloucestershire Map ref 2B1

★★★★
1 Unit

MALT HOUSE COTTAGE
Cheltenham
Contact: Mrs Charlotte Hutsby, Little Hill Farm, Wellesbourne, Warwick CV35 9EB
T: (01789) 840261
F: (01789) 842270
E: charhutsby@talk21.com
I: www.accomodata.co.uk/060999.htm

OPEN All Year
Payment accepted: Euros

Low season per wk
£300.00–£350.00
High season per wk
£450.00–£500.00

Grade II Listed property. Private parking. This pretty beamed, stone-walled cottage is in a quiet position close to river Eye.

LYDNEY, Gloucestershire Map ref 2B1

★★★
3 Units
Sleeping 2–5

HIGHBURY COACH HOUSE
Lydney
Contact: Mrs Maria-Inez Midgley, Highbury Coach House, Bream Road, Lydney GL15 5JH
T: (01594) 842339
F: (01594) 844948
E: midgleya1@aol.com

OPEN All Year
Payment accepted: Euros

Low season per wk
£150.00–£220.00
High season per wk
£250.00–£310.00

Apartments in a Listed coach house close to Lydney with panoramic views over the Forest of Dean and Severn Valley. Gardens, snooker and games rooms.

LYME REGIS, Dorset Map ref 1D2 Tourist Information Centre Tel: (01297) 442138

★★★
1 Unit
Sleeping 8

MARMALADE HOUSE
Lyme Regis
Contact: Mrs Pam Corbin
T: (01297) 442378
E: ozonepam@aol.com

OPEN All Year

Low season per wk
£400.00–£600.00
High season per wk
£600.00–£900.00

Centrally situated in historic Lyme Regis and with stunning views over the World Heritage coastline, Marmalade House provides light, bright, spacious and contemporary living.

★★★
2 Units

NORTHAY FARM COTTAGES

Axminster
Contact: Mrs Dee Olof, Northay Farm, Hawkchurch, Axminster EX13 5UU
T: (01297) 678591
F: (01297) 678591
E: deeolof@hotmail.com
I: www.northay.com

Relax in our cosy 16thC cottages, surrounded by the 200-acre, picturesque, working family farm. Enjoy the outdoor heated swimming pool, barbecue and children's adventure playground, ponies and shire horses. Log fires, central heating, video, dishwasher, microwave and old world charm all await you. Lyme Regis coast nearby.

OPEN All Year
Payment accepted: Delta, Switch, Visa

Weekend or mid-week breaks at £50 per night.

Low season per wk
£210.00–£280.00
High season per wk
£550.00–£650.00

★★★★
1 Unit
Sleeping 1–3

THE OLD WATCH HOUSE
Lyme Regis
Contact: Mrs Sarah Wilkinson, 1 Grey School Passage, Dorchester DT1 1XG
T: (01305) 262505
F: (01305) 259454
E: old-watch-house@lymeregis.com
I: www.lymeregis.com/old-watch-house

OPEN All Year

Low season per wk
£250.00–£350.00
High season per wk
£350.00–£500.00

Historic old coastguard's house at the Cobb Harbour of Lyme Regis; Grade II Listed building. 20yds from beach on World Heritage Coast site. Beautifully appointed flat.

347

SOUTH WEST ENGLAND

LYME REGIS continued

★★★★
2 Units
Sleeping 2-4

SEA TREE HOUSE
Lyme Regis
Contact: Mr David Parker, Sea Tree House,
18 Broad Street, Lyme Regis DT7 3QE
T: (01297) 442244
F: (01297) 442244
E: seatree.house@ukonline.co.uk
I: www.lymeregis.com/seatreehouse

Romantic, elegant apartments overlooking the sea, three minutes from the beach. Spacious living room with dining area overlooking the sea. Central position giving easy access to restaurants, pubs and walks in Area of Outstanding Natural Beauty. Warm, friendly welcome from owners.

OPEN All Year
Payment accepted: Euros

Low season per wk
£270.00-£410.00
High season per wk
£465.00-£595.00

Short breaks available in the low season.

★★★
4 Units
Sleeping 6-8

WESTOVER FARM COTTAGES
Bridport
Contact: Jon & Debby Snook, Westover Farm Cottages,
Westover Farm, Wootton Fitzpaine, Bridport DT6 6NE
T: (01297) 560111
E: wfcottages@aol.com
I: www.lymeregis.com/westover-farm-cottages

Lovely three-bedroomed cottages with woodburning stove, inglenook and open fires on edge of picturesque village. Additional three-bedroomed, stone-built cottages with adjoining games room overlooking gentle valley. Parking and large garden at all cottages. In an Area of Outstanding Natural Beauty, 1.5 miles from World Heritage Coastline.

OPEN All Year
Payment accepted: Euros

Low season per wk
£180.00-£295.00
High season per wk
£310.00-£650.00

Short-break bookings a speciality and very welcome, Nov-Apr (excl Christmas, New Year and Easter).

LYMPSHAM, Somerset Map ref 1D1

★★
4 Units
Sleeping 2-7

DULHORN FARM CARAVAN PARK
Weston-super-Mare
Contact: Mr & Mrs Bowden, Weston Road, Lympsham,
Weston-super-Mare BS24 0JQ
T: (01934) 750298
F: (01934) 750913

On working farm. Ideal touring and fishing, country surroundings. Beaches approximately four miles. Easy access to motorway. Pets welcome. Also campsite etc.

Payment accepted: Euros

Low season per wk
£110.00-£155.00
High season per wk
£240.00-£325.00

LYNTON, Devon Map ref 1C1 Tourist Information Centre Tel: 0845 660 3232 (national rate number)

★★★-★★★★★
7 Units
Sleeping 2-33

COASTAL EXMOOR HIDEAWAYS
Barnstaple
Contact: Mr Peter Hitchen, Coastal Exmoor Hideaways,
Heddon Valley Hill, Parracombe, Barnstaple EX31 4PU
T: (08717) 170772
F: (08717) 170773
E: info@coastalexmoorhideaways.co.uk
I: www.coastalexmoorhideaways.co.uk

Coastal Devon cottages on Exmoor in private 50-acre valley with heated indoor pool and jacuzzi. Four-posters, log fires, dogs welcome. Short breaks also available.

OPEN All Year
Payment accepted: Amex, Delta, Mastercard, Switch, Visa, Euros

Low season per wk
£248.00-£398.00
High season per wk
£698.00-£998.00

 Prices Please check prices and other details at the time of booking.

SOUTH WEST ENGLAND

LYNTON continued

★★★★
1 Unit
Sleeping 1-2

ROYAL CASTLE LODGE
Lynton
Contact: Mr M Wolverson, c/o Stag Cottage,
Holdstone Down, Combe Martin EX34 0PF
T: (01271) 882449

Something special! High-quality, 16thC, detached, thatched stone cottage with rustic balcony, stable door, real fire, garden. Idyllic coastal setting in England's 'Little Switzerland'. Exmoor National Park, wooded outlook with harbour, pubs, restaurants, shops within walking distance. Spectacular walks. Spotless, warm and cosy. Off-season short breaks. Perfect honeymoon/anniversaries.

OPEN All Year
Payment accepted: Euros

De-stressing breaks Nov-Mar.
All welcome who appreciate quality, privacy and no petty restrictions.

Low season per wk
Min £235.00
High season per wk
Max £545.00

MALMESBURY, Wiltshire Map ref 2B2 Tourist Information Centre Tel: (01666) 823748

★★★
2 Units
Sleeping 2-3

COW BYRE AND BULL PEN
Malmesbury
Contact: Mrs Edna Edwards, Cow Byre and Bull Pen, Stonehill, Charlton, Malmesbury SN16 9DY
T: (01666) 823310
F: (01666) 823310
E: johnedna@stonehillfarm.fsnet.co.uk
I: www.smoothhound.co.uk/hotels/stonehill.html

Superbly located on the Wiltshire/Gloucestershire border on the edge of the Cotswolds in lush, rolling countryside. Explore quiet villages, stately homes, market towns, walk in the beautiful countryside, visit fantastic gardens, or just stay at the farm and watch the cows come home. The perfect place for a holiday.

OPEN All Year

Low season per wk
Min £200.00
High season per wk
Max £280.00

MANACCAN, Cornwall Map ref 1B3

★★-★★★★★
3 Units
Sleeping 2-18

LESTOWDER FARM
Helston
Contact: Mrs Janet Martin, Lestowder Farm, Manaccan, Helston TR12 6ES
T: (01326) 231400
F: (01326) 231400
E: lestowderfarm@hotmail.com
I: www.lestowderfarmcottages.co.uk

OPEN All Year

Low season per wk
Min £150.00
High season per wk
£350.00-£685.00

Lestowder Farm Cottages nestle in a very quiet unspoilt part of Cornwall, on the south of the Helford River, near coastal footpath and beach.

Check the maps

The colour maps at the front of this guide show all the cities, towns and villages for which you will find accommodation entries. Refer to the town index to find the page on which they are listed.

SOUTH WEST ENGLAND

MARAZION, Cornwall Map ref 1B3

★★–★★★★
13 Units
Sleeping 1–5

Converted from an Edwardian hotel in the prime Mount's Bay location. 50yds from beach. Superb panoramic bay views of St Michael's Mount, Mousehole, Newlyn, Penzance. A selection of the finest self-catering accommodation available. One to five minute walk to safe sandy beach, playground, pubs, restaurants, galleries, shops, bus routes for Land's End, St Ives, Penzance.

TREVARTHIAN HOLIDAY HOMES
Marazion
Contact: Trevarthian Holiday Homes, West End, Marazion TR17 0EG
T: (01736) 710100
F: (01736) 710111
E: info@trevarthian.co.uk
I: www.trevarthian.co.uk

OPEN All Year

Payment accepted: Amex, Delta, Mastercard, Switch, Visa

Low season per wk
£195.00–£370.00
High season per wk
£375.00–£795.00

MELCOMBE BINGHAM, Dorset Map ref 2B3

★★★★
1 Unit
Sleeping 1–7

Rural peace in spacious, well-equipped stone cottage with delightful views. Hardy country, on edge of friendly village with well-known pub. Four bedrooms, one on ground floor. Log fire. Wendy house in garden. In an Area of Outstanding Natural Beauty, just off Wessex Ridgeway walkers' path. Coast, abbeys, castles, gardens, many attractions within 30 minutes' drive.

GREYGLES
Dorchester
Contact: Mr Paul Sommerfeld, 22 Tiverton Road, London NW10 3HL
T: (020) 8969 4830
F: (020) 8960 0069
E: enquiry@greygles.co.uk
I: www.greygles.co.uk

OPEN All Year

Payment accepted: Euros

Short breaks available outside summer peak, Christmas and Easter. Minimum 3-night stay. All linen, towels, heating included.

Low season per wk
£375.00–£525.00
High season per wk
£575.00–£725.00

MELPLASH, Dorset Map ref 2A3

★★★
2 Units
Sleeping 3

BINGHAMS FARM VALLEY VIEW APARTMENTS
Bridport
Contact: Mrs Lisa Herbert, Binghams Farm, Melplash, Bridport DT6 3TT
T: (01308) 488234
F: (01308) 488426
E: enquiries@binghamsfarm.co.uk
I: www.binghamsfarm.co.uk

OPEN All Year

Payment accepted: Amex, Delta, Mastercard, Switch, Visa

Low season per wk
Min £195.00
High season per wk
Max £395.00

Self-contained apartments in attractive barn conversion. Extensive countryside views in quiet location, excellent for walking. Restaurant/bar on site.

Important note Information on accommodation listed in this guide has been supplied by the proprietors. As changes may occur you are advised to check details at the time of booking.

SOUTH WEST ENGLAND

MEVAGISSEY, Cornwall Map ref 1B3

★★★
13 Units
Sleeping 2-6

TRELOEN HOLIDAY APARTMENTS
Mevagissey
Contact: Mrs Pat Seamark, Treloen Holiday Apartments, Polkirt Hill, Mevagissey PL26 6UX
T: (01726) 842406
F: (01726) 842406
E: holidays@treloen.co.uk
I: www.treloen.co.uk

OPEN All Year
Payment accepted: Delta, Mastercard, Switch, Visa

Low season per wk
£180.00-£245.00
High season per wk
£360.00-£630.00

Quality apartments in secluded clifftop setting, all with spectacular sea views and private balconies/patios. 450 metres picturesque harbour, shops, beach. Ten miles Eden Project.

MILTON ABBAS, Dorset Map ref 2B3

★★★★★
1 Unit
Sleeping 1-4

Converted 150-year-old brick and flint barn in lovely rural setting. Spacious open plan living/dining area features original beams, woodburning stove and fully equipped kitchen. There are two double bedrooms, both fully en suite, and full central heating. Fresh flowers, wine and first day breakfast included. Children welcome, well-behaved pets by arrangement.

LITTLE HEWISH BARN
Blandford Forum
Contact: Mr Terry Dunn, 2 Little Hewish Cottages, Milton Abbas, Blandford Forum DT11 0DP
T: (01258) 881235
F: (01258) 881393
E: terry@littlehewish.co.uk
I: www.littlehewish.co.uk

OPEN All Year

"Per person per night" pricing outside peak periods.

Low season per wk
Min £280.00
High season per wk
Max £560.00

★★★★
1 Unit
Sleeping 2-6

PRIMROSE COTTAGE
Blandford Forum
Contact: Mrs G D Garvey
T: (01300) 341352
F: (01300) 341352
E: tgarvey@ragtime99.freeserve.co.uk
I: www.miltonabbas-primrosecottage.co.uk

OPEN All Year

Low season per wk
£195.00-£245.00
High season per wk
£345.00-£465.00

Grade II Listed 18thC thatched cob cottage, set on the street in the unique village of Milton Abbas created by Lord Milton. Centre of Hardy country. Ideal for walkers and romantics.

MINCHINHAMPTON, Gloucestershire Map ref 2B1

★★★★
1 Unit
Sleeping 2

A cosy first floor coach house in a peaceful, rural position. Exposed timber beams throughout. Comfortable lounge with TV and radio and uninterrupted views over open countryside. Double en suite bedroom. Fitted kitchen with cooker, fridge, microwave and a drop-leaf oak dining table. Utility room with automatic washing machine. Central for touring the Cotswolds.

THE WOOLSACK
Stroud
Contact: Mrs E Hayward, Hyde Wood House, Cirencester Road, Minchinhampton, Stroud GL6 8PE
T: (01453) 885504
F: (01453) 885504
E: info@hydewoodhouse.co.uk
I: www.hydewoodhouse.co.uk

OPEN All Year

Low season per wk
Min £150.00
High season per wk
Max £325.00

351

SOUTH WEST ENGLAND

MINEHEAD, Somerset Map ref 1D1 Tourist Information Centre Tel: (01643) 702624

★★★★
3 Units
Sleeping 2-6

HUNTINGBALL LODGE
Minehead
Contact: Mr Brian & Mrs Kim Hall, Huntingball Lodge, Blue Anchor, Minehead TA24 6JP
T: (01984) 640076
F: (01984) 640076
I: www.huntingball-lodge.co.uk

Elegant country house with spectacular views over the Somerset coastline and Exmoor countryside. Luxurious and spacious self-catering apartments furnished and equipped to a very high standard, each with own private terrace and balcony. Pubs/restaurant, farm shop/tea rooms and convenience store within easy walking distance. Guaranteed warm welcome from the resident owners.

OPEN All Year
Payment accepted: Euros

Short breaks available Oct-Mar (excl Christmas and New Year).

Low season per wk
£200.00-£225.00
High season per wk
£260.00-£450.00

MISERDEN, Gloucestershire Map ref 2B1

★★★
3 Units
Sleeping 4-6

SUDGROVE COTTAGES
Stroud
Contact: Martin and Carol Ractliffe, Sudgrove, Miserden, Stroud GL6 7JD
T: (01285) 821322
F: (01285) 821322
E: enquiries@sudgrovecottages.co.uk
I: www.sudgrovecottages.co.uk

Attractive Cotswold-stone cottages with views across fields, in a peaceful hamlet on a no-through road. Footpaths lead through valleys, woods and pasture to picturesque villages while Cirencester, Stroud, Cheltenham and Gloucester are easily reached by car. You will find Sudgrove a place to relax and unwind.

OPEN All Year

Short breaks available Oct-Apr. Minimum 2 nights. Special offer: 3 nights for the price of 2.

Low season per wk
£210.00-£290.00
High season per wk
£250.00-£415.00

MORETON, Dorset Map ref 2B3

★★
1 Unit
Sleeping 4

GLEBE COTTAGE
Dorchester
Contact: Mrs Gibbens, Glebe Cottage, Moreton, Dorchester DT2 8RQ
T: (01929) 462468

Peaceful, detached cottage in quiet village full of history and wildlife paradise. Excellent walks and sea six miles away.

OPEN All Year
Payment accepted: Euros

Low season per wk
£150.00-£250.00
High season per wk
£250.00-£330.00

MORETON-IN-MARSH, Gloucestershire Map ref 2B1

★★★
1 Unit
Sleeping 3

THE LAURELS
Moreton-in-Marsh
Contact: Mrs Sandra Billinger, Blue Cedar House, Stow Road, Moreton-in-Marsh GL56 0DW
T: (01608) 650299
E: gandsib@dialstart.net

Modern well-equipped bungalow with private garden situated in the north Cotswolds. Ideal touring centre, convenient for shops and services.

OPEN All Year

Low season per wk
Min £231.00
High season per wk
Min £378.00

Location Complete addresses for properties are not given and the town(s) listed may be a distance from the actual establishment. Please check the precise location at the time of booking.

SOUTH WEST ENGLAND

MORETON-IN-MARSH continued

★★★
1 Unit
Sleeping 1–4

LITTLE PINNERS
Moreton-in-Marsh
Contact: Mrs Mariam Gilbert, Country House Interiors,
High Street, Moreton-in-Marsh GL56 0AT
T: (01608) 650007
F: (01608) 650007

OPEN All Year

Low season per wk
Max £225.00
High season per wk
Max £350.00

A 200-year-old Cotswold-stone cottage with double and twin bedrooms. Beautiful garden in a quiet location but within walking distance of all town facilities.

MORETONHAMPSTEAD, Devon Map ref 1C2

★★–★★★★★
7 Units
Sleeping 2–6

BUDLEIGH FARM
Newton Abbot
Contact: Mrs Harvey, Budleigh Farm, Moretonhampstead,
Newton Abbot TQ13 8SB
T: (01647) 440835
F: (01647) 440436
E: harvey@budleighfarm.co.uk
I: www.budleighfarm.co.uk

OPEN All Year
Payment accepted:
Mastercard, Visa

Low season per wk
£145.00–£215.00
High season per wk
£205.00–£475.00

Properties created with flair from granite barns, on a farm at the end of a stunning valley – rural but not remote. Easy to find. Superb gardens, pubs of character, beaches and castles are all accessible. Superb walking country. In Dartmoor National Park.

MOTHECOMBE, Devon Map ref 1C3

★★★★–★★★★★★
7 Units
Sleeping 5–12

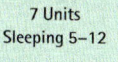

THE FLETE ESTATE HOLIDAY COTTAGES
Plymouth
Contact: Miss Josephine Webb, The Flete Estate Holiday Cottages, Pamflete, Holbeton, Plymouth PL8 1JR
T: (01752) 830234
F: (01752) 830500
I: www.flete.co.uk

OPEN All Year

Winter breaks Nov-Mar (excl Christmas and New Year) from £130pn, minimum 3 nights.

Low season per wk
£440.00–£850.00
High season per wk
£1,120.00–£1,785.00

The Flete Estate is undoubtedly the Jewel in the Crown of the beautiful South Hams. This private 5000-acre estate is designated an Area of Outstanding Natural Beauty, encompassing large, broadleaf woodlands, rolling pastures, cliff paths and sandy beaches, secluded cottages, little hamlets and a tantalising lacework of private drives and pathways.

Quality Assurance Standard

For an explanation of the quality and facilities represented by the stars please refer to the front of this guide. A more detailed explanation can be found in the information pages at the back.

SOUTH WEST ENGLAND

MOUSEHOLE, Cornwall Map ref 1A3

★★★
1 Unit
Sleeping 2–6

POLDARK COTTAGE
Mousehole
Contact: Ms Christine Brown-Miller, An-Benolva,
Fore Street, Newlyn, Penzance TR18 5JU
T: (01736) 330609
I: www.visitwestcountry.com/Poldark

Grade II Listed cosy cottage next to Mousehole harbour with open plan lounge/kitchen/dining, storage heaters, open fire, one double bedroom, one with single beds, shower room. Cosy netloft with double bed, shower room, dining area. Bed linen, towels and electricity, all inclusive. Sunny flower-filled courtyard. Parking permit.

OPEN All Year
Payment accepted: Mastercard, Switch, Visa

Out-of-season short breaks 8 Jan-2 Apr 05. 4-day breaks: £120 for 4 people.

Low season per wk
£210.00–£288.00
High season per wk
£262.00–£645.00

MYLOR, Cornwall Map ref 1B3

★★★★
2 Units
Sleeping 2–6

ALBION HOUSE COTTAGES
Falmouth
Contact: Mr Patrick & Mrs Penelope Polglase, Bells Hill,
Mylor Bridge, Falmouth TR11 5SQ
T: (01326) 373607
F: (01326) 377607
I: www.cottageholidayscornwall.co.uk

OPEN All Year

Low season per wk
£200.00–£380.00
High season per wk
£380.00–£695.00

Comfortable cottage with woodburning stove, separate apartment and yurt. Trampolines, grass tennis court. Close to beautiful gardens, beaches and walks. The best location for exploring all of Cornwall.

NAUNTON, Gloucestershire Map ref 2B1

★★
1 Unit
Sleeping 2

MILL BARN COTTAGE
Cheltenham
Contact: Mrs Madeleine Hindley, Mill Barn Cottage,
Mill Barn, Naunton, Cheltenham GL54 3AF
T: (01451) 850417
F: (01451) 850196

OPEN All Year

Low season per wk
£130.00–£180.00
High season per wk
Min £200.00

Well-appointed flat adjoining converted barn in peaceful Cotswolds village. Twin-bedded room, shower room, sitting/dining room, kitchenette.

★★★★
1 Unit
Sleeping 2–8

YEW TREE HOUSE COTTAGE
Naunton
Contact: Mrs Patricia Smith, White Gables,
4 Woodcote Park Road, Epsom KT18 7EX
T: (01372) 723166
F: (01372) 723166
I: www.yewtreehouse.com

Yew Tree House c1650, is one of the oldest properties in the village and used to be the barber's shop. Tastefully furnished, with inglenook fireplace, oak beams and Cotswold stone floors. Centrally situated to enjoy walking, lovely gardens and National Trust properties. Also Oxford, Stratford and other attractions.

OPEN All Year

Low season per wk
£395.00–£475.00
High season per wk
£475.00–£625.00

Map references The map references refer to the colour maps at the front of this guide. The first figure is the map number; the letter and figure which follow indicate the grid reference on the map.

SOUTH WEST ENGLAND

NEW POLZEATH, Cornwall Map ref 1B2

★★★
1 Unit
Sleeping 6

TREHEATHER
Wadebridge
Contact: Dr Mayall, Osmond House, Chestnut Crescent,
Stoke Canon, Exeter EX5 4AA
T: (01392) 841219

Low season per wk
Min £350.00
High season per wk
Max £680.00

Spacious, modern bungalow. About 200yds from sandy surfing beach with rock pools. Garden, coastal walks. Open March to November.

NEWQUAY, Cornwall Map ref 1B2 Tourist Information Centre Tel: (01637) 854020

★★★★
4 Units
Sleeping 2–8

CHEVIOT HOLIDAY APARTMENTS
Newquay
Contact: Mr Brian & Mrs Jill Biscard,
26 Chyverton Close, Newquay TR7 2AR
T: (01637) 872712
F: (01637) 872712
E: info@cheviotnewquay.co.uk
I: www.cheviotnewquay.co.uk

OPEN All Year

Low season per wk
£180.00–£560.00
High season per wk
£336.00–£1,120.00

The Cheviot holiday apartments are set in their own grounds containing three spacious, good quality, comfortable self-contained holiday apartments.

★★
9 Units
Sleeping 2–6

CROFTLEA HOLIDAY FLATS
Newquay
Contact: Croftlea Holiday Flats, Wild Flower Lane,
Newquay TR7 2QB
T: (01637) 852505
F: (01637) 877183
E: enquiries @croftlea.co.uk
I: www.croftlea.co.uk

Croftlea flats are fully self-contained and are ideally situated close to beaches, shops, station, leisure and sports facilities. Croftlea overlooks Trenance Leisure Park with zoo, tennis courts, bowls, boating, crazy golf and skateboarding. Croftlea stands in its own grounds with swimming pool, barbecue area, gardens and ample car parking.

OPEN All Year
Payment accepted:
Mastercard, Switch, Visa

Low season per wk
£150.00–£350.00
High season per wk
£350.00–£750.00

★★★★
3 Units
Sleeping 1–6

TREGURRIAN HOTEL APARTMENTS
Nr Newquay
Contact: Mr Paul Mills, Tregurrian Hotel Apartments,
Watergate Bay, Newquay TR8 4AB
T: (01637) 860280
F: (01637) 860540
E: tregurrian@holidaysincornwall.net
I: www.holidaysincornwall.net

OPEN All Year
Payment accepted: Delta,
Mastercard, Switch, Visa,
Euros

Low season per wk
£200.00–£360.00
High season per wk
£450.00–£750.00

Superb apartments just 100yds from beach, four miles from Newquay. Access to hotel amenities (same ownership), including bar, restaurant and pool, 50yds away.

At-a-glance symbols

Symbols at the end of each entry give useful information about services and facilities. A key to symbols can be found inside the back cover flap. Keep this open for easy reference.

SOUTH WEST ENGLAND

NORTH MOLTON, Devon Map ref 1C1

3 Units
Sleeping 2–8

WEST MILLBROOK FARM
South Molton
Contact: Mrs Courtney, West Millbrook Farm,
West Millbrook, Twitchen, South Molton EX36 3LP
T: (01598) 740382
E: wmbselfcatering@aol.com
I: www.westmillbrook.co.uk

Farm bordering Exmoor surrounded by pleasant gardens and beautiful, peaceful countryside. Situated a mile from North Molton village with easy access from North Devon link road. Ideal for touring Exmoor and North Devon/Somerset coast and beaches. Games room, play area. Out-of-season short breaks. Colour brochure available.

OPEN All Year

Low season per wk
Min £90.00
High season per wk
Max £390.00

NORTH WHILBOROUGH, Devon Map ref 1D2

4 Units
Sleeping 2–29

LONG BARN LUXURY HOLIDAY COTTAGES
Newton Abbot
Contact: Mr Peter Tidman, Long Barn Luxury Holiday Cottages, North Whilborough, Newton Abbot TQ12 5LP
T: (01803) 875044
F: (01803) 875705
E: tidman@lineone.net

Our cottages enjoy a rural and peaceful setting but are located just four miles from Torquay and 10 miles from Dartmoor. Fully equipped, central heating, logburning stoves, gardens and barbecues. Luxury indoor heated swimming pool with changing rooms and showers. Indoor and outdoor children's play areas. Open all year.

OPEN All Year

Short breaks available autumn, winter and spring, 3/4/5 nights, any day start, subject to availability. Colour brochure available.

Low season per wk
£355.00–£1,250.00
High season per wk
£550.00–£2,300.00

NYMPSFIELD, Gloucestershire Map ref 2B1

1 Unit
Sleeping 1–4

CROSSWAYS
Stonehouse
Contact: Mr & Mrs Bowen, Crossways, Tinkley Lane, Stonehouse GL10 3TU
T: (01453) 860309

OPEN All Year except Christmas and New Year

Low season per wk
Max £140.00
High season per wk
Max £150.00

Annexe to house, large living room, French window on to garden, fitted kitchen. Twin-bedded room, bathroom. Own entrance. Fully self-contained. Private garden.

OAKHILL, Somerset Map ref 2B2

1 Unit
Sleeping 6

THE CHAPEL
Nettlebridge
Contact: Mrs Jeanne Kirby, 166 West Street, Marlow SL7 2BU
T: (01628) 481239
E: kirbyjeanne@hotmail.com

Low season per wk
Max £250.00
High season per wk
Max £375.00

Delightfully converted Victorian chapel by nature reserve in beautiful Mendip Hills. Large kitchen with range, log-burning stove in sitting room. Patio for summer evenings.

Ratings All accommodation in this guide has been rated, or is awaiting a rating, by a trained VisitBritain assessor.

SOUTH WEST ENGLAND

OKEHAMPTON, Devon Map ref 1C2

★★★★
4 Units
Sleeping 4-6

BEER FARM
Okehampton
Contact: Mr & Mrs Annear, Beer Farm, Okehampton
EX20 1SG
T: (01837) 840265
F: (01837) 840245
E: beerfarm.oke@which.net
I: www.beerfarm.co.uk

Enjoy a peaceful holiday on our small farm situated on the northern edge of Dartmoor in mid-Devon. Comfortable and well-equipped two- and three-bedroomed cottages with VCRs and CD-players. One offers accessibility for the less mobile. Games room, some covered parking. Dogs/horses by arrangement. Good walking, cycling and touring base.

OPEN All Year

5% discount on second (lower price) cottage if booked together. Short breaks available (excl school holidays), minimum 3 nights.

Low season per wk
£180.00-£250.00
High season per wk
£450.00-£650.00

★★★★
3 Units
Sleeping 2-9

BOWERLAND
Okehampton
Contact: Mr Ray Quirke, East Bowerland Farm, Okehampton EX20 4LZ
T: (01837) 55979
E: bowerland@devonhols.com
I: www.devonhols.com

Bowerland is an ancient farmhouse and courtyard conversion on Dartmoor's doorstep. Ideally situated for a relaxing holiday in beautiful countryside but within easy reach of the many attractions of Devon and Cornwall. Good local food, superb walking, fishing, golf, cycling, tennis etc.

Payment accepted:
Mastercard, Switch, Visa

Short breaks available out of high season.

Low season per wk
£175.00-£235.00
High season per wk
£245.00-£700.00

★★★★
4 Units
Sleeping 1-2

THE COACH HOUSE – HAYRISH FARM
Okehampton
Contact: Mr David Judge, 1 Telegraph Street, London EC2R 7AR
T: (020) 7256 9013
F: (020) 7588 2051
E: hayrish@easynet.co.uk
I: www.hayrish.co.uk

Self-contained cottages suitable for the discerning couple. Each is unique in style with one large, beamed double bedroom, en suite bathroom and lounge with woodburning stove.

OPEN All Year

Low season per wk
£295.00-£344.00
High season per wk
£384.00-£508.00

Town index
This can be found at the back of the guide. If you know where you want to stay the index will give you the page number listing accommodation in your chosen town, city or village.

SOUTH WEST ENGLAND

OKEHAMPTON continued

★★★★★
1 Unit
Sleeping 2–8

THE LONGHOUSE – HAYRISH FARM
Okehampton
Contact: Mr David Judge, Hayrish Ltd, 1 Telegraph Street, London EC2R 7AR
T: (020) 7256 9013
F: (020) 7588 2051
E: hayrish@easynet.co.uk
I: www.hayrish.co.uk

OPEN All Year

Low season per wk
£786.00–£915.00
High season per wk
£1,039.00–£1,374.00

Listed Devon longhouse with four bedrooms en suite on the banks of the river Taw, near Dartmoor. Extensively refurbished providing luxury accommodation. The dining room can comfortably seat 22 people with catering arranged. Open fire and heated Cotswold-stone floors. The farmhouse style kitchen is fully equipped with all modern appliances.

OWLPEN, Gloucestershire Map ref 2B1

★★★★
9 Units
Sleeping 2–8

OWLPEN MANOR
Dursley
Contact: Mrs Julia Webb, Owlpen, Dursley GL11 5BZ
T: (01453) 860261
F: (01453) 860819
I: www.owlpen.com

OPEN All Year
Payment accepted: Amex, Delta, Mastercard, Switch, Visa

Low season per wk
£200.00–£560.00
High season per wk
£345.00–£935.00

A variety of historic cottages managed in the style of a country-house hotel. Offering antiques and four-posters.

PADSTOW, Cornwall Map ref 1B2 Tourist Information Centre Tel: (01841) 533449

★★★
6 Units
Sleeping 4–6

COACHYARD MEWS
Padstow
Contact: Mr Stephen Andrews, Raidean Ltd, 25 Bentley Close, Rectory Farm, Northampton NN3 5JS
T: (01841) 521198
E: raideanltd@aol.com
I: www.holidayinpadstow.co.uk

OPEN All Year

Low season per wk
£166.00–£249.00
High season per wk
£476.00–£891.00

Modern cottages, built, equipped and maintained to a high standard with adjacent parking and within yards of Padstow's picturesque harbour, shops and restaurants.

★★★-★★★★★
4 Units
Sleeping 2–12

THE LAURELS HOLIDAY PARK
Wadebridge
Contact: Mr Alan Nicholson, The Laurels Holiday Park, Padstow Road, Whitecross, Wadebridge PL27 7JQ
T: (01208) 813341
F: (01208) 816590
E: anicholson@thelaurelsholidaypark.co.uk
I: www.thelaurelsholidaypark.co.uk

OPEN All Year

Daily rates available Oct-Mar (excl Christmas and New Year): from £25 per night. Ideal for weekend break.

Low season per wk
£150.00–£460.00
High season per wk
£385.00–£675.00

Situated in an Area of Outstanding Natural Beauty near Padstow, these stone and slate cottages have been refurbished to provide a high standard of accommodation. An excellent location for touring, walking, cycling or just relaxing. Children and pets welcome. Daily rates for winter bookings available. Ample parking.

358

PADSTOW continued

★★★-★★★★★
6 Units
Sleeping 2-7

POLS PIECE HOLIDAYS
Padstow
Contact: Mrs J E Olivey, Dobbin Lane, Trevone, Padstow
PL28 8QP
T: (01841) 520372
F: (01841) 520372
I: www.polspieceholidays.co.uk

Low season per wk
£225.00–£4??.??
High season per wk
£450.00–£780.00

Delightful, well-equipped apartments, set in own grounds, enjoying panoramic sea views. Short walk to natural swimming pool and Trevone Beach. Twenty-five minutes to Eden Project.

★★★
1 Unit
Sleeping 1-5

34 SARAH'S VIEW
Padstow
Contact: Mrs Margaret Thomas, 31 Dennis Road,
Padstow PL28 8DF
T: (01841) 532243

OPEN All Year except Christmas

Low season per wk
£195.00–£275.00
High season per wk
£350.00–£435.00

Modern, well-equipped cottage on edge of town (Tesco nearby). Open all year. Owner supervised. Close to Camel Trail, lovely coastal walks. Off-street parking.

PAIGNTON, Torbay Map ref 1D2 *Tourist Information Centre Tel: 0906 680 1268 (Premium rate number)*

★★★★
4 Units
Sleeping 2-6

'Ideal location, very clean, comfortable and home from home' as frequently quoted by our guests. Our apartments are all non-smoking, have parking and are situated on level ground close to the beach, shops, coach, rail and bus stations. All apartments have lounge, double bedroom(s), separate kitchens and full size bathrooms.

ALL SEASONS HOLIDAY APARTMENTS
Paignton
Contact: Mr Mike Dessi, All Seasons Holiday Apartments, 18 Garfield Road, Paignton TQ4 6AX
T: (01803) 552187
F: (01803) 552187
E: mikedessi@allseasonsholiday.freeserve.co.uk
I: www.allseasonsholidayapartments.co.uk

OPEN All Year

Low season per wk
£150.00–£250.00
High season per wk
£225.00–£460.00

Short breaks available from Oct-Apr and last minute at all other times, subject to availability.

★★★★
5 Units
Sleeping 1-6

For over 45 years the Gorman family has specialised in friendly personal service at the Harwin. Panoramic sea views and balconies from the majority of our beautifully appointed fully self-contained holiday apartments – all with every home comfort. Ground floor apartments available. Linen included. No meters, no hidden extras.

HARWIN APARTMENTS
Paignton
Contact: Mr & Mrs S Gorman, Alta Vista Road, Goodrington Sands, Paignton TQ4 6DA
T: (01803) 558771
F: (08708) 313998
E: harwin@blueyonder.co.uk
I: www.harwinapartments.co.uk

OPEN All Year
Payment accepted: Delta, Mastercard, Switch, Visa

Low season per wk
£199.00–£440.00
High season per wk
£295.00–£700.00

Short breaks available Sep-Apr, minimum 3 nights.

 Enjoy England official guides to quality
Please mention this guide when making your booking.

WEST ENGLAND

PAIGNTON continued

★★★
9 Units
Sleeping 1–6

HUDSON'S BAY
Paignton
Contact: Mr J & Mrs T Somers, 5 Wye Dean Drive, Wigston LE18 3UE
T: (0116) 257 1740
F: (0116) 257 1740

OPEN All Year

Low season per wk
£90.00–£230.00
High season per wk
£230.00–£385.00

Superb level location, close to beaches, shops and attractions. Train and coach stations five minutes' walk. Parking. Ground floor apartments.

PANCRASWEEK, Devon Map ref 1C2

★★★
1 Unit
Sleeping 7

TAMARSTONE FARM
Holsworthy
Contact: Mrs Megan Daglish, Tamarstone Farm, Bude Road, Pancrasweek, Holsworthy EX22 7JT
T: (01288) 381734
E: cottage@tamarstone.co.uk
I: www.tamarstone.co.uk

OPEN All Year

Low season per wk
Min £230.00
High season per wk
Max £520.00

Tastefully extended, centrally-heated, three-bedroomed cob cottage. Peacefully situated on the Devon/Cornwall borders, ideal for touring both counties.

PARRACOMBE, Devon Map ref 1C1

★★★★
3 Units
Sleeping 1–2

MARTINHOE CLEAVE COTTAGES
Barnstaple
Contact: Mr & Mrs R M J Deville, Martinhoe Cleave Cottages, Parracombe, Barnstaple EX31 4PZ
T: (01598) 763313
E: info@hgate.co.uk
I: www.hgate.co.uk

Within the Exmoor National Park and set below the hamlet of Martinhoe, this row of three delightful cottages enjoy views across the Heddon Valley. Equipped to the highest standard throughout, with many extras included, they offer the perfect getaway location. Dogs welcome at no extra cost.

OPEN All Year

3-night breaks available from Sep-May (excl Bank Holidays).

Low season per wk
£280.00–£350.00
High season per wk
£350.00–£450.00

PELYNT, Cornwall Map ref 1C2

★★–★★★★
11 Units
Sleeping 2–8

TREMAINE GREEN COUNTRY COTTAGES
Looe
Contact: Mr & Mrs Spreckley, Tremaine Green Country Cottages, Tremaine Green, Pelynt, Looe PL13 2LT
T: (01503) 220333
F: (01503) 220633
E: stay@tremainegreen.co.uk
I: www.tremainegreen.co.uk

A private hamlet of beautiful romantic traditional Cornish stone cottages. Set around their own green in 3.5 acres of award-winning grounds. Warm, friendly atmosphere in the countryside. Beaches, coastal and moor walks in abundance, Eden Project nearby. Walk through the fields or lanes to village pub/shops. Brochure available.

OPEN All Year

Payment accepted: Amex, Delta, Mastercard, Switch, Visa

Low season per wk
£130.00–£227.00
High season per wk
£387.00–£825.00

Quality Assurance Standard

Star ratings and awards are explained at the back of this guide.

SOUTH WEST ENGLAND

PENSELWOOD, Somerset Map ref 2B3

★★★★
1 Unit
Sleeping 6–7

PEN MILL COTTAGE
Wincanton
Contact: Peter & Sarah Fitzgerald, Pen Mill Farm,
Coombe Street, Penselwood, Wincanton BA9 8NF
T: (01747) 840895
F: (01747) 840429
E: fitzgeraldatpen@aol.com

Relax on the terrace beside the ponds in the tranquillity of the rural corner of England with views of chickens, grazing sheep and horses. Good walks over the farm/adjacent National Trust land, yet close to Stourhead, Longleat, Bath and famous gardens. This spacious barn conversion is cosy with a log fire and Aga. Open March to October.

Low season per wk
£300.00–£450.00
High season per wk
£450.00–£675.00

PENSFORD, Bath and North East Somerset Map ref 2A2

★-★★
6 Units
Sleeping 2–6

LEIGH FARM
Bristol
Contact: Mrs Smart, Leigh Farm, Old Road, Pensford, Bristol BS39 4BA
T: (01761) 490281
F: (01761) 490281

Located between Bath and Bristol in a rural area. One, two and three-bedroomed, natural stone built conversion.

OPEN All Year
Payment accepted:
Mastercard, Switch, Visa

Low season per wk
£200.00–£300.00
High season per wk
£325.00–£425.00

PENTEWAN, Cornwall Map ref 1B3

★★★
1 Unit
Sleeping 4

CROFTERS END
St Austell
Contact: Mr & Mrs Radmore, Higher Penrose, Tregony, Truro TR2 5SS
T: (01872) 501269

Pretty, well-equipped cottage. Peaceful, yet close to village amenities. Minutes from the long sandy beach. The coastal footpath and cycle trail lead from the village. Ideally positioned for a quiet break or for visiting many of Cornwall's attractions: Lost Gardens of Heligan, Eden Project, Mevagissey, Charlestown etc.

OPEN All Year

Short breaks available Oct-Mar.

Low season per wk
£120.00–£300.00
High season per wk
£300.00–£450.00

PENZANCE, Cornwall Map ref 1A3 Tourist Information Centre Tel: (01736) 362207

★★★★★
1 Unit
Sleeping 6

THE OLD FARMHOUSE
Penzance
Contact: Mrs Vivienne Hall, Chegwidden Farm, St Levan, Penzance TR19 6LP
T: (01736) 810516
F: (01736) 810516
I: www.chegwidden.fsnet.co.uk

OPEN All Year
Payment accepted:
Mastercard, Switch, Visa

Low season per wk
£300.00–£500.00
High season per wk
£650.00–£900.00

A 17thC farmhouse on Land's End peninsula. Listed in Book of Legends. Near beaches and coastal paths and Minack Theatre. Hot tub. Tennis courts nearby.

Accessibility Look for the symbols which indicate National Accessible Scheme standards for hearing and visually impaired guests in addition to standards for guests with mobility impairment. You can find an index of all scheme participants at the back of this guide.

SOUTH WEST ENGLAND

PENZANCE continued

★★★
2 Units
Sleeping 3-8

ROSPANNEL FARM
Penzance
Contact: Mr Bernard Hocking, Rospannel Farm,
St Buryan, Penzance TR19 6HS
T: (01736) 810262
E: gbernard@v21.me.uk
I: www.rospannel.com

OPEN All Year

Low season per wk
£200.00-£300.00
High season per wk
£300.00-£450.00

Old-fashioned, very quiet and peaceful farm. Own pool and hide for bird-watchers. Moth light for insect enthusiasts. Badgers, foxes and lots of wildlife.

PERRANPORTH, Cornwall Map ref 1B2

★★★
4 Units
Sleeping 2-7

GULL ROCK HOLIDAY APARTMENTS
Perranporth
Contact: Mr Richard & Mrs Ann Snow, Gull Rock
Holiday Apartments, 25 Tywarnhayle Road,
Perranporth TR6 0DX
T: (01872) 573289
F: 0870 131 2570
E: holiday@gullrock.com
I: www.gullrock.com

OPEN All Year

Low season per wk
£89.00-£155.00
High season per wk
£250.00-£445.00

Self-catering apartments enjoying panoramic views. Two minutes to beach, town and cliff-top walks. For two to seven people. Dogs welcome. Open all year.

★★★★
1 Unit
Sleeping 1-6

TRETH COTTAGE
Perranporth
Contact: Mr John & Mrs Jenny Cuthill, Claremont,
St Georges Hill, Perranporth TR6 0JS
T: (01872) 573624

OPEN All Year

Low season per wk
£195.00-£360.00
High season per wk
£370.00-£550.00

Early Victorian cottage in a quiet, private location with a sheltered garden, 150m from a sandy surfing beach. Close to all amenities.

PILLATON, Cornwall Map ref 1C2

★★★★
2 Units
Sleeping 2-3

Character barn conversion. Own parking within four acres of grounds. Close St Mellion Golf and Leisure Centre. We provide many extra items you will not find elsewhere included in reasonable rates. No hidden extras. Local fishing, horse-riding. Short drive several National Trust properties, Moors, seaside and Plymouth. Eden Project 27 miles.

UPALONG & DOWNALONG

Nr Saltash
Contact: Mr Geoffrey & Mrs Ann Barnicoat, Trefenten,
Pillaton, Saltash PL12 6QX
T: (01579) 350141
F: (01579) 351520
E: trefenten@beeb.net
I: www.trefenten.co.uk

OPEN All Year
Payment accepted:
Mastercard, Switch, Visa

Low season per wk
£215.00-£240.00
High season per wk
£225.00-£295.00

Use your *i*s

There are more than 550 Tourist Information Centres throughout England offering friendly help with accommodation and holiday ideas as well as suggestions of places to visit and things to do. You'll find addresses in the local phone book.

SOUTH WEST ENGLAND

PLYMOUTH, Plymouth Map ref 1C2 *Tourist Information Centre Tel: (01752) 266030 or 304849*

★★★★
5 Units
Sleeping 1–6

HADDINGTON HOUSE APARTMENTS
Plymouth
Contact: Mr Fairfax Luxmoore, 42 Haddington Road, Stoke, Plymouth PL2 1RR
T: (01752) 500383 & 07966 256984
E: luxmooref@hotmail.com
I: www.abudd.co.uk

A warm welcome awaits you at our elegant, self-contained apartments set within a large Victorian house. Lovingly converted to a high standard offering well-appointed modern facilities, tasteful decoration and furnishings. Complimentary pick-up service at Plymouth stations, secure parking, and courtyard gardens. Price includes bills, bedlinen and towels. Pets welcome by arrangement. Broadband available.

OPEN All Year

Low season per wk
£195.00–£275.00
High season per wk
£255.00–£375.00

POLPERRO, Cornwall Map ref 1C3

★★★★-★★★★★
16 Units
Sleeping 1–16

CLASSY COTTAGES
Looe
Contact: Mr Martin & Mrs Fiona Nicolle, Blanches Windsor, Polperro, Looe PL13 2PT
T: (01720) 423000 & (07000) 423000
E: nicolle@classycottages.co.uk
I: www.classycottages.co.uk

Cottages feet from beach in Polperro. Along coast, isolated cottages with sea views and farm cottages. Cosy log fires, pictures and plants. You need not worry, we promise that your cottage will be beautifully clean and homely. Private indoor pool with sauna, spa etc and a Cornish cream tea completes our welcome.

OPEN All Year
Payment accepted:
Mastercard, Switch, Visa

Weekend breaks – out of season, mid-week breaks.

Low season per wk
£95.00–£800.00
High season per wk
£520.00–£3,400.00

POOLE, Poole Map ref 2B3 *Tourist Information Centre Tel: (01202) 253253*

★★-★★★
2 Units
Sleeping 6–7

FLATS 5 & 6 SANDACRES
Poole
Contact: Mrs Rosemary Bond, Blandford Road North, Nr Lytchett Minster, Poole BH16 6AB
T: (01202) 631631
F: (01202) 625749
I: www.beaconhilltouringpark.co.uk

Two first floor, two-bedroom flats, situated a stone's throw from beach, only minutes from Poole/Bournemouth.

OPEN All Year

Low season per wk
£198.00–£295.00
High season per wk
£440.00–£595.00

★★★-★★★★★
3 Units
Sleeping 1–5

QUAYSIDE, LAKESIDE, BOATHOUSE
Baiter Park
Contact: Mrs Suzanne Fuller, Holtwood, Holt, Wimborne BH21 7DR
T: (01258) 840377
F: (08701) 672994
E: baiter.holidays@btinternet.com
I: www.baiter.holidays.btinternet.co.uk

Luxury one- and two-bed centrally heated houses. Open sea/lake/harbour views. Sunny patios. Level walk to town/quay. All mod cons. Serviced by owner.

Low season per wk
£250.00–£300.00
High season per wk
£350.00–£500.00

Visitor attractions For ideas on places to visit refer to the introduction at the beginning of this section. Look out for the VisitBritain Quality Assured Visitor Attraction signs.

SOUTH WEST ENGLAND

PORLOCK, Somerset Map ref 1D1

★★★★
1 Unit
Sleeping 1-4

GREEN CHANTRY
Minehead
Contact: Mrs Margaret Payton, Home Farm, Burrowbridge, Bridgwater TA7 0RF
T: (01823) 698330
F: (01823) 698169
E: maggie_payton@hotmail.com

Pretty Victorian cottage in a tranquil setting, close to the high street of this charming village with its range of shops and restaurants. Pretty fabrics, wooden floors downstairs, brightly coloured rugs and co-ordinating bed linen make this a perfect place to unwind. Suntrap garden. Garage nearby.

OPEN All Year

Short breaks Nov-Easter, minimum 2 nights. Special offers for Christmas and New Year.

Low season per wk
Min £190.00
High season per wk
Max £400.00

PORT GAVERNE, Cornwall Map ref 1B2

★★★-★★★★★
10 Units
Sleeping 2-8

GREEN DOOR COTTAGES
Port Isaac
Contact: Mrs Oldrieve, Green Door Cottages, Port Gaverne, Port Isaac PL29 3SQ
T: (01208) 880293
F: (01208) 880151
I: www.greendoorcottages.co.uk

A delightful collection of restored 18thC Cornish buildings built around a sunny enclosed courtyard and two lovely apartments with stunning sea views. Picturesque, tranquil cove ideal for children. Half a mile from Port Isaac, on the coast path. Polzeath beach and Camel Trail nearby. Traditional pub opposite. Dogs welcome.

OPEN All Year

Payment accepted: Amex, Delta, Diners, Mastercard, Switch, Visa

3-night weekend or 4-night mid-week short breaks available Jan-May, Sep-Dec.

Low season per wk
£300.00-£491.00
High season per wk
£491.00-£1,027.00

PORT ISAAC, Cornwall Map ref 1B2

★★★
1 Unit
Sleeping 4-5

LOCARNO
Port Isaac
Contact: Mrs Hicks, 7 New Road, Haven Park, Port Isaac PL29 3SD
T: (01208) 880268

Spacious ground floor apartment close to beach, harbour, coastal footpath, shops, pubs. Central for touring. Warm and cosy open fire in lounge. Golf, surfing beach six miles.

OPEN All Year

Low season per wk
£200.00-£260.00
High season per wk
£300.00-£350.00

★★★★-★★★★★★
10 Units
Sleeping 2-12

TREVATHAN FARM
Port Isaac
Contact: Mrs Symons, St Endellion, Port Isaac PL29 3TT
T: (01208) 880248
F: (01208) 880248
E: symons@trevathanfarm.com
I: www.trevathanfarm.com

Beautiful cottages with countryside views, games room, fishing lake, tennis court, set on working farm. Beaches, golf, riding within three miles. Also large period house available.

OPEN All Year

Low season per wk
£130.00-£400.00
High season per wk
£460.00-£1,300.00

Credit card bookings
If you book by telephone and are asked for your credit card number it is advisable to check the proprietor's policy should you cancel your reservation.

SOUTH WEST ENGLAND

PORTLAND, Dorset Map ref 2B3

★★★
1 Unit
Sleeping 1–4

LILAC COTTAGE
Portland
Contact: Ms Shelagh Hepple, 9 Kestrel Drive, Sandal, Wakefield WF2 6SB
T: (01924) 252522
I: www.portlandholiday.co.uk

OPEN All Year

Low season per wk
Min £130.00
High season per wk
Max £360.00

A delightful Victorian terraced cottage with modern amenities but which retains many of its original features. Located in a highly scenic area five minutes from Church Ope Cove.

PORTREATH, Cornwall Map ref 1B3

★★★
8 Units
Sleeping 1–8

CORNWALL HOLIDAY HOMES
Portreath
Contact: Mrs Diana Cousins, Cornwall Holiday Homes, 34 Station Road, Pool, Redruth TR15 3QG
T: (01209) 715358
F: (01209) 715358
E: cwllholidayhomes@talk21.com
I: www.cornwall-holidayhomes.co.uk

OPEN All Year

Payment accepted: Delta, Mastercard, Switch, Visa

Low season per wk
£225.00–£295.00
High season per wk
£255.00–£780.00

Portreath – by beautiful sandy beach. Well-equipped properties in superb positions – some with unrivalled sea or harbour views. Suitable small/large groups. Ideal touring centre.

★★★★★
3 Units
Sleeping 1–5

HIGHER LAITY FARM
Redruth
Contact: Mrs Lynne Drew, Higher Laity Farm, Higher Laity, Portreath Road, Redruth TR16 4HY
T: (01209) 842317
F: (01209) 842317
E: info@higherlaityfarm.co.uk
I: www.higherlaityfarm.co.uk

Come and relax in our tastefully converted luxury barns. En suite bedrooms, central heating, linen provided, gas cooker, fridge/freezer, microwave, dishwasher, washer/dryer, hi-fi, video, pets corner. Close to beaches and the breathtaking North Cornish coast. Ideal for walking, relaxing and exploring Cornwall. A friendly welcome is guaranteed.

OPEN All Year

Short breaks available Oct-Mar, also discounted rates for couples, out of season.

Low season per wk
Min £220.00
High season per wk
Max £640.00

★★★
7 Units
Sleeping 2–7

TRENGOVE FARM COTTAGES
Redruth
Contact: Mrs Lindsey Richards, Illogan, Redruth TR16 4PU
T: (01209) 843008
F: (01209) 843682

Traditional, well-equipped cottages and farmhouse on a 140-acre arable farm. Close to beautiful beaches, cliffs and countryside park, yet within easy reach of the main towns. Centrally heated, some with woodburners – ideal for inexpensive winter breaks. A superb location for walking, swimming, touring or just switching off.

OPEN All Year

Payment accepted: Delta, Mastercard, Switch, Visa

Short breaks available from £90 during low season.

Low season per wk
£150.00–£350.00
High season per wk
£250.00–£675.00

 Prices Please check prices and other details at the time of booking.

SOUTH WEST ENGLAND

PUDDLETOWN, Dorset Map ref 2B3

★★★
1 Unit
Sleeping 5

THE RAMBLERS RETREAT
Puddletown
Contact: Mrs Clare Stokes, 8 Bathsheba Terrace, Dorchester DT1 2JU
T: (01305) 259588 & 07745 064556
E: ramblersretreat@ukonline.co.uk
I: web.ukonline.co.uk/ramblersretreat

High season per wk
£257.00–£469.00

Beautiful three-bedroomed end terrace house. Idyllic for exploring Hardy country. South-west facing garden, centrally heated and double glazed. Front parking. Double and single bedrooms have lovely views over countryside. Historic town of Dorchester only a 10-minute drive away. Open April to end September.

PUNCKNOWLE, Dorset Map ref 2A3

★★★★–★★★★★★
1 Unit
Sleeping 20

BERWICK MANOR
Dorchester
Contact: Mrs Lyn Hopkins, Puncknowle Manor Estate, c/o Hazel Lane Farmhouse, Dorchester DT2 9BU
T: (01308) 898107
E: cottages@pknlest.com
I: www.dorset-selfcatering.co.uk

Low season per wk
£900.00–£1,200.00
High season per wk
£1,800.00–£2,200.00

Berwick Manor is an expansive, historical property set in the delightful Bride Valley of West Dorset. Only four minutes' drive from the Jurassic coast.

RADSTOCK, Bath and North East Somerset Map ref 2B2

★★★★
1 Unit
Sleeping 4–6

CHARLTON FARM COTTAGE
Radstock
Contact: Mr Anthony & Mrs Vanessa Dutton, Charlton Farm Cottage, Charlton, Radstock BA3 5TN
T: (01761) 437761
F: (01761) 436410
E: anthony@charltonfarm.com
I: www.charltonfarm.com

OPEN All Year

Low season per wk
£200.00–£250.00
High season per wk
£250.00–£350.00

Very tasteful two-bedroom, single-storey cottage. Stunning setting. Family farm environment. Highly friendly and flexible hosts.

RAMPISHAM, Dorset Map ref 2A3

★★★★
1 Unit
Sleeping 2

STABLE COTTAGE
Dorchester
Contact: Mr James & Mrs Diane Read, School House, Rampisham, Dorchester DT2 0PR
T: (01935) 83555
E: usatschoolhouse@aol.com
I: www.usatschoolhouse.com

OPEN All Year except Christmas and New Year

Low season per wk
Max £210.00
High season per wk
£280.00–£310.00

Charming stone cottage surrounded by fields and woodland. Birds and wildlife abound. Fully heated and carpeted. Within easy reach of World Heritage Coast and many towns.

REDRUTH, Cornwall Map ref 1B3

★★–★★★★
2 Units
Sleeping 4–5

MORTHANA FARM HOLIDAYS
Redruth
Contact: Mrs Sally Pearce, Morthana Farm Holidays, Wheal Rose, Scorrier, Redruth TR16 5DF
T: (01209) 890938
F: (01209) 890938

OPEN All Year

Low season per wk
£135.00–£300.00
High season per wk
£345.00–£420.00

Modern, semi-detached cottages. Equipped to a high standard. Suntrap patios and rural views. Friendly animals. Central for all attractions. Beaches nearby. Couples and children welcome.

SOUTH WEST ENGLAND

RUAN HIGH LANES, Cornwall Map ref 1B3

★★★★
2 Units
Sleeping 6–8

The former farmhouse, together with an old stone workshop, have been tastefully converted to provide quality accommodation with modern furnishings and appliances for relaxing and peaceful holidays on a mixed working farm on the beautiful Roseland Peninsula. Private gardens and patios. Many public gardens and attractions nearby. Children/pets welcome.

TRENONA FARM HOLIDAYS – CHY TYAK AND CHY WHEL

Truro
Contact: Mrs Pamela Carbis, Trenona Farm Holidays, Trenona Farm, Ruan High Lanes, Truro TR2 5JS
T: (01872) 501339
F: (01872) 501253
E: pam@trenonafarmholidays.co.uk
I: www.trenonafarmholidays.co.uk

OPEN All Year

Payment accepted: Amex, Mastercard, Switch, Visa

Short breaks available Oct-Mar.

Low season per wk
£220.00–£350.00
High season per wk
£350.00–£640.00

ST AGNES, Cornwall Map ref 1B3

★★★★★
1 Unit
Sleeping 1–5

Spacious detached cottage enjoying the seclusion of woodland with meandering stream. Superbly equipped and with its own private patio, The Owl House is a luxurious base from which to explore Cornwall. Sleeps five. Walks from the doorstep. The lovely village of St Agnes is less than one mile away. Brochure available.

THE OWL HOUSE

St Agnes
Contact: Ms Lyn Hicks, Chy Ser Rosow, Barkla Shop, St Agnes TR5 0XN
T: (01872) 553644
E: enquiries@the-owl-house.co.uk
I: www.the-owl-house.co.uk

OPEN All Year

Payment accepted: Mastercard, Visa

Short breaks available in low season from £180.

Low season per wk
£255.00–£325.00
High season per wk
£325.00–£695.00

★★★-★★★★★
9 Units
Sleeping 2–6

PALMVALE HOLIDAYS

St Agnes
Contact: Mr K Williams & Mrs R Hobson, Duchy Holidays, 11 Boscawen Road, Perranporth TR6 0EP
T: (01872) 552234
F: (01872) 552690
E: enquiries@duchyholidays.co.uk

Semi-detached bungalows in five acres overlooking National Trust coastline and open countryside. Peace and tranquillity. Stunning views. Open all year. Three-bedroomed detached cottage available.

OPEN All Year

Payment accepted: Mastercard, Switch, Visa

Low season per wk
£155.00–£380.00
High season per wk
£390.00–£995.00

WEB

www.visitengland.com

Log on for information and inspiration. The latest information on places to visit, events and quality assessed accommodation.

SOUTH WEST ENGLAND

ST AUSTELL, Cornwall Map ref 1B3 *Tourist Information Centre Tel: (01726) 879500*

★★★★
4 Units
Sleeping 2–6

POLTARROW FARM
St Austell
Contact: Judith Nancarrow, Poltarrow Farm, St Mewan,
St Austell PL26 7DR
T: (01726) 67111
F: (01726) 67111
E: enquire@poltarrow.co.uk
I: www.poltarrow.co.uk

Set in superb countryside, the comfortable and welcoming cottages are well furnished and equipped, with central heating and log fires making them warm and cosy for any season. An all-year, indoor swimming pool, fishing from the lake, friendly animals and farm walks make Poltarrow your ideal holiday spot.

OPEN All Year
Payment accepted:
Switch, Visa

Low season per wk
£150.00–£350.00
High season per wk
£400.00–£900.00

★★★★
7 Units
Sleeping 2–6

TREGONGEEVES FARM HOLIDAY COTTAGES
St Austell
Contact: John & Judith Clemo, Tregongeeves Farm Holiday Cottages, Polgooth, St Austell PL26 7DS
T: (01726) 68202
F: (01726) 68202
E: tregongeeves@tesco.net
I: www.cornwall-holidays.co.uk

Tregongeeves combines quality accommodation with excellent leisure facilities. Guests enjoy exclusive, all year round use of the indoor heated swimming pool, spa bath, gym, recreation room and a professional tennis court. Being located in mid-Cornwall just off the A390 at St Austell, both coastlines are within easy reach.

OPEN All Year
Payment accepted: Delta, Mastercard, Switch, Visa

Low season per wk
£250.00–£450.00
High season per wk
£475.00–£950.00

Short breaks available Nov-Mar inclusive.

ST BLAZEY, Cornwall Map ref 1B2

★★★★
4 Units
Sleeping 2

THE MILL
Par
Contact: Mr John Tipper & Mrs Caroline Wey, The Mill, Prideaux Road, St Blazey, Par PL24 2SR
T: (01726) 810171
F: (01726) 810171
E: enquiries@woodmill-farm.co.uk
I: www.woodmill-farm.co.uk

Payment accepted: Mastercard, Switch, Visa

Low season per wk
£180.00–£190.00
High season per wk
£320.00–£330.00

The Mill – one-bedroomed cottages in former 17thC flour mill tastfully converted. Eden one mile, Lost Gardens six miles. Two local pubs within easy walking. Ideally situated to tour Cornwall.

Special breaks

Many establishments offer special promotions and themed breaks. These are highlighted in red. (All such offers are subject to availability.)

SOUTH WEST ENGLAND

ST CLETHER, Cornwall Map ref 1C2

★★★★
2 Units
Sleeping 2–6

FORGET-ME-NOT COTTAGE
Launceston
Contact: Mr James & Mrs Sheila Kempthorne, St Clether, Trefranck, Launceston PL15 8QN
T: (01566) 86284
E: holidays@trefranck.co.uk
I: www.trefranck.co.uk

Superb location between Bodmin Moor and spectacular North Cornwall Heritage Coastline. On family farm. Tastefully decorated, spacious, yet warm and cosy, real log fire. Well-equipped kitchen, large conservatory, secluded garden. Ideal base for outdoor activities. New for this season: a well-equipped barn conversion. Welcome retreat all year.

OPEN All Year

Long weekends or short breaks welcome – out of school holidays at short notice.

Low season per wk
Min £150.00
High season per wk
Max £600.00

ST ISSEY, Cornwall Map ref 1B2

1 Unit
Sleeping 25

THE MANOR HOUSE
Wadebridge
Contact: Mrs Kirk, The Manor House, St Issey, Wadebridge PL27 7QB
T: (01841) 540346
F: (01841) 540139
E: enquiries@manoractivitycentre.co.uk
I: www.manoractivitycentre.co.uk

Beautiful Grade II Listed Georgian manor-house in village setting, three miles from sandy beaches, Camel Estuary and Padstow. Nine bedrooms, two bathrooms, four shower rooms, luxurious lounge with DVD and widescreen TV and a formal dining room. Full board and activities available for groups. Weekend bookings welcome.

OPEN All Year

Weekend bookings welcome. Christmas and New Year packages, family activity holidays, surfing holidays. Retreat weekends. Hen and stag parties arranged.

Low season per wk
£800.00–£1,350.00
High season per wk
£1,350.00–£2,150.00

ST IVES, Cornwall Map ref 1B3 Tourist Information Centre Tel: (01736) 796297

Rating Applied For

12 Units
Sleeping 2–6

CHY AN EGLOS
St Ives
Contact: Mr David Eddy, Chy An Eglos, 1 St Andrews Street, St Ives TR26 1AH
T: (01736) 795542
F: (01736) 752996
E: david.eddy@chy-an-eglos.co.uk
I: www.chy-an-eglos.co.uk

Superb apartments on the harbour entrance, sleeping from two to six people. Double glazed, centrally heated and with TV and video recorders. Laundry facilities and car parking (in separate car park). Bed linen supplied. Open all year

OPEN All Year

Payment accepted: Delta, Mastercard, Switch, Visa, Euros

Low season per wk
£225.00–£425.00
High season per wk
£375.00–£850.00

Important note Information on accommodation listed in this guide has been supplied by the proprietors. As changes may occur you are advised to check details at the time of booking.

369

SOUTH WEST ENGLAND

ST IVES continued

★★★
7 Units
Sleeping 1–7

CHY MOR AND PREMIER APARTMENTS
St Ives
Contact: Mr Michael Gill, Beach House, The Wharf,
St Ives TR26 1QA
T: (01736) 798798
F: (01736) 796831
I: www.stivesharbour.com

OPEN All Year
Payment accepted: Delta, Mastercard, Switch, Visa

Low season per wk
£155.00–£175.00
High season per wk
£455.00–£650.00

Situated on St Ives harbour front with uninterrupted views of the harbour and bay. Visit our website, www.stivesharbour.com.

ST JUST, Cornwall Map ref 1A3

★★★
1 Unit
Sleeping 1–5

CASPLE COTTAGE
Penzance
Contact: Mr Ken & Mrs Jeni Smith, Higherhouse,
Higherland, Callington PL17 8LD
T: (01579) 370608

OPEN All Year

Low season per wk
Min £195.00
High season per wk
Max £400.00

Miner's cottage, garden, barbecue facilities. Close to village, beaches, prehistoric sites, coastal footpath, Minack. Ideal for bird-watchers and walkers.

ST KEVERNE, Cornwall Map ref 1B3

★★★★
3 Units
Sleeping 2–4

FATTY OWLS
Helston
Contact: Ms Yvonne Cole, Fatty Owls, St Keverne, Helston
TR12 6QQ
T: (01326) 280199
E: trenowethhouse@aol.com

Converted from old stone farm buiildings, these attractive and well-appointed, single-storey cottages are set around a courtyard within a four-acre garden in a peaceful conservation valley. Streamside footpaths to sea/village, coastal/country walks, splendid gardens to visit. Non-smoking, pets welcome. Personally supervised by resident owner.

Low season per wk
Min £160.00
High season per wk
£210.00–£360.00

ST MAWES, Cornwall

See display advertisement on opposite page

 **Location** Complete addresses for properties are not given and the town(s) listed may be a distance from the actual establishment. Please check the precise location at the time of booking.

tregenna CASTLE
St. Ives - Cornwall

Luxury Cottages and Apartments set in a private estate overlooking the fishing harbour of St Ives. Fabulous leisure facilities including indoor/outdoor pools, steam room, sauna, jacuzzi, badminton, squash, tennis and 18 hole golf course.

Phone 01736 795588 or visit www.tregenna-castle.co.uk

SOUTH WEST ENGLAND

SALCOMBE, Devon Map ref 1C3 Tourist Information Centre Tel: (01548) 843927

★★★
1 Unit
Sleeping 1–6

Delightfully-appointed period residence, with magnificent views over harbour and estuary and lying close to shops, pubs, restaurants and ferry to beaches, in this superb sailing resort. Hall, cloaks/shower room, lounge, kitchen/breakfast room, laundry, three bedrooms, bathroom, patio, central heating. Free use of indoor swimming pool.

COXSWAIN'S WATCH

Salcombe
Contact: Mr A Oulsnam, Robert Oulsnam & Co,
79 Hewell Road, Barnt Green, Birmingham B45 8NL
T: (0121) 445 3311
F: (0121) 445 6026
E: barntgreen@oulsnam.net
I: www.oulsnam.net

OPEN All Year

Payment accepted: Delta, Mastercard, Switch, Visa

Low season per wk
£500.00–£550.00
High season per wk
£900.00–£1,300.00

SALISBURY, Wiltshire Map ref 2B3 Tourist Information Centre Tel: (01722) 334956

Rating
Applied For

2 Units
Sleeping 1–2

Freedom to do as you please, in your own time, in your own space, for business, for pleasure, for visiting friends and family or escaping for two days, two weeks or longer – 4TEEN has it all. Rachel said: 'it was a pleasure to return home to 4TEEN each day.'

4TEEN

Salisbury
Contact: Mrs Mary Webb, 11 Hartington Road, Salisbury
SP2 7LG
T: (01722) 340892
F: (01722) 421903
E: enquiries@4teen.biz
I: www.4teen.biz

OPEN All Year

Payment accepted:
Mastercard, Switch, Visa,
Euros

Special rates for 2-night minimum stay: £55pn – 2 nights, £50pn – 3 nights, £48pn – 4 nights.

Low season per wk
Min £285.00
High season per wk
Min £285.00

Map references The map references refer to the colour maps at the front of this guide. The first figure is the map number; the letter and figure which follow indicate the grid reference on the map.

VISITBRITAIN 3-5 STARS ALL PROPERTIES INSPECTED

specialplaces CORNWALL

www.specialplacescornwall.co.uk
Self-catering at its Best

Beautiful waterside and countryside locations including St Mawes, Falmouth, Feock and Truro. A warm welcome awaits you at any time of the year. Convenient for Eden and well-placed for exploring our beautiful area of cornwall.

SPECIAL PLACES IN CORNWALL   TELEPHONE 01872 864400

SOUTH WEST ENGLAND

SALISBURY continued

★★★★
1 Unit
Sleeping 2–4

Newly refurbished, spacious apartment, part of a 19thC Gothic house, five minutes' walk from market square. A contemporary mix of French antiques and modern furnishings with lovely views over mature gardens and the city. Double/twin bedroom, sitting room with sofa bed, fully-equipped kitchen and large bathroom, decorated to the highest standards.

GARDEN FLAT, RAMSEY HOUSE
Salisbury
Contact: Vivien Brown, Ramsey House, 34 Fowlers Road, Salisbury SP1 2QU
T: (01722) 327166 & 07960 993746
E: ramseyhouse@hotmail.com

OPEN All Year

Payment accepted: Mastercard, Switch, Visa, Euros

Baby-sitting by arrangement. Grocery packs to order. Bed and breakfast option. Short breaks available.

Low season per wk
£275.00–£350.00
High season per wk
£350.00–£450.00

★★★★
1 Unit
Sleeping 2–5

SYCAMORE COTTAGE
Salisbury
Contact: Mr Richard & Mrs Cilla Pickett, Melrose Cottage, Lower Road, Quidhampton, Salisbury SP2 9AS
T: (01722) 743160
E: cilla@sycamorecottage.biz
I: www.sycamorecottage.biz

A recently converted stable offering high-quality accommodation in a lovely countryside setting. Salisbury city centre very easily accessible.

OPEN All Year

Low season per wk
£225.00–£275.00
High season per wk
£275.00–£350.00

SALISBURY PLAIN

See under Amesbury, Great Cheverell, Salisbury

SEATON, Devon Map ref 1D2 *Tourist Information Centre Tel: (01297) 21660*

★★★
1 Unit
Sleeping 1–5

Comfortably furnished bungalow on elevated ground in 1.5 acres of gardens. Beautiful, panoramic views of Axe Estuary and sea. Close by are Beer and Branscombe. Lyme Regis seven miles, Sidmouth 10 miles. Excellent centre for touring, walking, sailing, fishing, golf. Full gas central heating, double glazing throughout. Open March to October.

WEST RIDGE BUNGALOW
Seaton
Contact: Mrs Hildegard Fox, West Ridge, Harepath Hill, Seaton EX12 2TA
T: (01297) 22398
F: (01297) 22398
E: foxfamily@westridge.fsbusiness.co.uk
I: www.cottageguide.co.uk/westridge

10% reduction for 2 persons only, throughout booking period.

Low season per wk
£195.00–£295.00
High season per wk
£325.00–£450.00

Quality Assurance Standard

Star ratings and awards were correct at time of going to press but are subject to change. Please check at the time of booking.

372

SOUTH WEST ENGLAND

SHAFTESBURY, Dorset Map ref 2B3 *Tourist Information Centre Tel: (01747) 853514*

★★★–★★★★★

5 Units
Sleeping 2–5

A real family farm in stunning Thomas Hardy countryside. Beautifully equipped, award-winning cottages, full of character, with old beams, log fires etc. Swimming, tennis court, games barn. Children welcome to help feed animals and watch milking. Easy reach Jurassic coast and lovely beaches. Pretty thatched villages and good pubs. Disabled guests welcome.

HARTGROVE FARM
Shaftesbury
Contact: Mrs Susan Smart, Hartgrove Farm, Shaftesbury SP7 0JY
T: (01747) 811830
F: (01747) 811066
E: cottages@hartgrovefarm.co.uk
I: www.hartgrovefarm.co.uk

OPEN All Year

Payment accepted: Amex, Delta, Diners, Mastercard, Switch, Visa

Low season per wk
£250.00–£525.00
High season per wk
£430.00–£695.00

★★★★

2 Units
Sleeping 2–6

VALE FARM HOLIDAY COTTAGES
Blandford Forum
Contact: Mrs Sarah Drake, Vale Farm, Sutton Waldron, Blandford Forum DT11 8PG
T: (01747) 811286
F: (01747) 811286
E: sarah.drake@ukonline.co.uk
I: www.valeholidays.co.uk

OPEN All Year

Low season per wk
£135.00–£245.00
High season per wk
£300.00–£550.00

Luxury barn conversions tucked away on a picturesque dairy farm in one of the prettiest pockets of rural Dorset. A warm welcome awaits.

SHEPTON MALLET, Somerset Map ref 2A2 *Tourist Information Centre Tel: (01749) 345258*

★★★★

4 Units
Sleeping 2–6

Four self-catering cottages converted from traditional farm buildings set around a pretty communal garden, located in a peaceful secluded valley. All cottages fully equipped, central heating and open fires. Ideal centre for exploring Somerset, close to Wells, Glastonbury, Bath and local family attractions. No pets.

KNOWLE FARM COTTAGES
Shepton Mallet
Contact: Mrs Helen Trotman, Knowle Farm, West Compton, Shepton Mallet BA4 4PD
T: (01749) 890482
F: (01749) 890405
E: helen@knowle-farm-cottages.co.uk
I: www.knowle-farm-cottages.co.uk

OPEN All Year

Low season per wk
£155.00–£335.00
High season per wk
£290.00–£470.00

SHEPTON MONTAGUE, Somerset Map ref 2B2

★★★★

1 Unit
Sleeping 1–3

HIGHER FARM
Wincanton
Contact: Mrs C Dimond, Higher Farm, Wincanton BA9 8JJ
T: (01749) 812373
F: (01749) 812373
E: dimond@farm24771.fsnet.co.uk

OPEN All Year

Low season per wk
£200.00–£250.00
High season per wk
£300.00–£350.00

Tastefully converted from an old seed house with oak beams and stone and brick features, this cottage is situated in a delightfully rural village.

SOUTH WEST ENGLAND

SHERBORNE, Dorset Map ref 2B3 *Tourist Information Centre Tel: (01935) 815341*

★★★
1 Unit
Sleeping 4

BLACKBERRY COTTAGE
Sherborne
Contact: Mr John Michael Farr, 17 Marsh Lane, Yeovil
BA21 3BX
T: (01935) 423148

OPEN All Year

Low season per wk
£170.00–£200.00
High season per wk
£260.00–£310.00

An ideal base for discovering the delights of Dorset. This 19thC stone cottage is close to the centre of the historic town of Sherborne.

SIDMOUTH, Devon Map ref 1D2 *Tourist Information Centre Tel: (01395) 516441*

★★★★
7 Units
Sleeping 4–6

Two miles from the World Heritage Coastline and beaches, cradled in 45 acres of idyllic, peaceful valley. Listed, 17thC farmhouse with period cottages, lovingly converted from original farm buildings, each with own delightful, enclosed garden. Studio facilities in restored Victorian kennels. Tennis court, trout pond. 14thC inn and amenities within walking distance.

BOSWELL FARM COTTAGES
Sidmouth
Contact: Mr Brian & Mrs Linda Dillon, Boswell Farm Cottages, Boswell Farm, Harcombe, Sidmouth EX10 0PP
T: (01395) 514162
F: (01395) 514162
E: dillon@boswell-farm.co.uk
I: www.boswell-farm.co.uk

OPEN All Year
Payment accepted:
Mastercard, Visa

25% reduction – 2 people (or 2 people and baby) Nov-Mar (for full week only, excl Bank Holidays).

Low season per wk
£191.00–£282.00
High season per wk
£700.00–£984.00

1 Unit
Sleeping 1–4

HIGHER THORN BARN
Sidmouth
Contact: Mrs Louise Stout, Higher Thorn Cottage, Salcombe Regis, Sidmouth EX10 0PA
T: (01395) 519046

Stone-built barn, converted c1990. Part of Higher Thorn Cottage which has several medieval features. Cottage Grade II Listed.

Low season per wk
Min £170.00
High season per wk
Max £350.00

SIMONSBATH, Somerset Map ref 1C1

★★★–★★★★★
2 Units
Sleeping 2–16

Winstitchen is located in the centre of Exmoor National Park and occupies an outstanding position on the moor, completely secluded yet easily accessible. Simonsbath, a well known Exmoor landmark, is barely a mile with pub and hotel, and Exford with post office, store, newsagent, pub and hotel, a five minute drive away.

WINSTITCHEN FARM
Exmoor
Contact: Jane Organ, Lowerfield Farm, Willersey, Broadway WR11 7HF
T: (01386) 858273
F: (01386) 854608
E: info@exmoor-country-cottages.com
I: www.exmoor-country-cottages.com

OPEN All Year
Payment accepted:
Mastercard, Switch, Visa

Short breaks available minimum 3 nights (excl Christmas and New Year).

Low season per wk
£250.00–£800.00
High season per wk
£375.00–£1,600.00

Accessibility Look for the symbols which indicate National Accessible Scheme standards for hearing and visually impaired guests in addition to standards for guests with mobility impairment. You can find an index of all scheme participants at the back of this guide.

SOUTH WEST ENGLAND

SLAPTON, Devon Map ref 1D3

1 Unit
Sleeping 2–4

MAPLE COTTAGE
Kingsbridge
Contact: Toad Hall Cottages, Elliot House,
Church Street, Kingsbridge TQ7 1BY
T: (01548) 853089
F: (01548) 853086
E: thc@toadhallcottages.com
I: www.toadhallcottages.co.uk

OPEN All Year
Payment accepted: Delta,
Mastercard, Switch, Visa

Low season per wk
£220.00–£280.00
High season per wk
£315.00–£570.00

Comfortable, self-contained first floor apartment within barn conversion. Two bedrooms, bathroom and open plan living/kitchen area. Attractive courtyard setting in rural location.

SOUTH MOLTON, Devon Map ref 1C1

5 Units
Sleeping 2–8

NORTH LEE FARM HOLIDAY COTTAGES
South Molton
Contact: Miss Rebecca Evans, North Lee Farm Holiday
Cottages, Hacche Lane, South Molton EX36 3EH
T: (01598) 740248
F: (01598) 740045
E: beck@northlee.com
I: www.northlee.com

OPEN All Year
Payment accepted:
Mastercard, Visa, Euros

Low season per wk
£220.00–£550.00
High season per wk
£330.00–£800.00

Barn conversions in courtyard setting. Close to Exmoor and North Devon coast. Tranquil location on working dairy farm. Pets welcome. Short breaks available.

SOUTH PETHERTON, Somerset Map ref 1D2

1 Unit
Sleeping 4

TANWYN
South Petherton
Contact: Mr Rodney & Mrs Ann Tanswell,
St Brides Major, Bridgend CF32 0SB
T: (01656) 880524
F: (01656) 880524
E: rodney.tanswell@btinternet.com

OPEN All Year except
Christmas and New Year

Low season per wk
£160.00–£220.00
High season per wk
£250.00–£320.00

Delightful semi-detached cottage in quiet picturesque village. Bathroom and shower room. Sleeps four in three bedrooms. Well-equipped kitchen. Large garden and orchard.

SOUTHAM, Gloucestershire Map ref 2B1

1 Unit
Sleeping 2–4

PRIORY COTTAGE
Southam
Contact: Mr I S Mant, Church Gate, Southam Lane,
Southam, Cheltenham GL52 3NY
T: (01242) 584693
F: (01242) 584693
E: iansmant@hotmail.com

OPEN All Year
Payment accepted: Euros

Short breaks available all year from £120.

Low season per wk
£190.00–£250.00
High season per wk
£250.00–£290.00

Old Cotswold stone cottage in own garden overlooking apple orchard. Cosy and warm in winter with woodburning stove. Two bedrooms, one double, one twin; sitting room, dining room, modern fitted kitchen. Ideal base for Cotswolds, Cheltenham and Area of Outstanding Natural Beauty. Good walking country including Cotswold Way.

Credit card bookings

If you book by telephone and are asked for your credit card number it is advisable to check the proprietor's policy should you cancel your reservation.

SOUTH WEST ENGLAND

STANTON, Gloucestershire Map ref 2B1

★★★
1 Unit
Sleeping 6

CHARITY COTTAGE
Broadway
Contact: Mrs Ryland, Charity Farm, Stanton, Broadway WR12 7NE
T: (01386) 584339
F: (01386) 584270
E: kennethryland@ukonline.co.uk
I: www.myrtle-cottage.co.uk/ryland.htm

Charming Cotswold-stone cottage in picturesque village. Three bedrooms, two bathrooms, spacious accommodation. The pretty garden offers al fresco dining. Village pub five minutes' walk from cottage, and Broadway (two miles) has a selection of pubs and restaurants. Enjoy walking the Cotswold hills, or visit National Trust houses and gardens.

OPEN All Year

Payment accepted: Mastercard, Euros

Short breaks available.

Low season per wk
Min £320.00
High season per wk
Max £550.00

STICKER, Cornwall Map ref 1B3

★★★★★
1 Unit
Sleeping 1–4

GLENLEIGH FARM FISHERY
St Austell
Contact: Mrs Claire Tregunna, Glenleigh Farm Fishery, Sticker, St Austell PL26 7JB
T: (01726) 73154
F: (01726) 77465
E: fishglenleigh@aol.com

OPEN All Year

Low season per wk
£275.00–£500.00
High season per wk
£350.00–£750.00

Beautiful, luxury barn conversion in mid-Cornwall, free coarse fishing for residents, disabled access, patio garden and games room. Sleeps four.

STITHIANS, Cornwall Map ref 1B3

★★★
9 Units
Sleeping 2–8

HIGHER TREWITHEN
Truro
Contact: Mr Neil Pardoe, Higher Trewithen, Truro TR3 7DR
T: (01209) 860863
F: (01209) 860785
E: trewithen@talk21.com
I: www.trewithen.com

Attractive converted cottages and apartments, delightfully situated deep in the Cornish countryside. Ideal central location for discovering Cornwall and within easy reach of north and south coasts. Footpath to Stithians village for pubs and shops. Dogs welcome. Brochure available.

OPEN All Year

Payment accepted: Euros

Short breaks available Oct-Jan (excl Bank Holidays).

Low season per wk
£160.00–£205.00
High season per wk
£355.00–£690.00

STOKE SUB HAMDON, Somerset Map ref 1D2

★★★
1 Unit
Sleeping 2

TOP O HILL
Stoke sub Hamdon
Contact: Mrs Mary Gane, Percombe, Stoke sub Hamdon
TA14 6RD
T: (01935) 822089

Annexe of 150-year-old house in private road, close to A303. Excellent touring base for many places of interest. Garden with garden furniture, own entrance. Open spring-autumn.

Low season per wk
£90.00–£150.00
High season per wk
£150.00–£200.00

Important note Information on accommodation listed in this guide has been supplied by the proprietors. As changes may occur you are advised to check details at the time of booking.

376

SOUTH WEST ENGLAND

STOW-ON-THE-WOLD, Gloucestershire Map ref 2B1 *Tourist Information Centre Tel: (01451) 831082*

★★★
1 Unit
Sleeping 2–3

BOX COTTAGE
Broadwell
Contact: Mr Bob Johnston, Poplars Barn, Evenlode, Moreton-in-Marsh GL56 0NN
T: (01608) 650816
F: (01608) 652996
I: www.cottagesinstow.com

Charming well equipped cottage in quiet village, exposed beams throughout. Good pub in a few hundred yards. Woodburning stove, logs supplied in the winter.

OPEN All Year
Payment accepted: Delta, Diners, Mastercard, Switch, Visa

Low season per wk
£200.00–£250.00
High season per wk
£300.00–£350.00

★★★★★
4 Units
Sleeping 1–4

BROAD OAK COTTAGES
Cheltenham
Contact: Mrs Wilson, The Counting House, Stow-on-the-Wold, Cheltenham GL54 1AL
T: (01451) 830794
F: (01451) 830794
E: mary@broadoakcottages.fsnet.co.uk
I: www.broadoakcottages.fsnet.co.uk

Delightful cottages situated within a few minutes' walk of the centre of Stow. The cottages are furnished and equipped to the highest standard comprising both double and twin bedrooms, full central heating, log fires, and fully modernised bathrooms and kitchens; parking, south facing patios, gardens and lovely views.

OPEN All Year

Short breaks available (except in high season).

Low season per wk
Min £275.00
High season per wk
Max £540.00

★★★
1 Unit
Sleeping 4

HORSESHOES
Stow-on-the-Wold
Contact: Mr Bob Johnston, Poplars Barn, Evenlode, Moreton-in-Marsh GL56 0NN
T: (01608) 650816
F: (01608) 652996
I: www.cottagesinstow.com

Tucked away from the hustle and bustle on a quiet, no-through lane with private parking. Recently refurbished to a high standard. Near local pubs and restaurants.

OPEN All Year
Payment accepted: Delta, Diners, Mastercard, Switch, Visa

Low season per wk
£200.00–£250.00
High season per wk
£350.00–£450.00

★★★
1 Unit
Sleeping 2–5

JOHNSTON COTTAGE
Stow-on-the-Wold
Contact: Mrs Yvonne Johnston, Poplars Barn, Evenlode, Moreton-in-Marsh GL56 0NN
T: (01608) 650816
F: (01608) 652996
I: www.cottagesinstow.com

Charming stone terraced cottage with exposed beams and inglenook. Hanging baskets and tubs with garden furniture on terrace. Five minutes' walk from local pubs and restaurants.

OPEN All Year
Payment accepted: Delta, Diners, Mastercard, Switch, Visa

Low season per wk
£200.00–£250.00
High season per wk
£350.00–£400.00

SOUTH WEST ENGLAND

STOW-ON-THE-WOLD continued

★★★★–★★★★★
5 Units
Sleeping 2-6

PARK FARM HOLIDAY COTTAGES
Cheltenham
Contact: Mrs Tiana Ricketts, Park Farm, Maugersbury, Cheltenham GL54 1HP
T: (01451) 830227
F: (01451) 870568
E: parkfarm.cottages@virgin.net

Situated on owners' mixed farm in small hamlet. Less than 10 minutes' walk from Stow-on-the-Wold where there are excellent pubs and restaurants. Four south-facing, single-storey detached cottages with wonderful views. Romantic four-poster beds in double rooms. Also cosy, two-bedroomed wing to farmhouse. Logburning stoves. Linen, towels, electricity, heating included.

OPEN All Year

Payment accepted: Amex, Delta, Mastercard, Switch, Visa

Short breaks available.

Low season per wk £200.00–£300.00
High season per wk £350.00–£600.00

★★★★
1 Unit
Sleeping 4

2 UNION STREET
Stow-on-the-Wold
Contact: Ms Spiers, Cottage in the Country, Forest Gate, Frog Lane, Milton-under-Wychwood OX7 6JZ
T: (01993) 831495
F: (01993) 831095
E: info@cottageinthecountry.co.uk
I: www.cottageinthecountry.co.uk

Delightful Victorian Cotswold-stone semi-detached cottage, in a quiet street just five minutes' walk from the Market Square. Recently renovated and comfortably furnished, but retaining many original features including stripped pine doors, flagstone floors and an original range in the breakfast kitchen. Conservatory at the rear overlooks pleasant enclosed garden.

OPEN All Year

Payment accepted: Mastercard, Switch, Visa

Low season per wk Min £270.00
High season per wk £460.00–£485.00

★★★
1 Unit
Sleeping 4

WELLS COTTAGE
Cheltenham
Contact: Mr A G Williams, Woodlands, 5 Glebe Close, Stow-on-the-Wold, Cheltenham GL54 1DJ
T: (01451) 830045

Delightful house in an Area of Outstanding Natural Beauty, close to town centre, shops and restaurants.

OPEN All Year

Low season per wk £270.00–£300.00
High season per wk £300.00–£395.00

SUTTON POYNTZ, Dorset Map ref 2B3

★★★★
1 Unit
Sleeping 1-4

EBENEZER COTTAGE
Weymouth
Contact: Cathy Varley, Hiscocks Farm, Moorside, Sturminster Newton DT10 1HF
T: 07778 524199
E: info@ebenezercottage.co.uk
I: www.ebenezercottage.co.uk

Three-bedroom terraced cottage on picturesque millstream lane. Sutton Poyntz lies in a horseshoe of hills, along which runs the South West Coastal Path. Rolling downs and secret valleys provide access to beautiful scenery. At the heart of the World Heritage Site, there are spectacular views towards the Jurassic coastline.

OPEN All Year

Low season per wk £305.00–£465.00
High season per wk £520.00–£680.00

SOUTH WEST ENGLAND

SUTTON WALDRON, Dorset Map ref 2B3

★★★
1 Unit
Sleeping 1–4

DAIRY COTTAGE
Blandford Forum
Contact: Mary Pope, Broadlea Farm, Sutton Waldron,
Blandford Forum DT11 8NS
T: (01747) 811330
F: (01747) 811330
E: maryp2@tinyworld.co.uk

OPEN All Year

Low season per wk
Max £250.00
High season per wk
Max £300.00

Fully-equipped cottage amidst lovely countryside, south of Shaftesbury. Two bedrooms, spacious lounge/dining room, separate kitchen and bathroom. Good base for visiting tourist attractions.

SWANAGE, Dorset Map ref 2B3 Tourist Information Centre Tel: (01929) 422885

★★★★
1 Unit
Sleeping 6

PURBECK CLIFFS
Swanage
Contact: Mrs Sue McWilliams, Purbeck Cliffs,
3 Boundary Close, Swanage BH19 2JY
T: (01929) 424352
I: www.purbeckcliffs.co.uk

OPEN All Year

Low season per wk
£525.00–£595.00
High season per wk
£795.00–£995.00

Ground floor apartment with exclusive use of own swimming pool, sauna, snooker room. In 1.5-acre garden next to 300-acre country park. Jurassic coastal path.

TAUNTON, Somerset Map ref 1D1 Tourist Information Centre Tel: (01823) 336344

★★★
1 Unit
Sleeping 5

HIGHER HOUSE
Taunton
Contact: Mrs Kirsten Horton, Higher House, Hillcommon,
Taunton TA4 1DU
T: (01823) 400570
F: (01823) 400765
E: tedandkirsten@tiscali.co.uk
I: www.visitwestcountry.com/higherhouse

A spacious, airy apartment on the second floor of a converted barn standing in five acres, featuring a lake, lovely gardens, as well as fields and woodland areas. Fully equipped, centrally heated, and within walking distance of the pub serving tasty meals. Excellent touring base, with easy access to north and south coasts, and Taunton.

OPEN All Year except
Christmas and New Year

Short breaks available.

Low season per wk
£200.00–£245.00
High season per wk
£245.00–£365.00

TAVISTOCK, Devon Map ref 1C2 Tourist Information Centre Tel: (01822) 612938

★★★
1 Unit
Sleeping 2–5

CEDAR LODGE
Tavistock
Contact: Mr & Mrs Ashe, Cedar Lodge, Heathfield,
Tavistock PL19 0LQ
T: (01822) 810038
E: sandra@acorncot1.fsnet.co.uk
I: www.geocities.com/acorncottage

OPEN All Year

Low season per wk
£90.00–£120.00
High season per wk
£350.00–£380.00

Cedar Lodge, a spacious, colonial-style bungalow set in quiet rural location central to beaches and many recreational activities. Close Dartmoor National Park. Send for brochure.

Location Complete addresses for properties are not given and the town(s) listed may be a distance from the actual establishment. Please check the precise location at the time of booking.

SOUTH WEST ENGLAND

TAVISTOCK continued

★★★★
1 Unit
Sleeping 1–4

EDGEMOOR COTTAGE
Tavistock
Contact: Mrs Mary Susan Fox, Edgemoor, Middlemoor, Tavistock PL19 9DY
T: (01822) 612259
F: (01822) 617625

Attractive country cottage in peaceful hamlet. Two en suite bedrooms (one twin, one double, both with TV), kitchen/dining room, upstairs living room leading into a sun lounge/diner with patio overlooking fields. Perfect base to explore Dartmoor, Devon and Cornwall. North and south coasts are within an hour's drive.

OPEN All Year

£25 discount to holidaymakers booking a second week with us. £25 discount to holidaymakers booking a subsequent holiday with us.

Low season per wk
£200.00–£300.00
High season per wk
£300.00–£400.00

★★★
1 Unit
Sleeping 2–4

HIGHER CHADDLEHANGER FARM
Tavistock
Contact: Mrs Cole, Higher Chaddlehanger Farm, Tavistock PL19 0LG
T: (01822) 810268
F: (01822) 810268

Holiday flatlet in farmhouse on beef and sheep farm, close to moors. Own entrance, private garden.

OPEN All Year

Low season per wk
Min £140.00
High season per wk
Min £140.00

★★★★
1 Unit
Sleeping 1–6

MOORVIEW COTTAGE
Tavistock
Contact: Mrs Elaine Mackintosh, Moorview Cottage, Moorview, Cudlipptown, Peter Tavy, Tavistock PL19 9LZ
T: (01822) 810271
F: (01822) 810082
E: wts@dartmoor-holidays.fsnet.co.uk
I: www.dartmoor-holidays.com

Comfortable, well-furnished cottage in quiet, rural location with two double bedrooms, one twin-bedded room and two WCs. An ideal base for exploring Devon and Cornwall, for walking or simply relaxing. Historic market town of Tavistock within a 10-minute drive.

OPEN All Year

Short breaks available from 1 Nov 2004–18 Mar 2005. Reduced rates when only 2 people occupying the cottage – please quote 5WTS.

Low season per wk
£180.00–£300.00
High season per wk
£300.00–£525.00

TAYNTON, Gloucestershire Map ref 2B1

★★★★
1 Unit
Sleeping 1–2

OWLS BARN
Gloucester
Contact: Mrs Barbara Goodwin, Owls Barn, Coldcroft Farm, Glasshouse Lane, Gloucester GL19 3HJ
T: (01452) 831290
F: (01452) 831544
E: goodies@coldcroft.freeserve.co.uk
I: www.coldcroft.freeserve.co.uk

Coldcroft Farm has an equestrian centre, all-weather arena, livery yard. Tastefully converted barn, twin beds, shower included. Kitchen/diner, sitting room. Excellent views from French windows/balcony.

OPEN All Year

Low season per wk
£195.00–£295.00
High season per wk
£195.00–£295.00

Symbols The symbols in each entry give information about services and facilities. A key to these symbols appears at the back of this guide.

SOUTH WEST ENGLAND

TEIGNGRACE, Devon Map ref 1D2

★★★
2 Units
Sleeping 4–5

TWELVE OAKS HOLIDAY COTTAGES
Newton Abbot
Contact: Mrs Gale, Twelve Oaks Farm, Newton Abbot
TQ12 6QT
T: (01626) 352769
F: (01626) 352769

Low season per wk
£230.00–£280.00
High season per wk
£300.00–£410.00

220-acre beef farm. Working farm bordered by the River Teign, on the edge of the village of Teigngrace. Carefully converted cottages, each with own patio. Outdoor heated swimming pool. Open May to September.

TEMPLE GUITING, Gloucestershire Map ref 2B1

★★★★
4 Units
Sleeping 3–6

All of our luxuriously appointed 19thC cottages are spacious and centrally located, each having its own enclosed garden and parking and situated in a quiet area of Bourton-on-the-Water. They are a short walk to the many attractions of this lovely historic town. Children and pets welcome.

HATTIE'S, LUCY'S, CHAPEL AND JACK'S

Bourton-on-the-Water
Contact: Miss Pippa Arnott, Cotswold Cottage Company, Wells Head, Temple Guiting, Cheltenham GL54 5RR
T: (01451) 850560
F: 08701 280033
E: cotscotco@msn.com
I: www.cotswoldcottage.co.uk

OPEN All Year

Payment accepted: Amex, Delta, Mastercard, Switch, Visa

Low season per wk
£340.00–£475.00
High season per wk
£475.00–£595.00

Short breaks available out of season – minimum 3-night stay.

THORVERTON, Devon Map ref 1D2

★★★
1 Unit
Sleeping 6

RATCLIFFE FARM
Exeter
Contact: Mr & Mrs Ayre, Ratcliffe Farm, Thorverton, Exeter EX5 5PN
T: (01392) 860434
E: ayre.ratcliffe@virgin.net

OPEN All Year

Payment accepted: Delta, Mastercard, Switch, Visa

Low season per wk
Min £280.00
High season per wk
Max £500.00

Thatched farmhouse, spacious and comfortable, full of original features. One mile from pretty cobbled village in Exe Valley. Central for West Country coasts and moors.

TINTAGEL, Cornwall Map ref 1B2

★★★
1 Unit
Sleeping 6

SUNNYSIDE
Tintagel
Contact: Mr & Mrs Hansen, Bramblegate, West Green Common, Hartley Wintney, Hook RG27 8JD
T: (01252) 843986 & 07960 356428
E: hansen_harry@hotmail.com

OPEN All Year except Christmas and New Year

Low season per wk
£150.00–£275.00
High season per wk
£300.00–£500.00

Four-bedroomed traditional Cornish cottage near spectacular coastline and Tintagel castle. Footpath to Trebarwith Strand – sand and surfing. Excellent pubs nearby. Enclosed garden. Private parking.

★★★
1 Unit
Sleeping 1–5

TREGEATH COTTAGE
Tintagel
Contact: Mrs Edwina Broad, Davina, Trevillett, Tintagel
PL34 0HL
T: (01840) 770217
F: (01840) 770217

OPEN All Year

Low season per wk
Min £110.00
High season per wk
Max £410.00

Old modernised detached cottage, built of stone and slate. Coal grate, six night-storage heaters, TV/video, payphone, microwave. One dog, no cats. Parking space. Washing machine. Separate tumble dryer.

SOUTH WEST ENGLAND

TIVERTON, Devon Map ref 1D2 *Tourist Information Centre Tel: (01884) 255827*

★★★★
1 Unit
Sleeping 1–6

LILAC COTTAGE
Tiverton
Contact: Mrs Venner, Lilac Cottage, Battens Farm, Sampford Peverell, Tiverton EX16 7EE
T: (01884) 820226
I: www.cottageguide.co.uk/battensfarm

Lovely secluded country cottage with large mature walled garden. Large farm kitchen, cosy beamed sitting room, three comfortable bedrooms. The Grand Western Canal runs through our farm, with pleasant walks and cycling to local village pubs. Central for Exmoor, Dartmoor, north and south coasts and National Trust properties.

OPEN All Year

Low season per wk
£190.00–£250.00
High season per wk
£250.00–£475.00

★★★★
13 Units
Sleeping 2–10

OLD BRIDWELL HOLIDAY COTTAGES
Cullompton
Contact: Ms Jackie Kind, Old Bridwell Holiday Cottages, Uffculme, Cullompton EX15 3BU
T: (01884) 841464
E: jackie@oldbridwell.co.uk
I: www.oldbridwell.co.uk

Clustered around the thatched pumphouse, each of our spacious, individually styled cottages offers home from home comfort. Our extensive grounds have a safe children's play area, a restored, walled fruit garden, and with the whole of Devon awaiting your discovery, where better?

OPEN All Year

Discounts for reduced occupancy.

Low season per wk
£200.00–£325.00
High season per wk
£500.00–£1,034.00

★★★–★★★★★
5 Units
Sleeping 1–9

WEST PITT FARM
Tiverton
Contact: Ms Susanne Westgate, West Pitt Farm, Whitnage, Tiverton EX16 7DU
T: (01884) 820296
F: (01884) 820818
E: susannewestgate@yahoo.com
I: www.fisheries.co.uk/westpitt

Delightful stable conversions and 16thC cottage with recently fitted farmhouse kitchen, living room with open fireplace. Set in glorious farmland, West Pitt offers an indoor heated pool and sauna, fishing, walking, tennis and an excellent games room. Well placed for Exmoor, Dartmoor and North and South Devon.

OPEN All Year
Payment accepted: Euros

Short breaks available – 3 or 4 nights.

Low season per wk
£250.00–£460.00
High season per wk
£410.00–£900.00

Map references The map references refer to the colour maps at the front of this guide. The first figure is the map number; the letter and figure which follow indicate the grid reference on the map.

SOUTH WEST ENGLAND

TIVINGTON, Somerset Map ref 1D1

★★★★
1 Unit
Sleeping 1–5

TETHINSTONE COTTAGE
Minehead
Contact: Mr Nicholas Challis, Tethinstone Cottage, Minehead TA24 8SX
T: (01643) 706757
F: (01643) 706757

Very comfortable thatched cottage, secluded but not isolated, in idyllic position between Minehead and Porlock. Charges include all electricity, hot water and heating.

OPEN All Year

Low season per wk
£350.00–£410.00
High season per wk
£430.00–£500.00

TODENHAM, Gloucestershire Map ref 2B1

★★★★
1 Unit
Sleeping 1–2

APPLEGATE
Todenham
Contact: Mrs Crump, Applegate, The Retreat, Springbank, Moreton-in-Marsh GL56 9PA
T: (01608) 651307

Self contained Cotswold-stone cottage annex furnished to high standard. Twin beds, power shower, garden furniture, off-road parking next to cottage. Conveniently placed for visiting Stratford-upon-Avon, Warwick Castle, Batsford Arboretum, Chipping Campden and many other beauty spots. Trains to London and Oxford run from Moreton-in-Marsh.

OPEN All Year

Low season per wk
£220.00–£260.00
High season per wk
£260.00–£310.00

TORQUAY, Torbay Map ref 1D2 Tourist Information Centre Tel: 0906 680 1268 (Premium rate number)

★★
5 Units
Sleeping 2–4

ATHERTON HOLIDAY FLATS
Torquay
Contact: Mrs Kaye, 41 Morgan Avenue, Torquay TQ2 5RR
T: (01803) 296884

Centrally located, our clean, modern, fully equipped flats offer excellent value for money.

OPEN All Year

Low season per wk
£80.00–£150.00
High season per wk
£145.00–£250.00

★★★
9 Units
Sleeping 2–6

BARRAMORE HOLIDAY FLATS
Torquay
Contact: Mr & Mrs Trevor Ward, Barramore Holiday Flats, Solsbro Road, Chelston, Torquay TQ2 6PF
T: (01803) 607105
E: holidays@barramore.co.uk
I: www.barramore.co.uk

Friendly, welcoming, well-equipped, self-contained holiday flats. Heated outdoor swimming pool, garden. Near train station, beach, Riviera Centre. Short stroll to Cockington, Torquay town/harbour.

OPEN All Year
Payment accepted: Delta, Mastercard, Switch, Visa

Low season per wk
£115.00–£230.00
High season per wk
£235.00–£485.00

Quality Assurance Standard
Star ratings and awards were correct at time of going to press but are subject to change. Please check at the time of booking.

383

SOUTH WEST ENGLAND

TORQUAY continued

★★★
5 Units
Sleeping 2–6

An elegant, Tudor-style house built in 1888 and set in a sunny, pleasant garden. Well situated in a conservation area, only 500m from harbour, shops and entertainment. Comfortable, self-contained and well-equipped apartments. Colour TV and microwaves. Bath or shower room. Bed linen. Guest laundry. Central heating. Private car park.

BEDFORD HOUSE
Torquay
Contact: Mrs MacDonald-Smith, Bedford House, 517 Babbacombe Road, Torquay TQ1 1HJ
T: (01803) 296995
F: (01803) 296995
E: bedfordhotorquay@btconnect.com
I: www.bedfordhousetorquay.co.uk

OPEN All Year

Payment accepted: Delta, Mastercard, Switch, Visa

Short breaks available Oct–Apr, minimum 3 nights.

Low season per wk
£147.00–£170.00
High season per wk
£305.00–£430.00

★★★★★
17 Units
Sleeping 1–8

A new concept in quality suite accommodation. Purpose-built quality suites with one to three bedrooms and one to three bathrooms, 12-hour reception service. Dining concessions at nearby award-winning restaurants. Seafront location. 1995 'England for Excellence' Self-Catering Holiday of the Year award winners.

THE CORBYN SUITES AND PENTHOUSES
Torquay
Contact: The Corbyn Suites And Penthouses, Torbay Road, Torquay TQ2 6RH
T: (01803) 215595
F: (01803) 200568
I: www.thecorbyn.co.uk

OPEN All Year

Payment accepted: Mastercard, Switch, Visa

Low season per wk
£413.00–£815.00
High season per wk
£650.00–£1,373.00

★★★
5 Units
Sleeping 1–2

LINDEN HOUSE HOLIDAYS
Torquay
Contact: Keran Reilly, Linden House Holidays, Ruckamore Road, Chelston, Torquay TQ2 6HF
T: (01803) 607333
E: info@lindenholidays.com
I: www.lindenholidays.com

Tucked away in a secluded area of Torquay. Views across the bay, close to harbour, seafront and town centre. Short breaks available Oct–Mar.

OPEN All Year

Low season per wk
£100.00–£200.00
High season per wk
£200.00–£318.00

Town index

This can be found at the back of the guide. If you know where you want to stay the index will give you the page number listing accommodation in your chosen town, city or village.

384

SOUTH WEST ENGLAND

TORQUAY continued

★★★
24 Units
Sleeping 1–6

Well-appointed, self-contained apartments providing superior accommodation. Close to shops and seafront and an ideal base for touring. Superb leisure facilities including indoor/outdoor pools, spa, sauna and gymnasium. Beauty salon, solarium, games room, licensed bar and restaurant also available.

MAXTON LODGE HOLIDAY APARTMENTS
Torquay
Contact: Mr Richard Hassell, Rousdown Road, Torquay
TQ2 6PB
T: (01803) 607811
F: (01803) 605357
E: stay@redhouse-hotel.co.uk
I: www.redhouse-hotel.co.uk

OPEN All Year

Payment accepted: Delta, Mastercard, Switch, Visa

Fully-serviced apartments available with a choice of meals built into an inclusive tariff.

Low season per wk
£178.00–£280.00
High season per wk
£240.00–£750.00

★★★
6 Units
Sleeping 2–6

Beautifully appointed, spacious, Victorian, self-contained apartments in level woodland setting in exclusive, peaceful conservation area. Walks through woods to beaches, close to excellent shops. One mile from harbour. Regular bus service. Gardens, off-road parking. All accommodation is well equipped, tastefully decorated and immaculately maintained. Pets and children welcome.

MOORCOT SELF-CONTAINED HOLIDAY APARTMENTS
Torquay
Contact: Mrs Margaret Neilson, Moorcot Self-Contained Holiday Apartments, Kents Road, Wellswood, Torquay
TQ1 2NN
T: (01803) 293710
E: holidayflats@moorcot.com
I: www.moorcot.com

OPEN All Year

Short breaks Oct-Apr, 4 nights for the price of 3.

Low season per wk
£120.00–£210.00
High season per wk
£220.00–£400.00

★★★★
8 Units
Sleeping 2–6

MUNTHAM LUXURY HOLIDAY APARTMENTS
Torquay
Contact: Mr Peter & Mrs Trudie Cross, Muntham Luxury Holiday Apartments, Barrington Road, Wellswood, Torquay TQ1 1SG
T: (01803) 292958
F: (01803) 291715
E: muntham@btinternet.com
I: www.theenglishriviera.co.uk

OPEN All Year

Payment accepted: Delta, Mastercard, Switch, Visa

Low season per wk
£140.00–£290.00
High season per wk
£200.00–£420.00

Gracious Victorian villa with large gardens and car park. Quiet residential area close to local shops, beaches and Torbay. Resident proprietors.

Accessibility Look for the symbols which indicate National Accessible Scheme standards for hearing and visually impaired guests in addition to standards for guests with mobility impairment. You can find an index of all scheme participants at the back of this guide.

SOUTH WEST ENGLAND

TORQUAY continued

★★★
18 Units
Sleeping 1–5

SOUTH SANDS APARTMENTS
Torquay
Contact: Mr Paul & Mrs Deborah Moorhouse, South Sands Apartments, Torbay Road, Torquay TQ2 6RG
T: (01803) 293521
F: (01803) 293502
E: info@southsands.co.uk
I: www.southsands.co.uk

OPEN All Year

Payment accepted: Delta, Mastercard, Switch, Visa, Euros

Low season per wk
£120.00–£200.00
High season per wk
£235.00–£440.00

Short breaks and mid-week bookings in low season. Holiday cancellation insurance included. Discount available 2 weeks or more.

Specifically designed holiday apartments offering a high degree of comfort and cleanliness. Spacious and tastefully decorated with fitted kitchens. Apartments with bath or shower. No meters. Towels available upon request. Ground and first floor only. Seafront location. Beach 100yds. Main bus route. Families and couples only. Parking available.

★★★
19 Units
Sleeping 1–6

SUNNINGDALE APARTMENTS
Torquay
Contact: Mr Allan Carr, Sunningdale Apartments, 11 Babbacombe Downs Road, Torquay TQ1 3LF
T: (01803) 325786
F: (01803) 329611
I: www.sunningdaleapartments.co.uk

OPEN All Year

Payment accepted: Euros

Low season per wk
£175.00–£295.00
High season per wk
£350.00–£625.00

Spacious apartments, many with stunning sea views. Self-contained with bathroom and shower, fitted kitchen and lounge with dining area. Large car park, laundry room, gardens. All double glazed with sun patio and central heating. Level walk to shops, restaurants, bar and theatre. Excellent touring centre.

★★–★★★
4 Units
Sleeping 1–6

WESTCOURT HOLIDAY FLATS
Torquay
Contact: Mr John Lawton, Westcourt Holiday Flats, 108 Westhill Road, Torquay TQ1 4NT
T: (01803) 311703
E: westcourtholidayflats@hotmail.com
I: www.westcourtholidayflats.co.uk

OPEN All Year

Low season per wk
£95.00–£395.00
High season per wk
£300.00–£480.00

Westcourt is a large, Georgian house that has been tastefully converted into spacious self contained holiday flats; easy walk to St Marychurch shopping precinct, model village, Babbacombe Downs and Cliff Railway to Oddicombe Beach. Heated swimming pool, poolside barbecue and on-site parking.

Credit card bookings
If you book by telephone and are asked for your credit card number it is advisable to check the proprietor's policy should you cancel your reservation.

SOUTH WEST ENGLAND

TORRINGTON, Devon Map ref 1C2 Tourist Information Centre Tel: (01805) 626140

★★★★
1 Unit
Sleeping 1–10

2 LITTLE SILVER
Torrington
Contact: Mrs A Taylor, 67 Torwood Lane, Whyteleafe CR3 0HD
T: (020) 8763 0796
F: (020) 8763 0796
E: admin@devonshire-cottages.co.uk
I: www.devonshire-cottages.co.uk

OPEN All Year
Payment accepted: Mastercard, Visa

Low season per wk £325.00–£395.00
High season per wk £595.00–£695.00

Superb six-bedroomed Georgian home, sleeps 10. Minutes from RHS Rosemoor and close to Bideford and beaches.

★★★
6 Units
Sleeping 4–6

STOWFORD LODGE & SOUTH HILL COTTAGES
Torrington
Contact: Mrs Sally Milsom, Stowford Lodge & South Hill Cottages, Langtree, Torrington EX38 8NU
T: (01805) 601540
F: (01805) 601487
E: stowford@dial.pipex.com
I: www.stowford.dial.pipex.com

OPEN All Year
Payment accepted: Delta, Mastercard, Switch, Visa

Low season per wk £210.00–£340.00
High season per wk £270.00–£540.00

Delightful cottages converted from Victorian stone farm buildings. Heated indoor pool. Also, pair of period cottages on edge of farm. Pets welcome.

TOTNES, Devon Map ref 1D2 Tourist Information Centre Tel: (01803) 863168

★★★★
1 Unit
Sleeping 1–8

CASTLE FOOT
Totnes
Contact: Mr Hales, 18 South Street, Totnes TQ9 5DZ
T: (01803) 865282
E: davidg.r.hales@sagainternet.co.uk

OPEN All Year

Low season per wk £195.00–£285.00
High season per wk £390.00–£500.00

Four-bedroomed house right in the centre of this Elizabethan town, set in rolling South Hams countryside. Near castle. Dartmoor and many beaches all within a short drive.

TREBETHERICK, Cornwall Map ref 1B2

★★–★★★★
1 Unit
Sleeping 14

EVERGREEN LODGE
Wadebridge
Contact: Mr Wright, Nyetimber, Chiltern Road, Amersham HP6 5PH
T: (01494) 726453
F: (01494) 726453
I: www.selfcatering-evergreenlodge.com

Situated on the Trebetherick headland just behind the magnificent Greenaway cliffs, Evergreen Lodge is a spacious, well-equipped, recently refurbished seaside family house. Easy walk to safe beach and to surfing beach. Nearby golf, windsurfing, cliff walking and many attractions within easy reach. Ideal for small children.

OPEN All Year

3-night stays available Sep-May (excl Christmas, New Year, Easter and half-term weeks).

Low season per wk £900.00–£1,100.00
High season per wk £1,300.00–£2,100.00

TRURO, Cornwall

See display advertisement on page 388

UPTON ST LEONARDS, Gloucestershire Map ref 2B1

★★
2 Units
Sleeping 1–4

HILL FARM COTTAGES
Gloucester
Contact: Ms Margaret McLellan, Hill Farm, Upton Hill, Gloucester GL4 8DA
T: (01452) 614081

OPEN All Year

Low season per wk Min £180.00
High season per wk Min £260.00

Two miles from Gloucester with panoramic views of the Cotswolds. Close to dry ski slope and golfing facilities. Ideal for walking. Country pub nearby providing food.

387

SOUTH WEST ENGLAND

WATCHET, Somerset Map ref 1D1

★★★★
6 Units
Sleeping 2–8

THE CROFT HOLIDAY COTTAGES
Watchet
Contact: Mr & Mrs Musgrave, The Croft Holiday
Cottages, The Croft, Anchor Street, Watchet TA23 0BY
T: (01984) 631121
F: (01984) 631134
E: croftcottages@talk21.com
I: www.cottagessomerset.com

OPEN All Year

Low season per wk
£130.00–£230.00
High season per wk
£360.00–£580.00

Cottages and bungalows in quiet backwater location. Lawned children's play area. Heated indoor pool. Individual barbecues. Easy level walking to shops and harbour/ marina etc.

WATERROW, Somerset Map ref 1D1

★★★
8 Units
Sleeping 1–5

EXMOOR GATE LODGES
Taunton
Contact: Mrs Sue Gallagher, Whipcott Heights,
Holcombe Rogus, Wellington TA21 0NA
T: (01823) 672339
F: (01823) 672339
E: bookings@oldlimekiln.freeserve.co.uk

OPEN All Year

Low season per wk
Max £170.00
High season per wk
Max £520.00

Lodges set on wooded hillside with panoramic views, stream and abundant wildlife. Modern interiors, comfortably furnished; pets welcome in some units.

WELLS, Somerset Map ref 2A2 *Tourist Information Centre Tel: (01749) 672552*

★★★★
2 Units
Sleeping 2–4

THE POTTING SHED HOLIDAYS
Glastonbury
Contact: Mr & Mrs Van Bergen-Henegouwen, Potting Shed Holidays, Harters Hill Cottage, Pillmoor Lane, Wells BA5 1RF
T: (01749) 672857
F: (01749) 679925
I: www.pottingshedholidays.co.uk

OPEN All Year

Short breaks – 3 and 4 nights. See website for special promotions.

Low season per wk
£250.00–£350.00
High season per wk
£350.00–£750.00

We all know what a potting shed is – a place to withdraw and potter. Within the surroundings of Glastonbury and Wells, we offer a haven to hide in, a respite from the stresses of everyday life and, most importantly, a place to nurture, renew and restore the spirit. Ideal for dog owners and mature guests.

 Colour maps Colour maps at the front of this guide pinpoint all places under which you will find accommodation listed.

...a secluded hamlet of contemporary holiday cottages

An oasis of serenity in the centre of Cornwall's beauty and life... wherever the mood takes you is only a pebbles throw away.

Relax in contemporary cottages in spectacular countryside. Leisure facilities and Café Bar on your doorstep; golf, sailing and cycling close by.

Cornwall's new secret. Opening Whitsun 2005.

Ring for a brochure now.

01872 862194
www.the-valley.co.uk

SOUTH WEST ENGLAND

WELLS continued

★★★
1 Unit
Sleeping 6

VICARS' CLOSE HOLIDAY HOUSE
Wells
Contact: Mrs Debbie Jones, Cathedral Office, Chain Gate, Cathedral Green, Wells BA5 2UE
T: (01749) 674483
F: (01749) 832210
E: visits@wellscathedral.uk.net

OPEN All Year

Payment accepted: Amex, Delta, Mastercard, Switch, Visa

Low season per wk
£500.00–£625.00
High season per wk
£625.00–£750.00

Beautiful 14thC house in the oldest continuously inhabited street in Europe. In the shadow of Wells Cathedral and a short walk from the city centre and the Bishop's Palace. Short drive to Cheddar, Wookey Hole, Glastonbury, 35 minutes' drive to Bath or Bristol. Wonderful walks on the Mendip Hills.

WEMBURY, Devon Map ref 1C3

★★★–★★★★★
5 Units
Sleeping 2–7

TRAINE FARM
Plymouth
Contact: Mrs Rowland, Traine Farm, Wembury, Plymouth PL9 0EW
T: (01752) 862264
F: (01752) 862264
E: traine.cottages@btopenworld.com
I: www.traine-holiday-cottages.co.uk

OPEN All Year

Payment accepted: Amex, Delta, Mastercard, Switch, Visa, Euros

Low season per wk
£160.00–£250.00
High season per wk
£190.00–£550.00

Enjoy a relaxing holiday in lovely surroundings on farm overlooking Wembury village and coast, in an Area of Outstanding Natural Beauty. Close to Plymouth and Dartmoor.

WEST ANSTEY, Devon Map ref 1D1

★★★★
1 Unit
Sleeping 2–9

BRIMBLECOMBE
South Molton
Contact: Mrs Charlotte Hutsby, Little Hill Farm, Wellesbourne, Warwick CV35 9EB
T: (01789) 840261
F: (01789) 842270
I: www.brimblecombe-exmoor.co.uk

OPEN All Year

Payment accepted: Euros

Low season per wk
£600.00–£1,200.00
High season per wk
£600.00–£1,200.00

Devon longhouse on edge of Exmoor National Park. Four double rooms ensuite, well-equipped farmhouse kitchen, sitting room with inglenook. Stabling, eight acres, trout ponds.

WEST BAY, Dorset Map ref 2B3

★★★–★★★★★
7 Units
Sleeping 2–8

WESTPOINT APARTMENTS
Bridport
Contact: Mr & Mrs Slade, Westpoint Apartments, Esplanade, West Bay, Bridport DT6 4HE
T: (01308) 423636
F: (01308) 458871
E: bea@westpointapartments.co.uk
I: www.westpointapartments.co.uk

OPEN All Year

Payment accepted: Delta, Mastercard, Switch, Visa

Low season per wk
£170.00–£320.00
High season per wk
£345.00–£560.00

Quality self-catering apartments on seafront overlooking sea and harbour. Fishing, 18-hole golf course, beautiful cliff walks, Thomas Hardy country. Three-and four-day breaks available.

Important note Information on accommodation listed in this guide has been supplied by the proprietors. As changes may occur you are advised to check details at the time of booking.

SOUTH WEST ENGLAND

WEYMOUTH, Dorset Map ref 2B3 *Tourist Information Centre Tel: (01305) 785747*

★★★★★
6 Units
Sleeping 4–8

BAY LODGE SELF-CATERING ACCOMMODATION
Weymouth
Contact: Mr & Mrs Dubben, c/o Bay Lodge, 27 Greenhill, Weymouth DT4 7SW
T: (01305) 782419
F: (01305) 782828
E: barbara@baylodge.co.uk
I: www.baylodge.co.uk

OPEN All Year

Payment accepted: Delta, Mastercard, Switch, Visa, Euros

Early booking discount. Winter breaks available: Fri-Mon or Mon-Fri, from £8.34pppn for maximum occupancy of cottage.

Low season per wk
Min £200.00
High season per wk
Max £925.00

Seafront homes with garage or private parking, 18thC cottages with garage and seafront parking, all newly refurbished. Bedrooms with king-size beds, the majority with en suite bathrooms, some with jacuzzi. Beamed ceilings, open fires, designer kitchens with every modern convenience. Indoor and outdoor swimming pools and tennis courts nearby.

★★★★
1 Unit
Sleeping 2–6

CRESCENT COTTAGE
Weymouth
Contact: Mrs Tracy Buckwell, 38 Cleveland Avenue, Weymouth DT3 5AG
T: (01305) 771881
F: (01305) 768491

OPEN All Year

Low season per wk
Min £150.00
High season per wk
Max £595.00

Refurbished Grade II Listed cottage, one minute from sandy beach, close to town and harbour. Large lounge/diner. Two bathrooms. Great for summer and winter breaks.

★★
1 Unit
Sleeping 1–6

HOLIDAY HOUSE
Weymouth
Contact: Mr Saunders, 8 Sutcliffe Avenue, Weymouth DT4 9SA
T: (01305) 773307

OPEN All Year

Payment accepted: Euros

Low season per wk
£160.00–£260.00
High season per wk
£260.00–£500.00

Spacious three-bedroomed mid-terrace cottage. Parking. Five minute walk town/beach. Low season discounts. Pets welcome. Near marina.

★★★
1 Unit
Sleeping 1–4

SEA SHELLS HOLIDAY FLAT
Weymouth
Contact: Mr Duncan & Mrs Ramona Rosser, 26 High Street, Wyke Regis, Weymouth DT4 9NZ
T: (01305) 778540

OPEN All Year except Christmas and New Year

Payment accepted: Euros

Low season per wk
£169.00–£245.00
High season per wk
£255.00–£350.00

Picturesque village with local pub and shop. Short walk to Chesil Beach, Fleet Lagoon and Weymouth seafront. Tastefully furnished. Snooker/games/music room.

Country Code Always follow the Country Code

• Enjoy the countryside and respect its life and work • Guard against all risk of fire • Fasten all gates • Keep your dogs under close control • Keep to public paths across farmland • Use gates and stiles to cross fences, hedges and walls • Leave livestock, crops and machinery alone • Take your litter home • Help to keep all water clean • Protect wildlife, plants and trees • Take special care on country roads • Make no unnecessary noise.

SOUTH WEST ENGLAND

WIMBORNE MINSTER, Dorset Map ref 2B3 *Tourist Information Centre Tel: (01202) 886116*

3 Units
Sleeping 2–4

Barns, recently converted to a high standard, enjoying a courtyard setting in a countryside location one mile from the market town of Wimborne. These well-equipped cottages are within easy reach of the New Forest and the resorts of Bournemouth, Poole, Christchurch and the award-winning beaches of Studland.

GRANGE HOLIDAY COTTAGES

Grange, Wimborne
Contact: English Country Cottages, Stony Bank, Earby, Barnoldswick BB94 0AA
T: 0870 191 7700
F: (0128) 284 1539
E: eec.enquiry@holidaycottagesgroup.com
I: www.english-country-cottages.co.uk

OPEN All Year

Payment accepted: Amex, Delta, Diners, Mastercard, Switch, Visa, Euros

Low season per wk
£294.00–£453.00
High season per wk
£397.00–£605.00

WINCHCOMBE, Gloucestershire Map ref 2B1

★★★
1 Unit
Sleeping 1–4

DUNBAR COTTAGE
Cheltenham
Contact: Linda Andrews, 73 Gloucester Street, Cheltenham GL54 5LX
T: (01242) 604946

OPEN All Year

Low season per wk
Min £250.00
High season per wk
Min £250.00

A cottage in the Cotswolds, near to the Cotswold Way. Ideal for walking and sightseeing.

★★★★-★★★★★
5 Units
Sleeping 2–5

Courtyard setting of old traditional barns of individual style and character, finely restored to provide spacious, high-quality accommodation. Original features, quality facilities and furnishings. Gardens and patios, countryside views and private parking. Also stone detached cottage nearby. All family supervised. Ideal touring base. Regret no pets. Brochures available.

TRADITIONAL ACCOMMODATION

Winchcombe, Cheltenham
Contact: Mr & Mrs Wilson, 60 Pershore Road, Evesham WR11 2PQ
T: (01386) 446269
F: (01386) 446269
E: trad.accom@virgin.net
I: http://freespace.virgin.net/trad.accom

OPEN All Year

Payment accepted: Amex, Delta, Diners, Mastercard, Switch, Visa, Euros

Low season per wk
£230.00–£450.00
High season per wk
£450.00–£550.00

Check the maps

The colour maps at the front of this guide show all the cities, towns and villages for which you will find accommodation entries. Refer to the town index to find the page on which they are listed.

SOUTH WEST ENGLAND

WINGFIELD, Wiltshire Map ref 2B2

★★
5 Units
Sleeping 2–4

ROMSEY OAK COTTAGES
Trowbridge
Contact: Mr Alan Briars, Romsey Oak Farmhouse, Frome Road, Wingfield, Trowbridge BA14 9LS
T: (01225) 753950
F: (01225) 753950
E: enquiries@romseyoakcottages.co.uk
I: www.romseyoakcottages.co.uk/intro.htm

Converted farm building around courtyard of main house in open countryside. Bath 10 miles, Bradford on Avon three miles. Fully equipped kitchen, TV, heating, pay phone, laundry. Bed linen provided. Dogs accepted. Residents' garden and tennis court (professional coaching can be provided). Numerous good eating places and public houses nearby. Brochure available.

OPEN All Year

Payment accepted: Amex, Delta, Mastercard, Switch, Visa

Low season per wk
£185.00–£250.00
High season per wk
£225.00–£295.00

Special deals for tennis weeks to include professional coaching. Short breaks available – call for prices.

WOOKEY, Somerset Map ref 2A2

★★★★
1 Unit
Sleeping 2–5

MILL LODGE
Wells
Contact: Lesley Burt, Burcott Mill, Wookey, Wells BA5 1NJ
T: (01749) 673118
F: (01749) 677376
E: theburts@burcottmill.com
I: www.burcottmill.com

Newly converted unique apartment within working water-mill at small family-run attraction. Tours with the miller a feature. Playground, animals, tearoom. Ideal for Wells, Wookey Hole, Glastonbury, Cheddar, Bath, Bristol. Opposite country pub/restaurant. Post office stores in Wookey. Children: help feed our animals and collect eggs. Baby sitting available.

OPEN All Year

Payment accepted: Mastercard, Switch, Visa

Low season per wk
£135.00–£300.00
High season per wk
£265.00–£500.00

Short breaks available 3-night stay.

WOOLACOMBE, Devon Map ref 1C1 Tourist Information Centre Tel: (01271) 870553

★★
1 Unit
Sleeping 5

COVE COTTAGE FLAT
Woolacombe
Contact: Ms Vivien Lawrence, Cove Cottage Flat, Sharp Rock, Mortehoe, Woolacombe EX34 7EA
T: (01271) 870403
E: vivien@lawrence6232.fsnet.co.uk

Self-contained, first floor, well-furnished flat with sea views. Overlooking Sandy Combesgate beach/Barricane (10 minutes' walk – Blue Flag). Colour TV/video, fridge/freezer, microwave, washer/drier, garden, new kitchen. Bathroom with bath, Mira shower and shaver point. Close National Trust coastal path. Central heating included early/late season. Dogs welcome.

OPEN All Year

Short breaks early/late season with full central heating included.

Low season per wk
£185.00–£250.00
High season per wk
£300.00–£499.00

Location Complete addresses for properties are not given and the town(s) listed may be a distance from the actual establishment. Please check the precise location at the time of booking.

Self-catering agencies

This section of the guide lists agencies which have a selection of holiday homes to let in various parts of the country. Some agencies specialise in a particular area or region while others have properties in all parts of England.

The agencies listed here are grouped first into those who have had all properties assessed by VisitBritain, secondly into those who have had at least 75% of their properties assessed and thirdly those who have had at least 50% of their properties assessed.

To obtain further information on individual properties please contact the agency or agencies direct, indicating the time of year when the accommodation is required, the number of people to be accommodated and any preferred locations.

* The agencies listed in green have an advertisement in this guide.

Totally quality assessed

These agencies promote only properties which have been assessed under VisitBritain's National Quality Assurance Standard.

Appledore Holiday Letting Agency
T: (01237) 476191
F: (01237) 479621
E: enquiries@appledore-letting.co.uk
I: www.appledore-letting.co.uk
Offering accommodation in Appledore, Devon

Bath Centre-Stay Holidays
T: (01225) 313205
F: (01225) 313205
E: holidays@bathcentrestay.freeserve.co.uk
I: www.bcsh.co.uk
Offering accommodation in Bath

Quality Accredited Agency
Policies, Practices & Procedures Assessed

New for 2004
Quality Accredited Agency Standard

As a further step towards achieving quality not only in accommodation, VisitBritain has launched a new Quality Accredited Agency Standard. Agencies who are awarded the Quality Accredited Agency Marque by VisitBritain are recognised as offering good customer service and peace of mind, following an assessment of their office policies, practices and procedures.

Bath Holiday Homes
T: (01225) 332221
E: bhh@virgin.net
I: www.bathholidayhomes.co.uk
Offering accommodation in Bath

The Coppermines & Coniston Lakes Cottages
T: (015394) 41765
F: (015394) 41944
E: info@coppermines.co.uk
I: www.coppermines.co.uk
Offering accommodation in Cumbria – The Lake District

Cornish Holiday Cottages
T: (01326) 250339
F: (01326) 250339
E: postmaster@cornishholidaycottages.net
I: www.cornishholidaycottages.net
Offering accommodation in and around Falmouth, Cornwall

Above Island Cottage Holidays, Isle of Wight

Enjoy England official guides to quality

Cornish Horizons Holiday Cottages
T: (01841) 520889/521333
F: (01841) 521523
E: cottages@cornishhorizons.co.uk
I: www.cornishhorizons.co.uk
Offering accommodation in North Cornwall

Cottages South West
T: (01626) 872314
F: (01626) 872314
E: lets@cottagessw.vir.co.uk
I: www.cottagesw.co.uk
Offering accommodation in Shaldon and Teignmouth, Devon

Country Hideaways
T: (01969) 663559
F: (01969) 663559
E: ubr@countryhidaways.co.uk
I: www.countryhideaways.co.uk
Offering accommodation in the Yorkshire Dales

Cumbrian Cottages Ltd
T: (01228) 599950/599960
F: (01228) 599970
E: enquiries@cumbrian-cottages.co.uk
I: www.cumbrian-cottages.co.uk
Offering accommodation in Cumbria – The Lake District

Dartmouth Cottages
T: (01803) 839499
E: holidays@dartmouthcottages.com
I: www.dartmouthcottages.com
Offering accommodation in and around Dartmouth, Devon

Diana Bullivant Holidays
T: (01208) 831336
F: (01208) 831336
E: diana@bullivant.fsnet.co.uk
I: www.cornwall-online.co.uk/diana-bullivant
Offering accommodation in North Devon

Dream Cottages
T: (01305) 789000
F: (01305) 761346
E: admin@dream-cottages.co.uk
I: www.dream-cottages.co.uk
Offering accommodation in Dorset, Devon, Wiltshire and Hampshire

Freedom Holiday Homes
T: (01580) 720770
F: (01580) 720771
E: mail@freedomholidayhomes.co.uk
I: www.freedomholidayhomes.co.uk
Offering accommodation in Kent and East Sussex

Garden of England Cottages Limited
T: (01732) 369168
F: (01732) 358817
E: holidays@gardenofenglandcottages.co.uk
I: www.gardenofenglandcottages.co.uk
Offering accommodation in Kent and East Sussex

Harbour Holidays, Padstow
T: (01841) 533402
F: (01841) 533115
E: contact@harbourholidays.co.uk
I: www.harbourholidays.co.uk
Offering accommodation in and around Padstow, Cornwall

Heart of the Lakes and Cottage Life
T: (015394) 32321
F: (015394) 33251
E: info@heartofthelakes.co.uk
I: www.heartofthelakes.co.uk
Offering accommodation in Cumbria – The Lake District

Helford River Cottages
T: (01326) 231666
E: onfo@helfordcottages.co.uk
I: www.helfordcottages.co.uk
Offering accommodation in and around Helford, Cornwall

Holiday Home Services (Seaview)
T: (01983) 811418
F: (01983) 616900
E: mail@seaviewholidayhomes.co.uk
I: www.seaview-holiday-homes.co.uk
Offering accommodation in Seaview, Isle of Wight

Holiday Homes and Cottages SW
T: (01803) 663650
F: (01803) 664037
E: holcotts@aol.com
I: www.swcottages.co.uk
Offering accommodation in Devon and Cornwall

Holiday Homes Owners Services (West Wight)
T: (01983) 753423
Offering accommodation in the Isle of Wight

Home from Home Holidays
T: (01983) 854340
F: (01983) 855524
E: admin@hfromh.co.uk
I: www.hfromh.co.uk
Offering accommodation in the Isle of Wight

SELF-CATERING AGENCIES

In the English Manner (London Apartments)
T: (01559) 371600
F: (01559) 371601
E: london@english-manner.com
I: www.english-manner.com
Offering accommodation in London

Island Cottage Holidays
T: (01929) 480080
F: (01929) 481070
E: enq@islandcottageholidays.com
I: www.islandcottageholidays.com
Offering accommodation in the Isle of Wight

Jean Bartlett Cottage Holidays Ltd
T: (01297) 23221 / (01297) 20973
F: (01297) 23303
E: holidays@jeanbartlett.com
I: www.jeanbartlett.com
Offering accommodation in East Devon and West Dorset

Lakeland Cottage Company
T: 0870 442 5826
F: 0870 442 5828
E: john@lakelandcottageco.com
I: www.lakelandcottagecompany.com
Offering accommodation in Cumbria – The Lake District

Lakeland Cottage Holidays
T: (017687) 76065
F: (017687) 76869
E: info@lakelandcottages.co.uk
I: www.lakelandcottages.co.uk
Offering accommodation in Cumbria – The Lake District

Lakelovers Holiday Homes
T: (015394) 88855/88856
F: (015394) 88857
E: bookings@lakelovers.co.uk
I: www.lakelovers.co.uk
Offering accommodation in Cumbria – The Lake District

AQA APPLIED FOR

Linstone Chine Holiday Services Ltd
T: (01983) 755933/752015
F: (01983) 755933
E: enquiries@linstone-chine.co.uk
I: www.linstone-chine.co.uk
Offering accommodation in the Isle of Wight

Mackay's Agency
T: (0131) 225 3539/226 4364
F: (0131) 226 5284
E: patricia@mackays-scotland.co.uk
I: www.mackays-scotland.co.uk
Offering accommodation in the north of England

Marsdens Cottage Holidays
T: (01271) 813777
F: (01271) 813664
E: holidays@marsdens.co.uk
I: www.marsdens.co.uk
Offering accommodation in North Devon

Milkbere Cottage Holidays
T: (01297) 20729
F: (01297) 22925
E: info@milkberehols.com
I: www.milkberehols.com
Offering accommodation in Devon

Millers of Hayling
T: (023) 9246 5951
F: (023) 9246 1321
E: millers@haylingproperty.co.uk
I: www.millers@haylingproperty.co.uk
Offering accommodation in Hayling Island, Hampshire

Miraleisure Ltd
T: (01424) 730298
F: (01424) 212500
Offering accommodation in Bexhill-on-Sea, East Sussex

Red Rose Cottages
T: (01200) 420101
F: (01200) 420103
E: info@redrosecottages.co.uk
I: www.redrosecottages.co.uk
Offering accommodation in Lancashire

Special Places in Cornwall
T: (01872) 864400
E: office@specialplacescornwall.co.uk
I: www.specialplacescornwall.co.uk
Offering accommodation in Cornwall

Suffolk Country Cottages
T: (01603) 873378
F: (01603) 870304
E: info@suffolkcountrycottages.co.uk
I: www.suffolkcountrycottages.co.uk
Offering accommodation in Suffolk and South Norfolk

Suffolk Secrets
T: (01379) 651297
F: (01379) 650116
E: holidays@suffolk-secrets.co.uk
I: www.suffolk-secrets.co.uk
Offering accommodation in Suffolk

Town or Country Serviced Apartments and Houses
T: (023) 8088 1000
F: (023) 8088 1010
E: info@town-or-country.co.uk
I: www.town-or-country.co.uk
Offering accommodation in and around Southampton

Valley Villas Ltd
T: (01752) 774900
E: sales@valleyvillas.com
I: www.valleyvillas.com
Offering accommodation in Cornwall

Wheelwrights
T: (015394) 37635/37571
F: (015394) 37618
E: enquiries@wheelwrights.com
I: www.wheelwrights.com
Offering accommodation in Cumbria – The Lake District

Whitby Holiday Cottages
T: (01947) 603010
F: (01947) 821133
E: enquiries@whitby-cottages.co.uk
I: www.whitby-cottages.co.uk
Offering accommodation in Yorkshire

Yealm Holidays
T: 0870 747 2987
F: (01752) 873173
E: info@yealm-holidays.co.uk
I: www.yealm-holidays.co.uk
Offering accommodation in South West Devon

York Holiday Homes
T: (01904) 641997
F: (01904) 613453
I: www.yorkshirenet.co.uk/accgde/yorkholidayhomes
Offering accommodation in York

At least 75% quality assessed

At least 75% of the properties promoted by each of these agencies has been assessed under VisitBritain's National Quality Assurance Scheme.

Best of Brighton and Sussex Cottages Ltd
T: (01273) 308779
F: (01273) 390211
E: enquiries@bestofbrighton.co.uk
I: www.bestofbrighton.co.uk
Offering accommodation in Brighton and East and West Sussex

Birds Norfolk Holiday Homes
T: (01485) 534210
F: (01485) 535230
E: shohol@birdsnorfolkholidayhomes.co.uk
I: www.norfolkholidayhomes-birds.co.uk
Offering accommodation in Norfolk

The Cottage Collection
T: (01206) 262261
F: (01206) 263001
E: admin@the-cottage-collection.co.uk
I: www.the-cottage-collection.co.uk
Offering accommodation throughout the UK

Homefinders Holidays
T: (01904) 632660/655200
F: (01904) 651388
E: c.thomas-letters.of.york@btinternet.com
I: www.letters-of-york.co.uk
Offering accommodation in York

Rock Holidays
T: (01208) 863399
F: (01208) 862218
E: rockhols@aol.com
I: www.rockholidays.co.uk
Offering accommodation in Cornwall

Rumsey Holiday Homes
T: 0845 644 4852
F: (01202) 701955
E: info@rhh.org
I: www.rhh.org
Offering accommodation in Poole, Bournemouth and South Dorset

Shoreline Cottages Ltd
T: (0113) 244 8410
F: (0113) 244 9826
E: reservations@shoreline-cottages.com
I: www.shoreline-cottages.com
Offering accommodation in and around Whitby, Yorkshire

At least 50% quality assessed

At least 50% of the properties promoted by each of these agencies has been assessed under VisitBritain's National Quality Assurance Scheme.

Albion Rose Properties
T: (01763) 249999
F: (01763) 247793
E: albioncottages@aol.com
I: www.albionrose.co.uk
Offering accommodation in Norfolk and Suffolk

Cottage in the Country & Cottage Holidays
T: (01993) 831495/831743
F: (01993) 831095
E: info@cottageinthecountry.co.uk
I: www.cottageinthecountry.co.uk
Offering accommodation throughout England

SELF-CATERING AGENCIES

Dales Holiday Cottages
T: (01756) 799821/790919
F: (01756) 797012
E: Enq@dales-holiday-cottages.com
I: www.dales-holiday-cottages.com
Offering accommodation in the north of England

Fowey Harbour Cottages (W J B Hill & Son)
T: (01726) 832211
F: (01726) 832901
E: hillandson@talk21.com
Offering accommodation in Fowey, Cornwall

Island Holiday Homes
T: (01983) 616644
F: (01983) 616640
E: enquiries@island-holiday-homes.net
I: www.island-holiday.homes.net
Offering accommodation in the Isle of Wight

Lambert & Russell
T: (01263) 513139/511105
F: (01263) 513139
E: property@lamberttw.fslife.co.uk
Offering accommodation in Norfolk

Manor Cottages
T: (01993) 824252
F: (01993) 824443
E: mancott@netcomuk.co.uk
I: www.manorcottages.co.uk
Offering accommodation in the Cotswolds

Mullion Cottages
T: (01326) 240315 / 0845 066 7766
F: (01326) 241090
E: enquiries@mullioncottages.com
I: www.mullioncottages.com
Offering accommodation in Cornwall

Peak Cottages
T: (0114) 262 0777
F: (0114) 262 0777
E: enquiries@peakcottages.com
I: www.peakcottages.com
Offering accommodation in the Peak District

Above sea breezes at colourful Southwold

Enjoy England official guides to **quality**

enjoyEngland™
official guides to **quality**

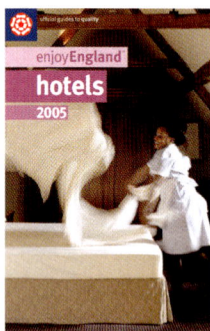

Hotels, Townhouses, Travel Accommodation and Restaurants with Rooms in England 2005
£10.99

Bed & Breakfasts, Small Hotels, Bed & Breakfasts, Farmhouses, Inns, Campus Accommodation and Hostels in England 2005
£11.99

Self-Catering Holiday Homes and Boat Accommodation in England 2005
£11.99

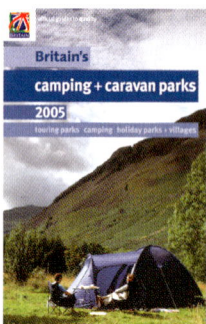

Touring Parks, Camping, Holiday Parks and Villages in Britain 2005
£8.99

Somewhere Special in England 2005
£8.99

Families and Pets Welcome in England 2005
£11.99

INFORMATIVE • EASY TO USE • GREAT VALUE FOR MONEY

The guides include:
- **Accommodation entries packed with information**
- **Full colour maps**
- **Places to visit**
- **Tourist Information Centres**

From all good bookshops or by mail order from:

VisitBritain Fulfilment Centre,
c/o Westex Ltd, 7 St Andrews Way,
Devons Road, Bromley-by-Bow, London E3 3PA
Tel: 0870 606 7204
Fax: (020) 7987 6505
Email: fulfilment@visitbritain.org

NOTES

NOTES

VisitBritain's
assessed accommodation

On the following pages you will find an exclusive listing of every self-catering establishment in England that has been assessed for quality by VisitBritain.

The information includes brief contact details for each place to stay, together with its star rating, and quality award if appropriate. The listing also shows if an establishment has a National Accessible rating (see the front of the guide for further information). Accommodation is listed by region and then alphabetically by place name. Establishments may be located in, or a short distance from, the places in blue bands.

More detailed information on all the places shown in blue can be found in the regional sections (where establishments have paid to have their details included). To find these entries please refer to the appropriate regional section, or look in the town index at the back of this guide.

The list which follows was compiled slightly later than the regional sections. For this reason you may find that, in a few instances, a diamond rating and quality award may differ between the two sections. This list contains the most up-to-date information and was correct at the time of going to press.

Boat accommodation

This section includes details of boat accommodation quality-rated by VisitBritain.

LONDON

LONDON

INNER LONDON E11

S.T.A.Y! ★★★
Contact: Mrs Teresa Farnham
17 Greenstone Mews, London
E11 2RS
T: (020) 8530 6729
F: (020) 8530 6729
E: stayfarnham@aol.com

E14

Bridge House-London Docklands ★★★★★
Contact: Mr John Graham
31 Falcon Way, London E14 9UP
T: (020) 7538 8980
E: johnkgraham@hotmail.com
I: www.johnkgraham.com

River Thames Apartment ★★★★
Contact: Greta Paull
35 Cheyne Avenue, South Woodford, London E18 2DP
T: (020) 85302336
F: (020) 8530 2336
E: gretapaull@aol.com
I: www.riverthamesapartment.co.uk

Riverside ★★★★
Contact: Christine James
18 Capstan Square, London E14 3EU
T: (01902) 843545
F: (01902) 843545
E: christine@capstansq.fsnet.co.uk
I: www.capstansq.fsnet.co.uk

N7

Carena Holiday Accommodation ★★★
Contact: Mr M Chouthi
98 St George's Avenue, London N7 0AH
T: (020) 7607 7453
F: (020) 7607 7453
E: deo.chouthi@btopenworld.com

N10

Hamlet UK ★★★
Contact:
Hamlet UK, 20 Granville Road, Barnet EN5 4DS
T: (020) 8440 2469
F: (020) 8440 4832
E: hamlet_uk@globalnet.co.uk
I: www.hamletuk.com

N21

Firs Apartments ★★★★
Contact:
28 Firs Lane, London N21 3ES
T: (020) 8360 3890
F: (020) 8364 2232
E: information@firsapartments.com
I: www.firsapartments.com

SE1

London Riverside Apartments ★★★★
Contact: Mr John Dillon
Flat 566 Manhattan Building, Fairfield Road, London E3 2UL
T: (020) 8983 1160
F: (020) 8983 1160
I: www.londonriverside.co.uk

SE3

Sunfields ★★
Contact: Mrs Jacqui Poole
135 Shooters Hill Road, London SE3 8UQ
T: (020) 8858 1420
E: jacqui.poole@nhs.net

SE6

Glenthurston Holiday Apartments ★★★-★★★★★
Contact: Ms Sue Halliday
27 Canadian Avenue, London SE6 3AU
T: (020) 8690 3992
F: (020) 8265 6872
E: mail@glenthurston.co.uk
I: www.glenthurston.co.uk

SE10

Harbour Master's House ★★★★
Contact: Mr Chris French
T: (020) 8293 9597
E: harbourmaster@lineone.net
I: website.lineone.net/~harbourmaster

SE13

Studio Cottage ★★★
Contact: Ms Pamela Burke
21 Kellerton Road, London SE13 5RB
T: (020) 8265 1212
F: (020) 8852 3243
E: info@welcomehomes.co.uk
I: www.welcomehomes.co.uk

SW1

The Apartments Knightsbridge ★★★★-★★★★★
Contact:
Flat 1, 49 Hans Place, London SW1X 0LA
F: (020) 7589 3274
E: maureen@theapartments.co.uk
I: www.theapartments.co.uk

Club Suites ★★★★
Contact: Ms Rosemary Earl
52 Lower Sloane Street, London SW1W 8BS
T: (020) 7730 9131
F: (020) 7730 6146
E: reservations@sloaneclub.co.uk
I: www.sloaneclub.co.uk

Regency Apartments ★★★★★
Contact:
Serviced Letting Ltd, Dolben Court, Montaigne Close, London SW1P 4BJ
T: 0800 093 5383
E: louise@servicedlet.com
I: www.london-stays.com

SW3

The Apartments ★★★★
Contact: Ms Maureen Boyle
41 Draycott Place, London SW3 2SH
T: (020) 7589 3271
F: (020) 7589 3274
E: alex@prestigeapartments.co.uk
I: www.theartments.co.uk

Beaufort House ★★★★★
Contact: Ms Bettina Hoff
Flat 1, 46-47 Beaufort Gardens, London SW3 1PN
T: (020) 7584 2600
F: (020) 7584 6532
E: info@beauforthouse.co.uk
I: www.beauforthouse.co.uk

Flat 362 ★★★
Contact:
Serviced Lettings Ltd, Chelsea Cloisters, Sloane Avenue, London SW3 3DW
T: (029) 2041 7344
F: (029) 2041 7347
E: louise@servicedlet.com
I: www.london-stays.com

SW5

Emperors Gate Short Stay Apartments ★★★
Contact:
8 Knaresborough Place, London SW5 0TG
T: (020) 7244 8409
F: (020) 7373 6455
E: info@apartment-hotels.com
I: www.apartment-hotels.com

SW7

Flat 16 ★★★★
Contact:
Serviced Lettings Ltd, Flat 16, 16-17 Manson Place, London SW7 5LT
T: (029) 2041 7344
F: (029) 2041 7347
E: louise@servicedlet.com
I: www.london-stays.com

Snow White Properties ★★-★★★
Contact: Maxine White
55 Ennismore Gardens, London SW7 1AJ
T: (020) 7584 3307
F: (020) 7581 4686
E: snow.white@virgin.net
I: www.snowwhitelondon.com

SW8

6 Oliver House ★★
Contact: Mr Ramesh Bhadresha
28-29 Wilcox Close, Lambeth, London SW8 2UD
T: (020) 7622 2821
F: (020) 7652 0033
E: rbhadresha@hotmail.com

SW14

East Sheen Studio Flat ★★★
Contact: Mr Angela Butt
Flat 1, 1 Monroe Drive, London SW14 7AR
T: (020) 8876 0584
F: (020) 8876 0584

SW18

Beaumont Apartments ★★★★
Contact: Mr Alan Afriat
24 Combemartin Road, London SW18 5PR
T: (020) 8789 2663
F: (020) 8265 5499
E: alan@beaumont-london-apartments.co.uk
I: www.beaumont-london-apartments.co.uk

SW19

Honey Cottage ★★★
Contact: Mrs Jenny Humphries
5 Homefield Road, London SW19 4QE
T: (020) 8947 9636
E: mikejenny@compuserve.com
I: www.honeycottage.com

SW20

Thalia & Hebe Holiday Homes ★★★-★★★★
Contact: Peter and Ann Briscoe-Smith
Thalia and Hebe Holiday Homes, 150 Westway, London SW20 9LS
T: (020) 8542 0505
E: peter@briscoe-smith.org.uk
I: www.briscoe-smith.org.uk/thalia

W1

The Ascott Mayfair ★★★★-★★★★★
Contact:
49 Hill Street, London W1J 5NB
T: (020) 7313 6190
F: (020) 7313 6189
E: enquiry.london@the-ascott.com
I: www.the-ascott.com

23 Greengarden House ★★★★
Serviced Apartments
Contact: Ms Nikki Pybus
St Christopher's Place, London W1U 1NL
T: (020) 7935 9191
F: (020) 7935 8858
E: info@greengardenhouse.com
I: www.greengardenhouse.com

Marylebone Apartment ★★★★
Contact:
Marylebone Apartment, 9 Molyneux Street, London W1H 5HP
T: (020) 7262 9843
F: (020) 7262 9843
E: rsutherland@ayli.com

Tustin Holiday Flats ★★-★★★
Contact: Mr Bruce Tunstin
P C Tustin and Co Limited, 94 York Street, London W1H 1QX
T: (020) 7723 9611
F: (020) 7724 0224
E: pctustinuk@btconnect.com
I: www.pctustin.com

LONDON

W2
Royal Court Apartments ★★
Contact:
51 Gloucester Terrace, London
W2 3DQ
T: (020) 7402 5077
F: (020) 7724 0286
E: info@royalcourtapartments.co.uk
I: www.royalcourtapartments.co.uk

W5
Clarendon House Apartments ★★★★
Contact: Mrs A Pedley
48 Ranelagh Road, Ealing,
London W5 5RJ
T: (020) 8567 0314
F: (020) 8566 3241
E: clarendon.house@lineone.net
I: www.clarendonhouseapartments.co.uk

W8
51 Kensington Court ★★★★
Contact: Reservations
Flat 1, 51 Kensington Court,
London W8 5DB
T: (020) 7937 2030
F: (020) 7938 5312
E: bookings@kensingtoncourt.co.uk
I: www.kensingtoncourt.co.uk

W13
Apartments West London ★★★
Contact: Mr W G Smith
Apartments West London,
94 Gordon Road, Ealing, London
W13 8PT
T: (020) 8566 8187
F: (020) 8566 7670
E: info@apartmentswestlondon.com
I: www.apartmentswestlondon.com

OUTER LONDON
Beckenham
Oakfield Apartments ★★-★★★★
Contact: Mr Deane
Oakfield Apartments, Flat 1,
107 South Eden Park Road,
Beckenham BR3 3AX
T: (020) 8658 4441 & 8658 9198
E: john@oakfield.co.uk
I: www.oakfield.co.uk

CROYDON
Ballards Cottage ★★★
Contact: Mr & Mrs McDermott
2 Ballards Farm Road, Croydon
CR0 5RL
T: (020) 8657 1080

S N D Apartments ★★★-★★★★★
Contact: Pamela Pereira
1 Mulgrave Road, Croydon
CR0 1BL
T: (020) 8686 7870
F: (020) 8686 7835
I: www.sndapartments.com

HAMPTON COURT
Moore's Place
Rating Applied For
Contact: Mr Mark Barnes
4 King Charles Road, Surbiton
KT5 8PY
T: (020) 8979 1792
F: (020) 8399 6639

HAMPTON WICK
Wick Cottage & The Barn
Rating Applied For
Contact: Mrs Dove
10 Park Road, Kingston upon
Thames KT1 4AS
T: (020) 8943 1862
F: (020) 8943 1862
E: info@chaselodgehotel.com
I: www.surreyhotels.com

HOUNSLOW
London Cottage ★★★★
Contact: Mr Sreemal Perera
26 Inverness Road, Hounslow
TW3 3LS
T: (020) 8570 1103
E: sreemalperera@aol.com
I: www.srlettings.com

KINGSTON UPON THAMES
Sunny House ★
Contact: Mrs Denise Haworth
10 Park Road, Kingston upon
Thames KT1 4AS
T: (020) 8943 1862
F: (020) 8943 9363
E: info@chaselodgehotel.com
I: www.surreyhotels.com

PETTS WOOD
3 Maple Close ★★
Contact: Mrs Debra Sutch
3 Maple Close, Orpington
BR5 1LP
T: (01689) 603037

PINNER
Moss Cottage ★★★★
Contact:
T: (020) 8868 5507
F: (020) 8868 5507
E: info@moss-lane-cottages.com
I: www.moss-lane-cottages.com

RICHMOND
Flat 4 Friston House ★★★
Contact: Mr Arthur Shipp
25 Larkfield Road, Richmond
TW9 2PG
T: (020) 8948 6620
E: shipplets@ukgateway.net
I: www.shipplets.com

Richmond Mews House ★★★★
Contact: Mr Tim Harris
Richmond Mews House, 3 Friars
Stile Place, Richmond TW10 6NL
T: (020) 8948 7419

SOUTH CROYDON
64a St Augustines Avenue ★★★
Contact: Mrs Lynn Starling
64a St Augustines Avenue,
South Croydon CR2 6JJ
T: (020) 8760 0371

ENGLAND'S NORTHWEST

ABBEYSTEAD
Lancashire
Higher Lee ★★★★
Contact: Hoseasons Cottages,
Higher Lee, Lowestoft NR32 2LW
T: (0150) 250 0505

Whitemoor Cottage ★★★★
Contact: Mr Martin McShane
Red Rose Cottages, 6 King
Street, Clitheroe BB7 2EP
T: (0120) 042 0101
F: (0120) 042 0103
I: www.redrosecottages.co.uk

ACCRINGTON
Lancashire
Low Moorside Farm Cottage ★★★
Contact: Mr C & Mrs E Hallworth
Low Moorside Farm Cottage,
Elcliffe Cottage, Accrington
BB5 5UG
T: (0125) 423 7053

ADLINGTON
Cheshire
Carr Cottage ★★★★
Contact: Mrs Isobel Worthington
Carr Cottage, Mill Lane,
Macclesfield SK10 4LG
T: (01625) 828137
F: (01625) 828137
E: isobel@carrhousefarm.fsnet.co.uk
I: www.topfarms.co.uk

ALDERLEY EDGE
Cheshire
The Hayloft ★★★★
Contact: Mrs Jenny Dawson
6 The Sycamores & 7 The Cedars,
Croft Cottage, Hough Lane,
Alderley Edge SK9 7JE
T: (01625) 599802
F: (01625) 599802
E: info@interludes-uk.com
I: www.interludes-uk.com

Interludes ★★★★
Contact: Mrs Jenny Dawson
Interludes, Croft Cottage, Hough
Lane, Alderley Edge SK9 7JE
T: (01625) 599802
F: (01625) 599802
E: info@interludes-uk.com
I: www.interludes-uk.com

2 Royles Square ★★★★
Contact: Jenny Dawson
Interludes, Croft Cottage, Hough
Lane, Alderley Edge SK9 7JE
T: (01625) 599802
F: (01625) 599802

ARKHOLME
Lancashire
Redwell Fisheries ★★★
Contact: Mrs Campbell-Barker & Mr Hall
Redwell Fisheries, Mere House,
Kirkby Lonsdale Road, Carntorth
LA6 1BQ
T: (015242) 21979
E: kenanddiane@redwellfisheries.co.uk
I: www.redwellfisheries.co.uk

BACUP
Lancashire
Oakenclough Farm ★★★
Contact: Mr Martin Mcshane
Red Rose Cottages, 6 King
Street, Clitheroe BB7 2EP
T: (0120) 042 0101
F: (0120) 042 0103
E: info@redrosecottages.co.uk
I: www.redrosecottages.co.uk

BARROWFORD
Lancashire
Toll House ★★★
Contact: Mr Dyson
Heritage Trust for North West
Pendle Heritage Centre, Park
Hill, Nelson BB9 6JQ
T: (01282) 661704
I: www.country-holidays.co.uk

BASHALL EAVES
Lancashire
The Coach House ★★★★
Contact: Country Holidays
The Coach House, Barnoldswick
BB94 0AA
T: 0870 078 1280

BEESTON
Cheshire
The Lodge - Whitegate Farm ★★★★
Contact: Mr & Mrs Davies
Handbridge Self Catering,
Whitegate Farm, Peckforton Hall
Lane, Spurston, Tarporley
CW6 9TG
T: (01829) 261601
F: (01829) 261602
E: stevedavies@euphony.net

BILLINGTON
Lancashire
Riverview ★★★★
Contact: Mr Martin Mcshane
Red Rose Cottages, 6 King
Street, Clitheroe BB7 2EP
T: (01200) 420101
F: (01200) 420103
E: info@redrosecottages.co.uk
I: www.redrosecottages.co.uk

Establishments printed in blue have a detailed entry in this guide

ENGLAND'S NORTHWEST

Weavers Cottage ★★★
Contact: Mr Martin McShane
Red Rose Cottages, 6 King Street, Clitheroe BB7 2EP
T: (01200) 420101
F: (01200) 420103
E: info@redrosecottages.co.uk

BISPHAM
Blackpool

Burbage Holiday Lodge ★★★★
Contact: Mrs Sheila Chick
Burbage Holiday Lodge, 198 Queens Promenade, Blackpool FY2 9JS
T: (0125) 356657
E: enquiries@burbageholidaylodge.co.uk
I: www.burbageholidaylodge.co.uk

BLACKO
Blackburn with Darwen

Malkin Tower Farm ★★★★
Contact: Mrs Rachel Turner
Malkin Tower Farm, Barnoldswick Road, Nelson BB9 6RQ
T: (01282) 699992
F: (01282) 613886
E: malkintower@msn.com
I: www.malkintowerfarm.co.uk

BLACKPOOL
Blackpool

Abingdon Holiday Flats ★★
Contact: Mr Douglas Nelson
Abingdon Holiday Apartments, 33 Holmfield Road, Blackpool FY2 9TB
T: (0125) 335 6181
I: www.accommodation-blackpool.co.uk

The Beach House
Rating Applied For
Contact: Mrs Estelle Livesey
The Beach House, Blackpool FY2 9JS
T: (0125) 335 2699
F: (0125) 359 1164
E: info@thebeachhouseblackpool.co.uk
I: www.thebeachhouseblackpool.co.uk

Beachcliffe Holiday Flats ★★★
Contact: Mr Terry Large
Beachcliffe Holiday Flats, Blackpool FY2 9TD
T: (0125) 335 1306
E: stay@beachcliffe.com
I: www.beachcliffe.com

Crystal Lodge Holiday Flats ★★
Contact: Mr T & Mrs C Cray
Crystal Lodge, 10-12 Crystal Road, Blackpool FY1 6BS
I: www.blackpool1.com/crystallodge

Donange ★★-★★★
Contact: Mrs Myra Hasson
Donange, 29 Holmfield Road, Blackpool FY2 9TB
T: (01253) 355051
E: don-ange@bushinternet.com
I: www.donange.cjb.net

Grand Hotel Holiday Flats ★★-★★★★
Contact: Mr Smith
Station Road, Blackpool FY4 1EU
T: (01253) 343741
F: (01253) 408228
I: www.grandholidayflats.co.uk

The Holiday Lodge
Rating Applied For
Contact: Mr B Haynes
115 Homefield Road, Blackpool FY2 9RF
T: (01253) 352934
F: (01253) 353252
I: www.holidaylodge.co.uk

San Remo Holiday Flats ★★
Contact: Mrs June Morgan
San Remo Holiday Flats, Apartments and Bungalows, Blackpool FY2 9SE
T: (0125) 335 3487
E: sanremoapartment@aol.com
I: www.sanremoapartments.com

Sea Cote Holiday Flats ★★★
Contact: Mrs Anne Cunningham
Sea Cote Holiday Flats, 172 Queens Promenade, Blackpool FY2 9JN
T: (0125) 335 4435

Stratford Holiday Apartments ★★-★★★
Contact: Mr Chris Taylor
Stratford Apartments, 36-38 Empress Drive, Blackpool FY2 9SD
T: (0125) 350 0150
F: (0125) 359 1004
E: tonorthdene@hotmail.com
I: www.500150.com

Thorncliffe Holiday Flats ★★-★★★
Contact: Mr Al Badani
Thorncliffe Holiday Flats, 1 Holmfield Road, Gynn Square, Blackpool FY2 9SL
T: (0125) 357561
F: (0125) 508770

BOLLINGTON
Cheshire

Higher Ingersley Barn ★★★★★
Contact: Mr Peacock
Higher Ingersley Barn, Higher Ingersley Farm, Oakenbank Lane, Macclesfield SK10 5RP
T: (01625) 572245
E: bw.peacock@ntlword.com
I: www.higheringerleyfarm.co.uk

BOLTON-BY-BOWLAND
Lancashire

Springhead Farm Holiday Cottages ★★★★
Contact: Mr Martin Mcshane
Red Rose Cottages, 6 King Street, Clitheroe BB7 2EP
T: (0120) 042 0101
F: (0120) 042 0103
E: info@redrosecottages.co.uk
I: www.redrosecottages.co.uk

BOLTON-LE-SANDS
Lancashire

Jasmine Cottage
Rating Applied For
Contact: Mr & Mrs Baker
Rosedene, 6 Hornby Bank, Carnforth LA6 1EJ
T: (01524) 733532

BOSLEY
Cheshire

The Old Byre ★★★
Contact: Mrs Dorothy Gilman
The Old Byre, Pye Ash Farm, Leek Road, Macclesfield SK11 0PN
T: (01260) 223293
F: (01260) 223293

Strawberry Duck Holidays ★★★
Contact: Mr Bruce Carter & Emma Cowley
Strawberry Duck Holidays, Bryher Cottage, Bullgate Lane, Macclesfield SK11 0PP
T: (01260) 223591
F: (01260) 223591

BRIERCLIFFE
Lancashire

Delph Cottage ★★★
Contact: Mr Martin McShane
Red Rose Cottages, 6 King Street, Clitheroe BB7 2EP
T: (0120) 042 0101
F: (0120) 042 0103
I: www.redrosecottages.co.uk

BRINSCALL
Lancashire

Moors View Cottage ★★★
Contact: Mrs Sheila Smith
Four Seasons Guest House, 9 Cambridge Road, Thornton, Cleveleys FY5 1EP
T: (01253) 853537 & 07747 808406
F: (01624) 662190

BUNBURY
Cheshire

Woodworth Lodge ★★
Contact: Mr Dykes
Woodworth House, Birds Lane, Tarporley CW6 9PU
T: (01829) 260581

BURROW
Lancashire

River Bank Cottage ★★★★
Contact: Dales Holiday Cottages
River Bank Cottage, Dales Holiday Cottages, Skipton BD23 2AA
T: (0175) 679 9821
F: (0175) 679 7012
E: info@dalesholcot.com
I: www.dalesholcot.com

BURTON
Cheshire

Honeysuckle Cottage ★★★★
Contact: Mrs C E Nevett
Honeysuckle Cottage, Warren House Farm, Burton Road, Tarporley CW6 0ES
T: (01829) 781178
E: nevettcb@hotmail.com

CARNFORTH
Lancashire

Coppernob Mews ★★★
Contact: Mr Peter Durbin
Cumbrian Cottages, 2 Lonsdale Street, Carlisle CA1 1DB
T: (01228) 599960
F: (01228) 599970
E: enquiries@cumbriancottages.co.uk

Deroy Cottage ★★★
Contact: Mr & Mrs Cross
Deroy, The Heights, Carnforth LA5 9LA
T: (01524) 733196
E: colin@colincross.co.uk
I: www.colincross.co.uk

Mansergh Farm House Cottages ★★★★
Contact: Mr & Mrs Morphy
Mansergh Farm House Cottages, Carnforth LA6 1JS
T: (01524) 732586
E: linda@manserghcottages.co.uk
I: www.manserghcottages.co.uk

Pine Lake Lodges ★★★★
Contact: Mr Tony Commons
2 Lonsdale Street, Carlisle CA1 1DB
T: (01228) 599960
F: (01228) 599970
I: www.cumbrian-cottages.co.uk

CATON
Lancashire

4 The Croft (Ground Floor Apartment) ★★★★
Contact: Sue Brierly-Hampton
4 The Croft (Ground Floor Apartment), Lancaster LA2 9QG
I: www.holiday-rentals.com/10721

Marybank Barn ★★★
Contact: Mrs Julie Fisher
Marybank Barn, Caton Green, Lancaster LA2 9JG
T: (01524) 770339

CHESTER
Cheshire

The Almshouse ★★★★
Contact: Ms Karen Mann
Crowmere House, Drovers Lane, Frodsham WA6 6HA
T: (01928) 733096

Cherry Tree Cottage & Damson Cottage ★★★★
Contact: Mr and Mrs R Menzies
Cheshire Country Cottages, Poplar House, Sandy Lane, Tarvin, Chester CH3 8JQ
T: (01829) 740732
F: (01829) 740722
E: info@cheshirecottages.com
I: www.cheshirecottages.com

Chester Apartment ★★★
Contact: Mrs Susan Marshall
Chester Apartment, 27 Grey Friars, Chester CH1 2NW
T: (01244) 400225
F: (01244) 400225

Look out for establishments participating in the National Accessible Scheme

ENGLAND'S NORTHWEST

The City Apartments ★★★★
Contact: Moira Martland
The City Apartment, Upton Lodge, Wealstone Lane, Upton, Chester CH2 1HD
T: (01244) 372091
F: (01244) 374779
E: chesterhols@btinternet.com
I: www.chesterholidays.co.uk

City Walls Apartments ★★★
Contact: Mr Rod Cox
1 City Walls, Rufus Court, Chester CH1 2JG
T: (01244) 313400
F: (01244) 400414

Domini Mews ★★★
Contact: Mr & Mrs Massey
Domini Mews, 46 York Road, Connahs Quay, Deeside CH5 4YE
T: (01244) 815664
F: (01244) 815664

Duchess Apartment ★★★★★
Contact: Mrs W J Appleton
Blakemere Lane, Warrington WA6 6NW
T: (01928) 788355
F: (01928) 788507
E: ches@williamj99.freeserve.co.uk

Fir Tree Cottage ★★★
Contact: Mrs Ursula Owen
Fir Tree House, 71 Heath Road, Upton, Chester CH2 1HT
T: (01244) 382681

Handbridge Village ★★★
Contact: Mrs R A Owen
Handbridge Village, Eaton Road, Chester CH4 7EN
T: (01244) 676159
F: (01244) 676159

Ivy Cottage ★★★
Contact: Joseph H D Barry
RMD Heritage, Dee Fords Avenue, Chester CH3 5UP
T: (01244) 403534
E: rmd.heritage@btconnect.com
I: www.rmd-heritage.co.uk

Kingswood Coach House ★★★
Contact: Mrs C Perry
Kingswood Coach House, Parkgate Road, Kingswood, Chester CH1 6JS
T: (01244) 851204
F: (01244) 851244
E: caroline.m.perry@btopenworld.com

Little Mayfield ★★
Contact: Mr Michael John Cullen
Mayfield House, Warrington Road, Hoole Village CH2 4EX
T: (01244) 300131
F: (01244) 300131

Mews Style Cottages ★★★★★
Contact: Karen Buchan
Accredited Property Rentals of Chester, Auchmacoy House, Llanfair Road, Abergele LL22 8DH
T: (01745) 825880
F: (01745) 825880
E: k.buchan@btinternet.com
I: www.chesterholidaycottages.com

Queen's Park ★★★
Contact: Mrs Lilian Maddock
Queen's Park, 24 Elizabeth Crescent, Queen's Park, Chester CH4 7AZ
T: (01244) 676141

RMD Heritage ★★★
Contact: Mr & Mrs J H D Barry
RMD Heritage, Woodsorrel, 18 Dee Fords Avenue, Chester CH3 5UP
T: (01244) 403630
F: (01244) 403699
E: rmd.heritage@btconnect.com
I: www.rmd-heritage.co.uk

Russia House ★★
Contact: Ian Bennion
Oldfield Crescent, Chester CH4 7PE
T: (01244) 629177

Spireview Apartment ★★★★
Contact: Mr Mike Pimlott
14 Beckenham Road, New Brighton, Wallasey CH45 2NR
E: corkeyhomes@hotmail.com

Stapleford Hall Cottage ★★★
Contact: M J Winward
Stapleford Hall Cottage, Stapleford Hall, Chester CH3 8HH
T: (01829) 740202
F: (01829) 740202
E: staplefordcottage@hotmail.com
I: www.staplefordhallcottage.com

York House ★★★★
Contact: Mr & Mrs Davies
Handbridge Self Catering, Whitegate Farm, Peckforton Hall Lane, Spurston, Tarporley CW6 9TG
T: (01829) 261601
F: (01829) 261602
E: stevedavies@euphony.net

CHIPPING
Lancashire

Fell View ★★★★
Contact: Mr Martin McShane
Red Rose Cottages, 6 King Street, Clitheroe BB7 2EP
T: (0120) 042 0101
F: (0120) 042 0103
I: www.redrosecottages.co.uk

Hall Trees Barn West ★★★★
Contact: Mr & Mrs Lesley Lloyd
Hall Trees Barn West, Turnleys Farm, Preston PR3 2TD
T: (0177) 278 3294
F: (0177) 278 3294

Pale Farm Cottages ★★★★
Contact: Mrs Lynn Ollerton
Pale Farm Cottages, 113 Halfpenny Lane, Preston PR3 2EA
T: (0177) 278 3082
I: www.palefarmcottages.co.uk

Rakefoot Barn ★★★-★★★★
Contact: Mrs Gifford
Rakefoot Farm, Thornley Road, Nr Clitheroe BB7 3LY
T: (01995) 61332
F: (01995) 61296
E: info@rakefootfarm.co.uk
I: www.rakefootfarm.co.uk

CHURCHTOWN
Merseyside

Mews Cottage
Rating Applied For
Contact: Mrs Palmer
Mews Cottage, 76A Botanic Road, Southport PR9 7NE

CLITHEROE
Lancashire

Five Fells Cottage ★★★
Contact: Mr & Mrs Hailwood
Albion House, Kirkmoor Road, Clitheroe BB7 2DU
T: (01200) 424240
E: roland.hailwood@talk21.com

Hawk Cottage ★★★★
Contact: Mr Martin Mcshane
Red Rose Cottages, 6 King Street, Clitheroe BB7 2EP
T: (0120) 042 0101
F: (0120) 042 0103
E: info@redrosecottages.co.uk
I: www.redrosecottages.co.uk

Higher Gills Farm ★★★★
Contact: Mrs Freda Pilkington
Higher Gills Farm, Clitheroe BB7 4DA
T: (0120) 044 5370
I: www.highergills.co.uk

&

Hydes Farm Holiday Cottages ★★★
Contact: Mrs Jean Howard
Hydes Farm, Clitheroe BB7 3DY
T: (01200) 446353

Number 10 ★★★
Contact: Mrs Newhouse
Number 10, 18 Church Street, Clitheroe BB7 3ER
T: (0120) 044 6620
F: (0120) 044 6620

Ribble Cottage ★★★
Contact: Mr Martin Mcshane
Red Rose Cottages, 6 King Street, Clitheroe BB7 2EP
T: (0120) 042 0101
F: (0120) 042 0103
E: info@redrosecottages.co.uk
I: www.redrosecottages.co.uk

Saetr Cottage ★★★
Contact: Mrs Victoria Wood
Harrod Fold, Clitheroe BB7 4PJ
T: (01200) 447600

COCKERHAM
Lancashire

Near Moss Farm Holidays ★★★
Contact: Mr Sutcliffe
Near Moss Farm Holidays, Lancaster LA2 0ER
T: (0125) 379 0504
F: (0125) 379 0043
I: www.nearmossfarm.co.uk

Patty's Farm Barn ★★★★
Contact: Mr Chris Parry
Patty's Farm Barn, Hillam Lane Farm, Hillman Lane, Lancaster LA2 0DY
T: (01524) 751285
F: (01524) 751285

COLNE
Lancashire

White Syke Farm ★★★
Contact: Mrs Elizabeth Jean Haythornthwaite
Aynhams Farm, Brogden Lane, Barnoldswick BB18 5XE
T: (01282) 815731

CONGLETON
Cheshire

Acorn Cottages ★★★★
Contact: Mr & Mrs Mark Bullock
Acorn Cottages, Oaklands, Congleton CW12 2PH
T: (01260) 223388
F: (01260) 223085
E: mark.bullock@lineone.net
I: www.acorncottages-england.co.uk

Yew Tree Farm Cottage ★★★★
Contact: Ann Syson
Yew Tree Farm Cottage, North Rode, Congleton CW12 2PF
T: (01260) 223547
E: syson@ukonline.co.uk

COW ARK
Lancashire

Marl Hill House ★★★★
Contact: Mr Martin Mcshane
Red Rose Cottages, 6 King Street, Clitheroe BB7 2EP
T: (01200) 420101
F: (01200) 420103
E: info@redrosecottages

CROSTON
Lancashire

Cockfight Barn ★★★★
Contact: Mr Martin Mcshane
Red Rose Cottages, 6 King Street, Clitheroe BB7 2EP
T: (0120) 042 0101
F: (0120) 042 0103
E: info@redrosecottages.co.uk
I: www.redrosecottages.co.uk

CUDDINGTON
Cheshire

Coach House at the Mount
Rating Applied For
Contact: Ms Annete Elwell
Coach House at the Mount, Cuddington Lane - The Mount, Northwich CW8 2SZ
T: (01606) 884278

Establishments printed in blue have a detailed entry in this guide   403

ENGLAND'S NORTHWEST

DELAMERE
Cheshire

Wicken Tree Farm ★★★
Contact: Mrs W J Appleton
Wicken Tree Farm, Blakemere
Lane, Warrington WA6 6NW
T: (01928) 788355
F: (01928) 788507
E: ches@williamj99.freeserve.co.uk
I: www.wickentreefarm.co.uk

DISLEY
Cheshire

Plattwood Farm Cottage ★★★★
Contact: Mrs Jill Emmott
Plattwood Farm Lyme Park,
Stockport SK12 2NT
T: (01625) 872738
F: (01625) 872738
E: plattwoodfarm@talk21.com
I: www.plattwoodfarm.com

DOWNHAM
Lancashire

Stables Lodge Cottage ★★★
Contact: Mr Taylor
Stables Lodge Cottage, The Post Office, Clitheroe BB7 4BJ
T: (01200) 441242

ECCLESTON
Cheshire

Riverside Cottage ★★★★
Contact: Suzanne Butterfield
Riverside Cottage, Riverside House, Church Road, Eccleston, Chester CH4 9HT
T: (01244) 675705

EGERTON
Cheshire

Manor Farm Holiday Cottages ★★★
Contact: J Dilworth
Manor Farm, Cholmondeley, Malpas SY14 8AW
T: (01829) 720261

FADDILEY
Cheshire

Old Cart House ★★★★★
Contact: Mrs Ruth Robinson
Old Cart House, Wood Hey Hall, Wood Hey Hall Lane, Nantwich CW5 8JH
T: (01270) 524215
F: (01270) 524677

FARNDON
Cheshire

Woodpecker Cottage ★★★★
Contact: Sue Heyworth
Woodpecker Cottage, Higher House, Caldecott Green, Farndon, Chester CH3 6PE
T: (01829) 270927

GARSTANG
Lancashire

Barnacre Cottages ★★★★★
Contact: Mr Terence Sharples
Barnacre Cottages, The Old Shippon, Arkwright Farm, Eidsforth Lane, Preston PR3 1GN
T: (01995) 600918
F: (01995) 600918
I: www.barnacre-cottages.co.uk

GISBURN
Lancashire

Coverdale Farm
Rating Applied For
Contact: Mrs Mandy Pilkington
Coverdale Farm, Clitheroe BB7 4JL
T: (0120) 044 5265

GREAT BARROW
Cheshire

Hawthorn Cottage ★★★
Contact: E. M. Pratt
Hawthorn Cottage, Woodlea, 44 Guilden Sutton Lane, Guilden Sutton, Chester CH3 7EY
T: (01344) 317287

GREAT ECCLESTON
Lancashire

Townside House ★★★
Contact: Mrs Judith Arnold
Townside House, Raikes Road, Preston PR3 0ZA
T: (01995) 670086
F: (01995) 670086

GRESSINGHAM
Lancashire

Garden Cottage ★★★
Contact: Mrs Margaret Burrow
Garden Cottage, Lancaster LA2 8LS
T: (01524) 221347
E: gardencottage@highsnab.freeserve.co.uk
I: www.highsnab.freeserve.co.uk

GRINDLETON
Lancashire

Crossfold House Holiday Cottage ★★★
Contact: Mrs Sheila Hailwood
Crossfold House Holiday Cottage, Crossfold House, Clitheroe BB7 4QT
T: (0120) 044 0178
F: (0120) 044 0587
E: rodney@rhailwood.freeserve.co.uk

HARROP FOLD
Lancashire

Harrop Fold Cottages ★★-★★★
Contact: Mr Frank Robinson
Dales Holiday Cottages, Harrop Fold, Clitheroe BB7 4PJ
T: (01200) 447665
I: www.cottagesdirect.com/cottagedetails.asp?searchId=yoa149

HIGH LANE
Greater Manchester

Ty Coch ★★★
Contact: Jane Beard
1 Huron Crescent, Lakeside, Cardiff CF23 6DT
T: (02920) 761888
E: townsendsom@hotmail.com

HOOLE
Cheshire

St James Apartments ★★★★
Contact: June & William Smith
Ba Ba Guest House, 65, Hoole Road, Chester CH2 3NJ
T: (01244) 315047
F: (01244) 315046
E: reservations@chesterholidayrentals.co.uk
I: www.chesterholidayrentals.co.uk

HOYLAKE
Wirral

AAA North Villa Apartments ★★★★
Contact:
AAA North Villa Apartments, 33 Cable Road, Wirral CH47 2AY
T: (0151) 632 3982
F: (0151) 632 3982
E: sandraverkade@tiscali.co.uk
I: www.northvilla.com

KELSALL
Cheshire

Northwood Hall ★★★
Contact: Mr Andrew Nock
Northwood Hall, Dog Lane, Tarporley CW6 0RP
T: (01829) 752569
F: (01829) 751157
E: enquiries@northwood-hall.co.uk
I: www.northwood-hall.co.uk

KETTLESHULME
Greater Manchester

Townfield Farm
Rating Applied For
Contact: Mrs Christine Hallam
Townfield Farm, Macclesfield Road, High Peak SK23 7EJ
T: (01663) 733450

KNUTSFORD
Cheshire

Danebury Serviced Apartments ★★★★
Contact: Mr Stephen & Mrs Pauline West
Danebury Apartments, 8 Tabley Road, Knutsford WA16 0NB
T: (01565) 755219
E: info@daneburyapartments.co.uk
I: www.daneburyapartments.co.uk

Mile End Apartment
Rating Applied For
Contact: Ms Diane Graziano
Mile End, 9 Tabley Road, Knutsford WA16 0NB
T: (01565) 632079
F: (01606) 44417
E: david.graziano@ntlworld.com
I: www.mile-end.co.uk

6 The Sycamores & 7 The Cedars ★★★★
Contact: Mrs Jenny Dawson
6 The Sycamores & 7 The Cedars, Croft Cottage, Hough Lane, Alderley Edge SK9 7JE
T: (01625) 599802
F: (01625) 599802
E: info@interludes-uk.com

LANCASTER
Lancashire

Langthwaite Farm Cottages ★★★★
Contact: Donald and Joan Deering
Langthwaite Farm Cottages, Langthwaite Farm, Lancaster LA2 9EB
T: (0152) 462 388
F: (0152) 434 143
E: info@langthwaitefarmcottages.co.uk
I: www.langthwaitefarmcottages.co.uk/

Mulberry Cottage ★★★
Contact: Mrs Catherine Fatkin
Mulberry Cottage, 8 Castle Park, Lancaster LA1 1YQ
T: (0152) 464 755
I: www.mulberrycottages.uk.com

The Stables ★★★
Contact: Mr & Mrs Quinn
The Stables, Conder Green Cottage, Lancaster LA2 0BG
T: (0152) 475 1568
F: (0152) 475 1568
E: thestable@conder-green.freeserve.co.uk

LANESHAW BRIDGE
Lancashire

Spaw Cottage ★★★★
Contact: Mr Martin McShane
Red Rose Cottages, 6 King Street, Clitheroe BB7 2EP

LIVERPOOL
Merseyside

City Quay ★★★
Contact: Mrs Eileen Jones
City Quay, Apt 316 Ellerman Road, Liverpool L3 4FH
T: (0151) 7277134
E: jeileenjones@aol.com.uk

Days Serviced Appartments (Howard Johnson) ★★★
Contact: Mr Richard Howard
Premier Apartments, L3 Complex, 15 Hatton Garden, Liverpool L3 2HB
T: 07951 539040
F: (0151) 2279468
E: sales@liverpool.premgroup.com
I: www.liverpool-apartments.com

Liverpool City Apartments
Rating Applied For
Contact: Mr Keith Baldwin
Apartment 65 Hudson Gardens, 136 Duke Street, Liverpool L1 5BB
T: (0151) 7081805

Medici Building
Rating Applied For
Contact: Ms Julie Gardiner
Medici Building, 36 Upper Paliment Street, Liverpool L8 1TE
T: (0186) 532 1106
F: (0186) 532 1101
E: greenhavenoxford@btconnect.com
I: www.holidayhomeoxford.co.uk

ENGLAND'S NORTHWEST

Mersey Waterfront Apartments ★★★★
Contact: Mr Ian & Mrs Janet Shields
Mersey Waterfront Apartments, 135 Royal Quay, Kings Dock, Liverpool L3 4EX
T: (0151) 7440
E: merseywaterfrontapartments@aol.com
I: www.merseywaterfrontapartments.co.uk

Quay Flat ★★★
Contact:
Quay Flat, 2 Royal Quay, Liverpool L3 4ET
T: (0151) 625 7298

Trafalgar Warehouse Apartments ★★★★
Contact: Mr Ray Gibson
25 Rosedale Road, Liverpool L18 5JD
T: (0151) 734 4924 & 07715 118419
F: (0151) 734 4924

Waterfront Penthouse ★★★★
Contact: Mrs Muriel Simpson
Waterfront Penthouse, 424 South Ferry Quay, Clippers Quay, Liverpool L2 4EZ
T: 07860 351684
F: (01695) 727877
E: rod+muir@stayinginliverpool.com
I: www.stayinginliverpool.com

LYTHAM ST ANNES
Lancashire

The Chymes Holiday Flats ★★★
Contact: Mrs Winstanley
The Chymes Holiday Flats, 21 Fairhaven Road, Lytham St Annes FY8 1NN
T: (01253) 726942
F: (01253) 726942

Cobble Cottage
Rating Applied For
Contact: Mrs Doreen Cryer
Cobble Cottage, Ribble Nurseries, Lodge Lane, Lytham St Annes FY8 5RP
T: (01253) 736138

Merlewood Holiday Apartments ★★★
Contact: Sharon
Merlewood Holiday Apartments, 383 Clifton Drive North, Lytham St Annes FY8 2PA
T: (01253) 726082

MACCLESFIELD
Cheshire

Holiday Cottages North East Cheshire ★★
Contact: Mr Longden
Holiday Cottages North East Cheshire, 34 Shaw Street, Macclesfield SK11 6QY
T: (01625) 875137
E: hcnecaccommodation@msn.com

Mellow Brook Cottage ★★★★
Contact: Susan Stevenson
Mellow Brook Cottage, Harrop Fold Farm, Macclesfield Road, Macclesfield SK10 5UU
T: (01625) 560085
E: susan@harropstudio.fsnet.co.uk

Mill House Farm Cottage ★★★
Contact: Mrs Lynne Whittaker
Mill House Farm, Bosley, Macclesfield SK11 0NZ
T: (01260) 226265
I: http://www.geocities.com/farm_cottage

The Teachers Cottage ★★★
Contact: Mr & Mrs Harrop
The Teachers Cottage, School House, Macclesfield SK11 0AR
T: (01260) 252674
F: (01260) 252674
E: enquiries@peakcottages.com
I: www.peakcottages.com

MANCHESTER
Greater Manchester

Days Serviced Apartments ★★★
Contact: Mrs Valerie Smith
Days Serviced Apartments, 3, Dale Street, Manchester M1 1JA
T: (0161) 236 8963
F: (0161) 238 8762
E: vsmith@premgroup.com
I: www.premgroup.com

La Suisse Service Apartments (Bury Old Road) ★★★
Contact: Mr Michael Phillips
La Suisse Service Apartments (Bury Old Road), 444 Bury Old Road, Manchester M25 1PQ
T: (0161) 796 0545
F: (0161) 796 0545
E: reservations@lasuisse.co.uk
I: www.lasuisse.co.uk

The Place Apartment Hotel ★★★★
Contact: Ms Clare Johnson
The Place Apartment Hotel, Ducie Street, Piccadilly M1 2TP
T: (0161) 778 7500
F: (0161) 778 7507
E: reservations@theplaceforliving.com
I: www.theplacehotel.com

MIDDLEWICH
Cheshire

Forge Mill Farm Cottages ★★★-★★★★★
Contact: Mrs Susan Moss
Forge Mill Farm Cottages, Forge Mill Farm, Forge Mill Lane, Warmingham, Middlewich CW10 0HQ
T: (01270) 526204
F: (01270) 526204
E: forgemill2@msn.com

MILNROW
Greater Manchester

Butterworth Hall ★★★★
Contact: Mrs Judith Hirst
31 Butterworth Hall, Rochdale OL16 3PE
T: (01706) 633342
F: (01706) 354890
E: gatehouse@springmill414.fsnet.co.uk
I: www.springmill.co.uk

MOBBERLEY
Cheshire

5 The Cedars ★★★★
Contact: Ms Jenny Dawson
Interludes, Croft Cottage, Hough Lane, Alderley Edge SK9 7JE
T: (01625) 599802
F: (01625) 599802

MORECAMBE
Lancashire

Eden Vale Luxury Holiday Flats ★★★
Contact: Mr Jason Coombs
Eden Vale Luxury Holiday Flats, 338 Marine Road, Morecambe LA4 5AB
T: (01524) 415544

Lakeland View Holiday Flat ★★
Contact: Mr Derek Morgan
Lakeland View Holiday Flat, 10 Princes Crescent, Morecambe LA4 6BX
T: (01524) 831355
F: (01524) 831244
E: derek@flowershop.org.uk

Mountfield Holiday Flats ★★
Contact: Mrs Janet Mayers
Mountfield Holiday Flats, 67 Balmoral Road, Morecambe LA4 4JS
T: (01524) 423518

Northumberland House ★★
Contact: Mr Neil Briggs
Northumberland House, 42 Northumberland Street, Morecambe LA4 4BA
T: (01524) 412039
E: j.s.shaw@tesco.net

St Ives and Rydal Mount ★
Contact: Mrs Holmes
St Ives and Rydal Mount, Morecambe LA4 5AQ
T: (0152) 441 1858

Sandown Holiday Flats ★★
Contact: Mr & Mrs Colin Matthews
Sandown Holiday Flats, Sandown Holiday Flats, Morecambe LA4 5AQ
T: (0152) 441 0933

NANTWICH
Cheshire

Bank Farm Cottages ★★★
Contact: Margaret Vaughan
Bank Farm Cottages, Newcastle Road, Hough, Nr Crewe CW2 5JG
T: (01270) 841809
F: (01270) 841809

Fields Farm ★★
Contact: Mr David Heys
Fields Farm, Off Queens Drive, Nantwich CW5 5JL
T: (01270) 625769
F: (01270) 625769

NESTON
Cheshire

The Field House ★★★★
Contact: Mrs Anna Wild
The Field House, Upper Raby Road, Wirral CH64 7TZ
T: (0151) 336 1728
I: www.the-field-house.uk.com

NETHER KELLET
Lancashire

The Apartment ★★★
Contact: Mr Richardson
10 Meadowcroft, Nether Kellet, Carnforth LA6 1HN
T: (01524) 734969 & 736331

Ashlea Cottage ★★★★
Contact:
Ashlea Cottage, Carnforth LA6 1ET
T: (0152) 473 6324

OLDHAM
Greater Manchester

Clifton Cottage ★★★
Contact: Mrs Wood
113 Chew Valley Road, Greenfield, Saddleworth, Oldham OL3 7JJ
T: (01457) 872098
F: (01457) 870760
E: ced117@aol.com

ORMSKIRK
Lancashire

Tristrams Farm Holiday Cottages ★★★
Contact: Mr David Swift
Tristrams Farm Holiday Cottages, Ormskirk L39 8RL
T: (0170) 484 0323

OSCROFT
Cheshire

Ash Cottage ★★★
Contact: Bookings Manager
Country Holidays, Spring Mill, Barnoldswick BB94 0AA
T: (01282) 445096
F: (01282) 844288
E: ownerservices@holidaycottagesgroup.com
I: www.country-holidays.co.uk

OVER KELLET
Lancashire

Lime Tree Cottage ★★
Contact: Mrs Greaves
Lime Tree Cottage, The Green, Carnforth LA6 1DA
T: (01524) 732165

PAYTHORNE
Lancashire

The Hawthorns ★★★
Contact: Mr Allan & Mrs Sarah Martin
The Hawthorns, Clitheroe BB7 4JD
T: (01200) 445911
E: slipdisc@tiscali.co.uk
I: www.hawthorns.me.uk

ENGLAND'S NORTHWEST

POULTON
Cheshire

Half Mile Cottage ★★★
Contact: Mrs Margaret Walker
Half Mile Cottage, 6 Straight
Mile, Chester CH4 9EQ
T: (01244) 570435
F: (01244) 570435
E: wallpoul@bytecraft.net

POULTON-LE-FYLDE
Lancashire

Swans Rest Holiday Cottages ★★★★
Contact: Mrs Irene O'Connor
Swans Rest Holiday Cottages,
Garstang Road East, Poulton-le-Fylde FY6 8LX
T: (0125) 388 6617
F: (0125) 389 2563
E: swansrest@btconnect.com
I: www.swansrest.co.uk

QUERNMORE
Lancashire

Daisy Bank Cottage ★★★
Contact: Mrs Janette Callon
Daisy Bank Cottage, Lancaster LA1 3JN
T: (0152) 435 493

Lodge View Cottages ★★★
Contact: Mr David Gardner
Far Lodge, Lancaster LA2 9EF
T: (01524) 63109
E: djkagardner@ukgateway.net

RIBCHESTER
Lancashire

Sunny Nook Cottage ★★★★
Contact: Mr Martin McShane
Red Rose Cottages, 6 King Street, Clitheroe BB7 2EP
T: (01200) 420101
F: (01200) 420103
E: info@redcottages.co.uk

RIMINGTON
Lancashire

Raikes Barn ★★★★
Contact: Mrs Robinson
Raikes Barn, Beckside Farm, Clitheroe BB7 4EE
T: (0120) 044 5287
F: (0120) 044 5287
I: www.raikesbarn.co.uk

Tewit and Badger Cottages ★★★★
Contact: Mrs Anne Smith
No. 1 Howcroft Cottages,
Stopper Lane, Clitheroe BB7 4EJ
T: (01200) 445598
F: (01200) 444188
I: www.ruralcottage.co.uk

ROCHDALE
Greater Manchester

The Gatehouse ★★★★
Contact: Mr David Hirst
The Gatehouse, Ogden Lane,
Lower Ogden, Newhey, Rochdale OL16 3TQ
T: (01706) 633342
F: (01706) 643432
E: gatehouse@springmill.fsnet.co.uk
I: www.springmill.co.uk

SABDEN
Lancashire

Kingfisher Cottage ★★★★
Contact: Mr Gordon Greenwood
Kingfisher Cottage, Greenbank Farm, Whalley Road, Clitheroe BB7 9DT
T: (01254) 823064
E: gordon.greenwood@virgin.net

SALFORD
Greater Manchester

30 The Gallery
Rating Applied For
Contact: Kash Ijaz
1 Old Town, London SW4 0JT
T: (020) 7388993
F: (020) 7388994
E: info@kash.co.uk
I: www.kash.co.uk

SAWLEY
Lancashire

Riverside Barn ★★★★
Contact: Mr Martin Mcshane
Red Rose Cottages, 6 King Street, Clitheroe BB7 2EP
T: (0120) 042 0101
F: (0120) 042 0103
E: info@redrosecottages.co.uk
I: www.btinternet.com/~sawley.holidaycottage/index.html

SILVERDALE
Lancashire

Old Waterslack Farmhouse Caravan Cottages ★★★
Contact: Mrs Hevey
Old Waterslack Farmhouse Caravan Cottages, Old Waterslack Farmhouse, Carnforth LA5 0UH
T: (01524) 701108
F: (01524) 844280
E: n.hevey@oldwaterslackfarm.ukf.net
I: www.oldwaterslackfarm.ukf.net

Pheasant Field ★★★
Contact: Sykes Cottages Ref: 684
Sykes Cottages, York House, York Street, Chester CH1 3LR
T: (01244) 345700
F: (01244) 321442
E: info@sykescottages.co.uk
I: www.sykescottages.co.uk

The Stables ★★★★
Contact: Mrs Ranford
The Stables, Lindeth House, Lindeth Road, Carnforth LA5 0TT
T: (01524) 702121
F: (01524) 702226
E: conquerors.maryk@virgin.net

Swallows End
Rating Applied For
Contact: Fiona Moody
Dales Holiday Cottages, Carleton Business Centre, Carleton New Road, Skipton BD23 2AA
T: (01756) 790919
F: (01756) 797012
E: info@dales-holiday-cottages.com
I: www.dales-holiday-cottages.com/

Virginia Cottage ★★★★
Contact: Mr Peter Durbin
Cumbrian Cottages, 2 Lonsdale Street, Carlisle CA1 1DB
T: (01228) 599960
F: (01228) 599970
E: enquiries@cumbrian-cottages.co.uk
I: www.cumbrian-cottages.co.uk

Wolf House Cottage ★★★-★★★★
Contact: Mrs Denise Dowbiggin
Wolf House Cottage, Gibraltar, Carnforth LA5 0TX
T: (01524) 701573
F: (01524) 701573
E: denise@wolfhouse-gallery.co.uk
I: www.wolfhouse-gallery.co.uk

SLAIDBURN
Lancashire

Laythams Farmhouse & Cottage ★★★★
Contact: Mr Ian Roger Driver
1 Laythams Farm, Back Lane, Clitheroe BB7 3AJ
T: (01200) 446454
F: (01200) 446454
E: iandriver@talk21.com
I: www.slaidburn.com/laythams

The Olde Stables ★★★★
Contact: Mrs Margaret Robinson
The Olde Stables, Clitheroe BB7 3AQ
T: (0120) 044 6240
F: (0120) 044 6412

SOUTHPORT
Merseyside

Barford House Apartments ★★★
Contact: Mr Graham Watson
Barford House Apartments, 32 Avondale Road, Southport PR9 0ND
F: (0170) 453 0735
E: graham@barfordhouse.co.uk
I: www.barfordhouse.co.uk

Beaucliffe Holiday Flats ★★★
Contact: Mrs Linda Lewis
Beaucliffe Holiday Flats, 9 Leicester Street, Southport PR9 0ER
T: (0170) 453 7207
E: linda@beaucliffeholidayflats.co.uk
I: www.beaucliffeholidayflats.co.uk

Carlmerl Apartments
Rating Applied For
Contact: Mr Harrison Clive
Carlmerl Apartments, 36 Bath Street, Southport PR9 0DA
E: carlmerl@bushinternet.com
I: www.carlmerl.homestead.com

Castle Mews ★★★
Contact: Mr Graham Watson
Castle Mews, 32 Avondale Road, Southport PR9 0ND
F: (0170) 453 0735
E: graham@barfordhouse.co.uk
I: www.barfordhouse.co.uk

Den-Rae Holiday Flats
Rating Applied For
Contact: Mr Warscher
87 King Street, Southport PR8 1LQ
T: (01704) 530918

Martin Lane Farmhouse Holiday Cottages ★★★★
Contact: Mrs Stubbs
Martin Lane Farmhouse, Martin Lane, Burscough L40 8JH
T: (01704) 893527
F: (01704) 893527
E: mlfhc@btinternet.com
I: www.martinlanefarmhouse.btinternet.co.uk

Sandcroft Holidy Flats ★
Contact: Mr Ralph Best
Sandcroft Holiday Flats, 13 Albany Road, Southport PR9 0JF
T: (0170) 453 7497

Sandy Brook Farm ★★★
Contact: Mr Core
Sandy Brook Farm, 52 Wyke Cop Road, Scarisbrick, Southport PR8 5LR
T: (01704) 880337
F: (01704) 880337
E: sandybrookfarm@lycos.com

Southport Holiday Apartments
Rating Applied For
Contact: Mrs Susan Lea
Southport Holiday Apartments, 34 Bold Street, Southport PR9 0ED
T: (0170) 453 0792
E: susan-lea@btconnect.com
I: www.southportholidayapartments.co.uk

STOCKPORT
Greater Manchester

Lake View ★★★
Contact: Mrs M Sidebottom
Shire Cottage, Benches Lane, Marple Bridge, Stockport SK6 5RY
T: (01457) 866536
F: (01457) 866536
E: monica@lakeviewscstockport6.fsbusiness.co.uk

STONYHURST
Blackburn with Darwen

Alden Cottage ★★★★
Contact: Mr B Carpenter
Alden Cottage, Kemple End, Birdy Brow, Clitheroe BB7 9QY
T: (01254) 826468
F: (01254) 826468
E: carpenter@aldencottagef9.co.uk
I: fp.aldencottage.f9.co.uk

SUTTON
Cheshire

Lower Pethills Farm Cottage ★★★★
Contact: Mr & Mrs Greg Rowson
Lower Pethills Farm Cottages, Lower Pethills Farm, Macclesfield SK11 0NJ
T: (01260) 252410

TABLEY
Cheshire

3 Waterless Brook Cottages ★★★
Contact: Mr Roger Thorp
3 Waterless Brook Cottages, Pickermere Lane, Knutsford WA16 0LN
T: (01565) 734159
F: (0161) 9297088
E: rthorp@tinyworld.co.uk

ENGLAND'S NORTHWEST

TARVIN
Cheshire
Cheese Makers Cottage ★★★
Contact: Elaine Sherwin
Cross Lanes Farm, Broomheath Lane, Stapleford, Chester CH3 8HE
T: (01829) 740439
E: jc.em.sherwin@agricontractors.fsnet.co.uk

THORNLEY
Lancashire
Thornley Hall ★★★
Contact: Mrs Airey
Thornley Hall, Thornley Hall Farm, Preston PR3 2TN
T: (0199) 561 243

TOSSIDE
Lancashire
Primrose Cottage, Jenny Wren, Wagtail, Swallows, Lower Gill Farm House ★★★★
Contact: Mr Roger Wales
Holiday Cottages (Yorkshire), Water Street, Skipton BD23 1PB
T: (01756) 700510
E: brochure@holidaycotts.co.uk
I: www.holidaycotts.co.uk

WADDINGTON
Lancashire
Hedgehog Cottage ★★★★
Contact: Mr Stephen Tasker
Hedgehog Cottage, Cuttock Clough Barn, Clitheroe BB7 3JJ
T: (0120) 042 9557
F: (0120) 042 9557
E: stephen_tasker@btinternet.com
I: www.hedgehogcottage.co.uk

WATERLOO
Merseyside
Liverpool Holiday Flats ★★★-★★★★★
Contact: Mr Michael Rothwell
Liverpool Holiday Flats, 24 - 26 North John Street, Liverpool L2 2AW
T: (0151) 928 4231
I: www.liverpoolholidayflats.co.uk

WENNINGTON
Lancashire
Easter Cottage ★★★★
Contact: Mrs Jenny Herd
Easter Cottage, Mill Farm, Lancaster LA2 8NU
T: (0152) 422 1690
I: www.easter-cottage.net

WESTHOUSE
Lancashire
Hillcrest ★★
Contact: Mr Brown
West House, Ingleton, Carnforth LA6 3PA
T: (015242) 41331

WHALLEY
Lancashire
Woodside ★★★
Contact: Mrs Hilary Whittaker
Woodside, 31 Sydney Avenue, Clitheroe BB7 9TF
T: (01254) 201658

WIGAN
Greater Manchester
Oysterber Farm Cottage Holidays ★★★
Contact: Mrs Cathy Cartledge
Oysterber Farm Cottage Holidays, Oysterber Farm, Burton Road, Wigan LA2 7ET
T: (015242) 61567
F: (015242) 62885
I: www.oysterberfarm.co.uk

WILDBOARCLOUGH
Cheshire
Lower House Cottage ★★
Contact: Mrs C. Waller
Lower House Cottage, Macclesfield SK11 0BL
T: (01260) 227266
F: (01260) 227266
E: sheponthehill@aol.com
I: www.lowerhousecottage.co.uk

WILLINGTON
Cheshire
Delamere Cottage ★★★★
Contact: Mr & Mrs Sidebotham
Delamere Cottage, Willington Road, Tarporley CW6 0ND
T: (01829) 751628
E: jhs@sebden.com

WINCLE
Cheshire
Clough Brook Cottage ★★★★
Contact: Mr John Henshall
Clough Brook Cottage, Almeadows Farm, Macclesfield SK11 0QU
T: (01260) 227209
F: (01260) 227209
E: henshalls@btinternet.com
I: www.allmeadows.co.uk

Lamborn Cottage ★★★★
Contact: Mrs Pam Bailey
Lamborn Cottage, Mill End Lane, Macclesfield SK11 0QG
T: (01260) 227291
F: (01260) 227291

WISWELL
Blackburn with Darwen
New Row Cottage ★★★
Contact: Mr Martin Mcshane
Red Rose Cottages, 6 King Street, Clitheroe BB7 2EP
T: (01200) 420101
F: (01200) 420103
E: info@redrosecottages.co.uk
I: www.redrosecottages.co.uk

WORSLEY
Greater Manchester
The Cottage - Worsley ★★★
Contact: Mr John Atherton
60 Worsley Road, Manchester M28 2SH
T: (0161) 7934157
F: (0161) 7934157

WORSTHORNE
Lancashire
Lower Bottin Cottage ★★★
Contact: Mr Martin McShane
Red Rose Cottages, 6 King Street, Clitheroe BB7 2EP
T: (01200) 420101
F: (01200) 420103
E: info@redrosecottages

YEALAND REDMAYNE
Lancashire
Brackenthwaite Cottages ★★★
Contact: Mrs Susan Clarke
Brackenthwaite Farm, Carnforth LA5 9TE
T: (015395) 63276
F: (015395) 63276
I: www.brackenthwaitecottages.co.uk

CUMBRIA – THE LAKE DISTRICT

AINSTABLE
Cumbria
The Old Dairy Cottage ★★★★
Contact: JE Moffat
The Old Dairy Cottage, Rowfoot, Carlisle CA4 9PZ
T: (01768) 896409
E: jackie@rowfoot.fsnet.co.uk
I: www.rowfoot-dairycottage.co.uk

ALLITHWAITE
Cumbria
Shamrock Cottage ★★★
Contact: Mr Peter Durbin
Cumbrian Cottages, 2 Lonsdale Street, Carlisle CA1 1DB
T: (01228) 599960
F: (01228) 599970
E: enquiries@cumbrian-cottages.co.uk
I: www.cumbrian-cottages.co.uk

ALLONBY
Cumbria
Crookhurst Farm ★★★★
Contact: Brenda Wilson
Crookhurst Farm, Bowscale Farm, Maryport CA15 6RB
T: (01900) 881228
E: brendawilson@zoom.co.uk
I: www.crookhurst.com

Red Howe
Rating Applied For
Contact: Mr Peter Durbin
Cumbrian Cottages, 2 Lonsdale Street, Carlisle CA1 1DB
T: (01228) 599960
F: (01228) 599970
E: enquiries@cumbrian-cottages.co.uk
I: www.cumbrian-cottages.co.uk

Spring Lea ★★★★
Contact: John Williamson
Spring Lea Caravan Park, Maryport CA15 6QF
T: (01900) 881331
F: (01900) 881209
E: mail@springlea.co.uk
I: www.springlea.co.uk

ALSTON
Cumbria
Connelly ★★★
Contact: Mr Timms
Connelly, 51 Silver Street, Ely CB7 4JB
T: (01353) 662171

Ghyll Burn Cottage ★★★
Contact: Mrs S Huntley
Ghyll Burn Cottage, Hartside Nursery Garden, Alston CA9 3BL
T: (01434) 381372
F: (01434) 381372
E: ghyllburn@macunlimited.net

Rock House Estate ★★★★
Contact: Mr Paul & Mrs Carol Huish
Valley View, Rock House Estate, Nenthead, Alston CA9 3NA
T: (01434) 382684
F: (01434) 382685
E: Paul@RockHouseEstate.co.uk
I: www.RockHouseEstate.co.uk

Stone Barn Cottage ★★★★★
Contact: Mrs Dee Ellis
Stone Barn Cottage, Low Galligill Farm, Alston CA9 3LW
T: (01434) 381672
I: www.hillfarmer.com

AMBLESIDE
Cumbria
1,2,3 Riverside Cottages ★★★
Contact: Mr Paul Liddell
Lakelovers, Belmont House, Lake Road, Bowness-on-Windermere, Windermere LA23 3BJ
T: (015394) 88855
F: (015394) 88857
E: bookings@lakelovers.co.uk
I: www.lakelovers.co.uk

Above Stock ★★★★
Contact: Paul Liddell
Lakelovers, Belmont House, Lake Road, Bowness-on-Windermere, Windermere LA23 3BJ
T: (015394) 88855
F: (015394) 88857

Establishments printed in blue have a detailed entry in this guide

CUMBRIA – THE LAKE DISTRICT

Acorns ★★★★
Contact: Susan Jackson
Heart of the Lakes, Fisherbeck Mill, Old Lake Road, Ambleside LA22 0DH
T: (015394) 32321
F: (015394) 33251
E: info@heartofthelakes.co.uk
I: www.heartofthelakes.co.uk

Altar End ★★★★
Contact: Susan Jackson
Heart of the Lakes, Fisherbeck Mill, Old Lake Road, Ambleside LA22 0DH
T: (015394) 32321
F: (015394) 33251
E: info@heartofthelakes.co.uk
I: www.heartofthelakes.co.uk

Amblers Rest ★★★★
Contact: Mr Peter Durbin
Cumbrian Cottages, 2 Lonsdale Street, Carlisle CA1 1DB
T: (01228) 599960
F: (01228) 599970
E: enquiries@cumbrian-cottages.co.uk
I: www.cumbrian-cottages.co.uk

20 and 21 The Falls ★★★
Contact: Mr Paul Liddell
Lakelovers, Belmont House, Lake Road, Bowness-on-Windermere, Windermere LA23 3BJ
T: (015394) 88855
F: (015394) 88857
E: bookings@lakelovers.co.uk
I: www.lakelovers.co.uk

Appletree Cottage ★★★
Contact: Mr Peter Durbin & Tony Commons
Cumbrian Cottages, 2 Lonsdale Street, Carlisle CA1 1DB
T: (01228) 599960
F: (01228) 599970
E: enquiries@cumbrian-cottages.co.uk
I: www.cumbrian-cottages.co.uk

Appletree Cottage ★★★★
Contact: Mrs Susan Jackson
Heart of the Lakes, Fisherbeck Mill, Old Lake Road, Ambleside LA22 0DH
T: (015394) 32321
F: (015394) 33251
E: info@heartofthelakes.co.uk
I: www.heartofthelakes.co.uk

Ashburne Cottage ★★
Contact: Susan Jackson
Heart of the Lakes, Fisherbeck Mill, Old Lake Road, Ambleside LA22 0DH
T: (015394) 32321
F: (015394) 33251

Ashness ★★★★
Contact: Mrs Susan Jackson
Heart of the Lakes, Fisherbeck Mill, Old Lake Road, Ambleside LA22 0DH
T: (015394) 32321
F: (015394) 33251
E: info@heartofthelakes.co.uk
I: www.heartofthelakes.co.uk

Babbling Brook ★★★★
Contact: Susan Jackson
Heart of the Lakes, Fisherbeck Mill, Old Lake Road, Ambleside LA22 0DH
T: (015394) 32321
F: (015394) 33251
E: info@heartofthelakes.co.uk
I: www.heartofthelakes.co.uk

7 Badgers Rake (The Garden Flat) ★★★
Contact: Mr Peter Durbin
Cumbrian Cottages, 2 Lonsdale Street, Carlisle CA1 1DB
T: (01228) 599960
F: (01228) 599970
E: enquiries@cumbrian-cottages.co.uk
I: www.cumbrian-cottages.co.uk

10 Badgers Rake ★★★★
Contact: Mr Peter Durbin
Cumbrian Cottages, 2 Lonsdale Street, Carlisle CA1 1DB
T: (01228) 599960
F: (01228) 599970
E: enquiries@cumbriancottages.co.uk
I: www.cumbrian-cottages.co.uk

9 Badgers Rake ★★★★
Contact: Mr Peter Durbin
Cumbrian Cottages, 2 Lonsdale Street, Carlisle CA1 1DB
T: (01228) 599960
F: (01228) 599970
E: enquiries@cumbriancottages.co.uk
I: www.cumbrian-cottages.co.uk

Bakestones Cottage ★★★★
Contact: Susan Jackson
Heart of the Lakes, Fisherbeck Mill, Old Lake Road, Ambleside LA22 0DH
T: (015394) 32321
F: (015394) 33251
E: info@heartofthelakes.co.uk
I: www.heartofthelakes.co.uk

Barn Waterhead ★★★★
Contact: Susan Jackson
Heart of the Lakes, Fisherbeck Mill, Old Lake Road, Ambleside LA22 0DH
T: (015394) 32321
F: (015394) 33251

Beck, Hillside and Couter Cottages ★★★
Contact: Mrs Morris
Beck, Hillside and Couter Cottages, 11 Maple Grove, Manchester M28 7ED
T: (0161) 790 8023
I: www.amblesideselfcatering.co.uk

Birch Cottage ★★★
Contact: Dr Nash
47 Goring Road, Bounds Green, London N11 2BT
T: (020) 8888 1252 &
(0115) 969 2190
E: birch@vithani.freeserve.co.uk

Birch Knoll ★★★★
Contact: Mr Paul Liddell
Lakelovers, Belmont House, Lake Road, Bowness-on-Windermere, Windermere LA23 3BJ
T: (015394) 88855
F: (015394) 88857
E: bookings@lakelovers.co.uk
I: www.lakelovers.co.uk

Birchcroft ★★★★
Contact: Susan Jackson
Heart of the Lakes, Fisherbeck Mill, Old Lake Road, Ambleside LA22 0DH
T: (015394) 32321
F: (015394) 33251
E: info@heartofthelakes.co.uk
I: www.heartofthelakes.co.uk

Blelham Tarn at Neaum Crag ★★★★
Contact: Andy Witts
PAD-LOK Products Ltd, Po Box 73, Newport TF10 8BP
T: (01952) 810101
F: (01952) 810102
E: enquiries@logcabin.bz
I: www.logcabin.bz

Blue Hill Cottage ★★★
Contact: Mr Peter Durbin
Cumbrian Cottages, 2 Lonsdale Street, Carlisle CA1 1DB
T: (01228) 599960
F: (01228) 599970
E: enquiries@cumbriancottages.co.uk
I: www.cumbrian-cottages.co.uk

Bobbin Cottage ★★★
Contact: Paul Liddell
Lakelovers, Belmont House, Lake Road, Bowness-on-Windermere, Windermere LA23 3BJ
T: (015394) 88855
F: (015394) 88857

Borrans View Cottage ★★★
Contact: Mr Peter Durbin
Cumbrian Cottages, 2 Lonsdale Street, Carlisle CA1 1DB
T: (01228) 599960
F: (01228) 599970
E: enquiries@cumbrian-cottages.co.uk
I: www.cumbrian-cottages.co.uk

Bowfell ★★
Contact: Susan Jackson
Heart of the Lakes, Fisherbeck Mill, Old Lake Road, Ambleside LA22 0DH
T: (015394) 32321
F: (015394) 33251
E: info@heartofthelakes.co.uk
I: www.heartofthelakes.co.uk

Brae Cottage ★★★
Contact: Paul Liddell
Lakelovers, Belmont House, Lake Road, Bowness-on-Windermere, Windermere LA23 3BJ
T: (015394) 88855
F: (015394) 88857

Braebeck ★★★★
Contact: Paul Liddell
Lakelovers, Belmont House, Lake Road, Bowness-on-Windermere, Windermere LA23 3BJ
T: (015394) 88855
F: (015394) 88857

Brathay 15 ★★★★
Contact: Susan Jackson
Heart of the Lakes, Fisherbeck Mill, Old Lake Road, Ambleside LA22 0DH
T: (015394) 32321
F: (015394) 33251
E: info@heartofthelakes.co.uk
I: www.heartofthelakes.co.uk

Briar Nook ★★★★
Contact: Mr Peter Durbin
Cumbrian Cottages, 2 Lonsdale Street, Carlisle CA1 1DB
T: (01228) 599960
F: (01228) 599970
E: enquiries@cumbrian-cottages.co.uk
I: www.cumbrian-cottages.co.uk

Briardale Cottage ★★★
Contact: Susan Jackson
Heart of the Lakes, Fisherbeck Mill, Old Lake Road, Ambleside LA22 0DH
T: (015394) 32321
F: (015394) 33251
E: info@heartofthelakes.co.uk
I: www.heartofthelakes.co.uk

Broad Oak Cottage ★★★
Contact: Susan Jackson
Heart of the Lakes, Fisherbeck Mill, Old Lake Road, Ambleside LA22 0DH
T: (015394) 32321
F: (015394) 33251
E: info@heartofthelakes.co.uk
I: www.heartofthelakes.co.uk

Brunt How ★★★
Contact: Mrs Susan Jackson
Heart of the Lakes, Fisherbeck Mill, Old Lake Road, Ambleside LA22 0DH
T: (015394) 32321
F: (015394) 33251
E: info@heartofthelakes.co.uk
I: www.heartofthelakes.co.uk

Brydewood ★★★★
Contact: Mrs Susan Jackson
Heart of the Lakes, Fisherbeck Mill, Old Lake Road, Ambleside LA22 0DH
T: (015394) 33110
F: (015394) 33251
E: info@heartofthelakes.co.uk
I: www.heartofthelakes.co.uk

Buttermere ★★★
Contact: Mr Paul Liddell
Lakelovers, Belmont House, Lake Road, Bowness-on-Windermere, Windermere LA23 3BJ
T: (015394) 88855
F: (015394) 88857
E: bookings@lakelovers.co.uk
I: www.lakelovers.co.uk

Byways ★★
Contact: Susan Jackson
Heart of the Lakes, Fisherbeck Mill, Old Lake Road, Ambleside LA22 0DH
T: (015394) 32321
F: (015394) 33251
E: info@heartofthelakes.co.uk
I: www.heartofthelakes.co.uk

Cairn Cottage
Rating Applied For
Contact: Mr Peter Durbin
Cumbrian Cottages, 2 Lonsdale Street, Carlisle CA1 1DB
T: (01228) 599960
F: (01228) 599970
E: enquiries@cumbrian-cottages.co.uk
I: www.cumbrian-cottage.co.uk

CUMBRIA – THE LAKE DISTRICT

Cedar House ★★★★
Contact: Paul Liddell
Lakelovers, Belmont House, Lake Road, Bowness-on-Windermere, Windermere LA23 3BJ
T: (015394) 88855
F: (015394) 88857
E: bookings@lakelovers.co.uk
I: www.lakelovers.co.uk

Chestnuts, Beeches and The Granary ★★★★
Contact: Mr Benson
High Sett, Sun Hill Lane, Windermere LA23 1HJ
T: (015394) 42731
F: (015394) 42731
E: sbenson@talk21.com
I: www.accommodationlakedistrict.com

Church View ★★★
Contact: Mr Peter Durbin
Cumbrian Cottages, 2 Lonsdale Street, Carlisle CA1 1DB
T: (01228) 599960
F: (01228) 599970
E: enquiries@cumbrian-cottages.co.uk
I: www.cumbrian-cottages.co.uk

Clover Cottage ★★★
Contact: Susan Jackson
Heart of the Lakes, Fisherbeck Mill, Old Lake Road, Ambleside LA22 0DH
T: (015394) 32321
F: (015394) 33251
E: info@heartofthelakes.co.uk
I: www.heartofthelakes.co.uk

The Coach House ★★★★
Contact: Mrs Susan Jackson
Heart of the Lakes, Fisherbeck Mill, Old Lake Road, Ambleside LA22 0DH
T: (015394) 32321
F: (015394) 33251
E: info@heartofthelakes.co.uk
I: www.heartofthelakes.co.uk

Cobblestone House ★★★★
Contact: Mr Peter Durbin
Cumbrian Cottages, 2 Lonsdale Street, Carlisle CA1 1DB
T: (01228) 599960
F: (01228) 599970
E: enquiries@cumbrian-cottages.co.uk
I: www.cumbrian-cottages.co.uk

Cobblestones ★★★★
Contact: Mr Peter Durbin
Cumbrian Cottages, 2 Lonsdale Street, Carlisle CA1 1DB
T: (01228) 599960
F: (01228) 599970
E: enquiries@cumbrian-cottage.co.uk
I: www.cumbrian-cottages.co.uk

Conifers ★★★
Contact: Mrs Susan Jackson
Heart of the Lakes, Fisherbeck Mill, Old Lake Road, Ambleside LA22 0DH
T: (015394) 32321
F: (015394) 33251
E: info@heartofthelakes.co.uk
I: www.heartofthelakes.co.uk

Cooksons Garth ★★★★
Contact: Mrs Susan Jackson
Heart of the Lakes, Fisherbeck Mill, Old Lake Road, Ambleside LA22 0DH
T: (015394) 32321
F: (015394) 33251
E: info@heartofthelakes.co.uk
I: www.heartofthelakes.co.uk

Copt How ★★★★
Contact: Paul Liddell
Lakelovers, Belmont House, Lake Road, Bowness-on-Windermere, Windermere LA23 3BJ
T: (015394) 88855
F: (015394) 88857
E: bookings@lakelovers.co.uk
I: www.lakelovers.co.uk

Cornerstones ★★★★
Contact: Mr Paul Durbin
Cumbrian Cottages, 2 Lonsdale Street, Carlisle CA1 1DB
T: (01228) 599960
F: (01228) 599970
E: enquiries@cumbriancottages.co.uk
I: www.cumbrian-cottages.co.uk

The Courtyard ★★★
Contact: Mrs Susan Jackson
Heart of the Lakes, Fisherbeck Mill, Old Lake Road, Ambleside LA22 0DH
T: (015394) 32321
F: (015394) 33251
E: info@heartofthelakes.co.uk
I: www.heartofthelakes.co.uk

Couter Cottage ★★★
Contact: Paul Liddell
Lakelovers, Belmont House, Lake Road, Bowness-on-Windermere, Windermere LA23 3BJ
T: (015394) 88855
F: (015394) 88857
E: bookings@lakelovers.co.uk
I: www.lakelovers.co.uk

Crag View ★★★
Contact: Mrs Davies
21 Dowhills Road, Liverpool L23 8SH
T: (0151) 9246995
F: (0151) 2859107
E: pfdavies@blueyonder.co.uk

Cranford Cottage ★★
Contact: Clive Sykes
Sykes Cottages, York House, York Street, Cheshire, Chester CH1 3LR
T: (01244) 345700
F: (01244) 321442

Cringol Cottage ★★★
Contact: Susan Jackson
Heart of the Lakes, Fisherbeck Mill, Old Lake Road, Ambleside LA22 0DH
T: (015394) 32321
F: (015394) 33251
E: info@heartofthelakes.co.uk
I: www.heartofthelakes.co.uk

Crinkle Crags ★★★
Contact: Susan Jackson
Heart of the Lakes, Fisherbeck Mill, Old Lake Road, Ambleside LA22 0DH
T: (015394) 32321
F: (015394) 33251
E: info@heartofthelakes.co.uk
I: www.heartofthelakes.co.uk

Cuckoo's Nest ★★★★★
Contact: Anthony & Christine Harrison
Smallwood House Hotel, Compston Road, Ambleside LA22 9DJ
T: (015394) 32330
F: (015394) 33764
E: cuckoosnest@cottagesambleside.co.uk
I: www.cottagesambleside.co.uk

Derby Cottage ★★★
Contact: Mr Peter Durbin
Cumbrian Cottages, 2 Lonsdale Street, Carlisle CA1 1DB
T: (01228) 599960
F: (01228) 599970
E: enquiries@cumbriancottages.co.uk
I: www.cumbrian-cottages.co.uk

Dower House Cottage ★★★
Contact: Mrs Margaret Rigg
Dower House Cottage, Dower House, Wray Castle, Ambleside LA22 0JA
T: (015394) 33211
F: (015394) 33211

Dwarf Studio ★★★
Contact: Mr Peter Durbin
Cumbrian Cottages, 2 Lonsdale Street, Carlisle CA1 1DB
T: (01228) 599960
F: (01228) 599970
E: enquiries@cumbrian-cottages.co.uk
I: www.cumbrian-cottages.co.uk

Ecclerigg Cottage ★★★★
Contact: Susan Jackson
Heart of the Lakes, Fisherbeck Mill, Old Lake Road, Ambleside LA22 0DH
T: (015394) 32321
F: (015394) 33251
E: info@heartofthelakes.co.uk
I: www.heartofthelakes.co.uk

Ecclerigg Old farm ★★★
Contact: Mrs Susan Jackson
Heart of the Lakes, Fisherbeck Mill, Old Lake Road, Ambleside LA22 0DH
T: (015394) 32321
F: (015394) 33251
E: info@heartofthelakes.co.uk
I: www.heartofthelakes.co.uk

Edelweiss ★★★★
Contact: Susan Jackson
Heart of the Lakes, Fisherbeck Mill, Old Lake Road, Ambleside LA22 0DH
T: (015394) 32321
F: (015394) 33251
E: info@heartofthelakes.co.uk
I: www.heartofthelakes.co.uk

Edenbridge ★★★
Contact: Mrs Susan Jackson
Heart of the Lakes, Fisherbeck Mill, Old Lake Road, Ambleside LA22 0DH
T: (015394) 32321
F: (015394) 33251
E: info@heartofthelakes.co.uk

Ellerview ★★★
Contact: Paul Liddell
Lakelovers, Belmont House, Lake Road, Bowness-on-Windermere, Windermere LA23 3BJ
T: (015394) 88855
F: (015394) 88857

Eskdale ★★★★
Contact: Mr Peter Durbin
Cumbrian Cottages, 2 Lonsdale Street, Carlisle CA1 1DB
T: (01228) 599960
F: (01228) 599970
E: enquiries@cumbrian-cottages.co.uk
I: www.cumbrian-cottages.co.uk

Evening Primrose Cottage ★★★
Contact: Mr Peter Durbin
Cumbrian Cottages, 2 Lonsdale Street, Carlisle CA1 1DB
T: (01228) 599960
F: (01228) 599970
E: enquiries@cumbrian-cottages.co.uk
I: www.cumbrian-cottages.co.uk

Fairview ★★★★★
Contact: Mrs Susan Jackson
Heart of the Lakes, Fisherbeck Mill, Old Lake Road, Ambleside LA22 0DH
T: (015394) 33110
F: (015394) 33251
E: info@heartofthelakes.co.uk
I: www.heartofthelakes.co.uk

Falls View Cottage ★★★
Contact: Susan Jackson
Heart of the Lakes, Fisherbeck Mill, Old Lake Road, Ambleside LA22 0DH
T: (015394) 32321
F: (015394) 33251
E: info@heartofthelakes.co.uk
I: www.heartofthelakes.co.uk

Fell View ★★★★
Contact: Mr Peter Durbin
Cumbrian Cottages, 2 Lonsdale Street, Carlisle CA1 1DB
T: (01228) 599960
F: (01228) 599970
E: enquiries@cumbriancottages.co.uk
I: www.cumbrian-cottages.co.uk

Fellcroft ★★★★
Contact: Mrs Susan Jackson
Heart of the Lakes, Fisherbeck Mill, Old Lake Road, Ambleside LA22 0DH
T: (015394) 32321
F: (015394) 33251
E: info@heartofthelakes.co.uk
I: www.heartofthelakes.co.uk

Fellside ★★★
Contact: Paul Liddell
Lakelovers, Belmont House, Lake Road, Bowness-on-Windermere, Windermere LA23 3BJ
T: (015394) 88855
F: (015394) 88857

Fern Ghyll ★★★★
Contact: Susan Jackson
Heart of the Lakes, Fisherbeck Mill, Old Lake Road, Ambleside LA22 0DH
T: (015394) 32321
F: (015394) 33251
E: info@heartofthelakes.co.uk
I: www.heartofthelakes.co.uk

Establishments printed in blue have a detailed entry in this guide

CUMBRIA – THE LAKE DISTRICT

Field Foot Cottage ★★★★
Contact: Mrs Susan Jackson
Heart of the Lakes, Fisherbeck Mill, Old Lake Road, Ambleside LA22 0DH
T: (015394) 32321
F: (015394) 33251
E: info@heartofthelakes.co.uk
I: www.heartofthelakes.co.uk

The Flat ★★★
Contact: Susan Jackson
Heart of the Lakes, Fisherbeck Mill, Old Lake Road, Ambleside LA22 0DH
T: (015394) 32321
F: (015394) 33251

Forge Side ★★★
Contact: Susan Jackson
Heart of the Lakes, Fisherbeck Mill, Old Lake Road, Ambleside LA22 0DH
T: (015394) 32321
F: (015394) 33251
E: info@heartofthelakes.co.uk
I: www.heartofthelakes.co.uk

Four Seasons Cottage ★★★
Contact: Susan Jackson
Heart of the Lakes, Fisherbeck Mill, Old Lake Road, Ambleside LA22 0DH
T: (015394) 32321
F: (015394) 33251
E: info@heartofthelakes.co.uk
I: www.heartofthelakes.co.uk

Gable End ★★★★
Contact: Mr Peter Durbin
Cumbrian Cottages, 2 Lonsdale Street, Carlisle CA1 1DB
T: (01228) 599960
F: (01228) 599970
E: enquiries@cumbrian-cottage.co.uk
I: www.cumbrian-cottages.co.uk

Gale House Cottage ★★★★
Contact: Mrs Susan Jackson
Heart of the Lakes, Fisherbeck Mill, Old Lake Road, Ambleside LA22 0DH
T: (015394) 32321
F: (015394) 33251
E: info@heartofthelakes.co.uk
I: www.heartofthelakes.co.uk

Gale Howe Barn ★★★★
Contact: Mrs Susan Jackson
Heart of the Lakes, Fisherbeck Mill, Old Lake Road, Ambleside LA22 0DH
T: (015394) 32321
F: (015394) 33251
E: info@heartofthelakes.co.uk
I: www.heartofthelakes.co.uk

Gale Lodge Cottage ★★★★
Contact: Mrs Vivien Bass
Wheelwrights Holiday Cottages, Langdale, Ambleside LA22 9HS
T: (015394) 37635
F: (015394) 37618
E: enquiries@wheelwrights.com
I: www.wheelwrights.com

Gale Lodge Stables ★★★★
Contact: Mr Paul Liddell
Lakelovers, Belmont House, Windermere LA23 3BJ
T: (015394) 88855
F: (015394) 88857
E: enquiries@lakelovers.co.uk
I: www.lakelovers.co.uk/listings/l0064.html

Gale Mews ★★★★
Contact: Susan Jackson
Heart of the Lakes, Fisherbeck Mill, Old Lake Road, Ambleside LA22 0DH
T: (015394) 32321
F: (015394) 33251
E: info@heartofthelakes.co.uk
I: www.heartofthelakes.co.uk

The Garden Flat ★★★
Contact: Mr & Mrs Alan Wardle
Bateman Fold Barn, Kendal LA8 8LN
T: (015395) 68074
I: www.lakedistrictholidays.net

The Gate ★★★★
Contact: Mrs Susan Jackson
Heart of the Lakes, Fisherbeck Mill, Old Lake Road, Ambleside LA22 0DH
T: (015394) 32321
F: (015394) 33251
E: info@heartofthelakes.co.uk
I: www.heartofthelakes.co.uk

Ghyll Bank ★★★★
Contact: Susan Jackson
Heart of the Lakes, Fisherbeck Mill, Old Lake Road, Ambleside LA22 0DH
T: (015394) 32321
F: (015394) 33251
E: info@heartofthelakes.co.uk
I: www.heartofthelakes.co.uk

Ghyll Heights ★★★
Contact: Mr Peter Durbin
Cumbrian Cottages, 2 Lonsdale Street, Carlisle CA1 1DB
T: (01228) 599960
F: (01228) 599970
E: enquiries@cumbrian-cottages.co.uk
I: www.cumbrian-cottages.co.uk

Ghyll View ★★★
Contact: Susan Jackson
Heart of the Lakes, Fisherbeck Mill, Old Lake Road, Ambleside LA22 0DH
T: (015394) 32321
F: (015394) 33251
E: info@heartofthelakes.co.uk
I: www.heartofthelakes.co.uk

3 Ghyllside ★★
Contact: Paul Liddell
Lakelovers, Belmont House, Lake Road, Bowness-on-Windermere, Windermere LA23 3BJ
T: (015394) 88855
F: (015394) 88857

Gillybeck, The Falls ★★★★
Contact: Susan Jackson
Heart of the Lakes, Fisherbeck Mill, Old Lake Road, Ambleside LA22 0DH
T: (015394) 32321
F: (015394) 33251
E: info@heartofthelakes.co.uk
I: www.heartofthelakes.co.uk

Glenmore Cottage ★★★
Contact: Mr Peter Durbin
Cumbrian Cottages, 2 Lonsdale Street, Carlisle CA1 1DB
T: (01228) 599960
F: (01228) 599970
E: enquiries@cumbriancottages.co.uk
I: www.cumbrian-cottages.co.uk

The Granny Flat ★★★
Contact: Susan Jackson
Heart of the Lakes, Fisherbeck Mill, Old Lake Road, Ambleside LA22 0DH
T: (015394) 32321
F: (015394) 33251

Green Moss ★★★★
Contact: Mrs Susan Jackson
Heart of the Lakes, Fisherbeck Mill, Old Lake Road, Ambleside LA22 0DH
T: (015394) 32321
F: (015394) 33251
E: info@heartofthelakes.co.uk
I: www.heartofthelakes.co.uk

Greenways ★★★★
Contact: Mr Paul Liddell
Lakelovers, Belmont House, Lake Road, Bowness-on-Windermere, Windermere LA23 3BJ
T: (015394) 88855
F: (015394) 88857
E: bookings@lakelovers.co.uk
I: www.lakelovers.co.uk

The Grove Cottages ★★★★-★★★★★
Contact: Mrs Zee Thompson
The Grove Cottages, The Grove Farm, Stockghyll Lane, Ambleside LA22 9LG
T: (015394) 33074
F: (015394) 31881
E: grovecottages@clara.co.uk
I: www.grovecottages.com

Halfway House ★★★★
Contact: Mr Peter Durbin
Cumbrian Cottages, 2 Lonsdale Street, Carlisle CA1 1DB
T: (01228) 599960
F: (01228) 599970
E: enquiries@cumbrian-cottages.co.uk
I: www.cumbrian-cottages.co.uk

Hayrake ★★★
Contact: Susan Jackson
Heart of the Lakes, Fisherbeck Mill, Old Lake Road, Ambleside LA22 0DH
T: (015394) 32321
F: (015394) 33251
E: info@heartofthelakes.co.uk
I: www.heartofthelakes.co.uk

Hazelhurst ★★★
Contact: Mr Peter Durbin
Cumbrian Cottages, 2 Lonsdale Street, Carlisle CA1 1DB
T: (01228) 599960
F: (01228) 599970
E: enquiries@cumbrian-cottages.co.uk
I: www.cumbrian-cottages.co.uk

Heather Cottage ★★★
Contact: Paul Liddell
Lakelovers, Belmont House, Lake Road, Bowness-on-Windermere, Windermere LA23 3BJ
T: (015394) 88855
F: (015394) 88857

Herald Cottage ★★★★
Contact: Mr Peter Durbin
Cumbrian Cottages, 2 Lonsdale Street, Carlisle CA1 1DB
T: (01228) 599960
F: (01228) 599970
E: enquiries@cumbriancottages.co.uk
I: www.cumbrian-cottages.co.uk

High Bank ★★★
Contact: Susan Jackson
Heart of the Lakes, Fisherbeck Mill, Old Lake Road, Ambleside LA22 0DH
T: (015394) 32321
F: (015394) 33251
E: info@heartofthelakes.co.uk
I: www.heartofthelakes.co.uk

High Bank Cottage ★★★
Contact: Mrs Susan Jackson
Heart of the Lakes, Fisherbeck Mill, Old Lake Road, Ambleside LA22 0DH
T: (015394) 32321
F: (015394) 33251
E: info@heartofthelakes.co.uk
I: www.heartofthelakes.co.uk

High Nook ★★★
Contact: Susan Jackson
Heart of the Lakes, Fisherbeck Mill, Old Lake Road, Ambleside LA22 0DH
T: (015394) 32321
F: (015394) 33251
E: info@heartofthelakes.co.uk
I: www.heartofthelakes.co.uk

High Pike Cottage ★★★
Contact: Mrs Susan Jackson
Heart of the Lakes, Fisherbeck Mill, Old Lake Road, Ambleside LA22 0DH
T: (015394) 32321
F: (015394) 33251
E: info@heartofthelakes.co.uk
I: www.heartofthelakes.co.uk

Hilber Cottage ★★★
Contact: Mrs Susan Jackson
Heart of the Lakes, Fisherbeck Mill, Old Lake Road, Ambleside LA22 0DH
T: (015394) 33110
F: (015394) 33251
E: info@heartofthelakes.co.uk
I: www.heartofthelakes.co.uk

Hillside Cottage ★★★
Contact: Susan Jackson
Heart of the Lakes, Fisherbeck Mill, Old Lake Road, Ambleside LA22 0DH
T: (015394) 32321
F: (015394) 33251
E: info@heartofthelakes.co.uk
I: www.heartofthelakes.co.uk

Holbeck ★★★★
Contact: Susan Jackson
Heart of the Lakes, Fisherbeck Mill, Old Lake Road, Ambleside LA22 0DH
T: (015394) 32321
F: (015394) 33251
E: info@heartofthelakes.co.uk
I: www.heartofthelakes.co.uk

Hole House ★★★
Contact: Clare Irvine
Tock How Farm, Ambleside LA22 0JF
T: (015394) 36106
E: info@tock-how-farm.com
I: www.tock-how-farm.com

The Hollies ★★★
Contact: Mr Peter Durbin
Cumbrian Cottages, 2 Lonsdale Street, Carlisle CA1 1DB
T: (01228) 599960
F: (01228) 599970
E: enquiries@cumbrian-cottages.co.uk
I: www.cumbrian-cottages.co.uk

CUMBRIA – THE LAKE DISTRICT

Holly Cottage ★★★
Contact: Mrs Susan Jackson
Heart of the Lakes, Fisherbeck
Mill, Old Lake Road, Ambleside
LA22 0DH
T: (015394) 32321
F: (015394) 33251
E: info@heartofthelakes.co.uk
I: www.heartofthelakes.co.uk

Hollybrook ★★★★
Contact: Mr Peter Durbin
Cumbrian Cottages, 2 Lonsdale
Street, Carlisle CA1 1DB
T: (01228) 599960
F: (01228) 599970
E: enquiries@
cumbrian-cottages.co.uk
I: www.cumbrian-cottages.co.uk

Honeypot Cottage ★★★★
Contact: Susan Jackson
Heart of the Lakes, Fisherbeck
Mill, Old Lake Road, Ambleside
LA22 0DH
T: (015394) 32321
F: (015394) 33251
E: info@heartofthelakes.co.uk
I: www.heartofthelakes.co.uk

Horseshoe Cottage ★★★
Contact: Susan Jackson
Heart of the Lakes, Fisherbeck
Mill, Old Lake Road, Ambleside
LA22 0DH
T: (015394) 32321
F: (015394) 33251
E: info@heartofthelakes.co.uk
I: www.heartofthelakes.co.uk

4 How Head ★★★
Contact: Mr & Mrs Holland
How Head Cottages, How Head
Cottage, East of Lake, Coniston
LA21 8AA
T: (015394) 41594
E: howhead@lineone.co.uk
I: www.howheadcottages.co.uk

How Head Barn ★★★
Contact: Mrs Susan Jackson
Heart of the Lakes, Fisherbeck
Mill, Old Lake Road, Ambleside
LA22 0DH
T: (015394) 32321
F: (015394) 33251
E: info@heartofthelakes.co.uk
I: www.heartofthelakes.co.uk

How Head Cottage ★★★
Contact: Susan Jackson
Heart of the Lakes, Fisherbeck
Mill, Old Lake Road, Ambleside
LA22 0DH
T: (015394) 32321
F: (015394) 33251
E: info@heartofthelakes.co.uk
I: www.heartofthelakes.co.uk

Iona ★★★
Contact: Susan Jackson
Heart of the Lakes, Fisherbeck
Mill, Old Lake Road, Ambleside
LA22 0DH
T: (015394) 32321
F: (015394) 33251
E: info@heartofthelakes.co.uk
I: www.heartofthelakes.co.uk

Juniper Cottage ★★★
Contact: Paul Liddell
Lakelovers, Belmont House, Lake
Road, Bowness-on-Windermere,
Windermere LA23 3BJ
T: (015394) 88855
F: (015394) 88857

Kelsick Heights
Rating Applied For
Contact: Mr Peter Durbin
Cumbrian Cottages, 2 Lonsdale
Street, Carlisle CA1 1DB
T: (01228) 599960
F: (01228) 599970
E: enquiries@
cumbrian-cottages.co.uk
I: www.cumbrian-cottages.co.uk

Kiln Cottage ★★★★
Contact: Paul Liddell
Lakelovers, Belmont House, Lake
Road, Bowness-on-Windermere,
Windermere LA23 3BJ
T: (015394) 88855
F: (015394) 88857
E: bookings@lakelovers.co.uk
I: www.lakelovers.co.uk

Kirkstone Cottage ★★★
Contact: Peter Durbin & Tony
Commons
Cumbrian Cottages, 2 Lonsdale
Street, Carlisle CA1 1DB
T: (01228) 599960
F: (01228) 599970
E: enquiries@
cumbrian-cottages.co.uk
I: www.cumbrian-cottages.co.uk

**Kirkstone Foot Cottages
and Apartments
★★★★-★★★★★**
Contact: Mr Norfolk
Kirkstone Foot Cottages and
Apartments, Kirkstone Pass
Road, Ambleside LA22 9EH
T: (015394) 32232
F: (015394) 32805
E: info@kirkstonefoot.co.uk
I: www.kirkstonefoot.co.uk

Lakeland Cottage ★★★★
Contact: Paul Liddell
Lakelovers, Belmont House, Lake
Road, Bowness-on-Windermere,
Windermere LA23 3BJ
T: (015394) 88855
F: (015394) 88857

The Lakelands ★★★★
Contact: Jackie Kingdom
The Lakelands, Lower Gale,
Ambleside LA22 0BD
T: (015394) 33777
F: (015394) 31301
E: lakeland@globalnet.co.uk
I: www.the-lakelands.com

19 The Lakelands ★★★★
Contact: Paul Liddell
Lakelovers, Belmont House, Lake
Road, Bowness-on-Windermere,
Windermere LA23 3BJ
T: (015394) 88855
F: (015394) 88857

The Larches ★★★
Contact: Mrs Susan Jackson
Heart of the Lakes, Fisherbeck
Mill, Old Lake Road, Ambleside
LA22 0DH
T: (015394) 32321
F: (015394) 33251
E: info@heartofthelakes.co.uk
I: www.heartofthelakes.co.uk

Leafy Nook ★★★★
Contact: Susan Jackson
Heart of the Lakes, Fisherbeck
Mill, Old Lake Road, Ambleside
LA22 0DH
T: (015394) 32321
F: (015394) 33251
E: info@heartofthelakes.co.uk
I: www.heartofthelakes.co.uk

Lingmell Gale Lodge ★★★
Contact: Mrs Susan Jackson
Heart of the Lakes, Fisherbeck
Mill, Old Lake Road, Ambleside
LA22 0DH
T: (015394) 32321
F: (015394) 33251
E: info@heartofthelakes.co.uk
I: www.heartofthelakes.co.uk

Little Robin Cottage ★★★
Contact: Mr Peter Durbin
Cumbrian Cottages, 2 Lonsdale
Street, Carlisle CA1 1DB
T: (01228) 599960
F: (01228) 599970
E: enquiries@
cumbrian-cottages.co.uk
I: www.cumbrian-cottages.co.uk

Littlegarth ★★★★
Contact: Mrs Vivien Bass
Wheelwrights Holiday Cottages,
Langdale, Ambleside LA22 9HS
T: (015394) 37635
E: enquiries@wheelwrights.com
I: www.wheelwrights.com

Long Mynd ★★★
Contact: Mr Peter Durbin
Cumbrian Cottages, 2 Lonsdale
Street, Carlisle CA1 1DB
T: (01228) 599960
F: (01228) 599970
E: enquiries@
cumbrian-cottages.co.uk
I: www.cumbrian-cottages.co.uk

Longmeadow ★★★★
Contact: Mr Peter Durbin
Cumbrian Cottages, 2 Lonsdale
Street, Carlisle CA1 1DB
T: (01228) 599960
F: (01228) 599970
E: enquiries@
cumbrian-cottages.co.uk
I: www.cumbrian-cottages.co.uk

The Lookout ★★★★★
Contact: Susan Jackson
Heart of the Lakes, Fisherbeck
Mill, Old Lake Road, Ambleside
LA22 0DH
T: (015394) 32321
F: (015394) 33251

Loughrigg ★★★★
Contact: Mr Paul Liddell
Lakelovers, Belmont House, Lake
Road, Bowness-on-Windermere,
Windermere LA23 3BJ
T: (015394) 88855
F: (015394) 88857
E: bookings@lakelovers.co.uk
I: www.lakelovers.co.uk

Loughrigg ★★★★
Contact: Mrs Susan Jackson
Heart of the Lakes, Fisherbeck
Mill, Old Lake Road, Ambleside
LA22 0DH
T: (015394) 32321
F: (015394) 33251
E: info@heartofthelakes.co.uk
I: www.heartofthelakes.co.uk

Loughrigg Suite ★★★★★
Contact: Susan Jackson
Heart of the Lakes, Fisherbeck
Mill, Old Lake Road, Ambleside
LA22 0DH
T: (015394) 32321
F: (015394) 33251
E: info@heartofthelakes.co.uk
I: www.heartofthelakes.co.uk

Loughrigg View
Rating Applied For
Contact: Mr Peter Durbin
Cumbrian Cottages, 2 Lonsdale
Street, Carlisle CA1 1DB
T: (01228) 599960
F: (01228) 599970
I: www.cumbriancottages.co.uk

Loughrigg View ★★★
Contact: Mrs Susan Jackson
Heart of the Lakes, Fisherbeck
Mill, Old Lake Road, Ambleside
LA22 0DH
T: (015394) 32321
F: (015394) 33251
E: info@heartofthelakes.co.uk
I: www.heartofthelakes.co.uk

Low Brow Barn ★★★★
Contact: Mrs Susan Jackson
Heart of the Lakes, Fisherbeck
Mill, Old Lake Road, Ambleside
LA22 0DH
T: (015394) 32321
F: (015394) 33251
E: info@heartofthelakes.co.uk
I: www.heartofthelakes.co.uk

Low Grove Cottage ★★★★
Contact: Susan Jackson
Heart of the Lakes, Fisherbeck
Mill, Old Lake Road, Ambleside
LA22 0DH
T: (015394) 32321
F: (015394) 33251
E: info@heartofthelakes.co.uk
I: www.heartofthelakes.co.uk

Low White Stones ★★★★
Contact: Susan Jackson
Heart of the Lakes, Fisherbeck
Mill, Old Lake Road, Ambleside
LA22 0DH
T: (015394) 32321
F: (015394) 33251
E: info@heartofthelakes.co.uk
I: www.heartofthelakes.co.uk

Lyndhurst ★★★
Contact: Mrs Susan Jackson
Heart of the Lakes, Fisherbeck
Mill, Old Lake Road, Ambleside
LA22 0DH
T: (015394) 33110
F: (015394) 33251
E: info@heartofthelakes.co.uk
I: www.heartofthelakes.co.uk

Martin's Nest ★★★★
Contact: Susan Jackson
Heart of the Lakes, Fisherbeck
Mill, Old Lake Road, Ambleside
LA22 0DH
T: (015394) 32321
F: (015394) 33251
E: info@heartofthelakes.co.uk
I: www.heartofthelakes.co.uk

Establishments printed in blue have a detailed entry in this guide

CUMBRIA – THE LAKE DISTRICT

Melverley ★★★
Contact: Susan Jackson
Heart of the Lakes, Fisherbeck
Mill, Old Lake Road, Ambleside
LA22 0DH
T: (015394) 32321
F: (015394) 33251
E: info@heartofthelakes.co.uk
I: www.heartofthelakes.co.uk

Milestones ★★★
Contact: Paul Liddell
Lakelovers, Belmont House, Lake
Road, Bowness-on-Windermere,
Windermere LA23 3BJ
T: (015394) 88855
F: (015394) 88857

**Mill Brow Farm Cottage
★★★★**
Contact: Pat Long
Mill Brow Farm Cottage, Mill
Brow Farm, Ambleside
LA22 9NH
T: (015394) 33253

**Mountain View Cottage
★★★**
Contact: Paul Liddell
Lakelovers, Belmont House, Lake
Road, Bowness-on-Windermere,
Windermere LA23 3BJ
T: (015394) 88855
F: (015394) 88857
E: bookings@lakelovers.co.uk
I: www.lakelovers.co.uk

Nab Cottage
Rating Applied For
Contact: Mr Peter Durbin
Cumbrian Cottages, 2 Lonsdale
Street, Carlisle CA1 1DB
T: (01228) 599960
F: (01228) 599970
E: enquiries@
cumbrian-cottages.co.uk
I: www.cumbrian-cottages.co.uk

Nook End Annexe ★★★
Contact: Mr John Serginson
The Lakeland Cottage Company,
Waterside House, Ulverston
LA12 8AN
T: (015395) 30024
F: (015395) 31932
E: john@lakelandcottageco.com
I: www.lakelandcottageco.com

Nook End Farm ★★★★
Contact: Barbara Humphreys
Nook End Farm, Nook Lane,
Ambleside LA22 9BH
T: (015394) 31324

Nook End Studio ★★★
Contact: Mr John Serginson
The Lakeland Cottage Company,
Waterside House, Ulverston
LA12 8AN
T: (015395) 30024
F: (015395) 31932
E: john@lakelandcottageco.com
I: www.lakelandcottageco.com

North Cottage ★★★★
Contact: Susan Jackson
Heart of the Lakes, Fisherbeck
Mill, Old Lake Road, Ambleside
LA22 0DH
T: (015394) 32321
F: (015394) 33251
E: info@heartofthelakes.co.uk
I: www.heartofthelakes.co.uk

Oak Cottage ★★★
Contact: Susan Jackson
Heart of the Lakes, Fisherbeck
Mill, Old Lake Road, Ambleside
LA22 0DH
T: (015394) 32321
F: (015394) 33251

Oaklands's ★★★
Contact: Mr Peter Durbin
Cumbrian Cottages, 2 Lonsdale
Street, Carlisle CA1 1DB
T: (01228) 599960
F: (01228) 599970
E: enquiries@
cumbrian-cottages.co.uk
I: www.cumbrian-cottages.co.uk

The Old Bakehouse ★★★
Contact: Mr Peter Durbin
Cumbrian Cottages, 2 Lonsdale
Street, Carlisle CA1 1DB
T: (01228) 599960
F: (01228) 599970
E: enquiries@
cumbrian-cottages.co.uk
I: www.cumbrian-cottages.co.uk

Old Coach House ★★★
Contact: Mr Peter Durbin & Tony
Commons
Cumbrian Cottages, 2 Lonsdale
Street, Carlisle CA1 1DB
T: (01228) 599960
F: (01228) 599970
E: enquiries@cumbria-cottages.
co.uk
I: www.cumbrian-cottages.co.uk

**Old Coach House, Riverside
and Garden Cottages
★★★★**
Contact: Mr Vyner-Brooks
Old Coach House, Riverside and
Garden Cottages, Middle
Barrows Green, Kendal LA8 0JG
T: (0151526) 5451/9321
F: (0151) 526 1331
E: vyner-brooks@btconnect.
com
I: www.primecottages.co.uk

**Old Coachman's Cottage
★★★★**
Contact: Paul Liddell
Lakelovers, Belmont House, Lake
Road, Bowness-on-Windermere,
Windermere LA23 3BJ
T: (015394) 88855
F: (015394) 88857
E: bookings@lakelovers.co.uk
I: www.lakelovers.co.uk

Old Gale Farmhouse ★★★
Contact: Mr Peter Durbin
Cumbrian Cottages, 2 Lonsdale
Street, Carlisle CA1 1DB
T: (01228) 599960
F: (01228) 599970
E: enquiries@
cumbrian-cottages.co.uk
I: www.cumbrian-cottages.co.uk

Old Mill Cottage ★★★
Contact: Susan Jackson
Heart of the Lakes, Fisherbeck
Mill, Old Lake Road, Ambleside
LA22 0DH
T: (015394) 32321
F: (015394) 33251

Orchard House ★★★★★
Contact: Mrs Susan Jackson
Heart of the Lakes, Fisherbeck
Mill, Old Lake Road, Ambleside
LA22 0DH
T: (015394) 33110
F: (015394) 33251
E: info@heartoflakes.co.uk
I: www.heartofthelakes.co.uk

Overghyll ★★★★
Contact: Susan Jackson
Heart of the Lakes, Fisherbeck
Mill, Old Lake Road, Ambleside
LA22 0DH
T: (015394) 32321
F: (015394) 33251

Parkwood ★★★★
Contact: Mrs Susan Jackson
Heart of the Lakes, Fisherbeck
Mill, Old Lake Road, Ambleside
LA22 0DH
T: (015394) 32321
F: (015394) 33251
E: info@heartofthelakes.co.uk
I: www.heartofthelakes.co.uk

Printers Cottage ★★★
Contact: Susan Jackson
Heart of the Lakes, Fisherbeck
Mill, Old Lake Road, Ambleside
LA22 0DH
T: (015394) 32321
F: (015394) 33251

Pudding Cottage ★★★★★
Contact: Jacky Morrison
Pudding Cottage, Boundary
House, 18 Boundary Lane,
Heswall, Wirral CH60 5RR
T: (0151) 342 1234
E: jacky.morrison@btinternet.
com
I: www.pudding-cottage.com

Raaesbeck ★★★★
Contact: Paul Liddell
Lakelovers, Belmont House, Lake
Road, Bowness-on-Windermere,
Windermere LA23 3BJ
T: (015394) 88855
F: (015394) 88857
E: bookings@lakelovers.co.uk
I: www.lakelovers.co.uk

Ramsteads ★-★★
Contact: Mr Evans
Ramsteads, Ambleside
LA22 0NH
T: (015394) 36583

Redwoods ★★★★
Contact: Mrs Susan Jackson
Heart of the Lakes, Fisherbeck
Mill, Old Lake Road, Ambleside
LA22 0DH
T: (015394) 32321
F: (015394) 33251
E: info@heartofthelakes.co.uk
I: www.heartofthelakes.co.uk

The Retreat ★★★★
Contact: Susan Jackson
Heart of the Lakes, Fisherbeck
Mill, Old Lake Road, Ambleside
LA22 0DH
T: (015394) 32321
F: (015394) 33251

River Falls View ★★★★
Contact: Paul Liddell
Lakelovers, Belmont House, Lake
Road, Bowness-on-Windermere,
Windermere LA23 3BJ
T: (015394) 88855
F: (015394) 88857

Riverside Lodge ★★★★
Contact: Alan Rhone
Riverside Lodge, Rothay Bridge,
Ambleside LA22 0EH
T: (015394) 34208
F: (01539) 431884
E: alanrhone@riversidelodge.
co.uk
I: www.riversidelodge.co.uk

Riverside Retreat ★★★★
Contact: Paul Liddell
Lakelovers, Belmont House, Lake
Road, Bowness-on-Windermere,
Windermere LA23 3BJ
T: (015394) 88855
F: (015394) 88857
E: bookings@lakelover.co.uk
I: www.lakelovers.co.uk

The Rock Shop Flat ★★★★
Contact: Ms Louise Burhouse
Burhouse Ltd, Quarmby Mills,
Tanyard Road, Oakes,
Huddersfield HD3 4YD
T: (01484) 485104
F: (01484) 460036
E: flat@rock-shop.co.uk
I: www.rock-shop.co.uk/flat

Rose Cottage ★★★
Contact: Susan Jackson
Heart of the Lakes, Fisherbeck
Mill, Old Lake Road, Ambleside
LA22 0DH
T: (015394) 32321
F: (015394) 33251

Roselea ★★★★
Contact: Mr Peter Durbin
Cumbrian Cottages, 2 Lonsdale
Street, Carlisle CA1 1DB
T: (01228) 599960
F: (01228) 599970
E: enquiries@cumbriancottages.
co.uk
I: www.cumbrian-cottages.co.uk

Rushbrook Cottage ★★★★
Contact: Susan Jackson
Heart of the Lakes, Fisherbeck
Mill, Old Lake Road, Ambleside
LA22 0DH
T: (015394) 32321
F: (015394) 33251

Rydal ★★★★
Contact: Mrs Susan Jackson
Heart of the Lakes, Fisherbeck
Mill, Old Lake Road, Ambleside
LA22 0DH
T: (015394) 32321
F: (015394) 33251
E: info@heartofthelakes.co.uk
I: www.heartofthelakes.co.uk

Rydale ★★★★
Contact: Mrs Susan Jackson
Heart of the Lakes, Fisherbeck
Mill, Old Lake Road, Ambleside
LA22 0DH
T: (015394) 32321
F: (015394) 33251
E: info@heartofthelakes.co.uk
I: www.heartofthelakes.co.uk

CUMBRIA – THE LAKE DISTRICT

Sarum ★★★
Contact: Jane Hughes
Sarum, c/o 95 Larkhill Lane,
Liverpool L37 1LU
T: (01704) 831558
F: (01704) 874866

Scafell Gale Lodge ★★★
Contact: Mrs Susan Jackson
Heart of the Lakes, Fisherbeck
Mill, Old Lake Road, Ambleside
LA22 0DH
T: (015394) 32321
F: (015394) 33251
E: info@heartofthelakes.co.uk
I: www.heartofthelakes.co.uk

Scandale Bridge Cottage ★★★
Contact: Mr Derek Sweeney
Kings Head Hotel, Thirlspot,
Keswick CA12 4TN
T: (017687) 72393
F: (017687) 72309
E: stay@lakedistrictinns.co.uk
I: www.lakedistrictinns.co.uk

Sheenfell ★★★
Contact: Mrs Susan Jackson
Heart of the Lakes, Fisherbeck
Mill, Old Lake Road, Ambleside
LA22 0DH
T: (015394) 32321
F: (015394) 33251
E: info@heartofthelakes.co.uk
I: www.heartofthelakes.co.uk

Shepherds Fold ★★★★
Contact: Mrs Susan Jackson
Heart of the Lakes, Fisherbeck
Mill, Old Lake Road, Ambleside
LA22 0DH
T: (015394) 32321
F: (015394) 33251
E: info@heartofthelakes.co.uk
I: www.heartofthelakes.co.uk

The Spinney ★★★★
Contact: Paul Liddell
Lakelovers, Belmont House, Lake
Road, Bowness-on-Windermere,
Windermere LA23 3BJ
T: (015394) 88855
F: (015394) 88857
E: bookings@lakelovers.co.uk
I: www.lakelovers.co.uk

Spring Cottage ★★★
Contact: Mr Paul Liddell
Lakelovers, Belmont House, Lake
Road, Bowness-on-Windermere,
Windermere LA23 3BJ
T: (015394) 88855
F: (015394) 88857
E: bookings@lakelovers.co.uk
I: www.lakelovers.co.uk

Spring Cottage ★★★★
Contact: Susan Jackson
Heart of the Lakes, Fisherbeck
Mill, Old Lake Road, Ambleside
LA22 0DH
T: (015394) 32321
F: (015394) 33251

Squirrel Bank ★★★
Contact: Mrs Susan Jackson
Heart of the Lakes, Fisherbeck
Mill, Old Lake Road, Ambleside
LA22 0DH
T: (015394) 32321
F: (015394) 33251
E: info@heartofthelakes.co.uk
I: www.heartofthelakes.co.uk

Squirrel's Nest ★★★★
Contact: Susan Jackson
Heart of the Lakes, Fisherbeck
Mill, Old Lake Road, Ambleside
LA22 0DH
T: (015394) 32321
F: (015394) 33251

Steeple View ★★★
Contact: Susan Jackson
Heart of the Lakes, Fisherbeck
Mill, Old Lake Road, Ambleside
LA22 0DH
T: (015394) 32321
F: (015394) 33251

Stepping Stones ★★★★
Contact: Susan Jackson
Heart of the Lakes, Fisherbeck
Mill, Old Lake Road, Ambleside
LA22 0DH
T: (015394) 32321
F: (015394) 33251

Stockghyll Court ★★★
Contact: Mr Peter Durbin
Cumbrian Cottages, 2 Lonsdale
Street, Carlisle CA1 1DB
T: (01228) 599960
F: (01228) 599970
E: enquiries@
cumbrian-cottages.co.uk
I: www.cumbrian-cottages.co.uk

Striding Home ★★★★
Contact: Mrs Susan Jackson
Heart of the Lakes, Fisherbeck
Mill, Old Lake Road, Ambleside
LA22 0DH
T: (015394) 32321
F: (015394) 33251
E: info@heartofthelakes.co.uk
I: www.heartofthelakes.co.uk

Studio Cottage ★★★★
Contact: Mrs Susan Jackson
Heart of the Lakes, Fisherbeck
Mill, Old Lake Road, Ambleside
LA22 0DH
T: (015394) 32321
F: (015394) 33251
E: info@heartofthelakes.co.uk
I: www.heartofthelakes.co.uk

Sunny Bank Cottages ★★★
Contact: Susan Jackson
Heart of the Lakes, Fisherbeck
Mill, Old Lake Road, Ambleside
LA22 0DH
T: (015394) 32321
F: (015394) 33251
E: info@heartofthelakes.co.uk
I: www.heartofthelakes.co.uk

Sunset Cottage ★★★★
Contact: Paul Liddell
Lakelovers, Belmont House, Lake
Road, Bowness-on-Windermere,
Windermere LA23 3BJ
T: (015394) 88855
F: (015394) 88857
E: bookings@lakelovers.co.uk
I: www.lakelovers.co.uk

Swallowdale ★★★★
Contact: Susan Jackson
Heart of the Lakes, Fisherbeck
Mill, Old Lake Road, Ambleside
LA22 0DH
T: (015394) 32321
F: (015394) 33251

Sweden Bank ★★★
Contact: Susan Jackson
Heart of the Lakes, Fisherbeck
Mill, Old Lake Road, Ambleside
LA22 0DH
T: (015394) 32321
F: (015394) 33251

Tethera ★★★
Contact: Mrs Susan Jackson
Heart of the Lakes, Fisherbeck
Mill, Old Lake Road, Ambleside
LA22 0DH
T: (015394) 32321
F: (015394) 33251
E: info@heartofthelakes.co.uk
I: www.heartofthelakes.co.uk

Thomas Fold Cottage ★★★★
Contact: Susan Jackson
Heart of the Lakes, Fisherbeck
Mill, Old Lake Road, Ambleside
LA22 0DH
T: (015394) 32321
F: (015394) 33251

1 Tom Fold ★★★
Contact: Paul Liddell
Lakelovers, Belmont House, Lake
Road, Bowness-on-Windermere,
Windermere LA23 3BJ
T: (015394) 88855
F: (015394) 88857

Tree Tops ★★★★
Contact: Mr Durbin
Cumbrian Cottages, 2 Lonsdale
Street, Carlisle CA1 1DB
T: (01228) 599960
F: (01228) 599970
E: enquiries@
cumbrian-cottages.co.uk
I: www.cumbrian-cottages.co.uk

Troutbeck ★★★★
Contact: Mrs Susan Jackson
Heart of the Lakes, Fisherbeck
Mill, Old Lake Road, Ambleside
LA22 0DH
T: (015394) 32321
F: (015394) 33251
E: info@heartofthelakes.co.uk
I: www.heartofthelakes.co.uk

Upper Sycamore Cottage ★★★★
Contact: Mrs Susan Jackson
Heart of the Lakes, Fisherbeck
Mill, Old Lake Road, Ambleside
LA22 0DH
T: (015394) 32351
F: (015394) 33251
E: info@heartofthelakes.co.uk
I: www.heartofthelakes.co.uk

Walkers Cottage ★★★
Contact: Mr Durbin
Cumbrian Cottages, 2 Lonsdale
Street, Carlisle CA1 1DB
T: (01228) 599960
F: (01228) 599970
E: enquiries@
cumbrian-cottages.co.uk
I: www.cumbrian-cottages.co.uk

Wansfell ★★★★★
Contact: Mrs Susan Jackson
Heart of the Lakes, Fisherbeck
Mill, Old Lake Road, Ambleside
LA22 0DH
T: (015394) 32321
F: (015394) 33251
E: info@heartofthelakes.co.uk
I: www.heartofthelakes.co.uk

Waterfalls ★★★★
Contact: Mrs Susan Jackson
Heart of the Lakes, Fisherbeck
Mill, Old Lake Road, Ambleside
LA22 0DH
T: (015394) 32321
F: (015394) 33251
E: info@heartofthelakes.co.uk
I: www.heartofthelakes.co.uk

Wayside Cottage ★★★★
Contact: Dr Leech
Wayside Cottage, 22 Styvechale
Avenue, Warwickshire, Coventry
CV5 6DX
T: (02476) 677549
F: 0870 0512818
E: waysidecottage@lineone.net
I: www.toddcrag.co.uk

West View ★★★★
Contact: Mr Peter Durbin
Cumbrian Cottages, 2 Lonsdale
Street, Carlisle CA1 1DB
T: (01228) 599960
F: (01228) 599970
E: enquiries@cumbriancottages.
co.uk
I: www.cumbrian-cottages.co.uk

Wetherlam ★★★★
Contact: Mr Paul Liddell
Lakelovers, Belmont House, Lake
Road, Bowness-on-Windermere,
Windermere LA23 3BJ
T: (015394) 88855
F: (015394) 88857
E: bookings@lakelovers.co.uk
I: www.lakelovers.co.uk

Wheelwrights Holiday Cottages ★★–★★★★★★
Contact: Mr Bass
Wheelwrights, Elterwater,
Ambleside LA22 9HS
T: (015394) 37635
F: (015394) 37618
E: enquiries@wheelwrights.com
I: www.wheelwrights.com

Wilmar Cottage ★★
Contact: Susan Jackson
Heart of the Lakes, Fisherbeck
Mill, Old Lake Road, Ambleside
LA22 0DH
T: (015394) 32321
F: (015394) 33251

Winander ★★★★★
Contact: Mrs Susan Jackson
Heart of the Lakes, Fisherbeck
Mill, Old Lake Road, Ambleside
LA22 0DH
T: (015394) 32321
F: (015394) 33251
E: info@heartofthelakes.co.uk
I: www.heartofthelakes.co.uk

Windermere Suite ★★★★★
Contact: Susan Jackson
Heart of the Lakes, Fisherbeck
Mill, Old Lake Road, Ambleside
LA22 0DH
T: (015394) 32321
F: (015394) 33251

Woolly End ★★★★
Contact: Paul Liddell
Lakelovers, Belmont House, Lake
Road, Bowness-on-Windermere,
Windermere LA23 3BJ
T: (015394) 88855
F: (015394) 88857
E: bookings@lakelovers.co.uk
I: www.lakelovers.co.uk

Establishments printed in blue have a detailed entry in this guide

CUMBRIA – THE LAKE DISTRICT

Wren Cottage ★★★
Contact: Susan Jackson
Heart of the Lakes, Fisherbeck Mill, Old Lake Road, Ambleside LA22 0DH
T: (015394) 32321
F: (015394) 33151

Yew Tree Cottage ★★★
Contact: Mrs Susan Jackson
Heart of the Lakes, Fisherbeck Mill, Old Lake Road, Ambleside LA22 0DH
T: (015394) 32321
F: (015394) 33151
E: info@heartofthelakes.co.uk
I: www.heartofthelakes.co.uk

APPLEBY-IN-WESTMORLAND
Cumbria

Black Bull ★★★
Contact: Mr Peter Durbin
Cumbrian Cottages, 2 Lonsdale Street, Carlisle CA1 1DB
T: (01228) 599960
F: (01228) 599970
E: enquiries@cumbrian-cottages.co.uk
I: www.cumbrian-cottages.co.uk

Dunkirk ★★★★
Contact: Paul Crosbie
Dunkirk Partnership, 30 Eagle Wharf Court, Lafone Street, London SE1 2LZ
T: (020) 7403 7346
E: paulcrosbie147@msn.com
I: www.dunkirk.20m.com

Glebe Hayloft and Glebe Stable ★★★★
Contact: Mr Martin Wardle
Goosemire Cottages, Bateman Fold Barn, Crook, Nr Kendal LA8 8LN
T: (015395) 68102
F: (015395) 68104
E: goosemirecottage@aol.com
I: www.glebeholidays.co.uk

Holly Lodge ★★★
Contact: Mr Nigel Hodgkinson
Holly Lodge, Roman Road, Appleby-in-Westmorland CA16 6JH
T: (017683) 51850

Ivy Cottage ★★★
Contact: The Proprietor
Ivy Cottage, Penerin, Appleby-in-Westmorland CA16 6BN
T: (017683) 61233

The Little House ★★★★
Contact: Mr Roger & Mrs Lesley Hiscox
Bradshaw Gate Main Street, Hackthorn, Lincoln LN2 3PF
T: (01673) 860047
F: (01673) 861380
E: rogerhiscox@beeb.net
I: www.thelittlehouseappleby.com

Long Marton Station ★★★
Contact: David and Madeleine Adams
The Station, Milburn Road, Long Marton, Appleby-in-Westmorland CA16 6BU
T: (0161) 775 5669
E: info@LongMartonStation.fsnet.co.uk
I: www.LongMartonStation.co.uk

Milburn Grange Holiday Cottages ★★★
Contact: Mr Peter G Baker
Milburn Grange Holidays, Milburn Grange, Appleby-in-Westmorland CA16 6DR
T: (017683) 61867
F: (017683) 62337
E: holidays@milburngrange.co.uk
I: www.milburngrange.co.uk

The Old Smithy ★★★★
Contact: Mrs Kay E Smith
The Old Smithy, Far Close, Appleby-in-Westmorland CA16 6DN
T: (017683) 61333
E: smithies.com@talk21.com

Owl Cottage ★★★
Contact: The Manager
Ref:2923, Dales Holiday Cottages, Carleton Business Park, Carleton New Road, Skipton BD23 2AA
T: (01756) 799821
F: (01756) 797012
E: info@dalesholcot.com
I: www.dalesholcot.com

APPLETHWAITE
Cumbria

Applethwaite Country House ★★★★
Contact: Tom & Gail Ryan
Applethwaite Country House, Gale Cottage, Keswick CA12 4PL
T: (017687) 72413
F: (017687) 75706
E: ryan@applethwaite.com
I: www.applethwaite.com

Applewick Cottage ★★★★
Contact: Mr Peter Durbin
Cumbrian Cottages, 2 Lonsdale Street, Carlisle CA1 1DB
T: (01228) 599960
F: (01228) 599970
E: enquiries@cumbrian-cottages.co.uk
I: www.cumbrian-cottages.co.uk

Emily's Escape ★★★★
Contact: David Miller
Harriets Hideaway, 81 Whaggs Lane, Newcastle upon Tyne NE16 4PQ
T: (0191) 4880549
F: (0191) 4223303
E: dm81@blueyonder.co.uk
I: www.dm81.pwp.blueyonder.co.uk

The Manesty ★★★★
Contact: Mr Peter Durbin
Cumbrian Cottages, 2 Lonsdale Street, Carlisle CA1 1DB
T: (01228) 599960
F: (01228) 599970
E: enquiries@cumbrian-cottages.co.uk
I: www.cumbrian-cottages.co.uk

Sarah's Secret ★★★★
Contact: David Miller
Harriets Hideaway, 81 Whaggs Lane, Newcastle upon Tyne NE16 4PQ
T: (0191) 4880549
F: (0191) 4223303
E: dm81@blueyonder.co.uk
I: www.dm81.pwp.blueyonder.co.uk

Whiteside ★★★
Contact: Mr David Burton
Lakeland Cottage Holidays, Melbecks, Keswick CA12 4QX
T: (017687) 76065
F: (017687) 76869
E: info@lakelandcottages.co.uk
I: www.lakelandcottages.co.uk

ARMATHWAITE
Cumbria

Coombs Cottage ★★★★
Contact: Mr Peter Durbin
Cumbrian Cottages, 2 Lonsdale Street, Carlisle CA1 1DB
T: (01228) 599960
F: (01228) 599970
E: enquiries@cumbrian-cottages.co.uk
I: www.cumbrian-cottages.co.uk

Longdales Cottage ★★★
Contact: Mr Peter Durbin
Cumbrian Cottages, 2 Lonsdale Street, Carlisle CA1 1DB
T: (01228) 599960
F: (01228) 599970
E: enquiries@cumbriancottages.co.uk
I: www.cumbrian-cottages.co.uk

ASKHAM
Cumbria

Park View ★★★★
Contact: Mrs Lyn Page
Lowther Estate Office, Penrith CA10 2HG
T: (01931) 712577
F: (01931) 712679
E: lyn.page@lowther.co.uk
I: lowther-estatecottages.co.uk

ASPATRIA
Cumbria

Halls Bank Farm ★★★★★
Contact: Messrs Wilkinson
Arkleby House, Arkleby, Carlisle CA5 2BP
T: (016973) 20374

BACKBARROW
Cumbria

Cark Cottage ★★★
Contact: Mr Peter Durbin
Cumbrian Cottages, 2 Lonsdale Street, Carlisle CA1 1DB
T: (01228) 599960
F: (01228) 599970
E: enquiries@cumbrian-cottages.co.uk
I: www.cumbrian-cottages.co.uk

Kate's Cottage ★★★
Contact: Irene Zuniga
Bowness Lakeland Holidays, 131 Radcliffe New Road, Manchester M45 7RP
T: (0161) 7963896
F: (0161) 2721841

Lynwood Cottage ★★★
Contact: Mr Peter Durbin
Cumbrian Cottages, 2 Lonsdale Street, Carlisle CA1 1DB
T: (01228) 599960
F: (01228) 599970
E: enquiries@cumbrian-cottages.co.uk
I: www.cumbrian-cottages.co.uk

Megan's Retreat ★★★★
Contact: Mrs Julia Foy
Megan's Retreat, 300 Brooklands Road, Brooklands, Manchester M23 9HB
T: (0161) 962 0685
E: enquiries@megansretreat.com
I: www.megansretreat.com

BAILEY
Cumbria

Saughs Farm Cottages ★★★★
Contact: Kevin & Jane Gray
Saughs Farm Cottages, Saughs Farm, Newcastleton TD9 0TT
T: (016977) 48346
F: (016977) 48180
E: kiving.fraykm@btopenworld.com
I: www.skylarkcottages.co.uk

BAMPTON
Cumbria

Tethera ★★★★
Contact: Mr Martin Wardle
Lakes and Valleys, Bateman Fold Barn, Kendal LA8 8LN
T: (015394) 68103
F: (015394) 68104
E: lakesandvalleys@aol.com
I: www.lakesandvalleys.co.uk

BASSENTHWAITE
Cumbria

Apple Tree Cottage ★★★★
Contact: Jill Pointon
Apple Tree Cottage, The Lodge, Cockermouth CA13 9UP
T: (01900) 85011

Brook Cottage ★★★★
Contact: Mr Peter Durbin
Cumbrian Cottages, 2 Lonsdale Street, Carlisle CA1 1DB
T: (01228) 599960
F: (01228) 599970
E: enquiries@cumbriancottages.co.uk
I: www.cumbrian-cottages.co.uk

Brookfield ★★★★
Contact: Mr Peter Durbin
Cumbrian Cottages, 2 Lonsdale Street, Carlisle CA1 1DB
T: (01228) 599960
F: (01228) 599970
E: enquiries@cumbriancottages.co.uk
I: www.cumbrian-cottages.co.uk

Castle Hill Cottage ★★★★
Contact: The Owner
Castle Hill Cottage, Keswick CA12 4RL
T: (017687) 76091

CUMBRIA – THE LAKE DISTRICT

Garries Cottage ★★★
Contact: Mr Durbin
Cumbrian Cottages, 2 Lonsdale Street, Carlisle CA1 1DB
T: (01228) 599960
F: (01228) 599970
E: enquiries@cumbrian-cottages.co.uk
I: www.cumbrian-cottages.co.uk

Glencrest ★★
Contact: Mr Peter Durbin
Cumbrian Cottages, 2 Lonsdale Street, Carlisle CA1 1DB
T: (01228) 599960
F: (01228) 599970
E: enquiries@cumbrian-cottages.co.uk
I: www.cumbrian-cottages.co.uk

The Granary ★★★
Contact: Margaret Crooks
Road Farm, Ruthwaite, Ireby, Wigton CA7 1HG
T: (016973) 71524
E: mcrooks.roadfarm@btopenworld.com

High Spy ★★★
Contact: Mr Peter Durbin
Cumbrian Cottages, 2 Lonsdale Street, Carlisle CA1 1DB
T: (01228) 599960
F: (01228) 599970
E: enquiries@cumbrian-cottages.co.uk
I: www.cumbrian-cottages.co.uk

Irton House Farm ★★★★
Contact: Mr & Mrs Almond
Isel, Cockermouth CA13 9ST
T: (017687) 76380
E: almond@farmersweekly.net
I: www.irtonhousefarm.com

6 Low Kiln Court ★★★
Contact: Mr Peter Durbin
Cumbrian Cottages, 2 Lonsdale Street, Carlisle CA1 1DB
T: (01228) 599960
F: (01228) 599970
E: enquiries@cumbriancottages.co.uk
I: www.cumbrian-cottages.co.uk

Melbecks Holidays Homes: Skiddaw, Dodd, Dash, Randel ★★★-★★★★
Contact: Mr Burton
Melbecks Holidays Homes, Melbecks, Keswick CA12 4QX
T: (017687) 76065
F: (017687) 76869
E: info@lakelandcottages.co.uk
I: www.lakelandcottages.co.uk

Peter House Farm Cottage ★★★★
Contact: Mrs Trafford
Peter House Farm Cottage, Peter House Farm, Keswick CA12 4QX
T: (017687) 76278
I: www.peterhousefarm.co.uk

Random Stones ★★★★
Contact: Mrs Susan Jackson
Heart of the Lakes, Fisherbeck Mill, Old Lake Road, Ambleside LA22 0DH
T: (015394) 32321
F: (015394) 33251
E: info@heartofthelakes.co.uk
I: www.heartofthelakes.co.uk

Riggs Cottage ★★★★
Contact: Mr Peter Durbin
Cumbrian Cottages, 2 Lonsdale Street, Carlisle CA1 1DB
T: (01228) 599960
F: (01228) 599970
E: enquiries@cumbrian-cottages.co.uk
I: www.cumbrian-cottages.co.uk

The Ruddings ★★★
Contact: Mr Peter Durbin
Cumbrian Cottages, 2 Lonsdale Street, Carlisle CA1 1DB
T: (01228) 599960
F: (01228) 599970
E: enquiries@cumbrian-cottages.co.uk
I: www.cumbrian-cottages.co.uk

South View ★★★
Contact: Mr Peter Durbin
Cumbrian Cottages, 2 Lonsdale Street, Carlisle CA1 1DB
T: (01228) 599960
F: (01228) 599970
E: enquiries@cumbrian-cottages.co.uk
I: www.cumbrian-cottages.co.uk

Uldale ★★★★
Contact: Mr David Burton
Lakeland Cottage Holidays, Melbecks, Keswick CA12 4QX
T: (017687) 76065
F: (017687) 76869
E: info@lakelandcottages.co.uk
I: www.lakelandcottages.co.uk

BERRIER
Cumbria

Bells Farm ★★★
Contact: Peter Durbin & Tony Commons
Cumbrian Cottages, 2 Lonsdale Street, Carlisle CA1 1DB
T: (01228) 599960
F: (01228) 599970
E: enquiries@cumbrian-cottages.co.uk
I: www.cumbrian-cottages.co.uk

The Cruck Barn ★★★
Contact: Mr Peter Durbin
Cumbrian Cottages, 2 Lonsdale Street, Carlisle CA1 1DB
T: (01228) 599960
F: (01228) 599970
E: enquiries@cumbrian-cottages.co.uk
I: www.cumbrian-cottages.co.uk

BEWCASTLE
Cumbria

Arch View Cottages ★★★-★★★★★
Contact: Jean James
Arch View, Midtodhills Farm, Bew Castle, Carlisle CA6 6PF
T: (016977) 48213
F: (016977) 48213
E: jjames@v21mail.co.uk
I: www.holidaycottagescarlisle.co.uk

BLAWITH
Cumbria

Birchbank Cottage ★★★★
Contact: Linda Nicholson
Birchbank Cottage, Birchbank, Ulverston LA12 8EW
T: (01229) 885277
E: birchbank@btinternet.com
I: www.lakedistrictfarmhouseholidays.co.uk/birchbankcottage

Blea Brows Cottage ★★★
Contact: Mr Philip Johnston
The Coppermines & Coniston Lakes Cottages, The Estate Office, The Bridge, Coniston LA21 8HJ
T: (015394) 41765
F: (015394) 41944
E: info@@coppermines.co.uk
I: www.coppermines.co.uk

Brown Howe Cottage ★★★★
Contact: Mr Philip Johnston
The Coppermines & Coniston Lakes Cottages, The Estate Office, The Bridge, Coniston LA21 8HJ
T: (015394) 41765
F: (015394) 41944
E: info@@coppermines.co.uk
I: www.coppermines.co.uk

BLEATARN
Cumbria

Sawbridge Hall ★★★★
Contact: Mrs Paul
Sawbridge Hall, Appleby-in-Westmorland CA16 6PY
T: (017683) 41201

BORROWDALE
Cumbria

Barrowgate ★★★
Contact: Mr David Burton
Lakeland Cottage Holidays, Melbecks, Keswick CA12 4QX
T: (017687) 76065
F: (017687) 76869
E: info@lakelandcottages.co.uk
I: www.lakelandcottages.co.uk

Chapelfield Cottage ★★★
Contact: Mr Peter Durbin
Cumbrian Cottages, 2Lonsdale Street, Carlisle CA1 1DB
T: (01228) 599960
F: (01228) 599970
E: enquiries@cumbrian-cottages.co.uk
I: www.cumbrian-cottages.co.uk

Derwent Farmhouse ★★★
Contact: Mr David Burton
Lakeland Cottage Holidays, Melbecks, Keswick CA12 4QX
T: (017687) 76065
F: (017687) 76869
E: info@lakelandcottages.co.uk
I: www.lakelandcottages.co.uk

Grange Cottage ★★★
Contact: Mr Peter Durbin
Cumbrian Cottages, 2 Lonsdale Street, Carlisle CA1 1DB
T: (01228) 599960
F: (01228) 599970
E: enquiries@cumbriancottages.co.uk
I: www.cumbrian-cottages.co.uk

Hazel Bank Cottage ★★★★
Contact: Glen & Brenda Davies
Hazel Bank Country House, Rosthwaite, Keswick CA12 5XB
T: (01768) 777248
F: (01767) 877373
E: enquiries@hazelbankhotel.co.uk
I: www.hazelbankhotel.co.uk

The Hollies ★★★★
Contact: Mrs Waksman
The Hollies Rosthwaite, 8 Erskine Hill, London NW11 6HB
T: (020) 8455 1260
F: (020) 8455 2768
E: j.waksman@btopenworld.com
I: holliesholidays.co.uk

Rose Cottage Holiday Apartments ★★★
Contact: Steve Cooke
Rose Cottage Holiday Apartments, Keswick CA12 5XB
T: (017687) 77678
E: stevecooke@rosthwaite.freeserve.co.uk
I: www.borrowdalecottages.co.uk

Scale Force ★★★
Contact: Mr David Burton
Lakeland Cottage Holidays, Melbecks, Keswick CA12 4QX
T: (017687) 76065
F: (017687) 76869
E: info@lakelandcottages.co.uk
I: www.lakelandcottages.co.uk

7 Twentymans Court ★★★
Contact: Mr Peter Durbin
Cumbrian Cottages, 2 Lonsdale Street, Carlisle CA1 1DB
T: (01228) 599960
F: (01228) 599970
E: enquiries@cumbriancottages.co.uk
I: www.cumbrian-cottages.co.uk

BOTHEL
Cumbria

The Lodge ★★★★
Contact: Diane Shankland
The Lodge, Quarry House, Carlisle CA7 2HH
T: (016973) 21674
E: lodge@lake-district.fsbusiness.co.uk
I: www.lodge-bothel.co.uk

Meadow View ★★★
Contact: Mr David Burton
Lakeland Cottage Holidays, Melbecks, Keswick CA12 4QX
T: (017687) 76065
F: (017687) 76869
E: info@lakelandcottages.co.uk
I: www.lakelandcottages.co.uk

Rose Cottage ★★★★
Contact: The Manager
Dales Holiday Cottages, Carleton Business Park, Carleton New Road, Skipton BD23 2AA
T: (01756) 790919
F: (01756) 797012
E: info@dalesholcot.com
I: www.dales-holiday-cottages.com

Establishments printed in blue have a detailed entry in this guide

CUMBRIA – THE LAKE DISTRICT

BOUTH
Cumbria

Crag House Cottage ★★★★
Contact: Mr John Serginson
The Lakeland Cottage Company,
Waterside House, Ulverston
LA12 8AN
T: (015395) 30024
F: (015395) 31932
E: john@lakelandcottageco.com
I: www.lakelandcottageco.com

Kiln Cottage ★★★★
Contact: Mr John Serginson
Lakeland Cottage Company,
Waterside House, Ulverston
LA12 8AN
T: (015395) 30024
F: (015395) 31932
E: john@lakelandcottageco.com
I: www.lakelandcottageco.com

No 1 Rose Cottage ★★★★
Contact: Mr John Serginson
The Lakeland Cottage Company,
Waterside House, Ulverston
LA12 8AN
T: (015395) 30024
F: (015395) 31932
E: john@lakelandcottageco.com
I: www.lakelandcottageco.com

BOWMANSTEAD
Cumbria

No 2 Lake View ★★★★
Contact: Mr Philip Johnston
The Coppermines & Coniston
Lakes Cottages, The Estate
Office, The Bridge, Coniston
LA21 8HJ
T: (01539) 441765
F: (01539) 441944
E: info@coppermines.co.uk
I: www.coppermines.
co.uk/property/show

BOWSTON
Cumbria

Kent View ★★★
Contact: Mr Peter Durbin
Cumbrian Cottages, 2 Lonsdale
Street, Carlisle CA1 1DB
T: (01228) 599960
F: (01228) 599970
E: enquiries@cumbriancottages.
co.uk
I: www.cumbrian-cottages.co.uk

Winstanley Cottage ★★★
Contact: Mr Peter Durbin
Cumbrian Cottages, 2 Lonsdale
Street, Carlisle CA1 1DB
T: (01228) 599960
F: (01228) 599970
E: enquiries@cumbriancottages.
co.uk
I: www.cumbrian-cottages.co.uk

BRAITHWAITE
Cumbria

Barrow View and Cedar Cottages ★★★★
Contact: Mr Horton
Barrow View and Cedar
Cottages, 5 St John's Street,
Keswick CA12 5AP
T: (017687) 74627
F: (017687) 74627
E: c.c.horton@talk21.com
I: www.bnminteractive.
co.uk/clients/cedarbarrowview/

Beech End ★★★
Contact: Mr David Burton
Lakeland Cottage Holidays,
Melbecks, Keswick CA12 4QX
T: (017687) 76065
F: (017687) 76869
E: info@lakelandcottages.co.uk
I: www.lakelandcottages.co.uk

Coledale House ★★★★
Contact: Mr Peter Durbin
Cumbrian Cottages, 2 Lonsdale
Street, Carlisle CA1 1DB
T: (01228) 599960
F: (01228) 599970
E: enquiries@cumbrian-cottage.
co.uk
I: www.cumbrian-cottages.co.uk

Cosy Cottage ★★★
Contact: Mr David Burton
Lakeland Cottage Holidays,
Melbecks, Keswick CA12 4QX
T: (017687) 76065
F: (017687) 76869
E: info@lakelandcottages.co.uk
I: www.lakelandcottages.co.uk

Eastern Cottage ★★
Contact: The Owner
Eastern Cottage, Keswick
CA12 5SX

Highbridge Cottages ★★★★
Contact: Peter Rigg
Highbridge Cottage, Manor
Crest, Manor Brow, Keswick
CA12 4AW
T: (017687) 80561
E: riggpeter@ntlworld.com
I: www.braithwaite-cottage.
co.uk

Olives Cottage ★★★★
Contact: Mr Peter Durbin
Cumbrian Cottages, 2 Lonsdale
Street, Carlisle CA1 1DB
T: (01228) 599960
F: (01228) 599970
E: enquiries@cumbriancottages.
co.uk
I: www.cumbrian-cottages.co.uk

The Shieling ★★★
Contact: Mr David Burton
Lakeland Cottage Holidays,
Melbecks, Keswick CA12 4QX
T: (017687) 76065
F: (017687) 76869
E: info@lakelandcottages.co.uk
I: www.lakelandcottages.co.uk

Windrush ★★★★
Contact: Mr David Burton
Lakeland Cottage Holidays,
Melbecks, Keswick CA12 4QX
T: (017687) 76065
F: (017687) 76869
E: info@lakelandcottages.co.uk
I: www.lakelandcottages.co.uk

Wychwood ★★★
Contact: Mr David Burton
Lakeland Cottage Holidays,
Melbecks, Keswick CA12 4QX
T: (017687) 76065
F: (017687) 76869
E: info@lakelandcottages.co.uk
I: www.lakelandcottages.co.uk

BRAMPTON
Cumbria

Chapel House ★★★
Contact: Dorothy Potts
Chapel House, Brampton
CA8 1LP
T: (01228) 670535
F: (01228) 670535
E: potts@chapelhouse10.fsnet.
co.uk
I: www.chapelhouse10.fsnet.
co.uk

Hay Barn Cottage ★★★★
Contact: Paul & Judith Barton
Bush Nook, Upper Denton,
Brampton CA8 7AF
T: (016977) 47194
F: (016977) 47790
E: info@bushnook.co.uk
I: www.bushnook.co.uk

Long Byres at Talkin Head ★★-★★★
Contact: Harriet Sykes
Long Byres at Talkin Head, Talkin
Head, Brampton CA8 1LT
T: (016977) 3435
E: harriet@talkinhead.co.uk
I: www.talkinhead.co.uk

South View Cottage ★★★★
Contact: Marie Hodgson
141 Nell Lane, West Didsbury,
Manchester M20 2LG
T: (0161) 374 0110
E: mariehodgson@
southviewbanks.f9.co.uk
I: www.southviewbanks.f9.
co.uk/cottage/index.htm

Stonerigg Barn ★★★★
Contact: Mr Peter Durbin
Cumbrian Cottages, 2 Lonsdale
Street, Carlisle CA1 1DB
T: (01228) 599960
F: (01228) 599970
E: enquiries@
cumbrian-cottages.co.uk
I: www.cumbrian-cottages.co.uk

Warren Bank Cottage ★★★★★
Contact: Margie Douglas
Warren Bank Cottage, The Coach
House, Halliwell Dene, Hexham
NE46 1HW
T: (01434) 607544
E: margie@warrenbankcottage.
com
I: www.warrenbankcottage.com

BRIDEKIRK
Cumbria

Ellwood ★★★
Contact: Mr Peter Durbin
Cumbrian Cottages, 2 Lonsdale
Street, Carlisle CA1 1DB
T: (01228) 599960
F: (01228) 599970
E: enquiries@
cumbrian-cottages.co.uk
I: www.cumbrian-cottages.co.uk

BRIGHAM
Cumbria

West Croft Holiday Cottages
Rating Applied For
Contact: Mrs Helen Buckingham
West Croft Holiday Cottages,
126 High Brigham, Cockermouth
CA13 0TJ
T: (01900) 822103
E: Westcroft.holidays@virgin.
net
I: www.westcroftcottages.co.uk

BRIGSTEER
Cumbria

Garden Cottage ★★★★
Contact: Mr Peter Durbin
Cumbrian Cottages, 2 Lonsdale
Street, Carlisle CA1 1DB
T: (01228) 599960
F: (01228) 599970
E: enquiries@
cumbrian-cottages.co.uk
I: www.cumbrian-cottages.co.uk

Moss Rigg ★★★
Contact: Mr Peter Durbin
Cumbrian Cottages, 2 Lonsdale
Street, Carlisle CA1 1DB
T: (01228) 599960
F: (01228) 599970
E: enquiries@cumbriancottages.
co.uk
I: www.cumbrian-cottages.co.uk

The Old Barn
Rating Applied For
Contact: Mr Paul Liddell
Lakelovers, Belmont House, Lake
Road, Bowness-on-Windermere,
Windermere LA23 3BJ
T: (015394) 88855
F: (015394) 88857
E: bookings@lakelovers.co.uk
I: www.lakelovers.co.uk

BROUGHTON IN FURNESS
Cumbria

Holebeck Farm Cottages ★★★-★★★★
Contact: Mr Philip Johnston
The Coppermines & Coniston
Lakes Cottages, Coppermines
Valley, Coniston LA21 8HX
T: (015394) 41765
F: (015394) 41765
E: bookings@coppermines.co.uk
I: www.coppermines.co.uk

The Old Millers Cottage ★★★★
Contact: Mr Philip Johnston
The Coppermines & Coniston
Lakes Cottages, The Estate
Office, The Bridge, Coniston
LA21 8HJ
T: (015394) 41765
I: www.coppermines.
co.uk/property/show_details.
cgi?id=82

Ring House Cottages ★★★-★★★★
Contact: Stuart & Lynda
Harrison
Ring House Cottages, Ring
House Farm, Woodland,
Broughton-in-Furness
LA20 6DG
T: (01229) 716578
F: (01229) 716850
E: info@ringhouse.co.uk
I: www.ringhouse.co.uk

CUMBRIA – THE LAKE DISTRICT

Rose Cottage & Honeysuckle Cottage ★★★★
Contact: Mrs M Harrison
Lane End Farm, Broughton-in-Furness LA20 6AX
T: (01229) 716332
I: www.lakesbreaks.co.uk

Thornthwaite Farm ★★★
Contact: Jean Jackson
Thornthwaite Farm, Woodland Hall, Woodland, Broughton-in-Furness LA20 6DF
T: (01229) 716340
F: (01229) 716340
E: info@lakedistrictcottages.co.uk
I: www.lakedistrictcottages.co.uk

BROUGHTON MILLS
Cumbria

Hobkin Cottage ★★★
Contact: Mr Philip Johnston
The Coppermines & Coniston Lakes Cottages, The Estate Office, The Bridge, Coniston LA21 8HJ
T: (015394) 41765
E: bookings@coppermines.co.uk
I: www.coppermines.co.uk

Lind End Farm Cottages
Rating Applied For
Contact: Mrs Janet Johnson
Hobkinground Farm, Broughton-in-Furness LA20 6AU
T: (01229) 716338
F: (01229) 716338
E: lindend@btinternet.com

BURNESIDE
Cumbria

St Oswald's View ★★★
Contact: Mr Peter Durbin
Cumbrian Cottages, 2 Lonsdale Street, Carlisle CA1 1DB
T: (01228) 599960
F: (01228) 599970
E: enquiries@cumbrian-cottages.co.uk
I: www.cumbrian-cottages.co.uk

BURTON-IN-KENDAL
Cumbria

East Wing ★★★★
Contact: Mr Peter Durbin
Cumbrian Cottages, 2 Lonsdale Street, Carlisle CA1 1DB
T: (01228) 599960
F: (01228) 599970
E: enquiries@cumbriancottages.co.uk
I: www.cumbrian-cottages.co.uk

BUTTERMERE
Cumbria

Beck House ★★★★
Contact: Simon Hughes
Beck House, 13 St Leonards Close, Oxford OX49 5PQ
T: (014916) 12841
F: (014916) 14668
E: shelagh@beckhouseholidays.co.uk
I: www.beckhouseholidays.co.uk

Bridge Hotel Self Catering Apartments ★★★★
Contact: Mr John McGuire
Bridge Hotel, Buttermere, Cockermouth CA13 9UZ
T: (017687) 70252
F: (017687) 70215
I: www.bridge-hotel.com

Lanthwaite Green Farm Cottage ★★★★
Contact: Mr John McGuire
Bridge Hotel, Buttermere, Cockermouth CA13 9UZ
T: (017687) 70252
F: (017687) 70215
E: enquiries@bridge-hotel.com
I: www.bridge-hotel.com

Rannerdale Cottages ★★★★
Contact: Mrs P E Beard
Rannerdale Cottages, Rannerdale Farm, Cockermouth CA13 9UY
T: (017687) 70232

CALDBECK
Cumbria

The Barn, Manor Cottage ★★★★
Contact: Mrs Ann Wade
The Barn, Manor Cottage, Fellside, Caldbeck, Wigton CA7 8HA
T: (016974) 78214
E: walterwade@tiscali.co.uk

Ellwood House ★★★★
Contact: Mr Durbin
Cumbrian Cottages, 2 Lonsdale Street, Carlisle CA1 1DB
T: (01228) 599960
F: (01228) 599970
E: enquiries@cumbrian-cottages.co.uk
I: www.cumbrian-cottages.co.uk

Greenside ★★★
Contact: Mr Peter Durbin
Cumbrian Cottages, 2 Lonsdale Street, Carlisle CA1 1DB
T: (01228) 599960
F: (01228) 599970
E: enquiries@cumbrian-cottages.co.uk
I: www.cumbrian-cottages.co.uk

High Greenrigg House Country Cottages ★★★★★
Contact: Mrs Sonia Hill
High Greenrigg House Country Cottages, High Greenrigg House, Wigton CA7 8HD
T: (016974) 78430
F: (016974) 78430
E: info@highgreenrigghouse.co.uk
I: www.highgreenrigghouse.co.uk

Monkhouse Hill Cottages ★★★★-★★★★★
Contact: Mr Andy Collard
Monkhouse Hill Cottages, Carlisle CA15 7HW
T: (016974) 76254
F: (016974) 76254
E: cottages@monkhousehill.co.uk
I: www.monkhousehill.co.uk

1 Riverside Cottage ★★★★
Contact: Mr Peter Durbin
Cumbrian Cottages, 2 Lonsdale Street, Carlisle CA1 1DB
T: (01228) 599960
F: (01228) 599970
I: www.cumbrian-cottages.co.uk

CARK IN CARTMEL
Cumbria

Batters Cottage ★★★
Contact: Mr John Serginson
The Lakeland Cottage Company, Waterside House, Ulverston LA12 8AN
T: (015395) 30024
F: (015395) 31932
E: john@lakelandcottageco.com
I: www.lakelandcottageco.com

The Mill Apartment ★★★
Contact: Mrs Teresa Watson
The Mill Apartment, 12 Millstream Court, Grange-over-Sands LA11 7NW
T: (015395) 58519
E: neiwatson@lineone.net
I: www.millholidayapartment.co.uk

Salesbrook ★★★★
Contact: Mr John Serginson
The Lakeland Cottage Company, Waterside House, Ulverston LA12 8AN
T: (015395) 30024
F: (015395) 31932
E: john@lakelandcottageco.com
I: www.lakelandcottageco.com

CARLETON
Cumbria

Newbiggin Hall ★★★★
Contact: Mr David & Mrs June Bates
Newbiggin Hall, Carlisle CA4 0AJ
T: (01228) 527549

CARLISLE
Cumbria

Bessiestown Farm Country Cottages ★★★★
Contact: Mr John Sisson
Bessiestown Farm Country Cottages, Catlowdy, Carlisle CA6 5QP
T: (01228) 577219
F: (01228) 577219
E: info@bessiestown.co.uk
I: www.bessiestown.co.uk

Meadow View, Burn Cottage & Ald Pallyards ★★★★
Contact: Mrs Elwen
Meadow View, Burn Cottage & Ald Pallyards, New Pallyards, Carlisle CA6 6HZ
T: (01228) 577308
F: (01228) 577308
E: info@newpallyards.freeserve.co.uk
I: www.newpallyards.freeserve.co.uk

Old Brewery Residences ★★★
Contact: Dee Carruthers
University of Northumbria (Carlisle Campus), Old Brewery Residences, Bridge Lane, Caldewgate, Carlisle CA2 5SR
T: (01228) 597352
F: (01228) 597352

West Cottage ★★★★
Contact: Mrs Allison Stamper
Cringles, Cumwhinton, Carlisle CA4 8DL
T: (01228) 561600

CARTMEL
Cumbria

2 Beckside Barn
Rating Applied For
Contact: Amy Hargreaves
2 Beckside Barn, The Spinney, Rosemary Lane, Bartle, Preston PR4 0HB
T: (01772) 691053
E: enquiries@cartmelholidays.co.uk
I: www.beckside.co.uk

Grange End Cottages ★★★★
Contact: Mr Simon Cleasby
45 The Row, Silverdale, Lancashire LA5 0UG
T: (01524) 702955 & 07770 301709
E: simoncleasby@aol.com
I: www.holidaycottagescumbria.com

Longlands at Cartmel ★★★★
Contact: Martin Ainscough
Longlands at Cartmel, Grange-over-Sands LA11 6HG
T: (015395) 36475
F: (015395) 36172
E: longlands@cartmel.com
I: www.cartmel.com

Longlands Farm Cottage ★★★
Contact: Valerie Dixon
Longlands Farm Cottage, Longlands Farm, Grange-over-Sands LA11 6HJ
T: (015395) 36406
I: www.longlandsfarmcottage.co.uk

The Old Vicarage ★★★★
Contact: Mrs Sharphouse
The Old Vicarage, Cartmel, Grange-over-Sands LA11 6HW
T: (015395) 36540
E: theflat@sharphouse.co.uk
I: www.sharphouse.co.uk/theflat

Springfield Lodge ★★★
Contact: Maureen & Jack Craig
Springfield Lodge, c/o Plane Tree Cottage, Milnthorpe LA7 7EX
T: (015395) 64787

Wharton Cottage ★★★★
Contact: Mr John Serginson
The Lakeland Cottage Company, Waterside House, Ulverston LA12 8AN
T: (015395) 30024
F: (015395) 31932
E: john@lakelandcottageco.com
I: www.lakelandcottageco.com

Wharton House ★★★★
Contact: Mr James Forbes
Wharton House, c/o Cornbrook-House, Clogger Beck, Cartmel, Cumbria, Grange-over-Sands LA11 6PN
T: (015395) 36314

Establishments printed in blue have a detailed entry in this guide

CUMBRIA – THE LAKE DISTRICT

CARTMEL FELL
Cumbria

Lightwood Barn ★★★★
Contact: Mr John Serginson
Lakeland Cottage Company,
Waterside House, Ulverston
LA12 8AN
T: (015395) 30024
F: (015395) 31932
E: john@lakelandcottageco.com

CASTLE CARROCK
Cumbria

Tottergill Farm
★★★★-★★★★★
Contact: Alison Bridges
Tottergill Farm, Castle Carrock,
Brampton CA8 9DP
T: (01228) 670615
F: (01228) 670727
E: alison@tottergill.demon.co.uk
I: www.tottergill.demon.co.uk

CHAPEL STILE
Cumbria

Anns Cottage ★★★
Contact: Mrs Vivien Bass
Wheelwrights Holiday Cottages,
Langdale, Ambleside LA22 9HS
T: (015394) 37635
E: enquiries@wheelwrights.com
I: www.wheelwrights.com

Bank View ★★★
Contact: Peter Durbin & Tony Commons
Cumbrian Cottages, 2 Lonsdale
Street, Carlisle CA1 1DB
T: (01228) 599960
F: (01228) 599970
E: sales@cumbrian-cottages.co.uk
I: www.cumbrian-cottages.co.uk

Birdie Fell ★★★
Contact: Mrs Vivien Bass
Wheelwrights Holiday Cottages,
Langdale, Ambleside LA22 9HS
T: (015394) 37635
E: enquiries@wheelwrights.com
I: www.wheelwrights.com

Church Bank ★★★
Contact: Mrs Vivien Bass
Wheelwrights Holiday Cottages,
Langdale, Ambleside LA22 9HS
T: (015394) 37635
F: (015394) 37618
E: enquiries@wheelwrights.com
I: www.wheelwrights.com

Daw Bank ★★★
Contact: Mrs Vivien Bass
Wheelwrights Holiday Cottages,
Langdale, Ambleside LA22 9HS
T: (015394) 37635
E: enquiries@wheelwrights.com
I: www.wheelwrights.com

Dulcanter ★★★
Contact: Mr Peter Durbin
Cumbrian Cottages, 2 Lonsdale
Street, Carlisle CA1 1DB
T: (01228) 599960
F: (01228) 599970
E: enquiries@cumbrian-cottage.co.uk
I: www.cumbrian-cottages.co.uk

End Cottage ★★
Contact: Mrs Vivien Bass
Wheelwrights Holiday Cottages,
Langdale, Ambleside LA22 9HS
T: (015394) 37635
E: enquiries@wheelwrights.com
I: www.wheelwrights.com

Fir Garth ★★★
Contact: Mr Peter Durbin
Cumbrian Cottages, 2 Lonsdale
Street, Carlisle CA1 1DB
T: (01228) 599960
F: (01228) 599970
E: enquiries@cumbrian-cottages.co.uk
I: www.cumbrian-cottages.co.uk

14 Firgarth ★★★
Contact: Mrs Vivien Bass
Wheelwrights Holiday Cottages,
Langdale, Ambleside LA22 9HS
T: (015394) 37635
E: enquiries@wheelwrights.com
I: www.wheelwrights.com

16 Firgarth ★★★
Contact: Mrs Vivien Bass
Wheelwrights Holiday Cottages,
Langdale, Ambleside LA22 9HS
T: (015394) 37635
F: (015394) 37618
E: enquiries@wheelwrights.com
I: www.wheelwrights.com

7 Firgarth ★★★★
Contact: Mrs Vivien Bass
Wheelwrights Holiday Cottages,
Langdale, Ambleside LA22 9HS
T: (015394) 37635
E: enquiries@wheelwrights.com
I: www.wheelwrights.com

Fold Cottage ★★★
Contact: Mrs Vivien Bass
Wheelwrights Holiday Cottages,
Langdale, Ambleside LA22 9HS
T: (015394) 37635
E: enquiries@wheelwrights.com
I: www.wheelwrights.com

Greenmire ★★★★
Contact: Mrs Vivien Bass
Wheelwrights Holiday Cottages,
Langdale, Ambleside LA22 9HS
T: (015394) 37635
E: enquiries@wheelwrights.com
I: www.wheelwrights.com

Inglewood Cottage ★★★
Contact: Mrs Vivien Bass
Wheelwrights Holiday Cottages,
Langdale, Ambleside LA22 9HS
T: (015394) 37635
E: enquiries@wheelwrights.com
I: www.wheelwrights.com

Inglewood House ★★★★
Contact: Mrs Vivien Bass
Wheelwrights Holiday Cottages,
Langdale, Ambleside LA22 9HS
T: (015394) 37635
E: enquiries@wheelwrights.com
I: www.wheelwrights.com

Jacks Nook ★★★
Contact: Mrs Vivien Bass
Wheelwrights Holiday Cottages,
Langdale, Ambleside LA22 9HS
T: (015394) 37635
E: enquiries@wheelwrights.com
I: www.wheelwrights.com

Jenny's Cottage ★★★
Contact: Mrs Vivien Bass
Wheelwrights Holiday Cottages,
Langdale, Ambleside LA22 9HS
T: (015394) 37635
E: enquiries@wheelwrights.com
I: www.wheelwrights.com

1 Lingmoor View ★★★
Contact: Pauline Robinson
1 Lingmoor View, 3 Whinfield
Road, Ulverston LA12 7HG
T: (01229) 583889
E: paulinerobinson@lakelandcottage.com
I: www.lakelandcottage.com

10 Lingmoor View ★★★
Contact: Mrs Vivien Bass
Wheelwrights Holiday Cottages,
Langdale, Ambleside LA22 9HS
T: (015394) 37635
F: (015394) 37618
E: enquiries@wheelwrights.com
I: www.wheelwrights.com

3 Lingmoor View ★★★
Contact: Mr Geoffrey & Mrs Sheila Smith
21 Cross Bank, Skipton
BD23 6AH
T: (01756) 791779
E: g.s.smith@btinternet.com

5 Lingmoor View ★★★
Contact: Mrs Vivien Bass
Wheelwrights Holiday Cottages,
Langdale, Ambleside LA22 9HS
T: (015394) 37635
F: (015394) 37618
E: enquiries@wheelwrights.com
I: www.wheelwrights.com

9 Lingmoor View ★★★★
Contact: Mrs Vivien Bass
Wheelwrights Holiday Cottages,
Langdale, Ambleside LA22 9HS
T: (015394) 37635
E: enquiries@wheelwrights.com
I: www.wheelwrights.com

Meadow View ★★★
Contact: Mrs Vivien Bass
Wheelwrights Holiday Cottages,
Langdale, Ambleside LA22 9HS
T: (015394) 37635
F: (015394) 37618
E: enquiries@wheelwrights.com
I: www.wheelwrights.com

Myrtle Cottage ★★★
Contact: Mrs Vivien Bass
Wheelwrights Holiday Cottages,
Langdale, Ambleside LA22 9HS
T: (015394) 37635
E: enquiries@wheelwrights.com
I: www.wheelwrights.com

Oak Cottage ★★★★
Contact: Mrs Vivien Bass
Wheelwrights Holiday Cottages,
Langdale, Ambleside LA22 9HS
T: (015394) 37635
F: (015394) 37618
E: enquiries@wheelwrights.com
I: www.wheelwrights.com

Oakdene Cottage ★★★★
Contact: Mrs Vivien Bass
Wheelwrights Holiday Cottages,
Langdale, Ambleside LA22 9HS
T: (015394) 37635
F: (015394) 37618
E: enquiries@wheelwrights.com
I: www.wheelwrights.com

Oakdene House ★★★★
Contact: Mrs Vivien Bass
Wheelwrights Holiday Cottages,
Langdale, Ambleside LA22 9HS
T: (015394) 37635
F: (015394) 37618
E: enquiries@wheelwrights.com
I: www.wheelwrights.com

The Old Post Office ★★★★
Contact: Mrs Vivien Bass
Wheelwrights Holiday Cottages,
Langdale, Ambleside LA22 9HS
T: (015394) 37635
E: enquiries@wheelwrights.com
I: www.wheelwrights.com

Old White Lion ★★★
Contact: Mrs Vivien Bass
Wheelwrights Holiday Cottages,
Langdale, Ambleside LA22 9HS
T: (015394) 37635
E: enquiries@wheelwrights.com
I: www.wheelwrights.com

Orchard Cottage ★★★
Contact: Mrs Vivien Bass
Wheelwrights Holiday Cottages,
Langdale, Ambleside LA22 9HS
T: (015394) 37635
E: enquiries@wheelwrights.com
I: www.wheelwrights.com

Plumblands ★★★★
Contact: Mr Peter Durbin
Cumbrian Cottages, 2 Lonsdale
Street, Carlisle CA1 1DB
T: (01228) 599960
F: (01228) 599970
E: enquiries@cumbrian-cottages.co.uk
I: www.cumbrian-cottages.co.uk

Priest End ★★★★
Contact: Mrs Vivien Bass
Wheelwrights Holiday Cottages,
Langdale, Ambleside LA22 9HS
T: (015394) 37635
E: enquiries@wheelwrights.com
I: www.wheelwrights.com

Spedding Fold ★★★
Contact: Mrs Vivien Bass
Wheelwrights Holiday Cottages,
Langdale, Ambleside LA22 9HS
T: (015394) 37635
E: enquiries@wheelwrights.com
I: www.wheelwrights.com

16 Thrang Brow ★★★
Contact: Mrs Vivien Bass
Wheelwrights Holiday Cottages,
Langdale, Ambleside LA22 9HS
T: (015394) 37635
F: (015394) 37618
E: enquiries@wheelwrights.com
I: www.wheelwrights.com

18 Thrang Brow ★★★
Contact: Mrs Vivien Bass
Wheelwrights Holiday Cottages,
Langdale, Ambleside LA22 9HS
T: (015394) 37635
E: enquiries@wheelwrights.com
I: www.wheelwrights.com

20 Thrang Brow ★★★
Contact: Mrs Vivien Bass
Wheelwrights Holiday Cottages,
Langdale, Ambleside LA22 9HS
T: (015394) 37635
E: enquiries@wheelwrights.com
I: www.wheelwrights.com

CUMBRIA – THE LAKE DISTRICT

7 Thrang Brow ★★★
Contact: Mrs Vivien Bass
Wheelwrights Holiday Cottages,
Langdale, Ambleside LA22 9HS
T: (015394) 37635
F: (015394) 37618
E: enquiries@wheelwrights.com
I: www.wheelwrights.com

White Lion Cottage ★★★★
Contact: Mrs Vivien Bass
Wheelwrights Holiday Cottages,
Langdale, Ambleside LA22 9HS
T: (015394) 37635
F: (015394) 37618
E: enquiries@wheelwrights.com
I: www.wheelwrights.com

CLAPPERSGATE
Cumbria

Blackcombe, Whitecrags ★★★★
Contact: Susan Jackson
Heart of the Lakes, Fisherbeck
Mill, Old Lake Road, Ambleside
LA22 0DH
T: (015394) 32321
F: (015394) 33251
E: info@heartofthelakes.co.uk
I: www.heartofthelakes.co.uk

The Clock ★★★★
Contact: Mr Paul Liddell
Lakelovers, Belmont House, Lake
Road, Bowness-on-Windermere,
Windermere LA23 3BJ
T: (015394) 88855
F: (015394) 88857
E: bookings@lakelovers.co.uk
I: www.lakelovers.co.uk

Courtyard Cottage
Rating Applied For
Contact: Mrs Susan Jackson
Heart of the Lakes, Fisherbeck
Mill, Old Lake Road, Ambleside
LA22 0DH
T: (015394) 33110
F: (015394) 33251
I: www.heartofthelakes.co.uk

Crag Head Cottage ★★★★★
Contact: Paul Liddell
Lakelovers, Belmont House, Lake
Road, Bowness-on-Windermere,
Windermere LA23 3BJ
T: (015394) 88855
F: (015394) 88857
E: bookings@lakelovers.co.uk
I: www.lakelovers.co.uk

Fell View ★★★
Contact: Susan Jackson
Heart of the Lakes, Fisherbeck
Mill, Old Lake Road, Ambleside
LA22 0DH
T: (015394) 32321
F: (015394) 33251
E: info@heartofthelakes.co.uk
I: www.heartofthelakes.co.uk

The Hayloft ★★★
Contact: Susan Jackson
Heart of the Lakes, Fisherbeck
Mill, Old Lake Road, Ambleside
LA22 0DH
T: (015394) 32321
F: (015394) 33251

Park Cottage ★★★
Contact: Mrs Susan Jackson
Heart of the Lakes, Fisherbeck
Mill, Old Lake Road, Ambleside
LA22 0DH
T: (015394) 32321
F: (015394) 33251
E: info@heartofthelakes.co.uk
I: www.heartofthelakes.co.uk

The Pavilion ★★★★
Contact: Mr Hogarth
Cumbrian Cottages, 7 The
Crescent, Carlisle CA1 1QW
T: (01228) 599960
F: (01228) 599970
E: enquiries@
cumbrian-cottages.co.uk
I: www.cumbrian-cottages.co.uk

Rock Cottage ★★★
Contact: Susan Jackson
Heart of the Lakes, Fisherbeck
Mill, Old Lake Road, Ambleside
LA22 0DH
T: (015394) 32321
F: (015394) 33251

Scafell Pike, White Crags ★★★★
Contact: Susan Jackson
Heart of the Lakes, Fisherbeck
Mill, Old Lake Road, Ambleside
LA22 0DH
T: (015394) 32321
F: (015394) 33251

Skiddaw, Whitecrags ★★★★
Contact: Mrs Susan Jackson
Heart of the Lakes, Fisherbeck
Mill, Old Lake Road, Ambleside
LA22 0DH
T: (015394) 32321
F: (015394) 33251
E: info@heartofthelakes.co.uk
I: www.heartofthelakes.co.uk

COCKERMOUTH
Cumbria

Corner Cottage ★★★
Contact: Susan Hannah
W. S & S Hannah, c/o
Limelighting, Grand Theatre,
Station Road, Cockermouth
CA13 9PZ
T: (01900) 822480
F: (01900) 823105
E: suehannah@limelighting.
demon.co.uk
I: www.cottageguide.
co.uk/greatbroughton

Fellside ★★★
Contact: The Owner
Fellside, Wythop Mill,
Cockermouth CA13 9YP

Garden Cottage ★★★
Contact: Colin Wornham
Dower Cottage, Pardshaw Hall,
Cockermouth CA13 0SP
T: (01900) 823531
F: (01900) 823531
E: wornham2@aol.com
I: www.lakesnw.
co.uk/gardencottage

Ghyll Yeat ★★★★
Contact: Anne Haworth
Ghyll Yeat, 1 Park Villas, Keswick
CA12 5LQ
T: (017687) 80321
E: peter_anneghyllyeat@
lineone.net
I: www.ghyllyeat.co.uk

Highside Cottage ★★★★
Contact: Mr Peter Durbin
Cumbrian Cottages, 2 Lonsdale
Street, Carlisle CA1 1DB
T: (01228) 599960
F: (01228) 599970
E: enquiries@cumbriancottages.
co.uk
I: www.cumbrian-cottages.co.uk

Jenkin Cottage ★★★★
Contact: Mrs Margaret Teasdale
Jenkin Cottage, Cockermouth
CA13 9TN
T: (017687) 76387
I: www.jenkinfarm.co.uk

37 Kirkgate ★★★
Contact: Mr Nelson & Mrs
Valerie Chicken
39 Kirkgate, Cockermouth
CA13 9PJ
T: (01900) 823236
F: (01900) 825983
E: valandnelson@btopenworld.
com
I: www.37kirkgate.com

46 Kirkgate ★★★★
Contact: Mrs Livesey
Fawcett House, High Brigham,
Cockermouth CA13 0TG
T: (01900) 825442
F: (01900) 825442
E: tricia.livesey@euphony.net
I: www.46kirkgate.co.uk

Moorside ★★★
Contact: Mr Peter Durbin
Cumbrian Cottages, 2 Lonsdale
Street, Carlisle CA1 1DB
T: (01228) 599960
F: (01228) 599970
E: enquiries@cumbriancottages.
co.uk
I: www.cumbrian-cottages.co.uk

**Southwaite Mill Holiday
Cottages** ★★★★
Contact: Mr David Warner
Southwaite Holidays Limited,
Greysouthern House, The Went
Greysouthen, Cockermouth
CA13 0UQ
T: (01900) 827270
F: (01900) 821168

The Stable ★★★★
Contact: Carolyn Heslop
The Stable, Cockermouth
CA13 9TS
T: (01900) 824222
F: (01900) 824222

Watersmeet ★★★★
Contact: Mr David Burton
Lakeland Cottage Holidays,
Melbecks, Keswick CA12 4QX
T: (017687) 76065
F: (017687) 76869
E: info@lakelandcottages.co.uk
I: www.lakelandcottages.co.uk

Wood Hall ★★★
Contact: Mrs Jackson
Wood Hall, Cockermouth
CA13 0NX
T: (01900) 823585
E: wood.hall@ukonline.co.uk
I: www.wood-hall.co.uk

COLTHOUSE
Cumbria

Croft Foot Barn ★★★
Contact: Susan Jackson
Heart of the Lakes, Fisherbeck
Mill, Old Lake Road, Ambleside
LA22 0DH
T: (015394) 32321
F: (015394) 33251
E: info@heartofthelakes.co.uk
I: www.heartofthelakes.co.uk

Croft Head Cottage ★★★★
Contact: Mr Peter Durbin
Cumbrian Cottages, 2 Lonsdale
Street, Carlisle CA1 1DB
T: (01228) 599960
F: (01228) 599970
E: enquiries@
cumbrian-cottages.co.uk
I: www.cumbrian-cottages.co.uk

COLTON
Cumbria

Bracken Ground ★★★★
Contact: Mr Peter Durbin
Cumbrian Cottages, 2 Lonsdale
Street, Carlisle CA1 1DB
T: (01228) 599960
F: (01228) 599970
E: enquiries@cumbriancottages.
co.uk
I: www.cumbrian-cottages.co.uk

CONISTON
Cumbria

Acorn Cottage ★★★★
Contact: Mrs Susan Jackson
Heart of the Lakes, Fisherbeck
Mill, Old Lake Road, Ambleside
LA22 0DH
T: (015394) 32321
F: (015394) 33251
I: www.heartofthelakes.co.uk

1 and 2 Ash Gill Cottages ★★★★
Contact: Mrs Dorothy Cowburn
Lyndene, Pope Lane, Whitestake,
Preston PR4 4JR
T: (01772) 612832

Atkinson Ground Cottage ★★★
Contact: Mr John Serginson
The Lakeland Cottage Company,
Waterside House, Ulverston
LA12 8AN
T: (015395) 30024
F: (015395) 31932
E: john@lakelandcottageco.com
I: www.lakelandcottageco.com

Bank Ground Farm Cottages ★★★★
Contact: Mrs Lucy Batty
Bank Ground Farm Cottages,
Bank Ground, Coniston
LA21 8AA
T: (015394) 41264
F: (015394) 41900
I: www.bankground.com

Banks Ghyll Cottage ★★★★
Contact: Mr Philip Johnston
The Coppermines & Coniston
Lakes Cottages, The Estate
Office, The Bridge, Coniston
LA21 8HJ
T: (015394) 41765
E: bookings@coppermines.co.uk
I: www.coppermines.co.uk

Establishments printed in blue have a detailed entry in this guide

CUMBRIA – THE LAKE DISTRICT

The Barn ★★
Contact: Susan Jackson
Heart of the Lakes, Fisherbeck
Mill, Old Lake Road, Ambleside
LA22 0DH
T: (015394) 32321
F: (015394) 33251
E: info@heartofthelakes.co.uk
I: www.heartofthelakes.co.uk

The Barn
Rating Applied For
Contact: Mrs Susan Jackson
Heart of the Lakes, Fisherbeck
Mill, Old Lake Road, Ambleside
LA22 0DH
T: (015394) 33110
F: (015394) 33251
E: contactus@heartofthelakes.co.uk
I: www.heartofthelakes.co.uk

Beck Yeat Cottage ★★★
Contact: Mr Philip Johnston
The Coppermines & Coniston
Lakes Cottages, The Estate
Office, The Bridge, Coniston
LA21 8HJ
T: (015394) 41765
F: (015394) 41944
E: info@coppermines.co.uk
I: www.coppermines.co.uk

Beech Grove ★★★★
Contact: Jean Johnson
Coniston Holidays, Orchard
Cottage, 18 Yewdale Road,
Coniston LA21 8DU
T: (015394) 41319
F: (015394) 41373
E: jean.orchardcottage@virgin.net
I: www.conistonholidays.com

Bramble Cottage ★★★★
Contact: Mr Philip Johnston
The Coppermines & Coniston
Lakes Cottages, The Estate
Office, The Bridge, Coniston
LA21 8HJ
T: (01539) 823450
E: bookings@coppermines.co.uk
I: www.lakesabout.co.uk

The Bridge Cottages ★★★★
Contact: Mr Philip Johnston
The Coppermines & Coniston
Lakes Cottages, Coppermines
Valley, Coniston LA21 8HX
T: (015394) 41765
F: (015394) 41944
E: bookings@coppermines.co.uk
I: www.coppermines.co.uk

Brow Close Cottage ★★★
Contact: Mr Philip Johnston
The Coppermines & Coniston
Lakes Cottages, The Estate
Office, The Bridge, Coniston
LA21 8HJ
T: (015394) 41765
I: www.coppermines.co.uk/property/show_details.cgi?id=79

Carries Gate ★★★★
Contact: Mrs Susan Jackson
Heart of the Lakes, Fisherbeck
Mill, Old Lake Road, Ambleside
LA22 0DH
T: (015394) 32321
F: (015394) 33251
E: info@heartofthelakes.co.uk
I: www.heartofthelakes.co.uk

Cherry Tree Cottage ★★★
Contact: Mr Philip Johnston
The Coppermines & Coniston
Lakes Cottages, The Estate
Office, The Bridge, Coniston
LA21 8HJ
T: (015394) 41765
F: (015394) 41944
E: info@coppermines.co.uk
I: www.coppermines.co.uk

The Coach House ★★★★
Contact: Gillian Newport
The Coach House, Bannisdale
Head, Kendal LA8 9JZ
T: (015394) 41592
E: info@lakesabout.co.uk
I: www.lakesabout.co.uk

Coniston Country Cottages ★★★-★★★★
Contact: Mr & Mrs Abbott
Coniston Country Cottages,
Coniston LA21 8AU
T: (015394) 41418
F: (015394) 41114
E: enquiry@conistoncottages.co
I: www.conistoncottages.co.uk

Coniston View Cottage ★★★
Contact: Susan Jackson
Heart of the Lakes, Fisherbeck
Mill, Old Lake Road, Ambleside
LA22 0DH
T: (015394) 32321
F: (015394) 33251
E: info@heartofthelakes.co.uk
I: www.heartofthelakes.co.uk

The Coppermines Coniston Cottages ★★-★★★★
Contact: Mr Philip Johnston
The Coppermines & Coniston
Lakes Cottages, Coniston
LA21 8HJ
T: (015394) 41765
F: (015394) 41944
E: bookings@coppermines.co.uk
I: www.coppermines.co.uk

4 Coppermines Cottages ★★★
Contact: Mr Philip Johnston
The Coppermines & Coniston
Lakes Cottages, Coppermines
Valley, Coniston LA21 8HX
T: (015394) 41765
E: bookings@coppermines.co.uk
I: www.coppermines.co.uk

Curdle Dub ★★★
Contact: Paul Liddell
Lakelovers, Belmont House, Lake
Road, Bowness-on-Windermere,
Windermere LA23 3BJ
T: (015394) 88855
F: (015394) 88857

Damson Cottage ★★★★
Contact: Mr Peter Durbin
Cumbrian Cottages, 2 Lonsdale
Street, Carlisle CA1 1DB
T: (01228) 599960
F: (01228) 599970
E: enquiries@cumbriancottages.co.uk
I: www.cumbria-cottages.co.uk

25 Days Bank ★★★
Contact: Mrs Thornton
43 Dovedale Gardens, Pendas
Fields, Cross Gates, Leeds
LS15 8UP
T: (0113) 260 2455

Dixon Ground ★★★
Contact: Mr Philip Johnston
The Coppermines & Coniston
Lakes Cottages, The Estate
Office, The Bridge, Coniston
LA21 8HJ
T: (015394) 41765
E: bookings@coppermines.co.uk
I: www.coppermines.co.uk

Fair Snape Cottage ★★★★
Contact: Mr Philip Johnston
The Coppermines & Coniston
Lakes Cottages, The Estate
Office, The Bridge, Coniston
LA21 8HJ
T: (015394) 41765
E: bookings@coppermines.co.uk
I: www.coppermines.co.uk

1 Far End Cottages ★★★
Contact: Mrs Andrea Batho
High Hollin Bank, Coniston
LA21 8AG
T: (015394) 41680
E: a.batho@virgin.net
I: www.cottagescumbria.com

Fisherbeck Fold ★★★★
Contact: Mr Paul Liddell
Lakelovers, Belmont House, Lake
Road, Bowness-on-Windermere,
Windermere LA23 3BJ
T: (015394) 88855
F: (015394) 88857
E: bookings@lakelovers.co.uk
I: www.lakelovers.co.uk

Fisherbeck Fold & Fisherbeck Nest ★★★
Contact: Paul Liddell
Lakelovers, Belmont House, Lake
Road, Bowness-on-Windermere,
Windermere LA23 3BJ
T: (015394) 88855
F: (015394) 88857
E: bookings@lakelovers.co.uk
I: www.lakelovers.co.uk

Forest Cottage ★★★★
Contact: Mr John Serginson
The Lakeland Cottage Company,
Waterside House, Ulverston
LA12 8AN
T: (015395) 30024
F: (015395) 31932
E: john@lakelandcottageco.com
I: www.lakelandcottageco.com

Gable Cottage ★★★
Contact: Mr Philip Johnston
The Coppermines & Coniston
Lakes Cottages, The Estate
Office, The Bridge, Coniston
LA21 8HJ
T: (015394) 41765
E: bookings@coppermines.co.uk
I: www.coppermines.co.uk

Gable End ★★★
Contact: Mr John Serginson
The Lakeland Cottage Company,
Waterside House, Ulverston
LA12 8AN
T: (015395) 30024
F: (015395) 31932
E: john@lakelandcottageco.com
I: www.lakelandcottageco.com

Grange Cottage ★★★
Contact: Mr Philip Johnston
The Coppermines & Coniston
Lakes Cottages, The Estate
Office, The Bridge, Coniston
LA21 8HJ
T: (015394) 41765
I: www.coppermines.co.uk/property/show_details.cgi?id=80

10 Green Cottages ★★★★
Contact: Mr Philip Johnston
Coppermines & Lakes Cottages,
The Estate Office, The Bridge,
Coniston LA21 8HJ
T: (015394) 41765
E: bookings@coppermines.co.uk

Grizedale
Rating Applied For
Contact: Mr John Serginson
The Lakeland Cottage Company,
Waterside House, Ulverston
LA12 8AN
T: (015395) 30024
F: (015395) 31932
E: john@lakelandcottageco.com
I: www.lakelandcottageco.com

Heathwaite Farm Cottages Heathwaite Farm House, The Old ★★★-★★★★
Contact: Mr Philip Johnston
The Coppermines & Coniston
Lakes Cottages, The Estate
Office, The Bridge, Coniston
LA21 8HJ
T: (015394) 41765
E: bookings@coppermines.co.u
I: www.coppermines.co.uk

High Arnside ★★★
Contact: Jan Meredith
High Arnside, High Arnside
Farm, Coniston LA21 8DW
T: (01539) 432261
E: janMeredith@bigwig.net
I: www.higharnsidefarm.co.uk

High Dixon Ground ★★★
Contact: Susan Jackson
Heart of the Lakes, Fisherbeck
Mill, Old Lake Road, Ambleside
LA22 0DH
T: (015394) 32321
F: (015394) 33251
E: info@heartofthelakes.co.uk
I: www.heartofthelakes.co.uk

Hollin & Richmond House Apartments ★★★
Contact: Jean Johnson
Coniston Holidays, Orchard
Cottage, 18 Yewdale Road,
Coniston LA21 8DU
T: (015394) 41319
F: (015394) 41373
E: jean.orchardcottage@virgin.net
I: www.conistonholidays.com

Holly Garth ★★★★
Contact: Susan Jackson
Heart of the Lakes, Fisherbeck
Mill, Old Lake Road, Ambleside
LA22 0DH
T: (015394) 32321
F: (015394) 33251
E: info@heartofthelakes.co.uk
I: www.heartofthelakes.co.uk

CUMBRIA – THE LAKE DISTRICT

5 Holme Ground Cottages ★★★
Contact: Mrs Kate Bradshaw
The Rookery, Oaklands, Riding Mill NE44 6AR
T: (01434) 682526
E: rookery1@tiscali.co.uk

How Head Cottage ★★★
Contact: Mr & Mrs Holland
How Head Cottages, How Head Cottage, East of Lake, Coniston LA21 8AA
T: (015394) 41594
E: howhead@lineone.net
I: www.howheadcottages.co.uk

Howhead ★★★★
Contact: Mr John Serginson
The Lakeland Cottage Company, Waterside House, Ulverston LA12 8AN
T: (015395) 30024
F: (015395) 31932
E: john@lakelandcottageco.com
I: www.lakelandcottageco.com

Lake View Cottage ★★★
Contact: Susan Jackson
Heart of the Lakes, Fisherbeck Mill, Old Lake Road, Ambleside LA22 0DH
T: (015394) 32321
F: (015394) 33251
E: info@heartofthelakes.co.uk
I: www.heartofthelakes.co.uk

Low Brow ★★★
Contact: Mrs Susan Jackson
Heart of the Lakes, Fisherbeck Mill, Old Lake Road, Ambleside LA22 0DH
T: (015394) 32321
F: (015394) 33251
E: info@heartofthelakes.co.uk
I: www.heartofthelakes.co.uk

Lower Barn ★★★
Contact: Mr John Serginson
The Lakeland Cottage Company, Waterside House, Ulverston LA12 8AN
T: (015395) 30024
F: (015395) 31932
E: john@lakelandcottageco.com
I: www.lakelandcottageco.com

Middlefield Cottage ★★★★
Contact: Mr Philip Johnston
The Coppermines & Coniston Lakes Cottages, The Estate Office, The Bridge, Coniston LA21 8HJ
T: (015394) 41765
I: www.coppermines.co.uk/property/show_details.cgi?id=81

Mountain Ash Cottage ★★★
Contact: Mr Philip Johnston
The Coppermines & Coniston Lakes Cottages, The Estate Office, The Bridge, Coniston LA21 8HJ
T: (015394) 41765
E: bookings@coppermines.co.uk
I: www.coppermines.co.uk

No 1 Silverbank
Rating Applied For
Contact: Mr Anthony Hext and Ms Faye Gorman
14 Devonia Road, Islington, London N1 8JH
T: (020) 7049071
E: no1silverbank@aol.com

Poppy Cottage ★★★
Contact: Mr Philip Johnston
The Coppermines & Coniston Lakes Cottages, The Estate Office, The Bridge, Coniston LA21 8HJ
T: (015394) 41765
F: (015394) 41944
E: info@coppermines.co.uk
I: www.coppermines.co.uk

Rascal Howe Cottage ★★★
Contact: Mr Philip Johnston
The Coppermines & Coniston Lakes Cottages, The Estate Office, The Bridge, Coniston LA21 8HJ
T: (015394) 41765
I: www.coppermines.co.uk/property/show_details.cgi?id=78

Red Dell Cottage ★★★★
Contact: Mr Philip Johnston
The Coppermines & Coniston Lakes Cottages, The Estate Office, The Bridge, Coniston LA21 8HJ
T: (015394) 41765
F: (015394) 41944
E: info@coppermines.co.uk
I: www.coppermines.co.uk

River Cottage ★★★
Contact: Mr Philip Johnston
The Coppermines & Coniston Lakes Cottages, The Estate Office, The Bridge, Coniston LA21 8HJ
T: (015394) 41765
F: (015394) 41944
E: info@coppermines.co.uk
I: www.coppermines.co.uk

Rivington ★★★
Contact: Mr Peter Durbin
Cumbrian Cottages, 2 Lonsdale Street, Carlisle CA1 1DB
T: (01228) 599960
F: (01228) 599970
E: enquiries@cumbrian-cottages.co.uk
I: www.cumbrian-cottages.co.uk

Rock Cottage ★★★
Contact: Mr Philip Johnston
The Coppermines & Coniston Lakes Cottages, The Estate Office, The Bridge, Coniston LA21 8HJ
T: (015394) 41765
I: www.coppermines.co.uk/property/show_details.cgi?id=85

Rockleigh ★★★★
Contact: Paul Liddell
Lakelovers, Belmont House, Lake Road, Bowness-on-Windermere, Windermere LA23 3BJ
T: (015394) 88855
F: (015394) 88857
E: bookings@lakelovers.co.uk
I: www.lakelovers.co.uk

Rose Cottage ★★★★
Contact: Mr John Serginson
The Lakeland Cottage Company, Waterside House, Ulverston LA12 8AN
T: (015395) 30024
F: (015395) 31932
E: john@lakelandcottageco.com
I: www.lakelandcottageco.com

Shelt Gill ★★★
Contact: Mrs Rosalind Dean
9 The Fairway, Sheffield S10 4LX
T: (0114) 230 8077
F: (0114) 230 8077
E: holiday@sheltgill.co.uk
I: www.sheltgill.co.uk

The Shieling ★★★
Contact: Paul Liddell
Lakelovers, Belmont House, Lake Road, Bowness-on-Windermere, Windermere LA23 3BJ
T: (015394) 88855
F: (015394) 88857

Sunbeam Cottage ★★★
Contact: Paul Liddell
Lakelovers, Belmont House, Lake Road, Bowness-on-Windermere, Windermere LA23 3BJ
T: (015394) 88855
F: (015394) 88857

Sunny Bank Farm ★★★★
Contact: Daphne Libby
Sunny Bank Farm, St James Vicarage, Goschen Road, Carlisle CA2 5PF
T: (01228) 515639
F: (01228) 524569
E: sunnybankfarm@btinternet.com
I: www.bbbweb.com/sunnybank

Tent Lodge Cottage ★★★★
Contact: Mr John Serginson
The Lakeland Cottage Company, Waterside House, Ulverston LA12 8AN
T: (015395) 30024
F: (015395) 31932
E: john@lakelandcottageco.com
I: www.lakelandcottageco.com

Three Springs ★★★
Contact: Mr John Serginson
The Lakeland Cottage Company, Waterside House, Ulverston LA12 8AN
T: (015395) 30024
F: (015395) 31932
E: john@lakelandcottageco.com
I: www.lakelandcottageco.com

Thurston House & Thurston View ★★-★★★★★
Contact: Mr & Mrs Jefferson
21 Chale Green, Harwood, Bolton BL2 3NJ
T: (01204) 419261
E: alan@jefferson99.freeserve.co.uk
I: www.jefferson99.freeserve.co.uk

Tilberthwaite Farm Cottage ★★★
Contact: Mrs Wilkinson
Tilberthwaite Farm Cottage, Tilberthwaite Farm, Coniston LA21 8DG
T: (015394) 37281

Tinkler Beck Farm ★★★★★
Contact: Mr John Serginson
The Lakeland Cottage Company, Waterside House, Ulverston LA12 8AN
T: (015395) 30024
F: (015395) 31932
E: john@lakelandcottageco.com
I: www.lakelandcottageco.com

Townson Ground House ★★★★
Contact: Mr John Serginson
The Lakeland Cottage Company, Waterside House, Ulverston LA12 8AN
T: (015395) 30024
F: (015395) 31932
E: john@lakelandcottageco.com
I: www.lakelandcottageco.com

Townson Ground Self Catering ★★★-★★★★★
Contact: Richard Nelson
Townson Ground, Tent Lodge, East of the Lake, Coniston LA21 8AA
T: (015394) 41272
E: barbara@townsonground.freeserve.co.uk
I: www.townsonground.co.uk

Wetherlam ★★★
Contact: Mr John Serginson
The Lakeland Cottage Company, Waterside House, Ulverston LA12 8AN
T: (015395) 30024
F: (015395) 31932
E: john@lakelandcottageco.com
I: www.lakelandcottageco.com

Windrush ★★★★
Contact: Mr John Serginson
Lakeland Cottage Company, Waterside House, Ulverston LA12 8AN
T: (015395) 30024
F: (015395) 31932
E: john@lakelandcottageco.com
I: www.lakelandcottageco.com

COUPLAND BECK
Cumbria

Westmorland Cottages ★★★★
Contact: C Patterson
Westmorland Cottages, Coupland Beck Farm, Appleby-in-Westmorland CA16 6LN
T: (01768) 351449
F: (01768) 352873
E: westmorlandcott@btconnect.com

COWAN HEAD
Cumbria

River View ★★★
Contact: Mr Peter Durbin
Cumbrian Cottages, 2 Lonsdale Street, Carlisle CA1 1DB
T: (01228) 599960
F: (01228) 599970
E: enquiries@cumbriancottages.co.uk
I: www.cumbrian-cottages.co.uk

Establishments printed in blue have a detailed entry in this guide

CUMBRIA – THE LAKE DISTRICT

CROOK
Cumbria

Brackenrigg ★★★
Contact: Mr Peter Durbin
Cumbrian Cottages, 2 Lonsdale Street, Carlisle CA1 1DB
T: (01228) 599960
F: (01228) 599970
E: enquiries@cumbrian-cottages.co.uk
I: www.cumbrian-cottages.co.uk

Lyth View Cottage ★★★
Contact: Mr Peter Durbin
Cumbrian Cottages, 2 Lonsdale Street, Carlisle CA1 1DB
T: (01228) 599960
F: (01228) 599970
E: enquiries@cumbriancottages.co.uk
I: www.cumbrian-cottages.co.uk

Mitchelland Farm Bungalow
Rating Applied For
Contact: Stuart Higham & Jane Farrer
Mitchelland Farm Bungalow, Off Crook Road, Nr Bowness-on-Windermere, Kendal LA8 8LL
T: (015394) 47421

Old Mill Cottage ★★★
Contact: Mr Peter Durbin
Cumbrian Cottages, 2 Lonsdale Street, Carlisle CA1 1DB
T: (01228) 599960
F: (01228) 599970
E: enquiries@cumbrian-cottage.co.uk
I: www.cumbrian-cottages.co.uk

Tan Smithy Cottage ★★★★
Contact: Mr Peter Durbin
Cumbrian Cottages, 2 Lonsdale Street, Carlisle CA1 1DB
T: (01228) 599960
F: (01228) 599970
E: enquiries@cumbriancottages.co.uk
I: www.cumbrian-cottages.co.uk

CROOKLANDS
Cumbria

Hillview Cottage ★★★★
Contact: Mrs Simpson
Craig Mount, 10 Kentrigg, Kendal LA9 6EE
T: (015395) 67467
F: (01539) 728528
E: bouncershire6746@aol.com
I: www.cottageguide.co.uk/hillviewcottage

CROSBY-ON-EDEN
Cumbria

Crosby House Cottages ★★★★
Contact: Deidre Dickson
Crosby House Cottages, Crosby House, Carlisle CA6 4QZ
T: (01228) 573139
F: (01228) 573338
E: crosby@norbyways.demon.co.uk
I: www.northumbria-byways.com/crosby

CROSBY RAVENSWORTH
Cumbria

The Stable ★★★★
Contact: Mrs Christine Jackson
Wickerslack Farm, Penrith CA10 2LN
T: (01931) 715236

CROSTHWAITE
Cumbria

Acorn Lodge ★★★★
Contact: Mr Peter Durbin
Cumbrian Cottages, 2 Lonsdale Street, Carlisle CA1 1DB
T: (01228) 599960
F: (01228) 599970
E: enquiries@cumbriancottages.co.uk
I: www.cumbrian-cottages.co.uk

Barf Lodge ★★★★
Contact: Mr Peter Durbin
Cumbrian Cottages, 2 Lonsdale Street, Carlisle CA1 1DB
T: (01228) 599960
F: (01228) 599970
E: enquiries@cumbriancottages.co.uk
I: www.cumbrian-cottages.co.uk

Dega ★★★★
Contact: Mr Peter Durbin
Cumbrian Cottages, 2 Lonsdale Street, Carlisle CA1 1DB
T: (01228) 599960
F: (01228) 599970
E: enquiries@cumbriancottages.co.uk
I: www.cumbrian-cottages.co.uk

Bobbin Mill Cottage ★★★★
Contact: Mr Roger Green
Waterways, Starnthwaite Ghyll, Kendal LA8 8JN
T: (01274) 551552
F: (01274) 551554
I: www.enjoythelakes.com/

Corner Cottage
Rating Applied For
Contact: Mary Smith
Corner Cottage, 51 Rennie Court, 11 Upper Ground, London SE1 9LP
T: (020) 76339500
E: mary@sgcornercottage.co.uk
I: www.sgcornercottage.co.uk

Crosthwaite Cottages ★★★
Contact: Mr John Serginson
The Lakeland Cottage Company, Waterside House, Ulverston LA12 8AN
T: (015395) 30024
F: (015395) 31932
E: john@lakelandcottageco.com
I: www.lakelandcottageco.com

Crosthwaite Spring Cottage ★★★
Contact: Mr Paul Liddell
Lakelovers, Belmont House, Lake Road, Bowness-on-Windermere, Windermere LA23 3BJ
T: (015394) 88855
F: (015394) 88857
E: bookings@lakelovers.co.uk
I: www.lakelovers.co.uk

Damson Barn ★★★
Contact: Mr Peter Durbin
Cumbrian Cottages, 2 Lonsdale Street, Carlisle CA1 1DB
T: (01228) 599960
F: (01228) 599970
E: enquiries@cumbriancottages.co.uk
I: www.cumbrian-cottages.co.uk

Ennerdale ★★★★
Contact: Mr Peter Durbin
Cumbrian Cottages, 2 Lonsdale Street, Carlisle CA1 1DB
T: (01228) 599960
F: (01228) 599970
E: enquiries@cumbriancottages.co.uk
I: www.cumbrian-cottages.co.uk

Ghyllbank ★★★★
Contact: Mr Paul Liddell
Lakelovers, Belmont House, Lake Road, Bowness-on-Windermere, Windermere LA23 3BJ
T: (015394) 88855
F: (015394) 88857
E: bookings@lakelovers.co.uk
I: www.lakelovers.co.uk

Gilpin View ★★★
Contact: Paul Liddell
Lakelovers, Belmont House, Lake Road, Bowness-on-Windermere, Windermere LA23 3BJ
T: (015394) 88855
F: (015394) 88857

Greenbank ★★★★
Contact: Jackie Gaskell
Crosthwaite, Kendal LA8 8JD
T: (015395) 68598
E: greenbank@nascr.net
I: www.greenbank-cumbria.co.uk

High Beck Cottage ★★★★
Contact: Mr Paul Liddell
Lakelovers, Belmont House, Lake Road, Bowness-on-Windermere, Windermere LA23 3BJ
T: (015394) 88855
F: (015394) 88857
E: bookings@lakelovers.co.uk
I: www.lakelovers.co.uk

Low Cartmel Fold ★★★★
Contact: Mr Peter Durbin
Cumbrian Cottages, 2 Lonsdale Street, Carlisle CA1 1DB
T: (01228) 599960
F: (01228) 599970
E: enquiries@cumbrian-cottages.co.uk
I: www.cumbrian-cottages.co.uk

6 Starnthwaite Ghyll ★★★★
Contact: Mr John Serginson
The Lakeland Cottage Company, Waterside House, Ulverston LA12 8AN
T: (015395) 30024
F: (015395) 31932
E: john@lakelandcottageco.com
I: www.lakelandcottageco.com

CUMWHINTON
Cumbria

Rosecote ★★★★
Contact: Mr Peter Durbin
Cumbrian Cottages, 2 Lonsdale Street, Carlisle CA1 1DB
T: (01228) 599960
F: (01228) 599970
E: enquiries@cumbrian-cottages.co.uk
I: www.cumbrian-cottages.co.uk

CUNSEY
Cumbria

Deer Holm ★★★★
Contact: Mr John Serginson
The Lakeland Cottage Company, Waterside House, Ulverston LA12 8AN
T: (015395) 30024
F: (015395) 31932
E: john@lakelandcottageco.com
I: www.lakelandcottageco.com

DACRE
Cumbria

Blaes Crag Cottage ★★★
Contact: Mr Peter Durbin
Cumbrian Cottages, 2 Lonsdale Street, Carlisle CA1 1DB
T: (01228) 599960
F: (01228) 599970
E: enquiries@cumbrian-cottages.co.uk
I: www.cumbrian-cottages.co.uk

DEARHAM
Cumbria

Bendale Cottage ★★★★
Contact: Susan Harper
Bendale Cottage, West House Farm, Maryport CA15 7LD
T: (01900) 816763
F: (01900) 816763
E: stay@bendalecottage.co.uk
I: www.bendalecottage.co.uk

DEEPDALE
Cumbria

Willans ★★
Contact: Mrs Kathleen Bentham
Willans, Outrake Foot, Deepdale, Dent, Sedbergh LA10 5QZ
T: (01539) 625285
E: kathbentham@hotmail.com
I: www.cottageguide.co.uk/willans

DENT
Cumbria

Brooks Barn ★★★★
Contact: The Manager
Ref 3306, Dales Holiday Cottages, Carleton Business Centre, Carleton New Road, Skipton BD23 2AA
T: (01756) 799821
F: (01756) 797012
E: info@dalesholcot.com
I: www.dentdale.com

Buzzard's Cottage ★★★★
Contact: The Manager
Ref:2865, Dales Holiday Cottages, Carleton Business Park, Carleton New Road, Skipton BD23 2AA
T: (01756) 799821
F: (01756) 797012
E: info@dalesholcot.com
I: www.dalesholcot.com

High Chapel Cottage ★★★★
Contact: The Manager
Ref:2074, Dales Holiday Cottages, Carleton Business Park, Carleton New Road, Skipton BD23 2AA
T: (01756) 799821
F: (01756) 797012
E: info@dalesholcot.com
I: www.dalesholcot.com

Look out for establishments participating in the National Accessible Scheme

CUMBRIA – THE LAKE DISTRICT

Middleton's Cottage and Fountain Cottage ★★★
Contact: Mr & Mrs Ayers
The Old Rectory, Litlington, Polegate BN26 5RB
T: (01323) 870032
F: (01323) 870032
E: candpayers@mistral.co.uk
I: www.dentcottages.co.uk

Mire Garth ★★★
Contact: Jean Middleton
Mire Garth, Sedbergh LA10 5RA
T: (015396) 25235

Stonecroft ★★★
Contact: Mr Robert Gornall
Croft House, Cowgill Dent, Sedbergh LA10 5TH
T: (015396) 25219

Wilsey House ★★★
Contact: Joan Saunders
Wilsey House, 21 Church Street, Huntingdon PE28 3EG
T: (01487) 841556
E: enquiries@wilsey.co.uk
I: www.wilsey.co.uk

DOCKRAY
Cumbria

Lookin How ★★★★★
Contact: Mr Peter Durbin
Cumbrian Cottages, 2 Lonsdale Street, Carlisle CA1 1DB
T: (01228) 599960
F: (01228) 599970
E: enquiries@cumbrian-cottages.co.uk
I: www.cumbrian-cottages.co.uk

DOVENBY
Cumbria

Sunnybrae Bungalow ★★★
Contact: Mr Peter Durbin
Cumbrian Cottages, 2 Lonsdale Street, Carlisle CA1 1DB
T: (01228) 599960
F: (01228) 599970
E: enquiries@cumbriancottages.co.uk

DRUMBURGH
Cumbria

The Grange ★★★-★★★★★
Contact: Sarah Hodgson
Grange Cottages, Carlisle CA7 5DW
T: (01228) 576551
E: messrs.hodgson@tesco.net
I: www.thegrangecottage.co.uk

EDDERSIDE
Cumbria

Centre Farm ★★★
Contact: Mr Peter Durbin
Cumbrian Cottages, 2 Lonsdale Street, Carlisle CA1 1DB
T: (01228) 599960
F: (01228) 599970
E: enquiries@cumbrian-cottages.co.uk
I: www.cumbrian-cottages.co.uk

ELTERWATER
Cumbria

Bottom Shop ★★★★
Contact: Mrs Vivien Bass
Wheelwrights Holiday Cottages, Langdale, Ambleside LA22 9HS
T: (015394) 37635
E: enquiries@wheelwrights.com
I: www.wheelwrights.com

Bridge End Cottage ★★★★
Contact: Mr Paul Liddell
Lakelovers, Belmont House, Lake Road, Bowness-on-Windermere, Windermere LA23 3BJ
T: (015394) 88855
F: (015394) 88857
E: bookings@lakelovers.co.uk
I: www.lakelovers.co.uk

Bridge Syke Cottage ★★★★
Contact: Paul Liddell
Lakelovers, Belmont House, Lake Road, Bowness-on-Windermere, Windermere LA23 3BJ
T: (015394) 88855
F: (015394) 88857
E: bookings@lakelovers.co.uk
I: www.lakelovers.co.uk

Eltermere Old Barn ★★★
Contact: Mrs Susan Jackson
Heart of the Lakes, Fisherbeck Mill, Old Lake Road, Ambleside LA22 0DH
T: (015394) 32321
F: (015394) 33251
E: info@heartofthelakes.co.uk
I: www.heartofthelakes.co.uk

Gunpowder Cottage ★★★★
Contact: Paul Liddell
Lakelovers, Belmont House, Lake Road, Bowness-on-Windermere, Windermere LA23 3BJ
T: (015394) 88855
F: (015394) 88857
E: bookings@lakelovers.co.uk
I: www.lakelovers.co.uk

Lane Ends Cottages ★★★
Contact: Mrs Rice
Fellside, 3 & 4 Lane Ends, Elterwater, Ambleside LA22 9HN
T: (015394) 37678

Maple Tree Corner ★★★★
Contact: Mrs Susan Jackson
Heart of the Lakes, Fisherbeck Mill, Old Lake Road, Ambleside LA22 0DH
T: (015394) 33110
F: (015394) 33251
E: info@heartofthelakes.co.uk
I: www.heartofthelakes.co.uk

Mill Race Cottage ★★★
Contact: Mrs Susan Jackson
Heart of the Lakes, Fisherbeck Mill, Old Lake Road, Ambleside LA22 0DH
T: (015394) 33110
F: (015394) 33251
E: info@heartofthelakes.co.uk
I: www.heartofthelakes.co.uk

Oakbank ★★★★
Contact: Susan Jackson
Heart of the Lakes, Fisherbeck Mill, Old Lake Road, Ambleside LA22 0DH
T: (015394) 32321
F: (015394) 33251

Peter Place
Rating Applicd For
Contact: Mrs Vivien Bass
Wheelwrights Holiday Cottages, Langdale, Ambleside LA22 9HS
T: (015394) 37635
E: enquiries@wheelwrights.com
I: www.wheelwrights.com

Pippins Cottage ★★★★
Contact: Mrs Vivien Bass
Wheelwrights Holiday Cottages, Langdale, Ambleside LA22 9HS
T: (015394) 37635
F: (015394) 37618
E: enquiries@wheelwrights.com
I: www.wheelwrights.com

Rose Cottage ★★★★
Contact: Mrs Vivien Bass
Wheelwrights Holiday Cottages, Langdale, Ambleside LA22 9HS
T: (015394) 37635
F: (015394) 37618
E: enquiries@wheelwrights.com
I: www.wheelwrights.com

St Giles ★★★
Contact: Susan Jackson
Heart of the Lakes, Fisherbeck Mill, Old Lake Road, Ambleside LA22 0DH
T: (015394) 32321
F: (015394) 33251

Sawpit Flat ★★★★
Contact: Mrs Vivien Bass
Wheelwrights Holiday Cottages, Langdale, Ambleside LA22 9HS
T: (015394) 37635
E: enquiries@wheelwrights.com
I: www.wheelwrights.com

Wistaria Cottage and 3 Main Street ★★★
Contact: Mr Geoffrey & Mrs Doreen Beardmore
2 Beech Drive, Kidsgrove, Stoke-on-Trent ST7 1BA
T: (01782) 783170
F: (01782) 783170
E: geoff.doreen.beardmore@ntlword.com

EMBLETON
Cumbria

Sunny Bank Cottage ★★★
Contact: Margaret Bell
Sunny Bank Cottage, 2 Rakefoot, Cockermouth CA13 9XU
T: (017687) 76273

ENDMOOR
Cumbria

Calvert Cottage ★★★★
Contact: Mr Peter Durbin
Cumbrian Cottages, 2 Lonsdale Street, Carlisle CA1 1DB
T: (01228) 599960
F: (01228) 599970
E: enquiries@cumbrian-cottages.co.uk
I: www.cumbrian-cottages.co.uk

West View Flat ★★★
Contact: Mrs Bainbridge
West View Flat, West View Farm, Kendal LA8 0HY
T: (015395) 67278

ESKDALE
Cumbria

Bridge End Farm Cottages ★★★★-★★★★★
Contact: Mr Poole
Bridge End Farm Cottages, Eskdale, Holmrook CA19 1TG
T: 0870 0 735328
F: 0870 0 735328

The Chalets ★★★★
Contact: Philip Hayden & Lisa Borrowdale
The Chalets, Boot, Eskdale CA19 1TF
T: (019467) 23128
E: info@thechalets.co.uk
I: www.thechalets.co.uk

Fisherground Farm Holidays ★★★
Contact: Mrs Hall
Fisherground Farm Holidays, Fisherground Farm, Eskdale, Holmrook CA19 1TF
T: (01946) 723319
E: holidays@fisherground.co.uk
I: www.fisherground.co.uk

Longrigg Green ★★★★★
Contact: Mrs Christine Carter
Forest How, Eskdale, Holmrook CA19 1TR
T: (019467) 23201
F: (019467) 23190
E: fcarter@easynet.co.uk
I: www.longrigg.green.btinternet.co.uk

Old Brantrake ★★★★
Contact: Mr Tyson
Old Brantrake, Brant Rake, Eskdale, Holmrook CA19 1TT
T: (019467) 23340
F: (019467) 23340
E: tyson@eskdale1.demon.co.uk

FAR SAWREY
Cumbria

1 & 2 Church Cottage ★★★★
Contact: Mrs Susan Jackson
Heart of the Lakes, Fisherbeck Mill, Old Lake Road, Ambleside LA22 0DH
T: (015394) 32321
F: (015394) 33251
E: info@heartofthelakes.co.uk
I: www.heartofthelakes.co.uk

Brimstock Cottage ★★★★
Contact: Mr Philip Johnston
The Coppermines & Coniston Lakes Cottages, The Estate Office, The Bridge, Coniston LA21 8HJ
T: (015394) 41765
I: www.coppermines.co.uk/property/show_details.cgi?id=83

Claife Cottage ★★★
Contact: Mr Peter Durbin
Cumbrian Cottages, 2 Lonsdale Street, Carlisle CA1 1DB
T: (01228) 599960
F: (01228) 599970
E: enquiries@cumbrian-cottage.co.uk
I: www.cumbrian-cottages.co.uk

Rowan Cottage ★★★★
Contact: Mrs Susan Jackson
Heart of the Lakes, Fisherbeck Mill, Old Lake Road, Ambleside LA22 0DH
T: (015394) 32321
F: (015394) 33251
E: info@heartofthelakes.co.uk
I: www.heartofthelakes.co.uk

Establishments printed in blue have a detailed entry in this guide

CUMBRIA – THE LAKE DISTRICT

Stables Cottage ★★★★
Contact: Paul Liddell
Lakelovers, Belmont House, Lake Road, Bowness-on-Windermere, Windermere LA23 3BJ
T: (015394) 88855
F: (015394) 88857
E: bookings@lakelovers.co.uk
I: www.lakelovers.co.uk

Tower Cottage and Knott Cottage ★★★★
Contact: Mr Philip Johnston
The Coppermines & Coniston Lakes Cottages, The Estate Office, The Bridge, Coniston LA21 8HJ
T: (01539) 441265
F: (01539) 441944
E: bookings@coppermines.co.uk
I: www.coppermines.co.uk

FARLAM
Cumbria

Calf Close Cottage ★★★★★
Contact: Mr & Mrs Seddon
Calf Close Cottage, Boon Hill Farmhouse, Brampton CA8 1TA
T: (016977) 46818

FIELD BROUGHTON
Cumbria

The Byre ★★★★
Contact: Mrs Penny Crowe
The Byre, Broughton House Farm, Grange-over-Sands LA11 6HN
T: (015395) 36577
E: p_crowe@talk21.com
I: http://lakedistrictcottage.mysite.freeserve.com

FINSTHWAITE
Cumbria

The Barn ★★★★★
Contact: Mr John Serginson
The Lakeland Cottage Company, Waterside House, Ulverston LA12 8AN
T: (015395) 30024
F: (015395) 31932
E: john@lakelandcottageco.com
I: www.lakelandcottageco.com

Sheiling Barn ★★★★
Contact: Mr Paul Liddell
Lakelovers, Belmont House, Lake Road, Bowness-on-Windermere, Windermere LA23 3BJ
T: (015394) 88855
F: (015394) 88857
E: bookings@lakelovers.co.uk
I: www.lakelovers.co.uk

GAMBLESBY
Cumbria

Church Court Cottages ★★★-★★★★★
Contact: Mark Cowell
Church Villa, Gamblesby, Penrith CA10 1HR
T: (01768) 881682
F: (01768) 889055
E: markcowell@tiscali.co.uk
I: www.gogamblesby.co.uk

GARNETT BRIDGE
Cumbria

Cocks Close ★★★
Contact: Mrs Denny
Cocks Close, Lindens, Ashley Park Road, Walton-on-Thames KT12 1JU
T: (01932) 246432
F: (01932) 253174

GARSDALE HEAD
Cumbria

Dandry Cottage ★★★
Contact: Dales Hol Cot Ref:1637
Dales Holiday Cottages, Carleton Business Park, Carleton New Road, Skipton BD23 2AA
T: (01756) 799821
F: (01756) 797012
E: info@dalesholcot.com
I: www.dalesholcot.com

GILCRUX
Cumbria

Ellen Hall ★★-★★★★
Contact: Alison Dunlop
Ellen Hall, Carlisle CA7 2QB
T: (016973) 21439
F: (016973) 22675
E: data.dunlop@virgin.net
I: www.cottagesmadefortwo.co.uk

GILSLAND
Cumbria

Working Dales Pony Centre ★★★
Contact: Mr & Mrs Parker
Working Dales Pony Centre, Clarks Hill Farm, Gilsland, Brampton CA8 7DF
T: (016977) 47208
E: Dales_Logger@clarkshill.fsnet.co.uk
I: www.daleslogger.com

GLASSONBY
Cumbria

Chapel House ★★★★
Contact: Mr Lowis
Chapel House, Drovers Ghyll, Penrith CA10 1DU
T: (01768) 898747
I: www.glassonbycottages.co.uk

GLENRIDDING
Cumbria

Beech House Apartments 1 & 2 ★★★
Contact: Paul Liddell
Lakelovers, Belmont House, Lake Road, Bowness-on-Windermere, Windermere LA23 3BJ
T: (015394) 88855
F: (015394) 88857
E: bookings@lakelovers.co.uk
I: www.lakelovers.co.uk

Birkside Cottage ★★★
Contact: Mr Peter Durbin
Cumbrian Cottages, 2 Lonsdale Street, Carlisle CA1 1DB
T: (01228) 599960
F: (01228) 599970
E: enquiries@cumbriancottages.co.uk
I: www.cumbrian-cottages.co.uk

Chapel Cottage ★★★★
Contact: Susan Jackson
Heart of the Lakes, Fisherbeck Mill, Old Lake Road, Ambleside LA22 0DH
T: (015394) 32321
F: (015394) 33251
E: info@heartofthelakes.co.uk
I: www.heartofthelakes.co.uk

Chapel House ★★★★
Contact: Susan Jackson
Heart of the Lakes, Fisherbeck Mill, Old Lake Road, Ambleside LA22 0DH
T: (015394) 32321
F: (015394) 33251
E: info@heartofthelakes.co.uk
I: www.heartofthelakes.co.uk

Crag Close ★★★★★
Contact: Mr Paul Liddell
Lakelovers, Belmont House, Lake Road, Bowness-on-Windermere, Windermere LA23 3BJ
T: (015394) 88855
F: (015394) 88857
E: bookings@lakelovers.co.uk
I: www.lakelovers.co.uk

Fell View Holidays ★★★★
Contact: Mr & Mrs Burnett
Fell View Holidays, Fell View, Grisedale Bridge, Penrith CA11 0PJ
T: (017684) 82342 &
(017688) 67420
F: (017688) 67420
E: enquiries@fellviewholidays.com
I: www.fellviewholidays.com

Grassthwaite How ★★★★
Contact: Susan Jackson
Heart of the Lakes, Fisherbeck Mill, Old Lake Road, Ambleside LA22 0DH
T: (015394) 32321
F: (015394) 33251
E: info@heartofthelakes.co.uk
I: www.heartofthelakes.co.uk

Grisedale Cottage ★★★
Contact: Mrs Susan Jackson
Heart of the Lakes, Fisherbeck Mill, Old Lake Road, Ambleside LA22 0DH
T: (015394) 32321
F: (015394) 33251
E: info@heartofthelakes.co.uk
I: www.heartofthelakes.co.uk

Halton Cottage ★★★
Contact: Mr Peter Durbin
Cumbrian Cottages, 2 Lonsdale Street, Carlisle CA1 1DB
T: (01228) 599960
F: (01228) 599970
E: enquiries@cumbrian-cottages.co.uk
I: www.cumbrian-cottages.co.uk

Mistal Cottage ★★★★
Contact: Susan Jackson
Heart of the Lakes, Fisherbeck Mill, Old Lake Road, Ambleside LA22 0DH
T: (015394) 32321
F: (015394) 33251
E: info@heartofthelakes.co.uk
I: www.heartofthelakes.co.uk

The Old Coach House Glenridding ★★★★
Contact: Mr Peter Durbin
Cumbrian Cottages, 2 Lonsdale Street, Carlisle CA1 1DB
T: (01228) 599960
F: (01228) 599970
E: enquiries@cumbrian-cottages.co.uk
I: www.cumbrian-cottages.co.uk

Rathmore ★★★
Contact: Susan Jackson
Heart of the Lakes, Fisherbeck Mill, Old Lake Road, Ambleside LA22 0DH
T: (015394) 32321
F: (015394) 33251

Stybarrow Cottage ★★★
Contact: Mr Peter Durbin
Cumbrian Cottages, 2 Lonsdale Street, Carlisle CA1 1DB
T: (01228) 599960
F: (01228) 599970
E: enquiries@cumbrian-cottages.co.uk
I: www.cumbrian-cottages.co.uk

Walkers Retreat
Rating Applied For
Contact: Mrs Susan Jackson
Heart of the Lakes, Fisherbeck Mill, Old Lake Road, Ambleside LA22 0DH
T: (015394) 32321
F: (015394) 33251
I: www.heartofthelakes.co.uk

GOSFORTH
Cumbria

Kell Bank Cottage ★★★
Contact: The Owner
Kell Bank Cottage, 1 Kell Bank, Keswick CA12 4XZ

Potters Barn ★★★★
Contact: Mrs Barbara Wright
Potters Barn, Gosforth Pottery, Seascale CA20 1AH
T: (019467) 25296
E: mail@potters-barn.co.uk
I: www.potters-barn.co.uk

GRANGE-OVER-SANDS
Cumbria

The Chalet Studio & Chalet Garden Flat ★★★
Contact: Margaret Wilson
The Chalet Studio & Chalet Garden Flat, Highfield Road, Grange-over-Sands LA11 7JA
T: (015395) 34695
E: thechalet@freeuk.com

Cornerways Bungalow ★★★
Contact: Mrs Eunice Rigg
Prospect House, Barber Green, Grange-over-Sands LA11 6HU
T: (015395) 36329

Dyer Dene ★★★
Contact: Mrs Andrews
121 Dorchester Road, Garstang, Preston PR3 1FE
T: (01995) 602769
E: dyerdene@fish.co.uk
I: www.dyerdene.com

CUMBRIA – THE LAKE DISTRICT

Hazelwood Court Country House ★★★★
Contact: Martin Stilling
Hazelwood Court Country House Self-Catering, Lindale Road, Grange-over-Sands LA11 6SP
T: (015395) 34196
F: (01539) 534196

The Nook ★★★
Contact: Mr John Serginson
The Lakeland Cottage Company, Waterside House, Ulverston LA12 8AN
T: (015395) 30024
F: (015395) 31932
E: john@lakelandcottageco.com
I: www.lakelandcottageco.com

Spring Bank Cottage ★★★★
Contact: Mrs Brocklebank
Spring Bank Cottage, Spring Bank Farm, Grange-over-Sands LA11 6HA
T: (015395) 32606

Swimmers Farm ★★★★★
Contact: Mr Peter Durbin
Cumbrian Cottages, 2 Lonsdale Street, Carlisle CA1 1DB
T: (01228) 599960
F: (01228) 599970
E: enquiries@cumbriancottages.co.uk
I: www.cumbrian-cottages.co.uk

Wycombe Holiday Flats ★★★
Contact: Mr Benson
Wycombe Holiday Flats, Wycombe, The Esplanade, Grange-over-Sands LA11 7HH
T: (015395) 32297
F: (015395) 32295

GRASMERE
Cumbria

Acorn Cottage ★★★★
Contact: Mr Paul Liddell
Lakelovers, Belmont House, Lake Road, Bowness-on-Windermere, Windermere LA23 3BJ
T: (015394) 88855
F: (015394) 88857
E: bookings@lakelovers.co.uk
I: www.lakelovers.co.uk

April Cottage ★★★★
Contact: Paul Liddell
Lakelovers, Belmont House, Lake Road, Bowness-on-Windermere, Windermere LA23 3BJ
T: (015394) 88855
F: (015394) 88857
E: bookings@lakelovers.co.uk
I: www.lakelovers.co.uk

Badger Cottage ★★
Contact: Mrs Vivien Bass
Wheelwrights Holiday Cottages, Langdale, Ambleside LA22 9HS
T: (015394) 37635
F: (015394) 37618
E: enquiries@wheelwrights.com
I: www.wheelwrights.com

Beck Allans Self Catering Apartments ★★★-★★★★★
Contact: Brian & Pat Taylor
Beck Allans, College Street, Ambleside LA22 9SZ
T: (015394) 35563
F: (015394) 35563
E: mail@beckallans.com
I: www.beckallans.com

Becksteps ★★★★
Contact:
Becksteps, Ambleside LA22 9SY
T: (015394) 32321
F: (015394) 33251
E: info@leisuretime.co.uk
I: www.leisuretime.co.uk

Beechghyll ★★★★
Contact: Mrs Susan Jackson
Heart of the Lakes, Fisherbeck Mill, Old Lake Road, Ambleside LA22 0DH
T: (015394) 32321
F: (015394) 33251
E: info@heartofthelakes.co.uk
I: www.heartofthelakes.co.uk

Bellfoot ★★★★
Contact: Mrs Susan Jackson
Heart of the Lakes, Fisherbeck Mill, Old Lake Road, Ambleside LA22 0DH
T: (015394) 32321
F: (015394) 33251
E: info@heartofthelakes.co.uk
I: www.heartofthelakes.co.uk

Blind Tarn ★★★
Contact: Mrs Susan Jackson
Heart of the Lakes, Fisherbeck Mill, Old Lake Road, Ambleside LA22 0DH
T: (015394) 32321
F: (015394) 33251
E: info@heartofthelakes.co.uk
I: www.heartofthelakes.co.uk

Bramrigg House ★★★★
Contact: Mr Derek Sweeney
Lakeland Inns & Cottages, Kings Head Hotel, Thirlspot, Keswick CA12 4TN
T: (017687) 72393
F: (017687) 72309
I: www.lakedistrictinns.co.uk

Broad Oak ★★★★
Contact: Mrs Susan Jackson
Heart of the Lakes, Fisherbeck Mill, Old Lake Road, Ambleside LA22 0DH
T: (015394) 32321
F: (015394) 33251
E: info@heartofthelakes.co.uk
I: www.heartofthelakes.co.uk

Broadrayne Farm Cottages ★★★★
Contact: Mrs Jo Dennison Drake
Broadrayne Farm Cottages, Broadrayne Farm, Grasmere, Ambleside LA22 9RU
T: (015394) 35055
F: (015394) 35733
E: jo@grasmere-accommodation.co.uk
I: www.grasmere-accommodation.co.uk

Coachmans Cottage ★★★★
Contact: Mrs Susan Jackson
Heart of the Lakes, Fisherbeck Mill, Old Lake Road, Ambleside LA22 0DH
T: (015394) 32321
F: (015394) 33251
E: info@heartofthelakes.co.uk
I: www.heartofthelakes.co.uk

The Cottage ★★★
Contact: Mr Peter Durbin
Cumbrian Cottages, 2 Lonsdale Street, Carlisle CA1 1DB
T: (01228) 599960
F: (01228) 599970
E: enquiries@cumbriancottages.co.uk
I: www.cumbrian-cottages.co.uk

Crummock Cottage ★★★★
Contact: Mrs Vivien Bass
Wheelwrights Holiday Cottages, Langdale, Ambleside LA22 9HS
T: (015394) 37635
F: (015394) 37618
E: enquiries@wheelwrights.com
I: www.wheelwrights.com

3 Dale End ★★★
Contact: Anne Truelove
3 Dale End, Dale End, Ambleside LA22 9PY
T: (015394) 35200
E: p.f.truelove@o2.co.uk
I: www.daleend.co.uk

Dale End Barn ★★★★
Contact: Mrs Vivien Bass
Wheelwrights Holiday Cottages, Langdale, Ambleside LA22 9HS
T: (015394) 37635
F: (015394) 37618
E: enquiries@wheelwrights.com
I: www.wheelwrights.com

Dale End Cottage ★★★★★
Contact: Susan Jackson
Heart of the Lakes, Fisherbeck Mill, Old Lake Road, Ambleside LA22 0DH
T: (015394) 32321
F: (015394) 33251
E: info@heartofthelakes.co.uk
I: www.heartofthelakes.co.uk

Dale End Farm ★★★★
Contact: Mrs Vivien Bass
Wheelwrights Holiday Cottages, Langdale, Ambleside LA22 9HS
T: (015394) 37635
E: enquiries@wheelwrights.com
I: www.wheelwrights.com

Dale Head Cottage ★★★
Contact: Mrs Susan Jackson
Heart of the Lakes, Fisherbeck Mill, Old Lake Road, Ambleside LA22 0DH
T: (015394) 32321
F: (015394) 33251
E: info@heartofthelakes.co.uk
I: www.heartofthelakes.co.uk

Dippers Bank ★★★★
Contact: Susan Jackson
Heart of the Lakes, Fisherbeck Mill, Old Lake Road, Ambleside LA22 0DH
T: (015394) 32321
F: (015394) 33251
E: info@heartofthelakes.co.uk
I: www.heartofthelakes.co.uk

Dove Holme ★★★
Contact: Mr Peter Durbin
Cumbrian Cottages, 2 Lonsdale Street, Carlisle CA1 1DB
T: (01228) 599960
F: (01228) 599970
E: enquiries@cumbrian-cottages.co.uk
I: www.cumbrian-cottages.co.uk

Dovecot Cottage ★★★★
Contact: Mr Philip Johnston
The Coppermines & Coniston Lakes Cottages, The Estate Office, The Bridge, Coniston LA21 8HJ
T: (015394) 41765
I: www.coppermines.co.uk/property/show_details.cgi?id=91

Dunnabeck ★★★★
Contact: Susan Jackson
Heart of the Lakes, Fisherbeck Mill, Old Lake Road, Ambleside LA22 0DH
T: (015394) 32321
F: (015394) 33251
E: info@heartofthelakes.co.uk
I: www.heartofthelakes.co.uk

Easedale ★★★
Contact: Susan Jackson
Heart of the Lakes, Fisherbeck Mill, Old Lake Road, Ambleside LA22 0DH
T: (015394) 32321
F: (015394) 33251
E: info@heartofthelakes.co.uk
I: www.heartofthelakes.co.uk

Eller Close, Wisteria & Garden Cottage
Rating Applied For
Contact: Paul Liddell
Lakelovers, Belmont House, Lake Road, Bowness-on-Windermere, Windermere LA23 3BJ
T: (015394) 88855
F: (015394) 88857
E: bookings@lakelovers.co.uk
I: www.lakelovers.co.uk

Eller Close House
Rating Applied For
Contact:
Holiday Cottages Group, Spring Mill, Barnoldswick BB94 0AA

Fairfield ★★★★
Contact: Susan Jackson
Heart of the Lakes, Fisherbeck Mill, Old Lake Road, Ambleside LA22 0DH
T: (015394) 32321
F: (015394) 33251
E: info@heartofthelakes.co.uk
I: www.heartofthelakes.co.uk

Fairfield Cottage ★★★★
Contact: Susan Jackson
Heart of the Lakes, Fisherbeck Mill, Old Lake Road, Ambleside LA22 0DH
T: (015394) 32321
F: (015394) 33251

Fellside Cottage ★★★★
Contact: Susan Jackson
Heart of the Lakes, Fisherbeck Mill, Old Lake Road, Ambleside LA22 0DH
T: (015394) 32321
F: (015394) 33251

Establishments printed in blue have a detailed entry in this guide

CUMBRIA – THE LAKE DISTRICT

1 Field Foot ★★★
Contact: Mrs J Morrison
1 Field Foot, 11 Park Crescent,
Wigan, Lancashire, Wigan
WN1 1R2
T: (01942) 236350

Glen Dene ★★★★
Contact: Susan Jackson
Heart of the Lakes, Fisherbeck
Mill, Old Lake Road, Ambleside
LA22 0DH
T: (015394) 32321
F: (015394) 33251
E: info@heartofthelakes.co.uk
I: www.heartofthelakes.co.uk

Glen View Cottage ★★★★
Contact: Paul Liddell
Lakelovers, Belmont House, Lake
Road, Bowness-on-Windermere,
Windermere LA23 3BJ
T: (015394) 88855
F: (015394) 88857
E: bookings@lakelovers.co.uk
I: www.lakelovers.co.uk

Goody Bridge Barn ★★★★
Contact: Susan Jackson
Heart of the Lakes, Fisherbeck
Mill, Old Lake Road, Ambleside
LA22 0DH
T: (015394) 32321
F: (015394) 33251
E: infor@heartofthelakes.co.uk
I: www.heartofthelakes.co.uk

Goody Bridge Cottage ★★★★
Contact: Susan Jackson
Heart of the Lakes, Fisherbeck
Mill, Old Lake Road, Ambleside
LA22 0DH
T: (015394) 32321
F: (015394) 33251
E: info@heartofthelakes.co.uk
I: www.heartofthelakes.co.uk

Grasmere Cottages ★★★★
Contact: Martin Wood
Grasmere Cottages, Lane End,
College Street, Grasmere,
Ambleside LA22 9SZ
T: (015394) 35395
E: martinw@globalnet.co.uk
I: www.grasmerecottage
accommodation.co.uk

Grasmere Self Catering ★★★★
Contact: Ann Dixon
Grasmere Self Catering
Accommodation, Tongue Ghyll,
Ambleside LA22 9RU
T: (015394) 35571
F: 0870 706 3180
E: ann@grasmere-holidays.co.uk
I: www.grasmere-holidays.co.uk

Grasmere View ★★★
Contact: Mr Peter Durbin
Cumbrian Cottages, 2 Lonsdale
Street, Carlisle CA1 1DB
T: (01228) 599960
F: (01228) 599970
E: enquiries@cumbriancottages.co.uk
I: www.cumbrian-cottages.co.uk

Grey Crag Barn ★★★★★
Contact: Paul Liddell
Lakelovers, Belmont House, Lake
Road, Bowness-on-Windermere,
Windermere LA23 3BJ
T: (015394) 88855
F: (015394) 88857
E: bookings@lakelovers.co.uk
I: www.lakelovers.co.uk

Helm Crag ★★★★
Contact: Mr & Mrs Alan Wardle
Bateman Fold Barn, Kendal
LA8 8LN
T: (015395) 68074
I: www.lakedistrictholidays.net

Heron View Cottage ★★★★
Contact: Mr Peter Durbin
Cumbrian Cottages, 2 Lonsdale
Street, Carlisle CA1 1DB
T: (01228) 599960
F: (01228) 599970
E: enquiries@cumbriancottages.co.uk
I: www.cumbrian-cottages.co.uk

Heronsyde ★★★★
Contact: Susan Jackson
Heart of the Lakes, Fisherbeck
Mill, Old Lake Road, Ambleside
LA22 0DH
T: (015394) 32321
F: (015394) 33251
E: info@heartofthelakes.co.uk
I: www.heartofthelakes.co.uk

Hollens Farm
Rating Applied For
Contact: Mr Peter Durbin
Cumbrian Cottages, 2 Lonsdale
Street, Carlisle CA1 1DB
T: (01228) 599960
F: (01228) 599970
E: enquiries@cumbriancottages.co.uk
I: www.cumbrian-cottages.co.uk

Holly Cottage ★★★★
Contact: Mr Peter Durbin
Cumbrian Cottages, 2 Lonsdale
Street, Carlisle CA1 1DB
T: (01228) 599960
F: (01228) 599970
E: enquiries@cumbriancottages.co.uk
I: www.cumbrian-cottages.co.uk

Huntingstile South ★★★★
Contact: Susan Jackson
Heart of the Lakes, Fisherbeck
Mill, Old Lake Road, Ambleside
LA22 0DH
T: (015394) 32321
F: (015394) 33251
E: info@heartofthelakes.co.uk
I: www.heartofthelakes.co.uk

Juniper Cottage ★★★★
Contact: Mrs Susan Jackson
Heart of the Lakes, Fisherbeck
Mill, Old Lake Road, Ambleside
LA22 0DH
T: (015394) 32321
F: (015394) 33251
E: info@heartofthelakes.co.uk
I: www.heartofthelakes.co.uk

Lake View Holiday Apartments ★★★
Contact: Mr Stephen & Mrs Michelle King
Lake View Holiday Apartments,
Lake View Drive, Grasmere,
Ambleside LA22 9TD
T: (015394) 35167
I: www.lakeview-grasmere.com

Lamb Cottage ★★★★
Contact: Mrs Susan Jackson
Heart of the Lakes, Old Lake
Road, Ambleside LA22 0DH
T: (015394) 34321
F: (015394) 33251
E: info@heartofthelakes.co.uk
I: www.heartofthelakes.co.uk

Le Tholonet ★★★★
Contact: Susan Jackson
Heart of the Lakes, Fisherbeck
Mill, Old Lake Road, Ambleside
LA22 0DH
T: (015394) 32321
F: (015394) 33251
E: info@heartofthelakes.co.uk
I: www.heartofthelakes.co.uk

Lion Cottage ★★★★
Contact: Mrs Susan Jackson
Heart of the Lakes, Old Lake
Road, Ambleside LA22 0DH
T: (015394) 34321
F: (015394) 33251
E: info@heartofthelakes.co.uk
I: www.heartofthelakes.co.uk

Little Beeches ★★★
Contact: Susan Jackson
Heart of the Lakes, Fisherbeck
Mill, Old Lake Road, Ambleside
LA22 0DH
T: (015394) 32321
F: (015394) 33251
E: info@heartofthelakes.co.uk
I: www.heartofthelakes.co.uk

14 Meadowcroft ★★★★
Contact: Mr Paul Liddell
Lakelovers, Belmont House, Lake
Road, Bowness-on-Windermere,
Windermere LA23 3BJ
T: (015394) 88855
F: (015394) 88857
E: bookings@lakelovers.co.uk
I: www.lakelovers.co.uk

Mews Cottage ★★★★
Contact: David Perrem
Mews Cottage, Fairfield Villa,
Broadgate, Ambleside LA22 9TA
T: (015394) 35627

North Lodge ★★★
Contact: Susan Jackson
Heart of the Lakes, Fisherbeck
Mill, Old Lake Road, Ambleside
LA22 0DH
T: (015394) 32321
F: (015394) 33251
E: info@heartofthelakes.co.uk
I: www.heartofthelakes.co.uk

Oak Bank Apartment ★★★
Contact: Mr Peter Durbin
Cumbrian Cottages, 2 Lonsdale
Street, Carlisle CA1 1DB
T: (01228) 599960
F: (01228) 599970
E: enquiries@cumbriancottages.co.uk
I: www.cumbrian-cottages.co.uk

Old Bakers Cottage ★★★★
Contact: Peter Durbin & Tony Commons
Cumbrian Cottages, 2 Lonsdale
Street, Carlisle CA1 1DB
T: (01228) 599960
F: (01228) 599970
E: enquiries@cumbrian-cottages.co.uk
I: www.cumbrian-cottages.co.uk

Old Hallsteads ★★★★
Contact: Paul Liddell
Lakelovers, Belmont House, Lake
Road, Bowness-on-Windermere,
Windermere LA23 3BJ
T: (015394) 88855
F: (015394) 88857
E: bookings@lakelovers.co.uk
I: www.lakelovers.co.uk

The Old Police House ★★★★
Contact: Mrs Susan Jackson
Heart of the Lakes, Fisherbeck
Mill, Old Lake Road, Ambleside
LA22 0DH
T: (015394) 32321
F: (015394) 33251
E: info@heartofthelakes.co.uk
I: www.heartofthelakes.co.uk

Overmere ★★★★
Contact: Susan Jackson
Heart of the Lakes, Fisherbeck
Mill, Old Lake Road, Ambleside
LA22 0DH
T: (015394) 32321
F: (015394) 33251

Poets View Cottage ★★★★
Contact: Mr Peter Durbin
Cumbrian Cottages, 2 Lonsdale
Street, Carlisle CA1 1DB
T: (01228) 599960
F: (01228) 599970
E: enquiries@cumbrian-cottages.co.uk
I: www.cumbrian-cottages.co.uk

Riverbank ★★★★
Contact: Paul Liddell
Lakelovers, Belmont House, Lake
Road, Bowness-on-Windermere,
Windermere LA23 3BJ
T: (015394) 88855
F: (015394) 88857
E: bookings@lakelovers.co.uk
I: www.lakelovers.co.uk

Rothay Lodge Garden Apartment ★★★★
Contact: Mrs Lindsay Rogers
54A Trevor Road, West
Bridgford, Nottingham NG2 6FT
T: (0115) 923 2618
F: (0115) 923 3984
I: www.rothay-lodge.co.uk

CUMBRIA – THE LAKE DISTRICT

Rowan Cottage ★★★★
Contact: Peter Durbin & Tony Commons
Cumbrian Cottages, 2 Lonsdale Street, Carlisle CA1 1DB
T: (01228) 599960
F: (01228) 599970
E: enquiries@cumbrian-cottages.co.uk
I: www.cumbrian-cottages.co.uk

Rowanberry Cottage ★★★
Contact: Paul Liddell
Lakelovers, Belmont House, Lake Road, Bowness-on-Windermere, Windermere LA23 3BJ
T: (015394) 88855
F: (015394) 88857
E: bookings@lakelovers.co.uk
I: www.lakelovers.co.uk

Silvergarth ★★★
Contact: Mrs Susan Coward
Silvergarth, 1 Low Riddings, Grasmere, Ambleside LA22 9QY
T: (015394) 35828
F: (015394) 35828
E: cowards.silvergarth@btinternet.com
I: www.cowards.silvergarth.btinternet.co.uk

Spinners ★★★★
Contact: Susan Jackson
Heart of the Lakes, Fisherbeck Mill, Old Lake Road, Ambleside LA22 0DH
T: (015394) 32321
F: (015394) 33251

Stonebeck ★★★★
Contact: Susan Jackson
Heart of the Lakes, Fisherbeck Mill, Old Lake Road, Ambleside LA22 0DH
T: (015394) 32321
F: (015394) 33251

Swallows Cottage ★★★★
Contact: Paul Liddell
Lakelovers, Belmont House, Lake Road, Bowness-on-Windermere, Windermere LA23 3BJ
T: (015394) 88855
F: (015394) 88857

3 Tarn Cottages ★★★
Contact: Mrs Isobel Yates
Brookside, Kendal LA8 8HH
T: (015395) 68843
E: iayates@btopenworld.com
I: www.tarncottage.co.uk

Thirlmere Cottage ★★★★
Contact: Susan Jackson
Heart of the Lakes, Fisherbeck Mill, Old Lake Road, Ambleside LA22 0DH
T: (015394) 32321
F: (015394) 33251

Tilly's Cottage ★★★★
Contact: Paul Liddell
Lakelovers, Belmont House, Lake Road, Bowness-on-Windermere, Windermere LA23 3BJ
T: (015394) 88855
F: (015394) 88857
E: bookings@lakelovers.co.uk
I: www.lakelovers.co.uk

2 Townhead Cottages ★★★
Contact: Paul Liddell
Lakelovers, Belmont House, Lake Road, Bowness-on-Windermere, Windermere LA23 3BJ
T: (015394) 88855
F: (015394) 88857

Underheron ★★★★
Contact: Susan Jackson
Heart of the Lakes, Fisherbeck Mill, Old Lake Road, Ambleside LA22 0DH
T: (015394) 32321
F: (015394) 33251

The West House ★★★
Contact: Susan Jackson
Heart of the Lakes, Fisherbeck Mill, Old Lake Road, Ambleside LA22 0DH
T: (015394) 32321
F: (015394) 33251
E: info@heartofthelakes.co.uk
I: www.heartofthelakes.co.uk

Willowbank ★★★
Contact: Susan Jackson
Heart of the Lakes, Fisherbeck Mill, Old Lake Road, Ambleside LA22 0DH
T: (015394) 32321
F: (015394) 33251

Woodland Crag Cottage ★★★★
Contact: Susan Jackson
Heart of the Lakes, Fisherbeck Mill, Old Lake Road, Ambleside LA22 0DH
T: (015394) 32321
F: (015394) 33251

GRAYRIGG
Cumbria

Punchbowl House ★★★
Contact: Mrs Johnson
Punchbowl House, Kendal LA8 9BU
T: (01539) 824345
F: (01539) 824345
E: enquiries@punchbowlhouse.co.uk
I: www.punchbowlhouse.co.uk

GREAT ASBY
Cumbria

Scalebeck Holiday Cottages ★★★★
Contact: Keith & Diane
Scalebeck, Great Asby, Appleby-in-Westmorland CA16 6TH
T: (01768) 351006
F: (01768) 353532
E: mail@scalebeckholidaycottages.com
I: www.scalebeckholidaycottages.com

Town Head Farm Cottages ★★★★
Contact: Ms Debbie Lucas
Town Head Farm Cottages, Town Head Farm, Appleby-in-Westmorland CA16 6EX
T: (017683) 51499
E: info@townheadfarm.co.uk
I: www.townheadfarm.co.uk

Wray Cottage ★★★
Contact: Mrs P Cowey
Wray Cottage, The Hunting House, Appleby-in-Westmorland CA16 6HD
T: (01768) 352485

GREAT BROUGHTON
Cumbria

Fern Cottage ★★★
Contact: Dr Logan
179 Eccleshall Road, Stafford ST16 1PD
T: (01785) 661365

GREAT CORBY
Cumbria

Clint Head Cottage ★★★★
Contact: Peter Durbin & Tony Commons
Cumbrian Cottages, 2 Lonsdale Street, Carlisle CA1 1DB
T: (01228) 599960
F: (01228) 599970
E: enquiries@cumbrian-cottages.co.uk
I: www.cumbrian-cottages.co.uk

GREAT LANGDALE
Cumbria

Elterwater Hall ★★★★★
Contact: Mrs Kath Morton
The Langdale Estate, Great Langdale, Ambleside LA22 9JD
T: (015394) 38012
F: (015394) 37394
E: sales@langdale.co.uk
I: www.langdale.co.uk

Harry Place Farm Cottage ★★★
Contact: Susan Jackson
Heart of the Lakes, Fisherbeck Mill, Old Lake Road, Ambleside LA22 0DH
T: (015394) 32321
F: (015394) 33251
E: info@heartofthelakes.co.uk
I: www.heartofthelakes.co.uk

Heron Place ★★★★★
Contact: Mrs Vivien Bass
Wheelwrights Holiday Cottages, Langdale, Ambleside LA22 9HS
T: (015394) 37635
E: enquiries@wheelwrights.com
I: www.wheelwrights.com

Langdale Estate Chapel Stile Apartments ★★★★
Contact: Mrs Kath Morton
Langdale Estate Chapel Stile Apartments, The Langdale Estate, Great Langdale, Ambleside LA22 9JD
T: (015394) 38012
F: (015394) 37394
E: sales@langdale.co.uk
I: www.langdale.co.uk

Langdale Estate Lodges ★★★★★
Contact: Mrs Kath Morton
Langdale Estate Lodges, Great Langdale, Ambleside LA22 9JD
T: (015394) 38012
F: (015394) 37394
E: sales@langdale.co.uk
I: www.langdale.co.uk

Middlefell Farm Cottage ★★★
Contact: Susan Jackson
Heart of the Lakes, Fisherbeck Mill, Old Lake Road, Ambleside LA22 0DH
T: (015394) 32321
F: (015394) 33251
E: info@heartofthelakes.co.uk
I: www.heartofthelakes.co.uk

Rawfell ★★★★
Contact: Susan Jackson
Heart of the Lakes, Fisherbeck Mill, Old Lake Road, Ambleside LA22 0DH
T: (015394) 32321
F: (015394) 33251

Stickle Cottage ★★★★
Contact: Mrs Vivien Bass
Wheelwrights Holiday Cottages, Langdale, Ambleside LA22 9HS
T: (015394) 37635
E: enquiries@wheelwrights.com
I: www.wheelwrights.com

GREAT MUSGRAVE
Cumbria

Blandswath Cottage ★★★
Contact: The Manager
Ref:1914, Dales Holiday Cottages, Carleton Business Park, Carleton New Road, Skipton BD23 2AA
T: (01756) 799821
F: (01756) 797012
E: info@dalesholcot.com
I: www.dalesholcot.com

GREAT STRICKLAND
Cumbria

The Old Cow Byre ★★★★
Contact: Mr Mark Melling
Taylors Farm Cottages, Taylors Farm, Penrith CA10 3DF
T: (01931) 712205
F: (01931) 712966
E: mark@taylorsfarm.co.uk
I: www.taylorsfarm.co.uk

GREYSOUTHEN
Cumbria

Swallow Barn Cottage ★★★★
Contact: Mr & Mrs James
Swallow Barn Cottage, 6 Evening Hill View, Brigham Road, Cockermouth CA13 0BB
T: (01900) 823016
F: (01900) 821446
E: enquiry@swallowbarn.co.uk
I: www.swallowbarn.co.uk

GREYSTOKE
Cumbria

Duck Down Cottage ★★★★
Contact: Kevin Duckenfield
Duck Down Cottage, 10 Leconfield Garth, Harrogate HG3 1NF
T: (01423) 870490
E: bookings@duckdowncottage.co.uk
I: www.duckdowncottage.co.uk

The Orchard & The Granary ★★★★
Contact: The Manager
Dales Holiday Cottages, Carleton Business Park, Carleton New Road, Skipton BD23 2AA
T: (01756) 799821
F: (01756) 797012
E: fiona@dalesholcot.com
I: www.dalesholcot.com

Thanetwell Lodge ★★★★
Contact: Ms Judith Robson
The Office, Mardale, Penrith CA11 9EH
I: www.thanetwell-lodge.co.

Establishments printed in blue have a detailed entry in this guide

CUMBRIA – THE LAKE DISTRICT

GRIZEBECK
Cumbria

The Cart House ★★★★
Contact: Mr John Serginson
The Lakeland Cottage Company,
Waterside House, Ulverston
LA12 8AN
T: (015395) 30024
F: (015395) 31932
E: john@lakelandcottageco.com
I: www.lakelandcottageco.com

GRIZEDALE
Cumbria

High Dale Park Barn ★★★
Contact: Mr Peter Brown
High Dale Park Farm, High Dale,
Ulverston LA12 8LJ
T: (01229) 860226
I: www.lakesweddingmusic.com/accomm

HARTLEY
Cumbria

The Barn ★★★
Contact: The Manager
Ref:2852, Dales Holiday
Cottages, Carleton Business
Park, Carleton New Road,
Skipton BD23 2AA
T: (01756) 799821
F: (01756) 797012
E: info@dalesholcot.com
I: www.dalesholcot.com

Hartley Castle ★★★★
Contact: Sally Dixon
Hartley Castle, Kirkby Stephen
CA17 4JJ
T: (017683) 71331
E: djs@hartleycastle.freeserve.co.uk

HARTSOP
Cumbria

Caudale Beck ★★★
Contact: Susan Jackson
Heart of the Lakes, Fisherbeck
Mill, Old Lake Road, Ambleside
LA22 0DH
T: (015394) 32321
F: (015394) 33251
E: info@heartofthelakes.co.uk
I: www.heartofthelakes.co.uk

Dovedale ★★
Contact: Susan Jackson
Heart of the Lakes, Fisherbeck
Mill, Old Lake Road, Ambleside
LA22 0DH
T: (015394) 32321
F: (015394) 33251
E: info@heartofthelakes.co.uk
I: www.heartofthelakes.co.uk

Greenbank ★★★★
Contact: Susan Jackson
Heart of the Lakes, Fisherbeck
Mill, Old Lake Road, Ambleside
LA22 0DH
T: (015394) 32321
F: (015394) 33251
E: info@heartofthelakes.co.uk
I: www.heartofthelakes.co.uk

High Beckside ★★★
Contact: Susan Jackson
Heart of the Lakes, Fisherbeck
Mill, Old Lake Road, Ambleside
LA22 0DH
T: (015394) 32321
F: (015394) 33251
E: info@heartofthelakes.co.uk
I: www.heartofthelakes.co.uk

Low Beckside ★★★
Contact: Shirley Thompson
CSH Absolute Escapes, 1 Little
Dockray, Penrith CA11 7HL
T: (01768) 868989
F: (01768) 865578
E: shirley.thompson@csh.co.uk
I: www.csh.co.uk

Weavers Cottage ★★★
Contact: Mrs Susan Jackson
Heart of the Lakes, Fisherbeck
Mill, Old Lake Road, Ambleside
LA22 0DH
T: (015394) 32321
F: (015394) 33251
E: contactus@heartofthelakes.co.uk
I: www.heartofthelakes.co.uk

HAVERIGG
Cumbria

Haverings ★★★
Contact: Mrs Nutting
1 Meadow Park, Milford Haven
SA73 1NZ
T: (01646) 602119

Lazey Cottage ★★★★★
Contact: Mrs Gloria Parsons and
Mrs P Jenkinson
Orchard House, The Hill, Millom
LA18 5HE
T: (01229) 772515 & 773291

Quiet Cottage ★★★
Contact: Mr & Mrs Haston
Quiet Cottage, 2 Pool Side,
Millom LA18 4HW
T: (01229) 772974
E: quietcottage@tiscali.co.uk
I: www.quietcottage.golakes.co.uk

HAVERTHWAITE
Cumbria

Close Cottage ★★★★
Contact: Mr John Serginson
The Lakeland Cottage Company,
Waterside House, Ulverston
LA12 8AN
T: (015395) 30024
F: (015395) 31932
E: john@lakelandcottageco.com
I: www.lakeland-cottage-company.co.uk

Heights View ★★★★
Contact: Ms Janet Dean
Heights View, Ulverston
LA12 8AL
T: (0161) 9290819
E: janetmariedean@yahoo.ie
I: www.immelia.com/heightsview

2 Kiln Houses ★★★★
Contact: Mr John Serginson
The Lakeland Cottage Company,
Waterside House, Ulverston
LA12 8AN
T: (015395) 30024
F: (015395) 31932
E: john@lakelandcottageco.com
I: www.lakelandcottageco.com

4 Woodcroft ★★★★
Contact: Mr John Serginson
Lakeland Cottage Company,
Waterside House, Ulverston
LA12 8AN
T: (015395) 30024
F: (015395) 31932
E: john@lakelandcottageco.com
I: www.lakelandcottageco.com

Woodcroft House ★★★★
Contact: Mr John Serginson
The Lakeland Cottage Company,
Waterside House, Ulverston
LA12 8AN
T: (015395) 30024
F: (015395) 31932
E: john@lakelandcottageco.com
I: www.lakelandcottageco.com

HAWKSHEAD
Cumbria

Above Beck ★★★
Contact: Mr Peter Durbin
Cumbrian Cottages, 2 Lonsdale
Street, Carlisle CA1 1DB
T: (01228) 599960
F: (01228) 599970
E: enquiries@cumbrian-cottages.co.uk
I: www.cumbrian-cottages.co.uk

The Barn, Stable & Crosslands Cottages
Rating Applied For
Contact: Mrs J Haddow
Broomriggs, Ambleside LA22 0JX
T: (015394) 36280
E: info@broomriggs.co.uk
I: www.broomriggs.co.uk

Barn Syke ★★★★
Contact: Mr Paul Liddell
Lakelovers, Belmont House, Lake
Road, Bowness-on-Windermere,
Windermere LA23 3BJ
T: (015394) 88855
F: (015394) 88857
E: bookings@lakelovers.co.uk
I: www.lakelovers.co.uk

Ben Fold ★★★★
Contact: Mrs Anne Gallagher
Hideaways, The Minstrels
Gallery, The Square Hawkshead,
Ambleside LA22 0NZ
T: (015394) 42435
F: (015394) 36178
E: bookings@lakeland-hideaways.co.uk
I: www.lakeland-hideaways.co.uk

Birkwray Farmhouse ★★★★
Contact: Paul Liddell
Lakelovers, Belmont House, Lake
Road, Bowness-on-Windermere,
Windermere LA23 3BJ
T: (015394) 88855
F: (015394) 88857

Bridge View ★★★
Contact: Mrs Dewhurst
Bridge View, 1 Bridge View,
Ambleside LA22 0PL
T: (015394) 36340

Broomriggs ★★★-★★★★
Contact: Mrs Wilson
Nr Sawrey, Hawkshead,
Ambleside LA22 0JX
T: (015394) 36280
E: broomriggs@zoom.co.uk
I: www.broomriggs.co.uk

Columbine Cottage ★★★
Contact: Mr Paul Liddell
Lakelovers, Belmont House, Lake
Road, Bowness-on-Windermere,
Windermere LA23 3BJ
T: (015394) 88855
F: (015394) 88857
E: bookings@lakelovers.co.uk
I: www.lakelovers.co.uk

The Croft Holiday Flats ★★★
Contact: Mrs Barr
The Croft Holiday Flats, North
Lonsdale Road, Hawkshead,
Ambleside LA22 0NX
T: (015394) 36374
F: (015394) 36544
E: enquiries@hawkshead-croft.com
I: www.hawkshead-croft.com

Fair Cop ★★★★
Contact: Susan Jackson
Heart of the Lakes, Fisherbeck
Mill, Old Lake Road, Ambleside
LA22 0DH
T: (015394) 32321
F: (015394) 33251
E: info@heartofthelakes.co.uk
I: www.heartofthelakes.co.uk

Gilpin Cottage ★★★
Contact: Susan Jackson
Heart of the Lakes, Fisherbeck
Mill, Old Lake Road, Ambleside
LA22 0DH
T: (015394) 32321
F: (015394) 33251
E: info@heartofthelakes.co.uk
I: www.heartofthelakes.co.uk

Goosifoot ★★★
Contact: Susan Jackson
Heart of the Lakes, Fisherbeck
Mill, Old Lake Road, Ambleside
LA22 0DH
T: (015394) 32321
F: (015394) 33251
E: info@heartofthelakes.co.uk
I: www.heartofthelakes.co.uk

Greenbank House ★★★
Contact: Mrs Susan Jackson
Heart of the Lakes, Fisherbeck
Mill, Old Lake Road, Ambleside
LA22 0DH
T: (015394) 32321
F: (015394) 33251
E: info@heartofthelakes.co.uk
I: www.heartofthelakes.co.uk

Hatter's Cottage ★★★
Contact: Mr & Mrs Gunner
Hatter's Cottage, Ambleside
LA22 0PW
T: (015394) 36203
E: mail22@hatters-cottage.freeserve.co.uk
I: www.hatters-cottage.freeserve.co.uk

Helm Cottage ★★★★
Contact: Mr Paul Liddell
Lakelovers, Belmont House, Lake
Road, Bowness-on-Windermere,
Windermere LA23 3BJ
T: (015394) 88855
F: (015394) 88857
E: bookings@lakelovers.co.uk
I: www.lakelovers.co.uk

Heron Cottage ★★★★
Contact: Mrs Susan Jacksosn
Heart of the Lakes, Fisherbeck
Mill, Old Lake Road, Ambleside
LA22 0DH
T: (015394) 32321
F: (015394) 33251
E: info@heartofthelakes.co.uk
I: www.heartofthelakes.co.uk

CUMBRIA – THE LAKE DISTRICT

High Orchard ★★★★
Contact: Mrs Anne Gallagher
Hideaways, The Minstrels
Gallery, The Square, Hawkshead,
Ambleside LA22 0NZ
T: (015394) 42435
F: (015394) 36178
E: bookings@
lakeland-hideaways.co.uk
I: www.lakeland-hideaways.co.uk

Hillcrest ★★★★★
Contact: Mrs Susan Jackson
Heart of the Lakes, Fisherbeck
Mill, Old Lake Road, Ambleside
LA22 0DH
T: (015394) 32321
F: (015394) 33251
E: info@heartofthelakes.co.uk
I: www.heartofthelakes.co.uk

Keen Ground Cottage ★★★
Contact: Mr John Serginson
The Lakeland Cottage Company,
Waterside House, Ulverston
LA12 8AN
T: (015395) 30024
F: (015395) 31932
E: john@lakelandcottageco.com
I: www.lakelandcottageco.com

Kings Yard Cottage ★★★
Contact: Mr Peter Durbin
Cumbrian Cottages, 2 Lonsdale
Street, Carlisle CA1 1DB
T: (01228) 599960
F: (01228) 599970
E: enquiries@
cumbrian-cottages.co.uk
I: www.cumbrian-cottages.co.uk

Lantern Cottage ★★★
Contact: Mr Peter Durbin
Cumbrian Cottages, 2 Lonsdale
Street, Carlisle CA1 1DB
T: (01228) 599960
F: (01228) 599970
E: enquiries@cumbriancottages.co.uk
I: www.cumbrian-cottages.co.uk

Larch Cottage ★★★
Contact: Susan Jackson
Heart of the Lakes, Fisherbeck
Mill, Old Lake Road, Ambleside
LA22 0DH
T: (015394) 32321
F: (015394) 33251
E: info@heartofthelakes.co.uk
I: www.heartofthelakes.co.uk

Meadow View ★★★
Contact:
Blakes Country Cottages, Spring
Mill, Earby BB94 0AA
T: 08700 708090
F: 0870 5851150
I: www.blakes-cottages.co.uk

The Nook Cottage ★★★★
Contact: Mrs Vivien Bass
Wheelwrights Holiday Cottages,
Langdale, Ambleside LA22 9HS
T: (015394) 37635
F: (015394) 37618
E: enquiries@wheelwrights.com
I: www.wheelwrights.com

Oak Apple Barn ★★★★
Contact: Nancy Penrice
Violet Bank, Ambleside LA22 0PL
T: (015394) 36222
E: chp@violetbank.freeserve.co.uk
I: www.oak-apple.co.uk

The Old Barn & Barn End Cottage ★★★★
Contact: Mrs Anne Gallagher
Hideaways, The Minstrels
Gallery, The Square, Hawkshead,
Ambleside LA22 0NZ
T: (015394) 42435
F: (015394) 36178
E: bookings@
lakeland-hideaways.co.uk
I: www.lakeland-hideaways.co.uk

Old Farm ★★★★
Contact: Mr John Serginson
The Lakeland Cottage Company,
Waterside House, Ulverston
LA12 8AN
T: (015395) 30024
F: (015395) 31932
E: john@lakelandcottageco.com
I: www.lakelandcottageco.com

Ramblers Roost ★★★
Contact: Howard King
Ramblers Roost, 38 The Drive,
Newcastle upon Tyne NE3 4AH
T: 0797 3 420179
F: (01429) 233105
E: hk.developments@virgin.net
I: www.hk.developmentslakes.co.uk

Rigges Wood Cottage ★★★★
Contact: Paul Liddell
Lakelovers, Belmont House, Lake
Road, Bowness-on-Windermere,
Windermere LA23 3BJ
T: (015394) 88855
F: (015394) 88857

The Rockery Suite ★★★★
Contact: Mrs Susan Jackson
Heart of the Lakes, Fisherbeck
Mill, Old Lake Road, Ambleside
LA22 0DH
T: (015394) 32321
F: (015394) 33251
E: info@heartofthelakes.co.uk
I: www.heartofthelakes.co.uk

Rose Howe ★★★★
Contact: Susan Jackson
Heart of the Lakes, Fisherbeck
Mill, Old Lake Road, Ambleside
LA22 0DH
T: (015394) 32321
F: (015394) 33251

Sand Ground Barn ★★★
Contact: Susan Jackson
Heart of the Lakes, Fisherbeck
Mill, Old Lake Road, Ambleside
LA22 0DH
T: (015394) 32321
F: (015394) 33251

Sandy Wyke ★★★
Contact: Susan Jackson
Heart of the Lakes, Fisherbeck
Mill, Old Lake Road, Ambleside
LA22 0DH
T: (015394) 32321
F: (015394) 33251

Sergeant Man ★★★★
Contact: Susan Jackson
Heart of the Lakes, Fisherbeck
Mill, Old Lake Road, Ambleside
LA22 0DH
T: (015394) 32321
F: (015394) 33251

Shepherds Cottage ★★★★
Contact: Mrs Anne Gallagher
Hideaways, Minstrels' Gallery,
The Square, Hawkshead,
Ambleside LA22 0NZ
T: (015394) 42435
F: (015394) 36178
E: bookings@
lakeland-hideaways.co.uk
I: www.lakeland-hideaways.co.uk

Summerhill Country House ★★★
Contact: Mr Philip Johnston
The Coppermines & Coniston
Lakes Cottages, The Estate
Office, The Bridge, Coniston
LA21 8HJ
T: (015394) 41765
F: (015394) 41944
E: info@coppermines.co.uk

Swallow's Nest ★★★
Contact: Susan Jackson
Heart of the Lakes, Fisherbeck
Mill, Old Lake Road, Ambleside
LA22 0DH
T: (015394) 32321
F: (015394) 33251

Swallows Nest Cottage ★★★
Contact: Mr Philip Johnston
The Coppermines & Coniston
Lakes Cottages, The Estate
Office, The Bridge, Coniston
LA21 8HJ
T: (015394) 41765
F: (015394) 41944
E: info@coppermines.co.uk
I: www.coppermines.co.uk

Syke Cottage ★★★★
Contact: Mrs Susan Jackson
Heart of the Lakes, Fisherbeck
Mill, Old Lake Road, Ambleside
LA22 0DH
T: (015394) 32321
F: (015394) 33251
E: info@heartofthelakes.co.uk
I: www.heartofthelakes.co.uk

Tarn Hows ★★★
Contact: Mrs Susan Jackson
Heart of the Lakes, Fisherbeck
Mill, Old Lake Road, Ambleside
LA22 0DH
T: (015394) 32321
F: (015394) 33251
E: info@heartofthelakes.co.uk
I: www.heartofthelakes.co.uk

Walker Ground Barn ★★★★
Contact: Mrs Susan Jackson
Heart of the Lakes, Fisherbeck
Mill, Old Lake Road, Ambleside
LA22 0DH
T: (015394) 32321
F: (015394) 33251
E: info@heartofthelakes.co.uk
I: www.heartofthelakes.co.uk

Walker Ground Cottage ★★★★
Contact: Mr Peter Durbin
Cumbrian Cottages, 2 Lonsdale
Street, Carlisle CA1 1DB
T: (01228) 599960
F: (01228) 599970
I: www.cumbrian-cottages.co.uk

Wheelwrights Holiday Cottages ★★-★★★★★
Contact: Mr Bass
Wheelwrights, Elterwater,
Ambleside LA22 9HS
T: (015394) 37635
F: (015394) 37618
E: enquiries@wheelwrights.com
I: www.wheelwrights.com

Woodlands, Roger Ground ★★★★
Contact: Susan Jackson
Heart of the Lakes, Fisherbeck
Mill, Old Lake Road, Ambleside
LA22 0DH
T: (015394) 32321
F: (015394) 33251

Yew Trees ★★★
Contact: Susan Jackson
Heart of the Lakes, Fisherbeck
Mill, Old Lake Road, Ambleside
LA22 0DH
T: (015394) 32321
F: (015394) 33251

HAWKSHEAD HILL
Cumbria

The Coachman's Loft ★★★
Contact: Mrs Susan Jackson
Heart of the Lakes, Fisherbeck
Mill, Old Lake Road, Ambleside
LA22 0DH
T: (015394) 33110
F: (015394) 33251
E: contactus@heartofthelakes.co.uk
I: www.heartofthelakes.co.uk

HAWS BANK
Cumbria

Beckside House ★★★★
Contact: Miss K Walton
Coniston Breaks, 2 Fitz Steps,
Ambleside LA22 9PA
T: (015394) 37379
E: info@conistonbreaks.com
I: www.conistonbreaks.com

HELTON
Cumbria

Talbot House & Talbot Studio ★★★★
Contact: Mark Cowell
Church Court Cottages, Church
Villa, Penrith CA10 1HR
T: (01768) 881682
F: (01768) 889055
E: markcowell@amserve.com
I: www.gogamblesby.co.uk

HESKET NEWMARKET
Cumbria

Beech Cottage ★★★
Contact: Mr Peter Durbin
Cumbrian Cottages, 2 Lonsdale
Street, Carlisle CA1 1DB
T: (01228) 599960
F: (01228) 599970
E: enquiries@
cumbrian-cottages.co.uk
I: www.cumbrian-cottages.co.uk

Establishments printed in blue have a detailed entry in this guide

CUMBRIA – THE LAKE DISTRICT

Ostlers Barn ★★★★
Contact: Mr Peter Durbin & Tony Commons
Cumbrian Cottages, 2 Lonsdale Street, Carlisle CA1 1DB
T: (01228) 599960
F: (01228) 599970
E: enquiries@cumbrian-cottages.co.uk
I: www.cumbrian-cottages.co.uk

Syke House ★★★
Contact: Clive Sykes
Sykes Cottages, York House, York Street, Chester CH1 3LR
T: (01244) 345700
F: (01244) 321442

HETHERSGILL
Cumbria

Newlands Farmhouse ★★★★
Contact: Peter Durbin & Tony Commons
Cumbrian Cottages, 2 Lonsdale Street, Carlisle CA1 1DB
T: (01228) 599960
F: (01228) 599970
E: enquires@cumbrian-cottages.co.uk
I: www.cumbrian-cottages.co.uk

HIGH LORTON
Cumbria

1&2 Midtown Cottages ★★★★
Contact: Mr Burrell
Midtown Cottages, 20 Hillside, Andover SP11 7DF
T: (01264) 710165
E: info@midtown-cottages.co.uk
I: www.midtown-cottages.co.uk

Acorn Cottage ★★★
Contact: Mr Peter Durbin
Cumbrian Cottages, 2 Lonsdale Street, Carlisle CA1 1DB
T: (01228) 599960
F: (01228) 599970
E: enquiries@cumbrian-cottages.co.uk
I: www.cumbrian-cottages.co.uk

Brewery House ★★★★★
Contact: Mr Peter Durbin
Cumbrian Cottages, 2 Lonsdale Street, Carlisle CA1 1DB
T: (01228) 599960
F: (01228) 599970
E: enquiries@cumbrian-cottages.co.uk
I: www.cumbrian-cottages.co.uk

Dale House ★★★
Contact: Peter Durbin & Tony Commons
Cumbrian Cottages, 2 Lonsdale Street, Carlisle CA1 1DB
T: (01228) 599960
F: (01228) 599970
E: enquiries@cumbrian-cottages.co.uk
I: www.cumbrian-cottages.co.uk

Groom Cottage ★★★
Contact: Peter Durbin & Tony Commons
Cumbrian Cottages, 2 Lonsdale Street, Carlisle CA1 1DB
T: (01228) 599960
F: (01228) 599970

High Swinside Holiday Cottages
Rating Applied For
Contact: Jacques Hankin
High Swinside Holiday Cottages, High Swinside Farm, Cockermouth CA13 9UA
T: (01900) 85206
F: (01900) 85076
E: bookings@highswinside.demon.co.uk
I: www.highswinside.demon.co.uk

Holemire House Barn ★★★★
Contact: Mrs Angela Fearfield
Holemire House Barn, Holemire House, High Lorton, Cockermouth CA13 9TX
T: (01900) 85225
E: enquiries@lakelandbarn.co.uk
I: www.lakelandbarn.co.uk

Wayside Cottage ★★★
Contact: The Manager
Ref:2376, Dales Holiday Cottages, Carleton Business Park, Carleton New Road, Skipton BD23 2AA
T: (01756) 799821
F: (01756) 797012
E: info@dalesholcot.com
I: www.dalesholcot.com

HIGH WRAY
Cumbria

Stable Cottage ★★★★
Contact: Sheila Briggs
High Wray Farm, Ambleside LA22 0JE
T: (015394) 32280
F: (015394) 32280
E: sheila@highwrayfarm.co.uk
I: www.highwrayfarm.co.uk

HOLMROOK
Cumbria

Randle How ★★★★
Contact: Susan Wedley
Randle How, Long Yocking How, Holmrook CA19 1UA
T: (01946) 723126
F: (01946) 723490
E: js.wedley@btopenworld.com

Yattus ★★★★★★
Contact: Mr Peter Durbin
Cumbrian Cottages, 2 Lonsdale Street, Carlisle CA1 1DB
T: (01228) 599960
F: (01228) 599970
E: enquiries@cumbriancottages.co.uk
I: www.cumbrian-cottages.co.uk

HOWGILL
Cumbria

Blandsgill Cottage ★★★
Contact: Mr Peter Durbin
Cumbrian Cottages, 2 Lonsdale Street, Carlisle CA1 1DB
T: (01228) 599960
F: (01228) 599970
E: enquiries@cumbrian-cottages.co.uk
I: www.cumbrian-cottages.co.uk

Crook-O-Lune Farm ★★★
Contact: Mrs B Bailey
Crook-O-Lune Farm, Kendal LA8 0BP
T: (01539) 824270
F: (01539) 824270

Drawell ★★★★
Contact: Janet Postlethwaite
Drawell, Bramaskew, Sedbergh LA10 5HX
T: (015396) 21529
E: drawell@pentalk.org
I: www.drawellcottage.co.uk

HUTTON ROOF
Cumbria

Barn Cottage ★★★
Contact: Arthur Newton
Barn Cottage, Hegglehead, Penrith CA11 0XS
T: (017684) 84566
F: (017684) 84460
E: hegglehead@aol.com
I: www.hegglehead.co.uk

Carrock Cottages ★★★★★
Contact: Mr Malcolm & Mrs Gillian Iredale
Carrock House, Howhill, Penrith CA11 0XY
T: (01768) 484111
F: (01768) 488850
E: info@carrockcottages.co.uk
I: www.carrockcottages.co.uk

INGS
Cumbria

Ings Mill Park Cottages ★★★★
Contact: Mr Peter Durbin
Cumbrian Cottages, 2 Lonsdale Street, Carlisle CA1 1DB
T: (01228) 599960
F: (01228) 599970
E: enquiries@cumbrian-cottages.co.uk
I: www.cumbrian-cottages.co.uk

Little Ghyll Cottage
Rating Applied For
Contact: Mrs Christine Omerod
Little Ghyll Cottage, Ghyll Cottage, Kendal LA8 9PU
T: (01539) 821274

Topiary Cottage ★★★★
Contact: Mr Paul Liddell
Lakelovers, Belmont House, Lake Road, Bowness-on-Windermere, Windermere LA23 3BJ
T: (015394) 88855
F: (015394) 88857
E: bookings@lakelovers.co.uk
I: www.lakelovers.co.uk

IREBY
Cumbria

Daleside Farm ★★★★
Contact: Isabel Teasdale
Daleside Farm, Carlisle CA7 1EW
T: (016973) 71268
E: info@dalesidefarm.co.uk
I: www.dalesidefarm.co.uk

Fell Cottage ★★★★★
Contact: Mr Peter Durbin
Cumbrian Cottages, 2 Lonsdale Street, Carlisle CA1 1DB
T: (01228) 599960
F: (01228) 599970
E: enquiries@cumbrian-cottages.co.uk
I: www.cumbrian-cottages.co.uk

Laundry Cottage ★★★★
Contact: Mr Peter Durbin & Tony Commons
Cumbrian Cottages, 2 Lonsdale Street, Carlisle CA1 1DB
T: (01228) 599960
F: (01228) 599970
E: enquiries@cumbrian-cottages.co.uk
I: www.cumbrian-cottages.co.uk

Old Saddlers Cottage ★★★★
Contact: Mr Peter Durbin
Cumbrian Cottages, 2 Lonsdale Street, Carlisle CA1 1DB
T: (01228) 599960
F: (01228) 599970
E: enquiries@cumbrian-cottages.co.uk
I: www.cumbrian-cottages.co.uk

Old Stables ★★★★
Contact: Mr Peter Durbin
Cumbrian Cottages, 2 Lonsdale Street, Carlisle CA1 1DB
T: (01228) 599960
F: (01228) 599970
E: enquiries@cumbrian-cottages.co.uk
I: www.cumbrian-cottages.co.uk

KENDAL
Cumbria

Barkinbeck Cottage ★★★
Contact: Mrs A Hamilton
Barkin House, Gatebeck, Kendal LA8 0HX
T: (015395) 67122
E: ann@barkin.fsnet.co.uk
I: www.barkinbeck.co.uk

Dora's Cottage ★★★
Contact: Mrs Val Sunter
Dora's Cottage, Oxenholme Lane, Kendal LA9 7QH
T: (015395) 61177

Field End Barns & Shaw End Mansion ★★★-★★★★
Contact: Mr & Mrs Robinson
Field End Barns & Shaw End Mansion, Patton, Kendal LA8 9DU
T: (01539) 824220
F: (01539) 824464
E: robinson@fieldendholidays.co.uk
I: www.fieldendholidays.co.uk

Great Gable ★★★★★
Contact: Mr Peter Durbin
Cumbrian Cottages, 2 Lonsdale Street, Carlisle CA1 1DB
T: (01228) 599960
F: (01228) 599970
E: enquiries@cumbrian-cottages.co.uk
I: www.cumbrian-cottages.co.uk

High Swinklebank Farm ★★★
Contact: Olive Simpson
High Swinklebank Farm, Kendal LA8 9BD
T: (01539) 823682
E: www.lakedistrictfarmhouseholidays.co.uk/highswinklebank

CUMBRIA – THE LAKE DISTRICT

Middle Swinklebank ★★★
Contact: Mary Todd
Middle Swinklebank,
Swinklebank House, Kendal
LA8 9BD
T: (01539) 823256

Moresdale Bank Cottage
★★★★
Contact: Helen Parkins
Moresdale Bank Cottage, Kendal
LA8 0DH
T: (01539) 824227
E: mclamb@ukonline.co.uk
I: www.
moresdale-bank-cottage.co.uk

Todd Meadow ★★★★
Contact: Mr Durbin
Cumbrian Cottages, 2 Lonsdale
Street, Carlisle CA1 1DB
T: (01228) 599960
F: (01228) 599970
E: enquiries@
cumbrian-cottages.co.uk
I: www.cumbrian-cottages.co.uk

KENTMERE
Cumbria

High Fold ★★★★
Contact: Mr Peter Durbin
Cumbrian Cottages, 2 Lonsdale
Street, Carlisle CA1 1DB
T: (01228) 599960
F: (01228) 599970
E: enquiries@
cumbrian-cottages.co.uk
I: www.cumbrian-cottages.co.uk

**Nook Cottage - Kentmere
Valley** ★★★
Contact: Mr John Serginson
The Lakeland Cottage Company,
Waterside House, Ulverston
LA12 8AN
T: (015395) 30024
F: (015395) 31932
E: john@lakelandcottageco.com
I: www.
lakelandcottagecompany.com

Rawe Cottage ★★★★
Contact: Mr John Serginson
The Lakeland Cottage Company,
Waterside House, Ulverston
LA12 8AN
T: (015395) 30024
F: (015395) 31932
E: john@lakelandcottageco.com
I: www.lakelandcottageco.com

KESWICK
Cumbria

**Acorn Apartments and
Acorn View**
★★★★-★★★★★
Contact: Mr J W Miller
Acorn Apartments and Acorn
View, South Barn, Fort Putnam,
Greystoke, Penrith CA11 0UP
T: (017684) 80310
E: info@acornselfcatering.co.uk
I: www.acornselfcatering.co.uk

Alice's Nook ★★★★
Contact: Mr Peter Durbin
Cumbrian Cottages, 2 Lonsdale
Street, Carlisle CA1 1DB
T: (01228) 599960
F: (01228) 599970
E: enquiries@
cumbrian-cottages.co.uk
I: www.cumbrian-cottages.co.uk

**Alison's Cottage/View/Laal
Yan/High Spy** ★★★-★★★★★
Contact: Alison Milner
Alison's Cottage, Alison's View,
Laal Yan and High Spy, 9 Fearon
Close, Nottingham NG14 7FA
T: (0115) 9664049

Amba ★★★★
Contact: Mr Peter Durbin
Cumbrian Cottages, 2 Lonsdale
Street, Carlisle CA1 1DB
T: (01228) 599960
F: (01228) 599970
E: enquiries@
cumbrian-cottages.co.uk
I: www.cumbrian-cottages.co.uk

Amberley ★★★★
Contact: Mr T Lowe
Amberley, 44 Windebrowe
Avenue, Keswick CA12 4JA
T: (017687) 71292
E: hillwalker@uku.co.uk
I: www.keswickrambles.co.uk

Amphora ★★★
Contact: Mr Peter Durbin
Cumbrian Cottages, 2 Lonsdale
Street, Carlisle CA1 1DB
T: (01228) 599960
F: (01228) 599970
E: enquiries@cumbriancottages.
co.uk
I: www.cumbrian-cottages.co.uk

Applemere ★★★★
Contact: Mr Peter Durbin
Cumbrian Cottages, 2 Lonsdale
Street, Carlisle CA1 1DB
T: (01228) 599960
F: (01228) 599970
E: enquiries@
cumbrian-cottages.co.uk
I: www.cumbrian-cottages.co.uk

Appleside ★★★
Contact: Mr Peter Durbin
Cumbrian Cottages, 2 Lonsdale
Street, Carlisle CA1 1DB
T: (01228) 599960
F: (01228) 599970
E: enquiries@cumbriancottages.
co.uk
I: www.cumbrian-cottage.co.uk

Appletree ★★★★
Contact: Mr Peter Durbin
Cumbrian Cottages, 2 Lonsdale
Street, Carlisle CA1 1DB
T: (01228) 599960
F: (01228) 599970
E: enquiries@cumbriancottages.
co.uk
I: www.cumbrian-cottages.co.uk

Ashbrooke ★★★
Contact: Mr Peter Durbin
Cumbrian Cottages, 2 Lonsdale
Street, Carlisle CA1 1DB
T: (01228) 599960
F: (01228) 599970
E: enquiries@
cumbrian-cottages.co.uk
I: www.cumbrian-cottages.co.uk

Ashlyn House ★★★
Contact: Mr Peter Durbin
Cumbrian Cottages, 2 Lonsdale
Street, Carlisle CA1 1DB
T: (01228) 599960
F: (01228) 599970
E: enquiries@
cumbrian-cottages.co.uk
I: www.cumbrian-cottages.co.uk

Ashmore ★★★★
Contact: Mr Peter Durbin
Cumbrian Cottages, 2 Lonsdale
Street, Carlisle CA1 1DB
T: (01228) 599960
F: (01228) 599970
E: enquiries@cumbriancottages.
co.uk
I: www.cumbrian-cottages.co.uk

Aura and Aaron ★★★★
Contact: Mr Robert & Mrs Linda
Au
The Stanners, 41 Lakeland Park,
Keswick CA12 4AT
T: (017687) 72541
E: aurabau@hotmail.com
I: www.keswickb.com

**6 Balmoral House
(Mountain View)** ★★★
Contact: Mr Peter Durbin
Cumbrian Cottages, 2 Lonsdale
Street, Carlisle CA1 1DB
T: (01228) 599960
F: (01228) 599970
E: enquiries@
cumbrian-cottages.co.uk
I: www.cumbrian-cottages.co.uk

3 Balmoral House ★★★
Contact: Mr Peter Durbin
Cumbrian Cottages, 2 Lonsdale
Street, Carlisle CA1 1DB
T: (01228) 599960
F: (01228) 599970
E: enquiries@
cumbrian-cottages.co.uk
I: www.cumbrian-cottages.co.uk

Bannerdale ★★★★
Contact: Ms Hazel Hutton
Springs Farm, Keswick
CA12 4AN
T: 07816 824253
F: (017687) 72546
E: info@bannerdale.co.uk
I: www.bannerdale.co.uk

Beagle Cottage ★★★
Contact: Mr Peter Durbin & Tony
Commons
Cumbrian Cottages, 2 Lonsdale
Street, Carlisle CA1 1DB
T: (01228) 599960
F: (01228) 599970
E: enquiries@
cumbrian-cottages.co.uk
I: www.cumbrian-cottages.co.uk

3 Beech ★★★
Contact: Mrs Johnstone
6 Nethertown Close, Clitheroe
BB7 9SF
T: (01254) 822733

Beech Nut ★★★
Contact: Mr Peter Durbin
Cumbrian Cottages, 2 Lonsdale
Street, Carlisle CA1 1DB
T: (01228) 599960
F: (01228) 599970
E: enquiries@
cumbrian-cottages.co.uk
I: www.cumbrian-cottages.co.uk

Belle Vue ★★★-★★★★★
Contact: Mrs Lexie Ryder
Hillside, Portinscale, Keswick
CA12 5RS
T: (017687) 71065
E: lexieryder@hotmail.com

Bleach Green Cottages
★★★
Contact: Mr Peter Durbin
Cumbrian Cottages, 2 Lonsdale
Street, Carlisle CA1 1DB
T: (01228) 599960
F: (01228) 599970
E: enquiries@
cumbrian-cottages.co.uk
I: www.cumbrian-cottages.co.uk

The Blencathra ★★★
Contact: Mr Peter Durbin
Cumbrian Cottages, 2 Lonsdale
Street, Carlisle CA1 1DB
T: (01228) 599960
F: (01228) 599970
E: enquiries@cumbriancottages.
co.uk
I: www.cumbrian-cottages.co.uk

Blencathra Cottage ★★★★
Contact: Mr Peter Durbin
Cumbrian Cottages, 2 Lonsdale
Street, Carlisle CA1 1DB
T: (01228) 599960
F: (01228) 599970
E: enquiries@
cumbrian-cottages.co.uk
I: www.cumbrian-cottages.co.uk

Blencathra House ★★★★
Contact: Mr Peter Durbin
Cumbrian Cottages, 2 Lonsdale
Street, Carlisle CA1 1DB
T: (01228) 599960
F: (01228) 599970
E: enquiries@
cumbrian-cottages.co.uk
I: www.cumbrian-cottages.co.uk

Bobbin Cottage ★★★★
Contact: Mr Durbin
Cumbrian Cottages, 2 Lonsdale
Street, Carlisle CA1 1DB
T: (01228) 599960
F: (01228) 599970
E: enquiries@
cumbrian-cottages.co.uk
I: www.cumbrian-cottages.co.uk

Bonshaw ★★★
Contact: Mr Peter Durbin
Cumbrian Cottages, 2 Lonsdale
Street, Carlisle CA1 1DB
T: (01228) 599960
F: (01228) 599970
E: enquiries@
cumbrian-cottages.co.uk
I: www.cumbrian-cottages.co.uk

Bracken Lodge ★★★★
Contact: Mr Peter Durbin
Cumbrian Cottages, 2 Lonsdale
Street, Carlisle CA1 1DB
T: (01228) 599960
F: (01228) 599970
E: enquiries@cumbriancottages.
co.uk
I: www.cumbrian-cottages.co.uk

Brandelhow ★★★★
Contact: Mrs Susan Jackson
Heart of the Lakes, Fisherbeck
Mill, Old Lake Road, Ambleside
LA22 0DH
T: (015394) 32321
F: (015394) 33251
E: info@heartofthelakes.co.uk
I: www.heartofthelakes.co.uk

Establishments printed in blue have a detailed entry in this guide

CUMBRIA – THE LAKE DISTRICT

Brigham Farm ★★★★
Contact: Mr Green
The Studio, Fornside House,
Keswick CA12 4TS
T: (017687) 79666
E: selfcatering@
keswickholidays.co.uk
I: www.keswickholidays.co.uk

Brundholme Keswick ★★★★
Contact: Mr Peter Durbin
Cumbrian Cottages, 2 Lonsdale
Street, Carlisle CA1 1DB
T: (01228) 599960
F: (01228) 599970
E: enquiries@
cumbrian-cottages.co.uk
I: www.cumbrian-cottages.co.uk

Bunbury Cottage ★★★★
Contact: Mr Peter Durbin
Cumbrian Cottages, 2 Lonsdale
Street, Carlisle CA1 1DB
T: (01228) 599960
F: (01228) 599970
E: enquiries@cumbria-cottages.co.uk
I: www.cumbrian-cottages.co.uk

11 Burnside Park ★★★★
Contact: Mr Peter Durbin
Cumbrian Cottages, 2 Lonsdale
Street, Carlisle CA1 1DB
T: (01228) 599960
F: (01228) 599970
E: enquiries@cumbriancottages.co.uk
I: www.cumbrian-cottages.co.uk

Cairnway ★★★★
Contact: Mr Peter Durbin
Cumbrian Cottages, 2 Lonsdale
Street, Carlisle CA1 1DB
T: (01228) 599960
F: (01228) 599970
E: enquiries@
cumbrian-cottages.co.uk
I: www.cumbrian-cottages.co.uk

Candlemas ★★★
Contact: David Burton
Lakeland Cottage Holidays,
Melbecks, Keswick CA12 4QX
T: (017687) 76065
F: (017687) 76869
E: info@lakelandcottages.co.uk
I: www.lakelandholidays.co.uk

Carlton Cottage ★★★★
Contact: Mr Peter Durbin
Cumbrian Cottages, 2 Lonsdale
Street, Carlisle CA1 1DB
T: (01228) 599960
F: (01228) 599970
E: enquiries@cumbriancottages.co.uk
I: www.cumbrian-cottages.co.uk

Carolyn's Cottage ★★★
Contact: Mr Peter Durbin
Cumbrian Cottages, 2 Lonsdale
Street, Carlisle CA1 1DB
T: (01228) 599960
F: (01228) 599970
E: enquiries@
cumbrian-cottages.co.uk
I: www.cumbrian-cottages.co.uk

Castlerigg Manor Lodge ★★★★
Contact: Mr Durbin
Cumbrian Cottages, 2 Lonsdale
Street, Carlisle CA1 1DB
T: (01228) 599960
F: (01228) 599970
E: enquiries@
cumbrian-cottages.co.uk
I: www.cumbrian-cottages.co.uk

3 Catherine Cottages ★★★
Contact: Mr Peter & Mrs
Margaret Hewitson
17 Cedar Lane, Cockermouth
CA13 9HN
T: (01900) 828039
E: peter.hewitson1@btinternet.com

Causey View ★★★
Contact: Mr David Etherden
Keswick Holidays Ltd, Keswick
Bridge, Brundholme Road,
Keswick CA12 4NL
T: (017687) 73200
F: (017687) 75811
E: enquiries@keswickb.com
I: www.keswickb.com/self-catering/causey-view-keswick

The Coach House ★★★★★
Contact: Mrs Susan Jackson
Heart of the Lakes, Fisherbeck
Mill, Old Lake Road, Ambleside
LA22 0DH
T: (015394) 32321
F: (015394) 33251
E: info@heartofthelakes.co.uk
I: www.heartofthelakes.co.uk

Coachmans Cottage ★★★
Contact: Mr Peter Durbin
Cumbrian Cottages, 2 Lonsdale
Street, Carlisle CA1 1DB
T: (01228) 599960
F: (01228) 599970
E: enquiries@
cumbrian-cottages.co.uk
I: www.cumbrian-cottages.co.uk

Cosy Nook ★★★
Contact: Mr Peter Durbin
Cumbrian Cottages, 2 Lonsdale
Street, Carlisle CA1 1DB
T: (01228) 599960
F: (01228) 599970
E: enquiries@cumbriancottages.co.uk
I: www.cumbrian-cottages.co.uk

The Cottage ★★★★
Contact: Susan Jackson
Heart of the Lakes, Fisherbeck
Mill, Old Lake Road, Ambleside
LA22 0DH
T: (015394) 32321
F: (015394) 33251

The Cottage ★★★
Contact: Mrs Margaret Beaty
The Cottage, Birkrigg, Newlands
Valley, Keswick CA12 5TS
T: (017687) 78278

Crag Lea ★★★
Contact: Mr Peter Durbin
Cumbrian Cottages, 2 Lonsdale
Street, Carlisle CA1 1DB
T: (01228) 599960
F: (01228) 599970
E: enquiries@cumbriancottages.co.uk
I: www.cumbrian-cottages.co.uk

The Croft ★★★
Contact: Mr Peter Durbin
Cumbrian Cottages, 2 Lonsdale
Street, Carlisle CA1 1DB
T: (01228) 599960
F: (01228) 599970
E: enquiries@
cumbrian-cottages.co.uk
I: www.cumbrian-cottages.co.uk

Croft House Holidays ★★★★
Contact: Mrs Jan Boniface
Croft House Holidays, Croft
House, Applethwaite, Keswick
CA12 4PN
T: (017687) 73693
E: holidays@crofthouselakes.co.uk
I: www.crofthouselakes.co.uk

Croftlands Cottages ★★★★★
Contact: Mrs Susan McGarvie
Croftlands Cottages, Croftlands,
Thornthwaite, Keswick
CA12 5SA
T: (017687) 78300
F: (017687) 78300
E: robmcgarvie@lineone.net
I: www.croftlands-cottages.co.uk

Dale Head Hall Lakeside Hotel ★★★★-★★★★★
Contact: Mr Hans Bonkenburg
Dale Head Hall Lakeside Hotel,
Keswick CA12 4TN
T: (017687) 72478
F: (017687) 71070
E: selfcater@dale-head-hall.co.uk
I: www.daleheadhall.info

Dalrymple ★★★
Contact: Mr David Burton
Lakeland Cottage Holidays,
Melbecks, Keswick CA12 4QX
T: (017687) 76065
F: (017687) 76869
E: info@lakelandcottages.co.uk
I: www.lakelandcottages.co.uk

Darwin Cottage ★★★
Contact: Mr Peter Durbin
Cumbrian Cottages, 2 Lonsdale
Street, Carlisle CA1 1DB
T: (01228) 599960
F: (01228) 599970
E: enquiries@
cumbrian-cottages.co.uk
I: www.cumbrian-cottages.co.uk

Denholm ★★★
Contact: Mr Peter Durbin
Cumbrian Cottages, 2 Lonsdale
Street, Carlisle CA1 1DB
T: (01228) 599960
F: (01228) 599970
E: enquiries@
cumbrian-cottages.co.uk
I: www.cumbrian-cottages.co.uk

Derwent Cottage ★★★
Contact: Mr Peter Durbin
Cumbrian Cottages, 2 Lonsdale
Street, Carlisle CA1 1DB
T: (01228) 599960
F: (01228) 599970
E: enquiries@cumbriancottages.co.uk
I: www.cumbrian-cottages.co.uk

Derwent Cottage Mews ★★★★★
Contact: Mrs Susan Newman
Derwent Cottage Mews,
Portinscale, Keswick CA12 5RF
T: (017687) 74838
E: enquiries@dercott.demon.co.uk
I: www.dercott.demon.co.uk

Derwent House and Brandelhowe ★★★
Contact: Mr & Mrs Oliver Bull
Derwent House Holidays, Stone
Heath, Hilderstone ST15 8SH
T: (01889) 505678
F: (01889) 505679
I: www.dhholidays-lakes.com

Derwent Manor ★★★★
Contact: Mrs C Denwood
Derwent Manor, Portinscale,
Keswick CA12 5RE
T: (017687) 72538
F: (017687) 71002
E: info@derwentwater-hotel.co.uk
I: www.derwent-manor.co.uk

Dove House ★★★
Contact: Susan Jackson
Heart of the Lakes, Fisherbeck
Mill, Old Lake Road, Ambleside
LA22 0DH
T: (015394) 32321
F: (015394) 33251
E: info@heartofthelakes.co.uk
I: www.heartofthelakes.co.uk

Dowthwaite ★★★★
Contact: Susan Jackson
Heart of the Lakes, Fisherbeck
Mill, Old Lake Road, Ambleside
LA22 0DH
T: (015394) 32321
F: (015394) 33251
E: info@heartofthelakes.co.uk
I: www.heartofthelakes.co.uk

Duck Pool ★★★
Contact: Mr David Burton
Lakeland Cottage Holidays,
Melbecks, Keswick CA12 4QX
T: (017687) 76065
F: (017687) 76869
E: info@lakelandcottages.co.uk
I: www.lakelandcottages.co.uk

Dunmallet ★★★
Contact: Mr Peter Durbin
Cumbrian Cottages, 2 Lonsdale
Street, Carlisle CA1 1DB
T: (01228) 599960
F: (01228) 599970
E: enquiries@cumbriancottages.co.uk
I: www.cumbrian-cottages.co.uk

14 Elm Court ★★★
Contact: Mr Peter Durbin
Cumbrian Cottages, 2 Lonsdale
Street, Carlisle CA1 1DB
T: (01228) 599960
F: (01228) 599970
E: enquiries@
cumbrian-cottages.co.uk
I: www.cumbrian-cottages.co.uk

CUMBRIA – THE LAKE DISTRICT

15 Elm Court ★★★★
Contact: Mr Peter Durbin
Cumbrian Cottages, 2 Lonsdale Street, Carlisle CA1 1DB
T: (01228) 599960
F: (01228) 599970
E: enquiries@cumbriancottages.co.uk
I: www.cumbrian-cottages.co.uk

9 Elm Court ★★★
Contact: Mr Peter Durbin
Cumbrian Cottages, 2 Lonsdale Street, Carlisle CA1 1DB
T: (01228) 599960
F: (01228) 599970
E: enquiries@cumbrian-cottages.co.uk
I: www.cumbrian-cottages.co.uk

Elmcot & Little Haven ★★★★
Contact: Mr Arun & Ajoy Roy
48 Geary Road, Dollis Hill, London NW10 1HH
T: (020) 84523695
F: (020) 8452 3695
E: info.keswickholiday@btopenworld.com
I: www.keswickholiday.co.uk

Fell View ★★★
Contact: Mr Peter Durbin
Cumbrian Cottages, 2 Lonsdale Street, Carlisle CA1 1DB
T: (01228) 599960
F: (01228) 599970
E: enquiries@cumbriancottages.co.uk
I: www.cumbrian-cottages.co.uk

Fell View Lodge ★★★★
Contact: Mr Peter Durbin
Cumbrian Cottages, 2 Lonsdale Street, Carlisle CA1 1DB
T: (01228) 599960
F: (01228) 599970
E: enquiries@cumbrian-cottages.co.uk
I: www.cumbrian-cottages.co.uk

The Fells ★★★★
Contact: Mr Peter Durbin
Cumbrian Cottages, 2 Lonsdale Street, Carlisle CA1 1DB
T: (01228) 599960
F: (01228) 599970
E: enquiries@cumbrian-cottages.co.uk
I: www.cumbrian-cottages.co.uk

Fernbank House ★★★★★
Contact: Stephen Mason
Stonegarth Guest House, 2 Eskin Street, Keswick CA12 4DH
T: (017687) 72436
E: info@fernbankhouse.com
I: www.fernbankhouse.com

Ferndale ★★★
Contact: Mr David Burton
Lakeland Cottage Holidays, Melbecks, Keswick CA12 4QX
T: (017687) 76065
F: (017687) 76869
E: info@lakelandcottages.co.uk
I: www.lakelandcottages.co.uk

Fieldside Grange ★★★-★★★★
Contact: Nicholas Gillham
Kingsfell and Kingstarn, 3 Salisbury House, Abbey Mills, Abbey Mill Lane, St Albans AL3 4HG
T: (01727) 853531
F: (01727) 851338

Fieldside Lodge ★★★★★
Contact: Mr Peter Durbin
Cumbrian Cottages, 2 Lonsdale Street, Carlisle CA1 1DB
T: (01228) 599960
F: (01228) 599970
E: enquiries@cumbrian-cottages.co.uk
I: www.cumbrian-cottages.co.uk

Fornside Farm Cottages ★★★★
Contact: Mr & Mrs Hall
Fornside Farm Cottages, Fornside Farm, Keswick CA12 4TS
T: (017687) 79173
E: cottages@fornside.co.uk
I: www.fornside.co.uk

Fountain Cottage ★★★★
Contact: Dr & Mrs Preston
Bannest Hill Cottage & Fountain Cottage, Bannest Hill House, Haltcliff Heskett Newmarket, Wigton CA7 8JT
T: (01768) 484394
F: (01768) 484394
E: stay@bannesthill.co.uk
I: www.bannesthill.co.uk

Friars Cottage ★★★★
Contact: Mr Peter Durbin
Cumbrian Cottages, 2 Lonsdale Street, Carlisle CA1 1DB
T: (01228) 599960
F: (01228) 599970
E: enquiries@cumbrian-cottages.co.uk
I: www.cumbrian-cottages.co.uk

Friars Crag ★★★
Contact: Mr Peter Durbin
Cumbrian Cottages, 2 Lonsdale Street, Carlisle CA1 1DB
T: (01228) 599960
F: (01228) 599970
E: enquiries@cumbriancottages.co.uk
I: www.cumbrian-cottages.co.uk

Gable Cottage ★★★
Contact: Mr Peter Durbin
Cumbrian Cottages, 2 Lonsdale Street, Carlisle CA1 1DB
T: (01228) 599960
F: (01228) 599970
E: enquiries@cumbriancottages.co.uk
I: www.cumbrian-cottages.co.uk

Gable Cottage ★★★★
Contact: David Burton
Lakeland Cottage Holidays, Melbecks, Keswick CA12 4QX
T: (017687) 76065
F: (017687) 76869
E: info@lakelandcottages.co.uk
I: www.lakelandcottages.co.uk

Gabriel's Cottage ★★★★
Contact: Mr Peter Durbin
Cumbrian Cottages, 2 Lonsdale Street, Carlisle CA1 1DB
T: (01228) 599960
F: (01228) 599970
E: enquiries@cumbrian-cottages.co.uk

Glaramara ★★★★
Contact: Mr Peter Durbin
Cumbrian Cottages, 2 Lonsdale Street, Carlisle CA1 1DB
T: (01228) 599960
F: (01228) 599970
E: enquiries@cumbriancottages.co.uk
I: www.cumbrian-cottages.co.uk

Glendera ★★★
Contact: Mr David Burton
Lakeland Cottage Holidays, Melbecks, Keswick CA12 4QX
T: (017687) 76065
F: (017687) 76869
E: info@lakelandcottages.co.uk
I: www.lakelandcottages.co.uk

Glenmore ★★★
Contact: Mr Peter Durbin
Cumbrian Cottages, 2 Lonsdale Street, Carlisle CA1 1DB
T: (01228) 599960
F: (01228) 599970
E: enquiries@cumbrian-cottages.co.uk
I: www.cumbrian-cottages.co.uk

Greenbank ★★★
Contact: Mr Peter Durbin
Cumbrian Cottages, 2 Lonsdale Street, Carlisle CA1 1DB
T: (01228) 599960
F: (01228) 599970
E: enquiries@cumbrian-cottages.co.uk
I: www.cumbrian-cottages.co.uk

17 Greta Grove House ★★★★
Contact: Mr Peter Durbin
Cumbrian Cottages, 2 Lonsdale Street, Carlisle CA1 1DB
T: (01228) 599960
F: (01228) 599970
E: enquiries@cumbriancottages.co.uk
I: www.cumbrian-cottages.co.uk

2 Greta Grove House ★★★★
Contact: Mr Peter Durbin
Cumbrian Cottages, 2 Lonsdale Street, Carlisle CA1 1DB
T: (01228) 599960
F: (01228) 599970
E: enquiries@cumbriancottages.co.uk
I: www.cumbrian-cottages.co.uk

Greta Side Court ★★★
Contact: John & Laura Atkinson
Greta Side Court, 3 Felsted, Lancashire, Bolton BL1 5EY
T: (01204) 493138
E: johnlaura3@btopenworld.com

1 Greta Side Court ★★★
Contact: Mr Peter Durbin
Cumbrian Cottages, 2 Lonsdale Street, Carlisle CA1 1DB
T: (01228) 599960
F: (01228) 599970
E: enquiries@cumbriancottages.co.uk
I: www.cumbrian-cottages.co.uk

2 Greta Side Court ★★★
Contact: Mr Peter Durbin
Cumbrian Cottages, 2 Lonsdale Street, Carlisle CA1 1DB
T: (01228) 599960
F: (01228) 599970
E: enquiries@cumbrian-cottage.co.uk
I: www.cumbrian-cottages.co.uk

4 Greta Side Court ★★★
Contact: Mr Peter Durbin
Cumbrian Cottages, 2 Lonsdale Street, Carlisle CA1 1DB
T: (01228) 599960
F: (01228) 599970
E: enquiries@cumbrian-cottage.co.uk
I: www.cumbrian-cottages.co.uk

Gretaside ★★★
Contact: Mr Cowman
10 The Forge, High Hill, Keswick CA12 5NX
T: (017687) 72650
E: ajcowman@hotmail.com

Haystacks ★★★
Contact: Mr Peter Durbin
Cumbrian Cottages, 2 Lonsdale Street, Carlisle CA1 1DB
T: (01228) 599960
F: (01228) 599970
E: enquiries@cumbrian-cottages.co.uk
I: www.cumbrian-cottages.co.uk

Herries ★★★
Contact: Mr David Burton
Lakeland Cottage Holidays, Melbecks, Keswick CA12 4QX
T: (017687) 76065
F: (017687) 76869
E: info@lakelandcottages.co.uk
I: www.lakelandcottages.co.uk

High Hill Farm Cottage ★★★★
Contact: Mr Peter Durbin
Cumbrian Cottages, 2 Lonsdale Street, Carlisle CA1 1DB
T: (01228) 599960
F: (01228) 599970
E: enquiries@cumbrian-cottages.co.uk
I: www.cumbrian-cottages.co.uk

High Rigg ★★★★
Contact: Mr Sayer
High Rigg, Fasnakyle, Oldhill Wood, Dunstable LU6 2NF
T: (01582) 872574

High Spy
Rating Applied For
Contact: Mr David Burton
Lakeland Cottage Holidays, Melbecks, Keswick CA12 4QX
T: (017687) 76065
F: (017687) 76869
E: info@lakelandcottages.co.uk
I: www.lakelandcottages.co.uk

Highbank ★★★★
Contact: Mr Peter Durbin
Cumbrian Cottages, 2 Lonsdale Street, Carlisle CA1 1DB
T: (01228) 599960
F: (01228) 599970
E: enquiries@cumbriancottages.co.uk
I: www.cumbrian-cottages.co.uk

Establishments printed in blue have a detailed entry in this guide

CUMBRIA – THE LAKE DISTRICT

Holly Cottage ★★★★
Contact: Richard Wilson
Holly Cottage, 92 Banner Cross
Road, Ecclesall, Sheffield
S11 9HR
T: (0114) 296 0491
F: (0114) 296 0491
E: r.e.t.wilson@btinternet.com
I: www.hollycottage.info

11 Howrah's Court ★★★★
Contact: Mr Peter Durbin
Cumbrian Cottages, 2 Lonsdale
Street, Carlisle CA1 1DB
T: (01228) 599960
F: (01228) 599970
E: enquiries@cumbriancottages.co.uk
I: www.cumbrian-cottages.co.uk

Keswick Cottages ★★★-★★★★★
Contact: Lynn Rimmer
Keswick Cottages, Broughton
Park, Cockermouth CA13 0XW
T: (017687) 73895
E: info@keswickcottages.co.uk
I: www.keswickcottages.co.uk

Keswick Timeshare ★★★★
Contact: Mr David Etherden
Keswick Timeshare Limited,
Keswick Bridge, Brundholme
Road, Keswick CA12 4NL
T: (017687) 73591
F: (017687) 75811
E: enquiries@keswickb.com
I: www.keswickb.com

Kiln Hill Barn Self-Catering ★★★
Contact: J K Armstrong
Cumbrian Cottages, Keswick
CA12 4RG
T: (017687) 76454
E: ken@kilnhillbarn.freeserve.co.uk
I: www.kilnhillbarn.co.uk

Kingsfell and Kingstarn ★★★★
Contact: Nicholas Gillham
Kingsfell and Kingstarn, 3
Salisbury House, Abbey Mills,
Abbey Mill Lane, St Albans
AL3 4HG
T: (01727) 853531
F: (01727) 851338

Kintail ★★★★★
Contact: Mr Peter Durbin
Cumbrian Cottages, 2 Lonsdale
Street, Carlisle CA1 1DB
T: (01228) 599960
F: (01228) 599970
E: enquiries@cumbrian-cottages.co.uk
I: www.cumbrian-cottages.co.uk

Kylesku ★★★
Contact: Mr Peter Durbin
Cumbrian Cottages, 2 Lonsdale
Street, Carlisle CA1 1DB
T: (01228) 599960
F: (01228) 599970
E: enquiries@cumbrian-cottages.co.uk
I: www.cumbrian-cottages.co.uk

Latrigg View ★★★★
Contact: Mr Peter Durbin
Cumbrian Cottages, 2 Lonsdale
Street, Carlisle CA1 1DB
T: (01228) 599960
F: (01228) 599970
E: enquiries@cumbrian-cottages.co.uk
I: www.cumbrian-cottages.co.uk

Leander ★★★★
Contact: Mr Peter Durbin
Cumbrian Cottages, 2 Lonsdale
Street, Carlisle CA1 1DB
T: (01228) 599960
F: (01228) 599970
E: enquiries@cumbrian-cottages.co.uk
I: www.cumbrian-cottages.co.uk

Little Chestnut Hill ★★★
Contact: Mr David Burton
Lakeland Cottage Holidays,
Melbecks, Keswick CA12 4QX
T: (017687) 76065
F: (017687) 76869
E: info@lakelandcottages.co.uk
I: www.lakelandcottages.co.uk

1 Lonsdale House ★★★★
Contact: Mr Durbin
Cumbrian Cottages, 2 Lonsdale
Street, Carlisle CA1 1DB
T: (01228) 599960
F: (01228) 599970
E: enquiries@cumbrian-cottages.co.uk
I: www.cumbrian-cottages.co.uk

5 Lonsdale House ★★★★
Contact: Mr Peter Durbin
Cumbrian Cottages, 2 Lonsdale
Street, Carlisle CA1 1DB
T: (01228) 599960
F: (01228) 599970
E: enquiries@cumbrian-cottages.co.uk
I: www.cumbrian-cottages.co.uk

Low Briery Holiday Village ★★★★
Contact: Mr Michael Atkinson
Low Briery Holiday Village,
Penrith Road, Keswick
CA12 4RN
T: (017687) 72044
F: (017687) 72044
I: www.keswick.uk.com

Loweswater ★★★★
Contact: Mr Paul Durbin
Cumbrian Cottages, 2 Lonsdale
Street, Carlisle CA1 1DB
T: (01228) 599960
F: (01228) 599970
E: enquiries@cumbriancottages.co.uk
I: www.cumbrian-cottage.co.uk

Luxurious Lakeland ★★-★★★
Contact: John Mitchell
Luxurious Lakeland, 6
Crosthwaite Gardens, Keswick
CA12 5QF
T: (017687) 72790
F: (017687) 75750

8 Lydia's Cottages ★★★★
Contact: Jean Hutchinson
8 Lydia's Cottages, 6 Mountain
View, Keswick CA12 5XH
T: (017687) 77631
E: jean@jhutch.demon.co.uk
I: www.jhutch.demon.co.uk/jean/lydias.htm

Meadow Cottage ★★★
Contact: Mr David Burton
Lakeland Cottage Holidays,
Melbecks, Keswick CA12 4QX
T: (017687) 76065
F: (017687) 76869
E: info@lakelandcottages.co.uk
I: www.lakelandcottages.co.uk

Michaels Cottage ★★★★
Contact: Mr Peter Durbin & Tony
Commons
Cumbrian Cottages, 2 Lonsdale
Street, Carlisle CA1 1DB
T: (01228) 599960
F: (01228) 599970
E: enquiries@cumbrian-cottages.co.uk
I: www.cumbrian-cottages.co.uk

Mill House ★★★★
Contact: Mr Peter Durbin
Cumbrian Cottages, 2 Lonsdale
Street, Carlisle CA1 1DB
T: (01228) 599960
F: (01228) 599970
E: enquiries@cumbrian-cottages.co.uk
I: www.cumbrian-cottages.co.uk

Millbeck Cottages ★★★★
Contact: Mr Peter Durbin
Cumbrian Cottages, 2 Lonsdale
Street, Carlisle CA1 1DB
T: (01228) 599960
F: (01228) 599970
E: enquiries@cumbrian-cottages.co.uk
I: www.cumbrian-cottages.co.uk

Mountain View ★★★
Contact: Mr Peter Durbin
Cumbrian Cottages, 2 Lonsdale
Street, Carlisle CA1 1DB
T: (01228) 599960
F: (01228) 599970
E: enquiries@cumbriancottages.co.uk
I: www.cumbrian-cottages.co.uk

Newlands View ★★★★
Contact: Mr David Burton
Lakeland Cottage Holidays,
Melbecks, Keswick CA12 4QX
T: (017687) 76065
F: (017687) 76869
E: info@lakelandcottages.co.uk
I: www.lakelandcottages.co.uk

Olivet ★★★
Contact: Mr Peter Durbin
Cumbrian Cottages, 2 Lonsdale
Street, Carlisle CA1 1DB
T: (01228) 599960
F: (01228) 599970
E: enquiries@cumbriancottages.co.uk
I: www.cumbrian-cottages.co.uk

Orchard Barn ★★★
Contact: Mr & Mrs Hall
Fisherground Farm, Eskdale
CA19 1TF
T: (01946) 723319
E: holidays@fisherground.co.uk
I: www.orchardhouseholidays.co.uk

Packhorse ★★★
Contact: Mr Peter Durbin
Cumbrian Cottages, 2 Lonsdale
Street, Carlisle CA1 1DB
T: (01228) 599960
F: (01228) 599970
E: enquiries@cumbrian-cottages.co.uk
I: www.cumbrian-cottages.co.uk

Peak View ★★★★
Contact: The Owner
Peak View, 9 Royal Oak Appt,
Station Street, Keswick
CA12 5HH

10 The Plosh ★★★★
Contact: Mr Peter Durbin
Cumbrian Cottages, 2 Lonsdale
Street, Carlisle CA1 1DB
T: (01228) 599960
F: (01228) 599970
E: enquiries@cumbrlan-cottages.co.uk
I: www.cumbrian-cottages.co.uk

Poet's Corner ★★★★
Contact: Mr Paul Liddell
Lakelovers, Belmont House, Lake
Road, Bowness-on-Windermere,
Windermere LA23 3BJ
T: (015394) 88855
F: (015394) 88857
E: bookings@lakelovers.co.uk
I: www.lakelovers.co.uk

Poplar Cottage ★★★
Contact: Mr Peter Durbin
Cumbrian Cottages, 2 Lonsdale
Street, Carlisle CA1 1DB
T: (01228) 599960
F: (01228) 599970
E: enquiries@cumbrian-cottages.co.uk
I: www.cumbrian-cottages.co.uk

Primrose Cottage ★★★★
Contact: Mr Geoff & Mrs Julia
Holloway
Bramble Cottage, Helmingham
Road, Ipswich IP6 9NS
T: (01473) 890035
E: primrose.cott@btinternet.com
I: www.primrose.cott.btinternet.co.uk

Ptarmigan House ★★★
Contact: Mr Peter Durbin
Cumbrian Cottages, 2 Lonsdale
Street, Carlisle CA1 1DB
T: (01228) 599960
F: (01228) 599970
E: enquiries@cumbrian-cottages.co.uk
I: www.cumbrian-cottages.co.uk

Quintok ★★★★
Contact: Mr David Burton
Lakeland Cottage Holidays,
Melbecks, Keswick CA12 4QX
T: (017687) 76065
F: (017687) 76869
E: info@lakelandcottages.co.uk
I: www.lakelandcottages.co.uk

24 Ratcliffe Place ★★★
Contact: Mrs W Plant
24 Ratcliffe Place, 102 Church
Lane, Leeds LS25 1NR
T: (0113) 286 3737
E: wendy@plant.go-legend.net

CUMBRIA – THE LAKE DISTRICT

The Retreat ★★★
Contact: Mr Peter Durbin
Cumbrian Cottages, 2 Lonsdale Street, Carlisle CA1 1DB
T: (01228) 599960
F: (01228) 599970
E: enquiries@cumbrian-cottages.co.uk
I: www.cumbrian-cottages.co.uk

Rheda Cottage ★★★★
Contact: Mr Peter Durbin
Cumbrian Cottages, 2 Lonsdale Street, Carlisle CA1 1DB
T: (01228) 599960
F: (01228) 599970
E: enquiries@cumbrian-cottages.co.uk
I: www.cumbrian-cottages.co.uk

Rivendell ★★★
Contact: Mr David Burton
Lakeland Cottage Holidays, Melbecks, Keswick CA12 4QX
T: (017687) 76065
F: (017687) 76869
E: info@lakelandcottages.co.uk
I: www.lakelandcottages.co.uk

Riverside Cottage ★★★★
Contact: Daphne Barron
Riverside Cottage, Fell View, Keswick CA12 4QP
T: (017687) 76007
E: info@riversideholidays.com
I: www.riversideholidays.com

Riverside Cottage ★★★
Contact: Mrs Susan Jackson
Heart of the Lakes, Fisherbeck Mill, Old Lake Road, Ambleside LA22 0DH
T: (015394) 32321
F: (015394) 33251
E: info@heartofthelakes.co.uk
I: www.heartofthelakes.co.uk

Robin's Nest ★★★★
Contact: Mr Peter Durbin
Cumbrian Cottages, 2 Lonsdale Street, Carlisle CA1 1DB
T: (01228) 599960
F: (01228) 599970
E: enquiries@cumbriancottages.co.uk
I: www.cumbrian-cottages.co.uk

Rock House ★★★★
Contact: Mrs Susan Jackson
Heart of the Lakes, Fisherbeck Mill, Old Lake Road, Ambleside LA22 0DH
T: (015394) 32321
F: (015394) 33251
E: info@heartofthelakes.co.uk
I: www.heartofthelakes.co.uk

Rosemary Cottage ★★★★
Contact: Mrs Susan Jackson
Heart of the Lakes, Fisherbeck Mill, Old Lake Road, Ambleside LA22 0DH
T: (015394) 33110
F: (015394) 33251
E: info@heartofthelakes.co.uk
I: www.heartofthelakes.co.uk

The Rowans ★★★
Contact: Mr Peter Durbin
Cumbrian Cottages, 2 Lonsdale Street, Carlisle CA1 1DB
T: (01228) 599960
F: (01228) 599970
E: enquiries@cumbriancottages.co.uk
I: www.cumbrian-cottages.co.uk

Rowanwood & Beechwood ★★★
Contact: Mr & Mrs Davison
Rowanwood & Beechwood, Northfield House, Northfield Drive, Mansfield NG18 3DD
T: (01623) 627370

Saddleback Cottage ★★★
Contact: Mr Peter Durbin
Cumbrian Cottages, 2 Lonsdale Street, Carlisle CA1 1DB
T: (01228) 599960
F: (01228) 599970
E: enquiries@cumbrian-cottages.co.uk
I: www.cumbrian-cottages.co.uk

St Herbert's Cottage ★★★
Contact: Mr David Etherden
Keswick Holidays Ltd, Keswick Bridge, Brundholme Road, Keswick CA12 4NL
T: (017687) 73200
F: (017687) 75811
E: enquiries@keswickb.com
I: www.keswick.com/self-catering/st-herberts-cottage

Sandburne Cottage ★★★★
Contact: Susan Jackson
Heart of the Lakes, Fisherbeck Mill, Old Lake Road, Ambleside LA22 0DH
T: (015394) 32321
F: (015394) 33251

Shelter Stone ★★★
Contact: Mr David Burton
Lakeland Cottage Holidays, Melbecks, Keswick CA12 4QX
T: (017687) 76065
F: (017687) 76869
E: info@lakelandcottages.co.uk
I: www.lakelandcottags.co.uk

The Shieling ★★★★
Contact: Mr Peter Durbin
Cumbrian Cottages, 2 Lonsdale Street, Carlisle CA1 1DB
T: (01228) 599960
F: (01228) 599970
E: enquiries@cumbrian-cottages.co.uk
I: www.cumbrian-cottages.co.uk

Skiddaw View ★★★
Contact: Mr Peter Durbin
Cumbrian Cottages, 2 Lonsdale Street, Carlisle CA1 1DB
T: (01228) 599960
F: (01228) 599970
E: enquiries@cumbrian-cottages.co.uk
I: www.cumbrian-cottages.co.uk

Slate Cottage ★★★★
Contact: Mr Peter Durbin
Cumbrian Cottages, 2 Lonsdale Street, Carlisle CA1 1DB
T: (01228) 599960
F: (01228) 599970
E: enquiries@cumbriancottages.co.uk
I: www.cumbrian-cottages.co.uk

South View ★★★★★
Contact: Mrs Susan Jackson
Heart of the Lakes, Fisherbeck Mill, Old Lake Road, Ambleside LA22 0DH
T: (015394) 32321
F: (015394) 33251
E: info@heartofthelakes.co.uk
I: www.heartofthelakes.co.uk

Sprys View Cottage ★★★
Contact: Mr Peter Durbin
Cumbrian Cottages, 2 Lonsdale Street, Carlisle CA1 1DB
T: (01228) 599960
F: (01228) 599970
E: enquiries@cumbrian-cottages.co.uk
I: www.cumbrian-cottages.co.uk

Squirrel Cottage ★★★
Contact: Mr David Burton
Lakeland Holiday Cottages, Melbecks, Keswick CA12 4QX
T: (017687) 76065
F: (017687) 76869
E: info@lakelandcottages.co.uk
I: www.lakelandcottages.co.uk

The Steps ★★★★
Contact: The Owner
The Steps, 15 The Plosh, Borrowdale Road, Keswick CA12 5DE

Stone Ledges ★★★
Contact: Mr Peter Durbin
Cumbrian Cottages, 2 Lonsdale Street, Carlisle CA1 1DB
T: (01228) 599960
F: (01228) 599970
E: enquiries@cumbriancottages.co.uk
I: www.cumbrian-cottages.co.uk

Stone Steps ★★★
Contact: Mr Peter Durbin
Cumbrian Cottages, 2 Lonsdale Street, Carlisle CA1 1DB
T: (01228) 599960
F: (01228) 599970
E: enquiries@cumbrian-cottages.co.uk
I: www.cumbrian-cottages.co.uk

Sunnybank Cottage ★★★
Contact: Mr Peter Durbin
Cumbrian Cottages, 2Lonsdale Street, Carlisle CA1 1DB
T: (01228) 599960
F: (01228) 599970
E: enquiries@cumbrian-cottage.co.uk
I: www.cumbrian-cottages.co.uk

Threeways ★★★★
Contact: Mr Peter Durbin
Cumbrian Cottages, 2 Lonsdale Street, Carlisle CA1 1DB
T: (01228) 599960
F: (01228) 599970
E: enquiries@cumbriancottages.co.uk
I: www.cumbrian-cottages.co.uk

Topsey Turvey ★★★★
Contact: Mr Peter Durbin
Cumbrian Cottages, 2 Lonsdale Street, Carlisle CA1 1DB
T: (01228) 599960
F: (01228) 599970
E: enquiries@cumbrian-cottages.co.uk
I: www.cumbrian-cottages.co.uk

Twentymans Court ★★★
Contact: Mr Peter Durbin
Cumbrian Cottages, 2 Lonsdale Street, Carlisle CA1 1DB
T: (01228) 599960
F: (01228) 599970
E: enquiries@cumbrian-cottages.co.uk
I: www.cumbrian-cottages.co.uk

Underne ★★★
Contact: Mr David Burton
Lakeland Cottage Holidays, Melbecks, Keswick CA12 4QX
T: (017687) 76065
F: (017687) 76869
E: info@lakelandcottages.co.uk
I: www.lakelandcottages.co.uk

Underscar ★★★★★
Contact: Susan Jackson
Heart of the Lakes, Fisherbeck Mill, Old Lake Road, Ambleside LA22 0DH
T: (015394) 32321
F: (015394) 33251

Upton Glen ★★★
Contact: Mr Peter Durbin
Cumbrian Cottages, 2 Lonsdale Street, Carlisle CA1 1DB
T: (01228) 599960
F: (01228) 599970
E: enquiries@cumbrian-cottages.co.uk
I: www.cumbrian-cottages.co.uk

Wendover ★★★
Contact: Mr Peter Durbin
Cumbrian Cottages, 2 Lonsdale Street, Carlisle CA1 1DB
T: (01228) 599960
F: (01228) 599970
E: enquiries@cumbrian-cottages.co.uk
I: www.cumbrian-cottages.co.uk

Westies ★★★
Contact: Mr David Burton
Lakeland Cottage Holidays, Melbecks, Keswick CA12 4QX
T: (017687) 76065
F: (017687) 76869
E: info@lakelandcottages.co.uk
I: www.lakelandcottages.co.uk

Whinridge ★★★
Contact: Mr David Burton
Lakeland Cottage Holidays, Melbrecks, Keswick CA12 4QX
T: (017687) 76065
F: (017687) 76869
E: info@lakelandcottages.co.uk
I: www.lakelandcottages.co.uk

White Wicket ★★★
Contact: Mr Peter Durbin
Cumbrian Cottages, 2 Lonsdale Street, Carlisle CA1 1DB
T: (01228) 599960
F: (01228) 599970
E: enquiries@cumbrian-cottages.co.uk
I: www.cumbrian-cottages.co.uk

Woodleigh ★★★★
Contact: Mr Peter Durbin
Cumbrian Cottages, 2 Lonsdale Street, Carlisle CA1 1DB
T: (01228) 599960
F: (01228) 599970
E: enquiries@cumbrian-cottages.co.uk
I: www.cumbrian-cottages.co.uk

KILLINGTON
Cumbria

Ghyll Stile Mill Cottage ★★★
Contact: Janet & Nick Chetwood
Ghyll Stile Mill Cottage, Sedbergh LA10 5EH
T: (015396) 21715
E: janetghyll@aol.com
I: www.ghyll-stile-mill-cottage.co.uk

Establishments printed in blue have a detailed entry in this guide

CUMBRIA – THE LAKE DISTRICT

Valley View & The Granary ★★★
Contact: Mr Isabel & Mrs Peter Sugden
Greenholme, Sedbergh LA10 5EP
T: (015396) 21153
E: peter@greenholme.fsnet.co.uk
I: www.greenholme.fsnet.co.uk

KING'S MEABURN
Cumbria

Lyvennet Cottages ★★★-★★★★
Contact: Mrs Margaret & Wendy & Janet Addison
Lyvennet Cottages, Keld, King's Meaburn, Penrith CA10 3BS
T: (01931) 714226
F: (01931) 714598
E: info@lyvennetcottages.co.uk
I: www.lyvennetcottages.co.uk

KIRKBY LONSDALE
Cumbria

Nutshell Barn
Rating Applied For
Contact: Mr Stephen Wightman
Keerdale Barn, Carnforth LA6 1AD
T: (01524) 733865
F: (01524) 733948
E: sj@nutshell-barn.fsnet.co.uk
I: www.nutshell-barn.fsnet.co.uk

The Old Stables ★★★★
Contact: Mr Peter Durbin
Cumbrian Cottages, 2 Lonsdale Street, Carlisle CA1 1DB
T: (01228) 599960
F: (01228) 599970
E: enquiries@cumbrian-cottages.co.uk
I: www.cumbrian-cottages.co.uk

Sellet Hall Cottages ★★★★
Contact: Mrs Hall
Sellet Hall Cottages, Sellet Hall, Hosticle Lane, Carnforth LA6 2QF
T: (01524) 271865
E: sellethall@hotmail.com
I: www.sellethall.com

Wisteria Cottage ★★★★
Contact: Mr Peter Durbin
Cumbrian Cottages, 2 Lonsdale Street, Carlisle CA1 1DB
T: (01228) 599960
F: (01228) 599970
E: enquiries@cumbrian-cottages.co.uk
I: www.cumbrian-cottages.co.uk

KIRKBY STEPHEN
Cumbria

Hatygill Cottage ★★★
Contact: The Manager
Ref: 1459, Dales Holiday Cottages, Carleton Business Park, Carleton New Road, Skipton BD23 2AA
T: (01756) 790919
F: (01756) 797012
E: info@dalesholcot.com
I: www.dalesholcot.com

Pennistone Green ★★★★
Contact: Mrs Susan Jackson
Ashmere, Rakes Road, Bakewell DE45 1JL
T: (01629) 815683
E: jackson@ashmere.fsnet.co.uk
I: www.uk-holiday-cottages.info

Swallows Barn ★★★★
Contact: Mrs Atkinson
Swallows Barn, Augill House Farm, Kirkby Stephen CA17 4DX
T: (017683) 41272 & 62321
F: (017683) 41272
E: edengrove.cumbria@aol.com
I: www.ukworld.net/swallowsbarn

KIRKBY THORE
Cumbria

Holme Lea ★★★
Contact: Mr Alan Price
27 Church Close, Norwich NR10 5ER
T: (01603) 279713
E: jprice@albatross.co.uk

KIRKLINTON
Cumbria

Dovecote ★★★★
Contact: Sherann Chandley
Dovecote, Cleughside Farm, Carlisle CA6 6BE
T: (01228) 675650
F: (01228) 675870
E: slc@cleughside.co.uk
I: www.cleughside.co.uk

Keepers Cottage ★★★★
Contact: Pat Armstrong
Keepers Cottage, Slealands, Carlisle CA6 5RQ
T: (01228) 791378
E: info@keepers-cottage.co.uk
I: www.keepers-cottage.co.uk

KIRKOSWALD
Cumbria

Crossfield Cottages ★★★
Contact: Mrs Susan Bottom
Crossfield Cottages, Staffield, Penrith CA10 1EU
T: (01768) 898711
F: (01768) 898711
E: info@crossfieldcottages.co.uk
I: www.crossfieldcottages.co.uk

Howscales ★★★★
Contact: Liz Webster
Howscales, Penrith CA10 1JG
T: (01768) 898666
F: (01768) 898710
E: liz@howscales.co.uk
I: www.howscales.co.uk

LAKESIDE
Cumbria

Deer Rise ★★★★
Contact: Paul Liddell
Lakelovers, Belmont House, Lake Road, Bowness-on-Windermere, Windermere LA23 3BJ
T: (015394) 88855
F: (015394) 88857
E: bookings@lakelovers.co.uk
I: www.lakelovers.co.uk

Fir Tree Lodge ★★★★
Contact: Paul Liddell
Lakelovers, Belmont House, Lake Road, Bowness-on-Windermere, Windermere LA23 3BJ
T: (015394) 88855
F: (015394) 88857
E: bookings@lakelovers.co.uk
I: www.lakelovers.co.uk

Nutwood ★★★★
Contact: Paul Liddell
Lakelovers, Belmont House, Lake Road, Bowness-on-Windermere, Windermere LA23 3BJ
T: (015394) 88855
F: (015394) 88857
E: bookings@lakelovers.co.uk
I: www.lakelovers.co.uk

2 Stock Park Mansion ★★★
Contact: Diane Watson
17 Argarmeols Road, Formby, Merseyside, Liverpool L37 7BX
T: (01704) 871144
E: rogerwatson@ic24.net

LAMONBY
Cumbria

Half Crown Cottage ★★★★
Contact: Mr Paul Durbin
Cumbrian Cottages, 2 Lonsdale Street, Carlisle CA1 1DB
T: (01228) 599960
F: (01228) 599970
I: www.cumbrian-cottages.co.uk

LAMPLUGH
Cumbria

2 Folly ★★★★
Contact: Alison Wilson
2 Folly, Dockray Nook, Workington CA14 4SH
T: (01946) 861151

LANGDALE
Cumbria

2 & 7 Lingmoor View ★★★
Contact: Mr Batho
High Hollin Bank, Coniston LA21 8AG
T: (015394) 41680
E: a.batho@virgin.net
I: www.cottagescumbria.com

Long House Cottages ★★★
Contact: Mr Grayston
Long House, Ambleside LA22 9JS
T: (015394) 37222
E: enquiries@longhousecottages.co.uk
I: www.longhousecottages.co.uk

The Maple Loft ★★★
Contact: Mrs Susan Jackson
Heart of the Lakes, Fisherbeck Mill, Old Lake Road, Ambleside LA22 0DH
T: (015394) 33110
F: (015394) 33251
E: info@heartofthelakes.co.uk
I: www.heartofthelakes.co.uk

Maple Tree Holiday Cottages ★★★-★★★★★
Contact: Mrs Judith Fry
Maple Tree Holiday Cottages, Contrast, Ambleside LA22 9HW
T: (015394) 37210
F: (015394) 37311

Meadow Bank ★★★-★★★★★
Contact: Pat & Robert Locke
Elterwater Investments Ltd, 17 Shay Lane, Hale Barns, Altrincham WA15 8NZ
T: (0161) 904 9445
F: (0161) 904 9877
E: lockemeadow@aol.com
I: www.langdalecottages.co.uk

Tabitha's Cottage ★★★★
Contact: Mrs Susan Jackson
Heart of the Lakes, Fisherbeck Mill, Old Lake Road, Ambleside LA22 0DH
T: (015394) 32321
F: (015394) 33251
E: info@heartofthelakes.co.uk
I: www.heartofthelakes.co.uk

Weir Cottage ★★★
Contact: Mrs Susan Jackson
Heart of the Lakes, Fisherbeck Mill, Old Lake Road, Ambleside LA22 0DH
T: (015394) 33110
F: (015394) 33251
E: info@heartofthelakes.co.uk
I: www.heartofthelakes.co.uk

LANGWATHBY
Cumbria

Byre Cottage ★★★★
Contact: Frances Flower
Byre Cottage, Nibthwaite Eden Garth, Penrith CA10 1NT
T: (01768) 881923
E: francesflower@tiscali.co.uk
I: www.byrecottage.co.uk

LEASGILL
Cumbria

The Cottage ★★★★
Contact: Beverly Keatings
The Cottage, 1 Eversley Gardens, Milnthorpe LA7 7EY
T: (015395) 63008
F: (015395) 62920
E: eversleycottage@going-away.co.uk

LEVENS
Cumbria

Gilpin Farmhouse Cottage ★★★
Contact: Ms Fiona Moody
Dales Holiday Cottages, Carlton Business Park, Carleton New Road, Skipton BD23 2AA
T: (01756) 790919

Greystones East ★★★★
Contact: Mr Paul Durbin
Cumbrian Cottages, 2 Lonsdale Street, Carlisle CA1 1DB
T: (01228) 599960
F: (01228) 599970
E: enquiries@cumbriancottages.co.uk
I: www.cumbrian-cottages.co.uk

The Orchard ★★★
Contact: Mr Peter Durbin
Cumbrian Cottages, 2 Lonsdale Street, Carlisle CA1 1DB
T: (01228) 599960
F: (01228) 599970
E: enquiries@cumbriancottages.co.uk
I: www.cumbrian-cottages.co.uk

Underhill Cottage ★★★★
Contact: Christine Phillips
Underhill Cottage, Underhill, Kendal LA8 8PH
T: (015395) 60298
E: underhillcottage@aol.com
I: www.cottage-in-cumbria.com

---

436 Look out for establishments participating in the National Accessible Scheme

CUMBRIA – THE LAKE DISTRICT

LINDALE
Cumbria

Horseshoe Cottage ★★★★
Contact: Mr Peter Durbin
Cumbrian Cottages, 2 Lonsdale Street, Carlisle CA1 1DB
T: (01228) 599960
F: (01228) 599970
E: enquiries@cumbrian-cottages.co.uk
I: www.cumbrian-cottages.co.uk

The Institute ★★★★
Contact: Mr John Serginson
The Lakeland Cottage Company, Waterside House, Ulverston LA12 8AN
T: (015395) 30024
F: (015395) 31932
E: john@lakelandcottageco.com
I: www.lakelandcottagesco.com

Lavender Cottage ★★★★
Contact: Mr John Serginson
Lakeland Cottage Co, Waterside House, Ulverston LA12 8AN
T: (015395) 30024
F: (015395) 31932
E: john@lakelandcottageco.com

Millers Loft ★★★
Contact: Mr John Serginson
Lakeland Cottage Company, Waterside House, Ulverston LA12 8AN
T: (015395) 30024
F: (015395) 31932
E: john@lakelandcottageco.com
I: www.lakelandcottageco.com

7 New Cottages ★★★
Contact: Mr David & Mrs Margaret Potts
Lindale Property, 37 Egerton Road, Davenport, Stockport SK3 8TQ
T: (0161) 2856867
E: mip10@tiscali.co.uk

Stonebeck ★★★★
Contact: Mr Peter Durbin
Cumbrian Cottages, 2 Lonsdale Street, Carlisle CA1 1DB
T: (01228) 599960
F: (01228) 599970
E: enquiries@cumbrian-cottages.co.uk
I: www.cumbrian-cottages.co.uk

LITTLE LANGDALE
Cumbria

The Bield ★★★★
Contact: Mrs Susan Jackson
Heart of the Lakes, Fisherbeck Mill, Old Lake Road, Ambleside LA22 0DH
T: (015394) 32321
F: (015394) 33251
E: info@heartofthelakes.co.uk
I: www.heartofthelakes.co.uk

Birch House ★★★★
Contact: Paul Liddell
Lakelovers, Belmont House, Lake Road, Bowness-on-Windermere, Windermere LA23 3BJ
T: (015394) 88855
F: (015394) 88857
E: bookings@lakelovers.co.uk
I: www.lakelovers.co.uk

Farra Grain ★★★★
Contact: Susan Jackson
Heart of the Lakes, Fisherbeck Mill, Old Lake Road, Ambleside LA22 0DH
T: (015394) 32321
F: (015394) 33251
E: info@heartofthelakes.co.uk
I: www.heartofthelakes.co.uk

Hacket Forge ★★★
Contact: Judith Amos
Hacket Forge, Ambleside LA22 9NU
T: (015394) 37630
I: www.amblesideonline.co.uk/adverts/hacket/main.html

Highfold Cottage ★★★
Contact: Mrs Blair
8 The Glebe, Chapel Stile, Ambleside LA22 9JT
T: (015394) 37686
I: www.highfoldcottage.co.uk

Lang Parrock ★★★
Contact: Susan Jackson
Heart of the Lakes, Fisherbeck Mill, Old Lake Road, Ambleside LA22 0DH
T: (015394) 32321
F: (015394) 33251
E: info@heartofthelakes.co.uk
I: www.heartofthelakes.co.uk

The Peat House ★★★★
Contact: Mrs Vivien Bass
Wheelwrights Holiday Cottages, Langdale, Ambleside LA22 9HS
T: (015394) 37635
E: enquiries@wheelwrights.com
I: www.wheelwrights.com

Wilson Place Farm ★★★★
Contact: Mrs Vivien Bass
Wheelwrights Holiday Cottages, Langdale, Ambleside LA22 9HS
T: (015394) 37635
E: enquiries@wheelwrights.com
I: www.wheelwrights.com

LITTLE STRICKLAND
Cumbria

Spring Bank ★★★★
Contact: Mrs Joan Ostle
Meadowfield, Little Strickland, Penrith CA10 3EG
T: (01931) 716246
E: springbank17@hotmail.com
I: www.holidaycumbria.co.uk

LONGSLEDDALE
Cumbria

The Coach House ★★★
Contact: Mrs Farmer
The Coach House, Capplebarrow House, Longsleddale, Kendal LA8 9BB
T: (01539) 823686
E: jenyfarmer@aol.com
I: www.capplebarrowcoachhouse.co.uk

Mill Cottage ★★★★
Contact: Mrs Jeanie Thom
Mill Cottage, Kendal LA8 9AZ
T: (01539) 823030
F: (01539) 823030
E: jeanie@corn-mill.fsnet.co.uk

LONGTHWAITE
Cumbria

Castle Lodge
Rating Applied For
Contact: Mrs Susan Jackson
Heart of the Lakes, Fisherbeck Mill, Old Lake Road, Ambleside LA22 0DH
T: (015394) 33110
F: (015394) 33251
I: www.heartofthelakes.co.uk

LORTON
Cumbria

Swaledale Cottage ★★★
Contact: Miss Christine England
Swaledale Cottage, Hope Farm, Cockermouth CA13 9UD
T: (01900) 85226
F: (01900) 85226
I: www.hope-farm-holiday-cottages.co.uk

LOUGHRIGG
Cumbria

Lane head ★★★★
Contact: Mrs Susan Jackson
Heart of the Lakes, Fisherbeck Mill, Old Lake Road, Ambleside LA22 0DH
T: (015394) 32321
F: (015394) 33251
E: info@heartofthelakes.co.uk
I: www.heartofthelakes.co.uk

The Poppies ★★★
Contact: Mrs Susan Jackson
Heart of the Lakes, Fisherbeck Mill, Old Lake Road, Ambleside LA22 0DH
T: (015394) 33110
F: (015394) 33251
E: info@heartofthelakes.co.uk
I: www.heartofthelakes.co.uk

LOW COTEHILL
Cumbria

Oakville Cottage ★★★★★
Contact: Mr Peter Durbin
Cumbrian Cottages, 2 Lonsdale Street, Carlisle CA1 1DB
T: (01228) 599960
F: (01228) 599970
E: enquiries@cumbrian-cottage.co.uk
I: www.cumbrian-cottages.co.uk

Oakville Garden Cottage ★★★★★
Contact: Peter Durbin & Tony Commons
Cumbrian Cottages, 2 Lonsdale Street, Carlisle CA1 1DB
T: (01228) 599960
F: (01228) 599970
E: enquiries@cumbrian-cottages.co.uk
I: www.cumbrian-cottages.co.uk

LOWESWATER
Cumbria

The Coach House ★★★★★
Contact: Mrs Naomi Kerr
Looking Stead, Cockermouth CA13 0RS
T: (01900) 85660
E: lookingstead@aol.com
I: www.cottageguide.co.uk/loweswater/index.html

Crummockwater Cottages
Rating Applied For
Contact: Joan Warren
Crummockwater Cottages, Grove House, Little Tew, Chipping Norton OX7 4JB
T: (01608) 683643
E: cjt@crummockcottages.co.uk
I: www.crummockcottages.co.uk

High Mosser Gate ★★★★
Contact: Mrs Alison Evens
High Mosser Gate, Russetts, Highfield Road, Tring HP23 6EB
T: (01442) 825855
F: (01442) 828227
E: alison@highmossergate.co.uk
I: www.highmossergate.co.uk

The Howe ★★★★
Contact: Millie Townson
The Howe, Cockermouth CA13 0RA
T: (01900) 823660
E: millie@mosserhowe.freeserve.co.uk
I: www.mosserhowe.co.uk

Low Park Cottage ★★★
Contact: Robert Watkins
Low Park Cottage, Low Park, Cockermouth CA13 0RU
T: (01900) 85242

Loweswater Holiday Cottages ★★★★-★★★★★
Contact: Mr Thompson
Loweswater Holiday Cottages, Scale Hill, Cockermouth CA13 9UX
T: (01900) 85232
F: (01900) 85321
E: thompson@scalehillloweswater.co.uk
I: www.loweswaterholidaycottages.co.uk

LOWICK
Cumbria

Bark Cottage ★★★
Contact: Jenny Tancock
Bark Cottage, Tannery Barn, The Meadows, Lowick Green, Ulverston LA12 8DX
T: (01229) 885416
E: joeandjenny@tannerybarn.freeserve.co.uk
I: www.tannerybarn.freeserve.co.uk

Tsukudu ★★★★
Contact: Mr Martin Wardle
Lakes and Valleys, Bateman Fold Barn, Kendal LA8 8LN
T: (015394) 68103
F: (015394) 68104
E: lakesandvalleys@aol.com
I: www.lakesandvalleys.co.uk

LOWICK BRIDGE
Cumbria

Langholme Cottage ★★★
Contact: Mr Philip Johnston
The Coppermines & Coniston Lakes Cottages, The Estate Office, The Bridge, Coniston LA21 8HJ
T: (015394) 41765
F: (015394) 41944
E: info@coppermines.co.uk
I: www.coppermines.co.uk

Establishments printed in blue have a detailed entry in this guide

CUMBRIA – THE LAKE DISTRICT

LOWICK GREEN
Cumbria

The Hidden Cottage ★★★
Contact: Mr Philip Johnston
The Coppermines & Coniston
Lakes Cottages, The Estate
Office, The Bridge, Coniston
LA21 8HJ
T: (015394) 41765
E: bookings@coppermines.co.uk
I: www.coppermines.co.uk

LYTH
Cumbria

Fellside Farm ★★★
Contact:
Bowness Lakeland Holidays, 131
Radcliffe New Road, Manchester
M45 7RP
T: (0161) 7963896

The Peat House
Rating Applied For
Contact: Mr Steven Brierley
Michael Yeat Farmhouse, The
Row, Lyth, Kendal LA8 8DD
T: (015395) 68172
E: enquiries@peathouse.co.uk
I: www.peathouse.co.uk

MALLERSTANG
Cumbria

Old Faw Cottage ★★★
Contact: Mr & Mrs Hamilton
Old Faw Cottage, The Thrang,
Kirkby Stephen CA17 4JX
T: (01768) 371889
E: thrang@mallerstang.com
I: www.mallerstang.com

MANESTY
Cumbria

The Coppice ★★
Contact: Mr David Burton
Lakeland Cottage Holidays,
Melbecks, Keswick CA12 4QX
T: (017687) 76065
F: (017687) 76869
E: info@lakelandcottages.co.uk
I: www.lakelandcottages.co.uk

High Ground ★★★
Contact: Mr David Burton
Lakeland Cottage Holidays,
Melbecks, Keswick CA12 4QX
T: (017687) 76065
F: (017687) 76869
E: info@lakelandcottages.co.uk
I: www.lakelandcottages.co.uk

Manesty Holiday Cottages
★★★-★★★★★
Contact: Mr & Mrs Leyland
Manesty Holiday Cottages,
Youdale Knot, Keswick
CA12 5UG
T: (017687) 77216
F: (017687) 77384
E: cottages@manesty.co.uk
I: www.manesty.co.uk

MARTINDALE
Cumbria

Beckside Cottage ★★★★
Contact: Mrs Caroline Ivinson
A & C Ivinson, Beckside Farm,
Sandwick, Penrith CA10 2NF
T: (017684) 86239
F: (017684) 86239
E: ivinson_becksidefarm@
hotmail.com

TOWNHEAD
Townhead Cottage ★★★★
Contact: Mr John Serginson
The Lakeland Cottage Company,
Waterside House, Ulverston
LA12 8AN
T: (015395) 30024
F: (015395) 31932
E: john@lakelandcottageco.com
I: www.lakelandcottageco.com

MAULDS MEABURN
Cumbria

Chestnuts ★★★★
Contact: Ms Annie Kindleysides
Meaburn Hill Farmhouse,
Penrith CA10 3HN
T: (01931) 715168

Harrys Barn ★★★★
Contact: Julie Hatton
Harrys Barn, Coat Flatt Mill,
Penrith CA10 3RE
T: (01539) 624664
F: (01539) 624527
E: hattonjulie@hotmail.com
I: www.harrysbarn.co.uk

MEALSGATE
Cumbria

West Court and East Court
★★★
Contact: The Manager
Ref:2315/2075, Dales Holiday
Cottages, Carleton Business
Park, Carleton New Road,
Skipton BD23 2AA
T: (01756) 799821
F: (01756) 797012
E: info@dalesholcot.com
I: www.dalesholcot.com

MILBURN
Cumbria

Bramley Cottage ★★★★
Contact: The Proprietor
Bramley Cottage, Orchard
Cottage, Penrith CA10 1TN
T: (01768) 361074
F: (01768) 895528
E: guyheelis@aol.com
I: www.oas.
co.uk/ukcottages/bramley

Gullom Cottage ★★★
Contact: Mr Peter Durbin
Cumbrian Cottages, 2 Lonsdale
Street, Carlisle CA1 1DB
T: (01228) 599960
F: (01228) 599970
E: enquiries@cumbrian-cottage.
co.uk
I: www.cumbrian-cottages.co.uk

High Slakes ★★★★
Contact: Mrs J Taylor
Low Howgill Farm, Low Howgill,
Penrith CA10 1TL
T: (01768) 361595
F: (01768) 361598
E: holidays@low-howgill.co.uk
I: www.lowhowgill.f9.co.uk

MILLBECK
Cumbria

Millbeck Cottages ★★★★
Contact: Richard Watson
Millbeck Cottages, 20 Hebing
End, Stevenage SG2 7DD
T: (01438) 359311
F: (01438) 740127

MORLAND
Cumbria

**Shorrocks House, Torbock
House & The Coach House**
★★★★★
Contact: Mrs Crossley
Morland Hall, Penrith CA10 3BB
T: (01931) 714029
F: (01931) 714714

MOTHERBY
Cumbria

**Nettle How Cottage &
Annex** ★★★
Contact: Mr & Mrs Hill
Nettle How Cottage & Annex,
Nettle How, Penrith CA11 0RJ
T: (017684) 83544
E: doreen@jims99.freeserve.
co.uk

MUNGRISDALE
Cumbria

The Garth ★★★★
Contact: Mrs Susan Jackson
Heart of the Lakes, Fisherbeck
Mill, Old Lake Road, Ambleside
LA22 0DH
T: (015394) 32321
F: (015394) 33251
E: info@heartofthelakes.co.uk
I: www.heartofthelakes.co.uk

Grisedale View, Howe Top
★★★★
Contact: Mrs Weightman
Near Howe Hotel and Cottages,
Troutbeck, Penrith CA11 0SH
T: (017687) 79678
F: (017687) 79462

NADDLE
Cumbria

The Bungalow ★★★
Contact: Mrs Jane Nicholson
Causeway Foot Farm, Keswick
CA12 4TF
T: (017687) 72290
E: jackie@causewayfoot.co.uk
I: www.causewayfoot.co.uk

NATLAND
Cumbria

Stonegable ★★★
Contact: Mr Peter Durbin
Cumbrian Cottages, 2 Lonsdale
Street, Carlisle CA1 1DB
T: (01228) 599960
F: (01228) 599970
E: enquiries@cumbriancottages.
co.uk
I: www.cumbrian-cottages.co.uk

NEAR SAWREY
Cumbria

Number Nine ★★★
Contact: Mr Philip Johnston
The Coppermines & Coniston
Lakes Cottages, The Estate
Office, The Bridge, Coniston
LA21 8HJ
T: (015394) 41765
I: www.coppermines.
co.uk/property/show_details.
cgi?id=88

Smithy Cottage ★★★
Contact: Paul Liddell
Lakelovers, Belmont House, Lake
Road, Bowness-on-Windermere,
Windermere LA23 3BJ
T: (015394) 88855
F: (015394) 88857

NENTHEAD
Cumbria

**The Stable & Keepers
Cottage** ★★★★-★★★★★★
Contact: Fiona Moody
Dales Holiday Cottages, Carleton
Business Park, Carleton New
Road, Skipton BD23 2AA
T: (01756) 790919
F: (01756) 797012
E: info@dales-holiday-cottages.
com
I: www.dales-holiday-cottages.
com

NEWBIGGIN-ON-LUNE
Cumbria

Green Bell View ★★★
Contact: The Manager
Ref: 2076, Dales Holiday
Cottages, Carleton Business
Park, Carleton New Road,
Skipton BD23 2AA
T: (01756) 790919
F: (01756) 797012
E: info@dalesholcot.com
I: www.dalesholcot.com

Pleasant View ★★★
Contact: The Manager
Ref: 2392, Dales Holiday
Cottages, Carleton Business
Park, Carleton New Road,
Skipton BD23 2AA
T: (01756) 790919
F: (01756) 797012
E: info@dalesholcot.com
I: www.dalesholcot.com

NEWBY
Cumbria

**Midtown Cottage & Dairy
Cottage** ★★★★-★★★★★
Contact: Wardle Family
Goosemire Cottages, Bateman
Fold Barn, Kendal LA8 8LN
T: (015395) 68102
F: (015395) 68104
E: goosemirecottage@aol.com
I: www.midtowncottage.co.uk

NEWBY BRIDGE
Cumbria

Fellcroft Cottage ★★★★
Contact: Cath Hale
Fellcroft Cottage, 1 Low Row,
Brow Edge Road, Ulverston
LA12 8QH
T: (015395) 30316
E: info@fellcroft.fsnet.co.uk

Woodland Cottage ★★★★
Contact: Mr Peter Newton
Fellside Lodge, Newby Bridge
Caravan Park, Canny Hill, Newby
Bridge LA12 8NF
T: (015395) 31030
F: (015395) 30105
E: info@cumbriancaravans.
co.uk
I: www.cumbriancaravans.co.uk

Woodside ★★★
Contact: Mr Peter Durbin
Cumbrian Cottages, 2 Lonsdale
Street, Carlisle CA1 1DB
T: (01228) 599960
F: (01228) 599970
E: enquiries@
cumbrian-cottages.co.uk
I: www.cumbrian-cottages.co.uk

CUMBRIA – THE LAKE DISTRICT

NEWLAND
Cumbria

Curlew Rise and Heron Beck ★★★★
Contact: Mr John Serginson
The Lakeland Cottage Company, Waterside House, Ulverston LA12 8AN
T: (015395) 30024
F: (015395) 31932
E: john@lakelandcottageco.com
I: www.lakelandcottageco.com

NEWLANDS
Cumbria

Aikin ★★★
Contact: Mr Peter Durbin
Cumbrian Cottages, 2 Lonsdale Street, Carlisle CA1 1DB
T: (01228) 599960
F: (01228) 599970
E: enquiries@cumbriancottages.co.uk
I: www.cumbrian-cottages.co.uk

Fell Cottage ★★★
Contact: Mr David Burton
Lakeland Cottage Holidays, Melbecks, Keswick CA12 4QX
T: (017687) 76065
F: (017687) 76869
E: info@lakelandcottages.co.uk
I: www.lakelandcottages.co.uk

The Oaks Apartment ★★★
Contact: Mr Peter Durbin
Cumbrian Cottages, 2 Lonsdale Street, Carlisle CA1 1DB
T: (01228) 599960
F: (01228) 599970
E: enquiries@cumbriancottages.co.uk
I: www.cumbrian-cottages.co.uk

NIBTHWAITE
Cumbria

Fell View ★★★
Contact: Mrs Susan Jackson
Heart of the Lakes, Fisherbeck Mill, Old Lake Road, Ambleside LA22 0DH
T: (015394) 32321
F: (015394) 33251
E: info@heartofthelakes.co.uk
I: www.heartofthelakes.co.uk

The Hovel ★★★★
Contact: Mr John Serginson
The Lakeland Cottage Company, Waterside House, Ulverston LA12 8AN
T: (015395) 30024
F: (015395) 31932
E: john@lakelandcottageco.com
I: www.lakelandcottageco.com

The Peat House ★★★★
Contact: Mr John Serginson
Lakeland Cottage Company, Waterside House, Ulverston LA12 8AN
T: (015395) 30024
F: (015395) 31932
E: john@lakelandcottageco.com
I: www.lakelandcottageco.com

ORTON
Cumbria

Chapel Beck Cottage ★★★★
Contact: Mrs L Hodgson
Chapel Beck Cottage, Coat Flatt Hall, Penrith CA10 3SZ
T: (015396) 24179

OUSBY
Cumbria

Hole Bank ★★★★
Contact: Mrs Lesley McVey
10 Helvellyn Court, Penrith CA11 8PZ
T: (01768) 892247
F: (01768) 892247

OUTGATE
Cumbria

Borwick Fold Cottages ★★★★
Contact: Mr & Mrs Johnson
Borwick Fold Cottages, Borwick Fold, Ambleside LA22 0PU
T: (015394) 36742
F: (015394) 36094
E: borwickfoldcottages@firenet.uk.net
I: www.borwickfold.com

Claife Cottage ★★★★
Contact: Paul Liddell
Lakelovers, Belmont House, Lake Road, Bowness-on-Windermere, Windermere LA23 3BJ
T: (015394) 88855
F: (015394) 88857
E: bookings@lakelovers.co.uk
I: www.lakelovers.co.uk

Honey Pot Cottage (Currier) ★★★★
Contact: Mr Philip Johnston
The Coppermines & Coniston Lakes Cottages, The Estate Office, The Bridge, Coniston LA21 8HJ
T: (015394) 41765
F: (015394) 41944
E: info@coppermines.co.uk
I: www.coppermines.co.uk

Honister Cottage ★★★★
Contact: Paul Liddell
Lakelovers, Belmont House, Lake Road, Bowness-on-Windermere, Windermere LA23 3BJ
T: (015394) 88855
F: (015394) 88857
E: bookings@lakelovers.co.uk
I: www.lakelovers.co.uk

Kirkstone Cottage ★★★★
Contact: Paul Liddell
Lakelovers, Belmont House, Lake Road, Bowness-on-Windermere, Windermere LA23 3BJ
T: (015394) 88855
F: (015394) 88857
E: booking@lakelovers.co.uk
I: www.lakelovers.co.uk

Latterbarrow ★★★★
Contact: Mrs Vivien Bass
Wheelwrights Holiday Cottages, Langdale, Ambleside LA22 9HS
T: (015394) 37635
F: (015394) 37618
E: enquiries@wheelwrights.com
I: www.wheelwrights.com

Moss Beck ★★★★★
Contact: Mr John Serginson
Lakeland Cottage Company, Waterise House, Ulverston LA12 8AN
T: (015395) 30024
F: (015395) 31932
E: john@lakelandcottageco.com
I: www.lakelandcottageco.com

Peacock ★★★★
Contact: Mrs Susan Jackson
Heart of the Lakes, Fisherbeck Mill, Old Lake Road, Ambleside LA22 0DH
T: (015394) 32321
F: (015394) 33251
E: info@heartofthelakes.co.uk
I: www.heartofthelakes.co.uk

Pepper Cottage ★★★★
Contact: Mr Paul Liddell
Lakelovers, Belmont House, Lake Road, Bowness-on-Windermere, Windermere LA23 3BJ
T: (015394) 88855
F: (015394) 88857
E: bookings@lakelovers.co.uk
I: www.lakelovers.co.uk

OUTHGILL
Cumbria

Ing Hill Barn Apartments ★★★★
Contact: Country Holidays ref:14815
Alnham, Alnwick NE66 4TJ
T: (01282) 445096
F: (01282) 844288

PAPCASTLE
Cumbria

Sunny Brae ★★★
Contact: Mr Peter Durbin
Cumbrian Cottages, 2 Lonsdale Street, Carlisle CA1 1DB
T: (01228) 599960
F: (01228) 599970
E: enquiries@cumbrian-cottage.co.uk
I: www.cumbrian-cottages.co.uk

PARDSHAW
Cumbria

Stoneygate Cottage ★★★★
Contact: Dr Gordon Pearson
Stoneygate Cottage, Stoneygate, Cockermouth CA13 0SP
T: (01900) 823595
I: www.btinternet.com/~G.W. PEARSON

PARK GATE
Cumbria

Line Cottage ★★★
Contact: Mr Philip Johnston
The Coppermines & Coniston Lakes Cottages, The Estate Office, The Bridge, Coniston LA21 8HJ
T: (015394) 41765
I: www.coppermines.co.uk/property/show_details.cgi?id=93

PATTERDALE
Cumbria

Bleaze End ★★★★
Contact: Susan Jackson
Heart of the Lakes, Fisherbeck Mill, Old Lake Road, Ambleside LA22 0DH
T: (015394) 32321
F: (015394) 33251

Broad How ★★★★
Contact:
Country Holidays
T: 0870 197 0600
I: www.country-holidays.co.uk

Deepdale Hall Cottage ★★★
Contact: Chris Brown
Deepdale Hall, Penrith CA11 0NR
T: (017684) 82369
F: (017684) 82608
E: brown@deepdalehall.freeserve.co.uk
I: www.deepdalehall.co.uk

Elm How, Cruck Barn & Eagle Cottage ★★★-★★★★
Contact: Miss M Scott & Mrs J Marsden
Matson Ground Estate Company Ltd, Estate Office, Matson Ground, Windermere LA23 2NH
T: (015394) 45756
F: (015394) 47892
E: info@matsonground.co.uk
I: www.matsonground.co.uk

Fellside Farm Cottage ★★★
Contact: Anne-Marie Knight
Fellside, Hartsop, Penrith CA11 0NZ
T: (017684) 82532

Hartsop Fold Holiday Lodges ★★★
Contact: Mrs L Hennedy
Hartsop Fold Holiday Lodges, Merlin Cragg, Sedbergh LA10 5HU
T: (015396) 22069
F: (015396) 20899
E: bookings@hartsop-fold.co.uk
I: www.hartsop-fold.co.uk

Lower Grisedale Lodge ★★★★
Contact: Susan Jackson
Heart of the Lakes, Fisherbeck Mill, Old Lake Road, Ambleside LA22 0DH
T: (015394) 32321
F: (015394) 33251
E: info@heartofthelakes.co.uk
I: www.heartofthelakes.co.uk

PENRITH
Cumbria

Bankside ★★★★
Contact: Mr Peter Durbin
Cumbrian Cottages, 2 Lonsdale Street, Carlisle CA1 1DB
T: (01228) 599960
F: (01228) 599970
E: enquiries@cumbrian-cottages.co.uk
I: www.cumbrian-cottages.co.uk

Barn End & Barn Croft ★★★★
Contact: Brenda Walton
Barn End & Barn Croft, Carthanet, Soulby, Dacre, Penrith CA11 0JF
T: (017684) 86376
F: (017684) 86376
E: brenda@waltoncottages.fsnet.co.uk
I: barnend-cottages.co.uk

Bracken Bank Lodge & Bracken Bank Cottage ★★★★
Contact: Mrs Hilary Burton
Bracken Bank Lodge & Bracken Bank Cottage, Lazonby, Penrith CA10 1AX
T: (01768) 898241
F: (01768) 898221
E: info@brackenbank.co.uk
I: www.brackenbank.co.uk

Establishments printed in blue have a detailed entry in this guide

CUMBRIA – THE LAKE DISTRICT

Croft House ★★
Contact: The Manager
Ref:3007, Dales Holiday Cottages, Carleton Business Park, Carleton New Road, Skipton BD23 2AA
T: (01756) 799821
F: (01756) 797012
E: info@dalesholcot.com
I: www.dalesholcot.com

Daisy Cottage ★★★★
Contact: Mr David Burton
Lakeland Cottage Holidays, Melbecks, Keswick CA12 4QX
T: (017687) 76065
F: (017687) 76869
E: info@lakelandcottages.co.uk
I: www.lakelandcottages.co.uk

Elind
Rating Applied For
Contact: Mrs Susan Jackson
Heart of the Lakes, Fisherbeck Mill, Old Lake Road, Ambleside LA22 0DH
I: (015394) 32321
F: (015394) 33251
E: info@heartofthelakes.co.uk
I: www.heartofthelakes.co.uk

Lavender Cottage ★★★★
Contact: Mr David Burton
Lakeland Cottage Holidays, Melbecks, Keswick CA12 4QX
T: (017687) 76065
F: (017687) 76869
E: info@lakelandcottages.co.uk
I: www.lakelandcottages.co.uk

Oak View Cottage ★★★★
Contact: Ms Dearling
Oak View Cottage, Millcrags, Penrith CA10 2RQ
T: (01931) 713121
F: (01931) 713121

Skirwith Hall Cottage & Smith Cottage ★★★★
Contact: Laura Wilson
Skirwith Hall Cottages, Skirwith Hall, Penrith CA10 1RH
T: (01768) 88241
F: (01768) 88241
E: stay@skirwithhallcottages.co.uk
I: www.skirwithhallcottages.co.uk

Stonefold ★★★★
Contact: Mrs Harrington
Stonefold Cottages, Stainton, Penrith CA11 0HP
T: (01768) 866383
F: (01768) 866383
E: gill@stonefold.co.uk
I: www.stonefold.co.uk

Wetheral Cottages ★★★★
Contact: Mr John Lowrey
Great Salkeld, Penrith CA11 9NA
T: (01768) 898779
E: wetheralcottages@btopenworld.com
I: www.wetheralcottages.co.uk

PENRUDDOCK
Cumbria

Beckses Cottage ★★★★
Contact: Mr Peter Durbin
Cumbrian Cottages, 2 Lonsdale Street, Carlisle CA1 1DB
T: (01228) 599960
F: (01228) 599970
E: enquiries@cumbrian-cottage.co.uk
I: www.cumbrian-cottages.co.uk

Green Barn ★★★
Contact: Mr Peter Durbin
Cumbrian Cottages, 2 Lonsdale Street, Carlisle CA1 1DB
T: (01228) 599960
F: (01228) 599970
E: enquiries@cumbrian-cottages.co.uk
I: www.cumbrian-cottages.co.uk

Low Garth Cottage ★★★★
Contact: The Manager
Ref: 3317, Dales Holiday Cottages, Carleton Business Park, Carleton New Road, Skipton BD23 2AA
T: (01756) 790919
F: (01756) 797012
E: info@dalesholcot.com
I: www.dalesholcot.com

Nab End ★★★★
Contact: Mr David Burton
Lakeland Cottage Holidays, Melbeck, Keswick CA12 4QX
T: (017687) 76065
F: (017687) 76869
E: info@lakelandcottages.co.uk
I: www.lakelandcottages.co.uk

PENTON
Cumbria

Liddel Park Holiday Cottage
Rating Applied For
Contact: Ms Linda Johnson
Liddel Park Holiday Cottage, Liddel Park, Carlisle CA6 5QW
T: (01228) 577440
I: business.thisisyork.co.uk/liddelpark/

POOLEY BRIDGE
Cumbria

Barton Hall FarmHoliday Cottages ★★★★
Contact: Amanda Strong
Barton Hall Farm Holiday Cottages, Penrith CA10 2NG
T: (017684) 86034

Beauthorn Coach House ★★★
Contact: Mr Martin Wardle
Lakes and Valleys, Bateman Fold Barn, Kendal LA8 8LN
T: (015394) 68103
F: (015394) 68104
E: lakesandvalleys@aol.com

Blacksmith's Cottages ★★★★
Contact: Mr Peter Durbin
Cumbrian Cottages, 2 Lonsdale Street, Carlisle CA1 1DB
T: (01228) 599960
F: (01228) 599970
E: enquiries@cumbriancottages.co.uk
I: www.cumbrian-cottages.co.uk

High Winder Cottages ★★★★
Contact: Mrs Moss
High Winder Cottages, High Winder House, Celleron, Tirril, Penrith CA10 2LS
T: (017684) 86997
F: (017684) 86997
E: mosses@highwinderhouse.co.uk
I: www.highwindercottages.co.uk

Waterfoot Lodge
Rating Applied For
Contact: Mrs Sheila Hewartson
Waterfoot Caravan Park, Penrith CA1 0JF
T: (017684) 86302
F: (017684) 86728

Windy Nook ★★★
Contact: Mr Peter Durbin
Cumbrian Cottages, 2 Lonsdale Street, Carlisle CA1 1DB
T: (01228) 599960
F: (01228) 599970
E: enquiries@cumbriancottages.co.uk
I: www.cumbrian-cottages.co.uk

Winn's Cottage ★★★★
Contact: Mrs C Fortescue
Winn's Cottage, Bowerbank House, Penrith CA10 2NG
T: (017684) 86642
F: (017684) 86977

PORTINSCALE
Cumbria

The Cottage and Cosey Cottage, Twentyman Court ★★★-★★★★
Contact: Mr David Brown
Morven, Ambleside Road, Keswick CA12 4DD
T: (017687) 74324
E: information@keswickholidaycottages.co.uk
I: www.keswickholidaycottages.co.uk

Grizedale View ★★★
Contact: Mr Peter Durbin
Cumbrian Cottages, 2 Lonsdale Street, Carlisle CA1 1DB
T: (01228) 599960
F: (01228) 599970
E: enquiries@cumbriancottages.co.uk
I: www.cumbrian-cottages.co.uk

High Portinscale ★★★★
Contact: Mr Peter Durbin
Cumbrian Cottages, 2 Lonsdale Street, Carlisle CA1 1DB
T: (01228) 599960
F: (01228) 599970
E: enquiries@cumbrian-cottages.co.uk
I: www.cumbrian-cottages.co.uk

Jasmine Cottage ★★★
Contact: Mr Peter Durbin
Cumbrian Cottages, 2 Lonsdale Street, Carlisle CA1 1DB
T: (01228) 599960
F: (01228) 599970
E: enquiries@cumbrian-cottage.co.uk
I: www.cumbrian-cottages.co.uk

Middle Howe ★★★★
Contact: Mr Peter Durbin
Cumbrian Cottages, 2 Lonsdale Street, Carlisle CA1 1DB
T: (01228) 599960
F: (01228) 599970
E: enquiries@cumbriancottages.co.uk
I: www.cumbrian-cottages.co.uk

Osprey Heights ★★★★
Contact: Mr Peter Durbin
Cumbrian Cottages, 2 Lonsdale Street, Carlisle CA1 1DB
T: (01228) 599960
F: (01228) 599970
E: enquiries@cumbrian-cottages.co.uk
I: www.cumbrian-cottages.co.uk

Rickerby Cottage ★★★
Contact: Mr Peter Durbin
Cumbrian Cottages, 2 Lonsdale Street, Carlisle CA1 1DB
T: (01228) 599960
F: (01228) 599970
E: enquiries@cumbrian-cottages.co.uk
I: www.cumbrian-cottages.co.uk

Smithy Cottage ★★★
Contact: Mr Peter Durbin
Cumbrian Cottages, 2 Lonsdale Street, Carlisle CA1 1DB
T: (01228) 599960
F: (01228) 599970
E: enquiries@cumbriancottages.co.uk
I: www.cumbrian-cottages.co.uk

Stable Cottage ★★★
Contact: Margaret Pope
Stable Cottage, Thirnbeck, Keswick CA12 5RD
T: (017687) 75161

Watendlath ★★★★
Contact: Mr Peter Durbin
Cumbrian Cottages, 2 Lonsdale Street, Carlisle CA1 1DB
T: (01228) 599960
F: (01228) 599970
E: enquiries@cumbriancottages.co.uk
I: www.cumbrian-cottages.co.uk

Whitegates ★★★
Contact: Mr Peter Durbin
Cumbrian Cottages, 2 Lonsdale Street, Carlisle CA1 1DB
T: (01228) 599960
F: (01228) 599970
E: enquiries@cumbrian-cottages.co.uk
I: www.cumbrian-cottages.co.uk

RAVENSTONEDALE
Cumbria

Moss Cottages ★★★
Contact: Mr George & Mrs Doreen Moynihan
Moss Cottages, The Moss, Kirkby Stephen CA17 4NB
T: (015396) 23316
E: moymoss@btinternet.com
I: www.cottageguide.co.uk/mosscottages

CUMBRIA – THE LAKE DISTRICT

REDMAIN
Cumbria

Huddlestone Cottage and The Hayloft ★★★★
Contact: Christine Neale
Country Ayres, Pooley House, Cockermouth CA13 0PZ
T: (01900) 825695
E: hudcot@lakesnw.co.uk
I: www.lakesnw.co.uk/hudcot

ROSTHWAITE
Cumbria

Borrowdale Self Catering Holidays ★★★
Contact: Peter & Nicola Davis-Merry
Borrowdale Self-Catering Holidays, Kiln How, Keswick CA12 5XB
T: (017687) 77356
E: info@kilnhow.com
I: www.kilnhow.com

Castle How ★★★
Contact: Mr Peter Durbin
Cumbrian Cottages, 2 Lonsdale Street, Carlisle CA1 1DB
T: (01228) 599960
F: (01228) 599970
E: enquiries@cumbrian-cottage.co.uk
I: www.cumbrian-cottages.co.uk

Clare's Cottage ★★
Contact: Janice Diamond
Clare's Cottage, 20 James Street, Bolton BL6 7QS
T: (01204) 668681
E: dms@clarescottage.com
I: www.clarescottage.com

High Knott ★★★★
Contact: Mr Peter Durbin
Cumbrian Cottages, 2 Lonsdale Street, Carlisle CA1 1DB
T: (01228) 599960
F: (01228) 599970
E: enquiries@cumbriancottages.co.uk
I: www.cumbrian-cottages.co.uk

Larch Cottage ★★★
Contact: Mr David Burton
Lakeland Cottage Holidays, Melbecks, Keswick CA12 4QX
T: (017687) 76065
F: (017687) 76869
E: info@lakelandcottages.co.uk
I: www.lakelandcottages.co.uk

Nokka and Lobstone Cottages ★★★
Contact: Mr Peter Durbin
Cumbrian Cottages, 2 Lonsdale Street, Carlisle CA1 1DB
T: (01228) 599960
F: (01228) 599970
E: enquiries@cumbrian-cottage.co.uk
I: www.cumbrian-cottages.co.uk

Thwaite How ★★★
Contact: Mr & Mrs Brewerton
Thwaite How, c/o 3 Sycamore Way, Market Bosworth, Nuneaton CV13 0LU
T: (01455) 290168
E: cematproperties@hotmail.com

RUCKCROFT
Cumbria

Ruckcroft Cottage ★★★
Contact: Mr Peter Durbin
Cumbrian Cottages, 2 Lonsdale Street, Carlisle CA1 1DB
T: (01228) 599960
F: (01228) 599970
E: enquiries@cumbrian-cottages.co.uk
I: www.cumbrian-cottages.co.uk

RYDAL
Cumbria

Daffodils ★★★
Contact: Mrs Susan Jackson
Heart of the Lakes, Fisherbeck Mill, Old Lake Road, Ambleside LA22 0DH
T: (015394) 32321
F: (015394) 33251
E: info@heartofthelakes.co.uk
I: www.heartofthelakes.co.uk

Fox Cottage ★★★★
Contact: Susan Jackson
Heart of the Lakes, Fisherbeck Mill, Old Lake Road, Ambleside LA22 0DH
T: (015394) 32321
F: (015394) 33251
E: info@heartofthelakes.co.uk
I: www.heartofthelakes.co.uk

Hall Bank Cottage ★★★
Contact: Mrs Janet Horne
Rydal Estate, Carter Jonas, 52 Kirkland, Kendal LA9 5AP
T: (01539) 814902
F: (01539) 729587
E: janet.horne@carterjonas.co.uk

Hart Head Barn ★★★★
Contact: Mrs Susan Jackson
Heart of the Lakes, Fisherbeck Mill, Old Lake Road, Ambleside LA22 0DH
T: (015394) 32321
F: (015394) 33251
E: info@heartofthelakes.co.uk
I: www.heartofthelakes.co.uk

1 Hart Head Barn ★★★★
Contact: Mrs Vivien Bass
Wheelwrights Holiday Cottages, Langdale, Ambleside LA22 9HS
T: (015394) 37635
F: (015394) 37618
E: enquiries@wheelwrights.com
I: www.wheelwrights.com

Loughrigg Cottage
Rating Applied For
Contact: Mr Graham Warrender
The Coach House - Templedean, Florabank Road, Lincoln EH41 3LR
T: (01620) 824357

Rydal Mount Cottage ★★★★
Contact: Susan Jackson
Heart of the Lakes, Fisherbeck Mill, Old Lake Road, Ambleside LA22 0DH
T: (015394) 32321
F: (015394) 33251

ST BEES
Cumbria

Tarn Flatt Cottage ★★★
Contact: Mrs Janice Telfer
Tarn Flatt Cottage, Sandwith, Whitehaven CA28 9UX
T: (01946) 692162
E: stay@tarnflattfarm.co.uk
I: www.tarnflattfarm.co.uk

ST JOHNS-IN-THE-VALE
Cumbria

Lowthwaite Cottage ★★★★
Contact: Mr Peter Durbin
Cumbrian Cottages, 2 Lonsdale Street, Carlisle CA1 1DB
T: (01228) 599960
F: (01228) 599970
E: enquiries@cumbrian-cottages.co.uk
I: www.cumbrian-cottages.co.uk

Pine Cottage ★★★
Contact: Mr David Burton
Lakeland Cottage Holidays, Melbecks, Keswick CA12 4QX
T: (017687) 76065
F: (017687) 76869
E: info@lakelandcottages.co.uk
I: www.lakelandcottages.co.uk

The Studio ★★★★
Contact: Mr Green
The Studio, Fornside House, Keswick CA12 4TS
T: (017687) 79666
E: selfcatering@keswickholidays.co.uk
I: www.keswickholidays.co.uk

SATTERTHWAITE
Cumbria

Church Cottage ★★★★
Contact: Mrs Susan Jackson
Heart of the Lakes, Fisherbeck Mill, Old Lake Road, Ambleside LA22 0DH
T: (015394) 32321
F: (015394) 33251
E: info@heartofthelakes.co.uk
I: www.heartofthelakes.co.uk

Hawkrigg House ★★★★
Contact: Mrs Susan Jackson
Heart of the Lakes, Fisherbeck Mill, Old Lake Road, Ambleside LA22 0DH
T: (015394) 32321
F: (015394) 33251
E: info@heartofthelakes.co.uk
I: www.heartofthelakes.co.uk

Tanwood Barn ★★★★
Contact: Susan Jackson
Heart of the Lakes, Fisherbeck Mill, Old Lake Road, Ambleside LA22 0DH
T: (015394) 32321
F: (015394) 33251

SAWREY
Cumbria

Anvil Cottage ★★★★
Contact: Mr Peter Durbin
Cumbrian Cottages, 2 Lonsdale Street, Carlisle CA1 1DB
T: (01228) 599960
F: (01228) 599970
E: enquiries@cumbriancottages.co.uk
I: www.cumbrian-cottages.co.uk

Apple Tree Cottage ★★★
Contact: Mr Paul Liddell
Lakelovers, Belmont House, Lake Road, Bowness-on-Windermere, Windermere LA23 3BJ
T: (015394) 88855
F: (015394) 88857
E: bookings@lakelovers.co.uk
I: www.lakelovers.co.uk

Derwentwater Cottage ★★★
Contact: Mrs Anne Gallagher
The Minstrels Gallery, The Square, Hawkshead, Ambleside LA22 0NZ
T: (015394) 42435
F: (015394) 36178
E: bookings@lakeland-hideaways.co.uk
I: www.lakeland-hideaways.co.uk

The Forge ★★★
Contact: Paul Liddell
Lakelovers, Belmont House, Lake Road, Bowness-on-Windermere, Windermere LA23 3BJ
T: (015394) 88855
F: (015394) 88857

Fountain Cottage ★★★
Contact: Mr Paul Liddell
Lakelovers, Belmont House, Lake Road, Bowness-on-Windermere, Windermere LA23 3BJ
T: (015394) 88855
F: (015394) 88857
E: bookings@lakelovers.co.uk
I: www.lakelovers.co.uk

Lakefield ★★★-★★★★
Contact: John Taylor
Lakefield, Ambleside LA22 0JZ
T: (015394) 36635
F: (015394) 36635
E: lakefieldacom@aol.com
I: www.lakefield.golakes.co.uk

Meadowside ★★★★
Contact: Paul Liddell
Lakelovers, Belmont House, Lake Road, Bowness-on-Windermere, Windermere LA23 3BJ
T: (015394) 88855
F: (015394) 88857

Sawrey Stables ★★★★★
Contact: Mrs Anne Gallagher
Hideaways, The Minstrels Gallery, The Square, Hawkshead, Ambleside LA22 0NZ
T: (015394) 42435
F: (015394) 36178
E: bookings@lakeland-hideaways.co.uk
I: www.lakeland-hideaways.co.uk

Sunnyside Cottage ★★★★
Contact: Mr John Serginson
The Lakeland Cottage Company, Waterside House, Ulverston LA12 8AN
T: (015395) 30024
F: (015395) 31932
E: john@lakelandcottageco.com
I: www.lakelandcottgeco.com

Establishments printed in blue have a detailed entry in this guide

CUMBRIA – THE LAKE DISTRICT

Top Garden Suite ★★★★
Contact: Mrs Susan Jackson
Heart of the Lakes, Fisherbeck Mill, Old Lake Road, Ambleside LA22 0DH
T: (015394) 32321
F: (015394) 33151
E: info@heartoflakes.co.uk
I: www.heartoflakes.co.uk

Town End Cottage
Rating Applied For
Contact: Paul Liddell
Lakelovers, Belmont House, Lake Road, Bowness-on-Windermere, Windermere LA23 3BJ
T: (015394) 88855
F: (015394) 88857
E: bookings@lakelovers.co.uk
I: www.lakelovers.co.uk

West Vale Cottage ★★★
Contact: Mr & Mrs Pennington
West Vale Country House & Restaurant, Hawkshead, Ambleside LA22 0LQ
T: (015394) 42817
F: (01539) 45302
E: enquiries@westvalecountryhouse.co.uk
I: www.westvalecountryhouse.co.uk

SEATHWAITE
Cumbria

Cockley Beck Cottage ★★★
Contact: Mrs Vivien Bass
Wheelwrights Holiday Cottages, Langdale, Ambleside LA22 9HS
T: (015394) 37635
F: (015394) 37618
I: www.wheelwrights.com

Hall Dunnerdale Farm Holiday Cottages
Rating Applied For
Contact: Ms Anne Brockbank
Dove Bank House, Kirkby-in-Furness LA17 7XD
T: (01229) 889281
F: (01229) 889776
E: anne@hall-dunnerdale.co.uk
I: www.hall-dunnerdale.co.uk/

2 High Moss House
Rating Applied For
Contact: Mrs Helen Barnard
13 Herries Road, Glasgow G41 4DE
T: (0141) 423 1060
F: (0141) 424 1441
E: helen@cognit.co.uk

Rose Cottage ★★★★
Contact: Mr John Serginson
The Lakeland Cottage Company, Waterside House, Ulverston LA12 8AN
T: (015395) 30024
F: (015395) 31932
E: john@lakelandcottageco.com
I: www.lakelandcottageco.com

SEATOLLER
Cumbria

The Barn ★★★★
Contact: Mr Peter Durbin
Cumbrian Cottages, 2 Lonsdale Street, Carlisle CA1 1DB
T: (01228) 599960
F: (01228) 599970
E: enquiries@cumbrian-cottages.co.uk
I: www.cumbrian-cottages.co.uk

Bell Crags ★★★
Contact: Mr David Burton
Lakeland Cottage Holidays, Melbecks, Keswick CA12 4QX
T: (017687) 76065
F: (017687) 76869
E: info@lakelandcottages.co.uk
I: www.lakelandcottages.co.uk

Brasscam ★★★★
Contact: Mr Peter Durbin
Cumbrian Cottages, 2 Lonsdale Street, Carlisle CA1 1DB
T: (01228) 599960
F: (01228) 599970
E: enquiries@cumbrian-cottages.co.uk
I: www.cumbrian-cottages.co.uk

Ghyllside ★★★
Contact: Mr Peter Durbin
Cumbrian Cottages, 2 Lonsdale Street, Carlisle CA1 1DB
T: (01228) 599960
F: (01228) 599970
E: enquiries@cumbriancottages.co.uk
I: www.cumbrian-cottages.co.uk

Hause Gill ★★★
Contact: Mr David Burton
Lakeland Cottage Holidays, Melbecks, Keswick CA12 4QX
T: (017687) 76065
F: (017687) 76869
E: info@lakelandcottages.co.uk
I: www.lakelandcottages.co.uk

High Stile ★★★
Contact: Mr David Burton
Lakeland Cottage Holidays, Melbecks, Keswick CA12 4QX
T: (017687) 76065
F: (017687) 76869
E: info@lakelandcottages.co.uk
I: www.lakelandcottages.co.uk

Honister ★★★
Contact: Mr Peter Durbin
Cumbrian Cottages, 2 Lonsdale Street, Carlisle CA1 1DB
T: (017687) 71071
F: (017687) 75036
E: info@cumbrian-cottages.co.uk
I: www.cumbrian-cottages.co.uk

Littlebeck ★★★★
Contact: Mr Peter Durbin
Cumbrian Cottages, 2 Lonsdale Street, Carlisle CA1 1DB
T: (01228) 599960
F: (01228) 599970
E: enquiries@cumbriancottages.co.uk
I: www.cumbrian-cottages.co.uk

SEDBERGH
Cumbria

Carriers Cottage ★★★
Contact: Mr & Mrs Ellis
Sun Ridge, Joss Lane, Sedbergh LA10 5AS
T: (015396) 20566

Fell House ★★★★
Contact: Mr Stephen Wickham
14 Home Meadows, Billericay CM12 9HQ
T: (01277) 652746 & 07974 028901
E: steve@higround.co.uk
I: www.higround.co.uk

Ingmire Hall ★★★★
Contact: Mr & Mrs Gardner
Ingmire Hall, Sedbergh LA10 5HR
T: (015396) 21012
F: (015396) 21116

Merlin Cottage ★★★★
Contact: Christine Linley
Merlin Cottage, 31 Greenside, Kendal LA9 5DU
T: (01539) 738677
F: (01539) 740615

The Mount ★★★★
Contact: Mrs Suzan Sedgwick
Howgill Lane, Sedbergh LA10 5HE
T: (015396) 20252
E: lockbank@uk4free.net
I: www.holidaysedbergh.co.uk

4 Railway Cottages ★★★
Contact: Mrs Mills
131 Glendale Gardens, Leigh-on-Sea SS9 2BE
T: (01702) 478846
F: (01702) 482088
E: trewen@clara.co.uk
I: www.dalescottages.com

Randall Hill Cottage ★★★
Contact: Mr Wilkinson
Dales Holiday Cottages, Station Road, Sedbergh LA10 5HJ
T: (015396) 21346
E: ha@wilkinson24.fsnet.co.uk

Thwaite Cottage ★★★★
Contact: Mrs Parker
Thwaite Cottage, Thwaite Farm, Sedbergh LA10 5JD
T: (01539) 620493
F: (01539) 620493

SEDGWICK
Cumbria

High House Barn ★★★★★
Contact: Mr Peter Durbin
Cumbrian Cottages, 2 Lonsdale Street, Carlisle CA1 1DB
T: (01228) 599960
F: (01228) 599970
E: enquiries@cumbrian-cottage.co.uk
I: www.cumbrian-cottages.co.uk

Woodside Cottage ★★★★
Contact: Mr Peter Durbin
Cumbrian Cottages, 2 Lonsdale Street, Carlisle CA1 1DB
T: (01228) 599960
F: (01228) 599970
E: enquiries@cumbrian-cottages.co.uk
I: www.cumbrian-cottages.co.uk

SETMURTHY
Cumbria

Derwent View ★★★
Contact: Mr Peter Durbin
Cumbrian Cottages, 2 Lonsdale Street, Carlisle CA1 1DB
T: (01228) 599960
F: (01228) 599970
E: enquiries@cumbriancottages.co.uk
I: www.cumbrian-cottages.co.uk

SILECROFT
Cumbria

Lowsha Cottage ★★★
Contact: The Manager
Ref:3126, Dales Holiday Cottages, Carleton Business Park, Carleton New Road, Skipton BD23 2AA
T: (01756) 799821
F: (01756) 797012
E: info@dalesholcot.com
I: www.dalesholcot.com

SKELWITH BRIDGE
Cumbria

Brathay View ★★★
Contact: Susan Jackson
Heart of the Lakes, Fisherbeck Mill, Old Lake Road, Ambleside LA22 0DH
T: (015394) 32321
F: (015394) 33151
E: info@heartoflakes.co.uk
I: www.heartoflakes.co.uk

Brow Foot ★★★★
Contact: Mrs Susan Jackson
Heart of the Lakes, Fisherbeck Mill, Old Lake Road, Ambleside LA22 0DH
T: (015394) 32321
F: (015394) 33151
E: info@heartoflakes.co.uk
I: www.heartoflakes.co.uk

The Coach House ★★★★
Contact: Mrs Vivien Bass
Wheelwrights Holiday Cottages, Langdale, Ambleside LA22 9HS
T: (015394) 37635
F: (015394) 37618
E: enquiries@wheelwrights.com
I: www.wheelwrights.com

Colwith ★★★★
Contact: Jane Heaney
Colwith, c/o 10 Scarsdale Avenue, Derby DE23 6ER
T: (01332) 343727
E: colwith.neaumcrag@ntlworld.com

Edna's Cottage ★★★
Contact: Mrs Vivien Bass
Wheelwrights Holiday Cottages, Langdale, Ambleside LA22 9HS
T: (015394) 37635
F: (015394) 37618
E: enquiries@wheelwrights.com
I: www.wheelwrights.com

Ghyll Pool Lodge ★★★
Contact: Mr Peter Durbin
Cumbrian Cottages, 2 Lonsdale Street, Carlisle CA1 1DB
T: (01228) 599960
F: (01228) 599970
E: enquiries@cumbriancottages.co.uk
I: www.cumbrian-cottages.co.uk

Greenbank Holiday Apartments ★★★★
Contact: Lilian Green
Greenbank Holiday Apartments, Greenbank, Ambleside LA22 9NW
T: (015394) 33236
E: info@visitgreenbank.co.uk
I: www.visitgreenbank.co.uk

CUMBRIA – THE LAKE DISTRICT

Heatherlea ★★★
Contact: Mrs Vivien Bass
Wheelwrights Holiday Cottages,
Langdale, Ambleside LA22 9HS
T: (015394) 37635
F: (015394) 37618
E: enquiries@wheelwrights.com
I: www.wheelwrights.com

Ivy Cottage ★★★★
Contact: Mr Peter Durbin
Cumbrian Cottages, 2 Lonsdale
Street, Carlisle CA1 1DB
T: (01228) 599960
F: (01228) 599970
E: enquiries@
cumbrian-cottages.co.uk
I: www.cumbrian-cottages.co.uk

Little Garth ★★★★★
Contact: Mrs Susan Jackson
Heart of the Lakes, Fisherbeck
Mill, Old Lake Road, Ambleside
LA22 0DH
T: (015394) 32321
F: (015394) 33251
E: info@heartofthelakes.co.uk
I: www.heartofthelakes.co.uk

Merlins ★★★★
Contact: Susan Jackson
Heart of the Lakes, Fisherbeck
Mill, Old Lake Road, Ambleside
LA22 0DH
T: (015394) 32321
F: (015394) 33251
E: info@heartofthelakes.co.uk
I: www.heartofthelakes.co.uk

Mockerkin Tarn ★★★
Contact: Mr Peter Durbin
Cumbrian Cottages, 2 Lonsdale
Street, Carlisle CA1 1DB
T: (01228) 599960
F: (01228) 599970
E: enquiries@cumbriancottages.
co.uk
I: www.cumbrian-cottages.co.uk

2 Neaum Crag Court ★★★
Contact: Mr Peter Durbin
Cumbrian Cottages, 2 Lonsdale
Street, Carlisle CA1 1DB
T: (01228) 599960
F: (01228) 599970
E: enquiries@cumbriancottages.
co.uk
I: www.cumbrian-cottages.co.uk

3 Neaum Crag Court ★★★★
Contact: Mrs Vivien Bass
Wheelwrights Holiday Cottages,
Langdale, Ambleside LA22 9HS
T: (015394) 37635
E: enquiries@wheelwrights.com
I: www.wheelwrights.com

Oakdene ★★★★
Contact: Susan Jackson
Heart of the Lakes, Fisherbeck
Mill, Old Lake Road, Ambleside
LA22 0DH
T: (015394) 32321
F: (015394) 33251

Ramblers Rest ★★★★
Contact: Paul Liddell
Lakelovers, Belmont House, Lake
Road, Bowness-on-Windermere,
Windermere LA23 3BJ
T: (015394) 88855
F: (015394) 88857
E: bookings@lakelovers.co.uk
I: www.lakelovers.co.uk

Riverbank Cottage ★★★★
Contact: Mrs Vivien Bass
Wheelwrights Holiday Cottages,
Langdale, Ambleside LA22 9HS
T: (015394) 37635
E: enquiries@wheelwrights.com
I: www.wheelwrights.com

Tarn Hows ★★
Contact: Mr Paul Liddell
Lakelovers, Belmont House, Lake
Road, Bowness-on-Windermere,
Windermere LA23 3BJ
T: (015394) 88855
F: (015394) 88857
E: bookings@lakelovers.co.uk
I: www.lakelovers.co.uk

Tarn Moss ★★★
Contact: Mr Peter Durbin
Cumbrian Cottages, 2 Lonsdale
Street, Carlisle CA1 1DB
T: (01228) 599960
F: (01228) 599970
E: enquiries@cumbriancottages.
co.uk
I: www.cumbrian-cottages.co.uk

Wordsworth, Neaum Crag ★★★
Contact: Susan Jackson
Heart of the Lakes, Fisherbeck
Mill, Old Lake Road, Ambleside
LA22 0DH
T: (015394) 32321
F: (015394) 33251

SKELWITH FOLD
Cumbria

The Hobbit ★★★
Contact: Mr Peter Durbin
Cumbrian Cottages, 2 Lonsdale
Street, Carlisle CA1 1DB
T: (01228) 599960
F: (01228) 599970
E: enquiries@
cumbrian-cottages.co.uk
I: www.cumbrian-cottages.co.uk

Rivendell Cottage ★★★
Contact: Susan Jackson
Heart of the Lakes, Fisherbeck
Mill, Old Lake Road, Ambleside
LA22 0DH
T: (015394) 32321
F: (015394) 33251

Swallows House ★★★★★
Contact: Mrs Vivien Bass
Wheelwrights Holiday Cottages,
Langdale, Ambleside LA22 9HS
T: (015394) 37635
E: enquiries@wheelwrights.com
I: www.wheelwrights.com

SKINBURNESS
Cumbria

Lucknow ★★★★
Contact: Mrs Joy Ross
10 Brittons Close, Bedford
MK44 1PN
T: 07774 888480
F: 07860 275142
E: lucknowcottage@btinternet.
com
I: www.btinternet.
com/~lucknowcottage

SMARDALE
Cumbria

Leases ★★★
Contact: Mrs Christina Galloway
Leases, Swardale, Kirkby Stephen
CA17 4HQ
T: (017683) 71198
E: leasesgal@aol.com

SOCKBRIDGE
Cumbria

Eastwards Cottage ★★★
Contact: Mr Paul Durbin
Cumbrian Cottages, 2 Lonsdale
Street, Carlisle CA1 1DB
T: (01228) 599960
F: (01228) 599970
E: enquiries@cumbriancottages.
co.uk
I: www.cumbrian-cottages.co.uk

SOUTHWAITE
Cumbria

Serendipity Cottage ★★★
Contact: The Manager
Ref:2814, Dales Holiday
Cottages, Carleton Business
Park, Carleton New Road,
Skipton BD23 2AA
T: (01756) 799821
F: (01756) 797012
E: info@dalesholcot.com
I: www.dalesholcot.com

SPARK BRIDGE
Cumbria

Riversdale ★★★
Contact: Mr John Serginson
The Lakeland Cottage Company,
Waterside House, Ulverston
LA12 8AN
T: (015395) 30024
F: (015395) 31932
E: john@lakelandcottageco.com
I: www.lakelandcottageco.com

Riverside Cottage ★★★
Contact: Mr Peter Durbin
Cumbrian Cottages, 2 Lonsdale
Street, Carlisle CA1 1DB
T: (01228) 599960
F: (01228) 599970
E: enquiries@
cumbrian-cottages.co.uk
I: www.cumbrian-cottage.co.uk

Summer Hill Holidays ★★★
Contact: Mrs R. Campbell
Summer Hill Holidays, Summer
Hill, Ulverston LA12 7SS
T: (01229) 861510
F: (01229) 861090
E: rosemary@summerhill.co.uk
I: www.summerhill.co.uk

Thurstonville High Lodge ★★
Contact: Mr Nigel Lord
Thurstonville High Lodge,
Ulverston LA12 7SX
T: (01229) 861271
F: (01229) 861271

The Turners Cottage ★★★
Contact: Mr Philip Johnston
The Coppermines & Coniston
Lakes Cottages, The Estate
Office, The Bridge, Coniston
LA21 8HJ
T: (015394) 41765
E: bookings@coppermines.co.uk
I: www.coppermines.co.uk

STAINTON
Cumbria

The Cottage at Andrew House ★★★
Contact: The Manager
Ref:2098, Dales Holiday
Cottages, Carleton Business
Park, Carleton New Road,
Skipton BD23 2AA
T: (01756) 799821
F: (01756) 797012
E: info@dalesholcot.com
I: www.dalesholcot.com

Mill Race View ★★★
Contact: The Manager
Ref:2264, Dales Holiday
Cottages, Carleton Business
Park, Carleton New Road,
Skipton BD23 2AA
T: (01756) 799821
F: (01756) 797012
E: info@dalesholcot.com
I: www.dalesholcot.com

STAIR
Cumbria

Clairgarth ★★★
Contact: Peter Durbin & Tony Commons
Cumbrian Cottages, 2 Lonsdale
Street, Carlisle CA1 1DB
T: (01228) 599960
F: (01228) 599970
E: enquiries@
cumbrian-cottages.co.uk
I: www.cumbrian-cottages.co.uk

Grizedale Cottage ★★★
Contact: Mr David Burton
Lakeland Cottage Holidays,
Melbecks, Keswick CA12 4QX
T: (017687) 76065
F: (017687) 76869
E: info@lakelandcottages.co.uk
I: www.lakelandcottages.co.uk

Stair Mill ★★★
Contact: Jacqueline Williams
Stair Mill, Keswick CA12 5UF
T: (017687) 78333
E: peterwilliams@stairmill.com
I: www.stairmill.com

STAPLETON
Cumbria

Drove Cottage ★★★
Contact: Mr Kenneth & Mrs Anne Hope
Drove Inn Public House,
Roweltown, Stapleton CA6 6LB
T: (01697) 748202
F: (01697) 748054
E: droveinn@hotmail.com

STAVELEY
Cumbria

Ashleigh ★★★★
Contact: Mr John Serginson
The Lakeland Cottage Company,
Waterside House, Ulverston
LA12 8AN
T: (015395) 30024
F: (015395) 31932
E: john@lakelandcottageco.com
I: www.lakelandcottageco.com

Establishments printed in blue have a detailed entry in this guide

CUMBRIA – THE LAKE DISTRICT

Avondale ★★★
Contact: Mrs Hughes
2 Lynstead, Thornbarrow Road,
Windermere LA23 2DG
T: (015394) 45713
E: enquiries@avondale.uk.net
I: www.avondale.uk.net

Bobbin Cottage ★★★
Contact: The Manager
Ref:2284, Dales Holiday
Cottages, Carleton Business
Park, Carleton New Road,
Skipton BD23 2AA
T: (01756) 799821
F: (01756) 797012
E: info@dalesholcot.com
I: www.dalesholcot.com

Brunt Knott Farm Holiday Cottages ★★★
Contact: Mr William & Mrs Margaret Beck
Brunt Knott Farm, Staveley,
Kendal LA8 9QX
T: (01539) 821030
F: (01539) 821221
E: margaret@bruntknott.demon.co.uk
I: www.bruntknott.demon.co.uk

The Chapel ★★★
Contact: Mr Peter Durbin
Cumbrian Cottages, 2 Lonsdale
Street, Carlisle CA1 1DB
T: (01228) 599960
F: (01228) 599970
E: enquiries@cumbriancottages.co.uk
I: www.cumbrian-cottages.co.uk

Ghyll Bank House ★★★
Contact: Mrs Beaty
Garnett House Farm, Kendal
LA9 5SF
T: (01539) 724542
F: (01539) 724542
E: info@garnetthousefarm.co.uk
I: www.garnetthousefarm.co.uk

Littlewood Farm
Rating Applied For
Contact: Fiona Moody
Dales Holiday Cottages, Carleton
Business Park, Carleton New
Road, Skipton BD23 2AA
T: (01756) 790919
F: (01756) 797012
E: info@dales-holiday-cottages.com
I: www.dales-holiday-cottages.com

Marsden ★★★
Contact: Peter Durbin & Tony Commons
Cumbrian Cottages, 2 Lonsdale
Street, Carlisle CA1 1DB
T: (01228) 599960
F: (01228) 599970

Mill House ★★★
Contact: Mr Peter Durbin
Cumbrian Cottages, 2 Lonsdale
Street, Carlisle CA1 1DB
T: (01228) 599960
F: (01228) 599970
E: enquiries@cumbrian-cottages.co.uk
I: www.cumbrian-cottages.co.uk

Millies Cottage ★★★
Contact: Mr Peter Durbin
Cumbrian Cottages, 2 Lonsdale
Street, Carlisle CA1 1DB
T: (01228) 599960
F: (01228) 599970
E: enquiries@cumbriancottages.co.uk
I: www.cumbrian-cottages.co.uk

Nook House ★★★
Contact: Mr John Serginson
The Lakeland Cottage Company,
Waterside House, Ulverston
LA12 8AN
T: (015395) 30024
F: (015395) 31932
E: john@lakelandcottageco.com
I: www.lakelandcottageco.com

Weasel Cottage ★★★
Contact: Mr Peter Durbin
Cumbrian Cottages, 2 Lonsdale
Street, Carlisle CA1 1DB
T: (01228) 599960
F: (01228) 599970
E: enquiries@cumbriancottages.co.uk
I: www.cumbrian-cottages.co.uk

STAVELEY-IN-CARTMEL
Cumbria

April Cottage ★★★
Contact: Mr Peter Durbin
Cumbrian Cottages, 2 Lonsdale
Street, Carlisle CA1 1DB
T: (01228) 599960
F: (01228) 599970
E: enquiries@cumbriancottages.co.uk
I: www.cumbrian-cottages.co.uk

Croft Cottage ★★★
Contact: Mr Paul Liddell
Lakelovers, Belmont House, Lake
Road, Bowness-on-Windermere,
Windermere LA23 3BJ
T: (015394) 88855
F: (015394) 88857
E: bookings@lakelovers.co.uk
I: www.lakelovers.co.uk

Staveley House Cottage ★★★★
Contact: Mr John Serginson
The Lakeland Cottage Company,
Waterside House, Ulverston
LA12 8AN
T: (015395) 30024
F: (015395) 31932
E: john@lakelandcottageco.com
I: www.lakelandcottageco.com

THORNTHWAITE
Cumbria

Barf Cottage ★★★
Contact: Mrs Susan Jackson
Heart of the Lakes, Fisherbeck
Mill, Old Lake Road, Ambleside
LA22 0DH
T: (015394) 32321
F: (015394) 33251
E: info@heartofthelakes.com
I: www.heartofthelakes.co.uk

Beck View ★★★★
Contact: Mr Peter Durbin
Cumbrian Cottages, 2 Lonsdale
Street, Carlisle CA1 1DB
T: (01228) 599960
F: (01228) 599970
E: enquiries@cumbriancottages.co.uk
I: www.cumbrian-cottages.co.uk

Hallgarth ★★★★
Contact: Mr Peter Durbin
Cumbrian Cottages, 2 Lonsdale
Street, Carlisle CA1 1DB
T: (01228) 599960
F: (01228) 599970
E: enquiries@cumbriancottages.co.uk
I: www.cumbrian-cottages.co.uk

Harriet's Hideaway ★★★★
Contact: David Miller
Harriets Hideaway, 81 Whaggs
Lane, Newcastle upon Tyne
NE6 4PQ
T: (0191) 4880549
F: (0191) 4223303
E: dm81@blueyonder.co.uk
I: www.dm81.pwp.blueyonder.co.uk

Holly Bank Cottage ★★★★
Contact: Kate Danchin
Holly Bank Cottage, Keswick
CA12 5SA
T: (017687) 78192
E: enquiries@hollybankcottage.co.uk
I: www.hollybankcottage.co.uk

Joans Cottage ★★★★
Contact: Mr Peter Durbin
Cumbrian Cottages, 2 Lonsdale
Street, Carlisle CA1 1DB
T: (01228) 599960
F: (01228) 599970
E: enquiries@cumbriancottages.co.uk
I: www.cumbrian-cottages.co.uk

Old School House ★★★
Contact: Mr Peter Durbin
Cumbrian Cottages, 2 Lonsdale
Street, Carlisle CA1 1DB
T: (01228) 599960
F: (01228) 599970
E: enquiries@cumbrian-cottages.co.uk
I: www.cumbrian-cottages.co.uk

Seat Howe ★★★
Contact: Mrs Dorothy Bell
Seat Howe, Keswick CA12 5SQ
T: (017687) 78371

Talcomb ★★★
Contact: Mr Howard King
Talcomb, 38 The Drive,
Newcastle upon Tyne NE3 4AH
T: (0191) 2268656
E: hkdevelopments@virgin.net
I: www.hkdevelopmentslakes.co.uk

Thwaite Hill Barn ★★★
Contact: Mrs SE Walls
Thwaite Hill Barn, Thwaite Hill,
Thornthwaite, Keswick CA3 8TP
T: (017687) 78412

Thwaite Hill Cottage ★★★
Contact: Mr David Burton
Lakeland Cottage Holidays,
Melbecks, Keswick CA12 4QX
T: (017687) 76065
F: (017687) 76869
E: info@lakelandcottages.co.uk
I: www.lakelandcottages.co.uk

Woodside Cottage ★★★★
Contact: Mr Peter Durbin
Cumbrian Cottages, Lonsdale
Street, Carlisle CA1 1DB
T: (01228) 599960
F: (01228) 599970
E: enquiries@cumbrian-cottages.co.uk
I: www.cumbrian-cottages.co.uk

THRELKELD
Cumbria

1 The Barns ★★★
Contact: Mrs Joan Browne
One The Barns, Merritts Hill,
Redruth TR16 4DF
T: (01209) 215553
E: tom.joan@lineone.net

Blease Barn ★★★★
Contact: Mr Peter Durbin
Cumbrian Cottages, 2 Lonsdale
Street, Carlisle CA1 1DB
T: (01228) 599960
F: (01228) 599970
E: enquiries@cumbriancottages.co.uk
I: www.cumbrian-cottages.co.uk

Blease Cottage ★★★★
Contact: Mr Peter Durbin
Cumbrian Cottages, 2 Lonsdale
Street, Carlisle CA1 1DB
T: (01228) 599960
F: (01228) 599970
E: enquiries@cumbrian-cottages.co.uk
I: www.cumbrian-cottages.co.uk

Blencathra Centre ★★★
Contact: Paul Richards
Blencathra Centre - Latrigg
View, Derwent View, Bo,
Blencathra Centre, Keswick
CA12 4SG
T: (017687) 79601
F: (017687) 79264
E: enquiries.bl@field-studies-council.org

Cropple How ★★★
Contact: Mr Peter Durbin
Cumbrian Cottages, 2 Lonsdale
Street, Carlisle CA1 1DB
T: (01228) 599960
F: (01228) 599970
E: enquiries@cumbrian-cottages.co.uk
I: www.cumbrian-cottages.co.uk

Fell View ★★★
Contact: Clive Sykes
Sykes Cottages, York House,
York Street, Chester CH1 3LR
T: (01244) 345700
F: (01244) 321442

Heather View ★★★
Contact: Mr Peter Durbin
Cumbrian Cottages, 2 Lonsdale
Street, Carlisle CA1 1DB
T: (01228) 599960
F: (01228) 599970
E: enquiries@cumbrian-cottages.co.uk
I: www.cumbrian-cottages.co.uk

Katellen Cottage ★★★
Contact: Mr Peter Durbin
Cumbrian Cottages, 2 Lonsdale
Street, Carlisle CA1 1DB
T: (01228) 599960
F: (01228) 599970
E: enquiries@cumbrian-cottages.co.uk
I: www.cumbrian-cottages.co.uk

CUMBRIA – THE LAKE DISTRICT

Latcrag Cottage and Caravan ★★★★
Contact: D Benson
Latcrag Cottage and Caravan, High Row, Keswick CA12 4SF
T: (017687) 79256

Lingclose Cottage ★★★★
Contact: The Manager
Ref:2469, Dales Holiday Cottages, Carleton Business Park, Carleton New Road, Skipton BD23 2AA
T: (01756) 799821
F: (01756) 797012
E: info@dalesholcot.com
I: www.dalesholcot.com

The Old Manse Barn ★★★
Contact: Mrs L Deadman
Old Manse Barn, The Old Manse, Keswick CA12 4SQ
T: (017687) 79270
E: jon@deadman.freeserve.co.uk
I: www.deadman.freeserve.co.uk

The Old School House ★★★★
Contact: Lucy Swarbrick
The Old School House, 12 Bonville Chase, Altrincham WA14 4QA
T: (0161) 9286290
E: info@cottageinthrelkeld.co.uk
I: www.theoldschoolhousethrelkeld.co.uk

Taylors Cottage ★★★
Contact: Mr Peter Durbin & Tony Commons
Cumbrian Cottages, 2 Lonsdale Street, Carlisle CA1 1DB
T: (01228) 599960
F: (01228) 599970
E: enquiries@cumbrian-cottages.co.uk
I: www.cumbrian-cottages.co.uk

Townhead Barn ★★★
Contact: Mr David Burton
Lakeland Cottage Holidays, Melbecks, Keswick CA12 4QX
T: (017687) 76065
F: (017687) 76869
E: info@lakelandcottages.co.uk
I: www.lakelandcottages.co.uk

Townhead Byre ★★★
Contact: Mr David Burton
Lakeland Cottage Holidays, Melbecks, Keswick CA12 4QX
T: (017687) 76065
F: (017687) 76869
E: info@lakelandcottages.co.uk
I: www.lakelandcottages.co.uk

White Pike ★★★★
Contact: Mr Peter Durbin
Cumbrian Cottages, 2 Lonsdale Street, Carlisle CA1 1DB
T: (01228) 599960
F: (01228) 599970
E: enquiries@cumbrian-cottages.co.uk
I: www.cumbrian-cottages.co.uk

THURSTONFIELD
Cumbria

The Tranquil Otter ★★★★-★★★★★
Contact: Richard & Wendy Wise
The Tranquil Otter Lodges, The Lough, Carlisle CA5 6HB
T: (01228) 576661
F: (01228) 576662
E: tranquilotter@aol.com
I: www.thetranquilotter.co.uk

TIRRIL
Cumbria

Tirril Farm Cottages ★★★★
Contact: Mr David Owens
Tirril Farm Cottages, Tirril View, Penrith CA10 2JE
T: (01768) 864767
F: (01768) 864767
E: enquiries@tirrilfarmcottages.co.uk
I: www.tirrilfarmcottages.co.uk

TORVER
Cumbria

Brigg House ★★★
Contact: Mr John Serginson
The Lakeland Cottage Company, Waterside House, Ulverston LA12 8AN
T: (015395) 30024
F: (015395) 31932
E: john@lakelandcottageco.com
I: www.lakelandcottageco.com

Brocklebank Ground Cottages Old Pottery, Old Stable, Old Dairy ★★★-★★★★
Contact: Mr Philip Johnston
The Coppermines & Coniston Lakes Cottages, The Estate Office, The Bridge, Coniston LA21 8HJ
T: (015394) 41765
E: bookings@coppermines.co.uk
I: www.coppermines.co.uk

Ellice Howe ★★★★
Contact: Mr Paul Liddell
Lakelovers, Belmont House, Lake Road, Bowness-on-Windermere, Windermere LA23 3BJ
T: (015394) 88855
F: (015394) 88857
E: bookings@lakelovers.co.uk
I: www.lakelovers.co.uk

High Park Cottage ★★★★
Contact: Mr Philip Johnston
The Coppermines & Coniston Lakes Cottages, The Estate Office, The Bridge, Coniston LA21 8HJ
T: (015394) 41765
I: www.coppermines.co.uk/property/show_details.cgi?id=94

Scarr Head Cottage ★★★★
Contact: Mr Peter Durbin
Cumbrian Cottages, 2 Lonsdale Street, Carlisle CA1 1DB
T: (01228) 599960
F: (01228) 599970
E: enquiries@cumbrian-cottages.co.uk
I: www.cumbrian-cottages.co.uk

Station House & Station Cottage ★★★
Contact: Mr Philip Johnston
The Coppermines & Coniston Lakes Cottages, The Estate Office, The Bridge, Coniston LA21 8HJ
T: (015394) 41765
F: (015394) 41944
E: info@coppermines.co.uk
I: www.coppermines.co.uk

Sunny Bank Mill ★★★
Contact: Paul Liddell
Lakelovers, Belmont House, Lake Road, Bowness-on-Windermere, Windermere LA23 3BJ
T: (015394) 88855
F: (015394) 88857

TROUTBECK
Cumbria

1 and 2 Butt Hill Cottage ★★★-★★★★
Contact: Paul Liddell
Lakelovers, Belmont House, Lake Road, Bowness-on-Windermere, Windermere LA23 3BJ
T: (015394) 88855
F: (015394) 88857

Barn Cottage ★★★
Contact: Mr Paul Liddell
Lakelovers, Belmont House, Lake Road, Bowness-on-Windermere, Windermere LA23 3BJ
T: (015394) 88855
F: (015394) 88857
E: bookings@lakelovers.co.uk
I: www.lakelovers.co.uk

Betty's Cottage ★★★★
Contact: Susan Jackson
Heart of the Lakes, Fisherbeck Mill, Old Lake Road, Ambleside LA22 0DH
T: (015394) 32321
F: (015394) 33251
E: info@heartofthelakes.co.uk
I: www.heartofthelakes.co.uk

Fell Cottage ★★★★
Contact: Mr Paul Liddell
Lakelovers, Belmont House, Lake Road, Bowness-on-Windermere, Windermere LA23 3BJ
T: (015394) 88855
F: (015394) 88857
E: bookings@lakelovers.co.uk
I: www.lakelovers.co.uk

Glenside ★★★
Contact: Susan Jackson
Heart of the Lakes, Fisherbeck Mill, Old Lake Road, Ambleside LA22 0DH
T: (015394) 32321
F: (015394) 33251
E: info@heartofthelakes.co.uk
I: www.heartofthelakes.co.uk

Granary Cottage ★★★
Contact: Mr Peter Durbin
Cumbrian Cottages, 2 Lonsdale Street, Carlisle CA1 1DB
T: (01228) 599960
F: (01228) 599970
E: enquiries@cumbriancottages.co.uk
I: www.cumbrian-cottages.co.uk

Holbeck Ghyll Lodge ★★★★
Contact: Mrs Maggie Kaye
Holbeck Ghyll Lodge, Holmdene, Stoney Bank Road, Huddersfield HD9 7SL
T: (01484) 684605
F: (01484) 684605
E: info@holbecklodge.com
I: www.holbecklodge.com

Ivy Cottage ★★★
Contact: Mr Paul Liddell
Lakelovers, Belmont House, Lake Road, Bowness-on-Windermere, Windermere LA23 3BJ
T: (015394) 88855
F: (015394) 88857
E: bookings@lakelovers.co.uk
I: www.lakelovers.co.uk

Knotts Cottage ★★★
Contact: Susan Jackson
Heart of the Lakes, Fisherbeck Mill, Old Lake Road, Ambleside LA22 0DH
T: (015394) 32321
F: (015394) 33251
E: info@heartofthelakes.co.uk
I: www.heartofthelakes.co.uk

Knotts Farmhouse ★★★
Contact: Susan Jackson
Heart of the Lakes, Fisherbeck Mill, Old Lake Road, Ambleside LA22 0DH
T: (015394) 32321
F: (015394) 33251
E: info@heartofthelakes.co.uk
I: www.heartofthelakes.co.uk

Long Mire Yeat ★★★
Contact: Susan Jackson
Heart of the Lakes, Fisherbeck Mill, Old Lake Road, Ambleside LA22 0DH
T: (015394) 32321
F: (015394) 33251
E: info@heartofthelakes.co.uk
I: www.heartofthelakes.co.uk

Low House & The Studio ★★★★
Contact: Eileen Dale
Low House & The Studio Low House, Moorend, Penrith CA11 0SX
T: (017687) 79388
I: www.holidaycottages-lakedistrict.co.uk

Myley Ghyll ★★★★★
Contact: Paul Liddell
Lakelovers, Belmont House, Lake Road, Bowness-on-Windermere, Windermere LA23 3BJ
T: (015394) 88855
F: (015394) 88857
E: bookings@lakelovers.co.uk
I: www.lakelovers.co.uk

Old Coach House
Rating Applied For
Contact: Mr Ben Price
Wheelwrights Holiday Cottages, Langdale, Ambleside LA22 9HS
T: (015394) 37635
E: enquiries@wheelwrights.com
I: www.wheelwrights.com

CUMBRIA – THE LAKE DISTRICT

Orchard Cottage ★★★★
Contact: Paul Liddell
Lakelovers, Belmont House, Lake Road, Bowness-on-Windermere, Windermere LA23 3BJ
T: (015394) 88855
F: (015394) 88857

South View ★★★
Contact: Mr Peter Durbin
Cumbrian Cottages, 2 Lonsdale Street, Carlisle CA1 1DB
T: (01228) 599960
F: (01228) 599970
E: enquiries@cumbrian-cottage.co.uk
I: www.cumbrian-cottages.co.uk

Stamp Howe ★★★★
Contact: Susan Jackson
Heart of the Lakes, Fisherbeck Mill, Old Lake Road, Ambleside LA22 0DH
T: (015394) 32321
F: (015394) 33251

Storeythwaite ★★★★
Contact: Mrs Susan Jackson
Heart of the Lakes, Fisherbeck Mill, Old Lake Road, Ambleside LA22 0DH
T: (015394) 32321
F: (015394) 33251
E: info@heartofthelakes.co.uk
I: www.heartofthelakes.co.uk

Syke Villa ★★★
Contact: Mr Paul Liddell
Lakelovers, Belmont House, Lake Road, Bowness-on-Windermere, Windermere LA23 3BJ
T: (015394) 88855
F: (015394) 88857
E: bookings@lakelovers.co.uk
I: www.lakelovers.co.uk

Wee Fell Cottage ★★★★
Contact: Mr Paul Liddell
Lakelovers, Belmont House Lake Road, Windermere LA23 3BJ
T: (015394) 88855
F: (015394) 88857
E: bookings@lakelovers.co.uk
I: www.lakelovers.co.uk

Wetherlam ★★★
Contact: Susan Jackson
Heart of the Lakes, Fisherbeck Mill, Old Lake Road, Ambleside LA22 0DH
T: (015394) 32321
F: (015394) 33251

TROUTBECK BRIDGE
Cumbria

Beckside Cottage ★★★
Contact: Mr Peter Durbin
Cumbrian Cottages, 2 Lonsdale Street, Carlisle CA1 1DB
T: (01228) 599960
F: (01228) 599970
E: enquiries@cumbrian-cottages.co.uk
I: www.cumbrian-cottages.co.uk

Briery Lodge ★★★
Contact: Susan Jackson
Heart of the Lakes, Fisherbeck Mill, Old Lake Road, Ambleside LA22 0DH
T: (015394) 32321
F: (015394) 33251
E: info@heartofthelakes.co.uk
I: www.heartofthelakes.co.uk

Grooms Cottage ★★★★
Contact: Mr Peter Durbin
Cumbrian Cottages, 2 Lonsdale Street, Carlisle CA1 1DB
T: (01228) 599960
F: (01228) 599970
E: enquiries@cumbrian-cottages.co.uk
I: www.cumbrian-cottages.co.uk

Howarth Cottage ★★★
Contact: Mr Peter Durbin
Cumbrian Cottages, 2 Lonsdale Street, Carlisle CA1 1DB
T: (01228) 599960
F: (01228) 599970
E: enquiries@cumbriancottages.co.uk
I: www.cumbrian-cottages.co.uk

Lowther Cottage ★★★
Contact: Mrs Susan Jackson
Heart of the Lakes, Fisherbeck Mill, Old Lake Road, Ambleside LA22 0DH
T: (015394) 32321
F: (015394) 33251
E: info@heartofthelakes.co.uk
I: www.heartofthelakes.co.uk

Quarry Garth Lodge ★★★★
Contact: Mr Richard Bee
Lakeland Estates, Ambleside Road, Windermere LA23 1LF
T: (015394) 45222
F: (015394) 45333
E: lakelandestates@nascr.net

School Cottage ★★★
Contact: Susan Jackson
Heart of the Lakes, Fisherbeck Mill, Old Lake Road, Ambleside LA22 0DH
T: (015394) 32321
F: (015394) 33251

ULDALE
Cumbria

Coach House and Groom Cottage ★★★
Contact: Mr Durbin
Cumbrian Cottages, 2 Lonsdale Street, Carlisle CA1 1DB
T: (01228) 599960
F: (01228) 599970
E: enquiries@cumbrian-cottages.co.uk
I: www.cumbrian-cottages.co.uk

Knaifot Cottage ★★★★
Contact: The Owner
Knaifot Cottage, 3 The Terrace, Cockermouth CA7 1EY

Trusmadoor ★★★★
Contact: The Owner
Trusmadoor, Garden Cottage, Wigton CA7 1JR

ULLOCK
Cumbria

Tree Tops ★★★★
Contact: The Manager
Ref:2884, Dales Holiday Cottages, Carleton Business Park, Carleton New Road, Skipton BD23 2AA
T: (01756) 799821
F: (01756) 797012
E: info@dalesholcot.com
I: www.dalesholcot.com

ULLSWATER
Cumbria

Cherry Holm Bungalow ★★★★
Contact: Mrs S Sheard
7 Bark Lane, Ilkley LS29 0RA
T: (01943) 830766

Ghyll Cottage ★★★★
Contact: Elizabeth Darbyshire
Ghyll Cottage, Crossgates Farm, Hartsop, Patterdale, Penrith CA11 0NZ
T: (017684) 82566
F: (017684) 82566
E: erdarbyshire@aol.com
I: www.ghyllcottage.co.uk

Lakefield ★★★★
Contact: Susan Jackson
Heart of the Lakes, Fisherbeck Mill, Old Lake Road, Ambleside LA22 0DH
T: (015394) 32321
F: (015394) 33251
E: info@heartofthelakes.co.uk
I: www.heartofthelakes.co.uk

Land Ends ★★★
Contact: Ms Barbara Holmes
Land Ends, Watermillock, Nr Ullswater, Penrith CA11 0NB
T: (017684) 86438
F: (017684) 86959
E: infolandends@btinternet.com
I: www.landends.co.uk

Low Wood View ★★★
Contact: Mrs J Wear
Low Wood View, Green Lane, Hartsop, Patterdale, Penrith CA11 0NQ
T: (017684) 82396

Patterdale Hall Estate ★★-★★★★
Contact: Ms Sue Kay
Patterdale Hall Estate, Estate Office, Glenridding, Penrith CA11 0PJ
T: (017684) 82308
F: (017684) 82867
E: mail@patterdalehallestate.com
I: www.patterdalehallestate.com

Swarthbeck Farm Holiday Cottages ★★★
Contact: Mr & Mrs Parkin
Swarthbeck Farm Holiday Cottages, Swarthbeck Farm, Howtown, Penrith CA10 2ND
T: (017684) 86432
E: whparkin@ukonline.co.uk
I: www.horseholidaysincumbria.co.uk

ULPHA
Cumbria

Brigg House Cottage ★★★★
Contact: Mr Philip Johnston
The Coppermines & Coniston Lakes Cottages, The Estate Office, The Bridge, Coniston LA21 8HJ
T: (015394) 41765
E: bookings@coppermines.co.uk
I: www.coppermines.co.uk

Fishermans Cottage (Church House) ★★★★
Contact: Mr Philip Johnston
The Coppermines & Coniston Lakes Cottages, The Estate Office, The Bridge, Coniston LA21 8HJ
T: (015394) 41765
F: (015394) 41944
E: info@coppermines.co.uk
I: www.coppermines.co.uk

High Kiln Bank Cottage ★★★★
Contact: Mr Philip Johnston
The Coppermines & Lakes Cottages, The Estate Office, The Bridge, Coniston LA21 8HJ
T: (015394) 41765
F: (015394) 41944
I: www.coppermines.co.uk/

Low Birks ★★★★
Contact: Mr John Serginson
The Lakeland Cottage Company, Waterside House, Ulverston LA12 8AN
T: (015395) 30024
F: (015395) 31932
E: john@lakelandcottageco.com
I: www.lakelandcottageco.com

ULVERSTON
Cumbria

Ashlack Cottages ★★★★
Contact: Amanda Keegan
Ashlack Cottages, Ashlack Hall, Kirkby-in-Furness LA17 7XN
T: (01229) 889108
F: (01229) 889111
E: enquiries@ashlackcottages.co.uk
I: www.ashlackcottages.co.uk

The Falls ★★-★★★
Contact: Mrs Cheetham and Mrs Unger
Mansriggs, Ulverston LA12 7PX
T: (01229) 583781
I: www.thefalls.co.uk

Lile Cottage at Gleaston Water Mill ★★★★
Contact: Vicky Brereton
Gleaston Water Mill, Ulverston LA12 0QH
T: (01229) 869244
F: (01229) 869764
E: pigsty@watermill.co.uk
I: www.watermill.co.uk

The Old School House ★★★★
Contact: Mr John Serginson
The Lakeland Cottage Company, Waterside House, Ulverston LA12 8AN
T: (015395) 30024
F: (015395) 31932
E: john@lakelandcottageco.com
I: www.lakelandcottageco.com

Orchard Cottage ★★★
Contact: Brian Martin
Orchard Cottage, Mascalles Bungalow, Ulverston LA12 0TQ
T: (01229) 463591
E: brianmartin@orchardcottageulverston.co.uk
I: www.orchardcottageulverston.co.uk

CUMBRIA – THE LAKE DISTRICT

3 Rosside Cottages ★★★
Contact: Clive Sykes
Sykes Cottages, York House,
York Street, Chester CH1 3LR
T: (01244) 345700
F: (01244) 321442

Swarthmoor Hall ★★★-★★★★★
Contact: Mr Bill Shaw
Swarthmoor Hall, Swarthmoor
Hall Lane, Swarthmoor,
Ulverston LA12 0JQ
T: (01229) 583204
F: (01229) 583283
E: swarthmrhall@gn.apc.org
I: www.swarthmoorhall.co.uk

Waters Yeat Mill ★★★
Contact: Mr Peter Durbin
Cumbrian Cottages, 2 Lonsdale
Street, Carlisle CA1 1DB
T: (01228) 599960
F: (01228) 599970
E: enquiries@
cumbrian-cottages.co.uk
I: www.cumbrian-cottages.co.uk

Wood View & Stable End ★★★★
Contact: Mr John Serginson
The Lakeland Cottage Company,
Waterside House, Ulverston
LA12 8AN
T: (015395) 30024
F: (015395) 31932
E: john@lakelandcottageco.com
I: www.lakelandcottageco.com

UNDERBARROW
Cumbria

Honey Pot ★★★★★
Contact: Mr Peter Durbin
Cumbrian Cottages, 2 Lonsdale
Street, Carlisle CA1 1DB
T: (01228) 599960
F: (01228) 599970
E: enquiries@
cumbrian-cottages.co.uk
I: www.cumbrian-cottages.co.uk

Nanny Goat ★★★★★
Contact: Mr Peter Durbin
Cumbrian Cottages, 2 Lonsdale
Street, Carlisle CA1 1DB
T: (01228) 599960
F: (01228) 599970
E: enquiries@cumbriancottages.co.uk
I: www.cumbrian-cottages.co.uk

UNDERSKIDDAW
Cumbria

Apartment 1, Oakfield House ★★★★
Contact: Mr Hogarth
Cumbrian Cottages Limited, 2
Lonsdale Street, Carlisle
CA1 1DB
T: (01228) 599960
F: (01228) 599970
E: enquiries@
cumbrian-cottages.co.uk
I: www.cumbrian-cottages.co.uk

Artists View ★★★★
Contact: Mr Peter Durbin
Cumbrian Cottages, 2 Lonsdale
Street, Carlisle CA1 1DB
T: (01228) 599960
F: (01228) 599970
E: enquiries@
cumbrian-cottages.co.uk
I: www.cumbrian-cottages.co.uk

Garth Cottage ★★★★
Contact: Mr Peter Durbin
Cumbrian Cottages, 2 Lonsdale
Street, Carlisle CA1 1DB
T: (01228) 599960
F: (01228) 599970
E: enquiries@
cumbrian-cottages.co.uk
I: www.cumbrian-cottages.co.uk

Squirrels Leap ★★★★
Contact: Mr Peter Durbin
Cumbrian Cottages, 2 Lonsdale
Street, Carlisle CA1 1DB
T: (01228) 599960
F: (01228) 599970
E: enquiries@
cumbrian-cottages.co.uk
I: www.cumbrian-cottages.co.uk

Whinny Brow ★★★★
Contact: Mr Peter Durbin
Cumbrian Cottages, 2 Lonsdale
Street, Carlisle CA1 1DB
T: (01228) 599960
F: (01228) 599970
E: enquiries@
cumbrian-cottages.co.uk
I: www.cumbrian-cottages.co.uk

WASDALE
Cumbria

Sundial Cottage ★★★
Contact: Mr Michael & Mrs
Christine McKinley
Sundial Cottage, Galesyke,
Wasdale CA20 1ET
T: (01946) 726267

Woodhow Farm Cottages ★★★
Contact: Dr Kaminski
The Squirrels, 55 Broadway,
Cheadle SK8 1LB
T: (0161) 428 9116
E: woodhow_farm@kaminsk.fsnet.co.uk
I: www.kaminski.fsnet.co.uk

Yewtree Farm ★★★-★★★★★
Contact: Pauline Corley
Yewtree Farm, Seascale
CA20 1EU
T: (019467) 26285
E: pauline@corleyp.freeserve.co.uk
I: www.yewtreeholidays.co.uk

WATER YEAT
Cumbria

Bee Bole House/The Farmstead/The Garden Cottage/Horseshoe Cottage ★★★-★★★★★
Contact: Mr Philip Johnston
The Coppermines & Coniston
Lakes Cottages, The Estate
Office, The Bridge, Coniston
LA21 8HJ
T: (015394) 41765
F: (015394) 41944
E: info@coppermines.co.uk
I: www.coppermines.co.uk

WATERHEAD
Cumbria

Betamere ★★★★
Contact: Susan Jackson
Heart of the Lakes, Fisherbeck
Mill, Old Lake Road, Ambleside
LA22 0DH
T: (015394) 32321
F: (015394) 33251
E: info@heartofthelakes.co.uk
I: www.heartofthelakes.co.uk

High Borrans ★★★★
Contact: Susan Jackson
Heart of the Lakes, Fisherbeck
Mill, Old Lake Road, Ambleside
LA22 0DH
T: (015394) 32321
F: (015394) 33251
E: info@heartofthelakes.co.uk
I: www.heartofthelakes.co.uk

Jenkins Crag ★★★★★
Contact: Susan Jackson
Heart of the Lakes, Fisherbeck
Mill, Old Lake Road, Ambleside
LA22 0DH
T: (015394) 32321
F: (015394) 33251
E: info@heartofthelakes.co.uk
I: www.heartofthelakes.co.uk

Latterbarrow ★★★★
Contact: Susan Jackson
Heart of the Lakes, Fisherbeck
Mill, Old Lake Road, Ambleside
LA22 0DH
T: (015394) 32321
F: (015394) 33251
E: info@heartofthelakes.co.uk
I: www.heartofthelakes.co.uk

Romney 17 ★★★★
Contact: Mrs Susan Jackson
Heart of the Lakes, Fisherbeck
Mill, Old Lake Road, Ambleside
LA22 0DH
T: (015394) 32321
F: (015394) 33251
E: info@heartofthelakes.co.uk
I: www.heartofthelakes.co.uk

Romney Grange ★★★★
Contact: Susan Jackson
Heart of the Lakes, Fisherbeck
Mill, Old Lake Road, Ambleside
LA22 0DH
T: (015394) 32321
F: (015394) 33251

Skelghyll ★★★★
Contact: Susan Jackson
Heart of the Lakes, Fisherbeck
Mill, Old Lake Road, Ambleside
LA22 0DH
T: (015394) 32321
F: (015394) 33251

WATERMILLOCK
Cumbria

Beauthorn Cottage ★★★
Contact: Mr Martin Wardle
Lakes and Valleys, Bateman Fold
Barn, Kendal LA8 8LN
T: (015394) 68103
F: (015394) 68104
E: lakesandvalleys@aol.com
I: www.lakesandvalleys.co.uk

Fair Place Cottage ★★★
Contact: The Owner
Fair Place Cottage, Penrith
CA11 0LR
T: (01768) 486235
F: (01768) 486235

Gatesgarth Cottage ★★★
Contact: The Manager
Ref:2297, Dales Holiday
Cottages, Carleton Business
Park, Carleton New Road,
Skipton BD23 2AA
T: (01756) 790919
F: (01756) 797012
E: info@dalesholcot.com
I: www.dalesholcot.com

Low House ★★★★★
Contact: Mrs Susan Jackson
Heart of the Lakes, Fisherbeck
Mill, Old Lake Road, Ambleside
LA22 0DH
T: (015394) 32321
F: (015394) 33251
E: info@heartofthelakes.co.uk
I: www.heartofthelakes.co.uk

Middlegate ★★★
Contact: Susan Jackson
Heart of the Lakes, Fisherbeck
Mill, Old Lake Road, Ambleside
LA22 0DH
T: (015394) 32321
F: (015394) 33251
E: info@heartofthelakes.co.uk
I: www.heartofthelakes.co.uk

8 Wreay Mansions ★★★★★
Contact: Ms Angela Atkinson
The Paddock 3 Riverside Close,
Selby YO8 8QZ
T: (01405) 816664

WESTWARD
Cumbria

High Hall Cottage ★★★
Contact: Jane Thompson
High Hall Cottage, High Hall,
Wigton CA7 8NQ
T: (016973) 42584

WETHERAL
Cumbria

Geltsdale ★★★★★
Contact: Peter Durbin & Tony
Commons
Cumbrian Cottages, 2 Lonsdale
Street, Carlisle CA1 1DB
T: (01228) 599960
F: (01228) 599970
E: enquiries@
cumbrian-cottages.co.uk
I: www.cumbrian-cottages.co.uk

Sarahs Cottage ★★★★★
Contact: Peter Durbin & Tony
Commons
Cumbrian Cottages, 2 Lonsdale
Street, Carlisle CA1 1DB
T: (01228) 599960
F: (01228) 599970
E: enquiries@
cumbrian-cottages.co.uk
I: www.cumbrian-cottages.co.uk

WHALE
Cumbria

Whale Farm Cottage ★★★★★
Contact: Mrs Lyn Page
Estate Office, Penrith CA10 2HG
T: (01931) 712577
F: (01931) 712679
E: lyn.page@lowther.co.uk
I: www.lowther-estatecottages.co.uk

Establishments printed in blue have a detailed entry in this guide

CUMBRIA – THE LAKE DISTRICT

WHITE MOSS
Cumbria

Ladywood Lodge ★★★
Contact: Susan Jackson
Heart of the Lakes, Fisherbeck Mill, Old Lake Road, Ambleside LA22 0DH
T: (015394) 32321
F: (015394) 33251
E: info@heartofthelakes.co.uk
I: www.heartofthelakes.co.uk

WHITEHAVEN
Cumbria

Rosmerta & Brighida Cottages ★★★★
Contact: Mrs Jane Saxon
Rosmerta & Brighida Cottages, Moresby Hall, Moresby, Whitehaven CA28 6PJ
T: (01946) 696317
F: (01946) 694385
E: etc@moresbyhall.co.uk
I: www.moresbyhall.co.uk

Swallows Return and Owls Retreat ★★★★
Contact: James & Joyce Moore
Swallows Return and Owls Retreat, Moresby Hall Cottage, Moresby, Whitehaven CA28 6PJ
T: (01946) 64078
E: mhc.moresby@virgin.net
I: www.cottageguide.co.uk/moresby

WIGTON
Cumbria

Croftlands Court ★★★★
Contact: Mr Peter Durbin
Cumbrian Cottages, Lonsdale Street, Carlisle CA1 1DB
T: (01228) 599960
F: (01228) 599970
F: enquiries@cumbriancottages.co.uk
I: www.cumbrian-cottages.co.uk

Foxgloves ★★★★
Contact: Mr & Mrs Kerr
Foxgloves, Greenrigg Farm, Westward, Wigton CA7 8AH
T: (016973) 42676
F: (016973) 42676
E: kerr_greenrigg@hotmail.com

Lane Head Apartment ★★★★
Contact: Mr David Colborn
Lane Head Apartment, c/o Lane Head Farm House, Wigton CA7 8PA
T: (016973) 43888
E: info@laneheadapartment.co.uk
I: www.laneheadapartment.co.uk

Leegate House Cottage ★★★
Contact: The Manager
Ref:2658, Dales Holiday Cottages, Carleton Business Park, Carleton New Road, Skipton BD23 2AA
T: (01756) 799821
F: (01756) 797012
E: info@dalesholcot.com
I: www.dalesholcot.com

WINDERMERE
Cumbria

The Abbey Coach House ★★★
Contact: Mrs Pamela Bell
The Abbey Coach House, St Mary's Park, Windermere LA23 1AZ
T: (015394) 44027
F: (015394) 44027
E: abbeycoach@aol.com
I: www.oas.co.uk/ukcottages

Above Cot ★★★
Contact: Peter Durbin & Tony Commons
Cumbrian Cottages, 2 Lonsdale Street, Carlisle CA1 1DB
T: (01228) 599960
F: (01228) 599970
E: enquiries@cumbrian-cottages.co.uk
I: www.cumbrian-cottages.co.uk

Almaria ★★
Contact: Mr Peter Durbin
Cumbrian Cottages, 2 Lonsdale Street, Carlisle CA1 1DB
T: (01228) 599960
F: (01228) 599970
E: enquiries@cumbrian-cottages.co.uk
I: www.cumbrian-cottage.co.uk

Annisgarth ★★★
Contact: Mr Paul Liddell
Lakelovers, Belmont House, Lake Road, Bowness-on-Windermere, Windermere LA23 3BJ
T: (015394) 88855
F: (015394) 88857
E: bookings@lakelovers.co.uk
I: www.lakelovers.co.uk

April Cottage ★★★★
Contact: Sam Lindley
April Cottage, Pontey Farm, Meltham Road, Honley, Huddersfield HD7
T: (01484) 661723
F: (01484) 663839

Bank Cottage ★★★★
Contact: Capt and Mrs Beighton
Bank Cottage, The Gables, 180 Singlewell Road, Gravesend DA11 7RB
T: (01474) 533028

Bears Den ★★★★
Contact: Mr Peter Durbin
Cumbrian Cottages, 2 Lonsdale Street, Carlisle CA1 1DB
T: (01228) 599960
F: (01228) 599970
E: enquiries@cumbriancottages.co.uk
I: www.cumbrian-cottages.co.uk

Beau Penny ★★★
Contact: Mr Paul Liddell
Lakelovers, Belmont House, Lake Road, Bowness-on-Windermere, Windermere LA23 3BJ
T: (015394) 88855
F: (015394) 88857
E: bookings@lakelovers.co.uk
I: www.lakelovers.co.uk

Beaumont ★★★
Contact: Mr Robert Theobald
Beaumont, Thornbarrow Road, Windermere LA23 2DG
T: (015394) 45521
E: dms@beaumont-holidays.co.uk
I: www.beaumont-holidays.co.uk

Bedes Cottage ★★★★
Contact: Mr Peter Durbin
Cumbrian Cottages, 2 Lonsdale Street, Carlisle CA1 1DB
T: (01228) 599960
F: (01228) 599970
E: enquiries@cumbrian-cottages.co.uk
I: www.cumbrian-cottages.co.uk

Beech How Cottage ★★★
Contact: Mr Paul Liddell
Lakelovers, Belmont House, Lake Road, Windermere LA23 3BJ
T: (015394) 88855
F: (015394) 88857
E: bookings@lakelovers.co.uk
I: www.lakelovers.co.uk

Beechmount ★★★★
Contact: Mrs Susan Jackson
Heart of the Lakes, Fisherbeck Mill, Old Lake Road, Ambleside LA22 0DH
T: (015394) 33110
F: (015394) 33251
E: info@heartofthelakes.co.uk
I: www.heartofthelakes.co.uk

Beechwood Apartment ★★★
Contact: Mr Peter Durbin
Cumbrian Cottages, 2 Lonsdale Street, Carlisle CA1 1DB
T: (01228) 599960
F: (01228) 599970
E: enquiries@cumbriancottages.co.uk
I: www.cumbrian-cottages.co.uk

Belle View ★★★
Contact: Mr Peter Durbin
Cumbrian Cottages, 2 Lonsdale Street, Carlisle CA1 1DB
T: (01228) 599960
F: (01228) 599970
E: enquiries@cumbriancottages.co.uk
I: www.cumbrian-cottage.co.uk

1 Birchmill Cottages ★★★★
Contact: Mr Paul Liddell
Lakelovers, Belmont House, Lake Road, Bowness-on-Windermere, Windermere LA23 3BJ
T: (015394) 88855
F: (015394) 88857
E: bookings@lakelovers.co.uk
I: www.lakelovers.co.uk

The Birds Nest ★★★
Contact: Susan Jackson
Heart of the Lakes, Fisherbeck Mill, Old Lake Road, Ambleside LA22 0DH
T: (015394) 32321
F: (015394) 33251

Birthwaite Edge ★★★
Contact: Mr Bruce Dodsworth
Birthwaite Road, Windermere LA23 1BS
T: (015394) 42861
I: www.lakedge.com

Biskey Rise ★★★★
Contact: Susan Jackson
Heart of the Lakes, Fisherbeck Mill, Old Lake Road, Ambleside LA22 0DH
T: (015394) 32321
F: (015394) 33251
E: info@heartofthelakes.co.uk
I: www.heartofthelakes.co.uk

Black Beck Cottage ★★★★★
Contact: Mr Peter Durbin
Cumbrian Cottages, 2 Lonsdale Street, Carlisle CA1 1DB
T: (01228) 599960
F: (01228) 599970
E: enquiries@cumbrian-cottages.co.uk
I: www.cumbrian-cottages.co.uk

The Bothy ★★★
Contact: Mr Peter Durbin
Cumbrian Cottages, 2 Lonsdale Street, Carlisle CA1 1DB
T: (01228) 599960
F: (01228) 599970
E: enquiries@cumbriancottages.co.uk
I: www.cumbrian-cottages.co.uk

Bowmere ★★★★
Contact: Mr Peter Durbin
Cumbrian Cottages, 2 Lonsdale Street, Carlisle CA1 1DB
T: (01228) 599960
F: (01228) 599970
E: enquiries@cumbrian-cottages.co.uk
I: www.cumbrian.cottages.co.uk

Brackenrigg Lodge
Rating Applied For
Contact: Miss Lynne Bush
Brackenrigg Lodge, Windy Hall Road, Windermere LA23 3HY
T: (015394) 47770
E: lynne@brackenriggs.co.uk
I: www.brackenriggs.co.uk

4 Brantfell Cottages ★★★
Contact: Mr Peter Durbin
Cumbrian Cottages, 2 Lonsdale Street, Carlisle CA1 1DB
T: (01228) 599960
F: (01228) 599970
E: enquiries@cumbriancottages.co.uk
I: www.cumbrian-cottages.co.uk

Brantfield Cottage ★★★
Contact: Mr Paul Liddell
Lakelovers, Belmont House, Lake Road, Bowness-on-Windermere, Windermere LA23 3BJ
T: (015394) 88855
F: (015394) 88857
E: bookings@lakelovers.co.uk
I: www.lakelovers.co.uk

Brent Cottage ★★★★
Contact: Paul Liddell
Lakelovers, Belmont House, Lake Road, Bowness-on-Windermere, Windermere LA23 3BJ
T: (015394) 88855
F: (015394) 88857

CUMBRIA – THE LAKE DISTRICT

Briarwood ★★★
Contact: Mr Peter Durbin
Cumbrian Cottages, 2 Lonsdale Street, Carlisle CA1 1DB
T: (01228) 599960
F: (01228) 599970
E: enquiries@cumbriancottages.co.uk
I: www.cumbrian-cottages.co.uk

Briscoe Lodge ★★★
Contact: Margaret Cook
Briscoe Lodge, Ellerthwaite Road, Windermere LA23 2AH
T: (015394) 42928

Brow Edge ★★★
Contact: Mr Peter Durbin
Cumbrian Cottages, 2 Lonsdale Street, Carlisle CA1 1DB
T: (01228) 599960
F: (01228) 599970
E: enquiries@cumbriancottages.co.uk
I: www.cumbrian-cottages.co.uk

Brunton Lodge ★★★★
Contact: Paul Liddell
Lakelovers, Belmont House, Lake Road, Bowness-on-Windermere, Windermere LA23 3BJ
T: (015394) 88855
F: (015394) 88857
E: bookings@lakelovers.co.uk
I: www.lakelovers.co.uk

Burkesfield Cottage ★★★★
Contact: Mr Paul Liddell
Lakelovers, Belmont House, Lake Road, Bowness-on-Windermere, Windermere LA23 3BJ
T: (015394) 88855
F: (015394) 88857
E: bookinghs@lakelovers.co.uk
I: www.lakelovers.co.uk

Burnside Park ★★★★
Contact: Candy Philip
Burnside Park, The Lodge, Kendal Road, Windermere LA23 3EW
T: 0870 0 468624
F: 0870 0 468649
E: cottages@burnsidehotel.com
I: www.burnsidehotel.com

The Burrow ★★★
Contact: Mr Paul Durbin
Cumbrian Cottages, 2 Lonsdale Street, Carlisle CA1 1DB
T: (01228) 599960
F: (01228) 599970
E: enquiries@cumbriancottages.co.uk
I: www.cumbrian-cottages.co.uk

Calgarth ★★★
Contact: Mr Peter Durbin
Cumbrian Cottages, 2 Lonsdale Street, Carlisle CA1 1DB
T: (01228) 599960
F: (01228) 599970
E: enquiries@cumbriancottages.co.uk
I: www.cumbrian-cottages.co.uk

Canons Craig ★★★★
Contact: Mr A or Mrs L Salter
52 Bromleigh Drive, Stoke, Coventry CV2 5LX
T: (024) 7645 7141
E: dougie@freeneasy.net
I: web.ukonline.co.uk/dougiedoo/Index.htm

Canterbury Flats ★★★
Contact: Mr & Mrs Zuniga
Bowness Holidays, 131 Radcliffe New Road, Manchester M45 7RP
T: (0161) 796 3896
F: (0161) 272 1841
E: info@bownesslakelandholidays.co.uk
I: www.bownesslakelandholidays.co.uk

The Carriage House ★★★★★
Contact: Mrs Susan Jackson
Heart of the Lakes, Fisherbeck Mill, Old Lake Road, Ambleside LA22 0DH
T: (015394) 32321
F: (015394) 33251
E: info@heartofthelakes.co.uk
I: www.heartofthelakes.co.uk

Chapel House & Rest ★★★★
Contact: Mr Paul Liddell
Lakelovers, Belmont House, Lake Road, Bowness-on-Windermere, Windermere LA23 3BJ
T: (015394) 88855
F: (015394) 88857
E: bookings@lakelovers.co.uk
I: www.lakelovers.co.uk

Cherry Tree Cottage ★★★★
Contact: Mr Peter Durbin
Cumbrian Cottages, 2 Lonsdale Street, Carlisle CA1 1DB
T: (01228) 599960
F: (01228) 599970
E: enquiries@cumbriancottages.co.uk
I: www.cumbrian-cottages.co.uk

Cherry Vale ★★★★
Contact: Mr Peter Durbin
Cumbrian Cottages, 2 Lonsdale Street, Carlisle CA1 1DB
T: (01228) 599960
F: (01228) 599970
E: enquiries@cumbriancottages.co.uk
I: www.cumbrian-cottages.co.uk

Cinnamon Cottage ★★★★
Contact: Mrs Susan Jackson
Heart of the Lakes, Fisherbeck Mill, Old Lake Road, Ambleside LA22 0DH
T: (015394) 33110
F: (015394) 33251
E: info@heartofthelakes.co.uk

Cinnamon Cottage
Rating Applied For
Contact: Mrs Susan Jackson
Heart of the Lakes, Fisherbeck Mill, Old Lake Road, Ambleside LA22 0DH
T: (015394) 32321
F: (015394) 33251
E: info@heartofthelakes.co.uk
I: www.heartofthelakes.co.uk

Claife View ★★★
Contact: Mr Peter Durbin
Cumbrian Cottages, 2 Lonsdale Street, Carlisle CA1 1DB
T: (01228) 599960
F: (01228) 599970
E: enquiries@cumbrian-cottages.co.uk
I: www.cumbrian-cottages.co.uk

Clara's Cottage ★★★
Contact: Paul Liddell
Lakelovers, Belmont House, Lake Road, Bowness-on-Windermere, Windermere LA23 3BJ
T: (015394) 88855
F: (015394) 88857
E: bookings@lakelovers.co.uk
I: www.lakelovers.co.uk

Claremont ★★★
Contact: Susan Jackson
Heart of the Lakes, Fisherbeck Mill, Old Lake Road, Ambleside LA22 0DH
T: (015394) 32321
F: (015394) 33251

The Coach House ★★★
Contact: Fiona McCulloch
The Coach House, 16 Turpins Chase, Welwyn AL6 0RA
T: (01438) 717077
F: (01438) 717287
E: fiona99@ukonline.co.uk
I: windermere-accommodation.co.uk

Cobblers Cottage ★★★★
Contact: Paul Liddell
Lakelovers, Belmont House, Lake Road, Bowness-on-Windermere, Windermere LA23 3BJ
T: (015394) 88855
F: (015394) 88857
E: bookings@lakelovers.co.uk
I: www.lakelovers.co.uk

Cobblestones ★★★
Contact: Mr Paul Liddell
Lakelovers, Belmont House, Lake Road, Bowness-on-Windermere, Windermere LA23 3BJ
T: (015394) 88855
F: (015394) 88857
E: bookings@lakelovers.co.uk
I: www.lakelovers.co.uk

Cockshott Wood ★★★★
Contact: Mrs Susan Jackson
Heart of the Lakes, Fisherbeck Mill, Old Lake Road, Ambleside LA22 0DH
T: (015394) 32321
F: (015394) 33251
E: info@heartofthelakes.co.uk
I: www.heartofthelakes.co.uk

4 College Court ★★★
Contact: Paul Liddell
Lakelovers, Belmont House, Lake Road, Bowness-on-Windermere, Windermere LA23 3BJ
T: (015394) 88855
F: (015394) 88857

8 College Court ★★★
Contact: Mr Paul Liddell
Lakelovers, Belmont House, Lake Road, Bowness-on-Windermere, Windermere LA23 3BJ
T: (015394) 88855
F: (015394) 88857
E: bookings@lakelovers.co.uk
I: www.lakelovers.co.uk

8 College Gate ★★★
Contact: Mr Peter Durbin
Cumbrian Cottages, 2 Lonsdale Street, Carlisle CA1 1DB
T: (01228) 599960
F: (01228) 599970
E: enquiries@cumbriancottages.co.uk
I: www.cumbrian-cottage.co.uk

Coppice Corner ★★★★★
Contact: Mr Paul Liddell
Lakelovers, Belmont House, Lake Road, Bowness-on-Windermere, Windermere LA23 3BJ
T: (015394) 88855
F: (015394) 88857
E: bookings@lakelovers.co.uk
I: www.lakelovers.co.uk

Coppice View ★★★★
Contact: Paul Liddell
Lakelovers, Belmont House, Lake Road, Bowness-on-Windermere, Windermere LA23 3BJ
T: (015394) 88855
F: (015394) 88857
E: bookings@lakelovers.co.uk
I: www.lakelovers.co.uk

Corner Cottage ★★★
Contact: Mr Peter Durbin
Cumbrian Cottages, 2 Lonsdale Street, Carlisle CA1 1DB
T: (01228) 599960
F: (01228) 599970
E: enquiries@cumbrian-cottages.co.uk
I: www.cumbrian-cottages.co.uk

Craglands ★★★★
Contact: Paul Liddell
Lakelovers, Belmont House, Lake Road, Bowness-on-Windermere, Windermere LA23 3BJ
T: (015394) 88855
F: (015394) 88857
E: bookings@lakelovers.co.uk
I: www.lakelovers.co.uk

Cragside ★★★★
Contact: Paul Liddell
Lakelovers, Belmont House, Lake Road, Bowness-on-Windermere, Windermere LA23 3BJ
T: (015394) 88855
F: (015394) 88857

Cross Cottage ★★★
Contact: Mr Durbin
Cumbrian Cottages, 2 Lonsdale Street, Carlisle CA1 1DB
T: (01228) 599960
F: (01228) 599970
E: enquiries@cumbrian-cottages.co.uk
I: www.cumbrian-cottages.co.uk

Crowmire Wood ★★★★
Contact: Mrs Susan Jackson
Heart of the Lakes, Fisherbeck Mill, Old Lake Road, Ambleside LA22 0DH
T: (015394) 33110
F: (015394) 33251
E: info@heartofthelakes.co.uk
I: www.heartofthelakes.co.uk

Daisy Bank Cottage ★★★
Contact: Mr Peter Durbin
Cumbrian Cottages, 2 Lonsdale Street, Carlisle CA1 1DB
T: (01228) 599960
F: (01228) 599970
E: enquiries@cumbrian-cottages.co.uk
I: www.cumbrian-cottages.co.uk

Establishments printed in blue have a detailed entry in this guide

CUMBRIA – THE LAKE DISTRICT

Deloraine ★★★
Contact: Mrs Fanstone
Deloraine, Helm Road,
Windermere LA23 2HS
T: (015394) 45557
F: 0870 0 517981
E: info@deloraine.demon.co.uk
I: www.deloraine.demon.co.uk

Elim Cottage ★★★
Contact: Mr Peter Durbin
Cumbrian Cottages, 2 Lonsdale
Street, Carlisle CA1 1DB
T: (01228) 599960
F: (01228) 599970
E: enquiries@cumbriancottages.co.uk
I: www.cumbrian-cottages.co.uk

Fair View ★★★★
Contact: Susan Jackson
Heart of the Lakes, Fisherbeck
Mill, Old Lake Road, Ambleside
LA22 0DH
T: (015394) 32321
F: (015394) 33251
E: info@heartofthelakes.co.uk
I: www.heartofthelakes.co.uk

9 Fairfield ★★★★
Contact: Mr Peter Durbin
Cumbrian Cottages, 2 Lonsdale
Street, Carlisle CA1 1DB
T: (01228) 599960
F: (01228) 599970
E: enquiries@cumbrian-cottage.co.uk
I: www.cumbrian-cottages.co.uk

Fairhaven ★★★
Contact: Mr Peter Durbin
Cumbrian Cottages, 2 Lonsdale
Street, Carlisle CA1 1DB
T: (01228) 599960
F: (01228) 599970
E: enquiries@cumbrian-cottages.co.uk
I: www.cumbrian-cottages.co.uk

2 Fellside Cottages ★★★★
Contact: Mr John Serginson
Lakeland Cottage Co, Waterside
House, Ulverston LA12 8AN
T: (015395) 30024
F: (015395) 31932
E: john@lakelandcottageco.com
I: www.lakelandcottageco.com

Fir Cones ★★★★
Contact: Mr Peter Durbin
Cumbrian Cottages, 2 Lonsdale
Street, Carlisle CA1 1DB
T: (01228) 599960
F: (01228) 599970
E: enquiries@cumbrian-cottages.co.uk
I: www.cumbrian-cottages.co.uk

Firbank ★★★
Contact: Mr Peter Durbin
Cumbrian Cottages, 2 Lonsdale
Street, Carlisle CA1 1DB
T: (01228) 599960
F: (01228) 599970
E: enquiries@cumbrian-cottages.co.uk
I: www.cumbrian-cottages.co.uk

The Gallery ★★★★★
Contact: Mrs Susan Jackson
Heart of the Lakes, Fisherbeck
Mill, Old Lake Road, Ambleside
LA20 0DH
T: (015394) 32321
F: (015394) 33251
E: info@heartofthelakes.co.uk
I: www.heartofthelakes.co.uk

Gardens View ★★★
Contact: Mr Paul Liddell
Lakelovers, Belmont House, Lake
Road, Bowness-on-Windermere,
Windermere LA23 3BJ
T: (015394) 88855
F: (015394) 88857
E: bookings@lakelovers.co.uk
I: www.lakelovers.co.uk

Gavel Cottage ★★★★
Contact:
Screetons, 25 Bridgegate,
Howden, Goole DN14 7AA
T: (01430) 431201
F: (01430) 432114
E: howden@screetons.co.uk
I: screetons.co.uk

Gildabrook Cottage ★★★
Contact: Mrs Susan Jackson
Heart of the Lakes, Fisherbeck
Mill, Old Lake Road, Ambleside
LA22 0DH
T: (015394) 32321
F: (015394) 33251
E: info@heartofthelakes.co.uk
I: www.heartofthelakes.co.uk

Glebe Holme ★★★★
Contact: Mr Peter Durbin
Cumbrian Cottages, 2 Lonsdale
Street, Carlisle CA1 1DB
T: (01228) 599960
F: (01228) 599970
E: enquiries@cumbriancottages.co.uk
I: www.cumbrian-cottages.co.uk

Grace Cottage ★★★★
Contact: Helen May
Grace Cottage, 79 High Garth,
Kendal LA9 5NR
T: (01539) 732602
E: cottage@mays-in-grace.co.uk
I: www.mays-in-grace.co.uk

Greenrigg ★★★★
Contact: Mr Peter Durbin
Cumbrian Cottages, 2 Lonsdale
Street, Carlisle CA1 1DB
T: (01228) 599960
F: (01228) 599970
E: enquiries@cumbrian-cottage.co.uk
I: www.cumbrian-cottages.co.uk

Greystones ★★★
Contact: Mr Peter Durbin
Cumbrian Cottages, 2 Lonsdale
Street, Carlisle CA1 1DB
T: (01228) 599960
F: (01228) 599970
E: enquiries@cumbrian-cottages.co.uk
I: www.cumbrian-cottages.co.uk

The Hayloft ★★★
Contact: Mr Peter Durbin
Cumbrian Cottages, 2 Lonsdale
Street, Carlisle CA1 1DB
T: (01228) 599960
F: (01228) 599970
E: enquiries@cumbrian-cottages.co.uk
I: www.cumbrian-cottages.co.uk

The Heaning ★★★
Contact: Hazel Moulding
The Heaning, Heaning Lane,
Windermere LA23 1JW
T: (015394) 43453
F: (015394) 43453
E: info@theheaning.co.uk
I: www.theheaning.co.uk

Heatherbank ★★★
Contact: Mr Peter Durbin
Cumbrian Cottages, 2 Lonsdale
Street, Carlisle CA1 1DB
T: (01228) 599960
F: (01228) 599970
E: enquiries@cumbrian-cottages.co.uk
I: www.cumbrian-cottages.co.uk

Helm Farm ★★★
Contact: Mrs J Marsden
Matson Ground Estate Co Ltd,
Estate Office, Matson Ground,
Windermere LA23 2NH
T: (015394) 45756
F: (015394) 47892
E: info@matsonground.co.uk
I: www.matsonground.co.uk

5 Helm Rigg ★★★
Contact: Mr Paul Liddell
Lakelovers, Belmont House, Lake
Road, Bowness-on-Windermere,
Windermere LA23 3BJ
T: (015394) 88855
F: (015394) 88857
E: bookings@lakelovers.co.uk
I: www.lakelovers.co.uk

Hidden Depths ★★★★★
Contact: Paul Liddell
Lakelovers, Belmont House, Lake
Road, Bowness-on-Windermere,
Windermere LA23 3BJ
T: (015394) 88855
F: (015394) 88857
E: bookings@lakelovers.co.uk
I: www.lakelovers.co.uk

High Croft ★★★★
Contact: Susan Jackson
Heart of the Lakes, Fisherbeck
Mill, Old Lake Road, Ambleside
LA22 0DH
T: (015394) 32321
F: (015394) 33251
E: info@heartofthelakes.co.uk
I: www.heartofthelakes.co.uk

Hill View Cottage ★★★
Contact: Mr Peter Durbin
Cumbrian Cottages, 2 Lonsdale
Street, Carlisle CA1 1DB
T: (01228) 599960
F: (01228) 599970
E: enquiries@cumbrian-cottages.co.uk
I: www.cumbrian-cottages.co.uk

2 Hodge How ★★★
Contact: Mr John Serginson
The Lakeland Cottage Company,
Waterside House, Ulverston
LA12 8AN
T: (015395) 30024
F: (015395) 31932
E: john@lakelandcottageco.com
I: www.lakelandcottageco.com

Hodge Howe ★★★★★
Contact: Mrs Susan Jackson
Heart of the Lakes, Fisherbeck
Mill, Old Lake Road, Ambleside
LA22 0DH
T: (015394) 32321
F: (015394) 33251
E: info@heartofthelakes.co.uk
I: www.heartofthelakes.co.uk

Holborn House ★★★
Contact: Mr Peter Durbin
Cumbrian Cottages, 2 Lonsdale
Street, Carlisle CA1 1DB
T: (01228) 599960
F: (01228) 599970
E: enquiries@cumbriancottages.co.uk
I: www.cumbrian-cottages.co.uk

Hollin Field ★★★★
Contact: Susan Jackson
Heart of the Lakes, Fisherbeck
Mill, Old Lake Road, Ambleside
LA22 0DH
T: (015394) 32321
F: (015394) 33251
E: info@heartofthelakes.co.uk
I: www.heartofthelakes.co.uk

Honeysuckle Cottage ★★★
Contact: Mr Peter Durbin
Cumbrian Cottages, 2 Lonsdale
Street, Carlisle CA1 1DB
T: (01228) 599960
F: (01228) 599970
E: enquiries@cumbriancottages.co.uk
I: www.cumbrian-cottages.co.uk

Honeysuckle Cottage ★★★
Contact: Mr Paul Liddell
Lakelovers, Belmont House, Lake
Road, Bowness-on-Windermere,
Windermere LA23 3BJ
T: (015394) 88855
F: (015394) 88857
E: bookings@lakelovers.co.uk
I: www.lakelovers.co.uk

Howe Cottage ★★★
Contact: Mr Peter Durbin
Cumbrian Cottages, 2 Lonsdale
Street, Carlisle CA1 1DB
T: (01228) 599960
F: (01228) 599970
E: enquiries@cumbrian-cottages.co.uk
I: www.cumbrian-cottages.co.uk

Hunters Moon ★★★★
Contact: Paul Liddell
Lakelovers, Belmont House, Lake
Road, Bowness-on-Windermere,
Windermere LA23 3BJ
T: (015394) 88855
F: (015394) 88857

CUMBRIA – THE LAKE DISTRICT

Hydaway ★★★
Contact: Mr Peter Durbin
Cumbrian Cottages, 2 Lonsdale Street, Carlisle CA1 1DB
T: (01228) 599960
F: (01228) 599970
E: enquiries@cumbriancottages.co.uk
I: www.cumbrian-cottages.co.uk

Karis Cottage ★★★
Contact: Mr Peter Durbin
Cumbrian Cottages, 2 Lonsdale Street, Carlisle CA1 1DB
T: (01228) 599960
F: (01228) 599970
E: enquiries@cumbriancottages.co.uk
I: www.cumbrian-cottages.co.uk

Kent Cottage ★★★
Contact: Mr Paul Liddell
Lakelovers, Belmont House, Lake Road, Bowness-on-Windermere, Windermere LA23 3BJ
T: (015394) 88855
F: (015394) 88857
E: bookings@lakelovers.co.uk
I: www.lakelovers.co.uk

Kerris Place ★★★
Contact: Mr Peter Durbin
Cumbrian Cottages, 2 Lonsdale Street, Windermere LA23 3BG
T: (01228) 599960
F: (01228) 599970
E: enquiries@cumbriancottages.co.uk
I: www.cumbrian-cottages.co.uk

Knotts View ★★★★
Contact: Mr Paul Liddell
Lakelovers, Belmont House, Lake Road, Bowness-on-Windermere, Windermere LA23 3BJ
T: (015394) 88855
F: (015394) 88857
E: bookings@lakelovers.co.uk
I: www.lakelovers.co.uk

Lake Lodge Studio ★★★
Contact: Mr Paul Liddell
Lakelovers, Belmont House, Windermere LA23 3BJ
T: (015394) 88855
F: (015394) 88857
E: bookings@lakelovers.co.uk
I: www.lakelovers.co.uk

Lake Lodge Studio ★★★★
Contact: Paul Liddell
Lakelovers, Belmont House, Lake Road, Bowness-on-Windermere, Windermere LA23 3BJ
T: (015394) 88855
F: (015394) 88857
E: bookings@lakelovers.co.uk
I: www.lakelovers.co.uk

Lake View ★★★★
Contact: Paul Liddell
Lakelovers, Belmont House, Lake Road, Bowness-on-Windermere, Windermere LA23 3BJ
T: (015394) 88855
F: (015394) 88857

Lakeside View ★★★★
Contact: Mr Paul Liddell
Lakelovers, Belmont House, Lake Road, Bowness-on-Windermere, Windermere LA23 3BJ
T: (015394) 88855
F: (015394) 88857
E: bookings@lakelovers.co.uk
I: www.lakelovers.co.uk

Lakeview ★★★
Contact: Mr Peter Durbin
Cumbrian Cottages, 2 Lonsdale Street, Carlisle CA1 1DB
T: (01228) 599960
F: (01228) 599970
E: enquiries@cumbrian-cottages.co.uk
I: www.cumbrian-cottages.co.uk

Langdale View Holiday Apartments ★★★
Contact: Mrs Julie Marsh
112 Craig Walk, Bowness-on-Windermere, Windermere LA23 3AX
T: (015394) 46655
E: enquiries@langdale-view.co.uk
I: www.langdale-view.co.uk

Langrigge Cottage ★★★★★
Contact: Mr Paul Liddell
Lakelovers, Belmont House, Lake Road, Bowness-on-Windermere, Windermere LA23 3BJ
T: (015394) 88855
F: (015394) 88857
E: bookings@lakelovers.co.uk
I: www.lakelovers.co.uk

Langrigge Cottage & High Langrigge ★★★★★
Contact: Paul Liddell
Lakelovers, Belmont House, Lake Road, Bowness-on-Windermere, Windermere LA23 3BJ
T: (015394) 88855
F: (015394) 88857
E: bookings@lakelovers.co.uk
I: www.lakelovers.co.uk

Larch House ★★★★
Contact: Mr Paul Liddell
Lakelovers, Belmont House, Lake Road, Bowness-on-Windermere, Windermere LA23 3BJ
T: (015394) 88855
F: (015394) 88857
E: bookings@lakelovers.co.uk
I: www.lakelovers.co.uk

Ling Howe ★★★★★
Contact: Mr Peter Durbin
Cumbrian Cottages, 2 Lonsdale Street, Carlisle CA1 1DB
T: (01228) 599960
F: (01228) 599970
E: enquiries@cumbrian-cottages.co.uk
I: www.cumbrian-cottages.co.uk

Little Ghyll ★★★★
Contact: Mr Peter Durbin
Cumbrian Cottages, 2 Lonsdale Street, Carlisle CA1 1DB
T: (01228) 599960
F: (01228) 599970
E: enquiries@cumbrian-cottages.co.uk
I: www.cumbrian-cottages.co.uk

Little Ivy ★★★
Contact: Mr Peter Durbin
Cumbrian Cottages, 2 Lonsdale Street, Carlisle CA1 1DB
T: (01228) 599960
F: (01228) 599970
E: enquiries@cumbrian-cottages.co.uk
I: www.cumbrian-cottages.co.uk

Little Rowan ★★★
Contact: Mr Peter Durbin
Cumbrian Cottages, 2 Lonsdale Street, Carlisle CA1 1DB
T: (01228) 599960
F: (01228) 599970
E: enquiries@cumbrian-cottages.co.uk
I: www.cumbrian-cottages.co.uk

Low Fell Cottage ★★★
Contact: Mr Peter Durbin
Cumbrian Cottages, 2 Lonsdale Street, Carlisle CA1 1DB
T: (01228) 599960
F: (01228) 599970
E: enquiries@cumbrian-cottages.co.uk
I: www.cumbrian-cottages.co.uk

Low How ★★★★
Contact: Mrs Susan Jackson
Heart of the Lakes, Fisherbeck Mill, Old Lake Road, Ambleside LA22 0DH
T: (015394) 32321
F: (015394) 33251
E: info@heartofthelakes.co.uk
I: www.heartofthelakes.co.uk

Marsh Cottage ★★★
Contact: Mr Peter Durbin
Cumbrian Cottages, 2 Lonsdale Street, Carlisle CA1 1DB
T: (01228) 599960
F: (01228) 599970
E: enquiries@cumbrian-cottages.co.uk
I: www.cumbrian-cottages.co.uk

Marybank ★★★
Contact: Mr Peter Durbin
Cumbrian Cottages, 2 Lonsdale Street, Carlisle CA1 1DB
T: (01228) 599960
F: (01228) 599970
E: enquiries@cumbriancottages.co.uk
I: www.cumbrian-cottages.co.uk

1 Meadowcroft ★★★★
Contact: Mr Peter Durbin
Cumbrian Cottages, 2 Lonsdale Street, Carlisle CA1 1DB
T: (01228) 599960
F: (01228) 599970
E: enquiries@cumbriancottages.co.uk
I: www.cumbrian-cottages.co.uk

3 Meadowcroft ★★★★
Contact: Mr Peter Durbin
Cumbrian Cottages, 2 Lonsdale Street, Carlisle CA1 1DB
T: (01228) 599960
F: (01228) 599970
E: enquiries@cumbriancottages.co.uk
I: www.cumbrian-cottages.co.uk

4 Meadowcroft ★★★★
Contact: Mr Peter Durbin
Cumbrian Cottages, 2 Lonsdale Street, Carlisle CA1 1DB
T: (01228) 599960
F: (01228) 599970
E: enquiries@cumbrian-cottages.co.uk
I: www.cumbrian-cottages.co.uk

6 Meadowcroft ★★★★
Contact: Mr Paul Liddell
Lakelovers, Belmont House, Lake Road, Windermere LA23 3BJ
T: (015394) 88855
F: (015394) 88857
E: bookings@lakelovers.co.uk
I: www.lakelovers.co.uk

7 Meadowcroft ★★★★
Contact: Mr Peter Durbin
Cumbrian Cottages, 2 Lonsdale Street, Carlisle CA1 1DB
T: (01228) 599960
F: (01228) 599970
E: enquiries@cumbriancottages.co.uk
I: www.cumbrian-cottages.co.uk

8 Meadowcroft ★★★★
Contact: Mr Peter Durbin
Cumbrian Cottages, 2 Lonsdale Street, Carlisle CA1 1DB
T: (01228) 599960
F: (01228) 599970
E: enquiries@cumbriancottages.co.uk
I: www.cumbrian-cottages.co.uk

Meadows End ★★★
Contact: Mr Peter Durbin
Cumbrian Cottages, 2 Lonsdale Street, Carlisle CA1 1DB
T: (01228) 599960
F: (01228) 599970
E: enquiries@cumbriancottages.co.uk
I: www.cumbrian-cottages.co.uk

Mere View ★★★★
Contact: Mr Paul Liddell
Lakelovers, Belmont House, Lake Road, Bowness-on-Windermere, Windermere LA23 3BJ
T: (015394) 88855
F: (015394) 88857
E: bookings@lakelovers.co.uk
I: www.lakelovers.co.uk

Merewood Stables ★★★★★
Contact: Mrs Susan Jackson
Heart of the Lakes, Fisherbeck Mill, Old Lake Road, Ambleside LA22 0DH
T: (015394) 32321
F: (015394) 33251
E: info@heartofthelakes.co.uk
I: www.heartofthelakes.co.uk

Middlerigg ★★★★
Contact: Mrs Susan Jackson
Heart of the Lakes, Fisherbeck Mill, Old Lake Road, Ambleside LA22 0DH
T: (015394) 32321
F: (015394) 33251
E: info@heartofthelakes.co.uk
I: www.heartofthelakes.co.uk

Mill Beck
Rating Applied For
Contact: Mrs Farmer
Mill Beck, The Rookery, Tamworth B78 2EZ
T: (01827) 330941
E: pb.farmer@virgin.net

Establishments printed in blue have a detailed entry in this guide

CUMBRIA – THE LAKE DISTRICT

Moss Bank Cottage ★★★★
Contact: Mr Peter Durbin
Cumbrian Cottages, 2 Lonsdale Street, Carlisle CA1 1DB
T: (01228) 599960
F: (01228) 599970
E: enquiries@cumbrian-cottages.co.uk
I: www.cumbrian-cottages.co.uk

North Lodge & Cottage ★★★★
Contact: Alan & Margaret Wardle
Lake District Holidays, Bateman Fold Barn, Crook, Nr. Kendal LA8 8LN
T: (015395) 68074
F: (015395) 68104
E: lakedistrictnols@aol.com
I: www.lakedistrictholidays.net

Oakdene ★★★★
Contact: Mrs I Baker
Oakdene, 98 Oak Street, Windermere LA23 1EN
T: (015394) 44575
F: (015394) 42784
E: tonybakerw@aol.com
I: www.windermereholidays.co.uk

The Oaks ★★★★
Contact: Mr Peter Durbin
Cumbrian Cottages, 2 Lonsdale Street, Carlisle CA1 1DB
T: (01228) 599960
F: (01228) 599970
E: enquiries@cumbriancottages.co.uk
I: www.cumbrian-cottages.co.uk

Octavia Cottage ★★★
Contact: Mr Clive Sykes
Sykes Cottages, York House, York Street, Chester CH1 3LR
T: (01244) 345700
F: (01244) 321442
E: info@sykescottages.co.uk
I: www.sykescottages.co.uk

1 Old College Cottage ★★★★
Contact: Paul Liddell
Lakelovers, Belmont House, Lake Road, Bowness-on-Windermere, Windermere LA23 3BJ
T: (015394) 88855
F: (015394) 88857
E: bookings@lakelovers.co.uk
I: www.lakelovers.co.uk

Old Fallbarrow Cottage ★★★★
Contact: Mrs Susan Jackson
Heart of the Lakes, Fisherbeck Mill, Old Lake Road, Ambleside LA22 0DH
T: (015394) 32321
F: (015394) 33251
E: info@heartofthelakes.co.uk
I: www.heartofthelakes.co.uk

The Old Picture House ★★★
Contact: Mr Nicholas Thompson
Cumbrian Cottages, Flat 3, 511 Barlow Moor Road, Chorlton, Manchester M21 8AQ
T: (01618) 617574
F: 0795 7 661362

Olde Coach House and Stables ★★★
Contact: Mr Alan & Mrs Margaret Wardle
Bateman Fold Barn, Kendal LA8 8LN
T: (015395) 68074
E: lakedistricthols@aol.com
I: www.lakedistrictholidays.net

Orchard Fold ★★★
Contact: Mr Peter Durbin
Cumbrian Cottages, 2 Lonsdale Street, Carlisle CA1 1DB
T: (01228) 599960
F: (01228) 599970
E: enquiries@cumbriancottages.co.uk
I: www.cumbrian-cottages.co.uk

Partridge Holme ★★★
Contact: Mr Paul Durbin
Cumbrian Cottages, 2 Lonsdale Street, Carlisle CA1 1DB
T: (01228) 599960
F: (01228) 599970
E: enquiries@cumbriancottages.co.uk
I: www.cumbrian-cottage.co.uk

Pear Tree Cottage ★★★
Contact: Mr Peter Durbin
Cumbrian Cottages, 2 Lonsdale Street, Carlisle CA1 1DB
T: (01228) 599960
F: (01228) 599970
E: enquiries@cumbriancottages.co.uk
I: www.cumbrian-cottages.co.uk

Penny Place ★★★★
Contact: Paul Liddell
Lakelovers, Belmont House, Lake Road, Bowness-on-Windermere, Windermere LA23 3BJ
T: (015394) 88855
F: (015394) 88857

Penny's Nest ★★★★
Contact: Paul Liddell
Lakelovers, Belmont House, Lake Road, Bowness-on-Windermere, Windermere LA23 3BJ
T: (015394) 88855
F: (015394) 88857

Pilgrim's Rest ★★★
Contact: John & Anne Ruck
Pilgrim's Rest, c/o 121 Bournbrook Road, Selly Park, Birmingham B29 7BY
T: (0121) 415 4036
E: johnanne@ruckja.freeserve.co.uk
I: mysite.freeserve.com/pilgrimsrest

Pine Lodge ★★★★
Contact: Mr Paul Liddell
Lakelovers, Belmont House, Lake Road, Bowness-on-Windermere, Windermere LA23 3BJ
T: (015394) 88855
F: (015394) 88857
E: bookings@lakelovers.co.uk
I: www.lakelovers.co.uk

Pine Rigg ★★★
Contact: Mr Begg
Pine Rigg, 28 Quarry Rigg, Windermere LA23 3DU
I: www.cumbrian-cottages.co.uk

Pine View ★★★
Contact: Mr Peter Durbin
Cumbrian Cottages, 2 Lonsdale Street, Carlisle CA1 1DB
T: (01228) 599960
F: (01228) 599970
E: enquiries@cumbrian-cottages.co.uk
I: www.cumbrian-cottages.co.uk

Pinethwaite Holiday Cottages ★★★
Contact: P B Legge
Pinethwaite Holiday Cottages, Lickbarrow Road, Windermere LA23 2NQ
T: (015394) 44558
E: info@pinecottages.co.uk
I: www.pinecottages.co.uk

Pipers Howe ★★★★
Contact: Paul Liddell
Lakelovers, Belmont House, Lake Road, Bowness-on-Windermere, Windermere LA23 3BJ
T: (015394) 88855
F: (015394) 88857

Post Masters House ★★★★
Contact: Mr Peter Durbin
Cumbrian Cottages, 2 Lonsdale Street, Carlisle CA1 1DB
T: (01228) 599960
F: (01228) 599970
E: enquiries@cumbriancottages.co.uk
I: www.cumbrian-cottages.co.uk

Primrose Cottage ★★★
Contact: Mr Peter Durbin
Cumbrian Cottages, 2 Lonsdale Street, Carlisle CA1 1DB
T: (01228) 599960
F: (01228) 599970
E: enquiries@cumbriancottages.co.uk
I: www.cumbrian-cottages.co.uk

The Priory
Rating Applied For
Contact: Mrs Susan Jackson
Heart of the Lakes, Fisherbeck Mill, Old Lake Road, Ambleside LA22 0DH
T: (015394) 32321
I: www.heartofthelakes.co.uk

Priory Coach House ★★★★
Contact: Paul Liddell
Lakelovers, Belmont House, Lake Road, Bowness-on-Windermere, Windermere LA23 3BJ
T: (015394) 88855
F: (015394) 88857

Priory Lodge ★★★★
Contact: Mr Paul Liddell
Lakelovers, Belmont House, Lake Road, Bowness-on-Windermere, Windermere LA23 3BJ
T: (015394) 88855
F: (015394) 88857
E: bookings@lakelovers.co.uk
I: www.lakelovers.co.uk

2 Priory Manor ★★★★
Contact: Mr Paul Liddell
Lakelovers, Belmont House, Lake Road, Bowness-on-Windermere, Windermere LA23 3BJ
T: (015394) 88855
F: (015394) 88857
E: bookings@lakelovers.co.uk
I: www.lakelovers.co.uk

48A Quarry Rigg ★★★
Contact: Mr Paul Liddell
Lakelovers, Belmont House, Lake Road, Bowness-on-Windermere, Windermere LA23 3BJ
T: (015394) 88855
F: (015394) 88857
E: bookings@lakelovers.co.uk
I: www.lakelovers.co.uk

35A Quarry Rigg-Lookout Post ★★★
Contact: Mr Peter Durbin
Cumbrian Cottages, 2 Lonsdale Street, Carlisle CA1 1DB
T: (01228) 599960
F: (01228) 599970
E: enquiries@cumbrian-cottages.co.uk
I: www.cumbrian-cottages.co.uk

Rainbows End ★★★
Contact: The Manager
Ref: 3338, Dales Holiday Cottages, Carleton Business Park, Carleton New Road, Skipton BD23 2AA
T: (01756) 799821
F: (01756) 797012
E: info@dalesholcot.com
I: www.dalesholcot.com

Rattle Beck ★★★
Contact: Mr Peter Durbin
Cumbrian Cottages, 2 Lonsdale Street, Carlisle CA1 1DB
T: (01228) 599960
F: (01228) 599970
E: enquiries@cumbriancottages.co.uk
I: www.cumbrian-cottages.co.uk

Rayrigg Roost ★★★
Contact: Mr Peter Durbin
Cumbrian Cottages, 2 Lonsdale Street, Carlisle CA1 1DB
T: (01228) 599960
F: (01228) 599970
E: enquiries@cumbriancottages.co.uk
I: www.cumbrian-cottages.co.uk

Revelstones ★★★
Contact: Mr Peter Durbin
Cumbrian Cottages, 2 Lonsdale Street, Carlisle CA1 1DB
T: (01228) 599960
F: (01229) 599970
E: enquiries@cumbriancottages.co.uk
I: www.cumbrian-cottages.co.uk

Rivendell ★★★
Contact: Mr Peter Durbin
Cumbrian Cottages, 2 Lonsdale Street, Carlisle CA1 1DB
T: (01228) 599960
F: (01228) 599970
E: enquiries@cumbriancottages.co.uk
I: www.cumbrian-cottages.co.uk

Robin Cottage ★★★★
Contact: Paul Liddell
Lakelovers, Belmont House, Lake Road, Bowness-on-Windermere, Windermere LA23 3BJ
T: (015394) 88855
F: (015394) 88857
E: bookings@lakelover.co.uk
I: www.lakelovers.co.uk

CUMBRIA – THE LAKE DISTRICT

Rogerground ★★★★
Contact: Mr Paul Liddell
Lakelovers, Belmont House, Lake Road, Bowness-on-Windermere, Windermere LA23 3BJ
T: (015394) 88855
F: (015394) 88857
E: bookings@lakelovers.co.uk
I: www.lakelovers.co.uk

Rose Cottage ★★★★
Contact: Mr Peter Durbin
Cumbrian Cottages, 2 Lonsdale Street, Carlisle CA1 1DB
T: (01228) 599960
F: (01228) 599970
E: enquiries@cumbriancottages.co.uk
I: www.cumbrian-cottages.co.uk

Rose Cottage ★★★
Contact: Mr & Mrs Alan Wardle
Bateman Fold Barn, Kendal
LA8 8LN
T: (015395) 68074
I: www.lakedistrictholidays.net

Rustic Cottage ★★★
Contact: Paul Liddell
Lakelovers, Belmont House, Lake Road, Bowness-on-Windermere, Windermere LA23 3BJ
T: (015394) 88855
F: (015394) 88857
E: bookings@lakelovers.co.uk
I: www.lakelovers.co.uk

Saw Mill Cottage ★★★
Contact: Mrs Susan Jackson
Heart of the Lakes, Fisherbeck Mill, Old Lake Road, Ambleside
LA22 0DH
T: (015394) 32321
F: (015394) 33251
E: info@heartofthelakes.co.uk
I: www.heartofthelakes.co.uk

Skylark ★★★★
Contact: Mr Peter Durbin
Cumbrian Cottages, 2 Lonsdale Street, Carlisle CA1 1DB
T: (01228) 599960
F: (01228) 599970
E: enquiries@cumbrian-cottages.co.uk
I: www.cumbrian-cottages.co.uk

Solstice Cottage ★★★
Contact: Mr Paul Liddell
Lakelovers, Belmont House, Lake Road, Bowness-on-Windermere, Windermere LA23 3BJ
T: (015394) 88855
F: (015394) 88857
E: bookings@lakelovers.co.uk
I: www.lakelovers.co.uk

Spinnery Cottage ★★★
Contact: Mr & Mrs Hood
Spinnery Holiday Cottage Apartments, c/o Sylvan Wood, Underbarrow Road, Kendal
LA8 8HA
T: (01539) 725153
F: (01539) 725153
E: raynbarb@spinnerycottage.co.uk
I: www.spinnerycottage.co.uk

Squirrels Nest ★★★★
Contact: Paul Liddell
Lakelovers, Belmont House, Lake Road, Bowness-on-Windermere, Windermere LA23 3BJ
T: (015394) 88855
F: (015394) 88857
E: bookings@lakelovers.co.uk
I: www.lakelovers.co.uk

Stable Cottage ★★★★★
Contact: Mrs Susan Jackson
Heart of the Lakes, Fisherbeck Mill, Old Lake Road, Ambleside
LA22 0DH
T: (015394) 32321
F: (015394) 33251
E: info@heartofthelakes.co.uk
I: www.heartofthelakes.co.uk

Storrs Hall ★★★
Contact: Mr Peter Durbin
Cumbrian Cottages, 2 Lonsdale Street, Carlisle CA1 1DB
T: (01228) 599960
F: (01228) 599970
E: enquiries@cumbriancottages.co.uk
I: www.cumbrian-cottages.co.uk

Sunny Brook Cottage ★★★
Contact: Mr Peter Durbin
Cumbrian Cottages, 2 Lonsdale Street, Carlisle CA1 1DB
T: (01228) 599960
F: (01228) 599970
E: enquiries@cumbrian-cottages.co.uk
I: www.cumbrian-cottages.co.uk

Swallows Rest ★★★
Contact: Paul Liddell
Lakelovers, Belmont House, Lake Road, Bowness-on-Windermere, Windermere LA23 3BJ
T: (015394) 88855
F: (015394) 88857
E: bookings@lakelovers.co.uk
I: www.lakelovers.co.uk

The Thimble ★★★
Contact: Paul Liddell
Lakelovers, Belmont House, Lake Road, Bowness-on-Windermere, Windermere LA23 3BJ
T: (015394) 88855
F: (015394) 88857
E: bookings@lakelovers.co.uk
I: www.lakelovers.co.uk

Thwaites Cottage ★★★
Contact: Mr Peter Durbin
Cumbrian Cottages, 2 Lonsdale Street, Carlisle CA1 1DB
T: (01228) 599960
F: (01228) 599970
E: enquiries@cumbrian-cottages.co.uk
I: www.cumbrian-cottages.co.uk

Tourelle ★★★★
Contact: Paul Liddell
Lakelovers, Belmont House, Lake Road, Bowness-on-Windermere, Windermere LA23 3BJ
T: (015394) 88855
F: (015394) 88857
E: bookings@lakelovers.co.uk
I: www.lakelovers.co.uk

Tree Tops ★★★★
Contact: Mr Paul Liddell
Lakelovers, Belmont House, Lake Road, Bowness-on-Windermere, Windermere LA23 3BJ
T: (015394) 88855
F: (015394) 88857
E: bookings@lakelovers.co.uk
I: www.lakelovers.co.uk

Treetops ★★★★
Contact: John Alcock
Treetops, 6 Ghyllside, Ambleside
LA22 0QU
T: (015394) 32819
E: treetops@lakedistrictcumbria.co.uk
I: www.lakedistrictcumbria.co.uk

Troutbeck Barn ★★★
Contact: Mr Paul Liddell
Lakelovers, Belmont House, Lake Road, Bowness-on-Windermere, Windermere LA23 3BJ
T: (015394) 88855
F: (015394) 88857
E: bookings@lakelovers.co.uk
I: www.lakelovers.co.uk

24 Victoria Terrace ★★
Contact: Mrs Lishman
Lishmans, 22 Victoria Terrace, Windermere LA23 1AB
T: (015394) 42982

Waterfall Cottage ★★★
Contact: Mr Durbin
Cumbrian Cottages, 2 Lonsdale Street, Carlisle CA1 1DB
T: (01228) 599960
F: (01228) 599970
E: enquiries@cumbrian-cottages.co.uk
I: www.cumbrian-cottages.co.uk

Waters Edge Villa ★★★★
Contact: Bernard Twitchett & Weir
Waters Edge Villa, Gilly's Landing's, Windermere
LA23 3HE
T: (015394) 43415
F: (015394) 88721

Wayside Cottage ★★★★
Contact: Paul Liddell
Lakelovers, Belmont House, Lake Road, Bowness-on-Windermere, Windermere LA23 3BJ
T: (015394) 88855
F: (015394) 88857
E: bookings@lakelovers.co.uk
I: www.lakelovers.co.uk

The Wendy House ★★★
Contact: Paul Liddell
Lakelovers, Belmont House, Lake Road, Bowness-on-Windermere, Windermere LA23 3BJ
T: (015394) 88855
F: (015394) 88857
E: bookings@lakelovers.co.uk
I: www.lakelovers.co.uk

Westwood ★★★★★
Contact: Mr Paul Liddell
Lakelovers, Belmont House, Lake Road, Bowness-on-Windermere, Windermere LA23 3BJ
T: (015394) 88855
F: (015394) 88857
E: bookings@lakelovers.co.uk
I: www.lakelovers.co.uk

White Moss ★★★★
Contact: Susan Jackson
Heart of the Lakes, Fisherbeck Mill, Old Lake Road, Ambleside
LA22 0DH
T: (015394) 32321
F: (015394) 33251

Wind Force ★★★★
Contact: Mr Paul Liddell
Lakelovers, Belmont House, Lake Road, Bowness-on-Windermere, Windermere LA23 3BJ
T: (015394) 88855
F: (015394) 88857
E: bookings@lakelovers.co.uk
I: www.lakelovers.co.uk

Windermere Marina Village ★★★★
Contact: Jason Dearden
Windermere Marina Village, Windermere LA23 3JQ
T: (015394) 46551
F: (015394) 43233
E: info@wmv.co.uk
I: www.wmv.co.uk

Winster Fields ★★★★★
Contact: Mrs Susan Jackson
Heart of the Lakes, Fisherbeck Mill, Old Lake Road, Ambleside
LA22 0DH
T: (015394) 33110
F: (015394) 33251
E: info@heartofthelakes.col.uk
I: www.heartofthelakes.co.uk

Winster House ★★★
Contact: Mrs Shirley Jump
Winster House, Sunny Bank Road, Windermere LA23 2EN
T: (015394) 44723
E: enquiries@winsterhouse.co.uk
I: www.winsterhouse.co.uk

3 Woodland Grove ★★★
Contact: Mr Paul Liddell
Lakelovers, Belmont House, Lake Road, Bowness-on-Windermere, Windermere LA23 3BJ
T: (015394) 88855
F: (015394) 88857
E: bookings@lakelovers.co.uk
I: www.lakelovers.co.uk

Woodland View ★★★
Contact: Mr Peter Durbin
Cumbrian Cottages, 2 Lonsdale Street, Carlisle CA1 1DB
T: (01228) 599960
F: (01228) 599970
E: enquiries@cumbriancottages.co.uk
I: www.cumbrian-cottages.co.uk

Woodside ★★★★
Contact: Mrs Susan Jackson
Heart of the Lakes, Fisherbeck Mill, Old Lake Road, Ambleside
LA22 0DH
T: (015394) 32321
F: (015394) 33251
E: info@heartofthelakes.co.uk
I: www.heartofthelakes.co.uk

Establishments printed in blue have a detailed entry in this guide

CUMBRIA – THE LAKE DISTRICT

WINSTER
Cumbria

Head of Winster ★★★
Contact: Paul Liddell
Lakelovers, Belmont House, Lake Road, Bowness-on-Windermere, Windermere LA23 3BJ
T: (015394) 88855
F: (015394) 88857
E: bookings@lakelovers.co.uk
I: www.lakelovers.co.uk

WINTON
Cumbria

Manor House ★★★
Contact: Mrs E Beckwith
Manor House, New Hall, Kirkby Stephen CA17 4JD
T: (017683) 41366
I: www.country-holidays.co.uk

WITHERSLACK
Cumbria

Fern Lea Rose Mount Mole End Ingle Nook Primrose Cottage Delph Cottage ★★-★★★
Contact: Mr Armour
Waddicar House, Waddicar Lane, Liverpool L31 1DR
T: (0151) 5460680

The Forge ★★★
Contact: Mr John Serginson
Lakeland Cottage Company, Waterside House, Ulverston LA12 8AN
T: (015395) 30024
F: (015395) 31932
E: john@lakelandcottageco.com
I: www.lakelandcottageco.com

The Old Coachouse ★★★★
Contact: Mr John Serginson
The Lakeland Cottage Company, Waterside House, Ulverston LA12 8AN
T: (015395) 30024
F: (015395) 31932
E: john@lakelandcottageco.com
I: www.lakelandcottageco.com

Spa Inn House ★★★★
Contact: Peter Durbin & Tony Commons
Cumbrian Cottages, 2 Lonsdale Street, Carlisle CA1 1DB
T: (01228) 599960
F: (01228) 599970
E: enquiries@cumbrian-cottages.co.uk
I: www.cumbrian-cottages.co.uk

Thornbarrow Hill Cottage ★★★
Contact: Mr John Serginson
The Lakeland Cottage Company, Waterside House, Ulverston LA12 8AN
T: (015395) 30024
F: (015395) 31932
E: john@lakelandcottageco.com
I: www.lakelandcottageco.com

WYTHOP
Cumbria

Sty Cottage ★★★
Contact: Mr Peter Durbin
Cumbrian Cottages, 2 Lonsdale Street, Carlisle CA1 1DB
T: (01228) 599960
F: (01228) 599970
E: enquiries@cumbriancottages.co.uk
I: www.cumbrian-cottages.co.uk

YANWATH
Cumbria

Copper Beech Cottage ★★★★
Contact: Beattie
2 Barnside, Glendowlin Park, Penrith CA10 2LA
T: (01768) 892855

YEARNGILL
Cumbria

Hill House ★★★
Contact: Mrs Mary Kinsella
Hill House, Wigton CA7 3JX
T: (016973) 22399
E: mary@mkinsella.fsbusiness.co.uk
I: www.mkinsella.fsbusiness.co.uk

NORTHUMBRIA

ACKLINGTON
Northumberland

The Railway Inn ★★★
Contact: Mrs Linda Osborne
The Railway Inn, Morpeth NE65 9BP
T: (01670) 760320
E: linda.osborne1@btopenworld.com
I: www.wishingwellcottages.co.uk

ALLENDALE
Northumberland

Allen Mill Cottages ★★★★
Contact: Mrs Kerry Crellin
Ashby Bank, Hexham NE47 9LQ
T: (01434) 683358
E: crellin@ukgateway.net
I: www.allenmill.com

ALLENHEADS
Northumberland

Englewood ★★★
Contact: Sykes Cottages
Ref:291, Sykes Cottages, York House, York Street, Chester CH1 3LR
T: (01244) 345700
F: (01244) 321442
E: info@sykescottages.co.uk
I: www.sykescottages.co.uk

ALNMOUTH
Northumberland

Bilton Barns ★★★★
Contact: Mrs Dorothy Jackson
Bilton Barns Farmhouse, Bilton Barns, Alnwick NE66 2TB
T: (01665) 830427
F: (01665) 833909
E: dorothy@biltonbarns.com
I: www.biltonbarns.com

Curlew's Calling ★★★
Contact: Alan and Sheila Worsley
Curlew's Calling, Rear of 10 Riverside Road, Alnmouth, Alnwick NE66 2SD
T: (01665) 830888
F: (01665) 830888

Garden Cottage ★★★★
Contact: Mr Robin Winder
Garden Cottage, 4 Garden Terrace, Alnwick NE66 2SF
T: (01665) 830352

Grange Cottages - Old Watch Tower & The Coach House ★★★★
Contact: Ms Nicola Brierley
Grange Cottages - Old Watch Tower & The Coach House, 20 Northumberland Street, Alnwick NE66 2RJ
T: (01665) 830783
F: (01665) 830783
E: enquiries@thegrange-alnmouth.com
I: www.northumbria-cottages.co.uk

Old Hall Cottage, High Buston Hall ★★★★★
Contact: Mrs Therese Atherton
High Buston Hall, High Buston, Alnwick NE66 3QH
T: (01665) 830606
F: (01665) 830707
E: highbuston@aol.com
I: www.highbuston.com

The Old Stables, High Buston Hall ★★★★
Contact: Miss Emma Gordon
High Buston Hall, High Buston, Alnwick NE66 3QH
T: (01665) 830341
F: (01665) 830005
E: johnedwards94@btinternet.com
I: www.holiday-cottages-northumberland.com

Prospect House ★★★
Contact: Mrs Yeadon
2 Prospect Place, Alnwick NE66 2RL
T: (01665) 830649
E: prospect.holidays@talk21.com
I: www.cottageguide.co.uk/alnmouth

Quality Self Catering ★★★★
Contact: Mrs Vicki Taylor
Letton Lodge, Alnwick NE66 2RJ
T: (01665) 830633
F: (01665) 830122
E: NTB@QSCmail.co.uk
I: www.alnmouth.co.uk

Shepherds House ★★★
Contact: Mrs Lyn Frater
High Buston Farm, Alnwick NE66 3QH
T: (01665) 830361
F: (01665) 830361
E: lynpfrater@aol.com
I: www.shepherdshouse.ntb.org.uk

Sunnyside Cottage ★★★★
Contact: Mrs Mary Hollins
2 The Grove, Newcastle upon Tyne NE16 4QY
T: (0191) 4883939
F: (0191) 4883939
E: sunnysidecott@lineone.net
I: www.sunnysidecottage.visitnorthumbria.com

Wooden Farm Holiday Cottages ★★-★★★
Contact: Mr Farr
Wooden Farm Holiday Cottages, Lesbury, Alnmouth, Alnwick NE66 2TW
T: (01665) 830342

ALNWICK
Northumberland

Alndyke Farm Cottages ★★★★
Contact: Mrs Laura Davison
Alndyke Farm Cottages, Alndyke Farmhouse, Alnmouth Road, Alnwick NE66 3PB
T: (01665) 510252
E: alndyke@fsmail.net
I: www.alndyke.co.uk

Alnwick Angel ★★★
Contact: Mr Colin McLean
Bondgate Cottage, Bondgate Without, Alnwick NE66 1PP
T: (01665) 602315
E: alnwickangel@tesco.net

Barbican View ★★★★
Contact: Mrs Frances Draper
10 Springwood Road, Thongsbridge, Huddersfield HD9 7SJ
T: (01484) 683705
E: fran.draper@virgin.net
I: www.barbicanview.plus.com

NORTHUMBRIA

Bog Mill Farm Holiday Cottages ★★★★-★★★★★
Contact: Mrs Ann Mason
Bog Mill Farm Holiday Cottages, Bog Mill Farm, Alnwick
NE66 3PA
T: (01665) 604529
F: (01665) 606972
E: stay@bogmill.co.uk
I: www.bogmill.co.uk

The Buie ★★★
Contact: Ms Diana Norris
Cosaig, Kyle of Lochalsh
IV40 8LB
T: (01599) 522365
F: (01599) 522365
E: diana_norris@hotmail.com

Cheviot View and Dipper Cottage ★★★-★★★★★
Contact: Mr Richard & Mrs Susan Green
Cheviot View and Dipper Cottage, Heckley High House, Alnwick NE66 2LQ
T: (01665) 602505

Dene View Cottage and Moor Croft Cottage ★★★★
Contact: Mrs Margaret McGregor
Dene View Cottage and Moor Croft Cottage, Broome Hill Farm, Alnwick NE66 2BA
T: (01665) 574460
F: (01665) 574460
E: margaret@broomehillfarm.co.uk
I: www.broomehillfarm.co.uk

Dunelm
Rating Applied For
Contact: Mrs Val Greene
Dunelm, 1 Crag View, Alnmouth Road, Alnwick NE66 2QQ
T: (01529) 413148
E: gvalgreene@aol.com

Farm Cottage ★★★
Contact: Mrs Renner
Farm Cottage, Shipley Hill, Alnwick NE66 2LX
T: (01665) 579266
I: www.cottageguide.co.uk/shipleyhill

Garden Cottages ★★★★
Contact: Mr & Mrs Harrison
Garden Cottages, Lemmington Hall, Alnwick NE66 2BH
T: (01665) 574129
F: (01665) 574129
E: gardencottage@lemmington.fsbusiness.co.uk
I: www.alnwickgardencottages.co.uk

Green Batt Cottages ★★★
Contact: Dr Emma Wady
Green Batt House, The Pinfold, Alnwick NE66 1TY
T: (01665) 602429
F: (01665) 602429
E: wadyone@aol.com
I: www.greenbattcottages.co.uk

Green Batt Studio ★★★
Contact: Mrs Clare Mills
1 Percy Street, Alnwick
NE66 1AE
T: (01665) 602742
E: paul@mills84.freeserve.co.uk

Henhill and Birchwood Hall Cottages ★★★★
Contact: Mrs Jane Mallen
Northumberland Estates, Alnwick Castle, Alnwick
NE66 1NQ
T: (01665) 602094
F: (01665) 608126
E: jane@nehc.co.uk
I: www.alnwickcastle.com/holidaycottages/

Hotspur Apartment ★★★
Contact: Mr Kevin Bremner
Coastal Retreats, P O Box 56, Alnwick NE66 3WZ
T: (01665) 830267
F: (01501) 753493
I: www.coastalretreat.com

1 Howick Street ★★★
Contact: Mr Thomas Payton
Austrey House, 3 Grosvenor Terrace, Alnwick NE66 1LG
T: (01665) 510484
E: tompayton@whsmithnet.co.uk
I: www.howickhols.fsnet.co.uk

Limpet Cottage ★★★★
Contact: Mrs Jane Mallen
Northumberland Estates, Alnwick Castle, Alnwick
NE66 1NQ
T: (01665) 602094
F: (01665) 608126
E: jane@nehc.co.uk
I: www.alnwickcastle.com/holidaycottages/

Lumbylaw & Garden Cottages ★★★★
Contact: Mrs S Lee
Lumbylaw & Garden Cottages, Alnwick NE66 2BW
T: (01665) 574277
F: (01665) 574277
E: holidays@lumbylaw.co.uk
I: www.lumbylaw.co.uk

Mole End
Rating Applied For
Contact: Mrs Joan Sanderson
14 St Marys Grove, Tudhoe Village, Spennymoor DL16 6LR
T: (01388) 815143
E: mrs.sanderson@gp-a83001.nhs.uk

The Pebble ★★★
Contact: Clare Laughton
Okelands, Pickhurst Road, Chiddingfold GU8 4TS
T: (01428) 683941
F: (01428) 683967
E: anthony.laughton@soc.soton.ac.uk

31 Pottergate ★★★★★
Contact: Mrs Jackie Galilee
The Northumberland Holiday Co, 33 Castle Street, Morpeth
NE65 0UN
T: (01665) 711353
E: northumberlandholidays@btinternet.com
I: www.thenorthumberlandholidaycompany.com

Reiver Cottage - Ref 3607 ★★★
Contact: Ms Hannah Cook
Dales Holiday Cottages, Carleton Business Park, Carleton New Road, Skipton BD23 2AA
T: (01756) 799821
E: info@dales-holiday-cottages.com
I: www.dales-holiday-cottages.com

Sawmill Cottage ★★★
Contact: Ms Alison Wrangham
Harehope Hall, Alnwick
NE66 2DP
T: (01668) 217329
F: (01668) 217346
E: aliwrangham@bt.connect.com

Stamford & Embleton Mill Farm Cottages ★★★★
Contact: Mrs Grahamslaw
The Farmhouse, Gallowmoor, Alnwick NE66 3SB
T: (01665) 579425
F: (01665) 579425

Thorn Rigg ★★★★
Contact: Mr & Mrs Potter
P O Box 5091, Dubai
T: +97 1439 44328

Tidal Watch ★★★★
Contact: Mr Kevin Bremner
Coastal Retreats, P O Box 56, Alnwick NE66 3WZ
T: (01665) 830267
F: (01312) 284309
E: kevinbremner@btopenworld.com

Village Farm ★★★-★★★★★★
Contact: Mrs Crissy Stoker
Town Foot Farm, Shilbottle, Alnwick NE66 2HG
T: (01665) 575591
F: (01665) 575591
E: crissy@villagefarmcottages.co.uk
I: www.villagefarmcottages.co.uk

Walkergate House
Rating Applied For
Contact: Dr Maryanne Freer
3 Lovaine Terrace, Alnwick
NE66 2RQ
T: (01665) 830139
E: maryanne.freer@pcpartners.org
I: www.alnwicktown.co.uk

2 White House Folly Cottages ★★★
Contact: Mrs Joan Gilroy
White House Folly Farm, Alnwick NE66 2LW
T: (01665) 579265

ALWINTON
Northumberland

Stonecrop Cottage ★★★
Contact: Mrs Mason
Flat 2, 1 Percy Gardens, North Shields NE30 4HG
T: (0191) 2570892

AMBLE
Northumberland

Acarsaid
Rating Applied For
Contact: Mrs Lynne Gray
17 West Avenue, Morpeth
NE65 0PD
T: (01665) 711737

Seashells ★★★
Contact: Mr Ian & Mrs Sue Rochester
22 Hauxley Way, Morpeth
NE65 0AL
T: (01665) 713448
F: (01665) 713448
E: ian@roch11.freeserve.co.uk

Warkworth Castle View ★★★
Contact: Mr Peter & Mrs Anne Jameson
34 Gynn Lane, Honley, Holmfirth HD9 6LF
T: (01484) 665627 & 07817 495556
E: peterjameson@gynn34.freeserve.co.uk
I: www.warkworthcastleview.co.uk

AMBLE-BY-THE-SEA
Northumberland

Braid View ★★★
Contact: Mrs Joyce Crass
11 Morwick Road, Morpeth
NE65 0TG
T: (01665) 711623
E: northumbriabreaks@hotmail.com

Brent Cottage ★★★
Contact: Mr Mike Clarke
18 The Green, Leicester LE7 4UH
T: (01664) 424480
E: mikeanddianaclarke@thrussington.fsworld.co.uk

Coastguard Cottage ★★★★
Contact: Mr & Mrs N Aitchison
Birchlands, Lords Moor Lane, York YO32 5XF
T: (01904) 490408
E: neville@aitchison.co.uk
I: coastguardcottage.co.uk

BALDERSDALE
County Durham

Clove Lodge Cottage ★★★
Contact: Mrs Ann Heys
Clove Lodge Farm, Barnard Castle DL12 9UP
T: (01833) 650030
E: ann@heys70.freeserve.co.uk
I: www.clovelodge.co.uk

Lartington Hall ★★★★
Contact: Mr Robin Rackham
Lartington Lettings, Barnard Castle DL12 9BW
T: (01833) 650495
F: (01833) 650419
E: robin.rackham@btconnect.com
I: www.lartington.com

The Old Chapel and Bluebell Barn ★★★★-★★★★★★
Contact: Mrs Moore
The Old Chapel and Bluebell Barn, Briscoe Farm, Barnard Castle DL12 9UL
T: (01833) 650822
E: robertehd@aol.com

Establishments printed in blue have a detailed entry in this guide

NORTHUMBRIA

BAMBURGH
Northumberland

Adderstone Hall Country Cottages ★★★-★★★★
Contact: Dr David Ratliff
Country Cottages, Adderstone Hall, Market Place, Belford NE70 7NE
T: (01668) 213543
F: (01668) 213787
E: davidratliff1@hotmail.com
I: www.adderstonehall.co.uk

The Blacksmiths ★★★★
Contact: Mrs Rachel Cole
Applecote, Goverton, Nottingham NG14 7FN
T: (01636) 830864
E: rachelstevecole@hotmail.com

Bradford Country Cottages ★★★-★★★★
Contact: Mr L W Robson
Bradford Country Cottages, Bradford House, Bamburgh, Belford NE70 7JT
T: (01668) 213432
F: (01668) 213891
E: lwrob@tiscali.co.uk
I: www.bradford-leisure.co.uk

Bridge End ★★★★
Contact: Mr Roger & Mrs Linda Topping
98 Dowanhill Street, Glasgow G12 9EG
T: (0141) 334 4833

The Bungalow ★★★
Contact: Miss Eve Humphreys
Burton Hall, Bamburgh NE69 7AR
T: (01668) 214213
F: (01668) 214538
E: evehumphreys@aol.com
I: www.burtonhall.co.uk

Castle View Bungalow ★★★★
Contact: Mr & Mrs I Nicol
Springwood, South Lane, Seahouses NE68 7UL
T: (01665) 720320
F: (01665) 720146
E: ian@slatehall.freeserve.co.uk
I: www.slatehallridingcentre.com

The Cottage ★★★
Contact: Mrs Turnbull
1 Friars Court, Bamburgh NE69 7AE
T: (01668) 214494

Dukesfield Farm Holiday Cottages ★★★★
Contact: Mrs Maria Eliana Robinson
The Glebe, Radcliffe Road, Bamburgh NE69 7AE
T: (01668) 214456
F: (01668) 214354
E: eric_j_robinson@compuserve.com
I: www.secretkingdom.com/dukes/field.htm

The Fairway ★★★
Contact: Mrs Diana Middleton
High Close House, Wylam NE41 8BL
T: (01661) 852125
E: rsmiddleton@talk21.com

Glebe House and Glebe Cottage ★★★★★
Contact: Mrs Maria Eliana Robinson
The Glebe, Radcliffe Road, Bamburgh NE69 7AE
T: (01668) 214456
F: (01668) 214354
E: eric_j_robinson@compuserve.com
I: www.secretkingdom.com/glebe/house.htm

The Granary ★★★
Contact: Mrs Patricia Cowen
Thornleigh, Carlisle CA4 8ES
T: (01228) 560245
E: cowen-home@hotmail.com

Harelaw House ★★★★
Contact: Mr Robert Turnbull
Church House, New Road, Chatton NE66 5PU
T: (01668) 215494
F: (01668) 215494
E: harelaw@fsmail.net
I: www.harelawhouse.ntb.org.uk

The Haven and Sandham ★★★★
Contact: Miss Lynn Gregory
Earsdon Hill Farm, Morpeth NE61 3ES
T: (01670) 787392
F: (01670) 787392
E: pg@africaselect.com
I: www.cottageguide.co.uk/thehaven/

High Tutlaw House ★★★★★
Contact: Mrs Jane Mallen
Park Farm House, Hulne Park, Alnwick NE66 3HZ
T: (01665) 602094
F: (01665) 608126
E: tutlaw@farming.co.uk
I: www.tutlaw.ntb.org.uk

Hillside ★★★★
Contact: Ms Michelle Mattinson
Hillside Bed & Breakfast, 25 Lucker Road, Bamburgh NE69 7BS
T: (01668) 214674
F: (01668) 214674
E: enquiries@hillside-bamburgh.com
I: www.hillside-bamburgh.com

Hoppen Hall Farm Cottages ★★★★
Contact: Mrs Jane Mallen
Northumberland Estates Holiday Cottages, Alnwick Castle, Alnwick NE66 1NQ
T: (01665) 602094
F: (01665) 608126
E: jane@nehc.co.uk
I: www.alnwickcastle.com/holidaycottages/

Inglenook Cottage ★★★★
Contact: Mrs Amanda J Moore
Swallow Cottage, Stripe Lane, Harrogate HG3 3EY
T: (01423) 772211
E: inglenookcottage@aol.com

Millhouse Cottage ★★★★
Contact: Mrs Sarah Nelson
Low Bleakhope, Alnwick NE66 4NZ
T: (01665) 578361
F: (01665) 578845
E: sarah.nelson@ukonline.co.uk

Nineteen ★★★★
Contact: Mr John McDougal
Whitestacks, Ingram Road, Bamburgh NE69 7BT
T: (01668) 214395
F: (01668) 214100
E: clem500@btinternet.com

The Old Coach House ★★★★
Contact: Carolynn & David Croisdale-Appleby
Abbotsholme, Hervines Road, Amersham HP6 5HS
T: (01494) 725194
F: (01494) 725474
E: croisdaleappleby@aol.com
I: www.selfcateringluxury.co.uk

Outchester & Ross Farm Cottages ★★★★
Contact: Mrs Shirley McKie
1 Cragview Road, Belford NE70 7NT
T: (01668) 213336
F: (01668) 219385
E: enquiry@rosscottages.co.uk
I: www.rosscottages.co.uk

Point Cottages ★★★
Contact: Mrs Sanderson
30 The Oval, Newcastle upon Tyne NE12 9PP
T: (0191) 2662800
T: (0191) 2151630
E: info@bamburgh-cottages.co.uk
I: www.bamburgh-cottages.co.uk

Saint Oswald's ★★-★★★
Contact: Mr Anthony Smith
10 Aldbourne Road, London W12 0LN
T: (020) 82489589
F: (020) 8248 9587
E: anthonysmith@hotmail.com

Smugglers Court ★★★★
Contact: Mr Gordon Begg
Belford NE70 7EE
T: (01665) 721477
F: (01665) 721477
E: gordon@budle-bay.com
I: www.budle-bay.com

Springhill Farm Cottages ★★★★
Contact: Mrs Julie Gregory
Springhill Farm Holiday Cottages, Springhill Farm House, Springhill Farm, Seahouses NE68 7UR
T: (01665) 721820
F: (01665) 721820
E: enquiries@springhill-farm.co.uk
I: www.springhill-farm.co.uk

Struan ★★★
Contact: Mr Charles Wilkie-Smith
27 Ridley Place, Newcastle upon Tyne NE1 8Lb
T: (0191) 2305471
F: (0191) 2221391
E: pfm.rcp@daviesbellreed.co.uk

Swallows Nest ★★★★
Contact: Ms Jo Tattersall
19 Belle Vue Avenue, Newcastle upon Tyne NE3 1AH
T: (0191) 2853334
F: (0191) 2853334

Waren Lea Hall ★★★★★
Contact: Carolynn & David Croisdale-Appleby
Abbotsholme, Hervines Road, Amersham HP6 5HS
T: (01494) 725194
F: (01494) 725474
E: croisdaleappleby@aol.com
I: www.selfcateringluxury.co.uk

Whinstone Cottage ★★★
Contact: Mrs Philippa Tait
Lyndale, 15 Kenton Road, Newcastle upon Tyne NE3 4NE
T: (0191) 2851363

Wynding Down ★★★★★
Contact: Mrs Dianne Stanger
6 Cottingwood Lane, Morpeth NE61 1EA
T: (01670) 511162
E: distanger@hotmail.com

BARDON MILL
Northumberland

The Hott ★★★
Contact: Mrs Noreen Harding
West End Town Farm, Hexham NE47 7JJ
T: (01434) 344258

BARNARD CASTLE
County Durham

Boot and Shoe Cottage ★★★★
Contact: Mrs Rachel Peat
Waterside Cottage, Barnard Castle DL12 9TR
T: (01833) 627200
F: (01833) 627200
E: info@bootandshoecottage.co.uk
I: www.bootandshoecottage.co.uk

East Briscoe Farm Cottages ★★★★
Contact: Mr Chris Tarpey
East Briscoe Farm Cottages, East Briscoe Farm, Barnard Castle DL12 9UL
T: (01833) 650087
F: (01833) 650027
E: vb@eastbriscoe.co.uk
I: www.eastbriscoe.co.uk

Hauxwell Grange Cottages (The Stone Byre and Curlew Cottage) ★★★★
Contact: Mrs Val Pearson
Hauxwell Cottages, Hauxwell Grange, Barnard Castle DL12 8QU
T: (01833) 695022
F: (01833) 695022
E: hauxwellvmp@supaworld.com

Lanquitts Cottage ★
Contact: Mrs Brenda Kidd
Strathmore Arms Farm, Barnard Castle DL12 9UR
T: (01833) 650345

NORTHUMBRIA

5A Market Place ★★★
Contact: Mr & Mrs C Armstrong
77 Galgate, Barnard Castle
DL12 8ES
T: (01833) 690726
E: cajamara@aol.com

Staindrop House Mews & The Arches ★★★★
Contact: Mrs Dorothy Walton
Staindrop House, 14 Front Street, Darlington DL2 3NH
T: (01833) 660951
E: shmholidays@hotmail.com

Thorngate Coach House ★★★★
Contact: Mrs Clare Terry
Thorngate Coach House, Thorngate House, Thorngate, Barnard Castle DL12 8PY
T: (01833) 637791
F: (01833) 637791
E: info@thorngatecoachhouse.co.uk
I: www.thorngatecoachhouse.com

Village Green Cottage ★★★★
Contact: Mr Robert & Mrs Mary Green
Village Green Cottage, Village Green, Richmond DL11 7BW
T: (01833) 627331
I: www.teesdaleholidays.co.uk/villagegreencottage.htm

Wackford Squeers Cottage ★★★
Contact: Mr John Braithwaite
Wackford Squeers Cottage, Wodencroft, Cotherstone, Barnard Castle DL12 9UQ
T: (01833) 650032
F: (01833) 650909

Woodland House Cottage ★★★
Contact: Mr Harding
Woodland House, Bishop Auckland DL13 5RH
T: (01388) 710836
E: cottage@woodland-house.freeserve.co.uk
I: www.cottageguide.co.uk/woodlandhouse

BARNINGHAM
County Durham

The Cottage ★★★★
Contact: Mrs Helen Lowes
The Cottage, Wilson House, Richmond DL11 7EB
T: (01833) 621218
F: (01833) 621110

Dove Cottage ★★★
Contact: Miss Sheila Catton
Dove Cottage, Heath House, Richmond DL11 7DU
T: (01833) 621374
E: dove@smithj90.fsnet.co.uk
I: www.cottageguide.co.uk/dove-cottage

BARRASFORD
Northumberland

Barrasford Arms Cottage ★★★
Contact: Mr Thomas & Mrs Joyce Milburn
Barrasford Arms, Hexham NE48 4AA
T: (01434) 681237
F: (01434) 681237

BEADNELL
Northumberland

Annstead Farm ★★★★
Contact: Mrs Susan Mellor
Annstead Farm, Chathill NE67 5BT
T: (01665) 720387
F: (01665) 721494
E: susan@annstead.co.uk
I: www.annstead.co.uk

Beechley ★★★
Contact: Mrs Deborah Baker
22 Upper Green Way, Tingley, Wakefield WF3 1TA
T: (0113) 218 9176
F: (0113) 218 9176
E: deb_n_ade@hotmail.com

Benthall ★★★★
Contact: Mr & Mrs Davidson
6 Benthall, Chathill NE67 5BQ
T: (01665) 720269

The Bothy ★★★★
Contact: Mrs Beryl Seaward-Birchall
The Bothy, Shepherds Cottage, Chathill NE67 5AD
T: (01665) 720497
F: (01665) 720497
I: www.thebothy.ntb.org.uk

The Dells ★★★
Contact: Mr Iain & Mrs Andrea Slater
25 Northumberland Gardens, Newcastle upon Tyne NE2 1HA
T: (0191) 2399934
E: andreaslater@beadnell.fsnet.co.uk

Driftwood ★★★
Contact: Mrs Carole Field
Beach Court, Harbour Road, Chathill NE67 5BJ
T: (01665) 720225
F: (01665) 721499
E: info@beachcourt.com
I: www.beachcourt.com/driftwood

Low Dover Beadnell Bay ★★★★
Contact: Mrs Kath Thompson
Low Dover Beadnell Bay, Harbour Road, Chathill NE67 5BJ
T: (01665) 720291
E: enquiries@lowdover.co.uk
I: www.lowdover.co.uk

Mapleleaf Cottage ★★★
Contact: Mrs Susan McKenzie
18 Murston Avenue, Cramlington NE23 3XH
T: (01670) 738422 & 07950 173570
F: (01670) 733399

Nook End Cottage ★★★★★
Contact: Ms Fiona McKeith
Coastal Retreats, 174 Warkworth Woods, Newcastle Great Park, Newcastle upon Tyne NE3 5RD
T: (0191) 2365971
E: info@coastalretreats.co.uk
I: www.coastalretreats.co.uk

Seaspray ★★★
Contact: Ms Sheila Armstrong
10 Fernville Road, Newcastle upon Tyne NE3 4HT
T: (0191) 2848771

Torwoodlee & Shorestone ★★★
Contact: Dales Hol Cot Ref:1892,1893
Dales Holiday Cottages, Carleton Business Park, Carleton New Road, Skipton BD23 2AA
T: (01756) 799821
F: (01756) 797012
E: info@dalesholcot.com
I: www.dalesholcot.com

Town Farm Cottages ★★★-★★★★
Contact: Mr & Mrs Thompson
South Lodge, Morpeth NE65 9JA
T: (01665) 604110
F: (01670) 786188
E: paul.thompson@marishalthompson.co.uk
I: www.northumberland-holidays.com

BEAL
Northumberland

Bee Hill Properties ★★★★-★★★★★
Contact: Mr David Nesbitt
Bee Hill Properties, Berwick-upon-Tweed TD15 2PB
T: (01289) 381102
F: (01289) 381418
E: info@beehill.co.uk
I: www.beehill.co.uk

BEAMISH
County Durham

Chapel House Studio Apartments ★★★
Contact: Mr MacLennan
Chapel House, Causey Row, Marley Hill, Newcastle upon Tyne NE16 5EJ
T: (01207) 290992

BELFORD
Northumberland

3, 4 and 5 Swinhoe Cottages ★★★
Contact: Mrs Valerie Nixon
Swinhoe Farm House, Belford NE70 7LJ
T: (01668) 213370
I: www.swinhoecottages.co.uk

Belford Court ★★★★
Contact:
Belford Court, Old Magistrates Building, High Street, Belford NE70 7NA
T: (01668) 213543
F: (01668) 213787
E: bluebel@globalnet.co.uk
I: www.belfordcourt.com

Church View ★★★
Contact: Mrs Susan Oates
West Lodge, 31 Holywood, Bishop Auckland DL13 3HE
T: (01388) 527127
F: (01377) 526547
E: johnoates@pro-streamlimited.co.uk

Elwick Farm Cottages ★★★★
Contact: Mrs Roslyn Rcay
Elwick Farm Cottages, Elwick Farm, Belford NE70 7EL
T: (01668) 213242
F: (01668) 213783
E: w.r.reay@talk21.com
I: www.elwickcottages.co.uk

Gardener's Cottage Rating Applied For
Contact: Mrs Susan Comber
2 Hepburn Cottages, Alnwick NE66 4EG
T: (01668) 215443
F: (01668) 215443
E: comber@hepburn2.fsnet.co.uk

Hollyhock House ★★★★
Contact: Miss Alison Turnbull
95 St Matthew's Road, London SW2 1NE
T: (020) 77334904
E: ali_turnbull@hotmail.com
I: www.hollyhockhouse.co.uk

Owls Rest ★★★★
Contact: Ms Christine Brown
The Old Manse, New Road, Alnwick NE66 5PU
T: (01668) 215343
F: (01668) 215343
E: chattonbb@aol.com
I: www.owlsrestbelford.co.uk

Shepherds Cottage ★★★★
Contact: Mrs Iris Oates
Easington Farm, Belford NE70 7EG
T: (01668) 213298

Teal Cottage ★★★★
Contact: Mrs Katie Burn
Teal Cottage, 2 Fenham-le-Moor, Belford NE70 7PN
T: (01668) 213247
F: (01668) 213247
E: enquiries@fenham-le-moor.co.uk
I: www.fenham-le-moor.co.uk

BELLINGHAM
Northumberland

Boat Farm Cottages ★★★★
Contact: Mrs Young
Boat Farm, Bellingham, Hexham NE48 2AR
T: (01434) 220989
E: barbaraattheboat@hotmail.com
I: www.boatfarm.co.uk

Buteland Bothy ★★
Contact: Mrs Alison Williams
Buteland Bothy, Buteland House, Hexham NE48 2EX
T: (01434) 220389
F: (01434) 220389
E: buteland@aol.com

Castle Hill View ★★★
Contact: Mr Len & Mrs Joan Batey
Castle Hill View, Front Street, Hexham NE48 2AA
T: (01434) 220263

Conheath Cottage ★★★★
Contact: Mrs Zaina Riddle
Blakelaw Farm, Bellingham, Hexham NE48 2EF
T: (01434) 220250
F: (01434) 220250
E: stay@conheath.co.uk
I: www.conheath.co.uk

Riverdale Court ★★★★
Contact: John and Iben Cocker
Riverdale Court, Bellingham, Hexham NE48 2JT
T: (01434) 220254
F: (01434) 220457
I: www.riverdalehall.demon.co.uk

Establishments printed in blue have a detailed entry in this guide

NORTHUMBRIA

BERWICK-UPON-TWEED
Northumberland

Broadstone Cottage ★★★
Contact: Mr Edward Chantler
Broadstone Farm, Grafty Green,
Maidstone ME17 2AT
T: (01622) 850207
F: (01622) 851750

2 The Courtyard ★★★
Contact: Mrs Joan Morton
1 The Courtyard, Church Street,
Berwick-upon-Tweed TD15 1EE
T: (01289) 308737
F: (01706) 817382
E: jim@patmosphere.uklinux.net

Courtyard Cottage ★★★★
Contact:
Reiver Properties, 30 Great Lime
Road, Newcastle upon Tyne
NE12 7AH
T: (0191) 2680788
E: enquiries@reiverproperties.com
I: www.reiverproperties.com

Gainslawhill Farm Cottage ★★★
Contact: Mrs Susan Wight
Gainslaw Farm, Berwick-upon-Tweed TD15 1SZ
T: (01289) 386210
E: susan@gainslawhill.co.uk
I: www.gainslawhill.co.uk

Honeysuckle Cottage and Bluebell Cottage ★★★★
Contact: Mr Robert Whitten
Honeysuckle Cottage and
Bluebell Cottage, West
Longridge Farm, Berwick-upon-Tweed TD15 2JX
T: (01289) 331112
F: (01289) 304591
E: robert@westlongridge.co.uk
I: www.westlongridge.co.uk

Kingsway Cottage ★★★★
Contact: Mrs Judith King
East Ord Farmhouse, Berwick-upon-Tweed TD15 2NS
T: (01289) 306228
E: jking4kingsway@aol.com
I: www.kingswaycottage.co.uk

Lark Rise ★★★★
Contact: Mrs Deirdre Dickson
8 Holme Eden Hall, Carlisle
CA4 8RD
T: (016977) 41800
F: (01228) 573338
I: www.northumbrian-cottages.co.uk

Mill Lane Apartments ★★★★
Contact: Mr John Haswell
Mill Lane Apartments, 2A Palace
Street East, Berwick-upon-Tweed TD15 1HT
T: (01289) 304492
F: 0870 7061496
E: john@millane.fsnet.co.uk
I: www.millane.co.uk

The Old Barn ★★★★
Contact: Mr Richard & Mrs
Susan Persse
High Letham Farmhouse, High
Letham, Berwick-upon-Tweed
TD15 1UX
T: (01289) 306585
F: (01289) 304194
E: hlfb@fantasyprints.co.uk
I: www.ntb.org.uk

1 The Old Smokehouse ★★★
Contact: Mrs Jackie Sell
46 Queenhythe Road, Jacobs
Well, Guildford GU4 7NX
T: (01483) 533757

6 Palace Green
Rating Applied For
Contact: Mr Louis Heward-Mills
73 Bengeo Street, Hertford
SG14 3ET
T: (01992) 534828
F: (01992) 534858
E: louis@cctr-london.demon.co.uk

The Retreat ★★★★
Contact: Mrs Muckle
40 Ravensdowne, Berwick-upon-Tweed TD15 1DQ
T: (01289) 306992
F: (01289) 331606
E: petedot@dmuckle.freeserve.co.uk
I: www.ravensdowne.co.uk

South Ord Farm Bungalow ★★★★
Contact: Dales Hol Cot Ref:2203
Dales Holiday Cottages, Carleton
Business Park, Carleton New
Road, Skipton BD23 2AA
T: (01756) 799821
F: (01756) 797012
E: info@dalesholcot.com
I: www.dalesholcot.com

Tigh Na Rudh ★★★★
Contact: Sykes Ref 891
Sykes Cottages, York House,
York Street, Chester CH1 3LR
T: (01244) 345700
F: (01244) 321442
E: info@sykescottages.co.uk
I: www.sykescottages.co.uk

Trevone ★★★★
Contact: Mr Peter Herdman
Devonia, 13 Bankhill, Berwick-upon-Tweed TD15 1BE
T: (01289) 307524

Unthank Farm Cottage ★★★★
Contact: Mrs Patricia Hart
1 Unthank Farm Cottages,
Berwick-upon-Tweed TD15 2NG
T: 0788 5 454962
I: www.hartscountrycottages.co.uk

West Kyloe Cottages ★★★
Contact: Mrs Teresa Smalley
Garden Cottage, 1 West Kyloe,
Berwick-upon-Tweed TD15 2PG
T: (01289) 381279
F: (01289) 381279
E: teresamalley@westkyloe.demon.co.uk
I: www.westkyloe.co.uk

West Ord Holiday Cottages ★★★★
Contact: Mrs Carol Lang
West Ord Holiday Cottages,
West Ord Farm, Berwick-upon-Tweed TD15 2XQ
T: (01289) 386631
F: (01289) 386800
E: stay@westord.co.uk
I: www.westord.co.uk

Whitecroft ★★★
Contact: Mrs Moira Kay
Tweed Cottage, Berwick-upon-Tweed TD15 2XW
T: (01289) 386066
F: (01289) 386066
E: enquiries@whitecroftcottage.co.uk
I: www.whitecroftcottage.co.uk

BISHOP AUCKLAND
County Durham

Five Gables Cottage ★★★★
Contact: Mr & Mrs Weston
Five Gables Guest House,
Granville Terrace, Bishop
Auckland DL14 8AT
T: (01388) 608204
F: (01388) 663092
E: cottage@fivegables.co.uk
I: www.fivegables.co.uk

Gill Bank Farm Cottage ★★★
Contact: Mrs Anne Marley
Gill Bank Farm, Bishop Auckland
DL13 5QF
T: (01388) 718614

Meadow View ★★★
Contact: Dales Hol Cot Ref:1462
Dales Holiday Cottages, Carleton
Business Park, Carleton New
Road, Skipton BD23 2AA
T: (01756) 799821
F: (01756) 797012
E: info@dalesholcot.com
I: www.dalesholcot.com

West Cottage ★★★★
Contact: Mrs Elizabeth
Wilkinson
West Cottage, Carrsides Lane,
Ferryhill DL17 0NJ
T: (01388) 720252
F: (01388) 720252
E: carrsides@farming.co.uk

BISHOP MIDDLEHAM
County Durham

Bee Eater Cottage ★★★
Contact: Mrs Daphne Anderson
Farnless Farm Cottage, Bishop
Middleham DL17 9EB
T: (0191) 377 1428
I: www.bee-eater-cottage.co.uk

BLANCHLAND
Northumberland

Bail Hill ★★★
Contact: Mrs Jennifer Graham
Allenshields, Consett DH8 9PP
T: (01434) 675274
F: (01434) 675274

Boltsburn Holiday Cottages ★★
Contact: Mr Cecil Ernest Davison
Bolts Brae, 10 Watergate Road,
Consett DH8 9QS
T: (01207) 583076

Boltslaw Cottage ★★★★
Contact: Mrs Nicola Smith
6 Selborne Avenue, Gateshead
NE9 6ET
T: (0191) 4879456
F: (01670) 510300
E: asmith6000@aol.com
I: www.uk-holiday-cottages.co.uk/boltslaw

BOULMER
Northumberland

North Cottage ★★★★
Contact: Mrs Madeleine Frater
North Cottage, Boulmer, Alnwick
NE66 3BX
T: (01665) 577308
E: madeleine_frater@hotmail.com
I: www.northcottage.boulmer.co.uk

BOWSDEN
Northumberland

Swallow Cottage ★★★
Contact: Mr & Mrs John Dunn
The Bungalow, Lickar Lea,
Berwick-upon-Tweed TD15 2TP
T: (01289) 388500
F: (01289) 388507
E: janet.dunn@lickarlea.co.uk
I: www.lickarlea.co.uk

BRANTON
Northumberland

Breamish Valley Cottages ★★★★-★★★★★
Contact: Mrs Michele Moralee
Breamish Valley Cottages,
Powburn, Alnwick NE66 4LW
T: (01665) 578263
F: (01665) 578263
E: peter@breamishvalley.co.uk
I: www.breamishvalley.co.uk

BYRNESS
Northumberland

Catcleugh Farm ★★★
Contact: Mr Walter Nieuwkoop
Catcleugh Farm, Byrness,
Newcastle upon Tyne NE19 1TX
T: (01670) 772607
F: (01670) 772607
E: catcleugh@hotmail.com
I: www.catcleugh.com

The Old School House ★★★★
Contact: Dales Holiday Cottages
Carleton Business Park,
Sandylands Business Centre,
Carleton New Road, Skipton
BD23 2DG
T: (01756) 799821
F: (01756) 797012

CALLALY
Northumberland

Dene Cottage ★★★★
Contact: Mrs Maureen Winn
Dene Cottage, Dene House,
Alnwick NE66 4TA
T: (01665) 574513

CARLTON IN CLEVELAND
Middlesbrough

Stables Cottage ★★★
Contact: Dales Hol Cot Ref:2697
Dales Holiday Cottages, Carleton
Business Park, Carleton New
Road, Skipton BD23 2AA
T: (01756) 799821
F: (01756) 797012
E: info@dalesholcot.com
I: www.dalesholcot.com

NORTHUMBRIA

CARRVILLE
County Durham

62 Wantage Road ★★
Contact: Mr Norman & Mrs Anne Walker
62 Wantage Road, Durham
DH1 1LR
T: (0191) 3862290
I: www.cottageguide.co.uk/carrville

CASTLESIDE
County Durham

The Cottage, The Dairy & The Forge ★★-★★★
Contact: Mr & Mrs Elliot
Derwent Grange Farm, Consett DH8 9BN
T: (01207) 508358
E: ekelliot@aol.com

Manor Park Cottage (Manor Park Ltd) ★★★
Contact: Mr Brian Elstrop
Manor Park Ltd, Broadmeadows, Ripon Burn, Consett DH8 9HD
T: (01207) 501000
F: (01207) 599179

Pondfield Villa Farm Cottages ★★★
Contact: Mrs Margaret Steel
Pondfield Villa Farm Cottages, Pondfield Villa Farm, Millersville Lane, Consett DH8 9HF
T: (01207) 582703
E: k.a.steel@btinternet.co.uk
I: www.pondfieldvillafarm.ntb.org.uk

CATTON
Northumberland

Station House Flat ★★★
Contact: Mr & Ms Mike & Verona Woodhouse
Station House Flat, Station House, Hexham NE47 9QF
T: (01434) 683362
F: 0870 4323432
E: info@allendale-holidays.co.uk

CAWBURN
Northumberland

Rowan Cottage ★★★★
Contact: Mrs Margaret Swallow
Rowan Cottage, High Edges Green, Haltwhistle NE49 9PP
T: (01434) 320352
F: (01434) 320352
E: swallow@rowan78.freeserve.co.uk
I: www.rowan78.freeserve.co.uk

CHATHILL
Northumberland

Charlton Hall Holiday Cottages ★★★★
Contact: Mr Robert Thorp
Charlton Hall Holiday Cottages, Charlton Hall, Chathill NE67 5DZ
T: (01665) 579378
I: www.charltonhall.co.uk

The Lodge and Head Gardener's House ★★★★
Contact: Mrs J. Shirley Burnie
The Lodge and Head Gardener's House, Doxford Hall, Chathill NE67 5DN
T: (01665) 589499
F: (01665) 589499
E: doxfordhall@aol.com

Newstead Cottage ★★
Contact: Mrs Riddell
Newstead Cottage, Newstead Farm, Chathill NE67 5LH
T: (01665) 589263

Tower Cottage ★★
Contact: Mrs Cresswell
Preston Tower, Chathill NE67 5DH
T: (01665) 589227

CHATTON
Northumberland

Mill Cottage ★★★★
Contact: Ms Kim Stewart
Coastal Accommodation, Ros View, 14 Mill Hill, Alnwick NE66 5PR
T: (01668) 215289
E: info@coastal-accommodation.co.uk
I: www.coastal-accommodation.co.uk

Percy Cottage
Rating Applied For
Contact: Miss Helen Cunningham
The Property Investments, The Barn House, Milfield Hill, Wooler NE71 6JE
T: (01668) 216556

CHESTER-LE-STREET
County Durham

The Old Stables ★★★★
Contact: Mr & Mrs Cutter
Hollycroft, 11 The Parade, Chester-le-Street DH3 3LR
T: (0191) 3887088
E: cutter@hollycroft11.freeserve.co.uk

Plawsworth Hall Farm ★★★★
Contact: Mr Harry Johnson
Plawsworth Hall Farm, Chester-le-Street DH2 3LD
T: (0191) 3710251
F: (0191) 3712101
E: plawsworth@aol.com
I: www.plawsworth.com

CHILLINGHAM
Northumberland

Chillingham Castle ★★★
Contact:
Chillingham Castle, Chillingham, Alnwick NE66 5NJ
T: (01668) 215359
F: (01668) 215463
E: enquiries@chillingham-castle.com
I: www.chillingham-castle.com

CHOLLERTON
Northumberland

The Old Church ★★★★
Contact: Mrs Marilyn Framrose
Old Church Cottage, Hexham NE46 4TF
T: (01434) 681930
E: oldchurch@supanet.com
I: chollerton.urscene.net

CHOPWELL
Tyne and Wear

High Pasture Cottage ★★★★
Contact: Mr Allan Low
High Pasture Cottage, Bowser Hill Farm, Newcastle upon Tyne NE17 7AY
T: (01207) 560881
E: alow@btinternet.com

COANWOOD
Northumberland

Mill Hill Farmhouse ★★★
Contact: Mrs Wigham
Hargill House, Haltwhistle NE49 0PQ
T: (01434) 320256
E: millhill@fsmail.net
I: www.cottageguide.co.uk/millhill

COCKFIELD
County Durham

New Cottage ★★★
Contact: Mrs Margaret Partridge
New Cottage, Hollymoor Farm, Bishop Auckland DL13 5HF
T: (01388) 718567
F: (01388) 718567

Rose Cottage ★★★
Contact: Mrs Elstob
Rose Cottage, Highlands, Bishop Auckland DL13 5BG
T: (01388) 718941

Stonecroft and Swallows Nest ★★★★
Contact: Mrs Alison Tallentire
Low Lands Farm, Cockfield, Bishop Auckland DL13 5AW
T: (01388) 718251
F: (01388) 718251
E: info@farmholidaysuk.com
I: www.farmholidaysuk.com

COLWELL
Northumberland

Lance-Surtees Cottage ★★★
Contact: Mrs Dorothea Nelson
Chapel Cottage, Prescott, Cullompton EX15 3BA
T: (01884) 841320

COPLEY
County Durham

Sandbed Cottages ★★
Contact: Mrs Barbara Dodd
Black Horse, Front Street, Darlington DL2 3HS
T: (01325) 730374
E: blackhorseuk@yahoo.com

CORBRIDGE
Northumberland

April Cottage ★★★
Contact: Mrs Kate Dean
21 Woodland Close, Macclesfield SK11 9BZ
T: (01625) 861718
E: peterandkatedean@btopenworld.com

The Hayes ★★★
Contact: Mrs Monica Matthews
The Hayes, Newcastle Road, Corbridge NE45 5LP
T: (01434) 632010
F: (01434) 633069
E: mjct@mmatthews.fsbusiness.co.uk
I: www.hayes-corbridge.co.uk

Nosbor Cottage ★★★
Contact: Mrs Veronica Robson
7 Runnymede Road, Darras Hall, Ponteland, Newcastle upon Tyne NE20 9HE
T: (01661) 871135
F: (01661) 871135
E: nosboruk@yahoo.co.uk
I: www.nosbor.co.uk

Oswald Cottage ★★★★
Contact: Mrs Harriman
Swarden House, Kyloe House Farm, Newcastle upon Tyne NE18 0BB
T: (01661) 852909
F: (01661) 854106
E: paul.harriman@littonproperties.co.uk

14 Princes Street ★★★★
Contact: Mrs Hendry
The Old Post Office, Consett DH8 9RW
T: (01207) 255283
E: olwen.hendry@btopenworld.com

Wallhouses South Farm Cottage ★★★★
Contact: Mrs Eileen Lymburn
South Farm, Military Road, Corbridge NE45 5PU
T: (01434) 672388
E: loraip@aol.com

West Fell Cottage ★★★
Contact: Mrs Smith
West Fell House, Corbridge NE45 5RZ
T: (01434) 632044

CORNHILL-ON-TWEED
Northumberland

Birch Cottage ★★★
Contact: Mr Robin Lathangle
East Moneylaws Farm Cottage, No 4 Cottage, East Moneylaws, Cornhill-on-Tweed TD12 4QD
T: (01890) 850328

Herds Hoose, Cherry Cottage ★★★
Contact: Mrs Diana Tweedie
Herds Hoose, Cherry Cottage, Tithe Hill, Cornhill-on-Tweed TD12 4QD
T: (01890) 850286
E: info@tithehill.co.uk
I: www.tithehill.co.uk

Jasmine Cottage ★★★
Contact: Dales Hol Cot Ref:2257
Dales Holiday Cottages, Carleton Business Park, Carleton New Road, Skipton BD23 2AA
T: (01756) 799821
F: (01756) 797012
E: info@dalesholcot.com
I: www.dalesholcot.com

Establishments printed in blue have a detailed entry in this guide

NORTHUMBRIA

Melkington Lodge ★★★★★
Contact: Mrs Veronica Barber
Melkington Lodge, Cornhill-on-Tweed TD12 4UP
T: (01890) 882313
F: (01890) 882300
E: barber@melkington.demon.co.uk
I: www.melkington.co.uk

Orchard Cottage ★★★★
Contact: Mrs Lucy Carroll
Old Egypt, Tiptoe, Cornhill-on-Tweed TD12 4XD
T: (01890) 882177
F: (01890) 883060
E: fish@till-fishing.co.uk
I: www.till-fishing.co.uk

The Stables ★★★★
Contact: Mrs Margaret Buckle
Tor Cottage, Cornhill-on-Tweed TD12 4QA
T: (01890) 882390
F: (01890) 883438
E: david.buckle@btinternet.com
I: www.thestables.cornhill.btinternet.co.uk/

Tillmouth Cottage ★★★★
Contact: Mrs Binnie
Tillmouth Cottage, Tillmouth Farm, Cornhill-on-Tweed TD12 4XA
T: (01289) 382482
F: (01289) 342482

COTHERSTONE
County Durham

Farthings ★★★
Contact: Mr Christopher John Bainbridge
Glen Leigh, Cotherstone, Barnard Castle DL12 9QW
T: (01833) 650331

Thwaite Hall ★★★
Contact: Mrs Audrey Wickham
Hillcrest, 6 Front Street, Sunderland SR6 7JD
T: (0191) 5293793
F: (0191) 5292362
E: keith@gate7.co.uk
I: www.thwaitehall.com

COWSHILL
County Durham

Dales Farm Cottage ★★★
Contact: Dales Hol Cot Ref:1322
Dales Holiday Cottages, Carleton Business Park, Carleton New Road, Skipton BD23 2AA
T: (01756) 799821
F: (01756) 797012
E: info@dalesholcot.com
I: www.dalesholcot.com

CRAMLINGTON
Northumberland

Burradon Farm Cottages ★★★★
Contact: Mrs Judith Younger
Burradon Farm Cottages, Burradon Farm, Cramlington NE23 7ND
T: (0191) 268 3203
E: judy_younger@burradonfarm.freeserve.co.uk
I: www.burradonfarm.freeserve.co.uk

CRASTER
Northumberland

Craster Pine Lodges ★★★★
Contact: Mr & Mrs Robson
Craster Pine Lodges, 9 West End, Alnwick NE66 3TS
T: (01665) 576286
E: pinelodges@barkpots.co.uk
I: www.crasterpinelodges.co.uk

Harbourside House and 2 Old Farm Buildings ★★★★
Contact: Mr Geoffrey Brewis-Levie
10 The Severals, Bury Road, Newmarket CB8 7YN
T: (01638) 604304
F: (01638) 604304
E: brewislevie@aol.com

Proctor's Stead Cottages ★★★
Contact: Mrs Ruth Anne Davidson
Proctor's Stead Cottages, Dunstan Village, Alnwick NE66 3TF
T: (01665) 576613
F: (01665) 576311
I: www.proctorsstead.ntb.org.uk

Rock Ville ★★★★
Contact: Mr & Mrs Robson
9 West End, Alnwick NE66 3TS
T: (01665) 576286
F: (01665) 576286
E: rockville@barkpots.co.uk
I: www.rockvillecraster.co.uk

Seahaven ★★★
Contact: Mrs Imrie
Seahaven, 90 Allerburn Lea, Alnwick NE66 2NQ
T: (01665) 602275
E: miriamimrie@sagainternet.co.uk

CROOKHAM
Northumberland

Askew Cottage ★★★★
Contact: Mrs Heather Pentland
32 Crookham Village, Cornhill-on-Tweed TD12 4SY
T: (01890) 820201
F: (01890) 820201
E: hjpentland@waitrose.com

DARLINGTON
Darlington

63 Cumberland Street ★★
Contact: Mrs Kathleen Reeve
63 Cumberland Street, 130 St Margarets Avenue, Rushden NN10 9PW
T: (01933) 387945
F: (01933) 350203
E: barry.reeve1@ntlworld.com

High House Farm Cottages ★★★-★★★★
Contact: Mr Harry & Mrs Peggy Wood
High House Farm, Houghton-le-Side, Darlington DL2 2UU
T: (01388) 834879
F: (01388) 834879
E: wood@houghtonleside.fsnet.co.uk
I: www.farmstaynorth.co.uk / www.highhousefarm.com

Pegasus Cottage ★★★
Contact: Mr Stuart & Mrs Denise Chapman
Pegasus Cottage, 4 Tees View, Hurworth Place, Darlington DL2 2DH
T: (01325) 722542
F: (01325) 722542
E: stuart1948@msn.com
I: www.pegasuscottage.co.uk

DENWICK
Northumberland

Riverside Cottage ★★★★
Contact: Ms Alison Wrangham
Harehope Hall, Alnwick NE66 2DP
T: (01668) 217329
F: (01668) 217346
E: aliwrangham@farming.co.uk

Waterside Cottage ★★★
Contact: Mrs Deborah Philipson
Waterside House, Alnwick NE66 3RA
T: (01665) 603082
F: (01665) 603082
E: debbiephilipson@hopeandanchorholidays.fsnet.co.uk
I: www.hopeandanchorholidays.co.uk

DETCHANT
Northumberland

Peace Cottage ★★★
Contact: Mr William Quinn
Peace Cottage, 1 Kettleburn Farm Cottages, Belford NE70 7PQ
T: (01668) 219459
E: victorquinn@l12.com

DURHAM
County Durham

26a and 26b Hallgarth Street ★★
Contact: Ms Sue Pitts
27 Hallgarth Street, Durham DH1 3AT
T: (0191) 384 1611

Arbour House Bungalow and Cottage ★★★
Contact: Mrs Rena Hunter
Arbour House Bungalow and Cottage, Arbour House Farm, Durham DH1 4TQ
T: (0191) 3842418
F: (0191) 3860738
E: enquiries@arbourhouse.co.uk
I: www.arbourhouse.ntb.org.uk

Baxter Wood Cottages ★★★★
Contact: Mr Trevor & Mrs Tricia Jones
Baxter Wood Cottages, Baxter Wood Farm, Durham DH1 4TG
T: (0191) 3865820
F: (0191) 3865820
E: info@baxterwood.co.uk
I: www.baxterwood.co.uk

Bourne Cottage ★★★★
Contact: Mrs Judith Heron
Bourne House Farm, Church Villas, Shadforth, Durham DH6 1LQ
T: (0191) 372 0730
F: (0191) 372 0730
E: judithheron@aol.com
I: www.bournecottagedurham.com

Crook Hall ★★★★
Contact: Mrs Lesley Greenwell
Crook Hall, Sidegate, Durham DH1 5SZ
T: (0191) 3848028
F: (0191) 3864521
E: lesley@kbacrookhall.co.uk
I: www.crookhallgardens.co.uk

Dove Cottage ★★★★
Contact: Mrs Eileen Woods
25 Orchard Drive, Durham DH1 1LA
T: (0191) 3864176
E: durhamcottages@aol.com
I: www.durhamcottages.com

The Old Power House ★★★★
Contact: Mrs Anne Hall
The Old Power House, Garden Cottage, Southill Hall, Chester-le-Street DH3 4EQ
T: (0191) 387 3001
F: (0191) 389 3569
E: g.s.hall@talk21.com

Sands Cottage ★★★
Contact: Mrs Greta Hodgson
Sands House, The Sands, Durham DH1 1JY
T: (0191) 3844731
F: (0191) 3844731
E: greta@sandshouse.fsnet.co.uk

Stowhouse Farm Cottages ★★★
Contact: Mr Peter Swinburne
Stowhouse Farm Cottages, Stowhouse Farm, Old Cornsay, Durham DH7 9EN
T: (0191) 373 9990

Swallow's Barn ★★★★
Contact: Mrs Caroline Broome
Swallow's Barn, Biggin House Farm, Durham DH7 9RP
T: (0191) 3737864
F: (0191) 3739130
I: www.holidaycotts.co.uk

EAGLESCLIFFE
Stockton-on-Tees

Aislaby Grange Farm Cottages ★★★
Contact: Mr Hutchinson
Aislaby Grange Farm Cottages, Stockton-on-Tees TS16 0QP
T: (01642) 782170
F: (01642) 782170

EASTFIELD
Northumberland

Seafield Lodge
Rating Applied For
Contact: Mrs Jennifer Cossins
Seafield Holidays, Strother House, Alnwood, Alnmouth, Alnwick NE66 3NN
T: (01665) 830597
E: jd.cossins@virgin.net

EDLINGHAM
Northumberland

Briar, Rose and Clematis Cottage ★★★★
Contact: Mrs Helen Wyld
Briar, Rose and Clematis Cottage, New Moor House, Alnwick NE66 2BT
T: (01665) 574638
E: stay@newmoorhouse.co.uk
I: www.newmoorhouse.co.uk

NORTHUMBRIA

Hazelnuthouse ★★★★
Contact: Ms Hazel Bennett
61 Portsmouth Road, Guildford
GU2 4BS
T: (01483) 569346
F: (01483) 569346
E: hazelnuthouse@dial.pipex.com
I: www.bigfoot.com/~hazelnuthouse

EGGLESTON
County Durham

The Granary ★★★★
Contact: Mrs Gray
The Cottage, Eggleston Hall,
Barnard Castle DL12 0AG
T: (01833) 650403
F: (01833) 650378

The Stobbs ★★★
Contact: Mrs D Bainbridge
East Carnigill, Barnard Castle
DL12 9UX
T: (01833) 650472
E: madbain@ukonline.co.uk
I: www.thestobbs.ntb.org.uk

Swinkly Cottage ★★★★
Contact: Mrs Mary Robinson
3 Dene Hall Drive, Bishop
Auckland DL14 6UF
T: (01388) 605620
E: info@swinklycottage.co.uk
I: www.swinklycottage.co.uk

ELSDON
Northumberland

Dunns Farm & Bilsmoorfoot
★★★-★★★★★
Contact: Mrs Mary Carruthers
Dunns Farm, Newcastle upon
Tyne NE19 1AL
T: (01669) 640219
I: www.dunnsfarm.ntb.org.uk

EMBLETON
Northumberland

Cra-na-ge ★★★
Contact: Sykes Cottages Ref: 694
York House, York Street, Chester
CH1 3LR
T: (01244) 345700
F: (01244) 321442
E: info@sykescottages.co.uk
I: www.sykescottages.co.uk

Doxford Farm Cottages
★★-★★★★★
Contact: Mrs Sarah Shell
Doxford Farm Cottages, Doxford
Farm, Doxford, Chathill
NE67 5DY
T: (01665) 579348 & 579477
F: (01665) 579331
E: doxfordfarm@hotmail.com
I: www.doxfordfarmcottages.com

**Dunstanburgh Castle
Courtyard Cottages** ★★★
Contact: Mrs Allison Licence
6A Greensfield Court, Alnwick
NE66 2DE
T: (01665) 604110
T: (08702) 414339
E: paul.thompson@marishalthompson.co.uk
I: www.northumberland-holidays.co.uk

Eider ★★★★
Contact: Mrs Jan Straughan
Crofter's Green, Riverside,
Alnwick NE66 3SG
T: (01665) 830032

Embleton Cottage & The Nook ★★★
Contact: Mrs Ella Unwin
Lynecroft, Alnwick NE66 3XN
T: (01665) 576639

Glebe Cottage ★★★
Contact: Mrs Sybil Goldthorpe
Glebe Farmhouse, Alnwick
NE66 3UX
T: (01665) 576465

The Haberdashers, 2A Front Street ★★★
Contact: Mrs Mary Axelby
86 Crimicar Lane, Sheffield
S10 4FB
T: (0114) 230 5090
F: (01141) 2305090
E: mary.axelby@btinternet.com
I: www.haberdashers-alnwickc.o.uk

Mansard Cottage ★★★★
Contact: Mr Nic & Mrs Pauline Grant
11 Holeyn Hall Road, Wylam
NE41 8BB
T: (01661) 853513
F: (01661) 852152
E: pauline.grant@btinternet.com
I: www.mansard.cottage.btinternet.co.uk

Northumbrian Holiday Cottages ★★★★
Contact: Mr & Mrs Chris Seal
1 Westfield, Newcastle upon
Tyne NE3 4YE
T: (0191) 2856930
F: (0191) 2856930
E: seal@northumbrian-holiday-cottages.co.uk
I: www.northumbrian-holiday-cottages.co.uk

ESCOMB
County Durham

Muskoka ★★★★
Contact: Dales Hol Cot Ref:3372
Dales Holiday Cottages, Carleton
Business Park, Carleton New
Road, Skipton BD23 2AA
T: (01756) 790919
F: (01756) 797012
E: info@dalesholcot.com
I: www.dalesholcot.com

FALSTONE
Northumberland

Station Cottage ★★★★
Contact: Mrs June Banks
Station House, Falstone,
Hexham NE48 1AB
T: (01434) 240311

FELTON
Northumberland

Eshottheugh Farm Cottage ★★★
Contact: Ms Fay Shead
Eshottheugh Farm, Morpeth
NE65 9QH
T: (01670) 787817
F: (01670) 787817

FOREST-IN-TEESDALE
County Durham

Laneside ★★★★
Contact: Mrs N J Liddle
Raby Estate Office, Barnard
Castle DL12 0QH
T: (01833) 640209
F: (01833) 640963
E: teesdaleestate@rabycastle.com
I: www.rabycastle.com

FOXTON
Northumberland

Greybarns ★★★★
Contact: Ms Jane Mallen
Northumberland Estates Holiday
Cottages, Alnwick Castle,
Alnwick NE66 1NQ
T: (01665) 602094
F: (01665) 608126
E: jane@nehc.co.uk
I: www.alnwickcastle.com/holidaycottages

Out of Bounds ★★★★
Contact: Mrs Hazel Tate
19 Lawhead Road West, St
Andrews KY16 9NE
T: (01334) 470200
E: golftate@aol.com

FROSTERLEY
County Durham

The Old Sunday School
★★★★
Contact: Mrs Pat Blayney
The Old Sunday School, Bridge
End, Bishop Auckland DL13 2SN
T: (01388) 528913
F: (01388) 528913
E: pat@theoss.freeserve.co.uk

Wearview Cottage
Rating Applied For
Contact: Mr Brian Sales
29 Front Street, Bishop Auckland
DL13 2QP
T: (01388) 527357
E: wearviewcottages@aol.com

GAINFORD
County Durham

Barn House Mews ★★★
Contact: Dales Hol Cot
Ref:1283/1285
Dales Holiday Cottages, Carleton
Business Park, Carleton New
Road, Skipton BD23 2AA
T: (01756) 799821
F: (01756) 797012
E: info@dalesholcot.com
I: www.dalesholcot.com

East Greystone Farm Cottages ★★★★
Contact: Mrs Sue Hodgson
East Greystone Farm Cottages,
East Greystone Farm, Main
Road, Darlington DL2 3BL
T: (01325) 730236
F: (01325) 730236
E: sue@holidayfarmcottages.co.uk
I: www.holidayfarmcottages.co.uk

GILESGATE
County Durham

Fern Cottage and Rose Cottage ★★★★
Contact: Mrs Eileen Woods
25 Orchard Drive, Durham
DH1 1LA
T: (0191) 3864176
E: durhamcottages@aol.com
I: www.durhamcottages.com

GLANTON
Northumberland

Coniston Cottage ★★★
Contact: Mrs Helen Jean Mossman
Coniston House, Whittingham
Road, Alnwick NE66 4AS
T: (01665) 578305

Holly Cottage ★★★
Contact: Mr Robert Johnston
Crag View Cottage, Alnwick
NE66 4AU
T: (01665) 578200
F: (01665) 578336
E: glantonvillagestore@yahoo
I: www.hollycottage-glanton.com

GREENHAUGH
Northumberland

Bought-Hill Mill ★★★★
Contact: Mrs A Cowan
Bimmer-Hill, Hexham NE48 1PG
T: (01434) 240373

GREENHEAD
Northumberland

Holmhead Farm Cottage
★★★
Contact: Mrs Pauline Staff
Holmhead Farm Cottage,
Thirlwall Castle Farm, Hadrian's
Wall, Brampton CA8 7HY
T: (016977) 47402
F: (016977) 47402
E: Holmhead@hadrianswall.freeserve.co.uk
I: www.holmhead.com

Stanegate Cottage Ref 902
★★★★
Contact: Mr Clive Sykes
Sykes Cottages, York House,
York Street, Chester CH1 3LR
T: (01244) 345700
F: (01244) 321442
E: info@sykescottages.co.uk
I: www.sykescottages.co.uk

GUYZANCE
Northumberland

Garden Cottage ★★★
Contact: Lady Milburn
Guyzance Hall, Morpeth
NE65 9AG
T: (01665) 513047
F: (01665) 513042
E: armilburn@guyzance1.fsnet.co.uk

HALTON LEA GATE
Northumberland

The Old Chapel ★★★★★
Contact: Mr Stephen Jackson
18 Grange Road, Newcastle
upon Tyne NE4 9LD
T: (0191) 2746125
F: (0191) 2746125
E: info@theoldcountychapel.com
I: www.theoldcountrychapel.com

Establishments printed in blue have a detailed entry in this guide

NORTHUMBRIA

HALTWHISTLE
Northumberland

Ald White Craig Farm Cottages ★★★-★★★★
Contact: Mrs Cherine Zard
Ald White Craig Farm, Shield Hill, Haltwhistle NE49 9NW
T: (01434) 320565
F: (01434) 322004
E: whitecraigfarm@yahoo.co.uk
I: www.hadrianswallholidays.com

Bracken & Meadow View Cottage ★★★
Contact: Mrs Dawson
Riverway House, 4 Wydon Avenue, Haltwhistle NE49 0AS
T: (01434) 320378

Gibbs Hill Farm Cottages ★★★★
Contact: Mrs Valerie Gibson
Gibbs Hill Farm Cottages, Once Brewed, Hexham NE47 7AP
T: (01434) 344030
F: (01434) 344030
E: val@gibbshillfarm.co.uk
I: www.gibbshillfarm.co.uk

Kellah Farm Cottages ★★★-★★★★
Contact: Mrs Lesley Teasdale
Kellah Farm, Haltwhistle NE49 0JL
T: (01434) 320816
E: teasdale@ukonline.co.uk
I: www.kellah.co.uk

Scotchcoulthard ★★★★
Contact: Mr Andrew & Mrs Susan Saunders
Scotchcoulthard, Haltwhistle NE49 9NH
T: (01434) 344470
F: (01434) 344020
E: cottages@scotchcoulthard.co.uk
I: www.scotchcoulthard.co.uk

HAMSTERLEY
County Durham

Edge Knoll Farm Cottages ★★★
Contact: Mr M G Edmonds
Edge Knoll Farm Cottages, Bishop Auckland DL13 3PF
T: (01388) 488537
E: vacationfarm@hotmail.com

Hoppyland House ★★★
Contact: Mr & Mrs John Bainbridge
Hoppyland House, West Hoppyland Farm, Bishop Auckland DL13 3NP
T: (01833) 660430

Jasmine Cottage ★★★
Contact: Mrs Roberts
Jessamine House, Bishop Auckland DL13 3QF
T: (01388) 488630

West Hoppyland Cabins ★★
Contact: Mr Bill & Mrs Carole Atkinson
West Hoppyland Cabins, West Hoppyland Trekking Centre, Hoppyland, Bishop Auckland DL13 3NP
T: (01388) 488196
E: westhoppyland@hotmail.com
I: www.geocities.com/westhoppyland

HARBOTTLE
Northumberland

Hillview and Woodbine Cottage ★★★-★★★★
Contact: Mrs Deirdre Dickson
8 Holme Eden Hall, Carlisle CA8 8RD
T: (01228) 573239
F: (01228) 573338
E: stay@northumbrian-cottages.co.uk
I: www.northumbrian-cottages.co.uk

Honeysuckle Cottage ★★
Contact: Mrs Bickmore
Wayside, Morpeth NE65 7DQ
T: (01669) 650348
I: www.honeysuckleharbottle.ntb.org.uk

Woodhall Farm Holiday Cottage ★★★
Contact: Mrs J D Blakey
Woodhall Farm Holiday Cottage, Morpeth NE65 7AD
T: (01669) 650245
F: (01669) 650245
E: blakey@woodhall65.freeserve.co.uk
I: www.woodhallcottage.co.uk

HARPERLEY
County Durham

Bushblades Farm Cottage ★★★
Contact: Mrs Pamela Gibson
Bushblades Farm Cottage, Bushblades Farm, Stanley DH9 9UA
T: (01207) 232722

HARWOOD
County Durham

Frog Hall Cottage ★★★
Contact: Ms Kath Toward
Herd Ship Farm, Barnard Castle DL12 0YB
T: (01833) 622215
F: (01833) 622215
E: kath@herdship.freeserve.co.uk
I: www.herdship.co.uk

Honey Pot Cottage ★★
Contact: Ms Elaine Nixon
Peghorn Lane, Barnard Castle DL12 0HX
T: (01833) 622247
E: enixon6189@aol.com
I: www.honeypotcottage.com

HAYDON BRIDGE
Northumberland

Airlea Bungalow ★★★
Contact: Dales Hol Cot Ref:3230
Dales Holiday Cottages, Carleton Business Park, Carleton New Road, Skipton BD23 2AA
T: (01756) 799821
F: (01756) 797012
E: info@dalesholcot.com
I: www.dalesholcot.com

Braemar ★★★★
Contact: Mrs Cynthia Bradley
Edenholme, John Martin Street, Hexham NE47 6AA
T: (01434) 684622
E: edenholme@btinternet.com
I: www.edenholme.btinternet.co.uk

Hadrian's Wall Country Cottages ★★★
Contact: Mrs Ruth Hunneysett
Hadrian's Wall Country Cottages, Hindshield Moss, North Road, Hexham NE47 6NF
T: (01434) 688688
F: (01434) 688688
I: www.hadrianswall.co.uk

Scotch Corner ★★★★
Contact: Mrs Pauline Wallis
Scotch Arms, Shaftoe Street, Hexham NE47 6BJ
T: (01434) 684061
E: wallis@scotcharms.fsnet.co.uk
I: www.scotcharms.com

HEBBURN
Tyne and Wear

26 Hazelmoor ★★★★
Contact: Mr Peter Goodall
18 Coleridge Square, Hebburn NE31 1QD
T: 0794 1 611551
E: peter.goodhall7@virgin.net

HEDDON-ON-THE-WALL
Northumberland

2 East Town House ★★★
Contact: Mr Ridley & Mrs Beryl Amos
1 East Town House, Heddon-on-the-Wall, Newcastle upon Tyne NE15 0DR
T: (01661) 852277
F: (01661) 853063

HEPPLE
Northumberland

The Barn ★★★★
Contact: Mrs Robinson
Hepple Tower, Morpeth NE65 7LQ
T: (01669) 640228
F: (01282) 844288
E: sales@holidaycottagesgroup.com

Beech Cottage ★★★
Contact: Mrs Elizabeth Rogerson
Beech Cottage, Morpeth NE65 7LH
T: (01669) 640216
E: erogerson@btopenworld.com
I: www.visitrothbury.co.uk

HEXHAM
Northumberland

Brokenheugh Lodge ★★★★
Contact: Mrs Renee Jamieson
Brokenheugh Lodge, Brokenheugh Hall, Hexham NE47 6JT
T: (01434) 684206
F: (01434) 684557
E: stay@brokenheugh.co.uk
I: www.brokenheugh.co.uk

Chapel House ★★★★
Contact: Mrs Joan Liddle
Chapel House, Whitley Chapel, Hexham NE47 0HD
T: (01434) 673286
F: (01434) 673038
E: tedliddle@compuserve.com
I: www.chapel-house.info

The Granary ★★★★★
Contact: Mrs Eileen Willey
Greystones, Hexham NE46 4LF
T: (01434) 607314
F: (01434) 607864
E: eileenwilley@lineone.net

Holy Island House ★★★★★
Contact: Mrs Judith Youens
Holy Island House, Gilesgate, Hexham NE46 3QL
T: (01434) 609386
E: stay@holyislandhouse.co.uk
I: www.holyislandhouse.co.uk

Moorgair Cottage ★★★★
Contact: Mrs Vicki Ridley
Moorgair Cottage, Hexham NE47 0AN
T: (01434) 673473
E: g_ridley@lineone.net
I: www.moorgair.co.uk

Rye Hill Farm, The Old Byre ★★★★
Contact: Mrs Elizabeth Courage
Rye Hill Farm, The Old Byre, Rye Hill Farm, Hexham NE47 0AH
T: (01434) 673259
F: (01434) 673259
E: info@ryehillfarm.co.uk
I: www.ryehillfarm.co.uk

Sammy's Place ★★★★★
Contact: Mr T A Sisterson
High Mead, Leazes Lane, Hexham NE46 3AE
T: (01434) 604656
F: (01434) 604656
E: relax@sammyshideaway.com
I: www.sammyshideaway.com

23 St Wilfrid's Road ★★★★
Contact: Mr G Greensitt
23 St Wilfrid's Road, 55 Apperley Road, Stocksfield NE43 7PQ
T: (01661) 842186
F: (01661) 843381

HOLY ISLAND
Northumberland

Britannia House and The Cottage ★★★★
Contact: Mrs Katharine Tiernan
St Andrews House, College Place, Berwick-upon-Tweed TD15 1DA
T: (01289) 309826
E: ktiernan@onetel.net.uk
I: www.lindisfarne-cottages.co.uk

NORTHUMBRIA

Farne Court Cottages, Farne View Cottage ★★★
Contact: Mrs Batty
Waterside House, Dalton by Lockerbie DG11 1AT
T: (01387) 840122
E: angelabatty@ukonline.co.uk

The Haven ★★★
Contact: Mr Christopher Souter
30 Brandling Place South, Newcastle upon Tyne NE2 4RU
T: (0191) 2817421
F: (0191) 2120600
E: csouter@souter-trading.com

Ivy Cottage ★★★
Contact: Mr Keith Mitcheson
18 Melkridge Gardens, Newcastle upon Tyne NE7 7GQ
T: (0191) 2664661
E: go.mitch@ic24.net

Memnon Cottage ★★★★
Contact: Ms Shirley Douglas
T: (0161) 9411963
E: shirleyandouglas@aol.com

HOWICK
Northumberland

South Cottage ★
Contact: Sykes Cottages Ref:625
York House, York Street, Chester CH1 3LR
T: (01244) 345700
F: (01244) 321442
E: info@sykescottages.co.uk
I: www.sykescottages.co.uk

HUMSHAUGH
Northumberland

East Farm Cottage ★★★
Contact: Mrs Gwen Dodds
East Farm House, Hexham NE46 4AT
T: (01434) 689150
E: charles.dodds2@btopenworld.com

ILDERTON
Northumberland

Coach House & Coach House Cottage ★★★
Contact: Mrs Margaret Sale
Ilderton Glebe, Alnwick NE66 4YD
T: (01668) 217293
E: margaretsale@amserve.com

INGRAM
Northumberland

Cheviot Holiday Cottages ★★★★★
Contact: Mrs Trysha Stephenson
Cheviot Holiday Cottages, The Old Rectory, Alnwick NE66 4LT
T: (01665) 578236
E: trysha@cheviotholidaycottages.co.uk
I: www.cheviotholidaycottages.co.uk

IRESHOPEBURN
County Durham

High Barnes Holiday Cottage ★★★★
Contact: Mr John & Mrs Frederique Wilson
High Barnes Holiday Cottage, Wearhead, Bishop Auckland DL13 1PY
T: (01388) 537556
E: jwilsonis@yahoo.co.uk

Hillside Cottage ★★★
Contact: Mrs Sadie McMullon
203 Fletton Avenue, Peterborough PE2 8DE
T: (01733) 892888

KIELDER
Northumberland

Kielder Lodges ★★★★-★★★★★
Contact:
Kielder Lodges, Leaplish Waterside Park, Kielder Water and Forest Park, Hexham NE48 1BT
T: (01434) 250294
F: (01434) 250806
E: kielder.holidays@nwl.co.uk
I: www.nwl.co.uk/kielder

KIELDER WATER
Northumberland

Calvert Trust Kielder ★★★★
Contact:
Calvert Trust Kielder, Kielder Water, Hexham NE48 1BS
T: (01434) 250232
F: (01434) 250015
E: enquiries@calvert-kielder.com
I: www.calvert-trust.org.uk

KIRKNEWTON
Northumberland

Coldburn Cottage ★★★★
Contact: Mrs Jane Matheson
College Valley Estates Ltd, East Lilburn House, Alnwick NE66 4ED
T: (01668) 217070
E: macdonaldsmith@btinternet.com
I: www.saleandpartners.co.uk

Hillview Cottage ★★★★
Contact: Dales Hol Cot Ref:2043
Dales Holiday Cottages, Carleton Business Park, Carleton New Road, Skipton BD23 2AA
T: (01756) 799821
F: (01756) 797012
E: info@dalesholcot.com
I: www.dalesholcot.com

LANCHESTER
County Durham

Browney Cottage & Browney Close ★★★
Contact: Mrs Ann Darlington
Hall Hill Farm, Durham DH7 0TA
T: (01207) 521476
F: (01388) 730300
E: hhf@freenetname.co.uk
I: www.hallhillfarm.co.uk

Stable Cottage ★★★★
Contact: Dales Hol Cot Ref: 3358
Dales Holiday Cottages, Carleton Business Park, Carleton New Road, Skipton BD23 2AA
T: (01756) 799821
F: (01756) 797012
E: info@dalesholcot.com
I: www.dalesholcot.com

LANGLEY-ON-TYNE
Northumberland

West Deanraw Bungalow ★★★
Contact: Mr John Drydon
West Deanraw Farm, Hexham NE47 5LY
T: (01434) 684228
F: (01434) 684228

LESBURY
Northumberland

Lesbury Glebe Cottage ★★★★★
Contact: Mrs D. Gillian Brunton
Lesbury Glebe Cottage, Glebe Garden Cottage, Alnwick NE66 3AU
T: (01665) 830732
E: gillieray@tiscali.co.uk

LOFTUS
Redcar and Cleveland

Liverton Lodge ★★
Contact: Dales Hol Cot Ref:1778
Dales Holiday Cottages, Carleton Business Park, Carleton New Road, Skipton BD23 2AA
T: (01756) 799821
F: (01756) 797012
E: info@dalesholcot.com
I: www.dalesholcot.com

LONGFRAMLINGTON
Northumberland

Dene House Farm Cottages Poppy, Bluebell, Primrose, Buttercup ★★★
Contact: Mrs Wilson
Dene House Farm Cottages, Dene House, Morpeth NE65 8EE
T: (01665) 570549
F: (01665) 570549

Picklewood Cottage ★★★★★
Contact: Mrs Di Jevons
Picklewood Cottage, Felton Road, Morpeth NE65 8BD
T: (01665) 570221
F: (01665) 570221
E: di@picklewood.info
I: www.picklewood.info

LONGHORSLEY
Northumberland

Beacon Hill Farm Holidays ★★★★-★★★★★
Contact: Mr Alun Moore
Beacon Hill House, Morpeth NE65 8QW
T: (01670) 780900
F: (01670) 780901
E: alun@beaconhill.co.uk
I: www.beaconhill.co.uk

Cartwheel Cottage ★★★
Contact: Mr James & Mrs Sarah Chisholm
Cartwheel Cottage, Westerheugh Farm, Morpeth NE65 8RH
T: (01665) 570661
E: sarah@cartwheelcottage.com
I: www.cartwheelcottage.com

Garrett Lee Cottage ★★★★
Contact: Ms Linda Wilson
Garrett Lee Cottage, Garrett Lee Farm, Morpeth NE65 8RJ
T: (01670) 788474
E: info@garrettleefarm.com
I: www.garrettleefarm.com

LONGHOUGHTON
Northumberland

Harlaw Hill Farm Cottages ★★★
Contact: Mrs Joan Pringle
Harlaw Hill Farm Cottages, Harlaw Hill, Alnwick NE66 3AA
T: (01665) 577215
I: www.harlaw-hill.co.uk

Rose Cottage & Croft Cottage ★★★
Contact: Mrs Margaret Forsyth
Low Steads Farm, Alnwick NE66 3AL
T: (01665) 577227
I: www.lowsteads.co.uk

LOWICK
Northumberland

Barmoor Ridge Cottage ★★★★
Contact: Mrs Patricia Adrienne Reavley
Barmoor Ridge Cottage, Barmoor Ridge, Berwick-upon-Tweed TD15 2QD
T: (01289) 388226
F: (01289) 388688
E: jimpyreavley@aol.com

Barmoor South Moor ★★★
Contact: Mrs Ann Gold
Barmoor South Moor, Berwick-upon-Tweed TD15 2QF
T: (01289) 388205
F: (01289) 388205
E: barryandanngold@aol.com

Granary Cottage
Rating Applied For
Contact: Mr Clive Sykes
York House, York Street, Chester CH1 3LR
T: (01244) 345700
F: (01244) 321442
E: info@sykescottages.co.uk

South View Cottage ★★★★
Contact: Mrs Carol Waugh
8 South Road, Berwick-upon-Tweed TD15 2TX
T: (01289) 388640

LUCKER
Northumberland

Lucker Hall Steading ★★★★-★★★★★
Contact: Mrs Jane Mallen
Northumberland Estates Holiday Cottage, Alnwick Castle, Alnwick NE66 1NQ
T: (01665) 602094
F: (01665) 608126
E: jane@nehc.co.uk
I: www.alnwickcastle.com/holidaycottages

Lucker Mill ★★★★★
Contact: Mrs Jane Mallen
Northumberland Estates Holiday Cottages, Alnwick Castle, Alnwick NE66 1NQ
T: (01665) 602094
F: (01665) 608126
E: jane@nehc.co.uk
I: www.alnwickcastle.com/holidaycottages/

NORTHUMBRIA

MAINSFORTH
County Durham

Swallow Cottage
Rating Applied For
Contact: Mrs Shirley Hindmarch
Swallow Cottage, Ferryhill
DL17 9AA
T: (01740) 656709
E: maudes@maudefamily.
freeserve.co.uk
I: www.swallowcottage.
visitnorthumbria.com

MARSKE-BY-THE-SEA
Redcar and Cleveland

4 Church Street ★★★
Contact: Mrs Barbara Mosey
27 The Avenue, Billericay
CM12 9HG
T: (01277) 652778
E: brmosey@yahoo.co.uk

White Rose Cottage ★★★
Contact: Mr & Mrs Philip Phillips
21 Church Howle Crescent,
Marske-by-the-Sea TS11 7EJ
T: (01642) 481064
F: (01642) 481064
E: phillipspcp@aol.com

MARWOOD
County Durham

Hauxwell Grange
Rating Applied For
Contact: Mrs Val Pearson
Hauxwell Grange, Barnard Castle
DL12 8QU
T: (01833) 695022
F: (01833) 695022
E: hauxwellvmp@supaworld.
com

MELKRIDGE
Northumberland

**Common House Farm
Cottages** ★★★
Contact: Mr Richard & Mrs
Louise Currie
Common House Farm Cottages,
Haltwhistle NE49 9PF
T: (01434) 321680
E: stay@commonhousefarm.
com
I: www.commonhousefarm.com

MICKLETON
County Durham

Bankside Cottage ★★★
Contact: Mr George Crooks
8 Polwarth Road, Newcastle
upon Tyne NE3 5ND
T: (0191) 2365163
F: (0191) 2365163
E: george.crooks@btinternet.
com

Blackthorn Cottage ★★★
Contact: Mrs Diane Garrett
3 Mariam Gardens, Hornchurch
RM12 6QA
T: (01708) 447260
E: coldigar@btinternet.com
I: www.teesdalecottages.co.uk

Kirkcarrion Cottage ★★★
Contact: Mrs Gail Foster
1 Syke Cottage, Barnard Castle
DL12 0LH
T: (01833) 640132
E: gailfoster.sykecott@virgin.
net

The Old Dairy
Rating Applied For
Contact: Mrs Tracey Cook
The Old Dairy, West Pasture
Farm, Kelton Road, Mickleton,
Barnard Castle DL12 0PW
T: (01833) 640248
F: (01833) 640491
E: cookes@tesco.net

West Tofts ★★★★
Contact: Mrs Stoddart
Wemmergill Hall Farm, Lunedale,
Barnard Castle DL12 0PA
T: (01833) 640379
E: wemmergill@freenet.co.uk
I: www.wemmergill-farm.co.uk

MIDDLETON-IN-TEESDALE
County Durham

The Barn ★★★
Contact: Mrs Ann Whitfield
Garden House, Low Side,
Barnard Castle DL12 0JR
T: (01833) 640759
I: www.thebarn.4t.com

Brock Scar Cottage ★★★★
Contact: Mrs Winfred Gargate
Brock Scar Farm, West Pasture,
Barnard Castle DL12 0PW
T: (01833) 640495
F: (01833) 640495
E: wyngargate@btopenworld.
com
I: www.brockscar.co.uk

The Coach House ★★★★
Contact: Mrs Finn
54 Market Place, Barnard Castle
DL12 0QH
T: (01833) 640884
F: (01883) 640884
E: info@thecoachhouse.net
I: www.thecoachhouse.net

Country Cottage ★★★
Contact: Mr Burman
1 Thorn Road, Bramhall,
Stockport SK7 1HG
T: (0161) 860 7123
E: enquiries@robinburman.com

Daisy Cottage (3729) ★★★★
Contact: Ms Fiona Moody
Dales Holiday Cottages, Carleton
Business Park, Carleton New
Road, Skipton BD23 2AA
T: (01756) 790919
F: (01756) 797012
E: fiona@
dales-holiday-cottages.com
I: www.dales-holiday-cottages.
com

Firethorn Cottage ★★★
Contact: Mrs June Thompson
Cutbush Farmhouse,
Hardingham Road, Norwich
NR9 4LY
T: (01953) 850364

**Green Acres, Meadow's
Edge, Shepherds Cottage** ★★★
Contact: Mrs Glennis Scott
Low Way Farm, Holwick, Barnard
Castle DL12 0NJ
T: (01833) 640506

**Grooms Cottage and The
Stables** ★★★★
Contact: Mr Nicholas Hamer
25 Village Way, Northallerton
DL7 0TW
T: (01609) 748938
F: (01609) 748938
E: clocktower@supanet.com

Hush Cottage ★★
Contact: Mrs Mulholland
Knapp Cottage, Warminster
BA12 0SZ
T: (01985) 850450
E: mul.cort@btinternet.com

North Wythes Hill ★★★
Contact: Mrs Eileen Dent
Wythes Hill, Middleton-in-
Teesdale, Barnard Castle
DL12 0NX
T: (01833) 640349
E: eileendent@teesdaleonline.
co.uk

Snaisgill Farm Cottage ★★★
Contact: Mrs Susan Parmley
Snaisgill Farm Cottage, Snaisgill
Road, Barnard Castle DL12 0RP
T: (01833) 640343

Summerville Cottage ★★★
Contact: Mr Fletcher
Friar House Farm, Forest in
Teesdale, Barnard Castle
DL12 0XG
T: (01833) 622202
I: www.summervillecottage.
co.uk

Town View Cottage ★★★
Contact: Mrs Marshall
The Bungalow, The Green,
Darlington DL2 3HA
T: (01325) 730989
F: (01325) 730989

Westfield Cottage ★★★★
Contact: Mrs Doreen Scott
Westfield House, Laithkirk,
Barnard Castle DL12 0PN
T: (01833) 640942
F: (01833) 640942

Willow Cottage ★★
Contact: Mrs Diane Garrett
3 Mariam Gardens, Hornchurch
RM12 6QA
T: (01708) 447260
E: coldigar@btinternet.com

MIDDLETON-ON-LEVEN
Stockton-on-Tees

Harvest Cottage ★★★★
Contact: Mrs Caroline
Bainbridge
Middleton Grange Farm, Yarm
TS15 0JU
T: (01642) 599669

MILFIELD
Northumberland

Barley Hill Cottage ★★★
Contact: Mr David Bell
20 Balmoral Terrace, Newcastle
upon Tyne NE3 1YH
T: (0191) 2852526
E: rosemary.bell@newcastle.
gov.uk

Milfield Hill Cottage ★★★★
Contact: Mrs Judith Craig
Milfield Hill House, Wooler
NE71 6JE
T: (01668) 216338
F: (01668) 216095
E: craig@milfield1.freeserve.
co.uk
I: www.milfield1.freeserve.co.uk

MINDRUM
Northumberland

Bowmont Cottage ★★
Contact: Mr & Mrs Orpwood
Bowmont Cottage, Bowmont
Hill, Mindrum TD12 4QW
T: (01890) 850266
F: (01890) 850245
E: s.orpwood@farmline.com
I: www.cottageguide.
co.uk/bowmonthill

The Longknowe ★★★
Contact: Jo Andrews
10 Yerbury Road, London
N19 4RL
T: (020) 7281 9579
E: longknowe@hotmail.com
I: www.cottageguide.
co.uk/longknowe

MITFORD
Northumberland

**The Old Blacksmiths
Cottage** ★★★★
Contact: Mrs Glass
The Old Blacksmiths Cottage,
Morpeth NE61 3PR
T: (01670) 512074
E: emma@emglass.freeserve.
co.uk

MORLEY
County Durham

Calf Close Cottage ★★★
Contact: Mrs Sandra Redfearn
Calf Close Cottage, Bishop
Auckland DL14 0PG
T: (01388) 718561
F: (01388) 718561
E: sandra@redfearn1208.
freeserve.co.uk

MORPETH
Northumberland

Barnacre ★★★★
Contact: Mrs Linda Rudd
Warren Cottage, Longhirst
Village, Morpeth NE61 3LX
T: (01670) 790116
E: linda@mrudd.fslife.co.uk

The Carriage House ★★★★★
Contact: Mr Joseph Evans
The Old Vicarage, Ulgham
Village, Morpeth NE61 3AR
T: (01670) 790225
E: joe@ulgham.demon.co.uk

5 Copper Chare ★★★
Contact: Mr G.M. Gagie
Hillside Cottage, Wood Lane,
Uttoxeter ST14 8JR
T: (01889) 562838

NORTHUMBRIA

High Barn Cottage ★★★
Contact: Mr Martin Downing
MDA, Waterside Cottage,
Morpeth NE65 9EG
T: (01670) 783398
F: (01670) 783398
E: downing@mdaconsultancy.co.uk
I: mdaconsultancy.tripod.com/highbarn

Meldon Park ★★★
Contact: Mrs Janet Wilson
Flat 1, Meldon Park, Morpeth
NE61 3SW
T: (01670) 772622
F: (01670) 772341
E: mrscookson@compuserve.com
I: www.cottageguide.co.uk/meldonpark

Morpeth Court ★★★★
Contact: Ms Carol Edmundson
Morpeth Court, Castle Bank,
Morpeth NE61 1YJ
T: (01670) 517217
F: (01670) 517217
E: carol_edmundson@hotmail.com
I: www.morpethcourt.com

Netherwitton Hall Cottages ★★★
Contact: Mrs Anne-Marie Trevelyan
Netherwitton Hall Cottages,
Netherwitton Hall, Morpeth
NE61 4NW
T: (01670) 772249
F: (01670) 772510
E: anne-marie@netherwitton.com

Old Barn Cottages ★★★
Contact: Mrs Jo Mancey
Old Barn Cottages, Benridge
Hagg, Morpeth NE61 3SB
T: (01670) 518507
I: benridge_cottages_uk.tripod.com/

Peigh Hills Farm Cottages ★★★★-★★★★★
Contact: Mr Tench
Peigh Hills Farm, Morpeth
NE61 3EU
T: (01670) 790332
F: (01670) 791390
E: info@peighhillsfarmcottages.co.uk
I: peighhillsfarmcottages.co.uk

NEWCASTLE UPON TYNE
Tyne and Wear

135 Audley Road ★★★
Contact: Miss Linda Wright
137 Audley Road, South
Gosforth, Newcastle upon Tyne
NE3 1QH
T: (0191) 285 6374
E: lkw@audleyender.fsnet.co.uk
I: www.audleyender.fsnet.co.uk

Bavington Hall, Stable Court ★★★
Contact: Mr Patrick
Bavington Hall, Stable Court,
Little Bavington, Newcastle
upon Tyne NE19 2BA
T: (01830) 530394
F: (01830) 530394
E: enquiries@bavingtonhall.co.uk
I: www.bavingtonhall.co.uk

Newcastle City Self-Catering Apartment ★★
Contact: Mrs Anne Cohen
Yard Art, 37 Sidney Grove,
Newcastle upon Tyne NE4 5PD
T: (0191) 2413015
E: annecohen@handbag.com

Walbottle Farm House ★★★★★
Contact: Mr & Mrs Dominic Aston
Walbottle Farm House,
Newcastle upon Tyne NE15 8JD
T: (0191) 2671368
E: aston@walbottle.fsnet.co.uk
I: www.walbottlefarmhouse.co.uk

Walbottle House ★★★★★★
Contact: Mrs Sharon Kent
Walbottle House, Newcastle
upon Tyne NE15 8JD
T: (0191) 2641108

NEWTON-BY-THE-SEA
Northumberland

3A & 3B Coastguard Cottages ★★★
Contact: Mr & Mrs Cottam
13 St Georges Crescent, Whitley
Bay NE25 8BJ
T: (0191) 251 2506
F: (0191) 222 1017
E: mbc@bradleyhall.co.uk
I: www.geocities.com/coastguardcottages.

Link House Farm ★★★★
Contact: Mrs Jayne Hellmann
The Granary, Link House Farm,
Alnwick NE66 3DF
T: (01665) 576820
F: (01665) 576821
E: jayne.hellman@virgin.net

Newton Hall Cottages ★★★★
Contact: Mrs Shirley Patterson
Newton Hall Cottages, Newton
Hall, Alnwick NE66 3DZ
T: (01665) 576239
F: (01665) 576900
E: patterson@newtonholidays.co.uk
I: www.newtonholidays.co.uk

Seawinds ★★★★
Contact: Miss Jo Park
Low Buston Hall, Warkworth,
Morpeth NE65 0XY
T: (01665) 714805
F: (01665) 711345
E: jopark@farming.co.uk
I: www.buston.co.uk/seawinds.htm

NORHAM
Northumberland

The Boathouse ★★★
Contact: Mrs Mair Chantler
Great Humphries Farm, Grafty
Green, Maidstone ME17 2AX
T: (01622) 859672
F: (01622) 859672
E: chantler@humphreys46.fsnet.co.uk
I: www.recommended-cottages.co.uk

Boathouse Cottage ★★★★
Contact: Mrs Susan Dalgety
The Columns, Berwick-upon-
Tweed TD15 2JZ
T: (01289) 382300
F: (01289) 382334
E: susan@boathousecottage.co.uk
I: www.boathousecottage.co.uk

Falcon's Gate, 5 Grievestead Farm Cottages ★★★★
Contact: Mrs Margaret Wright
19 Houghton Avenue, North
Shields NE30 3NQ
T: (0191) 2520627
F: (0191) 2971984
E: ron.wright2@virgin.net

**Norcot Cottage
Rating Applied For**
Contact: Mrs Cheryl Potter
12 Dobson Crescent, St Peter's
Basin, Newcastle upon Tyne
NE6 1TT
T: (0191) 2766505
E: cheryl@silverleafsoftware.co.uk

**Rosemary Cottage
Rating Applied For**
Contact: Mrs Barbara Piercy
Rosemary Cottage, 14 West
Street, Berwick-upon-Tweed
TD15 2LB
T: (01289) 382247

NORTH SUNDERLAND
Northumberland

The Shieling ★★★★
Contact: Mrs Susanna Hodgson
The Shieling, 97 Main Street,
Seahouses NE68 7TS
T: (01665) 721309

NORTH TOGSTON
Northumberland

Orchard Cottage ★★★★
Contact: Mr Matthew & Mrs Joy Pettifer
Orchard Cottage, Togston
House, Morpeth NE65 0HR
T: (01665) 710145
F: (01665) 714428
E: matthew.pettifer@btinternet.com

OAKENSHAW
County Durham

Stockley Fell Farm Cottages ★★★★
Contact: Mrs Jane Carter
Stockley Fell Farm Cottages, 1
Abbots Green, Crook DL15 0QY
T: (01388) 747381
F: (01388) 745938
I: www.stockleyfell.co.uk

OTTERBURN
Northumberland

Woodhill ★★★★★
Contact: Mrs Corrinne Knight
Woodhill, Newcastle upon Tyne
NE19 1JX
T: (01830) 520657
E: christopher@knightc41.fsbusiness.co.uk

OUSTON
County Durham

Katie's Cottage ★★★★
Contact: Mrs Hilary Johnson
Katie's Cottage, Low Urpeth
Farm, Chester-le-Street
DH2 1BD
T: (0191) 4102901
F: (0191) 4100088
E: stay@lowurpeth.co.uk
I: www.lowurpeth.co.uk

OVINGTON
Northumberland

Appletree Cottage ★★★★
Contact: Mrs Lesley Rowell
Appletree Cottage, Prudhoe
NE42 6ED
T: (01661) 832355

High Fewster Gill Cottage ★★★
Contact: Dales Hol Cot Ref:3228
Dales Holiday Cottages, Carleton
Business Park, Carleton New
Road, Skipton BD23 2AA
T: (01756) 799821
F: (01756) 797012
E: info@dalesholcot.com
I: www.dalesholcot.com

Porch Cottage ★★★
Contact: Mrs Patricia Craggs
5 Glendyn Close, Jesmond Park
West, Newcastle upon Tyne
NE7 7DZ
T: (0191) 2811302

Westgarth Cottage ★★★★
Contact: Mrs Claire Graham
Stonecroft, Ovington NE42 6EB
T: (01661) 832202

PIERCEBRIDGE
Darlington

The Bungalow ★★★
Contact: Mrs Jean Lowe
The Bungalow, Bolam Grange,
Darlington DL2 3UL
T: (01388) 832779

POWBURN
Northumberland

The Cottage ★★★
Contact: Mrs Helen Arnott
21 Cottonwood, Biddick Woods,
Houghton-le-Spring DH4 7TA
T: (0191) 3857167
E: harnott@talk21.com

Shepherd's Cottage ★★★
Contact: Mrs Sarah Wilson
Shepherd's Cottage, Ingram
Farm, Alnwick NE66 4LT
T: (01665) 578243
F: (01665) 578243
E: swingram@ukonline.co.uk
I: www.ingramfarm.co.uk

REDCAR
Redcar and Cleveland

Dove House ★★★
Contact: Mrs Carol McGovern
8 Kirkleatham Lane, Redcar
TS10 1NS
T: (01642) 479311
E: themcgoverns@ntlworld.com
I: www.dovehouses.co.uk

Establishments printed in blue have a detailed entry in this guide

NORTHUMBRIA

ROMALDKIRK
County Durham

Romaldkirk Self Catering Cottages ★★★-★★★★★
Contact: Mrs Gwen Wall
Romaldkirk Self Catering Cottages, Kleine Cottage, Barnard Castle DL12 9ED
T: (01833) 650794
E: richard@wall8309.freeserve.co.uk
I: www.cottageguide.co.uk/romaldkirk

Sycamore Cottage ★★★★
Contact: Dales Hol Cot Ref:698
Dales Holiday Cottages, Carleton Business Park, Carleton New Road, Skipton BD23 2AA
T: (01756) 799821
F: (01756) 797012
E: info@dalesholcot.com
I: www.dalesholcot.com

ROTHBURY
Northumberland

April Cottage ★★★★
Contact: Mr Peter & Mrs Karina Biggers
Hope Lodge, Hope Terrace, Alnwick NE66 1AJ
T: (01665) 603233
E: hope.biggers@tiscali.co.uk
I: www.april-cottage-rothbury.com

The Cottage ★★★
Contact: Mrs Isabelle Anthea Wilbie-Chalk
The Cottage, Well Close, Morpeth NE65 7NZ
T: (01669) 620430
E: visitors@wellclose.com
I: www.wellclose.com

Garden Cottage ★★★★★
Contact: Mr Roger & Mrs Dorothy Newman
Longfield, New Road, Aylesbury HP27 0LA
T: (01844) 274101
E: rogerdnewman@hotmail.com
I: www.silvertonlodge.co.uk

The Granary ★★★★★
Contact: Ms Mandy Lance and Mr George Snaith
The Granary, Charity Hall Farm, Morpeth NE65 7AG
T: (01669) 650219
F: (01669) 650219
E: mandy@charityhallfarm.com
I: www.charityhallfarm.com

Low Alwinton Holiday Cottages ★★★★
Contact: Mrs Jackie Stothard
Glen View, Queens Road, Wooler NE71 6DR
T: (01668) 283572
E: jackie@lowalwinton.co.uk
I: www.lowalwinton.co.uk

Milburn Mews ★★★★
Contact: Mr John McCall
Sunningdale, Cragside View, Morpeth NE65 7YU
T: (01669) 621927
E: jmccall@milburn150.fsnet.co.uk
I: www.rothbury-sunningdale.co.uk

The Old Telephone Exchange ★★★★
Contact: Mrs K Scott-Foreman
Sunnyville Cottage, Backcrofts, Rothbury, Morpeth NE65 7XY
T: (01669) 621858
E: info@theoldtelephoneexchange.com
I: www.theoldtelephoneexchange.com

The Pele Tower ★★★★★★
Contact: Mr David Malia
Whitton, Rothbury, Morpeth NE65 7RL
T: (01669) 620410
F: (01669) 621006
E: davidmalia@aol.com
I: www.thepeletower.com

Riverside Lodge ★★★★
Contact: Mr Eric Jensen
Edgecombe, Hillside Road, Morpeth NE65 7PT
T: (01669) 620464
F: (01669) 621031
E: eric.jensen@virgin.net
I: www.theriversidelodge.com

Tosson Tower Farm ★★★-★★★★
Contact: Mrs Ann Foggin
Tosson Tower Farm, Rothbury, Morpeth NE65 7NW
T: (01669) 620228
F: (01669) 620228
E: stay@tossontowerfarm.com
I: www.tossontowerfarm.com

Whitton Lodge ★★★★
Contact: Mrs Maggie Monaghan
Whitton Grange, Nr Rothbury, Morpeth NE65 7RL
T: (01669) 620929
F: (01669) 620471
E: john.monaghan@ukonline.co.uk
I: www.visit-rothbury.co.uk/members

ROWLANDS GILL
Tyne and Wear

The Stables ★★★★
Contact: Mrs Jenny Dicks
Barton, Low Thornley, Rowlands Gill NE39 1BE
T: (01207) 544486
E: jennydicks@bartonstables.freeserve.co.uk

ST JOHN'S CHAPEL
County Durham

Burnbrae ★★★★
Contact: Mrs Ann Robson
37 Park Drive, Deuchar Park, Morpeth NE61 2SX
T: (01670) 518129
E: ann@robsonmorpeth.freeserve.co.uk

SALTBURN-BY-THE-SEA
Redcar and Cleveland

Coastguard Cottages ★★★
Contact: Mrs Cecilia Daly
1 Coastguard Cottage, Huntcliffe, Saltburn-by-the-Sea TS12 1HG
T: (01287) 625235

Seagal Holiday Bungalow ★★★★
Contact: Ms Chris Priestman
61 High Street, Whitby YO21 2DB
T: (01287) 660099
E: chrissiepriestman@hotmail.com
I: www.northyorkshirecottages.com

The Zetland ★★★
Contact: Mrs Joan Carter
1 Hawthorne Grove, Yarm TS15 9EZ
T: (01642) 782507
E: graham@howard95.freeserve.co.uk
I: www.carter-steel.co.uk

SEAHOUSES
Northumberland

Cliff House Cottages ★★★
Contact: Mrs Jackie Forsyth
c/o Beadnell House, Beadnell NE67 5AT
T: (01665) 720161
E: wts.info@cliffhousecottages.co.uk
I: www.cliffhousecottages.co.uk

Crewe Cottage ★★★
Contact: Mrs Sarah Steed
3 Grants Crescent, Paisley PA2 6BD
T: (0141) 884 1064
F: (0141) 884 1064
E: msdfsteed@aol.com

31 Dunstan View
Rating Applied For
Contact: Mr Mark & Mrs Amanda Butler
139 Kepier Chare, Ryton NE40 4UY
T: (0191) 4138933
F: (0191) 4913883
E: mrb911@hotmail.com

Fahren Cottage
Rating Applied For
Contact: Mrs Rachel Dawson Shiel
40 North Lane, Seahouses NE68 7UQ
T: (01665) 721297
E: rachel.dawson@virgin.net
I: www.farne-islands.com

Fisherlasses Flat ★★★
Contact: Mrs Karen Wilkin
Fisherlasses Flat, Swallow Fish Ltd., 2 South Street, Seahouses NE68 7RB
T: (01665) 720470
F: (01665) 721177
E: wilkin@swallowfish.co.uk
I: www.swallowfish.co.uk

Fishermans Mid Cottage ★★★★
Contact: Mrs Dorothy Jackson
Bilton Barns Farmhouse, Bilton, Alnwick NE66 2TB
T: (01665) 830427
F: (01665) 833909
E: dorothy@biltonbarns.com
I: www.biltonbarns.com

Fisherman's Retreat ★★★★★
Contact: Ms Fiona McKeith
Northumberland Coastal Retreats, 174 Warkworth Woods, Newcastle Great Park, Newcastle upon Tyne NE3 5RD
T: (0191) 2365971
F: (0191) 2364586
E: info@coastalretreats.co.uk
I: www.coastalretreats.co.uk

The Lobster Pots ★★★★
Contact: Julia Steel
T: (0113) 239 1130
E: julia@thelobsterpots.co.uk
I: www.thelobsterpots.co.uk

Lynbank ★★★
Contact: Mrs Louise Donaldson
4 Broad Road, Seahouses NE68 7UP
T: (01665) 721066
F: (01665) 721066
E: islandproperties@uk6.net
I: www.dalfaber-lynbank.ntb.org.uk

Peregrine ★★★
Contact: Miss Ursula. D. Wanglin
Bolton Mill, Alnwick NE66 2EH
T: (01665) 574304
F: (01665) 574304

Quarry Cottage ★★★
Contact: Mrs Mary Alston
Woodlea, St Aidans, Seahouses NE68 7SS
T: (01665) 720235
F: (01665) 720235
E: george.alston@ic24.net

Rose Cottages ★★★★
Contact: Mr Michael Townsend
Dunstanburgh Castle Hotel, Alnwick NE66 3UN
T: (01665) 576111
F: (01665) 576203
E: stay@dunstanburghcastlehotel.co.uk
I: www.dunstanburghcastlehotel.co.uk

Sparrowhawk ★★★★
Contact: Miss Ursula D Wanglin
Bolton Mill, Alnwick NE66 2EH
T: (01665) 574304
F: (01665) 574304

SEDGEFIELD
County Durham

The Granary ★★★
Contact: Mr & Mrs Edgoose
The Granary, Todds House Farm, Stockton-on-Tees TS21 3EL
T: (01740) 620244
F: (01740) 620244
E: edgoosej@aol.com
I: www.toddshousefarm.co.uk

Sprucely Farm Cottage ★★
Contact: Mr Stewart Harris
Sprucely Farm, Stockton-on-Tees TS21 2BD
T: (01740) 620378
E: barbara@sprucely.fsnet.co.uk

NORTHUMBRIA

SHARPERTON
Northumberland

North Sharperton Farm Cottage ★★★★
Contact: Ms Carolyn Banks
North Sharperton Farm Cottage, Rothbury, Morpeth NE65 7AE
T: (01669) 650321
F: (01669) 650321
E: ormnthsharperton@bushinternet.com
I: www.northsharperton.co.uk

Ryecroft Cottage ★★★
Contact: Mrs Rosalind Kerven
Swindonburn Cottage West, Morpeth NE65 7AP
T: (01669) 640291
E: roskerven@hotmail.com

SHILBOTTLE
Northumberland

Sea View ★★★★
Contact: Miss Joy Ann Davidson
28 Lee Avenue, Alnwick NE66 2UW
T: (01665) 575281
E: keithandjudiththompson@hotmail.com

Sycamore and Honeysuckle Cottages ★★★
Contact: Mrs Janet Brewis
Sycamore and Honeysuckle Cottages, Woodhouse, Alnwick NE66 2HR
T: (01665) 575222
I: www.woodhousefarmholidays.co.uk

SHOTLEY BRIDGE
County Durham

Rivers Edge Cottage ★★★★
Contact: Mrs Jean Johnson
7 Shotley Grove Road, Consett DH8 8SF
T: (01207) 501194
E: jean.johnson1@tesco.net

SKELTON
Redcar and Cleveland

Barn Cottage and Newbrook Cottage ★★★★
Contact: Mr Ron & Mrs Eileen Goodenough
English Country Holidays, Newbrook Farmhouse, Trout Hall Lane, Saltburn-by-the-Sea TS12 2DE
T: (01287) 650288
F: (01287) 205496
E: r.goodenough1@ntlworld.com
I: www.english-country-cottages.co.uk

SLALEY
Northumberland

Clairmont Cottage ★★★★
Contact: Mrs Evelyn Allsop
Clairmont Cottage, Hexham NE47 0AD
T: (01434) 673686
F: (01434) 673921
E: david.allsop4@which.net
I: www.clairmontslaley.freeserve.co.uk

Combhills Farm ★★★
Contact: Mrs Ogle
Slaley, Hexham NE47 0AQ
T: (01434) 673475
F: (01434) 673778
E: m.ogle@lineone.net

SOUTH SHIELDS
Tyne and Wear

Eccleston Road ★★★
Contact: Mrs Kath Cole
9 Sea Way, South Shields NE33 2NQ
T: (0191) 4561802

22 Hartington Terrace ★★★
Contact: Mrs Patricia Capps
Cheer Me Up Barn, Thirsk YO7 3QZ
T: (01845) 578657
E: m.capps@aol.com

Sandhaven Beach Chalets ★★★
Contact: Mrs Christine Rowell
Sandhaven Beach Chalets, South Promenade, Sea Road, South Shields NE33 2LD
T: (0191) 4558319
F: (0191) 4558319
E: crowell@btconnect.com
I: www.sandhavenchalets.co.uk

Seawynnings ★★★★
Contact: Mrs Christine Whincop
2 Sea Wynnings Way, Westoe Crown Village, South Shields NE33 3NE
T: (0191) 4541876

Westoe Crown Village
Rating Applied For
Contact: Mr Ronald Cairns
North Farm, High Usworth Village, Washington NE37 1NT
T: (0191) 4163960
F: (0191) 4163960
E: bookings@execlets.net
I: www.execlets.net

SPARTY LEA
Northumberland

Isaac's and Hannah's Cottages ★★★
Contact: Mrs Heather Robson
Allenheads Farm, Hexham NE47 9HJ
T: (01434) 685312

SPENNYMOOR
County Durham

The Green Tree ★★★★
Contact: Mrs Yvonne Parker
The Green Tree, 41 Tudhoe Village, Spennymoor DL16 6LE
T: (01388) 818557
F: (01388) 813243

Highview Country House -Apartment ★★★
Contact: Mr Thompson
Highview Country House, Kirkmerrington, Spennymoor DL16 7JT
T: (01388) 811006

SPITTAL
Northumberland

21 Billendean Terrace ★★★
Contact: Mrs Ingham
8 Burnaby Crescent, Chiswick, London W4 3LH
T: (020) 87470425
E: inghamfive@hotmail.com

Silvester Properties ★★★
Contact: Mrs Fiona Silvester
Silvester Properties, The Old Manse, Horncliffe, Berwick-upon-Tweed TD15 2XW
T: (01289) 306666
E: silprops@aol.com

STAINTON
County Durham

The Old Granary ★★★★
Contact: Dales Hol Cot Ref:1691
Dales Holiday Cottages, Carleton Business Park, Carleton New Road, Skipton BD23 2AA
T: (01756) 790919
F: (01756) 797012
E: info@dalesholcot.com
I: www.dalesholcot.com

STANHOPE
County Durham

Primrose Cottage ★★
Contact: Mrs Dickson
Northumbria Byways, Unit 2, Brampton Business Centre, The Irthing Centre, Union Lane, Brampton CA8 1BX
T: (016977) 41600
F: (016977) 41800

STOCKSFIELD
Northumberland

The Granary and Stable Cottage ★★★
Contact: Mrs Susan Astbury
The Granary and Stable Cottage, Old Ridley Farm, Stocksfield NE43 7RU
T: (01661) 842043
F: (01661) 842043
I: www.country-holidays.co.uk

The Old Bakery Cottages ★★★★
Contact: Mr Ron & Mrs Vivien Bolton
Greencroft, New Ridley Road, Stocksfield NE43 7EE
T: (01661) 843217

Old Ridley Hall ★★★
Contact: Mrs Josephine Aldridge
Old Ridley Hall, Stocksfield NE43 7RU
T: (01661) 842816
E: oldridleyhall@talk21.com

The Wash House ★★★
Contact: Mrs Harrison
The Wash House, Eltringham Farm, Stocksfield NE43 7DF
T: (01661) 842833

SUNDERLAND
Tyne and Wear

Mill View - 45 Poplar Drive ★★
Contact: Mrs Bethan Farrar
50 Beechhill Road, Eltham, London SE9 1HH
T: (020) 88504863
E: cass.farrar@virgin.net

22 Topcliff ★★★
Contact: Mr & Mrs M B Farrar
50 Beechhill Road, Eltham, London SE9 1HH
T: (020) 88504863
E: cass.farrar@virgin.net

SWARLAND
Northumberland

Swarland Hall Golf Club ★★★
Contact: Mrs Doreen Havis
Swarland Hall Golf Club, Coast View, Morpeth NE65 9JG
T: (01670) 787940
F: (01670) 787214
E: info@swarlandgolf.co.uk
I: www.swarlandgolf.co.uk

SWINHOE
Northumberland

East House ★★★
Contact: Ms Amanda Hodgson
East House, Chathill NE67 5AA
T: (01665) 574015

TARSET
Northumberland

Highfield Farm Cottage ★★
Contact: Mrs Miriam Elizabeth Tweddle
Highfield Farm Cottage, Highfield, Hexham NE48 1RT
T: (01434) 240219

THROPTON
Northumberland

Black Chirnells, The Cottage ★★★★
Contact: Mrs Liz Juppenlatz
Po Box 97, Leimuiden, Netherlands
T: +31 172506020
E: 100663.1174@compuserve.com

Mordue's Cottage & Grandma's Cottage ★★★
Contact: Mrs Helen Farr
Mordue's Cottage & Grandma's Cottage, Lorbottle West Steads, Morpeth NE65 7JT
T: (01665) 574672
F: (01665) 574672
E: Helen.Farr@farming.co.uk
I: www.lorbottle.com

North Croft ★★★★
Contact: Mrs Marilyn Chalk
The Old School, Morpeth NE65 8RW
T: (01670) 788655
E: northcroftMC@aol.com
I: www.visit-rothbury.co.uk/accom/sc_northcroft.htm

Physic Cottage ★★★★
Contact: Mrs Helen Duffield
River View, Physic Lane, Morpeth NE65 7HU
T: (01669) 620450
E: physiccottage@aol.com
I: www.visit-rothbury.co.uk

Westfield Cottage ★★★★
Contact: Mr Alastair & Mrs Catherine Hardie
Westfield House Farm, Thropton, Rothbury, Morpeth NE65 7LB
T: (01669) 640263
E: alicat@btinternet.com
I: www.visit-rothbury.co.uk/accom/sc_westfield.htm

TOW LAW
County Durham

Binks Cottage
Rating Applied For
Contact: Mrs Amanda Simpson
Oaklea, Thornley Village, Bishop Auckland DL13 4PA
T: (01388) 731121
F: (01388) 731121
E: amanda.simpson@totalise.co.uk

Establishments printed in blue have a detailed entry in this guide

NORTHUMBRIA

Greenwell Farm Cottages ★★★
Contact: Mrs Linda Vickers
Greenwell Farm Cottages,
Greenwell Farm, Nr
Wolsingham, Bishop Auckland
DL13 4PH
T: (01388) 527248
E: greenwell@farming.co.uk
I: www.greenwellfarm.co.uk

Pennine View ★★★★
Contact: Mrs Dawn Paterson
Pennine View, Thornley, Bishop
Auckland DL13 4PQ
T: (01388) 731329
E: enquiries@bracken-hill.com
I: www.bracken-hill.com

TUDHOE COLLIERY
County Durham

Miner's Cottage ★★★★
Contact: Mrs Jacqueline Galvin
1 Well House, Ferryhill
DL17 0NA
T: (01388) 721913
E: lgalvin@talk21.com
I: www.miners.cottage.
btinternet.co.uk

TWEEDMOUTH
Northumberland

Rowandene ★★★★
Contact: Lorna Chappell
1 Ravensdowne, Berwick-upon-
Tweed TD15 1HX
T: (01289) 331300
E: lornachappell127@hotmail.
com
I: www.rowandene.co.uk

WARDEN
Northumberland

Boatside Inn & Holiday Cottages ★★★-★★★★★
Contact: Mr Geoff Myers
Boatside Inn & Holiday Cottages,
Hexham NE46 4SQ
T: (01434) 602233
F: (01434) 601061
I: www.boatsideinn.co.uk

WAREN MILL
Northumberland

Eider Cottage ★★★★
Contact: Mrs Turnbull
1 Friars Court, Bamburgh
NE69 7AE
T: (01668) 214494
E: theturnbulls2k@btinternet.
com

WARENFORD
Northumberland

Etive Cottage ★★★★
Contact: Mr David & Mrs Jan
Thompson
The Cott, Belford NE70 7HZ
T: (01668) 213233

WARK
Northumberland

Coachmans and Stable Cottages ★★★
Contact: Mr Bruce & Mrs Sally
Napier
Coachmans and Stable Cottages,
The Old Rectory, Hexham
NE48 3PP
T: (01434) 230223
E: bruce.napier@talk21.com
I: www.
northumberland-self-catering.
co.uk

The Green ★★★★
Contact: Sykes Cottages Ref:683
York House, York Street, Chester
CH1 3LR
T: (01244) 345700
F: (01244) 321442
E: info@sykescottages.co.uk
I: www.sykescottages.co.uk

The Hemmel ★★★★
Contact: Mrs Nichol
The Hemmel, Hetherington,
Wark, Hexham NE48 3DR
T: (01434) 230260
F: (01434) 230260
E: alan_nichol@hotmail.com
I: www.hetheringtonfarm.co.uk

Rainbow Cottage ★★★
Contact: Mr Sydney & Mrs
Susan Thorkildsen
Tweedbank Cottage, Cornhill-
on-Tweed TD12 4RH
T: (01890) 882218
F: (01890) 882218
E: winston44@ntlworld.com

Riverside Cottage ★★★
Contact: Mrs Stella Jackson
16 Moss Side, Gateshead
NE9 7UU
T: (0191) 4876531
E: jands@wrekenton.freeserve.
co.uk

Roses Bower ★★★★
Contact: Mr Lewis & Mrs Susan
Watson
Roses Bower Farm, Hexham
NE48 3DX
T: (01434) 230779
F: (01434) 230779
E: sandlwatson@rosesbower.
fsworld.co.uk
I: www.roses-bower.co.uk

WARKWORTH
Northumberland

Birling Vale ★★★
Contact: Mrs Janet Brewis
Woodhouse, Alnwick NE66 2HR
T: (01665) 575222
I: www.
woodhousefarmholidays.co.uk

Buston Farm Holiday Cottages ★★★★
Contact: Miss Jo Park
Low Buston Hall, Warkworth,
Morpeth NE65 0XY
T: (01665) 714805
F: (01665) 711345
E: stay@buston.co.uk
I: www.buston.co.uk

Coquet Cottage ★★★★
Contact: Mrs Barbara Jean
Purvis
Fynder, 3 Dovecote Steadings,
Morpeth NE61 6DN
T: (01670) 789516
F: (01670) 789520

**Mahonia Lodge
Rating Applied For**
Contact: Mr Paul Smith
2 Carlbury Vale, Darlington
DL2 3SL
T: (01325) 374070
E: bookings@mahonialodge.
co.uk
I: www.mahonia-lodge.co.uk

Old Barns Farmhouse Holiday Cottage ★★★★
Contact: Mrs Jane Wilkes
Old Barns Farmhouse Holiday
Cottage, Morwick Road,
Morpeth NE65 0TH
T: (01665) 713427
E: scott.wilkes@virgin.net
I: www.oldbarnsholidaycottage.
co.uk

Riverview Cottage ★★★★★
Contact: Mr Paul & Mrs Helen
Skuse
20 Bristol Road, Bristol
BS36 1RG
T: (01454) 775441
E: pmskuse@hotmail.com
I: www.riverview-warkworth.
co.uk

Southmede Cottage ★★★★
Contact: Mr Mike & Mrs Carol
Smith
Southmede Cottage, Beal Bank,
Morpeth NE65 0TB
T: (01665) 711360
E: info@southmede.co.uk
I: www.southmede.co.uk

Stanners Stable ★★★
Contact: Mr Kevin Bremner
Coastal Retreats, P O Box 56,
Alnwick NE66 3WZ
T: (01665) 830267
E: kevinbremner@btopenworld.
com

WESTGATE-IN-WEARDALE
County Durham

Craggy Barn ★★★★
Contact: Mrs Angela Hackett
Craggy Barn, High Kitty Crag,
Westgate, Bishop Auckland
DL13 1LF
T: (01388) 517562
F: (01388) 526122
E: matthackett@talk21.com

WHITBURN
Tyne and Wear

Seawynds ★★★
Contact: Mrs Christine Whincop
2 Sea Winnings Way, Westow
Crown Village, South Shields
NE33 3NE
T: (0191) 5293578

WHITLEY BAY
Tyne and Wear

Seafront Apartments ★★★
Contact: Mrs Rosemary Webb
Seafront Apartments, 46
Beverley Terrace, Cullercoats,
North Shields NE30 4NU
T: 07977 203379
E: stay@seafront.info
I: www.seafront.info

WHITTINGHAM
Northumberland

**Bluebell Cottage
Rating Applied For**
Contact: Mrs Marian Charleton
Bluebell Cottage, The Grange,
Alnwick NE66 4BE
T: (01665) 574380
F: (01665) 574380
E: cottage@
whittingham-grange.co.uk

The Lodge and the Gatehouse ★★★★
Contact: Mrs Jenny Sordy
Alnham House, Alnwick
NE66 4TJ
T: (01669) 630210
F: (01669) 630310
E: jenny@alnhamfarm.co.uk
I: www.alnhamfarm.co.uk

WHORLTON
County Durham

Lavender Cottage ★★★★
Contact: Mr Anthony Johnson
Po Box 169, Redcar TS10 2WW
T: (01642) 483690
E: enquiries@lavender-cottage.
co.uk
I: www.lavender-cottage.co.uk

WIDDRINGTON
Northumberland

Seaspray Cottage ★★★
Contact: Mrs Carole Wood
Tudor House, Parkway,
Wilmslow SK9 1LS
T: (01625) 525857
E: carole.woodc43.fsnet.co.uk

WINSTON
County Durham

Highcliffe Waters ★★★★
Contact: Mr & Mrs Marie
Hodson
Highcliffe Waters, Highcliffe
Farm, Darlington DL2 3PJ
T: (01325) 730427
F: (01325) 730740
E: mrshodson@aol.com
I: www.countryholiday.co.uk

Strathmore Barns ★★★★
Contact: Mrs Marion Boyes
Strathmore Barns, Strathmore
House, Darlington DL2 3QS
T: (01833) 660302
F: 0709 2285603
E: info@strathmore.co.uk
I: www.strathmorebarns.co.uk

WITTON-LE-WEAR
County Durham

Carrs Terrace ★★★★
Contact: Miss Merlyn Law
93-99 Upper Richmond Road,
London SW15 2TG
T: (020) 87801084
F: (020) 87899199
E: merlynlaw@aol.com

WOLSINGHAM
County Durham

Ardine and Elvet Cottages ★★★
Contact: Mrs Gardiner
3 Melbourne Place, Wolsingham,
Bishop Auckland DL13 3EQ
T: (01388) 527538

Bradley Burn Holiday Cottages ★★★
Contact: Mrs Judith Stephenson
Bradley Burn Holiday Cottages,
Bradley Burn Farm, Bishop
Auckland DL13 3JH
T: (01388) 527285
F: (01388) 527285
E: jas@bradleyburn.co.uk
I: www.bradleyburn.co.uk

NORTHUMBRIA

Sandycarr Farm Cottage ★★★★
Contact: Mrs Marjorie Love
Holywell Farm, Holywell Lane,
Bishop Auckland DL13 3HB
T: (01388) 527249
F: (01388) 527249

Whitfield House Cottage ★★★
Contact: Mrs Margaret Shepheard
25 Front Street, Wolsingham,
Bishop Auckland DL13 3DF
T: (01388) 527466
E: enquiries@whitfieldhouse.clara.net
I: www.whitfieldhouse.clara.net

WOODLAND
County Durham

Mayland Farm Cottage ★★★
Contact: Mrs Susan Mortimer
Mayland Farm, Bishop Auckland
DL13 5NH
T: (01388) 718237
E: susan_mortimer@msn.com

WOOLER
Northumberland

Bushyfield Cottage and Airidh Bhan ★★★★
Contact: Mrs Liz Turnbull
4 Wood Terrace, South Shields
NE33 4UU
T: (0191) 4276203
F: (0191) 4206987
E: turnbullliz@aol.com

Byram House ★★★
Contact: Mrs Catherine Easton
Byram House, High Humbleton,
Wooler NE71 6SU
T: (01668) 281647

Castle Hill Cottage ★★★
Contact: Mr James Nall-Cain
Rarick Ltd, Waterend House,
Waterend Lane, St Albans
AL4 8EP
T: (01582) 831083
F: (01582) 831081
E: manussj@aol.com

Coldgate Mill ★★★★
Contact: Mr & Mrs Diana Stone
Coldgate Mill, Wooler NE71 6QZ
T: (01668) 217259
F: (01668) 217053
E: diana_coldgatemill@hotmail.com
I: www.coldgatemill.co.uk

Fenton Hill Farm Cottages ★★★★
Contact: Mrs Margaret Logan
Fenton Hill Farm Cottages,
Fenton Hill, Wooler NE71 6JJ
T: (01668) 216228
F: (01668) 216169
E: stay@fentonhillfarm.co.uk
I: www.fentonhillfarm.co.uk

Harehope Hall ★★★★
Contact: Ms Alison Wrangham
Harehope Hall, Cresswell Wing,
Alnwick NE66 2DP
T: (01668) 217329
F: (01688) 217346
E: aliwrangham@btconnect.com

Hayloft & Yearle Tower ★★★★
Contact: CH ref:N377,N376
21A Roydon Road, Ware
SG12 8HQ
T: 0870 0 723723
F: (01282) 844288
E: sales@holidaycottagesgroup.com
I: www.country-holidays.co.uk

Kimmerston Riding Centre ★★★
Contact: Mr Jeffreys
Kimmerston Riding Centre,
Kimmerston Farm, Wooler
NE71 6JH
T: (01668) 216283
E: jane@kimmerston.com
I: www.kimmerston.com

28 Oliver Road ★★
Contact: Davidson/Pearson
21 Roselands Avenue, Sale
M33 4BH
T: (0161) 973 0894
F: (0161) 973 0894
E: aitken777@hotmail.com

Peth Head Cottage ★★★★
Contact: Mr Peter & Mrs Clare Jeffreys
Eaver Cottage, 5 Green Acres,
Morpeth NE61 2AD
T: (01670) 514900
E: peter@phcjeffreys.freeserve.co.uk
I: www.pethheadcottage.co.uk

Rose Cottage ★★★
Contact: Mrs Christine Andrews
1 Littleworth Lane, Esher
KT10 9PF
T: (01372) 464284
F: (01372) 467715
E: andrews@playfactors.demon.co.uk

Swallowfields
Rating Applied For
Contact: Mr Malcolm Pringle
Swallowfields, Coldmartin,
Wooler NE71 6QN
T: (01668) 283488
E: malcolm@coldmartin.co.uk
I: www.coldmartin.co.uk

Westnewton Estate ★★★
Contact: Mrs Jean Davidson
Westnewton Estate,
Westnewton, Wooler NE71 6XL
T: (01668) 216077
E: jd@westnewtonestate.com
I: www.westnewtonestate.com

YARM
Stockton-on-Tees

Yarm Holiday Homes ★★★★
Contact: Mr Geoff Rowley
Yarm Holiday Homes, Far End Farm, Worsall Road, Yarm
TS15 9PE
T: (01642) 787017
E: enquiries@yarmholidayhomes.co.uk
I: www.yarmholidayhomes.co.uk

YORKSHIRE

ACKLAM
North Yorkshire

Beck Side Cottage @ Trout Pond Barn ★★★★
Contact: Mrs Margaret Phillips
Trout Pond Barn, Malton
YO17 9RG
T: (01653) 658468
F: (01653) 698688
E: troutpondbarn@aol.com
I: www.troutpondbarn.co.uk

ADDINGHAM
West Yorkshire

Number Nine ★★★★
Contact: Mr Ian & Mrs Jean Francis
The Counting House, Old Lane,
Ilkley LS29 0SA
T: (01943) 831254

AIKE
East Riding of Yorkshire

The Old Chapel Ref:323 ★★★
Contact: Mr S Boardman
Sykes Cottages, York House,
York Street, Chester CH1 3LR
T: (01244) 345700
F: (01244) 321442
E: info@sykescottages.co.uk
I: www.sykescottages.co.uk

AIRTON
North Yorkshire

13 Riverside Walk ★★★★★
Contact: Agent
Welcome Holidays Ltd, Embsay Mills, Skipton BD23 6QR
T: (01756) 696868
F: (01756) 702235
I: www.welcomecottages.com

AISKEW
North Yorkshire

The Courtyard ★★★★
Contact: Mr James & Mrs Jill Cartman
The Courtyard, The Nurseries,
Bedale DL8 1BN
T: (01677) 423689
F: (01677) 425762
E: jill@courtyard.ndirect.co.uk
I: www.courtyard.ndirect.co.uk

AISLABY
North Yorkshire

Aislaby Hall Cottage ★★★★
Contact: Mrs Janet Hartshorne
Aislaby Hall, Pickering YO18 8PE
T: (01751) 477777
F: (01751) 477766

Eskbridge Cottage ★★★★
Contact: Mrs Julie Tuby
54 Carr Hill Lane, Whitby
YO21 1RS
T: (01947) 810388
F: (01947) 820466
I: www.eskbridgecottage.co.uk

Granary Cottage
Rating Applied For
Contact: Mrs Adele Thompson
Whitby Holiday Cottages, 47
Flowergate, Whitby YO21 3BB
T: (01947) 603010
F: (01947) 821133
E: enquiries@whitby-cottages.co.uk
I: www.whitby-cottages.co.uk

Low Newbiggin House ★★★-★★★★★
Contact: Miss Charlotte Etherington
Low Newbiggin House, Whitby
YO21 1TQ
T: (01947) 811811
F: (01947) 810348
E: holidays@lownewbiggin.co.uk
I: www.lownewbiggin.co.uk

Stable Cottage & Byre Cottage ★★★-★★★★★
Contact: Mrs Adele Thompson
Whitby Holiday Cottages, 47
Flowergate, Whitby YO21 3BB
T: (01947) 603010
F: (01947) 821133
E: enquiries@whitby-cottages.co.uk
I: www.whitby-cottages.co.uk

ALDBROUGH
North Yorkshire

Greencroft Cottage ★★★
Contact: Mrs Mary Baxter
Greencroft Cottage, Aldbrough
St John, Richmond DL11 7TJ
T: (01325) 374550
E: ray.baxter@btinternet.com
I: www.greencroft.org.uk

Lilac Cottage ★★★★
Contact: Mrs Helen Stubbs
19 Seaside Road, Hull HU11 4RX
T: (01964) 527645
E: helen@seasideroad.freeserve.co.uk
I: www.aer96.dial.pipex.com/lilac-cottage

Establishments printed in blue have a detailed entry in this guide

YORKSHIRE

ALDFIELD
North Yorkshire
Trips Cottage ★★★
Contact: Mrs Leeming
Trips Cottage, Bay Tree Farm, Ripon HG3 4BE
T: (01765) 620394
I: www.yorkshirebandb.co.uk

ALKBOROUGH
North Lincolnshire
Corner Cottage ★★★★
Contact: Ms Annette Dexter
169 Abbots Road, Watford WD5 0BN
T: (01923) 330022
F: (01923) 330022
E: annette.dexter@ntlworld.com

ALLERSTON
North Yorkshire
The Old Station ★★★★
Contact: Mr Mark & Mrs Carol Benson
The Old Station, Main Street, Pickering YO18 7PG
T: (01723) 859024
E: mcrbenson@aol.com
I: www.theoldstationallerston.co.uk

Rains Farm ★★★★
Contact: Mrs L Allanson
Rains Farm, Pickering YO18 7PQ
T: (01723) 859333
E: allan@rainsfarm.freeserve.co.uk
I: www.rains-farm-holidays.co.uk

ALLERTHORPE
East Riding of Yorkshire
The Old Gravel Pits ★★★★
Contact: Dr Edward Moll
The Old Gravel Pits, York YO42 4RW
T: (01759) 302192

ALNE
North Yorkshire
Sylvia Dene ★★★
Contact: Mr Brian Kenny
Sylvia Dene, Main Street, York YO61 1TA
T: (01347) 838278
E: jameskenny@btinternet.com

AMPLEFORTH
North Yorkshire
Brackensyke Cottage ★★★★
Contact: Mr Peter Davis
22 Rishworth Grove, Clifton Moor, York YO30 4XS
T: (01904) 690465
E: peter.davis@uk.nestle.com
I: www.brackensyke-ampleforth.com

Brook House ★★★★
Contact: Mrs Mary Sturges
Brook House Cottage, West End, Ampleforth, York YO62 4DY
T: (01439) 788563
F: (01439) 788563
E: mpsturge@aol.com

2 Carmel Cottage ★★★
Contact: Miss Clare Jennings
2 Carmel Cottage, West End, York YO62 4DU
T: (01439) 788467
F: (01439) 788467
E: carmelcott@onetel.net.uk

Hillside Cottage ★★★★
Contact: Mrs Pam Noble
Hillside, West End, Ampleforth, York YO62 4DY
T: (01439) 788303
F: (01439) 788303
E: hillsidecottage@westend-ampleforth.co.uk
I: www.cottageguide.co.uk/hillsidecottage

APPERSETT
North Yorkshire
The Coach House ★★★
Contact: Mr Head
The Coach House, Rigg House, High Abbotside, Hawes DL8 3LR
T: (01969) 667375
F: (01969) 667375
E: walterhead@rigghouse.freeserve.co.uk

APPLETON-LE-MOORS
North Yorkshire
The Carthouse ★★★
Contact: Mrs Diane Peirson
The Carthouse, Cockpit Farmhouse, Appleton-le-Moors, York YO62 6TF
T: (01751) 417363
F: (01751) 417636
E: bob.peirson@tiscali.co.uk
I: www.cottageguide.co.uk/thecarthouse

Darley Cottage ★★★★
Contact: Mr & Mrs James Brooke
The Pottery, York YO62 6TE
T: (01751) 417514
E: jbrooke@pottery1.fsnet.co.uk

Hamley Hagg Cottage ★★★
Contact: Mrs Feaster
Hamley Hagg Cottage, Hamley Hagg Farm, York YO62 6TG
T: (01751) 417413
F: (01751) 417413
I: www.appletonlemoors.fsnet.co.uk

Three Faces Cottage ★★★★
Contact: Mrs Firth
4 West End Lane, Leeds LS18 5JP
T: (0113) 258 8940
E: the3faces@hotmail.com
I: www.cottageguide.co.uk/the3faces

APPLETREEWICK
North Yorkshire
Fell Cottage ★★★★
Contact: Mr Nigel & Mrs Tracey Wain
Andras Farm, Skipton BD23 6DA
T: (01756) 720286
F: (01756) 720286
E: fellcottage@appletreewick.net
I: www.appletreewick.net/fellcottage

Fell View Ref:817 ★★★
Contact: Mr S Boardman
Sykes Cottages, York House, York Street, Chester CH1 3LR
T: (01244) 345700
F: (01244) 321442
E: info@sykescottages.co.uk
I: www.sykescottages.co.uk

Fellside ★★★
Contact: Mrs Murphy
Three Peaks, 5 Barns Close, Leicester LE9 2BA
T: (0116) 2395713
F: (0116) 2395713
E: murphyjayne@hotmail.com
I: mysite.freeserve.com/AppletreewickCottage/

ARKENGARTHDALE
North Yorkshire
Low Lock Slack Cottage Ref:62 ★★★
Contact: Mr S Boardman
Sykes Cottages, York House, York Street, Chester CH1 3LR
T: (01244) 345700
F: (01244) 321442
E: info@sykescottages.co.uk
I: www.sykescottages.co.uk

ARNCLIFFE
North Yorkshire
Green Farm Cottage Ref:1523 ★★★
Contact: Ms H Cook
Dales Holiday Cottages, Carleton Business Park, Carleton New Road, Skipton BD23 2AA
T: (01756) 799821
F: (01756) 797012
E: info@dalesholcot.com
I: www.dalesholcot.com

ASKRIGG
North Yorkshire
Askrigg Cottage Holidays ★★★★
Contact: Mr & Mrs Ken Williamson
Askrigg Cottage Holidays, Thwaite House, Moor Road, Leyburn DL8 3HH
T: (01969) 650022
E: stay@askrigg.com
I: www.askrigg.com

Askrigg Cottages ★★★-★★★★★
Contact: Mrs Kate Empsall
Whitfield/Askrigg Cottages, Leyburn DL8 3JF
T: (01969) 650565
F: (01969) 650565
E: info@askrigg-cottages.co.uk
I: www.askrigg-cottages.co.uk

Carr End Cottage Ref:2467 ★★★
Contact: Ms H Cook
Dales Holiday Cottages, Carleton Business Park, Carleton New Road, Skipton BD23 2AA
T: (01756) 799821
F: (01756) 797012
E: info@dalesholcot.com
I: www.dalesholcot.com

Cowlingholme Cottage ★★★★
Contact: Mrs Nadine Bell
Country Hideaways, Margaret's Cottage, Leyburn DL8 4JN
T: (01969) 663559
F: (01969) 663559
E: nadine@countryhideaways.co.uk
I: www.countryhideaways.co.uk

Elm Hill Holiday Cottages ★★★
Contact: Mr & Mrs Peter Haythornthwaite
Hargill Garth, Hargill Road, Leyburn DL8 4ER
T: (01969) 624252
F: (01969) 624252
E: enquiries@elmhillholidaycottages.co.uk
I: www.elmhillholidaycottages.co.uk

Faith Hill Cottage ★★★
Contact: Ms Jennifer Kirkbride
Town Head Farm, Moor Road, Leyburn DL8 3HH
T: (01969) 650325
E: allenkirkbride@hotmail.com

Greystones ★★★
Contact: Mrs Nadine Bell
Country Hideaways, Margaret's Cottage, Leyburn DL8 4JN
T: (01969) 663559
F: (01969) 663559
E: nadine@countryhideaways.co.uk
I: www.countryhideaways.co.uk

Lavender Cottage Ref: 729
Rating Applied For
Contact: Mr Clive Sykes
Sykes Cottages, York House, York Street, Chester CH1 3LR
T: (01244) 345700
F: (01244) 321442
E: info@sykescottages.co.uk
I: www.sykescottages.co.uk

Lukes Barn Ref:1675 ★★★
Contact: Ms H Cook
Dales Holiday Cottages, Carleton Business Park, Carleton New Road, Skipton BD23 2AA
T: (01756) 799821
F: (01756) 797012
E: info@dalesholcot.com
I: www.dalesholcot.com

Meadowsweet ★★★★
Contact: Mr Alan Rose
33 Burton Stone Lane, Bootham, York YO30 6BT
T: (01904) 626009
E: acrose@waitrose.com

Old Mill II ★★★
Contact: Mrs Nadine Bell
Country Hideaways, Margaret's Cottage, Leyburn DL8 4JN
T: (01969) 663559
F: (01969) 663559
E: nadine@countryhideaways.co.uk
I: www.countryhideaways.co.uk

School House ★★★
Contact: Mrs Nadine Bell
Country Hideaways, Margaret's Cottage, Leyburn DL8 4JN
T: (01969) 663559
F: (01969) 663559
E: nadine@countryhideaways.co.uk
I: www.countryhideaways.co.uk

Shaw Cote Cottage Ref: 218 ★★★
Contact: Mr S Boardman
Sykes Cottages, York House, York Street, Chester CH1 3LR
T: (01244) 345700
F: (01244) 321442
E: info@sykescottages.co.uk
I: www.sykescottages.co.uk

YORKSHIRE

The Shippon ★★★
Contact: Mrs Nadine Bell
Country Hideaways, Margaret's Cottage, Leyburn DL8 4JN
T: (01969) 663559
F: (01969) 663559
E: nadine@countryhideaways.co.uk
I: www.countryhideaways.co.uk

Yoredale Cottage ★★
Contact: Mrs Elizabeth Miller
The Orchard, Leyburn DL8 4JN
T: (01969) 663359
E: bmiller@wensleydale.n-yorks.sch.uk

AUSTWICK
North Yorkshire

Eldroth House ★★★★
Contact: Mr Roger Wales
Yorkshire Cottages Yorkshire Ltd, Water Street, Skipton BD23 1PB
T: (01756) 700510
E: brochure@holidaycotts.co.uk

Rawlinshaw Farm Ref:3335 ★★★★
Contact: Ms H Cook
Dales Holiday Cottages, Carleton Business Park, Carleton New Road, Skipton BD23 2AA
T: (01756) 799821
F: (01756) 797012
E: info@dalesholcot.com
I: www.dalesholcot.com

Spoutscroft Cottage ★★★★★
Contact: Mrs Christine Hartland
Leigh Cottage, Lancaster LA2 8BN
T: (01524) 251052
E: thehartlands@onetel.net.com
I: www.cottageguide.co.uk/spoutscroft

BAINBRIDGE
North Yorkshire

Courtyard Cottage Ref 3708 ★★★★
Contact:
Dales Holiday Cottages, Carleton Business Park, Carleton New Road, Skipton BD23 2AA
T: (01756) 799821
F: (01756) 797012
E: info@dalesholcot.com
I: www.dales-holiday-cottages.com

The Old Hall ★★★
Contact: Mr Keith Lucas
222 Ryebank Road, Chorlton Cum Hardy, Manchester M21 9LU
T: (0161) 8618187
F: (0161) 8618187
E: keith.lucas50@ntlworld.com

BARMBY MOOR
East Riding of Yorkshire

Northwood House ★★★★
Contact: Mrs Gregory
Northwood House, St Helens Square, Barmby Moor, York YO42 4HF
T: (01759) 302305
E: annjgregory@hotmail.com
I: www.northwoodcoachhouse.co.uk

BARNOLDBY-LE-BECK
North East Lincolnshire

Grange Farm Cottages & Riding School ★★★★
Contact: Ms Jo & Sue Jenkins
Grange Farm Cottages & Riding School, Waltham Road, Barnoldby-le-Beck, Grimsby DN37 0AR
T: (01472) 822216
F: (01472) 233550
E: sueuk4000@netscape.net
I: www.grangefarmcottages.com

BARTON-LE-WILLOWS
North Yorkshire

The Old Granary ★★★★
Contact: Mrs Hudson
The Old Granary, Green Farm, Barton Le Willows, York YO60 7PD
T: (01653) 618387
F: (01653) 618387
E: bartonlewillows@netscapeonline.co.uk
I: www.oldgranary.com

BARTON-UPON-HUMBER
North Lincolnshire

Pasture House Fisheries ★★★
Contact: Mrs Martine Smith
Pasture House Fisheries Ltd, Pasture Road North, Barton-upon-Humber DN18 5RB
T: (01652) 636369
F: (01652) 636369
E: pasturehousefish@aol.com
I: www.pasturehouse.co.uk

BAYSDALE
North Yorkshire

Baysdale Abbey ★★★
Contact: English Country Cottages, Stoney Bank, Barnoldswick BB94 0AA
T: 0870 5851155
F: (01282) 841539
I: www.english-country-cottages.co.uk

BECKWITHSHAW
North Yorkshire

The Old Mistal Cottage ★★★★
Contact: Mrs Christine Williams
The Old Mistal Cottage, Bluecoat Farm, Howhill Road, Beckwithshaw, Harrogate HG3 1QJ
T: (01423) 561385
F: (01423) 561385
E: c.williams@mistal.fsnet.co.uk
I: www.mistal.fsnet.co.uk

BEDALE
North Yorkshire

High Grange Holiday Cottages ★★★★
Contact: Mr Trevor & Mrs Janet Ripley
High Grange Holiday Cottages, High Grange, Bedale DL8 2HQ
T: (01677) 422740
E: highgrange@yorks.net
I: www.highgrange.yorks.net

BELLERBY
North Yorkshire

Boar Cottage ★★★★
Contact: Mr & Mrs Gray
The Boar Inn House, Bellerby, Leyburn DL8 5QP
T: (01969) 622220
F: (01969) 622220
E: graydales@aol.com
I: www.boarcottage.co.uk

Eastvale Cottage ★★★
Contact: Ms Trish Borrill
Eastvale Cottage, Stores Cottage, Moor Road, Bellerby, Leyburn DL8 5QT
T: (01969) 623152
E: trish@eastvalecottage.fslife.co.uk

Scott Cottage ★★★
Contact: Mrs Maughan
Scott Cottage, Leyburn DL8 5QP
T: (01969) 622498
F: (01969) 622498

BEMPTON
East Riding of Yorkshire

Primrose Cottage Ref:2122 ★★★★
Contact: Ms H Cook
Dales Holiday Cottages, Carleton Business Park, Carleton New Road, Skipton BD23 2AA
T: (01756) 799821
F: (01756) 797012
E: info@dalesholcot.com
I: www.dalesholcot.com

BEVERLEY
East Riding of Yorkshire

Apple Tree Cottages ★★★★
Contact: Mrs Linda Chamberlain
Apple Tree House, Norwood, Beverley HU17 9HN
T: (01482) 873615
F: (01482) 866666
I: www.appletreehouse.co.uk

Beckside Cottage ★★★
Contact: Mr King
Beckside Cottage, 66 Beckside, Beverley HU17 0PD
T: (01482) 872291
E: kings@three.karoo.co.uk

Beverley Holiday Cottages ★★
Contact: Mr Paul Eastburn
32 Wood Lane, Beverley HU17 8BS
T: (01482) 882699
E: eastburn@eastburn1066.karoo.co.uk
I: www.eastburn1066.karoo.net

Chapel View ★★★
Contact: Mr Philip Hillman
Chapel View, 138 Norwood, Beverley HU17 8RY
T: (01482) 867465
E: pooliverhillman@hotmail.com

The Cottage ★★★★
Contact: Mr Kenneth Hearne
25 All Hallows Road, Beverley HU17 8SH
T: (01482) 868310
E: knhearne@talk21.com
I: www.akcottage.com

Foremans Cottage ★★★
Contact: Mrs Hayward
Lane House, Beverley Road, Beverley HU17 8QY
T: (01964) 550821
F: (01964) 550898
E: heathermhay@aol.com

Lempicka Cottage ★★★★
Contact: Mrs Linda Boyeson
Lempicka Cottage, 13 Wednesday Market, Beverley HU17 0DH
T: (01482) 863665
F: (01482) 866960

Old Walkergate & The Cabin ★★★
Contact: Mrs Margaret Abbey
Beverley Self-Catering, 5 Laughton Road, Beverley HU17 9JR
T: (01482) 860005
F: (01482) 860005
E: margaretabbey@beverleyselfcatering.freeserve.co.uk
I: www.beverleyselfcatering.freeserve.co.uk

Rudstone Walk Country Accommodation ★★★★
Contact: Mrs Laura Greenwood
Rudstone Walk Country Accommodation, Brough HU15 2AH
T: (01430) 422230
F: (01430) 424552
E: admin@rudstone-walk.co.uk
I: www.rudstone-walk.co.uk

BEWERLEY
North Yorkshire

Bewerley Hall Farm ★★★★
Contact: Mrs Eileen Smith
Bewerley Hall Farm, Harrogate HG3 5JA
T: (01423) 711636
E: chris@farmhouseholidays.freeserve.co.uk
I: www.bewerleyhallfarm.co.uk

4 The Green ★★★
Contact: Mr Wales
Holiday Cottages (Yorkshire) Ltd, Water Street, Skipton BD23 1PB
T: (01756) 700510
E: brochure@holidaycotts.co.uk
I: www.holidaycotts.co.uk

BIELBY
East Riding of Yorkshire

Sunnyside Cottage
Rating Applied For
Contact: Mrs Debbie Britton
Sunnyside Cottage, Main Street, Bielby, York YO42 4JL
T: (01759) 318611
F: (01759) 319057
E: britton@supanet.com
I: www.sunnysidecottage.co.uk

BIRSTWITH
North Yorkshire

3 The Square ★★★★
Contact: Mr Wales
Holiday Cottages (Yorkshire) Ltd, Water Street, Skipton BD23 1PB
T: (01756) 700510
E: brochure@holidaycotts.co.uk
I: www.holidaycotts.co.uk

Establishments printed in blue have a detailed entry in this guide

YORKSHIRE

BISHOP MONKTON
North Yorkshire

Granary Cottage ★★★
Contact: Ms Allison Hewson
Granary Cottage, Laurel Bank Farm, Hungate Lane, Bishop Monkton, Harrogate HG3 3QL
T: (01765) 677677

Hall Farm Cottage ★★★★
Contact: Mrs Jennifer Barker
Hall Farm Cottage, Boroughbridge Road, Harrogate HG3 3QN
T: (01765) 677200
E: jenkenhallfarm@onetel.com
I: www.yorkshirebandb.co.uk

BISHOP THORNTON
North Yorkshire

The Courtyard at 'Dukes Place' ★★★-★★★★
Contact: Mrs Jaki Moorhouse
The Courtyard at 'Dukes Place', Harrogate HG3 3JY
T: (01765) 620229
F: (01765) 620454
E: jakimoorhouse@onetel.net.uk
I: www.dukesplace-courtyard.co.uk

BISHOP WILTON
East Riding of Yorkshire

Low Callis Granary ★★★★
Contact: Stringer & Sons
Low Callis Granary, Low Callis Wold, York YO42 1TD
T: (01759) 368831
E: thegranary@lowcallis.plus.com

BISHOPDALE
North Yorkshire

Fell View ★★★
Contact: Mrs Nadine Bell
Country Hideaways, Margaret's Cottage, West Burton, Leyburn DL8 4JN
T: (01969) 663559
F: (01969) 663559
E: nadine@countryhideaways.co.uk
I: www.countryhideaways.co.uk

BOLSTERSTONE
South Yorkshire

Nook Farm Holiday Cottage ★★★
Contact: Ms Jane Wainwright
Nook Farm Holiday Cottage, Nook Farm, Sunny Bank Road, Bolsterstone, Sheffield S36 3ST
T: (0114) 288 3335

BOLTBY
North Yorkshire

The Coach House ★★★
Contact:
Blakes Cottages, 21A Roydon Road, Ware SG12 8HQ
T: 0870 4 446603
F: (01282) 841539
I: www.boltbytrekking.co.uk

BOLTON ABBEY
North Yorkshire

The Beamsley Project ★★★★
Contact: Mr John & Mrs Margaret Tomlinson
The Beamsley Project, Skipton BD23 6JA
T: (01756) 710255
F: (01756) 710255
E: beamsley.project@virgin.net
I: www.beamsleyproject.org.uk

Low Laithe Barn ★★★★★
Contact: Mrs Susan Gray
Beech House Barns, Ilkley LS29 0EP
T: (01943) 609819
F: (01943) 609377
E: info@beechhousebarns.co.uk
I: www.beechhousebarns.co.uk

BORROWBY
North Yorkshire

Muttling Corner Cottage ★★★★
Contact: Mrs Jane McBretney
Rawcar, Northallerton DL7 0AL
T: (01325) 378297
E: muttlingcorner@dial.pipex.com
I: www.yorkshireescapes.com

BRADFIELD
South Yorkshire

Rickett Field Farm ★★★★
Contact: Mrs Shepherd
Rickett Field Farm, Sidlings Hollow, Sheffield S6 6HA
T: (0114) 285 1218
E: shepherd@rickettlathe.freeserve.co.uk

Rickettfield Barn
Rating Applied For
Contact: Mrs Connie Shepherd
Rickettfield Barn, Dungworth, Sheffield S6 6HA
T: (0114) 285 1218
I: www.rickettlathe.freeserve.co.uk

BRADSHAW
West Yorkshire

Popples Cottage ★★★
Contact: Mr Colin & Mrs Jan Huntley
3 Popples, School Lane, Bradshaw, Halifax HX2 9QP
T: (01422) 244788
E: janhuntley67@yahoo.co.uk

BRAWBY
North Yorkshire

The Old Cart House ★★★★
Contact: Mrs Anne Muir
The Old Cart House, Deepwell Cottages, Brawby, Malton YO17 6QA
T: (01653) 668252

BRIDLINGTON
East Riding of Yorkshire

Acorn House ★★★
Contact: Mr & Mrs Morton
Acorn House, 9 Belgrave Road, Bridlington YO15 3JP
T: (01262) 672451
E: marieoak24@hotmail.com

Angie's Imp-press Holiday Apartments ★★★★
Contact: Mrs Angela Boxer
Angie's Imp-press Holiday Apartments, 17 Blackburn Avenue, Bridlington YO15 2ER
T: (01262) 608838

Arncliffe ★-★★★
Contact: Mrs Shirley Drew
Arncliffe, 39 Blackburn Avenue, Bridlington YO15 2ER
T: (01262) 677945

Ash Lee Holiday Apartments ★★-★★★
Contact: Mrs Greatorex
Ash Lee Holiday Apartments, 4 Vernon Road, Bridlington YO15 2HQ
T: (01262) 400485
I: www.bridlington-flats.co.uk

Ashton Holiday Flats ★
Contact: Mr Samuel & Mrs Helen Levitt
Ashton Holiday Flats, 5 Belgrave Road, Bridlington YO15 3JP
T: (01262) 675132

Bay Side Holidays ★★★★
Contact: Mr Barry & Mrs Anne Hatfield
c/o 25 Victoria Road, Bridlington YO15 2AT
T: (01262) 609431
F: (01262) 609431
E: bayside.bridlington@virgin.net
I: www.baysideholidays.co.uk

Beach House ★★★
Contact: Doreen Hirst
47 Bond Road, Barnsley S75 2TW
T: (01226) 206847

Beaconsfield House ★★★
Contact: Mrs Loraine Stuart
5 Park Avenue, Bridlington YO15 2HL
T: (01262) 401482
I: www.beaconsfieldholidayapartments.co.uk

Bluebell Holiday Apartment ★★★
Contact: Mrs Lorna Shaw
8A Sands Lane, Bridlington YO15 2JE
T: (01262) 401445

East Coast Holiday Cottages ★★★
Contact: Mrs Cynthia Dean
East Coast Holiday Cottages, 23 Scarborough Crescent, Bridlington YO16 7PA
T: (01262) 601543
E: eastcoastholidaycottages@hotmail.com
I: www.bridlington.net/business.eastcoast

Ellwyn Holiday Flats ★★
Contact: Mr James & Mrs Susan Thornton
Ellwyn Holiday Flats, 47 Wellington Road, Bridlington YO15 2AX
T: (01262) 606896
E: elliethodsq@supanet.com
I: www.bridlington.net/ellwyn/business

Fairholme Holiday Flats ★★★
Contact: Mr Nicholas Geraghty
Fairholme Holiday Flats, 12 Pembroke Terrace, Bridlington YO15 3BX
T: (01262) 676269
E: nicholasscott@geraghty2.fsnet.co.uk

Finley Cottages ★★★
Contact: Mrs Pauline Halstead
Finley Cottages, 33 Beverley Road, Driffield YO25 6RZ
T: (01377) 253985
F: (01377) 253232
E: winston.halstead@virgin.net

Fir Lodge Holiday Apartments ★★★
Contact: Mr Les & Mrs Chris Day
Fir Lodge Holiday Apartments, 14 Sands Lane, Bridlington YO15 2JE
T: (01262) 671400
E: firlodge@bridlington.co.uk

Fountain House ★-★★
Contact: Mr Shuttleworth
Fountain House, 4 Marlborough Terrace, Bridlington YO15 2PA
T: (01262) 604850

The Grosvenor Holiday Flats ★★★★
Contact: Mrs Elizabeth Otulakowski
High House Farm, Skipton BD23 3QX
T: (01535) 272172
F: (01535) 272172
E: nicehols@aol.com

Hemsley Holiday Flats ★-★★
Contact: Mrs Christine Tranmer
Hemsley Holiday Flats, 5 Alexandra Drive, Bridlington YO15 2HZ
T: (01262) 672603

Highcliffe Holiday Apartments ★-★★★
Contact: Mrs Pat Willcocks
Highcliffe Holiday Apartments, 19 Albion Terrace, Bridlington YO15 2PJ
T: (01262) 674127

Lauralee Villa ★★★
Contact: Mr James William Hilton
6 Kendal Drive, Bolton-upon-Dearne, Rotherham S63 8NJ
T: (01709) 897606
E: bill@Lauraleeholidays.freeserve.co.uk
I: www.lauraleeholidays.co.uk

Marina Holiday Apartments ★★★
Contact: Mrs Shaw
8A Sands Lane, Bridlington YO15 2JE
T: (01262) 401445

Marina View ★-★★★
Contact: Ms Geraldine Ross
Holiday Flats, Pembroke Terrace, Bridlington YO15 3BX
T: (01262) 676565

472 Look out for establishments participating in the National Accessible Scheme

YORKSHIRE

Marton Manor Cottages ★★★★
Contact: Mrs Jane Waind
Marton Manor Cottages, Marton Manor, Flamborough Road, Bridlington YO15 1DU
T: (01262) 672552
F: (01262) 672552
E: martonmanor@btopenworld.com
I: www.martonmanor.fsnet.co.uk

23 Mount Drive ★★★
Contact: Mrs Helen Gudgeon
6 Westfield Avenue, Leeds LS12 3SJ
T: (0113) 226 1298
E: rkgudgeon@hotmail.com

Mowbray Holiday Flats ★-★★
Contact: Mr Carl Chambers
Mowbray Holiday Flats, 8 The Crescent, Bridlington YO15 2NX
T: (01262) 676218
E: mowbrayflats@amserve.com
I: www.mowbrayflats.co.uk

Pembroke Holiday Flats ★★★
Contact: Mr & Mrs Eaton
Pembroke Holiday Flats, 18 Pembroke Terrace, Bridlington YO15 3BX
T: (01262) 677376
E: ampembroke@btopenworld.com

The Rialto
Rating Applied For
Contact: Mr Ian & Mrs Michelle Stoddard
The Rialto, 63-65 Trinity Road, Bridlington YO15 2HF
T: (01262) 677653

St Margarets Holiday Apartments ★★-★★★
Contact: Mr John & Mrs Liz Stuart
St Margarets Holiday Apartments, 5/6 Marlborough Terrace, Bridlington YO15 2PA
T: (01262) 673698

San Remo ★★-★★★
Contact: Mrs Ann Jackson
3 Kingston Road, Bridlington YO15 3NF
T: (01262) 676585

Sea View Holiday Flats ★-★★
Contact: Mr Stanley & Mrs Margaret Benson
Sea View Holiday Flats, 8 Belgrave Road, Bridlington YO15 3JR
T: (01262) 676974

Winston Court Holiday Apartments ★-★★
Contact: Mr Ian Reed & Catherine Cook
7-8 Fort Terrace, Bridlington YO15 2PE
T: (01262) 677819
E: tedshep@sagainternet.co.uk
I: www.winston-court.fsbusiness.co.uk

York Holiday Flats ★★
Contact: Mrs Joan Cash
York Holiday Flats, York Road, Bridlington YO15 2PQ
T: (01262) 675956
F: (01262) 675956

BRIGSLEY
North East Lincolnshire

Prospect Farm Cottages ★★★★★
Contact: Mrs Janet Speight
Prospect Farm Cottages, Prospect Farm, Waltham Road, Brigsley, Grimsby DN37 0RQ
T: (01472) 826491
F: (01472) 826471
E: prospectfarm@btconnect.com
I: www.prospectfarm.co.uk

BROUGHTON
North Yorkshire

Summertree Granary & The Studio, Summertree Farm ★★★
Contact: Mr Bob & Mrs Bridget Eldridge
Summertree Farm, High Marishes, Malton YO17 6UH
T: (01751) 474355
E: bridget.m.eldridge@talk21.com
I: www.dales-holiday-cottages.com

BUCKDEN
North Yorkshire

Dalegarth and The Ghyll Cottages ★★★★
Contact: Mr David & Mrs Susan Lusted
9 Dalegarth, Buckden, Skipton BD23 5JU
T: (01756) 760877
F: (01756) 760877
E: info@dalegarth.co.uk
I: www.dalegarth.co.uk

East Farm Ref: 1542
Rating Applied For
Contact: Miss Fiona Moody
Dales Holiday Cottages, Carleton Business Park, Carleton New Road, Skipton BD23 2AA
T: (01756) 790919
F: (01756) 797012
E: fiona@dales-holiday-cottages.com

Woods Barn Ref: 3164
Rating Applied For
Contact: Miss Fiona Moody
Dales Holiday Cottages, Carleton Business Park, Carleton New Road, Skipton BD23 2AA
T: (01756) 790919
F: (01756) 797012
E: fiona@dales-holiday-cottages.com
I: www.dales-holiday-cottages.com

BULMER
North Yorkshire

Ashwall House
Rating Applied For
Contact: Mr Tony Thomas
Ashwall House, Wandales Lane, York YO60 7ES
T: (01845) 597614
F: (01845) 597630
E: enquiriesytb@ashwallhouse.co.uk
I: www.ashwallhouse.co.uk

BURNSALL
North Yorkshire

Bland Place and Manor Cottage ★★★
Contact: Ms Diana Rosemary Lodge
Bland Place and Manor Cottage, Main Street, High Croft, Skipton BD23 6BP
T: (01756) 720668

Oatcroft Farm Barn Apartment ★★★
Contact: Mrs Jane Stockdale
Oatcroft Farm Barn Apartment, Oatcroft Farm, Skipton BD23 6BN
T: (01756) 720268

Pipit Cottage Ref:1430 ★★★
Contact: Ms H Cook
Dales Holiday Cottages, Carleton Business Park, Carleton New Road, Skipton BD23 2AA
T: (01756) 799821
F: (01756) 797012
E: info@dalesholcot.com
I: www.dalesholcot.com

Riversyde Cottage Ref: 214 ★★★★
Contact: Mr S Boardman
Sykes Cottages, Sykes House, York Street, Chester CH1 3LR
T: (01244) 345700
F: (01244) 321442
E: info@sykescottages.co.uk
I: www.sykescottages.co.uk

The Sycamores ★★★★
Contact: Mrs Sheila Carr
Moor Green Farm, Threshfield, Skipton BD23 5NR
T: (01756) 752435
F: (01756) 752435
E: carr@totalise.co.uk

BURNT YATES
North Yorkshire

The Barn @ Fir Tree Farm
Rating Applied For
Contact: Mrs Rebecca Donnelly
The Barn @ Fir Tree Farm, High Winsley, Brimham Rocks Road, Harrogate HG3 3EP
T: (01423) 779708
F: (01895) 861959
E: rdonnelly@ge.cokecce.com

North Gate Cottage Ref:3045 ★★★
Contact: Ms H Cook
Dales Holiday Cottages, Carleton Business Park, Carleton New Road, Skipton BD23 2AA
T: (01756) 799821
F: (01756) 797012
E: info@dalesholcot.com
I: www.dalesholcot.com

BURTERSETT
North Yorkshire

2 Middlegate ★★★
Contact: Mrs V Punchard
Beckstones, Woodburn Yard, Main Street, Leyburn DL8 3HQ
T: (01969) 650607
E: tpunchard@aol.com

BURTON-IN-LONSDALE
North Yorkshire

Brentwood Farm Cottages ★★★★
Contact: Mrs Anita Taylor
Barnoldswick Lane, Burton-in-Lonsdale LA6 3LZ
T: (015242) 62155
F: (015242) 62155
E: info@brentwoodfarmcottages.co.uk
I: www.brentwoodfarmcottages.co.uk

Greta Cottage ★★★★
Contact: Mrs Jane Burns
Bridge Cottage, Bridge End, Burton in Lonsdale, Carnforth LA6 3LJ
T: (015242) 61081
E: janeandalbanburns@supanet.com

Riverside Cottage ★★★★★
Contact: Ms Patricia Leverton
1 Manor Fold, Bingley BD16 1TE
T: (01274) 560542
E: riversidecott@whsmith.net
I: members.aol.com/riversidecott

BURTON LEONARD
North Yorkshire

Park House Holiday Cottages ★★★★
Contact: Mr Russell Hammond
Park House, Station Lane, Burton Leonard, Harrogate HG3 3RX
T: (01765) 677387
I: www.parkhouseholidays.com

BURYTHORPE
North Yorkshire

Derwent Cottage ★★★★
Contact: Mr Christopher Turner
Low Penhowe, Malton YO17 9LU
T: (01653) 658336
F: (01653) 658619
E: holidaycottages@aol.com

The Granary ★★★★
Contact: Mrs Margaret Raines
The Granary, The Hermitage, Malton YO17 9LF
T: (01653) 658201
E: sallyvaines@btconnect.com
I: www.granaryholidays.co.uk

Primrose Cottage ★★★★
Contact: Mr Christopher Turner
Low Penhowe, Malton YO17 9LU
T: (01653) 658336
F: (01653) 658619
E: holidaycottages@aol.com

Establishments printed in blue have a detailed entry in this guide

YORKSHIRE

CARLETON
North Yorkshire

Ivy Cottage Ref:2713 ★★★
Contact: Ms H Cook
Dales Holiday Cottages, Carleton Business Park, Carleton New Road, Skipton BD23 2AA
T: (01756) 799821
F: (01756) 797012
E: info@dalesholcot.com
I: www.dalesholcot.com

Rombalds Cottage and Crookrise Cottage Ref:786 & 787 ★★★
Contact: Ms H Cook
Dales Holiday Cottages, Carleton Business Park, Carleton New Road, Skipton BD23 2AA
T: (01756) 799821
F: (01756) 797012
E: info@dalesholcot.com
I: www.dalesholcot.com

CARLTON
North Yorkshire

Coverdale Lodge Cottage ★★★★
Contact: Mrs Daphne Joy Beardsmore
Coverdale Lodge, Leyburn DL8 4BA
T: (01969) 640602

CARLTON MINIOTT
North Yorkshire

Holly Barn ★★★★
Contact: Mr William Edward Lawson
Holly House, Thirsk YO7 4NJ
T: (01845) 522099

10 Thirlmere Close
Rating Applied For
Contact: Mrs Joan Pounder
21 Kirkgate, Thirsk YO7 1PL
T: (01845) 511265

CARPERBY
North Yorkshire

Barnbrook Ref:567 ★★★
Contact: Mr S Boardman
Sykes Cottages, York House, York Street, Chester CH1 3LR
T: (01244) 345700
F: (01244) 321442
E: info@sykescottages.co.uk
I: www.sykescottages.co.uk

The Old Post Office ★★★
Contact: Mrs Nadine Bell
Country Hideaways, Margaret's Cottage, Leyburn DL8 4JN
T: (01969) 663559
F: (01969) 663559
E: nadine@countryhideaways.co.uk

Woodsomme Cottage Ref:3305 ★★★★
Contact: Ms H Cook
Dales Holiday Cottages, Carleton Business Park, Carleton New Road, Skipton BD23 2AA
T: (01756) 799821
F: (01756) 797012
E: info@dalesholcot.com
I: www.dalesholcot.com

CATTERICK
North Yorkshire

Gallery Cottage Ref:1993 ★★★
Contact: Ms H Cook
Dales Holiday Cottages, Carleton Business Park, Carleton New Road, Skipton BD23 2AA
T: (01756) 799821
F: (01756) 797012
E: info@dalesholcot.com
I: www.dalesholcot.com

CHAPEL LE DALE
North Yorkshire

Netherscar Ref: 281 ★★
Contact: Mr S Boardman
Sykes Cottages, York House, York Street, Chester CH1 3LR
T: (01244) 345700
F: (01244) 321442
E: info@sykescottages.co.uk
I: www.sykescottages.co.uk

4 Salt Lake Cottages ★★★
Contact: Mrs H.G Lees
Barnstead, New Houses, Settle BD24 0JE
T: (01729) 860485

CHOP GATE
North Yorkshire

Broadfields Cottage ★★★★
Contact: Mrs Judith Staples
Broadfields Cottage, Broadfields, Middlesbrough TS9 7JB
T: (01642) 778384
I: www.diamond.org/broadfields

Lavrock Hall Farmhouse Cottage ★★★
Contact: Mrs Jane Brack
Lavrock Hall Farmhouse Cottage, Bilsdale, Middlesbrough TS9 7LQ
T: (01439) 798275
F: (01439) 798337
E: info@lavrockhall.co.uk
I: www.lavrockhall.co.uk

CLAYTON
West Yorkshire

Brow Top Farm ★★★★★
Contact: Mrs Margaret Priestley
Brow Top Farm, Brow Top, Bandwin Lane, Clayton, Bradford BD14 6PS
T: (01274) 882178
F: (01274) 882178
E: ruthpriestley@farmersweekly.net
I: www.browtopfarm.co.uk

CLOUGHTON
North Yorkshire

Gowland Farm Holiday Cottages ★★★★
Contact: Mrs F J Bull
Gowland Farm Holiday Cottages, Gowland Lane, Scarborough YO13 0DU
T: (01723) 870924
F: (01723) 870524
E: www.gowlandfarm.co.uk

Station House ★★★★
Contact: Mr Steve & Mrs Barbara Hargreaves
Station House, Station Lane, Scarborough YO13 0AD
T: (01723) 870896

COMMONDALE
North Yorkshire

Fowl Green Farm ★★★
Contact: Mrs Susan Muir
Fowl Green Farm, Commondale, Whitby YO21 2HN
T: (01287) 660742
E: info@fowlgreenfarm.com
I: www.fowlgreenfarm.com

CONISBROUGH
South Yorkshire

Cosy Terrace Cottage ★★
Contact: Mr John Perrin
8 Denaby Lane, Doncaster DN12 4LA
T: (01709) 580612
E: john@cosyterrace.fsnet.co.uk
I: www.cosyterrace.fsnet.co.uk

CONONLEY
North Yorkshire

The Cottage Ref:521 ★★★
Contact: Ms H Cook
Dales Holiday Cottages, Carleton Business Park, Carleton New Road, Skipton BD23 2AA
T: (01756) 799821
F: (01756) 797012
E: info@dalesholcot.com
I: www.dalesholcot.com

CONSTABLE BURTON
North Yorkshire

Park Gate Cottage Ref:1785 ★★★★
Contact: Ms H Cook
Dales Holiday Cottages, Carleton Business Park, Carleton New Road, Skipton BD23 2AA
T: (01756) 799821
F: (01756) 797012
E: info@dalesholcot.com
I: www.dalesholcot.com

Sun Hill Cottage & Fextor House ★★★-★★★★
Contact: Mrs Ann Duffield
Fextor House, Market Place, Leyburn DL8 4NP
T: (01677) 450303
F: (01677) 450993
E: ann.duffield@virgin.net
I: www.annduffield.co.uk

COUNTERSETT
North Yorkshire

Bee-Bole Cottage Ref:353 ★★★
Contact: Mr S Boardman
Sykes Cottages, York House, York Street, Chester CH1 3LR
T: (01244) 345700
F: (01244) 321442
E: info@sykescottages.co.uk
I: www.sykescottages.co.uk

COWLING
North Yorkshire

Swallow Cottage Ref:2643 ★★★★
Contact: Ms H Cook
Dales Holiday Cottages, Carleton Business Park, Carleton New Road, Skipton BD23 2AA
T: (01756) 799821
F: (01756) 797012
E: info@dalesholcot.com
I: www.dalesholcot.com

CRAGG VALE
West Yorkshire

Robin Hood Cottage
Rating Applied For
Contact: Mrs Isabel Woznicki
18 Cooperfields, Luddendenfoot, Halifax HX2 6AT
T: (01422) 884840
E: liz@robinhoodcottage.co.uk
I: www.robinhoodcottage.co.uk

Rudd Clough Holiday Cottages ★★★★★
Contact: Mr James & Mrs Juliet Barker
The Old Vicarage, Hebden Bridge HX7 5TB
T: (01422) 882755
F: (01422) 886044
E: james.barker@hemscott.net

CRAKEHALL
North Yorkshire

St Edmund's Country Cottages ★★-★★★★
Contact: Ms Sue Cooper
St Edmund's Country Cottages, St Edmund's, The Green, Bedale DL8 1HP
T: (01677) 423584
F: (01677) 427397
E: stedmundscountrycottages@hotmail.com
I: www.crakehall.org.uk

CROPTON
North Yorkshire

Beckhouse Cottages ★★★★
Contact: Mrs Smith
Beckhouse Farm, Cropton, Pickering YO18 8ER
T: (01751) 417235
F: (01751) 417218
E: beckhousecottages@hotmail.com
I: www.beckhousecottages.co.uk

2 Corner Cottage ★★
Contact: Mrs Mary Rowlands
1 Corner Cottage, Pickering YO18 8HH
T: (01751) 417562
E: Rowlands.mary@talk21.com

High Farm Holiday Cottages ★★★★
Contact: Mrs Ruth Feaster
High Farm Holiday Cottages, High Farm, Pickering YO18 8HL
T: (01751) 417461
E: highfarmcropton@aol.com
I: www.hhml.com/cottages/highfarmcropton.htm

Keldy Forest Cabins
Rating Applied For
Contact: Ms Lisa Milne
Forest Holidays, 231 Corstorphine Road, Edinburgh EH12 7AT
T: (0131) 3146505
I: www.forestholidays.co.uk

YORKSHIRE

DALTON
North Yorkshire
Badgerway Stoop Cottage Ref:3119 ★★★
Contact: Ms H Cook
Dales Holiday Cottages, Carleton Business Park, Carleton New Road, Skipton BD23 2AA
T: (01756) 799821
F: (01756) 797012
E: info@dalesholcot.com
I: www.dalesholcot.com

Hilltop Cottage ★★★★
Contact: Mr Farr
Hilltop Cottage, Richmond DL11 7HU
T: (01833) 621234
F: (01833) 621092
E: hilltopcottage@rfarr.freeserve.co.uk
I: www.hilltopcottage.co.uk

Keepers Cottage ★★★
Contact: Dorothy Lewis
Keepers Cottage, Dalton Hall, Dalton, Richmond DL11 7GU
T: (01833) 621446
E: yaz66@dial.pipex.com

DANBY
North Yorkshire
Ainthorpe Farm Cottage ★★★★
Contact: Mrs Sheila Hide
Ainthorpe Farm House, Easton Lane, Ainthorpe, Whitby YO21 2JW
T: (01287) 660358

Beckwith House ★★★
Contact: Mrs Heather Mather
Davison House, Ainthorpe Lane, Whitby YO21 2NG
T: (01287) 669104
E: chmather@onetel.com

Blackmires Farm ★★★
Contact: Mrs Gillian Rhys
Blackmires Farm, Danby Head, Danby, Whitby YO21 2NN
T: (01287) 660352
E: gl.rhys@freenet.co.uk

Clitherbecks Farm ★★
Contact: Mr Neil Harland
Clitherbecks Farm, Whitby YO21 2NT
T: (01287) 660321
E: nharland@clitherbecks.freeserve.co.uk
I: www.clitherbecks.freeserve.co.uk

Margold Cottage Ref:2505 ★★★
Contact: Ms H Cook
Dales Holiday Cottages, Carleton Business Park, Carleton New Road, Skipton BD23 2AA
T: (01756) 799821
F: (01756) 797012
E: info@dalesholcot.com
I: www.dalesholcot.com

DENBY DALE
West Yorkshire
Ivy Holiday Cottage ★★★
Contact: Ms Susan Tombs
16 Illey Close, Holly Gardens Estate, Birmingham B31 5EW
T: (0121) 4537622

DENHOLME
West Yorkshire
Blacksmith's Cottages ★★
Contact: Mrs Janet Nella Ackroyd
Blacksmith's Cottages, Forge End, 2 Edge Bottom, Bradford BD13 4JW
T: (01274) 832850
F: (01274) 832850

DONCASTER
South Yorkshire
The Green Gable ★★★★
Contact: Mr Smeaton
The Green Gable, 161 Carr House Road, Doncaster DN4 5DP
T: (01302) 327782
F: (01302) 327774
E: qjs@btconnect.com

DOWNHOLME
North Yorkshire
Coldstorms Farm ★★★
Contact: Mrs Diana Greenwood
Walburn Hall, Richmond DL11 6AF
T: (01748) 822152
F: (01748) 822152

DRIFFIELD
East Riding of Yorkshire
Manor Farm Cottages ★★★
Contact: Mr & Mrs Byass
Manor Farm Cottages, North Dalton Manor, North Dalton, Driffield YO25 9UX
T: (01377) 217324
F: (01377) 217840
E: lanpulses@aol.com

DRINGHOUSES
York
Knavesmire Cottage
Rating Applied For
Contact: Mr John Slater
Knavesmire Cottage, 52 Tadcaster Road, York YO24 1LR
T: (01904) 798272

Mayfield
Rating Applied For
Contact: Mrs Joyce Schofield & Mrs Leslie
4 Leadley Croft, York YO23 3YX
T: (01904) 704571
E: davidleslie@mcmail.com
I: www.cottageholidaysonline.co.uk

DUGGLEBY
North Yorkshire
Highbury Farm Cottage ★★★★
Contact: Mr John & Mrs Christine Sawdon
Highbury Farm Cottage, Highbury Farm, Malton YO17 8BN
T: (01944) 738664
E: highburyfarmcott@aol.com
I: www.highbury-farm-holiday-cottage.co.uk

DUNSLEY
North Yorkshire
The Shippon & The Stable Ref:188&1989 ★★★
Contact: Ms H Cook
Dales Holiday Cottages, Carleton Business Park, Carleton New Road, Skipton BD23 2AA
T: (01756) 799821
F: (01756) 797012
E: info@dalesholcot.com
I: www.dalesholcot.com

EASINGWOLD
North Yorkshire
Allerton Cottage ★★★
Contact: Mrs Angela Thornton
Allerton Cottage, 34 Uppleby, York YO61 3BB
T: (01347) 821912

Mooracres Bungalow Ref:753 ★★★
Contact: Ms H Cook
Dales Holiday Cottages, Carleton Business Park, Carleton New Road, Skipton BD23 2AA
T: (01756) 799821
F: (01756) 797012
E: info@dalesholcot.com
I: www.dalesholcot.com

EAST WITTON
North Yorkshire
Wayland Cottage Ref:2379 ★★★
Contact: Ms F Moody
Dales Holiday Cottages, Carleton Business Park, Carleton New Road, Skipton BD23 2AA
T: (01756) 799821
F: (01756) 797012
E: fiona@dalesholcot.com
I: www.dalesholcot.com

EBBERSTON
North Yorkshire
Cliff House ★★★★
Contact: Mr Simon Morris
Cliff House, Scarborough YO13 9PA
T: (01723) 859440
F: (01723) 850005
E: cliffhouseebberston@btinternet.com
I: www.cliffhouse-cottageholidays.co.uk

Cow Pasture and Swallow Tail Cottages ★★★-★★★★
Contact: Mrs Green
Studley House, 67 Main Street, Scarborough YO13 9NR
T: (01723) 859285
F: (01723) 850624
E: ernie@jhodgson.fsnet.co.uk
I: www.studley-house.co.uk

Nesfield Cottage ★★★★
Contact: Mrs Janet Wood
Nesfield Cottage, Ingleside, Burton Road, Annswell, Ashby-De-La-Zouch LE65 2TF
T: (01530) 416094
E: chris.wood4@virgin.net

EGTON
North Yorkshire
Barn Cottages ★★★★
Contact: Mrs Barbara Howard
Deepdale House, Malton YO17 8HX
T: (01944) 758910
F: (01944) 758910
E: enquiries@barncottages.com
I: www.barncottages.com

The Hayloft & Pine Cottage ★★★
Contact: Mrs Hilary Walker
The Nurseries, Whitby YO21 1TT
T: (01947) 895640
E: hilary_phenix@hotamil.com

Westonby Cottage ★★
Contact: Mrs Joan Flintoft
Westonby Farm, Whitby YO21 1UH
T: (01947) 895296

EGTON BRIDGE
North Yorkshire
Broom Cottage ★★★★
Contact: Mrs Maria White
Broom Cottage, Whitby YO21 1XD
T: (01947) 895279
F: (01947) 895657
E: mw@broom-house.co.uk

EMBSAY
North Yorkshire
Elm Garth Cottage ★★★
Contact: Mrs Margaret Mewies
The Craggs, Kirk Lane, Skipton BD23 6SH
T: (01756) 799188
E: m.mewies@talk21.com
I: www.elmgarth.co.uk

FADMOOR
North Yorkshire
North Farm Cottages ★★★★
Contact: Mr David & Mrs Gill Broadbent
North Farm Cottages, North Farm, Main Street, Fadmoor, York YO62 7HY
T: (01751) 431934
F: (01751) 431934

FEIZOR
North Yorkshire
Scar Close Barn Ref:2953 ★★★★
Contact: Ms H Cook
Dales Holiday Cottages, Carleton Business Park, Carleton New Road, Skipton BD23 2AA
T: (01756) 799821
F: (01756) 797012
E: info@dalesholcot.com
I: www.dalesholcot.com

FELLBECK
North Yorkshire
1 and 2 North Oaks Farm Cottages ★★★★
Contact: Mrs Sue Loveless
1 and 2 North Oaks Farm Cottages, North Oaks Farm, Harrogate HG3 5EP
T: (01423) 712446
F: (01423) 712457
E: cottages@loveless.co.uk
I: www.loveless.co.uk

YORKSHIRE

South Oaks Cottage
Ref:3820 ★★★
Contact: Mrs Fiona Moody
Dales Holiday Cottages, Carleton Business Park, Carleton New Road, Skipton BD23 2AA
T: (01756) 790919
F: (01756) 797012
E: fiona@dales-holiday-cottages.com
I: www.dales-holiday-cottages.com

Troutbeck Cottage ★★★★
Contact: Mrs Nelson
Nidderdale Lodge Farm, Harrogate HG3 5EU
T: (01423) 711677

FILEY
North Yorkshire

Baxter House ★★★★
Contact: Mrs Anne Cooper
41 Northstead Manor Drive, Scarborough YO12 6AF
T: (01723) 365263

Beach Holiday Flats
★★-★★★
Contact: Mr David Tindall
9-10 The Beach, Filey YO14 9LA
T: (01723) 513178
E: anntindall@aol.com
I: www.thebeach-holidayflats.co.uk

The Cottages ★★★
Contact: Mr & Mrs David Teet
The Cottages, Muston Grange, Muston Road, Filey YO14 0HU
T: (01723) 516620
F: (01723) 516620
I: www.mustongrangefiley.co.uk

Crescent Apartment ★★★
Contact: Mr Jack Speight
2 Cad Beeston Mews, Leeds LS11 8AF
T: (0113) 277 5853

Ennerdale Holiday Flats
★-★★
Contact: Mr Chris Thompson
Ennerdale Holiday Flats, 31-33 Station Avenue, Filey YO14 9AE
T: (01723) 513798

84 Queen Street ★★★★
Contact: Ms Suzan Brown
26 Church Close, Chesterfield S42 6QA
T: (01246) 200780
I: www.filey.biz

FITLING
East Riding of Yorkshire

Stables Cottage ★★★★
Contact: Mrs Patricia Cockshutt
Fitling Garth, Humbleton Road, Hull HU12 9AJ
I: www.scope.karoo.net/fitling

FOLLIFOOT
North Yorkshire

Marlin Cottage ★★★★
Contact: Mrs Evelyn Clayton
Crimple Lane, Harrogate HG3 1DF
T: (01423) 883696
E: clayton.clayton@virgin.net

FRAISTHORPE
East Riding of Yorkshire

North Kingsfield Holiday Cottages ★★★★-★★★★★
Contact: Mr & Mrs Milner
North Kingsfield Holiday Cottages, North Kingsfield Farm, Bridlington YO15 3QP
T: (01262) 673743
E: helen@northkingsfield.co.uk
I: www.northkingsfield.co.uk

FYLINGDALES
North Yorkshire

Demesne Farm ★★★★
Contact: Mr Alan & Mrs June Bancroft
Demesne Farm, Whitby YO22 4QF
T: (01947) 880448
E: jhb49@hotmail.com
I: www.demesnefarm.co.uk

Swallows Cottage & The Granary ★★★
Contact: Mrs Adele Thompson
Whitby Holiday Cottages, 47 Flowergate, Whitby YO21 3BB
T: (01947) 603010
F: (01947) 821133
E: enquiries@whitby-cottages.co.uk
I: www.whitby-cottages.co.uk

FYLINGTHORPE
North Yorkshire

Croft Farm Cottage ★★★
Contact: Mrs Joanne Braithwaite
Croft Farm Cottage, Croft Farm, Church Lane, Fylingthorpe, Whitby YO22 4PW
T: (01947) 880231
F: (01947) 880231
E: croftfarmbb@aol.com
I: www.robinhoodsbay.co.uk/croftfarm

The Peat House ★★★★
Contact: Mrs Adele Thompson
Whitby Holiday Cottages, 47 Flowergate, Whitby YO21 3BB
T: (01947) 603010
F: (01947) 821133
E: enquiries@whitby-cottages.co.uk
I: www.whitby-cottages.co.uk

GARTON-ON-THE-WOLDS
East Riding of Yorkshire

Rolella ★★★
Contact: Mr Garvey
10 Main Street, Garton-on-the-Wolds, Driffield YO25 3ET
T: (01377) 253656 & 257570
F: (01377) 241408
E: stella@sssiteservices.co.uk

GAYLE
North Yorkshire

Aysgill Cottage ★★★
Contact: Mrs Deborah Allen
Aysgill Cottage, Scaur Head Farm, Hawes DL8 3SF
T: (01969) 667477

Foss Cottage ★★★
Contact: Mrs Brenda Watering
Foss Cottage, Force Head Farm, Hawes DL8 3RZ
T: (01969) 667518
F: (01969) 667518

Gayle Farmhouse ★★
Contact: Ms H Cook
Dales Holiday Cottages, Ref:636, Carleton Business Park, Carleton New Road, Skipton BD23 2AA
T: (01756) 799821
F: (01756) 797012
I: www.dalesholcot.com

GIGGLESWICK
North Yorkshire

Bookend Cottage Ref: 713 ★★★
Contact: Mr S Boardman
Sykes Cottages, York House, York Street, Chester CH1 3LR
T: (01244) 345700
F: (01244) 321442
E: info@sykescottages.co.uk
I: www.sykescottages.co.uk

Close House Cottage Holidays ★★★★
Contact: Mrs Sue Hargreaves
Close House Cottage Holidays, Close House, Settle BD24 0EA
T: (01729) 822778
F: (01729) 822778
E: chcottages@aol.com
I: www.close-house.co.uk

Foxholes Lodge ★★★
Contact: Mrs Lynn Scruton
Foxholes Lodge, Station Road, Settle BD24 0AB
T: (01729) 823505
F: (01729) 823505

2 Gildersleets ★★★★
Contact: Griffiths
9 Polefield Road, Manchester M9 6FN
T: (0161) 7959713
F: (0161) 6536570
E: doctor.g@gconnect.com

Ivy Cottage ★★★★
Contact: Fiona Moody
Dales Holiday Cottages, Ref:629, Carleton Business Park, Carleton New Road, Skipton BD23 2AA
T: (01756) 799821
F: (01756) 797012
I: www.dalesholcot.com

Rowan House, Willow Cottage Ref: 398&652 ★★★★
Contact: Mr S Boardman
Sykes Cottages, York House, York Street, Chester CH1 3LR
T: (01244) 345700
F: (01244) 321442
E: info@sykescottages.co.uk
I: www.sykescottages.co.uk

Stanton Cottage ★★★
Contact: Mrs Alison Boswell
3 Bankwell Close, Settle BD24 0BX
T: (01729) 822400
F: (01729) 822400
E: pboswell@ukonline.co.uk

Sutcliffe Cottage Ref: 31 ★★
Contact: Mr S Boardman
Sykes Cottages, York House, York Street, Chester CH1 3LR
T: (01244) 345700
F: (01244) 321442
E: info@sykescottages.co.uk
I: www.sykescottages.co.uk

GILLAMOOR
North Yorkshire

Gales House Farm ★★★★
Contact: Mr & Ms David & Kathy Ward
Gales House Farm, Kirkby Lane, York YO62 7HT
T: (01751) 431258
F: 0705 0 650741
E: ward@galeshousefarm.freeserve.co.uk
I: www.gillamoor.com

Hen House ★★★★★
Contact: Mr Stephen & Mrs Georgina Hackett
Hen House, Church View, Main Street, York YO62 7HX
T: (01751) 430135

GILLING EAST
North Yorkshire

Sunset Cottages
★★★-★★★★
Contact: Mr & Mrs Kelsey
Sunset Cottages, Grimston Manor Farm, York YO62 4HR
T: (01347) 888654
F: (01347) 888347
E: info@sunsetcottages.co.uk
I: www.sunsetcottages.co.uk

GILLING WEST
North Yorkshire

Gilling Old Mill Cottages ★★★★
Contact: Mr Hugh & Mrs Joyce Bird
Gilling Old Mill Cottages, Waters Lane, Gilling West, Richmond DL10 5JD
T: (01748) 822771
F: (01748) 821734
E: admin@yorkshiredales-cottages.com
I: www.yorkshiredales-cottages.com

GILSTEAD
West Yorkshire

Thimble, Bobbin & Shuttle
★★★-★★★★
Contact: Mrs L Jean Warin
March Cote Farm, Lee Lane, Bingley BD16 1UB
T: (01274) 487433
F: (01274) 561074
E: jean.warin@nevisuk.net
I: www.yorkshirenet.co.uk/accgde/marchcote

GLAISDALE
North Yorkshire

Lanes Cottage ★★
Contact: Mr John & Mrs Nancy Dale
Lanes Cottage, Whitby YO21 2PS
T: (01947) 897316

London Lodge ★★★
Contact: Mrs Mary Danaher
London Lodge, London House Farm, Whitby YO21 2PZ
T: (01947) 897166
F: (01947) 897166
E: gdanaherg@aol.com
I: www.londonhousefarm.com

YORKSHIRE

The Studio Flat ★★★★
Contact: Mr John & Mrs Mary Thompson
The Studio Flat, Postgate Farm, Whitby YO21 2PZ
T: (01947) 897353
F: (01947) 897353
E: j-m.thompson.bandb@talk21.com
I: www.eskvalley.com/postgate/postgate.html

Tailors Cottage Ref:457 ★★★
Contact: Mr S Boardman
Sykes Cottages, York House, York Street, Chester CH1 3LR
T: (01244) 345700
F: (01244) 321442
E: info@sykescottages.co.uk
I: www.sykescottages.co.uk

Underhill Cottage ★★★★
Contact: Mrs Vanessa Hicking
Whitby Holiday Cottages, 47 Flowergate, Whitby YO21 3BB
T: (01947) 603010
F: (01947) 6821133
E: enquiries@whitby-cottages.co.uk
I: www.whitby-cottages.co.uk

GOATHLAND
North Yorkshire

Eskholme ★★★★
Contact: Mrs Jim Hodgson
Woodlands, 31 Shillbank View, Mirfield WF14 0QG
T: (01924) 498154
E: ffsjan@aol.com

14 Oakfield Avenue ★★★
Contact: Mrs Adele Thompson
Whitby Holiday Cottages, 47 Flowergate, Whitby YO21 3BB
T: (01947) 603010
F: (01947) 821133
E: enquiries@whitby-cottages.co.uk
I: www.whitby-cottages.co.uk

Orchard Cottage Ref:1418 ★★★★★
Contact: Miss Fiona Moody
Dales Holiday Cottages, Carleton Business Park, Carleton New Road, Skipton BD23 2AA
T: (01756) 799821
F: (01756) 797012
E: info@dalesholcot.com
I: www.theorchardcottages.co.uk

The Stone Cottage ★★★
Contact: Dales Holiday Cottages
Carleton Business Park, Sandylands Business Centre, Carleton N, Skipton BD23 2DG
T: (01756) 799821
F: (01756) 799821

Woodpecker Cottage Ref:3125 ★★★★
Contact: Ms F Moody
Dales Holiday Cottages, Carleton Business Park, Carleton New Road, Skipton BD23 2AA
T: (01756) 799821
F: (01756) 797012
E: fiona@dalesholcot.com
I: www.dalesholcot.com

GOXHILL
North Lincolnshire

Butters Wood Holiday Cottage
Rating Applied For
Contact: Mrs Marshall
Larch Lodge, Howe Lane, Barrow upon Humber DN19 7JG
T: (01469) 530644

GRASSINGTON
North Yorkshire

The Barn ★★★★
Contact: Mrs Gail Evans
The Outpost, Sedber Lane, Skipton BD23 5LQ
T: (01756) 753390
E: grassington@ukonline.co.uk
I: www.dalestay.co.uk/thebarn

The Coach House Ref:3176 ★★★
Contact: Ms H Cook
Dales Holiday Cottages, Carleton Business Park, Carleton New Road, Skipton BD23 2AA
T: (01756) 799821
F: (01756) 797012
E: info@dalesholcot.com
I: www.dalesholcot.com

Garrs House Apartment ★★★
Contact: Mr Malcolm & Mrs Ann Wadsworth
25 Watson Road, Blackpool FY4 1EG
T: (01253) 404726
E: mw001F3365@blueyonder.co.uk

6A Garrs Lane ★★★
Contact: Mr Borrill
The Fish Shop, Garrs Lane, Grassington, Skipton BD23 5AT
T: 07709 313716
E: paborrill@supanet.com
I: www.grassingtonapartment.co.uk

Manna Cottage ★★★★
Contact: Mrs Sheila Carr
Moor Green Farm, Tarns Lane, Threshfield, Skipton BD23 5NR
T: (01756) 752435
F: (01756) 752435
E: carr@totalise.co.uk
I: www.yorkshirenet.co.uk/stayat/mannacottage

Riverside ★★★
Contact: Mrs Marilyn Brown
Riverside, 12 Bridge End, Skipton BD23 5NH
T: (01756) 753886
I: www.dales.accommodation.com

Sunnyside Cottage ★★★★
Contact: Mrs Carolyn Butt
Garris Lodge, Rylstone, Skipton BD23 6LJ
T: (01756) 730391 & 07720 294391
E: info@cosycottages.com
I: www.cosycottages.com

Theatre Cottage Ref:2214 ★★★
Contact: Ms H Cook
Dales Holiday Cottages, Carleton Business Park, Carleton New Road, Skipton BD23 2AA
T: (01756) 799821
F: (01756) 797012
E: info@dalesholcot.com
I: www.dalesholcot.com

Wellhead Cottage & Hilltop Fold Cottage ★★★★
Contact: Mr & Mrs Lesley Halliday
Halliday Holidays, P O Box 177, Leeds LS18 5WZ
T: (0113) 258 4212
F: (0113) 2819455
E: lesleyhalliday@hotmail.com

GREAT AYTON
North Yorkshire

Flat 2 ★★
Contact: Mrs Metcalfe
89 Newton Road, Middlesbrough TS9 6DY
T: (01642) 722935

Mallard Cottage ★★★
Contact: Mr Esmond Watson
Great Ayton Holiday Cottages Ltd, 28 Battersby Junction, Middlesbrough TS9 6LS
T: (01642) 711459
F: (01642) 241368

The Old Stables ★★★★
Contact: Mrs Catherine Hawman
Park House, Easby Hall, Easby, Great Ayton TS9 6JQ
T: (01642) 722560
E: theoldstables@btopenworld.com

The Stable Cottage Ref: 3490 ★★★
Contact: Miss Fiona Moody
Dales Holiday Cottages, Carleton Business Park, Carleton New Road, Skipton BD23 2AA
T: (01756) 799821
E: info@dalesholcot.com

GREAT EDSTONE
North Yorkshire

Cowldyke Farm ★★★-★★★★★
Contact: Mrs Janet Benton
Cowldyke Farm, Salton Road, York YO62 6PE
T: (01751) 431242
E: info@cowldyke-farm.co.uk
I: www.cowldyke-farm.co.uk

GREAT LANGTON
North Yorkshire

Stanhow Bungalow ★★★★
Contact: Mary Furness
Stanhow Farm, Great Langton, Northallerton DL7 0TJ
T: (01609) 748614
F: (01609) 748614
E: mary.stanhow@freenet.co.uk

GREETLAND
West Yorkshire

The Barn, Lower High Trees Farm ★★★
Contact: Mrs Kate Griffiths
The Barn, Lower High Trees Farm, High Trees Lane, Halifax HX4 8PP
T: (01422) 375205
F: (01422) 375205
E: griffs@freeuk.com
I: www.greetland.org.uk

GREWELTHORPE
North Yorkshire

Crown Cottage Ref:718 ★★★
Contact: Ms H Cook
Dales Holiday Cottages, Carleton Business Park, Carleton New Road, Skipton BD23 2AA
T: (01756) 799821
F: (01756) 797012
E: info@dalesholcot.com
I: www.dalesholcot.com

Sunnyside Cottage ★★★★
Contact: Mrs Jane Shuttleworth
224 Bradway Road, Sheffield S17 4PE
T: (0114) 235 2783

GRINDALE
East Riding of Yorkshire

Smithy Cottage ★★★★
Contact: Mrs Charlotte Davey
The Forge, 7 Front Street, Bridlington YO16 4XU
T: (01262) 602367
E: scjrm@msn.com
I: www.smithycottage.moonfruit.com

GRISTHORPE
North Yorkshire

Anchorage Holiday Flats ★★
Contact: Mr John Haywood
Anchorage Holiday Flats, 11 The Beach, Filey YO14 9LA
T: (01723) 513805

Dove Cottage Ref:3035 ★★★★
Contact: Ms H Cook
Dales Holiday Cottages, Carleton Business Park, Carleton New Road, Skipton BD23 2AA
T: (01756) 799821
F: (01756) 797012
E: info@dalesholcot.com
I: www.dalesholcot.com

GRISTHORPE BAY
North Yorkshire

58 Clarence Drive ★★★
Contact: Mrs Mary Graves
5 Whiston Drive, Filey YO14 0DB
T: (01723) 512791
E: graves19@freeserve.co.uk
I: www.fileybungalow.com

St Kitts ★★★★
Contact: Mrs K Rook
Manor House Farm, York YO43 4XE
T: (01430) 827661
I: www.stkittsselfcateringholidayflats.co.uk

Establishments printed in blue have a detailed entry in this guide

YORKSHIRE

GROSMONT
North Yorkshire

East Farm Cottage ★★★
Contact: Mrs Adele Thompson
Whitby Holiday Cottages, 47 Flowergate, Whitby YO21 3BB
T: (01947) 603010
F: (01947) 821133
E: enquiries@whitby-cottages.co.uk
I: www.whitby-cottages.co.uk

Engineman's Lodge ★★
Contact: Mrs Adele Thompson
Whitby Holiday Cottages, 47 Flowergate, Whitby YO21 3BB
T: (01947) 603010
F: (01947) 821133
E: enquiries@whitby-cottages.co.uk
I: www.whitby-cottages.co.uk

Porter's Lodge ★★
Contact: Mrs Adele Thompson
Whitby Holiday Cottages, 47 Flowergate, Whitby YO21 3BB
T: (01947) 603010
F: (01947) 821133
E: enquiries@whitby-cottages.co.uk
I: www.whitby-cottages.co.uk

Signalman's Lodge ★★
Contact: Mrs Adele Thompson
Whitby Holiday Cottages, 47 Flowergate, Whitby YO21 3BB
T: (01947) 603010
F: (01947) 821133
E: enquiries@whitby-cottages.co.uk
I: www.whitby-cottages.co.uk

Valley View Cottage ★★★★
Contact: Mrs Maggie Andrews
5 New Houses, Eskdaleside, Whitby YO22 5PP
T: (01582) 462157
E: magsandrews@hotmail.com
I: www.valleyviewcottage.co.uk

GUNNERSIDE
North Yorkshire

Appletons ★★★★
Contact: Mr John Burnham
Great Becketts, Duddenhoe End Road, Arkesden, Saffron Walden CB11 4HG
T: (01799) 550661

Croft Cottage ★★
Contact: Mrs Margaret Batty
Croft House, Low Row, Gunnerside, Richmond DL11 6ND
T: (01748) 886460
I: yorkshirecottage.org.uk

Dene Holme ★★★★
Contact: Mrs Annie Porter
Oxnop Hall, Richmond DL11 6JJ
T: (01748) 886253
F: (01748) 886253

Dufton House ★★★★
Contact: Mrs Annie Porter
Oxnop Hall, Richmond DL11 6JJ
T: (01748) 886253
F: (01748) 886253

High Oxnop ★★★★
Contact: Mrs Annie Porter
Oxnop Hall, Richmond DL11 6JJ
T: (01748) 886253
F: (01748) 886253

Sundale ★★
Contact: Mr Wales
Holiday Cottages (Yorkshire) Ltd, Water Street, Skipton BD23 1PB
T: (01756) 700510
E: brochure@holidaycotts.co.uk
I: www.holidaycotts.co.uk

HACKNESS
North Yorkshire

Poachers ★★★★
Contact: Mr & Mrs Howarth
Poachers, Hunters Cottage, Wrench Green, Hackness, Scarborough YO13 9AB
T: (01723) 882266
E: robert.elaine@lineone.net
I: www.cottageguide.co.uk/poachers

HALIFAX
West Yorkshire

Cherry Tree Cottages ★★★★
Contact: Stan & Elaine Shaw
Cherry Tree Cottages, Wall Nook, Barkisland, Halifax HX4 0BL
T: (01422) 372662
F: (01422) 372662
E: cherrytree@yorkshire-cottages.co.uk
I: www.yorkshire-cottages.co.uk

The Fall ★★★★
Contact: Mrs Ann Knight
4 Lane Ends, Halifax HX3 7UW
T: (01422) 363346

Nina's Cottage ★★★
Contact: Mr Kevin Hellowell
The Barn Moorside, Old Lindley, Holywell Green, Halifax HX4 9DF

HAMBLETON
North Yorkshire

Casten Cottage Ref:549 ★★★
Contact: Mr S Boardman
Sykes Cottages, York House, York Street, Chester CH1 3LR
T: (01244) 345700
F: (01244) 321442
E: info@sykescottages.co.uk
I: www.sykescottages.co.uk

HARMBY
North Yorkshire

1,2,3 and 4 Harmby Grange Cottages ★★★★
Contact: Dales Holiday Cottages, Carleton Business Park, New Road, Skipton BD23 2AA
T: (01756) 799821
F: (01756) 790919

Hillfoot House ★★★★
Contact: Mrs Gertrud Jones
Hillfoot House, Hillfoot, Leyburn DL8 5PH
T: (01969) 623632

Park Grange Cottage Farm ★★
Contact: Miss Pamela Sheppard
Low Gill Farm, Leyburn DL8 4TN
T: (01969) 640258
E: pamsheppardlgf@aol.com

HARROGATE
North Yorkshire

Apartment 1, Holmedale ★★★★
Contact: Mr Graham & Mrs Amanda Lloyd
Apartments of Distinction, Muncaster House, 18 Swan Road, Harrogate HG1 2SA
T: (01423) 538742
F: (01423) 538765
E: amanda@lloyd379.freeserve.co.uk
I: www.harrogateholidayapartments.co.uk

Apartments of Distinction ★★★★
Contact: Graham and Amanda Lloyd
Muncaster House, 18 Swan Road, Harrogate HG1 2SA
T: (01423) 538742
F: (01423) 538765
E: info@harrogateholidayapartments.co.uk
I: www.harrogateholidayapartments.co.uk

Ashness Apartments ★★★★
Contact: Mr Spinlove & Miss H Spinlove
Ashness Apartments, 15 St Marys Avenue, Harrogate HG2 0LP
T: (01423) 526894
F: (01423) 700038
E: office@ashness.com
I: www.ashness.com

Astoria Cottage ★★★★
Contact: Mr Joe & Mrs Ellen McCullogh
Astoria Cottage, 43 Kent Road, Harrogate HG1 2EU
T: (01423) 560223
E: Innuk@hotmail.com

Brimham Rocks Cottages ★★★★
Contact: Mrs Martin
Brimham Rocks Cottages, High North Farm, Fellbeck, Harrogate HG3 5EY
T: (01765) 620284
F: (01765) 620477
E: brimham@nascr.net
I: www.brimham.co.uk

Cheltenham Apartments ★★★
Contact: Mr Andrew Moss
20 Hollins Lane, Harrogate HG3 2EF
T: (01423) 770864
F: (01423) 770864
E: andrew_moss@ic24.net

days2go.com ★★★★
Contact: Mrs Kish
days2go.com, Harrogate
T: (01423) 780661
F: (01423) 780661
E: info@days2go.com
I: www.days2go.com

Dinmore Cottages ★★★★
Contact: Mrs Susan Chapman
Dovecote Cottage, Dinmore House, Pateley Bridge Road, Burnt Yates, Harrogate HG3 3ET
T: (01423) 770860
F: (01423) 770860
E: aib@dinmore-cottages.freeserve.co.uk
I: www.dinmore-cottages.co.uk

Duchy Mews ★★★★
Contact: Mrs Sandra Sykes
Duchy Mews, 16 Duchy Road, Harrogate HG1 2EP
T: (01423) 565109
E: sandra.sykes@btopenworld.com

Flat 1 ★★★★
Contact: Mrs Pamela Wright
Applegarth House, Sleingford Grange, Ripon HG4 3HX
T: (01765) 635367

Harrogate Holiday Cottages ★★★
Contact: Mrs Alison Hartwell
Harrogate Holiday Cottages, Crimple Head House, Beckwithshaw, Harrogate HG3 1QU
T: (01423) 523333
F: (01423) 526683
E: info@harrogateholidays.co.uk
I: www.harrogateholidays.co.uk

Holly House Farm Cottages ★★★
Contact: Miss Mary Owen
Holly House Farm Cottages, Holly House Farm, Moorcock Lane, Darley, Harrogate HG3 2QL
T: (01423) 780266
F: (01423) 780299
E: hollyhousecottages@supanet.com
I: www.hollyhousecottages.co.uk

Holmedale - Apartment 2 Rating Applied For
Contact: Mr Graham Lloyd
Apartments of Distinction, Muncaster House, 18 Swan Road, Harrogate HG1 2SA
T: (01423) 538742
F: (01423) 538765
E: amanda@lloyd379.freeserve.co.uk
I: www.harrogateholidayapartments.co.uk

Moor View Cottage ★★★
Contact: Mrs Sweeting
45 Kingsley Drive, Harrogate HG1 4TH
T: (01423) 885498
I: www.mvcottage.netfirms.com

Old Swan View ★★★★
Contact: Mr Graham & Mrs Amanda Lloyd
Apartments of Distinction, Muncaster House, 18 Swan Road, Harrogate HG1 2SA
T: (01423) 538742
F: (01423) 538765
E: amanda@lloyd379.freeserve.co.uk
I: www.harrogateholidayapartments.co.uk

YORKSHIRE

Regent Cottage ★★★★
Contact: Mr Robert Blake
1A Moorfield Road, Woodbridge
IP12 4JN
T: (01394) 382565
E: deben@btclick.com

Rudding Estate Cottages ★★★
Contact:
Rudding Estate Cottages, Haggs Farm, Haggs Road, Follifoot, Harrogate HG3 1EQ
T: (01423) 844844
F: (01423) 844803
E: info@rudding.com
I: www.rudding.com

Rudding Holiday Park ★★★
Contact: Mr Martin Hutchinson
Rudding Park, Harrogate
HG3 1JH
T: (01423) 870439
F: (01423) 870859
E: holiday-park@ruddingpark.com
I: www.ruddingpark.com

Strawberry House
Rating Applied For
Contact: Mrs Alison Hartwell
Harrogate Holiday Cottages, Crimple Head House, Harrogate HG3 1QU
T: (01423) 523333
E: bookings@harrogateholidays.co.uk

Studley View Apartment
Rating Applied For
Contact: Mrs Amanda Lloyd
Apartments of Distinction, Muncaster House, 18 Swan Road, Harrogate HG1 2SA
T: (01423) 538742
F: (01423) 538765

HARTON
North Yorkshire

W Todd & Sons ★★★
Contact: Mr & Mrs Todd
W Todd & Sons, York YO60 7NP
T: (01904) 468487
F: (01904) 468487
E: colin.todd@ukgateway.com
I: www.visityorkshire.com

HARTWITH
North Yorkshire

Cow Close Barn ★★★★
Contact: Mrs Diana Kitzing
Cow Close Barn, Stripe Lane, Harrogate HG3 3EY
T: (01423) 770850
F: (01423) 770993
E: rainerkitzing@aol.com
I: www.cowclose-barn.co.uk

HATFIELD WOODHOUSE
South Yorkshire

Cosy Executive Accommodation ★★★
Contact: Mr John Perrin
8 Denaby Lane, Doncaster
DN12 4LA
T: (01709) 580612
F: (01709) 585149
E: john@cosyterrace.fsnet.co.uk
I: www.cosyexecutive.fsnet.co.uk

HAWES
North Yorkshire

Chapel House Ref:2320 ★★★
Contact: Ms H Cook
Dales Holiday Cottages, Carleton Business Park, Carleton New Road, Skipton BD23 2AA
T: (01756) 799821
F: (01756) 797012
E: info@dalesholcot.com
I: www.dalesholcot.com

Cherry Tree Cottage ★★★
Contact: Mrs Nadine Bell
Country Hideaways, Margaret's Cottage, Leyburn DL8 4JN
T: (01969) 663559
F: (01969) 663559
E: nadine@countryhideaways.co.uk
I: www.countryhideaways.co.uk

Gaudy House Farm ★★★
Contact: Mrs Jane Allison
Gaudy House Farm, Hawes
DL8 3NA
T: (01969) 667231
I: www.gaudyhousefarm.co.uk

Jane Ann Cottage ★★
Contact: Mrs E Irene Sunter
Overdales View, Simonstone, Hawes DL8 3LY
T: (01969) 667186
E: irene.sunter@tiscali.co.uk
I: www.cloud-nine.org.uk/dales

Mile House Farm Country Cottages ★★★★
Contact: Mrs Anne Fawcett
Mile House Farm, Hawes
DL8 3PT
T: (01969) 667481
F: (01969) 667425
E: milehousefarm@hotmail.com
I: www.wensleydale.uk.com

Sandy Sike ★★★
Contact: Mrs Margaret Hill
Widdale Foot, Hawes DL8 3LX
T: (01969) 667383
F: (01969) 667417
E: widdalefoot@talk21.com
I: www.wensleydale.org

Yore View ★★★
Contact: Mrs Elizabeth Pedley
Yore House, Sedbergh LA10 5PX
T: (01969) 667358
E: yoreviewcottage@talk21.com

Yorkshire Dales Country Cottages ★★★-★★★★
Contact: Mrs Brenda Stott
Yorkshire Dales Country Cottages, Shaw Ghyll, High Shaw, Simonstone, Hawes
DL8 3LY
T: (01969) 667359
F: (01969) 667894
E: rogerstott@aol.com
I: www.yorkshirenet.co.uk/accgde/ydcotts.htm

HAWKSWICK
North Yorkshire

Redmire Farm ★★★★★
Contact: Mr Neil Tomlinson
Shaw Farm, Shaw Lane, Oxenhope BD22 9QL
T: (01535) 648791
F: (01535) 643671
E: neil@mckeighley.co.uk
I: www.redmire-farm.com

HAWORTH
West Yorkshire

Balcony Farm ★★★★
Contact: Mrs Raine
Balcony Farm, Balcony, Keighley
BD22 8QR
T: (01535) 643627

Bottoms Farm Cottages ★★★★
Contact: Mrs Littler
Bottoms Farm Cottages, Grey Stones Lane, Keighley BD22 0QD
T: (01535) 607720
F: (01535) 607720
I: www.bottomsfarm.co.uk

Bronte Country Cottages ★★★-★★★★
Contact: Ms Clare Pickles
Bronte Country Cottages, Westfield Farm, Tim Lane, Haworth, Keighley BD22 7SA
T: (01535) 644568
F: (01535) 646686
E: clare@brontecountrycottages.co.uk
I: www.brontecountrycottages.co.uk

Heathcliffe Cottage ★★★★
Contact: Mrs Vicky Walker
35 Norr Lane, Bradford
BD15 0DL
T: 0798 9 557201
F: 0798 9 557201

Heather, Bilberry Cottage ★★★★
Contact: Mrs Janet Milner
Heather, Bilberry Cottage, Hole Farm, Hole, Haworth, Keighley
BD22 8QT
T: (01535) 644755
F: (01535) 644755
E: janet@bronteholidays.co.uk
I: www.bronteholidays.co.uk

Heron Cottage ★★★★
Contact: Mr Richard & Mrs Jan Walker
Heron Cottage, Vale Barn, Mytholmes Lane, Haworth, Keighley BD22 0EE
T: (01535) 648537
E: jan_w@tinyworld.com

Hewenden Mill Cottages ★★★★
Contact: Mrs Janet Emanuel, W Lancaster & Co Ltd, Hewenden Mill, Cullingworth, Bradford BD13 5BP
T: (01535) 274259
F: (01535) 273943
E: info@hewendenmillcottages.co.uk
I: www.hewendenmillcottages.co.uk

Little Nook ★★★
Contact: Mr Anton & Mrs Sheila Murray
50 West Lane, Keighley
BD22 8DU
T: (01535) 607013
F: (01535) 690110
E: info@littlenook.co.uk
I: www.littlenook.co.uk

Penny Cottage ★★★
Contact: Ms Lynn Majakas & Mrs Sara Packham
5 Charles Court, Station Road, Oxenhope, Keighley BD22 9HG
T: (01535) 647796
E: pennycottage@haworth-cottage.co.uk
I: www.haworth-cottage.co.uk

September Cottage ★★★★
Contact: Mrs Joy Page
Heathcliff, Providence Lane, Oakworth, Keighley BD22 7QR
T: (01535) 644091
E: robjoypagecromer@supanet.com

Spring Cottage Ref:2389 ★★★
Contact: Ms H Cook
Dales Holiday Cottages, Carleton Business Park, Carleton New Road, Skipton BD23 2AA
T: (01756) 799821
F: (01756) 797012
E: info@dalesholcot.com
I: www.dalesholcot.com

Tanera Ref:751 ★★★
Contact: Ms H Cook
Dales Holiday Cottages, Carleton Business Park, Carleton New Road, Skipton BD23 2AA
T: (01756) 799821
F: (01756) 797012
E: info@dalesholcot.com
I: www.dalesholcot.com

Weavers Cottage and Loft ★★★
Contact: Gaye Bond
Latch Cottage, Lyon Road, Keighley BD20 8UY
T: (01535) 211184
E: g.j.bond@blueyonder.co.uk
I: www.weaverscottage-web.co.uk

Woolcombers Cottage ★★★
Contact: Ms Kay Doyle Johnson
276 Broad Street, San Luis Obispo, Wokingham 93405
T: (01535) 646778
E: woolcombers@clara.co.uk
I: www.bronte-country.com/accomm/woolcombers

HAWSKER
North Yorkshire

Ling Hill Farm ★★
Contact: Mr Tordoff and Miss A Trotter
Ling Hill Farm, Whitby Laithes, Whitby YO22 4JY
T: (01947) 603914

Summerfield Cottage ★★★★
Contact: Mr Richard Noble & Ms Jayne Williams
Summerfield Farm, Whitby
YO22 4LA
T: (01947) 602677
F: (01947) 602677
E: info@summerfieldfarm.co.uk
I: www.summerfieldfarm.co.uk

Establishments printed in blue have a detailed entry in this guide

YORKSHIRE

West End Farm Cottage Ref:1228 ★★★★
Contact: Ms F Moody
Dales Holiday Cottages, Carleton Business Park, Carleton New Road, Skipton BD23 2AA
T: (01756) 799821
F: (01756) 797012
E: fiona@dalesholcot.com
I: www.dalesholcot.com

HEALEY
North Yorkshire

Grange End. Ref (3446) ★★★
Contact: Ms H Cook
Dales Holiday Cottages, Carleton Business Park, Carleton New Road, Skipton BD23 2AA
T: (01756) 799821
F: (01756) 790919
E: info@dalesholcot.com
I: www.dalesholcot.com

HEATON
West Yorkshire

Honeysuckle Cottage ★★★
Contact: Mrs Pamela Stobart
29 Haworth Road, Bradford BD9 5PB
T: (01274) 541181
F: (01274) 496169

HEBDEN
North Yorkshire

High Dene House Ref:3503 ★★★★
Contact: Ms H Cook
Dales Holiday Cottages, Carleton Business Park, Carleton New Road, Skipton BD23 2AA
T: (01756) 799821
F: (01756) 797012
E: info@dalesholcot.com
I: www.dalesholcot.com

HEBDEN BRIDGE
West Yorkshire

3 Birks Hall Cottage ★★★
Contact: Mrs Wilkinson
1 Birks Hall Cottage, Upper Birks, Cragg Vale, Hebden Bridge HX7 5SB
T: (01422) 882064

Lumb Cottage ★★★
Contact: Mrs Maureen Audsley
14 Myrtle Grove, Hebden Bridge HX7 8HL
T: (01422) 846078
E: myrtlegrove@btinternet.com
I: www.myrtlegrove.btinternet.co.uk

15 Oldgate ★★★
Contact: Mrs Jan Barker
Cobweb Cottage, Banks Farm, Hebden Bridge HX7 5RF
T: (01422) 845929
F: (01422) 846354
E: janatcobweb@aol.com

HELMSLEY
North Yorkshire

Beadlam Farm Cottage ★★★
Contact: Mrs Jenny Rooke
Beadlam Farm Cottage, Beadlam Grange, York YO62 7TD
T: (01439) 770303
E: mark.rooke@farming.co.uk
I: www.farmstayuk.co.uk

Bell Cottage ★★★
Contact: Mrs Liz Hudson-Forster
Low House, Slingsby Walk, Harrogate HG2 7RZ
T: (01423) 884774

Bondgate Flat ★★★★
Contact: Mrs Margaret Kilby
The Bungalow, Langton Road, Malton YO17 9PX
T: (01653) 691576
F: (01653) 691576
E: wakilby@tiscali.co.uk

Church View ★★★★
Contact: Mrs Sally Ann Foster
Chestnut Tree Farm, Doncaster Road, Thrybergh, Rotherham S65 4NS
T: (01709) 852929
E: sally.f@ntlworld.com
I: www.foster1.force9.co.uk

Fleur-de-lys ★★★★
Contact: Mrs Pat Anderson
Mrs Anderson's Country Cottages, Boonhill Cottage, Pickering YO18 8QF
T: (01751) 472172
F: (01751) 472172
E: bookings@boonhill69.freeserve.co.uk
I: www.swiftlink.pnc-uk.net/sc/1236a.htm

Honeysuckle Cottage ★★★
Contact: Mrs Margaret Stringer
Cornfield House, Bransdale, York YO62 7JW
T: (01751) 431983
E: stringer@cornfield.go-legend.net

Osbourne & Orchard Cottage ★★★
Contact: Miss Wilcox & Mrs J Beckwith
Nice Things Cafe, 10 Market Place, York YO62 5BL
T: (01439) 770632
F: (01439) 770632
I: www.castlecottages.com

Rose Beck ★★★★
Contact: Ms Steph Woolhouse
9 Main Street, Ravenfield, Rotherham S65 4NA
T: (01709) 852483
E: steph.woolhouse@yahoo.co.uk

Townend Cottage ★★★★
Contact: Mrs Margaret Begg
Townend Farmhouse, High Lane, Beadlam, Nawton, York YO62 7SY
T: (01439) 770103
E: margaret.begg@ukgateway.net
I: www.visityorkshire.com

Wardy's ★★★
Contact: Miss Joanne Ward
1 Storey Close, York YO62 5DP
T: (01439) 770124

HELPERTHORPE
North Yorkshire

The Old Dairy & The Granary Ref:3194 & 3195 ★★★★
Contact: Ms H Cook
Dales Holiday Cottages, Carleton Business Park, Carleton New Road, Skipton BD23 2AA
T: (01756) 799821
F: (01756) 797012
E: info@dalesholcot.com
I: www.dalesholcot.com

HEPTONSTALL
West Yorkshire

5 Draper Corner ★★
Contact: Mrs Taylor
4 Northfield Terrace, Hebden Bridge HX7 7NG
T: (01422) 844323

The Hayloft Flat ★★★
Contact: Mrs H M Harrison
The Hayloft Flat, Fields Farm, Hebden Bridge HX7 7PD
T: (01422) 843145

HEPWORTH
West Yorkshire

Uppergate Farm ★★★★
Contact: Mrs Alison Booth
Uppergate Farm, Uppergate, Hepworth, Huddersfield HD9 1TG
T: (01484) 681369
F: (01484) 687343
E: stevenal.booth@virgin.net
I: www.uppergatefarm.co.uk

HIGH BENTHAM
North Yorkshire

Batty Farm Ref:1362 ★★★
Contact: Ms H Cook
Dales Holiday Cottages, Carleton Business Park, Carleton New Road, Skipton BD23 2AA
T: (01756) 799821
F: (01756) 797012
E: info@dalesholcot.com
I: www.dalesholcot.com

Holmes Farm Cottage ★★★★
Contact: Mrs Story
Holmes Farm Cottage, Holmes Farm, Lancaster LA2 7DE
T: (015242) 61198
E: lucy@clucy.demon.co.uk

HOLMBRIDGE
West Yorkshire

Ivy Cottage ★★★
Contact: Mr Ian & Mrs Joyce Bangham
Ivy Cottage, Woodhead Road, Holmbridge, Huddersfield HD9 2NQ
T: (01484) 682561
E: bangham77@hotmail.com

HOLMFIRTH
West Yorkshire

1 Cross Barn ★★★
Contact: Mr John & Mrs Janet Armitage
1 Cross Barn, Cross Farm, Dunford Road, Huddersfield HD9 2RR
T: (01484) 683664

Cuish Cottages ★★★★
Contact: Mrs Mairi Binns
5 Cliff Hill Court, Holmfirth HD9 1JF
T: (01484) 682722
E: martin@crepes.freeserve.co.uk

Dal-a-fr-sa ★★★★
Contact: Mr & Mrs David Babbings
52 Meltham Road, Huddersfield HD9 6HL
T: (01484) 666545
F: (01484) 323990
E: davidbabbings@ntlworld.com

Fern Mount Cottage ★★★
Contact: Mr Roger & Mrs Sally Carrier
36 Back Lane, Huddersfield HD9 1HG
T: (01484) 688755
F: (01484) 689378

The Studio & Victoria Flats ★★★-★★★★
Contact: Mrs Newby
Foxhill Keepers Cottage, Skipton Road, Hampsthwaite, Harrogate HG3 2LZ
T: (01423) 771730
F: (01423) 771730

Summerwine Cottages ★★★
Contact: Mrs Susan Meakin
Summerwine Cottages, West Royd Farm, Marsh Lane, Shepley, Huddersfield HD8 8AY
T: (01484) 602147
F: (01484) 609427
E: summerwinecottages@lineone.net
I: www.summerwinecottages.co.uk

Weavers Cottage ★★★★
Contact: Mrs Gillian Blewett
Weavers Cottage, 96 Woodhead Road, Holmbridge, Huddersfield HD9 2NL
T: (01484) 666319
F: (01484) 665715
E: martinblewett@aol.com

HOLTBY
York

Garden Cottage Ref:1472 ★★★★
Contact: Ms H Cook
Dales Holiday Cottages, Carleton Business Park, Carleton New Road, Skipton BD23 2AA
T: (01756) 799821
F: (01756) 797012
E: info@dalesholcot.com
I: www.dalesholcot.com

HORNSEA
East Riding of Yorkshire

Cobble Cottage ★★★
Contact: Mrs Mary Everington
Risingfield, Strawberry Gardens, Hornsea HU18 1US
T: (01964) 536159

Horseshoe Cottage ★★★
Contact: Mr & Mrs Barron
Horseshoe Cottage, Suffolk House, Suffolk Road, Hornsea HU18 1RT
T: (01964) 532088
E: a.barron1@talk21.com

YORKSHIRE

Little Arram Barn ★★★★
Contact: Mr Alan & Mrs Ann Coates
Little Arram Farm, Hull
HU11 5SX
T: (01964) 533169
E: alan@arram.karoo.co.uk
I: www.yorkshireholidays.com

Westgate Mews ★★★
Contact: Mrs Walker
27 Westgate, Hornsea HU18 1BP
T: (01964) 533430
E: lettings@walkerhornsea.plus.com
I: www.cottagesdirect.co.uk

HORTON-IN-RIBBLESDALE
North Yorkshire

Blind Beck Holiday Cottage ★★★
Contact: Mrs Huddleston
Blind Beck Holiday Cottage, Horton-in-Ribblesdale, Settle BD24 0HT
T: (01729) 860396
E: h.huddleston@daelnet.co.uk
I: www.blindbeck.co.uk

The Flat ★★★
Contact: Mrs Sheila Fleming
The Flat, South View, New Houses, Settle BD24 0JE
T: (01729) 860394
F: (01729) 860394
E: info@south-view.org.uk
I: www.south-view.org.uk

Fourways Cottage ★★★
Contact: Mr Dermot & Mrs Deborah Griffin
2 Openview, London SW18 3PF
T: (020) 8870 6784
F: (020) 8870 7668
E: enquiries@escapetothedales.co.uk
I: www.escapetothedales.co.uk

Selside Farm Holiday Cottages ★★★-★★★★
Contact: Mrs Shirley Lambert
Selside Farm Holiday Cottages, Selside Farm, Settle BD24 0HZ
T: (01729) 860367
F: (01729) 860367
E: shirley@lam67.freeserve.co.uk
I: www.cottageguide.co.uk/selsidefarm

HOVINGHAM
North Yorkshire

Beck Cottage ★★★
Contact: Mrs Penelope Day
Beck Cottage, Brookside, York YO62 4LG
T: (01653) 628607
E: popday@onetel.net.uk

Westwood ★★★
Contact: Mrs Weston
Elemore Grange Farm, Durham DH6 1QE
T: (0191) 3721785

HOWDEN
East Riding of Yorkshire

101 Hailgate ★★★
Contact: Mrs Karen Formon
101 Hailgate, 167 Lichfield Lane, Mansfield NG18 4RP
T: (01623) 484537
F: (01623) 484539
E: karen.formon@ntl.world

HOWSHAM
North Lincolnshire

Willow Cottages ★★★★
Contact: Mr Roy Holstein & Ms Linda Smith
The Grange, Brigg Road, Market Rasen LN7 6LF
T: (01652) 652549
F: (01652) 652549
E: linda@willowcottages.co.uk
I: www.willowcottages.co.uk

HUBY
North Yorkshire

Fir Tree Cottage ★★★★
Contact: Mr Martin Owen
Fir Tree Cottage, Fir Tree House, Strait Lane, Leeds LS17 0EA
T: (01423) 734817
E: martinhubyowen@btopenworld.com

HUDDERSFIELD
West Yorkshire

Ashes Farm Cottages ★★★-★★★★
Contact: Mrs Barbara Lockwood
Ashes Farm Cottages, Ashes Common Farm, Ashes Lane, Huddersfield HD4 6TE
T: (01484) 426507
F: (01484) 426507
E: enquiries@ashescommonfarm.co.uk
I: www.ashescommonfarm.co.uk

Castle House Farm Cottages ★★★★
Contact: Mr & Mrs Philip Coates
Castle House Farm Cottages, Castle House Farm, Castle Hill, Huddersfield HD4 6TS
T: (01484) 663808
F: (01484) 661464
E: philip@castlehousefarm.co.uk
I: www.castlehousefarm.co.uk

Elam & Coates ★★★
Contact: Mrs Anne Mullany
49 Lowerhouses Lane, Huddersfield HD5 8JP
T: (01484) 431432
E: mullany@tesco.net

Swallow Cottage ★★★★
Contact: Mrs Margaret Kucharczyk
Rockley House, High Flatts, Huddersfield HD8 8XU
T: (01484) 607072
F: (01484) 607072
E: swallow@care4free.net

HULL
Kingston upon Hull

Queens Court
Rating Applied For
Contact: Mrs LeighAnn Clark
1 Sands Lane, Brough HU15 1JH
T: (01482) 666460
E: john@clark.karoo.co.uk

Waters Edge Executive Apartments ★★★★
Contact: Mrs J L Langton
Acorn Guest House, 719 Beverley Road, Hull HU6 7JN
T: (01482) 853248
F: (01482) 853148

HUNMANBY
North Yorkshire

2 Courtside Cottage
Rating Applied For
Contact: Mrs Karen Cawthorn
2 Courtside Cottage, Hunmanby Hall, Filey YO14 0HZ
T: (01723) 892882
F: (01723) 892185
E: karen@kcawthorn.fsnet.co.uk

Honeysuckle Cottage Ref:1984 ★★★
Contact: Ms H Cook
Dales Holiday Cottages, Carleton Business Park, Carleton New Road, Skipton BD23 2AA
T: (01756) 799821
F: (01756) 797012
E: info@dalesholcot.com
I: www.dalesholcot.com

Orchard Farm Holiday Village ★★★
Contact: Mrs Sharon Dugdale
Orchard Farm Holiday Village, Stonegate, Hunmanby, Filey YO14 0PU
T: (01723) 891582
F: (01723) 891582
E: s.dugdale@virgin.net

HUNTON
North Yorkshire

Emberton ★★
Contact: Mr Trevor & Mrs Wendy Mills
131 Glendale Gardens, Leigh-on-Sea SS9 2BE
T: (01702) 478846
F: (01702) 482088
E: info@dalescottages.com
I: www.dalescottages.com

HURST
North Yorkshire

Shiney Row Cottage Ref:2786 ★★★
Contact: Ms H Cook
Dales Holiday Cottages, Carleton Business Park, Carleton New Road, Skipton BD23 2AA
T: (01756) 799821
F: (01756) 797012
E: info@dalesholcot.com
I: www.dalesholcot.com

HUSTHWAITE
North Yorkshire

Greg's Cottage ★★★
Contact: Mr Greg Harrand
Hedley House Hotel, 3 Bootham Terrace, York YO30 7DH
T: (01904) 637404
F: (01904) 639774
E: greg@hedleyhouse.com
I: www.hedleyhouse.com

Kate's Cottage ★★
Contact: Mrs Anne Cox
Kate's Cottage, The Nookin, York YO61 4PY
T: (01845) 526550
F: (01347) 821291
E: c.anne.cox@virgin.net

HUTTON-LE-HOLE
North Yorkshire

Waterswallow Cottage & Swallow Barn ★★★
Contact: Mrs Barbara Grabowski
Halfway House, Hutton-le-Hole, York YO62 6UQ
T: (01751) 431596
F: (01751) 431596
E: waterswallow.cottage@virgin.net

HUTTON SESSAY
North Yorkshire

White Rose Holiday Cottages ★★★
Contact: Mrs Z Williamson
White Rose Holiday Cottages, Thirsk YO7 3BA
T: (01845) 501180
F: (01845) 501180

IBURNDALE
North Yorkshire

Yarrow End ★★★
Contact: Mrs Vanessa Hicking
Whitby Holiday Cottages, 47 Flowergate, Whitby YO21 3BB
T: (01947) 603010
E: enquiries@whitby-cottages.co.uk
I: www.whitby-cottages.co.uk

ILKLEY
West Yorkshire

The Grange ★★★★-★★★★★
Contact: Mrs Debbie Skinn
The Grange, Sconce Lane, High Eldwick, Bingley BD16 3BL
T: (01943) 878777
F: (01943) 878777
E: skinn@attglobal.net
I: www.faweathergrange.com

Westwood Lodge, Ilkley Moor ★★★★-★★★★★
Contact: Mr Tim & Mrs Paula Edwards
Westwood Lodge, Ilkley Moor, Wells Road, Ilkley LS29 9JF
T: (01943) 433430
F: (01943) 433431
E: welcome@westwoodlodge.co.uk
I: www.westwoodlodge.co.uk

INGLEBY CROSS
North Yorkshire

The Cottage at Hill House ★★★★
Contact: Mr Richard & Mrs Vee Kitteridge
The Cottage at Hill House, Northallerton DL6 3NH
T: (01609) 882109
E: kitteridge@ukgateway.net

INGLEBY GREENHOW
North Yorkshire

Ingleby Manor ★★★★
Contact: Mrs Christine Bianco
Ingleby Manor, Ingleby Greenhow, Middlesbrough TS9 6RB
T: (01642) 722170
F: (01642) 722170
E: christine@inglebymanor.co.uk
I: www.inglebymanor.co.uk

Establishments printed in blue have a detailed entry in this guide   481

YORKSHIRE

INGLETON
North Yorkshire

Kingsdale Head Cottage ★★★
Contact: Mrs Stephanie Faraday
Kingsdale Head Cottage,
Westhouse, Carnforth LA6 3PH
T: (015242) 41393
F: (015242) 41393

Little Storrs & Flaggs Cottage ★★★★
Contact: Mrs Debby Kuhlmann
Storrs Dale, Carnforth LA6 3AN
T: (015242) 41843
F: (015242) 41690
E: debbykuhlmann@aol.com
I: www.littlestorrs.co.uk

Primrose Cottage ★★★
Contact: Mr John & Mrs Celia Jones
Ingleborough WMC, Spring View, Carnforth LA6 3HE
T: (015242) 41407
F: (015242) 41407
E: topclub.john@virgin.net

KEARBY WITH NETHERBY
North Yorkshire

Nethercroft Cottage ★★★★
Contact: Mrs Webb
Maustin Park Ltd, The Riddings,
Spring Lane, Kearby, Wetherby LS22 4DA
T: (0113) 288 6234
F: (0113) 2886234
E: info@maustin.co.uk
I: www.maustin.co.uk

KELD
North Yorkshire

Hillcrest Holiday Cottage ★★★
Contact: Mrs Barbara Rukin
Park Lodge, Richmond DL11 6LJ
T: (01748) 886274
E: babrarukin@ukonline.co.uk

Keld Cottages ★★★
Contact: Mr Stuart Brier
Keld Cottages, Richmond DL11 6LJ
T: (01748) 886436
I: www.keld.info

KETTLENESS
North Yorkshire

Eastwater Cottage Ref:1537 ★★★
Contact: Ms H Cook
Dales Holiday Cottages, Carleton Business Park, Carleton New Road, Skipton BD23 2AA
T: (01756) 799821
F: (01756) 797012
E: info@dalesholcot.com
I: www.dalesholcot.com

KETTLEWELL
North Yorkshire

Fold Farm Cottages ★★★★
Contact: Mrs Barbara Lambert
Fold Farm, Kettlewell, Skipton BD23 5RH
T: (01756) 760886
F: (01756) 760464
E: info@foldfarm.co.uk
I: www.foldfarm.co.uk

Heathlands Ref:931 ★★★
Contact: Ms H Cook
Dales Holiday Cottages, Carleton Business Park, Carleton New Road, Skipton BD23 2AA
T: (01756) 799821
F: (01756) 797012
E: info@dalesholcot.com
I: www.dalesholcot.com

Primrose Cottage Ref:2504 ★★★★
Contact: Ms H Cook
Dales Holiday Cottages, Carleton Business Park, Carleton New Road, Skipton BD23 2AA
T: (01756) 799821
F: (01756) 797012
E: info@dalesholcot.com
I: www.dalesholcot.com

Wayside Cottage ★★★
Contact: Mrs Georgina Drew
5 The Coombe, Dartmouth TQ6 9PG
T: (01803) 839295
E: craig.drew@tesco.net

KILDALE
North Yorkshire

Bernard's Barn Ref:1566 ★★★★
Contact: Ms F Moody
Dales Holiday Cottages, Carleton Business Park, Carleton New Road, Skipton BD23 2AA
T: (01756) 799821
F: (01756) 797012
E: fiona@dalesholcot.com
I: www.dalesholcot.com

KILHAM
East Riding of Yorkshire

Raven Hill Holiday Farmhouse ★★★★
Contact: Mrs Patricia Savile
Raven Hill Holiday Farmhouse,
Raven Hill Farm, Driffield YO25 4EG
T: (01377) 267217
F: (01377) 267217

KIPLIN
North Yorkshire

Maryland Cottage ★★★
Contact: Ms Elaine Bird
Maryland Cottage, Kiplin Hall,
Richmond DL10 6AT
T: (01748) 812863
F: (01748) 818178
E: info@kiplinhall.co.uk
I: www.kiplinhall.co.uk

KIRBY HILL
North Yorkshire

Manor Cottage ★★★
Contact: Mrs Diana Whitby
Manor House, Richmond DL11 7JH
T: (01748) 825634
E: dianawhitby@hotmail.com

KIRBY MISPERTON
North Yorkshire

2 Rose Cottages ★★★
Contact: Mrs Kathryn Greenwood
95 Dyson Road, Halifax HX1 4RL
T: (01422) 364880
E: kathryngreenwood@tiscali.co.uk
I: www.cottageguide.co.uk/kirbymisperton

KIRKBY MALZEARD
North Yorkshire

Alma Cottage ★★★★
Contact: Mrs Janet Barclay
12 St Stephens Road,
Chelmsford CM3 6JE
T: (01621) 828576
F: (01621) 828539
E: janet@lbarclay.demon.co.uk
I: www.almacottage.co.uk

The Cottage Ref:3146 ★★★
Contact: Ms H Cook
Dales Holiday Cottages, Carleton Business Park, Carleton New Road, Skipton BD23 2AA
T: (01756) 799821
F: (01756) 797012
E: info@dalesholcot.com
I: www.dalesholcot.com

The Woodpeckers ★★★
Contact: Mrs Elizabeth Drewery
The Woodpeckers, Main Street,
Ripon HG4 3SE
T: (01765) 658206

KIRKBYMOORSIDE
North Yorkshire

Burton House ★★★
Contact: Mrs J Susan Gozney
Burton House, 50 Piercy End,
York YO62 6DF
T: (01777) 838246
F: (01777) 838246
E: burtonhousekm@aol.com

Catterbridge Farm Cottage ★★★★
Contact: Mrs Jayne Peace
Catterbridge Farm Cottage,
Catterbridge Farm, York YO62 6NF
T: (01751) 433271

Cherry View Cottage ★★★★
Contact: Mrs Drinkel
Starfitts Lane, Kirkbymoorside, York YO62 7JF
T: (01751) 431714

The Cornmill ★★★★
Contact: Mr Chris & Mrs Karen Tinkler
The Cornmill, Kirby Mills,
Kirkbymoorside, York YO62 6NP
T: (01751) 432000
F: (01751) 432300
E: cornmill@kirbymills.demon.co.uk
I: www.kirbymills.demon.co.uk

Ellerslie ★★★
Contact: Mrs Elizabeth Davison
26 Castlegate, York YO62 6BJ
T: (01751) 431112
E: mail@lizdavison.co.uk

Feversham Arms ★★★★
Contact: Mrs Frances Debenham
Feversham Arms, Church Houses, Farndale,
Kirkbymoorside, York YO62 7LF
T: (01751) 433206
E: fevershamfarndale@hotmail.com

Keldholme Cottages ★★★
Contact: Mr Hughes
Keldholme Cottages, Keldholme, Kirkbymoorside, York YO62 6NA
T: (01751) 431933

Monket Cottage
Rating Applied For
Contact: Mrs Vicki Mitchell
Monket House, Farndale, York YO62 7LA
T: (01751) 432402

Oak Lodge ★★★
Contact: Mrs Andrea Turnbull
Oak Lodge, Whitethorn Farm,
Rook Barugh, York YO62 6PF
T: (01751) 431298

The Retreat Apartment ★★★★
Contact: Mrs A J Schulze
Mill Cottage, The Grange,
Sinnington, York YO62 6RB
T: (01751) 430806
F: (01751) 430369
E: kingfisher.mill@virgin.net
I: www.the-retreat-yorkshire.co.uk

Sinnington Common Farm ★★★
Contact: Mrs Felicity Wiles
Sinnington Common Farm,
Cartoft, York YO62 6NX
T: (01751) 431719
F: (01751) 431719
E: felicity@scfarm.demon.co.uk
I: www.scfarm.demon.co.uk

Sleightholmedale Cottages ★★★★
Contact: Mrs James
Sleightholmedale Cottages,
Sleightholmedale, York YO62 7JG
T: (01751) 431942
F: (01751) 430106
E: wshoot@aol.com
I: www.shdcottages.co.uk

Surprise View Cottage & Field Barn Cottage ★★★★
Contact: Mrs Ruth Wass
Sinnington Lodge, Sinnington, York YO62 6RB
T: (01751) 431345
F: (01751) 433418
E: info@surpriseviewcottages.co.uk
I: www.surpriseviewcottages.co.uk

KIRKSTALL
West Yorkshire

The Tops ★★–★★★
Contact: Mr Merton Miles
21 Wadlands Drive, Pudsey LS28 5JS
T: (0113) 257 2197
F: (0113) 2572197
E: mertonmiles@thetops.co.uk
I: www.thetops.co.uk

KNARESBOROUGH
North Yorkshire

Badger Hill Properties ★★★–★★★★
Contact: Mr McGrath
Dropping Well Village Ltd,
Badger Hill Properties,
Harrogate Road, Knaresborough HG5 8DP
T: (01423) 862352
F: (01423) 868021
E: manager@badgerhill.co.uk
I: www.badgerhill.co.uk

YORKSHIRE

6 Cheapside ★★
Contact: Mrs Doreen Cook
21 Manor Road, Knaresborough
HG5 0BN
T: (01423) 862641

Garden Apartment ★★★
Contact: Mrs Rowinski
Garden Apartment, 3 Aspin Way,
Knaresborough HG5 8HL
T: (01423) 860463
E: david.rowinski@ntlworld.com

The Granary ★★★★
Contact: Mrs Rachel Thornton
Gibbet House Farm, Farnham
Lane, Farnham, Knaresborough
HG5 9JP
T: (01423) 862325 &
07970 000068
F: (01423) 862271

Knaresborough Holiday Apartments ★★★
Contact: Mr & Mrs J Cheney
2A Aspin Lane, Knaresborough
HG5 8ED
T: (01423) 862629
F: (01423) 862629

Uncle Tom's Holiday Cabins ★★★
Contact: Mrs Pat Ridsdale
Uncle Tom's Holiday Cabins, 22
Waterside, Knaresborough
HG5 8DF
T: (01423) 867045
F: (01423) 867045
E: uncletoms@rapidial.co.uk

Watergate Lodge Holiday Apartments ★★★-★★★★
Contact: Mr Peter & Mrs Lesley
Guest
Watergate Lodge Holiday
Apartments, Ripley Road,
Knaresborough HG5 9BU
T: (01423) 864627
F: (01423) 861087
E: info@watergatehaven.com
I: www.watergatehaven.com

LANGTHWAITE
North Yorkshire

Arklehurst ★★★
Contact: Mrs Julie Bissicks
Arklehurst, Richmond DL11 6RE
T: (01748) 884912
I: www.arkengarthdalecottage.co.uk

LASTINGHAM
North Yorkshire

Lastingham Holiday Cottages ★★★-★★★★
Contact: Mrs Andrea Cattle
Lastingham Holiday Cottages,
Littlegarth, Low Street,
Lastingham, York YO62 6TJ
T: (0175) 1417223
E: lastinghamhols@aol.com
I: www.members.aol.com/lastinghamhols

Rose Cottage ★★★
Contact: Mrs Caroline Ashworth
Bridge Farm, Low Street, York
YO62 6TJ
T: (01751) 417896
F: (01751) 417403
E: cottages@lastinghamleisure.freeserve.co.uk

LEALHOLM
North Yorkshire

Greenhouses Farm Cottages ★★★
Contact: Mr & Mrs Nick
Eddleston
Greenhouses Farm,
Greenhouses, Lealholm, Whitby
YO21 2AD
T: (01947) 897486
F: (01947) 897486
E: n_eddleston@yahoo.com
I: www.greenhouses-farm-cottages.co.uk

Poets Cottage Holiday Flat ★★
Contact: Mrs Blanche Rees
25 Roseberry Road, Stockton-on-Tees TS20 1JZ
T: (01642) 532413
E: rees@btinternet.com

West Banks Farmhouse Ref:1671 ★★★
Contact: Ms F Moody
Dales Holiday Cottages, Carleton
Business Park, Carleton New
Road, Skipton BD23 2AA
T: (01756) 799821
F: (01756) 797012
E: fiona@dalesholcot.com
I: www.dalesholcot.com

LEEDS
West Yorkshire

Harman Suites ★★★★
Contact: Miss Kavpreet Kaur
Harman Suites, 48 St Martins
Avenue, Leeds LS7 3LG
T: (0113) 295 5886
F: (0113) 2955886
E: info@harmansuite.co.uk
I: www.harmansuite.co.uk

LEVEN
East Riding of Yorkshire

Leven Park Lake ★★★★
Contact: Mr Graham & Mrs Lisa
Skinner
Leven Park Lake, South Street,
Leven, Beverley HU17 5NY
T: (01964) 544510
I: www.levenparklake.co.uk

LEVISHAM
North Yorkshire

Lilac Farm ★★★
Contact: Mrs Heather Eddon
Lilac Farm, Main Street,
Pickering YO18 7NL
T: (01751) 460281
E: heather@lilacfarm.f9.co.uk
I: www.lilacfarm.f9.co.uk

Moorlands Cottage ★★★★★
Contact: Mr Ron & Mrs Gill
Leonard
The Moorlands Country House,
Main Street, Pickering YO18 7NL
T: (01751) 460229
F: (01751) 460470
E: ronaldoleonardo@aol.com
I: www.moorlandscottage.co.uk

LEYBURN
North Yorkshire

Calverts of Leyburn ★★★
Contact: Mrs Ann Calvert
Smithy Lane, Leyburn DL8 5DZ
T: (01969) 623051
F: (01969) 624345
E: cottages@calverts.co.uk
I: www.shawlmews.co.uk

2 Crown Court Cottage ★★★
Contact: Mr Roland & Mrs Diane
Terry
Old Farm, Leyburn DL8 5JS
T: (01969) 624448
F: (01969) 624448
E: dalescottages@uku.co.uk
I: www.yorkshiredalesholidaycottages.co.uk

Dales View Holiday Homes ★★★-★★★★★
Contact: Messrs Chilton
Dales View Holiday Homes,
Jenkins Garth, Leyburn DL8 5SP
T: (01969) 623707
F: (01969) 623707
E: daleshols@aol.com
I: www.daleshols.co.uk

Eastburn Cottage ★★★★
Contact: Mrs Nadine Bell
Country Hideaways, Margaret's
Cottage, Leyburn DL8 4JN
T: (01969) 663559
F: (01969) 663559
E: nadine@countryhideaways.co.uk
I: www.countryhideaways.co.uk

Foal Barn ★★★
Contact: Mrs Canham
Hayloft Suite, Foal Barn, Leyburn
DL8 5PR
T: (01969) 622580

Low Riseborough ★★
Contact: Mr John Rowntree
95 Chiswick Village, London
W4 3BZ
T: (020) 89949837
F: (020) 89954674

Thorney Cottages ★★★
Contact: Mrs Nadine Bell
Country Hideaways, Margaret's
Cottage, Leyburn DL8 4JN
T: (01969) 663559
F: (01969) 663559
E: nadine@countryhideaways.co.uk
I: www.countryhideaways.co.uk

Throstlenest Holiday Cottages ★★★
Contact: Mrs Tricia Smith
Throstlenest Holiday Cottages,
Walk Mill Lane, Leyburn DL8 5HF
T: (01969) 623694
F: (01969) 624755
E: info@throstlenestcottages.co.uk
I: www.throstlenestcottages.co.uk

LINTON
North Yorkshire

Wharfedene ★★★★
Contact: Miss Liquorish
6 Hope Street, Nottingham
NG9 1DR
T: (0115) 922 3239
E: eliquorish@avernish.fsnet.co.uk

LINTON-ON-OUSE
North Yorkshire

Nursery View & Fuchsia Cottage Ref:1463 & 1464 ★★★
Contact: Ms H Cook
Dales Holiday Cottages, Carleton
Business Park, Carleton New
Road, Skipton BD23 2AA
T: (01756) 799821
F: (01756) 797012
E: info@dalesholcot.com
I: www.dalesholcot.com

LITTLE OUSEBURN
North Yorkshire

Hawtree Cottage ★★★★
Contact: Mrs Anne Llewellyn
Hawtree House, Main Street,
Little Ouseburn, York YO26 9TD
T: (01423) 331526
E: cgllewellyn@fsmail.net

LITTLE THIRKLEBY
North Yorkshire

Old Oak Cottages ★★★★
Contact: Mrs Tattersall
Old Oak Cottages, High House
Farm, Little Thirkleby, Thirsk
YO7 2BB
T: (01845) 501258
F: (01845) 501258
E: amanda@oldoakcottages.com
I: www.oldoakcottages.com

LITTLEBECK
North Yorkshire

Kelp House ★★★★
Contact: Mr Ray Flute
Ingrid Flute, 1 Hillcrest Avenue,
Scarborough YO12 6RQ
T: (01723) 376777
F: (01723) 376777
E: info@ingridflute.co.uk

LITTON
North Yorkshire

Stonelands ★★★★
Contact: Mrs Cowan
Stonelands Farm Yard Cottages,
Skipton BD23 5QE
T: (01756) 770293
I: www.stonelands.co.uk

LOCKTON
North Yorkshire

Ashfield Cottage ★★★
Contact: Mrs Carol Fisk
Ashfield Cottage, Pickering
YO18 7PZ
T: (01751) 460397
E: ashfieldcottage@beeb.net

Barn Cottage ★★★
Contact: Mrs Gill Grant
Lincoln LN3 5AQ
T: (01673) 842283
E: emmalouise.grant@btopenworld.co.uk

Establishments printed in blue have a detailed entry in this guide

YORKSHIRE

Bell Cottage Ref 3466 ★★★★
Contact: Ms H Cook
Dales Holiday Cottages, Carleton
Business Park, Carleton New
Road, Skipton BD23 2AA
T: (01756) 799821
F: (01756) 797012
E: info@dalesholcot.com
I: www.dalesholcot.com

The Little Barn ★★★
Contact: Mr James Fisk
The Little Barn, The Courtyard,
Ivy Cottage, Pickering YO18 7PY
T: (01751) 460325

1 Moor View Cottage ★★★
Contact: Mr Shirley Greenwood
Westholme, Bewholme Road,
Driffield YO25 8DP
T: (01964) 533491
F: (01964) 533491
E: shirley@westholmeatwick.fs.
net.co.uk

Old Barn Cottage Ref:3237 ★★★★
Contact: Ms H Cook
Dales Holiday Cottages, Carleton
Business Park, Carleton New
Road, Skipton BD23 2AA
T: (01756) 799821
F: (01756) 797012
E: info@dalesholcot.com
I: www.dalesholcot.com

West View Farm ★★★
Contact: Mrs J Welburn
West View Farm, Pickering
YO18 7QB
T: (01751) 460286
F: (01751) 460286

LOFTHOUSE
North Yorkshire

Acorn Quality Cottages ★★★★
Contact: Mrs Kerr
82 Trafalgar Road, Southport
PR8 2NJ
T: (01704) 568941
E: acornqualitycottages@
supanet.com
I: www.acornqualitycottages.
co.uk

Blayshaw Farmhouse ★★★★
Contact: Mr Ian Walker
Studfold Farm, Harrogate
HG3 5SG
T: (01423) 755399
I: www.blayshawfarm.co.uk

Kirklea Cottage ★★★★
Contact: Mrs Elizabeth Anne
Challis
Cobblestone Top, Studfold Farm,
Harrogate HG3 5SG
T: (01423) 755228
E: elizabeth@challis-kirklea.
fsworld.co.uk
I: www.kirkleacottage.co.uk

Thrope Farm Cottage ★★★
Contact: Mr Stephen Harker
Thrope Farm Cottage, Harrogate
HG3 5SN
T: (01423) 755607

LONG MARSTON
North Yorkshire

The Cottage ★★★
Contact: Mrs Gilmour
The Cottage, Old Lane, York
YO26 7LF
T: (01904) 738535
T: (01904) 738535
E: bob.gilmour@btopenworld.
com
I: www.bob.gilmour.btinternet.
co.uk

LOTHERSDALE
North Yorkshire

Great Gib Cottage Ref:1859 ★★★
Contact: Ms H Cook
Dales Holiday Cottages, Carleton
Business Park, Carleton New
Road, Skipton BD23 2AA
T: (01756) 799821
F: (01756) 797012
E: info@dalesholcot.com
I: www.dalesholcot.com

Street Head Farm ★★★★★
Contact: Mrs Gooch
Tow Top Farm, Skipton
BD20 8HY
T: (01535) 632535
F: (01535) 632535
E: streethead@towtop.fsnet.
co.uk
I: www.towtop.co.uk

LOW LAITHE
North Yorkshire

Springside ★★★★
Contact: Mrs Cathie Murrell
The Old Barn, Old Coach Road,
Harrogate HG3 4DE
T: (01423) 781383
F: (01423) 781383

LOW MARISHES
North Yorkshire

Sheepfoot Cottage Ref: 3721 ★★★
Contact: Mrs Fiona Moody
Dales Holiday Cottages, Carleton
Business Park, Carleton New
Road, Skipton BD23 2AA
T: (01756) 790919
F: (01756) 797012
E: fiona@
dales-holiday-cottages.com
I: www.dales-holiday-cottages.
com

LOW ROW
North Yorkshire

High Smarber ★★★
Contact: Mr John Sharp
Trough House, Richmond
DL11 6PH
T: (01748) 886738
F: (01748) 886738
E: rentals@swaledalecottage.
com
I: www.swaledalecottage.com

MALHAM
North Yorkshire

The Old School ★★★★
Contact: Ms Victoria Spence
King House, Skipton BD23 4DD
T: (01729) 830445
E: oldschoolmalham@
btopenworld.com
I: www.yorkshirenet.
co.uk/stayat/oldschoolmalham/

Waterside Cottage Ref:641 ★★★★
Contact: Mr S Boardman
Sykes Cottages, York House,
York Street, Chester CH1 3LR
T: (01244) 345700
F: (01244) 321442
E: info@sykescottages.co.uk
I: www.sykescottages.co.uk

MALTON
North Yorkshire

Rowgate Cottage ★★★★
Contact: Mrs Janet Clarkson
Rowgate Farm, Malton
YO17 8LU
T: (01944) 758277
F: (01944) 758277
E: janet@rowgatecottage.fsnet.
co.uk

Swans Nest Cottage ★★★★
Contact: Mrs Yvonne Dickinson
Abbotts Farm House, Ryton,
Malton YO17 6SA
T: (01653) 694970
E: swansnestcottage@hotmail.
com
I: www.uk-holiday-cottages.
co.uk/swans-nest

4 Wellgarth ★★
Contact: Mrs Dianne Waudby
5 Wellgarth, Malton YO17 6SS
T: (01653) 697548
E: diannewaudby@onetel.net.uk

MARISHES
North Yorkshire

Bellafax Holiday Cottage Ref:2798 ★★★★
Contact: Ms H Cook
Dales Holiday Cottages, Carleton
Business Park, Carleton New
Road, Skipton BD23 2AA
T: (01756) 799821
F: (01756) 797012
E: info@dalesholcot.com
I: www.dalesholcot.com

MARSKE
North Yorkshire

Home Farm ★★★★
Contact: Mrs Simpson
Home Farm, Richmond DL11 7LT
T: (01748) 824770
F: (01748) 826357

MARTON
North Yorkshire

Orchard House ★★★★
Contact: Mr & Mrs Paul
Richardson
Orchard House, Marton, York
YO62 6RD
T: (01751) 432904
T: (01751) 430733
E: orchardhouse@tinyworld.
co.uk
I: www.
thebestbritishbedandbreakfast.
com

Wildsmith Court ★★★★
Contact: Mr David & Mrs Joan
Milner
Wildsmith Court, The Granary,
Marton, Sinnington, York
YO62 6RD
T: (01751) 431358
E: milner@wildsmithcourt.
freeserve.co.uk

MARTON CUM SEWERBY
East Riding of Yorkshire

Grange Farm Cottages ★★★★
Contact: Mr Richard & Mrs Jane
Dibb
Ryal, Flamborough Road,
Bridlington YO15 1DU
T: (01262) 671137
E: richard.dibb@btclick.com
I: www.grangefarmcottages.net

MASHAM
North Yorkshire

Barn Owl Cottage Ref:1178 ★★★
Contact: Ms H Cook
Dales Holiday Cottages, Carleton
Business Park, Carleton New
Road, Skipton BD23 2AA
T: (01756) 799821
F: (01756) 797012
E: info@dalesholcot.com
I: www.dalesholcot.com

Dales View Cottages ★★★★
Contact: Mr H Moyes
Dales View Cottages, Fearby,
Masham, Ripon HG4 4NF
T: (01765) 688820
E: hrmoyes@aol.com

Daleside ★★★★★
Contact: Mrs Pam Usher
Allendale, Swinton Terrace,
Ripon HG4 4HS
T: (01765) 688277
I: www.self-catering-masham.
co.uk

Masham Cottages ★★★
Contact: Mr John Airton
Masham Cottages, 27 Red Lane,
Ripon HG4 4HH
T: (01765) 689327
F: (01765) 689327
E: airton@bronco.co.uk
I: www.mashamcottages.co.uk

The Mews ★★★★
Contact: Mrs Jameson
The Mews, Sutton Grange, Ripon
HG4 4PB
T: (01765) 689068
E: jameson1@ukf.net
I: www.themews-masham.com

Mews Cottage ★★★
Contact: Mrs Catherine
Hallsworth
5 Bridge Close, Harleston
IP20 9HW
T: (01379) 853020
E: mashamcottage@hotmail.
com

Yoredale ★★★★
Contact: Ms J R Simon
The Barns, 42 Market Place,
Ripon HG4 4EF
T: (01765) 688707

YORKSHIRE

MELTHAM
West Yorkshire
Constance Cottage ★★★★
Contact: Mr Esposito & Ms J B Jackman
148 Huddersfield Road, Meltham, Huddersfield HD9 4AL
T: (01484) 851811

MENWITH HILL
North Yorkshire
Delves Ridge Cottages ★★★
Contact: Mrs Karen MacLaverty
Delves Ridge Cottages, Menwith Hill Road, Harrogate HG3 2RA
T: (01943) 880346
E: rossmacl@lineone.net

MIDDLEHAM
North Yorkshire
Briar Cottage
Rating Applied For
Contact: Mrs Nadine Bell
Country Hideaways, Margarets Cottage, Leyburn DL8 4JN
T: (01969) 663559
F: (01969) 663559
E: nadine@countryhideaways.co.uk
I: www.countryhideaways.co.uk

Castle Hill Cottage Ref:1506 ★★★
Contact: Ms H Cook
Dales Holiday Cottages, Carleton Business Park, Carleton New Road, Skipton BD23 2AA
T: (01756) 799821
F: (01756) 797012
E: info@dalesholcot.com
I: www.dalesholcot.com

The Cottage ★★★
Contact: Mr P Ralph
1 New Hall Road, Chesterfield S40 1HE
T: (01246) 224260

The Garth ★★★
Contact: Mrs Nadine Bell
Country Hideaways, Margaret's Cottage, Leyburn DL8 4JN
T: (01969) 663559
F: (01969) 663559
E: nadine@countryhideaways.co.uk
I: www.countryhideaways.co.uk

Honeykiln Cottage Ref:3197 ★★★
Contact: Ms H Cook
Dales Holiday Cottages, Carleton Business Park, Carleton New Road, Skipton BD23 2AA
T: (01756) 799821
F: (01756) 797012
E: info@dalesholcot.com
I: www.dalesholcot.com

Jade Cottage Ref:805 ★★★★
Contact: Mr Clive Sykes
Sykes Cottages, York House, York Street, Chester CH1 3LR
T: (01244) 345700
F: (01244) 321442
E: info@sykescottages.co.uk
I: www.sykescottages.co.uk

Middle Cottage
Rating Applied For
Contact: Mrs Jennie Perren
2 North Park Grove, Leeds LS8 1JJ
T: (0113) 237 1817
E: jennifer.perren@btinternet.com

Stonecroft ★★★★
Contact: Mrs Best
Chapel Farmhouse, Whaw, Richmond DL11 6RT
T: (01748) 884062
E: chapelfarmbb@aol.com
I: www.middlehamcottage.co.uk

Sunnyside Cottage Ref:2531 ★★★
Contact: Ms H Cook
Dales Holiday Cottages, Carleton Business Park, Carleton New Road, Skipton BD23 2AA
T: (01756) 799821
F: (01756) 797012
E: info@dalesholcot.com
I: www.dalesholcot.com

West Hill ★★★★
Contact: Mrs Nadine Bell
Country Hideaways, Margaret's Cottage, Leyburn DL8 4JN
T: (01969) 663559
F: (01969) 663559
E: nadine@countryhideaways.co.uk
I: www.countryhideaways.co.uk

MIDDLESMOOR
North Yorkshire
Abbey Holiday Cottages ★★★★
Contact: Mrs Katrina Holmes
Abbey Holiday Cottages, 12 Panorama Close, Harrogate HG3 5NY
T: (01423) 712062
F: (01423) 712776
E: abbeyholiday.cottages@virgin.net
I: abbeyholidaycottages.co.uk

MOOR MONKTON
North Yorkshire
Red House Estate
Rating Applied For
Contact: Mrs Jill Gordon
Red House Estate, York YO26 8JQ
T: (01904) 738256
F: (01904) 738256
E: redhouse@argonet.co.uk
I: www.redhouseyork.com

MUKER
North Yorkshire
Corner Cottage Ref:914 ★★★
Contact: Ms H Cook
Dales Holiday Cottages, Carleton Business Park, Carleton New Road, Skipton BD23 2AA
T: (01756) 799821
F: (01756) 797012
E: info@dalesholcot.com
I: www.dalesholcot.com

Stoneleigh ★★★
Contact: Mr Michael Peacock
Stoneleigh, Stoneleigh Cottage, Richmond DL11 6QQ
T: (01748) 886375
F: (01748) 886375

NAFFERTON
East Riding of Yorkshire
Heapfield Cottage Ref:2047 ★★★
Contact: Ms H Cook
Dales Holiday Cottages, Carleton Business Park, Carleton New Road, Skipton BD23 2AA
T: (01756) 799821
F: (01756) 797012
E: info@dalesholcot.com
I: www.dalesholcot.com

NEWSHAM
North Yorkshire
Dyson House Barn ★★★★
Contact: Mr & Mrs Clarkson
Dyson House, Newsham, Richmond DL11 7QP
T: (01833) 627365
E: dysonbarn@tinyworld.co.uk
I: www.cottageguide.co.uk/dysonhousebarn

High Dalton Hall Cottage ★★★★
Contact: Mrs Elizabeth Jopling
High Dalton Hall, Richmond DL11 7RG
T: (01833) 621450
F: (01833) 621450
I: www.highdaltonhallcottage.co.uk

The Mill Cottage ref:323 ★★★
Contact: Ms H Cook
Dales Holiday Cottages, Carleton Business Park, Carleton New Road, Skipton BD23 2AA
T: (01756) 799821
F: (01756) 797012
E: info@dalesholcot.com
I: www.dalesholcot.com

NEWTON-LE-WILLOWS
North Yorkshire
The Shippon ★★★
Contact: Mrs Valerie Nelson
The Shippon, Newton Le Willows, Bedale DL8 1TG
T: (01677) 450227
E: andrew.nelson3@virgin.net
I: www.theshippon.co.uk

NEWTON-ON-OUSE
North Yorkshire
Village Farm Holidays ★★★★
Contact: Mr Wales
Holiday Cottages (Yorkshire) Ltd, Water Street, Skipton BD23 1PB
T: (01756) 700510
E: brochure@holidaycotts.co.uk
I: www.holidaycotts.co.uk

NEWTON-ON-RAWCLIFFE
North Yorkshire
Hill Rise Cottage Ref:1617 ★★★★
Contact: Ms H Cook
Dales Holiday Cottages, Carleton Business Park, Carleton New Road, Skipton BD23 2AA
T: (01756) 799821
F: (01756) 797012
E: info@dalesholcot.com
I: www.dalesholcot.com

Hillcrest Cottage ★★★★
Contact: Mrs Pat Orgill
November Cottage, Melton Constable NR24 2ED
T: (01263) 862917

Manor Farm Cottages ★★★★
Contact: Lady Elizabeth Kirk
Manor Farm Cottages, Manor Farm, Pickering YO18 8QA
T: (01751) 472601
F: (01751) 472601
E: emkirkmanorfarm@aol.com
I: www.members.aol.com/ManorfarmNewton

Stable Cottage ★★★
Contact: Mr & Mrs Gardner
The Old Vicarage, Toftly View, Pickering YO18 8QD
T: (01751) 476126
E: sueashburn2007@aol.com

Sunset Cottage ★★★★
Contact: Mrs Pat Anderson
Mrs Anderson's Country Cottages, Boonhill Cottage, Pickering YO18 8QF
T: (01751) 472172
F: (01751) 472172
E: bookings@boonhill69.freeserve.co.uk
I: www.swiftlink.pnc-uk.net/sc/1236.htm

NORTH COWTON
North Yorkshire
Millstone Ref:613 ★★★
Contact: Mr S Boardman
Sykes Cottages, York House, York Street, Chester CH1 3LR
T: (01244) 345700
F: (01244) 321442
E: info@sykescottages.co.uk
I: www.sykescottages.co.uk

NORTH DALTON
East Riding of Yorkshire
Old Cobblers Cottage ★★★
Contact: Miss Chris Wade
2 Star Row, North Dalton, Driffield YO25 9UR
T: (01377) 217523 & 217662
F: (01377) 217754
E: chris@adastey.demon.co.uk

NORTHALLERTON
North Yorkshire
The Byre ★★★★
Contact: Mrs Crowe
The Byre, Hill View Farm, Bullamoor, Northallerton DL6 3QW
T: (01609) 776072

Hill House Farm Cottages ★★★★
Contact: Mr James Griffith
Hill House Farm, Northallerton DL7 0PZ
T: (01609) 770643
E: info@hillhousefarmcottages.com

2 Summerfield Cottage ★★★
Contact: Mrs Sally Holmes
Summerfield House Farm, Welbury, Northallerton DL6 2SL
T: (01609) 882393
F: (01609) 882393
E: sallyhholmes@aol.com

Establishments printed in blue have a detailed entry in this guide

YORKSHIRE

NORTON
North Yorkshire

Anson House ★★★★
Contact: Mrs Susan Camacho
Star Cottage, Welham Road,
Norton, Malton YO17 9DU
T: (01653) 694916
F: (01653) 694901
I: www.ansonhouseholidays.
co.uk

The Cottage ★★★★
Contact: Mrs Patricia Barber
The Cottage, 69 Welham Road,
Malton YO17 9DS
T: (01653) 693409
E: Patricia.barber@Btinternet.
com

NUNNINGTON
North Yorkshire

The Cottage Ref:200 ★★★
Contact: Ms H Cook
Dales Holiday Cottages, Carleton
Business Park, Carleton New
Road, Skipton BD23 2AA
T: (01756) 799821
F: (01756) 797012
E: info@dalesholcot.com
I: www.dalesholcot.com

Orchard Cottage ★★
Contact: Mr & Mrs Foxton
Ness Farm, Ness, Nunnington,
York YO62 5XE
T: (01439) 748226

Strawberry Cottage ★★★★
Contact: Mrs Angela Ward
Strawberry Cottage, c/o
Rosedene, Church Street, York
YO62 5US
T: (01439) 748399

OLD BYLAND
North Yorkshire

Tylas Lodge ★★★
Contact: Mrs Jane Holmes
Tylas Farm, York YO62 5LH
T: (01439) 798308
F: (01439) 798461
E: holmesivan@btinternet.com

Valley View Farm ★★★★
Contact: Mrs Robinson
Valley View Farm, York
YO62 5LG
T: (01439) 798221
E: sally@valleyviewfarm.com
I: www.valleyviewfarm.com

OLD MALTON
North Yorkshire

Coronation Cottage ★★★★
Contact: Mr David Beeley
Forge Valley Cottages, Barn
House, Westgate, Malton
YO17 7HE
T: (01653) 698251
F: (01653) 691962
E: enquiries@
forgevalleycottages.co.uk
I: www.forgevalleycottages.
co.uk

OSGODBY
North Yorkshire

**Sea Views and Sea Views
Too ★★★★-★★★★★**
Contact: Mr & Mrs O'Connor
15 Halifax Road, Brighouse
HD62AA
T: (01484) 401757
E: pat@oconn100.freeserve.
co.uk
I: www.sea-views-scarborough.
co.uk

OSMOTHERLEY
North Yorkshire

**Monk's Walk Ref:2041
★★★★**
Contact: Ms H Cook
Dales Holiday Cottages, Carleton
Business Park, Carleton New
Road, Skipton BD23 2AA
T: (01756) 799821
F: (01756) 797012
E: info@dalesholcot.com
I: www.dalesholcot.com

OSWALDKIRK
North Yorkshire

Angel Cottage ★★★★
Contact: Mrs Jane Sweeney
Angel Cottage, Wheatfield,
Newton Grange, York YO62 5YG
T: (01439) 788493
E: jane.sweeney@lineone.net
I: www.pb-design.
com/swiftlink/sc/1325.htm

Honeysuckle Cottage ★★★
Contact: Mrs Judith Bowles
Vale House, St Oswalds Close,
York YO62 5YH
T: (01439) 788980
F: (01439) 788226
E: jude@specialplacestours.
co.uk
I: www.country-holidays.co.uk

OXENHOPE
West Yorkshire

**The Cottage
Rating Applied For**
Contact: Mrs Anita Holland
The Cottage, Old Oxenhope Hall,
Keighley BD22 9RL
T: (01535) 643270
F: (01535) 643270

Hawksbridge Cottage ★★★
Contact: Mrs Hazel Holmes
2 Hawksbridge Lane, Keighley
BD22 9QU
T: (01535) 642203

**Lynden Barn Cottage
★★★★**
Contact: Mrs I Spencer
Lynden Barn, Sawood Lane,
Keighley BD22 9SP
T: (01535) 645074
E: lyndenbarn@ukonline.co.uk
I: members.netscapeonline.
co.uk/lyndenbarn/index.html

**2 Mouldgreave Cottages
★★★★**
Contact: Mrs Mackrell
Mouldgreave House,
Mouldgreave, Oxenhope,
Keighley BD22 9RT
T: (01535) 642325
F: (01535) 640370
E: mackrells@lineone.net
I: www.mouldgreave.plus.com

**Well Head Cottage
★★★★★**
Contact: Mrs Sheena McBryde
Hanging Gate Lane, Keighley
BD22 9RJ
T: (01535) 647966
E: sheena@brontecottages.com
I: www.brontecottages.co.uk

Yate Cottage ★★★
Contact: Mrs Jean M M Dunn
Yate House, Yate Lane,
Oxenhope, Keighley BD22 9HL
T: (01535) 643638
I: www.uk-holiday-cottages.
co.uk/yatecottage

PATELEY BRIDGE
North Yorkshire

Ashfield House ★★★
Contact: Mr & Mrs Myers
Ashfield House, Harrogate
HG3 5HJ
T: (01423) 711491
F: (01423) 711491
E: john.myers@virgin.net
I: freespace.virgin.net/john.
myers

**Bruce Cottage
Rating Applied For**
Contact: Mr Michael Jarosz
25 Lister Street, Ilkley LS29 9ET
T: (01943) 607392
F: (01943) 817099
E: enquiries@brucecottage.
co.uk
I: www.brucecottage.co.uk

**Helme Pasture, Old Spring
Wood ★★★★**
Contact: Mrs Rosemary Helme
Helme Pasture, Old Spring
Wood, Hartwith Bank,
Summerbridge, Harrogate
HG3 4DR
T: (01423) 780279
F: (01423) 780994
E: info@helmepasture.co.uk
I: www.helmepasture.co.uk

Rainbows End Ref:61 ★★★
Contact: Mr S Boardman
Sykes Cottages, York House,
York Street, Chester CH1 3LR
T: (01244) 345700
F: (01244) 321442
E: info@sykescottages.co.uk
I: www.sykescottages.co.uk

**Rolling Mill Stable Ref: 244
★★★**
Contact: Mr S Boardman
Sykes Cottages, York House,
York Street, Chester CH1 3LR
T: (01244) 345700
F: (01244) 321442
E: info@sykescottages.co.uk
I: www.sykescottages.co.uk

Terrace House ★★★
Contact: Mrs Tanya Jones
W W Accountants, Sandrock Hill
Road, Farnham GU10 4RJ
T: (01252) 820220
E: tanya@mtkm.freeserve.co.uk

PICKERING
North Yorkshire

**Amelia Cottage
Rating Applied For**
Contact: Mr Paul Hickabottom
16 The Parade, Pearson Park,
Hull HU5 2UH
T: (01482) 441175
F: (01482) 441175
E: hotham@hothamshipping.
co.uk

Barker Stakes Farm ★★★
Contact: Mrs Susannah Hardy
Barker Stakes Farm, Lendales
Lane, Pickering YO18 8EE
T: (01751) 476759
F: (01751) 476759
E: info@bakerstakes.co.uk
I: www.barkerstakes.co.uk

**Beech Farm Cottages
★★★★-★★★★★**
Contact: Mrs Pat Massara
Beech Farm Cottages, Wrelton,
Pickering YO18 8PG
T: (01751) 476612
F: (01751) 475032
E: holiday@beechfarm.com
I: www.beechfarm.com

**Bramwood Cottages
★★★★**
Contact: Mr John Butler
Bramwood Guest House &
Cottages, 19 Hall Garth,
Pickering YO18 7AW
T: (01751) 473446
F: (01751) 475849
E: bramwood@fsbdial.co.uk
I: www.bramwoodguesthouse.
co.uk/cottages.html

Dandelion Cottage ★★★
Contact: Mr Mark & Mrs Sandra
Ward
Dandelion Cottage, 22 Eastgate,
Pickering YO18 7DU
T: (01751) 473349

Eastgate Cottages ★★★★
Contact: Mr Kevin & Mrs Elaine
Bedford
Eastgate Cottages, 117 Eastgate,
Pickering YO18 7DW
T: (01751) 476653
F: (01751) 471310
E: info@
northyorkshirecottages.co.uk
I: www.northyorkshirecottages.
co.uk

**Easthill Farm House and
Gardens ★★★★**
Contact: Mrs Diane Stenton
Easthill Farm House, Wilton
Road, Thornton Dale, Pickering
YO18 7QP
T: (01751) 474561
E: info@easthill-farm-holidays.
co.uk
I: www.easthill-farm-holidays.
co.uk

Eastside Cottage ★★★
Contact: Mrs E Evans
Eastside Farm, Pickering
YO18 8QA
T: (01751) 477204

486 Look out for establishments participating in the National Accessible Scheme

YORKSHIRE

The Hayloft ★★★
Contact: Ms Karen Auker
The Granary, Pickering
YO18 8QA
T: (01851) 477075
E: granaryhayloft@hotmail.com

Hungate Cottages
Rating Applied For
Contact: Mr Richard Robertson
Hungate Cottages, Recreation
Road, Pickering YO18 7ET
T: (017514) 76382
F: (017514) 76382
E: holidays@hungatecottages.co.uk
I: www.hungatecottages.co.uk

Joiners Cottage ★★★
Contact: Mr Phil & Mrs Cynthia Fisher
Farndale House, 103 Eastgate, Pickering YO18 7DW
T: (01751) 475158

Keld Head Farm Cottages ★★★★
Contact: Mr Julian & Mrs Penny Fearn
Keld Head Farm Cottages, Keld Head, Pickering YO18 8LL
T: (01751) 473974
E: julian@keldheadcottages.com
I: www.keldheadcottages.com

Let's Holiday ★★★★
Contact: Mr John Wicks
Let's Holiday, Mel House, Newton-on-Rawcliffe, Pickering YO18 8QA
T: (01751) 475396
F: (01751) 475396
E: holiday@letsholiday.com
I: www.letsholiday.com

Lilac Cottage ★★★
Contact: Mr & Mrs Munn
Lilac Cottage, 23 Westgate, Pickering YO18 8BA
T: (01751) 472193

Low Costa Mill Cottages ★★★★
Contact: Mrs Eileen Thomas
Low Costa Mill, Costa Lane, Pickering YO18 8LP
T: (01751) 472050
E: thomas@lowcostamill.freeserve.co.uk
I: www.lowcostamill.co.uk

Lynton Cottage Ref:2800 ★★★
Contact: Ms H Cook
Dales Holiday Cottages, Carleton Business Park, Carleton New Road, Skipton BD23 2AA
T: (01756) 799821
F: (01756) 797012
E: info@dalesholcot.com
I: www.dalesholcot.com

New Meadows ★★★
Contact: Mrs Hill
New Meadows, 66 Ruffa Lane, Pickering YO18 7HT
T: (01751) 473258

Newton Cottage ★★★
Contact: Mr Tony Danks
Rosamund Avenue, Pickering YO18 7HF
T: (01751) 477913
E: mal.danks@btinternet.com

One Oak Lodge ★★★
Contact: Mr Baker
One Oak Lodge, Kirkham Lane, Pickering YO18 7AS
T: (01751) 472200

11 Potter Hill ★★★
Contact: Mr Michael Jones
Cheeseboard, 26 Royal Hill, London SE10 8RT
T: (020) 8305 0401
F: (020) 8305 0401
E: michael@cheese-board.co.uk

Rawcliffe House Farm ★★★★
Contact: Mr Duncan & Mrs Jan Allsopp
Rawcliffe House Farm, Pickering YO18 8JA
T: (01751) 473292
F: (01751) 473292
E: office@yorkshireaccommodation.com
I: www.yorkshireaccommodation.com

Sands Farm Cottages ★★★★
Contact: Mr Michael & Mrs Susan Parkin & Mrs Price
Sands Farm Cottages, Wilton, Pickering YO18 7JY
T: (01751) 474405
E: info@sandsfarmcottages.co.uk
I: www.sandsfarmcottages.co.uk

The Sidings ★★★
Contact: Mr Lloyd & Mrs Liz Varley
21 Redwood, Compton Acres, West Bridgford, Nottingham NG2 7UL
T: (0115) 945 5543
F: (0115) 9455543
E: varleyfm@supanet.com

Skelton Cottage & Rowntree Cottages ★★★★
Contact: Mr Kevin & Mrs Elaine Bedford
Eastgate Cottages, 117 Eastgate, Pickering YO18 7DW
T: (01751) 476653
F: (01751) 471310
E: info@northyorkshirecottages.co.uk
I: www.northyorkshirecottages.co.uk

South View Cottages ★★★-★★★★★
Contact: Mr Simpson
107 Church Street, Whitby YO22 4DE
T: (01937) 832192
E: info@southviewcottage.co.uk
I: www.southviewcottages.co.uk

2 Spring Gardens ★★★★
Contact: Mrs Sandra Pickering
Nabgate, Wilton Road, Pickering YO18 7QP
T: (01751) 474279

1 Tannery Cottages ★★★
Contact: Mr Robert & Mrs Diana Ellis
29 Hartington Close, Solihull B93 8SU
T: (015464) 779573
E: diana@tanneryholidays.co.uk
I: www.tanneryholidays.co.uk

Town End Farm Cottage ★★★
Contact: Mr Peter Holmes
Town End Farm Cottage, Eastfield Road, Pickering YO18 7HU
T: (01751) 472713

Upper Carr Chalet and Touring Park ★★★
Contact: Mr Martin Harker
Upper Carr Chalet and Touring Park, Upper Carr Lane, Malton Road, Pickering YO18 7JP
T: (01751) 473115
F: (01751) 473115
E: harker@uppercarr.demon.co.uk
I: www.uppercarr.demon.co.uk

1 Westgate ★★★★
Contact: Mr & Mrs S Toothill
2 Summerfields Drive, Doncaster DN9 3BG
T: (01302) 770601

White Lodge Cottage ★★★
Contact: Mrs Briggs
White Lodge Cottage, 54 Eastgate, Pickering YO18 7DU
T: (01751) 473897

PORT MULGRAVE
North Yorkshire

Cleveland Cottage ★★★
Contact: Mrs Adele Thompson
Whitby Holiday Cottages, 47 Flowergate, Whitby YO21 3BB
T: (01947) 603010
F: (01947) 821133
E: enquiries@whitby-cottages.co.uk
I: www.whitby-cottages.co.uk

PRESTON-UNDER-SCAR
North Yorkshire

Anna's Cottage at Rocky View ★★★
Contact: Mrs Nadine Bell
Country Hideaways, Margaret's Cottage, Leyburn DL8 4JN
T: (01969) 663559
F: (01969) 663559
E: nadine@countryhideaways.co.uk
I: www.countryhideaways.co.uk

Croxford Cottage Ref:2034 ★★★
Contact: Ms H Cook
Dales Holiday Cottages, Carleton Business Park, Carleton New Road, Skipton BD23 2AA
T: (01756) 799821
F: (01756) 797012
E: info@dalesholcot.com
I: www.dalesholcot.com

Mallyan Wynd ★★
Contact: Mrs Nadine Bell
Country Hideaways, Margaret's Cottage, Leyburn DL8 4JN
T: (01969) 663559
F: (01969) 663559
E: nadine@countryhideaways.co.uk
I: www.countryhideaways.co.uk

PRIMROSE VALLEY
North Yorkshire

Calm Waters Bungalow Ref:2478 ★★★
Contact: Ms H Cook
Dales Holiday Cottages, Carleton Business Park, Carleton New Road, Skipton BD23 2AA
T: (01756) 799821
F: (01756) 797012
E: info@dalesholcot.com
I: www.dalesholcot.com

RATHMELL
North Yorkshire

Layhead Farm Cottages ★★★★
Contact: Mrs Hyslop
Field House, Settle BD24 0LD
T: (01729) 840234
F: (01729) 840775
E: rosehyslop@layhead.co.uk
I: www.layhead.co.uk

RAVENSCAR
North Yorkshire

Raven Lea ★★★★
Contact: Mrs Turner
Raven Lea, Station Road, Scarborough YO13 0LX
T: (01723) 870949
E: ravenlea@ic24.net

Smugglers Rock Country House ★★★-★★★★
Contact: Mrs Sharon Gregson
Smugglers Rock Country House, Staintondale Road, Ravenscar, Scarborough YO13 0ER
T: (01723) 870044
E: info@smugglersrock.co.uk
I: www.smugglersrock.co.uk

RAVENSWORTH
North Yorkshire

Beckside Barn Ref:893 ★★★
Contact: Mr S Boardman
Sykes Cottages, York House, York Street, Chester CH1 3LR
T: (01244) 345700
F: (01244) 321442
E: info@sykescottages.co.uk
I: www.sykescottages.co.uk

REETH
North Yorkshire

Barn End Cottage Ref:3639 ★★★
Contact: Ms H Cook
Dales Holiday Cottages, Carleton Business Park, Carleton New Road, Skipton BD23 2AA
T: (01756) 799821
F: (01756) 797012
E: info@dalesholcot.com
I: www.dalesholcot.com

Braeside ★★★★
Contact: Ms Kate Empsall
Whitfield/Askrigg Cottages, Helm, Askrigg, Leyburn DL8 3JF
T: (01969) 650565
E: empsall@askrigg-cottages.co.uk
I: www.askrigg-cottages.co.uk

Establishments printed in blue have a detailed entry in this guide

YORKSHIRE

Burton House, Greystones, Turbine House and Charlies Stable ★★★★
Contact: Mrs Patricia Procter
Hill Cottage, Richmond
DL11 6SQ
T: (01748) 884273
E: cprocter@aol.com
I: www.uk-cottages.com

St Andrews Chapel ★★★
Contact: Dr David & Sarah Bown
The Old Wesleyan Chapel,
Richmond DL11 7LQ
T: (01748) 884792
E: sarah@twochapels.
free-online.co.uk
I: www.twochapels.free-online.co.uk

Swaledale Cottages ★★★★
Contact: Mrs Janet Hughes
Swaledale Cottages,
Thiernswood Hall, Richmond
DL11 6UJ
T: (01748) 884526
E: thiernswood@talk21.com
I: www.swaledale-cottages.co.uk

Winmaur Cottage Ref:2995 ★★★★
Contact: Ms F Moody
Dales Holiday Cottages, Carleton
Business Park, Carleton New
Road, Skipton BD23 2AA
T: (01756) 799821
F: (01756) 797012
E: fiona@dalesholcot.com
I: www.dalesholcot.com

Wraycroft Holiday Cottages ★★★★
Contact: Mrs F Hodgson
Wraycroft Holiday Cottages,
Wraycroft, Richmond DL11 6SU
T: (01748) 884497
F: (01748) 884497

REIGHTON
North Yorkshire

St Helen's Cottage ★★★★★
Contact: Mrs Janice T Carter
Hilla Green Farm, Scarborough
YO13 0BS
T: (01723) 882274
F: (01723) 882274

RICHMOND
North Yorkshire

Barn Owl Cottage and Kingfisher Cottage Ref:3225/2224 ★★★★
Contact: Ms Fiona Moody
Dales Holiday Cottages, Carleton
Business Park, Carleton New
Road, Skipton BD23 2AA
T: (01756) 799821
F: (01756) 797012
E: info@dalesholcot.com
I: www.dalesholcot.com

Blacksmiths Cottage ★★★
Contact: Mr James & Mrs Susan Melville
50 Whitefield Road, Warrington
WA4 6NA
T: (01925) 268691
E: js.melville@virgin.net

The Bungalow ★★★
Contact: Ms R Delf
The Bungalow, St Martin's
Priory, Richmond DL10 4LQ
T: (01748) 823122

Castle View ★★★★
Contact:
English Country Cottages,
Stoney Bank, Barnoldswick
BB94 0AA
T: 0870 5851155
F: 0870 5851150

Coach House ★★★★
Contact: Mrs Turnbull
Coach House, Whashton Springs
Farm, Whashton, Richmond
DL11 7JS
T: (01748) 822884
F: (01748) 826285
E: whashton@turnbullg.
freeserve.co.uk
I: www.whashtonsprings.co.uk

Croft Cottage ★★
Contact: Mrs Wakeling-Stretton
5 Vermont Grove, Leamington
Spa CV31 1SE
T: (01926) 428784
E: stretton7@aol.com
I: yorkshirecottage.org.uk

16 Culloden Mews ★★★
Contact: Mr Robert Holmes
72 Ronaldshay Drive, Richmond
DL10 5BW
T: (01748) 823043

Dillons Cottage ★★★
Contact: Mrs Kay Gibson
West Cottage, Victoria Road,
Richmond DL10 4AS
T: (01748) 824046
E: rickayuk@hotmail.com

Flowery Dell Luxury Lodges
Rating Applied For
Contact: Mrs Cullen
Flowery Dell Luxury Lodges,
Hudswell Lane, Richmond
DL11 6BD
T: (01748) 822406
F: (01748) 824150
E: flowerydell@clara.co.uk

Fox Cottage ★★★
Contact: Mr & Mrs Fryer
17 High Green, Richmond
DL10 7LN
T: (01748) 811772

Fryers Cottage ★★★
Contact: Mr Oliver & Mrs Valerie
Blease
26 Newbiggin, Richmond
DL10 4DT
T: (01748) 823344
F: (01748) 821319

Nuns Cottage Yard ★★★
Contact: Mrs Susan Parks
Nuns Cottage Yard, 5 Hurgill
Road, Richmond DL10 4AR
T: (01748) 822809
F: (01429) 864320
E: nunscottage@richmond.org.uk
I: richmond.org.uk/business/nunscottage

Rose Cottage ★★★★
Contact: Mr David Hunt
11 Richmond Road, Richmond
DL10 5DR
T: (01748) 823080
E: huntsholidays@hotmail.com
I: www.huntsholidays.co.uk

Thornlea Cottage Ref:249 ★★★
Contact: Mr S Boardman
Sykes Cottages, York House,
York Street, Chester CH1 3LR
T: (01244) 345700
F: (01244) 321442
E: info@sykescottages.co.uk
I: www.sykescottages.co.uk

Tish Toms Cottages ★★-★★★
Contact: Mrs Ann Hall
Mount Arrarat, Sleegill,
Richmond DL10 4RH
T: (01748) 822167
F: (01748) 850396
E: pete@catermech.co.uk
I: www.tishtomscottages.com

RILLINGTON
North Yorkshire

Thorpe-Rise ★★★
Contact: Mrs Marilyn Legard
Thorpe-Rise, 10 High Street,
Malton YO17 8LA
T: (01944) 758446

RIPLEY
North Yorkshire

The Old Smithy ★★★★★
Contact: Mrs Lesley Halliday
Halliday Holidays, Po Box 177,
Leeds LS18 5WZ
T: (0113) 258 4212
F: (0113) 2819455
E: lesleyhalliday@hotmail.com

RIPON
North Yorkshire

Byre Cottage & Swallow Cottage ★★★★
Contact: Mr Philip & Mrs Pamela Coldwell
Byre Cottage & Swallow
Cottage, Moor End Farm, Ripon
HG4 3LU
T: (01765) 677419
I: www.yorkshirebandb.co.uk

Intake ★★★★
Contact: Mrs Fiona McConnell
3 Hippingstones Lane, Corbridge
NE45 5JP
T: (01434) 632812
F: (01434) 633825
E: kfiona@tiscali.co.uk

Mallorie Bungalow Ref:2176 ★★
Contact: Ms H Cook
Dales Holiday Cottages, Carleton
Business Park, Carleton New
Road, Skipton BD23 2AA
T: (01756) 799821
F: (01756) 797012
E: info@dalesholcot.com
I: www.dalesholcot.com

Waterfront House
Rating Applied For
Contact: Mrs Lesley Halliday
Halliday Holidays, Po Box 177,
Leeds LS18 5WZ
T: (0113) 258 4212
F: (0113) 2819455

RISHWORTH
West Yorkshire

Kit Hill Cottage at Pike End Farm ★★★★
Contact: Mrs Caroline Ryder
Kit Hill Cottage at Pike End
Farm, Pike End Road, Sowerby
Bridge HX6 4QS
T: (01422) 823949
F: (01422) 824626
E: carolinerydr@pikeendfarm.net
I: www.pikeendfarm.net

The Old Post Office
Rating Applied For
Contact: Mr Steven Edwards
Calder House, 264 Oldham Road,
Sowerby Bridge HX6 4QB
T: (01422) 823840

ROBIN HOOD'S BAY
North Yorkshire

1 and 2 Wragby Barn ★★★★
Contact: Mrs Fenby
Whin Sill, Station Road, Robin
Hood's Bay, Whitby YO22 4RA
T: (01947) 880719
F: (01947) 880719
E: marilyn@fenby.fsbusiness.co.uk
I: www.wragbycottages.co.uk

Farsyde Farm Cottages ★★★-★★★★★
Contact: Mrs Angela Green
Farsyde Farm Cottages, Robin
Hood's Bay, Whitby YO22 4UG
T: (01947) 880249
F: (01947) 880877
E: farsydestud@talk21.com
I: www.farsydefarmcottages.co.uk

Heather Croft Ref:925 ★★
Contact: Mr S Boardman
Sykes Cottages, York House,
York Street, Chester CH1 3LR
T: (01244) 345700
F: (01244) 321442
E: info@sykescottages.co.uk
I: www.sykescottages.co.uk

Inglenook ★★★
Contact: Mrs Lesley Abbott
7 Goodwood Grove, York
YO24 1ER
T: (01904) 622059
F: (01904) 622059
I: www.inglenook-cottage.co.uk

Lingers Hill ★★★
Contact: Mrs Frances Harland
Lingers Hill Farm, Thorpe Lane,
Robin Hood's Bay, Whitby
YO22 4TQ
T: (01947) 880608

4 Martin's Row ★★★
Contact: Mrs Adele Thompson
Whitby Holiday Cottages, 47
Flowergate, Whitby YO21 3BB
T: (01947) 603010
F: (01947) 821133
E: enquiries@whitby-cottages.co.uk
I: www.whitby-cottages.co.uk

YORKSHIRE

Meadowcroft ★★★★
Contact: Mrs Adele Thompson
Whitby Holiday Cottages, 47 Flowergate, Whitby YO21 3BB
T: (01947) 603010
F: (01947) 821133
E: enquiries@whitby-cottages.co.uk
I: www.whitby-cottages.co.uk

St Roberts Chantry ★★
Contact: Mrs Adele Thompson
Whitby Holiday Cottages, 47 Flowergate, Whitby YO21 3BB
T: (01947) 603010
F: (01947) 821133
E: enquiries@whitby-cottages.co.uk
I: www.whitby-cottages.co.uk

South House Farmhouse & Cottages ★★★-★★★★★
Contact: Mrs Nealia Pattinson
South House Farmhouse & Cottages, Mill Beck, Fylingthorpe, Whitby YO22 4UQ
T: (01947) 880243
F: (01947) 880243
E: kmp@bogglehole.fsnet.co.uk
I: www.southhousefarm.co.uk

The White Owl Holiday Apartments ★★★
Contact: Mr David Higgins
The White Owl Holiday Apartments, Station Road, Robin Hoods Bay, Whitby YO22 4RL
T: (01947) 880879
E: higgins@whiteowlrhb.freeserve.co.uk
I: www.SmoothHound.co.uk/hotels/whiteowl.html

ROSEDALE ABBEY
North Yorkshire

Coach House ★★★★
Contact: Mrs Sugars
Coach House, Sevenford House, Pickering YO18 8SE
T: (01751) 417283
F: (01751) 417505
E: sevenford@aol.com
I: www.sevenford.com

Craven Garth Holiday Cottages ★★★
Contact: Mrs Ena Dent
Craven Garth Holiday Cottages, Craven Garth Farm, Pickering YO18 8RH
T: (01751) 417506
F: (01751) 417506
E: ena@cravengarth.com
I: www.cravengarth.com

The Grange Farm Cottages ★★★★
Contact: Mr & Mrs David Brown
The Grange Farm Cottages, The Grange, Rosedale Abbey, Pickering YO18 8RD
T: (01751) 417329
F: (01751) 417329
E: dbrown329@tiscali.co.uk
I: www.thegrangecottages.co.uk

Stable Cottage ★★★
Contact: Mrs Christine Ewinging
Stable Cottage, Medds Farmhouse, Pickering YO18 8SQ
T: (01751) 417583
E: holidays@medds.co.uk
I: www.medds.co.uk

Woodlea ★★★★
Contact: Mrs Pauline Belt
2 Low Green, York YO23 3SB
T: (01904) 705549
F: (01904) 709420
E: daviscoleman2@btopenworld.com
I: www.rosedaleholidaycottage.co.uk

ROSEDALE EAST
North Yorkshire

East Coast Holiday Bungalows ★★★
Contact: Mrs Lorraine Drake
8 Florence Terrace, Pickering YO18 8RJ
T: (01751) 417785

Hill Farm ★★★★
Contact: Mr Richard & Mrs Val Cook
Hill Farm, Pickering YO18 8RH
T: (01751) 417404
E: holidays@hillfarm-rosedale.co.uk
I: www.hillfarm-rosedale.co.uk

1 Hill Houses ★★★
Contact: Mrs Harrison
28 George Street, Driffield YO25 6RA
T: (01377) 253042
E: mary.harrison@btinternet.com
I: www.geocities.com/maryknitwit/rosedale.html

RUSWARP
North Yorkshire

Croft Farm Holiday Cottages ★★★★
Contact: Ms Emma Carpenter
1 Croft Farm, Whitby YO21 1NY
T: (01947) 825853
E: emma@croftfarm.com
I: www.croftfarm.com

Egton Cottage Ref:734 ★★★
Contact: Mr S Boardman
Sykes Cottages, York House, York Street, Chester CH1 3LR
T: (01244) 345700
F: (01244) 321442
E: info@sykescottages.co.uk
I: www.sykescottages.co.uk

Esk Moor Cottage ★★★
Contact: Mrs Marion Corner & Pauline Walker
15 Mulgrave Road, Whitby YO21 3JS
T: (01947) 605836

Esk View Cottage Ref:1912 ★★★
Contact: Ms H Cook
Dales Holiday Cottages, Carleton Business Park, Carleton New Road, Skipton BD23 2AA
T: (01756) 799821
F: (01756) 797012
E: info@dalesholcot.com
I: www.dalesholcot.com

Maybeck Cottage Ref:1674 ★★★
Contact: Ms H Cook
Dales Holiday Cottages, Carleton Business Park, Carleton New Road, Skipton BD23 2AA
T: (01756) 799821
F: (01756) 797012
E: info@dalesholcot.com
I: www.dalesholcot.com

Skipper Lodge ★★★
Contact: Mrs Adele Thompson
Whitby Holiday Cottages, 47 Flowergate, Whitby YO21 3BB
T: (01947) 603010
F: (01947) 821133
E: enquiries@whitby-cottages.co.uk
I: www.whitby-cottages.co.uk

Turnerdale Cottage ★★★★★
Contact: Mr David Haycox & Mrs Sue Brooks
Shoreline Cottages Ltd, Po Box 135, Leeds LS14 3XJ
T: (0113) 244 8410
F: (0113) 2449826
E: reservations@shoreline-cottages.com
I: www.shoreline-cottages.com

SALTAIRE
West Yorkshire

Glen Knoll ★★★★
Contact: Mr Norman Pilsworth
Glen Knoll, 5 and 5A Carlton Road, Shipley BD18 4NE
T: (01274) 825303

Mill Workers Cottage ★★★
Contact: Fiona Morgan
32 Titus Street, Saltaire Village, Shipley BD18 4LU
T: (01274) 589271

Overlookers Cottage ★★★★
Contact: Mrs Anne Heald
2 Victoria Road, Shipley BD18 3LA
T: (01274) 774993
F: (01274) 774464
I: www.saltaire.yorks.com/touristinfo/overlookers.html

SALTON
North Yorkshire

Dove Court ★★★★
Contact: Mrs Helen Earnshaw
Dove Court, Sparrow Hall, York YO62 6RW
T: (01751) 431697
F: (01751) 433455
E: helen@dovecourt.com
I: www.dovecourt.com

SALTWICK BAY
North Yorkshire

Brook House Barn Ref:1340 ★★★
Contact: Ms H Cook
Dales Holiday Cottages, Carleton Business Park, Carleton New Road, Skipton BD23 2AA
T: (01756) 799821
F: (01756) 797012
E: info@dalesholcot.com
I: www.dalesholcot.com

SANDSEND
North Yorkshire

Caedmon House ★★★★★
Contact: Mr David Haycox & Mrs Sue Brooks
Shoreline Cottages Ltd, Po Box 135, Leeds LS14 3XJ
T: (0113) 244 8410
F: (0113) 2449826
E: reservations@shoreline-cottages.com
I: www.shoreline-cottages.com

Harlow Cottage ★★★★
Contact: Mr David Haycox & Mrs Sue Brooks
Shoreline Cottages Ltd, Po Box 135, Leeds LS14 3XJ
T: (0113) 244 8410
F: (0113) 2449826
E: reservations@shoreline-cottages.com
I: www.shoreline-cottages.com

Howdale Cottage ★★★★
Contact: Mrs Adele Thompson
Whitby Holiday Cottages, 47 Flowergate, Whitby YO21 3BB
T: (01947) 603010
F: (01947) 821133
E: enquiries@whitby-cottages.co.uk
I: www.whitby-cottages.co.uk

Melrose ★★★
Contact: Mrs Adele Thompson
Whitby Holiday Cottages, 47 Flowergate, Whitby YO21 3BB
T: (01947) 603010
F: (01947) 821133
E: enquiries@whitby-cottages.co.uk
I: www.whitby-cottages.co.uk

Pebble Cottage Ref 3502 ★★★★
Contact: Miss Ruth Henderson
Dales Holiday Cottages, Carleton Business Park, Carleton New Road, Skipton BD23 2AA
T: (01756) 799821
F: (01756) 797012
I: www.dales-holiday-cottages.com

Plovers Nest Ref:2785 ★★★★
Contact: Ms H Cook
Dales Holiday Cottages, Carleton Business Park, Carleton New Road, Skipton BD23 2AA
T: (01756) 799821
F: (01756) 797012
E: info@dalesholcot.com
I: www.dalesholcot.com

Prospect House, Flats 1 & 3 ★★★★
Contact: Mrs Adele Thompson
Whitby Holiday Cottages, 47 Flowergate, Whitby YO21 3BB
T: (01947) 603010
F: (01947) 821133
E: enquiries@whitby-cottages.co.uk
I: www.whitby-cottages.co.uk

2 Sunnyside ★★★
Contact: Mrs Adele Thompson
Whitby Holiday Cottages, 47 Flowergate, Whitby YO21 3BB
T: (01947) 603010
F: (01947) 821133
E: enquiries@whitby-cottages.co.uk
I: www.whitby-cottages.co.uk

Toll Bar Ref:2243 ★★★★
Contact: Ms H Cook
Dales Holiday Cottages, Carleton Business Park, Carleton New Road, Skipton BD23 2AA
T: (01756) 799821
F: (01756) 797012
E: info@dalesholcot.com
I: www.dalesholcot.com

Establishments printed in blue have a detailed entry in this guide

YORKSHIRE

Vancouver Cottage
Rating Applied For
Contact: Mrs Vanessa Hicking
Vancouver Cottage, St Marys Hill, The Valley, Sandsend, Whitby YO21 3TQ
T: (01947) 603010
F: (01947) 821122
E: enquiries@whitby-cottages.co.uk
I: www.whitby-cottages.co.uk

Woodbine Cottage ★★★
Contact: Mrs Adele Thompson
Whitby Holiday Cottages, 47 Flowergate, Whitby YO21 3BB
T: (01947) 603010
F: (01947) 821133
E: enquiries@whitby-cottages.co.uk
I: www.whitby-cottages.co.uk

SAWLEY
North Yorkshire

Sawley Arms Cottages ★★★★
Contact: Mrs June Hawes
Sawley Arms Cottages, Sawley Arms, Ripon HG4 3EQ
T: (01765) 620642
F: (01765) 620642

SCALBY
North Yorkshire

Away From The Madding Crowd ★★★★
Contact: Mr & Mrs Peter Ward
Away From The Madding Crowd, Spring Farm, Scalby Nabs, Scalby, Scarborough YO13 0SL
T: (01723) 360502
E: peterandstella@scalbynabs99.fsnet.co.uk

Barmoor Farmhouse Holiday Cottages ★★★★
Contact: Mr Sharp
16 Throxenby Lane, Scarborough YO12 5HW
T: (01723) 363256

SCARBOROUGH
North Yorkshire

Abbey Holiday Flats ★★
Contact: Mrs Catherine Cook
7-8 Fort Terrace, Bridlington YO15 2PE
T: (01262) 677819
E: holiday-flats@abbey-flats.fsnet.co.uk

Atlantis Holiday Flats ★★
Contact: Mrs Ros Dyson
Atlantis Holiday Flats, 73 Queen's Parade, Scarborough YO12 7HT
T: (01723) 375087
F: (01723) 375087

Avenwood Apartments ★★★
Contact: Mr Atkinson
Avenwood Apartments, 129 Castle Road, Scarborough YO11 1HX
T: (01723) 374640
E: dave@avenwood.freeserve.co.uk

Avondale Holiday Flats ★★-★★★
Contact: Mr Roger Greaves
Avondale Holiday Flats, 75 Queens Parade, Scarborough YO12 7HY
T: (01723) 364836

Bay View Cottages ★★★★
Contact: Ms Sally Jubb
43 North Street, Scarborough YO13 0RP
T: (01723) 378711

Bayview Holiday Flatlets ★★
Contact: Mrs Ellen Johnson
Bayview Holiday Flatlets, 77 Queens Parade, Scarborough YO12 7HY
T: (01723) 373217
F: (01723) 375139

Bedwyn's Holiday Accommodation
Rating Applied For
Contact: Mrs Diane Callaghan
Bedwyn's Holiday Accommodation, 161 Old Scalby Road, Scarborough YO12 6TB
T: (01723) 373217
F: (01723) 501064
E: muckduck500@aol.com

Blenheim Holiday Flats ★★-★★★
Contact: Mr & Mrs Denis Middleton
Blenheim Holiday Flats, 7 Blenheim Terrace, Scarborough YO12 7HF
T: (01723) 363643
F: (01723) 363767

Brialene Holiday Apartments ★★-★★★
Contact: Mrs Marlene Witty
Brialene Holiday Apartments, 35-37 Valley Road, Scarborough YO11 2LX
T: (01723) 367158
E: reservations@scarborough-brialene.co.uk
I: www.scarborough-brialene.co.uk

Brompton Holiday Flats ★★★
Contact: Mr Kenneth Broadbent
Selomar Hotel, 23 Blenheim Terrace, Scarborough YO12 7HD
T: (01723) 364964
F: (01723) 364964
E: info@bromptonholidayflats.co.uk
I: www.bromptonholidayflats.co.uk

Cherry Trees Holiday Flats ★-★★
Contact: Mrs Helen Sanderson
Cherry Trees Holiday Flats, 72 North Marine Road, Scarborough YO12 7PE
T: (01723) 501433
E: info@cherrytrees.vholiday.co.uk
I: www.cherrytrees.vholiday.co.uk

Chomley Self-contained Holiday Apartments ★★★
Contact: Mr & Mrs Witty
Chomley Self-contained Holiday Apartments, 68 Columbus Ravine, Scarborough YO12 7QU
T: (01723) 367292
E: chomley@yahoo.co.uk
I: www.scarborough.co.uk

Cravendale Holiday Flats
Rating Applied For
Contact: Mrs Shirley Smith
3 Broomfield Terrace, Cleckheaton BD19 6AH
T: (01274) 871069
E: shirleysflats@hotmail.com
I: www.cravendaleflats.co.uk

Cresta House Flats ★★★★
Contact: Ms Dobie
10 Bridgewater Park Drive, Doncaster DN6 8RL
T: (01904) 799703
E: crestahouse@hotmail.com

Cromwell Court ★★★
Contact: Mrs Walker
9 The Garlands, Scarborough YO11 2SU
T: (01723) 376008
I: www.yorkshirecoast.co.uk/cromwell

Crown Holiday Apartments ★★★★
Contact: Miss Melinda Dowson
Crown Holiday Apartments, Apartments 2 & 3, 13, Crown Terrace, Scarborough YO11 2BL
T: (01723) 341786
E: holiday@crownaparts.fsnet.co.uk
I: mysite.freeserve.com/crownhols

East Farm Country Cottages ★★★★
Contact: Ms J Hutchinson & Mr M Fozard
East Farm Country Cottages, 6 Jameson Crescent, Scarborough YO12 5BZ
T: (01723) 506406
E: info@eastfarmcottages.co.uk
I: www.eastfarmcottages.co.uk

Elizabethan Court ★★★
Contact: Mrs Paula Randall
43 Church Avenue, Harrogate HG1 4HG
T: (01423) 549436

Glaisdale Holiday Flats and Cottage ★★★
Contact: Mr Michael Holliday FHCIMA
Glaisdale Holiday Flats and Cottage, 49 West Street, Scarborough YO11 2QR
T: (01723) 372728
F: (01723) 372728
E: michael.holliday@tesco.net
I: www.s-h-a.co.uk/glaisdale

Green Gables Hotel Holiday Flats ★★-★★★
Contact: Mrs McGovern
Green Gables Hotel Holiday Flats, West Bank, Scarborough YO12 4DX
T: (01723) 361005
E: ggables@netcomuk.co.uk

Harbour View Holiday Flats ★★
Contact: Mr Andrew Gordon Jenkinson
Harbour View Holiday Flats, 37/37A Sandside, Scarborough YO11 1PG
T: (01723) 361162

The Hayloft ★★★★
Contact: Mr Ray & Mrs Lucette Flute
Ingrid Flute Holiday Accommodation, 1 Hillcrest Avenue, Scarborough YO12 6RQ
T: (01723) 376777
F: (01723) 376777
E: info@ingridflute.co.uk

Honeysuckle Cottage ★★★★
Contact: Mr David Beeley
Forge Valley Cottages, Barn House, Westgate, Malton YO17 7HE
T: (01653) 698251
F: (01653) 691962
E: enquiries@forgevalleycottages.co.uk
I: www.forgevalleycottages.co.uk

Hydeaway Haven ★
Contact: Mr & Mrs John Hyde
18 Roslyn Close, Broxbourne EN10 7DA
T: (01992) 465509
F: (020) 8270 6451
E: hydehaven@ntlworld.com

Killerby Old Hall ★★★★
Contact: Mrs Margery Middleton
Killerby Old Hall, Killerby, Cayton, Scarborough YO11 3TW
T: (01723) 583799
F: (01723) 583799
I: www.killerby.com

Kimberley Holiday Flats ★★-★★★
Contact: Mr S Costello & Mr G Quilter
Q C Associates, The Gatehouse, Barker Lane, Scarborough YO13 9BG
T: (01723) 850552
F: (01723) 859362
E: stagedoorsteve@yahoo.co.uk
I: www.kimberleyholidayflats.com

Lendal House ★★★★
Contact: Mrs Petra Scott
Lendal House, 34 Trafalgar Square, Scarborough YO12 7PY
T: (01723) 372178
E: info@lendalhouse.co.uk
I: www.lendalhouse.co.uk

Marlborough Flats ★★
Contact: Mrs Julie Ellard
Marlborough Flats, 22 Blenheim Terrace, Scarborough YO12 7HD
T: (01723) 373116
E: julieellard@hotmail.com

Meenagoland Holiday Flats ★★-★★★
Contact: Mrs Samantha Pickering
Meenagoland Holiday Flats, 44 Shelton Avenue, Scarborough YO13 9HB
T: 0794 0 316313
E: flats@meenagoland.co.uk
I: www.meenagoland.co.uk

Neville House Apartments ★★★
Contact: Mr & Mrs Smailes
The Rise, 27 Seamer Road, Scarborough YO12 4DU
T: (01723) 366123
E: lindasmailes@ukf.net

YORKSHIRE

Parade Holiday Flats ★★
Contact: Mrs Sue Sayers
31 Cornelian Avenue,
Scarborough YO11 3AN
T: (01723) 374207

Rambling Rose Sea View Flats ★★★
Contact: Mrs Helen Benson
Rambling Rose Holiday Flats, 3 Marlborough Street,
Scarborough YO12 7HG
T: (01723) 351171
E: helenrose283@hotmail.com

Redford House ★★★★
Contact: Mr J Pearson
59 Northstead Manor Drive,
Scarborough YO12 6AF
T: (01723) 361088

Rosewood Holiday Flat ★★★
Contact: Mrs Lynne Redley
Rosewood Holiday Flat, 1 Scholes Park Road, Scarborough YO12 6RE
T: (01723) 367696
E: lynne.redley@talk21.com
I: www.rosewoodflats.plus.com

Sea Vista Holiday Bungalow ★★★★
Contact: Mr & Mrs Alan Roper
Merlewood, Bradford Road,
Bingley BD16 1TT
T: (01274) 564741
F: (01274) 548525
E: info@sea-vista.com
I: www.sea-vista.com

Seacliffe Holiday Flats ★★
Contact: Mrs Elizabeth Lumley
Manor Farm, Malton YO17 8RN
T: (01944) 728271
F: (01944) 728177
E: dclumley@scarborough.co.uk
I: www.seaviewflats.co.uk

Seascape
Rating Applied For
Contact: Mrs Julie Eborall
29 Cornelian Drive, Scarborough YO11 3AL
T: (01723) 379858
F: (01723) 376637
E: seascapebungalow@aol.com

Spikers Hill Country Cottages ★★★
Contact: Mrs Janet Hutchinson
Spikers Hill Country Cottages,
Spikers Hill Farm, Cockrah Road, West Ayton, Scarborough YO13 9LB
T: (01723) 862537
F: (01723) 865511
E: janet@spikershill.ndo.co.uk
I: www.spikershill.ndo.co.uk

Town Farm Cottages ★★★★
Contact: Mr & Mrs Joe Green
Town Farm Cottages, Town Farm, High Street, Cloughton, Scarborough YO13 0AE
T: (01723) 870278
E: mail@greenfarming.co.uk
I: www.greenfarming.co.uk

Valley View Holiday Flats ★★
Contact: Mr David Wilkinson
Valley View Holiday Flats, 13 Grosvenor Road, Scarborough YO11 2LZ
T: (01723) 364709
F: (01723) 364709
E: valleyview@btconnect.com
I: www.valleyview.org.uk

Victoria House Select Self-contained Holiday Apartments ★★★
Contact: Miss Ann Mason
Coverdale House, 1 Granville Road, South Cliff, Scarborough YO11 2RA
T: (01723) 368854

The Villa Esplanade - Holiday Apartment ★★-★★★★★
Contact: Mrs Pauline Gent
The Villa Esplanade - Holiday Apartment, Esplanade, Scarborough YO11 2AQ
T: (01723) 375571

Vincent Holiday Complex ★★★
Contact: Mr Alan & Mrs Sandra Hopkins
Vincent Holiday Complex, 42-43 Sandside, Scarborough YO11 1PG
T: (01723) 500997
E: vincents.scarborough@btinternet.com
I: yorkshireholidays.com

Wayside Farm Holiday Cottages ★★-★★★★
Contact: Mr & Mrs Peter Halder
Wayside Farm Holiday Cottages, Whitby Road, Scarborough YO13 0DX
T: (01723) 870519

52 Westbourne Grove ★★★
Contact: Mr Daniel Stone
52 Westbourne Grove, Scarborough YO11 2DL
T: (01723) 355431

Wheatlands Holiday Flats ★★★
Contact: Mr John & Mrs Josie Perry
Wheatlands Holiday Flats, 1-4 Blenheim Street, Scarborough YO12 7HB
T: (01723) 500440

White Acre ★★★-★★★★
Contact: Mr Squire
J G Squire (Holidays) Ltd, 54 Falsgrave Road, Scarborough YO12 5AX
T: (01723) 374220
F: (01723) 366693
E: squiresc@clara.co.uk
I: www.squiresc.clara.co.uk

White Gable ★★★★
Contact: Mr Squire
J G Squire (Holidays) Ltd, 54 Falsgrave Road, Scarborough YO12 5AX
T: (01723) 374220
F: (01723) 366693
E: squiresc@clara.co.uk
I: www.squiresc.clara.co.uk

Windsor Holiday Flats ★
Contact: Mr Andrew Eadie
6 Newlands Drive, Manchester M20 5NW
T: (01723) 375986
E: andrew@windsorholidayflats.com
I: www.windsorholidayflats.com

Wrea Head Country Cottages ★★★★
Contact: Mr Steve Marshall
Wrea Head Country Cottages, Barmoor Lane, Scalby, Scarborough YO13 0PG
T: (01723) 375844
F: (01723) 375911
E: ytb@wreahead.co.uk
I: www.wreahead.co.uk

SCAWTON
North Yorkshire

Forresters Cottage ★★★
Contact: Mrs Charlotte de Klee
Lockiehead Farm, Cupar KY14 7EH
T: (01337) 828217
F: (01337) 828686
E: charlotte@lcokiehead.freeserve.co.uk

SCOTCH CORNER
North Yorkshire

5 Cedar Grove ★★★
Contact: Mr & Mrs James P Lawson
The Close, Mill Lane, Cloughton, Scarborough YO13 0AB
T: (01723) 870455
E: jim@lawson5270fsnet.co.uk

SEDBUSK
North Yorkshire

The Coach House Ref: 2016 ★★★
Contact: Ms H Cook
Dales Holiday Cottages, Carleton Business Park, Carleton New Road, Skipton BD23 2AA
T: (01756) 799821
F: (01756) 797012
E: info@dalesholcot.com
I: www.dalesholcot.com

Wagtail Cottage ★★★★
Contact: Mrs Annette Riley
Leyburn DL8 3AN
T: (01969) 663716
E: info@oldgoatholidays.co.uk
I: www.cottageguide.co.uk/wagtail/

West Cottage ★★★
Contact: Mrs Nadine Bell
Country Hideaways, Margaret's Cottage, Leyburn DL8 4JN
T: (01969) 663559
F: (01969) 663559
E: nadine@countryhideaways.co.uk
I: www.countryhideaways.co.uk

SELBY
North Yorkshire

Lund Farm Cottages ★★★-★★★★
Contact: Mr Chris & Mrs Helen Middleton
Lund Farm Cottages, Lund Farm, Selby YO8 9LE
T: (01757) 228775
F: (01757) 228775
E: chris.middleton@farmline.com
I: www.lundfarm.co.uk

Rusholme Cottage ★★★
Contact: Mrs Anne Roberts
Rusholme Cottage, Rusholme Grange, Selby YO8 8PW
T: (01757) 618257
F: (01757) 618257
E: anne@rusholmegrange.co.uk
I: www.rusholmegrange.co.uk

SETTLE
North Yorkshire

Cragdale Cottage ★★★★
Contact: Mr Paul Whitehead
75 New North Road, Reigate RH2 8LZ
T: (01737) 247179
F: (020) 8288 1505
E: paul@cragdalecottage.co.uk
I: www.cragdalecottage.co.uk

Devonshire Flat ★★★
Contact: Mr Allan Aspden
Devonshire House, 27 Duke Street, Settle BD24 9DJ
T: (01729) 825781

Hazel Cottage ★★★
Contact: Mrs Jennie Crawford
T: (01274) 832368
E: rogercrawford@greenclough.freeserve.co.uk
I: www.geocities.com/moorsideuk/

Lock Cottage Ref: 816 ★★★★
Contact: Mr S Boardman
Sykes Cottages, York House, York Street, Chester CH1 3LR
T: (01244) 345700
F: (01244) 321442
E: info@sykescottages.co.uk
I: www.sykescottages.co.uk

Old Brew House, Brewhouse Cottage & Robin Hill ★★★★
Contact: Mrs Jeanne Carr
17 Midland Terrace, Skipton BD23 4HJ
T: (01729) 850319
E: jmcarr@tesco.net
I: www.settle-selfcatering.co.uk

4 St John's Row ★★★
Contact: Mrs Mary Sowerby
15 Netherfield Road, Leeds LS20 9DN
T: (01943) 875552
F: (01924) 267341
E: marysowerby@yahoo.com

Establishments printed in blue have a detailed entry in this guide

YORKSHIRE

SEWERBY
East Riding of Yorkshire

Field House Farm Cottages ★★★★-★★★★★
Contact: Mrs Angela Foster
Field House, Jewison Lane,
Bridlington YO16 6YG
T: (01262) 674932
F: (01262) 608688
E: john.foster@farmline.com
I: www.fieldhousefarmcottages.co.uk

Oakwood ★★★★
Contact: Mrs Josephine Hodgson
5 Fairways Court, Pontefract
WF8 3DH
T: (01977) 704942
F: (01977) 704942

Park Cottage ★★★
Contact: Mrs Sue Ashby
The Old Manse, Pontefract
WF8 3EB
T: (01977) 620359

Peach Tree Cottage ★★★
Contact: Mrs Adams
15 Redwing Drive, Driffield
YO25 5HJ
T: (01377) 240650
F: (01377) 272220
I: www.peachtreecottage.co.uk

Sunnyside Cottages ★★★★
Contact: Mr Andrew & Mrs Caroline Pond
Manor Farm, Newsham Hill Lane, Bridlington YO15 1HL
T: (01262) 850680
F: (01262) 850680
E: allponds@btopenworld.com
I: www.eastyorkshireholidaycottages.co.uk

SHEFFIELD
South Yorkshire

Apartment Nine ★★★★
Contact: Mr Walker-Kane
The Parsonage House,
Manchester Road, Sheffield
S36 8QS
T: (01226) 761408

The Clough ★★★★
Contact: Mrs King & Mr N Ritchie
The Clough, Mayfield House,
Mayfield Road, Sheffield
S10 4PR
T: (0114) 230 1949
F: (0114) 2302014
E: breking@hotmail.com

The Flat ★★★
Contact: Mrs Cox
The Flat, 152 Whirlowdale Road,
Sheffield S7 2NL
T: (0114) 221 5553

Foxholes Farm ★★★
Contact: Rachel Hague
Parkside adjacent to Prospect Farm, Bradfield, Sheffield S6 6LJ
T: (0114) 285 1551
F: (0114) 285 1559
E: hagueplant@farmersweekly.net

Hangram Lane Farmhouse ★★★★
Contact: Mrs Clark
Hangram Lane Farmhouse,
Hangram Lane Grange, Hangram Lane, Sheffield S11 7TQ
T: (0114) 230 3570
F: (0114) 230 6573

Mill Lane Farm Cottage and Orchard Cottage ★★★★★
Contact: Miss Jayne Middleton
Mill Lane Farm Cottage and Orchard Cottage, Mayfield Road, Sheffield S10 4PR
T: (0114) 263 0188
F: (0114) 2306647
E: milllanefarmcottages@hotmail.com
I: milllanefarmcottages.tripod.com

Moor Royd House ★★★-★★★★
Contact: Mrs Janet Hird
Moor Royd House, Manchester Road, Millhouse Green, Sheffield
S36 9FG
T: (01226) 763353
F: (01226) 763353
E: janet@moorroydhouse.freeserve.uk
I: www.moorroydhouse.com

SHERBURN
North Yorkshire

Housemartins ★★★
Contact: Mrs Elissa Massie
Housemartins, Millfield House,
Millfield, Malton YO17 8QF
T: (01944) 710259

Westfield Granary ★★★-★★★★
Contact: Mr Wales
Holiday Cottages (Yorkshire) Ltd,
Water Street, Skipton BD23 1PB
T: (01756) 700510
E: brochure@holidaycotts.co.uk
I: www.holidaycotts.co.uk

SHERIFF HUTTON
North Yorkshire

Grooms Cottage ★★★
Contact: Mrs Lynne Fawcett
Grooms Cottage, Castle Farm House, York YO60 6ST
T: (01347) 878311
E: lfawcett@personneltraining.freeserve.co.uk
I: www.castlefarmhouse.co.uk

SIGGLESTHORNE
East Riding of Yorkshire

Peggy's Cottage ★★★★
Contact: Jude Collingwood
Peggy's Cottage, Nr Hornsea
HU11 5QH
T: (01964) 535395
E: p.collingwood@btinternet.com

SILSDEN
West Yorkshire

Croft Cottage Ref:1622 ★★★★
Contact: Ms H Cook
Dales Holiday Cottages, Carleton Business Park, Carleton New Road, Skipton BD23 2AA
T: (01756) 799821
F: (01756) 797012
E: info@dalesholcot.com
I: www.dalesholcot.com

Ford Cottage Ref:89 ★★★
Contact: Ms H Cook
Dales Holiday Cottages, Carleton Business Park, Carleton New Road, Skipton BD23 2AA
T: (01756) 799821
F: (01756) 797012
E: info@dalesholcot.com
I: www.dalesholcot.com

SINNINGTON
North Yorkshire

Goose End of Seven House Ref:1779 ★★★
Contact: Ms H Cook
Dales Holiday Cottages, Carleton Business Park, Carleton New Road, Skipton BD23 2AA
T: (01756) 799821
F: (01756) 797012
E: info@dalesholcot.com
I: www.dalesholcot.com

Pear Tree Barn Ref: 3427 ★★★★
Contact: Ms H Cook
Dales Holiday Cottages, Carleton Business Park, Carleton New Road, Skipton BD23 2AA
T: (01756) 799821
F: (01756) 797012
E: info@dalesholcot.com
I: www.dalesholcot.com

Sevenside Holiday Bungalow ★★★
Contact: Mrs Elizabeth Allan
Station House, York YO62 6RA
T: (01751) 431812
E: jdallan@care4free.net

SKIPSEA
East Riding of Yorkshire

Sea Holme Cottage ★★★
Contact: Mrs Susan Allen
Chapel House, Beeford Road,
Skipsea, Driffield YO25 8TG
T: (01262) 468663
E: sumic@seaholme.fsnet.co.uk

SKIPTON
North Yorkshire

Airedale Flat
Rating Applied For
Contact: Mr Barrie & Mrs Carole Thomas
Airedale Flat, 20 Gargrave Road,
Skipton BD23 1PJ
T: (01756) 709581

Cawder Hall Cottages ★★★-★★★★
Contact: Mr Graham Pearson
Cawder Hall Cottages, Cawder Lane, Skipton BD23 2TD
T: (01756) 791579
F: (01756) 797036
E: info@cawderhallcottages.co.uk
I: www.cawderhallcottages.co.uk

Dales Flat ★★
Contact: Mrs Margaret Little
Dale House, Skipton Road,
Keighley BD20 6PD
T: (01535) 791688
F: (01535) 653637

Dalestone ★★★
Contact: Mr Malcolm & Mrs Ann Wadsworth
25 Watson Road, Blackpool
FY4 1EG
T: (01253) 404726
E: mw001F3365@blueyonder.co.uk

7 Elliot Street ★★★
Contact: Mr Wales
Holiday Cottages (Yorkshire) Ltd,
Water Street, Skipton BD23 1PB
T: (01756) 700510
E: brochure@holidaycotts.co.uk
I: www.holidaycotts.co.uk

Garden Cottage ★★★★
Contact: Mrs Barbara Anne Ross
Garden Cottage, 56 Otley Street,
Skipton BD23 1ET
T: (01756) 799867

Ginnel Mews Ref:46 ★★★
Contact: Mr S Boardman
Sykes Cottages, York House,
York Street, Chester CH1 3LR
T: (01244) 345700
F: (01244) 321442
E: info@sykescottages.co.uk
I: www.sykescottages.co.uk

Hallams Yard Ref:255 ★★★★
Contact: Ms H Cook
Dales Holiday Cottages, Carleton Business Park, Carleton New Road, Skipton BD23 2AA
T: (01756) 799821
F: (01756) 797012
E: info@dalesholcot.com
I: www.dalesholcot.com

The Hide Ref:617 ★★★
Contact: Mr S Boardman
Sykes Cottages, York House,
York Street, Chester CH1 3LR
T: (01244) 345700
F: (01244) 321442
E: info@sykescottages.co.uk
I: www.sykescottages.co.uk

High Malsis Farmhouse ★★★
Contact: Mrs Sheila Fort
High Malsis Farmhouse, High Malsis, Keighley BD20 8DU
T: (01535) 633309
I: www.jfort.co.uk/holiday/

The Lodge ★★★★
Contact: Mrs Edith Ann Thwaite
The Lodge, Horton Hall Farm,
Skipton BD23 3JT
T: (01200) 445300
E: ediththwaite@hotmail.com
I: www.thelodgehorton.co.uk

Low Skibeden Farm Cottage ★★★
Contact: Mrs Heather Simpson
Low Skibeden Farmhouse,
Harrogate Road, Skipton
BD23 6AB
T: (01756) 793849
F: (01756) 793804
I: www.yorkshirenet.co.uk/accgde.lowskibeden

Lower Heugh Cottage ★★★★★
Contact: Mr Trevor Nash
Lower Heugh Cottage, 16 Kirk Lane, Skipton BD23 6SH
T: (01756) 793702
E: heughcottage@talk21.com

492 Look out for establishments participating in the National Accessible Scheme

YORKSHIRE

Maypole Cottage ★★★★
Contact: Mrs Elizabeth Gamble
Blackburn House, Skipton
BD23 6BJ
T: (01756) 720609
E: gamble@daelnet.co.uk

None-go-Bye Farm Cottage ★★★
Contact: Mrs Lawn
None Go Bye Farm, Grassington Road, Skipton BD23 3LB
T: (01756) 793165
F: (01756) 793203
E: booking.nonegobye@virgin.net
I: www.yorkshiredales.net/stayat/nonegobyefarm/index.htm

7 Pasture Road ★★★
Contact: Mr J S & Mrs C Lunnon
17 Cherry Tree Way, Rossendale BB4 4JZ
T: (01706) 230653
E: chris.lunnon@barlo.co.uk
I: www.cjlunnon.co.uk

Thisledo
Rating Applied For
Contact: Mrs Shelley Green
Thisledo, 16 Woodman Terrace, Skipton BD23 1PX
T: (01756) 795024
E: mail@thisledo.co.uk

SLEDMERE
East Riding of Yorkshire

Life Hill Farm ★★★★
Contact: Mr Andrew & Mrs Fay Grace
Life Hill Farm, Driffield YO25 3EY
T: (01377) 236214
F: (01377) 236685
E: info@lifehillfarm.co.uk
I: www.lifehillfarm.co.uk

SLEIGHTS
North Yorkshire

April Cottage ★★★
Contact: Mrs Adele Thompson
Whitby Holiday Cottages, 47 Flowergate, Whitby YO21 3BB
T: (01947) 603010
F: (01947) 821133
E: enquiries@whitby-cottages.co.uk
I: www.whitby-cottages.co.uk

Bracken Edge Ref:887 ★★★
Contact: Mr S Boardman
Sykes Cottages, York House, York Street, Chester CH1 3LR
T: (01244) 345700
F: (01244) 321442
E: info@sykescottages.co.uk
I: www.sykescottages.co.uk

Groves Dyke ★★★
Contact: Mr Niall Carson
Groves Dyke, Woodlands Drive, Whitby YO21 1RY
T: (01947) 811404
E: relax@grovesdyke.co.uk
I: www.grovesdyke.co.uk

Rose Nook
Rating Applied For
Contact: Mrs Stephanie Thompson
Copperstone Cottages and Flats, The Riggs, Stainsacre, Whitby YO22 4LR
T: (01947) 603262
F: (01947) 603271
E: copperstonecott@aol.com

The Stable Ref:2892 ★★★★
Contact: Ms H Cook
Dales Holiday Cottages, Carleton Business Park, Carleton New Road, Skipton BD23 2AA
T: (01756) 799821
F: (01756) 797012
E: info@dalesholcot.com
I: www.dalesholcot.com

SLINGSBY
North Yorkshire

Dawson Cottage ★★★
Contact: Mrs Julia Snowball
Harlsey House, Railway Street, Slingsby, York YO62 4AL
T: (01653) 628136
F: (01653) 628413
E: julia.snowball@amserve.com

Home Farm Holiday Cottages ★★★★
Contact: Mr & Mrs Prest
Castle Farm, High Street, Slingsby, York YO62 4AE
T: (01653) 628277
F: (01653) 628277
E: sgprest@farming.co.uk
I: www.yorkshire-holiday-cottage.co.uk

Keepers Cottage Holidays ★★★
Contact: Mrs Joanna Pavey
Keepers Cottage Holidays, Railway Street, York YO62 4AN
T: (01653) 628656

SNAINTON
North Yorkshire

Foxglove Cottage ★★★★★
Contact: Mrs Sandra Simpson
Foxglove Cottage, Beswicks Yard, Scarborough YO13 9AT
T: (01944) 758047
F: (01944) 758047
E: ssimpsoncottages@aol.com
I: www.ssimpsoncottages.co.uk

SNAPE
North Yorkshire

Jasmine Cottage ★★★
Contact: Mr & Mrs Colette Leyshon
131 Shackleton Close, Warrington WA5 9QG
T: (01925) 413907
E: jasminecottage@ntlworld.com

SNEATON
North Yorkshire

Raygill Cottage ★★★
Contact: Mr John Knell
25 Beckwith Crescent, Harrogate HG2 0BH
T: (01423) 566280

Rose Cottage ★★★
Contact: Mrs Adele Thompson
Whitby Holiday Cottages, 47 Flowergate, Whitby YO21 3BB
T: (01947) 603010
F: (01947) 821133
E: enquiries@whitby-cottages.co.uk
I: www.whitby-cottages.co.uk

SNEATON THORPE
North Yorkshire

Rose Cottage Apartment ★★★
Contact: Mrs Eirene Toshach
Rose Cottage Apartment, Rose Cottage, Whitby YO22 5JG
T: (01947) 881192
E: info@rosecottageapartment.co.uk
I: www.rosecottageapartment.co.uk

Sorrel Cottage ★★★★★
Contact: Mr David Haycox & Mrs Sue Brooks
Shoreline Cottages Ltd, Po Box 135, Leeds LS14 3XJ
T: (0113) 244 8410
F: (0113) 2449826
E: reservations@shoreline-cottages.com
I: www.shoreline-cottages.com

SOUTH KILVINGTON
North Yorkshire

Mowbray Stable Cottages ★★★
Contact: Mrs Margaret Backhouse
Mowbray, Stockton Road, Thirsk YO7 2LY
T: (01845) 522605

SOWERBY
North Yorkshire

Long Acre Lodge ★★★★
Contact: Mrs Dawson
The Lodge, 86A Topcliffe Road, Thirsk YO7 1RY
T: (01845) 522360

SOWERBY BRIDGE
West Yorkshire

Shield Hall Holiday Cottage ★★★
Contact: Mr John R Broadbent
Shield Hall, Shield Hall Lane, Sowerby Bridge HX6 1NJ
T: (01422) 832165

SPEETON
North Yorkshire

Woodbine Farm Holiday Cottages ★★★★
Contact: Mrs Karen Dyson
Woodbine Farm, Filey YO14 9TG
T: (01723) 890783

SPROXTON
North Yorkshire

Lavender Cottage ★★★★
Contact: Mr Robin & Mrs Sue Houlston
3 Roseacres, Goole DN14 5PP
T: (01405) 764598
E: robin.houlston@which.net
I: homepages.which.net/~robin.houlston/index.html

Sproxton Hall Cottages ★★★
Contact: Mr David Bowens
Sproxton Hall Cottages, Bondgate, York YO62 5EZ
T: (01439) 770980
E: sproxtonhallcott@btopenworld.com
I: www.helmsley.biz

STACKHOUSE
North Yorkshire

Langcliffe Locks ★★★★
Contact: Mr Colin Hibbert
8 Undercliffe Rise, Ilkley LS29 8RF
T: (01943) 601729
E: catherine.hibbert@blueyonder.co.uk
I: www.holidaycottage.pwp.blueyonder.co.uk

STAINTONDALE
North Yorkshire

White Hall Farm Holiday Cottages ★★★
Contact: Mr James & Mrs Celia White
White Hall Farm Holiday Cottages, White Hall Farm, Staintondale, Scarborough YO13 0EY
T: (01723) 870234
E: celia@white66.fsbusiness.co.uk
I: www.whitehallcottages.co.uk

STAITHES
North Yorkshire

The Cottage ★★
Contact: Mrs Adele Thompson
Whitby Holiday Cottages, 47 Flowergate, Whitby YO21 3BB
T: (01947) 603010
F: (01947) 821133
E: enquiries@whitby-cottages.co.uk
I: www.whitby-cottages.co.uk

11 Cowbar Cottages, Miner's Rest ★★★
Contact: Mr Close
27 High Street, Stamford PE3 3PW
T: 0718 0 444245
I: www.country-holidays.co.uk

Glencoe ★★
Contact: Mr David Purdy
Church Street, Kirkbymoorside, York YO62 6AZ
T: (01751) 431452

Roxby Cottage ★★★
Contact: Mrs Adele Thompson
Whitby Holiday Cottages, 47 Flowergate, Whitby YO21 3BB
T: (01947) 603010
F: (01947) 821133
E: enquiries@whitby-cottages.co.uk
I: www.whitby-cottages.co.uky

Springfields ★★★
Contact: Mrs Watson
Springfields, 42 Staithes Lane, Saltburn-by-the-Sea TS13 5AD
T: (01947) 841865

Establishments printed in blue have a detailed entry in this guide

493

YORKSHIRE

STAMFORD BRIDGE
East Riding of Yorkshire
The Cottage ★★★★
Contact: Mrs Foster
The Cottage, High Catton
Grange, York YO41 1EP
T: (01759) 371374
F: (01759) 371374

STANBURY
West Yorkshire
Higher Scholes Cottage ★★★★★
Contact: Mrs Catherine O'Leary
Higher Scholes Barn, Higher
Scholes, Keighley BD22 0RP
T: (01535) 646793
E: olly@mopsy66552.freeserve.co.uk

Sarah's Cottage ★★★★
Contact: Mr Brian Fuller
101 Stanbury, Keighley
BD22 0HA
T: (01535) 643015
E: brian.fuller2@btinternet.com
I: www.sarahs-cottage.co.uk

Upper Heights Farm ★★★★
Contact: Mr Gordon & Mrs Barbara Baxter
Upper Heights Farm, Haworth,
Keighley BD22 0HH
T: (01535) 644592
I: www.brontemoor-breaks.co.uk

STANNINGTON
South Yorkshire
Wesley Cottage ★★★
Contact: Colin MacQueen
Peak Cottages, Strawberry Lee
Lane, Sheffield S17 3BA
T: (0114) 262 0777
F: (0114) 2620666
E: enquiries@peakcottages.com
I: www.peakcottages.com

STARBOTTON
North Yorkshire
Horseshoe Cottage ★★★
Contact: Mr Kevin & Mrs Lynn May
7 The Street, Tetbury GL8 8UN
T: (01666) 890336
E: kevin@may1561.fsnet.co.uk

Ivy Cottage Ref: 3390 ★★★★
Contact: Ms H Cook
Dales Holiday Cottages, Carleton
Business Park, Carleton New
Road, Skipton BD23 2AA
T: (01756) 799821
F: (01756) 797012
E: info@dalesholcot.com
I: www.dalesholcot.com

STILLINGTON
North Yorkshire
Rose Cottage & Holly Cottage ★★★★
Contact: Mrs Susie Hamilton
Stillington Grange Farm,
Easingwold Road, York YO61 1LT
T: (01347) 822631

STIRTON
North Yorkshire
Cockpit Corner Ref: 1699 ★★★
Contact: Ms H Cook
Dales Holiday Cottages, Carleton
Business Park, Carleton New
Road, Skipton BD23 2AA
T: (01756) 799821
F: (01756) 797012
E: info@dalesholcot.com
I: www.dalesholcot.com

STORWOOD
East Riding of Yorkshire
Paradise Leisure ★★★
Contact: Mrs Valerie Cranmer-Gordon
Paradise Leisure, Ballhall Lane,
York YO42 4TD
T: (01759) 318452
F: (01759) 318368
E: info@paradiseleisure.com
I: www.paradiseleisure.com

SUTTON-ON-THE-FOREST
North Yorkshire
K M Knowlson Holiday Cottages ★★★
Contact: Mrs Heather Knowlson
K M Knowlson Holiday Cottages,
Thrush House, Well Lane, York
YO61 1ED
T: (01347) 810225
F: (01347) 810225
E: kmkholcottyksuk@aol.com
I: www.holidayskmkholcotts-yks.uk.com

TERRINGTON
North Yorkshire
Terrington Holiday Cottages ★★★-★★★★★
Contact: Mrs Sally Goodrick
Terrington Holiday Cottages, 3
Springfield Court, York
YO60 6PY
T: (01653) 648370
E: goodrick@terrington10.freeserve.co.uk
I: www.terrington.com/sallycottages.html

THIRSK
North Yorkshire
Briar Cottage & Bramble Cottage ★★★
Contact: Audrey Saye
Thirsk YO7 2QA
T: (01845) 597309
E: jim.dickinson@btinternet.com

The Granary ★★★★
Contact: Mrs Mary Harrison
East Farm, Thirsk YO7 2DJ
T: (01845) 597554
E: mary@thegranary36.fsnet.co.uk
I: www.thegranary.20m.com

The Old School House ★★★
Contact: Mrs Gabrielle Readman
Catton, Thirsk YO7 4SG
T: (01845) 567308

Pasture Field House ★★
Contact: Mrs Emma Hunter
Pasture Field House, Thirsk
YO7 4DE
T: (01845) 587230
F: (01845) 587230

Poplars Holiday Cottages ★★★★
Contact: Mrs Chris Chilton
Poplars Holiday Cottages, Thirsk
YO7 4LX
T: (01845) 522712
F: (01845) 522712
E: the_poplars_cottages@btopenworld.com
I: www.yorkshirebandb.co.uk

Shires Court ★★★
Contact: Mrs Judy Rennie
Shires Court, Moor Road, Thirsk
YO7 4BS
T: (01845) 537494

Skipton Hall ★★★★
Contact: Mrs Audrey Skipsey
Swale House, Skipton on Swale,
Thirsk YO7 4SB
T: (01845) 567037
F: (01845) 567733
E: audrey@askipsey.psnet.co.uk
I: www.hireskiptonhall.co.uk

80 St James Green ★★★
Contact: Mrs Joanna Todd
79 St James Green, Thirsk
YO7 1AJ
T: (01845) 523522

THONGSBRIDGE
West Yorkshire
Mytholmbridge Studio Cottage ★★★★
Contact: Mrs Clay
Mytholmbridge Farm, Luke Lane,
Thongsbridge, Huddersfield
HD9 7TB
T: (01484) 686642
E: cottages@mytholmbridge.co.uk
I: www.mytholmbridge.co.uk

THORALBY
North Yorkshire
Coach House
Rating Applied For
Contact: Mrs Nadine Bell
Country Hideaways, Margaret's
Cottage, Leyburn DL8 4JN
T: (01969) 663559
F: (01969) 663559
E: nadine@countryhideaways.co.uk
I: www.countryhideaways.co.uk

The Garden Flat, The Old Corn Mill ★★★
Contact: Mrs Nadine Bell
Country Hideaways, Margaret's
Cottage, Leyburn DL8 4JN
T: (01969) 663559
F: (01969) 663559
E: nadine@countryhideaways.co.uk
I: www.countryhideaways.co.uk

High Green Cottage ★★★
Contact: Mr Clive Sykes
Sykes Holiday Cottages, York
House, York Street, Chester
CH1 3LR
T: (01244) 345700
F: (01244) 321442
E: info@sykescottages.co.uk
I: www.sykescottages.co.uk

Meadowcroft ★★★
Contact: Mr Mason
43 Llythrid Avenue, Swansea
SA2 0JJ
T: (01792) 280068
F: (01792) 280068
E: mcmason@globalnet.co.uk

Woodpecker Cottage ★★★★
Contact: Mrs Nadine Bell
Country Hideaways, Margaret's
Cottage, Leyburn DL8 4JN
T: (01969) 663559
F: (01969) 663559
E: nadine@countryhideaways.co.uk
I: www.countryhideaways.co.uk

THORGILL
North Yorkshire
Appledore Cottage ★★★★
Contact: Mrs Emma Glover
St Margaret's Rectory, South
Street, Durham DH1 4QP
T: (0191) 3843623
E: emmag@fish.co.uk

THORNTON DALE
North Yorkshire
Brookwood ★★★★
Contact: Mrs Balderson & Claire Lealman
Brookwood, Welcome Cafe,
Pickering YO18 7RW
T: (01751) 474272
F: (01751) 472372
E: baldersons@hotmail.com

Hillcroft ★★★
Contact: Mrs Lily Brookfield
Braemar, Roxby Road, Pickering
YO18 7TJ
T: (01751) 474342
I: www.country-holidays.co.uk

Station House Holiday Cottages ★★★
Contact: Mrs Hilary Scales
Station House Holiday Cottages,
Maltongate, Pickering YO18 7SE
T: (01751) 474417
F: (01751) 473373
E: overbrook@breathe.com

THORNTON IN CRAVEN
North Yorkshire
The Cottage Ref: 2166 ★★★
Contact: Ms H Cook
Dales Holiday Cottages, Carleton
Business Park, Carleton New
Road, Skipton BD23 2AA
T: (01756) 799821
F: (01756) 797012
E: info@dalesholcot.com
I: www.dalesholcot.com

THORNTON RUST
North Yorkshire
The Old Goat House ★★★★
Contact: Mrs Annette Riley
South View, Leyburn DL8 3AN
T: (01969) 663716
E: info@oldgoathouse.co.uk
I: www.oldgoathouse.co.uk

Outgang Cottage Ref: 1468 ★★★
Contact: Ms H Cook
Dales Holiday Cottages, Carleton
Business Park, Carleton New
Road, Skipton BD23 2AA
T: (01756) 799821
F: (01756) 797012
E: info@dalesholcot.com
I: www.dalesholcot.com

Look out for establishments participating in the National Accessible Scheme

YORKSHIRE

THORPE BASSETT
North Yorkshire
The Old Post Office ★★★★
Contact: Mrs Sandra Simpson
The Old Post Office, Malton
YO17 8LU
T: (01944) 758047
F: (01944) 758047
E: ssimpsoncottages@aol.com
I: www.ssimpsoncottages.co.uk

THRESHFIELD
North Yorkshire
Brazengate Ref:55 ★★★
Contact: Mr S Boardman
Sykes Cottages, York House,
York Street, Chester CH1 3LR
T: (01244) 345700
F: (01244) 321442
E: info@sykescottages.co.uk
I: www.sykescottages.co.uk

Wharfe Lodge ★★★
Contact: Mrs J Mitton
Hay House, Narcot Lane,
Chalfont St Giles HP8 4DX
T: (01494) 872572

THURLSTONE
South Yorkshire
The Parsonage House ★★★★★
Contact: Mr Walker-Kane
The Parsonage House,
Manchester Road, Sheffield
S36 9QS
T: (01226) 761408
F: (01226) 761044

THWAITE
North Yorkshire
The Cottage ★★★
Contact: Mrs Nadine Bell
Country Hideaways, Margaret's
Cottage, Leyburn DL8 4JN
T: (01969) 663559
F: (01969) 663559
E: nadine@countryhideaways.co.uk
I: www.countryhideaways.co.uk

Greystones & Stockdale ★★★
Contact: Mr Ken Williamson
Askrigg Cottage Holidays,
Thwaite House, Moor Road,
Leyburn DL8 3HH
T: (01969) 650022
E: stay@askrigg.com
I: www.askrigg.com

Thwaite Farm Cottages ★★★-★★★★★
Contact: Mrs Gillian Whitehead
Thwaite Farm Cottages, Thwaite
Farm, Richmond DL11 6DR
T: (01748) 886444
F: (01748) 886444
E: info@thwaitefarmcottages.co.uk
I: www.thwaitefarmcottages.co.uk

Thwaitedale Cottages ★★★★
Contact: Miss Valerie Hunter
Thwaitedale Cottages, 52 Moira
Road, Donisthorpe, Swadlincote
DE12 7QE
T: (01530) 272794
F: (01530) 272794
E: valerie@theturret.freeserve.co.uk
I: www.thwaitecottages.co.uk

Turfy Gill Hall ★★★★
Contact: Mr Keith & Mrs Ivy
Moseley
Turfy Gill Hall, Richmond
DL11 6DT
T: (01748) 886369
F: (01748) 886593
E: info@turfygill.com
I: www.turfygill.com

TICKTON
East Riding of Yorkshire
Bridge House Cottage ★★★
Contact: Mr Peter White & Ms
Adele Wilkinson
Bridge House Cottage, Hull
Bridge House, Weel Road,
Tickton, Beverley HU17 9RY
T: (01964) 542355
E: alw@amj.co.uk

TIMBLE
North Yorkshire
The Old Dairy ★★★★
Contact: Mrs Dawn Meeks
The Old Dairy, Southcroft, Otley
LS21 2NN
T: (01943) 880363
E: meeksdawn@hotmail.com
I: www.theolddairy.info

TOCKWITH
North Yorkshire
Ben's Cottage ★★★★
Contact: Mrs Julie Terry
Broad Oak Farm, Tockwith Lane,
York YO26 7QQ
T: (01423) 358304
F: (01484) 608763
E: jterry@benscottage.fsnet.co.uk
I: www.benscottage.harrogate.net

TODMORDEN
West Yorkshire
Butterworth Cottage ★★★
Contact: Mr Neil & Mrs Patricia
Butterworth
Butterworth Cottage, Cinder Hill
Farm, Cinderhill Road,
Todmorden OL14 8AA
T: (01706) 813067
F: 0870 0 884807
E: bookings@cottage-holiday.co.uk
I: www.cottage-holiday.co.uk

The Cottage ★★★
Contact: Mr & Mrs Bentham
The Cottage, Causeway East
Farmhouse, Lee Bottom Road,
Todmorden OL14 6HH
T: (01706) 815265
E: andrew@bentham5.freeserve.co.uk

Stannally Farm Cottage ★★★★
Contact: Mrs Dineen Ann Brunt
Stannally Farm Cottage,
Stannally Farm, Stoney Royd
Lane, Todmorden OL14 8EP
T: (01706) 813998
F: (01706) 813998
E: Bruntdennis@aol.com

Staups Barn Holiday Cottage ★★★
Contact: Mr & Mrs Crabtree
Staups Cottage, Staups Lane,
Higher Eastwood, Todmorden
OL14 8RU
T: (01706) 812730
F: (01706) 812730

TOLLERTON
North Yorkshire
Gill Cottage Ref:1977 ★★★★
Contact: Ms H Cook
Dales Holiday Cottages, Carleton
Business Park, Carleton New
Road, Skipton BD23 2AA
T: (01756) 799821
F: (01756) 797012
E: info@dalesholcot.com
I: www.dalesholcot.com

TOTLEY RISE
South Yorkshire
Swallow Cottage ★★★★
Contact: Mrs D Hill-Pickford
Swallow Cottage, Bents Farm,
Penny Lane, Totley Rise,
Sheffield S17 3AZ
T: (0114) 236 7806
I: www.swallowcottage.com

UGGLEBARNBY
North Yorkshire
Howlet Hall Farm Cottage Ref:1556 ★★★
Contact: Ms H Cook
Dales Holiday Cottages, Carleton
Business Park, Carleton New
Road, Skipton BD23 2AA
T: (01756) 799821
F: (01756) 797012
E: info@dalesholcot.com
I: www.dalesholcot.com

WARLEY
West Yorkshire
Greystones Farm Cottage ★★★★
Contact: Mrs Alison Phillips
Greystones Farm Cottage,
Greystones Road,
Luddendenfoot, Halifax HX2 6BY
T: (01422) 882445

WASS
North Yorkshire
High Woods Farm Holiday Cottages ★★★★
Contact: Mr Jonathan & Mrs
Susan Evans
High Woods Farm Holiday
Cottages, High Woods Farm,
York YO61 4AY
T: (01347) 868188
F: (01347) 868163
E: jon&sue@highwoodsfarm.co.uk
I: www.highwoodsfarm.co.uk

WELBURN
North Yorkshire
Castle View ★★★
Contact: Mr & Mrs Michael
Cockerill
Castle View, West End, York
YO60 7DX
T: (01653) 618344

Oak Tree Cottage ★★★★
Contact: Mr Mark Rees
Oak Tree Cottage, York
YO60 7DX
E: mark.rees@northyorkshire.pnn.police.uk

WEST BRETTON
West Yorkshire
Parkside Cottage ★★★★
Contact: Mr Philip & Mrs Joyce
Platts
Parkside Cottage, 31 Park Lane,
Wakefield WF4 4JT
T: (01924) 830215
F: (01924) 830215
E: jmplatts@hotmail.com
I: www.parksidecottage.co.uk

WEST BURTON
North Yorkshire
Cherry Tree Cottage ★★★
Contact: Mrs Nadine Bell
Country Hideaways, Margaret's
Cottage, Leyburn DL8 4JN
T: (01969) 663559
F: (01969) 663559
E: nadine@countryhideaways.co.uk
I: www.countryhideaways.co.uk

Craggley Cottage ★★★★
Contact: Mrs Nadine Bell
Country Hideaways, Margarets
Cottage, Leyburn DL8 4JN
T: (01969) 663559
F: (01969) 663559
E: nadine@countryhideaways.co.uk
I: www.countryhideaways.co.uk

First Floor Apartment, The Mill ★★★
Contact: Mrs Nadine Bell
Country Hideaways, Margaret's
Cottage, Leyburn DL8 4JN
T: (01969) 663559
F: (01969) 663559
E: nadine@countryhideaways.co.uk
I: www.countryhideaways.co.uk

The Garden Level Apartment, The Mill ★★★
Contact: Mrs Nadine Bell
Country Hideaways, Margaret's
Cottage, Leyburn DL8 4JN
T: (01969) 663559
F: (01969) 663559
E: nadine@countryhideaways.co.uk
I: www.countryhideaways.co.uk

Grange House ★★★★
Contact: Mrs Zoe Mort
Grange House, Walden, Leyburn
DL8 4LF
T: (01969) 663641
E: zoe.zeepee@virgin.net

Establishments printed in blue have a detailed entry in this guide

YORKSHIRE

Green Bank ★★★
Contact: Mrs Nadine Bell
Country Hideaways, Margaret's Cottage, Leyburn DL8 4JN
T: (01969) 663559
F: (01969) 663559
E: nadine@countryhideaways.co.uk
I: www.countryhideaways.co.uk

The Ground Floor Apartment, The Mill ★★★
Contact: Mrs Nadine Bell
Country Hideaways, Margaret's Cottage, Leyburn DL8 4JN
T: (01969) 663559
F: (01969) 663559
E: nadine@countryhideaways.co.uk
I: www.countryhideaways.co.uk

Ivy Cottage ★★★
Contact: Mrs Nadine Bell
Country Hideaways, Margaret's Cottage, Leyburn DL8 4JN
T: (01969) 663559
F: (01969) 663559
E: nadine@countryhideaways.co.uk
I: www.countryhideaways.co.uk

Jesmond Cottage ★★★
Contact: Mrs Nadine Bell
Country Hideaways, Margaret's Cottage, Leyburn DL8 4JN
T: (01969) 663559
F: (01969) 663559
E: nadine@countryhideaways.co.uk
I: www.countryhideaways.co.uk

Penny Farthings ★★★
Contact: Mrs Nadine Bell
Country Hideaways, Margaret's Cottage, Leyburn DL8 4JN
T: (01969) 663559
F: (01969) 663559
E: nadine@countryhideaways.co.uk
I: www.countryhideaways.co.uk

Studio Apartment, The Mill ★★
Contact: Mrs Nadine Bell
Country Hideaways, Margaret's Cottage, Leyburn DL8 4JN
T: (01969) 663559
F: (01969) 663559
E: nadine@countryhideaways.co.uk
I: www.countryhideaways.co.uk

WEST HESLERTON
North Yorkshire

Whin Moor Cottage Ref:1575 ★★★
Contact: Ms F Moody
Dales Holiday Cottages, Carleton Business Park, Carleton New Road, Skipton BD23 2AA
T: (01756) 799821
F: (01756) 797012
E: fiona@dalesholcot.com
I: www.dalesholcot.com

WEST WITTON
North Yorkshire

Arnolds Holiday Cottages ★★★
Contact: Mr and Mrs Arnold
Chantry Farmhouse, Main Street, West Witton, Leyburn DL8 4LU
T: (01969) 624303
F: (01969) 624303
E: holidaycottage2004@yahoo.com
I: www.arnoldsholidaycottages.com

1 Chestnut Garth Ref: 779 ★★★
Contact: Mr S Boardman
Sykes Cottages, York House, York Street, Chester CH1 3LR
T: (01244) 345700
F: (01244) 321442
E: info@sykescottages.co.uk
I: www.sykescottages.co.uk

Dairy Cottage ★★★
Contact: Mrs Nadine Bell
Country Hideaways, Margaret's Cottage, Leyburn DL8 4JN
T: (01969) 663559
F: (01969) 663559
E: nadine@countryhideaways.co.uk
I: www.countryhideaways.co.uk

Ivy Dene Cottage ★★★
Contact: Mr Bob Dickinson
Ivy Dene Cottage, Main Street, Leyburn DL8 4LP
T: (01969) 622785
F: (01969) 622785
E: info@ivydeneguesthouse.co.uk
I: www.ivydeneguesthouse.co.uk

WHASHTON
North Yorkshire

Mount Pleasant Farm ★★★-★★★★★★
Contact: Mrs Pittaway
Mount Pleasant Farm, Whashton, Richmond DL11 7JP
T: (01748) 822784
F: (01748) 822784
E: info@mountpleasantfarmhouse.co.uk
I: www.mountpleasantfarmhouse.co.uk

WHITBY
North Yorkshire

Abbey Holiday Apartments ★-★★★★
Contact: Mr Ted & Mrs Sandra Smith
17 Esk Terrace, Whitby YO21 1PA
T: (01947) 820025
E: smiths@tedsandra.co.uk

Abbey View ★★★★
Contact: Mrs Adele Thompson
Whitby Holiday Cottages, 47 Flowergate, Whitby YO21 3BB
T: (01947) 603010
F: (01947) 821133
E: enquiries@whitby-cottages.co.uk
I: www.whitby-cottages.co.uk

Abbey View ★★★★
Contact: Mr Peter Simpson
107 Church Street, Whitby YO22 4DE
T: (01947) 604406

Abbey View Rating Applied For
Contact: Mr David Hattersley
Abbey View, 4 Albert Place, Whitby YO21 3EX
T: (01629) 820273
E: reservations@debrettonestates.co.uk
I: www.debrettonestates.co.uk

Abbey View Cottage ★★★★
Contact: Mr David Haycox & Mrs Sue Brooks
Shoreline Cottages Ltd, Po Box 135, Leeds LS14 3XJ
T: (0113) 244 8410
F: (0113) 2449826
E: reservations@shoreline-cottages.com
I: www.shoreline-cottages.com

Acacia House ★★★★
Contact: Mrs Adele Thompson
Whitby Holiday Cottages, 47 Flowergate, Whitby YO21 3BB
T: (01947) 603010
F: (01947) 821133
E: enquiries@whitby-cottages.co.uk
I: www.whitby-cottages.co.uk

Admirals Lookout ★★★★
Contact: Mrs Vanessa Hicking
Whitby Holiday Cottages, 47 Flowergate, Whitby YO21 3BB
T: (01947) 603010
F: (01947) 821133
E: enquiries@whitby-cottages.co.uk
I: www.whitby-cottages.co.uk

Albany House ★★★★
Contact: Mrs Adele Thompson
Whitby Holiday Cottages, Flowergate, Whitby YO21 3BB
T: (01947) 603010
F: (01947) 821133
E: enquiries@whitby-cottages.co.uk
I: www.whitby-cottages.co.uk

Ambler Mews ★★★
Contact: Mrs Adele Thompson
Whitby Holiday Cottages, 47 Flowergate, Whitby YO21 3BB
T: (01947) 603010
F: (01947) 821133
E: enquiries@whitby-cottages.co.uk
I: www.whitby-cottages.co.uk

The Anchorage Ref:360 ★★
Contact: Mr S Boardman
Sykes Cottages, York House, York Street, Chester CH1 3LR
T: (01244) 345700
F: (01244) 321442
E: info@sykescottages.co.uk
I: www.sykescottages.co.uk

Appleton Cottage Rating Applied For
Contact: Mrs Vanessa Hicking
Appleton Cottage, 1 Hydings Yard, Whitby YO21 1DF
T: (01947) 603010
F: (01947) 821133
E: enquiries@whitby-cottages.co.uk
I: www.whitby-cottages.co.uk

Awd Tuts Cottage ★★★★
Contact: Mr Michael Peacock
45 Beverley Road, Redcar TS10 3RZ
T: (01642) 484547
E: awdtuts.information@ntlworld.com
I: www.whitby-cottage.co.uk

Bakehouse Cottage ★★★★
Contact: Mr David Haycox & Mrs Sue Brooks
Shoreline Cottages Ltd, Po Box 135, Leeds LS14 3XJ
T: (0113) 244 8410
F: (0113) 2449826
E: reservations@shoreline-cottages.com
I: www.shoreline-cottages.com

Bennison House Farm ★★★★
Contact: Mr R G & Mrs H E Thompson
Bennison House Farm, Beacon Way, Whitby YO22 5HS
T: (01947) 820292

1 Bensons Yard ★★★
Contact: Mrs Lonsdale
1 Bensons Yard, Meadowcroft, Oakley Walls, Whitby YO21 2AU
T: (01947) 897472

Bosuns Cottage Rating Applied For
Contact: Mrs Vanessa Hicking
47 Flowergate, Whitby YO21 3BB
T: (01947) 603010
F: (01947) 821133
E: enquiries@whitby-cottages.co.uk
I: www.whitby-cottages.co.uk

Breckon Cottage ★★★
Contact: Mrs Adele Thompson
Whitby Holiday Cottages, 47 Flowergate, Whitby YO21 3BB
T: (01947) 603010
F: (01947) 821133
E: enquiries@whitby-cottages.co.uk
I: www.whitby-cottages.co.uk

Brook House Farm Holiday Cottages ★★★★
Contact: Mrs Sallie White
Brook House Farm Holiday Cottages, Brook House Farm, Whitby YO21 2LH
T: (01287) 660064

Bumblebee Cottage ★★★
Contact: Mrs Julie Asher
Bumblebee Cottage, 4 Princess Place, Whitby YO21 1DZ
T: (01947) 821803
E: jash@dracula68.fsnet.co.uk

5 Burns Yard ★★★★
Contact: Mrs Adele Thompson
Whitby Holiday Cottages, 47 Flowergate, Whitby YO21 3BB
T: (01947) 603010
F: (01947) 821133
E: enquiries@whitby-cottages.co.uk
I: www.whitby-cottages.co.uk

YORKSHIRE

Calypso Cottage ★★
Contact: Mrs Adele Thompson
Whitby Holiday Cottages, 47 Flowergate, Whitby YO21 3BB
T: (01947) 603010
F: (01947) 821133
E: enquiries@whitby-cottages.co.uk
I: www.whitby-cottages.co.uk

Captain Cook's Haven ★★★-★★★★★
Contact: Mrs Anne Barrowman
Holiday Homes Ltd, Upton Hall, Whitby YO21 3RU
T: (01947) 893573
F: (01947) 893573
I: www.hoseasons.co.uk

Captains Cottage
Rating Applied For
Contact: Mrs Vanessa Hicking
Captains Cottage, Henrietta Street, Whitby YO22 4DW
T: (01947) 603010
F: (01947) 821133
E: enquiries@whitby-cottages.co.uk
I: www.whitby-cottages.co.uk

Captain's Quarters ★★★★★
Contact: Mr David Haycox & Mrs Sue Brooks
Shoreline Cottages Ltd, Po Box 135, Leeds LS14 3XJ
T: (0113) 244 8410
F: (0113) 2449826
E: reservations@shoreline-cottages.com
I: www.shoreline-cottages.com

The Captains View ★★★
Contact: Mrs Vanessa Hicking
Whitby Holiday Cottages, 47 Flowergate, Whitby YO21 3BB
T: (01947) 603010
F: (01947) 821133
E: enquiries@whitby-cottages.co.uk

Carlton House Holiday Accommodation ★-★★
Contact: Mrs Susan Brookes
Carlton House Holiday Accommodation, 5 Royal Crescent, West Cliff, Whitby YO21 3EJ
T: (01947) 602868
F: (01947) 602868

The Chapter House ★★★★
Contact: Mrs Adele Thompson
Whitby Holiday Cottages, 47 Flowergate, Whitby YO21 3BB
T: (01947) 603010
F: (01947) 821133
E: enquiries@whitby-cottages.co.uk
I: www.whitby-cottages.co.uk

Chatteris House ★★★
Contact: Mrs Adele Thompson
Whitby Holiday Cottages, 47 Flowergate, Whitby YO21 3BB
T: (01947) 603010
F: (01947) 821133
E: enquiries@whitby-cottages.co.uk
I: www.whitby-cottages.co.uk

Cherry Trees ★★★
Contact: Mr P Dowson
Newbiggin High Farm, Whitby YO21 1SX
T: (01947) 810324
F: (01947) 810324
I: www.cherrytreeswhitby.co.uk

Church Cottage ★★★
Contact: Mrs Adele Thompson
Whitby Holiday Cottages, 47 Flowergate, Whitby YO21 3BB
T: (01947) 603010
F: (01947) 821133
E: enquiries@whitby-cottages.co.uk
I: www.whitby-cottages.co.uk

Cliff House ★★
Contact: Mrs Pat Beale
Ryedale House, Coach Road, Sleights, Whitby YO22 5EQ
T: (01947) 810534
F: (01947) 810534

5A Cliff Street ★★★
Contact: Mrs Adele Thompson
Whitby Holiday Cottages, 47 Flowergate, Whitby YO21 3BB
T: (01947) 603010
F: (01947) 821133
E: enquiries@whitby-cottages.co.uk
I: www.whitby-cottages.co.uk

Cobble Cottage Ref:1808 ★★★
Contact: Ms H Cook
Dales Holiday Cottages, Carleton Business Park, Carleton New Road, Skipton BD23 2AA
T: (01756) 799821
F: (01756) 797012
E: info@dalesholcot.com
I: www.dalesholcot.com

Coble Cottage ★★★
Contact: Mrs Adele Thompson
Whitby Holiday Cottages, 47 Flowergate, Whitby YO21 3BB
T: (01947) 603010
F: (01947) 821133
E: enquiries@whitby-cottages.co.uk
I: www.whitby-cottages.co.uk

Copper Beeches ★★-★★★
Contact: Mrs Hilary Walker
The Nurseries, Whitby YO21 1TT
T: (01947) 895640
F: (01947) 895641
E: hilary_phenix@hotmail.com

Corner Cottage ★★★★
Contact: Mrs Adele Thompson
Whitby Holiday Cottages, 47 Flowergate, Whitby YO21 3BB
T: (01947) 603010
F: (01947) 821133
E: enquiries@whitby-cottages.co.uk
I: www.whitby-cottages.co.uk

The Cottage ★★★
Contact: Mrs Adele Thompson
Whitby Holiday Cottages, 47 Flowergate, Whitby YO21 3BB
T: (01947) 603010
F: (01947) 821133
E: enquiries@whitby-cottages.co.uk
I: www.whitby-cottages.co.uk

1 The Croft ★★★
Contact: Mrs Adele Thompson
Whitby Holiday Cottages, 47 Flowergate, Whitby YO21 3BB
T: (01947) 603010
F: (01947) 821133
E: enquiries@whitby-cottages.co.uk
I: www.whitby-cottages.co.uk

Crows Nest ★★★
Contact: Mr Eric Tayler
28 Cambrian Avenue, Redcar TS10 4HF
T: (01642) 492144
E: crowsnest.whitby@ntlworld.com
I: www.crowsnestwhitby.co.uk

Cuddy Cottage ★★★★
Contact: Mr David Haycox & Mrs Sue Brooks
Shoreline Cottages Ltd, Po Box 135, Leeds LS14 3XJ
T: (0113) 244 8410
F: (0113) 2449826
E: reservations@shoreline-cottages.com
I: www.shoreline-cottages.com

Discovery Accommodation ★★★★
Contact: Mrs Pam Gilmore
Discovery Accommodation, 11 Silver Street, Whitby YO21 3BX
T: (01947) 821598
F: (01947) 600406
E: info@discoveryaccommodation.com
I: www.discoveryaccommodation.com

East Cliff Cottages, Hardwick Cottage ★★★
Contact: Dr Thornton
Brookhouse, Dam Lane, Leavening, Malton YO17 9SF
T: (01653) 658249
E: enquiries@seasideholiday.co.uk
I: www.seasideholiday.co.uk

Elizabeth House Holiday Flats ★-★★★★
Contact: Mrs Rosaline Cooper
Park View, 14 Chubb Hill Road, Whitby YO21 1JU
T: (01947) 604213
E: jakanann@btopenworld.com
I: www.elizabeth-house.biz

Endeavour Cottage ★★★
Contact: Mrs Adele Thompson
Whitby Holiday Cottages, 47 Flowergate, Whitby YO21 3BB
T: (01947) 603010
F: (01947) 821133
E: enquiries@whitby-cottages.co.uk
I: www.whitby-cottages.co.uk

24 Endeavour Court ★★★
Contact: Mrs Adele Thompson
Whitby Holiday Cottages, 47 Flowergate, Whitby YO21 3BB
T: (01947) 603010
F: (01947) 821133
E: enquiries@whitby-cottages.co.uk
I: www.whitby-cottages.co.uk

7 Esk Terrace ★★★
Contact: Mrs Adele Thompson
Whitby Holiday Cottages, 47 Flowergate, Whitby YO21 3BB
T: (01947) 603010
F: (01947) 821133
E: enquiries@whitby-cottages.co.uk
I: www.whitby-cottages.co.uk

Esk View Apartment ★★★★
Contact: Mrs Adele Thompson
Whitby Holiday Cottages, 47 Flowergate, Whitby YO21 3BB
T: (01947) 603010
F: (01947) 821133
E: enquiries@whitby-cottages.co.uk
I: www.whitby-cottages.co.uk

Fayvan Holiday Apartments ★★★★
Contact: Mr Ian & Mrs Pauline Moore
Fayvan Holiday Apartments, 43 Crescent Avenue, West Cliff, Whitby YO21 3EQ
T: (01947) 604813
F: (01947) 604813
E: info@fayvan.co.uk
I: www.fayvan.co.uk

Flat 12 ★★★
Contact: Mrs Mohammed
1 Marine Parade, Whitby YO21 3PR
T: (01947) 604727

Forget-Me-Not ★★★
Contact: Mrs Adele Thompson
Whitby Holiday Cottages, 47 Flowergate, Whitby YO21 3BB
T: (01947) 603010
F: (01947) 821133
E: enquiries@whitby-cottages.co.uk
I: www.whitby-cottages.co.uk

Glencoe - Garden Flat ★★★★
Contact: Mrs Julie Charlton
Glencoe Holiday Flats, 18 Linden Close, Briggs Wath, Whitby YO21 1TA
T: (01947) 811531
F: (01947) 602474

Glencoe Holiday Flats ★-★★★
Contact: Mrs Julie Charlton
18 Linden Close, Whitby YO21 1TA
T: (01947) 811531
I: www.holidayflat.co.uk

Grange Farm Holiday Cottage ★★★★
Contact: Miss D Hooning
Grange Farm, Whitby YO22 4LF
T: (01947) 881080
F: (01947) 881080
E: info@grangefarm.net
I: www.grangefarm.net

Greencroft ★★
Contact: Mrs Susan Welford
Greencroft, 9 Esplanade, Whitby YO21 3HH
T: (01947) 603019

Establishments printed in blue have a detailed entry in this guide

YORKSHIRE

4 Halls Place ★★★★
Contact: Mr Peter Goff
65 Longmead, Letchworth
SG6 4HR
T: (01462) 641651
E: peter.goff@ntlworld.com

Harbour Lights ★★★★
Contact: Mrs Adele Thompson
Whitby Holiday Cottages, 47
Flowergate, Whitby YO21 3BB
T: (01947) 603010
F: (01947) 821133
E: enquiries@whitby-cottages.co.uk
I: www.whitby-cottages.co.uk

Harbourside Apartments ★★★-★★★★★
Contact: Mr Ian & Mrs June Roberts
Harbourside Apartments, 51 Church Street, Whitby YO22 4AS
T: (01947) 810763
E: marketing@whiterosecottages.co.uk

Harbourside Cottage ★★★
Contact: Mrs Adele Thompson
Whitby Holiday Cottages, 47
Flowergate, Whitby YO21 3BB
T: (01947) 603010
F: (01947) 821133
E: enquiries@whitby-cottages.co.uk
I: www.whitby-cottages.co.uk

Henrietta Cottage ★★★★
Contact: Mr David Haycox & Mrs Sue Brooks
Shoreline Cottages Ltd, Po Box 135, Leeds LS14 3XJ
T: (0113) 244 8410
F: (0113) 2449826
E: reservations@shoreline-cottages.com
I: www.shoreline-cottages.com

7 Henrietta Street ★★★
Contact: Mr Usher
2 Southlands Avenue, Whitby YO21 3DY
T: (01947) 605868

Hideaway Cottage ★★★
Contact: Mrs Terese Corner
Hideaway Cottage, Cliff Street, Whitby YO21 3DD
T: (01947) 603463

Hightrees Garden Apartment ★★★
Contact: Miss Sarah Elizabeth Clancy
Hightrees Garden Apartment, 34A Bagdale, Whitby YO21 1QL
T: (01947) 601926
E: seclancy@yahoo.co.uk

Hillside Sandsend ★★★★
Contact: Mrs Adele Thompson
Whitby Holiday Cottages, 47
Flowergate, Whitby YO21 3BB
T: (01947) 603010
F: (01947) 821133
E: enquiries@whitby-cottages.co.uk
I: www.whitby-cottages.co.uk

5 Hydings Yard ★★★
Contact: Mrs Adele Thompson
Whitby Holiday Cottages, 47
Flowergate, Whitby YO21 3BB
T: (01947) 603010
F: (01947) 821133
E: enquiries@whitby-cottages.co.uk
I: www.whitby-cottages.co.uk

Jet Cottage ★★★
Contact: Mrs Adele Thompson
Whitby Holiday Cottages, 47
Flowergate, Whitby YO21 3BB
T: (01947) 603010
F: (01947) 821133
E: enquiries@whitby-cottages.co.uk
I: www.whitby-cottages.co.uk

Kiln Cottage ★★★★
Contact: Mr David Haycox & Mrs Sue Brooks
Shoreline Cottages Ltd, Po Box 135, Leeds LS14 3XJ
T: (0113) 244 8410
F: (0113) 2449826
E: reservations@shoreline-cottages.com
I: www.shoreline-cottages.com

Kingfisher Cottage Ref:2588 ★★★
Contact: Ms H Cook
Dales Holiday Cottages, Carleton Business Park, Carleton New Road, Skipton BD23 2AA
T: (01756) 799821
F: (01756) 797012
E: info@dalesholcot.com
I: www.dalesholcot.com

Kipper Cottage ★★★★
Contact: Mrs Adele Thompson
Whitby Holiday Cottages, 47
Flowergate, Whitby YO21 3BB
T: (01947) 603010
F: (01947) 821133
E: enquiries@whitby-cottages.co.uk
I: www.whitby-cottages.co.uk

The Lamp House ★★★★
Contact: Mrs Adele Thompson
Whitby Holiday Cottages, 47
Flowergate, Whitby YO21 3BB
T: (01947) 603010
F: (01947) 821133
E: enquiries@whitby-cottages.co.uk
I: www.whitby-cottages.co.uk

Lauralee Cottage ★★★
Contact: Mr James William Hilton
6 Kendal Drive, Bolton-upon-Dearne, Rotherham S63 8NJ
T: (01709) 897606
E: bill@lauraleeholidays.freeserve.co.uk
I: www.lauraleeholidays.co.uk

2 Linskill Square
Rating Applied For
Contact: Mrs Vanessa Hicking
2 Linskill Square, Linskill Square, Baxtergate, Whitby YO21 1DA
T: (01947) 603010
F: (01947) 821133
E: enquiries@whitby-cottages.co.uk
I: www.whitby-cottages.co.uk

4 Linskill Square
Rating Applied For
Contact: Mrs Vanessa Hicking
Whitby Holiday Cottages, 47
Flowergate, Whitby YO21 3BB
T: (01947) 603010
F: (01947) 821133
E: enquiries@whitby-cottages.co.uk
I: www.whitby-cottages.co.uk

Little Venice Ref:2642 ★★★
Contact: Ms H Cook
Dales Holiday Cottages, Carleton Business Park, Carleton New Road, Skipton BD23 2AA
T: (01756) 799821
F: (01756) 797012
E: info@dalesholcot.com
I: www.dalesholcot.com

Little Whitehall
Rating Applied For
Contact: Mrs Vanessa Hicking
Whitby Holiday Cottages, 47
Flowergate, Whitby YO21 3BB
T: (01947) 603010
F: (01947) 821133
E: enquiries@whitby-cottages.co.uk
I: www.whitby-cottages.co.uk

Lobster Pot Cottage ★★★
Contact: Mrs Anne Forbes
Whitby Fishermens Amateur Rowing Club, 10 Castle Road, Whitby YO21 3NJ
T: (01947) 605846
E: anne.forbes2@btopenworld.com

Loen Cottage Ref:3418 ★★★
Contact: Ms H Cook
Dales Holiday Cottages, Carleton Business Park, Carleton New Road, Skipton BD23 2AA
T: (01756) 799821
F: (01756) 797012
E: info@dalesholcot.com
I: www.dalesholcot.com

The Lookout ★★★
Contact: Mrs Adele Thompson
Whitby Holiday Cottages, 47
Flowergate, Whitby YO21 3BB
T: (01947) 603010
F: (01947) 821133
E: enquiries@whitby-cottages.co.uk
I: www.Whitby-cottages.co.uk

Lupine Cottage
Rating Applied For
Contact: Mrs Vanessa Hicking
Lupine Cottage, 33A Flowergate, Whitby YO21 3BB
T: (01947) 603010
F: (01947) 821133
E: enquiries@whitbh-cottages.co.uk
I: www.Whitby-cottages.co.uk

Magenta House ★-★★★
Contact: Mr Jeffrey Roy Fox
Magenta House, 7 Esplanade, Whitby YO21 3HH
T: (01947) 820915
I: www.magenta-house.co.uk

Mallard ★★★★
Contact: Mr & Mrs Granger
Gunpowder House, Wades Lane, East Barnby, Whitby YO21 3SB
T: (01947) 893444
F: (01947) 893777
E: mgranger@eastbarnby.freeserve.co.uk
I: www.mallardwhitby.co.uk

Manor Cottage Ref:2448 ★★★★
Contact: Ms H Cook
Dales Holiday Cottages, Carleton Business Park, Carleton New Road, Skipton BD23 2AA
T: (01756) 799821
F: (01756) 797012
E: info@dalesholcot.com
I: www.dalesholcot.com

Marina Cottage
Rating Applied For
Contact: Mrs Vanessa Hicking
Marina Cottage, 8 Horners Terrace, Off Church Street, Whitby YO22 4EJ
T: (01947) 603010
F: (01947) 821133
E: enquiries@whitby-cottages.co.uk
I: www.whitby-cottages.co.uk

Marina View & Riverside Ref:3321 & 3322 ★★★-★★★★★
Contact: Ms H Cook
Dales Holiday Cottages, Carleton Business Park, Carleton New Road, Skipton BD23 2AA
T: (01756) 799821
F: (01756) 797012
E: info@dalesholcot.com
I: www.dalesholcot.com

Mariners Cottage ★★★
Contact: Mrs Adele Thompson
Whitby Holiday Cottages, 47
Flowergate, Whitby YO21 3BB
T: (01947) 603010
F: (01947) 821133
E: enquiries@whitby-cottages.co.uk
I: www.whitby-cottages.co.uk

Mariner's Cottage ★★★★
Contact: Mr David Haycox & Mrs Sue Brooks
Shoreline Cottages Ltd, Po Box 135, Leeds LS14 3XJ
T: (0113) 244 8410
F: (0113) 2449826
E: reservations@shoreline-cottages.com
I: www.shoreline-cottages.com

Midships ★★★
Contact: Mrs Adele Thompson
Whitby Holiday Cottages, 47
Flowergate, Whitby YO21 3BB
T: (01947) 603010
F: (01947) 821133
E: enquiries@whitby-cottages.co.uk
I: www.whitby-cottages.co.uk

YORKSHIRE

Nans Cottage
Rating Applied For
Contact: Mrs Vanessa Hicking
Nans Cottage, Henrietta Street,
Whitby YO22 4DW
T: (01947) 603010
F: (01947) 821133
E: enquiries@whitby-cottages.co.uk
I: www.whitby-cottage.co.uk

New Hills Ref:2586 ★★★
Contact: Ms H Cook
Dales Holiday Cottages, Carleton Business Park, Carleton New Road, Skipton BD23 2AA
T: (01756) 799821
F: (01756) 797012
E: info@dalesholcot.com
I: www.dalesholcot.com

Nobles Cottage
Rating Applied For
Contact: Mrs Vanessa Hicking
Nobles Cottage, Nobles Cottage, Henrietta Street, Whitby YO22 4DW
T: (01947) 603010
F: (01947) 821133
E: enquiries@whitby-cottages.co.uk
I: www.whitby-cottages.co.uk

Old Boatman's Shelter ★★★★
Contact: Mrs Alison Halidu
50 Carr Hill Lane, Whitby YO21 1RS
T: (01947) 811089
E: oldboatshelter@aol.com

Old Brewery Cottage
Rating Applied For
Contact: Mrs Vanessa Hicking
Old Brewery Cottage, White Horse Yard, Church Street, Whitby YO22 4BW
T: (01947) 603010
F: (01947) 821133
E: enquiries@whitby-cottages.co.uk
I: www.whitbycottages.co.uk

6 Old Coastguard Cottages ★★★★
Contact: Ms Noble
Howdale House, Browside, Whitby YO22
T: (01947) 881064

The Old Granary
Rating Applied For
Contact: Mrs Jackie Richardson
The Old Granary, Raven Hill Farm, Dunsley Nr Sandsend, Whitby YO21 3TJ
T: (01947) 893331
F: (01947) 893331
E: jackie.richardson6@btopenworld.com

Olive Tree Cottage ★★★★
Contact: Mrs Adele Thompson
Whitby Holiday Cottages, 47 Flowergate, Whitby YO21 3BB
T: (01947) 603010
F: (01947) 821133
E: enquiries@whitby-cottages.co.uk
I: www.whitby-cottages.co.uk

Paddock Cottage ★★★
Contact: Miss Jeana Shippey
12 Waterloo Place, Flowergate, Whitby YO21 3BN
T: (01947) 820370
E: jshippey159@aol.com
I: www.directwhitbyaccom.co.uk

Pantiles ★★★★
Contact: Mr Peter & Mrs Alison Lawson
51 Greenbank Crescent, Edinburgh EH10 5TD
T: (0131) 4460225
E: holidays@mountsquarewhitby.fsnet.co.uk
I: www.pantiles.mysite.freeserve.com/

2 Pear Tree Cottages ★★★★
Contact: Mrs Adele Thompson
Whitby Holiday Cottages, 47 Flowergate, Whitby YO21 3BB
T: (01947) 603010
F: (01947) 821133
E: enquiries@whitby-cottages.co.uk
I: www.whitby-cottages.co.uk

Penny Hedge House Ref:2994 ★★★★
Contact: Ms H Cook
Dales Holiday Cottages, Carleton Business Park, Carleton New Road, Skipton BD23 2AA
T: (01756) 799821
F: (01756) 797012
E: info@dalesholcot.com
I: www.dalesholcot.com

Perkins Cottage ★★★★
Contact: Mrs Adele Thompson
Whitby Holiday Cottages, 47 Flowergate, Whitby YO21 3BB
T: (01947) 603010
F: (01947) 821133
E: enquiries@whitby-cottages.co.uk
I: www.whitby-cottages.co.uk

Primrose & Bluebell Cottages ★★★★
Contact: Mr Robin & Mrs Barbara Hopps
Primrose & Bluebell Cottages, Low Newbiggin North Farm, Whitby YO21 1TQ
T: (01947) 810948
F: (01947) 810948
E: barbara@bhopps.freeserve.co.uk
I: www.stilwell.co.uk

Prince of Wales Cottage ★★★★
Contact: Mr David Haycox & Mrs Sue Brooks
Shoreline Cottages Ltd, Po Box 135, Leeds LS14 3XJ
T: (0113) 244 8410
F: (0113) 2449826
E: reservations@shoreline-cottages.com
I: www.shoreline-cottages.com

1 Princess Place ★★★★
Contact: Mr John Whitton
Brook House, Brook Lane, Ainthorpe, Whitby YO21 2JR
T: (01287) 660118
E: jonwhitton@ntlworld.com
I: www.holidayinwhitby.co.uk

8 Prospect Place ★★★
Contact: Mrs Adele Thompson
Whitby Holiday Cottages, 47 Flowergate, Whitby YO21 3BB
T: (01947) 603010
F: (01947) 821133
E: enquiries@whitby-cottages.co.uk
I: www.whitby-cottages.co.uk

Quayside Cottage ★★★★
Contact: Mr Paul & Mrs Di Wicks
Orchard Cottage, High Street, Scarborough YO13 0AE
T: (01723) 871028
F: (01723) 871379
E: di@whitbycottages.com
I: www.whitbycottages.com

Quayside Cottage ★★★★
Contact: Mr David Haycox & Mrs Sue Brooks
Shoreline Cottages Ltd, Po Box 135, Leeds LS14 3XJ
T: (0113) 244 8410
F: (0113) 2449826
E: reservations@shoreline-cottages.com
I: www.shoreline-cottages.com

River Esk Apartments
Rating Applied For
Contact: Mr Pauline Foran
River Esk Apartments, Spital Bridge, Whitehall Landing, Whitby YO22 4AE
T: (01947) 811264
E: foran9827@freeserve.co.uk

Robin Hood's Bay Cottages ★★★
Contact: Mrs Jean Speight
2 Cad Beeston Mews, Leeds LS11 8AF
T: (0113) 277 5853

Sailing By ★★★
Contact: Mrs Adele Thompson
Whitby Holiday Cottages, 47 Flowergate, Whitby YO21 3BB
T: (01947) 603010
F: (01947) 821133
E: enquiries@whitby-cottages.co.uk
I: www.whitby-cottages.co.uk

St Joseph's Cottage ★★★★★
Contact: Mr David Haycox & Mrs Sue Brooks
Shoreline Cottages Ltd, Po Box 135, Leeds LS14 3XJ
T: (0113) 244 8410
F: (0113) 2449826
E: reservations@shoreline-cottages.com
I: www.shoreline-cottages.com

Sandglass Cottage ★★★★
Contact: Mr David Haycox & Mrs Sue Brooks
Shoreline Cottages Ltd, Po Box 135, Leeds LS14 3XJ
T: (0113) 244 8410
F: (0113) 2449826
E: reservations@shoreline-cottages.com
I: www.shoreline-cottages.com

Scoresby Cottage ★★★
Contact: Mrs Vanessa Hicking
Whitby Holiday Cottages, 47 Flowergate, Whitby YO21 3BB
T: (01947) 603010
E: enquiries@whitby-cottages.co.uk
I: www.whitby-cottages.co.uk

Scoresby Lodge ★★★
Contact: Mr Eric Tayler
Crows Nest Apartments, 28 Cambrian Avenue, Redcar TS10 4HF
T: (01642) 492144
E: crowsnest.whitby@ntlworld.com
I: www.crowsnestwhitby.co.uk

Seagull Cottage ★★★★
Contact: Mrs Adele Thompson
Whitby Holiday Cottages, 47 Flowergate, Whitby YO21 3BB
T: (01947) 603010
F: (01947) 821133
E: enquiries@whitby-cottages.co.uk
I: www.whitby-cottages.co.uk

Seagull Cottage ★★★★
Contact: Mr David Haycox & Mrs Sue Brooks
Shoreline Cottages Ltd, Po Box 135, Leeds LS14 3XJ
T: (0113) 244 8410
F: (0113) 2449826
E: reservations@shoreline-cottages.com
I: www.shoreline-cottages.com

Seashell Cottage Ref: 1075
Rating Applied For
Contact: Mr Clive Sykes
Sykes Cottages, York House, York Street, Chester CH1 3LR
T: (01244) 345700
F: (01244) 321442
E: info@sykescottages.co.uk
I: www.sykescottages.co.uk

Slipway House ★★★★
Contact: Mrs Adele Thompson
Whitby Holiday Cottages, 47 Flowergate, Whitby YO21 3BB
T: (01947) 603010
F: (01947) 821133
E: enquiries@whitby-cottages.co.uk
I: www.whitby-cottages.co.uk

Southern Cross
Rating Applied For
Contact: Mrs Vanessa Hicking
Southern Cross, 8 Bog Hall, Whitby YO21 1PG
T: (01947) 603010
F: (01947) 821133
E: enquiries@whitby-cottages.co.uk
I: www.whitby-cottages.co.uk

Spring Cottage Ref: 3422 ★★★★
Contact: Ms H Cook
Dales Holiday Cottages, Carleton Business Park, Carleton New Road, Skipton BD23 2AA
T: (01756) 799821
F: (01756) 797012
E: info@dalesholcot.com
I: www.dalesholcot.com

Establishments printed in blue have a detailed entry in this guide

YORKSHIRE

Spring Vale ★★★★
Contact: Mr David Haycox & Mrs Sue Brooks
Shoreline Cottages Ltd, Po Box 135, Leeds LS14 3XJ
T: (0113) 244 8410
F: (0113) 2449826
E: reservations@shoreline-cottages.com
I: www.shoreline-cottages.com

Stable Cottage ★★★★
Contact: Mr Martin & Mrs Chrissie Warner
Stable Cottage, Sandfield House Farm, Sandsend Road, Whitby YO21 3SR
T: (01947) 602660
E: info@sandfieldhousefarm.co.uk

Steps Cottage ★★★
Contact: Mrs Adele Thompson
Whitby Holiday Cottages, 47 Flowergate, Whitby YO21 3BB
T: (01947) 603010
F: (01947) 821133
E: enquiries@whitby-cottages.co.uk
I: www.whitby-cottages.co.uk

Stoneleigh ★★★★★
Contact: Mrs Adele Thompson
Whitby Holiday Cottages, 47 Flowergate, Whitby YO21 3BB
T: (01947) 603010
F: (01947) 821133
E: enquiries@whitby-cottages.co.uk
I: www.whitby-cottages.co.uk

Storm Cottage ★★
Contact: Mrs Adele Thompson
Whitby Holiday Cottages, 47 Flowergate, Whitby YO21 3BB
T: (01947) 603010
F: (01947) 821133
E: enquiries@whitby-cottages.co.uk
I: www.whitby-cottages.co.uk

Studio Flat 6 ★★★
Contact: Mrs Adele Thompson
Whitby Holiday Cottages, 47 Flowergate, Whitby YO21 3BB
T: (01947) 603010
F: (01947) 821133
E: enquiries@whitby-cottages.co.uk
I: www.whitby-cottages.co.uk

Sunnydene
Rating Applied For
Contact: Mrs Kim Parry
14 Galtres Avenue, Stockton Lane, York YO31 1JT
T: (01904) 413956

Swallow Cottage ★★★★
Contact: Mrs Adele Thompson
Whitby Holiday Cottages, 47 Flowergate, Whitby YO21 3BB
T: (01947) 603010
F: (01947) 821133
E: enquiries@whitby-cottages.co.uk
I: www.whitby-cottages.co.uk

Swallow Holiday Cottages ★★-★★★★★
Contact: Mr & Mrs McNeil
Long Lease Farm, Hawsker, Whitby YO22 4LA
T: (01947) 603790
I: www.swallowcottages.co.uk

Swallows Nest & Wheelhouse Cottages ★★★★
Contact: Mr Peter Hamilton
Greystones Farm, Newholm, Whitby YO21 3QR
T: (01947) 605886

Swan Cottage ★★★
Contact: Mrs Smith
Swan Farm, Whitby YO22 4LH
T: (01947) 880682

Thimble Cottage, 15 Loggerhead Yard ★★
Contact: Mr Paul & Mrs Janet Breeze
The Barn, Gun End, Heaton, Rushton Spencer, Macclesfield SK11 0SJ
T: (01260) 227391
E: pbreeze@tiscali.co.uk

Tyremans Return ★★★
Contact: Mrs Adele Thompson
Whitby Holiday Cottages, 47 Flowergate, Whitby YO21 3BB
T: (01947) 603010
F: (01947) 821133
E: enquiries@whitby-cottages.co.uk
I: www.whitby-cottages.co.uk

108 Upgang Lane ★★★
Contact: Mrs Adele Thompson
Whitby Holiday Cottages, 47 Flowergate, Whitby YO21 3BB
T: (01947) 603010
F: (01947) 821133
E: enquiries@whitby-cottages.co.uk
I: www.whitby-cottages.co.uk

Vine House
Rating Applied For
Contact: Mr David Hattersley
DeBretton Estates Ltd, Po Box 6489, Matlock DE4 4WL
F: (01629) 820273
E: reservations@debrettonestates.co.uk
I: www.debrettonestates.co.uk

Walkers Cottage
Rating Applied For
Contact: Mrs Suzanne Walker
12 Lingfield Drive, Crawley RH10 7XQ
T: (01293) 885285
F: (01293) 885285
E: a&tswalker@walkerscottage.com
I: www.walkerscottage.com

Waverley ★★★
Contact: Mrs Adele Thompson
Whitby Holiday Cottages, 47 Flowergate, Whitby YO21 3BB
T: (01947) 603010
F: (01947) 821133
E: enquiries@whitby-cottages.co.uk
I: www.whitby-cottages.co.uk

West End Cottage ★★★★
Contact: Mr David Haycox & Mrs Sue Brooks
Shoreline Cottages Ltd, Po Box 135, Leeds LS14 3XJ
T: (0113) 244 8410
F: (0113) 2449826
E: reservations@shoreline-cottages.com
I: www.shoreline-cottages.com

Whitby Retreats - Grape Lane
Rating Applied For
Contact: Mr Nick & Mrs Emma Jaques
18 Gledhow Park Crescent, Leeds LS7 4JY
T: (0113) 225 0798
E: info@whitbyretreats.co.uk

White Horse Cottage ★★★
Contact: Mr George & Mr Steven Walker
The Shakespeare Inn, 120 Eldon Road, Rotherham S65 1RD
T: (01709) 367031

6 White Horse Yard ★★★
Contact: Mrs Adele Thompson
Whitby Holiday Cottages, 47 Flowergate, Whitby YO21 3BB
T: (01947) 603010
F: (01947) 821133
E: enquiries@whitby-cottages.co.uk
I: www.whitby-cottages.co.uk

White Rose Holiday Cottages ★★★-★★★★
Contact: Mrs June Roberts
Greenacres, Brook Park, Briggswath, Whitby YO21 1RT
T: (01947) 810763
F: (01947) 811739
I: www.whiterosecottages.co.uk

Whitehall Landing Apartment
Rating Applied For
Contact: Mrs Amanda Cowen
Whitehall Landing Apartment, Spital Bridge, Whitehall Landing, Whitby YO22 4AE
T: (01947) 810315

Windrush Cottage ★★★
Contact: Mrs Adele Thompson
Whitby Holiday Cottages, 47 Flowergate, Whitby YO21 3BB
T: (01947) 603010
F: (01947) 821133
E: enquiries@whitby-cottages.co.uk
I: www.whitby-cottages.co.uk

WHITWELL-ON-THE-HILL
North Yorkshire

The Hay Loft ★★★
Contact: Mrs Anne Polley
The Hay Loft, El Paso, York YO60 7JX
T: (01653) 618324
E: anne.polley1@btopenworld.com

WILSILL
North Yorkshire

Manor Farm Barn ★★★★
Contact: Mr William & Mrs Kellie LaBonte
Wilsill, Harrogate HG3 5EB
T: (01423) 711386
F: (01423) 711069
E: b.labonte@btopenworld.com

WILTON
North Yorkshire

The Old Forge Cottages ★★★
Contact: Mrs Bernice Graham
The Old Forge Cottages, The Old Forge, Pickering YO18 7JY
T: (01751) 477399
F: (01751) 473122
E: theoldforge@themutual.net
I: www.forgecottages.themutual.net/fc.html

WINKSLEY
North Yorkshire

Meadow View Cottage ★★★
Contact: Mr Les Broadbent
8 Sandymoor, Sandy Lane, Allerton, Bradford BD15 9LF
T: (01274) 541622

WINTERTON
North Lincolnshire

Tate Cottage ★★★★
Contact: Mrs Rachel Colecchia
107 Manor Road, Scunthorpe DN16 3JT
T: (01724) 347261
E: rcol@postmaster.co.uk

WOLD NEWTON
East Riding of Yorkshire

The Curate's Cottage Ref: 3669 ★★★★
Contact: Mrs Fiona Moody
Dales Holiday Cottages, Carleton Business Park, Carleton New Road, Skipton BD23 2AA
T: (01756) 790919
F: (01756) 797012
E: fiona@dalesholcot.com

Owl Cottage Ref: 2325 ★★★★
Contact: Ms H Cook
Dales Holiday Cottages, Carleton Business Park, Carleton New Road, Skipton BD23 2AA
T: (01756) 799821
F: (01756) 797012
E: info@dalesholcot.com
I: www.dalesholcot.com

WOMBLETON
North Yorkshire

Rosebud Cottage ★★★★
Contact: Ms L Smith & Mr D Barnacle
Carlton House, 48 Piercy End, York YO62 6DF
T: (01751) 433452
F: (01751) 430778
I: www.penhillviewleyburn.co.uk

WORSBROUGH
South Yorkshire

Delf Cottage ★★★★
Contact: Mrs Julie Elmhirst
Delf Cottage, Delf Cottages, Houndhill Lane, Worsbrough, Barnsley S70 6TX
T: (01226) 282430
F: (01226) 282430
E: t.elmhirst@btinternet.com
I: www.delfcottage.co.uk

YORKSHIRE

WORTLEY
South Yorkshire

Pennine Equine ★★★
Contact: Mrs Lynn Berry
Bromley Farm, Bromley,
Sheffield S35 7DE
T: (0114) 284 7140
F: (0114) 2847644
E: alex@tuefarming.freeserve.co.uk
I: www.pennine-equine.co.uk

WORTON
North Yorkshire

Stoney End Holidays ★★★-★★★★
Contact: Mr Mike & Mrs Pamela Hague
Stoney End Holidays, Stoney End, Leyburn DL8 3ET
T: (01969) 650652
F: (01969) 650077
E: pmh@stoneyend.co.uk
I: www.stoneyend.co.uk

WRELTON
North Yorkshire

Croft Head Cottage ★★★★
Contact: Mr Chris & Mrs Sue Halstead
Croft Head, Pickering YO18 8PF
T: (01751) 477918
F: (01751) 477918
E: susie@crofthead.co.uk

Hallgarth ★★★★
Contact: Mrs Carol Marsh
Orchard House, Main Street, Wrelton, Pickering YO18 8PG
T: (01751) 476081
F: (01751) 476081

Vale Cottage ★★★★
Contact: Mr Thomas & Mrs Jean Scaling
Cliff Farm, York YO62 6SS
T: (01751) 473792
F: (01751) 473792
E: jeanscaling@btinternet.com
I: www.cottageguide.co.uk/valecottage

WROOT
North Lincolnshire

Brook Lodge Cottage ★★★
Contact: Mrs E Bayes
Brook Lodge Cottage, High Street, Doncaster DN9 2BT
T: (01302) 772285
F: (01302) 772285
E: bayes1@aol.com

Rye House Granary ★★★
Contact: Mr Robin Aconley
Rye House Granary, Rye House, High Street, Wroot, Doncaster DN9 2BT
T: (01302) 770196
E: janeaconley@tinyworld.co.uk

YAPHAM
East Riding of Yorkshire

Wolds View Holiday Cottages ★★★★
Contact: Mrs Woodliffe
Wolds View Holiday Cottages, Mill Farm, York YO42 1PH
T: (01759) 302172

YEADON
West Yorkshire

Gillcroft Cottage ★★★★
Contact: Mrs Croft
Gillcroft, 41 Gill Lane, Leeds LS19 7DE
T: (0113) 250 4198

YORK
York

Abbeygate House ★★★★★
Contact: Mr & Mrs Halliday
1 Grange Drive, Horsforth, Leeds LS18 5EQ
T: (0113) 258 9833

Acer Bungalow ★★★
Contact: Mrs Sandra Wreglesworth
The Acer Hotel, 52 Scarcroft Hill, York YO24 1DE
T: (01904) 653839
F: (01904) 677017
E: info@acerhotel.co.uk
I: www.acerbungalow.co.uk

Apartment No 9 ★★★★
Contact: Mrs Hilary Atha
Tower Guest House, 2 Feversham Crescent, York YO31 8HQ
T: (01904) 655571
E: reservations@towerguesthouse.fsnet.co.uk
I: www.yorkholidayhome.com

Apple Cottage ★★★
Contact: Mrs Jean Corrigan
Highfields, Beckdale Road, Helmsley, York YO62 5AS
T: (01439) 770705
F: (01439) 770705

Ashling House ★★★★★
Contact: Mr Ian Addyman
5 Cherry Hill House, 149 Tadcaster Road, York YO24 1QJ
T: (01904) 706083
F: (01904) 636921
E: info@yorkselfcatering.fsnet.co.uk
I: www.yorkselfcatering.co.uk

Baile Hill Cottage ★★★
Contact: Mr & Mrs Paul Hodgson
Baile Hill Cottage, Avalon, North Lane, York YO19 6AY
T: (01904) 448670
E: enquiries@holiday-cottage.org.uk
I: www.holiday-cottage.org.uk

Barbican Mews ★★★
Contact: Mrs Helen Jones
Homefinders Holidays, 11 Walmgate, York YO1 9TX
T: (01904) 632660
F: (01904) 615388
E: agents@homefindersholidays.co.uk
I: www.homefindersholidays.co.uk

Bishopgate Pavilion-Bishops Wharf ★★★★★
Contact: Mr John Graham
31 Falcon Way, Clippers Quay, London E14 9UP
T: (020) 75388980
E: john@johnkgraham.com
I: www.johnkgraham.com

The Blue Rooms ★★★★★
Contact: Ms Lorraine Woodmansey
4 Franklins Yard, Fossgate, York YO1 9TN
T: (01904) 673990
F: (01904) 658147
E: blue-rooms@blue-bicycle.co.uk
I: www.thebluebicycle.com

Carlton House ★★★★
Contact: Mrs Sheila Kathryn Nevell
4 Harbledown Park, Canterbury CT2 8NR
T: (01227) 763308
F: (01227) 763308
E: knevell@aol.com

Centre York Cottages ★★-★★★
Contact: Mr William Richardson
Catton Park, York YO41 5QA
T: (01759) 388280
F: (01759) 388280
E: william@centre-yorkcottages.fsnet.co.uk
I: www.centre-yorkcottages.fsnet.co.uk

Chestnut Farm Holiday Cottages ★★★★
Contact: Mrs Alison Smith
Chestnut Farm Holiday Park, York YO23 2UQ
T: (01904) 704676
F: (01904) 704676
E: enquiries@chestnutfarmholidaypark.co.uk
I: www.yorkholidaycottages.co.uk

Classique Select Holiday Accommodation ★★-★★★
Contact: Mr Rodney Inns
21 Larchfield, Stockton Lane, York YO31 1JS
T: (01904) 421339
F: (01904) 421339
E: rodela_2194_inns@hotmail.com
I: www.classique-york.co.uk

Clementhorpe Cottages and Apartments ★★★★
Contact: Mrs Denise Magson
7 Holgate Bridge Gardens, York y024 4Ba
T: (01904) 658515
F: (01904) 628111
E: denise.magson@btopenworld.com

1 Cloisters Walk ★★★
Contact: Mrs Helen Jones
11 Walmgate, York YO1 9TX
T: (01904) 632660
F: (01904) 651388
E: agents@homefindersholidays.co.uk
I: www.homefindersholidays.co.uk

Cloisters Walk Holiday Accommodation ★★★
Contact: Mrs Susan Burrows
15 Knapton Close, York YO32 5ZF
T: (01904) 490729

Colonia Holidays ★★★
Contact: Mrs Margaret Booth
Kenilworth, Hutton Street, York YO26 7ND
T: (01904) 738579

Crambeck Court ★★★★
Contact: Mrs Helen Jones
Homefinders Holidays, 11 Walmgate, York YO1 9TX
T: (01904) 632660
F: (01904) 651388
E: agents@homefindersholidays.co.uk
I: www.homefindersholidays.co.uk

21 Emperors Wharf
Rating Applied For
Contact: Mrs Helen Jones
11 Walmgate, York YO1 9TX
T: (01904) 632660
F: (01904) 651388
E: agents@homefindersholidays.co.uk
I: www.homesfindersholidays.co.uk

17 Escrick Street ★★★
Contact: Mrs Helen Jones
Homefinders Holidays, 11 Walmgate, York YO1 9TX
T: (01904) 632660
F: (01904) 651388
E: agents@homefindersholidays.co.uk
I: www.homefindersholidays.co.uk

Fairfax Corner
Rating Applied For
Contact: Bill & Shan Rigby
Fairfax Corner, Fairfax Street, Bishophill, York YO1 6EB
T: (01482) 862085
E: rigby@york.netkonect.co.uk

Flat 24 Middleton House ★★★★
Contact: Mrs Carole Bowes
Melrose House Farm, Thirsk YO7 2ES
T: (01845) 597334
E: rce.bowes@lineone.net
I: www.yorkcityflat.co.uk

25 Fulford Place
Rating Applied For
Contact: Mrs Belinda Hepher
Off Keele Road, Whitmore, Newcastle ST5 5HN
T: (01782) 680035
E: belinda.hepher@btinternet.com
I: www.eboracum.co.uk

The Garden Cottage ★★★★
Contact: Mr & Mrs Ann Hart
Meadowville, Grimstone Bar, York YO19 5LA
T: (01904) 413353
F: (01904) 431559
E: ann@yorkgardencottage.co.uk
I: www.yorkgardencottage.co.uk

Garden Cottage ★★★
Contact: Mrs Katy Harvey
Moat View House, 28 Lord Mayors Walk, York YO31 7HA
T: (01904) 623329
E: katy.harvey1@ntlworld.com

Establishments printed in blue have a detailed entry in this guide

YORKSHIRE

Grosvenor and Grosvenor York Holiday Let
Rating Applied For
Contact: Mr Antony & Mrs Wendy Grosvenor
Grosvenor and Grosvenor York Holiday Let, 52 St Paul's Mews, Holgate, York YO24 4BR
T: (01904) 691171
F: (01904) 691171

Hilary's Holiday Homes (Riverhaven & The Moorings) ★★★★
Contact: Mrs Hilary Kernohan
Duncanne House, Roecliffe Lane, York YO51 9LN
T: 0771 0 147665
E: hak@btconnect.com
I: www.hilarysholidayhomes.co.uk

The Juniper
Rating Applied For
Contact: Mrs Helen Jones
11 Walmgate, York YO1 9TX
T: (01904) 632160
F: (01904) 651388
E: agents@homefindersholidays.co.uk
I: www.homefindersholidays.co.uk

Knowle House Apartments ★★-★★★
Contact: Mr Greg Harrand
Hedley House, 3 Bootham Terrace, York YO30 7DH
T: (01904) 637404
F: (01904) 639774
E: greg@hedleyhouse.com
I: www.hedleyhouse.com

Merchants Gate ★★★★
Contact: Mr Stephen Osborne
Oaklands Wetherby Ltd, Harewood Road, Wetherby LS22 5BZ
T: (01937) 574836

Merricote Cottages ★★★
Contact: Mr Andrew Williamson
Merricote Cottages, Malton Road, York YO32 9TL
T: (01904) 400256
F: (01904) 400846
E: merricote@hotmail.com
I: www.merricote-holiday-cottages.co.uk

Minster View
Rating Applied For
Contact: Mrs Helen Jones
11 Walmgate, York YO1 9TX
T: (01904) 632160
F: (01904) 651388
E: agents@homefindersholidays.co.uk
I: www.homefindersholidays.co.uk

Monkbridge Court
Rating Applied For
Contact: Mrs Angela Bush
Burtonfields Hall, Bridlington Road, YO41 1SA
T: (01759) 371308
E: angelabush@monkbridge.co.uk

12 Monkbridge Court ★★★★
Contact: Mrs Angela Bush
Burtonfields Hall, Bridlington Road, Stamford Bridge, York YO41 1SA
T: (01759) 371308
F: (01759) 371308
E: angelabush@monkbridge.co.uk
I: www.monkbridge.co.uk

145 Mount Vale ★★★★
Contact: Mrs Helen Jones
Homefinders Holidays, 11 Walmgate, York YO1 9TX
T: (01904) 632160
F: (01904) 651388
E: agents@homefindersholidays.co.uk
I: www.homefindersholidays.co.uk

No 10 York City Arms Apartment
Rating Applied For
Contact: Mrs Andrea Baugh
Yorkshire Cottages, 2 Lonsdale Street, Carlisle CA1 1DB
T: (01228) 599960
F: (01228) 599970
E: andrea@yorkshire-cottages.info

No 14 York City Arms Apartment
Rating Applied For
Contact: Mrs Andrea Baugh
Yorkshire Cottages, 2 Lonsdale Street, Carlisle CA1 1DB
T: (01228) 599960
F: (01228) 599970
E: andrea@yorkshire-cottages.info

Number 22 Bootham Terrace ★★★★★
Contact: Mrs Helen Jones
Homefinders Holidays, 11 Walmgate, York YO1 9TJ
T: (01904) 632160
F: (01904) 651388
E: agents@homefindersholidays.co.uk
I: www.homefindersholidays.co.uk

Owl Cottage ★★★
Contact: Mrs Rosemary Fletcher
Owl Cottage, Long Acres, The Village, York YO10 3NP
T: (01904) 410438
F: (01904) 414404
E: rjf@cfga.co.uk

The Penthouse ★★★★★
Contact: Mrs Kim Hodgson
1 Postern House, Postern Close, York YO23 1PH
T: (01904) 610351
F: (01904) 613687
E: hodgsonschoice@hotmail.com
I: www.hodgsons-choice.co.uk

The Penthouse, Westgate ★★★★★
Contact: Mr Ian Berg
1 Kenwood Avenue, Stockport SK7 1BP
T: (0161) 4398964
E: rtib@currantbun.com

43 Postern Close ★★★★★
Contact: Mr Gordon & Mrs Hilary Jones
2 Chalfonts, York YO24 1EX
T: (01904) 702043
F: (01904) 702043
E: hilary@yorkcloisters.com
I: www.yorkcloisters.com

44 Postern Close ★★★★
Contact: Mrs Christine Turner
Meadowcroft, Millfield, Willingham, Cambridge CB4 5HD
T: (01954) 201218
E: c.turner@gurdon.cam.ac.uk
I: www.yorkholidayflat.co.uk

60 Postern Close ★★★★★
Contact: Mrs Hilary Jones
York City Holidays, 2 Chalfonts, York YO24 1EX
T: (01904) 702043
F: (01904) 702043
E: hilary@yorkcloisters.com
I: www.yorkcloisters.com

29 Richardson Street ★★★
Contact: Mrs Helen Jones
Homefinders Holidays, 11 Walmgate, York YO1 9TX
T: (01904) 632160
F: (01904) 651388
E: agents@homefindersholidays.co.uk
I: www.homefindersholidays.co.uk

Riverside Holiday Flat ★★★★
Contact: Mr Peter & Mrs Elizabeth Jackson
17 Great Close, Selby YO8 3UG
T: (01757) 268207
E: pajack@lineone.net
I: www.yorkriversideholidayflat.co.uk

Roman Retreat ★★★★
Contact: Mr Hedderick
4 Crummock, York YO24 2SU
T: (01904) 331803
E: hedderick@ntlworld.com

St Peter's Quarter - 33 Bishopfields Drive
Rating Applied For
Contact: Mrs Jane Wilson
The Wytchwoods, Stowmarket IP14 6TB
T: (01473) 890056
E: janem.wilson@btopenworld.com

Shambles Holiday Apartments ★★★★
Contact: Mr & Mrs Fletcher
Shambles Holiday Apartments, The Art Shop, 27-27A Shambles, York YO1 7LX
T: (01904) 623898
F: (01904) 671283
E: shamblesholiday-york@tinyworld.co.uk

Sparrow Hall Cottages ★★★
Contact: Mr Nick & Mrs Pam Gaunt
Sparrow Hall Cottages, Sparrow Hall, Scrayingham, York YO41 1JE
T: (01759) 372917
E: holidays@yorkcott-pool.freeuk.com
I: www.yorkcott-pool.freeuk.com

Stakesby Holiday Flats ★★
Contact: Mr Anthony Bryce
Stakesby Holiday Flats, 4 St Georges Place, Mount Vale, York YO24 1DR
T: (01904) 611634
E: ant@stakesby.co.uk
I: www.stakesby.co.uk

Stonegate Court ★★★★★
Contact: Mrs Susan Kitchener
11 Earswick Chase, Old Earswick, York YO32 9FZ
T: 0774 6 552478
E: sue@yorkluxuryholidays.co.uk
I: www.yorkluxuryholidays.co.uk

Swallow Hall ★★★
Contact: Mrs Christine Scutt
Swallow Hall, Wheldrake Lane, York YO19 4SG
T: (01904) 448219
E: jtscores@hotmail.com
I: www.swallowhall.co.uk

Thornfield House ★★★
Contact: Ms Regina Longjaloux
14 Thirlmere Drive, York YO31 0LZ
T: (01904) 415478
E: r.d@longjaloux.freeserve.co.uk

9 Waterfront House, York
Rating Applied For
Contact: Mrs Veronica Lotbiniere
The Piggery, Brandon IP27 0SA
T: (01842) 814215
E: info@lignacite.co.uk

414 Westgate ★★★★
Contact: Mrs Helen Jones
Homefinders Holidays, 11 Walmgate, York YO1 9TX
T: (01904) 632160
F: (01904) 651388
E: agents@homefindersholidays.co.uk
I: www.homefindersholidays.co.uk

Westgate Apartments ★★★★★
Contact: Mr Kenneth Irving
142 Bonnyton Drive, Glasgow G76 0LU
T: (01355) 302508

Within the Walls Cottage ★★★
Contact: Mr Barry Giles
Willow House, 12 Willow Wong, Nottingham NG14 5FD
T: (0115) 931 2070

YORKSHIRE

24 Woodsmill Quay ★★★★
Contact: Mrs Helen Jones
Homefinders Holidays, 11
Walmgate, York YO1 9TX
T: (01904) 632660
F: (01904) 651388
E: agents@
homefindersholidays.co.uk
I: www.homefindersholidays.
co.uk

York Holiday Apartments ★★★★
Contact: Mr Malcolm & Mrs
Margaret Bradley
York Holiday Apartments,
Mulberry Farm, Old Quarry Lane,
Lumby, South Milford, Leeds
LS25 5JA
T: (01977) 683499
F: (01977) 680110
E: malcolmrbradley@btintenet.com
I: www.yorkholidayapartments.co.uk

York Holiday Homes ★★★-★★★★
Contact: Mrs Dorothy Preece &
Mrs D Widdicombe
York Holiday Homes, 53
Goodramgate, York YO1 7LS
T: (01094) 641997
F: (01904) 613453
E: info@yorkholidayhomes.co.uk
I: www.yorkshirenet.co.uk/accgde/yorkholidayhomes

York Lakeside Lodges ★★★★-★★★★★
Contact: Mr Manasir
York Lakeside Lodges Ltd, Moor Lane, York YO24 2QU
T: (01904) 702346
F: (01904) 701631
E: neil@yorklakesidelodges.co.uk
I: www.yorklakesidelodges.co.uk

York Luxury Breaks
Rating Applied For
Contact: Mrs Linda Waddington
York Luxury Breaks, Lowther
Street, York YO31 7ED
T: (01904) 768569
F: (01904) 768569
I: www.yorkluxurybreaks.co.uk

HEART OF ENGLAND

ABBERLEY
Worcestershire

Old Yates Cottages ★★★
Contact: Mr Richard & Mrs
Sarah Goodman
Old Yates Cottages, Stockton
Road, Worcester WR6 6AT
T: (01299) 896500
F: (01299) 896065
E: oldyates@aol.com
I: www.oldyatescottages.co.uk

ABBEY DORE
Herefordshire

Tan House Farm Cottage ★★★
Contact: Ms Glenys Powell
JP Powell & Son, Tan House
Farm, Abbeydore, Hereford
HR2 0AA
T: (01981) 240204
F: (01981) 240204
E: jppowell@ereal.net
I: www.golden-valley.co.uk/tanhouse

ACTON BURNELL
Shropshire

Rosehay ★★★★
Contact: Mr S Boardman
Sykes Cottages, York House,
York Street, Chester CH1 3LR
T: (01244) 345700
F: (01244) 321442
E: info@sykescottages.co.uk
I: www.sykescottages.co.uk

ADMASTON
Staffordshire

Blithfield Lakeside Barns ★★★★
Contact: Mr Richard Brown
St Stephens Hill Farm,
Steenwood Lane, Admaston,
Rugeley WS15 3NQ
T: (01889) 500458
F: (01889) 500288
E: reser2000@aol.com
I: www.blithfieldlakesidebarns.co.uk

ADMINGTON
Warwickshire

Mole End ★★★★
Contact: Mrs Liz Hale
Willow Tree Farm, Admington
Lane, Shipston-on-Stour
CV36 4JJ
T: (01789) 450881
E: liz-hale@willowtreefarm.fslife.co.uk
I: www.mole-end-cottage.co.uk

ALCESTER
Warwickshire

The Croft Cottage ★★★★
Contact: Mrs Catherine Harris
The Croft Cottage, Bidford Road,
Alcester B50 4HH
T: (01789) 490543
E: cathy@thecroftcottage.co.uk
I: www.thecroftcottage.co.uk

Dorset House Cottage and Dorset House ★★★★
Contact: Mrs Plummer
Dorset House Cottage and
Dorset House, Church Street,
Alcester B49 5AJ
T: (01789) 762856
F: (01789) 766165
E: dorsethac@aol.com

HeronView ★★★★
Contact: Mr Mike & Mrs Heather
Bosworth
HeronView, Cross Guns Cottage,
Mill Lane, Oversley Green,
Alcester B49 6LF
T: (01789) 766506
F: (01789) 400851
E: heather@heronview.net
I: www.heronview.net

ALL STRETTON
Shropshire

The Pottery ★★★
Contact: Mr Chris Cotter
Overbatch House, Castle Hill, All
Stretton SY6 6JX
T: (01694) 723511
F: (01694) 722397
E: chrisjcotter@yahoo.co.uk
I: www.churchstretton.co.uk/acpottery.htm

ALSTONEFIELD
Staffordshire

Ancestral Barn & Church Farm Cottage ★★★★-★★★★★
Contact: Mrs Sue Fowler
Ancestral Barn & Church Farm
Cottage, Church Farm,
Ashbourne DE6 2AD
T: (01335) 310243
F: (01335) 310243
E: sue@dovedalecottages.fsnet.co.uk
I: www.dovedalecottages.co.uk

Dove Cottage Fishing Lodge ★★★★★
Contact: Mrs M Hignett
Foxleaze Court, Preston,
Cirencester GL7 5PS
T: (01285) 655875
F: (01285) 655885
E: info@dovecottages.co.uk
I: www.dovecottages.co.uk

The Gables ★★★
Contact: Mr McKee
Timewell Estates Plc, Po Box 15,
Wirral CH48 1QQ
T: (0151) 6253264
E: timewell@rtconnect.com
I: www.dovedale.org.uk

Gateham Grange Cottage & The Coach House ★★★-★★★★★
Contact: Mrs Teresa Flower
Gateham Grange Cottage & The
Coach House, Gateham Grange,
Ashbourne DE6 2FT
T: (01335) 310349
E: gateham.grange@btinternet.com
I: www.cressbrook.co.uk/harting/gateham/

The Haybarn ★★★★
Contact: Mrs Coralie Smith
The Haybarn, Hope Green Farm,
Ashbourne DE6 2GE
T: (01335) 310328
I: www.cottageguide.com.uk/haybarn

Hope Farm House Barn ★★★★
Contact: Ms Su Hanson
4 Stone Row, Ashbourne
DE6 1LW
T: (01335) 347757
F: (01335) 342717
E: su.hanson@virgin.net

Rowlands Cottage ★★★★
Contact: Mrs Ellen Wibberley
Hope Farm, Ashbourne DE6 2GE
T: (01335) 310370

ALTON
Staffordshire

Dale Farm Cottage ★★★
Contact: Mrs Moult
Dale Farm Cottage, Dale Farm,
The Dale, Stoke-on-Trent
ST10 4BG
T: (01538) 702022
F: (01538) 702022
E: njmoult@aol.com

The Homesteads ★★★
Contact: Mrs Ann Smith
24 Dove Lane, Uttoxeter
ST14 5LA
T: (01889) 590062

The Raddle Inn ★★-★★★
Contact: Mr Wilkinson
The Raddle Inn, Quarry Bank,
Stoke-on-Trent ST10 4HQ
T: (01889) 507278
F: (01889) 507520
I: www.logcabin.co.uk

ALVESTON
Warwickshire

Elm Cottage ★★★★
Contact: Mr & Mrs Baker
Penny Well Cottage, 4 Lower
End, Stratford-upon-Avon
CV37 7QH
T: (01789) 299101
F: (01789) 262998
E: petro_baker@compuserve.com

Tods Earth ★★★★
Contact: Mr & Mrs Selby
88 Old Town Mews, Stratford-upon-Avon CV37 6GR
T: (01789) 414626

Establishments printed in blue have a detailed entry in this guide

HEART OF ENGLAND

ASTON CANTLOW
Warwickshire

Cantlow Cottage ★★★
Contact: Mr John & Mrs Jane Nickless
The Corner House, Henley Road, Alcester B49 6HX
T: (01789) 488513
I: www.stratford-upon-avon.co.uk/cantlow.htm

ASTON ON CLUN
Shropshire

The Granary ★★★★
Contact: Mrs Morgan
The Granary, Rowton Grange, Aston on Clun, Craven Arms SY7 0PA
T: (01588) 660217
F: (01588) 660217
E: all@rowtongrange.freeserve.co.uk
I: www.rowtongrange.co.uk

ATHERSTONE
Warwickshire

Hipsley Farm Cottages ★★★★
Contact: Contact: Mrs Ann Prosser
Waste Farm, Hurley, Atherstone CV9 2LR
T: (01827) 872437
F: (01827) 875433
E: ann@hipsley.co.uk
I: www.hipsley.co.uk

AVON DASSETT
Warwickshire

The Limes Cottage ★★★
Contact: Mrs Diane Anderson
The Limes Cottage, The Limes, Southam CV47 2AR
T: (01295) 690245
E: andrsndiane@aol.com

AYMESTREY
Herefordshire

The Bungalow ★★★
Contact: Mr & Mrs Price
The Bungalow, Sussex Acres, Lower Lye, Leominster HR6 9TA
T: (01568) 770582
E: price2k@fsmail.net

BAGNALL
Stoke-on-Trent

Cordwainer Cottage ★★★
Contact: Mrs Muriel Buckle
Cordwainer Cottage, Stoney Villa Farm, Salters Wells, Stoke-on-Trent ST9 9JY
T: (01782) 302575
I: www.cordwainercottage.co.uk

BARNT GREEN
Worcestershire

Sandon Self Catering
Rating Applied For
Contact: Ms Valerie Price
Sandon Self Catering, 4 Kimbolton Drive, Bromsgrove B60 1QF
T: (0121) 4556797
F: (0121) 4456797
E: sandon@apartments.fsworld.co.uk
I: www.sandonselfcatering.co.uk

BAYTON
Worcestershire

The Mill House ★★★
Contact: Mrs Jane Chance
The Mill House, Clows Top, Kidderminster DY14 9LP
T: (01299) 832608
F: (01299) 832137
E: millhousebayton@aol.com
I: www.themillhouse-bayton.co.uk

BEOLEY
Worcestershire

The Granary ★★★★
Contact: Mrs Lang
The Granary, Dagnell End Farm, Dagnell End Road, Redditch B98 9BE
T: (01527) 596406
E: donnalang@aol.com
I: hometown.aol.com/donnalang/granary.html

BEWDLEY
Worcestershire

The Brant ★★★★
Contact: Mrs Helen Robson
Chapel House, Bewdley DY12 2XY
T: (01299) 825603
F: (01299) 825603
E: paulandhelen@hotmail.com

Manor Holding ★★★
Contact: Mr Nigel & Mrs Penny Dobson-Smyth
32 Church Street, Stourbridge DY9 0NA
T: 07970 260010
E: nds@landscapeconsultancy.freeserve.co.uk

Peacock Coach House ★★★★
Contact: Mrs Prisca Hall
Peacock House, Lower Park, Bewdley DY12 2DP
T: (01299) 400149
E: priscahall@hotmail.com

Riverview Cottage ★★★
Contact: Mr & Mrs Giles
The Lodge, Station Road, Bewdley DY12 1BT
T: (01299) 403481
E: jgilesm81@aol.com
I: www.riverview-bdy.co.uk

The White Cottage Garden Flat ★★★★
Contact: Mrs Tallents
The White Cottage, Kinlet, Bewdley DY12 3BD
T: (01299) 841238
F: (01299) 841482

BIDFORD-ON-AVON
Warwickshire

Corner Cottage and Pathway Cottage
★★★★-★★★★★
Contact: Mr W A Lucas
Tanglewood, Park Close, Stratford-upon-Avon CV37 9XE
T: (01789) 293932
T: (01789) 261855
E: lucasstratford@aol.com
I: www.lucasstratford.co.uk

BIRCHER
Herefordshire

Brook House Farm Flat
Rating Applied For
Contact: Mrs Shan Smith
Brook House Farm, Leys Lane, Leominster HR6 0AY
T: (01568) 780520
F: (01568) 780491
E: shanmsmith@aol.com

BIRTLEY
Shropshire

Hinds Cottage ★★★★
Contact: Mrs Hazel Newby
Hinds Cottage, c/o White House Farm, Deerfold, Birtley, Bucknell SY7 0EF
T: (01568) 770242
E: geof.newby@lycos.com
I: www.hindscottage.co.uk

BISHOP'S CASTLE
Shropshire

Claremont ★★★
Contact: Mrs Price
Claremont, Claremont Holiday Cottages, Bull Lane, Bishop's Castle SY9 5BW
T: (01588) 638170
F: (01588) 638170
E: price@claremontcottages.freeserve.co.uk
I: www.priceclaremont.co.uk

The Firs ★★★
Contact: Mr Sykes
Sykes Cottage, York House, York Street, Chester CH1 3LR
T: (01244) 345700
F: (01244) 321442
E: info@sykescottages.co.uk
I: www.sykescottages.co.uk

Mount Cottage ★★★★
Contact: Mrs Heather Willis
Bull Lane, Bishop's Castle SY9 5DA
T: (01588) 638288
F: (01588) 638288
E: adamheather@btopenworld.com
I: www.mountcottage.co.uk

The Old Chapel ★★★
Contact: Mrs Jane Traies
Simply Shropshire Cottage Holidays, Lower Farm, Shelve, Shrewsbury SY5 0JF
T: (01743) 891117
E: jane.traies@btopenworld.com

The Porch House ★★★
Contact: Mrs Gill Lucas
The Porch House, High Street, Bishop's Castle SY9 5BE
T: (01588) 638854
E: info@theporchhouse.com
I: www.theporchhouse.com

Walkmill Cottage ★★★
Contact: Mr Barry Preston
Walkmill Cottage, Wentnor, Bishop's Castle SY9 5DZ
T: (01588) 650671

BISHOPS FROME
Herefordshire

Five Bridges Inn ★★★★
Contact: Mr Mark & Mrs Bea Chatterton
Five Bridges Inn, Five Bridges, Worcester WR6 5BX
T: (01531) 640340
E: mark@5bridges.freeserve.co.uk
I: www.fivebridgescottage.co.uk

BITTERLEY
Shropshire

Angel House ★★★
Contact: Mr Henry & Mrs Doreen Mears
Angel House, Angel Bank, Near Bitterley, Ludlow SY8 3HT
T: (01584) 890755
F: (01584) 890755

BLACKBROOK
Staffordshire

Nags Head Farm Cottages ★★★
Contact: Mr David William Leathem
Nags Head Farm Cottages, Nantwich Road, Newcastle-under-Lyme ST5 5EH
T: (01782) 680334
F: (01782) 680334
E: nagsheadfarm.@aol.com

BOCKLETON
Worcestershire

1 Grafton Cottage ★★★
Contact: Mrs Sue Thomas
Grafton Farm, Tenbury Wells WR15 8PT
T: (01568) 750602
F: (01568) 750602
E: grafton.farm@btinternet.com

BODENHAM
Herefordshire

Bodenham Forge ★★★★
Contact: Mrs Mary Nickols
Bodenham Forge, The Forge, Bodenham, Hereford HR1 3JZ
T: (01568) 797144
E: sgnickols@yahoo.co.uk
I: www.bodenhamforge.co.uk

BORESFORD
Herefordshire

Hicks Farm Holidays-Rose Cottage ★★★★
Contact: Mrs Susan Bywater
Hicks Farm, Boresford, Presteigne LD8 2NB
T: (01544) 260237
E: holidays@hicksfarm.fsbusiness.co.uk
I: www.stmem.com/rosecottage

BRADNOP
Staffordshire

Millstones ★★★
Contact: Mrs Edwards
Millstones, Ashbourne Road, Bottomhouse, Leek ST13 7NZ
T: (01538) 304548
F: (01538) 304101
E: stephan@swepme.fsnet.co.uk

---

504 Look out for establishments participating in the National Accessible Scheme

HEART OF ENGLAND

School House ★★★★★
Contact: Mr Sykes
Sykes Cottages, York House,
York Street, Chester CH1 3LR
T: (01244) 345700
F: (01244) 321442
E: info@sykescottages.co.uk
I: www.sykescottages.co.uk

BRAILES
Warwickshire

Mill Holm Cottage and Mill Flat ★★★
Contact: Mr Rod Case
Mill Holm Cottage and Mill Flat, Whichford Mill, Shipston-on-Stour CV36 5JB
T: (01608) 686537
E: rodcase29@hotmail.com
I: www.cottageguide.co.uk/whichfordmill

BREDON
Worcestershire

The Moretons Vacation Houses ★★★★★
Contact: Mrs Karen Webb
The Moretons Vacation Houses, Tewkesbury GL20 7EN
T: (01684) 772294
F: (01684) 772262
E: soutar@moretonsbredon.co.uk
I: www.moretons-soutar.co.uk

BRIDGNORTH
Shropshire

Bulls Head Cottages ★★★
Contact: Mr David Baxter
The Bulls Head, Chelmarsh, Bridgnorth WV16 6BA
T: (01746) 861469
F: (01746) 862646
E: dave@bullshead.fsnet.co.uk
I: www.virtual-shropshire.co.uk/bulls-head-inn

Eudon Burnell Cottages ★★★★
Contact: Mrs Margaret Crawford Clarke
Eudon Burnell Cottages, Eudon Burnell Farm, Bridgnorth WV16 6UD
T: (01746) 789235
F: (01746) 789550
E: eudon-burnell@talk21.com
I: www.eudon.co.uk

The Granary ★★★
Contact: Mrs Sarah Allen
The Granary, The Old Vicarage, Ditton Priors, Bridgnorth WV16 6SQ
T: (01746) 712272
F: (01746) 712288
E: allens@oldvicditton.freeserve.co.uk

Jacob's Cottage ★★★★
Contact: Mrs Gilly Wooldridge
2 Allscott, Nr Worfield, Bridgnorth WV15 5JX
T: (01746) 716687
F: (01746) 716687
I: www.virtual-shropshire.co.uk/jacob

Lobby Stables ★★★★
Contact: Mrs Helen Danks
Lobby Stables, Lobby Farm, Oldfield, Bridgnorth WV16 6AQ
T: (01746) 789218
E: lobby_farm@lineone.net
I: shropshire-cottage.co.uk

Severn Rest ★★★
Contact: Mrs Cartwright
36 Farley, Croydon CR0 5DQ
T: (01746) 718093
E: jacky.cartwright@virgin.net

Tudor Cottage ★★
Contact: Mrs Henshaw
The White Cottage, 17 High Street, Claverley, Bridgnorth WV5 7DR
T: (01746) 710262

BRIERLEY
Herefordshire

Walnut Tree Cottage ★★★★
Contact: Ms Elaine Johnson
Walnut Tree Cottage, Leominster HR6 0NU
T: (01568) 620033
F: (01568) 620011
E: elaine@walnuttreecottage.net
I: www.walnuttreecottage.net

BROADWAY
Worcestershire

Hesters House ★★★
Contact: Mrs Liz Dungate
Inglenook, Brokengate Lane, Denham, Uxbridge UB9 4LA
T: (01895) 834357
F: (01895) 832904
E: pdungate@aol.com

Mellowstone ★★★★
Contact: Mrs Gillian Barker
Cotswold Property Lettings, 4 Keil Close, High Street, Broadway WR12 7DP
T: (01386) 858147
E: gill@cotswoldpropertylettings.com
I: www.cotswoldpropertylettings.com

BROADWELL
Warwickshire

Little Biggin ★★★
Contact: Mr Adrian & Mrs Linda Denham
Little Biggin, Rugby CV23 8HF
T: (01926) 812347
F: (01926) 812347
E: broadwellhouse@fieldtrack.net

BROBURY
Herefordshire

Brobury House Cottages ★★★-★★★★★
Contact: Mrs Pru Cartwright
Brobury House Cottages, Brobury House, Hereford HR3 6BS
T: (01981) 500229
F: (01981) 500229
E: enquiries@broburyhouse.co.uk
I: www.broburyhouse.co.uk

BROCKTON
Shropshire

Skimblescott Barn
Rating Applied For
Contact: Mrs Rowena Jones
Skimblescott Barn, Much Wenlock TF13 6QS
T: (01746) 785664

BROMSGROVE
Worcestershire

East View Apartment ★★★
Contact: Mrs Alma Westwood
East View Apartment, Little Shortwood, Brockhill Lane, Tardebigge, Bromsgrove B60 1LU
T: (01527) 63180
F: (01527) 63180
E: westwoodja@hotmail.com

BROMYARD
Herefordshire

Boyce Holiday Cottages ★★★★
Contact: Alison Richards
Boyce Holiday Cottages, Boyce Farm, Stanford Bishop, Worcester WR6 5UB
T: (01886) 884248
F: (01886) 884187
E: ah.richards@btopenworld.com

Mintridge ★★★★
Contact: Mr Richard & Mrs Sally Barrett
Hodgebatch Manor, Bromyard HR7 4QQ
T: (01885) 483262
F: (01885) 483262
E: hodgebatch@aol.com
I: www.mintridge.co.uk

BROSELEY
Shropshire

Aynsley Cottages ★★★
Contact: Mr Keith & Mrs Elsie Elcock
Shalimar, 4 Fox Lane, Broseley TF12 5LR
T: (01952) 882695
E: aynsleycottages@hotmail.com

BROXWOOD
Herefordshire

The Coach House ★★★★★
Contact: Mr Mike & Mrs Anne Allen
The Coach House, Leominster HR6 9JJ
T: (01544) 340245
F: (01544) 340573
E: mikeanne@broxwood.kc3.co.uk
I: www.broxwoodcourt.co.uk

BURLEY GATE
Herefordshire

Holly Lodge ★★★
Contact: Mr Barry Lawrence
Holly Tree Cottage, Hereford HR1 3QS
T: (01432) 820493
E: lawrence3@supanet.com
I: www.cottageguide.co.uk/hollylodge.html

BUTTERTON
Staffordshire

Swainsley Farm ★★★★★
Contact: Mr & Mrs Snook
Swainsley Farm, Leek ST13 7SS
T: (01298) 84530

CALLOW
Herefordshire

The Loft at Cold Nose ★★★★
Contact: Mr John Evans
Cottage Life, Cold Nose Cottage, Hereford HR2 8DE
T: (01432) 340954
E: john@cottagelife.freeserve.co.uk

CARDINGTON
Shropshire

Plaish Park Farm Barns - Turnip House and Corn House ★★★★★
Contact: Mrs Sara Jones
Plaish Park Farm Barns, Park Farm, Plaish, Church Stretton SY6 7HX
T: (01694) 771262
F: (01694) 771847

CAREY
Herefordshire

Carey Dene and Rock House ★★★
Contact: Mrs Slater
Ruxton Farm, Hereford HR1 4TX
T: (01432) 840493
F: (01432) 840493
E: milly@ruxton.co.uk

CHELMARSH
Shropshire

Duck, Drake & Cart Cottages ★★★
Contact: Mrs Roberts
Dinney Farm, Bridgnorth WV16 6AU
T: (01746) 861070
F: (01746) 861002
I: www.smoothhound.co.uk/hotels/dinncy.html

CHERINGTON
Warwickshire

Steele's Cottage ★★★★
Contact: Mrs Russell
Home Farm House, Shipston-on-Stour CV36 5HL
T: (01608) 686540
F: (01608) 686333

CHURCH STRETTON
Shropshire

The Barn, Daisy's Place and Goose Yard ★★★★
Contact: Mr Sykes
Sykes Cottage, York House, York Street, Chester CH1 3LR
T: (01244) 345700
F: (01244) 321442
E: info@sykescottage.co.uk
I: www.sykescottge.co.uk

Berry's Coffee House ★★★★
Contact: Mr John Gott
Berry's Coffee House, 17 High Street, Church Stretton SY6 6BU
T: (01694) 724452
F: (01694) 724460
E: all@berryscoffeehouse.co.uk
I: www.berryscoffeehouse.co.uk

Establishments printed in blue have a detailed entry in this guide

505

HEART OF ENGLAND

Botvyle Farm ★★★-★★★★★
Contact: Mrs Gill Bebbington
Botvyle Farm, Church Stretton
SY6 7JN
T: (01694) 722869
F: (01694) 722869
E: tlmgill@bebbington28.fsnet.co.uk
I: www.botvylefarm.co.uk

Brook House Cottage ★★
Contact: Mr & Mrs J Worley
Rosehill, Chestnut Walk,
Felcourt, East Grinstead
RH19 2LB
T: (01342) 870444

Broome Farm Cottages ★★★★★
Contact: Mr & Mrs Cavendish
Broome Farm Cottages, Broome Farm, Church Stretton SY6 7LD
F: (01694) 771778
E: sarah@sarahcavendish.demon.co.uk
I: www.broomefarm.co.uk

Caradoc Cottage ★★★★
Contact: Mrs Wendy Lewis
Caradoc Cottage, Caradoc House, Comley, Church Stretton SY6 7JS
T: (01694) 751488
F: (01694) 751488
E: w-lewis@lineone.net

The Garden Flat ★★★
Contact: Mrs Carol Hembrow
The Garden Flat, Ashfield House, Wndle Hill, Church Stretton
SY6 7AF
T: (01694) 723715
E: cj.hembrow@ukonline.co.uk

Granary Cottage and The Long Barn ★★★★
Contact: Mr & Mrs Kirkwood
Granary Cottage and The Long Barn, Lower Day House, Church Preen, Church Stretton SY6 7LH
T: (01694) 771521
E: bookings@lowerdayhouse.com
I: www.lowerdayhouse.com

Hodghurst Cottage ★★★
Contact: Mrs Chris Forsyth
Hodghurst Farm, Lower Wood, Church Stretton SY6 6LF
T: (01694) 751403

Jasleigh Cottage and Eliza's Cottage ★★★-★★★★
Contact: Mrs Wendy Lewis
Caradoc House, Comley, Church Stretton SY6 7JS
T: (01694) 751488
F: (01694) 751488
E: w-lewis@lineone.net
I: www.churchstrettoncottages.co.uk

Leasowes Cottage ★★★★
Contact: Mrs Margaret Harris
Leasowes, Watling Street, Longnor, Shrewsbury SY5 7QG
T: (01694) 751351
E: paul-harris@c-stretton.fsnet.co.uk
I: www.virtual-shropshire.co.uk/leasowes

Longmynd Hotel ★★★
Contact: Mr Chapman
Longmynd Hotel, Cunnery Road, Church Stretton SY6 6AG
T: (01694) 722244
F: (01694) 722718
E: reservations@longmynd.co.uk
I: www.longmynd.co.uk

Parkgate Cottages ★★★
Contact: Mrs Audrey Hill
Parkgate Cottages, Parkgate Farmhouse, Shrewsbury
SY5 8DH
T: (01694) 751303
E: park-gate@lineone.net
I: www.shropshiretourism.info

The Retreat ★★★
Contact: Mr & Mrs Bennett
The Retreat, 72 Watling Street South, Church Stretton SY6 7BH
T: (01694) 723370
I: www.stmcm.com/theretreat

The Sapling at Oakwood Cottage ★★★
Contact: Mrs Jan Oram
Oakwood Cottage, Marshbrook, Church Stretton SY6 6RG
T: (01694) 781347
E: oakwoodcottage01@aol.com

The Stables ★★★★
Contact: Mrs Maureen Burd
Station House, Church Stretton
SY6 6AX
T: (01694) 722057
I: www.churchstretton.co.uk/acburd.htm

Woodview ★★★
Contact: Mrs Brereton
Woolston Farm, Church Stretton
SY6 6QD
T: (01694) 781201
F: (01694) 781201
I: www.breretonhouse.fg.co.uk

Ye Olde Stables at Jinlye ★★★★
Contact: Miss Kate Tory
Ye Olde Stables at Jinlye, Jinlye, Castle Hill, Church Stretton
SY6 6JP
T: (01694) 723243
F: (01694) 723243
E: info@jinlye.co.uk
I: www.jinlye.co.uk

CLEOBURY MORTIMER
Shropshire

Hop Barn ★★★★
Contact: Mrs Birgit Jones
Neen Court, Neen Sollars, Kidderminster DY14 0AH
T: (01299) 271204
F: (01299) 271916
E: birgitanne@aol.com
I: www.virtual-shropshire.co.uk/hopbarn

Prescott Mill ★★★
Contact: Mrs Wendy Etchells
Prescott Mill, Prescott, Kidderminster DY14 8RR
T: (01746) 718721
F: (01746) 718718
E: mail@prescott-mill-cottage.co.uk
I: www.prescott-mill-cottage.co.uk

CLIFTON UPON TEME
Worcestershire

Pitlands Farm ★★★★
Contact: Mrs Diane Mann
Pitlands Farm, Clifton-on-Teme, Worcester WR6 6DX
T: (01886) 812220
F: (01886) 812220
E: pitlandsfarmholidays@btopenworld.com
I: www.pitlandsfarm.co.uk

CLUN
Shropshire

Bramleys ★★★★
Contact: Ms Fiona Bentley
Bramleys, Whitcott Keysett, Craven Arms SY7 8QE
T: (01252) 715428
E: bentley.fiona@virgin.net
I: www.cottageguide.co.uk/bramleys

Dick Turpin Cottage at Cockford Hall ★★★★★
Contact: Mr Roger Wren
Dick Turpin Cottage at Cockford Hall, Cockford Hall, Cockford Bank, Craven Arms SY7 8LR
T: (01588) 640327
F: (01588) 640881
E: cockford.hall@virgin.net
I: www.dickturpincottage.com

Lake House Cottages ★★★
Contact: Mr & Mrs Berry
Lake House Cottages, Lake House, Guilden Down Road, Craven Arms SY7 8NY
T: (01588) 640148
F: (01588) 640152
E: graham.berry5@btopenworld.com

The Miller's House ★★★★
Contact: Ms Gill Della Casa
Birches Mill, Craven Arms
SY7 8NL
T: (01588) 640409
F: (01588) 640409
E: gill@birchesmill.fsnet.co.uk
I: www.virtual-shropshire.co.uk/mullerhouse

Wagtail Cottage ★★★★
Contact: Mrs Williams
Wagtail Cottage, Hurst Mill Farm, Craven Arms SY7 0JA
T: (01588) 640224
F: (01588) 640224
E: hurstmillholidays@tinyworld.co.uk

Woolbury Barn ★★★★
Contact: Mrs Morris
Woolbury Barn, Hollybush Farm, Woodside, Craven Arms SY7 0JB
T: (01588) 640481

CLUNBURY
Shropshire

Brookside ★★★
Contact: Mr & Mrs S Seabury
Brookside, Craven Arms
SY7 0HG
T: (01588) 660494
I: www.brooksidecottage.co.uk

Nuthatch Cottage ★★★★
Contact: The Manager
Rural Retreats, Draycott Business Park, Moreton-in-Marsh GL56 9JY
T: (01386) 701177
F: (01386) 701178
E: info@ruralretreats.co.uk
I: www.ruralretreats.co.uk

CLUNTON
Shropshire

Clunton Farm Granary ★★★
Contact: Mrs Pauline Edie
Clunton Farmhouse, Craven Arms SY7 0HZ
T: (01588) 660120
F: (01588) 660121
E: info@clunvalleyretreat.com
I: www.clunvalleyretreat.com

Kingfisher Apartment ★★★
Contact: Mrs Pittam
Kingfisher Apartment, Tawny Cottage, Craven Arms SY7 0HP
T: (01588) 660327
F: (01588) 660327

COALBROOKDALE
Telford and Wrekin

Coalbrookdale, Tea Kettle Row Cottages ★★★-★★★★
Contact: Mrs Mary Jones
34 Darby Road, Telford TF8 7EW
T: (01952) 433202
E: mary@teakettlecottages.co.uk
I: www.teakettlecottages.co.uk

COALPORT
Telford and Wrekin

Station House Holiday Lets ★★★★
Contact: Mrs Helen Irvine
Station House Holiday Lets, Station House, Telford TF8 7JF
T: (01952) 591575
F: (01952) 881107
E: enquiries@coalportstation.com
I: www.coalportstation.com

COLWALL
Herefordshire

Threshing Barn ★★★★
Contact: Mr Coates
Lower House Farm, Evendine Lane, Malvern WR13 6DT
T: (01684) 540284

CORLEY
West Midlands

St Ives Lodge ★★★★
Contact: Mr Tim Ruffett
St Ives Lodge, St Ives Cottage, Church Lane, Coventry CV7 8BA
T: (01676) 542994
F: (01676) 549088
E: tim@ruffett.co.uk
I: www.st-ives-lodge.co.uk

COUND
Shropshire

The Cottage ★★★
Contact: Mr & Mrs Willetts
The Cottage, Severnside, Shrewsbury SY5 6AF
T: (01952) 510352

HEART OF ENGLAND

CRAVEN ARMS
Shropshire

Gwynfa ★★★
Contact: Mrs Delysia Wall
The Balkans, Longmeadow End,
Craven Arms SY7 8ED
T: (01588) 673375

Halford Holiday Homes ★★★-★★★★★
Contact: Mr & Mrs James
Halford Holiday Homes, Halford
Farm, Craven Arms SY7 9JG
T: (01588) 672382
I: www.go2.co.uk/halford

Malt House ★★★★★
Contact: Mrs Margaret Mellings
Long Meads, Lower Barns Road,
Ludford, Ludlow SY8 4DS
T: (01584) 873315
E: jean@mellings.freeserve.co.uk
I: www.mellings.freeserve.co.uk

Orchard Cottage ★★★★
Contact: Mr Peter & Mrs Olga Lewis
Orchard Cottage, Strefford
House, Craven Arms SY7 8DE
T: (01588) 673340
F: (01588) 673340
E: pdlewisuk@aol.com
I: www.cottageguide.co.uk/orchardcottage

Swallows Nest and Robin's Nest ★★★★★
Contact: Mrs Caroline Morgan
Strefford Hall, Craven Arms
SY7 8DE
T: (01588) 672383
E: strefford@btconnect.com
I: www.streffordhall.co.uk

Upper Onibury Cottages ★★★★
Contact: Mrs Hickman
Upper Onibury Cottages, Upper
Onibury, Craven Arms SY7 9AW
T: (01584) 856206
F: (01584) 856236
E: info@shropshirecottages.com
I: www.information-britain.co.uk/www.shropshirecottages.com

CRESSAGE
Shropshire

Jasmine Lodge ★★
Contact: Ms Kate Hogwood
Jasmine Lodge, Wood Lane,
Shrewsbury SY5 6DY
T: (01952) 510375
F: (01952) 510350
E: shrop.mus@lineone.net
I: www.stmem.com/jasmine

DENSTONE
Staffordshire

Keepers Cottage ★★★★
Contact: Mr Christopher Ball
Keepers Cottage, Manor House
Farm, Denstone, Uttoxeter
ST14 5DD
T: (01889) 590415
F: (01335) 342198
E: cm_ball@yahoo.co.uk
I: 4posteraccom.com

DILHORNE
Stoke-on-Trent

Birchenfields Farm ★★★
Contact: Mr & Mrs Peter Edge
Birchenfields Farm, Birchenfields
Lane, Stoke-on-Trent ST10 2PX
T: (01538) 753972
F: (01538) 753972

DOCKLOW
Herefordshire

Docklow Manor Holiday Cottages ★★★
Contact: Mrs Jane Viner
Docklow Manor Holiday
Cottages, Docklow Manor,
Leominster HR6 0RX
T: (01568) 760668
F: (01568) 760572
E: jane@docklowmanor.freeserve.co.uk
I: www.docklow-manor.co.uk

DORSINGTON
Warwickshire

Windmill Grange Cottage ★★★★
Contact: Mrs Lorna Hollis
Windmill Grange, Stratford-upon-Avon CV37 8BQ
T: (01789) 720866
F: (01789) 721872
E: lornah_windmillgrange@hotmail.com
I: www.windmillgrange.co.uk

DRAYCOTT-IN-THE-CLAY
Staffordshire

Granary Court Holiday Cottages ★★★★
Contact: Mrs Lynne Statham
Granary Court Holiday Cottages,
Stubby Lane, Ashbourne
DE6 5BU
I: www.granarycourt.demon.co.uk

EARDISLAND
Herefordshire

The Stables ★★★★
Contact: Mr Albert Priday
The Stables, The Old Vicarage,
Leominster HR6 9BP
T: (01544) 388570
F: (01544) 388570
E: pridays@aol.com

EATON-UNDER-HEYWOOD
Shropshire

Eaton Manor Rural Escapes ★★★★
Contact: Miss Nichola Madeley
Eaton Manor Rural Escapes,
Church Stretton SY6 7DH
T: (01694) 724814
F: (01694) 722048
E: ruralescapes@eatonmanor.co.uk
I: www.eatonmanor.co.uk

ELKSTONE
Staffordshire

Stable Cottage ★★★
Contact: Mrs Veronica Lawrenson
Grove House, Elkstones, Buxton
SK17 0LU
T: (01538) 300487
E: elkstone@talk21.com

ELMLEY CASTLE
Worcestershire

The Cottage Manor Farm House ★★
Contact: Mr Brian & Mrs Pat Lovett
The Cottage Manor Farm House,
Main Street, Elmley Castle,
Pershore WR10 3HS
T: (01386) 710286
F: (01386) 710112

EVESHAM
Worcestershire

Thatchers End ★★★★
Contact: Mr & Mrs Wilson
60 Pershore Road, Evesham
WR11 2PQ
T: (01386) 446269
F: (01386) 446269
E: trad.accom@virgin.net
I: http://freespace.virgin.net/trad.accom

FELTON
Herefordshire

The Green Farm Cottage ★★★★
Contact: Mrs Shirley Simcock
The Green Farm Cottage, The
Green Farm, Hereford HR1 3PH
T: (01432) 820234
F: (01432) 820437

FLASH
Staffordshire

Northfield Farm ★★★
Contact: Mrs Elizabeth Andrews
Northfield Farm, Flash, Buxton
SK17 0SW
T: (01298) 22543
F: (01298) 27849
E: northfield@btinternet.com
I: www.northfieldfarm.co.uk

FORD
Shropshire

Longmore Cottage ★★★★
Contact: Mrs Mary Powell
Home Farm, Rowton,
Shrewsbury SY5 9EN
T: (01743) 884201
I: www.stem.com/longmorecottage

FOWNHOPE
Herefordshire

Birds Farm Cottage ★★★
Contact: Mrs Margaret Edwards
White House, Hereford HR1 4SR
T: (01989) 740644
F: (01989) 740388
E: birdscottage@yahoo.com
I: www.holidaybank.co.uk/uk/heuk/h0529.htm

FRODESLEY
Shropshire

The Haven ★★★
Contact: Mr Richard & Mrs Jenifer Pickard
The Haven, Frodesley, Nr
Dorrington, Shrewsbury SY5 7EY
T: (01694) 731672
E: the-haven@frodesley.fsnet.co.uk
I: www.cottageguide.co.uk/the-haven

FROGHALL
Stoke-on-Trent

Foxtwood Cottages ★★★★
Contact: Mr Clive & Mrs Alison Worrall
Foxtwood Cottages, Foxt Road,
Stoke-on-Trent ST10 2HJ
T: (01538) 266160
E: info@foxtwood.co.uk
I: www.foxtwood.co.uk

GLEWSTONE
Herefordshire

Coldwell ★★★
Contact: Mrs Karen Jackson
Coldwell, Ross-on-Wye HR9 6AT
T: (01989) 770294
F: (01989) 770087
E: jacksonbeerhouse@aol.com

GREAT COMBERTON
Worcestershire

The Granary ★★★★
Contact: Mr & Mrs Newbury
The Granary, Tibbitts Farm,
Pershore WR10 3DT
T: (01386) 710210
F: (01386) 710210

GRIMLEY
Worcestershire

The Whitehouse Annex ★★★★
Contact: Mrs O'Neill
The Whitehouse Annex, The
Whitehouse, Monkwood Green,
Worcester WR2 6NX
T: (01886) 888743

GRINDON
Staffordshire

Manifold Retreat ★★★★
Contact: Mr Robert Magnier
Manifold Retreat, Cawbrook
Cottage, Leek ST13 7TP
T: (01538) 304535
E: bwmag@freeuk.com

GRINSHILL
Shropshire

Barleycorn Barns ★★★★
Contact: Mr Neil Lewis & Ms Kerry Taylor
Barleycorn Barns, 71 High
Street, Shrewsbury SY4 3BH
T: (01939) 220333
F: (01952) 608275
E: booking@barleycornbarns.com
I: www.barleycornbarns.co.uk

Chestnut Croft Self-Catering Cottage ★★★
Contact: Mr Good
Chestnut Croft Self-Catering
Cottage, 61 The Hill, Shrewsbury
SY4 3BU
T: (01939) 220573
F: (01939) 220573
E: roger@goodrj.fsnet.co.uk
I: www.chestnutcroft.co.uk

Underwood Cottage ★★★★
Contact: Mrs Vanessa Wycherley
Underwood Cottage, The
Vineyard, Shrewsbury SY4 3BW
T: (01939) 220214
E: vantomwood@hotmail.com

Establishments printed in blue have a detailed entry in this guide

HEART OF ENGLAND

HALLOW
Worcestershire
The New Cottage ★★★★
Contact: Mr Michael & Mrs Doreen Jeeves
The New Cottage, Bridles End House, Greenhill Lane, Worcester WR2 6LG
T: (01905) 640953
E: jeeves@thenewcottage.co.uk
I: www.thenewcottage.co.uk

HANLEY CASTLE
Worcestershire
Orchard Cottage ★★★★
Contact: Mrs Nicola Whittaker
Orchard Cottage, Whitehall Farm, Brotheridge Green, Worcester WR8 0BB
T: (01684) 310376
F: (01684) 310376
E: nicki@aol.com

HANLEY SWAN
Worcestershire
Little Merebrook ★★★★
Contact: Mr Bishop
Little Merebrook, Worcester WR8 0EH
T: (01684) 310899
F: (01684) 310899

HATTON
Shropshire
The Stable ★★★
Contact: Mr & Mrs Hall
White House, Church Stretton SY6 6RL
T: (01694) 781202
E: raysarahhall@aol.com

HENLEY-IN-ARDEN
Warwickshire
Irelands Farm ★★★★
Contact: Mr & Mrs Williams
Irelands Farm, Irelands Lane, Solihull B95 5SA
T: (01564) 792476
F: (01564) 792476
E: stephanie.williams1@btinternet.com
I: www.irelandsfarmcottages.com

HEREFORD
Herefordshire
Anvil Cottage ★★★★
Contact: Mrs Jennie Layton
Grafton Villa Farmhouse, Hereford HR2 8ED
T: (01432) 268689
F: (01432) 268689
E: jennielayton@ereal.net
I: www.graftonvilla.co.uk

Barton West ★★★★★
Contact: Mrs Teresa Godbert
Hereford Hopes..You Enjoy Your Stay, 24 Broomy Hill, Hereford HR4 0LH
E: teresagodbert@hereford-hopes.co.uk
I: www.hereford-hopes.co.uk

Breinton Court ★★★
Contact: Mrs Hands
Breinton Court, Lower Breinton, Hereford HR4 7PG
T: (01432) 268156
F: (01432) 265134
E: hentaparkhotel@talk21.com

Castle Cliffe East ★★★★
Contact: Mr Mark Hubbard and Mr P Wilson
Castle Cliffe West, 14 Quay Street, Hereford HR1 2NH
T: (01432) 272096
E: mail@castlecliffe.net
I: www.castlecliffe.net

Cross In Hand Farm Cottage ★★★★
Contact: Dr Thornton
Cross In Hand Farm Cottage, Cross In Hand Farm, Hereford HR2 8EF
T: (01981) 540957
E: julia@crossinhand.com
I: www.crossinhand.com

Longwood Cottage ★★★★
Contact: Mrs Veronica Harris
Longwood Cottage, Ashfield House, Hereford HR1 4RL
T: (01989) 740248
F: (01989) 740214
E: kenverharris@aol.com

The Old Warehouse ★★★★
Contact: Mrs Gill Saunders
31 Kernal Road, St Nicholas Gate, Hereford HR4 0PR
T: (01432) 272545
E: theoldwarehouse@yahoo.com

Rushford ★★★★
Contact: Mrs Roberts
Rushford, 7 Belle Bank Avenue, Hereford HR4 9RL
T: (01432) 273380
F: (01432) 273380

HIMBLETON
Worcestershire
The Granary ★★★
Contact: Mr David & Mrs Trica Havard
The Granary, Phepson Farm, Droitwich WR9 7JZ
T: (01905) 391205
F: (01905) 391338
E: havard@globalnet.co.uk
I: www.phepsonfarm.co.uk

HOARWITHY
Herefordshire
Old Mill Cottage ★★★
Contact: Mrs Carol Probert
Old Mill, Hereford HR2 6QH
T: (01432) 840602
F: (01432) 840602
I: www.theoldmillhoarwithy.co.uk

HOLLINGTON
Stoke-on-Trent
Rowan Cottage ★★★
Contact: Mr & Mrs P Campbell
The Bungalow, Abbotsholme School, Uttoxeter ST14 5BS
T: (01889) 594379

HOPESAY
Shropshire
Hesterworth Holidays ★★-★★★
Contact: Mr Roger Davies
Hesterworth Holidays, Craven Arms SY7 8EX
T: (01588) 660487
F: (01588) 660153
I: www.hesterworth.co.uk

HULME END
Staffordshire
East & West Cawlow Barn ★★★★
Contact: Mr Clive Sykes
Sykes Cottages, York House, York Street, Chester CH1 3LR
T: (01244) 345700
F: (01244) 321442
E: info@sykescottages.co.uk
I: www.sykescottages.co.uk

The Old Dairy ★★★
Contact: Mrs Marianne Grayson
The Old Dairy, Endon House Farm, Buxton SK17 0HG
T: (01298) 84515
F: (01298) 84476
E: mariannechalcraft@endonhouse.fsnet.co.uk
I: www.peakdistrict-nationalpark.com

ILAM
Staffordshire
Beechenhill Cottage and The Cottage by the Pond ★★★★
Contact: Mrs Sue Prince
Beechenhill Cottage and The Cottage by the Pond, Beechenhill Farm, Ashbourne DE6 2BD
T: (01335) 310274
F: (01335) 310467
I: www.beechenhill.co.uk

Casterne Hall ★★
Contact: Susannah Hurt
Casterne Hall, Ashbourne DE6 2BA
T: (01335) 310489
I: www.casterne.co.uk

Throwley Hall Farm ★★★-★★★★★
Contact: Mrs Richardson
Throwley Hall Farm, Ashbourne DE6 2BB
T: (01538) 308202
F: (01538) 308243
E: throwleyhall@talk21.com
I: throwleyhallfarm.co.uk

ILMINGTON
Warwickshire
Cotswold Retreats at Folly Farm Cottage ★★★★
Contact: Mr Malcolm Lowe
Cotswold Retreat at Folly Farm Cottage, Folly Farm Cottage, Back Street, Shipston-on-Stour CV36 4LJ
T: (01608) 682425
F: (01608) 682425
E: slowe@follyfarmcottage.co.uk
I: www.cotswolds-retreats.co.uk

Featherbed Cottage ★★★★
Contact: Mr David Price
Featherbed Cottage, Featherbed Lane, 8 Nellands Close, Shipston-on-Stour CV36 4NF
T: (01608) 682215
E: featherbedcottage@hotmail.com

IPSTONES
Staffordshire
Coach House Stables ★★★
Contact: Mrs Susan Wyncoll
Coach House Stables, The Noggin, Stoke-on-Trent ST10 2LQ
T: (01538) 266579
E: susan@the-noggin.freeserve.co.uk

Meadow Place ★★★★
Contact: Mr Sykes
Sykes Cottages, York House, York Street, Chester CH1 3LR
T: (01244) 345700
F: (01244) 321442
E: info@sykescottages.co.uk
I: www.sykescottages.co.uk

Old Hall Farm Cottages ★★
Contact: Mr & Mrs Glover
Old Hall Farm Cottages, Old Hall Farm, Church Lane, Stoke-on-Trent ST10 2LF
T: (01538) 266465

The Stables & The Cart Shed ★★★
Contact: Mr Michael & Mrs Hilary Hall
The Stables & The Cart Shed, Clough Head Farm, Stoke-on-Trent ST10 2LZ
T: (01538) 266259
I: www.cloughhead.co.uk

IRONBRIDGE
Shropshire
Bottom End Cottage ★★★★
Contact: Mr Ottley
8 Ladywood, Telford TF8 7JR
T: (01952) 883770
F: (01952) 884647
E: ironbridge@theironbridge.co.uk
I: www.theironbridge.co.uk

Eleys of Ironbridge ★★★-★★★★
Contact: Ms Jayne Mountford
Eleys of Ironbridge, 13 Tontine Hill, Telford TF8 7AL
T: (01952) 684249
F: (01952) 432030
I: www.eleys-ironbridge.co.uk

Langdale Cottage ★★★
Contact: Mr Keith Blight
30 Kingswood Place, Boundary Walk, Knowle, Fareham PO17 5FQ
T: (01329) 830171

Marnwood Lodge and School House ★★★★★
Contact: Mrs Jenny Morgan
Marnwood Properties Ltd, Marnwood Hall, Buildwas Road, Telford TF8 7BJ
T: (01952) 432281
F: (01952) 432281
I: www.marnwoodproperty.co.uk

HEART OF ENGLAND

Martha's Cottage ★★★
Contact: Mr Brian Richards
Thorpe House, High Street,
Coalport, Telford TF8 7HP
T: (01952) 586789
F: (01952) 586789
E: thorpehouse@tiscali.co.uk

Murton Cottage ★★★
Contact: Mrs Shan Murton
Mickleden, Sutherland Avenue,
Telford TF1 3BL
T: (01952) 415019
E: shanmurton@aol.com

Paradise House ★★-★★★
Contact: Mrs Gilbride
Paradise House, 3 Paradise,
Telford TF8 7NR
T: (01952) 433379
E: marjorie@gilbride.co.uk

The Uplands Flat ★★★
Contact: Mrs Eccleston
The Uplands, Buildwas Road,
Telford TF8 7BJ
T: (01952) 433408

KENILWORTH
Warwickshire

Castle Cottage ★★★★
Contact: Mrs Sheila Tomalin
7 Castle Green, Kenilworth
CV8 1NE
T: (01926) 852204
E: sheilatomalin@tinyonline.co.uk

Jackdaw Cottage and Wren's Nest ★★★★
Contact: Mrs Lynn Grierson
The White Bungalow, 6
Canterbury Close, Kenilworth
CV8 2PU
T: (01926) 855616
F: (01926) 513189
E: kgrierson@ukonline.co.uk

The Little Barn ★★★
Contact: Mrs Oliver
Crewe Farm Barns, Crewe Lane,
Kenilworth CV8 2LA
T: (01926) 850692

The Old Church House ★★★★
Contact: Mr & Mrs T Bray
The Old Church House, 1 Spring
Lane, Kenilworth CV8 2HB
T: (01926) 859290
F: (01926) 732126
E: info@theoldchurchhouse.co.uk

KENLEY
Shropshire

No 1 & 2 Courtyard Cottages ★★★★
Contact: Mrs Annabel Gill
Lower Springs Farm, Courtyard
Cottages, Shrewsbury SY5 6PA
T: (01952) 510841
F: (01952) 510841
E: a-gill@lineone.net
I: www.courtyardcottages.com

KIMBOLTON
Herefordshire

Rowley Farm ★★★
Contact: Jean & Sue Pugh
A M & L T Pugh, Rowley Farm,
Leominster HR6 0EX
T: (01568) 616123
F: (01568) 611101
E: rowley@farmersweekley.net
I: www.rowleyholidaypark.co.uk

KINGS CAPLE
Herefordshire

Ruxton Mill ★★★★
Contact: Mrs Slater
Ruxton Farm, Hereford HR1 4TX
T: (01432) 840493
F: (01432) 840493
E: milly@ruxton.co.uk

KINGTON
Herefordshire

Cider Press Cottage ★★★★
Contact: Mrs Lorraine Wright
Cider Press Cottage, Bredward
Farm, Kington HR5 3HP
T: (01544) 231462

KINWARTON
Warwickshire

The Granary ★★★
Contact: Mr David Kinnersley
The Granary, Glebe Farm,
Alcester B49 6HB
T: (01789) 762554
F: (01789) 762554
E: johnandsusan@kinnersley.fsworld.co.uk

KNIGHTCOTE
Warwickshire

Knightcote Farm Cottages ★★★★★
Contact: Mrs Fiona Walker
Knightcote Farm Cottages, The
Bake House, Southam CV47 2EF
T: (01295) 770637
F: (01295) 770135
E: fionawalker@farmcottages.com
I: www.farmcottages.com

KNOWBURY
Shropshire

Old Vicarage Coach House ★★★
Contact: Mr Adrian Phillips
Old Vicarage Coach House, The
Old Vicarage, Ludlow SY8 3JU
T: (01584) 891749
F: 0870 163905
E: adrianphillips@aol.com
I: www.knowburyoldvicarage.co.uk

LEA
Herefordshire

Moorlands ★★★
Contact: Mrs White
Moors Farm, Ross-on-Wye
HR9 7JY
T: (01989) 750230

LEA CROSS
Shropshire

Ranulf Holiday Cottage ★★★
Contact: Mrs Sue Collins
Linden House, Shrewsbury Road,
Shrewsbury SY4 4AG
T: (01939) 210873
E: info@ranulfholidaycottage.co.uk
I: www.ranulfholidaycottage.co.uk

LEAMINGTON SPA
Warwickshire

Barn Owl Cottage ★★★★
Contact: Mrs Beatrice Norman
Fosseway Barns, Fosse Way,
Offchurch, Leamington Spa
CV33 9BQ
T: (01926) 614647
F: (01926) 614647
E: bnorman@fossebarn.prestel.co.uk
I: barnowlcottage.co.uk

Blackdown Farm Cottages ★
Contact: Mr & Mrs R Solt
Blackdown Farm, Sandy Lane,
Leamington Spa CV32 6QS
T: (01926) 422522
F: (01926) 450996
E: bobby@solt.demon.co.uk

Furzen Hill Farm ★★★★
Contact: Mrs Christine Whitfield
Furzen Hill Farm, Cubbington
Heath, Leamington Spa
CV32 7UJ
T: (01926) 424791
F: (01926) 424791

Riplingham ★★★★
Contact: Ms Shevlin
1 The Old Courtyard, Alderman
Way, Leamington Spa CV33 9GF
T: (01926) 633790
E: riplingham@hotmail.com

LEATON
Telford and Wrekin

Vicarage Cottage ★★★★★
Contact: Mrs Joan Mansell-Jones
Vicarage Cottage, The Old
Vicarage, Leaton, Shrewsbury
SY4 3AP
T: (01939) 290989
F: (01939) 290989
E: m-j@oldvicleaton.com
I: www.oldvicleaton.com

LEDBURY
Herefordshire

Coach House Apartment ★★★
Contact: Mr & Mrs Williams
Ross Road, Ledbury HR8 2LP
T: (01531) 631199
F: (01531) 631476
E: leadon.house@amserve.net
I: www.leadonhouse.net

Homend Bank Cottage ★★★
Contact: Mrs Hughes
R H & R W Clutton, The Estate
Office, Leighton Court, Ledbury
HR8 2UN
T: (01531) 640262
F: (01531) 640719

The Old Kennels Farm ★★★-★★★★★
Contact: Mrs Jeanette Wilce
The Old Kennels Farm, Bromyard
Road, Ledbury HR8 1LG
T: (01531) 635024
F: (01531) 635241
E: wilceoldkennelsfarm@btinternet.com
I: www.oldkennelsfarm.co.uk

The Studio ★★★
Contact: Mr & Mrs David Riley
The Studio, Kynaston Place,
Ledbury HR8 2PD
T: (01531) 670321
E: david@criley56.freeserve.co.uk

White House Cottages ★★★-★★★★★
Contact: Mrs Marianne Hills
White House Cottages, The
White House, Aylton, Ledbury
HR8 2RQ
T: (01531) 670349
F: (01531) 670057
E: hills1477@aol.com
I: www.whitehousecottages.co.uk

LEEK
Staffordshire

Blackshaw Grange ★★★-★★★★
Contact: Mr & Mrs Williams
Blackshaw Grange, Leek
ST13 8TL
T: (01538) 300165
E: kevwilliams@btinternet.com
I: website.lineone.net/~blackshawgrange

Broomyshaw Country Cottages Lower Broomyshaw Farm ★★★
Contact: Mr & Mrs Saul
Broomyshaw Country Cottages
Lower Broomyshaw Farm,
Winkhill, Leek ST13 7QZ
T: (01538) 308298

Candy Cottage ★★★★
Contact: Mrs Sylvia Plant
Candy Cottage, Upper Cadlow
Farm, Winkhill, Leek ST13 7QX
T: (01538) 266243
E: splantuppercadlow@hotmail.com
I: www.cottageguide.co.uk/candycottage/

Larks Rise ★★★
Contact: Mrs Laura Melland
Larks Rise, New House Farm,
Bottom House, Leek ST13 7PA
T: (01538) 304350
E: newhousefarm@btinternet.com
I: www.staffordshiremoorlandsfarmholidays.co.uk

Rosewood ★★★
Contact: Mr T & Mrs E Mycock
Rosewood, Lower Berkhamsytch
Farm, Bottom House, Leek
ST13 7QP
T: (01538) 308213
F: (01538) 308213

Wren Cottage ★★★★
Contact: Mr Robert & Mrs
Elizabeth Lowe
Rudyard, Leek ST13 8PR
T: (01260) 226341
F: (01260) 226341
E: fairboroughs@talk21.co.uk
I: www.fairboroughs.co.uk

Establishments printed in blue have a detailed entry in this guide

HEART OF ENGLAND

LEINTWARDINE
Herefordshire

Badgers Bluff Holiday Cottages ★★★★
Contact: Mr Norton
Badgers Bluff Holiday Cottages, The Todding Farmhouse, Craven Arms SY7 0LX
T: (01547) 540648
F: (01547) 540648
E: reg@badgersbluff.co.uk
I: www.badgersbluff.co.uk

Dower Cottage ★★★★
Contact: Ms Anne & Susan Douthwaite
Dower House, Whitton, Craven Arms SY7 0LS
T: (01547) 540446
E: info@dower-cottage.co.uk
I: www.dower-cottage.co.uk

Oak Cottage ★★★
Contact: Mrs Vivienne Faulkner
24 Watling Street, Craven Arms SY7 0LW
T: (01547) 540629
F: (01547) 540181
E: fmjones@skg.co.uk

Oaklands Farm ★★-★★★
Contact: Mrs Sally Ann Swift
Kinton, Leintwardine, Craven Arms SY7 0LT
T: (01547) 540635
E: mrpaswift@aol.co.uk

LEOMINSTER
Herefordshire

Ashton Court Farm ★★★
Contact: Mrs Edwards
Ashton Court Farm, Leominster HR6 0DN
T: (01584) 711245

The Buzzards ★★★★
Contact: Ms E Povey
The Buzzards, Leominster HR6 9QE
T: (01568) 708941
E: holiday@thebuzzards.co.uk
I: www.thebuzzards.co.uk

Eaton Farm Cottage ★★★
Contact: Mrs Audrey Pritchard
Eaton Farm Cottage, Eaton Court Farm, Stoke Prior Road, Leominster HR6 0NA
T: (01568) 612095
I: www.cottageguide.co.uk/eatonfarmcottage

Ford Abbey ★★★★★
Contact: Mr Ken Garrood-Bailey
Ford Abbey, Leominster HR6 0RZ
T: (01568) 760700
F: (01568) 760264
E: info@fordabbey.co.uk
I: www.fordabbey.co.uk

Ledicot Granary ★★★
Contact: Mr Crawford & Mrs Vanessa Gibbons
Ledicot Granary, Ledicot Farm, Leominster HR6 9NX
T: (01568) 709245

LITTLE DEWCHURCH
Herefordshire

The Granary ★★★★
Contact: Mrs Tibbetts
The Granary, Henclose Farm, Hereford HR2 6PP
T: (01432) 840826
F: (01432) 840826

LITTLE TARRINGTON
Herefordshire

Stock's Cottage ★★★★
Contact: Mrs Angela Stock
Stock's Cottage, Hereford HR1
T: (01432) 890243
F: (01432) 890243
E: stay@stockscottage.co.uk
I: www.stockscottage.co.uk

LLANFAIR WATERDINE
Shropshire

Llandinship ★★★★
Contact: Mr Andrew & Mrs Sharon Beavan
Blackhall, Llanfairwaterdine, Knighton LD7 1TU
T: (01547) 528909
F: (01547) 528909
E: andrew.beavan@telco4u.net
I: www.blackhallfarm.com

LLANGARRON
Herefordshire

Little Trereece Holiday Cottages ★★★★
Contact: Mr & Mrs Cinderey
Little Trereece Holiday Cottages, Little Trereece Farmhouse, Ross-on-Wye HR9 6NH
T: (01989) 770145
E: trereece@nasuwt.net
I: homepages.nasuwt.net/trereece

LLANYBLODWEL
Shropshire

The Coach House ★★★★
Contact: Mr Malcolm & Mrs Sylvia Perks
The Coach House, Huntsmans Lodge, Llanyblodwell, Oswestry SY10 8NF
T: (01691) 828038
E: coach.house@micro-plus-web.net
I: www.thecoachhouse.micro-plus-web.net

LLAWNT
Shropshire

Olde Cross Foxes ★★★
Contact: Mr Trevor Upshall
Olde Cross Foxes, Oswestry SY10 7PR
T: (01691) 657933
F: (01691) 656300
E: allenbydouglas@tiscali.co.uk

LONGNOR
Staffordshire

Heathylee Holiday Cottages ★★★★
Contact: Mr Paul Hancock
The Old Schoolhouse, School Green, Stoke-on-Trent ST10 2LX
T: (01538) 266977
E: paul.cathie@virgin.net

Rewlach Chapel ★★★
Contact: Mr Colin MacQueen
Peak Cottages, Strawberry Lee Lane, Totley Bents, Sheffield S17 3BA
T: (0114) 262 0777
F: (0114) 2620666
E: enquiries@peakcottages.com
I: www.peakcottages.com

LUDLOW
Shropshire

Angel Barn ★★★
Contact: Ms Jennifer Roberts
Angel Gardens, Springfield, Bitterley, Ludlow SY8 3HZ
T: (01584) 890381
F: (01584) 890381
E: angelgardens@sy83hz.fsnet.co.uk

Ashford Farm Cottages ★★★★
Contact: Mr & Mrs Norman Tudge
Ashford Farm Cottages, Ashford Farm, Ludlow SY8 4DB
T: (01584) 831243
F: (01584) 831243
E: ashfordfarms@aol.com
I: www.ashfordfarms.co.uk

The Avenue Flat ★★★★
Contact: Mr Meredith
The Avenue Flat, The Avenue, Ashford Carbonell, Ludlow SY8 4DA
T: (01584) 831616
E: ronmeredithavenue@talk21.com

The Bakery Apartment ★★★
Contact: Mrs Deborah Cook
16 Vashon Close, Ludlow SY8 1XG
T: (01584) 877051

9 Brand Lane ★★★★
Contact: Mrs Angela Wells
Trappe House, Evenjobb, Presteigne LD8 2PA
T: (01547) 560436
F: (01547) 560436
E: brandwell@holcott.freeserve.co.uk
I: www.9brandlane.co.uk

Bribery Cottage ★★★
Contact: Mr Richard & Mrs Juliet Caithness
2 Dinham, Ludlow SY8 1EJ
T: (01584) 872828
F: (01584) 872828
E: richard.caithness@virgin.net
I: www.virtual-shropshire.co.uk/bribery-cottage

Cariad Holiday Cottages ★★★
Contact: Mrs Fitzmaurice
16 Morden Road, Newport NP19 7EU
T: (01633) 666732
F: (01633) 666732
E: carol.fitzmaurice@ntlworld.com
I: www.southshropshire.org.uk/cariad

Casa Dona Marcella ★★★★
Contact: Mrs Mills-Pereira
Middlewood Stables, Lowerwood Road, Ludlow SY8 2JG
T: (01584) 856401
F: (01584) 856512
E: casadonamarcella@msn.com
I: www.casadonamarcella.co.uk

Chimney Pots ★★★
Contact: Mr Chris Williams
Chimney Pots, The Cross, Buttercross, Ludlow SY8 1AW
T: (01584) 875069
F: (01584) 877692
E: ludlow@chriswilliams.fsnet.co.uk
I: www.chimneypots.net

Church Bank ★★
Contact: Mrs Rosemary Laurie
Church Bank, Burrington, Ludlow SY8 2HT
T: (01568) 770426
E: laurie2502@lineone.net

Criterion Cottage ★★★
Contact: Mrs Christine Hodgson
Criterion House, Ludlow SY8 3NZ
T: (01584) 890344

Elm Lodge Apartment and The Coach House Apartment ★★★-★★★★
Contact: Mrs Barbara Weaver
Elm Lodge Apartment and The Coach House Apartment, Ludlow SY8 3DP
T: (01584) 877394
F: (01584) 877397
E: apartments@sjweaver.fsnet.co.uk
I: www.elm-lodge.org.uk

Emily Place ★★★★
Contact: Mrs Melanie Chetwood
1 Duke Street, Buxton SK17 9AB
T: (01298) 73807
E: paul.chetwood@royalmail.com

Garden Apartment ★★★
Contact: Ms Sue Walsh
Holloway Farm, Craven Arms SY7 9HG
T: (01584) 841225
F: (01584) 841225
E: suewalsh@tesco.net
I: www.virtual-shropshire.co.uk/greenwich

Garden Cottage ★★★★
Contact: Mr Pash
Hideaways, Chapel House, Luke Street, Berwick St John, Shaftesbury SP7 0HQ
T: (01747) 828170
F: (01747) 829090
E: enq@hideaways.co.uk
I: www.hideaways.co.uk/property2.cfm?ref=H182

Goosefoot Barn Cottages ★★★★
Contact: Mrs Sally Loft
Goosefoot Barn Cottages, Pinstones, Diddlebury, Craven Arms SY7 9LB
T: (01584) 861326
E: sally@goosefoot.freeserve.co.uk
I: www.goosefootbarn.co.uk

HEART OF ENGLAND

The Granary ★★★
Contact: Mr & Mrs Mercer
The Granary, Tana Leas Farm, Craven Arms SY7 9DZ
T: (01584) 823272
F: (01584) 823272
E: r.mercer@tinyworld.co.uk
I: www.southshropshire.org.uk/granary

Hazel Cottage ★★★★
Contact: Mrs Rachel Sanders
Duxmoor Farm, Craven Arms SY7 9BQ
T: (01584) 856342
F: (01584) 856696
E: RachelSanders@mac.com
I: www.stmem.com/hazelcottage

Horseshoe Cottage ★★★★
Contact: Mr & Mrs Gill
3 Fosse Close, Hinckley LE10 3PQ
T: (01455) 272874
F: (01455) 272874
E: trgill@btinternet.com
I: www.cottageguide.co.uk/horseshoecottage

Lilac Cottage ★★★★
Contact: Mrs Elizabeth Grant
Wheelers Hope Cottage Farm, Much Wenlock TF13 6DN
T: (01746) 785564
E: cottagefarm@farmersweekly.co.uk

Ludford View ★★★
Contact: Mr Christopher & Mrs Laura Birkett & Rutty
Ludlowlife, 22A Temeside, Ludlow SY81PB
T: (01584) 873249
F: (01584) 873249
E: ludlowlet@aol.com
I: www.ludlowlife.co.uk

Maryvale Lodge ★★★★
Contact: Mrs Alison Cundall
Palmers House, 7 Corue Street, Ludlow SY8 1DB
T: (01584) 878353
F: (01584) 873010
E: mail@maryvalecottages.co.uk
I: www.maryvalecottages.co.uk

The Mews Flat ★★★
Contact: Mrs Linda Taylor
8 Friars Garden, Ludlow SY8 1RX
T: (01584) 873609
E: mrs.miggs@virgin.net

24 Mill Street ★★★★
Contact: Mrs Debbie Brodie
Craven Arms SY7 8DQ
T: (01588) 672074
F: (01588) 672074

Mocktree Barns Holiday Cottages ★★★
Contact: Mr Clive & Mrs Cynthia Prior
Mocktree Barns Holiday Cottages, Mocktree Barns, Craven Arms SY7 0LY
T: (01547) 540144
I: www.mocktreeholidays.co.uk

Post Horn Cottage ★★
Contact: Ms Helen Davis
32 Leamington Drive, Chilwell, Nottingham NG9 5LJ
T: (0115) 922 2383

Ravenscourt Manor ★★★★
Contact: Mrs Elizabeth Purnell
Ravenscourt Manor, Ludlow SY8 4AL
T: (01584) 711905
E: ravenscourtmanor@amsgrve.com
I: www.virtual-shropshire.co.uk/ravencourt-manor

Shropshire Knights ★★★
Contact: Mrs Carole Miller
Tinkers Hill House, Tinkers Hill, Ludlow SY8 4BW
T: (01584) 876256
F: (01584) 876256

The Studio The Rhyse Farm ★★★
Contact: Mr & Mrs Barnard
The Rhyse Farm, Ludlow SY8 4AE
T: (01584) 831128
E: cbarn1937@aol.com

Sutton Court Farm Cottages ★★★★
Contact: Mrs S J Cronin
Sutton Court Farm, Little Sutton, Ludlow SY8 2AJ
T: (01584) 861305
F: (01584) 861441
E: suttoncourtfarm@hotmail.com
I: www.suttoncourtfarm.co.uk

Toad Hall ★★★
Contact: Mrs Jean Taylor
Lindidfarne, 2 Vashon Close, Ludlow SY8 1XG
T: (01584) 874161
F: (01584) 874161

The Town Flat ★★★
Contact: Mr Kidd
12 Corve Street, Ludlow SY8 1DA
T: (01584) 877946
F: (01584) 878256
E: gk@nka.co.uk
I: www.thetownflat.com

Wandering William Barn ★★★★
Contact: Mr Richard Maddicott
Wandering William Barn, Foldgate Farm, Foldgate Lane, Ludlow SY8 4BN
T: (01584) 877899
F: (01584) 878480
E: richard@maddicott.com

The Wool Shop ★★
Contact: Mr & Mrs Richard Mercer
Tana Leas Farm, Clee St Margaret, Craven Arms SY7 9DZ
T: (01584) 823272
F: (01584) 823272
E: r.mercer@tinyworld.co.uk

LYDBURY NORTH
Shropshire

Walcot Hall Holiday Apartments ★★★-★★★★
Contact: Miss Maria Higgs
Walcot Hall Holiday Apartments, Walcot Hall, Lydbury North SY7 8AZ
T: (01588) 680570
F: (01568) 680361
E: maria@walcothall.com
I: www.walcothall.com

LYONSHALL
Herefordshire

Field Cottage, The Sherriffs & Gardeners Cottage ★★★★-★★★★★
Contact: Mrs Joanna Hilditch
Whittern Farms Ltd, Lyonshall, Kington HR5 3JA
T: (01544) 340241
F: (01544) 340253
E: info@whiteheronproperties.com
I: www.whiteheronproperties.com

MADLEY
Herefordshire

Canon Bridge House ★★★★
Contact: Mrs Anscomb
Canon Bridge House, Canon Bridge, Hereford HR2 9JF
T: (01981) 251104
F: (01981) 251412
E: timothy.anscomb4@virgin.net
I: www.cottageguide.co.uk/canonbridge

MALVERN
Worcestershire

Annexe to Blue Cedars ★★★
Contact: Mrs Longmire
Blue Cedars, Peachfield Close, Malvern Wells, Malvern WR14 4AN
T: (01684) 566689

April Cottage ★★★
Contact: Mrs Longmire
2 Peachfield Close, Malvern WR14 4AN
T: (01684) 566689
E: pml@peachfield.freeserve.co.uk

The Coach House
Rating Applied For
Contact: Mrs Bury
David E J Prosser, 71 Church Street, Malvern WR14 2AE
T: (01684) 561411
F: (01684) 564748
E: dprosser@supanet.com

The Coach House ★★★
Contact: Mrs Jill Jones
58 North Malvern Road, Malvern WR1 4LX
T: (01684) 569562
E: jjmalvern@onetel.com

The Dell House ★★★
Contact: Mr Ian Burrage
The Dell House, Green Lane, Malvern Wells, Malvern WR14 4HU
T: (01684) 564448
F: (01684) 893974
E: burrage@dellhouse.co.uk
I: www.dellhouse.co.uk

Farmhouse Cottage ★★★
Contact: Mrs Sue Stringer
Farmhouse Cottage, Cowleigh Park Farm, Cowleigh Road, Malvern WR13 5HJ
T: (01684) 566750
E: cowleighpark@ukonline.co.uk
I: www.cowleighparkfarm.co.uk

Greenbank House Garden Flat ★★★
Contact: Mr David Matthews
Greenbank House Garden Flat, 236 West Malvern Road, Malvern WR14 4BG
T: (01684) 567328
E: matthews.greenbank@virgin.net

Hidelow House Cottages ★★★★-★★★★★
Contact: Mrs Pauline Diplock
Hidelow House Cottages, Acton Green, Worcester WR6 5AH
T: (01886) 884547
F: (01886) 884658
E: stay@hidelow.co.uk
I: www.hidelow.co.uk

Hillside Cottage
Rating Applied For
Contact: Mr Richard Ditchburn
Arosfa, Upper Welland Road, Malvern WR14 4JU
T: (01684) 562306
E: reditchburn@hotmail.com

Maynard Lodge ★★★★★★
Contact: Mr Michael & Elaine Roberts
Maynard Lodge, Croft Bank, Malvern WR14 4DU
T: (01684) 564568
F: (01684) 563201
E: info@maynardlodge.co.uk
I: www.maynardlodge.co.uk

The Old Bakery ★★★
Contact: Mrs Aldridge
The Old Bakery, West End House, Lower Dingle, West Malvern Road, Malvern WR14 4BQ
T: (01684) 566044
F: (01684) 566044
E: enquiry@oldbakerymalvern.co.uk
I: www.oldbakerymalvern.co.uk

The Studio ★★★
Contact: Mrs Gwyneth Sloan
The Studio, Rosehill Cottage, Holywell Road, Malvern WR14 4LF
T: (01684) 561074
F: (01684) 561074
E: sloaniain@hotmail.com

16 Warwick House
Rating Applied For
Contact: Mr Nick Beard
Leigh Sinton Farm & Nurseries Ltd, Lower Interfields, Malvern WR14 1UU
T: (01886) 832305
F: (01886) 833446
E: leighsinton@virgin.net

Wayfarers Cottage ★★★
Contact: Mr John & Mrs Caroline Roslington
Wayfarers Cottage, Park Road, Malvern WR14 4BJ
T: (01684) 575758
E: jroslington@mac.com
I: www.wayfarerscottage.co.uk

HEART OF ENGLAND

Whitewells Farm Cottages ★★★★
Contact: Mr & Ms Denis & Kate Kavanagh
Whitewells Farm Cottages, Whitewells Farm, Malvern WR13 5JR
T: (01886) 880607
F: (01886) 880360
E: info@whitewellsfarm.co.uk
I: www.whitewellsfarm.co.uk

MARKET DRAYTON
Shropshire

The Old Smithy Holiday Cottages ★★★★
Contact: Mrs Carmel Simpson
The Old Smithy Holiday Cottages, The Lightwoods, Market Drayton TF9 2LR
T: (01630) 661661

MARTON
Shropshire

Highgate Cottage ★★★
Contact: Mr Sykes
Sykes Cottage, York House, York Street, Chester CH1 3LR
T: (01244) 345700
F: (01244) 321442
E: info@sykescottages.co.uk
I: www.sykescottages.co.uk

MAVESYN RIDWARE
Staffordshire

Stable Cottage ★★★★
Contact: Mrs Susan Clift
Manor Farm Cottage, Church Lane, Rugeley WS15 3QE
T: (01543) 491579
F: (01543) 491579
E: dmsaclift@farming.co.uk

MEOLE BRACE
Shropshire

Stable Cottage ★★
Contact: Mrs Baugh
Stable Cottage, Glebe House, Vicarage Road, Shrewsbury SY3 9EZ
T: (01743) 236914
E: s.baugh@virgin.net

MIDDLETON SCRIVEN
Shropshire

Harry's House ★★★★
Contact: Mrs Patrica Round
Coates Farm, Bridgnorth WV16 6AG
T: (01746) 789224
I: www.coatesfarm.co.uk

MILWICH
Staffordshire

Summerhill Farm ★★★★
Contact: Mrs Patricia Milward
Summerhill Farm, Summer Hill, Milwich, Stafford ST18 0EL
T: (01889) 505546
F: (01889) 505692
E: p.milward@btinternet.com
I: www.summerhillfarmapartment.co.uk

MINSTERLEY
Shropshire

Brookland ★★★
Contact: Mrs Davies
New Moor Farm, Shrewsbury SY5 0HR
T: (01743) 791217

Fishpool Farm ★★
Contact: Mrs J Y Shelley
Fishpool Farm, White Gritt, Shrewsbury SY5 0JN
T: (01588) 650337

Lower Farm Cottage ★★★★
Contact: Mrs Jane Traies
Lower Farm Cottage, Shelve, Shrewsbury SY5 0JF
T: (01743) 891117
E: jane.traies@btopenworld.com

Luckley Cottage ★★★★
Contact: Mrs Angela O'Brien
Luckley Cottage, Bromlow, Minsterley, Shrewsbury SY5 0ED
T: (01743) 891469
F: (01743) 891469
E: angela.obrien@surfanytime.co.uk

Ovenpipe Cottage ★★★
Contact: Mr & Mrs A Thornton
Tankerville Lodge, Stiperstones, Shrewsbury SY5 0NB
T: (01743) 791401
F: (01743) 792305
E: tankervillelodge@supanet.com

Upper House Farm Cottage ★★★★
Contact: Mrs Kait Stanhope
Upper House Farm Cottage, Shrewsbury SY5 0AA
T: (01743) 792831
F: (01743) 792831
E: k.stanhope1@virgin.net

MONTFORD BRIDGE
Shropshire

Mytton Mill Flat ★★★
Contact: Mrs Patrica Minshall
Mytton Mill House, Forton Heath, Shrewsbury SY4 1HA
T: (01743) 850497

MORTON BAGOT
Warwickshire

Manor Farm Cottages Royland Farms ★★★★
Contact: Mrs Lydia Green
Manor Farm Cottages Royland Farms Ltd, Manor Farm, Studley B80 7ED
T: (01527) 852219
F: (01527) 852219
E: roylands@farmersweekly.net
I: www.manorfarmcottages.co.uk

MORVILLE
Shropshire

Hurst Farm Cottages ★★★★
Contact: Mr & Mrs Brick
Hurst Farm, Bridgnorth WV16 4TF
T: (01746) 714375
F: (01746) 714375
E: hurstfarm@talk21.com

MUCH COWARNE
Herefordshire

Cowarne Hall Cottages ★★★★
Contact: Mr Richard Bradbury
Cowarne Hall Cottages, Bromyard HR7 4JQ
T: (01432) 820317
E: rm@cowarnehall.co.uk
I: www.cowarnehall.co.uk

Old Bridgend Cottage ★★★★
Contact: Mrs Angela Morgan
32 Chestnut Grove, New Malden KT3 3JN
T: (020) 89420702
F: (020) 89494950

MUCH MARCLE
Herefordshire

Shepherds Rest ★★★★
Contact: Mrs Fiona Wilcox
Shepherds Rest, Hill Farm, Ledbury HR8 2PH
T: (01531) 660285
E: fjwilcox@waitrose.com
I: www.herefordshireholidaycottage.co.uk

MUCH WENLOCK
Shropshire

The Oaks ★★★
Contact: Mrs Denise Goodson
The Oaks, 2 Barrow Street, Much Wenlock TF13 6ES
T: (01952) 728637
F: (01952) 728355
E: kingdenigoodson@aol.com
I: www.theoaks.tk

The Priory ★★★
Contact: Mrs Annabel Croft
The Priory, Bull Ring, Much Wenlock TF13 6HS
T: (01952) 728280
E: aa@croftpriory.fslife.co.uk
I: www.stmem.com/thepriory

Priory Cottage ★★★★
Contact: Mrs Cumberland
Priory Cottage, Bull Ring, Much Wenlock TF13 6HS
T: (01952) 727386
I: www.priorycot.bridgnorthshropshire.com

Queen Street ★★★
Contact: Mrs Elizabeth Ann Williams
68 Church Hill, Penn, Wolverhampton WV4 5JD
T: (01902) 341399
E: williams_letting@hotmail.com

2 St Marys Lane ★★★★★
Contact: Mr & Mrs Gray
Penkridge Cottage, Sheinton Road, Much Wenlock TF13 6NS
T: (01952) 728169
F: (01952) 728415
E: dgray@dgray96.fsnet.co.uk
I: www.mortoncottage.co.uk

Stokes Cottage ★★★★
Contact: Mrs Suzanne Hill
Stokes Cottage, Newtown House Farm, Much Wenlock TF13 6DB
T: (01952) 727293
F: (01952) 728130
E: stokesbarn@hotmail.com
I: www.stokesbarn.co.uk

NEEN SOLLARS
Shropshire

Cider House ★★★★
Contact: Ms Priscilla Kennedy
Cider House, Tetstill, Kidderminster DY14 9AH
T: (01299) 270414
F: (01299) 271156
E: priscillahann@lineone.net

Garden Cottage ★★★
Contact: Mr & Mrs P Luff
Garden Cottage, Pear Tree Cottage, Kidderminster DY14 0AN
T: (01299) 271082

Live and Let Live ★★★
Contact: Mr & Mrs Ferguson
Live and Let Live, Kidderminster DY14 9AB
T: (01299) 832391

NETHERSEAL
Staffordshire

Grangefields ★★★★
Contact: Mrs Rita Hill
Grangefields, Clifton Road, Netherseal, Swadlincote DE12 8BT
T: (01827) 373253
F: (01827) 373253

NORBURY
Staffordshire

Oulton House Farm Garden Cottages ★★★★
Contact: Mrs Judy Palmer
Oulton House Farm, Stafford ST20 0PG
T: (01785) 284264
F: (01785) 284264
E: judy@oultonhousefarm.co.uk
I: www.oultonhousefarm.co.uk

Shuttocks Lodge ★★★
Contact: Mrs Ann Williams
Shuttocks Lodge, Shuttocks Wood, Bishop's Castle SY9 5EA
T: (01588) 650433
F: (01588) 650492
E: shuttockswood@btconnect.com

OAKAMOOR
Staffordshire

The Annexe at The Old Furnace ★★★
Contact: Annette and John Higgins
The Annexe at The Old Furnace, Greendale, Oakamoor ST10 3AP
T: (01538) 703331
I: www.oldfurnace.co.uk

ORCOP
Herefordshire

The Burnett Farmhouse ★★★★
Contact: Mr & Mrs Gooch
The Burnett Farmhouse, Hereford HR2 8SF
T: (01981) 540999
F: (01981) 540999
E: burnett.farmhouse@talk21.com
I: www.burnettfarmhouse.co.uk

Bury Farm ★★
Contact: Mrs Goodwin
Old Kitchen Farm, Hereford HR2 0DE
T: (01981) 240383
F: (01981) 241475

ORLETON
Worcestershire

The Forge Cottage ★★★
Contact: Mrs Rosemary Cox
The Forge Cottage, The Forge, Ludlow SY8 4HR
T: (01508) 780373
F: (01568) 780373

512 Look out for establishments participating in the National Accessible Scheme

HEART OF ENGLAND

OSWESTRY
Shropshire

The Cross Keys ★★★
Contact: Mr & Mrs Philip Rothera
The Cross Keys, Oswestry SY10 7DH
T: (01691) 650247

Hinsdale
Rating Applied For
Contact: Mrs Barbara Roberts
Hinsdale, Twmpath Lane, Oswestry SY10 7AH
T: (01691) 650408

The Old Rectory Cottage ★★
Contact: Mrs Maggie Barnes
The Old Rectory Cottage, The Old Rectory, Glyn Road, Selattyn, Oswestry SY10 7DH
T: (01691) 659708
F: (01691) 661366

PEMBRIDGE
Herefordshire

The Cottage ★★★
Contact: Mr & Mrs Jones
The Cottage, Clearbrook, Leominster HR6 9HL
T: (01544) 388569
E: jonescottage@aol.com
I: www.cottageguide.co.uk/clearbrook

The Granary and The Dairy ★★★
Contact: Mrs Owens
The Grove, Leominster HR6 9HP
T: (01544) 388268
F: (01544) 388154

Luntley Court Farm ★★★★
Contact: Mrs Sandra Owens
Luntley Court Farm, Leominster HR6 9EH
T: (01544) 388422
F: (01544) 388422
E: luntley.court.farm@faarming.co.uk

Rowena Cottage ★★
Contact: Mrs Diana Malone
The Cottage, Holme, Newark NG23 7RZ
T: (01636) 672914
E: dianamalone56@hotmail.com

Winyard Lodge & Tippet's Lodge Tibhall Lodges ★★★★
Contact: Mr & Mrs Gwatkin
Tibhall Lodge, Tibhall, Leominster HR6 9JR
T: (01544) 388428

PENKRIDGE
Staffordshire

Dalraddy Cottage ★★★★★
Contact: Mrs Sonia Young
Pottal Pool House, Pottal Pool, Teddesley Hay, Stafford ST19 5RR
T: (01785) 715700
F: (01785) 712216
E: sonia@adamsyoung.fsnet.co.uk
I: dalraddycottage.mysite.freeserve.com

PERSHORE
Worcestershire

Court Close Farm ★★★
Contact: Mrs Eileen Fincher
Court Close Farm, Manor Road, Pershore WR10 3BH
T: (01386) 750297
F: (01386) 750297
E: fincher@ukonline.co.uk

PILLERTON HERSEY
Warwickshire

Roman Acres Cottage ★★★
Contact: Mrs Williams
Roman Acres Cottage, Roman Acres, Oxhill Bridle Road, Warwick CV35 0QB
T: (01789) 740360

PONTRILAS
Herefordshire

Station House ★★
Contact: Ms Jo Russell
Station House, Hereford HR2 0EH
T: (01981) 240564
F: (01981) 240564
E: john.pring@tesco.net
I: www.golden-valley.co.uk/stationhouse

PONTSHILL
Herefordshire

The Coach House ★★★
Contact: Mr & Mrs Hoare
Croome Hall, Ross-on-Wye HR9 5TB
T: (01989) 750335
E: brendan@croomehall.freeserve.co.uk

PRESTON GUBBALS
Shropshire

Gubbals House Cottage ★★★
Contact: Mrs Valerie Nunn
Gubbals House Cottage, Shrewsbury SY4 3AN
T: (01939) 290644
F: (01939) 290644
E: mike_nunn@btinternet.com
I: www.stmem.com/gubbalscottage/

PRESTON WYNNE
Herefordshire

Wisteria Cottage ★★★
Contact: Mrs Jenni Maund
Lower Town, Hereford HR1 3PB
T: (01432) 820608
F: (01432) 820608
E: lowertown@onetel.net.uk

PRESTWOOD
Staffordshire

Swallows Loft ★★★★
Contact: Mrs Joyce Beeson
Swallows Loft, Brook Cottage, Quixhill Lane, Uttoxeter ST14 5DD
T: (01889) 590464
F: (01335) 300093
E: bookings@swallows-loft.fsnet.co.uk
I: www.swallows-loft.fsnet.co.uk

PRINCETHORPE
Warwickshire

Stretton Lodge Barns ★★★
Contact: Mrs Best
Stretton Lodge Barns, Stretton Lodge, Oxford Road, Rugby CV23 9QD
T: (01926) 632351
F: (01926) 456209
E: c.best@btinternet.com

PRIORS HARDWICK
Warwickshire

Pepperpot Lodge
Rating Applied For
Contact: Mrs Prophet
School Cottage, London End, Southam CV47 7SL
T: (01327) 262015
F: (01327) 264663

PULVERBATCH
Shropshire

Crossways Holiday Cottage ★★★
Contact: Mrs Gill Swain
The Granary, Wilderley Lane Farm, Shrewsbury SY5 8DF
T: (01743) 718152
E: gill@crosswaysstud.com
I: www.crosswaysstud.com

2 Holly Grove Cottages ★★★★
Contact: Mrs Sue Morris
Holly Grove Farm, Shrewsbury SY5 8DD
T: (01743) 718300
E: pulverbatch@farmersweekly.net
I: www.hollygrovecottage.co.uk

RICHARDS CASTLE
Shropshire

The Barn ★★★★
Contact: Mr Peter & Mrs Sue Plant
The Barn, Ryecroft, Ludlow SY8 4EU
T: (01584) 831224
F: (01584) 831224
E: ryecroftbarn@hotmail.com
I: www.ludlow.org.uk/ryecroft

ROCK
Worcestershire

The Barn ★★★
Contact: Mr Deall
Chinook, Bliss Gate, Kidderminster DY14 9YE
T: (01299) 266047

ROSS-ON-WYE
Herefordshire

The Ashe ★★★
Contact: Mrs M.R Ball
The Ashe, Ashe Holiday Cottages, Ross-on-Wye HR9 6QA
T: (01989) 563336
I: www.ashe-holiday-cottages.com

Barn House and Oaklands ★★★
Contact: Mrs Angela Farr
Farr Cottages, Southwell Court, Broad Oak, Hereford HR2 8RA
T: (01600) 750333
E: farrcottages@yahoo.com
I: www.farrcottages.co.uk

Columbine Cottage ★★★
Contact: Mrs Sue Wall
Radcliffe House, Wye Street, Ross-on-Wye HR9 7BS
T: (01989) 563895
E: radcliffegh@bt.internet.com

Fairview ★★★
Contact: Mrs Jones
Stoneleigh, Fourth Avenue, Ross-on-Wye HR9 7HR
T: (01989) 566301

The Game Larders and The Old Bakehouse ★★★
Contact: Miss Anthea McIntyre
Wythall Estate, Ross-on-Wye HR9 5SD
T: (01989) 562688
F: (01989) 763225
E: wythall@globalnet.co.uk
I: www.wythallestate.com

Highview ★★
Contact: Mr Perry
Westfield House, Wye Street, Ross-on-Wye HR9 7BT
T: (01989) 564149
F: (01989) 566884

Little Hatpins ★★★
Contact: Mrs Mary Waller
Hatpins, Bosham Lane, Old Bosham, Chichester PO18 8HG
T: (01243) 572644
F: (01243) 572644
E: mary@littlehatpins.co.uk
I: www.littlehatpins.co.uk

Mainoaks Farm Cottages ★★★-★★★★★
Contact: Mrs Unwin
Hill House, Chase End, Ledbury HR8 1SE
T: (01531) 650448
E: mainoaks@lineone.net
I: www.mainoaks.co.uk

Man of Ross House ★★
Contact: Mr David Campkin
8 Maitland Road, Reading RG1 6NL
T: (0118) 9572561
F: (0118) 9594867

Old Cider House ★★★★
Contact: Mrs Heather Jackson
Lowcop, Glewstone, Ross-on-Wye HR9 6AN
T: (01989) 562827
F: (01989) 563877
E: man.of.ross.ltd@farming.co.uk

Old Forge Cottage ★★★
Contact: Mrs Jennings
The Tower House, Priory Road, Bromsgrove B61 9DF
T: (01527) 833880
F: (01527) 833880

The Old Hall ★★★
Contact: Mrs Heather Lovett
The Old Hall, 7 Hom Green, Ross-on-Wye HR9 7TG
T: (01989) 567864
F: (01989) 567869
E: grather.lovett@btopenworld.com
I: homgreen.co.uk

Establishments printed in blue have a detailed entry in this guide

HEART OF ENGLAND

The Olde House ★★★
Contact: Mr & Mrs P Fray
Keepers Cottage, Ross-on-Wye
HR9 7UE
T: (01989) 780383
F: (01989) 780383
E: peter@pjfray.co.uk
I: www.oldehouse.com

Orchard View ★★★
Contact: Mr & Mrs Powell
Underhill Farm, Ross-on-Wye
HR9 6RD
T: (01989) 567950

Paddocks Farm ★★★★★
Contact: Ms Catherine Gaskell
Paddocks Farm, Deep Dean,
Ross-on-Wye HR9 5SQ
T: (01989) 768699
F: (01989) 768699
E: info@pakkocksfarm.co.uk

Perrystone Cottage ★★★
Contact: Mrs Jenny Sanders
Woodlands Farm, Hereford
HR2 6QD
T: (01432) 840488
F: (01432) 840700
E: perrystonecottages@hotmail.com
I: www.perrystonecottages.co.uk

Plymouth House ★★★
Contact: Mr Robert Green
Pembroke House, Ross-on-Wye
HR9 5QX
T: (01600) 891322
F: (01600) 891322
E: rgreen5929@aol.com
I: www.wyeholidaylets.co.uk

Riverview Apartment ★★★
Contact: Ms Jane Roberts
Riverview Apartment, Edde
Cross House, Edde Cross Street,
Ross-on-Wye HR9 7BZ
T: (01989) 563299
E: info-tb@riverviewapartment.co.uk
I: www.riverviewapartment.co.uk

Watchmaker's Cottage
★★★★
Contact: Mrs Jennifer Clark
Watchmaker's Cottage,
Daffaluke House, Ross-on-Wye
HR9 6BB
T: (01989) 770369
F: (01989) 770369
E: watchmakerscottage@madasafish.com

Wharton Lodge Cottages
★★★★★
Contact: Mrs Nicky Cross
Wharton Lodge Cottages, Ross-on-Wye HR9 7JX
T: (01989) 750140
F: (01989) 750140
E: ncross@whartonlodge.co.uk
I: www.whartonlodge.co.uk

Y Crwys ★★★
Contact: Mr Colin & Mrs Angie
Fuller
3 The Square, Goodrich, Ross-on-Wye HR9
T: (01600) 890799
E: colinfuller@hotmail.com
I: www.pimlico.demon.co.uk

RUGBY
Warwickshire

Lawford Hill Farm ★★★★
Contact: Mr & Mrs Susan Moses
Lawford Hill Farm, Lawford
Heath Lane, Rugby CV23 9HG
T: (01788) 542001
F: (01788) 537880
E: lawford.hill@talk21.com
I: www.lawfordhill.co.uk

The Saddlery ★★★★★
Contact: Mrs Heckford
Manor Farm, Brooks Close,
Willoughby, Rugby CV23 8BY
T: (01788) 890256
E: office@thesaddlery.org.uk
I: thesaddlery.org.uk

RUSHBURY
Shropshire

Lilywood Cottage ★★★★
Contact: Mrs Lole
Lilywood Cottage, Lilywood
Barn, Holloway Lane, Church
Stretton SY6 7EA
T: (01694) 771286
E: ruth.lole@ukonline.co.uk
I: www.stem.com/lilywoodcottage

RUSHTON SPENCER
Staffordshire

Cosy Nook ★★★★★
Contact: Mrs Jackie Matravers
Cosy Nook, Ivydene,
Macclesfield SK11 0QU
T: (01260) 226570
F: (01260) 226570
E: 106366.3376@compuserve.com
I: www.cottageguide.co.uk/cosynook

Toft Hall ★★★★
Contact: Ms Sue Norgrove-Moore
Toft Hall, Heaton, Macclesfield
SK11 0SJ
T: (01260) 226609
E: suenorgrove@hotmail.com
I: tofthall.com

SEVERN STOKE
Worcestershire

Roseland Annexe ★★★★
Contact: Mr Guy & Mrs Mary
Laurent
Roseland Annexe, Roseland,
Clifton, Worcester WR8 9JF
T: (01905) 371463
F: (01905) 371463
E: guy@guy-laurent.demon.co.uk
I: www.roselandworcs.demon.co.uk

SHEEN
Staffordshire

Bank Top Lodge ★★★★
Contact: Mrs Birch
Bank Top Farm, Buxton
SK17 0HN
T: (01298) 84768

Ferny Knowle ★★★★★
Contact: Mr George & Mrs
Pauline Grindon
Ferny Knowle, Buxton SK17 0ER
T: (01298) 83264

SHIFNAL
Shropshire

The Old Stable ★★★
Contact: Mr & Mrs R Wild
The Old Stable, 4 Church Street,
Shifnal TF11 9AA
T: (01952) 461136
E: wildthings@raphaelsrestaurant.co.uk
I: www.raphaelsrestaurant.co.uk

SHIPSTON-ON-STOUR
Warwickshire

Little Barn ★★★★
Contact: Mrs Karen Lawrence
Little Barn, Shipston-on-Stour
CV36 5PP
T: (01608) 684240
E: johnandkaren.lawrence@ic24.net
I: littlebarn.members.easyspace.com/index.htm

SHOBDON
Herefordshire

Tyn-y-Coed ★★★★
Contact: Mr & Mrs Diana
Andrews
Tyn-y-Coed, Leominster
HR6 9NY
T: (01568) 708277
F: (01568) 708277
E: jandrews@shobdondesign.kc3.co.uk

SHREWSBURY
Shropshire

Barn Cottages ★★★★
Contact: Mrs Susan Good
Barn Cottages, 1 Red Barn Lane,
Shrewsbury SY3 7HR
T: (01743) 355594
E: jgood70712@aol.com
I: www.cottageguide.co.uk/barncottages

Inglenook ★★
Contact: Mrs J.M Mullineux
Fach-Hir, Brooks, Welshpool
SY21 8QP
T: (01686) 650361

Mill House Farm ★★★
Contact: Mrs Christine Burton
Mill House Farm, Cruckmeole,
Shrewsbury SY5 8JN
T: (01743) 860325
E: christine@millhousefarmholidays.fsnet.co.uk

Yews Barn ★★★★
Contact: Ms Hiorns
5 Humbers Way, Telford TF2 8LH
T: (01952) 605915
E: gpassant@aol.com
I: www.yewsbarn.co.uk

SNAILBEACH
Shropshire

The Blessing ★★★
Contact: Mr & Mrs Dennis
3 Farm Cottages, Shrewsbury
SY5 0LP
T: (01743) 791489

STAFFORD
Staffordshire

No 4 The Row ★★★★
Contact: Miss Shirley Moore
Downtop Farm, Sandon Bank,
Stafford ST18 9TB
T: (01889) 508300

STANFORD BRIDGE
Worcestershire

The Riseling ★★★★
Contact: Mrs Margaret Lane
The Rise, Worcester WR6 6SP
T: (01886) 853438

STANSHOPE
Staffordshire

**Lower Damgate
Barns, Reuben's Roost,
Bremen's Barn, Hope's
Hideaway** ★★★★
Contact: Mr & Mrs Wilderspin
Lower Damgate Farm,
Ashbourne DE6 2AD
T: (01335) 310367
F: (01335) 310001
E: DAMGATE@HOTMAIL.COM
I: www.damgate.com

STIPERSTONES
Shropshire

The Resting Hill ★★★
Contact: Mrs Rowson
The Resting Hill, 46 Snailbeach,
Shrewsbury SY5 0LT
T: (01743) 791219

STOKE-ON-TRENT
Stoke-on-Trent

Bank End Farm Cottages
★★★
Contact: Mr Ken & Mrs Evelyn
Meredith
Bank End Farm, Hammond
Avenue, Stoke-on-Trent
ST6 8QU
T: (01782) 502160
E: pete502@btopenworld.com
I: www.alton-village.com

Coach House ★★★
Contact: Mrs Janet Lowery
Coach House, 2 Moss Cottage,
Mossfields, Stoke-on-Trent
ST7 1EL
T: (01782) 786821

**Field Head Farm House
Holidays** ★★★★
Contact: Ms Janet Hudson
Stoney Rock Farm, Waterhouses,
Stoke-on-Trent ST10 3LH
T: (01538) 308352
F: (01538) 308352
E: janet@field-head.co.uk
I: www.field-head.co.uk

Jay's Barn ★★★
Contact: Mrs Christine Babb
Rest Cottage, Bradley in the
Moor, Stoke-on-Trent ST10 4DF
T: (01889) 507444
E: jaysbarn@lineone.net
I: www.jaysbarn.co.uk

Lockwood Hall Farm
★★★★
Contact: Mrs Rebecca Sherratt
Lockwood Hall Farm, Lockwood
Road, Kingsley Holt, Stoke-on-Trent ST10 2DH
T: (01538) 752270
F: (01538) 752270
E: sherratt@lockwoodhall.freeserve.co.uk
I: www.cottageguide.co.uk/lockwoodhall

HEART OF ENGLAND

Low Roofs ★★★
Contact: Mrs Malkin
62 Albert Terrace, Newcastle-under-Lyme ST5 8AY
T: (01782) 627087
F: (01782) 627087

Moor Court Cottages Moor Court House ★★★★
Contact: Mr Vanessa & Mrs Les Bradshaw
Moor Court Cottages Moor Court House, Upper Leigh, Stoke-on-Trent ST10 4NU
T: (01538) 723008
F: (01538) 723008
I: www.moorcourtcottages.co.uk

STOURPORT-ON-SEVERN
Worcestershire

Winnall House Cottage and Caravan Park ★★★★
Contact: Mrs Sheila Wilson
Winnall House Cottage and Caravan Park, Winnall House, Stourport-on-Severn DY13 9RG
T: (01299) 250389

STRATFORD-UPON-AVON
Warwickshire

20-21 Bancroft Place ★★★★
Contact: Mrs Stella Carter
Park View, 57 Rother Street, Stratford-upon-Avon CV37 6LT
T: (01789) 266839
F: (01789) 266839

Anne's House ★★★★
Contact: Mrs Cauvin
34 Evesham Place, Stratford-upon-Avon CV37 6HT
T: (01789) 550197
F: (01789) 295322
E: karenc@anneshouse.com
I: www.anneshouse.com

As You Like It ★★★
Contact: Mrs Reid
Inwood House, New Road, Stratford-upon-Avon CV37 8PE
T: (01789) 450266
F: (01789) 450266
I: www.alderminster99.freeserve.co.uk

55 Bull Street ★★★★
Contact: Mr John Barlow
JSB Consulting Ltd, 2 Old Town, Statford-upon-Avon CV37 6BG
T: (01789) 268378
F: (01789) 268715
E: info@55bullstreet.com
I: www.55bullstreet.com

66 Bull Street ★★★
Contact: Sir William Lawrence
The Knoll, Alcester B49 6LZ
T: 0783 6 636932
F: 0797 1 434810
I: www.stratforduponavonselfcatering.co.uk

Carpenters Barn ★★★★
Contact: Mrs Lynn Harrop
25 Bickenhill Road, Birmingham B37 7EL
T: (0121) 7795664
F: (0121) 7795664
E: lynn.harrop@btopenworld.com
I: www.stratford-upon-avon.co.uk/carpentersbarn.htm

Charlecote Cottage 2 Willicote Pastures ★★★★
Contact: Mr John Lea
6 Oak Wharf Mews, Birchdale Road, Appleton, Warrington WA4 5AS
T: (01925) 604106
F: (0151) 4246785
E: jplea@aol.com

Chestnut Cottage ★★★
Contact: Mrs Joyce Rush
Gospel Oak House, Gospel Oak Lane, Pathlow, Stratford-upon-Avon CV37 0JA
T: (01789) 292764

1 College Mews ★★★★
Contact: Mr Reid
Inwood House, New Road, Stratford-upon-Avon CV37 8PE
T: (01789) 450266
F: (01789) 450266
I: www.alderminster99.freeserve.co.uk

Crimscote Downs Farm Holiday Cottages ★★★
Contact: Mrs Joan James
The Old Coach House, Whitchurch Farm, Wimpstone CV37 8NS
T: (01789) 450275
F: (01789) 450275
I: www.stratford-upon-avon.co.uk/crimscote.htm

Elmhurst ★★★★
Contact: Mrs Davenport
Lygon Arms Hotel, High Street, Chipping Campden GL55 6HB
T: (01386) 840318
F: (01386) 841088
E: sandra@elmhurstcottage.co.uk
I: www.elmhurstcottage.co.uk

Ely Street ★★★★
Contact: Mr Pash
Hideaways, Chapel House, Luke Street, Berwick St John, Shaftesbury SP7 0HQ
T: (01747) 828170
F: (01747) 829090
E: enq@hideaways.co.uk
I: www.hideaways.co.uk/property2.cfm?ref=H180

Flower Court ★★★★
Contact: Mrs Rachel Liddell
Settlestones, Chipping Campden GL55 6UJ
T: (01386) 438833
F: (01386) 438833
E: liddellrachel@aol.com
I: www.flowercourt.freeservers.com

Fosbroke Cottage ★★★
Contact: Mrs Susan Swift
4 High Street, Bidford-on-Avon, Alcester B50 4BU
T: (01789) 772327
E: mark@swiftvilla.fsnet.co.uk
I: www.smoothhound.co.uk/hotels/fosbroke.html

Guild Court ★★★-★★★★
Serviced Apartments
Contact: Miss Tanya Moss
Guild Court, 3 Guild Street, Stratford-upon-Avon CV37 6QZ
T: (01789) 293007
F: (01789) 296301
E: info@guildcourt.co.uk
I: www.guildcourt.co.uk

Loaf Cottage ★★★
Contact: Sir William Lawrence
The Knoll, Alcester B49 6LZ
T: 0783 6 636932
F: 0797 1 434810
E: sirwlawrence@cix.co.uk
I: www.stratforduponavonselfcatering.co.uk

The Mill House ★★★-★★★★★
Contact: Mrs Sheila Greenwood
The Mill House, Mill Lane, Stratford-upon-Avon CV37 8EW
T: (01789) 750267
F: (01789) 750267
I: www.stratford-upon-avon.co.uk/millhouse.htm

No 7 Bull Street ★★★
Contact: Mrs Sally-Ann Salmon
80 Fentham Road, Hampton-in-Arden, Solihull B92 0AY
T: (01675) 443613
F: (01675) 443613
E: sallyannsalmon@talk21.com

3 Queens Cottage ★★★
Contact: Sir William Lawrence
The Knoll, Alcester B49 6LZ
T: 0783 6 636932
F: 0797 1 434810
I: www.stratforduponavonselfcatering.co.uk

Rollright Cottage ★★★★
Contact: Mr Alun Thomas
8 The Carpathian, Chamberlain Court, Spencer Street, Hockley, Birmingham B18 6JT
T: (01675) 460269
E: info@rollrightcottage.co.uk
I: www.rollrightcottage.co.uk

42 Shakespeare Street ★★★★
Contact: Mr Field
Avon House, Mulberry Street, Stratford-upon-Avon CV37 6RS
T: (01789) 298141
F: (01789) 262272
E: info@fieldholidaycottages.com
I: www.fieldholidaycottages.com

61 Waterside ★★★★
Contact: Mrs Valerie Lewis
65 Longdon Close, Redditch B98 7UZ
T: (01527) 527407
E: valerie@lewis2730.freeserve.co.uk

Woodcote ★★★★★
Contact: Mr & Mrs Lucas
Tanglewood, Park Close, Stratford-upon-Avon CV37 9XE
T: (01789) 293932
F: (01789) 261855
E: lucasstratford@aolco.uk
I: www.lucasstratford.co.uk

STRETTON
Staffordshire

Silvermere Cottages ★★★★
Contact: Mrs Sylvia Blake
Silvermere Cottages, Hawkshutt Farm, Stafford ST19 9QU
T: (01785) 840808
I: www.silvermere.co.uk

STRETTON ON FOSSE
Warwickshire

Woodfield Cottage ★★★
Contact: Mr John & Mrs Anna Best
Arden Cottage, 109 High Street, Solihull B95 5AU
T: (01564) 793354
F: (01564) 793472
E: john@johnbest.demon.co.uk

SUCKLEY
Worcestershire

Tundridge Mill ★★★★
Contact: Mrs Penny Beard
Tundridge Mill, Blackhouse Lane, Worcester WR6 5DP
T: (01886) 884478
F: (01886) 884478
I: www.tundridgemill.co.uk

SYMONDS YAT
Herefordshire

Old Court Farm ★★★★
Contact: Mrs Edwina Gee
Old Court Farm, Ross-on-Wye HR9 6DA
T: (01600) 890316
F: (01600) 890316
E: teddy.gee@breathemail.net
I: www.holidaybank.co.uk/uk/heuk/ho587.htm

TEAN
Staffordshire

Oakhill Holiday Homes ★★★★
Contact: Mrs Hilary Williams
Oakhill Holiday Homes, Oakhill Farm, Upper Tean, Stoke-on-Trent ST10 4JH
T: (01538) 722213

The Old Smithy ★★★
Contact: Mrs Judy Dronzek
Woodlands, Quarry Bank, Stoke-on-Trent ST10 4HQ
T: (01889) 507249

The Rockery ★★★★
Contact: Mrs Rushton
The Rockery, Abbey View Cottage, Quarry Road, Stoke-on-Trent ST10 4HP
T: (01889) 507434
E: dinah@abbey-view.fsnet.co.uk
I: www.cottageguide.co.uk/therockery

TELFORD
Telford and Wrekin

Church Farm Cottages ★★★
Contact: Mrs Virginia Evans
Church Farm Cottages, Rowton, Wellington, Telford TF6 6QY
T: (01952) 770381
F: (01952) 770381
E: church.farm@bigfoot.com
I: www.virtual-shropshire.co.uk/churchfarm

Morrells Wood Farm ★★★-★★★★
Contact: Mr Derek Harper
Morrells Wood Farm, Shrewsbury SY5 6RU
T: (01952) 510273

Establishments printed in blue have a detailed entry in this guide

HEART OF ENGLAND

Old Stables Cottage ★★★
Contact: Mrs Ferriday
4 Laburnum Drive, Telford
TF7 5SE
T: (01952) 684238
E: alex@ferriday7131.freeserve.co.uk

Witchwell Cottage ★★★★
Contact: Mrs Carter
Witchwell Cottage, Church Lane, Telford TF6 5BB
T: (01952) 505573
E: rcarter@wenboro.freeserve.co.uk
I: www.witchwellcottage.co.uk

TENBURY WELLS
Worcestershire

Colleybatch Pine Lodges ★★★★
Contact: Mr & Mrs Tebbett
Colleybatch Pine Lodges, Colleybatch, Boraston Bank, Tenbury Wells WR15 8LQ
T: (01584) 810153
F: (01299) 827011

TREFONEN
Shropshire

Little Barn ★★★★
Contact: Mrs Sue Batley
Wulfruna Cottage, Old Post Office Lane, Oswestry SY10 9DL
T: (01691) 653387
E: info@little-barn.co.uk
I: www.little-barn.co.uk

TRUMPET
Herefordshire

The Trumpet Inn ★★★
Contact: Mr Riga
The Trumpet Inn, Ledbury HR8 2RA
T: (01531) 670277
F: (01531) 670277
I: www.trumpetinn.com

TUGFORD
Shropshire

Brookside Cottage ★★
Contact: Mrs Bronwen Williams
Brookside Cottage, Tugford Farm, Craven Arms SY7 9HS
T: (01584) 841259
F: (01584) 841259
E: williamstugford@supanet.com
I: www.corvedale.com

UFTON
Warwickshire

Wood Farm ★★★★
Contact: Mr Derek Hiatt
Wood Farm, Leamington Road, Leamington Spa CV33 9PH
T: (01926) 612270

UPPER HULME
Staffordshire

Field House Cottage ★★★
Contact: Mr David Roberts
Field House Cottage, Upper Hulme, Leek ST13 8TZ
T: (01538) 300023
F: (01538) 300023
E: lesleyroberts@field-house.fsnet.co.uk

Hurdlow Cottage ★★★★
Contact: Mrs Belfield
Hurdlow Cottage, Hurdlow Farm, Leek ST13 8TX
T: (01538) 300406
F: (01538) 300406
E: robertruth@hurdlowfarm.fsnet.co.uk
I: www.hurdlowfarm.fsnet.co.uk

Little Ramshaw
Rating Applied For
Contact:
Peak Cottages, Strawberry Lee Lane, Totley Bents, Sheffield S17 3BA
T: (0114) 262 0777
F: (0114) 2620666
E: enquiries@peakcottages.com
I: www.peakcottages.com

The Old Chapel ★★★★
Contact: Mr Paul Hancock
The Old Schoolhouse, Schoolgreen, Stoke-on-Trent ST10 2LX
T: (01538) 266977
E: paul.cathie@virgin.net

Paddock Farm Holiday Cottages ★★★★
Contact: Mr & Mrs Barlow
Paddock Farm, Leek ST13 8TY
T: (01538) 300345

UPPER QUINTON
Warwickshire

Gable Cottage ★★★★
Contact: Ms Angela Richards
Manor Cottages, Priory Mews, 33A Priory Lane, Oxford OX18 4SG
T: (01993) 824252
F: (01993) 824443
E: mancott@netcomuk.co.uk
I: www.manorcottages.co.uk

1 Meon View ★★★★
Contact: Mrs Rimell
1 Meon View, Taylors Lane, Stratford-upon-Avon CV37 8LG
T: (01789) 720080
I: www.meonview.co.uk

Winton House Cottage ★★★★
Contact: Mrs Lyon
Winton House Cottage, The Green, Stratford-upon-Avon CV37 8SX
T: (01789) 720500
E: gail@wintonhouse.com
I: www.wintonhouse.com

UPTON-UPON-SEVERN
Worcestershire

Captains Retreat ★★★★
Contact: Mr Michael & Mrs Julie-Ann Cranton
White Cottage, Church End, Hanley Castle, Worcester WR8 0BL
T: (01684) 592023
F: (01684) 592328
E: michael@cranton.freeserve.co.uk

UPTON WARREN
Worcestershire

The Durrance ★★★★
Contact: Mrs Helen Hirons
The Durrance, Berry Lane, Upton Warren, Bromsgrove B61 9EL
T: (01562) 777533
F: (01562) 777533
E: helenhirons@thedurrance.fsnet.co.uk
I: www.hedurrance.co.uk

UTTOXETER
Staffordshire

Woodland Views Holiday Cottages ★★★★
Contact: Mrs Kate Tomlinson
Woodland Views Holiday Cottages, Dambridge Farm, Marchington Woodlands, Uttoxeter ST14 8PB
T: (01283) 820012
F: (01283) 820816
E: enquiries@woodlandviews.co.uk
I: www.woodlandviews.co.uk

VOWCHURCH
Herefordshire

The Dingle ★★★★
Contact: Mrs Ruth Watkins
Upper Gilvach Farm, St Margarets, Hereford HR2 0QY
T: (01981) 510618
E: ruth@uppergilvach.freeserve.co.uk
I: www.golden-valley.co.uk/dingle

The Front Dore ★★★
Contact: Mrs Layton
The Front Dore, Ponty Pinna Farm, Hereford HR2 0QE
T: (01981) 550266

WARSLOW
Staffordshire

Shay Side Barn and Cottage ★★★★
Contact: Mr Sykes
Sykes Cottage, York House, York Street, Chester CH1 3LR
T: (01244) 345700
F: (01244) 321442
E: info@sykescottages.co.uk
I: www.sykescottages.co.uk

WARWICK
Warwickshire

Copes Flat ★★★
Contact: Mrs Draisey
Forth House, 44 High Street, Warwick CV34 4AX
T: (01926) 401512
F: (01926) 490809
E: info@forthhouseuk.co.uk
I: www.forthhouseuk.co.uk

Whitley Elm Cottages ★★★★
Contact: Mr Clive & Mrs Pat Bevins
Whitley Elm Cottages, Case Lane, Mousley End, Warwick CV35 7JE
T: (01926) 484577
F: (01926) 484577
E: clive.bevins@btclick.com
I: www.whitleyelmcottages.co.uk

WATERHOUSES
Staffordshire

Broadhurst Farm ★★★★
Contact: Mr Clowes
Broadhurst Farm, Stoke-on-Trent ST10 3LQ
T: (01538) 308261
E: enquires@broadhurstfarm.com
I: www.broadhurstfarm.com

Greenside and Greenside Cottage ★★★-★★★★
Contact: Mr Sykes
Sykes Cottage, York House, York Street, Chester CH1 3LR
T: (01244) 345700
F: (01244) 321442
E: info@sykescottages.co.uk
I: www.sykescottages.co.uk

Limestone View Cottage ★★★
Contact: Mrs Wendy Webster
Limestone View Farm, Stoney Lane, Cauldon, Stoke-on-Trent ST10 3EP
T: (01538) 308288
E: wendywebster@limestoneviewfarm.freeserve.co.uk
I: www.peakdistrictfarmhols.co.uk

WELFORD-ON-AVON
Warwickshire

The Granary ★★★★
Contact: Mr & Mrs Spink
The Granary, Rumer Hall Cottage, Welford on Avon, Stratford-upon-Avon CV37 8AF
T: (01789) 750752
F: (01789) 750752
E: bruce_spink@btopenworld.com

Peacock Thatch ★★★★
Contact: Mr Peter Holden
The Little Cottage, 3 Siddals Lane, Allestree, Derby DE22 2DY
T: (01332) 551155
F: (01332) 551155
E: peterpeacockthatch@dmserve.com

WELLINGTON
Telford and Wrekin

The Coach House ★★★★
Contact: Mrs Fellows
Old Vicarage, Wrockwardine, Telford TF6 5DG
T: (01952) 244859
F: (01952) 255066
E: mue@mfellows0.freeserve.co.uk
I: www.the-coach-house-wrockwardine.co.uk

WEM
Shropshire

Soulton Hall Cottages ★★★
Contact: Mrs Ashton
Soulton Hall Cottages, Soulton Hall, Shrewsbury SY4 5RS
T: (01939) 232786
F: (01939) 234097
E: jiashton@soultonhall.fsbusiness.co.uk

HEART OF ENGLAND

WEOBLEY
Herefordshire

Ella's Cottage ★★★★
Contact: Mrs Angie Vaughan
Briarley, Stepstile, Kington
HR5 3LG
T: (01544) 340543
F: (01544) 340543

WEST FELTON
Shropshire

The Stables ★★★★
Contact: Mr Edward & Mrs
Kirsten Nicholas
The Stables, Sutton Farm,
Rednal, Oswestry SY11 4HX
T: (01691) 610230
E: edwardnicholas@freeuk.com

WESTBURY
Shropshire

Garden Cottage ★★★
Contact: Mrs Halliday
Garden Cottage, Whitton Hall,
Shrewsbury SY5 9RD
T: (01743) 884270
F: (01743) 884158
E: whittonhall@farmersweekly.net
I: www.shropshiretourism.com

WESTON-ON-AVON
Warwickshire

March Font, Hurnberry, Brickall and The Arbales ★★★★
Contact: Mr & Mrs Richard
Bluck
Weston Farm, Weston-on-Avon,
Stratford-upon-Avon CV37 8JY
T: (01789) 750688
E: r.bluckwestonfarm@amserve.net
I: www.westonfarm.co.uk

WESTON RHYN
Shropshire

Mill Cottage ★★★
Contact: Mr & Mrs Brannick
Mill Cottage, Mill House, The
Wern, Oswestry SY10 7ER
T: (01691) 659738

WETTON
Staffordshire

Manor Barn ★★★
Contact: Mr & Mrs Higton
Manor Barn, Manor House Farm,
Ashbourne DE6 2AF
T: (01335) 310223
I: www.peakcottages.com

Old Sunday School ★★★★
Contact:
Peak Cottages, Strawberry Lee
Lane, Totley Bents, Sheffield
S17 3BA
T: (0114) 262 0777
F: (0114) 2620666
E: enquiries@peakcottages.com
I: www.peakcottages.com

Stable Barn ★★★
Contact: Mrs Higton
Stable Barn, The Old Post Office,
Ashbourne DE6 2AF
T: (01335) 310312

Wetton Barns Holiday Cottages ★★★★-★★★★★
Contact: Mrs T Reason
Chatsworth Estate Office,
Bakewell DE45 1PJ
T: (01246) 565379
F: (01246) 583464
E: wettonbarns@chatsworth.org
I: www.chatsworth.org

WHATELEY
Staffordshire

33 Rosemary Cottage ★★★
Contact: Mrs Voilet Coles
31 Old Forge Cottage, Tamworth
B78 2ET
T: (01827) 280826

WHICHFORD
Warwickshire

Hillside Cottage ★★★★
Contact: Mrs Janet Haines
Ascott House Farm, Shipston-on-Stour CV36 5PP
T: (01608) 684655
F: (01608) 684539
E: djhaines@ascott6.fsnet.co.uk
I: www.hillside-cottage.co.uk

Horseshoe Cottage ★★★
Contact: Mrs Gore
Holly Cottage, The Green,
Whichford, Shipston-on-Stour
CV36 5PE
T: (01608) 684310
F: (01608) 684310
E: suevaudin@community.co.uk

WHITBOURNE
Herefordshire

Crumplebury Farmhouse ★★★
Contact: Mrs Anne Evans
Crumplebury Farmhouse,
Worcester WR6 5SG
T: (01886) 821534
F: (01886) 821534
E: a.evans@candaevans.fsnet.co.uk
I: www.whitbourne-estate.co.uk

Elcocks Cottage ★★★
Contact: Mr Mike Hogg
61 Pereira Road, Birmingham
B17 9JB
T: (0121) 4271395
E: mikehogguk@aol.com
I: www.elcocks.net

The Olde Rectory ★★★★-★★★★★
Contact: Mr Gilly & Mrs Cliff
Poultney
The Olde Rectory, Boat Lane,
Worcester WR6 5RS
T: (01886) 822000
F: (01886) 822100
E: stay@olde-rectory.co.uk
I: www.olde-rectory.co.uk

Stone House ★★★★★
Contact: Mr Patrick Priest
High Lea, Worcester WR6 5SP
T: (01886) 821648
I: www.stonehouseholidays.co.uk

WHITCHURCH
Shropshire

Combermere Abbey Cottages ★★★★★
Contact: Mrs Fiona Grundy
Combermere Abbey Cottages,
Whitchurch SY13 4AJ
T: (01948) 662876
F: (01948) 660920
E: cottages@combermereabbey.co.uk
I: www.combermereabbey.co.uk

Norton Cottages Rating Applied For
Contact: Mr Richard & Mrs Su
Jackson
Norton Cottages, Norton House,
Ross-on-Wye HR9 6DJ
T: (01600) 890046
F: (01600) 890045
E: su@norton.wyenet.co.uk
I: www.norton-cottages.com

The Park (Holiday Cottage) ★★★★
Contact: Mr & Mrs Wright
The Park (Holiday Cottage),
Whitchurch SY13 3NL
T: (01948) 880669
F: (01948) 880669

WILMCOTE
Warwickshire

Apple Loft ★★★★
Contact: Mrs Margaret Mander
Apple Loft, Peartree Cottage, 5
Church Road, Wilmote,
Stratford-upon-Avon CV37 9UX
T: (01789) 205889
F: (01789) 262862
E: peartree3@hotmail.com
I: www.peartreecot.co.uk

WILTON
Herefordshire

Benhall Farm ★★★
Contact: Mrs Carol Brewer
Benhall Farm, Ross-on-Wye
HR9 6AG
T: (01989) 563900
F: (01989) 563900
E: info@benhallfarm.co.uk
I: www.benhallfarm.co.uk

WINKHILL
Staffordshire

Alma Cottage ★★★★
Contact: Mrs Diana Cope
Alma Cottage, Little Paradise
Farm, Blackbrook, Leek ST13 7QR
T: (01538) 308909
F: (01538) 308910
I: www.almacottage.com

WOONTON
Herefordshire

Marches Holiday Lets Rating Applied For
Contact: Mr David Bufton
Marches Holiday Lets, The
Stables, Stocks Court, Hereford
HR3 6QU
T: (01544) 340719
E: dvdbftn@aol.com

WORCESTER
Worcestershire

College Street Apartments ★★★★
Contact: Mr & Mrs A Manning
Malvern View, Broadgreen,
Worcester WR6 5NW
T: (01886) 822114
E: info@primaproperties.co.uk
I: www.primaproperties.co.uk

Honeysuckle Cottages ★★★
Contact: Mr Gilchrist
32 Barbourne Road, Knights
Rest, Worcester WR1 1HU
T: (01905) 24257
F: (01905) 26202

Little Lightwood Farm ★★★
Contact: Mrs Rogers
Hazeldene, Little Lightwood
Farm, Lightwood Lane,
Cotheridge, Worcester WR6 5LT
T: (01905) 333236
F: (01905) 333236
E: lightwood.holidays@virgin.net
I: www.lightwoodfarm.co.uk

Maybury and Malvern View ★★★
Contact: Mr & Mrs Houghton
Upper Lightwood Farm,
Worcester WR2 6RL
T: (01905) 333202
E: jph6@hotmail.com
I: www.upperlightwood.co.uk

Mill Cottage ★★★★
Contact: Mrs Valerie Baylis
Mill Cottage, Mildenham Mill,
Egg Lane, Worcester WR3 7SA
T: (01905) 451554

The Orangery at Little Boynes ★★★★
Contact: Mr Chris Martin
The Orangery at Little Boynes,
Upper Hook Road, Worcester
WR8 0SB
T: (01684) 594788
E: chris.w.martin@ukonline.co.uk
I: www.little-boynes.co.uk

Peter Jackson Apartments ★★★★
Contact: Mr Peter & Mrs Marilyn
Jackson
1 Birchwood, Peachley Lane,
Worcester WR6 6QR
T: (01905) 25822
I: www.peterjacksonapartments.com

Stildon Manor Cottage ★★★★
Contact: Mr & Mrs Wilding-Davies
Stildon Manor, Menith Wood,
Worcester WR6 6UL
T: (01299) 832720
F: (01299) 832720
I: www.blakes-cottages.co.uk

WORMELOW
Herefordshire

Old Forge Cottage ★★★
Contact: Mrs Shirley Wheeler
Old Forge Cottage, Lyston
Smithy, Hereford HR2 8EL
T: (01981) 540625

Establishments printed in blue have a detailed entry in this guide

HEART OF ENGLAND

WYRE PIDDLE
Worcestershire
Peaceavon ★★★★
Contact: Mr & Mrs Price
15 The Paddock, Leicester
LE9 9NW
T: (01455) 821723
E: pricenr@aol.com
I: www.peaceavon.co.uk

WYTHALL
Worcestershire
Inkford Court Cottages
★★★-★★★★
Contact: Mr Bedford
Inkford Court Cottages, Alcester Road, Whythall B47 6DL
T: (01564) 822304
F: (01564) 829618

EAST MIDLANDS

ALDERWASLEY
Derbyshire
Church View ★★★
Contact: Mr Mihulka
Knob Cottage, Belper DE56 2RA
T: (01629) 823728
F: (01629) 823728

ALDWARK
Derbyshire
The Old Coach House ★★★★
Contact: Mr Nigel John Smith
94 Northwood Lane, Darley Dale, Matlock DE4 2HR
T: (01629) 733114

ALFORD
Lincolnshire
Manor Farm Cottage ★★★
Contact: Mrs Mary Farrow
Manor Farm Cottage, Grove House, The Green, Alford LN13 0LW
T: (01507) 450228

Woodthorpe Hall Country Cottage ★★★★
Contact: Mrs Stubbs
Woodthorpe Hall Country Cottage, Alford LN13 0DD
T: (01507) 450294
F: (01507) 450885
E: enquiries@woodthorpehall.com
I: www.woodthorpehall.com

ALFRETON
Derbyshire
The Coach House ★★★★
Contact: Mr & Mrs Whitaker
The Old Vicarage, 136 Derby Road, Swanwick, Alfreton DE55 1AD
T: (01773) 605116
F: (01773) 528703
E: pwhitaker@dial.pipex.com

ALKMONTON
Derbyshire
The Looseboxes Dairy House Farm ★★★★
Contact: Mr Andy Harris
The Looseboxes Dairy House Farm, Ashbourne DE6 3DG
T: (01335) 330159
F: (01335) 330359
E: b&b@dairyhousefarm.org.uk
I: www.dairyhousefarm.org.uk/

ALSOP-EN-LE-DALE
Derbyshire
Church Farm Cottages ★★★★
Contact: Mrs Christine Duffell
Church Farm, Ashbourne DE6 1QP
T: (01335) 390216
F: (01335) 390216
E: churchfarmcottages.alsop@virgin.net
I: www.cressbrook.co.uk/ashborn/churchfarm

ALTON
Derbyshire
Wildflower Cottages ★★★★
Contact: Mrs S Fewtrell
Candlelight Cottage, Quarry Lane, Chesterfield S42 6AT
T: (01246) 590052
E: sue@wildflowercottages.co.uk
I: www.wildflowercottages.co.uk

ARNOLD
Nottinghamshire
The Grannary ★★★
Contact: Mrs Lamin
The Grannary, Top House Farm, Mansfield Road, Nottingham NG5 8PH
T: (0115) 926 8330

ASFORDBY
Leicestershire
Amberley Gardens Self-catering ★★★★
Contact: Mr Bruce Brotherhood
Amberley Gardens Self-catering, 4 Church Lane, Melton Mowbray LE14 3RU
T: (01664) 812314
F: (01664) 813740
E: doris@amberleygardens.net
I: www.amberleygardens.net

Stable Cottage ★★★★
Contact:
The Old Rectory, Church Lane, Melton Mowbray LE14 3RU
T: (01664) 813679
F: (0115) 9242450

ASHBOURNE
Derbyshire
Ashfield And Dove Cottages ★★★
Contact: Mr Tatlow
Ashfield Farm, Ashbourne DE6 2EB
T: (01335) 324279

Borrowdale Cottage ★★★
Contact: Mrs W Parratt
24 Weydon Lane, Farnham GU9 8UP
T: (01252) 712562
E: w.parratt@btinternet.com
I: www.cottagewide.co.uk/borrowdalecottage

Callow Top Cottages 1 and 2 ★★★
Contact: Mrs Sue Deane
Callow Top Cottages 1 and 2, Callow Top Holiday Park, Buxton Road, Ashbourne DE6 2AQ
T: (01335) 344020
F: (01335) 343726
E: enquiries@callowtop.co.uk
I: www.callowtop.co.uk

Dove Farm
Rating Applied For
Contact: Mrs Jane Stretton
Dove Farm, Ashbourne DE6 2GY
T: (01335) 324357
E: jane@dovefarm.co.uk
I: www.dovefarm.co.uk

The Groom's Quarters ★★★★★
Contact: Mr Ray & Mrs Ann Thompson
The Old Coach House, The Hall Lane, Wootton, Ashbourne DE6 2GW
T: (01335) 324549
E: ann@groomsquarters.co.uk
I: www.groomsquarters.co.uk

Haifa ★★★★
Contact: Mr David Dudley
8 Esher Court, The Arbours, Northampton NN3 3RN
T: (01604) 403625
F: (01604) 403646

Hillside Croft ★★★★★
Contact: Mrs Pat Walker
Offcote Grange Cottage Holidays, Offcote, Ashbourne DE6 1JQ
T: (01335) 344795
F: (01335) 348358
E: cottages@hillsidecroft.co.uk
I: www.hillsidecroft.co.uk

Home Farm Cottages ★★★★-★★★★★
Contact: Mrs Pat Longley
Home Farm Cottages, Hall Lane, Wootton, Ashbourne DE6 2GW
T: (01335) 324433
E: homefarm@hipp-demon.co.uk
I: www.hipp.demon.co.uk

Moore's Cottage Farm ★★★-★★★★
Contact: Ms Janet Watson
Moore's Cottage Farm, Slack Lane, Ashbourne DE6 2JX
T: (01335) 346121
E: janetwatson@waitrose.com
I: www.cressbrook.co.uk

The Nook ★★★★
Contact: Mrs Susan Osborn
Barracca, Ivydene Close, Leicester LE9 7NR
T: (01455) 842609
F: (01455) 842609
E: susan.osborn@virgin.net
I: www.come.to/thenook

The Old Laundry ★★★★★
Contact: Mrs Patricia Cust
The Old Laundry, Sturston Hall, Ashbourne DE6 1LN
T: (01335) 346711
E: p.cust@virgin.net
I: www.sturston.com

Old Miller's Cottage ★★★
Contact: Mrs P.M. Hewitt
45 Portway Drive, Burton upon Trent DE13 9HU
T: (01283) 815895

The Orchards ★★★★
Contact: Mrs Vanessa Holland
Rushley Farm, Ashbourne DE6 2BA
T: (01538) 308205
E: rushley.farm@btopenworld.com
I: www.cottageguide.co.uk/theorchards

Sandybrook Country Park ★★★-★★★★★
Contact: Reception
Sandybrook Country Park, Buxton Road, Ashbourne DE6 2AQ
T: (01335) 300000
F: (01335) 342679
E: enquiries@pinelodgeholidays.co.uk
I: www.pinelodgeholidays.co.uk/sandybrook.ihtml

Slade House Farm ★★★★-★★★★★
Contact: Mr Alan & Mrs Pat Philp
Slade House Farm, Ashbourne DE6 2BB
T: (01538) 308123
F: (01538) 308777
E: alanphilp@sladehousefarm.co.uk
I: www.sladehousefarm.co.uk

EAST MIDLANDS

Strawberry Cottage ★★★★
Contact: Mrs Wendy Boddy
The Old Schoolhouse, Ashbourne
DE6 2DQ
T: (01335) 343152
E: wendyboddy@handbag.com

The Tannery ★★★★
Contact: Mrs C G Spencer
The Tannery, Mapleton Road,
Ashbourne DE6 2AA
T: (01335) 342387

Thorpe Cloud View Cottage
★★★★★
Contact: Mr Ray Neilson
Thorpe Cloud View Cottage,
Thorpe House, Thorpe,
Ashbourne DE6 2AW
T: (01335) 350215
E: rayneilson@aol.com
I: www.thorpecloudview.com

Yeldersley Hall
★★★★-★★★★★★
Contact: Mr Andrew Bailey
Yeldersley Hall, Ashbourne
DE6 1LS
T: (01335) 343432

ASHBY-DE-LA-ZOUCH
Leicestershire

Badger's Sett ★★★
Contact: Aileen Wood
16 Sandpiper Close, South
Beach, Blyth NE24 3QN
T: (01670) 367723 &
07718 905251
E: graham-aileen@16sandpiper.
freeserve.co.uk
I: www.badgers-sett.com

Norman's Barn ★★★★
Contact: Mrs Isabel Stanley
Ingles Hill Farm, Burton Road,
Ashby-de-la-Zouch LE65 2TE
T: (01530) 412224
E: isabel_stanley@hotmail.com
I: www.normansbarn.co.uk

Sylvan ★★★
Contact: Mrs Doreen Gasson
13 Babelake Street, Ashby-De-
La-Zouch LE65 1WD
T: (01530) 412012
E: egg-deg@packington.
freeserve.co.uk
I: www.a-place-to-stay.co.uk

**Upper Rectory Farm
Cottages ★★★★★**
Contact: Mrs Jean Corbett
Cottage Farm, Norton-Juxta-
Twycross, Atherstone CV9 3QH
T: (01827) 880448
E: info@
upperrectoryfarmcottages.co.uk
I: www.
upperrectoryfarmcottages.co.uk

ASHFORD IN THE WATER
Derbyshire

Ashford Barns ★★★★
Contact: Mr MacQueen
Peak Cottages, Strawberry Lee
Lane, Tontley Bents, Sheffield
S17 3BA
T: (0114) 262 0777
F: (0114) 2620666
E: enquiries@peakcottages.com

Churchdale Holidays
★★★★★
Contact: Mrs Sarah Winkworth-
Smith
Churchdale Holidays,
Churchdale Farm, Ashford-in-
the-Water, Bakewell DE45 1NX
T: (01629) 640269
F: (01629) 640608
E: info@churchdaleholidays.
co.uk
I: www.churchdaleholidays.co.uk

Clematis Cottage ★★★
Contact: Mr Bernard & Mrs Kate
Armstrong
Holmedene, Ashford Road,
Bakewell DE45 1GL
T: (01629) 813448
E: bernard-armstrong@lineone.
net

The Coach House ★★★★
Contact: Mrs Shala Kay
The Coach House, Rowdale
House, Ashford-in-the-Water,
Bakewell DE45 1NX
T: (01629) 640260
F: (01629) 640260
E: shala@caan.freeserve.co.uk

Corner Cottage ★★★★★
Contact: Mrs Staley
The Seven Rakes, Salters Lane,
Matlock DE4 2PA
T: (01629) 56494
E: tonystaley@hotmail.com
I: www.littlegemcottages.co.uk

End Cottage ★★★★
Contact: Mrs Wright
Stancil House, Barn Furlong,
Bakewell DE45 1TR
T: (01629) 640136

Foxglove Cottage ★★★★
Contact: Mr MacQueen
Peak Cottages, Strawberry Lee
Lane, Totley Bents, Sheffield
S17 3BA
T: (0114) 262 0777
F: (0114) 2620666

Green Gates ★★★
Contact: Mr Colin MacQueen
Peak Cottages, Strawberry Lee
Lane, Totley Bents, Sheffield
S17 3BA
T: (0114) 262 0777
F: (0114) 2620666
E: enquiries@peakcottages.com
I: www.peakcottages.com

Nanny Peggy's Cottage
★★★★
Contact: Mrs Ros Marsden
Willow Croft, Station Road,
Bakewell DE45 1TS
T: (01629) 640576
E: rosylnm@aol.com
I: www.nannypeggy.com

Orchard House ★★★★
Contact: Mr MacQueen
Peak Cottages, Strawberry Lee
Lane, Totley Bents, Sheffield
S17 3BA
T: (0114) 262 0777
F: (0114) 2620666
E: enquiries@peakcottages.com
I: www.peakcottages.com

The Smithy ★★★★
Contact: Mrs Susan Akeroyd
Devonshire Weir, Watts Green,
Ashford-in-the-Water, Bakewell
DE45 1QE
T: (01629) 812693
E: akeroydsusie@aol.com

Sunny Lea ★★★★
Contact: Mrs D Furniss
Sunny Lea, Greaves Lane,
Ashford-in-the-Water, Bakewell
DE45 1QH
T: (01629) 815285
I: www.peakcottages.com

**Thorpe Cottage and Lilac
Cottage ★★★★**
Contact: Mrs Margaret Newman
14 Pool Drive, Doncaster
DN4 6UX
T: (01302) 536763
E: msnewman@care4free.co.uk

Thyme Cottage ★★★★★
Contact: Mrs Bell
Nether Croft, Eaton Place,
Bakewell DE45 1RW
T: (01246) 583564
E: nethercroftbandb@aol.com
I: www.nethercroft.co.uk

ASHOVER
Derbyshire

Hay Ho Cottage ★★★★
Contact: Mrs Susan Howe
Hay House, The Hay, Milltown,
Ashover, Chesterfield S45 0HB
T: (01246) 590538
F: (01246) 590538

Holestone Moor Barns
★★★★-★★★★★★
Contact: Mr Steve & Mrs Vicki
Clemerson
Holestone Moor Barns,
Holestone Moor Farm,
Holestone Moor, Ashover,
Chesterfield S45 0JS
T: (01246) 591263
F: (01246) 591263
E: hmbarns@aol.com
I: www.hmbarns.co.uk

ASHTON
Northamptonshire

Vale Farm House ★★★★
Contact: Mrs Zanotto
Vale Farm House, Stoke Road,
Northampton NN7 2JN
T: (01604) 863697
F: (01604) 862859

AVERHAM
Nottinghamshire

Wynberg ★★★
Contact: Mrs Maureen Justice
Wynberg, Staythorpe Road,
Newark NG23 5RA
T: (01636) 702874
F: (01636) 702874

BAKEWELL
Derbyshire

**Anne Cottage and Barn
Cottage ★★★★-★★★★★★**
Contact: Mrs Adrienne Howarth
Bakewell Holidays, Long
Meadow House, Coombs Road,
Bakewell DE45 1AQ
T: (01629) 812500
E: amshowarth@aol.com
I: www.bakewellholidays.co.uk

**Bakewell Holiday Cottage
(Coach Cottage) ★★★★**
Contact: Mr & Mrs J Gough
The Gatehouse, Riverside Court,
Hope Valley S32 3YW
T: (01433) 639582
E: john@gough57.fsnet.co.uk
I: www.bakewellcottages.co.uk

Ball Cross Farm Cottages
★★★★
Contact: Mrs Edwards
Ball Cross Farm Cottages,
Chatsworth Estate, Bakewell
DE45 1PE
T: (01629) 815215
E: info@ballcrossfarm.com
I: www.ballcrossfarm.com

The Barn ★★★★
Contact: Mr Raymont
44 Newland Lane, Ash Green,
Coventry CV7 9BA
T: (024) 76644173

Bay Tree Cottage ★★★★
Contact: Mr Philip Ryder
Bay Tree Cottage, 8 Old Lumford
Cottages, Bakewell DE45 1GG
T: (01663) 762724
F: (01663) 762724
E: baytree@smartone.co.uk

**Bolehill Farm Holiday
Cottages ★★★-★★★★**
Contact: Mr Chris & Mrs Shirley
Swaap
Bolehill Farm Holiday Cottages,
Bole Hill Farm, Monyash Road,
Bakewell DE45 10W
T: (01629) 812359
I: www.bolehillfarm.co.uk

Butts Cottage ★★★
Contact: Mr MacQueen
Peak Cottages, Strawberry Lee
Lane, Totley Bents, Sheffield
S17 3BA
T: (0114) 262 0777
F: (0114) 2620666
E: enquiries@peakcottages.com
I: www.peakcottages.com

Carter's Mill Cottage
★★★★
Contact: Mr & Mrs Marsden
Mill Farm, Haddon Grove,
Bakewell DE45 1JF
T: (01629) 812013
F: (01629) 814734
E: marsden.millfarm@
btinternet.com

The Cottage ★★★★
Contact: Mrs Barbara Nash
The Cottage, Castle Street,
Bakewell DE45 1DU
T: (01246) 583067
F: (01246) 583067
E: robbienash@birchfieldhall.
fsnet.co.uk

Dale End Farm ★★★
Contact: Mrs Elizabeth Hague
Dale End Farm, Gratton Dale,
Bakewell DE45 1LN
T: (01629) 650453
E: john.elizabeth.hague@talk21.
com
I: daleendfarm.users.
btopenworld.com

Establishments printed in blue have a detailed entry in this guide   519

EAST MIDLANDS

Dale View Farm
Rating Applied For
Contact: Mrs Janet Frost
Dale View Farm, Bakewell
DE45 1LN
T: (01629) 650670

Edge View ★★★★
Contact: Mrs Gillian Rogers
Penylan, Monyash Road,
Bakewell DE45 1FG
T: (01629) 813336
F: (01629) 813336

Four Winds ★★★
Contact: Mr Sykes
Sykes Cottages, York House,
York Street, Chester CH1 3LR
T: (01244) 345700
F: (01244) 321142
E: info@sykescottages.co.uk
I: www.sykescottages.co.uk

Gingerbread Cottage ★★★★
Contact: Mrs Jane Bond
The Shooting Lodge, Derwent,
Hope Valley S33 0AQ
T: (01433) 659767
F: (01433) 659767

Haddon Grove Farm Cottages ★★★
Contact: Mr John & Mrs Barbara Boxall
Haddon Grove Farm Cottages,
Haddon Grove Farm, Monyash Road, Bakewell DE45 1JF
T: (01629) 813551
F: (01629) 815684

Halfway House
Rating Applied For
Contact: Mrs Lesley Smithurst
Meadow Bank, Baslow Road,
Bakewell DE45 1AB
T: (01629) 815846

Mayfly Cottage ★★★★
Contact: Mr Colin MacQueen
Peak Cottages, Strawberry Lee Lane, Totley Bents, Sheffield
S17 3BA
T: (0114) 262 0777
F: (0114) 2620666
E: enquiries@peakcottages.com
I: www.peakcottages.com

36 North Church Street ★★★
Contact: Mr Phillip Dobbin
Home Farm House, Bryants Bottom Road, Great Missenden
HP16 0JU
T: (01494) 488463
E: phillip.dobbin@pipemedia.co.uk

Rozel ★★★★
Contact: Mr Colin MacQueen
Peak Cottages, Strawberry Lee Lane, Totley Bents, Sheffield
S17 3BA
T: (0114) 262 0777
F: (0114) 2620666
E: enquiries@peakcottages.com
I: www.peakcottages.com

Spout Farm ★★★
Contact: Mrs Ena Patterson
The Bungalow, Elton, Matlock
DE4 2BY
T: (01629) 650358

Yuletide Cottage ★★★
Contact: Mr & Mrs Figg
Yuletide Cottage, Church Street,
Youlgrave, Bakewell DE45 1UR
T: (01629) 636234

BALLIDON
Derbyshire

Ballidon Moor Farmhouse ★★★★
Contact: Mrs Vicki Lambert
Ballidon Moor Farmhouse,
Matlock DE4 4HP
T: (01629) 540327
F: (01629) 540661

Rachels Croft ★★★★
Contact: Mrs Alison Edge
Rachels Croft, Oldfield House,
Ashbourne DE6 1QX
T: (01335) 390587

BAMFORD
Derbyshire

Derwent View ★★★★
Contact: Mrs Joyce Mannion
12 Ashopton Drive, Hope Valley
S33 0BU
T: (01433) 651637
E: jamcottage@talk21.com
I: www.cottagesdirect.com.yoa096

Shatton Hall Farm ★★★★
Contact: Mrs Angela Kellie
Shatton Hall Farm, Bamford,
Hope Valley S33 0BG
T: (01433) 620635
F: (01433) 620689
E: ahk@peakfarmholidays.co.uk
I: www.peakfarmholidays.co.uk

Thornhill View ★★★
Contact: Mrs Joyce Fairbairn
Thornhill View, Hope Road, Hope Valley S33 0AL
T: (01433) 651823

BARLOW
Derbyshire

Mill Farm Holiday Cottages ★★★
Contact: Mr & Mrs Ward
Mill Farm Holiday Cottages,
Crow Hole, Dronfield S18 7TJ
T: (0114) 289 0543
F: (0114) 2891473
E: cottages@barfish.fsnet.co.uk
I: www.millfarmcottages.com

PCB Holiday Cottages ★★★-★★★★★
Contact: Mr & Mrs Moffatt
PCB Holiday Cottages, Oxton Rakes Hall Farm, Dronfield
S18 7SE
T: (0114) 289 9290
F: (0114) 2899260
E: bookings@heron-lodge.hypermart.net
I: heron-lodge.hypermart.net

BARROW UPON SOAR
Leicestershire

Kingfisher Cottage ★★★★
Contact: Mr Matthews
114 Main Street, Loughborough
LE12 8RZ
T: (01509) 890244
E: nikkidavid@aol.com
I: www.englishcottage.com

BASLOW
Derbyshire

Goose Green Apartment ★★★★
Contact: Mr Bailey
Goose Green Apartment, c/o Goose Green Tearooms, Nether End, Bakewell DE45 1SR
T: (01246) 583000

Goose Green Cottage ★★★★★
Contact: Mr & Mrs Levick
19 Peascliffe Drive, Grantham
NG31 8EN
T: (01476) 571025 & 07979 004579
E: levick2@btopenworld.com
I: www.peakdistrict-nationalpark.com

Hall Cottage ★★★★
Contact: Mr & Mrs Griffiths
Beechcroft, School Lane,
Bakewell DE45 1RZ
T: (01246) 582900
F: (01246) 583675
E: hallcottage@btinternet.com

Stable Cottage ★★★★
Contact: Ms Anne O'Connor
Woodside Cottage, Nether End,
Bakewell DE45 1SR
T: (01246) 582285
F: (01246) 583007
E: ourstablecottage@aol.com
I: www.stablecottagebaslow.com

Tom's Cottage ★★★★
Contact: Ms Hazel Bell
Nether Croft, Eaton Place,
Bakewell DE45 1RW
T: (01246) 583564
E: nethercroftBandB@aol.com

Wrose Cottage ★★★
Contact: Mrs Cartledge
Bramley Court, Waterside,
Calver Road, Bakewell DE45 1RR
T: (01246) 583131
F: (01246) 583131

BAUMBER
Lincolnshire

Gathman's Cottage ★★★
Contact: Mrs Wendy Harrison
Manor Farm, Horncastle
LN9 5QF
T: (01507) 578352
F: (01507) 578417
E: gathmans@freenetname.co.uk
I: www.gathmanscottage.co.uk

BEESBY
Lincolnshire

Walk Villa ★★★
Contact: Sue & Joanne
Manor Farm, Beesby, Alford
LN13 0JG
T: (01507) 450323 & 450392
E: j0anne66@yahoo.com

BELCHFORD
Lincolnshire

Poachers Hideaway ★★★★
Contact: Mr Andrew Tuxworth
Poachers Hideaway, Flintwood Farm, Belchford, Horncastle
LN9 6QN
T: (01507) 533555
F: (01507) 534264
E: andrewtuxworth@poachershideaway.com
I: poachershideaway.com

BELMESTHORPE
Rutland

Elder Flower Cottage ★★★
Contact: Mr & Mrs Wilkinson
Meadow View, Shepherds Walk,
Stamford PE9 4JG
T: (01780) 757188
F: (01780) 757188

BELPER
Derbyshire

Chevin House Farm Cottages Chevin House Farm ★★★
Contact: Mr & Mrs Jordan
Chevin House Farm Cottages,
Chevin House Farm, Chevin Road, Belper DE56 2UN
T: (01773) 823144
F: (01773) 823144

Wiggonlea Stable ★★★★
Contact: Mrs S. Ruth Spendlove
Wiggonlea Stable, Wiggonlea Farm, Belper DE56 2RE
T: (01773) 852344
E: ruth@wiggonlea.fsnet.co.uk
I: www.wiggonlea.fsnet.co.uk

BIGGIN-BY-HARTINGTON
Derbyshire

Cheese Press Cottage, The Old Farrowings & Courtyard Creamery ★★★★
Contact: Mr MacQueen
Peak Cottages, Strawberry Lee Lane, Totley Bents, Sheffield
S17 3BA
T: (0114) 262 0777
F: (0114) 2620666
E: enquiries@peakcottages.com
I: www.peakcottages.com

BIRCH VALE
Derbyshire

Hallishaw Cote ★★★★
Contact: Mrs Jennifer Hallam
Cold Harbour Farm, High Peak
SK22 4QJ
T: (01663) 746155
E: jenny@coldharbour.fslife.co.uk
I: www.hallishawcote.co.uk

BIRCHOVER
Derbyshire

Birchover Cottages ★★★
Contact: Mr MacQueen
Peak Cottages, Strawberry Lee Lane, Totley Bents, Sheffield
S17 3BA
T: (0114) 262 0777
F: (0114) 2620666

BLOXHOLM
Lincolnshire

The Lodge ★★
Contact: Mrs Helen Gillatt
Woodend Farm, Lincoln
LN4 3NG
T: (01526) 860347

EAST MIDLANDS

BONSALL
Derbyshire
Croft Cottage ★★★★
Contact: Mr Colin MacQueen
Peak Cottages Ltd, Strawberry
Lee Lane, Totley Bents, Sheffield
S17 3BA
T: (0114) 262 0777
F: (0114) 2620666
E: enquiries@peakcottages.com
I: www.peakcottages.com

Hollies Cottage ★★★
Contact: Mrs Mountney
38 High Street, Matlock DE4 2AR
T: (01629) 823162

BOSTON
Lincolnshire
The Annexe ★★★
Contact: Mrs Lindsey McBarron
The Annexe, Walnuts
Farmhouse, Frampton Bank,
Boston PE20 1SW
T: (01205) 290067
E: mcbcastle@aol.com

The Lodge at Pinewood ★★★
Contact: Ms Sylvia Kilshaw
Pinewood, Ralphs Lane, Boston
PE20 1QZ
T: (01205) 723739
F: (01205) 723739

BRACKENFIELD
Derbyshire
Ruardean ★★★
Contact: Mr S Boardman
Sykes Cottages, York House,
York Street, Chester CH1 3LR
T: (01244) 345700
F: (01244) 321442
E: info@sykescottages.co.uk
I: www.sykescottages.co.uk

BRACKLEY
Northamptonshire
Iletts Courtyard ★★★★
Contact: Mrs Sally Bellingham
Iletts Courtyard, Iletts Farm,
Northampton Road, Brackley
NN13 7TY
T: (01280) 703244
F: (01280) 703244
E: iletts@clara.co.uk
I: home.clara.net/iletts

BRADLEY
Derbyshire
**Briar, Primrose and Bluebell
Cottages ★★★-★★★★**
Contact: Mrs Janet Hinds
Briar, Primrose and Bluebell
Cottages, Yeldersley Old Hall
Farm, Yeldersley Lane, Bradley,
Ashbourne DE6 1PH
T: (01335) 344504
F: (01335) 344504
E: janethindsfarm@yahoo.co.uk
I: www.yeldersleyoldhallfarm.co.uk

Shepherds Folly ★★★★
Contact: Mrs Kathy Cowley
Shepherds Folly, Belper Road,
Ashbourne DE6 1LL
T: (01335) 343315

BRADWELL
Derbyshire
Bridge End Barn ★★★★
Contact: Mrs Gill Gascoyne
Bridge End Barn, Brough, Hope
Valley S33 9HG
T: (01433) 621258

**The Croft and Edge View
★★★-★★★★★**
Contact: Mr Sykes
Sykes Cottage, York House, York
Street, Chester CH1 3LR
T: (01244) 345700
F: (01244) 321442
E: info@sykescottage.co.uk
I: www.sykescottge.co.uk

Derwent Cottage ★★★
Contact: Mr Mark Gilbertson
124 Cranbrook Road, Chiswick,
London W4 2LJ
T: (020) 87479450
E: markanddoona@hotmail.com

Smalldale ★★★★
Contact: Mr Sykes
Sykes Cottages, York House,
York Street, Chester CH1 3LR
T: (01244) 345700
F: (01244) 321442
E: info@sykescottages.co.uk
I: www.sykescottages.co.uk

BRAILSFORD
Derbyshire
The Cottage ★★★★
Contact: Mrs Phillips
The Cottage, Culland Mount
Farm, Ashbourne DE6 3BW
T: (01335) 360313

BRASSINGTON
Derbyshire
The Coach House ★★★★
Contact: Mr Andrew Colclough
26 Southridge Drive, Mansfield
NG18 4RL
T: (01623) 465437
E: patandandycole@ntlworld.com

Hillocks Barn ★★★★
Contact: Mr Christopher
Gorman
The Cottage, Hillside, Matlock
DE4 4HL
T: (01629) 540435
E: chrisgorman@freenet.co.uk
I: www.hillocksbarn.co.uk

Jack's Cottage ★★★★
Contact: Mrs Rodrigues
48 Grove Avenue, Chilwell,
Nottingham NG9 4DZ
T: (0115) 925 1441
E: jacks.cottage@tinyworld.co.uk

BRIGSTOCK
Northamptonshire
The Gable End ★★★
Contact: Mrs Helen Clarke
The Gables, 2 Benefield Road,
Kettering NN14 3ES
T: (01536) 373674
F: (01536) 373674
E: Marcus@Clarke.1999.freeserve.co.uk

BURGH-LE-MARSH
Lincolnshire
**The Hollies Country
Cottages
Rating Applied For**
Contact: Mrs Janet Dodsworth
The Hollies Country Cottages,
West End, Burgh Le Marsh,
Skegness PE24 5EF
T: (01754) 810866
F: (01754) 810866
E: jldodsworth@supanet.com
I: www.holliescountrycottages.co.uk

**Sycamore Fishing Lakes
★★-★★★**
Contact: Mrs Joy Giraldez
Sycamore Fishing Lakes,
Skegness Road, Burgh Le Marsh,
Skegness PE24 5LN
T: (01754) 811411
I: www.sycamorelakes.co.uk

BURGH-ON-BAIN
Lincolnshire
Bainfield Lodge ★★★★
Contact: Mr & Mrs D Walker
Bainfield House, Main Road,
Market Rasen LN8 6JY
T: (01507) 313540
E: dennis.walker1@btinternet.com
I: www.bainfieldholidaylodge.co.uk

BURTON
Lincolnshire
**The Conifers Guest Annexe
★★★★**
Contact: Mr Martin Gray
The Conifers Guest Annexe,
Occupation Lane, Lincoln
LN1 2NB
T: (01522) 703196
E: mjgtheconifers@supanet.com

BUXTON
Derbyshire
Glen Apartment ★★★
Contact:
Peak Cottages, Strawberry Lee
Lane, Totley Bents, Sheffield
S17 3BA
T: (0114) 262 0777
F: (0114) 2620666
E: enquries@peakcottages.com
I: www.peakcottages.com

**Harefield Garden Flat
★★★★**
Contact: Mr & Mrs Hardie
Harefield Garden Flat, 15
Marlborough Road, Buxton
SK17 6RD
T: (01298) 24029
F: (01298) 24029
E: hardie@harefield1.freeserve.co.uk
I: www.harefield1.freeserve.co.uk

Hargate Hall ★★★
Contact: Mr J Jackson
Hargate Hall, Buxton SK17 8TA
T: (01298) 872591
E: info@hargate-hall.co.uk
I: www.hargate-hall.co.uk

**High Needham Cottage
★★★★**
Contact: Mrs Paula Bradbury
High Needham Cottage, High
Needham Farm, Earl Sterndale,
Buxton SK17 0OD
T: (01298) 83242

Hill Side House ★★★★
Contact: Mrs M Swain
1 Spencer Road, Buxton
SK17 9DX
T: (01298) 25451

Lake View ★★★
Contact: Mr MacQueen
Peak Cottages, Strawberry Lee
Lane, Totley Bents, Sheffield
S17 3BA
T: (0114) 262 0777
F: (0114) 2620666

**Meadow Barn Cottage
★★★★**
Contact: Mr Colin MacQueen
Peak Cottages, Strawberry Lee
Lane, Totley Bents, Sheffield
S17 3BA
T: (0114) 262 0777
F: (0114) 2620666
E: enquiries@peakcottages.com
I: www.peakcottages.com

The Old Stables ★★★
Contact: Mrs J Cowlishaw
136 Green Lane, Buxton
SK17 9DQ
T: (01298) 71086
F: (01298) 77678
E: j.cowlishaw@endeavour.co.uk

Outlow ★★★
Contact: Mr Colin MacQueen
Peak Cottages, Strawberry Lee
Lane, Totley Bents, Sheffield
S17 3BA
T: (0114) 262 0777
F: (0114) 2620666
E: enquiries@peakcottages.com
I: www.peakcottages.com

**Priory Lea Holiday Flats
★-★★★**
Contact: Mrs Gillian Taylor
Priory Lea Holiday Flats, 50
White Knowle Road, Buxton
SK17 9NH
T: (01298) 23737

Establishments printed in blue have a detailed entry in this guide

EAST MIDLANDS

Silverlands Holiday Flats 2 & 3 ★★
Contact: Mrs Gillian Kitchen
156 Brown Edge Road, Buxton SK17 7AA
T: (01298) 79381
F: (01298) 72212

Sittinglow Farm Cottage ★★★
Contact: Mrs Ann S Buckley
Sittinglow Farm Cottage, Meadow Lane, Buxton SK17 8DA
T: (01298) 812271
E: louise@sittinglow.freeserve.co.uk

Smithy's Cottage ★★★
Contact: Mrs Pam Livesley
136 Hillside Road, Nottingham NG9 3BD
T: (0115) 922 5582
F: (0115) 9225582
E: pam@smithyscottage.co.uk
I: www.buxtontown.freeserve.co.uk

CALDECOTT
Rutland

Magnolia Cottage ★★★
Contact: Mel Hudson
22 Main Street, Caldecott, Market Harborough LE16 8RS
T: (01536) 771357
E: enquiries@rutland-cottages.co.uk
I: www.rutland-cottages.co.uk

Rose Cottage ★★★★
Contact: Mrs Jill Bartlett
The Dog House, 7 The Green, Market Harborough LE16 8RR
T: (01536) 770149
E: mcldoghouse@aol.com
I: www.northamptonshire.co.uk/hotels/rosecottage.htm

Wisteria Cottage ★★★
Contact: Mel Hudson
22 Main Street, Caldecott, Market Harborough LE16 8RS
T: (01536) 771357
E: wisteria@rutland-cottages.co.uk
I: www.rutland-cottages.co.uk

CALVER
Derbyshire

Barn Cottage ★★★★
Contact: Mr Finney
The Barn, Lowside, Hope Valley S32 3XQ
T: (01433) 631672
E: enquiries@barncottage.com
I: www.barncottage.com

Foxglove Cottage
Rating Applied For
Contact: Mrs Dorota Holden
Foxglove Cottage, Main Street, Hope Valley S32 3XR
T: (01629) 812198
E: peaklets@fsmail.net
I: www.peakholidaycottages.com

Knouchley Cottage ★★★★
Contact:
Peak Cottages, Paddock Cottage, Strawberry Lee Lane, Totley Bents, Sheffield S17 3BA
T: (0114) 262 0777
F: (0114) 2620666

The Old Vicarage ★★★★
Contact: Mr MacQueen
Peak Cottages, Strawberry Lee Lane, Totley Bents, Sheffield S17 3BA
T: (0114) 262 0777
F: (0114) 2620666
E: enquiries@peakcottages.com

Sunnyside ★★★
Contact:
Peak Cottages, Strawberry Lee Lane, Totley Bents, Sheffield S17 3BA
T: (0114) 262 0777
F: (0114) 2620666
E: enquiries@peakcottages.com
I: www.peakcottages.com

CAREBY
Lincolnshire

Linnet Cottage ★★★
Contact: Mrs Barbara Cooper
Maazledene, Careby, Stamford PE9 4EA
T: (01780) 410580
F: (01780) 410580
E: haresleap@supanet.com

CARSINGTON
Derbyshire

Breach Farm ★★★★
Contact: Mrs Michelle Wilson
Breach Farm, Matlock DE4 4DD
T: (01629) 540265
I: www.breachfarm.co.uk

Knockerdown Holiday Cottages ★★★-★★★★
Contact: Ms Cathy Lambert
Knockerdown, Ashbourne DE6 1NQ
T: (01629) 540525
F: (01629) 540525
E: cathy@knockerdown-cottages.co.uk
I: www.derbyshireholidaycottages.co.uk

Owslow ★★★
Contact: Mr Peter Oldfield
Owslow, Owslow Farm, Matlock DE4 4DD
T: (01629) 540510
F: (01629) 540445
E: peter.oldfield@ukonline.co.uk
I: www.peakdistrictfarmhols.co.uk

CASTLETON
Derbyshire

Cave End Cottage ★★★★
Contact: Mr Colin MacQueen
Peak Cottages, Strawberry Lee Lane, Totley Bents, Sheffield S17 3BA
T: (0114) 262 0777
F: (0114) 2620666
E: enquiries@peakcottages.com
I: www.peakcottages.com

Eastry Cottage ★★★★
Contact: Mrs Webster
Eastry Cottage, Pindale Road, Hope Valley S33 8WU
T: (01433) 620312
F: (01433) 620312

High View Cottage ★★★
Contact: Mr MacQueen
Peak Cottages, Strawberry Lee Lane, Totley Bents, Sheffield S17 3BA
T: (0114) 262 0777
F: (0114) 2620666
E: enquiries@peakcottages.com
I: www.peakcottages.com

Honeysuckle Cottage ★★★
Contact: Mrs Maura Ward
Honeysuckle Cottage, Market Place, Hope Valley S33 8WQ
T: (01433) 623227
E: maura@castletoncottages.co.uk
I: www.castletoncottages.co.uk

Llamedos ★★★
Contact: Mrs S Johnson
Llamedos, Bargate, Market Place, Hope Valley S33 8WQ
T: (01433) 623048
I: www.castletoncottages.co.uk

Millbridge Cottage ★★★★
Contact: Mrs Cutts
Millbridge House, Millbridge, Hope Valley S33 8WR
T: (01433) 621556
E: cuttssue@aol.com

Mullions ★★★★★
Contact: Mrs Christine Bell
Spring House Farm, Hope Valley S33 8WB
T: (01433) 620962
F: 0870 1371046
E: christine@peak-district-holiday-cottages.co.uk
I: www.peak-district-holiday-cottages.co.uk

CHAPEL-EN-LE-FRITH
Derbyshire

Herb View at Newlyn ★★★
Contact: Mr Mike & Mrs Helen Cullen
Newlyn, Crossings Road, Chapel-en-le-Frith, High Peak SK23 9RY
T: (01298) 814775
E: culherbs@ukonline.co.uk

Keepers Cottage ★★★
Contact: Mrs Mary Hayward
Keepers Cottage, Castleton Road, High Peak SK23 0QS
T: (01298) 812845
F: (01298) 812845

Sweetpiece Cottage ★★★★
Contact: Mr Colin MacQueen
Peak Cottages, Strawberry Lee Lane, Totley Bents, Sheffield S17 3BA
T: (0114) 262 0777
F: (0114) 2620666
E: enquiries@peakcottages.com
I: www.peakcottages.com

CHELMORTON
Derbyshire

The Hall ★★★
Contact: Mrs Lucilla Marsden
The Hall, Town End Farm, Buxton SK17 9SH
T: (01298) 85249
E: charles.marsden@nottingham.ac.uk

Swallow Barn ★★★★
Contact: Mrs Gill Chapman
Swallow Barn, The Green, Buxton SK17 9SL
T: (01298) 85355
E: enquiries@swallowbarn.com
I: www.swallowbarn.com

CHESTERFIELD
Derbyshire

Chryslinash ★★★
Contact: Mrs Tina Cave
Chryslinash, Chesterfield S45 8DG
T: (01246) 853467
E: chryslinash@aol.com

Pear Tree Cottage ★★★
Contact: Mrs Beckett
Laburnum Cottage, 46 Hardstoft Road, Chesterfield S45 8BL
T: (01773) 872767

Ploughmans Cottage ★★★★
Contact: Mr & Mrs Fry
Ploughmans Cottage, Low Farm, Main Road, Marsh Lane, Chesterfield S21 5RH
T: (01246) 435328
E: ploughmans.cottage@virgin.net

CHINLEY
Derbyshire

Fernbank ★★★
Contact: Mrs J Storer
34 Beresford Road, High Peak SK23 0NY
T: (01298) 813458
E: jeanstorer@btopenworld.com

Monks Meadow Cottage ★★★★
Contact: Mrs Pauline Gill
Monks Meadow Cottage, Hayfield Road, Chinley Head, High Peak SK23 6AL
T: (01663) 751267
E: MurielJackson1@btopenworld.com
I: www.monksmeadow.co.uk

CLAXBY
Lincolnshire

The Coach House ★★★
Contact: Mrs Elizabeth Wilson
Claxby Manor, Alford LN13 0HJ
T: (01507) 466374
F: (01507) 466374
E: liffa@claxby.fsnet.co.uk

CLAY CROSS
Derbyshire

Ridgewell Farm ★★★★
Contact: Mrs Ann Kerry
Ridgewell Farm, Handley Lane, Handley, Clay Cross, Chesterfield S45 9AT
T: (01246) 590698
F: (01246) 590698
E: ridgewellfarm@tiscali.co.uk

CLAYWORTH
Nottinghamshire

The Shambles ★★★★
Contact: Mrs Roberts
143 Bawtry Road, Doncaster DN4 7AH
T: (01302) 537110

522 Look out for establishments participating in the National Accessible Scheme

EAST MIDLANDS

COMBS
Derbyshire
Pyegreave Cottage
★★★★★
Contact: Mr Noel & Mrs Rita Pollard
Pyegreave Cottage, Combs, High Peak SK23 9UX
T: (01298) 813444
F: (01298) 815381
E: n.pollard@allenpollard.co.uk
I: www.holidayapartments.org

COSTOCK
Nottinghamshire
Costock Manor Luxury Cottages ★★★★★
Contact: Mr & Mrs Simblet
Costock Manor Luxury Cottages, The Manor, Church Lane, Loughborough LE12 6UZ
T: (01509) 852250
F: (01509) 853337
E: simblet@costock-manor.co.uk
I: www.costock-manor.co.uk

COTTESMORE
Rutland
Thompson's Barn ★★★
Contact: Mrs Cheetham
Thompson's Barn, 12 The Leas, Oakham LE15 7DG
T: (01572) 812231

CRESSBROOK
Derbyshire
8 Bobbin Mill ★★★★
Contact: Mrs Wendy Hicks
Chert Cottage, Main Road, Bakewell DE45 1TG
T: (01629) 640410

Cressbrook Hall Cottages
★★★
Contact: Mrs Bobby Bailey
Cressbrook Hall Cottages, Cressbrook Hall, Buxton SK17 8SY
T: (01298) 871289
F: (01298) 871845
E: stay@cressbrookhall.co.uk
I: www.cressbrookhall.co.uk

CRICH
Derbyshire
Clover Stable ★★★★
Contact: Mr David Worthy
Clover Stable, Crich Pottery, Market Place, Matlock DE4 5DD
T: (01773) 853171
F: (01773) 857325
E: davidworthy@hotmail.com
I: www.peakcottages.com

CROMFORD
Derbyshire
1 High Peak Cottages ★★★
Contact: Mr David & Mrs Lorraine Wolsey
5 High Peak Cottages, High Peak Junction, Matlock DE4 5HN
T: (01629) 823402
E: stay@highpeakcottage.co.uk
I: www.highpeakcottage.co.uk

CROPWELL BISHOP
Nottinghamshire
Corner Cottage ★★★★
Contact: Ms Hilary Hawkins
Corner Cottage, 1 Kinoulton Road, Nottingham NG12 3BH
T: (0115) 9899243
E: hilary.j.hawkins@btinternet.com
I: www.cornercottage.cjb.com

CURBAR
Derbyshire
Jack's Cottage ★★★★
Contact: Mrs North
Green Farm, Hope Valley S32 3YH
T: (01433) 630120
F: (01433) 631829
E: enquiries@peakdistrictholiday.co.uk
I: www.peakdistrictholiday.co.uk

The Mullions ★★★★★
Contact: Mrs North
Green Farm, Hope Valley S32 3YH
T: (01433) 630120
F: (01433) 631829
E: enquiries@peakdistrictholiday.co.uk
I: www.peakdistrictholidays.co.uk

Upper Barn and Lower Barn
★★★
Contact: Mr & Mrs Pierce
Upper Barn and Lower Barn, Orchard House, Curbar, Hope Valley S32 3YJ
T: (01433) 631885
F: (0114) 290 3309
E: info@curbarcottages.com
I: www.curbarcottages.com

CUTTHORPE
Derbyshire
Cow Close Farm Cottages
★★★
Contact: Mr & Mrs Gaskin
Cow Close Farm, Overgreen, Chesterfield S42 7BA
T: (01246) 232055
E: cowclosefarm.cottages@virgin.net

DARLEY DALE
Derbyshire
Housekeepers Cottage
★★★★★
Contact: Mrs Rudkin
Housekeepers Cottage, The Winnatts, Long Hill, Matlock DE4 2HE
T: (01629) 733270
F: (01629) 733270
E: enquires@housekeeperscottage.co.uk
I: www.housekeeperscottage.co.uk

Meadow Cottage ★★★
Contact: Mrs Cynthia Davies
The Spinney, Lincombe Drive, Torquay TQ1 2HH
T: (01803) 294218
E: calice@meadow382.fsnet.co.uk

Nether End c/o Nether Hall
★★★★
Contact: Mrs Lynne Wilson
Nether End c/o Nether Hall, Hallmoor Road, Daley Dale, Matlock DE4 2HF
T: (01629) 732131
F: (01629) 735716
E: lynne.netherhall@dial.pippex.com
I: www.cottageguide.co.uk/netherend

DERBY
Derby
Bank Cottage ★★★
Contact: Mrs Pym
Bank Cottage, 2 The Hollow, Derby DE3 0DG
T: (01332) 515607

DONINGTON
Lincolnshire
The Barn ★★★
Contact: Mrs Margaret A Smith
The Barn, 110 Quadring Road, Spalding PE11 4SJ
T: (01775) 821242

DUNSTON
Lincolnshire
Garden Cottage Holiday Home ★★★★
Contact: Mr Michael Swinburn
Garden Cottage Holiday Home, Willow Lane, Lincoln LN4 2EP
T: (01526) 321565
E: michael@swinburn.fsworld.co.uk

EAGLE
Lincolnshire
Eagle and Thorpe Crossing Cottage ★★★
Contact: Mr Patrick Britton
95 Lauriston Road, Victoria Park, London E9 7HJ
T: (020) 89865601
F: (020) 89865601
E: p.j.britton@amserve.net

EARL STERNDALE
Derbyshire
Wheeldon Trees Farm Holiday Cottages ★★★★
Contact: Mr Hollands
Wheeldon Trees Farm Holiday Cottages, Wheeldon Trees Farm, Buxton SK17 0AA
T: (01298) 83219
F: (01298) 83219
E: hollands@earlsterndale.fsnet.co.uk
I: www.wheeldontreesfarm.co.uk

EAST FIRSBY
Lincolnshire
The Log Cabins ★★★
Contact: Mr Robert Cox
The Log Cabins, Manor Farm, Market Rasen LN8 2DB
T: (01673) 878258
F: (01673) 878310
E: info@lincolnshire-lanes.com
I: www.lincolnshire-lanes.com

EAST HADDON
Northamptonshire
East Haddon Grange
★★★★
Contact: Mr & Mrs Pike
East Haddon Grange, Northampton NN6 8DR
T: (01604) 770368
F: (01604) 770368
E: ged.pike@u.genie.co.uk
I: www.easthaddongrange.co.uk

Mulberry Cottage ★★★★★
Contact: Mr & Mrs Smerin
Lane Cottage, St Andrews Road, Northampton NN6 8DE
T: (01604) 770244
F: (01327) 844822
E: liz@smerin.freeserve.co.uk

Rye Hill Country Cottages
★★★★
Contact: Mrs Margaret Widdowson
Rye Hill Country Cottages, Holdenby Road, Northampton NN6 8JR
T: (01604) 770990
F: (01604) 770990
E: ryehillcottages@btinternet.com
I: www.ryehillcottages.co.uk

EAST MARKHAM
Nottinghamshire
Stables Cottage ★★★★★
Contact: Mrs Juliet Hagger
York House, York Street, Newark NG22 0QW
T: (01777) 870683

EASTON ON THE HILL
Northamptonshire
The Old Bakery ★★★
Contact: Mrs Yogasundram
The Old Bakery, 25 West Street, Stamford PE9 3LS
T: (01780) 753898
E: yogiandmel@theoldbakery25.freeserve.co.uk
I: www.eastonoldbakery.co.uk

EDALE
Derbyshire
Grindslow House ★★★
Contact: Mrs Crook
c/o Meller Braggins, The Estate Office, Knutsford WA16 6SW
T: (01565) 830395
F: (01565) 830241

Hathaway and Heath Cottages ★★★
Contact: Mrs Gee
Cotefield Farm, Ollerbrook, Hope Valley S33 2ZG
T: (01433) 670273
F: (01433) 670273

Ollerbrook Cottages
★★★★
Contact: Mrs Paula Greenlees
Ollerbrook Cottages, Middle Ollerbrook House, Ollerbrook, Hope Valley S33 7LG
T: (01433) 670083
I: www.ollerbrook-cottages.co.uk

Establishments printed in blue have a detailed entry in this guide

EAST MIDLANDS

Taylor's Croft ★★★★★
Contact: Mrs Susan Favell
Taylor's Croft, Skinners Hall,
Hope Valley S33 7ZE
T: (01433) 670281
F: (01433) 670481
E: sue@skinnershall.freeserve.co.uk
I: www.skinnershall.freeserve.co.uk

Upper Holt Cottage ★★★★
Contact: Mr Richard Code
Upper Holt Farm, Barber Booth,
Hope Valley S33 7ZL
T: (01433) 670420
E: uppperholtcottage@uku.co.uk
I: www.upperholtcottage.com

EDLASTON
Derbyshire

Church Farm Cottages ★★★
Contact: Mrs Lois Blake
Church Farm Cottages, Church Farm, Ashbourne DE6 2DQ
T: (01335) 348776
E: adeblake@aol.com
I: www.churchfarm-holidays.freeserve.co.uk

EDWINSTOWE
Nottinghamshire

Crow Hollow ★★★★
Contact: Mrs Helen Proctor
18 Mackleys Lane, Newark
NG23 6EY
T: (01636) 677847
E: shp18@lineone.net

ELKINGTON
Northamptonshire

Manor Farm ★★★★
Contact:
Elkington Farm Partnership,
Manor Farm, Northampton
NN6 6NH
T: (01858) 575245
F: (01858) 575213

ELTON
Derbyshire

Barn Croft Cottage ★★★
Contact: Mr S Boardman
Sykes Cottages, York House,
York Street, Chester CH1 3LR
T: (01244) 345700
F: (01244) 321442
E: info@sykescottages.co.uk
I: www.sykescottages.co.uk

The Stable ★★★★
Contact: Mrs Jean Carson
The Stable, Homestead Farm,
Main Street, Matlock DE4 2BW
T: (01629) 650359

Swallow Cottage ★★★★
Contact: Mrs Lois Clark
51 Telegraph Street, Cottenham,
Cambridge CB4 8QU
T: (01954) 251004 & 07932 644287
E: lois@swallow-cottage.co.uk
I: www.swallow-cottage.co.uk

EPPERSTONE
Nottinghamshire

The Mews ★★★
Contact: Mrs Susan Santos
Eastwood Farm, Hagg Lane,
Nottingham NG14 6AX
T: (0115) 9663018
E: santosthemews@hotmail.com
I: www.farmstaydirect.com#347

EYAM
Derbyshire

Alice Cottage ★★★★
Contact: Mrs Judy Downes
Cliffe Cottage, Jaggers Lane,
Hathersage, Hope Valley
S32 1AZ
T: (01433) 650364
E: judy@alice-cottage.co.uk
I: www.alice-cottage.co.uk

Dalehead Court Cottages ★★★★-★★★★★
Contact: Mrs Neary
Laneside Farm, Hope Valley
S33 6RR
T: (01433) 620214
F: (01433) 620214
E: laneside@lineone.net
I: www.laneside.fsbusiness.co.uk

Fern and Brosterfield Cottage Brosterfield Hall ★★★★
Contact: Mrs Jenny Vickers
Fern and Brosterfield Cottage
Brosterfield Hall, Bakewell Road,
Foolow, Hope Valley S32 5QB
T: (01433) 631254
F: (01433) 639180
E: rcv@bvandp.co.uk
I: www.peak-cottages.com

The Flat Bramblegate ★★★
Contact: Mr Stafford Rowland
The Flat Bramblegate, Tideswell
Lane, Hope Valley S32 5RD
T: (01433) 631004
F: (01433) 639539
E: staffordrowland@supanet.com

Lark Cottage ★★★★★
Contact: Mrs Hazel Bell
Peak District Holidays, Nether
Croft, Eaton Place, Bakewell
DE45 1RW
T: (01246) 583564
E: hazel@peak-district-holidays.co.uk
I: www.peak-district-holidays.co.uk

1 Lydgate Cottages ★★★★
Contact: Mrs Harrop
Townfield House, Townfield
Lane, Warburton, Lymm
WA13 9SR
T: (01925) 752118
E: lydgatecottage@townfieldhouse.freeserve.co.uk

Steeple Barn ★★★★
Contact: Mrs Yvonne Pursglove
The Well House, Highcliff, Hope
Valley S32 5QN
T: (01433) 639030
E: info@onetorent.com
I: www.onetorent.com

The Trap House ★★★★
Contact:
Peak Cottages, Strawberry Lee
Lane, Totley Bents, Sheffield
S17 3BA
T: (0114) 262 0777
F: (0114) 2620666
E: enquiries@peakcottages.com
I: www.peakcottages.com

Watchmakers Cottage ★★★★
Contact: Mrs Carmichael
Croft View Cottage, Foolow,
Hope Valley S32 5QA
T: (01433) 630711
E: carmichael@msn.com

FENNY BENTLEY
Derbyshire

Church Barn ★★★★
Contact: Mr Kenneth & Mrs June
John Pearson
Church Barn, Church Cottage,
Ashes Lane, Ashbourne DE6 1LD
T: (01335) 350499
F: (01335) 350499
I: www.peakcottages.com

Swallows Cottage ★★★
Contact: Mrs Angela Hughes
The Priory, Woodleaves,
Ashbourne DE6 1LF
T: (01335) 350238
E: hughes.priory@virgin.net

FLECKNEY
Leicestershire

Elms Farm Cottage
Rating Applied For
Contact: Mrs Greta Bentley
Elms Farm Cottage, Arnesby
Road, Leicester LE8 8AQ
T: (01162) 402238
F: (01162) 402238
E: info@elms-farm.co.uk
I: www.elms-farm.co.uk

FLORE
Northamptonshire

Brewer's Cottage ★★★★
Contact: Mrs Loasby
Brewer's Cottage, Old Baker's
Arms (No 16), Kings Lane,
Northampton NN7 4LQ
T: (01327) 349737
F: (01327) 349747
E: mloasby@btinternet.com

FOOLOW
Derbyshire

Sycamore Cottage ★★★
Contact: Mrs Maveen Norton
The Rest, Foolow, Hope Valley
S32 5QR
T: (01433) 630186
E: mnortonfoolow@aol.com

FRITHVILLE
Lincolnshire

Carrington Court Holiday Cottages ★★★★
Contact: Mr Steven Lunn
Hawthorne House, Westville
Road, Boston PE22 7HL
T: (01205) 750441
F: (01205) 750441
I: www.carringtoncourt.co.uk

FROGGATT
Derbyshire

Bridgefoot Cottage ★★★★★
Contact: Mrs Marsha North
Green Farm, Curbar, Hope Valley
S32 3YH
T: (01433) 630120
E: enquiries@peakdistrictholiday.co.uk
I: www.peakdistrictholiday.co.uk

FULLETBY
Lincolnshire

High Beacon Cottage ★★★★
Contact: Mr Andrew & Mrs
Susan Walker
High Beacon Cottage, High
Beacon Farm, Horncastle
LN9 6LB
T: (01507) 534009
F: (01507) 534009
E: beacon.cottage@virgin.net
I: www.highbeaconcottage.co.uk

FULSTOW
Lincolnshire

Enfield Farm Cottages ★★★★
Contact: Mrs Joyce Marshall
Enfield Farm Cottages, Main
Street, Louth LN11 0XF
T: (01507) 363268
E: enquiries@enfieldfarmcottages.co.uk
I: www.enfieldfarmcottages.co.uk

Waingrove Farm Country Cottages ★★★★
Contact: Mr & Mrs P Tinker
Waingrove Farm Country
Cottages, Station Road, Louth
LN11 0XQ
T: (01507) 363704
E: ptinker.tinkernet@virgin.net
I: www.lincolnshirecottages.com

GLENTHAM
Lincolnshire

Laburnum Cottage ★★★
Contact: Mrs Imelda Hall
Laburnum Cottage, Middlefield
Lane, Market Rasen LN8 2ET
T: (01427) 614570
F: (01427) 614570
E: laburnumcottage@hotmail.com
I: www.laburnumcottage.netfirms.com

GONALSTON
Nottinghamshire

The Studio Cottage ★★★★
Contact: Mike and Ann
Carradice
The Studio Cottage, Hill House,
Gonalston, Nottingham
NG14 7JA
T: (0115) 966 4551
E: carradice@btinternet.com
I: www.carradice.btinternet.co.uk

Look out for establishments participating in the National Accessible Scheme

EAST MIDLANDS

GOULCEBY
Lincolnshire

Bay Tree Cottage ★★★★
Contact: Mr Gordon Reid
Bay Tree Cottage, Goulceby Post,
Ford Way, Louth LN11 9WD
T: (01507) 343230
F: (01507) 343920
E: info@goulcebypost.co.uk
I: www.goulcebypost.co.uk

GRANTHAM
Lincolnshire

Belvoir Cottage
Contact: Mrs Ursula Soar
Old Millhouse, Branston Road,
Eaton, Grantham NG32 1SF
T: (01476) 870797

Granary Cottage
Rating Applied For
Contact: Miss Marion Pepper
Granary Cottage, The Farm
House, Little Humby, Grantham
NG33 4HW
T: (01476) 585311

GRATTON
Derbyshire

The Managers House ★★★★
Contact: Mr Jonathon & Mrs
Jane Snodgrass
The Cheese Factory, Bakewell
DE45 1LN
T: (01629) 650489
E: enquiries@
cheesefactory-cottages.co.uk
I: www.cheesefactory-cottages.co.uk

GREAT CARLTON
Lincolnshire

Willow Farm ★★★
Contact: Mr James Clark
Willow Farm, Great Carlton,
Louth LN11 8JT
T: (01507) 338540

GREAT HALE
Lincolnshire

The Old Stable ★★★★
Contact: Mr Nigel & Mrs
Caroline Redmond
The Old Stable, 9 Church Street,
Sleaford NG34 9LF
T: (01529) 460307
E: c.redmond@virgin.net
I: www.theoldstable-greathale.co.uk

GREAT HUCKLOW
Derbyshire

Burrs Cottage ★★★
Contact: Mr Sykes
Sykes Cottages, York House,
York Street, Chester CH1 3LR
T: (01244) 345700
F: (01244) 321442
E: info@sykescottages.co.uk
I: www.sykescottages.co.uk

The Hayloft ★★★★
Contact: Mrs Margot Darley
Stanley House Farm, Buxton
SK17 8RL
T: (01298) 871044
E: margot.darley@btinternet.com
I: www.peakdistrictfarmhols.co.uk

South View Cottage ★★★★
Contact: Mrs Waterhouse
Holme Cottage, Windmill, Great
Hucklow, Buxton SK17 8RE
T: (01298) 871440
E: mo@mmwaterhouse.demon.co.uk
I: www.cottageguide.co.uk/southviewcottage

GREAT LONGSTONE
Derbyshire

Two Bears Cottage ★★★★
Contact: Mrs Valerie Squire
185 Crimicar Lane, Sheffield
S10 4EH
T: (0114) 230 3274
E: roger.squire@virgin.net
I: www.twobearscottage.co.uk

Wildflower ★★★★
Contact: Mrs Bell
Nether Croft, Eaton Place,
Bakewell DE45 1RW
T: (01246) 583564
E: hazel@peak-district-holidays.co.uk
I: www.peak-district-holidays.co.uk

GREAT PONTON
Lincolnshire

Witham Barn ★★★★
Contact: Mr Stephen Jackson
Witham Barn, Mill Farm,
Grantham NG33 5DP
T: (01476) 530502
F: (01476) 530344
E: steve@jackson3985.fslife.co.uk
I: www.withambarn.4t.com

GREAT STURTON
Lincolnshire

Old Barn Cottages ★★★★
Contact: Mr Dan Dobson
Old Barn Cottages, Beech House,
Horncastle LN9 5NX
T: (01507) 578435
E: danandko@dobson78.freeserve.co.uk
I: www.dobson78.freeserve.co.uk

GRIMBLETHORPE
Lincolnshire

Grimblethorpe Hall Country Cottages ★★★★★
Contact: Mrs Annie Codling
Grimblethorpe Hall Country
Cottages, Louth LN11 0RB
T: (01507) 313671
F: (01507) 313854
E: enquiries@
shepherdsholidaycottage.co.uk
I: www.shepherdsholidaycottage.co.uk

GRINDLEFORD
Derbyshire

Middle Cottage ★★★
Contact:
Peak Cottages, Paddock Cottage,
Strawberry Lee Lane, Totley
Bents, Sheffield S17 3BA
T: (0114) 262 0777
F: (0114) 262 0666
E: enquiries@peakcottages.com
I: www.peakcottages.com

GUNTHORPE
Nottinghamshire

Glebe Farm Cottages ★★★★
Contact: Mr Phil Warrior
Glebe Farm Cottages, Peck Lane,
Nottingham NG14 7EX
T: (0115) 9663836
F: (0115) 9663216
E: philwarrior@aol.com
I: www.glebefarmcottages.com

HAGWORTHINGHAM
Lincolnshire

Kingfisher Lodge ★★★★
Contact: Mr Nick Bowser
E W Bowser & Son Ltd, The
Estate Office, Boston PE22 0AA
T: (01205) 870210 &
07970 128531
F: (01205) 870602
E: office@ewbowser.com

HALLINGTON
Lincolnshire

The Paddy House and Blacksmiths Shop ★★★★
Contact: Mrs Heather Canter
The Paddy House and
Blacksmiths Shop, Louth
LN11 9QX
T: (01507) 605864
F: (01472) 250365
E: canter.hallington@virgin.net
I: www.canter-hallington.co.uk

HALSE
Northamptonshire

Hill Farm ★★★★
Contact: Mrs Robinson
Hill Farm, Brackley NN13 6DY
T: (01280) 703300
F: (01280) 704999
E: jg.robinson@btinternet.com

HARBY
Leicestershire

New Farm Cottage ★★★
Contact: Mrs Jeon Stanley
New Farm Cottage, Waltham
Road, Melton Mowbray
LE14 4DB
T: (01949) 860640
F: (01949) 861165

HARTINGTON
Derbyshire

Beech Cottage ★★★
Contact: Mrs Lesley Birch
Dale House, The Dale, Buxton
SK17 0AS
T: (01298) 84532
E: lesley@beechcottage99.freeserve.co.uk
I: www.beechcottage99.freeserve.co.uk

Church View ★★★
Contact: Miss Bassett
Digmer, Hartington, Buxton
SK17 0AQ
T: (01298) 84660

Cotterill Farm Cottages ★★★★
Contact: Mrs Frances Skemp
Cotterill Farm Cottages, Cotterill
Farm, Buxton SK17 0DJ
T: (01298) 84447
F: (01298) 84664
E: enquire@cotterillfarm.co.uk
I: www.cotterillfarm.co.uk

Cruck & Wolfscote Cottages ★★★★
Contact: Mrs Jane Gibbs
Cruck & Wolfscote Cottages,
Wolfscote Grange Farm,
Hartington, Buxton SK17 0AX
T: (01298) 84342
E: wolfscote@btinternet.com
I: www.wolfscotegrangecottages.com

Dairy Cottage, Piggery Place, Shire's Rest ★★★-★★★★
Contact: Mrs Flower
Dairy Cottage, Piggery Place,
Shire's Rest, Newhaven, Buxton
SK17 0DY
T: (01629) 636268
F: (01629) 636268
E: s.flower1@virgin.net
I: freespace.virgin.net/s.flower1

Dalescroft Cottage and Apartment ★★★★-★★★★★
Contact: Mr Brian Leese
Bishops Grange, Bishops Lane,
Buxton SK17 6UP
T: (01298) 24263
E: mail@dalescroft.co.uk
I: www.dalescroft.co.uk

Dove Valley Centre ★★★★
Contact: Mr & Mrs Walker
Dove Valley Centre, Under
Whitle, Sheen, Buxton SK17 0PR
T: (01298) 83282
E: walker@dovevalleycentre.co.uk
I: www.dovevalleycentre.co.uk

Hall Cottage ★★★
Contact: Mr Colin MacQueen
Peak Cottages, Strawberry Lee
Lane, Totley Bents, Sheffield
S17 3BA
T: (0114) 262 0777
F: (0114) 2620666
E: enquiries@peakcottages.com
I: www.peakcottages.com

Hartington Cottages ★★★★-★★★★★
Contact: Mr Patrick & Mrs
Frances Skemp
Cotterill Farm, Biggin by
Hartington, Buxton SK17 0DJ
F: (01298) 84447
E: enquiries@
hartingtoncottages.co.uk
I: www.hartingtoncottages.co.uk

Raikes Barn ★★★★
Contact: Mr MacQueen
Peak Cottages, Strawberry Lee
Lane, Totley Bents, Sheffield
S17 3BA
T: (0114) 262 0777
F: (0114) 2620666
E: enquiries@peakcottages.com
I: www.peakcottages.com

1 Staley Cottage and Victoria House ★★★★
Contact: Mr & Mrs Oliver
Carr Head Farm, Penistone,
Sheffield S36 7GA
T: (01226) 762387

Establishments printed in blue have a detailed entry in this guide

EAST MIDLANDS

HASLAND
Derbyshire

Sunshine Cottage ★★★
Contact: Mrs Suzannah Richardson
14 Alexandra Road East, Spital, Chesterfield S41 0HF
T: (01246) 209579
E: annah@peaksunshine.fslife.co.uk
I: www.peaksunshinecottage.co.uk

HATHERSAGE
Derbyshire

Oaks Farm ★★★
Contact: Mrs Bardwell
Oaks Farm, Highlow, Hope Valley S32 1AX
T: (01433) 650494
E: oaksfarm@fsdial.co.uk

The Old Barn ★★★★
Contact: Kathleen Stewart
Booths Farm, Highfield Road, Hope Valley S32 1DA
T: (01433) 650667
F: (01433) 650667
I: www.theoldbarn.co.uk

Pat's Cottage ★★★
Contact: Mr John Drakeford
110 Townhead Road, Sheffield S17 3GB
T: (0114) 236 6014 & 07850 200711
F: (0114) 236 6014
E: johnmdrakeford@hotmail.com
I: www.patscottage.co.uk

St Michael's Cottage ★★★
Contact: Miss Turton
Saint Michael's Environmental Education Centre, Main Road, Hope Valley S32 1BB
T: (01433) 650309
F: (01433) 650089
E: stmichaels@education.nottscc.gov.uk
I: www.eess.org.uk

HATTON
Lincolnshire

The Gables ★★★★★
Contact: Mrs Merivale
The Gables, Hatton Hall Farm, Market Rasen LN8 5QG
T: (01673) 858862
I: www.thegables-hatton.co.uk

HAYFIELD
Derbyshire

Bowden Bridge Cottage ★★★★
Contact: Mrs Margrith Easter
Bowden Bridge Cottage, Bowden Bridge, High Peak SK22 2LH
T: (01663) 743975
F: (01663) 743812
E: j_easter@talk21.com

Kinder Cottage ★★★
Contact: Mr Colin MacQueen
Peak Cottages, Strawberry Lee Lane, Totley Bents, Sheffield S17 3BA
T: (0114) 262 0777
F: (0114) 2620666
E: enquiries@peakcottages.com
I: www.peakcottages.com

HAZELWOOD
Derbyshire

Duck Pond View ★★★★★
Contact: Mrs Liz Chisman
Knowle Farm, Nether Lane, Belper DE56 4AP
T: (01773) 550686
F: (01773) 550686
E: liz@chisman.co.uk
I: www.duckpondview.co.uk

HOGNASTON
Derbyshire

The Flintstones - Barney's Cottage and Fred's Place ★★★★
Contact: Mrs Gillian Pearson
4 Bank House Court, Ashbourne DE6 1PR
T: (01335) 372189
F: (01335) 372189
E: gillian.pearson@virgin.net
I: www.theflintstones.info

HOLBEACH
Lincolnshire

Poachers Den ★★★
Contact: Mr Flynn
34 Fen Road, Spalding PE12 8QA
T: (01406) 423625
F: (01406) 423625
E: MFlynn8748@aol.com
I: www.SmoothHound.co.uk/hotels/poachers.html

HOLLOWAY
Derbyshire

1 Yew Tree Cottage ★★★
Contact: Mr Colin MacQueen
Peak Cottages, Strawberry Lee Lane, Totley Bents, Sheffield S17 3BA
T: (0114) 262 0777
F: (0114) 2620666
E: enquiries@peakcottages.com
I: www.peakcottages.com

HOLMESFIELD
Derbyshire

Millthorpe Cottage ★★★★
Contact: Mr Nich & Mrs Liz Barrett
Sleaford Property Services Ltd, Sleaford House, Cordwell Lane, Dronfield S18 7WH
T: (0114) 289 1071
F: (0114) 2891071
E: cottage.holidays@btopenworld.com
I: www.cottage-vacations.co.uk

HOLYMOORSIDE
Derbyshire

Chander Cottages ★★★
Contact: Mrs Margaret Smith
Chander Cottages, Chander Hill Barn, Chesterfield S42 7BW
T: (01246) 569416
E: margaretesmith@totalise.co.uk

Millclose Cottage ★★★★
Contact: Mr & Mrs Stockton
Millclose Cottage, Millclose Farm, Nether Loads, Chesterfield S42 7HW
T: (01246) 567624
F: (01246) 567624
E: allan.stockton@btinternet.com
I: www.millclosefarm.co.uk

HOPE
Derbyshire

Farfield Farm Cottages ★★★★
Contact: Mrs Elliott
Farfield Farm Cottages, Farfield Farm, Hope Valley S33 6RA
T: (01433) 620640
F: (01433) 620640
I: www.farfield.gemsoft.co.uk

Keepers Lodge ★★★★★
Contact: Mrs Christine Bell
Keeper's Lodge, Spring House Farm, Hope Valley S33 8WB
T: (01433) 620962
F: 0870 1 371046
E: thebells@btinternet.com
I: www.peak-district-holiday-cottages.co.uk

Laneside Farm Cottages ★★★★
Contact: Mrs Neary
Laneside Farm, Hope Valley S33 6RR
T: (01433) 620214
F: (01433) 620214
E: laneside@lineone.net
I: www.laneside.fsbusiness.co.uk

Oaker Farm Holiday Cottages ★★★★
Contact: Mrs Julie Ann Hadfield
Oaker Farm Holiday Cottages, Off Edale Road, Hope Valley S33 6RF
T: (01433) 621955
F: (01433) 621955
E: julieannhadfield@hotmail.com
I: www.oakerfarm.fsnet.co.uk

HOPE VALLEY
Derbyshire

Dene Cottage ★★★★
Contact: Mr Colin MacQueen
Peak Cottages, Strawberry Lee Lane, Totley Bents, Sheffield S17 3BA
T: (0114) 262 0777
F: (0114) 2620666
E: enquiries@peakcottages.com
I: www.peakcottages.com

Win Hill Cottage ★★★
Contact: Mr Colin MacQueen
Peak Cottages, Strawberry Lee Lane, Totley Bents, Sheffield S17 3BA
T: (0114) 262 0777
F: (0114) 2620666
E: enquiries@peakcottages.com
I: www.peakcottages.com

HOPTON
Derbyshire

Peakside ★★★
Contact: Mr Colin MacQueen
Peak Cottages, Strawberry Lee Lane, Totley Bents, Sheffield S17 3BA
T: (0114) 262 0777
F: (0114) 2620666
E: enquiries@peakcottages.com
I: www.peakside.co.uk

HORNCASTLE
Lincolnshire

The Pottery ★★★
Contact: Mrs Emmerson
7 Moores Yard, Lincoln Road, Horncastle LN9 5AN
T: (01507) 525810
E: jaspkme@aol.com

Southolme Cottage ★★★
Contact: Mr David Gresham
Glebe Cottage, Valenders Lane, Shipston-on-Stour CV36 4LB
T: (0121) 4495666
E: david@gartongresham.co.uk
I: www.southolmecottage.connectfree.co.uk

HORSINGTON
Lincolnshire

Wayside Cottage ★★★
Contact: Mr Ian & Mrs Jane Williamson
72 Mill Lane, Horsington, Woodhall Spa LN10 6QZ
T: (01526) 353101
E: janewill89@hotmail.com
I: www.cottagesdirect.com

HUBBERTS BRIDGE
Lincolnshire

Elms Farm Cottages ★★★★
Contact: Mr John Carol Emerson
The Elms, Boardsides, Hubberts Bridge, Boston PE20 3QP
T: (01205) 290840
F: (01205) 290840
E: elmsfarm@ukf.net

HULLAND WARD
Derbyshire

Valley View ★★★
Contact: Mrs Audrcy Gray
Valley View, Hayes Farm, Biggin by Hulland, Ashbourne DE6 3FJ
T: (01335) 370204
F: (01333) 70204
E: hayes.farm@lineone.net
I: www.valleyview.tk

IBSTOCK
Leicestershire

Lavender Cottage ★★★★
Contact: Mrs Lorraine Rajput
The Cottage, 155 High Street, Ibstock, Leicester LE67 6JQ
T: (01530) 450451

INGHAM
Lincolnshire

3 Anyans Row ★★★
Contact: Mr & Mrs T Taylor
Ivy Cottage, Stow Road, Sturton by Stow, Lincoln LN1 2BZ
T: (01427) 788023

INGOLDSBY
Lincolnshire

Little Scotland Farm ★★★★
Contact: Mrs Angela Jasinski
Little Scotland Farm, Scotland Lane, Grantham NG33 4ES
T: (01476) 585494
F: (01476) 585014

526   Look out for establishments participating in the National Accessible Scheme

EAST MIDLANDS

KERSALL
Nottinghamshire
Rose and Sweetbriar Cottages ★★★
Contact: Mrs Brenda Wood
Rose and Sweetbriar Cottages, Hill Farm, Kersall, Newark NG22 0BJ
T: (01636) 636274
I: www.roseandsweetbriar.fsbusiness.co.uk

KETTERING
Northamptonshire
The Villiers Suite, Cranford Hall ★★★
Contact: Mr & Mrs John Robinson
The Villiers Suite, Cranford Hall, Cranford, Kettering NN14 4AL
T: (01536) 330248
F: (01536) 330203
E: cranford@farmline.com
I: cranfordhall.co.uk

KETTON
Rutland
Dove Cottage ★★★
Contact: Mr Don & Mrs Margaret Bradley
27 High Street, Stamford PE9 3TA
T: (01780) 720248

Randolph Cottage ★★★★
Contact: Mrs Forster
Randolph Cottage, 11 Church Road, Stamford PE9 3RD
T: (01780) 720802
E: forster.ketton@virgin.net

KING'S CLIFFE
Northamptonshire
Maltings Cottage ★★★★
Contact: Mrs Jenny Dixon
19 West Street, King's Cliffe, Peterborough PE8 6XA
T: (01780) 470365
F: (01780) 470623

KIRK IRETON
Derbyshire
Bluebell, Buttercup and Clover Barn ★★★★
Contact: Mr & Mrs Pollard
Bluebell, Buttercup and Clover Barn, Alton Nether Farm, Tinkerley Lane, Kirk Ireton, Ashbourne DE6 3LF
T: (01335) 370270
F: (01335) 370270
E: ben@redpepperpictures.freeserve.co.uk
I: www.peakcottages.co.uk

Grange Holidays ★★★★
Contact: Mr Malcolm Race
Grange Holidays, Tinkerley Lane, Derby DE6 3LF
T: (01335) 370880
E: cottages@w33.co.uk
I: www.ashbourne-accommodation.co.uk

Ivy Cottage ★★★
Contact:
Peak Cottages Ltd, Strawberry Lee Lane, Totley Bents, Sheffield S17 3BA
T: (0114) 262 0177
F: (0114) 2620666

KIRK LANGLEY
Derbyshire
The Cart Hovel and The Stables ★★★★
Contact: Mrs Sue Gibbs
The Cart Hovel and The Stables, Brun Farm View, Brun Lane, Kirk Langley, Ashbourne DE6 4LU
T: (01332) 824214
I: www.cottageguide.co.uk/thecarthovel

KIRKLINGTON
Nottinghamshire
The Gatehouse ★★
Contact: Mr & Mrs Crane
The Gatehouse, Belle Eau Park, Newark NG22 8TX
T: (01623) 871605
F: (01623) 411103
E: gatehouse@belleeau.freeserve.co.uk
I: www.belleeau.freeserve.co.uk

KNAITH
Lincolnshire
Central Park Farm ★★★★
Contact: Mrs Anne Fenwick
Walford House, Hillside, Gainsborough DN21 5LT
T: (01427) 613259
F: (01427) 611820
E: anne.fenwick1@virgin.net

KNIVETON
Derbyshire
Willow Bank ★★★★
Contact: Mrs Vaughan
Willow Bank, Kniveton, Ashbourne DE6 1JJ
T: (01335) 343308
F: (01335) 347859
E: willowbank@kniveton.net
I: www.kniveton.net

LAMBLEY
Nottinghamshire
Dickman's Cottage ★★★
Contact: Mr William Marshall Smith
Springsyde, Birdcage Walk, Otley LS21 3HB
T: (01943) 462719
F: (01943) 850925
E: marshallsmithuk@hotmail.com
I: http://mywebpage.netscape.com/wmarshallsmith/default.html

LANGWORTH
Lincolnshire
The Barn
Rating Applied For
Contact: Mrs Susie Fleetwood
The Barn, Ferry House Farm, Low Barlings, Lincoln LN3 5DG
T: (01522) 751939
F: (01522) 751959
E: ifleet@barlings.demon.co.uk
I: www.barlings.demon.co.uk

LEA
Derbyshire
The Coach House ★★★
Contact: Mr & Mrs M Helme
Coach House, Main Road, Matlock DE4 5GJ
T: (01629) 534346
F: (01629) 534346
I: www.coachhouselea.co.uk

The Old Stable and Hollybrook Cottage ★★★
Contact: Mr Philip Waterfall
The Old Stable and Hollybrook Cottage, 5 Main Road, Matlock DE4 5GJ
T: (01629) 534546

LEICESTER
Leicester
Harrisons Self-Catering Properties ★★★
Contact: Ms Susan Howell
49 Oakcroft Avenue, Leicester LE9 2DH
E: info@harrisonsselfcateringproperties.com
I: www.harrisonsselfcateringproperties.com

Romany ★★
Contact: Mrs Evelyn Harris
86 Station Lane, Leicester LE7 9UF
T: (0116) 2927161
E: romany1@talk21.com

LINCOLN
Lincolnshire
Bight House ★★★★
Contact: Mrs Mavis Sharpe
Bight House, 17 East Bight, Lincoln LN2 1QH
T: (01522) 534477

Burton Mews ★★★
Contact: Mrs Karen Rastall
30 Burton Road, Lincoln LN1 3LB
T: (01522) 524990
F: (01522) 560845
E: karen@rastallandco.com

Cliff Farm Cottage ★★★★
Contact: Mrs Rae Marris
Cliff Farm, North Carlton, Lincoln LN1 2RP
T: (01522) 730475
E: rae.marris@farming.co.uk
I: www.cliff-farm-cottage.co.uk
&

D'isney Place Cottage ★★★★
Contact: Judy or Sarah
D'isney Place Cottage, Lincoln LN2 4AA
T: (01522) 542411
F: (01522) 511321
E: info@disneyplacehotel.co.uk

9 Dorron Court ★★★
Contact: Mr Barry Dean
Cedar Lodge, Thackers Lane, Lincoln LN4 1LT
T: (01522) 791442
F: (01522) 523067

The Flat ★★★
Contact: Mrs E A Slingsby
The Flat, 3 Greestone Place, Lincoln LN2 1PP
T: (01522) 560880
F: (01522) 535600
E: auction@thosmawer.co.uk
I: www.greestoneplace.com

Jubilee Farm ★★★
Contact: Mr David Richardson
Jubilee Farm, Lincoln Lane, Thorpe-on-the-Hill, Lincoln LN6 9BH
T: (01522) 681241
E: davidandelaine53@aol.com

Kenton ★★★
Contact: Mr Michael Taylor
2 Ventnor Terrace, Ventnor Terrace, Lincoln LN2 1LZ
T: (01522) 532136
E: mikefs@compuserve.com

Lilac Cottage ★★★
Contact: Mrs Veronica Verner
1B Danes Terrace, Lincoln LN2 1LP
T: (01522) 533347

19a Lindum Hill ★★★★
Contact: Mr Stuart Richardson
Elder House, The Green, Welbourn, Lincoln LN5 0NJ
T: (01400) 272793 &
07957 622583
E: therichardsons@lindumhill.fsnet.co.uk
I: www.lindum-hill.co.uk

Martingale Cottage ★★★
Contact: Mrs Patsy Pate
19 East Street, Nettleham, Lincoln LN2 2SL
T: (01522) 751795
E: patsy.pate@ntlworld.com

The Needleworkers ★★★★
Contact: Mr & Mrs Rochester
1 Padley Road, Lincoln LN2 4WB
T: (01522) 522113
E: john@jrochester.fsnet.co.uk

Old Vicarage Cottage ★★★★
Contact: Mrs Downs
Old Vicarage Cottage, East Street, Lincoln LN2 2SL
T: (01522) 750819
F: (01522) 750819
E: susan@oldvic.net

Old Vicarage Cottages ★★★★
Contact: Mrs Susan Downs
The Old Vicarage, East Street, Lincoln LN2 2SL
T: (01522) 750819
F: (01522) 750819
E: susan@oldvic.net

Pingles Cottage ★★★
Contact: Mrs Sutcliffe
Pingles Cottage, Grange Farm, Broxholme, Lincoln LN1 2NG
T: (01522) 702441

Saint Clements ★★★
Contact: Mrs Gill Marshall
Saint Clements, Langworthgate, Lincoln LN2 4AD
T: (01522) 538087
F: (01522) 560642
E: jroywood@aol.com
I: www.stayatstclements.co.uk

South Cliff Farm Log Cabins ★★★★
Contact: Mrs Jennifer Marris
South Cliff Farm Log Cabins, Middle Street, South Carlton Cliff, Lincoln LN1 2RW
T: (01522) 730236
F: (01522) 730853
I: www.southcliffarmlogcabins.ports.com

The Stable ★★★★
Contact: Mr Jerry & Chris Scott
Sunnyside, Lincoln Road, Brattleby, Lincoln LN1 2SQ
T: (01522) 730561
E: jmsco@lineone.net
I: www.lincolncottages.co.uk

Establishments printed in blue have a detailed entry in this guide

EAST MIDLANDS

Tennyson Court ★★
Contact: Mr Andrew Carnell
Tennyson Court, Tennyson House, 3 Tennyson Street, Lincoln LN1 1LZ
T: (01522) 569892
F: (01522) 887997
E: andrew@tennyson-court.co.uk
I: www.tennyson-court.co.uk

31 Union Road
Rating Applied For
Contact: Mr Stuart Richardson
Elder House, The Green, Lincoln LN5 0NJ
T: (01400) 272793
E: therichardsons@lindumhill.fsnet.co.uk
I: www.lindum-hill.co.uk

LITTLE HUCKLOW
Derbyshire

Glider View Cottage ★★★★
Contact: Mrs C Sherman
Two Barns, Main Street, Matlock DE4 2BW
T: (01629) 650196
I: www.english-country-cottages.co.uk

The Parlour and The Dairy ★★★★
Contact: Mrs Wendy Mycock
The Parlour and The Dairy, Forest Lane Farm, Buxton SK17 8JE
T: (01298) 871226
F: (01298) 871226

LITTLE LONGSTONE
Derbyshire

The Lodge and Dove Cottage ★★★-★★★★★
Contact: Mrs Davey
Chestnut House, Bakewell DE45 1NN
T: (01629) 640542
F: (01629) 640450
E: annie@littlelongstone.freeserve.co.uk

Orrs Barn ★★★★
Contact:
Peak Cottages, Strawberry Lee Lane, Totley Bents, Sheffield S17 3BA
T: (0114) 262 0777
F: (0114) 2620666
E: enquires@peakcottages.com
I: www.peakcottages.com

LITTON
Derbyshire

Cross View ★★★
Contact: Mrs Rowan-Olive
44 Burnham Road, St Albans AL1 4QW
T: (01727) 844169
E: enquiries@cross-view.co.uk
I: www.cross-view.co.uk

Farm Hands Cottage ★★★★
Contact: Mrs Annette Scott
Hall Farm House, Buxton SK17 8OP
T: (01298) 872172
E: jfscott@waitrose.com
I: www.users.waitrose.com/~jfscott

LOBTHORPE
Lincolnshire

Old Moat Barn ★★★
Contact: Mrs Grindal
Hall Farm, Grantham NG33 5LS
T: (01476) 860350
F: (01476) 861724
E: grindal@freeuk.com

LONG BUCKBY
Northamptonshire

Meadowview Cottages ★★★★
Contact: Mrs Judith Jelley
Meadowview Cottages, Perkins Lodge Farm, Brington Road, Northampton NN6 7NT
T: (01327) 842205
F: (01327) 842205
E: meadowview.cottages@farming.com
I: www.oas.co.uk/ukcottages/meadowview

LOUGHBOROUGH
Leicestershire

The Woodlands ★★★
Contact: Mr & Mrs Grudgings
14 Beacon Drive, Loughborough LE11 2BD
T: (01509) 214596
E: thewoodlands@onetel.com

LOUTH
Lincolnshire

Ashwater House ★★★-★★★★★
Contact: Mrs Holly Mapletoft
Ashpot Cottage, Willow Drive, Louth LN11 0AH
T: 0845 126 0442
E: enquiries@ashwaterhouse.co.uk
I: www.ashwaterhouse.co.uk

Canal Farm Cottages ★★★★
Contact: Mr & Mrs Richard Drinkel
Canal Farm, Austen Fen, Grainthorpe, Louth LN11 0NX
T: (01472) 388825
F: (01472) 388825
E: canalfarm@ukhome.net
I: www.canalfarmcottages.co.uk

2 Kenwick Park Lodge ★★★★
Contact: Mrs Jan Matthews
Windmill Garage, Main Road, Louth LN11 7SB
T: (01507) 338429
E: windg@fsbdial.co.uk

Kenwick Woods
Rating Applied For
Contact:
Kenwick Woods, Kenwick Estate, Louth LN11 8NR
T: (01507) 608806 & 353003
F: (01507) 608027
E: enquiries@kenwick-park.co.uk
I: www.kenwickwoods.com

Mill Lodge ★★★
Contact: Mrs Cade
Mill Lodge, Benniworth House Farm, Donington-on-Bain, Louth LN11 9RD
T: (01507) 343265
E: pamela@milllodge995fsnet.co.uk

LOWER BENEFIELD
Northamptonshire

Granary Cottage ★★★
Contact: Mrs Judith Singlehurst
Granary Cottage, Brook Farm, Peterborough PE8 5AE
T: (01832) 205215

LULLINGTON
Derbyshire

Aubrietia Cottage ★★★★
Contact: Mrs Rita Cooper
Aubrietia Cottage, Lullington, Swadlincote DE12 8ED
T: (01827) 373219
F: (01283) 515885
E: r.cooper@care4free.net

MABLETHORPE
Lincolnshire

Dunes Cottage
Rating Applied For
Contact: Mrs Sheila Morrison
Bank House, Brickyard Lane, Theddlethorpe, Mablethorpe LN12 1NR
T: (01507) 338342
F: (01507) 338359
E: sheila.a.morrison@btopenworld.com
I: www.dunesholidaycottage.co.uk

MALTBY LE MARSH
Lincolnshire

Yew Tree Cottage and The Granary ★★★★
Contact: Mrs Ann Graves
Yew Tree Cottage and The Granary, Grange Farm, Alford LN13 0JP
T: (01507) 450267
E: grangefarm@beeb.net
I: www.grange-farmhouse.co.uk

MANSFIELD
Nottinghamshire

Blue Barn Cottage ★★★
Contact: Mrs June Ibbotson
Blue Barn Cottage, Langwith, Mansfield NG20 9JD
T: (01623) 742248
F: (01623) 742248
E: bluebarnfarm@supanet.com
I: www.bluebarnfarm-notts.co.uk

MAPPLETON
Derbyshire

Hawthorn Cottage ★★★★
Contact: Mrs Judy Lawrence
Hawthorn Cottage, Ashbourne DE6 2AB
T: (01925) 752220
I: www.caldecotthomes.co.uk

MARKET HARBOROUGH
Leicestershire

The Hollies ★★★★
Contact: Mrs Frances Fray
The Hollies, Hollies Barn, Main Street, Market Harborough LE16 7SY
T: (01858) 545271
F: (01858) 545885
E: frances@mfray.com
I: www.mfray.com

Newbold Farm Holiday Cottages ★★★★
Contact: Mr & Mrs Gilbert
Newbold Farm Holiday Cottages, Newbold Farm, Dicks Hill, Clipston, Market Harborough LE16 9TT
T: (01858) 525272
F: (01858) 525565
E: enquiries@nbfhc.co.uk
I: www.nbfhc.co.uk

Short Lodge ★★★
Contact: Ms Durham
Short Lodge, Oxendon Road, Market Harborough LE16 8LB
T: (01858) 525323

MARKET RASEN
Lincolnshire

Meadow Farm House ★★★★
Contact: Mr Nick Grimshaw
Meadow Farm House, Bleasby Moor, Market Rasen LN8 3QL
T: (01673) 885909
F: (01673) 885909
E: nickgrimshaw@btconnect.com
I: www.meadowfarmhouse.co.uk

Papermill Cottages ★★★-★★★★★
Contact: Mr Peter & Mrs Joyce Rhodes
Papermill Cottages, Vale Farm, Caistor Lane, Market Rasen LN8 3XN
T: (01673) 838010
F: (01673) 838127
E: peter.rhodes1@btinternet.com
I: www.papermillcottages.co.uk

Pelham Arms Farm ★★★★
Contact: Mrs Margaret Henderson
Pelham Arms Farm, Market Rasen LN8 3YP
T: (01673) 828261
E: pelhamarmsfarm@btinternet.com
I: www.pelhamarmsfarm.co.uk

MARSH LANE
Derbyshire

Fold Farm ★★★
Contact: Mr & Mrs Ryan
10 Hawkshead Avenue, Dronfield S18 8NB
T: (01246) 415143
E: foldfarm@fwryan.freeserve.co.uk
I: www.fwryan.freeserve.co.uk

MARSHCHAPEL
Lincolnshire

Dove Cottage ★★★★
Contact: Mrs J Houghton
Dove Cottage, c/o Sedgebeck, West End Lane, Grimsby DN36 5TN
T: (01472) 388520
E: june.houghton@tesco.net
I: www.dovecottage-lincs.co.uk

EAST MIDLANDS

MATLOCK
Derbyshire

The Bird's Nest Holiday Apartment ★★★★★
Contact: Mr Abid Shah
The Bird's Nest Holiday Apartment, 5 Portland Mews, Clifton Road, Matlock DE4 3PW
T: (01629) 584549
E: birdsnest@peakdistrictholidays.co.uk
I: www.peakdistrictholidays.co.uk

Carpenter's Cottage ★★★★
Contact: Mrs Iris Wilmot
8 Croft Road, Nottingham NG12 4BW
T: (0115) 923 3455
F: (0115) 9233455
E: bobwilmot@edwalton.fslife.co.uk

Carsington Cottages ★★★
Contact: Mrs Valerie Riach
Carsington Cottages, Swiers Farm, Matlock DE4 4DE
T: (01629) 540513
F: (01629) 540513
E: riachclan@btinternet.com
I: www.carsingtoncottages.co.uk

Clematis Cottage ★★★★
Contact: Mr J Lomas
Middle Hills Farm, Grange Mill, Matlock DE4 4HY
T: (01629) 650368
F: (01629) 650368
E: l.lomas@btinternet.com
I: www.peakdistrictfarmhols.co.uk

Croft Edge ★★★★
Contact: Dr Miller
21 Plover Wharf, Castle Marina, Nottingham NG7 1TL
T: (0115) 9582766
E: info@croftedge.co.uk
I: www.croftedge.co.uk

Darwin Forest Country Park ★★★-★★★★★
Contact: Reception
Darwin Forest Country Park, Darley Moor, Two Dales, Matlock DE4 5LN
T: (01629) 732428
F: (01629) 735015
E: enquiries@pinelodgeholidays.co.uk
I: www.pinelodgeholidays.co.uk/darwin_forest.ihtml

&

Darwin Lake ★★★★
Contact: Miss Nikki Manning
Peak Village Ltd, Darwin Lake, Jaggers Lane, Darley Moor, Matlock DE4 5LH
T: (01629) 735859
F: (01629) 735859
E: enquiries@darwinlake.co.uk
I: www.darwinlake.co.uk

Dene Cottage ★★★★
Contact: Ms Amanda Latham
11 The Charters, Lichfield WS13 7LX
T: (01543) 319440
F: (01543) 319441
E: amanda@threespires.net
I: www.peakdistrictcottage.co.uk

Eagle Cottage ★★★★
Contact: Mrs Mary Prince
Haresfield House, Keeling Lane, Birchover, Matlock DE4 2BL
T: (01629) 650634
E: maryprince@msn.com
I: www.cressbrook.co.uk/youlgve/eagle/

End Cottage ★★★
Contact: Mrs Dorotia Holden
End Cottage, 1 The Lane, Stanton-in-the-Peak, Matlock DE4 2LX
T: (01629) 812198
E: peaklets@fsmail.net
I: www.peakholidaycottages.com

Florence Nightingale Chapel ★★★★
Contact: Mrs Susan Metcalf
14 Chapel Lane, Matlock DE4 5AU
T: (01629) 534652
F: (01629) 534977
E: paulmetcalf@tiscali.co.uk
I: www.derbyshireholiday.co.uk

Hadfield House ★★
Contact: Mrs Marie Evans
Christ Church Vicarage, Doncaster Road, Barnsley S71 5EF
T: (01226) 203784
E: rgrevans@compuserve.com

Ivonbrook Grange Farm Cottage ★★★
Contact: Ms Christine Heathcote
Ivonbrook Grange Farm Cottage, Grange Mill, Matlock DE4 4HU
T: (01629) 650221
F: (01629) 650221
E: ivonbrokgrangefarm@amserve.com

Ivy Cottage ★★★
Contact: Mrs Potter
Highfields, Pounder Lane, Matlock DE4 2AT
T: (01629) 823018
E: ivy.cottage@ukgateway.net

Little Hallmoor Castle ★★★★
Contact: The Manager
Derbyshire Country Cottages, 90 Cavendish Road, Matlock DE4 3HD
T: (01629) 583545
F: (01629) 583545
E: enquiries@derbyshirecountrycottages.co.uk

Masson Leys Farm ★★★★
Contact: Mrs Brenda Dawes
Masson Leys Farm, Salters Lane, Matlock DE4 2PA
T: (01629) 582944
I: www.massonleys.co.uk

Mooredge Barns ★★★★-★★★★★
Contact: Mr Barratt
Mooredge Farm, Knabb Hall Lane, Matlock DE4 5FS
T: (01629) 583701
F: (01629) 583701
E: enquiries@mooredgefarm.co.uk
I: www.mooredgefarmcottages.co.uk

The Studio ★★
Contact: Mrs Reuss
247 Starkholmes Road, Matlock DE4 5JE
T: (01629) 584622

Swiss View ★★★
Contact: Mr William Lennox
Treetops, 111 Cavendish Road, Matlock DE4 3HE
T: (01629) 582568

Thimble Cottage ★★★
Contact: Mr & Mrs Armstrong
Holmedene, Ashford Road, Bakewell DE45 1GL
T: (01629) 813448
E: bernard-armstrong@lineone.net

Tinkersley Barn ★★★★
Contact: Mrs Bradford
Tinkersley Barn, Tinkersley, Rowsley, Matlock DE4 2NJ
T: (01629) 735451

MATLOCK BATH
Derbyshire

Derwent View ★★★
Contact: Mr Tim Heathcote
3 Wellington House, Waterloo Road, Matlock DE4 3PH
T: (01629) 57473
F: (01629) 57473

Nonsuch Apartment ★★★★
Contact: Mr Dennis Smith
Wilson Lane Farm House, Main Street, Heath Village, Chesterfield S44 5SA
T: (01246) 851421

Rambler Cottage ★★★
Contact: Mrs Singer
Peak Cottages, Strawberry Lee Lane, Totley Bents, Sheffield S17 3BA
T: (0114) 262 0777
F: (0114) 2620666
E: enquiries@peakcottages.com
I: www.peakcottages.com

Weavers Cottage ★★★
Contact: Mr Colin MacQueen
Peak Cottages, Strawberry Lee Lane, Totley Bents, Sheffield S17 3BA
T: (0114) 262 0777
F: (0114) 2620666
E: enquiries@peakcottages.com
I: www.peakcottages.com

MELBOURNE
Derbyshire

Orchard Barn ★★★★
Contact: Mrs Hendley
7 Holm Avenue, Derby DE21 5DX
T: (01332) 833584
E: hendleysfour@aol.uk

MELTON MOWBRAY
Leicestershire

28 Melton Road ★★★★
Contact: Mrs Watchorn
Chester House, 26 Melton Road, Waltham on the Wolds, Melton Mowbray LE14 4AJ
T: (01664) 464255
E: awatchorn1314@yahoo.com

MIDDLE RASEN
Lincolnshire

East Farm Cottage
Rating Applied For
Contact: Mrs Gill Grant
East Farm Cottage, Mill Lane, Market Rasen LN3 5AQ
T: (01673) 842283
F: (01673) 849041
E: emmalouise.grant@btopenworld.co.uk
I: www.eastfarmholidaycottage.co.uk

MIDDLETON
Derbyshire

The Barn ★★★
Contact: Mr Peter John Smith
The Barn, 14 Main Street, Middleton by Wirksworth, Matlock DE4 4LQ
T: (01629) 824519
I: www.barnaccommodation.freeserve.co.uk

MIDDLETON-BY-YOULGREAVE
Derbyshire

The Coach House ★★★★
Contact: Mr Colin MacQueen
Peak Cottages, Strawberry Lee Lane, Totley Bents, Sheffield S17 3BA
T: (0114) 262 0777
F: (0114) 2620666
E: enquiries@peakcottages.com
I: www.peakcottages.com

Curlew Cottage ★★★★
Contact: Mrs Carole Brister
Lowfield Farm, Middleton-by-Youlgrave, Bakewell DE45 1LR
T: (01629) 636180
F: (01629) 636513
E: brister@quista.net
I: mysite.freeserve.com/lowfieldfarmcottages

Holly Homestead Cottage ★★★★
Contact: Mr David & Mrs Valerie Edge
Ridgeway House, Hillcliff Lane, Turnditch, Belper DE56 2EA
T: (01773) 550754
E: daveedge@turnditch82.freeserve.co.uk
I: www.holly-homestead.co.uk

MILLER'S DALE
Derbyshire

Miller's Dale Cottages & Monks Retreat ★★★-★★★★★
Contact: Mrs Pamela Wilkson
Miller's Dale Cottages & Monks Retrea, Monks Dale Farm, Millers Dale, Buxton SK17 8SN
T: (01298) 871306
F: (01298) 871306
E: pamwilkson@hotmail.com
I: www.cressbrook.co.uk/tidza/monksdale

MILLTOWN
Derbyshire

Greenfield Barn ★★★★
Contact: Mr & Mrs Page
Greenfield House, Oakstedge Lane, Milltown, Ashover S45 0HA
T: (01246) 590119

EAST MIDLANDS

MONSAL DALE
Derbyshire

Heron Cottage Upperdale Farm ★★★
Contact: Mr & Mrs Clarke
Heron Cottage Upperdale Farm, Upperdale, Buxton SK17 8SZ
T: (01629) 640536

Riversdale Farm Holiday Cottages ★★★★
Contact: Mrs Jackson
Riversdale Farm Holiday Cottages, Riversdale, Buxton SK17 8SZ
T: (01629) 640500
I: www.riversdalefarm.co.uk

MONYASH
Derbyshire

The Barn ★★★★
Contact: Mr Staley
Bole Hill, Monyash Road, Bakewell DE45 1QW
T: (01629) 56494
E: tonystaley@hotmail.com
I: www.bolehillfarmcottages.co.uk

Rose Cottage ★★★
Contact: Mr Brian & Mrs Heather Read
20 Church Street, Bakewell DE45 1JH
T: (01629) 813629

Sheldon Cottages ★★★★
Contact: Mrs Louise Fanshawe
Sheldon House, Chapel Street, Monyash, Bakewell DE45 1JJ
T: (01629) 813067
F: (01629) 815768
E: steveandlou.fanshawe@virgin.net
I: www.sheldoncottages.co.uk

NETTLEHAM
Lincolnshire

Luv-a-Duck Cottage ★★★★
Contact: Mrs Elizabeth Johnston
The Croft, 15 East Street, Lincoln LN2 2SL
T: (01522) 750746

The Stables ★★★★
Contact: Mrs Annette Dickens
Northfield Farm, Scothern Road, Nettleham, Lincoln LN2 2TX
T: (01673) 861866
F: (01673) 862629
E: info@sunwish.com
I: www.sunwish.com

NEW MILLS
Derbyshire

Shaw Farm ★★★
Contact: Mrs Nicky Burgess
Shaw Farm, Shaw Marsh, High Peak SK22 4QE
T: (0161) 4271841
E: nicky.burgess@talk21.com
I: www.shawfarmholidays.co.uk

NEWTON GRANGE
Derbyshire

New Hanson Bungalow ★★★★
Contact: Mrs Linda Bonsall
New Hanson Grange Farm, Ashbourne DE6 1NN
T: (01335) 310258
F: (01335) 310258
E: NHGFarmHoliday@tiscali.co.uk
I: www.cressbrook.co.uk/ashborn/newhanson

NORTH LUFFENHAM
Rutland

Old School Cottage ★★★★
Contact: Mrs Elaine Handley
Wytchley House, Empingham Road, Stamford PE9 3UP
T: (01780) 721768
F: (01780) 720214
E: emhand@hotmail.com
I: www.rutnet.co.uk/oldschoolcottage

NORTH WILLINGHAM
Lincolnshire

Brooks Cottage ★★★
Contact: Mrs Fiona Molloy
Brooks Cottage, Brooks Manor, Market Rasen LN8 3RA
T: (01673) 838035
F: (01673) 838035
I: www.lincsholidaycottages.fsnet.co.uk

NORTHAMPTON
Northamptonshire

The Long Barn ★★★★★
Contact: Mrs Carter
Broombank, Upper Harlestone, Northampton NN7 4EL
T: (01604) 583237
F: (01604) 751865
E: longbarn@carter2861.fsnet.co.uk

Mill Barn Cottage ★★★
Contact: Mr Roger Wolens
Mill Barn Cottage, The Mill House, Mill Lane, Northampton NN6 0NR
T: (01604) 810507
F: (01604) 810507
I: www.themillbarn.free-online.co.uk

NOTTINGHAM
Nottingham

Days Inn Serviced Apartments ★★★
Contact: Mr Paul Smith
Days Inn Serviced Apartments, Ropewalk Court, Derby Road, Nottingham NG1 5AD
T: (0115) 924 1900
F: (0115) 9471500
E: psmith@premgroup.com
I: www.premgroup.com

46 Riverview ★★★
Contact: Mrs Margaret Hallam
364 Loughborough Road, Nottingham NG2 7FD
T: (0115) 923 3372

Tree Tops ★★★
Contact: Mrs Ann Turner
Tree Tops, Castle Boulevard, Nottingham NG7 1FE
T: (0115) 911 7580
F: (0115) 9472819
E: ann.turner1@ntlworld.com
I: www.treetopsnottingham.co.uk

Woodview Cottages ★★★★
Contact: Mrs Judith Morley
Newfields Farm, Owthorpe, Nottingham NG12 3GF
T: (01949) 81279
F: (01949) 81279
E: enquiries@woodviewcottages.co.uk
I: www.woodviewcottages.co.uk

OLD BOLINGBROKE
Lincolnshire

1 Hope Cottage ★★★★
Contact: Mr & Mrs Taylor
Clowery Cottage, Craypool Lane, Scothern, Lincoln LN2 2UU
T: (01673) 861412
F: (01673) 863336
E: no1hopecottage@aol.com
I: www.no1hopecottage.co.uk

OLD BRAMPTON
Derbyshire

Chestnut Cottage and Willow Cottage ★★★★
Contact: Mr Jeffery & Mrs Patrica Green
Chestnut Cottage and Willow Cottage, Priestfield Grange, Hollins, Old Brampton, Chesterfield S42 7JH
T: (01246) 566159

OLD STRATFORD
Northamptonshire

33 and 35 Brookside Close ★★★
Contact: Mrs Hepher
The Old Bakery, 5 Main Street, Milton Keynes MK19 7JL
T: (01908) 562253
F: (01908) 562228
E: mksh@hepher.demon.co.uk
I: www.mksh.co.uk

OUNDLE
Northamptonshire

The Bolt Hole ★★★★
Contact: Mrs Anita Spurrell
Rose Cottage, 70 Glapthorne Road, Oundle, Peterborough PE8 4PT
T: (01832) 272298 & 07850 388109
E: nanda@spurrell.ocs-uk.com

13 Cotterstock Road ★★★
Contact: Mr & Mrs J S Czwortek
13 Cotterstock Road, Peterborough PE8 4PN
T: (01832) 273371

Oundle Cottage Breaks ★★★-★★★★★
Contact: Mr & Mrs Simmonds
Oundle Cottage Breaks, Market Place, Peterborough PE8 4BE
T: (01832) 273531
F: (01832) 274938
E: richard@simmondsatoundle.co.uk
I: www.oundlecottagebreaks.co.uk

OVER HADDON
Derbyshire

Burton Manor Barns ★★★★
Contact: Mr MacQueen
Peak Cottages, Strawberry Lee Lane, Totley Bents, Sheffield S17 3BA
T: (0114) 262 0777
F: (0114) 2620666

May Cottage ★★★★
Contact: Mrs Margaret Corbridge
Shutts Farm, Shutts Lane, Bakewell DE45 1JA
T: (01629) 813639

OXTON
Nottinghamshire

Wesley Farm Cottage ★★★★
Contact: Mr Des & Mrs Heather Palmer
Windmill Farm, Forest Road, Oxton, Southwell NG25 0SZ
T: (0115) 9652043
I: www.wesleycottage.com

PANTON
Lincolnshire

St Andrew's Church ★★★
Contact: Mrs J K Haller
St Andrew's Church, The Old Rectory, Market Rasen LN8 5LQ
T: (01673) 857302
E: janet_haller@hotmail.com
I: www.lincs-holiday.co.uk

PARWICH
Derbyshire

Brook Lodge ★★★★
Contact: Mr Colin MacQueen
Peak Cottages, Strawberry Lee Lane, Totley Bents, Sheffield S17 3BA
T: (0114) 262 0777
F: (0114) 2620666
E: enquiries@peakcottages.com
I: www.peakcottages.com

Church Gates Cottage ★★★
Contact: Mr MacQueen
Peak Cottages, Strawberry Lee Lane, Totley Bents, Sheffield S17 3BA
T: (0114) 262 0777
F: (0114) 2620666
E: enquiries@peakcottages.com
I: www.peakcottages.com

Croft Cottage ★★★★
Contact: Mrs Saskia Tallis
Croft Cottage, Creamery Lane, Ashbourne DE6 1QB
T: (01335) 390440
F: (01335) 390440
E: enquiries@croftcottage.co.uk
I: www.croftcottage.co.uk

EAST MIDLANDS

Curlew Wheatear and Redstart Cottages ★★★
Contact: Mr Colin McQueen
Peak Cottages, Paddock Cottage, Strawberry Lane, Totley Bents, Sheffield S17 3BA
T: (0114) 262 0777
F: (0114) 262 0666

Tom's Barn ★★★★★
Contact: Mr & Mrs J Fuller-Sessions
Tom's Barn, Orchard Farm, Parwich, Ashbourne DE6 1QB
T: (01335) 390519
E: tom@orchardfarm.demon.co.uk
I: www.tomsbarn.co.uk

PIKEHALL
Derbyshire

The Old Farmhouse and The Grange ★★★★
Contact: Mr & Mrs Mavin
The Old Farmhouse and The Grange, Roystone Grange, Matlock DE4 2PQ
T: (01335) 390382
I: www.roystonegrange.co.uk

PLUNGAR
Leicestershire

The Old Wharf ★★★★★
Contact: Mrs Elaine Pell
Grange Farm, Granby Lane, Nottingham NG13 0JJ
T: (01949) 860630
E: pellelaine@hotmail.com
I: www.oldwharf.com

POTTERHANWORTH
Lincolnshire

Skelghyll Cottage ★★★★
Contact: Mrs Hawes
Skelghyll Cottage, Moor Lane, Lincoln LN4 2DZ
T: (01522) 790043

QUARNFORD
Derbyshire

Black Clough Farmhouse ★★-★★★
Contact: Mrs Kate Farnworth
Black Clough Farmhouse, Buxton SK17 0TG
T: (01298) 23160
E: farnworth@totalise.co.uk
I: www.blackclough.co.uk

Colshaw Cottage ★★★
Contact:
Country Holidays ref: 5291 Sales, Holiday Cottages Group Limited, Spring Mill, Barnoldswick BB94 0AA
T: 08700 723723
F: (01282) 844288
E: sales@ttgihg.co.uk
I: www.country-holidays.co.uk

Greens Farm ★★★
Contact: Mrs Audrey Gould
Flash Head, Buxton SK17 0TE
T: (01298) 25172
E: skidd156@hotmail.com

New Colshaw Farm ★★★
Contact: Mr John Belfield
New Colshaw Farm, Hollinsclough, Buxton SK17 0SL
T: (01298) 73166

RANBY
Nottinghamshire

Spruce Cottage ★★★
Contact: Ms Penny Mason
58 Newbattle Terrace, Edinburgh EH10 4RX
T: (0131) 4476886
E: bpmason@blueyonder.co.uk

RETFORD
Nottinghamshire

Westhill Cottage ★★★
Contact: Mr David Hollingsworth
Westhill Farmhouse, Westhill Road, Retford DN22 7SH
T: (01777) 707034
E: dave@holly23.freeserve.co.uk
I: www.westhillcottage.mysite.freeserve.com

RIPLEY
Derbyshire

Heage Road Post Office ★★
Contact: Mr Graham Critchlow
Heage Road Post Office, 133 Heage Road, Ripley DE5 3GG
T: (01773) 743267
F: (01773) 743267
E: graham@dcritchlow.freeserve.co.uk

ROLLESTON
Nottinghamshire

Mill Cottage ★★★
Contact: Mrs Laura Murray
The Den Cottage, Main Street, Nottingham NG14 6AD
T: (0115) 9664015
E: laurajmurray@tiscali.co.uk
I: www.rollestonmill.co.uk

ROSTON
Derbyshire

Derbyshire Dales Holidays ★★★★
Contact: Mrs Beryl Wheeler
Derbyshire Dales Holidays, Town End Farm, Ashbourne DE6 2EH
T: (01335) 324062
F: (01335) 324062
E: wheelertef@supanet.com

ROWSLEY
Derbyshire

Bluebell Cottage ★★★★
Contact: Mrs Jane Henderson
67 Dalewood Avenue, Beauchief, Sheffield S8 0EG
T: (0114) 281 7217
F: (0114) 2817217
E: jane77@blueyonder.co.uk
I: www.bluebellcountrycottage.co.uk

RUSKINGTON
Lincolnshire

Orwell House Annex ★★★
Contact: Mrs Elizabeth Cartwright
Orwell House Annex, 67 Sleaford Road, Sleaford NG34 9BL
T: (01526) 834292
F: (01526) 830780
E: lelisian@aol.com

RUTLAND WATER
Rutland

Barn Owl House ★★★★★
Contact: Mr & Mrs Roger Page
33 Coniston Road, Oakham LE15 8HP
T: (01780) 720413
F: (01780) 720413

SELSTON
Nottinghamshire

Cottages in the Square ★★★-★★★★
Contact: Mr Keith Hill
Cottages in the Square, 62 Nottingham Road, Nottingham NG16 6DE
T: (01773) 812029
F: (01623) 559849
E: cottages2000@yahoo.com
I: www.cottages2000.com

Kinnaird ★★★
Contact: Mrs Karen Barton
10 Searwood Avenue, Nottingham NG17 8HL
T: (01623) 441278
F: (01623) 441278
E: karen.barton10@btopenworld.com

SHARDLOW
Derbyshire

The Old Workshop ★★★★
Contact: Mrs Hansen
24 Mill Green, The Wharf, Derby DE72 2WE
T: (01332) 799820
E: hansendorothy@hotmail.com

SHELDON
Derbyshire

Townend Cottage ★★★
Contact: Mrs Ethel Plumtree
Townend Cottage, Bakewell DE45 1QS
T: (01629) 813322

SHIRLEY
Derbyshire

Shirley Hall Farm ★★★
Contact: Mrs Sylvia Foster
Shirley Hall Farm, Ashbourne DE6 3AS
T: (01335) 360346
F: (01335) 360346
E: sylviafoster@shirleyhallfarm.com
I: shirleyhallfarm.com

SIBBERTOFT
Northamptonshire

Brook Meadow Holiday Chalets ★★★-★★★★
Contact: Mrs Mary Hart
Brook Meadow Holiday Chalets, The Wrongs, Welford Road, Market Harborough LE16 9UJ
T: (01858) 880886
F: (01858) 880485
E: brookmeadow@farmline.com
I: www.brookmeadow.com

SIBSEY
Lincolnshire

Sweetbriar ★★★
Contact: Mrs Alison Twiddy
Sweetbriar, Main Road, Boston PE22 0TT
T: (01205) 750837

SKEGNESS
Lincolnshire

Ingoldale Park ★★★★
Contact: Mrs Cathryn Whitehead
Ingoldale Park, Beach Estate, Skegness PE25 1LL
T: (01754) 872335
F: (01754) 873887
E: ingoldalepark@btopenworld.com
I: www.ingoldmells.net

Lyndene Holiday Apartments ★-★★★
Contact: Mr Bailey
11A St Margarets Avenue, Skegness PE25 2LX
T: (01754) 766108
E: info@lyndene-uk.com
I: www.lyndene-uk.com

Springfield & Island Holiday Apartments ★-★★★
Contact: Mr John & Mrs Carol Haines
Springfield & Island Holiday Apartments, 30-32 Scarborough Avenue, Skegness PE25 2TA
T: (01754) 762660
E: carol@springfield-island.fsnet.co.uk
I: www.skegness-resort.co.uk/springfield

SOUTH COCKERINGTON
Lincolnshire

West View Cottages ★★★
Contact: Mr Richard Nicholson and Mrs Judith Hand
West View, South View Lane, Louth LN11 7ED
T: (01507) 327209
E: richard@nicholson55.freeserve.co.uk

SOUTH LUFFENHAM
Rutland

Country View Holiday Home ★★★★
Contact: Mr Terry Langley
Hillberry, 6 Barrowden Lane, Oakham LE15 8NH
T: (01780) 721265

SOUTH WILLINGHAM
Lincolnshire

The Cottage ★★★★
Contact: Mrs Donocik
The Cottage, Church Farm, Station Road, Market Rasen LN8 6NJ
T: (01507) 313737

The Orchard Glasshouse ★★★★
Contact: Mrs Maureen Ferguson
The Orchard Glasshouse, The Old Rectory, Market Rasen LN8 6NG
T: (01507) 313584
F: 0870 1 916092
E: maureen.ferguson@uniquevenues.org.uk
I: www.uniquevenues.org.uk

Establishments printed in blue have a detailed entry in this guide

EAST MIDLANDS

SOUTHWELL
Nottinghamshire

The Hayloft and Little Tithe ★★★
Contact: Mrs Wilson
Lodge Farm, Morton, Southwell
NG25 0XH
T: (01636) 830497
I: www.lodgebarns.co.uk

The Nest ★★★★
Contact: Mrs Diana Dawes
The Nest, Cooks Lane, Morton-Cum-Fiskerton, Southwell
NG25 0XQ
T: (01636) 830140
E: rlgdawes@hotmail.com

SPARROWPIT
Derbyshire

Daisy Bank Cottage and Hope Cottage ★★★
Contact: Mrs Hilary Batterbee
Daisy Bank, Buxton SK17 8ET
T: (01298) 813027
F: (01298) 816012
E: batterbees@btopenworld.com
I: www.sparrowpit.com

Whitelee Cottage ★★★★
Contact: Mr Colin MacQueen
Peak Cottages, Strawberry Lee Lane, Totley Bents, Sheffield
S17 3BA
T: (0114) 262 0777
F: (0114) 2620666
E: enquiries@peakcottages.com
I: www.peakcottages.com

SPILSBY
Lincolnshire

Corner Farm Cottage ★★★
Contact: Mr Fitzpatrick
Corner Farm Cottage, Halton Holegate, Spilsby PE23
T: (01790) 753476
F: (01790) 752810
E: smrfitzp@ukonline.co.uk

Northfields Farm Cottages ★★★
Contact: Mr W P Miller
Northfields Farm Cottages, Spilsby PE23 4EW
T: (01507) 588251
F: (01507) 588251
E: chrismiller@tiscali.co.uk
I: www.northfieldsfarmcottages.co.uk

SPROXTON
Leicestershire

Appletree Cottage ★★★
Contact: Mrs Celia Slack
Appletree Cottage, The Green, 19 Main Street, Melton Mowbray
LE14 4QS
T: (01476) 860435
F: (01476) 860435
E: celia.slack@virgin.net

STAMFORD
Lincolnshire

Midstone House ★★★★
Contact: Mrs Anne Harrison-Smith
Midstone House, Stamford
PE9 3BX
T: (01780) 740136
F: (01780) 749294
E: midstonehouse@yahoo.co.uk
I: www.midstonehouse.com

STANLEY
Derbyshire

Yew Tree Farm ★★★★★
Contact: Mrs Gail Newman
Yew Tree Farm, Morley Lane, Stanley Village, Ilkeston DE7 6EZ
T: (0115) 932 9803
E: gailnewman@yewtreefarm94.freeserve.co.uk

STANTON-ON-THE-WOLDS
Nottinghamshire

Foxcote Cottage ★★★★
Contact: Mrs Joan Hinchley
Hill Farm (Foxcote), Melton Road, Stanton-on-the-Wolds, Keyworth NG12 5PJ
T: (0115) 937 4337
F: (0115) 937 4337

STATHERN
Leicestershire

Brambles Barn ★★★★
Contact: Mrs Newton
Brambles Barn, 6 Penn Lane, Melton Mowbray LE14 4JA
T: (01949) 860071
E: richard@bramblesbarn.co.uk
I: www.bramblesbarn.co.uk

Sycamore Farm ★★★★
Contact: Mrs Jean Stanley
New Farm, Waltham Road, Melton Mowbray LE14 4DB
T: (01949) 860640
F: (01949) 861165

STEWTON
Lincolnshire

Westfield Farm Cottages ★★★
Contact: Mr Darren Royle
Westfield Farm Cottages, Louth LN11 8SD
T: (01507) 607421
E: daz@thisvillage.com
I: www.thisvillage.com/westfield

STOKE BRUERNE
Northamptonshire

3 Canalside ★★★
Contact: Mr Trevor Morley
29 Main Road, Towcester
NN12 7RU
T: (01604) 862107
F: (01604) 864098
I: www.stokebruerneboats.co.uk

SUTTERTON
Lincolnshire

Somercotes ★★★
Contact: Dr Sharp
Irish Fail, Orchard Close, Wantage OX12 8JJ
T: (01235) 833367
F: (01235) 833367
E: j.v.sharp@btinternet.com
I: www.j.v.sharp.btinternet.co.uk/somercotes.htm

SUTTON-ON-SEA
Lincolnshire

Poplar Farm Holiday Cottages ★★★★
Contact: Mrs Helen Matthews
111 Rushmere Road, Ipswich
IP4 4LH
T: (01473) 711117
F: (01473) 711117
E: h-matthews@supanet.com
I: www.poplar-farm.co.uk

SUTTON ON THE HILL
Derbyshire

The Chop House and The Hay Loft ★★★★
Contact: Mr Keith & Mrs Joan Lennard
Windle Hill Farm, Ashbourne
DE6 5JH
T: (01283) 732377
F: (01283) 732377
E: windlehill@btinternet.com
I: www.windlehill.btinternet.co.uk

SUTTON ST JAMES
Lincolnshire

Foremans Bridge Caravan Park ★★★★
Contact: Mrs Ann Negus
Foreman's Bridge Caravan Park, Sutton Road, Spalding
PE12 0HU
T: (01945) 440346
F: (01945) 440346
I: www.foremans.bridge.co.uk

SWADLINCOTE
Derbyshire

Barne Cottage ★★★
Contact: Mrs M Fallon
Ivy Cottage, 96 Woodville Road, Hartshorne, Swadlincote
DE11 7EX
T: (01283) 221511
F: 0845 458 9632
E: mim@mims-holidaylets.co.uk
I: www.mims-holidaylets.co.uk

SWAYFIELD
Lincolnshire

Greystones Lodge ★★★★
Contact: Mrs Stanley
Greystones, Overgate Road, Grantham NG33 4LG
T: (01476) 550909
F: (01476) 550989
E: jslog@mcmail.com

5a High Street ★★★
Contact: Mrs Juliette Cooke
5a High Street, Grantham
NG33 4LL
T: (01476) 550120
F: (01476) 550120
E: jcooke@grantham.ac.uk

Woodview ★★★
Contact: Mrs Alison Bairsto
Woodview, c/o Lucklaw House, 13 Corby Road, Grantham
NG33 4LQ
T: (01476) 550097
E: bears178@aol.com

TADDINGTON
Derbyshire

Ash Barn ★★★
Contact: Ms Judith Hawley
Ash Barn, Main Street, Buxton
SK17 9UB
T: (01298) 85453
E: jah@ashtreebarn.fsnet.co.uk
I: www.cressbrook.co.uk/tidza/ashbarn/

Middle Farm Holiday Cottages ★★★★
Contact: Mr & Mrs Mullan
Middle Farm Holiday Cottages, Middle Farm, Brushfield, Buxton
SK17 9UQ
T: (01298) 85787
E: bmullan1@aol.com
I: www.cressbrook.co.uk/tidza/brushfield

TANSLEY
Derbyshire

Abbey Lane End House ★★★
Contact: Mr Dave Wilson
Abbey Lane End House, Green Lane, Matlock DE4 5FJ
T: (01629) 583981
E: dave@laneendhouse.co.uk
I: www.laneendhouse.co.uk

Acorn Place ★★★★
Contact: Mr & Mrs C Winder
Peak Cottages, Tawny, Alders Lane, Matlock DE4 5FB
T: (01629) 55330
I: www.peakcottages.com

Blakelow Cottages ★★★★
Contact: Mr Colin MacQueen
Peak Cottages, Strawberry Lee Lane, Totley Bents, Sheffield
S17 3BA
T: (0114) 262 0777
F: (0114) 2620666
E: enquiries@peakcottages.com
I: www.peakcottages.com

Lair Barn ★★★★★
Contact: Mrs Anne McLean
Roystone Lodge, Chesterfield Road, Matlock Moor, Matlock
DE4 5LZ
T: (01629) 580456
F: (01629) 580327
E: anne@pwltd.net

TEALBY
Lincolnshire

Field Cottage ★★
Contact: Mr R F Richardson
Greystone Cottage, Market Rasen LN8 3RJ
T: (01673) 838213
F: (01673) 838596
E: sanara@globalnet.co.uk

TEMPLE NORMANTON
Derbyshire

Rocklea Private House ★★★
Contact: Mr Roger & Mrs Tricia Stirling
8 Ranworth Road, Rotherham
S66 2SN
T: (01709) 543108

TETFORD
Lincolnshire

Grange Farm Cottages ★★★
Contact: Mr & Mrs Downes
Grange Farm, Horncastle
LN9 6QS
T: (01507) 534101
F: (01507) 534101
E: grangefarm@salmonby.wanadoo.co.uk

Little London Cottages ★★★★-★★★★★
Contact: Mrs Debbie Sutcliffe
The Mansion House, Little London, Horncastle LN9 6QL
T: (01507) 533697
E: debbie@sutclifell.freeserve.co.uk
I: www.littlelondoncottages.co.uk

532 Look out for establishments participating in the National Accessible Scheme

EAST MIDLANDS

Pine Lodge ★★★★
Contact: Mr Paddy Langdown
30 The Crescent, Canterbury
CT2 7AW
T: (01227) 454562
I: www.pinelodge-tetford.com

TETNEY
Lincolnshire

Beech Farm Cottages ★★★★
Contact: Mr & Mrs Smith
Beech Farm Cottages, Beech
Farm, Station Road, Grimsby
DN36 5HX
T: (01472) 815935
E: norman@beechfarm.fsworld.co.uk
I: www.beechfarmcottages.co.uk

THORGANBY
Lincolnshire

Little Walk Cottage
Rating Applied For
Contact: Mr James Milligan-Manby
Hall Farm Conservation,
Thorganby Hall, Grimsby
DN37 0SR
T: (01472) 398304
F: (01472) 398697
E: thorganby@lineone.net
I: www.littlewalkcottage.co.uk

THORPE
Derbyshire

Hawthorn Studio
Rating Applied For
Contact: Mrs Suzanne Walton
Hawthorn Cottage, Church Lane,
Ashbourne DE6 2AW
T: (01335) 350494

Paxtons Studio ★★★
Contact: Mrs Wilford
Paxtons Studio, Paxtons,
Ashbourne DE6 2AW
T: (01335) 350302
F: (01335) 350302
I: www.derbyshire-online.co.uk

THORPE WATERVILLE
Northamptonshire

The Loft ★★★★
Contact: Mrs Sue Goodall
Thorpe Castle House, Kettering
NN14 3ED
T: (01832) 720549
F: (01832) 720549
E: sugoodall@aol.com

TIDESWELL
Derbyshire

Geil Torrs ★★★
Contact: Ms Buttle
Geil Torrs, Buxton Road, Buxton
SK17 8QJ
T: (01298) 871302

Goldstraws ★★★
Contact: Mr & Mrs Sutherland
2 Curzon Terrace, Litton Mill,
Buxton SK17 8SR
T: (01298) 871100
F: (01298) 871641
E: eng@goldstrawshouse.co.uk
I: www.goldstrawshouse.co.uk

Lane End Cottage ★★★★
Contact: Mr John Snowden
6 Winterbank Close, Sutton in
Ashfield NG17 1LS
T: (01623) 557279

Markeygate Cottage and Barn ★★★★
Contact: Mrs Greening-James
Markeygate Cottage and Barn,
Markeygate House, Bank Square,
Buxton SK17 8NT
T: (01298) 871260
E: markeygatehouse@hotmail.com
I: www.markeygatecottages.co.uk

The Nook ★★★★
Contact:
Peak Cottages, Strawberry Lee
Lane, Totley Bents, Sheffield
S17 3BA
T: (0114) 262 0777
F: (0114) 2620666
E: enquiries@peakcottages.com
I: www.peakcottages.com

Stanley Barn ★★★
Contact: Ms Jean Hopkin
Stanley Barn, Stanley House,
Sherwood Road, Buxton
SK17 8HJ
T: (01298) 872327
E: jeanhopkin@aol.com

Stoneycroft ★★★★
Contact: Mr Clive Sykes
Sykes Cottages, York House,
York Street, Chester CH1 3LR
T: (01244) 345700
F: (01244) 321442
I: www.sykescottages.co.uk

TOWCESTER
Northamptonshire

Lodge Cottage ★★★★
Contact: Mrs June Webster
Slapton Lodge, Slapton,
Towcester NN12 8PE
T: (01327) 860221
E: cjpht@aol.com

TRUSTHORPE
Lincolnshire

The Old Garth Holiday Cottages ★★★
Contact: Mr Stephen Lewis
The Old Garth Holiday Cottages,
St Peters Lane, Mablethorpe
LN12 2PJ
T: (01507) 477380
F: (01507) 477807
E: shamrocnsy@aol.com
I: www.shamrocknurseries.co.uk

TWO DALES
Derbyshire

Piggery ★★★
Contact: Mr Colin MacQueen
Peak Cottages, Strawberry Lee
Lane, Totley Bents, Sheffield
S17 3BA
T: (0114) 262 0777
F: (0114) 2620666
E: enquiries@peakcottages.com
I: www.peakcottages.com

WADDINGWORTH
Lincolnshire

Redhouse Cottage ★★★★
Contact: Mr & Mrs Pritchard
Redhouse Farm, Waddingworth,
Woodhall Spa LN10 5EE
T: (01507) 578285
F: (01507) 578285

WARDLEY
Rutland

Pool House ★★★★
Contact: Mrs Ann Kanter
Pool House, Wardley House,
Oakham LE15 9AZ
T: (01527) 717671
F: (01527) 717401
E: annkanter@compuserve.com
I: www.wardleyhouse.com

WARMINGTON
Northamptonshire

Papley Farm Cottages ★★★★
Contact: Mrs Joyce Lane
Papley Farm Cottages, Slade
House, Papley Farm,
Peterborough PE8 6UU
T: (01832) 272583
F: (01832) 272583

WELBOURN
Lincolnshire

Well Cottage ★★★
Contact: Mrs Valerie Fischer
12 High Street, Lincoln LN5 0NH
T: (01400) 272976

WELLOW
Nottinghamshire

Foliat Cottages ★★★
Contact: Mr & Mrs Carr
Jordan Castle Farm, Newark
NG22 0EL
T: (01623) 861088
F: (01623) 861088
E: janet.carr@farmline.com
I: www.sherwoodforestholidaycottages.com

The White House and Studio ★★★
Contact: Mrs Angela Holding
Rose Cottage, Maypole Green,
Newark NG22 0FE
T: (01623) 835798
E: alan.holding@btinternet.com
I: www.whitehouseatwellow.co.uk

WELTON
Lincolnshire

Mill Cottage ★★★★
Contact: Mrs Gillian Gladwin
Mill House, Mill Lane, Lincoln
LN2 3PB
T: (01673) 860082
F: (01673) 863424
E: gill@millhousecottage.freeserve.co.uk
I: www.millcottageholidaylets.co.uk

WESTON UNDERWOOD
Derbyshire

Brook Cottage and Honeysuckle Cottage ★★★-★★★★★
Contact: Mrs Linda Adams
Parkview Farm, Ashbourne
DE6 4PA
T: (01335) 360352
F: (01335) 360352
E: enquires@parkviewfarm.co.uk
I: parkviewfarm.co.uk

WHALEY BRIDGE
Derbyshire

Cloud Cottage and Nimbus House ★★★★
Contact:
Country Holidays - 9405 Sales,
Spring Mill, Barnoldswick
BB94 0AA
T: 0870 0 723723
F: (01282) 844288
E: sales@ttgihg.co.uk
I: www.country-holidays.co.uk

Cote Bank Cottages ★★★★
Contact: Mrs Pamela Broadhurst
Cote Bank Cottages, Buxworth,
Whaley Bridge, High Peak
SK23 7NP
T: (01663) 750566
F: (01663) 750566
E: cotebank@btinternet.com
I: www.cotebank.co.uk

Horwich Barns ★★★★★
Contact: Mr Colin MacQueen
Peak Cottages, Strawberry Lee
Lane, Totley Bents, Sheffield
S17 3BA
T: (0114) 262 0777
F: (0114) 262 0666
I: www.peakcottages.com

WHATSTANDWELL
Derbyshire

Eden House and Eden Cottage ★★★★
Contact: Miss Louise Treanor
Eden House and Eden Cottage,
Main Road, Matlock DE4 5HE
T: (01773) 857143
F: (01773) 857143
E: louiset298@aol.com

Smithy Forge Cottages ★★★
Contact: Mr Chris Buxton
End Cottage, 32 Station Road,
Ripley DE5 8ND
T: (01332) 881758
F: (01332) 780232
E: chris@smithyforgecottages.co.uk
I: www.smithyforgecottages.co.uk

WHITTLEBURY
Northamptonshire

Dolly's Cottage ★★
Contact: Mrs Clapp
6 High Street, Towcester
NN12 8XJ
T: (01327) 857896
F: (01327) 857896
E: patcandalan@tesco.net

WINDLEY
Derbyshire

The Old Cheese Factory ★★★★★
Contact: Mrs Sally Wallwork
Belper DE56 2LP
T: (01773) 550947
F: (01773) 550944
E: sawallwork@aol.com
I: www.theoldcheesefactory.com

Establishments printed in blue have a detailed entry in this guide

EAST MIDLANDS

WINSTER
Derbyshire

Blakelow Farm Holiday Cottages ★★★★★
Contact: Mr Stephen Ogan
Blakelow Farm Holiday Cottages, Blakelow Farm, Bonsall Lane, Matlock DE4 2PD
T: (01629) 650814
F: (01629) 650814
E: blakelowfarm@aol.com
I: www.blakelowcottages.co.uk

Briar Cottage ★★★★
Contact: Mrs Anne Walters
Briar Cottage, Heathcote House, Main Street, Matlock DE4 2DJ
T: (01629) 650342

Gingerbread Cottage ★★★★
Contact: Mrs Jill Wild
September Cottage, East Bank, Matlock DE4 2DT
T: (01629) 650071
E: wildgray@hotmail.com
I: www.wildgray.fsnet.co.uk

The Headlands Fold ★★★
Contact: Mrs Janet Shiers
The Headlands Fold, The Headlands, East Bank, Matlock DE4 2DS
T: (01629) 650523
E: cottage@familyshier.org.uk
I: www.familyshier.org.uk

Jasmine Cottage ★★★★
Contact: Ms Ann Banister
Field Farm, Main Road, Matlock DE4 2LL
T: (01629) 732084
I: www.winster-cottages.co.uk

Rock Cottage ★★★★
Contact: Mr Christopher Higgs
Rock Cottage, West Bank, Matlock DE4 2DQ
T: (01629) 650020
F: (01629) 650488
E: info@peakrockcottages.co.uk
I: www.peakrockcottages.co.uk

WIRKSWORTH
Derbyshire

Hog Cottage ★★★★
Contact: Ms Anna Fern
Blue Lagoon, Po Box 294, Knutsford WA16 8YX
T: 0771 4 230118
F: 0845 2722444
E: hogcottage@bluelagoon.co.uk
I: www.bluelagoon.co.uk

Hopton Estates ★★★★-★★★★★
Contact: Mr Bill & Mrs Eddy Brogden
Hopton Estates, Hopton Hall, Hopton, Derby DE4 4DF
T: (01629) 540458
F: (01629) 540712
E: h.e@saqnet.co.uk
I: www.hoptonhall.co.uk

Snuffless Dip ★★★
Contact: Mrs Margaret Doxey
Chandlers, West End, Matlock DE4 4EG
T: (01629) 824466

Weathericks and Bradstone ★★★★
Contact: Mr MacQueen
Peak Cottages, Strawberry Lee Lane, Totley Bents, Sheffield S17 3BA
T: (0114) 262 0777
F: (0114) 2620666
E: enquiries@peakcottages.com
I: www.peakcottages.com

WITHERN
Lincolnshire

Park Farm Holidays ★★★
Contact: Mrs E H Burkitt
Park Farm Holidays, Aby Road, Withern, Alford LN13 0DF
T: (01507) 450331
F: (01507) 450331
E: alan@park-farm25.fsnet.co.uk

WOODHALL SPA
Lincolnshire

Cuckoo Land ★★★
Contact: Mr & Mrs Coates
16 The Broadway, Woodhall Spa LN10 6ST
T: (01526) 353336
E: cuckoo.land@ic24.net

Merrimoles ★★★
Contact: Mrs Margot Mills
The Vale, 50 Tor-O-Moor Road, Woodhall Spa LN10 6SB
T: (01526) 353022
E: thevale@amserve.net

Mill Lane Cottage ★★★
Contact: Mr Ian & Mrs Jane Williamson
72 Mill Lane, Horsington, Woodhall Spa LN10 6QZ
T: (01526) 353101
E: janewill89@hotmail.com
I: www.skegness.net/woodhallspa.htm

Old Forge Cottage ★★★★
Contact: Mr David Mawer
47 Witham Road, Woodhall Spa LN10 6RG
T: (01526) 353813
F: (01526) 353996
E: tanyamawer@hotmail.com
I: www.oldforgecottage.co.uk

YARDLEY GOBION
Northamptonshire

The Stable ★★
Contact: Mr Alan Paine
Old Wharf Farm, The Wharf, Towcester NN12 7UE
T: (01908) 542293
F: (01908) 542293

YELDERSLEY
Derbyshire

Ladyhole House - The Old Stables ★★★★★
Contact: Mrs Rosamond Woodrow
The Old Stables, Ladyhole House, Ashbourne DE6 1LR
T: (01335) 342670
F: (01335) 300320
E: rosamondwoodrow@boltblue.com
I: www.ladyholehouseholidays.co.uk

YOULGREAVE
Derbyshire

April Cottage ★★★
Contact: Mrs Lisa Lovell
Christmas Cottage, Church Street, Youlgreave, Bakewell DE45 1WL
T: (01629) 636151
F: (01629) 636151
E: l.lovell@whitepeakcottage.co.uk
I: www.whitepeakcottage.co.uk

Braemar Cottage ★★★★
Contact: Mrs Irene Shimwell
Crimble House, Main Street, Youlgrave, Nr Bakewell DE45 1UW
T: (01629) 636568 & 07929 396525
E: braemarcottage@fsmail.net
I: www.braemarcottage.co.uk

The Cottage ★★★★
Contact: Mr John & Mrs Carol Sutcliffe
The Old School House, Main Street, Youlgreave, Bakewell DE45 1UW
T: (01629) 636570
E: carolandjohn@coalmoor.fsnet.co.uk
I: www.thecottage-crimbleslane.co.uk

Knoll Cottage ★★★
Contact: Mr Colin MacQueen
Peak Cottages, Strawberry Lee Lane, Totley Bents, Sheffield S17 3BA
T: (0114) 262 0777
F: (0115) 2620666
E: enquiries@peakcottages.com
I: www.peakcottages.com

The Old Dairy & Buttermilk Cottage ★★★
Contact: Mrs Twose
Manor Cottage, Healaugh Manor Farm, Wighill Lane, Tadcaster LS24 8HG
T: 07798 830467
I: www.peakcottages.com

The Old Grocers Shop ★★★★
Contact: Mr Colin MacQueen
Peak Cottages, Strawberry Lee Lane, Totley Bents, Sheffield S17 3BA
T: (0114) 262 0777
F: (0114) 2620666
E: enquiries@peakcottages.com
I: www.peakcottages.com

Rose Cottages ★★★★
Contact: Mr John & Mrs Carol Upton
Rose Cottages, Copper Pot, Conksbury Lane, Youlgrave, Bakewell DE45 1WR
T: (01629) 636487
E: enquiries@rosecottages.co.uk
I: www.rosecottages.co.uk

Sunnydale ★★★★
Contact: Mrs June Marie Bradley
Sunnydale, Bank Top, Youlgrave, Bakewell DE45 1UZ
T: (01246) 558199
F: (01246) 558199
E: marie@birdholme.freeserve.co.uk
I: www.bradleysholidaycottages.co.uk

Sunnyside ★★★
Contact: Ms J Steed
Falkland House, 10 New Road, Bakewell DE45 1WP
T: (01629) 636195

Thyme Cottage ★★★★
Contact: Mrs H Mason
Riversley, Cunningham Place, Bakewell DE45 1DD
T: (01629) 813442
F: (01629) 815176
E: helenm@masonandco.co.uk

EAST OF ENGLAND

ACLE
Norfolk

Station Cottage ★★★★
Contact: Mrs Deborah Mann
Station Cottage, Station Road, Norwich NR13 3BZ
T: (01493) 751136
F: (01493) 752930
E: obmc@clara.net
I: www.uk-holiday-cottages.co.uk/station

ALDBOROUGH
Norfolk

Waverley ★★★
Contact: Mr Colin Skipper
Doctor's Corner, Norwich NR11 7NR
T: (01263) 761512

ALDBURY
Hertfordshire

Aldbury Cottage ★★★★
Contact: Mrs Pamela Dickens
Red Barn Farm, Tythe Close, Leighton Buzzard LU7 0HD
T: (01525) 242253
F: (01525) 242254
E: pam@dickens1.com
I: www.aldburycottage.co.uk

ALDEBURGH
Suffolk

Aldeburgh Court House & Aldeburgh Court The Cottage ★★★-★★★★
Contact: Mrs Susie Hayward
Poplar Farm Barn, Saxmundham IP17 2BW
T: (01728) 664014
E: susie@thefountain.co.uk

EAST OF ENGLAND

29 Aldeburgh Lodge ★★★
Contact: Ms Francoise Cresson
Hillsfoot Cottage, Eastridge Nr
Leiston, Leiston IP16 4SG
T: (01728) 830499

Amber Cottage & Crabbe Cottage ★★★-★★★★
Contact: Mr Roger Williams
The Court House, Tostock Place,
Church Road, Bury St Edmunds
IP30 9PG
T: (01359) 270444
F: (01359) 271226
E: roger.williams43@virgin.net
I: www.cottageguide.
co.uk/ambercottage

Avalon ★★★★
Contact:
Avalon, 63 King Street,
Aldeburgh IP15 5DA
T: (01379) 651297
I: www.suffolk-secrets.co.uk

Avon Cottage ★★★
Contact:
Suffolk Secrets, 7 Frenze Road,
Diss IP22 4PA
T: (01379) 651297
F: (01379) 641555
E: holidays@suffolk-secrets.
co.uk
I: www.suffolk-secrets.co.uk

Braid House ★★★
Contact: Miss Ying Tan
Yew Tree Farm, Saxmundham
IP17 2BU
T: (01728) 663432
F: (01728) 663532
E: tonying4488@aol.com

Bramcote ★★★
Contact: Mrs Diana Biddlecombe
1 Barley Lands, Aldeburgh
IP15 5LW
T: 0781 7 724643

15 Britten Close ★★★★
Contact: Mrs Heather Hunting
Saffron House, Aldeburgh
IP15 5LW
T: (01728) 454716
F: (01728) 454716
E: david@hunting6166.
freeserve.co.uk

8 Coastguard Court ★★★
Contact: Mr & Mrs John Mauger
Mount Pleasant Farmhouse,
Beccles NR34 8LU
T: (01502) 575896
F: (01502) 575896
E: john.mauger@blythweb.net
I: www.blythweb.
co.uk/coastguard-court

Cosy Corner ★★★
Contact: Mrs Fryer
Cosy Corner, 41 Mariners Way,
Aldeburgh IP15 5QH
T: (01728) 453121

The Cottage ★★★
Contact: Mr Alexander
The Old Rectory, Old Church
Road, Woodbridge IP13 6DH
T: (01394) 383822

21 Crag Path ★★★
Contact: Ms Lisabeth Hoad
5 King Street, Aldeburgh
IP15 5BY
T: (01728) 453933

Cragside ★★★★
Contact: Mrs Lesley Valentine
Rookery Farm, Cratfield,
Halesworth IP19 0QE
T: (01986) 798609
F: (01986) 798609
E: j.r.valentine@btinternet.com

Deben House ★★★★
Contact: Mrs Linda Price
52 Churchgate Street, Bury St
Edmunds IP33 1RH
T: (01284) 704780
E: pjlp@lineone.net

Dial Flat ★
Contact: Mrs Pam Harrison
Dial House, 5 Dial Lane,
Aldeburgh IP15 5AG
T: (01728) 453212
E: pam@harpd.freeserve.co.uk

The Dutch House Flat ★★★
Contact: Mr Christopher Bacon
Dodnash Priory Farm, Hazel
Shrub, Ipswich IP9 2DF
T: (01473) 310682
T: (01473) 311131
E: cbacon@freeuk.com

Fig Tree ★★★
Contact: Mr & Mrs Martin Jinks
94 Leiston Road, Aldeburgh
IP15 5PX
T: (01728) 453037
E: martin@jinsky.fsnet.co.uk

Hall Cottage ★★★★
Contact: Ms Buchanan
Loomsachool Farm, Woodbridge
IP13 6JW
T: (01473) 735456
T: (01473) 738887
E: miriam@greenlabel.co.uk
I: www.loomscottage.co.uk

290 High Street ★★★
Contact: Mr & Mrs Martin Jinks
94 Leiston Road, Aldeburgh
IP15 5PX
T: (01728) 453037
E: martin@jinksy.fsnet.co.uk

65 High Street ★★★★
Contact: Mr Richard Pither
Suffolk Secrets, / Frenze Road,
Diss IP22 4PA
T: (01379) 651297
F: (01379) 641555
I: www.suffolk-secrets.co.uk

Kingfisher & Swallow Cottages
Rating Applied For
Contact: Mr Robert Barr
Kingfisher & Swallow Cottages,
Manor Farm, Grove Road,
Saxmundham IP17 1TZ
T: (01728) 603196
T: (01728) 603196
E: manorfarmcottages@
hotmail.com

38 Lee Road ★★★★
Contact: Mrs Elizabeth Wagener
Cox Hill House, Cox Hill, Sudbury
CO10 5JG
T: (01787) 210223
E: lizwagener@aol.com

Magenta ★★★
Contact: Mr & Mrs Martin Jinks
94 Leiston Road, Aldeburgh
IP15 5PX
T: (01728) 453037
E: martin@jinksy.fsnet.co.uk

11B Market Cross Place ★★★
Contact: Mr Robert Prince
49 Park Road, Aldeburgh
IP15 5EN
T: (01728) 453659
E: robert@princebob.fsnet.co.uk

Mermaid Cottage ★★★★
Contact: Mrs Jacqueline Collier
Clopton Hall, Woodbridge
IP13 6QB
T: (01473) 735004

No 38 Aldeburgh Lodge ★★★
Contact: Mrs Carole Morley
No 38 Aldeburgh Lodge, St
Peters Road, Aldeburgh
IP15 5DF
T: (01728) 687999
F: (01728) 687999

Orlando ★★★
Contact: Mr Peter Hatcher
Martlesham Hall, Church Lane,
Woodbridge IP12 4PQ
T: (01394) 382126
F: (01394) 278600
E: orlando@hatcher.co.uk
I: www.hatcher.co.uk/orlando

Parklands ★★★★★
Contact: Mrs Sandra Allen
Garden Suite, 6 Aldringham
House, Leiston Road, Leiston
IP16 4PT
T: (01728) 830139
F: (01728) 831034
E: aldribghamhouse@aol.com

The Peach House ★★★★
Contact: Mrs J Alexander
The Old Rectory, Old Church
Road, Woodbridge IP13 6DH
T: (01394) 383822
F: (01394) 383822
E: jmalexander@onetel.net.uk

Regatta Apartment
Rating Applied For
Contact: Mrs Johanna Mabey
Regatta Apartment, 171-173
High Street, Aldeburgh IP15 5AN
T: (01728) 454417
F: (01728) 453324
E: regatta.restaurant@
aldeburgh.sagehost.co.uk
I: www.regattaaldeburgh.com

River Cottage ★★★★★
Contact: Kate Kilburn
River Cottage, Iken Cliff,
Woodbridge IP12 2EN
T: (01728) 688267
F: (01728) 688267
E: dkilburn@cmpinformation.
com

Suffolk House ★★★
Contact: Mr Tim Connolly
Reynard House, Castlefield
Road, Reigate RH2 0SA
T: (01737) 230734
F: (01737) 230701
E: timconnolly@ugly-duckling.
net
I: www.
suffolk-house-aldeburgh.co.uk

ALRESFORD
Essex

Creek Lodge ★★★
Contact: Mrs Patricia Mountney
Ford Lane, Colchester CO7 8BE
T: (01206) 825411

ASHDON
Essex

Whitensmere Farm Cottages ★★★★-★★★★★
Contact: Mrs Susan Ford
Whitensmere Farm, Saffron
Walden CB10 2JQ
T: (01799) 584244
F: (01799) 584244
E: gford@lineone.net
I: www.
holidaycottagescambridge.co.uk

AYLMERTON
Norfolk

Moorland Park ★★★
Contact: Mrs Elaine Field
Moorland Park, Holt Road,
Norwich NR11 8QA
T: (01263) 837508
F: (01263) 837508
E: moorlandpark@fsmail.net
I: www.moorlandpark.co.uk

Rodavia ★★★★
Contact: Mr David & Mrs
Rosemary Wilson
Rodavia, Church Road, Norwich
NR11 8PZ
T: (01263) 837338
E: rodavia@hotmail.com
I: www.villarodavia.co.uk

Thyme Untied ★★★
Contact: Mr Tony Mackay
70 Cromer Road, Sheringham
NR26 8RT
T: (01263) 824955
F: (01263) 824955
E: tonyandpat@pinecones.fsnet.
co.uk

AYLSHAM
Norfolk

Bay Cottage ★★★★
Contact: Mr Stuart Clarke
Bay Cottage, Colby Corner,
Colby, Norwich NR11 7EB
T: (01263) 734574
F: (01263) 734574
E: jsclarke@colbycorner.fsnet.
co.uk
I: www.cottagesdirect.com

Holly Cottage ★★★
Contact: Mr & Mrs Burr
Holly Cottage, Burgh House,
Burgh Road, Norwich NR11 6AT
T: (01263) 733567

The Old Windmill ★★★★★
Contact: Mr & Mrs Tim Bower
The Old Windmill, Cawston
Road, Norwich NR11 6NB
T: (01263) 732118
E: timatmill@aol.com
I: www.aylshamwindmill.co.uk

BABRAHAM
Cambridgeshire

Brick Row Cottage ★★★★
Contact: Mr & Mrs Ian Kime
25 Brick Row, Cambridge
CB2 4AJ
T: (01223) 836045
E: ian@brickrowcottage.co.uk
I: www.brickrowcottage.co.uk

Establishments printed in blue have a detailed entry in this guide

EAST OF ENGLAND

The Granary ★★★
Contact: Mrs Gill Kotschy
The Granary, Chalk Farm, High Street, Cambridge CB2 4AG
T: (01223) 837783
F: (01223) 834113
E: kotschy@dial.pipex.com
I: www.granaryvisit.co.uk

BACTON
Norfolk
Swiss Cottage ★★★★
Contact: Mrs Linda Weinberg
Buehl Str 6, 8113 Boppelsen, Switzerland
T: 00 41 1844 2222
F: 00 41 1840 0222
E: info@swissonthebeach.com
I: www.swissonthebeach.com

BADINGHAM
Suffolk
The Nest ★★★
Contact: Mrs Susan Long
Wood Farm, Saxmundham IP17 2EZ
T: (01728) 660360
F: (01728) 660131

BALE
Norfolk
Chapel Field Cottage ★★★
Contact: Mrs Judith Everitt
Wheelcroft, Field Dalling Road, Fakenham NR21 0QS
T: (01328) 878419

BALSHAM
Cambridgeshire
Grannies Bungalow ★★★
Contact: Mrs Anne Kiddy
Grannies Bungalow, Lower Farm, Cambridge CB1 6EP
T: (01223) 893010

BANHAM
Norfolk
Olde Farm Cottage ★★★
Contact: Mrs Kathleen Girling
Olde Farm, New Buckenham Road, Norwich NR16 2DA
T: (01953) 860023
E: kathygirling@aol.com
I: www.banhamandthebucks.co.uk/oldefarm

BANNINGHAM
Norfolk
Bridge Bungalow ★★★★
Contact: Mrs Gail Armstrong
Norfolk Country Cottages, Carlton House, Market Place, Norwich NR10 4JJ
T: (01603) 871872
F: (01603) 870304
E: info@norfolkcottages.co.uk
I: www.norfolkcottages.co.uk

BARDWELL
Suffolk
Holly House ★★★★
Contact: Mrs Susette Bone
Holly House, The Green, Bury St Edmunds IP31 1AW
T: (01359) 250804
I: www.tel.w.com

BARNEY
Norfolk
The Stables ★★★
Contact: Mrs Christine Blackman
London House, The Street, Fakenham NR21 0AD
T: (01328) 878204

BAWDESWELL
Norfolk
Jotts Cottage ★★★★
Contact: Mrs Sue Clarke
Jasmine House, Dereham Road, Bawdeswell, Dereham NR20 4AA
T: (01362) 688444
F: (01362) 688444
E: clarkes.jasmine@virgin.net

BAWDSEY
Suffolk
Bawdsey Manor
★★★-★★★★
Contact: Mrs A Toettcher
Bawdsey Manor, Woodbridge IP12 3AZ
T: (01394) 411633
F: (01394) 410417
E: info@bawdseymanor.co.uk
I: www.bawdseymanor.co.uk

BAYLHAM
Suffolk
Baylham House Annexe & Baylham House Flat ★★★
Contact: Mrs Ann Storer
Baylham House Farm, Mill Lane, Ipswich IP6 8LG
T: (01473) 830264
F: (01473) 830264
E: ann@baylham-house-farm.co.uk
I: www.baylham-house-farm.co.uk

BEACHAMWELL
Norfolk
Carole Wilsons Rectory Holidays ★★★
Contact: Mrs Carole Wilson
Carole Wilsons Rectory Holidays, Old Hall Lane, Swaffham PE37 8BA
T: (01366) 328628
E: wilson@rectoryholidays.com
I: www.rectoryholidays.com

BECCLES
Suffolk
Redisham Hall ★★★★
Contact: Agent
Country Holidays, Spring Mill, Barnoldswick BB94 0AA
T: 0870 0 723723
I: www.country-holidays.co.uk

BEDFORD
Bedfordshire
The Dovecote ★★★★
Contact: Mrs Rosalind Northern
The Dovecote, Priory Farm, High Street, Bedford MK43 7EE
T: (01234) 720293
F: (01234) 720292
E: ros.northern@farmline.com
I: www.harroldholidays.com

BEESTON
Norfolk
Holmdene Farm ★★★
Contact: Mrs Davidson
Holmdene Farm, Syers Lane, King's Lynn PE32 2NJ
T: (01328) 701284
E: holmdenefarm@farmersweekly.net
I: www.northnorfolk.co.uk/holmdenefarm

BELCHAMP ST PAUL
Essex
Colefair Cottage ★★★★
Contact: Mr & Mrs John Doggett
Halycon Cottages, 25 Estuary Drive, Felixstowe IP11 9TL
T: (01394) 276590
E: halcyon.cottages@btinternet.com
I: www.colefaircottage.co.uk

BERKHAMSTED
Hertfordshire
Holly Tree & Jack's Cottage
★★★
Contact: Mrs Barrington
20 & 21 Ringshall, Berkhamsted HP4 1ND
T: (01442) 843464
F: (01442) 842051

Walnut Cottage ★★★★
Contact: Mrs Alison Knowles
Broadway Farm, Berkhamsted HP4 2RR
T: (01442) 866541
F: (01442) 866541
E: aknowles@broadway.nildram.co.uk
I: www.SmoothHound.co.uk/hotels/broad.html

BEYTON
Suffolk
Manorflat ★★★★
Contact: Mr Kay & Mrs Mark Dewsbury
Manorhouse, The Green, Bury St Edmunds IP30 9AF
T: (01359) 270960
E: manorhouse@beyton.com
I: www.beyton.com

BILDESTON
Suffolk
Christmas Hall & The Coach House ★★★★
Contact: Mrs Christina Hawkins
Christmas Hall & The Coach House, Market Place, Ipswich IP7 7EN
T: (01449) 741428
F: (01449) 744161
E: christmas.hall@macunlimited.net
I: www.christmashall.co.uk

Minto Cottage ★★★★
Contact: Mr & Mrs Andy Cox
Minto House, 74 High Street, Ipswich IP7 7EA
T: (01449) 744988
F: (01449) 740086
E: andycox@eidosnet.co.uk
I: www.mintoholidays.co.uk

BILLERICAY
Essex
The Pump House Apartment ★★★★★
Contact: Mr John Bayliss
Pump House, Church Street, Great Burstead, Billericay CM11 2TR
T: (01277) 656579
F: (01277) 631160
E: johnwbayliss@btinternet.com
I: www.thepumphouseapartment.co.uk

BINHAM
Norfolk
The Barn ★★★★
Contact: Mrs Gail Armstrong
Norfolk Country Cottages, Carlton House, Market Place, Norwich NR10 4JJ
T: (01603) 871872
F: (01603) 870304
E: info@norfolkcottages.co.uk

Betty's Cottage & Bob's Cottage ★★★★
Contact: Ms Fiona Thompson
Betty's Cottage & Bob's Cottage, Field House, Walsingham Road, Fakenham NR21 0BU
T: (01328) 830639

Fairfield Cottage ★★★
Contact: Mrs Sheila Thornton
Apple Acre, Bleasby Road, Nottingham NG14 7FW
T: (01636) 830395
F: (0115) 9878011

BLAKENEY
Norfolk
The Friary ★★★
Contact: Mrs Cooke
31 Bracondale, Norwich NR1 2AT
T: (01603) 624827
E: cookehd@paston.co.uk
I: www.blakeney-friary.co.uk

51 High Street ★★
Contact: Mrs G Armstrong
Norfolk Country Cottages Ref. 674, Market Place, Norwich NR10 4JJ
T: (01603) 871872
F: (01603) 870304
E: info@norfolkcottages.co.uk
I: www.norfolkcottages.co.uk/blakeney_674.htm

Pimpernel Cottage ★★
Contact: Mrs G Armstrong
Norfolk Country Cottages Ref. 680, Market Place, Norwich NR10 4JJ
T: (01603) 871872
F: (01603) 870304
E: info@norfolkcottages.co.uk
I: www.norfolkcottages.co.uk/blakeney_680.htm

Quayside Cottages
★★-★★★★★
Contact: Mrs Alvarez
New Wellbury Farmhouse, Wellbury Park, Hitchin SG5 3BP
T: (01462) 768627
F: (01462) 768320
E: veronicaAlvarez@compuserve.com
I: www.blakeneycottages.co.uk

Roslyn ★★
Contact: Mrs Brenda Eke
Bermuda House, 169 Fakenham Road, Melton Constable NR24 2DN
T: (01263) 860111

EAST OF ENGLAND

Seagulls ★★★★
Contact: Holiday Cottages
Ref: CEU, Holiday Cottages Group, Spring Mill, Barnoldswick BB94 0AA
T: 0870 0 723723
F: (01282) 844288
E: sales@holidaycottagesgroup.com
I: www.english-country-cottages.co.uk

The Tanning House ★★★
Contact: Mrs Brigid Pope
The Lodge, Back Lane, Blakeney, Holt NR25 7NR
T: (01263) 740477
F: (01263) 741356
E: enquiries@marinershillcottages.com
I: www.marinershillcottages.com

Wren Cottage ★★★★
Contact: Mr & Mrs Ian Mashiter
11 Branksome Close, Norwich NR4 6SP
T: (01603) 457560
E: cleycottage@aol.com
I: www.internet-cottages.com

BLAXHALL
Suffolk

Willows ★★
Contact: Mrs Elizabeth Simmonds
54 St Augustines Road, Bedford MK40 2NA
T: (01234) 214686
E: liz@simmonds1941.freeserve.co.uk

BOURN
Cambridgeshire

Bay Tree Cottage
Rating Applied For
Contact: Mrs Caroline Botha
C J Botha Rental, 1 Riddy Lane, Cambridge CB3 7SP
T: (01954) 718428
F: (01954) 718428
E: baytree@bothas.co.uk
I: www.bothas.co.uk/rental-baytree.htm

BRAINTREE
Essex

1 Red Lion Cottages ★★
Contact: Mrs Moran McKellar Ratcliffe
1 Red Lion Cottages, Lanham Green Road, Braintree CM77 8DR
T: (01376) 584043
F: (01376) 584043
E: moran.ratcliffe@btconnect.com
I: www.stilwell.co.uk

BRAMFIELD
Suffolk

Japonica House ★★★
Contact:
Suffolk Secrets, 7 Frenze Road, Diss IP22 4PA
T: (01379) 651297
F: (01379) 641555
E: holidays@suffolk-secrets.co.uk
I: www.suffolk-secrets.co.uk

BRANCASTER
Norfolk

11 Anchorage View ★★★
Contact: Mrs Sandra Hohol
Birds Norfolk Holiday Homes, 62 Westgate, Hunstanton PE36 5EL
T: (01485) 534267
F: (01485) 535230
E: shohol@birdsnorfolkholidayhomes.co.uk
I: www.norfolkholidayhomes-birds.co.uk

Dunlin ★★
Contact: Mrs Sandra Hohol
Birds Norfolk Holiday Homes, 62 Westgate, Hunstanton PE36 5EL
T: (01485) 534267
F: (01485) 535230
E: shohol@birdsnorfolkholidayhomes.co.uk
I: www.norfolkholidayhomes-birds.co.uk

36 Mill Hill ★★★★
Contact: Mrs Susanne Chalcraft
The Malthouse, 39 London Street, Swaffham PE37 7DD
T: (01760) 724805
F: (01760) 720658
E: su.craft@virgin.net

The Old Stores ★★★
Contact: Mrs Gail Armstrong
Norfolk Country Cottages, Carlton House, Market Place, Norwich NR10 4JJ
T: (01603) 871872
F: (01603) 870304
E: info@norfolkcottages.co.uk
I: www.norfolkcottages.co.uk

Plunketts Cottage ★★★★
Contact: Mr Simon Barclay
Kett Country Cottages, 8 Oak Street, Fakenham NR21 9DY
T: (01328) 856853
F: (01328) 853903
E: info@kettcountrycottages.co.uk

Russett Lodge ★★★
Contact: Mrs Sandra Hohol
Norfolk Holiday Homes, 62 Westgate, Hunstanton PE36 5EL
T: (01485) 534267
F: (01485) 535230
E: shohol@birdsnorfolkholidayhomes.co.uk
I: www.norfolkholidayhomes-birds.co.uk

The Stalls ★★★
Contact: Mrs Judith Rippon
The Stalls, The Old Stables, Broad Lane, King's Lynn PE31 8AU
T: (01485) 210774
F: (01485) 210774
E: judyrippon@theoldstables123.fslife.co.uk
I: www.norfolk-holiday-cottages.co.uk

Stubton Cottage ★★★★
Contact: Mrs Sandra Hohol
Birds Norfolk Holiday Homes, 62 Westgate, Hunstanton PE36 5EL
T: (01485) 534267
F: (01485) 535230
E: shohol@birdsnorfolkholidayhomes.co.uk
I: www.norfolkholidayhomes-birds.co.uk

Thompson Brancaster Farms ★★★
Contact: Mrs Sue Lane
4 Stiffkey Road, Wells-next-the-Sea NR23 1NP
F: (01328) 710144
E: info@tbfholidaycottages.co.uk
I: www.tbfholidaycottages.co.uk

Whiteacres ★★★
Contact: Mr Simon Barclay
Kett Country Cottages, 8 Oak Street, Fakenham NR21 9DY
T: (01328) 856853
F: (01328) 853903
E: info@kettcountrycottages.co.uk
I: www.kettcountrycottages.co.uk

BRANCASTER STAITHE
Norfolk

21 Dale End ★★★★
Contact: Mrs Debbie Clark
Stone House, 19 Main Street, Oakham LE15 9HU
T: (01572) 747389
F: (01572) 747693
E: debbieclark@btopenworld.com
I: www.debbieclarklettings.com

Island Cottage ★
Contact: Mrs Sandra Hohol
Birds Norfolk Holiday Homes, 62 Westgate, Hunstanton PE36 5EL
T: (01485) 534267
F: (01485) 535230
E: shohol@birdsnorfolkholidayhomes.co.uk
I: www.norfolkholidayhomes-birds.co.uk

Oak Cottage ★★★★★
Contact: Mrs Sue Ormiston
Ashbee House, King's Lynn PE31 6HA
T: (01485) 543218
F: (01485) 540969
E: sue@ormiston4.freeserve.co.uk

Vista & Carpenters Cottages ★★★
Contact: Mrs Gloria Smith
Dale View, Main Road, Brancaster Staithe, King's Lynn PE31 8BY
T: (01485) 210497
F: (01485) 210497

Westbourne ★★★
Contact: Mrs Sandra Hohol
Norfolk Holiday Homes, 62 Westgate, Hunstanton PE36 5EL
T: (01485) 534267
F: (01485) 535230
E: shohol@birdsnorfolkholidayhomes.co.uk
I: www.norfolkholidayhomes-birds.co.uk

BRANDON
Suffolk

Deacons Cottage ★★
Contact: Mrs Deacon
Deacons Cottage, South Street, Thetford IP26 4JG
T: (01842) 828023

BRANTHAM
Suffolk

Brantham Hall ★★★★
Contact: Ms Caroline Williams
Brantham Lodge, Brantham, Manningtree CO11 1PT
T: (01473) 327090
F: (01473) 327090
E: hwilliams@branmann.freeserve.co.uk

BRAUGHING
Hertfordshire

Edwinstree Chapel ★★★★
Contact: Mrs Pamela Bradley
Edwinstree Chapel, Edwinstree, Dassels, Ware SG11 2RR
T: (01763) 289509
E: edwinstree@tesco.net
I: www.Edwinstree.com

BRININGHAM
Norfolk

Moriah Cottage ★★★★
Contact: Mrs Gail Armstrong
Norfolk Country Cottages Ref. 139, Market Place, Norwich NR10 4JJ
T: (01603) 871872
F: (01603) 870304
E: info@norfolkcottages.co.uk
I: www.norfolkcottages.co.uk

Old White Horse Cottage ★★★
Contact: Mr Simon Barclay
Kett Country Cottages, 8 Oak Street, Fakenham NR21 9DY
T: (01328) 856853
F: (01328) 853903
E: info@kettcountrycottages.co.uk
I: www.kettcountrycottages.co.uk

BRISLEY
Norfolk

Church Farm Cottages & Pond Farm Studio ★★★-★★★
Contact: Mrs G.V Howes
Church Farm Cottages & Pond Farm Studio, The Green, Brisley, Dereham NR20 5LL
T: (01362) 668332
F: (01362) 668332

Mill Farm Barn ★★★★
Contact:
Norfolk Country Cottages, Carlton House, Market Place, Norwich NR10 4JJ
T: (01603) 871872
F: (01603) 870304
E: info@norfolkcottages.co.uk
I: www.norfolkcottages.co.uk

Establishments printed in blue have a detailed entry in this guide

EAST OF ENGLAND

BRISTON
Norfolk

The Bolthole ★★★★
Contact: Mr Keith Richmond
286 Ordnance Road, Enfield
EN3 6HF
T: (020) 88072664
F: (020) 88078877
E: k.richmond@st-edmunds.enfield.sch.uk

45 Chequers Close ★★★
Contact: Mrs Gail Armstrong
Norfolk Country Cottages,
Carlton House, Market Place,
Norwich NR10 4JJ
T: (01603) 871872
F: (01603) 870304
E: info@norfolkcottages.co.uk
I: www.norfolkcottages.co.uk

BROME
Suffolk

The Homestead Barn ★★★★
Contact: Mr David & Mrs Diana Downes
The Homestead Barn, The Homestead, Brome, Eye
IP23 8AE
T: (01379) 870489
E: www.dianadownes@hotmail.com

BRUISYARD
Suffolk

Bruisyard Hall ★★★★
Contact: Mr Robert Rous
The Country House, Dennington,
Woodbridge IP13 8AU
T: (01728) 638712
F: (01728) 638712
E: dennington@farmline.com
I: www.bruisyardhall.co.uk

Shelley Lodge ★★★
Contact: Mrs Kathleen Bowman
Shelley Lodge, Saxmundham
IP17 2HB
T: (01728) 660312
E: bowmankmg@aol.com

BULCAMP
Suffolk

4 Whitehouse Farm Cottages ★★★★
Contact: Mrs Mischa Lester
Timberley Cottage, Beccles Road,
Beccles NR34 8AN
T: (01502) 578366
F: (01502) 578030
E: admin@blythcottages.com
I: www.blythcottages.com

BURNHAM MARKET
Norfolk

Barley Cottage ★★★
Contact: Mr Andrew & Mrs Susan Watley
26 Mount Crescent, Brentwood
CM14 5DB
T: (01277) 218116
E: a.s.watley@btinternet.com

Chapel Cottage ★★★
Contact: Mrs Gail Armstrong
Norfolk Country Cottages,
Carlton House, Market Place,
Norwich NR10 4JJ
T: (01603) 871872
F: (01603) 870304
E: info@norfolkcottages.co.uk
I: www.norfolkcottages.co.uk

Clippers Cottage ★★★
Contact: Mrs Kinsley
Norfolk Country Cottages,
Carlton House, Market Place,
Norwich NR10 4JJ
T: (01603) 871872
F: (01603) 870304
E: holidays@swallow-tail.com
I: www.swallow-tail.com

Easterly ★★
Contact: Mrs Gail Armstrong
Norfolk Country Cottages Ref. 675, Market Place, Norwich NR10 4JJ
T: (01603) 871872
F: (01603) 870304
E: info@norfolkcottages.co.uk
I: www.norfolkcottages.co.uk/burnham_market_675.htm

Field End ★★★
Contact: Mrs Suzannah Olivier
The Moorings, Tower Road,
King's Lynn PE31 8JB
T: (01328) 730248
E: mooringsnorfolk@aol.com
I: www.burnham-market.co.uk/fieldend/fieldend.html

Foundry Barn ★★★★
Contact: Mr & Mrs Mike Benson
Badgers Croft Nottwood Lane,
Henley-on-Thames RG9 5PU
T: (01491) 681644
F: (01491) 681644
E: mikebenson@btopenworld.com
I: www.foundrybarn.co.uk

Fuchsia Cottage ★★★
Contact: Mr Tinsley
6 The Green, Stanhoe, King's Lynn PE31 8QE
T: (01485) 518896
E: tinsley.co@virgin.net

Granary Cottage ★★★
Contact: Ms Julie Levitt
Castle Cottage, Polopit,
Kettering NN14 3DL
T: (01832) 735150
F: (01832) 735150
E: levitt.smarter@virgin.net

Merymeet
Rating Applied For
Contact: Mrs Sandra Hohol
Norfolk Holiday Homes, 62 Westgate, Hunstanton PE36 5EL
T: (01485) 534267
F: (01485) 535230
E: shohol@birdsnorfolkholidayhomes.co.uk
I: www.norfolkholidayhomes-birds.co.uk

Rose Cottage ★★★
Contact: Mrs Anne Manning
Steward's Cottage, Sussex Farm,
King's Lynn PE31 8JY
T: (01328) 730775
F: (01328) 738470

The Shielings and Ebenezer Cottage ★★★-★★★★
Contact: Mrs Gail Armstrong
Norfolk Country Cottages,
Market Place, Norwich NR10 4JJ
T: (01603) 871872
F: (01603) 870304
E: info@norfolkcottages.co.uk
I: www.norfolkcottages.co.uk

Stable Cottage ★★★★
Contact: Mrs Anne Cringle
Market Place, King's Lynn
PE31 8HD
T: (01328) 738456
E: pmcringle@aol.com

BURNHAM-ON-CROUCH
Essex

38 Petticrow Quays ★★★
Contact: Mr Paul Ayling
38 Petticrow Quays, Belvedere Road, Burnham-on-Crouch
CM0 8AJ
T: (01702) 522857
E: www.paulmayling@aol.com

BURNHAM THORPE
Norfolk

12 The Pightle ★★
Contact: Mr Pocock
Norfolk Country Cottages,
Carlton House, Market Place,
Norwich NR10 4JJ
T: (01603) 308108
F: (01603) 870304
E: holidays@swallow-tail.com
I: www.swallow-tail.com

BURY ST EDMUNDS
Suffolk

15 Bridewell Lane ★★★★
Contact: Mr Wesley Rawdon Cushing
4A Hawstead Lane, Bury St Edmunds IP30 0BT
T: (01284) 388117
E: hawkeye52uk@yahoo.co.uk
I: www.members.lycos.co.uk/bridewell/

Brook Villa ★★★
Contact: Mr David Manning
Brook Villa, Rushbrooke Lane,
Bury St Edmunds IP33 2RR
T: (01284) 764387
E: suffolksaddlery@supanet.com

The Court & The Granary Suites ★★★-★★★★
Contact: Mrs Roberta Truin
The Court & The Granary Suites, Melford Road, Bury St Edmunds IP29 4PX
T: (01284) 830385
F: (01284) 830674
E: info@brighthousefarm.fsnet.co.uk
I: www.brighthousefarm.fsnet.co.uk

Garden Corner ★★★★
Contact: Mr John Stemp
Garden Corner, 91A Kings Road,
Bury St Edmunds IP33 3DT
T: (01284) 702848

The Granary & The Cartlodge ★★★★
Contact: Mrs Sarah Worboys
Worboys Farms Ltd, Francis Farm, Upper Somerton, Bury St Edmunds IP29 4NE
T: (01284) 789241
F: (01284) 789643
E: francisfarmcottages@farmline.com
I: www.francisfarmcottages.co.uk

Kitchen Flat ★★★
Contact: Mrs Eileen Storey
15 Northgate Street, Bury St Edmunds IP33 1HP
T: (01284) 755744
F: (01284) 755744
E: eileen@queequeg.demon.co.uk
I: www.queequeg.demon.co.uk

95 Oliver Road ★★★
Contact: Mrs C Titcombe
95 Oliver Road, Bury St Edmunds IP33 3JG
T: (01284) 766432
E: jo@titcombe.fsworld.co.uk

Pump Lane House ★★★
Contact: Mr Neil & Mrs Lucy Taylor
Pump Lane House, Pump Lane, Bury St Edmunds IP33 1HN
T: (01284) 755248

BYLAUGH
Norfolk

Meadowview ★★★
Contact: Mrs Jenny Lake
Meadowview, Park Farm,
Bylaugh, Dereham NR20 4QE
T: (01362) 688584
E: lakeparkfm@aol.com

CALIFORNIA
Norfolk

Bella Vista T/A Beachside Holidays ★★★★
Contact: Mrs S J Sampson
Beachside Holidays, Wakefield Court, Rottenstone Lane, Great Yarmouth NR29 3QT
T: (01493) 730279
E: holidays@theseaside.org
I: www.beachside-holidays.co.uk

CAMBRIDGE
Cambridgeshire

The Annexe ★★★
Contact: Mr & Mrs Francis Durning
34 Nuttings Road, Cambridge
CB1 3HU
T: (01223) 415668
F: (01223) 248899
E: annexe_cb1@hotmail.com

Canonbury House & 53 Richmond Road ★★★-★★★★★
Contact: Mr Kiddy
Radwinter Park, Radwinter End, Saffron Walden CB10 2UE
T: (01799) 599272
F: (01799) 599172
E: ajkiddy@cambridge-vacation-homes.com
I: www.cambridge-vacation-homes.com

39 Castle Street
Rating Applied For
Contact: Mr & Mrs Tony Loizou
39 Castle Street, Cambridge
CB3 0AH
T: (01223) 323231
F: (01223) 323231
E: tony@deadgoodsoup.org

EAST OF ENGLAND

Clarence House ★★★★
Contact: Mr & Mrs Oliver Digney
9a Cambridge Road, Cambridge
CB2 5JE
T: (01223) 841294
F: (01223) 841294
E: sdigney@clarencehouse.
fsnet.co.uk
I: www.clarencehouse.org.uk

First Floor Apartment
★★★★
Contact: Mr Desmond Hirsch
31 Grantchester Street,
Cambridge CB3 9HY
T: (01223) 360200
F: (01223) 529699
E: cambridge.accommodation@
virgin.net

Glebe Cottage ★★★★
Contact: Mrs Key
Glebe Cottage, 44 Main Street,
Cambridge CB3 7QS
T: (01954) 212895
E: info@camcottage.co.uk
I: www.camcottage.co.uk

28 Hanover Court ★★
Contact: Mr Young
53 Devonshire Road, Cambridge
CB1 2BL
T: (01223) 529653
E: riyo50@yahoo.com
I: www.location-cambridge.com

**Home From Home
Apartments** ★★★★
Contact: Mrs Fasano
Home From Home Apartments,
78 Milton Road, Cambridge
CB4 1LA
T: (01223) 323555
F: (01223) 277612
E: homefromhome@tesco.net
I: www.
homefromhomecambridge.co.uk

J C Accommodation ★★★★
Contact: Mr Jose Carro
5 St Leonards Close, Chesterton
Road, Newport, Saffron Walden
CB11 3TQ
T: (01799) 540987
E: pepecarro@lycos.co.uk
I: www.jcaccommodation.
co.uk/jc/

Midsummer Apartments
Rating Applied For
Contact: Mrs Maria Fasano
Midsummer Apartments, 4
Poynters Lodge, Chesterton
Road, Cambridge CB4 1JB
T: +390 823787383
F: +390 823787383
E: midsummerapartments@
liberoit.it

The School House ★★★★
Contact: Mr Terry & Mrs Nicola
Mann
The School House, High Street,
Horningsea, Cambridge CB5 9JG
T: (01223) 440077
F: (01223) 441414
E: schoolhse1@aol.com
I: schoolhouse-uk.com

Tudor Cottage ★★
Contact: Mr George Lock
Tudor Cottage, 13 Castle Row,
Cambridge CB3 0BB
T: (01953) 681597
F: (01953) 681166

79a Victoria Road ★★★★
Contact: Mrs Anita Mills
40 High Street, Aldreth, Ely
CB6 3PG
T: (01353) 740022
F: (01353) 740022
E: trojan.david@virgin.net

Warkworth Villa ★★★
Contact: Ms Wendy Whistler
Selective Studios, Rose Lodge, 9
Boxworth End, Cambridge
CB4 5RA
T: (01954) 231850
F: (01954) 204100
E: selectivestudios@ntlworld.
com
I: www.selectivestudios.com

CASTLE ACRE
Norfolk

Cherry Tree Cottage
★★★★
Contact: Mr & Mrs Boswell
Cherry Tree Cottage, Back Lane,
King's Lynn PE32 2AR
T: (01760) 755000
F: (01760) 755000
E: boswell@paston.co.uk

Friars Croft ★★★
Contact: Mrs McGrath
Hillside, Mill Road, Thetford
IP25 7LU
T: (01362) 820408

Peddars Cottage ★★★
Contact: Mrs Angela Swindell
The Rectory, St Saviour, Jersey
JE2 7NP
T: (01534) 727480
F: (01534) 727480
E: info@thecastleacre.org
I: www.castleacre.org

1 Sandles Court ★★
Contact: Mrs Jane Wood
9 Brancaster Way, Swaffham
PE37 7RY
T: (01760) 722455
E: j.wood1@tinyonline.co.uk

CASTLE HEDINGHAM
Essex

Keepers Cottage ★★★★
Contact: Mr David Brown
Keepers Cottage, Rushley Green,
Halstead CO9 3AH
T: (01787) 462685
F: (01787) 462685
E: davidmbrown@btinternet.
com
I: www.keeperscottage.20m.com

Rosemary Farm ★★★★
Contact: Mr Garry Ian
Henderson
Rosemary Lane, Castle
Hedingham, Nr Halstead
CO9 3AJ
T: (01787) 461653

CAXTON
Cambridgeshire

Church Cottage ★★★
Contact: Mr Peter & Mrs
Margaret Scott
Church Farm, Gransden Road,
Cambridge CB3 8PL
T: (01954) 719543
F: (01954) 718999
E: churchfarm@aol.com

CHEDGRAVE
Norfolk

Barn Owl Holidays ★★★
Contact: Mrs Rosemary Beattie
Barn Owl Holidays, Big Back
Lane, Norwich NR14 6BH
T: (01508) 528786
F: (01508) 528698
E: barnowls@bt.clara.co.uk
I: www.barnowlholidays.co.uk

CHELMONDISTON
Suffolk

Charlie's Cottage
Rating Applied For
Contact: Mr Eddie Coyle
7 Little Gulls, Capel St Mary,
Ipswich IP9 2EZ
T: (01473) 310851
F: (01473) 310851
E: virginia@littlegulls.freeserve.
co.uk

CHELMSFORD
Essex

Bury Barn Cottage ★★★★
Contact: Mr Richard Morris
Bury Barn Cottage, Bury Road,
Chelmsford CM3 1HB
T: (01245) 237384
F: (01245) 237327
E: rmorris@
richardmorrisfurniture.com
I: www.burybarncottage.co.uk

CLACTON-ON-SEA
Essex

Brunton House ★★
Contact: Mr & Mrs Kirk
Brunton House, 15 Carnarvon
Road, Clacton-on-Sea CO15 6PH
T: (01255) 420431

Taylors Self-contained Flats
★★
Contact: Mr Terence Taylor
Taylors Self-Contained Flats, 41
Thoroughgood Road, Clacton-
on-Sea CO15 6DD
T: (01255) 431646

CLEY NEXT THE SEA
Norfolk

Archway Cottage ★★★
Contact: Mrs Vickey Jackson
3A Brickendon Lane, Hertford
SG13 8NU
T: (01992) 511303 & 503196
F: (01992) 511303

Dolphin Cottage ★★★★
Contact: Mr & Mrs Ian Mashiter
11 Branksome Close, Norwich
NR4 6SP
T: (01603) 457560
E: cleycottage@aol.com
I: www.internet-cottages.com

Little Cottage ★★★
Contact: Mrs Gail Armstrong
Norfolk Country Cottages,
Carlton House, Market Place,
Norwich NR10 4JJ
T: (01603) 871872
F: (01603) 870304
E: info@norfolkcottages.co.uk
I: www.norfolkcottages.co.uk

Orchard Cottage ★★★★
Contact: Mrs Sarah Godfrey
Town House, Easthorpe,
Southwell NG25 0HY
T: (01636) 816398
F: (01636) 816398
E: sarah@spaces.demon.co.uk
I: www.spaces.demon.
co.uk/norfolk.htm

South Knoll ★★★
Contact: Mrs Jo Trench
186 New North Road, London
N1 7BJ
T: (020) 73596093
E: jo-trench@lineone.net

Thurn Cottage ★★★★
Contact: Mr Chris & Mrs Carol
Smith
15 South Hanningfield Way,
Wickford SS11 7DR
T: (01268) 769801
E: cjcksmith@btinternet.com

Tickers and Skylarks
★★★★
Contact: Mrs Nicola
Arrowsmith-Brown
Forge Cottage, The Street,
Norwich NR13 6DQ
T: (01603) 270457
F: (01603) 270142
E: arrows270@aol.com
I: www.cottageguide.
co.uk/tickers

CLIPPESBY
Norfolk

Clippesby Hall ★★★
Contact: Mrs Jean Lindsay
Clippesby Hall, Hall Road,
Clippesby, Great Yarmouth
NR29 3BL
T: (01493) 367800
F: (01493) 367803
E: holidays@clippesby.com
I: www.clippesby.com

COLCHESTER
Essex

Castle Road Cottages
★★★★-★★★★★
Contact: Mrs Patsie Ford
Castle Road Cottages, 19 High
Street, Colchester CO6 4JG
T: (01206) 262210
F: (01206) 262210
I: www.castleroadcottages.com

Glinska House ★★★★
Contact: Mrs Angela Hawkins
2 Queens Road, Colchester
CO3 3NP
T: (01206) 540881
F: (01206) 503406
E: rhawki@msn.com
I: www.glinskahouse.co.uk

50 Rosebery Avenue ★★★
Contact: Mrs Webb
51 Rosebery Avenue, Colchester
CO1 2UP
T: (01206) 866888
E: rosebery.avenue@ntlworld.
com

Establishments printed in blue have a detailed entry in this guide   539

EAST OF ENGLAND

The Tea House ★★★★
Contact: Mr Nicholas Charrington
The Tea House, Layer Marney Tower, Colchester CO5 9US
T: (01206) 330784
F: (01206) 330884
E: info@layermarneytower.co.uk
I: www.layermarneytower.co.uk

COLKIRK
Norfolk

Saddlery and Hillside Cottage ★★★
Contact: Mrs Catherine Joice
Nelson Cottage, Hall Lane, Fakenham NR21 7ND
T: (01328) 862261
F: (01328) 856464
E: catherine.joice@btinternet.com
I: www.colkirk.com

COLMWORTH
Bedfordshire

Colmworth Golf Course Holiday Cottages ★★★
Contact: Mrs Julie Vesely
Colmworth Golf Course Holiday Cottages, New Road, Bedford MK44 2NN
T: (01234) 378181
T: (01234) 376678
E: colmworthgc@btopenworld.co.uk
I: www.colmworthgolfclub.co.uk

COLTISHALL
Norfolk

Broadgates ★★★★
Contact: Mrs Dack
Broadgates, Wroxham Road, Norwich NR12 7DU
T: (01603) 737598
E: 2.richard@4broads.fsnet.co.uk
I: www.norfolkbroads.com/broadgates

COPDOCK
Suffolk

The Briars & Mansard Cottage ★★★★
Contact: Mrs Steward
High View, Back Lane, Ipswich IP8 3JA
T: (01473) 730494
E: rosanna.steward@virgin.net
I: www.suffolkholidays.com

CORPUSTY
Norfolk

Daisy Cottage ★★★
Contact: Mrs Gail Armstrong
Norfolk Country Cottages, Carlton House, Market Place, Norwich NR10 4JJ
T: (01603) 871872
T: (01603) 870304
E: info@norfolkcottages.co.uk
I: www.norfolkcottages.co.uk

COTTON
Suffolk

Coda Cottages ★★★★
Contact: Mrs Kate Sida-Nicholls
Poplar Farm, Dandy Corner, Cotton, Stowmarket IP14 4QX
T: (01449) 780076
T: (01449) 780180
I: www.codacottages.co.uk

CRANMER
Norfolk

Home Farm / Cranmer Country Cottages ★★★★-★★★★★
Contact: Mr John & Mrs Lynne Johnson
Home Farm, Fakenham NR21 9HY
T: (01328) 823135
F: (01328) 823136
E: booking@homefarmcranmer.co.uk
I: www.homefarmcranmer.co.uk

CRATFIELD
Suffolk

Cherry Trees ★★★★
Contact: Mrs Chris Knox
Cratfield Hall, Halesworth IP19 0DR
T: (01379) 586709
F: (01379) 588033
E: J.L.Knox@farming.co.uk
I: www.cratfield-hall.co.uk

School Farm Cottages ★★★★
Contact: Mrs Claire Sillett
School Farm, Church Road, Halesworth IP19 0BU
T: (01986) 798844
F: (01986) 798394
E: schoolfarmcotts@aol.com
I: www.schoolfarmcottages.com

CROMER
Norfolk

Albion House ★★★
Contact: Mrs Angela Forsyth
Thornfield Acre, Pudding Lane, Tarporley CW6 9SN
T: (01829) 733467
F: (01829) 733467
E: forsythleisure@aol.com
I: www.albion-house.com

Allseasons ★★-★★★
Contact: Mr & Mrs Teagle
Ashgrove, Sustead Road, Norwich NR11 8RE
T: (01263) 577205
E: sue@allseasons-cromer-co.uk

Avenue Holiday Flats ★★★
Contact: Mr John Bradley
Avenue Holiday Flats, Cliff Avenue, Cromer NR27 0AN
T: (01263) 513611
F: (01263) 515009

Beverley House Holiday Apartments ★-★★★
Contact: Mr Peter & Mrs Gill Day
Beverley House Holiday Apartments, 17 Alfred Road, Cromer NR27 9AN
T: (01263) 512787
F: (01263) 512787
I: www.broadland.com/beverleyhouse

Broadgates Cottages ★★-★★★
Contact: Mrs Julie Bryant
Broadgates Cottages, Forest Park Caravan Site, Northrepps Road, Cromer NR27 0JR
T: (01263) 513290
F: (01263) 511992
E: forestpark@netcom.co.uk
I: www.broadgates.co.uk

Chalet No 130 ★★
Contact: Ms Tanya Hickman
Lambert Watts Self Catering Holidays, 15 West Street, Cromer NR27 9HZ
T: (01263) 513139
F: (01263) 513139
E: property@lambertw.fslife.co.uk

Chalets 28, 151, 152 ★★
Contact:
Russells Self Catering Holidays, 15 West Street, Cromer NR27 9HZ
T: (01263) 513139
F: (01263) 513139
E: property@lambertw.fslife.co.uk

Cliff Hollow ★★
Contact: Miss L Willins
Cliff Hollow, 35 Overstrand Road, Cromer NR27 0AL
T: (01263) 512447
F: (01263) 512447

Cliffside at King's Chalet Park
Rating Applied For
Contact: Mrs S A Jones
Sloley Farm, High Street, Norwich NR12 8HJ
T: (01692) 536281
F: (01692) 535162
E: sloley@farmhotel.u-net.com
I: www.norfolkbroads.co.uk/sloleyfarm

15 Clifton Park ★★★★
Contact:
Norfolk Country Cottages, Carlton House, Market Place, Norwich NR10 4JJ
T: (01603) 871872
F: (01603) 870304

Coach House Cottage ★★★
Contact: Mrs Dorothy Casburn
Grove House, 81 Station Road, King's Lynn PE32 2JQ
T: (01485) 520569
F: (01485) 520569
E: ccasburn@britishsugar.com

Drift Barn Cottage ★★★
Contact: Mr Payne
Drift Cottage Farm, Norwich NR11 8PL
T: (01263) 513765

Flat 2 Bernard House ★★★
Contact:
Lambert Watts Self Catering Holidays, 15 West Street, Cromer NR27 9HZ
T: (01263) 513139
F: (01263) 513139
I: www.seaglimpse.demon.co.uk

Foxglade Lodge ★★★
Contact:
Russells Self Catering Holidays, Russell & Company, 15 West Street, Cromer NR27 9HZ
T: (01263) 511028
F: (01263) 513139

2 The Gangway ★★
Contact: Mrs Price
Misterton, Kendal Avenue, Epping CM16 4PN
T: (01992) 572672

Greenwood Holiday Cottage ★★★
Contact: Mrs Hemming
The Lookout, 11 Cliff Drive, Cromer NR27 0AW
T: (01263) 514139

The Grove ★★★
Contact: Mrs Graveling
The Grove, 95 Overstrand Road, Cromer NR27 0DJ
T: (01263) 512412
E: thegrovecromer@btopenworld.com
I: www.thegrovecromer.co.uk

King's Chalet Park ★★
Contact: Mrs Scotlock
Shangri-La, Little Cambridge, Duton Hill, Dunmow CM6 3QU
T: (01371) 870482

Kings Chalet Park ★★
Contact: Mr Arthur Pritchard
The Barn House, Norwich NR11 8RP
T: (01692) 409906
F: (01263) 824736
E: arthur@afjpritchard.fsnet.co.uk

Kings Chalet Park ★★
Contact: Mrs Bateman
Stenson, 32 Overstrand Road, Cromer NR27 0AJ
T: (01263) 511308

119 Kings Chalet Park ★★
Contact:
Russells Self Catering Holidays, 15 West Street, Cromer NR27 9HZ
T: (01263) 513139
F: (01263) 513139

123 King's Chalet Park ★★
Contact: Mrs Lotta Fox
Lambert Watts Self Catering Holidays, 15 West Street, Cromer NR27 9HZ
T: (01263) 513139
F: (01263) 513139
E: property@lambertw.fslife.co.uk

150 Kings Chalet Park ★★
Contact: Mrs Cole
201 Roughton Road, Cromer NR27 9LN
T: (01263) 513932

Maynard House ★★★
Contact: Mr Adam Cade
Brewery House, High Street, Stamford PE9 3TA
T: (01780) 720521
E: adam@studentforce.org.uk

The Old Forge ★★
Contact:
Lambert and Russell Self Catering Holidays, 15 West Street, Cromer NR27 9HZ
T: (01263) 513139

Suncourt Holiday Flats ★★
Contact: Mr & Mrs A R Hams
The Officers House, Walcott Road, Bacton, Norwich NR12 0HB
T: (01692) 650022
E: suncourtflats@mail.com
I: www.suncourt1.fsnet.co.uk

EAST OF ENGLAND

Thorpewood Cottages ★★★
Contact: Mr David Howarth
Nursery Farm, Cromer Road, Norwich NR11 8TU
T: (01263) 834493
E: davidhowarth@thorpegate. fsnet.co.uk
I: www.thorpewoodcottages. co.uk

CULFORD
Suffolk
Culford Farm Cottages ★★★★-★★★★★
Contact: Mrs Rosemary Flack
Culford Farm Cottages, Bury St Edmunds IP28 6DS
T: (01502) 500505
F: (01502) 514298
E: cottages@hoseasons.co.uk
I: www.hoseasons.co.uk

DALLINGHOO
Suffolk
The Carpenter's Shop at Robins Nest ★★★★
Contact: Mr Robert Blake
1A Moorfield Road, Woodbridge IP12 4JN
T: (01394) 382565 & 07907 773545
F: (01394) 389370
E: robert@blake4110.fsbusiness. co.uk

DARSHAM
Suffolk
The Granary & The Mallards ★★★
Contact: Mrs S Bloomfield
The Granary & The Mallards, Priory Farm, Darsham, Saxmundham IP17 3QD
T: (01728) 668459

Rolletts Marsh ★★★
Contact:
Suffolk Secrets, 7 Frenze Road, Diss IP22 4PA
T: (01379) 651297
F: (01379) 641555
E: holidays@suffolk-secrets. co.uk
I: www.suffolk-secrets.co.uk

DEBDEN
Essex
The Old Granary ★★★★
Contact: Ms Jessica Sperryn
Deynes House, Deynes Road, Saffron Walden CB11 3LG
T: (01799) 540232
E: sperryn@nascr.net

DEDHAM
Essex
The Tallow Factory ★★★★
Contact: Mrs Christine Thompson
14 School Lane, Manningtree CO11 2HZ
T: (01206) 393711
I: www.tallowfactory.com

DENHAM
Suffolk
Low Farm
Rating Applied For
Contact: Mr Nigel Blandford
Low Farm, Low Road, Eye IP21 5ET
T: (01379) 873068
F: (01379) 870062
E: nigel.carol@virgin.net

DENVER
Norfolk
West Hall Farm Holidays and Lakeside Fisheries ★★★
Contact: Mrs Riches
West Hall Lodge, Sandy Lane, Downham Market PE38 0EB
T: (01366) 383291
F: (01366) 387074
I: www.west-hall-farm-holidays. co.uk

DEREHAM
Norfolk
Bylaugh Hall ★★★★
Contact: Mrs Sarah Jeary
Bylaugh Hall, Bylaugh Park, Bylaugh, Dereham NR20 4RL
T: (01362) 688828
F: (01362) 688838
E: info@bylaugh.com
I: www.bylaugh.com

DERSINGHAM
Norfolk
Cowslip Cottage ★★★★
Contact: Mrs Karen Kennedy-Hill
9 Wheatfields, King's Lynn PE31 6BH
T: (01485) 600850
E: kennedyhill@tesco.net

Magnolia Cottage ★★★
Contact: Mrs Sandra Hohol
Birds Norfolk Holiday Homes, 62 Westgate, Hunstanton PE36 5EL
T: (01485) 534267
F: (01485) 535230
E: shohol@ birdsnorfolkholidayhomes.co.uk
I: www. norfolkholidayhomes-birds. co.uk

Oaks Cottage ★★★★
Contact: Mr & Mrs Ben Mullarkey
46 Chapel Road, King's Lynn PE31 6PN
T: (01485) 540761
E: jb.mullarkey@eidosnet.co.uk
I: www.oakscottage.co.uk

Quince Cottage ★★★★
Contact: Mrs Karen Kennedy-Hill
Cottage Breaks, 9 Wheatfields, King's Lynn PE31 6BH
T: (01485) 600850
E: kennedyhill@tesco.net
I: www.cottageguide. co.uk/quincecottage

Sandacre ★★★★
Contact: Mrs Sandra Hohol
Birds Norfolk Holiday Homes, 62 Westgate, Hunstanton PE36 5EL
T: (01485) 534267
F: (01485) 535230
E: shohol@ birdsnorfolkholidayhomes.co.uk

Silver Birches ★★★★
Contact: Mrs Jacqueline Garrett
11 Woodside Avenue, King's Lynn PE31 6QE
T: (01485) 540329
F: (01485) 540329
E: alan@blackball7.fsnet.co.uk

DILHAM
Norfolk
Dairy Farm Cottages ★★★★
Contact: Mr James Paterson
Rumford Limited, Manor Farm, North Walsham NR28 9PZ
T: (01692) 536883
F: (01692) 536723
E: japdilman@farmline.com
I: www.dairyfarmcottages.co.uk

DISS
Norfolk
Honey Bee Cottage ★★★
Contact: Mrs Rachel Davy
Honey End, Upper Street, Diss IP21 4HR
T: (01379) 741449
F: (01379) 741449
E: chrisjdavy@freenetname. co.uk
I: www.honeybeecott.co.uk

Norfolk Cottages Malthouse Farm ★★★★
Contact: Mrs Sue Austin
Malthouse Lane, Diss IP22 5UT
T: (01379) 677512
F: (01379) 677510
E: bookings@norfolkcottages. net
I: www.norfolkcottages.net

Old Mill Farm ★★★
Contact: Mrs Pauline Ward
Old Mill Farm, Hopton Road, Diss IP22 2RJ
T: (01953) 681350
E: lward@mmkarton.fsnet.co.uk
I: www.oldmillfarm.co.uk

Walcot Green Farm Cottage ★★★★
Contact: Mrs Nannette Catchpole
Walcot Green Farm Cottage, Walcot Green Farm, Diss IP22 5SU
T: (01379) 652806
F: (01379) 652806
E: walcotgreenfarm@fsmail.net
I: www.walcotgreenfarm.co.uk

DOCKING
Norfolk
Honeysuckle Cottage ★★★★
Contact: Miss Amanda Cox
49 Chertsey Road, Byfleet, Weybridge KT14 7AP
T: 07901 822621

Norfolk House & Courtyard Cottage ★★★★★
Contact: Mr Tim & Mrs Liz Witley
17 Peddars Way South, Ringstead PE36 5LF
T: (01485) 525341
F: (01485) 532715
E: info@escapetonorfolk.com

White Cottage ★★★
Contact: Mrs Sandra Hohol
Birds Norfolk Holiday Homes, 62 Westgate, Hunstanton PE36 5EL
T: (01485) 534267
F: (01485) 535230
E: shohol@ birdsnorfolkholidayhomes.co.uk
I: www. norfolkholidayhomes-birds. co.uk

Woodbine Cottage ★★★★
Contact: Mrs Karen Kennedy-Hill
Cottage Breaks, 9 Wheatfields, King's Lynn PE31 6BH
T: (01485) 600850
E: kennedyhill@tesco.net
I: www.cottageguide. co.uk/woodbinecottage

DUDDENHOE END
Essex
Cosh Cottage ★★★★
Contact: Mrs Perks
Cosh Cottage, Saffron Walden CB11 4UX
T: (01763) 838880
E: susan.perks@virgin.net

DUNMOW
Essex
Bury Farm Cottages
Rating Applied For
Contact: Mrs Sarah Clarke
Bury Farm Cottages, Bury Farm, Great Canfield, Dunmow CM6 1JS
T: (01371) 872213

DUNWICH
Suffolk
Apple Tree & Walnut Tree Cottages ★★
Contact: Mrs Claire Guppy
Acanthus Property Letting Services Ltd, 9 Trinity Street, Southwold IP18 6JH
T: (01502) 724033
F: (01502) 725168
E: sales@southwold-holidays. co.uk
I: www.southwold-holidays. co.uk

Lodge Cottage ★★★
Contact: Mrs Maureen Nielson
The Dairy House, High Street, Saxmundham IP17 3DN
T: (01728) 648388
E: drbcargill@farming.co.uk

Tinkers Cottage ★★★
Contact:
Suffolk Secrets, 7 Frenze Road, Diss IP22 4PA
T: (01379) 651297
F: (01379) 641555
E: holidays@suffolk-secrets. co.uk
I: www.suffolk-secrets.co.uk

Tower Bungalow
Rating Applied For
Contact: Mrs Eleanor Barnes
Conifers, Church Road, Sudbury CO10 7NA
T: (01787) 269916
F: (01787) 269665
E: info@towerbungalow.co.uk
I: www.towerbungalow.co.uk

Establishments printed in blue have a detailed entry in this guide

EAST OF ENGLAND

EARSHAM
Norfolk

Dukes Cottage ★★★
Contact: Mrs Gail Armstrong
Norfolk Country Cottages,
Carlton House, Market Place,
Norwich NR10 4JJ
T: (01603) 871872
F: (01603) 870304
E: info@norfolkcottages.co.uk
I: www.norfolkcottages.co.uk

EAST BERGHOLT
Suffolk

Flatford Cottage
Rating Applied For
Contact: Mr Paul & Mrs Debbie Goddard
Flatford Farmhouse, Flatford Lane, Colchester CO7 6UN
T: (01206) 298985

Woodstock Wing Woodstock ★★★
Contact: Mr Keith & Mrs Janet Alcoe
Woodstock Wing Woodstock, Gaston Street, East Bergholt, Colchester CO7 6SD
T: (01206) 298724
E: janetandkeith@familyalcoe.fsnet.co.uk

EAST DEREHAM
Norfolk

Clinton Cottage and Clinton House ★★★★
Contact: Mrs Margaret Searle
Clinton Willows, Cutthroat Lane, Yaxham, Dereham NR19 1RZ
T: (01362) 692079
F: (01362) 692079
E: clintonholidays@tesco.net
I: www.norfolkcountrycottage.co.uk

EAST HARLING
Norfolk

Berwick Cottage ★★★
Contact: Mrs Miriam Toosey
The Lin Berwick Trust, 5 List House, Hall Street, Sudbury CO10 9JL
T: (01787) 372343
F: (01787) 372343
E: info@thelinberwicktrust.org.uk
I: www.thelinberwicktrust.org.uk

Dolphin Lodge ★★★★
Contact: Mrs Ellen Jolly
Dolphin Lodge, Roudham Farm, Norwich NR16 2RJ
T: (01953) 717126
F: (01953) 718593
E: jolly@roudhamfarm.co.uk
I: www.roudhamfarm.co.uk

Tapestry Cottage ★★★
Contact: Mr Michael Dolling
Tapestry Cottage, 44 White Hart Street, Norwich NR16 2NE
T: (01953) 718658
F: (01953) 717443
E: ok_to.mark_it@virgin.net
I: www.tapestrycottage.com

EAST RUDHAM
Norfolk

Bumble Barn ★★
Contact: Mr David Kernon
Bramble Cottage, Broomsthorpe Road, King's Lynn PE31 8RG
T: (01485) 528717

Rose Cottage Annex ★★
Contact: Mrs E. Maureen Mawby
Rose Cottage Annex, Bagthorpe Road, King's Lynn PE31 8RA
T: (01485) 528274

EAST RUNTON
Norfolk

Mallards Rest ★★★
Contact: Mrs Nicola Thompson
Mallards Rest, Lower Common, Cromer NR27 9PG
T: (01263) 512496

Poplars Caravan and Chalet Park ★★-★★★★
Contact: Mr Kevin & Mrs Dena Parfitt
Poplars Caravan and Chalet Park, Brick Lane, Cromer NR27 9PL
T: (01263) 512892

Woodhill House ★★★
Contact: Ms Denise Lewis
Lambert Watts self catering holidays, 15 West Street, Cromer NR27 9HZ
T: (01263) 511028
E: property@lambertw.fslife.co.uk

EAST RUSTON
Norfolk

Swallowtail Cottage ★★★
Contact: Mrs Brenda Taylor
21A Roydon Road, Ware SG12 8HQ
T: (01920) 070079
E: swallowtailcottage@hotmail.com
I: www.swallowtailcottage.co.uk

EASTBRIDGE
Suffolk

Holly Cottage ★★★★
Contact: Mr Richard Pither
Suffolk Secrets, 7 Frenze Road, Diss IP22 4PA
T: (01379) 651297
F: (01379) 641555
E: holidays@suffolk-secrets.co.uk

ELMSTEAD MARKET
Essex

Birds Farm ★★★-★★★★
Contact: Mrs Joanna Burke
Birds Farm, School Road, Colchester CO7 7EY
T: (01206) 823838
E: birdsfarm@btinternet.com
I: www.birdsfarm.com

ELMSWELL
Suffolk

Hill Farm
Rating Applied For
Contact: Mrs Amanda Roberts
The Willows, Willow Drive, Long Thurlow, Bury St Edmunds IP31 3JA
T: (01359) 258544
E: roberts.ar@tiscali.co.uk
I: www.english-country-cottages.co.uk

Kiln Farm ★★★
Contact: Mrs Jacqueline Macaree
Kiln Farm, Kiln Lane, Bury St Edmunds IP30 9QR
T: (01359) 240442
E: paul-jacky@kilnfarm.fsnet.co.uk
I: www.smoothhound.co.uk/bury-st-edmunds

Oak Farm ★★★★★
Contact: Mr & Mrs Dyball
Willow Farm, Ashfield Road, Elmswell, Bury St Edmunds IP30 9HG
T: (01359) 240263
F: (01359) 240263

ELY
Cambridgeshire

47 Brooke Grove
Rating Applied For
Contact: Mr Patrick Fisher
47 Brooke Grove, Ely CB6 3WT
T: 0800 0857763
F: 0800 0857763
E: streetsaheadselfcatering@hotmail.com
I: www.streetsaheadselfcatering.co.uk

Cathedral House Coach House ★★★★
Contact: Mrs Jenny Farndale
17 St Marys Street, Ely CB7 4ER
T: (01353) 662124
F: (01353) 662124
E: farndale@cathedralhouse.co.uk
I: www.cathedralhouse.co.uk

19 Chiefs Street ★★★
Contact: Mrs Coates
Cheviot House, Church End, Cambridge CB1 5PE
T: (01223) 290842
F: (01223) 290529
E: cheviotbob@aol.com

Hill House Farm Cottage and The Old Granary ★★★★★
Contact: Mrs Hilary Nix
Hill House Farm Cottage and The Old Granary, 9 Main Street, Ely CB6 2DJ
T: (01353) 778369
F: (01353) 778369
E: hilary@hillhousefarmely.co.uk
I: www.hillhousefarmely.co.uk

47a Waterside ★★★
Contact: Mrs Florence Nolan
47a Waterside, Ely CB7 4AU
T: (01353) 664377

ERISWELL
Suffolk

Church Cottage ★★★★★
Contact: Ms Yolande Goode
Elveden Farms Ltd, Estate Office, London Road, Thetford IP24 3TQ
T: 08704 441155
F: 08704 441150
E: elveden@farmline.com

Cranhouse ★★★★★
Contact: Ms Yolande Goode
Elveden Farms Ltd, Estate Office, London Road, Thetford IP24 3TQ
T: (01638) 533318
F: (01842) 890070
E: elveden@farmline.com

ERPINGHAM
Norfolk

Grange Farm ★★★
Contact: Mrs Jane Bell
Scarrow Beck Farm, Erpingham, Norwich NR11 7QU
T: (01263) 761241
F: (01263) 761241
E: jez.bell@btinternet.com
I: www.grangefarmholidays.co.uk

Keepers Cottage ★★★
Contact: Mrs Daniels
Keepers Cottage, Blacksmiths Lane, Norwich NR11 7QF
T: (01263) 761724

EYE
Suffolk

Athelington Hall ★★★★
Contact: Mr Peter Havers
Athelington Hall, Horham, Eye IP21 5EJ
T: (01728) 628233
F: (01379) 384491
E: peter@logcabinholidays.co.uk
I: www.logcabinholidays.co.uk

Manor House Cottages ★★★-★★★★
Contact: Mrs Yvonne Mason
Manor House Cottages, Yaxley Manor House, Mellis Road, Eye IP23 8DP
T: (01379) 788049
F: (01379) 788422
E: holiday@manorhousecottages.co.uk
I: www.manorhousecottages.co.uk

FAKENHAM
Norfolk

The Cottage ★★★
Contact: Mrs Gail Armstrong
Norfolk Country Cottages Ref. 672, Market Place, Norwich NR10 4JJ
T: (01603) 871872
F: (01603) 870304
E: info@norfolkcottages.co.uk
I: www.norfolkcottages.co.uk/fakenham_672.htm

Idyllic Cottages at Vere Lodge ★★★-★★★★
Contact: Jackie Nelson
Idyllic Cottages at Vere Lodge, South Raynham, Fakenham NR21 7HE
T: (01328) 838261
F: (01328) 838300
E: major@verelodge.co.uk
I: www.idylliccottages.co.uk

The Paddocks ★★★★
Contact: Mr & Mrs John Strahan
The Paddocks The Old Brick Kilns, Little Barney Lane, Fakenham NR21 0NL
T: (01328) 878305
F: (01328) 878948
E: oldbrickkilns@aol.com
I: www.paddocks-cottages.co.uk

EAST OF ENGLAND

Pollywiggle Cottage ★★★★
Contact: Mrs Marilyn Farnham-Smith
79 Earlham Road, Norwich
NR2 3RE
T: (01603) 471990
F: (01603) 612221
E: marilyn@pollywigglecottage.co.uk
I: www.pollywigglecottage.co.uk

Stables Cottage and Oxford Barn ★★★
Contact: Mr & Mrs John/Jill Matthews
The Old Ale House, Fakenham
NR21 7EZ
T: (01328) 838509
E: oldalehousecottages@hotmail.com

FELBRIGG
Norfolk

Boundary Farm Cottage ★★★
Contact: Mrs Wendy Congreve
Smiths Farm, Spalding PE12 0AZ
T: (01406) 363618

FELIXSTOWE
Suffolk

Fairlight Detached Bungalow ★★★
Contact: Mrs Daphne Knights
Priory View, 127 High Road East, Old Felixstowe, Felixstowe
IP11 9PS
T: (01394) 277730

Flat 2 ★★★
Contact: Mrs Gwen Lynch
Cedar House, 20 The Close, Tattingstone, Ipswich IP9 2PD
T: (01473) 328729

Honeypot Cottage ★★★
Contact: Mrs Theresa Adams
Deben Lodge, Falkenham, Ipswich IP10 0RA
T: (01394) 448564
E: adams99@btinternet.com

Kimberley Holiday Flats ★★
Contact: Mrs Valerie Reed
Kimberley Holiday Flats, 105-107 Undercliff Road West, Felixstowe IP11 2AF
T: (01394) 672157

Sea View Holiday Flat ★★★★
Contact: Mrs Sue Brady
Sea View, 50 St Georges Road, Felixstowe IP11 9PN
T: (01394) 274231
F: (01394) 279634
E: enquire@felixstoweholidayhomes.co.uk
I: www.felixstoweholidayhomes.co.uk

FIELD DALLING
Norfolk

The Annexe ★★★
Contact: Mrs Betty Ringer
The Annexe, Hedgerows, Binham Road, Holt NR25 7LJ
T: (01328) 830206

Eastcote Cottage ★★★★
Contact: Mrs Sally Grove
Eastcote Cottage, Holt Road, Field Dalling, Holt NR25 7LE
T: (01328) 830359
E: sally@eastcotecottage.co.uk
I: www.eastcotecottage.co.uk

Oak Barn ★★★★
Contact: Mrs Angela Harcourt
Hard Farm House, Little Marsh Lane, Holt NR25 7LL
T: (01328) 830655
F: (01328) 830257
E: harcog@farming.co.uk

FILBY
Norfolk

Wychwood ★★★★
Contact: Mrs Gail Armstrong
Norfolk Country Cottages, Carlton House, Market Place, Norwich NR10 4JJ
T: (01603) 871872
F: (01603) 870304
E: info@norfolkcottages.co.uk
I: www.norfolkcottages.co.uk

FINNINGHAM
Suffolk

Willow Cottage ★★★★
Contact:
The Cottage Collection, 17-23 Ber Street, Norwich NR1 3EU
T: (01603) 724804
E: bookings@the-cottage-collection.co.uk
I: www.the-cottage-collection.co.uk

FORNHAM ALL SAINTS
Suffolk

Fornham Hall Cottage ★★★★
Contact: Mrs Helene Sjolin
Fornham Hall, Bury St Edmunds IP28 6JJ
T: (01284) 703424
E: cottage@sjolin.demon.co.uk

FOXLEY
Norfolk

Moor Farm Stable Cottages ★★-★★★★
Contact: Mr Paul Davis
Moor Farm, Foxley, Dereham NR20 4QN
T: (01362) 688523
F: (01362) 688523
E: moorfarm@aol.com
I: www.moorfarmstablecottages.co.uk

FRAMLINGHAM
Suffolk

Boundary Farm ★★★-★★★★★
Contact: Mrs Susan Seabrook
Boundary Farm, Saxtead Road, Woodbridge IP13 9PZ
T: (01728) 621026
F: (01728) 621026

Wood Lodge ★★★
Contact: Mr Tim Kindred
Wood Lodge, High House Farm, Woodbridge IP13 9PD
T: (01728) 663461
F: (01728) 663409
E: woodlodge@highhousefarm.co.uk
I: www.highhousefarm.co.uk

FRETTENHAM
Norfolk

Glebe Farm ★★★
Contact: Mrs Rona Norton
Beck Farm, Off Pound Hill, Norwich NR12 7NF
T: (01603) 897641
F: (01603) 897641
E: r.norton99@ntlworld.com
I: www.freespace.virgin.net/glebefarm.cottages

FRING
Norfolk

Owl Barn ★★★★
Contact: Mrs Heather Habbin
4 Fir Tree Drive, King's Lynn PE33 0PR
T: (01553) 840655
E: owlbarnfring@aol.com
I: www.owlbarnfring.co.uk

FRINTON-ON-SEA
Essex

Quartette ★★★★
Contact: Mr Robert Bucke
Boydens, 73 Connaught Avenue, Frinton-on-Sea CO13 9PP
T: 0701 0 716013
F: 0870 7 653746
E: ipsw2@btinternet.com
I: www.ipsw.btinternet.co.uk/quartette.htm

FRISTON
Suffolk

Holly Cottage ★★★★
Contact:
Suffolk Secrets, 7 Frenze Road, Diss IP22 4PA
T: (01379) 651297
F: (01379) 641555
E: holidays@suffolk-secrets.co.uk

FULBOURN
Cambridgeshire

The Old Chapel ★★★
Contact: Mrs Denise Ryder
The Old Mangle, 41 Pierce Lane, Cambridge CB1 5DJ
T: (01223) 881427
E: denisearyder@hotmail.com
I: www.stayintheoldchapel.com

GARBOLDISHAM
Norfolk

Burnside & Hawthorn Lodge ★★★★
Contact: Mrs Connie Atkins
Burnside & Hawthorn Lodge, Alderwood, Hopton Road, Diss IP22 2RQ
T: (01953) 688376
F: (01953) 681743
E: douconatkins@waitrose.com

GAYTON
Norfolk

Field View ★★★
Contact: Mr & Mrs Steel
Aramir, Lynn Road, Gayton, King's Lynn PE32 1QJ
T: (01553) 636813

Jasmine Cottage ★★★★
Contact: Mr Michael Pooley
West Hall Farm, Winch Road, King's Lynn PE32 1QP
T: (01553) 636519
F: (01553) 636519
E: mike@westhallfarm.co.uk
I: www.westhallfarm.co.uk

Jenny's Cottage
Rating Applied For
Contact: Mrs Jennifer Salisbury
18 Hawes Lane, West Wickham BR4 0DB
T: (020) 87773926
E: jennysalno1@hotmail.com

GEDGRAVE
Suffolk

The Gedgrave Broom ★★★★
Contact: Mrs Ali Watson
Chillesford Lodge Estate, Newton Farm, Woodbridge IP12 2AG
T: (01394) 450488
E: geowat@farmersweekly.net

GORLESTON-ON-SEA
Norfolk

Manor Cottage ★★★
Contact: Mrs Margaret Ward
North Manor House, 12 Pier Plain, Gorleston, Great Yarmouth NR31 6PE
T: (01493) 669845
F: (01493) 669845
E: manorcottage@wardm4.fsnet.co.uk
I: www.wardm4.fsnet.co.uk

GOSFIELD
Essex

Casita ★★★
Contact: Mrs Christine Jones
Church Cottage, Church Road, Halstead CO9 1UD
T: (01787) 474863
F: (01787) 473449
E: christine.jones7@btinternet.com

GREAT BIRCHAM
Norfolk

The Guest Flat ★★★
Contact: Mrs Sandra Hohol
Birds Norfolk Holiday Homes, 62 Westgate, Hunstanton PE36 5EL
T: (01485) 534267
F: (01485) 535230
E: shohol@birdsnorfolkholidayhomes.co.uk
I: www.norfolkholidayhomes-birds.co.uk

Humphrey Cottage ★★★
Contact: Mrs Elly Chalmers
Bircham Windmill, King's Lynn PE31 6SJ
T: (01485) 578393
E: info@birchamwindmill.co.uk
I: www.birchamwindmill.co.uk

GREAT DUNMOW
Essex

The Granary ★★★★
Contact: Mr Philip & Mrs Cathy Burton
The Granary, Moor End Farm, Broxted, Dunmow CM6 2EL
T: (01371) 870821
F: (01371) 870170
E: moorendfarm@btconnect.com
I: www.moorendfarm.com

Old Piggeries ★★★
Contact: Mr Kirby
Old Piggeries, Grange Lane, Little Dunmow, Dunmow CM6 3HY
T: (01371) 820205
F: (01377) 820205

Establishments printed in blue have a detailed entry in this guide

EAST OF ENGLAND

GREAT EVERSDEN
Cambridgeshire

Rose Barn Cottages ★★★★
Contact: Mr Paul & Mrs Margaret Tebbit
Rose Barn Cottages, 44 High Street, Cambridge CB3 7HW
T: (01223) 262154
F: (01223) 264875
E: paul@pbgtebbit.plus.com
I: www.redhousefarmuk.com

GREAT HOCKHAM
Norfolk

Old School Cottage ★★★★
Contact: Mrs Gwen Flanders
Beechwood House, Wretham Road, Thetford IP24 1NY
T: (01953) 498177
E: oscott@clara.net
I: www.4starcottage.co.uk

GREAT MASSINGHAM
Norfolk

Eves Cottage ★★★
Contact: Mrs Gail Armstrong
Norfolk Country Cottages, Carlton House, Market Place, Norwich NR10 4JJ
T: (01603) 871872
F: (01603) 870304
E: info@norfolkcottages.co.uk
I: www.norfolkcottages.co.uk

Old Swan Cottage & The Stables at the Old Swan ★★★★
Contact: Mrs Sara Barns
The Old Swan, School Road, King's Lynn PE32 2JA
T: (01485) 520151
E: ssbarns@hotmail.com

Primrose Cottage ★★★
Contact: Mrs Christine Riches
Primrose Cottage (Christines Cottages), 21 Weasenham Road, King's Lynn PE32 2EY
T: (01485) 520216
E: christine-riches@supanet.com
I: www.christine-riches.supanet.com

GREAT PLUMSTEAD
Norfolk

Windfalls ★★★
Contact: Mrs Jane Jones
Hall Farm, Middle Road, Norwich NR13 5EF
T: (01603) 720235
F: (01603) 722008
E: hall.farm@btinternet.com

GREAT SHELFORD
Cambridgeshire

3 The Limes
Rating Applied For
Contact: Mrs Caroline Botha
C J Botha Rental, 1 Riddy Lane, Cambridge CB3 7SP
T: (01954) 718428
F: (01954) 718428
E: limes@bothas.co.uk

GREAT SNORING
Norfolk

Church View Cottage ★★★
Contact: Mrs Gail Armstrong
Norfolk Country Cottages Ref. 676, Market Place, Norwich NR10 4JJ
T: (01603) 871872
F: (01603) 870304
E: info@norfolkcottages.co.uk
I: www.norfolkcottages.co.uk/great_snoring_676.htm

Home Cottage ★★★
Contact: Mr Tony Rivett
Windmill Farm, Holt Road, Wood Norton, Dereham NR20 5BN
T: (01263) 860462

Rose Cottage ★★★★
Contact: Mrs Gilly Paramor
4 Hall Farm Cottages, Pedlars Lane, Fakenham NR21 0NH
T: (01328) 878867
F: (01328) 878867
E: gilly@gparamor.freeserve.co.uk
I: www.clevencycottages.co.uk

GREAT WALSINGHAM
Norfolk

The Tailor's House ★★★
Contact:
Norfolk Country Cottages, Carlton House, Market Place, Norwich NR10 4JJ
T: (01603) 871872
F: (01603) 870304
E: info@norfolkcottages.co.uk
I: www.norfolkcottages.co.uk/properties/849

GREAT WIGBOROUGH
Essex

Honeysuckle Cottage ★★★★
Contact: Mr Kevin Benner
Honeysuckle Cottage, Mistletoe Cottage, Maldon Road, Colchester CO5 7RH
T: (01206) 735282
E: kevinbenner@btopenworld.com
I: www.honeysucklecot.co.uk

GREAT YARMOUTH
Norfolk

Arrandale Apartments ★★★
Contact: Mr Peter Meah
Arrandale Apartments, 39 Wellesley Road, Great Yarmouth NR30 1EU
T: (01493) 855046
F: (01493) 300434
I: www.arrandaleapartments.co.uk

Cambridge Court Holiday Apartments ★★★-★★★★★
Contact: Ms Linda Dyble
Cambridge Court Holiday Apartments, 10 North Denes Road, Great Yarmouth NR30 4LW
T: (01493) 304913
F: (01493) 304913

Kenwood Holiday Flats ★★
Contact: Mrs V Forbes
82 North Denes Road, Great Yarmouth NR30 4LW
T: (01493) 852740

GRESHAM
Norfolk

Astalot and Avalon Cottages ★★
Contact: Mrs Jennifer Murray
Mariners Hard, High Street, Cley, Holt NR25 7RX
T: (01263) 740404
F: (01263) 740404

The Little Place ★★
Contact: Mr & Mrs Paul Hill
The Little Place, Loke End Cottage, The Loke, Gresham, Norwich NR11 8RJ
T: (01263) 577344
E: info@broadland.com/littleplace

GRUNDISBURGH
Suffolk

The Stable ★★★
Contact: Mrs Louisa Davies
Folly Cottage, The Green, Woodbridge IP13 6TA
T: (01473) 738827

GUNTHORPE
Norfolk

Chimney Cottage ★★★
Contact: Mr Roy Preston
10 Marryats Loke, Holt NR25 7AE
T: (01328) 830411
F: (01328) 830411

HADDENHAM
Cambridgeshire

Old Porch House ★★★★
Contact: Mrs Lesley Innes
Old Porch House, Hill Row, Ely CB6 3TJ
T: (01353) 741948
E: info@oldporchhouse.co.uk
I: www.oldporchhouse.com

HADLEIGH
Suffolk

The Lodge House
Rating Applied For
Contact: Mr Rod & Mrs Angela Rolfe
The Lodge, Station Road, High Street, Ipswich IP7 5AP
T: (01473) 822458
F: (01473) 827751

Stable Cottages ★★★★
Contact: Mrs Margaret Langton
Stable Cottages, The Granary, Chattisham Place, Ipswich IP8 3QD
T: (01473) 652210
F: (01473) 652210
E: margaret.langton@talk21.com
I: www.farmstayanglia.co.uk/chattisham

HALESWORTH
Suffolk

Bucks Farm ★★★★
Contact: Mrs Bradshaw
Bucks Farm, Halesworth IP19 0LX
T: (01986) 784216
F: (01986) 784216
E: jo@bucksfarm.freeuk.com
I: www.bucksfarm-holidays.co.uk

Stable End Cottage ★★★★
Contact: Ms Jo Jordan
Stable End Cottage, Wissett Place, Norwich Road, Halesworth IP19 8HY
T: (01986) 873124
F: (01986) 874114
E: jo@stable-end-cottage.co.uk
I: www.stable-end-cottage.co.uk

HALSTEAD
Essex

Froyz Hall Barn ★★★★
Contact: Mrs Judi Butler
Froyz Hall Farm, Halstead CO9 1RS
T: (01787) 476684
F: (01787) 474647
E: judibutler@dsl.pipex.com
I: www.froyzhallbarn.co.uk

HAPPISBURGH
Norfolk

Heather Cottage ★★★★
Contact: Mrs G Armstrong
Norfolk Country Cottages, Carlton House, Market Place, Norwich NR10 4JJ
T: (01603) 871872
F: (01603) 870304
E: info@norfolkcottages.co.uk
I: www.norfolkcottages.co.uk

Lanthorn Cottage ★★★★
Contact: Mr Brown
Mellows Brown & Co Ltd, 52 Granville Road, Berkhamsted HP4 3RN
T: (01442) 384473

HARPLEY
Norfolk

Rosedene ★★★★
Contact: Mr Roger Osborne
Duryard, 22 Westgate Green, Norwich NR10 5RF
T: (01603) 754349
F: 0870 1383280
E: rogero@pobox.com
I: pobox.com/~rogero

HAUGHLEY
Suffolk

The Cottage ★★★
Contact: Mrs Mary Noy
Red House Farm, Station Road, Stowmarket IP14 3QP
T: (01449) 673323
F: (01449) 675413
E: mary@noy1.fsnet.co.uk

HAUXTON
Cambridgeshire

Whitewall Cottage ★★★★
Contact: Mr Geoffrey Steel
Dorset House, 35 Newton Road, Cambridge CB2 5HL
T: (01223) 844440
F: (01223) 844440
E: dorsethouse@btopenworld.com
I: www.smoothhound.co.uk

HEACHAM
Norfolk

1 Canon Pott Close ★★★★
Contact: Mr Chris Saunders
14 Hurdles Way, Cambridge CB2 4PA
T: (01223) 832684
E: mail@westcrete.co.uk
I: www.norfolkcottages.co.uk

---

544 Look out for establishments participating in the National Accessible Scheme

EAST OF ENGLAND

Cedar Springs ★-★★★
Contact: Mrs A Howe
Owl Lodge, Jubilee Road, King's Lynn PE31 7AR
T: (01485) 570609
F: (01485) 579093
E: antoniahowe@aol.com

Cedar Springs Chalets ★★
Contact: Mr Michael & Mrs Ann Chestney
35 The Street, West Raynham, Fakenham NR21 7EY
T: (01328) 838341
F: (01328) 838341

Cheney Hollow Cottages ★★★★
Contact: Mrs Thelma Holland
Cheney Hollow, 3-5 Cheney Hill, King's Lynn PE31 7BX
T: (01485) 572625
F: (01485) 572625
E: thelma@cheneyhollow.co.uk
I: www.cheneyhollow.co.uk

Dora's Cottage ★★★★
Contact: Mrs Sandra Hohol
Birds Norfolk Holiday Homes, 62 Westgate, Hunstanton PE36 5EL
T: (01485) 534267
F: (01485) 535230
E: shohol@birdsnorfolkholidayhomes.co.uk
I: www.norfolkholidayhomes-birds.co.uk

Little Acorns ★★★
Contact: Mrs Sandra Hohol
Birds Norfolk Holiday Homes, 62 Westgate, Hunstanton PE36 5EL
T: (01485) 534267
F: (01485) 535230
E: shohol@birdsnorfolkholidayhomes.co.uk

Manor Farm Cottage ★★★
Contact: Mrs C. M. Wallace
Manor Farm, Hunstanton Road, King's Lynn PE31 7JX
T: (01485) 570567
F: (01485) 570567
I: www.heacham1.fsnet.co.uk

The Old Station Waiting Rooms ★★★
Contact: Mr & Mrs Clay
Station Road, King's Lynn PE31 7AW
T: (01485) 570712
I: www.cottageguide.co.uk/waitingrooms

Painters Corner ★★★★
Contact: Mrs N. J. O'Callaghan
The Hermitage, 2 Wilton Road, King's Lynn PE31 7AD
T: (01485) 525381
E: hideawaya1@aol.com
I: www.heacham1.fsnet.co.uk/hideaway/accommodation_07.htm

4 Pretoria Cottages ★★★
Contact: Mr Colin Barnes
58 High Drive, New Malden KT3 3UB
T: (020) 82558834
E: colinpbarnes@hotmail.com

2 Retreat Cottage ★★★
Contact: Mrs Rooth
32 Church Green, Hunstanton Road, King's Lynn PE31 7HH
T: (01485) 572072
E: sl.rooth@virgin.net
I: www.retreatcottage.com

Robin Hill ★★
Contact: Mrs Gidney
Robin Hill, Hunstanton Road, King's Lynn PE31 7JX
T: (01485) 570309

Roseleigh Villa ★★★
Contact: Mrs Sandra Hohol
Birds Norfolk Holiday Homes, 62 Westgate, Hunstanton PE36 5EL
T: (01485) 534267
F: (01485) 535230
E: shohol@birdsnorfolkholidayhomes.co.uk
I: www.norfolkholidayhomes-birds.co.uk

Staneve ★★★
Contact: Mr & Mrs Smith
2B Church Road, Bedford MK45 1AE
T: (01525) 634935
E: amandalsmith@ntlworld.com
I: www.staneve.biz

1 Sunnyside Cottages ★★★
Contact: Mrs Gail Armstrong
Norfolk Country Cottages, Carlton House, Market Place, Norwich NR10 4JJ
T: (01603) 871872
F: (01603) 870304
E: info@norfolkcottages.co.uk
I: www.norfolkcottages.co.uk

Tawny Cottage ★★★★
Contact: Mrs Gail Armstrong
Norfolk Country Cottages, Carlton House, Market Place, Norwich NR10 4JJ
T: (01603) 871872
F: (01603) 870304
E: info@norfolkcottages.co.uk

HEMSBY
Norfolk

Nuthatch Cottage ★★★★
Contact: Ms Stephanie Sampson
Beachside Holidays, Wakefield Court, Great Yarmouth NR29 3QT
T: (01493) 730279
E: holidays@theseaside.org
I: www.cottages-in-norfolk.co.uk

HERTFORD
Hertfordshire

Dalmonds Barns ★★★★
Contact: Mrs Ann Reay
Dalmonds Barns Ltd, Jepps Farm, Mangrove Lane, Hertford SG13 8QJ
T: (01992) 479151
F: (01992) 479151
E: ann.reay@virgin.net
I: www.dalmondsbarns.com+dalmonsbarns.co.ko

HESSETT
Suffolk

Heathfield ★★★★
Contact: Mrs Christine Whitton
Arcadia, Bury Road, Bury St Edmunds IP30 9AB
T: (01359) 271130
F: (01394) 448418
E: chriswhitton@aol.com
I: www.cottageguide.co.uk/heathfield

Wilwyn & Chapel Cottages ★★★
Contact: Mr Chris & Mrs Nicky Glass
Alwyd Cottage, The Street, Bury St Edmunds IP30 9AZ
T: (01359) 270736
F: (01359) 270736
E: chrisglass@hessettgrain.freeserve.co.uk
I: www.cottageguide.co.uk/hessett

HICKLING
Norfolk

The Conifers ★★★★
Contact: Mrs Gail Armstrong
Norfolk Country Cottages, Carlton House, Market Place, Norwich NR10 4JJ
T: (01603) 871872
F: (01603) 870304
E: info@norfolkcottages.co.uk
I: www.norfolkcottages.co.uk

The Cottage ★★★
Contact: Mrs Gail Armstrong
Norfolk Country Cottages, Carlton House, Market Place, Norwich NR10 4JJ
T: (01603) 871872
F: (01603) 870304
E: info@norfolkcottages.co.uk
I: www.norfolkcottages.co.uk

HIGH KELLING
Norfolk

Lynton Loft ★★★
Contact: Mrs Gail Armstrong
Norfolk Country Cottages, Carlton House, Market Place, Norwich NR10 4JJ
T: (01603) 871872
F: (01603) 870304
E: info@norfolkcottages.co.uk
I: www.norfolkcottages.co.uk

HILLINGTON
Norfolk

The Old Rectory ★★★
Contact: Mrs Sarah Thompsett
The Old Rectory, Station Road, King's Lynn PE31 6DE
T: (01485) 600177

HINDOLVESTON
Norfolk

Lavender Cottage ★★★★
Contact: Ms Jacqui Rose & Mr Phillip Archer
Thatches, Nedging Road, Ipswich IP7 7HL
T: (01473) 741396
E: philarcher_uk@yahoo.co.uk

Pine Cottage ★★★
Contact: Mr & Mrs Scammell
61 Ladbrooke Drive, Potters Bar EN6 1QW
T: (01707) 651734

HINDRINGHAM
Norfolk

Sundial House ★★★
Contact: Mr Simon Barclay
Kett Country Cottages, 8 Oak Street, Fakenham NR21 9DY
T: (01328) 856853
F: (01328) 853903
E: info@kettcountrycottages.co.uk
I: www.kettcountrycottages.co.uk

HINGHAM
Norfolk

The Granary ★★★★
Contact: Mrs Dunnett
College Farm, Norwich NR9 4PP
T: (01953) 850596
F: (01953) 851364
E: christine.dunnett@lineone.net

HISTON
Cambridgeshire

13 The Green ★★★
Contact: Mrs Pauline Wynn
4 Eversley Close, Cambridge CB4 8SG
T: (01954) 250729

HITCHAM
Suffolk

Mill House Holiday Cottages ★★-★★★
Contact: Ms Melanie Rieger
Mill House Holiday Cottages, c/o Water Run, Ipswich IP7 7LN
T: (01449) 740315
F: (01449) 740315
E: hitcham@aol.com
I: www.millhouse-hitcham.co.uk

HOLME
Cambridgeshire

2 Pig & Whistle Cottage ★★★
Contact: Mrs Susan Lynn
2 Pig & Whistle Cottage, 2 Station Road, Peterborough PE7 3PH
T: (01487) 830579

HOLME NEXT THE SEA
Norfolk

Beach Cottage ★★★★
Contact: Mrs Stephanie Jones
Beach Road, Hunstanton PE36 6LG
T: (01485) 525201
E: robertjones@samphire1.demon.co.uk

Brook Bungalow ★★★★
Contact: Mrs Whitsed
8 Holme Close, Ailsworth, Peterborough PE5 7AQ
T: (01733) 380028
F: (01733) 380028
E: john@jwhitsed.freeserve.co.uk
I: www.cottageguide.co.uk

Eastgate Barn ★★★
Contact: Mrs Shirley Simeone
Eastgate Barn, Eastgate Road, Holme-next-the-Sea, Hunstanton PE36 6LL
T: (01485) 525218

Establishments printed in blue have a detailed entry in this guide

EAST OF ENGLAND

Rose Cottage ★★★★
Contact: Mrs Stephanie Hedge
34 Rampton Road, Cambridge
CB4 8UL
T: (01954) 250470
F: (01954) 250470
I: www.ashtoncottages.co.uk

Sunnymead Corner ★★★★
Contact: Mrs Nicola O'Callaghan
The Hermitage, Wilton Road,
King's Lynn PE31 7AD
T: (01485) 525381
E: sunnymeadholpark@aol.com
I: www.heacham1.fsnet.
co.uk/hideaway/
accommodation_10.htm

Swift Cottage ★★★
Contact: Mr Richard Simmonds
Oundle Cottage Breaks, Market
Place, Peterborough PE8 4BE
T: (01832) 273531
F: (01832) 274938
E: richard@simmondsatoundle.
co.uk
I: www.oundlecottagebreaks.
co.uk

Tudor Lodge Cottage
★★★★
Contact: Mrs Sandra Hohol
Birds Norfolk Holiday Homes, 62
Westgate, Hunstanton PE36 5EL
T: (01485) 534267
F: (01485) 535230
E: shohol@
birdsnorfolkholidayhomes.co.uk
I: www.
norfolkholidayhomes-birds.
co.uk

HOLT
Norfolk

Arcadia ★★★
Contact: Mrs Elizabeth McGill
8 Sunmead Road, Shepperton
TW16 6PE
T: (01932) 770207
E: elizabethmcgill@dialstart.net

Askin
Rating Applied For
Contact: Mrs Nadzieja Askew
Askin, High Street, Cley, Holt
NR25 7AP
T: (01206) 273288

6 Carpenters Cottage ★★★
Contact: Mrs Sally Beament
36 Avranches Avenue, Crediton
EX17 2HB
T: (01363) 773789
E: sallybeament@hotmail.com

5 Carpenters Cottages
★★★
Contact: Mr Christopher Knights
The Hollies Farmhouse,
Rushmere, Lowestoft NR33 8EP
T: (01502) 742022 &
(01493) 842289
F: (01502) 742022

**1 Crowlands Cottage & 4
Carpenters Cottage** ★★★
Contact: Mrs Julie Pell
11 Birch Grove, Spalding
PE11 2HL
T: (01775) 725126
F: (01775) 725126
E: julie.pell@talk21.com

Halcyon House ★★★★
Contact: Mrs Judith Everitt
Wheelcroft, Field Dalling Road,
Fakenham NR21 0OS
T: (01328) 878419

1 Hawthorn Walk ★★★
Contact: Mr Simon Barclay
Kett Country Cottages, 8 Oak
Street, Fakenham NR21 9DY
T: (01328) 856853
F: (01328) 853903
E: info@kettcountrycottages.
co.uk

Hidden Talents ★★★★
Contact: Mr & Mrs Barker
The Anchor, 19 Quay Street,
Woodbridge IP12 1BX
T: (01394) 382649
F: (01394) 610212

Holly Cottage ★★★★
Contact: Mrs Sheila Nelson
Manor Farm, The Loke, Norwich
NR11 7JR
T: (01263) 570035
F: (01263) 570034

Honeysuckle Cottage ★★★
Contact: Miss Allison
Orchard House, Withers Close,
Holt NR25 6NH
T: (01263) 712457

Sunnyside Cottage ★★★
Contact: Mr Michael Drake
Broadland House, Station New
Road, Norwich NR13 5PQ
T: (01603) 712524
F: (01603) 712524
E: michael.drake@ukgateway.
net

Wood Farm Cottages
★★★-★★★★
Contact: Mrs Diana Jacob
Wood Farm Cottages, Plumstead
Road, Melton Constable
NR24 2AQ
T: (01263) 587347
F: (01263) 587347
E: info@wood-farm.com
I: www.wood-farm.com

HOLTON ST MARY
Suffolk

The Coach House ★★★★
Contact: Mrs Anne Selleck
Stratford House, Holton St Mary,
Colchester CO7 6NT
T: (01206) 298246
F: (01206) 298246
E: fjs.stratho@brutus.go-plus.
net
I: www.selfcatering-directory.
co.uk/info.asp?id=582/

HORHAM
Suffolk

Alpha Cottages ★★★
Contact: Mr & Mrs Brian Cooper
The Street, Horham, Eye
IP21 5DX
T: (01379) 384424
F: (01379) 384424

HORNING
Norfolk

Bittern ★★★★
Contact: Mrs Anne Wagstaff
Horning Holiday Homes, 1 Lower
Street, Norwich NR12 8PE
T: (01692) 630849
F: (01692) 630849
E: enquiries@
horningholidayhomes.co.uk
I: www.horningholidayhomes.
co.uk

**Boy's Own Cottage
Riverside** ★★★★
Contact: Ms Alison Atkins
Boys Own Cottage, Great Heath
Farm, Chelmsford Road, Bishop's
Stortford CM22 7BQ
E: alirick@daynet.co.uk
I: www.boysowncottage.co.uk

Bure House ★★★★
Contact: Mrs Bryan
The Manor House, Melton
Mowbray LE14 4SS
T: (01664) 444206
E: ebryan@rutland.gov.uk
I: www.norfolkcottages.co.uk

Ferry Marina ★★★
Contact:
Ferry Road, Norwich NR12 8PS
T: (01692) 630392
I: www.ferry-marina.co.uk

Heron Cottage ★★★★★
Contact: Mrs Gail Pitts
12 Eastfield Road, Royston
SG8 7ED
T: 0778 8 853332
E: info@heron-cottage.com
I: www.heron-cottage.com

**Horning Lodges 1,2,3,
Kates & Lady Lodge & Eagle
Cottage** ★★★-★★★★
Contact: Mr Robert King
King Line Cottages, 4 Pinewood
Drive, Norwich NR12 8LZ
T: (01692) 630849
F: (01692) 630849
E: enquiries@
horningholidayhomes.co.uk
I: www.horningholidayhomes.
co.uk

Little River View ★★★
Contact: Mrs Free
7 Magwitch Close, Newlands
Spring, Chelmsford CM1 4YE
T: (01245) 441981
E: victoria@littleriverview.co.uk
I: www.littleriverview.co.uk

HORNINGTOFT
Norfolk

The Old Stables ★★★
Contact: Mr Ivan Baker
The Old Stables, Church Farm,
Oxwich Road, Dereham
NR20 5DX
T: (01328) 700262
I: www.
theoldstableshorningtoft.com

HOUGHTON
Norfolk

Forester's Cottages ★★★★
Contact: Mrs Joanna Getley
Forester's Cottages, King's Lynn
PE31 6SU
T: (01485) 528609
F: (01485) 528609
E: info@getley.co.uk
I: www.getley.co.uk

HUNSTANTON
Norfolk

Albert House ★★★
Contact: Ms Sarah Flanagan
2 Station Cottages, Station
Road, Nottingham NG14 7GD
T: (01636) 831159
E: sarahflan20@aol.com

Altera ★★★★
Contact: Mrs Jean Larman
64 Hillview Road, Pinner
HA5 4PE
T: (020) 84213815
E: jean.larman@tinyworld.co.uk

Ashdale House ★★★★
Contact: Mrs Sandra Hohol
Birds Norfolk Holiday Homes, 62
Westgate, Hunstanton PE36 5EL
T: (01485) 534267
F: (01485) 535230
E: shohol@
birdsnorfolkholidayhomes.co.uk
I: www.
norfolkholidayhomes-birds.
co.uk

Beat 'n' Retreat ★★
Contact: Mrs Sandra Hohol
Birds Norfolk Holiday Homes, 62
Westgate, Hunstanton PE36 5EL
T: (01485) 534267
F: (01485) 535230
E: shohol@
birdsnorfolkholidayshomes.co.uk
I: www.
norfolkholidayhomes-birds.
co.uk

Beeches ★★★
Contact: Mr & Mrs Judd
Hunstanton Holidays, 64 Tudor
Road, Huntingdon PE29 2DW
T: (01480) 411509
F: (01480) 411509
E: hunstantonholidays@dsl.
pipex.com
I: www.hunstantonholidays.
co.uk

Belle Vue Apartment
★★★-★★★★★
Contact: Mrs Sandra Bowman
Belle Vue Apartment, 28 St
Edmunds Avenue, Hunstanton
PE36 6BW
T: (01485) 532826
F: (01485) 572287

Brincliffe ★★★★
Contact: Mrs Sandra Hohol
Birds Norfolk Holiday Homes, 62
Westgate, Hunstanton PE36 5EL
T: (01485) 534267
F: (01485) 535230
E: shohol@
birdsnorfolkholidayhomes.co.uk
I: www.
norfolkholidayhomes-birds.
co.uk

EAST OF ENGLAND

The Bungalow ★★★
Contact: Mrs Harris
Karivil, 3 Ratby Meadow Lane, St Johns Enderby, Leicester
LE19 2BN
T: (0116) 2862943

Cameo Cottage ★★
Contact: Ms Sandra Hohol
Norfolk Holiday Homes, 62 Westgate, Hunstanton PE36 5EL
T: (01485) 534267
F: (01485) 535230
E: shohol@birdsnorfolkholidayhomes.co.uk
I: www.norfolkholidayhomes.co.uk

Chalet 4 ★★
Contact: Mr Michael & Mrs Ann Chestney
35 West Raynham, 35 The Street, Fakenham NR21 7EY
T: (01328) 838341
F: (01328) 838341

Cleeks ★★★
Contact: Mrs Sandra Hohol
Birds Norfolk Holiday Homes, 62 Westgate, Hunstanton PE36 5EL
T: (01485) 534267
F: (01485) 535230
E: shohol@birdsnorfolkholidayhomes.co.uk
I: www.norfolkholidayhomes-birds.co.uk

70 Cliff Parade ★★★
Contact: Mrs Sandra Hohol
Norfolk Holiday Homes, 62 Westgate, Hunstanton PE36 5EL
T: (01485) 534267
F: (01485) 535230
E: shohol@birdsnorfolkholidayhomes.co.uk
I: www.norfolkholidayhomes-birds.co.uk

40 Collingwood Road ★★★
Contact: Mrs Sandra Hohol
Norfolk Holiday Homes, 62 Westgate, Hunstanton PE36 5EL
T: (01485) 534267
F: (01485) 535230
E: shohol@birdsnorfolkholidayhomes.co.uk
I: www.norfolkholidayhomes-birds.co.uk

End of the Road ★★
Contact: Mrs Sandra Hohol
Birds Norfolk Holiday Homes, 62 Westgate, Hunstanton PE36 5EL
T: (01485) 534267
F: (01485) 535230
E: shohol@birdsnorfolkholidayhomes.co.uk
I: www.norfolkholidayhomes-birds.co.uk

Firemans Cottage ★★★★
Contact: Ms Sandra Hohol
Norfolk Holiday Homes, 62 Westgate, Hunstanton PE36 5EL
T: (01485) 534267

Flat 11 ★★★
Contact: Mrs Sandra Hohol
Norfolk Holiday Homes, 62 Westgate, Hunstanton PE36 5EL
T: (01485) 534267
F: (01485) 535230
E: shohol@birdsnorfolkholhomes.co.uk
I: www.norfolkholidayhomes-birds.co.uk

Flat 3 Tolcarne House ★★★
Contact: Mrs Sandra Hohol
Birds Norfolk Holiday Homes, 62 Westgate, Hunstanton PE36 5EL
T: (01485) 534267
F: (01485) 535230
E: shohol@birdsnorfolkholidayhomes.co.uk

Flat 8 Ashley Gardens ★★★★
Contact: Mrs Sandra Hohol
Birds Norfolk Holiday Homes, 62 Westgate, Hunstanton PE36 5EL
T: (01485) 534267
F: (01485) 535230
E: shohol@birdsnorfolkholidayhomes.co.uk

Hermits Lea ★★★
Contact: Mrs Cheri Crosley
Glebe House, Cromer Road, Hunstanton PE36 6HW
T: (01485) 533332
F: (01485) 533332
E: chericrosley@aol.com

4 Homefields Road ★★★
Contact: Ms Elizabeth Anderson
Prospect House, 92 North End, Royston SG8 5PD
T: (01763) 243067

Honey House
Rating Applied For
Contact: Mr Pam & Mrs Dave McRoberts
Victoria House, Main Road, Hunstanton PE36 6LY
T: (01485) 512077
E: mcrobs@connectfree.co.uk

Horizons ★★★
Contact: Mrs Sandra Hohol
Birds Norfolk Holiday Homes, 62 Westgate, Hunstanton PE36 5EL
T: (01485) 534267
F: (01485) 535230
E: shohol@birdsnorfolkholidayhomes.co.uk

Jaskville ★★★
Contact: Mr John & Mrs Ann Smith
Jaskville, 11 Nene Road, Hunstanton PE36 5BZ
T: (01485) 533404

Jordans
Rating Applied For
Contact: Mrs Linda Smith
37 Melton Drive, Congleton CW12 4YF
T: (01260) 277955
F: (01260) 270435
E: info@stayinhunstanton.co.uk
I: www.stayinhunstanton.co.uk

Keepers Cottage ★★★
Contact: Mrs Sandra Hohol
Norfolk Holiday Homes, 62 Westgate, Hunstanton PE36 5EL
T: (01485) 534267
F: (01485) 534267
E: shohol@birdsnorfolkholidayhomes.co.uk

Lavender Lodge ★★★★
Contact: Mrs Sandra Hohol
Birds Norfolk Holiday Homes, 62 Westgate, Hunstanton PE36 5EL
T: (01485) 534267
F: (01485) 535230
E: shohol@birdsnorfolkholidayhomes.co.uk

1 Lower Lincoln Street ★★★
Contact: Mr Michael Emsden
Sutton House Hotel, 17 Evans Gardens, Hunstanton PE36 5DX
T: (01485) 535001
E: mike@emsden782.fsnet.co.uk

Malgwyn
Rating Applied For
Contact: Mrs Jackie Swift
Great Nortons Farm, Cornish Hall End Road, Halstead CO9 4PE
T: (01440) 785263
E: jackie@nortons.fsworld.co.uk

Midway ★★★
Contact: Mrs Sandra Hohol
Birds Norfolk Holiday Homes, 62 Westgate, Hunstanton PE36 5EL
T: (01485) 534267
F: (01485) 535230
E: shohol@birdsnorfolkholidayhomes.co.uk
I: www.norfolkholidayhomes-birds.co.uk

Minna Cottage ★★★
Contact: Mr Tony Cassie
21 The Green, Hunstanton PE36 5AH
T: (01485) 532448
E: tonycassie@btconnect.com
I: www.minnacottage.com

18 Nelson Drive ★★★
Contact: Mrs Sandra Hohol
Birds Norfolk Holiday Homes, 62 Westgate, Hunstanton PE36 5EL
T: (01485) 534267
F: (01485) 535230
E: shohol@birdsnorfolkholidayhomes.co.uk

No 2, 39 South Beach Road ★★
Contact: Mrs Sandra Hohol
Norfolk Holiday Homes, 62 Westgate, Hunstanton PE36 5EL
T: (01485) 534267
F: (01485) 535230
E: sholhol@birdsnorfolkholidayhomes.co.uk
I: www.norfolkholidayhomes-birds.co.uk

9 Peddars Close ★★★
Contact: Mrs Sandra Hohol
Birds Norfolk Holiday Homes, 62 Westgate, Hunstanton PE36 5EL
T: (01485) 534267
F: (01485) 535230
E: shohol@birdsnorfolkholidayhomes.co.uk

Roundstones ★★★
Contact: Mrs Sandra Hohol
Birds Norfolk Holiday Homes, 62 Westgate, Hunstanton PE36 5EL
T: (01485) 534267
F: (01485) 535230
E: shohol@birdsnorfolkholidayshomes.co.uk
I: www.norfolkholidayhomes-birds.co.uk

St Crispin ★★★
Contact: Mrs Lesley Poore
St Crispin, 3 Wodehouse Road, Old Hunstanton, Hunstanton PE36 6JD
T: (01485) 534036
E: st.crispins@btinternet.com

Sandbanks
Rating Applied For
Contact: Mrs Sandra Hohol
Norfolk Holiday Homes, 62 Westgate, Hunstanton PE36 5EL
T: (01485) 534267
F: (01485) 535230
E: shohol@birdsnorfolkholidayhomes.co.uk
I: www.norfolkholidayhomes-birds.co.uk

Sandpiper Cottage ★★★★
Contact: Mrs Sandra Hohol
Birds Norfolk Holiday Homes, 62 Westgate, Hunstanton PE36 5EL
T: (01485) 534267
F: (01485) 535230
E: shohol@birdsnorfolkholidayhomes.co.uk
I: www.norfolkholidayhomes-birds.co.uk

Sea Breeze ★★★
Contact: Mrs Sandra Hohol
Birds Norfolk Holiday Homes, 62 Westgate, Hunstanton PE36 5EL
T: (01485) 534267
F: (01485) 535230
E: shohol@birdsnorfolkholidaytage.co.uk
I: www.norfolkholidayhomes-birds.co.uk

1 Sea Lane ★★★
Contact: Mrs Kinsley
Norfolk Country Cottages, Carlton House, Market Place, Norwich NR10 4JJ
T: (01603) 308108
F: (01603) 870304
E: holidays@swallow-tail.com
I: www.swallow-tail.com

44 Sea Lane ★★★
Contact: Mrs Sandra Hohol
Birds Norfolk Holiday Homes, 62 Westgate, Hunstanton PE36 5EL
T: (01485) 534267
F: (01485) 535230
E: shohol@birdsnorfolkholidayhomes.co.uk
I: www.norfolkholidayhomes-birds.co.uk

Establishments printed in blue have a detailed entry in this guide

EAST OF ENGLAND

Sea View ★★
Contact: Mr Jeremy Roberts
51 Park Road, Peterborough
PE1 2TH
T: (01733) 342172
E: jeremyroberts.co@btconnect.com

Spindrift ★★★
Contact: Mrs Sandra Hohol
Birds Norfolk Holiday Homes, 62 Westgate, Hunstanton PE36 5EL
T: (01485) 534267
F: (01485) 535340
E: shohol@birdsnorfolkholidayhomes.co.uk
I: www.norfolkholidayhomes-birds.co.uk

Three Steps
Rating Applied For
Contact: Mrs Sandra Hohol
Norfolk Holiday Homes, 62 Westgate, Hunstanton PE36 5EL
T: (01485) 534267
F: (01485) 535340
E: shohol@birdsnorfolkholidayhomes.co.uk
I: www.norfolkholidayhomes-birds.co.uk

Victory Cottage ★★★
Contact: Mrs Sandra Hohol
Norfolk Holiday Homes, 62 Westgate, Hunstanton PE36 5EL
T: (01485) 534267
F: (01485) 535340
E: shohol@birdsnorfolkholidayhomes.co.uk
I: www.norfolkholidayhomes-birds.co.uk

75 Waveney Road
Rating Applied For
Contact: Mrs Sandra Hohol
Birds Norfolk Holiday Homes, 62 Westgate, Hunstanton PE36 5EL
T: (01485) 534267
F: (01485) 535340
E: shohol@birdsnorfolkholidayhomes.co.uk
I: www.norfolkholidayhomes-birds.co.uk

West Lodge ★★★
Contact: Mrs Geraldine Tibbs
West Lodge, Cole Green, Hunstanton PE36 5LS
T: (01485) 571770
F: (01485) 571770

Westacre ★★★
Contact: Mrs Sandra Hohol
Birds Norfolk Holiday Homes, 62 Westgate, Hunstanton PE36 5EL
T: (01485) 534267
F: (01485) 535340
E: shohol@birdsnorfolkholidayhomes.co.uk
I: www.norfolkholidayhomes-birds.co.uk

Westgate Flat ★★
Contact: Mrs Jean Chilleystone
27 Clarence Road, Hunstanton PE36 6HQ
T: (01485) 533646

HUNTINGDON
Cambridgeshire

The Forge White Gates ★★★
Contact: Mr Ian Campbell
T/A The Three Horseshoes Public House, Moat Lane, Huntingdon PE28 2PD
T: (01487) 773555
F: (01487) 773545
E: admin@arfco.co.uk

HUNWORTH
Norfolk

Green Farm Barn ★★★★
Contact: Mrs Patricia Hoskison
Green Farm Barn, The Green, Melton Constable NR24 2AA
T: (01263) 713177
F: (01263) 710083
E: alan@tagsy.freeserve.co.uk
I: www.greenfarmbarn.com

Spink's Nest ★★
Contact: Mrs Angela Hampshire
Riverbank, Kings Street, Melton Constable NR24 2EH
T: (01263) 713891

IKEN
Suffolk

Iken Barns
Rating Applied For
Contact:
Suffolk Secrets, 7 Frenze Road, Diss IP22 4PA
T: (01379) 651297

The Old Stable ★★★★
Contact: Mrs Gunilla Hailes
The Anchorage, Church Lane, Woodbridge IP12 2ES
T: (01728) 688263
F: (01728) 688262

INGOLDISTHORPE
Norfolk

Fox Cottage ★★★
Contact: Ms Eileen Fox
5 Handel Road, Canvey Island SS8 7HL
T: (01268) 680616

Foxes Croft ★★
Contact: Mrs Christine Riches
Foxes Croft (Christines Cottages), 21 Weasenham Road, King's Lynn PE32 2EY
T: (01485) 520216
E: christine-riches@supanet.com
I: www.christine-riches.supanet.com

Pond View ★★★
Contact: Mrs Joy Kelly
14 Robert Balding Road, King's Lynn PE31 6UP
T: (01485) 542751

Swan Cottage ★★★★
Contact: Mr Alex Swan
56 Hill Road, King's Lynn PE31 6NZ
T: (01485) 543882
F: (01485) 543882
E: swans.norfolk@virgin.net
I: www.swanholidays.co.uk

KEDINGTON
Suffolk

The Cottage at Rowans ★★★★
Contact: Mrs Cheryl Owen
Rowans House, Calford Green, Kedington, Haverhill CB9 7UN
T: (01440) 702408
F: (01440) 702408
E: cheryl@owen41.supanet.com
I: www.where2stay-uk.com/html/thecottageatrowans.html

KELLING
Norfolk

The Plough Wheel ★★★
Contact: Mrs Gail Armstrong
Norfolk Country Cottages, Carlton House, Market Place, Norwich NR10 4JJ
T: (01603) 871872
F: (01603) 870304
E: info@norfolkcottages.co.uk
I: www.norfolkcottages.co.uk

KELSALE
Suffolk

East Green Farm Cottages ★★★★
Contact: Mr Robbie & Mrs Claire Gawthrop
East Green, Kelsale, Saxmundham IP17 2PH
T: (01728) 602316
F: (01728) 604408
E: claire@eastgreenproperty.co.uk
I: www.eastgreencottages.co.uk

KESSINGLAND
Suffolk

Beach House Holidays ★★★★
Contact: Mrs Pat Griffin
3 Bakers Lane, Cambridge CB1 6NF
T: (01223) 891054
F: (01223) 891054
E: pat@griffin65.freeserve.co.uk

Church Road ★★★
Contact: Mr James Rayment
28 Woollards Lane, Great Shelford, Cambridge CB2 5LZ
T: (01223) 843048

74 The Cliff ★★
Contact: Mrs Saunders
Foxdale, 159 The Street, Norwich NR14 7HL
T: (01508) 538340

Four Winds Retreat ★★★★
Contact: Mr Peter & Mrs Jane Garner
Four Winds Retreat, Holly Grange Road, Lowestoft NR33 7RR
T: (01502) 740044
E: info@four-winds-retreat.co.uk
I: www.four-winds-retreat.co.uk

&

11 Kessingland Cottages ★★
Contact: Mrs Carol Keane
25 Bunnsfield, Panshanger, Welwyn Garden City AL7 2DZ
T: (01707) 330742

Kew Cottage ★★★
Contact: Mrs Joan Gill
46 St Georges Avenue, Northampton NN2 6JA
T: (01604) 717301
F: (01604) 791424
E: b.s.g@btopenworld.com

Knights Holiday Homes ★★★
Contact: Mr Michael Knights
Knights Holiday Homes, 198 Church Road, Lowestoft NR33 7SF
T: (01502) 588533
E: khols@suffolk70.freeserve.co.uk

5 Seaview ★★★
Contact: Mrs Carol Head
333 Long Road, Lowestoft NR33 9DG
T: (01502) 584880

Spindrift ★★★
Contact: Mrs Gail Armstrong
Norfolk Country Cottages, Carlton House, Market Place, Norwich NR10 4JJ
T: (01603) 871872
F: (01603) 870304
E: info@norfolkcottages.co.uk
I: www.norfolkcottages.co.uk

KETTLEBASTON
Suffolk

Rosie ★★★
Contact: Mrs Sylvia Tillotson
Rosie, Water Hall, Ipswich IP7 7QF
T: (01449) 740703
E: sylvia.tillotson@btopenworld.com

KETTLESTONE
Norfolk

Caretakers Cottage ★★★★
Contact: Mr Simon Barclay
Kett Country Cottages, 8 Oak Street, Fakenham NR21 9DY
T: (01328) 856853
F: (01328) 853903
E: info@kettcountrycottages.co.uk
I: www.kettcountrycottages.co.uk

KING'S LYNN
Norfolk

Granary ★★★
Contact: Mrs Ann Jones
Manor House, Churchgate Way, King's Lynn PE34 4LZ
T: (01553) 828700
E: rhj.akj@terrman1.fsnet.co.uk
I: www.cottagesdirect.com

The Stables Too ★★★
Contact: Ms Sue O'Brien
The Stables Too, 35A Goodwins Road, King's Lynn PE30 5QX
T: (01553) 774638
E: mikeandsueobrien@hotmail.com
I: www.cottageguide.co.uk/thestablestoo

548 Look out for establishments participating in the National Accessible Scheme

EAST OF ENGLAND

KNAPTON
Norfolk

Cornerstone Cottage ★★★★
Contact: Mr & Mrs Eves
Cornerstone Cottage, The Street, North Walsham NR28 0AD
T: (01263) 722884
E: evescornerstone@hotmail.com
I: www.broadland.com/cornerstone

White House Farm - The Granary and Wallages Cottage ★★★★
Contact: Mr & Mrs Goodhead
White House Farm, North Walsham NR28 0RX
T: (01263) 721344
E: info@whitehousefarmnorfolk.co.uk
I: www.whitehousefarmnorfolk.co.uk

KNODISHALL
Suffolk

Forget-Me-Not ★★★
Contact:
Suffolk Secrets, 7 Frenze Road, Diss IP22 4PA
T: (01379) 651297
F: (01379) 641555
E: holiday@suffolk-secrets.co.uk
I: www.suffolk-secrets.co.uk

LAMARSH
Essex

Hill Farm House Self Catering Accommodation ★★★★
Contact: Mrs Brenda Greenhill
Hill Farm House, Alphamstone Back Road, Bures CO8 5HB
T: (01787) 269905
E: greenhillaccom@tiscali.co.uk
I: www.hidden-treasures.co.uk

LANGHAM
Norfolk

Sunnyside Cottage ★★★★
Contact: Mr & Mrs Shephard
11 Faire Road, Leicester LE3 8EE
T: (0116) 2872739
E: jt.glenfield@btinternet.com

LAVENHAM
Suffolk

Blaize Cottages ★★★★★
Contact: Carol & Jim Keohane
Blaize Cottages, Church Street, Lavenham, Sudbury CO10 9QT
T: (01787) 247402
F: (01787) 247402
E: info@blaizecottages.com
I: www.blaizecottages.com

Glebe Cottage ★★★★★
Contact: Mrs Klair Bauly
Malting Farm, Bury St Edmunds IP30 9BJ
T: (01359) 271528
F: (01359) 271528
E: kbauly@waitrose.com
I: www.cottageguide.co.uk/glebecottage

Granary Cottage ★★★★
Contact: Mrs Wendy Williams
Granary Cottage, Mill Farm, Lavenham Road, Bury St Edmunds IP30 0HX
T: (01284) 828458

The Grove ★★★★
Contact: Mr Mark Scott
The Grove, Edwardstone, Lavenham CO10 5PP
T: (01787) 211115
E: mark@grove-cottages.co.uk
I: www.grove-cottages.co.uk

Hour Cottage ★★★★
Contact: Mrs Esther Perkins
118 Western Road, Billericay CM12 9JH
T: (01277) 651843
F: (01277) 650669
E: esther@hourcottage.co.uk
I: www.hourcottage.co.uk

Lavenham Cottages ★★★★★
Contact: Mrs Sheila Lane
Tile Barn, Bury St Edmunds IP29 4DW
T: (01284) 830771
F: (01284) 830771
E: sheila@lavenhamcottages.co.uk
I: www.lavenhamcottages.co.uk

Old Wetherden Hall ★★★
Contact: Mrs Julie Elsden
Old Wetherden Hall, Hitcham, Ipswich IP7 7PZ
T: (01449) 740574
F: (01449) 740574
E: farm@wetherdenhall.force9.co.uk
I: www.oldwetherdenhall.co.uk

Quakers Yard ★★★★
Contact: Mr David Aldous
Two A's Hoggards Green, Bury St Edmunds IP29 4RG
T: (01284) 827271
E: val@quakersyard.com
I: www.quakersyard.com

The Rector's Retreat ★★★
Contact: Mr & Mrs Peter Gutteridge
The Rector's Retreat, The Old Convent, The Street, Ipswich IP7 7QA
T: (01449) 741557
E: holidays@kettlebaston.fsnet.co.uk
I: www.kettlebaston.fsnet.co.uk/

12 Ropers Court ★★★
Contact: Mr Roger Arnold
Queen's House, Church Square, Bures CO8 5AB
T: (01787) 227760
F: (01787) 227078
E: queens-house@btconnect.com
I: www.queenscottages.com

Victoria Cottage ★★★★
Contact: Mr Nigel & Mrs Sheila Margo
5 Brockwell Park Row, London SW2 2YH
T: (020) 86715601
E: sheila@victoriacottage-lavenham.co.uk
I: www.victoriacottage-lavenham.co.uk

LAXFIELD
Suffolk

The Loose Box & The Old Stables ★★★
Contact: Mr John & Mrs Jane Reeve
Laxfield Leisure Ltd, High Street, Laxfield IP13 8DU
T: (01986) 798019
F: (01986) 798155
E: laxfieldleisure@talk21.com
I: www.villastables.co.uk

Meadow Cottage ★★★★
Contact: Mr William Ayers
Quinton House, Gorhams Mill Lane, Laxfield, Woodbridge IP13 8DN
T: (01986) 798345
F: (01986) 798345
E: will.ayers@btinternet.com

LEISTON
Suffolk

Abbey Cottage and The Annexe ★★★
Contact: Ms Sally Baker
6 Glensdale Road, Brockley, London SE4 1UE
T: (020) 84694679
E: info@abbeycottage.com
I: www.abbeycottage.com

Abbey View Lodges ★★★-★★★★★
Contact: Mrs Sally Stobbart
Abbey View Lodge, Abbey Road, Leiston IP16 4TA
T: (01728) 831128
F: (01728) 832633
E: info@abbeyviewlodges.co.uk
I: www.abbeyviewlodges.co.uk

Micawbers ★★★★
Contact: Mrs Joan Hockley
Piggotts Farm, Albury End, Ware SG11 2HS
T: (01279) 771281
F: (01279) 771517
E: j.hockley@whestates.com

The Studio Cottage ★★★
Contact: Mrs Janet Lister
Ivy Cottage, Eastbridge, Leiston IP16 4SG
T: (01728) 833034
F: (01728) 833034

LINDSEY
Suffolk

Heritage Holidays ★★★-★★★★★
Contact: Mrs Jeni White
Heritage Holidays, East View, Lindsey Road, Ipswich IP7 7BB
T: (01787) 247218
F: (01473) 834445
E: info@heritageholidays.com
I: www.heritageholidays.com

LITCHAM
Norfolk

4 Canaan Row ★★★
Contact: Mr David Court
Norfolk Country Cottages, Carlton House, Market Place, Norwich NR10 4JJ
T: (01603) 871872
F: (01603) 870304
E: cottages@paston.co.uk
I: www.norfolkcottages.co.uk/litcham.htm

The Old Farmhouse ★★★
Contact: Mrs Judith Archer
The Old Farmhouse, Druids Lane, King's Lynn PE32 2YA
T: (01328) 701331
F: (01328) 700719
E: judiarcher@aol.com

LITTLE ELLINGHAM
Norfolk

Horseshoes ★★★
Contact: Mrs Julie Abbs
Anchor Farm Cottage, Wood Lane, Attleborough NR17 1JZ
T: (01953) 454514
F: (01953) 454514
E: horseshoes@crackingdeal.com

LITTLE FRANSHAM
Norfolk

Lyons Green & Little Flint ★★★★-★★★★★
Contact: Mrs Jenny Mallon
Fransham Farm Co Ltd, The Old Hall, Little Fransham, East Dereham NR19 2AD
T: (01362) 687649
F: (01362) 687419
E: office@franshamfarm.co.uk
I: www.franshamfarm.co.uk

LITTLE HENHAM
Essex

Stable Cottage ★★★
Contact: Mrs Kate Muskett
Little Henham Hall, Saffron Walden CB11 3XR
T: (01279) 850228
F: (01279) 850397
E: kgmletting@aol.com

LITTLE SNORING
Norfolk

Jex Farm Barn ★★★★
Contact: Mr Stephen Harvey
Jex Farm, Fakenham NR21 0JJ
T: (01328) 878257
F: (01328) 878257
E: stephenharvey@supanet.com
I: www.broadland.com/jexfarmbarn.html

Sunset Cottage ★★★★
Contact: Mr & Mrs Fuller
Sunset Cottage, The Street, Fakenham NR21 0HU
T: (01328) 878836
F: (01328) 878836

The White House Cottage & Barn Lodge ★★★
Contact: Mrs Celia Lee
The White House Cottage & Barn Lodge, The Street, Fakenham NR21 0AJ
T: (01328) 878789
E: celia.lee@freenet.co.uk

LITTLE WALDEN
Essex

Orchard View Numbers 1 - 4 ★★★
Contact: Mrs Maureen Chapman-Barker
Orchard View Numbers 1 - 4, Little Bowsers Farm, Bowsers Lane, Saffron Walden CB10 1XQ
T: (01799) 527315
F: (01799) 527315
E: sales@farmerkit.co.uk
I: www.farmerkit.co.uk

Establishments printed in blue have a detailed entry in this guide

EAST OF ENGLAND

LITTLE WALSINGHAM
Norfolk

The Old Coach House ★★★★
Contact: Mr Geoff & Mrs Julia Holloway
Bramble Cottage, Helmingham Road, Ipswich IP6 9NS
T: (01473) 390035
E: theoldcoach.house@btinternet.com
I: www.theoldcoach.house.btinternet.com

LITTLEPORT
Cambridgeshire

Caves Farm Barns ★★★
Contact: Mr Stephen Kerridge
Caves Farm, 25 Hale Fen, Ely CB6 1EJ
T: (01353) 861423
F: (01353) 861423
E: cb6steve@aol.com
I: www.cavesfarmbarns.co.uk

LONG MELFORD
Suffolk

4 Church Walk ★★★
Contact: Mr Mark Thomas
4 Church Walk, 33 Patshull Road, Kentish Town, London NW5 2JX
T: (020) 72673653
F: (01932) 583206
E: mark.thomas@rmc-group.com

Hope Cottage ★★★★
Contact: Ms S Jamil
Hill Farm Cottage, Duffs Hill, Glemsford, Sudbury CO10 7PP
T: (01787) 282338 & 07970 808701
F: (01787) 282338
E: sns.jam@tesco.net
I: www.hope-cottage-suffolk.co.uk

LOWER GRESHAM
Norfolk

The Cottage ★★★★
Contact: Mrs Karen Battrick
Flint House, Sustead Road, Norwich NR11 8RE
T: (01263) 577725
E: pjkbatt@naser.net

The Roost ★★★
Contact: Mr & Mrs Entwistle
Brick Kiln Farmhouse, Sustead Road, Norwich NR11 8RE
T: (01263) 577388
E: keith.entwistle@supanet.com

LOWESTOFT
Suffolk

10 Banner Court ★★★
Contact: Mrs Aisha Khalaf
32A Kirkley Cliff Road, Lowestoft NR33 0DB
T: (01502) 511876
F: (01502) 580738
E: aishakhalaf@hotmail.com

Lowestoft Holiday Flat ★★
Contact: Mrs Courtauld
Pyes Hall, London Road, Wrentham, Beccles NR34 7HL
T: (01502) 675209
E: mcourtauld@onetel.net.uk

Lyka Sands ★★★
Contact: Ms Lynne Luettschwager
78 Worthing Road, Lowestoft NR32 4HA
T: (01502) 530631
F: (01502) 530631
E: lynne@luettschwager.freeserve.co.uk

Pebble Cottage ★★★
Contact: Mr Lisa & Mrs Shane Harris
Wisteria Cottage, 23 The Square, Reading R67 1BS
T: (0118) 9886858

Shaftsbury House ★★★★
Contact: Mrs Wigg
Jacaranda House & Home Services, Lowestoft
T: (01502) 568580

Suffolk Seaside & Broadlands ★★★
Contact: Mrs Collecott
282 Gorleston Road, Oulton, Lowestoft NR32 3AJ
T: (01502) 564396

Tides Reach Holiday Flats ★★
Contact: Mrs Tallamy
Marsh Farm, Hulver Road, Beccles NR34 7TP
T: (01502) 476658

16 Wilson Road ★★★
Contact: Mr & Mrs Andrew Murray
24 Maltese Road, Chelmsford CM1 2PA
T: (01245) 266018
F: (01245) 287000

LYNG
Norfolk

Holly Cottage ★★★
Contact: Mr Thomas
Collin Green Farm, Norwich NR9 5LH
T: (01603) 880158
F: (01603) 881228

Utopia Paradise ★★★
Contact: Mrs Suzan Jarvis
The Mallards, Farman Close, Lyng, Norwich NR9 5RD
T: (01603) 870812
E: holidays@utopia-paradise.co.uk

MALDON
Essex

Sunningdale ★★★
Contact: Mr Roger & Mrs Christine Beckett
Sunningdale, 49 Fambridge Road, Maldon CM9 6BG
T: (01621) 858235
E: roger.beckett@btinternet.com

MARLESFORD
Suffolk

Hollyhock Cottage ★★★
Contact: Mr John Hammond & Elizabeth Ardill
Suffolk Cottage Holidays, 34 Seckford Street, Woodbridge IP12 4LY
T: (01394) 384007
F: (01394) 386253
E: lizzie@suffolkcottageholidays.co.uk
I: www.suffolkcottageholidays.com

MARSWORTH
Hertfordshire

Field House ★★★★
Contact: Mr Pash
Hideaways, Chapel House, Luke Street, Berwick St John, Shaftesbury SP7 0HQ
T: (01747) 828170
F: (01747) 829090
E: enq@hideaways.co.uk
I: www.hideaways.co.uk/property.cfm/h704

MARTHAM
Norfolk

Greenside Cottage ★★★
Contact: Mrs Barbara Dyball
Greenside, 30 The Green, Great Yarmouth NR29 4PA
T: (01493) 740375

MAUTBY
Norfolk

Lower Wood Farm Country Cottages ★★★★
Contact: Ms Jill Nicholls
Lower Wood Farm Country Cottages, Browns Lane, Great Yarmouth NR29 3JQ
T: (01493) 722523
F: (01403) 722523
E: info@lowerwoodfarm.co.uk
I: www.lowerwoodfarm.co.uk

MENDHAM
Suffolk

Tom, Dick & Harry ★★★
Contact: Mrs Audrey Carless
Tom, Dick & Harry, Church Farm Barn, Withersdale Street, Harleston IP20 0JR
T: (01379) 588091
F: (01379) 586009
E: enquiries@bacatchurchfarm.co.uk
I: www.bacatchurchfarm.co.uk

MICKFIELD
Suffolk

Read Cottage
Rating Applied For
Contact: Mr Andrew & Mrs Andrea Stewart
Read Cottage, Read Hall, Stowmarket IP14 5LU
T: (01449) 711663
E: info@readhall.co.uk
I: www.readhall.co.uk

MIDDLETON
Suffolk

The Old Church Room ★★★★
Contact:
Suffolk Secrets, 7 Frenze Road, Diss IP22 4PA
T: (01379) 651297
F: (01379) 641555
E: holidays@suffolk-secrets.co.uk
I: www.suffolk-secrets.co.uk

Rose Farm Barns ★★★★
Contact: Mrs Janet Maricic
Rose Farm Barns, Mill Street, Saxmundham IP17 3NG
T: (01728) 648456
I: www.suffolk-secrets.co.uk

MILDENHALL
Suffolk

The Coach House & Stables
Rating Applied For
Contact: Mrs Anne Greenfield
The Coach House & Stables, 23 North Terrace, Bury St Edmunds IP28 7AA
T: (01638) 711237
E: orchardhouse23@aol.com
I: www.mildenhall-bed-breakfast.co.uk

MILEHAM
Norfolk

Mallards ★★★
Contact: Mrs Joscelin Colborne
Mallards, The Street, King's Lynn PE32 2RA
T: (01328) 700602
F: (01328) 700061
E: joscelin.colborne@mallards.co.uk

MUCH HADHAM
Hertfordshire

Blackcroft Farmhouse ★★★★
Contact: Mrs Gill Trundle
Blackcroft Farmhouse, Much Hadham SG10 6AD
T: (01279) 843832

MUNDESLEY
Norfolk

The Anchorage ★★★
Contact: Mrs Gail Armstrong
Norfolk Country Cottages, Market Place, Norwich NR10 4JJ
T: (01603) 871872
F: (01603) 870304
E: info@norfolkcottages.co.uk
I: www.norfolkcottages.co.uk

Holiday Properties (Mundesley) ★-★★★
Contact: Mr Mark & Mrs Nadine Gray
Holiday Properties (Mundesley) Ltd, 6A Paston Road, Mundesley, Norwich NR11 8BN
T: (01263) 720719
F: (01263) 720719
E: holidayproperties@tesco.net
I: www.holidayprops.freeuk.com

EAST OF ENGLAND

Paddock Bungalow ★★★
Contact: Mrs Christine Harding
The Hughes Farm, Gimingham
Road, Norwich NR11 8DG
T: (01263) 721060
F: (01263) 722998
E: christine.m.harding@
btinternet.com
I: www.cottageguide.
co.uk/paddockbungalow/

10 Royal Chalet Park ★★★
Contact: Mrs Gail Armstrong
Norfolk Country Cottages,
Carlton House, Market Place,
Norwich NR10 4JJ
T: (01603) 871872
F: (01603) 870304
E: info@norfolkcottages.com
I: www.norfolkcottages.co.uk

Schooner Cottage ★★★★
Contact: Mr & Mrs Martin Webb
Schooner Cottage, Victoria
Road, Mundesley, Norwich
NR11 8JG
T: (01692) 582290
E: thewebbs@macunlimited.net

Wild Rose Cottage ★★★
Contact: Mr Graham Tuckett
127 Writtle Road, Chelmsford
CM1 3BP
T: (01245) 252397
F: (01245) 252397
E: ruffelsandtuckett@hotmail.com

NARBOROUGH
Norfolk

Church Farm Holiday Homes ★★★★
Contact: Mrs Nicky St Lawrence
Church Farm Holiday Homes,
King's Lynn PE32 1TE
T: (01760) 337696
F: (01760) 337858
E: nickystlawrence@yahoo.com
I: www.
churchfarmholidayhomes.com

Cliff Barns
Rating Applied For
Contact: Mr Russell Hall
Po Box 47, Thetford IP26 5WS
T: (01366) 328342
F: (01366) 328942
E: shoutout@skmarket.co.uk
I: www.cliffbarns.com

Fairywood Cottage
Rating Applied For
Contact: Mrs Sandra Hohol
Norfolk Holiday Homes, 62
Westgate, Hunstanton PE36 5EL
T: (01485) 534267
F: (01485) 535230
E: shohol@
birdsnorfolkholidayhomes.co.uk
I: www.
norfolkholidayhomes-birds.
co.uk

NAYLAND
Suffolk

Gladwins Farm ★★★★-★★★★★
Contact: Mrs Pauline Dossor
Gladwins Farm, Harpers Hill,
Nayland, Colchester CO6 4NU
T: (01206) 262261
F: (01206) 263001
E: gladwinsfarm@aol.com
I: www.gladwinsfarm.co.uk

NEWMARKET
Suffolk

6 Belmont & 11 Ashbourne Court ★★
Contact: Mrs Jennie Collingridge
Harraton Court Stables, Chapel
Street, Newmarket CB8 7HA
T: (01638) 577952
F: (01638) 577952
E: jennie@harratonstables.
freeserve.co.uk

Gipsy Hall ★★★★
Contact: Mrs Francis Dow
Gipsy Hall, Dullingham Ley,
Newmarket CB8 9XF
T: (01638) 508443
E: gipsyhall@onetel.com

Swallows Rest ★★★★
Contact: Mrs Gill Woodward
Swallows Rest, 6 Ditton Green,
Woodditton, Newmarket
CB8 9SQ
T: (01638) 730823
E: gillian@swallowsrest.f9.co.uk

NORTH WALSHAM
Norfolk

April Cottage ★★★
Contact: Dr Elisabeth Le Strange
14 Fairfax Avenue, Oxford
OX3 0RP
T: (01865) 421834
I: www.autonomic.org.
uk/aprilcottage

NORTH WOOTTON
Norfolk

Winsdail ★★★★
Contact: Mr Andrew Booth
Tudorwood Fern Hill, King's Lynn
PE31 6HT
T: (01485) 543639
F: (01485) 543639
E: mail@winsdailcottage.com
I: www.winsdailcottage.com

NORTHREPPS
Norfolk

Acorn Cottage ★★★
Contact: Mrs Louise Strong
Acorn Cottage, Woodland
House, Cromer Road, Cromer
NR27 0JY
T: (01263) 579736
E: stephen.strong@virgin.net

Corder Cottage ★★★★
Contact: Mrs Heather McCraith
Norfolk Country Cottages,
Carlton House, Market Place,
Norwich NR10 4JJ
T: (01603) 871872
F: (01603) 870304
E: info@norfolkcottages.co.uk

Manor Studio ★★★★
Contact: Mrs Jane Hunt
Manor Studio, The Old Manor
House, 21 Church Street, Cromer
NR27 0AA
T: (01263) 579126
E: jane_d_hunt@yahoo.com

The Old Post Office ★★★
Contact: Mr Andrew Banner
Odd Fellows Hall, Black Street,
Great Yarmouth NR29 4PN
T: 0845 6 444018
E: info@norfolkcottageholidays.
com
I: www.norfolkcottageholidays.
com

Torridon & Yeomans Cottage ★★★★
Contact: Mrs Youngman
Shrublands Farm, Northrepps,
Cromer NR27 0AA
T: (01263) 579297
F: (01263) 579297
E: youngman@farming.co.uk
I: www.broadland.com/torridon

NORWICH
Norfolk

The Garden Flat ★★★
Contact: Mrs Eunice Edwards
Hatton House, 70 Earlham Road,
Norwich NR2 3DF
T: (01603) 612579
E: enquiries@gardenflat.co.uk
I: www.gardenflat70.co.uk

The Hideaway ★★★-★★★★
Contact: Mrs Reilly
The Hideaway, Woodbastwick
Road, Norwich NR13 4AB
T: (01603) 715052
E: pondside@talk21.com
I: www.norfolkbroads.
com/thehideaway

30 Kingsley Road ★★★
Contact: Miss Sally Clarke
9 Kingsley Road, Norwich
NR1 3RB
T: (01603) 473547
F: (01603) 473547
E: kingsley@paston.co.uk
I: www.selfcateringnorwich.
co.uk

Mabels Cottage ★★★
Contact: Mr & Mrs Randon
Mabels Cottage, Fritton
Common, Norwich NR15 2QS
T: (01508) 499279
F: (01508) 499279
E: judy.randon@virgin.net
I: www.mabels-cottage.co.uk

Mill House ★★★★
Contact: Ms Fay Godin
3 Mill Cottages, Hellesdon Mill
Lane, Norwich NR6 5AZ
T: (01603) 415061
E: villa.cott@virgin.net

Parlours ★★★★
Contact: Mr & Mrs Derek Wright
Earlham Guesthouse, 147
Earlham Road, Norwich
NR2 3RG
T: (01603) 454169
E: earlhamgh@hotmail.com
I: www.parlours.net

Poolside Lodges ★★★
Contact: Mrs Sally-Anne Hinkley
Poolside Lodges, South Lodge,
Woods End, Salhouse Road,
Rackheath Park, Norwich
NR13 6LD
T: (01603) 720000
F: (01603) 721483
E: sally.hinkley@btinternet.com
I: www.visitnorwich-area.co.uk

Sommersby ★★★
Contact: Miss Jackson
31 Guy Cook Close, Sudbury
CO10 0JX
T: (01787) 372903
E: djackson@sommersby.
freeserve.co.uk

Spixworth Hall Cottages ★★★-★★★★
Contact: Mrs Sheelah-Jane Cook
Spixworth Hall Cottages, Buxton
Road, Norwich NR10 3PR
T: (01603) 898190
F: (01603) 897176
E: hallcottages@btinternet.com
I: www.hallcottages.co.uk

Thyme Cottage ★★★★
Contact: Mr David Lythell
Town Pit Cottage,
Woodbastwick Road, Blofield
Heath, Norwich NR13 4AB
T: (01603) 414443
F: (01603) 789472
E: dave@lythell.demon.co.uk

OLD BUCKENHAM
Norfolk

Ox and Plough Cottages ★★★
Contact: Mrs Sally Bishop
Ox and Plough Cottages, The
Green, Attleborough NR17 1RN
T: (01953) 860004
F: (01953) 860004
E: oxandplough.bishop@barbox.
net
I: www.oxandploughcottages.
co.uk

ORFORD
Suffolk

Broom Cottage ★★★★
Contact: Mrs Suvi Pool
High House Fruit Farm, 69
Broom Cottages, High House
Farm Road, Woodbridge
IP12 2BL
T: (01394) 450378
F: (01394) 450124
E: cottage@high-house.co.uk

Brownies ★★★★
Contact: Mrs Sue Cartlidge
Orford Cottages, 10 Sandy Lane,
Woodbridge IP12 2HF
T: (01728) 687844
F: (01728) 687841
E: info@orford-cottages.co.uk
I: www.orford-cottages.co.uk

The Cart Lodge Studio Apartment ★★★
Contact: Mrs Susan Crane
The White House, Ferry Road,
Sudbourne, Woodbridge
IP12 2BQ
T: (01394) 450033
F: (01394) 450033
E: jasmcrane@aol.com

Establishments printed in blue have a detailed entry in this guide

EAST OF ENGLAND

47 Daphne Road ★★★
Contact: Mrs Sheila Hitchcock
Church Farm Cottage, Ferry Road, Sudbourne, Woodbridge IP12 2BP
T: (01394) 450714
F: (01394) 450714
E: barryhitchcock@tesco.com

Hawes Cottage ★★★
Contact: Mr Keble Paterson
Black Cottage, Quay Street, Woodbridge IP12 2NU
T: (01394) 450771
F: (01394) 450062
E: keblepaterson@vodafone.net

Vesta Cottage ★★★
Contact: Mrs Penny Kay
Orford, Woodbridge IP12 2NQ
T: (01394) 450652
F: (01394) 450097
E: kaycottages@pobox.com
I: www.vestacottage.com

ORWELL
Cambridgeshire

The Retreat ★★★★
Contact: Mrs M Meikle
The Retreat, Malton Road, Royston SG8 5QR
T: (01223) 208005

OULTON
Norfolk

Docking Farm Cottage ★★★★
Contact: Mrs Sally Harrold
Docking Farm Cottage, Norwich NR11 6QZ
T: (01603) 870715
F: (01603) 872952
E: efharrold@farming.co.uk

Willowbank Cottage ★★★
Contact: Mrs E. Poynder
25 Champneys Walk, Cambridge CB3 9AW
T: (01223) 462470
E: richard@smartex.com

OULTON BROAD
Suffolk

7 Holly Road ★★★
Contact: Mrs Tonia Moore
97A Normanston Drive, Lowestoft NR32 2PX
T: (01502) 563868
E: tonia@moore97a.fsnet.co.uk

Maltings Holiday Accommodation ★★★★
Contact: Miss Caroline Sterry
c/o Ivy House Country Hotel, Ivy Lane, Oulton Broad, Lowestoft NR33 8HY
T: (01502) 501353
F: (01502) 501530
E: etc@ivyhousefarm.co.uk
I: www.ivyhousefarm.co.uk

White House Farm ★★★
Contact: Mr & Mrs Andrew Hughes
White House Farm, Burnt Hill Lane, Carlton Colville Oulton Broad, Lowestoft NR33 8HU
T: (01502) 564049
E: mail@whitehousefarm.org.uk
I: www.whitehousefarm.org.uk

OVERSTRAND
Norfolk

Beaches ★★★
Contact: Miss Denise Lewis
Lambert & Watts Self Catering Holidays, Holiday Cottages, Chalets And Flats, 15 West Street, Cromer NR27 9HZ
T: (01263) 511028
F: (01263) 513139
E: property@lambertw.fslife.co.uk

Buckthorns ★★★★
Contact: Mrs Mandy Reeve
Crackers, Wignals Gate, Spalding PE12 7HR
T: (01406) 422953
F: (01406) 425192
E: mail@ealing74.fsnet.co.uk

17 Danish House Gardens ★★★★
Contact: Ms Denise Lewis
Lambert & Russell, 15 West Street, Cromer NR27 9HZ
T: (01263) 511028
F: (01263) 513139
E: property@lambertw.fslife.co.uk
I: uk.geocities.com/overstrand.cromer@btinternet.com

Flat 4 ★★★
Contact:
Lambert & Russell, 15 West Street, Cromer NR27 9HZ
T: (01263) 511028
F: (01263) 513139
E: property@lambertw.fslife.co.uk

31 Harbord Road ★★★★
Contact: Mrs Jane Langley
28 Esher Place Avenue, Esher KT10 8PY
T: (01372) 463063
F: (01372) 463063
E: jane@harbordholidays.co.uk
I: www.harbord.holidays.co.uk

Poppyland Holiday Cottages ★★★★
Contact: Mrs Riches
Poppyland Holiday Cottages, 21 Regent Street, Norwich NR11 7ND
T: (01263) 577473
F: (01263) 570087
E: poppyland@totalise.co.uk
I: www.broadland.com/poppyland

OXBOROUGH
Norfolk

Ferry Farm Cottage ★★★
Contact: Mrs Margaret Wilson
Ferry Farm, Ferry Road, King's Lynn PE33 9PT
T: (01366) 328287
E: ferryfarm@btinternet.com
I: www.ferryfarm.btinternet.co.uk

OXNEAD
Norfolk

Keepers Cottage ★★★
Contact:
Norfolk Country Cottages, Carlton House, Market Place, Norwich NR10 4JJ
T: (01603) 871872
F: (01603) 870304
E: cottages@paston.co.uk
I: www.norfolkcottages.co.uk

PAKEFIELD
Suffolk

Cliff Cottage ★★★
Contact: Mrs Thelma Bruce
Fishermans Cottage, Pakefield Street, Lowestoft NR33 0JS
T: (01502) 501955
F: (01502) 501955

Holiday Cottage ★★★★
Contact: Mrs Victoria Mead
Longshore, Coastguard Lane, Lowestoft NR33 9RE
T: (01502) 740304

PASTON
Norfolk

Garden Cottage ★★★★
Contact: Mr Nigel Cornwall
Heath Farm Cottage, North Walsham NR28 0SQ
T: (01692) 407008

PELDON
Essex

Rose Barn Cottage ★★★★
Contact: Mrs Ariette Everett
Mersea Road/Colchester Road, Peldon, Colchester CO5 7QJ
T: (01206) 735317
F: (01206) 735311
E: everettaj@aol.com

PENTNEY
Norfolk

Bradmoor Cottage ★★★★
Contact: Mrs Sandra Hohol
Birds Norfolk Holiday Homes, 62 Westgate, Hunstanton PE36 5EL
T: (01485) 534267
F: (01485) 535230
E: shohol@birdsnorfolkholidayhomes.co.uk
I: www.norfolkholidayhomes-birds.co.uk

PIN MILL
Suffolk

Alma Cottage ★★★
Contact: Mr John Pugh
Culver End, Stroud GL5 5AG
T: (01453) 872551
F: (01453) 843225
E: john.pugh@talk21.com

POLSTEAD
Suffolk

The Stables ★★★
Contact: Mr & Mrs Richard English
Sprotts Farm, Holt Road, Colchester CO6 5BT
T: (01787) 210368
E: R.J.English@btinternet.com

RADLETT
Hertfordshire

Constance ★★★
Contact: Mr & Mrs Clive Miles
Constance, 39 Homefield Road, Radlett WD7 8PX
T: (01923) 854444
E: CAYD@homefield39.fsnet.co.uk

RADWINTER
Essex

Plough Hill Farm ★★★★
Contact: Mr Richard Martin
Plough Hill Farm, Hempstead Road, Saffron Walden CB10 2TQ
T: (01799) 599411
E: richard.martin3@tesco.net
I: homepages.tesco.net/~richard.martin3/index.html

RATTLESDEN
Suffolk

The Dower House ★★★★
Contact: Mrs Hilary Voysey
The Dower House, Clopton Green, Bury St Edmunds IP30 0RN
T: (01449) 736332
E: all@voysey.freeserve.co.uk

REDBOURN
Hertfordshire

The Beeches ★★★★
Contact: Mrs June Surridge
The Beeches, Hemel Hempstead Road, St Albans AL3 7AG
T: (01582) 792638
F: (01582) 792638

REEDHAM
Norfolk

Norton Marsh Mill ★★★
Contact: Mrs Kinsley
Norfolk Country Cottages, Carlton House, Market Place, Norwich NR10 4JJ
T: (01603) 308108
F: (01603) 870304
E: holidays@swallow-tail.com
I: www.swallow-tail.com

REEPHAM
Norfolk

Church View ★★★★
Contact: Ms Marion Stiefel
Echo Lodge, 34 Ollands Road, Norwich NR10 4EJ
T: (01603) 872068

REPPS WITH BASTWICK

Grove Farm Holidays ★★★-★★★★
Contact: Mr & Mrs P W Pratt
Grove Farm Holidays, Great Yarmouth NR29 5JN
T: (01692) 670205
E: enquiries@grovefarmholidays.co.uk
I: www.grovefarmholidays.co.uk

REYDON
Suffolk

The Ark ★★★
Contact:
Suffolk Secrets, 7 Frenze Road, Diss IP22 4PA
T: (01379) 651297
F: (01379) 641555
E: holidays@suffolk.secrets.co.uk
I: www.suffolk-secrets.co.uk

Church Cottage ★★★
Contact:
Suffolk Secrets, 7 Frenze Road, Diss IP22 4PA
T: (01379) 651297
F: (01379) 641555
E: holidays@suffolk.secrets.co.uk
I: www.suffolk-secrets.co.uk

EAST OF ENGLAND

The Coach House
Rating Applied For
Contact:
The Coach House, 59 Wangford Road, Southwold IP18 6QA
T: (01379) 651297
F: (01379) 641555
E: holidays@suffolk-secrets.co.uk
I: www.suffolk-secrets.co.uk

Furze Patch ★★★★
Contact:
Suffolk Secrets, 7 Frenze Road, Diss IP22 4PA
T: (01379) 651297
F: (01379) 641555
E: holidays@suffolk-secrets.co.uk
I: www.suffolk-secrets.co.uk

Quay House Chalet ★★★
Contact: Mrs Claire Guppy
The Maltings, Woodleys Yard, High Street, Southwold IP18 6HP
T: (01502) 723323
F: (01502) 723323
E: reservations@southwold-quaychalet.co.uk
I: www.southwold-quayhouse.co.uk

Richmond ★★★
Contact:
Suffolk Secrets, 7 Frenze Road, Diss IP22 4PA
T: (01379) 651297
F: (01379) 641555
E: holidays@suffolk-secrets.co.uk
I: www.suffolk-secrets.co.uk

Sundial ★★
Contact: Mrs Claire Guppy
Acanthus Property Letting Services Ltd, 9 Trinity Street, Southwold IP18 6JH
T: (01502) 724033
F: (01502) 725168
E: sales@southwold-holidays.co.uk
I: www.southwold-holidays.co.uk

Whimbrel Cottage ★★★
Contact:
Suffolk Secrets, 7 Frenze Road, Diss IP22 4PA
T: (01379) 651297
F: (01379) 641555
E: holidays@suffolk-secrets.co.uk
I: www.suffolk-secrets.co.uk

RINGSTEAD
Norfolk

April Cottage & Tamarisk Cottage ★★★★
Contact: Ms Laurice Jarman
Jariard Ltd, Church Farm House, 33 Nursery Lane, King's Lynn PE30 3NG
T: (01553) 676060
F: (01553) 671211
E: bookings@jariard.fsnet.co.uk
I: www.jariardltd.co.uk

Crossways ★
Contact: Mrs Sandra Hohol
Birds Norfolk Holiday Homes, 62 Westgate, Hunstanton PE36 5EL
T: (01485) 534267
F: (01485) 535230
E: shohol@birdsnorfolkholidayhomes.co.uk
I: www.norfolkholidayhomes-birds.co.uk

7 Langford Cottages ★★★★
Contact: Mr Douglas Hill
Shootersway Lane, Woodstock, Berkhamsted HP4 3NW
T: (01442) 864387
F: (01442) 871589
E: djbhill@waitrose.com

Lindsay Cottage ★★★
Contact: Mrs Gail Armstrong
Norfolk Country Cottages Ref. 560, Market Place, Norwich NR10 4JJ
T: (01603) 871872
F: (01603) 870304
E: info@norfolkcottages.co.uk
I: www.norfolkcottages.co.uk/ringstea.htm

Orchard House ★★★
Contact: Mrs Sandra Hohol
Birds Norfolk Holiday Homes, 62 Westgate, Hunstanton PE36 5EL
T: (01485) 534267
F: (01485) 535230
E: shohol@birdsnorfolkholidayhomes.co.uk
I: www.norfolkholidayhomes-birds.co.uk

RISELEY
Bedfordshire

Coldham Cottages ★★★★
Contact: Ms Jean Felce
Risley Lodge Farm, Bowers Lane, Bedford MK44 1DL
T: (01234) 708489
F: (01234) 708372
E: info@coldhamcottages.co.uk
I: www.coldhamcottages.co.uk

ROCKLAND ST MARY
Norfolk

Oxnead Holiday Cottages ★★★
Contact: Mrs Helen Cook
Oxnead Holiday Cottages, 5 New Inn Hill, Rockland St Mary, Norwich NR14 7HP
T: (01508) 538295
E: oxnead@supanet.com
I: www.oxnead.com

ROUGHTON
Norfolk

Jonas Farm Holiday Barns Ltd ★★★★-★★★★★
Contact: Mr Sean Kelly
Jonas Farm Holiday Barns Ltd, Cromer Road, Cromer NR11 8PF
T: (01263) 515438
F: (01263) 515438
E: info@jonasfarmholidaybarns.co.uk
I: www.jonasfarmholidaybarns.co.uk

Nora Blogg's Cottage ★★
Contact: Mr Varden
Chalden Cottage, Felbrigg Road, Roughton, Norwich NR11 8PA
T: (01263) 513353

Pond Farm Cottages ★★★★
Contact: Mr Faiers
Argyll Group, Argyll House, 201 Holt Road, Cromer NR27 9JN
T: (01263) 513165
F: (01263) 513165
E: tonyfaiers@btinternet.com
I: www.blakes-cottages.co.uk

RUNCTON HOLME
Norfolk

Thorpland Manor Barns ★★★★
Contact: Mrs Mary Caley
Downham Road, King's Lynn PE33 0AD
T: (01553) 810409
F: (01553) 811831
E: w.p.caley@tesco.net

SAFFRON WALDEN
Essex

The Barn ★★★★
Contact: Mr John Goose & Mrs Minty Landeryou
Burntwood End, Saffron Walden CB10 1XE
T: (01799) 523202
E: burntwood@onetel.com
I: www.cottageguide.co.uk/the-barn

The Byre ★★★
Contact: Mrs Tineke Westerhuis
The Byre, Rockells Farm, Duddenhow End, Saffron Walden CB11 4UY
T: (01763) 838053
F: (01763) 838053
E: evert.westerhuis@tiscali.co.uk
I: www.rockellsfarm.co.uk

The Coach House ★★★★
Contact: Dr John Goose
Burntwood End, Saffron Walden CB10 1XE
T: (01799) 523202
E: burntwood@onetel.com
I: www.cottageguide.co.uk/the-coach-house

The Cottage ★★★★
Contact: Dr Michael Rigby
38 Gold Street, Saffron Walden CB10 1EJ
T: (01799) 501373
E: Mike@MCRigby.co.uk
I: www.mcrigby.co.uk

Little Bulls Farmhouse ★★★★
Contact: Mr Kiddy
Radwinter Park, Radwinter End, Saffron Walden CB10 2UE
T: (01799) 599272
F: (01799) 599172
E: ajkiddy@cambridge-vacation-homes.com
I: www.cambridge-vacation-homes.com

Newhouse Farm ★★★★
Contact: Mrs E Redcliffe
Newhouse Farm, Walden Road, Radwinter, Saffron Walden CB10 2SP
T: (01799) 599211
F: (01799) 599037
E: emmaredcliffe@hotmail.com

ST ALBANS
Hertfordshire

69 Albert Street & 20 Keyfield Terrace ★★
Contact: Mrs Carol Nicol
178 London Road, St Albans AL1 1PL
T: (01727) 846726
F: (01727) 831267
I: www.178londonroad.co.uk

High Meadows ★★★★
Contact: Mrs Jenny Hale
High Meadows, 32 Lancaster Road, St Albans AL1 4ET
T: (01727) 865092
E: family.hale@ntlworld.com
I: www.akomodation.co.uk

The Hollies ★★★★
Contact: Mrs Anne Newbury
11 Spencer Place, Sandridge, St Albans AL4 9DW
T: (01727) 859845
E: martin.newbury@ntlworld.co.uk

Holmes Court Apartment ★★★★
Contact: Ms Margot Choo
Monworth Limited, 12 Wyton, Welwyn Garden City AL7 2PF
T: (01707) 327977
E: margot@monworth.com
I: www.monworth.com

ST NEOTS
Cambridgeshire

Croxton Old Rectory ★★★
Contact: Mrs Margaret Williams
Croxton Old Rectory, Cambridge Road, Croxton, Huntingdon PE19 6SU
T: (01480) 880344
F: (01480) 880344

ST OSYTH
Essex

Park Hall Country Cottages ★★★★★
Contact: Mrs Trisha Ford
Park Hall Country Cottages, Park Farm, Clay Lane, St Osyth, Clacton-on-Sea CO16 8HG
T: (01255) 820922
E: Trish@parkhall.fslife.co.uk
I: www.parkhall-countrycottages.com

SALLE
Norfolk

Lodge Cottage ★★★
Contact: Mr Douglas Whitelaw
Salle Moor Hall Farm, Norwich NR10 4SB
T: (01603) 879046
F: (01603) 879047
E: douglas@salleoragnics.com
I: www.salleorganics.com

SALTHOUSE
Norfolk

Dun Cow Public House ★★★
Contact: Mrs Kay Groom
Dun Cow Public House, Coast Road, Holt NR25 7XA
T: (01263) 740467
I: www.theduncow-salthouse.co.uk

Establishments printed in blue have a detailed entry in this guide

EAST OF ENGLAND

White End ★★
Contact: Mr John Robbins
122 Yarmouth Road, Bungay
NR35 2PA
T: (01986) 893562

SANDRINGHAM
Norfolk

Folk on the Hill ★★★★
Contact: Mrs L. Skerritt
Mill Cottage, Mill Road,
Dersingham, King's Lynn
PE31 6HY
T: (01485) 544411
E: lili@skerritt-euwe.freeserve.co.uk

SANDY
Bedfordshire

Acorn Cottage ★★★★
Contact: Mrs Margaret Codd
Highfield Farm, Tempsford Road,
Great North Road, Sandy
SG19 2AQ
T: (01767) 682332
F: (01767) 692503
E: margaret@highfield-farm.co.uk
I: www.highfield-farm.co.uk

SAXMUNDHAM
Suffolk

Flora Cottage ★★★★
Contact: Mr Richard & Mrs Wendy Pither
Suffolk Secrets, 7 Frenze Road,
Diss IP22 4PA
T: (01379) 651297
F: (01379) 641553
E: holidays@suffolk-secrets.co.uk
I: www.suffolk-secrets.co.uk

Harvey's Mill ★★★★
Contact: Mrs Christine Baker
Harvey's Mill, Main Road,
Saxmundham IP17 2RD
T: (01728) 603212
F: (01728) 603637
E: mail@bensteadhouse.freeserve.co.uk
I: www.blythweb.co.uk/harveysmill

Quince Cottage ★★★
Contact: Mr & Mrs John Andrew
Barnabees, Mutton Lane,
Woodbridge IP13 7AR
T: (01728) 685953
E: tedischa@aol.com

Red Lodge Barn ★★★★
Contact: Mr Michael & Mrs Lesley Bowler
Red Lodge Barn, Middleton Moor, Saxmundham IP17 3LN
T: (01728) 668100

Riverside Cottage ★★★
Contact:
Suffolk Secrets, 7 Frenze Road,
Diss IP22 4PA
T: (01379) 651297
F: (01379) 641555
E: holidays@suffolk-secrets.co.uk
I: www.suffolk-secrets.co.uk

Rookery Park ★★★★
Contact: Mrs Eden McDonald
Rookery Park, Saxmundham
IP17 3HQ
T: (01728) 668740
F: (01728) 668102

SAXON STREET
Cambridgeshire

Syde House ★★★
Contact: Mrs Susan Greenwood
37 The Street, Newmarket
CB8 9RU
T: (01638) 730044

SCULTHORPE
Norfolk

Clarence's & Edna's Lodges ★★★
Contact: Mrs Beryl Engledow
Caxton House, Creake Road,
Fakenham NR21 9NG
T: (01328) 864785

The Cottage ★★★
Contact: Mrs Chapman
30 Lambert Cross, Saffron Walden CB10 2DP
T: (01799) 527287

Greenacre Bungalow ★★
Contact: Mrs Tuddenham
Greenacre Bungalow, 1 The Street, Fakenham NR21 9QD
T: (01328) 862858

1 Grove Farm Barns
Rating Applied For
Contact: Mrs Christine Banson
J Banson & A Herculson, 3 The Green, Grove Farm, Fakenham NR21 9QJ
T: (01328) 864427
F: (01328) 864427
E: johnny@banson.fslife.net

SEA PALLING
Norfolk

Spring Cottage ★★★
Contact: Mrs Jane Davidson
Priory Barn, Sea Palling Road,
Ingham, Norwich NR12 0TW
T: (01692) 582346

SEDGEFORD
Norfolk

Lavender Cottage ★★★★
Contact: Mrs Karen Kennedy-Hill
Lavender Cottage Holidays, 9 Wheatfields, King's Lynn
PE31 6BH
T: (01485) 600850
E: kennedyhill@tesco.net
I: www.lavendercottage.co.uk

Victoria Cottage ★★★
Contact: Ms Charlotte Forbes-Robertson
Heacham Road, Hunstanton
PE36 5LU
T: (01485) 571082
E: charlotte@charard.com
I: www.charard.com

SHARRINGTON
Norfolk

Daubeney Cottage ★★★
Contact: Ms Nina Ogier
Daubeney Hall Farm, Lower Hall Lane, Melton Constable
NR24 2PQ
T: (01263) 861412
E: ninaogier@hotmail.com

Gable Cottage ★★
Contact: Miss M Lakey
Ashyard, Melton Constable
NR24 2PH
T: (01263) 860393

Garden Cottage ★★★★
Contact: Mrs R M Kimmins
Chequers, Bale Road,
Sharrington, Melton Constable
NR24 2PG
T: (01263) 860308
E: rkimmins@netcomuk.co.uk

Stone Cottage ★★★★
Contact: Mrs Gail Armstrong
Norfolk Country Cottages,
Market Place, Norwich NR10 4JJ
T: (01603) 871872
F: (01603) 870304
E: info@norfolkcottages.co.uk
I: www.norfolkcottages.co.uk

SHELLEY
Suffolk

Ivy Tree Cottage Annexe ★★★
Contact: Mrs Lock
Ivy Tree Cottage, Ipswich
IP7 5RE
T: (01473) 827632

SHERINGHAM
Norfolk

Augusta & Bennett ★★★
Contact: Mr Trevor Claydon
Owlet House, Laurel Drive, Holt
NR25 6JR
T: (01263) 713998
E: trevor.claydon@which.net
I: www.broadland.com/augusta.html

Clifftop Cottages
Rating Applied For
Contact: Mrs Laura Fenn
Clifftop Cottages, 19A & 19B Vincent Road, Sheringham
NR26 8BP
T: (01263) 825409

The Croft ★★★
Contact: Mr Dale McKean
The Croft, 124 Eye Road,
Peterborough PE1 4SG
E: dalemck@ntlworld.com
I: www.cyberware.co.uk/dial/dmckean/thecroft.htm

**Fisherman's Cottage,
Fisherman's Hyde Cottage
and Fisherman's Rest** ★★
Contact: Mrs Bernadette Bennett
35 Sandilands Road, London
SW6 2BD
T: (020) 73810771

Flat 2 ★★
Contact: Mrs Valerie Muggridge
Laburnham, 8 Warren Close,
Holt NR25 6QX
T: (01263) 712688

Glendalough ★★★★
Contact: Mrs Janet Teather
8 Cromer Road, Sheringham
NR26 8RR
T: (01263) 825032
E: janetandbrian@telinco.com
I: www.broadland.com/glendalough

Hall Cottage ★★★
Contact: Mrs Gail Armstrong
Norfolk Country Cottages,
Market Place, Norwich NR10 4JJ
T: (01603) 871872
F: (01603) 870304
E: info@norfolkcottages.co.uk
I: www.norfolkcottages.co.uk

The Haven ★★★
Contact: Mrs Pam Pilkington
2 Moorgreen, Nottingham
NG16 2FB
T: (01773) 763010

The Haven ★★★
Contact: Mrs Irene Buck & Audrey Challoner
The Haven, 19 Marriotts Way,
Sheringham NR26 8RJ
T: (01263) 821281
E: irene@buck1065.fsnet.co.uk
I: www.thehavenholidayhomesheringham.com

High Lee ★★
Contact: Mr & Mrs Nelson
519 Galleywood Road,
Chelmsford CM2 8AA
T: (01245) 262436

Ivydene ★★★
Contact: Mrs Jenny Linder
Broadlea, Links Crescent,
Sheringham NR26 8HQ
T: (01263) 822990
E: ivydeneholidays@btopenworld.com

The Old Boathouse ★★★
Contact: Mr Roger Cooling
21 High Street, Spalding
PE11 1TX
T: (01775) 712100
F: (01775) 713125
E: house@gxn.co.uk

Pinecones ★★★
Contact: Mrs Pat Harvey
Pinecones, 70 Cromer Road,
Sheringham NR26 8RT
T: (01263) 824955
F: (01263) 824955
E: tonyandpat@pinecones.fsnet.co.uk
I: www.pine-cones.co.uk

Poppy Cottage ★★★
Contact: Mr Peter Crook
Manor Farm, School Road,
Norwich NR13 6DZ
T: (01603) 270451
F: (01603) 633638
E: peter.jacqui@virgin.net

Rogue's and Rascal's Barns ★★★★
Contact: Mrs Clare Wilson
Grove Farm, Back Lane,
Roughton, Norwich NR11 8QR
T: (01263) 761594
F: (01263) 761605
E: enquiries@grove-farm.com
I: www.grovefarm.com

4 Seaview ★★★★
Contact: Mrs Howes
28 Stanton Square, Hampton Hargate, Peterborough PE7 8BB
T: (01733) 315371

8 Seaview ★★★
Contact: Mrs Joan Munday
Keys Holidays, 18 Station Road,
Sheringham NR26 8RE
T: (01263) 823010
F: (01263) 821449
E: info@keys-holidays.co.uk
I: www.keys-holidays.co.uk

EAST OF ENGLAND

Victoria Court ★★★★
Contact: Mr Graham Simmons
Camberley, 62 Cliff Road,
Sheringham NR26 8BJ
T: (01263) 823101
F: (01263) 821433
E: graham@
camberleyguesthouse.co.uk
I: www.camberleyguesthouse.
co.uk

16 Wyndham Street ★★★
Contact: Mrs Joan Munday
Keys Holidays, 18 Station Road,
Sheringham NR26 8RE
T: (01263) 823010
F: (01263) 821449
E: info@keys-holidays.co.uk
I: www.keys-holidays.co.uk

SHOTLEY
Suffolk

The Apartment ★★★
Contact: Ms Deborah Baynes
Nether Hall, Main Road, Ipswich
IP9 1PW
T: (01473) 788300
F: (01473) 787055
E: deb@deborahbaynes.co.uk
I: www.netherhall.net

Box Iron Cottage ★★★
Contact: Mrs Broadway
Threefields, The Street, Ipswich
IP9 2PX
T: (01473) 327673
E: debroadway@macunlimited.
net

SIBLE HEDINGHAM
Essex

Brickwall Farm ★★★★
Contact: Mrs Jean Fuller
Brickwall Farm, Queen Street,
Halstead CO9 3RH
T: (01787) 460329
F: (01787) 462584
E: fuller@brickwallfarm.com

Pevors Farm Cottages
★★★★
Contact: Mr John & Mrs
Margaret Lewis
Southey Green, Halstead
CO9 3RN
T: (01787) 460830
E: naturist@pevorsfarm.co.uk
I: www.pevorsfarm.co.uk

SIBTON
Suffolk

Apple Tree Cottage ★★★★
Contact: Mr Donald Derrick
Owl Leisure, 15 Brookdale Close,
Upminster RM14 2LU
T: (01708) 250676
F: (01708) 250676
E: owlleisure@hotmail.com

**Bluebell, Bonny, Buttercup
& Bertie** ★★★★
Contact: Mrs Margaret Gray
Park Farm, Saxmundham
IP17 2LZ
T: (01728) 668324
E: margaret.gray@btinternet.
com
I: www.farmstayanglia.
co.uk/parkfarm

Cardinal Cottage ★★★★
Contact: Mr & Mrs Eric Belton
Cardinal Cottage, Pouy Street,
Sibton, Saxmundham IP17 2JH
T: (01728) 660111
E: jan.belton@btopenworld.com
I: www.cardinalcottageholidays.
co.uk

SLOLEY
Norfolk

Piggery Cottage ★★★★
Contact: Mrs Ann Jones
Piggery Cottage, High Street,
Norwich NR12 8HJ
T: (01692) 536281
F: (01692) 535162
E: sloley@farmhotel.u-net.com
I: www.norfolkbroads.
co.uk/sloleyfarm

SNAPE
Suffolk

The Granary & The Forge
★★★★
Contact: Mrs Sally Gillett
Croft Farm, Saxmundham
IP17 1QU
T: (01728) 688254
E: e.r.gillett@btinternet.com
I: www.croftfarmsnape.co.uk

Jubilee Cottage ★★★★
Contact:
Suffolk Secrets, 7 Frenze Road,
Diss IP22 4PA
T: (01379) 651297
F: (01379) 641555
E: holidays@suffolk-secrets.
co.uk
I: www.suffolk-secrets.co.uk

Mulberry Cottage ★★★★
Contact:
Suffolk Secrets, 7 Frenze Road,
Diss IP22 4PA
T: (01379) 651297
F: (01379) 641555
E: holidays@suffolk-secrets.
co.uk
I: www.suffolk-secrets.co.uk

Shoehorn Cottage
Rating Applied For
Contact: Mrs Louise Daley
34 Greenacres, South Benfleet
SS7 2JD
T: 0774 5 802091

Smithy Cottage ★★★★
Contact:
Suffolk Secrets, 7 Frenze Road,
Diss IP22 4PA
T: (01379) 651297
F: (01379) 641555
E: holidays@suffolk-secrets.
co.uk
I: www.suffolk-secrets.co.uk

Snape Maltings
★★★-★★★★★
Contact: Mrs Melaine Thurston
Snape Maltings, Snape Bridge,
Snape, Saxmundham IP17 1SR
T: (01708) 688303
F: (01708) 688930
E: accom@snapemaltings.co.uk
I: www.snapemaltings.co.uk

The Studio Flat ★★★
Contact: Ms Kathy Ball
Church Garage, Farnham Road,
Saxmundham IP17 1QW
T: (01728) 688327
F: (01728) 688500

Valley Farm Barns ★★★★
Contact: Mr Chris Nicholson
Valley Farm Barns, Aldeburgh
Road, Saxmundham IP17 1QH
T: (01728) 689071
E: chrisvalleyfarm@aol.com

Whitewalls ★★
Contact:
Suffolk Secrets, 7 Frenze Road,
Diss IP22 4PA
T: (01379) 651297
F: (01379) 641555
E: holidays@suffolk-secrets.
co.uk
I: www.suffolk-secrets.co.uk

SNETTISHAM
Norfolk

21 Brent Avenue ★★
Contact: Mrs Sandra Hohol
Birds Norfolk Holiday Homes, 62
Westgate, Hunstanton PE36 5EL
T: (01485) 534267
F: (01485) 535230
E: shohol@
birdsnorfolkholidayhomes.co.uk
I: www.
norfolkholidayhomes-birds.
co.uk

Carpenters Lodge ★★★
Contact: Mr Nigel Madgett
Carpenters Lodge, Norton Hill,
King's Lynn PE31 7LZ
T: (01485) 541580
E: nmmadgett@hotmail.com
I: www.carpenterslodge.co.uk

The Coach House ★★★
Contact: Mrs Marion Peters-
Loader
The Coach House, Snettisham
House, St Thomas's Lane, King's
Lynn PE31 7RZ
T: (01485) 544902
E: cliveloader@snettisham19.
fsnet.co.uk

Cobbe Court ★★★
Contact: Mr & Mrs James
Douglas
Cobbe Court, Snettisham House,
St Thomas Lane, King's Lynn
PE31 7RZ
T: (01485) 543986

4 The Courtyard ★★★
Contact: Mrs Jennifer Overson
9 Fakenham Chase, Spalding
PE12 7QU
T: (01406) 422569
E: jennifer.overson@ntlworld.
com
I: www.cottageguide.co.uk/4.
thecourtyard

Cursons Cottage ★★★★
Contact: Mrs Averil Campbell
Craven House, Lynn Road,
Snettisham, King's Lynn
PE31 7LW
T: (01485) 541179
F: (01485) 543259
E: ian.averilcampbell@
btinternet.com
I: www.cottageguide.
co.uk/cursonscottage

**Hollies Cottage & Grooms
Cottage** ★★★★
Contact: Mrs Elaine Aldridge
The Hollies, 12 Lynn Road, King's
Lynn PE31 7LS
T: (01485) 541294
F: (01485) 541294

Lavender Cottage ★★★
Contact: Mrs Rosa Barry
10 Jubilee Gardens, King's Lynn
PE31 7RN
T: (01485) 541280

The Old Barn ★★★★
Contact: Mrs Lynn Shannon
The Grove, 17 Collins Lane,
King's Lynn PE31 7DZ
T: (01485) 570513
E: tm.shannon@virgin.net
I: www.thegroveandoldbarn.
fsnet.co.uk

**The Old Farm House
Cottage** ★★★
Contact: Mrs Jacqueline Sandy
The Old Farm House Cottage,
Bircham Road, King's Lynn
PE31 7NG
T: (01485) 543106
E: jacqueline.sandy@tesco.net

Orangery Lodge ★★★★
Contact: Mrs Marion
Goldsworthy
East Wing, Snettisham House,
King's Lynn PE31 7RZ
T: (01485) 541187
E: mail@orangerylodge.co.uk
I: www.orangerylodge.co.uk

The Smithy ★★★
Contact: Mrs Sandra Hohol
Birds Norfolk Holiday Homes, 62
Westgate, Hunstanton PE36 5EL
T: (01485) 534267
F: (01485) 535230
E: shohol@
birdsnorfolkholidayhomes.co.uk
I: www.
norfolkholidayhomes-birds.
co.uk

Wagtail Cottage ★★★★
Contact: Mrs Sandra Hohol
Birds Norfolk Holiday Homes, 62
Westgate, Hunstanton PE36 5EL
T: (01485) 534267
F: (01485) 535230
E: shohol@
birdsnorfolkholidayhomes.co.uk
I: www.
norfolkholidayhomes-birds.
co.uk

SOHAM
Cambridgeshire

Poppies ★★★★
Contact: Ms Roseann Allum
Poppies, Eye Hill Drove, Ely
CB7 5XF
T: (01353) 624541
F: (01353) 624541

SOUTH BENFLEET
Essex

Alice's Place ★★★
Contact: Mr & Mrs Millward
43 Danesfield, South Benfleet
SS7 5EE
T: (01268) 756283
F: (01268) 756283
E: info@alices-place.co.uk
I: www.alices-place.co.uk

SOUTH CREAKE
Norfolk

Primrose Cottage ★★★
Contact: Mrs Jane Shulver
Norfolk Country Cottages,
Carlton House, Market Place,
Norwich NR10 4JJ
T: (01603) 871872
I: www.norfolk-cottages.co.uk

Establishments printed in blue have a detailed entry in this guide

EAST OF ENGLAND

SOUTH MIMMS
Hertfordshire

The Black Swan ★★-★★★
Contact: Mr Marsterson
62-64 Blanche Lane, Potters Bar
EN6 3PD
T: (01707) 644180
F: (01707) 642344

SOUTH WALSHAM
Norfolk

Charity Barn ★★★★
Contact: Mr Colin & Mrs Lynda Holmes
Charity Farm, 10 Wymers Lane, Norwich NR13 6EA
T: (01603) 270410
I: www.charitybarn.co.uk

SOUTHEND-ON-SEA
Southend-on-Sea

Everhome Apartments ★★
Contact: Mr Malcolm Taylor
26 Drake Road, Westcliff-on-Sea SS0 8LP
T: (01702) 343030
E: malcolmt@zoom.co.uk

Family Bungalow ★★★
Contact: Mrs Kim Frederick
199 Caufield Road, Southend-on-Sea SS3 9LU
T: (01702) 297328

Royal Apartments ★★★
Contact: Mrs Monk
Royal Apartments, 12 Royal Terrace, Southend-on-Sea SS1 1DY
T: (01702) 345323
F: (01702) 390415
E: patmmonk@hotmail.com

SOUTHMINSTER
Essex

Avonmore ★★★★
Contact: Mr & Mrs Bull
Rose House, Poole Street, Sudbury CO10 8BD
T: (01787) 280063
F: (01787) 282617
E: mrd@teambull.co.uk

SOUTHREPPS
Norfolk

Clipped Hedge Cottages ★★★-★★★★
Contact: Mr Tony Blyth
2 Vicarage Road, Sheringham NR26 8NH
T: (01263) 822817
F: (01263) 822817
E: tony.blyth@tiscali.co.uk
I: www.norfolka2z.co.uk/clippedhedgecottages.htm

SOUTHWOLD
Suffolk

Anchor Point ★★
Contact: Mrs Claire Guppy
Acanthus Property Letting Services Ltd, 9 Trinity Street, Southwold IP18 6JH
T: (01502) 724033
F: (01502) 725168
E: sales@southwold-holidays.co.uk
I: www.southwold-holidays.co.uk

Apartment 12
Rating Applied For
Contact: Mrs Clare Guppy
Acanthus Property Letting Services Ltd, 9 Trinity Street, Southwold IP18 6JH
T: (01502) 724033
E: sales@southwold-holidays.co.uk
I: www.southwold-holidays.co.uk

Blackshore Corner ★★★★
Contact:
Suffolk Secrets, 7 Frenze Road, Diss IP22 4PA
T: (01379) 651297
F: (01379) 641555
E: holidays@suffolk-secrets.co.uk
I: www.suffolk-secrets.co.uk

Blackshore Cottage ★★★
Contact:
Suffolk Secrets, 7 Frenze Road, Diss IP22 4PA
T: (01379) 651297
F: (01379) 641555
E: holidays@suffolk-secrets.co.uk
I: www.suffolk-secrets.co.uk

The Bolt Hole ★★★
Contact:
Suffolk Secrets, 7 Frenze Road, Diss IP22 4PA
T: (01379) 651297
F: (01379) 641555
E: holidays@suffolk-secrets.co.uk
I: www.suffolk-secrets.co.uk

Caterer House ★★★
Contact:
Suffolk Secrets, 7 Frenze Road, Diss IP22 4PA
T: (01379) 651297
F: (01379) 641555
E: holidays@suffolk-secrets.co.uk
I: www.suffolk-secrets.co.uk

Cherry Trees ★★★★
Contact:
Suffolk Secrets, 7 Frenze Road, Diss IP22 4PA
T: (01379) 651297
F: (01379) 641555
E: holidays@suffolk-secrets.co.uk
I: www.suffolk-secrets.co.uk

Corner Cottage ★★★
Contact: Mrs Daphne Hall
Adnams, 98 High Street, Southwold IP18 6DP
T: (01502) 723292
F: (01502) 724794

The Cottage ★★★★
Contact: Mr Thomas
2 Pier Court, Pier Avenue, Southwold IP18 6BL
T: (01502) 723561

Dolphin Cottage ★★★
Contact:
Suffolk Secrets, 7 Frenze Road, Diss IP22 3PA
T: (01379) 651297
F: (01379) 641555
E: holidays@suffolk-secrets.co.uk
I: www.suffolk-secrets.co.uk

8 Dunwich Road ★★★
Contact: Adnams
98 High Street, Southwold IP18
T: (01502) 723292
F: (01502) 724794

10a East Cliff ★★★
Contact: Mrs Claire Guppy
Acanthus Property Letting Services Ltd, 9 Trinity Street, Southwold IP18 6JH
T: (01502) 724033
F: (01502) 725168
E: sales@southwold-holidays.co.uk
I: www.southwold-holidays.co.uk

The Elms Mews ★★★
Contact: Mrs Claire Guppy
Acanthus Property Letting Services Ltd, 9 Trinity Street, Southwold IP18 6JH
T: (01502) 724033
F: (01502) 725168
E: sales@southwold-holidays.co.uk
I: www.southwold-holidays.co.uk

Garden Cottage ★★★
Contact: Mr & Mrs Wigg
162 Hall Road, Oulton Broad, Lowestoft NR32 3NR
T: (01502) 568580
F: (01502) 568580

Harbour Cottage ★★★
Contact:
Suffolk Secrets, 7 Frenze Road, Diss IP22 4PA
T: (01379) 651297
F: (01379) 641555
E: holidays@suffolk-secrets.co.uk
I: www.suffolk-secrets.co.uk

Heathside ★★★
Contact: Mrs Claire Guppy
Acanthus Property Letting Services Ltd, 9 Trinity Street, Southwold IP18 6JH
T: (01502) 724033
F: (01502) 725168
E: sales@southwold-holidays.co.uk
I: www.southwold-holidays.co.uk

Holly Cottage ★★★★
Contact: Mrs Claire Guppy
Acanthus PLS Limited, 9 Trinity Street, Southwold IP18 6JH
T: (01502) 722806
E: sales@southwold-holidays.co.uk
I: www.southwold-holidays.co.uk

Horseshoe Cottage ★★★
Contact: Ms Claire Guppy & Mrs J Tallon
9 Trinity Street, Southwold IP18 6JH
T: (01502) 724033
F: (01502) 725168
E: sales@southwold-holidays.co.uk
I: www.southwold-holidays.co.uk

Jersey Lodge
Rating Applied For
Contact:
Suffolk Secrets, 7 Frenze Road, Diss IP22 4PA
T: (01379) 651297
F: (01379) 641555
E: holidays@suffolk-secrets.co.uk
I: www.suffolksecrets.co.uk

Lighthouse View ★★★
Contact: Mrs Claire Guppy
Acanthus Property Letting Services Ltd, 9 Trinity Street, Southwold IP18 6JH
T: (01502) 724033
F: (01502) 725168
E: sales@southwold-holidays.co.uk
I: www.southwold-holidays.co.uk

The Little Blue House ★★
Contact: Mrs Diana Wright
The Kiln, The Folley, Colchester CO2 0HZ
T: (01206) 738003

Little Garth ★★★
Contact: Joe Tynan
30 Tovells Road, Ipswich IP4 4DY
I: www.southwold.ws/littlegarth.co.uk

Manor Lodge ★★★
Contact: Mrs Claire Guppy
Acanthus Property Letting Services Ltd, 9 Trinity Street, Southwold IP18 6JH
T: (01502) 724033
F: (01502) 725168
E: sales@southwold-holidays.co.uk
I: www.southwold-holidays.co.uk

The Nest ★★★
Contact: Mrs Daphne Hall
98 High Street, Southwold IP18 6DP
T: (01502) 723292
F: (01502) 724794
E: haadnams_lets@ic24.net
I: www.thenest-southwold.info

The Old Rope House ★★★★
Contact: Mrs Sian Mortlock
The Moorings, 16 Jermyns Road, Southwold IP18 6QB
T: (01502) 724769
E: sian@theoldropehouse.co.uk
I: www.theoldropehouse.co.uk

The Olde Banke House ★★★★
Contact: Mrs Claire Guppy
Acanthus Property Letting services Ltd, 9 Trinity Street, Southwold IP18 6JH
T: (01502) 724033
F: (01502) 725168
E: sales@southwold-holidays.co.uk
I: www.southwold-holidays.co.uk

EAST OF ENGLAND

Owl Cottage ★★
Contact: Mrs Claire Guppy
Acanthus Property Letting
Services Ltd, 9 Trinity Street,
Southwold IP18 6JH
T: (01502) 724033
F: (01502) 725168
E: sales@southwold-holidays.co.uk
I: www.southwold-holidays.co.uk

Pebbles ★★★
Contact: Mrs Claire Guppy
Acanthus Property Letting
Services Ltd, 9 Trinity Street,
Southwold IP18 6JH
T: (01502) 724033
F: (01502) 725168
E: sales@southwold-holidays.co.uk
I: www.southwold-holidays.co.uk

15 Pier Avenue ★★★
Contact:
Suffolk Secrets, 7 Frenze Road,
Diss IP22 4PA
T: (01379) 651297
F: (01379) 641555
E: holidays@suffolk-secrets.co.uk
I: www.suffolk-secrets.co.uk

1 Pier Court ★★★
Contact: Mrs Claire Guppy
Acanthus Property Lettings
Services Ltd, 9 Trinity Street,
Southwold IP18 6JH
T: (01502) 724033
F: (01502) 725168
E: sales@southwold-holidays.co.uk
I: www.southwold-holidays.co.uk

Pippins ★★★
Contact: Mrs Daphne Hall
H A Adnams, 98 High Street,
Southwold IP18 6DP
T: (01502) 723292
F: (01502) 724794

Poplar Hall ★★★★
Contact: Mrs Anna Garwood
Poplar Hall, Frostenden Corner,
Frostenden, Nr Southwold
NR34 7JA
T: (01502) 578549
I: www.southwold.ws/poplar-hall

Red Roofs ★★
Contact:
Suffolk Secrets, 7 Frenze Road,
Diss IP22 4PA
T: (01379) 651297
F: (01379) 641555
E: holidays@suffolk-secrets.co.uk
I: www.suffolk-secrets.co.uk

Rosemary Cottage ★★★
Contact: Mr Richard & Mrs Wendy Pither
Suffolk Secrets, 7 Frenze Road,
Diss IP22 4PA
T: (01379) 651297
F: (01379) 641553
E: holidays@suffolk-secrets.co.uk
I: www.suffolk-secrets.co.uk

Saffron & Church Green Cottages ★★★-★★★★
Contact: Mrs Claire Guppy
Acanthus Property Lettings
Services Ltd, 9 Trinity Street,
Southwold IP18 6JH
T: (01502) 724033
F: (01502) 725168
E: sales@southwold-holidays.co.uk
I: www.southwold-holidays.co.uk

Saltings ★★★
Contact:
Suffolk Secrets, 7 Frenze Road,
Diss IP22 4PA
T: (01379) 651297
F: (01379) 641555
E: holidays@suffolk-secrets.co.uk
I: www.suffolk-secrets.co.uk

Seabreeze ★★
Contact: Mrs Claire Guppy
Acanthus Property Letting
Services Ltd, 9 Trinity Street,
Southwold IP18 6JH
T: (01502) 724033
F: (01502) 725168
E: sales@southwold-holidays.co.uk
I: www.southwold-holidays.co.uk

Seaview House & Seaview Cottage ★★★
Contact: Mrs Claire Guppy
Acanthus Property Letting
Services Ltd, 9 Trinity Street,
Southwold IP18 6JH
T: (01502) 724033
F: (01502) 725168
E: sales@southwold-holidays.co.uk
I: www.southwold-holidays.co.uk

Seaward ★★★
Contact: Mrs Claire Guppy
Acanthus Property Letting
Services Ltd, 9 Trinity Street,
Southwold IP18 6JH
T: (01502) 724033
F: (01502) 725168
E: sales@southwold-holidays.co.uk
I: www.southwold-holidays.co.uk

September Cottage
Rating Applied For
Contact: Mrs Sylvia Hayward
September Cottage, 28 Victoria Street, Southwold IP18 6JF
T: (01502) 723215
E: sylvia@septembercottage.info
I: www.septembercottage.info

The Shed ★★
Contact:
Suffolk Secrets, 7 Frenze Road,
Diss IP22 3PA
T: (01379) 651297
F: (01379) 641555
E: holidays@suffolk-secrets.co.uk
I: www.suffolk-secrets.co.uk

Shrimp Cottage ★★★
Contact:
Suffolk Secrets, 7 Frenze Road,
Diss IP22 3PA
T: (01379) 651297
F: (01379) 641555
E: holidays@suffolk-secrets.co.uk
I: www.suffolk-secrets.co.uk

Solely Southwold ★★★
Contact: Miss Kathy Oliver
1 Sawyers Cottage, Norfolk Road, Beccles NR34 8RE
T: (01502) 578383
E: kathy@solely-southwold.co.uk
I: www.solely-southwold.co.uk

Southwold Holiday Home ★★★
Contact: Mr Wayne Thomas
Pippin House, Coxs Lane,
Southwold IP18 6QL
T: (01502) 724402
E: waynethomas60@aol.com
I: www.southwoldholidayhome.co.uk

20 St James Green ★★
Contact: Mrs Doris Burley
8 Long Marsh Close, Southwold IP18 6RS
T: (01502) 724096

Suffolk House ★★★
Contact: Mrs Betty Freeman
Suffolk House, 18 Dunwich Road, Southwold IP18 6LJ
T: (01502) 723742

Suton Cottage ★★
Contact:
Suffolk Secrets, 7 Frenze Road,
Diss IP22 4PA
T: (01379) 651297
F: (01379) 641555
E: holidays@suffolk-secrets.co.uk
I: www.suffolk-secrets.co.uk

10 Trinity Street ★★★
Contact: Mrs Claire Guppy
Acanthus Property Letting
Services Ltd, 9 Trinity Street,
Southwold IP18 6JH
T: (01502) 724033
F: (01502) 725168
E: sales@southwold-holidays.co.uk
I: www.southwold-holidays.co.uk

Victoria Cottage ★★
Contact: Mrs Claire Guppy
Acanthus Property Letting
Services Ltd, 9 Trinity Street,
Southwold IP18 6JH
T: (01502) 724033
F: (01502) 725168
E: sales@southwold-holidays.co.uk
I: www.southwold-holidays.co.uk

Weathervane
Rating Applied For
Contact:
Suffolk Secrets, 7 Frenze Road,
Diss IP22 4PA
T: (01379) 651297
F: (01379) 641555
E: holidays@suffolksecrets.co.uk
I: www.suffolk-secrets.co.uk

Whitehouse Barns ★★★★
Contact: Mrs Penelope Roskell-Griffiths
66 Queen Elizabeth's Walk,
London N16 5UQ
T: (020) 8802 6258
E: peneperoskell@yahoo.co.uk
I: www.whitehousebarns.co.uk

SPEXHALL
Suffolk

Rose Cottage ★★★
Contact: Mrs Hammond
South Lodge, Redisham Hall,
Beccles NR34 8LZ
T: (01502) 575894

SPROWSTON
Norfolk

Holme ★★
Contact: Mrs P Guyton
2 Recreation Ground Road,
Sprowston, Norwich NR7 8EN
T: (01603) 465703

STALHAM
Norfolk

144 Broadside Chalet Park ★★
Contact: Mr Crawford
5 Collingwood Avenue, Surbiton KT5 9PT
T: (020) 8337 4487
F: (020) 8337 4487
E: crawfcall@aol.com
I: www.norfolkholiday.co.uk

Chapelfield Cottage Flat ★★★
Contact: Mr Gary Holmes
Chapelfield Cottage Flat, Chapel Field, Stalham, Norwich NR12 9EN
T: (01692) 582173
F: (01692) 583009
E: gary@cinqueportsmarine.freeserve.co.uk
I: www.norfolkbroads.com/chapelfield

STANBRIDGE
Bedfordshire

Bluegate Farm Holiday Cottages ★★★★
Contact: Mrs Philippa Michie
Bluegate Farm Holiday Cottages, Peddars Lane, Leighton Buzzard LU7 9JD
T: (01525) 210621
F: (01525) 210621
E: michies@bluegate.freeserve.co.uk

STANHOE
Norfolk

Cherry Tree Cottage ★★★★
Contact: Mrs Gail Armstrong
Norfolk Country Cottages,
Carlton House, Market Place,
Norwich NR10 4JJ
T: (01603) 871872
F: (01603) 870304
E: info@norfolkcottages.co.uk

Pilgrims ★★★
Contact: Mrs Gail Armstrong
Norfolk Country Cottages,
Carlton House, Market Place,
Norwich NR10 4JJ
T: (01603) 871872
F: (01603) 870304
E: info@norfolkcottages.co.uk
I: www.norfolkcottages.co.uk

Establishments printed in blue have a detailed entry in this guide

EAST OF ENGLAND

Sarahs Cottage ★★
Contact: Mrs Sandra Hohol
Birds Norfolk Holiday Homes, 62 Westgate, Hunstanton PE36 5EL
T: (01485) 534267
F: (01485) 535230
E: shohol@birdsnorfolkholidayhomes.co.uk
I: www.norfolkholidayhomes-birds.co.uk

Vine Cottage
Rating Applied For
Contact: Mrs Alyson Aronson
The Crow's Nest, 5 Silver Close, Tadworth KT20 6QS
T: (01737) 832584
F: (01737) 832689
E: alyson.aronson@freeuk.com

STANSTED
Essex

Cedar Court Cottage & Apartment ★★★
Contact: Mrs Jean Windus
Anglesey House, 16 Grailands, Bishop's Stortford CM23 2RG
T: (01279) 653614
E: jeanwindus@ntlworld.com
I: www.angleseyhouse.com

STANSTED MOUNTFITCHET
Essex

Walpole Farm House ★★★-★★★★★
Contact: Mrs Jill Walton
Walpole Farm House, Cambridge Road, Stansted CM24 8TA
T: (01279) 812265
F: (01279) 812098

STIFFKEY
Norfolk

Apple Tree Cottage ★★★
Contact: Mr Brian & Mrs Carol Braid
23A Sandown Road, Stoneygate, Leicester LE2 3TN
T: (0116) 2716783

Grays Cottage ★★★
Contact: Mrs Gail Armstrong
Norfolk Country Cottages, Carlton House, Market Place, Norwich NR10 4JJ
T: (01603) 871872
F: (01603) 870304
E: info@norfolkcottages.co.uk
I: www.norfolkcottages.co.uk

Harbour House ★★★★
Contact: Mr Bindley
Hill House, 20 Hill House Road, Norwich NR1 4BQ
T: (01603) 270637

Hawthorns ★★★
Contact: Mrs M. Hickey-Smith
18 Poplar Road, Cambridge CB4 9LN
T: (01223) 572316
E: maddy@hawthorns.info

Manor Cottage ★★★
Contact: Mrs Cooke
The Manor, Wells-next-the-Sea NR23 1QP
T: (01328) 830439
E: chriscooke@aol.com
I: www.stiffkey.com

Mount Tabor ★★★
Contact: Mrs Pat Norris
30 Cotswold Drive, Cotswold Drive, Oldham OL2 5HD
T: (0161) 6336834
E: roger@stiffkeycottage.fsnet.co.uk
I: www.stiffkeycottage.co.uk

Primrose Cottage ★★★
Contact: Mrs Pearson
High Gables, Wells Road, Wells-next-the-Sea NR23 1AJ
T: (01328) 830303

2 Red Lion Cottages ★★★
Contact: Ms Jane Whitaker
8 Hollybank Cottages, The Avenue, Northwich CW9 6HT
T: (01606) 892368
E: jane.pathways@virgin.net

Shrimp Cottage ★★
Contact: Mrs Gail Armstrong
Norfolk Country Cottages Ref. 658, Carlton House, Market Place, Norwich NR10 4JJ
T: (01603) 871872
F: (01603) 870304
E: info@norfolkcottages.co.uk
I: www.norfolkcottages.co.uk/stiffkey_658.htm

STILTON
Cambridgeshire

Orchard Cottage ★★★★
Contact: Mrs Jennifer Higgo
22 Stocks Hill, Oakham LE15 8SY
T: (01572) 737420
E: jhiggo@freeuk.com
I: www.higgo.com/orchard

STISTED
Essex

Ballaglass ★★★★
Contact: Mrs Sally Dunn
Ballaglass, Coggeshall Road, Braintree CM77 8AB
T: (01376) 331409
F: (01376) 331405
E: ballaglass@btopenworld.com

STOKE-BY-NAYLAND
Suffolk

Cobbs Cottage ★★
Contact: Mr H. Engleheart
Cobbs Cottage, The Priory, Stoke by Nayland, Colchester CO6 4RL
T: (01206) 262216
F: (01206) 262373

STOVEN
Suffolk

Stringers Woodlands, Wood Farm Stables & Dairy ★★★★
Contact: Mrs Melody Kidner
North Green, Beccles NR34 8DF
T: (01502) 575744

STOWMARKET
Suffolk

Barn Cottages ★★★★
Contact: Mrs Tydeman
Goldings, East End Lane, Stonham Aspal, Stowmarket IP14 6AS
T: (01449) 711229
E: maria@barncottages.co.uk
I: www.barncottages.co.uk

Kimberley Cottage ★★★
Contact: Mr Brian Whiting
Kimberley Hall, Moats Tye, Stowmarket IP14 2EZ
T: (01449) 677766
F: (01449) 677766
E: brianwhiting.kimberleyhall@virgin.net
I: www.kimberleyhall.biz

STRADBROKE
Suffolk

Cornhouse Cottage ★★★★
Contact: Mrs Charmaine Cooper
Cornhouse Cottage, Hepwood Lodge, Wilby Road, Stradbroke, Eye IP21 5JN
T: (01379) 384256
F: (01379) 384256
E: cornhouse@hepwoodcottages.co.uk
I: www.hepwoodcottages.co.uk

STRATFORD ST ANDREW
Suffolk

Toad Hall Flat ★★★
Contact: Mr Perry & Mrs Bunty Hunt
Toad Hall Flat, Stratford Lodge, Stratford St Andrew, Saxmundham IP17 1LJ
T: (01728) 603463
F: (01728) 604501
E: peregrine.hunt@btinternet.com

SUDBURY
Suffolk

The Compasses ★★★
Contact: Mr & Mrs Mark Blows
The Compasses, High Street, Sudbury CO10 8LN
T: (01284) 789486
E: mark@thecompasses.com
I: www.thecompasses.com

Six Bells Barn ★★★
Contact: Mrs Janet Martin
Preston Hall, Sudbury CO10 9NQ
T: 0700 2782000
F: (01787) 248413
E: janet.martin@tesco.net

SUTTON
Norfolk

Sutton Staithe Boathouse ★★★
Contact: Mrs Patricia Holloway
Sutton Staithe Boathouse, Sutton Staithe Boatyard Ltd, Norwich NR12 9QS
T: (01692) 581653
F: (01692) 582938
E: ssboatyd@paston.co.uk
I: www.suttonstaitheleisure.co.uk

SWAFFHAM
Norfolk

Hall Barn ★★★
Contact: Ms Brenda Wilbourn
Hall Barn, Old Hall Lane, Swaffham PE37 8BG
T: (01366) 328794
F: (01366) 328794
E: brenda@hall-barn.freeserve.co.uk
I: www.cottageguide.co.uk/hallbarn

SWANTON ABBOT
Norfolk

Magnolia Cottage ★★
Contact: Mrs Christine Nockolds
Hill Farm House, Swanton Hill, Norwich NT10 5EA
T: (01692) 538481

Walnut Tree Barn ★★★★
Contact: Mr Mark & Mrs Sally Page
Walnut Tree Farm, Aylsham Road, Swanton Abbott, Norwich NR10 5DL
T: (01692) 538888
F: (01692) 538100

Willow Tree Cottage ★★★★★
Contact: Mrs Nixon
Willow Tree Cottage, Long Common Lane, Norwich NR10 5BH
T: (01692) 538169
F: (01692) 538169

SWANTON MORLEY
Norfolk

Teal, Heron & Grebe Cottage ★★★
Contact: Mrs Sally Marsham
Waterfall Farm, Worthing Road, Swanton Morley, East Dereham NR20 4QD
T: (01362) 637300
F: (01362) 637300
E: waterfallfarm@tesco.net

SYDERSTONE
Norfolk

Harrow Barn ★★★★
Contact: Miss Catherine Ringer
Buildings Farm, Creake Road, Syderstone, King's Lynn PE31 8SH
T: (01485) 578287
F: (01485) 576030
E: chringeris@hotmail.com
I: www.norfolk-holiday-cottages.co.uk/cottage/harrowbarn.html

TATTERSETT
Norfolk

Tatt Valley Holiday Cottages ★★★-★★★★
Contact: Mr Thomas Hurn
Tatt Valley Holiday Cottages, Lower Farm, King's Lynn PE31 8RT
T: (01485) 528506
E: enquiries@norfolkholidayhomes.co.uk
I: www.norfolkholidayhomes.co.uk

EAST OF ENGLAND

TATTINGSTONE
Suffolk

The Cowshed ★★★★
Contact: Mrs Annie Eaves
Park House, Tattingstone Park,
Ipswich IP9 2NF
T: (01473) 327000
F: 0870 7108550
E: annie@evere.co.uk
I: www.suffolk-cowshed.co.uk

TERRINGTON ST CLEMENT
Norfolk

Northgate Lodge Flat ★★★
Contact: Mrs Howling
21 Northgate Way, Terrington St Clement, King's Lynn PE34 4LG
T: (01553) 828428
E: jbh@interads.co.uk

THAXTED
Essex

Thaxted Holiday Cottages ★★★★
Contact: Mrs Yolanda De Bono
Thaxted Holiday Cottages,
Dunmow Road, Totmans Farm,
Thaxted, Dunmow CM6 2LU
T: (01371) 830233
E: enquiries@thaxtedholidaycottages.co.uk
I: www.thaxtedholidaycottages.co.uk

THEBERTON
Suffolk

Woodpecker Cottage ★★★
Contact: Mr Richard & Mrs Wendy Pither
Suffolk Secrets, 7 Frenze Road,
Diss IP22 4PA
T: (01379) 651297
F: (01379) 641553
E: holidays@suffolk-secrets.co.uk
I: www.suffolk-secrets.co.uk

THETFORD
Norfolk

River Lodge ★★★★
Contact: Mrs Susan Burton
River Lodge, River House, River Lane, Thetford IP25 7TQ
T: (01362) 821570
F: (01362) 820639
E: andy@abaltd.demon.co.uk
I: www.aburtonassociates.com

THORNAGE
Norfolk

Daisy Lodge ★★
Contact: Mrs Melanie Hickling
Primrose Farm Barns, Back Lane,
Cromer NR11 8QR
T: (01263) 761705
F: (01263) 761705
E: primrosefarmbarns@btinternet.co.uk
I: www.northnorfolkcountrycottages.co.uk

THORNDON
Suffolk

Manor Farm Barn ★★★★
Contact: Mrs Janet Edgecombe
Moat Farm, Eye IP23 7LX
T: (01379) 678437
F: (01379) 678023
E: gerald@clara.co.uk
I: www.moatfarm.co.uk

THORNHAM
Norfolk

Linzel Cottage ★★★★
Contact: Mrs Sandra Hohol
Birds Norfolk Holiday Homes, 62 Westgate, Hunstanton PE36 5EL
T: (01485) 534267
F: (01485) 535230
E: shohol@birdsnorfolkholidayhomes.co.uk
I: www.norfolkholidayhomes-birds.co.uk

Little Gull and Sanderling Cottages ★★★-★★★★★
Contact: Mr John Warham
Redbrick House, Hall Lane,
Hunstanton PE36 6NB
T: (01485) 512546
E: johnwarham@hotmail.com

1 Malthouse Cottages ★★
Contact: Mrs Rigby
6 Church Hill, Castor,
Peterborough PE5 7AU
T: (01733) 380399
F: (01733) 380399
E: leslierigby@castor.freeserve.co.uk

8 Malthouse Court ★★★
Contact: Sue Sadler
8 Malthouse Court, Malthouse Court, Hunstanton PE36 6NW
T: (01485) 512085
F: (01485) 512085
I: www.forsell-property.com

Manor Cottage ★★
Contact: Mrs Sandra Hohol
Birds Norfolk Holiday Homes, 62 Westgate, Hunstanton PE36 5EL
T: (01485) 534267
F: (01485) 535230
E: shohol@birdsnorfolkholidayhomes.co.uk
I: www.norfolkholidayhomes-birds.co.uk

Manor Farm Cottages ★★★-★★★★★
Contact: Mrs Margaret Goddard
Manor Farm House, Hunstanton PE36 6NB
T: (01485) 512272
F: (01485) 512241

The Old Maltings ★★★★
Contact: Mr Simon Barclay
Kett Country Cottages, 8 Oak Street, Fakenham NR21 9DY
T: (01328) 856853
F: (01328) 853903
E: info@kettcountrycottages.co.uk
I: www.kettcountrycottages.co.uk

Oyster Cottage ★★★
Contact: Mrs Geraldine Tibbs
Cole Green Cottage, Cole Green,
Hunstanton PE36 5LS
T: (01485) 571770
F: (01485) 571770

Rosemary Cottage ★★★★
Contact: Mrs Jane Shulver
Norfolk Country Cottages,
Carlton House, Market Place,
Norwich NR10 4JJ
T: (01603) 871872
I: www.norfolk-cottages.co.uk

Rushmeadow Studio ★★★
Contact: Mr & Mrs Wyett
Rushmeadow Studio, Main Road, Hunstanton PE36 6LZ
T: (01485) 512372
F: (01485) 512372
E: rushmeadow@lineone.net
I: www.rushmeadow.com

21 Shepherds Pightle ★★★★
Contact: Mrs Sue Sadler
Green Lane, Hunstanton
PE36 6NW
T: (01485) 512085
F: (01485) 512085

Thornham Holidays Rating Applied For
Contact: Mrs Jean B Wilson
Baytree Cottage, High Street,
Hunstanton PE36 6LY
T: (01485) 512204

1 West End Cottages ★★
Contact: Mr & Mrs Hardy
23 Kings Grove, Cambridge CB3 7AZ
T: (01223) 263859

THORPE MARKET
Norfolk

Poppylands & Puddleduck ★★★★
Contact: Jena Castleton
Poppy Cottage, Thorpe Market,
Norwich NR11 8AJ
T: (01263) 833219
E: poppylandholiday@aol.com
I: www.bravura.com

THORPE MORIEUX
Suffolk

Maltings Farm Holiday Cottages ★★★
Contact: Mrs Rachel Bell
Maltings Farm Holiday Cottages,
Bury St Edmunds IP30 0NG
T: (01284) 828843
F: (01284) 827444
E: tim-bell@fsbdial.co.uk
I: www.holidaycottagesinsuffolk.co.uk

THORPENESS
Suffolk

The Country Club Apartments ★★★★
Contact: Reception
Thorpeness Hotel & Golf Club,
Lakeside Avenue, Leiston
IP16 4NH
T: (01728) 452176
F: (01728) 453868
E: info@thorpeness.co.uk
I: www.thorpeness.co.uk

Hope Cove Cottage ★★★★
Contact: Mrs Irene Pearman
Piggotts Farm, Albury End, Ware SG11 2HS
T: (01279) 771281
F: (01279) 771517
E: ipearman@whestates.com

The House in the Clouds ★★★
Contact: Mrs Le Comber
4 Hinde House, 14 Hinde Street,
London W1U 3BG
T: (020) 7224 3615
F: (020) 7224 3615
E: houseintheclouds@btopenworld.com
I: www.houseintheclouds.co.uk

4 Old Homes ★★★★
Contact: Mrs Ellen Nall
High Barn, Gorams Mill Lane,
Woodbridge IP13 8DN
T: (01986) 798908
F: (01986) 798908

7 The Uplands ★★★
Contact: Mrs Diane Holmes
2 Red House Cottage, Uplands Road, Leiston IP16 4NG
T: (01728) 454648

THROCKING
Hertfordshire

Bluntswood Hall Cottages ★★★
Contact: Mrs Sally Smyth
Bluntswood Hall Cottages,
Bluntswood Hall, Buntingford SG9 9RN
T: (01763) 281204
F: (01763) 281204
I: www.bluntswoodhall.co.uk

THURLEIGH
Bedfordshire

Scald Farm ★
Contact: Mr Reg Towler
C V Towler & Sons, Scald End,
Mill Road, Thurleigh, Bedford MK44 2DP
T: (01234) 771996
F: (01234) 771996
E: scaldendfarm@tesco.net
I: www.scaldfarm.skynet.co.uk

THURSFORD
Norfolk

Hayloft ★★★
Contact: Mrs Ann Green
Old Coach House, Fakenham NR21 0BD
T: (01328) 878273

Ransome Lodge The Meadows ★★★★
Contact: Mrs Gail Armstrong
Norfolk Country Cottages,
Carlton House, Market Place,
Norwich NR10 4JJ
T: (01603) 871872
F: (01603) 870304
E: info@norfolkcottages.co.uk
I: www.norfolkcottages.co.uk

Wallis Lodge ★★★★
Contact: Mrs G Armstrong
Norfolk Country Cottages,
Carlton House, Market Place,
Norwich NR10 4JJ
T: (01603) 871872
F: (01603) 870304
E: info@norfolkcottages.co.uk
I: www.norfolkcottages.co.uk

TOLLESBURY
Essex

Fernleigh ★★★
Contact: Mrs Gillian Willson
Fernleigh, 16 Woodrolfe Farm Lane, Maldon CM9 8SX
T: (01621) 868245
F: (01621) 868245
E: gillwillson@onetel.com

TRIMLEY
Suffolk

Treacle Pot Cottage ★★★
Contact: Mr Richard Borley
69 Grimston Lane, Felixstowe IP11 0SA
T: (01394) 275367
I: www.suffolk-holiday-cottages.co.uk

Establishments printed in blue have a detailed entry in this guide

EAST OF ENGLAND

TRIMLEY ST MARTIN
Suffolk
Oak Cottage ★★★
Contact: Mrs Gillian Young
5 Waterside, Oldham OL3 7DP
T: (01457) 873313

TRUNCH
Norfolk
Bracken Cottage and Briar Cottage ★★★
Contact: Mr & Mrs Lomax
Malthouse Cottage, Mundesley Road, North Walsham NR28 0QB
T: (01263) 721973
E: ronbet@fdn.co.uk

TUNSTALL
Suffolk
Knoll Cottage ★★★★
Contact: Mrs Jill Robinson
Timbertop Farm, Stowmarket IP14 6NA
T: (01728) 685084
F: (01728) 685084
E: jill@timbertop.co.uk
I: www.timbertop.co.uk

Walnut Tree Cottage ★★★★
Contact:
Suffolk Secrets, 7 Frenze Road, Diss IP22 4PA
T: (01379) 651297
F: (01379) 641555
E: holidays@suffolk-secrets.co.uk
I: www.suffolk-secrets.co.uk

UPPER SHERINGHAM
Norfolk
Barn Owl Cottage ★★★
Contact: Mr & Mrs Rosemary Russell
Lodge Cottage, Lodge Hill, Sheringham NR26 8TJ
T: (01263) 821445
E: russells_norfolk@yahoo.co.uk
I: www.lodgecottage.co.uk

WALBERSWICK
Suffolk
1 Blackshore ★★★
Contact:
Suffolk Secrets, 7 Frenze Road, Diss IP22 4PA
T: (01379) 651297
F: (01379) 641555
E: holidays@suffolk-secrets.co.uk
I: www.suffolk-secrets.co.uk

2 Blackshore ★★★
Contact:
Suffolk Secrets, 7 Frenze Road, Diss IP22 4PA
T: (01379) 651297
F: (01379) 641555
E: holidays@suffolk-secrets.co.uk
I: www.suffolk-secrets.co.uk

Ferry Knoll
Rating Applied For
Contact: Mrs Claire Guppy
Acanthus Property Letting Services Ltd, 9 Trinity Street, Southwold IP18 6JH
T: (01502) 724033
F: (01502) 725168
E: sales@southwold-holidays.co.uk
I: www.southwold-holidays.co.uk

The Shieling ★★★
Contact:
Adnams, 98 High Street, Southwold IP18 6DP
T: (01502) 723292
F: (01502) 724794
E: h.a.adnams_lets@i.c.24.net

Stuckie Ben ★★★
Contact:
Suffolk Secrets, 7 Frenze Road, Diss IP22 4PA
T: (01379) 651297
F: (01379) 641555
E: holidays@suffolk-secrets.co.uk
I: www.suffolk-secrets.co.uk

White Cottage ★★★
Contact: Mrs Claire Guppy
Acanthus Property Letting Services Ltd, 9 Trinity Street, Southwold IP18 6JH
T: (01502) 724033
F: (01502) 725168
E: sales@southwold-holidays.co.uk
I: www.southwold-holidays.co.uk

WALCOTT
Norfolk
Tamarisk ★★★★
Contact: Mrs Jane Shulver
Point House, North Walsham NR28 9TY
T: (01692) 651126
E: pointhouse@hotmail.com
I: www.norfolkcottages.com

WALDRINGFIELD
Suffolk
Low Farm Estate Services ★★★
Contact: Mr Lee York
Low Farm Estate Services, Ipswich Road, Woodbridge IP12 4QU
T: (01473) 736475
F: (01473) 736387
E: cottages@lowfarm.fsbusiness.co.uk

WALTON HIGHWAY
Cambridgeshire
Espalier Cottage ★★★
Contact: Mrs Catherine Harvey
The Mill, St Pauls Road South, Wisbech PE14 7DD
T: (01945) 476627
F: (01945) 463937
E: espalier@pdh.co.uk

WANGFORD
Suffolk
Corner Cottage ★★★
Contact: Mrs Paula Mather
Harrogate
T: (01423) 525305

15 Elms Lane ★★★
Contact: Mr David Weight
4 Long Marsh Close, Southwold IP18 6RS
T: (01502) 724705
E: weight@onetel.net.uk

WANSFORD
Peterborough
Manor House Cottage ★★★★
Contact: Mrs Gillian Berry
Manor House Cottage, Yarwell Manor, Yarwell, Peterborough PE8 6PR
T: (01780) 783741
F: (01780) 783741
E: gillian@yarberrys.fsnet.co.uk

WASHBROOK
Suffolk
Stebbings Cottage ★★★
Contact: Mrs Caroline Fox
Stebbings, Back Lane, Ipswich IP8 3JA
T: (01473) 730216
E: caroline@foxworld.fsnet.co.uk

WATERBEACH
Cambridgeshire
New Farm Cottage ★★★
Contact: Mrs Susan Matthews
New Farm, Green End, Cambridge CB4 8ED
T: (01223) 863597
F: (01223) 860258
E: new_farm_@hotmail.com
I: www.newfarmcottages.co.uk

WELLS-NEXT-THE-SEA
Norfolk
Annie's ★★★★
Contact: Mrs Sarah Orford
Hall Farm, Bury St Edmunds IP31 3HF
T: (01359) 240340

Apartment 2 ★★★★
Contact: Mr John & Mrs Helen Ilsley
The Cottage by the Church, Church Lane, Hitchin SG4 7DJ
T: (01462) 790210
F: (01462) 790210
E: john_f_ilsley@yahoo.co.uk

Canary Cottage ★★★
Contact: Ms Sally Maufe
Branthill Farm, Branthill, Wells-next-the-Sea NR23 1SB
T: (01328) 710246
T: (01328) 711524
E: branthill.farms@macunlimited.net

Chantry ★★★
Contact: Mrs Jackson
3A Brickendon Lane, Hertford SG13 8NU
T: (01992) 511303
F: (01992) 511303

14 Church Street ★★
Contact: Mrs Rita Piesse
1 Longwater Lane, Norwich NR8 5AH
T: (01603) 744233
E: randjp2004@yahoo.co.uk

Cotman Cottage ★★★★
Contact: Mrs Gill Austen
Heacham Bottom Farm, Lynn Road, Snettisham, King's Lynn PE31 7PQ
T: (01485) 570004
F: (01485) 572468
E: gillausten@yahoo.co.uk

Fisherman's Cottage ★★★
Contact: Ms Lesley Whitby
170 Leighton Road, London NW5 2RE
T: (020) 76799477
E: l.whitby@ucl.ac.uk

Gabriel Cottage ★★★★
Contact: Dr Marie Strong
Saltings, East Quay, Wells-next-the-Sea NR23 1LE
T: (01328) 710743

The Glebe ★★★
Contact: Mrs Gail Armstrong
Norfolk Country Cottages Ref. 653, Market Place, Norwich NR10 4JJ
T: (01603) 871872
F: (01603) 870304
E: info@norfolkcottages.co.uk
I: www.norfolkcottages.co.uk/wells_653.htm

Honeypot Cottage ★★★
Contact: Mrs Joan Price
Shingles, Southgate Close, Wells-next-the-Sea NR23 1HG
T: (01328) 711982
F: (01328) 711982
E: walker.al@talk21.com
I: www.wells-honeypot.co.uk

4 Laylands Yard ★★★
Contact: Mrs Ann Heaton
5 Laylands Yard, Freeman Street, Wells-next-the-Sea NR23 1DA
T: (01328) 711361

Luggers Cottage ★★★★
Contact: Mrs Gail Armstrong
Norfolk Country Cottages, Market Place, Norwich NR10 4JJ
T: (01603) 871872
F: (01603) 870304
E: info@norfolkcottages.co.uk
I: www.norfolkcottages.co.uk

No 5 Coastguard Cottage ★★★
Contact: Mrs Wace
Eastgate Farm, Scarborough Road, Walsingham NR22 6AB
T: (01328) 820028
F: (01328) 821100

Oar House ★★★
Contact: Mrs Joanna Getley
Forester's Lodge, King's Lynn PE31 6SU
T: (01485) 528609
F: (01485) 528609
E: info@getley.co.uk
I: www.getley.co.uk

Poppy Cottage ★★★
Contact: Mrs Christine Curtis
Ship Cottage, East Quay, Wells-next-the-Sea NR23 1LF
T: (01328) 710395

Ranters Cottage ★★★
Contact: Mrs Hilary Marsden
St Phillips, 22 Charles Street, Berkhamsted HP4 3DF
T: (01442) 872486
E: hilaryamarsden@aol.com

Look out for establishments participating in the National Accessible Scheme

EAST OF ENGLAND

Rose Cottage ★★★
Contact: Mrs Madeline Rainsford
The Old Custom House, East Quay, Wells-next-the-Sea NR23 1LD
T: (01328) 711463
F: (01328) 710277
E: maddie@eastquay.co.uk
I: www.eastquay.co.uk

Seashell Cottage ★★★
Contact: Mrs Cecilia Fox
Middle Cottage, 72 Edinburgh Road, Norwich NR2 3RJ
T: (01603) 630232
F: (01603) 630232
I: www.seashellcottage.co.uk

Skylark Cottage ★★★
Contact: Mrs Bridget Jones
3 Broadgate, Bellaire, Barnstaple EX31 1QZ
T: (01271) 372225
E: bridget.jones@ukgateway.net
I: www.bridget.jones.ukgateway.net

Swamp Cottage ★★
Contact: Mrs Gail Armstrong
Norfolk Country Cottages Ref. 647, Market Place, Norwich NR10 4JJ
T: (01603) 871872
F: (01603) 870304
E: info@norfolkcottages.co.uk
I: www.norfolkcottages.co.uk/wells_647.htm

13 Tunns Yard ★★★
Contact: Ms Jean Clitheroe
14 Shop Lane, Wells-next-the-Sea NR23
T: (01328) 711362 & 07880 871733
E: jean@theoldexchange.fsnet.co.uk
I: www.the1950shop.com/accommodation.htm

Wherry Cottage ★★★
Contact: Mrs Gail Armstrong
Norfolk Country Cottages, Carlton House, Market Place, Norwich NR10 4JJ
T: (01603) 871872
F: (01603) 870304
E: info@norfolkcottages.co.uk
I: www.norfolkcottages.co.uk

WELWYN
Hertfordshire

Gamekeeper's Lodge, Shire Barn, Mill Farm Barn & Gate House ★★★★
Contact: Mr & Mrs Marinus Buisman
Welwyn Home Farm Enterprises Ltd, Lockley Farm, Welwyn AL6 0BL
T: (01438) 718641
F: (01438) 714238
E: liz@lockleyfarm.co.uk
I: www.lockleyfarm.co.uk

WENDENS AMBO
Essex

The Old Chapel ★★
Contact: Mrs Rosemary Barratt
35 Rudall Crescent, London NW3 1RR
T: (020) 74351126

WENHASTON
Suffolk

The Buntings ★★★
Contact: Mr L. E. Freeman
Suffolk House, Dunwich Road, Southwold IP18 8LJ
T: (01502) 722621
F: (01502) 722621

Poplar Cottage ★★★★
Contact: Mr Richard & Mrs Wendy Pither
Suffolk Secrets, 7 Frenze Road, Diss IP22 4PA
T: (01379) 651297
F: (01379) 641553
E: holidays@suffolk-secrets.co.uk
I: www.suffolk-secrets.co.uk

WEST BECKHAM
Norfolk

Flint Farm Cottages ★★-★★★★★
Contact: Mrs Judy Wilson
Flint Farm Cottages, Chestnut Farm, Church Road, Holt NR25 6NX
T: (01263) 822241
F: (01263) 822243
E: john@mcneil-wilson.freeserve.co.uk

Merry Cottage ★★★
Contact: Mrs Mo Teeuw
20 High Street, Spalding PE12 6QB
T: (01406) 370012
E: mo@moteeuw.co.uk
I: www.moteeuw.co.uk

WEST RUDHAM
Norfolk

North Cottage ★★-★★★
Contact: Blakes Holidays
Blakes, Stoney Bank Road, Barnoldswick BB94 0AA
T: 0870 0 708090

WEST RUNTON
Norfolk

8 & 13 Travers Court ★★★
Contact: Mrs Oliver
Maple Cottage, Arkesden Road, Saffron Walden CB11 4QU
T: (01799) 550265
F: (01799) 550396
E: louise44@btinternet.com

Beacon Hill ★★
Contact: Mrs Justina Morris
Beacon Hill, Sandy Lane, Cromer NR27 9NB
T: (01263) 838162

6 Cromer Road ★★★
Contact: Ms Lotta Fox
Lambert & Watts Self-Catering Holidays, 15 West Street, Cromer NR27 9HZ
T: (01263) 511028
E: property@lambertw.fslife.co.uk

Old Farm Cottage ★★★
Contact: Mrs Jackie Hack
1 Abbey Road, Sheringham NR26 8HH
T: (01263) 824729

Roman Camp Brick Chalets ★★★
Contact: Mr John Julian
Roman Camp Caravan Park, Cromer NR27 9ND
T: (01263) 837256

Roseacre Country House ★-★★
Contact: Mr & Mrs Lunken
Roseacre Country House, The Hurn, Cromer NR27 9QS
T: (01263) 837221
I: www.roseacrecountryhouse.co.uk

WEST WRATTING
Cambridgeshire

Bakery Cottage
Rating Applied For
Contact: Mr David Denny
Bakery Cottage, High Street, Cambridge CB1 5LU
T: (01223) 290492
F: (01223) 290845
E: davidstractors@aol.com
I: www.bakerycottage.co.uk

WESTCLIFF-ON-SEA
Southend-on-Sea

Thames Estuary Holiday Apartments ★★★
Contact: Mr Donald Watson
83 Vardon Drive, Leigh-on-Sea SS9 3SJ
T: (01702) 477255
F: (01702) 477255

WESTLETON
Suffolk

Apple Tree Cottage ★★★
Contact:
Suffolk Secrets, 7 Frenze Road, Diss IP22 4PA
T: (01379) 651297
F: (01379) 641555
E: holidays@suffolk-secrets.co.uk
I: www.suffolk-secrets.co.uk

Easter Cottage ★★★★
Contact:
Suffolk Secrets, 7 Frenze Road, Diss IP22 4PA
T: (01379) 651297
F: (01379) 641555
E: holidays@suffolk-secrets.co.uk
I: www.suffolk-secrets.co.uk

Ebenezer House, 1&3&5 Ebenezer Row ★★
Contact:
Suffolk Secrets, 7 Frenze Road, Diss IP22 4PA
T: (01379) 651297
F: (01379) 641555
E: holidays@suffolk-secrets.co.uk
I: www.suffolk-secrets.co.uk

Middle Cottage ★★★★
Contact: Mr Richard Pither
Suffolk Secrets, 7 Frenze Road, Diss IP22 4PA
T: (01379) 651297
F: (01379) 641555
E: holidays@suffolk-secrets.co.uk
I: www.suffolk-secrets.co.uk

Mulleys Cottage ★★★★
Contact: Mr & Mrs Richard Pither
Suffolk Secrets, 7 Frenze Road, Diss IP22 4PA
T: (01379) 651297
F: (01379) 641553
E: holidays@suffolk-secrets.co.uk
I: www.suffolk-secrets.co.uk

Spring Cottage ★★★★
Contact: Dr Ruth Whittaker
2 Clematis Close, Saxmundham IP17 3BN
T: (01728) 648380
F: (01728) 648380

WEYBOURNE
Norfolk

Appletree Cottage ★★★★
Contact: Mrs Gail Armstrong
Norfolk Country Cottages, Carlton House, Market Place, Norwich NR10 4JJ
T: (01603) 871872
F: (01603) 870304
E: info@norfolkcottages.co.uk
I: www.norfolkcottages.co.uk

Bolding Way Holiday Cottages ★★★★
Contact: Mr Charlie Harrison
Bolding Way Holiday Cottages, Bolding Way, Holt NR25 7SW
T: (01263) 588666
E: holidays@boldingway.co.uk
I: www.boldingway.co.uk

Home Farm Cottages ★★★
Contact: Mrs Sally Middleton
Home Farm Cottages, Home Farm, Holt Road, Holt NR25 7ST
T: (01263) 588334
E: sallymiddleton@virgin.com
I: www.weybourne-holiday-cottages.co.uk

Lower Byre ★★★
Contact: Ms Valerie James
5 Birch Grove, Spalding PE11 2HL
T: (01775) 760938
F: (01775) 762856
E: valeriejames@waitrose.com

The Old Stables ★★★
Contact: Mr & Mrs Roger Cooling
Holiday Cottages, 21 High Street, Spalding PE11 1TX
T: (01775) 712100

The Treehouse ★★★
Contact: Mrs Sharon Moss
Priory Barn, Harleston IP20 0JH
T: (01379) 854601
E: sharonmoss@pgen.net

Wayside Cottage ★★★
Contact:
Countryside Cottages, 5 Old Stable Yard, High Street, Holt NR25 6BN
T: (01263) 713133
I: www.waysidecottage.info

Weybourne Forest Lodges ★★-★★★★
Contact: Mr Chris & Mrs Sue Tansley
Weybourne Forest Lodges, Sandy Hill Lane, Holt NR25 7HW
T: (01263) 588440
F: (01263) 588588
E: chris_tansley@hotmail.com
I: www.weybourneforestlodges.co.uk

Establishments printed in blue have a detailed entry in this guide

EAST OF ENGLAND

WHEATACRE
Norfolk
Bluebell Cottage ★★★
Contact: Mrs Vera Thirtle
Playters Old Farm, Church Road,
Ellough, Beccles NR34 7TN
T: (01502) 712325
F: (01502) 712325
E: thirtle.playters@virgin.net
I: www.bluebellcottages.com

WHEPSTEAD
Suffolk
Rowney Cottage ★★★
Contact: Mrs Kati Turner
Rowney Farm, Bury St Edmunds
IP29 4TQ
T: (01284) 735842
E: nick.turner@farming.co.uk

WHITE RODING
Essex
Josselyns ★★★★
Contact: Mrs Dawn Becker
Josselyns, New Hall Farm, White
Roding, Dunmow CM6 1RY
T: (01279) 876734
F: (01279) 876938
E: nb@artbecco.co.uk
I: www.essexbungalow.co.uk

WICKHAM SKEITH
Suffolk
The Netus Barn ★★★
Contact: Mrs Joy Homan
Street Farm, Wickham Skeith,
Eye IP23 8LP
T: (01449) 766215
E: joygeoff@homansf.freeserve.co.uk

WICKMERE
Norfolk
Church Farm Barns ★★-★★★
Contact: Mr & Mrs McKenzie
Church Farm Barns, Owl &
Harvest Cottages, Norwich
NR11 7NB
T: (01263) 577332
E: tulloch.ard1@btopenworld.co.uk
I: www.churchfarmbarns.northnorfolk.co.uk

Swallow Cottages (Poppyland Holiday Cottages) ★★★★
Contact: Mr & Mrs Riches
21 Regent Street, Norwich
NR11 7ND
T: (01263) 577473
F: (01263) 570087
E: poppyland@totalise.co.uk
I: www.broadland.com/poppyland

WIGHTON
Norfolk
Malthouse ★★★
Contact: Mrs Linden Green
Copys Green, Wells-next-the-Sea NR23 1NY
T: (01328) 820204
F: (01328) 820175
E: t.b.green@lineone.net

Old Barn Cottage ★★★
Contact: Mrs Gail Armstrong
Norfolk Country Cottages Ref.
493, Market Place, Norwich
NR10 4JJ
T: (01603) 871872
F: (01603) 870304
E: info@norfolkcottages.co.uk
I: www.norfolkcottages.co.uk/wighton_493.htm

WILBURTON
Cambridgeshire
Australia Farmhouse ★★★★
Contact: Mrs Rebecca Howard
Australia Farmhouse,
Twentypence Road, Ely CB6 3PX
T: (01353) 740322
F: (01353) 740322
E: fenflat@hotmail.com
I: www.sakernet.com/jameshoward

WINGFIELD
Suffolk
Beech Farm Maltings ★★★★
Contact: Mrs Rosemary Gosling
Beech Farm, Eye IP21 5RG
T: (01379) 586630
F: (01379) 586630
E: maltings.beechfarm@virgin.net
I: www.beech-farm-maltings.co.uk

Keeley's Farm ★★★
Contact: Mrs Gloria Elsden
Keeley's Farm, Solomon Place,
Eye IP21 4LT
T: (01379) 668409

WISBECH
Cambridgeshire
Common Right Barns ★★★★
Contact: Mrs Teresa Fowler
Common Right Barns, Plash
Drove, Tholomas Drove, Wisbech
St Mary, Wisbech PE13 4SP
T: (01945) 410424
F: (01945) 410424
E: teresa@commonrightbarns.co.uk
I: www.commonrightbarns.co.uk

WISBECH ST MARY
Cambridgeshire
Fenland Self Catering Holidays ★★★
Contact: Mr Michael Southern
Fenland Self Catering Holidays,
Mandalay, Station Road,
Wisbech PE13 1RY
T: (01945) 410680
I: www.fenlandselfcateringholidays.co.uk

WIVETON
Norfolk
Laneway Cottage ★★★★
Contact: Mrs Catherine Joice
Nelson Cottage, Hall Lane,
Fakenham NR21 7ND
T: (01328) 862261
F: (01328) 856464
E: catherine.joice@btinternet.com
I: www.colkirk.com

WOOD NORTON
Norfolk
Acorn Cottages ★★★★
Contact: Ms Ann Pope
White House Farm, Foulsham
Road, Wood Norton, Dereham
NR20 5BG
T: (01362) 683615
F: (01362) 683615
E: rjpope@lineone.net
I: www.countrysideholidays.com

Hall Farm Cottage ★★★★
Contact: Mr Barry Mark Griss
Hall Farm House, Church Road,
Wood Norton, Dereham
NR20 5AR
T: (01362) 683341
E: barrygriss@anserve.com
I: www.cottageguide.co.uk

The Small Barn ★★★
Contact: Miss Jane Lister
The Small Barn, Severals Grange,
Holt Road, Dereham NR20 5BL
T: (01362) 684206
E: hoecroft@acedial.co.uk

WOODBRIDGE
Suffolk
The Coach House ★★★
Contact: Ms Nicola Deller
Hill House, Mill Hill, Framsden,
Stowmarket IP14 6HB
T: (01473) 890891
E: nicoladeller@yahoo.com
I: www.accommodationsuffolk.co.uk

Colston Cottage ★★★★
Contact: Mr John Bellefontaine
Colston Cottage, Colston Hall,
Woodbridge IP13 8LB
T: (01728) 638375
F: (01728) 638084
E: lizjohn@colstonhall.com
I: www.colstonhall.com

Easton Farm Park ★★★★
Contact: Miss Fiona Kerr
Easton Farm Park, Pound Corner,
Woodbridge IP13 0EQ
T: (01728) 746475
F: (01728) 747861
E: fionakerr@suffolkonline.net
I: www.eastonfarmpark.co.uk

The Old Forge ★★★★
Contact: Mr Robert Blake
1A Moorfield Road, Woodbridge
IP12 4JN
T: (01394) 382565
E: robert@bloke4110.fsbusiness.co.uk

Quayside Cottage ★★★
Contact: Mr Richard Leigh
Quayside Cottage, The Quay,
Woodbridge IP12 4QZ
T: (01473) 736724
E: quayside@waldringfield.org.uk

Sampsons Mill ★★★
Contact: Mr Gordon J. Turner
Sampsons Mill, Mill Lane,
Woodbridge IP13 0SF
T: (01728) 746791
F: (01728) 746791
E: sampsons.mill@ntlworld.com

Sunbeams ★★★
Contact: Mrs Penny Moon
Mrs Jane Good (Holidays)
Limited, Little Bass, Ferry Quay,
Woodbridge IP12 1BW
T: (01394) 382770
F: (01394) 382770
E: theoffice@mrsjanegoodltd.co.uk
I: www.mrsjanegoodltd.co.uk

Windmill Lodges ★★★★
Contact: Mrs Katie Coe
Windmill Lodges, Red House
Farm, Saxtead, Woodbridge
IP13 9RD
T: (01728) 685338
F: (01728) 684850
E: holidays@windmilllodges.co.uk
I: www.windmilllodges.co.uk

WOOLPIT
Suffolk
The Bothy ★★★★
Contact: Mrs Kathryn Parker
Grange Farm, Woolpit Green,
Bury St Edmunds IP30 9RG
T: (01359) 241143
F: (01359) 244296
E: grangefarm@btinternet.com
I: www.farmstayanglia.co.uk/grangefarm/

WOOTTON
Bedfordshire
The Stable Yard ★★★★
Contact: Mrs Rachael Thomas
Hunters Lodge, Wood Farm,
Wootton Green, Bedford
MK43 9EF
T: (01234) 765351
F: (01234) 764278
E: thestableyard@tiscali.co.uk
I: www.thestableyard.org.uk

WORSTEAD
Norfolk
Poppyfields Cottages ★★★
Contact: Mr Dennis Gilligan
Church View House, Westwick
Road, Worstead, North Walsham
NR28 9SD
T: (01692) 536863
E: dennis.gilligan1@btinternet.com
I: www.poppyfieldscottages.co.uk

Woodcarvers Barn ★★★★
Contact: Mr Simon Gray
Rose Cottage, Honing Row,
North Walsham NR28 9RH
T: (01692) 536662
E: si@worstead.co.uk
I: www.worstead.co.uk/barn

WORTHAM
Suffolk
Ivy House Farm ★★★★
Contact: Mr & Mrs Paul Bradley
Ivy House Farm, Long Green,
Diss IP22 1RD
T: (01379) 898395
F: (01379) 898395
E: prjsdrad@aol.com
I: www.ivyhousefarmcottages.co.uk

EAST OF ENGLAND

Olde Tea Shoppe Apartment ★★★★
Contact: Mrs Alison Dumbell
Post Office Stores, Long Green,
Diss IP22 1PP
T: (01379) 783210
E: teashop@wortham.freeserve.co.uk

WROXHAM
Norfolk

Daisy Broad Lodges ★★★★
Contact: Mr Daniel Thwaites
Riverside Road, Wroxham,
Norwich NR12 8UD
T: (01603) 782625
F: (01603) 784072
E: daniel@barnesbrinkcraft.co.uk
I: www.barnesbrinkcraft.co.uk

Helen's ★★★
Contact: Mrs G Armstrong
Norfolk Country Cottages,
Carlton House, Market Place,
Norwich NR10 4JJ
T: (01603) 871872
F: (01603) 870304
E: info@norfolkcottages.co.uk
I: www.norfolkcottages.co.uk

Nutmeg & Plum Tree Cottages ★★★★
Contact: Mrs Jane Pond
East View Farm, Stone Lane,
Ashmanhaugh, Norwich
NR12 8YW
T: (01603) 782225 &
07831 258258
F: (01603) 782225
E: john.pond@tinyworld.co.uk
I: www.eastviewfarm.co.uk

Old Farm Cottages ★★★★
Contact: Mrs Kay Paterson
Old Farm Cottages, Tunstead,
Norwich NR12 8HS
T: (01692) 536612
F: (01692) 536612
E: mail@oldfarmcottages.fsnet.co.uk
I: www.oldfarmcottages.com

20 Trail Quay Cottages ★★★
Contact: Mrs Gail Armstrong
Norfolk Country Cottages,
Carlton House, Market Place,
Norwich NR10 4JJ
T: (01603) 871872
F: (01603) 870304
E: info@norfolkcottages.co.uk
I: www.norfolkcottages.co.uk

Whitegates Apartment ★★★
Contact: Mrs Cheryl Youd
Whitegates, Norwich Road,
Norwich NR12 8RZ
T: (01603) 781037

YOXFORD
Suffolk

Wolsey Farm House ★★★★
Contact: Mrs Marion Anthony
Heritage Hideaways Ltd, 2
Westend Farm Cottages, Beccles
NR34 7NH
T: (01502) 675674
F: (01502) 676050
E: marion.anthony1@virgin.net
I: www.heritagehideaways.com

SOUTH EAST ENGLAND

ABINGDON
Oxfordshire

Brook Farm ★★★★
Contact: Mrs Pam Humphrey
Brook Farm, Abingdon OX14 4EZ
T: (01235) 820717
F: (01235) 820262
E: info@brookfarmcottages.com
I: www.brookfarmcottages.co.uk

Flat 1 ★★★
Contact: Mrs Stella Carter
The Old Bakehouse, Winterborne
Road, Abingdon OX14 1AJ
T: (01235) 520317
E: stella@bakehouse.supanet.com

Kingfisher Barn Holiday Cottages ★★★-★★★★★
Contact: Sarah
Culham, Abingdon OX14 3NN
T: (01235) 537538
F: (01235) 537538
E: info@kingfisherbarn.com
I: www.kingfisherbarn.com

ACRISE
Kent

Ladwood Farm Cottages ★★★
Contact: Mr Steve & Mrs Shirley Craigie
Ladwood Farm, Folkestone
CT18 8LL
I: www.ladwood.com

ADDERBURY
Oxfordshire

Hannah's Cottage at Fletcher's ★★★★
Contact: Mrs Charlotte Holmes
Fletchers, High Street,
Adderbury, Banbury OX17 3LS
T: (01295) 810308
E: charlotteaholmes@hotmail.com
I: www.holiday-rentals.com

ALBURY
Surrey

The Lodge at Overbrook ★★★★
Contact: Ms Rebecca Greayer
The Lodge at Overbrook, Farley Green, Guildford GU5 9DN
T: (01483) 209579
F: (01483) 209579

ALCISTON
East Sussex

Rose Cottage Flat ★★★
Contact: Mrs Brenda Beck
Freedom Holiday Homes, 15
High Street, Cranbrook
TN17 3EB
T: (01580) 720770
F: (01580) 720771
E: mail@freedomholidayhomes.co.uk
I: www.freedomholidayhomes.co.uk

Southdown Barn ★★★
Contact: Mr Richard Harris
Best of Brighton & Sussex
Cottages Ltd, Vicarage Lane,
Brighton BN2 7HD
T: (01273) 308779
F: (01273) 300266
E: brightoncottages@pavilion.co.uk
I: www.bestofbrighton.co.uk

The Studio ★★★
Contact: Mrs Brenda Beck
Freedom Holiday Homes, 15
High Street, Cranbrook
TN17 3EB
T: (01580) 720770
F: (01580) 720771
E: mail@freedomholidayhomes.co.uk
I: www.freedomholidayhomes.co.uk

ALDINGTON
Kent

Goldwell Manor Cottage ★★★★
Contact: Mrs Brenda Beck
Freedom Holiday Homes, 15
High Street, Cranbrook
TN17 3EB
T: (01580) 720770
F: (01580) 720771

Peacock
Rating Applied For
Contact: Mrs Gill Manwarin
Peacock, Giggers Green Road,
Ashford TN25 7BY
T: (01233) 720452
E: dmanwa4857@aol.com
I: www.peacockstudio.co.uk

ALFRISTON
East Sussex

Danny Cottage ★★★★★
Contact: Mr Michael Ann
Danny Cottage, Polegate
BN26 5XW
T: (01323) 870406
F: (01323) 870406
E: contact@dannycottage.co.uk
I: www.dannycottage.co.uk

Flint Cottage ★★★★
Contact: Mrs Shirley Moore
Renby Stables, Royal Tunbridge Wells TN3 9LG
T: (01892) 864811
F: (01322) 666476
E: flintcott@aol.com
I: www.flintcottagesussex.co.uk

The Pony House ★★★★
Contact: Mrs Sandy Hernu
The Pony House, Sloe Lane,
Polegate BN26 5UP
T: (01323) 870303
F: (01323) 871664
E: hernu@supanet.com
I: www.visitsussex.org/ponyhouse

Winton Barn ★★★
Contact: Mrs Fay Smith
Winton Barn, Winton Street,
Alfriston, Polegate BN26 5UJ
T: (01323) 870407
F: (01323) 870407

ALTON
Hampshire

Butts House Studio ★★★
Contact: Mrs Sue Webborn
Butts House Studio, Butts
House, The Butts, Alton
GU34 1RD
T: (01420) 87507
F: (01420) 87507
E: webbons@buttshouse.com
I: www.buttshouse.com

The Coach House ★★★★
Contact: Mrs Jean Stephens
The Coach House, Stubbs Farm,
Kingsley, Bordon GU35 9NR
T: (01420) 474906
F: (01420) 474906
E: info@stubbsfarm.co.uk
I: www.stubbsfarm.co.uk

ALVERSTOKE
Hampshire

28 The Avenue ★★
Contact: Mr Martin Lawson
18 Upper Paddock Road,
Watford WD19 4DZ
T: (01923) 244042
F: (01923) 244042
E: martinlawson8400@aol.com

ALVERSTONE
Isle of Wight

Combe View ★★★
Contact: Mrs Oliver
Kern Farm, Sandown PO36 0EY
T: (01983) 403721

The Dairy, The Forge & The Grange ★★★★
Contact: Mrs Lisa Baskill
31 Pier Street, Ventnor
PO38 1SX
T: (01983) 854340
F: (01983) 855524

West Wing Kern Farmhouse ★★★★
Contact: Mrs Oliver
Kern Farm, Sandown PO36 0EY
T: (01983) 403721

ALVERSTONE GARDEN VILLAGE
Isle of Wight

Garstone ★★★★
Contact: Mrs Lisa Baskill
31 Pier Street, Ventnor
PO38 1SX
T: (01983) 854340
F: (01983) 855524

AMBERLEY
West Sussex

Culver Cottage ★★
Contact: Mrs Beryl Cruttenden
Dornoch, 1 Bunbury Close,
Pulborough RH20 3PN
T: (01903) 746610
F: (01903) 743332
I: www.visitbritain.com

Establishments printed in blue have a detailed entry in this guide

SOUTH EAST ENGLAND

AMERSHAM
Buckinghamshire
Chiltern Cottages ★★★★
Contact: Mr Stephen Hinds
Hill Farm Lane, Chalfont St Giles HP8 4NT
T: (07973) 737107
F: (01494) 872421
E: bookings@chilterncottages.org.uk
I: www.chilterncottages.org.uk

AMPFIELD
Hampshire
The Den ★★★★
Contact: Mrs Beryl Knight
The Den, Birch House, Knapp Lane, Romsey SO51 9BT
T: (01794) 367903
F: (01794) 367291
E: beryl@knightworld.com

ANDOVER
Hampshire
Westmead
Rating Applied For
Contact: Mrs Dianna Leighton
Westmead, Amesbury Road, Andover SP11 8DU
T: (01264) 772513
F: (01204) 773003
E: westmeadweyhill@aol.com

APPLEDORE
Kent
Ashby Farms Ltd ★★-★★★
Contact: Mr Ashby
Ashby Farms Ltd, Place Farm, Ashford TN26 2LZ
T: (01233) 733332
F: (01233) 733326
I: www.ashbyfarms.com

ARDINGLY
West Sussex
Townhouse Bothy ★★★
Contact: Mrs Ann Campbell
Fairhaven Holiday Cottages, Derby House, 123 Watling Street, Gillingham ME7 2YY
T: (01634) 300089
F: (01634) 570157
E: enquiries@fairhaven-holidays.co.uk
I: www.fairhaven-holidays.co.uk

ARUNDEL
West Sussex
Arundel Town Cottage
Rating Applied For
Contact: Miss Sue Blaney
Littlefield West Drive, Littlehampton BN16 4NL
E: arundeltowncottage@hotmail.com

Castle View ★★★★
Contact: Ms Jeannie Gapp
16 Maltravers Street, Arundel BN18 9BU
T: (01903) 884713
E: jeanniegapp@yahoo.com.uk

The Coachman's Flat and The Cottage ★★★
Contact: Mrs Jan Fuente
The Coachman's Flat and The Cottage, Mill Lane House, Arundel BN18 0RP
T: (01243) 814440
F: (01243) 814436
E: jan.fuente@btopenworld.com
I: www.mill-lane-house.co.uk

Village Holidays ★★★-★★★★
Contact: Mrs Pilkington & Miss C Booker
Village Holidays, The Street, Arundel BN18 0PF
T: (01243) 551073
F: (01243) 551073
E: tb@villageholidays.com
I: www.villageholidays.com

ASH
Kent
Hawthorn Farm ★★★-★★★★★
Contact: Mr John Baker
Hawthorn Farm, Corner Drove, Ware, Canterbury CT3 2LU
T: (01304) 813560
F: (01304) 812482
E: info@hawthornfarm.co.uk
I: www.hawthornfarm.co.uk

ASHBURNHAM
East Sussex
The Folly ★★★
Contact: Mrs Brenda Beck
Freedom Holiday Homes, 15 High Street, Cranbrook TN17 3EB
T: (01580) 720770
F: (01580) 720771
E: mail@freedomholidayhomes.co.uk
I: www.freedomholidayhomes.co.uk

ASHEY
Isle of Wight
The Springs ★★★★
Contact: Mrs Honor Vass
Island Cottage Holidays, Godshill Park Farm House, Ventnor PO38 3JF
T: (01929) 480080
F: (01929) 481070
E: enq@islandcottagesholidays.com
I: www.cottageholidays.dmon.co.uk

Tithe Barn, Old Byre & The Cote ★★★★★
Contact: Mrs Alison Jane Johnson
Tithe Barn, Old Byre & The Cote, Little Upton Farm, Gatehouse Road, Ryde PO33 4BS
T: (01983) 563236
F: (01983) 563236
E: alison@littleuptonfarm.co.uk
I: www.littleuptonfarm.co.uk

ASHFORD
Kent
Dean Farm ★★★★
Contact: Mrs Brenda Beck
Freedom Holiday Homes, 15 High Street, Cranbrook TN17 3EB
T: (01580) 720770
F: (01580) 720771
E: mail@freedomholidayhomes.co.uk
I: www.freedomholidayhomes.co.uk

Eversleigh Woodland Lodges ★★★
Contact: Mrs Drury
Eversleigh House, Hornash Lane, Ashford TN26 1HX
T: (01233) 733248
F: (01233) 733248
E: cjdrury@freeuk.com
I: www.eversleighlodges.co.uk

Grove House Cottage ★★★★
Contact: Mr Stuart Winter
Grove House Cottage, Main Road, Ashford TN25 6JX
T: (01732) 369168
F: (01732) 358817
E: holidays@gardenofenglandcottages.co.uk
I: www.gardenofenglandcottages.co.uk

The Old Dairy ★★★
Contact: Mrs June Browning
Whatsole Street Farm, Ashford TN25 5JW
T: (01233) 750238
F: (01233) 750238
E: browning.elmstead@talk21.com

ASHLEY GREEN
Buckinghamshire
The Old Farm ★★★
Contact: Mrs Gillian Potter
The Old Farm, Hog Lane, Chesham HP5 3PY
T: (01442) 866430
F: (01442) 866430
E: tc.eng@virgin.net

AYLESFORD
Kent
Stable Cottage at Wickham Lodge ★★★★★
Contact: Mr & Mrs Richard Bourne
Wickham Lodge, The Quay, 73 High Street, Aylesford ME20 7AY
T: (01622) 717267
F: (01622) 792855
E: wickhamlodge@aol.com
I: www.wickhamlodge.co.uk

BAMPTON
Oxfordshire
Grafton Manor Wing ★★★
Contact: Ms Sandra Eddolls
Grafton Manor Wing, Manor Farm, Grafton, Bampton OX18 2RY
T: (01367) 810237

Haytor Cottage ★★★
Contact: Mrs Susan Phillips
Haytor, Lavender Square, Bampton OX18 2LR
T: (01993) 850321
E: smph@supanet.com

Tom's Barn ★★
Contact: Mr Thomas Freeman
Radcot Bridge House, Radcot, Bampton OX18 2SX
T: (01367) 810410
E: tmfreeman@btinternet.com

BANBURY
Oxfordshire
Little Good Lodge ★★★★
Contact: Ms Lynne Aries
Little Good Lodge, Banbury OX17 1QZ
T: (01295) 750069
F: (01295) 750069
E: bryan.aries@btopenworld.com
I: www.littlegoodfarm.users.btopenworld.com

BARNHAM
West Sussex
Welldiggers ★★★★★
Contact: Mrs Penelope Crawford
Church Farm Barns, Hill Lane, Bognor Regis PO22 0BN
T: (01243) 555119
F: (01243) 552779
E: welldiggers@hotmail.com
I: www.welldiggers.co.uk

West Cottage & Paddock Barn ★★★
Contact: Mrs Karen Blackman
Barnham Court Farm, Barnham PO22 0BP
T: (01243) 553223
F: (01243) 553223

BARTON ON SEA
Hampshire
Lanterns
Rating Applied For
Contact: Ms Rosina Bray
Lanterns, 6 Powerscourt Road, New Milton BH25 7DP

Rose Cottage ★★★★
Contact: Mr Patrick Higgins
Rafters, Dilly Lane, New Milton BH25 7DQ
T: (01425) 613406
F: (01425) 613406

Solent Heights ★★★★★
Contact: Mrs Dee Philpott
Solent Heights, 53 Marine Drive East, New Milton BH25 7DX
T: (01425) 616066
F: (01425) 616066

Westbury Apartment ★★★
Contact: Mr Les Williams
Westbury Apartment, 12 Greenacre, New Milton BH25 7BS
T: (01425) 620935
E: les@westbury-apartment.co.uk
I: www.westbury-apartment.co.uk/sc

BATTLE
East Sussex
Henley Bridge Stud ★★★
Contact: Mr & Mrs Martin White
Henley Bridge Stud, Lower Brays Hill, Battle TN33 9NZ
T: (01424) 892076
F: (01424) 893990
E: martan@hbstud.fsnet.co.uk

Highfields ★★★
Contact: Mr & Mrs Martin Holgate
Highfields, Telham Lane, Battle TN33 0SN
T: (01424) 774865

SOUTH EAST ENGLAND

Lonicera Lodge ★★★★
Contact: Mrs Annette Hedges
Lonicera, 114 Hastings Road,
Battle TN33 0TQ
T: (01424) 772835

Stiles Garage (Battle) Ltd
★★★
Contact: Mr John Stiles
Stiles Garage (Battle) Ltd, 2-3
Upper Lake, Battle TN33 0AN
T: (01424) 773155
F: (01424) 773155
E: stilesgarage@hotmail.com

BEACONSFIELD
Buckinghamshire

Roselands ★★★
Contact: Mrs June Koderisch
Roselands, 3 Beechwood Road,
Beaconsfield HP9 1HP
T: (01494) 676864
F: (01494) 676864
E: dkoderisch@iname.com

BEAULIEU
Hampshire

Hill Top House Cottage
★★★★
Contact: Mr & Mrs Brett
Johnson
Hill Top House, Palace Lane,
Brockenhurst SO42 7YG
T: (01590) 612731
F: (01590) 612743
E: bretros@aol.com

Ivy Cottage ★★★
Contact: Mr & Mrs Gibb
28 Church Street, Littlehampton
BN17 5PX
T: (01903) 715595
F: (01903) 719176
E: gibb28@breathemail.net

Mares Tails Cottage ★★★★
Contact: Mrs Alice Barber
Mares Tails Cottage, Furzey
Lane, Brockenhurst SO42 7WB
T: (01590) 612160
E: marestails1@ukonline.co.uk

Old Stables Cottage ★★★★
Contact: Mr Peter & Mrs Jo
Whapham
Myrtle Farm, Brockenhurst
SO42 7WU
T: (01590) 626707
E: oldstablescott@aol.com
I: www.oldstablescottage.co.uk

BECKLEY
East Sussex

Bixley ★★★
Contact: Ms Philippa Bushe
93 Balfour Road, London
N5 2HE
T: (020) 72269035
E: tim@busheassoc.com
I: www.bixleycottage.co.uk

**The Herdsman & The
Blacksmith's Cottage**
★★★-★★★★★
Contact: Mr Stuart Winter
Garden of England Cottages, The
Mews Office, 189A High Street,
Tonbridge TN9 1BX
T: (01732) 369168
F: (01732) 358817
E: holidays@
gardenofenglandcottages.co.uk
I: www.
gardenofenglandcottages.co.uk
♿

BEECH
Hampshire

4B Wellhouse Road ★★★★
Contact: Mr Norman Adams
4A Wellhouse Road, Alton
GU34 4AH
T: (01420) 542011

BEMBRIDGE
Isle of Wight

Allandale ★★★
Contact: Mrs Ellis
Bembridge Holiday Homes, 13
High Street, Bembridge
PO35 5SD
T: (01983) 872335

1 Bay Cottages ★★
Contact: Mrs Ellis
Bembridge Holiday Homes, 13
High Street, Bembridge
PO35 5SD
T: (01983) 872335

Bella Vista ★★★★
Contact: Mrs Ellis
Bembridge Holiday Homes, 13
High Street, Bembridge
PO35 5SD
T: (01983) 872335

Cara Cottage ★★★
Contact: Mrs Ellis
Bembridge Holiday Homes, 13
High Street, Bembridge
PO35 5SD
T: (01983) 872335

Casa Blanca ★★★★
Contact: Mrs Ellis
Bembridge Holiday Homes, 13
High Street, Bembridge
PO35 5SD
T: (01983) 872335

The Chalet ★★★
Contact: Mrs Ellis
Bembridge Holiday Homes, 13
High Street, Bembridge
PO35 5SD
T: (01983) 872335

Cliff Cottage ★★
Contact: Mrs Lisa Baskill
31 Pier Street, Ventnor
PO38 1SX
T: (01983) 854340
F: (01983) 855524

Crab Cottage ★★★
Contact: Mrs Ellis
Bembridge Holiday Homes, 13
High Street, Bembridge
PO35 5SD
T: (01983) 872335

Crossways ★★★
Contact: Mrs Ellis
Bembridge Holiday Homes, 13
High Street, Bembridge
PO35 5SD
T: (01983) 872335

Dolphin Cottage ★★★
Contact: Mrs Lisa Baskill
31 Pier Street, Ventnor
PO38 1SX
T: (01983) 854340
F: (01983) 855524

8 Downsview Road ★★
Contact: Mrs Ellis
Bembridge Holiday Homes, 13
High Street, Bembridge
PO35 5SD
T: (01983) 872335

3 Fairhaven Close ★★★
Contact: Mrs Ellis
Bembridge Holiday Homes, 13
High Street, Bembridge
PO35 5SD
T: (01983) 872335

The Finches ★★★
Contact: Mrs Ellis
Bembridge Holiday Homes, 13
High Street, Bembridge
PO35 5SD
T: (01983) 872335

Flat 3 Pump Mews ★★★★
Contact: Ms Catherine Hopper
Residential & Holiday Letting
Agents, 138 High Street,
Newport PO30 1TY
T: (01983) 521114
F: (01983) 822030
E: rental_office@
hose-Rhodes-Dickson.co.uk
I: www.island-holiday-homes.
net

Folly Hill Cottage ★★
Contact: Mrs Lisa Baskill
Home from Home Holidays, 31
Pier Street, Ventnor PO38 1SX
T: (01983) 854340
F: (01983) 855524
E: admin@hfromh.co.uk

Forelands Cottage ★★
Contact: Mrs Ellis
Bembridge Holiday Homes, 13
High Street, Bembridge
PO35 5SD
T: (01983) 872335

Green Oaks ★★★
Contact: Mrs Ellis
Bembridge Holiday Homes, 13
High Street, Bembridge
PO35 5SD
T: (01983) 872335

**Harbour Farm Cottage and
Harbour Farm Lodge** ★★★
Contact: Mr Kenneth Hicks
Harbour Farm Cottage and
Harbour Farm Lodge,
Embankment Road, Bembridge
PO35 5NS
T: (01983) 872610
F: (01983) 874080
I: www.harbourfarm.co.uk

3 Harbour Strand ★★★
Contact: Mrs Lisa Baskill
31 Pier Street, Ventnor
PO38 1SX
T: (01983) 854340
F: (01983) 855524

4 Highbury Court ★★★
Contact: Mrs Page
32 Mays Avenue, Carlton,
Nottingham NG4 1AU
T: (0115) 987 4420

Hilvana ★★
Contact: Mrs Ellis
Bembridge Holiday Homes, 13
High Street, Bembridge
PO35 5SD
T: (01983) 872335

Honeysuckle Haven ★★
Contact: Mrs Ellis
Bembridge Holiday Homes, 13
High Street, Bembridge
PO35 5SD
T: (01983) 872335

51 Howgate Road ★★★★
Contact: Mrs Ellis
Bembridge Holiday Homes, 13
High Street, Bembridge
PO35 5SD
T: (01983) 872335

Kestrel ★★★
Contact: Mrs Ellis
Bembridge Holiday Homes, 13
High Street, Bembridge
PO35 5SD
T: (01983) 872335

7 Kings Close ★★★
Contact: Mrs Ellis
Bembridge Holiday Homes, 13
High Street, Bembridge
PO35 5SD
T: (01983) 872335

Kingsmere ★★
Contact: Mrs Kersley
Kingsmere, Lane End, Bembridge
PO35 5TB
T: (01983) 872778

Little Forelands ★★★★
Contact: Mrs Ellis
Bembridge Holiday Homes, 13
High Street, Bembridge
PO35 5SD
T: (01983) 872335

Meadow Dairy ★★★
Contact: Mrs Lisa Baskill
31 Pier Street, Ventnor
PO38 1SX
T: (01983) 854340
F: (01983) 855524

Merryweather Cottage
★★★★
Contact: Mrs Debbie Stapleton
Peel House, 4 Steyne Road,
Bembridge PO35 5UH
T: (01983) 875459
E: debbiestapleton@aol.com
I: www.cottageguide.
co.uk/merryweather

Mimosa Cottage ★★★
Contact: Mrs Lisa Baskill
Home from Home Holidays, 31
Pier Street, Ventnor PO38 1SX
T: (01983) 854340
F: (01983) 855524
E: admin@hfromh.co.uk

Nine ★★★
Contact: Mrs Betty Cripps
High Point, Brook Green,
Cuckfield RH17 5JJ
T: (01444) 454474

Pippin
Rating Applied For
Contact: Ms Jacqui Ellis
Bembridge Holiday Homes, 13
High Street, Bembridge
PO35 5SD
T: (01983) 873163
F: (01983) 872279

Pitt Corner ★★★
Contact: Mrs Lisa Baskill
Home from Home Holidays, 31
Pier Street, Ventnor PO38 1SX
T: (01983) 854340
F: (01983) 855524
E: admin@hfromh.co.uk

Establishments printed in blue have a detailed entry in this guide

SOUTH EAST ENGLAND

11 Port St Helens ★★
Contact: Mrs Ellis
Bembridge Holiday Homes, 13 High Street, Bembridge
PO35 5SD
T: (01983) 872335

Portland House ★★★★★
Contact: Mrs Ellis
Bembridge Holiday Homes, 13 High Street, Bembridge
PO35 5SD
T: (01983) 872335

Princessa Cottage & Coastwatch Cottage ★★★
Contact: Mrs Hargreaves
1 Norcott Drive, Bembridge
PO35 5TX
T: (01983) 874403
F: (01983) 874403
E: ssnharg@aol.com
I: www.islandbreaks.co.uk

Rothsay Cottage ★★★★
Contact: Mrs Ellis
Bembridge Holiday Homes, 13 High Street, Bembridge
PO35 5SD
T: (01983) 872335

Seahorses ★★★
Contact: Mrs Ellis
Bembridge Holiday Homes, 13 High Street, Bembridge
PO35 5SD
T: (01983) 872335

September Cottage ★★
Contact: Mrs Saunders
Swan House Swanley Village, Swanley BR8 7NF
T: (01322) 662996

Ship-n-Shore ★★★★
Contact: Mr Chris Durham
The Butchers Arms, Dunmow Road, North End, Dunmow
CM6 3PJ
T: (01245) 237481
E: thebutchersarms@tesco.net

12a Solent Landings ★★★
Contact: Ms Catherine Hopper
Island Holiday Homes, 138 High Street, Newport PO30 1TY
T: (01983) 521114

18 Solent Landings
Rating Applied For
Contact: Ms Jacqui Ellis
Bembridge Holiday Homes, 13 High Street, Bembridge
PO35 5SD
T: (01983) 873163
F: (01983) 872279

4 Swains Villas ★★★
Contact: Mrs Ellis
Bembridge Holiday Homes, 13 High Street, Bembridge
PO35 5SD
T: (01983) 872335

Will-o-Cott ★★
Contact: Mrs Betty Cripps
High Point, Brook Green, Cuckfield RH17 5JJ
T: (01444) 454174

Windmill Inn, Hotel & Restaurant ★★★-★★★★
Contact: Mrs Elizabeth Miles
Windmill Inn, Hotel & Restaurant, 1 Steyne Road, Bembridge PO35 5UH
T: (01983) 872875
F: (01983) 874760
E: enquiries@windmill-inn.com
I: www.windmill-inn.com

BENENDEN
Kent

Bluebell Cottage ★★★
Contact: Mrs Brenda Beck
Freedom Holiday Homes, 15 High Street, Cranbrook
TN17 3EB
T: (01580) 720770
F: (01580) 720771
E: mail@freedomholidayhomes.co.uk
I: www.freedomholidayhomes.co.uk

Coopers Cottage ★★★★
Contact: Mr Stuart Winter
Garden of England Cottages, The Mews Office, 189A High Street, Tonbridge TN9 1BX
T: (01732) 369168
F: (01732) 358817
E: holidays@gardenofenglandcottages.co.uk
I: www.gardenofenglandcottages.co.uk

Standen Barn Cottage ★★★★
Contact: Mr Stuart Winter
Garden of England Cottages, Standen Street, Cranbrook
TN17 4LA
T: (01732) 369168
F: (01732) 358817
E: holidays@gardenofenglandcottages.co.uk
I: www.gardenofenglandcottages.co.uk

BEPTON
West Sussex

The Coach House ★★★
Contact: Dr Jennifer Randall
The Coach House, Midhurst
GU29 0HZ
T: (01730) 812351

BETHERSDEN
Kent

Mill Barn ★★★★
Contact: Mrs Brenda Beck
Freedom Holiday Homes, 15 High Street, Cranbrook
TN17 3EB
T: (01580) 720770
F: (01580) 720771
E: mail@freedomholidayhomes.co.uk
I: www.freedomholidayhomes.co.uk

Oast Mews ★★★
Contact: Mr Tim Bourne
Kent Holiday Cottages, Shepherd's View, Brissenden Court, Ashford TN26 3BE
T: (01233) 820746
F: (01233) 820746

BEXHILL
East Sussex

Beachcomber Flat ★★★
Contact: Mrs Mathews
Miraleisure Ltd, 51 Marina, Bexhill TN40 1BQ
T: (01424) 730298
F: (01424) 212500
E: infomira@waitrose.com

Boulevard Flat ★★★
Contact: Mrs Mathews
Miraleisure Ltd, 51 Marina, Bexhill TN40 1BQ
T: (01424) 730298
F: (01424) 212500
E: infomira@waitrose.com

Carlton Flat ★★★
Contact: Mrs Mathews
Miraleisure Ltd, 51 Marina, Bexhill TN40 1BQ
T: (01424) 730298
F: (01424) 212500
E: infomira@waitrose.com

Devonshire Flat ★★★
Contact: Mrs Mathews
Miraleisure Ltd, 51 Marina, Bexhill TN40 1BQ
T: (01424) 730298
F: (01424) 212500
E: infomira@waitrose.com

Eversley Flat ★★
Contact: Mrs Mathews
Miraleisure Ltd, 51 Marina, Bexhill TN40 1BQ
T: (01424) 730298
F: (01424) 212500
E: infomira@waitrose.com

Flat 1 Trent House ★★★
Contact: Mrs Brenda Beck
Freedom Holiday Homes, 15 High Street, Cranbrook
TN17 3EB
T: (01580) 720770
F: (01580) 720771
E: mail@freedomholidayhomes.co.uk
I: www.freedomholidayhomes.co.uk

Haven Flat ★★★
Contact: Mrs Mathews
Miraleisure Ltd, 51 Marina, Bexhill TN40 1BQ
T: (01424) 730298
F: (01424) 212500
E: infomira@waitrose.com

27 Linden Road ★★★
Contact: Mrs Mathews
Miraleisure Ltd, 51 Marina, Bexhill TN40 1BQ
T: (01424) 730298
F: (01424) 212500
E: infomira@waitrose.com

Mansion Flat ★★★★
Contact: Mrs Mathews
Miraleisure Ltd, 51 Marina, Bexhill TN40 1BQ
T: (01424) 730298
F: (01424) 212500
E: infomira@waitrose.com

Marina Flat ★★★
Contact: Mrs Mathews
Miraleisure Ltd, 51 Marina, Bexhill TN40 1BQ
T: (01424) 730298
F: (01424) 212500
E: infomira@waitrose.com

Mariners Flat ★★★
Contact: Mrs Mathews
Miraleisure Ltd, 51 Marina, Bexhill TN40 1BQ
T: (01424) 730298
F: (01424) 212500
E: infomira@waitrose.com

Miramar Holiday Flats ★★★
Contact: Mrs Carolyn Simmonds
Miramar Holiday Flats, De La Warr Parade, Bexhill TN40 1NR
T: (01424) 220360

Mulberry ★★★
Contact: Mrs Valerie Passfield
Mulberry, 31 Warwick Road, Bexhill TN39 4HG
T: (01424) 219204

Pavilion Flat ★★★
Contact: Mrs Mathews
Miraleisure Ltd, 51 Marina, Bexhill TN40 1BQ
T: (01424) 730298
F: (01424) 212500
E: infomira@waitrose.com

Promenade Flat ★★★
Contact: Mrs Mathews
Miraleisure Ltd, 51 Marina, Bexhill TN40 1BQ
T: (01424) 730298
F: (01424) 212500
E: infomira@waitrose.com

Riviera Flat ★★★
Contact: Mrs Mathews
Miraleisure Ltd, 51 Marina, Bexhill TN40 1BQ
T: (01424) 730298
F: (01424) 212500
E: infomira@waitrose.com

Sackville Hotel ★★★★
Contact: Ms Amanda Fiora
Sackville Hotel, De La Warr Parade, Bexhill-on-Sea, Bexhill TN40 1LS
T: (01424) 224694
F: (01424) 734132

Sea Whispers ★★★
Contact: Mrs Mathews
Miraleisure Ltd, 51 Marina, Bexhill TN40 1BQ
T: (01424) 730298
F: (01424) 212500
E: infomira@waitrose.com

Seaside Flat ★★★
Contact: Mrs Mathews
Miraleisure Ltd, 51 Marina, Bexhill TN40 1BQ
T: (01424) 730298
F: (01424) 212500
E: infomira@waitrose.com

Sovereign Flat ★★★
Contact: Mrs Mathews
Miraleisure Ltd, 51 Marina, Bexhill TN40 1BQ
T: (01424) 730298
F: (01424) 212500
E: infomira@waitrose.com

Sylvian ★★★
Contact: Adrian or Nicola Hazell
40 Fairfield Chase, Bexhill
TN39 3YD
T: (01424) 733955
F: (01424) 733955
E: nicola@ajcleaning.fsbusiness.co.uk

SOUTH EAST ENGLAND

Wilton Flat ★★★
Contact: Mrs Mathews
Miraleisure Ltd, 51 Marina,
Bexhill TN40 1BQ
T: (01424) 730298
F: (01424) 212500
E: infomira@waitrose.com

BICESTER
Oxfordshire

Pimlico Farm Country Cottages ★★★★
Contact: Mr John & Mrs Monica Harper
Pimlico Farm Country Cottages,
Pimlico Farm, Bicester OX27 7SL
T: (01869) 810306
F: (01869) 810309
E: enquiries@pimlicofarm.co.uk
I: www.pimlicofarm.co.uk

BIDDENDEN
Kent

Cart Barn
Rating Applied For
Contact: Ms Brenda Beck
Freedom Holiday Homes, 15
High Street, Cranbrook
TN17 3EB
T: (01580) 720770
F: (01580) 720771

The Den
Rating Applied For
Contact: Mrs Brenda Beck
Freedom Holiday Homes, 15
High Street, Cranbrook
TN17 3EB
T: (01580) 720770

Frogs Hole Barn ★★★★
Contact: Mrs Penny Pellett
Frogs Hole Barn, Sissinghurst Road, Ashford TN27 8EY
T: (01580) 291845
F: (01580) 291845
E: geo.pellett@btinternet.com

Garden Cottage ★★★★
Contact: Mrs Brenda Beck
Freedom Holiday Homes, 15
High Street, Cranbrook
TN17 3EB
T: (01580) 720770
F: (01580) 720771
E: mail@freedomholidayhomes.co.uk
I: www.freedomholidayhomes.co.uk

Tanyard Barn ★★★★
Contact: Mr Stuart Winter
Garden of England Cottages, The Mews Office, 189A High Street, Tonbridge TN9 1BX
T: (01732) 369168
F: (01732) 358817
E: holidays@gardenofenglandcottages.co.uk
I: www.gardenofenglandcottages.co.uk

BILSINGTON
Kent

Lanary Oast ★★★★★★
Contact: Mrs Brenda Beck
Freedom Holiday Homes, 15
High Street, Cranbrook
TN17 3EB
T: (01580) 720770
F: (01580) 720771
I: www.freedomholidayhomes.co.uk

Stonecross Farm Barn ★★★★
Contact: Mr John & Mrs Jane Hickman
Stonecross Farm Barn, Stonecross, Ashford TN25 7JJ
T: (01233) 720397
E: stonecrossbarn@tiscali.co.uk
I: myweb.tiscali.co.uk/stonecrossbarn/

BIRDHAM
West Sussex

The Old Dairy ★★★★
Contact: Mrs Diana Strange
Carthagena Farm, Bell Lane, Chichester PO20 7HY
T: (01243) 513885

BISHOPSTONE
East Sussex

144 Norton Cottage ★★★
Contact: Mrs Carol Collinson
Norton Farm, Bishopstone, Seaford BN25 2UW
T: (01323) 897544
F: (01323) 897544
E: norton.farm@farmline.com
I: members.farmline.com/collinson

BIX
Oxfordshire

Little Pightle
Rating Applied For
Contact: Mrs Camilla Shelley
Little Pightle, Old Bix Road,
Henley-on-Thames RG9 6BY
T: (01491) 574126
E: camillashelley@lineone.net

BLEAN
Kent

50 School Lane ★★★★
Contact: Mrs Brenda Beck
Freedom Holiday Homes, 15
High Street, Cranbrook
TN17 3EB
T: (01580) 720770
F: (01580) 720771
E: mail@freedomholidayhomes.co.uk
I: www.freedomholidayhomes.co.uk

BOGNOR REGIS
West Sussex

Aldwick Lodge ★★★★
Contact: Mrs Morag Bouterse
Aldwick Lodge, 40 Gossamer Lane, Bognor Regis PO21 3BY
T: (01243) 267445
F: (01243) 267445
E: kees@tinyworld.co.uk

BOLDRE
Hampshire

Close Cottage ★★★
Contact: Mr & Mrs White
Close Cottage, Brockenhurst Road, Battramsley, Lymington SO41 8PT
T: (01590) 675343

Orchard House
Rating Applied For
Contact: Mrs Valerie Barnes
Orchard House, Battramsley, Lymington SO41 8ND
T: (01590) 676686

Springfield Wing, Boldre ★★★
Contact: Mr & Mrs David or Rosemary Scott
Springfield Wing, Boldre, Spring Hill, Lymington SO41 8NG
T: (01590) 672491
E: david.scott@nfdc.gov.uk
I: www.vnewforest.co.uk

BONCHURCH
Isle of Wight

Ashcliff Holiday Apartments ★★★
Contact: Mrs Judith Lines
Ashcliff Holiday Apartments, The Pitts, Ventnor PO38 1NT
T: (01983) 853919
F: (01983) 853919
E: ashcliff.iow@virgin.net

Fernwood Cottage ★★★★
Contact: Mrs Lisa Baskill
31 Pier Street, Ventnor PO38 1SX
T: (01983) 854340
F: (01983) 855524

Hadfield Cottage ★★★★
Contact: Mrs Honor Vass
Island Cottage Holidays, The Old Vicarage, Kingston, Wareham BH20 5LH
T: (01929) 480080
F: (01929) 481070
E: enq@islandcottageholidays.com
I: www.islandcottageholidays.com

Regent Court Holiday Bungalows ★★★
Contact: Mrs Smith
Park Road, Ryde PO33 4RL
T: (01983) 883782
E: smith.windycroft@tinyworld.co.uk
I: www.cottageguide.co.uk/regentcourt

Uppermount ★★★★
Contact: Mrs Honor Vass
Island Cottage Holidays, The Old Vicarage, West Street, Kingston, Corfe Castle, Wareham BH20 5LH
T: (01929) 480080
F: (01929) 481070
E: enq@islandcottageholidays.com
I: www.islandcottageholidays.com

Wyndcliffe Holiday Apartments ★★★★
Contact: Mrs Rosalind Young
Wyndcliffe Holiday Apartments, 16 Spring Gardens, Ventnor PO38 1QX
T: (01983) 853458
F: (01983) 853272

BOOKHAM
Surrey

Woodlands ★★★
Contact: Mr Victor Edwards
Woodlands, 31 Woodlands Road, Leatherhead KT23 4HG
T: (01372) 453281
F: (01372) 453281
E: vicedwards@btopenworld.com
I: www.woodlandsselfcatering.btinternet.co.uk

BORDON
Hampshire

Tunford Cottage Lodge ★★
Contact: Mrs Anne Symon
Tunford Cottage Lodge, Tunford Cottage, Bordon GU35 9JE
T: (01420) 473159
E: symon@tunford.freeserve.co.uk

BORTHWOOD
Isle of Wight

Borthwood Cottages ★★★
Contact: Ms Anne Finch
Borthwood Cottages, c/o Sandlin Boarding Kennels, Sandown PO36 0HH
T: (01983) 402011

BOSHAM
West Sussex

The Warren ★★★
Contact: Mrs Gillian Odell
The Warren, Main Road, Chichester PO18 8PL
T: (01243) 573927
F: (01243) 573927
E: gillodell@aol.com

BOUGHTON MONCHELSEA
Kent

Dovecote ★★★★
Contact: Mrs Gill Beveridge
Dovecote, Wierton Oast, Wierton Hill, Maidstone ME17 4JT
T: (01622) 741935
F: (01622) 741935
E: gill.beveridge@lineone.net

BOWLHEAD GREEN
Surrey

The Barn Flat ★★
Contact: Mrs Grace Ranson
Bowlhead Green Farm, Bowlhead Green, Godalming GU8 6NW
T: (01428) 682687
E: Ranson@Bowlhead.fsnet.co.uk

BOXLEY
Kent

Styles Cottage ★★
Contact: Mrs Sue Mayo
Styles Cottage, Styles Lane, Maidstone ME14 3DZ
T: (01622) 757567
E: sue.mayo@virgin.net
I: www.freespace.virginnet.co.uk/styles.cottage/

BRACKLESHAM BAY
West Sussex

Broadwater ★★★★
Contact: Mr Michael & Mrs Susan Wright
Broadwater, West Bracklesham Drive, Chichester PO20 8PH
T: (01243) 670059
F: (01243) 670059

39 Marineside ★★★
Contact: Mrs Kirsten Spanswick
33 Cartier Close, Old Hall, Warrington WA5 5TD
T: (01925) 652334
F: (01925) 499552
E: chris.spanswick@ntlworld.com

Establishments printed in blue have a detailed entry in this guide

SOUTH EAST ENGLAND

Searide ★★★
Contact: Mrs Kevin Bailey
Baileys, 17 Shore Road,
Chichester PO20 8DY
T: (01243) 672217
F: (01243) 670100
E: info@baileys.uk.com
I: www.baileys.uk.com

BRADING
Isle of Wight

Anemoen ★★★
Contact: Mrs Lisa Baskill
31 Pier Street, Ventnor
PO38 1SX
T: (01983) 854340
F: (01983) 855524

5 Hawkins Close ★★★
Contact: Catherine Hopper
Island Holiday Homes, 138 High
Street, Newport PO30 1TY
T: (01983) 821113
F: (01983) 822050

Moles Leap ★★
Contact: Mrs Lisa Baskill
31 Pier Street, Ventnor
PO38 1SX
T: (01983) 854340
F: (01983) 855524

The Old Bakery ★★★
Contact: Mrs Lisa Baskill
Home from Home Holidays, 31
Pier Street, Ventnor PO38 1SX
T: (01983) 854340
F: (01983) 855524
E: admin@hfromh.co.uk

The Stables ★★★
Contact: Mrs Diane Morris
New Farm, Coach Lane,
Sandown PO36 0JQ

Thistlewaite ★★★★
Contact: Mrs Jan Hegarty
Rock Cottage, Melville Street,
Sandown PO36 9JW
T: (01983) 409707
E: jananddon-rock2@yahoo.com

BRAISHFIELD
Hampshire

Meadow Cottage & Rosie's Cottage ★★★
Contact: Mrs Wendy Graham
Meadow Cottage & Rosie's
Cottage, Farley Chamberlayne,
Romsey SO51 0QP
T: (01794) 368265
F: (01794) 367847

BRAMLEY
Surrey

Converted Stable at Juniper Cottage ★★★
Contact: Mr Bob Heyes
Juniper Cottage, 22 Eastwood
Road, Guildford GU5 0DS
T: (01483) 893706
F: (01483) 894001
E: heyes@tiscali.co.uk
I: myweb.tiscali.co.uk/heyes

Old Timbers ★★★
Contact: Mrs Taylor
Old Timbers, Snowdenham Links
Road, Old Timbers, Guildford
GU5 0BX
T: (01483) 893258
E: jpold_timbers@hotmail.com

BREDE
East Sussex

Eastwood Cottage ★★★★
Contact: Mr Stuart Winter
Eastwood Cottage, Stubb Lane,
Rye TN31 6BN
T: (01732) 369168
F: (01732) 358817
E: holidays@gardenofenglandcottages.co.uk
I: www.gardenofenglandcottages.co.uk

BRIGHSTONE
Isle of Wight

The Brew House ★★★★
Contact: Mrs Honor Vass
Island Cottage Holidays, The Old
Vicarage, Kingston, Wareham
BH20 5LH
T: (01929) 481555
I: www.islandcottageholidays.com

Carriers Stable ★★★★
Contact: Ms Catherine Hopper
Island Holiday Homes, 138 High
Street, Newport PO30 1TY
T: (01983) 521113
F: (01983) 822030

Casses - Brighstone - Isle of Wight ★★★★
Contact: Mr & Mrs J K Nesbitt
Kerrich House, Peartree Court,
Old Orchards, Lymington
SO41 3TF
T: (01590) 679601
E: jkn@casses.fsbusiness.co.uk

Chilton Farm Cottages ★★★
Contact: Mrs Susan Fisk
Chilton Farm, Chilton Lane,
Newport PO30 4DS
T: (01983) 740338
F: (01983) 741370
E: info@chiltonfarm.co.uk
I: www.chiltonfarm.co.uk

2 The Granary ★★★★
Contact: Teresa Herd
22 Westrope Way, Bedford
MK41 7YU
T: (01234) 328664 & 07795 078049
E: info@2thegranary.co.uk
I: http://2thegranary.co.uk

Grange Farm - Brighstone Bay ★★★
Contact: Mr Dunjay
Grange Farm - Brighstone Bay,
Military Road, Newport
PO30 4DA
T: (01983) 740296
F: (01983) 741233
E: grangefarm@brighstonebay.fsnet.co.uk
I: www.brighstonebay.fsnet.co.uk

Ivy Cottage ★★★★
Contact: Mr Matthew White
Island Holiday Homes, 138 High
Street, Newport PO30 1TY
T: (01983) 521114

The Mill House
Rating Applied For
Contact: Mrs Honor Vass
Island Cottage Holidays, West
Street, Kingston, Corfe Castle,
Wareham BH20 5LH
T: (01929) 480080
F: (01929) 481070

Pool Cottage ★★★★★
Contact: Mr John Russell
Thorncross Farm, Newport
PO30 4PN
T: (01983) 740291
F: (01983) 741408

Rose Cottage ★★★★★
Contact: Mr John Russell
Thorncross Farm, Newport
PO30 4PN
T: (01983) 740291

Stable Cottage ★★★★
Contact: Mrs Honor Vass
Island Cottage Holidays, The Old
Vicarage, Kingston, Wareham
BH20 5LH
T: (01929) 480080
F: (01929) 481070
E: enq@islandcottageholidays.com
I: www.islandcottageholidays.com

BRIGHTLING
East Sussex

Great Worge Farm Barn ★★★★
Contact: Mrs Brenda Beck
Freedom Holiday Homes, 15
High Street, Cranbrook
TN17 3EB
T: (01580) 720770
F: (01580) 720771
E: mail@freedomholidayhomes.co.uk
I: www.freedomholidayhomes.co.uk

BRIGHTON & HOVE
Brighton & Hove

The Abbey Self-Catering Flatlets ★-★★
Contact: Mr Smith
The Abbey Self-Catering Flatlets,
14-19 Norfolk Terrace, Brighton
BN1 3AD
T: (01273) 778771
F: (01273) 729147
E: theabbey@brighton.co.uk
I: www.brighton.co.uk/hotels/theabbey

11B Bedford Towers ★★★★★
Contact: Mr Richard Harris
Best of Brighton & Sussex
Cottages Ltd, Windmill Lodge,
Vicarage Lane, Brighton
BN2 7HD
T: (01273) 308779
F: (01273) 300266
E: enquiries@bestofbrighton.co.uk
I: www.bestofbrighton.co.uk

Brighton Holiday Flats ★★★
Contact: Veronica Cronin
English Language & Holiday
Bureau, 327 Portland Road,
Hove BN3 5SE
T: (01273) 410595 & 410944
F: (01273) 412662
E: office@cronin-accommodation.co.uk
I: www.cronin-accommodation.co.uk

Brighton Lanes ★★-★★★★
Contact: Miss Carol Coates
Brighton Lanes, 14A Ship Street,
Brighton BN1 1AD
T: (01273) 325315
F: (01273) 325315
E: brightonlanes@easynet.co.uk
I: www.brighton.co.uk/hotels/brightonlanes

Brighton Marina Apartments ★★
Contact: Mr Richard & Mrs
Lorna Gartside
16 Orchard Gardens, Brighton
BN3 7BJ
T: (01273) 737006
E: enquiries@brightonmarinaapartments.co.uk
I: www.brightonmarinaapartments.co.uk

Brighton Marina Holiday Apartments ★★★★
Contact: Mrs Wills
Brighton Marina Holiday
Apartments, 5 Marlborough
Road, Richmond, Surrey
TW10 6JT
T: (01273) 693569
F: (01273) 693569

18 Bristol Road ★★★
Contact: Mr Richard Harris
Best of Brighton & Sussex
Cottages Ltd, Vicarage Lane,
Brighton BN2 7HD
T: (01273) 308779
F: (01273) 300266
E: brightoncottages@pavilion.co.uk
I: www.bestofbrighton.co.uk

1 Britannia Court ★★★★
Contact: Mr Richard Harris
1 Britannia Court, The Strand,
Brighton Marina Village,
Brighton BN2 5SF
T: (01273) 308779
F: (01273) 300266

67 Britannia Court ★★★★
Contact: Mr Richard Harris
Best of Brighton & Sussex
Cottages Ltd, Vicarage Lane,
Brighton BN2 7HD
T: (01273) 308779
F: (01273) 300266
E: brightoncottages@pavilion.co.uk
I: www.bestofbrighton.co.uk

SOUTH EAST ENGLAND

9 Brunswick Mews ★★★
Contact: Mr Richard Harris
Best of Brighton & Sussex
Cottages Ltd, Vicarage Lane,
Brighton BN2 7HD
T: (01273) 308779
F: (01273) 300266
E: brightoncottages@pavilion.co.uk
I: www.bestofbrighton.co.uk

50 Brunswick Square Flat 4 ★★★
Contact: Mr Richard Harris
Best of Brighton & Sussex
Cottages Ltd, Vicarage Lane,
Brighton BN2 7HD
T: (01273) 308779
F: (01273) 300266
E: brightoncottages@pavilion.co.uk
I: www.bestofbrighton.co.uk

The Cabin ★★
Contact: Mr Richard Harris
Best of Brighton & Sussex
Cottages Ltd, Vicarage Lane,
Brighton BN2 7HD
T: (01273) 308779
F: (01273) 300266
E: brightoncottages@pavilion.co.uk
I: www.bestofbrighton.co.uk

The Cape Apartment
Rating Applied For
Contact: Ms Gail Latimer
446 South Coast Road,
Peacehaven BN10 7BE
T: (01273) 581495
E: gail.latimer@msbluk.co.uk
I: www.thecapeapartment.co.uk

Cobblers Cottage ★★★
Contact: Mr Richard Harris
Best of Brighton & Sussex
Cottages Ltd, Vicarage Lane,
Brighton BN2 7HD
T: (01273) 308779
F: (01273) 300266
E: brightoncottages@pavilion.co.uk
I: www.bestofbrighton.co.uk

2 Crown Gardens ★★★★
Contact: Mr Richard Harris
Best of Brighton & Sussex
Cottages Ltd, Windmill Lodge,
Vicarage Lane, Brighton
BN2 7HD
T: (01273) 308779
F: (01273) 300266
E: enquiries@bestofbrighton.co.uk
I: www.bestofbrighton.co.uk

5 Cumberland Court ★★★★
Contact: Mr Richard Harris
Best of Brighton & Sussex
Cottages Ltd, Windmill Cottage,
Vicarage Lane, Brighton
BN2 7HD
T: (01273) 308779
F: (01273) 300266
E: enquiries@bestofbrighton.co.uk
I: www.bestofbrighton.co.uk

Dale Court Family Holiday Flats ★★★
Contact: Ms Bettina Goodman
Dale Court Family Holiday Flats,
9 Florence Road, Brighton
BN1 6DL
T: (01273) 326963

36 Dorset Court ★★★
Contact: Mr Richard Harris
Best of Brighton & Sussex
Cottages Ltd, Vicarage Lane,
Brighton BN2 7HD
T: (01273) 308779
F: (01273) 300266
E: brightoncottages@pavilion.co.uk
I: www.bestofbrighton.co.uk

44 Eastern Concourse ★★★
Contact: Mrs Pat Lowe
Palms Property Sales & Letting,
16 Village Square, Brighton
Marina, Brighton BN2 5WA
T: (01273) 626000
F: (01273) 624449
E: enquiries@palmsagency.co.uk
I: www.palmsagency.co.uk

Flat 1
Rating Applied For
Contact: Mr Richard Harris
Flat 1, 24 Western Road,
Brighton BN3 1AF
T: (01273) 308779
F: (01273) 300266

Flat 1 22 Brunswick Square ★★★
Contact: Mr Richard Harris
Best of Brighton & Sussex
Cottages Ltd, Vicarage Lane,
Brighton BN2 7HD
T: (01273) 308779
F: (01273) 300266
E: brightoncottages@pavilion.co.uk
I: www.bestofbrighton.co.uk

Flat 1 68 Marine Parade ★★★
Contact: Mr Richard Harris
Best of Brighton & Sussex
Cottages Ltd, Vicarage Lane,
Brighton BN2 7HD
T: (01273) 308779
F: (01273) 300266
E: brightoncottages@pavilion.co.uk
I: www.bestofbrighton.co.uk

Flat 10 4 Adelaide Mansions ★★★★
Contact: Mr Richard Harris
Best of Brighton & Sussex
Cottages Ltd, Vicarage Lane,
Brighton BN2 7HD
T: (01273) 308779
F: (01273) 300266
E: brightoncottages@pavilion.co.uk
I: www.bestofbrighton.co.uk

Flat 11 4 Adelaide Mansions ★★★★
Contact: Mr Richard Harris
Best of Brighton & Sussex
Cottages Ltd, Vicarage Lane,
Brighton BN2 7HD
T: (01273) 308779
F: (01273) 300266
E: brightoncottages@pavilion.co.uk
I: www.bestofbrighton.co.uk

Flat 14, 37-38 Adelaide Crescent ★★★★
Contact: Mr Richard Harris
Best of Brighton & Sussex
Cottages Ltd, Vicarage Lane,
Brighton BN2 7HD
T: (01273) 308779
F: (01273) 300266
E: brightoncottages@pavilion.co.uk
I: www.bestofbrighton.co.uk

Flat 2 ★★★
Contact: Mr Richard Harris
Best of Brighton & Sussex
Cottages Ltd, Windmill Lodge,
Vicarage Lane, Brighton
BN2 7HD
T: (01273) 308779
F: (01273) 300266
E: enquiries@bestofbrighton.co.uk
I: www.bestofbrighton.co.uk

Flat 2, 7 Eastern Terrace ★★★★
Contact: Mr Richard Harris
Best of Brighton & Sussex
Cottages Ltd, Vicarage Lane,
Brighton BN2 7HD
T: (01273) 308779
F: (01273) 300266
E: enquiries@bestofbrighton.co.ukk
I: www.bestofbrighton.co.uk

Flat 2 34 Bedford Square ★★★
Contact: Mr Richard Harris
Best of Brighton & Sussex
Cottages Ltd, Vicarage Lane,
Brighton BN2 7HD
T: (01273) 308779
F: (01273) 300266
E: brightoncottages@pavilion.co.uk
I: www.bestofbrighton.co.uk

Flat 2 Glenside Court ★★★
Contact: Mr Richard Harris
Best of Brighton & Sussex
Cottages Ltd, Vicarage Lane,
Brighton BN2 7HD
T: (01273) 308779
F: (01273) 300266
E: enquiries@bestofbrighton.co.ukk
I: www.bestofbrighton.co.uk

Flat 3 ★★★★
Contact: Mr Harris
Best of Brighton & Sussex
Cottages Ltd, Vicarage Lane,
Brighton BN2 7HD
T: (01273) 308779
F: (01273) 300266

Flat 3, 4 Chichester Terrace ★★★★★
Contact: Mr Richard Harris
Best of Brighton & Sussex
Cottages Ltd, Vicarage Lane,
Brighton BN2 7HD
T: (01273) 308779
F: (01273) 300266
E: brightoncottages@pavilion.co.uk
I: www.bestofbrighton.co.uk

Flat 3, 9 Belgrave Place ★★★
Contact: Mr Richard Harris
Best of Brighton & Sussex
Cottages Ltd, Vicarage Lane,
Brighton BN2 7HD
T: (01273) 308779
F: (01273) 300266
E: enquiries@bestofbrighton.co.uk
I: www.bestofbrighton.co.uk

Flat 3 1 Third Avenue ★★★
Contact: Mr Richard Harris
Best of Brighton & Sussex
Cottages Ltd, Vicarage Lane,
Brighton BN2 7HD
T: (01273) 308779
F: (01273) 300266
E: brightoncottages@pavilion.co.uk
I: www.bestofbrighton.co.uk

Flat 3 127 Kings Road ★★★★
Contact: Mr Richard Harris
Best of Brighton & Sussex
Cottages Ltd, Vicarage Lane,
Brighton BN2 7HD
T: (01273) 308779
F: (01273) 300266
E: brightoncottages@pavilion.co.uk
I: www.bestofbrighton.co.uk

Flat 3 34 Brunswick Terrace ★★★★
Contact: Mr Richard Harris
Best of Brighton & Sussex
Cottages Ltd, Vicarage Lane,
Brighton BN2 7HD
T: (01273) 308779
F: (01273) 300266
E: brightoncottages@pavilion.co.uk
I: www.bestofbrighton.co.uk

Flat 3 35 First Avenue ★★
Contact: Mr Richard Harris
Best of Brighton & Sussex
Cottages Ltd, Vicarage Lane,
Brighton BN2 7HD
T: (01273) 308779
F: (01273) 300266
E: brightoncottages@pavilion.co.uk
I: www.bestofbrighton.co.uk

Flat 3 68 Marine Parade ★★★
Contact: Mr Richard Harris
Best of Brighton & Sussex
Cottages Ltd, Vicarage Lane,
Brighton BN2 7HD
T: (01273) 308779
F: (01273) 300266
E: brightoncottages@pavilion.co.uk
I: www.bestofbrighton.co.uk

Flat 4 Windsor Lodge
Rating Applied For
Contact: Mr Richard Harris
Best of Brighton & Sussex
Cottages Ltd, Windmill Lodge,
Vicarage Lane, Brighton
BN2 7HD
T: (01273) 308779
F: (01273) 300266
E: enquiries@bestofbrighton.co.uk
I: www.bestofbrighton.co.uk

Establishments printed in blue have a detailed entry in this guide

SOUTH EAST ENGLAND

Flat 5, 143 Western Road ★★★★
Contact: Mr Richard Harris
Best of Brighton & Sussex Cottages Ltd, Vicarage Lane, Brighton BN2 7HD
T: (01273) 308779
F: (01273) 300266
E: enquiries@bestofbrighton.co.ukk
I: www.bestofbrighton.co.uk

Flat 5, 52 The Drive ★★★
Contact: Mr Richard Harris
Best of Brighton & Sussex Cottages Ltd, Vicarage Lane, Brighton BN2 7HD
T: (01273) 308779
F: (01273) 300266
E: enquiries@bestofbrighton.co.ukk
I: www.bestofbrighton.co.uk

Flat 5 35 First Avenue ★★
Contact: Mr Richard Harris
Best of Brighton & Sussex Cottages Ltd, Vicarage Lane, Brighton BN2 7HD
T: (01273) 308779
F: (01273) 300266
E: brightoncottages@pavilion.co.uk
I: www.bestofbrighton.co.uk

Flat 5 37 Brunswick Terrace ★★★
Contact: Mr Richard Harris
Best of Brighton & Sussex Cottages Ltd, Vicarage Lane, Brighton BN2 7HD
T: (01273) 308779
F: (01273) 300266
E: brightoncottages@pavilion.co
I: www.bestofbrighton.co.uk

Flat 5 4 Medina Terrace ★★★
Contact: Mr Richard Harris
Best of Brighton & Sussex Cottages Ltd, Vicarage Lane, Brighton BN2 7HD
T: (01273) 308779
F: (01273) 300266
E: brightoncottages@pavilion.co
I: www.bestofbrighton.co.uk

Flat 5 Lansdowne Court ★★★★
Contact: Mr Richard Harris
Best of Brighton & Sussex Cottages Ltd, 21A Roydon Road, Ware SG12 8HQ
T: (01273) 308779
F: (01273) 300266

Flat 6, 63 Regency Square ★★★
Contact: Mr Richard Harris
Best of Brighton & Sussex Cottages Ltd, Vicarage Lane, Brighton BN2 7HD
T: (01273) 308779
F: (01273) 300266
E: brightoncottages@pavilion.co
I: www.bestofbrighton.co.uk

Flat 6 8 Regency Square ★★★
Contact: Mr Richard Harris
Best of Brighton & Sussex Cottages Ltd, Vicarage Lane, Brighton BN2 7HD
T: (01273) 308779
F: (01273) 300266
E: brightoncottages@pavilion.co.uk
I: www.bestofbrighton.co.uk

Flat 6 Glenside Court ★★★
Contact: Mr Richard Harris
Best of Brighton & Sussex Cottages Ltd, Vicarage Lane, Brighton BN2 7HD
T: (01273) 308779
F: (01273) 300266
E: brightoncottages@pavilion.co.uk
I: www.bestofbrighton.co.uk

Flat 6 Lansdowne Court ★★★★
Contact: Mr Harris
Best of Brighton & Sussex Cottages, Vicarage Lane, Brighton BN2 7HD
T: (01273) 308779
F: (01273) 300266
E: brightoncottages@pavilion.co.uk
I: www.bestofbrighton.co.uk

Flat 8 The Georgian House ★★★
Contact: Mr Richard Harris
Best of Brighton & Sussex Cottages Ltd, Vicarage Lane, Brighton BN2 7HD
T: (01273) 308779
F: (01273) 300266
E: brightoncottages@pavilion.co.uk
I: www.bestofbrighton.co.uk

Flat 9 28 Brunswick Terrace ★★★
Contact: Mr Richard Harris
Best of Brighton & Sussex Cottages Ltd, Vicarage Lane, Brighton BN2 7HD
T: (01273) 308779
F: (01273) 300266
E: brightoncottages@pavilion.co.uk
I: www.bestofbrighton.co.uk

Florence House ★★★
Contact: Mr Geoff Hart
Florence House, 18 Florence Road, Brighton BN1 6DJ
T: (01273) 506624
F: (01273) 506624
E: annexe@brightonlets.net

7 The French Apartments ★★★★★
Contact: Mr Richard Harris
Best of Brighton & Sussex Cottages Ltd, Windmill Lodge, Vicarage Lane, Brighton BN2 7HD
T: (01273) 308779
F: (01273) 300266
E: enquiries@bestofbrighton.co.uk
I: www.bestofbrighton.co.uk

The Garden Flat ★★★
Contact: Mr Richard Harris
Best of Brighton & Sussex Cottages Ltd, Vicarage Lane, Brighton BN2 7HD
T: (01273) 308779
F: (01273) 300266
E: brightoncottages@pavilion.co.uk
I: www.bestofbrighton.co.uk

Garden Flat ★★★★
Contact: Mr Richard Harris
Best of Brighton & Sussex Cottages Ltd, Vicarage Lane, Brighton BN2 7HD
T: (01273) 308779
F: (01273) 300266
E: brightoncottages@pavilion.co.uk
I: www.bestofbrighton.co.uk

Ground Floor Flat ★★★★
Contact: Mr Richard Harris
Best of Brighton & Sussex Cottages Ltd, Windmill Lodge, Vicarage Lane, Brighton BN2 7HD
T: (01273) 308779
F: (01273) 300266
E: enquiries@bestofbrighton.co.uk
I: www.bestofbrighton.co.uk

4 Hamilton Court ★★★
Contact: Mr Richard Harris
Best of Brighton & Sussex Cottages Ltd, Windmill Lodge, Vicarage Lane, Brighton BN2 7HD
T: (01273) 308779
F: (01273) 300266
E: enquiries@bestofbrighton.co.uk
I: www.bestofbrighton.co.uk

Hanover Cottage ★★★
Contact: Mrs Maureen Jackson
Lewes Road, Lewes BN8 5NB
T: (01273) 814254
E: mjackson@sunnyspells.biz

Holiday Flat 16 Lancaster Court ★★★
Contact: Mr Peter Anthony
Merrydown, 1A Fairfields, Huntingdon PE27 5QQ
T: (01480) 495914
F: (01480) 495914
E: pastives@aol.com

2 Ivy Mews ★★★
Contact: Mr Richard Harris
Best of Brighton & Sussex Cottages Ltd, Vicarage Lane, Brighton BN2 7HD
T: (01273) 308779
F: (01273) 300266
E: brightoncottages@pavilion.co.uk
I: www.bestofbrighton.co.uk

3 Kemp Town Mews ★★★
Contact: Mr Richard Harris
Best of Brighton & Sussex Cottages Ltd, Vicarage Lane, Brighton BN2 7HD
T: (01273) 308779
F: (01273) 300266
E: brightoncottages@pavilion.co.uk
I: www.bestofbrighton.co.uk

13c Kemp Town Place ★★★★
Contact: Mr Richard Harris
Best of Brighton & Sussex Cottages Ltd, Vicarage Lane, Brighton BN2 7HD
T: (01273) 308779
F: (01273) 300266
E: brightoncottages@pavilion.co.uk
I: www.bestofbrighton.co.uk

Kilcolgan Premier Bungalow ★★★★★
Contact: Mr J C St George
22 Baches Street, London N1 6DL
T: (020) 7250 3678
T: (020) 7250 1955
E: jc.stgeorge@virgin.net

Lower Ground Floor Flat ★★★
Contact: Mr Richard Harris
Best of Brighton & Sussex Cottages Ltd, Windmill Lodge, Vicarage Lane, Brighton BN2 7HD
T: (01273) 308779
F: (01273) 300266
E: enquiries@bestofbrighton.co.uk
I: www.bestofbrighton.co.uk

Lower Ground Floor Flat ★★★★
Contact: Mr Richard Harris
Best of Brighton & Sussex Cottages Ltd, Windmill Lodge, Vicarage Lane, Rottingdean, Brighton BN2 7HD
T: (01273) 308779
F: (01273) 300266
E: brightoncottages@pavilion.co.uk
I: www.bestofbrighton.co.uk

Lower Ground Floor Flat ★★★
Contact: Mr Richard Harris
Best of Brighton & Sussex Cottages Ltd, Vicarage Lane, Brighton BN2 7HD
T: (01273) 308779
F: (01273) 300266
E: brightoncottages@pavilion.co.uk
I: www.bestofbrighton.co.uk

Lower Ground Floor Flat, Preston House ★★★
Contact: Mr Richard Harris
Best of Brighton & Sussex Cottages Ltd, Windmill Lodge, Vicarage Lane, Brighton BN2 7HD
T: (01273) 308779
F: (01273) 300266
E: enquiries@bestofbrighton.co.uk
I: www.bestofbrighton.co.uk

82 Lowther Road ★★★
Contact: Mr Richard Harris
Best of Brighton & Sussex Cottages Ltd, Vicarage Lane, Brighton BN2 7HD
T: (01273) 308779
F: (01273) 300266
E: brightoncottages@pavilion.co.uk
I: www.bestofbrighton.co.uk

Look out for establishments participating in the National Accessible Scheme

SOUTH EAST ENGLAND

Lutyens Apartment ★★★
Contact: Mr Richard Harris
Best of Brighton & Sussex
Cottages Ltd, Windmill Lodge,
Vicarage Lane, Rottingdean,
Brighton BN2 7HD
T: (01273) 308779
F: (01273) 300266
E: enquiries@bestofbrighton.co.uk
I: www.bestofbrighton.co.uk

63 Marine Parade ★★★
Contact: Mr Richard Harris
Best of Brighton & Sussex
Cottages Ltd, Vicarage Lane,
Brighton BN2 7HD
T: (01273) 308779
F: (01273) 300266
E: enquiries@bestofbrighton.co.ukk
I: www.bestofbrighton.co.uk

19A Metropole Court ★★★★★
Contact: Mr Richard Harris
Best of Brighton & Sussex
Cottages Ltd, Vicarage Lane,
Brighton BN2 7HD
T: (01273) 308779
F: (01273) 390211
E: enquiries@bestofbrighton.co.uk
I: www.bestofbrighton.co.uk

3A Metropole Court ★★★
Contact: Mr Nigel & Mrs Viv Earwicker
Nivian Apartments, Acorn Cottage, Tudor Close,
Pulborough RH20 2EF
T: (01798) 875513
E: nivianinc@aol.com

4A Metropole Court ★★★★
Contact: Mr Richard Harris
Best of Brighton & Sussex
Cottages Ltd, Windmill Lodge,
Vicarage Lane, Brighton
BN2 7HD
T: (01273) 308779
F: (01273) 300266
E: enquiries@bestofbrighton.co.uk

5B Metropole Court ★★★
Contact: Mrs Catherine Draco
Mortlake Business Centre, 20
Mortlake High Street, London
SW14 8JN
T: (020) 82465664
F: (020) 8246 5663
E: enquie@brighton-apartments.com
I: www.brighton-apartments.com

19 North Gardens ★★★★
Contact: Mr Richard Harris
Best of Brighton & Sussex
Cottages Ltd, Vicarage Lane,
Brighton BN2 7HD
T: (01273) 308779
F: (01273) 300266
E: brightoncottages@pavilion.co.uk
I: www.bestofbrighton.co.uk

10 Oxford Mews ★★★★
Contact: Mr Richard Harris
Best of Brighton & Sussex
Cottages Ltd, Vicarage Lane,
Brighton BN2 7HD
T: (01273) 308779
F: (01273) 300266
E: enquiries@bestofbrighton.co.ukk
I: www.bestofbrighton.co.uk

Patio Flat 10 Brunswick Terrace ★★★★
Contact: Mr Rupert Riley
Riley Properties, 10 Brunswick Terrace, Brighton BN3 1HL
T: (01273) 203758
F: (01273) 205608

20 Portside ★★★★
Contact: Mr Richard Harris
Best of Brighton & Sussex
Cottages Ltd, Vicarage Lane,
Brighton BN2 7HD
T: (01273) 308779
F: (01273) 300266
E: brightoncottages@pavilion.co.uk
I: www.bestofbrighton.co.uk

Regency Seafront Holiday Flats ★★
Contact: Mrs Edwards
6 Highcroft Villas, Brighton
BN1 5PS
T: (01273) 556227

28 Royal Crescent Mansions ★★★★
Contact: Mr Richard Harris
Best of Brighton & Sussex
Cottages Ltd, Vicarage Lane,
Brighton BN2 7HD
T: (01273) 308779
F: (01273) 300266
E: brightoncottages@pavilion.co.uk
I: www.bestofbrighton.co.uk

Seapoint ★★★★
Contact: Mr Richard Harris
Best of Brighton & Sussex
Cottages Ltd, Vicarage Lane,
Brighton BN2 7HD
T: (01273) 308779
F: (01273) 390211
E: enquiries@bestofbrighton.co.uk
I: www.bestofbrighton.co.uk

South Lodge ★★★
Contact: Mr Richard Harris
Best of Brighton & Sussex
Cottages Ltd, Vicarage Lane,
Brighton BN2 7HD
T: (01273) 308779
F: (01273) 300266
E: brightoncottages@pavilion.co.uk
I: www.bestofbrighton.co.uk

65 St Georges Road ★★★
Contact: Mr Richard Harris
65 St Georges Road, Brighton
BN2 1EF
T: (01273) 308779
F: (01273) 300266

18 St Vincents Court ★★★★
Contact: Mr Richard Harris
Best of Brighton & Sussex
Cottages Ltd, Vicarage Lane,
Brighton BN2 7HD
T: (01273) 308779
F: (01273) 300266
E: brightoncottages@pavilion.co.uk
I: www.bestofbrighton.co.uk

9 Starboard ★★★★
Contact: Mrs Pat Lowe
Palms Property Sales & Letting,
16 Village Square, Brighton
Marina, Brighton BN2 5WA
T: (01273) 626000
F: (01273) 624449
E: enquiries@palmsagency.co.uk
I: www.palmsagency.co.uk

6 Starboard Court ★★★
Contact: Mr Richard Harris
Best of Brighton & Sussex
Cottages Ltd, Vicarage Lane,
Brighton BN2 7HD
T: (01273) 308779
F: (01273) 300266
E: brightoncottages@pavilion.co.uk
I: www.bestofbrighton.co.uk

Upper Market Street ★★
Contact: Ms Marcia Stanton
4 King Charles Road, Surbiton
KT5 8PY
T: (020) 8979 1792
F: (020) 8399 6639

93 Victory Mews ★★★
Contact: Mr Richard Harris
93 Victory Mews, The Strand,
Brighton Marina Village,
Brighton BN2 5XD
T: (01273) 308779
F: (01273) 300266

12 Western Concourse ★★★
Contact: Mrs Bowen
2 Lincoln Avenue, Peacehaven
BN10 7HL
T: (01273) 584347

Wild & Wonderful ★★★★★
Contact: Mrs Christine Bennett
24 Modena Road, Brighton
BN3 5QG
T: (01273) 734344
E: christine@wildwonderful.co.uk
I: www.wildwonderful.co.uk

BROAD OAK
East Sussex

Austens Wood Farm Annexe ★★★★
Contact: Mrs Brenda Beck
Freedom Holiday Homes, 15
High Street, Cranbrook
TN17 3EB
T: (01580) 720770
F: (01580) 720771
E: mail@freedomholidayhomes.co.uk
I: www.freedomholidayhomes.co.uk

Riding & Stable Cottage ★★★★
Contact: Mrs Jill Winter
Garden of England Cottages,
189A High Street, Tonbridge
TN9 1BX
T: (01732) 369168

BROADSTAIRS
Kent

Albert Cottage ★★★★
Contact: Mrs Brenda Beck
Freedom Holiday Homes, 15
High Street, Cranbrook
TN17 3EB
T: (01580) 720770
F: (01580) 720771
E: mail@freedomholidayhomes.co.uk
I: www.freedomholidayhomes.co.uk

Beacon Light Cottage ★★★★
Contact: Mr Patrick Vandervorst
Duinhelmlaan 11, B-8420
Wenduine, Belgium
T: +32 504 23207
F: +32 504 23207
E: beaconlight.cottage@worldonline.be
I: www.beaconlightcottage.com

Bray Holiday Homes ★★★
Contact: Mr Bray
34 Smithamdowns Road, Purley
CR8 4ND
T: (020) 86601925

Broadstairs Holiday House ★★★
Contact: Mrs Bull
Millstone Cottage, 16 Beulah
Road, Epping CM16 6RH
T: (01992) 576044
E: lynn.bull@btinternet.com

2 Church Square ★★★
Contact: Mr Philip Dennis
St Peters Footpath, Broadstairs
CT10 2RA
T: (01843) 601996

Coachman's Flat ★★★
Contact: Mrs Ellen Barrett
Manningham, 15 Western
Esplanade, Broadstairs CT10 1TD
T: (01843) 867925
F: (01843) 867925
E: ellen@stonar.com

1 Darren Gardens ★★★★
Contact: Mrs Jean Lawrence
24 Winterstoke Crescent,
Ramsgate CT11 8AH
T: (01843) 591422
F: (01843) 591422
E: jnancylawrence@aol.com

Fisherman's Cottage ★★★★
Contact: Ms Linda Spillane
5 Union Square, Broadstairs
CT10 1EX
T: (020) 8672 4150
E: linda.spillane@virgin.net
I: www.fishermanscottagebroadstairs.co.uk

Flat 1 ★★★
Contact: Mrs Linda Sear
Charity Farm, Leighton Buzzard
LU7 9PB
T: (01525) 210550

Establishments printed in blue have a detailed entry in this guide

SOUTH EAST ENGLAND

Flat 1, 2 Prospect Place ★★★★
Contact: Mrs Brenda Beck
Freedom Holiday Homes, 15 High Street, Cranbrook
TN17 3EB
T: (01580) 720770
F: (01580) 720771

Flat 3 ★★★
Contact: Mrs Linda Sear
Charity Farm, Leighton Buzzard
LU7 9PB
T: (01525) 210550

Homehaven House ★★★
Contact: Mrs Barbara Vandervord
13 Granville Avenue, Ramsgate CT12 6DX
T: (01843) 585798
E: bvandervord@hotmail.com
I: www.members.eunet.at/j.krautgartner

11 Inverness Terrace
Rating Applied For
Contact: Mrs Beatrice Jones
11 Inverness Terrace, 11 Inverness Terrace, The Vale, Broadstairs CT10 1QZ
T: (01843) 867116

Land & Life Self Catering Apartments
Rating Applied For
Contact: Mrs Simone Vince
Land & Life Self Catering Apartments, Holland Cottage, Kingsgate Bay Road, Broadstairs CT10 3QL
T: (01843) 867727
E: timvince@ukonline.co.uk

Martin Holiday Homes ★★★★
Contact: Mrs Penny Martin
21 Avebury Avenue, Ramsgate CT11 8BB
T: (01843) 592945
F: (01843) 599063
E: penny@martinholidays.co.uk
I: www.martinholidays.co.uk

Martin Holiday Homes ★★★★
Contact: Mrs Penny Martin
Martin Holiday Homes, 21 Avebury Avenue, Ramsgate CT11 8BB
T: (01843) 592945
F: (01843) 599063
E: penny@martinholidays.co.uk
I: www.martinholidays.co.uk

Secret Cottage ★★★★
Contact: Mr John Ferris
Blue Sky, 15 St Peters Park Road, Broadstairs CT10 2BG
T: (01843) 600650
F: (01843) 602656
E: info@bluesky-apart.com
I: www.secret-cottage.co.uk

Spero Court Apartments Flat 13 ★★★
Contact: Miss Carol Bowerman
28 Heather Drive, Dartford
DA1 3LE
T: (01322) 224869

BROCKENHURST
Hampshire

Annexe, Forest Lodge ★★★★
Contact: Miss Helen Haynes
Annex, Forest Lodge, Balmer Lawn Road, Brockenhurst
SO42 7TS
T: (01590) 622907
F: (01590) 622835
I: www.forestlodge.info

Brookley Dairy ★★★
Contact: Mrs Tracey Boulton
Mayfield, 77 Burley Road, Bockhampton, Christchurch
BH23 7AJ
T: (01425) 672013
F: (01425) 672013
E: tracey.boulton@btopenworld.com

Gorse Cottage ★★★★
Contact: Mr Julian Gilbert
Suite 4, Chiltern House, 180 High Street North, Dunstable
LU6 1AT
T: 0870 3210020
F: 0870 2330151
E: info@gorsecottage.co.uk
I: www.gorsecottage.co.uk

Jacmar Cottage ★★★
Contact: Mrs Melanie Ayres
Jacmar Cottage, Mill Lane, Brockenhurst SO42 7UA
T: (01590) 622019
E: jacmarcottage@aol.com

Latchmoor Corner ★★★
Contact: Ms Jacquie Taylor
Three Corners, Centre Lane, Lymington SO41 0JD
T: (01590) 645217
E: tommy.tiddles@virgin.net
I: www.halcyonholidays.com

BROOK
Isle of Wight

Brook Farm Cottages ★★★
Contact: Mrs Sonia Fry
Brook Farmhouse, Newport
PO30 4ES
T: (01983) 740387

Holiday Homes Owners Services Ref: B1 ★★★
Contact: Mr Colin Nolson
Holiday Homes Owners Services (West Wight), 18 Solent Hill, Freshwater PO40 9TG
T: (01983) 753423
F: (01983) 753423
E: holidayhomesiow@ic24.net

Holiday Homes Owners Services Ref: B2 ★★
Contact: Mr Colin Nolson
Holiday Homes Owners Services (West Wight), 18 Solent Hill, Freshwater PO40 9TG
T: (01983) 753423
F: (01983) 753423
E: holidayhomesiow@ic24.net

Holiday Homes Owners Services Ref: B3 ★★
Contact: Mr Colin Nolson
Holiday Homes Owners Services (West Wight), 18 Solent Hill, Freshwater PO40 9TG
T: (01983) 753423
F: (01983) 753423
E: holidayhomesiow@ic24.net

Holiday Homes Owners Services Ref: B4 ★★★
Contact: Mr Colin Nolson
Holiday Homes Owners Services (West Wight), 18 Solent Hill, Freshwater PO40 9TG
T: (01983) 753423
F: (01983) 753423
E: holidayhomesiow@ic24.net

Holiday Homes Owners Services Ref: B5 ★★★★
Contact: Mr Colin Nolson
Holiday Homes Owners Services (West Wight), 18 Solent Hill, Freshwater PO40 9TG
T: (01983) 753423
F: (01983) 753423
E: holidayhomesiow@ic24.net

Holiday Homes Owners Services Ref: B6 ★★★
Contact: Mr Colin Nolson
Holiday Homes Owners Services (West Wight), 18 Solent Hill, Freshwater PO40 9TG
T: (01983) 753423
F: (01983) 753423
E: holidayhomesiow@ic24.net

Holiday Homes Owners Services Ref: B7 ★★★★
Contact: Mr Colin Nolson
Holiday Homes Owners Services (West Wight), 18 Solent Hill, Freshwater PO40 9TG
T: (01983) 753423
F: (01983) 753423
E: holidayhomesiow@ic24.net

Sudmoor Cottage ★★★★
Contact: Mrs Honor Vass
Island Cottage Holidays, The Old Vicarage, Kingston, Wareham
BH20 5LH
T: (01929) 481555
I: www.islandcottageholidays.com

Wittensford Lodge ★★★
Contact: Ms Carol Smith
14 Hunts Mead, Billericay
CM12 9JA
T: (01277) 623997
F: (01277) 634976
E: mbmcarol@dircon.co.uk
I: www.wittensfordlodge.freeservers.com

BROOKLAND
Kent

Puddock Farm Pine Lodges ★★★★
Contact: Mrs Amanda Skinner
Puddock Farm Pine Lodges, Fairfield, Romney Marsh
TN29 9SA
T: (01797) 344440
F: (01797) 344440
E: amanda_skinner@talk21.com
I: www.cottageguide.co.uk/puddockfarmpinelodges.

BUCKINGHAM
Buckinghamshire

Huntsmill Holidays ★★★★
Contact: Mrs Fiona Hilsdon
Huntsmill Holidays, Huntsmill Farm, Buckingham MK18 5ND
T: (01280) 704852
F: (01280) 704852
E: fiona@huntsmill.com
I: www.huntsmill.com

BURFORD
Oxfordshire

Candlemas ★★★★
Contact:
Manor Cottages & Cotswolds Retreats, Priory Mews, 33A Priory Lane, Oxford OX18 4SG
T: (01993) 824252
F: (01993) 824443
E: mancott@netcomuk.co.uk
I: www.manorcottages.co.uk

The Pheasantry
Rating Applied For
Contact: Ms C Hamson
42 High Street, Alcester
T: 0780 2 929233

BURGATE
Hampshire

Burgate Farmhouse ★★★
Contact: Mrs Christine Bennett
Burgate Farmhouse, Burgate, Fordingbridge SP6 1LX
T: (01425) 655909
E: christine@burgatefarm.freeserve.co.uk
I: www.burgate.fslife.co.uk

BURGESS HILL
West Sussex

Farnaby ★★★
Contact: Mr Geoff Hart
18 Florence Road, Brighton
BN1 6DJ
T: (01296) 429139
E: geoffhart@eggconnect.net
I: www.brightonlets.com

BURLEY
Hampshire

Brackenwood ★★★★★
Contact: Mrs Carole Stewart
Great Wells House, Beechwood Lane, Ringwood BH24 4AS
T: (01425) 402302
F: (01425) 402302
E: greatwells@cs.com
I: www.smoothhound.co.uk/hotels/greatwel

Cherry Tree Cottage ★★★
Contact: Mr & Mrs Pannell
West Cliff Sands Hotel, 9 Priory Road, West Cliff, Bournemouth
BH2 5DF
T: (01202) 557013

The Dairy ★★★★
Contact: Mrs Carole Stewart
The Dairy, Beechwood Lane, Ringwood BH24 4AS
T: (01425) 402302
F: (01425) 402302
E: carolestewart@pobox.com
I: www.greatwells.com

Foxglove Cottage ★★
Contact: Mrs Wanda Williams
Oakapple Cottage, 5 Garden Road, Ringwood BH24 4EA
T: (01425) 402489
I: www.wandascottages.com

Honeysuckle Cottage ★★★
Contact: Mrs Wanda Williams
Oakapple Cottage, 5 Garden Road, Ringwood BH24 4EA
T: (01425) 402489
F: (01425) 402489
E: wanda@oakapplecottage.fsnet.co.uk
I: www.oakapplecottage.fsnet.co.uk

SOUTH EAST ENGLAND

BURSLEDON
Hampshire

62 Goodlands Vale ★★★
Contact: Mr Mike & Mrs Sue Batley
Town or Country Serviced Apartments & Houses, 60 Oxford Street, Southampton SO14 3DL
T: (023) 80881000
F: (023) 80881010
E: town@interalpha.co.uk
I: www.intent.co.uk/southampton/hotels/townorc/index.htm

BURWASH
East Sussex

Battenhurst Barn ★★★
Contact: Mr Stuart Winter
Battenhurst Barn, Battenhurst Road, Wadhurst TN5 7DU
T: (01732) 369168
F: (01732) 358817
E: holidays@gardenofenglandcottages.co.uk
I: www.gardenofenglandcottages.co.uk

Little Haycorns ★★★★
Contact: Mr Stuart Winter
Garden of England Cottages, The Mews Office, 189A High St, Tonbridge TN9 1BX
T: (01732) 369168
F: (01732) 358817
E: holidays@gardenofenglandcottages.co.uk
I: www.gardenofenglandcottages.co.uk

CALBOURNE
Isle of Wight

Holiday Homes Owners Services Ref: C1 ★★★★
Contact: Mr Colin Nolson
Holiday Homes Owners Services (West Wight), 18 Solent Hill, Freshwater PO40 9TG
T: (01983) 753423
F: (01983) 753423
E: holidayhomesiow@ic24.net

CAMBER
East Sussex

Bridle Cottage & Horseshoe Cottage & Poundfield Bungalow ★★★★
Contact: Mr Stuart Winter
Bridle Cottage & Horseshoe Cottage & Poundfield Bungalow, Farm Lane, Rye TN31 7QY
T: (01732) 369168
F: (01732) 358817
E: holidays@gardenofenglandcottages.co.uk
I: www.gardenofenglandcottages.co.uk

Camber Farmhouse Barn ★★★★
Contact: Ms Georgina Holt
Camber Farmhouse Barn, Farm Lane, Rye TN31 7QY
T: (01797) 225202

CANTERBURY
Kent

Canterbury Holiday Lets ★★★★
Contact: Mrs Kathryn Nevell
4 Harbledown Park, Harbledown, Canterbury CT2 8NR
T: (01227) 763308
F: (01227) 763308
E: rnevell@aol.com

11 Dunstan Court ★★★★
Contact: Mrs Maria Cain
39 London Road, Canterbury CT2 8LF
T: (01227) 769955

Ebury Hotel Cottages ★★★★
Contact: Mr Henry Mason
Ebury Hotel, 65-67 New Dover Road, Canterbury CT1 3DX
T: (01227) 768433
F: (01227) 459187
E: info@ebury-hotel.co.uk
I: www.ebury-hotel.co.uk

Knowlton Court ★★★-★★★★★
Contact: Miss Amy Froggatt
The Estate Office, Knowlton Court, Canterbury CT3 1PT
T: (01304) 842402
F: (01304) 842403
E: knowlton.cottages@farmline.com
I: www.knowltoncourt.co.uk

Oriel Lodge ★★★★
Contact: Mr Keith Rishworth
Oriel Lodge, 3 Queens Avenue, Canterbury CT2 8AY
T: (01227) 462845
F: (01227) 462845
E: info@oriel-lodge.co.uk
I: www.oriel-lodge.co.uk

Queensview Cottage ★★★★
Contact: Mrs Woodifield
Queensview Cottage, Braymor House, Queens Avenue, Canterbury CT2 8AY
T: (01227) 471914
F: (01227) 785348
I: www.cottageguide.co.uk/queensview/

St Mary's Cottage ★★★★
Contact: Mr R Allcorn
Abberley House, 115 Whitstable Road, Canterbury CT2 8EF
T: (01227) 450265
F: (01227) 478626
E: r.allcorn@discovercanterbury.com

14 St Michael's Place ★★★
Contact: Mrs Erica Drysdale
37 Effingham Road, Surbiton KT6 5JZ
T: (020) 83987036

Wagoners & Shepherds Cottage ★★★
Contact: Ms Hazel Long
Wagoners & Shepherds Cottage, Denstroude Farm, Denstroude Lane, Canterbury CT2 9JZ
T: (01227) 471513

CARISBROOKE
Isle of Wight

Alvington Manor Farm ★★
Contact: Mrs Margaret Marsh
Alvington Manor Farm, Newport PO30 5SP
T: (01983) 523463
F: (01983) 523463

Dairy Cottage ★★★★
Contact: Mrs Yapp
Luckington Farm, Bowcombe Road, Newport PO30 3HT
T: (01983) 822951

New Close Farm ★★★★
Contact: Mrs Fisher-McAllum
Technifind, New Close Farm, Nunnery Lane, Newport PO30 1YR
T: (01983) 523996
F: (01983) 537378
E: newclosefarm@42net.co.uk

Toll Cottage ★★★★
Contact: Mrs Siobhan Aubin
8 Shide Road, Newport PO30 1YQ
T: (01983) 523685

CASTLETHORPE
Milton Keynes

Orchard House ★★★-★★★★★
Contact: Mrs Mary Stacey
Orchard House, Hanslope Road, Milton Keynes MK19 7HD
T: (01908) 510208
F: (01908) 516119
E: mary.stacy@tesco.net
I: www.lets-stay-mk.co.uk

CATERHAM
Surrey

The White Cottage ★★★
Contact: Mrs Josephine Crux
3 Willow House, 8 East Parkside, Gt Park, Warlingham CR6 9OS
T: (01883) 621330
F: (01883) 620898
E: alan.crux@virgin.net
I: www.oas.co.uk/ukcottages

CATHERINGTON
Hampshire

Lone Barn ★★★★
Contact: Mrs Melanie Flint
Lone Barn, Waterlooville PO8 0SF
T: (023) 92632911
F: (023) 92632288
I: www.lonebarn.net

CAVERSFIELD
Oxfordshire

Grooms Cottage ★★★
Contact: Mr Albert Phipps
Banbury Road, Caversfield, Bicester OX27 8TG
T: (01869) 249307
F: (01869) 249307
E: odette@phippscottage.co.uk
I: www.phippscottage.co.uk

CHALE
Isle of Wight

Atherfield Green Farm Holiday Cottages ★★★★
Contact: Jupe
The Laurels, High Street, Sandown PO36 ONJ
T: (01983) 867613
F: (01983) 868214
E: alistair.jupe@btinternet.com

Chapel Cottage ★★★
Contact: Ms Catherine Hopper
Island Holiday Homes, 138 High Street, Newport PO30 1TY
T: (01983) 521113
F: (01983) 822030

The Old Rectory ★★★★
Contact: Mrs Mary Coward
The Old Rectory, Chale Street, Ventnor PO38 2HE

CHALE GREEN
Isle of Wight

Greenedge ★★★
Contact: Mrs Jacqueline Miles
Greenedge, Ventnor PO38 2JR
T: (01983) 551419

North Appleford Cottages ★★★
Contact: Mrs Jan Clarke
Cridmore Farm, Ryde PO33 3HH
T: (01983) 721206
I: www.appleford-cottages.co.uk

CHALFONT ST GILES
Buckinghamshire

Hilborough ★★
Contact: Mr & Mrs Peter Bentall
Hilborough, Mill Lane, Chalfont St Giles HP8 4NX
T: (01494) 872536
F: (01494) 872536

CHAPEL ROW
West Berkshire

The Flat
Rating Applied For
Contact: Mrs Rosemary Morris
Bracken Cottage, Bucklebury Common, Reading RG7 6PD
T: (0118) 9713394
F: (0118) 9713394

CHARLBURY
Oxfordshire

Banbury Hill Farm Cottages ★★★
Contact: Mrs Angela Widdows
Banbury Hill Farm, Oxford OX7 3JH
T: (01608) 810314
F: (01608) 811891
E: angelawiddows@gfwiddowsf9.co.uk
I: www.charlburyoxfordaccom.co.uk

CHARLTON
West Sussex

Orchard Cottage ★★★
Contact: Mrs Eve Jeffries
34 Foxhall Lane, Chichester PO18 0HU
T: (01243) 811338

CHART SUTTON
Kent

Brick Kiln Cottage ★★★★
Contact: Mrs Susan Spain
Brick Kiln Cottage, Green Lane, Maidstone ME17 3ES
T: (01622) 842490
F: (01622) 842490
E: sue.spain@totalise.co.uk
I: www.whitehousefarm-kent.co.uk

Establishments printed in blue have a detailed entry in this guide   573

SOUTH EAST ENGLAND

Orchard Cottage ★★★
Contact: Mrs Brenda Beck
Freedom Holiday Homes, 15
High Street, Cranbrook
TN17 3EB
T: (01580) 720770
F: (01580) 720771
E: mail@freedomholidayhomes.co.uk
I: www.freedomholidayhomes.co.uk

CHECKENDON
Oxfordshire

Livery Cottage ★★★★
Contact: Ms Linda Tarrant
Livery Cottage, c/o Checkendon
Equestrian Centre, Lovegrove's
Lane, Reading RG8 0NE
T: (01491) 680225
F: (01491) 682801
E: linda@checkendon.f9.co.uk
I: www.checkendon.f9.co.uk

CHICHESTER
West Sussex

24 & 26 Oaklands Court ★★★
Contact: Mr Ryan & Mr M Stait
Southern Counties Lettings, 42
Copthall Drive, Mill Hill, London
NW7 2NB
T: (020) 89594367
F: (020) 89061940
E: info@southerncountieslettings.com
I: www.southerncountieslettings.com

Apple Tree Cottage ★★★★
Contact: Mrs Daphne Vickers
34 King George Gardens,
Chichester PO19 6LB
T: (01243) 839770
F: (01243) 839771
E: vickersdaphne@aol.com
I: www.visitsussex.org/appletreecottage

1a Blackfriars House ★★★
Contact: Mr Laurie & Mrs Pat
Burrell
48 Stewart Avenue, Shepperton
TW17 0EH
T: (01932) 564556
E: patburrell@onetel.com

5 Caledonian Road ★★★★
Contact: Miss Victoria Chubb
33 Hillier Road, London
SW11 6AX
T: (020) 7924 5446 &
07786 674195
E: victoriachubb@hotmail.com
I: www.visitsussex.org/caledonianroad

Cornerstones ★★★★
Contact: Mrs Higgins
Greenacre, Goodwood Gardens,
Chichester PO20 1SP
T: (01243) 839096
E: vjrmhiggins@hotmail.com
I: www.visitsussex.org/cornerstones

Cygnet Cottage ★★★★
Contact: Mrs Higgins
Greenacre, Goodwood Gardens,
Chichester PO20 1SP
T: (01243) 839096
E: vjrmhiggins@hotmail.com
I: www.visitsussex.org/cygnetcottage

Flat 2, 4 Guildhall Street ★★★
Contact: Mr Ryan & Mr M Stait
Southern Counties Lettings, 7
Loretto Gardens, Harrow
HA3 9LY
T: (020) 89594307
F: (020) 89061940
E: info@southerncountieslettings.com
I: www.southerncountieslettings.com

Flats 1 & 5 West Broyle House
Rating Applied For
Contact: Mrs Penelope Gurland
Flat 6, 21 De Vere Gardens,
London W8 5AN
T: (020) 7937 6337
F: (020) 7938 2199

16 Goodwood Drive ★★★
Contact: Mrs Jackie Brading
5 Eastfield Close, Emsworth
PO10 8NJ
T: (01243) 375374

Honeysuckle Cottage ★★★★
Contact: Mr Noel & Mrs Jenny
Bettridge
Honeysuckle Cottage, Post
Office Lane, Chichester PO20 1JY
T: (01243) 779823
F: (01243) 779823
E: noeljenny@onetel.net.uk
I: www.visitsussex.org/honeysucklecottage

Hunston Mill ★★★
Contact: Mr & Mrs Potter
Selsey Road, Chichester
PO20 1AU
T: (01243) 783375
F: (01243) 785179
E: hunstonmillcottages@bushinternet.com
I: www.hunstonmill.co.uk

Lavender Cottage ★★★★
Contact: Mr Ron & Mrs Pam
Foden
4 York Road, Chichester
PO19 7TJ
T: (01243) 771314
F: (01243) 839171
E: rdfoden@talk21.com
I: www.visitsussex.org/lavendercottage

33 Melbourne Road ★★★
Contact: Mrs Jane Donnelly
Clevelands, Fordwater Road,
Chichester PO19 6PS
T: (01243) 537737

38 Mosse Gardens ★★★
Contact: Mrs Jennie Randall
The Coach House, Midhurst
GU29 0HZ
T: (01730) 812351

Oak Apple Barn ★★★★
Contact: Mrs Siobain Davies
Oak Apple Barn, The Lane,
Chichester PO19 5PY
T: (01243) 771669
E: siobain.davies@virgin.net
I: www.visitsussex.org/oakapplebarn

Poplars Farm House ★★★★
Contact: Mr & Mrs T Kinross
Batchmere Road, Almodington,
Chichester PO20 7LD
T: (01243) 514969
F: (01243) 512081
E: poplarsfarmhouse@tiscali.co.uk
I: www.poplarsfarmhouse.co.uk

Quay Quarters ★★★★★
Contact: Mrs Lorraine Sawday
Quay Quarters, Appledram
Manor Farm, Appledram Lane,
Chichester PO20 7EF
T: (01243) 839900
F: (01243) 782052
E: cottages@quayquarters.co.uk
I: www.quayquarters.co.uk

2 Rumbolds Close ★★★
Contact: Dr Ian White
35 Baldwin Avenue, Eastbourne
BN21 1UL
T: (01323) 648291
E: irwhite@nildram.co.uk

Walnut Tree Barn Cottage ★★★★
Contact: Mr Vernon D'Costa
Walnut Tree Barn Cottage, Old
Chimneys, Easthampnett Lane,
Chichester PO18 0JY
T: (01243) 773395
F: (01243) 780757
E: info@walnuttreebarn.co.uk
I: www.walnuttreebarn.co.uk

CHIDDINGFOLD
Surrey

Combe Court Farm ★★★
Contact: Mrs Thelma Lane
Combe Court Farm, Prestwick
Lane, Godalming GU8 4XW
T: (01428) 683375
F: (01428) 683375

Prestwick Byre ★★★★
Contact: Mrs Valerie Mills
Prestwick Byre, Prestwick Lane,
Godalming GU8 4XP
T: (01428) 654695
F: (01428) 654695
E: paul.prestwick@virgin.net

CHIDDINGLY
East Sussex

Dove Cottage ★★★★
Contact: Mr Stuart Winter
Garden of England Cottages, The
Mews Office, 189A High Street,
Tonbridge TN9 1BX
T: (01732) 369168
F: (01732) 358817
E: holiday@gardenofenglandcottages.co.uk
I: www.gardenofenglandcottages.co.uk

CHIDHAM
West Sussex

Canute Cottages ★★★★
Contact: Ms Diana Beale
Cobnor House, Chichester
PO18 8TE
T: (01243) 572123
E: taylorbeales@yahoo.co.uk
I: www.canutecottages.co.uk

CHILHAM
Kent

Monckton Cottages ★★★★
Contact: Mrs Helen Kirwan
Monckton Cottages, Mountain
Street, Chilham, Canterbury
CT4 8DG
T: (01227) 730256
F: (01227) 732423
E: monckton@rw-kirwan.demon.co.uk

CHILLERTON
Isle of Wight

Roslin Farm Annexe ★★
Contact: Mrs Evelyn Murdoch
Roslin Farm Annexe, Newport
PO30 3HG
T: (01983) 721662
E: bill.murdoch2@btopenworld.com

Sunnybank Cottage ★★★
Contact: Mrs Honor Vass
Island Cottage Holidays,
Godshill Park Farm House,
Ventnor PO38 3JF
T: (01929) 480080
F: (01929) 481070
E: enq@islandcottagesholidays.com
I: www.islandcottageholidays.com

The Willows ★★★
Contact: Mrs Muriel Burns
Dove Cottage, Brook Lane,
Newport PO30 3EW
T: (01983) 721630

CHILWORTH
Southampton

Lavender Cottage ★★★★
Contact: Mrs Susan Barnes
Holbrook House, Rugby
CV23 9BD
T: (01788) 543932

CHIPPING NORTON
Oxfordshire

Bruern Holiday Cottages ★★★★★
Contact: Ms Frances Curtin
Red Brick House, Chipping
Norton OX7 6PY
F: (01993) 831750
I: www.bruern-holiday-cottages.co.uk

Hedera Cottage ★★★★
Contact: Mrs Angela Richards
Manor Cottages & Cotswold
Retreats, 33A Priory Lane,
Oxford OX14 4SG
T: (01993) 824252
F: (01993) 824443
E: mancott@netcomuk.co.uk
I: www.manorcottages.co.uk

Washpool Cottage ★★★★
Contact: Mrs Angela Richards
Priory Mews, 33A Priory Lane,
Carterton OX18 4SG
T: (01993) 824252
F: (01993) 824443

SOUTH EAST ENGLAND

CHURCHILL
Oxfordshire
The Little Cottage ★★★★
Contact: Mr David Sheppard
Gables Cottage, Hackers Lane,
Chipping Norton OX7 6NL
T: (01608) 658674
E: enquiries@littlecottage.co.uk
I: www.littlecottage.co.uk

CLIFTONVILLE
Kent
19 Majestic Court ★★★★
Contact: Mrs Yvonne Forbes
Elonville Hotel, 70/72 Harold
Road, Margate CT9 2HS
T: (01843) 298635
F: (01843) 298635
E: enquiries@elonville-hotel.
demon.co.uk
I: www.elenvillehotel.com

CLIMPING
West Sussex
The Dairy Cottage ★★★
Contact: Mrs Sue Beckhurst
Brookpit Lane, Littlehampton
BN17 5QU
T: (01903) 724187
E: thedairy@tiscali.co.uk

COLWELL BAY
Isle of Wight
The Acorns ★★★
Contact: Mrs Lisa Baskill
Home from Home Holidays, 31
Pier Street, Ventnor PO38 1SX
T: (01983) 854340
F: (01983) 855524
E: admin@hfromh.co.uk

**Chalet 14 Island View
Chalet Park ★**
Contact: Ms Dorothea Lutticke
Unterer Hasselbach 14, 34359
Reinhardshagen, Germany
T: +49 5544 7328
F: +49 5544 7328
E: dorothealutticke@hotmail.
com

Solent Heights ★★★
Contact: Mrs Honor Vass
Island Cottage Holidays, The Old
Vicarage, Kingston, Wareham
BH20 5LH
T: (01929) 480080
F: (01929) 481070
E: enq@islandcottageholidays.
com
I: www.islandcottageholidays.
com

COMPTON
West Sussex
Yew Tree House Annexe ★★★
Contact: Mr & Mrs James
Buchanan
Yew Tree House Annexe, Yew
Tree House, Chichester
PO18 9HD
T: (023) 92631248
E: d.buchanan@btinternet.com

COWDEN
Kent
The Duck House ★★★★
Contact: Mrs Jill Winter
Garden of England Cottages,
189A High Street, Tonbridge
TN9 1BX
T: (01732) 369168
F: (01732) 358817
E: holidays@
gardenofenglandcottages.co.uk

COWES
Isle of Wight
Apartment Marivent ★★★
Contact: Mrs Segui
Apartment Marivent, 75 High
Street, Cowes PO31 7AJ
T: (01983) 292148
F: (01983) 280174
E: julia@marivent.co.uk
I: www.marivent.co.uk

Belharbour
Rating Applied For
Contact: Mrs Carys Kenna
8 Lattimer Place, London
W4 2UA
T: (020) 87478308

7 Cliff Road ★★★
Contact: Mrs Catherine Flury
34 Summerhill Way, Mitcham
CR4 2NJ
T: (020) 86481193
E: catherine@flury.fslife.co.uk

**Cutters & Marina Glimpse
★★★-★★★★★**
Contact: Mrs Valerie Caws
Cutters Accommodation, 4/5
Shooters Hill, Cowes PO31 7BE
T: (01983) 295697
F: (01983) 281203
E: caws@lineoe.net
I: www.cuttersaccommodation.
co.uk

Debourne Lodge ★★★
Contact: Mrs Lisa Baskill
31 Pier Street, Ventnor
PO38 1SX
T: (01983) 854340
F: (01983) 855524

Dolphin House ★★★
Contact: Mrs Kimiko Ure
c/o 58 Place Road, Cowes
PO31 7UB
T: (01983) 294788
F: (01983) 294788
E: dolphin_house_iow@yahoo.
co.uk
I: www.dolphinhousecowes.
co.uk

Dormers Cottage ★★★★
Contact: Mrs Honor Vass
Island Cottage Holidays,
Godshill Park Farm House,
Ventnor PO38 3JF
T: (01929) 480080
F: (01929) 481070
E: enq@islandcottagesholidays.
com
I: www.cottageholidays.dmon.
co.uk.

Farthings ★★★
Contact: Mr Michael Rabjohns
Firestone Cottage, Kite Hill, Ryde
PO33 4LE
T: (01983) 884122

Flat 2 ★★★
Contact: Catherine Hopper
Island Holiday Homes, 138 High
Street, Newport PO30 1TY
T: (01983) 521113
F: (01983) 822030

Greenside ★★★★
Contact: Mrs Kathy Domaille
Greenside, 124 Baring Road,
Cowes PO31 8DS
T: (01983) 840781
E: info@godshillparkfarm
I: www.islandcottageholidays.
com

Kingfisher
Rating Applied For
Contact: Mrs Linda Bek
Kingfisher, 222 Gurnard Pines,
Cockleton Lane, Cowes
PO31 8QE
T: (01983) 731761
E: tbek@onetel.net.uk
I: www.lynbrookholidays.co.uk

Mariners ★★★★
Contact: Mrs Suzanne Thomas
69 Airedale Avenue, Chiswick,
London W4 2NN
T: (020) 89940856
F: (020) 89940856

87 Medina View ★★★
Contact: Ms Catherine Hopper
Hose Rhodes Dickson, Island
Holiday Homes, 177 High Street,
Ryde PO33 2HW
T: (01983) 616644
F: (01983) 616640
E: enquiries@
island-holiday-homes.net
I: www.island-holiday-homes.
net

Point Cottages
Rating Applied For
Contact: Ms Laura Billings
Flying Fish, 25 Union Rad,
Cowes PO31 7RZ
T: (01983) 280641
F: (01983) 281821
I: www.pointcottages.co.uk

24 Seaview Road ★★★
Contact: Mrs Lisa Baskill
Home from Home Holidays, 31
Pier Street, Ventnor PO38 1SX
T: (01983) 854340
F: (01983) 855524
E: admin@hfromh.co.uk

**Skylark, Gurnard Pines
Holiday Village**
Rating Applied For
Contact: Mrs Linda Bek
Skylark, Gurnard Pines Holiday
Village , 224 Gurnard Pines,
Cockleton Lane, Cowes
PO31 8QE
T: (01983) 731761
E: tbek@onetel.net.uk
I: www.lynbrookholidays.co.uk

47 Victoria Road ★★★
Contact: Mr & Mrs Barker
75 Lowndes Avenue, Chesham
HP5 2HJ
T: (01494) 785948
E: v.barker@tiscali.co.uk

CRANBROOK
Kent
Bakersbarn ★★★★
Contact: Dr & Mrs Hooper
Bakersbarn, Golford Road,
Cranbrook TN17 3NW
T: (01580) 713344

Highwell Annexe
Rating Applied For
Contact: Mrs Johnson
Highwell Annexe, Highwell,
Heartenoak Road, Cranbrook
TN18 5EU
T: (01580) 752447
F: (01580) 754909

Little Dodges ★★★★
Contact: Mrs Brenda Beck
Freedom Holiday Homes, 15
High Street, Cranbrook
TN17 3EB
T: (01580) 720770
F: (01580) 720771
E: mail@freedomholidayhomes.
co.uk
I: www.freedomholidayhomes.
co.uk

Mill Cottage ★★★★
Contact: Mr Stuart Winter
Mill Cottage, The Hill, Cranbrook
TN17 3AH
T: (01732) 369168
F: (01732) 358817
E: holidays@
gardenofenglandcottages.co.uk
I: www.
gardenofenglandcottages.co.uk

Oak Cottage ★★★
Contact: Mrs Brenda Beck
Freedom Holiday Homes, 15
High Street, Cranbrook
TN17 3EB
T: (01580) 720770
F: (01580) 720771
E: mail@freedomholidayhomes.
co.uk
I: www.freedomholidayhomes.
co.uk

The Old Barn ★★★
Contact: Mrs Brenda Beck
Freedom Holiday Homes, 15
High Street, Cranbrook
TN17 3EB
T: (01580) 720770
F: (01580) 720771
E: mail@freedomholidayhomes.
co.uk
I: www.freedomholidayhomes.
co.uk

CROWBOROUGH
East Sussex
Cleeve Lodge ★★★★
Contact: Mr Edward & Mrs Nina
Sibley
The Old House, Harlequin Lane,
Crowborough TN6 1HS
T: (01892) 654331
E: nina@the-old-house.co.uk
I: www.the-old-house.co.uk

Hodges ★★★★★
Contact: Mrs Hazel Colliver
Hodges, Eridge Road,
Crowborough TN6 2SS
T: (01892) 652386
F: (01892) 667775
I: www.hodges.uk.com

Establishments printed in blue have a detailed entry in this guide

SOUTH EAST ENGLAND

CROWHURST
East Sussex

Old Shop Cottage ★★★★
Contact: Miss Denise P Webster
Old Shop Cottage, Sampsons Lane, Battle TN33 9AU
T: (01424) 830541
E: frank.73.sandgate@virgin.net
I: www.oldshopcottage.co.uk

Park Farm Holidays ★★★-★★★★★
Contact: Mrs Monica Butler
Park Farm Holidays, R & M Farming, Park Farm, Battle TN38 8EB
T: (01424) 852505
F: (01424) 852505
E: monicabutler2000@yahooo.co.uk

CRUNDALE
Kent

Farnley Little Barn ★★★★
Contact: Mrs Sylvia Hope
Farnley Little Barn, Denwood Street, Canterbury CT4 7EF
T: (01227) 730510
F: (01227) 730510
E: farnleylittlebarn@supaworld.com

Ripple Farm ★★★
Contact: Ms Maggie Baur
Ripple Farm, Canterbury CT4 7EB
T: (01227) 730748
F: (01227) 730748
E: ripplefarmhols@aol.com

CUDHAM
Kent

Fairmead Cottage ★★★★
Contact: Mrs Val Gillingham
Fairmead Cottage, Cudham Lane South, Sevenoaks TN14 7NZ
T: (01959) 532662
F: (01959) 534274
E: fairmeadfarm@aol.com

DAMERHAM
Hampshire

Nelson's Quarter Rating Applied For
Contact: Mr David Haydon
Wath Cottage, Fordingbridge SP6 3HD

DEAL
Kent

Chalet 88 ★★★
Contact: Rita Nadorf
Lunkegarten 6, Germany 45237
T: +49 201 585452
F: +49 201 585452
E: bnadorf@online.de

The Chequers ★★★
Contact: Mr David Sworder
The Chequers, Golf Road, Deal CT14 6RG
T: (01304) 362288

Shirley House ★★★★
Contact: Mrs Brenda Beck
Freedom Holiday Homes, 15 High Street, Cranbrook TN17 3EB
T: (01580) 720770
F: (01580) 720771
E: mail@freedomholidayhomes.co.uk
I: www.freedomholidayhomes.co.uk

DENMEAD
Hampshire

Flint Cottage ★★★
Contact: Mr John & Mrs Sheila Knight
High Trees, Ashling Close, Waterlooville PO7 6NQ
T: (023) 92266345
E: sheila@flintcottagehants.fsnet.co.uk

DINTON
Buckinghamshire

Wallace Farm Cottages ★★
Contact: Mrs Cook
Wallace Farm, Aylesbury HP17 8UF
T: (01296) 748660
F: (01296) 748851
E: jackiecook@wallacefarm.freeserve.co.uk
I: www.country-accom.co.uk

DITCHLING
East Sussex

Tovey Cottage ★★★★
Contact: Mr Richard Harris
Best of Brighton & Sussex Cottages Ltd, Vicarage Lane, Brighton BN2 7HD
T: (01273) 308779
F: (01273) 300266
E: brightoncottages@pavilion.co.uk
I: www.bestofbrighton.co.uk

Tovey Flat ★★★★
Contact: Mr Richard Harris
Best of Brighton & Sussex Cottages Ltd, Vicarage Lane, Brighton BN2 7HD
T: (01273) 308779
F: (01273) 300266
E: brightoncottages@pavilion.co.uk
I: www.bestofbrighton.co.uk

DODDINGTON
Kent

The Old School House ★★★★
Contact: Mr Stuart Winter
Garden of England Cottages, The Mews Office, 189A High Street, Tonbridge TN9 1BX
T: (01732) 369168
F: (01732) 358817
E: holidays@gardenofenglandcottages.co.uk
I: www.gardenofenglandcottages.co.uk

DORCHESTER ON THAMES
Oxfordshire

Vine Cottage ★★★★
Contact: Mr Robert & Mrs Jenny Booth
Well Place Road, Wallingford OX10 6QY
T: (01491) 681158
F: (01491) 681158
E: wellplacebarns@aol.com
I: www.holiday-rentals.co.uk (property number 8047)

DORKING
Surrey

Bulmer Farm ★★★
Contact: Mrs Gill Hill
Bulmer Farm, Holmbury St Mary, Dorking RH5 6LG
T: (01306) 730210

Milton Brook Cottage ★★★
Contact: Mrs Susan Scarrott
Milton Brook Cottage, Westcott Road, Dorking RH4 3PU
T: (01306) 877256
E: abacusue@aol.com

DOVER
Kent

Meggett Farm Cottage ★★★★
Contact: Mr Simon Price
Dover CT15 7BS
T: (01303) 252764
F: (01303) 252764
E: simon-price.dover@virgin.net
I: www.meggettfarmcottage.co.uk

DRAYTON
Oxfordshire

The Old School ★★★
Contact: Mrs Radburn
The Old School, 16 High Street, Abingdon OX14 4JL
T: (01235) 531557
E: gordon@theoldeschool.freeserve.co.uk

DYMCHURCH
Kent

Dymchurch House ★★★★★
Contact: Mrs J Uden
53 Crescent Road, Sidcup DA15 7HW
T: (020) 8300 2100
E: dymchurchhouse@btopenworld.com

Seabreeze Holiday Homes ★★-★★★
Contact: Mr Peter Checksfield
Seabreeze Holiday Homes, 1 Sea Wall, Romney Marsh TN29 0TG
T: (01303) 874116

EAST BOLDRE
Hampshire

Greycott ★
Contact: Ms Catherine Gray
The Bungalow, Main Road, Brockenhurst SO42 7WL
T: (01590) 612162
F: (01590) 612162

EAST COWES
Isle of Wight

Buttercup Cottage ★★★★
Contact: Mr G Newnham
Alberts Dairy, Heathfield Farm, Whippingham Road, East Cowes PO32 6NQ
T: (01983) 884553
F: (01983) 568822
E: post@newnhams.freeserve.co.uk

Harbour View ★★★★
Contact: Mrs Lisa Baskill
Home from Home Holidays, 31 Pier Street, Ventnor PO38 1SX
T: (01983) 854340
F: (01983) 855524
E: admin@hfromh.co.uk

21 Medina View Rating Applied For
Contact: Catherine Hopper
Island Holiday Homes, 138 High Street, Newport PO30 1TY
T: (01983) 521113
F: (01983) 822030

School House ★★★
Contact: Mr Matthew White
Island Holiday Homes, 138 High Street, Newport PO30 1TY
T: (01983) 521114

1 Seymour Court ★★★
Contact: Mrs Julia Maciw
5 Orchard Close, Reading RG31 6YS
T: (0118) 9419866
E: holiday@seymourcourt.co.uk
I: www.seymourcourt.co.uk

EAST FARLEIGH
Kent

Linden Cottage Rating Applied For
Contact: Mrs Jill Winter
Garden of England Cottages, 189A High Street, Tonbridge TN9 1BX
T: (01732) 369168
F: (01732) 358817
E: holidays@gardenofenglandcottages.co.uk

EAST GRINSTEAD
West Sussex

Boyles Farmhouse Self-Catering Holidays ★★★★
Contact: Mrs Emma Amos
Boyles Farmhouse, Harwoods Lane, East Grinstead RH19 4NQ
T: (01342) 315570
E: emmacamos@hotmail.com
I: www.sussexcountrycottages.co.uk

EAST HAGBOURNE
Oxfordshire

The Oast House ★★★★
Contact: Mr Harries
The Oast House, Manor Farm, Didcot OX11 9ND
T: (01235) 815005

EAST HOATHLY
East Sussex

Fern Cottage ★★★★
Contact: Mr Robert Wallace/Tracie Greenland
The Kings Head, 1 High Street, Lewes BN8 6DR
T: (01825) 840238
F: (01825) 880044
E: kingshead1648@hotmail.com
I: www.ferncottageholidays.co.uk

EAST PECKHAM
Kent

Middle Cottage, Pippins Barn & Oak Weir ★★★★
Contact: Mr Stuart Winter
Middle Cottage, Pippins Barn & Oak Weir, Tonbridge Road, Tonbridge TN12 5LQ
T: (01732) 369168
F: (01732) 358817
E: holidays@gardenofengland.co.uk
I: www.gardenofenglandcottages.co.uk

---

576 Look out for establishments participating in the National Accessible Scheme

SOUTH EAST ENGLAND

EAST PRESTON
West Sussex

Mariners House
Rating Applied For
Contact: Ms Jennie Spackman Brown
Skeg Limited, Rusper Road, Dorking RH5 5HG
T: (01293) 871937
F: (020) 8542 1647
E: derekedwards@sovereignprinters.co.uk
I: www.marinerhouse.net

EAST WITTERING
West Sussex

Fairhaven ★★★
Contact: Mrs Karen Dallaway
Baileys, 17 Shore Road, Chichester PO20 8DY
T: (01243) 672217
F: (01243) 670100
E: info@baileys.uk.com
I: www.baileys.uk.com

1 Seagate Court ★★★★
Contact: Ms Karen Brooker
Baileys Estate Agents, 17 Shore Road, Chichester PO20 8DY
T: (01243) 672217
F: (01243) 670100
E: info@baileys.uk.com

20 Seagate Court ★★★
Contact: Mr Ryan & Mr M Stait
Southern Counties Lettings, 42 Copthall Drive, Mill Hill, London NW7 2NB
T: (020) 82041188
F: (020) 89061940
E: info@southerncountieslettings.com
I: www.southerncountieslettings.com

Sunnyside ★★★
Contact: Kevin Bailey
Baileys, 17 Shore Road, Chichester PO20 8DY
T: (01243) 672217
E: info@baileys.uk.com
I: www.baileys.uk.com

EASTBOURNE
East Sussex

Black Robin Farm ★★★★
Contact: Mrs Jane Higgs
Black Robin Farm, Beachy Head Road, Beachy Head, Eastbourne BN20 7XX
T: (01323) 643357
F: (01323) 643357
E: jane_higgsbrb@yahoo.co.uk

Boathouse & The Beach House ★★★★★
Contact: Mr Richard Harris
Best of Brighton & Sussex Cottages Ltd, Vicarage Lane, Brighton BN2 7HD
T: (01273) 308779
F: (01273) 300266

4 Boship Cottages ★★★★
Contact: Country Hols Ref: 11983
Country Holidays, Spring Mill, Barnoldswick BB94 0AA
T: 0870 0 723723
F: (01282) 844288
E: sales@holidaycottagesgroup.com
I: www.country-holidays.co.uk

4 Clovelly ★★★
Contact: Mr Richard Harris
Best of Brighton & Sussex Cottages Ltd, Vicarage Lane, Brighton BN2 7HD
T: (01273) 308779
F: (01273) 390211
E: enquiries@bestofbrighton.co.uk
I: www.bestofbrighton.co.uk

Courtney House Holiday Flats ★★★★
Contact: Dr E Toner
Courtney House Holiday Flats, 53 Royal Parade, Eastbourne BN22 7AQ
T: (01323) 410202
E: holidays@courtneyhouse.org.uk
I: www.courtneyhouse.org.uk

Oysters ★★★★★
Contact: Mr Richard Harris
Best of Brighton & Sussex Cottages Ltd, Vicarage Lane, Brighton BN2 7HD
T: (01273) 308779
F: (01273) 300266
E: brightoncottages@pavilion.co.uk
I: www.bestofbrighton.co.uk

Quayside ★★★★★
Contact: Mr Richard Harris
Best of Brighton & Sussex Cottages Ltd, Vicarage Lane, Brighton BN2 7HD
T: (01273) 308779
F: (01273) 300266
E: brightoncottages@pavilion.co.uk
I: www.bestofbrighton.co.uk

Santana Waterfront Holiday House
Rating Applied For
Contact: Mrs Valerie Taylor
6 Kingston Quay, Sovereign Harbour, Eastbourne BN23 5UP
T: 0771 4 380966
F: (01323) 470632
E: santanahouse@onetel.com

Tom Thumb Cottages ★★
Contact: Mr & Mrs Roger Clark
52 Royal Parade, Eastbourne BN22 7AQ
T: (01323) 723248
F: (01323) 723248
E: info@eastbourne-holidayflats.co.uk
I: www.eastbourne-holidayflats.co.uk

EASTCHURCH
Kent

Connetts Farm Holiday Cottages ★★★-★★★★★
Contact: Mrs Maria Phipps
Connetts Farm Holiday Cottages, Plough Road, Sheerness ME12 4JL
T: (01795) 880358
F: (01795) 880358
E: connetts@btconnect.com
I: www.connettsfarm.co.uk

EASTERGATE
West Sussex

Eastmere ★★★
Contact: Mrs Sarah Wilkins
Eastmere, Eastergate Lane, Chichester PO20 3SJ
T: (01243) 574389
E: wilkins45@hotmail.com
I: www.eastmere.com

EGERTON
Kent

Box Farm Barn ★★★★
Contact: Mr Stuart Winter
Garden of England Cottages, The Mews Office, 189A High Street, Tonbridge TN9 1BX
T: (01732) 369168
F: (01732) 358817
E: holidays@gardenofenglandcottages.co.uk
I: www.gardenofenglandcottages.co.uk

Coldharbour Farm Oast & Pond Cottage ★★★★
Contact: Mrs Lisa Fraser
Coldharbour Farm Oast & Pond Cottage, Barhams Mill Road, Ashford TN27 9DD
T: (01233) 756548
F: (01233) 756770

The Dering Suite & The Old Bakery ★★★-★★★★
Contact: Mrs Brenda Beck
Freedom Holiday Homes, 15 High Street, Cranbrook TN17 3EB
T: (01580) 720770
F: (01580) 720771
E: mail@freedomholidayhomes.co.uk
I: www.freedomholidayhomes.co.uk

ELHAM
Kent

Lower Court Cottage ★★★★
Contact: Mrs Caunce
Lower Court, Shuttlesfield Lane, Canterbury CT4 6XJ
T: (01303) 862124
F: (01303) 864231
E: caunce@ottinge.fsnet.co.uk

ELMER
West Sussex

Pebble Cottage
Rating Applied For
Contact: Ms Sarah Barnes
11 Boxwell Road, Berkhamsted HP4 3EX
T: (01442) 863603

ELMSTED
Kent

The Dairy ★★★
Contact: Mrs Brenda Beck
Freedom Holiday Homes, 15 High Street, Cranbrook TN17 3EB
T: (01580) 720770
F: (01580) 720771
E: mail@freedomholidayhomes.co.uk
I: www.freedomholidayhomes.co.uk

The Shippen ★★★
Contact: Mr Stuart Winter
The Shippen, Ashford TN25 5JY
T: (01732) 369168
F: (01732) 358817
E: holidays@gardenofenglandcottages.co.uk
I: www.gardenofenglandcottages.co.uk

EMSWORTH
Hampshire

3 Avocet Quay ★★★
Contact: Mrs Jane Eastell
111 East Lane, Leatherhead KT24 6LJ
T: (01483) 281819
E: janeeastell@aol.com

Delta House ★★★★
Contact: Mr Ben Francis
Flat 1, 38 Mayfield Road, London N8 9LP
T: (020) 8340 8074
E: www.deltahouse-emsworth.co.uk
I: www.deltahouse-emsworth.co.uk

Flat A Dolphin House ★★★★
Contact: Mrs Michelle Leggatt
1 Laburnum Villas, South Bank, Chichester PO19 8DY
T: (01243) 775138
F: (01243) 775138
E: info@dolphinhideaway.co.uk
I: www.dolphinhideaway.co.uk

Hermitage Cottage ★★★-★★★★
Contact: Mrs Sarah Evans
Kimlas, School Lane, Chichester PO18 8RZ
T: (01243) 372554
E: hermitagecottage@btinternet.com
I: www.btinternet.com/~seeksystems

2 Heron Quay ★★★★
Contact: Mrs Linda Sprules
Tandriway, 15 Godstone Road, Old Oxted, Oxted RH8 9JS
T: (01883) 732144
F: (01883) 722510

Swan Cottage ★★★
Contact: Mr Richard Meager
70 Westbourne Avenue, Emsworth PO10 7QU
T: (01243) 370741
I: www.visit-oystercoast.co.uk

Westview Holiday Flat ★★★
Contact: Mrs Julia Oakley
61 Bath Road, Emsworth PO10 7ES
T: (01243) 373002
E: j.oakley@bigfoot.com

EPSOM
Surrey

7 Great Tattenhams ★★★
Contact: Mrs Mary Willis
7 Great Tattenhams, Epsom KT18 5RF
T: (01737) 354112

Establishments printed in blue have a detailed entry in this guide

SOUTH EAST ENGLAND

EPWELL
Oxfordshire

The Retreat of Church Farm ★★★★
Contact: Mrs Dawn Castle
Church Farm, Banbury OX15 6LD
T: (01295) 788473

ETCHINGHAM
East Sussex

Moon Cottage ★★★★
Contact: Mrs Jan Harrison
The White Cottage, Union Street, Wadhurst TN5 7NT
T: (01580) 879328
F: (01580) 879729
E: enquiries@harrison-holidays.co.uk
I: www.harrison-holidays.co.uk

EVERTON
Hampshire

Gothic Cottage ★★★-★★★★
Contact: Mrs Mary Brockett
The Old Boathouse, 13 Newlands Manor, Lymington SO41 0JH
T: (01590) 645141
E: gothic.everton@btopenworld.com

10 Newlands Manor ★★★
Contact: Mrs J A Rhoden
10 Newlands Manor, Lymington SO41 0JH
T: (01590) 642830
F: (01590) 642830
E: newlandsmanor@tiscali.co.uk

2 Uplay Cottages ★★★★
Contact: Ms Jacquie Taylor
Centre Lane, Everton, Lymington SO41 0JP
T: (01590) 641810
F: (01590) 671325
E: booking@halcyonholidays.com
I: www.halcyonholidays.com

Wheatley Cottage ★★★
Contact: Mrs Jacquie Taylor
Three Corners, Centre Lane, Lymington SO41 0JP
T: (01590) 645217
E: tommy.tiddles@virgin.net

EXTON
Hampshire

Beacon Hill Farm Cottages ★★★-★★★★
Contact: Mrs C Dunford
The Farm Office, Manor Farm, Beacon Hill Lane, Warnford Road, Southampton SO32 3NW
T: (01730) 829724
F: (01730) 829833
E: chris@martin4031.freeserve.co.uk
I: www.beaconhillcottages.co.uk

FAIRLIGHT
East Sussex

Little Oaks ★★★★
Contact: Mrs Janet Adams
Fairlight Cottage, Warren Road, (Via Coastguard Lane), Hastings TN35 4AG
T: (01424) 812145
F: (01424) 812145
E: fairlightcottage@supanet.com

FAREHAM
Hampshire

Manor Croft ★★★★
Contact: Mr Thomson
Manor Croft, Church Path, Fareham PO16 7DT
T: (01329) 280750
F: (01329) 280750
E: mcc-feedback@btconnect.com
I: www.manor-croft-health.co.uk/visitor_accom_1.htm

FARNHAM
Surrey

High Barn Annex & Summerhouse ★★
Contact: Ms Sandra Daplyn
High Barn Annex & Summerhouse, High Barn, Tilford Road, Farnham GU10 2LS
T: (01428) 605809
E: sdaplyn@enterprise.net
I: www.businesspartnersuk.co.uk/highbarn

High Wray ★★
Contact: Mrs Alexine G N Crawford
High Wray, 73 Lodge Hill Road, Farnham GU10 3RB
T: (01252) 715589
F: (01252) 715746
E: crawford@highwray73.co.uk

Kilnside Farm ★★
Contact: Mrs Ros Milton
Kilnside Farm, Moor Park Lane, Farnham GU10 1NS
T: (01252) 710325
E: b&tmilton@kilnsidefarm.fsnet.co.uk

Tilford Woods ★★★★
Contact: Mr Ede
Tilford Woods, Tilford Road, Tilford, Farnham GU10 2DD
T: (01252) 792199
F: (01252) 797040
I: www.tilfordwoods.co.uk

FAVERSHAM
Kent

The Country Retreat ★★★★
Contact: Mrs Maureen French
The Country Retreat, London Road, Faversham ME13 0RH
T: (01795) 531257
F: (01795) 531257
E: countryretreat1@aol.com
I: www.syndalepark.co.uk

Monks Cottage ★★★★
Contact: Mr Graham & Mrs Teresa Darby
Monks Cottage, Faversham ME13 0NP
T: (01233) 740419
F: (01233) 740187
E: info@selfcateringinkent.com
I: www.holidaycottagesinkent.com

Old Dairy ★★★
Contact: Mrs Gillian Falcon
Old Dairy, Shepherds Hill, Faversham ME13 9RS
T: (01227) 752212
F: (01227) 752212
E: ag@agfalcon.f9.co.uk

Uplees Farm ★★★★
Contact: Mr Chris & Mrs Heather Flood
Uplees Farm, Uplees Road, Faversham ME13 0QR
T: (01795) 532133

FELPHAM
West Sussex

Felpham Bungalow ★★★
Contact: Mrs Janet Yabsley
4 Nicholas Road, Croydon CR0 4QS
T: (020) 86804761

FERRING
West Sussex

Lamorna Gardens ★★★
Contact: Mrs Elsden & Mary Fitzgerald
Ferring-by-Sea, Worthing BN12 5QD
T: (01903) 238582 & 07860 699268
F: (01903) 330266

FINCHDEAN
Hampshire

Wagtails ★★★★
Contact: Mrs Libby Guess
Wagtails, Finchdean Farm, Waterlooville PO8 0AU
T: (023) 92413838
F: (023) 92413569
E: roger.guess@btinternet.com
I: www.wagtailscottage.co.uk

FINGEST
Oxfordshire

**Barnfields
Rating Applied For**
Contact: Mr Guy Prince
Nottingham Mansions, Nottingham Street, London W1U 5EN
T: 0785 0 095233
F: (020) 7224 1839

FINSTOCK
Oxfordshire

Wychwood ★★★
Contact: Mrs Bodil Grain
40 School Road, Oxford OX7 3DJ
T: (01993) 868249
E: bgrain@wychwoodcottage.co.uk
I: www.wychwoodcottage.co.uk

FISHBOURNE
West Sussex

The Tidings ★★★
Contact: Mrs Davies
The Tidings, Appledram Lane North, Chichester PO19 3RW
T: (01243) 773958

FIVE OAK GREEN
Kent

Stable Cottage ★★★★
Contact: Mrs Brenda Beck
Freedom Holiday Homes, 15 High Street, Cranbrook TN17 3EB
T: (01580) 720770
F: (01580) 720771
E: mail@freedomholidayhomes.co.uk
I: www.freedomholidayhomes.co.uk

FOLKESTONE
Kent

Bybrook Cottage ★★★
Contact: Mrs Gwendoline Baker
Bybrook House, The Undercliffe, Folkestone CT20 3AT
T: (01303) 248255

**Clifton Crescent The Leas
Rating Applied For**
Contact: Mrs Louise Scillitoe-Brown
Chartfield, Dorking RH4 3LG
T: (01306) 883838
F: (01306) 883838
E: cliftoncrescent@chartfield.biz

Flat 4 Leas House ★★★
Contact: Mr James Kitson
Flat 3 Leas House, 3 Castle Hill Avenue, Folkestone CT20 2TD
T: (01303) 248905

The Grand ★★-★★★★
Contact: Mr Michael Stainer
The Grand, The Leas, Folkestone CT20 2XL
T: (01303) 222222
F: (01303) 220220
E: info@grand.uk.com
I: www.grand.uk.com

Merriwinds ★★★★
Contact: Country Holidays
Merriwinds, 147 Old Dover Road, Capel-le-Ferne, Folkestone CT18 7HX
T: 0870 0 726726
F: (01282) 841539
E: ownerservices@holidaycottagesgroup.com
I: www.varne-ridge.co.uk

Meyrick Court Studio Apartments ★★
Contact: Mr Julio Santos Hilario
Meyrick Court Studio Apartments, 8-10 Trinity Crescent, Folkestone CT20 2ET
T: (01303) 275388
F: (01303) 275325

FOLKINGTON
East Sussex

**1 Frederick House
Rating Applied For**
Contact: Mr Richard Harris
Best of Brighton & Sussex Cottages Ltd, Vicarage Lane, Brighton BN2 7HD
T: (01273) 308779
F: (01273) 300266
E: brightoncottages@pavilion.co.uk
I: www.bestofbrighton.co.uk

Wood Barn at The Old Rectory ★★★
Contact: Mrs Janet Macdonald
Wood Barn at The Old Rectory, Polegate BN26 5SD
T: (01323) 483367
E: gerard@pobox.com

Look out for establishments participating in the National Accessible Scheme

SOUTH EAST ENGLAND

FORDINGBRIDGE
Hampshire

Alderholt Mill ★★★
Contact: Mr Richard & Mrs Sandra Harte
Alderholt Mill, Fordingbridge SP6 1PU
T: (01425) 653130
F: (01425) 652868
E: alderholt-mill@zetnet.co.uk
I: www.alderholtmill.co.uk

Burgate Manor Farm Holidays ★★★★-★★★★★
Contact: Mrs Bridget Stallard
Burgate Manor Farm Holidays, Burgate Manor Farm, Fordingbridge SP6 1LX
T: (01425) 653908
F: (01425) 653908
E: info@newforestcottages.com
I: www.newforestcottages.com

Fir Tree Farm Cottage ★★★★
Contact: Mr Colin & Mrs Sarah Proctor
Fir Tree Farm Cottage, Fir Tree Farm, Frogham Hill, Fordingbridge SP6 2HH
T: (01425) 654001
E: cjproctor@onetel.net.uk
I: www.firtreefarmcottage.co.uk

Garden Cottage ★★★
Contact: Mrs Adele Holmes
The Dial House, Fordingbridge SP6 3NA
T: (01725) 518083
F: (01725) 518083
E: rockbourneprop@freeuk.com
I: www.rockbourneproperties.co.uk

Glencairn ★★★
Contact: Mrs Tiller
2 Fernlea, Fordingbridge SP6 1PN
T: (01425) 652506

Hucklesbrook Farm ★★★★
Contact: Mrs Debbie Sampson
Hucklesbrook Farm, Fordingbridge SP6 2PN
T: (01425) 653180
E: jcl.samson@btinternet.com
I: www.newforestfarmcottages.com

FRESHWATER
Isle of Wight

A House in Cowes ★★★
Contact: Mr Graham Halls
TSF Management Ltd, 6 Catmose Street, Oakham LE15 6HW
T: 0777 1 880378
E: bookings@ahouseincowes.co.uk
I: www.ahouseincowes.c.uk

Afton Thatch ★★★★
Contact: Mrs Mylene Curtis
Afton Thatch, The Causeway, Freshwater PO40 9TN
T: (020) 8995 9288
F: (020) 8580 3911
E: mylene@blueyonder.co.uk

Applebarns
Rating Applied For
Contact: Catherine Hopper
Island Holiday Homes, 138 High Street, Newport PO30 1TY
T: (01983) 521113
F: (01983) 822030

Applebarns House & Cottage ★★★-★★★★★
Contact: Mr David Poole
42 Frewin Road, London SW18 3LP

103 Brambles Chine ★★
Contact: The Lettings Administrator
Linstone Chine Holiday Services Ltd, Brambles Office, Monks Lane, Freshwater PO40 9NQ
T: (01983) 755933
F: (01983) 752015

107 Brambles Chine ★★★
Contact: The Lettings Administrator
Linstone Chine Holiday Services Ltd, Brambles Office, Monks Lane, Freshwater PO40 9SU
T: (01983) 755933
E: holidays@linstone-chine.co.uk

110 Brambles Chine ★★
Contact: The Lettings Administrator
Linstone Chine Holiday Services Ltd, Brambles Office, Monks Lane, Freshwater PO40 9SU
T: (01983) 755933
E: holidays@linstone-chine.co.uk

111 Brambles Chine ★★
Contact: The Lettings Administrator
Linstone Chine Holiday Services Ltd, Brambles Office, Freshwater PO40 9SU
T: (01983) 755933
F: (01983) 752015

129 Brambles Chine ★★★
Contact: The Lettings Administrator
Linstone Chine Holiday Services Ltd, Brambles Office, Monks Lane, Freshwater PO40 9SU
T: (01983) 755933
E: holidays@linstone-chine.co.uk

131 Brambles Chine ★★★
Contact: The Lettings Administrator
Linstone Chine Holiday Services Ltd, Brambles Office, Monks Lane, Freshwater PO40 9NQ
T: (01983) 755933
F: (01983) 752015

148 Brambles Chine ★★
Contact: Mr Colin Nolson
Holiday Homes Owners Services (West Wight), 18 Solent Hill, Freshwater PO40 9TG
T: (01983) 753423
F: (01983) 753423
E: holidayhomesiow@ic24.net

160 Brambles Chine ★★
Contact: The Lettings Administrator
Linstone Chine Holiday Services Ltd, Brambles Office, Monks Lane, Freshwater PO40 9SU
T: (01983) 755933
E: holidays@linstone-chine.co.uk

168 Brambles Chine ★★
Contact: Ms Suzanne Buckley
Brambles Chine 168, Monks Lane, Freshwater PO40 9SU
T: (01983) 755933
F: (01983) 752015

170 Brambles Chine ★★★
Contact: The Lettings Administrator
Linstone Chine Holiday Services Ltd, Brambles Office, Monks Lane, Freshwater PO40 9SU
T: (01983) 755933
F: (01983) 752015

171 Brambles Chine ★★★
Contact: The Lettings Administrator
Linstone Chine Holiday Services Ltd, Brambles Office, Freshwater PO40 9SU
T: (01983) 755933
F: (01983) 752015

176 Brambles Chine ★★
Contact: Mr Neil Andrew Cain
18 Osborn Gardens, Mill Hill East, London NW7 1DY
T: (020) 83466308

177 Brambles Chine ★★★
Contact: Ms Suzanne Buckley
Brambles Chine 177, Monks Lane, Freshwater PO40 9SU
T: (01983) 755933
F: (01983) 752015

196 Brambles Chine ★★★
Contact: The Lettings Administrator
Linstone Chine Holiday Services Ltd, Brambles Office, Monks Lane, Freshwater PO40 9SU
E: holidays@linstone-chine.co.uk

197 Brambles Chine ★★
Contact: The Lettings Administrator
Linstone Chine Holiday Services Ltd, Brambles Office, Monks Lane, Freshwater PO40 9SU
E: holidays@linstone-chine.co.uk

209 Brambles Chine ★★
Contact: The Lettings Administrator
Linstone Chine Holiday Services Ltd, Brambles Office, Freshwater PO40 9SU
T: (01983) 755933
F: (01983) 752015

210 Brambles Chine ★★★
Contact: The Lettings Administrator
Linstone Chine Holiday Services Ltd, Brambles Office, Freshwater PO40 9SU

222 Brambles Chine ★★★
Contact: The Lettings Administrator
Linstone Chine Holiday Services Ltd, Brambles Office, Freshwater PO40 9SU
T: (01983) 755933
F: (01983) 752015

226 Brambles Chine ★★
Contact: The Lettings Administrator
Linstone Chine Holiday Services Ltd, Brambles Office, Monks Lane, Freshwater PO40 9NQ
T: (01983) 755933
F: (01983) 752015

40 Brambles Chine ★★
Contact: The Lettings Administrator
Linstone Chine Holiday Services Ltd, Brambles Office, Monks Lane, Freshwater PO40 9SU
T: (01983) 755933
E: holidays@linstone-chine.co.uk

60 Brambles Chine ★★
Contact: The Lettings Administrator
Linstone Chine Holiday Services Ltd, Brambles Office, Freshwater PO40 9SU
T: (01983) 755933
F: (01983) 752015

67 Brambles Chine ★★
Contact: The Lettings Administrator
Linstone Chine Holiday Services Ltd, Brambles Office, Monks Lane, Freshwater PO40 9SU
T: (01983) 755933
E: holidays@linstone-chine.co.uk

87 Brambles Chine ★★
Contact: The Lettings Administrator
Linstone Chine Holiday Services Ltd, Brambles Office, Monks Lane, Freshwater PO40 9SU
T: (01983) 755933
E: holidays@linstone-chine.co.uk

92 Brambles Chine ★★
Contact: The Lettings Administrator
Linstone Chine Holiday Services Ltd, Brambles Office, Freshwater PO40 9SU
T: (01983) 755933
F: (01983) 752015

Brockley Barns Cottage ★★★★
Contact: Mrs Sally Mitchell
Brockley Barns Cottage, Manor Farm Lane, Calbourne Road, Newport PO30 5SR
T: (01983) 537276
F: (01983) 537276
E: mitchellbrockley@aol.com
I: www.brockleybarns.co.uk

1 Cliff End ★★
Contact: Ms Suzanne Buckley
Cliff End 1, Monks Lane, Freshwater PO40 9SU
T: (01983) 755933
F: (01983) 755933

12A Cliff End ★★
Contact: The Lettings Administrator
Linstone Chine Holiday Services Ltd, Brambles Office, Freshwater PO40 9SU
T: (01983) 755933
F: (01983) 752015

Establishments printed in blue have a detailed entry in this guide

SOUTH EAST ENGLAND

38 Cliff End ★★
Contact: The Lettings Administrator
Linstone Chine Holiday Services Ltd, Brambles Office, Freshwater PO40 9SU
T: (01983) 755933
F: (01983) 752015

52 Cliff End ★
Contact: The Lettings Administrator
Linstone Chine Holiday Services Ltd, Brambles Office, Freshwater PO40 9SU
T: (01983) 755933
F: (01983) 752015

71 Cliff End ★★
Contact: Ms Suzanne Buckley
Cliff End 71, Monks Lane, Freshwater PO40 9SU
T: (01983) 755933
F: (01983) 755933

10 Dolphin Court ★★★★
Contact: Catherine Hopper
Island Holiday Homes, 138 High Street, Newport PO30 1TY
T: (01983) 521113
F: (01983) 822050

Farringford Hotel ★★★
Contact: Miss Hollyhead
Farringford Hotel, Bedbury Lane, Freshwater PO40 9PE
T: (01983) 752500
F: (01983) 756515
E: enquiries@farringford.co.uk
I: www.farringford.co.uk

1 Finsbury Cottage ★★★
Contact: Mr Colin Nolson
Holiday Homes Owners Services (West Wight), 18 Solent Hill, Freshwater PO40 9TG
T: (01983) 753423
F: (01983) 753423
E: holidayhomesiow@ic24.net

Freshfields ★★★
Contact: Mr & Mrs Barry
26 Calbourne Road, Newport PO30 5AP
T: (01983) 529901
E: jo-isle-of-wight.fsbusiness.co.uk
I: www.cottageguide.co.uk/freshfields

Holiday Homes Owner Services Ref : F6 ★★★★
Contact: Mr Colin Nolson
Holiday Homes Owner Services Ref : F6, 18 Solent Hill, Freshwater PO40 9TG
T: (01983) 753423

Holiday Homes Owner Services Ref : T3 ★★★★
Contact: Mr Colin Nolson
Holiday Homes Owner Services Ref : T3, 18 Solent Hill, Freshwater PO40 9TG
T: (01983) 753423

Holiday Homes Owner Services Ref: T8 ★★★★
Contact: Mr Colin Nolson
Holiday Homes Owner Services Ref: T8, 18 Solent Hill, Freshwater PO40 9TG
T: (01983) 753423

Holiday Homes Owner Services Ref: Y1 ★★★
Contact: Mr Colin Nolson
Holiday Homes Owner Services Ref: Y1, 18 Solent Hill, Freshwater PO40 9TG
T: (01983) 753423

Holiday Homes Owners Services Ref: F1 ★★★
Contact: Mr Colin Nolson
Holiday Homes Owners Services (West Wight), 18 Solent Hill, Freshwater PO40 9TG
T: (01983) 753423
F: (01983) 753423
E: holidayhomesiow@ic24.net

Holiday Homes Owners Services Ref: F10 ★★★★
Contact: Mr Colin Nolson
Holiday Homes Owners Services (West Wight), 18 Solent Hill, Freshwater PO40 9TG
T: (01983) 753423
F: (01983) 753423
E: holidayhomesiow@ic24.net

Holiday Homes Owners Services Ref: F2/168 ★★
Contact: Mr Colin Nolson
Holiday Homes Owners Services (West Wight), 18 Solent Hill, Freshwater PO40 9TG
T: (01983) 753423
F: (01983) 753423
E: holidayhomesiow@ic24.net

Holiday Homes Owners Services Ref: F2/203 ★★★
Contact: Mr Colin Nolson
Holiday Homes Owners Services (West Wight), 18 Solent Hill, Freshwater PO40 9TG
T: (01983) 753423
F: (01983) 753423
E: holidayhomesiow@ic24.net

Holiday Homes Owners Services Ref: F2/30 ★★
Contact: Mr Colin Nolson
Holiday Homes Owners Services (West Wight), 18 Solent Hill, Freshwater PO40 9TG
T: (01983) 753423
F: (01983) 753423
E: holidayhomesiow@ic24.net

Holiday Homes Owners Services Ref: F2/32 ★★
Contact: Mr Colin Nolson
Holiday Homes Owners Services (West Wight), 18 Solent Hill, Freshwater PO40 9TG
T: (01983) 753423
F: (01983) 753423
E: holidayhomesiow@ic24.net

Holiday Homes Owners Services Ref: F2/48 ★★
Contact: Mr Colin Nolson
Holiday Homes Owners Services (West Wight), 18 Solent Hill, Freshwater PO40 9TG
T: (01983) 753423
F: (01983) 753423
E: holidayhomesiow@ic24.net

Holiday Homes Owners Services Ref: F2/51 ★★★
Contact: Mr Colin Nolson
Holiday Homes Owners Services (West Wight), 18 Solent Hill, Freshwater PO40 9TG
T: (01983) 753423
F: (01983) 753423
E: holidayhomesiow@ic24.net

Holiday Homes Owners Services Ref: F7 ★★★
Contact: Mr Colin Nolson
Holiday Homes Owners Services (West Wight), 18 Solent Hill, Freshwater PO40 9TG
T: (01983) 753423
F: (01983) 753423
E: holidayhomesiow@ic24.net

Holiday Homes Owners Services Ref: F8 ★★★
Contact: Mr Colin Nolson
Holiday Homes Owners Services (West Wight), 18 Solent Hill, Freshwater PO40 9TG
T: (01983) 753423
F: (01983) 753423
E: holidayhomesiow@ic24.net

Little Rabbits ★★★
Contact: Mrs Helen Long
Windrush, Yarmouth PO41 0TA
T: (01983) 761506
E: hugh7@bushinternet.com

Rose Cottage ★★★
Contact: Mrs Jo Gardner
12 New Barn Lane, Alton GU34 2RU
T: (01420) 543385
F: (01420) 84587
E: jlightfoot.knowkedgeexchange@btinternet.com

St Martins Holiday Flats ★★
Contact: Mr & Mrs John Finch
St Martins Holiday Flats, Afton Down, Freshwater Bay, Freshwater PO40 9TY
T: (01983) 752389
E: stmartins.holidayflats@virgin.net

Seascape ★★★
Contact: Mrs Sheila Rose
8 Woodland View, Ryde PO33 2DG
T: (01983) 563218

Soake Farm House ★★★★
Contact: Ms Annette Edmundson
Soake Farm House, Queens Road, Freshwater PO40 9ES
T: (01983) 752383

Sunkissed Haven
Rating Applied For
Contact: Mrs Elizabeth Shea
14 Queens Street, Stamford PE9 1QS
T: (01780) 754112
E: lizshea@hotmail.com

Sunnyside ★★★
Contact: Mrs Sara Yarwood
Waratah, Church Lane, Lymington SO41 6AD
T: (01590) 682863
I: www.waratah.fsworld.co.uk

Sunsets ★★
Contact: The Lettings Administrator
Linstone Chine Holiday Services Ltd, Brambles Office, Freshwater PO40 9SU
T: (01983) 755933
F: (01983) 752015

Tree Tops ★★★
Contact: Mrs Lisa Baskill
Home from Home Holidays, 31 Pier Street, Ventnor PO38 1SX
T: (01983) 854340
F: (01983) 855524
E: admin@hfromh.co.uk

FRESHWATER BAY
Isle of Wight

Holiday Homes Owners Services Ref: F3 ★★★
Contact: Mr Colin Nolson
Holiday Homes Owners Services (West Wight), 18 Solent Hill, Freshwater PO40 9TG
T: (01983) 753423
F: (01983) 753423
E: holidayhomesiow@ic24.net

Holiday Homes Owners Services Ref: F9 ★★★★
Contact: Mr Colin Nolson
Holiday Homes Owners Services (West Wight), 18 Solent Hill, Freshwater PO40 9TG
T: (01983) 753423
F: (01983) 753423
E: holidayhomesiow@ic24.net

10 Tennyson View ★★★★
Contact: Ms Catherine Hopper
Manager, Housing Letting Hose Rhodes Dickson, Island Holiday Homes, 177 High Street, Ryde PO33 2HW
T: (01983) 616644
F: (01983) 616640
E: enquiries@island-holiday-homes.net
I: www.island-holiday-homes.net

2 Tennyson View ★★★★★
Contact: Ms Catherine Hopper
Manager, Housing Letting Hose Rhodes Dickson, Island Holiday Homes, 177 High Street, Ryde PO33 2HW
T: (01983) 616644
F: (01983) 616640
E: enquiries@island-holiday-homes.net
I: www.island-holiday-homes.net

5 Tennyson View ★★★★
Contact: Mr Matthew White
Island Holiday Homes, 138 High Street, Newport PO30 1TY
T: (01983) 521114

FRITTENDEN
Kent

Cresslands
Rating Applied For
Contact: Ms Brenda Beck
Freedom Holiday Homes, 15 High Street, Cranbrook TN17 3EB
T: (01580) 720770
F: (01580) 720771

580 Look out for establishments participating in the National Accessible Scheme

SOUTH EAST ENGLAND

Weaversden Oast House ★★★★
Contact: Mr Stuart Winter
Weaversden Oast House,
Cranbrook TN17 2EP
T: (01732) 369168
F: (01732) 358817
E: holidays@
gardenofenglandcottages.co.uk
I: www.
gardenofenglandcottages.co.uk

FUNTINGTON
West Sussex

The Courtyard ★★★★
Contact: Mrs Claire Hoare
3 The Cottages, Adsdean Farm,
Chichester PO18 9DN
T: (01243) 575464
F: (01243) 575586
E: tim.hoare@farming.co.uk

Dellfield ★★★★
Contact: Mr Hall Hall
Dellfield, Downs Road,
Chichester PO18 9LS
T: (01243) 575244
E: holidays@dellfield.com
I: www.dellfield.com

FYFIELD
Hampshire

2 Rose Lane ★★★
Contact: Mr Jan & Mrs Paul
Martin
2 Rose Lane, Andover SP11 8ER
T: (01264) 771556

GATCOMBE
Isle of Wight

Newbarn Country Cottages
★★★★
Contact: Mrs Diane Harvey
Newbarn Country Cottages,
Newbarn Farm, Newport
PO30 3EQ
T: (01983) 721202
E: newbarnfarm@aol.com
I: www.wightfarmholidays.
co.uk/stable

GLYNDE
East Sussex

Caburn Cottages ★★★★
Contact: Mr & Mrs Philip Norris
Caburn Cottages, Ranscombe
Farm, Lewes BN8 6AA
T: (01273) 858062
I: www.caburncottages.co.uk

GODALMING
Surrey

Magpie Cottage ★★★
Contact: Mrs Gabrielle Mabley
Magpie Cottage, New Road,
Godalming GU8 5SU
T: (01428) 682702
E: Gabrielle.Mabley1@
btinternet.com

GODSHILL
Isle of Wight

Bagwich Cottage
Rating Applied For
Contact: Mrs Honor Vass
Island Cottage Holidays, The Old
Vicarage, Kingston, Wareham
BH20 5LH
T: (01929) 481555
I: www.islandcottageholidays.
com

Barwick Cottage
★★★-★★★★
Contact: Mrs P J Wickham
Barwick Cottage, Rookley Farm
Lane, Niton Road, Ventnor
PO38 3PA
T: (01983) 840787
F: (01983) 840787
E: pam@barwickcottages.co.uk
I: www.barwickcottages.co.uk

The Coach House Studio
★★★
Contact: Mrs Honor Vass
Island Cottage Holidays, The Old
Vicarage, Kingston, Wareham
BH20 5LH
T: (01929) 480080
F: (01929) 481070
E: enq@islandcottageholidays.
com
I: www.islandcottageholidays.
com

Demelza ★★★★
Contact: Mrs Honor Vass
Island Cottage Holidays, The Old
Vicarage, Sturminster Newton
BH20 5LH
T: (01929) 480080
F: (01929) 481070
E: enq@islandcottageholidays.
com
I: www.islandcottageholidays.
com

Glebelands Holiday
Apartments ★★★★
Contact: Mrs Iris Beardsall
Glebelands Holiday Apartments,
Church Hollow, Ventnor
PO38 3DR
T: (01983) 840371
F: (01983) 867482
I: www.glebelands.fsnet.co.uk

Godshill Park House ★★★★
Contact: Mrs Nora Down
Godshill Park House, Shanklin
Road, Ventnor PO38 3JF
T: (01983) 840271
F: (01983) 840960
E: noradown@godshillpark.
fsnet.co.uk
I: www.godshillpark.co.uk

Graylands Cottage ★★★
Contact: Professor Ian Bruce
54 Mall Road, Hammersmith,
London W6 9DG
T: (020) 8748 0611
F: (020) 8741 5621
E: tinab@cocoon.co.uk

Keepers Cottage ★★★★
Contact: Mrs Honor Vass
Island Cottage Holidays, The Old
Vicarage, Kingston, Wareham
BH20 5LH
T: (01929) 480080
I: www.islandcottageholidays.
com

Lambourn View Holiday
Annexe ★★
Contact: Mrs Maureen Plumbley
Lambourn View Holiday Annexe,
Beacon Alley, Ventnor PO38 3JX

Loves Cottage ★★★
Contact: Mrs Honor Vass
Island Cottage Holidays, The Old
Vicarage, West Street, Kingston,
Corfe Castle, Wareham
BH20 5LH
T: (01929) 480080
F: (01929) 481070
E: enq@islandcottageholidays.
com
I: www.islandcottageholidays.
com

Milk Pan Farm ★★★
Contact: Mr Tony & Mrs Leila
Morrish
Milk Pan Farm, Bagwich Lane,
Godshill, Ventnor PO38 3JY
T: (01983) 840570
E: tony@milkpanfarm.co.uk
I: www.milkpanfarm.co.uk

Pheasant Cottage ★★★★
Contact: Mrs Kathy Domaille
Pheasant Cottage, Godshill Park
Farm, Shanklin Road, Ventnor
PO38 3JF
T: (01983) 840781
E: info@godshillparkfarm.
uk.com
I: godshillparkfarm.uk.com

Pilgrims Lodge ★★★★
Contact: Mrs Honor Vass
Island Cottage Holidays, The Old
Vicarage, West Street, Kingston,
Corfe Castle, Wareham
BH20 5LH
T: (01929) 480080
F: (01929) 481070
E: enq@islandcottageholidays.
com
I: www.islandcottageholidays.
com

Rosemary Cottage ★★★★
Contact: Mrs Honor Vass
Island Cottage Holidays, The Old
Vicarage, Kingston, Wareham
BH20 5LH
T: (01929) 480080
I: www.islandcottageholidays.
com

Seymour Cottages ★★★
Contact: Mr Arthur & Mrs Pat
Lazenby
Seymour Cottages, Newport
Road, Ventnor PO38 3LY
T: (01983) 840536

Stag Cottage ★★★★
Contact: Mrs Honor Vass
Island Cottage Holidays, The Old
Vicarage, Kingston, Wareham
BH20 5LH
T: (01929) 480080
I: www.islandcottageholidays.
com

GODSHILL WOOD
Hampshire

The Lodge (Ref: H212)
★★★★
Contact: Mr Nick Pash
Hideaways, Chapel House, Luke
Street, Berwick St John,
Shaftesbury SP7 0HQ
T: (01747) 828170
F: (01747) 829090
E: enq@hideaways.co.uk
I: www.hideaways.co.uk/

GOODWOOD
West Sussex

Bay Cottage ★★★
Contact: Mrs Rosemary Wilks
58 North Acre, Banstead
SM7 2EG
T: (01737) 358863

GORING-BY-SEA
West Sussex

37 Harwood Avenue
Rating Applied For
Contact: Mrs Susan Fountain
56 Church Leys, Huntingdon
PE28 9QD
T: (01480) 370656

Sea Place ★★
Contact: Anne Wright
Promenade Holiday Homes, 44
Nepcote Lane, Worthing
BN14 0SL
T: (01903) 877047
F: (01903) 877047
I: www.
promenadeholidayhomes.co.uk

Spindrift
Rating Applied For
Contact: Mr & Mrs N C Wootton
The Channon, Grange Park,
Worthing BN12 5LS
T: (01903) 246940
F: (01903) 246940
E: mail@vanessawootton.com
I: www.kitesurfsussex.com

GOSPORT
Hampshire

Avenue Corner ★★★★
Contact: Mr Kevin Macaulay
21 Vernon Close, Gosport
PO12 3NU
T: (023) 92502222
F: (023) 92528338
E: enquiries@avenuecorner.
co.uk
I: www.avenuecorner.co.uk

Dolphins ★★★
Contact: Mrs Donnelly
28 Crescent Road, Gosport
PO12 2DJ
T: (023) 92588179

19 The Quarterdeck
★★★★★
Contact: Mr Dave Danns
197 Portsmouth Road, Gosport
PO13 9AA
T: (023) 9255 2550
F: (023) 9255 4657
E: dave@thequarterdeck.co.uk
I: www.thequarterdeck.co.uk

GOUDHURST
Kent

Blackthorn Barn ★★★★
Contact: Mrs Brenda Beck
Freedom Holiday Homes, 15
High Street, Cranbrook
TN17 3EB
T: (01580) 720770
F: (01580) 720771
E: mail@freedomholidayhomes.
co.uk
I: www.freedomholidayhomes.
co.uk

Establishments printed in blue have a detailed entry in this guide

SOUTH EAST ENGLAND

The Coach House ★★★
Contact: Mrs Brenda Beck
Freedom Holiday Homes, 15
High Street, Cranbrook
TN17 3EB
T: (01580) 720770
F: (01580) 720771
E: mail@freedomholidayhomes.co.uk
I: www.freedomholidayhomes.co.uk

The Stables ★★★★
Contact: Mrs Brenda Beck
Freedom Holiday Homes, 15
High Street, Cranbrook
TN17 3EB
T: (01580) 720770
F: (01580) 720771
E: mail@freedomholidayhomes.co.uk
I: www.freedomholidayhomes.co.uk

Three Chimneys Farm ★★★★
Contact: Mrs Marion Fuller
Three Chimneys Farm,
Bedgebury Road, Goudhurst,
Cranbrook TN17 2RA
T: (01580) 212175
F: (01580) 212175
E: marionfuller@threechimneysfarm.co.uk
I: www.threechimneysfarm.co.uk

3 Whitestocks Cottages ★★★★
Contact: Mrs Brenda Beck
Freedom Holiday Homes, 15
High Street, Cranbrook
TN17 3EB
T: (01580) 720770
F: (01580) 720771
E: mail@freedomholidayhomes.co.uk
I: www.freedomholidayhomes.co.uk

GRAFTY GREEN
Kent

Fermor Cottage ★★★
Contact: Mr Stuart Winter
Garden of England Cottages, The
Mews Office, 189A High Street,
Tonbridge TN9 1BX
T: (01732) 369168
F: (01732) 358817
E: holidays@gardenofenglandcottages.co.uk
I: www.gardenofenglandcottages.co.uk

The Old Chapel & Weirton Villa ★★★★
Contact: Mr Stuart Winter
The Old Chapel & Weirton Villa,
Headcorn Road, Maidstone
ME17 2AP
T: (01732) 369168
F: (01732) 358817
E: holidays@gardenofenglandcottages.co.uk
I: www.gardenofenglandcottages.co.uk

GRAVESEND
Kent

Russell Quay ★★★★
Contact: Mr Trevor Dickety
1 Brimstone Hill, Medpham,
Gravesend DA13 0BN
T: (01474) 573045
F: (01474) 573049
E: mikedickety@beeb.net
I: www.halcyon-gifts.co.uk/holidaylet.htm

GREAT MILTON
Oxfordshire

Views Farm Barns ★★★★
Contact: Mr & Mrs Peers
Views Farm Barns, Views Farm,
Great Milton, Oxford OX44 7NW
T: (01844) 279352
F: (01844) 279362
E: info@viewsfarmbarns.co.uk
I: www.viewsfarmbarns.co.uk

GREAT ROLLRIGHT
Oxfordshire

Blackbird Cottage ★★★★
Contact: Mrs Carol Dingle
Tyte End Cottage, Chipping
Norton OX7 5RU
T: (01608) 737676
F: (01608) 737330

Butlers Hill Farm ★★★
Contact: Mrs Campbell
Butlers Hill Farm, Chipping
Norton OX7 5SJ
T: (01608) 684430

GROOMBRIDGE
East Sussex

Sherlocks Cottage ★★★★
Contact: Mrs Brenda Beck
Freedom Holiday Homes, 15
High Street, Cranbrook
TN17 3EB
T: (01580) 720770
F: (01580) 720771
E: mail@freedomholidayhomes.co.uk
I: www.freedomholidayhomes.co.uk

GUILDFORD
Surrey

Cathedral View Self-Catering Flat ★★★
Contact: Mrs Caroline Salmon
Cathedral View Self-Catering
Flat, 7 Harvey Road, Guildford
GU1 3SG
T: (01483) 504915
E: cathedralview@supanet.com

4 Grove End ★★★
Contact: Mr Colin Stoneley
4 Grove End, 12 Pit Farm Road,
Guildford GU1 2JH
T: (01483) 560831
E: wtieurope@btclick.com

Lavender ★★★
Contact: Mr & Mrs Liew
Mandarin, Pewley Point, Pewley
Hill, Guildford GU1 3SP
T: (01483) 506819
F: (01483) 506819
E: shirleyliew9@hotmail.com

University of Surrey ★★
Contact:
University of Surrey, Guildford
GU2 7XH
T: (01483) 689157
F: (01483) 579266
E: conferences@surrey.ac.uk
I: www.surrey.ac.uk/conferences

GURNARD
Isle of Wight

The Stable ★★★★
Contact: Mr Peter & Mrs
Madeline Newton
17 Foxhills, Ventnor PO38 1LX
T: (01983) 853378
F: (01983) 853378

GUSTON
Kent

Owl Cottage ★★★★
Contact: Mr Michael & Mrs
Gloria Morgan
10 Cranleigh Drive, Dover
CT16 3NL
T: (01304) 825732
F: (01304) 825732
E: owlcottage@lineone.net

HADLOW
Kent

4 Castle View ★★★★★
Contact: Mrs Jill Winter
Garden of England Cottages,
189A High Street, Tonbridge
TN9 1BX
T: (01732) 369168
F: (01732) 358817
E: holidays@gardenofenglandcottages.co.uk

HAILSHAM
East Sussex

Little Marshfoot Farmhouse ★★★★
Contact: Ms Kathryn Webster
Little Marshfoot Farmhouse, Mill
Road, Hailsham BN27 2SJ
T: (01323) 844690
E: kew@waitrose.com
I: littlemarshfootfarmhouse.co.uk

The Old Orchard Bungalow ★★★
Contact: Mr Brian Bennett
The Old Orchard Bungalow, The
Platt, Caburn Way, Hailsham
BN27 3LX
T: (01323) 440977
F: (01323) 440977
E: bbrian985@AOL.com
I: www.sussexcoast.co.uk/old-orchard/

Pekes ★★★-★★★★
Contact: Ms Eva Morris
124 Elm Park Mansions, Park
Walk, London SW10 0AR
T: (020) 7352 8088
F: (020) 7352 8125
E: pekes.afa@virgin.net
I: www.pekesmanor.com

HALLAND
East Sussex

Little Tamberry ★★★★
Contact: Mrs Brenda Beck
Freedom Holiday Homes, 15
High Street, Cranbrook
TN17 3EB
T: (01580) 720770
F: (01580) 720771
E: mail@freedomholidayhomes.co.uk
I: www.freedomholidayhomes.co.uk

HARTLEY
Kent

Chestnuts Annex ★★★
Contact: Mrs Pamela Thomas
Chestnuts Annex, Quakers Close,
Longfield DA3 7EA
T: (01474) 704273

HARTLEY WINTNEY
Hampshire

Wintney Stable ★★★
Contact: Mr & Mrs Bernard
Kilroy
Wintney Stable, 10 Hunts
Common, Hook RG27 8NT
T: (01252) 843133
F: (01252) 843133
E: bernardkilroy@uk2.net

HASLEMERE
Surrey

The Creamery ★★★★
Contact: Mr Nick Pash
Hideaways, Luke Street, Berwick
St John, Shaftesbury SP7 0HQ
T: (01747) 828170
F: (01747) 829090
E: enq@hideaways.co.uk
I: www.hideaways.co.uk/property.cfm/h742

Guard Hill ★★
Contact: Mr Wimbush
Guard Hill, 13 Hill Road,
Haslemere GU27 2JP
T: (01428) 642166

HASTINGLEIGH
Kent

Staple Farm ★★★★
Contact: Mr & Mrs Martindale
Staple Farm, Hastingleigh,
Ashford TN25 5HF
T: (01233) 750248
F: (01233) 750249

HASTINGS
East Sussex

Brooklands Coach House ★★★
Contact: Mrs Caroline McNally
Brooklands Coach House, 61 Old
London Road, Hastings
TN35 5NB
T: (01424) 421957
F: (01424) 437003
E: brooklandscoachhouse@btinternet.com

Bryn-Y-Mor ★★★-★★★★
Contact: Mrs Doreen Karen-Alun
Bryn-Y-Mor, 12 Godwin Road,
Hastings TN35 5JR
T: (01424) 722744
F: (01424) 445933
E: karen-alun@brynymor.ndirect.co.uk

SOUTH EAST ENGLAND

12 The Coastguards ★★★
Contact: Mrs Janine Vallor-Doyle
Merton House, 11 Barrack Street, Bridport DT6 3LX
T: (01308) 423180

Lionsdown House ★★★★
Contact: Mrs Sharon Bigg
Lionsdown House, 116 High Street, Old Town, Hastings TN34 3ET
T: (01424) 420802
F: (01424) 420802
E: info@lionsdownhouse.co.uk
I: www.lionsdownhouse.co.uk

Number Six ★
Contact: Mr Chris & Mrs Pat Hart
Number Six, 6 Stanley Road, Hastings TN34 1UE
T: (01424) 431984
F: (01424) 432690
E: famhart@supanet.com
I: www.sixstanleyroad.co.uk

14 Old Humphrey Avenue ★★★
Contact: Mrs Chris Nixey
52 Woollerton Crescent, Wendover, Aylesbury HP22 6HT
T: (01296) 625780
F: (01296) 625780
E: cnixey@aol.com

Rocklands Holiday Park ★★★
Contact: Mr Len & Mrs Joan Guilliard
Rocklands Holiday Park, Rocklands Lane, Hastings TN35 5DY
T: (01424) 423097
E: rocklandspark@aol.com

Rose House ★★★
Contact: Mrs Susan Hill
1 Beauport Gardens, St Leonards-on-Sea, Hastings TN37 7PQ
T: (01424) 754812
F: (01424) 754812
E: hillbusybee@aol.com

St Marys Holiday Flats ★-★★
Contact: Mrs Edwards
6 Highcroft Villas, Brighton BN1 5PS
T: (01273) 556227

Tillys Cottage ★★★
Contact: Mrs Celia Conway
The Captain's Cabin, Solent Breezes, Hook Lane, Southampton SO31 9HG
T: (01494) 565493
I: www.hastings-holidays.com

35 Warrior Square ★★★★
Contact: Mr Walter Van Dijk
1 Eggshole Cottage, Starvecrow Lane, Rye TN31 6XN
T: (01797) 230145
F: (01797) 230366
E: wltrvandyk@aol.com

Wellington Holiday Apartments ★★-★★★
Contact: Mrs Joan Stevens
Wellington, Ashen Grove Road, East Hill, Sevenoaks TN15 6YE
T: (01959) 524160

Westcliff Lodge ★★★
Contact: Mrs Celia Conway
The Captain's Cabin, Solent Breezes, Hook Lane, Southampton SO31 9HG
T: (01494) 565493
I: www.hastings-holidays.com

HAWKHURST
Kent

Kent Bridge Croft ★★★★
Contact: Mrs Brenda Beck
Freedom Holiday Homes, 15 High Street, Cranbrook TN17 3EB
T: (01580) 720770
F: (01580) 720771
E: mail@freedomholidayhomes.co.uk
I: www.freedomholidayhomes.co.uk

The Stables ★★★★
Contact: Mr Stuart Winter
Garden of England Cottages, The Mews Office, 189A High Street, Tonbridge TN9 1BX
T: (01732) 369168
F: (01732) 358817
E: holidays@gardenofenglandcottages.co.uk
I: www.gardenofenglandcottages.co.uk

HAWKINGE
Kent

1 North Downs Cottage ★★★★
Contact: Mrs Brenda Beck
Freedom Holiday Homes, 15 High Street, Cranbrook TN17 3EB
T: (01580) 720770
F: (01580) 720771
E: mail@freedomholidayhomes.co.uk
I: www.freedomholidayhomes.co.uk

HAYLING ISLAND
Hampshire

15 Anchor Court ★★★
Contact: Mr Roy Pine
Millers, 19 Mengham Road, Hayling Island PO11 9BG
T: (023) 92465951
F: (023) 92461321
E: millers@haylingproperty.co.uk
I: www.haylingproperty.co.uk

Bay Cottage ★★★★
Contact: Miss Kate Cross
Cockle Warren Hotel, 36 Sea Front, Hayling Island PO11 9HL
T: (023) 92464961
F: (023) 92464838

8 Chandlers Close ★★★
Contact: Mr Roy Pine
Millers, 19 Mengham Road, Hayling Island PO11 9BG
T: (023) 9246 5951
F: (023) 9246 1321
E: millers@haylingproperty.co.uk

69 Creek Road ★★★
Contact: Mr Roy Pine
Millers, 19 Mengham Road, Hayling Island PO11 9BG
T: (023) 9246 5951
F: (023) 9246 1321
E: millers@haylingproperty.co.uk

30 Fairlight Chalets ★
Contact: Mr Roy Pine
Millers, 19 Mengham Road, Hayling Island PO11 9BG
T: (023) 92465951
F: (023) 92461321
E: millers@haylingproperty.co.uk
I: www.haylingproperty.co.uk

7 Fairlight Chalets ★★★
Contact: Mrs Janet Bulmer
9 Whitethorn Road, Hayling Island PO11 9LS
T: (023) 9246 0309

31 Itchenor Road ★★
Contact: Mr R L Pine
Millers, 19 Mengham Road, Hayling Island PO11 9BG
T: (023) 92465951
F: (023) 92461321
E: millers@haylingproperty.co.uk
I: www.haylingproperty.co.uk

1 Nab Court ★★
Contact: Mr Roy Pine
Millers of Hayling, 19 Mengham Road, Hayling Island PO11 9BG
T: (023) 92465951
F: (023) 92461321
E: millers@haylingproperty.co.uk

63 North Shore Road ★★★★
Contact: Mr Roy Pine
Millers, 19 Mengham Road, Hayling Island PO11 9BG
T: (023) 92465951
F: (023) 92461321
E: millers@haylingproperty.co.uk
I: www.haylingproperty.co.uk

1 Ramsey Road ★★
Contact: Mr Roy Pine
Millers, 19 Mengham Road, Hayling Island PO11 9BG
T: (023) 92465951
F: (023) 92461321
E: millers@haylingproperty.co.uk
I: www.haylingproperty.co.uk

78 Sandypoint Road ★★
Contact: Mr Roy Pine
Millers, 19 Mengham Road, Hayling Island PO11 9BG
T: (023) 92465951
F: (023) 92461321
E: millers@haylingproperty.co.uk
I: www.haylingproperty.co.uk

84 Sea Front ★★★
Contact: Mr R L Pine
Millers, 19 Mengham Road, Hayling Island PO11 9BG
T: (023) 92465951
F: (023) 92461321
E: millers@haylingproperty.co.uk
I: www.haylingproperty.co.uk

10 Sidlesham Close ★★★
Contact:
Millers, 19 Mengham Road, Hayling Island PO11 9BG
T: (023) 9246 5951
F: (023) 9246 1321

88 Southwood Road ★★
Contact: Mr Roy Pine
Millers, 19 Mengham Road, Hayling Island PO11 9BG
T: (023) 92465951
F: (023) 92461321
E: millers@haylingproperty.co.uk

88c Southwood Road ★★
Contact: Mr Roy Pine
Millers, 19 Mengham Road, Hayling Island PO11 9BG
T: (023) 92465951
F: (023) 92461321
E: millers@haylingproperty.co.uk
I: www.haylingproperty.co.uk

5 Webb Close ★★★
Contact: Mr Roy Pine
Millers, 19 Mengham Road, Hayling Island PO11 9BG
T: (023) 92465951
F: (023) 92461321
E: millers@haylingproperty.co.uk
I: www.haylingproperty.co.uk

3 Wight View ★★★
Contact: Mr R L Pine
Millers of Hayling, 19 Mengham Road, Hayling Island PO11 9BG
T: (023) 92465951
F: (023) 92461321
E: millers@haylingproperty.co.uk
I: www.haylingproperty.com

26 Wittering Road ★★★★
Contact: Mr Roy Pine
Millers of Hayling, 19 Mengham Road, Hayling Island PO11 9BG
T: (023) 92465951
F: (023) 92461321
E: millers@haylingproperty.co.uk
I: www.haylingproperty.co.uk

HAYWARDS HEATH
West Sussex

Stevens Barn ★★★
Contact: Mr Richard Harris
Best of Brighton & Sussex Cottages Ltd, Vicarage Lane, Brighton BN2 7HD
T: (01273) 308779
F: (01273) 300266
E: brightoncottages@pavilion.co.uk
I: www.bestofbrighton.co.uk

HEADINGTON
Oxfordshire

Mulberry Self-Catering ★★★
Contact: Mr Gojko & Mrs Nada Miljkovic
Mulberry Guest House, 265 London Road, Oxford OX3 9EH
T: (01865) 767114
F: (01865) 767114
E: mulberryguesthouse@hotmail.com
I: www.oxfordcity.co.uk/accom/mulberrysc

Establishments printed in blue have a detailed entry in this guide

SOUTH EAST ENGLAND

HEATHFIELD
East Sussex

Boring House Farm The Cottage ★★★
Contact: Mrs Anne Reed
Boring House Farm The Cottage, Nettlesworth Lane, Heathfield TN21 9AS
T: (01435) 812285
E: info@boringhousefarm.co.uk
I: www.boringhousefarm.co.uk

HENFIELD
West Sussex

New Hall Cottage & New Hall Holiday Flat ★★★
Contact: Mrs Marjorie Carreck
New Hall Cottage & New Hall Holiday Flat, New Hall, New Hall Lane, Henfield BN5 9YJ
T: (01273) 492546

HENLEY-ON-THAMES
Oxfordshire

The Clock Tower & Beechwood Cottage ★★★★
Contact: Mrs Liz Martin
The Clock Tower & Beechwood Cottage, Lovesgroves Barn, Wyfold Road, Reading RG4 9HS
T: (0118) 9722365

141 Greys Road ★★★★
Contact: Mrs Janet King
Jersey Farmhouse, Colmore Lane, Kingwood Common, Henley-on-Thames RG9 5LX
T: (01491) 628486
F: (01491) 628015
E: mjking@btinternet.com
I: www.holiday.btinternet.co.uk

Jersey Farmhouse ★★★
Contact: Mrs Janet King
Jersey Farmhouse, Colmore Lane, Kingwood Common, Henley-on-Thames RG9 5LX
T: (01491) 628486
E: mjking@btinternet.com
I: www.holiday.btinternet.co.uk

Rotherleigh House Annexe ★★★
Contact: Mrs Jane Butler
Rotherleigh House Annexe, Rotherleigh House, Harpsden Way, Henley-on-Thames RG9 1NS
T: (01491) 572776
E: jvbutler57@hotmail.com
I: www.rotherleighannexe.co.uk

HERNE BAY
Kent

Arlington Lodge ★★★★
Contact: Mr Adrian Webb
45A Warren Road, Reigate RH2 0BN
T: (01737) 244385

HERONS GHYLL
East Sussex

The Stables ★★★★
Contact: Mrs Brenda Beck
Freedom Holiday Homes, 15 High Street, Cranbrook TN17 3EB
T: (01580) 720770
F: (01580) 720771
E: mail@freedomholidayhomes.co.uk
I: www.freedomholidayhomes.co.uk

HIGH HALDEN
Kent

Arundel Oast ★★★★★
Contact: Mrs Serena Maundrell
Arundel Oast, Woodchurch Road, Ashford TN26 3JQ
T: (01233) 850248
F: (01233) 850871
E: serena@vintageyears.demon.co.uk
I: www.vintage-years.co.uk

Crampton Lodge ★★★★
Contact: Mrs Brenda Beck
Freedom Holiday Homes, 15 High Street, Cranbrook TN17 3EB
T: (01580) 720770
F: (01580) 720771
E: mail@freedomholidayhomes.co.uk
I: www.freedomholidayhomes.co.uk

The Granary & The Stables ★★★★
Contact: Mrs Serena Maundrell
The Granary & The Stables, Hales Place, Ashford TN26 3JQ
T: (01233) 850871

Heron Cottage ★★★
Contact: Mr Stuart Winter
Garden of England Cottages, The Mews Office, 189A High Street, Tonbridge TN9 1BX
T: (01732) 369168
F: (01732) 358817
E: holidays@gardenofenglandcottages.co.uk
I: www.gardenofenglandcottages.co.uk

Mallard Cottage ★★★
Contact: Mr Stuart Winter
Garden of England Cottages, The Mews Office, 189A High Street, Tonbridge TN9 1BX
T: (01732) 369168
F: (01732) 358817
E: holidays@gardenofenglandcottages.co.uk
I: www.gardenofenglandcottages.co.uk

Mark Haven Cottage ★★★★
Contact: Mrs Brenda Beck
Freedom Holiday Homes, 15 High Street, Cranbrook TN17 3EB
T: (01580) 720770
F: (01580) 720771
E: mail@freedomholidayhomes.co.uk
I: www.freedomholidayhomes.co.uk

HIGH HURSTWOOD
East Sussex

Sunnymead Farm Cottages Rating Applied For
Contact: Mrs Joan Cooper
Sunnymead Farm Cottages, Perrymans Lane, Uckfield TN22 4AG
T: (01825) 733168

HIGHCLERE
Hampshire

Glencross Annexe ★★★
Contact: Mr Martyn Alexander
Glencross Annexe, Glencross, Mount Road, Newbury RG20 9QZ
T: (01635) 253244
F: (01635) 253244
E: martyn@owenalex.freeserve.co.uk

HIGHMOOR
Oxfordshire

Bay Tree Cottage ★★★★
Contact: Ms Carolyn Wyndham
Witheridge Hill Farm, Witheridge Hill, Henley-on-Thames RG9 5PE
T: (01491) 641229
F: (01491) 642260
E: baytree@hotmail.com

HILDENBOROUGH
Kent

The Cottage ★★★
Contact: Mr Dudley Hurrell
The Cottage, Coldharbour Lane, Tonbridge TN11 9LE
T: (01732) 832081
F: (01732) 832081

HOLLINGBOURNE
Kent

Well Cottage Northdowns Country Cottages Rating Applied For
Contact: Mr Paul Dixon
Northdowns Country Cottages, Hollingbourne House, Maidstone ME17 1QJ
T: (01622) 880116
F: (01622) 880991
E: angela@pauldixonphotography.co.uk

HOO
Medway

Whitehall Farmhouse ★★★★
Contact: Mr Dennis Reavell
Whitehall Farmhouse, Stoke Road, Rochester ME3 9NP
T: (01634) 250251
F: (01634) 251112
E: reavell@waystarltd.freeserve.co.uk
I: www.selfkater.com

HORSHAM
West Sussex

Walnut Barn & Walnut Cottage ★★★★-★★★★★
Contact: Mr Julian Cole
Walnut Barn & Walnut Cottage, Kerves Lane, Horsham RH13 6RJ
T: (01405) 249159
I: www.sussexholidaycottages.com

HORSMONDEN
Kent

Field Cottage ★★★
Contact: Mrs Brenda Beck
Freedom Holiday Homes, 15 High Street, Cranbrook TN17 3EB
T: (01580) 720770
F: (01580) 720771
E: mail@freedomholidayhomes.co.uk
I: www.freedomholidayhomes.co.uk

HORTON HEATH
Hampshire

The Stable at Rambler Cottage Rating Applied For
Contact: Mrs H Collins
The Stable at Rambler Cottage, Rambler Cottage, Chapel Drove, Eastleigh
T: (023) 80602755

HUNSTON
West Sussex

Well Cottage ★★★★
Contact: Mrs Paula Fountain
Well Cottage, Church Lane, Chichester PO20 1AJ
T: (01243) 530889
F: (01243) 537689
E: tomandpaula@lineone.net
I: www.wellcottagechichester.co.uk

HYDE
Hampshire

Holly Lea ★★★
Contact: Mr & Mrs Havelock
Fordingbridge SP6
T: (01425) 652456
F: (01425) 652456

HYTHE
Kent

Hydene Cottage ★★★★
Contact: Mrs Brenda Beck
Freedom Holiday Homes, 15 High Street, Cranbrook TN17 3EB
T: (01580) 720770
F: (01580) 720771
E: mail@freedomholidayhomes.co.uk
I: www.freedomholidayhomes.co.uk

Hythe Period Cottage ★★★
Contact: Mrs Sophie James
73 Donald Street, Roath, Cardiff CF24 4TL
T: (029) 2048 0667
E: sophie-james123@hotmail.com

Uppermill ★★★
Contact: Mrs Nicola Hooshangpour
Marston Properties Ltd, 1 Stephendale Road, London SW6 2LU
T: (020) 77367133
F: (020) 7731 8412
E: nicky@marstonproperties.co.uk
I: www.marstonproperties.co.uk

Waterfront House ★★★★★
Contact: Mr & Mrs Cunningham
Lime Walk, Southampton SO45 4RA
T: (023) 80842460
E: alexcunningham@waitrose.com
I: www.users.waitrose.com/~alexcunningham

IBSLEY
Hampshire

Chocolate Box Cottage ★★★★★
Contact: Mrs Higham
T: 07768 075761
I: www.chocolateboxcottage.co.uk

SOUTH EAST ENGLAND

Crofton ★★★★★
Contact: Mrs Julie Hordle
Crofton, Mockbeggar Lane,
Ringwood BH24 3PR
T: (01425) 471829
E: crofton@tiscali.co.uk
I: www.croftonewforest.co.uk

ICKLESHAM
East Sussex

Broadstairs House ★★★
Contact: Mr Stuart Winter
Broadstairs House, Workhouse
Lane, Winchelsea TN36 4AJ
T: (01732) 369168
F: (01732) 358817
E: holiday@
gardenofenglandcottages.co.uk
I: www.
gardenofenglandcottages.co.uk

Garden Cottage ★★★
Contact: Mr Stuart Winter
Garden of England Cottages, The
Mews Office, 189A High Street,
Tonbridge TN9 1BX
T: (01732) 369168
F: (01732) 358817
E: holidays@
gardenofenglandcottages.co.uk
I: www.
gardenofenglandcottages.co.uk

The Oast Cottage ★★★★
Contact: Mrs Brenda Beck
Freedom Holiday Homes, 15
High Street, Cranbrook
TN17 3EB
T: (01580) 720770
F: (01580) 720771
E: mail@freedomholidayhomes.
co.uk
I: www.freedomholidayhomes.
co.uk

The Stable ★★★
Contact: Mr Stuart Winter
Garden of England Cottages, The
Mews Office, 189A High Street,
Tonbridge TN9 1BX
T: (01732) 369168
F: (01732) 358817
E: holidays@
gardenofenglandcottages.co.uk
I: www.
gardenofenglandcottages.co.uk

IFFLEY
Oxfordshire

13B Abberbury Road
★★★★
Contact: Mr Christopher
Griffiths
13B Abberbury Road, Oxford
OX4 4ET
T: (01865) 776904

INKPEN
West Berkshire

Beacon Cottage ★★★
Contact: Mr Nick Pash
Hideaways, Chapel House, Luke
Street, Shaftesbury SP7 0HQ
T: (01747) 828170
F: (01747) 829090
E: enq@hideaways.co.uk
I: www.hideaways.co.uk

IPING
West Sussex

River Meadow Flat ★★★
Contact: Mr Tim & Mrs Rowena
Hill
River Meadow Flat, Midhurst
GU29 0PE
T: (01730) 814713

The Studio ★★★
Contact: Claudia Callingham
The Studio, Kinrose House, Titty
Mill, Midhurst GU29 0PL
T: (01428) 741561
F: (01428) 741561

IPSDEN
Oxfordshire

**The Old Stables at
Wellplace Barns** ★★★★
Contact: Mr Robert & Mrs Jenny
Booth
Wellplace Barns, Wellplace,
Wallingford OX10 6QY
T: (01491) 681158
F: (01491) 681158
E: wellplacebarns@aol.com
I: www.holiday-rentals.co.uk
(property 2664)

ITCHEN ABBAS
Hampshire

Itchen Down Farm
Rating Applied For
Contact: Mr R Burge
Itchen Down Farm, Itchen Down,
Winchester SO21 1BS
T: (01962) 779388

IVINGHOE
Buckinghamshire

**Town Farm Holiday
Cottages** ★★★
Contact: Mrs Angie Leach
Town Farm Holiday Cottages,
Icknield Way, Leighton Buzzard
LU7 9EL
T: (01296) 668455
F: (01296) 668455
E: angie@unlimitedlets.com
I: www.unlimitedlets.com

KEMSING
Kent

6 Dippers Close ★★★
Contact: Mr & Mrs Ronald Rose
6 Dippers Close, Sevenoaks
TN15 6QD
T: (01732) 761937

KILMESTON
Hampshire

**College Down Farm Self
Catering Holidays** ★★★
Contact: Mr Eric Ruff
College Down Farm Self
Catering Holidays, College Down
Farm, Alresford SO24 0NS
T: (01962) 771345

KING'S SOMBORNE
Hampshire

By the Way Annexe ★★★
Contact: Dr Penny Morgan
By the Way Annexe, Romsey
Road, Kings Somborne,
Stockbridge SO20 6PR
T: (01794) 388469
E: penny@bytheway4.freeserve.
co.uk

2 Crown Cottages ★★★
Contact: Mrs Maureen Banks
3 Croft Lane, Banbury OX17 3NB
T: (01295) 810539
E: maureen.banks@tesco.net

KINGSTON
East Sussex

Nightingales ★★★★
Contact: Mrs Jean Hudson
Nightingales, The Avenue, Lewes
BN7 3LL
T: (01273) 475673
F: (01273) 475673
E: Nightingales@totalise.co.uk
I: www.user.totalise.
co.uk/nightingales/

Roman Way ★★★★
Contact: Mrs Pippa Campbell
Roman Way, Kingston Ridge,
Lewes BN7 3JX
T: (01273) 476583
F: (01273) 476583
E: camp1942@aol.com

LAKE
Isle of Wight

The Dolphins ★★★
Contact: Mrs Lisa Baskill
Home from Home Holidays, 31
Pier Street, Ventnor PO38 1SX
T: (01983) 854340
F: (01983) 855524
E: admin@hfromh.co.uk

LAMBERHURST
Kent

Goldings Barn ★★★
Contact: Mrs Brenda Beck
Freedom Holiday Homes, 15
High Street, Cranbrook
TN17 3EB
T: (01580) 720770
F: (01580) 720771
E: mail@freedomholidayhomes.
co.uk
I: www.freedomholidayhomes.
co.uk

The Hideaway ★★★
Contact: Mrs Brenda Beck
Freedom Holiday Homes, 15
High Street, Cranbrook
TN17 3EB
T: (01580) 720770
F: (01580) 720771
E: mail@freedomholidayhomes.
co.uk
I: www.freedomholidayhomes.
co.uk

**Oast Cottage, Orchard
Cottage & The Oast House -
Barnfield Oast Self**
★★★-★★★★
Contact: Mrs Brenda Beck
Freedom Holiday Homes, 15
High Street, Cranbrook
TN17 3EB
T: (01580) 720770
F: (01580) 720771
E: mail@freedomholidayhomes.
co.uk
I: www.freedomholidayhomes.
co.uk

Owls Castle Oast ★★★★
Contact: Mrs Sally Bingham
Owls Castle Oast, Hoghole Lane,
Royal Tunbridge Wells TN3 8BN
T: (01892) 890758
F: (01892) 890215
E: sally.bingham1@
btopenworld.com

LAUGHTON
East Sussex

Holly Cottage ★★★
Contact: Mr David & Mrs Pat
Fuller
Holly Cottage, Lewes Road,
Lewes BN8 6BL
T: (01323) 811309
F: (01323) 811106
E: hollycottage@tinyworld.
co.uk
I: www.smoothhound-co.uk

LAVANT
West Sussex

South Cottage ★★★★
Contact: Mr Graham Davies
South Cottage, Raughmere
Drive, Chichester PO18 0AB
T: (01243) 527120
E: gmd@cix.co.uk

LEAFIELD
Oxfordshire

King John's Barn ★★★★
Contact: Mrs Vicky Greves
Langley Lodge, Langley, Witney
OX29 9QD
T: (01993) 878075
F: (01993) 878774
E: info@kingjohnsbarn.co.uk
I: www.kingjohnsbarn.co.uk

LEE COMMON
Buckinghamshire

The Cottage ★★★
Contact: Mrs Bette Brumpton
High Beeches, Ballinger Road,
Great Missenden HP16 9NE
T: (01494) 837246

LEE ON THE SOLENT
Hampshire

Bay Tree Lodge ★★★
Contact: Mr Dave Danns
197 Portsmouth Road, Gosport
PO13 9AA
T: (023) 9255 2550
F: (023) 9255 4657
E: dave@baytreelodge.co.uk
I: www.baytreelodge.co.uk

The Beach House ★★★
Contact: Mrs Driver
The Beach House, 142
Portsmouth Road, Lee on the
Solent PO13 9AE
T: (023) 92554882

The Chart House ★★★
Contact: Mr Brook White
6 Cambridge Road, Lee on the
Solent PO13 9DH
T: (023) 9255 4145
F: (023) 9255 3847
E: marion_kinnear-white@
talk21.com
I: www.brook.white1.btinternet.
co.uk

Holly House
Rating Applied For
Contact: Mrs Jane Windsor
25 Raynes Road, Lee on the
Solent PO13 9AJ
T: (023) 92551016
F: (023) 92551016

Kinderton House ★★★
Contact: Mrs Jean Miller
Kinderton House, 13 Marine
Parade West, Lee on the Solent
PO13 9LW
T: (023) 92552056

Establishments printed in blue have a detailed entry in this guide

SOUTH EAST ENGLAND

LEEDS
Kent
1 & 2 Orchard View ★★★
Contact: Mr Stuart Winter
1 & 2 Orchard View, Eyhorne Street, Maidstone ME17 1TS
T: (01732) 369168
F: (01732) 358817
E: holidays@gardenofenglandcottages.co.uk
I: www.gardenofenglandcottages.co.uk

LEIGH
Kent
The Old Stables ★★★★
Contact: Mr & Mrs Nicholas Morris
Charcott Farmhouse, Charcott, Tonbridge TN11 8LG
T: (01892) 870024
F: (01892) 870158
E: nicholasmorris@charcott.freeserve.co.uk
I: www.smoothhound.co.uk/hotels/charcott

LENHAM
Kent
Apple Pye Cottage ★★★★
Contact: Mrs Patricia Diane Leat
Apple Pye Cottage, Bramley Knowle Farm, Eastwood Road, Maidstone ME17 1ET
T: (01622) 858878
F: (01622) 851121
E: diane@bramleyknowlefarm.co.uk
I: www.bramleyknowlefarm.co.uk

Court Lodge Cottage ★★
Contact: Mrs Brenda Beck
Freedom Holiday Homes, 15 High Street, Cranbrook TN17 3EB
T: (01580) 720770
F: (01580) 720771
E: mail@freedomholidayhomes.co.uk
I: www.freedomholidayhomes.co.uk

Holiday Cottage
Rating Applied For
Contact: Mrs Brenda Beck
Freedom Holiday Homes, 15 High Street, Cranbrook TN17 3EB
T: (01580) 720770
F: (01580) 720771
E: mail@freedomholidayhomes.co.uk
I: www.freedomholidayhomes.co.uk

5 Lime Tree Cottages ★★★
Contact: Mr Peter Hasler
4 Lime Tree Cottages, Pilgrims Way, Lenham, Maidstone ME17 2EY
T: (01622) 851310
F: (01622) 853186
E: pvhasler@hotmail.com
I: www.kentcottage.com

The Olde Shoppe ★★★
Contact: Mrs Brenda Beck
Freedom Holiday Homes, 15 High Street, Cranbrook TN17 3EB
T: (01580) 720770
F: (01580) 720771
E: mail@freedomholidayhomes.co.uk
I: www.freedomholidayhomes.co.uk

LEWES
East Sussex
5 Buckhurst Close ★★★
Contact: Mrs S Foulds
66 Houndean Rise, Lewes BN7 1EJ
T: (01273) 474755
F: (01273) 474755

66 Court Road ★★★
Contact: Mr Richard Harris
66 Court Road, Lewes BN7 2SA
T: (01273) 308779
F: (01273) 300266

The Finings
Rating Applied For
Contact: Ms Sara Gosling
The Cooperage, Castle Precincts, Lewes BN7 1YT
T: (01273) 480084

24 St Johns Terrace ★★★
Contact: Mr Richard Harris
Best of Brighton & Sussex Cottages Ltd, Vicarage Lane, Brighton BN2 7HD
T: (01273) 308779
F: (01273) 300266
E: brightoncottages@pavilion.co.uk
I: www.bestofbrighton.co.uk

Sussex Countryside Accommodation ★★★★
Contact: Mrs Hazel Gaydon
Sussex Countryside Accommodation, Barcombe Mills Road, Lewes BN8 5BJ
T: (01273) 400625
F: (01273) 401893
E: info@crinkhouse.co.uk
I: www.sussexcountryaccommodation.co.uk

LILLINGSTONE LOVELL
Buckinghamshire
Little Thatch ★★★★
Contact: Mrs Jane Scott
9 Brookside, Buckingham MK18 5BD
T: (01280) 860014
F: (01280) 860014
E: janegscott@lineone.net
I: www.thatchedholidaycottage.co.uk

LINTON
Kent
Loddington Oast ★★★★
Contact: Mr Richard & Mrs Valerie Martin
Loddington Oast, Loddington Lane, Maidstone ME17 4AG
T: (01622) 747777
F: (01622) 746991
E: rm_trsystems@btinternet.com
I: www.loddingtonoast.co.uk

LITTLE HORSTED
East Sussex
Crumps Corner
Rating Applied For
Contact: Mrs K Clark
10 East Street, Lewes BN7 2LJ
T: (01273) 473685

LITTLEHAMPTON
West Sussex
8 The Cape ★★★
Contact: Miss Mary Fitzgerald
Torrington Holiday Flats, 60 Manor Road, Worthing BN11 4SL
T: (01903) 238582

Dormer Cottage ★★★
Contact: Mrs Susan Ogrodnik
Victoria Holidays, 86 South Terrace, Littlehampton BN17 5LJ
T: (01903) 722644

Racing Greens ★★★
Contact: Mrs Eileen Thomas
Racing Greens, 70 South Terrace, Littlehampton BN17 5LQ
T: (01903) 732972
F: (01903) 732932

Victoria Holidays ★★★
Contact: Mrs Ogrodnik
Victoria Holidays, 86 South Terrace, Littlehampton BN17 5LJ
T: (01903) 722644

LOCKINGE
Oxfordshire
The Coach House ★★★★
Contact: Mrs Janine Beaumont
The Coach House, Andersey Farm, Grove Park Drive, Wantage OX12 8SG
T: (01235) 771866
F: (01235) 771866

LOCKS HEATH
Hampshire
Stepping Stones ★★★★
Contact: Mrs Barbara Habens
Stepping Stones, 126 Locks Heath Park Road, Locks Heath, Southampton SO31 6LZ
T: (01489) 572604
E: jimhabens@aol.com
I: http://members.lycos.co.uk/selfcateringannexe/

LONGPARISH
Hampshire
Cowleaze Cottage
Rating Applied For
Contact: Mrs Tracey Chuter
Moundsmere Estate Management Ltd, Basingstoke RG25 2HE
T: (01256) 389253
F: (01256) 389508
E: clive@moundsmere.co.uk
I: www.moundsmere.co.uk

LOOSE
Kent
Bockingford Steps Barn ★★★
Contact: Mrs Jennifer Buckley
Bockingford Steps, Bockingford Lane, Maidstone ME15 6DP
T: (01622) 756030

LOUDWATER
Buckinghamshire
Daisy's Cottage ★★★★
Contact: Mrs Julia Newman
Daisy's Cottage, Derehams Lane, High Wycombe HP10 9RR
T: (01494) 520964
F: (01494) 520964
E: newmanwill@aol.com

LOWER BEEDING
West Sussex
Black Cottage, the Little Barn & the Old Dairy
★★★-★★★★
Contact: Mrs Vicky Storey
Black Cottage, the Little Barn & the Old Dairy, Newells Lane, Horsham RH13 6LN
T: (01403) 891326
F: (01403) 891530
E: vicky.storey@btinternet.com

LOWER BOURNE
Surrey
Timberline ★★
Contact: Mrs Sandra Daplyn
Rockhopper Retreats Ltd, High Barn, Tilford Road, Farnham GU10 2LS
T: (01428) 605809
E: sandra@rockhopperretreats.co.uk
I: www.rockhopperretreats.co.uk

LYDD
Kent
1 & 2 Riddlers Cottages ★★★
Contact: Mr Glyn Swift
1 & 2 Riddlers Cottages, Romney Farm, Romney Road, Romney Marsh TN29 9LS
T: (01797) 361499

LYDD ON SEA
Kent
69 Coast Drive ★★★
Contact: Mrs Brenda Beck
Freedom Holiday Homes, 15 High Street, Cranbrook TN17 3EB
T: (01580) 720770
F: (01580) 720771
E: mail@freedomholidayhomes.co.uk
I: www.freedomholidayhomes.co.uk

LYMINGTON
Hampshire
8 Admirals Court ★★★★
Contact: Mrs Mayes
Ridgeway Rents New Forest Cottages, 4 Quay Hill, Lymington SO41 3AR
T: (01590) 679655
F: (01590) 670989
E: holidays@newforestcottages.co.uk
I: www.newforestcottages.co.uk

Badgers Holt ★★★★
Contact: Mrs Mary Brockett
Badgers Holt, Newlands Manor, Lymington SO41 0JH
T: (01590) 645941
E: gothic_cottage@hotmail.com

586 Look out for establishments participating in the National Accessible Scheme

SOUTH EAST ENGLAND

4 Belmore Lane ★★
Contact: Mrs Jacquie Taylor
Three Corners, Centre Lane,
Lymington SO41 0JP
T: (01590) 645217
E: tommy.tiddles@virgin.net
I: www.halcyonholidays.com

Bourne House ★★★★
Contact: Mr & Mrs Mare
Maybury Wood Cottage, The
Ridge, Woking GU22 7EG
T: (01483) 772086
F: (01483) 772086
E: jppmare@aol.com

Corner Cottages ★★★★
Contact: Mrs Ginny Neath
Courtyard Cottage, Main Road,
Brockenhurst SO42 7WD
T: (01590) 612080
E: rg.neath@virgin.net

3 Court Close ★★★
Contact: Mr Darren Roberts
Halcyon Holidays, 48 Church
Lane, Lymington SO41 3RD
T: (01590) 645217
F: (01590) 673633
E: tommy.tiddles@virgin.net
I: www.halcyonholidays.com

**De La Warr House
★★★-★★★★★**
Contact: Mrs Joanne Broadway
De La Warr House, All Saints
Road, Lymington SO41 8FB
T: (01590) 672785
F: (01590) 672785
E: delawarrhouse@aol.com
I: www.delawarrhouse.co.uk

Fir Tree Cottage ★★★
Contact: Mrs Saword
1 Merlewood Court, Lyon
Avenue, New Milton BH25 6AP
T: (01425) 617219

**No.17 Southampton Road
★★★★**
Contact: Miss Julie Stevens &
Andrew Baxendine
Elm Cottage, Pilley Bailey,
Lymington SO41 5QT
T: (01590) 676445
E: juleestevens@aol.com
I: www.17southamptonroad.
co.uk

**94 Queen Katherine Road
★★★**
Contact: Mrs Jan Anstey Hayes
2 Bonham Road, London
SW2 5HF
T: (020) 77712384
E: j.anstey-hayes@talk21.com

Rainbow Cottage ★★★
Contact: Mr & Mrs Mare
Maybury Wood Cottage, The
Ridge, Woking GU22 7EG
T: (01483) 772086
F: (01483) 772086
E: jppmare@aol.com

Saltmarsh ★★★★
Contact: Mr James Cecil-Wright
Garden Cottage, Kitwalls Lane,
Lymington SO41 0RJ
T: (01590) 642965
E: gardctg@aol.com
I: www.saltmarsh.biz

Silk Cottage ★★★★
Contact: Mrs Anne Paterson
Silkhouse, 77 Lower Buckland
Road, Lymington SO41 9DR
T: (01590) 688797
F: (01590) 688797
E: anne@silkcottage.com
I: www.silkcottage.com

Solent Reach Mews ★★★★
Contact: Ms Denise Farmer
Solent Reach Mews, Lower
Pennington Lane, Lymington
SO41 8AN
T: (01590) 671648
F: (01590) 689244
E: enquiries@hurstviewleisure.
co.uk
I: www.solentreachmews.co.uk

8 Station Street ★★★
Contact: Mrs Joanne Hill
J R Hill Residential Letting
Agency, 12 Stanford Road,
Lymington SO41 9GF
T: (01590) 679200
F: (01590) 677915
E: enquiries@jrhill.co.uk

Waterford Cottage ★★★★
Contact: Mrs Sally Sargeaunt
33 Barton Court Avenue, Barton
on Sea, New Milton BH25 7EP
T: (01425) 628970
F: (01425) 620399

LYNDHURST
Hampshire

Acorn Cottage ★★★★
Contact: Mrs April Robinson
Lyndhurst Cottages, Boltons
House, Princes Crescent,
Lyndhurst SO43 7BS
T: (023) 80283000
E: visit@lyndhurstcottages.
co.uk
I: www.lyndhurstcottages.co.uk

The Cottage ★★★
Contact: Mrs Sheila Robinson
The Cottage, The Old Stables,
Pikes Hill, Lyndhurst SO43 7AY
T: (023) 80283697

95B High Street ★★★
Contact: Mr & Mrs John
Langston
Monkton Cottage, 93 High
Street, Lyndhurst SO43 7BH
T: (023) 8028 2206
F: (023) 8028 2206

Holly Cottage ★★★★
Contact: Mr & Mrs F S Turner
Greensward, The Crescent,
Ashurst, Southampton
SO40 7AQ
T: (023) 8029 2374
F: (023) 8029 2374
E: sam@turner402.fsnet.co.uk
I: http://mysite.
wanadoo-members.
co.uk/hollycottnewforest

Link Place ★★★★
Contact: Mrs April Robinson
Lyndhurst Cottages, Boltons
House, Princes Crescent,
Lyndhurst SO43 7BS
T: (023) 80283000
E: enquiries@
lyndhurstcottages.co.uk
I: www.lyndhurstcottages.co.uk

**Penny Farthing Hotel &
Cottages ★★★★**
Contact: Mike/Linda/Sue
Penny Farthing Hotel &
Cottages, Romsey Road,
Lyndhurst SO43 7AA
T: (023) 8028 4422
F: (023) 8028 4488
I: www.pennyfarthinghotel.
co.uk

Puckpitts Cottage ★★★★
Contact: Mr & Mrs R H M
Stennett
36 Westwood Road,
Southampton SO17 1DP
T: (023) 80557426

Stable Cottage ★★
Contact: Mr Stephen Morris
Huntley Farm, Patch Elm Lane,
Bristol BS37 7LU
T: (01454) 227322
F: (01454) 227323
E: newforest.cottage@
btinternet.com
I: www.newforestcottages.net

MAIDENHEAD
Windsor and Maidenhead

11 Cadwell Drive ★★★
Contact: Mrs Vivien Williams
32 York Road, Maidenhead
SL6 1SF
T: (01628) 627370
F: (01628) 627370
E: rvwilliams@btopenworld.com

Courtyard Cottages ★★★★
Contact: Mrs Carol Bardo
Moor Farm, Ascot Road,
Maidenhead SL6 2HY
T: (01628) 633761
F: (01628) 636167
E: moorfm@aol.com
I: www.moorfarm.com

**Sheephouse Manor
★★-★★★★**
Contact: Mrs Caroline Street
Sheephouse Manor, Sheephouse
Road, Maidenhead SL6 8HJ
T: (01628) 776902
F: (01628) 625138
E: info@sheephousemanor.
co.uk
I: www.sheephousemanor.co.uk

MAIDSTONE
Kent

Kentish Court ★★★★
Contact: Mr Stuart Winter
Kentish Court, London Road,
Maidstone ME16 8AA
T: (01732) 369168
F: (01732) 358817
E: holidays@
gardenofenglandcottages.co.uk
I: www.
gardenofenglandcottages.co.uk

20 Kings Walk ★★★★
Contact: Mr Stuart Winter
Garden of England Cottages, The
Mews Office, 189A High Street,
Tonbridge TN9 1BX
T: (01732) 369168
F: (01732) 358817
E: holidays@
gardenofenglandcottages.co.uk
I: www.
gardenofenglandcottages.co.uk

Lavender Cottage ★★
T: (01622) 850287
E: lavender@nascr.net
I: www.oas.
co.uk/ukcottages/lavender

Orchard Flat ★★
Contact: Mrs Pamela Clark
Orchard Flat, Farlaga, Vicarage
Lane, Maidstone ME15 0LX
T: (01622) 726919
E: pamclark@ferlaga.freeserve.
co.uk

Twitchers ★★★★★
Contact: Mrs Brenda Beck
Freedom Holiday Homes, 15
High Street, Cranbrook
TN17 3EB
T: (01580) 720770
F: (01580) 720771
E: mail@freedomholidayhomes.
co.uk

MAPLEDURHAM
Oxfordshire

**Mapledurham Holiday
Cottages ★★-★★★★★**
Contact: Mrs Lola Andrews
Mapledurham Holiday Cottages,
The Estate Office, Reading
RG4 7TR
T: (0118) 9724292
F: (0118) 9724016
E: mtrust1997@aol.com
I: www.mapledurham.co.uk

MARDEN
Kent

Redstock ★★★★
Contact: Mr Stuart Winter
Redstock, Goudhurst Road,
Tonbridge TN12 9JT
T: (01732) 369168
F: (01732) 358817
E: holidays@
gardenofenglandcottages.co.uk
I: www.
gardenofenglandcottages.co.uk

MARGATE
Kent

House Palm Bay ★★★
Contact: Mrs Bowles
57 Rectory Lane North, West
Malling ME19 5HD
T: (01732) 843396
F: (01732) 843396
E: richardbowles@blueyonder.
co.uk

Lombard House ★★★★
Contact: Ms Janet Williams
71 Sea Road, Margate CT8 8QG
T: 07879 630257

Salmestone Grange ★★★
Contact: Mr William Whelan
Salmestone Grange, Nash Road,
Margate CT9 4BX
T: (01843) 231161
F: (01843) 231161
E: salmestongrange@aol.com
I: www.salmestongrange.co.uk

Establishments printed in blue have a detailed entry in this guide

SOUTH EAST ENGLAND

MARSH GREEN
Kent
Littleworth Cottage ★★★★
Contact: Mr Stuart Winter
Littleworth Cottage, Moor Lane,
Edenbridge TN8 5QU
T: (01732) 369168
F: (01732) 358817
E: holidays@
gardenofenglandcottages.co.uk
I: www.
gardenofenglandcottages.co.uk

MATFIELD
Kent
Chestnut Cottage
Rating Applied For
Contact: Mr Stuart Winter
Garden of England Cottages, The
Mews Office, 189A High Street,
Tonbridge TN9 1BX
T: (01732) 369168
F: (01732) 358817
E: holidays@
gardenofenglandcottages.co.uk
I: www.
gardenofenglandcottages.co.uk

MEDSTEAD
Hampshire
The Barn ★★★
Contact: Mrs Sarah Darch
Barford Farm House, Common
Hill, Alton GU34 5LZ
T: (01420) 562682
F: (01420) 562682

MERSHAM
Kent
Gill Farm ★★★★
Contact: Mrs Jan Bowman
Gill Farm, Gill Lane, Ashford
TN25 7HZ
T: (01303) 261247
F: (01233) 721622
E: gillfarm@studio2uk.com
I: www.studio2uk.com/gillfarm

MERSTONE
Isle of Wight
Chapel Cottage ★★★★
Contact: Mrs Honor Vass
Island Cottage Holidays, The Old
Vicarage, Kingston, Wareham
BH20 5LH
T: (01929) 480080
F: (01929) 481070
E: enq@islandcottagesholidays.
com

MICHELDEVER
Hampshire
Garden Cottage ★★★★
Contact: Mrs Elaine Walker
Garden Cottage, Hope Cottage,
Winchester Road, Winchester
SO21 3DG
T: (01962) 774221
F: (01962) 774818
E: hopeis@btinternet.com

MIDHURST
West Sussex
**Cowdray Park Holiday
Cottages ★★★★**
Contact: Mrs Sam Collins
Cowdray Park Holiday Cottages,
Cowdray Estate Office, Cowdray
Park, Midhurst GU29 0AQ
T: (01730) 812423
F: (01730) 815608
E: enquires@cowdray.co.uk
I: www.cowdray.co.uk

MILFORD ON SEA
Hampshire
Bethany ★★★★
Contact: Mrs J A Green
The Vicarage, Station Road,
Lymington SO41 6BA
T: (01590) 683389
F: (01590) 683389
E: jackiegreen@onetel.net.uk
I: www.bethany-milford.com

Curlew Cottage ★★★
Contact: Mrs Sally Edgar
Flexford Rise, Flexford Lane,
Lymington SO41 6DN
T: (01590) 683744

Forest Farm ★★★
Contact: Ms Pippa Jarman
Forest Farm, Barnes Lane,
Milford on Sea, Lymington
SO41 0RR
T: (01590) 644365
F: (01590) 644365
E: driving@ffarm.fsnet.co.uk
I: www.forestfarmdriving.com

3 Kingfisher Court ★★★
Contact: Mrs Olga Budden
111 Milford Road, Lymington
SO41 8DN
T: (01590) 671492
F: (01590) 672012
E: budden1@onetel.net.uk
I: www.kingfishers.info

Maryland Court
Rating Applied For
Contact: Mr Robin Drake
12 Glebe Fields, Milford on Sea,
Lymington SO41 0WW
T: (01590) 643624

The Old Bakery ★★★
Contact: Mrs Braithwaite
Bay Tree Cottage, Bashley
Common Road, New Milton
BH25 5SQ
T: (01425) 620733

Old Walls ★★★
Contact: Mrs Kate Danby
Old Walls, Church Hill,
Lymington SO41 0QJ
T: (01590) 642138
F: (01590) 642138
E: mrskatedanby@aol.com

Penny Pot ★★★★
Contact: Mr Roy Plummer
Penny Pot, Whitby Road, 16
Milford on Sea, Lymington
SO41 0ND
T: (01590) 641210
E: pennypot@hapennyhouse.
co.uk
I: www.hapennyhouse.
co.uk/pennypot.htm

Pine View Cottage ★★★★
Contact: Mrs Sheri Gadd
Cherry Trees, Lymington Road,
Lymington SO41 0QL
T: (01590) 643746
E: cherrytrees@beeb.net
I: www.theaa.
co.uk/region12/98653.
htmlnewforest.demon.
co.uk/cherrytrees.htm

Windmill Cottage ★★★
Contact: Mrs Perham
Danescourt, 14 Kivernell Road,
Milton on Sea, Lymington
SO41 0PQ
T: (01590) 643516
F: (01590) 641255

MINSTEAD
Hampshire
Minstead House ★★★★
Contact: Mrs Isabel Morton
Minstead House, School Lane,
Lyndhurst SO43 7GL
T: (023) 80813824
E: ismorton@aol.com
I: www.members.aol.
com/minsteadhouse/holidays

MINSTER-IN-THANET
Kent
Durlock Lodge ★★★
Contact: Mr David Sworder
Durlock Lodge, Durlock,
Ramsgate CT12 4HD
T: (01843) 821219
E: david@durlocklodge.co.uk
I: www.durlocklodge.co.uk

MOLLINGTON
Oxfordshire
**The Stables, The Shippon,
The Byre - Anita's Holiday
Cottages ★★★-★★★★★**
Contact: Mr Darrel & Mrs Anita
Gail Jeffries
Anita's Holiday Cottages, The
Yews, Church Farm, Banbury
OX17 1AZ
T: (01295) 750731
F: (01295) 750731

MONXTON
Hampshire
The Den at Millcroft ★★★★
Contact: Mrs Pat Hayward
The Den at Millcroft, Millcroft,
Chalkpit Lane, Andover
SP11 8AR
T: (01264) 710618
F: (01264) 710615
E: millcroft@aol.com

MORETON
Oxfordshire
**Meadowbrook Farm
Holiday Cottages ★★★★**
Contact: Mrs Diana Wynn
Meadowbrook Farm Holiday
Cottages, Moreton, Thame
OX9 2HY
T: (01844) 212116
F: (01844) 217503
E: rdwynn@ukonline.co.uk

MURSLEY
Buckinghamshire
The Barn ★★★★
Contact: Mrs Jenny Dobbs
Fourpenny Cottage, 23 Main
Street, Milton Keynes MK17 0RT
T: (01296) 720544
F: (01296) 720906
E: fourpennycottage@
tinyworld.co.uk
I: www.fourpennycottage.co.uk

NAPHILL
Buckinghamshire
High Gables ★★★★
Contact: Mr Stefan Zachary
High Gables, Stocking Lane, High
Wycombe HP14 4RE
T: (01494) 562591
F: (01494) 562592
E: zach@btinternet.com.
wwwzachary.co.uk

NEW MILTON
Hampshire
Appletree Cottage
Rating Applied For
Contact: Mr Mike Harding
33 The Ridgeway, Bracknell
RG12 9QU

Dahlia Cottage ★★★★
Contact: Mr Ken Claxton
19 Elmcroft Drive, Chessington
KT9 1DZ
T: (020) 83978825
E: freqabev@hotmail.com

The Granary ★★
Contact: Mr Daniel & Mrs Jane
Fish
Woodcutters, St Johns Road,
Bashley, New Milton BH25 5SD
T: (01425) 610332
F: (01425) 610332
E: danfishsurface@onetel.net.uk

NEWBRIDGE
Isle of Wight
Laurel Cottage ★★★★
Contact: Mrs Honor Vass
Island Cottage Holidays, The Old
Vicarage, Kingston, Wareham
BH20 5LH
T: (01929) 480080
F: (01929) 481070
E: enq@islandcottageholidays.
com
I: www.islandcottageholidays.
com

Lavender Cottage ★★★★
Contact: Mrs Lisa Baskill
31 Pier Street, Ventnor
PO38 1SX
T: (01983) 854340
F: (01983) 855524

Lower Calbourne Mill
Rating Applied For
Contact: Mr & Mrs P J French
Lower Calbourne Mill,
Caulbourne Lane, Yarmouth
PO41 0TZ
T: (01983) 531228

NEWBURY
West Berkshire
Barn House ★★★★
Contact: Mrs Edwards
Barn House, Enborne Street,
Newbury RG20 0JP
T: (01635) 253443
F: (01635) 253443

Peregrine Cottage ★★★★★
Contact: Mrs Elizabeth Knight
Peregrine House, Enborne Street,
Newbury RG14 6RP
T: (01635) 42585
F: (01635) 528775
E: lizknight@amserve.net

SOUTH EAST ENGLAND

Yaffles ★★★-★★★★★
Contact: Mr Tony & Mrs Jean Bradford
Yaffles, Red Shute Hill, Thatcham RG18 9QH
T: (01635) 201100
F: (01635) 201100
E: yaffles@ukonline.co.uk
I: www.cottagesdirect.com/yaffles & www.ukonline.co.uk/yaffles

NEWCHURCH
Isle of Wight

Barn Cottage ★★★
Contact: Mrs Anne Corbin
Knighton Barn, Knighton Shute, Sandown PO36 0NT
T: (01983) 865349
F: (01983) 865349
E: anne.cobin@virgin.net
I: www.wightfarmholidays.co.uk

Clematis ★★★
Contact: Mr A & Mrs B Jupe
The Laurels, High Street, Sandown PO36 0NJ
T: (01983) 867613
F: (01983) 868214
E: alistair.jupe@btinternet.com
I: www.btinternet.com/~alistair.jupe/

Knighton Farmhouse ★★★★
Contact: Mrs Honor Vass
Island Cottage Holidays, West Street, Kingston, Corfe Castle, Wareham BH20 5LH
T: (01929) 480080
F: (01929) 481070
E: enq@islandcottageholidays.com
I: www.islandcottageholidays.com

Knighton Gorges ★★★
Contact: Mrs Honor Vass
Island Cottage Holidays, The Old Vicarage, Kingston, Wareham BH20 5LH
T: (01929) 480080
F: (01929) 4810700
E: enq@islandcottageholidays.com
I: www.islandcottageholidays.com

Mersley Farm ★★★
Contact: Mrs Jennifer Boswell
Mersley Farm, Mersley Lane, Sandown PO36 0NR
T: (01983) 865213
F: (01983) 862294
E: jenny@mersleyfarm.co.uk
I: www.mersleyfarm.co.uk

Paper Barn & Squire Thatchers Barn ★★★★
Contact: Mrs Honor Vass
Island Cottage Holidays, The Old Vicarage, Kingston, Wareham BH20 5LH
T: (01929) 481555

NEWENDEN
Kent

The Bothy & The Barn ★★★-★★★★★
Contact: Mrs Brenda Beck
Freedom Holiday Homes, 15 High Street, Cranbrook TN17 3EB
T: (01580) 720770
F: (01580) 720771
E: mail@freedomholidayhomes.co.uk
I: www.freedomholidayhomes.co.uk

NEWHAVEN
East Sussex

The Old Farmhouse & Barn Owls Apartments ★★★-★★★★★
Contact: Mr Frank & Mrs Gill Canham
34 The Glade, Epsom KT17 2HB
T: (020) 87865868
F: (020) 87865868
E: gillcanham@yahoo.co.uk
I: www.visitsussex.org/theoldfarmhouse

NEWICK
East Sussex

Manor House Cottage ★★★★
Contact: Mrs Jane Roberts
Manor House Cottage, Church Road, Lewes BN8 4JZ
T: (01825) 722868
E: jane.roberts@tinyworld.co.uk
I: www.manorhousecottage.co.uk

NEWPORT
Isle of Wight

Bethel Cottage ★★★
Contact: Mrs Bridget Lewis
Channers Ltd, Blackbridge Brook House, Main Road, Ryde PO33 4DR
T: (01983) 884742
E: bridget.lewis@btinternet.com

The Cottage, Stone Farm ★★★★
Contact: Mrs Honor Vass
Island Cottage Holidays, The Old Vicarage, Kingston, Wareham BH20 5LH
T: (01929) 481555
I: www.islandcottageholidays.com

Marvel Cottage ★★★★
Contact: Mr Steven & Mrs Prudence Sweetman
Marvel Cottage, Marvel Farm, Marvel Lane, Newport PO30 3DT
T: (01983) 822691.
F: (01983) 822692
E: s@mys.uk.com
I: www.mys.uk.com

The Old Brew House ★★★★
Contact: Mrs Honor Vass
Island Cottage Holidays, West Street, Kingston, Corfe Castle, Wareham BH20 5LH
T: (01929) 480080
F: (01929) 481070

2 Sydney Lodge ★★★★
Contact: Mrs Carol Henley
2 Sydney Lodge, 44 Shide Road, Newport PO30 1YE
T: (01983) 537445

Therles Cottage ★★★★
Contact: Mrs Honor Vass
Island Cottage Holidays, West Street, Kingston, Corfe Castle, Wareham BH20 5LH
T: (01929) 480080
F: (01929) 481070
E: enq@islandcottageholidays.com

West Standen Farm ★★★★
Contact: Mr Edwin & Mrs Sally Burt
West Standen Farm, Blackwater Road, Newport PO30 3BD
T: (01983) 522099
I: www.weststandenfarm.co.uk

NINGWOOD
Isle of Wight

The Granary ★★★★
Contact: Mrs Honor Vass
Island Cottage Holidays, The Old Vicarage, West Street, Kingston, Corfe Castle, Wareham BH20 5LH
T: (01929) 480080
F: (01929) 481070
E: enq@islandcottageholidays.com
I: www.islandcottageholidays.com

NITON
Isle of Wight

Bridge Cottage ★★★
Contact: Mrs Lisa Baskill
Home from Home Holidays, 31 Pier Street, Ventnor PO38 1SX
T: (01983) 854340
F: (01983) 855524
E: admin@hfromh.co.uk

Enfield Cottage ★★
Contact: Mrs Lisa Baskill
31 Pier Street, Ventnor PO38 1SX
T: (01983) 854340
F: (01983) 855524

Fern Gully ★★★★
Contact: Mrs Honor Vass
Island Cottage Holidays, West Street, Kingston, Corfe Castle, Wareham BH20 5LH
T: (01929) 480080
F: (01929) 481070
E: enq@islandcottageholidays.com
I: www.islandcottageholidays.com

Gate Lodge ★★★
Contact: Mrs Lisa Baskill
31 Pier Street, Ventnor PO38 1SX
T: (01983) 854340
F: (01983) 855524

Hoyes Farmhouse ★★
Contact: Mr & Mrs Willis
Ladyacre Farm, Pan Lane, Ventnor PO38 2BU
T: (01983) 730015

Jobsons Farm Cottage ★★
Contact: Mrs Lisa Baskill
Home from Home Holidays, 31 Pier Street, Ventnor PO38 1SX
T: (01983) 854340
F: (01983) 855524
E: admin@hfromh.co.uk

Pictou ★★★
Contact: Mrs Lisa Baskill
31 Pier Street, Ventnor PO38 1SX
T: (01983) 854340
F: (01983) 855524

2 Puckaster Lodge ★★★
Contact: Mrs Lisa Baskill
Home from Home Holidays, 31 Pier Street, Ventnor PO38 1SX
T: (01983) 854340
F: (01983) 855524
E: admin@hfromh.co.uk

NITON UNDERCLIFF
Isle of Wight

Puckaster Cottage, Puckaster House & Puckaster Wing ★★★★
Contact: Mrs Honor Vass
Island Cottage Holidays, The Old Vicarage, Kingston, Wareham BH20 5LH
T: (01929) 480080
I: www.islandcottageholidays.com

NOKE
Oxfordshire

Manor Barn ★★★★
Contact: Ms Emma Righton
1St Floor Cranbrook House, Oxford OX3 9TX
T: 0870 1602325
E: er@oxfordshortlets.co.uk
I: isisnokelets.co.uk

NORLEYWOOD
Hampshire

The Bee Garden ★★★★
Contact: Mr Mayes
Ridgeway Rents New Forest Cottages, 4 Quay Hill, Lymington SO41 3AR
T: (01590) 679655
F: (01590) 670989
E: holidays@newforestcottages.co.uk
I: www.newforestcottages.co.uk

NORTH LEIGH
Oxfordshire

Wylcot Cottage ★★★★
Contact: Mrs Joy Crew
Hollywell Cottage, Witney OX29 6TF
T: (01993) 868614

NORTH NEWINGTON
Oxfordshire

Herrieff's Cottage ★★★★
Contact: Mrs Mary T Bentley
Herrieff's Farmhouse, The Green, North Newington, Banbury OX15 6AF
T: (01295) 738835
F: (01295) 738835
E: mary@herrieffsfarm.freeserve.co.uk
I: www.herrieffsfarm.freeserve.co.uk

Establishments printed in blue have a detailed entry in this guide

SOUTH EAST ENGLAND

NORTHBOURNE
Kent

New Mill ★★★
Contact: Mrs Brenda Beck
Freedom Holiday Homes, 15 High Street, Cranbrook TN17 3EB
T: (01580) 720770
F: (01580) 720771
E: mail@freedomholidayhomes.co.uk
I: www.freedomholidayhomes.co.uk

NORTHMOOR
Oxfordshire

Rectory Farm Cottages ★★★★
Contact: Mrs Mary Anne Florey
Rectory Farm, Oxford OX8 1SX
T: (01865) 300207
F: (01865) 300559
E: pj.florey@farmline.com

NUTLEY
East Sussex

The Old Cart Lodge
Rating Applied For
Contact: Mrs Pauline Graves
2 Victoria Cottages, Bell Lane, Uckfield TN22 3PD
T: (01825) 712475
F: (01825) 712475
E: grapauline@aol.com
I: www.theoldcartlodge.co.uk

Whitehouse Farm Holiday Cottages ★★-★★★
Contact: Mr K Wilson
Whitehouse Farm, Horney Common, Nutley, Uckfield TN22 3EE
T: (01825) 712377
F: (01825) 712377
E: keith.g.r.wilson@btinternet.com
I: www.streets-ahead.com/whitehousefarm

OFFHAM
East Sussex

Mill Laine Farm ★★★★
Contact: Mrs Susan Harmer
Mill Laine Farm, Lewes BN7 3QB
T: (01273) 475473
F: (01273) 475473
E: susan.harmer@farming.co.uk
I: www.milllainebarns.co.uk

OLD CHALFORD
Oxfordshire

Beech House ★★★★★
Contact: Mrs Dorothy Canty
Oak House, Chalford Park, Chipping Norton OX7 5QR
T: (01608) 641435
F: (01608) 641435

OLNEY
Milton Keynes

Hyde Farm Cottages ★★★★
Contact: Mrs Penny Reynolds
Hyde Farm Cottages, Warrington Road, Olney MK46 4DU
T: (01234) 711223
F: (01234) 714155
E: accomm@thehyde.fsbusiness.co.uk

The Old Stone Barn ★★★-★★★★★
Contact: Mr & Mrs G J Pibworth
The Old Stone Barn, Home Farm, Olney MK46 4HN
T: (01234) 711655
F: (01234) 711855
E: accommodation@oldstonebarn.co.uk
I: www.oldstonebarn.co.uk

OTTERDEN
Kent

Frith Farm House ★★★★
Contact: Mrs Susan Chesterfield
Frith Farm House, Faversham ME13 0DD
T: (01795) 890701
F: (01795) 890009
E: markham@frith.force9.co.uk

OWSLEBURY
Hampshire

The Fo'c'sle ★★★
Contact: Mrs Barbara Crabbe
Little Lodge, Hensting Lane, Owslebury, Winchester SO21 1LE
T: (01962) 777887
F: (01962) 777781

Hensting Valley Chalet ★★★
Contact: Mrs Diana Carter
Dell Croft, Hensting Lane, Winchester SO21 1LE
T: (01962) 777297

Lower Farm House Annexe ★★★★
Contact: Mrs Penelope Bowes
Lower Farm House Annexe, Lower Farm House, Whaddon Lane, Winchester SO21 1JL
T: (01962) 777676
F: (01962) 777675
E: pbowes@boltblue.com

OXFORD
Oxfordshire

Apartments in Oxford ★★★★★
Contact: Mrs Sheena Witney
St Thomas' Mews Apartments in Oxford Limited, 58 St Thomas Street, Oxford OX1 1JP
T: (01865) 254077
F: (01865) 254001
E: resasst@oxstay.co.uk
I: www.oxstay.co.uk

7 Bannister Close ★★★
Contact: Mrs Irene Priestly
7 Bannister Close, Bannister Close, Oxford OX4 1SH
T: (01865) 251095

Green Cottage ★★★★
Contact: Mr & Mrs P Hankey
Green Cottage, The Green, Northmoor, Witney OX29 5SX
T: (01865) 300740
E: lettings@thegreen.co.uk
I: www.oxtowns.co.uk/greencottage

17 Kingston Road ★★★
Contact: Mrs Pru Dickson
17 Kingston Road, Oxford OX2 6QR
T: (01865) 516913
F: (01865) 516913
E: pru.dickson@tesco.net
I: www.oxfordcity.co.uk/accom/studioflat/

Manor House Cottages ★★★★
Contact: Mr & Mrs Edward Hess
Manor House Cottages, High Street, Oxford OX33 1XX
T: (01865) 875022
F: (01865) 875023
E: chess@harcourtchambers.law.co.uk

Otmoor Holidays ★★★★
Contact: Mrs Emma Righton
Otmoor Holidays, Lower Farm, Noke, Oxford OX9 9TX
T: (01865) 373766
F: (01865) 371911
E: info@oxfordholidays.co.uk
I: www.oxfordholidays.co.uk

48 St Bernards Road ★★★
Contact: Ms Sian Lewis-Rippington
The Old Workshop, Bruncombe Lane, Abingdon OX13 6QU
T: (01865) 321100
E: greenhavenoxford@btconnect.com
I: www.holidayhomeoxford.co.uk

Weekly Home ★★★
Contact: Mr Kelvin Fowler
Weekly Home, Gordon House, 276 Banbury Road, Oxford OX2 7ED
T: (01865) 557555 & 07870 234725
F: (01865) 557545
E: info@weeklyhome.com
I: www.weeklyhome.com

PANGBOURNE
West Berkshire

Brambly Thatch ★★★
Contact: Mr & Mrs Hatt
Merricroft Farming, Ref: Brambly Thatch, Goring Heath, Reading RG8 7TA
T: (0118) 984 3121
F: (0118) 984 4662
E: hatts@merricroft.demon.co.uk

The Old Rectory Cottage ★★★
Contact: Mrs Short
The Old Rectory Cottage, Lower Basildon, Reading RG8 9NH

Soldalen Annexe ★★
Contact: Mr John & Mrs Bente Kirk
Soldalen Annexe, Riverview Road, Reading RG8 7AU
T: (0118) 9842924
F: (0118) 9842924

PEACEHAVEN
East Sussex

Highseas ★★★
Contact: Mr Richard Harris
Best of Brighton & Sussex Cottages Ltd, Vicarage Lane, Brighton BN2 7HD
T: (01273) 308779
F: (01273) 300266
E: brightoncottages@pavilion.co.uk
I: www.bestofbrighton.co.uk

PEASMARSH
East Sussex

Joywell Cottage
Rating Applied For
Contact: Brenda Beck
Freedom Holiday Homes, 15 High Street, Cranbrook TN17 3EB
T: (01580) 720770
F: (01580) 720771

Pond Cottage ★★★★
Contact: Mrs Jacqueline Reeve
Pond Cottage, Church Lane, Rye TN31 6XS
T: (01797) 230394
I: www.rye-tourism.co.uk/pondcottage

Sharvels Oast House ★★★★
Contact: Mrs Brenda Beck
Freedom Holiday Homes, 15 High Street, Cranbrook TN17 3EB
T: (01580) 720770
F: (01580) 720771
E: mail@freedomholidayhomes.co.uk
I: www.freedomholidayhomes.co.uk

PETHAM
Kent

Lime Tree Farmhouse ★★★★
Contact: Mrs Brenda Beck
Freedom Holiday Homes, 15 High Street, Cranbrook TN17 3EB
T: (01580) 720770
F: (01580) 720771
E: mail@freedomholidayhomes.co.uk
I: www.freedomholidayhomes.co.uk

PETT
East Sussex

Grace Dieu ★★★
Contact: L Morgan-Griffiths
3A Greville Place, London NW6 5JP
T: (020) 76240525

PETWORTH
West Sussex

The Old Dairy ★★★★
Contact: Mrs Rosaleen Waugh
The Old Dairy, Coultershaw Farm House, Station Road, Petworth GU28 0JE
T: (01798) 342900
I: www.theolddairy.com

Polo Cottage ★★★★
Contact: Mr Peter & Mrs Deirdre Cope
Polo Cottage, Rotherbridge Lane, Petworth GU28 0LL
T: (01798) 344286
F: (01798) 344286
E: demalpas@aol.com
I: www.cottage-by-the-river.co.uk

SOUTH EAST ENGLAND

PLAXTOL
Kent

Golding Hop Farm Cottage ★★★
Contact: Mrs Jacqueline Vincent
Bewley Lane, Plaxtol, Sevenoaks
TN15 0PS
T: (01732) 885432
F: (01732) 885432
E: info@goldinghopfarm.com
I: www.goldinghopfarm.com

PLUMPTON GREEN
East Sussex

Heath Farm
Rating Applied For
Contact: Mr Robin & Mrs Marilyn Hanbury
Heath Farm, South Road, Lewes
BN8 4EA
T: (01273) 890712
F: (01273) 890712
E: hanbury@heath-farm.com
I: www.heath-farm.com

POLEGATE
East Sussex

Barn Cottage ★★★★★
Contact: Mr Richard Harris
Best of Brighton & Sussex Cottages Ltd, Vicarage Lane, Brighton BN2 7HD
T: (01273) 308779
F: (01273) 300266
E: brightoncottages@pavilion.co.uk
I: www.bestofbrighton.co.uk

PORCHFIELD
Isle of Wight

Squirrels ★★★★
Contact: Mrs Bridget Lewis
Channers Ltd, Blackbridge Brook House, Main Road, Ryde
PO33 4DR
T: (01983) 884742
E: bridget.lewis@btinternet.com

PORTMORE
Hampshire

Rosemary Cottage ★★★★
Contact: Mrs Jacquie Taylor
Centre Lane, Lymington
SO41 0JP
T: (01590) 645217
E: tommy.tiddles@virgin.net
I: www.halcyonholidays.com

PORTSMOUTH & SOUTHSEA
Portsmouth

Alamar ★
Contact: Mr Alan Hyde
1 Eastlake Heights, Horse Sands Close, Southsea PO4 9UE
T: (023) 92826352

Atlantic Apartments ★★★
Contact: Mrs Dawn Sait
Atlantic Apartments, 61A Festing Road, Southsea
PO4 0NQ
T: (023) 9282 3606
F: (023) 9229 7046
I: www.portsmouth-apartments.co.uk/atlantic.htm

Geminair Holiday & Business Flats ★★★
Contact: Mrs Pamela Holman
Geminair Holiday & Business Flats, 1 Helena Road, Southsea
PO4 9RH
T: (023) 92821602
E: gemflat@aol.com
I: www.gemflat.co.uk

Greenhays Business/ Holiday Accommodation ★★★★
Contact: Mrs Christine Martin
Greenhays Business/Holiday Accommodation, 10 Helena Road, Portsmouth PO4 9RH
T: (023) 9273 7590
F: (023) 9273 7590

Helena Court Apartments ★★★
Contact: Mrs Wendy Haley
Helena Court Apartments, 3 Helena Road, Southsea PO4 9RH
T: (023) 92732116
F: (023) 92825793
E: tikitouch@hotmail.com

Kenilworth Court Holiday Flats ★★★★
Contact: Mrs Sparrowhawk
1 Kenilworth Road, Southsea
PO5 2PG
T: (023) 92734205
F: (023) 92734205
E: kenilworthcourt@onetel.net.uk

Lakeside Holiday & Business Apartments ★★★
Contact: Mrs Hamza
5 Helena Road, Southsea
PO4 9RH
T: 07810 436981
I: www.lakesidesouthsea.com

Ocean Apartments ★★★
Contact: Mrs Dawn Sait
8-10 St Helens Parade, Southsea
PO4 0RW
T: (023) 9273 4233
F: (023) 9229 7046
I: www.portsmouth-apartments.co.uk

Salisbury Apartments ★★★
Contact: Mrs Dawn Sait
Salisbury Apartments, 61A Festing Road, Southsea
PO4 0NQ
T: (023) 92823606
F: (023) 92297046
I: www.portsmouth-apartments.co.uk

South Parade Apartments ★★★
Contact: Mrs Dawn Sait
South Parade Apartments, 29B South Parade, Southsea
PO4 0SH
T: (023) 92734342
F: (023) 92297046
E: southparade@portsmouth-apartments.co.uk
I: www.portsmouth-apartments.co.uk/southparade.htm

Sovereign Holiday Flatlets ★
Contact: Mr & Mrs Michael Cummings
Sovereign Holiday Flatlets, 18 Victoria Grove, Portsmouth
PO5 1NE
T: (023) 9281 1398

University of Portsmouth ★★
Contact: Mr David Goodwin
University of Portsmouth, Langstone Centre, Furze Lane, Southsea PO4 8LW

Wallington Court ★-★★★
Contact: Mr Paul Stretton
Wallington Court, 64 Craneswater Avenue, Southsea
PO4 0PD

PRESTON
Brighton & Hove

13 The Parks ★★★★
Contact: Mr Richard Harris
13 The Parks, London Road, Brighton BN1 6YL
T: (01273) 308779
F: (01273) 300266

PRINCES RISBOROUGH
Buckinghamshire

Old Callow Down Farm ★★★
Contact: Mrs Nancy Gee
Old Callow Down Farm, Wigans Lane, High Wycombe HP14 4BH
T: (01844) 344416
F: (01844) 344703
E: oldcallow@aol.com
I: www.chilternscottage.co.uk

Windmill Farm ★★
Contact: Mrs Rosemarie Smith
Windmill Farm, Pink Road, Lacey Green, Aylesbury HP27 0PG
T: (01844) 343901
E: windmill_farm@hotmail.com

PRINSTED
West Sussex

4 The Square ★★
Contact: Mrs Anne Brooks
The Staddles, Emsworth
PO10 8HS
T: (01243) 377489
E: brooksems@btclick.com
I: www.fourthesquare.co.uk

PUNNETTS TOWN
East Sussex

The Bothy ★★★
Contact: Mrs Brenda Beck
Freedom Holiday Homes, 15 High Street, Cranbrook
TN17 3EB
T: (01580) 720770
F: (01580) 720771
E: mail@freedomholidayhomes.co.uk
I: www.freedomholidayhomes.co.uk

RAMSGATE
Kent

Hamilton House Holiday Flats ★★-★★★
Contact: Mrs Ann Burridge
Hamilton House Holiday Flats, 5 Nelson Crescent, Ramsgate
CT11 9JF
T: (01843) 582592

23 The Lawns ★★★★
Contact: Mrs Jean Lawrence
24 Winterstoke Crescent, Ramsgate CT11 8AH
T: (01843) 591422
F: (01843) 591422
E: jnancylawrence@aol.com

RINGWOOD
Hampshire

Glenavon ★★★
Contact: Mrs Wareham
Glenavon, 12 Boundary Lane, St Leonards, Ringwood BH24 2SE
T: (01202) 873868
E: enquiries@glenavonhol.co.uk
I: www.glenavonhol.co.uk

Heather Cottage ★★★
Contact: Mr & Mrs Peter Harper
The Gables, 93 Southampton Road, Ringwood BH24 1HR
T: (01425) 474567
F: (01425) 474567
E: pjh.hols@btinternet.com

Karelia Holidays ★★★
Contact: Mr Gleed
Karelia Holidays, c/o The Studio, Ringwood BH24 2EE
T: (01425) 478920
F: (01425) 480479
E: kareliahol@aol.com

Mallards
Rating Applied For
Contact: Mr John Whitcombe
47A Kings Stone Avenue, Steyning BN44 3FJ
T: (01903) 813803

ROBERTSBRIDGE
East Sussex

Butters Cottage ★★★★
Contact: Mrs Brenda Beck
Freedom Holiday Homes, 15 High Street, Cranbrook
TN17 3EB
T: (01580) 720770
F: (01580) 720771
E: mail@freedomholidayhomes.co.uk
I: www.freedomholidayhomes.co.uk

Garden Cottage ★★★
Contact: Mrs Brenda Beck
Freedom Holiday Homes, 15 High Street, Cranbrook
TN17 3EB
T: (01580) 720770
F: (01580) 720771
E: mail@freedomholidayhomes.co.uk
I: www.freedomholidayhomes.co.uk

Holly Cottage ★★★
Contact: Mrs Ann Campbell
Fairhaven Holiday Cottages, Derby House, 123 Watling Street, Gillingham ME7 2YY
T: (01634) 300089
F: (01634) 570157
E: enquiries@fairhaven-holidays.co.uk
I: www.fairhaven-holidays.co.uk

Establishments printed in blue have a detailed entry in this guide

SOUTH EAST ENGLAND

Rose Cottage Studio ★★★
Contact: Mrs Brenda Beck
Freedom Holiday Homes, 15
High Street, Cranbrook
TN17 3EB
T: (01580) 720770
F: (01580) 720771
E: mail@freedomholidayhomes.co.uk
I: www.freedomholidayhomes.co.uk

Tudor Cottage ★★★★
Contact: Mr Stuart Winter
Tudor Cottage, High Street,
Robertsbridge TN32 5AJ
T: (01732) 369168
F: (01732) 358817
E: holidays@gardenofenglandcottages.co.uk
I: www.gardenofenglandcottages.co.uk

ROCHESTER
Medway

Merton Villa ★★
Contact: Mrs Nicola Radford
Merton Villa, 38 Maidstone
Road, Rochester ME1 1RJ
T: (01634) 817190

Stable Cottages ★★★★
Contact: Mrs Debbie Symonds
Stable Cottages, Fenn Street, St
Mary Hoo, Rochester ME3 8QS
T: (01634) 272439
F: (01634) 272205
E: stablecottages@btinternet.com
I: www.stable-cottages.com

ROLVENDEN
Kent

The Little House
Rating Applied For
Contact: Mrs Jennifer Field
Coveneys Tenterden Road,
Cranbrook TN17 4NB
T: (01580) 241736
F: (01580) 241736
E: jfield.coveneys@virgin.net

ROMSEY
Hampshire

The Old Smithy Cottage ★★★
Contact: Mr Paul Reeves
The Old Smithy Cottage,
Awbridge Hill, Romsey SO51 0HF
T: (01794) 511778
F: (01794) 521446
E: paul@smithycottage.co.uk
I: www.smithycottage.co.uk

ROPLEY
Hampshire

Dairy Cottage ★★★★
Contact: Mr M Neal
Cowgrove Farm, Petersfield
Road, Alresford SO24 0EJ
T: (01962) 773348
E: theneals@virgin.net

ROTTINGDEAN
Brighton & Hove

38 Highcliff Court ★★
Contact: Mr Richard Harris
Best of Brighton & Sussex
Cottages Ltd, Vicarage Lane,
Brighton BN2 7HD
T: (01273) 308779
F: (01273) 300266
E: brightoncottages@pavilion.co.uk
I: www.bestofbrighton.co.uk

11 Highcliffe Court ★★
Contact: Mr Richard Harris
Best of Brighton & Sussex
Cottages Ltd, Vicarage Lane,
Brighton BN2 7HD
T: (01273) 308779
F: (01273) 300266
E: brightoncottages@pavilion.co.uk
I: www.bestofbrighton.co.uk

Horseshoe Cottage ★★★
Contact: Mr Richard Harris
Best of Brighton & Sussex
Cottages Ltd, Vicarage Lane,
Brighton BN2 7HD
T: (01273) 308779
T: (01273) 390211
E: enquiries@bestofbrighton.co.uk
I: www.bestofbrighton.co.uk

Kilcolgan Premier Bungalow ★★★★★
Contact: Mr J C St George
22 Baches Street, London
N1 6DL
T: (020) 7250 3678
F: (020) 7250 1955
E: jc.stgeorge@virgin.net

White Cliffs ★★★★
Contact: Mr Richard Harris
Best of Brighton & Sussex
Cottages Ltd, Vicarage Lane,
Brighton BN2 7HD
T: (01273) 308779
F: (01273) 300266
E: brightoncottages@pavilion.co.uk
I: www.bestofbrighton.co.uk

ROYAL TUNBRIDGE WELLS
Kent

Broad Oak House ★★★
Contact: Ms Tina Seymour
Broad Oak House, 9 Linden Park
Road, Royal Tunbridge Wells
TN2 5QL
T: (01892) 619065
F: (01892) 619066
E: tina@thctraining.co.uk
I: www.tunbridgewellsonline.com

Flat 4 76 London Road ★★★★
Contact: Mrs Brenda Beck
Freedom Holiday Homes, 15
High Street, Cranbrook
TN17 3EB
T: (01580) 720770
F: (01580) 720771
E: mail@freedomholidayhomes.co.uk
I: www.freedomholidayhomes.co.uk

Flat 6, Hamilton Court
Rating Applied For
Contact: Mr Tim Draper
38 Abbeyfields Close, London
NW10 7EF
T: (01892) 528950

Ford Cottage ★★★
Contact: Mrs Wendy Cusdin
Ford Cottage, Linden Park Road,
Royal Tunbridge Wells TN2 5QL
T: (01892) 531419
E: FordCottage@tinyworld.co.uk
I: www.fordcottage.co.uk

Garden Flat ★★★★
Contact: Mr Stuart Winter
Garden Flat, St James Road,
Royal Tunbridge Wells TN1 2JZ
T: (01732) 369168
F: (01732) 358817
E: holidays@gardenofenglandcottages.co.uk
I: www.gardenofenglandcottages.co.uk

22 Hawkenbury Mead ★★★
Contact: Mr R H Wright
T: (01892) 536977
F: (01892) 536200
E: rhwright1@aol.com

Hollambys ★★★
Contact: Mr Andrew Joad
Hollambys, Eridge Road, Royal
Tunbridge Wells TN3 9NJ
T: (01892) 864203
E: ajoad@hollambys.co.uk
I: www.hollambys.co.uk

Itaris Properties Limited ★★★★
Contact: Mrs Angela May
Itaris Properties Limited, 12
Mount Ephraim, Royal
Tunbridge Wells TN4 8AS
T: (01892) 511065
F: (01892) 540171
E: enquiries@itaris.co.uk
I: www.itaris.co.uk

Kennett ★★★★
Contact: Mrs Lesley Clements
Kennett, London Road, Royal
Tunbridge Wells TN4 0UJ
T: (01892) 533363
E: gravels@onetel.net.uk

St Peters View ★★★★
Contact: Mrs Jill Winter
Garden of England Cottages,
189A High Street, Tonbridge
TN9 1BX
T: (01732) 369168
F: (01732) 358817
E: holidays@gardenofenglandcottages.co.uk

Sion House ★★★★★
Contact: Mrs Caroline Crowther
Sion House, 15 Mount Sion,
Royal Tunbridge Wells TN1 1UD
T: (01273) 248888
E: caroline.crowther@atlantic-marine.co.uk
I: www.sion-house.com

1 Stable Mews ★★★
Contact: Mrs Brenda Beck
Freedom Holiday Homes, 15
High Street, Cranbrook
TN17 3EB
T: (01580) 720770
F: (01580) 720771
E: mail@freedomholidayhomes.co.uk
I: www.freedomholidayhomes.co.uk

RUCKINGE
Kent

The Old Granary ★★★★
Contact: Mrs Brenda Beck
Freedom Holiday Homes, 15
High Street, Cranbrook
TN17 3EB
T: (01580) 720770
F: (01580) 720771
E: mail@freedomholidayhomes.co.uk
I: www.freedomholidayhomes.co.uk

The Old Post Office ★★★
Contact: Mr Chris Cook
121 The Drive, Beckenham
BR3 1EF
T: (020) 86554466
F: (020) 86567755
E: c.cook@btinternet.com
I: www.ruckinge.info

Willow Court ★★★
Contact: Mrs Brenda Beck
Freedom Holiday Homes, 15
High Street, Cranbrook
TN17 3EB
T: (01580) 720770
F: (01580) 720771
E: mail@freedomholidayhomes.co.uk
I: www.freedomholidayhomes.co.uk

RUSHLAKE GREEN
East Sussex

The Coach House ★★★★
Contact: Mrs Julia Desch
The Coach House, Beech Hill
Farm, Cowbeech Road,
Heathfield TN21 9QB
T: (01435) 830203
F: (01435) 830203
E: julia@desch.go-plus.net
I: www.sussexcountryretreat.co.uk

Stone House Coach House ★★★★
Contact: Mr Peter Dunn
Stone House, Heathfield
TN21 9QJ
T: (01435) 830553
F: (01435) 830726

RUSTINGTON
West Sussex

79 Mallon Dene ★★★
Contact: Mrs Anne Wright
Promenade Holiday Homes, 44
Nepcote Lane, Worthing
BN14 0SL
T: (01903) 877047
F: (01903) 877047
E: anne@promenade-holidays.fsbusiness.co.uk
I: www.promenadeholidayhomes.co.uk

Papyrus ★★★
Contact: Mrs Joyce Smith
16 Meadow Way, Littlehampton
BN17 6BW
T: (01903) 725345
E: joyce@16meadow89.freeserve.co.uk

Seaway ★★★
Contact: Mrs Millidge
25 Evelyn Avenue, Rustington
BN16 2EJ
T: (01903) 772548

SOUTH EAST ENGLAND

RYDE
Isle of Wight

Benham Lodge & Forelands ★★★
Contact: Mrs Kathleen Yaxley
Bellair, East Hill Road, Ryde
PO33 1LB
T: (01983) 616841
E: kathy@appleyfarmcottages.co.uk
I: www.appleyfarmcottages.co.uk

Bramble Cottage ★★★★
Contact: Ms Lyn Cooper-Hall
Island Holiday Homes, Hose Rhodes Dickson, 177 High Street, Ryde PO33 2HW
T: (01983) 616655
F: (01983) 568822
I: www.island-holiday-homes.net

Claverton House ★★★-★★★★★
Contact: Dr Hartwig Metz
Claverton House, 12 The Strand, Ryde PO33 1JE
T: (01983) 613015
F: (01983) 613015
E: clavertonhouse@aol.com

Dungen ★★★
Contact: Mrs Bernadette Sessions
Hilltop Dairy Farm, Long Lane, Newport PO30 3NW
T: (01983) 564370
F: (01983) 528880

Flat 4, Wellwood House ★★★
Contact: Catherine Hopper
Flat 4, Wellwood House, Quarr Hill, Ryde PO33 4EH
T: (01983) 521113
F: (01983) 822050

Holmwood ★★★★
Contact: Mrs Nicola Newton
Holmwood, 7 Argyll Street, Ryde PO33 3BZ
T: (01983) 614852
E: nicola@holmwood-holidays.co.uk
I: www.holmwood-holidays.co.uk

Island Retreat ★★★
Contact: Mrs Lisa Baskill
Home from Home Holidays, 31 Pier Street, Ventnor PO38 1SX
T: (01983) 854340
F: (01983) 855524
E: admin@hfromh.co.uk

Jubilee Cottage ★★★★
Contact: Ms Catherine Hopper
Manager, Housing Letting Hose Rhodes Dickson, Island Holiday Homes, 177 High Street, Ryde PO33 2HW
T: (01983) 616644
F: (01983) 616640
E: enquiries@island-holiday-homes.net

Kemphill Barn & The Old Dairy ★★★★★
Contact: Mr Ron Holland
Kemphill Barn & The Old Dairy, Stroud Wood Road, Ryde PO33 4BZ
T: (01983) 563880
F: (01983) 563880
E: ronholland@btconnect.com
I: www.kemphill.com

Lionstone House ★★-★★★
Contact: Mrs June Hermiston-Hooper
Lionstone House, 13 The Strand, Ryde PO33 1JE
T: (01983) 563496
F: (01983) 563496

OakLawn Cottages ★★★★
Contact: Mrs Lynette Haywood
Corner House, Oak Lawn, Woodside, Ryde PO33 4JR
T: (01983) 884080
I: www.oaklawncottages.co.uk

The Oaks ★★-★★★
Contact: Mrs Christine Rossall
The Oaks, West Hill Road, Ryde PO33 1LW
T: (01983) 565769

Percy House ★★★
Contact: Ms Catherine Hopper
Manager, Housing Letting Hose Rhodes Dickson, Island Holiday Homes, 177 High Street, Ryde PO33 2HW
T: (01983) 616644
F: (01983) 616640
E: enquiries@island-holiday-homes.net
I: www.island-holiday-homes.net

Silver Birches
Rating Applied For
Contact: Mrs Kathy Domaille
Godshill Park Farm House, Shanklin Road, Ventnor PO38 3JF
T: (01983) 840781
E: info@godshillparkfarm.uk.com
I: godshillparkfarm.uk.com

Strand House ★★★
Contact: Ms Jan Johnston
Strand House, 17 The Strand, Ryde PO33 1JE
T: 07973 683722

The Victorian Lodge ★★★
Contact: Mrs Herbert
The Victorian Lodge, 8 Easthill Road, Ryde PO33 1LS
T: (01983) 563366

Westfield Park Lodge
Rating Applied For
Contact: Lady Rebecca Thompson
Appley Rise, Ryde PO33 1LE
T: (01983) 811467
E: westfieldparklodge@hotmail.com

RYE
East Sussex

Boat House ★★★
Contact: Mr Melville-Brown
107 Crescent Drive South, Woodingdean, Brighton BN2 6SB
T: 07803 189031
E: chris@ryeholidays.co.uk
I: www.ryeholidays.co.uk

The Boathouse ★★★★
Contact: Mr Stuart Winter
Garden of England Cottages, 189A High Street, Tonbridge TN9 1BX
T: (01732) 369168
T: (01732) 358817
E: holidays@gardenofenglandcottages.co.uk
I: www.gardenofenglandcottages.co.uk

10 The Boathouse ★★★
Contact: Mr Robert Lever
Seascape, Coastguard Lane, Hastings TN35 4AB
T: (01424) 813566
F: (01424) 813566
E: rslever@tn35ab.freeserve.co.uk
I: www.tn354ab.freeserve.co.uk

15 The Boathouse ★★★
Contact: Mr Mike Hickmott
Glynton Hurst, Penshurst Road, Royal Tunbridge Wells TN3 0PH
T: (01892) 863037
E: mike@rye4ukbreaks.co.uk
I: www.rye4ukbreaks.co.uk

Brandy's Cottage ★★★★
Contact: Mrs Jane Apperly
Brandy's Cottage, Cadborough Farm, Udimore Road, Rye TN31 6AA
T: (01797) 225426
F: (01797) 224097
E: info@cadborough.co.uk
I: www.cadborough.co.uk

Caer Glow ★★★
Contact: Mr Stuart Winter
Garden of England Cottages, 189A High Street, Tonbridge TN9 1BX
T: (01732) 369168
T: (01732) 358817
E: holidays@gardenofenglandcottages.co.uk
I: www.gardenofenglandcottages.co.uk

Chapel Cottage ★★★
Contact: Mr Stuart Winter
Garden of England Cottages, The Mews Office, 189A High Street, Tonbridge TN9 1BX
T: (01732) 369168
T: (01732) 358817
E: holidays@gardenofenglandcottages.co.uk
I: www.gardenofenglandcottages.co.uk

Chesterfield Cottage ★★★
Contact: Ms Sally Bayly
44 1/2 The Mint, Rye TN31 7EN
T: (01797) 222498
F: (01797) 222498
E: chesterfieldcottage@virgin.net

26 Church Square
Rating Applied For
Contact: Mrs Brenda Beck
Freedom Holiday Homes, 15 High Street, Cranbrook TN17 3EB
T: (01580) 720770
E: mail@freedomholidayhomes.co.uk
I: www.freedomholidayhomes.co.uk

Cinque Ports Corner
Rating Applied For
Contact: Mr George Parkins
Cinque Ports Corner, 2A Cinque Ports Street, Rye TN31 7AD
T: (01797) 227496
I: www.cinqueportscorner.co.uk

Crispins Arena Apartments ★★★
Contact: Mr David & Mrs Sarah Nixon
75 The Mint, Rye TN31 7EW
T: (01797) 226837
F: (01797) 226837
E: crispins@talk21.com

Driftwood ★★★
Contact: Mrs Brenda Beck
Freedom Holiday Homes, 15 High Street, Cranbrook TN17 3EB
T: (01580) 720770
F: (01580) 720771
E: mail@freedomholidayhomes.co.uk
I: www.freedomholidayhomes.co.uk

Ellis Bros (Ironmongers) Ltd ★★
Contact: Miss Harminder Gill
Ellis Bros (Ironmongers) Ltd, 1 High Street, Rye TN31 7JE
T: (01797) 222110

Froglets Cottage ★★★★
Contact: Mrs Brenda Haines
Little Frogs, Rye Road, Newenden, Cranbrook TN18 5PL
T: (01797) 252011
E: brenda@curtishaines.co.uk
I: www.froglets.uk.com

Homelands ★★★
Contact: Mrs Margaret Royle
Tutts Farm, Lewes BN8 4RS
T: (01825) 723294
F: (01825) 723294

2 Hucksteps Row ★★★
Contact: Mrs Brenda Beck
Freedom Holiday Homes, 15 High Street, Cranbrook TN17 3EB
T: (01580) 720770
F: (01580) 720771
E: mail@freedomholidayhomes.co.uk
I: www.freedomholidayhomes.co.uk

Larkin House ★★★
Contact: Ms Stella Larkin
31 London Road, Radlett WD7 9EP
T: (01923) 857095
E: stella.larkin@freenet.co.uk
I: www.interiorstylist.com

Establishments printed in blue have a detailed entry in this guide

SOUTH EAST ENGLAND

Mermaid Cottage ★★★★
Contact: Mrs Suzie Warren
Tanners, Freight Lane, Cranbrook
TN17 3PF
T: (01580) 712046
E: mermaidcottage@supanet.com
I: www.mermaidcottage.supanet.com

22 Mermaid Street ★★★
Contact: Mr Grimes
36 Poets Road, Highbury,
London N5 2SH
T: (020) 77048470
E: frankgrimes1@blueyonder.co.uk

41 Military Road ★★★
Contact: Mrs Valerie John
1 Chapel Row, Haverfordwest
SA62 4HR
T: (01437) 890370
E: vlouisej@yahoo.co.uk

Oakhurst Cottage ★★★
Contact: Mrs Kathryn Clarkson
36 Church Square, Rye
TN31 7HE
T: (01797) 223118
E: oakhurstcottage@aol.com
I: www.holidaycottagerye.co.uk

Ockman Cottage ★★★
Contact: Mrs Brenda Beck
Freedom Holiday Homes, 15
High Street, Cranbrook
TN17 3EB
T: (01580) 720770
F: (01580) 720771
E: mail@freedomholidayhomes.co.uk
I: www.freedomholidayhomes.co.uk

Providence Cottage ★★★★
Contact: Mrs Hilary White
Brainstorm Properties, 3 White
Hart Close, Sevenoaks TN13 1RH
T: (01732) 458559

Riverview Cottage ★★★
Contact: Mr & Mrs Henderson
18 Chipstead Park, Sevenoaks
TN13 2SN
T: (01732) 457837

Seaview Terrace ★★★
Contact: Mrs Pamela Pettigrew
Folly Road, Hungerford
RG17 8QE
T: (01488) 71569
F: (01488) 71569

RYE FOREIGN
East Sussex

Rose Cottage ★★★
Contact: Mr Anthony Reeve
A. Reeve & Son, Church Lane,
Rye TN31 6XS
T: (01797) 230394
E: jackiereeve@peasmarsh68.fsnet.co.uk
I: www.country-holidays.co.uk

RYE HARBOUR
East Sussex

1a Coastguard Square ★★★
Contact: Mrs Brenda Beck
Freedom Holiday Homes, 15
High Street, Cranbrook
TN17 3EB
T: (01580) 720770
F: (01580) 720771
E: mail@freedomholidayhomes.co.uk
I: www.freedomholidayhomes.co.uk

Harbour Lights ★★★
Contact: Mrs Penelope Webster
24 Moorcroft Close, Sheffield
S10 4GU
T: (0114) 230 6859
E: holidays@harbourlights.info
I: www.harbourlights.info

Harbour Point South ★★★
Contact: Mrs Brenda Beck
Freedom Holiday Homes, 15
High Street, Cranbrook
TN17 3EB
T: (01580) 720770
F: (01580) 720771
E: mail@freedomholidayhomes.co.uk
I: www.freedomholidayhomes.co.uk

ST HELENS
Isle of Wight

1 & 2 Glade House ★★★-★★★★★
Contact: Mrs Peggy Stephens
Old Mill Holiday Park, Mill Road,
Ryde PO33 1UE
T: (01983) 872507
E: oldmill@fsb.dial.co.uk
I: www.oldmill.co.uk

Carpenters Farm ★★
Contact: Mrs Mary Lovegrove
Carpenters Farm, Carpenters
Road, Ryde PO33 1YL
T: (01983) 872450

2 Hope Cottages
Rating Applied For
Contact: Ms Jacqui Ellis
Bembridge Holiday Homes, 13
High Street, Bembridge
PO35 5SD
T: (01983) 873163
F: (01983) 872279

Island Lights ★★
Contact: Mrs Lisa Baskill
Home from Home Holidays, 31
Pier Street, Ventnor PO38 1SX
T: (01983) 854340
F: (01983) 855524
E: admin@hfromh.co.uk

Isola ★★★★
Contact: Mr Tim & Mrs Anne Baker
19 Sandfield Road, Oxford
OX3 7RN
T: (01865) 761558
E: timbaker@isola-iow.freeserve.co.uk

The Little Shell House ★★★
Contact: Mrs Christina Hind
11 Byng Road, High Barnet,
Barnet EN5 4NW
T: (020) 8449 8867
F: (020) 8449 8867
E: thehinds@ntlworld.com

The Poplars ★★★
Contact: Mrs Honor Vass
Island Cottage Holidays, The Old
Vicarage, Kingston, Wareham
BH20 5LH
T: (01929) 480080
F: (01929) 481070
E: enq@islandcottageholidays.com
I: www.islandcottageholidays.com

9 Port St Helens ★★★
Contact: Mrs Peggy Stephens
Old Mill Holiday Park, Mill Road,
Ryde PO33 1UA
T: (01983) 872507
E: old_mill@netguides.co.uk
I: www.oldmill.co.uk

Seagull Cottage ★★★
Contact: Dr & Mrs Simon Baker
High Tree Cottage, Wood Lane,
Ongar CM5 0QU
T: (01277) 896364
F: (01920) 877513
E: kcf88@dial.pipex.co

ST LAWRENCE
Isle of Wight

Charles Wood House ★★★★
Contact: Mrs Lisa Baskill
Home from Home Holidays, 31
Pier Street, Ventnor PO38 1SX
T: (01983) 854340
F: (01983) 855524
E: admin@hfromh.co.uk

Copse Hill ★★
Contact: Mrs Lisa Baskill
Home from Home Holidays, 31
Pier Street, Ventnor PO38 1SX
T: (01983) 854340
F: (01983) 855524
E: admin@hfromh.co.uk

Heshcot ★★★
Contact: Mrs Lisa Baskill
31 Pier Street, Ventnor
PO38 1SX
T: (01983) 854340
F: (01983) 855524

The Spinnaker ★★★
Contact: Mr & Mrs Derek Morris
The Spinnaker, Undercliff Glen,
The Undercliffe Drive, Ventnor
PO38 1XY
T: (01983) 730261

1 St Rhadagunds Cottages ★★★★
Contact: Mrs Julie Banks-Thompson
The Garden House, Green Lane,
Woking GU24 8PH
T: (01276) 858168
F: (01276) 485821
E: JB-T@talk21.com

ST LEONARDS
East Sussex

Flat 4 42 Marina ★★★★
Contact: Mrs Brenda Beck
Freedom Holiday Homes, 15
High Street, Cranbrook
TN17 3EB
T: (01580) 720770
F: (01580) 720771
E: mail@freedomholidayhomes.co.uk
I: www.freedomholidayhomes.co.uk

Flats 5 & 6 ★★★
Contact: Mrs Brenda Beck
Freedom Holiday Homes, 15
High Street, Cranbrook
TN17 3EB
T: (01580) 720770
F: (01580) 720771
E: mail@freedomholidayhomes.co.uk
I: www.freedomholidayhomes.co.uk

Glastonbury Self-Catering ★★★
Contact: Mr Campbell
Glastonbury Self-Catering, 45
Eversfield Place, Hastings
TN37 6DB
T: (01424) 436186
E: glastonburyselfcatering@btinternet.com
I: www.hastings.gov.uk

Ground Floor Flat
Rating Applied For
Contact: Mr Richard Harris
Best of Brighton & Sussex
Cottages Ltd, Windmill Lodge,
Vicarage Lane, Rottingdean,
Brighton BN2 7HD
T: (01273) 308779
F: (01273) 300266
E: brightoncottages@pavilion.co.uk
I: www.bestofbrighton.co.uk

St Leonards Flat ★★★
Contact: Mrs Mathews
Miraleisure Ltd, 51 Marina,
Bexhill TN40 1BQ
T: (01424) 730298
F: (01424) 212500
E: infomira@waitrose.com

60 Warrior Square ★★★★
Contact: Mrs Brenda Beck
Freedom Holiday Homes, 15
High Street, Cranbrook
TN17 3EB
T: (01580) 720770
F: (01580) 720771
E: mail@freedomholidayhomes.co.uk
I: www.freedomholidayhomes.co.uk

ST MARGARET'S BAY
Kent

Reach Court Farm Cottages ★★★★
Contact: Mrs Jacqui Mitchell
Reach Court Farm Cottages,
Reach Court Farm, Reach Road,
Dover CT15 6AQ
T: (01304) 852159
F: (01304) 853902

ST MICHAELS
Kent

Rustlings
Rating Applied For
Contact: Brenda Beck
Freedom Holiday Homes, 15
High Street, Cranbrook
TN17 3EB
T: (01580) 720770
F: (01580) 720771

SOUTH EAST ENGLAND

6 The Terrace ★★★
Contact: Mrs Brenda Beck
Freedom Holiday Homes, 15 High Street, Cranbrook
TN17 3EB
T: (01580) 720770
F: (01580) 720771
E: mail@freedomholidayhomes.co.uk
I: www.freedomholidayhomes.co.uk

SALFORD
Oxfordshire

Mill Cottage ★★★★
Contact: Mr Charles & Mrs Liz Teall
Salford Mill, Worcester Road, Chipping Norton OX7 5YQ
T: (01608) 641304
F: (01608) 644442
E: teall@compuserve.com

Stable Cottage & The Granary ★★★★
Contact: Mrs Barbara Lewis
Stable Cottage & The Granary, Larches Farmhouse, Chipping Norton OX7 5YY
T: (01608) 643198
E: babbylew@supanet.com
I: www.cotswolds-retreats.com

SALTDEAN
Brighton & Hove

11b Nutley Avenue ★★★★★
Contact: Mr Richard Harris
Best of Brighton & Sussex Cottages Ltd, Vicarage Lane, Brighton BN2 7HD
T: (01273) 308779
F: (01273) 300266
E: brightoncottages@pavilion.co.uk
I: www.bestofbrighton.co.uk

Westpoint ★★★
Contact: Mr Richard Harris
Best of Brighton & Sussex Cottages Ltd, Vicarage Lane, Brighton BN2 7HD
T: (01273) 308779
F: (01273) 300266
E: brightoncottages@pavilion.co.uk
I: www.bestofbrighton.co.uk

SANDFORD
Isle of Wight

The Cottage ★★★
Contact: Mr David Owen
5 Heatherdale Close, Kingston upon Thames KT2 7SU
T: (020) 82881034
F: (020) 8288 1034
E: david.owen@csfb.com
I: www.iowcottage.com

Rose Cottage ★★★★
Contact: Mrs Honor Vass
Island Cottage Holidays, West Street, Kingston, Corfe Castle, Wareham BH20 5LH
T: (01929) 480080
F: (01929) 481070

SANDHURST
Kent

Little Brook ★★★
Contact: Mr Nick Pash
Hideaways, Chapel House, Luke Street, Berwick St John, Shaftesbury SP7 0HQ
T: (01747) 828170
F: (01747) 829090
E: enq@hideaways.co.uk

SANDLING
Kent

Dingley Cottage & Dell Cottage ★★★★
Contact: Mr Robert Lawty
Cobtree Manor House, Forstal Road, Maidstone ME14 3AX
T: (01622) 671160
F: (01622) 750378
E: Enquiries@cobtreemanor.co.uk
I: www.cobtreemanor.co.uk

SANDOWN
Isle of Wight

Beaulieu Cottage ★★★
Contact: Mrs Honor Vass
Island Cottage Holidays, Godshill Park Farm House, Ventnor PO38 3JF
T: (01929) 480080
F: (01929) 481070
E: enq@islandcottagesholidays.com
I: www.islandcottageholidays.com

Brackla Apartments ★★★★
Contact: Mrs Lindsay Heinrich
Brackla Apartments, 7 Leed Street, Sandown PO36 9DA
T: (01983) 403648
E: enquire@brackla-apartments.co.uk
I: www.brackla-apartments.co.uk

Bramley Cottage
Rating Applied For
Contact: Mr Purrington
Bramley Cottage, 73 The Fairway, Sandown PO36 9EQ
T: (01983) 402998

19 Copse End ★★★
Contact: Mrs Lisa Baskill
Home from Home Holidays, 31 Pier Street, Ventnor PO38 1SX
T: (01983) 854340
F: (01983) 855524
E: admin@hfromh.co.uk

71 Culver Way
Rating Applied For
Contact: Ms Jacqui Ellis
Bembridge Holiday Homes, 13 High Street, Bembridge PO35 5SD
T: (01983) 873163
F: (01983) 872279

Hope Cottage ★★★
Contact: Ms Gail Whiting
Hillrise House, 11 Vaughan Way, Shanklin PO37 6SD
T: (01983) 864103

Kintore Court Holiday Apartments ★★★
Contact: Mr Bass
Kintore Court Holiday Apartments, 15 Broadway, Sandown PO36 9BY
T: (01983) 402507

Little Parklands Holiday Apartments ★★★
Contact: Mrs Karen Hudson
Little Parklands Holiday Apartments, 7 Winchester Park Road, Sandown PO36 8HJ
T: (01983) 402883
E: info@sandownholidays.com
I: www.sandownholidays.co.uk

Mayfair ★★★★
Contact: Mrs Lisa Baskill
31 Pier Street, Ventnor PO38 1SX
T: (01983) 854340
F: (01983) 855524

No 21 Napoleon's Landing
Rating Applied For
Contact: Mr Colin Powell
Primrose Slip, Newchurch Road, Tadley RG26 4FA
T: (0118) 9813445

Ocean View Apartment 2 ★★★★
Contact: Mr Clive Pettit
125 High Street, Canvey Island SS8 7RF
T: (01268) 691444
F: (01268) 691444
E: oceanview@onthebeachiow.freeserve.co.uk
I: www.onthebeachiow.co.uk

Parklands Apartments ★★
Contact: Mr Hugh McGee
Parklands Apartments, 9 Winchester Park Road, Sandown PO36 8HJ
T: (01983) 409602
F: (01983) 407644

Parterre Holiday Flats ★★★
Contact: Mr Roger Hollis
Parterre Holiday Flats, 34 Broadway, Sandown PO36 9BY
T: (01983) 403555
E: roger@parterre.freeserve.co.uk

Royal Cliff Apartments ★★★
Contact: Mr Peter Smith
Royal Cliff Apartments, Beachfield Road, Sandown PO36 8NA
T: (01983) 402138
F: (01983) 402368
I: www.royalcliff.co.uk

Royal Court & Garden Apartments ★★★★
Contact: Mr Graham & Mrs Kathy Blake
The Town House, Beachfield Road, Sandown PO36 8ND
T: (01983) 405032
I: www.isleofwight.com

Victoria Lodge ★★★
Contact: Mr Gibbens & Mrs P Jackson
Victoria Lodge, 4-6 Victoria Road, Sandown PO36 8AP
T: (01983) 403209

SANDWICH
Kent

The Old Dairy ★★★★
Contact: Mrs Montgomery
Little Brooksend Farm, Birchington CT7 0JW
T: (01843) 841656
F: (01843) 841656

Quay Location ★★★
Contact: Mrs Janet Cross
Quay Location, 1 Kings Avenue, Sandwich CT13 9PH
T: (01304) 612880
E: janet@quaylocation.com
I: www.quaylocation.com

2 Worth Farm Cottages ★★★
Contact: Mrs Patricia Mallett
Vine Farm, Sandwich CT13 0PG
T: (01304) 812276
F: (01304) 812694
E: worthcotts@vinefarm.plus.com

SEAFORD
East Sussex

Cuilfail ★★★
Contact: Mrs Lois Fuller
Cuilfail, Firle Road, Seaford BN25 2JD
T: (01323) 898622

Dymock Farm ★★★
Contact: Mrs White
Dymock Farm, Chyngton Lane North, Seaford BN25 4AA
T: (01323) 892982

Hardy's Coffee House
Rating Applied For
Contact: Mrs Christine Nott
Hardy's Coffee House, Richmond Road, Seaford BN25 1DN
T: (01323) 894864

2 Kingsway Court ★★★★
Contact: Mrs Pauline Gower
6 Sunningdale Close, Southdown Road, Seaford BN25 4PF
T: (01323) 895233
E: sific@bgower.f9.co.uk

21 Marine Parade ★★★
Contact: Mr Richard Harris
Best of Brighton & Sussex Cottages Ltd, Vicarage Lane, Brighton BN2 7HD
T: (01273) 308779
F: (01273) 300266
E: brightoncottages@pavilion.co.uk
I: www.bestofbrighton.co.uk

SEAL
Kent

The Apartment ★★★★
Contact: Mr Stuart Winter
Garden of England Cottages, 189A High Street, Tonbridge TN9 1BX
T: (01732) 369168
F: (01732) 358817
E: holidays@gardenofenglandcottages.co.uk
I: www.gardenofenglandcottages.co.uk

Establishments printed in blue have a detailed entry in this guide

SOUTH EAST ENGLAND

SEAVIEW
Isle of Wight

The Bolt Hole at Linden ★★★★
Contact: Mrs Barbara Hughes
The Bolt Hole at Linden, Seaview Lane, Seaview PO34 5DJ
T: (01983) 810324
F: (01983) 810324
E: barbara_hughes@btinternet.com
I: www.thebotholeiow.co.uk

Flat 2 Fairlawn
Rating Applied For
Contact: Catherine Hopper
Island Holiday Homes, 138 High Street, Newport PO30 1TY
T: (01983) 521113
F: (01983) 822050

Glynn Cottage ★★★
Contact: Mrs Lisa Baskill
31 Pier Street, Ventnor PO38 1SX
T: (01983) 854340
F: (01983) 855524

44 Horestone Drive ★★★★
Contact: Mrs Honor Vass
Island Cottage Holidays, The Old Vicarage, Kingston, Wareham BH20 5LH
T: (01929) 480080
F: (01929) 481070
E: enq@islandcottagesholidays.com

Pepita ★★
Contact: Mrs Lisa Baskill
31 Pier Street, Ventnor PO38 1SX
T: (01983) 854340
F: (01983) 855524

1 Pond Lane ★★★
Contact: Mrs Sara Capon
11 Circular Road, Elmfield, Ryde PO33 1AL
T: (01983) 564267
F: (01983) 564267
E: smcapon@aol.com

7 Seaview Bay
Rating Applied For
Contact: Ms Jacqui Ellis
Bembridge Holiday Homes, 13 High Street, Bembridge PO35 5SD
T: (01983) 873163
F: (01983) 872279

SEDLESCOMBE
East Sussex

Acorn Chalet ★★★★
Contact: Mr Stuart Winter
Acorn Chalet, Churchlands Lane, Battle TN33 0PF
T: (01732) 369168
F: (01732) 358817
E: holidays@gardenofenglandcottages.co.uk
I: www.gardenofenglandcottages.co.uk

SELSEY
West Sussex

12 Fraser Close ★★★
Contact: Mrs Heather Birchall
Sea Spangles, West Street, Chichester PO20 9AG
T: (01243) 606892

2 Shore House ★★★★
Contact: Mr Richard Harris
2 Shore House, Hillfield Road, Chichester PO20 0LH
T: (01273) 308779
F: (01273) 300266

Stable Annexe ★★
Contact: Mr & Mrs Kenneth Child
Post Cottage, Rectory Lane, Chichester PO20 9DU
T: (01243) 604264

40 Toledo ★★
Contact: Mr & Mrs Robert Jones
47 Colne Avenue, West Drayton UB7 7AL
T: (01895) 446352

SEVENOAKS
Kent

Harveys ★★★
Contact: Mrs Pat Harvey
Harveys, 143 West End, Sevenoaks TN15 6QJ
T: (01732) 761862

Linden Beeches Cottages ★★★
Contact: Mr Peter & Lynda Gilbert
Linden Beeches Cottages, 81 Bradbourne Park Road, Sevenoaks TN13 3LQ
T: (01732) 461008
E: lindenbeeches@rmplc.co.uk
I: www.smoothhound.co.uk/hotels/linde.html

SHALFLEET
Isle of Wight

Shalfleet Manor Farmhouse & Cottage ★★★★
Contact: Mrs Honor Vass
Island Cottage Holidays Ltd., The Old Vicarage, Kingston, Wareham BH20 5LH
T: (01929) 480080

SHANKLIN
Isle of Wight

1 Apse Castle Cottages ★★
Contact: Mrs Lisa Baskill
Home from Home Holidays, 31 Pier Street, Ventnor PO38 1SX
T: (01983) 854340
F: (01983) 855524
E: admin@hfromh.co.uk

Broadslade Court ★★★
Contact:
Broadslade Court, Westhill Road, Shanklin PO37 6PZ
T: (01983) 865861

Byre Cottage ★★★★
Contact: Mrs Honor Vass
Island Cottage Holidays, The Old Vicarage, Kingston, Wareham BH20 5LH
T: (01929) 480080

Chestnut Mews ★★★★★
Contact: Mrs Carol Bowkis
Jasmine House, 14 Vaughan Way, Shanklin PO37 6SD
T: (01983) 861143
F: (01983) 861143
E: chestnut@isleofwight.co.uk
I: www.chestnutmews.co.uk

Dairymaid Cottage ★★★
Contact: Mrs Lisa Baskill
31 Pier Street, Ventnor PO38 1SX
T: (01983) 854340
F: (01983) 855524

Fair Winds ★★★
Contact: Mrs Lisa Baskill
Home from Home Holidays, 31 Pier Street, Ventnor PO38 1SX
T: (01983) 854340
F: (01983) 855524
E: admin@hfromh.co.uk

Fernhurst Holiday Apartments ★★★
Contact: Mrs Sandra Petcher
Fernhurst Holiday Apartments, 42 Western Road, Shanklin PO37 7NF
T: (01983) 862126
E: bpetcher@talk21.com
I: www.isle-of-wight-uk.com/fernhurst

Green Gable ★★★
Contact: Mrs Lisa Baskill
31 Pier Street, Ventnor PO38 1SX
T: (01983) 854340
F: (01983) 855524

Heatherdene ★★★★
Contact: Mrs Lisa Baskill
31 Pier Street, Ventnor PO38 1SX
T: (01983) 854340
F: (01983) 855524

Laramie ★★★
Contact: Mrs Sally Ranson
Laramie, Howard Road, Shanklin PO37 6HD
T: (01983) 862905
E: sally.ranson@tiscali.co.uk

Laurel Court Holiday Apartments ★★
Contact: Mr & Mrs Brash
Priory Road, Shanklin PO37 6SA
T: (01983) 868025
E: info@laurel-court.co.uk
I: www.laurel-court.co.uk

Lavender Cottage & Magnolia Cottage ★★★★
Contact: Mrs Honor Vass
Island Cottage Holidays, The Old Vicarage, Kingston, Wareham BH20 5LH
T: (01929) 480080
F: (01929) 481070
E: enq@islandcottageholidays.com
I: www.islandcottageholidays.com

Lovecombe Cottage ★★★
Contact: Mrs Anne Kennerley
Duxmore Farm, Newport PO30 2NZ
T: (01983) 883993

Luccombe Villa ★★★
Contact: Mrs Christine Williams
Luccombe Villa, 9 Popham Road, Shanklin PO37 6RF
T: (01983) 862825
F: (01983) 862362

4 Napier Apartments
Rating Applied For
Contact: Mr Paul Reeves
60 Station Road, Guildford GU5 9NP
T: (01483) 203838

9 Napier Apartments
Rating Applied For
Contact: Mr Paul Reeves
60 Station Road, Guildford GU5 9NP
T: (01483) 203838

Ninham House ★★★★
Contact: Mrs Veronica Harvey
Ninham House, Ninham, Shanklin PO37 7PL
T: (01983) 864243
F: (01983) 868881

Percy Cottage ★★★
Contact: Mr David Hirst
47 George Street, Barnsley S74 9AE
T: (01226) 744754

2 Rubstone Court ★★★★
Contact: Mrs Elaine Hedley
19 Palmerston Road, Shanklin PO37 6AU
T: (01983) 867695
E: rubstone2@aol.com

Shanklin Manor Mews ★★★★
Contact: Mr Thomas McLinden
Shanklin Manor Mews, Manor Road, Old Village, Shanklin PO37 6QX
T: (01983) 862777
F: (01983) 863464
I: www.shanklinmanor.co.uk

The Stables ★★★
Contact: Mr Rigby
The Stables, 29 Sandy Lane, Shanklin PO37
T: (01983) 866702

Upper Chine Holiday Cottages & Apartments ★★★★
Contact: Mr Danny Bowkis
Upper Chine Holiday Cottages & Apartments, 22A Church Road, Shanklin PO37 6QR
T: (01983) 867900
F: (01983) 861145
E: upperchine@btinternet.com
I: www.upperchinecottages.co.uk

Upper Hatch ★★★
Contact: Mrs Lisa Baskill
31 Pier Street, Ventnor PO38 1SX
T: (01983) 854340
F: (01983) 855524

Winchester House ★★★
Contact: Miss Kathryn Hayward
Winchester House, Sandown Road, Shanklin PO37 6HU
T: (01983) 862441
F: (01983) 863513
E: winchesterhouse@lineone.net
I: www.winchesterhouse.org.uk

SOUTH EAST ENGLAND

SHAWFORD
Hampshire
Kingsmere Cottage ★★★★
Contact: Mrs Caroline Daniels
Kingsmere Cottage, Kingsmere Acres, Bridge Lane, Winchester SO21 2BL
T: (01962) 714876
F: (01962) 717398

SHELDWICH
Kent
Littles Manor Farmhouse ★★★★
Contact: Mr Tim Bourne
Kent Holiday Cottages, Shepherd's View, Brissenden Court, Ashford TN26 3BE
T: (01233) 820425
F: (01233) 820746

SHERE
Surrey
Five Pines ★★
Contact: Ms Gill Gellatly
Lockhurst Hatch Farm, Lockhurst Hatch Lane, Guildford GU5 9JN
T: (01483) 202689

SHILTON
Oxfordshire
The Chestnuts ★★★★
Contact: Miss Christine Burton
The Chestnuts, Oxford OX18 4AB
T: (01993) 844905
F: (01993) 841508

SHIPBOURNE
Kent
The Old Stables ★★★★
Contact: Mrs Cohen
The Old Stables, Great Oaks House, Puttenden Road, Tonbridge TN11 9RX
T: (01732) 810739
F: (01732) 810738
E: kent.lets@virgin.net
I: www.kent-lets.co.uk

SHIPTON-UNDER-WYCHWOOD
Oxfordshire
Plum Cottage ★★★★
Contact: Mrs Angela Richards
Manor Cottages & Cotswold Retreats, Priory Mews, 33A Priory Lane, Oxford OX18 4SG
T: (01993) 824252
F: (01993) 824443
E: mancott@netcomuk.co.uk
I: www.manorcottages.co.uk

Turkey Cottage ★★★★
Contact: Cottage in the Country
Forest Gate, Frog Lane, Chipping Norton OXY 6JZ
T: (01993) 831495
F: (01993) 831095
E: cottage@cottageinthecountry.co.uk
I: www.cottageinthecountry.co.uk

6 Westgate ★★★★
Contact: Mrs Helen Harrison
Northgat, Shipton Court, Shipton-under-Wychwood, Chipping Norton OX7 6DG
T: (01993) 830202
F: (01993) 830202

SHOREHAM-BY-SEA
West Sussex
140 Old Fort Road ★★★★
Contact: Mr Richard Harris
Best of Brighton & Sussex Cottages Ltd, Windmill Lodge, Vicarage Lane, Rottingdean, Brighton BN2 7HD
T: (01273) 308779
F: (01273) 390211
E: brightoncottages@pavilion.co.uk
I: www.bestofbrighton.co.uk

SHORTGATE
East Sussex
White Lion Farm Cottages ★★★
Contact: Mrs Diana Green
White Lion Farm Cottages, White Lion Farm, Lewes BN8 6PJ
T: (01825) 840288
F: (01825) 840288

SHORWELL
Isle of Wight
Cheverton Farm Cottage & Brummell Barn ★★★★-★★★★★
Contact: Mrs Sheila Hodgson
Cheverton Farm Cottage & Brummell Barn, Cheverton Farm, Cheverton Shute, Newport PO30 3JE
T: (01983) 741017
F: (01983) 741017

Marylands ★★★
Contact: Mrs Honor Vass
Island Cottage Holidays, The Old Vicarage, West Street, Kingston, Corfe Castle, Wareham BH20 5LH
T: (01929) 480080
F: (01929) 481070
E: enq@islandcottageholidays.com
I: www.islandcottageholidays.com

Sandfoot ★★★★
Contact: Mrs Kathy Domaille
Sandfoot, Sandy Way, Newport PO30 3LN
T: (01983) 840781
E: info@godshillparkfarm
I: www.islandcottageholidays.com

Stone Place Cottage ★★★
Contact: Ms Lisa Baskill
Home from Home Holidays, 31 Pier Street, Ventnor PO38 1SX
T: (01983) 854340
F: (01983) 855524

SIDLESHAM
West Sussex
Tombrec ★★
Contact: Mrs Christine Morris
The Old Bakery, Mill Lane, Chichester PO20 7LZ
T: (01243) 641379
F: (01243) 641129
E: chris_morris@onetel.net.uk
I: www.tombrec.com

SIDLESHAM COMMON
West Sussex
Lockgate Dairy Cottages ★★★★
Contact: Mrs Jean Buchanan
Lockgate Dairy Cottages, Lockgate Road, Chichester PO20 7QH
T: (01243) 641452
F: (01243) 641452
E: buchanan.j@virgin.net
I: www.lockgatedairy.co.uk

SMARDEN
Kent
Bakehouse ★★★
Contact: Mrs Brenda Beck
Freedom Holiday Homes, 15 High Street, Cranbrook TN17 3EB
T: (01580) 720770
F: (01580) 720771
E: mail@freedomholidayhomes.co.uk
I: www.freedomholidayhomes.co.uk

The Cobbles ★★★
Contact: Mrs Brenda Beck
Freedom Holiday Homes, 15 High Street, Cranbrook TN17 3EB
T: (01580) 720770
F: (01580) 720771
E: mail@freedomholidayhomes.co.uk
I: www.freedomholidayhomes.co.uk

Dering Cottage ★★★★
Contact: Mrs Brenda Beck
Freedom Holiday Homes, 15 High Street, Cranbrook TN17 3EB
T: (01580) 720770
F: (01580) 720771
E: mail@freedomholidayhomes.co.uk

SOUTH CHAILEY
East Sussex
Tile Cottage ★★★
Contact: Mr Stuart Winter
Tile Cottage, Kilnwood Lane, Lewes BN8 4AU
T: (01732) 369168
F: (01732) 358817
E: holidays@gardenofenglandcottages.co.uk
I: www.gardenofenglandcottages.co.uk

SOUTH WONSTON
Hampshire
'Burwood' ★★★★
Contact: Mrs Alice Lowery
Burwood, 128 Downs Road, Winchester SO21 3EH
T: (01962) 881690
E: lowery@euphonyzone.com

SOUTHAMPTON
Southampton
Bridge Terrace Apartments ★★
Contact: Mr Mike & Mrs Sue Batley
Town or Country Serviced Apartments & Houses, 60 Oxford Street, Southampton SO14 3DL
T: (023) 80881000
F: (023) 80881010
E: town@interalpha.co.uk
I: www.intent.co.uk/southampton/hotels/townorc/index.htm

Bridge Terrace Studio Apartments ★★
Contact: Mr Mike & Mrs Sue Batley
Town or Country Serviced Apartments & Houses, 60 Oxford Street, Southampton SO14 3DL
T: (023) 80881000
F: (023) 80881010
E: town@interalpha.co.uk
I: www.intent.co.uk/southampton/hotels/townorc/index.htm

4 Canada Place ★★★
Contact: Mr Mike & Mrs Sue Batley
Town or Country Serviced Apartments & Houses, 60 Oxford Street, Southampton SO14 3DL
T: (023) 80881000
F: (023) 80881010
E: town@interalpha.co.uk
I: www.intent.co.uk/southampton/hotels/townorc/index.htm

7 Canada Place ★★★
Contact: Mr Mike & Mrs Sue Batley
Town or Country Serviced Apartments & Houses, 60 Oxford Street, Southampton SO14 3DL
T: (023) 80881000
F: (023) 80881010
E: town@interalpha.co.uk
I: www.intent.co.uk/southampton/hotels/townorc/index.htm

27 The Grenwich ★★★★
Contact: Mr Mike & Mrs Sue Batley
Town or Country Serviced Apartments & Houses, 60 Oxford Street, Southampton SO14 3DL
T: (023) 8088 1000
F: (023) 8088 1010
E: town@interalpha.co.uk

45 The Grenwich ★★★★
Contact: Mr Mike & Mrs Sue Batley
Town or Country Serviced Apartments & Houses, 60 Oxford Street, Southampton SO14 3DL
T: (023) 8088 1000
F: (023) 8088 1010
E: town@interalpha.co.uk

Establishments printed in blue have a detailed entry in this guide

SOUTH EAST ENGLAND

307 Imperial Apartments ★★★★
Contact: Mr Mike & Mrs Sue Batley
Town or Country Serviced Apartments & Houses, 60 Oxford Street, Southampton SO14 3DL
T: (023) 8088 1000
F: (023) 8088 1010
E: town@interalpha.co.uk

315 Imperial Apartments ★★★★
Contact: Mr Mike & Mrs Sue Batley
Town or Country Serviced Apartments & Houses, 60 Oxford Street, Southampton SO14 3DL
T: (023) 8088 1000
F: (023) 8088 1010
E: town@interalpha.co.uk

Pinewood Lodge Apartments ★★★
Contact: Bradberry
Pinewood Lodge Apartments, Kanes Hill, Southampton SO19 6AJ
T: (023) 80402925
E: stan.bradberry@tesco.net

STANDLAKE
Oxfordshire

Wheelwrights Cottage ★★★★
Contact: Mr & Mrs JR Hunt
Acham Farm, 29 Rack End, Witney OX29 7SA
T: (01865) 300536
E: bobnora@huntb1.fsnet.co.uk
I: www.oxtowns.co.uk/wheelwrights

STANFORD IN THE VALE
Oxfordshire

The Paddock ★★★★
Contact: Cottage in the Country
Forest Gate, Frog Lane, Oxford OX7 6JZ
T: (01993) 831495
F: (01993) 831095
E: cottage@cottageinthecountry.co.uk
I: www.cottageinthecountry.co.uk

STAPLE
Kent

Piglet Place ★★★★
Contact: Mr Richard & Mrs Bronwen Barber
Greengage Cottage, Lower Road, Barnsole, Canterbury CT3 1LG
T: (01304) 813321
F: (01304) 812312
E: richbarber@lineone.net
I: www.pigletplace.co.uk

STAPLECROSS
East Sussex

York Cottage
Rating Applied For
Contact: Mrs Jill Winter
Garden of England Cottages, 189A High Street, Tonbridge TN9 1BX
T: (01732) 369168
F: (01732) 358817
E: holidays@gardenofenglandcottages.co.uk

STAPLEHURST
Kent

Gardeners Cottage ★★★★
Contact: Mrs Brenda Beck
Freedom Holiday Homes, 15 High Street, Cranbrook TN17 3EB
T: (01580) 720770
F: (01580) 720771
E: mail@freedomholidayhomes.co.uk
I: www.gardenofenglandcottages.co.uk

6 Headcorn Road ★★
Contact: Mrs Maxted
6 Headcorn Road, Tonbridge TN12 0BT
T: (01580) 891219

Rose Cottage Oast ★★★
Contact: Mrs Brenda Beck
Freedom Holiday Homes, 15 High Street, Cranbrook TN17 3EB
T: (01580) 720770
F: (01580) 720771
E: mail@freedomholidayhomes.co.uk
I: www.freedomholidayhomes.co.uk

Tudor Hurst Cottage ★★★★
Contact: Mrs Brenda Beck
Freedom Holiday Homes, 15 High Street, Cranbrook TN17 3EB
T: (01580) 720770
F: (01580) 720771
E: mail@freedomholidayhomes.co.uk
I: www.freedomholidayhomes.co.uk

STEEPLE ASTON
Oxfordshire

Westfield Farm Motel ★★★
Contact: Mrs Julie Hillier
Westfield Farm Motel, Fenway, Oxford OX25 4SS
T: (01869) 340591
F: (01869) 347594
E: info@westfieldmotel.u-net.com

STOCKBURY
Kent

The Old Dairy ★★★
Contact: Mrs Anthony
The Old Dairy, Wheatsheaf Farm, Hazel Street, Sittingbourne ME9 7SA
T: (01622) 884222

STONEGATE
East Sussex

Coopers Farm Cottage ★★★★★
Contact: Ms Jane Howard
Coopers Farm Cottage, Coopers Farm, Stonegate TN5 7EH
T: (01580) 200386
E: jane@coopersfarmstonegate.co.uk
I: www.coopersfarmstonegate.co.uk

STONESFIELD
Oxfordshire

Laughtons Retreat ★★★
Contact: Mr Dave Holloway
Callow Farm, The Ridings, Stonesfield, Witney OX29 8EG
T: (01993) 891172

STONOR
Oxfordshire

White Pond Farm ★★★★
Contact: Mrs Lindy Stracey
White Pond Farm, Henley-on-Thames RG9 6HG
T: (01491) 638224
F: (01491) 638428
I: www.whitepondfarm.co.uk

STORRINGTON
West Sussex

Byre Cottages ★★★-★★★★
Contact: Mr Grahame Kittle
Byre Cottages, Sullington Manor Farm, Sullington Lane, Pulborough RH20 4AE
T: (01903) 745754

STOWTING
Kent

Cavalry Farm ★★★
Contact: Mrs Marion Britton
Cavalry Farm, Ashford TN25 6BG
T: (01233) 750319
F: (01233) 750225

STREAT
West Sussex

The Gote Lodge ★★★
Contact: Mrs Caroline Tower
The Gote Lodge, Streat, Hassocks BN6 8RN
T: (01273) 890976
F: (01273) 891656
E: tower@gote.freeserve.co.uk

SUTTON VALENCE
Kent

1 Trafalgar Cottage ★★★★
Contact: Mrs Ruth Wise
1 Trafalgar Cottage, Chart Road, Maidstone ME17 3RB
T: 0796 7 009509
I: www.colesco.co.uk/hoildayletts

SWAY
Hampshire

Hackney Park ★★★
Contact: Mrs Helen Beale
Hackney Park, Mount Pleasant Lane, Lymington SO41 8LS
T: (01590) 682049

High Bank ★
Contact: Mr Stuart Bailey
Homefield, Silver Street, Lymington SO41 6DG
T: (01590) 682025
F: (01590) 683782
E: cottages@stuartbailey.net
I: www.stuartbailey.net

4 Laurel Close ★★★★
Contact: Mrs Jacquie Taylor
Three Corners, Centre Lane, Lymington SO41 0JP
T: (01590) 645127
E: tommy.tiddles@virgin.net

Little Corner Cottage ★★★★
Contact: Mrs Maureen Jones
315 Vale Road, Aldershot GU12 5LN
T: (01252) 664428
E: maureengaryl@hotmail.com
I: www.littlecornercottage.co.uk

The Old Exchange ★★★
Contact: Mrs Sarah Alborino
Gabetti Cottage, Priestlands Lane, Lymington SO41 8HZ
T: (01590) 679228
E: arcobaleno_1@hotmail.com

SWERFORD
Oxfordshire

Heath Farm Holiday Cottages ★★★★-★★★★★★
Contact: Mr David & Mrs Nena Barbour
Heath Farm Holiday Cottages, Swerford, Chipping Norton OX7 4BN
T: (01608) 683270
F: (01608) 683222
I: www.heathfarm.com

TELSCOMBE
East Sussex

The Coach House ★★★★
Contact: Mr Richard Harris
Best of Brighton & Sussex Cottages Ltd, Windmill Lodge, Vicarage Lane, Brighton BN2 7HD
T: (01273) 308779
F: (01273) 300266
E: enquiries@bestofbrighton.co.ukk

TENTERDEN
Kent

Cromwell Cottage ★★★
Contact: Mrs Valerie Ernst Aventine, Ingleden Park Road, Tenterden TN30 6NS
T: (01580) 762958
F: (01580) 762958
E: val@cromwellcottage.fsnet.co.uk

Meadow Cottage & Tamworth Cottage ★★★★
Contact: Mrs Cooke
Great Prawls Farm, Stone in Oxney, Tenterden TN30 7HB
T: (01797) 270539
E: info@prawls.co.uk
I: www.prawls.co.uk

Quince Cottage ★★★★
Contact: Mrs Heather E S Crease
Laurelhurst, 38 Ashford Road, Tenterden TN30 6LL
T: (01580) 765636
E: quincott@zetnet.co.uk
I: www.quincecottage.co.uk

44 Rogersmead ★★★★
Contact: Mrs Brenda Beck
Freedom Holiday Homes, 15 High Street, Cranbrook TN17 3EB
T: (01580) 720770
F: (01580) 720771
E: mail@freedomholidayhomes.co.uk
I: www.freedomholidayhomes.co.uk

SOUTH EAST ENGLAND

THAME
Oxfordshire

Goldsworthy Cottage ★★★
Contact: Mrs Janet Eaton
Cuttle Cottage, 17 Southern Road, Thame OX9 2EE
T: (01844) 213035
E: janet-eaton@virgin.net
I: www.cottageinthecountry.co.uk

The Hollies ★★★★
Contact: Ms Julia Tanner
Little Acre, 4 High Street, Thame OX9 7AT
T: (01844) 281423
E: info@thehollisthame.co.uk
I: www.thehollisthame.co.uk

Honeysuckle Cottage ★★★
Contact: Mr & Mrs Lester
Honeysuckle Cottage, Frogmore Lane, Aylesbury HP18 9DZ

THORLEY
Isle of Wight

Holiday Homes Owners Services Ref: Y20 ★★★
Contact: Mr Colin Nolson
Holiday Homes Owners Services (West Wight), 18 Solent Hill, Freshwater PO40 9TG
T: (01983) 761193
F: (01983) 753423
E: holidayhomesiow@ic24.net

Southlee ★★★★
Contact: Mr Steve & Mrs Jill Cowley
Coast and Country, Lee Farm, Yarmouth PO41 0SY
T: (01983) 760327
F: (01983) 760327

TIPTOE
Hampshire

Brockhill Farm ★★★-★★★★★
Contact: Mr David Turner
Brockhill Farm, Sway Road, Lymington SO41 6FQ
T: (01425) 627 457

TONBRIDGE
Kent

88 Avebury Avenue ★★★★★
Contact: Mr Ragnhild Baker
88 Avebury Avenue, Tonbridge TN9 1TQ
T: (01732) 353298
E: charles@cgbaker.eclipse.co.uk
I: www.cgbaker.eclipse.co.uk

Goldhill Mill Cottages ★★★★★
Contact: Mr & Mrs Cole
Goldhill Mill Cottages, Goldhill Mill, Tonbridge TN11 0BA
T: (01732) 851626
F: (01732) 851881
E: vernon.cole@virgin.net
I: www.goldhillmillcottages.com

Grapevine Lodge ★★★
Contact: Mr Stuart Winter
Grapevine Lodge, 1 Grapevine Cottages, Old Whetsted Road, Tonbridge TN12 6QB
T: (01732) 369168
F: (01732) 358817
E: holidays@gardenofenglandcottages.co.uk
I: www.gardenofenglandcottages.co.uk

High Barn Farm Cottage ★★★★
Contact: Mrs Sue Brooks
High Barn Farm Cottage, High Barn Farm, Tonbridge Road, Tonbridge TN11 9JR
T: (01732) 832490
F: (01732) 832490

The Little Dairy ★★★
Contact: Mr Stuart Winter
Garden of England Cottages, The Mews Office, 189A High Street, Tonbridge TN9 1BX
T: (01732) 369168
I: www.gardenofenglandcottages.co.uk

Oast Barn ★★★★
Contact: Mr Ragnhild Baker
Oast Barn, Royal Tunbridge Wells TN9 1TQ
T: (01732) 353298
E: charles@cgbaker.eclipse.co.uk
I: www.cgbaker.eclipse.co.uk

The Roundel ★★★
Contact: Mrs Brenda Beck
Freedom Holiday Homes, 15 High Street, Cranbrook TN17 3EB
T: (01580) 720770
F: (01580) 720771
E: mail@freedomholidayhomes.co.uk
I: www.freedomholidayhomes.co.uk

Takoradi ★★★★
Contact: Mr Stuart Winter
Takoradi, 2B Orchard Drive, Tonbridge TN10 4LU
T: (01732) 369168
F: (01732) 358817
E: holidays@gardenofenglandcottages.co.uk
I: www.gardenofenglandcottages.co.uk

Waters Edge ★★★★
Contact: Mr Stuart Winter
Waters Edge, 22 Mortley Close, Tonbridge TN9 1ET
T: (01732) 369168
F: (01732) 358817
E: holidays@gardenofenglandcottages.co.uk
I: www.gardenofenglandcottages.co.uk

TOTLAND BAY
Isle of Wight

The Coach House ★★★
Contact: Mr Boatfield
Frenchman's Cove, Alum Bay Old Road, Totland Bay PO39 0HZ
T: (01983) 752227
F: (01983) 755125
E: boatfield@frenchmanscove.co.uk

Holiday Homes Owners Services Ref: T1 ★★★
Contact: Mr Colin Nolson
Holiday Homes Owners Services (West Wight), 18 Solent Hill, Freshwater PO40 9TG
T: (01983) 753423
F: (01983) 753423
E: holidayhomesiow@ic24.net

Holiday Homes Owners Services Ref: T6 ★★★
Contact: Mr Colin Nolson
Holiday Homes Owners Services (West Wight), 18 Solent Hill, Freshwater PO40 9TG
T: (01983) 753423
F: (01983) 753423
E: holidayhomesiow@ic24.net

Holiday Homes Owners Services Ref: T7 ★★★★
Contact: Mr Colin Nolson
Holiday Homes Owners Services (West Wight), 18 Solent Hill, Freshwater PO40 9TG
T: (01983) 753423
F: (01983) 753423
E: holidayhomesiow@ic24.net

Holiday Homes Owners Services Ref: T8 ★★★
Contact: Mr Colin Nolson
Holiday Homes Owners Services (West Wight), 18 Solent Hill, Colwell Bay PO40 9TG
T: (01983) 753423
F: (01983) 753423
E: holidayhomesiow@ic24.net

5 Manor Villas ★★
Contact: Mrs Lisa Baskill
Home from Home Holidays, 31 Pier Street, Ventnor PO38 1SX
T: (01983) 854340
F: (01983) 855524
E: admin@hfromh.co.uk

Seawinds Self-Catering Bungalows ★★
Contact: Mrs Jacquie Simmonds
Norton Lodge, Granville Road, Totland Bay PO39 0AZ
T: (01983) 752772

Stonewind Farm ★★★
Contact: Mrs Pat Hayles
Barn Cottage, Middleton, Freshwater PO40 9RW
T: (01983) 752912
F: (01983) 752912

Summers Lodge ★★★★
Contact: Mrs Honor Vass
Island Cottage Holidays, The Old Vicarage, Kingston, Wareham BH20 5LH
T: (01929) 480080
F: (01929) 481070
E: enq@islandcottagesholidays.com

TUDELEY
Kent

Latters Farm Barn ★★★★
Contact: Mr Stuart Winter
Latters Farm Barn, Hartlake Road, Tonbridge TN11 0PG
T: (01732) 369168
F: (01732) 358817
E: holidays@gardenofenglandcottages.co.uk
I: www.gardenofenglandcottages.co.uk

Latters Oast ★★★★
Contact: Mr Stuart Winter
Garden of England Cottages, The Mews Office, 189A High Street, Tonbridge TN9 1BX
T: (01732) 369168
F: (01732) 358817
E: holidays@gardenofenglandcottages.co.uk
I: www.gardenofenglandcottages.co.uk

TWYFORD
Hampshire

Embessy Cottage ★★★
Contact: Mrs Caroline Rees
Highfield Cottage, Old Rectory Lane, Winchester SO21 1NS
T: (01962) 712921
F: (01962) 712921
E: reescj@hotmail.com
I: www.holidayrentals.com

UCKFIELD
East Sussex

Keen's Lodge ★★★★
Contact: Mr Bill & Mrs Sue Keen
Keen's Lodge, Uckfield TN22 5TT
T: (01825) 750616

UDIMORE
East Sussex

Billingham Byre ★★★★
Contact: Mrs Nanette Hacking
Billingham Farm, Rye TN31 6BD
T: (01424) 882348
E: hackingnan@aol.com

Devonia House ★★★★
Contact: Mr Stuart Winter
Garden of England Cottages, The Mews Office, 189A High Street, Tonbridge TN9 1BX
T: (01732) 369168
F: (01732) 358817
E: holidays@gardenofenglandcottages.co.uk
I: www.gardenofenglandcottages.co.uk

Finlay Cottage ★★★★
Contact: Mr Stuart Winter
Finlay Cottage, Rye TN31 6AX
T: (01732) 369168
F: (01732) 358817
E: holidays@gardenofenglandcottages.co.uk
I: www.gardenofenglandcottages.co.uk

Establishments printed in blue have a detailed entry in this guide

SOUTH EAST ENGLAND

The Jays ★★★★
Contact: Mrs Brenda Beck
Freedom Holiday Homes, 15
High Street, Cranbrook
TN17 3EB
T: (01580) 720770
F: (01580) 720771
E: mail@freedomholidayhomes.co.uk
I: www.freedomholidayhomes.co.uk

ULCOMBE
Kent

Oast ★★★★
Contact: Mrs Brenda Beck
Freedom Holiday Homes, 15
High Street, Cranbrook
TN17 3EB
T: (01580) 720770
F: (01580) 720771
E: mail@freedomholidayhomes.co.uk
I: www.freedomholidayhomes.co.uk

UPCHURCH
Kent

The Old Stable ★★★
Contact: Mr Stuart Winter
The Old Stable, Poot Lane,
Sittingbourne ME9 7HJ
T: (01732) 369168
F: (01732) 358817
E: holidays@gardenofenglandcottages.co.uk
I: www.gardenofenglandcottages.co.uk

VENTNOR
Isle of Wight

Bay Lodge ★★★
Contact: Mrs Lisa Baskill
Home from Home Holidays, 31
Pier Street, Ventnor PO38 1SX
T: (01983) 854340
F: (01983) 855524
E: admin@hfromh.co.uk

Bush Cottage ★★★
Contact: Mrs Lisa Baskill
31 Pier Street, Ventnor
PO38 1SX
T: (01983) 854340
F: (01983) 855524

Bywell
Rating Applied For
Contact: Catherine Hopper
Island Holiday Homes, 138 High
Street, Newport PO30 1TY
T: (01983) 521113
F: (01983) 822050

Clarence House ★★★★
Contact: Mrs Sue Lawson
Clarence House, Park Avenue,
Ventnor PO38 1LE
T: (01983) 852875
F: (01983) 855006
E: c.a.c@btinternet.com
I: www.iowholidayapartments.co.uk

1 Cleeve Court ★★★
Contact: Ms Catherine Hopper
Hose Rhodes Dickson, Island
Holiday Homes, 177 High Street,
Ryde PO33 2HW
T: (01983) 616644
F: (01983) 616640
E: enquiries@island-holiday-homes.net

Cliff Cottage ★★★
Contact: Mrs Lisa Baskill
Home from Home Holidays, 31
Pier Street, Ventnor PO38 1SX
T: (01983) 854340
F: (01983) 855524
E: admin@hfromh.co.uk

Cliff Cottage ★★★★
Contact: Mrs Honor Vass
Island Cottage Holidays, West
Street, Kingston, Corfe Castle,
Wareham BH20 5LH
T: (01929) 480080
F: (01929) 481070

The Clock House ★★★★
Contact: Mrs Honor Vass
Island Cottage Holidays, West
Street, Kingston, Corfe Castle,
Wareham BH20 5LH
T: (01929) 480080
F: (01929) 481070

Cove Cottage ★★★
Contact: Mrs Lisa Baskill
Home from Home Holidays, 31
Pier Street, Ventnor PO38 1SX
T: (01983) 854340
F: (01983) 855524
E: admin@hfromh.co.uk

Daisy Cottage ★★★
Contact: Mrs Valerie Anderson
Mari Laetare, Esplanade, Ventnor
PO38 1JX
T: (01983) 855189
F: (01983) 855189
E: samval@marilaetare.freeserve.co.uk

Dudley House ★★★
Contact: Mrs Lisa Baskill
31 Pier Street, Ventnor
PO38 1SX
T: (01983) 854340
F: (01983) 855524

Garfield Holiday Flats ★★★
Contact: Mrs Susan Stead
Garfield Holiday Flats, 13 Spring
Gardens, Ventnor PO38 1QX
T: (01983) 854084

Gatcliff ★★★★
Contact: Mrs Lisa Baskill
Home from Home Holidays, 31
Pier Street, Ventnor PO38 1SX
T: (01983) 854340
F: (01983) 855524
E: admin@hfromh.co.uk

Glenlyn ★★★
Contact: Mr Louis Stritton
c/o Eversley Hotel, Park Avenue,
Ventnor PO38 1LB
T: (01983) 852244
F: (01983) 856534
E: eversleyhotel@fsbdial.co.uk
I: www.eversleyhotel.com

Halcyon ★★★
Contact: Mrs Lisa Baskill
Home from Home Holidays, 31
Pier Street, Ventnor PO38 1SX
T: (01983) 854340
F: (01983) 855524
E: admin@hfromh.co.uk

Haven Under Hill ★★★★
Contact: Mrs J D Banks
Thompson
The Gorde House, Green Lane,
Woking GU24 8PH
T: (01276) 858168
E: jb-t@tak21.com

Holiday Homes Owners Services Ref: V1 ★★★
Contact: Mr Colin Nolson
Holiday Homes Owners Services
(West Wight), 18 Solent Hill,
Freshwater PO40 9TG
T: (01983) 753423
F: (01983) 753423
E: holidayhomesiow@ic24.net

Ivy Cottage ★★★
Contact: Mr Madeline & Mrs
Peter Newton
17 Foxhills, Ventnor PO38 1LX
T: (01983) 853378
F: (01983) 853378

Jules Cottage ★★★★
Contact: Mrs Lisa Baskill
31 Pier Street, Ventnor
PO38 1SX
T: (01983) 854340
F: (01983) 855524

Marina Apartments ★★★★
Contact: Mr Redding
Marina Apartments, Marine
Parade, Ventnor PO38 1JN
T: (01983) 852802
E: information@marinaapartments.co.uk
I: www.marinaapartments.co.uk

Marula
Contact: Mrs Lisa Baskill
31 Pier Street, Ventnor
PO38 1SX
T: (01983) 854340
F: (01983) 855524

Old Park Hotel ★★★★
Contact: Mrs Sharp
Old Park Hotel, Old Park Road,
Ventnor PO38 1XS
T: (01983) 852583
I: oldparkhotel.com

2 Palmerston House ★★★
Contact: Mrs Lisa Baskill
31 Pier Street, Ventnor
PO38 1SX
T: (01983) 854340
F: (01983) 855524

Park Lodge ★★★★
Contact: Mrs Honor Vass
Island Cottage Holidays, West
Street, Kingston, Corfe Castle,
Wareham BH20 5LH
T: (01929) 480080

Petit Tor ★★★
Contact: Mrs Lisa Baskill
Home from Home Holidays, 31
Pier Street, Ventnor PO38 1SX
T: (01983) 854340
F: (01983) 855524
E: admin@hfromh.co.uk

Richmond Arms and Apartments
Rating Applied For
Contact: Dawn Bothwell
Richmond Arms and
Apartments, Esplanade, Ventnor
PO38 1JX
T: (01983) 855674
F: (01983) 855674

Royal Marine House ★★★
Contact: Mr Richard Wetherill
Aventa Properties, Sylvatica,
Park Road, Winchester SO23 7BE
T: (01962) 878722
F: (01962) 878722
E: aventaarchitects@btconnect.com
I: www.royalmarinehouse.co.uk

Russet Spinney ★★★
Contact: Mrs Lisa Baskill
Home from Home Holidays, 31
Pier Street, Ventnor PO38 1SX
T: (01983) 854340
F: (01983) 855524
E: admin@hfromh.co.uk

St Lawrence Rare Breeds Farm ★★★★
Contact: Mrs Honour Vaff
Island Cottage Holiday, West
Street, Kingston, Corfe Castle,
Wareham BH20 5LH
T: (01929) 481555
F: (01929) 481070
E: eng@islandcottageholiday.com

Sea Haze ★★★
Contact: Mrs Lisa Baskill
31 Pier Street, Ventnor
PO38 1SX
T: (01983) 854340
F: (01983) 855524

Seagate Lodge ★★★
Contact: Ms Julia Warr
8 Dartmouth Park Road, London
NW5 1SY
T: (020) 74854809

3 Seaview ★★★
Contact: Mr & Mrs Smithers
Dykebeck Farm, Wymondham
NR18 9PL
T: (01953) 602477
F: (01953) 602157
E: peter@isleofwightholidays.com
I: www.isleofwightholidays.com

64 South Street ★★★
Contact: Catherine Hopper
Island Holiday Homes, 138 High
Street, Newport PO30 1TY
T: (01983) 521113
F: (01983) 822050

1 St Catherines View ★★
Contact: Mrs Lisa Baskill
Home from Home Holidays, 31
Pier Street, Ventnor PO38 1SX
T: (01983) 854340
F: (01983) 855524
E: admin@hfromh.co.uk

Stoneplace Cottage ★★★
Contact: Mrs Lisa Baskill
31 Pier Street, Ventnor
PO38 1SX
T: (01983) 854340
F: (01983) 855524

Trelawney ★★
Contact: Mrs Lisa Baskill
31 Pier Street, Ventnor
PO38 1SX
T: (01983) 854340
F: (01983) 855524

Valerian ★★★
Contact: Mrs Lisa Baskill
31 Pier Street, Ventnor
PO38 1SX
T: (01983) 854340
F: (01983) 855524

SOUTH EAST ENGLAND

Ventnor Holiday Villas ★-★★
Contact: Mr Stephen King
Ventnor Holiday Villas, Old Fort Place (Reception), Wheelers Bay Road, Ventnor PO38 1HR
T: (01983) 852973
F: (01983) 855401
E: steve@ventnor-holidayvillas.co.uk

Verbena ★★★
Contact: Mrs Lisa Baskill
31 Pier Street, Ventnor PO38 1SX
T: (01983) 854340
F: (01983) 855524

Victoria Villa ★★★
Contact: Ms Hopper Catherine
Island Holiday Homes, 138 High Street, Newport PO30 1TY
T: (01983) 521113
F: (01983) 822050

Western Lines ★★★
Contact: Mrs Lisa Baskill
Home from Home Holidays, 31 Pier Street, Ventnor PO38 1SX
T: (01983) 854340
F: (01983) 855524
E: admin@hfromh.co.uk

Westfield Lodges & Apartments ★★★
Contact: Ms Christine Conwell
14 Maple Wood, Bedhampton Hill, Havant PO9 3JB
T: 0796 8795987
F: (023) 92450378
E: info@westfieldlodges.co.uk
I: www.westfieldlodges.co.uk

Westwood ★★
Contact: Mr Douglas Shrubsole
2 Waddon Way, Croydon CR0 4HU
T: (020) 86861120
F: (020) 86861120
E: ann@annshrubsole.freeserve.co.uk

Woodcliffe Holiday Apartments ★★★
Contact: Mr Bryce Wilson
Woodcliffe Holiday Apartments, The Undercliffe Drive, Ventnor PO38 1XJ
T: (01983) 852397
F: (01983) 852397
E: bryce.wilson@virgin.net
I: www.business.virgin.net/bryce.wilson

VINES CROSS
East Sussex

Cannon Barn ★★★★
Contact: Mrs Anne Reed
Cannon Barn, Boring House Farm, Nettlesworth Lane, Heathfield TN21 9AS
T: (01435) 812285
E: info@boringhousefarm.co.uk
I: www.boringhousefarm.co.uk

WADHURST
East Sussex

Bewl Water Cottages ★★★★
Contact: Mr & Mrs Bentsen
Bewl Water Cottages, Wards Lane, Wadhurst TN5 6HP
T: (01892) 782042
E: bentsen@bewlwatercottages.com
I: www.bewlwatercottages.com

The Old Stables ★★★
Contact: Mrs Edwina Le May
Old Stables, Ladymeads Farm, Lower Cousley Wood, Wadhurst TN5 6HH
T: (01892) 783240
F: (01892) 783562
E: enquiries@camrosa.co.uk

WALLINGFORD
Oxfordshire

Oak Cottage ★★★★
Contact: Mr Philip & Mrs Wendy Burton
Oak Cottage, Oak House, New Road, Wallingford OX10 0AU
T: (01491) 836200
E: pburton@dircon.co.uk

WALMER
Kent

Cottage In Deal ★★
Contact: Mr Alan Hay
Leipziger Str 13D, 91058 Erlangen, Germany
T: +49 9131 65921
F: +49 9131 65733
E: alan.hay@t-online.de

Fisherman's Cottage ★★★
Contact: Dr & Mrs Angela Morris
39 Dorset Road, London SW19 3EZ
T: (020) 85425086
F: (020) 8540 9443

The Gulls & Sea Watch ★★★★
Contact: Mr Sandra & Mrs Kenneth Upton
51 The Strand, Deal CT14 7DP
T: (01304) 371449
F: (01304) 371449
E: palmers3@freenetname.co.uk

Holm Oaks ★★★★
Contact: Mrs Annie Spencer-Smith
Holm Oaks, 72 The Strand, Deal CT14 7DL
T: (01304) 367365
E: holm_oaks@hotmail.com

32 York Road ★★★
Contact: Mrs Janice Twaits
44 Mayfield Road, Chingford, London E4 7JA
T: (020) 85243320

WALTHAM
Kent

Springfield Cottage and Springfield Barn ★★★
Contact: Mr Stuart Winter
Springfield Cottage and Springfield Barn, Ansdore, Canterbury CT4 5QB
T: (01732) 369168
F: (01732) 358817
E: holidays@gardenofenglandcottages.co.uk
I: www.gardenofenglandcottages.co.uk

WALTON-ON-THAMES
Surrey

Guest Wing ★★★★
Contact: Mr Richard Dominy
Guest Wing, 30 Mayfield Gardens, Walton-on-Thames KT12 5PP
T: (01932) 241223

WARBLETON
East Sussex

Well Cottage ★★★★
Contact: Mr Stuart Winter
Well Cottage, Warbleton, Heathfield TN21 9PX
T: (01732) 369168
F: (01732) 358817
E: holidays@gardenofenglandcottages.co.uk
I: www.gardenofenglandcottages.co.uk

WAREHORNE
Kent

Tuckers Farm ★★★★
Contact: Mrs Bernadette Restorick
Tuckers Farm, Warehorne, Ashford TN26 2ER
T: (01233) 733433 & 07796 878733
F: (01233) 733700
E: prestorick@aol.com

WATCHFIELD
Oxfordshire

The Coach House ★★★★★
Contact:
Cottage in the Country Cottage Holidays, Forest Gate, Frog Lane, Oxford OX7 6JZ
T: (01993) 831495
F: (01993) 831095
E: info@cottageinthecountry.co.uk

WELLOW
Isle of Wight

Blakes Barn & Dairy Cottages ★★★★
Contact: Mr & Mrs Alan Milbank
Mattingley Farm, Main Road, Yarmouth PO41 0SZ
T: (01983) 760503
F: (01983) 760503
E: i.milbank@btinternet.com

Brook Cottage & Mrs Tiggywinkles Cottage ★★★★
Contact: Mrs Anne Longford
Warren Holidays, The Warren, 1 Elenors Grove, Ryde PO33 4HE
T: (01983) 883364
F: (01983) 884980
E: anne.longford@btinternet.com
I: www.warrenholidays.com

Jubilee Villa ★★★★
Contact: Mr Steve & Mrs Jill Cowley
Lee Farm, Yarmouth PO41 0SY
T: (01983) 760327
F: (01983) 760327

Tudor Lee
Rating Applied For
Contact: Mrs Jill Cowley
Tudor Lee, Lee Farm, Yarmouth PO41 0SY
T: (01983) 760327
F: (01983) 760327
E: coast@country.co.uk

WEST ASHLING
West Sussex

Hills Cottage ★★★★
Contact: Mrs Virginia Jack
Down Street, Chichester PO18 8DP
T: (01243) 574382
F: 0709 2 217358
E: hills.cottage@btinternet.com
I: www.hillscottage.com

WEST HORSLEY
Surrey

West View ★★★
Contact: Mrs Janet Steer
West View, Shere Road, Leatherhead KT24 6EW
T: (01483) 284686
E: cliveandjan@aol.com
I: www.homestead.com/2westview

WEST MALLING
Kent

The Shire ★★★★
Contact: Mr & Mrs S Garrard
The Shire, Manor Farm, West Malling ME19 6RE
T: (01732) 842091
F: (01732) 873784
E: barbaralambert@lineone.net

WEST MARDEN
West Sussex

Barley Cottage ★★★★
Contact: Mr & Mrs Martin Edney
West Marden Farmhouse, West Marden Farm, Chichester PO18 9ES
T: (023) 92631382
E: carole.edney@btopenworld.com
I: www.barleycottage.co.uk

Cabragh Cottage ★★★★
Contact: Mrs Lesley Segrave
Cabragh House, West Marden, Chichester PO18 9EJ
T: (023) 9263 1267
E: lsegrave@tinyworld.co.uk

The Coach House
Rating Applied For
Contact: Mr R & Mrs J Hawes
The Coach House, Horsley Farm, Chichester PO18 9PB
T: (023) 92631261

The Old Stables ★★★★★
Contact: Mr & Mrs Martin Edney
West Marden Farmhouse, West Marden Farm, Chichester PO18 9ES
T: (023) 92631382
E: carole.edney@btopenworld.com
I: www.theoldstables.net

WEST PECKHAM
Kent

Beech Farmhouse ★★★★
Contact: Mr & Mrs Wooldridge
Beech Farmhouse, Stan Lane, Maidstone ME18 5JT
T: (01622) 812360
F: (01622) 814659

WEST WELLOW
Hampshire

Forest View Cottage
Rating Applied For
Contact: Mrs P Field
Pineview, Canada Common, Romsey SO51 6DH
T: (01794) 324383

Establishments printed in blue have a detailed entry in this guide

SOUTH EAST ENGLAND

The Granary ★★
Contact: Mrs Jean Haworth
Lukes Barn, Maurys Lane,
Romsey SO51 6DA
T: (01794) 324431
F: (01794) 324431
E: bookings@lukesbarn.com

WEST WITTERING
West Sussex

The Breeze ★★★★
Contact:
Baileys Estate Agents, 17 Short
Road, Chichester PO20 8DY
T: (01243) 672217
F: (01243) 670100
E: info@baileys.uk.com

Brendon ★★★
Contact: Mr Michael Palmer
15 Downs Way, Epsom KT18 5LU
T: (01372) 739150
E: info@wittering.info/
I: www.wittering.info/

WESTBOURNE
West Sussex

2 Longcopse Cottages ★★★★
Contact: Mrs Diana Ashe
2 Longcopse Cottages, Long
Copse Lane, Emsworth
PO10 8SU
T: (01243) 379296
F: (01243) 378697

WESTBROOK
Kent

The Cottage ★★★
Contact: Mr & Mrs R T Smith
The Cottage, 190 Canterbury
Road, Margate CT9 5JW
T: (01843) 834545
F: (01843) 834545

WESTCOTT
Surrey

The Garden Flat ★★★★
Contact: Ms Louise Scillitoe
Brown
The Garden Flat, Chartfield,
Guildford Road, Dorking
RH4 3LG
T: (01306) 883838
F: (01306) 883838

WESTERHAM
Kent

The Barn at Bombers ★★★★★
Contact: Mr & Mrs Roy or
Brigitte Callow
The Barn at Bombers, Bombers
Lane, Westerham TN16 2JA
T: (01959) 573471
F: (01959) 540035
E: roy@bombers-farm.co.uk
I: www.bombers-farm.co.uk

WESTFIELD
East Sussex

Mashe Foldes Stable ★★★
Contact: Mr Stuart Winter
Garden of England Cottages, The
Mews Office, 189A High Street,
Tonbridge TN9 1BX
T: (01732) 369168
F: (01732) 358817
E: holidays@
gardenofenglandcottages.co.uk
I: www.
gardenofenglandcottages.co.uk

WHIPPINGHAM
Isle of Wight

Daisy Cottage ★★★★
Contact: Mr G Newnham
Alberts Dairy, Heathfield Farm,
Whippingham Road, East Cowes
PO32 6NQ
T: (01983) 884553
F: (01983) 568822
E: post@newnhams.freeserve.co.uk

WHITSTABLE
Kent

Fairway View ★★★★
Contact: Mrs Maria Hudson
35 Cedar Road, Romford
RM7 7JS
T: (01708) 766599
E: brian_hudson@novar.com

Flat 31 Grand Pavilion ★★★★
Contact: Mr Robert Gough
Alliston House, 1 Joy Lane,
Whitstable CT5 4LS
T: (01227) 779066
F: (01227) 779066
E: bobgough57@aol.com

3 Harbour Mews ★★★★
Contact: Mr & Mrs John Kaye
46 Marine Parade, Whitstable
CT5 2BE
T: (01227) 280391
E: jkaye46@hotmail.com
I: www.harbourmews.co.uk

Harbour Rest ★★★
Contact: Mr & Mrs Avery-Smith
21 Argyle Road, Whitstable
CT5 1JS
T: (01227) 261449 &
07932 410343

38 Marine Parade ★★★★
Contact: Mrs Janet Adams
98 Northwood Road, Whitstable
CT5 2HA
T: (01227) 282095
E: janetwadams@btinternet.com

Oyster Mews
Rating Applied For
Contact: Mrs Ray Jones
28 Castle Road, Tankerton,
Whitstable CT5 2DY
T: (01227) 273225
E: j.oyster@virgin.net

4 Saxon Shore ★★★★
Contact: Mrs Bryant
29 Summerfield Avenue,
Whitstable CT5 1NR
T: (01227) 263958

Trappers End ★★★
Contact: Mrs Janette Reed
11 Woodlands Avenue, New
Malden KT3 3UL
T: (020) 89420342
F: (020) 89420344
E: janette.reed07@btopenworld.com
I: www.kenttourism.co.uk/trappers

WHITWELL
Isle of Wight

43 Bannock Road ★★★
Contact: Mrs Sally Morris
1 Upper Ash Drive, Ventnor
PO38 2PD
T: (01983) 730153

Castleview Flat ★★★
Contact: Mr Matthew White
Island Holiday Homes, 138 High
Street, Ryde PO33 1TY
T: (01983) 521114

2 Farm Cottages ★★★
Contact: Mrs Lisa Baskill
31 Pier Street, Ventnor
PO38 1SX
T: (01983) 854340
F: (01983) 855524

Fossil Cottage ★★★
Contact: Mrs Honor Vass
Island Cottage Holidays, The Old
Vicarage, West Street, Kingston,
Corfe Castle, Wareham
BH20 5LH
T: (01929) 480080
F: (01929) 481070
E: enq@islandcottageholidays.com
I: www.islandcottageholidays.com

Greystone Cottage ★★
Contact: Mrs Steele
Mardon, 79 New Road, Sandown
PO36 0AG
T: (01983) 407221

Nettlecombe Farm ★★★-★★★★
Contact: Mrs Jose Morris
Nettlecombe Farm, Nettlecombe
Lane, Ventnor PO38 2AF
T: (01983) 730783
F: (01983) 730783

The Old Dairy ★★★
Contact: Mrs Denham
Lower Dolcoppice Farm,
Dolcoppice Lane, Ventnor
PO38 2PB
T: (01983) 551445
F: (01983) 551445

Pyrmont Cottage ★★
Contact:
Hose Rhodes Dickson,
Residential And Holiday Letting
Agents, 177 High Street, Ryde
PO33 2HW
T: (01983) 616644
F: (01983) 568822
E: rental_office@
hose-rhodes-dickson.co.uk

Sunglaze ★★★★
Contact: Mrs Evans
Kingsmede, Kemming Road,
Ventnor PO38 2QX
T: (01983) 730867

Whitwell Station ★★★
Contact: Mrs Julia Carter
Old Station House, Nettlecombe
Lane, Ventnor PO38 2QA
T: (01983) 730667
F: (01983) 730667
E: enqs@whitwellstation.co.uk
I: www.whitwellstation.co.uk

Willow Bank ★★★
Contact: Eldridge
Mill View, Ricketts Lane,
Sturminster Newton DT10 1BY
T: (01258) 473327

The Wing, Dean Farm ★★★★
Contact: Mrs Honor Vass
Island Cottage Holidays,
Godshill Park Farm House,
Ventnor PO38 3JF
T: (01983) 730236
F: (01983) 730202
E: enq@islandcottageholidays.com
I: www.islandcottageholidays.com

WICKHAM
Hampshire

Meonwood Annexe ★★★
Contact: Mrs Susan Wells
Meonwood, Heath Road,
Fareham PO17 6JZ
T: (01329) 834130
F: (01329) 834380

WILMINGTON
East Sussex

Old Inn House ★★★★
Contact: Mrs Annette Whamond
Old Inn House, The Street,
Polegate BN26 5SN
T: (01323) 871331
F: (01323) 871331
E: awhamond@netscape.net
I: www.tourismsoutheast.com/member/webpages/M0302.htm

Wishing Well Cottage ★★★★
Contact: Mr Stuart Winter
Garden of England Cottage,
189A High Street, Tonbridge
TN9 1BX
T: (01732) 369168
F: (01732) 358817
E: holidays@
gardenofenglandcottages.co.uk
I: www.
gardenofenglandcottages.co.uk

WINCHELSEA
East Sussex

Landgate Cottage ★★★★
Contact: Mrs Gill Stringer
1 Russell Villas, Willoughby
Road, Twickenham TW1 2QG
T: (020) 8921417

WINCHELSEA BEACH
East Sussex

Tamarix ★★★
Contact: Mr & Mrs Miller
Plovers Barrows, Uckfield
TN22 4JP
T: (01825) 732034

WINCHESTER
Hampshire

87 Christchurch Road ★★★★
Contact: Mrs Elisabeth Peacocke
87 Christchurch Road,
Winchester SO23 9QY
T: (01962) 854902
F: (01962) 843458
E: the_peacockes@hotmail.com
I: www.cottageguide.co.uk/christchurch/

Flat 7 Kingsway Court ★★
Contact: Mr Peter Bulmer
Flat 14 Kingsway Court,
Kingsway Gardens, Eastleigh
SO53 1FG
T: (023) 80253159

SOUTH EAST ENGLAND

Gyleen ★★★★★
Contact: Mr Paul & Mrs Elizabeth Tipple
9 Mount View Road, Oliver's Battery, Winchester SO22 4JJ
T: (01962) 861918
F: 08700 542801
E: pauliz@tipple.demon.co.uk
I: www.cottageguide.co.uk/gyleen

Little Acres ★★★
Contact: Mrs Joy Welch
Marsfield, Kennel Lane, Winchester SO22 6PT
T: (01962) 882295
F: (01892) 882295
E: littleacres@door.gear.co.uk

Mallard Cottage ★★★
Contact: Mrs Tricia Simpkin
Mallard Cottage, 64 Chesil Street, Winchester SO23 0HX
T: (01962) 853002
F: (01962) 853002
E: mallardsimpkin@aol.com
I: www.mallardcottage.co.uk

Milnthorpe ★★★★★
Contact: Mrs Alison Dudgeon
Milnthorpe, Sleepers Hill, Winchester SO22 4NF
T: (01962) 850440
F: (01962) 890114
E: alison@milnthorpehouse.demon.co.uk

18 Swanmore Close ★★
Contact: Mrs Carole Wilkins
18 Swanmore Close, Winchester SO22 6LX
T: (01962) 883141

WINDSOR
Windsor and Maidenhead

Amberley Place ★★★
Contact: Mrs Nikki Tehel
175 Oxford Road, Windsor SL4 5DX
T: (01753) 865144
E: stripey@attglobal.net

Castle Mews Apartment ★★★★
Contact: Mr Duncan Gordon
17 Spencers Road, Maidenhead SL6 6LJ
T: (01628) 632092
F: (01628) 626631
E: bookings@royalwindsorlets.com
I: www.royalwindsorlets.com

9 The Courtyard ★★★
Contact: Mrs Hitchcock
1 Agar's Place, Slough SL3 9AH
T: (01753) 545005
F: (01753) 545005
E: jhhitchcock@btinternet.com

Dorney Holiday Apartments ★★
Contact: Sarah Everitt
Dorney Holiday Apartments, Nr Windsor SL4 6QQ
T: (01753) 827037
F: (01753) 855022
E: enquiries@troppo.uk.com
I: www.troppo.uk.com

Flat 6 The Courtyard ★★★
Contact: Mr Gavin Gordon
5 Temple Mill Island, Marlow SL7 1SG
T: (01628) 824267
F: (01628) 828949
E: gavingordon@totalise.co.uk
I: www.windsor-selfcatering.co.uk

House in the Courtyard ★★★★★
Contact: Mrs Eva Brooks
Belmont House, 64 Bolton Road, Windsor SL4 3JL
T: (01753) 860860
F: (01753) 830330

Manor View Apartment ★★★
Contact: Mrs Clare Smith
32 Matthews Chase, Bracknell RG42 4UR
T: (01344) 485658
E: manorview@care4free.net
I: www.manorview.care4free.net

Riverviewaccommodation ★★★★
Contact: Mrs Janet Noakes
Riverviewaccommodation, 7 Stovell Road, Windsor SL4 5JB
T: (01753) 863628

WINGHAM
Kent

Charolais Cottages ★★★★
Contact: Mr & Mrs Pagdin
Dambridge Oast, Staple Road, Canterbury CT3 1LU
T: (01227) 720082
F: (01227) 720082
E: info@pagoast.co.uk
I: www.pagoast.co.uk

WITNEY
Oxfordshire

Grove Farm ★★★
Contact: Mr & Mrs J R Bowtell
Grove Farm, Brize Norton Road, Minster Lovell, Witney OX29 0SJ
T: (01993) 843755
E: jrbowtell@aol.com

Little Barn ★★★
Contact: Mrs Sissel Harrison
Little Barn, c/o Stable Barn, New Yatt Road, Witney OX29 6TA
T: (01993) 706632
F: (01993) 706689
E: booking@stablebarn.co.uk

Melrose Villa & Mews ★★★
Contact: Mrs Susan Petty
Melrose Villa & Mews, 74 Corn Street, Witney OX28 6BS
T: (01993) 703035
F: (01993) 771014
E: petty@witneyserve.net
I: www.witneycottages.co.uk

Sighs Cottage ★★
Contact: Mr Peter Crowther
Sighs Cottage, 11 Bridge Street, Witney OX28 1BY
T: (01993) 709596
F: (01993) 709596
F: pjccrowth@hotmail.com

Swallows Nest ★★★★
Contact: Mrs Janet Strainge
Springhill Farm Swallows Nest, High Cogges, Witney OX29 6UL
T: (01993) 704919
E: jan@strainge.fsnet.co.uk

WOODCHURCH
Kent

The Stable ★★★★
Contact: Mrs Carol Vant
The Stable, Coldblow Lodge, Ashford TN26 3PH
T: (01233) 860388
F: (01233) 860388
E: carol.vant@btinternet.com
I: www.thestablecottage.co.uk

WOODLANDS
Hampshire

Purlins ★★★
Contact: Mrs Kay Lindsell
Purlins, 159 Woodlands Road, Southampton SO40 7GL
T: (023) 80293833
F: (023) 80293855
E: Kay@purlins.net
I: www.purlins.net

WOODMANCOTE
West Sussex

Woodhouse Cottages ★★★
Contact: Mrs Sally Brown
Woodhouse Cottages, Wheatsheaf Road, Henfield BN5 9BA
T: (01273) 491142
F: (01273) 491141
E: sally@woodhouse-cottages.co.uk
I: woodhouse-cottages.co.uk

WOODNESBOROUGH
Kent

Sonnet Cottage ★★
Contact: Mrs Brenda Beck
Freedom Holiday Homes, 15 High Street, Cranbrook TN17 3EB
T: (01580) 720770
F: (01580) 720771
E: mail@freedomholidayhomes.co.uk
I: www.freedomholidayhomes.co.uk

WOOLSTONE
Oxfordshire

Cartwheel Cottage ★★★
Contact: Mrs A K Walker
Cartwheel Cottage, Oxleaze Farm, Faringdon SN7 7QS
T: (01367) 820116
F: (01367) 820116
E: ridgewayholidays@amserve.net

WOOTTON
Kent

Captains & Colonels ★★★
Contact: Mrs Brenda Beck
Freedom Holiday Homes, 15 High Street, Cranbrook TN17 3EB
T: (01580) 720770
F: (01580) 720771
E: mail@freedomholidayhomes.co.uk
I: www.freedomholidayhomes.co.uk

WOOTTON BRIDGE
Isle of Wight

Alpine Cottage ★★★
Contact: Mrs Honor Vass
Island Cottage Holidays, The Old Vicarage, Kingston, Wareham BH20 5LH
T: (01929) 480080
F: (01929) 481070
E: enq@islandcottagesholidays.com
I: www.islandcottageholidays.com

The Barn ★★★★
Contact: Mrs Lisa Baskill
Home from Home Holidays, 31 Pier Street, Ventnor PO38 1SX
T: (01983) 854340
F: (01983) 855524
E: admin@hfromh.co.uk

Grange Farm ★★★
Contact: Mrs Rosemarie Horne
Grange Farm, Staplers Road, Ryde PO33 4RW
T: (01983) 882147
I: www.wightfarmholidays.co.uk/grange

The Hayloft ★★★★
Contact: Mrs Lisa Baskill
31 Pier Street, Ventnor PO38 1SX
T: (01983) 854340
F: (01983) 855524

The Hayloft & New Barn Cottage ★★★★
Contact: Mrs Honor Vass
Island Cottage Holidays, Godshill Park Farm House, Ventnor PO38 3JF
T: (01929) 480080
F: (01929) 481070
E: enq@islandcottagesholidays.com
I: www.cottageholidays.demon.co.uk.

The Orangery ★★★★
Contact: Mrs Honor Vass
Island Cottage Holidays, The Old Vicarage, Kingston, Wareham BH20 5LH
T: (01929) 480080
F: (01929) 481070
E: enq@islandcottagesholidays.com
I: www.islandcottageholidays.com

Palmers Farm
Rating Applied For
Contact: Mr T Rogers
The Old Farmhouse, Brocks Copse Road, Ryde PO33 4NP
T: (01983) 880124

West Wing Westwood House ★★★★
Contact: Mrs Honor Vass
Island Cottage Holidays Ltd., The Old Vicarage, Kingston, Wareham BH20 5LH
T: (01929) 480080
I: www.islandcottageholidays.com

Establishments printed in blue have a detailed entry in this guide

SOUTH EAST ENGLAND

Wootton Keepers Cottage ★★★
Contact: Mrs Honor Vass
Island Cottage Holidays, The Old Vicarage, Kingston, Wareham BH20 5LH
T: (01929) 480080
F: (01929) 481070
E: enq@islandcottageholidays.com
I: www.islandcottageholidays.com

WORTHING
West Sussex

Aldine House ★★★
Contact: Mr & Mrs Hills
311 South Farm Road, Worthing BN14 7TL
T: (01903) 266980
E: hills.aldine@supanet.com

Exmoor House ★
Contact: Mr & Mrs Harrison
Exmoor House, 32 Chesswood Road, Worthing BN11 2AD
T: (01903) 208856

Flat 4 6 Heene Terrace ★★★★
Contact: Mrs Anne Wright
Promenade Holiday Homes, Nepcote Lane, Worthing BN14 0SL
T: (01903) 877047
F: (01903) 877047
E: anne@promenade-holidays.fsbusiness.co.uk
I: www.promenadeholidayhomes.co.uk

Flat 7, Waverley Court ★★★
Contact: Anne Wright
Promenade Holiday Homes, 44 Nepcote Lane, Worthing BN14 0SL
T: (01903) 877047
F: (01903) 877047

Flat A ★★
Contact: Mrs Anne Wright
Promenade Holiday Homes, Nepcote Lane, Worthing BN14 0SL
T: (01903) 877047
F: (01903) 877047
E: anne@promenade-holidays.fsbusiness.co.uk
I: www.promenadeholidayhomes.co.uk

Garden Flat ★★
Contact: Mrs Anne Wright
4 Nepcote Lane, Worthing BN14 0SL
T: (01903) 877047
F: (01903) 877047
E: anne@promenade-holidays.fsbusiness.co.uk
I: www.promenadeholidayhomes.co.uk

2 Harley Court ★★★
Contact: Mr Robert Brew
Promenade Holiday Homes, 165 Dominion Road, Worthing BN14 8LD
T: (01903) 201426
F: (01903) 201426
E: robert@promhols.fsbusiness.co.uk
I: www.promenadeholidayhomes.co.uk

6 Heene Terrace ★★★
Contact: Ms Anne Wright
Promenade Holiday Homes, 44 Netcote Lane, Findon, Worthing BN14 0SL
T: (01903) 877047
I: www.promenadeholidayhomes.co.uk

Holiday Bungalow ★★★
Contact: Mr & Mrs Graham Haynes
Bahnstrasse 59, 3008 Bern, Switzerland
T: +4131 381 1876
F: +4131 381 1876
E: grahamhaynes@tiscalinet.ch

2 Knightsbridge House ★★★
Contact: Ms Greta Paull
35 Cheyne Avenue, South Woodford, London E18 2DP
T: (020) 85302336
F: (020) 8530 2336
E: gretapaull@aol.com

8 Mariners Walk ★★
Contact: Mrs A Wright
Promenade Holiday Homes, 44 Nepcote Lane, Findon BN14 0SL
T: (01903) 877047
F: (01903) 877047
I: www.promenadeholidayhomes.co.uk

Navarino Flat ★★★
Contact: Mrs Cynthia Hanton
Navarino Flat, 46 Navarino Road, Worthing BN11 2NF
T: (01903) 205984
F: (01903) 520620
E: chantan@cwctv.net

Park Cottage ★★★
Contact: Ms Tina Williams
27 Madeira Avenue, Worthing BN11 2AX
T: (01903) 521091

17 Pendine Avenue ★★★
Contact: Mrs Sue Harding
17 Pendine Avenue, Pendine Avenue, Worthing BN11 2NA
T: (01903) 202833
E: sue.harding@catlover.com

Torrington Holiday Flats ★★
Contact: Mrs Elsden & Mary Fitzgerald
Torrington Holiday Flats, 60 Manor Road, Worthing BN11 4SL
T: (01903) 238582 & 07860 699268
F: (01903) 230266
I: www.visitsussex.org/torrington

WROXALL
Isle of Wight

Appuldurcombe Holiday Cottages ★★★-★★★★★
Contact: Mrs Jane Owen
Appuldurcombe Farm, Appuldurcombe Road, Wroxall, Ventnor PO38 3EW
T: (01983) 840188
F: (01983) 840188
I: www.appuldurcombe.co.uk

The Brewhouse & Stable Cottage ★★★
Contact: Mrs Felcity Corry
Little Span Farm, Rew Lane, Ventnor PO38 3AU
T: (01983) 852419
F: (01983) 852419
E: info@spanfarm.co.uk
I: www.spanfarm.co.uk

Clevelands House ★★★
Contact: Mrs Nicolette Roberts
Clevelands House, Clevelands Road, Ventnor PO38 3DZ
T: (01983) 853021
F: (01983) 852340

Malmesbury Cottage ★★★★
Contact: Mrs Lisa Baskill
31 Pier Street, Ventnor PO38 1SX
T: (01983) 854340
F: (01983) 855524

Malmesbury Cottage ★★★★
Contact: Mrs Honor Vass
Island Cottage Holidays, West Street, Kingston, Corfe Castle, Wareham BH20 5LH
T: (01929) 480080
F: (01929) 481070
E: enq@islandcottageholidays.com
I: www.islandcottageholidays.com

Poppies ★★★
Contact: Mrs Lisa Baskill
31 Pier Street, Ventnor PO38 1SX
T: (01983) 854340
F: (01983) 855524

Sundown ★★★
Contact: Mrs Lisa Baskill
31 Pier Street, Ventnor PO38 1SX
T: (01983) 854340
F: (01983) 855524

Wroxall Manor Farmhouse ★★★
Contact: Mrs Virginia Grace
Wroxall Manor Farmhouse, Manor Road, Ventnor PO38 3DN
T: (01983) 854033

WYE
Kent

Downs Farm Granary ★★★★
Contact: Mrs Wendy Barnes
Downs Farm Granary, Ashford TN25 5DJ
T: (01233) 812555
F: (01233) 812555
E: barnes@downsfarm.fsworld.co.uk

YARMOUTH
Isle of Wight

Alma Cottage ★★★★
Contact: Mr Matthew White
Island Holiday Homes, 138 High Street, Newport PO30 1TY
T: (01983) 521114

Holiday Homes Owners Services Ref: Y11 ★★★★
Contact: Mr Colin Nolson
Holiday Homes Owners Services (West Wight), 18 Solent Hill, Freshwater PO40 9TG
T: (01983) 753423
F: (01983) 753423
E: holidayhomesiow@ic24.net

Holiday Homes Owners Services Ref: Y12 ★★★
Contact: Mr Colin Nolson
Holiday Homes Owners Services (West Wight), 18 Solent Hill, Freshwater PO40 9TG
T: (01983) 753423
F: (01983) 753423
E: holidayhomesiow@ic24.net

Holiday Homes Owners Services Ref: Y13 ★★★
Contact: Mr Colin Nolson
Holiday Homes Owners Services (West Wight), 18 Solent Hill, Freshwater PO40 9TG
T: (01983) 753423
F: (01983) 753423
E: holidayhomesiow@ic24.net

Holiday Homes Owners Services ref: Y15 ★★★
Contact: Mr Colin Nolson
Holiday Homes Owners Services (West Wight), 18 Solent Hill, Freshwater PO40 9TG
T: (01983) 753423
F: (01983) 753423
E: holidayhomesiow@ic24.net

Holiday Homes Owners Services Ref: Y17 ★★★
Contact: Mr Colin Nolson
Holiday Homes Owners Services (West Wight), 18 Solent Hill, Freshwater PO40 9TG
T: (01983) 753423
F: (01983) 753423
E: holidayhomesiow@ic24.net

Holiday Homes Owners Services Ref: Y18 ★★★
Contact: Mr Colin Nolson
Holiday Homes Owners Services (West Wight), 18 Solent Hill, Freshwater PO40 9TG
T: (01983) 753423
F: (01983) 753423
E: holidayhomesiow@ic24.net

Holiday Homes Owners Services Ref: Y21 ★★★
Contact: Mr Colin Nolson
Holiday Homes Owners Services (West Wight), 18 Solent Hill, Freshwater PO40 9TG
T: (01983) 753423
F: (01983) 753423
E: holidayhomesiow@ic24.net

Holiday Homes Owners Services Ref: Y3 ★★★
Contact: Mr Colin Nolson
Holiday Homes Owners Services (West Wight), 18 Solent Hill, Freshwater PO40 9TG
T: (01983) 753423
F: (01983) 753423
E: holidayhomesiow@ic24.net

SOUTH EAST ENGLAND

Holiday Homes Owners Services Ref: Y5 ★★★
Contact: Mr Colin Nolson
Holiday Homes Owners Services (West Wight), 18 Solent Hill, Freshwater PO40 9TG
T: (01983) 753423
F: (01983) 753423
E: holidayhomesiow@ic24.net

Holiday Homes Owners Services Ref: Y6 ★★★★★
Contact: Mr Colin Nolson
Holiday Homes Owners Services (West Wight), 18 Solent Hill, Freshwater PO40 9TG
T: (01983) 753423
F: (01983) 753423
E: holidayhomesiow@ic24.net

Holiday Homes Owners Services Ref: Y8 ★★★
Contact: Mr Colin Nolson
Holiday Homes Owners Services (West Wight), 18 Solent Hill, Freshwater PO40 9TG
T: (01983) 753423
F: (01983) 753423
E: holidayhomesiow@ic24.net

Holiday Homes Owners Services Ref: Y9 ★★★
Contact: Mr Colin Nolson
Holiday Homes Owners Services (West Wight), 18 Solent Hill, Freshwater PO40 9TG
T: (01983) 753423
F: (01983) 753423
E: holidayhomesiow@ic24.net

Portside, Sail Loft Annexe, Sail Loft and Starboard ★★★
Contact: Mr John Brady
Manor House, Church Hill, Totland Bay PO39 0EU
T: (01983) 754718

Prosper Cottage ★★★
Contact: Mrs Susan Robinson
The Loft, High Street, Yarmouth PO41 0PL
T: (01983) 760987
F: (01983) 760245

River Cottage ★★★★
Contact: Mr Nigel Howell
River Cottage, Station Road, Yarmouth PO41 0QX
T: (01983) 760553
F: (01983) 760553
E: nigel@isle-wight.co.uk
I: www.isle-wight.co.uk

SOUTH WEST ENGLAND

ABBOTSBURY
Dorset

The Cottage ★★★
Contact: Mrs Val Dredge
The Cottage, Grove Lane, Weymouth DT3 4JH
T: (01305) 871462
E: val@thecottage-abbotsbury.co.uk
I: www.thecottage-abbotsbury.co.uk

Elworth Farmhouse and Poppy's Cottage ★★★★-★★★★★
Contact: Mrs Christine Wade
Elworth Farmhouse and Poppy's Cottage, Elworth, Weymouth DT3 4HF
T: (01305) 871693
E: elworthfarmhouse@aol.com
I: www.members.aol.com/elworthfarmhouse

Gorwell Farm Cottages ★★★★-★★★★★
Contact: Mrs Mary Pengelly
Gorwell Farm Cottages, Gorwell, Weymouth DT3 4JX
T: (01305) 871401
F: (01305) 871441
E: mary@gorwellfarm.co.uk
I: www.gorwellfarm.co.uk

Lawrence's Cottage ★★★
Contact: Mr Zachary Stuart-Brown
Dream Cottages, 5 Hope Square, Weymouth DT4 8TR
T: (01305) 789000
F: (01305) 761346
E: admin@dream-cottages.co.uk
I: www.dream-cottages.co.uk

The Old Coastguards ★★★★
Contact: Mr John & Mrs Cheryl Varley
The Old Coastguards, Weymouth DT3 4LB
T: (01305) 871335
F: (01305) 871766
E: enquiries@oldcoastguards.com
I: www.oldcoastguards.com

ABBOTSHAM
Devon

Bowood Farm Cottages ★★★★
Contact: Toad Hall Cottages, Elliot House, Church Street, Kingsbridge TQ7 1BY
T: (01548) 853089
F: (01548) 853086
E: thc@toadhallcottages.com
I: www.toadhallcottages.com

ADVENT
Cornwall

Aldermoor ★★★-★★★★
Contact: Mrs Golding
Aldermoor, Camelford PL32 9QQ
T: (01840) 213366
F: (01840) 213366

Widewalls Cottage ★★★
Contact: Mrs Pauline Metters
Widewalls Cottage, Widewalls Farm, Camelford PL32 9PY
I: www.widewalls.fsnet.co.uk

ALDERLEY
Gloucestershire

La Vacherie and The Gunroom ★★★★
Contact: Mr & Mrs Shearer
Awssome Partnership, The Old Farmhouse, Wotton-under-Edge GL12 7QT
T: 07930 367621
E: awssomeuk@aol.com
I: www.awssome.com

ALDERTON
Gloucestershire

Rectory Farm Cottages ★★★★
Contact: Mr Peter & Mrs Margaret Burton
Rectory Farm Cottages, Tewkesbury GL20 8NW
T: (01242) 620455
F: (01242) 620456
E: peterannabel@hotmail.com
I: www.rectoryfarmcottages.co.uk

ALDSWORTH
Gloucestershire

Aldwyns Cottage ★★★
Contact: Mrs Judy Munson-Kingham
Pheasant Run, Swyre Farm, Cheltenham GL54 3RE
T: (01451) 844461
F: (01451) 844871

ALLERFORD
Somerset

Lynch Country House Holiday Apartments ★★★★
Contact: Mr & Mrs Tacchi
Lynch Country House Holiday Apartments, Exmoor National Park, Minehead TA24 8HJ
T: (01643) 862800
F: (01643) 862800
E: anntacchi@beeb.net
I: www.lynchcountryhouse.co.uk

Orchard Cottage ★★★
Contact: Mrs Diana Williams
Orchard Cottage, Brandish Street Farm, Allerford, Minehead TA24 8HR
T: (01643) 862383

The Pack Horse ★★★
Contact: Mr Brian & Mrs Linda Garner
The Pack Horse, Allerford, Minehead TA24 8HW
T: (01643) 862475
F: (01643) 862475
I: www.thepackhorse.net

ALTON PANCRAS
Dorset

Bookham Court ★★★★-★★★★★
Contact: Mr & Mrs Andrew Foot
Whiteways, Bookham, Dorchester DT2 7RP
T: (01300) 345511
F: (01300) 345511
E: andy.foot1@btinternet.com
I: www.bookhamcourt.co.uk

AMBERLEY
Gloucestershire

The Squirrels ★★★
Contact: Mrs Valerie Bowen
The Squirrels, Theescombe, Stroud GL5 5AU
T: (01453) 836940
E: valerie.bowen@btinternet.com

AMESBURY
Wiltshire

The Cottage ★★★★
Contact: Mrs Joan Robathan
The Cottage, Maddington House, Maddington Street, Shrewton, Salisbury SP3 4JD
T: (01980) 620406
E: rsrobathan@freenet.co.uk
I: www.maddingtonhouse.co.uk

The Stables ★★★★
Contact: Mrs Anna Thatcher
Ivy Cottage, High Street, Salisbury SP4 9QW
T: (01980) 670557
F: (01980) 670557
E: anna.thatcher@ntlworld.com
I: www.cottageguide.co.uk/thestables-netheravon

Wilsford Cottage H108 ★★★
Contact:
Hideaways, Chapel House, Luke Street, Berwick St John, Shaftesbury SP7 0HQ
T: (01747) 828170
F: (01747) 829090
E: enq@hideaways.co.uk
I: www.hideaways.co.uk

APPLEDORE
Devon

Appledown ★★★
Contact:
Farm & Cottage Holidays, Victoria House, 12 Fore Street, Bideford EX39 1AW
T: (01237) 479146
F: (01237) 421512
E: enquiries@farmcott.co.uk
I: www.farmcott.co.uk

Establishments printed in blue have a detailed entry in this guide

SOUTH WEST ENGLAND

Crab Apple Cottage ★★★
Contact: Agent
Marsden's Cottage Holidays, 2 The Square, Braunton EX33 2JB
T: (01271) 813777
F: (01271) 813664
E: holidays@marsdens.co.uk
I: www.marsdens.co.uk

Jolly Cottage ★★★
Contact:
Farm & Cottage Holidays, Victoria House, 15 Fore Street, Bideford EX39 1AW
T: (01237) 479146
F: (01237) 421512
I: www.farmcott.co.uk

Lyntor ★★★★
Contact:
Farm & Cottage Holidays, Victoria House, 34 Fore Street, Bideford EX39 1AW
T: (01237) 479146
F: (01237) 421512
E: bookings@farmcott.co.uk
I: www.farmcott.co.uk

Meander, Bimbo's and Two Rivers ★★★
Contact:
Farm & Cottage Holidays, Victoria House, 12 Fore Street, Bideford EX39 1AW
T: (01237) 479146
F: (01237) 421512
E: enquiries@farmcott.co.uk
I: www.farmcott.co.uk

Nanashaven ★★
Contact:
Farm & Cottage Holidays, Victoria House, 12 Fore Street, Bideford EX39 1AW
T: (01237) 479146
F: (01237) 421512
E: bookings@farmcott.co.uk

The Sail Loft ★★★
Contact:
Farm & Cottage Holidays, Victoria House, 28 Fore Street, Bideford EX39 1AW
T: (01237) 479146
F: (01237) 421512
E: bookings@farmcott.co.uk

Sailmakers ★★
Contact: Mrs Palmer
179 Old Woking Road, Maybury, Woking GU22 8HP
T: (01483) 761982

The Waterfront ★★★★
Contact:
Farm & Cottage Holidays, Victoria House, 12 Fore Street, Bideford EX39 1AW
T: (01237) 479146
F: (01237) 421512
E: enquiries@farmcott.co.uk
I: www.farmcott.co.uk

Waters Reach ★★★
Contact: Mrs Foley
Mandevyll, The Ridgeway, Potters Bar EN6 5QS
T: (01707) 657644
E: viv@vfoley.freeserve.co.uk

APPLEY
Somerset

Stone Barn Cottages ★★★★
Contact: Mrs A Champion
Stone Barn Cottages, Court Farm, Appley, Wellington TA21 0HJ
T: (01823) 673263
F: (01823) 673287
E: goappleycourt@aol.com

ASHBURTON
Devon

Stares Nest Cottage ★★
Contact: Mrs Hemingway
188 Sutton Court Road, London O20
T: (020) 89955676

Wooder Manor Holiday Homes ★★★-★★★★
Contact: Mrs Angela Bell
Wooder Manor Holiday Homes, Widecombe-in-the-Moor, Dartmoor, Newton Abbot TQ13 7TR
T: (01364) 621391
F: (01364) 621391
E: angela@woodermanor.com
I: www.woodermanor.com

Wren & Robin Cottages ★★★★
Contact: Mrs Margaret Phipps
New Cott Farm, Poundsgate, Newton Abbot TQ13 7PD
T: (01364) 631421
F: (01364) 631421
E: enquiries@newcott-farm.co.uk
I: www.newcott-farm.co.uk

ASHFORD
Devon

Ashford Holt Cottage ★★
Contact:
Toad Hall Cottages, Elliot House, Church Street, Kingsbridge TQ7 1BY
T: (01548) 853089
F: (01548) 853086
E: thc@toadhallcottages.com
I: www.toadhallcottages.com

Garden Cottage ★★★
Contact:
Marsden's Cottage Holidays, 2 The Square, Braunton EX33 2JB
T: (01271) 813777
F: (01271) 813664
E: holidays@marsdens.co.uk
I: www.marsdens.co.uk

Helliers Farm ★★★★
Contact: Mrs Lancaster
Helliers Farm, Kingsbridge TQ7 4NB
T: (01548) 550689
F: (01548) 550689
I: www.helliersfarm.co.uk

Incledon Barn ★★★
Contact: Mr & Mrs Cornwell
Marsden's Cottage Holidays, 2 The Square, Braunton EX33 2JB
T: (01271) 813777
F: (01271) 813664
E: holidays@marsdens.co.uk
I: www.marsdens.co.uk

ASHILL
Devon

Glen Cottage ★★★★
Contact: Miss Caroline Denton
Glen Cottage, Gaddon Down, Cullompton EX15 3NR
T: (01884) 840331
F: (01884) 840331
E: caroline@glencott.co.uk
I: www.glencott.co.uk

ASHINGTON
Dorset

Fripps Cottage ★★★★
Contact: Mrs Helen Edbrooke
Stoneleigh House, 2 Rowlands Hill, Wimborne Minster BH21 1AN
T: (01202) 848312
F: (01202) 848349
E: john@stoneleighhouse.com
I: www.stoneleighhouse.com/frippscottage

ASHLEWORTH
Gloucestershire

Little Manor ★★★★
Contact: Mrs Sylvia Mary Barnes
Little Manor, Ashleworth Manor, Gloucester GL19 4LA
T: (01452) 700350
F: (01452) 700350
E: rjb@ashleworthmanor.fsnet.co.uk

ASHLEY
Gloucestershire

Wisteria Cottage ★★★
Contact: Mrs Alison Smith
4 Manor Farm Cottages, Tetbury GL8 8ST
T: (01666) 577540

ASHPRINGTON
Devon

Hill Quay ★★★★
Contact:
Toad Hall Cottages, Elliot House, Church Street, Kingsbridge TQ7 1BY
T: (01548) 853089
F: (01548) 853086
E: thc@toadhallcottages.com

ASHREIGNEY
Devon

Colehouse Farm ★★★★
Contact:
Farm & Cottage Holidays, Victoria House, 12 Fore Street, Bideford EX39 1AW
T: (01237) 479146
F: (01237) 421512
E: enquiries@farmcott.co.uk
I: www.farmcott.co.uk

Northcott Barton Farm Holiday Cottage ★★★★
Contact: Mrs Gay
Northcott Barton Farm Holiday Cottage, Northcott Barton, Chulmleigh EX18 9PR
T: (01769) 520259
E: sandra@northcottbarton.co.uk
I: www.northcottbarton.co.uk

ASHTON
Cornwall

Chycarne Farm Cottages ★★★
Contact: Mrs P. J. Ross
Chycarne Farm Cottages, Balwest, Helston TR13 9TE
T: (01736) 762473
F: (01736) 762473
E: chycarnefarmcottages@hotmail.com
I: www.chycarne-farm-cottages.co.uk

Gwennol Cottage
Rating Applied For
Contact: Mrs Hughes
10 Rowan Lane, Ashurst, Skelmersdale WN8 6UL
T: (01695) 724485

ASHWATER
Devon

Blagdon Farm Country Holidays ★★★★-★★★★★
Contact: Mr & Mrs Tucker
Blagdon Farm Country Holidays, Beaworthy EX21 5DF
T: (01409) 211509
F: (01409) 211510
I: www.blagdon-farm.co.uk

Braddon Cottages and Forest ★★★
Contact: Mr George & Mrs Anne Ridge
Ashwater, Beaworthy EX21 5EP
T: (01409) 211350
E: holidays@braddoncottages.co.uk
I: www.braddoncottages.co.uk

ASKERSWELL
Dorset

Court Farm Cottages ★★★★-★★★★★
Contact: Mrs Rebecca Bryan
Court Farm Cottages, Dorchester DT2 9EJ
T: (01308) 485668
E: courtfarmcottages@eclipse.co.uk
I: www.eclipse.co.uk/courtfarmcottages/webpg2

Little Court ★★★★★
Contact: Mr Leonard Vickery
The Barn House, Moens Farm, Bridport DT6 4PH
T: (01308) 421933
E: vicklen@tesco.net

West Hembury Farm ★★★★
Contact: Dr & Mrs Hunt
West Hembury Farm, Dorchester DT2 9EN
T: (01308) 485289
F: (01308) 485041
E: hunt@westhembury.com
I: www.westhembury.com

ATHELHAMPTON
Dorset

River Cottage ★★★★
Contact: Miss Tracy Winder
River Cottage, Dorchester DT2 7LG
T: (01305) 848363
F: (01305) 848135
E: enquiry@athelhampton.co.uk
I: www.athelhampton.co.uk

606 Look out for establishments participating in the National Accessible Scheme

SOUTH WEST ENGLAND

AWLISCOMBE
Devon

Godford Farm ★★★★
Contact: Mrs Sally Lawrence
Godford Farm, Otter Holt And Owl Hayes, Godford Farm, Honiton EX14 3PW
T: (01404) 42825
F: (01404) 42825
E: lawrencesally@hotmail.com
I: www.devon-farm-holidays.co.uk

AXBRIDGE
Somerset

Springbanks ★★
Contact: Mrs Celia Wilkinson
Orchard Farm, Cheddar Road, Wedmore BS28 4JA
T: (01934) 713356
E: mcw@kergouet.freeserve.co.uk

AXMINSTER
Devon

Beckford Cottage ★★★★
Contact: Mrs Jill Bellamy
Dalwood, Axminster EX13 7HQ
T: (01404) 881641
F: (01404) 881108
I: www.beckford-cottage.co.uk

Cider Room Cottage ★★★★
Contact: Mrs Steele
Cider Room Cottage, Hasland Farm, Tolcis, Axminster EX13 7JF
T: (01404) 881558
F: (01404) 881834
E: ciderroomcottage@rscontracting.co.uk

Furzeleigh House Country Cottages and Gardens ★★★★
Contact: Mr Rob & Mrs Shirley Blatchford
Furzeleigh House Country Cottages and Gardens, Lyme Road, Axminster EX13 5SW
T: (01297) 34448
E: shirley.blatchford@tesco.net
I: www.devoncottages-furzeleigh.co.uk

Primrose Cottage ★★★★
Contact: Ms Louise Hayman
Milkbere Holidays, 3 Fore Street, Seaton EX12 2LE
T: (01297) 20729
E: info@milkberehols.com
I: www.milkberehols.com

Symondsdown Cottages ★★★-★★★★★
Contact: Mr Stuart & Mrs Jenny Hynds
Symondsdown Cottages, Woodbury Lane, Woodbury Cross, Axminster EX13 5TL
T: (01297) 32385
I: www.symondsdownholidaycottages.co.uk

AXMOUTH
Devon

Anchor Cottage ★★★★
Contact:
Milkbere Cottage Holidays, 3 Fore Street, Seaton EX12 2LE
T: (01297) 20729
F: (01297) 22925
E: info@milkberehols.com
I: www.milkberehols.com

Combe Farm Cottages ★★-★★★
Contact: Ms Bows
Combe Farm Cottages, Combe Farm, Seaton EX12 4AU
T: (01297) 23822

Lattenbells ★★★★
Contact:
Milkbere Cottage Holidays, 3 Fore Street, Seaton EX12 2LE
T: (01297) 20729
F: (01297) 22925
E: info@milkberehols.com
I: www.milkberehols.com

3 Old Coastguards Cottages ★★★★
Contact:
Milkbere Holidays, 3 Fore Street, Seaton EX12 2LE
T: (01297) 20729
F: (01297) 22925
E: info@milkbere.com
I: www.milkbere.com

Stepps Barn ★★★★★
Contact:
Jean Bartlett Cottage Holidays, The Old Dairy, Fore Street, Seaton EX12 3JB
T: (01297) 23221
F: (01297) 23303
E: holidays@jeanbartlett.com
I: www.netbreaks.com/jeanb

Stepps Cross Cottage ★★★★
Contact: Ms Kate Bartlett
Jean Bartlett Cottage Holidays, The Old Dairy, Fore Street, Seaton EX12 3JB
T: (01297) 23221
F: (01297) 23303
E: holidays@jeanbartlett.com
I: www.jeanbartlett.com

Stepps Orchard ★★★★
Contact: Ms Kate Bartlett
Jean Bartlett Cottage Holidays, The Old Dairy, Fore Street, Seaton EX12 3JB
T: (01297) 23221
F: (01297) 23303
E: holidays@jeanbartlett.com
I: www.jeanbartlett.com

AYLESBEARE
Devon

Alpine Park Cottages ★★★
Contact: Mrs Wendy Atkin
Alpine Park Cottages, Sidmouth Road, Exeter EX5 2JW
T: (01395) 233619
T: (01395) 239096
E: alpinians@eclipse.co.uk
I: www.cottageguide.co.uk/alpineparkcottages

AYR
Cornwall

9 Ayr Lane ★★★
Contact: Ms Sue Kibby
115 Earlsfield Road, London SW18 3DD
T: (020) 88703228
F: (020) 8488 9192
E: sue.kirby@btinternet.com
I: www.btinternet.com/~stives.cottage

BABBACOMBE
Torbay

Rose Court Holiday Apartments ★★★
Contact: Mrs J Henshall
Rose Court Holiday Apartments, York Road, Torquay TQ1 3SG
T: (01803) 327203
E: holidays@rosecourtorquay.co.uk
I: www.rosecourtorquay.co.uk

Sunnybank ★★★
Contact:
Holiday Homes & Cottages South West, 365A Torquay Road, Paignton TQ3 2BT
T: (01803) 663650
F: (01803) 664037
E: holcotts@aol.com
I: www.swcottages.co.uk

Willow Cottage ★★★
Contact:
Holiday Homes & Cottages South West, 365A Torquay Road, Paignton TQ3 2BT
T: (01803) 663650
F: (01803) 664037
E: holcotts@aol.com
I: www.swcottages.co.uk

BACKWELL
North Somerset

The Coach House ★★★★
Contact: Mrs Iola Solari
The Coach House, 73 West Town Road, Bristol BS48 3BH
T: (01275) 464635
E: info@coachhousebackwell.co.uk
I: www.coachhousebackwell.co.uk

BAMPTON
Devon

Three Gates Farm ★★★★
Contact: Mrs Alison Spencer
Three Gates Farm, Huntsham, Tiverton EX16 7QH
T: (01398) 331280
F: (01398) 332476
E: threegatesfarm@hotmail.com
I: www.threegatesfarm.co.uk

Veltham Cottages ★★★
Contact: Mrs Pauline Krombas
Veltham Cottages, Veltham House, Morebath, Tiverton EX16 9AL
T: (01398) 331465
F: (01398) 331465

Westbrook House ★★★
Contact: Mrs Patricia Currie
Westbrook House, Tiverton EX16 9HU
T: (01398) 331418
F: (01398) 331418
E: info@westbrookhouse.co.uk
I: www.westbrookhouse.co.uk

Wonham Barton ★★★
Contact: Clifford Williams & Anne McLean Williams
Wonham Barton, Bampton, Tiverton EX16 9JZ
T: (01398) 331312
F: (01398) 331312
I: www.wonham-country-holidays.co.uk

BANTHAM
Devon

Sloopside ★★★★
Contact:
Toad Hall Cottages, Elliot House, Church Street, Kingsbridge TQ7 1BY
T: (01548) 853089
F: (01548) 853086
E: thc@toadhallcottages.com
I: www.toadhallcottages.com

Whiddons ★★★★
Contact:
Toad Hall Cottages, Elliot House, Church Street, Kingsbridge TQ7 1BY
T: (01548) 853089
F: (01548) 853086
E: thc@toadhallcottages.com
I: www.toadhallcottages.com

BARBICAN
Plymouth

Barbican Hideaway ★★★★★
Contact: Ms Julie Burdett
A home from Home Holidays, 58 Fulcher Avenue, Cromer NR27 9SG
T: (01263) 515208
F: (01263) 519220
E: info@home-from-home-holidays.com
I: www.hfhh.co.uk

The Harlequin ★★★★★
Contact: Ms Julie Burdett
A Home from Home Holidays Ltd., 58 Fulcher Avenue, Cromer NR27 9SG
T: (01263) 515208
F: (01263) 519220
E: info@home-from-home-holidays.com
I: www.home-from-home-holidays.co.uk

BARBROOK
Devon

New Mill Farm ★★★-★★★★
Contact: Mr Bingham
Outovercott Riding Stables, Lynton EX35 6JR
T: (01598) 753341
E: susan@exmoor-outdoors.co.uk
I: www.outovercott.co.uk

Woodside ★★★
Contact: Mrs Sally Gunn
Woodside, Lynton EX35 6PD
T: (01598) 753298
E: woodside@salian.fsnet.co.uk

BARNSTAPLE
Devon

Country Ways ★★★★
Contact: Mrs Kate Price
Country Ways, Little Knowle Farm, Umberleigh EX37 9BJ
T: (01769) 560503
F: (01769) 560503
E: kate@country-ways.net
I: www.country-ways.net

SOUTH WEST ENGLAND

Hartpiece Farm ★★★★
Contact: Mr Chris Baker
c/o JFA Ltd, Riverside, Mill Lane,
Taplow, Maidenhead SL6 0AA
T: (01628) 637111
F: (01628) 773030
E: chris@hartpiece.co.uk
I: www.hartpiece.co.uk

Humes Farm Cottages ★★★-★★★★★
Contact:
Marsden's Cottage Holidays, 2
The Square, Braunton EX33 2JB
T: (01271) 813777
F: (01271) 813664
E: holidays@marsdens.co.uk
I: www.marsdens.co.uk

Lower Yelland Farm ★★★
Contact: Mr Peter Day
Lower Yelland Farm, Yelland,
Barnstaple EX31 3EN
T: (01271) 860101
E: pday@loweryellandfarm.co.uk
I: www.loweryellandfarm.co.uk

Meadow Cottage ★★★
Contact: Mr Peter & Mrs Janet Cornwell
Marsden's Cottage Holidays, 2
The Square, Braunton EX33 2JB
T: (01271) 813777
F: (01271) 813664
E: holidays@marsdens.co.uk
I: www.marsdens.co.uk

North Hill Cottages ★★★
Contact: Mrs Joan Hassall
North Hill Cottages, North Hill,
Barnstaple EX31 4LG
T: (01271) 850611
F: (01271) 850693
E: enquiries@bestleisure.co.uk
I: www.bestleisure.co.uk

Willesleigh Farm ★★★★
Contact: Mr & Mrs Esmond-Cole
Willesleigh Farm, Barnstaple
EX32 7NA
T: (01271) 343763
F: (01271) 343763

BARTON ST DAVID
Somerset

Windyash
Rating Applied For
Contact: Mr Nick & Mrs Mandy Ladd
Windyash, Mill Road, Somerton
TA11 6DF
T: (01458) 851005

BATCOMBE
Somerset

The Coach House at Boords Farm ★★★★
Contact: Mr Michael & Mrs Anne Page
Batcombe, Shepton Mallet
BA4 6HD
T: (01749) 850372
F: (01749) 850372
E: boordsfarm@michaelp.demon.co.uk
I: www.boordsfarm.co.uk

BATH
Bath and North East Somerset

Bath Centre Stay Holidays ★★★
Contact: Mr Gerald Davey
163 Newbridge Hill, Bath
BA1 3PX
T: (01225) 313205
F: (01225) 313205
E: holidays@bathcentrestay.freeserve.co.uk
I: www.bcsh.co.uk

Bath Holiday Breaks
Rating Applied For
Contact: Mr Chris & Mrs Suzanne Kille
Bath Holiday Breaks, 41
Bloomfield Park, Bath BA2 2BX
T: (01225) 428944
F: (01225) 428944
E: christopher.kille@tiscalli.co.uk
I: www.bathholidaybreaks.co.uk

Beau Street Apartments 1-3 ★★★
Contact: Mr Brian Taylor
49 Reynolds Road, Beaconsfield
HP9 2NQ
T: (01494) 681212
F: (01494) 681231
E: bath.heritage@which.net
I: www.bath-selfcatering.co.uk

The Beeches Farmhouse - Pig Wig Cottages ★★★★★★
Contact: Mr Kevin & Mrs Sharon Gover
The Beeches Farmhouse - Pig Wig Cottages, Holt Road,
Bradford-on-Avon BA15 1TS
T: (01225) 865170
F: (01225) 863996
E: beeches-farmhouse@netgates.co.uk
I: www.beeches-farmhouse.co.uk

Calverley Wing ★★★
Contact: Mrs Jenny John
Calverley Wing, South Stoke
Hall, Southstoke, Bath BA2 7DL
T: (01225) 833387
F: (01225) 833387
E: tandjjohn@aol.com
I: www.calverleywing.co.uk

Camden Garden Apartment ★★★
Contact: Mrs Ros Pritchard
Camden Garden Apartment, 5
Upper Camden Place, Camden
Road, Bath BA1 5HX
T: (01225) 338730

Church Farm Country Cottages ★★★★
Contact: Mrs Trish Bowles
Church Farm Country Cottages,
Bath, Bradford-on-Avon
BA15 2JH
T: (01225) 722246
F: (01225) 722246
E: stay@churchfarmcottages.com
I: www.churchfarmcottages.com

Circus View ★★★★
Contact: Mrs Deborah Challinor
The Garden Flat, 11 Collingham
Gardens, London SW5 0HS
T: (020) 78351962
F: (020) 7437 1167
E: deborah@circusview.co.uk
I: www.circusview.co.uk

The Coach House (Bath) ★★★★
Contact: Mrs Marilyn Quiggin
The Coach House (Bath),
Lansdown Road, Bath BA1 5TJ
T: (01225) 331341
F: (01225) 482202
E: mq@bathselfcatering.fsnet.co.uk
I: www.bathselfcatering.fsnet.co.uk

Courtyard Apartment ★★★★★
Contact: Ms Karen Werrett
Bath Vacation Rentals, Po Box
3100, Bath BA2 6WA
T: 07817 306934
F: 0870 1 321656
E: enquiries@bathvacationrentals.com
I: www.bathvacationrentals.com

2 Devonshire Villas ★★★
Contact: Mr & Mrs Daniel Wall
2 Devonshire Villas, Wellsway,
Bath BA2 4SX
T: (01225) 331539
E: daniel@wallsbath.freeserve.co.uk
I: www.visirtbath.co.uk

Flat 2 ★★
Contact: Miss Sophie Rosser-Rees
Glenhazel, 3 Warminster Road,
Bath BA2 7HZ
T: (01225) 723545
E: srosserrees@hotmail.com

Georgian Maisonette ★★★
Contact: Mrs Susanne Cragg
Georgian Maisonette, 16
Margarets Buildings, Bath
BA1 2LP
T: (01761) 415655
F: (01761) 419706
E: info@rentingplaces.com
I: www.rentingplaces.com

Greyfield Farm Cottages ★★★★★
Contact: Mrs June Merry
Greyfield Farm Cottages,
Greyfield Road, High Littleton,
Bristol BS39 6YQ
T: (01761) 471132
F: (01761) 471152
E: june@greyfieldfarm.com
I: www.greyfieldfarm.com

Margaret's Building Apartment ★★★★
Contact: Mr Pash
Hideaways, Luke Street, Berwick
St John, Shaftesbury SP7 0HQ
T: (01747) 828170
F: (01747) 829090
E: enq@hideaways.co.uk
I: www.hideaways.co.uk

Nailey Cottages ★★★★
Contact: Mrs Brett Gardner
Nailey Cottages, Nailey Farm, St
Catherines Valley, Bath BA1 8HD
T: (01225) 852989
F: (01225) 852989
E: cottages@naileyfarm.co.uk
I: www.naileyfarm.co.uk

Riverside Apartment ★★★
Contact: Mr Graham Wilson
Riverside Apartment, 1 Norfolk
Buildings, Bath BA1 2BP
T: (01225) 337968

Riverside Cottage ★★
Contact: Mr Barrie & Valerie Trezise
1 High Street, Bristol BS30 5QJ
T: (0117) 9372304
F: (0117) 9372304
E: b.trezise@btopenworld.com

Russel Street Apartment ★★★★★
Contact: Mrs Clare Margaret Travers
9 Prior Park Buildings, Bath
BA2 4NP
T: (01225) 312011
E: traversa@aol.com
I: www.bathbreaks.co.uk

Second Floor Flat ★★★★
Contact: Mrs Lindsay Bishop
15 Heatherdale Road, Camberley
GU15 2LR
T: (01276) 29033
E: lindsay.bishop@btopenworld.com

Sheylors Farm ★★★★★
Contact: Mrs S Sanders
Sheylors Farm, Sheylors Barn,
Ashley, Box, Corsham SN13 8AN
T: (01225) 743922
F: (01225) 743998
E: sam@sheylorsfarm.co.uk
I: www.sheylorsfarm.co.uk

Spring Farm Holiday Cottages ★★★-★★★★
Contact: Mrs Sue Brown
Spring Farm Holiday Cottages,
Carlingcott, Peasedown St John,
Bath BA2 8AP
T: (01761) 435524
F: (01761) 439461
I: www.springfarmcottages.co.uk

Time-2-Relax-Holidays ★★★★★
Contact: Ms Sue Thornton
Time-2-Relax-Holidays,
Eastwood House, Stroudley
Crescent, Weymouth DT3 6NT
T: (01305) 837474
F: (01305) 777515
E: sue@eastwoodquay.freeserve.co.uk

BATHEALTON
Somerset

Woodlands Farm ★★★
Contact: Mrs Joan Greenway
Woodlands Farm, Taunton
TA4 2AH
T: (01984) 623271

SOUTH WEST ENGLAND

BATHEASTON
Bath and North East Somerset

Avondale Riverside
★★★★-★★★★★★
Contact: Mr & Mrs Pecchia
Avondale Riverside, 104 Lower
Northend, North End,
Batheaston, Bath BA1 7HA
T: (01225) 852226
F: (01225) 852226
E: sheilapex@questmusic.co.uk
I: www.riversapart.co.uk

BATHFORD
Bath and North East Somerset

Avon Cottage Studio
Rating Applied For
Contact: Mr Henrik Bebber
Avon Cottage Studio, 22 Northend
Street, Bath BA1 7TU
T: (01225) 858490
F: 0709 2 151943
E: info@avoncottagestudio.co.uk
I: www.avoncottagestudio.co.uk

BATHWICK
Bath and North East Somerset

Flat 1, 17 Argyle Street
★★★★★
Contact: Mr Tim Doyle
Flat 1, 17 Argyle Street, Bath
BA2 4BQ
T: 0793 2 075175
E: bathluxuryapt@aol.com

BEAMINSTER
Dorset

The Cottage ★★★
Contact: Ms Trish Mitchell
The Cottage, North Buckham
Farm, Beaminster dt8 3sh
T: (01308) 863054
F: (01308) 863054
E: trish@northbuckham.fsnet.co.uk

Greens Cross Farm ★★★
Contact: Mr David & Mrs Lora Baker
Greens Cross Farm, Stoke Road, Beaminster DT8 3JL
T: (01308) 862661
E: greenscross@btopenworld.com

Lewesdon Farm Holidays
★★★★
Contact: Mr Micheal & Mrs Linda Smith
Lewesdon Farm Holidays, Lewesdon Farm, Beaminster DT8 3JZ
T: (01308) 868270
E: lewesdonfarmholiday@tinyonline.co.uk
I: www.lewesdonfarmholidays.co.uk

Orchard End ★★★★
Contact: Mrs Wallbridge
Watermeadow House, Bridge Farm, Beaminster DT8 3PD
T: (01308) 862619
F: (01308) 862619
E: enquiries@watermeadowhouse.co.uk
I: www.watermeadowhouse.co.uk

Stable Cottage ★★★★
Contact: Mrs Diana Clarke
Meerhay Manor, Beaminster DT8 3SB
T: (01308) 862305
F: (01308) 863972
E: meerhay@aol.com
I: www.meerhay.co.uk

BEAWORTHY
Devon

Tillislow Barn ★★★★
Contact:
Farm & Cottage Holidays,
Victoria House, 12 Fore Street,
Bideford EX39 1AW
T: (01237) 479146
F: (01237) 421512
E: bookings@farmcott.co.uk

BEER
Devon

The Admirals View ★★★★
Contact:
Jean Bartlett Cottage Holidays,
The Old Dairy, Fore Street,
Seaton EX12 3JB
T: (01297) 23221
F: (01297) 23303
E: holidays@jeanbartlett.com
I: www.netbreaks.com/jeanb

Bakery Cottage ★★★★
Contact: Ms Kate Bartlett
Jean Bartlett Cottage Holidays,
The Old Dairy, Fore Street,
Seaton EX12 3JB
T: (01297) 23221
F: (01297) 23303
E: holidays@jeanbartlett.com
I: www.jeanbartlett.com

Beer View and New Nookies
★★★★
Contact: Mrs Jean Forbes-Harriss
Beer View and New Nookies, Berry Lane, Seaton EX12 3JS
T: (01297) 20096
F: (01297) 20096
E: forbesh@globalnet.co.uk

Brooksyde ★★
Contact:
Jean Bartlett Cottage Holidays,
The Old Dairy, Fore Street,
Seaton EX12 3JB
T: (01297) 23221
F: (01297) 23303
E: holidays@jeanbartlett.com
I: www.netbreaks.com/jeanb

Bung Ho ★★★★
Contact:
Jean Bartlett Cottage Holidays,
The Old Dairy, Fore Street,
Seaton EX12 3JB

Captains Cabin ★★★★
Contact: Ms Kate Bartlett
Jean Bartlett Cottage Holidays,
The Old Dairy, Fore Street,
Seaton EX12 3JB
T: (01297) 23221
F: (01297) 23303
E: holidays@jeanbartlett.com
I: www.jeanbartlett.com

Church View ★★★★
Contact:
Milkbere Holidays, 3 Fore Street,
Seaton EX12 2LE
T: (01297) 20729
F: (01297) 22925
E: info@milkberehols.com
I: www.milkberehols.com

Craft Cottage ★★★★
Contact: Ms Kate Bartlett
Jean Bartlett Cottage Holidays,
The Old Dairy, Fore Street,
Seaton EX12 3JB
T: (01297) 23221
F: (01297) 23303
E: holidays@jeanbartlett.com
I: www.netbreaks.com/jeanb

Farnham House ★★★
Contact: Ms Kate Bartlett
Jean Bartlett Cottage Holidays,
The Old Dairy, Fore Street,
Seaton EX12 3JB
T: (01297) 23221
F: (01297) 23303
E: holidays@jeanbartlett.com
I: www.netbreaks.com/jeamb

Hardergraft ★★★
Contact:
Jean Bartlett Cottage Holidays,
The Old Dairy, Fore Street,
Seaton EX12 3JB
T: (01297) 23221
F: (01297) 23303
E: holidays@jeanbartlett.com
I: www.netbreaks.com/jeanb

Hollyhocks ★★★★
Contact:
Jean Bartlett Cottage Holidays,
The Old Dairy, Fore Street,
Seaton EX12 3JB
T: (01297) 23221
F: (01297) 23303
E: holidays@jeanbartlett
I: www.netbreaks.com/jeanb

Hooknell House ★★★★
Contact:
Milkbere Holidays, 3 Fore Street,
Seaton EX12 2LE
T: (01297) 20729
F: (01297) 22925
E: info@milkbere.com
I: www.milkbere.com

Hope Cottage and Creole Cottage ★★★★
Contact:
Jean Bartlett Cottage Holidays,
The Old Dairy, Fore Street,
Seaton EX12 3JB
T: (01297) 23221
F: (01297) 23303
E: holidays@jeanbartlett.com
I: www.netbreaks.com/jeanb

Images ★★★
Contact: Ms Kate Bartlett
Jean Bartlett Cottage Holidays,
The Old Dairy, Fore Street,
Seaton EX12 3JB
T: (01297) 23221
F: (01297) 23303
E: holidays@jeanbartlett.com
I: www.jeanbartlett.com

Jubilee Cottage ★★★★
Contact: Ms Kate Bartlett
Jean Bartlett Cottage Holidays,
The Old Dairy, Fore Street,
Seaton EX12 3JB
T: (01297) 23221
E: holidays@jeanbartlett.com
I: www.jeanbartlett.com

Little Jacks Corner ★★★
Contact:
Jean Bartlett Cottage Holidays,
The Old Dairy, Fore Street,
Seaton EX12 3JB

Marine House Apartments & Twyford Cottage
★★★★-★★★★★★
Contact: Ms Kate Bartlett
Jean Bartlett Cottage Holidays,
The Old Dairy, Fore Street,
Seaton EX12 3JB
T: (01297) 23221
F: (01297) 23303
E: holidays@jeanbartlett.com
I: www.jeanbartlett.com

No 2 Jubilee Cottage
Rating Applied For
Contact: Ms Kate Bartlett
Jean Bartlett Cottage Holidays,
The Old Dairy,fore Street, Seaton EX12 3JB
T: (01297) 23221
E: holidays@jeanbartlett.com
I: www.jeanbartlett.com

Old Dairy
Rating Applied For
Contact:
Jean Bartlett Cottage Holidays,
The Old Dairy,fore Street, Seaton EX12 3JA
T: (01297) 23221
F: (01297) 23303
E: holidays@jeanbartlett.com
I: www.jeanbartlett.com

The Old Lace Shop ★★★
Contact: Ms Kate Bartlett
Jean Bartlett Cottage Holidays,
The Old Dairy, Fore Street,
Seaton EX12 3JB
T: (01297) 23221
F: (01297) 23303
E: holidays@jeanbartlett.com
I: www.jeanbartlett.com

12 Pioneer Cottage ★★★
Contact: Ms Kate Bartlett
Jean Bartlett Cottage Holidays,
The Old Dairy, Fore Street,
Seaton EX12 3JB
I: www.jeanbartlett.com

3 Pioneer Cottage ★★★
Contact: Ms Kate Bartlett
Jean Bartlett Cottage Holidays,
The Old Dairy, Fore Street,
Seaton EX12 3JB
I: www.jeanbartlett.com

6 Pioneer Cottages ★★★
Contact: Ms Kate Bartlett
Jean Bartlett Cottage Holidays,
The Old Diary, Fore Street,
Seaton EX12 3JB
T: (01297) 23221
I: www.jeanbartlett.com

Establishments printed in blue have a detailed entry in this guide

SOUTH WEST ENGLAND

7 Pioneer Cottages ★★★
Contact: Ms Kate Bartlett
Jean Bartlett Cottage Holidays,
The Old Dairy, Fore Street,
Seaton EX12 3JB
T: (01297) 23221
F: (01297) 23303
E: holidays@jeanbartlett.com
I: www.jeanbartlett.com

Purley
Rating Applied For
Contact: Ms Kate Bartlett
Jean Bartlett Cottage Holidays,
The Old Dairy, Fore Street,
Seaton EX12 3JB
T: (01297) 23221
F: (01297) 23303
E: holidays@jeanbartlett.com
I: www.jeanbartlett.com

Ramblers ★★★
Contact:
Jean Bartlett Cottage Holidays,
The Old Dairy, Fore Street,
Seaton EX12 3JB
T: (01297) 23221
F: (01297) 23303
E: holidays@jeanbartlett.com
I: www.netbreaks.com/jeanb

Rattenbury Cottage ★★★
Contact: Ms Kate Bartlett
Jean Bartlett Cottage Holidays,
The Old Dairy, Fore Street,
Seaton EX12 3JB
T: (01297) 23221
F: (01297) 23303
E: holidays@jeanbartlett.com
I: www.jeanbartlett.com

Rock Cottage ★★★★
Contact: Ms Kate Bartlett
Jean Bartlett Cottage Holidays,
The Old Dairy, Fore Street,
Seaton EX12 3JB
T: (01297) 23221
F: (01297) 23303
E: holidays@jeanbartlett.com
I: www.netbreaks.com/jeanb

Rock Cottage
Rating Applied For
Contact:
Jean Bartlett Cottage Holidays,
The Old Dairy,fore Street, Seaton EX12 3JB
T: (01297) 23221
E: holidays@jeanbartlett.com
I: www.jeanbartlett.com

Rock Farm ★★★★
Contact: Ms Kate Barlett
Jean Bartlett Holiday Cottages,
The Old Dairy, Fore Street,
Seaton EX12 3JB
T: (01297) 23221
E: holidays@jeanbartlett.com
I: www.jeanbartlett.com

5 Rose Cottage ★★
Contact: Ms Kate Bartlett
Jean Bartlett Cottage Holidays,
The Old Dairy, Fore Street,
Seaton EX12 3JB
T: (01297) 23221
I: www.jeanbartlett.com

Sea Mist ★★★
Contact: Ms Kate Bartlett
Jean Bartlett Cottage Holidays,
The Old Dairy, Fore Street,
Seaton EX12 3JB
T: (01297) 23221
F: (01297) 23303
E: holidays@jeanbartlett.com
I: www.jeanbartlett.com

Sea View ★★★
Contact: Ms Kate Bartlett
Jean Bartlett Cottage Holidays,
The Old Dairy, Fore Street,
Seaton EX12 3JB
T: (01297) 23221
F: (01297) 23303
E: holidays@jeanbartlett.com
I: www.jeanbartlett.com

Shannon Cottage ★★★★
Contact: Ms Kate Bartlett
Jean Bartlett Cottage Holidays,
The Old Dairy, Fore Street,
Seaton EX12 3JB
T: (01297) 23221
I: www.jeanbartlett.com

Snowdrops ★★★
Contact: Ms Kate Bartlett
Jean Bartlett Cottage Holidays,
The Old Dairy, Fore Street,
Seaton EX12 3JB
T: (01297) 23221
F: (01297) 23303
E: holidays@jeanbartlett.com
I: www.jeanbartlett.com

Spring Garden ★★★
Contact: Ms Kate Bartlett
Jean Bartlett Cottage Holidays,
The Old Dairy, Fore Street,
Seaton EX12 3JB
T: (01297) 23221
F: (01297) 23303
E: holidays@jeanbartlett.com
I: www.jeanbartlett.com

Starre Cottage ★★★★
Contact: Ms Kate Bartlett
Jean Bartlett Cottage Holidays,
The Old Dairy, Fore Street,
Seaton EX12 3JB
T: (01297) 23221
F: (01297) 23303
E: holidays@jeanbartlett.com
I: www.jeanbartlett.com

Tanglewood ★★★★
Contact: Ms Kate Bartlett
Jean Bartlett Cottage Holidays,
The Old Dairy, Fore Street,
Seaton EX12 3JB
T: (01297) 23221
F: (01297) 23303
E: holidays@jeanbartlett.com
I: www.netbreaks.com/jeamb

West View Cottage ★★★★
Contact: Ms Kate Bartlett
Jean Bartlett Cottage Holidays,
The Old Dairy, Fore Street,
Seaton EX12 3JB
T: (01297) 23221
F: (01297) 23303
E: holidays@jeanbartlett.com
I: www.jeanbartlett.com

BEESANDS
Devon

Kimberley Cottage ★★★
Contact:
Toad Hall Cottages, Elliot House, Church Street, Kingsbridge
TQ7 1BY
T: (01548) 853089
F: (01548) 853086

BEESON
Devon

Andryl ★★★
Contact: Ms Beryl Wotton
Andryl, Lower Farm, Kingsbridge
TQ7 2HW
T: (01548) 580527

Beeson Farm Holiday Cottages ★★★★
Contact: Mr Robin & Mrs Veronica Cross
Beeson Farm Holiday Cottages, Beeson Farm, Kingsbridge
TQ7 2HW
T: (01548) 581270
F: (01548) 581270
I: www.beesonhols.co.uk

Gull Cry ★★★★
Contact:
Toad Hall Cottages, Elliot House, Church Street, Kingsbridge
TQ7 1BY
T: (01548) 853089
F: (01548) 853086
E: thc@toadhallcottages.com
I: www.toadhallcottages.com

BERE REGIS
Dorset

Troy, Bathsheba, Oak and Dairy Cottages ★★★★
Contact: Mr Ian Ventham
Troy, Bathsheba, Oak and Dairy Cottages, Shitterton Farmhouse, Wareham BH20 7HU
T: (01929) 471480
E: info@shitterton.com
I: www.shitterton.com

BERRY HEAD
Torbay

Berry Head Cottage
Rating Applied For
Contact:
Brixham Holiday Homes, 121A New Road, Brixham TQ5 8BY
T: (01803) 854187
F: (01803) 851773
E: info@brixhamholidayhomes.co.uk
I: www.brixhamholidayhomes.co.uk

BERRYNARBOR
Devon

Adventure Cottage ★★★★
Contact: Mr & Mrs Cornwell
Marsden's Cottage Holidays, 2 The Square, Braunton EX33 2JB
I: www.marsdens.co.uk

Cairn Cottage ★★★★
Contact:
Marsdens Cottage Holidays, 2 The Square, Braunton EX33 2JB
T: (01271) 813777
F: (01271) 813664
E: holidays@marsdens.co.uk
I: www.marsdens.co.uk

Forge Cottage ★★★★
Contact:
Marsden's Cottage Holidays, 2 The Square, Braunton EX33 2JB
T: (01271) 813777
F: (01271) 813664
E: holidays@marsdens.co.uk
I: www.marsdens.co.uk

Glebe House & Coach House ★★★★
Contact:
Marsden's Cottage Holidays, 2 The Square, Braunton EX33 2JB
T: (01271) 813777
F: (01271) 813664
E: holidays@marsdens.co.uk
I: www.marsdens.co.uk

Lee Copse ★★★
Contact: Mr Peter & Mrs Janet Cornwell
Marsden's Cottage Holidays, 2 The Square, Braunton EX33 2JB
T: (01271) 813777
F: (01271) 813664
E: holidays@marsdens.co.uk
I: www.marsdens.co.uk

Ropes End ★★★
Contact: Mrs Davey
Ropes End, Newberry Hill, Ilfracombe EX34 9SS
T: (01271) 883476
E: yvonne@ropesend.eclipse.co.uk

Smythen Farm Coastal Holiday Cottages ★★★-★★★★★
Contact: Mr & Ms Thompson & Elstone
Symthen, Sterridge Valley, Berrynarbor, Ilfracombe EX34 9TB
T: (01271) 882875
F: (01271) 882875
E: jayne@smythenfarmholidaycottages.co.uk
I: www.smythenfarmholidaycottages.co.uk

Watermouth Cove Cottages ★★★
Contact: Mrs Janette Menday
Coastal Valley Hideaways, Narracott Down, Honiton Road, South Molton EX36 4JA
T: 08702 413168
F: (01769) 573921
E: stay@watermouthcove.co.uk
I: www.watermouthcove.co.uk

BERWICK ST JAMES
Wiltshire

Rose Cottage ★★★
Contact: Mr John & Mrs Mildred Read
124 Greenwood Avenue, Salisbury SP1 1PE
T: (01722) 328934

BERWICK ST JOHN
Wiltshire

Easton Farm ★★★★
Contact: Mr Nicholas Pash
Hideaways, Chapel House, Luke Street, Berwick St John, Shaftesbury SP7 0HQ
T: (01747) 828170
F: (01747) 829090
E: enq@hideaways.co.uk
I: www.hideaways.co.uk

610 Look out for establishments participating in the National Accessible Scheme

SOUTH WEST ENGLAND

BETTISCOMBE
Dorset
Conway Bungalow ★★★
Contact: Mrs Margaret Smith
Conway Bungalow, Bridport
DT6 5NT
T: (01308) 868313
F: (01308) 868313
E: info@conway-bungalow.co.uk
I: www.conway-bungalow.co.uk

BIBURY
Gloucestershire
Bibury Holiday Cottages ★★★-★★★★★
Contact: Mrs J Hedgeland
Bibury Holiday Cottages, Coln Court, Arlington, Cirencester GL7 5NL
T: (01285) 740314
F: (01285) 740314
E: info@biburyholidaycottages.com
I: www.biburyholidaycottages.com

Cotteswold House Cottages ★★★★
Contact: Mrs Judith Underwood
Cotteswold House, Bibury, Cirencester GL7 5ND
T: (01285) 740609
F: (01285) 740609
E: cotteswold.house@btconnect.com
I: http://home.btconnect.com/cotteswold.house

BICKINGTON
Devon
East Burne Farm ★★★
Contact: Mr Mike & Emma Pallett
East Burne Farm, Newton Abbot TQ12 6PA
T: (01626) 821496
F: (01626) 821105
E: eastburnefarm@screaming.net
I: www.eastburnefarm.8k.com

BIDDESTONE
Wiltshire
Barn End ★★★★
Contact: Mrs Jenny Davis
Barn End, The Barn, Manor Farm, Biddestone, Chippenham SN14 7DH
T: (01249) 712104
E: jennyandbob@biddestone.com

BIDEFORD
Devon
Britannia House ★★★
Contact:
Farm & Cottage Holidays, Victoria House, 12 Fore Street, Bideford EX39 1AW
T: (01237) 479146
F: (01237) 421512
E: enquiries@farmcott.co.uk
I: www.farmcott.co.uk

Coachmans Cottage ★★★
Contact: Mr Tom & Mrs Sue Downie
Coachmans Cottage, Monkleigh, Bideford EX39 5JR
T: (01805) 623670
E: tom.downie@ukonline.co.uk
I: www.creamteacottages.co.uk

Copinger's Cottage ★★★★
Contact: Mr Dennis & Mrs Sonia Heard
Copinger's Cottage, Galsham Farm, Bideford EX39 6DN
T: (01237) 441262
I: www.galsham.co.uk

Little Melville Holiday Cottage ★★★★
Contact: Mr Bernard Moore
Melville Cottage, Heywood Road, Bideford EX39 3QB
T: (01237) 471140
F: (01237) 471140
E: anb@melvillecot.freeserve.co.uk
I: www.litmel.freeserve.co.uk

Pillhead Farm ★★★-★★★★
Contact: Mr Richard Hill
Pillhead Farm, Old Barnstaple Road, Bideford EX39 4NF
T: (01237) 479337
F: (01237) 479337
E: hill@pillheadfarm.fsnet.co.uk

BIGBURY-ON-SEA
Devon
Apartment 19
Rating Applied For
Contact: Mrs Sue Bowater
Helpful Holidays, Mill Street, Newton Abbot TQ13 8AW
T: (01647) 43359
E: help@helpfulholidays.com
I: www.helpfulholidays.com

Apartment 2 ★★★★★
Contact: Mr S Middleton
Whitewood, Redhill Road, Cobham KT11 1EF
T: (01932) 866387

Apartment 29, Burgh Island Causeway ★★★★★
Contact: Mrs R Street
Waverley House, Kingsbridge TQ7 4HT
T: (01548) 810942

Apartment 5, Burgh Island Causeway ★★★★★
Contact:
Helpful Holidays, Mill Street, Chagford, Devon TQ13 8AW
T: (01647) 433593
F: (01647) 433694
E: help@helpfulholidays.com
I: www.helpfulholidays.com

Ferrycombe ★★★★
Contact: Mrs Juliet Fooks
15 Mouchton Close, Biggin Hill, Westerham TN16 3ES
T: 07050 030231

1 Sharpland Crest ★★★
Contact: Mrs Amanda Hough
7 Oriole Drive, Pennsylvania, Exeter EX4 4SJ
T: (01392) 438234
E: amandahough@talk21.com

Thornbury ★★★★
Contact: Mrs J Tagent
Challaborough Cottage, Kingsbridge TQ7 4HW
T: (01548) 810520
E: met@cix.co.uk
I: www.cottagesdirect.co.uk/thornbury

BINEGAR
Somerset
Spindle Cottage ★★★★
Contact: Ms Angela Bunting
Spindle Cottage, Binegar Green, Binegar, Radstock BA3 4UE
T: (01749) 840497
E: spindle.cottage@ukonline.co.uk
I: www.spindlecottagelets.co.uk

BISHOP SUTTON
Bath and North East Somerset
The Trebartha ★★★★
Contact: Edward & Sally Catchpole
The Trebartha, The Street, Bishop Sutton, Bristol BS39 5UU
T: (01275) 333845
E: sally@thetrebartha.co.uk
I: www.thetrebartha.co.uk

BISHOP'S CAUNDLE
Dorset
Ryalls Stud Cottage ★★★
Contact: Mr John & Mrs Lavinia Rawlins
Ryalls Stud Cottage, Bishops Caundle, Sherborne DT9 5NG
T: (01963) 23036
F: (01963) 23179
I: www.english-country-cottages.co.uk

BISHOP'S NYMPTON
Devon
Crosse Farm ★★★
Contact: Mrs Verney
Crosse Farm, Wing of Farmhouse, South Molton EX36 4PB
T: (01769) 550288

BISHOPS DOWN
Dorset
Monks Barn ★★★★
Contact: Mrs Caryll Perry
Glebe Farm House, Stakes Lane, Sherborne DT9 5PN
T: (01963) 23259

BISHOPS HULL
Somerset
Leat Cottage ★★★★★
Contact: Mr William Beaumont
Leat Cottage, Longaller Mill, Taunton TA4 1AD
T: (01823) 326071
E: jo.beaumont@btopenworld.com

1 Old School Cottages ★★
Contact: Mrs Randle
Shute Cotttage,shutewater Hill, Taunton TA1 5EQ
T: (01823) 331189

BISHOPSTEIGNTON
Devon
Rose Cottage ★★
Contact:
Holiday Homes & Cottages South West, 365A Torquay Road, Paignton TQ3 2BT
T: (01803) 663650
F: (01803) 664037
E: holcotts@aol.com
I: www.swcottages.com

BISHOPSTROW
Wiltshire
Eastleigh Farm ★★★★
Contact: Mr Roz Walker
Eastleigh Farm, Warminster BA12 7BE
T: (01985) 212325

BISLEY
Gloucestershire
Coopers Cottage ★★★
Contact: Mr Michael & Mrs Liz Flint
Wells Cottage, Wells Road, Stroud GL6 7AG
T: (01452) 770289
E: flint.bisley@btinternet.com

BITTON
South Gloucestershire
The Gate House ★★
Contact: Mr Stone
The Gate House, Green Gables, Redfield BS30 6NX
T: (0117) 9325303
F: (0117) 9325303
E: thegatehouse@houseofstone.co.uk
I: www.houseofstone.co.uk

BLACK TORRINGTON
Devon
Kingsley Mill ★★★★
Contact:
Farm & Cottage Holidays, Victoria House, 12 Fore Street, Bideford EX39 1AW
T: (01237) 479146
F: (01237) 421512
E: enquiries@farmcott.co.uk
I: www.farmcott.co.uk

BLACKAWTON
Devon
Chuckle Too ★★★
Contact: Ms Jill Hanlon
Chuckle Cottage, Main Street, Totnes TQ9 7BG
T: (01803) 712455
F: (01803) 712455
E: jillyhanlon@beeb.net
I: www.stay-in-devon.co.uk

Lower Collaton Farmhouse ★★★★
Contact: Mr James & Mrs Rosie Mussen
Lower Collaton Farmhouse, Totnes TQ9 7DW
T: (01803) 712260
E: Mussen@lower-collaton-farm.co.uk
I: www.lower-collaton-farm.co.uk

BLACKBOROUGH
Devon
Bodmiscombe Farm ★★★
Contact: Mrs Northam
Bodmiscombe Farm, Cullompton EX15 2HR

Establishments printed in blue have a detailed entry in this guide

SOUTH WEST ENGLAND

South Farm Holiday Cottages & Fishery ★★★
Contact: Mrs Susan Chapman
South Farm Holiday Cottages & Fishery, Cullompton EX15 2JE
T: (01823) 681078
F: (01823) 680483
E: chapman@southfarm.co.uk
I: www.southfarm.co.uk

BLACKDOWN
Dorset

The Grooms Quarters - W4183 ★★★
Contact:
Lyme Bay Holidays, Bos House, 44 Church Street, Lyme Regis DT7 3DA
T: (01297) 443363
F: (01297) 445176
E: email@lymebayholidays.co.uk
I: www.lymebayholidays.co.uk

BLANDFORD FORUM
Dorset

Bluebell Cottage ★★★
Contact: Mr Stuart-Brown
Dream Cottages, 41 Maiden Street, Weymouth DT4 8TR
T: (01305) 789000

Hillcrest ★★★
Contact: Mrs Salisbury
Orchard Cottage, Duck Street, Blandford Forum DT11 8ET
T: (01258) 861476
E: mikesal66@yahoo.co.uk
I: www.heartofdorset.easynet.co.uk

The Lodge, The Stable, Plumtree Cottage and Jasmine Cottage ★★★
Contact: Mrs Penny Cooper
Dairy House Farm, Woolland, Blandford Forum DT11 0EY
T: (01258) 817501
F: (01258) 818060
E: penny.cooper@farming.co.uk
I: www.self-cateringholidays4u.co.uk

Old Rectory Cottage ★★★
Contact: Mrs Margaret Waldie
Old Rectory Cottage, Lower Blandford St Mary, Blandford Forum DT11 9ND
T: (01258) 453120

Orchard House Cottage ★★★★
Contact: Ms Fiona Chapman
Orchard House, Everetts Lane, Blandford Forum DT11 0SJ
T: (01258) 860257
F: (01258) 863784
E: fiona@chapman1807.fsnet.com

Shepherds Cottage ★★★
Contact: CH ref; 8002, 8003, 8322
Country Holidays, Spring Mill, Barnoldswick BB94 0AA
T: 0870 0723723
F: (01282) 844288
E: sales@holidaycottagesgroup.com
I: www.country-holidays.co.uk

Underwood ★★★
Contact: Mrs Belbin
Underwood, Home Farm, Blandford Forum DT11 8JW
T: (01258) 830208
E: rod@rbelbin.fsnet.co.uk

BLATCHBRIDGE
Somerset

Mill Cottage ★★★★
Contact: Mrs Thelma Morris
Mill Cottage, Blatchbridge Mill, Frome BA11 5EJ
T: (01373) 464784

BLISLAND
Cornwall

Beech View
Rating Applied For
Contact: Mr Len Croney
Beech View, Higher Pengelly, Bodmin PL30 4HR
T: (01208) 821116
E: len@pengellyconsult.com

Bridge Pool Cottage ★★★★
Contact: Mr Kathryn & Mrs Trevor Sobey
Higher Trevartha Farm, Liskeard PL14 3NJ
T: (01579) 343382

Torr House Cottages ★★★★
Contact: Mr Martin & Mrs Carolyn Wilson
Torr House Cottages, Bodmin PL30 4JH
T: (01208) 851601
F: (01208) 851601
E: wilson@millbanks.fsworld.co.uk
I: www.torrhouseholidays.co.uk

BLOCKLEY
Gloucestershire

Angel Cottage ★★
Contact: Mr Peter & Mrs Sue Knights
25 Blackroot Road, Sutton Coldfield B74 2QP
T: (0121) 3550575
E: sue_knights@hotmail.com

Arreton Cottage
Rating Applied For
Contact: Mrs Gloria Bayliss
Arreton House, Station Road, Moreton-in-Marsh GL56 9DT
T: (01386) 701077
E: bandb@arreton.demon.co.uk

Briar Cottage ★★★★
Contact: Miss Sheila Rolland
Campden Cottages, Folly Cottage, Chipping Campden GL55 6XG
T: (01386) 593315
F: (01386) 593057
E: info@campdencottages.co.uk
I: www.campdencottages.co.uk

Cinquefoil Cottage ★★★
Contact: Mrs Patricia Hinksman
45 Brookmans Avenue, Hatfield AL9 7QH
T: (01707) 652485
I: www.cinquefoilcottage.co.uk

Julianas Court ★★★★
Contact: Mr Timothy Lomas
The Cedars, 92 Prestbury Road, Macclesfield SK10 3BN
T: (01625) 613701
E: erl@daniels.uk.com

Lower Farm Cottages ★★★★
Contact: Mrs Katie Batchelor
Lower Farm Cottages, Lower Farmhouse, Moreton-in-Marsh GL56 9DP
T: (01386) 700237
F: (01386) 700237
E: lowerfarm@hotmail.com
I: www.lower-farm.co.uk

Michaelmas Cottage ★★★★
Contact: Mr M J Gaffney
Mulberry, Shrubs Hill Lane, Ascot SL5 0LD
T: (01344) 624833
F: (01344) 624693
E: michael@spoonerco.com
I: www.country-cottages.org.uk

BODIEVE
Cornwall

Cornish Cottage ★★★
Contact: Mrs Holder
Roseley, Wadebridge PL27 6EG
T: (01208) 813024

BODMIN
Cornwall

Glynn Barton Cottages ★★★★
Contact: Ms Lucy Orr
Glynn Barton Cottages, Glynn Barton, Glynn, Bodmin PL30 4AX
T: (01208) 821375
F: (01208) 821104
E: cottages@glynnbarton.fsnet.co.uk
I: www.glynnbarton.co.uk

Great Brightor Farm ★★★★★
Contact: Mr Frank & Mrs Kay Chapman
Great Brightor Farm, St Kew Highway, Bodmin PL30 3DR
T: (01208) 850464
F: (01208) 850464

Gwel Myre ★★★★
Contact: Mr John Carthew
Gwel Myre, 1 Halgavor Park, Bodmin PL31 1DL
T: (01208) 269292
E: john@gwelmyre.fsnet.co.uk
I: www.gwelmyre.co.uk

The Honeypot ★★★★
Contact: Mrs Gill Jenkins
The Honeypot, Polgwyn, Castle Street, Bodmin PL31 2DX
T: (01208) 77553
F: (01208) 77885
E: gill@bedknobs.co.uk
I: thehoneypot-bodmin.co.uk

Lanjew Park ★★★★
Contact: Mrs Elanie Biddick
Lanjew Park, Lanjew Farm, Bodmin PL30 5PB
T: (01726) 890214
F: (01726) 890214
E: biddick@lanjew.co.uk
I: www.lanjew.co.uk

Mount Pleasant Cottages ★★★
Contact: Mrs Capper
Mount Pleasant Cottages, Mount Pleasant Farm, Bodmin PL30 4EX
T: (01208) 821342
E: collette@capper61.fsnet.co.uk
I: www.peacefulholiday.co.uk

Outer Colvannick ★★★
Contact:
Farm & Cottage Holidays, Victoria House, 12 Fore Street, Bideford EX39 1AW
T: (01237) 479146
F: (01237) 421512
E: enquiries@farmcott.co.uk
I: www.farmcott.co.uk

Penrose Burden Holiday Cottages ★★★-★★★★
Contact: Ms Hall
Penrose Burden Holiday Cottages, St Breward, Bodmin PL30 4LZ
T: (01208) 850277
I: www.penroseburden.co.uk

Tor View ★★★-★★★★
Contact: Mr Rob & Mrs Helen Watson
Tor View, Trebell Green, Bodmin PL30 5HR
T: (01208) 831472
F: (01208) 831472

Trethorne Cottage ★★★★★
Contact: Mr Stephen Chidgey
Cornwall Quality Cottages, The Old Barn, Tregonetha, St Columb TR9 6EL
T: (01637) 880630
E: oldbarncornwall@btinternet.com
I: www.trethorne-cottage-cornwall.co.uk

BODREAN
Cornwall

Apple Orchard Bungalow ★★★★
Contact: Mr Peter Morris
Farm & Cottage Holidays, Victoria House, 12 Fore Street, Bideford EX39 1AW
T: (01237) 479146
F: (01237) 421512
E: farmcott@cix.co.uk
I: www.farmcott.co.uk

BOSCASTLE
Cornwall

Anneth Lowen ★★★★
Contact: Mr Dougan
Kernow Holidays, 40A Oriental Road, Woking GU22 7AR
T: (01483) 765446
F: 0870 321 4658
E: info@annethlowen.co.uk
I: www.annethlowen.co.uk

Barn Park Gallery ★★★★
Contact: Mr Holliday
Drewenna, Manor Close, Somerton TA11 7LW
T: (01935) 842089
E: kingsdonman@aol.com

The Boathouse ★★★★
Contact: Mrs Webster
Seagulls, The Harbour, Boscastle PL35 0AG
T: (01840) 250413
I: business.thisiscornwall.co.uk/boathouse/

Boscastle Holidays ★★★★
Contact: Mrs Congdon
Boscastle Holidays, Tremorle, Boscastle PL35 0BU
T: (01840) 250233
I: boscastleholidays.co.uk

SOUTH WEST ENGLAND

Cargurra Farm ★★★★
Contact: Mrs Gillian Elson
Cargurra Farm, Hennett, St Juliot, Boscastle PL35 0BT
T: (01840) 261206
F: (01840) 261206
E: gillian@cargurra.co.uk
I: www.cargurra.co.uk

Courtyard Farm and Cottages ★★★-★★★★
Contact: Mr Compton
Courtyard Farm and Cottages, Boscastle PL35 0HR
T: (01840) 261256
F: (01840) 261794
E: courtyard.farm@virgin.net
I: www.courtyardfarmcottages.com

The Garden Place ★★★★
Contact: Ms Celia Knox
Penagar Solutions, Penagar, Boscastle PL35 0AB
T: (01840) 250817
E: celia.knox@btinternet.com

Gull Cottage ★★★
Contact: Mr Chris & Mrs Ann Gooderham
Fir Cottage, 16 Church Close, Melton Mowbray LE14 4JJ
T: (01949) 860564
F: (01949) 860084
E: cottages@gooderham44.freeserve.co.uk
I: www.cornwalltouristboard.co.uk/gullcottage

Harbour Holidays ★★★★
Contact: Mrs Christine Morgan
Harbour Holidays, The Harbour Restaurant, Riverside Walk, Boscastle PL35 0HD
T: (01840) 250380

Home Farm Cottage ★★★★
Contact: Mrs Haddy
Home Farm Cottage, Boscastle PL35 0BN
T: (01840) 250195
F: (01840) 250195
E: jackie.haddy@btclick.com

Honeysuckle Cottage ★★★
Contact: Mr & Mrs Bunker
89 Austin Road, Luton LU3 1TZ
T: (01582) 619314

1 Jordan Vale ★★★-★★★★★
Contact: Mrs Scott
1 Jordan Vale, Old Road, Boscastle PL35 0AJ
T: (01840) 250463

Lewarne ★★★
Contact: Mr Purvis
4 Alder Lane, Coventry CV7 7DZ
T: (01676) 534648

Little Cobwebs ★★★★
Contact: Mr Jeff & Mrs Judi Covelle
Little Cobwebs, Cobwebs, Camelford PL32 9YN
T: (01840) 261766
F: 0709 2 363351
E: jeff@jcovelle.freeserve.co.uk
I: www.cottagesdirect.com/coa081

No 4 Pennally Cottage ★★★
Contact: Mrs Janet Welch
104 Rochester Drive, Bexley DA5 1QF
T: (01322) 522240
F: (01322) 522240

The Olde Carpenters Shop ★★★★★
Contact: Mrs Jackie Haddy
Home Farm, Boscastle PL35 0BN
T: (01840) 250195
F: (01840) 250195
E: jackie.haddy@btclick.com
I: www.cornwall-online.co.uk

Paradise Farm Cottage ★★★
Contact: Mrs Delia Hancock
Paradise Farm Cottage, Paradise Road, Boscastle PL35 0BL
T: (01840) 250528

Shepherd's Cottage ★★★
Contact: Mr Jenkins
Endellion House, Parc Road, Usk NP15 1NL
T: (01633) 450417
E: jenkins@choicecornishcottages.com
I: www.choicecornishcottages.com

Tregatherall Farm ★★★★
Contact: Mrs Seldon
Tregatherall Farm, Boscastle PL35 0EQ
T: (01840) 250277
F: (01804) 250277

Trehane House ★★
Contact: Mrs Cynthia Taylor
Gwel-An-Mor, Tintagel Road, Boscastle PL35 0DS
T: (01840) 250052

Trewannett Bungalow ★★★
Contact: Mr & Mrs James Sleep
Trewannett Bungalow, Boscastle PL35 0HJ
T: (01840) 250295

Venn Down Farmhouse Apartments ★★★★
Contact: Mrs Diane Bentall
Venn Down Farmhouse, Minster, Boscastle PL35 0EG
T: (01840) 250599
F: (01840) 250599
E: venndownfarmhouse@uk2.net
I: www.venndownfarmhouse.co.uk

Welltown Farmhouse ★★★
Contact: Mrs Diane Kehoe
Welltown Farmhouse, Boscastle PL35 0DY
T: (01840) 250718
E: stella210@hotmail.com

Westerings ★★★
Contact: Mrs Shirley Wakelin
Westerings, Boscastle PL35 0DJ
T: (01840) 250314
E: shirley@westeringsholidays.co.uk
I: www.westeringsholidays.co.uk

BOSCOMBE
Bournemouth

Sea Road Holiday Apartments ★★★
Contact: Mr Lees
581 Christchurch Road, Bournemouth BH1 4BU
T: (01202) 721666
F: (01202) 303490

BOSSINEY
Cornwall

Bramble Nook ★★★★
Contact: Mrs Janet Bate
117 Tamworth Road, Atherstone CV9 2QQ
T: (01827) 873084

BOURNEMOUTH
Bournemouth

The Black House ★★★
Contact:
The Black House, 51 Carbery Avenue, Bournemouth BH6 3LN
T: 07855 280191
F: (01202) 483555
E: theblackhouse@hotmail.com
I: www.theblackhouse.co.uk

Woodview Holiday Apartments ★★★★
Contact: Mr Shane Busby
Woodview Holiday Apartments, 6 St Anthony's Road, Meyrick Park, Bournemouth BH2 6PD
T: (01202) 290027
F: (01202) 295959
E: woodview.holidays@virgin.net
I: www.SmoothHound.co.uk/hotels/woodview.html

BOURTON-ON-THE-WATER
Gloucestershire

Acorn Cottage ★★★★
Contact: Mrs Ann Oakes
White Rails Farm, Evesham WR11 4SZ
T: (01386) 870727
F: (01386) 870727
E: oakescottages@bigfoot.com
I: www.oakescottages.co.uk

Annes Cottage ★★★★
Contact: Mrs Ann Oakes
White Rails Farm, Evesham WR11 4SZ
T: (01386) 870727
F: (01386) 870727
E: oakescottages@bigfoot.com
I: www.oakescottages.co.uk

The Coach House of the Dower House ★★
Contact: Mrs Philomena Adams
The Dower House, Cheltenham GL54 2AP
T: (01451) 820629

Farncombe Apartment ★★★★
Contact: Mrs Julia Wright
Farncombe Apartment, Clapton, Farncombe, Cheltenham GL54 2LG
T: (01451) 820120
F: (01451) 820120
E: julia@farncombecotswolds.com
I: www.farncombecotswolds.com

Greenleighs ★★★★
Contact: Mrs Joyce Tombs
The Old Forge, Wotton-under-Edge GL12 8UH
T: (01454) 419760

Inglenook Cottage ★★★
Contact: Mrs Vicki Garland
Mythe Farm, Pinwall Lane, Atherstone CV9 3PF
T: (01827) 712367
F: (01827) 715738

Magnolia Cottage Apartment ★★★★
Contact: Mr Janice & Mrs Michael Cotterill
Magnolia Cottage, Lansdown, Cheltenham GL54 2AR
T: (01451) 821841
F: (01451) 821841
E: cotterillmj@hotmail.com
I: www.cottageguide.co.uk/magnolia

Oxleigh Cottages ★★★★
Contact: Mrs Barbara Smith
12 Moore Road, Bourton-on-the-Water, Cheltenham GL54 2AZ
T: 07773 474108
E: cdsmith.annexe@fsmail.net

Tagmoor Hollow Apartment ★★★★
Contact: Mrs Bennett
Tagmoor Hollow, Marshmouth Lane, Cheltenham GL54 2EE
T: (01451) 821307

Well Cottage ★★★★
Contact: Mr & Mrs Roberts
Wayside Cottage, Letch Lane, Cheltenham GL54 2DG
T: (01451) 824059

Wrights Cottage ★★★★
Contact: Mr & Mrs Marsh
Applegarth, Hilcote Drive, Cheltenham GL54 2DU
T: (01451) 820568

BOVEY TRACEY
Devon

Lower Elsford Farm ★★★★
Contact:
Helpful Holidays, Mill Street, Newton Abbot TQ13 8AN
T: (01647) 433593

Stickwick Farm ★★★
Contact: Mrs Harvey
Frost Farm, Newton Abbot TQ13 9PP
T: (01626) 833266
E: linda@frostfarm.co.uk
I: www.frostfarm.co.uk

Tracey Cottage ★★★
Contact: Mr Ian Butterworth
Holiday Homes & Cottages South West, 365A Torquay Road, Paignton TQ3 2BT
T: (01803) 663650

Warmhill Farm ★★★★
Contact: W B Marnham
Hennock, Bovey Tracey, Newton Abbot TQ13 9QH
T: (01626) 833229
E: marnham@agriplus.net

Establishments printed in blue have a detailed entry in this guide

SOUTH WEST ENGLAND

BOWERCHALKE
Wiltshire
Pennywort Cottage ★★★
Contact: Mr Nicholas Pash
Hideaways, Chapel House, Luke Street, Berwick St John, Shaftesbury SP7 0HQ
T: (01747) 828170
F: (01747) 829090
E: enq@hideaways.co.uk
I: www.hideaways.co.uk

BOX
Wiltshire
Henley Farmhouse ★★★
Contact: Mrs Cordle
Henley Farmhouse, Corsham SN13 8BX
T: (01225) 742417
E: penart@onetel.net.uk

BRADFORD ABBAS
Dorset
The Studio ★★★
Contact: Mrs Wendy Dann
The Studio, Heartsease Cottage, North Street, Sherborne DT9 6SA
T: (01935) 475480
F: (01935) 475480

BRADFORD-ON-AVON
Wiltshire
Fairfield Barns ★★★★★
Contact: Mr Taff & Mrs Gilly Thomas
Fairfield Barns, Bradford Road, Atworth SN12 8HZ
T: (01225) 703585 & 07768 625868
F: 0870 051490
E: gilly@fairfieldbarns.com
I: www.fairfieldbarns.com

BRADNINCH
Devon
Highdown Organic Farm ★★★★
Contact: Mrs Vallis
Highdown Organic Farm, Cranishaies Lane, Exeter EX5 4LJ
T: (01392) 881028
F: (01392) 881272
E: svallis@highdownfarm.co.uk
I: www.highdownfarm.co.uk

BRADWORTHY
Devon
Lympscott Farm Holidays ★★★★
Contact: Mrs Caroline Furse
Lympscott Farm Holidays, Holsworthy EX22 7TR
T: (01409) 241607
F: (01409) 241607
I: www.lympscott.co.uk

Teddies ★★★
Contact: Mr Peter & Mrs Janet Cornwell
Marsden's Cottage Holidays, 2 The Square, Braunton EX33 2JB
T: (01271) 813777
F: (01271) 813664
E: holidays@marsdens.co.uk
I: www.marsdens.co.uk

Waterland Mill ★★★
Contact:
Farm & Cottage Holidays, Victoria House, 21 Fore Street, Bideford EX39 1AW
T: (01237) 479146
F: (01237) 421512
E: bookings@farmcott.co.uk
I: www.farmcott.co.uk

BRANKSOME PARK
Poole
Dolphin Cottage, Seahorse & Starfish Apartments ★★★
Contact: Mrs Middler
The Grovefield Manor Hotel, 18 Pinewood Road, Poole BH13 6JS
T: (01202) 766798

BRANSCOMBE
Devon
Bank Cottage ★★★
Contact: Ms Kate Bartlett
Jean Bartlett Cottage Holidays, The Old Dairy, Fore Street, Seaton EX12 3JB
T: (01297) 23221
F: (01297) 23303
E: holidays@jeanbartlett.com
I: www.jeanbartlett.com

The Chapel at Borcombe Farm ★★★
Contact: Ms Kate Bartlett
Jean Bartlett Cottage Holidays, The Old Dairy, Fore Street, Seaton EX12 3JB
T: (01297) 23221
F: (01297) 23303
E: holidays@jeanbartlett.com
I: www.jeanbartlett.com

Chapel Row ★★★★
Contact: Ms Kate Bartlett
Jean Bartlett Cottage Holidays, The Old Dairy, Fore Street, Seaton EX12 3JB
T: (01297) 23221
F: (01297) 23303
E: holidays@jeanbartlett.com
I: www.jeanbartlett.com

Cliffhayes ★★★
Contact: Ms Kate Bartlett
Jean Bartlett Cottage Holidays, The Old Dairy, Fore Street, Seaton EX12 3JB
T: (01297) 23221
F: (01297) 23303
E: holidays@jeanbartlett.com
I: www.jeanbartlett.com

Combe Way ★★★
Contact: Ms Kate Bartlett
Jean Bartlett Cottage Holidays, The Old Dairy, Fore Street, Seaton EX12 3JB
T: (01297) 23221
F: (01297) 23303
E: holidays@jeanbartlett.com
I: www.jeanbartlett.com

Gill Cottage ★★★
Contact: Ms Kate Bartlett
Jean Bartlett Cottage Holidays, The Old Dairy, Fore Street, Seaton EX12 3JB
T: (01297) 23221
F: (01297) 23303
E: holidays@jeanbartlett.com
I: www.jeanbartlett.com

Hole House ★★★★
Contact: Ms Kate Bartlett
Jean Bartlett Cottage Holidays, The Old Dairy, Fore Street, Seaton EX12 3JB
T: (01297) 23221
F: (01297) 23303
E: holidays@jeanbartlett.com
I: www.jeanbartlett.com

Jasmine Cottage ★★
Contact: Ms Kate Bartlett
Jean Bartlett Cottage Holidays, The Old Dairy, Fore Street, Seaton EX12 3JB
T: (01297) 23221
F: (01297) 23303
E: holidays@jeanbartlett.com
I: www.jeanbarton.com

The Old Sunday School ★★★★
Contact:
Jean Bartlett Cottage Holidays, The Old Dairy, Fore Street, Seaton EX12 3JB
T: (01297) 23221
F: (01297) 23303
E: holidays@jeanbartlett.com
I: www.netbreaks.com/jeanb

Pitt Farm Lodge ★★★
Contact: Ms Kate Bartlett
Jean Bartlett Cottage Holidays, The Old Dairy, Fore Street, Seaton EX12 3JB
T: (01297) 23221
F: (01297) 23303
E: holidays@jeanbartlett.com
I: www.jeanbartlett.com

Roslyn Cottage ★★★
Contact: JEAN BARTLETT
Roslyn Cottage, Seaton
I: www.jeanbartlett.com

Terry Holt, Nook ★★★★
Contact: Ms Kate Bartlett
Jean Bartlett Cottage Holidays, The Old Dairy, Fore Street, Seaton EX12 3JB
T: (01297) 23221
F: (01297) 23303
E: holidays@jeanbartlett.com
I: www.jeanbartlett.com

BRATTON
Somerset
Woodcombe Lodges ★★★★
Contact: Mrs Hanson
Woodcombe Lodges, Bratton Lane, Minehead TA24 8SQ
T: (01643) 702789 & 07860 667325
F: (01643) 702789
E: nicola@woodcombelodge.co.uk
I: www.woodcombelodge.co.uk

BRATTON CLOVELLY
Devon
Lavender Cottage ★★
Contact: Mrs Carol Blatchford
Laveddon Cottage, Blowinghouse Lane, Bodmin PL30 5JU
T: (01208) 74278

BRATTON FLEMING
Devon
Bracken Roost ★★★★
Contact: Mr Lawrie Scott
Bracken Roost, Barnstaple EX31 4TG
T: (01598) 710320
F: (01598) 710115
E: lawrie@brackenhousehotel.com
I: www.brackenhousehotel.com

Capelands Farm ★★★
Contact:
Toad Hall Cottages, Elliot House, Church Street, Kingsbridge TQ7 1BY
T: (01548) 521366
F: (01548) 853086
E: thc@toadhallcottages.com
I: www.toadhallcottages.com

The Tops ★★★
Contact: Mrs Hamner
Toad Hall Cottages, Elliot House, Church Street, Kingsbridge TQ7 1BY
T: (01548) 853089
I: www.toadhallcottages.com

Wallover Barton Cottages ★★★
Contact:
Marsden's Cottage Holidays, 2 The Square, Braunton EX33 2JB
T: (01271) 813777
F: (01271) 813664
E: holidays@marsdens.co.uk
I: www.marsdens.co.uk

BRAUNTON
Devon
Bowden House ★★★★
Contact:
Marsdens Cottage Holidays, 2 The Square, Braunton EX33 2JB
T: (01271) 813777
F: (01271) 813664
E: info@marsdens.co.uk

Britton Lodge ★★★
Contact: Mr Peter & Mrs Janet Cornwell
Marsden's Cottage Holidays, 2 The Square, Braunton EX33 2JB
T: (01271) 813777
F: (01271) 813664
E: holidays@marsdens.co.uk
I: www.marsdens.co.uk

Buckland Manor Cottage ★★★
Contact:
Marsden's Cottage Holidays, 2 The Square, Braunton EX33 2JB
T: (01271) 813777
F: (01271) 813664
E: holidays@marsdens.co.uk
I: www.marsdens.co.uk

Buckland Mews ★★★
Contact:
Marsden's Cottage Holidays, 2 The Square, Braunton EX33 2JB
T: (01271) 813777
F: (01271) 813664
E: holidays@marsdens.co.uk
I: www.marsdens.co.uk

SOUTH WEST ENGLAND

Casquets ★★★★
Contact:
Marsden's Cottage Holidays, 2 The Square, Braunton EX33 2JB
T: (01271) 813777
F: (01271) 813664
E: holidays@marsdens.co.uk
I: www.marsdens.co.uk

Courtyard, Cob & Coach House ★★★
Contact:
Marsden's Cottage Holidays, 2 The Square, Braunton EX33 2JB
T: (01271) 813777
F: (01271) 813664
E: holidays@marsdens.co.uk
I: www.marsdens.co.uk

Farmhouse Cottage ★★★
Contact:
Marsden's Cottage Holidays, 2 The Square, Braunton EX33 2JB
T: (01271) 813777
F: (01271) 813664
E: holidays@marsdens.co.uk
I: www.marsdens.co.uk

Garden Flat ★★★
Contact:
Marsden's Cottage Holidays, 2 The Square, Braunton EX33 2JB
T: (01271) 813777
F: (01271) 813664
E: holidays@marsdens.co.uk
I: www.marsdens.co.uk

Goadgates ★★★
Contact:
Marsden's Cottage Holidays, 2 The Square, Braunton EX33 2JB
T: (01271) 813777
F: (01271) 813664
E: holidays@marsdens.co.uk
I: www.marsdens.co.uk

Higher Spreacombe Farm ★★★
Contact: Mrs Colleen McCammond
Higher Spreacombe Farm, Higher Spreacombe, Braunton EX33 1JA
T: (01271) 870443
E: mccamondgc@aol.com

Hope Cottage ★★★★★
Contact:
Marsdens Cottage Holidays, 2 The Square, Braunton EX33 2JB
T: (01271) 813777
F: (01271) 813664
E: holidays@marsdens.co.uk

Incledon Farmhouse ★★★
Contact:
Marsden's Cottage Holidays, 2 The Square, Braunton EX33 2JB
T: (01271) 813777
F: (01271) 813664
E: holidays@marsdens.co.uk
I: www.marsdens.co.uk

Leacroft ★★★
Contact:
Marsden's Cottage Holidays, 2 The Square, Braunton EX33 2JB
T: (01271) 813777
F: (01271) 813664
E: holidays@marsdens.co.uk
I: www.marsdens.co.uk

Lime Tree Nursery ★★★★
Contact:
Marsden's Cottage Holidays, 2 The Square, Braunton EX33 2JB
T: (01271) 813777
F: (01271) 813664
E: holidays@marsdens.co.uk
I: www.marsdens.co.uk

Little Comfort Farm ★★★
Contact: Mrs Jackie Milsom
Little Comfort Farm, Braunton EX33 2NJ
T: (01271) 812414
F: (01271) 817975
E: jackie.milsom@btclick.com
I: www.littlecomfortfarm.co.uk

1 Millhouse Cottage ★★★
Contact:
Marsden's Cottage Holidays, 2 The Square, Braunton EX33 2JB
T: (01271) 813777
F: (01271) 813664
E: holidays@marsdens.co.uk
I: www.marsdens.co.uk

2 Millhouse Cottage ★★★
Contact:
Marsden's Cottage Holidays, 2 The Square, Braunton EX33 2JB
T: (01271) 813777
F: (01271) 813664
E: holidays@marsdens.co.uk
I: www.marsdens.co.uk

The Nook ★★★★
Contact:
Marsden's Cottage Holidays, 2 The Square, Braunton EX33 2JB
T: (01271) 813777
F: (01271) 813664
E: holidays@marsdens.co.uk
I: www.marsdens.co.uk

The Old Byre ★★★★
Contact:
Marsden's Cottage Holidays, 2 The Square, Braunton EX33 2JB
T: (01271) 813777
F: (01271) 813664
E: holidays@marsdens.co.uk
I: www.marsdens.co.uk

Orchard House ★★★
Contact:
Marsden's Cottage Holidays, 2 The Square, Braunton EX33 2JB
T: (01271) 813777
F: (01271) 813664
E: holidays@marsdens.co.uk
I: www.marsdens.co.uk

Ramblers Return ★★★
Contact:
Marsden's Cottage Holidays, 2 The Square, Braunton EX33 2JB
T: (01271) 813777
F: (01271) 813664
E: holidays@marsdens.co.uk
I: www.marsdens.co.uk

Saunton Beach Villas ★★
Contact: Mr David Marshall
Broadfield Holidays, 1 Park Villas, Taw Vale, Barnstaple EX32 8NJ
T: (01271) 322033
F: (01271) 378558

Score Farm House and Annexe ★★★★
Contact: Mrs Helen Knight
Score Farm House and Annexe, Chapel Street, Braunton EX33 1EL
T: (01271) 814815
F: (01271) 815257
E: sunshinenel@btinternet.com
I: www.scorefarmholidays.co.uk

Waverley ★★★
Contact:
Marsden's Cottage Holidays, 2 The Square, Braunton EX33 2JB
T: (01271) 813777
F: (01271) 813664
E: holidays@marsdens.co.uk
I: www.marsdens.co.uk

Well Cottage ★★★★
Contact: Mr Peter & Mrs Janet Cornwell
Marsden's Cottage Holidays, 2 The Square, Braunton EX33 2JB
T: (01271) 815266
F: (01271) 813664
E: holidays@marsdens.co.uk
I: www.marsdens.co.uk

Willoways ★★★
Contact: Mr & Mrs Cornwell
Marsden's Cottage Holidays, 2 The Square, Braunton EX33 2JB
T: (01271) 813777
F: (01271) 813664
E: holidays@marsdens.co.uk
I: www.marsdens.co.uk

Windspray ★★★
Contact:
Marsden's Cottage Holidays, 2 The Square, Braunton EX33 2JB
T: (01271) 813777
F: (01271) 813664
E: holidays@marsdens.co.uk
I: www.marsdens.co.uk

BRAYFORD
Devon

Kedworthy
Rating Applied For
Contact:
Farm & Cottage Holidays, Victoria House, 12 Fore Street, Bideford EX39 1AW
T: (01237) 479146
F: (01237) 421512
E: enquiries@farmcott.co.uk
I: www.farmcott.co.uk

Muxworthy Cottage ★★
Contact: Mrs G M Bament
Muxworthy Farm, Brayford, Barnstaple EX32 7QP
T: (01598) 710342

Rockley Farmhouse - The Stable Barn ★★★★
Contact: Mrs Renee Dover
Rockley Farmhouse - The Stable Barn, Rockley Farmhouse, Simansbath, Exmoor, Barnstaple EX32 7QR
T: (01598) 710429
F: (01598) 710429
E: info@rockley.co.uk
I: www.rockley.co.uk

BREAGE
Cornwall

Pump House ★★★★
Contact:
Cornish Cottage Holidays, Godolphin Road, Helston TR13 8AA
T: (01326) 573808
F: (01326) 564992
E: enquiry@cornishcottageholidays.co.uk
I: www.cornishcottageholidays.co.uk

BREAN
Somerset

Gadara Bungalow ★★
Contact: Mr Trevor Hicks
Gadara Bungalow, Diamond Farm, Weston Road, Burnham-on-Sea TA8 2RL
T: (01278) 751263
E: trevor@diamondfarm42.freeserve.co.uk
I: www.diamondfarm.co.uk

BRENT KNOLL
Somerset

West Croft Farm Dairy Cottage ★★★
Contact: Mrs Janet Harris
West Croft Farm Dairy Cottage, Brent Street, Highbridge TA9 4BE
T: (01278) 760259

BRENTOR
Devon

The Smithy ★★★
Contact: Mrs Wetherbee
Thorn Cottage, Burn Lane, Tavistock PL19 0ND
T: (01822) 810285

BRIDESTOWE
Devon

Knole Farm ★★★★
Contact:
Farm & Cottage Holidays, Victoria House, 12 Fore Street, Bideford EX39 1AW
T: (01237) 479146
F: (01237) 421512
E: enquiries@farmcott.co.uk
I: www.farmcott.co.uk

Way Barton Barn ★★★
Contact: Mr Doug & Mrs Deb Valentine
Way Barton Barn, Okehampton EX20 4QH
T: (01837) 861513
E: dougv777@aol.com
I: www.waybarton.co.uk

BRIDGWATER
Somerset

Ash-Wembdon Farm Cottages ★★★★
Contact: Mr Clarence Rowe
Ash-Wembdon Farm Cottages, Ash-Wembdon Farm, Hollow Lane, Bridgwater TA5 2BD
T: (01278) 453097
F: (01278) 445856
E: c.a.rowe@btinternet.com
I: www.ukcottageholiday.com

Establishments printed in blue have a detailed entry in this guide

SOUTH WEST ENGLAND

Grange Barn ★★★★★
Contact: Mr Matthew Wheeler
Grange Barn, Cannington,
Bridgwater TA5 2LD
T: (01278) 652216
F: (01278) 653611
E: grangehols@aol.com
I: www.grangehols.co.uk

BRIDPORT
Dorset

Clearview Bungalow ★★★
Contact: Mr Zachary Stuart-Brown
Dream Cottages, 5 Hope Square,
Weymouth DT4 8TR
T: (01305) 789000
E: admin@dream-cottages.co.uk
I: www.dream-cottages.co.uk

Coneygar Close ★★★
Contact: Mrs Janet Grimwood
Coneygar Close, 24 Coneygar
Close, Bridport DT6 3AR
T: (01308) 485314

Coniston Holiday Apartments ★★★
Contact: Mrs Jackie Murphy
Coniston Holiday Apartments,
Coniston House, Victoria Grove,
Bridport DT6 3AE
T: (01308) 424049
F: (01308) 424049

Crockhaven Cottage ★★★
Contact: Mr & Mrs Slade
Westpoint Apartments, The
Esplanade, Bridport DT6 4HG
T: (01308) 423636
F: (01308) 458871
E: bea@westpoint-apartments.co.uk
I: www.westpoint-apartments.co.uk

Fern Down Farm ★★★
Contact: Mrs Solly
Fern Down Farm, Shatcombe
Lane, Dorchester DT2 0EZ
T: (01300) 320810
E: pdnsolly@hotmail.com

Ganders Cottage ★★★
Contact: Mrs Pauline Bale
Ganders Cottage, Highway Farm,
West Road, Bridport DT6 6AE
T: (01308) 424321
F: (01308) 424321
E: bale@highwayfarm.co.uk
I: www.highwayfarm.co.uk

Hayday ★★★★
Contact: Mrs Day
Hayday, 29 Howard Road,
Bridport DT6 4SG
T: (01308) 424438
F: (01308) 424438

Highlands End Holiday Park ★★★
Contact: Mr Martin Cox
Highlands End Holiday Park,
Eype, Bridport DT6 6AR
T: (01308) 422139
F: (01308) 425672
E: holidays@wdlh.co.uk
I: www.wdlh.co.uk

Holiday Cottages Numbers 1 and 3 Stanley Place ★★
Contact: Mrs Barford
Bowood, Post Lane, Honiton
EX14 9HZ
T: (01404) 861566

Hoskins
Rating Applied For
Contact:
Dream Cottages, 5 Hope Square,
Weymouth DT4 8TR
T: (01305) 789000
F: (01305) 761346
E: admin@dream-cottages.co.uk
I: www.dreamcottages.co.uk

Lancombes House ★★★
Contact: Mr & Mrs Mansfield
Lancombes House, Bridport
DT6 3TN
T: (01308) 485375

Lavender Cottage
Rating Applied For
Contact: Mr & Mrs Hawes
Horsley Farm, Chichester
PO18 9PB
T: (023) 92631261

10 Meadowlands: X4411 ★★★
Contact:
Lyme Bay Holidays, Bos House,
44 Church Street, Lyme Regis
DT7 3DA
T: (01297) 443363
F: (01297) 445576
E: email@lymebayholidays.co.uk

Rope Cottage ★★★
Contact: Mrs Reichter
Rope Cottage, Rope Walks,
Bridport DT6 3RH
T: (01308) 425122
F: (01308) 425122
E: ropecott22@lycos.com

Rudge Farm ★★★★
Contact: Mrs Sue Diment
Rudge Farm, Bridport DT6 4NF
T: (01308) 482630
E: sue@rudgefarm.co.uk
I: www.rudgefarm.co.uk

Strongate Cottage ★★★
Contact: Mrs Sandra Huxter
Strongate Cottage, Salwayash,
Strongate Cottage, Bridport
DT6 5JD
T: (01308) 488295
F: (01380) 488295
E: sandrat.charnley@freeserve.co.uk

Sunset ★★★
Contact: Mr Dan Walker FHCIMA
Sunset, c/o Eypeleaze, 117 West
Bay Road, Bridport DT6 4EQ
T: (01308) 423363
F: (01308) 420228
E: cdan@walker42.freeserve.co.uk

30 Victoria Grove ★★
Contact: Mr & Mrs Brook
30 Victoria Grove, Victoria
Grove, Bridport DT6 3AD
T: (01308) 424605

West Bay Road - X3460 ★★★
Contact:
Lyme Bay Holidays, Bos House,
44 Church Street, Lyme Regis
DT7 3DA
T: (01297) 443363
F: (01297) 445576
E: email@lymebayholidays.co.uk
I: www.lymebayholidays.co.uk

Wooth Manor Cottage ★★★
Contact: Mrs Gaby Martelli
The Old Workhouse, St James
Road, Bridport DT6 5LW
T: (01308) 488348
E: amyasmartelli40@hotmail.com

Yew Tree House - Y4317 ★★★
Contact: Mr Dave Matthews
Lyme Bay Holiday Cottages, Bos
House, 44 Church Street, Lyme
Regis DT7 3DA
T: (01297) 443363

BRIMPSFIELD
Gloucestershire

Brimpsfield Farmhouse (West Wing) ★★★
Contact: Mrs Valerie Partridge
Brimpsfield Farmhouse (West
Wing), Brimpsfield Farm,
Brimpsfield, Gloucester GL4 8LD
T: (01452) 863568

BRISTOL
City of Bristol

Avonside ★★★
Contact: Mrs Ridout
Avonside, 19 St Edyth's Road,
Bristol BS9 2EP
T: (0117) 968 1967

Days Serviced Apartments ★★★
Contact: Miss Emma Potter
Days Serviced Apartments,
30-38 St Thomas Street, Bristol
BS1 6JZ
T: (01179) 544800
F: (01179) 544900
I: www.daysinn.com

Harbourside Apartment ★★★★
Contact: Mrs Flick Selway
Savernake, 11 Hillside Road,
Bristol BS41 9LG
T: 0779 2 503604
E: flickSelway@Pselway.freeserve.co.uk
I: www.harbourlet.co.uk

Harbourside View ★★★★★
Contact: Mr Kevin & Mrs Alison Davies
Bridesmead, Shipton Lane,
Bridport DT6 4NQ
T: (01308) 897457
F: (01308) 898782
E: alisondavies21@hotmail.com

Marine Apartments ★★★★
Contact: Ms Kay Hicken
18 Pier Road, Bristol BS20 7EA
T: (01275) 847928
E: bookings@marineapartments.co.uk

Redland Flat ★★★
Contact: Mr Jones
Flat 1, Elm Lodge, Elm Grove,
London NW2 3AE
T: (020) 8450 6761
E: redlandflat.btc@onmail.co.uk

Waterside ★★★★★
Contact: Mr Pete Hodges
Waterside, 37 Montague Court,
Bristol BS2 8HT
E: pete.hodges@virgin.net
I: www.watersidebristol.co.uk

BRIXHAM
Torbay

Anchorage
Rating Applied For
Contact:
Brixham Holiday Homes, 121A
New Road, Brixham TQ5 8BY
T: (01803) 854187
F: (01803) 851773
E: info@brixhamholidayhomes.co.uk
I: www.brixhamholidayhomes.co.uk

Arlington Holiday Flats ★★★
Contact: Ms Denise Buggins
14 Station Road, Bromsgrove
B60 1PZ
T: (0121) 4477387
E: denise.bugins@btinternet.com
I: www.selfcateringtorbay.co.uk

BEACHCOMBER ★★★
Contact:
Holiday Homes & Cottages
South West, 365A Torquay Road,
Paignton TQ3 2BT
T: (01803) 663650
F: (01803) 664037
E: holcotts@aol.co.uk
I: www.swcottages.co.uk

BERRY HEAD ★★★
Contact:
Holiday Homes & Cottages
South West, 365A Torquay Road,
Paignton TQ3 2BT
T: (01803) 663650
F: (01803) 664037
E: holcotts@aol.com
I: www.swcottages.co.uk

Blue Chip Vacations - Moorings Reach ★★★★★
Contact: Blue Chip Vacations, 3
Marina Walk, Berry Head Road,
Brixham TQ5 9AF
T: (01803) 855282
F: (01803) 881029
E: info@bluechipdevelopments.com
I: www.bluechipvacations.com

Brixham Harbourside Flats
Rating Applied For
Contact: Mrs Stone
13 Cambridge Road, Brixham
TQ5 8JW
T: (01803) 851919
F: (01803) 854244

Captain's Quarters ★★★★★
Contact: Mrs Gretchen Tricker
The Hill House, 23 St Peter's Hill,
Brixham TQ5 9TE
T: (01803) 857937
E: gtricker@aol.com
I: www.brixhamhistorichouses.co.uk

Caravella ★★★
Contact: Mr Ian Butterworth
Holiday Homes & Cottages
South West, 365A Torquay Road,
Paignton TQ3 2BT
T: (01803) 663650
F: (01803) 664037
E: holcotts@aol.com
I: www.swcottages.co.uk

SOUTH WEST ENGLAND

Celeste Cottage
Rating Applied For
Contact:
Brixham Holiday Homes, 121A New Road, Brixham TQ5 8BY
T: (01803) 854187
F: (01803) 851773
E: info@brixhamholidayhomes.co.uk
I: www.brixhamholidayhomes.co.uk

Coastguard Cottage
Rating Applied For
Contact:
Brixham Holiday Homes Ltd, 121A New Road, Brixham TQ5 8BY
T: (01803) 854187
F: (01803) 851773
E: info@brixhamholidaycottages.co.uk
I: www.brixhamholidayhomes.co.uk

Compass Cottage
Rating Applied For
Contact:
Brixham Holiday Homes Ltd, 121A New Road, Brixham TQ5 8BY
T: (01803) 854187
F: (01803) 851773
E: info@brixhamholidayhomes.co.uk
I: www.brixhamholidayhomes.co.uk

Crabbers Cottage ★★★★
Contact: Ms Tegan Cornish
8 The Queensway, Chalfont St Peter, Gerrards Cross SL9 8NF
T: (01753) 882482
F: (01753) 882546
E: info@cornish-cottage.com
I: www.cornish-cottage.com

Devoncourt Holiday Flats ★★
Contact: Mr Robin Hooker
Devoncourt Holiday Flats, Berry Head Road, Brixham TQ5 9AB
T: (01803) 853748
F: (01803) 855775
E: robinhooker@devoncoast.com
I: www.devoncourt.net

Elm Road
Rating Applied For
Contact:
Brixham Holiday Homes Ltd, 121A New Road, Brixham TQ5 8BY
T: (01803) 854187
F: (01803) 851773
E: info@brixhamholidayhomes.co.uk
I: www.brixhamholidayhomes.co.uk

Fairview Cottage ★★★
Contact:
Holiday Homes & Cottages Sw, 365A Torquay Road, Paignton TQ3 2BT
T: (01803) 663650
F: (01803) 664037
E: holcotts@aol.com
I: www.swcottages.co.uk

Fortune Cottage
Rating Applied For
Contact:
Brixham Holiday Homes Ltd, 121A New Road, Brixham TQ5 8BY
T: (01803) 854187
F: (01803) 851773
E: info@brixhamholidayhomes.co.uk
I: www.brixhamholidayhomes.co.uk

Gulls' Nest ★★★★★
Contact: Mrs Gretchen Tricker
The Hill House, 23 St Peter's Hill, Brixham TQ5 9TE
T: (01803) 857937
F: (01803) 857937
E: gtricker@aol.com
I: www.brixhamhistorichouses.co.uk

Harbour Heights
Rating Applied For
Contact:
Holiday Homes & Cottages SW, 365A Torquay Road, Paignton TQ3 2BT
T: (01803) 663650
F: (01803) 664037
E: holcotts@aol.com
I: www.swcottages.co.uk

Harbour Lights Holiday Flats ★-★★
Contact: Mr Robert Walker
Harbour Lights Holiday Flats, 69 Berry Head Road, Brixham TQ5 9AA
T: (01803) 854816
F: (01803) 854816
E: harbourlights@compuserve.com

Harbour Reach ★★★
Contact: Mrs Jenny Pocock
Totley Hall Farm, Totley Hall Lane, Sheffield S17 4AA
T: (0114) 236 4761
F: (0114) 2364761

Harbour View
Rating Applied For
Contact:
Brixham Holidays Homes Ltd, 121A New Road, Brixham TQ5 8BY
T: (01803) 854187
F: (01803) 851773
E: info@brixhamholidayhomes.co.uk
I: www.brixhamholidayhomes.co.uk

Harbour View ★★★★
Contact:
Holiday Homes & Cottages South West, 365A Torquay Road, Paignton TQ3 2BT
T: (01803) 663650
F: (01803) 664037
E: holcotts@aol.com
I: www.swcottages.co.uk

The Harbour's Edge ★★★
Contact: Mr & Mrs Booth
24 The Close, Brixham TQ5 8RF
T: (01803) 859859

The Hatchway and the Porthole ★★★
Contact:
Holiday Homes and Cottages SW, 365A Torquay Road, Paignton TQ3 2BT
T: (01803) 663650
F: (01803) 664037
E: holcotts@aol.com

Heath Cote
Rating Applied For
Contact:
Brixham Holiday Homes Ltd, 121A New Road, Brixham TQ5 8BY
T: (01803) 854187
F: (01803) 851773
E: info@brixhamholidayhomes.co.uk
I: www.brixhamholidayhomes.co.uk

Hideaway Cottage
Rating Applied For
Contact:
Brixham Holiday Homes Ltd, 121A New Road, Brixham TQ5 8BY
T: (01803) 854187
F: (01803) 851773
E: info@brixhamholidayhomes.co.uk
I: www.brixhamholidayhomes.co.uk

Jericho Cottage ★★★★
Contact:
Blue Chip Vacations, 3 Marina Walk, Brixham TQ5 9BW
T: (01803) 855282
F: (01803) 881029
E: info@bluechipdevelopments.com

Keel House
Rating Applied For
Contact:
121A New Road, Brixham TQ5 8BY
T: (01803) 854187
F: (01803) 851773
E: info@brixhamholidayhomes.co.uk
I: www.brixhamholidayhomes.co.uk

Kings Barton Cottage ★★★
Contact:
Holiday Homes & Cottages South West, 365A Torquay Road, Paignton TQ3 2BT
T: (01803) 663650
F: (01803) 664037
E: holcotts@eol.com
I: www.swcottages.co.uk

Lantern Cottage
Rating Applied For
Contact:
Brixham Holiday Homes Ltd, 121A New Road, Brixham TQ5 8BY
T: (01803) 854187
F: (01803) 851773
E: info@brixhamholidayhomes.co.uk
I: www.brixhamholidayhomes.co.uk

Lily Cottage ★★★
Contact:
Holiday Homes & Cottages South West, 365A Torquay Road, Paignton TQ3 2BT
T: (01803) 663650
F: (01803) 664307
E: holcotts@aol.com

Linden Court Holiday Apartments ★★★
Contact: Mr Brian & Mrs Carol McCandlish
Linden Court Holiday Apartments, South Furzeham Road, Brixham TQ5 8JA
T: (01803) 851491
F: (01803) 558761
E: linden_court@mail.com

Lobster Pot Cottage
Rating Applied For
Contact:
Brixham Holiday Homes Ltd, 121A New Road, Brixham TQ5 8BY
T: (01803) 854187
F: (01803) 851773
E: info@brixhamholidayhomes.co.uk
I: www.brixhamholidaycottages.co.uk

Lorna
Rating Applied For
Contact:
Brixham Holiday Homes Ltd, 121A New Road, Brixham TQ5 8BY
T: (01803) 854187
F: (01803) 851773
E: info@brixhamholidayhomes.co.uk
I: www.brixhamholidayhomes.co.uk

Lytehouse Cottage ★★★
Contact: Mr Ian Butterworth
Holiday Homes & Cottages South West, 365A Torquay Road, Paignton TQ3 2BT
T: (01803) 663650
F: (01803) 664037
E: holcotts@aol.com
I: www.swcottages.co.uk

Mariners Cottage ★★★
Contact:
Holiday Homes & Cottages SW, 365A Torquay Road, Paignton TQ3 2BT
T: (01803) 663650
F: (01803) 664037
E: holcotts@aol.com
I: www.swcottages.co.uk

Monkbarns Annexe
Rating Applied For
Contact:
Brixham Holiday Homes Ltd, 121A New Road, Brixham TQ5 8BY
T: (01803) 854187
F: (01803) 851773
E: info@brixhamholidayhomes.co.uk
I: www.brixhamholidayhomes.co.uk

SOUTH WEST ENGLAND

Moonlit Waters
Rating Applied For
Contact:
Brixham Holiday Homes Ltd,
121A New Road, Brixham
TQ5 8BY
T: (01803) 854187
F: (01803) 851773
E: info@brixhamholidayhomes.co.uk
I: www.brixhamholidayhomes.co.uk

Mudberry House ★★★
Contact:
Holiday Homes & Cottages
South West, 365A Torquay Road,
Paignton TQ3 2BT
T: (01803) 663650
F: (01803) 664037
E: holcotts@aol.com
I: www.swcottages.co.uk

Newlands
Rating Applied For
Contact:
Brixham Holiday Homes Ltd,
121A New Road, Brixham
TQ5 8BY
T: (01803) 854187
F: (01803) 851773
E: info@brixhamholidayhomes.co.uk
I: www.brixhamholidayhomes.co.uk

Outlook ★★★
Contact:
Holiday Homes & Cottages
South West, 365A Torquay Road,
Paignton TQ3 2BT
T: (01803) 663650
F: (01803) 664037
E: holcotts@aol.com
I: www.swcottages.co.uk

Sailor's Haunt ★★★★
Contact: Mr Richard Haycock
Beaumont House, 25 Siston
Common, Bristol BS15 4NY
T: (0117) 9676659
F: (0117) 9676659
E: beaumont.cottages@virgin.net
I: www.beaumontcottages.co.uk

Sea View Terrace
Rating Applied For
Contact:
Brixham Holiday Homes Ltd,
121A New Road, Brixham
TQ5 8BY
T: (01803) 854187
F: (01803) 851773
E: info@brixhamholidayhomes.co.uk
I: www.brixhamholidayhomes.co.uk

Seacat Cottage ★★★★
Contact:
Holiday Homes & Cottages
South West, 365A Torquay Road,
Paignton TQ3 2BT
T: (01803) 663650
F: (01803) 664037
E: holcotts@aol.co.uk
I: www.swcottages.co.uk

Seashell Cottage ★★★
Contact: Mr Ian Butterworth
Holiday Homes & Cottages
South West, 365A Torquay Road,
Paignton TQ3 2BT
T: (01803) 663650
F: (01803) 664037
E: holcotts@aol.com
I: www.swcottages.co.uk

Spyglass
Rating Applied For
Contact:
Brixham Holiday Homes Ltd,
121A New Road, Brixham
TQ5 8BY
T: (01803) 854187
F: (01803) 851773
E: info@brixhamholidayhomes.co.uk
I: www.brixhamholidays.co.uk

The Studios ★★★★
Contact:
Holiday Homes & Cottages SW,
365A Torquay Road, Paignton
TQ3 2BT
T: (01803) 664037
E: holcotts@aol.com

Sundial Cottage
Rating Applied For
Contact:
Brixham Holiday Homes Ltd,
121A New Road, Brixham
TQ5 8BY
T: (01803) 854187
F: (01803) 851773
E: info@brixhamholidayhomes.co.uk
I: www.brixhamholidayhomes.co.uk

Sunset Cottage
Rating Applied For
Contact:
Brixham Holiday Homes Ltd,
121A New Road, Brixham
TQ5 8BY
T: (01803) 854187
F: (01803) 851773
E: info@brixhamholidayhomes.co.uk

Tide's Reach
Rating Applied For
Contact:
Brixham Holiday Homes, 151A
New Road, Brixham TQ5 8BY
T: (01803) 854187
F: (01803) 851773
E: info@brixhamholidayhomes.co.uk
I: www.brixhamholidayhomes.co.uk

Top Deck
Rating Applied For
Contact:
Brixham Holiday Homes, 121A
New Road, Brixham TQ5 8BY
T: (01803) 854187
F: (01803) 851773
E: info@brixhamholidayhomes.co.uk
I: www.brixhamholidayhomes.co.uk

Torbay Holiday Chalets ★★
Contact: Mr Martyn & Mrs Jane
Swift
Torbay Holiday Chalets,
Fishcombe Cove, Brixham
TQ5 8RA
T: (01803) 853313

Torbay House
Rating Applied For
Contact:
Brixham Holiday Homes Ltd,
121A New Road, Brixham
TQ5 8BY
T: (01803) 854187
F: (01803) 851773
E: info@brixhamholidayhomes.co.uk
I: www.brixhamholidayhomes.co.uk

Torfrey Cottage
Rating Applied For
Contact:
Brixham Holiday Homes Ltd,
121A New Road, Brixham
TQ5 8BY
T: (01803) 854187
F: (01803) 851773
E: info@brixhamholidayhomes.co.uk
I: www.brixhamholidayhomes.co.uk

Trade Winds
Rating Applied For
Contact:
Brixham Holiday Homes Ltd,
121A New Road, Brixham
TQ5 8BY
T: (01803) 854187
F: (01803) 851773
E: info@brixhamholidayhomes.co.uk
I: www.brixhamholidayhomes.co.uk

Watchman's Cottage
Rating Applied For
Contact:
Brixham Holiday Homes Ltd,
121A New Road, Brixham
TQ5 8BY
T: (01803) 854187
F: (01803) 851773
E: info@brixhamholidayhomes.co.uk
I: www.brixhamholidayhomes.co.uk

White Sails
Rating Applied For
Contact:
Brixham Holiday Homes Ltd,
121A New Road, Brixham
TQ5 8BY
T: (01803) 854187
F: (01803) 851773
E: info@brixhamholidayhomes.co.uk
I: www.brixhamholidayhomes.co.uk

Windjammer Apartment ★★★
Contact: Mr & Mrs Skeggs
Windjammer Apartment,
Windjammer Lodge, Parkham
Road, Brixham TQ5 9BU
T: (01803) 854279
E: info@windjammer.org.uk
I: www.windjammer.org.uk

BROAD CAMPDEN
Gloucestershire

Lion Cottage ★★★
Contact: Mrs Barbara Rawcliffe
Lion Cottage, Broad Campden,
Chipping Campden GL55 6UR
T: (01386) 840077

BROADCLYST
Devon

Hue's Piece ★★★★
Contact: Mrs Anna Hamlyn
Hue's Piece, Paynes Farm,
Broadclyst, Exeter EX5 3BJ
T: (01392) 466720
E: nchamlyn@fsbdial.co.uk
I: www.visitwestcountry.com/huespiece

Wares Cottage ★★★★
Contact:
Farm & Cottage Holidays,
Victoria House, 12 Fore Street,
Bideford EX39 1AW
T: (01237) 479146
F: (01237) 421512
E: bookings@farmcott.co.uk
I: www.farmcott.co.uk

BROADMAYNE
Dorset

Holcombe Valley Cottages ★★★
Contact: Mr Peter & Mrs Jane
Davies
Holcombe Valley Cottages,
Chalky Road, Dorchester
DT2 8PW
T: (01305) 852817
E: holvalcots@aol.com
I: www.holcombe-cottages.co.uk

BROADOAK
Dorset

Stoke Mill Farm ★★-★★★
Contact: Mrs Anthea Bay
Stoke Mill Farm, Bridport
DT6 5NR
T: (01308) 868036
F: (01308) 868036
I: www.stokemillholidays.20m.com

BROMHAM
Wiltshire

The Byres ★★
Contact: Mr & Mrs G, B Myers
The Byres, 84 Westbrook,
Chippenham SN15 2EE
T: (01380) 850557

Farthings ★★★
Contact: Mrs Gloria Steed
Farthings, The Cottage,
Westbrook, Chippenham
SN15 2EE
T: (01380) 850255
E: richard_gloriasteed@hotmail.com

Park Farm Cottages ★★★
Contact: Mrs Valerie Bourne
Park Farm Cottages, Westbrook,
Chippenham SN15 2EE
T: (01380) 850966
E: valandtom2003@aol.com

SOUTH WEST ENGLAND

BROMPTON REGIS
Somerset

Weatherham Farm Cottages ★★★★
Contact: Mrs Anne Caldwell
Weatherham Farm Cottages, Brompton Regis, Weather Farm, Dulverton TA22 9LG
T: (01398) 371303
F: (01398) 371104
E: enquiries@weatherhamfarm.co.uk
I: www.weatherhamfarm.co.uk

BROMSBERROW
Gloucestershire

Perrins Court Holiday Cottages ★★★
Contact: Mr & Mrs A Stow
Stow House, Chase End Street, Bromesberrow, Ledbury HR8 1SD
T: (01531) 650670
E: stow@perrinscourt.org

BROMSBERROW HEATH
Gloucestershire

Honeysuckle Cottage ★★★★
Contact: Wendy Hooper
Greenlands, Bromsberrow Heath, Ledbury HR8 1PG
T: (01531) 650360
E: ws.hooper@btopenworld.com

BROUGHTON GIFFORD
Wiltshire

Church Farm Holiday Cottages ★★★★
Contact: Mrs Sharon Hooper
J Hooper and Son, Church Farm, Melksham SN12 8PR
T: (01225) 783413
F: (01225) 783467
E: shooper@churchfarmcottages.fsnet.co.uk
I: www.smoothhound.co.uk

BRUSHFORD
Somerset

Orchard Cottage ★★★
Contact: Mr Peter & Mrs Janet Cornwell
Marsden's Cottage Holidays, 2 The Square, Braunton EX33 2JB
T: (01271) 813777
F: (01271) 813664
E: holidays@marsdens.co.uk
I: www.marsdens.co.uk

BRUTON
Somerset

78 High Street
Rating Applied For
Contact: Mrs Lisa Pickering
78 High Street, 78 High Street, Bruton BA10 0AJ
T: (01749) 813772

BRYHER
Isles of Scilly

Atlanta Holiday Accommodation ★★★
Contact: Mrs Langdon
Atlanta Holiday Accommodation, Bryher TR23 0PR
T: (01720) 422823

Glenhope ★★★
Contact: Mr Langdon
Glenhope, Bryher TR23 0PR
T: (01720) 423136
F: (01720) 423166
E: glenhope@ukonline.co.uk

Hebe, Fernside & Shippen Cottage ★★★
Contact: Mrs Taylor
Veronica Farm, Bryher TR23 0PR
T: (01720) 422862

Hillside Farm ★★★★
Contact: Mrs Ruth Jenkins
Hillside Farm, Bryher TR23 0PR
T: (01720) 423156
E: ruthbryher@aol.com
I: www.bryher-ios.co.uk/hf

South Hill ★★★
Contact: Mrs Bennett
Firmans, Bryher TR23
T: (01720) 422411
E: marianbennett@excite.co.uk

The White House Flat ★★★
Contact: Mr Bushell
The White House, Bryher TR23 0PR
T: (01720) 422010
F: (01720) 422010

BUCKLAND
Gloucestershire

Hillside Cottage and The Bothy ★★★★
Contact: Mr Edmondson
Burhill, Buckland, Broadway WR12 7LY
T: (01386) 853426
F: (01386) 833211
E: bob.e@tesco.net
I: www.burhill.co.uk

BUCKLAND BREWER
Devon

Adipit ★★★★
Contact:
Powell's Cottage Holidays, High Street, Saundersfoot SA69 9EJ
T: (01834) 812791
F: (01834) 811731
E: info@powells.co.uk
I: www.powells.co.uk

Craneham Court ★★★★
Contact:
North Devon Holiday Homes, 19 Cross Street, Barnstaple EX31 1BD
T: (01271) 376322

BUCKLAND IN THE MOOR
Devon

Pine Lodge ★★★
Contact:
Holiday Homes & Cottages South West, 365A Torquay Road, Paignton TQ3 2BT
T: (01803) 663650
F: (01803) 664037
E: holcotts@aol.com
I: www.swcottages.co.uk

BUCKLAND NEWTON
Dorset

Church Farm Stables ★★★★
Contact: Mr & Mrs Neville Archer
Church Farm Stables, Dorchester DT2 7BX
T: (01300) 345315
F: (01300) 345320
E: enquiries@staydorset.co.uk
I: www.staydorset.co.uk

Domineys Cottages ★★★★
Contact: Mrs Jeanette Gueterbock
Domineys Cottages, Domineys Yard, Buckland Newton, Dorchester DT2 7BS
T: (01300) 345295
F: (01300) 345596
E: cottages@domineys.com
I: www.domineys.com

BUCKLAND ST MARY
Somerset

The Apartment ★★★★
Contact: Mr Roy Harkness
Hillside Guest Accommodation, Buckland St Mary, Chard TA20 3TQ
T: (01460) 234599
F: (01460) 234599
E: royandmarge@hillsidebsm.freeserve.co.uk
I: www.theaa.com/hotels/103591.html

Leveret Cottage ★★★
Contact: Mrs Suzie Float
Leveret Cottage, Hare House, Blackwater, Buckland St Mary, Chard TA20 3LE
T: (01460) 234638
E: info@leveretcottage.co.uk

BUDE
Cornwall

Atlantic View Bungalows ★★★
Contact: Mr Chris & Mrs Brenda Raven
Atlantic View Bungalows, Marine Drive, Bude EX23 0AG
T: (01288) 361716
E: enquiries@atlanticview.co.uk
I: www.atlanticview.co.uk

Bithecutt Cottage ★★★★
Contact: Christine
Bude EX23 8EN
T: (01288) 352199
E: mikejur@aol.com

Bramble Cottage ★★★★
Contact: Mrs Jane Campbell
Lime Cottage, Lime Walk, Southampton SO45 4RB
T: (023) 80844425
E: jane.campbell@talk21.com

Brannel Cottage ★★★
Contact: Mrs Christine Parker
The Crescent, Yelverton PL20 7PS
T: (01822) 855614
E: hannafordpc@Aol.com

4 Brightlands Apartments ★★★
Contact: Mrs Gill Tawse
Naseby, Sebastopol Lane, Sandhills, Wormley, Godalming GU8 5UG
T: (01428) 682565

Broomhill Manor Country Estate ★★★★-★★★★★
Contact: Mr Mower
Broomhill Manor Country Estate, Broomhill Manor, Bude EX23 9HA
T: (01288) 352940
F: (01288) 356526
E: chris@broomhill-manor.demon.co.uk
I: www.broomhillmanor.co.uk

Coast View ★★★
Contact:
Holiday Homes & Cottages SW, 365A Torquay Road, Paignton TQ3 2BT
T: (01803) 663650
F: (01803) 664037
E: holcotts@aol.com
I: www.swcottages.co.uk

Conna-Mara ★★★
Contact: Mrs Tina Collins
Conna-Mara, Maer Down, Bude EX23 8NG
T: (01288) 356354
F: (01288) 356354
E: conna-mara@btconnect.com
I: www.visitwestcountry.com/connamara

Downlands ★★★
Contact: Mr Clive Bloy
Downlands, Maer Lane, Bude EX23 9EE
T: (01288) 356920
E: sonia@downlands.net
I: www.downlands.net

The Falcon Hotel ★★★
Contact: Mr & Mrs Browning
The Falcon Hotel, Breakwater Road, Bude EX23 8SD
T: (01288) 352005
F: (01288) 356359
E: reception@falconhotel.com
I: www.falconhotel.com

Flat 16 Kiming ★★★
Contact: Mrs Chris Ellis
10 Parkfield Road, Exeter EX3 0DR
T: (01392) 873666

Forda Lodges & Cottages ★★★★-★★★★★
Contact: Mr Jim & Mrs Gillian Chibbett
Forda Lodges & Cottages, Bude EX23 9RZ
T: (01288) 321413
F: (01288) 321413
E: forda.lodges@virgin.net
I: www.fordalodges.co.uk

Frys ★★★★-★★★★★
Contact: Mr John & Mrs Gillian Stone
Frys, Rosecare, St Gennys, Bude EX23 0BE
T: (01840) 230375
E: gilljohn@rosecare.freeserve.co.uk
I: www.cottageguide.co.uk/rosecare

Establishments printed in blue have a detailed entry in this guide   619

SOUTH WEST ENGLAND

Glebe House Cottages ★★★★
Contact: Mr & Mrs Varley
Glebe House Cottages Limited,
Bridgerule, Holsworthy
EX22 7EW
T: (01288) 381272
E: etc@glebehousecottages.co.uk
I: www.glebehousecottages.co.uk

Hilton Farm Holiday Cottages ★★★-★★★★
Contact: Mr Ian & Mrs Fiona Goodman
Hilton Farm Holiday Cottages,
Hilton Road, Bude EX23 0HE
T: (01288) 361521
F: (01288) 361521
E: ian@hiltonfarmhouse.freeserve.co.uk
I: www.hiltonfarmhouse.co.uk

Houndapitt Farm Cottages ★★★
Contact: Mr Heard
Houndapitt Farm Cottages,
Sandymouth Bay, Bude
EX23 9HW
T: (01288) 355455
E: info@houndapitt.co.uk
I: www.houndapitt.co.uk

Ivyleaf Barton Cottages ★★-★★★★★
Contact: Mr Robert Barrett
Ivyleaf Barton Cottages, Ivyleaf Hill, Bude EX23 9LD
T: (01288) 321237
F: (01288) 321937
E: info@ivyleafbarton.co.uk
I: www.ivyleafbarton.co.uk

Karibu ★★★
Contact: Mrs Anna Rutlidge
Karibu, 3 Downs View, Bude
EX23 8RF
T: (01288) 356519
E: benmafo@aol.com

Kennacott Court ★★★★★
Contact: Mr Philip & Mrs Mary Myers
Kennacott Court, Bude
EX23 0ND
T: (01288) 362000
F: (01288) 361434
I: www.kennacottcourt.co.uk

Langfield Manor ★★★
Contact: Mr Keith Freestone
Langfield Manor, Broadclose,
Bude EX23 8DP
T: (01288) 352415
E: info@langfieldmanor.co.uk
I: www.langfieldmanor.co.uk

Little Orchard ★★★
Contact: Mrs Patricia Gosney
Little Orchard, Old Orchard,
Bude EX23 0LR
T: (01288) 355617

Lower Northcott Farmhouse ★★★
Contact: Mrs Mary Trewin
Court Farm, Bude EX23 0EN
T: (01288) 361494
F: (01288) 361494
E: mary@courtfarm-holidays.co.uk
I: www.courtfarm-holidays.co.uk

Manby ★★★
Contact: Mrs Hoole
54 Western Road, Oxford
OX1 4LG
T: (01865) 245268
E: hoole@patrol.1-way.co.uk

Mornish Holiday Apartments ★★★★
Contact: Mr John & Mrs Julia Hilder
Mornish Holiday Apartments, 20 Summerleaze Crescent, Bude
EX23 8HJ
T: (01288) 352972
F: (01288) 352972
E: mornishholidays@btconnect.com
I: www.bude.co.uk/mornish-apartments

Neet Cottage
Rating Applied For
Contact: Mrs Carolyn Harrison
Higher Widemouth Farm, Bude
EX23 0DE
T: (01288) 361877
E: widemouthfarm@tiscali.co.uk

Old Lifeboat House ★★-★★★
Contact: Ms Bader
Old Lifeboat House, c/o Brendon Arms, Falcon Terrace, Bude
EX23 8SD
T: (01288) 354542
F: (01288) 354542
E: enquiries@brendonarms.co.uk
I: www.brendonarms.co.uk

Penhalt Farm ★★★
Contact: Mr Den & Mrs Jennie Marks
Widemouth Bay, Poundstock,
Bude EX23 0DG
T: (01288) 361210
F: (01288) 361210
I: www.holidaybank.co.uk/penhaltfarm

Penrhyn ★★★
Contact: Mr Brett
Penrhyn, 1 Flexbury Avenue,
Bude EX23 8RE
T: (01288) 355039

Riverview ★★★
Contact: Mr Martin Challans
15 Percheron Close, Impington,
Cambridge CB4 9YX
T: (01223) 235072
E: mchallans@hotmail.com

St Annes ★★★
Contact: Mr & Mrs Butler
97 Great Tattenhams, Epsom
KT18 5RB
T: (01737) 362117

St Annes Bungalow ★★★
Contact: Mrs Britten
6 Woodside Avenue N, Green Lane, Coventry CV3 6BB
T: (02476) 692410

South Lynstone Barns ★★★
Contact: Mrs Armstrong
Back Lane, Paddockhurst Road,
Crawley RH10 4SF
T: (01342) 716355
E: armstrongsydney@aol.co.uk

Stable Cottages ★★★
Contact: Ms Gregory
10 Pathfields, Bude EX23 8DW
T: (01288) 354237

Trelay Farm Holiday Cottages ★★★★
Contact: Mr Robert Watson
Trelay Farm Holiday Cottages, St Gennys, Bude EX23 0NJ
T: (01840) 230378
F: (01840) 230423
E: info@trelayfarm.co.uk
I: www.trelayfarm.co.uk

Trevalgas Manor ★★★★
Contact: Mr Richard & Mrs Anita Smith
Trevalgas Manor, Pughill, Bude
EX23 9EX
T: (01288) 359777
E: accounts@exsel5.freeserve.co.uk

Widemouth Bay
Rating Applied For
Contact:
Holiday Homes & Cottages SW,
365A Torquay Road, Paignton
TQ3 2BT
T: (01803) 663650
F: (01803) 664037
E: holcotts@ao.com
I: www.swcottages.co.uk

Wild Pigeon Holidays ★★
Contact: Mrs Anne Longley
Wild Pigeon Holidays, 8 Breakwater Road, Bude
EX23 8LQ
T: (01288) 353839

Woodlands Farm ★★★★
Contact: Mrs S M Webb
Woodlands Farm, Woodford,
Bude EX23 9HU
T: (01288) 331689
F: (01288) 331689
E: woodlandsholiday@aol.com
I: www.woodlandsfarmholidays.co.uk

Woolstone Manor Farm ★★★★
Contact:
Farm & Cottage Holidays,
Victoria House, 12 Fore Street,
Bideford EX39 1AW
T: (01237) 479146
F: (01237) 421512
E: enquiries@farmcott.co.uk
I: www.farmcott.co.uk

BUDLEIGH SALTERTON
Devon

Aysgarth ★★★★
Contact:
Holiday Cottages & Cottages SW, 365A Torquay Road,
Paignton TQ3 2BT
T: (01803) 663650
F: (01803) 664037
E: holcotts@aol.com

Christophers ★★★★★
Contact: Mrs Barlow
The Thatched Cottage Company,
56 Fore Street, Budleigh
Salterton EX9 7HB
T: (01395) 567676
F: (01395) 567440
E: info@thethatchedcottagecompany.com
I: www.thethatchedcottagecompany.co.uk

Lufflands ★★★★
Contact: Mr & Mrs Goode
Lufflands, Yettington, Budleigh
Salterton EX9 7BP
T: (01395) 568422
F: (01395) 568810
E: cottages@lufflands.co.uk
I: www.lufflands.co.uk

Pebbles ★★
Contact:
Jean Bartlett Cottage Holidays,
The Old Dairy, Fore Street,
Seaton EX12 3JB
T: (01297) 23221
F: (01297) 23303
E: holidays@jeanbartlett.com
I: www.netbreaaks.com/jeanb

BUDOCK WATER
Cornwall

Penmorvah Manor Hotel and Courtyard Cottages
Rating Applied For
Contact: Mrs Cheryl Risely
Penmorvah Manor Hotel and Courtyard Cottages, Falmouth
TR11 5ED
T: (01326) 250277
F: (01326) 250509
E: reception@penmorvah.co.uk
I: www.penmorvah.co.uk

BUGLE
Cornwall

Higher Menadew Farm Cottages ★★★★
Contact: Mr Andrew & Mrs Anita Higman
Higher Menadew Farm Cottages,
Higher Menaden, St Austell
PL26 8QW
T: (01726) 850310
F: (01726) 850310
E: mail@stayingincornwall.com
I: www.stayingincornwall.com

BULL PITCH
Gloucestershire

The Garden Flat
Rating Applied For
Contact: Mr John & Mrs Louisa Rubin
The Garden Flat, Ormond House,
Dursley GL11 4NG
T: (01453) 545312
E: jjrubin@lineone.net

BURLAWN
Cornwall

The Old Chapel ★★★
Contact: Mrs Angela Byrne
The Old Chapel, Wadebridge
PL27 7LA
T: (01208) 812075
F: (01208) 815421

SOUTH WEST ENGLAND

Wren Cottage ★★★
Contact:
Rock Holidays inc. Harbour Holidays Rock Ltd., Trebetherick House, Wadebridge PL27 6SB
T: (01208) 863399
F: (01208) 862218
E: rockhols@aol.com
I: www.rockholidays.co.uk

BURNHAM-ON-SEA
Somerset

Hurn Farm ★★★
Contact: Mrs Holdom
Hurn Farm, Hurn Lane, Burnham-on-Sea TA8 2QT
T: (01278) 751418
E: hurnfarm@hurnfarmcottages.co.uk
I: www.hurnfarmcottages.co.uk

Kingsway ★★★
Contact:
Land & Law, PO Box 24930, London SE23 2YD
T: (020) 8699 1000
F: (020) 8699 1022

Prospect Farm ★★★-★★★★★
Contact: Mrs Gillian Wall
Strowlands, East Brent, Highbridge TA9 4JH
T: (01278) 760507

Stable Cottage and Coach House ★★★-★★★★
Contact: Mr & Mrs Bigwood
Brean Farm, Brean Down, Burnham-on-Sea TA8 2RR
T: (01278) 751055
F: (01278) 751055

Stoddens Farm Holiday Cottages ★★★
Contact: Mrs Sandra Tipling
Stoddens Farm Holiday Cottages, Stoddens Farm, Stoddens Road, Burnham-on-Sea TA8 2DE
T: (01278) 782505
F: (01278) 792221
E: stoddens-cottage@btconnect.com

BURROWBRIDGE
Somerset

Hillview ★★★
Contact: Mrs Rosalind Griffiths
Hillview, Stanmoor Road, Burrowbridge, Bridgwater TA7 0RX
T: (01823) 698308
F: (01823) 698308

BURSTOCK
Dorset

Whetham Farm The Flat ★★★
Contact: Mrs Curtis
Whetham Farm The Flat, Beaminster DT8 3LH
T: (01308) 868293

BURTLE
Somerset

Catcott Burtle Farm Cottage ★★
Contact: Mrs Rosemary Tucker
Catcott Burtle Farm Cottage, Westhay Road, Bridgwater TA7 8NE
T: (01278) 722321
F: (01278) 722321
E: rosemary@catcottburtlefarm.totalserve.co.uk

Glebe Farm Cottage ★★★★
Contact:
Farm & Cottage Holidays, Victoria House, 19 Fore Street, Bideford EX39 1AW
T: (01237) 479146
F: (01237) 421512
E: bookings@farmcott.co.uk
I: www.farmcott.co.uk

BURTON BRADSTOCK
Dorset

Apple Tree Cottage ★★★
Contact:
Dream Cottages, 5 Hope Square, Weymouth DT4 8TR
T: (01305) 789000
F: (01305) 761347
I: www.dream-cottages.co.uk

Bramble Cottage ★★★
Contact: Mr Zachary Stuart-Brown
Dream Cottages, 5 Hope Square, Weymouth DT4 8TR
T: (01305) 789000
E: admin@dream-cottages.co.uk
I: www.dream-cottages.co.uk

Bryer Lea ★★★
Contact: Mr Zachary Stuart-Brown
Dream Cottages, 5 Hope Square, Weymouth DT4 8TR
T: (01305) 789000
F: (01305) 761346
E: admin@dream-cottages.co.uk
I: www.dream-cottages.co.uk

Cliff Farm ★★★
Contact: Mr Zachary Stuart-Brown
Dream Cottages, 5 Hope Square, Weymouth DT4 8TR
T: (01305) 789000
F: (01305) 761346
E: admin@dream-cottages.co.uk
I: www.dream-cottages.co.uk

The Doves ★★★
Contact: Mr Zachary Stuart-Brown
Dream Cottages, 5 Hope Square, Weymouth DT4 8TR
T: (01305) 789000
F: (01305) 761346
E: admin@dream-cottages.co.uk
I: www.dream-cottages.co.uk

2 High Street ★★★★
Contact: Ms Celia Crosby
The Orchard, Rhode Lane, Lyme Regis DT7 3TX
T: (01297) 444641
F: (01297) 444263
E: celia.crosby@virgin.net

Hillview Bungalow ★★★
Contact: Mr Zachary Stuart-Brown
Dream Cottages, 5 Hope Square, Weymouth DT4 8TR
T: (01305) 789000
F: (01305) 761346
E: admin@dream-cottages.co.uk
I: www.dream-cottages.co.uk

Jasmine Cottage ★★★
Contact: Mr Zachary Stuart-Brown
Dream Cottages, 5 Hope Square, Weymouth DT4 8TR
T: (01305) 789000
F: (01305) 761346
E: admin@dream-cottages.co.uk
I: www.dream-cottages.co.uk

Little Berwick & Berwick House ★★★-★★★★
Contact: Mr Zachary Stuart-Brown
Dream Cottages, 5 Hope Square, Weymouth DT4 8TR
T: (01305) 789000
F: (01305) 761346
E: admin@dream-cottages.co.uk
I: www.dream-cottages.co.uk

Pebble Beach Lodge ★★★
Contact: Mrs Jan Hemingway
Pebble Beach Lodge, Bridport DT6 4RJ
T: (01308) 897428
I: www.burtonbradstock.org.uk

Primrose Hill ★★
Contact:
Dream Cottages, 5 Hope Square, Weymouth DT4 8TR
T: (01305) 789000
F: (01305) 761346
E: admin@dream-cottages.co.uk
I: www.dream-cottages.co.uk

Smugglers Cottage ★★★★
Contact:
Dream Cottages, 5 Hope Square, Weymouth DT4 8TR
T: (01305) 789000
F: (01305) 761347

BUTCOMBE
North Somerset

Butcombe Farm ★★★
Contact: Ms Sandra Moss
Butcombe Farm, Aldwick Lane, Bristol BS40 7UW
T: (01761) 462380
F: (01761) 462300
E: info@butcombe-farm.demon.co.uk
I: www.butcombe-farm.demon.co.uk

BUTLEIGH WOOTTON
Somerset

Little Broadway ★★
Contact: Mrs Mary Butt
Little Broadway, Glastonbury BA6 8TX
T: (01458) 442824
F: (01458) 442824

CADGWITH
Cornwall

Pennard ★★★
Contact: Mr Martin Raftery
Mullion Cottages, Mullion Meadows, Helston TR12 7HB
T: (01326) 240315
F: (01326) 241090
E: martin@mullioncottages.com
I: www.mullioncottages.com

CALLINGTON
Cornwall

Cadson Manor Farm ★★★★
Contact: Mrs Brenda Crago
Cadson Manor Farm, Callington PL17 7HW
T: (01579) 383969
F: (01579) 383969
E: brenda.crago@btclick.com
I: www.cadsonmanor.com

CAMBORNE
Cornwall

Mill Cottage ★★★★
Contact: Mr Colin & Mrs Rebecca Campbell
Drym Mill, Drym, Praze, Camborne TR14 0NU
T: (01209) 832276
F: (01209) 832276
E: colincam@dialstart.net
I: www.drymmill.com

CAMELFORD
Cornwall

Juliot's Well Holiday Park ★★★★
Contact: Mrs Kim Boundy
Juliot's Well Holiday Park, Camelford PL32 9RF
T: (01840) 213302
F: (01840) 212700
E: juliotswell@holidaysincornwall.net
I: www.holidaysincornwall.net

Lane End Farm Bungalow ★★★
Contact: Mr Keith Vasey
Lane End Farm Bungalow, Victoria Road, Camelford PL32 9XB
T: (01840) 212452
F: (01840) 212452
E: keith@laneend47.fsnet.co.uk

The Swallows ★★★★
Contact: Mrs Juliet Elsey
The Swallows, Trekeek Farm, Camelford PL32 9UB
T: (01840) 212212
F: (01840) 213054
E: info@jumbocolor.co.uk

Vilnius ★★★
Contact: CH ref: 66068
Holiday Cottages Group Owner Services Dept, Stoney Bank Road, Barnoldswick BB18 6RN
T: 0870 0723723
F: (01282) 844288
E: sales@holidaycottagesgroup.com
I: www.country-holidays.co.uk

CANNINGTON
Somerset

The Courtyard ★★★★
Contact: Mrs Dyer
Blackmore Farm, Blackmore Lane, Bridgwater TA5 2NE
T: (01278) 653442
F: (01278) 653427
E: dyerfarm@aol.com
I: www.dyerfarm.co.uk

Establishments printed in blue have a detailed entry in this guide

SOUTH WEST ENGLAND

CANNOP
Gloucestershire

Woodside Cottage ★★★
Contact: Mrs Helen Evans
Peaked Rocks Cottage, The Rocks, Lydbrook GL17 9RF
T: (01594) 861119
F: (01594) 823408
E: evens@evansholidays.freeserve.co.uk

CARBIS BAY
Cornwall

Argent
Rating Applied For
Contact:
Barbis Bay Holidays, 8 Marl Road, Nottingham NG12 6GY
T: (01159) 491593
F: (01159) 491593
E: enquiries@carbisbayholidays.co.uk
I: www.carbisbayholidays.co.uk

Azure
Rating Applied For
Contact: Mrs Sheena Brindley
Carbis Bay Holidays, 8 Marl Road, Nottingham NG12 2GY
T: (01159) 334870
F: (01159) 491593
E: enquiries@carbisbayholidays.co.uk
I: www.carbisbayholidays.co.uk

Boskenza Court ★★★
Contact:
Powells Cottage Holidays, Dolphin House, High Street, Saundersfoot SA69 9EJ
T: (01834) 813232
F: (01834) 811731
E: info@powells.co.uk

Godrevy view
Rating Applied For
Contact: Mrs Sheena Brindley
Carbis Bay Holidays, 8 Marl Road, Nottingham NG12 2GY
T: (01159) 334870
F: (01159) 491593
E: enquiries@carbisbayholidays.co.uk

The Lookout ★★★★★
Contact:
Powells Cottage Holidays, Dolphin House, High Street, Saundersfoot SA69 9EJ
T: (01834) 813232
F: (01834) 811731
E: info@powells.co.uk
I: www.powells.co.uk

Lowena & Kevran ★★★★
Contact: Mrs Beverley Rigby
120 Leander Drive, Castleton, Rochdale OL11 2XE
T: (01706) 525554
E: dave.rigby3@ntlworld.com
I: www.godrevycourt.co.uk/lowena/index.htm

Menhir Cottage ★★★★
Contact:
Powells Cottage Holidays, Dolphin House, High Street, Saundersfoot SA69 9EJ
T: (01834) 813232
F: (01834) 813731
E: info@powells.co.uk

Rose Cottage
Rating Applied For
Contact: Mrs Lesley Sumner
St Ives Road, Oceanis, St Ives TR26 2JS
T: (01736) 794147
E: lesleysumner@yahoo.com
I: www.rosecottagecarbisbay.co.uk

Rotorua Apartments ★★★★
Contact: Mrs Linda Roach
Rotorua Apartments, Trencrom Lane, St Ives TR26 2TD
T: (01736) 795419
F: (01736) 795419
E: rotorua@btconnect.com
I: www.stivesapartments.com

Sandpiper
Rating Applied For
Contact:
Sandpiper, Apt. No 25 Compass Point Apartments, Boskerris Road, Carbis Bay, St Ives TR26 2PU
T: (01159) 334870
F: (01159) 491593
E: enquiries@carbisbayholidays.co.uk
I: www.carbisbayholidays.co.uk

Topaz & Azure ★★★★
Contact:
Powells Cottage Holidays, High Street, Saundersfoot SA69 9EJ
T: 0870 5143076
F: (01834) 811731
E: info@powells.co.uk
I: www.powells.co.uk

Turquarze
Rating Applied For
Contact:
Carbis Bay Holidays, Carbis Beach Apartments, St Ives TR26 2JL
T: (01159) 334870
F: (01159) 491593
E: enquiries@carbisbayholidays.co.uk
I: www.carbisbayholidays.co.uk

CARDINHAM
Cornwall

The Linhay ★★★
Contact: Mr Gerald Moseley
The Linhay, The Stables, Welltown, Bodmin PL30 4EG
T: (01208) 821316

Welltown ★★★
Contact: Mr David Williams
Welltown, Bodmin PL30 4EG
T: (01208) 821653
E: daveange@telco4u.net
I: www.corncott.com www.thebestofbodmin.co.uk

CARHARRACK
Cornwall

Olde Alma Stores Bosuns Locker Holiday Apartment ★★★
Contact: Mr & Mrs M L Holmes
Olde Alma Stores Bosuns Locker Holiday Apartment, Alma Terrace, Redruth TR16 5RT
T: (01209) 820417
E: bosnsickr@aol.com
I: www.cornwalltouristboard.co.uk/oldalmastores

CARKEEL
Cornwall

Lower Coombe Apartment ★★★★
Contact: Mrs M J Clarke
Lower Coombe Apartment, Combe Rise, Saltash PL12 6NR
T: (01752) 849419
F: (01752) 849419
E: mikemjc@lineonenet
I: www.lowercoombe.co.uk

CARLYON BAY
Cornwall

Sea Haze ★★★★★
Contact:
Valley Villas, Sales Office, City Business Park, Office 38, Somerset Place, Plymouth PL3 4BB
T: (01752) 605605
E: sales@valleyvillas.co.uk
I: www.valleyvillas.co.uk

CARNON DOWNS
Cornwall

Higher Tresithick Barn ★★★★
Contact:
Special Places in Cornwall, Poachers Reach, Truro TR3 6SQ
T: (01872) 864400
E: office@specialplacescornwall.co.uk
I: www.specialplacescornwall.co.uk

CASTLE CARY
Somerset

The Ancient Barn and The Old Stables ★★★★
Contact: Ms Anthea Peppin
The Ancient Barn and The Old Stables, Lower Cockhill Farm, Cockhill, Castle Cary BA7 7NZ
T: (01963) 351288
F: (01963) 351288
E: bookings@medievalbarn.co.uk
I: www.medievalbarn.co.uk

Clanville Manor Tallet ★★★★
Contact: Mrs Snook
Clanville Manor Tallet, Clanville Manor, Clanville, Castle Cary BA7 7PJ
T: (01963) 350124
F: (01963) 350719
E: info@clanvillemanor.co.uk
I: www.clanvillemanor.co.uk

Orchard Farm Cottages ★★★
Contact: Mr Dave & Mrs Helen Boyer
Orchard Farm Cottages, Cockhill, Castle Cary BA7 7NY
T: (01963) 350418
F: (01963) 350418
E: boyer@orchardfarm.wanadoo.co.uk
I: www.orchardfm.freeuk.com

The Weaver's Cottage ★★★★
Contact: Ms Anthea Peppin
Lower Cockhill Farm, Castle Cary BA7 7NZ
T: (01963) 351288
E: enquiries@medievalbarn.co.uk
I: www.medievalbarn.co.uk

CATTISTOCK
Dorset

4 The Rocks ★★★★
Contact: Mrs Ann Stockwell
The Old Vicarage, Honiton EX14 9BD
T: (01404) 861594
F: (01404) 861594
E: jonannstockwell@aol.com

CERNE ABBAS
Dorset

Old Gaol Cottage ★★★★★
Contact: Ms Nicky Willis
Lamperts Cottage, 10 Dorchester Road, Dorchester DT2 9NU
T: (01300) 341659
F: (01300) 341699
E: nickywillis@tesco.net

CHAFFCOMBE
Somerset

Summer House ★★★
Contact:
Farm & Cottage Holidays, Victoria House, 20 Fore Street, Bideford EX39 1AW
T: (01237) 479146
F: (01237) 421512
E: bookings@farmcott.co.uk
I: www.farmcott.co.uk

CHAGFORD
Devon

Hunters Moon ★★★★
Contact: Dr & Mrs David Spear
Hunters Moon, Manor Road, Newton Abbot TQ13 8AW
T: (01647) 433323
E: woof@mail.eclipse.co.uk

Springfield Cottage ★★★★
Contact:
Helpful Holidays, Mill Street, Newton Abbot TQ13 8AW
T: (01647) 433593
F: (01647) 433694
E: help@helpfulholidays.com
I: www.helpfulholidays.com

Yelfords ★★★★★
Contact: Mrs Ghislaine Caine
Yelfords, Newton Abbot TQ13 8ES
T: (01647) 432856

CHALLACOMBE
Devon

Home Place Farm Cottages ★★★
Contact: Mr Mark Ravenscroft
Home Place Farm Cottages, Barnstaple EX31 4TS
T: (01598) 763283
F: (01598) 763745
E: mark@holidayexmoor.co.uk
I: www.holidayexmoor.co.uk

Town Tenement ★★★
Contact: Mr & Mrs Yendell
Town Tenement, Barnstaple EX31 4TS
T: (01598) 763320

Whitefield Barton ★★★
Contact: Mrs Rosemarie Kingdon
Whitefield Barton, Barnstaple EX31 4TU
T: (01598) 763271
I: www.exmoorholidays.co.uk

SOUTH WEST ENGLAND

CHAPEL AMBLE
Cornwall

Ambledown Cottage ★★★★★
Contact: Bookings and Enquire
English Country Cottages
Stoney Bank, Barnoldswick
BB94 0AA
T: 0870 5851155
F: 0870 5851150
I: www.english-country-cottages.co.uk

Carclaze Cottages ★★★★
Contact: Mrs Jean Nicholls
Carclaze Cottages, Wadebridge
PL27 6EP
T: (01208) 813886
E: enquire@carclaze.dabsol.co.uk
I: www.carclaze.co.uk

Down Below ★★★
Contact: Mrs Davey
Carns Farm, Wadebridge
PL27 6ER
T: (01208) 880398

Homeleigh Farm ★★★★
Contact: Mrs Ann Rees
Homeleigh Farm, Chapel Amble,
Wadebridge PL27 6EU
T: (01208) 812411
F: (01208) 815025
I: www.eclipse.co.uk/homeleigh

The Olde House ★★★
Contact: Mr & Mrs Hawkey
The Olde House, Wadebridge
PL27 6EN
T: (01208) 813219
F: (01208) 815689
E: info@theoldehouse.co.uk
I: www.theoldehouse.co.uk

The Parlour ★★★★★
Contact: Mrs Margaret Hosegood
The Parlour, Kivells, Chapel
Amble, Wadebridge PL27 6EP
T: (01208) 841755
F: (01208) 841182
E: info@acornishcottage.co.uk
I: www.acornishcottage.co.uk

Rooke Country Cottages ★★★★★
Contact: Mrs Gill Reskelly
Rooke Country Cottages, Rooke
Farm, Wadebridge PL27 6ES
T: (01208) 880368
F: (01208) 880600
E: info@rookefarm.com
I: www.rookecottages.com

Rooke Mill ★★★★
Contact: Mrs Diana Bullivant
Diana Bullivant Holidays, South
Winds, Trebell Green, Bodmin
PL30 5HR
T: (01208) 831336
F: (01208) 831336
E: diana@dbullivant.fsnet.co.uk
I: www.cornwall-online.co.uk/diana-bullivant

CHARDSTOCK
Devon

Barn Owls Cottage ★★★★
Contact: Mrs Jean Hafner
Barn Owls Cottage, Axminster
EX13 7BY
T: (01460) 220475
F: (01460) 220475
E: Jean.hafnet@BTinternet.com
I: www.cottageguide.co.uk/barnowlscottage

Cherryhazel ★★★★
Contact:
Milkbere Holidays, 3 Fore Street,
Seaton EX12 2LE
T: (01297) 20729
E: info@milkberehols.com
I: www.milkberehols.com

CHARLTON MUSGROVE
Somerset

Pigsty, Cowstall & Bullpen Cottages ★★★
Contact: Mrs Chilcott
Pigsty, Cowstall & Bullpen
Cottages, Barrow Lane Farm,
Wincanton BA9 8HJ
T: (01963) 33217
F: (01963) 31449
E: chrischilcott@farmersweekly.net

CHARMOUTH
Dorset

1 & 2 Albury Cottages - J4376 & J4377 ★★★
Contact:
Lyme Bay Holidays, Bos House,
44 Church Street, Lyme Regis
DT7 3DA
T: (01297) 443363
F: (01297) 445576
E: email@lymebayholidays.co.uk

The Barn - W4368 ★★★★
Contact: Mr Dave Matthews
Lyme Bay Holidays, Bos House,
44 Church Street, Lyme Regis
DT7 3DA
T: (01297) 443363
F: (01297) 445576
E: email@lymebayholidays.co.uk
I: www.lymebayholidays.co.uk

11 Barney's Close- L4226 ★★★★
Contact:
Lyme Bay Holidays, Bos House,
44 Church Street, Lyme Regis
DT7 3DA
T: (01297) 443363
F: (01297) 445576
E: email@lymebayholidays.co.uk
I: www.lymebayholidays.co.uk

Beachcomber ★★★★
Contact: Mr Zachary Stuart-Brown
Dream Cottages, 5 Hope Square,
Weymouth DT4 8TR
T: (01305) 789000
E: admin@dream-cottages.co.uk
I: www.dream-cottages.co.uk

Befferlands Farm ★★★★★
Contact: Mr & Mrs Andrews
Befferlands Farm, Bridport
DT6 6RD
T: (01297) 560203
E: befferlands@netscape.net

Bridge House - K4271 ★★★
Contact:
Lyme Bay Holidays, Bos House,
44 Church Street, Lyme Regis
DT7 3DA
T: (01297) 443363
F: (01297) 445576
E: email@lymebayholidays.co.uk
I: www.lymebayholidays.co.uk

Calderbrook - K3401 ★★★
Contact:
Lyme Bay Holidays, Bos House,
44 Church Street, Lyme Regis
DT7 3DA
T: (01297) 443363
E: email@lymebayholidaycottages.co.uk
I: www.lymebayholidays.co.uk

Charleston Holiday Cottages ★★★
Contact: Mrs Kim Wood
Grosvenor Cottage, The Street,
Bridport DT6

Claremont Apartment - K4325 ★★★★
Contact: Mr Dave Matthews
Lyme Bay Holidays, Bos House,
44 Church Street, Lyme Regis
DT7 3DA
T: (01297) 443363
F: (01297) 445576
E: email@lymebayholidays.co.uk
I: www.lymebayholidays.co.uk

The Coach House - K4398 ★★★
Contact: Mr Dave Matthews
Lyme Bay Holidays, Bos House,
44 Church Street, Lyme Regis
DT7 3DA
T: (01297) 443363
F: (01297) 445576
E: email@lymebayholidays.co.uk
I: www.lymebayholidays.co.uk

Coach House Flat J4175 ★★★
Contact: Mr Dave Matthews
Lyme Bay Holidays, Bos House,
44 Church Street, Lyme Regis
DT7 3DA
T: (01297) 443363
F: (01297) 445576
E: email@lymebayholidays.co.uk
I: www.lymebayholidays.co.uk

Dolphin House - M4383 ★★★★
Contact:
Lyme Bay Holidays, Bos House,
44 Church Street, Lyme Regis
DT7 3DA
T: (01297) 443363
F: (01297) 445576
E: email@lymebayholidays.co.uk
I: www.lymebayholidays.co.uk

9 Double Common - K4229 ★★★★
Contact: Mr Dave Matthews
Lyme Bay Holidays, Bos House,
44 Church Street, Lyme Regis
DT7 3DA
T: (01297) 443363
F: (01297) 445576
E: email@lymebayholidays.co.uk
I: www.lymebayholidays.co.uk

Double Common - K4385 ★★★★
Contact:
Lyme Bay Holidays, Bos House,
44 Church Street, Lyme Regis
DT7 3DA
T: (01297) 444756
F: (01297) 445576
E: email@lymebayholidays.co.uk
I: www.lymebayholidays.co.uk

7 Double Common - K4426 ★★★
Contact:
Lyme Bay Holidays, Bos House,
44 Church Street, Lyme Regis
DT7 3DA
T: (01297) 443363
F: (01297) 445576
E: email@lymebayholidays.co.uk
I: www.lymebayholidays.co.uk

11 Double Common - L4222 ★★★★
Contact: Mr Dave Matthews
Lyme Bay Holidays, Bos House,
44 Church Street, Lyme Regis
DT7 3DA
T: (01297) 443363
F: (01297) 445576
E: email@lymebayholidays.co.uk
I: www.lymebayholidays.co.uk

3 Double Common - L4223 ★★★★
Contact:
Lyme Bay Holidays, Bos House,
44 Church Street, Lyme Regis
DT7 3DA
T: (01297) 443363
F: (01297) 445576
E: email@lymebayholidays.co.uk
I: www.lymebayholidays.co.uk

40 Fernhill - Q5005 ★★★
Contact: Mr Dave Matthews
Lyme Bay Holidays, Bos House,
44 Church Street, Lyme Regis
DT7 3DA
T: (01297) 443363
F: (01297) 445576
E: email@lymebayholidays.co.uk
I: www.lymebayholidays.co.uk

Fernhill - Q5010 ★★★
Contact: Mr Dave Matthews
Lyme Bay Holidays, Bos House,
44 Church Street, Lyme Regis
DT7 3DA
T: (01297) 443363
F: (01297) 445576
E: email@lymebayholidays.co.uk
I: www.lymebayholidays.co.uk

Establishments printed in blue have a detailed entry in this guide

SOUTH WEST ENGLAND

41 Fernhill - Q5018 ★★★
Contact: Mr Jim Matthews
Lyme Bay Holidays, Bos House,
44 Church Street, Lyme Regis
DT7 3DA
T: (01297) 443363
F: (01297) 445576
E: email@lymebayholidays.co.uk
I: www.lymebayholidays.co.uk

2 Fernhill Heights - Q5017 ★★★★
Contact:
Lyme Bay Holidays, Bos House,
44 Church Street, Lyme Regis
DT7 3DA
T: (01297) 443363
F: (01297) 445576
E: email@lymebayholidays.co.uk

Fernhill Heights - R5004 ★★★★
Contact: Mr Dave Matthews
Lyme Bay Holidays, Bos House,
44 Church Street, Lyme Regis
DT7 3DA
T: (01297) 443363
F: (01297) 445576
E: email@lymebayholidays.co.uk
I: www.lymebayholidays.co.uk

45 Fernhill Heights - R5011 ★★★★
Contact:
Lyme Bay Holidays, Bos House,
44 Church Street, Lyme Regis
DT7 3DA
T: (01297) 443363
F: (01297) 445576
E: email@lymebayholidays.co.uk
I: www.lymebayholidays.co.uk

23 Fernhill Heights ★★★★
Contact: Mrs Webb
Uplands Cottages, Shipham Lane, Winscombe BS25 1PX
T: (01934) 842257

51 Fernhill: R5016 ★★★★
Contact:
Lyme Bay Holidays, Bos House,
44 Church Street, Lyme Regis
DT7 3DA
T: (01297) 443363
F: (01297) 445576
E: email@lymebayholidays.co.uk
I: www.lymebayholidays.co.uk

Fleur - K4243 ★★★
Contact:
Lime Bay Holidays, Bos House,
44 Church Street, Lyme Regis
DT7 3DA
T: (01297) 443363
F: (01297) 445576
E: email@lymebayholidays.co.uk
I: www.lymebayholidays.co.uk

Georges Close - K4305 ★★★★
Contact:
Lyme Bay Holidays, Bos House,
44 Church Street, Lyme Regis
DT7 3DA
T: (01297) 443363
E: email@lymebayholidays.co.uk
I: www.lymebayholidays.co.uk

Greenhayes - L4342 ★★★
Contact: Mr Dave Matthews
Lyme Bay Holidays, Bos House,
44 Church Street, Lyme Regis
DT7 3DA
T: (01297) 443363
F: (01297) 445576
E: email@lymebayholidays.co.uk
I: www.lymebayholidays.co.uk

Honeycot - K4295 ★★★
Contact:
Lyme Bay Holidays, Bos House,
44 Church Street, Lyme Regis
DT7 3DA
T: (01297) 443363
E: email@lymebayholidays.co.uk

Knapp Cottages - K4313 ★★★★
Contact: Mr Dave Matthews
Lyme Bay Holidays, Bos House,
44 Church Street, Lyme Regis
DT7 3DA
T: (01297) 443363
F: (01297) 445576
E: email@lymebayholidays.co.uk
I: www.lymebayholidays.co.uk

Lias Lea - L3501 ★★★
Contact:
Lyme Bay Holidays, Bos House,
44 Church Street, Lyme Regis
DT7 3DA
T: (01297) 443363
F: (01297) 445576
E: email@lymebayholidays.co.uk
I: www.lymebayholidays.co.uk

Little Catherston Farm ★★★
Contact: Mrs R J White
Little Catherston Farm, Charmouth, Bridport DT6 6LZ
T: (01297) 560550
I: www.catherstonfarm-bungalows.co.uk

The Lodge - V4367 ★★★★
Contact: Mr Dave Matthews
Lyme Bay Holidays, Bos House,
44 Church Street, Lyme Regis
DT7 3DA
T: (01297) 443363
F: (01297) 445576
E: email@lymebayholidays.co.uk
I: www.lymebayholidays.co.uk

Luttrell House - J4298 ★★★
Contact:
Lyme Bay Holidays, Bos House,
44 Church Street, Lyme Regis
DT7 3DA
T: (01297) 443363
E: email@lymebayholidays.co.uk

Manor Farm Holiday Centre ★★
Contact: Mr Robin Loosmore
Manor Farm Holiday Centre, The Street, Bridport DT6 6QL
T: (01297) 560226
E: enq@manorfarmholidaycentre.co.uk
I: www.manorfarmholidaycentre.co.uk

Nookies ★★★★
Contact: Ms Kate Bartlett
Jean Bartlett Cottage Holidays, The Old Dairy, Fore Street, Seaton EX12 3JB
T: (01297) 23221
F: (01297) 23303
E: holidays@jeanbartlett.com
I: www.netbreaks.com/jeanb

Nutwood - L4423 ★★★★
Contact: Mr Dave Matthews
Lyme Bay Holidays, Bos House,
44 Church Street, Lyme Regis
DT7 3DA
T: (01297) 443363
F: (01297) 445576
E: email@lymebayholidays.co.uk
I: www.lymebayholidays.co.uk

Penderel - L3958 ★★★★
Contact:
Lyme Bay Holidays, Bos House,
44 Church Street, Lyme Regis
DT7 3DA
T: (01297) 443363
F: (01297) 445576
E: email@lymebayholidays.co.uk
I: www.lymebayholidays.co.uk

The Poplars ★★★
Contact: Mrs Jane Pointing
The Poplars, Wood Farm Caravan Park, Axminster Road, Bridport DT6 6BT
T: (01297) 560697
F: (01297) 561243
E: holiday@woodfarm.co.uk
I: www.woodfarm.co.uk

Portland House - K4219 ★★★
Contact:
Lyme Bay Holidays, Bos House,
44 Church Street, Lyme Regis
DT7 3DA
T: (01297) 443363
F: (01297) 445576
E: email@lymebayholidays.co.uk
I: www.lymebayholidays.co.uk

Queens Walk - L4345 ★★★★
Contact:
Lyme Bay Holidays, Bos House,
44 Church Street, Lyme Regis
DT7 3DA
T: (01297) 443363
F: (01297) 445576
E: email@lymebayholidays.co.uk
I: www.lymebayholidays.co.uk

11 Queens Walk - L4361 ★★★★
Contact:
Lyme Bay Holidays, Bos House,
44 Church Street, Lyme Regis
DT7 3DA
T: (01297) 443363
F: (01297) 445576
E: email@lymebayholidays.co.uk
I: www.lymebayholidays.co.uk

2 Queens Walk ★★★★
Contact: Mrs Jane Simmonds-Short
Butts Cottage, Ilminster TA19 9LG
T: (01460) 52832
F: (01460) 259619
E: jane@simmonds-short.fsnet.co.uk

Riverway - K3557 ★★★
Contact:
Lyme Bay Holidays, Bos House,
44 Church Street, Lyme Regis
DT7 3DA
T: (01297) 443363
E: email@lymebayholidays.co.uk

Rosern - K4064 ★★★
Contact:
Lyme Bay Holidays, Bos House,
44 Church Street, Lyme Regis
DT7 3DA
T: (01297) 443363
F: (01297) 445576
E: email@lymebayholidays.co.uk
I: www.lymebayholidays.co.uk

Seaspray - L4306 ★★★
Contact:
Lyme Bay Holiday Cottages, Bos House, 44 Church Street, Lyme Regis DT7 3DA
T: (01297) 443363
E: email@lymebayholidays.co.uk
I: www.lymebayholidays.co.uk

Shadows ★★★
Contact: I Ward
Shadows, Lower Sea Lane, Charmouth, Bridport DT6 6LW
T: (01297) 489609
F: (01297) 489609

2 Southwinds - K4332 ★★★★
Contact: Mr Dave Matthews
Lyme Bay Holidays, Bos House,
44 Church Street, Lyme Regis
DT7 3DA
T: (01297) 443363
F: (01297) 445576
E: email@lymebayholidays.co.uk
I: www.lymebayholidays.co.uk

The Stone House - N3911 ★★★★★
Contact:
Lyme Bay Holidays, Bos House,
44 Church Street, Lyme Regis
DT7 3DA
T: (01297) 443363
F: (01297) 445576
E: email@lymebayholidays.co.uk
I: www.lymebayholidays.co.uk

Thalatta M3988 ★★
Contact:
Lyme Bay Holidays, Bos House,
44 Church Street, Lyme Regis
DT7 3DA
T: (01297) 443363
F: (01297) 445576
E: email@lymebayholidays.co.uk
I: www.lymebayholidays.co.uk

SOUTH WEST ENGLAND

Tillicum - M3927 ★★★
Contact:
Lyme Bay Holidays, Bos House,
44 Church Street, Lyme Regis
DT7 3DA
T: (01297) 443363
F: (01297) 445576
E: email@lymebayholidays.co.uk
I: www.lymebayholidays.co.uk

Uphill Apartment - K4363 ★★★
Contact:
Lyme Bay Holidays, Bos House,
44 Church Street, Lyme Regis
DT7 3DA
T: (01297) 443363
F: (01297) 445576
E: email@lymebayholidays.co.uk

Uplands - M4304 ★★★
Contact:
Lyme Bay Holidays, Bos House,
44 Church Street, Lyme Regis
DT7 3DA
T: (01297) 443363
F: (01297) 445576
E: email@lymebayholidays.co.uk
I: www.lymebayholidays.co.uk

Wheelers Cottage - V4386 ★★★★
Contact:
Lyme Bay Holidays, Bos House,
44 Church Street, Lyme Regis
DT7 3DA
T: (01297) 444756
F: (01297) 445576
E: email@lymebayholidays.co.uk
I: www.lymebayholidays.co.uk

Willows - K3909 ★★★
Contact:
Lyme Bay Holidays, Bos House,
44 Church Street, Lyme Regis
DT7 3DA
T: (01297) 443363
F: (01297) 445576
E: email@lymebayholidays.co.uk
I: www.lymebayholidays.co.uk

CHEDDAR
Somerset

Applebee South Barn Cottage ★
Contact: Mrs Kay Richardson
Applebee South Barn Cottage,
The Hayes, Cheddar BS27 3AN
T: (01934) 743146
F: (01934) 743146

Cheddar Lodge ★★★
Contact: Mr Jon Rawlings
Cheddar Lodge, Draycott Road,
Cheddar BS27 3RP
T: (01934) 743859
F: (01934) 741550
E: jon@1rawlings.freeserve.co.uk
I: www.cheddarlodge.pwp.blueyonder.co.uk

Home Farm Cottages ★★★★
Contact: Mr Chris Sanders
Home Farm Cottages, Barton,
Winscombe BS25 1DX
T: (01934) 842078
F: (01934) 842500
E: enquiries@homefarmcottages.com
I: www.homefarmcottages.com

Millyard Cottage ★★★★
Contact: Mr Stuart Fisher
Millyard Cottage, Stoke Street,
Cheddar BS27 3UP
T: (01749) 870704
E: stuartfisher2@aol.com
I: www.cheddar-cottages.com

Orchard Court & Bungalow ★★★★
Contact: Mrs Carol Roberts
Orchard Lodge, Tweentown,
Cheddar BS27 3HY
T: (01934) 742116

Spring Cottages ★★★★
Contact: Mrs Jennifer Buckland
Spring Cottages, Spring Cottage,
Venns Gate, Cheddar BS27 3LW
T: (01934) 742493
F: (01934) 742493
E: buckland@springcottages.co.uk
I: www.springcottages.co.uk

Sungate Holiday Apartments ★★★
Contact: Mrs M M Fieldhouse
Pyrenmount, Parsons Way,
Winscombe BS25 1BU
T: (01934) 842273
F: (01934) 844994
E: sunholapart@aol.com

Uplands Cottages ★★★
Contact: Mrs Webb
Uplands Cottages, Shipham
Lane, Winscombe BS25 1PX
T: (01934) 842257

CHEDWORTH
Gloucestershire

Littlecote
Rating Applied For
Contact: Miss Jennifer Walker
Cheriot House, 20 Stockwell
Road, Wolverhampton WV6 9PQ
T: (01902) 751197
F: (01902) 750044
E: Jenni101@yahoo.com

Tiddley Dyke ★★★★
Contact: Mrs Jenny Bull
Tiddley Dyke, School Lane,
Middle Chedworth, Cheltenham
GL54 4AJ
T: (01285) 720673

CHEDZOY
Somerset

Nelson Cottage ★★★★
Contact: Mr & Mrs Robbins
Nelson Lodge, Chezoy Lane,
Bridgwater TA7 8QR
T: (01278) 453492
E: robbinsm@bridgwater.ac.uk

CHELSTON
Torbay

Chelston Hall Holiday Apartments ★★★
Contact: Mr Peter & Mrs Shirley Archer-Moy
Chelston Hall Holiday
Apartments, Old Mill Road,
Torquay TQ2 6HW
T: (01803) 605520

CHELTENHAM
Gloucestershire

The Annexe ★★★
Contact: Mrs Corbett
The Annexe, 11 Oldfield
Crescent, St Marks, Cheltenham
GL51 7BB
T: (01242) 524608

Bakery Cottage ★★★
Contact: Mrs Weller
Wortheal House, Southam Lane,
Cheltenham GL52 3NY
T: (01242) 236765

Balcarras Farm Holiday Cottages ★★★
Contact: Mr Judith & Mrs David Ballinger
Balcarras Farm, London Road,
Cheltenham GL52 6UT
T: (01242) 584837
E: cottage@balcarras-farm.co.uk
I: www.balcarras-farm.co.uk

Barn Cottages ★★★★
Contact: Mr Paul Tilley
Barn Cottages, Moat Farm, 34
Malleson Road, Cheltenham
GL52 9ET
T: (01242) 672055
F: 07050 665639
E: jo@moatfarm.free-online.co.uk
I: www.moatfarm.free-online.co.uk

Beechgarden Apartments ★★★
Contact: Miss Denise Holman
Beechgarden Apartments,
Beechcroft, 295 Gloucester
Road, Cheltenham GL51 7AD
T: (01242) 519564
F: (01242) 519564
E: beechcroft.cheltenham@dial.pipex.com
I: www.geocities.com/beechcroftuk

Butlers
Rating Applied For
Contact: Mr Guy Hunter
Butlers, Western Road,
Cheltenham GL50 3RN
T: (01242) 570771
F: (01242) 528724
E: info@butlers-hotel.co.uk
I: www.butlers-hotel.co.uk

College Farm ★★★
Contact: Mrs Julia Van Gils
College Farm, Cheltenham
GL54 4JQ
T: (01242) 820366
F: (01242) 820017
E: thevangils@aol.com

The Courtyard ★★★★
Contact: Mrs Jane Reynolds
The Austwick Traddock,
Lancaster LA2 8BY
T: (015242) 51224
F: (015242) 51796
E: jane@22montpellier.co.uk
I: www.22montpellier.co.uk

Coxhorne Farm ★★★
Contact: Mr & Mrs Close
Coxhorne Farm, London Road,
Cheltenham GL52 6UY
T: (01242) 236599

Flat 8 ★★★
Contact: Mr & Mrs Richard Moseley
56B Copers Cope Road,
Beckenham BR3 1RJ
T: (020) 83256251
I: www.cottageguide.co.uk

The Furrow ★★★★
Contact: Mrs Valerie Hughes
The Furrow, The Ploughmans
Cottage, Cheltenham GL54 5RW
T: (01451) 850733
F: (01451) 850733
I: www.cotswoldholiday.co.uk

The Garden Flat ★★★★
Contact: Ms Jenny Wardle
Change Forum Ltd, 20 Lansdown
Parade, Cheltenham GL50 2LH
T: (01242) 577450
E: jennyw@changeforum.co.uk

The Garden Studio ★★★★
Contact: Mrs Ellams
The Garden Studio, 53 Gratton
Road, Cheltenham GL50 2BZ
T: (01242) 575572

Holmer Cottages ★★★★
Contact: Mrs Jill Collins
Holmer Cottages, Haines
Orchard, Woolstone,
Cheltenham GL52 9RG
T: (01242) 672848
F: (01242) 672848
E: holmercottages@talk21.com
I: www.cottageguide.co.uk/holmercottages

Hotels Apart ★★★★★
Contact: Mrs Bernadette Fairclough
Hotels Apart Ltd, Arch Mews, 22
Lansdown Terrace Lane,
Cheltenham GL50 2JU
T: (01242) 510523
F: (01242) 523163
E: mail@hotels-apart.com
I: www.hotels-apart.com

The Maisonette ★★★★
Contact: Mrs Jane Reynolds
The Austwick Traddock,
Lancaster LA2 8BY
T: (015242) 51224
F: (015242) 51796
E: jane@22montpellier.co.uk
I: www.22montpellier.co.uk

Oakfield Rise ★★★★
Contact: Mr Tony Russell
Oakfield Rise, Ashley Road,
Battledown, Cheltenham
GL52 6NU
T: (01242) 222220
E: oakfieldrise@hotmail.com
I: www.oakfieldrise.com

SOUTH WEST ENGLAND

The Old Dairy ★★★★
Contact: Mr Rickie & Mrs Jennie Gauld
The Old Dairy, Slades Farm, Bushcombe Lane, Cheltenham GL52 3PN
T: (01242) 676003
F: (01242) 676003
E: rickieg@btinternet.com
I: www.cotswoldscottages.btinternet.co.uk

Spring Hill Stable Cottages ★★★
Contact: Mrs Smail
Spring Hill, Cheltenham GL54 4DU
T: (01242) 890263
F: (01242) 890166

Top Flat ★★★
Contact: Mr & Mrs Morris
Huntley Farm, Patch Elm Lane, Bristol BS37 7LU
T: (01454) 227322
F: (01454) 227323
E: cotswold.cottage@btopenworld.com
I: www.cotswoldcottage.net/

The Vergus ★★★
Contact: Mrs Rita Preen
Ashley, Cheltenham GL51 0TW
T: (01242) 680511
E: ritapreen@aol.com
I: www.vergus.co.uk

Vine Court ★★★★
Contact: Mrs Linda Hennessy
Vine Court, Leckhampton Road, Cheltenham GL53 0BS
T: (01242) 222403
E: lindyhennessy@hotmail.com

Willoughby House Hotel and Apartments ★★★-★★★★★
Contact: Mr & Mrs F P Eckermann
Willoughby House Hotel and Apartments, 1 Suffolk Square, Cheltenham GL50 2DR
T: (01242) 522798
E: bookings@willoughbyhouse.com
I: www.willoughbyhouse.com

CHESTERBLADE
Somerset

Millhouse Farm ★★★★
Contact: Mrs Margo Green
Millhouse Farm, Shepton Mallet BA4 4EQ
T: (01749) 830295

CHEW MAGNA
Bath and North East Somerset

Chew Hill Farm ★★★
Contact: Mrs Lyons
Chew Hill Farm, Bristol BS40 8QP
T: (01275) 332496
F: (01275) 332496

Woodbarn Farm Cottages ★★★-★★★★★
Contact: Mrs Judi Hasell
Woodbarn Farm, Denny Lane, Bristol BS40 8SZ
T: (01275) 332599
F: (01275) 332599
E: woodbarnfarm@hotmail.com

CHICKERELL
Dorset

Tidmoor Stables ★★★★
Contact: Mr & Mrs Townsend/Wills
Tidmoor Stables, 431 Chickerell Road, Weymouth DT3 4DG
T: (01305) 787867
E: sarah@tidmoorstables.co.uk
I: www.tidmoorstables.co.uk

CHIDEOCK
Dorset

Chideock Coachouse ★★★★
Contact: Mr Zachary Stuart-Brown
Dream Cottages, 5 Hope Square, Weymouth DT4 8TR
T: (01305) 789000
E: admin@dream-cottages.co.uk
I: www.dream-cottages.co.uk

Greystones Cottage - X4438 ★★★★
Contact:
Lyme Bay Holidays, Bos House, 44 Church Street, Lyme Regis DT7 3DA
T: (01297) 443363
F: (01297) 445576
E: email@lymebayholidays.co.uk
I: www.lymebayholidays.co.uk

Guard House Cottage ★★★★
Contact: Mrs Joyce Whittaker
Guard House Cottage, Seatown House, Seatown, Chideock, Bridport DT6 6JU
T: (01297) 489417
F: (01297) 489151
E: info@guardhouse.co.uk
I: www.guardhouse.co.uk

Prester - V4353 and Laneside - X4354 ★★★
Contact: Mr Dave Matthews
Lyme Bay Holidays, Bos House, 44 Church Street, Lyme Regis DT7 3DA
T: (01297) 443363
F: (01297) 445576
E: email@lymebayholidays.co.uk
I: www.lymebayholidays.co.uk

CHILCOMBE
Dorset

Cherry Tree Cottage ★★★
Contact: Mr Zachary Stuart-Brown
Dream Cottages, 5 Hope Square, Weymouth DT4 8TR
T: (01305) 789000
F: (01305) 761346
E: admin@dream-cottages.co.uk
I: www.dream-cottages.co.uk

CHILLINGTON
Devon

Friends Cottage ★★★
Contact:
Powell's Cottage Holidays, High Street, Saundersfoot SA69 9EJ
T: (01834) 812791
F: (01834) 811731
E: info@powells.co.uk
I: www.powells.co.uk

CHILTON TRINITY
Somerset

Chilton Farm ★★★★
Contact: Mr Warman
Farm & Cottage Holidays, Bridgwater TA5 2BL
T: (01278) 421864
I: www.farmcott.co.uk

CHIPPENHAM
Wiltshire

Nut Tree Cottage ★★★
Contact: Mrs Margaret Payne
Nut Tree Cottage, Longdean, Chippenham SN14 7EX
T: (01249) 782354

Olivemead Farm Holidays ★★★★
Contact: Mrs Suzanne Candy
Olivemead Farm, Olivemead Lane, Chippenham SN15 4JQ
T: (01666) 510205
F: (01666) 510864
E: olivemeadfarmholidays@tesco.net
I: www.olivemeadfarmholidays.com

Roward Farm ★★★★
Contact: Mr David Humphrey
Roward Farm, The Old Dairy, Roward Farm, Draycot Cerne, Chippenham SN15 4SG
T: (01249) 758147
F: (01249) 758149
E: d.humphrey@roward.demon.co.uk
I: www.roward.demon.co.uk

CHIPPING CAMPDEN
Gloucestershire

Bank Cottage ★★★★
Contact: Mr Robert Hutsby
Middle Hill Farm, Warwick CV35 9EH
T: (01789) 841525
F: (01789) 841523
E: robert.hutsby@btinternet.com
I: www.chipping-campden-holiday-cottages.co.uk

Barnstones ★★★★★
Contact: Mr & Mrs Jones
Barnstones, Aston Road, Chipping Campden GL55 6HR
T: (01386) 840975
F: (01386) 840975
E: jonesbarnstones@aol.com

Box Tree Cottage ★★★
Contact: Mr Robert Hutsby
Middle Hill Farm, Warwick CV35 9EH
T: (01789) 841525
F: (01789) 841523
E: robert.hutsby@btinternet.com
I: www.chipping-campden-holiday-cottages.co.uk/boxtree.htm

Chapter Cottage ★★★★
Contact: Mr Revers
The Tyning, Blind Lane, Chipping Campden GL55 6ED
T: (01386) 841450
E: admin@perpetuare.com
I: www.perpetuare.com

Cosy Corner
Rating Applied For
Contact: Mrs Pearl Brandreth
Pearl Investments Ltd, Tally Ho Cottage, Dyers Lane, Noel Court, Calf Lane, Chipping Campden GL55 6BS
T: (01386) 841752
F: (01386) 841752
E: pearl@mdina03.fsnet.co.uk

Cotswold Charm ★★★★
Contact: Mr & Miss Margaret & Michael Haines
Cotswold Charm, Top Farm, Blind Lane, Chipping Campden GL55 6ED
T: (01386) 840164
F: (01386) 841883
E: cotswoldcharm@fsmail.net
I: www.cotswoldcharm.co.uk

Cowfair ★★★★
Contact: Mrs Whitehouse
Weston Park Farm, Dovers Hill, Chipping Campden GL55 6UW
T: (01386) 840835
E: jane_whitehouse@hotmail.com
I: www.cotswoldcottages.uk.com

Grafton Mews ★★★★
Contact: Ms Sheila Rolland
Campden Cottages, Folly Cottage, Chipping Campden GL55 6XG
T: (01386) 593315
F: (01386) 593057
E: info@campdencottages.co.uk
I: www.campdencottages.co.uk

Honeysuckle Cottage ★★★★
Contact: Mrs Kate Daly
13 Serpentine Road, Harborne, Birmingham B17 9RD
T: (0121) 426 6310 & 07905 497211
F: (0121) 426 6310
E: stjohn.daly@virgin.net
I: www.thecountrycottage.co.uk

Little Thatch ★★★★
Contact: Mrs Gadsby
'Hillsdown', Aston Road, Chipping Campden GL55 6PL
T: (01386) 840234

Millers Cottage ★★★★
Contact: Mrs Susan Jessup
Old Palace Cottage, Hatfield Park, Hatfield AL9 5NE
T: (01707) 287042
F: (01707) 287033
E: info@millerscottage.co.uk
I: www.millerscottage.co.uk

Orchard Cottage ★★★★
Contact: Ms Sheila Rolland
Campden Cottages, Folly Cottage, Paxford, Chipping Campden GL55 6XG
T: (01386) 593315
F: (01386) 593057
E: info@campdencottages.co.uk
I: www.campdencottages.co.uk

SOUTH WEST ENGLAND

Over the Arches
Rating Applied For
Contact: Mrs Pearl Brandreth
Tally Ho Cottage, Park Road,
Chipping Campden GL55 6EB
T: (01386) 841752
F: (01386) 841752
E: pearl@mdina03.fsnet.co.uk
I: www.chippingcampden.
co.uk/overthearches.htm

Sansons Cottage ★★★★
Contact: Miss Sheila Rolland
Campden Cottages, Folly
Cottage, Chipping Campden
GL55 6XG
T: (01386) 593315
F: (01386) 593057
E: info@campdencottages.co.uk
I: www.campdencottages.co.uk

Shepherd's Cottage ★★★★
Contact: Miss Sheila Rolland
Campden Cottages, Folly
Cottage, Chipping Campden
GL55 6XG
T: (01386) 593315
F: (01386) 593057
E: info@campdencottages.co.uk
I: www.campdencottages.co.uk

Walkers Retreat ★★★
Contact: Mrs Whitehouse
Weston Park Farm, Dovers Hill,
Chipping Campden GL55 6UW
T: (01386) 840835
I: www.cotswoldcottages.uk.
com

Whistlers Corner Cottage
★★★★
Contact: Mr Robert Hutsby
Middle Hill Farm, Warwick
CV35 9EH
T: (01789) 841525
F: (01789) 841523
E: robert.hutsby@btinternet.
com
I: www.
chipping-campden-holiday-
cottages.co.uk/whistlers.htm

CHIPPING SODBURY
South Gloucestershire

Tan House Farm Cottage
★★★
Contact: Mrs James
Tan House Farm, Tanhouse Lane,
Yate, Bristol BS37 7QL
T: (01454) 228280
F: (01454) 228777

CHISELBOROUGH
Somerset

One Fair Place ★★★★
Contact: Mrs Adrienne Wright
39 The Avenue, Crowthorne
RG45 6PB
T: (01344) 772461
F: (01344) 778389
E: info@
somersetcottageholidays.co.uk
I: www.
somersetcottageholidays.co.uk

CHITTLEHAMHOLT
Devon

Simmons Farm Cottage
★★★
Contact:
Marsden's Cottage Holidays, 2
The Square, Braunton EX33 2JB
T: (01271) 813777
F: (01271) 813664
E: holidays@marsdens.co.uk
I: www.marsdens.co.uk

Treetops ★★★★
Contact:
Marsden's Cottage Holidays, 2
The Square, Braunton EX33 2JB
T: (01271) 813777
F: (01271) 813664
E: holidays@marsdens.co.uk
I: www.marsdens.co.uk

CHITTLEHAMPTON
Devon

Greendown Farm Cottages
★★★-★★★★
Contact: Mr Morley Heal
Greendown Farm, Umberleigh
EX37 9QR
T: (01769) 540441
I: devonfarmcottages.co.uk

Thatch Cottage ★★★★
Contact:
Marsdens Cottage Holidays, 2
The Square, Braunton EX33 2JB
T: (01271) 813777
F: (01271) 813664
E: holidays@marsdens.co.uk

CHRISTCHURCH
Dorset

Burton Farm House Annexe
★★★
Contact: Mrs Marylyn Etheridge
Burton Farm House, 159
Salisbury Road, Christchurch
BH23 5HF
T: (01202) 484475

The Causeway ★-★★
Contact: Mrs Tomkinson
The Causeway, 32-34 Stanpit,
Christchurch BH23 3LZ
T: (01202) 470149
F: (01202) 477558
E: thecauseway@nascr.net

Cumberland Lodge
★★-★★★★
Contact: Mr Paul Williamson
Flat 1, Cumberland Lodge, 424
Lymington Road, Highcliffe
BH23 5HF
T: (01425) 280275
E: enquiries@
cumberland-lodge.co.uk
I: www.cumberland-lodge.
co.uk/info

The Flat Briarwood ★★★
Contact: Mrs Stella Ward
Briarwood, 1 Dunbar Crescent,
Christchurch BH23 5RY
T: (01425) 275523

Glenwood ★★★
Contact: Mr Keith & Mrs Joan
Harvey
Woodland Road, Coleford
GL16 7NR
T: (01594) 833128
F: (01594) 833128

The Holiday Cottage ★★★
Contact: Mr & Mrs John Brewer
61 Southwick Road,
Bournemouth BH6 5PR
T: (01202) 420673

Mallard Cottage ★★★
Contact: Mr & Mrs David Pearce
Swan Lodge, 17 Willow Way,
Christchurch BH23 1JJ
T: (01202) 480805
F: (01202) 480805

Pedralves ★★★
Contact: Mrs Kenney
Pedralves, Nea Road,
Christchurch BH23 4NB
T: (01425) 273858

Riverbank Holidays ★★★
Contact: Mr & Mrs Gibson
Riverbank Holidays, Toad Hall, 8
Willow Way, Christchurch
BH23 1JJ
T: (01202) 477813

Riverbank House ★★★★
Contact: Mr Terry Hayden
Riverbank House, 5 Swan Green,
Willow Way, Christchurch
BH23 1JJ
T: (01202) 828487
F: (01202) 828487
E: handbleisure@amserve.net
I: riverbankholidays.co.uk

Riverside Park ★★★
Contact: Mrs Lisa Booth
Riverside Park, Paddlegrade
Limited, 28 Willow Way,
Christchurch BH23 1JJ
T: (01202) 471090
E: holidays@riversidepark.biz
I: www.riversidepark.biz

Saffron ★★★
Contact: Mrs Rosemary Broadey
Mallow Close, Christchurch
BH23 4UL
T: (01425) 277507
E: rosemary@broadey.net

Wingfield Holiday
Bungalow ★★★
Contact: Mrs Josephine Stevens
15 Wingfield Avenue,
Christchurch BH23 4NR
T: (01425) 278583
E: josephinemstevens@hotmail.
com
I: www.wingfieldholiday.co.uk

CHUDLEIGH
Devon

Coombeshead Farm ★★★
Contact: Mr Robert & Mrs Anne
Smith
Coombeshead Farm,
Combeshead Cross, Chudleigh,
Newton Abbot TQ13 0NQ
T: (01626) 853334
E: anne-coombeshead@
supanet.com

Farmborough House
★★★★
Contact: Mrs Deirdre Aldridge
Farmborough House, Old Exeter
Road, Chudleigh, Newton Abbot
TQ13 0DR
T: (01626) 853258
F: (01626) 853258
E: holidays@
farmborough-house.com
I: www.farmborough-house.
com

Silver Cottage ★★★
Contact: Mr Eric Gardner
75 Old Exeter Street, Chudleigh,
Newton Abbot TQ13 0JX
T: (01626) 854571
F: (01626) 854571
E: ejgardner@care4free.net

CHULMLEIGH
Devon

Bealy Court Holiday
Cottages ★★★★
Contact: Mr Richard & Mrs Jane
Lea
Bealy Court Holiday Cottages,
Bealy Court, Chulmleigh
EX18 7EG
T: (01769) 580312
F: (01769) 508986
E: bealycourt@msn.com
I: www.beatycourt.com

Deer Cott ★★★★
Contact: Mr & Mrs George
Simpson
Deer Cott, Middle Garland,
Chulmleigh EX18 7DU
T: (01769) 580461
F: (01769) 580461
E: enquiries@deercott.co.uk
I: www.deercott.co.uk

CHURCH KNOWLE
Dorset

Denorah ★★★
Contact: Mr Ronald & Mrs Mary
Wrixon
The Old Post Office, 16 Church
Knowle, Wareham BH20 5NG
T: (01929) 480234

CHURCHINFORD
Somerset

Mow Barton ★★★★
Contact: Ms Louise Hayman
Milkbere Cottage Holidays, 3
Fore Street, Seaton EX12 2LE
T: (01297) 20729
F: (01297) 22925
E: info@milkberehols.com
I: www.milkberehols.com

South Cleeve Bungalow
★★★★
Contact: Mrs V D Manning
South Cleeve Bungalow,
Taunton TA3 7PR
T: (01823) 601378

CHURSTON FERRERS
Torbay

Alston Farm Cottages
★★★★★
Contact: Mrs Claire Hockaday
Alston Farm Cottages, Alston
Lane, Brixham TQ5 0HT
T: (01803) 845388
F: (01803) 842065
E: alstonnch@aol.com
I: www.alstonfarm.co.uk

CIRENCESTER
Gloucestershire

Flowers Barn ★★★★
Contact: Mrs Tina Barton
Flowers Barn, Manor Farm,
Middle Duntisbourne,
Cirencester GL7 7AR
T: (01285) 658145
F: (01285) 641504
E: duntisbourne@aol.com
I: www.SmoothHound.
co.uk/hotels/manorfar.html

Establishments printed in blue have a detailed entry in this guide

SOUTH WEST ENGLAND

Glebe Farm Holiday Lets ★★★★
Contact: Mrs Handover
Glebe Farm Holiday Lets, Glebe Farm, Barnsley Road, Cirencester GL7 5DY
T: (01285) 659226
F: (01285) 642622

The Tallet ★★★
Contact: Mrs Susan Spivey
Cirencester GL7 5PR
T: (01285) 653405
F: (01285) 651152
E: howard@theoldfarmhouse.fsbusiness.co.uk

The Tallet Cottage ★★★★★
Contact: Mrs Arbuthnott
The Tallet, Calmsden, Cirencester GL7 5ET
T: (01285) 831437
F: (01285) 831437
E: vanessa@thetallet.demon.co.uk
I: www.thetallet.co.uk

Warrens Gorse Cottages ★★
Contact: Mrs Nanette Randall
Warrens Gorse Cottages, Home Farm, Warrens Gorse, Cirencester GL7 7JD
T: (01285) 831261

CLAWTON
Devon

The Coach House ★★★
Contact: Mrs Carolyn Pix
The Coach House, The Old Vicarage, Holsworthy EX22 6PS
T: (01409) 271100
E: enquiries@oldvicarageclawton.co.uk
I: www.oldvicarageclawton.co.uk

CLIFTON
City of Bristol

Bristol Serviced Apartments ★★★★
Contact: Mrs Kim Whife
Bristol Serviced Apartments, 8 Lansdown Place, Bristol BS8 3AE
T: (0117) 9741414
E: bsapartments@aol.com
I: www.bristolservicedapartments.co.uk

COBERLEY
Gloucestershire

Seven Springs Cottages ★★★
Contact: Miss Marcie Stokes
Seven Springs Cottages, Seven Springs, Cheltenham GL53 9NG
T: (01242) 870385
F: (01242) 870385
E: mail@sevenspringscottages.com
I: www.sevenspringscottages.com

COCKINGTON
Torbay

Spyglass ★★★
Contact: Mr Ian Butterworth
Holiday Homes & Cottages South West, 365A Torquay Road, Paignton TQ3 2BT
T: (01803) 663650
F: (01803) 664037
E: holcotts@aol.com
I: www.swcottages.co.uk

COFFINSWELL
Devon

Willa Cottage ★★★★
Contact: Mr Tim Whitehouse
Court Barton Cotage, Newton Abbot TQ12 4SR
T: (01803) 875078
E: tim@willacottage.com
I: www.willacottage.com

COLAN
Cornwall

Little Barton ★★★★
Contact:
Cornish Horizons, The Cottage, 19 New Street, Padstow PL28 8EA
T: (01841) 533331
F: (01841) 533933
E: cottages@cornishhorizons.co.uk

COLD ASTON
Gloucestershire

Pheasant Walk ★★★★
Contact: Mrs Penny Avery
Pheasant Walk, Grove Farm, Cheltenham GL54 3BJ
T: (01451) 810942
F: (01451) 810942
E: grovefarm@coldaston.fsnet.co.uk
I: www.coldaston.fsnet.co.uk

COLEFORD
Gloucestershire

Little Millend ★★★
Contact: Mr Nicholas Pash
Hideaways, Chapel House, Luke Street, Berwick St John, Shaftesbury SP70 0HQ
T: (01747) 828170
E: enq@hideaways.co.uk
I: www.hideaways.co.uk

32 Tudor Walk ★★★
Contact: Mr Beale
82 Park Road, Christchurch, Coleford GL16 7AZ
T: (01594) 832061

COLERNE
Wiltshire

Thickwood House (Garden Cottages) ★★★
Contact: Mr Colin Agombar
Thickwood House, Thickwood Lane, Chippenham SN14 8BN
T: (01225) 744377
F: (01225) 742329
I: www.westcountrynow.com

COLLATON ST MARY
Torbay

Newbarn Farm Cottages and Angling Centre ★★★★
Contact: Mrs Sharon Ryan
Newbarn Farm Cottages and Angling Centre, Totnes Road, Collaton St Mary, Paignton TQ3 7PT
T: (01803) 553602
F: (01803) 553637
E: nbf@newbarnfarm.com
I: www.newbarnfarm.com

COLYFORD
Devon

Chequers ★★★
Contact: Ms Louise Hayman
Milkbere Holidays, 3 Fore Street, Seaton EX12 2LE
T: (01297) 20729
F: (01297) 22925
E: info@milkberehols.com
I: www.milkberehols.com

Riverside ★★★★
Contact: Ms Louise Hayman
Milkbere Cottage Holidays Ltd, 3 Fore Street, Seaton EX12 2LE
T: (01297) 20729
F: (01297) 22925
E: info@milkberehols.com
I: www.milkberehols.com

Whitwell Farm Cottages ★★★★★
Contact: Mr Mike Williams
Whitwell Farm Cottages, Whitwell Lane, Colyton EX24 6HS
T: 0800 0920419
F: (01297) 552911
E: 100755.66@compuserve.com
I: www.a5star.co.uk

COLYTON
Devon

Barritshayes Farm Cottages Rating Applied For
Contact: Mr Gordon & Mrs Liz Lindsay
Barrithayes Farm Cottages, Northleigh Road, Colyton EX24 6DU
T: (01297) 552485
E: info@barritshayes.co.uk
I: www.barritshayes.co.uk

Bonehayne Farm Cottage ★★★
Contact: Mrs Gould
Bonehayne Farm Cottage, Bonehayne Farm, Colyton EX24 6SG
T: (01404) 871416
E: gould@bonehayne.co.uk
I: www.bonehayne.co.uk

Coles House ★★★★
Contact: Ms Kate Bartlett
Jean Bartlett Cottage Holidays, The Old Dairy, Fore Street, Seaton EX12 3JB
T: (01297) 23221
F: (01297) 23303
E: holidays@jeanbartlett.com
I: www.jeanbartlett.com

Colycroft ★★
Contact: Ms Kate Bartlett
Jean Bartlett Cottage Holidays, The Old Dairy, Fore Street, Seaton EX12 3JB
T: (01297) 23221
F: (01297) 23303
E: holidays@jeanbartlett.com
I: www.jeanbartlett.com

Hill End Bungalow ★★★★
Contact: Ms Kate Bartlett
Jean Bartlett Cottage Holidays, The Old Dairy, Fore Street, Seaton EX12 3JB
T: (01297) 23221
I: www.jeanbartlett.com

Lavender Cottage ★★★
Contact: Ms Kate Bartlett
Jean Bartlett Cottage Holidays, The Old Dairy, Fore Street, Seaton EX12 3JB
T: (01297) 23221
E: holidays@jeanbartlett.com
I: www.jeanbartlett.com

Lovehayne Farm Cottages ★★★★
Contact: Mrs Philippa Bignell
Lovehayne Farm Cottages, Lovehayne Farm, Colyton EX24 6JE
T: (01404) 871216
F: (01404) 871216
E: cottages@fairway.globalnet.co.uk
I: www.lovehayne.co.uk

Malt House ★★★
Contact: Ms Louise Hayman
Milkbere Holidays, 3 Fore Street, Seaton EX12 2LE
T: (01297) 20729
F: (01297) 22925
E: info@milkberehols.com
I: www.milkberehols.com

Millstream ★★★
Contact: Ms Kate Bartlett
Jean Bartlett Cottage Holidays, The Old Dairy, Fore Street, Seaton EX12 3JB
T: (01297) 23221
F: (01297) 23303
E: holidays@jeanbartlett.com
I: www.netbreaks.com/jeamb

Quiet Corner Cottage ★★★
Contact: Ms Kate Bartlett
Jean Bartlett Cottage Holidays, The Old Dairy, Fore Street, Seaton EX12 3JB
T: (01297) 23221
E: holidays@jeanbartlett.com
I: www.jeanbartlett.com

St Andrews Cottage ★★★
Contact: Ms Kate Bartlett
Jean bartlett Cottage Holidays, The Old Dairy, Fore Street, Seaton EX12 3JB
T: (01297) 23221
E: holidays@jeanbartlett.com

Smallicombe Farm ★★★★
Contact: Mrs Todd
Smallicombe Farm, Colyton EX24 6BU
T: (01404) 831310
F: (01404) 831431
E: maggie_todd@yahoo.com
I: www.smallicombe.com

Southcot ★★★★
Contact: Ms Kate Bartlett
Jean Bartlett Cottage Holidays, The Old Dairy, Fore Street, Seaton EX12 3JB
T: (01297) 23221
F: (01297) 23303
E: holidays@jeanbartlett.com
I: www.netbreaks.com/jeamb

Look out for establishments participating in the National Accessible Scheme

SOUTH WEST ENGLAND

Sunnyside ★★★★
Contact: Ms Kate Bartlett
Jean Bartlett Cottage Holidays,
The Old Dairy, Fore Street,
Seaton EX12 3JB
T: (01297) 23221
F: (01297) 23303
E: holidays@jeanbartlett.com
I: www.jeanbartlett.com

Valley View ★★★
Contact: Ms Kate Bartlett
Jean Bartlett Cottage Holidays,
The Old Dairy, Fore Street,
Seaton EX12 3JB
T: (01297) 23221
F: (01297) 23303
E: holidays@jeanbartlett.com
I: www.jeanbartlett.com

COMBE DOWN
Bath and North East Somerset

Kingham Cottage ★★★★
Contact: Mr Peter & Mrs
Christine Davis
Kingham Cottage, Summer Lane,
Bath BA2 7EU
T: (01225) 837909
F: (01225) 837909
E: kinghamcottage@aol.com
I: www.kinghamcottage.co.uk

COMBE MARTIN
Devon

Beech & Ash Cottages ★★★★
Contact:
Marsden's Cottage Holidays, 2
The Square, Braunton EX33 2JB
T: (01271) 813777
F: (01271) 813664
E: holidays@marsdens.co.uk
I: www.marsdens.co.uk

Bosun's Cottage ★★★
Contact: Mr Martin & Mrs
Margaret Wolverson
Primespot Character Cottages,
c/o Stag Cottage, Holdstone
Down, Combe Martin,
Ilfracombe EX34 0PF
T: (01271) 882449

Coulscott ★★★★-★★★★★
Contact: Ms Trish Twigger
Coulscott, Nutcombe Hill,
Ilfracombe EX34 0PQ
T: (01271) 883339
E: stay@coulscott.co.uk
I: www.coulscott.co.uk

Ebrington Holiday Cottage ★★★
Contact: Mrs Hilary Markland
Belmont House, Belmont
Avenue, Combe Martin
EX34 0PR
T: (01271) 882292
F: (01271) 882391
E: mail@ebringtoncottage.co.uk
I: www.ebringtoncottage.co.uk

Grassmere House Apartments ★★★★-★★★★★
Contact: Mr Peter Taft
125 Allumbridge Cottage, Allum
Bridge, Bridgnorth WV15 6HL
T: (01746) 780902
E: paulinetaft@msn.com
I: www.grassmerehouse.net

Indicknowle Farm ★★★★
Contact: Mrs Susan West
Indicknowle Farm, Long Lane,
Ilfracombe EX34 0PA
T: (01271) 883980
E: mark.sue@indicknowle.plus.com
I: www.indicknowlefarmholidays.co.uk

Jewells Holiday Villas ★★★★★
Contact: Ms Katie Jewell
37 - 39 King Street, Reading
RG7 3RS
T: (01189) 333935
F: (01189) 332737
E: katie-kewell@talk21.com
I: www.holiday-rentals.com

Newberry View ★★★★
Contact:
Marsens Holiday cottages, 2 The
Square, Braunton EX33 2JB
T: (01271) 813777
F: (01271) 813664
E: holidays@marsdens.co.uk
I: www.marsdens.co.uk

Pretoria ★★★★
Contact: Mrs Heather Trueman
8 Drapers Close, Ilfracombe
EX34 0PP
T: (01271) 882590
E: JanolHtrueman@aol.com

Prospect Cottage ★★★
Contact:
Marsdens Cottage Holidays, 2
The Square, Braunton EX33 2JB
T: (01271) 813777
F: (01271) 813664
E: holidays@marsdens.co.uk
I: www.marsdens.co.uk

1 Stattens Cottages ★★★
Contact: Mrs Peggy Crees
47 Kingcup Drive, Bisley, Woking
GU24 9HH
T: (01483) 488790
F: (01932) 562638
E: peggy.crees@virgin.net
I: www.cottagesindevon.com

Wheel Farm Country Cottages ★★★★
Contact: Mr & Mrs John
Robertson
Wheel Farm Country Cottages,
Berry Down, Ilfracombe
EX34 0NT
T: (01271) 882100
F: (01271) 883120
E: holidays@wheelfarmcottages.co.uk
I: wheelfarmcottages.co.uk

Wood Sorrell ★★★
Contact:
Marsden's Cottage Holidays, 2
The Square, Braunton EX33 2JB
T: (01271) 813777
F: (01271) 813664
E: holidays@marsdens.co.uk
I: www.marsdens.co.uk

Yetland Farm Cottages ★★★★
Contact: Alan & Alison
Balcombe
Yetland Farm Holiday Cottages,
Berry Down, Combe Martin,
Ilfracombe EX34 0NT
T: (01271) 883655
F: (01271) 883655
E: enquiries@yetlandcottages.co.uk
I: www.yetlandcottages.co.uk

COMBEINTEIGNHEAD
Devon

Little Westborough
Rating Applied For
Contact:
Holiday Homes & Cottages SW,
365A Torquay Road, Paignton
TQ3 2BT
T: (01803) 663650
E: holcotts@aol.com

The Old Bakery ★★★
Contact:
Holiday Homes & Cottages
South West, 365A Torquay Road,
Paignton TQ3 2BT
T: (01803) 663650
F: (01803) 664037
E: holcotts@aol.com
I: www.swcottages.co.uk

Thorn Cottage ★★★
Contact: Mr Ian Butterworth
Holiday Homes & Cottages
South West, 365A Torquay Road,
Paignton TQ3 2BT
T: (01803) 663650
F: (01803) 664037
E: holcotts@aol.com
I: www.swcottages.co.uk

COMPTON ABDALE
Gloucestershire

Southwold Barn
Rating Applied For
Contact: Mrs Emma Doyle
Southwold Barn, Cheltenham
GL54 4DS
T: (01242) 890147
E: emma@southwoldfarm.co.uk
I: www.southwoldbarn.co.uk

COMPTON DUNDON
Somerset

Castlebrook Holiday Cottages ★★★
Contact: Mr & Mrs Smith
Castlebrook Holiday Cottages,
Castlebrook, Somerton TA11 6PR
T: (01458) 841680
F: (01458) 441680

Wisteria Cottage ★★★★
Contact: Mrs Georgina Baston
Wisteria Cottage, The Old
Farmhouse, Compton Street,
Somerton TA11 6PS
T: (01458) 242848

CONNOR DOWNS
Cornwall

Trevaskis Dairy ★★★★
Contact: Ms Julie Strachey
Trevaskis Barn, 12 Gwinear
Road, Hayle TR27 5JQ
T: (01209) 613750

CONSTANTINE
Cornwall

Anneth Lowen ★★★★
Contact:
Cornish Cottage Holidays,
Godolphin Road, Helston
TR13 8AA
T: (01326) 573808
F: (01326) 564992
E: enquiry@cornishcottageholidays.co.uk
I: www.cornishcottageholidays.co.uk

Chynoweth ★★★
Contact: Mrs E. W. Combellack
Chynoweth, Seworgan,
Falmouth TR11 5QN
T: (01326) 340196

The Fuchsia's ★★★
Contact:
Cornish Traditional Cottages,
Bodmin PL30 4HS
T: (01208) 821666
F: (01208) 821766

Green Bank Cottage ★★★
Contact: Mrs Carol Scobie-Allin
Selective Cornish Retreats, Bath
BA2 7BG
T: (01225) 466720
F: (01225) 466720
E: carole@selectiveretreats.co.uk
I: www.connexions.co.uk

Jackdaw Cottage ★★★★
Contact: Mrs Castling
Rock Farm, Usk NP15 1DL
T: (01291) 690069
E: jill.castling@tesco.net
I: www.availablecottages.com

Nantrissack Farm
Rating Applied For
Contact: Miss Wendy Palmer
Nantrissack Farm, Trebarvah
Woon, Falmouth TR11 5QJ
T: (01326) 341161

Sail Loft ★★★★
Contact:
Cornish Cottage Holidays,
Killibrae, West Bay Maenporth
Road, Falmouth TR11 5HP
T: (01326) 250339
F: (01326) 250339
E: postmaster@cornishholidaycottages.net
I: www.cornishholidaycottages.net/property/helford-river/sailloft.html

Swallow Barn ★★★★
Contact:
Cornish Cottage Holidays, The
Old Turnpike Dairy, Godolphin
Road, Helston TR13 8AA
T: (01326) 573808
F: (01326) 564992
E: enquiry@cornishcottageholidays.co.uk
I: www.cornishcottageholidays.co.uk

Trewince, Flat 4 ★★★
Contact: Mr Martin Rafferty
Mullion Cottages, Mullion
Meadows, Helston TR12 7HB
T: (01326) 240315
F: (01326) 241090
E: enquiries@mullioncottages.com
I: www.mullioncottages.com

Establishments printed in blue have a detailed entry in this guide

SOUTH WEST ENGLAND

CONSTANTINE BAY
Cornwall

1 & 2 Tremawr ★★★
Contact:
Cornish Horizons, The Cottage,
19 New Street, Padstow
PL28 8EA
T: (01841) 533331
F: (01841) 533933
E: cottages@cornishhorizons.co.uk
I: www.cornishhorizons.co.uk

Costilloes
Rating Applied For
Contact:
Cornish Horizons, The Cottage,
19 New Street, Padstow
PL28 8EA
T: (01841) 533331
F: (01841) 533933
E: cottages@cornishhorizons.co.uk

Cowries ★★★
Contact:
Cornish Horizons, The Cottage,
19 New Street, Padstow
PL28 8EA
T: (01841) 533331
F: (01841) 533933
E: cottages@cornishhorizons.co.uk
I: www.cornishhorizons.co.uk

Flat 12 Sandhills ★★★
Contact: Mr Keith & Mrs Marie Hull
18 Caernarvon Gardens,
Plymouth PL2 2RY
T: (01752) 772519

Flat 7, Sandhills ★★★
Contact: Mrs Vaughan
Chestnut Lodge, Oulton, Stone
ST15 8UR
T: (01785) 813864
F: (01785) 813864
E: tim-and-jen@chestnut1.freeserve.co.uk

The Garden Cottage Holiday Flats ★★★
Contact: Mrs Elizabeth Harris
Constantine Bungalow, Padstow
PL28 8JJ
T: (01841) 520262
F: (01741) 520262
E: gardencottage@cornwall-county.com

The Greens ★★★
Contact:
Cornish Horizons, The Cottage,
19 New Street, Padstow
PL28 8EA
T: (01841) 533331
F: (01841) 533933
E: cottages@cornishhorizons.co.uk
I: www.cornishhorizons.co.uk

Kalundu ★★★★
Contact:
Cornish Horizons, The Cottage,
19 New Street, Padstow
PL28 8EA
T: (01841) 533331
F: (01841) 533933
E: cottages@cornishhorizons.co.uk
I: www.cornishhorizons.co.uk

Kittiwake ★★★★
Contact:
Cornish Horizons, The Cottage,
19 New Street, Padstow
PL28 8EA
T: (01841) 533331
F: (01841) 533933
E: cottages@cornishhorizons.co.uk
I: www.cornishhorizons.co.uk

Lees Nook ★★-★★★
Contact: Mrs Stuttaford
Lees Nook, Padstow PL28 8JJ
T: (01841) 520344
I: www.cornwall-online.co.uk/lees-nook

Little Trevelyan ★★★
Contact: Ms Nicky Stanley
Harbour Holidays - Padstow, 1
North Quay, Padstow PL28 8AF
T: (01841) 532555
F: (01841) 533115
E: sales@jackie-stanley.co.uk
I: www.harbourholidays.co.uk

Moonraker ★★★
Contact:
Harbour Holidays Ltd, 1 North
Quay, Padstow PL28 8AF
T: (01841) 533402
F: (01841) 533115
E: contact@harbourholidays.co.uk
I: www.harbourholidays.co.uk

Ocean View ★★★
Contact: Mrs Julie Carter
Ocean View, 15 Sandhills,
Padstow PL28 8JJ
T: (01425) 654180
E: julie@jcarterj.fsnet.co.uk
I: oceanview.mysite.freeserve.com

Pippins & Dinas View ★★★
Contact:
Cornish Horizons, The Cottage,
19 New Street, Padstow
PL28 8EA
T: (01841) 533331
F: (01841) 533933
E: cottages@cornishhorizons.co.uk
I: www.cornishhorizons.co.uk

Porth Clyne ★★★★
Contact:
Cornish Horizons, The Cottage,
19 New Street, Padstow
PL28 8EA
T: (01841) 533331
F: (01841) 533933
E: cottages@cornishhorizons.co.uk
I: www.cornishhorizons.co.uk

Portol ★★★
Contact: Mr Grayson
Alcester, Sunhill, Hook Heath
Road, Woking GU22 0QL
T: (01483) 755539
E: alecjenny@aol.com

Quilletts ★★★★
Contact:
Cornish Horizons, The Cottage,
19 New Street, Padstow
PL28 8EA
T: (01841) 533331
F: (01841) 533933
E: cottages@cornishhorizons.co.uk
I: www.cornishhorizons.co.uk

Rose Campion ★★★
Contact:
Cornish Horizons, The Cottage,
19 New Street, Padstow
PL28 8EA
T: (01841) 533331
F: (01841) 533933
E: cottages@cornishhorizons.co.uk
I: www.cornishhorizons.co.uk

Stone's Throw ★★★
Contact: Mr & Mrs Temple
4 Gwendrock Villas, Fernleigh
Road, Wadebridge PL27 7AZ
T: (01208) 812612
F: 08701 325817
E: iantemple@bigfoot.com
I: www.northcornwall.fsnet.co.uk

Trefebus ★★★★
Contact:
Cornish Horizons, The Cottage,
19 New Street, Padstow
PL28 8EA
T: (01841) 533331
F: (01841) 533933
E: cottages@cornishhorizons.co.uk
I: www.cornishhorizons.co.uk

Treglos ★★★
Contact: Mr Barlow
Treglos, Padstow PL28 8JH
T: (01841) 520727
E: enquiries@treglos-hotel.co.uk
I: www.treglos-hotel.co.uk

Treglyn ★★
Contact:
Cornish Horizons, The Cottage,
19 New Street, Padstow
PL28 8EA
T: (01841) 533331
F: (01841) 533933
E: cottages@cornishhorizons.co.uk
I: www.cornishhorizons.co.uk

Treless ★★★★
Contact:
Cornish Horizons, The Cottage,
19 New Street, Padstow
PL28 8EA
T: (01841) 533331
F: (01841) 533933
E: cottages@cornishhorizons.co.uk
I: www.cornishhorizons.co.uk

Trescore ★★★
Contact:
Cornish Horizons, The Cottage,
19 New Street, Padstow
PL28 8EA
T: (01841) 533331
F: (01841) 533933
E: cottages@cornishhorizons.co.uk
I: www.cornishhorizons.co.uk

Trevanion ★★★
Contact: Ms Nicky Stanley
Harbour Holidays - Padstow, 1
North Quay, Padstow PL28 8AF
T: (01841) 532555
F: (01841) 533115
E: sales@jackie-stanley.co.uk
I: www.harbourholidays.co.uk

Trevose Golf & Country Club ★★-★★★★
Contact: Miss Angela Wise
Trevose Golf & Country Club,
Constantine Bay, Padstow
PL28 8JB
T: (01841) 520208
F: (01841) 521057
E: info@trevose-gc.co.uk
I: www.trevose-gc.co.uk

Turnstones ★★★
Contact:
Cornish Horizons, The Cottage,
19 New Street, Padstow
PL28 8EA
T: (01841) 533331
F: (01841) 533933
E: cottages@cornishhorizons.co.uk

COOMBE BISSETT
Wiltshire

Cross Farm Cottage ★★★
Contact: Mrs Kittermaster
Cross Farm Cottage, Cross Farm,
Salisbury SP5 4LY
T: (01722) 718293
F: (01722) 718665
E: s.j.kittermaster@talk21.com

CORFE CASTLE
Dorset

Hartland Stud ★★★★
Contact:
Dream Cottages, 5 Hope Square,
Weymouth DT4 8TR
T: (01305) 789000
F: (01305) 761346
E: admin@dream-cottages.co.uk
I: www.dreamcottages.co.uk

Kingston Country Courtyard ★★★
Contact: Mrs Ann Fry
Kingston Country Courtyard,
Greystone Court, Kingston,
Wareham BH20 5LR
T: (01929) 481066
F: (01929) 481256
E: annfry@kingstoncountrycourtyard.co.uk
I: www.kingstoncountrycourtyard.co.uk

Knaveswell Farm ★★
Contact: Mrs Valerie Murray
Knaveswell Farm, Knitson,
Wareham BH20 5JB
T: (01929) 424184
F: (01929) 424184

Scoles Manor ★★★★
Contact: Mr & Mrs Peter Bell
Scoles Manor, Kingston, Corfe
Castle, Wareham BH20 5LG
T: (01929) 480312
F: (01929) 481237
E: peter@scoles.co.uk
I: www.scoles.co.uk

CORFE MULLEN
Dorset

Hillberry ★
Contact: Mr & Mrs Cheyne
Hillberry, Blandford Road,
Wimborne Minster BH21 3HF
T: (01202) 658906

630 Look out for establishments participating in the National Accessible Scheme

SOUTH WEST ENGLAND

CORSCOMBE
Dorset
Underhill Farm Holidays Meadow Rise ★★★★
Contact: Mrs Joanna Vassie
Underhill Farm Holidays
Meadow Rise, Underhill Farm,
Dorchester DT2 0PA
T: (01935) 891245
F: (01935) 891245
E: vassie@underhillfarm.co.uk
I: www.underhillfarm.co.uk

CORSHAM
Wiltshire
Linleys Farm Cottages ★★★★★
Contact: Ms Han Warr
Linleys Farm Cottages, Linleys,
Corsham SN13 9PG
T: (01249) 715578
F: (01249) 715578
E: linleysfarm@aol.com

Wadswick Barns ★★★★★
Contact: Mr Tim & Mrs Carolyn Barton
Wadswick Barns, Wadswick,
Corsham SN13 8JB
T: (01225) 810733
F: (01225) 810307
E: barns@wadswick.co.uk
I: www.wadswick.co.uk

COSSINGTON
Somerset
Cossington Park
Rating Applied For
Contact: Ms Lesley Marshman
Cossington Park, Middle Road,
Bridgwater TA7 8LH
T: (01278) 684923
E: enq@cossingtonpark.com
I: www.cossingtonpark.com

COTLEIGH
Devon
Authers Cottage ★★★★
Contact: Ms Louise Hayman
Milkbere Holidays, 3 Fore Street,
Seaton EX12 2LE
T: (01297) 20729
F: (01297) 22925
E: enq@milkberehols.com
I: www.milkberehols.com

COVERACK
Cornwall
14 Coverack Headland ★★★
Contact: Mrs Anne Bradley-Smith
Dorland Cottage, The Mint,
Church Lane, Bletchingley,
Redhill RH1 4LP
T: (01883) 743442
F: (01883) 743442

Heath Farm Cottages ★★-★★★★
Contact: Mr Andy Goodman
Heath Farm Cottages, Heath
Farm, Ponsongath, Helston
TR12 6SQ
T: (01326) 280521
F: (01326) 281272
E: info@heath-farm-holidays.co.uk
I: www.heath-farm-holidays.co.uk

Little Fernleigh ★★
Contact:
Cornish Cottage Holidays, The
Old Turnpike Dairy, Godolphin
Road, Helston TR13 8AA
T: (01326) 573808
F: (01326) 564992
E: enquiry@cornishcottageholidays.co.uk
I: www.cornishcottageholidays.co.uk

Polcoverack Farm Cottages ★★★
Contact: Mr Trevor & Mrs Pat Angell
Polcoverack Farm Cottages,
Polcoverack, Helston TR12 6SP
T: (01326) 281021
F: (01326) 280683
E: angells@polcoverack.co.uk
I: www.polcoverack.co.uk

Treprenn ★★★★
Contact: Mr Martin Raftery
Mullion Cottages, Mullion
Meadows, Helston TR12 7HB
T: (01326) 240315
F: (01326) 241090
E: enquiries@mullioncottages.com
I: www.mullioncottages.com

COXLEY WICK
Somerset
Cowstalls
Rating Applied For
Contact:
Farm & Cottage Holidays,
Victoria House, 31 Fore Street,
Bideford EX39 1AW
T: (01237) 479146
F: (01237) 421512

CRACKINGTON HAVEN
Cornwall
Bremor Holiday Bungalows and Cottages ★★★
Contact: Mr & Mrs Rogers
Bremor Holiday Bungalows and
Cottages, Bude EX23 0JN
T: (01840) 230340

Cleave Farm Cottages ★★-★★★
Contact: Mrs Carole Zoeftig
Cleave Farm Cottages, St
Gennys, Bude EX23 0NQ
T: (01840) 230426
E: carole@cleavefm.force9.co.uk

The Coopers Lodge
Rating Applied For
Contact: Mr Stephen Bennett
Fresh Breaks Ltd, 64 Park Drive,
London W3 8NA
T: (020) 89932628
E: booking@freshbreaks.co.uk

Higher Hill House
Rating Applied For
Contact: Mr Stephen Bennett
Fresh Breaks Ltd, 64 Park Drive,
London W3 8NA
T: (020) 89932628
E: booking@freshbreaks.co.uk

Longstones ★★★★
Contact: Mrs Pat Bird
Longstones, Middle Crackington
Farm, Bude EX23 0JW
T: (01840) 230445
F: (01840) 230445
E: pat.bird@btinternet.com
I: www.cottagesdirect.com/coa018

9 Lundy Drive ★★★★
Contact: Mrs Anderson
1 Long-A-Row Close, Bude
EX23 0PG
T: (01840) 230504
E: paul@panderson60.freeserve.co.uk

The Old Cider Press ★★★★
Contact: Mr Stephen Bennett
The Old Cider Press, Bude
EX23 0LF
T: (020) 89932628
F: 08709 223563
E: booking@theoldciderpress.co.uk
I: www.theoldciderpress.co.uk

Trenannick Cottages ★★★
Contact: Ms Lorraine Harrison
Trenannick Farm House,
Warbstow, Launceston PL15 8RP
T: (01566) 781443
F: (01566) 781443
E: lorraine.trenannick@i12.com
I: www.trenannickcottages.co.uk

Trevigue Cottages ★★★-★★★★★
Contact: Mr Francis Crocker
Barton Cottage, Bude EX23
T: (01840) 230492
I: www.trevigue.co.uk

Trevigue Cottages ★★★★
Contact: Ms Gayle Crocker
Trevigue Cottages, Trevigue
Farm, Bude EX23 0LQ
T: (01840) 230418
E: trevigue@talk21.com
I: www.trevigue.co.uk

Treworgie Barton
Rating Applied For
Contact: Mrs Norma Warner
Treworgie Barton, St Gennys,
Bude EX23 0NL
T: (01840) 230233
F: (01840) 230738
E: info@treworgie.co.uk

CRAFTHOLE
Cornwall
Little Eden
Rating Applied For
Contact: Mrs Sarah Chisnell
43C Bycullah Road, Enfield
EN2 8PH
T: (020) 82450191
F: (020) 8482 0307
E: scchisnall@hotmail.com
I: www.littleedencornwall.com

CRAPSTONE
Devon
Midway
Rating Applied For
Contact: Mrs Eggins
Leigh Farm, Plymouth PL6 7BS
T: (01752) 733221

CREDITON
Devon
Creedy Manor ★★★★
Contact: Ms Sandra Turner
Creedy Manor, Long Barn Farm,
Crediton EX17 4AB
T: (01363) 772684
E: sandra@creedymanor.com
I: www.creedymanor.com

Eastacott Farm ★★★
Contact:
Farm & Cottage Holidays,
Victoria House, 12 Fore Street,
Bideford EX39 1AW
T: (01237) 479146
F: (01237) 421512
E: enquiries@farmcott.co.uk
I: www.farmcott.co.uk

Rudge Rew Cottage & Colts Hill Barn ★★★★
Contact: Mrs Christine Bailey
Rudge Rew Cottage & Colts Hill
Barn, Morchard Bishop, Crediton
EX17 6NG
T: (01363) 877309
F: (01363) 877309
E: rudgerew@talk21.com
I: www.rudgerewfarm.btinternet.com

White Witches and Stable Lodge ★★★-★★★★
Contact: Mrs Gillbard
White Witches and Stable Lodge,
Hele Barton, Crediton EX17 4QJ
T: (01884) 860278
F: (01884) 860278
E: gillbard@eclipse.co.uk
I: www.eclipse.co.uk/helebarton

CREECH
Dorset
The Cottage ★★★★
Contact: Mr & Mrs Evans
The Cottage, Creech Bottom,
Wareham BH20 5DQ
T: (01929) 556241

CROCKERTON
Wiltshire
Glebe Lodge ★★★
Contact: Mrs Margaret Askew
Easter Cottage, Foxholes,
Warminster BA12 7DB
T: (01985) 219367
E: askew.easter@btinternet.com

CROWLAS
Cornwall
Cuckoo Cottage ★★★
Contact: Mrs Jackman
Mowshurst Farmhouse, Swan
Lane, Edenbridge TN8 6AH
T: (01732) 862064

Millers Loft ★★★
Contact:
Farm & Cottage Holidays,
Victoria House, 12 Fore Street,
Bideford EX39 1AW
T: (01237) 479146
F: (01237) 421512
E: bookings@farmcott.co.uk

Establishments printed in blue have a detailed entry in this guide

SOUTH WEST ENGLAND

CROYDE
Devon

Baggy Point Apartment ★★★
Contact:
Marsden's Cottage Holidays, 2 The Square, Braunton EX33 2JB
T: (01271) 813777
F: (01271) 813664
E: holidays@marsdens.co.uk
I: www.marsdens.co.uk

Bramleys ★★★
Contact:
Marsden's Cottage Holidays, 2 The Square, Braunton EX33 2JB
T: (01271) 813777
F: (01271) 813664
E: holidays@marsdens.co.uk
I: www.marsdens.co.uk

Bridge Cottage ★★★★
Contact: Mr Peter & Mrs Janet Cornwell
Marsden's Cottage Holidays, 2 The Square, Braunton EX33 2JB
T: (01271) 813777
F: (01271) 813664
E: holidays@marsdens.co.uk
I: www.marsdens.co.uk

The Bungalow ★★★★
Contact:
Marsden's Cottage Holidays, 2 The Square, Braunton EX33 2JB
T: (01271) 813777
F: (01271) 813664
E: holidays@marsdens.co.uk
I: www.marsdens.co.uk

Cock Rock Cottage ★★★★★
Contact:
Marsden's Cottage Holidays, 2 The Square, Braunton EX33 2JB
T: (01271) 813777
F: (01271) 813664
E: holidays@marsdens.co.uk
I: www.marsdens.co.uk

Croyde Bay Lodge Apartments 1 & 2 ★★★★
Contact: Mrs Jenny Penny
Croyde Bay House Hotel, Moor Lane, Braunton EX33 1PA
T: (01271) 890270

Cubbies Corner ★★★
Contact:
Marsden's Cottage Holidays, 2 The Square, Braunton EX33 2JB
T: (01271) 813777
F: (01271) 813664
E: holidays@marsdens.co.uk
I: www.marsdens.co.uk

Denham House ★★★
Contact: Mr Hugh Bond
Denham House, Braunton EX33 1HY
T: (01271) 890297
F: (01271) 890297
I: www.denhamhouse.co.uk

Dunehaven ★★★★
Contact:
Marsden's Cottage Holidays, 2 The Square, Braunton EX33 2JB
T: (01271) 813777
F: (01271) 813664
E: holidays@marsdens.co.uk
I: www.marsdens.co.uk

The Dunes ★★★★
Contact:
Marsden's Cottage Holidays, 2 The Square, Braunton EX33 2JB
T: (01271) 813777
F: (01271) 813664
E: holidays@marsdens.co.uk
I: www.marsdens.co.uk

Duneside ★★★★
Contact:
Marsdens Cottage Holidays, 2 The Square, Braunton EX33 2JB
T: (01271) 813777
F: (01271) 813664
E: holidays@marsdens.co.uk
I: www.marsdens.co.uk

Embleton ★★★★
Contact:
Marsden's Cottage Holidays, 2 The Square, Braunton EX33 2JB
T: (01271) 813777
F: (01271) 813664

Fujikawa ★★★
Contact: Mr Peter & Mrs Janet Cornwell
Marsden's Cottage Holidays, 2 The Square, Braunton EX33 2JB
T: (01271) 813777
F: (01271) 813664
E: holidays@marsdens.co.uk
I: www.marsdens.co.uk

Hillview ★★★★
Contact:
Marsden's Cottage Holidays, 2 The Square, Braunton EX33 2JB
T: (01271) 813777
F: (01271) 813664
E: holidays@marsdens.co.uk
I: www.marsdens.co.uk

Hobbs House ★★★★
Contact:
Marsdens Cottage Holidays, 2 The Square, Braunton EX33 2JB
T: (01271) 813777
E: holidays@marsdens.co.uk
I: www.marsdens.co.uk

Honeycott ★★★
Contact:
Marsdens Cottage Holidays, 2 The square, Braunton EX33 2JB
T: (01271) 813777
E: holidays@marsdens.co.uk
I: www.marsdens.co.uk

Keats Lodge ★★★★
Contact:
Marsden's Cottage Holidays, 2 The Square, Braunton EX33 2JB
T: (01271) 813777
F: (01271) 813664
E: holidays@marsdens.co.uk
I: www.marsdens.co.uk

Little Doone ★★★★
Contact:
Marsden's Cottage Holidays, 2 The Square, Braunton EX33 2JB
T: (01271) 813777
F: (01271) 813664
E: holidays@marsdens.co.uk
I: www.marsdens.co.uk

Lundy Lodge ★★★★
Contact: Mr & Mrs Cornwell
Marsden's Cottage Holidays, 2 The Square, Braunton EX33 2JB
I: www.marsdens.co.uk

The Mallows ★★★
Contact:
Marsden's Cottage Holidays, 2 The Square, Braunton EX33 2JB
T: (01271) 813777
F: (01271) 813664
E: holidays@marsdens.co.uk
I: www.marsdens.co.uk

Montana ★★★
Contact: Mr & Mrs Cornwell
Marsden's Cottage Holidays, 2 The Square, Braunton EX33 2JB
I: www.marsdens.co.uk

Mountain Ash ★★★
Contact: Mr Peter & Mrs Janet Cornwell
Marsden's Cottage Holidays, 2 The Square, Braunton EX33 2JB
T: (01271) 813777
F: (01271) 813664
E: holidays@marsdens.co.uk
I: www.marsdens.co.uk

Myrtle Cottage ★★★★
Contact:
Marsden's Cottage Holidays, 2 The Square, Braunton EX33 2JB
T: (01271) 813777
F: (01271) 813664
E: holidays@marsdens.co.uk
I: www.marsdens.co.uk

Nauwai ★★★★
Contact: Mr Peter & Mrs Janet Cornwell
Marsden's Cottage Holidays, 2 The Square, Braunton EX33 2JB
T: (01271) 813777
F: (01271) 813664
E: holidays@marsdens.co.uk
I: www.marsdens.co.uk

Oceanus & Poseidon ★★★
Contact:
Marsden's Cottage Holidays, 2 The Square, Braunton EX33 2JB
T: (01271) 813777
F: (01271) 813664
E: holidays@marsdens.co.uk
I: www.marsdens.co.uk

Oyster Falls ★★★★
Contact:
Marsden's Cottage Holidays, 2 The Square, Braunton EX33 2JB
T: (01271) 813777
F: (01271) 813664
E: holidays@marsdens.co.uk
I: www.marsdens.co.uk

Rose Villa ★★★★
Contact:
Marsden's Cottage Holidays, 2 The Square, Braunton EX33 2JB
T: (01271) 813777
F: (01271) 813664
E: holidays@marsdens.co.uk
I: www.marsdens.co.uk

Sands End ★★★★
Contact:
Marsden's Cottage Holidays, 2 The Square, Braunton EX33 2JB
T: (01271) 813777
F: (01271) 813664
E: holidays@marsdens.co.uk
I: www.marsdens.co.uk

Seahaven ★★★★
Contact:
Marsden's Cottage Holidays, 2 The Square, Braunton EX33 2JB
T: (01271) 813777
F: (01271) 813664
E: holidays@marsdens.co.uk
I: www.marsdens.co.uk

Sennen Cottage ★★★
Contact:
Marsden's Cottage Holidays, 2 The Square, Braunton EX33 2JB
T: (01271) 813777
F: (01271) 813664
E: holidays@marsdens.co.uk
I: www.marsdens.co.uk

Sunny Skies ★★★★
Contact:
Marsden's Cottage Holidays, 2 The Square, Braunton EX33 2JB
T: (01271) 813777
F: (01271) 813664
E: holidays@marsdens.co.uk
I: www.marsdens.co.uk

Sunnyside ★★★★
Contact:
Marsden's Cottage Holidays, 2 The Square, Braunton EX33 2JB
T: (01271) 813777
F: (01271) 813664
E: holidays@marsdens.co.uk
I: www.marsdens.co.uk

Sunset View ★★★
Contact:
Marsden's Cottage Holidays, 2 The Square, Braunton EX33 2JB
T: (01271) 813777
F: (01271) 813664
E: holidays@marsdens.co.uk
I: www.marsdens.co.uk

Suntana ★★★
Contact:
Marsden's Cottage Holidays, 2 The Square, Braunton EX33 2JB
T: (01271) 813777
F: (01271) 813664
E: holidays@marsdens.co.uk
I: www.marsdens.co.uk

Sweets Cottage ★★★★
Contact:
Marsden's Cottage Holidays, 2 The Square, Braunton EX33 2JB
T: (01271) 813777
F: (01271) 813664
E: holidays@marsdens.co.uk
I: www.marsdens.co.uk

Swell ★★★★
Contact:
Marsdens Cottage Holidays, 2 The Square, Braunton EX33 2JB
T: (01271) 813777
F: (01271) 813664
E: holidays@marsdens.co.uk
I: www.marsdens.co.uk

Wayside ★★★★
Contact: Mr & Mrs Cornwell
Marsden's Cottage Holidays, 2 The Square, Braunton EX33 2JB
I: www.marsdens.co.uk

Withyside ★★★★
Contact:
Marsden's Cottage Holidays, 2 The Square, Braunton EX33 2JB
T: (01271) 813777
F: (01271) 813664
E: holidays@marsdens.co.uk
I: www.marsdens.co.uk

Look out for establishments participating in the National Accessible Scheme

SOUTH WEST ENGLAND

CROYDE BAY
Devon

Cotilla ★★★
Contact:
Marsdens Cottage Holidays, 2 The Square, Braunton EX33 2JB
T: (01271) 813777
F: (01271) 813664
E: holidays@marsdens.co.uk

Hilbre ★★★★
Contact:
Marsdens Cottage Holidays, 2 The Square, Braunton EX33 2JB
T: (01271) 813777
F: (01271) 813664
E: holidays@marsdens.co.uk
I: www.marsdens.co.uk

Sundowner ★★★★
Contact:
Marsdens Cottage Holidays, 2 The Square, Braunton EX33 2JB
T: (01271) 813777
F: (01271) 813664
E: holidays@marsdens.co.uk
I: www.marsdens.co.uk

CRUGMEER
Cornwall

Old Lifeboat Station ★★★
Contact: Ms Nicky Stanley
Harbour Holidays - Padstow, 1 North Quay, Padstow PL28 8AF
T: (01841) 532555
F: (01841) 533115
E: sales@jackie-stanley.co.uk
I: www.harbourholidays.co.uk

Webbers ★★★
Contact: Ms Nicky Stanley
Harbour Holidays - Padstow, 1 North Quay, Padstow PL28 8AF
T: (01841) 532555
F: (01841) 533115
E: sales@jackie-stanley.co.uk
I: www.harbourholidays.co.uk

CUBERT
Cornwall

Elfadore ★★★
Contact: Mrs Valerie Clegg
8 Ellenglaze Meadow, Newquay TR8 5QU
T: (01637) 830640
F: (01637) 830013

CUCKLINGTON
Somerset

Hale Farm ★★★
Contact: Mrs David
Hale Farm, Wincanton BA9 9PN
T: (01963) 31342

CULMHEAD
Somerset

Culmhead House ★★★
Contact: Mrs Timothy & Mrs Susan Rodgers
Culmhead House, Culmhead, Taunton TA3 7DU
T: (01823) 421073
I: www.culmheadhouse.com

CURRY MALLET
Somerset

Buzzards View ★★★★
Contact:
Country Holidays, Spring Mill, Barnoldswick BB94 0AA
T: 0870 0 723723
I: www.crimsonhillfarm.co.uk

♿

CURY
Cornwall

Nanplough Farm ★★★
Contact: Mr William Lepper
Nanplough Farm, Helston TR12 7BQ
T: (01326) 241088
E: william.lepper@btopenworld.com
I: www.nanplough.co.uk

Treloskan Farm ★★★
Contact: Mrs Lane
Treloskan Farm, Porthallow, St Keverne, Helston TR12 6PW
T: (01326) 240493

DAGLINGWORTH
Gloucestershire

Corner Cottage ★★★★★
Contact: Mrs Mary Bartlett
23 Farm Court, Daglingworth, Cirencester GL7 7AF
T: (01285) 653478
F: (01285) 653478

DALWOOD
Devon

Millwater 1 & 2 ★★★★
Contact: Mr Zachary Stuart-Brown
Dream Cottages, 5 Hope Square, Weymouth DT4 8TR
T: (01305) 789000
F: (01305) 761346
E: admin@dream-cottages.co.uk
I: www.dream-cottages.co.uk

Old Symes Cottages ★★★★
Contact: Mr John & Mrs Kathleen Brennan
Old Symes Cottages, The Green, Axminster EX13 7RG
T: (01297) 35982
F: (01297) 34982
E: brennans@oldsymes.fsnet.co.uk

DARTINGTON
Devon

Billany ★★★
Contact:
Farm & Cottage Holidays, Victoria House, 12 Fore Street, Bideford EX39 1AW
T: (01237) 479146
F: (01237) 421512
E: enquiries@farmcott.co.uk
I: www.farmcott.co.uk

DARTMEET
Devon

Coachman's Cottage ★★★★
Contact: Mr John Evans
Coachman's Cottage, Hunters Lodge, Dartmeet, Princetown PL20 6SG
T: (01364) 631173
E: mail@dartmeet.com
I: www.dartmeet.com

DARTMOUTH
Devon

Beauford House ★★★★
Contact:
Dartmouth Cottages .Com, 14 Mayors Avenue, Dartmouth TQ6 9NG
T: (01803) 839499

Cairn Cottage ★★★
Contact: Mr & Mrs Cawley
Dartmouth Cottages, 14 Mayors Avenue, Dartmouth TQ6 9NG
T: (01803) 839499
E: holidays@dartmouthcottages.com
I: www.dartmouthcottages.com

Chipton House ★★★
Contact: Mr & Mrs Cawley
Dartmouth Cottages, 14 Mayors Avenue, Dartmouth TQ6 9NG
T: (01803) 839499
E: holidays@dartmouthcottages.com
I: www.dartmouthcottages.com

33 Clarence Hill ★★★★
Contact: Mrs Sally Pool
6 Copyground Court, Copyground Lane, High Wycombe HP12 3XB
T: (01494) 727687
E: poolfamily@btinternet.com

Cornwood ★★★
Contact:
Dartmouth Cottages .Com, 14 Mayors Avenue, Dartmouth TQ6 9NG
T: (01803) 839499

Cotterbury ★★★
Contact:
Dartmouth Cottages .Com, 14 Mayors Avenue, Dartmouth TQ6 9NG
T: (01803) 839499

Fairview ★★★★
Contact: Mr & Mrs Cawley
Dartmouth Cottages, 14 Mayors Avenue, Dartmouth TQ6 9NG
T: (01803) 839499
E: holidays@dartmouthcottages.com
I: www.dartmouthcottages.com

Foss View ★★★
Contact:
Dartmouth Cottages .Com, 14 Mayors Avenue, Dartmouth TQ6 9NG
T: (01803) 839499

Freshford ★★★★
Contact:
Dartmouth Cottages .Com, 14 Mayors Avenue, Dartmouth TQ6 9NG
T: (01803) 839499

Full Deck ★★★
Contact: Mr & Mrs Cawley
Dartmouth Cottages, 14 Mayors Avenue, Dartmouth TQ6 9NG
T: (01803) 839499
E: holidays@dartmouthcottages.com
I: www.dartmouthcottages.com

Fulmar Cottage ★★★
Contact: Mr & Mrs Cawley
Dartmouth Cottages, 14 Mayors Avenue, Dartmouth TQ6 9NG
T: (01803) 839499
E: holidays@dartmouthcottages.com
I: www.dartmouthcottages.com

The Gallery ★★★★★
Contact: Mrs James
43 Faraday Drive, Shenley Lodge, Milton Keynes MK5 7DD
T: (01908) 604449

Green Meadows ★★★
Contact:
Dartmouth Cottages .Com, 14 Mayors Avenue, Dartmouth TQ6 9NG
T: (01803) 839499

Harbour Lights ★★★★
Contact: Mr & Mrs Cawley
Dartmouth Cottages, 14 Mayors Avenue, Dartmouth TQ6 9NG
T: (01803) 839499
E: holidays@dartmouthcottages.com
I: www.dartmouthcottages.com

Harbour Views ★★★★
Contact: Mr & Mrs Cawley
Dartmouth Cottages, 14 Mayors Avenue, Dartmouth TQ6 9NG
T: (01803) 839499
E: holidays@dartmouthcottages.com
I: www.dartmouthcottages.com

Harbourside ★★★★★
Contact: Mr & Mrs Cawley
Dartmouth Cottages, 14 Mayors Avenue, Dartmouth TQ6 9NG
T: (01803) 839499
E: holidays@dartmouthcottages.com
I: www.dartmouthcottages.com

Herons ★★★
Contact: Mr & Mrs Cawley
Dartmouth Cottages, 14 Mayors Avenue, Dartmouth TQ6 9NG
T: (01803) 839499
E: holidays@dartmouthcottages.com
I: www.dartmouthcottages.com

Higher Bowden Holiday Cottages ★★★★
Contact: Mrs Linda Horne
Higher Bowden Holiday Cottages, Dartmouth TQ6 0LH
T: (01803) 770745
F: (01803) 770262
E: lin@higherbowden.com
I: www.higherbowden.com

Higher Venice ★★★★
Contact: Mr Ian Butterworth
Holiday Homes & Cottages South West, 365A Torquay Road, Paignton TQ3 2BT
T: (01803) 663650
F: (01803) 664037
E: holcotts@aol.com

Huffin ★★★★★
Contact:
Dartmouth Cottages .Com, 14 Mayors Avenue, Dartmouth TQ6 9NG
T: (01803) 839499

Island Cottage ★★★
Contact: Mr & Mrs Cawley
Dartmouth Cottages, 14 Mayors Avenue, Dartmouth TQ6 9NG
T: (01803) 839499
E: holidays@dartmouthcottages.com
I: www.dartmouthcottages.com

Lake Victoria Cottage ★★★
Contact:
Dartmouth Cottages .Com, 14 Mayors Avenue, Dartmouth TQ6 9NG
T: (01803) 839499

Establishments printed in blue have a detailed entry in this guide

SOUTH WEST ENGLAND

Lily Cottage ★★★
Contact:
Dartmouth Cottages .Com, 14 Mayors Avenue, Dartmouth TQ6 9NG
T: (01803) 839499

Little Coombe Cottage ★★★★★
Contact: Mr Phil & Mrs Ann Unitt
Little Coombe Cottage, Dittisham, Dartmouth TQ6 0JB
T: (01803) 722599
F: (01803) 722599
I: www.dartmouth-information.co.uk

The Little White House ★★★★
Contact: Mr & Mrs Cawley
Dartmouth Cottages, 14 Mayors Avenue, Dartmouth TQ6 9NG
T: (01803) 839499
E: holidays@dartmouthcottages.com
I: www.dartmouthcottages.com

Lower Swannaton Farm ★★
Contact:
Farm & Cottage Holidays, Victoria House, 12 Fore Street, Bideford EX39 1AW
T: (01237) 479146
F: (01237) 421512
E: enquiries@farmcott.co.uk
I: www.farmcott.co.uk

Mews Cottage ★★★
Contact: Mr & Mrs Cawley
Dartmouth Cottages, 14 Mayors Avenue, Dartmouth TQ6 9NG
T: (01803) 839499
E: holidays@dartmouthcottages.com
I: www.dartmouthcottages.com

Middle Clifton ★★★★
Contact: Mr & Mrs Cawley
Dartmouth Cottages, 14 Mayors Avenue, Dartmouth TQ6 9NG
T: (01803) 839499
E: holidays@dartmouthcottages.com
I: www.dartmouthcottages.com

Moonrakers ★★★★
Contact:
Dartmouth Cottages .Com, 14 Mayors Avenue, Dartmouth TQ6 9NG
T: (01803) 839499

No 67 ★★★★
Contact: Ms Elizabeth Harvey
Glen Helen, Elmsdale Road, Ledbury HR8 2EG
T: (01684) 896325

The Old Bakehouse ★★★-★★★★★
Contact: Mrs Sylvia Ridalls
The Old Bakehouse, 7 Broadstone, Dartmouth TQ6 9NR
T: (01803) 834585
F: (01803) 834585
E: gparker@pioneer.ps.co.uk
I: www.oldbakehousedartmouth.co.uk

Old Globe House ★★★
Contact: Mr & Mrs Cawley
Dartmouth Cottages, 14 Mayors Avenue, Dartmouth TQ6 9NG
T: (01803) 839499
E: holidays@dartmouthcottages.com
I: www.dartmouthcottages.com

Palladium Mews ★★★★
Contact:
Dartmouth Cottages .Com, 14 Mayors Avenue, Dartmouth TQ6 9NG
T: (01803) 839499

The Penthouse at Barrington House ★★★★★
Contact: Mrs Elizabeth Twigg
Barrington House, 33 Old Bath Road, Cheltenham GL53 7QE
T: (01242) 539678
I: www.barrington-house.co.uk

Puffin ★★★★★
Contact:
Dartmouth Cottages .Com, 14 Mayors Avenue, Dartmouth TQ6 9NG
T: (01803) 839499

The Quay ★★
Contact: Mr & Mrs Cawley
Dartmouth Cottages, 14 Mayors Avenue, Dartmouth TQ6 9NG
T: (01803) 839499
E: holidays@dartmouthcottages.com
I: www.dartmouthcottages.com

Rose Cottage ★★★★
Contact: Mr Ian Butterworth
Holiday Homes & Cottages South West, 365A Torquay Road, Paignton TQ3 2BT
T: (01803) 663650

Serica ★★★★★
Contact:
Dartmouth Cottages .Com, 14 Mayors Avenue, Dartmouth TQ6 9NG
T: (01803) 839499

Speedwell ★★★
Contact:
Dartmouth Cottages .Com, 14 Mayors Avenue, Dartmouth TQ6 9NG
T: (01803) 839499

Sunny Bank ★★★★
Contact: Mr & Mrs Cawley
Dartmouth Cottages, 14 Mayors Avenue, Dartmouth TQ6 9NG
T: (01803) 839499
E: holidays@dartmouthcottages.com
I: www.dartmouthcottages.com

Top View ★★★
Contact: Mr & Mrs Cawley
Dartmouth Cottages, 14 Mayors Avenue, Dartmouth TQ6 9NG
T: (01803) 839499
E: holidays@dartmouthcottages.com
I: www.dartmouthcottages.com

Town View ★★★
Contact: Mr & Mrs Cawley
Dartmouth Cottages, 14 Mayors Avenue, Dartmouth TQ6 9NG
T: (01803) 839499
E: holidays@dartmouthcottages.com
I: www.dartmouthcottages.com

Upper Tremorvah ★★
Contact:
Toad Hall Cottages, Elliot House, Church Street, Kingsbridge TQ7 1BY
T: (01548) 853089
F: (01548) 853086
E: thc@toadhallcottages.com

DAVIDSTOW
Cornwall

Treworra Stables ★★★★
Contact:
Farm & Cottage Holidays, Victoria House, 14 Fore Street, Bideford EX39 1AW
T: (01237) 479146
F: (01237) 421512
I: www.farmcott.co.uk

DAWLISH
Devon

Brookdale ★★★★
Contact: Mr Ian Butterworth
Holiday Homes & Cottages South West, 365A Torquay Road, Paignton TQ3 2BT
T: (01803) 663650
F: (01803) 664037
E: holcotts@aol.com
I: www.swcottages.co.uk

Cofton Country Cottage Holidays ★★★★
Contact:
Cofton Country Cottage Holidays, Cofton, Exeter EX6 8RP
T: (01626) 890111
F: (01626) 891572
E: valarie@croftonholidays.co.uk
I: www.coftonholidays.co.uk

Erminhurst ★★★★
Contact:
Holiday Homes & Cottages South West, 365A Torquay Road, Paignton TQ3 2BT
T: (01803) 663650
F: (01803) 664037
E: holcotts@aol.com
I: www.swcottages.co.uk

Rockstone ★★★★
Contact:
Holiday Homes & Cottages South West, 365A Torquay Road, Paignton TQ3 2BT
T: (01803) 663650
F: (01803) 664037
E: holcotts@aol.com
I: www.swcottages.co.uk

Shell Cove House ★★★★
Contact: Ms Jameson
Shell Cove House, Old Teignmouth Road, Dawlish EX7 0NJ
T: (01626) 862523
F: (01626) 862523

DAWLISH WARREN
Devon

Baichal on Welcome Family Holiday Park ★★
Contact: Mr Robert Bailey
10 Canons Close, Teignmouth TQ14 9RU
T: (01626) 773737
I: www.baichal.com

Devondale ★★★
Contact:
Holiday Homes & Cottages South West, 365A Torquay Road, Paignton TQ3 2BT
T: (01803) 663650
F: (01803) 664037
E: holcotts@aol.com
I: www.swcottages.co.uk

Eastdon Estate ★★★★
Contact:
Crofton Country Holidays, Cofton, Exeter EX6 8RP
T: (01626) 890111
F: (01626) 891572
E: info@coftonholidays.co.uk
I: www.coftonholidays.co.uk

DELABOLE
Cornwall

The Mill House ★★★★
Contact: Richard & Rebecca Daglish
The Mill House, Helland Barton, Delabole PL33 9ED
T: (01840) 212526
F: (01840) 212526
E: richard@daglish8141.freeserve.co.uk
I: www.themill-house.co.uk

DEVIOCK
Cornwall

Deviock Barns ★★★
Contact: Ms Theresa Irwin-Bowen
Deviock Barns, Bodmin PL30 4DA
T: (01208) 821208
E: tandc@deviockbarns.freeserve.co.uk

DEVIZES
Wiltshire

The Derby ★★★
Contact: Mrs Janet Tyler
The Derby, Calne SN11 0PL
T: (01380) 850523
F: (01380) 850523
E: W.S.Tyler@farmline.com

2 Eastfield Cottages ★★★
Contact: Mr David & Mrs Nina Lamb
Eastfield House, London Road, Devizes SN10 2DW
T: (01380) 721562
F: (01380) 721562
E: david@devizes.force9.co.uk

The Gate House ★★★★
Contact: Mrs Laura Stratton
The Gate House, Wick Lane, Devizes SN10 5DW
T: (01380) 725283
F: (01380) 722382
E: info@visitdevizes.co.uk
I: www.visitdevizes.co.uk

The Old Stables ★★★★
Contact: Mr Jon & Mrs Judy Nash
The Old Stables, Tichborne's Farm, Etchilhampton, Devizes SN10 3JL
T: (01380) 862971
F: (01380) 862971
E: info@tichbornes.co.uk
I: www.tichbornes.co.uk

SOUTH WEST ENGLAND

Owls Cottage ★★★★
Contact: Mrs Gill Whittome
Owls Cottage, 48 White Street, Easterton, Devizes SN10 4PA
T: (01380) 818804
F: (01380) 818804
E: gill_whittome@yahoo.com
I: www.owlscottage.homestead.com

Rendells Farm Holiday Cottages ★★★★
Contact: Mr Keith & Mrs Sue Baron
The Barn, Devizes SN10 3PA
T: (01380) 860243
F: (01895) 270708
E: sroper@waitrose.com
I: www.rendellsfarmcottages.com

DEVORAN
Cornwall

Anne's Cottage ★★★★
Contact: Mrs Margie Lumby
Special Places in Cornwall, Poachers Reach, Harcourt, Truro TR3 6SQ
T: (01872) 864400
E: office@specialplacescornwall.co.uk
I: www.specialplacescornwall.co.uk

Tinners ★★★
Contact: Mrs Margie Lumby
Special Places in Cornwall, Poachers Reach, Harcourt, Truro TR3 6SQ
T: (01872) 864400
E: office@specialplacescornwall.co.uk
I: www.specialplacescornwall.co.uk

DIDWORTHY
Devon

Didworthy House ★★★★
Contact: Mr & Ms Jeff & Fiona Beer
Didworthy House, South Brent TQ10 9EF
T: (01364) 72655
F: (01364) 73022
E: didworthhouse@aol.com
I: www.didworthyhouse.co.uk

DINTON
Wiltshire

The Cottage, Marshwood Farm ★★★★
Contact: Mrs Fiona Lockyer
Marshwood Farm, Dinton, Salisbury SP3 5ET
T: (01722) 716334
F: (01722) 716334

Fitz Farm Cottage ★★★
Contact: Mr Nicholas Pash
Hideaways, Chapel House, Luke Street, Berwick St John, Shaftesbury SP7 0HQ
T: (01747) 828170
F: (01747) 829090
E: enq@hideaways.co.uk
I: www.hideaways.co.uk

The Flat Honeysuckle Homestead ★★
Contact: Mr David Kirby
The Flat Honeysuckle Homestead, Catherine Ford Road, Salisbury SP3 5HA
T: (01722) 717887
F: (01722) 716036
E: honeysuckle@dinton21.freeserve.co.uk

DIPTFORD
Devon

Higher Beneknowle ★★★★★
Contact:
Toad Hall Cottages, Elliot House, Church Street, Kingsbridge TQ7 1BY
T: (01548) 853089
F: (01548) 853086
E: thc@toadhallcottages.com
I: www.toadhalcottages.com

Ley Farm ★★★
Contact: Mrs Sophia Hendy
Ley Farm, Totnes TQ9 7NN
T: (01548) 821200

DITCHEAT
Somerset

Long Batch Cottage ★★★★
Contact: Mrs Christine Smallbone
Long Batch Cottage, Wraxall Road, Shepton Mallet BA4 6RE
T: (01749) 860421
E: chrissmallbone@aol.com
I: uk.geocities.com/somersetretreat

DITTISHAM
Devon

Cobwebs ★★★★
Contact: Mrs Christine Clark
Dart Valley Cottages, Parklands, Dartmouth Road, Dartmouth TQ6 0QY
T: (01803) 771127
F: (01803) 771128
E: enquiries@dartvalleycottages.co.uk
I: www.dartvalleycottages.co.uk

Ollie's Cottage ★★★★
Contact:
Dart Valley Cottages, Parklands, Dartmouth Road, Dartmouth TQ6 0QY
T: (01803) 771127
F: (01803) 771128
E: enquiries@dartvalleycottages.co.uk
I: www.dartvalleycottages.co.uk

Orchard House ★★★★
Contact:
Toad Hall Cottages, Elliot House, Church Street, Kingsbridge TQ7 1BY
T: (01548) 853089
F: (01548) 853086
E: thc@toadhallcottages.com

Sarah Elliots ★★★★
Contact: Mrs Christine Clark
Dart Valley Cottages, Parklands, Dartmouth Road, Dartmouth TQ6 0QY
T: (01803) 771127
F: (01803) 771128
E: enquiries@dartvalleycottages.co.uk
I: www.dartvalleycottages.co.uk

Smugglers Cottage ★★★★
Contact:
Toad Hall Cottages, Elliot House, Church Street, Kingsbridge TQ7 1BY
T: (01548) 853089
F: (01548) 853089
E: thc@toadhallcottages.com
I: www.toadhallcottages.com

DOBWALLS
Cornwall

An Penty ★★★★
Contact:
Farm & Cottage Holidays, Victoria House, 12 Fore Street, Bideford EX39 1AW
T: (01237) 479146
F: (01237) 421512
E: enquiries@farmcott.co.uk
I: www.farmcott.co.uk

DODDISCOMBSLEIGH
Devon

Shippen Barton ★★★
Contact:
Farm & Cottage Holidays, Victoria House, 12 Fore Street, Bideford EX39 1AW
T: (01237) 479146
F: (01237) 421512
E: enquiries@farmcott.co.uk
I: www.farmcott.co.uk

DOLTON
Devon

Ham Farm ★★★★-★★★★★
Contact: Mr & Mrs Cobbledick
Hebron, Calf Street, Torrington EX38 8EG
T: (01805) 624000
F: (01805) 623058

DONHEAD ST ANDREW
Wiltshire

Sparrow Cottage ★★★
Contact: Mr Nicholas Pash
Hideaways, Chapel House, Luke Street, Berwick St John, Shaftesbury SP7 0HQ
T: (01747) 828170
F: (01747) 829090
E: enq@hideaways.co.uk
I: www.hideaways.co.uk

DORCHESTER
Dorset

Bridle House ★★★★
Contact:
Dream Cottages, 5 Hope Square, Weymouth DT4 8TR
T: (01305) 789000
F: (01305) 761347

Damers Cottage ★★★
Contact: Mrs Rosemary Hodder
Damers Cottage, Dorchester DT2 8DN
T: (01305) 852829
F: (01305) 852025
E: RH@cottage-holidays-dorset.co.uk
I: www.cottage-holidays-dorset.co.uk

Dove House and Swallows ★★★★★
Contact: Mrs Pippa James
Holiday Lettings, Pigeon House, Hampton, Dorchester DT2 9DZ
T: (01305) 889338
F: (01305) 889887
E: hugojames@ukonline.co.uk
I: www.dovehousedorset.co.uk

Greenwood Grange Farm Cottages ★★★★-★★★★★
Contact: Mr R P O'Brien
Greenwood Grange, Higher Bockhampton, Dorchester DT2 8QH
T: (01305) 268874
E: enquiries@greenwoodgrange.co.uk
I: www.greenwoodgrange.co.uk

Hardy Country Cottages ★★★★
Contact: Mrs Frances Carroll
Hardy Country Cottages, Rew Manor, Rew, Dorchester DT2 9HB
T: (01305) 889222
I: www.hardycountrycottages.co.uk

Hastings Farm Cottages ★★★★
Contact: Mr David Hills
Hastings Farm Cottages, Dorchester DT2 8QP
T: (01305) 848627
E: djh@hastingsfarm.freeserve.co.uk
I: www.hastingsfarm.freeserve.co.uk

Lower Wrackleford Farm ★★★
Contact: Mr Steve & Mrs Caroline Foot
Lower Wrackleford Farm, Dorchester DT2 9SN
T: (01305) 265390
E: footsteve@aol.com

Molly's Cottage ★★★
Contact: Mr Tim & Mrs Sue Stiles
Molly's Cottage, 41 High Street, Sydling St Nicholas, Dorchester DT2 9PD
T: (01300) 341514
F: (01300) 341944

The Stables ★★★★
Contact: Mrs Elizabeth Peckover
The Barn, Dorchester DT2 8QU
T: (01305) 849344
E: stables@epeckover.fsnet.co.uk

Wolfeton Lodge ★★★
Contact: Mrs Thimbleby
Wolfeton House, Dorchester DT2 9QN
T: (01305) 263500
F: (01305) 265090
E: kthimbley@wolfeton.freeserve.co.uk

Woodlands Cottage ★★★
Contact:
Dream Cottages, 5 Hope Square, Weymouth DT4 8TR
T: (01305) 789000
F: (01305) 761347

DOULTING
Somerset

Brottens Lodge ★★★
Contact: Mrs Caroline Gent
Brottens Lodge, Shepton Mallet BA4 4RB
T: (01749) 880601
F: (01749) 880601
E: brottens@ukgateway.net
I: www.cottagesdirect.co.uk

SOUTH WEST ENGLAND

DOWLISH FORD
Somerset

Number 3 New Buildings ★★★
Contact: Mrs Hillary Mead
Greenclose Cottage, Chard
TA20 4AX
T: (01460) 61996

DOWN THOMAS
Devon

Bayfield ★★★
Contact: Mrs M Doody
Manor Bourne, Plymouth
PL9 0AS
T: (01752) 862202
F: (01752) 221886
I: www.country-holidays.co.uk

DOWNDERRY
Cornwall

The Chalet
Rating Applied For
Contact: Mrs Nicholas Burns
6 Rollis Park Road, Plymouth
PL9 7LY
T: (01752) 404750

Greengates ★★★★
Contact:
Valley Villas, Brook House, Old
Warleigh Lane, Plymouth
PL5 4ND
T: (01752) 774900
E: sales@valleyvillas.co.uk
I: www.valleyvillas.co.uk

Laburnum Cottage ★★★
Contact:
Valley Villas, Sales Office, City
Business Park, Office 38
Somerset Park, Plymouth
PL3 4BB
T: (01752) 605605
E: sales@valleyvillas.co.uk
I: www.valleyvillas.co.uk

Morweth 32 ★★★
Contact:
Valley Villas, Brook Cottage, Old
Warleigh Lane, Plymouth
PL5 4ND
T: (01752) 774900
E: sales@valleyvillas
I: www.valleyvillas.co.uk

Morweth 36 ★★★
Contact:
Valley Villas, Brook Cottage, Old
Warleigh Lane, Plymouth
PL5 4ND
T: (01752) 774900
E: sales@valleyvillas.co.uk
I: www.valleyvillas.co.uk

6 Morweth Cottage
Rating Applied For
Contact:
Valley Villas, Sales Office, City
Business Park, Office 38
Somerset Park, Plymouth
PL3 4BB
T: (01752) 605605
E: sales@valleyvillas.co.uk

29 Morweth Court ★★★
Contact:
Valley Villas, Office 38, City
Business Park, Somerset Place,
Stoke, Plymouth PL3 4BB
T: (01752) 605605
E: sales@valleyvillas.com
I: www.valleyvillas.com

3 Morweth Court ★★
Contact:
Valley Villas Sales Office, Trerieve
Estate, Torpoint PL11 3LX
T: (01752) 605605
E: sales@valleyvillas.com
I: www.valleyvillas.com

34 Morweth Court ★★★
Contact:
Valley Villas, Sales Office, City
Business Park, Office 38
Somerset Park, Plymouth
PL3 4BB
T: (01752) 605605
E: sales@valleyvillas.co.uk
I: www.valleyvillas.co.uk

Sea Vista ★★★
Contact:
Valley Villas, Sales Office, City
Business Park, Office
38,Somerset Place, Plymouth
PL3 4BB
T: (01752) 605605
E: sales@valleyvillas.co.uk
I: www.valleyvillas.co.uk

Treguna Cottages ★★★
Contact:
Valley Villas, Sales Office, City
Business Park, Office 38,
Somerset Place, Plymouth
PL3 4BB
T: (01752) 774900
E: sales@valleyvillas.co.uk
I: www.valleyvillas.co.uk

DRAYCOTT
Somerset

Martindale ★★★
Contact: Mr & Mrs Dance
Leighhurst, The Street, Cheddar
BS27 3TH
T: (01934) 742811
E: helge@tesco.net

DRAYNES
Cornwall

South Draynes Farm
Rating Applied For
Contact: Mrs Debbie Abbott
South Draynes Farm, South
Draynes Farm, Liskeard
PL14 6RX
T: (01579) 321512
F: (01579) 321402
E: debbie@southdraynesfarm.co.uk
I: www.southdraynesfarm.co.uk

DREWSTEIGNTON
Devon

East Underdown ★★★★★
Contact: Mr Tim Clarke
East Underdown, Exeter EX6 6PE
T: (01647) 231339
F: (01647) 231339

Michaelmas & Gardeners Cottages ★★★★★
Contact: Mr & Mrs Thomas
Netherton Vine, Exeter EX6 6RB
T: (01647) 281602

DRIFFIELD
Gloucestershire

The Stables ★★★★
Contact: Margaret Smith
The Grange, Driffield,
Cirencester GL7 5PY
T: (01285) 850641
E: simonsmith@thegrangedriffield.freeserve.co.uk

DRYBROOK
Gloucestershire

Coach House ★★★
Contact: Mrs Gillian Marfell
Springfields Bungalow,
Springfields, Hawthorne Cross,
Drybrook GL17 9BW
T: (01594) 542278

DULVERTON
Somerset

Anstey Mills Cottages ★★★★
Contact: Mrs Doris Braukmann-Pugsley
Anstey Mills Cottages, East
Liscombe, Dulverton TA22 9RZ
T: (01398) 341329
F: 0709 2 386955
E: ansteymills@yahoo.com
I: www.ansteymillscottagedevon.co.uk

Ashway Cottage ★★★
Contact: Mr George Vellacott
Ashway Cottage, Ashway Farm,
Dulverton TA22 9QD
T: (01398) 323577
F: (01398) 323577

Northmoor House & Lodge ★★★★
Contact: Mr Tim Tarling
Northmoor House & Lodge,
Northmoor, Dulverton TA22 9QG
T: (01398) 323720
F: (01398) 324537
E: timtarling@northmoor.fsnet.co.uk
I: www.northmoorhouse.co.uk

Paddons ★★★
Contact: Mrs Mary McMichael
Paddons, Northmoor Road,
Dulverton TA22 9PW
T: (01398) 323514
F: (01398) 324283
E: marymm@padons.fsnet.co.uk

Venford Cottage ★★★★
Contact: Mr Harley Stratton
Venford Cottage, Venford,
Dulverton TA22 9QH
T: (01398) 341308
E: harleyhstratton@aol.com
I: www.venfordcottage.co.uk

Whitehall House ★★★
Contact: Mr Kevin Reeves
22 Fitzwilliam Avenue, Fareham
PO14 3SD
T: (01329) 665792
E: kevin.reeves4@ntlworld.com
I: www.whitehallhouse.f9.co.uk

DUNSFORD
Devon

Poppy Cottage ★★★
Contact: Miss Hazel Cant
23 Fox Brook, Swindon SN4 8QD
T: (01793) 850555
E: hazel@hcart.freeserve.co.uk

DUNSTER
Somerset

Cedar House Cottages ★★★-★★★★★
Contact: Mr David & Mrs Christine Holmes
Cedar House Cottages, Cedar House, Old Cleeve, Minehead
TA24 6HH
T: (01984) 640437
F: (01984) 640437
E: enquiries@cedarhousesomerset.co.uk
I: www.cedarhousesomerset.co.uk

5 Chapel Row ★★★
Contact: Ms Hall
12 Rue Gabriel Faure, 78290
Croissy-Sur-Seine, France
T: (01305) 130536730
E: familydavidmhall@compuserve.com

Duddings Country Holidays ★★★★
Contact: Mr Richard Tilke
Duddings Country Holidays,
Minehead TA24 7TB
T: (01643) 841123
F: (01643) 841165
E: richard@duddings.co.uk
I: www.duddings.co.uk

Grooms Cottage ★★★★
Contact: Ms Disney
Grooms Cottage, Minehead
TA24 6TX
T: (01643) 821497

Little Quarme Cottages ★★★★-★★★★★
Contact: Mrs Tammy Cody-Boutcher
Little Quarme Cottages, Exmoor,
Minehead TA24 7EA
T: (01643) 841249
F: (01643) 841249
E: info@littlequarme-cottages.co.uk
I: www.littlequarme-cottages.co.uk

Pound ★★★
Contact: Mrs Sherrin
The Bungalow, Orchard Road,
Minehead TA24 6NW
T: (01643) 821366
F: (01643) 821366

The Studio and Courtyard Flats ★★★
Contact: Mrs Harwood
1 Church Street, Minehead
TA24 6SH
T: (01643) 821485

DUNTISBOURNE ABBOTS
Gloucestershire

The Old Cottage ★★★★
Contact: Mrs Simpson
Hawling House, Cheltenham
GL54 5TA
T: (01451) 850118
F: (01451) 850118
E: simpson@glos68.fsnet.co.uk
I: www.cottageguide.co.uk/cotswold-cottages

---

636 Look out for establishments participating in the National Accessible Scheme

SOUTH WEST ENGLAND

DUNTISBOURNE ROUSE
Gloucestershire
Swallow Barns ★★★★★
Contact: Mr Anthony & Mrs Jean Merrett
Swallow Barns, Cirencester GL7 7AP
T: (01285) 651031
I: www.cottageinthecountry.co.uk

DURSLEY
Gloucestershire
Badgers Mead Downhouse Farm ★★★
Contact: Mrs Maureen Marsh
Badgers Mead Downhouse Farm, Springhill, Upper Cam, Dursley GL11 5HQ
T: (01453) 546001
E: marsh52@clara.co.uk

The Stable ★★★★
Contact: Mrs Sarah Randall
The Stable, The Granary, Silver Street, Dursley GL11 5AX
T: (01453) 860728
E: thegranary@fsmail.net

Two Springbank ★★★
Contact: Mrs Jones
32 Everlands, Cam, Dursley GL11 5NL
T: (01453) 543047
E: lhandfaj32lg@surefish.co.uk

EAST ALLINGTON
Devon
Flear Farm Cottages ★★★★-★★★★★★
Contact: Mrs Julie Ford
Flear Farm Cottages, Flear Farm, Totnes TQ9 7RF
T: (01548) 521227
E: flearfarm@btinternet.com
I: www.flearfarm.co.uk

Honeysuckle Barn ★★★★★
Contact: Mrs Rita Jeanette Pickering
Honeysuckle Barn, Hutcherleigh Barn, Hutcherleigh, Blackawton, Totnes TQ9 7AD
T: (01548) 521309
F: (01548) 521593
E: info@honeysucklebarn.com
I: www.honeysucklebarn.com

Pitt Farm ★★★★
Contact: Mr Christopher & Mrs Denise Bates
Pitt Farm, Green Lane, East Allington, Totnes TQ9 7QD
T: (01548) 521234
F: (01548) 521518
E: info@pitt-farm.co.uk
I: www.pitt-farm.co.uk

EAST ANSTEY
Devon
Knapp House ★★★★
Contact: Mr Evert & Mrs Veronique Veltnik
Knapp House, Tiverton EX16 9JL
T: (01398) 341163
F: (01398) 341163
E: info@knapp-house.com
I: www.knapp-house.com

EAST BRENT
Somerset
Knoll Farm ★★★
Contact: Mrs Jeanne Champion
Knoll Farm, Jarvis Lane, Highbridge TA9 4HS
T: (01278) 760227

EAST BUDLEIGH
Devon
Brook Cottage ★★★★
Contact: Mrs Jo Simons
Foxcote, Noverton Lane, Prestbury, Cheltenham GL52 5BB
T: (01242) 574031
E: josimons@tesco.net
I: www.BrookCottageBudleigh.co.uk

EAST CHALDON
Dorset
Kay's Cottage ★★★
Contact: Mrs Noel Hosford
Heart of Dorset, Mill Cottage, Dorchester DT2 7QA
T: (01258) 880248
F: (01258) 880248
I: www.heartofdorset.easynet.co.uk/

EAST CHINNOCK
Somerset
Weston House ★★★★
Contact: Mrs Susan Gliddon
Weston House, Yeovil BA22 9EL
T: (01935) 863712
E: westonhouseuk@netscapeonline.co.uk

EAST HILL
Devon
The Hay House
Rating Applied For
Contact: Mrs Catherine Oates
The Hay House, Blacklake Farm, Ottery St Mary EX11 1QA
T: (01404) 812122
F: (01404) 812478
E: catherine@blacklakefarm.com
I: www.blacklakefarm.com

EAST KNIGHTON
Dorset
Dairy House Cottage ★★★
Contact: Mr Stuart-Brown
Dream Cottages, 41 Maiden Street, Weymouth DT4 8TR
T: (01305) 789000

Lovers Knot ★★★
Contact: Mr Stuart-Brown
Dream Cottages, 41 Maiden Street, Weymouth DT4 8TR
T: (01305) 789000

Oaktree Cottage ★★★
Contact: Mr Stuart-Brown
Dream Cottages, 41 Maiden Street, Weymouth DT4 8TR
T: (01305) 789000

EAST KNOYLE
Wiltshire
Spring Cottage ★★★★★
Contact: Mr Nicholas Pash
Hideaways, Chapel House, Luke Street, Berwick St John, Shaftesbury SP7 0HQ
T: (01747) 828170
F: (01747) 829090
E: enq@hideaways.co.uk
I: www.hideaways.co.uk

EAST LOOE
Cornwall
Admiralty Court Apartments ★★★★
Contact: Mrs Sheila Summers
Admiralty Court Apartments, Apartment 5, Church End, Looe PL13 1BU
T: (01503) 264617

Endymion ★★★★★
Contact: Mr David Pearn
2 Lower Street, Looe PL13 1DA
T: (01503) 262244
F: (01503) 262244
E: endymion@exclusivevacations.co.uk
I: www.exclusivevactions.co.uk/endymion

EAST PORTLEMOUTH
Devon
Ferryside ★★★★
Contact: Mrs Sally Cardnell
Portlemouth Estates Ltd, 41 Round Berry Drive, Salcombe TQ8 8LY
T: (01548) 842210
F: (01548) 842210
E: portlemouth.estates@virgin.net

Two West Waterhead ★★★★
Contact: Mr & Mrs Stokes
12 Elmcroft Crescent, Bristol BS7 9NF
T: (0117) 9516333

EAST PRAWLE
Devon
Higher House Farm ★★★
Contact: Mrs Vicky Tucker
Higher House Farm, East Prawle, Kingsbridge TQ7 2BU
T: (01548) 511332
F: (01548) 511332
E: tuckersatprawle@btconnect.com
I: www.eastprawlefarmholidays.co.uk

EAST STOUR
Dorset
Crown Inn ★★★★
Contact: Mr Samuel Holmes
Crown Inn, Gillingham SP8 5JS
T: (01747) 838866
E: crown.inn@o2.co.uk
I: www.go.to/thecrowninn

EBRINGTON
Gloucestershire
Pump Cottage ★★★
Contact: Mr Robert Hutsby
Middle Hill Farm, Warwick CV35 9EH
T: (01789) 841525
F: (01789) 841523
E: robert.hutsby@btinternet.com
I: www.chipping-campden-holiday-cottages.co.uk/pump.htm

Tythe Barn Cottage
Rating Applied For
Contact: Mrs Michelle Sharp
Mayfield Cottage, 7 Church Street, Church Street, Willersey, Broadway WR12 7PN
T: (01386) 854824
E: info@tythebarn.co.uk
I: www.tythebarn.co.uk

EDINGTON
Wiltshire
Greengrove Cottage ★★★★
Contact: Ref: E2483
Hoseasons Country Cottages, Raglan Road, Lowestoft NR32 2LW
T: 0870 5 342342
F: 0870 9 022090
I: www.hoseasons.co.uk/images/2002/ukcottages/cottages/aa98.html

Moor House Farm ★★★
Contact: Ms Angela Bastable
Moor House Farm, Bridgwater TA7 9LA
T: (01278) 722329
I: www.idass.com/moor_house/index.htm

EDMONTON
Cornwall
Honey and Cowrie Cottages ★★★
Contact: Mr Robert Hoole
Camel Cottages, 19 Hallam Road, Rotherham S60 3BT
T: (01709) 370034
E: bobhoole@blueyonder.co.uk

16 Quarrymans ★★
Contact: Ms Nicky Stanley
Harbour Holidays - Padstow, 1 North Quay, Padstow PL28 8AF
T: (01841) 532555
F: (01841) 533115
E: sales@jackie-stanley.co.uk
I: www.harbourholidays.co.uk

Quarryman's Cottages No 20 & No 1 ★★★
Contact: Mr Huw Jenkins
Endellion House, Parc Road, Usk NP15 1NL
T: (01633) 450417
E: jenkins@choicecornishcottages.com

EGLOSHAYLE
Cornwall
Watermill Cottage ★★★
Contact: Mrs Ruth Varcoe
Watermill Cottage, Lemail Quinnies, Wadebridge PL27 6JQ
T: (01208) 895127
F: (01208) 895127
E: varcoeuk@aol.com
I: www.watermillcottage.co.uk

EGLOSKERRY
Cornwall
Treburtle Cottage ★★★★
Contact: Mrs Wyldbore-Smith
Bremhill Manor, Calne SN11 9LA
T: (01249) 814969

ELKSTONE
Gloucestershire
The Dolls House ★★★
Contact: Mrs Cooch
The Dolls House, Cheltenham GL53 9PB
T: (01242) 870244

ENGLISH BICKNOR
Gloucestershire
Upper Tump Farm ★★★
Contact: Mrs Merrett
Upper Tump Farm, Tump Lane, Eastbak, Coleford GL16 7EU
T: (01594) 860072

Establishments printed in blue have a detailed entry in this guide

SOUTH WEST ENGLAND

ETLOE
Gloucestershire
Oatfield Country Cottages ★★★★
Contact: Mr Julian & Mrs Pennie Berrisford
Oatfield Country Cottages, Oatfield House Farm, Blakeney GL15 4AY
T: (01594) 510372
F: (01594) 510372
I: www.oatfieldfarm.co.uk

EVENLODE
Gloucestershire
2 Rose Terrace ★★★★
Contact: Ms Richards
Manor Cottages, 33A Priory Lane, Oxford OX18 4SG
T: (01993) 824252
F: (01993) 824443
E: mancott@netcomuk.co.uk
I: www.cottageinthecountry.co.uk

Swallow Cottage ★★★
Contact: Ms Cheryl Lamb
32 Persiaran Duta, Taman Duta, Malaysia
T: 0852 2 8137504
F: 0852 2 8137504
E: chlamb@netvigator.com
I: www.cottageinthecountry.co.uk

EXETER
Devon
Augusta Court ★★★★★
Contact: Ms Juliet Ware
Augusta Court, 9-10 Augusta Court, Smythen Street, Exeter EX1 1DL
T: (01392) 477727
F: (01392) 477727
E: enquiries@wareedwards.co.uk

Bussells Farm Cottages ★★★★
Contact: Lucy and Andy Hines
Bussells Farm Cottages, Bussells Farm, Huxham, Exeter EX5 4EN
T: (01392) 841238
F: (01392) 841345
E: bussellsfarm@aol.com
I: www.bussellsfarm.co.uk

Coach House Farm ★★★★★
Contact: Mr John & Miss Polly Bale
Coach House Farm, Moor Lane, Broadclyst, Exeter EX5 3JH
T: (01392) 461254
F: (01392) 460931
E: selfcatering@mpprops.co.uk

45 Compass Quays ★★★★★
Contact: Mrs Diane Harvey
22 Storrs Close, Newton Abbot TQ13 9HR
T: (01626) 834120

Fairwinds Holiday Bungalow ★★★★
Contact: Mrs Price
Fairwinds Hotel, Exeter EX6 7UD
T: (01392) 832911
E: FAIRWINDSHOTBUN@AOL.COM

The Garden House ★★★★
Contact: Mr Hugh & Mrs Anna Evans
The Garden House, Anne's Park, Cowley, Exeter EX5 5EN
T: (01392) 211286
E: anna@realcakes.co.uk
I: www.exeterholidayhouse.co.uk

Mr & Mrs W Sage, Exeter Holiday Homes ★★★
Contact: Mrs Pauline Sage
Exeter Holiday Homes, 4 Spicer Road, Exeter EX1 1SX
T: (01392) 271668

Regent House ★★★★
Contact: Mrs Jewel Goss
Regent House, The Strand, Starcross, Exeter EX6 8PA
T: (01626) 891947
F: (01626) 899126
E: regenthouse@eclipse.co.uk
I: www.selfcateringflats.co.uk

Rixlade Farm - The Old Well House & Drakes Barn
Rating Applied For
Contact:
Farm & Cottage Holidays, Victoria House, 36 Fore Street, Bideford EX39 1AW
T: (01237) 479146
F: (01237) 421512
E: bookings@farmcott.co.uk
I: www.farmcott.co.uk

EXFORD
Somerset
2 Auction Field Cottages ★★★
Contact: Mr & Mrs Batchelor
Bulbarrow Farm, Bulbarrow, Blandford Forum DT11 0HQ
T: (01258) 817801
F: (01258) 817004

Bailiffs Cottage ★★★
Contact: Mr Martin Burnett
Bailiffs Cottage, Muddicombe Lane, Minehead TA24 7NH
T: (01643) 831342
F: (01643) 831342
E: jycburnett@aol.com
I: www.bailiffscottage.f9.co.uk

Court Farm ★★★★
Contact: Mrs Beth Horstmann
Court Farm, Minehead TA24 7LY
T: (01643) 831207
F: (01643) 831207
E: beth@courtfarm.co.uk
I: www.courtfarm.co.uk

Riscombe Farm Holiday Cottages and Stabling ★★★★
Contact: Mr Brian & Mrs Leone Martin
Riscombe Farm Holiday Cottages and Stabling, Minehead TA24 7NH
T: (01643) 831480
F: (01643) 831480
E: info@riscombe.co.uk
I: www.riscombe.co.uk

Rocks Bungalow ★★★★
Contact: Mrs Kathryn Tucker
Stetfold Rocks Farm, Minehead TA24 7NZ
T: (01643) 831213
F: (01643) 831426
E: tucker@exfordfsbusiness.co.uk
I: www.rocksbungalow.f9.co.uk

Stilemoor Bungalow ★★★★
Contact: Mrs Joan Atkins
2 Edgcott Cottages, Exford, Minehead TA24 7QG
T: (01643) 831564
F: (01643) 831564
E: info@stilemoorexmoor.co.uk
I: www.stilemoorexmoor.co.uk

Westermill Farm ★★★-★★★★
Contact: Mr & Mrs Oliver & Edwards
Westermill Farm, Minehead TA24 7NJ
T: (01643) 831238
F: (01643) 831216
E: holidays@westermill-exmoor.co.uk
I: www.exmoorfarmholidays.co.uk

EXMOUTH
Devon
2 & 4 Channel View ★★★-★★★★★
Contact: Mr Cliff & Mrs Sandra Lenn
St Andrews Holiday Homes, Channel View, Esplanade, Exmouth EX8 2AZ
T: (01395) 222555
F: (01395) 270766
E: st-andrews@lineone.net

Pilot Cottage ★★★★
Contact: Mr & Mrs Woods
131 Victoria Road, Exmouth EX8 1DR
T: (01395) 222882
E: seahorse@exmouth.net
I: www.exmouth.net

Queenswood ★★★★
Contact:
Holiday Homes & Cottages SW, 365A Torquay Road, Paignton TQ3 2BT
T: (01803) 663650
F: (01803) 664037
E: holcotts@aol.com
I: www.swcottages.co.uk

Saxonbury Annexe ★★★
Contact: Mrs Elliott
Saxonbury Annexe, 43 Seymour Road, Exmouth EX8 3JG
T: (01395) 264323
E: jojohn@elliott.fsnet.co.uk

EXTON
Somerset
Oakley Lodge ★★★
Contact: Mrs Anne Pantall
Upper House, Staunton-on-Wye, Hereford HR4 7LW
T: (01981) 500249
E: anne.pantall@amserve.net
I: www.oakley-lodge.co.uk

FAIRFORD
Gloucestershire
The Cottage, East End House ★★★★★
Contact: Mrs Ewart
East End House, Fairford GL7 4AP
T: (01285) 713715
F: (01285) 713505
E: eastendho@cs.com
I: www.eastendhouse.co.uk

FALMOUTH
Cornwall
Baywatch ★★★
Contact:
Cornish Cottage Holidays, Godolphin Road, Helston TR13 8AA
T: (01326) 573808
F: (01326) 564992
E: enquiry@cornishcottageholidays.co.uk
I: www.cornishcottageholidays.co.uk

Captains Corner, Sunrise & The Brig ★★★-★★★★
Contact: Mrs Margie Lumby
Special Places in Cornwall, Poachers Reach, Harcourt, Truro TR3 6SQ
T: (01872) 864400
E: office@specialplacescornwall.co.uk
I: www.specialplacescornwall.co.uk

Captain's Lookout ★★★
Contact: Mr Mark Fishwick
The Log Cabin, Oban PA34 4SX
T: (01631) 563883
E: mfishwick@aol.com

Castle Lodge Ground Floor Flat ★★★★
Contact:
Cornish Holiday Cottages, Killibrae, West Bay Maenporth Road, Falmouth TR11 5HP
T: (01326) 250339
F: (01326) 250339
E: postmaster@cornishholidaycottages.net
I: www.cornishholidaycottages.net/property/falmouth/castlelodge.html

The Foredeck ★★★★★
Contact: Mr Derek Paget
Little Barn, Wells Road, Cheddar BS27 3XB
T: (01749) 870230
F: (01749) 870230
E: derekpages@aol.com

Good-Winds Apartments ★★★
Contact: Mrs Jean Goodwin
Good-Winds Apartments, 13 Stratton Terrace, Falmouth TR11 2SY
T: (01326) 313200
F: (01326) 313200
E: goodwinds13@aol.com

Little Avalon ★★★★
Contact: Mrs Joan McCartney
Little Avalon, 30 Kimberley Park Road, Falmouth TR11 2DB
T: (01326) 311119
E: joanpete@nildram.co.uk
I: www.little-avalon.co.uk

SOUTH WEST ENGLAND

Maenheere Hotel & Self Catering ★★-★★★
Contact: Mr John Dilley
Maenheere Hotel & Self Catering, Grove Place, Falmouth TR11 4AU
T: (01326) 312009
I: www.maenheere.co.uk

The Moorings ★★★★
Contact: Mrs Margie Lumby
Special Places In Cornwall, Poachers Reach, Harcourt, Truro TR3 6SQ
T: (01872) 864400
E: office@specialplacescornwall.co.uk
I: www.specialplacescornwall.co.uk

Mylor Yacht Harbour Ltd. Holiday Accomodation
Rating Applied For
Contact: Ms Celeste Cagnon
Mylor Yacht Harbour Ltd. Holiday Accomodation, Mylor Yacht Harbour, Mylor, Churchtown, Falmouth TR11 5UF

Pantiles ★★★
Contact: Mr Colin Kemp
Pantiles, 6 Stracey Road, Falmouth TR11 4DW
T: (01326) 211838
F: (01326) 211668
E: colinkemp@lineone.net
I: www.colinkemp.plus.com

Parklands ★★★
Contact: Mrs Simmons
215A Perry Street, Billericay CM12 0NZ
T: (01277) 654425
E: parklands@fsmail.net

Pendra Loweth Holiday Cottages ★★★★
Contact: Ms Janet Dawes
Pendra Loweth Holiday Cottages, Maen Valley, Falmouth TR11 5BJ
T: (01326) 312190
F: (01326) 211120
E: maenvalley@aol.com
I: www.pendraloweth.co.uk

Pennant Cottage ★★★★
Contact:
Cornish Cottage Holidays, The Old Turnpike Dairy, Godolphin Road, Helston TR13 8AA
T: (01326) 573808
F: (01326) 564992
E: enquiry@cornishcottageholidays.co.uk
I: www.cornishcottageholidays.co.uk

Pontoon
Rating Applied For
Contact:
Farm & Cottage Holidays, Victoria House, 30 Fore Street, Bideford EX39 1AW
T: (01237) 479146
F: (01237) 421512
I: www.farmcott.co.uk

Seagulls ★★★★
Contact:
Seagulls, 2 Pelham Court, Port Pendennis Harbour Village, Falmouth TR11 3XT
T: (01326) 250339
F: (01326) 250339
E: postmaster@cornishholidaycottages.net
I: www.cornishholidaycottages.net/property/port_pendennis/seagulls.html

Seaworthy ★★★★
Contact: Mr & Mrs Hinton
Cornish Cottage Holidays, The Old Turnpike Dairy, Godolphin, Meneage Street, Helston TR13 8AA
T: (01326) 573808
F: (01326) 564992
E: enquiry@cornishcottageholidays.co.uk
I: www.cornishcottageholidays.co.uk

Smugglers Reach ★★★★★
Contact: Mr Russell Jones
6 Place Stables, Fowey PL23 1DR
T: (01726) 833727
F: (01726) 833727
E: russell@jones9223.fsnet.co.uk
I: www.smugglersreach.co.uk

Tall Ships ★★★★★
Contact: Mr Couldry
8 Campbeltown Way, Port Pendennis, Falmouth TR11 3YE
T: (01326) 311440
F: (01326) 316781
E: mike.couldry@virgin.net
I: www.cornwall-online.co.uk/tallships

Toldeen Waterside Studio ★★★
Contact: Mrs Margie Lumby
Special Places in Cornwall, Poachers Reach, Harcourt, Truro TR3 6SQ
T: (01872) 864400
E: office@specialplacescornwall.co.uk
I: www.specialplacescornwall.co.uk

West Winds ★★★-★★★★
Contact: Mrs Patricia Watmore
West Winds, Stracey Road, Falmouth TR11 4DW
T: (01326) 211707
F: (01326) 319158
I: www.cornwall-online.co.uk/west-winds

Wodehouse Place ★★★
Contact: Shelagh Spear
Wodehouse Place, 31 Woodlane, Falmouth TR11 4RA
T: (01326) 314311

FARWAY
Devon

Church Approach Cottage ★★★
Contact: Mrs Sheila Lee
Church Approach Cottage, Colyton EX24 6EQ
T: (01404) 871383
F: (01404) 871233
E: lizlee@eclipse.co.uk

Perryhill Farm ★★★
Contact: Ms Louise Hayman
Milkbere Holidays, 3 Fore Street, Seaton EX12 2LE
T: (01297) 20729
E: info@milkberehols.com
I: www.milkberehols.com

FAULKLAND
Somerset

The Green Farm ★★★★★
Contact: Mrs Anne Gatley
The Green Farm, The Green, Faulkland, Radstock BA3 5UY
T: (01373) 834331
F: (01373) 834331
E: AnneGatley@greenfarmhouse.fsworld.co.uk

Lime Kiln Farm ★★★★★
Contact: Mrs Merinda Kendall
Lime Kiln Farm, Faulkland, Radstock BA3 5XE
T: (01373) 834305
F: (01373) 834026
E: lime_kiln@hotmail.com
I: www.limekilnfarm.co.uk

FENNY BRIDGES
Devon

Skinners Ash Farm ★★★★
Contact: Mrs Jill Godfrey
Skinners Ash Farm, Honiton EX14 3BH
T: (01404) 850231
F: (01404) 850231
I: www.cottageguide.co.uk/skinnersash/

FEOCK
Cornwall

Brambles ★★★
Contact:
Cornish Cottage Holidays, The Old Turnpike Dairy, Godolphin, Meneage Street, Helston TR13 8AA
T: (01326) 573808
F: (01326) 564992
E: enquiry@cornishcottageholidays.co.uk
I: www.cornishcottageholidays.co.uk

Seaview Farm Cottage ★★★
Contact: Mrs Margie Lumby
Special Places in Cornwall, Poachers Reach, Harcourt, Truro TR3 6SQ
T: (01872) 864400
E: office@specialplacescornwall.co.uk
I: www.specialplacescornwall.co.uk

FERNDOWN
Dorset

The Bungalow ★★★
Contact: Mrs Annette Leach
22 West Drive, Sutton SM2 7NA
T: (020) 82417498
E: annette.leach@blueyonder.co.uk
I: www.geocities.com/bournemouth3/

Church Farm ★★-★★★
Contact: Mr Andrew Ross
Church Farm, Church Lane, West Parley, Ferndown BH22 8TR
T: (01202) 579515
F: (01202) 591763
I: www.churchfarmcottages.co.uk

FIFEHEAD MAGDALEN
Dorset

Middle Farm Holiday Cottages ★★★-★★★★★
Contact: Mrs Denise Trevor
Middle Farm Holiday Cottages, Middle Farm, Gillingham SP8 5RR
T: (01258) 820163
E: trevorsmiddlefm@aol.com

Top Stall ★★★
Contact: Mrs Kathleen Jeanes
Top Stall, Factory Farm, Gillingham SP8 5RS
T: (01258) 820022
F: (01258) 820022
E: factoryfarm@agriplus.net

FISHPOND
Dorset

Coombe Ridge - X4344 ★★★★
Contact:
Lyme Bay Holidays, Bos House, 44 Church Street, Lyme Regis DT7 3DA
T: (01297) 443363
F: (01297) 445576
E: email@lymebayholidays.co.uk
I: www.lymebayholidays.co.uk

FIVE LANES
Cornwall

The Little Barn ★★★★
Contact: Ms Sheila Taylor
The Little Barn, Thorn Cottage, Launceston PL15 7RX
T: (01566) 86689
F: (01566) 86936
E: sheilataylor@littlebarn.demon.co.uk
I: www.littlebarn.demon.co.uk

FLEET
Dorset

The Lugger Inn ★★★★
Contact: Mr John Parker
The Lugger Inn, 30 West Street, Weymouth DT3 4DY
T: (01305) 766611
E: john@theluggerinn.co.uk
I: www.theluggerinn.co.uk

FLUSHING
Cornwall

Clottage ★★★
Contact:
Special Places in Cornwall, Poachers Reach, Truro TR3 6SQ
T: (01872) 864400
F: (01872) 864400
E: office@specialplacescornwall.co.uk
I: www.specialplacescornwall.co.uk

Quay Cottage ★★★
Contact: Mrs Margie Lumby
Special Places in Cornwall, Poachers Reach, Harcourt, Truro TR3 6SQ
T: (01872) 864400
E: office@specialplacescornwall.co.uk
I: www.specialplacescornwall.co.uk

Establishments printed in blue have a detailed entry in this guide

SOUTH WEST ENGLAND

Sea Pie Cottage ★★★★
Contact: Mrs Margie Lumby
Special Places in Cornwall,
Poachers Reach, Harcourt, Truro
TR3 6SQ
T: (01872) 864400
E: office@
specialplacescornwall.co.uk
I: www.specialplacescornwall.
co.uk

Waterside House ★★★★
Contact: Mrs Margie Lumby
Special Places in Cornwall,
Poachers Reach, Harcourt, Truro
TR3 6SQ
T: (01872) 864400
E: office@
specialplacescornwall.co.uk
I: www.specialplacescornwall.
co.uk

FOLKE
Dorset

Glebe House - Guests' Suite ★★★★
Contact: Mr S Friar
Glebe House - Guests' Suite,
Glebe House, Sherborne
DT9 5HP
T: (01963) 210337
F: (01963) 210337
E: glebehouse.dorset@
btinternet.com
I: www.glebehouse-dorset.co.uk

FONTHILL BISHOP
Wiltshire

Rose Cottage ★★★
Contact: Mr Nicholas Pash
Hideaways, Chapel House, Luke
Street, Berwick St John,
Shaftesbury SP7 0HQ
T: (01747) 828170
F: (01747) 829090
E: enq@hideaways.co.uk
I: www.hideaways.co.uk

FORSTON
Dorset

Watcombe House ★★★★
Contact: Mr Zachary Stuart-Brown
Dream Cottages, 5 Hope Square,
Weymouth DT4 8TR
T: (01305) 789000
F: (01305) 761346
E: admin@dream-cottages.co.uk
I: www.dream-cottages.co.uk

FORTUNESWELL
Dorset

Cama Cottage ★★★★
Contact: Mr Zachary Stuart-Brown
Dream Cottages, 5 Hope Square,
Weymouth DT4 8TR
T: (01305) 789000
F: (01305) 761346
E: admin@dream-cottages.co.uk
I: www.dream-cottages.co.uk

Ocean Views ★★★
Contact: Mr Charles Gollop
93 Graham Road, London
SW19 3SP
T: (020) 84089800
F: (020) 8408 9804
E: charles@oceanviews.uk.com
I: www.oceanviews.uk.com

Parkers Cottage ★★★★★
Contact: Ms Lesley Gyte
Amhurst Lodge Cottages and
Apartments, 4 Spring Gardens,
Portland DT5 1JG
T: (01305) 860960
F: (01305) 860960

Quiet Nook ★★★
Contact:
Dream Cottages, 5 Hope Square,
Weymouth DT4 8TR
T: (01305) 789000
F: (01305) 761347

Sues Cottage ★★★
Contact: Mr Zachary Stuart-Brown
Dream Cottages, 5 Hope Square,
Weymouth DT4 8TR
T: (01305) 789000
F: (01305) 761346
E: admin@dream-cottages.co.uk
I: www.dream-cottages.co.uk

FOWEY
Cornwall

1 & 2 Harbour Cottages ★★-★★★
Contact:
Estuary Cottages, Estuary House,
Fore Street, Fowey PL23 1AH
T: (01726) 832965
F: (01726) 832866
E: info@estuarycottages.co.uk
I: www.estuarycottages.co.uk

Chy Vounder and Rose Villa ★★
Contact: Mr David Hill
Fowey Harbour Cottages (WJB Hill & Son), 3 Fore Street, Fowey PL23 1AH
T: (01726) 832211
F: (01726) 832901
E: hillandson@talk21.com
I: www.foweyharbourcottages.co.uk

Crow's Nest & West Wing ★★★★
Contact:
Estuary Cottages, Estuary House,
Fore Street, Fowey PL23 1AH
T: (01726) 832965
F: (01726) 832866
E: info@estuarycottages.co.uk
I: www.estuarycottages.co.uk

Estuary Heights ★★★★
Contact:
Estuary Cottages, Fore Street,
Fowey PL23 1AH
T: (01726) 832965
F: (01726) 832866
E: info@estuarycottages.co.uk
I: www.estuarycottages.co.uk

Harbour Cottage ★★★
Contact: Mr David Hill
Fowey Harbour Cottages (W J B Hill & Son), 3 Fore Street, Fowey PL23 1AH
T: (01726) 832211
F: (01726) 832901
E: hillandson@talk21.com
I: www.foweyharbourcottages.co.uk

Palm Trees ★★
Contact: Mr David Hill
Fowey Harbour Cottages WJB Hill & Son, 3 Fore Street, Fowey PL23 1AH
T: (01726) 832211
F: (01726) 832901
E: hillandson@talk21.com

The Penthouse ★★★
Contact: Mr David Hill
Fowey Harbour Cottages (W J B Hill & Son), 3 Fore Street, Fowey PL23 1AH
T: (01726) 832211
F: (01726) 832901
E: hillandson@talk21.com

River Watch ★★★★
Contact:
Estuary Cottages, Estuary House,
Fore Street, Fowey PL23 1AH
T: (01726) 832965
F: (01726) 832866
E: info@estuarycottages.co.uk
I: www.estuarycottages.co.uk

Sideways Cottage ★★★★
Contact: Mr David Hill
Fowey Harbour Cottages (W J B Hill & Son), 3 Fore Street, Fowey PL23 1AH
T: (01726) 832211
F: (01726) 832901
E: hillandson@talk21.com

The Square Rig ★★★★
Contact: Mrs Stuart
Ladybird House, 26 The Avenue,
Birmingham B45 9AL
T: (0121) 457 6664
F: (0121) 457 6685
E: info@sqrighol.co.uk
I: www.sqrighol.co.uk

17a St Fimbarrus Road ★★★
Contact: Mr David Hill
Fowey Harbour Cottages (WJB Hill & Son), 3 Fore Street, Fowey PL23 1AH
T: (01726) 832211
F: (01726) 832901
E: hillandson@talk21.com
I: www.foweyharbourcottages.co.uk

Star Cottage ★★★★
Contact:
Estuary Cottages, Estuary House,
Fore Street, Fowey PL23 1AH
T: (01726) 832965
F: (01726) 832866
E: info@estuarycottages.co.uk
I: www.estuarycottages.co.uk

9 Troy Court ★★★★★
Contact: Mrs Sarah Wateridge
Estuary Cottages, Estuary House,
Fowey PL23 1AH
T: (01726) 832965
F: (01726) 832866
E: info@estuarycottages.co.uk
I: www.estuarycottages.co.uk

Waterfront Apartment ★★★
Contact:
Estuary Cottages, Estuary House,
Fore Street, Fowey PL23 1AH
T: (01726) 832965
F: (01726) 832866
E: info@estuarycottages.co.uk
I: www.estuarycottages.co.uk

FRAMPTON
Dorset

Wingreen Manor Farm Cottages ★★
Contact: Mr Jon & Mrs Sandra Desborough
354 Hatfield Road, St Albans AL4 0DU
T: (01727) 853853
E: afe24@dial.pipex.com

FRAMPTON-ON-SEVERN
Gloucestershire

Clair Cottage ★★★★
Contact: Mrs Cullen
Church Court Cottage, Church End, Frampton on Severn,
Gloucester GL2 7EH
T: (01452) 740289
E: claircottage@waitrose.com
I: www.claircottage.co.uk

Old Priest Cottage and Old Stable Cottage ★★★★-★★★★★
Contact: Mr Mike & Mrs Caroline Williams
Tan House Farm, Gloucester GL2 7EH
T: (01452) 741072
F: (01452) 741072
E: tanhouse.farm@lineone.net
I: www.tanhouse-farm.co.uk

FRESHFORD
Bath and North East Somerset

The Barton Cottage ★★★
Contact: Mrs Foster
57 Hillcrest Drive, Bath BA2 1HD
T: (01225) 429756

Dolphin Cottage ★★★★★
Contact: Mrs Rowena Wood
Dolphin Cottage, Park Corner, Bath BA2 7UQ
T: (01225) 722100
E: rowena_wood@compuserve.com
I: www.dolphincottage.com

FRITHELSTOCK
Devon

Honeysuckle Cottage ★★★★
Contact:
Farm & Cottage Holidays,
Victoria House, 12 Fore Street,
Bideford EX39 1AW
T: (01237) 479146
F: (01237) 421512
E: enquiries@farmcott.co.uk
I: www.farmcott.co.uk

FROME
Somerset

Bollow Hill Farm ★★★★
Contact: Mr Mark & Mrs Emma Kaye
Bollow Hill Farm, Friggle Street, Frome BA11 5LJ
T: (01373) 463007
I: www.farmhousecottages.com

Executive Holidays ★★★★-★★★★★
Contact: Mr R A Gregory
Executive Holidays, Whitemill Farm, Iron Mills Lane, Frome BA11 2NR
T: (01373) 452907 &
07860 147525
F: (01373) 453353
E: info@executiveholidays.co.uk
I: www.executiveholidays.co.uk

640 Look out for establishments participating in the National Accessible Scheme

SOUTH WEST ENGLAND

Hill View ★★
Contact: Mrs Margaret House
Forest View, Gare Hill, Frome
BA11 5EZ
T: (01985) 844276
E: wells@packsaddle11.
freeserve.co.uk

St Katharine's Lodge
★★★★
Contact: Mrs Tania Maynard
St Katharine's Cottage, Frome
BA11 5LQ
T: (01373) 471434
F: (01373) 474499
E: rogermaynard@csi.com
I: www.stkaths.com

GALMPTON
Devon

Dart View ★★★
Contact: Mr Ian Butterworth
Holiday Homes & Cottages
South West, 365A Torquay Road,
Paignton TQ3 2BT
T: (01803) 663650
F: (01803) 664037
E: holcotts@aol.com
I: www.swcottages.co.uk

Georgia ★★★
Contact:
Holiday Homes & Cottages
South West, 365A Torquay Road,
Paignton TQ3 2BT
T: (01803) 663650
F: (01803) 664037
E: holcotts@aol.com
I: www.swcottages.co.uk

GEORGE NYMPTON
Devon

East Trayne Cottage ★★★★
Contact:
Marsden's Cottage Holidays, 2
The Square, Braunton EX33 2JB
T: (01271) 813777
F: (01271) 813664
E: holidays@marsdens.co.uk
I: www.marsdens.co.uk

GEORGEHAM
Devon

Bryher ★★★★
Contact:
Marsden's Cottage Holidays, 2
The Square, Braunton EX33 2JB
T: (01271) 813777
F: (01271) 813664
E: holidays@marsdens.co.uk
I: www.marsdens.co.uk

Burver Cottage ★★★★
Contact:
Marsden's Cottage Holidays, 2
The Square, Braunton EX33 2JB
T: (01271) 813777
F: (01271) 813664
E: holidays@marsdens.co.uk
I: www.marsdens.co.uk

Callum Cottage ★★★
Contact:
Marsden's Cottage Holidays, 2
The Square, Braunton EX33 2JB
T: (01271) 813777
F: (01271) 813664
E: holidays@marsdens.co.uk
I: www.marsdens.co.uk

16 David's Hill ★★★
Contact:
Marsden's Cottage Holidays, 2
The Square, Braunton EX33 2JB
T: (01271) 813777
F: (01271) 813664
E: holidays@marsdens.co.uk
I: www.marsdens.co.uk

Little Dene ★★★★
Contact:
Marsden's Cottage Holidays, 2
The Square, Braunton EX33 2JB
T: (01271) 813777
F: (01271) 813664
E: holidays@marsdens.co.uk
I: www.marsdens.co.uk

Pickwell Barton Cottages
★★-★★★★
Contact: Mrs Sheila Cook
Pickwell Barton Cottages,
Pickwell Barton, Braunton
EX33 1LA
T: (01271) 890987
F: (01271) 890987
I: www.pickwellbarton.co.uk

Rock Cottage ★★
Contact:
Marsden's Cottage Holidays, 2
The Square, Braunton EX33 2JB
T: (01271) 813777
F: (01271) 813664
E: holidays@marsdens.co.uk
I: www.marsdens.co.uk

Westcliff Cottage ★★★★
Contact:
Marsdens Cottage Holidays, 2
The Square, Braunton EX33 2JB
T: (01271) 813777
F: (01271) 813664
E: holidays@marsdens.co.uk
I: www.marsdens.co.uk

Wester David ★★★★
Contact:
Marsden's Cottage Holidays, 2
The Square, Braunton EX33 2JB
T: (01271) 813777
F: (01271) 813664
E: holidays@marsdens.co.uk
I: www.marsdens.co.uk

Westfield ★★★★★
Contact:
Marsdens Cottage Holidays, 2
The Square, Braunton EX33 2JB
T: (01271) 813777
F: (01271) 813664
E: holidays@marsdens.co.uk
I: www.marsdens.co.uk

GILLINGHAM
Dorset

Meads Farm ★★★★
Contact: June Wallis
Meads Farm, Stour Provost,
Gillingham SP8 5RX
T: (01747) 838265
F: (01258) 821123

Whistley Waters
★★★-★★★★★
Contact: Mrs Cleo Campbell
Whistley Waters, Milton on
Stour, Gillingham SP8 5PT
T: (01747) 840666
F: (01747) 840666
E: campbell.whistley@virgin.net
I: www.whistleywaters.com

Woolfields Barn ★★★★
Contact: Mr & Mrs Thomas
Woolfields Barn, Woolfields
Farm, Milton on Stour,
Gillingham SP8 5PX
T: (01747) 824729
F: (01747) 824986
E: OThomas453@aol.com
I: www.woolfieldsbarn.co.uk

GITTISHAM
Devon

Westgate Cottage ★★★★
Contact:
Jean Bartlett Cottage Holidays,
The Old Dairy, Fore Street,
Seaton EX12 3JB
T: (01297) 23221
F: (01297) 23303
E: holidays@jeanbartlett.com
I: www.jeanbartlett.com

GLANVILLES WOOTTON
Dorset

Churchill Cottage ★★★★
Contact: Mrs Rachel Rich
Churchill Cottage, Round
Chimneys Farm, Sherborne
DT9 5QQ
T: (01963) 210827

The Stables
Rating Applied For
Contact: Mr & Mrs Bernard Rich
Brookmead, Sherborne DT9 5QQ
T: (01963) 210209

GLASTONBURY
Somerset

The Lightship ★★★
Contact: Ms Rose
The Lightship, 82 Bove Town,
Glastonbury BA6 8JG
T: (01458) 833698
E: roselightship2001@yahoo.
co.uk
I: www.lightship.ukf.net

**Middlewick Holiday
Cottages** ★★★★
Contact: Mr Martin & Mrs
Shirley Kavanagh
Middlewick Holiday Cottages,
Wick Lane, Middlewick,
Glastonbury BA6 8JW
T: (01458) 832351
F: (01458) 832351
E: info@
middlewickholidaycottages.
co.uk
I: www.
middlewickholidaycottages.
co.uk

St Edmunds Cottage
★★★★
Contact: Mrs Jeannette
Heygate-Browne
St Edmunds Cottage, 26 Wells
Road, Glastonbury BA6 9BS
T: (01458) 830461
E: rheygatebrowne@aol.com
I: www.members.aol.
com/rheygatebrowne/
stedmundscottage/homepage.
html

GLOUCESTER
Gloucestershire

Norfolk House ★★★
Contact: Mrs Jackson
3 Wood Street, Wellingborough
NN9 8DL
T: (01452) 300997
E: nor39@fsmail.net

Number Ten ★★★
Contact: Mr M A Lampkin
Number Ten, 10 Albion Street,
Gloucester GL1 1UE
T: (01452) 304402
E: lampkinternet.com@
bushinternet.com

Sydenham House ★★★★
Contact: Mrs Jennifer Treasure
31 Theobalds Road, Leigh-on-
Sea SS9 2NE
T: (01702) 474318
E: jktreasure@msn.com

GODNEY
Somerset

Swallow Barn ★★★★
Contact: Mrs Hilary Millard
Swallow Barn, Double Gate
Farm, Godney, Wells BA5 1RX
T: (01458) 832217
F: (01458) 835612
E: doublegatefarm@aol.com
I: www.doublegatefarm.com

**Tor View & Church
Cottages** ★★★
Contact: Mr Michael & Mrs
Jenny Churches
Godney Farm Holiday Cottages,
Wells BA5 1RX
T: (01458) 831141
F: (01458) 831141
E: m.churches@farmersweekly.
net.co.uk

GOLANT
Cornwall

Coaches Rest ★★★★★
Contact: Mrs Ruth Varco
Penquite, Fowey PL23 1LB
T: (01726) 833319
F: (01726) 833319
E: varco@farmersweekly.net
I: www.penquitefarm.co.uk

Penquite Farm
★★★★-★★★★★
Contact: Mrs Ruth Varco
Penquite Farm, Fowey PL23 1LB
T: (01726) 833319
F: (01726) 833319
E: varco@farmersweekly.net
I: www.penquitefarm.co.uk

South Torfrey Farm ★★★★
Contact: Mrs Andrews
South Torfrey Farm, Fowey
PL23 1LA
T: (01726) 833126
F: (01726) 832625
E: southtorfreyfarm@Macace.
co.uk

GOLDSITHNEY
Cornwall

Chy-an-bal
Rating Applied For
Contact: Mrs Joanna Richards
52 Hollins Lane, Stockport
SK6 5BD
T: (01614) 271426
F: (01614) 279316
E: sricha407@ao.com
I: www.stayincornwall.
co.uk/chyanbal.htm

Establishments printed in blue have a detailed entry in this guide

641

SOUTH WEST ENGLAND

GOODLEIGH
Devon
Bampfield Cottages ★★★★
Contact: Ms Lynda Thorne
Bampfield Cottages, Bampfield Farm, Barnstaple EX32 7NR
T: (01271) 346566
I: www.bampfieldfarm.co.uk

GOODRINGTON
Torbay
43 Louville Close ★★★
Contact:
Holiday Homes & Cottages SW, 365A Torquay Road, Paignton TQ3 2BT
T: (01803) 663650
F: (01803) 664037
E: holcotts@aol.com

GOONOWN
Cornwall
Goonown Barn Cottages ★★★
Contact: Mrs Deirdre Butson
Goonown Farmhouse, St Agnes TR5 0XG
T: (01872) 553654

GORRAN
Cornwall
The Dovecote
Rating Applied For
Contact: Mrs Myra Welsh
The Dovecote, Treveague Farm, St Austell PL26 6NY
T: (01726) 842295
E: treveague@btconnect.com

GORRAN HAVEN
Cornwall
Haven Cottage and Seamew
Rating Applied For
Contact: Mr Malcolm Debbage
4 Eastdale Road, Bakersfield, Nottingham NG3 7GE
T: (01159) 879184
I: www.gorranhavencottages.co.uk

Morwenna House ★★★★
Contact: Mrs Pamela Kendall
39 Perhaver Park, Gorran Haven, St Austell PL26 6NZ
T: (01726) 843015
I: morwennaholidays.co.uk

Tregillan ★★★
Contact: Mr KF & Mrs S Pike
Tregillan, Trewollock Lane, St Austell PL26 6NT
T: (01726) 842452

GRAMPOUND ROAD
Cornwall
The Garden Cottage ★★★★★
Contact:
Niche Retreats, Banns Road, Truro TR4 8BW
T: (01209) 890272
F: (01209) 891695
E: info@nicheretreats.co.uk

Ralphs Barn ★★★
Contact: Mr Alan Blake
Ralphs Barn, Grampound Road, Truro TR2 4EH
T: (01726) 882222
E: ralphscottage@tinyworld.co.uk

GREAT CHEVERELL
Wiltshire
Downswood ★
Contact: Mrs Ros Shepherd
Downswood, Devizes SN10 5TW
T: (01380) 813304

GREAT RISSINGTON
Gloucestershire
The Dairy Barn ★★★★
Contact: Manor Cottages
Manor Cottages, 33A Priory Mews, Oxford OX18 4SG
T: (01993) 824252
E: mancott@netcomuk.co.uk
I: www.manorcottages.co.uk

Daisy's Cottage ★★★★★
Contact: Ms Kate Cleverly
Meadow Barn, Cheltenham GL54 2LP
T: (01451) 820129

GREAT WITCOMBE
Gloucestershire
Witcombe Park Holiday Cottages ★★★
Contact: Mrs Cecilia Hicks-Beach
Witcombe Park Holiday Cottages, Witcombe Farm, Gloucester GL3 4TR
T: (01452) 863591
F: (01452) 863591

GRITTENHAM
Wiltshire
Orchard View ★★★★
Contact: Mr & Mrs Cary
Orchard View, Chippenham SN15 4JX
T: (01666) 510747

GUITING POWER
Gloucestershire
Little Barnfield ★★★★
Contact: Ms Anne Dawson
Little Barnfield, Kineton, Cheltenham GL54 5UG
T: (01451) 850664

GULVAL
Cornwall
Barton Woods Cottage ★★★★
Contact: Mr Chris & Mrs Margaret Townsend
2 The Bungalow, Mortimer Lane, Mortimer, Reading RG7 3AN
T: (01189) 332136
E: chris@mortimer.demon.co.uk

Mount View ★★
Contact: Mrs Helen Evans
Peacked Rocks Cottage, The Rocks, Lydbrook GL17 9RF
T: (01594) 861119
F: (01594) 861119
E: helen@peakedrockscottage.fsnet

The Retreat ★★★
Contact: Mrs Helen Evans
Peaked Rocks Cottage, The Rocks, Lydbrook GL17 9RF
T: (01594) 861119
F: (01594) 861119
E: helen@peakedrockscottage.fsnet
I: www.evansholidays.co.uk

Rosemorran Holiday Cottages ★★★
Contact: Mrs Shirley Leah
Rosemorran Holiday Cottages, Penzance TR20 8YS
T: (01736) 361479

GUNWALLOE
Cornwall
Hingey Farm ★★★★
Contact:
Cornish Cottage Holidays, The Old Turnpike Dairy, Godolphin, Meneage Street, Helston TR13 8AA
T: (01326) 573808
F: (01326) 564992
E: enquiry@cornishcottageholidays.co.uk
I: www.cornishcottageholidays.co.uk

GWEEK
Cornwall
Anderrows ★★★★
Contact:
Farm & Cottage Holidays, Victoria House, 22 Fore Street, Bideford EX39 1AW
T: (01237) 479146
F: (01237) 421512
E: bookings@farmcott.co.uk
I: www.farmcott.co.uk

Old Mill Studio
Rating Applied For
Contact: Mrs Anne Nicholas
Old Mill Studio, Old Mill Studio, Priors Lane, Gweek, Helston TR12 6UA
T: (01326) 221217

Pheasants' Lodge
Rating Applied For
Contact: Mrs Ruth Pascoe
Pheasants' Lodge, Lower Boskenwyn Farm, Helston TR13 0QQ
T: (01326) 573248
E: ruthpascoe@hotmail.com

HALWILL
Devon
Anglers Paradise ★★★★
Contact: Mr Zyg Gregorek
Anglers Paradise, The Gables, Winsford, Beaworthy EX21 5XT
T: (01409) 221559
F: (01409) 221559
I: www.anglers-paradise.co.uk

Westcroft Coach House & Wheelwright Cottage ★★★★
Contact: Mrs Barbara Dalton
Westcroft Coach House & Wheelwright Cottage, Westcroft Farm, Beaworthy EX21 5UL
T: (01409) 221328
F: (01409) 221836
E: bdalton@waitrose.com
I: www.westcroftholidaycottages.co.uk

HAMWORTHY
Poole
71 Harkwood Drive ★★★
Contact: Mrs Liz Keirl
9 Townsend Rise, Bruton BA10 0JA
T: (01749) 812212

HARCOMBE
Devon
Chapel Cottage ★★★
Contact: Ms Kate Bartlett
Jean Bartlett Cottage Holidays, The Old Dairy, Fore Street, Seaton EX12 3JB
T: (01297) 23221
F: (01297) 23303
E: holidays@jeanbartlett.com
I: www.netbreaks.com/jeanb

HARDINGTON MANDEVILLE
Somerset
Stable Cottage ★★★
Contact:
Farm & Cottage Holidays, Victoria House, 12 Fore Street, Bideford EX39 1AW
T: (01237) 479146
F: (01237) 421512
E: enquiries@farmcott.co.uk
I: www.farmcott.co.uk

HARLYN BAY
Cornwall
The Croft ★★
Contact: Ms Nicky Stanley
Harbour Holidays - Padstow, 1 North Quay, Padstow PL28 8AF
T: (01841) 532555
F: (01841) 533115
E: sales@jackie-stanley.co.uk
I: www.harbourholidays.co.uk

Harlyn Farmhouse ★★★★
Contact: Mrs Hazel Perry
35 Westbury Hill, Westbury on Trym, Bristol BS9 3AG
T: (0117) 9624831
F: (0117) 9624831
E: harlynfarmhouse@blueyonder.co.uk

4 Polmark Drive ★★★
Contact: Mr Neville Powell
7 Pellew Close, Padstow PL28 8EY
T: (01841) 532156

Polmark House ★★★-★★★★
Contact: Miss Rebecca Moncaster
Polmark House, Padstow PL28 8SB
T: (01841) 520206
F: (01841) 521395
E: reception@polmarkhotel.co.uk
I: www.polmark.co.uk

Yellow Sands Holiday Apartments & House ★★★
Contact: Mr Martin Dakin
Yellow Sands Holiday Apartments & House, Padstow PL28 8SE
T: (01841) 520376

HARTLAND
Devon
Mettaford Farm Cottages ★★★-★★★★
Contact: Mr Peter & Mrs Janet Cornwell
Marsden's Cottage Holidays, 2 The Square, Braunton EX33 2JB
T: (01271) 813777
F: (01271) 813664
E: holidays@marsdens.co.uk
I: www.marsdens.co.uk

642 Look out for establishments participating in the National Accessible Scheme

SOUTH WEST ENGLAND

The Old Dairy & Polly's Cottage ★★★-★★★★
Contact: Mrs Heywood
East Milford, Hartland, Bideford
EX39 6EA
T: (01237) 441268
E: sue@gorvincottages.com

HARTPURY
Gloucestershire

The Old Coach House
Rating Applied For
Contact: Miss Wendy Houldey
The Old Coach House, Cooks Hill, Gloucester Road, Hartpury, Gloucester GL19 3BT
T: (01452) 700324
E: nannyknowsbest@hotmail.com

HATHERLEIGH
Devon

Prudence Cottage ★★★
Contact: Ms Stoner
Light Rock Systems Ltd, 67 Dorking Road, Epsom KT18 7JU
T: (01372) 741123
E: info@yourcountrycottages.co.uk
I: www.yourcountrycottage.co.uk

HAWKCHURCH
Devon

Angel Farm Apartment - X4277 ★★★
Contact:
Lyme Bay Holidays, Bos House, 44 Church Street, Lyme Regis DT7 3DA
T: (01297) 443363
F: (01297) 445576
E: email@lymebayholidays.co.uk
I: www.lymebayholidays.co.uk

Angels Farm Apartment ★★★
Contact: Mrs Anne Gibbins
Angels Farm Apartment, Angels Farm, Axminster EX13 5UA
T: (01297) 678295
F: (01297) 678295
E: angels.farm@virgin.net
I: www.cottageguide.co.uk/angelsfarm

Pound House Wing: W4414
Rating Applied For
Contact:
Lyme Bay Holidays, Bos House, 44 Church Street, Lyme Regis DT7 3DA
T: (01297) 443363
F: (01297) 445576
E: email@lymebayholidays.co.uk
I: www.lymebayholidays.co.uk

Sandford Cottage ★★★★
Contact: Mr & Mrs Golding
Sandford Cottage, Southmoor Farm, Axminster EX13 5UF
T: (01297) 678440
F: (01297) 678668
E: petergolding@ic24.net

HAWKRIDGE
Somerset

West Hollowcombe Cottages ★★★★
Contact:
Farm & Cottage Holidays, Victoria House, 12 Fore Street, Bideford EX39 1AW
T: (01237) 479146
F: (01237) 421512
E: enquiries@farmcott.co.uk
I: www.farmcott.co.uk

HAWLING
Gloucestershire

The Bothy ★★★★
Contact: Mrs Watters
Brocklehurst, Cheltenham GL54 5TA
T: (01451) 850772
E: hawling@aol.com

HAYLE
Cornwall

Brunnion Barns H620 & H621 ★★★★
Contact:
Hideaways, Chapel House, Luke Street, Berwick St John, Shaftesbury SP7 0HQ
T: (01747) 828170
F: (01747) 829090
E: enq@hideaways.co.uk
I: www.hideaways.co.uk

Chyreene Court Holiday Flats ★★★
Contact: Mr Bailie
Heva, Riviere Towans, Hayle TR27 5AF
T: (01736) 756651

74 Gwithian Towans ★★★
Contact: Mr Ray & Mrs Nicola Skinner
7 The Gardens, Brentwood CM15 0LU
T: (01277) 822924

Manor House ★★★★
Contact:
Powell's Cottage Holidays, High Street, Saundersfoot SA69 9EJ
T: (01834) 812791
F: (01834) 811731
E: info@powells.co.uk
I: www.powells.co.uk

Penellen ★★★
Contact: Mr Peter Beare
Penellen, Penellen Hotel, Riviere Towans, Hayle TR27 5AF
T: (01736) 753777
E: pjbeare@aol.com
I: www.penellen.co.uk

Truthwall Farm ★★★
Contact: Mrs Goldsworthy
Truthwall Farm, Hayle TR27 5EU
T: (01736) 850266
I: www.farmcott.co.uk

HAZELBURY BRYAN
Dorset

The Old Malthouse ★★
Contact: Ms Sandra Davidson
The Old Malthouse, Droop, Sturminster Newton DT10 2ED
T: (01258) 450696

HEAMOOR
Cornwall

Crankan Flat
Rating Applied For
Contact: Mrs Elspeth Braybrooks
Crankan Flat, Penzance TR20 8UJ
T: (01736) 351388
E: braybroo@fish.co.uk

HEANTON
Devon

Grange House ★★★★
Contact:
Marsden's Cottage Holidays, 2 The Square, Braunton EX33 2JB
T: (01271) 813777
F: (01271) 813664
E: holidays@marsdens.co.uk
I: www.marsdens.co.uk

HEDDINGTON
Wiltshire

Harley Bungalow ★★
Contact: Mrs Mary Fox
Harley Bungalow, Harley Farm, Stockley Road, Calne SN11 0PS
T: (01380) 850214
F: (01380) 850214
E: harley@luna.co.uk

HELE
Devon

Hele Payne Farm Cottages ★★★★
Contact: Mrs Maynard
Hele Payne Farm Cottages, Hele Payne Farm, Exeter EX5 4PH
T: (01392) 881530
F: (01392) 881530
E: info@helepayne.co.uk
I: www.helepayne.co.uk

HELFORD
Cornwall

The Barns ★★★★
Contact:
Helford River Cottages, Point, Helford, Helston TR12 6JY
T: (01326) 231666
E: info@helfordrivercottages.co.uk
I: www.helfordrivercottages.co.uk

Bridge Cottage ★★★
Contact:
Helford River Cottages, Point, Helford, Helston TR12 6JY
T: (01326) 231666
E: info@helfordcottages.co.uk
I: www.helfordcottages.co.uk

The Cottage ★★★
Contact:
Helford River Cottages, Point, Helford, Helston TR12 6JY
T: (01326) 231666
E: info@helfordcottages.co.uk
I: www.helfordcottages.co.uk

Creek Cottage ★★
Contact:
Helford River Cottages, Point, Helford, Helston TR12 6JY
T: (01326) 231666
E: info@helfordcottages.co.uk
I: www.helfordcottages.co.uk

Dowr Penty ★★★
Contact:
Helford River Cottages, Point, Helford, Helston TR12 6JY
T: (01326) 231666
E: info@helfordcottages.co.uk
I: www.helfordcottages.co.uk

Laloma Cottage ★★★
Contact:
Helford River Cottages, Point, Helford, Helston TR12 6JY
T: (01326) 231666
E: info@helfordcottages.co.uk
I: www.helfordcottages.co.uk

Popigale Cottage ★★★
Contact:
Helford River Cottages, Point, Helford, Helston TR12 6JY
T: (01326) 231666
E: info@helfordcottages.co.uk
I: www.helfordcottages.co.uk

River View ★★★
Contact:
Helford River Cottages, Point, Helford, Helston TR12 6JY
T: (01326) 231666
E: info@helfordcottages.co.uk
I: www.helfordcottages.co.uk

Rose Cottage ★★★★
Contact:
Helford River Cottages, Point, Helford, Helston TR12 6JY
T: (01326) 231666
E: info@helfordcottages.co.uk
I: www.helfordcottages.co.uk

Wednesday Cottage ★★★★
Contact:
Helford River Cottages, Point, Helford, Helston TR12 6JY
T: (01326) 231666
E: info@helfordcottages.co.uk

Well House ★★★
Contact:
Helford River Cottages, Point, Helford, Helston TR12 6JY
T: (01326) 231666
E: info@helfordcottages.co.uk
I: www.helfordcottages.co.uk

West View & Halvose Cottages ★★★★
Contact:
Helford River Cottages, Point, Helford, Helston TR12 6JY
T: (01326) 231666
E: info@helfordcottages.co.uk
I: www.helfordcottages.co.uk

HELLANDBRIDGE
Cornwall

Lower Helland Farm Cottages
Rating Applied For
Contact: Mrs Astrid Coad
Lower Helland Farm Cottages, Lower Helland Farm, Helland Bridge, Bodmin PL30 4QP
T: (01208) 72813

Silverstream Holidays ★★★
Contact: Mr Cameron
Silverstream Holidays, Bodmin PL30 4QR
T: (01208) 74408
F: (01208) 74408

Establishments printed in blue have a detailed entry in this guide

SOUTH WEST ENGLAND

HELLESVEOR
Cornwall

Padgy Vesa
Rating Applied For
Contact:
Powells Cottage Holidays,
Dolphin House, High Street,
Saundersfoot SA69 9EJ
T: (01834) 813232
F: (01834) 811731
E: info@powells.co.uk
I: www.powells.co.uk

HELSTON
Cornwall

Boswin
Rating Applied For
Contact: Mr Martin Raftery
Mullion Cottages, Mullion
Meadows, Helston TR12 7HB
T: (01326) 240315
F: (01326) 241090
E: martin@mullioncottages.com
I: www.mullioncottages.com

Burncoose Farmhouse ★★★
Contact: Mr Martin Raftery
Mullion Cottages, Mullion
Meadows, Helston TR12 7HB
T: (01326) 240315
F: (01326) 241090
E: enquiries@mullioncottages.com
I: www.mullioncottages.com

Carminowe View ★★★
Contact: Mr John Huddleston
3 Northfield Road, Bristol
BS20 8LE
T: (01275) 848899
E: jhuddl2144@aol.com

Church View ★★★★
Contact: Mr Martin Raftery
Mullion Cottages, Mullion
Meadows, Helston TR12 7HB
T: (01326) 240315
F: (01326) 241090
E: martin@mullioncottage.com
I: www.mullioncottages.com

5 Coastguard Cottage ★★★
Contact: Mr Martin Raftery
Mullion Cottages, Mullion
Meadows, Helston TR12 7HB
T: (01326) 240315
F: (01326) 241090
E: martin@mullioncottages.com
I: www.mullioncottages.com

The Crag ★★★★
Contact: Mr Martin Raftery
Mullion Cottages, Mullion
Meadows, Helston TR12 7HB
T: (01326) 240315
F: (01326) 241090
E: martin@mullioncottages.com
I: www.mullioncottages.com

Driftwood ★★★★
Contact: Mr Martin Raftery
Mullion Cottages, Mullion
Meadows, Helston TR12 7HB
T: (01326) 240315
F: (01326) 241090
E: martin@mullioncottages.com
I: www.mullioncottages.com

Flat 11a ★★★
Contact: Mr Tim Clifford
22 Trevallion Park, Truro
TR3 6RS
T: (01872) 863537

Ginentonic ★★★★
Contact:
Mullion Cottages, Sea View
Terrace, Churchtown, Mullion,
Helston TR12 7HN
T: (01326) 240315
F: (01326) 241090
E: martin@mullioncottages.com
I: www.mullioncottages.com

Little Criccieth ★★★
Contact: Mr Martin Raftery
Mullion Cottages, Sea View
Terrace, Churchtown, Mullion,
Helston TR12 7HN
T: (01326) 240315
F: (01326) 241090
E: martin@mullioncottages.com
I: www.mullioncottages.com

Lobster Pot ★★★
Contact: Mr & Mrs Hinton
Cornish Cottage Holidays, The
Old Turnpike Dairy, Godolphin
Road, Helston TR13 8AA

The Longbarn ★★★
Contact:
Mullion Cottages, Sea View
Terrace, Churchtown, Mullion,
Helston TR12 7HN
T: (01326) 240315
F: (01326) 241090
E: martin@mullioncottages.com

Mariners Flat
Rating Applied For
Contact: Mr Martin Raftery
Mullion Cottages, Mullion
Meadows, Helston TR12 7HB
T: (01326) 240315
F: (01326) 241090
E: martin@mullioncottages.com
I: www.mullioncottages.com

Midsummer Barn ★★★★
Contact: Mr Martin Raftery
Mullion Cottages, Mullion
Meadows, Helston TR12 7HB
T: (01326) 240315
F: (01326) 241090
E: martin@mullioncottage.com
I: www.mullioncottages.com

Moorlands
Rating Applied For
Contact: Mr Martin Rafferty
Mullion Cottages, Mullion
Meadows, Helston TR12 7HB
T: (01326) 240315
F: (01326) 241090
E: enquiries@mullioncottages.com
I: www.mullioncottages.com

Neid Cottage ★★★
Contact: Mr Martin Raftery
Mullion Cottages, Mullion
Meadows, Helston TR12 7HB
T: (01326) 240315
F: (01326) 241090
E: martin@mullioncottages.com
I: www.mullioncottages.com

The Nook ★★★
Contact: Mr Martin Raftery
Mullion Cottages, Mullion
Meadows, Helston TR12 7HB
T: (01326) 240315
F: (01326) 241090
E: martin@mullioncottages.com
I: www.mullioncottages.com

Pebble Dene
Rating Applied For
Contact: Mr Martin Raftery
Mullion Cottages, Mullion
Meadows, Helston TR12 7HB
T: (01326) 240315
F: (01326) 241090
E: martin@mullioncottages.com
I: www.mullioncottages.com

Pemboa Holiday Cottages ★★★-★★★★
Contact: Mrs Angela Crapp
Pemboa Holiday Cottages,
Pemboa Farm, Helston TR13 0QF
T: (01326) 572380

Poltesco Way ★★
Contact: Mr Martin Raftery
Mullion Cottages, Mullion
Meadows, Helston TR12 7HB
T: (01326) 240315
F: (01326) 241090
E: martin@mullioncottages.com
I: www.mullioncottages.com

Tregevis Farm ★★★★
Contact: Mrs Bray
Tregevis Farm, St Martin,
Helston TR12 6DN
T: (01326) 231265
F: (01326) 231265

Trelawney House Self Catering Holidays ★★★
Contact: Mr E J Cardnell
Gunwalloe, Helston TR12 7QB
T: (01326) 240260
F: (01326) 240260
E: ejcardnell@aol.com

Treyn'wyns ★★
Contact: Mr Martin Raftery
Mullion Cottages, Mullion
Meadows, Helston TR12 7HB
T: (01326) 240315
F: (01326) 241090
E: martin@mullioncottages.com
I: www.mullioncottages.com

Westward House & Mews ★★★
Contact: Mr Martin Raftery
Mullion Cottages, Mullion
Meadows, Helston TR12 7HB
T: (01326) 240315
F: (01326) 241090
E: martin@mullioncottages.com
I: www.mullioncottages.com

HELSTONE
Cornwall

Mayrose Farm ★★★-★★★★
Contact: Mrs Jane Maunder
Helstone, Camelford PL32 9RN
T: (01840) 213509
F: (01840) 213509
E: info@mayrosefarmcottages.co.uk
I: www.mayrosefarmcottages.co.uk

HENWOOD
Cornwall

Clouds Hill Cottage ★★★★★
Contact: Mr Stephen Bennett
64 Park Drive, London W3 8NA
T: (020) 89932628
F: 0870 9 223563
E: stephen@cloudshillcottage.co.uk
I: www.cloudshillcottage.co.uk

Henwood Barns ★★
Contact: Mrs C Crossey
Henwood Barns, Liskeard
PL14 5BP
T: (01579) 363576
F: (01579) 363576
E: henwoodbarns@aol.com

HESSENFORD
Cornwall

2 West End Cottages ★★★★
Contact:
Valley Villas, Sales Office, City
Business Park, Office 38
Somerset Park, Plymouth
PL3 4BB
T: (01752) 605605
E: sales@valleyvillas.co.uk
I: www.valleyvillas.co.uk

HEYWOOD
Wiltshire

Heywood Holiday Cottages and The Wilderness ★★★★★
Contact: Mr John Boyce
7A Huntingdon Street,
Bradford-on-Avon BA15 1RF
T: (01225) 868393
F: (01225) 868393
E: enquiries@ashecottage-holidaylets.co.uk
I: www.ashecottage-holidaylets.co.uk

Pine Lodge ★
Contact: Mrs Mary Prince
Lea Cottage, 12 Church Road,
Westbury BA13 4LP
T: (01373) 822949
E: Pinelodgex@aol.com

HIGH BICKINGTON
Devon

Barn Owl Cottage ★★★★
Contact:
Marsden's Cottage Holidays, 2
The Square, Braunton EX33 2JB
T: (01271) 813777
F: (01271) 813664
E: holidays@marsdens.co.uk
I: www.marsdens.co.uk

The Corn Mill & Lee Meadow ★★★★★
Contact: Mrs Glenda Tucker
The Corn Mill & Lee Meadow,
Lee Barton, Umberleigh
EX37 9BX
T: (01769) 560796
F: (01769) 560796
I: www.Lee-Barton.co.uk

Millbrook ★★★★
Contact:
Marsdens Cottage Holidays, 2
The Square, Braunton EX33 2JB
T: (01271) 813777
F: (01271) 813664
E: holidays@marsdens.co.uk

HIGHAMPTON
Devon

No 10 Lakeview Rise ★★★★
Contact: Mr Peter & Mrs
Margery Mathews
Kimberley, Bridge Street, Great
Kimble, Aylesbury HP17 9TN
T: (01844) 347204
E: margejulepete@aol.com
I: www.lakeviewrise.co.uk

Look out for establishments participating in the National Accessible Scheme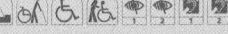

SOUTH WEST ENGLAND

Orchard House ★★★★★
Contact: Mrs Sames
28 Creslow Way, Aylesbury
HP17 8YW
T: (01296) 747425
E: j.l.pearce@tesco.net
I: www.lakeviewrise.co.uk

HIGHBRIDGE
Somerset

The Cottage ★★★★
Contact: Mrs Sarah Alderton
Grenacre Place, Bristol Road,
Edithmead, Highbridge TA9 4HA
T: (01278) 785227
F: (01278) 785227
E: sm.alderton@btopenworld.com
I: www.greenacreplace.com

HIGHLEADON
Gloucestershire

Highleadon Holiday Cottages
Rating Applied For
Contact: Mr Jonathan & Mrs Janet Corbett
Highleadon Holiday Cottages, New House Farm, Newent GL18 1HQ
T: (01452) 790209
F: (01452) 790209

HILPERTON
Wiltshire

Ashton Lodge Cottage ★★★
Contact: Mrs Daphne Richards
Ashton Lodge Cottage, Ashton Lodge, Ashton Road, Trowbridge BA14 7QY
T: (01225) 751420
E: daphne.richards@blueyonder.co.uk

HILTON
Dorset

Crown Farm ★★★
Contact: Mrs Pamela Crocker
Crown Farm, Duck Street, Blandford Forum DT11 0DQ
T: (01258) 880259

HINTON CHARTERHOUSE
Bath and North East Somerset

Church Cottage ★★★★
Contact: Mrs Barbara Crisp
47 Wolsey Road, East Molesey KT8 9EW
T: (020) 89419810

HINTON ST GEORGE
Somerset

Summer Hill Cottage ★★★★
Contact: Mr Leslie & Mrs Joan Farris
Summer Hill Cottage, Niddons House, Green Street, Hinton St George TA17 8SQ
T: (01460) 74475
E: lesfarris@cix.co.uk
I: summerhillcottage.co.uk

HOLBETON
Devon

Carswell Cottages ★★★
Contact: Mrs Zoe Sayers
Carswell Cottages, Carswell, Plymouth PL8 1HH
T: (01752) 830020
F: (01752) 830565
E: peggy@carswellfarm.co.uk
I: www.carswellcottages.com

HOLCOMBE
Devon

Manor Farm ★★★
Contact: Mr H & Mrs J Clemens
Manor Farm, Holcombe Village, Dawlish EX7 0JT
T: (01626) 863020
F: (01626) 863020
E: humphreyclem@aol.com

HOLCOMBE ROGUS
Devon

Whipcott Heights ★★★★
Contact: Mrs Gallagher
Whipcott Heights, Wellington TA21 0NA
T: (01823) 672339
F: (01823) 672339
E: bookings@oldlimekiln.freeserve.co.uk

HOLSWORTHY
Devon

Beech House ★★★★
Contact: Mrs Heard
Thorne Park, Holsworthy EX22 7BL
T: (01409) 253339
F: (01409) 253339

Colesmill ★★★
Contact:
Farm & Cottage Holidays, Victoria House, 23 Fore Street, Bideford EX39 1AW
T: (01237) 479146
F: (01237) 421512
E: bookings@farmcott.co.uk
I: www.farmcott.co.uk

Higher Sellick Farm Cottages ★★★★
Contact: Ms Denise Grafton
Higher Sellick Farm Cottages, Holsworthy EX22 6PS
T: (01409) 271456
F: (01409) 271144
E: denisegrafton@devonholidays.org
I: www.devonholidays.org

Leworthy Cottage ★★★
Contact: Mrs Patricia Jennings
Leworthy Cottage, Holsworthy EX22 6SJ
T: (01409) 259469

Thorne Manor Holiday Cottages ★★★-★★★★★
Contact: Mr Julian & Mrs Angela Plank
Thorne Manor, Holsworthy EX22 7JD
T: (01409) 253342
E: thornemanor@ex227jd.freeserve.co.uk
I: thorneover.co.uk

HOLWORTH
Dorset

Aura Holworth ★★★
Contact: Mr Zachary Stuart-Brown
Dream Cottages, 5 Hope Square, Weymouth DT4 8TR
T: (01305) 789000
F: (01305) 761346
E: admin@dream-cottages.co.uk
I: www.dream-cottages.co.uk

2 North Holworth Cottages ★★★
Contact: Mrs Celia Thorne
North Holworth Cottages, Dorchester DT2 8NH
T: (01305) 852922
F: (01305) 852282

HOLYWELL
Dorset

Pippins Cottage ★★★
Contact: Mr Zachary Stuart-Brown
Dream Cottages, 5 Hope Square, Weymouth DT4 8TR
T: (01305) 789000
E: admin@dream-cottages.co.uk
I: www.dream-cottages.co.uk

HOLYWELL BAY
Cornwall

Kelseys And Sailors Cove Bungalows
Rating Applied For
Contact: Mrs Joy Benney
Sandy Close, Newquay TR8 5PT
T: (01637) 830531

Ocean Sands ★★★-★★★★★
Contact: Mrs Penna
Ocean Sands, Newquay TR8 5PQ
T: (01637) 830447
F: (01637) 830447
E: www.sheilapenna@lineone.net

Pennasville Holidays
Rating Applied For
Contact: Mrs Joanne Penna
Pennasville Holidays, Newquay TR8 5PP
T: (01637) 830423
E: enquiries@pennasville.co.uk
I: www.pennasville.co.uk

The Studio ★★★
Contact:
Cornish Horizons, The Cottage, 19 New Street, Padstow PL28 8EA
T: (01841) 533331
F: (01841) 533933
E: cottages@cornishhorizons.co.uk
I: www.cornishhorizons.co.uk

Trevornick Cottages ★★★★
Contact: Mrs Lynne Lord
Trevornick Cottages, Trevornick, Newquay TR8 5PW
T: (01637) 830531
F: (01637) 831000
E: bookings@trevonick.co.uk
I: www.trevornickcottages.co.uk

HONITON
Devon

Abbots Cottage ★★★
Contact: Mr Douglas Acreman
Abbots Cottage, 13 Dark Lane, Waltham Cross EN7 5ED
T: (01992) 622685
F: (01992) 622685

Devon Cottage Holidays ★★★★-★★★★★
Contact: Mr Paul & Mrs Julia Hardy
Devon Cottage Holidays, Treaslake Cottages, Honiton EX14 3EP
T: (01404) 850292
F: (01404) 850292
E: info@devoncottage.com
I: www.devoncottage.com

The Haybarton ★★★★★
Contact: Mrs Wells
Bidwell Farm, Honiton EX14 9PP
T: (01404) 861122
F: 0870 055496
E: pat@bidwellfarm.co.uk
I: www.bidwellfarm.co.uk

March Cottage ★★★★
Contact: Ms Louise Hayman
Milkbere Cottage Holidays Ltd, 3 Fore Street, Seaton EX12 2LE
T: (01297) 20729
F: (01297) 24831
E: info@milkberehols.com
I: www.milkberehols.com

Pippins
Rating Applied For
Contact:
Jean Bartlett Cottage Holidays, The Old Dairy, fore Street, Seaton EX12 3JB
T: (01297) 23221
E: holidays@jeanbartlett.com
I: www.jeanbartlett.com

Red Doors Farm ★★★★★
Contact: Mr Chris Shrubb
Red Doors Farm, Beacon, Honiton EX14 4TX
T: (01404) 890067
F: (01404) 890067
E: info@reddoors.co.uk
I: www.reddoors.co.uk

Sutton Barton ★★★★★
Contact: Mrs Teresa Cooke
Sutton Barton, Widworthy, Honiton EX14 9SH
T: (01404) 831382
F: (01404) 831669
E: andycooke@suttonbartonfarm.co.uk
I: www.suttonbartonfarm.co.uk

HOOKE
Dorset

Greenlands Bungalow ★★
Contact: Mr Zachary Stuart-Brown
Dream Cottages, 5 Hope Square, Weymouth DT4 8TR
T: (01305) 789000
F: (01305) 761346
E: admin@dream-cottages.co.uk
I: www.dream-cottages.co.uk

HOPE COVE
Devon

Blue Bay Apartments ★★★-★★★★★
Contact: Mrs Moon
Little Orchard, Kellaton, Kingsbridge TQ7 2ES
T: (01548) 511400
F: (01548) 511400
E: bbayapts@aol.co.uk

Establishments printed in blue have a detailed entry in this guide

SOUTH WEST ENGLAND

Bolberry Farm Cottages ★★★★★
Contact: Mrs Hazel Hassall
Bolberry Farm Cottages,
Bolberry, Malborough,
Kingsbridge TQ7 3DY
T: (01548) 561384
E: info@bolberryfarmcottages.co.uk
I: www.bolberryfarmcottages.co.uk

Sanderlings ★★★
Contact: Mrs Diana Middleton
Reading Road, Woodley,
Reading RG5 3DB
T: (0118) 969 0958
E: diana_middleton@yahoo.com

Seascape ★★★
Contact: Mrs Hazel Kolb
57 The Whiteway, Cirencester
GL7 2HQ
T: (01285) 654781
F: (01285) 654781
E: kolb@btinternet.com
I: www.englishholidayhouses.co.uk

Thornlea Mews Holiday Cottages ★★★
Contact: Mr John & Mrs Ann Wilton
Thornlea Mews Holiday
Cottages, Hope Cove, Salcombe
TQ7 3HB
T: (01548) 561319
F: (01548) 561319
E: thornleamews@ukonline.co.uk
I: www.thornleamews-holidaycottages.co.uk

HORSINGTON
Somerset

Lois Country Cottages ★★★★
Contact: Mr Paul & Mrs Penny Constant
Lois Country Cottages, Lois
Farm, Templecombe BA8 0EW
T: (01963) 370496
F: (01963) 370496
E: info@loisfarm.com
I: www.loisfarm.com

HORTON
South Gloucestershire

Bridle Path Cottage ★★★
Contact: Mr Clive Sykes
Sykes Cottages, York House,
York Street, Chester CH1 3LR
T: (01244) 345700
F: (01244) 321442
E: info@sykescottages.co.uk
I: www.sykescottages.co.uk

HUISH CHAMPFLOWER
Somerset

The Cottage ★★★
Contact: Mrs Mary Reynolds
The Cottage, Manor Farmhouse,
Taunton TA4 2EY
T: (01984) 624915
F: (01984) 624915
E: reynoldsmary@aol.com

HUNTLEY
Gloucestershire

The Olde Brew House ★★★★
Contact: Mr Maurice Estop
The Olde Brew House, The
Farmers Arms, Ledbury Road,
Lower Apperly, Gloucester
GL19 3DR
T: (01452) 780307

The Vineary ★★★
Contact: Mrs Ann Snow
The Vineary, Vinetree Cottage,
Solomons Tump, Gloucester
GL19 3EB
T: (01452) 830006

HUNTSHAW
Devon

Bowood Barn
Rating Applied For
Contact:
Marsdens Cottage Holidays, 2
The Square, Braunton EX33 2JB
T: (01271) 813777
F: (01271) 813664
E: holidays@marsdens.co.uk

Forge Cottage ★★★★★
Contact:
Farm & Cottage Holidays,
Victoria House, 33 Fore Street,
Bideford EX39 1AW
T: (01237) 479146
F: (01237) 421512
E: bookings@farmcott.co.uk

HURN
Dorset

The Old Farmhouse ★★★
Contact: Mrs Jennifer Burford
The Old Farmhouse, Pitt House
Farm, Pitt House Lane,
Christchurch BH23 6AU
T: (01202) 479483

IBBERTON
Dorset

May Cottage ★★★
Contact: Mr Stuart-Brown
Dream Cottages, 41 Maiden
Street, Weymouth DT4 8TR
T: (01305) 789000

IDLESS
Cornwall

The Cottage
Rating Applied For
Contact: Mrs Patricia Dronfield
Cookbury Court, Holsworthy
EX22 7YG
T: (01409) 281869
F: (01409) 281869

ILFRACOMBE
Devon

The Admirals House ★★★★
Contact: Miss Marshall
Admirals House, Quayfield Road,
Ilfracombe EX34 9EN
T: (01271) 864666
E: enquiries@theadmiralshouse.co.uk
I: www.theadmiralshouse.co.uk

Bath Place
Rating Applied For
Contact:
Marsdens Cottage Holidays, 2
The Square, Braunton EX33 2JB
T: (01271) 813777
F: (01271) 813664
E: holidays@marsdens.co.uk
I: www.marsdens.co.uk

Benricks ★★★
Contact:
Marsden's Cottage Holidays, 2
The Square, Braunton EX33 2JB
T: (01271) 813777
F: (01271) 813664
E: holidays@marsdens.co.uk
I: www.marsdens.co.uk

Brookdale Lodge ★★★
Contact:
Marsden's Cottage Holidays, 2
The Square, Braunton EX33 2JB
T: (01271) 813777
F: (01271) 813664
E: holidays@marsdens.co.uk
I: www.marsdens.co.uk

Cheyne Flat ★★★
Contact:
Marsden's Cottage Holidays, 2
The Square, Braunton EX33 2JB
T: (01271) 813777
F: (01271) 813664
E: holidays@marsdens.co.uk
I: www.marsdens.co.uk

Cornmill Cottage ★★★★
Contact:
Marsden's Cottage Holidays, 2
The Square, Braunton EX33 2JB
T: (01271) 813777
F: (01271) 813664
E: holidays@marsdens.co.uk
I: www.marsdens.co.uk

Darnley Holiday Cottages ★★★
Contact: Mrs Susan Dale
Darnley Holiday Cottages, 3
Belmont Road, Ilfracombe
EX34 8DR
T: (01271) 863955
F: (01271) 864076
E: darnleyhotel@yahoo.co.uk
I: darnleyhotel.co.uk

Farthings Nest ★★★
Contact:
Marsden's Cottage Holidays, 2
The Square, Braunton EX33 2JB
T: (01271) 813777
F: (01271) 813664
E: holidays@marsdens.co.uk
I: www.marsdens.co.uk

Gull Cottage ★★★★
Contact:
Marsden's Cottage Holidays, 2
The Square, Braunton EX33 2JB
T: (01271) 813777
F: (01271) 813664
E: holidays@marsdens.co.uk
I: www.marsdens.co.uk

Horne Cottage ★★★
Contact:
Marsden's Cottage Holidays, 2
The Square, Braunton EX33 2JB
T: (01271) 813777
F: (01271) 813664
E: holidays@marsdens.co.uk
I: www.marsdens.co.uk

The Knapps ★★★★
Contact:
Marsdens Cottage Holidays, 2
The Square, Braunton EX33 2JB
T: (01271) 813777
F: (01271) 813664
E: holidays@marsdens.co.uk
I: www.marsdens.co.uk

The Lodge & Stables ★★★
Contact:
Marsden's Cottage Holidays, 2
The Square, Braunton EX33 2JB
T: (01271) 813777
F: (01271) 813664
E: holidays@marsdens.co.uk
I: www.marsdens.co.uk

Middle Lee Farm ★★★-★★★★★
Contact: Mr Robin & Mrs Jenny Downer
Middle Lee Farm, Ilfracombe
EX34 9SD
T: (01271) 882256
F: (01271) 882256
E: info@middleleefarm.co.uk
I: www.middleleefarm.co.uk

The Mill House ★★★★
Contact:
Marsden's Cottage Holidays, 2
The Square, Braunton EX33 2JB
T: (01271) 813777
F: (01271) 813664
E: holidays@marsdens.co.uk
I: www.marsdens.co.uk

Mimosa Cottage ★★★
Contact:
Marsden's Cottage Holidays, 2
The Square, Braunton EX33 2JB
T: (01271) 813777
F: (01271) 813664
E: holidays@marsdens.co.uk
I: www.marsdens.co.uk

Mostyn ★★★
Contact:
Marsden's Cottage Holidays, 2
The Square, Braunton EX33 2JB
T: (01271) 813777
F: (01271) 813664
E: holidays@marsdens.co.uk
I: www.marsdens.co.uk

Norwood Holiday Flats ★★★
Contact: Mrs Betty Bulled
Norwood Holiday Flats,
Highfield Road, Ilfracombe
EX34 9LH
T: (01271) 862370

Rockcliffe ★★★★
Contact:
Marsden's Cottage Holidays, 2
The Square, Braunton EX33 2JB
T: (01271) 813777
F: (01271) 813664
E: holidays@marsdens.co.uk
I: www.marsdens.co.uk

The Round House ★★★★
Contact: Mr & Mrs P Cornwell
Marsden's Cottage Holidays, 2
The Square, Braunton EX33 2JB
T: (01271) 813777
I: www.marsdens.co.uk

Look out for establishments participating in the National Accessible Scheme

SOUTH WEST ENGLAND

Somerset Villa ★★★★
Contact:
Marsdens Cottage Holidays, 2 The Square, Braunton EX33 2JB
T: (01271) 813777
F: (01271) 813664
E: holidays@marsdens.co.uk
I: www.marsdens.co.uk

Widmouth Farm Cottages ★★★
Contact: Mrs Elizabeth Sansom
Widmouth Farm Cottages, Watermouth, Ilfracombe EX34 9QR
T: (01271) 863743
F: (01271) 866479
E: holidays@widmouthfarmcottages.co.uk
I: www.widmouthfarmcottages.co.uk

Woodclose Cottage ★★★
Contact:
Toad Hall Cottages, Elliot House, Church Street, Kingsbridge TQ7 1BY
T: (01548) 853089
F: (01548) 853089
E: thc@toadhallcottages.com
I: www.toadhallcottages.com

ILMINSTER
Somerset

Myrtle House ★★★★
Contact: Mr Gordon & Mrs Marion Denman
16 Challis Green, Cambridge CB2 5RJ
T: (01223) 871294
E: denman@appleorchard.freeserve.co.uk
I: www.appleorchard.freeserve.co.uk

INSTOW
Devon

Bath House ★★★
Contact:
Marsden's Cottage Holidays, 2 The Square, Braunton EX33 2JB
T: (01271) 813777
F: (01271) 813664
E: holidays@marsdens.co.uk

Chandlers Court ★★★
Contact:
Farm & Cottage Holidays, Victoria House, 12 Fore Street, Bideford EX39 1AW
T: (01237) 479146
F: (01237) 421512
E: bookings@farmcott.co.uk
I: www.farmcott.co.uk

Driftwood ★★★★
Contact:
Marsden's Cottage Holidays, 2 The Square, Braunton EX33 2JB
T: (01271) 813777
F: (01271) 813664
E: holidays@marsdens.co.uk
I: www.marsdens.co.uk

Garden House ★★★★
Contact:
Marsden's Cottage Holidays, 2 The Square, Braunton EX33 2JB
T: (01271) 813777
F: (01271) 813664
E: holidays@marsdens.co.uk
I: www.marsdens.co.uk

Inglenook Cottage ★★★★
Contact:
Marsden's Cottage Holidays, 2 The Square, Braunton EX33 2JB
T: (01271) 813777
F: (01271) 813664
E: holidays@marsdens.co.uk
I: www.marsdens.co.uk

Oak Tree Cottage ★★★★
Contact: Mr Peter & Mrs Janet Cornwell
Marsden's Cottage Holidays, 2 The Square, Braunton EX33 2JB
T: (01271) 813777
F: (01271) 813664
E: holidays@marsdens.co.uk
I: www.marsdens.co.uk

The Old Dairy ★★★★
Contact:
Marsden's Cottage Holidays, 2 The Square, Braunton EX33 2JB
T: (01271) 813777
F: (01271) 813664
E: holidays@marsdens.co.uk
I: www.marsdens.co.uk

IPPLEPEN
Devon

Bulleigh Park ★★★
Contact: Mrs Angela Dallyn
Bulleigh Park, Bulleigh Park Farm, Newton Abbot TQ12 5UA
T: (01803) 872254
F: (01803) 872254
E: bulleigh@lineone.net

Dainton Lodge ★★★
Contact: Mr Ian Butterworth
Holiday Homes & Cottages South West, 365A Torquay Road, Paignton TQ3 2BT
T: (01803) 663650
F: (01803) 664037
E: holcotts@aol.com
I: www.swcottages.co.uk

Roselands Holiday Chalets ★★-★★★★
Contact: Mr Simon Whale
Roselands Holiday Chalets, Totnes Road, Newton Abbot TQ12 5TD
T: (01803) 812701
E: enquiries@roselands.net
I: www.roselands.net

ISLE BREWERS
Somerset

Old School House ★★★
Contact: Mrs Lynda Coles
Stoke Hill Barn, Stoke St Mary, Taunton TA3 5BT
T: (01823) 443759
F: (01823) 443759
E: ajcoles@supanet.com

ISLES OF SCILLY
Isles of Scilly

3 & 4 Well Cross ★★
Contact: Mr Perry
Treboeth Guest House, St Mary's TR21 0HX
T: (01720) 422548

An Oberva ★★
Contact: Mrs Berryman
Chy An Mor, 4 Fore Street, Helston TR13 9HQ
T: (01326) 574113

Harbour View ★★★-★★★★★
Contact: Mr Chris Hopkins
Harbour View, Bryher TR23 0PR
T: (01720) 422222
I: www.bryher-ios.co.uk/hv

Holy Vale Holiday Houses ★★★
Contact: Mr & Mrs Banfield
Holy Vale Holiday Houses, Holy Vale Farmhouse, St Mary's TR21 0NT
T: (01720) 422429
F: (01720) 422429
E: johnkay@holyvale.freeserve.co.uk

Leumeah House ★★
Contact:
Island Properties, Porthmellon, St Mary's
T: (01720) 422082
F: (01720) 422211
E: enquiries@islesofscillyholidays.com
I: www.islesofscillyholidays.com

Moonrakers Holiday Flats ★★★
Contact: Mr & Mrs R.J Gregory
Moonrakers Holiday Flats, St Mary's TR21 0JF
T: (01720) 422717
I: www.moonrakersholidayflats.fsnet.co.uk

Mount Flagon ★★★★
Contact: Mr & Mrs Crawford
Mount Flagon, Porthloo, St Mary's TR21 0NE
T: (01720) 422598
F: (01720) 422529

Pednbrose ★★★
Contact: Mrs Tugwell
Minalto, Macfarlands Down, St Mary's TR21 0NS
T: (01752) 423605

Puffin Burrow ★★★★
Contact: Mrs Carol Sargeant
Willow Tree House, Swindon SN6 8NG
T: (01793) 710062
F: (01793) 710387

Seaways Flower Farm ★★★-★★★★★
Contact: Mrs Juliet May
Seaways Flower Farm, St Mary's TR21 0NF
T: (01720) 422845
F: (01720) 423224

IVYBRIDGE
Devon

Beacon Cottage ★★★★
Contact: Mrs Edwards
Moorhedge Farm, David's Lane, Ivybridge PL21 0DP
T: (01752) 894820
F: (01752) 894820

The Forge ★★★★
Contact:
Toad Hall Cottages, Elliot House, Church Street, Kingsbridge TQ7 1BY
T: (01548) 853089
I: www.toadhallcottages.com

Ivybridge ★★★
Contact: Mr John & Mrs Christine Crew
40 Sheridan Way, Bristol BS30 9UE
T: (01179) 328968

KELSTON
Bath and North East Somerset

Coombe Barn Holidays ★★-★★★
Contact: Mr George Cullimore
Coombe Barn Holidays, Coombe Barn, Bath BA1 9AJ
T: (01225) 448757

KENNFORD
Devon

Tapstone Barn ★★★★
Contact:
Holiday Homes and Cottages SW, 365A Torquay Road, Paignton TQ3 2BT
T: (01803) 663650
F: (01803) 664037
E: holcotts@aol.com
I: www.swcottages.co.uk

KENTISBURY
Devon

Northcote Manor Farm Holiday Cottages ★★★★
Contact: Mrs Peter & Pat Bunch
Northcote Manor Farm Holiday Cottages, Barnstaple EX31 4NB
T: (01271) 882376
E: info@northcotemanorfarm.co.uk
I: www.northcotemanorfarm.co.uk

South Patchole Farm Cottage ★★★★
Contact: Mrs Heywood
South Patchole Farm Cottage, Barnstaple

KENTISBURY FORD
Devon

Friars Cottages
Rating Applied For
Contact: Mr Gary Donovan
Friars Cottages, 19 Lindsey Close, Brentwood CM14 4PN
T: (01277) 233776
E: relax@friarscottages.co.uk
I: friarscottages.co.uk

Old Stable Cottage ★★★★
Contact: Mrs Christine Hewitt
Old Stable Cottage, South Sandpark, Barnstaple EX31 4NG
T: (01271) 882305
E: christine@kentisburyford.fsnet.co.uk
I: www.oldstablecottage.ukgo.com

KILKHAMPTON
Cornwall

Carefree Holidays ★★
Contact: Mr Alan & Mrs Geraldine Glover
180 Gloucester Road, Bristol BS34 5BD
T: (0117) 9693699
F: (0117) 9760594
E: carefreeholsglover1@activemail.co.uk

East Thorne Cottages ★★★
Contact: Mrs Margaret Stears
East Thorne Cottages, Bude EX23 9RY
T: (01288) 321618

Establishments printed in blue have a detailed entry in this guide

SOUTH WEST ENGLAND

South Forda Holidays
★★★-★★★★★
Contact: Mr Rose
South Forda Holidays, South Forda, Bude EX23 9RZ
T: (01288) 321524
E: southforda@hotmail.com
I: www.southfordaholidays.co.uk

Spanish Villas 7&8 ★★
Contact: Mr & Mrs Sumner
4 Park Court, Bude EX23 9PA
T: (01288) 321832

KILLIOW
Cornwall

Nansavallon Farm House ★★★★
Contact:
Special Places, Poachers Reach, Truro TR3 6SQ
T: (01872) 864400
F: (01872) 864400
E: office@specialplaces.co.uk
I: www.specialplacescornwall.co.uk

KILMERSDON
Somerset

The Creamery ★★★★
Contact: Mr & Mrs Knatchbull & Sons
The Creamery, Batch Farm, Kilmersdon, Radstock BA3 5SP
T: (01373) 812337
F: (01373) 813781

KILMINGTON
Devon

Little Thatch - W4440 ★★★
Contact:
Lyme Bay Holidays, Bos House, 44 Church Street, Lyme Regis DT7 3DA
T: (01297) 443363
F: (01297) 445576
E: email@lymebayholidays.co.uk
I: www.lymebayholidays.co.uk

Stable Loft ★★
Contact: Mr Nicholas Pash
Hideaways, Chapel House, Luke Street, Berwick St John, Shaftesbury SP7 0HQ
T: (01747) 828170
F: (01747) 829090
E: enq@hideaways.co.uk
I: www.hideaways.co.uk

KING'S NYMPTON
Devon

The Old Rectory
Rating Applied For
Contact: Mrs Karen Robinson
The Old Rectory, Kings Nympton, Umberleigh EX37 9SS
T: (01769) 580456
F: (01769) 581519
E: info@oldrectorycottages.co.uk
I: www.theoldrectorycottages.co.uk

Venn Farm Cottages ★★★
Contact: Mrs Pauline Cain
Ducklett LTD, Kings Nympton, Umberleigh EX37 9JR
T: (01769) 572448
E: vennfarmcottages@msn.com
I: www.vennfarm.com

KINGSBRIDGE
Devon

Dairymans Corner and Shepherds Rest ★★★
Contact: Mrs Anne Rossiter
Burton Farmhouse & Garden Room Restaurant, Galmpton, Kingsbridge TQ7 3EY
T: (01548) 561210
F: (01548) 562257
I: www.burtonfarm.co.uk

The Laurels, Coach House & Coachmans Lodge
★★★-★★★★★
Contact: Mrs Barbara Baker
The Laurels, Coach House & Coachmans Lodge, Chivelstone, Kingsbridge TQ7 2NB
T: (01548) 511272
F: (01548) 511421
E: barbara@sthallingtonbnb.demon.co.uk
I: www.sthallingtonbnb.demon.co.uk

Malston Mill Farm Holiday Cottages ★★★★
Contact: Mr Tony & Mrs Linda Gresham
Malston Mill Farm Holiday Cottages, Malston Mill Farm, Kingsbridge TQ7 2DR
T: (01548) 852518
F: (01548) 854084
E: gresham@malstonmill.fsnet.co.uk
I: www.malstonmill.co.uk

Reads Farm ★★★
Contact: Mrs Pethybridge
Reads Farm, Loddiswell, Kingsbridge TQ7 4RT
T: (01548) 550317
F: (01548) 550317

Sloop Cottages ★★★★
Contact: Mr Girling
West Buckland Cottage, Kingsbridge TQ7 3AQ
T: (01548) 560489
F: (01548) 561940

Trouts Holiday Apartments
★★★-★★★★★
Contact: Mrs Jill Norman
Prospect Cottage Trouts Holiday Apartments, South Hallsands, Kingsbridge TQ7 2EY
T: (01548) 511296
F: (01548) 511296
E: trouts.holiday@virgin.net
I: www.selfcateringdevon.com

West Charleton Grange ★★★★★
Contact: Mrs Amanda Lubrani
West Charleton Grange, Kingsbridge TQ7 2AD
T: (01548) 531779
F: (01548) 531100
E: admin@westcharltongrange.com
I: www.westcharletongrange.com

KINGSDON
Somerset

The Lodge ★★★★
Contact: Mrs Jo Furneaux
The Lodge, Somerton TA11 7LE
T: (01935) 841194

KINGSHEANTON
Devon

The Coach House ★★★★
Contact:
Marsdens Cottage Holidays, 2 The Square, Braunton EX33 2JB
T: (01271) 813777
F: (01271) 813664
E: holidays@marsdens.co.uk
I: www.marsdens.co.uk

The Welkin ★★★★
Contact:
Marsden's Cottage Holidays, 2 The Square, Braunton EX33 2JB
T: (01271) 813777
F: (01271) 813664
E: holidays@marsdens.co.uk
I: www.marsdens.co.uk

KINGSTEIGNTON
Devon

Plumb Corner ★★★★
Contact:
Holiday Homes & Cottages South West, 365A Torquay Road, Paignton TQ3 2BT
T: (01803) 663650
T: (01803) 664037
E: holcotts@aol.com
I: www.swcottages.co.uk

KINGSTON DEVERILL
Wiltshire

Downsview Cottage ★★★
Contact: Ms Phyllis Linstone
Downsview Cottage, Warminster BA12 7HD
T: (01985) 844459
F: (01985) 844459

KINGSTON SEYMOUR
North Somerset

Bullock Farm & Fishing Lakes ★★★
Contact: Mr Philip & Mrs Jude Simmons
Bullock Farm & Fishing Lakes, Back Lane, Clevedon BS21 6XA
T: (01934) 835020
F: (01934) 835927
E: bullockfarm@kingstonseymour1.freeserve.co.uk
I: www.bullockfarm.co.uk

KNOWSTONE
Devon

West Cross Side Farm ★★★★
Contact: Mr Martin Begbie
West Cross Side Farm, South Molton EX36 4RT
T: (01398) 341288
F: (01398) 341288
E: enquiries@devoncountryholidays.com
I: www.devoncountryholidays.com

LACOCK
Wiltshire

Cyder House and Cheese House ★★★★
Contact: Mr Philip & Mrs Susan King
Cyder House and Cheese House, Wick Farm, Wick Lane, Lacock, Chippenham SN15 2LU
T: (01249) 730244
F: (01249) 730072
E: kingsilverlands2@btinternet.com
I: www.cheeseandcyderhouses.co.uk

LADOCK
Cornwall

Higher Hewas ★★★★
Contact: Mrs Pamela Blake
Lower Hewas, Truro TR2 4QH
T: (01726) 882318

LAMORNA
Cornwall

Camelot
Rating Applied For
Contact: Mrs Trudi Thomas
Trevear Farm, Penzance TR19 7BH
T: (01736) 871205
F: (01736) 871205
I: www.trevearfarm.co.uk

Lamorna Vean ★★★★
Contact: Mr M & Mrs S Searle
30 Church Street, York YO19 5PW
T: (01904) 481951
F: (01904) 481951
E: lamornavean@yorktrain.demon.co.uk
I: www.yorktrain.co.uk/lamornavean

Round Chapel Barn ★★★
Contact: Mr Ian Butterworth
Holiday Homes & Cottages South West, 365A Torquay Road, Paignton TQ3 2BT
T: (01803) 663650
F: (01803) 664037
E: holcotts@aol.com
I: www.swcottages.co.uk

LAMORNA COVE
Cornwall

Bal Red ★★
Contact: Miss Sarah Daniel
Sarah's Cottage, Penzance TR19 6XJ
T: (01736) 731227

LANDRAKE
Cornwall

The Coach House ★★★★
Contact: Mrs Nicky Walker
The Coach House, Lantallack Farm, Saltash PL12 5AE
T: (01752) 851281
F: (01752) 851281
E: lanyallack@ukgateway.net
I: www.lantallack.co.uk

LANGLEY BURRELL
Wiltshire

Cedarwood ★★★★
Contact: Mrs Helen Miflin
Grove Farm, Sutton Lane, Langley Burrell, Chippenham SN15 4LW
T: (01249) 721500
F: (01249) 720413
E: miflin@btinternet.com

648 Look out for establishments participating in the National Accessible Scheme

SOUTH WEST ENGLAND

LANGLEY MARSH
Somerset

Vickery View Cottages ★★★
Contact:
Farm & Cottage Holidays,
Victoria House, 12 Fore Street,
Bideford EX39 1AW
T: (01237) 479146
F: (01237) 421512

LANGPORT
Somerset

Hay Loft & Stables ★★★
Contact: Mrs Pauline Pickard
Hay Loft & Stables, Dairy House
Farm, Langport TA10 0DJ
T: (01458) 253113

Laurel Wharf ★★★★
Contact: Mr John Neale
Laurel Wharf, c/o Laurel Cottage,
Westport, Langport TA10 0BN
T: (01460) 281713
E: laurelwharf@hotmail.com
I: www.laurelwharf.co.uk

Muchelney Ham Farm
★★★-★★★★
Contact: Mr Jim Woodborne
Muchelney Ham Farm, Langport
TA10 0DJ
T: (01458) 250737

LANGRIDGE
Bath and North East Somerset

Langridge Studio ★★★★
Contact: Mr Brian Shuttleworth
Langridge House, Bath BA1 9BX
T: (01225) 338874
F: (01225) 338874
E: info@langridge-studio.co.uk
I: www.langridge-studio.co.uk

LANGTON HERRING
Dorset

Hazel Copse & Orchard View ★★★
Contact: Mr Zachary Stuart-Brown
Dream Cottages, 5 Hope Square,
Weymouth DT4 8TR
T: (01305) 789000
E: admin@dream-cottages.co.uk
I: www.dream-cottages.co.uk

Higher Farm Cottage ★★★★★
Contact: Mr Peter Cropper
Zephen Properties Limited,
Somerton Randle Farm,
Somerton TA11 7HW
T: (01458) 274767
F: (01458) 274901
E: peter@zephen.com
I: www.zephen.com

3 Lower Farm, Chelsea Cottage, The Brambles, The Sycamores, ★★★★
Contact: Mrs Mayo
Higher Farm, Weymouth DT3 4JE
T: (01305) 871347
F: (01305) 871347
E: jane@mayo.fsbusiness.co.uk

Saint Anthony's Cottage ★★★★★
Contact: Mr Peter Cropper
Zephen Properties Limited,
Somerton Randle Farm,
Somerton TA11 7HW
T: (01458) 274767
F: (01458) 274901
E: peter@zephen.com
I: www.zephen.com

LANGTON MATRAVERS
Dorset

Driftwood Cottage ★★★
Contact: Miss Leanne Hemingway
Dorset Cottage Holidays, 11
Tyneham Close, Wareham
BH20 7BE
T: (01929) 553443
F: (01929) 552714
E: enq@dhcottages.co.uk
I: dhcottages.
co.uk/driftwood%20cottage.htm

Flat 5 Garfield House ★★★
Contact: Susan Inge
Flat A, 147 Holland Road,
London W14 8AS
T: (020) 7602 4945
E: sueinge@hotmail.com
I: www.langton-matravers.co.uk

Forge Cottage ★★★
Contact: Ms Leanne Hemingway
Dorset Cottage Holidays, 11
Tyneham Close, Wareham
BH20 7BE
T: (01929) 553443
F: (01929) 552714
E: enquiries@dhcottages.co.uk
I: www.dhcottages.co.uk

Hyde View Cottage ★★★
Contact: Ms Leanne Hemingway
Dorset Cottage Holidays, 11
Tyneham Close, Wareham
BH20 7BE
T: (01929) 553443
F: (01929) 552714
E: enquiries@dhcottages.co.uk
I: www.dhcottages.
co.uk/hyde%20view%20cottage.
htm

Island View ★★★
Contact: Mr Zachary Stuart-Brown
Dream Cottage, 5 Hope Square,
Weymouth DT4 8TR
T: (01305) 789000
F: (01305) 761346
E: admin@dream-cottages.
co.uk
I: www.dream-cottages.co.uk

5 North Street ★★★
Contact: Mrs Ann Garratt
High Street, Brasted, Westerham
TN16 1JE
T: (01959) 565145

Roxeth Cottage ★★★
Contact: Ms Leanne Hemingway
Dorset Cottage Holidays, 11
Tyneham Close, Wareham
BH20 7BE
T: (01929) 553443
F: (01929) 552714
E: enquiries@dhcottages.co.uk

Westview House ★★★★
Contact:
Lodge Farm
T: (01788) 560193
F: (01788) 550603
E: alec@lodgefarm.com
I: www.westview.co.uk

LANHYDROCK
Cornwall

Little Cutmadoc Farm ★★★★★
Contact: Ms Helen Cobb
17 Waterside Tower, Imperial
Wharf, London SW6 2SW
T: (020) 73487532
E: helen@luxurybreaks.co.uk
I: www.luxurybreaks.co.uk

LANIVET
Cornwall

Vernons Retreat
Rating Applied For
Contact:
Vernons Retreat, 3 Honeys Hill,
Bodmin PL30 5HE
T: (01841) 533331
F: (01841) 533331
E: cottages@cornishhorizons.
co.uk

LANLIVERY
Cornwall

Higher Gready Farm ★★★★
Contact: Mrs Elizabeth Hemmings
Lower Tregantle, Bodmin
PL30 5DA
T: (01208) 872716
F: (01208) 872716
E: hemmings@farming.co.uk
I: www.farmcot.co.uk

LANNER
Cornwall

Little Shalom ★★★★
Contact:
Powell's Cottage Holidays, High
Street, Saundersfoot SA69 9EJ
T: (01834) 812791
F: (01834) 811731
E: info@powells.co.uk
I: www.powells.co.uk

LANREATH-BY-LOOE
Cornwall

The Old Rectory
Contact: Mr & Mrs Duncan
The Old Rectory, Looe PL13 2NU
T: (01503) 220247
F: (01503) 220108
E: info@oldrectory-lanreath.
co.uk
I: www.oldrectory-lanreath.
co.uk

LANSALLOS
Cornwall

West Kellow Farmhouse ★★★★
Contact: Mrs Evelyn Julian
West Kellow Farmhouse, Looe
PL13 2QL
T: (01503) 272089
F: (01503) 272089
E: westkellow@aol.com
I: www.westkellow.co.uk

LATCHLEY
Cornwall

The Apple Loft ★★★★
Contact: Mrs Margaret Blake
The Apple Loft, Old Solomons
Farm, Latchley, Gunnislake
PL18 9AX
T: (01822) 833242
F: (01822) 833242
E: info@oldsolomonsfarm.co.uk
I: www.oldsolomonsfarm.co.uk

LAUNCESTON
Cornwall

Bamham Farm Cottages ★★★★
Contact: Mrs Jackie Chapman
Bamham Farm Cottages, Higher
Bamham Farm, Launceston
PL15 9LD
T: (01566) 772141
F: (01566) 775266
E: jackie@bamhamfarm.co.uk
I: www.bamhamfarm.co.uk

Langdon Farm Holiday Cottages ★★★-★★★★
Contact: Mrs Rawlinson
Langdon Farm Holiday Cottages,
Langdon Farm, Boyton,
Launceston PL15 8NW
T: (01566) 785389
E: g.f.rawlinson@btinternet.com
I: www.langdonholidays.com

Platt Cottage ★★★★
Contact: Mrs Barbara Sleep
Platt Cottage, Trevadlock Farm,
Congdon's Shop, Launceston
PL15 7PW
T: (01566) 782239
F: (01566) 782239
E: trevadlockfarm@compuserve.
com
I: www.trevadlock.co.uk

Swallows ★★★
Contact: Mrs Kathryn Broad
Swallows, Lower Dutson Farm,
Dutson, Launceston PL15 9SP
T: (01566) 776456
F: (01566) 776456
E: francis.broad@farm-cottage.
co.uk
I: www.farm-cottage.co.uk

Ta Mill ★★★-★★★★
Contact: Mrs Helen Harvey
Ta Mill, St Clether, Launceston
PL15 8PS
T: (01840) 261797
F: (01840) 261381
E: helen@tamill.co.uk
I: www.tamill.co.uk

West Barton - Cider Annexe ★★★
Contact: Mr Brian & Mrs Fiona Perris
West Barton - Cider Annexe,
West Barton, North Petherwin,
Launceston PL15 8LR
T: (01566) 785710
E: enquiries@westbarton.co.uk
I: www.westbarton.co.uk

Establishments printed in blue have a detailed entry in this guide

SOUTH WEST ENGLAND

Wheatley Cottage and Barn ★★★★
Contact: Mrs Griffin
Wheatley Cottage and Barn,
Wheatley Farm, Launceston
PL15 8LY
T: (01566) 781232
F: (01566) 781232
E: valerie@wheatleyfrm.com
I: www.chycor.
co.uk/cottages/wheatley

LAVERSTOCK
Wiltshire

Church Cottage H090 ★★★★
Contact:
Hideaways, Chapel House, Luke Street, Berwick St John,
Shaftesbury SP7 0HQ
T: (01747) 828170
F: (01747) 829090
E: enq@hideaways.co.uk
I: www.hideaways.co.uk

LEE
Devon

Daymer Cottage
Rating Applied For
Contact:
Marsdens Cottage Holidays, 2
The Square, Braunton EX33 2JB
T: (01271) 813777
F: (01271) 813664
E: holidays@marsdens.co.uk

Eliot House ★★★-★★★★★
Contact:
Marsden's Cottage Holidays, 2
The Square, Braunton EX33 2JB
T: (01271) 813777
F: (01271) 813664
E: holidays@marsdens.co.uk
I: www.marsdens.co.uk

Grange Apartment ★★★★
Contact: Mr Peter & Mrs Janet
Cornwell
Marsden's Cottage Holidays, 2
The Square, Braunton EX33 2JB
T: (01271) 813777
F: (01271) 813664
E: holidays@marsdens.co.uk
I: www.marsdens.co.uk

Lincombe House ★★★
Contact: Mr Ian & Mrs Cynthia Stuart
Lincombe House, Lincombe,
Ilfracombe EX34 8LL
T: (01271) 864834
F: (01271) 864834
E: holidays@lincombehouse.co.uk
I: www.lincombehouse.co.uk

Lower Campscott Farm ★★★-★★★★★
Contact: Mrs Margaret Cowell
Lower Campscott Farm, Lee,
Ilfracombe EX34 8LS
T: (01271) 863479
F: (01271) 867639
E: holidays@lowercampscott.co.uk
I: www.lowercampscott.co.uk

Smugglers Cottage ★★★★
Contact:
Marsden's Cottage Holidays, 2
The Square, Braunton EX33 2JB
T: (01271) 813777
F: (01271) 813664
E: holidays@marsdens.co.uk
I: www.marsdens.co.uk

Vine Cottage ★★★★
Contact: Mr Peter & Mrs Janet
Cornwell
Marsden's Cottage Holidays, 2
The Square, Braunton EX33 2JB
T: (01271) 813777
F: (01271) 813664
E: holidays@marsdens.co.uk
I: www.marsdens.co.uk

LELANT
Cornwall

Trevalgan Holiday Barns
Rating Applied For
Contact: Mrs Jean Osborne
Trevalgan Holiday Barns, Beech Lea, Brush End, St Ives TR26 3EF
T: (01736) 756252
E: trevalganites@aol.com
I: www.trevalganites.co.uk

Trevethoe Farm Cottages ★★★
Contact: Mrs Rogers
Trevethoe Farm Cottages,
Trevethoe Farm, Trevethoe, St Ives TR26 3HG
T: (01736) 753279
F: (01736) 753279
E: holidaycottages@trevethoe.co.uk
I: www.trevethoe.co.uk

LERRYN
Cornwall

Puddleduck Cottage ★★★★
Contact:
Estuary Cottages, Estuary House, Fore Street, Fowey PL23 1AH
T: (01726) 832965
F: (01726) 832866
E: info@estuarycottages.co.uk
I: www.estuarycottages.co.uk

LEWDOWN
Devon

The Honey House ★★★★
Contact: Mr Richard Baker
The Honey House, Bidlake Mill,
Okehampton EX20 4ED
T: (01837) 861323
F: (01837) 861323
E: rrdb123@aol.com

LEZANT
Cornwall

East Penrest Barn ★★★★★
Contact: Mrs Rider
East Penrest Barn, East Penrest,
Launceston PL15 9NR
T: (01579) 370186
F: (01579) 370477
E: jorider@eastpenrest.freeserve.co.uk
I: www.eastpenrest.freeserve.co.uk

LIFTON
Devon

Frankaborough Farm Cottages
Rating Applied For
Contact: Mrs Linda Banbury
Frankaborough Farm Cottages,
Lifton PL16 0JS
T: (01409) 211308
E: banbury960@aol.com

LISKEARD
Cornwall

Beechleigh Cottage ★★★★
Contact: Mrs Stephanie Rowe
Tregondale Farm, Liskeard
PL14 3RG
T: (01579) 342407
F: (01579) 342407
E: tregondale@connectfree.co.uk
I: www.tregondalefarm.co.uk

Coach House Cottages ★★★★
Contact: Mr Jeremy & Mrs Jane Hall
Coach House Cottages,
Treworgey Manor, Liskeard
PL14 6RN
T: (01579) 347755
F: (01579) 347755
E: cotttages@treworgay.co.uk
I: www.treworgey.co.uk

Hopsland Holidays ★★★★
Contact: Mr Neil & Mrs Linda Hosken
Hopsland Holidays,
Commonmoor, Liskeard
PL14 6EJ
T: (01579) 344480
F: (01579) 344480
E: hopslandholidays@aol.com
I: www.hopslandholidays.co.uk

Ithaca ★★
Contact:
Valley Villas, Brook Cottage, Old Warleigh Lane, Plymouth
PL5 4ND
T: (01752) 774900
E: sales@valleyvillas.co.uk
I: www.valleyvillas.co.uk

Lodge Barton ★★★
Contact: Mrs Hodin
Lodge Barton, Lamellion,
Liskeard PL14 4JX
T: (01579) 344432
F: (01579) 344432
E: lodgebart@aol.com
I: www.selectideas.co.uk/lodgebarton

Lower Trengale Farm ★★★★
Contact: Mr Brian & Mrs Terri Shears
Lower Trengale Farm, Trengale,
Liskeard PL14 6HF
T: (01579) 321019
F: (01579) 321432
E: enquiries@trengale.co.uk
I: www.trengale.co.uk

Old Post Office ★★★
Contact:
Farm & Cottage Holidays,
Victoria House, 12 Fore Street,
Bideford EX39 1AW
T: (01237) 479146
F: (01237) 421512
E: bookings@farmcott.co.uk
I: www.farmcott.co.uk

LITTLE DRYBROOK
Gloucestershire

Middle Cottage
Rating Applied For
Contact: Miss Angela Flynn
Middle Cottage, Coleford
GL16 8LP
T: (01594) 562736

LITTLE PETHERICK
Cornwall

Driftwood ★★★★
Contact:
Cornish Horizons, The Cottage,
19 New Street, Padstow
PL28 8EA
T: (01841) 533331
F: (01841) 533933
E: cottages@cornishhorizons.co.uk

Petroc Lodge ★★★★
Contact:
Cornish Horizons, The Cottage,
19 New Street, Padstow
PL28 8EA
T: (01841) 533331
F: (01841) 533933
E: cottages@cornishhorizons.co.uk
I: www.cornishhorizons.co.uk

Pine Haven ★★★★
Contact:
Cornish Horizons, The Cottage,
19 New Street, Padstow
PL28 8EA
T: (01841) 533331
F: (01841) 533933
E: cottages@cornishhorizons.co.uk
I: www.cornishhorizons.co.uk

Quay House ★★★
Contact: Mrs Allison Hatcher
Quay House, Petherick Creek,
Wadebridge PL27 7QT
T: (01841) 540431
F: (01841) 540431
I: www.Quay-House-Holidays.co.uk

Swallow Court Cottages ★★★★
Contact: Mr Geoffrey French
Molesworth Manor, Wadebridge
PL27 7QT
T: (01841) 540292
E: molesworthmanor@aol.com
I: www.molesworthmanor.co.uk

Tregonna Farm Barn and Cottage ★★★★
Contact:
Cornish Horizons, The Cottage,
19 New Street, Padstow
PL28 8EA
T: (01841) 533331
F: (01841) 533331
E: cottages@cornishhorizons.co.uk
I: www.cornishhorizons.co.uk

Trenant ★★★★
Contact:
Cornish Horizons, The Cottage,
19 New Street, Padstow
PL28 8EA
T: (01841) 533331
F: (01841) 533933
E: cottages@cornishhorizons.co.uk

650 Look out for establishments participating in the National Accessible Scheme

SOUTH WEST ENGLAND

Westcreek
Rating Applied For
Contact:
Cornish Cottage Holidays, The Old Turnpike Dairy, Godolphin, Meneage Street, Helston TR13 8AA
T: (01326) 573808
F: (01326) 564992
E: enquiry@cornishcottageholidays.co.uk
I: www.cornishcottageholidays.co.uk

LITTLE RISSINGTON
Gloucestershire

Bobble Cottage ★★★
Contact:
Country Holidays reference: 15430, Spring Mill, Barnoldswick BB94 0AA
T: 0870 0 723723
E: ch.enquiry@holidaycottagesgroup.com

Southview, Courtyard and Tallet Cott ★★★★-★★★★★
Contact: Mr Nando & Mrs Joyce Fracasso
Southview, Courtyard and Tallet Cott, c/o Home Farm House, Cheltenham GL54 2NA
T: (01451) 820691

LITTLE TORRINGTON
Devon

Cream Tea Cottages ★★★★
Contact: Mr Tom & Mrs Sue Downie
Staddon House, Monkleigh, Bideford EX39 5JR
T: (01805) 623670
E: tom.downie@ukonline.co.uk
I: www.creamteacottages.co.uk

Torridge House Cottages ★★★
Contact: Mrs Terry
Torridge House Cottages, Torrington EX38 8PS
T: (01805) 622542
F: (01805) 622360
E: bookings@torridgehouse.co.uk
I: www.torrridgehouse.co.uk

LITTLEHAM
Devon

Robin Hill Farm Cottages ★★★★
Contact: Mr Robin & Mrs Sue Williams
Robin Hill Farm Cottages, Robin Hill Farm, Littleham, Bideford EX39 5EG
T: (01237) 473605
E: r.hillcotts@amserve.net
I: www.robinhillcottages.co.uk

LITTON CHENEY
Dorset

Baglake Barn and Brewery Cottage ★★★★-★★★★★
Contact: Mrs Barbour
Baglake Barn and Brewery Cottage, Baglake Farm, Dorchester DT2 9AD
T: (01308) 482222
F: (01308) 482226

Brambles ★★★★
Contact: Mrs Jackson
Oldbury Lane, Sevenoaks TN15 9DG
T: (01732) 884277
E: janet@kortoll.fsnet.co.uk
I: www.dorsetbrambles.com

Chimney Sweep ★★★★
Contact: Mr Zachary Stuart-Brown
Dream Cottages, 5 Hope Square, Weymouth DT4 8TR
T: (01305) 789000
F: (01305) 761346
E: admin@dream-cottages.co.uk
I: www.dream-cottages.co.uk

LIVERTON
Devon

Lookweep Farm Cottages ★★★
Contact: Mr John & Mrs Helen Griffiths
Lookweep Farm Cottages, Liverton, Newton Abbot TQ12 6HT
T: (01626) 833277
F: (01626) 834412
E: holidays@lookweep.co.uk
I: www.lookweep.co.uk

Moor Copse Farm Cottages ★★★
Contact: Mr & Mrs Cross
Moor Copse Farm Cottages, Newton Abbot TQ12 6HT
T: (01626) 833920
F: (01626) 833920
E: cross@moorcopse.fslife.co.uk

LOBB
Devon

South Lobb Cottage and House ★★★
Contact:
Farm & Cottage Holidays, Victoria House, 12 Fore Street, Bideford EX39 1AW
T: (01237) 479146
F: (01237) 421512
E: enquiries@farmcott.co.uk
I: www.farmcott.co.uk

LONDON APPRENTICE
Cornwall

Holly Bank
Rating Applied For
Contact: Mrs Linda McGuffie
Spindrift, St Austell PL26 7AR
T: (01726) 69316
E: enquiries@spindrift-guesthouse.co.uk
I: www.spindrift-guesthouse.co.uk

Levalsa Farm ★★★-★★★★
Contact: Mrs Gaye Julian
Levalsa Farm, St Austell PL26 7AW
T: (01726) 843505
F: (01726) 843505

LONG BREDY
Dorset

Whatcombe Stables ★★★
Contact: Mrs Jane Peretz
Whatcombe Stables, Dorchester DT2 9HN
T: (01308) 482762
F: (01308) 482762
E: janeperetz@compuserve.com

LONG ROCK
Cornwall

The Cottage ★★★★
Contact: Mr James Morris-Marsham
The Cottage, Heron House, Penzance TR20 9BJ
T: (01736) 711680
F: (01736) 711193
E: susiemm@freenet.co.uk

LONGBOROUGH
Gloucestershire

Cottage Barn ★★★★
Contact: Mr & Mrs Williams-Ellis
Cottage Barn, Sunnybank, Chapel Lane, Longborough, Moreton-in-Marsh GL56 0OR
T: (01451) 830695
F: (01451) 830695
E: rupert.williams-ellis@talk21.com
I: www.cotswoldscottage.co.uk

Luckley Holidays ★★★
Contact: Mr Robert Wharton
Luckley Holidays, Moreton-in-Marsh GL56 0RD
T: (01451) 870885
F: (01541) 831481
E: info@luckley-holidays.co.uk
I: www.luckley-holidays.co.uk

Studio Cottage ★★★
Contact: Mrs Green
Ganborough House, Moreton-in-Marsh GL56 0QZ
T: (01451) 830466

LONGBRIDGE DEVERILL
Wiltshire

Copperfield ★★★
Contact:
Farm & Cottage Holidays, Victoria House, 12 Fore Street, Bideford EX39 1AW
T: (01237) 479146
F: (01237) 421512
E: enquiries@farmcott.co.uk
I: www.farmcott.co.uk

Sturgess Farmhouse ★★★★
Contact: Mr Ramsay
Sturgess Farmhouse, The Marsh, Warminster BA12 7EA
T: (01985) 840329
F: (01985) 840331
E: info@sturgessbarns.co.uk
I: www.sturgessbarns.co.uk

LONGHOPE
Gloucestershire

The Old Farm ★★★★★
Contact: Ms Lucy Rodger
The Old Farm, Barrel Lane, Longhope GL17 0LR
T: (01452) 830252
F: (01452) 830255
E: lucy@the-old-farm.co.uk

LOOE
Cornwall

Alices Cottage ★★★★
Contact:
Cornish Cottage Holidays, The Old Turnpike Dairy, Godolphin Road, Helston TR13 8AA
T: (01326) 573808
F: (01326) 564992
E: enquiry@cornishcottageholidays.co.uk
I: www.cornishcottageholidays.co.uk

Badham Farm Holiday Cottages ★★★
Contact: Mr & Mrs Brown
The Old Chapel, White Lane, Truro TR2 5NA
T: (01872) 580211

Barclay House Cottages ★★★★★
Contact: Mr Barclay
Barclay House Cottages, St Martins Road, Looe PL13 1LP
T: (01503) 262929
F: (01503) 262632
E: info@barclayhouse.co.uk
I: www.barclayhouse.co.uk

Bocaddon Holiday Cottages ★★★★
Contact: Mrs Alison Maiklem
Bocaddon Holiday Cottages, Lanreath, Looe PL13 2PG
T: (01503) 220192
F: (01503) 220192
E: bocaddon@aol.com
I: www.bocaddon.com

Bucklawren Farm ★★★★-★★★★★
Contact: Mrs Henly
Bucklawren Farm, St Martins, Looe PL13 1NZ
T: (01503) 240738
F: (01503) 240481
E: bucklawren@btopenworld.com
I: www.bucklawren.com

Clipper House
Rating Applied For
Contact: Mrs Roper
Millpool Head, Herodsfoot, Liskeard PL14 4QX

Coldrinnick Cottages ★★★★
Contact: Mrs Kaye Chapman
Coldrinnick Cottages, Liskeard PL14 4QF
T: (01503) 220251
E: kaye@coldrinnick.fsnet.co.uk
I: www.cornishcottage.net

Crylla Valley Cottages ★★★★
Contact: Mr M Walsh
Crylla Valley Cottages, Notter Bridge, Saltash PL12 4RN
T: (01752) 851133
F: (01752) 851666
E: sales@cryllacottages.co.uk
I: www.cryllacottages.co.uk

Grantham Lodge ★★
Contact:
Valley Villas, Sales Office, City Business Park, Office 38, Somerset Park, Plymouth PL3 4BB
T: (01752) 605605
E: sales@valleyvillas.co.uk
I: www.valleyvillas.co.uk

Hawks View Cottage ★★
Contact:
Valley Villas, Sales Office, City Business Park, Office 38, Somerset Place, Plymouth PL3 4BB
T: (01752) 605605
E: sales@valleyvillas
I: www.valleyvillas.co.uk

Establishments printed in blue have a detailed entry in this guide

651

SOUTH WEST ENGLAND

Hendra Farm Cottages
Rating Applied For
Contact: Mrs Senara Higgs
Hendra Farm Cottages, Looe
PL13 2LU
T: (01503) 220701
F: (01503) 220701
E: senara@hendrafarmcottages.co.uk
I: www.hendrafarmcottages.co.uk

Highbank Log Cabin ★★★
Contact:
Valley Villas, Sales Office, City Business Park, Office 38
Somerset Park, Plymouth
PL3 4BB
T: (01752) 605605
E: sales@valleyvillas.co.uk
I: www.valleyvillas.co.uk

Highwood ★★★★
Contact: Mrs Beatrix Windle
118 Horsham Road, Cranleigh
GU6 8DY
T: (01483) 277894
E: beatrix@talk21.com
I: www.cornwall-online.co.uk/highwood

Jasmine Cottage ★★
Contact:
Valley Villas, Brook Cottage, Old Warleigh Lane, Plymouth
PL5 4ND
T: (01752) 774900
E: sales@valleyvillas.co.uk
I: www.valleyvillas.co.uk

Keepers Log Cabin
Rating Applied For
Contact:
Valley Villas, Sales Office, City Business Park, Office 38
Somerset Park, Plymouth
PL3 4BB
T: (01752) 605605
E: sales@valleyvillas.co.uk
I: www.valleyvillas.co.uk

Lakeside Log Cabin ★★★
Contact:
Valley Villas, Sales Office, City Business Park, Office 38
Somerset Park, Plymouth
PL3 4BB
T: (01752) 605605
E: sales@valleyvillas.co.uk
I: www.valleyvillas.co.uk

Lantau Cottage ★★★★
Contact:
Valley Villas Sales Office, Office 38, City Business Park, Somerset Place, Stoke, Plymouth pl3 4bb
T: (01752) 605605
E: sales@valleyvillas.com
I: www.valleyvillas.com

Lemain Garden Apartments
★★★-★★★★
Contact: Mr Alan & Mrs Dee Palin
Lemain Garden Apartments, Portuan Road, Looe PL13 2DR
T: (01503) 262073
F: (01503) 265288
E: sales@lemain.com
I: www.lemain.com

Little Cottage ★★★
Contact: Mrs Annette Tolputt
Little Cottage, Lesquite
Lansallos, Looe PL13 2QE
T: (01503) 220315
I: www.lesquite-polperro.fsnet.co.uk

Little Larnick Holiday Cottages
Rating Applied For
Contact: Mrs Irene Eastley
Little Larnick Holiday Cottages, Near Looe, Looe PL13 2NB
T: (01503) 220205

Nickelodeon ★★★
Contact:
Valley Villas, Brook Cottage, Old Warleigh Lane, Plymouth
PL5 4ND
T: (01752) 774900
E: sales@valleyvillas.co.uk
I: www.valleyvillas.co.uk

Penvith Cottages ★★★★
Contact: Mrs Beatrix Windle
118 Horsham Road, Cranleigh
GU6 8DY
T: (01483) 277894
E: beatrix@talk21.com
I: www.penvithcottages.co.uk

Rock Towers Apartments
★★★★
Contact: Mr Clive Dixon
Cornish Collection Ltd, 73 Bodrigan Road, Barbican, Looe
PL13 1EH
T: (01503) 262736
F: (01503) 262736
E: cornishcol@aol.com
I: www.cornishcollection.co.uk

Seaways Fishermans Cottage ★★
Contact:
Valley Villas Sales Office, Office 38 City Business Park, Somerset Place, Stoke, Plymouth PL3 4BB
T: (01752) 605605
E: sales@valleyvillas.com
I: www.valleyvillas.com

Spinnaker
Rating Applied For
Contact: Mrs Enid Hill
Island View, Marine Drive, Looe
PL13 2DJ
T: (01503) 263485

Summercourt Coastal Cottages ★★★★
Contact: Mr Steve & Mrs Lisa Rawlins
Summercourt Coastal Cottages, Bodigga Cliff, St Martin, Looe
PL13 1NZ
T: (01503) 263149
E: lisa.rawlins@virgin.net
I: www.holidaycottagescornwall.tv

Talehay ★★★★
Contact: Mr Paul Brumpton
Talehay, Tremaine, Pelynt, Looe
PL13 2LT
T: (01503) 220252
F: (01503) 220252
E: paul@talehay.co.uk
I: www.talehay.co.uk

Trecan Farm Cottages
★★★-★★★★
Contact: Mr Richard & Mrs Janet Pugh
Trecan Farm Cottages, Lanreath, Looe PL13 2PF
T: (01503) 220768
F: (01503) 220768
E: richardpugh@trecan.fsnet.co.uk

Trenant View ★★
Contact:
Valley Villas, Sales Office, City Business Park, Office 38
Somerset Park, Plymouth
PL3 4BB
T: (01752) 605605
E: sales@valleyvillas.co.uk
I: www.valleyvillas.co.uk

Trewith Holiday Cottages
★★★★
Contact: Mr Paul & Mrs Barbara Higgins
Trewith Holiday Cottages, Liskeard PL14 4PR
T: (01503) 262184
F: (01503) 265024
E: holiday-cottages@trewith.freeserve.co.uk
I: www.trewith.freeserve.co.uk

Treworgey Cottages
★★★★★
Contact: Mr Bevis & Mrs Linda Wright
Treworgey Cottages, Duloe, Liskeard PL14 4PP
T: (01503) 262730
F: (01503) 263767
E: treworgey@enterprise.net
I: www.cornishdreamcottages.co.uk

11 Woburn Lodge ★★★★
Contact:
Valley Villas, Brook Cottage, Old Warleigh Lane, Plymouth
PL5 4ND
T: (01752) 774900
E: sales@valleyvillas.co.uk
I: www.valleyvillas.co.uk

16 Woburn Lodge ★★★★
Contact:
Valley Villas, Sales Office, City Business Park, Office 38
Somerset Park, Plymouth
PL3 4BB
T: (01752) 605605
E: sales@valleyvillas.co.uk
I: www.valleyvillas.co.uk

Woodsaws Farm ★★★★
Contact: Mrs Ann Wills
Woodsaws Farm, Woodsaws Cross, Lanreath, Looe PL13 2NT
T: (01503) 220190
E: ann@woodsawsfarm.co.uk
I: www.woodsawsfarm.co.uk

LOSCOMBE
Dorset

Garden Cottage ★★★
Contact: Major Poe
Pear Tree Farm, Bridport DT6 3TL
T: (01308) 488223
E: poe@loscombe.freeserve.co.uk

LOSTWITHIEL
Cornwall

Chark Country Holidays
★★★★
Contact: Ms Jenny Littleton
Chark Country Holidays, Chark, Bodmin PL30 5AR
T: (01208) 871118
F: (01208) 871118
E: charkFARM@farmersweekly.net
I: www.charkcountryholidays.co.uk

Hartswheal Barn ★★★
Contact: Mrs Wendy Jordan
Hartswheal Barn, Saint Winnow, Downend, Lostwithiel PL22 0RB
T: (01208) 873419
F: (01208) 873419
E: hartswheal@connexions.co.uk
I: www.connexions.co.uk/hartswheal/index.htm

Lanwithan Manor, Farm & Waterside Cottages
★★★-★★★★
Contact: Mr Edward-Collins
Lanwithan Cottages, Lanwithan Road, Lostwithiel PL22 0LA
T: (01208) 872444
F: (01208) 872444
I: www.lanwithancottages.co.uk

Newham Farm Cottages
★★★★
Contact: Mrs Patricia Bolsover
Newham Farm Cottages, Newham Farm, Lostwithiel
PL22 0LD
T: (01208) 872262
F: (01208) 872262

Tredethick Farm Cottages
★★★★
Contact: Mr Tim & Mrs Nicky Reed
Tredethick Farm Cottages, Tredethick, Lostwithiel PL22 0LE
T: (01208) 873618
F: (01208) 873618
E: holidays@tredethick.co.uk
I: www.tredethick.co.uk

LOWER APPERLEY
Gloucestershire

Rofield Barn ★★★★★★
Contact: Mrs Hazel Lewis
Rofield Barn, Lower Apperley, Gloucester GL19 4DR
T: (01452) 780323
F: (01452) 780777
E: jeremy@tewkbury.freeserve.co.uk
I: www.rofieldbarn.com

LOWER ODCOMBE
Somerset

The Cottage ★★★
Contact: Mrs N C Worledge
The Cottage, Old Dairy House, Yeovil BA22 8TX
T: (01935) 862874
E: john.worledge@lineone.net

SOUTH WEST ENGLAND

LOWER SLAUGHTER
Gloucestershire

Malt House Cottage ★★★★
Contact: Mrs Charlotte Hutsby
Little Hill Farm, Wellesbourne,
Warwick CV35 9EB
T: (01789) 840261
F: (01789) 842270
E: charhutsby@talk21.com
I: www.accomodata.
co.uk/060999.htm

LOWER SOUDLEY
Gloucestershire

Beechwood Bungalow ★★★★
Contact: Mrs Judith Anderton
Brookside Cottage, Cinderford
GL14 2UB
T: (01594) 825864
E: raanderton@ntlworld.com

LUCCOMBE
Somerset

Wychanger ★★★-★★★★★
Contact: Mr David & Mrs Sue Dalton
Wychanger, Minehead TA24 8TA
T: (01643) 862526
E: holidays@wychanger.net
I: www.wychanger.net

LUDGVAN
Cornwall

Dowling Barn ★★★
Contact: Mr David Beer
West Cornwall Lets, Kelynack
Moor Farmhouse, Bosworlas, St Just, Penzance TR19 7RQ
T: (01736) 787011
E: db.properties@virgin.net

Mount View Cottage ★★★
Contact: Mrs Ruth Wallis
Eglos Corner Cottage, Penzance TR20 8HQ
T: (01736) 711425
I: www.eglos.co.uk

Nanceddan ★★★
Contact: Mrs Richards
Nanceddan, Penzance TR20 8AN

LUSTLEIGH
Devon

Lustleigh Mills ★★★-★★★★
Contact: Mrs Janet Rowe
Lustleigh Mills, Mill Road,
Lustleigh Mills, Newton Abbot
TQ13 9SS
T: (01647) 277357
E: lustleighmills@ukgateway.net
I: www.lustleighmills.btinternet.co.uk

LUXBOROUGH
Somerset

The Old Granary ★★★★
Contact: Mr Ivan & Mrs Anne Simpson
The Old Granary, Watchet
TA23 0SJ
T: (01984) 640909
E: theoldgranaryexmoor@talk21.com
I: www.granarycottage.co.uk

Pool farm Byres
Rating Applied For
Contact:
Marsdens Cottage Holidays, 2
The Square, Braunton EX33 2JB
T: (01271) 813777
F: (01271) 813664
E: holidays@marsdens.co.uk
I: www.marsdens.co.uk

Westcott Lodge and Mill Cottage ★★★★
Contact: Mr Sylvia Herbert
Westcott Lodge and Mill
Cottage, Westcott Farm,
Watchet TA23 0ST
T: (01984) 641285
F: (01984) 641285
E: westcottlodge@freeuk.com

LYDEARD ST LAWRENCE
Somerset

Oaklea House ★★★★
Contact: Mrs Peta-Elaine Barker
Oaklea House, Tolland, Lydeard
St Lawrence, Taunton TA4 3PW
T: (01984) 667373
F: (01984) 667373
E: Barker@Oakleahouse.fsnet.co.uk

LYDNEY
Gloucestershire

Bream Cross Farm ★★★
Contact: Mr Jock & Mrs Margaret Reeks
Bream Cross Farm, Lydney
GL16 6EU
T: (01594) 562208
F: (01594) 564399

Cider Press Cottage ★★★★
Contact: Mr & Mrs Hinton
Cider Press Cottage, 1 Westleigh
Villa, St Swithins Road, Lydney
GL15 4NF
T: (01594) 510285
F: (01594) 510285

The Coach House ★★★★
Contact: Mrs Yeatman
Deanfield, Royal Forest of Dean,
Lydney GL15
T: (01594) 562256

Highbury Coach House ★★★
Contact: Mrs Maria-Inez Midgley
Highbury Coach House, Bream Road, Lydney GL15 5JH
T: (01594) 842339
F: (01594) 844948
E: midgleya1@aol.com

The Old Pumphouse ★★★★
Contact: Mr Nicholas Pash
Hideaways, Chapel House, Luke
Street, Berwick St John,
Shaftesbury SP7 0HQ
T: (01747) 828170
I: www.hideaways.co.uk

LYME REGIS
Dorset

44/45 Coombe Street - B4341 ★★★★
Contact:
Lyme Bay Holiday Cottages, Bos
House, 44 Church Street, Lyme
Regis DT7 3DA
T: (01297) 443363
F: (01297) 445576
E: email@lymebayholidays.co.uk
I: www.lymebayholidays.co.uk

1 Alexandra Cottages - B4432
Rating Applied For
Contact: Mr Jim Matthews
Lyme Bay Holidays, Bos House,
44 Church Street, Lyme Regis
DT7 3HZ
T: (01297) 443363
F: (01297) 445576
E: email@lymebayholidays.co.uk
I: www.lymebayholidays.co.uk

Alwyns - B4002 ★★★
Contact:
Lyme Bay Holidays, Bos House,
44 Church Street, Lyme Regis
DT7 3DA
T: (01297) 443363
F: (01297) 445576
E: email@lymebayholidays.co.uk
I: www.lymebayholidays.co.uk

Anning Road - B4371 ★★★
Contact:
Lyme Bay Holiday, Bos House,
44 Church Street, Lyme Regis
DT7 3DA
T: (01297) 443363
F: (01297) 445576
E: email@lymebayholidays.co.uk
I: www.lymebayholidays.co.uk

Appletrees ★★★★
Contact: Mr Charles & Mrs Liz Teall
Salford Mill, Chipping Norton
OX7 5YQ
T: (01608) 641304
F: (01608) 644442
E: teall@compuserve.com

Aquae Sulis - B4287 ★★★
Contact:
Lyme Bay Holiday Cottages, Bos
House, 44 Church Street, Lyme
Regis DT7 3DA
T: (01297) 443363
E: email@lymebayholidays.co.uk
I: www.lymebayholidays.co.uk

The Arched House - F4045 ★★★
Contact:
Lyme Bay Holidays, Bos House,
44 Church Street, Lyme Regis
DT7 3DA
T: (01297) 443363
F: (01297) 445576
E: email@lymebayholidays.co.uk
I: www.lymebayholidays.co.uk

Argyle House - B4200 ★★★
Contact:
Lyme Bay Holiday Cottages, Bos
House, 44 Church Street, Lyme
Regis DT7 3DA
T: (01297) 443363
F: (01297) 445576
E: email@lymebayholidays.co.uk
I: www.lymebayholidays.co.uk

Banff - B4109 ★★★
Contact:
Lyme Bay Holidays, Bos House,
44 Church Street, Lyme Regis
DT7 3DA
T: (01297) 443363
F: (01297) 445576
E: email@lymebayholidays.co.uk
I: www.lymebayholidays.co.uk

Bay View Court - B4357 ★★★★
Contact:
Lyme Bay Holidays, Bos House,
44 Church Street, Lyme Regis
DT7 3DA
T: (01297) 443363
F: (01297) 445576
E: email@lymebayholidays.co.uk
I: www.lymebayholidays.co.uk

Bedrock - B4390 ★★★
Contact:
Lyme Bay Holidays, Bos House,
44 Church Street, Lyme Regis
DT7 3DA
T: (01297) 443363
F: (01297) 445576
E: email@lymebayholidays.co.uk
I: www.lymebayholidays.co.uk

Benwick - B4232 ★★★★
Contact:
Lyme Bay Holidays, Bos House,
44 Church Street, Lyme Regis
DT7 3DA
T: (01297) 443363
F: (01297) 445576
E: email@lymebayholidays.co.uk
I: www.lymebayholidays.co.uk

Blacksmith Cottage ★★★★
Contact: Mrs Su Jolley
Westward, Loves Lane, Bridport
DT6 6DZ
T: (01297) 489778
E: su@westward.fsbusiness.co.uk

Blue Horizons - B4314 ★★★
Contact: Mr Dave Matthews
Lyme Bay Holidays, Bos House,
44 Church Street, Lyme Regis
DT7 3DA
T: (01297) 443363
F: (01297) 445576
E: email@lymebayholidays.co.uk
I: www.lymebayholidays.co.uk

Establishments printed in blue have a detailed entry in this guide

SOUTH WEST ENGLAND

The Blue House - C4422 ★★★
Contact: Mr Dave Matthews
Lyme Bay Holidays, Bos House,
44 Church Street, Lyme Regis
DT7 3DA
T: (01297) 443363
F: (01297) 445576
E: email@lymebayholidays.co.uk
I: www.lymebayholidays.co.uk

The Boat House - B4081 ★★★
Contact:
Lyme Bay Holidays, Bos House,
44 Church Street, Lyme Regis
DT7 3DA
T: (01297) 443363
F: (01297) 445576
E: email@lymebayholidays.co.uk
I: www.lymebayholidays.co.uk

The Bookie - A4374 ★★★
Contact: Mr Dave Matthews
Lyme Bay Holidays, Bos House,
44 Church Street, Lyme Regis
DT7 3DA
T: (01297) 443363
F: (01297) 445576
E: email@lymebayholidays.co.uk
I: www.lymebayholidays.co.uk

Boston - D4326 ★★★★
Contact: Mr Dave Matthews
Lyme Bay Holidays, Bos House,
44 Church Street, Lyme Regis
DT7 3DA
T: (01297) 443363
F: (01297) 445576
E: email@lymebayholidays.co.uk
I: www.lymebayholidays.co.uk

Bosup - B4098 ★★★
Contact: Mr Dave Matthews
Lyme Bay Holidays, Bos House,
44 Church Street, Lyme Regis
DT7 3DA
T: (01297) 443363
F: (01297) 445576
E: email@lymebayholidays.co.uk
I: www.lymebayholidays.co.uk

1 The Bothy - w4391 ★★★★
Contact:
Lyme Bay Holidays, Bos House,
44 Church Street, Lyme Regis
DT7 3DA
T: (01297) 443363
F: (01297) 445576
E: email@lymebayholidays.co.uk
I: www.lymebayholidays.co.uk

Bramcote - A4415 ★★★★
Contact:
Lyme Bay Holidays, Bos House,
44 Church Street, Lyme Regis
DT7 3DA
T: (01297) 443363
F: (01297) 445576
E: email@lymebayholidays.co.uk
I: www.lymebayholidays.co.uk

Bramcote Apartment ★★★★
Contact: Mrs Rosalind Price
Bramcote Apartment, East Cliff,
Lyme Regis DT7 3DH
T: (01297) 442924
F: (01297) 442924
E: fnr.price@virgin.net
I: www.bramcotelymeregis.com

21c Broad Street - A4356 ★★★★
Contact:
Lyme Bay Holidays, Bos House,
44 Church Street, Lyme Regis
DT7 3DA
T: (01297) 443363
F: (01297) 445576
E: email@lymebayholidays.co.uk
I: www.lymebayholidays.co.uk

49a Broad Street - C4049 ★★★★
Contact:
Lyme Bay Holidays, Bos House,
44 Church Street, Lyme Regis
DT7 3DA
T: (01297) 443363
F: (01297) 445576
E: email@lymebayholidays.co.uk
I: www.lymebayholidays.co.uk

3 Chard House - A4312 ★★★
Contact: Mr Dave Matthews
Lyme Bay Holidays, Bos House,
44 Church Street, Lyme Regis
DT7 3DA
T: (01297) 443363
F: (01297) 445576
E: email@lymebayholidays.co.uk
I: www.lymebayholidays.co.uk

Church Cliff - B4308 ★★★★
Contact:
Lyme Bay Holidays, Bos House,
44 Church Street, Lyme Regis
DT7 3DA
T: (01297) 443363
F: (01297) 445576
E: email@lymebayholidays.co.uk
I: www.lymebayholidays.co.uk

Church Cliff - C4296 ★★★★
Contact:
Lyme Bay Holidays, Bos House,
44 Church Street, Lyme Regis
DT7 3DA
T: (01297) 443363
F: (01297) 445576
E: email@lymebayholidays.co.uk
I: www.lymebayholidays.co.uk

48 Church Street - C4335 ★★★★
Contact: Mr Dave Matthews
Lyme Bay Holidays, Bos House,
44 Church Street, Lyme Regis
DT7 3DA
T: (01297) 443363
F: (01297) 445576
E: email@lymebayholidays.co.uk
I: www.lymebayholidays.co.uk

Clappentail Court - B4141 ★★★★
Contact:
Lyme Bay Holidays, Bos House,
44 Church Street, Lyme Regis
DT7 3DA
T: (01297) 443363
F: (01297) 445576
E: email@lymebayholidays.co.uk
I: www.lymebayholidays.co.uk

Cleve House - B3437 ★★★
Contact: Mr Dave Matthews
Lyme Bay Holidays, Bos House,
44 Church Street, Lyme Regis
DT7 3DA
T: (01297) 443363
F: (01297) 445576
E: email@lymebayholidays.co.uk
I: www.lymebayholidays.co.uk

Cleveland - C4427 ★★★★
Contact:
Lyme Bay Holidays, Bos House,
44 Church Street, Lyme Regis
DT7 3DA
T: (01297) 443363
F: (01297) 445576
E: email@lymebayholidays.co.uk
I: www.lymebayholidays.co.uk

Cliff Cottage ★★★
Contact: Mrs Sue Rose
3 Rantfell House, 55 New Road,
Whitehill, Bordon GU35 9AX
T: (01420) 472512
E: cliffcottlyme@aol.com

The Coach House - End House ★★
Contact: Mrs Lucy Watt
Ware Wood, Ware Lane, Lyme
Regis DT7 3EL
T: (01297) 445100

Cobb House ★★
Contact: Ms Kate Bartlett
Jean Bartlett Cottage Holidays,
The Old Dairy, Fore Street,
Seaton EX12 3JB
T: (01297) 23221
F: (01297) 23303
E: holidays@jeanbartlett.com
I: www.netbreaks.com/jeanb

7 Cobb Road - C4358 ★★★
Contact:
Lyme Bay Holidays, Bos House,
44 Church Street, Lyme Regis
DT7 3DA
T: (01297) 443363
F: (01297) 445576
E: email@lymebayholidays.co.uk
I: www.lymebayholidays.co.uk

Cockwell Cross Cottage - V4285 ★★★★
Contact: Mr Dave Matthews
Lyme Bay Holidays, Bos House,
44 Church Street, Lyme Regis
DT7 3DA
T: (01297) 443363
F: (01297) 445576
E: email@lymebayholidays.co.uk
I: www.lymebayholidays.co.uk

Coolrus - B4349 ★★★
Contact:
Lyme Bay Holidays, Bos House,
44 Church Street, Lyme Regis
DT7 3DA
T: (01297) 443363
F: (01297) 445576
E: email@lymebayholidays.co.uk
I: www.lymebayholidays.co.uk

Coombe Cottage - C4346 ★★★★
Contact: Mr Dave Matthews
Lyme Bay Holidays, Bos House,
44 Church Street, Lyme Regis
DT7 3DA
T: (01297) 443363
F: (01297) 445576
E: email@lymebayholidays.co.uk
I: www.lymebayholidays.co.uk

Coombe House Flat ★★★
Contact: Mrs Dympna Duncan
Coombe House Flat, 41 Coombe
Street, Lyme Regis DT7 3PY
T: (01297) 443849
F: (01297) 443849
E: dymps@coombe-house.co.uk
I: www.coombe-house.co.uk

3 Coombe Street - 52700k ★★★
Contact:
Lyme Bay Holidays, Bos House,
44 Church Street, Lyme Regis
DT7 3DA
T: (01297) 444756
F: (01297) 445576
E: email@lymebayholidays.co.uk
I: www.lymebayholidays.co.uk

2 Coombe Street - B4278 ★★★
Contact: Mr Dave Matthews
Lyme Bay Holidays, Bos House,
44 Church Street, Lyme Regis
DT7 3DA
T: (01297) 443363
F: (01297) 445576
E: email@lymebayholidays.co.uk
I: www.lymebayholidays.co.uk

26 Coombe Street - C4424 ★★★
Contact:
Lyme Bay Holidays, Bos House,
44 Church Street, Lyme Regis
DT7 3DA
T: (01297) 443363
F: (01297) 445576
E: email@lymebayholidays.co.uk
I: www.lymebayholidays.co.uk

7 Coram Mews - C4351 ★★★★★
Contact:
Lyme Bay Holidays, Bos House,
44 Church Street, Lyme Regis
DT7 3DA
T: (01297) 443363
F: (01297) 445576
E: email@lymebayholidays.co.uk
I: www.lymebayholidays.co.uk

SOUTH WEST ENGLAND

Coram Tower Holidays ★★★
Contact: Mr John & Mrs Margaret McLaren
Coram Tower Holidays Ltd., Coram Tower, Pound Road, Lyme Regis DT7 3HX
T: (01297) 442012
E: jmmclaren@coramtower.co.uk
I: www.coramtower.co.uk

Crystal - A4433 ★★★
Contact:
Lyme Bay Holidays, Bos House, 44 Church Street, Lyme Regis DT7 3DA
T: (01297) 443363
F: (01297) 445576
E: email@lymebayholidays.co.uk
I: www.lymebayholidays.co.uk

Dolphin Cottage - B4340 ★★★
Contact: Mr Dave Matthews
Lyme Bay Holidays, Bos House, 44 Church Street, Lyme Regis DT7 3DA
T: (01297) 443363
F: (01297) 445576
E: email@lymebayholidays.co.uk
I: www.lymebayholidays.co.uk

3 Dolphin Cottages ★★
Contact: Mrs Daphne E Lindfield
Sunnyside, Horsham RH13 0NX
T: (01403) 791158

Faraway - C4436 ★★★★★
Contact: Mr Jim Matthews
Lyme Bay Holidays, Bos House, 44 Church Street, Lyme Regis DT7 3DA
T: (01297) 443363
F: (01297) 445576
E: email@lymebayholidays.co.uk
I: www.lymebayholidays.co.uk

Farwest - C4303 ★★★
Contact: Mr Dave Matthews
Lyme Bay Holidays, Bos House, 44 Church Street, Lyme Regis DT7 3DA
T: (01297) 443363
F: (01297) 445576
E: email@lymebayholidays.co.uk
I: www.lymebayholidays.co.uk

16 Fernhill - P5007 ★★★
Contact: Mr Dave Matthews
Lyme Bay Holidays, Bos House, 44 Church Street, Lyme Regis DT7 3DA
T: (01297) 443363
F: (01297) 445576
E: email@lymebayholidays.co.uk
I: www.lymebayholidays.co.uk

25 Fernhill - P5008 ★★★
Contact: Mr Dave Matthews
Lyme Bay Holidays, Bos House, 44 Church Street, Lyme Regis DT7 3DA
T: (01297) 443363
F: (01297) 445576
E: email@lymebayholidays.co.uk
I: www.lymebayholidays.co.uk

11 Fernhill - P5014 ★★★
Contact:
Lyme Bay Holidays, Bos House, 44 Church Street, Lyme Regis DT7 3DA
T: (01297) 443363
F: (01297) 445576
E: email@lymebayholidays.co.uk
I: www.lymebayholidays.co.uk

39 Fernhill - Q5006 ★★★★
Contact: Mr Dave Matthews
Lyme Bay Holidays, Bos House, 44 Church Street, Lyme Regis DT7 3DA
T: (01297) 443363
F: (01297) 445576
E: email@lymebayholidays.co.uk
I: www.lymebayholidays.co.uk

47 Fernhill - R5001 ★★★★
Contact:
Lyme Bay Holiday Cottages, Bos House, 44 Church Street, Lyme Regis DT7 3DA
T: (01297) 443363
F: (01297) 445576
E: email@lymebayholidays.co.uk
I: www.lymebayholidays.co.uk

38 Fernhill - R5002 ★★★★
Contact:
Lyme Bay Holiday Cottages, Bos House, 44 Church Street, Lyme Regis DT7 3DA
T: (01297) 443363
F: (01297) 445576
E: email@lymebayholidays.co.uk
I: www.lymebayholidays.co.uk

24 Fernhill - R5012 ★★★
Contact:
Lyme Bay Holidays, Bos House, 44 Church Street, Lyme Regis DT7 3DA
T: (01297) 443363
F: (01297) 445576
E: email@lymebayholidays.co.uk
I: www.lymebayholidays.co.uk

34 Fernhill - S5000 ★★★★
Contact: Mr Dave Matthews
Lyme Bay Holidays, Bos House, 44 Church Street, Lyme Regis DT7 3DA
T: (01297) 443363
F: (01297) 445576
E: email@lymebayholidays.co.uk
I: www.lymebayholidays.co.uk

49 Fernhill Heights Ref: S5015 ★★★
Contact: Mr David Matthews
49 Fernhill Heights Ref: S5015, Fernhill, Charmouth, Lyme Regis DT6 6BX
T: (01297) 443363
F: (01297) 445576
E: email@lymebayholidays.co.uk

35 Fernhill S5003 ★★★
Contact: Mr Dave Matthews
Lyme Bay Holidays, Bos House, 44 Church Street, Lyme Regis DT7 3DA
T: (01297) 443363
F: (01297) 445576
E: email@lymebayholidays.co.uk
I: www.lymebayholidays.co.uk

Fivepence - D4430
Rating Applied For
Contact:
Lyme Bay Holidays, Bos House, 44 Church Street, Lyme Regis DT7 3DA
T: (01297) 443363
F: (01297) 445576
E: email@lymebayholidays.co.uk
I: www.lymebayholidays.co.uk

Flat 1, Burton House ★★★
Contact: Mrs Elaine Windust
Flat 1, Burton House, 5 Pound Street, Lyme Regis DT7 3HZ
T: (01297) 443548
E: lymeregisflat1@aol.com

Flat 1 Pyne House ★★★
Contact: Ms Sue Dare
117 Leander Road, London SW2 2NB
T: (020) 86718587

The Gables Holiday Apartments ★★★
Contact: Mr Alan & Mrs Christine Simpson
The Gables Holiday Apartments, Church Street, Lyme Regis DT7 3BX
T: (01297) 442536
E: simpson100@tiscali.co.uk
I: www.thegableslymeregis.co.uk

Greystones ★★★★
Contact: Mrs Joan Gollop
Greystones, View Road, Lyme Regis DT7 3AA
T: (01297) 443678
E: greystones.flat@btopenworld.com
I: www.greystones-lymeregis.com

Gulls Nest - A4293 ★★★
Contact:
Lyme Bay Holiday Cottages, Bos House, 44 Church Street, Lyme Regis DT7 3DA
T: (01297) 443363
E: email@lymebayholidays.co.uk
I: www.lymebayholidays.co.uk

Hadleigh Villas - B3520 ★★★
Contact:
Lyme Bay Holidays, Bos House, 44 Church Street, Lyme Regis DT7 3DA
T: (01297) 443363
F: (01297) 445576
E: email@lymebayholidays.co.uk
I: www.lymebayholidays.co.uk

Harbour House Flats ★★★
Contact: Mrs Monica Cary
Briseham, Broadway Road, Newton Abbot TQ12 3EH
T: (01626) 364779

The Haven - D4096 ★★★
Contact:
Lyme Bay Holidays, Bos House, 44 Church Street, Lyme Regis DT7 3DA
T: (01297) 443363
F: (01297) 445576
E: email@lymebayholidays.co.uk
I: www.lymebayholidays.co.uk

Haye Farm Bungalow, Stables, Hayloft & Dairy ★★★-★★★★★
Contact: Mr Bob & Mrs Grace Anderson
Haye Farm, Haye Lane, Lyme Regis DT7 3UD
T: (01297) 442400
F: (01297) 442745

Highbanks - D4372 ★★★★
Contact:
Lyme Bay Holidays, Bos House, 44 Church Street, Lyme Regis DT7 3DA
T: (01297) 443363
F: (01297) 445576
E: email@lymebayholidays.co.uk
I: www.lymebayholidays.co.uk

Hobbs Cottage ★★★
Contact: Mr Zachary Stuart-Brown
Dream Cottages, 5 Hope Square, Weymouth DT4 8TR
T: (01305) 789000
E: admin@dream-cottages.co.uk
I: www.dream-cottages.co.uk

Honeymoon Cottage - C2627 ★★★★
Contact: Mr Dave Matthews
Lyme Bay Holidays, Bos House, 44 Church Street, Lyme Regis DT7 3DA
T: (01297) 443363
F: (01297) 445576
E: email@lymebayholidays.co.uk
I: www.lymebayholidays.co.uk

Hove To - C4364 ★★★★
Contact: Mr Jim Matthews
Lyme Bay Holidays, Bos House, 44 Church Street, Lyme Regis DT7 3DA
T: (01297) 443363
I: www.lymebayholidays.co.uk

Ilex House ★★★
Contact: Mr Royston Davies
Seven Springs Letting Agency, Fairfield Cottage, Charmouth Road, Lyme Regis DT7 3HH
T: (01297) 445362
F: (01297) 445362
I: www.lymeregis.com/seven-springs

Ivy Cottage - B4442
Rating Applied For
Contact:
Lyme Bay Holidays, Bos House, 44 Church Street, Lyme Regis DT7 3DA
T: (01297) 443363
F: (01297) 445576
E: email@lymebayholidays.co.uk
I: www.lymebayholidays.co.uk

Establishments printed in blue have a detailed entry in this guide

SOUTH WEST ENGLAND

Jasper - B4108 ★★★
Contact:
Lyme Bay Holidays, Bos House,
44 Church Street, Lyme Regis
DT7 3DA
T: (01297) 443363
F: (01297) 445576
E: email@lymebayholidays.
co.uk
I: www.lymebayholidays.co.uk

Kamloops and Nanaimo Apartments ★★★
Contact: Mr Sweet
Grove Cottage, Hollybush Lane,
Bristol BS9 1BH
T: (0117) 9681866
E: sw55t@msn.com

4 Kersbrook Gardens - B4437 ★★★
Contact: Mr Jim Matthews
Lyme Bay Holidays, Bos House,
44 Church Street, Lyme Regis
DT7 3DA
T: (01297) 443363
F: (01297) 445576
E: email@lymebayholidays.
co.uk
I: www.lymebayholidays.co.uk

2 Kersbrook Gardens - C4393 ★★★
Contact:
Lyme Bay Holidays, Bos House,
44 Church Street, Lyme Regis
DT7 3DA
T: (01297) 443363
F: (01297) 445576
E: email@lymebayholidays.
co.uk
I: www.lymebayholidays.co.uk

La Casa ★★★
Contact: Mr Royston Davies
Seven Springs Letting Agency,
Fairfield Cottage, Charmouth
Road, Lyme Regis DT7 3HH
T: (01297) 445362

Lentons - C4260 ★★★★
Contact:
Lyme Bay Holidays, Bos House,
44 Church Street, Lyme Regis
DT7 3DA
T: (01297) 443363
F: (01297) 445576
E: email@lymebayholidays.
co.uk
I: www.lymebayholidays.co.uk

Library Cottage - C4315 ★★★
Contact: Mr Dave Matthews
Lyme Bay Holidays, Bos House,
44 Church Street, Lyme Regis
DT7 3DA
T: (01297) 443363
F: (01297) 445576
E: email@lymebayholidays.
co.uk
I: www.lymebayholidays.co.uk

Little Cleve ★★★★
Contact: Mr Alister Mackenzie
Carters Cottage, Smithams Hill,
Bristol BS40 6BZ
T: (01761) 221554

Little Clovelly - A3602 ★★★★
Contact:
Lyme Bay Holidays, Bos House,
44 Church Street, Lyme Regis
DT7 3DA
T: (01297) 443363
F: (01297) 445576
E: email@lymebayholidays.
co.uk
I: www.lymebayholidays.co.uk

Little Jordan - C4300 ★★★★
Contact:
Lyme Bay Holidays, Bos House,
44 Church Street, Lyme Regis
DT7 3DA
T: (01297) 443363
F: (01297) 445576
E: email@lymebayholidays.
co.uk
I: www.lymebayholidays.co.uk

Little Rowan _ B4431
Rating Applied For
Contact: Mr Jim Matthews
Lyme Bay Holidays, Bos House,
44 Church Street, Lyme Regis
DT7 3DA
T: (01297) 443363
F: (01297) 445576
E: email@lymebayholidays.
co.uk
I: www.lymebayholidays.co.uk

Little Thatch - C3439 ★★★
Contact:
Lyme Bay Holidays, Bos House,
44 Church Street, Lyme Regis
DT7 3DA
T: (01297) 443363
F: (01297) 445576
E: email@lymebayholidays.
co.uk
I: www.lymebayholidays.co.uk

Long Path - D4370 ★★★★
Contact: Mr Dave Matthews
Lyme Bay Holidays, Bos House,
44 Church Street, Lyme Regis
DT7 3DA
T: (01297) 443363
F: (01297) 445576
E: email@lymebayholidays.
co.uk
I: www.lymebayholidays.co.uk

Lucerne Apartment ★★★★
Contact: Mr O Lovell
Lucerne, View Road, Lyme Regis
DT7 3AA
T: (01297) 443752

3 Lym Close - B4253 ★★★
Contact:
Lyme Bay Holidays, Bos House,
44 Church Street, Lyme Regis
DT7 3DA
T: (01297) 443363
F: (01297) 445576
E: email@lymebayholidays.
co.uk
I: www.lymebayholidays.co.uk

23 Lym Close - C4179 ★★★
Contact:
Lyme Bay Holidays, Bos House,
44 Church Street, Lyme Regis
DT7 3DA
T: (01297) 443363
F: (01297) 445576
E: email@lymebayholidays.
co.uk
I: www.lymebayholidays.co.uk

4 Lymbrook Cottages ★★★
Contact: Mrs Start
Monks Hall, Bowsers Lane,
Saffron Walden CB10 1XQ
T: (01799) 522096

Lymcroft - C4267 ★★★★
Contact:
Lyme Bay Holidays, Bos House,
44 Church Street, Lyme Regis
DT7 3DA
T: (01297) 443363
F: (01297) 445576
E: email@lymebayholidays.
co.uk
I: www.lymebayholidays.co.uk

Lymrush - D4355 ★★★
Contact:
Lyme Bay Holidays, Bos House,
44 Church Street, Lyme Regis
DT7 3DA
T: (01297) 443363
F: (01297) 445576
E: email@lymebayholidays.
co.uk
I: www.lymebayholidays.co.uk

Mad Hatters Apartment - B4369 ★★★
Contact:
Lyme Bay Holidays, Bos House,
44 Church Street, Lyme Regis
DT7 3DA
T: (01297) 443363
F: (01297) 445576
E: email@lymebayholidays.
co.uk
I: www.lymebayholidays.co.uk

Marmalade House ★★★
Contact: Mrs Pam Corbin
T: (01297) 442378
E: ozonepam@aol.com

Mermaid Cottage - C4281 ★★★★
Contact:
Lyme Bay Holidays, Bos House,
44 Church Street, Lyme Regis
DT7 3DA
T: (01297) 443363
F: (01297) 445576
E: email@lymebayholidays.
co.uk
I: www.lymebayholidays.co.uk

Mermaid House: E4412 ★★★★
Contact:
Lyme Bay Holidays, Bos House,
44 Church Street, Lyme Regis
DT7 3DA
T: (01297) 443363
F: (01297) 445576
E: email@lymebayholidays.
co.uk
I: www.lymebayholidays.co.uk

14 Mill Green - B4003 ★★★
Contact:
Lyme Bay Holidays, Bos House,
44 Church Street, Lyme Regis
DT7 3DA
T: (01297) 443363
F: (01297) 445576
E: email@lymebayholidays.
co.uk
I: www.lymebayholidays.co.uk

Milton Cottage - B4362 ★★★
Contact: Mr Dave Matthews
Lyme Bay Holidays, Bos House,
44 Church Street, Lyme Regis
DT7 3DA
T: (01297) 443363
F: (01297) 445576
E: email@lymebayholidays.
co.uk
I: www.lymebayholidays.co.uk

Monmouth Cottage ★★★
Contact: Mrs W R Fisk
28 Station Road, Crewkerne
TA18 8AJ
T: (01460) 73878

Naunton Cottage - B4375 ★★★
Contact:
Lyme Bay Holidays, Bos House,
44 Church Street, Lyme Regis
DT7 3DA
T: (01297) 443363
F: (01297) 445576
E: email@lymebayholidays.
co.uk
I: www.lymebayholidays.co.uk

Northay Farm Cottages ★★★★
Contact: Mrs Dee Olof
Northay Farm, Hawkchurch,
Axminster EX13 5UU
T: (01297) 678591
F: (01297) 678591
E: deeolof@hotmail.com
I: www.northay.com

Okanagen - B4107 ★★★
Contact:
Lyme Bay Holidays, Bos House,
44 Church Street, Lyme Regis
DT7 3DA
T: (01297) 443363
F: (01297) 445576
E: email@lymebayholidays.
co.uk
I: www.lymebayholidays.co.uk

The Old Watch House ★★★★
Contact: Mrs Sarah Wilkinson
1 Grey School Passage,
Dorchester DT1 1XG
T: (01305) 262505
F: (01305) 259454
E: old-watch-house@lymeregis.
com
I: www.lymeregis.
com/old-watch-house

Ozone Terrace - B4036 - A3603 ★★★
Contact:
Lyme Bay Holidays, Bos House,
44 Church Street, Lyme Regis
DT7 3DA
T: (01297) 443363
E: email@lymebayholidays.
co.uk
I: www.lymebayholidays.co.uk

Pucks Cottage - B4339 ★★★
Contact: Mr Dave Matthews
Lyme Bay Holidays, Bos House,
44 Church Street, Lyme Regis
DT7 3DA
T: (01297) 443363
F: (01297) 445576
E: email@lymebayholidays.
co.uk
I: www.lymebayholidays.co.uk

SOUTH WEST ENGLAND

Queen Ann's Lodge ★★★★
Contact: Mr Royson Davies
Fairfield Cottage, Charmouth Road, Lyme Regis DT7 3HH
T: (01297) 445362

47 Queens Walk - B4249 ★★★
Contact:
Lyme Bay Holidays, Bos House, 44 Church Street, Lyme Regis DT7 3DA
T: (01297) 443363
F: (01297) 445576
E: email@lymebayholidays.co.uk
I: www.lymebayholidays.co.uk

Radium - A4429 ★★★★
Contact:
Lyme Bay Holidays, Bos House, 44 Church Street, Lyme Regis DT7 3DA
T: (01297) 443363
F: (01297) 445576
E: email@lymebayholidays.co.uk
I: www.lymebayholidays.co.uk

Resthaven - A4373 ★★★
Contact:
Lyme Bay Holidays, Bos House, 44 Church Street, Lyme Regis DT7 3DA
T: (01297) 443363
F: (01297) 445576
E: email@lymebayholidays.co.uk
I: www.lymebayholidays.co.uk

The Retreat - A4273 ★★★
Contact:
Lyme Bay Holidays, Bos House, 44 Church Street, Lyme Regis DT7 3DA
T: (01297) 443363
F: (01297) 445576
E: email@lymebayholidays.co.uk
I: www.lymebayholidays.co.uk

Roselands: B/C4407 ★★★
Contact:
Lyme Bay Holidays, Bos House, 44 Church Street, Lyme Regis DT7 3DA
T: (01297) 443363
F: (01297) 445576
E: email@lymebayholidays.co.uk
I: www.lymebayholidays.co.uk

Ross House - B4394 ★★★
Contact:
Lyme Bay Holidays, Bos House, 44 Church Street, Lyme Regis DT7 3DA
T: (01297) 443363
F: (01297) 445576
E: email@lymebayholidays.co.uk
I: www.lymebaycottages.co.uk

St Agnes - A3601 ★★★
Contact:
Lyme Bay Holidays, Bos House, 44 Church Street, Lyme Regis DT7 3DA
T: (01297) 443363
F: (01297) 445576
E: email@lymebayholidays.co.uk
I: www.lymebayholidays.co.uk

St Andrews Holiday Flats ★★★
Contact: Mrs Cynthia Wendy McHardy
St Andrews Holiday Flats, Uplyme Road, Lyme Regis DT7 3LP
T: (01297) 445495
F: (01297) 445495

St Michaels Penthouse Apartment - B4352 ★★★★★
Contact:
Lyme Bay Holidays, Bos House, 44 Church Street, Lyme Regis DT7 3DA
T: (01297) 443363
F: (01297) 445576
E: email@lymebayholidays.co.uk

Sea Tree House ★★★★
Contact: Mr David Parker
Sea Tree House, 18 Broad Street, Lyme Regis DT7 3QE
T: (01297) 442244
F: (01297) 442244
E: seatree.house@ukonline.co.uk
I: www.lymeregis.com/seatreehouse

Seahorse Cottage - B4270 ★★★
Contact:
Lyme Bay Holidays, Bos House, 44 Church Street, Lyme Regis DT7 3DA
T: (01297) 443363
F: (01297) 445576
E: email@lymebayholidays.co.uk
I: www.lymebayholidays.co.uk

Seaview - C4302 ★★★
Contact: Mr Dave Matthews
Lyme Bay Holidays, Bos House, 44 Church Street, Lyme Regis DT7 3DA
T: (01297) 443363
F: (01297) 445576
E: email@lymebayholidays.co.uk
I: www.lymebayholidays.co.uk

Seaward - B4280 ★★★★
Contact:
Lyme Bay Holidays, Bos House, 44 Church Street, Lyme Regis DT7 3DA
T: (01297) 443363
F: (01297) 445576
E: email@lymebayholidays.co.uk
I: www.lymebayholidays.co.uk

30 Sherborne Lane - B4378 ★★★
Contact:
Lyme Bay Holidays, Bos House, 44 Church Street, Lyme Regis DT7 3DA
T: (01297) 443363
F: (01297) 445576
E: email@lymebayholidays.co.uk
I: www.lymebayholidays.co.uk

22a Sherborne Lane - C4197 ★★★
Contact:
Lyme Bay Holidays, Bos House, 44 Church Street, Lyme Regis DT7 3DA
T: (01297) 443363
F: (01297) 445576
E: email@lymebayholidays.co.uk
I: www.lymebayholidays.co.uk

35 Sherborne Lane - C4382 ★★★
Contact:
Lyme Bay Holidays, Bos House, 44 Church Street, Lyme Regis DT7 3DA
T: (01297) 443363
F: (01297) 445576
E: email@lymebayholidays.co.uk
I: www.lymebayholidays.co.uk

31 Sherborne Lane: B4406 ★★★
Contact:
Lyme Bay Holidays, Bos House, 44 Church Street, Lyme Regis DT7 3DA
T: (01297) 443363
F: (01297) 445576
E: email@lymebayholidays.co.uk
I: www.lymebayholidays.co.uk

57a Silver Street ★★
Contact: Ms Rhoda Elwick
Tigerhead House, Dorchester DT2 0PT
T: (01935) 83260
F: (01297) 443485
E: thethatch@lineone.net
I: www.holidaycottages-uk.com

Skagen Lodge - B3440 ★★★
Contact:
Lyme Bay Holidays, Bos House, 44 Church Street, Lyme Regis DT7 3DA
T: (01297) 443363
F: (01297) 44576
E: email@lymebayholidays.co.uk
I: www.lymebayholidays.co.uk

Snail House - B4291 ★★★★
Contact:
Lyme Bay Holiday Cottages, Bos House, 44 Church Street, Lyme Regis DT7 3DA
T: (01297) 443363
E: email@lymebayholidays.co.uk
I: www.lymebayholidays.co.uk

South Lawn: C4396 ★★★
Contact:
Lyme Bay Holidays, Bos House, 44 Church Street, Lyme Regis DT7 3DA
T: (01297) 443363
F: (01297) 445576
E: email@lymebayholidays.co.uk
I: www.lymebayholidays.co.uk

Spring Cottage ★★★
Contact: Mr Zachary Stuart-Brown
Dream Cottages, 5 Hope Square, Weymouth DT4 8TR
T: (01305) 789000
F: (01305) 761346
E: admin@dream-cottages.co.uk
I: www.dream-cottages.co.uk

Stable Cottage ★★★★
Contact: Mrs Penny Jones
Stable Cottage, The Coach House, Haye Lane, Lyme Regis DT7 3NQ
T: (01297) 442656
F: (01297) 442656

Stable Cottage - C4425 ★★★
Contact: Mr Dave Matthews
Lyme Bay Holidays, Bos House, 44 Church Street, Lyme Regis DT7 3DA
T: (01297) 443363
F: (01297) 445576
E: email@lymebayholidays.co.uk
I: www.lymebayholidays.co.uk

Sunnybank - C3442 ★★★★
Contact:
Lyme Bay Holidays, Bos House, 44 Church Street, Lyme Regis DT7 3DA
T: (01297) 443363
F: (01297) 445576
E: email@lymebayholidays.co.uk
I: www.lymebayholidays.co.uk

Valentine Cottage - B4350 ★★★★
Contact:
Lyme Bay Holidays, Bos House, 44 Church Street, Lyme Regis DT7 3DA
T: (01297) 443363
F: (01297) 445576
E: email@lymebayholidays.co.uk
I: www.lymebayholidays.co.uk

View House - D4100 ★★★
Contact:
Lyme Bay Holidays, Bos House, 44 Church Street, Lyme Regis DT7 3DA
T: (01297) 443363
F: (01297) 445576
E: email@lymebayholidays.co.uk
I: www.lymebayholidays.co.uk

Establishments printed in blue have a detailed entry in this guide

SOUTH WEST ENGLAND

The Walk C4006 ★★★
Contact:
Lyme Bay Holidays, Bos House,
44 Church Street, Lyme Regis
DT7 3DA
T: (01297) 443363
F: (01297) 445576
E: email@lymebayholidays.co.uk
I: www.lymebayholidays.co.uk

Waltham House - C4288 ★★★
Contact: Mr Matthews
Lyme Bay Holidays, Bos House,
44 Church Street, Lyme Regis
DT7 3DA
T: (01297) 443363
F: (01297) 445576
E: email@lymebayholidays.co.uk
I: www.lymebayholidays.co.uk

Water Cottage ★★★
Contact: Mrs Claire Laven-Morris
67 Montholme Road, London
SW11 6HX
T: (020) 79246194
F: (020) 7228 6779

Weavers Cottage - D4421 ★★★
Contact:
Lyme Bay Holidays, Bos House,
44 Church Street, Lyme Regis
DT7 3DA
T: (01297) 443363
F: (01297) 445576
E: email@lymebayholidays.co.uk
I: www.lymebayholidays.co.uk

Weighbridge Cottage - B4316 ★★★
Contact: Mr Dave Matthews
Lyme Bay Holidays, Bos House,
44 Church Street, Lyme Regis
DT7 3DA
T: (01297) 443363
F: (01297) 445576
E: email@lymebayholidays.co.uk
I: www.lymebayholidays.co.uk

Weirside: B4392 ★★★
Contact:
Lyme Bay Holidays, Bos House,
44 Church Street, Lyme Regis
DT7 3DA
T: (01297) 443363
F: (01297) 445576
E: email@lymebayholidays.co.uk
I: www.lymebayholidays.co.uk

1 Wellhayes- B4399 ★★★
Contact:
Lyme Bay Holidays, Bos House,
44 Church Street, Lyme Regis
DT7 3DA
T: (01297) 443363
F: (01297) 445576
E: email@lymebayholidays.co.uk
I: www.lymebayholidays.co.uk

2 Wellhayes Cottage ★★-★★★
Contact: Ms Sandra Hailes
The Granary, Harbourneford,
South Brent TQ10 9DT
T: (01364) 72515
E: shailes@freeuk.com
I: www.coinage.co.uk/wellhayes

Westfield
Rating Applied For
Contact: Mrs Stella Alford
Moonrakers, Claverton Down
Road, Bath BA2 6DZ
T: (01225) 465430
F: (01225) 465430

Westover Farm Cottages ★★★
Contact: Jon & Debby Snook
Westover Farm Cottages,
Westover Farm, Wootton
Fitzpaine, Bridport DT6 6NE
T: (01297) 560451
E: wfcottages@aol.com
I: www.lymeregis.com/westover-farm-cottages

Windyridge - C4359 ★★★
Contact:
Lyme Bay Holidays, Bos House,
44 Church Street, Lyme Regis
DT7 3DA
T: (01297) 443363
F: (01297) 445576
E: email@lymebayholidays.co.uk
I: www.lymebayholidays.co.uk

Woodville Apartment - B4338 ★★★
Contact: Mr Dave Matthews
Lyme Bay Holidays, Bos House,
44 Church Street, Lyme Regis
DT7 3DA
T: (01297) 443363
F: (01297) 445576
E: email@lymebayholidays.co.uk
I: www.lymebayholidays.co.uk

LYMPSHAM
Somerset

Dulhorn Farm Caravan Park ★★
Contact: Mr & Mrs Bowden
Weston Road, Lympsham,
Weston-super-Mare BS24 0JQ
T: (01934) 750298
F: (01934) 750913

Lower Wick Farm Cottages ★★★
Contact: Mr & Ms Nigel, Elaine
Bishop & Coles
Lower Wick Farm Cottages, Wick
Lane, Weston-super-Mare
BS24 0HG
T: (01278) 751333
F: (01278) 751909
E: info@lowerwickfarmcottages.co.uk
I: www.lowerwickfarmcottages.co.uk

LYNMOUTH
Devon

The Beacon ★★★★
Contact: Mr Michael & Mrs
Tracy Ann Burnside
The Beacon, Countisbury Hill,
Lynmouth EX35 6ND
T: (01598) 753268
F: (01598) 752340
E: thebeacon@btinternet.com
I: www.lynmouthaccomodation.co.uk

Clooneavin Holidays ★★★
Contact: Mrs Gill Davidson
Clooneavin Holidays, Clooneavin
Path, Lynmouth EX35 6EE
T: (01598) 753334
I: www.clooneavinholidays.co.uk

Clovelly House ★★★★
Contact: Mrs Linda Dobie
1 Ducks Meadow, Marlborough
SN8 4DE
T: (01672) 513621
F: (01488) 684824
E: clovelly@hotmail.com
I: www.clovellycottage.co.uk

Manorview ★★★★
Contact: Mr Peter & Mrs Janet
Cornwell
Marsden's Cottage Holidays, 2
The Square, Braunton EX33 2JB
T: (01271) 813777
F: (01271) 813664
E: holidays@marsdens.co.uk
I: www.marsdens.co.uk

Ottery Cottage ★★★★
Contact:
Marsdens Cottage Holidays, 2
The Square, Braunton EX33 2JB
T: (01271) 813777
F: (01271) 813664
E: holidays@marsdens.co.uk
I: www.marsdens.co.uk

Riverview ★★★
Contact:
Marsden's Cottage Holidays, 2
The Square, Braunton EX33 2JB
T: (01271) 813777
F: (01271) 813664

Water's Edge Cottage ★★★★
Contact: Mr M Wolverson
Primespot Character Properties,
c/o Stag Cottage, Holestone
Down, Combe Martin,
Ilfracombe EX34 0PF
T: (01271) 882449

Wilrose ★★★
Contact:
Marsden's Cottage Holidays, 2
The Square, Braunton EX33 2JB
T: (01271) 813777
F: (01271) 813664
E: holidays@marsdens.co.uk
I: www.marsdens.co.uk

LYNTON
Devon

Buttershaw Cottage ★★★★
Contact:
Marsden's Cottage Holidays, 2
The Square, Braunton EX33 2JB
T: (01271) 813777
F: (01271) 813664
E: holidays@marsdens.co.uk
I: www.marsdens.co.uk

Byways ★★★★
Contact:
Marsdens Cottage Holidays, 2
The Square, Braunton EX33 2JB
T: (01271) 813777
F: (01271) 813664
E: holidays@marsdens.co.uk
I: www.marsdens.co.uk

Cloud Farm ★★★
Contact: Mrs Jill Harman
Cloud Farm, Lynton EX35 6NU
T: (01598) 741234
F: (01598) 741234
E: doonevalleyholidays@hotmail.com
I: www.doonevalleyholidays.co.uk

Coastal Exmoor Hideaways ★★★-★★★★★
Contact: Mr Peter Hitchen
Coastal Exmoor Hideaways,
Heddon Valley Hill, Parracombe,
Barnstaple EX31 4PU
T: (08717) 170772
F: (08717) 170773
E: info@coastalexmoorhideaways.co.uk
I: www.coastalexmoorhideaways.co.uk

Lyn Cottage ★★★★
Contact: Mr Peter & Mrs Janet
Cornwell
Marsden's Cottage Holidays, 2
The Square, Braunton EX33 2JB
T: (01271) 813777
F: (01271) 813664
E: holidays@marsdens.co.uk
I: www.marsdens.co.uk

Nettlecombe Cottage ★★★
Contact:
Marsden's Cottage Holidays, 2
The Square, Braunton EX33 2JB
T: (01271) 813777
F: (01271) 813664
E: holidayds@marsdens.co.uk
I: www.marsdens.co.uk

Royal Castle Lodge ★★★★
Contact: Mr M Wolverson
c/o Stag Cottage, Holestone
Down, Combe Martin EX34 0PF
T: (01271) 882449

The Stables ★★★★
Contact: Mr Keith & Patricia
Luckhurst
Hammonds Farmhouse, Longpot
Lane, Barnstaple EX31 4SY
T: (01271) 850882
I: www.stablesatlynton.co.uk

Tillys One and Tillys Two ★★★
Contact:
Marsdens Cottage Holidays, 2
The Square, Braunton EX33 2JB
T: (01271) 813777
F: (01271) 813664
E: holidays@marsdens.co.uk
I: www.marsdens.co.uk

West Ilkerton Farm ★★★★
Contact: Mrs Eveleigh
West Ilkerton Farm, Lynton
EX35 6QA
T: (01598) 752310
F: (01598) 752310
E: eveleigh@westilkerton.co.uk
I: www.westilkerton.co.uk

Wringcliffe, Sillery ★★★-★★★★★
Contact: Mr Shimwell
Wringcliffe, Sillery, Burlington
House, 11 Lee Road, Lynton
EX35 6HW
T: (01598) 753352
F: (01598) 753352
E: art@gunnsgallery.co.uk
I: www.gunnsgallery.co.uk

SOUTH WEST ENGLAND

MAENPORTH
Cornwall

Tregullow ★★★★
Contact:
Cornish Cottage Holidays,
Killibrae, west Bay Maenporth
Road, Falmouth TR11 5HP
T: (01326) 250339
F: (01326) 250339
E: postmaster@
cornishholidaycottages.net
I: www.cornishholidaycottages.
net/property/maenporth/
tregullow.html

MAIDEN NEWTON
Dorset

Lancombe Country Cottages ★★★★
Contact: Mr Myles & Mrs Janet
Provis & Schofield
Lancombe Country Cottages,
Higher Chilfrome, Dorchester
DT2 0HU
T: (01300) 320562
F: (01300) 320562
E: info@lancombe.co.uk
I: www.lancombe.co.uk

MAIDENCOMBE
Torbay

Langley Manor ★★★
Contact:
Holiday Homes & Cottages
South West, 365A Torquay Road,
Paignton TQ3 2BT
T: (01803) 663650
F: (01803) 664037
E: holcotts@aol.com
I: www.swcottages.co.uk

MALMESBURY
Wiltshire

Cow Byre and Bull Pen ★★★
Contact: Mrs Edna Edwards
Cow Byre and Bull Pen,
Stonehill, Charlton, Malmesbury
SN16 9DY
T: (01666) 823310
F: (01666) 823310
E: johnedna@stonehillfarm.
fsnet.co.uk
I: www.smoothhound.
co.uk/hotels/stonehill.html

King's Cottage H139 ★★★
Contact:
Hideaways, Luke Street, Berwick
St John, Shaftesbury SP7 0HQ
T: (01747) 828170
F: (01747) 829090
E: enq@hideaways.co.uk
I: www.hideaways.co.uk

MALPAS
Cornwall

Curlews ★★★★
Contact: Mrs Margie Lumby
Special Places In Cornwall,
Poachers Reach, Harcourt, Truro
TR3 6SQ
T: (01872) 864400
E: office@
specialplacescornwall.co.uk
I: www.specialplacescornwall.
co.uk

The Quarterdeck ★★★★
Contact: Mrs Margie Lumby
Special Places in Cornwall,
Poachers Reach, Harcourt, Truro
TR3 6SQ
T: (01872) 864400
E: office@
specialplacescornwall.co.uk
I: www.specialplacescornwall.
co.uk

Trelowthas ★★★★
Contact: Mr Chris Churm
2 The Rookery, Tythby Road,
Nottingham NG12 3AA
T: (01159) 334707
F: (01159) 334707

MANACCAN
Cornwall

Discovery ★★★
Contact:
Cornish Cottage Holidays, The
Old Turnpike Dairy, Godolphin
Road, Helston TR13 8AA
T: (01326) 573808
F: (01326) 564992
E: enquiry@
cornishcottageholidays.co.uk
I: www.cornishcottageholidays.
co.uk

Flushing Cove Cottage ★★★★
Contact: Mrs Sally Ablewhite
Glebe House, Up Marden,
Chichester PO18 9JR
T: (01243) 535266
F: (01243) 535266
E: michael.ablewhite@
btopenworld.com
I: flushingcove-gillan.net

Hallowarren Barn
Rating Applied For
Contact:
Cornish Cottage Holidays, The
Old Turnpike Dairy, Godolphin
Road, Helston TR13 8AA
T: (01326) 573808
F: (01326) 564992
E: enquiry@
cornishcottageholidays.co.uk
I: www.cornishcottageholidays.
co.uk

Hallowarren Cottage ★★★★
Contact:
Cornish Cottage Holidays, The
Old Turnpike Dairy, Godolphin
Road, Helston TR13 8AA
T: (01326) 573808
F: (01326) 564992
E: enquiry@
cornishcottageholidays.co.uk
I: www.cornishcottageholidays.
co.uk

Hillside & Chy-Pyth ★★★-★★★★
Contact:
Cornish Cottage Holidays, The
Old Turnpike Dairy, Godolphin
Meneage Street, Helston
TR13 8AA
T: (01326) 573808
F: (01326) 564992
E: enquiry@
cornishcottageholidays.co.uk
I: www.cornishcottageholidays.
co.uk

Lestowder Farm ★★-★★★★★
Contact: Mrs Janet Martin
Lestowder Farm, Manaccan,
Helston TR12 6ES
T: (01326) 231400
F: (01326) 231400
E: lestowderfarm@hotmail.com
I: www.lestowderfarmcottages.
co.uk

Menifters Holiday Cottages ★★★
Contact: Mrs Wendy Baxter
Menifters Holiday Cottages,
Gillan, Helston TR12 6ER
T: (01326) 280711
E: menifters@tinyonline.co.uk
I: www.menifterscottages.co.uk

West Minster Cottage ★★★★
Contact:
Helford River Cottages, Point,
Helford, Helston TR12 6JY
T: (01326) 231666
E: info@helfordcottages.co.uk
I: www.helfordcottages.co.uk

MANATON
Devon

Beckaford Cottage ★★★★
Contact:
Toad Hall Cottages, Elliot House,
Church Street, Kingsbridge
TQ7 1BY
T: (01548) 853089
F: (01548) 853086
E: thc@toadhallcottages.com
I: www.toadhallcottages.com

Homer Heales ★★
Contact: Mrs Moreton
Great Houndtor, Newton Abbot
TQ13 9UW
T: (01647) 221202

MANNINGFORD ABBOTS
Wiltshire

The Old Tulip Barn ★★★
Contact: Mrs Margot Andrews
The Old Tulip Barn, c/o Huntlys,
Pewsey SN9 6HZ
T: (01672) 563663
F: (01672) 851249
E: meg@gimspike.fsnet.co.uk

MARAZION
Cornwall

Arizona & Tuscany ★★★
Contact: Mrs Dawn Senior
The Old Rectory, Green Lane,
Marazion TR17 0HQ
T: (01736) 710222

The Captain's House ★★★★★
Contact: Mr & Mrs Pettit
Tregullas, Truro TR3 6AJ
T: (01872) 865403
E: treduma@tiscali.co.uk
I: www.captainshousemarazion.
co.uk

Polgew ★★★★
Contact: Mrs Diane Hickman
Paddock Wood, Crenver Corner,
Camborne TR14 0PE
T: (01209) 831740
F: (01209) 832007
E: polgew1@ntlworld.com
I: www.westcornwallholidays.
co.uk

St Aubyn Estates ★★★-★★★★★
Contact: Ms Clare Sandry
St Aubyn Estates, The Manor
Office, West End, Marazion
TR17 0EF
T: (01736) 710507
F: (01736) 719930
E: godolphin@manor-office.
co.uk
I: www.staubynestates.co.uk

Tregew Holiday Bungalows ★★★
Contact: Mr Rodney Pool
Tregew Holiday Bungalows,
Rose Hill, Marazion TR17 0HB
T: (01736) 710247

Trevara ★★★★
Contact: Mrs Sally Laird
Pheasant Copse, Bere Court
Road, Reading RG8 8JU
T: (0118) 9845500
F: (0118) 9843966
E: sallylaird@talk21.com
I: www.bestcottageincornwall.
co.uk

Trevarthian Holiday Homes ★★-★★★
Contact:
Trevarthian Holiday Homes,
West End, Marazion TR17 0EG
T: (01736) 710100
F: (01736) 710111
E: info@trevarthian.co.uk
I: www.trevarthian.co.uk

The White House, Courtyard Cottage and Whitehouse Mews Flat ★★★
Contact: Mr Peter Hall
The White House, The Square,
Marazion TR17 0AP
T: (01736) 710424
F: (01736) 710424
E: info@
cornwall-holiday-cottages.com
I: www.
cornwall-holiday-cottages.com

MARHAMCHURCH
Cornwall

Budds Barns ★★★★
Contact: Mr David & Mrs Carol
Richardson
Budds Barns, Titson, Bude
EX23 0HQ
T: (01288) 361339
F: (01288) 361339
E: relax@buddsbarns.co.uk
I: www.buddsbarns.co.uk

Corner Cottage ★★★
Contact: Mr Colin & Mrs
Suzanne Burke
Two Waters, Park Road,
Dunstable LU5 6AB
T: (01525) 878100
F: (01525) 878119
E: colin@gardnerburke.co.uk
I: www.ourcornercottage.co.uk

Corner Cottage & Bluebell Cottage
Rating Applied For
Contact:
Cornish Cottage Holidays, The
Old Turnpike Dairy, Godolphin
Road, Helston TR13 8AA
T: (01326) 573808
E: enquiry@
cornishcottageholidays.co.uk

Establishments printed in blue have a detailed entry in this guide

SOUTH WEST ENGLAND

Court Farm ★★★-★★★★
Contact: Mrs Mary Trewin
Court Farm, Bude EX23 0EN
T: (01288) 361494
F: (01288) 361494
E: mary@courtfarm-holidays.co.uk
I: www.courtfarm-holidays.co.uk

Knowle Farm Cottage & Tallet Barn ★★★-★★★★
Contact: Mr & Mrs S Youldon
Knowle Farm Cottage & Tallet Barn, Bude EX23 0HG
T: (01288) 381215
F: (01288) 381215
E: youldon@knowle007.fsnet.co.uk

Sharlands Farm ★★★★
Contact:
Farm & Cottage Holidays, Victoria House, 12 Fore Street, Bideford EX39 1AW
T: (01237) 479146
F: (01237) 421512
E: enquiries@farmcott.co.uk
I: www.farmcott.co.uk

Trelay Farmhouse
Rating Applied For
Contact:
Farm & Cottage Holidays, Victoria House, 12 Fore Street, Bideford EX39 1AW
T: (01237) 479146
F: (01237) 421512
E: enquiries@farmcott.co.uk
I: www.farmcott.co.uk

Wooldown Farm Cottages ★★★-★★★★
Contact: Mrs Susan Blewett
Wooldown Farm Cottages, Wooldown Farm, Bude EX23 OHP
T: (01288) 361216
F: (01288) 361216
E: rogersueblewett@aol.com
I: www.wooldown.co.uk

MARK
Somerset

Pear Tree Cottage ★★★
Contact: Mrs Susan Slocombe
Pear Tree Cottage, Northwick Road, Highbridge TA9 4PG
T: (01278) 641228
E: northwickfarm@breathemail.net

MARKET LAVINGTON
Wiltshire

Hazel Cottage ★★★★
Contact: Mrs Janette Hodgkinson
Hazel Cottage, 5 Parsonage Lane, Devizes SN10 4AA
T: (01380) 813516
F: (01380) 813516
E: okasan@waitrose.com

MARLDON
Devon

Millmans Cottages ★★★-★★★★
Contact: Mr Edward & Mrs Tina Girard
Millmans Farm, Village Road, Paignton TQ3 1SJ
T: (01803) 558213
F: (01803) 558213
E: tina@millmanfarm.co.uk

Pottery Mews
Rating Applied For
Contact:
Holiday Homes & Cottages SW, 365A Torquay Road, Paignton TQ3 2BT
T: (01803) 663650
F: (01803) 664037
E: holcotts@aol.com
I: www.swcottages.co.uk

Wildwoods ★★
Contact: Mr Ian Butterworth
Holiday Homes & Cottages South West, 365A Torquay Road, Paignton TQ3 2BT
T: (01803) 663650
F: (01803) 664037
E: holcotts@aol.com
I: www.swcottages.co.uk

MARNHULL
Dorset

Trooper Farm ★★
Contact: Mr Cyril Bastable
Trooper Farm, Love Lane, Sturminster Newton DT10 1PT
T: (01258) 820753

MARSHFIELD
South Gloucestershire

The Old Inn ★★★
Contact: Mrs Judy Brason
The Old Inn, Market Place, Chippenham SN14 8NP
T: (01225) 891803
F: (01225) 891301
E: judy@theoldinnatmarshfield.co.uk
I: www.theoldinnatmarshfield.co.uk

MARSTON
Wiltshire

Barn Cottage & Stable Cottage ★★★★
Contact: Mrs Joy Reardon
Barn Cottage & Stable Cottage, Home Farm, Close Lane, Devizes SN10 5SN
T: (01380) 725484
E: maupicereardon@lineone.net

MARTINHOE
Devon

Hollowbrook Cottage ★★★★
Contact: Mr Christopher Richmond
Hollowbrook Cottage, Martinhoe, Barnstaple EX31 4QT
T: (01598) 763368
F: (01598) 763567
E: cottages@oldrectoryhotel.co.uk
I: www.exmoorcottages.co.uk

Ivy Cottage ★★★★
Contact:
Marsden's Cottage Holidays, 2 The Square, Braunton EX33 2JB
T: (01271) 813777
F: (01271) 813644
E: holidays@marsdens.co.uk
I: www.marsdens.co.uk

MARTINSTOWN
Dorset

Blackbird Cottage ★★★
Contact: Mr Zachary Stuart-Brown
Dream Cottages, 5 Hope Square, Weymouth DT4 8TR
T: (01305) 789000
F: (01305) 761346
E: admin@dream-cottages.co.uk
I: www.dream-cottages.co.uk

Greatstone Cottage ★★★
Contact:
Dream Cottages, 5 Hope Square, Weymouth DT4 8TR
T: (01305) 789000
F: (01305) 761347

Hope Cottage ★★★★
Contact:
Dream Cottages, 5 Hope Square, Weymouth DT4 8TR
T: (01305) 789000
F: (01305) 761347

MARTOCK
Somerset

Anne's Place ★★★
Contact:
Country Holidays, Spring Mill, Barnoldswick BB94 0AA
T: 0870 1970600

MARWOOD
Devon

The Pump House ★★★★
Contact:
Marsdens Cottage Holidays, 2 The Square, Braunton EX33 2JB
T: (01271) 813777
F: (01271) 813644
E: holidays@marsdens.co.uk

The Tallett ★★★
Contact:
Marsden's Cottage Holidays, 2 The Square, Braunton EX33 2JB
T: (01271) 813777
F: (01271) 813644
E: holidays@marsdens.co.uk
I: www.marsdens.co.uk

MAWGAN
Cornwall

The Cuckoos Nest ★★★
Contact: Mr Martin Raftery
Mullion Cottages, Mullion Meadows, Helston TR12 7HB
T: (01326) 240315
F: (01326) 241090
E: enquiries@mullioncottages.com

Le An Marghas ★★★
Contact:
Helford River Cottages, Point, Helford, Helston TR12 6JY
T: (01326) 231666
E: info@helfordcottages.co.uk
I: www.helfordcottages.co.uk

The Studio ★★★
Contact: Mr Martin Raftery
Mullion Cottages, Churchtown, Helston TR12 7HQ
T: (01326) 240315
F: (01326) 241090
E: martin@mullioncottages.com
I: www.mullioncottages.com

MAWGAN PORTH
Cornwall

Tredragon Lodges ★★★
Contact: Mr James Mcluskie
Tredragon Lodges, Newquay TR8 4BW
T: (01637) 860324
F: (01637) 860743
E: tredragonlodge@hotmail.com.uk
I: www.tredragonlodge.co.uk

Trelawns ★★★★
Contact:
Cornish Cottage Holidays, The Old Turnpike Dairy, Godolphin, Meneage Street, Helston TR13 8AA
T: (01326) 573808
F: (01326) 564992
E: enquiry@cornishcottageholidays.co.uk
I: www.cornishcottageholidays.co.uk

MAWNAN SMITH
Cornwall

Glen Avon ★★★
Contact: Mrs A Benney
Lower Penpol Farm, Budock Vean Lane, Falmouth TR11 5LJ
T: (01326) 250283

Helford Point ★★★★
Contact:
Cornish Holiday Cottages, Killibrae, West Bay Maenporth Road, Falmouth TR11 5HP
T: (01326) 250399
F: (01326) 250399
E: postmaster@cornishholidaycottages.com
I: www.cornishholidaycottages.net/property/helford_river/helfordpoint.html

No 3 Rose Cottages ★★★
Contact:
Cornish Cottage Holidays, Killibrae, West Bay Maenporth Road, Falmouth TR11 5HP
T: (01326) 250339
F: (01326) 250339
E: postmaster@cornishholidaycottages.net
I: www.cornishholidaycottages.net/property/helford_river/rosecottages3.html

MELCOMBE BINGHAM
Dorset

Greygles ★★★★
Contact: Mr Paul Sommerfeld
22 Tiverton Road, London NW10 3HL
T: (020) 8969 4830
F: (020) 8960 0069
E: enquiry@greygles.co.uk
I: www.greygles.co.uk

MELDON
Devon

Kerslake Cottage ★★★★
Contact: Ms Lizzie St George
Kerslake Cottage, Kerslake Farm, Okehampton EX20 4LU
T: (01837) 54892
F: (01837) 54892
E: booking@kerslakemeldon.co.uk
I: www.kerslakemeldon.co.uk

SOUTH WEST ENGLAND

MELKSHAM
Wiltshire

Moorlands Self Catering Holiday Homes ★★★★
Contact: Mrs Jackie Moore
Moorlands Self Catering Holiday Homes, The Coach House, Station Approach, Melksham SN12 8BN
T: (01225) 702155
F: (01225) 702155
E: moorlands@aol.com
I: www.moorlandsuk.com

MELPLASH
Dorset

Binghams Farm Valley View Apartments ★★★
Contact: Mrs Lisa Herbert
Binghams Farm, Melplash, Bridport DT6 3TT
T: (01308) 488234
F: (01308) 488426
E: enquiries@binghamsfarm.co.uk
I: www.binghamsfarm.co.uk

Mount Cottage - V4365 ★★★★
Contact: Mr Dave Matthews
Lyme Bay Holidays, Bos House, 44 Church Street, Lyme Regis DT7 3DA
T: (01297) 443363
F: (01297) 445576
E: email@lymebayholidays.co.uk
I: www.lymebayholidays.co.uk

MEMBURY
Devon

Bowditch Farm ★★★★
Contact: Mr Sarah & Mrs Michael Bell
Bowditch Farm, Axminster EX13 7TY
T: 0845 4560290
F: (01404) 881801

Bowditch Farm Lodge
Rating Applied For
Contact:
Milkbere Holidays, 3 Fore Street, Seaton EX12 2LE
T: (01297) 20729
E: info@milkbere.com

Oxenways Estate Cottages ★★★★-★★★★★
Contact: Mr Ken Beecham
Oxenways Estate Cottages, Oxenways, Chapelcroft Road, Axminster EX13 7JR
T: (01404) 881785
F: (01404) 881778
E: info@oxenways.com
I: www.oxenways.com

MENHENIOT
Cornwall

Hayloft Courtyard Cottages ★★★-★★★★
Contact: Mr & Mrs Hore
Hoseasons Country Cottages, Raglan Road, Lowestoft NR32 2LW
T: (01502) 501515
I: www.hoseasons.co.uk

Trewint Farm ★★★-★★★★
Contact: Mrs Elizabeth Rowe
Trewint Farm, Liskeard PL14 3RE
T: (01579) 347155
F: (01579) 347155
I: www.geocities.com/trewint_2000

MERE
Wiltshire

2 Chance Cottages ★★★★
Contact: Mr & Mrs White
Chance Cottage, Shaftesbury Road, Warminster BA12 6BW
T: (01747) 861401
F: (01747) 861401
E: mail@wiltshirecottageholidays.co.uk
I: www.wiltshirecottageholidays.co.uk

Lower Mere Park Farm ★★★★
Contact: Mrs Nicky Mitchell
Lower Mere Park Farm, Warminster BA12 6AD
T: (01747) 830771

MEVAGISSEY
Cornwall

Bay View ★★★
Contact: Mr William Truscott
Bay View, Jetty Street, St Austell PL26
T: (01726) 822727
F: (01726) 822685
E: truscott@ctfarm.freeserve.co.uk
I: www.chycon.co.uk

Pollys Apartments
Rating Applied For
Contact: Mrs Diana Littlejohns
Pollys Apartments, Stanwicke, School Hill, St Austell PL26 6TQ
T: (01726) 843352

The Poppins ★★★★
Contact:
Cornish Cottage Holidays, The Old Turnpike Dairy, Godolphin Road, Helston TR13 8AA
T: (01326) 573808

Treleaven Farm Cottages ★★★★
Contact: Mr Linda Hennah
Treleaven Farm Cottages, Treleaven Farm, Valley Road, St Austell PL26 6RZ
T: (01726) 843558
F: (01726) 843558
I: www.treleavenfarm.co.uk

Treloen Holiday Apartments ★★★
Contact: Mrs Pat Seamark
Treloen Holiday Apartments, Polkirt Hill, Mevagissey PL26 6UX
T: (01726) 842406
F: (01726) 842406
E: holidays@treloen.co.uk
I: www.treloen.co.uk

MIDDLE MARWOOD
Devon

Primrose House ★★★★
Contact:
Marsden's Cottage Holidays, 2 The Square, Braunton EX33 2JB
T: (01271) 813777
F: (01271) 813664
E: holidays@marsdens.co.uk
I: www.marsdens.co.uk

MIDDLECOMBE
Somerset

Periton Park Court & Riding Stables ★★-★★★★
Contact: Mr John Borland
Periton Park Court, Periton Road, Minehead TA24 8SN
T: (01643) 705970
F: (01643) 705970
E: peritonparkcourt@btinternet.com
I: peritonpark.co.uk

MIDDLEMARSH
Dorset

White Horse Farm ★★★★
Contact: Mr David Wilding
White Horse Farm, Sherborne DT9 5QN
T: (01963) 210222
F: (01963) 210222
E: enquiries@whitehorsefarm.co.uk
I: www.whitehorsefarm.co.uk

MILBORNE ST ANDREW
Dorset

Orchard Cottage ★★★
Contact: Mrs Charlotte Martin
2 Deverel Cottages, Deverel Farm, Milborne St Andrew, Blandford Forum DT11 0HX
T: (01258) 837195
E: deverel@dialstart78.fsnet.co.uk
I: www.oas.co.uk/ukcottages/orchardcottage/

The Retreat ★★★
Contact: Mrs June Jenkins
27 Fourgates Road, Dorchester DT1 2NL
T: (01305) 269194
E: junejenkins56@hotmail.com

MILLBROOK
Cornwall

The Retreat/The Studio ★★★-★★★★★
Contact: Mrs Sarah Blake
Stone Farm, Torpoint PL10 1JJ
T: (01752) 822267
I: www.farmcott.co.uk

MILLENDREATH
Cornwall

1 The Adit ★★★
Contact:
Valley Villas, Brook Cottage, Old Warleigh Lane, Plymouth PL5 4ND
T: (01752) 774900
E: sales@valleyvillas.co.uk
I: www.valleyvillas.co.uk

Bay View Villa ★★
Contact:
Valley Villas, Brook Cottage, Old Warleigh Lane, Plymouth PL5 4ND
T: (01752) 774900
E: sales@valleyvillas.co.uk
I: www.valleyvillas.co.uk

Beach Villa ★★
Contact:
Valley Villas, Brook Cottage, Old Warleigh Lane, Plymouth PL5 4ND
T: (01752) 774900
E: sales@valleyvillas.co.uk
I: www.valleyvillas.co.uk

Coastpath Villa ★★★
Contact:
Valley Villas, Sales Office, City Business Park, Office 38 Somerset Place, Plymouth PL3 4BB
T: (01752) 605605
E: sales@valleyvillas.co.uk
I: www.valleyvillas.co.uk

Eden II ★★★
Contact:
Valley Villas Sales Office, Office 38, City Business Park, Somerset Place, Stoke, Plymouth PL3 4BB
T: (01752) 605605
E: sales@valleyvillas.co.uk
I: www.valleyvillas.com

59 Hillside Villa ★★
Contact:
Valley Villas, Brook Cottage, Old Warleigh Lane, Plymouth PL5 4ND
T: (01752) 774900
E: sales@valleyvillas.co.uk
I: www.valleyvillas.co.uk

73 Hillside Villa ★★★
Contact:
Valley Villas, Brook Cottage, Old Warleigh Lane, Plymouth PL5 4ND
T: (01752) 774900
E: sales@valleyvillas.co.uk
I: www.valleyvillas.co.uk

74 Hillside Villa ★★
Contact:
Valley Villas, Brook House, Old Warleigh Lane, Plymouth PL5 4ND
T: (01752) 774900
E: sales@valleyvillas.co.uk
I: www.valleyvillas.co.uk

The Lobster Pot ★★★
Contact:
Valley Villas, Sales Office, City Business Park, Office 38 Somerset Park, Plymouth PL3 4BB
T: (01752) 605605
E: sales@valleyvillas.co.uk
I: www.valleyvillas.co.uk

Palm Villa ★★
Contact:
Valley Villas, Brook Cottage, Old Warleigh Lane, Plymouth PL5 4ND
T: (01752) 774900
E: sales@valleyvillas.co.uk
I: www.valleyvillas.co.uk

Riviera Villa ★★
Contact:
Valley Villas, Brook Cottage, Old Warleigh Lane, Plymouth PL5 4ND
T: (01752) 774900
E: sales@valleyvillas.co.uk
I: www.valleyvillas.co.uk

Robins Nest ★★
Contact:
Valley Villas, Brook Cottage, Old Warleigh Lane, Plymouth PL5 4ND
T: (01752) 774900
E: sales@valleyvillas.co.uk
I: www.valleyvillas.co.uk

Establishments printed in blue have a detailed entry in this guide

SOUTH WEST ENGLAND

Sea View Villa ★★
Contact:
Valley Villas, Brook Cottage, Old Warleigh Lane, Plymouth PL5 4ND
T: (01752) 774900
E: sales@valleyvillas.co.uk
I: www.valleyvillas.co.uk

Seaside Villa ★★★
Contact:
Valley Villas, Brook Cottage, Old Warleigh Lane, Plymouth PL5 4ND
T: (01752) 774900
E: sales@valleyvillas.co.uk
I: www.valleyvillas.co.uk

1 Valley Bungalow ★★
Contact:
Valley Villas, Brook Cottage, Old Warleigh Lane, Plymouth PL5 4ND
T: (01752) 774900
E: sales@valleyvillas.co.uk
I: www.valleyvillas.co.uk

Waterfront Villa ★★★
Contact:
Valley Villas, Brook Cottage, Old Warleigh Lane, Plymouth PL5 4ND
T: (01752) 774900
E: sales@valleyvillas.co.uk
I: www.valleyvillas.co.uk

MILLPOOL
Cornwall

Nutkin Lodge ★★★★
Contact: Mr John Bass
Nutkin Lodge, Millpool Grange, Bodmin PL30 4HZ
T: (01208) 821596
E: jsnbass@aol.com

MILTON ABBAS
Dorset

Little Hewish Barn ★★★★★
Contact: Mr Terry Dunn
2 Little Hewish Cottages, Milton Abbas, Blandford Forum DT11 0DP
T: (01258) 881235
F: (01258) 881393
E: terry@littlehewish.co.uk
I: www.littlehewish.co.uk

Luccombe Farm ★★★★
Contact: Mr Murray & Mrs Amanda Kayll
Luccombe Farm, Blandford Forum DT11 0BE

Park Farm ★★★★
Contact: Mrs Audrey Burch
Park Farm, Blandford Forum DT11 0AX
T: (01258) 880828
F: (01258) 881788
E: burch@parkfarmcottages.co.uk
I: www.parkfarmcottages.co.uk

Primrose Cottage ★★★★
Contact: Mrs G D Garvey
T: (01300) 341352
F: (01300) 341352
E: tgarvey@ragtime99.freeserve.co.uk
I: www.miltonabbas-primrosecottage.co.uk

Three the Maltings ★★★
Contact: Mr Stuart-Brown
Dream Cottages, 41 Maiden Street, Weymouth DT4 8TR
T: (01305) 789000

MILTON COOMBE
Devon

Tower Cottage ★★★★
Contact: Mrs Sarah Stone
Tower Cottage, Yelverton PL20 6EZ
T: (01822) 853285
E: sarah.stone@cider-house.co.uk
I: www.cider-house.co.uk

MINCHINHAMPTON
Gloucestershire

Vine House Flat ★★★★
Contact: Mrs Veronica Finn
Vine House, Friday Street, Stroud GL6 9JL
T: (01453) 884437
E: finnatminch@aol.com

The Woolsack ★★★★
Contact: Mrs E Hayward
Hyde Wood House, Cirencester Road, Minchinhampton, Stroud GL6 8PE
T: (01453) 885504
F: (01453) 885504
E: info@hydewoodhouse.co.uk
I: www.hydewoodhouse.co.uk

MINEHEAD
Somerset

Anchor Cottage ★★★★
Contact: Dr John Malin
3 The Courtyard, Bancks Street, Minehead TA24 5DJ
T: (01643) 707529
F: (01643) 708712
E: jmalin@btinternet.com

Combe Cottages ★★★★
Contact: Mrs Parks
Mead House, 104 Periton Lane, Minehead TA24 8DZ
T: (01643) 704939

Dome Flat ★★★★
Contact: Mr Lowin
176A Harefield Road, Uxbridge UB8 1PP
T: (01895) 236972

Dove Cottage ★★★
Contact: Mr Waterman
38 Fernleigh Road, Winchmore Hill, London N21 3AL
T: (020) 8882 4920
F: (020) 8882 4920

Fishermans Cottages ★★★
Contact: Mrs Martin
57 Quay Street, Minehead TA24 5UL
T: (01643) 704263

The Freight Shed ★★★
Contact: Mr Alison & Mrs Duncan Waller
The Freight Shed, Goosemore Station Cottage, Minehead TA24 7BY
T: (01643) 851386
F: (01643) 851532
E: barlevalley@hotmail.com
I: www.exmoor-barlevalley-safaris.co.uk

Harbour Cottage ★★★
Contact: Ms Hall
14 Rue De L'equerre, 78290 Croissy-Sur-Seine, France
T: +331 30536730
E: family davidm.hall@compuserve.com

The Haven Holiday Flats ★★
Contact: Mr Thorpe
The Haven Holiday Flats, 41 Blenheim Road, Minehead TA24 5QA
T: (01643) 705167

Higher Rodhuish Farm ★★
Contact: Mrs Thomas
Higher Rodhuish Farm, Minehead TA24 6QL
T: (01984) 640253
F: (01984) 640253

Hindon Organic Farm ★★★-★★★★
Contact: Mrs Webber
Hindon Organic Farm, Minehead TA24 8SH
T: (01643) 705244
F: (01643) 705244
E: info@hindonfram.co.uk
I: www.hindonfarm.co.uk

Holmbush ★★
Contact:
Toad Hall Cottages, Elliot House, Church Street, Kingsbridge TQ7 1BY
T: (01548) 853089
F: (01548) 853086
E: thc@toadhallcottages.com

Huntingball Lodge ★★★★
Contact: Mr Brian & Mrs Kim Hall
Huntingball Lodge, Blue Anchor, Minehead TA24 6JP
T: (01984) 640076
F: (01984) 640076
I: www.huntingball-lodge.co.uk

La Mer ★★★
Contact: Mrs Bowden
4 Tides Reach, Quay Street, Minehead TA24 5UL
T: (01643) 704405
F: (01643) 704405

Little Barn Cottage ★★★★
Contact: Mrs Marian Padgett
Little Barn Cottage, Selworthy, Minehead TA24 8TL
T: (01643) 862303

Luxury Flat ★★
Contact: Mr D J & Mrs E J Coward
28 Parks Lane, Minehead TA24 8BT
T: (01643) 705634

Marshfield Apartment ★★★★
Contact: Miss Dawn Leonard
4 First Avenue, Epsom KT19 9TP
T: (020) 87868406
E: c.lister7@ntl.world.com

Old Black Boy Cottage ★★★
Contact: Mr & Mrs Harvey
42 Bampton Street, Minehead TA24 5TT
T: (01643) 705016

The Old Kennels ★★★★
Contact: Mr Vivian Perkins
The Old Kennels, 4A Periton Lane, Minehead TA24 8AQ
T: (01643) 705754

Parkside ★★
Contact: Mrs Janet Bond
Parkside, 31 Blenheim Road, Minehead TA24 5PZ
T: (01643) 703720
I: www.travel.to/parkside

Peake Cottage ★★★
Contact: Mr H. J. Davies
Meadowcroft, Whitegate Road, Minehead TA24 8BB
T: (01643) 704634

Pella ★★★
Contact: Mrs Yendole
Pella, Western Lane, Minehead TA24 8BZ
T: (01643) 703277
E: hyendole@ukonline.co.uk
I: www.exmoorretreat.co.uk

Rosanda House ★★★
Contact: Mr Richard & Mrs Lorna Robbins
Rosanda House, 2 Northfield Road, Minehead TA24 5QQ
T: (01643) 704958
E: enquiries@rosanda.co.uk
I: www.rosanda.co.uk

Seagate Cottage ★★★★
Contact: Dr & Mr Eaton & Ball
Applegarth, Crewkerne TA18 7PW
T: (01935) 881436
E: meganeaton@ukonline.co.uk

Wydon Farm Cottages ★★★
Contact:
Farm & Cottage Holidays, Victoria House, 12 Fore Street, Bideford EX39 1AW
T: (01237) 479146
F: (01237) 421512
E: enquiries@farmcott.co.uk
I: www.farmcott.co.uk

MINIONS
Cornwall

Trewalla Farm ★★★★
Contact: Mr James Speed
Trewalla Farm, Commonmoor, Liskeard PL14 6ED
T: (01579) 342385
F: (01579) 342385

MISERDEN
Gloucestershire

Sudgrove Cottages ★★★
Contact: Martin and Carol Ractliffe
Sudgrove, Miserden, Stroud GL6 7JD
T: (01285) 821322
F: (01285) 821322
E: enquiries@sudgrovecottages.co.uk
I: www.sudgrovecottages.co.uk

SOUTH WEST ENGLAND

MITCHELDEAN
Gloucestershire

Church Farm Holidays
Church Farm ★★★
Contact: Mr John Verity
Church Farm Holidays Church Farm, Church Lane, Abenhall, Mitcheldean GL17 0DX
T: (01594) 541211
F: (01594) 541212
E: info@churchfarm.uk.net
I: www.churchfarm.uk.net

MODBURY
Devon

Hope Cottage ★★★★
Contact:
Powell's Cottage Holidays, High Street, Saundersfoot SA69 9EJ
T: (01834) 812791
I: www.westcountrycottages.co.uk

The Lodge ★★★★★
Contact: Mrs Sue Ward
The Lodge, Colmer Estate, California Cross, Ivybridge PL21 0SG
T: (01548) 821702
F: (01548) 853086
E: info@heavenlydevon.co.uk
I: www.heavenlydevon.co.uk

Old Traine Barn and Old Traine Cottage
★★★★-★★★★★
Contact:
Toad Hall Cottages, Elliot House, Church Street, Kingsbridge TQ7 1BY
T: (01548) 853089
F: (01548) 853086
E: thc@toadhallcottages.com
I: www.toadhallcottages.com

Oldaport Farm Cottages
★★★★
Contact: Miss Evans
Oldaport Farm Cottages, Ivybridge PL21 0TG
T: (01548) 830842
F: (01548) 830998
E: cathy@oldaport.com
I: www.oldaport.dial.pipex.com

The Popples ★★★★
Contact:
Toad Hall Cottages, Elliot House, Church Street, Kingsbridge TQ7 1BY
T: (01548) 853089
F: (01548) 853086
E: thc@toadhallcottages.com
I: www.toadhallcottages.com

MONKTON WYLD
Dorset

The Thatch - W4400
★★★★
Contact:
Lyme Bay Holidays, Bos House, 44 Church Street, Lyme Regis DT7 3DA
T: (01297) 443363
F: (01297) 445576
E: email@lymebayholidays.co.uk
I: www.lymebayholidays.co.uk

MONTACUTE
Somerset

Abbey Farm ★★★
Contact: Mrs Jenkins
Abbey Farm, Montacute TA15 6UA
T: (01935) 823572
E: xxe70@dial.pipex.com

MORCOMBELAKE
Dorset

Norchard Farmhouse ★★★
Contact: Mrs Mary Ollard
Norchard Farmhouse, Norchard Barn, Bridport DT6 6EP
T: (01297) 489263
F: (01297) 489661
E: norchardbarn@btinternet.com

Upalong Studio - V4395
★★★
Contact:
Lyme Bay Holidays, Bos House, 44 Church Street, Lyme Regis DT7 3DA
T: (01297) 443363
F: (01297) 445576
E: email@lymebayholidays.co.uk
I: www.lymebayholidays.co.uk

MORETON
Dorset

The Courtyard ★★★
Contact: Mrs Lofts
The Courtyard, Moreford Hall, Dorchester DT2 8BA
T: (01305) 853499
E: famlofts@aol.com

Glebe Cottage ★★
Contact: Mrs Gibbens
Glebe Cottage, Moreton, Dorchester DT2 8RQ
T: (01929) 462468

MORETON-IN-MARSH
Gloucestershire

The Flat ★★★★
Contact: Ms Sheila Rolland
Campden Cottages, Folly Cottage, Chipping Campden GL55 6XG
T: (01386) 593315
F: (01386) 593057
E: info@campdencottages.co.uk
I: www.campdencottages.co.uk

Hayloft ★★★
Contact: Mrs Jan Wright
Hayloft, Twostones, Moreton-in-Marsh GL56 0NY
T: (01608) 651104

Hope Cottage ★★★★★
Contact: Miss E.M Langton
Hope Cottage, School Square, Moreton-in-Marsh GL56 0QD
T: (01451) 830343
F: (01451) 832043
E: e.langton@200m.co.uk
I: www.hopecottage.com

Horseshoe Cottage ★★★★
Contact: Mr & Mrs McHale
Horseshoe Cottage, Forge House, Lower Oddington, Moreton-in-Marsh GL56 0UP
T: (01451) 831556

The Laurels ★★★
Contact: Mrs Sandra Billinger
Blue Cedar House, Stow Road, Moreton-in-Marsh GL56 0DW
T: (01608) 650299
E: gandsib@dialstart.net

Little Milton ★★★★
Contact: Mrs Heather Bates
Little Milton, High Street, Moreton-in-Marsh GL56 9ET
T: (01386) 701163
F: (01386) 701163
E: heb@henmarsh.freeserve.co.uk
I: www.miltonview.co.uk

Little Pinners ★★★
Contact: Mrs Mariam Gilbert
Country House Interiors, High Street, Moreton-in-Marsh GL56 0AT
T: (01608) 650007
F: (01608) 650007

Merlin Cottage ★★★★
Contact: Miss Sheila Rolland
Campden Cottages, Folly Cottage, Chipping Campden GL55 6XG
T: (01386) 593315
F: (01386) 593057
E: info@campdencottages.co.uk
I: www.campdencottages.co.uk

Michaelmas Daisy Cottage
★★★
Contact: Mrs Alexander
The Folly, Fifield, Chipping Norton OX7 6HW
T: (01993) 830484
F: (01993) 832022
E: rosemaryalex@onetel.net.uk

Old Corner Cottage ★★★★
Contact: Mrs Cathy Terry
St Helens Vicarage, St Helens Gardens, London W10 6LP
T: (020) 8960 5067
F: (020) 8965782
E: cathy@jcterry.go-plus.net
I: www.oldcornercottage.com

Rose's Cottage ★★★★
Contact: Mr Richard & Mrs Janice Drinkwater
Rose's Cottage, The Green, Broadwell, Moreton-in-Marsh GL56 0UF
T: (01451) 830007

Sarum ★★★★
Contact: Mrs Jo Brooks
Ashlar, Todenham Road, Moreton-in-Marsh GL56 9NJ
T: (01608) 650821
E: jobrooks41@btinternet.com

Stonecroft ★★★
Contact: Mr & Mrs Williams
Sitch Estates, Bell House, Salford, Chipping Norton OX7 5FE
T: (01608) 645397
F: (01608) 645397
E: sitchestate@aol.com

Toms Cottage ★★★★
Contact: Mrs Hall
Chanonry, St Leonards Hill, Windsor SL4 4AT
T: (01753) 855086

The Trees ★★★
Contact: Mrs Ward
15 Gisborough Way, Bailey's Meadow, Loughborough LE11 4FU
T: (01509) 646135
E: rosemaryanne.ward@virgin.net

Twinkle Toes Cottage
★★★★
Contact: Mrs Christine Gowing
Barley Cottage, Junction Road, Churchill, Chipping Norton OX7 6NW
T: (01608) 658579
E: kcgowing@talk21.com

Woodkeepers ★★★★★
Contact: Mrs Wendy Hicks
Woodkeepers, Barton-on-the-Heath, Moreton-in-Marsh GL56 0PL
T: (01608) 674236
E: wendy@woodkeepers.co.uk
I: www.woodkeepers.co.uk

MORETONHAMPSTEAD
Devon

Budleigh Farm ★★-★★★★★
Contact: Mrs Harvey
Budleigh Farm, Moretonhampstead, Newton Abbot TQ13 8SB
T: (01647) 440835
F: (01647) 440436
E: harvey@budleighfarm.co.uk
I: www.budleighfarm.co.uk

Great Doccombe Farm
★★★★
Contact: Mr & Mrs Oakey
Great Doccombe Farm, Doccombe, Newton Abbot TQ13 8SS
T: (01647) 440694

Yarningale ★★★
Contact: Mrs Sarah (Sally) Radcliffe
Yarningale, Exeter Road, Newton Abbot TQ13 8SW
T: (01647) 440560
F: (01647) 440560

MORTEHOE
Devon

Combesgate House ★★★
Contact: Mr Keith & Mrs Virginia Sprason
Ferndale Leisure, Hagley Mews, Hagley Hall, Hall Drive, Hagley, Stourbridge DY9 9LQ
T: (01562) 883038
F: (01562) 886592
E: combesgate.house@virgin.net
I: www.combesgate.fsnet.co.uk

Crows Nest & The Lookout
★★★
Contact:
Marsden's Cottage Holidays, 2 The Square, Braunton EX33 2JB
T: (01271) 813777
F: (01271) 813664
E: holidays@marsdens.co.uk
I: www.marsdens.co.uk

Establishments printed in blue have a detailed entry in this guide

SOUTH WEST ENGLAND

The Grange ★★★-★★★★
Contact: Mr Peter & Mrs Jill Lawley
The Grange, North Morte Road, Woolacombe EX34 7EG
T: (01271) 870580
E: the-grange-mortehoe@ supanet.com

Mailscot & Wykeham ★★-★★★
Contact:
Marsden's Cottage Holidays, 2 The Square, Braunton EX33 2JB
T: (01271) 813777
F: (01271) 813664
E: holidays@marsdens.co.uk
I: www.marsdens.co.uk

Rosemary Cottage ★★★★
Contact:
Marsdens Cottage Holidays, 2 The Square, Braunton EX33 2JB
T: (01271) 813777
F: (01271) 813664
E: holidays@marsdens.co.uk
I: www.marsdens.co.uk

Seaview ★★★
Contact: Mr Peter & Mrs Janet Cornwell
Marsden's Cottage Holidays, 2 The Square, Braunton EX33 2JB
T: (01271) 813777
F: (01271) 813664
E: holidays@marsdens.co.uk
I: www.marsdens.co.uk

Seaview Cottage ★★★
Contact:
Marsdens Cottage Holidays, 2 The Square, Braunton EX33 2JB
T: (01271) 813777
F: (01271) 813664
E: holidays@marsdens.co.uk
I: www.marsdens.co.uk

MORVAL
Cornwall

Wringworthy Holiday Cottages ★★★★
Contact: Mr Michael & Mrs Kim Spencer
Wringworthy Holiday Cottages, Wringworthy Farm, Looe PL13 1PR
T: (01503) 240685
F: (01503) 240830
E: holidays@wringworthy.co.uk
I: www.wringworthy.co.uk

MORWENSTOW
Cornwall

Cordena ★★★
Contact: Mr Peter Willoughby
Cordena, Shop, Bude EX23 9SL
T: (01732) 833196
E: cordena@bradley.org.uk
I: bradley.org.uk/cordena

Cory Farm Cottages ★★★★
Contact: Mrs Edwina Tape
Cory Farm Cottages, Bude EX23 9ST
T: (01288) 331735
F: (01288) 331758
E: info@coryfarmcottages.co.uk
I: www.coryfarmcottages.co.uk

Morningside - Annex ★★★
Contact: Mrs Patricia Burgess
Morningside - Annex, Shop, Bude EX23 9PE
T: (01288) 331178

West Woolley Barns ★★★-★★★★
Contact: Mr Chris & Mrs Jan Everard
West Woolley Barns, West Woolley Farm, Bude EX23 9PP
T: (01288) 331202
E: info@westwoolleyfarm.co.uk
I: www.westwoolleyfarm.co.uk

MOTCOMBE
Dorset

The Dairy House ★★★★★
Contact: Mr Gilbert Archdale
The Dairy House, Church Farm, Shaftesbury SP7 9NT
T: (01747) 850968
E: enquiries@thedairyhouse.com
I: www.thedairyhouse.com

MOTHECOMBE
Devon

The Flete Estate Holiday Cottages ★★★★-★★★★★
Contact: Miss Josephine Webb
The Flete Estate Holiday Cottages, Pamflete, Holbeton, Plymouth PL8 1JR
T: (01752) 830234
F: (01752) 830500
I: www.flete.co.uk

MOUNT HAWKE
Cornwall

Old Basset Cottage
Rating Applied For
Contact: Mr Furr Garrick
G A Furr, Old Basset Cottage, Truro TR4 8DJ
T: (01209) 890334
F: (01209) 890334
E: kfurr@whealbasset.fsnet.co.uk
I: www.geocities.com/whealbasset

MOUSEHOLE
Cornwall

Fern Cottage ★★★
Contact: Mr Phillip & Mrs Melanie Stephens
Fern Cottage, Fore Street, Penzance TR19 6TQ
T: (01736) 731363
E: stephens@churleys.freeserve.co.uk

Harbourside & Tides Reach Cottages ★★★★
Contact: Mrs Sandra Hall
The White House, The Square, Marazion TR17 0AP
T: (01736) 710424
F: (01736) 710424
E: info@cornwall-holiday-cottages.com
I: www.cornwall-holiday-cottages.com

Hoskins Meadows
Rating Applied For
Contact: Mrs Laura Jillian Leiworthy
Hoskins Meadows, Paul Lane, Penzance TR19 6TR
T: (01736) 331467

The Little Net Loft
Rating Applied For
Contact: Mr Martin King
22 Cotswold Gardens, Ilford IG2 7DW
T: (020) 82204538
E: martin.king90@ntlworld.com

Morwenna Cottage
Rating Applied For
Contact: Mr Barry & Mrs Natalie Johnson
Frog Hall Farm, Bury St Edmunds IP30 0PR
T: (01449) 736189
F: (01449) 736189
E: morwennacottage@tiscali.co.uk

The Old Standard ★★★
Contact: Mr & Mrs Underhill
The Old Vicarage, Brunton, Marlborough SN8 3SE
T: (01264) 850234
F: (01264) 850703
E: j.underhill@oldstandard.co.uk
I: www.oldstandard.co.uk

Poldark Cottage ★★★
Contact: Ms Christine Brown-Miller
An-Benolva, Fore Street, Newlyn, Penzance TR18 5JU
T: (01736) 330609
I: www.visitwestcountry.com/Poldark

Sea Whispers
Rating Applied For
Contact: Mrs Jane Robinson
Sunny Cottage, Rinsey Lane, Ashton, Helston TR13 9SG
T: (01736) 763695
E: jrobi54536@aol.com

Trevean Cottage ★★★
Contact: Mr David Coleman
Trevean Cottage, Raginnis Hill, Penzance TR19 6SR
T: (01736) 731699
E: jex5@hotmail.com

Wootton Gray ★★★
Contact: Mrs Jenifer Bower
4 Coldharbour Close, Henley-on-Thames RG9 1QF
T: (01491) 575297
F: (01491) 575297
I: www.henley-bb.freeserve.co.uk

MUCHELNEY
Somerset

Gothic House (The Old Dairy) ★★★
Contact: Mrs Joy Thorne
Gothic House (The Old Dairy), Langport TA10 0DW
T: (01458) 250626
E: joy-thorne@totalserve.co.uk

MUDDIFORD
Devon

Ashtree Cottage ★★★★
Contact:
Marsden's Cottage Holidays, 2 The Square, Braunton EX33 2JB
T: (01271) 813777
F: (01271) 813664
E: holidays@marsdens.co.uk
I: www.marsdens.co.uk

Rose Cottage ★★★★
Contact: Ms Helen Knight
Fircombe Hall, Seven Acres Park, Braunton EX33 2PD
T: (01271) 814815
F: (01271) 817973
E: sunshinenel@btinternet.com
I: scorefarmholidays.co.uk

MUDEFORD
Dorset

Avon Reach ★★★★
Contact: Mrs Wynne
Hollyoaks, 10 Ramley Road, Lymington SO41 8GQ
T: (01590) 670220

Burridge Lettings ★★-★★★
Contact: Mr Mark Pope
Burridge Lettings, 3 Mudeford, Christchurch BH23 3NQ
T: (01202) 481810
F: (01202) 476677
E: enquiries@burridge-property.co.uk
I: www.burridge-property.co.uk

Cherry Tree ★★★
Contact: Mrs Jean Bassil
6 Woodland Way, Christchurch BH23 4LQ
T: (01425) 271761

Crouch Cottage ★★★★
Contact: Mrs Julia Crouch
2 Firbank Road, Charminster, Bournemouth BH9 1EL
T: (01202) 530540

Flat 1 Digby Court ★★
Contact: Mrs Spreadbury
Merbury House, Vaggs Lane, Lymington SO41 0FP
T: (01425) 615605

Victoria Cottage ★★★★
Contact: Mr Stuart-Brown
Dream Cottages, 41 Maiden Street, Weymouth DT4 8TR
T: (01305) 789000

MULLION
Cornwall

Anchordown ★★★
Contact: Mr Martin Raftery
Mullion Cottages, Mullion Meadow, Helston TR12 7HB
T: (01326) 240315
F: (01326) 241090
E: martin@mullioncottages.com
I: www.mullioncottages.com

Angrouse Cottage
Rating Applied For
Contact: Mr Martin Raftery
Mullion Cottages, Mullion Meadows, Helston TR12 7HB
T: (01326) 240315
F: (01326) 241090
E: enquiries@mullioncottages.com

Atlantic Suite ★★★
Contact: Mr Martin Raftery
Mullion Cottages, Mullion Meadow, Helston TR12 7HB
T: (01326) 240315
F: (01326) 241090
E: martin@mullioncottages.com
I: www.mullioncottages.com

Barnwood Cottage ★★★
Contact: Mr Martin Raftery
Mullion Cottages, Mullion Meadows, Helston TR12 7HB
T: (01326) 240315
F: (01326) 241090
E: enquiries@mullioncottages.com
I: www.mullioncottages.com

SOUTH WEST ENGLAND

Cadgwith, Trewoon ★★★
Contact: Mr Martin Raftery
Mullion Cottages, Mullion
Meadows, Helston TR12 7HB
T: (01326) 240315
F: (01326) 241090
E: enquiries@mullioncottages.com
I: www.mullioncottages.com

Carleon, Trewoon ★★★
Contact: Mr Martin Raftery
Mullion Cottages, Mullion
Meadows, Helston TR12 7HB
T: (01326) 240315
F: (01326) 241090
E: enquiries@mullioncottage.com

Chy-an-Mor ★★★
Contact: Mr Martin Raftery
Mullion Cottages, Churchtown, Helston TR12 7HQ
T: (01326) 240315
F: (01326) 241090
E: martin@mullioncottages.com
I: www.mullioncottages.com

2 Coastguard Cottage ★★★
Contact: Mr Martin Raftery
Mullion Cottages, Mullion
Meadows, Helston TR12 7HB
T: (01326) 240315
F: (01326) 241090
E: martin@mullioncottages.com
I: www.mullioncottages.com

6 Coastguard Cottage ★★★
Contact: Mr Martin Raftery
Mullion Cottages, Mullion
Meadows, Helston TR12 7HB
T: (01326) 240315
F: (01326) 241090
E: martin@mullioncottages.com
I: www.mullioncottages.com

Cornerways ★★★
Contact: Mr Martin Raftery
Mullion Cottages, Mullion
Meadows, Helston TR12 7HB
T: (01326) 240315
F: (01326) 241090
E: martin@mullioncottages.com
I: www.mullioncottages.com

The Cottage ★★★
Contact: Mr Martin Raftery
Mullion Cottages, Mullion
Meadows, Helston TR12 7HB
T: (01326) 240315
F: (01326) 241090
E: martin@mullioncottages.com
I: www.mullioncottages.com

Creigan House ★★★
Contact: Mr Martin Raftery
Mullion Cottages, Mullion
Meadows, Helston TR12 7HB
T: (01326) 240315
F: (01326) 241090
E: martin@mullioncottages.com
I: www.mullioncottages.com

Cwary Vean ★★★
Contact:
Mullion Cottages, Mullion
Meadows, Helston TR12 7HB
T: (01326) 240315
E: enquiries@mullioncottages.com
I: www.mullioncottages.com

Deu-Try ★★★
Contact: Mr Martin Raftery
Mullion Cottages, Mullion
Meadows, Helston TR12 7HB
T: (01326) 240315
F: (01326) 241090
E: martin@mullioncottages.com
I: www.mullioncottages.com

The Garden Suite ★★★★
Contact: Mr Martin Raftery
Mullion Cottages, Mullion
Meadows, Helston TR12 7HB
T: (01326) 240315
F: (01326) 241090
E: martin@mullioncottages.com
I: www.mullioncottages.com

Glenmoor ★★★
Contact: Mr Martin Raftery
Mullion Cottages, Mullion
Meadows, Helston TR12 7HB
T: (01326) 240315
F: (01326) 241090
E: enquiries@mullioncottages.com

Green Cottage ★★★
Contact: Mr Martin Raftery
Mullion Cottages, Churchtown, Helston TR12 7HQ
T: (01326) 240315
F: (01326) 241090
E: martin@mullioncottages.com

Gulls ★★★
Contact: Mr Martin Raftery
Mullion Cottages, Mullion
Meadows, Helston TR12 7HB
T: (01326) 240315
F: (01326) 241090
E: martin@mullioncottages.com
I: www.mullioncottages.com

The Heathers and The Palms
Rating Applied For
Contact: Mr Martin Raftery
Mullion Cottages, Mullion
Meadows, Helston TR12 7HB
T: (01326) 240315
F: (01326) 241090
E: enquiries@mullioncottages.com
I: www.mullioncottages.com

Higher Lampra ★★★
Contact: Mr Martin Raftery
Mullion Cottages, Mullion
Meadows, Helston TR12 7HB
T: (01326) 240315
F: (01326) 241090
E: martin@mullioncottages.com
I: www.mullioncottages.com

Lampra Mill ★★★★
Contact: Mr Martin Raftery
Mullion Cottages, Mullion
Meadows, Helston TR12 7HB
T: (01326) 240512
F: (01326) 241090
E: martin@mullioncottages.com
I: www.mullioncottages.com

Mullion Mill Cottage ★★★
Contact: Mrs Lane
Trcloskan Farm, Helston TR12
T: (01326) 240493

Nythfa ★★★
Contact:
Cornish Cottage Holidays, The Old Turnpike Dairy, Godolphin Road, Helston TR13 8AA
T: (01326) 573808
F: (01326) 564992
E: enquiry@cornishcottageholidays.co.uk
I: www.cornishcottageholidays.co.uk

Ogo-Dour ★★★
Contact:
Cornish Cottage Holidays, The Old Turnpike Dairy, Godolphin Road, Helston TR13 8AA
T: (01326) 573808
F: (01326) 564992
E: enquiry@cornishcottageholidays.co.uk
I: www.cornishcottageholidays.co.uk

Poltesco, Trewoon ★★★
Contact: Mr Martin Rafferty
Mullion Cottages, Mullion
Meadows, Helston TR12 7HB
T: (01326) 240315
F: (01326) 241090
E: enquiries@mullioncottages.com
I: www.mullioncottages.com

Redannack Bungalow ★★★
Contact: Mr Martin Raftery
Mullion Cottages, Mullion
Meadows, Helston TR12 7HB
T: (01326) 240315
F: (01326) 241090
E: martin@mullioncottages.com
I: www.mullioncottages.com

Sea Breezes ★★★★
Contact: Mr Martin Raftery
Mullion Cottages, Mullion
Meadows, Helston TR12 7HB
T: (01326) 240315
F: (01326) 241090
E: martin@mullioncottages.com
I: www.mullioncottages.com

Stable Cottage ★★★
Contact: Mr Martin Raftery
Mullion Cottages, Mullion
Meadows, Helston TR12 7HB
T: (01326) 240315
F: (01326) 241090
E: martin@mullioncottages.com
I: www.mullioncottages.com

Tregonning ★★★
Contact:
Cornish Cottage Holidays, The Old Turnpike Dairy, Godolphin Road, Helston TR13 8AA
T: (01326) 573808
F: (01326) 564992
E: enquiry@cornishcottageholidays.co.uk
I: www.cornishcottageholidays.co.uk

Trenance Barton ★★★
Contact: Mr Martin Raftery
Mullion Cottages, Mullion
Meadows, Helston TR12 7HB
T: (01326) 240315
F: (01326) 241090
E: martin@mullioncottages.com
I: www.mullioncottages.com

Trenance Farm Cottages ★★★
Contact: Mr Richard & Mrs Jennifer Tyler Street
Trenance Farm Cottages, Trenance Farm, Helston TR12 7HB
T: (01326) 240639
F: (01326) 240639
E: info@trenancefarmholidays.co.uk
I: www.trenancefarmholidays.co.uk

Trencrom ★★★★
Contact: Mr Martin Raftery
Mullion Cottages, Mullion
Meadows, Helston TR12 7HB
T: (01326) 240315
F: (01326) 241090
E: martin@mullioncottages.com
I: www.mullioncottages.com

Trevaylor
Rating Applied For
Contact: Mr Martin Raftery
Mullion Cottages, Mullion
Meadows, Helston TR12 7HB
T: (01326) 240315
F: (01326) 241090
E: enquiries@mullioncottages.com
I: www.mullioncottages.com

Trewenna & Scrumpy Cottage ★★★★
Contact: Mr Martin Raftery
Mullion Cottages, Mullion
Meadows, Helston TR12 7HB
T: (01237) 479146
F: (01237) 421512
E: martin@mullioncottages.com
I: www.mullioncottages.com

The Vestry ★★
Contact: Mr Martin Raftery
The Vestry, Churchtown, Helston TR12 7HQ
T: (01326) 240315
F: (01326) 241090
E: martin@mullioncottages.com
I: www.mullioncottages.com

MUSBURY
Devon

Maidenhayne Farm Cottage ★★★★★
Contact: Mrs Trudi Colley
Maidenhayne Farmhouse, Maidenhayne Lane, Axminster EX13 8AG
T: (01297) 552469
F: (01297) 551109
E: graham@maidenhayne-farm-cottage.co.uk
I: www.Maidenhayne-farm-cottage.co.uk

Wood Cottage ★★★★
Contact: Ms Kate Bartlett
Jean Bartlett Cottage Holidays, The Old Dairy, Fore Street, Seaton EX12 3JB
T: (01297) 23221
F: (01297) 23303
E: holidays@jeanbartlett.com
I: www.jeanbartlett.com

Establishments printed in blue have a detailed entry in this guide

665

SOUTH WEST ENGLAND

MYLOR
Cornwall

Albion House Cottages ★★★★
Contact: Mr Patrick & Mrs Penelope Polglase
Bells Hill, Mylor Bridge, Falmouth TR11 5SQ
T: (01326) 373607
F: (01326) 377607
I: www.cottageholidayscornwall.co.uk

Carsawsan Cottage ★★★★
Contact: Mrs Victoria Whitworth
Overleat House, Water Lane, St Agnes TR5 0QZ
T: (01872) 552042
E: vic.whit@btinternet.com
I: www.homesteadcottages.co.uk/property/carsawsancottage

Trehovel ★★★★
Contact:
Cornish Holiday Cottages, Killibrae, West Bay Maenporth Road, Falmouth TR11 5HP
T: (01326) 250339
F: (01326) 250339
E: postmaster@cornishholidaycottages.net
I: www.cornishholidaycottages.net/property/mylor/trehovel.html

NANSTALLON
Cornwall

The Gate House ★★★★
Contact: Mr & Mrs Hamley
Nanscarne, Bodmin PL30 5LG
T: (01208) 74291
E: mikekathhamley@clara.co.uk
I: www.trailcottage.co.uk

Stables Cottage ★★★★
Contact: Mr Michael & Mrs Norma Hinde
Stables Cottage, Lower Mulberry Farm, Bodmin PL30 5LJ
T: (01208) 831636
E: hind831636@aol.com
I: members.aol.com/hind831636

Tregarthen Cottages
★★★★-★★★★★
Contact: Mrs Margaret Bealing
Tregarthen Cottages, Bodmin PL30 5LB
T: (01208) 831570
F: (01208) 831570
E: enquiries@tregarthencottages.co.uk
I: www.tregarthencottages.co.uk

NAUNTON
Gloucestershire

Mill Barn Cottage ★★
Contact: Mrs Madeleine Hindley
Mill Barn Cottage, Mill Barn, Naunton, Cheltenham GL54 3AF
T: (01451) 850417
F: (01451) 850196

Yew Tree House Cottage ★★★★
Contact: Mrs Patricia Smith
White Gables, 4 Woodcote Park Road, Epsom KT18 7EX
T: (01372) 723166
F: (01372) 723166
I: www.yewtreehouse.com

NETHER STOWEY
Somerset

The Old House ★★★-★★★★★
Contact: Mr J Douglas Gee
The Old House, St Mary Street, Bridgwater TA5 1LJ
T: (01278) 732392
E: dgeetheoldhouse@ision.co.uk
I: www.theoldhouse.ision.co.uk

NETHERBURY
Dorset

Little Thatch ★★★
Contact: Mr Zachary Stuart-Brown
Dream Cottages, 5 Hope Square, Weymouth DT4 8TR
T: (01305) 789000
F: (01305) 761346
E: admin@dream-cottages.co.uk
I: www.dream-cottages.co.uk

NETTLECOMBE
Dorset

Wren Cottage ★★★★
Contact: Mrs Eirlys Johnson
9 The Berkeleys, Leatherhead KT22 9DW
T: (01372) 378907
E: eirlys.johnson@tinyworld.co.uk

NEW POLZEATH
Cornwall

Atlantic View and Atlantic View Coach House New Polzeath ★★★-★★★★
Contact: Dr Sarah Garthwaite
Atlantic View Holidays, Matfield Oast, Chestnut Lane, Tonbridge TN12 7JJ
T: (01892) 722264
F: (01892) 724022
E: enquiries@atlanticview.net
I: www.atlanticview.net

No 7 Polzeath Court ★★★
Contact:
Rock Holidays inc. Harbour Holidays Rock Ltd., Trebetherick House, Wadebridge PL27 6SB
T: (01208) 863399
E: rockhols@aol.com
I: www.rockholidays.co.uk

Stepper View
Rating Applied For
Contact: Mr Paul Smith
38 The Chase, Romford RM1 4BE
T: (01708) 733966
E: paul@aveley.f9.co.uk
I: www.stepperview.co.uk

Treheather ★★★
Contact: Dr Mayall
Osmond House, Chestnut Crescent, Stoke Canon, Exeter EX5 4AA
T: (01392) 841219

Trehenlie
Rating Applied For
Contact: Mrs June Angwin
Trehenlie, 16 Tinners Way, Wadebridge PL27 6UH
T: (01208) 75243
F: (01208) 75243
E: steve@angwin.fsnet.co.uk

NEWLAND
Gloucestershire

Birchamp Coach House ★★★★
Contact: Mrs Karen Davies
Birchamp Coach House, Birchamp House, Coleford GL16 8NP
T: (01594) 833143
F: (01594) 836775
E: karen@wyedeancottages.co.uk
I: www.wyedeancottages.co.uk

NEWLYN
Cornwall

Silver Seas ★★★
Contact: Mrs Melanie Toms
Silver Seas, Gwavas Road, Penzance TR18 5LY
T: (01736) 368007

NEWQUAY
Cornwall

Apartment Treffry ★★★
Contact: Mrs Annabelle Bennetts
Apartment Treffry, Treffry, King Edward Crescent, Newquay TR7 1HJ
T: (01637) 875673
F: (01637) 859670
E: annabelle@bennettsa.freeserve.co.uk

B1 The Bay Apartments ★★★
Contact: Mr David Buckari & Ms Helen Gray
B1 The Bay Apartments, Fistral Crescent, Newquay TR7 1PH
T: 077 7 219458

Bezant Green Cottage ★★★
Contact: Mrs Jan Exell
Bezant Green Cottages, Penpol Farm, Newquay TR8 5RL
T: (01637) 831141

Cheviot Holiday Apartments ★★★★
Contact: Mr Brian & Mrs Jill Biscard
26 Chyverton Close, Newquay TR7 2AR
T: (01637) 872712
F: (01637) 872712
E: info@cheviotnewquay.co.uk
I: www.cheviotnewquay.co.uk

Cornwall Holiday Lets
Rating Applied For
Contact: Mr Michael Campbell
11 Emperor Close, Berkhamsted HP4 1TD
T: (01442) 871251
E: michael@cornwallholidaylets.net
I: www.cornwallholidaylets.net

Croftlea Holiday Flats ★★
Contact:
Croftlea Holiday Flats, Wild Flower Lane, Newquay TR7 2QB
T: (01637) 852505
F: (01637) 877183
E: enquiries@croftlea.co.uk
I: www.croftlea.co.uk

Driftwood Apartments ★★★
Contact: Mr & Mrs Tregunna
Farthings, Newquay TR8 5PT
T: (01637) 830093
F: (01637) 830093
I: www.holywell-bay-driftwood.co.uk

Ebb-Tide Holiday Homes
Rating Applied For
Contact: Mrs Barbara Anne Dearden
Ebb-Tide Holiday Homes, 44 Lewarne Road, Porth Beach, Newquay TR7 3JT
T: (01637) 873683
E: enquiries@ebbtide.co.uk
I: www.ebb-tide.co.uk

Eton Court ★★★
Contact: Mr Allan O'Dell
2 Playingfield Lane, Newquay TR7 2DB
T: (01637) 852545
F: (01637) 859999
E: fiona@holidaysinnewquay.com
I: holidaysinnewquay.com

Fistral Beach House
Rating Applied For
Contact: Mr Steve Harrison
Fistral Beach House, Camullas Way, Newquay TR7 1PP
T: (01637) 870955
E: steharrison@supanet.com
I: www.fistralbeachhouse.com

Gillyn ★★
Contact: Mrs Betty Barry
Gillyn, 21 Towan Blystra Road, Newquay TR7 2RP
T: (01637) 876104
E: betty.barry@BTinternet.com

Greenslade ★★★
Contact: Mr Stavros & Mrs Pat Stavrou
Greenslade, 165 Henver Road, Newquay TR7 3EJ
T: (01637) 871517

12 Harvest Moon Apartments ★★★★
Contact:
Cornish Horizons, The Cottage, Dane Road, Padstow PL28 8EA
T: (01841) 533331
F: (01841) 533933
E: cottages@cornishhorizons.co.uk

Hendra Paul Cottages ★★★★
Contact: Mrs Julia Schofield
Hendra Paul Cottages, Hendra Paul Farm, Newquay TR8 4JL
T: (01637) 874695
F: (01637) 874695
E: info@hendrapaul.co.uk
I: www.hendrapaul.co.uk

Kestle Mill
Rating Applied For
Contact: Mr Alex Weller
David Ball Holiday Lettings, 34 East Street, Newquay TR7 1BH
T: (01637) 852987
E: sales@davidballholidaylettings.co.uk

666   Look out for establishments participating in the National Accessible Scheme

SOUTH WEST ENGLAND

Manuels Farm ★★★★
Contact: Mr James & Mrs Tracy Wilson
Manuels Farm, Quintrell Downs, Newquay TR8 4NY
T: (01637) 878300
F: (01637) 878300
I: www.manuelsfarm.co.uk

Porth Apartments
Rating Applied For
Contact: Ms Catherine Concah
16 Creffield Road, London W5 3RP
T: (020) 89933910
I: www.porthapartments.co.uk

Retorrick Mill ★★-★★★
Contact: Mr Ross & Mrs Margaret Oliver
Retorrick Mill, Newquay TR8 4BH
T: (01637) 860460
F: (01637) 860460

Surf View
Rating Applied For
Contact: Miss Emma Skinner
Surf View, 33 Surf View, Camullas Way, Newquay TR7 1PP
T: (01327) 874681
F: (01872) 271886
E: emmaskinner21@hotmail.com

Tolcarne Beach Village ★★★★
Contact: Mr Jon & Mrs Linda Briant
Tolcarne Beach Village, Narrowcliff, Newquay TR7 2QN
T: (01209) 714771
E: info@tolcarnebeach.co.uk
I: www.tolcarnebeach.co.uk

Tregurrian Hotel Apartments ★★★★
Contact: Mr Paul Mills
Tregurrian Hotel Apartments, Watergate Bay, Newquay TR8 4AB
T: (01637) 860280
F: (01637) 860540
E: tregurrian@holidaysincornwall.net
I: www.holidaysincornwall.net

Trendrean Farm Barns ★★★★
Contact: Mr & Mrs I Marshall
Trendrean Farm Barns, St Newlyn East, Newquay TR8 5LY
T: (01208) 813228
E: ivor.gill@btopenworld.com

NEWTON ABBOT
Devon

Chipley Mill ★★★★
Contact: Mr Coleman
Chipley Mill, Newton Abbot TQ12 6JW
T: (01626) 821681
E: laurence@colemanx.org.uk
I: www.chipleymill.co.uk

Lower Bramble Farm ★★★★
Contact: Mr Howard Lewis
Lower Bramble Farm, Newton Abbot TQ13 0DU
T: (01626) 852294
F: (01626) 852294

Oak Cottage ★★
Contact:
Holiday Homes & Cottages South West, 365A Torquay Road, Paignton TQ3 2BT
T: (01803) 663650
F: (01803) 664037
E: holcotts@aol.com
I: www.swcottages.co.uk

2 Thorn Cottages ★★★
Contact: Ms Debbie Saunders
2 Thorn Cottages, Newton Abbot TQ12 4RB
T: (01626) 872779
E: debbie@saunders17.freeserve.co.uk
I: www.visitwestcountry.com/thorncottage

NEWTON FERRERS
Devon

Crown Yealm Apartment ★★
Contact:
Yealm Holidays, 8 Whittingham Road, Plymouth PL8 2NF
T: 0870 7472987
F: (01752) 873173
E: info@yealm-holidays.co.uk
I: www.yealm-holidays.co.uk

Glen Cottage ★★★
Contact:
Yealm Holidays, 8 Whittingham Road, Plymouth PL8 2NF
T: 0870 7472987
F: (01752) 873173
E: info@yealm-holidays.co.uk
I: www.yealm-holidays.co.uk

Lezant Pine Lodge ★★★★
Contact:
Yealm Holidays, 8 Whittingham Road, Plymouth PL8 2NF
T: 0870 7472987
F: (01752) 873173
E: info@yealm-holidays.co.uk
I: www.yealm-holidays.co.uk

NEWTON POPPLEFORD
Devon

21 Otter Reach ★★★
Contact:
Holiday Homes & Cottages South West, 365A Torquay Road, Paignton TQ3 2BT
T: (01803) 663650
F: (01803) 664037
E: holcott@aol.com
I: www.swcottages.co.uk

Umbrella Cottage ★★★
Contact: Mrs M Woodley
Umbrella Cottage, Burrow, Sidmouth EX10 0BP
T: (01395) 568687
F: (01395) 568883

NEWTON ST LOE
Bath and North East Somerset

Pennsylvania Farm ★★★-★★★★★
Contact: Mr Paul & Mrs Peggy Foster
Pennsylvania Farm, The Cheese House, The Stables, Bath BA2 9JD
T: (01225) 314912

NEWTON TRACEY
Devon

Acorn Cottage ★★★
Contact:
Marsdens Cottage Holidays, 2 The Square, Braunton EX33 2JB
T: (01271) 813777
F: (01271) 813664
E: holidays@marsdens.co.uk

NORTH CHERITON
Somerset

Fives Court Cottage
Rating Applied For
Contact: Mrs Heather Martin
Fives Court Cottage, Cheriton Hill, Templecombe BA8 0AB
T: (01963) 32777

NORTH CHIDEOCK
Dorset

Hell Barn Cottages ★★★
Contact: Mr Shigeaki & Mrs Diana Takezoe
Hell Barn Cottages, Hell Farmhouse, Hell Lane, Bridport DT6 6LA
T: (01297) 489589
F: (01297) 489043
E: diana@hellbarn.co.uk
I: www.hellbarn.co.uk

NORTH HILL
Cornwall

The Granary at Eastgate Barn ★★★★
Contact: Ms Jill Goodman
Eastgate Barn, Landreyne, North Hill, Launceston PL15 7LZ
T: (01566) 782573
E: jill@eastgatebarn.co.uk
I: www.eastgatebarn.co.uk

NORTH MOLTON
Devon

Bampfylde & Florence Cottages ★★★★★
Contact: Mr & Mrs P Cornwell
Marsden's Cottage Holidays, 2 The Square, Braunton EX33 2JB
T: (01271) 813777
F: (01271) 813664
E: holidays@marsdens.co.uk
I: www.marsdens.co.uk

Lambscombe Farm Cottages ★★★★
Contact: Mr Paul & Mrs Cathy Farenden
Lambscombe Farm Cottages, South Molton EX36 3JT
T: (01598) 740558
F: (01598) 740668
E: Farenden4@aol.com
I: www.lambscombefarm.co.uk

Pitt Farm ★★★★
Contact: Mrs Gladys Ayre
Pitt Farm, Stable Cottage, South Molton EX36 3JR
T: (01598) 740285
E: royayre@tiscali.co.uk
I: www.devonfarms.co.uk

West Millbrook Farm ★★-★★★★
Contact: Mrs Courtney
West Millbrook Farm, West Millbrook, Twitchen, South Molton EX36 3LP
T: (01598) 740382
E: wmbselfcatering@aol.com
I: www.westmillbrook.co.uk

NORTH PETHERWIN
Cornwall

Castle Milford Mill ★★★★
Contact:
Farm & Cottage Holidays, Victoria House, 12 Fore Street, Bideford EX39 1AW
T: (01237) 479146
F: (01237) 421512
E: enquiries@farmcott.co.uk
I: www.farmcott.co.uk

Waterloo Farm ★★★★
Contact:
Farm & Cottage Holidays, Victoria House, 12 Fore Street, Bideford EX39 1AW
T: (01237) 479146
F: (01237) 421512
E: enquiries@farmcott.co.uk
I: www.farmcott.co.uk

Woodside Cottage ★★★★★
Contact: Mrs Phyllis Reddock
Woodside Cottage, Stenhill Farm, Launceston PL15 8NN
T: (01566) 785686
E: e.reddock@btinternet.com
I: www.stenhill.com

NORTH TAMERTON
Cornwall

Eastcott Lodges ★★-★★★
Contact: Miss C Mitchell
Eastcott Lodges, Holsworthy EX22 6SB
T: (01409) 271308
E: mail@eastcott-lodges.co.uk
I: www.eastcott-lodges.co.uk

Hill Cottage ★★★★
Contact: Mr R & Mrs E Green
Beer Mill Farm, Holsworthy EX22 6PF
T: (01409) 253093
F: (01409) 253024
E: lgsg@supanet.com
I: www.selfcateringcottagesdevon.co.uk

Tamar Valley Cottages ★★★★
Contact: Mr Stephen & Mrs Jane Rhodes
Tamar Valley Cottages, North Tamerton House, Holsworthy EX22 6SA
T: (01409) 271284
E: smrhodes@btinternet.com
I: www.tamarvalleycottages.co.uk

NORTH TAWTON
Devon

Cider Cottage ★★★★
Contact: Mr Daniel & Mrs Sue Kirst & Bartlett
Cider Cottage, Yeo Lane, North Tawton EX20 2DD
T: (01837) 89002
F: (01837) 89237
E: dannysue@yeo-farm.com
I: www.yeo-farm.com

Westacott Barton Farm ★★★★
Contact:
Farm & Cottage Holidays, Victoria House, 13 Fore Street, Bideford EX39 1AW
T: (01237) 479146
E: enquiries@farmcott.co.uk
I: www.farmcott.co.uk

Establishments printed in blue have a detailed entry in this guide

SOUTH WEST ENGLAND

NORTH WHILBOROUGH
Devon

Long Barn Luxury Holiday Cottages ★★★★★
Contact: Mr Peter Tidman
Long Barn Luxury Holiday Cottages, North Whilborough, Newton Abbot TQ12 5LP
T: (01803) 875044
F: (01803) 875705
E: tidman@lineone.net

NORTH WRAXALL
Wiltshire

Home Farm ★★★★
Contact: Mr & Mrs Drew
Home Farm, Chippenham SN14 7AG
T: (01225) 891238

NORTHAM
Devon

Atlantic View ★★★
Contact:
Farm & Cottage Holidays, Victoria House, 32 Fore Street, Bideford EX39 1AW
T: (01237) 479146
F: (01237) 421512
E: bookings@farmcott.co.uk

The Cabin ★★★★
Contact:
Marsden's Cottage Holidays, 2 The Square, Braunton EX33 2JB
T: (01271) 813777
F: (01271) 813664
E: holidays@marsdens.co.uk
I: www.marsdens.co.uk

Lenwood ★★★
Contact:
Farm & Cottage Holidays, Victoria House, 12 Fore Street, Bideford EX39 1AW
T: (01237) 479146
F: (01237) 421512
E: bookings@farmcott.co.uk
I: www.farmcott.co.uk

River Knowle ★★★
Contact:
Farm & Cottage Holidays, Victoria House, 16 Fore Street, Bideford EX39 1AW
T: (01237) 479146
F: (01237) 421512
E: bookings@farmcott.co.uk
I: www.farmcott.co.uk

NORTHLEACH
Gloucestershire

1 College Row ★★★
Contact: Mr & Mrs Morris
Huntley Farm, Patch Elm Lane, Bristol BS37 7LU
T: (01454) 227322
F: (01454) 227323
E: cotswold.cottage@btopenworld.com
I: www.cotswoldcottage.net/

NORTHLEIGH
Devon

Chilcombe ★★★
Contact: Ms Louise Hayman
Milkbere Holidays, 3 Fore Street, Seaton EX12 2LE
T: (01297) 20729
F: (01297) 22925
E: info@milkberehols.com
I: www.milkberehols.com

The Cider Barn
Rating Applied For
Contact:
Jean Bartlett Cottage Holidays, The Old Dairy,fore Street, Seaton EX12 3JA
T: (01297) 23221
F: (01297) 23303
E: holidays@jeanbartlett.com
I: www.jeanbartlett.com

4 The Malt House ★★★
Contact: Ms Louise Hayman
Milkbere Cottage Holidays Ltd, 3 Fore Street, Seaton EX12 2LE
T: (01297) 20729
F: (01297) 22925
E: info@milkberehols.com
I: www.milkberehols.com

Northleigh Farm ★★★★
Contact: Mr Simon & Mrs Sue Potter
Northleigh Farm, Colyton EX24 6BL
T: (01404) 871217
F: (01404) 871217
E: simon-potter@msn.com
I: www.northleighfarm.co.uk

NORTHWOOD GREEN
Gloucestershire

Post Paddock ★★★★★
Contact: Mrs Angela Smuthwaite
Post Paddock, Ampney Lane, Westbury-on-Severn GL14 1LZ
T: (01452) 762086
E: info@postpaddock.co.uk
I: www.postpaddock.co.uk

NORTON SUB HAMDON
Somerset

Little Norton Mill ★★★★-★★★★★
Contact: Mrs Lynn Hart
Little Norton Mill, Little Norton, Stoke sub Hamdon TA14 6TE
T: (01935) 881337
F: (01935) 881337
E: tom.hart@dial.pipex.com
I: www.littlenortonmill.co.uk

NOSS MAYO
Devon

Swift Cottage ★★★★
Contact:
Farm & Cottage Holidays, Victoria House, 17 Fore Street, Bideford EX39 1AW
T: (01237) 479146
F: (01237) 421512
E: bookings@farmcott.co.uk
I: www.farmcott.co.uk

NOTTON
Dorset

Notton Hill Barn Holiday Cottages ★★★-★★★★
Contact: Mr & Mrs D Smith
Notton Hill Barn Holiday Cottages, Dorchester DT2 0BZ
T: (01300) 321299
F: (01300) 321299

NUNNEY
Somerset

Riverside Cottage ★★★★
Contact: Mrs Clare Hulley
1 Hill House, 37 Innox Hill Gardens, Frome BA11 2LN
T: (01373) 464712
I: www.nunney.free.new.net

NYMPSFIELD
Gloucestershire

Crossways ★★★
Contact: Mr & Mrs Bowen
Crossways, Tinkley Lane, Stonehouse GL10 3TU
T: (01453) 860309

OAKHILL
Somerset

The Chapel ★★★
Contact: Mrs Jeanne Kirby
166 West Street, Marlow SL7 2BU
T: (01628) 481239
E: kirbyjeanne@hotmail.com

OGWELL
Devon

Rydon Ball ★★★★
Contact: Mr Ian Butterworth
Holiday Homes & Cottages South West, 365A Torquay Road, Paignton TQ3 2BT
T: (01803) 663650
F: (01803) 664037
E: holcotts@aol.com
I: www.swcottages.co.uk

OKEHAMPTON
Devon

Beer Farm ★★★★
Contact: Mr & Mrs Annear
Beer Farm, Okehampton EX20 1SG
T: (01837) 840265
F: (01837) 840245
E: beerfarm.oke@which.net
I: www.beerfarm.co.uk

Bowerland ★★★★
Contact: Mr Ray Quirke
East Bowerland Farm, Okehampton EX20 4LZ
T: (01837) 55979
E: bowerland@devonhols.com
I: www.devonhols.com

The Coach House - Hayrish Farm ★★★★
Contact: Mr David Judge
1 Telegraph Street, London EC2R 7AR
T: (020) 7256 9013
F: (020) 7588 2051
E: hayrish@easynet.co.uk
I: www.hayrish.co.uk

East Hook Holiday Cottages ★★-★★★★
Contact: Mrs Ruth Maile
East Hook Cottages, West Hook Farm, Okehampton EX20 1RL
T: (01837) 52305
E: marystevens@westhookfarm.fsnet.co.uk
I: www.easthook-holiday-cottages.co.uk

Fourwinds Self-Catering Properties ★★★★
Contact: Miss Sue Collins
Fourwinds Self-Catering Properties, Tavistock Road, Okehampton EX20 4LX
T: (01837) 55785
F: (01837) 55785
E: four.winds@eclipse.co.uk
I: www.eclipse.co.uk/fourwinds

Little Bidlake Barns ★★★★
Contact: Mrs Joanna Down
Little Bidlake Barns, Okehampton EX20 4NS
T: (01837) 861233
F: (01837) 861233
E: bidlakefrm@aol.com
I: www.dartmoor-holiday-cottages.co.uk

The Longhouse - Hayrish Farm ★★★★★
Contact: Mr David Judge
Hayrish Ltd., 1 Telegraph Street, London EC2R 7AR
T: (020) 7256 9013
F: (020) 7588 2051
E: hayrish@easynet.co.uk
I: www.hayrish.co.uk

Meldon Cottages ★★★★
Contact: Mr Stuart & Mrs Bridie Plant & Roberts
Meldon Cottages, Okehampton EX20 4LU
T: (01837) 54363
E: enquiries@meldoncottages.co.uk
I: www.meldoncottages.co.uk

Week Farm Country Holidays ★★★★
Contact: Mrs Margaret Hockridge
Week Farm Country Holidays, Okehampton EX20 4HZ
T: (01837) 861221
F: (01837) 861221
E: accom@weekfarmonline.com
I: www.weekfarmonline.com

ORCHARDLEIGH
Somerset

Orchardleigh Estate
Rating Applied For
Contact: Mr Ed Vincent
Orchardleigh Estate, Frome BA11 2PH
T: (01373) 472550
F: (01373) 472298
I: www.orchardleighholidays.net

OSMINGTON
Dorset

Emmies Cottage ★★★★
Contact: Mr Zachary Stuart-Brown
Dream Cottages, 5 Hope Square, Weymouth DT4 8TR
T: (01305) 789000
F: (01305) 761346
E: admin@dream-cottages.co.uk
I: www.dream-cottages.co.uk

Gardeners Cottage ★★★
Contact: Mr Zachary Stuart-Brown
Dream Cottages, 5 Hope Square, Weymouth DT4 8TR
T: (01305) 789000
F: (01305) 761346
E: admin@dream-cottages.co.uk
I: www.dream-cottages.co.uk

Look out for establishments participating in the National Accessible Scheme

SOUTH WEST ENGLAND

Honeybun ★★★★
Contact: Mr Zachary Stuart-Brown
Dream Cottages, 5 Hope Square, Weymouth DT4 8TR
T: (01305) 789000
F: (01305) 761346
E: admin@dream-cottages.co.uk
I: www.dream-cottages.co.uk

Norden Cottage ★★★
Contact: Mr Zachary Stuart-Brown
Dream Cottages, 5 Hope Square, Weymouth DT4 8TR
T: (01305) 789000
F: (01305) 761346
E: admin@dream-cottages.co.uk
I: www.dream-cottages.co.uk

OSMINGTON MILLS
Dorset

Vine Cottage ★★
Contact:
Dream Cottages, 5 Hope Square, Weymouth DT4 8TR
T: (01305) 789000
E: admin@dream-cottages.co.uk
I: www.dream-cottages.co.uk

OTHERY
Somerset

Middlefield Farm Cottage ★★★
Contact: Mrs Anita Winslade
Elmgrove Bungalow, Holloway Road, Bridgwater TA7 0QF
T: (01823) 698368
F: (01823) 698368

Willows Cottage ★★★★
Contact: Mrs Christine Ellis
Willows Cottage, Bagenham Farm, Rye Lane, Bridgwater TA7 0PT
T: (01823) 698166

OTTERFORD
Somerset

Tamarack Lodge ★★★★
Contact: Mr Matthew Sparks
Tamarack Lodge, Fyfett Farm, Chard TA20 3QP
T: (01823) 601270
E: matthew.sparks@tamaracklodge.co.uk

OTTERHAM
Cornwall

Old Newham Farm ★★★
Contact: Mrs Mary Purdue
Old Newham Farm, Camelford PL32 9SR
T: (01840) 230470
F: (01840) 230303
E: cottages@old-newham.co.uk
I: www.old-newham.co.uk

Saint Tinney Farm Holidays ★★★★
Contact: Mrs Elizabeth Windley
Saint Tinney Farm Holidays, St Tinney Farm, Camelford PL32 9TA
T: (01840) 261174
E: info@st-tinney.co.uk
I: www.st-tinney.co.uk

OTTERTON
Devon

Jodies ★★★
Contact:
Jean Bartlett Cottage Holidays, The Old Dairy, Fore Street, Seaton EX12 3JB
T: (01297) 23221
F: (01297) 23303
E: holidays@jeanbartlett.com
I: www.netbreaks.com/jeanb

OTTERY ST MARY
Devon

Deblins Brook Farm Cottage ★★★★
Contact: Mrs Glynis Walker
Deblins Brook Farm, Sandgate Lane, Ottery St Mary EX11 1PX
T: (01404) 811331

OVER COMPTON
Dorset

Uplands ★★★
Contact: Mr & Mrs Suellen Brake
Uplands, Sherborne DT9 4QS
T: (01935) 477043

OWERMOIGNE
Dorset

Jasmine Cottage ★★
Contact: Mrs Lawton
9 Moreton Road, Dorchester DT2 8HT
T: (01305) 854457
F: (01305) 854457
I: www.cottagesindorset.co.uk

Wooden Tops & Vinney Cottage ★★★
Contact: Mr Zachary Stuart-Brown
Dream Cottages, 5 Hope Square, Weymouth DT4 8TR
T: (01305) 789000
F: (01305) 761346
E: admin@dream-cottages.co.uk
I: www.dream-cottages.co.uk

OWLPEN
Gloucestershire

Owlpen Manor ★★★★
Contact: Mrs Julia Webb
Owlpen, Dursley GL11 5BZ
T: (01453) 860261
F: (01453) 860819
I: www.owlpen.com

OZLEWORTH
Gloucestershire

Hill Mill Cottage ★★★★
Contact: Mrs Nash
Hill Mill Cottage, Hill Mill House, Wotton-under-Edge GL12 7QR
T: (01453) 842401
F: (01453) 842401
E: pnash@hillmillcottage.co.uk
I: www.hillmillcottage.co.uk

PADSTOW
Cornwall

7/9 Grove Place ★★★
Contact: Ms Nicky Stanley
Harbour Holidays - Padstow, 1 North Quay, Padstow PL28 8AF
T: (01841) 532555
F: (01841) 533115
E: sales@jackie-stanley.co.uk
I: www.harbourholidays.co.uk

Alexandra House ★★★★
Contact: Mrs Moreen Williams
Alexandra House, 30 Dennis Road, Padstow PL28 8DE
T: (01841) 532503

The Backs and Rhetts ★★★
Contact: Ms Nicky Stanley
Harbour Holidays - Padstow, 1 North Quay, Padstow PL28 8AF
T: (01841) 532555
F: (01841) 533115
E: sales@jackie-stanley.co.uk
I: www.harbourholidays.co.uk

7 Barry's Lane ★★★
Contact:
Harbour Holidays, 1 North Quay, Padstow PL28 8AF
T: (01841) 532555
E: contact@harbourholidays.co.uk
I: www.harbourholidays.co.uk

9 Barry's Lane ★★★
Contact: Ms Nicky Stanley
Harbour Holidays - Padstow, 1 North Quay, Padstow PL28 8AF
T: (01841) 532555
F: (01841) 533115
E: sales@jackie-stanley.co.uk
I: www.harbourholidays.co.uk

Beau Vista ★★★★
Contact: Mr Peter Haseldine
34 Raleigh Close, Padstow PL28 8BQ
T: (01841) 533270
F: (01841) 533270
E: peter@beauvista.co.uk
I: www.beauvista.co.uk

Bloomfield and The Old Post Office ★★★
Contact: Mr Michael Bennett
52 Church Street, Padstow PL28 8BG
T: (01841) 533804
E: mikeswave@onetel.net.uk

Bobbins ★★★
Contact: Ms Nicky Stanley
Harbour Holidays - Padstow, 1 North Quay, Padstow PL28 8AF
T: (01841) 532555
F: (01841) 533115
E: sales@jackie-stanley.co.uk
I: www.harbourholidays.co.uk

Bos Keun Lowen
Rating Applied For
Contact:
Cornish Horizons, The Cottage, 19 New Street, Padstow PL28 8EA
T: (01841) 533331
F: (01841) 533933
E: cottages@cornishhorizons.co.uk

Brambles ★★★
Contact:
Cornish Horizons, The Cottage, 19 New Street, Padstow PL28 8EA
T: (01841) 533331
F: (01841) 533933
E: cottages@cornishhorizons.co.uk
I: www.cornishhorizons.co.uk

10 Broad Street, 2 Mill Road, 5 Mill Road ★★★
Contact: Mrs Susan Farr
Sheepcombe House, Washingpool Hill Roa, Bristol BS32 4NZ
T: (01454) 614861
F: (01454) 613252

Broomleaf Cottage ★★★
Contact:
Cornish Horizons, The Cottage, 19 New Street, Padstow PL28 8EA
T: (01841) 533331
F: (01841) 533933
E: cottages@cornishhorizons.co.uk
I: www.cornishhorizons.co.uk

Camel Cottage ★★★
Contact:
Cornish Horizons, The Cottage, 19 New Street, Padstow PL28 8EA
T: (01841) 533331
F: (01841) 533933
E: cottages@cornishhorizons.co.uk
I: www.cornishhorizons.co.uk

Catherine's ★★★★
Contact: Mrs Olive Lovell
Catherine's, 13A Duke Street, Padstow PL28 8AB
T: (01841) 533859
E: bobandolive@padstow.force9.co.uk

Catty Clew ★★★
Contact:
Cornish Horizons, The Cottage, 19 New Street, Padstow PL28 8EA
T: (01841) 533331
F: (01841) 533933
E: cottages@cornishhorizons.co.uk
I: www.cornishhorizons.co.uk

10 Church Lane ★★★
Contact: Ms Nicky Stanley
Harbour Holidays - Padstow, 1 North Quay, Padstow PL28 8AF
T: (01841) 532555
F: (01841) 533115
E: sales@jackie-stanley.co.uk
I: www.harbourholidays.co.uk

23 Church Lane ★★★
Contact: Ms Nicky Stanley
Harbour Holidays - Padstow, 1 North Quay, Padstow PL28 8AF
T: (01841) 532555
F: (01841) 533115
E: sales@jackie-stanley.co.uk
I: www.harbourholidays.co.uk

26 Church Lane
Rating Applied For
Contact:
Cornish Horizons, The Cottage, 19 New Street, Padstow PL28 8EA
T: (01841) 533331
F: (01841) 533933
E: cottages@cornishhorizons.co.uk

Establishments printed in blue have a detailed entry in this guide

SOUTH WEST ENGLAND

Coachyard Mews ★★★
Contact: Mr Stephen Andrews
Raidean Ltd, 25 Bentley Close,
Rectory Farm, Northampton
NN3 5JS
T: (01841) 521198
E: raideanltd@aol.com
I: www.holidayinpadstow.com

Cobblers ★★★
Contact: Ms Nicky Stanley
Harbour Holidays - Padstow, 1
North Quay, Padstow PL28 8AF
T: (01841) 532555
F: (01841) 533115
E: sales@jackie-stanley.co.uk
I: www.harbourholidays.co.uk

Crabcatchers ★★★
Contact:
Cornish Horizons, The Cottage,
19 New Street, Padstow
PL28 8EA
T: (01841) 533331
F: (01841) 533933
E: cottages@cornishhorizons.co.uk

Crenella Barn ★★★
Contact: Ms Nicky Stanley
Harbour Holidays - Padstow, 1
North Quay, Padstow PL28 8AF
T: (01841) 532555
F: (01841) 533115
E: sales@jackie-stanley.co.uk
I: www.harbourholidays.co.uk

14 Cross Street ★★
Contact: Ms Nicky Stanley
Harbour Holidays - Padstow, 1
North Quay, Padstow PL28 8AF
T: (01841) 532555
F: (01841) 533115
E: sales@jackie-stanley.co.uk
I: www.harbourholidays.co.uk

Curlews ★★★
Contact: Ms Nicky Stanley
Harbour Holidays - Padstow, 1
North Quay, Padstow PL28 8AF
T: (01841) 532555
F: (01841) 533115
E: sales@jackie-stanley.co.uk
I: www.harbourholidays.co.uk

3 Dennis Cove ★★★
Contact: Ms Nicky Stanley
Harbour Holidays - Padstow, 1
North Quay, Padstow PL28 8AF
T: (01841) 532555
F: (01841) 533115
E: sales@jackie-stanley.co.uk
I: www.harbourholidays.co.uk

Dingly Dell ★★★
Contact: Ms Nicky Stanley
Harbour Holidays - Padstow, 1
North Quay, Padstow PL28 8AF
T: (01841) 532555
F: (01841) 533115
E: sales@jackie-stanley.co.uk
I: www.harbourholidays.co.uk

Dodo's Cottage ★★★
Contact:
Harbour Holidays - Padstow, 1
North Quay, Padstow PL28 8AF
T: (01841) 532555
F: (01841) 533115
E: sales@jackie-stanley.co.uk

Dove Cottage ★★★
Contact:
Harbour Holidays - Padstow, 1
North Quay, Padstow PL28 8AF
T: (01841) 532555

The Drang House ★★★
Contact: Ms Nicky Stanley
Harbour Holidays - Padstow, 1
North Quay, Padstow PL28 8AF
T: (01841) 532555
F: (01841) 533115
E: sales@jackie-stanley.co.uk
I: www.harbourholidays.co.uk

The Dukes ★★★
Contact: Mr Peter Howorth
Vine Cottage, Love Lane,
Newbury RG14 2JG
T: (01635) 30096
E: manancat@phowth.fsnet.co.uk

15 Egerton Road ★★★
Contact:
Harbour Holidays - Padstow, 1
North Quay, Padstow PL28 8AF
T: (01841) 532555
F: (01841) 533115
E: sales@jackie-stanley.co.uk
I: www.harbourholidays.co.uk

17 Egerton Road ★★
Contact: Ms Nicky Stanley
Harbour Holidays - Padstow, 1
North Quay, Padstow PL28 8AF
T: (01841) 532555
F: (01841) 533115
E: sales@jackie-stanley.co.uk
I: www.harbourholidays.co.uk

22 Egerton Road ★★★★
Contact: Ms Nicky Stanley
Harbour Holidays - Padstow, 1
North Quay, Padstow PL28 8AF
T: (01841) 532555
F: (01841) 533115
E: sales@jackie-stanley.co.uk
I: www.harbourholidays.co.uk

42 Egerton Road ★★★
Contact:
Harbour Holidays - Padstow, 1
North Quay, Padstow PL28 8AF
T: (01841) 532555
F: (01841) 533115
E: sales@jackie-stanley.co.uk

Estuary View ★★★
Contact: Mrs Pamela Thomas
Tilmore House, Reservoir Lane,
Petersfield GU32 2HX
T: (01730) 263135

Estuary View ★★★
Contact:
Harbour Holidays - Padstow, 1
North Quay, Padstow PL28 8AF
T: (01841) 532555

Felwyn
Rating Applied For
Contact: Mr Peter Osbourne
Cornish Horizons, 19 New
Street, Padstow PL28 8EA
T: (01841) 533331
F: (01841) 533933
E: cottages@cornishhorizons.co.uk

Ferndale ★★★
Contact:
Cornish Horizons, The Cottage,
19 New Street, Padstow
PL28 8EA
T: (01841) 533331
F: (01841) 533933
E: cottages@cornishhorizons.co.uk
I: www.cornishhorizons.co.uk

Fisherman's Cottage ★★
Contact: Mr & Mrs Angelinetta
18 Church Street, Banwell
BS29 6EA
T: (01934) 822688
F: (01934) 822688

Fishermans Cottage ★★★★
Contact: Ms Nicky Stanley
Harbour Holidays - Padstow, 1
North Quay, Padstow PL28 8AF
T: (01841) 532555
F: (01841) 533115
E: sales@jackie-stanley.co.uk
I: www.harbourholidays.co.uk

Fuchsia Cottage ★★★
Contact: Mrs Lumley
1 College Mews, Middlesbrough
TS9 5DJ
T: (01642) 710732
E: lumley@magnolia1.fsnet.co.uk
I: www.fuchsiacottage.co.uk

Garden Flat ★★★
Contact:
Cornish Horizons, The Cottage,
19 New Street, Padstow
PL28 8EA
T: (01841) 533331
F: (01841) 533933
E: cottages@cornishhorizons.co.uk
I: www.cornishhorizons.co.uk

Grove Cottage ★★★
Contact: Ms Claudia Dierks
6 Rosse Wehe 3, 26160 Bad
Zwischenahn, Germany
T: (01432) 275084
E: inquiries@padstowcottages.info
I: www.padstowcottages.info

Harbour View Holiday Flats ★★★
Contact: Mrs Oliver
Trewornan Manor, Wadebridge
PL27 6EX
T: (01208) 816422
E: beach.hols@dial.pipex.com

Harmony ★★★
Contact:
Cornish Horizons, The Cottage,
19 New Street, Padstow
PL28 8EA
T: (01841) 533331
F: (01841) 533933
E: cottages@cornishhorizons.co.uk
I: www.cornishhorizons.co.uk

Hidden Cottage ★★★★★
Contact: Ms Nicky Stanley
Harbour Holidays - Padstow, 1
North Quay, Padstow PL28 8AF
T: (01841) 532555
F: (01841) 533115
E: sales@jackie-stanley.co.uk
I: www.harbourholidays.co.uk

Hideaway Cottage ★★★★
Contact: Mr Nick Sutton
7 Dorchester Way, Bedford
MK42 9FF
T: (01234) 353499
E: dnl.holidays@ntlworld.com
I: www.dnlholidays.co.uk

19 High Street ★★★
Contact: Ms Nicky Stanley
Harbour Holidays - Padstow, 1
North Quay, Padstow PL28 8AF
T: (01841) 532555
F: (01841) 533115
E: sales@jackie-stanley.co.uk
I: www.harbourholidays.co.uk

Hollyhocks ★★★★
Contact: Mrs Jo Robinson
26 The Culvery, Trevanion Road,
Wadebridge PL27 7DX
T: (01208) 815746
E: info@westcountry-life.co.uk
I: www.westcountry-life.co.uk

Honey Cottage ★★★
Contact: Mr Ian & Mrs Jane
Trimmer
6 Greenacre Close, Hadley High
Stone, Barnet EN5 4QB
T: (020) 84416239
E: i.trimmer@btinternet.com
I: www.i.trimmer.users.btopenworld.com/honeycottagepadstow.htm

Honeysuckle Cottage ★★★
Contact:
Harbour Holidays - Padstow, 1
North Quay, Padstow PL28 8AF
T: (01841) 532555
F: (01841) 533115
I: www.harbourholidays.co.uk

Honeysuckle Cottage ★★★★
Contact: Mrs Clarke
Manor Croft, Crediton EX17 5DL
T: (01363) 84292
F: (01363) 84559
E: honeysucklecottage@cchaulage.com

Jasmine Cottage ★★★★
Contact: Ms Nicky Stanley
Harbour Holidays - Padstow, 1
North Quay, Padstow PL28 8AF
T: (01841) 532555
F: (01841) 533115
E: sales@jackie-stanley.co.uk
I: www.harbourholidays.co.uk

Kittiwake ★★★
Contact: Ms Nicky Stanley
Harbour Holidays - Padstow, 1
North Quay, Padstow PL28 8AF
T: (01841) 532555
F: (01841) 533115
E: sales@jackie-stanley.co.uk

Lamorva Cottage ★★★
Contact: Mr David & Mrs Anita
Plume
Lamorva Cottage, 13 Sarahs
View, Padstow PL28 8DU
T: (01841) 533841
F: (01841) 533841
E: lamorva@aol.com

Look out for establishments participating in the National Accessible Scheme

SOUTH WEST ENGLAND

Lantern House ★★★
Contact: Mr Alistair Wright
Lantern House, 38/40 Duke Street, Padstow PL28 8AD
T: (01841) 532566

The Laurels Holiday Park ★★★-★★★★★
Contact: Mr Alan Nicholson
The Laurels Holiday Park, Padstow Road, Whitecross, Wadebridge PL27 7JQ
T: (01208) 813341
F: (01208) 816590
E: anicholson@thelaurelsholidaypark.co.uk
I: www.thelaurelsholidaypark.co.uk

Lawn Cottage ★★★★
Contact: Ms Heather Buckingham
Buckingham Properties, 101 Coventry Road, Birmingham B46 3EX
T: 0870 4 423684
F: 0870 4 423685
E: heather@bprops.co.uk
I: www.bprops.co.uk

Lelissick ★★★
Contact: Ms Nicky Stanley
Harbour Holidays - Padstow, 1 North Quay, Padstow PL28 8AF
T: (01841) 532555
F: (01841) 533115
E: sales@jackie-stanley.co.uk
I: www.harbourholidays.co.uk

Little Dolphins ★★★
Contact:
Cornish Horizons, The Cottage, 19 New Street, Padstow PL28 8EA
T: (01841) 533331
F: (01841) 533933
E: cottages@cornishhorizons.co.uk
I: www.cornishhorizions.co.uk

Little Dukes ★★
Contact:
Cornish Horizons, The Cottage, 19 New Street, Padstow PL28 8EA
T: (01841) 533331
F: (01841) 533933
E: cottages@cornishhorizons.co.uk
I: www.cornishhorizons.co.uk

Little Haven
Rating Applied For
Contact: Mr Andrew Cousins
31 Carolina Place, Wokingham RG40 4PQ
T: (01189) 328116
E: andycousins@hotmail.com
I: www.stay-in-padstow.co.uk

Lobster House ★★★★
Contact:
Cornish Horizons, The Cottage, 19 New Street, Padstow Pl28 8EA
T: (01841) 533331
F: (01841) 533933
E: cottages@cornishhorizons.co.uk

The Lobster Pot ★★★
Contact: Ms Kay Wood
Trevillador Farm, St Issey, Wadebridge PL27 7SD
T: (01841) 540226
E: kaywood@onetel.net.uk

Lobsterpots ★★★
Contact:
Cornish Horizons, The Cottage, 19 New Street, Padstow PL28 8EA
T: (01841) 533331
F: (01741) 533933
E: cottages@cornishhorizons.co.uk

Louand ★★★
Contact: Mr & Mrs Osborne
Cornish Horizons Holiday Cottages, The Cottage, 19 New Street, Padstow PL28 8EA

Marina Villa - St Edmunds End
Rating Applied For
Contact: Ms Nicky Stanley
Harbour Holidays - Padstow, 1 North Quay, Padstow PL28 8AF
T: (01841) 532555
F: (01841) 533115
E: sales@jackie-stanley.co.uk
I: www.harbourholidays.co.uk

Marine Villa - Harbour End ★★★
Contact:
Harbour Holidays - Padstow, 1 North Quay, Padstow PL28 8AF
T: (01841) 532555
F: (01841) 533115
E: sales@jackie-stanley.co.uk
I: www.harbourholidays.co.uk

Market Square Holiday Apartments ★★★-★★★★★
Contact: Mrs Higgins
Tregolds, Wadebridge PL27 7JB
T: (01208) 813379
F: (01841) 533339
E: msh@padstow.com
I: www.padstow.com

Maypole Cottage ★★★
Contact:
Harbour Holidays - Padstow, 1 North Quay, Padstow PL28 8AF
T: (01841) 532555
F: (01841) 533115
E: sales@jackie-stanley.co.uk
I: www.harbourholidays.co.uk

3 Meadow Court ★★★★
Contact:
Harbour Holidays - Padstow, 1 North Quay, Padstow PL28 8AF
T: (01841) 532555

6 Meadow Court ★★★★
Contact:
Harbour Holidays - Padstow, 1 North Quay, Padstow PL28 8AF
T: (01841) 532555
E: contact@harbourholidays.co.uk

Mevagh ★★★
Contact: Ms Nicky Stanley
Harbour Holidays - Padstow, 1 North Quay, Padstow PL28 8AF
T: (01841) 532555
F: (01841) 533115
E: sales@jackie-stanley.co.uk
I: www.harbourholidays.co.uk

Middle Street Apartments ★★-★★★★
Contact: Mrs Joan Hull
24 Hawkins Road, Padstow PL28 3EU
T: (01841) 533545
F: (01841) 832630
E: jim@jwhull.fsnet.co.uk

14 Mill Road ★★★★
Contact: Mrs McCall
Upperdeck, Primrose Drive, St Merryn, Padstow PL28 8TE
T: (01841) 520998
I: www.padstowholidays.co.uk

3 Mill Road ★★★
Contact: Mrs Debbie Morris-Kirby
33 Barry's Lane, Padstow PL28 8AU
T: (01841) 533219
E: debbie.morriskirby@tesco.net
I: www.acottageinpadstow.com

Moonfleet and Tamarisk ★★★
Contact: Mrs Jenny O'Sullivan
12 Champion Road, Upminster RM14 2SY
T: (01708) 229872

The Mowhay ★★
Contact:
Harbour Holidays - Padstow, 1 North Quay, Padstow PL28 8AF
T: (01841) 532555
F: (01841) 533115
E: sales@jackie-stanley.co.uk

12 Netherton Road ★★★
Contact:
Cornish Horizons, The Cottage, 19 New Street, Padstow PL28 8EA
T: (01841) 533331
F: (01841) 533933
E: cottages@cornishhorizons.co.uk
I: www.cornishhorizons.co.uk

10 New Street ★★★
Contact: Ms Nicky Stanley
Harbour Holidays - Padstow, 1 North Quay, Padstow PL28 8AF
T: (01841) 532555
F: (01841) 533115
E: sales@jackie-stanley.co.uk
I: www.harbourholidays.co.uk

21 New Street ★★★★★
Contact:
Harbour Holidays Ltd, 1 North Quay, Padstow PL28 8AF
T: (01841) 533402
F: (01841) 533115
I: www.harbourholidays.co.uk

No 1 Cross Street ★★★
Contact: Mrs Susanne Hollest
The Old Malthouse, Bath Road, Melksham SN12 8EF
T: (01225) 707519
F: (01225) 709787
E: susanne.roger@virgin.net

Nooks Cottage ★★★
Contact:
Cornish Horizons, The Cottage, 19 New Street, Padstow PL28 8EA
T: (01841) 533331
F: (01841) 533933
E: cottages@cornishhorizons.co.uk
I: www.cornishhorizons.co.uk

The Old Bakery ★★★★
Contact: Mr Tony Tippett
The Old Bakery, T W Properties, 6 Cross Street, Padstow PL28 8AT
T: (01841) 532885
E: tony.twproperties@aol.com
I: www.TWPROPERTIES.co.uk

12 The Old Boatyard ★★★
Contact: Mrs McCall
Primrose Drive, St Merryn, Padstow PL28 8TE
T: (01841) 520998
I: www.padstowholidays.co.uk/

The Old Coach House ★★★
Contact: Ms Nicky Stanley
Harbour Holidays - Padstow, 1 North Quay, Padstow PL28 8AF
T: (01841) 532555
F: (01841) 533115
E: sales@jackie-stanley.co.uk
I: www.harbourholidays.co.uk

Old Custom House Barn ★★★★★
Contact:
Harbour Holidays Ltd, 1 North Quay, Padstow PL28 8AF
T: (01841) 533402
F: (01841) 533115
E: contact@harbourholidays.co.uk
I: www.harbourholidays.co.uk

25 Old School Court ★★★★
Contact: Ms Nicky Stanley
Harbour Holidays - Padstow, 1 North Quay, Padstow PL28 8AF
T: (01841) 532555
F: (01841) 533115
E: sales@jackie-stanley.co.uk
I: www.harbourholidays.co.uk

9 Old School Court ★★★
Contact: Mrs Vicki Windows
56 Shirehampton Road, Bristol BS9 2DL
T: (0117) 9626247
E: vickiwindows@yahoo.com

Old School House ★★★
Contact: Ms Stanley
Jackie Stanley Estate Agents, Ferry Point, Wadebridge PL27 6LD
T: (01208) 862424
F: (01841) 533115

Ossmill Cottage ★★★
Contact: Ms Nicky Stanley
Harbour Holidays - Padstow, 1 North Quay, Padstow PL28 8AF
T: (01841) 532555
F: (01841) 533115
E: sales@jackie-stanley.co.uk
I: www.harbourholidays.co.uk

Overcliff ★★★★
Contact: Mr John & Mrs Gillian Hammond
The Mount Farm, Foxton, Market Harborough LE16 7RD
T: (0116) 2517171
F: (01858) 545950
E: pjh@pjh.u-net.com

Padstow Holiday Cottages ★★★
Contact: Mrs Pat Walker
St Edwards, Little Petherick, Wadebridge PL27 7QT
T: (01841) 541180
F: (01841) 541180
I: www.padstow-holiday-cottages.co.uk

Establishments printed in blue have a detailed entry in this guide

SOUTH WEST ENGLAND

Padstow House ★★
Contact:
Valley Villas, Brook Cottage, Old Warleigh Lane, Plymouth
PL5 4ND
T: (01752) 774900
E: sales@valleyvillas.co.uk
I: www.valleyvillas.co.uk

Parnalls ★★★
Contact: Ms Nicky Stanley
Harbour Holidays - Padstow, 1 North Quay, Padstow PL28 8AF
T: (01841) 532555
F: (01841) 533115
E: sales@jackie-stanley.co.uk
I: www.harbourholidays.co.uk

Pebble Cottage ★★★
Contact: Ms Nicky Stanley
Harbour Holidays - Padstow, 1 North Quay, Padstow PL28 8AF
T: (01841) 532555
F: (01841) 533115
E: sales@jackie-stanley.co.uk
I: www.harbourholidays.co.uk

Pebbles
Rating Applied For
Contact:
Harbour Holidays, 1 North Quay, Padstow PL28 8AF
T: (01841) 532555
F: (01841) 533115
E: contact@harbourholidays.co.uk
I: www.harbourholidays.co.uk

Pensers ★★★★
Contact: Ms Nicky Stanley
Harbour Holidays - Padstow, 1 North Quay, Padstow PL28 8AF
T: (01841) 532555
F: (01841) 533115
E: sales@jackie-stanley.co.uk
I: www.harbourholidays.co.uk

Pentire Apartment ★★★★
Contact: Ms Nicky Stanley
Harbour Holidays - Padstow, 1 North Quay, Padstow PL28 8AF
T: (01841) 532555
F: (01841) 533115
E: sales@jackie-stanley.co.uk
I: www.harbourholidays.co.uk

Pinmill Cottage ★★★
Contact: Ms Nicky Stanley
Harbour Holidays - Padstow, 1 North Quay, Padstow PL28 8AF
T: (01841) 532555
F: (01841) 533115
E: sales@jackie-stanley.co.uk
I: www.harbourholidays.co.uk

Pippits ★★★
Contact:
Cornish Horizons, The Cottage, 19 New Street, Padstow
PL28 8EA
T: (01841) 533331
F: (01841) 533933
E: cottages@cornishhorizons.co.uk
I: www.cornishhorizons.co.uk

Pols Piece Holidays ★★★-★★★★
Contact: Mrs J E Olivey
Dobbin Lane, Trevone, Padstow
PL28 8QP
T: (01841) 520372
F: (01841) 520372
I: www.polspieceholidays.co.uk

Poppies ★★★
Contact:
Harbour Holidays - Padstow, 1 North Quay, Padstow PL28 8AF
T: (01841) 532555

Portloe ★★
Contact:
Harbour Holidays - Padstow, 1 North Quay, Padstow PL28 8AF
T: (01841) 532555

Primrose House ★★★★
Contact:
Cornish Horizons, The Cottage, 19 New Street, Padstow
PL28 8EA
T: (01841) 533331
F: (01841) 533933
E: cottages@cornishhorizons.co.uk
I: www.cornishhorizons.co.uk

Puffin Cottage ★★★
Contact: Ms Nicky Stanley
Harbour Holidays - Padstow, 1 North Quay, Padstow PL28 8AF
T: (01841) 532555
F: (01841) 533115
E: sales@jackie-stanley.co.uk
I: www.harbourholidays.co.uk

Quayside Cottage ★★★★
Contact: Mrs Andrea Richards
Petrocstowe, 30 Treverbyn Road, Padstow PL28 8DW
T: (01841) 532429

The Quies ★★★
Contact:
Harbour Holidays - Padstow, 1 North Quay, Padstow PL28 8AF
T: (01841) 532555

Raleigh ★★★★
Contact: Mrs Gillian Burgess
Raleigh, 19 Raleigh Close, Padstow PL28 8BQ
T: (01841) 532633

3 Red Brick Building ★★★
Contact:
Harbour Holidays - Padstow, 1 North Quay, Padstow PL28 8AF
T: (01841) 532555

4 Red Brick Building ★★★
Contact:
4 Red Brick Building, North Quay, Padstow PL28 8AF
T: (01841) 533402
F: (01841) 533115
E: contact@harbourholidays.co.uk

The Retreat & Sunrise Cottage ★★★-★★★★
Contact: Mrs Ann Walker
The Lodge, Bridgnorth Road, Stourbridge DY7 5JF
T: (01384) 221295
F: (01384) 221141

Robins Nest ★★★
Contact:
Cornish Horizons, The Cottage, 19 New Street, Padstow
PL28 8EA
T: (01841) 533331
F: (01841) 533933
E: cottages@cornishhorizons.co.uk
I: www.cornishhorizons.co.uk

Rockview ★★★
Contact:
Harbour Holidays, 1 North Quay, Padstow PL28 8AF
T: (01841) 532555
F: (01841) 533115
E: contact@harbourholidays.co.uk
I: www.harbourholidays.co.uk

Rose Cottage ★★★
Contact: Ms Nicky Stanley
Harbour Holidays - Padstow, 1 North Quay, Padstow PL28 8AF
T: (01841) 532555
F: (01841) 533115
E: sales@jackie-stanley.co.uk
I: www.harbourholidays.co.uk

Rosehill House ★★★
Contact: Ms Nicky Stanley
Harbour Holidays - Padstow, 1 North Quay, Padstow PL28 8AF
T: (01841) 532555
F: (01841) 533115
E: sales@jackie-stanley.co.uk
I: www.harbourholidays.co.uk

Rosevanion ★★★
Contact: Mrs Helen Mary Haller
Rosevanion, Sarahs Lane, Padstow PL28 8EL
T: (01841) 532227
F: (01841) 532227
E: mary@haller250.freeserve.co.uk
I: www.padstow-rosevanion.freeserve.co.uk

Sable Cottage & Chiff Chaff ★★★-★★★★
Contact: Ms Denise Daw
16 Harbury Road, Bristol
BS9 4PL
T: (0117) 9079348
E: mddaw@harbury56.co.uk
I: www.sablecottage.co.uk

Sail Loft ★★★
Contact: Ms Nicky Stanley
Harbour Holidays - Padstow, 1 North Quay, Padstow PL28 8AF
T: (01841) 532555
F: (01841) 533115
E: sales@jackie-stanley.co.uk
I: www.harbourholidays.co.uk

Saint Breock ★★★
Contact: Ms Nicky Stanley
Harbour Holidays - Padstow, 1 North Quay, Padstow PL28 8AF
T: (01841) 532555
F: (01841) 533115
E: sales@jackie-stanley.co.uk
I: www.harbourholidays.co.uk

St Ervan Manor and Country Cottages ★★★★
Contact: Mrs Lorraine Clarke
St Ervan Manor and Country Cottages, The Old Rectory, Wadebridge PL27 7TA
T: (01841) 540255
F: (01841) 540255
E: mail@stervanmanor.freeserve.co.uk
I: www.stervanmanor.co.uk

Sanderlings ★★★★
Contact: Mrs Gill Vivian
Holiday Padstow, 4 St Saviours Lane, Padstow PL28 8BD
T: (01841) 533791
F: (01841) 533843
E: neil.vivian@btopenworld.com
I: www.holiday-padstow.co.uk

2 Sarah's Court
Rating Applied For
Contact: Mrs Major
2 Sarah's Court, Padstow
PL28 8DZ
T: (01841) 533656

Sarahs View ★★★
Contact:
Harbour Holidays, 4 North Quay, Padstow PL28 8AF
T: (01841) 532555
F: (01841) 533115
E: contact@harbourholidays.co.uk
I: www.harbourholidays.co.uk

34 Sarah's View ★★★
Contact: Mrs Margaret Thomas
31 Dennis Road, Padstow
PL28 8DF
T: (01841) 532243

62 Sarah's View ★★★
Contact: Mrs Amey
45 Southern Road, Southborne, Bournemouth BH6 3SS
T: (01202) 258769

The School House ★★★★
Contact: Mr Martin & Mrs Jacqui Wilson
The Old Vicarage, Eglosmayle Road, Wadebridge PL27 6AQ
T: (01208) 812640
E: Martin.Jacqui@virgin.net

Seal Cottage ★★★
Contact: Ms Nicky Stanley
Harbour Holidays - Padstow, 1 North Quay, Padstow PL28 8AF
T: (01841) 532555
F: (01841) 533115
E: sales@jackie-stanley.co.uk
I: www.harbourholidays.co.uk

Serendipity ★★★
Contact: Ms Nicky Stanley
Harbour Holidays - Padstow, 1 North Quay, Padstow PL28 8AF
T: (01841) 532555
F: (01841) 533115
E: sales@jackie-stanley.co.uk
I: www.harbourholidays.co.uk

Shore Lodge ★★★★★
Contact: Mrs Vivian
Holiday-Padstow, 4 St Saviours Lane, Padstow PL28 8BD
T: (01841) 533791
F: (01841) 533843
E: Neil.Vivian@btopenworld.com
I: www.holiday-padstow.co.uk

Skipper Cottage ★★★
Contact: Mrs MacRae
Skipper Cottage, 18 Riverside, Padstow PL28 8BY
T: (01841) 540237

The Slate House ★★★
Contact: Ms Nicky Stanley
Harbour Holidays - Padstow, 1 North Quay, Padstow PL28 8AF
T: (01841) 532555
F: (01841) 533115
E: sales@jackie-stanley.co.uk
I: www.harbourholidays.co.uk

SOUTH WEST ENGLAND

Squirrels ★★★
Contact:
Cornish Horizons, The Cottage,
19 New Street, Padstow
PL28 8EA
T: (01841) 533331
F: (01841) 533933
E: cottages@cornishhorizons.co.uk
I: www.cornishhorizons.co.uk

10 St Petroc's Meadow ★★★
Contact: Mr Neville Powell
7 Pellew Close, Padstow PL2 8EY
T: (01841) 532156

Stable Cottage, Bay Tree Cottage & Clover Cottage ★★★★
Contact: Mrs Jill Hagley
Stable Cottage, Bay Tree Cottage & Clover Cottage, Trevethan Farm, Sarah's Lane, Padstow
PL28 8LE
T: (01841) 532874
F: (01841) 532874
E: info@padstowcottages.co.uk
I: www.padstowcottages.co.uk

Stone Cottage ★★
Contact: Dr Richardson
45A Cassiobury Park Avenue,
Watford WD18 7LD
T: (01923) 226218
F: (01923) 226218
E: jrichardson09@aol.com

Stonesthrow Cottage ★★★★
Contact:
Cornish Horizons, The Cottage,
19 New Street, Padstow
PL28 8EA
T: (01841) 533331
F: (01841) 533933
E: cottages@cornishhorizons.co.uk
I: www.cornishhorizons.co.uk

2 The Strand ★★★
Contact: Ms Nicky Stanley
Harbour Holidays - Padstow, 1
North Quay, Padstow PL28 8AF
T: (01841) 532555
F: (01841) 533115
E: sales@jackie-stanley.co.uk
I: www.harbourholidays.co.uk

Strand Flats ★★★
Contact: Mr Brown
Strand Flats, Treoell, Bodmin
PL30 4BL
T: (01208) 821611
F: (01208) 821611
E: Jill.P.Brown@btinternet.com
I: www.strandflats.co.uk

Summer Court ★★★★
Contact: Mr & Mrs Whitehead
Grange House, Great North Road, Leeds LS25 4AG
T: (0113) 286 0036

Sunbeam Cottage ★★★★
Contact: Ms Wendy Gidlow
Sunbeam Cottage, 39 Duke Street, Padstow PL28 8AD
T: (01841) 533634
F: (01841) 532271
E: wendy@wgidlow.fsnet.co.uk
I: www.sunbeam-cottage.co.uk/

Sundance ★★★
Contact:
Harbour Holidays Ltd, 1 North Quay, Padstow PL28 8AF
T: (01841) 532555
F: (01841) 533115
E: contact@harbourholidays.co.uk

Sunday Cottage & School Cottage ★★★★
Contact: Mrs Diane Hoe
Lower Cottage, Stratford-upon-Avon CV37 8NG
T: (01789) 450214
F: (01789) 730199
E: mail@sundaycottage.co.uk
I: www.sundaycottage.co.uk

Sunnyhill Cottage ★★★★
Contact: Ms Nicky Stanley
Harbour Holidays - Padstow, 1
North Quay, Padstow PL28 8AF
T: (01841) 532555
F: (01841) 533115
E: sales@jackie-stanley.co.uk
I: www.harbourholidays.co.uk

Teal ★★★
Contact: Ms Nicky Stanley
Harbour Holidays - Padstow, 1
North Quay, Padstow PL28 8AF
T: (01841) 532555
F: (01841) 533115
E: sales@jackie-stanley.co.uk
I: www.harbourholidays.co.uk

Teazers ★★★
Contact: Ms Nicky Stanley
Harbour Holidays - Padstow, 1
North Quay, Padstow PL28 8AF
T: (01841) 532555
F: (01841) 533115
E: sales@jackie-stanley.co.uk
I: www.harbourholidays.co.uk

Tregirls ★★★-★★★★★
Contact: Mrs Watson Smyth
Tregirls, Padstow PL28 8RR
T: (01841) 532648

Trenoder ★★★
Contact:
Cornish Horizons, The Cottage,
19 New Street, Padstow
PL28 8EA
T: (01841) 533331
F: (01841) 533933
E: cottages@cornishhorizons.co.uk

Treverbyn Road ★★★
Contact:
Harbour Holidays, 4 North Quay, Padstow PL28 8AF
T: (01841) 532555
F: (01841) 533115
E: contact@harbourholidays.co.uk
I: www.harbourholidays.co.uk

4 Treverbyn Road ★★★★
Contact: Mrs Vivian
Holiday - Padstow, 4 St Saviours Lane, Padstow PL28 8BD
T: (01841) 533791
F: (01841) 533843
E: Neil.Vivian@btopenworld.com
I: www.holiday-padstow.co.uk

Trevorrick Farm ★★★
Contact: Mr & Mrs Topliss & Benwell
Trevorrick Farm, Wadebridge
PL27 7QH
T: (01841) 540574
F: (01841) 540574
E: info@trevorrick.co.uk
I: www.trevorrick.co.uk

Valerian ★★★
Contact: Mrs Vivian
Holiday - Padstow, 4 St Saviours Lane, Padstow PL28 8BD
T: (01841) 533791
F: (01481) 533843
E: Neil.Vivian@btopenworld.com
I: www.holiday-padstow.co.uk

6 Waterside ★★★
Contact:
Harbour Holidays, 4 North Quay, Padstow PL28 8AF
T: (01841) 532555
F: (01741) 533115
E: contact@harbourholidays.co.uk
I: www.harbourholidays.co.uk

Wharf Cottage ★★★★
Contact:
Harbour Holidays, 1 North Quay, Padstow PL28 8AF
T: (01841) 533402
F: (01841) 533115
E: contact@harbourholidays.co.uk
I: www.harbourholidays.co.uk

The White Hart ★★★★
Contact: Ms Patricia Jacoby-Blake
The White Hart, New Street, Padstow PL28 8EA
T: (01841) 532350
E: whitehartpad@aol.com
I: www.whitehartpadstow.co.uk

Zefyros ★★★★
Contact: Mrs Harris
Hunters Gate, Much Wenlock
TF13 6BW
T: (01746) 785504

Zingiber ★★
Contact: Mrs Anna Gwilt
Laurel Cottage, Frome BA11 3QZ
T: (01373) 812640
F: (01373) 813540
E: annagwilt@primavera.co.uk

't Sandt ★★★
Contact:
Cornish Horizons, The Cottage,
19 New Street, Padstow
PL28 8EA
T: (01841) 533331
F: (01841) 533933
E: cottages@cornishhorizons.co.uk
I: www.cornishhorizons.co.uk

PAIGNTON
Torbay

Above Deck
Rating Applied For
Contact:
Holiday Homes & Cottages SW, 365A Torquay Road, Paignton
TQ3 2BT
T: (01803) 663650
F: (01803) 664037
E: holcotts@aol.com
I: www.swcottages.co.uk

All Seasons Holiday Apartments ★★★★
Contact: Mr Mike Dessi
All Seasons Holiday Apartments, 18 Garfield Road, Paignton
TQ4 6AX
T: (01803) 552187
F: (01803) 552187
E: mikedessi@allseasonsholiday.freeserve.co.uk
I: www.allseasonsholidayapartments.co.uk

Alpenrose Holiday Apartments ★★★★
Contact: Mrs Margaret Taylor
Alpenrose Holiday Apartments, 20 Polsham Park, Paignton
TQ3 2AD
T: (01803) 558430
F: (01803) 407959
E: alpenrose@blueyonder.co.uk
I: www.alpenrose.myby.co.uk

Bay View
Rating Applied For
Contact:
Holiday Homes & Cottages SW, 365A Torquay Road, Paignton
TQ3 2BT
T: (01803) 663650
F: (01803) 664037
E: holcotts@aol.com

Bay View ★★★
Contact:
Holday Homes and Cottages,
Torquay Road, Paignton TQ3 2BT
T: (01803) 663650
F: (01803) 664037
E: holcotts@aol.com

Beachway Holiday Flats ★★
Contact: Mr Edwin Toms
Beachway Holiday Flats, 11 Kernou Road, Paignton TQ4 6BA
T: (01803) 555717

Bedford Holiday Flats and Flatlets ★-★★★
Contact: Mr & Mrs S Dunster
Bedford Holiday Flats and Flatlets, 10 Adelphi Road, Paignton TQ4 6AW
T: (01803) 557737
E: info@bedfordholidayflats.co.uk
I: www.bedfordholidayflats.co.uk

Big Tree Holiday Flats ★★★
Contact: Mrs Pam Siddall
Big Tree Holiday Flats, 68 Fisher Street, Paignton TQ4 5ES
T: (01803) 559559
E: bigtree@eidosnet.co.uk
I: www.bigtreeholidayflats.co.uk

Bosuns Cottage ★★★★
Contact:
Holiday Homes & Cottages South West, 365A Torquay Road, Paignton TQ3 2BT
T: (01803) 663650
F: (01803) 664037
E: holcotts@aol.co.uk
I: www.swcottages.co.uk

Establishments printed in blue have a detailed entry in this guide

SOUTH WEST ENGLAND

Broadshade Holiday Flats ★-★★★
Contact: Mr John & Mrs Dot Barber
Broadshade Holid_/ Flats, 9 St Andrews Road, Paignton TQ4 6HA
T: (01803) 559647
F: (01803) 529400
E: broadshade@hotmail.com
I: www.broadshade.com

Brockhurst Lodge ★★★★
Contact:
Holiday Homes and Cottages SW, 365A Torquay Road, Paignton TQ3 2BT
T: (01803) 663650
F: (01803) 664037
E: holcotts@aol.com
I: www.swcottagesco.uk

Carlton Manor ★★★★★
Contact:
Blue Chip Vacations, 3 Marina Walk, Brixham TQ5 9BW
T: (01803) 855282
F: (01803) 881029
E: info@bluechipdevelopments.com

Casa Marina Holiday Apartments ★★★
Contact: Mr Bob & Mrs Andrea Wooller
Casa Marina Holiday Apartments, 2 Keysfield Road, Paignton TQ4 6EP
T: (01803) 558334

Compton Pool Farm ★★★-★★★★★
Contact: Mr & Mrs Phipps
Compton Pool Farm, Compton, Marldon, Paignton TQ3 1TA
T: (01803) 872241
F: (01803) 874012
E: enquiries@comptonpool.co.uk
I: www.comptonpool.co.uk

The Conifers ★★★
Contact:
Holiday Homes & Cottages South West, 365A Torquay Road, Paignton TQ3 2BT
T: (01803) 663650
F: (01803) 664037
E: holcotts@aol.com
I: www.swcottages.co.uk

Cranmore Lodge ★★★
Contact: Mr Deryck Edwards
Cranmore Lodge, 45 Marine Drive, Paignton TQ3 2NS
T: (01803) 556278
F: (01803) 665797
E: cranlodge@btopenworld.com
I: www.cranmorelodge.co.uk

Denby House Holiday Apartments ★★★
Contact: Mr Brian & Mrs Lina Ford
Denby House Holiday Apartments, Belle Vue Road, Paignton TQ4 6ES
T: (01803) 559121
E: lina@denbyhouse.co.uk
I: www.denbyhouse.co.uk

Fairsea Holiday Flats ★★-★★★
Contact: Mr John & Mrs Lesley Hallett & Farrand
Fairsea Holiday Flats, 12 St Andrews Road, Paignton TQ4 6HA
T: (01803) 556903
E: fairsea@amserve.net

Fortescue ★★★
Contact:
Holiday Homes & Cottages South West, 365A Torquay Road, Paignton TQ3 2BT
T: (01803) 663650
F: (01803) 664037
E: holcotts@aol.com
I: www.swcottages.co.uk

Glencoe Holiday Flats ★★★
Contact: Mrs Patricia Jill Ayles
Glencoe Holiday Flats, Seafront, 7 Esplanade Road, Paignton TQ4 6EB
T: (01803) 557727
F: (01803) 666512
E: info@glencoeapartments.com
I: www.glencoeapartments.com

Grassington Court Holiday Apartments ★★★
Contact: Mrs J M Crompton
Grassington Court Holiday Apartments, 28 Sands Road, Paignton TQ4 6EJ
T: (01803) 557979

Harbour Reach Holiday Flats ★★-★★★
Contact: Ms Christine Grindrod
Harbour Reach Holiday Flats, 33 Sands Road, Paignton TQ4 6EG
T: (01803) 525857

Harbourside Holiday Apartments ★★★
Contact: Ms Kathleen Quaid
Harbourside Holiday Apartments, 49 Roundham Road, Paignton TQ4 6DS
T: (01803) 550181
F: (01803) 550181
E: habourside@amserve.net

Harwin Apartments ★★★★
Contact: Mr & Mrs S Gorman
Alta Vista Road, Goodrington Sands, Paignton TQ4 6DA
T: (01803) 558771
F: (08708) 313998
E: harwin@blueyonder.co.uk
I: www.harwinapartments.co.uk

Harwood Lodge ★★★★
Contact: Mr & Mrs Holgate
Harwood Lodge, 14 Roundham Road, Paignton TQ4 6DN
T: (01803) 391538
F: (01803) 401357
E: denise@harwoodlodge.co.uk
I: www.harwoodlodge.co.uk

Headland Lodge ★★★★
Contact:
Holiday Homes & Cottages, 365A Torquay Road, Paignton TQ3 2BT
T: (01803) 663650
F: (01803) 664037
E: info@swcottages.co.uk
I: www.swcottages.co.uk

HENNOCK ★★★★
Contact:
Holiday Homes & Cottages South West, 365A Torquay Road, Paignton TQ3 2BT
T: (01803) 663650
F: (01803) 664037
E: holcotts@aol.com
I: www.swcottages.co.uk

Hudson's Bay ★★★
Contact: Mr J & Mrs T Somers
5 Wye Dean Drive, Wigston LE18 3UE
T: (0116) 257 1740
F: (0116) 257 1740

Julie Court Holiday Apartments ★★★
Contact: Mr Abu & Mrs Wahida Abdullah
Julie Court Holiday Apartments, 5 Colin Road, Paignton TQ2 2NR
T: (01803) 551012
E: info@juliecourt.co.uk
I: www.juliecourt.co.uk

Kimberley Holiday Flats ★★-★★★
Contact: Miss Frances Moreby
Kimberley Holiday Flats, 39 Sands Road, Paignton TQ4 6EG
T: (01803) 551576
E: nigelboon@blueyonder.co.uk
I: www.kimberleyholidayflats.co.uk

Lanhydrock ★★★★
Contact:
Holiday Homes & Cottages, 365A Torquay Road, Paignton TQ3 2BT
T: (01803) 663650
F: (01803) 664037
E: holcotts@aol.com
I: www.swcottages.co.uk

Laverna Palms ★★
Contact: Mr Michael Craft
Laverna Palms, 5 Kernou Road, Paignton TQ4 6BA
T: (01803) 557620
I: www.devonselfcatering.com

The Lawn Holiday Apartments ★★★
Contact: Mrs Linda Harrison
The Lawn Holiday Apartments, St Andrews Road, Paignton TQ4 6HA
T: (01803) 528983
F: (01803) 528983
E: the.lawn@4mymail.co.uk
I: www.thelawn.info

7 Louville Close ★★★
Contact:
Holiday Homes & Cottages South West, 365A Torquay Road, Paignton TQ3 2BT
T: (01803) 663650

24 Marine Parade ★★★
Contact:
Holiday Homes and Cottages SW, 365A Torquay Road, Paignton TQ3 2BT
T: (01803) 663650
F: (01803) 664037
E: holcotts@aol.com
I: www.swcottages.co.uk

Montana ★-★★★
Contact: Mr Roger Seaward
Montana, 10 Belle Vue Road, Paignton TQ4 6ER
T: (01803) 559783

Morin ★★★
Contact:
Holiday Homes & Cottages SW, 365A Torquay Road, Paignton TQ3 2BT
T: (01803) 663650
F: (01803) 664037
E: holcotts@aol.com
I: www.swcottages.co.uk

Preston Down ★★★
Contact:
Holiday Homes & Cottages South West, 365A Torquay Road, Paignton TQ3 2BT
T: (01803) 663650
F: (01803) 664037
E: holcotts@aol.com
I: www.swcottages.co.uk

148 Preston Down Road ★★★★
Contact:
Holiday Homes & Cottages South West, 365A Torquay Road, Paignton TQ3 2BT
T: (01803) 663650

Primley ★★★
Contact:
Holiday Homes & Cottages South West, 365A Torquay Road, Paignton TQ3 2BT
T: (01803) 663650
F: (01803) 664037
E: holcotts@aol.com
I: www.swcottages.co.uk

Roundham Heights
Rating Applied For
Contact:
Blue Chip Vacations, 3 Marina Walk, Brixham TQ5 9BW
T: (01803) 855282
F: (01803) 851825
E: info@bluechipdevelopment.com
I: www.bluchipvacations.com

San Remo Holiday Apartments ★★-★★★
Contact: Mr & Mrs Hannant
San Remo Holiday Apartments, 15 Marine Drive, Paignton TQ3 2NJ
T: (01803) 550293

Sandmoor Holiday Apartments ★★★
Contact: Mr Rita & Mrs Brian Ellis
Sandmoor Holiday Apartments, 29 St Andrews Road, Paignton TQ4 6HA
T: (01803) 525909
F: (01803) 525909
E: sandmoorholidayapt@amserve.com
I: www.sandmoorholidayapartment.co.uk

SOUTH WEST ENGLAND

Serena Lodge Holiday Apartments ★★★
Contact: Mrs Christine Grindrod
Serena Lodge Holiday Apartments, 15 Cliff Road, Paignton TQ4 6DG
T: (01803) 550330
F: (01803) 550330
I: www.serenalodge.com

Stanley House ★★★
Contact: Mr E & Mrs D Baldry
Stanley House, 17 Cliff Road, Paignton TQ4 6DG
T: (01803) 557173
E: stanley.house@btinternet.com

Suncrest ★★-★★★
Contact: Mr Neil Carr
Suncrest, Adelphi Lane, Paignton TQ4 6AS
T: (01803) 665571
E: neilcarr@fsmail.net

Sunnybeach Holiday Flats ★-★★★
Contact: Mr David & Mrs Jane Schaedl
Sunnybeach Holiday Flats, 6 Esplanade Road, Paignton TQ4 6EB
T: (01803) 558729
F: (01803) 558729
E: jshadll@btconnect.com
I: www.sunny-beach.co.uk

Thatcher View ★★★
Contact: Mr David Morey
Thatcher View, 25A Cliff Road, Paignton TQ4 6DH
T: (01803) 555759
E: moreyfamily@tiscali.co.uk

Torbay Holiday Motel ★★
Contact: Mr Booth
Torbay Holiday Motel, Totnes Road, Paignton TQ4 7PP
T: (01803) 558226
F: (01803) 663175
E: enquries@thm.co.uk
I: www.thm.co.uk

Tregarth ★-★★
Contact: Mr Barry Haskins
Tregarth, 8 Adelphi Road, Paignton TQ4 6AW
T: (01803) 558458

Vista Apartments
Rating Applied For
Contact:
Blue Chip Vacations, 3 Marina Walk, Brixham TQ5 9BW
T: (01803) 855282
F: (01803) 851825
E: info@bluechipdevelopments.com
I: www.bluechipvacations.com

PANBOROUGH
Somerset

Panborough Batch House ★★★
Contact: Mrs Sheila Booth
Panborough Batch House, Wells BA5 1PN
T: (01934) 712769
E: sdb.antiques@ukgateway.co.uk

PANCRASWEEK
Devon

Tamarstone Farm ★★★
Contact: Mrs Megan Daglish
Tamarstone Farm, Bude Road, Pancrasweek, Holsworthy EX22 7JT
T: (01288) 381734
E: cottage@tamarstone.co.uk
I: www.tamarstone.co.uk

PARKEND
Gloucestershire

Nagshead Cottage ★★★★
Contact: Mr Alistair & Mrs Gabrielle McCrindle
Forest Cottages, Thistle Cottage, Lydney GL15 4LX
T: (01594) 510695
E: info@forest-cottages.co.uk
I: www.forest-cottages.co.uk

Squirrel Cottage ★★★
Contact: Mr Alistair & Mrs Gabrielle McCrindle
Forest Cottages, Thistle Cottage, Lydney GL15 4LX
T: (01594) 510695
E: info@forest-cottages.co.uk
I: www.forest-cottages.co.uk

PARKHAM
Devon

Logans and The Granary
Rating Applied For
Contact:
Marsdens Cottage Holidays, 2 The Square, Braunton EX33 2JB
T: (01271) 813777
F: (01271) 813664
E: holidays@marsdens.co.uk
I: www.marsdens.co.uk

PARRACOMBE
Devon

Killington Farm House and Owls Rest Barns
Rating Applied For
Contact:
Farm & Cottage Holidays, Victoria House, 29 Fore Street, Bideford EX39 1AW
T: (01237) 479146
F: (01237) 421512
E: bookings@farmcott.co.uk
I: www.farmcott.co.uk

Martinhoe Cleave Cottages ★★★★
Contact: Mr & Mrs RM J Deville
Martinhoe Cleave Cottages, Parracombe, Barnstaple EX31 4PZ
T: (01598) 763313
E: info@hgate.co.uk
I: www.hgate.co.uk

Voley Farm ★★★★
Contact: Ms Judith Killen
Voley Farm, Barnstaple EX31 4PG
T: (01598) 763315
E: voleyfarm@tesco.net
I: www.voleyfarm.com

Woodcote ★★★★
Contact:
Marsden's Cottage Holidays, 2 The Square, Braunton EX33 2JB
T: (01271) 813777
F: (01271) 813664
E: holidays@marsdens.co.uk
I: www.marsdens.co.uk

PAUL
Cornwall

Susies Cottage ★★★
Contact: Mrs Susan Hales
14 Long Row, Sheffield, Paul, Penzance TR19 6UN
T: (01736) 731703
F: (01736) 731703

PAULTON
Bath and North East Somerset

The Coach House ★★★-★★★★
Contact: Mrs Jenny Ahlberg
The Coach House, Hanham Lane, Bristol BS39 7PF
T: (01761) 413121
F: (01761) 413121
E: jennyahlberg@aol.com

PAXFORD
Gloucestershire

Fox Cottage ★★★★
Contact: Miss Sheila Rolland
Campden Cottages, Folly Cottage, Chipping Campden GL55 6XG
T: (01386) 593315
F: (01386) 593057
E: info@campdencottages.co.uk
I: www.campdencottages.co.uk

PEDWELL
Somerset

Sunnyside ★★★★
Contact: Ms Sheila Caruso
Sunnyside, 34 Taunton Road, Bridgwater TA7 9BG
T: (01458) 210097
E: sunnyside@pedwell.freeuk.com

PELYNT
Cornwall

Cartole Cottages ★★★
Contact: Mr Michael & Mrs Carol Taylor
Cartole Cottages, Looe PL13 2QH
T: (01503) 220956
I: www.cornwalltouristboard.co.uk/cartolecottages

Penrose Cottage ★★★★
Contact: Mr Paul Brumpton
Penrose Cottage, 5 Summer Lane, Looe PL13 2LP
T: (01503) 220252
F: (01503) 220252
E: paul@talehay.co.uk
I: www.talehay.co.uk

Tower Lodge ★★★
Contact:
Valley Villas, Brook Cottage, Old Warleigh Lane, Plymouth PL5 4ND
T: (01752) 774900
E: sales@valleyvillas.co.uk
I: www.valleyvillas.co.uk

Tremaine Green Country Cottages ★★-★★★★
Contact: Mr & Mrs Spreckley
Tremaine Green Country Cottages, Tremaine Green, Pelynt, Looe PL13 2LT
T: (01503) 220333
F: (01503) 220633
E: stay@tremainegreen.co.uk
I: www.tremainegreen.co.uk

PENDEEN
Cornwall

Kerenza ★★
Contact:
Cornish Cottage Holidays, Godolphin Road, Helston TR13 8AA
T: (01326) 573808
F: (01326) 564992
E: enquiry@cornishcottageholidays.co.uk
I: www.cornishcottageholidays.co.uk

Trewellard Manor Farm ★★★-★★★★★
Contact: Mrs Marion Bailey
Trewellard Manor Farm, Levant Road, Trewellard, Pendeen, Penzance TR19 7SU
T: (01736) 788526
F: (01736) 788526
E: marionbbailey@hotmail.com
I: www.trewellardmanor.co.uk

PENHALLOW
Cornwall

Nutmeg & Peppercorn ★★★★
Contact:
Cornish Cottage Holidays, The Old Turnpike Dairy, Godolphin, Meneage Street, Helston TR13 8AA
T: (01326) 573808
F: (01326) 564992
E: enquiry@cornishcottageholidays.co.uk
I: www.cornishcottageholidays.co.uk

PENRYN
Cornwall

Pampaluna Cottage ★★
Contact: Mr Bernard & Mrs Patricia Lawrence
Pampaluna Cottage, Corpascus, Penryn TR10 9JB
T: (01326) 373203
E: pat-bern@tinyworld.co.uk

PENSELWOOD
Somerset

Pen Mill Cottage ★★★★
Contact: Peter & Sarah Fitzgerald
Pen Mill Farm, Coombe Street, Penselwood, Wincanton BA9 8NF
T: (01747) 840895
F: (01747) 840429
E: fitzgeraldatpen@aol.com

PENSFORD
Bath and North East Somerset

Leigh Farm ★-★★
Contact: Mrs Smart
Leigh Farm, Old Road, Pensford, Bristol BS39 4BA
T: (01761) 490281
F: (01761) 490281

PENTEWAN
Cornwall

Crofters End ★★★
Contact: Mr & Mrs Radmore
Higher Penrose, Tregony, Truro TR2 5SS
T: (01872) 501269

Establishments printed in blue have a detailed entry in this guide

SOUTH WEST ENGLAND

PENWITHICK
Cornwall

Penwithick ★★★★
Contact:
Holiday Homes and Cottages
SW, 365A Torquay Road,
Paignton TQ3 2BT
T: (01803) 663650
F: (01803) 664037
E: holcotts@aol.com
I: www.swcottages.co.uk

PENZANCE
Cornwall

Boskennal Farm ★★★★
Contact: Ms Beryl Richards
Boskennal Farm, Ludgvan,
Penzance TR20 8AR
T: (01736) 740293
F: (01736) 740293
E: alan@boskennal.fsnet.co.uk

Bosworlas Farm House
Rating Applied For
Contact: Mr Thomas Osborne
Bosworlas Farm House,
Bosworlas, St Just, Penzance
TR19 7RQ
T: (01736) 788709
F: (01736) 788709
E: info@bosworlas.co.uk
I: www.bosworlas.co.uk

Chy Nessa ★★★
Contact: Mrs Shirley Keene
2 Creeping Lane, Penzance
TR18 4PB
T: (01736) 366697
E: chynessa@netscape.net
I: www.uk.geocities.
com/blee83/Chynessa.
photopage.html

**Chyandaunce and
Chyancrowse ★★★**
Contact: Mrs Joan Sampson
Gulval Cottages, 55 Albemarle
Gate, Cheltenham GL50 4PH
T: (01242) 232769
F: (01242) 232769
E: tjwsampson@aol.com
I: www.gulvalcottages.co.uk

Countryview ★★★
Contact: Mrs C P Wright
Countryview, Richden, Upwell
Road, Wisbech PE14 9LF
T: (01354) 638282
E: tony@wright113.freeserve.
co.uk
I: www.wright113.freeserve.
co.uk

**The Old Farmhouse
★★★★★**
Contact: Mrs Vivienne Hall
Chegwidden Farm, St Levan,
Penzance TR19 6LP
T: (01736) 810516
F: (01736) 810516
I: www.chegwidden.fsnet.co.uk

**Portheras Farm Cottage
★★★★**
Contact:
Powells Cottage Holidays,
Dolphin House, High Street,
Saundersfoot SA69 9EJ
T: (01834) 813232
F: (01834) 811731
E: info@powells.co.uk

Rospannel Farm ★★★
Contact: Mr Bernard Hocking
Rospannel Farm, St Buryan,
Penzance TR19 6HS
T: (01736) 810262
E: gbernard@v21.me.uk
I: www.rospannel.com

**Saint Pirans Cottages
★★★-★★★★★**
Contact: Mrs Gresswell
The White House, Northbrook,
Winchester SO21 3AJ
T: (01962) 774379
E: perranhols@aol.com
I: www.stpiranscottages.co.uk

Seascape ★★★
Contact: Mr & Mrs Hinton
Cornish Cottage Holidays, The
Old Turnpike Dairy, Godolphin
Road, Helston TR13 8AA

Spindrift
Rating Applied For
Contact: Mr Peter Morgan
Spindrift, 1 Dock Cottages, Dock
Lane, Penzance TR18 4AS
T: (01467) 629597
E: spindrift45@tiscali.co.uk

Summer Breeze ★★★
Contact: Mrs Roberts
The Barn, Trewarveneth Vean,
Tredaude Lane, Penzance
TR18 5DL
T: (01736) 351949

Trevenen ★★★★
Contact:
Cornish Cottage Holidays, The
Old Turnpike Dairy, Godolphin
Road, Helston TR13 8AA
T: (01326) 573808
F: (01326) 564992
E: enquiry@
cornishcottageholidays.co.uk
I: www.cornishcottageholidays.
co.uk

**The Wharf Apartments
★★★★**
Contact: Mrs Penny O'Neill
The Wharf Apartments, The
Wharfhouse, Wharf Road,
Penzance TR18 2JY
T: (01736) 366888
F: (01736) 331129
E: info@wharfapartments.com
I: www.wharfapartments.com

PERRANPORTH
Cornwall

**Gull Rock Holiday
Apartments ★★★**
Contact: Mr Richard & Mrs Ann
Snow
Gull Rock Holiday Apartments,
25 Tywarnhayle Road,
Perranporth TR6 0DX
T: (01736) 573289
F: 0870 131 2570
E: holiday@gullrock.com
I: www.gullrock.com

Treth Cottage ★★★★
Contact: Mr John & Mrs Jenny
Cuthill
Claremont, St Georges Hill,
Perranporth TR6 0JS
T: (01872) 573624

PERRANWELL STATION
Cornwall

The Barn ★★★★
Contact: Mrs Margie Lumby
Special Places in Cornwall,
Poachers Reach, Harcourt, Truro
TR3 6SQ
T: (01872) 864400
E: office@
specialplacescornwall.co.uk
I: www.specialplacescornwall.
co.uk

Lymington Snug ★★★★
Contact: Mrs Margie Lumby
Special Places In Cornwall,
Poachers Reach, Harcourt, Truro
TR3 6SQ
T: (01872) 864400
E: office@
specialplacescornwall.co.uk
I: www.specialplacescornwall.
co.uk

Postbox Cottage ★★★★
Contact: Mrs Margie Lumby
Special Places in Cornwall,
Poachers Reach, Harcourt, Truro
TR3 6SQ
T: (01872) 864400
E: office@
specialplacescornwall.co.uk
I: www.specialplacescornwall.
co.uk

Woodpeckers ★★★
Contact: Mrs Margie Lumby
Special Places In Cornwall,
Poachers Reach, Harcourt, Truro
TR3 6SQ
T: (01872) 864400
E: office@
specialplacescornwall.co.uk
I: www.specialplacescornwall.
co.uk

PHILLACK
Cornwall

Chymoresk ★★★★★
Contact:
Powells Cottage Holidays,
Dolphin House, High Street,
Saundersfoot SA69 9EJ
T: (01834) 813232
F: (01834) 811731
E: info@powells.co.uk
I: www.powells.co.uk

Elova F71 ★★
Contact: Mrs Barbara Terrill
2 Vivian Park, Camborne
TR14 7TP
T: (01209) 612214

**Greenduke & Saltair
★★-★★★**
Contact: Mrs Pat Pascoe
18 Condurrow Road, Camborne
TR14 7SW
T: (01209) 716535
E: info@cornishbungalows.
co.uk

PIDDLETRENTHIDE
Dorset

Coach House ★★★★
Contact: Mr & Mrs Drewe
Coach House, Lackington
Farmhouse, Dorchester DT2 7QU
T: (01300) 348253
F: (01300) 348222
E: info@lackingtonfarmhouse.
co.uk
I: www.lackingtonfarmhouse.
co.uk

PILLATON
Cornwall

**Upalong & Downalong
★★★★**
Contact: Mr Geoffrey & Mrs Ann
Barnicoat
Trefenten, Pillaton, Saltash
PL12 6QX
T: (01579) 350141
F: (01579) 351520
E: trefenten@beeb.net
I: www.trefenten.co.uk

PIMPERNE
Dorset

Carters Cottage ★★★
Contact: Mrs Lucy Lake
Davis Farms, Shaston Road,
Blandford Forum DT11 8TD
T: (01258) 454628

PLAYING PLACE
Cornwall

Kernewek ★★★
Contact:
Cornish Cottage Holidays, The
Old Turnpike Dairy, Godolphin,
Meneage Street, Helston
TR13 8AA
T: (01326) 573808
F: (01326) 564992
E: enquiry@
cornishcottageholidays.co.uk
I: www.cornishcottageholidays.
co.uk

PLYMOUTH
Plymouth

22 Athenaeum Street
Rating Applied For
Contact: Mrs Laetitia Wittock
22 Athenaeum Street, 22
Athenaeum Street, Plymouth
PL1 2RH
T: (01503) 230922
F: (01503) 230922
E: amplitude@treboul.freeserve.
co.uk
I: www.amplitude.co.uk

Gatehouse Cottage ★★★★
Contact: Mr Ian Butterworth
Holiday Homes & Cottages
South West, 365A Torquay Road,
Paignton TQ3 2BT
T: (01803) 663650

**Haddington House
Apartments ★★★★**
Contact: Mr Fairfax Luxmoore
42 Haddington Road, Stoke,
Plymouth PL2 1RR
T: (01752) 500383 &
07966 256984
E: luxmooref@hotmail.com
I: www.abudd.co.uk

Hoeside Holiday Flats ★★★
Contact: Mrs Dianne Seymour
Old Rectory, 20 Penlee Way,
Plymouth PL3 4AW
T: (01752) 563504
F: (01752) 563504
E: hoeside.dsfs@virgin.net

POLBATHIC
Cornwall

Higher Tredis Farm ★★
Contact: Mrs Cindy Rice
Higher Tredis Farm, Torpoint
PL11 3ER
T: (01503) 230184
E: cindyrice@btopenworld.com

SOUTH WEST ENGLAND

POLPERRO
Cornwall

Classy Cottages ★★★★-★★★★★
Contact: Mr Martin & Mrs Fiona Nicolle
Blanches Windsor, Polperro, Looe PL13 2PT
T: (01720) 423000 &
(07000) 423000
E: nicolle@classycottages.co.uk
I: www.classycottages.co.uk

Crumplehorn Cottages ★★★-★★★★★
Contact: Mr Murray & Gloria Collings
Crumplehorn Cottages, The Anchorage, Portuan Road, Looe PL13 2DN
T: (01503) 262523
F: (01503) 262523
E: gloria@crumplehorncottages.co.uk
I: www.crumplehorncottage.co.uk

East Cliff Cottage
Rating Applied For
Contact: Mrs Ruth Puckey
East Cliff Cottage, The Warren, Looe PL13 2RD
T: (01503) 272324

Kirk House ★★★★★★
Contact: Ms Kay Boniface
Aspire Lifestyle Holidays Ltd, Greyswood, 9 The Ridgeway, Stratford-upon-Avon CV37 9JL
T: (01789) 205522
F: (01789) 298189
E: wts@kirkhouseholidays.co.uk
I: www.kirkhouseholidays.co.uk

Little Laney and Polhaven ★★★★
Contact: Mrs Tegan Cornish
8 The Queensway, Chalfont St Peter, Gerrards Cross SL9 8NF
T: (01753) 882482
F: (01753) 882546
E: tegan@cornish-cottage.com
I: www.cornish-cottage.com

Lucy's ★★★
Contact: Mrs Jackie Leftly
Pleydon Meadow, Talland Hill, Looe PL13 2JL
T: (01503) 272271
F: (01503) 272271
E: info@leftly.com
I: www.polperrocottages.com

Osprey Holidays ★★★
Contact: Mr Ian Ferguson
Osprey Holidays, Talland Hill, Looe PL13 2RX
T: (01503) 272819

Pier Inn House and Studio ★★★★★
Contact: Mr C & Mrs M Wood
Woodlands, 2 St Nicholas Close, Milton Keynes MK17 9EL
T: 0774 5 816647
I: www.pierinnholidays.co.uk

POLRUAN
Cornwall

The Hideaway ★★
Contact:
Fowey Harbour Cottages (W J B Hill & Son), 3 Fore Street, Fowey PL23 1AH
T: (01726) 832211
F: (01726) 832901
E: hillandson@talk21.com

POLRUAN-BY-FOWEY
Cornwall

Peppercorn Cottage ★★★
Contact: Mr David Hill
Fowey Harbour Cottages WJB Hill & Son, 3 Fore Street, Fowey PL23 1AH
T: (01726) 832211
F: (01726) 832901
E: hillandson@talk21.com
I: www.foweyharbourcottages.co.uk

Tremaine Cottage ★★★
Contact: Mr David Hill
Fowey Harbour Cottages(WJB Hill&Son, 3 Fore Street, Fowey PL23 1AH
T: (01726) 832211
F: (01726) 832901
E: hillandson@talk21.com
I: www.foweyharbourcottages.co.uk

POLYPHANT
Cornwall

Darkes Court Cottages ★★★
Contact: Mr Richard Sowerby
Darkes Court Cottages, Launceston PL15 7PS
T: (01566) 86598
F: (01566) 86795
E: sowerby@darkesfarm.fsnet.co.uk

Tregarth ★★★
Contact:
Farm & Cottage Holidays, Victoria House, 12 Fore Street, Bideford EX39 1AW
T: (01237) 479146
F: (01237) 421512
E: enquiries@farmcott.co.uk
I: www.farmcott.co.uk

POLZEATH
Cornwall

Bluebirds ★★★
Contact:
Harbour Holidays, Rock Ltd, Trebetherick House, Wadebridge PL27 6SB
T: (01208) 863399
F: (01208) 862218
E: rockhols@aol.com
I: www.rockholidays.co.uk

Chough ★★★
Contact:
Harbour Holidays, Rock Ltd, Trebetherick House, Wadebridge PL27 6SB
T: (01208) 863399
F: (01208) 862218
E: rockhols@aol.com
I: www.rockholidays.co.uk

Godolphin House ★★★★
Contact:
Rock Holidays inc. Harbour Holidays Rock Ltd., Trebetherick House, Wadebridge PL27 6SB
T: (01208) 863399
F: 07208 862218
E: rockhols@aol.com
I: www.rockholidays.co.uk

Honeysuckle Hill ★★★★★
Contact: Mrs Carolyn Crutcher
The Homestead, Rusper Road, Newdigate, Dorking RH5 5BX
T: (01306) 631568
E: carrie@crutchersfarm.freeserve.co.uk
I: www.honeysucklehill.co.uk

Jay ★★★
Contact:
Harbour Holidays, Rock Ltd, Trebetherick House, Wadebridge PL27 6SB
T: (01208) 863399
F: (01208) 862218
E: rockhols@aol.com
I: www.rockholidays.co.uk

The Lookout ★★★
Contact:
Rock Holidays inc. Harbour Holidays Rock Ltd., Trebetherick House, Wadebridge PL27 6SB
T: (01208) 863399
F: (01208) 862218
E: rockhols@aol.com
I: www.rockholidays.co.uk

Marmarra ★★★
Contact:
Rock Holidays inc. Harbour Holidays Rock Ltd., Trebetherick House, Wadebridge PL27 6SB
T: (01208) 863399
F: (01208) 862218
E: rockhols@aol.com
I: www.rockholidays.co.uk

Millbank ★★★
Contact:
Rock Holidays inc. Harbour Holidays Rock Ltd., Trebetherick House, Wadebridge PL27 6SB
T: (01208) 863399
F: (01208) 862218
E: rockhols@aol.com
I: www.rockholidays.co.uk

1 Pentire View ★★★★
Contact: Mrs Diana Bullivant
Diana Bullivant Holidays, Southwinds, Trebell Green, Bodmin PL30 5HR
T: (01208) 831336
F: (01208) 831336
E: diana@dbullivant.fsnet.co.uk
I: www.cornwall-online.co.uk/diana-bullivant

2 Pentire View ★★★
Contact: Mrs Diana Bullivant
Diana Bullivant Holidays, South Winds, Trebell Green, Bodmin PL30 5HR
T: (01208) 831336
F: (01208) 831336
E: diana@dbullivant.fsnet.co.uk
I: www.cornwall-online.co.uk/diana-bullivant

3 Pinewood Flats ★★★
Contact:
Rock Holidays inc. Harbour Holidays, Trebetherick House, Wadebridge PL27 6SB
T: (01208) 863399
F: (01208) 862218
E: rockhols@aol.com
I: www.rockholidays.co.uk

Polmeor
Rating Applied For
Contact: Mrs Jean Angwin
Polmeor, Dunder Close, Wadebridge PL27 6SX
T: (01208) 72684

Robin ★★★
Contact:
Harbour Holidays, Rock Ltd, Trebetherick House, Wadebridge PL27 6SB
T: (01208) 863399
F: (01208) 862218
E: rockhols@aol.com
I: www.rockholidyas.co.uk

Seaview ★★★★
Contact: Mrs Diana Bullivant
Diana Bullivant Holidays, South Winds, Trebell Green, Bodmin PL30 5HR
T: (01208) 831336
F: (01208) 831336
E: diana@d.bullivant.fsnet.co.uk
I: www.dbholidays.co.uk

Stonechat ★★★
Contact: Mrs Teresa Smith
The Starlings, 2 Sunnybank, Shilla Mill Lane, Wadebridge PL27 6SS
T: (01208) 863172
E: tesspete@tiscali.co.uk
I: www.polzeathcottages.com/stonechat.html

Sun Deck ★★★
Contact:
Harbour Holidays, Rock Ltd, Trebetherick House, Wadebridge PL27 6SB
T: (01208) 863399
F: (01208) 862218
E: rockhols@aol.com
I: www.rockholidays.co.uk

Trecreege Barn ★★★
Contact:
Rock Holidays inc. Harbour Holidays Rock Ltd., Trebetherick House, Wadebridge PL27 6SB
T: (01208) 863399
F: (01208) 862218
E: rockhols@aol.com
I: www.rockholidays.co.uk

Trehanoo ★★★
Contact: Mrs Kate Buckingham
9 Downsmead, Marlborough SN8 2LQ
T: (01672) 541120

Treleven ★★
Contact:
Rock Holidays inc. Harbour Holidays Rock Ltd., Trebetherick House, Wadebridge PL27 6SB
T: (01208) 863399
F: (01208) 862218
E: rockhols@aol.com
I: www.rockholidays.co.uk

SOUTH WEST ENGLAND

10 Trenant Close ★★★
Contact: Mr & Mrs Goodright
Camel Coast Holidays, 5
Marshalls Way, Port Isaac
PL29 3TE
T: (01208) 880509
E: goodright@ndirect.co.uk

Trevarthian ★★★★
Contact: Mrs Diana Bullivant
Diana Bullivant Holidays, South
Winds, Trebell Green, Bodmin
PL30 5HR
T: (01208) 831336
F: (01208) 831336
E: diana@dbullivant.fsnet.co.uk
I: www.cornwall-online/diana-bullivant

Tywardale Cottage ★★★
Contact: Mr & Mrs G Swann
Tywardale Cottage, West Rae
Road, Wadebridge PL27 6ST
T: (01208) 862721
F: (01208) 862721

Waders ★★★
Contact:
Rock Holidays inc. Harbour
Holidays, Trebetherick House,
Wadebridge PL27 6SB
T: (01208) 863399
F: (01208) 862218
E: rockhols@aol.com
I: www.rockholidays.co.uk

Waveley
Rating Applied For
Contact: Mr Joe Shepherd
Waveley, Flat 2 The Parade,
Wadebridge PL27 6SS
T: (01208) 862933
E: Joseph@waveley.fsnet.co.uk
I: www.cornwallonline.co.uk

West Point ★★★
Contact:
Rock Holidays inc. Harbour
Holidays Rock Ltd., Trebetherick
House, Wadebridge PL27 6SB
T: (01208) 863399
F: (01208) 862218
E: rockhols@aol.com
I: www.rockholidays.co.uk

White Rose ★★★
Contact:
Harbour Holidays - Rock,
Trebetherick House, Wadebridge
PL27 6SB
T: (01208) 863399
E: rockhols@aol.com

POOLE
Poole

Danehurst Holiday Flat ★★★
Contact: Mr John Richings
Danehurst Holiday Flat,
Brunstead Road, Poole BH12 1EJ
T: (01202) 768632

Dolphin Cottage ★★★
Contact: Mrs Jean Redsell
24 Heathclose Road, Dartford
DA1 2PU
T: (01322) 271848
F: (01322) 346817

Egret ★★★
Contact: Mr & Mrs Cocklin
46 Perry Gardens, Poole
BH15 1QA
T: (01202) 670046

Flat 8 Sandacres ★★
Contact: Miss M Barker-Smith
10 Gainsborough Road,
Littledown, Bournemouth
BH7 7BD
T: (01202) 395383

Flats 5 & 6 Sandacres ★★-★★★
Contact: Mrs Rosemary Bond
Blandford Road North, Nr
Lytchett Minster, Poole
BH16 6AB
T: (01202) 631631
F: (01202) 625749
I: www.beaconhilltouringpark.co.uk

17 Green Gardens ★★★
Contact: Ms Christina Harris
46 Bournemouth Road, Poole
BH14 0EY
T: (01202) 462485
E: christina.harris@breathemail.net

Harbour Holidays ★★
Contact: Mrs Beryl Saunders
Harbour Holidays, 1 Harbour
Shallows, 15 Whitecliff Road,
Poole BH14 8DU
T: (01202) 741637

Quayside ★★★
Contact: Mrs Mary Ball
59 Oakwood Avenue,
Beckenham BR3 6PT
T: (020) 86636426
F: (020) 86630038
E: quayside@oakwood59.freeserve.co.uk
I: www.uk-holiday-cottages.co.uk/quayside

Quayside, Lakeside, Boathouse ★★★-★★★★★
Contact: Mrs Suzanne Fuller
Holtwood, Holt, Wimborne
BH21 7DR
T: (01258) 840377
F: (08701) 672994
E: baiter.holidays@btinternet.com
I: www.baiter.holidays.btinternet.co.uk

Quayside Close Holiday Apartments ★★★
Contact: Mr David & Mrs Susan Ellison
Bromlea, 23 Leicester Road,
Poole BH13 6DA
T: (01202) 764107
F: (01202) 764107
E: quaysideclose@aol.co.uk
I: www.quayside.co.uk

Sandon House ★-★★
Contact: Mrs Whittingham
Sandon House, 641-643
Blandford Road, Poole
BH16 5ED
T: (01202) 622442

Sea Haven
Rating Applied For
Contact: Mrs Hayley Copley
44 Perry Gardens, Poole
BH15 1QA
T: (01202) 669469
F: (01202) 649587
E: seahaven58@aol.com

43 Vallis Close ★★★
Contact: Miss Patricia Thomas
65 Parr Street, Poole BH14 0JX
T: (01202) 743768

POOLE KEYNES
Gloucestershire

Old Mill Cottages ★★★★
Contact: Mrs Catherine Hazell
Ermin House Farm, Cheltenham
GL53 9PN
T: (01285) 821255
F: (01285) 821531
E: catherine@oldmillcottages.fsnet.co.uk
I: www.oldmillcottages.co.uk

PORKELLIS
Cornwall

Ivy's Cabin ★★★
Contact: Agent
Cornish Cottage Holidays,
Godolphin Road, Helston
TR13 8AA
T: (01326) 573808
F: (01326) 564992
E: enquiry@cornishcottageholidays.co.uk
I: www.cornishcottageholidays.co.uk

PORLOCK
Somerset

Church Farm ★★★★
Contact:
Toad Hall Cottages, Elliot House,
Church Street, Kingsbridge
TQ7 1BY
T: (01548) 853089
F: (01548) 853086
E: thc@toadhallcottages.com
I: www.toadhallcottages.com

Coach House Apartments The Old Coach House & Stables ★★★
Contact: Mrs Lloyd
Coach House Apartments The
Old Coach House & Stables,
Doverhay Place, Porlock
TA24 8HU
T: (01643) 862409
F: (01643) 862409
E: lloyd@oldcoachhouse.f9.co.uk
I: www.whatsonexmoor.co.uk/coachhouse

Green Chantry ★★★★
Contact: Mrs Margaret Payton
Home Farm, Burrowbridge,
Bridgwater TA7 0RF
T: (01823) 698330
F: (01823) 698169
E: maggie_payton@hotmail.com

Hartshanger Holidays ★★★★
Contact: Mrs Anna Edward
Hartshanger Holidays,
Hartshanger, Toll Road,
Minehead TA24 8JH
T: (01643) 862700
F: (01643) 862700
E: hartshanger@lineone.net
I: www.hartshanger.com

Hunters Rest ★★★
Contact: Mr Barry West
Hunters Rest, Mill Lane,
Hawkcombe, Minehead
TA24 8QW
T: (01643) 862349
F: (01643) 863295
E: west@huntersrest.info
I: www.huntersrest.info

The Watermill ★★★★
Contact: Mr John & Mrs Diane
Ames
12 The Mead, Longfield DA3 8EZ
T: (01474) 879810
F: (01474) 879810
E: john.ames1@btinternet.com
I: www.thewatermillporlock.com

Wellcombe ★★★
Contact: Mrs Barbara Healey
Dunkery View, Brandish Street,
Minehead TA24 8HR
T: (01643) 862966
F: (01643) 862966
I: www.wellcombe.co.uk

Woodside Cottage ★★★
Contact: Mr & Ms Lawrence &
Daley
28 Clarendon Road, Bristol
BS6 7EU
T: (01242) 261435
E: woodside_cottage@hotmail.com

PORT GAVERNE
Cornwall

Carn-Awn ★★★
Contact: Mrs May
Orcades House, Port Isaac
PL29 3SQ
T: (01208) 880716
F: (01208) 880716
E: jimmay@orcades.u-net.com
I: www.orcades.u-net.com

Green Door Cottages ★★★-★★★★
Contact: Mrs Oldrieve
Green Door Cottages, Port
Gaverne, Port Isaac PL29 3SQ
T: (01208) 880293
F: (01208) 880151
I: www.greendoorcottages.co.uk

PORT ISAAC
Cornwall

Atlantic House ★★★
Contact: Mr Dennis Knight
Atlantic House, 41 Fore Street,
Port Isaac PL29 3RE
T: (01208) 880498
F: (01208) 880934
E: info@cornishholidayhomes.co.uk
I: www.cornishholidayhomes.net

Cloam Cottage ★★★
Contact:
Valley Villas, Brook Cottage, Old
Warleigh Lane, Plymouth
PL5 4ND
T: (01782) 774900
E: sales@valleyvillas.co.uk
I: www.valleyvillas.co.uk

Locarno ★★★
Contact: Mrs Hicks
7 New Road, Haven Park, Port
Isaac PL29 3SD
T: (01208) 880268

SOUTH WEST ENGLAND

9a Lundy Road ★★
Contact: Mrs E. E. Taylor
9a Lundy Road, Port Isaac
PL29 3RR
T: (01208) 880283
I: www.Northcornwall.co.uk

57a Springside ★★★
Contact: Mrs Catherine Armstrong
66 Fore Street, Port Isaac
PL29 3RE
T: (01208) 880780
E: cath.armstrong@tesco.net

Tremanon ★★★
Contact:
Harbour Holidays Rock Ltd.,
Trebetherick House, Wadebridge
PL27 6SB
T: (01208) 863399
F: (01208) 862218
E: rockhols@aol.com
I: rockholidays.co.uk

Trevallion ★★★★
Contact: Mr F J Holpin
F J Holpin & Son Ltd., 1 Leaze Close, Berkeley GL13 9BZ
T: (01453) 810486

Trevathan Farm
★★★★-★★★★★
Contact: Mrs Symons
St Endellion, Port Isaac PL29 3TT
T: (01208) 880248
F: (01208) 880248
E: symons@trevathanfarm.com
I: www.trevathanfarm.com

The White House ★★★
Contact: Dr Anthony Hambly
Bodrean Manor, St Clements,
Bodrean, Truro TR4 9AG
T: (01872) 264400
F: (01872) 264400
E: anthonyhambly@hotmail.com
I: www.cornishholidays.com

PORT PENDENNIS
Cornwall

Marinaside ★★★★
Contact: Mrs Margie Lumby
Special Places in Cornwall,
Poachers Reach, Harcourt, Truro
TR3 6SQ
T: (01872) 864400
E: office@specialplacescornwall.co.uk
I: www.specialplacescornwall.co.uk

4 Royalist Court ★★★★
Contact:
Cornish Holiday Cottages,
Killibrae, West Bay Maenporth Road, Falmouth TR11 5HP
T: (01326) 250339
F: (01326) 250339
E: postmaster@cornishholidaycottages.net

PORTESHAM
Dorset

Rockfall Cottage ★★★
Contact: Mr Philippa Roper
Rockfall Cottage, 5 Portesham Hill, Weymouth DT3 4EU
T: (01305) 871879

Sleepers ★★★
Contact: Miss Parker
Gorselands Caravan Park,
Dorchester DT2 9DJ
T: (01308) 897232
F: (01308) 897239
I: www.gorselands-uk.com

PORTHALLOW
Cornwall

Bank Cottage ★★★
Contact:
Cornish Cottage Holidays, The
Old Turnpike Dairy, Godolphin
Road, Helston TR13 8AA
T: (01326) 573808
F: (01326) 564992
E: enquiry@cornishcottageholidays.co.uk
I: www.cornishcottageholidays.co.uk

Cockle Island Cottage ★★★★
Contact: Mr Ian Hawthorne
Porthallow, St Keverne, Helston
TR12 6PN
T: (01326) 280370
E: hawthorne@valleyviewhouse-freeserve.co.uk
I: www.smoothhound.co.uk/hotels/valleyvi

PORTHCOTHAN
Cornwall

Gull Cottage ★★★
Contact: Ms Nicky Stanley
Harbour Holidays - Padstow, 1
North Quay, Padstow PL28 8AF
T: (01841) 532555
F: (01841) 533115
E: sales@jackie-stanley.co.uk
I: www.harbourholidays.co.uk

Sunset ★★★
Contact: Ms Nicky Stanley
Harbour Holidays - Padstow, 1
North Quay, Padstow PL28 8AF
T: (01841) 532555
F: (01841) 533115
E: sales@jackie-stanley.co.uk
I: www.harbourholidays.co.uk

10 Tregella ★★★★
Contact:
Harbour Holidays, 1 North Quay,
Padstow PL28 8AF
T: (01841) 532555
E: contact@harbourholidays.co.uk
I: www.harbourholidays.co.uk

PORTHCURNO
Cornwall

Stargazey ★★★★
Contact: Ms Liz Trenary
First and Last Cottages, Treeve
Moor House, Penzance TR19 7AE
T: (01736) 871284
E: info@firstandlastcottages.co.uk
I: www.firstandlastcottages.co.uk

PORTHLEVEN
Cornwall

Above Beach Cottages
★★★★-★★★★★★
Contact: Mrs Janice Benney
Chy-An-Gwel, Torleven Road,
Helston TR13 9HR
T: (01032) 656 3198
E: motthouse@sandpebbles.com
I: www.abovebeachcottages.co.uk

An-Mordros ★★★★
Contact:
Cornish Cottage Holidays, The
Old Turnpike Dairy, Godolphin
Road, Helston TR13 8GL
T: (01326) 573808
F: (01326) 564992
E: inquirey@cornishcottageholidays.co.uk
I: www.cornishcottageholidays.co.uk

Atlantic Cottage ★★★
Contact:
Cornish Cottage Holidays, The
Old Turnpike Dairy, Godolphin
Road, Helston TR13 8AA
T: (01326) 573808
F: (01326) 564992
E: enquiry@cornishcottageholidays.co.uk
I: www.cornishcottageholidays.co.uk

Cliff House & Bay Cottage (Niche Retreats) ★★★★
Contact: Mrs J A Kitchen
Niche Retreats, Banns Road,
Truro TR4 8BW
T: (01209) 890272
F: (01209) 891695
E: info@nicheretreats.co.uk
I: www.nicheretreats.co.uk

Crabpot Cottage ★★★
Contact:
Cornish Cottage Holidays, The
Old Turnpike Dairy, Godolphin
Raod, Helston TR13 8GS
T: (01326) 573808
F: (01326) 564992
E: inquiry@cornishcottageholidays.co.uk
I: www.cornishcottageholidays.co.uk

Dai-Mar
Rating Applied For
Contact: Mrs Gillian Oxford
70 Holden Road, London
N12 7DY
T: (020) 84450090
F: (020) 8445 6663

Dolphin Cottages
Rating Applied For
Contact: Mrs Anne Russell
Dolphin Cottages, Yacht House,
Mount Pleasant Road, Helston
TR13 9JS
T: (01326) 562264
E: sundown2@freenetname.co.uk

The Haven ★★★★
Contact:
Cornish Cottage Holidays, The
Old Turnpike Dairy, Godolphin,
Meneage Street, Helston
TR13 8AA
T: (01326) 573808
F: (01326) 564992
E: enquiry@cornishcottageholidays.co.uk
I: www.cornishcottageholidays.co.uk

Kestrel House and Harbour View ★★★-★★★★
Contact:
Cornish Cottage Holidays, The
Old Turnpike Dairy, Godolphin
Road, Helston TR13 8GS
T: (01326) 573808
E: inquiry@cornishcottageholidays.co.uk
I: www.cornishcottageholidays.co.uk

Kyldenna
Rating Applied For
Contact: Mr Martin Rafferty
Mullion Cottages, Mullion
Meadows, Helston TR12 7HB
T: (01326) 240315
F: (01326) 241090
I: www.mullioncottages.com

The Lugger Apartment ★★★
Contact: Mr Martin Raftery
Mullion Cottages, Mullion
Meadows, Helston TR12 7HB
T: (01326) 240315
F: (01326) 241090
E: enquiries@mullioncottages.com
I: www.mullioncottages.com

The Manse ★★★
Contact:
Cornish Cottage Holidays, The
Old Turnpike Dairy, Godolphin,
Meneage Street, Helston
TR13 8AA
T: (01326) 573808

Meadowside ★★★★
Contact: Mr Christopher & Mrs
Margar Orchard
Glendale, Wellington Road,
Helston TR13 9AA
T: (01326) 572928

Mounts Bay & Morgolok ★★★
Contact: Mrs Karen Waters
Niche Retreats, Hunters Moon,
Banns Road, Truro TR4 8BW
T: (01209) 890272
F: (01209) 891695
E: info@nicheretreats.co.uk
I: www.nicheretreats.co.uk

Mounts Bay Villa ★★
Contact: Mr Martin Raftery
Mullion Cottages, Churchtown,
Helston TR12 7HQ
T: (01326) 240315
F: (01326) 241090
E: martin@mullioncottages.com
I: www.mullioncottages.com

Establishments printed in blue have a detailed entry in this guide

SOUTH WEST ENGLAND

Pegs ★★★
Contact:
Cornish Cottage Holidays, The Old Turnpike Dairy, Godolphin, Meneage Street, Helston TR13 8AA
T: (01326) 573808
F: (01326) 564992
E: enquiry@cornishcottageholidays.co.uk
I: www.cornishcottageholidays.co.uk

Pengarrick & Lodge Cottage ★★★-★★★★
Contact: Mrs Edith Blewett
Pengarrick, Mill Lane, Helston TR13 9LQ
T: (01326) 563789
F: (01326) 563789
E: sam.blewett@talk21.com
I: www.blewetts.fsbusiness.co.uk

Peverell ★★★
Contact:
Cornish Cottage Holidays, The Old Turnpike Dairy, Godolphin, Meneage Street, Helston TR13 8AA
T: (01326) 573808
F: (01326) 564992
E: enquiry@cornishcottageholidays.co.uk
I: www.cornishcottageholidays.co.uk

Porthcressa ★★★★
Contact: Mrs Barbara Arthur
Porthcressa, 13 Chapel Terrace, The Gue, Helston TR13 9DN
T: (01326) 574487

Porthleven Harbour & Dock Company
Rating Applied For
Contact: Kathy Tisdale
Porthleven Harbour & Dock Company, Celtic House, The Harbour Head, Helston TR13 9JY
T: (01326) 574270
F: (01326) 574125
E: kathy.phd@btconnect.com
I: www.porthlevenholidaycottages.co.uk

Roysdean ★★
Contact: Mrs Majorie Kitchen
Marrow, Salt Cellar Hill, Helston TR13 9DP
T: (01326) 574375

Sea Cottage ★★★★
Contact: Mrs Janice Benney
Chy-an-Gwel, Torleven Road, Helston TR13 9HR
T: (01326) 563198
E: seacottage@sandpebbles.com

Surf Cottage ★★★
Contact: Mr Martin Raftery
Mullion Cottages, Mullion Meadows, Helston TR12 7HB
T: (01326) 240315
F: (01326) 241090
E: martin@mullioncottages.com
I: www.mullioncottages.com

Trenance ★★★★
Contact:
Cornish Cottage Holidays, The Old Turnpike Dairy, Godolphin Road, Helston TR13 8AA
T: (01326) 573808
E: enquiry@cornishcottageholidays.co.uk
I: www.cornishcottageholidays.co.uk

W. Oliver Allen & Sons ★★
Contact: Mr Paul Allen
W. Oliver Allen & Sons, Loe Bar Road, Helston TR13 9EN
T: (01326) 562222
E: pwoe@porth-leven.com
I: www.porth-leven.com

PORTLAND
Dorset

Alpen Rose ★★★★
Contact:
Dream Cottages, 5 Hope Square, Weymouth DT4 8TR
T: (01305) 789000
F: (01305) 761346
E: admin@dream-cottages.co.uk
I: www.dream-cottage.co.uk

Beacon View ★★
Contact: Mrs Jen Wraight
Seascape, 11 Queens Road, Portland DT5 1AH
T: (01305) 860651
E: jen@djwraight.freeserve.co.uk

The Bell & Lighthouse ★★★
Contact: Mr Zachary Stuart-Brown
Dream Cottages, 5 Hope Square, Weymouth DT4 8TR
T: (01305) 789000
E: admin@dream-cottages.co.uk
I: www.dream-cottages.co.uk

Blue Horizon ★★★
Contact:
Dream Cottages, 5 Hope Square, Weymouth DT4 8TR
T: (01305) 789000
F: (01305) 761347

Chapel Cottage ★★★★
Contact: Ms Brenda Parker
Gorselands, Dorchester DT2 9DJ
T: (01308) 897232
F: (01308) 897239
I: www.gorselands-uk.com

Chesil Cottage ★★★★
Contact: Mrs Heather Parsons
Chesil Cottage, 10 Queens Road, Portland DT5 1AH
T: (01305) 820940
E: heparsons@tiscali.co.uk
I: www.portlandholiday.co.uk

Chesil Rise ★★★★
Contact: Miss Hannah Brain
Charm Properties Limited, 12 Stavordale Road, Weymouth DT4 0AB
T: (01305) 786514
F: (01305) 786556
E: hilary@tamariskhotel.co.uk
I: www.charmproperties.co.uk

Church Ope Cottage ★★
Contact: Mrs Margaret Hoyt
Church Ope Cottage, 1 Diprose Cottages, Hinksden Road, Cranbrook TN17 4LE
T: (01580) 240700
E: maggyrhoyt@tiscali.co.uk
I: www.dorset-coastal.co.uk

Endeavour ★★★★
Contact: Mr Zachary Stuart-Brown
Dream Cottages, 5 Hope Square, Weymouth DT4 8TR
T: (01305) 789000
E: admin@dream-cottages.co.uk

Fleet House ★★★
Contact: Mrs Margaret Beckett
The Gatehouse Cottage, Church Ope, Portland DT5 1GH
T: (01305) 823349
E: gaynorbeckett@hotmail.com

Greenhill Cottage ★★★
Contact: Mr Zachary Stuart-Brown
Dream Cottages, 5 Hope Square, Weymouth DT4 8TR
T: (01305) 789000
E: admin@dream-cottages.co.uk
I: www.dream-cottages.co.uk

Kivel Cottage, Bilbo Cottage, Hobbiton ★★★
Contact: Mrs Susan Boden
17 South Street, Fareham PO14 4DL
T: (01329) 841104
E: sue_richardboden@hotmail.com

Lilac Cottage ★★★
Contact: Ms Shelagh Hepple
9 Kestrel Drive, Sandal, Wakefield WF2 6SB
T: (01924) 252522
I: www.portlandholiday.co.uk

Old Coastguard Cottage ★★★
Contact: Mr John Bunday
Brierley, Knellers Lane, Southampton SO40 7EB
T: (023) 80866421

Old Customs House ★★★★
Contact:
Dream Cottages, 5 Hope Square, Weymouth DT4 8TR
T: (01305) 789000
F: (01305) 761347

The Old Higher Lighthouse ★★★★
Contact: Mrs Fran Lockyer
The Old Higher Lighthouse, Portland Bill, Portland DT5 2JT
T: (01305) 822300
F: (01305) 822300
E: f.lockyer@talk21.com
I: www.oldhigherlighthouse.com

Polly's Cottage ★★★
Contact: Leverton
Woodwater Causeway, Radipole Village, Weymouth DT4 9XX
T: (01305) 774360

Portland Holiday Home ★★★
Contact: Mrs Amanda Jones
Lloyds Cottage, Portland Bill, Portland DT5 2JT
T: (01305) 861044
F: (01305) 860970
E: mandy1311.jones@virgin.net

Sunset Cottage ★★★★
Contact: Mr Zachary Stuart-Brown
Dream Cottages, 5 Hope Square, Weymouth DT4 8TR
T: (01305) 789000
F: (01305) 761346
E: admin@dream-cottages.co.uk
I: www.dream-cottages.co.uk

Tompot Cottage ★★★
Contact: Mr David Cooper
91 Longfield Road, Tring HP23 4DF
T: (01442) 826344
E: info@portlandcottage.com
I: www.portland-cottage.com

Twybill Cottage ★★★
Contact: Mr Zachary Stuart-Brown
Dream Cottages, 5 Hope Square, Weymouth DT4 8TR
T: (01305) 789000
F: (01305) 761346
E: admin@dream-cottages.co.uk
I: www.dream-cottages.co.uk

Westcliff Cottage ★★★
Contact: Miss Hannah Brain
Charm Properties Limited, 12 Stavordale Road, Weymouth DT4 0AB
T: (01305) 786514
F: (01305) 786556
E: hilary@tamariskhotel.co.uk
I: www.charmproperties.co.uk

Wobblers ★★
Contact: Mr Zachary Stuart-Brown
Dream Cottages, 5 Hope Square, Weymouth DT4 8TR
T: (01305) 789000
E: admin@dream-cottages.co.uk
I: www.dream-cottages.co.uk

PORTLOE
Cornwall

Cove Cottage
Rating Applied For
Contact:
Roseland Holiday Cottages, Crab Apple Cottage, Truro TR2 5ET
T: (01872) 580480
F: (01872) 580480
E: enquiries@roselandholidaycottages.co.uk
I: www.roselandholidaycottages.co.uk

Dolphin Cottage
Rating Applied For
Contact:
Roseland Holiday Cottages, Crab Apple Cottage, Truro TR2 5ET
T: (01872) 580480
F: (01872) 580480
E: enquiries@roselandholidaycottages.co.uk
I: www.roselandholidaycottages.com

SOUTH WEST ENGLAND

Farm Cottage
Rating Applied For
Contact:
Roseland Holiday Cottages, Crab Apple Cottage, Truro TR2 5ET
T: (01872) 580480
F: (01872) 580480
E: enquiries@roselandholidaycottages.co.uk
I: www.roselandholidaycottages.co.uk

Middle Cottage
Rating Applied For
Contact:
Roseland Holiday Cottages, Crab Apple Cottage, Truro TR2 5ET
T: (01872) 580480
F: (01872) 580480
E: enquiries@roselandholidaycottages.co.uk
I: www.roselandholidaycottages.co.uk

Ocean View
Rating Applied For
Contact: Mrs Leonie Iddison
Roseland Holiday Cottages, Crab Apple Cottage, Truro TR2 5ET
T: (01872) 580480
F: (01872) 580480
E: enquiries@roselandholidaycottages.co.uk
I: www.roselandholidaycottages.co.uk

PORTREATH
Cornwall

Cliff View ★★★
Contact:
Powell's Cottage Holidays, High Street, Saundersfoot SA69 9EJ
T: (01834) 812791
F: (01834) 811731
E: info@powells.co.uk
I: www.powells.co.uk

Cornwall Holiday Homes ★★★
Contact: Mrs Diana Cousins
Cornwall Holiday Homes, 34 Station Road, Pool, Redruth TR15 3QG
T: (01209) 715358
F: (01209) 715358
E: cwllholidayhomes@talk21.com
I: www.cornwall-holidayhomes.co.uk

Dolphins & Harbourside ★★★★
Contact:
Cornish Harbourside Holidays, Loam Cottage, Redruth TR16 6BB
T: (01209) 820089
E: loam.cottage@btinternet.com
I: www.cornish-harbourside-holidays.co.uk

Gull View ★★★
Contact:
Holiday Homes & Cottages South West, 365A Torquay Road, Paignton TQ3 2BT
T: (01803) 663650

Higher Laity Farm ★★★★★
Contact: Mrs Lynne Drew
Higher Laity Farm, Higher Laity, Portreath Road, Redruth TR16 4HY
T: (01209) 842317
F: (01209) 842317
E: info@higherlaityfarm.co.uk
I: www.higherlaityfarm.co.uk

The Moorings ★★★
Contact:
Powell's Cottage Holidays, High Street, Saundersfoot SA69 9EJ
T: (01834) 812791
F: (01834) 811731
E: info@powells.co.uk
I: www.powells.co.uk

Sea Spray
Rating Applied For
Contact:
Powells Cottage Holidays, Dolphin House, High Street, Saundersfoot SA69 9EJ
T: (01834) 813232
F: (01834) 811731
E: info@powells.co.uk
I: www.powells.co.uk

Trengove Farm Cottages ★★★
Contact: Mrs Lindsey Richards
Illogan, Redruth TR16 4PU
T: (01209) 843008
F: (01209) 843682

PORTSCATHO
Cornwall

Alicias Barn
Rating Applied For
Contact:
Roseland Holiday Cottages, Crab Apple Cottage, Truro TR2 5ET
T: (01872) 580480
F: (01872) 580480
E: enquiries@roselandholidaycottages.co.uk
I: www.roselandholidaycottages.co.uk

Antigua
Rating Applied For
Contact:
Roseland Holiday Cottages, Crab Apple Cottage, Truro TR2 5ET
T: (01872) 580480
F: (01872) 580480
E: enquiries@roselandholidaycottages.co.uk
I: www.roselandholidaycottages.co.uk

Caroline Cottage ★★★★
Contact: Mr Stuart & Mrs Marianne Evans
Tregerein, New Road, Truro TR2 5HF
T: (01872) 580336
F: (01872) 580336
I: www.portscatho.com

Chick Cottage & The Beach House
Rating Applied For
Contact:
Roseland Holiday Cottages, Crab Apple Cottage, Truro TR2 5ET
T: (01872) 580480
F: (01872) 580480
E: enquiries@roselandholidaycottages.co.uk
I: www.roselandholidaycottages.co.uk

Coast Cottage
Rating Applied For
Contact:
Roseland Holiday Cottages, Crab Apple Cottage, Truro TR2 5ET
T: (01872) 580480
F: (01872) 580480
E: enquiries@roselandholidaycottages.co.uk
I: www.roselandholidaycottages.co.uk

Cowrie
Rating Applied For
Contact:
Roseland Holiday Cottages, Crab Apple Cottage, Truro TR2 5ET
T: (01872) 580480
F: (01872) 580480
E: enquiries@roselandholidaycottages.co.uk
I: www.roselandholidaycottages.co.uk

Cuilan ★★★★
Contact:
Roseland Holiday Cottages, Crab Apple Cottage, Truro TR2 5ET
T: (01872) 580480
F: (01872) 580480
E: enquiries@roselandholidaycottages.co.uk
I: www.roselandholidaycottages.co.uk

Dormer Cottage & Byways
Rating Applied For
Contact:
Roseland Holiday Cottages, Crab Apple Cottage, Truro TR2 5ET
T: (01872) 580480
F: (01872) 580480
E: enquiries@roselandholidaycottages.co.uk
I: www.roselandholidaycottages.co.uk

The Forge
Rating Applied For
Contact: Dr Glyn Stanley
6 Church Street, Banbury OX15 4DW
T: (01295) 700083
F: (01295) 700083
E: julia.stanley@tinyworld.co.uk

Garden Cottage & Gull Loft
Rating Applied For
Contact:
Roseland Holiday Cottages, Crab Apple Cottage, Truro TR2 5ET
T: (01872) 580480
F: (01872) 580480
E: enquiries@roselandholidaycottages.co.uk
I: www.roselandholidaycottages.co.uk

Hera
Rating Applied For
Contact:
Roseland Holiday Cottages, Crab Apple Cottage, Truro TR2 5ET
T: (01872) 580480
F: (01872) 580480
E: enquiries@roselandholidaycottages.co.uk
I: www.roselandholidaycottages.co.uk

Hillside Cottage
Rating Applied For
Contact:
Roseland Holiday Cottages, Crab Apple Cottage, Truro TR2 5ET
T: (01872) 580480
F: (01872) 580480
E: enquiries@roselandholidaycottages.co.uk
I: www.roselandholidaycottages.co.uk

Jacaranda Apartment & Bungalow
Rating Applied For
Contact:
Roseland Holiday Cottages, Crab Apple Cottage, Truro TR2 5ET
T: (01872) 580480
F: (01872) 580480
E: enquiries@roselandholidaycottages.co.uk
I: www.roselandholidaycottages.co.uk

Linhay Cottage ★★★★
Contact:
Holiday Homes & Cottages SW, 365A Torquay Road, Paignton TQ3 2BT
T: (01803) 663650
F: (01803) 664037
E: holcotts@aol.com
I: www.swcottages.co.uk

Lugger End
Rating Applied For
Contact:
Roseland Holiday Cottages, Crab Apple Cottage, Truro TR2 5ET
T: (01872) 580480
F: (01872) 580480
E: enquiries@roselandholidaycottages.co.uk
I: www.roselandholidaycottages.co.uk

Maralane
Rating Applied For
Contact:
Roseland Holiday Cottages, Crab Apple Cottage, Truro TR2 5ET
T: (01872) 580480
F: (01872) 580480
E: enquiries@roselandholidaycottages.co.uk
I: www.roselandholidaycottages.co.uk

Morgwyn
Rating Applied For
Contact:
Roseland Holiday Cottages, Crab Apple Cottage, Truro TR2 5ET
T: (01872) 580480
F: (01872) 580480
E: enquiries@roselandholidaycottages.co.uk

Establishments printed in blue have a detailed entry in this guide

SOUTH WEST ENGLAND

Nangwedhen
Rating Applied For
Contact:
Roseland Holiday Cottages, Crab Apple Cottage, Truro TR2 5ET
T: (01872) 580480
F: (01872) 580480
E: enquiries@roselandholidaycottages.co.uk
I: www.roselandholidaycottages.co.uk

The Old School House
Rating Applied For
Contact:
Roseland Holiday Cottages, Crab Apple Cottage, Truro TR2 5ET
T: (01872) 580480
F: (01872) 580480
E: enquiries@roselandholidaycottages.co.uk
I: www.roselandholidaycottages.co.uk

Opal Cottage
Rating Applied For
Contact:
Roseland Holiday Cottages, Crab Apple Cottage, Truro TR2 5ET
T: (01872) 580480
F: (01872) 580480
E: enquiries@roselandholidaycottages.co.uk
I: www.roselandholidaycottages.co.uk

Pengerein Cottage ★★★
Contact: Mr Stuart & Mrs Marianne Evans
Tregerein, New Road, Truro TR2 5HD
T: (01872) 580336
E: holidays@portscatho.com
I: www.portscatho.com

Pengerrans
Rating Applied For
Contact: Mrs Leonie Iddison
Roseland Holiday Cottages, Crab Apple Cottage, Truro TR2 5ET
T: (01872) 580480
F: (01872) 580480
E: enquiries@roselandholidaycottages.co.uk
I: www.roselandholidaycottages.co.uk

Pollaughan Farm Holidays
★★★★-★★★★★
Contact: Mrs Penny Pollaughan Farm Holidays,
Pollaughan Farm, Truro TR2 5EH
T: (01872) 580150
F: (01872) 58010
E: pollaughan@yahoo.co.uk
I: www.pollaughan.co.uk

Porthcurnick Lodge
Rating Applied For
Contact: Mrs Leonie Iddison
Roseland Holiday Cottages, Crab Apple Cottage, Truro TR2 5ET
T: (01872) 580480
F: (01872) 580480
E: enquiries@roselandholidaycottages.co.uk
I: roselandholidaycottages.co.uk

Puffins ★★★★
Contact: Mr Paul Riches
19 Wyvern Road, Sutton Coldfield B74 2PS
T: (0121) 3558785
E: RPaulflap@aol.com

Roseland Lodge
Rating Applied For
Contact: Mrs Leonie Iddison
Roseland Holiday Cottages, Crab Apple Cottage, Truro TR2 5ET
T: (01872) 580480
F: (01872) 580480
E: enquiries@roselandholidaycottages.co.uk
I: Roselandholidaycottages.co.uk

Rosevine Holiday Cottages
★★★★
Contact:
Roseland Holiday Cottages, Crab Apple Cottage, Truro TR2 5ET
T: (01872) 580480
F: (01872) 580480
E: enquires@roselandholidaycottages.co.uk
I: www.roselandholidaycottages.co.uk

Seacroft
Rating Applied For
Contact: Mrs Leonie Iddison
Roseland Holiday Cottages, Crab Apple Cottage, Truro TR2 5ET
T: (01827) 580480
F: (01827) 580480
E: enqueiries@roselandholidaycottages.co.uk
I: Roselandholidaycottages.co.uk

Shambles ★★★
Contact:
Roseland Holiday Cottages, Crab Apple Cottage, Truro TR2 5ET
T: (01872) 580480
F: (01872) 580480
E: enquiries@roselandholidaycottages.co.uk
I: www.roselandholidaycottages.co.uk

Sunday House East and West ★★★★
Contact:
Roseland Holiday Cottages, Crab Apple Cottage, Truro TR2 5ET
T: (01872) 580480
F: (01872) 580480
E: enquiries@roselandholidaycottages.co.uk
I: www.roselandholidaycottages.co.uk

Waterside
Rating Applied For
Contact:
Roseland Holiday Cottages, Crab Apple Cottage, Truro TR2 5ET
T: (01872) 580480
F: (01872) 580480
E: enquiries@roselandholidaycottages.co.uk
I: www.roselandholidaycottages.co.uk

10 Wellington Terrace
Rating Applied For
Contact:
Roseland Holiday Cottages, Crab Apple Cottage, Truro TR2 5ET
T: (01872) 580480
F: (01872) 580480
E: enquiries@roselandholidaycottages.co.uk
I: www.roselandholidaycottages.co.uk

9 Wellington Terrace
Rating Applied For
Contact:
Roseland Holiday Cottages, Crab Apple Cottage, Truro TR2 5ET
T: (01872) 580480
F: (01872) 580480
E: enquiries@roselandholidaycottages

Wilbury Cottage ★★★
Contact:
Roseland Holiday Cottages, Crab Apple Cottage, Truro TR2 5ET
T: (01872) 580480
F: (01872) 580480
E: enquiries@roselandholidaycottages.co.uk
I: www.roselandholidaycottages.co.uk

PORTWRINKLE
Cornwall

Westway ★★★
Contact: Ms Susan Irving
33 Greyhound Lane, Streatham Common, London SW16 5NP
T: (020) 8769 7988

POTTERNE
Wiltshire

Stroud Hill Farm Holidays ★★★
Contact: Mrs Helen Straker
Stroud Hill Farm Holidays, Stroud Hill Farm, Potterne Wick, Devizes SN10 5QR
T: (01380) 720371
F: (01380) 739643
E: hstraker@amserve.net

POUGHILL
Cornwall

1 Brightland Apartments ★★★★
Contact: Mrs J Sames
28 Creslow Way, Aylesbury HP17 8YW
T: (01296) 747425
E: j.l.pearce@tesco.net
I: www.lakeviewrise.co.uk

Moor Farm ★★★
Contact:
Farm & Cottage Holidays, Victoria House, 12 Fore Street, Bideford EX39 1AW
T: (01237) 479146
F: (01237) 421512
E: enquiries@farmcott.co.uk
I: www.farmcott.co.uk

Tregella ★★★★
Contact:
Farm & Cottage Holidays, Victoria House, 26 Fore Street, Bideford EX39 1AW
T: (01237) 479146
F: (01237) 421512
I: www.farmcott.co.uk

Trevalgas Cottages
★★★-★★★★
Contact: Mrs Sarah Banning
Candytuft Green, High Wycombe HP15 6BX
T: (01494) 711540
E: info@trevalgascottages.co.uk
I: www.trevalgascottages.co.uk

POUNDISFORD
Somerset

Old Mapp's Garden ★★★
Contact: Mrs Carole Bartleet
Old Mapp's Garden, Corner House, Taunton TA3 7AE
T: (01823) 421737
F: (01823) 421197
E: stephenbartleet@lineone.net

POUNDSGATE
Devon

Bramblemoor Cottage ★★★★
Contact: Mrs Helen Hull
Bramblemoor Cottage, Leusdon, Newton Abbot TQ13 7NU
T: (01364) 631410
E: helen.hull@eclipse.co.uk
I: www.bramblemoor.fsworld.co.uk

Oldsbrim Shippon ★★★★
Contact:
Toad Hall Cottages, Elliot House, Church Street, Kingsbridge TQ7 1BY
T: (01548) 853089
F: (01548) 853086
E: thc@toadhallcottages.com
I: www.toadhallcottages.com

POUNDSTOCK
Cornwall

Herds Cottage ★★★
Contact: Mrs Doris Toon
Herds Cottage, Bude EX23 0DN
T: (01288) 361448
F: (01288) 361448
E: herdscottage@tiscali.co.uk

Pegsdown ★★★
Contact:
Powell's Cottage Holidays, High Street, Saundersfoot SA69 9EJ
T: (01834) 812791
F: (01834) 811731
E: info@powells.co.uk
I: www.powells.co.uk

POXWELL
Dorset

Honeysuckle Cottage ★★★
Contact: Mr Zachary Stuart-Brown
Dream Cottages, 5 Hope Square, Weymouth DT4 8TR
T: (01305) 789000
F: (01305) 761346
E: admin@dream-cottages.co.uk
I: www.dream-cottages.co.uk

SOUTH WEST ENGLAND

PRAA SANDS
Cornwall
Sea Meads Holiday Homes ★★★
Contact: Mrs Joan Hassall
Best Leisure, North Hill,
Barnstaple EX31 4LG
T: (01271) 850611
F: (01271) 850655
E: enquiries@bestleisure.co.uk
I: www.bestleisure.co.uk

PRAZE-AN-BEEBLE
Cornwall
Cargenwen Farm Holiday Cottages ★★-★★★
Contact: Mr Tony & Mrs Sue Blumenau
Cargenwen Farm Holiday Cottages, Cargenwen Farm, Blackrock, Camborne TR14 9PL
T: (01209) 831151
F: (01209) 831151
E: cargenwen@freenet.co.uk

PRESTBURY
Gloucestershire
Home Farm ★★★★
Contact: Mr Charles Banwell
Home Farm, Mill Street, Cheltenham GL52 3BG
T: (01242) 583161
F: (01242) 583161
I: www.homefarm.clara.net/

PRESTON
Dorset
Bayview ★★★
Contact: Mr Zachary Stuart-Brown
Dream Cottages, 5 Hope Square, Weymouth DT4 8TR
T: (01305) 789000
F: (01305) 761346
E: admin@dream-cottages.co.uk
I: www.dream-cottages.co.uk

Bella Rosa, Bella Vista & Villa de la Mer ★★★
Contact: Mr Zachary Stuart-Brown
Dream Cottages, 5 Hope Square, Weymouth DT4 8TR
T: (01305) 789000
E: admin@dream-cottages.co.uk
I: www.dream-cottages.co.uk

Deers Leap ★★★
Contact:
Holiday Homes & Cottages South West, 365A Torquay Road, Paignton TQ3 2BT
T: (01803) 663650
F: (01803) 664037
E: holcotts@aol.com
I: www.swcottages.co.uk

Phoenix Holiday Flats ★★★★
Contact: Ms Janet Bennett
Phoenix Holiday Flats, 53 Coombe Valley Road, Weymouth DT3 6NL
T: (01305) 832134
F: (01305) 834955

Preston Heights ★★★
Contact: Mr Zachary Stuart-Brown
Dream Cottages, 5 Hope Square, Weymouth DT4 8TR
T: (01305) 789000
F: (01305) 761346
E: admin@dream-cottages.co.uk
I: www.dream-cottages.co.uk

Shingle Cottage ★★★
Contact:
Dream Cottages, 5 Hope Square, Weymouth DT4 8TR
T: (01305) 789000
F: (01305) 761347

PROBUS
Cornwall
Coal Harbour Cottage ★★★
Contact: Mrs Jill Lucas
Mount Pleasant Farm, Gorran High Lanes, St Austell PL26 6LR
T: (01726) 843918
E: jill@mpfarm.vispa.com

PUCKLECHURCH
South Gloucestershire
Fern Cottage ★★★★
Contact: Mrs Sue James
Fern Cottage Self Catering Accommodation, Fern Cottage, 188 Shortwood Hill, Bristol BS16 9PG
T: (0117) 937 4966

PUDDLETOWN
Dorset
The Ramblers Retreat ★★★
Contact: Mrs Clare Stokes
8 Bathsheba Terrace, Dorchester DT1 2JU
T: (01305) 259588 & 07745 064556
E: ramblersretreat@ukonline.co.uk
I: web.ukonline.co.uk/ramblersretreat

Weatherbury Cottages ★★★★
Contact: Mr & Mrs Clive Howes
Weatherbury Cottages, 7A High Street, Dorchester DT2 8RT
T: (01305) 848358
E: enquires@weatherburycottages.co.uk

PUNCKNOWLE
Dorset
Berwick Manor ★★★★-★★★★★
Contact: Mrs Lyn Hopkins
Puncknowle Manor Estate, c/o Hazel Lane Farmhouse, Dorchester DT2 9BU
T: (01308) 898107
E: cottages@pknlest.com
I: www.dorset-selfcatering.co.uk

Daisy Down Cottage, Berwick Manor and Puncknowle Manor Farmhouse ★★★★-★★★★★
Contact: Mrs Lyn Hopkins
Puncknowle Manor Estate, c/o Hazel Lane Farmhouse, Dorchester DT2 9BU
T: (01308) 898107
F: (01308) 898107
E: cottages@pxnlest.com
I: www.dorset-selfcatering.co.uk

Prosperous Cottage ★★★
Contact: Mr Zachary Stuart-Brown
Dream Cottages, 5 Hope Square, Weymouth DT4 8TR
T: (01305) 789000
E: admin@dream-cottages.co.uk
I: www.dream-cottages.co.uk

PUTSBOROUGH
Devon
11 Clifton Court ★★★★
Contact:
Marsden's Cottage Holidays, 2 The Square, Braunton EX33 2JB
T: (01271) 813777
F: (01271) 813664
E: holidays@marsdens.co.uk
I: www.marsdens.co.uk

17 Clifton Court ★★★★
Contact:
Marsden's Cottage Holidays, 2 The Square, Braunton EX33 2JB
T: (01271) 813777
F: (01271) 813664
E: holidays@marsdens.co.uk
I: www.marsdens.co.uk

25 Clifton Court ★★★★
Contact:
Marsden's Cottage Holidays, 2 The Square, Braunton EX33 2JB
T: (01271) 813777
F: (01271) 813664
E: holidays@marsdens.co.uk
I: www.marsdens.co.uk

Flat 1 Clifton Court ★★★★
Contact:
Marsden's Cottage Holidays, 2 The Square, Braunton EX33 2JB
T: (01271) 813777
F: (01271) 813664
E: holidays@marsdens.co.uk
I: www.marsdens.co.uk

Flat 18 Clifton Court ★★★★
Contact:
Marsdens Cottage Holidays, 2 The Square, Braunton EX33 2JB
T: (01271) 813777
F: (01271) 813664
E: holidays@marsdens.co.uk
I: www.marsdens.co.uk

Flat 22 Clifton Court ★★★★
Contact:
Marsden's Cottage Holidays, 2 The Square, Braunton EX33 2JB
T: (01271) 813777
F: (01271) 813664
E: holidays@marsdens.co.uk
I: www.marsdens.co.uk

Flat 24 Clifton Court ★★★★
Contact:
Marsden's Cottage Holidays, 2 The Square, Braunton EX33 2JB
T: (01271) 813777
F: (01271) 813664
E: holidays@marsdens.co.uk
I: www.marsdens.co.uk

Flat 27 Clifton Court ★★★★
Contact:
Marsdens Cottage Holidays, 2 The Square, Braunton EX33 2JB
T: (01271) 813777
F: (01271) 813664
E: holidays@marsdens.co.uk
I: www.marsdens.co.uk

Flat 32 Clifton Court ★★★★
Contact: Mr & Mrs Cornwell
Marsden's Cottage Holidays, 2 The Square, Braunton EX33 2JB
I: www.marsdens.co.uk

Flat 7 Clifton court ★★★★
Contact:
Marsden's Cottage Holidays, 2 The Square, Braunton EX33 2JB
T: (01271) 813777
F: (01271) 813664
E: holidays@marsdens.co.uk
I: www.marsdens.co.uk

Flat 8, Clifton Court ★★★★
Contact:
Marsdens Cottage Holidays, 2 The Square, Braunton EX33 2JB
T: (01271) 813777
F: (01271) 813664
E: holidays@marsdens.co.uk
I: www.marsdens.co.uk

Vention Cottage ★★★★
Contact: Mr Peter & Mrs Janet Cornwell
Marsden's Cottage Holidays, 2 The Square, Braunton EX33 2JB
T: (01271) 813777
F: (01271) 813664
E: holidays@marsdens.co.uk
I: www.marsdens.co.uk

RADSTOCK
Bath and North East Somerset
Charlton Farm Cottage ★★★★
Contact: Mr Anthony & Mrs Vanessa Dutton
Charlton Farm Cottage, Charlton, Radstock BA3 5TN
T: (01761) 437761
F: (01761) 436410
E: anthony@charltonfarm.com
I: www.charltonfarm.com

RAMPISHAM
Dorset
Stable Cottage ★★★★
Contact: Mr James & Mrs Diane Read
School House, Rampisham, Dorchester DT2 0PR
T: (01935) 83555
E: usatschoolhouse@aol.com
I: www.usatschoolhouse.com

RATTERY
Devon
Knowle Farm ★★★★
Contact: Mr Richard & Mrs Lynn Micklewright
Knowle Farm, Nr Totnes, South Brent TQ10 9JY
T: (01364) 73914
F: (01364) 73914
E: Holiday@knowle-farm.co.uk
I: www.knowle-farm.co.uk

Establishments printed in blue have a detailed entry in this guide

SOUTH WEST ENGLAND

READY TOKEN
Gloucestershire
Hartwell Farm Cottages ★★★★
Contact: Mrs Caroline Mann
Hartwell Farm, Cirencester
GL7 5SY
T: (01285) 740210
F: (01285) 740210
E: caroline@hartwell89.freeserve.co.uk
I: www.selfcateringcotswolds.com

REDMARLEY
Gloucestershire
Playley Green Cottages ★★★★
Contact: Mr McKechnie
Playley Green Cottages, Playley Green Farm, Gloucester
GL19 3NB
T: (01531) 650309
F: (01531) 650375
E: playley-cottages@lineone.net

REDRUTH
Cornwall
Morthana Farm Holidays ★★-★★★
Contact: Mrs Sally Pearce
Morthana Farm Holidays, Wheal Rose, Scorrier, Redruth
TR16 5DF
T: (01209) 890938
F: (01209) 890938

RESKADINNICK
Cornwall
Dromona ★★
Contact: Mr Brian & Mrs Elizabeth Jackson
Dromona, Camborne TR14 0BH
T: (01209) 713644
E: elizabeth@dromona.fsnet.co.uk

Reskadinnick Bungalow ★★★
Contact:
Farm & Cottage Holidays, Victoria House, 35 Fore Street, Bideford EX39 1AW
T: (01237) 479146
F: (01237) 421512
E: bookings@farmcott.co.uk
I: www.farmcott.co.uk

RESTRONGUET
Cornwall
Regatta Cottage ★★★★
Contact: Mrs Margie Lumby
Special Places in Cornwall, Poachers Reach, Harcourt, Truro
TR3 6SQ
T: (01872) 864400
E: office@specialplacescornwall.co.uk
I: www.specialplacescornwall.co.uk

RHODE
Somerset
1 Rhode Farm Cottages ★★★★
Contact: Mrs Mary Adams
1 Rhode Farm Cottages, Bridgwater TA5 2AD
T: (01278) 662178
E: adams@rhode.fslite.co.uk

RIDDLECOMBE
Devon
Manor Farm ★★★★
Contact: Mrs Gay
Manor Farm, Chulmleigh
EX18 7NX
T: (01769) 520335
F: (01769) 520335

RINGSTEAD
Dorset
The Creek ★★
Contact: Mrs Fisher
The Creek, Ground Floor Flat, Dorchester DT2 8NG
T: (01305) 852251
E: michaelandfredafisher@btinternet.com

Upton Farm ★★★★★
Contact: Mr & Mrs Davis
Upton Farm, Upton, Dorchester
DT2 8NE
T: (01305) 853970
F: (01305) 853970
E: alan@uptonfarm.co.uk
I: www.uptonfarm.co.uk

ROADWATER
Somerset
Tacker Street Cottage ★★
Contact: Mrs Thomas
Higher Rodhuish Farm, Minehead TA24 6QL
T: (01984) 640253
F: (01984) 640253

ROCHE
Cornwall
Owl's Reach ★★★★
Contact: Mrs Diana Pride
Owl's Reach, Colbiggan Farm, Old Coach Road, St Austell
PL26 8LJ
T: (01208) 831597
E: info@owlsreach.co.uk
I: www.owlsreach.co.uk

Treickle Barn ★★★★
Contact: Mrs dee Tracey-Smith
Three Chimneys, Belowda, St Austell PL26 8NQ
T: (01726) 890566
F: (01726) 891648

ROCK
Cornwall
Cant Cove ★★★★★
Contact: Mr Sleeman
The Cottage, Cant Farm, St Minver, Wadebridge PL27 6RL
T: (01208) 862841
F: (01208) 862142
E: info@cantcove.co.uk
I: www.cantcove.co.uk

22 Croftlands ★★★★
Contact: Mr & Ms James & Dee Smith & McCormack
Tredrizzick, St Minver, Wadebridge PL27 6PB
T: (01208) 862278
E: jimmer2000000@aol.com

Half Way Tree ★★★★
Contact: Mrs Diana Bullivant
Diana Bullivant Holidays, South Winds, Trebell Green, Bodmin
PL30 5HR
T: (01208) 831336
F: (01208) 831336
E: diana@dbullivant.fsnet.co.uk
I: www.cornwall-online.co.uk/diana-bullivant

Little Riggs ★★★
Contact: Mrs Diana Bullivant
Diana Bullivant Holidays, South Winds, Trebell Green, Bodmin
PL30 5HR
T: (01208) 831336
F: (01208) 831336
E: diana@dbullivant.fsnet.co.uk
I: www.cornwall-online.co.uk/diana-bullivant

Maidenover ★★★★
Contact: Mrs Diana Bullivant
Diana Bullivant Holidays, South Winds, Trebell Green, Bodmin
PL30 5HR
T: (01208) 831336
F: (01208) 831336
E: diana@dbullivant.fsnet.co.uk
I: www.cornwall-online.co.uk/diana-bullivant

Mariners Rock ★★★-★★★★★
Contact: Miss Claire Tordoff
Mariners Lettings Ltd, 1 Ranelagh Avenue, London
SW6 3PJ
T: (020) 73849105
I: www.marinersrock.com

Meadowside ★★★★★
Contact: Mrs Diana Bullivant
Diana Bullivant Holidays, Southwinds, Trebell Green, Bodmin PL30 5HR
T: (01208) 831336
F: (01208) 831336
E: diana@d.bullivant.fsnet.co.uk
I: www.cornwall-online.co.uk/diana-bullivant

Mullets ★★★★
Contact: Mrs Diana Bullivant
Diana Bullivant Holidays, Southwinds, Trebell Green, Bodmin PL30 5HR
T: (01208) 831336
F: (01208) 831336
E: diana@dbullivant.fsnet.co.uk
I: www.cornwall-online.co.uk/diana-bullivant

Musters ★★★
Contact: Mrs Diana Bullivant
Diana Bullivant Holidays, South Winds, Trebell Green, Bodmin
PL30 5HR
T: (01208) 831336
F: (01208) 831336
E: diana@dbullivant.fsnet.co.uk
I: www.cornwall-online.co.uk/diana-bullivant

17 Slipway Cottages ★★★
Contact: Mrs Diana Bullivant
Diana Bullivant Holidays, Southwinds, Trebell Green, Bodmin PL30 5HR
T: (01208) 831336
F: (01208) 831336
E: diana@dbullivant.fsnet.co.uk
I: www.cornwall-online.co.uk/diana-bullivant

The Studio ★★★
Contact: Mr & Mrs Gregan
The Studio, Porthilly, Wadebridge PL27 6JX
T: (01208) 862410

Tomhara ★★★★★
Contact: Mrs Diane Bullivant
Diana Bullivant Holidays, South Winds, Trebell Green, Bodmin
PL30 5HR
T: (01208) 831336
F: (01208) 831336
E: diana@dbullivant.fsnet.co.uk
I: www.cornwall-online.co.uk/diana-bullivant

Trevethan ★★★
Contact:
Rock Holidays inc. Harbour Holidays, Trebetherick House, Wadebridge PL27 6SB
T: (01208) 863399
F: (01208) 862218
E: rockhols@aol.com
I: www.rockholidays.co.uk

Tristan House ★★★
Contact:
Harbour Holidays - Rock, Trebetherick House, Wadebridge
PL27 6SB
T: (01208) 863399
F: (01208) 862218
I: www.rockholidays.com

Wheel Cottage ★★★★
Contact: Mrs Diana Bullivant
Diana Bullivant Holidays, South Winds, Trebell Green, Bodmin
PL30 5HR
T: (01208) 831336
F: (01208) 831336
E: diana@d.bullivant.fsnet.co.uk
I: www.cornwall-online.co.uk/diana-bullivant

ROCOMBE
Devon
Sunshine Cottage - V4132 ★★★
Contact:
Lyme Bay Holidays, Bos House, 44 Church Street, Lyme Regis
DT7 3DA
T: (01297) 443363
F: (01297) 445576
E: email@lymebayholidays.co.uk
I: www.lymebayholidays.co.uk

ROOKSBRIDGE
Somerset
Garden Cottage and Dairy Cottage ★★★★
Contact: Mrs Mandi Counsell
Rooksbridge House, Axbridge
BS26 2UL
T: (01934) 750630
E: rooksbridgehouse@btinternet.com

ROSE ASH
Devon
Nethercott Manor Farm ★★★
Contact: Mrs Carol Woollacott
Nethercott Manor Farm, South Molton EX36 4RE
T: (01769) 550483
F: (01769) 550483

ROSUDGEON
Cornwall
Thatched Cottage ★★★★
Contact: Welcome Cottages
Welcome Cottages, Stringmill, Stoney Bank Road, Barnoldswick
BB94 0AA
T: 0870 1 970990
F: 0870 2 389989

SOUTH WEST ENGLAND

ROUSDON
Devon

The Lodge House ★★★★
Contact: Ms Kate Bartlett
Jean Bartlett Cottage Holidays,
The Old Dairy, Fore Street,
Seaton EX12 3JB
T: (01297) 23221
F: (01297) 23303
E: holidays@jeanbartlett.com
I: www.jeanbartlett.com

Peek House
Rating Applied For
Contact: Ms Judith Ellard
Peek House, Rousdon Estate,
Lyme Regis DT7 3XR
T: (01297) 444734
F: (01297) 444332
E: mail@peekhouse.co.uk
I: www.peekhouse.co.uk

ROWDE
Wiltshire

Lakeside Rendezvous ★★★★
Contact: Mrs Sarah Gleed
Lakeside Rendezvous, Devizes
Road, Devizes SN10 2LX
T: (01380) 725447
E: enquiries@
lakesiderendezvous.co.uk
I: lakesiderendezvous.co.uk

RUAN HIGH LANES
Cornwall

The Little Barn
Rating Applied For
Contact:
Roseland Holiday Cottages, Crab
Apple Cottage, Truro TR2 5ET
T: (01872) 580480
F: (01872) 580480
E: enquiries@
roselandholidaycottages
I: www.roselandholidaycottages.
co.uk

Lower Penhallow Farm ★★★★
Contact: Mr Johan Balslev
Lower Penhallow Farm, Truro
TR2 5LS
T: (01872) 501105
F: (01872) 501105
E: enquiries@
lowerpenhallowfarm.co.uk
I: www.lowerpenhallowfarm.
co.uk

Martha's Cottage
Rating Applied For
Contact:
Martha's Cottage, Treworthal,
Truro TR2 5LR
T: (01872) 580480
F: (01872) 580480
E: enquiries@
roselandholidaycottages.co.uk
I: www.roselandholidaycottages.
co.uk

Trelagossick Farm ★★★
Contact: Mrs Rachel Carbis
Trelagossick Farm, Truro TR2 5JU
T: (01872) 501338

Trenona Farm Holidays - Chy Tyak and Chy Whel ★★★★
Contact: Mrs Pamela Carbis
Trenona Farm Holidays, Trenona
Farm, Ruan High Lanes, Truro
TR2 5JS
T: (01872) 501339
F: (01872) 501253
E: pam@trenonafarmholidays.
co.uk
I: www.trenonafarmholidays.
co.uk

RUAN MINOR
Cornwall

Adjewednack ★★★★
Contact: Mr Martin Raftery
Mullion Cottages, Mullion
Meadows, Helston TR12 7HB
T: (01326) 240315
F: (01326) 241090
E: enquiries@mullioncottages.
com
I: www.mullioncottages.com

Candle Cottage ★★★★
Contact: Mr Martin Raftery
Mullion Cottages, Churchtown,
Helston TR12 7HQ
T: (01326) 240315
F: (01326) 241090
E: martin@mullioncottages.com
I: www.mullioncottages.com

Gwavas Vean ★★★
Contact: Mr Martin Raftery
Mullion Cottages, Mullion
Meadows, Helston TR12 7HB
T: (01326) 240315
F: (01326) 241090
E: martin@mullioncottages.com
I: www.mullioncottages.com

Tanuf ★★★
Contact: Mr Martin Raftery
Mullion Cottages, Mullion
Meadows, Helston TR12 7HB
T: (01326) 240315
F: (01326) 241090
E: martin@mullioncottages.com
I: www.mullioncottages.com

RUARDEAN
Gloucestershire

Anne's Cottage ★★★★
Contact: Mrs Anne Seager
South View, Crooked End,
Ruardean GL17 9XF
T: (01594) 543217
F: (01594) 543217
E: anneseager@aol.com
I: www.annescottage.ik.com

The Old Post Office Annexe ★★★
Contact: Mr & Mrs Harrison
Hope Cottage, High Street, The
Pludds, Ruardean GL17 9JU
T: (01594) 860229

ST AGNES
Isles of Scilly

Covean Cottage Little House ★★★
Contact: Mrs Heather Sewell
Covean Cottage Little House, St
Agnes TR22 0PL
T: (01720) 422620
F: (01720) 422620

Croft Cottage ★★★★
Contact: Mrs Jane Sawle
Croft Cottage, Beacon Cottage
Farm, Beacon Drive, St Agnes
TR5 0NU
T: (01872) 553381
E: beaconcottagefarm@lineone.
net
I: www.
beaconcottagefarmholidays.
co.uk

Gothic Cottages ★★
Contact: Ms Amanda Torris
Woodbine Cottage, Greenwith
Road, Truro TR3 7LX
T: (01872) 870790
E: ameliahoney@aol.com
I: www.users.waitrose.
com/~gwillson

Lowertown Barn ★★★
Contact: Mrs Page
Garden Cottage, Willinghurst,
Guildford GU5 0SU
T: (01483) 273805
F: (01483) 271606
E: robert@gcpage.freeserve.
co.uk

Marna Cottage
Rating Applied For
Contact:
Cornish Cottage Holidays, The
Old Turnpike Dairy, Godolphin
Road, Helston TR13 8AA
T: (01326) 573808
F: (01326) 564992
E: Inquiry@
cornishcottageholidays.com
I: www.cornishcottageholidays.
co.uk

The Owl House ★★★★★
Contact: Ms Lyn Hicks
Chy Ser Rosow, Barkla Shop, St
Agnes TR5 0XN
T: (01872) 553644
E: enquiries@the-owl-house.
co.uk
I: www.the-owl-house.co.uk

Palmvale Holidays ★★★-★★★★★
Contact: Mr K Williams & Mrs R
Hobson
Duchy Holidays, 11 Boscawen
Road, Perranporth TR6 0EP
T: (01872) 552234
F: (01872) 552690
E: enquiries@duchyholidays.
co.uk

Periglis Cottage ★★★
Contact: Mr Paget-Brown
Periglis Cottage, St Agnes
TR22 0PL
T: (01720) 422366

Tregease
Rating Applied For
Contact: Mr John Simmons
15 Fall View, Barnsley S75 4LG
T: (01226) 790482

ST AUSTELL
Cornwall

Bosinver Farm Cottages ★★★-★★★★★
Contact: Mrs Pat Smith
Bosinver Farm Cottages,
Bosinver Farm, St Mewan, St
Austell PL26 7DT
T: (01726) 72128
F: (01726) 72128
E: reception@bosinver.co.uk
I: www.bosinver.co.uk

The Engine House ★★★★★
Contact: Mrs Kitchen
Niche Retreats, Hunters Moon,
Banns Road, Truro TR4 8BW
T: (01209) 890272

Lanjeth Farm Holiday Cottages ★★★★
Contact: Mrs Anita Webber
Lanjeth Farm Holiday Cottages,
Lanjeth, St Austell PL26 7TN
T: (01726) 68438
E: anita@cornwall-holidays.uk.
com
I: cornwall-holidays.uk.com

Nanjeath Farm ★★★★
Contact: Mrs Jill Sandercock
Nanjeath Farm, Lanjeth, St
Austell PL26 7TN
T: (01726) 70666
E: peter@sandercocks.freeserve.
co.uk
I: www.nanjeath.co.uk

Poltarrow Farm ★★★★
Contact: Judith Nancarrow
Poltarrow Farm, St Austell
PL26 7DR
T: (01726) 67111
F: (01726) 67111
E: enquire@poltarrow.co.uk
I: www.poltarrow.co.uk

Southfield ★★★
Contact: Mrs Pamela Treleaven
Trevissick Farm, St Austell
PL26 6BQ
T: (01726) 75819
F: (01726) 68052

Tor View ★★★★
Contact: Mrs Clare Hugo
Tor View, Corgee Farm, Bodmin
PL30 5DS
T: (01726) 850340
F: (01726) 850195
E: torview@btopenworld.com
I: www.torviewcentre.co.uk

Tregongeeves Farm Holiday Cottages ★★★★
Contact: John & Judith Clemo
Tregongeeves Farm Holiday
Cottages, Polgooth, St Austell
PL26 7DS
T: (01726) 68202
F: (01726) 68202
E: tregongeeves@tesco.net
I: www.cornwall-holidays.co.uk

Establishments printed in blue have a detailed entry in this guide

SOUTH WEST ENGLAND

ST BLAZEY
Cornwall

Cornhill Farm Cottages ★★★★
Contact: Mrs Kay Carne
Cornhill Farm Cottages, Cornhill Farm, St Blazey, Par PL24 2SP
T: (01726) 815700
F: (01726) 815700
E: cornhillfarmcottages@fsmail.net
I: www.cornhillfarmcottages.co.uk

Eden-Gates Apartments ★★★★★
Contact: Mr Stephen Chidgey
The Old Town Hall, Fore Street, St Blazey, Par PL24 2NH
T: (01726) 815560
F: (01726) 815560
E: stephen@eden-gate.co.uk
I: www.eden-gate.co.uk

The Mill ★★★★
Contact: Mr John Tipper & Mrs Caroline Wey
The Mill, Prideaux Road, St Blazey, Par PL24 2SR
T: (01726) 810171
F: (01726) 810171
E: enquiries@woodmill-farm.co.uk
I: www.woodmill-farm.co.uk

ST BLAZEY GATE
Cornwall

Windsworth Holiday Bungalow
Rating Applied For
Contact: Mrs Pat Wheeler
Windsworth Holiday Bungalow, Luxulyan Road, St Blazey Gate, Par PL24 2EH
T: (01726) 815352
E: info@windsworth.co.uk
I: www.windsworth.co.uk

ST BREOCK
Cornwall

Hustyns ★★★★★
Contact: Ms Katie Richards
Hustyns, St Breock, Wadebridge PL27 7LG
T: (01208) 893700
F: (01208) 893701
E: reception@hustyns.com
I: www.hustyns.com

ST BREWARD
Cornwall

Darrynane Cottages ★★★
Contact: Mrs Angela Clark
Darrynane, St Breward, Bodmin PL30 4LZ
T: (01208) 850885
E: enquiries@darrynane.co.uk
I: www.darrynane.co.uk

Irish Farm ★★★★
Contact: Ms Lisa Arcari
24 Albert Bridge Road, London SW11 4PY

Meadowside Cottage ★★★★
Contact: Mr Aileen & Mrs David Feasey
Meadowside Cottage, Mellon Farm, St Breward, Bodmin PL30 4PL
T: (01208) 851497
F: (01208) 851497
E: feaseymellon@aol.com
I: www.mellonfarm.co.uk

Swallow Hollow ★★★★
Contact: Mr John & Mrs Christine Gerring
Swallow Hollow, St Breward, Bodmin PL30 4QL
T: (01208) 851390
E: john.gerring@tiscali.co.uk
I: www.riverdale.me.uk

ST BURYAN
Cornwall

Choone Farm Holiday Cottages ★★★
Contact: Mr Eric Care
Downs Barn Farm, St Buryan, Penzance TR19 6DG
T: (01736) 810658
F: (01736) 810658
E: bonnar.care@talk21.com
I: www.choonefarm.co.uk

3 The Green
Rating Applied For
Contact: Sally Follett
3 North Parade, Penzance TR18 4SH
T: (01736) 364892

Lands End Cottages ★★★
Contact: Mrs Chris Wells
Millstone Barn, Lower Treave, St Buryan, Penzance TR19 6HZ
T: (01736) 810072
F: (01736) 810072
E: kwells6166@aol.com
I: landsendcottages.com

Tredinney Farm Holiday Cottage
Rating Applied For
Contact: Mrs Warren
Tredinney Farm Holiday Cottage, Tredinney Farm, Crows-An-Wra, Penzance TR19 6HX
T: (01736) 810352
F: (01736) 810352
E: rosemary.warren@btopenworld.com

ST CLEMENT
Cornwall

Churchtown Farm ★★★
Contact: Mrs Margie Lumby
Special Places in Cornwall, Poachers Reach, Harcourt, Truro TR3 6SQ
T: (01872) 864400
E: office@specialplacescornwall.co.uk
I: www.specialplacescornwall.co.uk

ST CLETHER
Cornwall

Forget-Me-Not Cottage ★★★★
Contact: Mr James & Mrs Sheila Kempthorne
St Clether, Trefranck, Launceston PL15 8QN
T: (01566) 86284
E: holidays@trefranck.co.uk
I: www.trefranck.co.uk

Treven Farmhouse ★★★
Contact:
Farm & Cottage Holidays, Victoria House, 12 Fore Street, Bideford EX39 1AW
T: (01237) 479146
F: (01237) 421512
E: enquiries@farmcott.co.uk
I: www.farmcott.co.uk

ST COLUMB
Cornwall

Retreat Court Apartment
Rating Applied For
Contact: Mrs Jo Whitrow-Coates
The Newstead, West Pentire Road, Newquay TR8 5RZ
T: (01637) 830508
F: (01637) 830639
E: info@holidayapartmentscornwall.co.uk
I: www.holidayapartmentcornwall.co.uk

Tregatillian Cottages ★★★
Contact:
Cornish Horizons, The Cottage, 19 New Street, Padstow PL28 8EA
T: (01841) 533331
F: (01841) 533933
E: cottages@cornishhorizons.co.uk
I: www.cornishhorizons.co.uk

Trembleath Farm & Cottage ★★-★★★
Contact:
Farm & Cottage Holidays, Victoria House, 25 Fore Street, Bideford EX39 1AW
T: (01237) 479146
F: (01237) 421512
I: www.farmcott.co.uk

ST COLUMB MAJOR
Cornwall

Trevellan ★★★★
Contact: Mr Corinne & Mrs Bob Medhurst
Trevellan, Arcadia Mill, Reterth, St Columb TR9 6DX
T: (01637) 889148

Walhalla Cottage ★★★
Contact: Ms Nicky Stanley
Harbour Holidays - Padstow, 1 North Quay, Padstow PL28 8AF
T: (01841) 532555
F: (01841) 533115
E: sales@jackie-stanley.co.uk
I: www.harbourholidays.co.uk

ST DAY
Cornwall

Manor Farmhouse Cottage ★★★
Contact: Mrs Zoe Nelson
Manor Farmhouse Cottage, Little Beside, St Day, Redruth TR16 5PX
T: (01209) 822066
F: (01209) 822066
E: muzoe@ntlworld.com

ST ENDELLION
Cornwall

Barton Cottage ★★-★★★★
Contact: Mrs Harris
Barton Cottage, Tolraggott Farm, St Endellion, Port Isaac PL29 3TP
T: (01208) 880927
F: (01208) 880927
I: www.rock-wadebridge.co.uk

Trentinney Farm Holiday Cottages ★★★
Contact: Mr Richard Mably
Trentinney Farm Holiday Cottages, St Endellion, Port Isaac PL29 3TS
T: (01208) 880564
E: info@trentinney.co.uk
I: www.trentinney.co.uk

ST ERME
Cornwall

Sunlight Cottages and Moonlight Studio ★★★★
Contact:
Special Places, Poachers Reach, Harcourt, Truro TR3 6SQ
T: (01872) 864400
F: (01872) 864400
E: office@specialplacescornwall.co.uk
I: www.specialplacescornwall.co.uk

ST ERTH
Cornwall

The Brambles ★★★
Contact: Mrs Alma Barnett
The Brambles, 50 Chenhalls Road, St Erth, Hayle TR27 6HJ
T: (01736) 753331
E: david.alma1@virgin.net

Trenedros Green ★★★
Contact:
Cornish Cottage Holidays, The Old Turnpike Dairy, Godolphin Road, Helston TR13 8AA
T: (01326) 573808
F: (01326) 564992
E: enquiry@cornishcottageholidays.co.uk
I: www.cornishcottageholidays.co.uk

Wisteria Cottage & Trehaven ★★★
Contact: Mrs Cynthia Lawson-Smith
42 Chenhalls Road, St Erth, Hayle TR27 6HJ
T: (01736) 753476
E: cynthia@lawsonsmith.freeserve.co.uk

ST ERVAN
Cornwall

Treleigh Manor Farm ★★★
Contact: Mr Andrew & Mrs Michelle Old
Treleigh Manor Farm, St Ervan, Wadebridge PL27 7RT
T: (01841) 540075

ST EVAL
Cornwall

Springfield ★★★
Contact:
Harbour Holidays, 1 North Quay, Padstow PL28 8AF
T: (01841) 532555
F: (01841) 533115
E: contact@harbourholidays.co.uk
I: www.harbourholidays.co.uk

Trelorna ★★★
Contact: Ms Lorna Knott
Treforna, Trevorgey Mowhay, Wadebridge PL27 7UJ
T: (01841) 520992

Look out for establishments participating in the National Accessible Scheme

SOUTH WEST ENGLAND

ST GENNYS
Cornwall

Penrowan Farmhouse ★★★★
Contact:
Farm & Cottage Holidays,
Victoria House, 12 Fore Street,
Bideford EX39 1AW
T: (01237) 479146
F: (01237) 421512
E: enquiries@farmcott.co.uk
I: www.farmcott.co.uk

Woodgate ★★★
Contact: Mr Francis Crocker
Woodgate, Barton Cottage,
Bude EX23
T: (01840) 230492
I: www.wild-trevigue.co.uk

ST GERMANS
Cornwall

The White House ★★★
Contact: Mrs Daw
The White House, Old Quay Lane,
St Germans, Saltash PL12 5LH
T: (01503) 230505
E: thewhitehouse_cornwall@
hotmail.com

ST GLUVIAS
Cornwall

Glengarth
Rating Applied For
Contact: Mrs Barbara Newing
Glengarth, Burnthouse, St
Gluvias, Penryn TR10 9AS
T: (01872) 863209

ST ISSEY
Cornwall

Blable Farm Barns ★★★★★
Contact: Mr Mike & Mrs Alison
Roberts
Blable Farm Barns, St Issey,
Wadebridge PL27 7RF
T: (01208) 815813
F: (01208) 814834
E: blablefarm@btclick.com
I: www.blablefarmbarns.co.uk

Cannallidgey Villa ★★★
Contact: Mr Old
Cannallidgey Villa Farm, St Issey,
Wadebridge PL27 7RB
T: (01208) 812276

Hawksland Mill ★★★★
Contact: Mr Richard Jenkins
Hawksland Mill, Hawkland, St
Issey, Wadebridge PL27 7RG
T: (01208) 815404
F: (01208) 816831
E: hjc@hawkslandmill.idps.co.uk
I: www.4starcottages.co.uk

Lotties Cottage ★★★★
Contact: Mrs Christine Searle
Lotties Cottage, Middle Halwyn,
Wadebridge PL27 7EL
T: (01841) 541116
F: (01841) 541116
E: christine.searle12@virgin.net

The Manor House ★
Contact: Mrs Kirk
The Manor House, St Issey,
Wadebridge PL27 7QB
T: (01841) 540346
F: (01841) 540139
E: enquiries@
manoractivitycentre.co.uk
I: www.manoractivitycentre.
co.uk

Marshall Barn ★★★
Contact: Ms Nicky Stanley
Harbour Holidays - Padstow, 1
North Quay, Padstow PL28 8AF
T: (01841) 532555
F: (01841) 533115
E: sales@jackie-stanley.co.uk
I: www.harbourholidays.co.uk

The Old Dairy ★★★
Contact: Ms Nicky Stanley
Harbour Holidays - Padstow, 1
North Quay, Padstow PL28 8AF
T: (01841) 532555
F: (01841) 533115
E: sales@jackie-stanley.co.uk
I: www.harbourholidays.co.uk

Pentire View ★★★
Contact: Mrs Sarah Brewer
Pentire View and Trewint Farm
Holiday Homes, Wadebridge
PL27 7RL
T: (01208) 816595

Rose End Cottage ★★★
Contact:
Harbour Holidays, 1 North Quay,
Padstow PL28 8AF
T: (01841) 533402
F: (01841) 533115
E: contact@harbourholidays.
co.uk
I: www.harbourholidays.co.uk

The Snug ★★★
Contact: Ms Nicky Stanley
Harbour Holidays - Padstow, 1
North Quay, Padstow PL28 8AF
T: (01841) 532555
F: (01841) 533115
E: sales@jackie-stanley.co.uk
I: www.harbourholidays.co.uk

**Tremain Cottage &
Hambley Cottage ★★★★**
Contact: Mrs Wynn & Miss Kate
House
Middle Halwyn Farm, St Issey,
Wadebridge PL27 7QL
T: (01208) 812434

Valencia Cottage ★★★
Contact:
Cornish Horizons, The Cottage,
19 New Street, Padstow
PL28 8EA
T: (01841) 533331
F: (01841) 533933
E: cottages@cornishhorizons.
co.uk
I: www.cornishhorizons.co.uk

ST IVES
Cornwall

Ayr Holiday Homes ★★★
Contact: Mrs Kerry Baragwanath
Ayr Holiday Homes, St Ives
TR26 1EJ
T: (01736) 795855
F: (01736) 798797
E: recept@ayrholidaypark.co.uk
I: www.ayrholidaypark.co.uk

Carrack Widden ★★★★
Contact: Mrs Perry
Tros-An-Mor, Treloyhan Manor
Drive, St Ives TR26 2AS
T: (01736) 793370

Casa Bella ★★★★
Contact: Mrs Perry
Tros-An-Mor, Treloyhan Manor
Drive, St Ives TR26 2AS
T: (01736) 793370

**Cheriton Self Catering
★★★**
Contact: Mr Alec Luke
Cheriton Self Catering, Cheriton
House, Market Place, St Ives
TR26 1RZ
T: (01736) 795083

Chy An Eglos
Rating Applied For
Contact: Mr David Eddy
Chy An Eglos, 1 St Andrews
Street, St Ives TR26 1AH
T: (01736) 795542
F: (01736) 752996
E: david.eddy@chy-an-eglos.
co.uk
I: www.chy-an-eglos.co.uk

**Chy Mor and Premier
Apartments ★★★**
Contact: Mr Michael Gill
Beach House, The Wharf, St Ives
TR26 1QA
T: (01736) 798798
F: (01736) 796831
I: www.stivesharbour.com

Gran's Cottage ★★★
Contact: Mrs Dorothy Edmond
Saveock Manor, Greenbottom,
Truro TR4 8QR
T: (01872) 560644
F: (01872) 560644

Lamorna Apartment ★★★★
Contact: Ms Judy Dale
Lamorna Apartment, Treloyhan
Park Road, St Ives TR26 2AH
T: (01736) 794384
F: (01736) 794384
E: judydale@fsmail.net

**Lower Carnstabba Farm
★★★**
Contact: Mrs Marie Short
Lower Carnstabba Farm, Lower
Carnstabba Farmhouse,
Carnstabba, St Ives TR26 3LS
T: (01736) 795920

Nanjizal Cottage ★★★★
Contact: Mrs Judy Dale
Lamorna, Treloyhan Park Road,
St Ives TR26 2AH
T: (01736) 794384
E: judydale@fsmail.net

8 Piazza
Rating Applied For
Contact: Mrs Jeanette Harling
Trecillian Barn, Trevalgan, St Ives
TR26 3BT
T: (01736) 795132

Smeatons Nook Cottage
Rating Applied For
Contact: Mrs Cowling
Carthew Vean, Orange Lane, St
Ives TR26 1RH
T: (01736) 795241

Star Gazy
Rating Applied For
Contact: Mrs Sandra Fenn
Northlands, Chitcombe Road,
Rye TN31 6EU
T: (01424) 882607
F: (01424) 883417
E: sandra@northlands.co.uk

The Studio ★★
Contact: Ms Carol Holland
Little Parc Owles, Pannier Lane,
St Ives TR26 2RQ
T: (01736) 793015
F: (01736) 793258

Suncrest Holiday Flats
Rating Applied For
Contact: Mrs Joy Williams
Suncrest Holiday Flats, Fernlea
Terrace, St Ives TR26 2BH
T: (01326) 572969
E: enquiries@suncrestholidays.
co.uk

Trecillian Barn
Rating Applied For
Contact: Mrs Jeanette Harling
Trecillian Barn, Trevalgan, St Ives
TR26 3BJ
T: (01736) 795132
I: www.stives-accommodation.
co.uk

**Tregenna Castle Self-
Catering, Tregenna Castle
Hotel ★★-★★★★**
Contact: Mr Tony Smith
Tregenna Castle Self-Catering,
Tregenna Castle Hot, Treloyan
Avenue, St Ives TR26 2DE
T: (01736) 795254
F: (01736) 796066
E: hotel@tregenna-castle.co.uk
I: www.tregenna-castle.co.uk

**Trevalgan Holiday Farm
★★★★**
Contact: Mrs Melanie Osborne
Trevalgan Holiday Farm,
Trevalgan, St Ives TR26 3BJ
T: (01736) 796529
E: holidays@trevalgan.co.uk
I: www.trevalgan.co.uk

ST JULIOT
Cornwall

The Hayloft ★★★★★
Contact: Mrs Nicola Collings
The Hayloft, Hillsborough, St
Juliot, Boscastle PL35 0HH
T: (01840) 250218
E: hayloftbarn@hotmail.com
I: www.
cornwallonline/hayloftbarn.
co.uk

ST JUST-IN-PENWITH
Cornwall

Nanquidno Vean ★★★
Contact: Mrs Gildea
15 College Street, Stratford-
upon-Avon CV37 6BN
T: (01789) 299338
F: (01789) 204554
E: pennyguildea@uku.co.uk

Swallows End ★★★★
Contact: Mr David Beer
Swallows End, Kelynack Moor
Farmhouse, Bosworlas, St Just,
Penzance TR19 7RQ
T: (01736) 787011
F: (01736) 787011
E: db.properties@virgin.net
I: www.westcornwalllets.co.uk

ST JUST IN ROSELAND
Cornwall

Brambly Cottage ★★★★
Contact: Mrs Margie Lumby
Special Places In Cornwall,
Poachers Reach, Harcourt, Truro
TR3 6SQ
T: (01872) 864400
E: office@
specialplacescornwall.co.uk
I: www.specialplacescornwall.
co.uk

Establishments printed in blue have a detailed entry in this guide

SOUTH WEST ENGLAND

Carrick View ★★★★
Contact: Mrs Margie Lumby
Special Places in Cornwall,
Poachers Reach, Harcourt, Truro
TR3 6SQ
T: (01872) 864400
E: office@
specialplacescornwall.co.uk
I: www.specialplacescornwall.co.uk

Carvinack Cottage
Rating Applied For
Contact:
Roseland Holiday Cottages, Crab Apple Cottage, Truro TR2 5ET
T: (01872) 580480
F: (01872) 580480
E: enquiries@
roselandholidaycottages.co.uk
I: www.roselandholidaycottages.co.uk

Churchtown Farm
Rating Applied For
Contact:
Roseland Holiday Cottages, Crab Apple Cottage, Truro TR2 5ET
T: (01872) 580480
F: (01872) 580480
E: enquiries@
roselandholidaycottages.co.uk
I: www.roselandholidaycottages.co.uk

ST JUST
Cornwall

Casple Cottage ★★★
Contact: Mr Ken & Mrs Jeni Smith
Higherhouse, Higherland, Callington PL17 8LD
T: (01579) 370608

ST KEVERNE
Cornwall

East End Cottage ★★★★
Contact:
Cornish Cottage Holidays, Godolphin Road, Helston
TR13 8AA
T: (01326) 573808
F: (01326) 564992
E: enquiry@
cornishcottageholidays.co.uk
I: www.cornishcottageholidays.co.uk

Eden House Wing ★★★
Contact:
Cornish Cottage Holidays, Godolphin Road, Helston
TR13 8AA
T: (01326) 573808
F: (01326) 564992
E: robertBOBhughes@aol.com
I: www.cornishcottageholidays.co.uk

Fatty Owls ★★★★
Contact: Ms Yvonne Cole
Fatty Owls, St Keverne, Helston
TR12 6QQ
T: (01326) 280199
E: trenowethhouse@aol.com

Pedn-Tiere ★★★
Contact: Mr Martin Raftery
Mullion Cottages, Mullion Meadows, Helston TR12 7HB
T: (01326) 240315
F: (01326) 241090
E: martin@mullioncottages.com
I: www.mullioncottages.com

Penrose Farm Cottage ★★★
Contact:
Cornish Cottage Holidays, The Old Turnpike Dairy, Godolphin Road, Helston TR13 8GS
T: (01326) 573808
F: (01326) 564992
E: enquiry@
cornishcottageholidays.co.uk
I: www.cornishcottageholidays.co.uk

Tarragon ★★★★
Contact:
Cornish Cottage Holidays, The Old Turnpike Dairy, Godolphin, Meneage Street, Helston
TR13 8AA
T: (01326) 573808
F: (01326) 564992
E: enquiry@
cornishcottageholidays.co.uk
I: www.cornishcottageholidays.co.uk

Trenoweth Mill ★★★★
Contact:
Cornish Cottage Holidays, The Old Turnpike Dairy, Godolphin Road, Helston TR13 8AA
T: (01326) 573808
F: (01326) 564992
E: enquiry@
cornishcottageholidays.co.uk
I: www.cornishcottageholidays.co.uk

Trevallack House ★★★
Contact:
Farm & Cottage Holidays, Victoria House, 12 Fore Street, Bideford EX39 1AW
T: (01237) 479146
F: (01237) 421512
E: bookings@farmcott.co.uk
I: www.farmcott.co.uk

ST KEW
Cornwall

The Barn House ★★★★
Contact: Mrs Janet Chancellor
Ashley, Forty Green Road, Beaconsfield HP9 1XL
T: (01494) 670696
E: jeremy.chancellar@which.net
I: www.visitbarnhouse.co.uk

Keats Cottage ★★
Contact: Mrs Susan Coster
Keats Cottage, Pendoggett Farm, St Kew, Bodmin PL30 3HH
T: (01208) 880332

Lana Vale ★★★★
Contact:
Rock Holidays inc. Harbour Holidays Rock Ltd., Trebetherick House, Wadebridge PL27 6SB
T: (01208) 863399
F: (01208) 862218

Lane End Farm Bungalow ★★★
Contact: Mrs Monk
Lane End Farm Bungalow, Pendoggett, St Kew, Bodmin PL30 3HH
T: (01208) 880013
F: (01208) 880013
E: nabmonk@tiscali.co.uk

Mays Cottage ★★★★★
Contact: Mrs Julia Payne
Manor Farm, Taunton TA4 1DL
T: (01823) 432615
F: (01823) 432615
E: enquiries@scarletgreen.com
I: www.scarletgreen.com

Ogas Pol ★★★★
Contact: Mr B Greenhalgh
43 Meadway, Southgate, London N14 6NJ
T: (020) 88821333
E: ogaspol_43@onetel.com

Paget & Every ★★★
Contact:
Rock Holidays inc. Harbour Holidays, Trebetherick House, Wadebridge PL27 6SB
T: (01208) 863399
F: (01208) 862218
E: rockholidays@aol.com
I: www.rockholidays.co.uk

Skisdon ★★★★
Contact: Mr Tim Honeywill
Skisdon, Bodmin PL30 3HB
T: (01208) 841372
E: Tim580208@aol.com
I: www.skisdon.com

Treharrock Farm Cottages ★★★★
Contact: Mrs Emerald Quinn
Treharrock Farm, Port Isaac
PL29 3TA
T: (01208) 880517
F: (01208) 881139
E: treharrockfarmcottages@btinternet.com
I: www.treharrock.co.uk

Trewethern Barn ★★★★
Contact:
Rock Holidays inc. Harbour Holidays Rock Ltd., Trebetherick House, Wadebridge PL27 6SB
T: (01208) 863399
F: (01208) 862218
E: rockhols@aol.com
I: www.rockholidays.co.uk

ST LEVAN
Cornwall

Bosistow Cottage ★★★★
Contact: Mrs Thomas
Lower Bosistow, Penzance
TR19 6JH
T: (01736) 871254
F: (01736) 871551
E: bosistow.farm@virgin.net

Kibblestone ★★★★
Contact: Mrs Barbara Ottway
4 Woodpecker Avenue, Midsomer Norton, Radstock
BA3 4NN
T: (01761) 410185
F: (01761) 410868
E: barbara_ottway@tiscali.co.uk

Lan-Pedn Garden Flat ★★
Contact: Mrs Barbara Atter
Lan-Pedn Garden Flat, Rospletha Cliff, Porthcurno, Penzance
TR19 6JS
T: (01736) 810153

The Land's End Vineries ★★
Contact: Mrs Clair Sutton
The Land's End Vineries, Polgigga, St Levan, Penzance
TR19 6LT
T: (01736) 871437
E: vineries@clara.co.uk
I: www.cornwalltouristboard.co.uk

Longships & Tater-Du ★★★★
Contact:
Cornish Cottage Holidays, The Old Turnpike Dairy, Godolphin, Meneage Street, Helston
TR13 8AA
T: (01326) 573808

The Lookout ★★★
Contact: Mrs Barbara Ottway
4 Woodpecker Avenue, Midsomer Norton, Radstock
BA3 4NN
T: (01761) 410185
E: barbara_ottway@tiscali.co.uk

Mercury House
Rating Applied For
Contact: Mr Roy Prouse
Mercury House, Porthcurno, St Levan, Penzance TR19 6JX
T: (01736) 811910
I: www.porthcurno.org.uk

The Piggery
Rating Applied For
Contact: Mr Stephen Walton
The Piggery, Molevenny, Porthcurno, St Levan, Penzance TR19 6LN
T: (01736) 810132
E: swalton@bolitho.biblio.net

Trebehor Cottages ★★★-★★★★
Contact: Mr Richard Jeffery
Trebehor Cottages, Trebehor, St Levan, Penzance TR19 6LX
T: (01736) 871263
F: (01736) 871263
E: rwjeffery@trebehor.fsnet.co.uk
I: www.trebehorcottages.co.uk

Treloggan Cottage
Rating Applied For
Contact: Mr Robert & Mrs Kay George
The Meadows, Treen, St Levan, Penzance TR19 6LQ
T: (01736) 810452
F: (01736) 810116
E: robertandkay@penberth.co.uk
I: www.sennen-cove.com

ST MARTIN
Cornwall

Bodigga ★★★
Contact:
Cornish Cottage Holidays, The Old Turnpike Dairy, Godolphin Road, Helston TR13 8AA
T: (01326) 573808
F: (01326) 564992
E: enquiry@
cornishcottageholidays.co.uk
I: www.cornishcottageholidays.co.uk

SOUTH WEST ENGLAND

The Bull House ★★★★
Contact:
Cornish Cottage Holidays, The Old Turnpike Dairy, Godolphin Road, Helston TR13 8AA
T: (01326) 573808
F: (01326) 564992
E: enquiry@cornishcottageholidays.co.uk
I: www.cornishcottageholidays.co.uk

Mudgeon Vean Farm Holiday Cottages
Rating Applied For
Contact: Mrs Sarah Trewhella
Mudgeon Vean Farm Holiday Cottages, Mudgeon Vean Farm, St Martin, Helston TR12 6DB
T: (01326) 231341
E: mudgeonvean@aol.com
I: www.cornwall-online.co.uk/mudgeon-vean/ctb.htm

Rosuick Farm Cottages
Rating Applied For
Contact: Mrs Jan Oates
Rosuick Farm Cottages, Rosuick Farm, St Martin, Helston TR12 6DZ
T: (01326) 231302
F: (01326) 231302
E: oates@rosuick.co.uk
I: www.rosuick.co.uk

1 School Cottage ★★★★
Contact:
Valley Villas, Office 38, City Business Park, Somerset Place, Stoke, Plymouth PL3 4BB
T: (01752) 605605
E: sales@valleyvillas.com
I: www.valleyvillas.com

Trewoon
Rating Applied For
Contact: Mrs Jan Oates
Rosuick Farm & Country Cottages, Rosuick, St Martin, Helston TR12 6DZ
T: (01326) 231302
F: (01326) 231302
E: oates@rosuick.co.uk

ST MARTIN'S
Isles of Scilly

Carron Farm ★★★
Contact: Mrs Julia Walder
Carron Farm, Higher Town, St Martin's TR25 0QL
T: (01720) 422893
I: www.carronfarm.co.uk

Churchtown Farm ★★★★-★★★★★
Contact: Mrs Julian
Churchtown Farm, Higher Town, St Martin's TR25 0QL
T: (01720) 422169
F: (01720) 422800
E: info@churchtownfarmholidays.co.uk
I: www.churchtownfarmholidays.co.uk

Connemara Farm ★★★
Contact: Mr T Perkins
2 Coastguard Cottage, Higher Town, St Martin's TR25 0QL
T: (01720) 422814
F: (01720) 422814
E: taperkins@btinternet.com

Grans Cottage and The Stable ★★★★
Contact: Mrs D Williams
Grans Cottage and The Stable, Middle Town, St Martin's TR25 0QN
T: (01720) 422810
F: (01720) 422810
E: middletownfarm@tesco.net

Merrion's Holiday cottage ★★★★
Contact: Mrs Valerie Thomas
Merrion's Holiday cottage, 3 Signal Row, Higher Town, St Martin's TR25 0QL
T: (01720) 423418
E: grahamw.thomas@tiscali.co.uk

The Stables ★★★
Contact: Mr John Boyle
Sunset, Salt Cellar Hill, Helston TR13 9DP
T: (01326) 563811
F: (01326) 563811
E: john@sharkbayfilms.demon.co.uk

ST MARY'S
Isles of Scilly

The Aft Cabin ★★★
Contact: Mr Terry & Mrs Elizabeth Parsons
The Aft Cabin, The Cabin, 2 The Bank, St Mary's TR21 0HY
T: (01720) 422393
F: (01720) 422393

Ajax ★★★
Contact:
Island Properties Holiday Lettings & Management, Porthmellon, St Mary's TR21 0JY
T: (01720) 422082
F: (01720) 422211
E: enquiries@islesofscillyholidays.com
I: www.islesofscillyholidays.com

Albany Flats & Thurleigh ★★-★★★
Contact: Mrs Isabel Trenear
Albany Flats & Thurleigh, Church Street, Thurleigh, St Mary's TR21 0JT
T: (01720) 422601

Allwinds ★★★
Contact: Mrs Lewis
Henhurst Farm, Foots Lane, Etchingham TN19 7LE
T: (01435) 883239
E: henhurst@hotmail.com.co.uk

Anchor Cottage ★★★
Contact:
Island Properties Holiday Lettings & Management, Porthmellon, St Mary's TR21 0JY
T: (01720) 422082
F: (01720) 422211
E: enquiries@islesofscillyholidays.com
I: www.islesofscillyholidays.com

1 and 2 Quay House ★★
Contact:
Island Properties Holidays Lettings & Management, Porthmellon, St Mary's TR21 0JY
T: (01720) 422082
F: (01720) 422211
E: enquiries@islesofscillyholidays.com
I: www.islesofscillyholidays.com

Anglesea House ★★★★
Contact:
Island Properties Holiday Lettings & Management, Porhtmellon, St Mary's TR21 0JY
T: (01720) 422082
F: (01720) 422211
E: enquiries@islesofscillyholidays.com
I: www.islesofscillyholidays.com

Ardwyn ★★★★
Contact: Mrs Gill Osborne
The Withies, Trench Lane, Old Town, St Mary's TR21 0PA
T: (01720) 422986

Armorel Cottage ★★★
Contact:
Island Properties Holiday Lettings & Management, Porthmellon, St Mary's TR21 0JY
T: (01720) 422082
F: (01720) 422211
E: enquiries@islesofscillyholidays.com
I: www.islesofscillyholidays.com

Avoca Holiday Homes ★★★★
Contact: Mr Colin & Mrs Elizabeth Ridsdale
Avoca, Hospital Lane, Church Road, St Mary's TR21 0LQ
T: (01720) 422656
I: www.avocaholidayhomes.co.uk

Bar Escapade ★★-★★★
Contact:
Island Properties, Church Street, St Mary's
T: (01720) 422082
F: (01720) 422111
E: enquiries@islesofscillyholidays.com
I: www.islesofscillyholidays.com

The Barn ★★★
Contact:
Island Properties Holiday Lettings & Management, Porthmellon, St Mary's TR21 0JY
T: (01720) 422082
F: (01720) 422211
E: enquiries@islesofscillyholidays.com
I: www.islesofscillyholidays.com

1 Bay View ★★★
Contact: Mr Tony Dingley
Island Properties, Church Street, St Mary's TR21 0PT
T: (01720) 422082
F: (01720) 422211

3 Bay View ★★
Contact:
Island Properties Holiday Lettings & Management, Porthmellon, St Mary's TR21 0JY
T: (01720) 422082
F: (01720) 422211
E: enquiries@islesofscillyholidays.com
I: www.islesofscillyholidays.com

Beach House Flat ★★★
Contact:
Island Properties Holiday Lettings & Management, Porthmellon, St Mary's TR21 0JY
T: (01720) 422082
F: (01720) 422211
E: enquiries@islesofscillyholidays.com
I: www.islesofscillyholidays.com

Beach Mooring Flat 1, Smugglers Ride ★★★★
Contact: Mrs Susan Eccles
Orchard Meadow, Well Lane, Truro TR2 5EG
T: (01872) 580997
E: norman_eccles@barclays.net

Beachside Maisonette Above Co-op ★★
Contact:
Island Properties Holiday Lettings & Management, Porthmellon, St Mary's TR21 0JY
T: (01720) 422082
F: (01720) 422211
E: enquiries@islesofscillyholidays.com
I: www.islesofscillyholidays.com

Beggars Roost ★★
Contact: Mr Kenneth Peay
19 Langley Avenue, Surbiton KT6 6QN
T: (020) 83998364

Bodilly Cottage ★★★
Contact:
Island Properties, Church Street, St Mary's TR21 0JY
T: (01720) 422082
F: (01720) 422211
E: enquiries@islesofscillyholidays.com

Bounty Ledge ★★★
Contact: Mr Jackman
Scillonian Estate Agency, 8 Lower Strand, St Mary's TR21 0PS
T: (01720) 422124

Buzza Ledge ★★★★
Contact: Mr Jeremy Phillips
Rose Cottage, Strand, St Mary's TR21 0PT
T: (01720) 422078
F: (01720) 423588
E: jeremyphillips@rosecottagescilly.freeserve.co.uk

Bylet Holiday Homes ★★★
Contact: Mr Williams
Bylet Holiday Homes, The Bylet, Church Road, St Mary's TR21 0NA
T: (01720) 422479
F: (01720) 422479
E: thebylet@bushinternet.com
I: www.geocities.com/bylet_holidays/

The Captains Cabin ★★★
Contact: Mrs Peggy Rowe
The Captains Cabin, Marine House, Church Street, St Mary's TR21 0JT
T: (01720) 422966
E: peggy@rowe55.freeserve.co.uk

Establishments printed in blue have a detailed entry in this guide

SOUTH WEST ENGLAND

Carnwethers Country House ★★★★
Contact: Mr Roy Harry Graham
Carnwethers Country House,
Pelistry, St Mary's TR21 0NX
T: (01720) 422415

Christmas House ★★★
Contact: Mrs Jane Chiverton
St Mary's TR21 0JE
T: (01720) 422002
E: chivy002@aol.com

Church Hall Cottage ★★★★
Contact: Mr David Townend
Trelawney Guest House, Church Street, St Mary's TR21 0JT
T: (01720) 422377
F: (01720) 422377
E: dtownend@netcomuk.co.uk

Chy Kensa ★★★★
Contact: Mr Dingley
Island Properties, Church Street, Lifton
T: (01720) 422082

Clemys Cottage ★★★
Contact: Miss C Cattran
Cattran & Sons Ltd, 59 Lower Queen Street, Penzance
TR18 4DF
T: (01736) 363493
E: cattran@onetel.net.uk

The Corner House Flat ★★★
Contact:
Island Properties Holiday Lettings & Management,
Porthmellon, St Mary's TR21 0JY
T: (01720) 422082
F: (01720) 422211
E: enquiries@
islesofscillyholidays.com
I: www.isleofscillyholidays.com

Cornerways ★★★★★
Contact: Mr & Mrs Pritchard
Cornerways, Jacksons Hill, St Mary's TR21 0JZ
T: (01720) 422757
F: (01720) 422797

The Crow's Nest ★★★
Contact: Mrs Stella Carter
The Old Bakehouse, Winterborne Road, Abingdon OX14 1AJ
T: (01235) 520317
F: (01235) 527495
E: stella@bakehouse.supanet.com

Dolphins ★★
Contact:
Island Properties Holiday Lettings & Management,
Porthmellon, St Mary's TR21 0JY
T: (01720) 422082
F: (01720) 422211
E: enquiries@
islesofscillyholidays.com
I: www.isleofscillyholidays.com

Dunmallard, Lower Flat ★★★
Contact: Mr & Mrs Elliot
2 Greenhill Mead, Pesters Lane, Somerton TA11 7AB
T: (01458) 272971

Ebor Cottage ★★★
Contact:
Island Properties Holiday Lettings & Management,
Porthmellon, St Mary's TR21 0JY
T: (01720) 422082
F: (01720) 422211
E: enquiries@
islesofscillyholidays.com
I: www.isleofscillyholidays.com

Escallonia ★★★★
Contact: Mrs Susan Quinton
31 Forest Ridge, Keston BR2 6EG
T: (01689) 850216

Fishermans Arms ★★★
Contact: Mrs Walker
Bute Lodge, 182 Petersham Road, Petersham, Richmond
TW10 7AD
T: (020) 8940 9808

The Flat ★★★★
Contact: Mrs Jill May
The Flat, The Sandpiper Shop, Hugh Town, St Mary's TR21 0HY
T: (01720) 422122
F: (01720) 422122

Flat 2 Buccabu ★★
Contact:
Island Properties, Porth Mellon, St Mary's TR21 0JY
T: (01720) 422082
F: (01720) 422221

Flat 2 Madura ★★★
Contact: Mrs Winifred A Davis
Hawkwell Chase, Hockley
SS5 4NH
T: (01702) 203515
E: fredadavis@v21.me.uk

Flat 3 Rosevean ★★★
Contact: Mrs Eileen Talbot
35 Barracks Lane, Macclesfield
SK10 1QJ
T: (01625) 427059
E: eileen@talbot4635.freeserve.co.uk

Flat 4 Kenwyn ★★★
Contact: Mrs Patricia Vian
Fourwinds, Telegraph, St Mary's TR21 0NR
T: (01720) 423100
E: vian@btinternet.com

Flat 6 Spanish Ledge Holiday Flats ★★★
Contact: Mrs Phillips
Guthers Church Road, St Mary's TR21 0NA
T: (01720) 422345

Flats 3 & 4 Pentland ★★★
Contact:
Island Properties Holiday Lettings & Management,
Porthmellon, St Mary's TR21 0JY
T: (01720) 422082
F: (01720) 422211
E: enquiries@
islesofscillyholidays.com
I: www.isleofscillyholidays.com

Garrison Holidays ★★★
Contact: Mr Ted & Mrs Barbara Moulson
Garrison Holidays, The Garrison, St Mary's TR21 0LS
T: (01720) 422670
F: (01720) 422625
E: tedmoulson@aol.com
I: www.isles-of-scilly.co.uk

Glandore Apartments ★★★★
Contact: Mr Stephen Morris
Glandore Apartments, Porthloo, St Mary's TR21 0NE
T: (01720) 422535
E: apartments@glandore.co.uk
I: www.glandore.co.uk

2 Godolphin Flats ★★★★
Contact: Mr Dingley
Island Properties, Church Street, St Mary's TR21 0JY
T: (01720) 422082
F: (01720) 422211
E: enquiries@
islesofscillyholidays.com

6 Godolphin House & 8 Buzza Street ★★★
Contact: Mrs Hogg
92 Brinklow Road, Coventry
CV3 2HY
T: (024) 7645 0455

1 Golden Bay Mansions ★★★
Contact:
Island Properties, Porth Mellon, St Mary's TR21 0JY
T: (01720) 422082
F: (01720) 422221

Greystones ★★
Contact: Mr Tony Dingley
Island Properties, Church Street, St Mary's TR21 0PT
T: (01720) 422082
F: (01720) 422211

Harbour Lights with Smugglers Ride ★★★
Contact: Mr Clifford
22 Trevallion Park, Feock, Truro
TR3 6RS
T: (01872) 863537
F: (01872) 863537
E: tcclif@globalnet.co.uk
I: www.users.globalnet.co.uk/~tcclif/

Haycocks ★★★
Contact:
Island Properties Holiday Lettings & Management,
Porthmellon, St Mary's TR21 0JY
T: (01720) 422082
F: (01720) 422211
E: enquiries@
islesofscillyholidays.com
I: www.isleofscillyholidays.com

The Hideaway ★★★★
Contact: Mr Tim Clifford
22 Trevallion Park, Truro
TR3 6RS
T: (01872) 863537
F: (01872) 863537
E: tcclif@globalnet.co.uk
I: www.selfcateringislesofscilly.co.uk

Hole in the Wall ★★
Contact:
Island Properties, Porth Mellon, St Mary's TR21 0JY
T: (01720) 422082
F: (01720) 422221

Inglenook ★★★
Contact: Mr White
36 Cotland Acres, Redhill
RH1 6JZ
T: (01737) 248890
F: (01737) 242770
E: jon@holidayinglenook.co.uk
I: www.holidayinglenook.co.uk

Katrine ★★★★
Contact: Mrs Patricia Hayden
2 Buzza Street, St Mary's
TR21 0HX
T: (01720) 422178

Kingston House ★★★
Contact:
Island Properties Holiday Lettings & Management,
Porthmellon, St Mary's TR21 0JY
T: (01720) 422082
F: (01720) 422211
E: enquiries@
islesofscillyholidays.com
I: www.isleofscillyholidays.com

Kirklees Holiday Flat ★★★
Contact: Mr & Mrs Coldwell
Kirklees, St Mary's TR21 0JL
T: (01720) 422623

Kistvaen ★★
Contact: Mrs Jane Chiverton
Kistvaen, St Mary's TR21 0JE
T: (01720) 422002
F: (01720) 422002
E: chivy002@aol.com

Lea View ★★★
Contact:
Island Properties Holiday Lettings & Management,
Porthmellon, St Mary's TR21 0JY
T: (01720) 422082
F: (01720) 422211
E: enquiries@
islesofscillyholidays.com
I: www.isleofscillyholidays.com

The Lighthouse ★★★
Contact:
Island Properties Holiday Lettings & Management,
Porthmellon, St Mary's TR21 0JY
T: (01720) 422082
F: (01720) 422211
E: enquiries@
islesofscillyholidays.com
I: www.isleofscillyholidays.com

Lower Ganilly Flat ★★★
Contact:
Island Properties, Church Street, St Mary's TR21 0JY
T: (01720) 422082
F: (01720) 422211
E: enquiries@
islesofscillyholidays.com
I: www.isleofscillyholidays.com

6 Lower Strand ★★★★
Contact: Mrs Susan Richards
Holy Vale, St Mary's TR21 0NT
T: (01720) 422904
F: (01720) 422904

Lunnon Cottage, The Quillet, Medlar ★★★
Contact: Mrs Rogers
Lunnon Cottage, The Quillet, Medlar, Lunnon, St Mary's
TR21 0NZ
T: (01720) 422422
F: (01720) 422422

SOUTH WEST ENGLAND

Madura I ★★★
Contact:
Island Properties Holiday
Lettings & Management,
Porthmellon, St Mary's TR21 0JY
T: (01720) 422082
F: (01720) 422211
E: enquiries@
islesofscillyholidays.com
I: www.islesofscillyholidays.com

Manilla Flats ★★★
Contact: Mrs Frances Grottick
Burgundy House, Rams Valley,
St Mary's TR21 0JX
T: (01720) 422424
F: (01720) 422424

Maypole Farm ★★-★★★
Contact:
Island Properties Holiday
Lettings & Management,
Porthmellon, St Mary's TR21 0JY
T: (01720) 422082
F: (01720) 422211
E: enquiries@
islesofscillyholidays.com
I: www.islesofscillyholidays.com

Mellyns Holiday Home ★★★★
Contact: Jill & Bill Wilson
The Laundry House, Church Way,
Northampton NN6 0QE
T: (01604) 414906
F: (01604) 414906

Minalto Holiday Flats ★★★-★★★★★
Contact: Mr Richard Vaughan
Minalto Holiday Flats, Church
Street, St Mary's TR21 0JT
T: (01720) 423159

Minmow Holiday Flats ★★★
Contact: Mr Simpson
Stoneraise, Old Town, St Mary's
TR21 0NH
T: (01720) 422561

Monaveen
Rating Applied For
Contact:
Island Properties, Porth Mellon,
St Mary's TR21 0JY
T: (01720) 422082
F: (01720) 422221

The Moos ★★★
Contact: Mrs Susan Williams
Polmenor, Pelistry, St Mary's
TR21 0NX
T: (01720) 422605

Morgelyn ★★★
Contact: Mrs Lishman
Morgelyn, Mcfarlands Down, St
Mary's TR21 0NS
T: (01720) 422897
E: info@morgelyn.co.uk
I: www.morgelyn.co.uk

The Mount ★★★★
Contact: Mr Peter Loxton
The Mount, Jerusalem Terrace, St
Mary's TR21 0JH
T: (01720) 422484

Mount Todden Farm ★★★
Contact: Miss Anna Ebert
Mount Todden Farm, St Mary's
TR21 0NY
T: (01720) 422311
E: annaebert@mounttodden.sol.co.uk

4 Myrtle Cottages ★★★
Contact:
Island Properties Holiday
Lettings & Management,
Porthmellon, St Mary's TR21 0JY
T: (01720) 422082
F: (01720) 422211
E: enquiries@
islesofscillyholidays.com
I: www.islesofscillyholidays.com

5 Myrtle Cottages ★★★
Contact:
Island Properties Holiday Letings
& Management, Porthmellont,
St Mary's TR21 0JY
T: (01720) 422082
F: (01720) 422211
E: enquiries@
islesofscillyholidays.com
I: www.islesofscillyholidays.com

Newfort House ★★★★
Contact:
Island Properties Holiday
Lettings & Management,
Porthmellon, St Mary's TR21 0JY
T: (01720) 422082
F: (01720) 422211
E: enquiries@
islesofscillyholidays.com
I: www.islesofscillyholidays.com

No. 3 Godolphin House ★★★
Contact:
Island Properties Holiday
Lettings & Management,
Porthmellon, St Mary's TR21 0JY
T: (01720) 422082
F: (01720) 422211
E: enquiries@
islesofscillyholidays.com
I: www.islesofscillyholidays.com

No 3 Bungalow ★★
Contact: Mrs Sherris
Content Farm, St Mary's
TR21 0NS
T: (01720) 422496

The Old Cottage ★★
Contact: Mrs Lethbridge
The Old Cottage, Garrison Hill, St
Mary's TR21 0HY
T: (01720) 422630

The Palms ★★
Contact: Mrs Lethbridge
The Palms, Maypole, St Mary's
TR21 0NU
T: (01720) 422404

Peacehaven ★★★
Contact: Mr Bennett
Borough Farm, St Mary's TR21
T: (01720) 422326

Pelistry Cottage ★★★
Contact: Mr John & Mrs Brenda
Ashford
Tean, Hugh Street, St Mary's
TR21 0LL
T: (01720) 422059

Pengarriss ★★★
Contact: Mrs A Walker
4 Copse View, Andover SP11 9AT
I: (01264) 772758

Penlee Boathouse ★★
Contact: Mr Rod Tugwell
Penlee Boathouse, Porthcressa
Road, St Mary's TR21 0JL
T: (01720) 423605
E: penleeboathouse_scilly@hotmail.com

Pennlyon ★★★
Contact: Mrs Majorie Feast
Sole Agent, Bryher Cottage,
Whitemoor Lane, Sambourne,
Redditch B96 6NT
T: (01527) 893619

1 Pentland ★★
Contact: Mr Dingley
Island Properties, Church Street,
St Mary's
T: (01720) 422082
F: (01720) 422211
E: enquiries@
islesofscillyholidays.com

Perran ★★★
Contact:
Island Properties Holiday
Lettings & Management, Church
Street, St Mary's TR21 0JY
T: (01720) 422082
F: (01720) 422211
E: enquiries@
islesofscillyholidays.com
I: www.islesofscillyholidays.com

Pharmacy Flat ★★★
Contact: Ms Helen Pearce
Rooftops, Jacksons Hill, St
Mary's TR21 0JZ
T: (01720) 422567

Pilots Gig Flat ★★★★
Contact: Mrs Jay Holliday
Daventry Road, Daventry
NN11 6JH
T: (01327) 871053

Plumb Cottage ★★★★
Contact:
Island Properties Holiday
Lettings & Management,
Porthmellon, St Mary's TR21 0JY
T: (01720) 422082
F: (01720) 422211
E: enquiries@
islesofscillyholidays.com
I: www.islesofscillyholidays.com

2 Porthcressa View ★★★★
Contact: Mrs Diana Peat
Pelorus, Church Road, St Mary's
TR21 0NA
T: (01720) 422376
E: cpeat@aol.com
I: www.scillyonline.
co.uk/accomm/porthview.html

Porthlow Farm ★-★★★
Contact: Mr Richard Woof
Porthlow Farm, St Mary's
TR21 0NF
T: (01720) 422082
F: (01720) 422211
E: enquiries@
islesofscillyholidays.com

Prospect House Flats ★★★★
Contact: Mr Peter & Mrs Nicola
Thompson
Prospect Lodge, Well Lane, St
Mary's TR21 0HZ
T: (01720) 422948

2 Quay House ★★
Contact: Mr Tony Dingley
Island Properties, Porth Mellon,
St Mary's TR21 0JY
T: (01720) 422082
E: enquiries@
islesofscillyholidays.com

The Retreat ★★★
Contact:
Island Properties Holiday
Lettings & Management,
Porthmellon, St Mary's TR21 0JY
T: (01720) 422082
F: (01720) 422211
E: enquiries@
islesofscillyholidays.com
I: www.islesofscillyholidays.com

Rocky Hill Chalets ★★★
Contact: Mrs Edwards
Rocky Hill Chalets, Rocky Hill, St
Mary's TR21 0NE
T: (01720) 422955

1 Rosevean ★★★
Contact: Raymond
1 Cart Lane, Kents Bank Road,
Grange-over-Sands LA11 7EF
T: (015395) 34780
F: (015395) 34780
E: gwyn.raymond@
btopenworld.com

4 Rosevean House ★★★★
Contact: Mr Mark Littleford
Halangy, Mcfarlands Down, St
Mary's TR21 0NS
T: (01720) 423102

The Round House ★★★
Contact:
Island Properties Holiday
Lettings & Management,
Porthmellon, St Mary's TR21 0JY
T: (01720) 422082
F: (01720) 422211
E: enquiries@
islesofscillyholidays.com
I: www.islesofscillyholidays.com

Sailcheck ★★★★
Contact: Miss Liz Hodges
Moor End Farmhouse, London
Road, Hemel Hempstead
HP1 2RE
E: sailcheck7@aol.com

Sallakee Farm ★★★
Contact: Mrs Mumford
Sallakee Farm, St Mary's
TR21 0NZ
T: (01720) 422391

22 Sally Port ★★
Contact:
Island Properties, Porth Mellon,
St Mary's TR21 0JY
T: (01720) 422082
F: (01720) 422221

Sea Spray ★★★
Contact:
Scilly Agency, 22 Trevallion Park,
Truro TR3 6RS

Shamrock ★★★
Contact: Ms Tracey Guy
Shamrock, St Mary's TR21 0NW
T: (01720) 423269

Shipwrights Cottage Maisonettes ★★★★
Contact: Mrs Margaret Lorenz
Rillston, Rams Valley, St Mary's
TR21 0JX
T: (01720) 422522

Establishments printed in blue have a detailed entry in this guide

SOUTH WEST ENGLAND

14 Silver Street ★★★
Contact:
Island Properties Holiday Lettings & Management, Porthmellon, St Mary's TR21 0JY
T: (01720) 422082
F: (01720) 422211
E: enquiries@islesofscillyholidays.com
I: www.islesofscillyholidays.com

12 Silver Street and 1 Porthcressa ★★★★
Contact: Mrs Mills
6 Highclere Drive, Longdean Park, Hemel Hempstead HP3 8BT
T: (01923) 270533
F: (01923) 268080

Smuggler's Den (flat 2) ★★★
Contact: Mrs Stella Carter
The Old Bakehouse, Winterborne Road, Abingdon OX14 1AJ
T: (01235) 520317
E: stella@bakehouse.supanet.com

2 Spanish Ledge ★★★
Contact:
Island Properties, Porthmellon, St Mary's TR21 0JY
T: (01720) 422082
F: (01720) 422211

3 Spanish Ledge ★★★
Contact:
Island Properties, Porthmellon, St Mary's TR21 0JY
T: (01720) 422082
F: (01720) 422211
E: enquiries@islesofscillyholidays.com

4 Spanish Ledge ★★
Contact:
Island Properties, Porthmellon, St Mary's TR21 0JY
T: (01720) 422082
F: (01720) 422211
E: enquiries@islesofscillyholidays.com

5, Spanish Ledge ★★★
Contact:
Island Properties, Porthmellon, St Mary's TR21 0JY
T: (01720) 422082
F: (01720) 422211
E: enquiries@islesofscillyholidays.com

7 Spanish Ledge Holiday Flats ★★★
Contact: Mr Tony Dingley
Island Properties, Church Street, St Mary's TR21 0PT
T: (01720) 422338
F: (01720) 422211

1 Springfield Court ★★★
Contact:
Island Properties, Porthmellon, St Mary's TR21 0JY
T: (01720) 422082
F: (01720) 422211
E: enquiries@islesofscillyholidays.com
I: www.isleofscillyholidays.com

7 Springfield Court ★★★★
Contact:
Island Properties Holiday Lettings & Management, Porthmellon, St Mary's TR21 0JY
T: (01720) 422082
F: (01720) 422211
E: enquiries@islesofscillyholidays.com
I: www.islesofscillyholidays.com

9 Springfield Court ★★★
Contact:
Island Properties Holiday Lettings & Management, Porthmellon, St Mary's TR21 0JY
T: (01720) 422082
F: (01720) 422211
E: enquiries@islesofscillyholidays.com
I: www.islesofscillyholidays.com

Spy Hole ★★
Contact:
Island Properties Holiday Lettings & Management, Porthmellon, St Mary's TR21 0JY
T: (01720) 422082
F: (01720) 422211
E: enquiries@islesofscillyholidays.com
I: www.islesofscillyholidays.com

10 The Strand ★★★★
Contact: Mrs Pamela Murray
The Barn, Westcott, Tremaine, Launceston PL15 8SA
T: (01566) 781270
E: cottage@madnmap.com
I: www.10thestrand.co.uk

Sunny Creek ★★
Contact:
Island Properties Holiday Lettings & Management, Porthmellon, St Mary's TR21 0JY
T: (01720) 422082
F: (01720) 422211
E: enquiries@islesofscillyholidays.com
I: www.islesofscillyholidays.com

Sunnyside Flats ★★-★★★
Contact: Mr Mike Brown
Sunnyside Flats, Rosemary Cottage, St Mary's TR21 0NW
T: (01720) 422903
E: mike@sunnysideflats.com
I: www.sunnysideflats.com

The Tardis ★★★
Contact: Mrs Margaret Helen Williams
The Tardis, c/o Briar Lea, Pelistry, St Mary's TR21 0NX
T: (01720) 422209

Teeki ★★★
Contact:
Island Properties, Church Street, St Mary's
T: (01720) 422211

2 Telegraph Bungalows and Lemon Tree ★★★
Contact: Mrs Mumford
Newford Farm, St Mary's TR21 0NS
T: (01720) 422650

Top Flat ★★★
Contact: Mrs Christine Hosken
Top Flat, Trenoweth Farm, St Mary's TR21 0NS
T: (01720) 422666

Treglesyn ★★★
Contact: Dr Richard Holden
88 Station Road, Ilkley LS29 7NS
T: (01943) 863260
E: rich@storeycroft27.freeserve.co.uk

Tremelethen Farm ★★★
Contact: Mrs Sarah Hale
Tremelethen Farm, St Mary's TR21 0NZ
T: (01720) 422436
F: (01720) 423226

Trevessa ★★★★
Contact: Mrs Browning
Wingletang Guest House, The Parade, St Mary's TR21 0LP
T: (01720) 422381

Upper Flat, Dunmallard ★★★★
Contact: Mr & Mrs Poynter
17 Braybrooke Road, Reading RG10 8DU
T: (0118) 940 3539

Verona ★★★
Contact:
Island Properties Holiday Lettings & Management, Porthmellon, St Mary's TR21 0JY
T: (01720) 422082
F: (01720) 422211
E: enquiries@islesofscillyholidays.com
I: www.islesofscillyholidays.com

Warleggan Holiday Flats ★★★
Contact: Mrs Hiron
Warleggan Holiday Flats, Church Street, St Mary's TR21 0JT
T: (01720) 422563
F: (01720) 422563
I: www.warleggan.com

The White Cottage ★★★
Contact: Mr Tony Dingley
Island Properties, Church Street, St Mary's TR21 0PT
T: (01720) 422082
F: (01720) 422211

Wisteria & Jasmine Cottages ★★★★
Contact: Claire Oyler
2 Hamewith, The Parade, St Mary's TR21 0LP
T: (01720) 422111

1 Wras ★★
Contact:
Island Properties Holiday Lettings & Management, Porthmellon, St Mary's TR21 0JY
T: (01720) 422082
F: (01720) 422211
E: enquiries@islesofscillyholidays.com
I: www.islesofscillyholidays.com

3 Wras ★★★
Contact: Mr Tony Dingley
Island Properties, Church Street, St Mary's TR21 0PT
T: (01720) 422082
F: (01720) 422211

ST MARYCHURCH
Torbay

Little Grange ★★★
Contact: Mr Edward & Mrs Jenifer Webber
Grange Cottage, Babbacombe Downs Road, Torquay TQ1 3LP
T: (01803) 313809
E: littlegrange@bushinternet.com

Ludwell House ★★-★★★★
Contact: Ms Karen Clark
Ludwell House, Cary Park, Torquay TQ1 3NH
T: (01803) 326032
F: (01803) 326032
E: sue.clark@ukonline.co.uk

ST MAWES
Cornwall

The Boathouse
Rating Applied For
Contact:
Roseland Holiday Cottages, Crab Apple Cottage, Truro TR2 5ET
T: (01872) 580480
F: (01872) 580480
E: enquiries@roselandholidaycottages.co.uk
I: www.roselandholidaycottages.co.uk

Captains Cottage ★★
Contact:
Roseland Holiday Cottages, Crab Apple Cottage, Truro TR2 5ET
T: (01872) 580480
F: (01872) 580480
E: enquiries@roselandholidaycottages.co.uk
I: www.roselandholidaycottages.co.uk

Chy Ryn ★★★
Contact: Mrs Margie Lumby
Special Places in Cornwall, Poachers Reach, Harcourt, Truro TR3 6SQ
T: (01872) 864400
E: office@specialplacescornwall.co.uk
I: www.specialplacescornwall.co.uk

Coppers & Peel Cottage ★★★★
Contact: Mrs Margie Lumby
Special Places in Cornwall, Poachers Reach, Harcourt, Truro TR3 6SQ
T: (01872) 864400
E: office@specialplacescornwall.co.uk
I: www.specialplacescornwall.co.uk

Dolphins ★★★
Contact: Mrs Margie Lumby
Special Places in Cornwall, Poachers Reach, Harcourt, Truro TR3 6SQ
T: (01872) 864400
E: office@specialplacescornwall.co.uk
I: www.specialplacescornwall.co.uk

Look out for establishments participating in the National Accessible Scheme

SOUTH WEST ENGLAND

The Gingerbread House
★★★★
Contact: Mrs Margie Lumby
Special Places in Cornwall,
Poachers Reach, Harcourt, Truro
TR3 6SQ
T: (01872) 864400
E: office@
specialplacescornwall.co.uk
I: www.specialplacescornwall.
co.uk

Gull Cottage
Rating Applied For
Contact:
Gull Cottage, Pedn-Moran, St
Mawes, Truro TR2 5BA
T: (01872) 580480
F: (01872) 580480
E: enquiries@
roselandholidaycottages.co.uk
I: www.roselandholidaycottages.
co.uk

Hillside Cottage
Rating Applied For
Contact:
Roseland Holiday Cottages, Crab
Apple Cottage, Truro TR2 5ET
T: (01872) 580480
F: (01872) 580480
E: enquiries@
roselandholidaycottages.co.uk
I: www.roselandholidaycottages.
co.uk

Manor Cottage ★★★
Contact:
Manor Cottage, 1 Kings Road, St
Mawes, Truro TR2 5DH
T: (01872) 580480
F: (01872) 580480
E: enquiries@
roselandholidaycottages.co.uk
I: www.roselandholidaycottages.
co.uk

5 Manor Court
Rating Applied For
Contact:
Roseland Holiday Cottages, Crab
Apple Cottage, Truro TR2 5ET
T: (01872) 580480
F: (01872) 580480
E: enquiries@
roselandholidaycottages.co.uk
I: www.roselandholidaycottages.
co.uk

Mariners ★★★★
Contact: Ms Margie Lumby
Special Places in Cornwall,
Poachers Reach, Harcourt, Truro
TR3 6SQ
T: (01872) 864400
E: office@
specialplacescornwall.co.uk
I: www.specialplacescornwall.
co.uk

The Old Dairy
Rating Applied For
Contact:
The Old Dairy, Newton Farm,
Newton Road, St Mawes, Truro
TR2 5BS
T: (01872) 580480
F: (01870) 580480
E: enquiries@
roselandholidaycottages.co.uk
I: www.roselandholidaycottages.
co.uk

Oyster Haven & Prydes
★★★★-★★★★★
Contact: Mrs Margie Lumby
Special Places in Cornwall,
Poachers Reach, Harcourt, Truro
TR3 6SQ
T: (01872) 864400
E: office@
specialplacescornwall.co.uk
I: www.specialplacescornwall.
co.uk

Penlee ★★★★
Contact: Mrs Margie Lumby
Special Places in Cornwall,
Poachers Reach, Harcourt, Truro
TR3 6SQ
T: (01872) 864400
E: office@
specialplacescornwall.co.uk
I: www.specialplacescornwall.
co.uk

Pier Cottage ★★★★
Contact:
Holiday Homes & Cottages SW,
365A Torquay Road, Paignton
TQ3 2BT
T: (01803) 663650
F: (01803) 664037
E: holcotts@aol.com
I: www.swcottages.co.uk

Rocklee House ★★★★
Contact: Mrs Margie Lumby
Special Places in Cornwall,
Poachers Reach, Harcourt, Truro
TR3 6SQ
T: (01872) 864400
F: (01872) 864400
E: office@
specialplacescornwall.co.uk
I: www.specialplacescornwall.
co.uk

Sail Cottage
Rating Applied For
Contact:
Roseland Holiday Cottages, Crab
Apple Cottage, Truro TR2 5ET
T: (01872) 580480
F: (01872) 580480
E: enquiries@
roselandholidaycottages.co.uk
I: www.roselandholidaycottages.
co.uk

Seagulls
Rating Applied For
Contact:
Roseland Holiday Cottages, Crab
Apple Cottage, Truro TR2 5ET
T: (01872) 580480
F: (01872) 580480
I: Roselandholidaycottages.co.uk

Seaward ★★★★
Contact: Mrs Margie Lumby
Special Places in Cornwall,
Poachers Reach, Harcourt, Truro
TR3 6SQ
T: (01872) 864400
E: office@
specialplacescornwall.co.uk
I: www.specialplacescornwall.
co.uk

September Cottage
Rating Applied For
Contact: Mrs Leonie Iddison
Roseland Holiday Cottages, Crab
Apple Cottage, Truro TR2 5ET
T: (01872) 580480
F: (01872) 580480
E: enquiries@
roselandholidaycottages.co.uk
I: Roselandholidaycottages.co.uk

Skippers
Rating Applied For
Contact:
Roseland Holiday Cottages, Crab
Apple Cottage, Truro TR2 5ET
T: (01872) 580480
F: (01872) 580480
E: enquiries@
roselandholidaycottages.co.uk
I: www.roselandholidaycottages.
co.uk

Starboard ★★★
Contact: Mrs Margie Lumby
Special Places In Cornwall,
Poachers Reach, Harcourt, Truro
TR3 6SQ
T: (01872) 864400
E: office@
specialplacescornwall.co.uk
I: www.specialplacescornwall.
co.uk

Sunnybanks ★★★★
Contact: Mrs Margie Lumby
Special Places In Cornwall,
Poachers Reach, Harcourt, Truro
TR3 6SQ
T: (01872) 864400
E: office@
specialplacescornwall.co.uk
I: www.specialplacescornwall.
co.uk

Sycamore
Rating Applied For
Contact:
Roseland Holiday Cottages, Crab
Apple Cottage, Truro TR2 5ET
T: (01872) 580480
F: (01872) 580480
E: enquiries@
roselandholidaycottages.co.uk
I: www.roselandholidaycottages.
co.uk

Tom Thumb Cottage
Rating Applied For
Contact:
Roseland Holiday Cottages, Crab
Apple Cottage, Truro TR2 5ET
T: (01872) 580480
F: (01872) 580480
I: www.roselandholidaycottages.
co.uk

Topdeck ★★★★
Contact: Mrs Margie Lumby
Special Places In Cornwall,
Poachers Reach, Harcourt, Truro
TR3 6SQ
T: (01872) 864400
E: office@
specialplacescornwall.co.uk
I: www.specialplacescornwall.
co.uk

2 Tregarth Cottages
Rating Applied For
Contact:
Roseland Holiday Cottages, Crab
Apple Cottage, Truro TR2 5ET
T: (01872) 580480
F: (01872) 580480
E: enquiries@
roselandholidaycottages.co.uk
I: www.roselandholidaycottages.
co.uk

3 Tregarth Cottages
Rating Applied For
Contact:
Roseland Holiday Cottages, Crab
Apple Cottage, Truro TR2 5ET
T: (01872) 580480
F: (01872) 580480
E: enquiries@
roselandholidaycottages.co.uk
I: www.roselandholidaycottages.
co.uk

Up a Loft
Rating Applied For
Contact:
Roseland Holiday Cottages, Crab
Apple Cottage, Truro TR2 5ET
T: (01872) 580480
F: (01872) 580480
E: enquiries@
roselandholidaycottages.co.uk
I: www.roselandholidaycottages.
co.uk

Uplands
Rating Applied For
Contact:
Roseland Holiday Cottages, Crab
Apple Cottage, Truro TR2 5ET
T: (01872) 580480
F: (01872) 580480
E: enquiries@
roselandholidaycottages.co.uk
I: www.roselandholidaycottages.
co.uk

White Lodge ★★★★
Contact:
Special Places, Poachers Reach,
Truro TR3 6SQ
T: (01872) 864400
F: (01872) 864400
E: office@
specialplacescornwall.co.uk
I: www.specialplacescornwall.
co.uk

Woodhambury House
Rating Applied For
Contact:
Roseland Holiday Cottages, Crab
Apple Cottage, Truro TR2 5ET
T: (01872) 580480
F: (01872) 580480
E: enquiries@
roselandholidaycottages.co.uk
I: www.roselandholidaycottages.
co.uk

The Workshop ★★★★
Contact: Mrs Margie Lumby
Special Places in Cornwall,
Poachers Reach, Harcourt, Truro
TR3 6SQ
T: (01872) 864400
E: office@
specialplacescornwall.co.uk
I: www.specialplacescornwall.
co.uk

SOUTH WEST ENGLAND

ST MAWGAN
Cornwall

Polgreen Manor ★★
Contact: Mrs Judith Ann Wake, NDD
Polgreen Manor, St Mawgan, Newquay TR8 4AG
T: (01637) 860700
F: (01637) 875165

ST MERRYN
Cornwall

Chalet 83 ★★
Contact: Miss Elizabeth Kerry
Church Cottage, Church Street, Swindon SN4 0NJ
T: (01793) 740284

Chyloweth ★★★
Contact: Mr Roger & Mrs Sally Vivian
Chyloweth, Padstow PL28 8JQ
T: (01841) 521012
E: roger.vivian@ukgateway.net
I: www.padstowlive.com

Curlew
Rating Applied For
Contact: Mr Peter Osbourne
Cornish Horizons, The Cottage, 19 New Street, Padstow PL28 8EA
T: (01841) 533331
F: (01841) 533933

Little Lancarrow ★★★
Contact:
Cornish Horizons, The Cottage, 19 New Street, Padstow PL28 8EA
T: (01841) 533331
F: (01841) 533933
E: cottages@cornishhorizons.co.uk
I: www.cornishhorizons.co.uk

Lower Trevorgus
Rating Applied For
Contact:
Harbour Holidays Ltd, 1 North Quay, Padstow PL28 8AF
T: (01841) 533402
F: (01841) 535115
I: www.harbourholidays.co.uk

Lower Trevorgus ★★★★
Contact:
Cornish Horizons, The Cottage, 19 New Street, Padstow PL28 8EA
T: (01841) 533331
F: (01841) 533933
E: cottages@cornishhorizons.co.uk
I: www.cornishhorizons.co.uk

132 Point Curlew ★★★
Contact: Mr Tony Allen
2 Church Cottage, Wadebridge PL27 7QT
T: (01841) 540871

Rozmerrow ★★★★
Contact:
Cornish Horizons, The Cottage, 19 New Street, Padstow PL28 8EA
T: (01841) 533331
F: (01841) 533933
E: cottages@cornishhorizons.co.uk

St Hilary ★★★
Contact:
Cornish Horizons, The Cottage, 19 New Street, Padstow PL28 8EA
T: (01841) 533331
F: (01841) 533933
E: cottages@cornishhorizons.co.uk
I: www.cornishhorizons.co.uk

Spindrift ★★
Contact:
Cornish Horizons, The Cottage, 19 New Street, Padstow PL28 8EA
T: (01841) 533331
F: (01841) 533933
E: cottages@cornishhorizons.co.uk
I: www.cornishhorizons.co.uk

Trearth ★★★★
Contact:
Cornish Horizons, The Cottage, 19 New Street, Padstow PL28 8EA
T: (01841) 533331
F: (01841) 533933
E: cottages@cornishhorizons.co.uk
I: www.trearth.com

Tregerrick
Rating Applied For
Contact: Mr Andy Stefanczyk
80 Westbrook End, Milton Keynes MK17 0DF
T: (01908) 374451

Trevose Lodge, 24 Trescore ★★★★
Contact: Miss Claudine Fontier
8 Treburgie Water, Liskeard PL14 4NB
T: 0783 7 571945
E: claudinefontier@hotmail.com

Twizzletwig ★★★
Contact:
Cornish Horizons, The Cottage, 19 New Street, Padstow PL28 8EA
T: (01841) 533331
F: (01841) 533933
E: cottages@cornishhorizons.co.uk
I: www.cornishhorizons.co.uk

Two Stiles ★★★★
Contact:
Cornish Horizons, The Cottage, 19 New Street, Padstow PL28 8EA
T: (01841) 533331
F: (01841) 533933
E: cottages@cornishhorizons.co.uk

Yellow Sands Cottages ★★★-★★★★
Contact: Mrs Sharron Keast
Yellow Sands Cottages, Harlyn Bay, Padstow PL28 8SE
T: (01637) 881548
E: yellowsands@btinternet.com
I: www.yellowsands.co.uk

ST MINVER
Cornwall

April Cottage ★★★★★
Contact:
Rock Holidays inc. Harbour Holidays Rock Ltd., Trebetherick House, Wadebridge PL27 6SB
T: (01208) 863399
F: (01208) 862218
E: rockhols@aol.com
I: www.rockholidays.co.uk

The Bothy ★★★★
Contact:
Rock Holidays inc. Harbour Holidays Rock Ltd., Trebetherick House, Wadebridge PL27 6SB
T: (01208) 863399
F: (01208) 862218
E: rockhols@aol.com
I: www.rockholidays.co.uk

Brook House ★★★★
Contact:
Rock Holidays inc. Harbour Holidays Rock Ltd., Trebetherick House, Wadebridge PL27 6SB
T: (01208) 863399
F: (01208) 862218
E: rockhols@aol.com
I: www.rockholidays.co.uk

Bunkers Cottage ★★★★
Contact:
Rock Holidays inc. Harbour Holidays Roack Ltd., Trebetherick House, Wadebridge PL27 6SB
T: (01208) 863399
F: (01208) 862218
E: rockhols@aol.com
I: www.rockholidays.co.uk

Caldarvan ★★★★
Contact:
Rock Holidays inc. Harbour Holidays Rock Ltd., Trebetherick House, Wadebridge PL27 6SB
T: (01208) 863399
F: (01208) 862218
E: rockhols@aol.com
I: www.rockholidays.co.uk

Casa Piedra Cottage ★★★★
Contact:
Rock Holidays inc. Harbour Holidays Rock Ltd., Trebetherick House, Wadebridge PL27 6SB
T: (01208) 863399
F: (01208) 862218
E: rockhols@aol.com
I: www.rockholidays.co.uk

Chy Petroc ★★★★
Contact:
Rock Holidays inc. Harbour Holidays Rock Ltd., Trebetherick House, Wadebridge PL27 6SB
T: (01208) 863399
F: (01208) 862218
E: rockhols@aol.com
I: www.rockholidays.co.uk

Cobwebs ★★★★
Contact:
Harbour Holidays - Rock, Trebetherick House, Wadebridge PL27 6SB
T: (01208) 863399
F: (01208) 862218
I: www.rockholidays.co.uk

Cowrie ★★★★
Contact:
Rock Holidays inc. Harbour Holidays Rock Ltd., Trebetherick House, Wadebridge PL27 6SB
T: (01208) 863399
F: (01208) 862218
E: rockhols@aol.com
I: www.rockholidays.co.uk

The Farmhouse Roserrow ★★★★
Contact:
Rock Holidays inc. Harbour Holidays Rock Ltd., Trebetherick House, Wadebridge PL27 6SB
T: (01208) 863399
F: (01208) 862218
E: rockhols@aol.com
I: www.rockholidays.co.uk

Gearys ★★★★
Contact:
Rock Holidays inc Harbour Holidays Rock Ltd., Trebetherick House, Wadebridge PL27 6SB
T: (01208) 863399
F: (01208) 862218
E: rockhols@aol.com
I: www.rockholidays.co.uk

Gore's Garisson ★★★★★
Contact:
Rock Holidays inc. Harbour Holidays Rock Ltd., Trebetherick House, Wadebridge PL27 6SB
T: (01208) 863399
F: (01208) 862218
E: rockhols@aol.com
I: www.rockholidays.co.uk

Gwella ★★★★
Contact:
Rock Holidays inc. Harbour Holidays Rock Ltd., Trebetherick House, Wadebridge PL27 6SB
T: (01208) 863399
F: (01208) 862218
E: rockhols@aol.com
I: www.rockholidays.co.uk

The Haven ★★★★★
Contact:
Rock Holidays inc. Harbour Holidays Rock Ltd., Trebetherick House, Wadebridge PL27 6SB
T: (01208) 863399
F: (01208) 862218
E: rockhols@aol.com
I: www.rockholidays.co.uk

The Hawthorns ★★★★
Contact:
Rock Holidays inc. Harbour Holidays Rock Ltd., Trebetherick House, Wadebridge PL27 6SB
T: (01208) 863399
F: (01208) 862218
E: rockhols@aol.com
I: www.rockholidays.co.uk

Idle Rocks ★★★★
Contact:
Rock Holidays inc. Harbour Holidays Rock Ltd., Trebetherick House, Wadebridge PL27 6SB
T: (01208) 863399
F: (01208) 862218
E: rockhols@aol.com
I: www.rockholidays.co.uk

SOUTH WEST ENGLAND

Janners Retreat ★★★★
Contact:
Rock Holidays inc. Harbour Holidays Rock Ltd., Trebetherick House, Wadebridge PL27 6SB
T: (01208) 863399
F: (01208) 862218
E: rockhols@aol.com
I: www.rockholidays.co.uk

Keepers ★★★★
Contact:
Rock Holidays inc. Harbour Holidays Rock Ltd., Trebetherick House, Wadebridge PL27 6SB
T: (01208) 863399
F: (01208) 862218
E: rockhols@aol.com
I: www.rockholidays.co.uk

Lundy Cottage ★★★★
Contact:
Rock Holidays inc. Harbour Holidays Rock Ltd., Trebetherick House, Wadebridge PL27 6SB
T: (01208) 863399
F: (01208) 862218
E: rockhols@aol.com
I: www.rockholidays.co.uk

Mayfield ★★★★
Contact:
Rock Holidays inc. Harbour Holidays Rock Ltd., Trebetherick House, Wadebridge PL27 6SB
T: (01208) 863399
F: (01208) 862218
E: rockhols@aol.com
I: www.rockholidays.co.uk

The Millhouse ★★★
Contact:
Rock Holidays inc. Harbour Holidays Rock Ltd., Trebetherick House, Wadebridge PL27 6SB
T: (01208) 863399
F: (01208) 862218
E: rockhols@aol.com
I: www.rockholidays.co.uk

The Millhouse Barn ★★★★
Contact:
Rock Holidays inc. Harbour Holidays Rock Ltd., Trebetherick House, Wadebridge PL27 6SB
T: (01208) 863399
F: (01208) 862218
E: rockhols@aol.com
I: www.rockholidays.co.uk

Mosseyoak ★★★★
Contact:
Rock Holidays inc. Harbour Holidays Rock Ltd., Trebetherick House, Wadebridge PL27 6SB
T: (01208) 863399
F: (01208) 862218
E: rockhols@aol.com
I: www.rockholidays.co.uk

The Nineteenth ★★★★
Contact:
Rock Holidays inc. Harbour Holidays Rock Ltd., Trebetherick House, Wadebridge PL27 6SB
T: (01208) 863399
F: (01208) 862218
E: rockhols@aol.com
I: www.rockholidays.co.uk

Numbers 3 & 4 Trevanger Cottages ★-★★★
Contact: Mrs Lisa Marsh
15 Woodside Avenue, Chislehurst BR7 6BX
T: (020) 82952901
E: lisamarsh@supanet.com

Oak Tree House ★★★★
Contact:
Rock Holidays inc. Harbour Holidays Rock Ltd., Trebetherick House, Wadebridge PL27 6SB
T: (01208) 863399
F: (01208) 862218
E: rockhols@aol.com
I: www.rockholidays.co.uk

2 The Old Dairy ★★★★
Contact:
Rock Holidays inc. Harbour Holidays Rock Ltd., Trebetherick House, Wadebridge PL27 6SB
T: (01208) 863399
F: (01208) 862218
E: rockhols@aol.com
I: www.rockholidays.co.uk

Pearl Springs ★★★
Contact: The Agent Blakes Country Cottages
Springmill, Earby, Saundersfoot BB94 0AA
T: 0870 0 708090
F: (01282) 841539

Pendragon Cottage ★★★
Contact: Mrs T J Smith
2 Sunnybank, Shilla Mill Lane, Wadebridge PL27 6SS
T: (01208) 863172
E: tesspete@tiscali.co.uk
I: www.polzeathcottages.com/pendragon.html

Penhayle ★★★★
Contact:
Rock Holidays inc. Harbour Holidays Rock Ltd., Trebetherick House, Wadebridge PL27 6SB
T: (01208) 863399
F: (01208) 862218
E: rockhols@aol.com
I: www.rockholidays.co.uk

Penkivel House ★★★★
Contact:
Rock Holidays inc. Harbour Holidays Rock Ltd., Trebetherick House, Wadebridge PL27 6SB
T: (01208) 863399
F: (01208) 862218
E: rockhols@aol.com
I: www.rockholidays.co.uk

Penteli ★★★★
Contact:
Rock Holidays inc. Harbour Holidays Rock Ltd., Trebetherick House, Wadebridge PL27 6SB
T: (01208) 863399
F: (01208) 862218
E: rockhols@aol.com
I: www.rockholidays.co.uk

Puffin House ★★★
Contact:
Rock Holidays inc. Harbour Holidays Rock Ltd., Trebetherick House, Wadebridge PL27 6SB
T: (01208) 863399
F: (01208) 862218
E: rockhols@aol.com
I: www.rockholidays.co.uk

Ridgewood ★★★★
Contact:
Rock Holidays inc. Harbour Holidays Rock Ltd., Trebetherick House, Wadebridge PL27 6SB
T: (01208) 863399
F: (01208) 862218
E: rockhols@aol.com
I: www.rockholidays.co.uk

Rosewin Barn ★★★
Contact:
Rock Holidays inc. Harbour Holidays Rock Ltd., Trebetherick House, Wadebridge PL27 6SB
T: (01208) 863399
F: (01208) 862218
E: rockhols@aol.com
I: www.rockholidays.co.uk

Rosewin Farmhouse ★★★★
Contact:
Rock Holidays inc. Harbour Holidays Ltd., Trebetherick House, Wadebridge PL27 6SB
T: (01208) 863399
F: (01208) 862218
E: rockhols@aol.com
I: www.rockholidays.co.uk

Ryth Hogh ★★★
Contact:
Rock Holidays inc. Harbour Holidays Rock Ltd., Trebetherick House, Wadebridge PL27 6SB
T: (01208) 863399
F: (01208) 862218
E: rockhols@aol.com
I: www.rockholidays.co.uk

St Andrew's Cottage ★★★★
Contact:
Rock Holidays inc. Harbour Holidays Rock Ltd., Trebetherick House, Wadebridge PL27 6SB
T: (01208) 863399
F: (01208) 862218
E: rockhols@aol.com
I: www.rockholidays.co.uk

Sandy Cottage ★★★★
Contact:
Rock Holidays inc. Harbour Holidays Rock Ltd., Trebetherick House, Wadebridge PL27 6SB
T: (01208) 863399
F: (01208) 862218
E: rockhols@aol.com
I: www.rockholidays.co.uk

September ★★★★
Contact:
Rock Holidays inc. Harbour Holidays Rock Ltd., Trebetherick House, Wadebridge PL27 6SB
T: (01208) 863399
F: (01208) 862218
E: rockhols@aol.com
I: www.rockholidays.co.uk

Streth Tu ★★★★★
Contact:
Rock Holidays inc. Harbour Holidays Rock Ltd., Trebetherickhouse, Wadebridge PL27 6SB
T: (01208) 863399
F: (01208) 862218
E: rockhols@aol.com
I: www.rockholidays.co.uk

Talamore ★★★★
Contact:
Rock Holidays inc. Harbour Holidays Rock Ltd., Trebetherick House, Wadebridge PL27 6SB
T: (01208) 863399
F: (01208) 862218
E: rockhols@aol.com
I: www.rockholidays.co.uk

Tamarisk ★★★★
Contact:
Rock Holidays inc. Harbour Holidays Rock Ltd., Trebetherick House, Wadebridge PL27 6SB
T: (01208) 863399
F: (01208) 862218
E: rockhols@aol.com
I: www.rockholidays.co.uk

The Taphouse ★★★★★
Contact:
Rock Holidays inc. Harbour Holidays Rock Ltd., Trebetherick House, Wadebridge PL27 6SB
T: (01208) 863399
F: (01208) 862218
E: rockhols@aol.com
I: www.rockholidays.co.uk

Thyme Cottage ★★★★
Contact:
Harbour Holidays Rock Ltd, Trebetherick House, Wadebridge PL27 6SB
T: (01208) 863399
F: (01208) 862218
E: rockhols@aol.com

Tremaine ★★★★★
Contact:
Rock Holidays inc. Harbour Holidays Rock Ltd., Trebetherick House, Wadebridge PL27 6SB
T: (01208) 863399
F: (01208) 862218
E: rockhols@aol.com
I: www.rockholidays.co.uk

Trevelver Farm Cottage ★★★
Contact: Mrs Avice Wills
Trevelver Farm Cottage, St Minver, Wadebridge PL27 6RJ
T: (01208) 863290

Trewint Farm ★★
Contact: Mrs Sarah Brewer
Pentire View and Trewint Farm Holiday Homes, Wadebridge PL27 7RL
T: (01208) 816595

Webbs Retreat ★★★★
Contact:
Rock Holidays inc. Harbour Holidays Rock Ltd., Trebetherick House, Wadebridge PL27 6SB
T: (01208) 863399
F: (01208) 862218
E: rockhols@aol.com
I: www.rockholidays.co.uk

Wedge Cottage ★★★
Contact:
Rock Holidays inc. Harbour Holidays Rock Ltd., Trebetherick House, Wadebridge PL27 6SB
T: (01208) 863399
F: (01208) 862218
E: rockhols@aol.com
I: www.rockholidays.co.uk

SOUTH WEST ENGLAND

Wenlock ★★★★
Contact:
Rock Holidays inc. Harbour Holidays Rock Ltd., Trebetherick House, Wadebridge PL27 6SB
T: (01208) 863399
F: (01208) 862218
E: rockhols@aol.com
I: www.rockholidays.co.uk

Woodbine House ★★★★★
Contact:
Harbour Holidays, Rock Ltd, Trebetherick House, Wadebridge PL27 6SB
T: (01208) 863399
F: (01208) 862218
E: rockhols@aol.com

Woodfin
Rating Applied For
Contact: Mrs Janet Edwards
Oak & Elm Cottage, Brook Lane, Guildford GU5 9DH
T: (01483) 202478

ST NEWLYN EAST
Cornwall

Chy an Melynwyns ★★★
Contact:
Cornish Horizons, The Cottage, 19 New Street, Padstow PL28 8EA
T: (01841) 533331
F: (01841) 533933

Degembris Cottage ★★★★
Contact: Mrs Kathy Woodley
Degembris Cottage, St Newlyn East, Newquay TR8 5HY
T: (01872) 510555
F: (01872) 510230
E: kathy@degembris.co.uk
I: www.degembris.co.uk

Penty Gwyn ★★★
Contact:
Powell's Cottage Holidays, High Street, Saundersfoot SA69 9EJ
T: (01834) 812791
F: (01834) 811731
E: info@powells.co.uk
I: www.powells.co.uk

ST STEPHEN
Cornwall

Court Farm Cottages ★★★★
Contact: Mr Bill Truscott
Court Farm Cottages, St Stephen, St Austell PL26 7LE
T: (01726) 823684
F: (01726) 823684
E: truscott@ctfarm.freeserve.co.uk
I: www.courtfarmcornwall.co.uk

ST TEATH
Cornwall

Barn Farm Holidays ★★★★
Contact: Mrs Valerie Goldie
Barn Farm Holidays, Trewennen Road, St Teath, Bodmin PL30 3JZ
T: (01208) 850912

Dinnabroad Cottage ★★★★
Contact:
Farm & Cottage Holidays, Victoria House, 24 Fore Street, Bideford EX39 1AW
T: (01237) 479146
F: (01237) 421512
E: bookings@farmcott.co.uk
I: www.farmcott.co.uk

Higher Hendra Cottages ★★★★
Contact: Mrs Roose
Higher Hendra Cottages, Higher Hendra, Bodmin PL30 3LP
T: (01208) 880341

Mill Barn & Stable Cottage
Rating Applied For
Contact: Mrs Julie Bailey
Mill Barn & Stable Cottage, Treveighan, St Teath, Bodmin PL30 3JN
T: (01208) 850994
E: Juliebaileycornw@aol.com
I: www.tredarrup.com

ST TUDY
Cornwall

The Linhay ★★★★★
Contact: Mrs C. Mavis Kingdon
The Linhay, The Oaks Barn, Redvale Road, Bodmin PL30 3PU
T: (01208) 851422

SALCOMBE
Devon

Coxswain's Watch ★★★
Contact: Mr A Oulsnam
Robert Oulsnam & Co, 79 Hewell Road, Barnt Green, Birmingham B45 8NL
T: (0121) 445 3311
F: (0121) 445 6026
E: barntgreen@oulsnam.net
I: www.oulsnam.net

Longridge ★★★★
Contact: Mr Curry
Meriden Cottage, Sherborne DT9 5PH
T: (01963) 210622
F: (01963) 210622
E: curryb@btinternet.com

SALISBURY
Wiltshire

The Bridge House Annex ★★★★
Contact: Mr John & Mrs Jane Waddington
10 Shady Bower, Salisbury SP1 2RG
T: (01722) 324731
F: (01722) 339983
E: medieval.hall@ntlworld.com

Charter Court ★★★★
Contact: Mr Nicholas Pash
Hideaways, Chapel House, Luke Street, Berwick St John, Shaftesbury SP7 0HQ
T: (01747) 828170
F: (01747) 829090
E: enq@hideaways.co.uk
I: www.hideaways.co.uk

12 Charter Court ★★★★
Contact: Mrs Moore
28 Riverside Close, Salisbury SP1 1QW
T: (01722) 320188
E: charterho@hotmail.com

80 Exeter Street ★★★
Contact: Mr Ashley & Mrs Sandra Browning
3 Nightingale Close, Romsey SO51 6BZ
T: (01794) 322766

4TEEN
Rating Applied For
Contact: Mrs Mary Webb
11 Hartington Road, Salisbury SP2 7LG
T: (01722) 340892
F: (01722) 421903
E: enquiries@4teen.biz
I: www.4teen.biz

Fowlers Road ★★★
Contact: Mr Nicholas Pash
Hideaways, Chapel House, Luke Street, Berwick St John, Shaftesbury SP7 0HQ
T: (01747) 828170
F: (01747) 829090
E: enq@hideaways.co.uk
I: www.hideaways.co.uk

Fowlers Road ★★★
Contact: Mr Nicholas Pash
Hideaways, Chapel House, Luke Street, Berwick St John, Shaftesbury SP7 0HQ
T: (01747) 828170
F: (01747) 829090
E: enq@hideaways.co.uk
I: www.hideaways.co.uk

Garden Flat, Ramsey House ★★★★
Contact: Vivien Brown
Ramsey House, 34 Fowlers Road, Salisbury SP1 2QU
T: (01722) 327166 & 07960 993746
E: ramseyhouse@hotmail.com

Hen View (The Fishing Lodge) ★★★★
Contact: Mrs Victoria Dakin
Church Farmhouse, Shaftesbury SP7 0EA
T: (01747) 855976
E: vdakin@skymarket.org

Love Lane ★★★
Contact: Mr Nicholas Pash
Hideaways, Chapel House, Luke Street, Berwick St John, Shaftesbury SP7 0HQ
T: (01747) 828170
F: (01747) 829090
E: enq@hideaways.co.uk
I: www.hideaways.co.uk

Manor Farm Cottages ★★★★
Contact: Ms Gillie Strang
Manor Farm Cottages, Manor Farm, Sutton Mandeville, Salisbury SP3 5NL
T: (01722) 714226
F: (01722) 714507
E: strangf@aol.com
I: www.strangcottages.com

The Old Stables ★★★★
Contact: Mr Giles Gould
The Old Stables, Bridge Farm, Lower Road, Salisbury SP5 4DY
T: (01722) 349002
F: (01722) 349003
E: mail@old-stables.co.uk
I: www.old-stables.co.uk

Rojoy ★★★
Contact: Mr Nicholas Pash
Hideaways, Chapel House, Luke Street, Berwick St John, Shaftesbury SP7 0HQ
T: (01747) 828170
F: (01747) 829090
E: enq@hideaways.co.uk
I: www.hideaways.co.uk

Saint Ann Street ★★★
Contact: Mr Nicholas Pash
Hideaways, Chapel House, Luke Street, Berwick St John, Shaftesbury SP7 0HQ
T: (01747) 828170
F: (01747) 829090
E: enq@hideaways.co.uk
I: www.hideaways.co.uk

Sycamore Cottage ★★★★
Contact: Mr Richard & Mrs Cilla Pickett
Melrose Cottage, Lower Road, Quidhampton, Salisbury SP2 9AS
T: (01722) 743160
E: cilla@sycamorecottage.biz
I: www.sycamorecottage.biz

Winterbourne Cottage ★★★★
Contact: Mr Nicholas Pash
Hideaways, Chapel House, Luke Street, Berwick St John, Shaftesbury SP7 0HQ
T: (01747) 828170
F: (01747) 829090
E: enq@hideaways.co.uk
I: www.hideaways.co.uk

SALWAY ASH
Dorset

Brinsham Farm Cottages ★★★★
Contact: Mrs Viv Harding
Brinsham Farm Cottages, Brinsham Farm, Pineapple Lane, Bridport DT6 5HY
T: (01308) 488196
F: (01308) 488196
E: Brinsham@aol.com

SANDHURST
Gloucestershire

Great Coverden
Rating Applied For
Contact: Mrs Deb Deyes
Bengrave Farm, Base Lane, Gloucester GL2 9NU
T: (01452) 730231
F: (01452) 730895
E: Debs@bengravefarm.fsnet.co.uk

SANDYWAY
Devon

Barkham Cottages ★★★★
Contact: Mr & Mrs Adie
Barkham Cottages, Sandyway, Exmoor, South Molton EX36 3LU
T: (01643) 831370
F: (01643) 831370
E: adie.exmoor@btinternet.com
I: www.holidays-exmoor.com

Look out for establishments participating in the National Accessible Scheme

SOUTH WEST ENGLAND

SAUNTON
Devon

Lower Lease ★★★★
Contact:
Marsden's Cottage Holidays, 2
The Square, Braunton EX33 2JB
T: (01271) 813777
F: (01271) 813664
E: holidays@marsdens.co.uk
I: www.marsdens.co.uk

**Rhu & Little Rhu
★★★-★★★★★**
Contact:
Marsden's Cottage Holidays, 2
The Square, Braunton EX33 2JB
T: (01271) 813777
F: (01271) 813664
E: holidays@marsdens.co.uk
I: www.marsdens.co.uk

Saunton Heath ★★★
Contact:
Marsden's Cottage Holidays, 2
The Square, Braunton EX33 2JB
T: (01271) 813777
F: (01271) 813664
E: holidays@marsdens.co.uk
I: www.marsdens.co.uk

Surf ★★★
Contact:
Marsden's Cottage Holidays, 2
The Square, Braunton EX33 2JB
T: (01271) 813777
F: (01271) 813664
E: holidays@marsdens.co.uk
I: www.marsdens.co.uk

**Thorn Close Cottage
★★★★**
Contact:
Marsdens Cottage Holidays, 2
The Square, Braunton EX33 2JB
T: (01271) 813777
F: (01271) 813664
E: holidays@marsdens.co.uk
I: www.marsdens.co.uk

SEATON
Devon

Badgers Holt ★★★
Contact: Ms Louise Hayman
Milkbere Holidays, 3 Fore Street,
Seaton EX12 2LE
T: (01297) 20729
F: (01297) 22925
E: info@milkberehols.com
I: www.milkberehols.com

California Glory ★★★★
Contact: Ms Kate Bartlett
Jean Bartlett Cottage Holidays,
The Old Dairy, Fore Street,
Seaton EX12 3JB
T: (01297) 23221
E: holidays@jeanbartlett.com
I: www.jeanbartlett.com

Caruso ★★★
Contact: Ms Louise Hayman
Milkbere Holidays, 3 Fore Street,
Seaton EX12 2LE
T: (01297) 20729
F: (01297) 22925
E: info@milkberehols.com
I: www.milkberehols.com

Cherry Trees
Rating Applied For
Contact:
Jean Bartlett Cottage Holidays,
Old Dairy, Fore Street, Seaton
EX12 3JA
T: (01297) 23221
F: (01297) 23303
E: holidays@jeanbartlett.com
I: www.jeanbartlett.com

Cliff Cottage ★★★
Contact: Ms Kate Bartlett
Jean Bartlett Cottage Holidays,
The Old Dairy, Fore Street,
Seaton EX12 3JB
T: (01297) 23221
E: holidays@jeanbartlett.com
I: www.jeanbartlett.com

Cliff View
Rating Applied For
Contact: Ms Louise Hayman
Milkbere Holidays, 3 Fore Street,
Seaton EX12 2LE
T: (01297) 20729
E: info@milkberehols.com
I: www.milkberehols.com

Conswalk ★★★
Contact: Ms Louise Hayman
Milkbere Cottage Holidays, 3
Fore Street, Seaton EX12 2LE
T: (01297) 20729
F: (01297) 22925
E: info@milkberehols.com
I: www.milkberehols.com

Deepdale ★★★
Contact:
Milkbere Holidays, 3 Fore Street,
Seaton EX12 2LE
T: (01297) 27029
F: (01297) 22925
E: info@milkberehols.com

Drakes Nest ★★★
Contact: Ms Louise Hayman
Milkbere Holidays, 3 Fore Street,
Seaton EX12 2LE
T: (01297) 20729
F: (01297) 22925
E: info@milkberehols.com
I: www.milkberehols.com

Farthings ★★★★
Contact: Ms Louise Hayman
Milkbere Cottage Holidays, 3
Fore Street, Seaton EX12 2LE
T: (01297) 20729
F: (01297) 22925
E: info@milkberehols.com
I: www.milkberehols.com

**Flat 2, 8 Westcliffe Terrace
★★★**
Contact:
Milkbere Holidays, 3 Fore Street,
Seaton EX12 2LE
T: (01297) 20729
E: info@milkberehols.com

Glynsall Cabin ★★
Contact: Ms Louise Hayman
Milkbere Holidays, 3 Fore Street,
Seaton EX12 2LE
T: (01297) 20729
F: (01297) 22925
E: info@milkberehols.com

**Harbour View and Harbour
Side ★★★★**
Contact: Mrs Hilary Bevis
Harbour View and Harbour Side,
Beach End, 8 Trevelyan Road,
Seaton EX12 2NL
T: (01297) 23388
F: (01297) 625604

The Haven (Flat 1)
Rating Applied For
Contact:
Jean Bartlett Cottage Holidays,
The Old Dairy,fore Street, Seaton
EX12 3JA
T: (01297) 23221
F: (01297) 23303
E: holidays@jeanbartlett.com
I: www.jeanbartlett.com

Homestead Flats ★★★
Contact: Ms Kate Bartlett
Jean Bartlett Cottage Holidays,
The Old Dairy, Fore Street,
Seaton EX12 3JB
T: (01297) 23221
I: www.jeanbartlett.com

Last Penny Cottage ★★★★
Contact:
Milkbere Holidays, 3 Fore Street,
Seaton EX12 2LE
T: (01297) 20729
F: (01297) 22925
E: info@milkbere.com
I: www.milkbere.com

Little Cot ★★★
Contact:
Jean Bartlett Cottage Holidays,
The Old Dairy, Fore Street,
Seaton EX12 3JB
T: (01297) 23221
F: (01297) 23303
E: holidays@jeanbartlett.com
I: www.netbreaks.com/jeanb

Little Oaks ★★★★
Contact: Ms Louise Hayman
Milkbere Holidays, 3 Fore Street,
Seaton EX12 2LE
T: (01297) 20729
F: (01297) 22925
E: info@milkberehols.com
I: www.milkberehols.com

The Loft ★★★
Contact: Ms Louise Hayman
Milkbere Cottage Holidays, 3
Fore Street, Seaton EX12 2LE
T: (01297) 20729
F: (01297) 22925
E: info@milkberehols.com
I: www.milkberehols.com

3 Lyme Mews ★★★
Contact: Ms Kate Bartlett
Jean Bartlett Cottage Holidays,
The Old Dairy, Fore Street,
Seaton EX12 3JB
T: (01297) 23221
F: (01297) 23303
E: holidays@jeanbartlett.com
I: www.jeanbartlett.com

**Manor Farm Cottages
★★★-★★★★★**
Contact: Mrs Parr
Manor Farm, Harepath Hill,
Seaton EX12 2TF
T: (01297) 625349

**Marine Place Apartments
★★★**
Contact:
Milkbere Cottage Holidays, 3
Fore Street, Seaton EX12 2LE
T: (01297) 20729
F: (01297) 22925
E: info@milkberehols.com
I: www.milkberehols.com

Mole Cottage ★★★★
Contact: Ms Louise Hayman
Milkbere Cottage Holidays Ltd, 3
Fore Street, Seaton EX12 2LE
T: (01297) 20729
F: (01297) 22925
E: info@milkberehols.com
I: www.milkberehols.com

The Nook ★★★★
Contact: Ms Louise Hayman
Milkbere Holidays, 3 Fore Street,
Seaton EX12 2LE
T: (01297) 20729
F: (01297) 22925
E: info@milkberehols.com
I: www.milkberehols.com

Owls Retreat ★★★
Contact: Ms Louise Hayman
Milkbere Holidays, 3 Fore Street,
Seaton EX12 2LE
T: (01297) 20729
F: (01297) 22925
E: info@milkberehols.com
I: www.milkberehols.com

Owls Twoo ★★★
Contact: Ms Louise Hayman
Milkbere Holidays, 3 Fore Street,
Seaton EX12 2LE
T: (01297) 20729
F: (01297) 22925
E: info@milkberehols.com
I: www.milkberehols.com

4 Pioneer Cottages ★★★
Contact: Ms Kate Bartlett
Jean Bartlett Cottage Holidays,
The Old Dairy, Fore Street,
Seaton EX12 3JB
T: (01297) 23221
E: holidays@jeanbartlett.com
I: www.jeanbartlett.com

Primrose ★★★
Contact: Ms Louise Hayman
Milkbere Holidays, 3 Fore Street,
Seaton EX12 2LE
T: (01297) 20729
F: (01297) 22925
E: info@milkberehols.com
I: www.milkberehols.com

Rosemead ★★★
Contact:
Milkbere Holidays, 3 Fore Street,
Seaton EX12 2LE
T: (01297) 20729
F: (01297) 22925
E: info@milkberehols.com
I: www.milkberehols.com

Sarnia ★★★
Contact: Ms Louise Hayman
Milkbere Cottage Holidays Ltd, 3
Fore Street, Seaton EX12 2LE
T: (01297) 20729
F: (01297) 22925
E: info@milkberehols.com
I: www.milkberehols.com

Establishments printed in blue have a detailed entry in this guide

SOUTH WEST ENGLAND

Sea Moon ★★★★
Contact: Ms Louise Hayman
Milkbere Cottage Holidays, 3
Fore Street, Seaton EX12 2LE
T: (01297) 20729
F: (01297) 22925
E: info@milkberehols.com
I: www.milkberehols.com

10 Seafield Road ★★★★
Contact: Ms Louise Hayman
Milkbere Holidays, 3 Fore Street,
Seaton EX12 2LE
T: (01297) 20729
F: (01297) 22925
E: info@milkberehols.com
I: www.milkberehols.com

Seagulls ★★★
Contact:
Milkbere Cottage Holidays, 3
Fore Street, Seaton EX12 2LE
T: (01297) 20729
F: (01297) 22925
E: info@milkberehols.com
I: www.milkberehols.com

Seaside Flat 3 ★★★
Contact:
Jean Bartlett Cottage Holidays,
The Old Dairy, Fore Street,
Seaton EX12 3JB
T: (01297) 23221
F: (01297) 23303
E: holidays@jeanbartlett.com
I: www.netbreaks.com/jeanb

Seaview Garden
Rating Applied For
Contact:
Jean Bartlett Cottage Holidays,
The Old Dairy,fore Street, Seaton
EX12 3JA
T: (01297) 23221
F: (01297) 23303
E: holidays@jeanbartlett.com
I: www.jeanbartlett.com

Shalom ★★★★
Contact:
Milkbere Holidays, 3 Fore Street,
Seaton EX12 2LE
T: (01297) 20729
F: (01297) 22925
E: info@milkbere.com
I: www.milkbere.com

Soo Soo San ★★★
Contact: Ms Louise Hayman
Milkbere Holidays, 3 Fore Street,
Seaton EX12 2LE
T: (01297) 20729
F: (01297) 22925
E: info@milkberehols.com
I: www.milkberehols.com

Spindrift ★★★
Contact:
Milkbere Holidays, 3 Fore Street,
Seaton EX12 2LE
T: (01297) 20729
F: (01297) 22925
E: info@milkberehols.com
I: www.milkberehols.com

Swans Nest ★★★★
Contact: Ms Louise Hayman
Milkbere Cottage Holidays, 3
Fore Street, Seaton EX12 2LE
T: (01297) 20729
F: (01297) 22925
E: info@milkberehols.com
I: www.milkberehols.com

Teazles
Rating Applied For
Contact: Ms Louise Hayman
Milkbere Cottages, 3 Fore Street,
Seaton EX12 2LE
T: (01297) 22925
F: (01297) 22925
E: info@milkberehols.com
I: www.milkberehols.com

27 West Acres ★★★★
Contact: Ms Louise Hayman
Milkbere Holidays, 3 Fore Street,
Seaton EX12 2LE
T: (01297) 20729
F: (01297) 22925
E: info@milkberehols.com
I: www.milkberehols.com

West Ridge Bungalow ★★★
Contact: Mrs Hildegard Fox
West Ridge, Harepath Hill,
Seaton EX12 2TA
T: (01297) 22398
F: (01297) 22398
E: foxfamily@westridge.
fsbusiness.co.uk
I: www.cottageguide.
co.uk/westridge

Westacres ★★★
Contact: Ms Kate Bartlett
Jean Bartlett Cottage Holidays,
The Old Dairy, Fore Street,
Seaton EX12 3JB
T: (01297) 23221
F: (01297) 23303
E: holidays@jeanbartlett.com
I: www.jeanbartlett.com

Windrush ★★★
Contact: Ms Kate Bartlett
Jean Bartlett Cottage Holidays,
The Old Dairy, Fore Street,
Seaton EX12 3JB
T: (01297) 23221
F: (01297) 23303
E: holidays@jeanbartlett.com
I: www.jeanbartlett.com

Yarty Cottage ★★★★
Contact:
Milkbere Holidays, 3 Fore Street,
Seaton EX12 2LE
T: (01297) 20729
E: info@milkberehols.com
I: www.milkberehols.com

SEATOWN
Dorset

Guard House ★★★★★
Contact: Mrs Joyce Whittaker
Guard House Cottages, Seatown
House, Seatown, Bridport
DT6 6JU
T: (01297) 489417
F: (01297) 489151
E: info@guardhouse.co.uk
I: www.guardhouse.co.uk

SECTOR
Devon

Brook Cottage ★★★★
Contact: Ms Kate Bartlett
Jean Bartlett Cottage Holidays,
The Old Dairy, Fore Street,
Seaton EX12 3JB
T: (01297) 23221
F: (01297) 23303
E: holidays@jeanbartlett.com
I: www.netbreaks.com/jeamb

SENNEN
Cornwall

3 & 4 Wesley Cottages ★★★
Contact: Mrs Jane Davey
Rosteague, Raginnis Farm,
Penzance TR19 6NJ
T: (01736) 731933
F: (01736) 732344
E: wesley@raginnis.demon.
co.uk
I: www.wesleyatnanquidno.
co.uk

Little Trevallack ★★★
Contact: Mrs Sue Nicholas
Trevallck, Mayon, Sennen,
Penzance TR19 7AD
T: (01736) 871451
F: (01736) 871451
E: suenicholas@hotmail.com

Surfers
Rating Applied For
Contact: Mr Brian & Mrs Wendy
Bishop
311 Longford Road, Cannock
WS11 1NF
T: (01543) 570901
E: wbishop@onetel.com

Trevorrian Farmhouse
Rating Applied For
Contact: Mrs Trudy Thomas
Trevorrian Farmhouse,
Trevorrian Farmhouse, Penzance
TR19 7BH
T: (01736) 871205
F: (01736) 871205
E: trevear.farm@farming.co.uk
I: www.trevearfarm.co.uk

Weavers ★★
Contact: Mrs Janet Harrison
8 Lodge Drive, Truro TR1 1TX
T: (01872) 273506

SENNEN COVE
Cornwall

Jubilee Cottage ★★★
Contact: Mr Nicholas
Harbour View, Penzance
TR19 7DE
T: (01736) 871206
F: (01736) 871206
E: susannecook@supanet.com

Lynwood House ★★★
Contact: Mr Nicholas
Harbour View, Penzance
TR19 7DE
T: (01736) 871206
F: (01736) 871206
E: susannecook@supanet.com

The Old Success Inn ★★★
Contact: Mr Martin Brookes
The Old Success Inn, Penzance
TR19 7DG
T: (01736) 871232
F: (01736) 871457
E: oldsuccess@sennencove.
fsbusiness.co.uk
I: www.oldsuccess.com

Riviera Apartments
Rating Applied For
Contact: Mr Robert & Mrs Kay
George
Riviera Apartments, The
Meadows, Treen, St Levan,
Penzance TR19 6LQ
T: (01736) 810452
F: (01736) 810116
E: robertandkay@penberth.com
I: www.sennen-cove.com

Tinker Taylor Cottage
Rating Applied For
Contact: Mr David Paget
Bridgwater Road, Weston-
super-Mare BS24 0BZ
T: (01934) 751306
E: davepagets@aol.com

SHAFTESBURY
Dorset

Allans Farm Cottage ★★★★
Contact: Ms Sally Nutbeem
T & S Nutbeem, Allans Farm,
Pitts Lane, Shaftesbury SP7 0BX
T: (01747) 852153
F: (01747) 852153
E: sally.nutbeem@tesco.net

Bowling Green Farm ★★★
Contact: Mr Ian Benefer
Bowling Green Farm,
Shaftesbury SP7 0LG
T: (01747) 811588
F: (01747) 811588
E: bowlinggreenfarm@aol.com
I: www.bowlinggreenfarm.co.uk

Hartgrove Farm
★★★-★★★★★
Contact: Mrs Susan Smart
Hartgrove Farm, Shaftesbury
SP7 0JY
T: (01747) 811830
F: (01747) 811066
E: cottages@hartgrovefarm.
co.uk
I: www.hartgrovefarm.co.uk

Lakeside Cottage ★★★
Contact: Mrs Jane Cecil
Lakeside Cottage, Incombe Farm,
Shaftesbury SP7 0LZ
T: (01747) 811081
F: (01747) 812029
E: info@cecil.com
I: www.incombe.co.uk

The Smithy ★★★★
Contact: Mrs Lucy Kerridge
The Smithy, The Old Forge,
Fanners Yard, Compton Abbas,
Shaftesbury SP7 0NQ
T: (01747) 811881
F: (01747) 811881
E: theoldforge@hotmail.com
I: www.smoothhound.
co.uk/hotels/oldforge

South View ★★★
Contact: Mr Keith Westcott
Stonebank, 14 West Street,
Weymouth DT3 4DY
T: (01305) 760120
F: (01305) 760871
E: elmvale@
stonebank-chickerell.co.uk
I: www.stonebank-chickerell.
com

SOUTH WEST ENGLAND

25 St James's Street ★★★
Contact: Mrs Jane Pyrgos
Prichard Hall, Port Regis,
Motcombe Park, Shaftesbury
SP7 9QA
T: (01747) 856343
E: pjp@portregis.com

Summer Cottage ★★★
Contact: Miss Suzanne Harding
Stockfield House, 41 High Street,
Salisbury SP5 5ND
T: (01725) 553161
F: (01725) 553161
E: roomreview@hotmail.com
I: www.summerinshaftesbury.co.uk

Thatch Cottage ★★★
Contact: Mrs Lynne Sekree
Four Seasons, Beech Road,
Chandler's Ford, Eastleigh
SO53 1LR
T: (023) 80265945
F: (023) 80486259
E: thatchcottage@ntlworld.com
I: www.thatchcottage.co.uk

Vale Farm Holiday Cottages ★★★★
Contact: Mrs Sarah Drake
Vale Farm, Sutton Waldron,
Blandford Forum DT11 8PL
T: (01747) 811286
F: (01747) 811286
E: sarah.drake@ukonline.co.uk
I: www.valeholidays.co.uk

SHALDON
Devon

Barton Cottage ★★★
Contact: Ms Susan Witt
Honeysuckle Cottage, Deane
Road, Newton Abbot TQ12 4QF
T: (01626) 872441
E: bartoncottage@
stokeinteignhead.freeserve.co.uk

Coombe Close Holidays ★★★
Contact: Mr & Mrs Huff
Coombe Close Holidays, Coombe
Close, Brim Hill, Torquay
TQ1 4TR
T: (01803) 327215
F: (01803) 327215
E: peterhuff@onetel.net.uk
I: www.shines.net/maidencombe

Longmeadow Farm ★★-★★★
Contact: Mrs Mann
Longmeadow Farm, Coombe
Road, Ringmore, Teignmouth
TQ14 0EX

Shoreside ★★★★★
Contact:
Blue Chip Vacations, 3 Marina
Walk, Brixham TQ5 9BW
T: (01803) 855282
F: (01803) 881029
E: info@bluechipdevelpments.com

SHEEPSCOMBE
Gloucestershire

Longridge Meend ★★★
Contact: Mr Cound
Longridge Meend, Bulls Cross,
Stroud GL7 7HU
T: (01452) 813225
F: (01452) 812006
E: richardcound@beeb.net

SHEEPSTOR
Devon

Burrator House ★★★-★★★★★
Contact: Ms Sarah Bridger
Biznot Ltd, Burrartor House,
Sheepstor, Yelverton PL20 6PF
T: (01822) 855669
E: sarah.bridger@btopenworld.com
I: www.burratorhouse.com

SHEEPWASH
Devon

Swardicott Farm ★★★
Contact: Mrs Purser
Swardicott Farm, Beaworthy
EX21 5PB
T: (01409) 231633
F: (01409) 231361
E: mpurser@btinternet.com
I: www.holidaycottages-devon.co.uk

SHELDON
Devon

Droughtwell Farm ★★★
Contact: Mrs Susan Cochrane
Droughtwell Farm, Honiton
EX14 4QW
T: (01404) 841349
F: (01404) 841349

SHEPTON MALLET
Somerset

Knowle Farm Cottages ★★★★
Contact: Mrs Helen Trotman
Knowle Farm, West Compton,
Shepton Mallet BA4 4PD
T: (01749) 890482
F: (01749) 890405
E: helen@knowle-farm-cottages.co.uk
I: www.knowle-farm-cottages.co.uk

Leigh Holt ★★★★★
Contact: Mrs Pamela Hoddinott
Leigh Holt, Burnt House Farm,
Waterlip, Shepton Mallet
BA4 4RN
T: (01749) 880280
F: (01749) 880004
E: pam@burnthousefarmbandb.co.uk
I: www.burnthousefarmbandb.co.uk

SHEPTON MONTAGUE
Somerset

Higher Farm ★★★★
Contact: Mrs C Dimond
Higher Farm, Wincanton BA9 8JJ
T: (01749) 812373
F: (01749) 812373
E: dimond@farm24771.fsnet.co.uk

SHERBORNE
Dorset

1 & 2 Trill Cottages ★★★
Contact: Mrs Warr
1 & 2 Trill Cottages, Trill House,
Sherborne DT9 6HF
T: (01935) 872305
E: trill.cottages@ic24.net

Blackberry Cottage ★★★
Contact: Mr John Michael Farr
17 Marsh Lane, Yeovil BA21 3BX
T: (01935) 423148

Grange Farm ★★★★
Contact: Mrs K Flannery
Grange Farm, Sherborne
DT9 4LA
T: (01935) 812793
F: (01935) 432765

Millers Loft ★★★
Contact: Mrs Bridget Buckland
Millers Loft, Sherborne DT9 5JD
T: (01963) 250380
E: bandebuckland@aol.com

Old Orchard Cottage ★★★★
Contact: Mrs Alexa Buckland
Old Orchard Cottage, Goathill
Farm, Sherborne DT9 5JD
T: (01963) 251365
F: (01963) 251365

Stable Cottage ★★★
Contact: Mrs Dimond
Stable Cottage, Bridleways,
Oborne Road, Sherborne
DT9 3RX
T: (01935) 814716
F: (01935) 814716
E: bridleways@tiscali.co.uk

SHERFORD
Devon

Keynedon Barton ★★★★
Contact: Mrs Angela Heath
Keynedon Barton, Kingsbridge
TQ7 2AS
T: (01548) 531273
I: www.keynedon.fsnet.co.uk

Valley Springs Cottages ★★★★★
Contact: Ms Lynne Bentley
Valley Springs Cottages, The
Spinney, Kingsbridge TQ7 2DR
T: (01548) 856005
F: (01548) 856005
E: valleyspringscottages@btopenworld.com
I: www.valley-springs.com

SHERRINGTON
Wiltshire

Gingerbread Cottage ★★★★
Contact: Mrs Gabrielle Lewis
Gingerbread Cottage, Sheepfold
Cottage, 12 Sherrington,
Warminster BA12 0SN
T: (01985) 850453
F: (01985) 850453
E: patlewis@lineone.net
I: www.gingerbreadcottage.co.uk

SHERSTON
Wiltshire

Homeview Cottages ★★★
Contact: Mr John & Mrs Julie
Curtis
Homeview Cottages, Tetbury
Road, Malmesbury SN16 0LU
T: (01666) 840303
E: jcurtis@btinternet.com
I: www.homeviewcottages.co.uk

May Cottage ★★★★
Contact: Mrs Sheila Bristow
Mill Cottage, Thompsons Hill,
Malmesbury SN16 0PZ
T: (01666) 840655

SHILLINGFORD
Devon

South Hayne Farm
Rating Applied For
Contact:
Farm & Cottage Holidays,
Victoria House, 12 Fore Street,
Bideford EX39 1AW
T: (01237) 479146
F: (01237) 421512
E: enquiries@farmcott.co.uk
I: www.farmcott.co.uk

SHIPTON GORGE
Dorset

Masons Cottage ★★★
Contact:
Dream Cottages, 5 Hope Square,
Weymouth DT4 8TR
T: (01305) 789000
E: admin@dream-cottages.co.uk
I: www.dream-cottages.co.uk

SHIPTON MOYNE
Gloucestershire

Street Farm Cottage
Rating Applied For
Contact: Mrs Beth Birdwood
Street Farm Cottage, The Street,
Tetbury GL8 8PN
T: (01666) 880523
F: (01666) 880541
E: beth@streetfarm.co.uk
I: www.streetfarm.co.uk

SHIPTON OLIFFE
Gloucestershire

Paddock Barn ★★★★★
Contact: Mrs Doyle
Southwold Farm, Cheltenham
GL54 4DS
T: (01242) 890147
E: emma@paddockbarn.co.uk
I: www.paddockbarn.co.uk

SHORNCOTE
Gloucestershire

The Oak Cabin ★★★
Contact: Mrs Philippa Knight
The Oak Cabin, Glebe Farm,
Cirencester GL7 6DE
T: (01285) 860206
F: (01285) 860206

SHREWTON
Wiltshire

Drovers' Barn ★★★★
Contact:
Hideaways, Chapel House, Luke
Street, Berwick St John,
Shaftesbury SP7 0HQ
T: (01747) 828170
F: (01747) 829090
E: enq@hideaways.co.uk
I: www.hideaways.co.uk

SHUTE
Devon

Higher Watchcombe Farmhouse and Country Cottages ★★★★
Contact: Mr Paul & Mrs Jane
Galloway
Higher Watchcombe Farmhouse
and Country Cottages,
Axminster EX13 7QN
T: (01297) 552424
F: (01297) 552424
E: galloways@ukgateway.net
I: www.higherwatchcombe.com

Establishments printed in blue have a detailed entry in this guide

SOUTH WEST ENGLAND

SIDFORD
Devon

6 Axe Vale ★★★
Contact:
Jean Bartlett Cottage Holidays,
The Old Dairy, Fore Street,
Seaton EX12 3JB
T: (01297) 23221

Porch Cottage ★★★
Contact: Ms Kate Bartlett
Jean Bartlett Cottage Holidays,
The Old Dairy, Fore Street,
Seaton EX12 3JB
T: (01297) 23221
I: www.jeanbartlett.com

SIDMOUTH
Devon

Bayview ★★★
Contact: Mrs Rosemary Sidwell
Little Mead, Beatlands Road,
Sidmouth EX10 8JH
T: (01395) 515668

Boswell Farm Cottages ★★★★
Contact: Mr Brian & Mrs Linda Dillon
Boswell Farm Cottages, Boswell Farm, Harcombe, Sidmouth EX10 0PP
T: (01395) 514162
F: (01395) 514162
E: dillon@boswell-farm.co.uk
I: www.boswell-farm.co.uk

Cherry Tree Cottage ★★★
Contact: Mrs Rosemary Sidwell
Little Mead, Beatlands Road,
Sidmouth EX10 8JH
T: (01395) 515668

Cliffe Cottage ★★★★
Contact: Ms Kate Bartlett
Jean Bartlett Cottage Holidays,
The Old Dairy, Fore Street,
Seaton EX12 3JB
T: (01297) 23221
F: (01297) 23303
E: holidays@jeanbartlett.com
I: www.jeanbartlett.com

Clovelly ★★★
Contact: Ms Kate Bartlett
Jean Bartlett Cottage Holidays,
The Old Dairy, Fore Street,
Seaton EX12 3JB
T: (01297) 23221
F: (01297) 23303
E: holidays@jeanbartlett.com
I: www.jeanbartlett.com

Farthings ★★
Contact: Ms Kate Bartlett
Jean Bartlett Cottage Holidays,
The Old Dairy, Fore Street,
Seaton EX12 3JB
T: (01297) 23221
F: (01297) 23303
E: holidays@jeanbartlett.com
I: www.netbreaks.com/jeamb

Flat 3, Fortfield Chambers ★★★★
Contact: Mrs Sylvia Brownlee
Flat 3, 5 Alexandria Road,
Sidmouth EX10 9HD
T: (01395) 577993
F: (01395) 577993
E: brownlee@clara.co.uk
I: www.fortfieldchambers.com

Higher Thorn Barn
Contact: Mrs Louise Stout
Higher Thorn Cottage, Salcombe Regis, Sidmouth EX10 0PA
T: (01395) 519046

Hill View ★★★
Contact: Ms Kate Bartlett
Jean Bartlett Cottage Holidays,
The Old Dairy, Fore Street,
Seaton EX12 3JB
T: (01297) 23221
E: holidays@jeanbartlett.com
I: www.jeanbartlett.com

Leigh Farm ★★★★
Contact: Mr Geoff & Mrs Gill Davis
Leigh Farm, Sidmouth EX10 0PH
T: (01395) 516065
F: (01395) 579582
E: leigh.farm@virgin.net
I: www.streets-ahead.com/leighfarm

Littlecourt Cottages ★★★★
Contact: Mr Selwyn Kussman
Littlecourt Cottages, Seafield Road, Sidmouth EX10 8HF
T: (01395) 515279
E: admin@littlecourtcottages.com
I: www.littlecourtcottages.com

Riverside Cottage ★★★
Contact: Ms Kate Bartlett
Jean Bartlett Cottage Holidays,
The Old Dairy, Fore Street,
Seaton EX12 3JB
T: (01297) 23221
F: (01297) 23303
E: holidays@jeanbartlett.com
I: www.jeanbartlett.com

Stonechat ★★★
Contact: Ms Louise Hayman
Milkbere Holidays, 3 Fore Street, Seaton EX12 2LE
T: (01297) 20729
F: (01297) 22925
E: info@milkberehols.com
I: www.milkberehols.com

Sunhaven ★★★
Contact: Ms Kate Bartlett
Jean Bartlett Cottage Holidays,
The Old Dairy, Fore Street,
Seaton EX12 3JB
T: (01297) 23221
E: holidays@jeanbartlett.com
I: www.jeanbartlett.com

SIMONSBATH
Somerset

Winstitchen Farm ★★★-★★★★
Contact: Jane Organ
Lowerfield Farm, Willersey, Broadway WR11 7HF
T: (01386) 858273
F: (01386) 854608
E: info@exmoor-country-cottages.com
I: www.exmoor-country-cottages.com

Wintershead Farm ★★★★
Contact: Mrs Styles
Wintershead Farm, Minehead TA24 7LF
T: (01643) 831222
I: www.wintershead.co.uk

SITHNEY
Cornwall

The Hideaway ★★★
Contact: Mrs Marlene Faull
The Hideaway, Trelissick Farm, Helston TR13 0RL
T: (01326) 573489
F: (01326) 573489
E: trellisick@hotmail.com

Tregathenan Country Cottages ★★★-★★★★★
Contact: Miss Liz Fairweather
Tregathenan Country Cottages, The Old Farmhouse, Tregathenen, Helston TR13 0RZ
T: (01326) 569840
F: (01326) 563362
E: tregathenan@hotmail.com
I: www.tregathenan.co.uk

SLAPTON
Devon

Dittiscombe Holiday Cottages ★★★★
Contact: Mrs Ruth Saunders
Dittiscombe Holiday Cottages, Kingsbridge TQ7 2QF
T: (01548) 521272
F: (01548) 521425
E: info@dittiscombe.co.uk
I: www.dittiscombe.co.uk

Maple Cottage ★★★
Contact:
Toad Hall Cottages, Elliot House, Church Street, Kingsbridge TQ7 1BY
T: (01548) 853089
F: (01548) 853086
E: thc@toadhallcottages.com
I: www.toadhallcottages.co.uk

Meadow Court Barn ★★★★
Contact:
Toad Hall Cottages, Elliot House, Church Street, Kingsbridge TQ7 1BY
T: (01548) 853089
F: (01548) 853086
E: thc@toadhallcottages.com

Pound Cottage ★★★★
Contact:
Holiday Homes & Cottages SW, 365A Torquay Road, Paignton TQ3 2BT
T: (01803) 663650
F: (01803) 664037
E: holcotts@aol.com
I: www.swcottages.co.uk

Willow Cottage ★★★
Contact:
Toad Hall Cottages, Elliot House, Church Street, Kingsbridge TQ7 1BY
T: (01548) 853089
F: (01548) 853086
E: thc@toadhallcottages.com
I: www.toadhallcottages.com

SLAUGHTERFORD
Wiltshire

Carters Cottage ★★★
Contact: Mrs Janet Jones
Carters Cottage, Chippenham SN14 8RE
T: (01249) 782243
F: (01249) 782243
E: hanfreeth@hotmail.com

SOMERTON
Somerset

Sleepy Hollow ★★★★
Contact: Mr & Mrs Raine
Sleepy Hollow, Double Gates Drove, Mill Road, Somerton TA11 6DF
T: (01458) 850584
F: (01458) 850584
E: paul&rhian@sleepyhollowcottages.com
I: www.sleepyhollowcottages.com

SOUDLEY
Gloucestershire

The Cottage ★★★
Contact: Mrs Helen Evans
Peaked Rocks Cottage, The Rocks, Joys Green, Lydbrook GL17 9RF
T: (01594) 861119
F: (01594) 823408
E: evans@evansholidays.freeserve.co.uk

SOUTH BRENT
Devon

Hillview ★★★
Contact:
Valley Villas, Brook Cottage, old Warleigh Lane, Plymouth PL5 4ND
T: (01752) 774900
I: www.devonaccommodationdirectory.co.uk

SOUTH BREWHAM
Somerset

Magpie Cottage & Jackdaw Cottage ★★★★
Contact: Mr David Dabinett
Magpie Cottage & Jackdaw Cottage, Haven Farm, Bruton BA10 0JZ
T: (01749) 850441
E: david@havenfarm.co.uk
I: www.havenfarm.co.uk

SOUTH CERNEY
Gloucestershire

Beau Lodge ★★★★
Contact: Ms Parfitt
Flat 1, 156/8 Wandsworth Bridge Road, Fulham, London SW6 2UH
T: 07976 610157
F: 07970 701378
E: gloria@parfittdirect.com

Orion Holidays ★★★★
Contact: Mr Mark Thomas
Orion Holidays, Cotswold Water Park, Gateway Centre, Spine Road East, Lake 6, Sine Road, South Cerney, Cirencester GL7 5TL
T: (01285) 861839
F: (01285) 869188
E: bookings@orionholidays.com
I: www.orionholidays.com

The Watermark Club ★★★-★★★★
Contact: Mr Robert Cowley
The Watermark Club, Isis Lake, Cirencester GL7 5TL
T: (01285) 862288
F: (01285) 862488
E: enquiries@watermarkclub.co.uk
I: www.watermarkclub.co.uk

SOUTH WEST ENGLAND

SOUTH MILTON
Devon

Nancy's Cottage
Rating Applied For
Contact: Mr Mark Jones
11 Woodland Avenue,
Kidderminster DY11 5AW
T: (01562) 824769
F: (01562) 747476
E: markjones.frics@virgin.net

SOUTH MOLTON
Devon

Drewstone Farm ★★★★
Contact: Mrs Ruth Ley
Drewstone Farm, South Molton
EX36 3EF
T: (01769) 572337
E: Ruth_ley@drewstonefarm.
fsnet.co.uk
I: www.devonself-catering.co.uk

**North Lee Farm Holiday
Cottages ★★★★**
Contact: Miss Rebecca Evans
North Lee Farm Holiday
Cottages, Hacche Lane, South
Molton EX36 3EH
T: (01598) 740248
F: (01598) 740045
E: beck@northlee.com
I: www.northlee.com

Vicarys Mews ★★★★
Contact:
Marsdens Cottage Holidays, 2
The Square, Braunton EX33 2JB
T: (01271) 813777
F: (01271) 813664
E: holidays@marsdens.co.uk
I: www.marsdens.co.uk

The Willows ★★★★
Contact:
Marsden's Cottage Holidays, 2
The Square, Braunton EX33 2JB
T: (01271) 813777
F: (01271) 813664
E: holidays@marsdens.co.uk
I: www.marsdens.co.uk

SOUTH PETHERTON
Somerset

**Brook House Cottage
★★★★**
Contact: Mrs Carolyne Entwistle
Brook House Cottage, Silver
Street, South Petherton
TA13 5BY
T: (01460) 242704
E: kevin.entwistle@
btopenworld.com

Tanwyn ★★★★
Contact: Mr Rodney & Mrs Ann
Tanswell
St Brides Major, Bridgend
CF32 0SB
T: (01656) 880524
F: (01656) 880524
E: rodney.tanswell@btinternet.
com

SOUTHAM
Gloucestershire

Priory Cottage ★★★
Contact: Mr I S Mant
Church Gate, Southam Lane,
Southam, Cheltenham GL52 3NY
T: (01242) 584693
F: (01242) 584693
E: iansmant@hotmail.com

SOUTHBOURNE
Bournemouth

**Shalbourne House Holiday
Flats ★★★**
Contact: Mr Tony Parker
Shalbourne House Holiday Flats
c/o Jay Cottage, Middle Road,
Poole BH16 6HJ
T: (01202) 624342
I: www.holidayflatsandvillas.
co.uk

SPRYTOWN
Devon

Herb Cottage ★★★
Contact: Mrs J Earl
Bottom Cottage, Portgate,
Lewdown, Okehampton
EX20 4PY
T: (01566) 783386

STANTON
Gloucestershire

Charity Cottage ★★★
Contact: Mrs Ryland
Charity Farm, Stanton,
Broadway WR12 7NE
T: (01386) 584339
F: (01386) 584270
E: kennethryland@ukonline.
co.uk
I: www.myrtle-cottage.
co.uk/ryland.htm

**Stanton Court Cottages
★★★★**
Contact: Mrs Sheila Campbell
Stanton Court Cottages, Stanton
Court, Broadway WR12 6SW
T: (01386) 584527
F: (01386) 584682
I: www.stantoncourt.co.uk

STAPLEGROVE
Somerset

The Barn ★★★★
Contact: Mrs Anita Harris
The Barn, Higher Yarde
Farmhouse, Staplegrove,
Taunton TA2 6SW
T: (01823) 451553
E: anitaharris@
higheryardefarm.co.uk

STARCROSS
Devon

Aster House ★★★★
Contact:
Holiday Homes & Cottages
South West, 365A Torquay Road,
Paignton TQ3 2BT
T: (01803) 663650
F: (01803) 664037
E: holcotts@aol.com
I: www.swcottages.co.uk

STATHE
Somerset

**Walkers Farm Cottages
★★★★**
Contact: Mr William & Mrs
Dianne Tiley
Walkers Farm Cottages, Walkers
Farm, Stathe, Bridgwater
TA7 0JL
T: (01823) 698229
E: bookings@
walkersfarmcottages.co.uk
I: www.walkersfarmcottages.
co.uk

STAVERTON
Devon

**The Kingston Estate
★★★★★**
Contact: Mr Mark Stevens
Kingston House, Totnes TQ9 6AR
T: (01803) 762235
F: (01803) 762444
E: info@kingston-estate.net
I: www.kingston-estate.net

STAWLEY
Somerset

Stawley Wood Farm ★★★★
Contact: Mr James & Mrs Julia
Luard
Stawley Wood Farm, Wellington
TA21 0HP
T: (01823) 672300
F: (01823) 672300
E: jandjluard@tiscali.co.uk
I: www.stawleywood.co.uk

STEEPLE ASHTON
Wiltshire

Elwyns Cottage ★★★★
Contact: Ref: E2484
Hoseasons Country Cottages,
Raglan Road, Lowestoft
NR32 2LW
T: 0870 5 342342
F: 0870 9 022090
I: www.hoseasons.
co.uk/images/2002/ukcottages/
cottages/aa99.html

Jasmine Cottage ★★★★
Contact: Mr Sharples
4 St Margarets, Sutton Coldfield
B74 4HU
T: (0121) 3535258
E: stay@jasminecottage.co.uk
I: www.jasminecottage.co.uk

STIBB
Cornwall

Claires Cottage ★★★
Contact: Mr Roger & Mrs Brenda
Dunstan
Claires Cottage, Strands, Bude
EX23 9HW
T: (01288) 353514

STICKER
Cornwall

**Glenleigh Farm Fishery
★★★★★**
Contact: Mrs Claire Tregunna
Glenleigh Farm Fishery, Sticker,
St Austell PL26 7JB
T: (01726) 73154
F: (01726) 77465
E: fishglenleigh@aol.com

STICKLEPATH
Devon

The Shippon ★★★
Contact: Mrs Jackie Day
The Shippon, Coombe Head
Farm, Okehampton EX20 1QL
T: (01837) 840108
F: (01837) 840789
E: jackie@coombeheadfarm.
co.uk
I: www.coombeheadfarm.co.uk

STITHIANS
Cornwall

Charis Cottage ★★★★
Contact: Mr Drees & Schneider
Charis Cottage, Treweege,
Trewithen Moor, Truro TR3 7DU
T: (01209) 861003
E: astondrees@hotmail.com
I: www.chariscottage.co.uk

The Dhorlin ★★★★
Contact: Mrs Margaret Richards
Davaar, Vellandrucia, Truro
TR3 7AA
T: (01209) 860640
E: enquiries@thedhorlin.co.uk
I: www.thedhorlin.co.uk

Higher Trewithen ★★★
Contact: Mr Neil Pardoe
Higher Trewithen, Truro TR3 7DR
T: (01209) 860863
F: (01209) 860785
E: trewithen@talk21.com
I: www.trewithen.com

STOGUMBER
Somerset

Periwinkle Cottage ★★★★
Contact: Miss Sheila Hubbard
Puzzle Tree, Minehead TA24 8RD
T: (01643) 841413
F: (01643) 841413

STOKE ABBOTT
Dorset

Canterburys Cottage ★★★
Contact: Mr Zachary Stuart-
Brown
Dream Cottages, 5 Hope Square,
Weymouth DT4 8TR
T: (01305) 789000
F: (01305) 761346
E: admin@dream-cottages.
co.uk
I: www.dream-cottages.co.uk

Fossil Cottage ★★★
Contact: Mr J L Roberts
Fossil Cottage, Chartknolle,
Beaminster DT8 3JN
T: (01306) 862220
F: (01306) 863989
E: john@jlro.demon.co.uk

Rectory Cottage ★★★
Contact: Mr Thomas
Harmsworth
The Old Rectory, Beaminster
DT8 3JT
T: (01308) 868118

STOKE GABRIEL
Devon

Jesters ★★★★
Contact:
Holiday Homes & Cottages
South West, 365A Torquay Road,
Paignton TQ3 2BT
T: (01803) 663650
F: (01803) 664037
E: holcotts@aol.com
I: www.swcottages.co.uk

Thatch Cottage ★★★★★
Contact: Ms Anita Chisolm
Belsford Farmhouse, Totnes
TQ9 7SP
T: (01803) 863341
F: (01803) 840208
E: anita@smoothtransition.
freeserve.co.uk

Establishments printed in blue have a detailed entry in this guide

SOUTH WEST ENGLAND

STOKE ST GREGORY
Somerset

Baileys Gallery ★★★
Contact: Mr Stanley Chedzoy
Fairholme, Stoke St Gregory,
Taunton TA3 6JQ
T: (01823) 490644

Holly Farm ★★★★
Contact: Mr & Mrs Hembrow & Smith
Holly Farm, Meare Green, Stoke St Gregory, Taunton TA3 6HS
T: (01823) 490828
F: (01823) 490590
E: robhembrow@btinternet.com
I: www.holly-farm.com

Lovells Farm ★★★-★★★★
Contact: Mr & Ms Oppenlander/Bolton
Lovells Farm, Dark Lane, Stoke Gregory, Taunton TA3 6EU
T: (01823) 491405
F: (01823) 491433
I: www.somersetholidays.com

STOKE ST MARY
Somerset

Centra ★★★★
Contact: Mrs Karen Freir
Centra, Stoke St Mary, Taunton TA3 5BS
T: (01823) 442443
E: info@centra-uk.com
I: www.centra-uk.com

Stoke Hill Barn ★★-★★★★
Contact: Mr Alan Coles
Stoke Hill Barn, Stoke St Mary, Taunton TA3 5BT
T: (01823) 443759
F: (01823) 443759
E: ajcoles@supanet.com

STOKE ST MICHAEL
Bath and North East Somerset

Pitcot Farm Barn Cottages ★★★★
Contact: Mrs Mary Coles
Pitcot Farm Barn Cottages, Pitcot Lane, Radstock BA3 4SX
T: (01761) 233108
F: (01761) 417710
I: www.pitcotfarm.co.uk

STOKE SUB HAMDON
Somerset

2 Blackspur Cottage ★★★★
Contact: Mr John Fisher
Brook House, Little Street, Stoke sub Hamdon TA14 6SR
T: (01935) 881789
F: (01935) 881789

Fairhaven ★★★★
Contact: Mrs Margaret Wilson
Fairhaven, Montacute Road, Stoke sub Hamdon TA14 6UQ
T: (01935) 823534
E: frank@fairhaven70.freeserve.co.uk
I: www.fairhavensomerset.co.uk

Top o Hill ★★★
Contact: Mrs Mary Gane
Percombe, Stoke sub Hamdon TA14 6RD
T: (01935) 822089

STOKEINTEIGNHEAD
Devon

Church Barn Cottage ★★★★
Contact: Mr Peter & Mrs Judy Rees
Congdon Farm Cottages, Newton Abbot TQ12 4QA
T: (01626) 872433

Dean Cottage ★★★★
Contact:
Holiday Homes & Cottages South West, 365A Torquay Road, Paignton TQ3 2BT
T: (01803) 663650
F: (01803) 664037
E: holcotts@aol.com
I: www.swcottages.co.uk

The Granary ★★★
Contact:
Holiday Homes & Cottages South West, 365A Torquay Road, Paignton TQ3 2BT
T: (01803) 663650

STOKENHAM
Devon

Tilly's Tuckaway ★★★★★
Contact:
Toad Hall Cottages, Elliot House, Church Street, Kingsbridge TQ7 1BY
T: (01548) 853089
F: (01548) 853086
E: thc@toadhallcottages.com
I: www.toadhallcottages.com

STONEY STRATTON
Somerset

Red Tiles ★★★★
Contact: Mr Richard Neill
Red Tiles, The Vicarage, Winkfield Street, Windsor SL4 4SW
T: (01344) 882322
E: neill.hall@care4free.net

Springfield Cottages ★★★★
Contact: Mrs Pat Allen
Springfield Cottages, Springfield House, Maesdown Hill, Shepton Mallet BA4 6EG
T: (01749) 830748
E: ted.allen@btinternet.com

STOW-ON-THE-WOLD
Gloucestershire

Barn Cottage ★★★★★
Contact: Mrs Lissa Mills
Blundells, Moreton-in-Marsh GL56 0TL
T: (01451) 830947
E: lissa-mills@ukonline.co.uk

Box Cottage ★★★
Contact: Mr Bob Johnston
Poplars Barn, Evenlode, Moreton-in-Marsh GL56 0NN
T: (01608) 650816
F: (01608) 652996
I: www.cottagesinstow.com

Broad Oak Cottages ★★★★★
Contact: Mrs Wilson
The Counting House, Stow-on-the-Wold, Cheltenham GL54 1AL
T: (01451) 830794
F: (01451) 830794
E: mary@broadoakcottages.fsnet.co.uk
I: www.broadoakcottages.fsnet.co.uk

Charlie's Cottage ★★★★
Contact: Mrs Veronica Woodford
21 Wyck Rissington, Cheltenham GL54 2PN
T: (01451) 821496
E: iwoodford@wyckriss.freeserve.co.uk

Foden Lodge ★★★
Contact: Mr & Mrs Beryl Gypps
77 Park Lane, Waltham Cross EN8 8AD
T: (01992) 301800
E: thefodenlodge@hotmail.com
I: www.come.to/fodenlodge

Glebe Cottage ★★★★
Contact: Mr Lesley Paler
Newlands Cottage, Guildford Lane, Guildford GU5 9BG
T: (01483) 203375
E: lesley@gbc-ca.co.uk

Greystoke Bungalow ★★★★★
Contact: Mr G Dobson
Middle Croft House, Bossington Lane, Minehead TA24 8HD
T: (01643) 862636
E: geodobson@hemscott.net
I: www.cottageguide.co.uk/elderbeck2

Horseshoes ★★★
Contact: Mr Bob Johnston
Poplars Barn, Evenlode, Moreton-in-Marsh GL56 0NN
T: (01608) 650816
F: (01608) 652996
I: www.cottagesinstow.com

Icomb Lodge ★★★★★
Contact: Mr Antony Batty
12 Dale Bank, Oakdale, Harrogate HG1 2LP
T: (01423) 502355

Johnston Cottage ★★★
Contact: Mrs Yvonne Johnston
Poplars Barn, Evenlode, Moreton-in-Marsh GL56 0NN
T: (01608) 650816
F: (01608) 652996
I: www.cottagesinstow.com

Kelross ★★★★
Contact: Mrs Kate McReynolds
Top Leather Mill Farm, Watling Street, Nuneaton CV10 0TQ
T: (024) 76350221
F: (024) 76373608
E: suehawkins@hawksmoor.fsbusiness.co.uk
I: www.goldenretrievers-uk.com

Lower Court Cottages ★★★-★★★★★
Contact: Mrs Juliet Pauling
Lower Court Farm, Oxford OX7 3NQ
T: (01608) 676422
F: (01608) 676422
E: jpauling@lineone.net

Maugersbury Manor ★★★
Contact: Mr Martin
Maugersbury Manor, Cheltenham GL54 1HP
T: (01451) 830581
F: (01451) 870902
I: www.manorholidays.co.uk

The Old School House ★★★★
Contact: Mrs Anita McKinney
Beresford, Cliveden Mead, Maidenhead SL6 8HE
T: (01628) 638190
E: information@heartofthecotswolds.com
I: www.heartofthecotswolds.com

Park Farm Holiday Cottages ★★★★-★★★★★
Contact: Mrs Tiana Ricketts
Park Farm, Maugersbury, Cheltenham GL54 1HP
T: (01451) 830227
F: (01451) 870568
E: parkfarm.cottages@virgin.net

Park House Cottage ★★★
Contact: Mr & Mrs G Sutton
Park House Cottage, Park House, Park Street, Stow on the Wold, Cheltenham GL54 1AQ
T: (01451) 830159
F: (01451) 870809
E: info@parkhousecottage.co.uk
I: www.parkhousecottage.co.uk

Stable Cottage ★★★★
Contact: Mrs Marie Hill
Stable Cottage, Stow-on-the-Wold, Cheltenham GL54 1EW
T: (01451) 830198
E: mariehill500@hotmail.com

Sycamore Cottage ★★★★
Contact: Mrs S Jones
Hill House, 111 Bicester Road, Aylesbury HP18 9EF
T: (01844) 208615
E: suejones16@hotmail.com

2 Union Street ★★★★
Contact: Ms Spiers
Cottage in the Country, Forest Gate, Frog Lane, Milton-under-Wychwood OX7 6JZ
T: (01993) 831495
F: (01993) 831095
E: info@cottageinthecountry.co.uk
I: www.cottageinthecountry.co.uk

Valley View ★★★
Contact: Mr & Mrs Craddock
25 Avenue Road, Dorridge, Solihull B93 8LD
T: (01564) 770143

Wells Cottage ★★★
Contact: Mr A G Williams
Woodlands, 5 Glebe Close, Stow-on-the-Wold, Cheltenham GL54 1DJ
T: (01451) 830045

702   Look out for establishments participating in the National Accessible Scheme

SOUTH WEST ENGLAND

STRATFORD SUB CASTLE
Wiltshire

Manor Cottage H107 ★★★★
Contact:
Hideaways, Chapel House, Luke Street, Berwick St John, Shaftesbury SP7 0HQ
T: (01747) 828170
F: (01747) 829090
E: enq@hideaways.co.uk
I: www.hideaways.co.uk

Millers Barn ★★★
Contact: Mr Nicholas Pash
Hideaways, Chapel House, Luke Street, Berwick St John, Shaftesbury SP7 0HQ
T: (01747) 828170
F: (01747) 829090
E: enq@hideaways.co.uk
I: www.hideaways.co.uk

STRATTON
Cornwall

The Granary ★★★
Contact: Mrs Deborah Chivers
The Granary, Marsh Farm Cottage, Howard Lane, Bude EX23 9TE
T: (01288) 355503
F: (01288) 355503
E: ncsigns@ncsigns.co.uk
I: www.cottagesdirect.com/coa197

Ivyleaf Combe ★★★★
Contact: Mr Tony Cheeseman
Ivyleaf Combe, Bude EX23 9LD
T: (01288) 321323
F: (01288) 321323
E: tony@ivyleafcombe.com
I: www.ivyleafcombe.com

Kitts Cottage ★★★
Contact:
Farm & Cottage Holidays, Victoria House, 12 Fore Street, Bideford EX39 1AW
T: (01237) 479146
F: (01237) 421512
E: enquiries@farmcott.co.uk
I: www.farmcott.co.uk

No. 2 Bideford Mews ★★★
Contact: Mr Neil Harrold
Greensleeves, Heathton, Wolverhampton WV5 7EB
T: (01746) 710147

Old Sanctuary Cottages ★★★★
Contact: Mrs Jane Berry
Old Sanctuary Cottages, Diddies Road, Bude EX23 9DW
T: (01288) 353159
F: (01288) 353159
E: kj.berry@virgin.net
I: www.oldsanctuarycottages.com

The Tithe Barn ★★★
Contact: Mrs S Gregory
High View Cottage, Townsend, Bude EX23 9DL
T: (01288) 353138

Tree Hill House ★★★
Contact: Mrs Christine Heybourn
9 Frances Road, Windsor SL4 3AE
T: (01753) 852512
F: (01753) 852512
E: robert@heybourn.freeserve.co.uk

STREET
Somerset

Blue Lias ★★★
Contact: Mr Mark Foot
8 Kingston Drive, Bristol BS48 4RB
T: (01275) 853612
F: (01275) 544936

STRETE
Devon

Sunsets ★★★★
Contact:
Powells Cottage Holidays, Springmill, Earby, Saundersfoot BB94 0AA
T: 0870 5 143076
F: (01834) 811731
E: info@powells.co.uk
I: www.powells.co.uk

STROUD
Gloucestershire

The Coach House c/o The Old Vicarage ★★★★
Contact: Mrs Stella Knight
The Old Vicarage, Rockness, Horsley, Stroud GL6 0PJ
T: (01453) 832265
F: (01453) 832865
E: stella.knight@tiscali.co.uk
I: www.cotswoldholidaycottage.co.uk

Little Vatch ★★★
Contact: Mr Hoy
Little Vatch, Upper Vatch Mill, The Vatch, Stroud GL6 7JY
T: (01453) 764270
F: (01453) 755233
E: i.hodgkins@dial.pipex.com
I: www.ianhodgkins.com

Lypiatt Hill House ★★-★★★
Contact: Mr Pyke
Lypiatt Hill House, Bisley Road, Stroud GL6 7LQ
T: (01453) 764785
F: (01453) 751782
E: john.pyke@virgin.net

Twissells Mill ★★
Contact: Mr Daphne & Mrs Martin Neville
Twissells Mill, Stroud GL6 8JH
T: (01285) 760234

Westley Farm ★★★
Contact: Mr Usborne
Westley Farm, Charlford, Stroud GL6 8HP
T: (01285) 760262
F: (01285) 760262
I: www.westleyfarm.co.uk

The Yew Tree ★★★★
Contact: Mrs Elizabeth Peters
The Yew Tree, Walls Quarry, Brimscombe, Stroud GL5 2PA
T: (01453) 887594
F: (01453) 883428
E: elizabeth.peters@tesco.net
I: www.preferredplaces.co.uk/explore/cotswolds

STURMINSTER NEWTON
Dorset

The Homestead ★★★
Contact: Mrs Carol Townsend
The Homestead, Holehouse Lane, Sturminster Newton DT10 2AA
T: (01258) 471390
E: townsend@dircon.co.uk
I: www.townsend.dircon.co.uk

Rivers Corner House ★★★★
Contact: Mr Paul Gardiner
5 The Old Dairy Farm, Sturminster Newton DT10 2ES
T: (01258) 817021
F: (01258) 817371
E: pg@twinserve.co.uk
I: www.heartofdorset.easynet.co.uk

SUTTON POYNTZ
Dorset

Ebenezer Cottage ★★★★
Contact: Cathy Varley
Hiscocks Farm, Moorside, Sturminster Newton DT10 1HF
T: 07778 524199
E: info@ebenezercottage.co.uk
I: www.ebenezercottage.co.uk

Magnolia Cottage ★★★
Contact: Mr Zachary Stuart-Brown
Dream Cottages, 5 Hope Square, Weymouth DT4 8TR
T: (01305) 789000
F: (01305) 761346
E: admin@dream-cottages.co.uk
I: www.dream-cottages.co.uk

SUTTON WALDRON
Dorset

Dairy Cottage ★★★
Contact: Mary Pope
Broadlea Farm, Sutton Waldron, Blandford Forum DT11 8NS
T: (01747) 811330
F: (01747) 811330
E: maryp2@tinyworld.co.uk

SWANAGE
Dorset

Alrose Villa Holiday Apartments ★★★
Contact: Mrs Jacqueline Wilson
Alrose Villa Holiday Apartments, 2 Highcliffe Road, Swanage BH19 1LW
T: (01929) 426318
E: enquiry@alrosevilla.co.uk
I: www.alrosevilla.co.uk

Ballard Lee & Ballard Ridge ★★★
Contact: Mr & Mrs Ian Lever
Old Stables, Grange Road, Wareham BH20 5AL
T: (01929) 551320

6 Cluny Crescent ★★★★
Contact: Mr David Smith
Miles & Son, Railway House, 2 Rempstone Road, Swanage BH19 1DW
T: (01929) 423333
F: (01929) 427533
E: info@milesandson.co.uk

Coastguards Return ★★★★
Contact: Mrs Anna Morrison
Coastguards Return, 6 Sunnydale Villas, Durlston Road, Swanage BH19 2HY
T: (01929) 424630
F: (01929) 424630
E: jamesrmorrison@aol.com

5 Durlston Mews ★★★★
Contact: Ms Leanne Hemingway
Dorset Cottage Holidays, 11 Tyneham Close, Wareham BH20 7BE
T: (01929) 553443
F: (01929) 552714
E: enquiries@dhcottages.co.uk
I: www.dhcottages.co.uk/durlston_mews.htm

Flat 32 ★★★★
Contact: Mrs Chris Hobson
17 Moorside Road, Wimborne Minster BH21 3NB
T: (01202) 696222
F: 0871 4334879
E: mel.hobson@lds.co.uk
I: www.lds.co.uk/holidayhome

Flat 7 Grand View
Rating Applied For
Contact: Ms Nicky Russ
Wyke Holiday Properties, 137A High Street, Swanage BH19 2NB
T: (01929) 422776
F: (01929) 422002
E: bookings@wykeholiday.co.uk
I: www.apexweb.co.uk/whp

Flat 8 Sandringham Court ★★★★
Contact: Mrs Nicola Russ
Wyke Holiday Properties Ltd, 137A High Street, Swanage BH19 2NB
T: (01929) 422776
F: (01929) 422002
I: www.wykeholiday.co.uk

1 Garwood ★★★
Contact: Ms Russ
Wyke Holiday Properties, 137A High Street, Swanage BH19 2NB
T: (01929) 422776

10 The Haven ★★★★
Contact: Mrs Russ
Wyke Holiday Properties, 137A High Street, Swanage BH19 2NB
T: (01929) 422776
F: (01929) 422002
E: bookings@wykeholiday.co.uk
I: www.wykeholiday.co.uk

13 The Haven ★★★★
Contact: Ms Nicky Russ
Wyke Holiday Properties, 137A High Street, Swanage BH19 2NB
T: (01929) 422776
F: (01929) 422002
E: bookings@wykeholiday.co.uk
I: www.wykeholiday.co.uk

Holiday Bungalow ★★★
Contact: Mrs Mary Brennan
Speedwell, 10 Hillsea Road, Swanage BH19 2QN
T: (01929) 425715
F: (01929) 425715

Island View ★★★
Contact: Mr & Mrs Jones
Island View, 19A Priests Road, Swanage BH19 2RG
T: (01929) 426614
E: ray.jones@btinternet.com

Establishments printed in blue have a detailed entry in this guide

SOUTH WEST ENGLAND

The Ketch
Rating Applied For
Contact: Ms Leanne Hemingway
Dorset Cottage Holidays, 11 Tyneham Close, Wareham
BH20 7BE
T: (01929) 553443
F: (01929) 552714
E: enq@dhcottages.co.uk
I: www.dhcottages.
co.uk/the%20ketch.htm

27 Manwell Road ★★★
Contact: Mrs Jill Henstridge
10 Moor Road, Swanage
BH19 1RG
T: (01929) 427276

No 3 Exeter Road ★★★★
Contact: Mrs Anna Morrison
6 Sunnydale Villas, Durlston Road, Swanage BH19 2HY
T: (01929) 424630
F: (01929) 424630
E: jamesrmorrison@aol.com

One London Row ★★★
Contact: Mr Philip & Mrs Monica Sanders
54 Hillway, Highgate, London N6 6EP
T: (020) 83489815
F: (020) 8347 7124
E: info@philamonic.com
I: www.philamonic.com

Pips Cottage ★★
Contact: Mr Michael Padfield
Greenways, Grubwood Lane, Maidenhead SL6 9UB
T: (01628) 472113
E: mike@thepadfields.com

Purbeck Cliffs ★★★★
Contact: Mrs Sue McWilliams
Purbeck Cliffs, 3 Boundary Close, Swanage BH19 2JY
T: (01929) 424352
I: www.purbeckcliffs.co.uk

1B Purbeck Terrace Road ★★★
Contact: Ms Nicky Russ
Wyke Holiday Properties, 137A High Street, Swanage BH19 2NB
T: (01929) 422776
F: (01929) 422002
E: bookings@wykeholiday.co.uk
I: www.wykeholiday.co.uk

The Quarterdeck ★★★
Contact: Ms Leanne Hemingway
Dorset Cottage Holidays, 11 Tyneham Close, Wareham
BH20 7BE
T: (01929) 553443
F: (01929) 552714
E: reservations@dhcottages.
co.uk
I: www.purbeckholidays.co.uk

2 Quayside Court ★★
Contact: Mr Michael Padfield
Greenways, Grubwood Lane, Maidenhead SL6 9UB
T: (01628) 472113
E: mike@thepadfields.com

St Mark's Cottage ★★★★
Contact: Mr David Evans
38 Blackborough Road, Reigate RH2 7BX
T: (01737) 224441
F: (01737) 240952
E: david@asdellevans.co.uk

Sea Wall ★★★
Contact: Ms Leanne Hemingway
Dorset Cottage Holidays, 11 Tyneham Close, Wareham
BH20 7BE
T: (01929) 553443
F: (01929) 552714
E: enquiries@dhcottages.co.uk
I: www.dhcottages.
co.uk/sea%20wall.htm

Seaviews ★★★
Contact: Mr Robert Moon
40 Bryanstone Lodge, Bryanstone Road, Talbot Woods, Bournemouth BH3 7JF
T: (01202) 513671
E: moon-enterprises@cwctv.net

Swanwic House ★★
Contact: Mrs Carole Figg
Swanwic House, 41A Kings Road West, Swanage BH19 1HF
T: (01929) 423517

Tanglewood ★★★★
Contact: Probert
9 Longfield Drive, Amersham HP6 5HD
T: (01494) 721849
F: (01494) 721849
E: audrey.probert@btopenworld.com

2 Wilksworth Cottage ★★
Contact: Mr Stuart-Brown
Dream Cottages, 41 Maiden Street, Weymouth DT4 8TR
T: (01305) 789000

SWANPOOL
Cornwall

Mobri ★★★★★
Contact: Mrs Broughton
Mobri, 1B Madeira Walk, Falmouth TR11 4EJ
T: (01326) 314348

SWIMBRIDGE
Devon

Lane End ★★★★
Contact:
Marsden's Cottage Holidays, 2 The Square, Braunton EX33 2JB
T: (01271) 813777
F: (01271) 813664
E: holidays@marsdens.co.uk
I: www.marsdens.co.uk

Lower Hearson Country Holidays ★★★-★★★★★
Contact: Mr John Donlan
Lower Hearson Country Holidays, Barnstaple EX32 0QH
T: (01271) 830246
E: john@aushndonlan.freeserve.co.uk
I: www.hearsoncottagesdevon.co.uk

SWINDON
Swindon

The Cottage ★★★★
Contact: Mrs Judith Stares
The Cottage, 101 Bath Road, Swindon SN1 4AX
T: (01793) 485461
F: (01793) 485462
E: judith@stares.co.uk
I: www.stares.co.uk

Minsters Chase ★★★★
Contact: Mr Bob & Mrs Pennie Astbury
26 Coln Crescent, Green Meadow, Swindon SN25 3NA
T: (01793) 726775
E: penniebob@tiscali.co.uk

SYDLING ST NICHOLAS
Dorset

Grace Cottage ★★★
Contact: Mrs Nicky Willis
Lamperts Cottage, Dorchester Road, Sydling St Nicholas, Dorchester DT2 9NU
T: (01300) 341659
F: (01300) 341699
E: nickywillis@tesco.net

SYMONDSBURY
Dorset

Bathsheba ★★★★
Contact: Mrs Shelagh Mullins
Bathsheba, 1 Shutes Farm Cottage, Bridport DT6 6HF
T: (01308) 425261
F: (01308) 425261
E: shelaghmullins@aol.com
I: www.shelaghsbathsheba.co.uk

Crepe Farmhouse ★★★★
Contact: Ms Catherine Chick
Symondsbury Farms Ltd, The Estate Office, Bridport DT6 6EX
T: 07940 839868
E: philip@holcot.com
I: www.holcot.com

TALATON
Devon

Westcot House Farm ★★★
Contact: Miss Melanie Peters
Westcot House Farm, Exeter EX5 2RN
T: (01404) 822320
F: (01404) 823847
E: m.peters@farming.co.uk

TAUNTON
Somerset

Higher House ★★★
Contact: Mrs Kirsten Horton
Higher House, Hillcommon, Taunton TA4 1DU
T: (01823) 400570
F: (01823) 400765
E: tedandkirsten@tiscali.co.uk
I: www.visitwestcountry.com/higherhouse

Masons Arms ★★
Contact: Mr Jeremy Leyton
Masons Arms, Magdalene Street, Taunton TA1 1SG
T: (01823) 288916
E: jjmax@jleyton.freeserve.co.uk
I: www.masonsarms.freeuk.com

Meadowsweet Farm Cottages
Rating Applied For
Contact: Miss Jacqueline McCann
Meadowsweet Farm Cottages, Meadowsweet Farm, Newton, Taunton TA4 4EU
T: (01984) 656323
F: (01984) 656933
E: info@meadowsweet-cottages.co.uk
I: www.meadowsweet-cottages.co.uk

Meare Court Holiday Cottages ★★★-★★★★
Contact: Mrs Elizabeth Bray
Meare Court Holiday Cottages, Meare Court, Meare Green, Taunton TA3 6DA
T: (01823) 480570
F: (01823) 481123
E: mearecourt@farming.co.uk
I: www.mearecourt.co.uk

TAVISTOCK
Devon

Cedar Lodge ★★★
Contact: Mr & Mrs Ashe
Cedar Lodge, Heathfield, Tavistock PL19 0LQ
T: (01822) 810038
E: sandra@acorncot1.fsnet.co.uk
I: www.geocities.com/acorncottage

Downhouse Farm ★★★★
Contact: Ms Sarah Heaps
Downhouse Farm, Mill Hill Lane, Tavistock PL19 8NH
T: (01822) 614521
F: (01822) 613675
E: downhousefarm@aol.com
I: www.downhousefarm.co.uk

Edgemoor Cottage ★★★★
Contact: Mrs Mary Susan Fox
Edgemoor, Middlemoor, Tavistock PL19 9DY
T: (01822) 612259
F: (01822) 617625

Higher Chaddlehanger Farm ★★★
Contact: Mrs Cole
Higher Chaddlehanger Farm, Tavistock PL19 0LG
T: (01822) 810268
F: (01822) 810268

Moorview Cottage ★★★★
Contact: Mrs Elaine Mackintosh
Moorview Cottage, Moorview, Cudlipptown, Peter Tavy, Tavistock PL19 9LZ
T: (01822) 810271
F: (01822) 810082
E: wts@dartmoor-holidays.fsnet.co.uk
I: www.dartmoor-holidays.com

Old Sowtontown ★★★
Contact: Mr Christopher Boswell
Old Sowtontown, Tavistock PL19 9JR
T: (01822) 810687
F: (01822) 810687
E: chrisboswe@aol.com
I: www.dartmoorholidays.co.uk

Tavistock Trout Fishery ★★★★
Contact: Miss A Underhill
Tavistock Trout Fishery, Parkwood Road, Tavistock PL19 9JW
T: (01822) 615441
F: (01822) 615401
E: abigail@tavistocktroutfishery.co.uk
I: www.tavistocktroutfishery.co.uk

SOUTH WEST ENGLAND

TAYNTON
Gloucestershire

Owls Barn ★★★★
Contact: Mrs Barbara Goodwin
Owls Barn, Coldcroft Farm,
Glasshouse Lane, Gloucester
GL19 3HJ
T: (01452) 831290
F: (01452) 831544
E: goodies@coldcroft.freeserve.co.uk
I: www.coldcroft.freeserve.co.uk

TEIGNGRACE
Devon

Twelve Oaks Holiday Cottages ★★★
Contact: Mrs Gale
Twelve Oaks Farm, Newton Abbot TQ12 6QT
T: (01626) 352769
F: (01626) 352769

TEIGNMOUTH
Devon

Clifton House
Rating Applied For
Contact:
Holiday Homes & Cottages SW, 365A Torquay Road, Paignton TQ3 2BT
T: (01808) 663650
F: (01808) 664037
E: holcotts@AOL.com
I: www.swcottages.co.uk

Grendons Holiday Apartments ★★★
Contact: Mr Charles Gray
Grendons Holiday Apartments, 58 Coombe Vale Road, Teignmouth TQ14 9EW
T: (01626) 773667
F: (01626) 773667
E: grendonsholidayapts@cix.co.uk

The Old Post office ★★★
Contact:
Holiday Homes and Cottages SW, 365A Torquay Road, Paignton TQ3 2BT
T: (01803) 663650
F: (01803) 664037
E: holcotts@aol.com
I: www.swcottages.co.uk

TELLISFORD
Somerset

Farleigh Wood ★★★★
Contact: Ms Bella Gingell
Farleigh Wood, Wood Cottage, Tellisford, Bath BA2 7RN
T: (01373) 831495
F: (01373) 830289
E: bellagingell@farleighwood.fsnet.co.uk
I: www.farleighwood.co.uk

TEMPLE GUITING
Gloucestershire

Hattie's, Lucy's, Chapel and Jack's ★★★★
Contact: Miss Pippa Arnott
Cotswold Cottage Company, Wells Head, Temple Guiting, Cheltenham GL54 5RR
T: (01451) 850560
F: 08701 280033
E: cotsxotco@msn.com
I: www.cotswoldcottage.co.uk

Springbank ★★★★★
Contact: Mrs Kate Mather
Springbank, Colman, Cheltenham GL54 5RT
T: (01451) 850571
F: (01451) 850614
E: springbank@landgatetg.co.uk
I: www.landgatetg.co.uk

TETBURY
Gloucestershire

Folly Farm Cottages ★★★
Contact: Mr Julian Benton
Folly Farm Cottages, Folly Farm Cottages, Tetbury GL8 8XA
T: (01666) 502475
F: (01666) 502358
E: info@gtb.co.uk
I: www.gtb.co.uk

TEWKESBURY
Gloucestershire

Courtyard Cottages ★★★★-★★★★★
Contact: Mr Herford
Upper Court, Tewkesbury GL20 7HY
T: (01386) 725351
F: (01386) 725472
E: diana@uppercourt.co.uk
I: www.uppercourt.co.uk

9 Millbank ★★
Contact: Mr Hunt
7 Mill Bank, Tewkesbury GL20 5SD
T: (01684) 276190
F: (01527) 875384
E: billhunt@9mb.co.uk
I: www.9mb.co.uk

The Old Stable Block ★★★
Contact: Mr & Mrs Geoff Stringer
The Old Stable Block, Beckford Stores, Main Street, Tewkesbury GL20 7AD
T: (01386) 881248
E: info@beckford-stores.co.uk

The Stables Rose Hill Farm ★★★
Contact: Mrs Elizabeth Collinson
The Stables Rose Hill Farm, Stokes Lane, Tewkesbury GL20 6HS
T: (01684) 293598

THE LIZARD
Cornwall

Bass Point Cottage
Rating Applied For
Contact: Mr Martin Raftery
Mullion Cottages, Mullion Meadows, Helston TR12 7HB
T: (01326) 240315
F: (01326) 241090
E: enquiries@mullioncottages.com

Dene House ★★★★
Contact: Mr Martin Raftery
Mullion Cottages, Mullion Meadows, Helston TR12 7HB
T: (01326) 240315
F: (01326) 241090
E: martin@mullioncottages.com
I: www.mullioncottages.com

The Haven ★★★
Contact: Mr Martin Raftery
Mullion Cottages, Mullion Meadows, Helston TR12 7HB
T: (01326) 240315
F: (01326) 241090
E: martin@mullioncottages.com
I: www.mullioncottages.com

The Roundhouse ★★★★
Contact: Mr Martin Raftery
Mullion Cottages, Mullion Meadow, Helston TR12 7HB
T: (01326) 240315
F: (01326) 241090
E: martin@mullioncottages.com
I: www.mullioncottages.com

Sunny Corner ★★
Contact: Mr Martin Raftery
Mullion Cottages, Mullion Meadows, Helston TR12 7HB
T: (01326) 240315
F: (01326) 241090
E: martin@mullioncottages.com
I: www.mullioncottages.com

Tregonoggy ★★★
Contact: Mr Martin Raftery
Mullion Cottages, Mullion Meadows, Helston TR12 7HB
T: (01326) 240315
F: (01326) 241090
E: enquiries@mullioncottages.com

THE PACKET QUAYS
Cornwall

6 Jane's Court ★★★★
Contact:
Cornish Holiday Cottages, Killibrae, West Bay Maenporth Road, Falmouth TR11 5HP
T: (01326) 250339
F: (01326) 250339
E: postmaster@cornishholidaycottages.net

THORNBURY
Devon

Dairy Cottage and Beech Barn ★★★★
Contact:
Farm & Cottage Holidays, Victoria House, 12 Fore Street, Bideford EX39 1AW
T: (01237) 479146
F: (01237) 421512
E: enquiries@farmcott.co.uk
I: www.selfcatering-devon.com

THORNCOMBE
Dorset

6 The Terrace - W4434 ★★★
Contact: Mr Jim Matthews
Lyme Bay Holidays, Bos House, 44 Church Street, Lyme Regis DT7 3DA
T: (01297) 443363
F: (01297) 445576
E: email@lymebayholidays.co.uk
I: www.lymebayholidays.co.uk

Thatch Cottage ★★★★★
Contact: Mr John Mercer
53 Heatherside Road, Epsom KT19 9QS
T: (020) 83938165
E: eileenjmercer@hotmail.com

THORVERTON
Devon

Fursdon Estate ★★★★
Contact: Mrs Catriona Fursdon
Fursdon Estate, Fursdon House, Cadbury, Exeter EX5 5JS
T: (01392) 860860
F: (01392) 860126
E: enquiries@fursdon.co.uk
I: www.fursdon.co.uk

Ratcliffe Farm ★★★
Contact: Mr & Mrs Ayre
Ratcliffe Farm, Thorverton, Exeter EX5 5PN
T: (01392) 860434
E: ayre.ratcliffe@virgin.net

THREE LEGGED CROSS
Dorset

The Gables ★★★
Contact: Mr & Mrs David Priest
The Gables, Verwood Road, Wimborne Minster BH21 6RW
T: (01202) 821322
F: (01202) 821322

THROWLEIGH
Devon

Sue's House & The Cottage ★★-★★★
Contact: Mrs Joan White
Sue's House & The Cottage, Aysh Farm, Okehampton EX20 2HY
T: (01647) 231266

THURLESTONE
Devon

April Cottage ★★★★
Contact:
Toad Hall Cottages, Elliot House, Church Street, Kingsbridge TQ7 1BY
T: (01548) 853089
F: (01548) 853086
E: thc@toadhallcottages.com

Jasmine Cottage ★★★★
Contact:
Toad Hall Cottages, Elliot House, Church Street, Kingsbridge TQ7 1BY
T: (01548) 853089
F: (01548) 853086
E: thc@toadhallcottages.com

Stable Cottage ★★★★★
Contact:
Toad Hall Cottages, Elliot House, Church Street, Kingsbridge TQ7 1BY
T: (01548) 853089
F: (01548) 853086
E: thc@toadhallcottages.com

THURLESTONE SANDS
Devon

Seamark ★★★-★★★★
Contact: Mr Robin & Mrs Angela Collyns
Seamark, Salcombe, Kingsbridge TQ7 3JY
T: (01548) 561300
F: (01548) 561285
E: collyns.seamark@virgin.net
I: www.seamarkdevon.co.uk

TIMBERSCOMBE
Somerset

Allercott Cottages ★★★★
Contact: Mr Julian Willford
Allercott Cottages, Allercott Farm, Minehead TA24 7BN
T: (01643) 841555
I: www.allercott-cottages.co.uk

Establishments printed in blue have a detailed entry in this guide

SOUTH WEST ENGLAND

TINCLETON
Dorset

The Old Dairy Cottage and Clyffe Dairy Cottage ★★★★
Contact: Mrs Rosemary Coleman
The Old Dairy Cottage and Clyffe Dairy Cottage, Clyffe Farm, Dorchester DT2 8QR
T: (01305) 848252
F: (01305) 848702
E: coleman.clyffe@virgin.net
I: www.heartofdorset.easynet.co.uk & www.the-old-barn.co.uk

TINTAGEL
Cornwall

Barras House ★★
Contact: Mr Sleep
Barras House, Castle View, Tintagel PL34 0DH
T: (01840) 770457

Clifden Farm Cottages ★★★
Contact: Mrs Margaret Nute
Clifden Farm Cottages, Halgabron, Tintagel PL34 0BD
T: (01840) 770437
E: mnute@clifdenfarm.fsnet.co.uk

Glen House ★★★★
Contact: Mrs White
Hazeldene, Bude EX23 0JQ
T: (01840) 230024
F: (01840) 230078
E: paul.bcfc@btinternet.com
I: www.cornwall-online.co.uk/glenhouse

Halgabron Mill ★★★
Contact: Mr Robin Evans
Halgabron Mill, St Nectans Glen, Tintagel PL34 0BB
T: (01840) 779099
F: (01840) 770661
E: robin@halgabronmill.co.uk
I: www.halgabronmill.co.uk

Newlands ★★★★
Contact: Mr Roger & Mrs Carol Wickett
Nancledra, Back Lane, Tintagel PL34 0AU
T: (01840) 770800

Penpethy Holiday Cottages ★★★
Contact: Mrs Morag Steadman
Penpethy Holiday Cottages, Lower Penpethy Farm, Tintagel PL34 0HH
T: (01840) 213903

Rosemary ★★★
Contact: Mrs Dyer
Rosemary, Bossiney Road, Tintagel PL34 0AH
T: (01840) 770472
F: (01840) 770472

Sunnyside ★★★
Contact: Mr & Mrs Hansen
Bramblegate, West Green Common, Hartley Wintney, Hook RG27 8JD
T: (01252) 843986 & 07960 356428
E: hansen_harry@hotmail.com

Tregeath Cottage ★★★
Contact: Mrs Edwina Broad
Davina, Trevillett, Tintagel PL34 0HL
T: (01840) 770217
F: (01840) 770217

TISBURY
Wiltshire

The Old Coach House ★★★
Contact: Mr Nicholas Pash
Hideaways, Chapel House, Luke Street, Berwick St John, Shaftesbury SP7 0HQ
T: (01747) 828170
F: (01747) 829090
E: enq@hideaways.co.uk
I: www.hideaways.co.uk

TIVERTON
Devon

Cider Cottage ★★★★
Contact: Mrs Sylvia Hann
Cider Cottage, Great Bradley Farm, Tiverton EX16 8JL
T: (01884) 256946
F: (01884) 256946
E: hann@agriplus.net
I: www.cider-cottage.co.uk

Coombe Cottage ★★★★
Contact: Mrs Mary Reed
Coombe Cottage, Tiverton EX16 9HF
T: (01398) 351281
F: (01398) 351211
E: coombehse@aol.com
I: www.exmoor-holiday-cottage.co.uk

Lilac Cottage ★★★★
Contact: Mrs Venner
Lilac Cottage, Battens Farm, Sampford Peverell, Tiverton EX16 7EE
T: (01884) 820226
I: www.cottageguide.co.uk/battensfarm

Old Bridwell Holiday Cottages ★★★★
Contact: Ms Jackie Kind
Old Bridwell Holiday Cottages, Uffculme, Cullompton EX15 3BU
T: (01884) 841464
E: jackie@oldbridwell.co.uk
I: www.oldbridwell.co.uk

Tiverton Castle ★★★★
Contact: Mrs Alison Gordon
Tiverton Castle, Park Hill, Tiverton EX16 6RP
T: (01884) 253200
F: (01884) 254200
E: tiverton.castle@ukf.net
I: www.tivertoncastle.com

West Pitt Farm ★★★-★★★★★
Contact: Ms Susanne Westgate
West Pitt Farm, Whitnage, Tiverton EX16 7DU
T: (01884) 820296
F: (01884) 820818
E: susannewestgate@yahoo.com
I: www.fisheries.co.uk/westpitt

TIVINGTON
Somerset

Tethinstone Cottage ★★★★
Contact: Mr Nicholas Challis
Tethinstone Cottage, Minehead TA24 8SX
T: (01643) 706757
F: (01643) 706757

TODENHAM
Gloucestershire

Applegate ★★★★
Contact: Mrs Crump
Applegate, The Retreat, Springbank, Moreton-in-Marsh GL56 9PA
T: (01608) 651307

TOLLER PORCORUM
Dorset

Dairy Maids Cottage ★★★★
Contact: Mrs Rosemary Gower
Dairy Maids Cottage, Frogmore Farm, Dorchester DT2 0DL
T: (01300) 320541
E: rosemarygower@hotmail.com

11 High Street ★★★
Contact: Mrs Dot Thornton
2 The George Yard, Broad Street, Alresford SO24 9EF
T: (01962) 732700
E: dot.thornton@virgin.net

TOLPUDDLE
Dorset

Cob Cottage ★★★★★
Contact: Miss Hilary Cobban
The Old Mill, Dorchester DT2 7EX
T: (01305) 848552
F: (01305) 848552
E: hlcobban@lineone.net

River View Cottage ★★★★
Contact: Miss Leanne Hemingway
11 Tyneham Close, Wareham BH20 7BE
T: (01929) 553443
F: (01929) 552714
E: enq@dhcottages.co.uk
I: www.dhcottages.co.uk/river%20view.htm

TORPOINT
Cornwall

Chough Cottage ★★★★
Contact:
Valley Villas Sales Office, Office 38, City Business Park, Somerset Place, Stoke, Plymouth PL3 4BB
T: (01752) 605605
E: sales@valleyvillas.com
I: www.valleyvillas.com

Jackdaw Cottage
Rating Applied For
Contact: Mrs Rachael Sartorius
Farquhar Road, Birmingham B15 3RE
T: (0121) 4540284
E: aes@alucast.co.uk
I: www.Jackdawcottagecornwall.co.uk

TORQUAY
Torbay

ABBEY MEWS ★★★★
Contact:
Holiday Homes & Cottages South West, 365A Torquay Road, Paignton TQ3 2BT
T: (01803) 663650
F: (01803) 664037
E: holcotts@aol.com
I: www.swcottages.co.uk

Abbey View Holiday Flats ★★★
Contact: Mr & Mrs Foss & Blockley
Abbey View, Rathmore Road, Torquay TQ2 6NZ
T: (01803) 293722
E: abbeyflats@tinyworld.co.uk

Alexandra Lodge ★★★
Contact: Mrs Heather Armes
Alexandra Lodge, Grafton Road, Torquay TQ1 1QJ
T: (01803) 213465
F: (01803) 390933
E: alexalodge@aol.com
I: www.alexandra-lodge.co.uk

Appletorre House ★★★
Contact: Mr Colin & Mrs Coleen Moon
Appletorre House, 20 Vansittart Road, Torquay TQ2 5BW
T: (01803) 296430
I: www.appletorreflats.co.uk

Aster House Apartments ★★-★★★
Contact: Mr Coleman
Aster House Apartments, Warren Road, Torquay TQ2 5TR
T: (01803) 292747
E: info@asterhouse.freeserve.co.uk
I: www.asterhouse.freeserve.co.uk

Atherton Holiday Flats ★★
Contact: Mrs Kaye
41 Morgan Avenue, Torquay TQ2 5RR
T: (01803) 296884

Atlantis Holiday Apartments ★★★
Contact: Mrs Pauline Roberts
Atlantis Holiday Apartments, Solsbro Road, Torquay TQ2 6PF
T: (01803) 607929
F: (01803) 391313
E: enquiry@atlantistorquay.co.uk
I: www.atlantistorquay.co.uk

The Atrium ★★★★
Contact:
Holiday Homes & Cottages SW, 365A Torquay Road, Paignton TQ3 2BT
T: (01803) 663650
F: (01803) 664037
E: holcotts@aol.com
I: www.swcottages.co.uk

SOUTH WEST ENGLAND

Babbacombe Downs ★★★
Contact: Mr Ian Butterworth
Holiday Homes & Cottages
South West, 365A Torquay Road,
Paignton TQ3 2BT
T: (01803) 663650
F: (01803) 664037
E: holcotts@aol.com
I: www.swcottaages.co.uk

Barramore Holiday Flats ★★★
Contact: Mr & Mrs Trevor Ward
Barramore Holiday Flats, Solsbro Road, Chelston, Torquay TQ2 6PF
T: (01803) 607105
E: holidays@barramore.co.uk
I: www.barramore.co.uk

Bay Fort Mansions ★★★★
Contact: Mr & Miss Paul & Maria Freeman & Young
Bay Fort Mansions, Warren Road, Torquay TQ2 5TN
T: (01803) 213810
F: (01803) 209057
E: freeman@bayfortapartments.co.uk
I: www.bayfortapartments.co.uk

Bedford House ★★★
Contact: Mrs MacDonald-Smith
Bedford House, 517 Babbacombe Road, Torquay TQ1 1HJ
T: (01803) 296995
F: (01803) 296995
E: bedfordhotorquay@btconnect.com
I: www.bedfordhousetorquay.co.uk

The Beulah Holiday Apartments ★★★
Contact: Mr David & Mrs Caroline Perry
The Beulah Holiday Apartments, Meadfoot Road, Torquay TQ1 2JP
T: (01803) 297471
E: enquiries@thebeulah.co.uk
I: www.thebeulah.co.uk

Bronshill Court Holiday Apartments ★★★
Contact: Mr Tony & Mrs Glenys Burden
Bronshill Court Holiday Apartments, Bronshill Road, Torquay TQ1 3HD
T: (01803) 324549
F: (01803) 324549
E: holidays@bronshillcourt.co.uk
I: www.bronshillcourt.co.uk

Brunel ★★★★
Contact:
Holiday Homes & Cottages
South West, 365A Torquay Road,
Paignton TQ3 2BT
T: (01803) 663650
F: (01803) 664037
E: holcotts@aol.com
I: www.swcottages.co.uk

Burley Court Apartments ★★★
Contact: Mr & Mrs S Palmer
Burley Court Apartments, Wheatridge Lane, Livermead, Torquay TQ2 6RA
T: (01803) 607879
F: (01803) 605516
E: simon@burleycourt.co.uk
I: www.burleycourt.co.uk

Chelston Dene ★★★
Contact: Mr Rod Payne
Chelston Dene, Chelston Road, Chelston, Torquay TQ2 6PU
T: (01803) 605180
F: (01803) 605180
E: info@chelstondene.com
I: www.chelstondene.com

Chestnut Lodge Holiday Apartments ★★★
Contact: Mr George Baxter
Chestnut Lodge Holiday Apartments, Rowdens Road, Torquay TQ2 5AZ
T: (01803) 297242
E: enquiries@chestnutlodgetorquay.co.uk
I: www.chestnutlodgetorquay.co.uk

Cliff Court Holiday Apartments ★★★
Contact: Mrs Denise Tudor
Cliff Court Holiday Apartments, Cliff Road, Livermead, Torquay TQ2 6RE
T: (01803) 294687
E: info@cliffcourt.co.uk
I: www.cliffcourt.co.uk

Clydesdale Holiday Flats ★★★
Contact: Mr Terry Watson
Clydesdale Holiday Flats, 32 Croft Road, Torquay TQ2 5UE
T: (01803) 292759
I: www.clydesdaleholidayflats.co.uk

The Coach House & Butlers Flat ★★★★
Contact: Mr Ian Butterworth
Holiday Homes & Cottages
South West, 365A Torquay Road,
Paignton TQ3 2BT
T: (01803) 663650
F: (01803) 664037
E: holcotts@aol.com
I: www.swcottages.co.uk

Corbyn Lodge ★★-★★★
Contact:
Holiday Homes & Cottages
South West, 365A Torquay Road,
Paignton TQ3 2BT
T: (01803) 663650
F: (01803) 664037
E: holcotts@aol.com
I: www.swcottages.co.uk

The Corbyn Suites and Penthouses ★★★★★★
Contact:
The Corbyn Suites And Penthouses, Torbay Road, Torquay TQ2 6RH
T: (01803) 215595
F: (01803) 200568
I: www.thecorbyn.co.uk

Cornerstone ★★★
Contact: Mr Ian Butterworth
Holiday Homes & Cottages
South West, 365A Torquay Road,
Paignton TQ3 2BT
T: (01803) 663650

Cranmere Court ★★★
Contact: Mrs Sally Noad
Cranmere Court, Kents Road, Torquay TQ1 2NL
T: (01803) 293173
F: (01803) 293173

Derwent Hill Holiday Apartments ★★★
Contact: Mr Gill & Mrs Derek Bryant
Derwent Hill Holiday Apartments, Greenway Road, Torquay TQ2 6JE
T: (01803) 606793
F: (01803) 606793
E: info@derwent-hill.co.uk
I: www.derwent-hill.co.uk

Evergreen Lodge ★★★★
Contact: Mr Louise Clifford
Evergreen Lodge, Ruckamore Road, Chelston, Torquay TQ2 6HF
T: (01803) 605519
F: (01803) 605519
E: evergreenlodge@dial.pipex.com
I: evergreenlodge.co.uk

Fairlawns Hall Holiday Apartments ★★-★★★
Contact: Mrs Emma Hanbury
Fairlawns Hall Holiday Apartments, 27 St Michaels Road, Torquay TQ1 4DD
T: (01803) 328904
E: fairlawnshall@btinternet.com
I: www.fairlawnshall.co.uk

Florence Holiday Apartments ★★
Contact: Mr Ian J King
Florence Holiday Apartments, 39 Morgan Avenue, Torquay TQ2 5RR
T: (01803) 297264
F: (01803) 297264
E: florenceflats@aol.com

Gainsborough ★★★
Contact:
Holiday Homes & Cottages
South West, 365A Torquay Road,
Paignton TQ3 2BT
T: (01803) 663650
F: (01803) 664037
E: holcotts@aol.com
I: www.swcottages.co.uk

Glebeland ★★★
Contact:
Holiday Homes & Cottages
South West, 365A Torquay Road,
Paignton TQ3 2BT
T: (01803) 663650
F: (01803) 664037
E: holcotts@aol.com
I: www.swcottages.co.uk

Hesketh Crescent ★★★
Contact:
Holiday Homes & Cottages SW, 365A Torquay Road, Paignton TQ3 2BT
T: (01803) 663650
F: (01803) 664037
E: holcotts@aol.com

Hesketh Mews ★★★★★
Contact:
Blue Chip Vacations, 3 Marina Walk, Brixham TQ5 9BW
T: (01803) 855282

5 Hesketh Mews ★★★★
Contact:
Holiday Homes & Cottages
South West, 365A Torquay Road,
Paignton TQ3 2BT
T: (01803) 663650
F: (01803) 664037
E: holcotts@aol.com
I: www.swcottages.co.uk

Kingswood Holiday Flats ★★
Contact: Mr Peter Skinns
Kingswood Holiday Flats, 22 Morgan Avenue, Torquay TQ2 5RS
T: (01803) 293164
E: peter@kingswoodholidayflats.co.uk
I: www.kingswoodholidayflats.co.uk

Linden House Holidays ★★★
Contact: Keran Reilly
Linden House Holidays, Ruckamore Road, Chelston, Torquay TQ2 6HF
T: (01803) 607333
E: info@lindenholidays.com
I: www.lindenholidays.com

Lisburne Place ★★★★-★★★★★★
Contact:
Lisburne Place, Lisburne Square, Torquay TQ1 2PS
T: (01803) 855282
F: (01803) 811825
E: bluechip@eclipse.co.uk

Little Walderlea ★★★
Contact:
Holiday Homes & Cottages
South West, 365A Torquay Road,
Paignton TQ3 2BT
T: (01803) 663650
F: (01803) 664037
E: holcotts@aol.com
I: www.swcottages.co.uk

The Lodge ★★★★
Contact:
Holiday Homes & Cottages
South West, 365A Torquay Road,
Paignton TQ3 2BT
T: (01803) 663650
F: (01803) 664037
E: holcotts@aol.com
I: www.swcottages.co.uk

Longdon Holiday Flats & Flatlets ★★-★★★
Contact: Mrs Jean Erdpresser
Longdon Holiday Flats & Flatlets, Higher Erith Road, Torquay TQ1 2NH
T: (01803) 297240
E: jean@longdonholidayflats.fsnet.co.uk

Marina Delight ★★★
Contact:
Holiday Homes & Cottages SW, 365A Torquay Road, Paignton TQ3 2BT
T: (01803) 663650
F: (01803) 664037
E: holcotts@aol.com

Establishments printed in blue have a detailed entry in this guide

SOUTH WEST ENGLAND

Marina View & Bay View ★★★
Contact:
Holiday Homes & Cottages
South West, 365A Torquay Road,
Paignton TQ3 2BT
T: (01803) 663650
F: (01803) 664037
E: holcotts@aol.com
I: www.swcottages.co.uk

Maxton Lodge Holiday Apartments ★★★
Contact: Mr Richard Hassell
Rousdown Road, Torquay
TQ2 6PB
T: (01803) 607811
F: (01803) 605357
E: stay@redhouse-hotel.co.uk
I: www.redhouse-hotel.co.uk

Meadcourt ★★★★
Contact:
Holiday Homes & Cottages
South West, 365A Torquay Road,
Paignton TQ3 2BT
T: (01803) 663650
F: (01803) 664037
E: holcotts@aol.com
I: www.swcottages.co.uk

Meadfoot Lodge Holiday Apartments ★★★
Contact: Mr Paul Shamlou
Meadfoot Lodge Holiday
Apartments, Meadfoot Sea
Road, Torquay TQ1 2LG
T: (01803) 293350
F: (01803) 293353
I: www.meadfootlodge.co.uk

Meadowside Holiday Flats ★★★
Contact: Mr Maurice & Mrs Iris Wilson
Meadowside Holiday Flats, 22
Vansittart Road, Torquay
TQ2 5BW
T: (01803) 295683
E: meadowside@torquay38.freeserve.co.uk

Moongate Cottages ★★★
Contact:
Holiday Homes & Cottages
South West, 365A Torquay Road,
Paignton TQ3 2BT
T: (01803) 663650
F: (01803) 664037
E: holcotts@aol.com
I: www.swcottages.co.uk

Moor Haven Holiday Flats ★★★-★★★★
Contact: Mr Terry & Mrs Jackie Chandler
Moor Haven Holiday Flats, 43
Barton Road, Torquay TQ1 4DT
T: (01803) 328567
E: eng@moorhaven.co.uk
I: www.moorhaven.co.uk

Moorcot Self-Contained Holiday Apartments ★★★
Contact: Mrs Margaret Neilson
Moorcot Self-Contained Holiday
Apartments, Kents Road,
Wellswood, Torquay TQ1 2NN
T: (01803) 293710
E: holidayflats@moorcot.com
I: www.moorcot.com

Moorings ★★★
Contact:
Holiday Homes & Cottages
South West, 365A Torquay Road,
Paignton TQ3 2BT
T: (01803) 663650
F: (01803) 664037
E: holcotts@aol.com
I: www.swcottages.co.uk

Muntham Luxury Holiday Apartments ★★★★
Contact: Mr Peter & Mrs Trudie Cross
Muntham Luxury Holiday
Apartments, Barrington Road,
Wellswood, Torquay TQ1 1SG
T: (01803) 292958
F: (01803) 291715
E: muntham@btinternet.com
I: www.theenglishriviera.co.uk

Newhaven ★★★
Contact: Mr Brian Wiltshire
Newhaven, 49 Morgan Avenue,
Torquay TQ2 5RR
T: (01803) 612836

The Preferred Apartment Company - Horizon and Skyline ★★★★★
Contact: Mrs Sue Vaughton
The Preferred Apartment
Company, 21 Bishops Close,
Torquay TQ1 2PL
T: (01803) 211116
F: (01803) 214023
E: enquiry@torbayapartments.com
I: www.torbayapartments.com

Richmond Court ★★★
Contact: Ms Leslie J Creber
Richmond Court, 1 Rowdens
Road, Torquay TQ2 5AZ
T: (01803) 293824

South Sands Apartments ★★★
Contact: Mr Paul & Mrs Deborah Moorhouse
South Sands Apartments, Torbay
Road, Torquay TQ2 6RG
T: (01803) 293521
F: (01803) 293502
E: info@southsands.co.uk
I: www.southsands.co.uk

Southern Comfort ★★★
Contact:
Holiday Homes & Cottages
South West, 365A Torquay Road,
Paignton TQ3 2BT
T: (01803) 663650
F: (01803) 664037
E: holcotts@aol.com
I: www.swcottages.co.uk

Spa Cottage ★★★
Contact:
Holiday Homes & Cottages
South West, 365A Torquay Road,
Paignton TQ3 2BT
T: (01803) 663650
F: (01803) 664037
E: holcotts@aol.com
I: www.swcottages.co.uk

Summerdyne Apartments ★★★
Contact: Mr Dale & Mrs Mandy Tanner
Summerdyne Apartments,
Greenway Road, Torquay
TQ2 6JE
T: (01803) 605439
F: (01803) 607441
E: stay@summerdyne.co.uk
I: www.summerdyne.co.uk

Suncourt ★★★
Contact:
Holiday Homes & Cottages
South West, 365A Torquay Road,
Paignton TQ3 2BT
T: (01803) 663650
F: (01803) 664037
E: holcotts@aol.com
I: www.swcottages.co.uk

Sunningdale Apartments ★★★
Contact: Mr Allan Carr
Sunningdale Apartments, 11
Babbacombe Downs Road,
Torquay TQ1 3LF
T: (01803) 325786
F: (01803) 329611
I: www.sunningdaleapartments.co.uk

Sunnyhill Mews ★★★★
Contact:
Holiday Homes & Cottages SW,
365A Torquay Road, Paignton
TQ3 2BT
T: (01803) 663650
F: (01803) 664037
E: holcotts@aol.com
I: www.swcottages.co.uk

Vane Tower ★★★★
Contact:
Holiday Homes & Cottages
South West, 365A Torquay Road,
Paignton TQ3 2BT
T: (01803) 663650
F: (01803) 664037
E: holcotts@aol.com
I: www.swcottages.co.uk

Villa Capri ★★★★
Contact: Mr Arthur Turner
Villa Capri, Daddyhole Road,
Meadfoot, Torquay TQ1 2ED
T: (01803) 297959
F: (01803) 297959
E: villcapr@btinternet.com
I: www.torbay.gov.uk./tourism/t-self-c/villcapr.htm

Vomero Holiday Apartments ★★★
Contact: Mr Anthony Brown
Vomero Holiday Apartments,
Stitchill Road, Torquay TQ1 1PZ
T: (01803) 293470
F: (01803) 293470
E: holidays@vomero.co.uk
I: www.vomero.co.uk

Waldon Court ★★★★
Contact: Mr Ian Butterworth
Holiday Homes & Cottages
South West, 365A Torquay Road,
Paignton TQ3 2BT
T: (01803) 663650
F: (01803) 664037
E: holcotts@aol.com
I: www.swcottages.co.uk

The Wayland Hotel & Belgravia Luxury Self Catering Holiday ★★★★
Contact: Mr Brian & Mrs Jacky Kirkaldy
The Wayland Hotel & Belgravia
Luxury Self Catering, 31
Belgrave Road, Torquay TQ2 5HX
T: (01803) 293417
F: (01803) 291911
E: info@waylandhotel.co.uk
I: www.waylandhotel.co.uk

Westcourt Holiday Flats ★★-★★★
Contact: Mr John Lawton
Westcourt Holiday Flats, 108
Westhill Road, Torquay TQ1 4NT
T: (01803) 311703
E: westcourtholidayflats@hotmail.com
I: www.westcourtholidayflats.co.uk

Woodfield Holiday Apartments ★★★
Contact: Mr Terence & Mrs Betty Gaylard
Woodfield Holiday Apartments,
Lower Woodfield Road, Torquay
TQ1 2JY
T: (01803) 295974

Wrenwood ★★★★
Contact:
Holiday Homes & Cottages
South West, 365A Torquay Road,
Paignton TQ3 2BT
T: (01803) 663650
F: (01803) 664037
E: holcotts@aol.com
I: www.swcottages.co.uk

TORRINGTON
Devon

Glebe Farm Cottage ★★★★
Contact: Mr Mike & Mrs Marilyn Cooper
Glebe Farm Cottage, Torrington
EX38 8PS
T: (01805) 622156
E: marilyn_mike@cornflowerblue.com
I: www.cornflowerblue.com

Hill Farm Cottages ★★★★
Contact: Mrs Mary Vickery
Hill Farm Cottages, Hill Farm,
Weare Trees Hill, Torrington
EX38 7EZ
T: (01805) 622432
F: (01805) 622432
E: info@hillfarmcottages.co.uk
I: www.hillfarmcottages.co.uk

2 Little Silver ★★★★
Contact: Mrs A Taylor
67 Torwood Lane, Whyteleafe
CR3 0HD
T: (020) 8763 0796
F: (020) 8763 0796
E: admin@devonshire-cottages.co.uk
I: www.devonshire-cottages.co.uk

SOUTH WEST ENGLAND

Stowford Lodge & South Hill Cottages ★★★
Contact: Mrs Sally Milsom
Stowford Lodge & South Hill Cottages, Langtree, Torrington EX38 8NU
T: (01805) 601540
F: (01805) 601487
E: stowford@dial.pipex.com
I: www.stowford.dial.pipex.com

Week Farm Flat ★★★
Contact: Mrs Della Bealey
Week Farm Flat, Week Farm, Torrington EX38 7HU
T: (01805) 623029
F: (01805) 623029
E: weekfarm.flat@btinternet.com
I: www.weekfarm.co.uk

TOTNES
Devon

The Annexe, The Talus ★★★
Contact: Mr & Mrs Pedley
The Annexe, The Talus, 12 Quarry Close, Follaton, Totnes TQ9 5FA
T: (01803) 865647
E: theannexe@talk21.com
I: www.theannexe-totnes.co.uk

Castle Foot ★★★★
Contact: Mr Hales
18 South Street, Totnes TQ9 5DZ
T: (01803) 865282
E: davidg.r.hales@sagainternet.co.uk

The Little Elbow Room ★★★
Contact: Mrs Savin
The Little Elbow Room, North Street, Totnes TQ9 5NZ
T: (01803) 863480
F: (01803) 863480
E: elbowroomtotnes@aol.com

Wedge Cottage ★★★★
Contact: Mrs Shirley Seymour
17 Bridgetown, Totnes TQ9 5BA
T: (01803) 862893

TREBETHERICK
Cornwall

Bars House ★★
Contact: Dr Anthony Hambly
Bodrean Manor, St Clements, Bodrean, Truro TR4 9AG
T: (01872) 264400
F: (01872) 264400
E: anthonyhambly@hotmail.com
I: www.cornishholidays.com

Boskenna
Rating Applied For
Contact: Mrs Diana Bullivant
Diana Bullivant Holidays, Southwinds, Trebell Green, Bodmin PL30 5HR
T: (01208) 831336
F: (01208) 831336
E: diana@d.bullivant.fsnet.co.uk
I: www.cornwall-online.co.uk/diana-bullivant

Church Lane House ★★★★
Contact: Mrs Painter
10 Chapel Street, Camelford PL32 9PJ
T: 07814 684822

Evergreen Lodge ★★-★★★
Contact: Mr Wright
Nyetimber, Chiltern Road, Amersham HP6 5PH
T: (01494) 726453
F: (01494) 726453
I: www.selfcatering-evergreenlodge.com

Highcliffe ★★★★
Contact: Mr Robert Mably
Highcliffe, Francis Lane, Wadebridge PL27 6TS
T: (01208) 863843
F: (01208) 863813
E: sales@highcliffeagency.com
I: www.highcliffeagency.com

Hillcroft Bungalow ★★★
Contact: Mr Diana & Mrs Piers Beach
Longwood, West Street, Hook RG29 1NX
T: (01256) 702650
E: dibeach@hotmail.com

2 The Martins ★★★
Contact: A P Duffield
2 The Martins, Dunder Hill, Wadebridge PL27 6SX
T: (01208) 863638
F: (01208) 862940
E: information@seascapehotel.co.uk
I: www.seascapehotel.co.uk

Saint Moritz Villas ★★★★
Contact:
Rock Holidays inc. Harbour Holidays Rock Ltd., Trebetherick House, Wadebridge PL27 6SB
T: (01208) 863399
I: www.stmoritzhotel.co.uk

Sanderlings ★★★
Contact:
Rock Holidays inc. Harbour Holidays Rock Ltd., Trebetherick House, Wadebridge PL27 6SB
T: (01208) 863399
E: rockhols@aol.com
I: www.rockholidays.co.uk

Sea Breezes ★★
Contact: Mrs Marion Brown
Gay Bowers, Deadmans Lane, Galleywood., Chelmsford CM2 8NA
T: (01245) 477206

White Rose
Rating Applied For
Contact:
Rock Holidays inc. Harbour Holidays Rock Ltd., Trebetherick House, Wadebridge PL27 6SB
T: (01208) 863399
E: rockhols@aol.com
I: www.rockholidays.co.uk

TREDETHY
Cornwall

Brinkywell Holiday Cottages ★★★
Contact: Mr & Mrs Tocknell
Treetops, Dursley GL11 5EW
T: (01453) 545184
E: brian.tocknell@treetopscam.freeserve.co.uk
I: www.brinkywell.co.uk

TREFULA
Cornwall

The Barn at Little Trefula ★★★
Contact: Mr William Higgins
Little Trefula, Redruth TR16 5ET
T: (01209) 820263
F: (01209) 820751
E: enquiries@trefula.com
I: www.trefula.com/holidays

TREGADA
Cornwall

Burdown Cottage ★★★★
Contact: Mr & Ms Terence & Janet Oxenbury
Burdown Cottage, Little Comfort, Launceston PL15 9NA
T: (01566) 772960
I: burdowncottage.users.btopenworld.com

TREGATTA
Cornwall

Beaver Cottage ★★★
Contact: Mr Alec & Mrs Barbara Luckin
Beaver Cottage, Tintagel PL34 0DY
T: (01840) 770265
F: (01840) 770265
E: beaver.cottages@virgin.net

TREGONY
Cornwall

The Bolt Hole ★★★★
Contact: Miss Rebecca Nash
43 Huntingtower Road, Banner Cross, Sheffield S11 7GT
T: (0114) 238 3966
E: rebnash@yahoo.com
I: www.cottageguide.co.uk/thebolthole

Trefern
Rating Applied For
Contact:
Roseland Holiday Cottages, Crab Apple Cottage, Truro TR2 5ET
T: (01872) 580480
F: (01872) 580480
E: enquiries@roselandholidaycottages.co.uk
I: www.roselandholidaycottages.co.uk

TREGURRIAN
Cornwall

Bay View ★★★
Contact:
Harbour Holidays, 1 North Quay, Padstow PL28 8AF
T: (01841) 543402
F: (01841) 533115
E: contact@harbourholidays.co.uk
I: www.harbourholidays.co.uk

Mandalay ★★★
Contact: Ms Nicky Stanley
Harbour Holidays - Padstow, 1 North Quay, Padstow PL28 8AF
T: (01841) 532555
F: (01841) 533115
E: sales@jackie-stanley.co.uk
I: www.harbourholidays.co.uk

TREKNOW
Cornwall

Kittiwake Cottage ★★★★
Contact: Mrs Jan Harwood
Kittiwake Cottage, Gull Rock, Tintagel PL34 0EP
T: (01840) 770438
F: (01840) 770406
E: jan@gullrock.eclipse.co.uk

Parwin ★★★
Contact:
Cornish Horizons, The Cottage, 19 New Street, Padstow PL28 8EA
T: (01841) 533331
F: (01841) 533933
E: cottages@cornishhorizons.co.uk
I: www.cornishhorizons.co.uk

TRELIGGA
Cornwall

Caradoc Barn ★★★★
Contact:
Rock Holidays inc. Harbour Holidays Rock Ltd., Trebetherick House, Wadebridge PL27 6SB
T: (01208) 863399
F: (01208) 862218
E: rockhols@aol.com
I: www.rockholidays.co.uk

TRELILL
Cornwall

The White House ★★★
Contact: Mr & Mrs Farmer
The White House, Bodmin PL30 3HX
T: (01208) 850883
F: (01208) 851914
E: richard@farmer46.freeserve.co.uk

TREMAINE
Cornwall

Tremaine Barn ★★★★★
Contact: Mr Alan & Mrs Jillie Lamb
Tremaine Barn, Launceston PL15 8SA
T: (01566) 781636
F: (01566) 781309
E: welcome@stay-in-cornwall.co.uk
I: www.stay-in-cornwall.co.uk

TRENANCE
Cornwall

11 Europa Court ★★★
Contact: Mr Frederick Blackmore
Trenalt, Mawgan Porth, Newquay TR8 4DB
T: (01637) 860296

Romanov
Rating Applied For
Contact:
Cornish Horizons, The Cottage, 19 New Street, Padstow PL28 8EA
T: (01841) 533331
F: (01841) 533933
E: cottages@cornishhorizons.co.uk

Establishments printed in blue have a detailed entry in this guide

SOUTH WEST ENGLAND

TRENARREN
Cornwall
East Wing Apartment ★★★
Contact: Mrs Anita Treleaven
East Wing Apartment, Trevissick Manor, St Austell PL26 6BQ
T: (01726) 72954
F: (01726) 72954
E: d.treleaven@farmline.com

TRENEGLOS
Cornwall
Tregerry Farm ★★★★
Contact:
Farm & Cottage Holidays, Victoria House, 12 Fore Street, Bideford EX39 1AW
T: (01237) 479146
F: (01237) 421512
E: enquiries@farmcott.co.uk
I: www.farmcott.co.uk

TRENTISHOE
Devon
The Old Farmhouse ★★★
Contact: Mr Ian & Mrs Ann Wright
The Old Farmhouse, Barnstaple EX31 4QD
T: (01598) 763495
E: ian@oldfarmhouse.co.uk
I: www.oldfarmhouse.co.uk

TRESCO
Isles of Scilly
Boro Chalets and Cottages
★★★-★★★★★
Contact: Mrs Margaret Christopher
Boro Chalets and Cottages, Boro Farm, Tresco TR24 0PX
T: (01720) 422843

Borough Farm Chalets ★★★
Contact: Mrs Ann Oyler
Borough Farm Chalets, The Bungalow, Borough, Tresco TR24 0PX
T: (01720) 422840

TRESPARRETT
Cornwall
Underlanes ★★
Contact: Mrs Prout
Penventon, Boscastle PL35 0DA
T: (01840) 250289

TREVANSON
Cornwall
The Old Cottage
Rating Applied For
Contact: Mrs Jill Brown
Tregel, Bodmin PL30 4BL
T: (01208) 821611
F: (01208) 821611
E: jill.p.brown@btinternet.com
I: www.old-cottage.com

TREVELGUE
Cornwall
2 Porth Valley Cottages
Rating Applied For
Contact: Mr Peter Osborne
Cornish Horizons, The Cottage, 19 New Street, Padstow PL28 8EA
T: (01841) 533331
F: (01841) 533933
E: cottages@cornishhorizons.co.uk

TREVELLAS
Cornwall
Quarry Farm ★★★
Contact: Mrs Pauline Johnson
Quarry Farm, St Agnes TR5 0XU
T: (01872) 573920
E: everett.johnson@btopenworld.com
I: www.homesandcottages.co.uk/property/quarryfarm

TREVIA
Cornwall
The Garden Flat ★★★
Contact: Ms Irene Hislop
The Garden Flat, Green Valley, Camelford PL32 9UX
T: (01840) 213415

TREVONE
Cornwall
5 Atlanta ★★★
Contact: Ms Nicky Stanley
Harbour Holidays - Padstow, 1 North Quay, Padstow PL28 8AF
T: (01841) 532555
F: (01841) 533115
E: sales@jackie-stanley.co.uk
I: www.harbourholidays.co.uk

1 Atlantic ★★★
Contact: Ms Nicky Stanley
Harbour Holidays - Padstow, 1 North Quay, Padstow PL28 8AF
T: (01841) 532555
F: (01841) 533115
E: sales@jackie-stanley.co.uk
I: www.harbourholidays.co.uk

Avon Cottage ★★★
Contact: Mr Hugo Woolley
Avon Cottage, Woodlands Country House, Padstow PL28 8RU
T: (01841) 532426
F: (01841) 533353
E: enquiries@avoncottage.com
I: www.padstowlive.com

The Bothy ★★★
Contact: Ms Nicky Stanley
Harbour Holidays - Padstow, 1 North Quay, Padstow PL28 8AF
T: (01841) 532555
F: (01841) 533115
E: sales@jackie-stanley.co.uk
I: www.harbourholidays.co.uk

The Bower ★★★
Contact: Ms Nicky Stanley
Harbour Holidays - Padstow, 1 North Quay, Padstow PL28 8AF
T: (01841) 532555
F: (01841) 533115
E: sales@jackie-stanley.co.uk
I: www.cornishhorizons.co.uk

Chy an Porth ★★
Contact:
Cornish Horizons, The Cottage, 19 New Street, Padstow PL28 8EA
T: (01841) 533331
F: (01841) 533933
E: cottages@cornishhorizons.co.uk
I: www.cornishhorizons.co.uk

Chy Vean ★★
Contact:
Cornish Horizons, The Cottage, 19 New Street, Padstow PL28 8EA
T: (01841) 533331
F: (01841) 533933
E: cottages@cornishhorizons.co.uk
I: www.cornishhorizons.co.uk

1 Dobbin House
Rating Applied For
Contact: Mr Peter Osbourne
Cornish Horizons, The Cottage, 19 New Street, Padstow PL28 8EA
T: (01841) 533331
F: (01841) 533933
E: cottages@cornishhorizons.co.uk

Hill Rise ★★★
Contact: Mr Peter Alvey
The Drive, Bristol BS9 4LD
T: (0117) 9625862
E: hillrise1@aol.com
I: www.cornwall-online.co.uk

Hope House ★★★★★
Contact:
Harbour Holidays, 1 North Quay, Padstow PL28 8AF
T: (01841) 533402
F: (01841) 533115
E: contact@harbourholidays.co.uk

Jacaranda ★★★
Contact: Ms Nicky Stanley
Harbour Holidays - Padstow, 1 North Quay, Padstow PL28 8AF
T: (01841) 532555
F: (01841) 533115
E: sales@jackie-stanley.co.uk
I: www.harbourholidays.co.uk

Lamorna Cottage ★★★
Contact: Ms Nicky Stanley
Harbour Holidays - Padstow, 1 North Quay, Padstow PL28 8AF
T: (01841) 532555
F: (01841) 533115
E: sales@jackie-stanley.co.uk
I: www.harbourholidays.co.uk

Lesal ★★★★
Contact:
Harbour Holidays - Padstow, 1 North Quay, Padstow PL28 8AF
T: (01841) 532555

Pentonwarra ★★★
Contact: Ms Nicky Stanley
Harbour Holidays - Padstow, 1 North Quay, Padstow PL28 8AF
T: (01841) 532555
F: (01841) 533115
E: sales@jackie-stanley.co.uk
I: www.harbourholidays.co.uk

Riviera ★★
Contact:
Harbour Holidays - Padstow, 1 North Quay, Padstow PL28 8AF
T: (01841) 532555
F: (01841) 533115
E: sales@jackie-stanley.co.uk
I: www.harbourholidays.co.uk

Rosben ★★★
Contact: Ms Nicky Stanley
Harbour Holidays - Padstow, 1 North Quay, Padstow PL28 8AF
T: (01841) 532555
F: (01841) 533115
E: sales@jackie-stanley.co.uk
I: www.harbourholidays.co.uk

Sintra ★★★-★★★★
Contact: Mrs Barrie Luscombe
Rushwood House, 173 Nine Ashes Road, Ingatestone CM4 0JY
T: (01277) 821339
I: www.btinternet.com/~trevoneholiday/index.html

Trelyn ★★★★
Contact:
Cornish Horizons, The Cottage, 19 New Street, Padstow PL28 8EA
T: (01841) 533331
F: (01841) 533933
E: cottages@cornishhorizons.co.uk
I: www.cornishhorizons.co.uk

Warnecliffe Flat ★★★
Contact:
Cornish Horizons, The Cottage, 19 New Street, Padstow PL28 8EA
T: (01841) 533331
F: (01841) 533933
E: cottages@cornishhorizons.co.uk
I: www.cornishhorizons.co.uk

Windmill Cottage ★★
Contact: Mr Christopher Hawkes
Loose Chippings, Lower Rads End, Milton Keynes MK17 9EE
T: (01525) 280385
F: (01525) 280385
E: hawkes@dial.pipex.com

Zanzibar ★★★★
Contact: Mr Tim & Mrs Vicky Stafford
Zanzibar, Cliff House, West View, Padstow PL28 8RD
T: (01841) 521828
E: enquiries@wave-scapes.com
I: www.wave-scapes.com/zanzibar.htm

TREVONE BAY
Cornwall
Atlanta Holiday Apartments
★★★-★★★★★
Contact: Mr Michael Alken
Askrigg, Dobbin Road, Padstow PL28 8QW
T: (01841) 520442
E: mikealken@mail.com
I: www.cornwall-seaside-holidays.com

TREVOSE
Cornwall
Coastguard Cottage West ★★★★
Contact:
Cornish Horizons, The Cottage, 19 New Street, Padstow PL28 8EA
T: (01841) 533331
F: (01841) 533933
E: cottages@cornishhorizons.co.uk
I: www.cornishhorizons.co.uk

SOUTH WEST ENGLAND

TREWIDLAND
Cornwall

Trehalvin Cottages ★★★★
Contact: Mrs Catherine Woollard
Trehalvin Cottages, Liskeard
PL14 4ST
T: (01503) 240334
F: (01503) 240334
E: cottages@trehalvin.co.uk
I: www.trehalvin.co.uk

TREYARNON BAY
Cornwall

Foxes ★★★
Contact: Mr Peter Tapper
Foxes, Padstow PL28 8JS
T: (01590) 674660

Glendurgan ★★★
Contact:
Harbour Holidays, 1 North Quay, Padstow PL28 8AF
T: (01841) 533402
F: (01841) 533115
E: contact@harbourholidays.co.uk

Primrose Cottage ★★★
Contact:
Harbour Holidays, 4 North Quay, Padstow PL28 8AF
T: (01841) 532555
F: (01841) 533115
E: contact@harbourholidays.co.uk
I: www.harbourholidays.co.uk

Saint Cadocs ★★★
Contact:
Cornish Horizons, The Cottage, 19 New Street, Padstow
PL28 8EA
T: (01841) 533331
F: (01841) 533933
E: cottages@cornishhorizons.co.uk
I: www.cornishhorizons.co.uk

Trebah ★★★
Contact:
Harbour Holidays, 1 North Quay, Padstow PL28 8AF
T: (01841) 533402
E: contact@harbourholidays.co.uk
I: www.harbourholidays.co.uk

TROWBRIDGE
Wiltshire

Hinton Lodge ★★★★
Contact: Mrs Gompels
Hinton House, Trowbridge
BA14 6BS
T: (01380) 871067
F: 0870 8 707026
E: sam@gompels.co.uk
I: www.hintonlodge.co.uk

TRULL
Somerset

Amberd Farmhouse - Old Barn ★★★★
Contact: Mr Tim Isaac
Amberd Farmhouse, Amberd Lane, Taunton TA3 7AA
T: (01823) 331744
F: (01823) 331744
E: amberd@btopenworld.com
I: amberd.users.btopenworld.com

TRURO
Cornwall

Ancarva Cottage ★★★
Contact: Mrs Margie Lumby
Special Places in Cornwall, Poachers Reach, Harcourt, Truro
TR3 6SQ
T: (01872) 864400
E: office@specialplacescornwall.co.uk
I: www.specialplacescornwall.co.uk

Clifford House Cottages ★★★-★★★★★
Contact: Mrs Anne Grant
Clifford House Cottages, Clifford House, Race Hill, Truro TR4 8RH
T: (01872) 863052
F: (01872) 862483
E: clifford.cottages@btopenworld.com
I: www.cliffordhousecottages.co.uk

The Coach House ★★★
Contact: Dr Hambly
The Coach House, Bodrean Manor, St Clements, Bodrean, Truro TR4 9AG
T: (01872) 264400
F: (01872) 264400
E: anthonyhambly@hotmail.com
I: www.cornishholidays.com

The Old Forge
Rating Applied For
Contact:
Roseland Holiday Cottages, Crab Apple Cottage, Truro TR2 5ET
T: (01872) 580480
F: (01872) 580480
E: enquiries@roselandholidays.co.uk
I: www.roselandholidaycottages.co.uk

Tremarner Lodge
Rating Applied For
Contact: Mrs Bellingham
Tremarner Lodge, Rope Walk, Penpol, Truro TR3 6NA

Trenerry Lodge ★★
Contact: Mrs Angela Parsons
Trenerry Lodge, Trenerry Farm, Mingoose, Truro TR4 8BX
T: (01872) 553755
F: (01872) 553755
E: info@babatrenerry.co.uk
I: www.babatrenerry.co.uk

The Valley
Rating Applied For
Contact: Mr Keith & Mrs Julie Horsfall
The Valley, Ringwell Hill, Bissoe Road, Carnon Downs, Truro
TR3 6LQ
T: (01872) 862194
F: (01872) 864343
E: keith@ringwell.co.uk
I: www.the-valley.co.uk

Westward & Mellangoose (Niche Retreats) ★★★-★★★★
Contact: Mrs J A Kitchen
Niche Retreats, Banns Road, Truro TR4 8BW
T: (01209) 890272
F: (01209) 891695
E: info@nicheretreats.co.uk
I: www.nicheretreats.co.uk

TWO WATERS FOOT
Cornwall

Bluebell Barn ★★★
Contact:
Valley Villas, Brook Cottage, Old Warleigh Lane, Plymouth
PL5 4ND
T: (01752) 774900
E: sales@valleyvillas.co.uk
I: www.valleyvillas.co.uk

Foxglove Barn ★★★
Contact:
Valley Villas, Brook Cottage, Old Warleigh Lane, Plymouth
PL5 4ND
T: (01752) 774900
E: sales@valleyvillas.co.uk
I: www.valleyvillas.co.uk

TWYFORD
Dorset

Anvil Cottage ★★
Contact: Mrs Susan Ryan
Anvil Cottage, Shaftesbury
SP7 0JG
T: (01747) 811553
E: sue.ryan@care4free.net

Buddens Farm Holidays ★★★-★★★★★
Contact: Mrs Sarah Gulliford
Buddens Farm Holidays, Buddens Farm, Shaftesbury
SP7 0JE
T: (01747) 811433
F: (01747) 811433
E: buddensfarm@eurolink.ltd.net
I: www.buddensfarm.co.uk

UGBOROUGH
Devon

Coombe House and Cottages ★★★★-★★★★★
Contact: Mr John & Mrs Faith Scharenguivel
Coombe House and Cottages, South Brent TQ10 9NJ
T: (01548) 821277
F: (01548) 821277
E: coombehouse@hotmail.com
I: www.coombehouse.uk.com

Donkey Cottage ★★★★
Contact: Mrs Gill Barker
5 Meade King Grove, Cheltenham GL52 9UD
T: (01242) 678568
E: gill@donkeycottage.co.uk
I: www.donkeycottage.co.uk

Venn Farm ★★★★
Contact: Mrs Stephens
Venn Farm, Ivybridge PL21 0PE
T: (01364) 73240
F: (01364) 73240

ULEY
Gloucestershire

Coopers Cottage ★★★★
Contact: Mrs Diana Griffiths
48 Orchard Leaze, Dursley
GL11 6HX
T: (01453) 542861
E: cooperscot@onetel.com

ULLENWOOD
Gloucestershire

Ullenwood Court Cottages ★★★★
Contact: Mrs Shand
90 Redgrove Park, Hatherley Lane, Cheltenham GL51 6YZ
T: (01242) 239751

UMBERLEIGH
Devon

Hansford Cottage ★★★
Contact:
Farm & Cottage Holidays, Victoria House, 27 Fore Street, Bideford EX39 1AW
T: (01237) 479146
F: (01237) 421512
E: bookings@farmcott.co.uk
I: www.farmcott.co.uk

Little Wick ★★★★
Contact:
Marsdens Cottage Holidays, 2 The Square, Braunton EX33 2JB
T: (01271) 813777
F: (01271) 813664
E: holidays@marsdens.co.uk
I: www.marsdens.co.uk

UPLEADON
Gloucestershire

Middletown Farm Cottages ★★★★
Contact: Mrs Judy Elkins
Middletown Farm Cottages, Middletown Farm, Middletown Lane, Upleadon, Newent
GL18 1EQ
T: (01531) 828237
F: (01531) 822850
E: cottages@middletownfarm.co.uk
I: www.middletownfarm.co.uk

UPLODERS
Dorset

Clematis Cottage ★★★
Contact:
Dream Cottages, 5 Hope Square, Weymouth DT4 8TR
T: (01305) 789000
E: admin@dream-cottages.co.uk
I: www.dream-cottages.co.uk

Moens Dairyhouse ★★★★
Contact: Mrs Marston
Moens Farmhouse, Uploders, Bridport DT6 4PH
T: (01308) 420631

Tiddlers Cottage ★★★
Contact: Mr Alan Spargo
Tiddlers Cottage, c/o Springside Cottage, Bridport DT6 4NU
T: (01308) 485478
E: alan@aspargo.freeserve.co.uk
I: www.tiddlerscottage.com

Establishments printed in blue have a detailed entry in this guide

SOUTH WEST ENGLAND

UPLYME
Devon

4 Barnes Meadow: C4401 ★★★★
Contact:
Lyme Bay Holidays, Bos House, 44 Church Street, Lyme Regis DT7 3DA
T: (01297) 443363
F: (01297) 445576
E: email@lymebayholidays.co.uk
I: www.lymebayholidays.co.uk

The Bower & The Bothy ★★★★
Contact: Mrs Paula Wyon-Brown
The Bower & The Bothy, Hill Barn, Gore Lane, Lyme Regis DT7 3RJ
T: (01297) 445185
F: (01297) 445185
E: jwb@lymeregis-accommodation.com
I: www.lymeregis-accommodation.com

9 Coram Court - C4366 ★★★★
Contact:
Lyme Bay Holidays, Bos House, 44 Church Street, Lyme Regis DT7 3DA
T: (01297) 443363
F: (01297) 445576
E: email@lymebayholidays.co.uk
I: www.lymebayholidays.co.uk

Garden Flat & Panorama, Westfield - B4381 ★★★
Contact: Mr Dave Matthews
Lyme Bay Holidays, Bos House, 44 Church Street, Lyme Regis DT7 3DA
T: (01297) 443363
F: (01297) 445576
E: email@lymebayholidays.co.uk
I: www.lymebayholidays.co.uk

Higher Holcombe Farm Cottage ★★★
Contact: Mrs Rosamund Duffin
Higher Holcombe Farm Cottage, Holcombe Lane, Lyme Regis DT7 3SN
T: (01297) 444078
E: ro3duffin@hotmail.com
I: www.lymeregis.com

Holmer Villas ★★★
Contact: Mrs Pamela Boyland
Holmer Villas, 3 Ozone Terrace, Lyme Regis DT7 3JY
T: (01404) 861297
E: pab@barnparkfarm.fsnet.co.uk

Little Westhill - A4409 ★★★
Contact:
Lyme Bay Holidays, Bos House, 44 Church Street, Lyme Regis DT7 3DA
T: (01297) 443363
F: (01297) 445576
E: email@lymebayholidays.co.uk
I: www.lymebayholidays.co.uk

Lyme Croft - D4227 ★★★★
Contact:
Lyme Bay Holidays, Bos House, 44 Church Street, Lyme Regis DT7 3DA
T: (01297) 443363
F: (01297) 445576
E: email@lymebayholidays.co.uk
I: www.lymebayholidays.co.uk

Mount View - C4343 ★★★
Contact:
Lyme Bay Holidays, Bos House, 44 Church Street, Lyme Regis DT7 3DA
T: (01297) 443363
F: (01297) 445576
E: email@lymebayholidays.co.uk
I: www.lymebayholidays.co.uk

The Old Barn - B4078 ★★★
Contact:
Lyme Bay Holidays, Bos House, 44 Church Street, Lyme Regis DT7 3DA
T: (01297) 443363
F: (01297) 445576
E: email@lymebayholidays.co.uk
I: www.lymebayholidays.co.uk

Old Orchard ★★★★
Contact: Mr Smith
Cannington Farm, Cannington Lane, Lyme Regis DT7 3SW
T: (01297) 443172
F: (01297) 445005
E: tvecs@aol.com

Pitt White House: E4410 ★★★★
Contact: Mr Dave Matthews
Lyme Bay Holidays, Bos House, 44 Church Street, Lyme Regis DT7 3DA
T: (01297) 443363
F: (01297) 445576
E: email@lymebayholidays.co.uk
I: www.lymebayholidays.co.uk

3 Sherwood Apartments - B4389 ★★★
Contact:
Lyme Bay Holidays, Bos House, 44 Church Street, Lyme Regis DT7 3DA
T: (01297) 443363
F: (01297) 445576
E: email@lymebayholidays.co.uk
I: www.lymebayholidays.co.uk

Spinney Cottage - B4329 ★★★★
Contact: Mr Dave Matthews
Lyme Bay Holidays, Bos House, 44 Church Street, Lyme Regis DT7 3DA
T: (01297) 443363
F: (01297) 445576
E: email@lymebayholidays.co.uk
I: www.lymebayholidays.co.uk

Stable Wing - B4307 ★★★★
Contact:
Lyme Bay Holidays, Bos House, 44 Church Street, Lyme Regis DT7 3DA
T: (01297) 443363
F: (01297) 445576
E: email@lymebayholidays.co.uk
I: www.lymebayholidays.co.uk

Yawl House - E4111 & Bramleys - W4384 ★★-★★★
Contact:
Lyme Bay Holidays, Bos House, 44 Church Street, Lyme Regis DT7 3DA
T: (01297) 443363
F: (01297) 445576
E: email@lymebayholidays.co.uk
I: www.lymebayholidays.co.uk

UPOTTERY
Devon

Courtmoor Farm ★★★★
Contact: Mrs Rosalind Buxton
Courtmoor Farm, Honiton EX14 9QA
T: (01404) 861565
E: courtmoor.farm@btinternet.com
I: www.courtmoor.farm.btinternet.co.uk

Hoemoor Bungalow ★★★
Contact: Mrs Phillips
Hoemoor Bungalow, Honiton EX14 9PB
T: (01823) 601265
E: holidays@hoemoor.freeserve.co.uk

UPPER SLAUGHTER
Gloucestershire

Home Farm Stable ★★★★★
Contact: Mrs Bayetto
Home Farm Stable, Home Farmhouse, The Square, Cheltenham GL54 2JF
T: (01451) 820487
F: (01451) 820487
E: maureen.bayetto@virgin.net
I: www.home-farm-stable.co.uk

UPTON
Somerset

West Withy Farm Holiday Cottages ★★★★
Contact: Mr Gareth & Mrs Mary Hughes
West Withy Farm Holiday Cottages, West Withy Farm, Taunton TA4 2JH
T: (01398) 371258
F: (01398) 371123
E: g.hughes@irisi.u-net.com
I: www.exmoor-cottages.com

UPTON ST LEONARDS
Gloucestershire

Hill Farm Cottages ★★
Contact: Ms Margaret McLellan
Hill Farm, Upton Hill, Gloucester GL4 8DA
T: (01452) 614081

UPTON TOWANS
Cornwall

Gwithian Sands Chalet Park
Rating Applied For
Contact: Mr Patchett
Gwithian Sands Chalet Park, Hayle TR27 5BJ
T: (01736) 753489
I: www.qwithiansands.co.uk

UPWEY
Dorset

Appleloft & Brook Springs ★★-★★★
Contact: Mr Zachary Stuart-Brown
Dream Cottages, 5 Hope Square, Weymouth DT4 8TR
T: (01305) 789000
F: (01305) 761346
E: admin@dream-cottages.co.uk
I: www.dream-cottages.co.uk

Buttermilk Cottage ★★★
Contact:
Dream Cottages, 5 Hope Square, Weymouth DT4 8TR
T: (01305) 789000
F: (01305) 761347
E: admin@dream-cottages.co.uk
I: www.dream-cottages.co.uk

Chapel Cottage & Old School Cottage ★★★
Contact: Mr Zachary Stuart-Brown
Dream Cottages, 5 Hope Square, Weymouth DT4 8TR
T: (01305) 789000
F: (01305) 761346
E: admin@dream-cottages.co.uk
I: www.dream-cottages.co.uk

Rock Rose Cottage ★★★
Contact: Mr Zachary Stuart-Brown
Dream Cottages, 5 Hope Square, Weymouth DT4 8TR
T: (01305) 789000
E: admin@dream-cottages.co.uk
I: www.dream-cottages.co.uk

Sixpenny Cottage ★★★★
Contact:
Dream Cottages, 5 Hope Square, Weymouth DT4 8TR
T: (01305) 789000
F: (01305) 761347

Strawberry Cottage ★★★
Contact: Mr Zachary Stuart-Brown
Dream Cottages, 5 Hope Square, Weymouth DT4 8TR
T: (01305) 789000
E: admin@dream-cottages.co.uk
I: www.dream-cottages.co.uk

Wey Valley House ★★★★
Contact:
Dream Cottages, 5 Hope Square, Weymouth DT4 8TR
T: (01305) 789000
F: (01305) 761347

SOUTH WEST ENGLAND

URCHFONT
Wiltshire

Breach Cottage and The Pottery ★★-★★★
Contact: Mr Philip & Mrs Clare Milanes
Breach Cottage and The Pottery, Cuckoo Corner, Devizes SN10 4RA
T: (01380) 840402
F: (01380) 840150
E: milanefoils@btopenworld.com
I: www.breachhouse.co.uk

VERWOOD
Dorset

West Farm Lodges & West Farm Cottage ★★★
Contact: Mr Roger & Mrs Penny Froud
West Farm Lodges & West Farm Cottage, West Farm, Romford, Wimborne Minster BH31 7LE
T: (01202) 822263
F: (01202) 821040
E: west.farm@virgin.net
I: www.westfarmholidays.co.uk

VERYAN
Cornwall

Mill Cottage ★★★
Contact:
Cornish Cottage Holidays, The Old Turnpike Dairy, Godolphin Road, Helston TR13 8AA
T: (01326) 573808
F: (01326) 564992
E: enquiry@cornishcottageholidays.co.uk
I: www.cornishcottageholidays.co.uk

1 Raglan Cottages
Rating Applied For
Contact: Mrs Leonie Iddison
Roseland Holiday Cottages, Crab Apple Cottage, Truro TR2 5ET
T: (01872) 580480
F: (01872) 580480
I: Roselandholidaycottages.co.uk

WADEBRIDGE
Cornwall

15 & 16 Michaelstow Manor Holiday Park ★★
Contact: Mr John & Mrs Pam Hartill
17 St Leonards, Bodmin PL31 1LA
T: (01208) 73676
F: (01208) 73676
E: pamhartill@ukonline.co.uk

The Barn ★★★
Contact:
Cornish Horizons, The Cottage, 19 New Street, Padstow PL28 8EA
T: (01841) 533331
F: (01841) 533933
E: cottages@cornishhorizons.co.uk
I: www.cornishhorizons.co.uk

Colesent Cottages ★★★★
Contact: Mrs Sue Zamaria
Colesent Cottages, Wadebridge, Bodmin PL30 4QX
T: (01208) 850112
F: (01208) 850112
E: holiday@colesent.co.uk
I: www.colesent.co.uk

Curlews ★★★★
Contact:
Harbour Holidays - Rock, Trebetherick House, Wadebridge PL27 6SB
T: (01208) 863399
F: (01841) 533115

Lowenna Holiday Apartment ★★★
Contact: Mrs Katy Holmes
Lowenna Holiday Apartment, Lowenna House, 35 Egloshayle Road, Wadebridge PL27 6AE
T: (01208) 815725
E: pablo.holmes@btinternet.com
I: www.northcornwalllive.com

Potters ★★★★
Contact: Ms Susan Enderby
48, Little Heath, Charlton, London SE7 8BH
T: (020) 8855 8532
F: (020) 8855 8532
E: susanenderby@aol.com

Rosehill Holiday Accommodation ★★★★
Contact:
Cornish Horizons, The Cottage, 19 New Street, Padstow PL28 8EA
T: (01841) 533331
E: cottages@cornishhorizons.co.uk
I: www.cornishhorizons.co.uk

117 Talmena Avenue ★★★★
Contact: Mr Knapp
9 Treforest Road, Wadebridge PL27 7NP
T: (01208) 813448

Tregolls Farm Cottages ★★★★
Contact: Mrs Marilyn Hawkey
Tregolls Farm Cottages, Tregolls Farm, St Wenn, Bodmin PL30 5PG
T: (01208) 812154
F: (01208) 812154
E: tregollsfarm@btclick.com
I: www.tregollsfarm.co.uk

West Park Farm Holiday Cottages ★★★
Contact: Miss Helen Fishenden
West Park Farm Holiday Cottages, No Mans Land, St Issey, Wadebridge PL27 7RF
T: (01208) 813882
E: helen@daymer.freeserve.co.uk
I: www.westparkfarm.com

WANBOROUGH
Swindon

The Garden Apartment ★★★
Contact: Mrs Julie Evans
The Garden Apartment, The Bungalow, Chapel Lane, Swindon SN4 0AJ
T: (01793) 791395
F: (01793) 791395
E: tom.m.evans@talk21.com
I: www.members.lycos.co.uk/gardenapartment

WARBSTOW
Cornwall

Cartmell Bungalow ★★★
Contact: Mrs Dawe
Cartmell Bungalow, Trelash, Launceston PL15 8RL
T: (01840) 261353

Fentrigan Manor Farm Cottage ★★★★
Contact:
Farm & Cottage Holidays, Victoria House, 12 Fore Street, Bideford EX39 1AW
T: (01237) 479146
F: (01237) 421512
E: enquiries@farmcott.co.uk
I: www.farmcott.co.uk

WAREHAM
Dorset

Bronte Cottage ★★★★
Contact: Mr Stuart-Brown
Dream Cottages, 41 Maiden Street, Weymouth DT4 8TR
T: (01305) 789000

Culeaze ★★★★
Contact: Major Christopher Barne
Culeaze, Wareham BH20 7NR
T: (01929) 471344
F: (01929) 472221
E: majorbarne@ukonline.co.uk
I: www.culeaze.com

The Dutch Barn ★★★★
Contact: Mrs Jill Lidgey
Dorset Wareham Holidays, 5 Hurst Lane, Freeland, Witney OX29 8JA
T: (01993) 882028
F: (01993) 882028
E: lidgey@boltblue.com
I: www.dorsetwarehamholidays.com

East Creech Farm House ★★★
Contact: Mrs Best
East Creech Farm House, East Creech Farm, East Creech, Wareham BH20 5AP
T: (01929) 480519
F: (01929) 481312
E: debbie.best@euphony.net

The Glen ★★★
Contact:
Dream Cottages, 5 Hope Square, Weymouth DT4 8TR
T: (01305) 789000
F: (01305) 761346
E: admin@dream-cottages.co.uk
I: www.dreamcottages.co.uk

Tavern Way ★★★
Contact: Mrs Stuart-Brown
Dream Cottages, 5 Hope Square, Weymouth DT4 8TR
T: (01305) 789000
F: (01305) 761347
E: admin@dream-cottages.co.uk

WARLEGGAN
Cornwall

Treveddoe & Barley Crush ★★★-★★★★★
Contact: Lady Hill-Norton
The Barns, Newton Valence, Alton GU34 3RB
T: (01420) 588302
F: (01420) 587387
E: jennic@hill-norton.freeserve.co.uk
I: www.cornwall-online.co.uk/treveddoe

WARMINSTER
Wiltshire

The Annex ★★
Contact: Mrs Allery
The Annex, 'Wayside', 64 Weymouth Street, Warminster BA12 9NT
T: (01985) 218158

The Coach House ★★★★
Contact: Mrs Lynn Corp
Sturford Mead Farm, Warminster BA12 7QU
T: (01373) 832213
F: (01373) 832213
E: lynn_sturford.cottage@virgin.net

Downside House H112 ★★★★
Contact:
Hideaways, Chapel House, Luke Street, Berwick St John, Shaftesbury SP7 0HQ
T: (01747) 828170
F: (01747) 829090
E: enq@hideaways.co.uk
I: www.hideaways.co.uk

Whey Cottage ★★★★
Contact: Mr Zachary Stuart-Brown
Dream Cottages, 5 Hope Square, Weymouth DT4 8TR
T: (01305) 789000
F: (01305) 761346
E: admin@dream-cottages.co.uk
I: www.dream-cottages.co.uk

WARMLEY
South Gloucestershire

The Byre ★★
Contact: Mr John Hallett
The Byre, Fairsea, 12 St Andrews Road, Paignton TQ4 6HA
T: (01179) 561387
E: mjac103581@aol.com

WARMWELL
Dorset

Apple Orchard ★★
Contact: Mr Geoffrey Stuart Murgatroyd
Apple Orchard, Skippet Heath, Warmwell Road, Dorchester DT2 8JD
T: (01305) 853702
F: (01305) 853702

Beech Farm ★★★
Contact: Mrs Ruth Goldsack
Beech Farm, Dorchester DT2 8LZ
T: (01305) 852414
F: (01305) 853138
E: rugold@lineone.net

Establishments printed in blue have a detailed entry in this guide

SOUTH WEST ENGLAND

Misery Farm ★★★
Contact: Mr Zachary Stuart-Brown
Dream Cottages, 5 Hope Square, Weymouth DT4 8TR
T: (01305) 789000
F: (01305) 761346
E: admin@dream-cottages.co.uk
I: www.dream-cottages.co.uk

WASHAWAY
Cornwall

Ferkins Barn ★★★
Contact:
Cornish Horizons, The Cottage, 19 New Street, Padstow PL28 8EA
T: (01841) 533331
F: (01841) 533933
E: cottages@cornishhorizons.co.uk
I: www.cornishhorizons.co.uk

WASHFIELD
Devon

Barn Court ★★★★
Contact: Ms Anne Rawlings
Barn Court, Tiverton EX16 9QU
T: (01884) 243041
F: (01884) 243041
E: relaxindevon@ukonline.co.uk
I: www.relaxindevon.co.uk

WASHFORD
Somerset

Monksway ★★★★★
Contact: Mr & Mrs Woolford
Parkside, Hailey, Wallingford OX10 6AD
T: (01491) 681229
E: barry.woolford@ntlworld.com
I: www.countrycottagesonline.com

WATCHET
Somerset

The Croft Holiday Cottages ★★★★
Contact: Mr & Mrs Musgrave
The Croft Holiday Cottages, The Croft, Anchor Street, Watchet TA23 0BY
T: (01984) 631121
F: (01984) 631134
E: croftcottages@talk21.com
I: www.cottagessomerset.com

The Square ★★★
Contact: Mrs Court
31 North Croft, Taunton TA4 4RP
T: (01984) 639089
E: clarecourt@supanet.com
I: www.somerset-cottage.com

WATERMOUTH
Devon

The Nut House ★★★
Contact:
Marsden's Cottage Holidays, 2 The Square, Braunton EX33 2JB
T: (01271) 813777
F: (01271) 813664
E: holidays@marsdens.co.uk
I: www.marsdens.co.uk

WATERROW
Somerset

Exmoor Gate Lodges ★★★
Contact: Mrs Sue Gallagher
Whipcott Heights, Holcombe Rogus, Wellington TA21 0NA
T: (01823) 672339
F: (01823) 672339
E: bookings@oldlimekiln.freeserve.co.uk

Halsdown Farm Holiday Cottages ★★★
Contact: Mrs James
Halsdown Farm Holiday Cottages, Taunton TA4 2QU
T: (01984) 623493
F: (01984) 623493
E: jamesathalsdown@tinyworld.co.uk

Handley Farm ★★★★
Contact: Mr George & Mrs Linda Leigh-Firbank
Handley Farm, Taunton TA4 2BE
T: (01398) 361516
F: (01398) 361516
E: leigh-firbank.george@ntlworld.com
I: www.handleyfarm.co.uk

WEARE GIFFARD
Devon

Honeycomb ★★★★
Contact:
Farm & Cottage Holidays, Victoria House, 12 Fore Street, Bideford EX39 1AW
T: (01237) 479146
F: (01237) 421512
E: enquiries@farmcott.co.uk
I: www.farmcott.co.uk

WEDMORE
Somerset

The Coach House ★★★★
Contact: Mr Mike Rippon
The Coach House, Holdenhurst, Cheddar Road, Wedmore BS28 4EQ
T: (01934) 713125
F: (01934) 710050
E: coach.house@holdenhurst.co.uk
I: www.holdenhurst.co.uk/coachhouse

WEEK ST MARY
Cornwall

Ranelagh ★★★★
Contact: Mrs Susan Dickenson
The Rectory, The Glebe, Week St Mary, Holsworthy EX22 6UY
T: (01288) 341134
F: (01288) 341134
E: shdickenson@aol.com

Stewart House Holiday Cottages ★★★
Contact: Mrs Cox
Stewart House Holiday Cottages, Stewart House, Holsworthy EX22 6XA
T: (01288) 341556
E: simon.gaynor2@tinyworld.co.uk

WELCOMBE
Devon

Mead Barn Cottages ★★★-★★★★
Contact: Mrs Valerie Price
Mead Barn Cottages, Bideford EX39 6HQ
T: (01288) 331721
E: meadbarns@aol.com
I: www.meadbarns.com

Olde Smithy Bungalows ★★★
Contact: Mrs Sandra Millbourne
Olde Smithy Bungalows Self Catering, 14 Foxhill, Bideford EX39 1BP
T: (01237) 421811
E: user@fearonsfsbusiness.co.uk
I: www.northdevon.com/oldesmithy

WELLINGTON
Somerset

Old Lime Kilns ★★★★
Contact: Mrs Gallagher
Whipcott Heights, Wellington TA21 0NA
T: (01823) 672339
F: (01823) 672339
E: whipcott@aol.com

Tone Dale House ★★★★★
Contact: Mrs Beverley Netley
Tone Dale House, Milverton Road, Tonedale, Wellington TA21 0EZ
T: (01823) 662673
F: (01823) 662177
E: party@thebighouseco.com
I: www.thebighouseco.com

WELLOW
Bath and North East Somerset

Holly Cottage ★★★★
Contact: Mr Alick & Mrs Mari Bartholomew
Holly Cottage, The Hollies, Mill Hill, Bath BA2 8QJ
T: (01225) 840889
F: (01225) 833150
E: enquiries@bath-holidays.co.uk
I: www.bath-holidays.co.uk

WELLS
Somerset

Hart Cottage ★★★
Contact: Mr Aaron Nandi
Hart Cottage, 21 St John Street, Wells BA5 1SW
T: (01749) 674897
E: nandi@clara.co.uk

Model Farm Cottages ★★★
Contact: Mrs Gill Creed
Model Farm Cottages, Model Farm, Wells BA5 3AE
T: (01749) 673363
F: (01749) 671566
E: gillcreed@aol.com

The Old Farm House ★★★
Contact: Mrs Jayne Wood
The Old Farm House, 62 Bath Road, Wells BA5 3LQ
T: (01749) 673087
F: (01749) 674689
E: frankjwood@aol.com

The Potting Shed Holidays ★★★★
Contact: Mr & Mrs Van Bergen-Henegouwen
Potting Shed Holidays, Harters Hill Cottage, Pillmoor Lane, Wells BA5 1RF
T: (01749) 672857
F: (01749) 679925
I: www.pottingshedholidays.co.uk

St Marys Lodge ★★★★
Contact: Mrs Jane Hughes
St Marys Lodge, St Mary Mead, Long Street, Wells BA5 3QL
T: (01749) 342157
E: janehughes@trtopbox.net

Shalom ★★
Contact: Mrs Rees
60 Eastgrove Avenue, Sharples, Bolton BL1 7HA
T: (01204) 418576

Somerleaze Lodge ★★★
Contact: Mrs Marlene & Miss Victo Carse Jones
Somerleaze Lodge, The Coach House, Somerleaze, Wells BA5 1JU
T: (01749) 673859
F: (01749) 674053
I: www.cottagesdirect.com

Spiders End ★★★★
Contact: Mr & Mrs Van Bergen-Henegouwen
Potting Shed Holidays, Harters Hill Cottage, Pillmoor Lane, Wells BA5 1RF
T: (01749) 672857
F: (01749) 679925
E: cjvbhhol@aol.com
I: www.pottingshedholidays.co.uk

Spindlewood Lodges ★★★★
Contact: Mr & Mrs Peter/Linda Norris
Spindlewood Lodges, Lower Westholme, Shepton Mallet BA4 4EL
T: (01749) 890367
F: (01749) 899101
E: info@spindlewoodlodges.co.uk
I: www.spindlewoodlodges.co.uk

Vicars' Close Holiday House ★★★
Contact: Mrs Debbie Jones
Cathedral Office, Chain Gate, Cathedral Green, Wells BA5 2UE
T: (01749) 674483
F: (01749) 832210
E: visits@wellscathedral.uk.net

Wrinkle Mead
Rating Applied For
Contact: Mrs Cynthia Glass
Wrinkle Mead, Islington Farm, Ilsington, Wells BA5 1US
T: (01749) 673445
F: (01749) 673445
E: ilsingtonfarm2004@yahoo.co.uk

SOUTH WEST ENGLAND

WEMBDON
Somerset

Grange Farm Cottage ★★★★
Contact:
English Country Cottages,
Stoney Bank, Barnoldswick
BB94 0AA
T: 0870 5 851155
F: 0870 5 851150
I: www.
english-country-cottages.co.uk

WEMBURY
Devon

Bovisand Lodge Estate ★★★-★★★★★
Contact: Mrs Rita Hart
Bovisand Lodge Estate,
Plymouth PL9 0AA
T: (01752) 403554
F: (01752) 482646
E: blodge@netcomuk.co.uk
I: www.bovisand-apartments.co.uk

Traine Farm ★★★-★★★★★
Contact: Mrs Rowland
Traine Farm, Wembury,
Plymouth PL9 0EW
T: (01752) 862264
F: (01752) 862264
E: traine.cottages@btopenworld.com
I: www.traine-holiday-cottages.co.uk

WEST ALVINGTON
Devon

Osborne Cottage
Rating Applied For
Contact:
Toad Hall Cottages, Elliot House,
Church Street, Kingsbridge
TQ7 1BY
T: (01548) 853089
F: (01548) 853086
E: thc@toadhallcottages.com
I: www.toadhallcottages.com

Sunshine Cottage ★★★★
Contact: Mr Nicholas Pash
Hideaways, Chapel House, Luke Street, Shaftesbury SP7 0HQ
T: (01747) 828170
F: (01747) 829090
E: enq@hideaways.co.uk
I: www.hideaways.co.uk

WEST ANSTEY
Devon

Brimblecombe ★★★★
Contact: Mrs Charlotte Hutsby
Little Hill Farm, Wellesbourne,
Warwick CV35 9EB
T: (01789) 840261
F: (01789) 842270
I: www.brimblecombe-exmoor.co.uk

Deer's Leap Country Cottages ★★★★
Contact: Mr Michael & Mrs Frances Heggadon
Deer's Leap Country Cottages,
South Molton EX36 3NZ
T: (01398) 341407
F: (01398) 341407
E: deersleapcottages@lineone.net
I: www.deersleap.com

Dunsley Farm ★★★
Contact: Mrs Mary Robins
Dunsley Farm, South Molton
EX36 3PF
T: (01398) 341246
F: (01398) 341246
E: dunsleyfarm@aol.com
I: dunsley-farm-devon.co.uk

Dunsley Mill ★★★★
Contact: Mr John & Mrs Helen Sparrow
Dunsley Mill, South Molton
EX36 3PF
T: (01398) 341374
F: (01398) 341374
E: helen@dunsleymill.co.uk
I: www.dunsleymill.co.uk

WEST BAY
Dorset

The Bay House ★★★
Contact: Mr Kimber
5 Flaxfield Court, Basingstoke
RG21 8FX
T: (01256) 470927

15 Bramble Drive ★★★
Contact: Mr Gerald & Mrs Janet Paget
15 Bramble Drive, Meadowlands, Bridport DT6 4SN
F: (01962) 877946
E: gerry.paget@hants.gov.uk

28 Chesil House ★★★
Contact: Mrs Frances Hunt
Spices, Stoney Lane, Langport
TA10 0HY
T: (01458) 251203
F: (01458) 251203
E: frances.hunt@curryrivel.freeserve.co.uk
I: www.somersetcook.freeserve.co.uk

Foxglove Cottage
Rating Applied For
Contact:
Dream Cottages, 5 Hope Square, Weymouth DT4 8TR
T: (01305) 789000
F: (01305) 789000
E: admin@dream-cottages.co.uk
I: www.dreamcottages.co.uk

Harbour Lights ★★★
Contact: Mr Zachary Stuart-Brown
Dream Cottages, 5 Hope Square, Weymouth DT4 8TR
T: (01305) 789000
F: (01305) 761346
E: admin@dream-cottages.co.uk
I: www.dream-cottages.co.uk

Heron Court- V4331 ★★★
Contact: Mr Dave Matthews
Lyme Bay Holidays, Bos House, 44 Church Street, Lyme Regis
DT7 3DA
T: (01297) 443363
F: (01297) 445576
E: email@lymebayholidays.co.uk
I: www.lymebayholidays.co.uk

13 Heron Court
Rating Applied For
Contact: Mrs Mary Fitzpatrick
Merlins Cottage, Looke Lane, Coast Road, Dorchester DT2 9DB
T: (01308) 898261
F: (01308) 898261
E: merlinscottage@aol.com

18 Heron Court ★★★
Contact: Mr Mary Fitzpatrick
Merlins Cottage, Looke Lane, Dorchester DT2
F: (01308) 898261
E: merlinscottage@aol.com

8 Meadowlands: X4416
Rating Applied For
Contact:
Lyme Bay Holidays, Bos House, 44 Church Street, Lyme Regis
DT7 3DA
T: (01297) 443363
F: (01297) 445576
E: email@lymebayholidays.co.uk

8 Poppy Way X4428 ★★★★
Contact:
Lyme Bay Holidays, Bos House, 44 Church Street, Lyme Regis
DT7 3DA
T: (01297) 443363
F: (01297) 445576
E: email@lymebayholidays.co.uk
I: www.lymebayholidays.co.uk

Seafront Chalet ★★
Contact: Mrs Teresa Visram
224 Perth Road, Gants Hill, Ilford IG2 6DZ
T: (020) 85541543
F: (020) 8554 1543
E: teresa.visram@btinternet.com
I: www.btinternet.com/~sadru.visram

Westpoint Apartments ★★★-★★★★★
Contact: Mr & Mrs Slade
Westpoint Apartments, Esplanade, West Bay, Bridport
DT6 4HE
T: (01308) 423636
F: (01308) 458871
E: bea@westpointapartments.co.uk
I: www.westpointapartments.co.uk

Winnie Bustles ★★
Contact: Ms Anne Francis
Mole Cottage, 31 Loders, Bridport DT6 3SA
T: (01308) 427741
E: mole@theboops.fsnet.co.uk

WEST BEXINGTON
Dorset

Gorselands ★★-★★★★
Contact: Mrs Pallister
Gorselands, Dorchester DT2 9DJ
T: (01308) 897232
F: (01308) 897239
I: www.gorselands-uk.com

Tamarisk Farm Cottages ★★★-★★★★★
Contact: Mrs Josephine Pearse
Tamarisk Farm Cottages, Beach Road, Dorchester DT2 9DF
T: (01308) 897784
F: (01308) 897784
E: holidays@tamariskfarm.com
I: www.tamariskfarm.co.uk

WEST CHINNOCK
Somerset

Weavers Cottage ★★★★
Contact: Lt Col Gordon Piper
Weavers Cottage, Higher Street, Crewkerne TA18 7QA
T: (01935) 881370
E: thepipers@btinternet.com

Yeoman Cottage ★★★★
Contact: Mrs Marie Wheatley
Yeoman Cottage, Yeoman Wake, Higher Street, Crewkerne
TA18 7QA
T: (01935) 881421
F: (01935) 881421
E: jonwheat@aol.com

WEST DOWN
Devon

Fairview Farm Cottages ★★★
Contact: Mr Kevin Walker
Fairview Farm Cottages, Ilfracombe EX34 8NE
T: (01271) 862249
E: info@fairviewfarm.co.uk
I: www.fairviewfarm.co.uk

Kings Close ★★★★
Contact: Mrs Toni Buchan
Kings Close, Ilfracombe
EX34 8NF
T: (01271) 865222
F: 0870 130133
I: www.devoncottages.net

Rock Cottage ★★★
Contact: Mrs Virginia Sprason
53 Middlefield Lane, Stourbridge
DY9 0PY
T: (01562) 883038
F: (01562) 886592
E: rock.cott@virgin.net
I: www.devoncottage.fsnet.co.uk

Tawny Cottage & Swallow Cottage ★★★★
Contact:
Marsden's Cottage Holidays, 2 The Square, Braunton EX33 2JB
T: (01271) 813777
F: (01271) 813664
E: holidays@marsdens.co.uk
I: www.marsdens.co.uk

WEST LOOE
Cornwall

Tideways
Rating Applied For
Contact: Mrs Susan Richardson
Tideways, Church Street, Looe
PL13 2EX
T: (01503) 264103
E: richardsonks@supanet.com

Establishments printed in blue have a detailed entry in this guide

SOUTH WEST ENGLAND

WEST LULWORTH
Dorset

Advantage Point ★★
Contact: Mr Zachary Stuart-Brown
Dream Cottages, 5 Hope Square, Weymouth DT4 8TR
T: (01305) 789000
F: (01305) 761346
E: admin@dream-cottages.co.uk

Flat 2 Chestnut Court ★★★
Contact: Mrs Patricia Coulson
Laleham, The Glade, Tadworth KT20 6JE
T: (01737) 832282
E: pat.coulson@talk21.com

Ivy Cottage ★★★
Contact: Mrs Patricia Hurcombe
Ivy Cottage, 10 Main Road, Wareham BH20 5RN
T: (01929) 400509
F: (01929) 400509
E: ivycottage@thecove.worldonline.co.uk

Villa Buena Vista ★★★
Contact: Mr Stuart-Brown
5 Hope Square, 41 Maiden Street, Weymouth DT4 8TR
T: (01305) 789000

WEST MILTON
Dorset

Garden Lodge
Rating Applied For
Contact: Ms Sarah Talbot-Ponsonby
Leopard Cottage, Ruscombe Lane, Bridport DT6 3SL
T: (01920) 464755

Gore Cottage ★★★
Contact: Mrs E.G. Maude
Sparrow Court, Chalk Hill Road, Deal CT14 8DP
T: (01304) 389253
F: (01304) 389016
E: gmaude@waitrose.com
I: www.heartofdorset.co.uk

Pear Tree Cottage
Rating Applied For
Contact: Mrs Rachel Gauntlet
Monument Farm, Swivelton Lane, Fareham PO17 6AX
T: (01329) 280683
F: (01329) 283131
E: monumentfarm@aol.com

WEST PENNARD
Somerset

Victoria Farm ★★
Contact: Mr & Mrs Rands
Victoria Farm, Glastonbury BA6 8LW
T: (01458) 850509

WEST STAFFORD
Dorset

Barton House Loft ★★★
Contact: Mrs Robertson
Barton House Loft, Barton Close, Dorchester DT2 8AD
T: (01305) 250472
F: (01305) 250472

Daisy Cottage ★★
Contact:
Dream Cottages, 5 Hope Square, Weymouth DT4 8TR
T: (01305) 789000
F: (01305) 761347
E: admin@dreamcottages.co.uk
I: www.dream-cottages.co.uk

WEST TYTHERLEY
Dorset

Brightside Cottage Annexe ★★★
Contact: Mrs Barbara Wilks
Brightside Cottage Annexe, 19 Church Lane, Salisbury SP5 1JY
T: (01794) 341391
F: (01794) 341775
E: bwilks@talk21.com

WESTBURY
Wiltshire

Iron Box Cottage ★★★★
Contact: Mrs Hansford
1 Carpenters Lane, Westbury BA13 4SS
T: (01380) 830169
E: sue.hansford@tesco.net
I: www.ironboxcottage.co.uk

WESTBURY-SUB-MENDIP
Somerset

The Dairy ★★★
Contact: Mrs Catherine Hancock
The Dairy, Cottage Farm, The Hollow, Westbury sub Mendip, Wells BA5 1HH
T: (01749) 870351
I: www.westbury-sub-mendip.org

Old Apple Loft ★★★
Contact: Mrs Anne Flintham
Old Apple Loft, Westbury Cross House, Crow Lane, Wells BA5 1HB
T: (01749) 870557
F: (01749) 870997
E: enquiries@swan-networks.co.uk
I: www.oldappleloft.co.uk

WESTHAY
Somerset

The Courtyard New House Farm ★★★★
Contact: Mr Bell
The Courtyard New House Farm, Shapwick Road, Glastonbury BA6 9TT
T: (01458) 860238
F: (01458) 860568
E: newhousefarm@farmersweekly.net

Riverside Farmhouse ★★★★
Contact: Mr & Mrs Graham Noel
Riverside Farmhouse, Main Road, Glastonbury BA6 9TN
T: (01458) 860408
E: gnoel@venividi.co.uk
I: www.go-see.co.uk/riversidefarmhouse

WESTLEIGH
Devon

Farleigh Cottage ★★★★
Contact:
Farm & Cottage Holidays, Victoria House, 12 Fore Street, Bideford EX39 1AW
T: (01237) 479146
F: (01237) 421512
E: enquiries@farmcott.co.uk
I: www.farmcott.co.uk

WESTON
Devon

Birdsong Bungalow ★★★
Contact: Ms Kate Bartlett
Jean bartlett Cottage Holidays, The Old Dairy, Fore Street, Seaton EX12 3JB
T: (01297) 23221
E: holidays@jeanbartlett.com
I: www.jeanbartlett.com

Robin's Nest ★★★
Contact:
Milkbere Cottage Holidays, 3 Fore Street, Seaton EX12 2LE
T: (01297) 20729
F: (01297) 22925
E: info@milkberehols.com
I: www.milkberehols.com

Sandways ★★★
Contact: Ms Kate Bartlett
Jean Bartlett Cottage Holidays, The Old Dairy, Fore Street, Seaton EX12 3JB
T: (01297) 23221
F: (01297) 23303
E: holidays@jeanbartlett.com
I: www.jeanbartlett.com

Sea View ★★★
Contact: Ms Kate Bartlett
Jean Bartlett Cottage Holidays, The Old Dairy, Fore Street, Seaton EX12 3JB
T: (01297) 23221
E: holidays@jeanbartlett.com
I: www.jeanbartlett.com

Seagulls ★★★
Contact: Ms Kate Bartlett
Jean Bartlett Cottage Holidays, The Old Dairy, Fore Street, Seaton EX12 3JB
T: (01297) 23221
F: (01297) 23303
E: holidays@jeanbartlett.com
I: www.jeanbartlett.com

8 Sidvale
Rating Applied For
Contact: Ms Kate Bartlett
Jean Bartlett Cottage Holidays, The Old Dairy, Fore Street, Seaton EX12 3JB
T: (01297) 23221
F: (01297) 23303
E: holidays@jeanbartlett.com
I: www.netbreaks.com/jeanb

Starfish ★★★
Contact:
Milkbere Cottage Holidays, 3 Fore Street, Seaton EX12 2LE
T: (01297) 20729
F: (01297) 20725
E: info@milkberehols.com
I: www.milkberehols.com

2 Stoneleigh
Rating Applied For
Contact: Ms Kate Bartlett
Jean Bartlett Cottage Holidays, The Old Dairy, Fore Street, Seaton EX12 3JB
T: (01297) 23221
F: (01297) 23303
E: holidays@jeanbartlett.com
I: www.netbreaks.com/jeanb

Wagtails ★★★
Contact:
Milkbere Holidays, 3 Fore Street, Seaton EX12 2LE
T: (01297) 20729
F: (01297) 23227
E: info@milkberehols.com

WESTON SUBEDGE
Gloucestershire

Buff's Cottage ★★★★
Contact: Mrs Nelson
The Old Baptist Manse, Sheep Street, Stow-on-the-Wold, Cheltenham GL54 1AA
T: (01451) 870813
E: caroline.nelson@virgin.net
I: www.buffscottage.co.uk

Lychgate Cottage ★★★★
Contact: Mr Robert Hutsby
Middle Hill Farm, Warwick CV35 9EH
T: (01789) 841525
F: (01789) 841523
E: robert.hutsby@btinternet.com
I: www.chipping-campden-holiday-cottages.co.uk/lychgate.htm

WESTON-SUPER-MARE
North Somerset

Batch Farm Cottage ★★
Contact: Mrs Isabel Wall
Batch Farm Cottage, Batch Farm, Batch Lane, Weston-super-Mare BS24 0EX
T: (01934) 750287
F: (01934) 750287

Champagne Lettings ★★★★
Contact: Mrs Alison Cantle
Champagne Holiday Lets, Broomrigg House, Broomrigg Road, Aldershot GU51 4LR
T: (01252) 622789
F: (01252) 812948
E: alison@champagnelettings.fsnet.co.uk
I: www.champagnelettings.co.uk

Doubleton Farm Cottages ★★★
Contact: Mr John & Mrs Victoria Southwood
Doubleton Farm Cottages, Weston-super-Mare BS24 6RB
T: (01934) 520225
F: (01934) 520225
E: info@doubleton.com
I: www.doubleton.com

Hope Farm Cottages ★★★★
Contact: Mrs Liz Stirk
Hope Farm Cottages, Brean Road, Weston-super-Mare BS24 0HA
T: (01934) 750506
F: (01934) 750506
E: stirkhopefarm@aol.com
I: www.hopefarmcottages.co.uk

SOUTH WEST ENGLAND

Manor House Cottages
★★★-★★★★★
Contact: Mrs Hart
Manor House, Bleadon Road,
Weston-super-Mare BS24 0PY
T: (01934) 812689
F: (01934) 812689
E: valerie@
manor-house-cottages.com
I: www.manor-house-cottages.
com

Westward Ho! Holiday Flats
★★-★★★
Contact: Mr Ken & Mrs Janet
Everard
Westward Ho! Holiday Flats, 39
Severn Road, Weston-super-
Mare BS23 1DP
T: (01934) 629294
F: (01934) 624168
E: kenandjanet@
westwardhohols.fsnet.co.uk

WESTPORT
Somerset

Riverside ★★★★
Contact: Mrs Caroline King
Cullompton EX15 3PT
T: (01823) 680447
F: (01823) 681008
E: cking@dunnsgreen.fsnet.
co.uk
I: www.dunnsgreen.fsnet.co.uk

**Wind in the Willows
Cottage** ★★★
Contact: Mr Baker
Hillside, Cooks Lane, Axminster
EX13 5SQ
T: (01297) 32051
F: (01297) 32051
E: cjbaker@eggconnect.net

WEYCROFT
Devon

The Willows ★★★★
Contact: Mr Mark & Mrs Anetta
Regan
The Willows, Weycroft Mill,
Axminster EX13 7LN
T: (01297) 34565
E: contactus@devonwillows.
com
I: www.devonwillows.com

WEYMOUTH
Dorset

**Acropolis Hotel &
Apartments** ★★
Contact: Mr & Mrs Afedakis
Plantours Ltd, Dorchester Road,
Weymouth DT4 7JT
T: (01305) 784282
F: (01305) 767172
E: acropolishotel@plantours.
fsnet.co.uk
I: www.acropolihotel.co.uk

Anvil House ★★★
Contact: Mr Zachary Stuart-
Brown
Dream Cottages, 5 Hope Square,
Weymouth DT4 8TR
T: (01305) 789000
F: (01305) 761346
E: admin@dream-cottages.
co.uk
I: www.dream-cottages.co.uk

Ashleigh Holiday Flats
★★-★★
Contact: Mr Roger Littler
Ashleigh Holiday Flats, 53
Abbotsbury Road, Weymouth
DT4 0AQ
T: (01305) 773715
E: ashleighhols@talk21.com

Ashwood ★★★★
Contact:
Dream Cottages, 5 Hope Square,
Weymouth DT4 8TR
T: (01305) 789000
F: (01305) 761347
E: admin@dream-cottages.co.uk

Bank View ★★★★
Contact: Miss Hannah Brain
Charm Properties Limited, 12
Stavordale Road, Weymouth
DT4 0AB
T: (01305) 786514
F: (01305) 786556
E: hilary@tamariskhotel.co.uk
I: www.charmproperties.co.uk

The Barbican ★★★★
Contact: Mr Zachary Stuart-
Brown
Dream Cottages, 5 Hope Square,
Weymouth DT4 8TR
T: (01305) 789000
F: (01305) 761346
E: admin@dream-cottages.
co.uk
I: www.dream-cottages.co.uk

**Bay Lodge Self-Catering
Accommodation** ★★★★★
Contact: Mr & Mrs Dubben
c/o Bay Lodge, 27 Greenhill,
Weymouth DT4 7SW
T: (01305) 782419
F: (01305) 782828
E: barbara@baylodge.co.uk
I: www.baylodge.co.uk

Bay Tree House ★★★
Contact: Mrs Dawn Rolls
12 Great Western Terrace,
Weymouth DT4 7LU
T: (01305) 772952
F: (01305) 772952
E: baytree@rollsco.com
I: www.rollsco.com/baytree

Baywatch ★★★
Contact: Mr Broadhead
Eastney Hotel, 15 Longfield
Hotel, Weymouth DT4 8RQ
T: (01305) 761347
I: www.eastneyhotel.co.uk

Beach View Apartment ★★
Contact: Mr Zachary Stuart-
Brown
Dream Cottages, 5 Hope Square,
Weymouth DT4 8TR
T: (01305) 789000
F: (01305) 761346
E: admin@dream-cottages.
co.uk
I: www.dream-cottages.co.uk

Blissco ★★
Contact: Mr Zachary Stuart-
Brown
Dream Cottages, 5 Hope Square,
Weymouth DT4 8TR
T: (01305) 789000
F: (01305) 761346
E: admin@dream-cottages.
co.uk
I: www.dream-cottages.co.uk

Bridges ★★★
Contact: Ms Lyndsey Diment
11 Love Lane, Weymouth
DT4 8JZ
T: (01305) 759565
E: lyndseyd@madasafish.com

Cassis Cottage ★★★
Contact: Mr Zachary Stuart-
Brown
Dream Cottages, 5 Hope Square,
Weymouth DT4 8TR
T: (01305) 789000
F: (01305) 761346
E: admin@dream-cottages.
co.uk
I: www.dream-cottages.co.uk

**Central Seafront
Apartments** ★★★
Contact: Mr & Mrs Wright
21 Greenhill, Weymouth
DT4 7SW
T: (01305) 766744

Chapelhay Cottage ★★★★
Contact: Mr Martin & Mrs Annie
Harman
45 Hendham Road, London
SW17 7DH
T: (020) 86777007
F: (020) 86727165
E: annie.kilington@masons.com
I: www.cottageinweymouth.com

Cherry Tree Cottage ★★★
Contact: Mr Martin Rolls
12 Great Western Terrace,
Lodmoor, Weymouth DT4 7LU
T: (01305) 772952
F: (01305) 772952
E: cottage@rollsco.com
I: www.rollsco.com/cottage

**Christopher Robin Holiday
Flats** ★★★
Contact: Mrs Davies
Christopher Robin Holiday Flats,
70 The Esplanade, Weymouth
DT4 7AA
T: (01305) 774870
I: www.
christopherrobinholidayflats.
co.uk

Cockleshells ★★
Contact: Mr Zachary Stuart-
Brown
Dream Cottages, 5 Hope Square,
Weymouth DT4 8TR
T: (01305) 789000
F: (01305) 761346
E: admin@dream-cottages.
co.uk
I: www.dream-cottages.co.uk

Corner Cottage
Rating Applied For
Contact: Miss Hannah Brain
Charm Properties, 12 Stavordale
Road, Weymouth DT4 0AB
T: (01305) 786514
F: (01305) 786556
E: hilary@tamariskhotel.co.uk
I: www.charmproperties.co.uk

Cove Corner ★★★★
Contact:
Dream Cottages, 5 Hope Square,
Weymouth DT4 8TR
T: (01305) 789000
F: (01305) 761346
E: admin@dream-cottages.
co.uk

Cove Walk Cottage ★★★★
Contact: Ms Rosemarie Latta
7 Coniston Crescent, Weymouth
DT3 5HA
T: (01305) 779144
E: dstone2880@aol.com

Crescent Cottage ★★★★
Contact: Mrs Tracy Buckwell
38 Cleveland Avenue,
Weymouth DT3 5AG
T: (01305) 771881
F: (01305) 768491

Crows Nest ★★★
Contact: Mr Zachary Stuart-
Brown
Dream Cottages, 5 Hope Square,
Weymouth DT4 8TR
T: (01305) 789000
F: (01305) 761346
E: admin@dream-cottages.
co.uk
I: www.dream-cottages.co.uk

Cygnets
Rating Applied For
Contact:
Dream Cottages, 5 Hope Square,
Weymouth DT4 8TR
T: (01305) 789000
F: (01305) 761346
E: admin@dream-cottages.
co.uk
I: www.dreamcottages.co.uk

Daintree ★★
Contact: Mrs Sheila Snook
Daintree, 46 Chelmsford Street,
Weymouth DT4 7HR
T: (01305) 782689

Dornare Holiday Flats
★-★★
Contact: Mrs Dorenne Fowler
Dornare Holiday Flats, 3
Newberry Road, Weymouth
DT4 8LP
T: (01305) 786359
E: dornare@fowler77.freeserve.
co.uk

Driftwood Cottage ★★★
Contact:
Dream Cottages, 41 Maiden
Street, Weymouth DT4 8AZ
T: (01305) 761347
E: admin@dream-cottages.
co.uk
I: www.dream-cottages.co.uk

Dunvegan Holiday Cottages
★★★
Contact: Mr Ian Boudier
1 Old Castle Road, Weymouth
DT4 8QB
T: (01305) 783188
F: (01305) 783181
E: trelawney@freeuk.com

Eastleigh House ★★
Contact: Mr Zachary Stuart-
Brown
Dream Cottages, 5 Hope Square,
Weymouth DT4 8TR
T: (01305) 789000
F: (01305) 761346
E: admin@dream-cottages.
co.uk
I: www.dream-cottages.co.uk

Establishments printed in blue have a detailed entry in this guide

SOUTH WEST ENGLAND

Ebb Tide ★★★
Contact: Mr Zachary Stuart-Brown
Dream Cottages, 5 Hope Square, Weymouth DT4 8TR
T: (01305) 789000
F: (01305) 761346
E: admin@dream-cottages.co.uk
I: www.dream-cottages.co.uk

Fairhaven Holiday Flats & Cottage ★★
Contact: Mr Peter Stark
Kings Hotel Group, 12 The Esplanade, Weymouth DT4 8EB
T: (01305) 760100
F: (01305) 760300
I: www.kingshotels.co.uk

Ferndale House ★★★
Contact: Mr Zachary Stuart-Brown
Dream Cottages, 5 Hope Square, Weymouth DT4 8TR
T: (01305) 789000
F: (01305) 761346
E: admin@dream-cottages.co.uk
I: www.dream-cottages.co.uk

The Ferryman
Rating Applied For
Contact:
Dream Cottages, 5 Hope Square, Weymouth DT4 8TR
T: (01305) 789000
F: (01305) 761346
E: admin@dream-cottages.co.uk

The Firs ★★★
Contact:
Dream Cottages, 5 Hope Square, Weymouth DT4 8TR
T: (01305) 789000
E: admin@dream-cottages.co.uk
I: www.dream-cottages.co.uk

Fishermans Cottage ★★★
Contact: Mr Zachary Stuart-Brown
Dream Cottages, 5 Hope Square, Weymouth DT4 8TR
T: (01305) 789000
F: (01305) 761346
E: admin@dream-cottages.co.uk
I: www.dream-cottages.co.uk

Footprints ★★★★
Contact: Mr Zachary Stuart-Brown
Dream Cottages, 5 Hope Square, Weymouth DT4 8TR
T: (01305) 789000
E: admin@dream-cottages.co.uk

Fuchsia's Edge ★★★
Contact:
Dream Cottages, 5 Hope Square, Weymouth DT4 8TR
T: (01305) 789000
F: (01305) 761347

The Gables ★★★★
Contact: Mr Zachary Stuart-Brown
Dream Cottages, 5 Hope Square, Weymouth DT4 8TR
T: (01305) 789000
E: admin@dream-cottages.co.uk
I: www.dream-cottages.co.uk

The Gatehouse & Malthouse ★★★★
Contact: Mr Zachary Stuart-Brown
Dream Cottages, 5 Hope Square, Weymouth DT4 8TR
T: (01305) 789000
E: admin@dream-cottages.co.uk
I: www.dream-cottages.co.uk

Georges House ★★★★
Contact: Mr Zachary Stuart-Brown
Dream Cottages, 5 Hope Square, Weymouth DT4 8TR
T: (01305) 789000
E: admin@dream-cottages.co.uk
I: www.dream-cottages.co.uk

Glen House ★★★★
Contact: Mrs Tracy Buckwell
Cleveland Avenue, Weymouth DT3 5AG
T: (01305) 771881
E: buckwell@btinternet.com

Grandview ★★★
Contact: Mr Downham
Grandview, 22 Greenhill, Weymouth DT4 7SG
T: (01305) 783796

Greenhill Lodge ★★★
Contact: Ms Marylou Delaplanque
Greenhill Lodge, 18 Greenhill, Weymouth DT4 7SG
T: (01305) 786351

Harbour Edge ★★★
Contact: Mr Zachary Stuart-Brown
Dream Cottages, 5 Hope Square, Weymouth DT4 8TR
T: (01305) 789000
F: (01305) 761346
E: admin@dream-cottages.co.uk
I: www.dream-cottages.co.uk

Harbour Retreat ★★★
Contact: Mr Zachary Stuart-Brown
Dream Cottages, 5 Hope Square, Weymouth DT4 8TR
T: (01305) 789000
F: (01305) 761346
E: admin@dream-cottages.co.uk
I: www.dream-cottages.co.uk

Harbour View Apartments ★★★
Contact: Mr Zachary Stuart-Brown
Dream Cottages, 5 Hope Square, Weymouth DT4 8TR
T: (01305) 789000
E: admin@dream-cottages.co.uk

Holiday House ★★
Contact: Mr Saunders
8 Sutcliffe Avenue, Weymouth DT4 9SA
T: (01305) 773307

Hops House ★★★★
Contact: Mr Zachary Stuart-Brown
Dream Cottages, 5 Hope Square, Weymouth DT4 8TR
T: (01305) 789000
F: (01305) 761346
E: admin@dream-cottages.co.uk
I: www.dream-cottages.co.uk

Howard Cottage ★★★
Contact: Mrs Barbara Willy
5 Helston Close, Weymouth DT3 4EY
T: (01305) 871799

Ivy Cottage ★★★★
Contact:
Dream Cottages, 5 Hope Square, Weymouth DT4 8TR
T: (01305) 789000
F: (01305) 761347
E: admin@dream-cottages.co.uk
I: www.dream-cottages.co.uk

Jacaranda ★★★
Contact: Mr Zachary Stuart-Brown
Dream Cottages, 5 Hope Square, Weymouth DT4 8TR
T: (01305) 789000
E: admin@dream-cottages.co.uk
I: www.dream-cottages.co.uk

Kenmuire Holiday Flats ★-★★★
Contact: Mr Cotterill
Kenmuire Holiday Flats, 28 Alexandra Road, Lodmoor, Weymouth DT4 7QQ
T: (01305) 785659

Kingsview ★★
Contact: Ms Anne Breen
The Old Rectory, Lorton Lane, Weymouth DT3 5DJ
T: (01305) 814741

Lavender Cottage ★★★★
Contact:
Dream Cottages, 5 Hope Square, Weymouth DT4 8TR
T: (01305) 789000
F: (01305) 761347

The Lawns
Rating Applied For
Contact:
Dream Cottages, 5 Hope Square, Weymouth DT4 8TR
T: (01305) 789000
F: (01305) 761346
E: admin@dream-cottages.co.uk
I: www.dreamcottages.co.uk

Lillie Cottage ★★★
Contact:
Lillie Cottage, 15 Springfield Road, Weymouth DT3 5DX
T: (01305) 789000
F: (01305) 761347
E: admin@dream-cottages.co.uk
I: www.dream-cottages.co.uk

The Little Coachouse ★★★
Contact: Mr Zachary Stuart-Brown
Dream Cottages, 5 Hope Square, Weymouth DT4 8TR
T: (01305) 789000
E: admin@dream-cottages.co.uk
I: www.dream-cottages.co.uk

Little Venice ★★★
Contact:
Dream Cottages, 5 Hope Square, Weymouth DT4 8TR
T: (01305) 789000
F: (01305) 761346
E: admin@dream-cottages.co.uk
I: www.dream-cottages.co.uk

Littlecoombe Flat 1 Coombe House ★★★
Contact: Stuart-Brown
Dream Cottages, 5 Hope Square, Weymouth DT4 8TR
T: (01305) 789000

Lobster Pot ★★★
Contact: Mrs Creed
Propect House, The Street, Chippenham SN14 7BQ
T: (01249) 782713

Lookout ★★★
Contact:
Dream Cottages, 5 Hope Square, Weymouth DT4 8TR
T: (01305) 789000
F: (01305) 761346
E: admin@dream-cottages.co.uk

Malt Cottage ★★★
Contact:
Dream Cottages, 5 Hope Square, Weymouth DT4 8TR
T: (01305) 789000
F: (01305) 761347
E: admin@dream-cottages.co.uk
I: www.dream-cottages.co.uk

Marina View Apartment ★★★★
Contact: Mr Zachary Stuart-Brown
Dream Cottages, 5 Hope Square, Weymouth DT4 8TR
T: (01305) 789000
F: (01305) 761346
E: admin@dream-cottages.co.uk
I: www.dream-cottages.co.uk

Mariners Way ★★★
Contact: Mr Zachary Stuart-Brown
Dream Cottages, 5 Hope Square, Weymouth DT4 8TR
T: (01305) 789000
F: (01305) 761346
E: admin@dream-cottages.co.uk

Marlow House ★★★
Contact:
Dream Cottages, 5 Hope Square, Weymouth DT4 8TR
T: (01305) 789000
F: (01305) 761347
E: admin@dream-cottages.co.uk
I: www.dream-cottages.co.uk

SOUTH WEST ENGLAND

Mulberry Cottage ★★★
Contact:
Dream Cottages, 5 Hope Square,
Weymouth DT4 8TR
T: (01305) 789000
F: (01305) 761346
E: admin@dream-cottages.
co.uk
I: www.dream-cottages.co.uk

**Newlands Holiday Flats
★-★★★**
Contact: Mr & Mrs Hazel
Brownsey
Newlands Holiday Flats, 10
Glendinning Avenue, Weymouth
DT4 7QF
T: (01305) 784949

The Oast House ★★★★
Contact: Mr Zachary Stuart-
Brown
Dream Cottages, 5 Hope Square,
Weymouth DT4 8TR
T: (01305) 789000
E: admin@dream-cottages.
co.uk
I: www.dream-cottages.co.uk

Ocean Wave ★★★★
Contact: Mr Zachary Stuart-
Brown
Dream Cottages, 5 Hope Square,
Weymouth DT4 8TR
T: (01305) 789000
E: admin@dream-cottages.
co.uk
I: www.dream-cottages.co.uk

**Old Beams
Rating Applied For**
Contact:
Dream Cottages, 5 Hope Square,
Weymouth DT4 8TR
T: (01305) 789000
F: (01305) 761347
E: admin@dream-cottages.
co.uk
I: www.dream-cottages.co.uk

90 Old Castle Road ★★★
Contact: Mrs Angela Mary Blake
Weymouth Bay Holiday
Apartments, 56 Greenhill,
Weymouth DT4 7SL
T: (01305) 785003

**Old Harbour Holiday Flats
★★**
Contact: Mrs Ida Goddard
451 Chickerell Road, Weymouth
DT3 4DG
T: (01305) 776674

**Orchard Cottage
Rating Applied For**
Contact: Miss Anne M Breen
Orchard Cottage, The Old
Rectory, Lorton Lane, Weymouth
DT3 5DJ
T: (01305) 814741
F: (01305) 812010

Oyster Cottage ★★★★
Contact: Mrs Burt
46 Greenhill, Weymouth
DT4 7SL
T: (01305) 761271
E: family@tburt.fsnet.co.uk

Panda Holiday Flats ★★★
Contact: Mrs Anne Rose
Panda Holiday Flats, 12
Grosvenor Road, Weymouth
DT4 7QL
T: (01305) 773817

Pear Tree Cottage ★★★
Contact: Mr Ian Boudier
Dunvegan Holiday Cottages, 1
Old Castle Road, Weymouth
DT4 8QB
T: (01305) 783188
F: (01305) 783181
E: trelawney@freeuk.com
I: www.trelawneyhotel.com

Pebble Cottage ★★★
Contact: Mr Zachary Stuart-
Brown
Dream Cottages, 5 Hope Square,
Weymouth DT4 8TR
T: (01305) 789000
E: admin@dream-cottages.
co.uk
I: www.dream-cottages.co.uk

The Pines ★★★★
Contact:
Dream Cottages, 5 Hope Square,
Weymouth DT4 8TR
T: (01305) 789000
E: admin@dream-cottages.
co.uk
I: www.dream-cottages.co.uk

Poppies Cottage ★★★★
Contact: Mr Zachary Stuart-
Brown
Dream Cottages, 5 Hope Square,
Weymouth DT4 8TR
T: (01305) 789000
E: admin@dream-cottages.
co.uk
I: www.dream-cottages.co.uk

Promenade Way ★★★
Contact:
Dream Cottages, 5 Hope Square,
Weymouth DT4 8TR
T: (01305) 789000
E: admin@dream-cottages.
co.uk
I: www.dream-cottages.co.uk

Quayside ★★★
Contact: Mr Heath
Heath Developments Ltd, 2 St
James Walk, Iver SL0 9EW
T: (01753) 654676
F: (01753) 653856
E: amhuk@aol.com

**Quayside Apartment
★★★★**
Contact: Mr Zachary Stuart-
Brown
Dream Cottages, 5 Hope Square,
Weymouth DT4 8TR
T: (01305) 789000
E: admin@dream-cottages.
co.uk
I: www.dream-cottages.co.uk

**Queensway Holiday Flats
★-★★★**
Contact: Mr Martin Kelly
46 Park Street, Weymouth
DT4 7DF
T: (01305) 760747
I: www.precision.clara.
net/queensway

**Queensway Holiday Flats
★★**
Contact: Mr Martin Kelly
46 Park Street, Weymouth
DT4 7DF
T: (01305) 760747
I: www.precision.clara.
net/queensway

**Randall's Net Loft & The
Old Boathouse (Phoenix
Holiday Flats) ★★★**
Contact: Mrs Janet Bennett
Phoenix Holiday Flats, 53
Coombe Valley Road, Weymouth
DT3 6NL
T: (01305) 832134
F: (01305) 834955

Sailing Waters ★★★★
Contact:
Dream Cottages, 5 Hope Square,
Weymouth DT4 8TR
T: (01305) 789000
F: (01305) 761347
E: admin@dream-cottages.
co.uk
I: www.dream-cottages.co.uk

Sandpipers ★★★★
Contact:
Dream Cottages, 5 Hope Square,
Weymouth DT4 8TR
T: (01305) 789000
F: (01305) 761347
E: admin@dream-cottages.
co.uk
I: www.dream-cottages.co.uk

Savoy Holiday Flats ★★★
Contact: Mr Mark Taylor
Savoy Holiday Flats, 112 The
Esplanade, Weymouth DT4 7EA
T: (01305) 783254

**Sea Horse Apartment
★★★★**
Contact: Mr Zachary Stuart-
Brown
Dream Cottages, 5 Hope Square,
Weymouth DT4 8TR
T: (01305) 789000
E: admin@dream-cottages.
co.uk

**Sea Shells Holiday Flat
★★★**
Contact: Mr Duncan & Mrs
Ramona Rosser
26 High Street, Wyke Regis,
Weymouth DT4 9NZ
T: (01305) 778540

**Sea Tower & Sea Watch
Rating Applied For**
Contact:
Dream Cottages, 5 Hope Square,
Weymouth DT4 8TR
T: (01305) 789000
F: (01305) 761346
E: admin@dream-cottages.
co.uk
I: www.dreamcottages.co.uk

Seabreeze ★★★
Contact: Mr Zachary Stuart-
Brown
Dream Cottages, 5 Hope Square,
Weymouth DT4 8TR
T: (01305) 789000
E: admin@dream-cottages.
co.uk
I: www.dream-cottages.co.uk

Seafields ★★★
Contact: Mr Zachary Stuart-
Brown
Dream Cottages, 5 Hope Square,
Weymouth DT4 8TR
T: (01305) 789000
E: admin@dream-cottages.
co.uk
I: www.dream-cottages.co.uk

Seafront Holiday Flats ★★★
Contact: Mr Stephen Taylor
225 Dorchester Road,
Weymouth DT3 5EQ
T: (01305) 780104
F: (01305) 780104

Seagull Cottage ★★★
Contact: Mr Zachary Stuart-
Brown
Dream Cottages, 5 Hope Square,
Weymouth DT4 8TR
T: (01305) 789000
F: (01305) 761346
E: admin@dream-cottages.
co.uk
I: www.dream-cottages.co.uk

Seaside House ★★★
Contact: Mr Zachary Stuart-
Brown
Dream Cottages, 5 Hope Square,
Weymouth DT4 8TR
T: (01305) 789000
F: (01305) 761346
E: admin@dream-cottages.
co.uk
I: www.dream-cottages.co.uk

Seaspray ★★★
Contact: Mr Zachary Stuart-
Brown
Dream Cottages, 5 Hope Square,
Weymouth DT4 8TR
T: (01305) 789000
E: admin@dream-cottages.
co.uk
I: www.dream-cottages.co.uk

**Seaview Cottage & Captains
Cabin ★★**
Contact: Mrs Wendy Evans
811 Wyke Road, Weymouth
DT4 9QN
T: (01305) 785037
E: wenjon@onetel.net.uk

The Shanty ★★★
Contact: Mr Zachary Stuart-
Brown
Dream Cottages, 5 Hope Square,
Weymouth DT4 8TR
T: (01305) 789000
F: (01305) 761346
E: admin@dream-cottages.
co.uk
I: www.dream-cottages.co.uk

Shire Horse Mews ★★★
Contact: Mr Zachary Stuart-
Brown
Dream Cottages, 5 Hope Square,
Weymouth DT4 8TR
T: (01305) 789000
E: admin@dream-cottages.
co.uk
I: www.dream-cottages.co.uk

Spinnaker House ★★★
Contact: Mr Zachary Stuart-
Brown
Dream Cottages, 5 Hope Square,
Weymouth DT4 8TR
T: (01305) 789000
E: admin@dream-cottages.
co.uk
I: www.dream-cottages.co.uk

**Stavordale House Holiday
Apartments ★★★**
Contact: Mr Mark Marriott
Little Compton, Fairmile Park
Road, Cobham KT11 2PG
T: (01932) 869932
E: stavordalehouse@ukonline.
co.uk

Establishments printed in blue have a detailed entry in this guide

SOUTH WEST ENGLAND

Stonebank Cottage ★★★★
Contact: Mrs Pru Westcott
Stonebank Cottage, 14 West Street, Weymouth DT3 4DY
T: (01305) 760120
F: (01305) 760871
E: annexe@stonebank-chickerell.com
I: www.stonebank-chickerell.co.uk

Sunnywey Apartments ★★★★
Contact: Mr & Mrs Bond
Sunnywey Apartments, 27 Kirtleton Avenue, Weymouth DT4 7PS
T: (01305) 781767
E: bond@sunnywey.co.uk
I: www.sunnywey.co.uk

4 Sutcliffe Avenue ★★★
Contact: Mr Saunders
8 Sutcliffe Avenue, Southill, Weymouth DT4 9SA
T: (01305) 773307

Tamarisk Apartment ★★★
Contact: Mr Zachary Stuart-Brown
Dream Cottages, 5 Hope Square, Weymouth DT4 8TR
T: (01305) 789000
F: (01305) 761346
E: admin@dream-cottages.co.uk
I: www.dream-cottages.co.uk

Timbers ★★★
Contact: Mr Zachary Stuart-Brown
Dream Cottages, 5 Hope Square, Weymouth DT4 8TR
T: (01305) 789000
F: (01305) 761346
E: admin@dream-cottages.co.uk
I: www.dream-cottages.co.uk

The Trawlerman
Rating Applied For
Contact:
Dream Cottages, 5 Hope Square, Weymouth DT4 8TR
T: (01305) 789000
F: (01305) 761346
E: admin@dream-cottages.co.uk
I: www.dream-cottages.co.uk

Treetops ★★★★
Contact: Mr Zachary Stuart-Brown
Dream Cottages, 5 Hope Square, Weymouth DT4 8TR
T: (01305) 789000
F: (01305) 761346
E: admin@dream-cottages.co.uk
I: www.dream-cottages.co.uk

Trezise Holiday Home ★★★
Contact: Mr Barrie & Valerie Trezise
1 High Street, Bristol BS30 5QJ
T: (0117) 9372304
E: b.trezise@btopenworld.com

Upsidedown House ★★★★
Contact:
Dream Cottages, 5 Hope Square, Weymouth DT4 8TR
T: (01305) 789000
I: www.dream-cottages.co.uk

Wagonwheels ★★★
Contact:
Dream Cottages, 5 Hope Square, Weymouth DT4 8TR
T: (01305) 789000
F: (01305) 761347
E: admin@dream-cottages.co.uk
I: www.dream-cottages.co.uk

Waters Edge ★★★
Contact: Mr Zachary Stuart-Brown
Dream Cottages, 5 Hope Square, Weymouth DT4 8TR
T: (01305) 789000
F: (01305) 761346
E: admin@dream-cottages.co.uk
I: www.dream-cottages.co.uk

Weyfarer Cottage ★★★
Contact: Mr Zachary Stuart-Brown
Dream Cottages, 5 Hope Square, Weymouth DT4 8TR
T: (01305) 789000
F: (01305) 761346
E: admin@dream-cottages.co.uk
I: www.dream-cottages.co.uk

Weymouth Bay Holiday Apartments ★★★
Contact: Mrs Angela Mary Blake
Weymouth Bay Holiday Apartments, 56 Greenhill, Weymouth DT4 7SL
T: (01305) 785003

The Weymouth Seafront Holiday Flat ★★★
Contact: Mr Don Whistance
Kilderkin, The Old Malthouse, Weymouth DT3 4BH
T: (01305) 813237
E: donwhistance@rmplc.co.uk
I: www.theflat.org.uk

Wheelwright House ★★★
Contact: Mr Zachary Stuart-Brown
Dream Cottages, 5 Hope Square, Weymouth DT4 8TR
T: (01305) 789000
E: admin@dream-cottages.co.uk
I: www.dream-cottages.co.uk

White Horse House ★★★
Contact: Mr Zachary Stuart-Brown
Dream Cottages, 5 Hope Square, Weymouth DT4 8TR
T: (01305) 789000
F: (01305) 761346
E: admin@dream-cottages.co.uk
I: www.dream-cottages.co.uk

White Waves
Rating Applied For
Contact:
Dream Cottages, 5 Hope Square, Weymouth DT4 8TR
T: (01305) 789000
F: (01305) 761346
E: admin@dream-cottages.co.uk
I: www.dreamcottages.co.uk

Whitesands Seafront Apartments ★-★★★
Contact: Mr Harvey Bailey
Whitesands Seafront Apartments, 23 The Esplanade, Weymouth DT4 8DN
T: (01305) 782202

Winkle Cottage ★★★
Contact: Mr Zachary Stuart-Brown
Dream Cottages, 5 Hope Square, Weymouth DT4 8TR
T: (01305) 789000
E: admin@dream-cottages.co.uk
I: www.dream-cottages.co.uk

WHEDDON CROSS
Somerset

Cutthorne ★★★★
Contact: Mrs Ann Durbin
Cutthorne, Minehead TA24 7EW
T: (01643) 831255
F: (01643) 831255
E: durbin@cutthorne.co.uk
I: www.cutthorne.co.uk

Mill Cottage ★★★★
Contact: Mrs Ratcliff
Mill Cottage, Ford Farm, Draypers Way, Minehead TA24 7EE
T: (01643) 841251
F: (01643) 841251
E: ratcliff@ford-farm.freeserve.co.uk
I: www.millcottage-exmoor.co.uk

North Wheddon Farm
Rating Applied For
Contact: Mr Julian Abraham
North Wheddon Farm, Minehead TA24 7EX
T: (01225) 461634
E: julian@go-exmoor.co.uk
I: www.go-exmoor.co.uk

Pembroke ★★★
Contact: Mrs Escott
Brake Cottage, Minehead TA24 7EX
T: (01643) 841550

Triscombe Farm ★★★★
Contact: Ruth Corby
Triscombe Farm, Minehead TA24 7HA
T: (01643) 851227
F: (01643) 851227
E: ruthattriscombe@aol.com
I: www.triscombefarm.co.uk

WHIMPLE
Devon

LSF Holiday Cottages ★★★
Contact: Mrs Angela Lang
LSF Holiday Cottages, Lower Southbrook Farm, Southbrook Lane, Exeter EX5 2PG
T: (01404) 822989
F: (01404) 822989
E: lowersouthbrookfarm@btinternet.com

WHITCHURCH CANONICORUM
Dorset

Berehayes Farm Cottages ★★★★
Contact: Mr & Mrs Winterbourne
Berehayes Farm Cottages, Whitchurch Canonicorum, Bridport DT6 6RQ
T: (01297) 489093
F: (01297) 489093
E: berehayes@tesco.net
I: www.berehayes.co.uk

Bonhayes Stable - Y4360 ★★★
Contact:
Lyme Bay Holidays, Bos House, 44 Church Street, Lyme Regis DT7 3DA
T: (01297) 443363
F: (01297) 445576
E: email@lymebayholidays.co.uk
I: www.lymebayholidays.co.uk

Hinkhams Farm Willow View ★★
Contact: Mrs Marion Ray
Hinkhams Farm Willow View, Whitchurch Canonicorum, Bridport DT6 6RJ
T: (01297) 489311

Taphouse Farmhouse, Courthouse Farmhouse & Courthouse Dairy ★★-★★★
Contact: Mrs Sue Johnson
Cardsmill Farm, Whitchurch Canonicorum, Bridport DT6 6RP
T: (01297) 489375
F: (01297) 489375
E: cardsmill@aol.com
I: www.farmhousedorset.com

Vale View & West Barn X42024/23 ★★★
Contact:
Lyme Bay Holidays, Bos House, 44 Church Street, Lyme Regis DT7 3DA
T: (01297) 443363
F: (01297) 445576
E: email@lymebayholidays.co.uk
I: www.lymebayholidays.co.uk

WHITECROSS
Cornwall

Endsleigh ★★★
Contact: Mr George & Mrs Sue Beresford
Endsleigh, Wadebridge PL27 7JD
T: (01208) 814477
I: www.gberesford.fsnet.co.uk

WHITESTAUNTON
Somerset

Little Barton, Higher Beetham Farm ★★★★
Contact: Mrs Hilary Cumming
Little Barton, Higher Beetham Farm, Chard TA20 3PZ
T: (01460) 234460
E: ianandhilary@higher-beetham.fsnet.co.uk

Look out for establishments participating in the National Accessible Scheme

SOUTH WEST ENGLAND

WHITMINSTER
Gloucestershire
The Stable ★★★
Contact: Mr & Mrs Beeby
The Stable, Jaxons Farm, Hyde Lane, Gloucester GL2 7LS
T: (01452) 740969
E: beebyac@onet.co.uk
I: homepage.ntlworld.com/beebyac

Whitminster House Cottages ★★-★★★
Contact: Mrs Teesdale
Whitminster House, Wheatenhurst, Gloucester GL2 7PN
T: (01452) 740204
F: (01452) 740204
E: millard@burwarton-estates.co.uk
I: www.whitminsterhousecottages..co.uk

WIDCOMBE
Bath and North East Somerset
Highclere ★★★-★★★★★
Contact: Mrs Elizabeth Daniel
Meadowland, 16 Cleveland Walk, Bath BA2 6JU
T: (01225) 465465
F: (01225) 465465
E: liz.daniel@tiscali.co.uk
I: www.holidayinbath.co.uk

WIDEGATES
Cornwall
Tresorya ★★★
Contact:
Valley Villas, Sales Office, City Business Park, Office 38 Somerset Place, Plymouth PL3 4BB
T: (01752) 605605
E: sales@valleyvillas.co.uk
I: www.valleyvillas.co.uk

WIDEMOUTH BAY
Cornwall
Freestyle at Widemouth Bay Holiday Village ★★
Contact: Mr Barker
14 Brook Road, Bristol BS6 5LN
E: freestyle4me@yahoo.com
I: www.visitbude.com

Quinceborough Farm Cottages ★★★
Contact:
Farm & Cottage Holidays, Victoria House, 12 Fore Street, Bideford EX39 1AW
T: (01237) 479146
F: (01237) 421512
E: enquiries@farmcott.co.uk
I: www.farmcott.co.uk

WILLERSEY
Gloucestershire
3 Cheltenham Cottages ★★
Contact: Mrs Gillian Malin
28 Bibsworth Avenue, Broadway WR12 7BQ
T: (01386) 853248
F: (01386) 853181
E: g.malin@virgin.net

Rex Cottage ★★
Contact: Mrs Baldwin
Rex House, Broadway WR12 7PJ
T: (01386) 852365

WILLITON
Somerset
Daisy Cottage ★★★★
Contact: Mrs Ann Bishop
6 North Street, Taunton TA4 4SL
T: (01984) 632657
F: (01984) 632657

WILLSBRIDGE
South Gloucestershire
Clack Mill Farm ★★★
Contact: Mrs Gaile Gay
Clack Mill Farm, Keynsham Road, Bristol BS30 6EH
T: (0117) 9322399
F: (0117) 9322399
E: gaile12331@aol.com

WIMBORNE MINSTER
Dorset
Grange Holiday Cottages ★★★★
Contact:
English Country Cottages, Stony Bank, Earby, Barnoldswick BB94 0AA
T: 0870 191 7700
F: (0128) 284 1539
E: eec.enquiry@holidaycottagesgroup.com
I: www.english-country-cottages.co.uk

Millstream ★★★★
Contact: Mrs Mary Ball
59 Oakwood Avenue, Beckenham BR3 6PT
T: (020) 86636426
E: millstream@oakwood59.freeserve.co.uk

The Old Exchange ★★★★
Contact: Mr & Mrs Holland
The Old Exchange, c/o High Lea Cottage, Witchampton Lane, Wimborne Minster BH21 5AF
T: (01258) 840809
I: www.heartofdorset.easynet.co.uk

Owls Lodge ★★★
Contact: Miss Mary King
Hope Farm, Holtwood, Wimborne Minster BH21 7DU
T: (01258) 840239
E: kinger@owls-lodge.freeservenet.co.uk

WINCHCOMBE
Gloucestershire
Briar Cottage ★★★★
Contact: Mrs Chambers
Castle Street, Cheltenham GL54 5JA
T: (01242) 704277
F: (01242) 704277
E: deniseparker@onetel-net.uk

Cockbury Court Cottages ★★★★
Contact: Mr & Mrs Charlton
Cotswold Cottages Limited, Rowan Lodge, Neata Farm, Cheltenham GL54 5BL
T: (01242) 604806
F: (01242) 604806
E: john@rowan-lodge.demon.co.uk
I: www.cotswoldcottagesltd.co.uk/bookings

Dunbar Cottage ★★★
Contact: Linda Andrews
73 Gloucester Street, Cheltenham GL54 5LX
T: (01242) 604946

Muir Cottage ★★★★
Contact: Mr Mark Grassick
Postlip Estate Co, Muir Cottage, Postlip, Cheltenham GL54 5AQ
T: (01242) 603124
F: (01242) 603602
E: enquiries@thecotswoldretreat.co.uk
I: www.thecotswoldretreat.co.uk

The Old Stables ★★★
Contact: Miss Jane Eayrs
The Old Stables, Hill View, Farmcote, Winchcombe, Cheltenham GL54 5AU
T: (01242) 603860
F: (01242) 603860

Orchard Cottage ★★★
Contact: Mrs S M Rolt
Orchard Cottage, Stanley Pontlarge, Cheltenham GL54 5HD
T: (01242) 602594
E: cottages@rolt99.freeserve.co.uk
I: www.cottageguide.co.uk/orchard-cottage

Orchard View ★★★
Contact: Mrs Pamela Lear
13 Huddleston Road, Cheltenham GL54 5HL
T: (01242) 609147
E: pam.lear@ukgateway.net

Styche Cottage ★★★★
Contact: Mrs Anne Bayston
276A Myton Road, Warwick CV34 6PT
T: (01926) 831508
E: stychecottage@bayston.f9.co.uk
I: www.cottageguide.co.uk/stychecottage

Sudeley Castle Country Cottages ★★★
Contact: Mrs Olive Byng
Sudeley Castle Country Cottages, Castle Street, Cheltenham GL54 5JA
T: (01242) 604181
F: (01242) 604181
E: olive.byng@sudeley.org.uk
I: www.sudeleycastle.co.uk

Traditional Accommodation ★★★★-★★★★★★
Contact: Mr & Mrs Wilson
60 Pershore Road, Evesham WR11 2PQ
T: (01386) 446269
F: (01386) 446269
E: trad.accom@virgin.net
I: http://freespace.virgin.net/trad.accom

WINFORD
North Somerset
Regilbury Farm ★★-★★★
Contact: Mrs Keedwell
Regilbury Farm, Regil, Bristol BS40 8BB
T: (01275) 472265
E: janekeedwell@yahoo.co.uk

WINGFIELD
Wiltshire
Romsey Oak Cottages ★★
Contact: Mr Alan Briars
Romsey Oak Farmhouse, Frome Road, Wingfield, Trowbridge BA14 9LS
T: (01225) 753950
F: (01225) 753950
E: enquiries@romseyoakcottages.co.uk
I: www.romseyoakcottages.co.uk/intro.htm

WINKLEIGH
Devon
Hen House & Donkeys Cottage ★★★
Contact:
Farm & Cottage Holidays, Victoria House, 12 Fore Street, Bideford EX39 1AW
T: (01237) 479146
F: (01237) 421512
E: enquiries@farmcott.co.uk
I: www.farmcott.co.uk

WINSCOMBE
North Somerset
Mulberry and Medlar ★★★★
Contact: Mrs Symons
Mulberry and Medlar, Winscombe Court, Winscombe Hill, Winscombe BS25 1DE
T: (01934) 842171
F: (01934) 842171
E: jsymons@winscombecourt.fsnet.co.uk
I: www.winscombecourt.co.uk

WINSFORD
Somerset
East Galliford ★★★
Contact: Mr Alexander
28 Friars Stile Road, Richmond TW10 6NE
T: (020) 8940 8078
F: (020) 8940 6871
E: malcolm.alexander@interregna.com

Little Folly ★★★
Contact: Mrs Pat Hewlett
Little Folly, Folly, Minehead TA24 7JL
T: (01643) 851391
F: (01643) 851391
E: adrianh@follyexmoor.f9.co.uk
I: www.follyexmoor.f9.co.uk

The Tufters ★★★★★
Contact: Mrs Katherine White
East Lodge Farm, Washbrook Lane, Northampton NN6 0QU
T: 0770 3 490876
E: robertwhite486@msn.com

WINSON
Gloucestershire
Swan House ★★★★★
Contact: Mrs Patricia Langley
Riverside House, Chiswick Mall, London W4 2PR
T: (020) 9959072
E: patriciavlangley@btinternet.com

Establishments printed in blue have a detailed entry in this guide

SOUTH WEST ENGLAND

WINTERBORNE HOUGHTON
Dorset
Downview Farm
Rating Applied For
Contact: Mrs Clarice Fiander-Norman
Downview Farm, Blandford Forum DT11 0PE
T: (01258) 882170
F: (01258) 882170
E: enquiries@downviewfarmcottages.co.uk
I: www.downviewcottages.co.uk

WINTERBORNE WHITECHURCH
Dorset
3 Rose Cottages ★★
Contact: Mrs Anne Macfarlane
Barn Court, West Street, Blandford Forum DT11 9AX
T: (01929) 471612
F: (01929) 472293
E: rosecottages5137@aol.com
I: www.cottageguide.co.uk/rose.cottage

WINTERBOURNE ABBAS
Dorset
Lavender Lodge
Rating Applied For
Contact: Mr Graham Tobitt
Lavender Lodge, Dorchester DT2 9LS
T: (01305) 889662

WINTERBOURNE STOKE
Wiltshire
Scotland Lodge ★★
Contact: Mrs Jane Singleton
Scotland Lodge, Salisbury SP3 4TF
T: (01980) 620943
F: (01980) 621403
E: scotland.lodge@virgin.net.co.uk
I: www.scotland-lodge.co.uk

WITHERIDGE
Devon
Maggies Cottage ★★★★
Contact:
Maggies Cottage, 8 West Street, Tiverton EX16 8AA
T: +351 251684107
E: enquiry@maggiecottage.co.uk
I: www.maggiescottage.co.uk

WITHINGTON
Gloucestershire
Ballingers Farmhouse Cottages ★★★★
Contact: Mrs Judith Pollard
Ballingers Farmhouse Cottages, Ballingers Farm House, Cheltenham GL54 4BB
T: (01242) 890335
E: pollardfam@compuserve.com
I: www.ballingersfarmhousecottages.co.uk

WITHYPOOL
Somerset
Hillway Lodge ★★★
Contact: Ms Gillian Lamble
Hillway Lodge, Hillway Farm, Minehead TA24 7SA
T: (01643) 831182
E: gillian@hillwayfarm.com
I: www.hillwayfarm.com

Leys Farm ★★★★★
Contact: Mr & Mrs Zurick
Leys Farm, Foxtwitchen, Minehead TA24 7RU
T: (01643) 831427

Westerclose House Cottages ★★★-★★★★★
Contact: Mrs Valerie Warner
Westerclose House Cottages, Westerclose House, Minehead TA24 7QR
T: (01643) 831302
F: (01643) 831302
E: val@westerclose.co.uk
I: www.westerclose.f9.co.uk

Westwater Cottage ★★★★
Contact: Mrs Sue Branfield
Westwater Cottage, Minehead TA24 7RQ
T: (01643) 831360

WIVELISCOMBE
Somerset
Pinkhouse Farm Cottages ★★★★
Contact: Mrs Deborah Davey
Higher Pinkhouse Farm, Waterrow, Taunton TA4 2QX
T: (01398) 361428
F: (01398) 361428

WOODBURY
Devon
The Coach House ★★★★
Contact: Mr Paul Slade
The Coach House, Furze Close, Sanctuary Lane, Exeter EX5 1EX
T: (01395) 233704

Squirrel ★★★★★
Contact: Mrs Barlow
The Thatched Cottage Company, 56 Fore Street, Budleigh Salterton EX9 7HB
T: (01395) 567676
F: (01395) 567440
E: info@thethatchedcottagecompany.co.uk
I: www.thethatchcottagecompany.co.uk

WOODLANDS
Dorset
Meadow Cottage ★★★★
Contact: Mrs Vicki Brickwood
Meadow Cottage, Horton Road, Wimborne Minster BH21 8NB
T: (01202) 825002

WOOKEY
Somerset
Honeysuckle Cottage ★★★★
Contact: Mrs Luana Law
Honeysuckle Cottage, Worth, Wells BA5 1LW
T: (01749) 678971
E: honeycroft2@aol.com

Mill Lodge ★★★★
Contact: Lesley Burt
Burcott Mill, Wookey, Wells BA5 1NJ
T: (01749) 673118
F: (01749) 677376
E: theburts@burcottmill.com
I: www.burcottmill.com

WOOLACOMBE
Devon
The Apartment ★★★★
Contact:
Marsden's Cottage Holidays, 2 The Square, Braunton EX33 2JB
T: (01271) 813777
F: (01271) 813664
E: holidays@marsdens.co.uk
I: www.marsdens.co.uk

Apartment 1 ★★★★★
Contact:
Marsdens Cottage Holidays, 2 The Square, Braunton EX33 2JB
T: (01271) 813777
F: (01271) 813664
E: holidays@marsdens.co.uk

Apartment 10 ★★★★★
Contact:
Marsdens Cottage Holidays, 2 The Square, Braunton EX33 2JB
T: (01271) 813777
F: (01271) 813664
E: holidays@marsdens.co.uk

Apartment 2 ★★★★★
Contact:
Marsdens Cottage Holidays, 2 The Square, Braunton EX33 2JB
T: (01271) 813777
F: (01271) 813664
E: holidays@marsdens.co.uk
I: www.marsdens.co.uk

Apartment 4 ★★★★★
Contact:
Marsdens Cottage Holidays, 2 The Square, Braunton EX33 2JB
T: (01271) 813777
F: (01271) 813644
E: holidays@marsdens.co.uk

Apartment 7 ★★★★★
Contact:
Marsdens Cottage Holidays, 2 The Square, Braunton EX33 2JB
T: (01271) 813777
F: (01271) 813664
E: holidays@marsdens.co.uk

Baggy Leap ★★★★★
Contact:
Marsdens Cottage Holidays, 2 The Square, Braunton EX33 2JB
T: (01271) 813777
F: (01271) 813664
E: holidays@marsdens.co.uk
I: www.marsdens.co.uk

Barricane Sands ★★★★
Contact:
Marsden's Cottage Holidays, 2 The Square, Braunton EX33 2JB
T: (01271) 813777
F: (01271) 813664
E: holidays@marsdens.co.uk
I: www.marsdens.co.uk

Bayview ★★★★
Contact: Mr & Mrs Cornwell
Marsden's Cottage Holidays, 2 The Square, Braunton EX33 2JB
I: www.marsdens.co.uk

Beachcomber ★★★★
Contact:
Marsdens Cottage Holidays, 2 The Square, Braunton EX33 2JB
T: (01271) 813777
F: (01271) 813644
E: holidays@marsdens.co.uk

Beachcroft Holiday Apartments ★★-★★★
Contact: Mrs Gill Barr
Beachcroft Holiday Apartments, Beach Road, Woolacombe EX34 7BT
T: (01271) 870655
F: (01271) 870655
E: robert@rbarr.freeserve.co.uk

40 Chichester Park ★★★
Contact: Mr & Mrs Cornwell
Marsden's Cottage Holidays, 2 The Square, Braunton EX33 2JB
I: www.marsdens.co.uk

Cove Cottage Flat ★★
Contact: Ms Vivien Lawrence
Cove Cottage Flat, Sharp Rock, Mortehoe, Woolacombe EX34 7EA
T: (01271) 870403
E: vivien@lawrence6232.fsnet.co.uk

5 Devon Beach ★★★★
Contact: Mr Peter & Mrs Janet Cornwell
Marsden's Cottage Holidays, 2 The Square, Braunton EX33 2JB
T: (01271) 813777
F: (01271) 813664
E: holidays@marsdens.co.uk
I: www.marsdens.co.uk

1 Devon Beach Court ★★★★
Contact:
Marsdens Cottage Holidays, 2 The Square, Braunton EX33 2JB
T: (01271) 813777
F: (01271) 813664
E: holidays@marsdens.co.uk
I: www.marsdens.co.uk

Dolphin Court ★★★★
Contact:
Marsden's Cottage Holidays, 2 The Square, Braunton EX33 2JB
T: (01271) 813777
F: (01271) 813664
E: holidays@marsdens.co.uk
I: www.marsdens.co.uk

2 Dolphin Court ★★★★★
Contact:
Marsden's Cottage Holidays, 2 The Square, Braunton EX33 2JB
T: (01271) 813777
F: (01271) 813664
E: holidays@marsdens.co.uk
I: www.marsdens.co.uk

1 Europa Park ★★
Contact: Mrs Rosemary Ann Facey
Sticklepath Lodge, Old Sticklepath Hil, Sticklepath, Barnstaple EX31 2BG
T: (01271) 343426
E: rosemary.facey@talk21.com
I: www.rosemaryandderek.co.uk

Footsteps ★★★★
Contact:
Marsdens Cottage Holidays, 2 The Square, Braunton EX33 2JB
T: (01271) 813777
F: (01271) 813664
E: holiday@marsdens.co.uk
I: www.marsdens.co.uk

SOUTH WEST ENGLAND

Kirton ★★★
Contact:
Marsdens Cottage Holidays, 2 The Square, Braunton EX33 2JB
T: (01271) 813777
F: 813664
E: holidays@marsdens.co.uk
I: www.marsdens.co.uk

Lundy Set ★★★★
Contact: Mr & Mrs P Cornwell
Marsden's Cottage Holidays, 2 The Square, Braunton EX33 2JB
T: (01271) 813777
F: (01271) 813664
E: holidays@marsdens.co.uk
I: www.marsdens.co.uk

Malo ★★★
Contact:
Marsdens Cottage Holidays, 2 The Square, Braunton EX33 2JB
T: (01271) 813777
F: (01271) 813664
E: holidays@marsdens.co.uk
I: www.marsdens.co.uk

Narracott Apartment 9 ★★★★★
Contact:
Marsdens Cottage Holidays, 2 The Square, Braunton EX33 2JB
T: (01271) 813777
F: (01271) 813664
E: holidays@marsdens.co.uk
I: www.marsdens.co.uk

No 3 Narracott Apartments ★★★★★
Contact:
Marsdens Cottage Holidays, 2 The Square, Braunton EX33 2JB
T: (01271) 813777
F: (01271) 813664
E: holidays@marsdens.co.uk
I: www.marsdens.co.uk

Ocean View ★★★★
Contact:
Marsden's Cottage Holidays, 2 The Square, Braunton EX33 2JB
T: (01271) 813777
F: (01271) 813664
E: holidays@marsdens.co.uk
I: www.marsdens.co.uk

Oysters ★★★★
Contact:
Marsden's Cottage Holidays, 2 The Square, Braunton EX33 2JB
T: (01271) 813777
F: (01271) 813664
E: holidays@marsdens.co.uk
I: www.marsdens.co.uk

The Palms ★★★
Contact:
Marsden's Cottage Holidays, 2 The Square, Braunton EX33 2JB
T: (01271) 813777
F: (01271) 813664
E: holidays@marsdens.co.uk
I: www.marsdens.co.uk

4 Pandora Court ★★★★
Contact:
Marsden's Cottage Holidays, 2 The Square, Braunton EX33 2JB
T: (01271) 813777
F: (01271) 813664
E: holidays@marsdens.co.uk
I: www.marsdens.co.uk

5 Pandora Court ★★★★
Contact:
Marsden's Cottage Holidays, 2 The Square, Braunton EX33 2JB
T: (01271) 813777
F: (01271) 813664

Potters View ★★★★
Contact:
Marsdens Cottage Holidays, 2 The Square, Braunton EX33 2JB
T: (01271) 813777
F: (01271) 813664
E: holidays@marsdens.co.uk

Seawatch ★★★
Contact:
Marsden's Cottage Holidays, 2 The Square, Braunton EX33 2JB
T: (01271) 813777
F: (01271) 813664
E: holidays@marsdens.co.uk
I: www.marsdens.co.uk

Stouts Cottage ★★★★
Contact:
Marsden's Cottage Holidays, 2 The Square, Braunton EX33 2JB
T: (01271) 813777
F: (01271) 813664
E: holidays@marsdens.co.uk
I: www.marsdens.co.uk

Swallows Nest ★★★★
Contact:
Marsden's Cottage Holidays, 2 The Square, Braunton EX33 2JB
T: (01271) 813777
F: (01271) 813664
E: holidays@marsdens.co.uk
I: www.marsdens.co.uk

Swiss Cottage ★★★★
Contact:
Marsden's Cottage Holidays, 2 The Square, Braunton EX33 2JB
T: (01271) 813777
F: (01271) 813664
E: holidays@marsdens.co.uk
I: www.marsdens.co.uk

Tamarin ★★★★
Contact:
Marsden Cottage Holidays, 2 The Square, Braunton EX33 2JB
T: (01271) 813777
F: (01271) 813664
E: holidays@marsdens.co.uk
I: www.marsdens.co.uk

Tysoe ★★★★
Contact:
Marsden's Cottage Holidays, 2 The Square, Braunton EX33 2JB
T: (01271) 813777
F: (01271) 813664
E: holidays@marsdens.co.uk
I: www.marsdens.co.uk

WOOLFARDISWORTHY
Devon

Fairchild Cottage ★★★★★
Contact: Mrs Doreen Cox
Fairchild Cottage, Gorrel Farm, Bideford EX39 5QZ
T: (01237) 431503
F: (01237) 431503
E: cox5.gorrel@virgin.net

WOOTTON COURTENAY
Somerset

Bridge Cottage ★★★
Contact: Mrs E. M. Hawksford
Bridge Cottage, Crockford House, Minehead TA24 8RE
T: (01643) 841286

Exmoor View ★★★★
Contact: Mrs Carole Turner
Exmoor View, Green Close, Minehead TA24 8RA
T: (01643) 841482
E: info@exmoorview.co.uk
I: www.exmoorview.co.uk

Old Parlour Cottage ★★★★
Contact: Mr Bishop
Old Parlour Cottage, Hanny Cottage, Minehead TA24 8RE
T: (01643) 841440
E: bishop.dunn@virgin.net

Rose Cottage ★★★
Contact: Mr Bryan Fawcett
Pilgrims Way, Bristol BS40 8TZ
T: (01275) 331123
E: bryanfawcett@lineone.net
I: www.exmoorose.co.uk

WOOTTON FITZPAINE
Dorset

Champernhayes Cottages ★★★★★
Contact: Mrs Tina Le-Clercq
Champernhayes, Bay Tree Cottage, Old Lyme Road, Bridport DT6 6BW
T: (01297) 560853
E: champernhayes@aol.com
I: www.champernhayes.com

Cider & Barn Cottages ★★★★
Contact: Mrs Debby Snook
Cider & Barn Cottages, Bridport DT6 6NE
I: (01297) 560541
E: wfcottages@aol.com

Dairy Farm Holiday Homes ★★★
Contact: Mr Dave Matthews
Lyme Bay Holidays, Bos House, 44 Church Street, Lyme Regis DT7 3DA
T: (01297) 443363
F: (01297) 445576
E: email@lymebayholidays.co.uk
I: www.lymebayholidays.co.uk

Higher Wyld Farmhouse Annexe ★★
Contact: Mrs Jo Day
Higher Wyld Farm, Bridport DT6 6DE
T: (01297) 560479

Marsh Farm ★★★
Contact: Mrs Fabia Mansbridge
Marsh Farm, Bridport DT6 6DF
T: (01297) 560600

Natterjacks ★★★★★
Contact: Mr Steve & Mrs Tracy Day
Bowshot Holidays, 1 Bowshot Farm, Bridport DT6 6DE
T: (01297) 560113

41a Silver Street: A4397 ★★★
Contact:
Lyme Bay Holidays, Bos House, 44 Church Street, Lyme Regis DT7 3DA
T: (01297) 443363
F: (01297) 445576
E: email@lymebayholidays.co.uk
I: www.lymebayholidays.co.uk

Stable Cottage - X4347 ★★★
Contact:
Lyme Bay Holidays, Bos House, 44 Church Street, Lyme Regis DT7 3DA
T: (01297) 443363
F: (01297) 445576
E: email@lymebayholidays.co.uk
I: www.lymebayholidays.co.uk

WORTH MATRAVERS
Dorset

Drovers Cottage ★★★★
Contact: Mrs Ann Cockerell
Weston Farm Cottage, Swanage BH19 3LJ
T: (01929) 439254
F: (01929) 439254
E: drovers@worthmatravers.freeserve.com
I: www.drovers-cottage.co.uk

WRAFTON
Devon

Owencott ★★★★
Contact:
Marsdens Cottage Holidays, 2 The Square, Braunton EX33 2JB
T: (01271) 813777
F: (01271) 813664
E: holidays@marsdens.co.uk
I: www.marsdens.co.uk

WRANTAGE
Somerset

Ludwells Barn ★★★
Contact: Mr Dodd
Ludwells Barn, Wrantage, Taunton TA3 6DQ
T: (01823) 480316

WYCK RISSINGTON
Gloucestershire

Garden Cottage ★★★★
Contact: Mrs Catherine Lukas
Garden Cottage, Stone House, Cheltenham GL54 2PN
T: (01451) 810337
E: katelukas@globalnet.co.uk

WYKE REGIS
Dorset

Church View ★★★
Contact: Mr Zachary Stuart-Brown
Dream Cottages, 5 Hope Square, Weymouth DT4 8TR
T: (01305) 789000
F: (01305) 761346
E: admin@dream-cottages.co.uk
I: www.dream-cottages.co.uk

41 Dowman Place
Rating Applied For
Contact: Ms Julia Larcom
Berkeley Lettings, 78 Broomfield Road, Chelmsford CM1 1SS
T: (01245) 211974
F: (01245) 496110
I: www.berkeleymarine.co.uk/weymouth.htm

Serendipity ★★★★
Contact: Mr Zachary Stuart-Brown
Dream Cottages, 5 Hope Square, Weymouth DT4 8TR
T: (01305) 789000
F: (01305) 761346
E: admin@dream-cottages.co.uk
I: www.dream-cottages.co.uk

SOUTH WEST ENGLAND

Still Waters ★★★
Contact: Mr Zachary Stuart-Brown
Dream Cottages, 5 Hope Square, Weymouth DT4 8TR
T: (01305) 789000
F: (01305) 761346
E: admin@dream-cottages.co.uk
I: www.dream-cottages.co.uk

The Victorian House ★★★
Contact:
Dream Cottages, 5 Hope Square, Weymouth DT4 8TR
T: (01305) 789000
F: (01305) 761347
E: admin@dream-cottages.co.uk
I: www.dream-cottages.co.uk

YARCOMBE
Devon

Heaven's Mouth ★★★
Contact: Mrs Ruth Everitt
Heaven's Mouth, Beacon, Honiton EX14 9LU
T: (01404) 861517
E: ruth-everitt@supanet.com

YEALMPTON
Devon

Gnaton Holiday Cottages
Rating Applied For
Contact: Mrs Josegphine Webb
The Fleet Estate, Plymouth PL8 1JR
T: (01752) 830253
E: cottages@flete.co.uk
I: www.flete.co.uk

YELVERTON
Devon

Greenwell Farm ★★★★
Contact: Mrs Bridget Cole
Greenwell Farm, Nr Clear Brook, Yelverton PL20 6PY
T: (01822) 853563
F: (01822) 853563
E: greenwellfarm@btconnect.com
I: www.greenwell-farm.co.uk

ZELAH
Cornwall

Little Callestock Farm
★★★-★★★★★
Contact: Mrs Liz Down
Little Callestock Farm, Truro TR4 9HB
T: (01872) 540445
F: (01872) 540445
E: liznick@littlecallestockfarm.co.uk
I: www.littlecallestockfarm.co.uk

Little Lowarth ★★★★
Contact:
Farm & Cottage Holidays, Victoria House, 18 Fore Street, Bideford EX39 1AW
T: (01237) 479146
F: (01237) 421512
E: bookings@farmcott.co.uk
I: www.farmcott.co.uk

The Old Chapel ★★★★
Contact: Mrs V M Arthur
The Old Chapel, Truro TR4 9HP
T: (01872) 561566
F: (01872) 561566
E: office@varthur-associates.co.uk

724 Look out for establishments participating in the National Accessible Scheme

Boat accommodation

Follow the stars for the assurance of a rating system you know you can trust. VisitBritain's Quality Assurance Standards for water-based accommodation have been developed to give customers the reassurance that real efforts have been made to set, maintain and improve standards, not only in terms of fixtures and fittings but also in areas such as cleanliness, comfort, hospitality, efficiency and service provided.

So, when choosing your boat, the VisitBritain ratings will give you a clear and trustworthy guide as to what you can expect, and one which makes comparing one boat with another so much easier. Craft are assessed annually by trained, impartial assessors, so you can be confident that your accommodation has been thoroughly checked and rated before you make a booking.

For more information and the latest list of operators which have attained a quality rating, look on:
www.visitheartofengland.co.uk
www.waterwayholidaysuk.com

Star ratings to look out for

Five grades of award reflect the range of quality standards and facilities provided by a craft, and they are indicated by a simple one to five star system. The rating is awarded after assessing a combination of facilities and the overall quality of accommodation – so the more stars, the higher the overall level of quality and comfort you can expect to find. Please note that many boats may provide some of the facilities/equipment/quality also found at a higher star rating.

What to expect

NARROWBOAT AND CRUISER ACCOMMODATION

ONE STAR (minimum requirements)
Acceptable overall level of quality. Clean craft with good standards of customer care provided, along with an adequate provision and quality of furniture, furnishings and fittings. Television available. Galley equipped to meet all essential requirements. Pricing and conditions of booking made clear, and information available to help you make the best of your stay.

TWO STAR (in addition to what is provided at one star)
Quite good to good overall level of quality and customer care in all areas. Radio fitted.

THREE STAR (in addition to what is provided at two star)
Good to very good overall level of quality. Good standard of maintenance and decoration along with a good quality and range of furniture, furnishings and fittings. Generally more space available. Colour TV available. Lighting for each berth.

FOUR STAR (in addition to what is provided at three star)
Very good to excellent overall level of quality. High level of care and attention to detail is evident throughout with higher comfort levels provided for guests. Maximum of two persons sleeping in cabins.

BOAT ACCOMMODATION

FIVE STAR (in addition to what is provided at four star)
Excellent to exceptional overall level of quality. Highest levels of décor, fixtures and fittings, together with excellent standards of management efficiency and guest care. Higher range of accessories and personal touches provided. Saloon/living area not used as sleeping cabin. 240volts AC electrical power supply available.

HOTEL BOAT ACCOMMODATION

ONE STAR (minimum requirements)
Clean craft with good standards of customer care and acceptable comfort provided, along with an adequate provision and quality of furniture, furnishings and fittings. All meals will be available and freshly cooked. Comfortable bed with clean bed linen and towels, and fresh soap. Adequate heating and hot water available at all times. A wide range of guest and tourist information made available by knowledgeable crew.

TWO STAR (in addition to what is provided at one star)
A good overall level of quality and customer care in all areas.

THREE STAR (in addition to what is provided at two star)
Good to very good overall level of quality. Comfortable cabins and saloons with well maintained, practical décor, furniture, furnishings and fittings. A wider choice of quality items available for breakfast and all other meals, freshly cooked from good quality ingredients. A good degree of comfort provided, with good levels of customer care.

FOUR STAR (in addition to what is provided at three star)
Very good to excellent overall level of quality. High level of care and attention to detail is evident throughout with higher comfort and service levels provided for guests.

FIVE STAR (in addition to what is provided at four star)
Excellent to exceptional overall level of quality. Highest levels of décor, fixtures and fittings, together with excellent standards of management efficiency and guest care anticipating guests needs. Higher range of accessories and personal touches provided. All meals prepared with highest quality, fresh ingredients including seasonal and local produce where appropriate.

CRUISERS

Barnes Brinkcraft
★★★-★★★★★
Cruiser
Riverside Road, Wroxham, Norwich NR12 8UD
T: (01603) 782625

C J Broom & Sons Ltd
★★★-★★★★★
Cruiser
Brundall, Norwich NR13 5PX
T: (01603) 712334
E: broom-boats@200.co.uk

Castle Craft Ltd
★★★-★★★★
Cruiser
Reeds Lane, St Olaves, Great Yarmouth NR31 9HG
T: (01493) 488675
E: alex@bostock40.fsnet.co.uk

Caversham Boat Service
★★-★★★
Cruiser
Frys Island, Thameside RG1 8DG
T: (0118) 9574323
E: wicks@cavershamboats.co.uk

City Boats (Highcraft)
★-★★★
Cruiser
Highcraft Marina, Griffin Lane, Thorpe St Andrew, Norwich NR7 0SL
T: (01603) 701701
E: enquires@cityboats.co.uk

Fencraft Ltd
★★★-★★★★
Cruiser
Riverside Estate, Brundall, Norwich NR13 5PS
T: (01603) 715011

Kris Cruisers
★★★-★★★★★
Cruiser
The Waterfront, Southlea Road, Datchet SL3 9BU
T: (01753) 543930
E: sales@kriscruisers.co.uk

J P C
★★★★-★★★★★
Cruiser
Staitheway Road, Wroxham, Norwich NR12 8RN
T: (01603) 783311

Norfolk Broads Direct
★★★-★★★★★
Cruiser
The Bridge, Wroxham, Norwich NR12 8RX
T: (01603) 782207

Sanderson Marine Craft Ltd
★★-★★★
Cruiser
Riverside, Reedham, Norwich NR13 3TE
T: (01493) 70024

Swancraft Boat Services
★★★-★★★★★
Cruiser
Benson Water Front, Benson OX10 6SJ
T: (01491) 836700
F: (01491) 836738

BOAT ACCOMMODATION

HOTEL BOATS

Duke & Duchess Hotel Boats
★★★★
Hotel Boat
9 Lyndale Close, Coventry
CV5 8AE
T: (0771) 1836441

H & H Narrowboat Hotels
★★★★
Hotel Boat
7 Bramshill Gardens, London
NW5 1JJ
T: (0207) 272 0033

Inland Waterway Holiday Cruises
★★★★★
Hotel Boat
Greenham Lock Cottage,
London Road, Newbury
RG14 5SN
T: (0783) 1110811

Narrowboat Hotel Company
★★★★
Hotel Boat
c/o Dorking Business Centre,
51 South Street, Dorking,
Guildford RH4 2JX
T: (0783) 6600029

Thames & Chilterns Holiday Cruises
★★★★
Hotel Boat
Rothbury House, High Street,
Staithes TS13 5BQ
T: (0796) 6248079

NARROW BOATS

Alvechurch Boat Centres
★★-★★★★★
Narrow Boat
Scarfield Wharf, Alvechurch
B48 7SQ
T: (0121) 445 2909
E: edward@helps.f9.co.uk

Andersen Boats
★★★-★★★★★
Narrow Boat
Wych House Lane, Middlewich
CW10 9BQ
T: (01606) 833668
E: Info@andersonboats.com

Anglowelsh Boats
★★-★★★★★
Narrow Boat
2 The Hyde Market, West Street,
St Phillips, Bristol BS2 0BH
T: (0117) 3041122
F: (0117) 304 1133

Black Prince Holidays
★★★★
Narrow Boat
Hanbury Road, Stoke Prior,
Bromsgrove B60 4LA
T: (01527) 575115
F: (01527) 575116

Canalboat Holiday Ltd
★★★★
Narrow Boat
The Boatyard, High Street,
Weedon NN7 4QD
T: (01327) 340739
E: info@canalboat-holidays.com

Canal Cruising Company
★★★-★★★★★
Narrow Boat
Crown Street, Stone ST15 8QN
T: (01785) 813982
E: kwyatt5745@aol.com

Charterline
Rating Applied For
Narrow Boat
Penton Hook Marina, (Gate 5)
Staines Road Chertsey, Chertsey
KT16 8PY
T: (01932) 567541

Claymoore Navigation Ltd
★★-★★★★★
Narrow Boat
The Wharf, Preston Brook,
Warrington WA4 4BA
T: (01928) 717273
E: email@claymoore.co.uk

Copt Heath Wharf
★★★★
Narrow Boat
19 Church Lane, Bingham
NG13 8AL
T: (0121) 704 4464
E: breaks@coptheathwharf.co.uk

Countrywide Cruisers (Brewood) Ltd
★★★-★★★★★
Narrow Boat
The Wharf, Off Kiddemore Road,
Brewood ST19 9BG
T: (01902) 850166
F: (01902) 851662

Evesham Boats
★★-★★★★
Narrow Boat
Evesham Marina, Kings Road,
Evesham WR11 3KZ
T: (01386) 48906

Fox Boats
★★★★-★★★★★
Narrow Boat
10 Marina Drive, March
PE15 0AU
T: (01354) 652770
E: foxboats@dial.pipex.com

Heritage Narrowboats Ltd
★★★
Narrow Boat
The Marina, Kent Green, Scholar
Green ST7 3JT
T: (01782) 785700
E: heritage@sherbournewharf.co.uk

Lee Valley Boat Centre
★★-★★★★★
Narrow Boat
Old Nazeing Road, Broxbourne
EN10 6LX
T: (01992) 462085
F: (01992) 440235

Maestermyn Hire Cruisers
★★-★★★★★
Narrow Boat
Maestermyn Marine, Ellesmere
Road, Whittington, Oswestry
SY11 4NU
T: (01691) 662424
F: (01691) 662424

Marine Services
★★★★
Narrow Boat
Chirk Marina, Whitehurst, Chirk
LL14 5AD
T: (01691) 774558
F: (0169) 772255

Middlewich Narrowboats
Rating Applied For
Narrow Boat
Canal Terrace, Middlewich
CW10 9BD
T: (01606) 832460

Mid-Wales Narrowboats
★★★-★★★★★
Narrow Boat
Maestermyn Marine, Ellesmere
Road, Whittington Owestry
SY11 4NJ
T: (01691) 650243
F: (01691) 662424

Oxfordshire Narrowboats
★★★-★★★★★
Narrow Boat
Canal Wharf, Station Road,
Lower Heyford OX25 5PD
T: (01869) 340348
E: enquiries@oxfordshire-narrowboats.co.uk

Penton Hook Marina
Rating Applied For
Narrowboat
(Gate 5) Staines Road Chertsey,
Chertsey KT16 8PY
T: (01932) 567541

Rose Narrowboats
★★-★★★★★
Narrow Boat
Stretton under Fosse, Rugby
CV23 0PU
T: (01788) 832449
E: rose@rose-narrowboats.co.uk

Sally Boats Ltd
★★-★★★★★
Narrow Boat
Bradford on Avon Marina,
Trowbridge Road, Bradford on
Avon BA15 1UD
T: (01225) 864923
E: chris@sallyboats.ltd.uk

Shepley Bridge Marina
★-★★★★
Narrow Boat
Huddersfield Road, Mirfield
WF14 9HR
T: (01924) 491872

Shire Cruisers
★★★-★★★★★
Narrow Boat
The Wharf, Sowerby Bridge
HX6 2AG
T: (01422) 832712
E: nigel@shirecruisers.co.uk

Silsden Boats
★★★-★★★★★
Narrow Boat
Canal Wharf, Keighley
BD20 0DE
T: (01535) 653675
F: (01535) 670101

Swan Lane Wharf/Clubline Cruisers
★-★★★
Narrow Boat
Swan Lane, Stoke Heath,
Coventry CV2 4QN
T: (02476) 258864
E: swanlanewharf@hotmail.com

Teddesley Boat Company
★★★-★★★★★
Narrow Boat
Park Gate Lock, Teddesley Road,
Penkridge ST19 5RH
T: (01785) 714692
E: teddesley.boat@eclipse

Union Canal Carriers (Adventure Fleet)
★★-★★★★★
Narrow Boat
Braunston Pump House, Dark
Lane, Braunston,Daventry
NN11 7HJ
T: (01788) 890784
E: bo@unioncanalcarriers.co.uk

Valley Cruises
★★-★★★★★
Narrow Boat
Springwood Haven, Mancetter
Road, Nuneaton CV10 0RZ
T: (02476) 393333
F: (02476) 393928

Viking Afloat
★★★★
Narrow Boat
Lowesmoor Wharf, Worcester
WR1 2RS
T: (01905) 610660
E: rob@viking.co.uk

Weltonfield
★★★★-★★★★★
Narrow Boat
Narrowboats, Welton Hythe,
Daventry NN1 5LF
T: (01327) 842282
E: sarahjane@weltonfield.co.uk

Willow Wren Cruising Holidays
★★-★★★
Narrow Boat
Rugby Wharf, Consul Road,
Rugby CV21 1PB
T: (01788) 569153
F: (01788) 540540

The Wyvern Shipping Co Ltd
★★★-★★★★★
Narrow Boat
Rothschild Road, Linslade,
Leighton Buzzard LU7 7TF
T: (01525) 373379
E: james@canalholidays.co.uk

Establishments printed in blue have an advertisement in this guide

Finding **accommodation**
is as easy as 1 2 3

Enjoy England official guides to quality accommodation make it quick and easy to find a place to stay. There are several ways to use this guide.

1 TOWN INDEX
The town index at the back lists all the places with accommodation featured in the regional sections. The index gives a page number where you can find full accommodation and contact details.

2 COLOUR MAPS
All the place names in black on the colour maps at the front have an entry in the regional sections. Refer to the town index for the page number where you will find one or more establishments offering accommodation in your chosen town or village.

3 ACCOMMODATION LISTING
Contact details for all VisitBritain assessed accommodation throughout England, together with their national star rating are given in the listing section of this guide. Establishments with a full entry in the regional sections are shown in blue. Look in the town index for the page number on which their full entry appears.

Further information

The National Quality Assurance Standard	730
General advice and information	731
About the guide entries	734
Travel information by car and by train	736
A selection of events for 2005	738
In which region is the county I wish to visit?	744
National Accessible Scheme index	746
Town index	751

Left, from top Brunt Knott Farm Holiday Cottages, Staveley; seaside stroll, Southwold

Enjoy England official guides to quality

The National Quality Assurance Standard

Wherever you see a national rating sign, you can be sure that one of our trained, impartial assessors has been there before you, checking the place on your behalf – and will be there again, because every place with a national rating is assessed annually. The star ratings reflect the quality that you're looking for when booking accommodation. All properties have to meet an extensive list of minimum requirements to take part in the scheme. From there, increased levels of quality apply. For instance, you'll find acceptable quality at one star, good to very good quality at three star and exceptional quality at five star establishments.

Quite simply, the more stars, the higher the overall level of quality you can expect to find. Establishments at higher rating levels also have to meet some additional requirements for facilities.

Minimum entry requirements include the following:

- High standards of cleanliness throughout
- Pricing and conditions of booking made clear
- Local information to help you make the best of your stay
- Comfortable accommodation with a range of furniture to meet your needs
- Colour television (where signal available) at no extra charge
- Kitchen equipped to meet all essential requirements.

What to expect

The brief explanations of the star ratings outlined below show what is included at each rating level.

ONE STAR
An acceptable overall level of quality with adequate provision of furniture, furnishings and fittings.

TWO STAR (in addition to what is provided at one star):
A good overall level of quality. All units self-contained.

THREE STAR (in addition to what is provided at one and two star):
A good to very good overall level of quality with good standard of maintenance and decoration. Ample space, good-quality furniture. All double beds have access from both sides. Microwave.

FOUR STAR (in addition to what is provided at one, two and three star):
An excellent overall level of quality with very good care and attention to detail throughout. Access to a washing machine and drier if not provided in the unit, or a 24-hour laundry service.

FIVE STAR (in addition to what is provided at one, two, three and four star):
An exceptional overall level of quality with high levels of décor, fixtures and fittings with personal touches. Excellent standards of management, efficiency and guest services.

The rating awarded to an establishment is a reflection of the overall standard, taking everything into account. It is a balanced view of what is provided and, as such, cannot acknowledge individual areas of excellence. Quality ratings are not intended to indicate value for money. A high-quality product can be over-priced; a product of modest quality, if offered at a low price, can represent good value. The information provided by the quality rating will enable you to determine for yourself what represents good value for money.

Many self-catering establishments have a range of accommodation units in the building or on the site, and in some cases the individual units may have different star ratings. In such cases, the entry shows the range available.

Above Clippesby Hall, Clippesby **Right** Old Brantrake, Eskdale

730

INFORMATION

General advice and information

Making a booking

When enquiring about accommodation, make sure you check prices and other important details. You will also need to state your requirements, clearly and precisely, for example:

- Arrival and departure dates, with acceptable alternatives if appropriate.
- The accommodation you need.
- Number of people in your party, and the ages of any children.
- Special requirements, such as ground-floor bathroom, garden, cot.

Booking by letter or email

Misunderstandings can easily happen over the telephone, so we strongly advise you to confirm your booking in writing if there is time.

Please note that VisitBritain does not make reservations – you should write direct to the accommodation.

Deposits

When you book your self-catering holiday, the proprietor will normally ask you to pay a deposit immediately, and then to pay the full balance before your holiday date.

The reason for asking you to pay in advance is to safeguard the proprietor in case you decide to cancel at a late stage, or simply do not turn up. He or she may have turned down other bookings on the strength of yours, and may find it hard to re-let if you cancel.

Cancellations
Legal contract

When you accept accommodation that is offered to you, by telephone or in writing, you enter a legally binding contract with the proprietor.

This means that if you cancel your booking, fail to take up the accommodation or leave early, you will probably forfeit your deposit, and may expect to be charged the balance at the end of the period booked if the place cannot be re-let.

You should be advised at the time of the booking of what charges would be made in the event of cancelling the accommodation or leaving early. If this does not happen you should ask, to avoid any further disputes. Where you have already paid the full amount before cancelling, the proprietor is likely to retain the money. If the accommodation is re-let, the proprietor will make a refund, normally less the amount of the deposit.

And remember, if you book by telephone and are asked for your credit card number, you should check whether the proprietor intends charging your credit card account should you later cancel your reservation. A proprietor should not be able to charge your credit card account with a cancellation unless he or she has made this clear at the time of your booking and you have agreed. However, to avoid later disputes, we suggest you check with the proprietor whether he or she intends to charge your credit card account if you cancel.

Insurance

There are so many reasons why you might have to cancel your holiday, which is why we strongly advise people to take out a cancellation insurance policy. In fact, many self-catering agencies now insist their customers take out a policy when they book their holiday.

Arriving late

If you know you will be arriving late in the evening, it is a good idea to say so when you book. If you are delayed on your way, a telephone call to say that you will be late will help prevent any problems when you arrive.

Bringing pets to England

The quarantine laws have changed in England, and a Pet Travel Scheme (PETS) is currently in operation. Under this scheme pet dogs, cats and ferrets are able to come into Britain from over 50 countries via certain sea, air and rail routes into England as long as they meet the rules. Dogs, cats and ferrets that have been resident in these countries for more than six months may enter the UK under the scheme, providing they are accompanied by the appropriate documentation. Pets from other countries will still have to undergo six months' quarantine. For dogs, cats and ferrets to be able

Enjoy England official guides to **quality**

to enter the UK without quarantine under PETS they will have to meet certain conditions and travel with official documentation.

On 3 July 2004 a new European Regulation on moving pets between European Union (EU) countries and into the EU took effect. The UK will continue to operate the Pet Travel Scheme, but there will be some changes to the scheme in terms of documentation, countries involved and types of animals covered.

For details of the rules, participating countries, routes, operators and further information about the scheme and the new EU Regulation, please contact the PETS Helpline or write to DEFRA (Department for Environment, Food and Rural Affairs), 1a Page Street, London SW1P 4PQ
Tel: + 44 (0) 870 241 1710
Fax: +44 (0) 20 7904 6206
Email: pets.helpline@defra.gsi.gov.uk
or visit their website at
www.defra.gov.uk/animalh/quarantine/index.htm

Code of conduct and conditions of participation

The proprietor/management is required to undertake and observe the following Code of Conduct:

- To maintain standards of guest care, cleanliness, and service appropriate to the type of establishment;
- To describe accurately in any advertisement, brochure, or other printed or electronic media, the facilities and services provided;
- To make clear to visitors exactly what is included in all prices quoted for accommodation, including taxes, and any other surcharges. Details of charges for additional services/facilities should also be made clear;
- To give a clear statement of the policy on cancellations to guests at the time of booking ie by telephone, fax, email as well as information given in a printed format;
- To adhere to, and not to exceed prices quoted at the time of booking for accommodation and other services;
- To advise visitors at the time of booking, and subsequently of any change, if the accommodation offered is in an unconnected annexe or similar and to indicate the location of such accommodation and any difference in comfort and/or amenities from accommodation in the establishment;
- To give each visitor on request details of payments due and a receipt, if required;
- To deal promptly and courteously with all enquiries, requests, bookings and correspondence from visitors;
- Ensure complaint handling procedures are in place and that complaints received are investigated promptly and courteously and that the outcome is communicated to the visitor;
- To give due consideration to the requirements of visitors with disabilities and visitors with special needs, and to make suitable provision where applicable;
- To provide public liability insurance or comparable arrangements and to comply with all applicable planning, safety and other statutory requirements;
- To allow a VisitBritain representative reasonable access to the establishment, on request to confirm the Code of Conduct is being observed.

Conditions for participation

All establishments participating in the National Quality Assurance Standard (NQAS) are required to:

- Meet or exceed the VisitBritain minimum entry requirements for a rating in the relevant accommodation sector;
- Observe the VisitBritain Code of Conduct;
- Be assessed annually, and in the event of complaints by authorised representatives of VisitBritain;
- Pay an annual participation fee;
- Complete an annual information collection questionnaire either online or by post as required.

Change of ownership

When an establishment is sold, the existing rating cannot be transferred to the new owner, unless otherwise agreed by VisitBritain in writing. The new owner is required to make an application for participation in the VisitBritain National Quality Assurance Standard.

Signage

Where an establishment, for whatever reason, ceases to participate in the NQAS, all relevant display signs and print material must be removed. Use of ratings should always be accompanied by the VisitBritain quality marque. Any listing in a VisitBritain publication/website and within the Tourist Information Centre network is conditional on continued participation in the NQAS. Failure to observe these conditions may result in the establishment becoming ineligible to display or use the VisitBritain endorsement in any form whatsoever.

Comments and complaints
Information

The proprietors themselves supply the descriptions of their establishments and other information for the entries (except VisitBritain Ratings). They have all signed a declaration that their information conforms to the Trade Description Acts 1968 and 1972.

INFORMATION

VisitBritain cannot guarantee the accuracy of information in this guide, and accepts no responsibility for any error or misrepresentation.

All liability for loss, disappointment, negligence or other damage caused by reliance on the information contained in this guide, or in the event of bankruptcy or liquidation or cessation of trade of any company, individual or firm mentioned, is hereby excluded. We strongly recommend that you carefully check prices and other details when you book your accommodation.

Problems

Of course, we hope you will not have cause for complaint, but problems do occur from time to time.

If you are dissatisfied with anything, make your complaint to the management immediately. Then the management can take action at once to investigate the matter and put things right. The longer you leave a complaint, the harder it is to deal with it effectively.

In certain circumstances, VisitBritain may look into complaints. However, VisitBritain has no statutory control over establishments or their methods of operating. VisitBritain cannot become involved in legal or contractual matters or in seeking financial compensation.

If you do have problems that have not been resolved by the proprietor and which you would like to bring to our attention, please write to: Quality Standards Department, VisitBritain, Thames Tower, Blacks Road, Hammersmith, London W6 9EL.

Above discover rock pools near Dunstanburgh Castle, Northumberland

Enjoy England official guides to **quality**

About the guide entries

Entries
All the accommodation featured in this guide has been assessed or has applied for assessment under VisitBritain's Quality Assurance Standard. Assessment automatically entitles establishments to a listing in this guide. Additionally proprietors may pay to have their establishment featured in either a standard entry (includes description, facilities and prices) or enhanced entry (photographs and extended details).

Locations
Places to stay are listed under the town, city or village where they are located. If a place is in the countryside, you may find it listed under a nearby village or town.

Place names are listed alphabetically within each regional section of the guide, along with the name of the county or unitary authority they are in and their map reference. Complete addresses for rental properties are not given and the town(s) listed may be a distance from the actual establishment. Please check the precise location at the time of booking.

Map references
These refer to the colour location maps at the front of the guide. The first figure shown is the map number, the following letter and figure indicate the grid reference on the map. Only place names under which standard or enhanced entries (see above) are included appear on the maps. Some entries were included just before the guide went to press, so they do not appear on the maps.

Telephone numbers
Booking telephone numbers are listed below the contact address for each entry. Area codes are shown in brackets.

Prices
The prices shown in the Enjoy England guide are only a general guide; they were supplied to us by proprietors in summer 2004. Remember, changes may occur after the guide goes to press, so we strongly advise you to check prices when you book your accommodation.

Prices are shown in pounds sterling, including VAT where applicable, and are per unit per week.

Prices often vary through the year, and may be significantly lower outside peak holiday weeks. You can get details of other bargain packages that may be available from the establishments themselves, the regional tourism organisations or your local Tourist Information Centre (TIC). Your local travel agent may also have information, and can help you make bookings.

Opening period
If an entry does not indicate when it is open, please check directly with the establishment.

Symbols
The at-a-glance symbols included at the end of each entry show many of the services and facilities available at each establishment. You will find the key to these symbols on the back-cover flap. Open out the flap and you can check the meanings of the symbols as you go.

Smoking
Some places prefer not to accommodate smokers, and in such cases the descriptions or symbols in each entry make this clear.

Pets
Many places accept guests with dogs, but we do advise that you check this when you book, and ask if there are any extra charges or rules about exactly where your pet is allowed. The acceptance of dogs is not always extended to cats, and it is strongly advised that cat owners contact the establishment well in advance. Some establishments do not accept pets at all. Pets are welcome where you see this symbol 🐕.

The quarantine laws have changed in England, and dogs, cats and ferrets are able to come into Britain from over 50 countries. For details of the Pet Travel Scheme (PETS) please turn to page 731.

INFORMATION

Payment accepted

The credit and charge cards accepted by an establishment are listed in the payment accepted section. If you do plan to pay by card, check that the establishment will take your card before you book. Some proprietors will charge you a higher rate if you pay by credit card rather than cash or cheque. The difference is to cover the percentage paid by the proprietor to the credit card company. When you book by telephone, you may be asked for your credit card number as confirmation. But remember, the proprietor may then charge your credit card account if you cancel your booking. See under Cancellations on page 731.

Over the next few years Switch debit cards will be phased out and replaced by the globally recognised Maestro. Almost all establishments will also accept payment by cash or cheque. Many now accept Euros which is indicated in the payment accepted section.

Awaiting confirmation of rating

At the time of going to press some establishments featured in this guide had not yet been assessed for their rating for the year 2005 and so their new rating could not be included. Rating Applied For indicates this.

Left cooling off in St Ives **Above** cycle around Kielder Water

Enjoy England official guides to **quality**

Travel information by car and by train

Distance chart

The distances between towns on the chart below are given to the nearest mile, and are measured along routes based on the quickest travelling time, making maximum use of motorways or dual-carriageway roads. The chart is based upon information supplied by the Automobile Association.

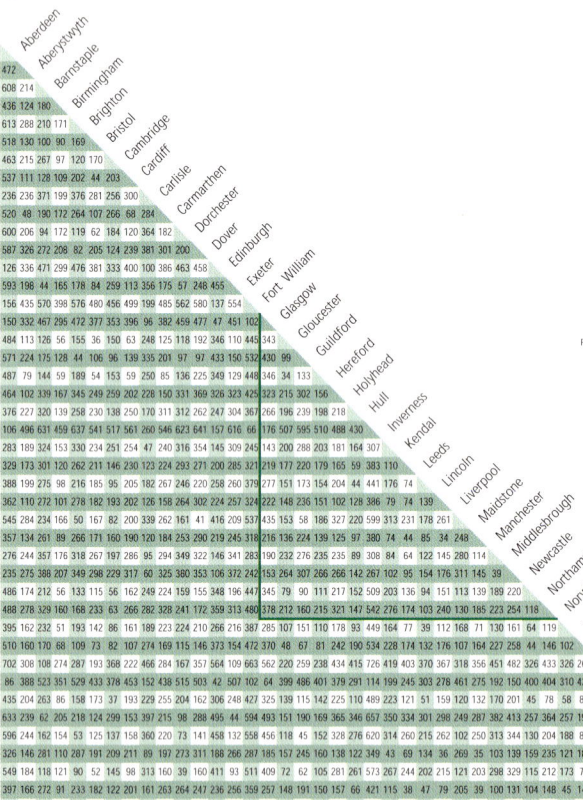

To calculate the distance in kilometres multiply the mileage by 1.6

For example: Brighton to Dover
82 miles x 1.6
=131.2 kilometres

736

TRAVEL

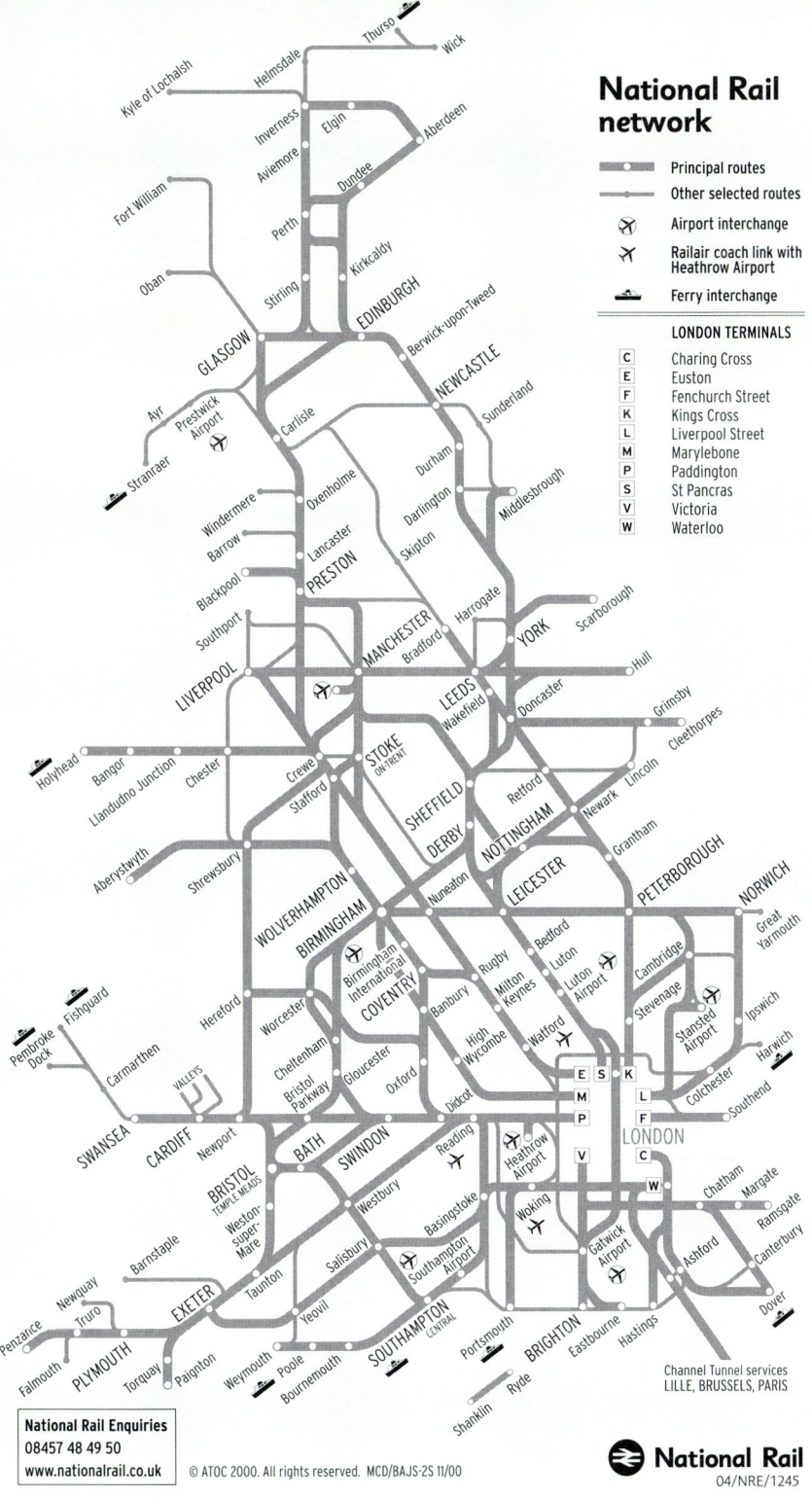

A selection of events for 2005

This is a selection of the many cultural, sporting and other events that will be taking place throughout England during 2005. Please note, as changes often occur after press date, it is advisable to confirm the date and location before travelling.

JANUARY

1 Jan – 9 Jan
Lakeside World Professional Darts Championships
Lakeside Country Club
Wharf Road, Frimley Green, Camberley, Surrey
Tel: (020) 8883 5544
Bookings: (01252) 836464
www.bdodarts.com

15 Jan – 16 Jan
Autosports International 2005
National Exhibition Centre
Birmingham, West Midlands
Tel: 0870 902 0444
www.autosport-international.com

15 Jan – 16 Jan
Motorbike 2005
Springfields Exhibition Centre
Camelgate, Spalding, Lincolnshire
Tel: (01775) 724843
www.springfields.mistral.co.uk

16 Jan
Antique and Collectors' Fair
Alexandra Palace
Alexandra Palace Way, London
Tel: (020) 8883 7061
www.allypally-uk.com

30 Jan
Charles I Commemoration
Banqueting House
Whitehall, London
Tel: (01430) 430695

FEBRUARY

13 Feb
Chinese New Year Celebrations
Chinatown, London
Tel: (020) 7292 2877
www.chinatownchinese.com

13 Feb
Youth Brass Band Entertainment Festival of Great Britain
Winter Gardens, Opera House and Empress Ballroom
Church Street, Blackpool, Lancashire
Tel: (01706) 373911
Bookings: (01706) 373911 x 213

MARCH

1 Mar – 6 Mar
Fine Art and Antiques Fair
Olympia
Hammersmith Road, London
Tel: 0870 736 3105
www.olympia-antiques.co.uk

2 Mar – 28 Mar
Daily Mail Ideal Home Show
Earls Court Exhibition Centre
Warwick Road, London
Tel: 0870 606 6080

13 Mar
Antique and Collectors' Fair
Alexandra Palace and Park
Alexandra Palace Way, Wood Green, London
Tel: (020) 8883 7061
www.allypally-uk.com

Above Chinese New Year 2004, Chinatown, London

* provisional date at time of going to press

EVENTS

25 Mar – 28 Mar
Easter Trails
Petworth House and Park
Petworth, West Sussex
Tel: (01798) 342207
www.nationaltrust.org.uk/petworth

28 Mar
Trigg Morris Men's Easter Monday Tour
Various venues starting in the Market Square
Launceston, Cornwall
Tel: (01637) 880394
www.triggmorris.freeserve.co.uk

APRIL

17 Apr
Flora London Marathon
Greenwich Park to The Mall
London
Tel: (020) 7902 0199
www.london-marathon.co.uk

28 Apr – 1 May
Harrogate Spring Flower Show
Great Yorkshire Showground
Harrogate, North Yorkshire
Tel: (01423) 561049
www.flowershow.org.uk

MAY

1 May
Old Custom: Mayday Celebrations
Town Centre
Padstow, Cornwall
Tel: (01841) 533449

1 May – 2 May*
Carlisle and Borders Spring Flower Show
Bitts Park, Carlisle
Tel: (01228) 817359

7 May – 21 May
Newbury Spring Festival
Various venues
Newbury, Berkshire
Tel: (01635) 528766
Bookings: (01635) 522733
www.newburyspringfestival.org.uk

8 May
Antique and Collectors' Fair
Alexandra Palace and Park
Alexandra Palace Way, Wood Green, London
Tel: (020) 8883 7061
www.allypally-uk.com

14 May – 15 May
Newark and Nottinghamshire County Show
County Showground
Drove Lane, Winthorpe, Newark
Tel: (01636) 702627
www.newarkshowground.com

24 May – 27 May*
Chelsea Flower Show
Royal Hospital Chelsea
Royal Hospital Road, Chelsea, London
Tel: (020) 7649 1885
Bookings: 0870 906 3781
www.rhs.org.uk

27 May – 3 Jun 2005
Blackpool Dance Festival
Winter Gardens, Opera House and Empress Ballroom
Church Street, Blackpool, Lancashire
Tel: (01253) 625252

28 May – 30 May
Kent Garden Show
Kent County Showground
Detling, Maidstone, Kent
Tel: (01795) 474660
www.kentgardenshow.com

29 May – 4 Jun
Pennine Spring Music Festival
Parish Church
Heptonstall, Hebden Bridge, West Yorkshire
Tel: (01422) 845023
Bookings: (01422) 843831

30 May
Northumberland County Show
Tynedale Park
Corbridge, Northumberland
Tel: (01697) 747848
Bookings: 0870 011 5007
www.northcountyshow.co.uk

JUNE

3 Jun
Robert Dover's Cotswold Olimpick Games
Dovers Hill
Weston Subedge, Chipping Campden, Gloucestershire
Tel: (01384) 274041
www.olimpickgames.co.uk

3 Jun – 5 Jun
The Garden Festival at Holker Hall
Holker Hall and Gardens
Cark in Cartmel, Grange-over-Sands, Cumbria
Tel: (015395) 58328
www.holker-hall.co.uk

Enjoy England official guides to **quality**

739

JUNE continued

9 Jun – 12 Jun
Blenheim Palace Flower Show
Blenheim Palace
Woodstock, Oxfordshire
Tel: 0845 644 5145
Bookings: 0870 906 3805
www.blenheimpalaceflowershow.co.uk

18 Jun*
Trooping the Colour – The Queen's Birthday Parade
Horse Guards Parade Headquarters Household Division
Horse Guards, Whitehall, London
Tel: (020) 7414 2479

18 Jun – 26 Jun
Otley Walking Festival 2005
Various locations around Otley
Otley, West Yorkshire
Tel: (01943) 851166
www.chevintrek.co.uk

20 Jun – 3 Jul
Tennis: Wimbledon Lawn Tennis Championships
All England Lawn Tennis & Croquet Club
Church Road, Wimbledon
Bookings: (020) 8946 2244
www.wimbledon.org

24 Jun – 27 Jun
The Mersey River Festival
Albert Dock
Edward Pavilion, Albert Dock, Liverpool, Merseyside
Tel: (0151) 233 3007

25 Jun – 26 Jun
Whitehaven Maritime Festival
Whitehaven Harbour
Whitehaven, Cumbria
Tel: (01946) 696346

29 Jun – 3 Jul
Henley Royal Regatta
Henley Reach
Regatta Headquarters, Henley-on-Thames, Oxfordshire
Tel: (01491) 572153
www.hrr.co.uk

JULY

1 Jul – 10 Jul
Ledbury Poetry Festival
Various venues
Church Street, Ledbury, Herefordshire
Tel: 0845 458 1743
www.poetry-festival.com

2 Jul*
Alnwick Fair
Market Square
Alnwick, Northumberland
Tel: (01665) 711397

2 Jul – 3 Jul
Chiltern Traction Engine Steam Rally
The Hangings
Honor End Road, Prestwood, Great Missenden, Buckinghamshire
Tel: 07889 965604

2 Jul – 3 Jul*
Sunderland International Kite Festival
Northern Area Playing Fields
Stephenson, Washington,
Tyne and Wear
Tel: (0191) 514 1235
www.sunderland.gov.uk/kitefestival

5 Jul – 10 Jul
Hampton Court Palace Flower Show
Hampton Court Palace
Hampton Court, East Molesey, Surrey
Tel: (020) 7649 1885
Bookings: 0870 906 3791
www.rhs.org.uk

Left Hampton Court Palace, London **Right** Mersey River Festival, Liverpool

* provisional date at time of going to press

EVENTS

8 Jul - 17 Jul
Lichfield Festival
Throughout City of Lichfield
Lichfield, Staffordshire
Tel: (01543) 306270
Bookings: (01543) 306543
www.lichfieldfestival.org

9 Jul – 10 Jul
Americana International
County Showground
Drove Lane, Winthorpe, Newark,
Tel: (0115) 939 0595
www.americana-international.co.uk/

9 Jul – 10 Jul*
Beaulieu 4 x 4 Show
National Motor Museum
John Montagu Building, Beaulieu, Brockenhurst,
Hampshire
Tel: (01590) 612345
Bookings: (01590) 612888
www.beaulieu.co.uk

9 Jul – 16 Jul*
Carlisle International Summer Festival
Carlisle Cathedral
The Abbey, Castle Street, Carlisle, Cumbria
Bookings: (01228) 625600

10 Jul
Burton Constable Country Fair
Burton Constable Hall
Burton Constable, Hull, East Yorkshire
Tel: (01964) 562400
www.burtonconstable.com

12 Jul – 14 Jul
Great Yorkshire Show
Great Yorkshire Showground
Harrogate, North Yorkshire
Tel: (01423) 541000
www.yas.co.uk

15 Jul – 17 Jul
Kent County Show
Kent County Showground
Detling, Maidstone, Kent
Tel: (01622) 630975
Bookings: (01622) 630030
www.kentshowground.co.uk

15 Jul – 10 Sep*
The Proms
Royal Albert Hall
Kensington Gore, London
Tel: (020) 7765 5575
www.bbc.co.uk/proms

15 Jul – 31 Jul*
Ryedale Festival
Various venues in the Ryedale area
North Yorkshire
Tel: (01751) 475777
www.ryedalefestival.co.uk

16 Jul
Beaulieu Village Fete
Palace House Lawns
Beaulieu, Brockenhurst, Hampshire
Tel: (01590) 614621

17 Jul
Battle Abbey Classic Car and Motorcycle Show
Battle Abbey and Battlefield
High Street, Battle, East Sussex
Tel: (01424) 211334

29 Jul – 2 Aug
Class 1 Powerboats World Championships
Plymouth Sound
Plymouth, Devon
Tel: (01752) 304849

29 Jul – 31 Jul
Gateshead Summer Flower Show
Gateshead Central Nurseries
Whickham Highway, Lobley Hill, Gateshead,
Tyne and Wear
Tel: (0191) 433 3838

29 Jul – 31 Jul*
Potfest in the Park
Hutton-in-the-Forest
Penrith, Cumbria
Tel: (017684) 83820
www.potfest.co.uk

30 Jul – 31 Jul*
Cumbria Steam Gathering
Cark Airfield
Flookburgh, Grange-over-Sands, Cumbria
Tel: (015242) 71584

30 Jul – 6 Aug 2005
Skandia Cowes Week 2005
The Solent
Cowes, Isle of Wight
Tel: (01983) 293303

30 Jul – 31 Jul*
Sunderland International Air Show Promenade
Sea Front, Seaburn, Sunderland
Tel: (0191) 553 2000
www.sunderland.gov.uk/airshow

Enjoy England official guides to **quality**

AUGUST

4 Aug
Burwarton Show
Burwarton Showground
Cleobury North, Bridgnorth, Shropshire
Tel: (01746) 787535
www.burwartonshow.co.uk

5 Aug – 7 Aug
Lowther Horse Driving Trials and Country Fair
Lowther Castle
Lowther Estate, Lowther, Penrith, Cumbria
Tel: (01931) 712378
www.lowther.co.uk

7 Aug – 13 Aug
Falmouth Regatta Week
Helford River
Carrick Roads and Falmouth Bay, Cornwall
Tel: (01326) 211555
www.falmouth-week.co.uk

12 Aug – 14 Aug
Weymouth Sailing Regatta
Weymouth Bay
Weymouth, Dorset
Tel: (01305) 838501
www.weymouth.gov.uk

20 Aug – 21 Aug
Saddleworth Rushcart Festival
Saddleworth Villages of Uppermill, Greenfield,
Dobcross and Delph Uppermill, Saddleworth
Tel: (01457) 876198
www.saddleworthrushcart.mysite.
freeserve.com

27 Aug – 29 Aug*
England's Medieval Festival
Gardens and Grounds of Herstmonceux Castle
Herstmonceux, Hailsham, East Sussex
Tel: (020) 8416 0398
Bookings: (01323) 834489 (Advance ticket sales)
www.mgel.com

28 Aug
Grasmere Lakeland Sports and Show
Sports Field
Stock Lane, Grasmere, Ambleside, Cumbria
Tel: (015394) 32127

28 Aug – 29 Aug
Notting Hill Carnival
Streets around Ladbroke Grove
London
Tel: (020) 8964 0544

29 Aug
Corsley Show
Corsley Showfield
Corsley, Warminster, Wiltshire
Tel: (01373) 832418

29 Aug
Keswick Agricultural Show
Keswick Showground
Crossings Field, High Hill, Keswick, Cumbria
Tel: (016973) 23418

29 Aug – 1 Sep
International Beatles Festival
Various venues
Liverpool
Tel: (0151) 236 9091
www.caverncitytours.com

31 Aug*
Port of Dartmouth Royal Regatta
Various venues
Dartmouth, Devon
www.dartmouthregatta.co.uk

Left Notting Hill Carnival, London **Right** Herstmonceux Castle, Herstmonceux

* provisional date at time of going to press

EVENTS

SEPTEMBER

1 Sep*
Leeds Conductors' Competition
Town Hall
The Headrow, Leeds, West Yorkshire
Tel: (0113) 247 8332
Bookings: (0113) 224 3801 x 2
www.leedsconcertseason.com

2 Sep – 6 Nov
Blackpool Illuminations
Blackpool Promenade
Blackpool
Tel: (01253) 478222
www.blackpooltourism.com

8 Sep*
Westmorland County Show
Westmorland County Showfield
Lane Farm, Crooklands, Milnthorpe, Cumbria
Tel: (015395) 67804
www.westmorland-county-show.co.uk

9 Sep*
36th Annual Kendal Torchlight Carnival
Town Centre Streets
Kendal, Cumbria
Tel: (015395) 63018
www.kendaltorchlightcarnival.co.uk

10 Sep – 11 Sep*
Beaulieu International Autojumble and Automart
National Motor Museum
John Montagu Building, Beaulieu, Brockenhurst, Hampshire
Tel: (01590) 612345
Bookings: (01590) 612888
www.beaulieu.co.uk

10 Sep – 11 Sep
Caravan Extravaganza
The Lawns
University of Hull, Harland Way, Cottingham, East Riding of Yorkshire
Tel: (01276) 686654
www.hercma.co.uk

15 Sep
Thame and Oxfordshire County Show
The Showground
Kingsey Road, Thame, Oxfordshire
Tel: (01844) 212737
www.thameshow.co.uk

16 Sep – 18 Sep
Harrogate Autumn Flower Show
Great Yorkshire Showground
Harrogate, North Yorkshire
Tel: (01423) 561049
www.flowershow.org.uk

17 Sep – 18 Sep
Mayor's Thames Festival
River Thames
London
Tel: (020) 7928 0960
www.ThamesFestival.org

17 Sep – 18 Sep*
The Royal County of Berkshire Show
Newbury Showground
Priors Court, Hermitage, Thatcham, Berkshire
Tel: (01635) 247111
www.newburyshowground.co.uk

24 Sep – 25 Sep
Malvern Autumn Garden and Country Show
Three Counties Showground
The Showground, Malvern, Worcestershire
Tel: (01684) 584900
www.threecounties.co.uk

OCTOBER

7 Oct – 15 Oct
Hull Fair
Walton Street Fairground
Walton Street, Hull
Tel: (01482) 615625

13 Oct – 16 Oct
Falmouth Oyster Festival
Falmouth, Cornwall
Tel: (01326) 375309

23 Oct 2005*
Trafalgar Day Parade
Trafalgar Square
London
Tel: (020) 7928 8978

NOVEMBER

5 Nov
The City of Liverpool Fireworks Display
Sefton Park, Liverpool
Tel: (0151) 233 3007

12 Nov
Lord Mayor's Show
London
Tel: (020) 7606 3030
www.lordmayorsshow.org

In which region is the county I wish to visit?

County/Unitary Authority	Region
Bath and North East Somerset (U)	South West England
Bedfordshire	East of England
Blackburn with Darwen (U)	England's Northwest
Blackpool (U)	England's Northwest
Bournemouth (U)	South West England
Bracknell Forest (U)	South East England
Brighton & Hove (U)	South East England
Buckinghamshire	South East England
Cambridgeshire	East of England
Cheshire	England's Northwest
City of Bristol (U)	South West England
Cornwall	South West England
County Durham	Northumbria
Cumbria	Cumbria – The Lake District
Darlington (U)	Northumbria
Derby (U)	East Midlands
Derbyshire	East Midlands
Devon	South West England
Dorset	South West England
Durham	Northumbria
East Riding of Yorkshire (U)	Yorkshire
East Sussex	South East England
Essex	East of England
Gloucestershire	South West England
Greater London	London
Greater Manchester	England's Northwest
Halton (U)	England's Northwest

County/Unitary Authority	Region
Hampshire	South East England
Hartlepool (U)	Northumbria
Herefordshire (U)	Heart of England
Hertfordshire	East of England
Isle of Wight (U)	South East England
Isles of Scilly	South West England
Kent	South East England
Kingston upon Hull (U)	Yorkshire
Lancashire	England's Northwest
Leicester (U)	East Midlands
Leicestershire	East Midlands
Lincolnshire	East Midlands
Luton (U)	East of England
Medway (U)	South East England
Merseyside	England's Northwest
Middlesbrough (U)	Northumbria
Milton Keynes (U)	South East England
Norfolk	East of England
North East Lincolnshire (U)	Yorkshire
North Lincolnshire (U)	Yorkshire
North Somerset (U)	South West England
North Yorkshire	Yorkshire
Northamptonshire	East Midlands
Northamptonshire	East Midlands
Northumberland	Northumbria
Nottingham City (U)	East Midlands
Nottinghamshire	East Midlands

Above Rochdale Canal, Greater Manchester **Right** seaside family fun, Southwold

COUNTIES AND REGIONS

County/Unitary Authority	Region
Oxfordshire	South East England
Peterborough (U)	East of England
Plymouth (U)	South West England
Poole (U)	South West England
Portsmouth (U)	South East England
Reading (U)	South East England
Redcar and Cleveland (U)	Northumbria
Rutland (U)	East Midlands
Shropshire	Heart of England
Slough (U)	South East England
Somerset	South West England
South Gloucestershire (U)	South West England
South Yorkshire	Yorkshire
Southampton (U)	South East England
Southend-on-Sea (U)	East of England
Staffordshire	Heart of England
Stockton-on-Tees (U)	Northumbria
Stoke-on-Trent (U)	Heart of England
Suffolk	East of England

County/Unitary Authority	Region
Surrey	South East England
Swindon (U)	South West England
Telford and Wrekin (U)	Heart of England
Thurrock (U)	East of England
Torbay (U)	South West England
Tyne and Wear	Northumbria
Warrington (U)	England's Northwest
Warwickshire	Heart of England
West Berkshire (U)	South East England
West Midlands	Heart of England
West Sussex	South East England
West Yorkshire	Yorkshire
Wiltshire	South West England
Windsor and Maidenhead (U)	South East England
Wirral	England's Northwest
Wokingham (U)	South East England
Worcestershire	Heart of England
York (U)	Yorkshire

(U) Unitary Authority

Enjoy England official guides to **quality**

National Accessible Scheme index

Establishments taking part in the National Accessible Scheme are listed below. For full details of accessible ratings please see pages 10 & 11. Listings in green have a detailed entry in this guide. Use the town index at the back to find the page numbers for their full entries.

Mobility level 1

Old Byre, The	Bosley	**England's Northwest**
Strawberry Duck Holidays	Bosley	**England's Northwest**
Higher Gills Farm	Clitheroe	**England's Northwest**
Forge Mill Farm Cottages	Middlewich	**England's Northwest**
Eden Vale Luxury Holiday Flats	Morecambe	**England's Northwest**
Lower House Cottage	Wildboarclough	**England's Northwest**
The Larches	Ambleside	**Cumbria – The Lake District**
Glebe Hayloft and Glebe Stable	Appleby-in-Westmorland	**Cumbria – The Lake District**
Monkhouse Hill Cottages	Caldbeck	**Cumbria – The Lake District**
Greenbank	Crosthwaite	**Cumbria – The Lake District**
Leases	Smardale	**Cumbria – The Lake District**
Avondale	Staveley	**Cumbria – The Lake District**
Beaumont	Windermere	**Cumbria – The Lake District**
Deloraine	Windermere	**Cumbria – The Lake District**
Bog Mill Farm Holiday Cottages	Alnwick	**Northumbria**
Village Farm	Alnwick	**Northumbria**
Dukesfield Farm Holiday Cottages	Bamburgh	**Northumbria**
East Greystone Farm Cottages	Gainford	**Northumbria**
Fenton Hill Farm Cottages	Wooler	**Northumbria**
Rudstone Walk Country Accommodation	Beverley	**Yorkshire**
The Barn	Grassington	**Yorkshire**
Brimham Rocks Cottages	Harrogate	**Yorkshire**
Bronte Country Cottages	Haworth	**Yorkshire**
Helme Pasture, Old Spring Wood	Pateley Bridge	**Yorkshire**
Beech Farm Cottages	Pickering	**Yorkshire**
Easthill Farm House and Gardens	Pickering	**Yorkshire**
Keld Head Farm Cottages	Pickering	**Yorkshire**
Byre Cottage & Swallow Cottage	Ripon	**Yorkshire**
Groves Dyke	Sleights	**Yorkshire**
The Old Post Office	Thorpe Bassett	**Yorkshire**
York Lakeside Lodges	York	**Yorkshire**
Old Yates Cottages	Abberley	**Heart of England**
Hipsley Farm Cottages	Atherstone	**Heart of England**

746

NATIONAL ACCESSIBLE SCHEME

Upper Onibury Cottages	Craven Arms	**Heart of England**
Anvil Cottage	Hereford	**Heart of England**
The Old Kennels Farm	Ledbury	**Heart of England**
The Granary	Little Dewchurch	**Heart of England**
Stock's Cottage	Little Tarrington	**Heart of England**
The Riseling	Stanford Bridge	**Heart of England**
Church Farm Cottages	Telford	**Heart of England**
Crumplebury Farmhouse	Whitbourne	**Heart of England**
Haddon Grove Farm Cottages	Bakewell	**East Midlands**
Cressbrook Hall Cottages	Cressbrook	**East Midlands**
Nether End c/o Nether Hall	Darley Dale	**East Midlands**
Bay Tree Cottage	Goulceby	**East Midlands**
Kingfisher Lodge	Hagworthingham	**East Midlands**
Wayside Cottage	Horsington	**East Midlands**
Yew Tree Cottage and The Granary	Maltby le Marsh	**East Midlands**
Chestnut Cottage and Willow Cottage	Old Brampton	**East Midlands**
Oundle Cottage Breaks	Oundle	**East Midlands**
Mill Lane Cottage	Woodhall Spa	**East Midlands**
Cherry Tree Cottage	Castle Acre	**East of England**
School Farm Cottages	Cratfield	**East of England**
Dairy Farm Cottages	Dilham	**East of England**
Moor Farm Stable Cottages	Foxley	**East of England**
Boundary Farm	Framlingham	**East of England**
Wood Farm Cottages	Holt	**East of England**
Horning Lodges 1,2,3 Kates & Lady Lodge & Eagle Cottage	Horning	**East of England**
Bluebell, Bonny, Buttercup & Bertie	Sibton	**East of England**
Stringers Woodlands, Wood Farm Stables & Dairy	Stoven	**East of England**
Common Right Barns	Wisbech	**East of England**
Pimlico Farm Country Cottages	Bicester	**South East England**
Cornerstones	Chichester	**South East England**
Bulmer Farm	Dorking	**South East England**
High Wray	Farnham	**South East England**
The Old Dairy	Sandwich	**South East England**
Laramie	Shanklin	**South East England**
Goldhill Mill Cottages	Tonbridge	**South East England**
Wooder Manor Holiday Homes	Ashburton	**South West England**
Wren & Robin Cottages	Ashburton	**South West England**
Greyfield Farm Cottages	Bath	**South West England**
Stable Cottage	Beaminster	**South West England**
Conway Bungalow	Bettiscombe	**South West England**
Lympscott Farm Holidays	Bradworthy	**South West England**
Ash-Wembdon Farm Cottages	Bridgwater	**South West England**
Park Farm Cottages	Bromham	**South West England**
Pine Lodge	Buckland in the Moor	**South West England**
The Olde House	Chapel Amble	**South West England**
Pigsty, Cowstall & Bullpen Cottages	Charlton Musgrove	**South West England**
Whitwell Farm Cottages	Colyford	**South West England**
Northmoor House & Lodge	Dulverton	**South West England**
Westermill Farm	Exford	**South West England**
The Creamery	Kilmersdon	**South West England**

Enjoy England official guides to **quality**

Mobility level 1 continued

Whatcombe Stables	Long Bredy	South West England
Bocaddon Holiday Cottages	Looe	South West England
Budleigh Farm	Moretonhampstead	South West England
Rydon Ball	Ogwell	South West England
Haddington House Apartments	Plymouth	South West England
Trengove Farm Cottages	Portreath	South West England
Trenona Farm Holidays – Chy Tyak and Chy Whel	Ruan High Lanes	South West England
Hartgrove Farm	Shaftesbury	South West England
Trenerry Lodge	Truro	South West England
Venn Farm	Ugborough	South West England
Traine Farm	Wembury	South West England

Mobility level 2

Burbage Holiday Lodge	Bispham	England's Northwest
4 The Croft (Ground Floor Apartment)	Caton	England's Northwest
The Stables	Silverdale	England's Northwest
Red Dell Cottage	Coniston	Cumbria – The Lake District
Barkinbeck Cottage	Kendal	Cumbria – The Lake District
Howscales	Kirkoswald	Cumbria – The Lake District
Swarthmoor Hall	Ulverston	Cumbria – The Lake District
Craster Pine Lodges	Craster	Northumbria
East Greystone Farm Cottages	Gainford	Northumbria
Dalegarth and The Ghyll Cottages	Buckden	Yorkshire
Brentwood Farm Cottages	Burton-in-Lonsdale	Yorkshire
Fowl Green Farm	Commondale	Yorkshire
Cow Pasture and Swallow Tail Cottages	Ebberston	Yorkshire
Brimham Rocks Cottages	Harrogate	Yorkshire
Angel Cottage	Oswaldkirk	Yorkshire
Let's Holiday	Pickering	Yorkshire
Rawcliffe House Farm	Pickering	Yorkshire
Lund Farm Cottages	Selby	Yorkshire
Field House Farm Cottages	Sewerby	Yorkshire
Life Hill Farm	Sledmere	Yorkshire
Mowbray Stable Cottages	South Kilvington	Yorkshire
Captain Cook's Haven	Whitby	Yorkshire
Bulls Head Cottages	Bridgnorth	Heart of England
Swainsley Farm	Butterton	Heart of England
Botvyle Farm	Stretton	Heart of England
Swallows Nest and Robin's Nest	Craven Arms	Heart of England
Northfield Farm	Flash	Heart of England
Foxtwood Cottages	Froghall	Heart of England
The New Cottage	Hallow	Heart of England
Beechenhill Cottage and The Cottage by the Pond	Ilam	Heart of England
Knightcote Farm Cottages	Knightcote	Heart of England
The Old Kennels Farm	Ledbury	Heart of England
Larks Rise	Leek	Heart of England
Hidelow House Cottages	Malvern	Heart of England
Jay's Barn	Stoke-on-Trent	Heart of England
Dove Farm	Ashbourne	East Midlands
Holestone Moor Barns	Ashover	East Midlands

Dairy Cottage, Piggery Pl, Shire's Rest	Hartington	**East Midlands**
Darwin Forest Country Park	Matlock	**East Midlands**
Ingoldale Park	Skegness	**East Midlands**
Holmdene Farm	Beeston	**East of England**
Coda Cottages	Cotton	**East of England**
Norfolk Cottages Malthouse Farm	Diss	**East of England**
Stable Cottages	Hadleigh	**East of England**
Alpha Cottages	Horham	**East of England**
Horning Lodges 1,2,3 Kates & Lady Lodge & Eagle Cottage	Horning	**East of England**
Four Winds Retreat	Kessingland	**East of England**
Gladwins Farm	Nayland	**East of England**
Acorn Cottage	Sandy	**East of England**
The Netus Barn	Wickham Skeith	**East of England**
Common Right Barns	Wisbech	**East of England**
The Herdsman & The Blacksmith's Cottage	Beckley	**South East England**
Pimlico Farm Country Cottages	Bicester	**South East England**
High Wray	Farnham	**South East England**
The Granary & The Stables	High Halden	**South East England**
Apple Pye Cottage	Lenham	**South East England**
The Old Dairy	Sandwich	**South East England**
Goldhill Mill Cottages	Tonbridge	**South East England**
Gorwell Farm Cottages	Abbotsbury	**South West England**
Bookham Court	Alton Pancras	**South West England**
Wooder Manor Holiday Homes	Ashburton	**South West England**
Wren & Robin Cottages	Ashburton	**South West England**
Blagdon Farm Country Holidays	Ashwater	**South West England**
Country Ways	Barnstaple	**South West England**
Church Farm Country Cottages	Bath	**South West England**
Lewesdon Farm Holidays	Beaminster	**South West England**
Woodcombe Lodges	Bratton	**South West England**
Woodbarn Farm Cottages	Chew Magna	**South West England**
Creedy Manor	Crediton	**South West England**
White Witches and Stable Lodge	Crediton	**South West England**
Buzzards View	Curry Mallet	**South West England**
Coach House Farm	Exeter	**South West England**
Top Stall	Fifehead Magdalen	**South West England**
Penquite Farm	Golant	**South West England**
Anglers Paradise	Halwill	**South West England**
Hay Loft & Stables	Langport	**South West England**
Bocaddon Holiday Cottages	Looe	**SouthWest England**
Bucklawren Farm	Looe	**South West England**
Hartswheal Barn	Lostwithiel	**South West England**
Cider Press Cottage	Lydney	**South West England**
Beer Farm	Okehampton	**South West England**
Higher Laity Farm	Portreath	**South West England**
Barton Cottage	St Endellion	**South West England**
The Old Stables	Salisbury	**South West England**
Hartgrove Farm	Shaftesbury	**South West England**
Holly Farm	Stoke St Gregory	**South West England**
Whitminster House Cottages	Whitminster	**South West England**

Mobility level 3

Stonecroft and Swallows Nest	Cockfield	Northumbria
Calvert Trust Kielder	Kielder Water	Northumbria
Fowl Green Farm	Commondale	Yorkshire
Brimham Rocks Cottages	Harrogate	Yorkshire
Dove Court	Salton	Yorkshire
Knightcote Farm Cottages	Knightcote	Heart of England
Hidelow House Cottages	Malvern	Heart of England
Ingoldale Park	Skegness	East Midlands
Cliff Farm Cottage	Lincoln	East Midlands
Blagdon Farm Country Holidays	Ashwater	South West England
Monks Barn	Bishops Down	South West England
Hue's Piece	Broadclyst	South West England
Forda Lodges & Cottages	Bude	South West England
The Poplars	Charmouth	South West England
Smallicombe Farm	Colyton	South West England
Swallow Barn	Godney	South West England
Barton Cottage	St Endellion	South West England
Swallows End	St Just-in-Penwith	South West England
Hartgrove Farm	Shaftesbury	South West England
Tamarisk Farm Cottages	West Bexington	South West England

Mobility level 4

Ingoldale Park	Skegness	East Midlands
Berwick Cottage	East Harling	East of England
Spixworth Hall Cottages	Norwich	East of England
Grange Holiday Cottages	Wimborne Minster	South West England

Hearing impairment level 1

Calvert Trust Kielder	Kielder Water	Northumbria
Fowl Green Farm	Commondale	Yorkshire
Cow Pasture and Swallow Tail Cottages	Ebberston	Yorkshire
Easthill Farm House and Gardens	Pickering	Yorkshire
Life Hill Farm	Sledmere	Yorkshire
Wolds View Holiday Cottages	Yapham	Yorkshire
Ancestral Barn & Church Farm Cottage	Alstonefield	Heart of England
Bainfield Lodge	Burgh-on-Bain	East Midlands

Hearing impairment level 2

Berwick Cottage	East Harling	East of England

Visual impairment level 1

4 The Croft (Ground Floor Apartment)	Caton	England's Northwest
Fowl Green Farm	Commondale	Yorkshire
Easthill Farm House and Gardens	Pickering	Yorkshire
Life Hill Farm	Sledmere	Yorkshire

Visual impairment level 2

Calvert Trust Kielder	Kielder Water	Northumbria
Berwick Cottage	East Harling	East of England

Town index

The following cities, towns and villages all have detailed entries in the regional pages of this guide. If the place where you wish to stay is not shown, the location maps (starting on page 22) will help you to find somewhere to stay in the area.

A	PAGE
Abbotsham *Devon*	299
Abingdon *Oxfordshire*	259
Adderbury *Oxfordshire*	260
Admaston *Staffordshire*	166
Aldeburgh *Suffolk*	220
Alfriston *East Sussex*	261
All Stretton *Shropshire*	166
Allerford *Somerset*	299
Alnmouth *Northumberland*	102
Alnwick *Northumberland*	102
Alresford *Essex*	221
Alston *Cumbria*	65
Alstonefield *Staffordshire*	167
Alton *Staffordshire*	167
Alverstoke *Hampshire*	261
Ambleside *Cumbria*	65
Amersham *Buckinghamshire*	261
Amesbury *Wiltshire*	302
Ampleforth *North Yorkshire*	126
Appleby-in-Westmorland *Cumbria*	68
Arundel *West Sussex*	261
Ashbourne *Derbyshire*	192
Ashburton *Devon*	302
Ashby-de-la-Zouch *Leicestershire*	193
Ashdown Forest (See under Nutley)	
Ashford *Kent*	262
Ashwater *Devon*	302
Atherstone *Warwickshire*	168
Axminster *Devon*	303

B	PAGE
Bacton *Norfolk*	221
Bakewell *Derbyshire*	193
Bamburgh *Northumberland*	103
Bamford *Derbyshire*	194
Bampton *Devon*	303
Barmby Moor *East Riding of Yorkshire*	126
Barnard Castle *County Durham*	106
Barnham *West Sussex*	262
Barnoldby-le-Beck *North East Lincolnshire*	127
Barnstaple *Devon*	304
Barton-upon-Humber *North Lincolnshire*	127
Baslow *Derbyshire*	194
Bassenthwaite *Cumbria*	68
Batcombe *Somerset*	304
Bath *Bath and North East Somerset*	305
Beadnell *Northumberland*	106
Beaminster *Dorset*	305
Beamish *County Durham*	107
Beaulieu *Hampshire*	262
Beckenham *Outer London*	45
Beesby *Lincolnshire*	195
Belchford *Lincolnshire*	195
Belford *Northumberland*	107
Bellingham *Northumberland*	107

Bembridge *Isle of Wight*	262
Berrynarbor *Devon*	306
Berwick-upon-Tweed *Northumberland*	108
Bewdley *Worcestershire*	168
Bibury *Gloucestershire*	306
Bideford *Devon*	307
Bigbury-on-Sea *Devon*	307
Billericay *Essex*	222
Bishop Middleham *County Durham*	108
Bishop Sutton *Bath and North East Somerset*	308
Bishop's Castle *Shropshire*	168
Bishopstone *East Sussex*	263
Blackpool *Blackpool*	52
Blakeney *Norfolk*	223
Blanchland *Northumberland*	108
Blandford Forum *Dorset*	308
Blockley *Gloucestershire*	308
Bodenham *Herefordshire*	169
Boresford *Herefordshire*	169
Boscastle *Cornwall*	308
Boulmer *Northumberland*	108
Bournemouth *Bournemouth*	309
Bourton-on-the-Water *Gloucestershire*	309
Bovey Tracey *Devon*	309
Bowlhead Green *Surrey*	263
Bradford-on-Avon *Wiltshire*	310
Brancaster Staithe *Norfolk*	223
Brantham *Suffolk*	223
Bratton *Somerset*	310
Brayford *Devon*	310
Bridgnorth *Shropshire*	169
Bridlington *East Riding of Yorkshire*	127
Bridport *Dorset*	311
Brighstone *Isle of Wight*	263
Brighton & Hove *Brighton & Hove*	264
Brimpsfield *Gloucestershire*	311
Brinscall *Lancashire*	52
Brixham *Torbay*	311
Broad Campden *Gloucestershire*	313
Broadstairs *Kent*	265
Broadway *Worcestershire*	170
Brockenhurst *Hampshire*	265
Brome *Suffolk*	224
Bromsberrow Heath *Gloucestershire*	313
Bromsgrove *Worcestershire*	170
Bromyard *Herefordshire*	170
Brook *Hampshire*	265
Bruisyard *Suffolk*	224
Buckden *North Yorkshire*	128
Buckland *Gloucestershire*	313
Buckland Newton *Dorset*	313
Buckland St Mary *Somerset*	314
Bude *Cornwall*	314
Burnham Market *Norfolk*	224
Burnham-on-Sea *Somerset*	316
Burnsall *North Yorkshire*	128
Burrowbridge *Somerset*	316
Burton-in-Lonsdale *North Yorkshire*	128
Burton Leonard *North Yorkshire*	129

Buttermere *Cumbria*	69
Byrness *Northumberland*	108

C	PAGE
Caldbeck *Cumbria*	69
Caldecott *Rutland*	196
Cambridge *Cambridgeshire*	225
Camelford *Cornwall*	317
Canterbury *Kent*	265
Carlisle *Cumbria*	69
Carsington *Derbyshire*	196
Cartmel *Cumbria*	70
Castle Hedingham *Essex*	225
Castleside *County Durham*	109
Caversfield *Oxfordshire*	266
Chapel Amble *Cornwall*	317
Charmouth *Dorset*	317
Chathill *Northumberland*	109
Cheddar *Somerset*	318
Cheltenham *Gloucestershire*	319
Chester *Cheshire*	53
Chesterfield *Derbyshire*	196
Chichester *West Sussex*	266
Chilham *Kent*	268
Chillingham *Northumberland*	109
Chippenham *Wiltshire*	319
Chipping *Lancashire*	53
Chipping Campden *Gloucestershire*	320
Chipping Sodbury *South Gloucestershire*	320
Chiselborough *Somerset*	321
Christchurch *Dorset*	321
Chudleigh *Devon*	322
Chulmleigh *Devon*	322
Church Stretton *Shropshire*	170
Cirencester *Gloucestershire*	322
Cley next the Sea *Norfolk*	226
Clippesby *Norfolk*	226
Cockermouth *Cumbria*	70
Cockfield *County Durham*	109
Colchester *Essex*	226
Coleford *Gloucestershire*	323
Colyton *Devon*	323
Combe Martin *Devon*	323
Combs *Derbyshire*	197
Commondale *North Yorkshire*	129
Congleton *Cheshire*	53
Coniston *Cumbria*	70
Constantine Bay *Cornwall*	324
Corbridge *Northumberland*	110
Corfe Castle *Dorset*	324
Cotherstone *County Durham*	110
Cotswolds *Heart of England* (See under Broadway) See also Cotswolds in the South East England and South West England sections)	
Cotswolds *South East England* (See under Finstock) See also Cotswolds in Heart of England and South West England sections)	

751

Cotswolds *South West England*	
(See under Bibury, Blockley, Bourton-on-the-Water, Broad Campden, Cheltenham, Chipping Campden, Cirencester, Daglingworth, Dursley, Lower Slaughter, Minchinhampton, Miserden, Moreton-in-Marsh, Naunton, Nympsfield, Owlpen, Stanton, Stow-on-the-Wold, Temple Guiting, Upton St Leonards, Winchcombe	
See also Cotswolds in Heart of England and South East England sections)	
Cotton *Suffolk*	226
Coverack *Cornwall*	324
Crackington Haven *Cornwall*	324
Cramlington *Northumberland*	110
Cratfield *Suffolk*	227
Craven Arms *Shropshire*	172
Cromer *Norfolk*	227
Cropton *North Yorkshire*	129
Crosthwaite *Cumbria*	72
Crowborough *East Sussex*	268
Croyde *Devon*	325
Culmhead *Somerset*	326
Curbar *Derbyshire*	197

D	PAGE
Daglingworth *Gloucestershire*	326
Dallinghoo *Suffolk*	227
Dalton *North Yorkshire*	129
Danby *North Yorkshire*	129
Darlington *Darlington*	111
Darsham *Suffolk*	227
Dartmeet *Devon*	326
Dartmoor	
(See under Ashburton, Bovey Tracey, Dartmeet, Moretonhampstead, Okehampton, Tavistock)	
Dartmouth *Devon*	326
Delabole *Cornwall*	327
Dent *Cumbria*	72
Devizes *Wiltshire*	327
Dinton *Wiltshire*	327
Docking *Norfolk*	228
Dorchester *Dorset*	327
Dorking *Surrey*	268
Driffield *East Riding of Yorkshire*	130
Driffield *Gloucestershire*	328
Dunster *Somerset*	328
Durham *County Durham*	111
Dursley *Gloucestershire*	328
Dymchurch *Kent*	269

E	PAGE
East Allington *Devon*	329
East Bergholt *Suffolk*	228
East Budleigh *Devon*	329
Edale *Derbyshire*	198
Edlingham *Northumberland*	112
Elkington *Northamptonshire*	198
Elmley Castle *Worcestershire*	172
Elmswell *Suffolk*	228
Elterwater *Cumbria*	72
Elton *Derbyshire*	198
Embleton *Northumberland*	112
Emsworth *Hampshire*	269
English Bicknor *Gloucestershire*	329
Epsom *Surrey*	269
Erpingham *Norfolk*	228

752

Eskdale *Cumbria*	73
Everton *Hampshire*	270
Evesham *Worcestershire*	173
Exeter *Devon*	330
Exford *Somerset*	331
Exmoor	
(See under Allerford, Bratton, Brayford, Combe Martin, Dunster, Exford, Lynton, Minehead, North Molton, Parracombe, Porlock, Simonsbath, West Anstey)	
Exton *Hampshire*	270
Eye *Suffolk*	229

F	PAGE
Fakenham *Norfolk*	229
Falmouth *Cornwall*	331
Falstone *Northumberland*	113
Fareham *Hampshire*	270
Farnham *Surrey*	271
Felixstowe *Suffolk*	229
Ferring *West Sussex*	271
Field Broughton *Cumbria*	74
Field Dalling *Norfolk*	230
Filey *North Yorkshire*	130
Finstock *Oxfordshire*	271
Folkestone *Kent*	272
Fordingbridge *Hampshire*	272
Forest of Dean	
(See under Coleford, English Bicknor, Lydney)	
Fowey *Cornwall*	332
Foxley *Norfolk*	230
Freshwater *Isle of Wight*	272
Froggatt *Derbyshire*	198
Frome *Somerset*	332

G	PAGE
Gamblesby *Cumbria*	74
Garton-on-the-Wolds *East Riding of Yorkshire*	130
Gayle *North Yorkshire*	130
Gayton *Norfolk*	231
Giggleswick *North Yorkshire*	131
Gilling West *North Yorkshire*	131
Gillingham *Dorset*	332
Gilsland *Cumbria*	74
Glastonbury *Somerset*	333
Glenridding *Cumbria*	74
Glynde *East Sussex*	273
Godshill *Isle of Wight*	273
Gonalston *Nottinghamshire*	199
Gorleston-on-Sea *Norfolk*	231
Gorran Haven *Cornwall*	333
Goudhurst *Kent*	273
Grange-over-Sands *Cumbria*	74
Grantham *Lincolnshire*	199
Grasmere *Cumbria*	75
Grassington *North Yorkshire*	131
Great Asby *Cumbria*	76
Great Ayton *North Yorkshire*	132
Great Carlton *Lincolnshire*	199
Great Cheverell *Wiltshire*	333
Great Hucklow *Derbyshire*	199
Great Langdale *Cumbria*	76
Great Langton *North Yorkshire*	132
Great Milton *Oxfordshire*	273
Gresham *Norfolk*	231
Grizedale *Cumbria*	77
Grosmont *North Yorkshire*	132
Guildford *Surrey*	274

H	PAGE
Hagworthingham *Lincolnshire*	200
Hailsham *East Sussex*	274
Halesworth *Suffolk*	231
Halifax *West Yorkshire*	133
Halstead *Essex*	232
Hamsterley Forest	
(See under Barnard Castle, Stanhope, Wolsingham)	
Harrogate *North Yorkshire*	133
Hartington *Derbyshire*	200
Hastingleigh *Kent*	274
Hastings *East Sussex*	275
Hathersage *Derbyshire*	201
Haverigg *Cumbria*	77
Hawkshead *Cumbria*	77
Hawkswick *North Yorkshire*	136
Haworth *West Yorkshire*	136
Hayling Island *Hampshire*	275
Heacham *Norfolk*	232
Hebden Bridge *West Yorkshire*	137
Heddon-on-the-Wall *Northumberland*	113
Helmsley *North Yorkshire*	137
Helston *Cornwall*	333
Helstone *Cornwall*	334
Henfield *West Sussex*	275
Heptonstall *West Yorkshire*	137
Hereford *Herefordshire*	173
Hexham *Northumberland*	114
High Lane *Greater Manchester*	54
High Lorton *Cumbria*	79
Highampton *Devon*	334
Holcombe Rogus *Devon*	334
Holme next the Sea *Norfolk*	232
Holmfirth *West Yorkshire*	137
Holsworthy *Devon*	335
Holt *Norfolk*	232
Holy Island *Northumberland*	114
Honiton *Devon*	335
Hope Cove *Devon*	336
Horham *Suffolk*	232
Horsington *Lincolnshire*	202
Horton-in-Ribblesdale *North Yorkshire*	137
Hove	
(See under Brighton & Hove)	
Hunmanby *North Yorkshire*	138
Hunstanton *Norfolk*	233
Huntley *Gloucestershire*	337
Hutton-le-Hole *North Yorkshire*	138
Hutton Roof *Cumbria*	80
Hythe *Kent*	276

I	PAGE
Ibsley *Hampshire*	276
Ilfracombe *Devon*	337
Ironbridge *Shropshire*	174
Isle of Wight	276
(See under Bembridge, Brighstone, Brook, Freshwater, Godshill, Porchfield, Ryde, Sandown, Seaview, Totland Bay, Wroxall)	

K	PAGE
Kedington *Suffolk*	233
Kelsale *Suffolk*	233
Kendal *Cumbria*	80
Kenilworth *Warwickshire*	174
Kenley *Shropshire*	174
Kessingland *Suffolk*	234

Keswick *Cumbria*	80
Kettlewell *North Yorkshire*	138
Kielder Forest (See under Bellingham, Falstone, Wark)	
King's Cliffe *Northamptonshire*	202
King's Lynn *Norfolk*	234
King's Meaburn *Cumbria*	83
Kingsbridge *Devon*	338
Kirkby Lonsdale *Cumbria*	83
Kirkbymoorside *North Yorkshire*	138
Knaresborough *North Yorkshire*	140
Kniveton *Derbyshire*	202
Knutsford *Cheshire*	54

L	PAGE
Lacock *Wiltshire*	338
Lambley *Nottinghamshire*	203
Langdale *Cumbria*	84
Langport *Somerset*	338
Langton Herring *Dorset*	339
Langton Matravers *Dorset*	339
Lanreath-by-Looe *Cornwall*	340
Launceston *Cornwall*	341
Lavenham *Suffolk*	234
Laxfield *Suffolk*	235
Lealholm *North Yorkshire*	140
Leamington Spa *Warwickshire*	175
Ledbury *Herefordshire*	175
Lee *Devon*	341
Lee on the Solent *Hampshire*	276
Leek *Staffordshire*	176
Leicester *Leicestershire*	203
Leintwardine *Herefordshire*	176
Leiston *Suffolk*	236
Leven *East Riding of Yorkshire*	140
Lewes *East Sussex*	276
Leyburn *North Yorkshire*	141
Lincoln *Lincolnshire*	203
Liskeard *Cornwall*	342
Little Fransham *Norfolk*	236
Little Langdale *Cumbria*	85
Little Snoring *Norfolk*	236
Little Strickland *Cumbria*	85
Little Thirkleby *North Yorkshire*	141
Little Torrington *Devon*	342
Litton *Derbyshire*	206
Liverpool *Merseyside*	54
Liverton *Devon*	342
Locks Heath *Hampshire*	277
London	43
Long Melford *Suffolk*	236
Longsleddale *Cumbria*	85
Looe *Cornwall*	343
Lostwithiel *Cornwall*	346
Louth *Lincolnshire*	206
Lower Apperley *Gloucestershire*	346
Lower Slaughter *Gloucestershire*	347
Lowestoft *Suffolk*	237
Loweswater *Cumbria*	86
Ludlow *Shropshire*	176
Lydney *Gloucestershire*	347
Lyme Regis *Dorset*	347
Lymington *Hampshire*	277
Lympsham *Somerset*	348
Lyndhurst *Hampshire*	278
Lyng *Norfolk*	237
Lynton *Devon*	348
Lyonshall *Herefordshire*	178
Lytham St Annes *Lancashire*	54

M	PAGE
Macclesfield *Cheshire*	54
Maidenhead *Windsor and Maidenhead*	278
Maidstone *Kent*	278
Malmesbury *Wiltshire*	349
Malton *North Yorkshire*	141
Malvern *Worcestershire*	179
Manaccan *Cornwall*	349
Manchester *Greater Manchester*	55
Manchester Airport (See under Knutsford, Manchester, Stockport)	
Marazion *Cornwall*	350
Masham *North Yorkshire*	142
Matlock *Derbyshire*	207
Melcombe Bingham *Dorset*	350
Melplash *Dorset*	350
Mevagissey *Cornwall*	351
Middleham *North Yorkshire*	142
Middleton-by-Youlgreave *Derbyshire*	209
Middleton-in-Teesdale *County Durham*	114
Middlewich *Cheshire*	55
Milford on Sea *Hampshire*	279
Milton Abbas *Dorset*	351
Milwich *Staffordshire*	179
Minchinhampton *Gloucestershire*	351
Mindrum *Northumberland*	115
Minehead *Somerset*	352
Minsterley *Shropshire*	179
Miserden *Gloucestershire*	352
Mollington *Oxfordshire*	279
Monyash *Derbyshire*	209
Moreton *Dorset*	352
Moreton *Oxfordshire*	279
Moreton-in-Marsh *Gloucestershire*	352
Moretonhampstead *Devon*	353
Morpeth *Northumberland*	115
Mothecombe *Devon*	353
Mousehole *Cornwall*	354
Much Wenlock *Shropshire*	179
Mylor *Cornwall*	354

N	PAGE
Nantwich *Cheshire*	55
Naphill *Buckinghamshire*	279
Naunton *Gloucestershire*	354
Nayland *Suffolk*	237
Nether Kellet *Lancashire*	55
Nettleham *Lincolnshire*	209
New Forest (See under Beaulieu, Brockenhurst, Brook, Fordingbridge, Godshill, Hythe, Lymington, Lyndhurst, Milford on Sea, Sway)	
New Polzeath *Cornwall*	355
Newbury *West Berkshire*	280
Newby Bridge *Cumbria*	86
Newcastle upon Tyne *Tyne and Wear*	115
Newmarket *Suffolk*	237
Newquay *Cornwall*	355
Newsham *North Yorkshire*	142
Newton-by-the-Sea *Northumberland*	115
Norfolk Broads (See under Clippesby, Gorleston-on-Sea, Lowestoft, Oulton Broad, Sprowston, Stalham, Wroxham)	
Norham *Northumberland*	116

North Dalton *East Riding of Yorkshire*	142
North Molton *Devon*	356
North Newington *Oxfordshire*	280
North Whilborough *Devon*	356
Northallerton *North Yorkshire*	143
Northampton *Northamptonshire*	209
Northrepps *Norfolk*	238
Norton *North Yorkshire*	143
Nottingham *Nottingham*	210
Nutley *East Sussex*	280
Nympsfield *Gloucestershire*	356

O	PAGE
Oakamoor *Staffordshire*	180
Oakhill *Somerset*	356
Okehampton *Devon*	357
Old Bolingbroke *Lincolnshire*	210
Oldham *Greater Manchester*	56
Olney *Milton Keynes*	280
Orcop *Herefordshire*	180
Orford *Suffolk*	238
Oulton Broad *Suffolk*	239
Oundle *Northamptonshire*	210
Ovington *Northumberland*	116
Owlpen *Gloucestershire*	358
Owslebury *Hampshire*	281
Oxenhope *West Yorkshire*	143
Oxford *Oxfordshire*	281

P	PAGE
Padstow *Cornwall*	358
Paignton *Torbay*	359
Pancrasweek *Devon*	360
Pangbourne *West Berkshire*	281
Parracombe *Devon*	360
Parwich *Derbyshire*	211
Patterdale *Cumbria*	86
Peak District *Heart of England* (See under Alstonefield See also Peak District in East Midlands section)	
Peak District *East Midlands* (See under Ashbourne, Bakewell, Bamford, Baslow, Edale, Froggatt, Great Hucklow, Hartington, Hathersage, Litton, Middleton-by-Youlgreave, Monyash, Parwich See also Peak District in Heart of England section)	
Peldon *Essex*	239
Pelynt *Cornwall*	360
Pembridge *Herefordshire*	180
Penrith *Cumbria*	87
Penselwood *Somerset*	361
Pensford *Bath and North East Somerset*	361
Pentewan *Cornwall*	361
Penzance *Cornwall*	361
Perranporth *Cornwall*	362
Pickering *North Yorkshire*	143
Pillaton *Cornwall*	362
Pinner *Outer London*	45
Plaxtol *Kent*	281
Plymouth *Plymouth*	363
Polperro *Cornwall*	363
Poole *Poole*	363
Porchfield *Isle of Wight*	282
Porlock *Somerset*	364
Port Gaverne *Cornwall*	364
Port Isaac *Cornwall*	364
Portland *Dorset*	365

753

Portreath *Cornwall*	365
Portsmouth & Southsea *Portsmouth*	282
Priors Hardwick *Warwickshire*	181
Puddletown *Dorset*	366
Puncknowle *Dorset*	366

R	PAGE
Radstock *Bath and North East Somerset*	366
Rampisham *Dorset*	366
Ravenscar *North Yorkshire*	145
Redruth *Cornwall*	366
Ribble Valley (See under Chipping)	
Robin Hood's Bay *North Yorkshire*	146
Ross-on-Wye *Herefordshire*	181
Rothbury *Northumberland*	116
Rottingdean *Brighton & Hove*	283
Royal Tunbridge Wells *Kent*	283
Ruan High Lanes *Cornwall*	367
Rugby *Warwickshire*	181
Rustington *West Sussex*	284
Rydal *Cumbria*	87
Ryde *Isle of Wight*	284
Rye *East Sussex*	284

S	PAGE
Saffron Walden *Essex*	239
St Agnes *Cornwall*	367
St Albans *Hertfordshire*	240
St Austell *Cornwall*	368
St Bees *Cumbria*	88
St Blazey *Cornwall*	368
St Clether *Cornwall*	369
St Issey *Cornwall*	369
St Ives *Cornwall*	369
St Just *Cornwall*	370
St Keverne *Cornwall*	370
St Mawes *Cornwall*	370
Salcombe *Devon*	371
Salisbury *Wiltshire*	371
Salisbury Plain (See under Amesbury, Great Cheverell, Salisbury)	
Sandling *Kent*	285
Sandown *Isle of Wight*	285
Sandringham *Norfolk*	240
Sawrey *Cumbria*	88
Scarborough *North Yorkshire*	146
Sea Palling *Norfolk*	240
Seaford *East Sussex*	285
Seahouses *Northumberland*	117
Seaton *Devon*	372
Seaview *Isle of Wight*	286
Sedbergh *Cumbria*	88
Settle *North Yorkshire*	147
Shaftesbury *Dorset*	373
Sharrington *Norfolk*	240
Sheffield *South Yorkshire*	148
Shepton Mallet *Somerset*	373
Shepton Montague *Somerset*	373
Sherborne *Dorset*	374
Sheringham *Norfolk*	241
Sherwood Forest (See under Gonalston, Southwell)	
Shrewsbury *Shropshire*	182
Sibton *Suffolk*	241
Sidmouth *Devon*	374
Sigglesthorne *East Riding of Yorkshire*	148
Simonsbath *Somerset*	374
Skipton *North Yorkshire*	148

Slaley *Northumberland*	118
Slapton *Devon*	375
Snape *Suffolk*	242
Snettisham *Norfolk*	242
South Benfleet *Essex*	242
South Cockerington *Lincolnshire*	211
South Mimms *Hertfordshire*	242
South Molton *Devon*	375
South Petherton *Somerset*	375
Southam *Gloucestershire*	375
Southport *Merseyside*	56
Southsea (See under Portsmouth & Southsea)	
Southwell *Nottinghamshire*	211
Southwold *Suffolk*	242
Sprowston *Norfolk*	244
Staintondale *North Yorkshire*	149
Staithes *North Yorkshire*	149
Stalham *Norfolk*	244
Stanhope *County Durham*	118
Stanton *Gloucestershire*	376
Stanton-on-the-Wolds *Nottinghamshire*	212
Staple *Kent*	286
Stapleton *Cumbria*	89
Staveley *Cumbria*	89
Sticker *Cornwall*	376
Stithians *Cornwall*	376
Stockport *Greater Manchester*	56
Stoke-on-Trent *Stoke-on-Trent*	182
Stoke sub Hamdon *Somerset*	376
Stonegate *East Sussex*	286
Stow-on-the-Wold *Gloucestershire*	377
Stowmarket *Suffolk*	245
Stradbroke *Suffolk*	245
Stratford-upon-Avon *Warwickshire*	182
Streat *West Sussex*	287
Sutton Poyntz *Dorset*	378
Sutton St James *Lincolnshire*	212
Sutton Waldron *Dorset*	379
Swadlincote *Derbyshire*	212
Swanage *Dorset*	379
Swanton Morley *Norfolk*	245
Sway *Hampshire*	287
Syderstone *Norfolk*	245

T	PAGE
Taunton *Somerset*	379
Tavistock *Devon*	379
Taynton *Gloucestershire*	380
Teigngrace *Devon*	381
Temple Guiting *Gloucestershire*	381
Tenterden *Kent*	287
Thame *Oxfordshire*	288
Thirsk *North Yorkshire*	149
Thornham *Norfolk*	246
Thorpe Market *Norfolk*	246
Thorpeness *Suffolk*	246
Thorverton *Devon*	381
Thursford *Norfolk*	247
Tickton *East Riding of Yorkshire*	150
Tintagel *Cornwall*	381
Tirril *Cumbria*	90
Tiverton *Devon*	382
Tivington *Somerset*	383
Todenham *Gloucestershire*	383
Todmorden *West Yorkshire*	150
Torquay *Torbay*	383
Torrington *Devon*	387
Tosside *Lancashire*	57
Totland Bay *Isle of Wight*	288
Totley Rise *South Yorkshire*	150
Totnes *Devon*	387

Towcester *Northamptonshire*	212
Trebetherick *Cornwall*	387
Truro *Cornwall*	387
Tunbridge Wells (See under Royal Tunbridge Wells)	

U	PAGE
Ullswater *Cumbria*	90
Ulverston *Cumbria*	91
Upper Hulme *Staffordshire*	183
Upton St Leonards *Gloucestershire*	387

W	PAGE
Walton-on-Thames *Surrey*	288
Wangford *Suffolk*	247
Warehorne *Kent*	288
Wark *Northumberland*	118
Warkworth *Northumberland*	118
Warwick *Warwickshire*	183
Wasdale *Cumbria*	91
Watchet *Somerset*	388
Waterrow *Somerset*	388
Wellington *Telford and Wrekin*	183
Wells *Somerset*	388
Wells-next-the-Sea *Norfolk*	247
Wembury *Devon*	389
West Anstey *Devon*	389
West Bay *Dorset*	389
West Beckham *Norfolk*	248
West Marden *West Sussex*	289
West Witton *North Yorkshire*	150
Wetton *Staffordshire*	184
Weymouth *Dorset*	390
Whaley Bridge *Derbyshire*	212
Whashton *North Yorkshire*	151
Wheatacre *Norfolk*	248
Whitbourne *Herefordshire*	184
Whitby *North Yorkshire*	151
Whitley Bay *Tyne and Wear*	119
Whitstable *Kent*	289
Wickham Skeith *Suffolk*	248
Wighton *Norfolk*	248
Wigton *Cumbria*	92
Wilsill *North Yorkshire*	153
Wimborne Minster *Dorset*	391
Winchcombe *Gloucestershire*	391
Winchester *Hampshire*	289
Windermere *Cumbria*	92
Windsor *Windsor and Maidenhead*	290
Wingfield *Suffolk*	249
Wingfield *Wiltshire*	392
Withern *Lincolnshire*	213
Wolsingham *County Durham*	119
Woodbridge *Suffolk*	249
Woodhall Spa *Lincolnshire*	213
Wookey *Somerset*	392
Woolacombe *Devon*	392
Wooler *Northumberland*	119
Worcester *Worcestershire*	184
Worthing *West Sussex*	291
Wroxall *Isle of Wight*	291
Wroxham *Norfolk*	249
Wye Valley (See under Hereford, Ross-on-Wye)	
Wythall *Worcestershire*	184

Y	PAGE
Yardley Gobion *Northamptonshire*	213
York *York*	154

enjoyEngland™
official guides to **quality**

Published by: VisitBritain, Thames Tower, Blacks Road, London W6 9EL in partnership with England's tourism industry www.visitengland.com
Publishing Manager: Tess Lugos
Production Manager: Iris Buckley
Compilation, design, copywriting, production and advertisement sales: Jackson Lowe Marketing, 173 High Street, Lewes, East Sussex BN7 1YE
Tel: (01273) 487487 www.jacksonlowe.com
Typesetting: Tradespools Ltd, Somerset and Jackson Lowe Marketing
Maps: Based on digital map data © ESR Cartography, 2004
Printing and binding: Emirates Printing Press, Dubai, United Arab Emirates
Cover design: Eugenie Dodd Typographics

Photography credits: Cumbria Tourist Board; Drayton Manor; East Midlands Tourism; East of England Tourist Board; Heart of England Tourism; Zac Macaulay; Northwest Development Agency; One Northeast Tourism Team/Carlton Reid/Alex Telfer; Portsmouth Historic Dockyard; South West Tourism; Tourism South East; Visit London; www.britainonview.com/Martin Brent/Rod Edwards/ Graham Gough/Klaus Hagmeier/David Hal/Grant Pritchard/ Ingrid Rasmussen; Yorkshire Tourist Board

Important note: The information contained in this guide has been published in good faith on the basis of information submitted to VisitBritain by the proprietors of the premises listed, who have paid for their entries to appear. VisitBritain cannot guarantee the accuracy of the information in this guide and accepts no responsibility for any error or misrepresentation. All liability for loss, disappointment, negligence or other damage caused by reliance on the information contained in this guide, or in the event of bankruptcy, or liquidation, or cessation of trade of any company, individual or firm mentioned, is hereby excluded to the fullest extent permitted by law. Please check carefully all prices, ratings and other details before confirming a reservation.

© British Tourist Authority (trading as VisitBritain) 2005
ISBN 0 7095 7933 0

A VisitBritain Publishing guide

Finding **accommodation**
is as easy as **1 2 3**

Enjoy England official guides to quality accommodation make it quick and easy to find a place to stay. There are several ways to use this guide.

1
TOWN INDEX
The town index at the back lists all the places with accommodation featured in the regional sections. The index gives a page number where you can find full accommodation and contact details.

2
COLOUR MAPS
All the place names in black on the colour maps at the front have an entry in the regional sections. Refer to the town index for the page number where you will find one or more establishments offering accommodation in your chosen town or village.

3
ACCOMMODATION LISTING
Contact details for all VisitBritain assessed accommodation throughout England, together with their national star rating are given in the listing section of this guide. Establishments with a full entry in the regional sections are shown in blue. Look in the town index for the page number on which their full entry appears.

NOTES

NOTES